BELIEVER'S BIBLE COMMENTARY

NEW TESTAMENT

WILLIAM MacDONALD

Contributions by Art Farstad

THOMAS NELSON PUBLISHERS
Nashville

ISBN 0-8407-7576-8

Library of Congress Catalog Card Number: 87-073459

Printed in the United States of America

1 2 3 4 5 6 7 — 95 94 93 92 91 90

CONTENTS

4

Author's Preface

The Believers Bible Commentary is designed to help the average Christian become a serious student of the Word of God. No commentary, however, can take the place of the Bible. The best it can hope to do is to explain the general meaning in an understandable manner, then send the reader back to the Scriptures for further study.

The Commentary is written in simple, non-technical language. It does not profess to be scholarly or deeply theological. Most believers are not versed in the original languages of the Old and New Testaments, but this does not cut them off from the practical benefits of the Word. I am convinced that through the systematic study of the Scriptures, any Christian can become "a worker who does not need to be ashamed, rightly dividing the word of truth" (2 Tim. 2:15).

The comments are brief, concise, and to the point. In order to get help on a passage, the reader does not have to wade through long pages of explanation.

The pace of modern life makes it essential that the truth be served in digest portions.

The notes do not avoid difficult passages. In many cases, alternative explanations are given, leaving the reader to decide which one best fits the context and the rest of Scripture.

Knowledge of the Bible is not enough. There must be the practical application of the Word to the life. So the BBC seeks to suggest how the Scriptures can be fleshed out in the lives of God's people.

If the book is used as an end in itself, it will become a snare rather than a help; if it is used to stimulate personal study of the Sacred Scriptures and prompt obedience to the precepts of the Lord, then it will achieve its goal.

May the Holy Spirit, who inspired the Bible, illuminate the reader's mind in this wonderful pursuit — to know God through His Word.

Editor's Introduction

"Don't despise the commentaries." This was the advice of a Bible teacher to his class at Emmaus Bible School (now College) in the late 1950's. At least one student remembered those words through three decades. The teacher was William MacDonald, the author of *Believers Bible Commentary*. The student was the editor, Arthur Farstad, at that time a callow freshman. He had only read one commentary in his life — *In the Heavenlies* (Ephesians) by Harry A. Ironside. Reading the commentary every night one summer as a teenager, Art Farstad found out what a commentary is.

What a Commentary Is

Exactly what is a commentary and why should we not despise one? Recently a prominent Christian publisher listed *fifteen* types of Bible-related books. If some people don't know exactly how a commentary differs from a Study Bible, e.g., or even from a concordance, an atlas, a Bible dictionary — to name four — it should be no surprise.

A commentary *comments*, or makes (hopefully) helpful remarks on the text, either verse by verse or paragraph by paragraph. Some Christians sneer at commentaries and say, "I only want to hear the spoken word and read the Bible itself!" Sounds pious, but it is not. A commentary merely puts in print the best (*and hardest!*) type of Bible exposition — the verse by verse teaching and preaching of the Word of God. Some commentaries (such as Ironside's) are quite literally sermons put into print. What's more, the greatest Bible expositions of all ages and tongues are available in English. Unfortunately many are so long, so dated, and so difficult that the ordinary Christian gets discouraged, not to say overwhelmed. Hence, *The Believers Bible Commentary*.

Kinds of Commentaries

Theoretically, anyone interested in the Bible could write a commentary. For this reason they range from extremely liberal to very conservative — with every shade of thought in between. The BBC is a very conservative one, accepting the Bible as the inspired and flawless Word of God, totally sufficient for faith and practice.

A commentary can range all the way from highly technical (minute details of Greek and Hebrew syntax, e.g.) to a very breezy sketch. The BBC is somewhere in between. What technicalities are needed are largely relegated to the endnotes, but a serious interaction with the details of the text is given with no dodging of difficult passages or convicting applications. Mr. MacDonald's writing is *rich in exposition*. Its aim is to help produce, not merely garden-variety, lowest common denominator Christians, but *disciples*.

Commentaries also differ as to theological camp — conservative or liberal, Protestant or Roman Catholic, premillennial or amillennial. The BBC is conservative, Protestant, and premillennial.

How to Use This Book

There are several approaches to the BBC. We suggest the following, pretty much in this order:

Browsing — If you like or love the Bible you will enjoy leafing through this book, reading bits and pieces here and there to get the flavor of the whole work.

Specific Passage — You may have a question on a verse or paragraph that you need help on. Look it up in the appropriate place in context and you will surely find good material.

A Doctrine — If you are studying the Sabbath, baptism, election, or the Trinity, look up the passages that deal with that subject. The table of contents lists essays, or "excurses," on many of these topics. Use a concordance to help locate key words that guide to central passages for topics other than the thirty-seven excurses.

Bible Book — Perhaps your Sunday school class or congregation is going through a book of the New Testament. You will greatly enrich yourself (and have something to add, if there is a discussion) if you read ahead each week the passage to be covered. (Of course, if the leader is *also* using the BBC as a main study help, you may want to have *two* different commentaries!)

The Whole Book — Eventually every Christian should read through the *entire Bible*. There are hard texts scattered throughout, and a careful, conservative book like the BBC will greatly enhance your study.

Bible study may start out in the "shredded wheat" stage — "nutritious but dry," but as you progress it will become "chocolate pie!"

Mr. MacDonald's advice to me thirty years ago was, "Don't despise the commentaries." Having studied his Commentary on the New Testament with great care while editing it for the New King James text, I can go a step further. My advice: "Enjoy!"

Abbreviations

Abbreviations of Books of the Bible

Old Testament Books

Gen.	Genesis	2 Chron.	2 Chronicles	Dan.	Daniel
Ex.	Exodus	Ezra	Ezra	Hos.	Hosea
Lev.	Leviticus	Neh.	Nehemiah	Joel	Joel
Num.	Numbers	Est.	Esther	Amos	Amos
Deut.	Deuteronomy	Job	Job	Obad.	Obadiah
Josh.	Joshua	Ps. (Pss.)	Psalms	Jon.	Jonah
Judg.	Judges	Prov.	Proverbs	Mic.	Micah
Ruth	Ruth	Eccl.	Ecclesiastes	Nah.	Nahum
1 Sam.	1 Samuel	Song	Song of Songs	Hab.	Habakkuk
2 Sam.	2 Samuel	Isa.	Isaiah	Zeph.	Zephaniah
1 Kgs.	1 Kings	Jer.	Jeremiah	Hag.	Haggai
2 Kgs.	2 Kings	Lam.	Lamentations	Zech.	Zechariah
1 Chron.	1 Chronicles	Ezek.	Ezekiel	Mal.	Malachi

New Testament Books

Matt.	Matthew	Eph.	Ephesians	Heb.	Hebrews
Mark	Mark	Phil.	Philippians	Jas.	James
Luke	Luke	Col.	Colossians	1 Pet.	1 Peter
John	John	1 Thess.	1 Thessalonians	2 Pet.	2 Peter
Acts	Acts	2 Thess.	2 Thessalonians	1 Jn.	1 John
Rom.	Romans	1 Tim.	1 Timothy	2 Jn.	2 John
1 Cor.	1 Corinthians	2 Tim.	2 Timothy	3 Jn.	3 John
2 Cor.	2 Corinthians	Tit.	Titus	Jude	Jude
Gal.	Galatians	Phmn.	Philemon	Rev.	Revelation

Abbreviations of Bible Versions, Translations, and Paraphrases

ASV	American Standard Version	LB	Living Bible
FWG	F. W. Grant's *Numerical Bible*	NASB	New American Standard Bible
JND	John Nelson Darby's *New Translation*	NEB	New English Bible
JBP	J. B. Phillips' Paraphrase	NIV	New International Version
KJV	King James Version	NKJV	New King James Version
KSW	Kenneth S. Wuest's *An Expanded Translation*	RSV	Revised Standard Version
		RV	Revised Version (England)

Other Abbreviations

A.D.	*Anno Domini,* in the year of our Lord
Aram.	Aramaic
BBC	*Believers Bible Commentary*
B.C.	Before Christ
c.	*circa,* about
cf.	*confer,* compare
chap.	chapter
chaps.	chapters
ed.	edited, edition, editor
eds.	editors
e.g.	*exempli gratia,* for example
et al.	*et allii, aliae, alia,* and others
fem.	feminine
Gk.	Greek
ICC	International Critical Commentary
ibid.	*ibidem,* in the same place
i.e.	*id est,* that is
lit.	literal, literally
LXX	Septuagint (ancient Gk. Version of the OT)
marg.	margin, marginal reading
masc.	masculine
ms., mss.	manuscript(s)
M	Majority Text
MT	Masoretic Text
n.d.	no date
NIC	New International Commentary
n.p.	no publisher, no place of publication
NT	New Testament
NU	Nestle-Aland/United Bible Societies Greek NT
OT	Old Testament
p., pp.	page(s)
TBC	Tyndale Bible Commentary
trans.	translated, translator
vol(s).	volume(s)
v., vv.	verse(s)
vs.	versus

Transliteration of Greek Words

Greek Name	Greek Letter	English Equivalent	Greek Name	Greek Letter	English Equivalent
alpha	α	a	nu	ν	n
beta	β	b	xi	ξ	x
gamma	γ	g, ng	omicron	ο	o (short)
delta	δ	d	pi	π	p
epsilon	ε	e (short)	rho	ρ	r
zeta	ζ	z	sigma	σ (ς)	s
eta	η	e (long)	tau	τ	t
theta	θ	th	upsilon	υ	u, y
iota	ι	i	phi	φ	ph
kappa	κ	k	chi	χ	ch (hard)
lambda	λ	l	psi	ψ	ps
mu	μ	m	omega	ω	o (long)

INTRODUCTION TO
THE NEW TESTAMENT

"The value of these Writings, historical and spiritual, is out of all proportion to their number and length, and their influence upon life and history is incalculable. Here is the noontide of the day which began to dawn in Eden. The Christ of Prophecy in the Old Testament becomes the Christ of History in the Gospels; the Christ of Experience in the Epistles; and the Christ of Glory in the Revelation."   W. Graham Scroggie

I. The Name "New Testament"

Before launching out into the deep seas of NT studies, or even the comparatively small area of studying a particular book, it will prove helpful to outline briefly some general facts about the Sacred Book we call "The New Testament."

"Testament" and "covenant" both translate the same Greek word (*diathēkē*), and in one or two places in Hebrews it is debatable which translation is better. In the title of the Christian Scriptures the meaning "covenant" seems definitely preferable because the Book constitutes a pact, alliance, or *covenant* between God and His people.

It is called the *New* Testament (or Covenant) to contrast it with the Old (or "Older") one.

Both Testaments are inspired by God and therefore profitable for all Christians. But naturally the believer in Christ is more often likely to turn to that part of the Bible that specifically tells of our Lord and His church, and how He wishes His disciples to live.

The relationship between the OT and the NT is nicely expressed by Augustine:
  The New is in the Old concealed;
  The Old is in the New revealed.

II. The NT Canon

The word *canon* (Gk. *kanōn*) refers to a "rule" by which something is measured or evaluated. The canon of the NT is the collection of inspired books. How do we know that these are the *only* books that should be in the canon or that all of these twenty-seven writings should be there? Since there were other Christian epistles and writings (also heretical ones) from early days, how can we be sure these are the right ones?

It is often said that a church council drew up the canonical list in the late 300's of our era. Actually, the books were *canonical* as soon as they were written. Godly and discerning disciples recognized inspired Scriptures from the start, as Peter did Paul's writings (2 Pet. 3:15, 16). However, there was dispute over some of the books (Jude, 2 and 3 John, e.g.) in some churches for a time.

Generally if a book was by an apostle, such as Matthew, Peter, John, or Paul, or one of the apostolic circle, such as Mark or Luke, there was no doubt about that book's canonicity.

The council that officially recognized our canon was actually *confirming* what had been generally accepted for many, many years. The council drew up not an *inspired list* of books, but a list of *inspired books*.

III. Authorship[†]

The Divine Author of the NT is the Holy Spirit. He inspired Matthew, Mark, Luke, John, Paul, James, Peter, Jude and the anonymous author of Hebrews (see Introduction to Hebrews) to write. The best and correct understanding of this question of how the NT books were produced is "dual authorship." The NT is not partly human and partly divine, but totally human and totally divine at the same time. The divine element kept the human element from making any errors. The result is an inerrant or flawless book in the original manuscripts.

A helpful analogy to the written Word is the dual nature of the Living Word, our Lord Jesus Christ. He is not partly human and partly divine (like a Greek myth) but completely human and completely divine at the same time. The divine nature made it impossible for the human to err or sin in any way.

IV. Dates

Unlike the OT, which took about a millennium to complete (c. 1400–400 B.C.), the NT took only half a century to write (c. A.D. 50–100).

The present order of the NT books is best suited for the church for all time. It starts with the life of Christ, then tells of the church, then gives instructions to that church, and finally reveals the future of the church and the world. However, the books do not occur in order of writing. They were written as the need for them arose.

The first books were "Letters to young churches," as Phillips calls the Epistles. James, Galatians, and Thessalonians are probably the first written, near the middle of our first Christian century.

The Gospels are next in order of writing, Matthew or Mark first, Luke next, and John last. Finally comes the Revelation, probably near the end of the first century A.D.

V. Contents

The contents of the NT may be summarized concisely as follows:

Historical
  Gospels
  Acts
Epistolary
  Paul's Epistles
  General Epistles
Apocalyptic
  Revelation

A Christian who gets a good grasp of these books will be "thoroughly furnished for every good work."

It is our prayer that the BBC will greatly aid many believers to be just that.

VI. Language

The NT was written in *everyday language* (called *koinē*, or "common Greek"). This was a nearly universal second language in the first century of the Faith, as well-known and as widely used as English is today.

Just as the Hebrew language's warm and colorful style perfectly fits the prophecy, poetry, and narrative of the OT, so Greek was providentially prepared as a marvelous vehicle for the NT. The Greek language spread far abroad through Alexander the Great's conquests, his soldiers simplifying and popularizing the language for the masses.

The precision of Greek verb tenses, cases, vocabulary, and other details makes it ideal for communicating the important doctrinal truths found in the Epistles — especially in such a book as Romans.

While not an elite literary language, the *koinē* Greek is not "street language" or poor Greek either. A few parts of the NT — Hebrews, James, 2 Peter — do approximate the literary level. Also, Luke, at times, waxes almost classical and even Paul writes with great beauty on occasion (1 Cor. 13, 15, e.g.).

VII. Translation

English is blessed with many (perhaps too many!) translations. These fall into four general types:

1. Very literal

The "New" (in 1871) Translation of J. N. Darby and the English Revised Version (1881) and its U.S. variant, the American Standard Version (1901) are extremely literal. This makes them helpful for study but weak for worship, public reading, and memorization. The masses of Christians have never abandoned the majesty and beauty of the KJV for these versions.

2. Complete Equivalence

Versions that are quite literal and follow the Hebrew or Greek closely when English allows it, yet still permit a freer translation where good style and idiom demand it, include the KJV, the RSV, the NASB, and the NKJV. Unfortunately, the RSV, while generally reliable in the NT, is wedded to an OT that plays down many Messianic prophecies. This dangerous trend is seen today even among some previously sound scholars. The BBC was edited to conform to the NKJV as the most viable position between the beautiful (but archaic) KJV and today's usage, yet without using any "thee's" and "thou's." It also retains many verses and words eliminated in most modern Bibles (see notes on text throughout the BBC.)

3. Dynamic Equivalence

This type of translation is freer than the complete equivalence type, and sometimes resorts to paraphrase, a valid technique as long as the reader is made aware of it. The Moffatt Translation, NEB, NIV, and the Jerusalem Bible all fall into this category. An attempt is made to put whole thoughts into the structure that John and Paul might have used if they were writing today — and in English. When done conservatively, this methodology can be a helpful tool.

4. Paraphrase

A paraphrase seeks to transmit the text thought by thought, yet it often takes great liberties in *adding* material. Since it is far removed from the original text in wording there is always the danger of *too much interpretation*. The Living Bible, e.g., while evangelical, makes many interpretive decisions that are *at best* debatable.

The paraphrase of J. B. Phillips (he calls it a translation) is very well done from a literary viewpoint. He also usually says in *his* words what he believes Peter and Paul meant in *theirs*.

It is good to have a Bible from at least three of these categories for purposes of comparison. However, we believe that the complete equivalence translation is safest for detailed Bible study, such as is presented in the BBC.

INTRODUCTION TO THE GOSPELS†

"The Gospels are the firstfruits of all writings." — Origen

I. Our Glorious Gospels

Everyone who has studied literature is familiar with the story, the novel, the play, the poem, and the biography, as well as other literary forms. But when our Lord Jesus Christ came to earth, a whole new category of literature was needed — the *Gospel*. The Gospels are not biographies, though they have strong biographical material. They are not stories, though they contain parables such as the Prodigal Son and the Good Samaritan that are as interesting as any story in all literature. Some parables have even been adapted into novels or short stories. The Gospels are not documentary reports, yet they contain accurate, though obviously condensed, accounts of many conversations and discourses of our Lord.

Not only is the "Gospel" a unique literary category, but after the four evangelists wrote Matthew, Mark, Luke, and John, the canonical mold was broken. Four Gospels and only these four have been recognized by orthodox Christians for nearly two thousand years. Various heretics wrote books they *called* gospels, but these were shabby vehicles to promote some heresy, such as Gnosticism.

But why four Gospels? Why not five, to match the five books of Moses to form a Christian Pentateuch? Or why not just one long Gospel, omitting all repetitions and having room for more miracles and parables? Actually, attempts to "harmonize" or put all four together go as far back as Tatian's second century *Diatessaron* (Greek for "through four".)

Irenaeus theorized that there were four Gospels to match the four quarters of the world and the four winds, four being the number of universality.

II. The Four Symbols

Many, especially artistic people, appreciate the parallel proposed between the four Gospels and the four symbols of Ezekiel and Revelation: the lion, the ox (or calf), the man, and the eagle. They, however, have been matched up quite differently with the Gospels by different Christians. If there is validity to these *attributes*, as they are called in art, the lion best fits Matthew, the royal Gospel of the Lion of Judah. The ox, as a beast of burden, fits Mark well, the Gospel of the Servant. The man is definitely the key figure of Luke, the Gospel of the Son of Man. Even the *Standard Handbook of Synonyms, Antonyms & Prepositions* says that "the eagle is the *attribute* of St. John as an *emblem* of lofty spiritual vision."[1]

III. The Four Readerships

Probably the best explanation for the fact that there are four Gospels is that the Holy Spirit is seeking to reach four different groups of people — four ancient types that still have clear modern counterparts.

Everyone agrees that Matthew is the most Jewish Gospel. The OT quotations, detailed discourses, genealogy of our Lord, and general Semitic tone are noticed by even a new reader.

Mark, probably writing from the imperial capital itself, is aiming at Romans, and also the millions of similar people who like action more than thought. His Gospel is thus long on miracles and short on parables. This Gospel needs no genealogy, because what Roman would care about Jewish genealogies for an active Servant?

†*See pp. iii–viii.*

Luke is clearly the Gospel for the Greeks and the many Romans who loved and emulated Greek literature and art. Such people love beauty, humanity, cultural style, and literary excellence. Dr. Luke supplies all of these. Along with the modern Greeks, the most obvious counterparts are the French. It is no surprise that it was a *Frenchman* who said that Luke was "the most beautiful book in the world" (see Introduction to Luke).

Who is left for John? John is the universal Gospel, with something for everyone. It is evangelistic (20:30, 31), yet also cherished by deep Christian thinkers. Perhaps this is the key: John is for "the third race" — a name given by the pagans to the early Christians as being neither Jews nor Gentiles.

IV. Other Fourfold Motifs

There are a few other fourfold motifs in the OT that dovetail beautifully with the emphases of the four Gospels.

"The Branch" as a title of our Lord occurs in the following contexts:

". . . to David a Branch . . . a King"
(Jer. 23:5, 6)
"My Servant, the BRANCH"
(Zech. 3:8)
"The Man . . . the BRANCH"
(Zech. 6:12)
"The Branch of the LORD" (Jehovah)
(Isa. 4:2)

There are also four "Beholds" in the OT that exactly match the Gospels' main themes:

"Behold, your King" (Zech. 9:9)
"Behold, my Servant" (Isa. 42:1)
"Behold, the Man" (Zech. 6:12)
"Behold your God" (Isa. 40:9)

A final parallel is one that is a little less obvious but has proved a blessing to many. The four colors of materials in the tabernacle with their symbolic meanings also seem to fit the evangelists' fourfold presentation of the attributes of our Lord:

Purple is an obvious choice for *Matthew*, the Gospel of the King. Judges 8:26 shows the regal nature of this color.

Scarlet dye was derived in ancient times from crushing a cochineal worm. This suggests *Mark*, the Gospel of the bondservant, "a worm and no man" (Ps. 22:6).

White speaks of the righteous deeds of the saints (Rev. 19:8). *Luke* stresses the perfect humanity of Christ.

Blue represents the sapphire dome we call the heavens (Ex. 24:10), an attractive representation of the Deity of Christ, a key note in *John*.

V. Order and Emphasis

In the Gospels, we find the events are not always listed in the order in which they occurred. It is good to know at the outset that the Spirit of God often groups events according to their moral teaching. Kelly says:

It will be proved, as we proceed, that Luke's is essentially a moral order, and that he classfies the facts, conversations, questions, replies, and discourses of our Lord according to their inward connection, and not the mere outward succession of events, which is in truth the rudest and most infantile form of record. But to group events together with their causes and consequences, in their moral order, is a far more difficult task for the historian, as distinguished from the mere chronicler. God can use Luke to do it perfectly.[2]

These different emphases and approaches help explain the variations in the Gospels. While the first three Gospels, the so-called "Synoptics" (meaning "taking a common view") are similar in their approach to the life of Christ, John is different. He wrote later and didn't want to repeat what had already been well covered. His is a more reflective and theological presentation of the life and words of our Lord.

VI. The Synoptic Question

Why there are so many *similarities* — even to almost identical wording of relatively long passages — and yet also so many *differences* among the first three Gospels is usually called the "Synoptic problem." It is much more of a problem for those who deny inspiration than for conservative Christians. Many complex theories have been formulated, often involving theoretical lost documents that have left no trace in manuscript form. Some of these ideas fit in with Luke 1:1 and are at least *possible* from an orthodox standpoint. However, some of these theories have reached the point where they assert that the first century church pieced together "myths" about Jesus Christ. Aside from the infidelity to all Christian Scriptures and church history that these alleged "form-critical" theories represent, it should be pointed out that there is no documentary proof for any of them. Also, *no two scholars agree* on how they categorize and fragment the Synoptic Gospels.

A better solution to the question lies in our Lord's words in John 14:26: "But the Helper, the Holy Spirit, whom the Father will send in My name, He will teach you all things, and bring to your remembrance all things that I said to you."

This takes care of the eyewitness reminiscences of Matthew and John, and probably includes Mark as well, assuming he records Peter's remembrances, as church history says. Add to this direct help from the Holy Spirit the written documents mentioned in Luke 1:1, the outstanding verbally accurate *oral tradition* of Semitic peoples, and the Synoptic question is answered. Any necessary truths, details or interpretations beyond these sources can have been directly revealed "(in words) which the Holy Spirit teaches" (1 Cor. 2:13).

Thus, when finding an *apparent* contradiction or differences in details we do well to ask, "Why does *this* Gospel leave out, include, or emphasize *this* event or speech?" For example, twice Matthew records two people being healed (of blindness and from a demon), while Mark and Luke mention only one. Some see this as a contradiction. Better to see Matthew, the Jewish Gospel, mentioning both men, since the law demanded "two or three witnesses," and the others mentioning, for example, the prominent, *named* person (blind Bartimaeus).

The following selections illustrate that some of the seeming duplications in the Gospels actually highlight significant differences:

Luke 6:20-23 seems to duplicate the Sermon on the Mount, but the former is a Sermon on the plain (Luke 6:17). The Beatitudes describe the character of the ideal citizen of the kingdom, whereas Luke traces the lifestyle of those who are Christ's disciples.

Luke 6:40 seems to be the same as Matthew 10:24. But in Matthew, Jesus is the Master and we are His disciples. In Luke, the discipler is the master, and the person he teaches is the disciple. Matthew 7:22 emphasizes service for the King; whereas Luke 13:25-27 describes fellowship with the Master.

Whereas Luke 15:4-7 is a barbed denunciation of the Pharisees, Matthew 18:12, 13 is concerned with children and God's love for them.

When only believers were present, John said, "He will baptize you with the Holy Spirit" (Mark 1:8; John 1:33). When there was a mixed multitude, especially including Pharisees, he said, "He will baptize you with the Holy Spirit and fire" (a baptism of judgment) (Matt. 3:11; Luke 3:16).

The expression "With the measure you use . . ." applies to our *judgmental attitude* toward others in Matthew 7:2, our *appropriation of the Word* in Mark 4:24, and our *liberality* in Luke 6:38.

These differences, then, are not contradictions, but purposeful, suggesting spiritual food for thought to the meditative believer.

VII. The Authorship of the Books[†]

It is standard in discussing who wrote the Gospels — in fact, all of the books of the Bible — to divide the testimonies into *external* and *internal* evidence. This we propose to do in all the twenty-seven New Testament books. Under *external* evidence, writers who lived nearer the times of the books — generally second and third century "church fathers" and a few heretics, or false teachers — are referred to. These men quote, allude to, and sometimes specifically tell us about the books and authors who interest us. For example, if Clement of Rome quotes 1 Corinthians near the end of the first century, it obviously cannot be a second century forg-

[†]*See p. i.*

ery written under Paul's name. Under *internal* evidence we note the style, vocabulary, history, and contents of a book to see if it supports or contradicts what the outside documents and authors claim. For example, the style of Luke and Acts sustains the view that the author was a cultured Gentile physician.

In many books the "canon" or list of approved books of the second century heretic Marcion is quoted. He only accepted a stripped-down edition of Luke and ten of Paul's Epistles, but he nevertheless is a helpful witness to which books were standard in his time. The Muratorian Canon (named after the Italian Cardinal Muratori, who found the document) is an orthodox, though sometimes fragmentary, list of canonical Christian books.

ENDNOTES

[1]James C. Fernald, ed., "Emblem," *Funk & Wagnalls Standard Handbook of Synonyms, Antonyms, and Prepositions*, p. 175.

[2]William Kelly, *An Exposition of the Gospel of Luke*, p. 16.

THE GOSPEL
ACCORDING TO MATTHEW†

Introduction

"In grandness of conception and in the power with which a mass of material is subordinated to great ideas no writing in either Testament, dealing with a historical theme, is to be compared with Matthew."

— Theodor Zahn.

I. Unique Place in the Canon

Matthew's Gospel is the perfect bridge between the Old and the New Testaments. Its very first words throw us back to the forefather of the OT people of God, Abraham, and to the first *great* king of Israel, David. In its emphasis, strong Jewish flavor, its many quotations from the Hebrew Scriptures, and its position at the head of the NT books, Matthew is the logical place to start the Christian message to the world.

Matthew has long held this first position in the order of the four Gospels. This is because until very modern times, it was universally believed to be the first Gospel *written*. Also, Matthew's clear, orderly style made it most suitable for congregational reading. Hence it was the most popular Gospel, sometimes vying for that place with John.

It is not necessary to believe that Matthew was the first Gospel written in order to be orthodox. However, the earliest Christians were nearly all of Jewish extraction, and there were many thousands of them. Meeting the needs of the first Christians *first* does seem quite logical.

II. Authorship††

The *external evidence* is ancient and universal that Matthew the tax collector, also called Levi, wrote the First Gospel. Since he was not a prominent member of the apostolic band it would be strange to attribute the First Gospel to him if indeed he had nothing to do with it.

Besides the ancient document known as the "Didache" (*Teaching of the Twelve Apostles*), Justin Martyr, Dionysius of Corinth, Theophilus of Antioch, and Athenagoras, the Athenian quote the Gospel as authentic. Eusebius, the church historian, quotes Papias as saying that "Matthew composed the *Logia* in the Hebrew language, and everyone interpreted them as he was able." Irenaeus, Pantaenus, and Origen basically agree with this. "Hebrew" is widely thought to mean the dialect of Aramaic used by the Hebrews in our Lord's time, as the word is used in the NT. But what are the "*Logia*"? Usually this Greek word means "oracles," as the OT contains the *oracles* of God. It cannot mean that in Papias' statement. There are three main views on his statement: (1) It refers to the *Gospel* of Matthew as such. That is, Matthew wrote an Aramaic edition of his Gospel especially to win the Jews to Christ and edify Hebrew Christians, and only later did a Greek edition appear. (2) It refers to *sayings* of Jesus only, which later became incorporated into his Gospel. (3) It refers to *testimonia*, i.e., citations of OT Scriptures to show that Jesus is the Messiah. Views 1 and 2 are more likely than view 3.

The Greek of Matthew does not read like a mere translation, but such a widespread tradition (with no early dissent) must have some factual basis. Tradition says that Matthew preached for fifteen years in Palestine and then left to evangelize in foreign parts. It is possible that about A.D. 45 he left behind for the Jews who had accepted Jesus as their Messiah a first draft of his Gospel in Aramaic (or just the *discourses* of Christ), and later made a *Greek* edition for *universal* use. A similar thing was done by Matthew's contemporary, Josephus. This Jewish historian made an Aramaic first draft of his *Jewish Wars* and then the final form of the book in Greek.

The *internal evidence* of the First Gospel does fit well with a devout Jew who loved the OT and was gifted as a careful writer and editor. As a civil servant of Rome, Matthew would have to be proficient in both the language of his people (Aramaic) and of the ruling authorities. (The Romans used Greek, not Latin, in the East.) The numerical details, parables regarding money, and the monetary terms all fit in with a tax collector. So does the concise, orderly style. Goodspeed, a nonconservative scholar, accepted the Matthaean authorship of this Gospel partly from this corroborating internal evidence.

In spite of such universal external evidence and favorable internal evidence, most nonconservative scholars *reject* the traditional view that Matthew the tax collector wrote this book. They do so on two main grounds.

First of all, *assuming* that Mark was the first Gospel written (taught as "Gospel truth" in many circles today), how could an apostle and eyewitness use so much of Mark's material (93% of Mark occurs also in other Gospels)? To answer this, first of all, it is not *proven* that Mark was first. Ancient testimony says Matthew was first, and since the early Christians were nearly all Jewish, this makes a great deal of sense. But even if we accept the so-called Marcan priority (and many conservatives do so), Matthew could have recognized that Mark's work was largely the reminiscences of the dynamic Simon Peter, Matthew's fellow-apostle, as early church tradition maintains (see Introduction to Mark).

The second argument against the book being by Matthew (or any eyewitness) is that it lacks vivid details. Mark, who no one claims witnessed Christ's ministry, has colorful details that suggest he was there. How could an eyewitness write so matter-of-factly? Perhaps the personality of a tax collector explains it quite well. In order to have room for more of our Lord's discourses, Levi could have cut down on needless details. This would especially be so if Mark wrote first and Matthew saw that Peter's first-hand reminiscences were well represented.

III. Date

If the widespread belief that Matthew made an Aramaic first edition of his Gospel (or at least of the sayings of Jesus) is so, a date for that of A.D. 45, fifteen years after the Ascension, would fit in with ancient tradition. He could have brought out the fuller, canonical Gospel in Greek in 50 or 55, or even later.

The view that the Gospel *must* have been written after the destruction of Jerusalem (A.D. 70) rests largely on disbelief in Christ's ability to predict that future event in detail, and other rationalistic theories that ignore or deny divine inspiration.

IV. Background and Theme

Matthew was a young man when Jesus called him. A Jew by birth, and a tax collector by training and practice, he forsook all to follow Christ. One of his many compensations was that he became one of the twelve apostles. Another was that he was chosen as the writer of what we know as the First Gospel. It is generally believed that Matthew was the same as Levi (Mark 2:14; Luke 5:27).

In his Gospel, Matthew sets out to show that Jesus is the long-expected Messiah of Israel, the only lawful Claimant to the throne of David.

The book does not profess to be a complete narrative of the life of Christ. It begins with His genealogy and early years, then jumps to the beginning of His public ministry when He was about thirty. Guided by the Holy Spirit, Matthew selects those aspects of the Savior's life and ministry which attest Him as God's *Anointed One* (that is what *Messiah* and *Christ* mean). The book moves toward a climax: the trial, death, burial, resurrection, and ascension of the Lord Jesus. And in that climax, of course, is laid the foundation for man's salvation. That is why the book is called a Gospel — not so much because it sets forth the way by which sinful people may receive salvation, but rather because it describes the sacrificial work of Christ by which salvation was made possible.

The Believers Bible Commentary is not intended to be exhaustive or technical, but rather to stimulate independent study and meditation. And most of all it is aimed at creating in the reader's heart an intense longing for the return of the King.

> So even I, and with a heart more burning,
> So even I, and with a hope more sweet,
> Groan for the hour, O Christ! of Thy
>   returning,
> Faint for the flaming of Thine advent feet.
> — *from St. Paul, by F. W. H. Myers*

OUTLINE

Commentary†

I. GENEALOGY AND BIRTH OF THE MESSIAH-KING (Chap. 1)

A. The Genealogy of Jesus Christ (1:1–17)

A casual reading of the NT may cause a person to wonder why it begins with something as seemingly dull as a family tree. One might conclude that there is little significance to be drawn from this catalog of names and, thus, skip over it to where the action begins.

However, the genealogy is indispensable. It lays the foundation for all that follows. Unless it can be shown that Jesus is a legal descendant of David through the royal line, it is impossible to prove that He is the Messiah-King of Israel. Matthew begins his account where he must — with the documentary evi-

†*See p. ix.*

dence that Jesus inherited the legal right to the throne of David through His stepfather, Joseph.

This genealogy traces the *legal* descent of Jesus as King of Israel; the genealogy in Luke's Gospel traces His *lineal* descent as Son of David. Matthew's genealogy follows the *royal* line from David through his son, Solomon, the next king; Luke's genealogy follows the *blood* line from David through another son, Nathan. This genealogy concludes with Joseph, of whom Jesus was the *adopted* Son; the genealogy in Luke 3 probably traces the ancestry of Mary, of whom Jesus was the *real* Son.

A millennium earlier, God had made an unconditional agreement with David, promising him a kingdom that would last forever and a perpetually ruling line (Ps. 89:4, 36, 37). That covenant is now fulfilled in Christ: He is legal heir to the throne of David through Joseph and the actual seed of David through Mary. Because He lives forever, His kingdom will last forever and He will reign forever as David's greater Son. Jesus united in His Person the only two bases for claims to the throne of Israel (the legal and the lineal); since He still lives, there can be no other claimant.

1:1–15† The formula **the book of the genealogy of Jesus Christ, the Son of David, the Son of Abraham** is similar to the expression in Genesis 5:1: "This is the book of the genealogy of Adam." Genesis introduces the first Adam; Matthew, the last Adam. The first Adam was head of the first, or physical, creation. Christ, as the last Adam, is Head of the new, or spiritual, creation.

The subject of this Gospel is **Jesus Christ**. The name **Jesus** presents Him as Jehovah-Savior;[1] the title **Christ** ("Anointed"), as the long awaited Messiah of Israel. The title **Son of David** is associated with the roles of both Messiah and King in the OT. The title **Son of Abraham** presents our Lord as the One who is the ultimate fulfillment of the promises made to the progenitor of the Hebrew people.††

The genealogy is divided into three historical sections: from Abraham to Jesse, from David to Josiah, and from Jeconiah to Joseph. The first section leads up to David; the second covers the king-dom period; the third preserves the record of royal descent during the exile (586 B.C. and following).

There are many interesting features in this register. For example, in this paragraph, four women are mentioned: **Tamar, Rahab, Ruth,** and Bathsheba **(her who had been the wife of Uriah)**. Since women are seldom mentioned in eastern genealogical tables, the inclusion of these women is all the more astonishing in that two of them were harlots (Tamar and Rahab), one had committed adultery (Bathsheba), and two were Gentiles (Rahab and Ruth). Their inclusion in Matthew's introduction is perhaps a subtle suggestion that the coming of Christ would bring salvation to sinners, grace to Gentiles, and that in Him, barriers of race and sex would be torn down.

Of interest too is the mention of a king named **Jeconiah**. In Jeremiah 22:30 God pronounced a curse on this man:

Thus says the LORD:
"Write this man down as childless,
A man who shall not prosper in
　his days;
For none of his descendants
　shall prosper,
Sitting on the throne of David,
And ruling anymore in Judah."

If Jesus had been the *real* son of Joseph, He would have come under this curse. Yet He had to be the legal son of Joseph in order to inherit the rights to the throne of David. The problem was solved by the miracle of the virgin birth: Jesus was the *legal* heir to the throne through Joseph. He was the *real* Son of David through Mary. The curse on Jeconiah did not fall on Mary or her children since she did not descend from Jeconiah.

1:16 Of whom in English could be construed as referring to both Joseph and Mary. However, in the original Greek, **whom** is singular and in the feminine gender, thus indicating that Jesus was born **of Mary**, but not of **Joseph**. But in addition to these interesting features of the genealogy, mention must also be made of the difficulties which it presents.

1:17 Matthew draws special attention to the fact that there are three sections of **fourteen generations** each. However, we know from the OT that

---

†See p. xviii.
††See p. xviii.

certain names are missing from his list. For example, between Joram and Uzziah (v. 8), Ahaziah, Joash, and Amaziah reigned as kings (see 2 Kgs. 8–14; 2 Chron. 21–25).

The genealogies of Matthew and Luke seem to overlap in mentioning two names: Shealtiel and Zerubbabel (Matt. 1:12, 13; Luke 3:27). It is strange that the ancestry of Joseph and Mary should merge in these two men, and separate again. The difficulty is increased when we notice that both Gospels follow Ezra 3:2 in listing Zerubbabel as the son of Shealtiel, whereas in 1 Chronicles 3:19 he is listed as the son of Pedaiah.

A third difficulty is that Matthew counts twenty-seven generations from David to Jesus, while Luke gives forty-two. Even though the evangelists are outlining different family trees, it still seems odd that there should be such a difference in the number of generations.

What attitude should the Bible student take toward these difficulties and seeming discrepancies? First, our foundational premise is that the Bible is the inspired Word of God. Therefore, it cannot contain errors. Second, it is infinite because it reflects the infinity of the Godhead. We can understand the fundamental truths of the Word, but we can never fully comprehend all there is in it.

So, our approach to these difficulties leads us to conclude that the problem lies in our lack of knowledge rather than in the Bible's fallibility. Bible problems should challenge us to study and search for the answers. "It is the glory of God to conceal a matter, but the glory of kings is to search out a matter" (Prov. 25:2).

Careful research by historians and excavations by archaeologists have not been able to demonstrate that the statements of the Bible are false. What seem to us like difficulties and contradictions all have reasonable explanations, and these explanations are filled with spiritual significance and profit.

B. Jesus Christ Is Born of Mary (1:18–25)

1:18 The birth of Jesus Christ was different from any of the births mentioned in the genealogy. There we found the repeated formula: "A begot B." But now we have the record of a birth without a human father. The facts surrounding this miraculous conception are stated with dignity and simplicity. **Mary** had been promised in marriage **to Joseph**, but the wedding had not yet taken place. In NT times, betrothal was a form of engagement (but more binding than engagement today) and it could be broken only by divorce. Although an engaged couple did not live together until the marriage ceremony, unfaithfulness on the part of the betrothed was treated as adultery and punishable by death.

During the time of her betrothal, the Virgin Mary became pregnant by a miracle of **the Holy Spirit**. An angel had previously announced this mysterious event to Mary: "The Holy Spirit will come upon you, and the power of the Highest will overshadow you" (Luke 1:35). A cloud of suspicion and scandal hung over Mary. In all of human history there had never been a virgin birth. When people saw an unwed woman who was pregnant, they had only one possible explanation.

1:19 Even **Joseph** did not yet know the true explanation of Mary's condition. He might have been indignant at his fiancée on two counts: First, her apparent unfaithfulness to him; and second, though innocent, he would almost inevitably be accused of complicity. His love for Mary and desire for justice led him to decide to break the betrothal by a quiet divorce. He wished to avoid the public disgrace which normally accompanied such an action.

1:20 While this gentle and deliberate man was mapping his strategy to protect Mary, **an angel of the Lord appeared to him in a dream**. The salutation, **"Joseph, son of David,"** was doubtless designed to stir up the consciousness of his royal pedigree and to prepare him for the unusual advent of Israel's Messiah-King. He should have no misgivings about marrying **Mary**. Any suspicions concerning her purity were groundless. Her pregnancy was a miracle of **the Holy Spirit**.

1:21 The angel then revealed the unborn Child's sex, name, and mission. Mary would bear **a Son**. He was to be named **JESUS**, (which means "Jehovah is salvation" or "Jehovah, the Savior").

True to His Name, He would **save His people from their sins**. This Child of destiny was Jehovah Himself, visiting earth to save people from the penalty of sin, from the power of sin, and eventually from the very presence of sin.

1:22 As Matthew recorded these events, he realized that a new era had dawned in the history of God's dealings with the human race. The words of a messianic prophecy, long dormant, had now sprung to life. Isaiah's cryptic prophecy was now fulfilled in Mary's Child: **So all this was done that it might be fulfilled which was spoken by the Lord through the prophet**. Matthew claims divine inspiration for the words of Isaiah — the Lord had spoken by the prophet at least 700 years before Christ.

1:23 The prophecy of Isaiah 7:14 included the foretelling of a unique birth ("Behold, the virgin shall conceive"), the sex of the Child ("and bear a Son"), and the name of the child ("and [she] shall call His name Immanuel"). Matthew adds the explanation that **Immanuel** means **God with us**. There is no record of Christ ever being called "Immanuel" while on earth; He was always called "Jesus." However, the meaning of the name *Jesus* (see above on v. 21) implies the presence of **God with us**. Immanuel might also be a designation for Christ which will be used primarily in His Second Advent.

1:24 As a result of the angel's intervention, Joseph abandoned his plan to divorce Mary. He continued to recognize their betrothal until Jesus' birth, after which he married her.

1:25 The teaching that Mary remained a virgin all of her life is disproved by the consummation of their marriage mentioned in this verse. Other references which indicate that Mary had children by Joseph are Matthew 12:46; 13:55, 56; Mark 6:3; John 7:3, 5; Acts 1:14; 1 Corinthians 9:5; and Galatians 1:19.

In taking Mary as his wife, Joseph also took her Child as his adopted Son. This is how Jesus became legal heir to the throne of David. In obedience to the angelic visitor, **he called** the Baby's **name Jesus**.

Thus the Messiah-King was born. The Eternal One entered time. The Omnipotent became a tiny Infant. The Lord of glory veiled that glory in a human body, and "in Him dwells all the fullness of the Godhead bodily" (Col. 2:9).

II. EARLY YEARS OF THE MESSIAH-KING (Chap. 2)

A. Wise Men Come to Worship the King (2:1–12)

2:1, 2 It is easy to be confused about the chronology of the events surrounding Christ's birth. While verse 1 may appear to indicate that Herod tried to kill Jesus during Mary and Joseph's stay in the stable at Bethlehem,† the combined evidence points to a time one or two years later. Matthew says in verse 11 that the wise men saw Jesus in a house. The order by Herod to execute all male children under two years old (v. 16) also is an indication of the passage of an unspecified period of time since the royal birth.

Herod the Great was a descendant of Esau and, therefore, a traditional enemy of the Jews. He was a convert to Judaism, but his conversion was perhaps politically motivated. It was toward the close of his reign that **wise men from the East came** in search of the **King of the Jews**. These men might have been pagan priests whose ritual centered around the elements of nature. Because of their knowledge and predictive powers, they were often chosen as counselors to kings. We do not know where they lived in the East, how many there were, nor how long their journey lasted.

It was the **star in the East** that somehow made them aware of the birth of a **King, whom they came to worship**. Possibly they were familiar with OT prophecies concerning the Messiah's arrival. Perhaps they knew of Balaam's prediction that a Star would come out of Jacob (Num. 24:17) and connected this with the prophecy of seventy weeks which foretold the time of Christ's first coming (Dan. 9:24, 25). But it seems more probable that the knowledge was communicated to them supernaturally.

Various scientific explanations have been offered to account for the star. Some say, for instance, that it was a conjunction of planets. But the course of this star was highly irregular; it went before

†*See pp. x–xi.*

the wise men, leading them from Jerusalem to the house where Jesus was living (v. 9). Then it stopped. In fact, it was so unusual that it can only be accounted for as a miracle.

2:3 When Herod the king heard that a Baby had been born who was to be king of the Jews, **he was troubled**. Any such Baby was a threat to his uneasy rule. **All Jerusalem** was troubled **with him**. The city that should have received the news with joy was disturbed by anything that might upset its status quo or risk the displeasure of the hated Roman rulers.

2:4–6 Herod assembled the Jewish religious leaders to find out **where the Christ was to be born**. The **chief priests** were the high priest and his sons (and perhaps other members of his family). The **scribes of the people** were lay experts in the Law of Moses. They preserved and taught the law and served as judges in the Sanhedrin. These priests and scribes promptly quoted Micah 5:2 which identified **Bethlehem of Judea** as the King's birthplace. The text of the prophecy in Micah calls the city "Bethlehem Ephrathah." Since there was more than one town called Bethlehem in Palestine, this identifies it as the one in the district of Ephrathah within the tribal boundaries of Judah.

2:7, 8 King Herod . . . secretly called the wise men to determine **what time the star** first **appeared**. This secrecy betrayed his sadistic motive: he would need this information if he was unable to locate the right Child. To cover up his real intention, **he sent** the magi on their **search** and requested that they send **back word** to him of their success.

2:9 As the wise men set out, **the star which they had seen in the East** reappeared. This indicates that the star had not guided them all the way from the East. But now it did guide them to the house **where the young Child was.**

2:10 Special mention is made of the **exceedingly great joy** of the wise men **when they saw the star**. These Gentiles diligently sought for Christ; Herod planned to kill Him; the priests and scribes were (as yet) indifferent; the people of Jerusalem were troubled. These attitudes were omens of the way in which the Messiah would be received.

2:11 When they entered the house, the magi saw **the young Child with Mary His mother**. They **fell down and worshiped Him,** offering costly **gifts** of **gold, frankincense, and myrrh**. Notice that they saw Jesus with His mother. Ordinarily mention would be made of a mother first, then her child, but this Child is unique and must be given first place (see also vv. 13, 14, 20, 21). The wise men worshiped Jesus, *not* Mary or Joseph. (Joseph is not even mentioned in this account; he will soon disappear entirely from the Gospel record.) It is Jesus who deserves our praise and worship, not Mary or Joseph.

The treasures they brought spoke volumes. **Gold** is a symbol of deity and glory; it speaks of the shining perfection of His divine Person. **Frankincense** is an ointment or perfume; it suggests the fragrance of the life of sinless perfection. **Myrrh** is a bitter herb; it presages the sufferings He would endure in bearing the sins of the world. The bringing of gifts by Gentiles is reminiscent of the language of Isaiah 60:6. Isaiah predicted that Gentiles would come to the Messiah with gifts, but mentioned only gold and frankincense: ". . . they shall bring gold and incense. And they shall proclaim the praises of the Lord." Why was myrrh omitted? Because Isaiah was speaking of Christ's second advent — His coming in power and great glory. There will be no myrrh then because He will not suffer then. But in Matthew the myrrh is included because His first coming is in view. In Matthew we have the sufferings of Christ; in this passage of Isaiah, the glories that shall follow.

2:12 The wise men were **divinely warned in a dream . . .** not to **return to Herod,** and so they obediently returned to their homes by another route. No one who meets Christ with a sincere heart ever returns the same way. True encounter with Him transforms all of life.

B. Joseph, Mary, and Jesus Flee to Egypt (2:13–15)

2:13, 14† From infancy the threat of death hung over our Lord. It is apparent that He was born to die, but only at the appointed time. Anyone, who walks in God's will is immortal until his work is done. **An angel of the Lord** warned Jo-

†*See p. xvix.*

seph in a dream to flee to Egypt with his family. Herod was ready to embark on his "search and destroy" mission. The family became refugees from the wrath of Herod. We do not know how long they stayed, but with the death of Herod, the coast was clear for their repatriation.

2:15 Thus, another OT prophecy became clothed with new meaning. God had said **through the prophet** Hosea: **"Out of Egypt I called My Son"** (Hos. 11:1). In its original setting this referred to Israel's deliverance from Egypt at the time of the exodus. But the statement is capable of a double meaning — the Messiah's history would closely parallel that of Israel. The prophecy was fulfilled in the life of Christ by His return to Israel from Egypt.

When the Lord returns to reign in righteousness, Egypt will be one of the countries sharing in the blessings of the Millennium (Isa. 19:21–25; Zeph. 3:9, 10; Ps. 68:31). Why should that nation, a traditional enemy of Israel, be so favored? Could it be a token of divine gratitude for its granting sanctuary to the Lord Jesus?

C. Herod Massacres the Babies of Bethlehem (2:16–18)[†]

2:16 When the wise men failed to return, **Herod** realized that he had been **deceived** in his plot to locate the young King. In senseless rage, he ordered the **death** of **all the male children** under the age of **two in Bethlehem and in all its districts**. Estimates vary as to the number slain; one writer suggests about twenty-six. It is not likely that hundreds were involved.

2:17, 18 The **weeping** which followed the killing of the children was a fulfillment of the words of **Jeremiah the prophet**:

Thus says the LORD:
"A voice was heard in Ramah,
Lamentation and bitter weeping,
Rachel weeping for her children,
Refusing to be comforted for her
        children,
Because they are no more"
        (Jer. 31:15).

In the prophecy, **Rachel** represents the nation Israel. The grief of the nation is attributed to Rachel, who was buried

in **Ramah** (near Bethlehem, where the massacre took place). As the bereaved parents passed her tomb, she is pictured as **weeping** with them. In his effort to eliminate this young Rival, Herod gained nothing but dishonorable mention in the annals of infamy.

D. Joseph, Mary, and Jesus Settle in Nazareth (2:19–23)

After Herod's death, **an angel of the Lord** assured **Joseph** that it was now safe to return. When he reached **the land of Israel,** however, **he heard that** Herod's son **Archelaus** had succeeded **his father** as king of **Judea.** Joseph was reluctant to venture into this region and so, after his fears were confirmed **by God in a dream,** he traveled north to **the region of Galilee** and settled in **Nazareth.**

For the fourth time in this chapter, Matthew reminds us that prophecy was being **fulfilled.** He mentions none of **the prophets** by name, but says that the prophets had foretold that the Messiah would **be called a Nazarene.** No OT verse says this directly. Many scholars suggest Matthew is referring to Isaiah 11:1: "There shall come forth a Rod from the stem of Jesse, and a Branch shall grow out of his roots." The Hebrew word translated "Rod" is *netzer,* but the connection seems remote. A more probable explanation is that "Nazarene" is used to describe anyone who lived in Nazareth, a town viewed with contempt by the rest of the people. Nathaniel expresses this by the proverbial question, "Can anything good come out of Nazareth?" (John 1:46). The scorn heaped upon this "unimportant" town fell upon its inhabitants as well. So when verse 23 says **He shall be called a Nazarene**, it means that He would be treated with contempt. Although we cannot find any prophecy that Jesus would be called a Nazarene, we can find one that says He would be "despised and rejected by men" (Isa. 53:3). Another says that He would be a worm and not a man, scorned and rejected by people (Ps. 22:6). So while the prophets did not use the exact words, this was undeniably the spirit of several prophecies.

It is amazing that when the mighty God came to earth, He was given a nickname of reproach. Those who follow Him are privileged to share His reproach (Heb. 13:13).

III. PREPARATIONS FOR THE MESSIAH'S MINISTRY AND HIS INAUGURATION (Chaps. 3, 4)

A. John the Baptist Prepares the Way (3:1–12)

Between chapters 2 and 3 is an interval of twenty-eight or twenty-nine years which Matthew does not mention. During this time, Jesus was in Nazareth, preparing for the work which lay ahead. They were years in which He performed no miracles, yet in which He found perfect delight in the eyes of God (Matt. 3:17). With this chapter we come to the threshold of His public ministry.

3:1, 2 John the Baptist was six months older than his cousin Jesus (see Luke 1:26, 36). He stepped onto the stage of history to serve as forerunner for the King of Israel. His unlikely parish was **the wilderness of Judea** — an arid area extending from Jerusalem to the Jordan. John's message was, **"Repent, for the kingdom of heaven is at hand!"** The King would soon appear, but He could not and would not reign over people who clung to their sins. They must change directions, must confess and forsake their sins. God was calling them from the kingdom of darkness to **the kingdom of heaven.**

THE KINGDOM OF HEAVEN

In verse 2 we have the first occurrence of the phrase the kingdom of heaven, which is used thirty-two times in this Gospel. Since a person cannot rightly understand Matthew without comprehending this concept, a definition and description of the term are in order here.

The kingdom of heaven is the sphere is which God's rule is acknowledged. The word "heaven" is used to denote God. This is shown in Daniel 4:25, where Daniel said that "the Most High" rules in the kingdom of men. In the next verse he says that "heaven" rules. Wherever people submit to the rule of God, there the kingdom of heaven exists.

There are two aspects of the kingdom of heaven. In its broadest sense it includes everyone who *professes* to acknowledge God as Supreme Ruler. In its narrower aspect it includes only those who have been genuinely *converted*. We may picture this by two concentric circles.

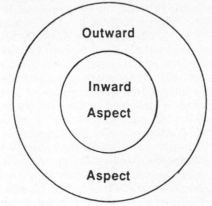

The big circle is the sphere of profession; it includes all who are genuine subjects of the King, and also those who only profess allegiance to Him. This is seen in the parables of the sower (Matt. 13:3–9), the mustard seed (Matt. 13:31, 32), and the leaven (Matt. 13:33). The little circle includes only those who have been born again through faith in the Lord Jesus Christ. The kingdom of heaven in its inward aspect can be entered only by those who are converted (Matt. 18:3).

By putting together all the references to the kingdom in the Bible, we can trace its historical development in five distinct phases:

First, the kingdom was *prophesied* in the OT. Daniel predicted that God would set up a kingdom that would never be destroyed nor yield its sovereignty to another people (Dan. 2:44). He also foresaw the coming of Christ to wield universal and everlasting dominion (Dan. 7:13, 14; see also Jer. 23:5, 6).

Second, the kingdom was described by John the Baptist, Jesus, and the twelve disciples as being *at hand* or *present* (Matt. 3:2; 4:17; 10:7). In Matthew 12:28, Jesus said, " . . . if I cast out demons by the Spirit of God, surely the kingdom of God has come upon you." In Luke 17:21, He said, "For indeed, the kingdom of God is within you" or in your midst. The kingdom was present in the Person of the King. As we shall show later, the terms kingdom of God and kingdom of heaven are used interchangeably.

Third, the kingdom is described in an *interim* form. After He was rejected by the nation of Israel, the King returned to heaven. The kingdom exists today, while the King is absent, in the hearts of all who acknowledge His kingship, and its moral and ethical principles, including the Sermon on the Mount, are applicable to us today. This interim phase of the kingdom is described in the parables of Matthew 13.

The fourth phase of the kingdom is what might be called its *manifestation*. This is the thousand-year reign of Christ on earth which was pictured by the Transfiguration of Christ when He was seen in the glory of His coming reign (Matt. 17:1–8). Jesus referred to this phase in Matthew 8:11 when He said, ". . . many will come from east and west, and sit down with Abraham, Isaac, and Jacob in the kingdom of heaven."

The final form will be the *everlasting* kingdom. It is described in 2 Peter 1:11 as "the everlasting kingdom of our Lord and Savior Jesus Christ."

The phrase "kingdom of heaven" is found only in Matthew's Gospel, but "kingdom of God" is found in all four Gospels. For all practical purposes there is no difference — the same things are said about both. For example, in Matthew 19:23 Jesus said that it would be hard for a rich man to enter the kingdom of *heaven*. Both Mark (10:23) and Luke (18:24) record that Jesus said this about the kingdom of *God* (see also Matt. 19:24 which has a similar maxim using "kingdom of God").

We mentioned above that the kingdom of heaven has an outward aspect and an inner reality. That the same is true of the kingdom of God is further proof that the two terms indicate the same thing. The kingdom of God, too, includes the real and the false. This is seen in the parables of the sower (Luke 8:4–10), the mustard seed (Luke 13:18, 19), and the leaven (Luke 13:20, 21). As to its true, inward reality, the kingdom of God can be entered only by those who are born again (John 3:3, 5).

One final point: the kingdom is not the same as the church. The kingdom began when Christ embarked on His public ministry; the church began on the day of Pentecost (Acts 2). The kingdom will continue on earth till the earth is destroyed; the church continues on earth till the Rapture (the catching away or removal of the church from earth when Christ descends from heaven and takes all believers home with Him — 1 Thess. 4:13–18). The church will return with Christ at His Second Advent to reign with Him as His bride. At present the people who are in the kingdom in its true, inner reality are also in the church. ‡

3:3 To return to the exposition of Matthew 3, note that the preparatory ministry of John had been prophesied by **Isaiah** over seven hundred years before his time:

The voice of one crying in the
    wilderness:
"Prepare the way of the LORD;
Make straight in the desert
A highway for our God" (40:3).

John was **the voice**. The nation of Israel, spiritually speaking, was **the wilderness** — dry and barren. John called on the people to **prepare the way of the LORD** by repenting of, and forsaking, their sins and to **make His paths straight** by removing from their lives anything that would hinder His complete dominion.

3:4 The Baptizer's garment was made of **camel's hair** — not the soft, luxurious camel's hair cloth of our day, but the coarse fabric of an outdoorsman. He also wore a **leather belt**. This was the same attire as that of Elijah (2 Kgs. 1:8) and perhaps served to alert believing Jews to the similarity between John's mission and that of Elijah (Mal. 4:5; Luke 1:17; Matt. 11:14; 17:10–12). John ate **locusts and wild honey**, the subsistence diet of one so consumed by his mission that the normal comforts and pleasures of life were sublimated.

It must have been a convicting, scalding experience to meet John — a man who cared for none of the things that people ordinarily live for. His absorption with spiritual realities must have made others realize how poor they were. His self-renunciation was a stinging rebuke to the worldliness of his day.

3:5, 6 People flocked to hear him from **Jerusalem, all Judea**, and the trans-Jordan area. Some of the people responded to his message and **were baptized by him in the Jordan**, saying in effect that they were ready to give full allegiance and obedience to the coming King.

3:7 With **the Pharisees and Sadducees** it was a different story. When they came to listen to him, John knew that they were not sincere. He recognized their true nature: **the Pharisees** professed great devotion to the law, but they were inwardly corrupt, sectarian, hypocritical, and self-righteous; the **Sadducees** were social aristocrats and religious skeptics who denied such basic doctrines as the resurrection of the body, the existence of angels, the immortality of the soul, and eternal punishment. Therefore he denounced both sects as a **brood of vipers**, who pretended to desire to escape **from the wrath to come**, but exhibited no signs of true repentance.

3:8 He challenged them to prove their sincerity by bearing **fruits worthy of repentance**. True repentance, as J. R. Miller wrote, "amounts to nothing whatever if it produces only a few tears, a spasm of regret, a little fright. We must leave the sins we repent of and walk in the new, clean ways of holiness."

3:9 The Jews should stop presuming on their descent from **Abraham** as a passport to heaven. The grace of salvation is not transmitted in natural birth. God could make the **stones** of the Jordan into **children** of **Abraham** by a less violent process than the conversion of the Pharisees and Sadducees.

3:10 By stating that **the ax is laid to the root of the trees**, John was saying that a work of divine judgment was about to begin. Christ's arrival and presence would test all men. Those found fruitless would be destroyed just as a fruitless tree . . . **is cut down and thrown into the fire**.

3:11, 12 In verses 7–10, John had been speaking exclusively to the Phari-sees and Sadducees (see. v. 7), but now he apparently addresses his entire audience, which included both the true and the false. He explained that there was a significant difference between his ministry and that of the Messiah who would soon arrive. John baptized **with water unto repentance**: the **water** was ceremonial and had no cleansing power; the **repentance**, though real, did not bring a person to full salvation. John viewed his ministry as preparatory and partial. The Messiah would completely overshadow John. He would be **mightier**, He would be more worthy, His work would reach farther, for He would **baptize . . . with the Holy Spirit and fire.**

The baptism **with the Holy Spirit** is distinct from the baptism with **fire**. The former is a baptism of blessing, the latter of judgment. The former took place at Pentecost, the latter is still future. The former is enjoyed by all true believers in the Lord Jesus, the latter will be the fate of all unbelievers. The former would be for those Israelites whose baptism was an outward sign of inward repentance, the latter would be for the Pharisees, Sadducees, and all who showed no evidence of true repentance.

Some teach that the baptism with the Holy Spirit and the baptism with fire are the same event, i.e., could not the baptism with fire refer to the tongues of fire that appeared when the Spirit was given at Pentecost? In light of verse 12 which equates fire with judgment, it probably does not.

Immediately after his reference to the baptism of fire, John speaks of judgment. The Lord is pictured using a **winnowing fan** to toss the threshed grain into the wind. The **wheat** (true believers) falls directly to the ground and is carried **into the barn. The chaff** (unbelievers) is carried a short distance away by the wind and then gathered and burned **with unquenchable fire**. The fire in verse 12 means judgment, and since this verse is an amplification of verse 11, it is reasonable to conclude that the baptism with fire is a baptism of judgment.

B. John Baptizes Jesus (3:13–17)

3:13 Jesus walked approximately sixty miles **from Galilee** to **the** lower **Jordan** River **to be baptized by** John. This indicates the importance which He attached to this ceremony and it should indicate the significance of baptism for His followers today.

3:14, 15 Realizing that Jesus had no sins of which to repent, **John** protested against baptizing Him. It was a true instinct that led him to suggest that the proper order would be for Jesus to baptize him. Jesus did not deny this; He simply repeated His request for baptism as a **fitting** way in which **to fulfill all righteousness**. He felt it appropriate that in baptism He identify Himself with those godly Israelites who were coming to be baptized unto repentance.

But there was an even deeper meaning. Baptism for Him was a ritual symbolizing the way in which He would fulfill all the righteous claims of God against man's sin. His immersion typified His baptism in the waters of God's judgment at Calvary. His emergence from the water foreshadowed His resurrection. By death, burial, and resurrection, He would satisfy the demands of divine justice and provide a righteous basis by which sinners could be justified.

3:16, 17† As soon as He came up **from the water**, Jesus **saw the Spirit of God descending** from heaven **like a dove and alighting upon Him**. Just as persons and things in the OT were consecrated to sacred purposes by "the holy anointing oil" (Ex. 30:25–30), so He was anointed Messiah by the Holy Spirit.

It was a hallowed occasion, when all three members of the Trinity were evident. The **beloved Son** was there. The Holy **Spirit** was there in **dove** form. The Father's **voice** was heard **from heaven** pronouncing His blessing on Jesus. It was a memorable event because the voice of God was heard quoting Scripture: **"This is My beloved Son** (from Ps. 2:7) **in whom I am well pleased"** (from Isa. 42:1). This is one of three occasions when the Father spoke from heaven in delighted acknowledgment of His unique Son (the other places are Matt. 17:5 and John 12:28).

C. Jesus Is Tempted by Satan (4:1–11)

4:1 It may seem strange that Jesus should be **led up by the Spirit** into temptation. Why should the Holy Spirit lead Him into such an encounter? The answer is that this temptation was necessary to demonstrate His moral fitness to do the work for which He had come into the world. The first Adam proved his unfitness for dominion when he met the adversary in the Garden of Eden. Here the last Adam meets the devil in a head-on confrontation and emerges unscathed.

The Greek word translated "tempt" or "test" has two meanings: (1) to test or prove (John 6:6; 2 Cor. 13:5; Heb. 11:17); and (2) to solicit to evil. The Holy Spirit tested or proved Christ. The devil sought to lure Him to do evil.

There is deep mystery connected with the temptation of our Lord. Inevitably the question arises, "Could He have sinned?" If we answer "No," then we must face the further question, "How could it be a real temptation if He could not yield?" If we answer "Yes," we are faced with the problem of how God incarnate could sin.

It is of first importance to remember that Jesus Christ is God and that God cannot sin. It is true that He is also human; however, to say that He could sin as a human but not as God is to build a case without scriptural foundation. The NT writers wrote of the sinlessness of Christ on several occasions. Paul wrote that He "knew no sin" (2 Cor. 5:21); Peter says that He "committed no sin" (1 Pet. 2:22); and John says, "in Him there is no sin" (1 Jn. 3:5).

Like us, Jesus could be tempted from without: Satan came to Him with suggestions contrary to the will of God. But unlike us, He could not be tempted from within — no sinful lusts or passions could originate in Him. Furthermore, there was nothing in Him that would respond to the devil's seductions (John 14:30).

Despite Jesus' inability to sin, the temptation was very real. It was possible for Him to be faced with enticements to sin, but it was morally impossible for Him to yield. He could only do what He saw the Father doing (John 5:19), and it is inconceivable that He would ever see the Father sinning. He could do nothing on His own authority (John 5:30), and the Father would never give Him the authority to yield to temptation.

The purpose of the temptation was not to see if He would sin, but to prove that even under tremendous pressure He could do nothing but obey the Word of God.

If Jesus could sin as a human being, we are faced with the problem of His still being a human in heaven. Could He still sin? Obviously, no.

4:2, 3 After fasting **forty days and forty nights**, Jesus **was hungry**. (The number **forty** in Scripture is frequently used in contexts of testing or probation.) This natural appetite provided **the tempter** with an advantage which in many people he could exploit. He suggested that Jesus use His miraculous power to convert the **stones** of the desert into loaves of **bread**. The introductory words, **"If You are the Son of God,"** do not imply doubt. They actually mean "Since You are the Son of God." The devil is alluding to the words of the Father to Jesus at the baptism, "This is My beloved Son." He uses a Greek construction[2] which assumes the statement to be true and, thereby, he calls on Jesus to exercise His power to appease His hunger.

To fulfill a natural appetite by using divine power in response to Satan's prompting is in direct disobedience to God. The idea behind Satan's suggestion is an echo of Genesis 3:6 ("good for food"). John classifies this temptation as "the lust of the flesh" (1 Jn. 2:16). Our corresponding temptation is to live for the gratification of natural desires, to choose a pathway of comfort instead of seeking the kingdom of God and His righteousness. The devil says, "You have to live, don't you?"

4:4 Jesus **answered** the temptation by quoting the Word of God. Our Lord's example teaches that we *don't* have to live, but we *do* have to obey God! Getting **bread** is *not* the most important thing in life. Obedience to **every word** of **God** is. Since Jesus had received no instructions from the Father to turn stones into bread, He would not act on His own and thus obey Satan, no matter how intense His hunger.

4:5, 6 The second temptation took place in Jerusalem on the **pinnacle of the temple. The devil** challenged Jesus to **throw** Himself **down** as a spectacular display of His divine Sonship. Again, the opening word **if** does not imply doubt,

as is seen in Satan's reference to the protection promised to the Messiah by God in Psalm 91:11, 12.

The temptation was for Jesus to demonstrate that He was Messiah by performing a sensational stunt. He could achieve glory without suffering; He could bypass the cross and still reach the throne. But this action would be outside the will of God. John describes this appeal as "the pride of life" (1 Jn. 2:16). It resembles the "tree desirable to make one wise" (Gen. 3:6) in the Garden of Eden, as both were a means of achieving personal glory in disregard of God's will. This temptation comes to us in the desire to attain religious prominence apart from the fellowship of His suffering. We seek great things for ourselves, then run and hide when difficulties come our way. When we ignore God's will and exalt ourselves, we tempt God.

4:7 Again, **Jesus** resisted the attack by quoting Scripture: **"It is written again, 'You shall not tempt the Lord your God'"** (see Deut. 6:16). God had promised to preserve the Messiah, but that guarantee presupposed living in God's will. To claim the promise in an act of disobedience would be tempting God. The time would come when Jesus would be revealed as Messiah, but the cross must come first. The altar of sacrifice must precede the throne. The crown of thorns must precede the crown of glory. Jesus would await God's time and would accomplish God's will.

4:8, 9 In the third temptation **the devil took** Jesus **up on an exceedingly high mountain, and showed Him all the kingdoms of the world**. He offered them to Jesus in exchange for His **worship**. Although this temptation had to do with **worship**, an exercise of the spirit, it was an effort to induce our Lord to grasp imperial power over the world by worshiping Satan. The reward offered, **all the kingdoms of the world** with their grandeur, appealed to "the lust of the eyes" (1 Jn. 2:16).

In a sense, the kingdoms of the world *do* belong to the devil at present. He is spoken of as "the god of this age" (2 Cor. 4:4), and John tells us that "the whole world lies under the sway of the wicked one" (1 Jn. 5:19). When Jesus appears at the Second Advent as King of kings (Rev. 19:16), then "the kingdoms of this world" become His (Rev. 11:15). Jesus would not violate the divine timetable, and certainly He would never worship Satan!

For us the temptation is twofold: to barter our spiritual birthright for the passing glory of this world, and to worship and serve the creature rather than the Creator.

4:10 For the third time, Jesus resisted temptation by using the OT: **"You shall worship the LORD your God, and Him only you shall serve."** Worship and the service that flows from it are for God alone. To worship Satan would be tantamount to acknowledging him as God.

The order of the temptations as recorded by Matthew varies from that in Luke (4:1–13). Some have suggested that Matthew's order parallels the order of the temptations that Israel faced in the wilderness (Ex. 16; 17; 32). Jesus showed Himself in perfect contrast to Israel's response to hardship.

4:11 When Jesus had successfully rebutted Satan's temptations, **the devil left Him**. Temptations come in waves rather than in a steady flow. "When the enemy comes in like flood, the Spirit of the Lord will lift up a standard against him" (Isa. 59:19). What an encouragement for God's tested saints!

We are told that **angels came and ministered to Him**, but no explanation is given for this supernatural assistance. It probably means that they provided the physical nourishment for Him which He had refused to provide at Satan's suggestion.

From the temptation of Jesus, we learn that the devil can attack those who are controlled by the Holy Spirit, but that he is powerless against those who resist him with the Word of God.

D. Jesus Begins His Galilean Ministry (4:12–17)†

The Judean ministry of Jesus, which lasted almost one year, is not discussed by Matthew. This one year period is covered in John 1–4 and fits between Matthew 4:11 and 4:12. Matthew takes us from the temptation directly to the Galilean ministry.

4:12 When Jesus heard that **John** the Baptist **had been put in prison**, He rea-

†See p. xii.

lized that this was an omen of His own rejection. In rejecting the King's forerunner, the people were, for all practical purposes, rejecting the King also. But it was not fear that drove Him north **to Galilee**. Actually He was going right into the center of Herod's kingdom — the same king who had just imprisoned John. In moving to Galilee of the Gentiles, He was showing that His rejection by the Jews would result in the gospel going out to the Gentiles.

4:13†† Jesus remained in **Nazareth** until the populace tried to kill Him for proclaiming salvation for the Gentiles (see Luke 4:16–30). Then He moved to **Capernaum** by the Sea of Galilee, an area originally populated by the tribes of **Zebulun and Napthali**. From this time, Capernaum became His headquarters.

4:14–16 Jesus' move to Galilee was a fulfillment of **Isaiah** 9:1, 2. The ignorant, superstitious **Gentiles** living in **Galilee** saw **a great light** — that is Christ, the **Light** of the world.

4:17 From then on **Jesus** took up the message which John had preached: **"Repent, for the kingdom of heaven is at hand."** It was a further call for moral renewal in preparation for His kingdom. The kingdom was near in the sense that the King was present.

E. Jesus Calls Four Fishermen (4:18–22)

4:18, 19 This is actually the second time Jesus called **Peter and Andrew**. In John 1:35–42 they were called to salvation; here they are called to service. The first took place in Judea; this one in Galilee. Peter and Andrew **were fishermen**, but Jesus called them to be **fishers of men**. Their responsibility was to **follow** Christ. His responsibility was to **make** them successful fishermen. Their following of Christ involved more than physical nearness. It included their imitation of the character of Christ. Theirs was to be a ministry of character. What they were was more important than what they said or did. Just as with Peter and Andrew, we are to avoid the temptation to substitute eloquence, personality, or clever arguments for true spirituality. In following Christ, the disciple learns to go where the fish are swimming, to use the proper lure, to endure discomfort and

††See p. xx.

inconvenience, to be patient, and to keep out of sight.

4:20 Peter and Andrew heard the call and responded **immediately**. In true faith, they **left their nets**. In true commitment and devotion they **followed** Jesus.

4:21, 22 The call came next to **James** and **John**. They, too, became instant disciples. Leaving not only their means of livelihood but **their father** as well, they acknowledged the priority of Jesus over all earthly ties.

By responding to the call of Christ, these fishermen became key figures in the evangelization of the world. Had they remained at their nets, we would never have heard of them. Recognition of the lordship of Christ makes all the difference in the world.

F. Jesus Heals a Great Multitude (4:23–25)

The ministry of the Lord Jesus was threefold: He taught God's Word **in** the **synagogues**; He preached **the gospel of the kingdom**; and He healed the sick. One purpose of the miracles of healing was to authenticate His person and ministry (Heb. 2:3, 4). Chapters 5–7 are an example of His teaching ministry and chapters 8–9 describe His miracles.

4:23 Verse 23 is the first use of **gospel** in the NT. The term means "good news of salvation." In every age of the world's history there has been only one gospel, only one way of salvation.

THE GOSPEL

The gospel originates in the grace of God (Eph. 2:8). That means that God gives eternal life freely to sinful people who don't deserve it.

The basis of the gospel is the work of Christ on the cross (1 Cor. 15:1–4). Our Savior fulfilled all the claims of divine justice, enabling God to justify believing sinners. Old Testament believers were saved through the work of Christ, even though it was still future. They probably did not know much about the Messiah, but God did — and He imputed the value of Christ's work to their account. In a sense they were saved "on credit." We, too, are saved through the work of Christ, but in our case, the work has already been finished.

The gospel is received by faith alone (Eph. 2:8). In the OT, people were saved by believing whatever God had told them. In this age, people are saved by believing God's testimony concerning His Son as the only way of salvation (1 Jn. 5:11, 12). The ultimate goal of the gospel is heaven. We have the hope of eternity in heaven (2 Cor. 5:6–10), just as OT saints did (Heb. 11:10, 14–16).

While there is only one gospel, there are different features of the gospel in different times. For instance, there is a different emphasis between the gospel of the kingdom and the gospel of the grace of God. The gospel of the kingdom says, "Repent and receive the Messiah; then you will enter His kingdom when it is set up on earth." The gospel of grace says, "Repent and receive Christ; then you will be taken up to meet Him and to be with Him forever." Fundamentally, they are the same gospel — salvation by grace through faith — but they show that there are different administrations of the gospel according to God's dispensational purposes.

When Jesus preached the gospel of the kingdom, He was announcing His coming as King of the Jews and explaining the terms of admission into His kingdom. His miracles showed the wholesome nature of the kingdom.[3] ‡

4:24, 25 **His fame** spread **throughout all Syria** (the territory north and northeast of Israel). All the **sick people, demon-possessed**, and disabled felt His healing touch. People thronged to Him from **Galilee**, the **Decapolis** (a confederation of ten Gentile cities in northeastern Palestine), **Jerusalem, Judea** and the region east of **the Jordan** River. As. B. B. Warfield wrote: "Disease and death must have been almost eliminated for a brief season from . . . the region." No wonder the public was greatly astonished at the reports they were hearing from Galilee!

IV. THE CONSTITUTION OF THE KINGDOM (Chaps. 5–7)

It is no accident that the Sermon on the Mount is placed near the beginning of the NT. Its position indicates its importance. In it the King summarizes the character and conduct expected of His subjects.

This sermon is *not* a presentation of the plan of salvation; nor is its teaching intended for unsaved people. It was addressed to the disciples (5:1, 2) and was intended to be the constitution, or the system of laws and principles, which was to govern the King's subjects during His reign. It was meant for all — past, present, or future — who acknowledge Christ as King. When Christ was on earth, it had direct application to His disciples. Now, while our Lord reigns in heaven, it applies to all who crown Him King in their hearts. Finally, it will be the code of behavior for Christ's followers during the Tribulation and during His reign on earth.

The Sermon has a distinct Jewish flavor, as seen in allusions to the council (i.e., the Sanhedrin) in 5:22, the altar (5:23, 24), and Jerusalem (5:35). Yet it would be wrong to say that its teaching is exclusively for believing Israelites in the past or future; it is for those of every age who acknowledge Jesus Christ as King.

A. The Beatitudes (5:1–12)

5:1, 2 The sermon opens with the Beatitudes, or blessings. These set forth the ideal citizen of Christ's kingdom. The qualities described and approved are the opposite of those that the world values. A. W. Tozer describes them thus: "A fairly accurate description of the human race might be furnished one unacquainted with it by taking the Beatitudes, turning them wrong side out, and saying, 'Here is your human race.' "

5:3 This first blessing is pronounced on **the poor in spirit**. This does not refer to natural disposition, but to one's deliberate choice and discipline. **The poor in spirit** are those who acknowledge their own helplessness and rely on God's omnipotence. They sense their spiritual need and find it supplied in the Lord. **The kingdom of heaven**, where self-sufficiency is no virtue and self-exaltation is a vice, belongs to such people.

5:4 Those who mourn are **blessed**; a day of comfort awaits them. This does not refer to mourning because of the vicissitudes of life. It is the sorrow which one experiences because of fellowship

with the Lord Jesus. It is an active sharing of the world's hurt and sin with Jesus. Therefore, it includes, not only sorrow for one's own sin, but also sorrow because of the world's appalling condition, it's rejection of the Savior, and the doom of those who refuse His mercy. These mourners **shall be comforted** in the coming day when "God shall wipe away every tear from their eyes" (Rev. 21:4). Believers do all their mourning in this life; for unbelievers, today's grief is only a foretaste of eternal sorrow.

5:5 A third blessing is pronounced on **the meek**: **they shall inherit the earth**. By nature these people might be volatile, temperamental, and gruff. But by purposefully taking Christ's spirit on them, they become **meek** or gentle (compare Matthew 11:29). Meekness implies acceptance of one's lowly position. **The meek** person is gentle and mild in his own cause, though he may be a lion in God's cause or in defending others.

The meek do not *now* inherit the earth; rather they inherit abuse and dispossession. But they *will* literally **inherit the earth** when Christ, the King, reigns for a thousand years in peace and prosperity.

5:6 Next, a blessing is pronounced on **those who hunger and thirst for righteousness**: they are promised satisfaction. These people have a passion **for righteousness** in their own lives; they long to see honesty, integrity, and justice in society; they look for practical holiness in the church. Like the people of whom Gamaliel Bradford wrote, they have "a thirst no earthly stream can satisfy, a hunger that must feed on Christ or die." These people will be abundantly satisfied in Christ's coming kingdom: **they shall be filled**, for righteousness will reign and corruption will give way to the highest moral standards.

5:7 In our Lord's kingdom, **the merciful** are **blessed . . . for they shall obtain mercy**. To be **merciful** means to be actively compassionate. In one sense it means to withhold punishment from offenders who deserve it. In a wider sense it means to help others in need who cannot help themselves. God showed mercy in sparing us from the judgment which our sins deserved and in demonstrating kindness to us through the saving work of Christ. We imitate God when we have compassion.

The merciful **shall obtain mercy**. Here, Jesus is not referring to the mercy of salvation which God gives to a believing sinner; *that* mercy is not dependent on a person's being merciful — it is a free, unconditional gift. Rather the Lord is speaking of the daily **mercy** needed for Christian living and of **mercy** in that future day when one's works will be reviewed (1 Cor. 3:12–15). If one has not been merciful, that person will not receive mercy; that is, one's rewards will decrease accordingly.

5:8 The pure in heart are given the assurance that **they shall see God**. A pure-hearted person is one whose motives are unmixed, whose thoughts are holy, whose conscience is clean. The expression **they shall see God** may be understood in several ways. First, **the pure in heart see God** now through fellowship in the Word and the Spirit. Second, they sometimes have a supernatural appearance, or vision, of the Lord presented to them. Third, **they shall see God** in the Person of Jesus when He comes again. Fourth, **they shall see God** in eternity.

5:9 A blessing is pronounced on **the peacemakers**: **they shall be called sons of God**. Notice that the Lord is not speaking about people with a peaceful disposition or those who love peace. He is referring to those who actively intervene to make peace. The natural approach is to watch strife from the sidelines. The divine approach is to take positive action toward creating **peace**, even if it means taking abuse and invective.

Peacemakers are **called sons of God**. This is not how they *become* sons of God — that can only happen by receiving Jesus Christ as Savior (John 1:12). By making peace, believers *manifest* themselves as **sons of God**, and God will one day acknowledge them as people who bear the family likeness.

5:10 The next beatitude deals with those **who are persecuted**, not for their own wrongdoings, but **for righteousness' sake**. **The kingdom of heaven** is promised to those believers who suffer for doing right. Their integrity condemns the ungodly world and brings out its hostility. People hate a righteous life because it exposes their own unrighteousness.

5:11 The final beatitude seems to be a repetition of the preceding one. However, there is one difference. In the previous verse, the subject was persecution because of righteousness; here it is persecution **for** Christ's **sake**. The Lord knew that His disciples would be maltreated because of their association with, and loyalty to, Him. History has confirmed this: from the outset the world has persecuted, jailed, and killed followers of Jesus.

5:12 To suffer for Christ's sake is a privilege that should cause joy. A **great reward** awaits those who thus become companions of **the prophets** in tribulation. Those OT spokesmen for God stood true in spite of persecution. All who imitate their loyal courage will share their present exhilaration and future exaltation.

The Beatitudes present a portrait of the ideal citizen in Christ's kingdom. Notice the emphases on *righteousness* (v. 6), *peace* (v. 9), and *joy* (v. 12). Paul probably had this passage in mind when he wrote: "For the kingdom of God is not eating and drinking, but righteousness and peace and joy in the Holy Spirit" (Rom. 14:17).

B. Believers Are Salt and Light (5:13–16)

5:13 Jesus likened His disciples to **salt**. They were to the world what salt is in everyday life: salt seasons food; it hinders the spread of corruption; it creates thirst; it brings out the flavor. So His followers add piquancy to human society, serve as a preservative, and make others long for the righteousness described in the preceding verses.

If the salt loses its flavor, how can its saltiness be restored? There is no way to restore the true, natural taste. Once it has lost its flavor, salt is **good for nothing**. It is discarded on a footpath. Albert Barnes's comment on this passage is illuminating:

The salt used in this country is a chemical compound — and if the *saltiness* were lost, or it were to lose its *savor*, there would be nothing remaining. In eastern countries, however, the salt used was impure, mingled with vegetable and earthly substances; so that it might lose the whole of its saltiness, and a considerable quantity [of salt without flavor] remain. This was good for nothing except that it was used, as it is said, to place in paths, or walks, as we use gravel.⁴

The disciple has one great function — to be **the salt of the earth** by living out the terms of discipleship listed in the Beatitudes and throughout the rest of the Sermon. If he fails to exhibit this spiritual reality, men will tread his testimony under their feet. The world has only contempt for an undedicated believer.

5:14 Jesus also calls Christians **the light of the world**. He spoke of Himself as "the light of the world" (John 8:12; 12:35, 36, 46). The relationship between these two statements is that Jesus is the source of light; Christians are the reflection of His light. Their function is to shine for Him just as the moon reflects the glory of the sun.

The Christian is like **a city that is set on a hill**: it is elevated above its surroundings and it shines in the midst of darkness. Those whose lives exhibit the traits of Christ's teaching **cannot be hidden**.

5:15, 16 People do not **light a lamp and put it under a basket**. Instead, they put it **on a lampstand** so that it will give **light to all who are in the house**. He did not intend that we hoard the light of His teaching for ourselves, but that we share it with others. We should **let** our **light so shine** that as people **see** our **good works**, they will **glorify** our **Father in heaven**. The emphasis is on the ministry of Christian character. The winsomeness of lives in which Christ is seen speaks louder than the persuasion of words.

C. Christ Fulfills the Law (5:17-20)

5:17, 18 Most revolutionary leaders sever all ties with the past and repudiate the traditional, existing order. Not so the Lord Jesus. He upheld the Law of Moses and insisted that it must be fulfilled. Jesus had not come to abolish **the Law or the Prophets**, but **to fulfill** them. He clearly insisted that not **one jot or one tittle** would **pass from the law** until it

was completely fulfilled. The **jot**, or *yod*, is the smallest letter in the Hebrew alphabet; the **tittle** is a small mark or projection that serves to distinguish one letter from another, much as the bottom stroke of a capital *E* distinguishes it from a capital *F*. Jesus believed in the literal inspiration of the Bible, even in what might seem small unimportant details. Nothing in Scripture, even the smallest stroke, is without significance.

It is important to notice that Jesus did *not* say that the law would *never* pass away. He said it would not pass away **till all** was **fulfilled**. This distinction has ramifications for the believer today, and since the believer's relation to the law is rather complicated, we are going to take time to summarize the Bible's teaching on this subject.

THE BELIEVER'S RELATION TO THE LAW

The law is that system of legislation given by God through Moses to the nation of Israel. The entire body of the law is found in Exodus 20-31, Leviticus, and Deuteronomy, though its essence is embodied in the Ten Commandments.

The law was not given as a means of salvation (Acts 13:39; Rom. 3:20a; Gal. 2:16, 21; 3:11); it was designed to show people their sinfulness (Rom. 3:20b; 5:20; 7:7; 1 Cor. 15:56; Gal. 3:19) and then drive them to God for His gracious salvation. It was given to the nation of Israel, even though it contains moral principles which are valid for people in every age (Rom. 2:14, 15). God tested Israel under the law as a sample of the human race, and Israel's guilt proved the world's guilt (Rom. 3:19).

The law had attached to it the penalty of death (Gal. 3:10); and to break one command was to be guilty of all (Jas. 2:10). Since people had broken the law, they were under the curse of death. God's righteousness and holiness demanded that the penalty be paid. It was for this reason that Jesus came into the world: to pay the penalty by His death. He died as a Substitute for guilty lawbreakers, even though He Himself was sinless. He did not wave the law aside; rather He met the full demands of the law by fulfilling its strict requirements in His life and in His death. Thus, the gospel does not overthrow the law; it upholds the law and shows how the law's demands have been fully satisfied by Christ's redemptive work.

Therefore, the person who trusts in Jesus is no longer under the law; he is under grace (Rom. 6:14). He is dead to the law through the work of Christ. The penalty of the law must be paid only once; since Christ paid the penalty, the believer does not have to. It is in this sense that the law has faded away for the Christian (2 Cor. 3:7–11). The law was a tutor until Christ came, but after salvation, this tutor is no longer needed (Gal. 3:24, 25).

Yet, while the Christian is not under the law, that doesn't mean he is lawless. He is bound by a stronger chain than law because he is under the law of Christ (1 Cor. 9:21). His behavior is molded, not by fear of punishment, but by a loving desire to please his Savior. Christ has become his rule of life (John 13:15; 15:12; Eph. 5:1, 2; 1 Jn. 2:6; 3:16).

A common question in a discussion of the believer's relation to the law is, "Should I obey the Ten Commandments?" The answer is that certain principles contained in the law are of lasting relevance. It is always wrong to steal, to covet, or to murder. Nine of the Ten Commandments are repeated in the NT, with an important distinction — they are not given as law (with penalty attached), but as training in righteousness for the people of God (2 Tim. 3:16b). The one commandment not repeated is the Sabbath law: Christians are *never* taught to keep the Sabbath (i.e., the seventh day of the week, Saturday).

The ministry of the law to unsaved people has not ended: "But we know that the law is good if one uses it lawfully" (1 Tim. 1:8). Its lawful use is to produce the knowledge of sin and thus lead to repentance. But the law is not for those who are already saved: "The law is not made for a righteous person" (1 Tim. 1:9).

The righteousness demanded by the law is fulfilled in those "who do not walk according to the flesh but according to the Spirit" (Rom. 8:4). In fact, the teachings of our Lord in the Sermon on the Mount set a higher standard than that set by the law. For instance, the law

said, "Do not murder"; Jesus said, "Do not even hate." So the Sermon on the Mount not only upholds the Law and the Prophets but it amplifies them and develops their deeper implications. ‡

5:19   In returning to the Sermon, we notice that Jesus anticipated a natural tendency to relax God's commandments. Because they are of such a supernatural nature, people tend to explain them away, to rationalize their meaning. But **whoever breaks one** part of the law, and **teaches** other people to do the same, **shall be called least in the kingdom of heaven**. The wonder is that such people are permitted in the kingdom at all — but then, entrance *into* the kingdom is by faith in Christ. A person's position *in* the kingdom is determined by his obedience and faithfulness while on earth. The person who obeys the law of the kingdom — that person **shall be called great in the kingdom of heaven**.

5:20   To gain entrance into the kingdom, our **righteousness** must surpass **the righteousness of the scribes and Pharisees** (who were content with religious ceremonies which gave them an outward, ritual cleansing, but which never changed their hearts). Jesus uses hyperbole (exaggeration) to drive home the truth that external righteousness without internal reality will not gain entrance into the kingdom. The only righteousness that God will accept is the perfection that He imputes to those who accept His Son as Savior (2 Cor. 5:21). Of course, where there is true faith in Christ, there will also be the practical righteousness that Jesus describes in the remainder of the Sermon.

D. Jesus Warns Against Anger (5:21–26)

5:21   The Jews of Jesus' time knew that murder was forbidden by God and that the murderer was liable to punishment. This was true before the giving of the law (Gen. 9:6) and it was later incorporated into the law (Ex. 20:13; Deut. 5:17). With the words, **"But I say to you,"** Jesus institutes an amendment to the teaching on murder. No longer could a person take pride in having never committed murder. Jesus now says, "In My kingdom, you must not even have murderous thoughts." He traces the act of murder to its source and warns against three forms of unrighteous anger.

5:22 The first is the case of a person who **is angry with his brother without a cause.**[5] One accused of this crime would be **in danger of the judgment** — that is, he could be taken to court. Most people can find what they think is a valid cause for their anger, but anger is justified only when God's honor is at stake or when someone else is being wronged. It is never right when expressed in retaliation for personal wrongs.

Even more serious is the sin of insulting a brother. In Jesus' day, people used the word **Raca** (an Aramaic term meaning "empty one") as a word of contempt and abuse. Those who used this epithet were **in danger of the council** —that is, they were subject to trial before the Sanhedrin, the highest court in the land.

Finally, to call someone a **fool** is the third form of unrighteous anger that Jesus condemns. Here the word **fool** means more than just a dunce. It signifies a moral **fool** who ought to be dead and it expresses the wish that he were. Today it is common to hear a person cursing another with the words, "God damn you!" He is calling on God to consign the victim to hell. Jesus says that the one who utters such a curse is **in danger of hell fire**. The bodies of executed criminals were often thrown into a burning dump outside Jerusalem known as the Valley of Hinnom or Gehenna. This was a figure of the fires of hell which shall never be quenched.

There is no mistaking the severity of the Savior's words. He teaches that anger contains the seeds of murder, that abusive language contains the spirit of murder, and that cursing language implies the very desire to murder. The progressive heightening of the crimes demand three degrees of punishment: the *judgment*, the *council*, and *hell fire*. In the kingdom, Jesus will deal with sins according to severity.

5:23, 24 If a person offends another, whether by anger or any other cause, there is no use in his bringing a gift to God. The Lord will not be pleased with it. The offender should first go and make the wrong right. Only then will the gift be acceptable.

Even though these words are written in a Jewish context, that does not mean there is no application today. Paul interprets this concept in relation to the Lord's Supper (see 1 Cor. 11). God receives no worship from a believer who is not on speaking terms with another.

5:25, 26 It is against a litigious spirit and a reluctance to admit guilt that Jesus warns here. It is better to promptly settle with an accuser rather than run the risk of a court trial. If that happens, we are bound to lose. While there is some disagreement among scholars about the identity of the people in this parable, the point is clear: if you are wrong, be quick to admit it and make things right. If you remain unrepentant, your sin will eventually catch up with you and you will not only have to make full restitution but suffer additional penalties as well. And don't be in a hurry to go to court. If you do, the law will find you out, and you will pay the last penny.

E. Jesus Condemns Adultery (5:27–30)

5:27, 28 The Mosaic Law clearly prohibited adultery (Ex. 20:14; Deut. 5:18). A person might be proud that he had never broken this commandment, and yet have his "eyes full of adultery" (2 Pet. 2:14). While outwardly respectable, his mind might be constantly wandering down labyrinths of impurity. So Jesus reminded His disciples that mere abstinence from the physical act was not enough — there must be inward purity. The law forbade the act of adultery; Jesus forbids the desire: **Whoever looks at a woman to lust for her has already committed adultery with her in his heart**. E. Stanley Jones caught the import of this verse when he wrote: "If you think or act adultery, you do not satisfy the sex urge; you pour oil on a fire to quench it." Sin begins in the mind, and if we nourish it, we eventually commit the act.

5:29, 30 Maintaining an undefiled thought life demands strict self-discipline. Thus, Jesus taught that if any part of our body causes us to sin, it would be better to lose that member during life rather than to lose one's soul for eternity. Are we to take Jesus' words literally? Was He actually advocating self-mutilation? The words are literal to this extent: *if it were necessary* to lose a member rather than one's soul, then we should gladly part with the member. *Fortunately it is never necessary*, since the Holy Spirit empowers the believer to live a holy life. However, there must be co-operation and rigid discipline on the believer's part.

F. Jesus Censures Divorce (5:31, 32)

5:31 Under OT law, divorce was permitted according to Deuteronomy 24:1–4. This passage was not concerned with the case of an adulterous wife (the penalty for adultery was death, see Deut. 22:22). Rather, it deals with divorce because of dislike or "incompatibility."

5:32 However, in the kingdom of Christ, **whoever divorces his wife for any reason except sexual immorality causes her to commit adultery**. This does not mean that she automatically becomes an adulteress; it presupposes that, having no means of support, she is forced to live with another man. In so doing she becomes an adulteress. Not only is the former wife living in adultery, **whoever marries a woman who is divorced commits adultery**.

The subject of divorce and remarriage is one of the most complicated topics in the Bible. It is virtually impossible to answer all the questions that arise, but it may be helpful to survey and summarize what we believe the Scriptures teach.

DIVORCE AND REMARRIAGE

Divorce was never God's intention for man. His ideal is that one man and one woman remain married until their union is broken by death (Rom. 7:2, 3). Jesus made this clear to the Pharisees by appealing to the divine order at creation (Matt. 19:4–6).

God hates divorce (Mal. 2:16), that is, unscriptural divorce. He does not hate all divorce because He speaks of Himself as having divorced Israel (Jer. 3:8). This was because the nation forsook Him to worship idols. Israel was unfaithful.

In Matthew 5:31, 32 and 19:9, Jesus taught that divorce was forbidden except when one of the partners had been guilty of sexual immorality. In Mark 10:11, 12 and Luke 16:18, the exception clause is omitted.

The discrepancy is probably best explained as that neither Mark nor Luke record the entire saying. Therefore, even though divorce is not the ideal, it is permitted in the case where one's partner has been unfaithful. Jesus *allows* divorce in this case, but He does not *command* it.

Some scholars see 1 Corinthians 7:12–16 as teaching that divorce is acceptable when a believer is deserted by an unbeliever. Paul says that the remaining person is "not under bondage in such cases," i.e., he or she is free to obtain a divorce (for desertion). The present writer's opinion is that this case is the same exception granted in Matthew 5 and 19; namely, the unbeliever departs to live with someone else. Therefore, the believer can be granted a divorce on the scriptural grounds only if the other party commits adultery.

It is often contended that, although divorce is permitted in the NT, remarriage is never contemplated. However, this argument begs the question. Remarriage is not condemned for the innocent party in the NT — only for the offending person. Also, one of the main purposes of a scriptural divorce is to permit remarriage; otherwise, separation would serve the purpose just as well.

In any discussion of this topic, the question inevitably arises, "What about people who were divorced before they were saved?" There should be no question that unlawful divorces and remarriages contracted before conversion are sins which have been fully forgiven (see, for example, 1 Cor. 6:11 where Paul includes adultery in the list of sins in which the Corinthian believers had formerly participated). Pre-conversion sins do not bar believers from full participation in the local church.

A more difficult question concerns Christians who have divorced for unscriptural reasons and then remarry. Can they be received back into the fellowship of the local church? The answer depends on whether adultery is the initial act of physical union or a continued state. If these people are living in a state of adultery, then they would not only have to confess their sin but also forsake their present partner. But God's solution for a problem is never one that creates worse problems. If, in order to untangle a marital snarl, men or women are driven into sin, or women and children are left homeless and penniless, the cure is worse than the disease.

In the writer's opinion, Christians who have been divorced unscripturally and then remarried can truly repent of their sin and be restored to the Lord and to the fellowship of the church. In the matter of divorce, it seems that almost every case is different. Therefore, the elders of a local church must investigate each case individually and judge it according to the Word of God. If, at times, disciplinary action has to be taken, all concerned should submit to the decision of the elders. ‡

G. Jesus Condemns Oaths (5:33–37)

5:33–36 The Mosaic Law contained several prohibitions against swearing **falsely** by the name of God (Lev. 19:12; Num. 30:2; Deut. 23:21). To swear by God's Name meant that He was your witness that you were telling the truth. The Jews sought to avoid the impropriety of swearing falsely by God's Name by substituting **heaven**, **earth**, **Jerusalem**, or their **head** as that by which they swore.

Jesus condemns such circumvention of the law as sheer hypocrisy and forbids any form of swearing or oaths in ordinary conversation. Not only was it hypocritical, it was useless to try to avoid swearing by God's Name by merely substituting another noun for His Name. To swear **by heaven** is to swear by **God's throne**. To swear **by the earth** is to swear by **His footstool**. To swear **by Jerusalem** is to swear by the royal capital. Even to swear by one's own **head** involves God because He is the Creator of all.

5:37 For the Christian, an oath is unnecessary. His **Yes** should mean **Yes**, and his **No** should mean **No**. To use stronger language is to admit that Satan — **the evil one** — rules our lives. There are no circumstances under which it is proper for a Christian to lie.

This passage also forbids any shading of the truth or deception. It does not, however, forbid taking an oath in a court of law. Jesus Himself testified under oath before the High Priest (Matt. 26:63ff). Paul also used an oath to call God as his witness that what he was writing was true (2 Cor. 1:23; Gal. 1:20).

H. Going the Second Mile (5:38–42)

5:38 The law said, **"An eye for an eye and a tooth for a tooth"** (Ex. 21:24; Lev. 24:20; Deut. 19:21). This was both a command to punish and a limitation on punishment — the penalty must not exceed the crime. However, according to the OT, authority for punishment was vested in the government, *not* in the individual.

5:39–41 Jesus went beyond the law to a higher righteousness by abolishing retaliation altogether. He showed His disciples that, whereas revenge was once legally permissible, now non-resistance was graciously possible. Jesus instructed His followers to offer no resistance to **an evil person**. If they were slapped on one **cheek** by someone, they were to **turn the other to him also**. If they were sued for their **tunic** (an inner garment), they were to surrender their **cloak** (an outer garment used for covering at night) as well. If an official compelled them to carry his baggage for **one mile**, they were to voluntarily carry it **two** miles.

5:42 Jesus' last command in this paragraph seems the most impractical to us today. **Give to him who asks you, and from him who wants to borrow from you do not turn away**. Our obsession with material goods and possessions makes us recoil at the thought of giving away what we have acquired. However, if we were willing to concentrate on the treasures of heaven and be content with only necessary food and clothing, we would accept these words more literally and willingly. Jesus' statement presupposes that the person who asks for help has a genuine need. Since it is impossible to know whether the need is legitimate in all cases, it is better (as someone said), "to help a score of fraudulent beggars than to risk turning away one man in real need."

Humanly speaking, such behavior as the Lord calls for here is impossible. Only as a person is controlled by the

Holy Spirit can he live a self-sacrificing life. Only as the Savior is allowed to live His life in the believer can insult (v. 39), injustice (v. 40), and inconvenience (v. 41) be repaid with love. This is "the gospel of the second mile."

I. Love Your Enemies (5:43–48)

5:43 Our Lord's final example of the higher righteousness demanded in His kingdom concerns the treatment of one's enemies, a topic which grows naturally out of the previous paragraph. The law had taught the Israelites to **love** their **neighbor** (Lev. 19:18). Although they were never explicitly commanded to **hate** their **enemy**, this spirit underlay much of their indoctrination. This attitude was a summary of the OT's outlook toward those who persecuted God's people (see Ps. 139:21, 22). It was a righteous hostility directed against the enemies of God.

5:44–47 But now Jesus announces that we are to **love** our **enemies** and to **pray for those who . . . persecute** us. The fact that **love** is commanded shows that it is a matter of the will and not primarily of the emotions. It is not the same as natural affection because it is not natural to love those who hate and harm you. It is a supernatural grace and can be manifested only by those who have divine life.

There is no reward if we **love those who love us**; Jesus says that even unconverted **tax collectors**[6] do that! That type of love requires no divine power. Neither is there any virtue in greeting our **brethren**[7] **only**, i.e., our relatives and friends. The unsaved can do that; there is nothing distinctively Christian about it. If our standards are no higher than the world's, it is certain that we will never make an impact on the world.

Jesus said that His followers should return good for evil so that they might be **sons of** their **Father in heaven**. He was not saying that this was the way to *become* sons of God; rather, it is how we *show* that we are God's children. Since God shows no partiality to either **the evil** or **the good** (in that both benefit from **sun** and **rain**), so we should deal graciously and fairly with all.

5:48 Jesus closes this section with the admonition: **Therefore you shall be perfect, just as your Father in heaven is perfect**. The word **perfect** must be understood in the light of the context. It does not mean sinless or flawless. The previous verses explain that to be perfect means to love those who hate us, to pray for those who persecute us, and to show kindness to both friend and foe. Perfection here is that spiritual maturity which enables a Christian to imitate God in dispensing blessing to everybody without partiality.

J. Give with Sincerity (6:1–4)

6:1 In the first half of this chapter, Jesus deals with three specific areas of practical righteousness in an individual's life: charitable deeds (vv. 1–4), prayer (vv. 5–15), and fasting (vv. 16–18). The name **Father** is found ten times in these eighteen verses and is the key to understanding them. Practical deeds of righteousness should be done for His approval, not for people's.

He begins this portion of His sermon with a warning against the temptation to parade our piety by performing **charitable deeds** for the purpose of being **seen by** others. It is not the deed that He condemns, but the motive. If public notice is the motivating factor then it is the only **reward**, for God will not reward hypocrisy.

6:2 It seems incredible that **hypocrites** would noisily attract attention to themselves as they gave offerings **in the synagogues** or handouts to beggars **in the streets**. The Lord dismissed their conduct with the terse comment: **"They have their reward"** (i.e., their only reward is the reputation they gain while on earth).

6:3, 4 When a follower of Christ does **a charitable deed**, it is to be done **in secret**. It should be so secret that Jesus told His disciples: **"Do not let your left hand know what your right hand is doing."** Jesus uses this graphic figure of speech to show that our **charitable deed** should be for the **Father**, and not to gain notoriety for the giver.

This passage should not be pressed to prohibit any gift that might be seen by others, since it is virtually impossible to make all one's contributions strictly anonymous. It simply condemns the blatant display of giving.

K. Pray with Sincerity (6:5–8)

6:5 Next Jesus warns His disciples against hypocrisy **when** they **pray**. They should not purposely position themselves in public areas so that others will see them praying and be impressed by their piety. If the love for prominence is the only motive in prayer, then, Jesus declares, the prominence gained is the only **reward**.

6:6 In verses 5 and 7, the Greek pronoun translated **you** is plural. But in verse 6, in order to emphasize private communion with God, *you* switches to singular. The key to answered prayer is to do it in **secret** (i.e., **go into your room** and **shut your door**). If our real motive is to get through to God, He will hear and answer.

It is reading too much into the passage to use it to prohibit public prayer. The early church met together for collective prayer (Acts 2:42; 12:12; 13:3; 14:23; 20:36). The point is not *where* we pray. At issue here is, *why* we pray — to be seen by people or to be heard by God.

6:7 Prayer should not consist of **vain repetitions**, i.e., stock sentences or empty phrases. Unsaved people pray like that, but God is not impressed by the mere multiplication of **many words**. He wants to hear the sincere expressions of the heart.

6:8 Since our **Father knows the things** we **have need of**, even **before** we **ask Him**, then it is reasonable to ask, "Why pray at all?" The reason is that, in prayer, we acknowledge our need and dependence on Him. It is the basis of our communicating with God. Also God does things in answer to prayer that He would not have done otherwise (Jas. 4:2d).

L. Jesus Teaches the Model Prayer (6:9–15)

6:9 In verses 9–13 we have what is generally called "The Lord's Prayer." In using this title, however, we should remember that Jesus never prayed it Himself. It was given to His disciples as a model after which they could pattern their prayers. It was not given as the exact words they were to use (v. 7 seems to rule this out), because many words repeated by rote memory can become empty phrases.

Our Father in heaven. Prayer should be addressed to God the Father in acknowledgment of His sovereignty over the universe.

Hallowed be Your name. We should begin our prayers with worship, ascribing praise and honor to Him who is so worthy of it.

6:10 Your kingdom come. After worship, we should pray for the advancement of God's cause, putting His interests first. Specifically, we should pray for the day when our Savior-God, the Lord Jesus Christ, will set up His kingdom on earth and reign in righteousness.

Your will be done. In this petition we acknowledge that God knows what is best and that we surrender our will to His. It also expresses a longing to see His will acknowledged throughout the world.

On earth as it is in heaven. This phrase modifies all three preceding petitions. The worship of God, the sovereign rule by God, and the performance of His **will** are all a reality of **heaven**. The prayer is that these conditions might exist **on earth as** they do **in heaven**.

6:11 Give us this day our daily bread. After putting God's interests first, we are permitted to present our own needs. This petition acknowledges our dependence on God for daily food, both spiritual and physical.

6:12 And forgive us our debts, as we forgive our debtors. This does not refer to judicial forgiveness from the penalty of sin (that forgiveness is obtained by faith in the Son of God). Rather this refers to the parental forgiveness that is necessary if fellowship with our Father is to be maintained. If believers are unwilling to forgive those who wrong them, how can they expect to be in fellowship with their Father who has freely forgiven them for their wrongdoings?

6:13 And do not lead us into temptation. This request may appear to contradict James 1:13, which states that God would never tempt anyone. However, God does allow His people to be tested and tried. This petition expresses a healthy distrust of one's own ability to resist temptations or to stand up under trial. It acknowledges complete dependence on the Lord for preservation.

But deliver us from the evil one. This is the prayer of all who desperately desire to be kept from sin by the power of God. It is the heart's cry for daily salvation from the power of sin and Satan in one's life.

For Yours is the kingdom and the power and the glory forever. Amen. The last sentence of the prayer is omitted in the Roman Catholic and most modern Protestant Bibles since it is lacking in many ancient manuscripts. However, such a doxology is the perfect ending to the prayer and is in the majority of manuscripts.[8] It should, as John Calvin writes, "not only warm our hearts to press toward the glory of God . . . but also to tell us that all our prayers . . . have no other foundation than God alone."

6:14, 15 This serves as an explanatory footnote to verse 12. It is not part of the prayer, but added to emphasize that the parental forgiveness mentioned in verse 12 is conditional.

M. Jesus Teaches How to Fast (6:16–18)

6:16 The third form of religous hypocrisy that Jesus denounced was the deliberate attempt to create an appearance of **fasting. The hypocrites** disfigured **their faces** when they fasted in order to look gaunt, haggard, and doleful. But Jesus says it is ridiculous to attempt to **appear** holy.

6:17, 18 True believers should **fast** in secret, giving no outward appearance of it. **To anoint your head and wash your face** was a means of appearing in one's normal manner. It is enough that **the Father** knows; His **reward** will be better than people's approval.

FASTING

To fast is to abstain from gratifying any physical appetite. It may be voluntary, as in this passage, or involuntary (as in Acts 27:33 or 2 Cor. 11:27). In the NT it is associated with mourning (Matt. 9:14, 15) and prayer (Luke 2:37; Acts 14:23). In these passages fasting accompanied prayer as an acknowledgment of

one's earnestness in discerning the will of God.

Fasting has no merit as far as salvation is concerned; neither does it give a Christian special standing before God. A Pharisee once boasted that he fasted twice a week; however, it failed to bring him the justification he sought (Luke 18:12, 14). But when a Christian fasts secretly as a spiritual exercise, God sees and rewards. While not commanded in the NT, it is *encouraged* by promise of reward. It can aid in one's prayer life by taking away dullness and drowsiness. It is valuable in times of crisis when one wishes to discern the will of God. And it is of value in promoting self-discipline. Fasting is a matter between an individual and God and should be done only with a desire to please Him. It loses its value when it is imposed from outside or displayed from a wrong motive. ‡

N. Lay Up Treasures in Heaven (6:19–21)

This passage contains some of the most revolutionary teachings of our Lord — and some of the most neglected. The theme of the rest of the chapter is how to find security for the future.

6:19, 20 In verses 19–21 Jesus contravenes all human advice to provide for a financially secure future. When He says, **"Do not lay up for yourselves treasures on earth,"** He is indicating that there is no security in material things. Any type of material treasure **on earth** can be either destroyed by elements of nature (**moth or rust**) or stolen by **thieves**. Jesus says that the only investments not subject to loss are **treasures in heaven**.

6:21 This radical financial policy is based on the underlying principle that **where your treasure is, there your heart will be also**. If your money is in a safe-deposit box, then your heart and desire are also there. If your treasures are in heaven, your interests will be centered there. This teaching forces us to decide if Jesus meant what He said. If He did, then we face the question, "What are we going to do with our earthly treasures?" If He didn't, then we face the question, "What are we going to do with our Bible?"

O. The Lamp of the Body (6:22, 23)

Jesus realized that it would be difficult for His followers to see how His unconventional teaching on security for the future could possibly work. So He used an analogy of the human **eye** to teach a lesson on spiritual sight. He said that **the eye** is **the lamp of the body**. It is through the eye that the body receives illumination and can see. **If the eye is good**, the **whole body** is flooded with **light**. **But if** the **eye is bad**, then vision is impaired. Instead of light, there is **darkness**.

The application is this: The good eye belongs to the person whose motives are pure, who has a single desire for God's interests, and who is willing to accept Christ's teachings literally. His whole life is flooded with light. He believes Jesus' words, he forsakes earthly riches, he lays up treasures in heaven, and he knows that this is the only true security. On the other hand, the bad eye belongs to the person who is trying to live for two worlds. He doesn't want to let go of his earthly treasures, yet he wants treasures in heaven too. The teachings of Jesus seems impractical and impossible to him. He lacks clear guidance since he is full of darkness.

Jesus adds the statement that **if therefore the light that is in you is darkness, how great is that darkness!** In other words, if you know that Christ forbids trusting earthly treasures for security, yet you do it anyway, then the teaching you have failed to obey becomes darkness — a very intense form of spiritual blindness. You cannot see riches in their true perspective.

P. You Cannot Serve God and Mammon (6:24)

The impossibility of living for **God** and for money is stated here in terms of **masters** and slaves. **No one can serve two masters. One** will inevitably take precedence in his loyalty and obedience. So it is with **God and mammon**. They present rival claims and a choice must be made. Either we must put God first and reject the rule of materialism or we must live for temporal things and refuse God's claim on our lives.

Q. Do Not Worry (6:25–34)

6:25 In this passage Jesus strikes at the tendency to center our lives around food and clothing, thus missing life's real meaning. The problem is not so much what we eat and wear *today*, but what we shall eat and wear ten, twenty, or thirty years from now. Such worry about the future is sin because it denies the love, wisdom, and power of God. It denies the love of God by implying that He doesn't care for us. It denies His wisdom by implying that He doesn't know what He is doing. And it denies His power by implying that He isn't able to provide for our needs.

This type of worry causes us to devote our finest energies to making sure we will have enough to live on. Then before we know it, our lives have passed, and we have missed the central purpose for which we were made. God did not create us in His image with no higher destiny than that we should consume food. We are here to love, worship, and serve Him and to represent His interests on earth. Our bodies are intended to be our servants, not our masters.

6:26 **The birds of the air** illustrate God's care for His creatures. They preach to us how unnecessary it is for us to worry. They **neither sow nor reap**, yet God **feeds them**. Since, in God's hierarchy of creation, we are **of more value than** the birds, then we can surely expect God to take care of our needs.

But we should not infer from this that we need not work for the supply of our present needs. Paul reminds us: "If anyone will not work, neither shall he eat" (2 Thess. 3:10). Nor should we conclude that it is wrong for a farmer to sow, reap, and harvest. These activities are a necessary part of his providing for his current needs. What Jesus forbids here is multiplying barns in an attempt to provide future security independent of God (a practice He condemns in His story of the rich farmer in Luke 12: 16–21.) The *Daily Notes of the Scripture Union* succinctly summarize verse 26:

The argument is that if God sustains, *without* their conscious participation, creatures of a lower order, He will all the more sustain, *with* their active participation, those for whom creation took place.

6:27 Worry about the future is not only a dishonor to God — it is also futile. The Lord demonstrates this with a question: **"Which of you by worrying can add one cubit to his stature?"** A short person cannot worry himself eighteen inches taller. Yet, relatively speaking, it would be far easier to perform this feat than to worry into existence all the provisions for one's future needs.

6:28–30 Next the Lord deals with the unreasonableness of worrying that we will not have enough **clothing** in the future. **The lilies of the field** (probably wild anemones) **neither toil nor spin,** yet their beauty surpasses that of Solomon's royal garments. If God can provide such elegant apparel for wildflowers, which have a brief existence and are then used as fuel in the baking **oven,** He will certainly care for His people who worship and serve Him.

6:31, 32 The conclusion is that we should not spend our lives in anxious pursuit of food, drink, and clothing for the future. The unconverted **Gentiles** live for the mad accumulation of material things, as if food and clothing were the whole of life. But it should not be so with Christians, who have a **heavenly Father** who **knows** their basic needs.

If Christians were to set before them the goal of providing in advance for all their future needs, then their time and energy would have to be devoted to the accumulation of financial reserves. They could never be sure that they had saved enough, because there is always the danger of market collapse, inflation, catastrophe, prolonged illness, paralyzing accident. This means that God would be robbed of the service of His people. The real purpose for which they were created and converted would be missed. Men and women bearing the divine image would be living for an uncertain future on this earth when they should be living with eternity's values in view.

6:33 The Lord, therefore, makes a covenant with His followers. He says, in effect, "If you will put God's interests first in your life, I will guarantee your future needs. If you **seek first the kingdom of God and His righteousness,** then I

will see that you never lack the necessities of life."

6:34 This is God's "social security" program. The believer's responsibility is to live for the Lord, trusting God for the future with unshakable confidence that He will provide. One's job is simply a means of providing for current needs; everything above this is invested in the work of the Lord. We are called to live one day at a time: **tomorrow** can **worry about its own things**.

R. Do Not Judge (7:1–6)

This section on judging immediately follows our Lord's provocative teaching concerning earthly riches. The connection between these two themes is important. It is easy for the Christian who has forsaken all to criticize wealthy Christians. Conversely, Christians who take seriously their duty to provide for the future needs of their families tend to downplay the literalness that some place on Jesus' words in the last chapter. Since no one lives completely by faith, such criticism is out of order.

This command not to judge others includes the following areas: we should not judge motives; only God can read them; we should not judge by appearance (John 7:24; Jas. 2:1–4); we should not judge those who have conscientious scruples about matters that are not in themselves right or wrong (Rom. 14:1–5); we should not judge the service of another Christian (1 Cor. 4:1–5); and, we should not judge a fellow believer by speaking evil about him (Jas. 4:11, 12).

7:1 Sometimes these words of our Lord are misconstrued by people to prohibit all forms of judgment. No matter what happens, they piously say, **"Judge not, that you be not judged."** But Jesus is not teaching that we are to be undiscerning Christians. He never intended that we abandon our critical faculty or discernment. The NT has many illustrations of legitimate judgment of the condition, conduct, or teaching of others. In addition, there are several areas in which the Christian is commanded to make a decision, to discriminate between good and bad or between good and best. Some of these include:

1. When disputes arise between be-

lievers, they should be settled in the church before members who can decide the matter (1 Cor. 6:1-8).

2. The local church is to judge serious sins of its members and take appropriate action (Matt. 18:17; 1 Cor. 5:9-13).

3. Believers are to judge the doctrinal teaching of teachers and preachers by the Word of God (Matt. 7:15–20; 1 Cor. 14:29; 1 Jn. 4:1).

4. Christians have to discern if others are believers in order to obey Paul's command in 2 Corinthians 6:14.

5. Those in the church must judge which men have the qualifications necessary for elders and deacons (1 Tim. 3:1-13).

6. We have to discern which people are unruly, fainthearted, weak, etc., and treat them according to the instructions in the Bible (e.g., 1 Thess. 5:14).

7:2 Jesus warned that unrighteous judgment would be repaid in kind: **"For with what judgment you judge, you will be judged."** This principle of reaping what we sow is built into all human life and affairs. Mark applies the principle to our appropriation of the Word (4:24) and Luke applies it to our liberality in giving (6:38).

7:3–5 Jesus exposed our tendency to see a small fault in someone else while ignoring the same fault in ourselves. He purposely exaggerated the situation (using a figure of speech known as hyperbole) to drive home the point. Someone with a **plank** in his **eye** often finds fault with the **speck** in the eye of another, not even noticing his own condition. It is hypocritical to suppose that we could help someone with a fault when we ourselves have a greater fault. We must remedy our own faults before criticizing them in others.

7:6 Verse 6 proves that Jesus did not intend to forbid *every* kind of judgment. He warned His disciples not to **give** holy things to **dogs** or to **cast . . . pearls before swine**. Under the Mosaic Law dogs and swine were unclean animals and here the terms are used to depict wicked people. When we meet vicious people who treat divine truths with utter contempt and respond to our preaching of

the claims of Christ with abuse and violence, we are not obligated to continue to share the gospel with them. To press the matter only brings increased condemnation to the offenders.

Needless to say, it requires spiritual perception to discern these people. Perhaps that is why the next verses take up the subject of prayer, by which we can ask for wisdom.

S. Keep Asking, Seeking, Knocking (7:7–12)

7:7, 8 If we think that we can live out the teachings of the Sermon on the Mount by our own strength, we have failed to realize the supernatural character of the life to which the Savior calls us. The wisdom or power for such a life must be given to us from above. So here we have an invitation to **ask** and keep on asking; to **seek** and keep on seeking; to **knock** and keep on knocking. Wisdom and power for the Christian life will be given to all who earnestly and persistently pray for it.

Taken out of context, verses 7 and 8 might seem like a blank check for believers, i.e., we can get anything we ask for. But this is simply not true. The verses must be understood in their immediate context and in light of the whole Bible's teaching on prayer. Therefore, what seems like unqualified promises here are actually restricted by other passages. For example, from Psalm 66:18 we learn that the person praying must have no unconfessed sin in his life. The Christian must pray in faith (Jas. 1:6–8) and in conformity with the will of God (1 Jn. 5:14). Prayer must be offered persistently (Luke 18:1–8) and sincerely (Heb. 10:22a).

7:9, 10 When the conditions for prayer are met, the Christian can have utter confidence that God will hear and answer. This assurance is based on the character of God, our Father. On the human level, we know that if a **son asks for bread**, his father will not **give him a stone**. Neither would he **give him a serpent** if he had asked for **a fish**. An earthly father would neither deceive his hungry son nor give him anything that might inflict pain.

7:11 The Lord argues from the

lesser to the greater. If human parents reward their children's requests with what is best for them, **how much more will** our **Father who is in heaven** do so.

7:12 The immediate connection of verse 12 with the preceding seems to be this: since our Father is a giver of good things to us, we should imitate Him in showing kindness to others. The way to test whether an action is beneficial to others is whether we would want to receive it ourselves. The "Golden Rule" had been expressed in negative terms at least one hundred years before this time by Rabbi Hillel. However, by stating the rule in positive terminology, Jesus goes beyond passive restraint to active benevolence. Christianity is not simply a matter of abstinence from sin; it is positive goodness.

This saying by Jesus **is the Law and the Prophets**, that is, it summarizes the moral teachings of the **Law** of Moses and the writings of the **Prophets** of Israel. The righteousness demanded by the OT is fulfilled in converted believers who thus walk according to the Spirit (Rom. 8:4). If this verse were universally obeyed, it would transform all areas of international relationships, national politics, family life, and church life.

T. The Narrow Way (7:13, 14)

The Lord now warns that the **gate** of Christian discipleship is **narrow** and the **way** is **difficult**.[9] But those who faithfully follow His teachings find the abundant **life**. On the other hand, there is the **wide gate** — the life of self-indulgence and pleasure. The end of such a life is **destruction**. This is not a discussion of losing one's soul, but of a failure to live out the purpose of one's existence.

These verses also have an application to the gospel by depicting the two roads and destinies of the human race. The wide gate and broad way lead to destruction (Prov. 16:25). The narrow gate and difficult way lead to life. Jesus is both the gate (John 10:9) and the way (John 14:6). But while this is a valid *application* of the passage, the *interpretation* is for believers. Jesus is saying that to follow Him would require faith, discipline, and endurance. But this **difficult** life is the only life worth living. If you choose

the easy way, you will have plenty of company, but you will miss God's best for you.

U. By Their Fruits You Shall Know Them (7:15–20)

7:15 Wherever the stern demands of true discipleship are taught, there are **false prophets** who advocate the wide gate and easy way. They water down the truth until, as C. H. Spurgeon said, "There is not enough left to make soup for a sick grasshopper." These men who profess to be speaking for God come in **sheep's clothing**, giving the appearance of being true believers. But **inwardly they are ravenous wolves**, i.e., they are vicious unbelievers who prey on the immature, the unstable, and the gullible.

7:16–18 Verses 16–18 deal with the detection of the false prophets: **you will know them by their fruits**. Their licentious lives and destructive teachings betray them. A tree or plant produces **fruit** according to its character. **Thornbushes** cannot bear **grapes**; **thistles** do not bear **figs**. **A good tree** bears **good fruit** and **a bad tree** bears **bad fruit**. This principle is true in the natural world and in the spiritual world. The life and teaching of those who claim to speak for God should be tested by the Word of God: "If they do not speak according to this word, it is because there is no light in them" (Isa. 8:20).

7:19, 20 The destiny of the false prophets is to be **thrown into the fire**. The doom of false teachers and prophets is "swift destruction" (2 Pet. 2:1). They can be known by their fruits.

V. I Never Knew You (7:21–23)

7:21 The Lord Jesus next warns against people who falsely profess to acknowledge Him as Savior, but have never been converted. **Not everyone** who calls Jesus, **"Lord, Lord," shall enter the kingdom of heaven**. Only those who do **the will** of God enter the kingdom. The first step in doing the will of God is to believe on the Lord Jesus (John 6:29).

7:22, 23 On judgment **day** when unbelievers stand before Christ (Rev. 20:11–15), **many will** remind Him that they **prophesied**, or **cast out demons**, or performed **many wonders** — all in His **name**. But their protestation will be in vain. Jesus **will declare to them** that He **never knew** them or acknowledged them as His own.

From these verses we learn that not all miracles are of divine origin and that not all miracle workers are divinely accredited. A miracle simply means that a supernatural power is at work. That power may be divine or satanic. Satan may empower his workers to cast out demons *temporarily*, in order to create the illusion that the miracle is divine. He is not dividing his kingdom against itself in such a case, but is plotting an even worse invasion of demons in the future.

W. Build on the Rock (7:24–29)

7:24, 25 Jesus closes His sermon with a parable that drives home the importance of obedience. It is not enough to hear **these sayings**; we must put them into practice. The disciple who **hears** and **does** Jesus' commands is like **a wise man who built his house on the rock**. His house (life) has a solid foundation and, when it is battered by **rain** and **winds**, it will **not fall**.

7:26, 27 The person who **hears** Jesus' **sayings** and **does not do** them is **like a foolish man who built his house on the sand**. This man will not be able to stand against the storms of adversity: when **the rain descended** and **the winds blew**, the house **fell** because it had no solid base.

If a person lives according to the principles of the Sermon on the Mount, the world calls him a fool; Jesus calls him a **wise man**. The world considers a wise man to be someone who lives by sight, who lives for the present, and who lives for self; Jesus calls such a person a fool. It is legitimate to use the wise and foolish builders to illustrate the gospel. The wise man puts his full confidence in the Rock, Christ Jesus, as Lord and Savior. The foolish man refuses to repent and rejects Jesus as his only hope of salvation. But the interpretation of the parable actually carries us beyond salvation to its practical outworking in the Christian life.

7:28, 29 As our Lord **ended** His message, **the people were astonished**. If we read the Sermon on the Mount and are not astonished at its revolutionary character, then we have failed to grasp its meaning.

The people recognized a difference between Jesus' teaching and that of the scribes. He spoke with authority; their words were powerless. His was a voice; theirs was an echo. Jamieson, Fausset and Brown comment,

> The consciousness of divine authority, as Lawgiver, Expounder and Judge, so beamed through His teaching, that the scribes' teaching could not but appear drivelling in such a light.[10]

V. THE MESSIAH'S MIRACLES OF POWER AND GRACE, AND VARYING REACTIONS TO THEM (8:1–9:34)

In chapters 8–12 the Lord Jesus presents conclusive evidence to the nation of Israel that He was indeed the Messiah of whom the prophets had written. Isaiah, for example, had foretold that Messiah would open the eyes of the blind, unstop the ears of the deaf, heal the lame, and make the mute sing (35:5, 6). Jesus, by fulfilling all these prophecies, proved that He was Messiah. Israel, by referring to her Scriptures, should have had no difficulty in identifying Him as the Christ. But none are so blind as those who will not see.

The events recorded in these chapters are presented according to a thematic scheme, rather than in strict chronological order. This is not a complete account of the Lord's ministry, but a presentation of events selected by the Holy Spirit to portray certain motifs in the Savior's life. Included in this presentation are the following:

1. Christ's absolute authority over disease, demons, death, and the elements of nature.
2. His claim to absolute lordship in the lives of those who would follow Him.
3. The mounting rejection of Jesus by the nation of Israel, particularly by the religious leaders.
4. The ready reception of the Savior by individual Gentiles.

A. Power Over Leprosy (8:1–4)

8:1 Though the teaching of Jesus was radical and extreme, it had a drawing power — so much so that **great multitudes followed Him**. Truth is self-verifying and, though people may not like it, they can never forget it.

8:2 A leper knelt before Jesus with a desperate appeal for healing. This leper had faith that the Lord could cure him, and true faith is never disappointed. Leprosy is an appropriate picture of sin because it is loathsome, destructive, infectious, and, in some forms, humanly incurable.[11]

8:3 Lepers were untouchables. Physical contact with them might expose a person to infection. In the case of the Jews, this contact made the person ceremonially unclean, that is, unfit to worship with the congregation of Israel. But when Jesus **touched** the leper and spoke the healing words, the **leprosy** vanished **immediately**. Our Savior has power to cleanse from sin and to qualify the cleansed person to be a worshiper.

8:4 This is the first instance in Matthew's Gospel where it is recorded that Jesus commanded someone to **tell no one** of the miracle done for them or of what they had seen (see also 9:30; 12:16; 17:9; Mark 5:43; 7:36; 8:26). This was probably because He was aware that many people, interested only in deliverance from the Roman yoke, wanted to make Him King. But He knew that Israel was still unrepentant, that the nation would reject His spiritual leadership, and that He must first go to the cross.

Under the Law of Moses, **the priest** also served as physician. When a leper was cleansed, he was obligated to bring an offering and to appear before the priest in order to be pronounced clean (Lev. 14:4–6). It was no doubt a rare event for a leper to be healed, so extraordinary, in fact, that it should have alerted this priest to investigate whether the Messiah had appeared at last. But we read of no such reaction. Jesus told the leper to obey the law in this matter.

The spiritual implications of the miracle are clear: The Messiah had come to Israel with power to heal the nation of its illness. He presented this miracle as one of His credentials. But the nation was not yet ready for her Deliverer.

B. Power Over Paralysis (8:5–13)

8:5, 6 The faith of a Gentile **centurion** is introduced in striking contrast to the unreceptiveness of the Jews. If Israel will not acknowledge her King, the despised pagans will. The centurion was a Roman military officer in charge of about one hundred men, and was stationed in or near Capernaum. He **came to** Jesus to seek healing for his **servant** who had suffered a violent and painful paralysis. This was an unusual display of compassion — most officials would not have shown such concern for a servant.

8:7–9 When the Lord **Jesus** offered to visit the sick servant, **the centurion** showed the reality and depth of his faith. He said, in effect, **"I am not worthy that You should** enter my house. Anyway, it isn't necessary, because You could easily heal him by saying the **word**. I know about **authority**. I take orders from my superiors, and give order to those under me. My commands are obeyed implicitly. How much more would Your words have power over my servant's illness!"

8:10–12 Jesus **marveled** at the faith of this Gentile. This is one of two times when Jesus is said to have marveled; the other time was at the unbelief of the Jews (Mark 6:6). He had **not found such great faith** among God's chosen people, **Israel**. This led Him to point out that in His coming kingdom, Gentiles would flock from all over the world to enjoy fellowship with the Jewish patriarchs while **the sons of the kingdom** would be thrown **into outer darkness** where they would weep and gnash their **teeth. Sons of the kingdom** are those who were Jews by birth, who professed to acknowledge God as King, but who were never truly converted. But the principle applies today. Many children privileged to be born and raised in Christian families will perish in hell because they reject Christ, while jungle savages will enjoy the eternal glories of heaven because they believed the gospel message.

8:13 Jesus said to the centurion, **"Go your way; and as you have believed, so let it be done for you."** Faith is rewarded in proportion to its confidence in the character of God. The **servant was healed** instantly, even though Jesus was some distance away. We may see in this a picture of Christ's present ministry; healing the non-privileged Gentiles from the paralysis of sin, though He Himself is not bodily present.

C. Power Over Fever (8:14, 15)

Entering **Peter's house**, Jesus found the mother-in-law **sick with a fever. He touched her hand, and the fever** vanished. Ordinarily fever leaves a person greatly weakened, but this cure was so instantaneous and complete that she was able to get out of bed and **serve** Him — a fitting expression of gratitude for what the Savior had done for her. We should imitate her, whenever we are healed, by serving Him with renewed dedication and vigor.

D. Power over Demons and Various Sicknesses (8:16, 17)

At **evening**, when the Sabbath was over (see Mark 1:21–34), the people surged to Him with **many** victims of demon-possession. These pathetic individuals were indwelt and controlled by evil spirits. Often they exhibited superhuman knowledge and power; at other times they were tormented. Their behavior sometimes resembled that of insane persons, but the cause was demonic rather than physical or mental. Jesus **cast out the spirits with a word**.

He also **healed all who were sick**, fulfilling the prophecy of Isaiah 53:4: **"He Himself took our infirmities and bore our sicknesses."** Verse 17 is often used by faith-healers to show that healing is in the atonement, and that therefore physical healing is something the believer can claim by faith. But here the Spirit of God applies the prophecy to our Savior's earthly healing ministry and *not* to His work on the cross.

So far in this chapter we have seen four miracles as follows:

1. Healing of the Jewish leper, with Christ present.
2. Healing of the centurion's servant, with Christ at a distance.
3. Healing of Peter's mother-in-law, with Jesus there in the house.
4. Healing of all the demon-possessed and sick, with Jesus present.

Gaebelein suggests that these typify four stages of our Lord's ministry:

1. Christ in His First Advent, ministering to His people Israel.
2. The Gentile dispensation, with Jesus absent.
3. His Second Advent, when He will enter the house, restoring His relations with Israel and heal the sick daughter of Zion.
4. The Millennium when all the demon-possessed and sick will be healed.[12]

This is an intriguing analysis of the progress of teaching in the miracles, and should alert us to the hidden depths of meaning in the sacred Scriptures. We should be warned, however, not to carry this method to extremes by forcing meanings to the point where they are ridiculous.

E. The Miracle of Human Refusal (8:18–22)

We have seen Christ exercising authority over disease and demons. It is only when He comes in contact with men and women that He meets with resistance — the miracle of human refusal.

8:18–20 As **Jesus** prepared to cross the Sea of Galilee from Capernaum to the east side, a self-confident **scribe** stepped forward pledging to follow Him "all the way." The Lord's answer challenged him to count the cost — a life of self-denial. **"Foxes have holes and birds of the air have nests, but the Son of Man has nowhere to lay His head."** In His public ministry, He had no home of His own; however, there were homes where He was a welcome guest and He ordinarily had a place to sleep. The true force of His words seems to be spiritual: this world could not provide Him with true, lasting rest. He had a work to do and could not rest till it was accomplished. The same is true of His followers; this world is not their resting place — or at least, it shouldn't be!

8:21 **Another** well-meaning follower expressed a willingness to follow Him, but had a higher priority: **"Lord, let me first go and bury my father."** Whether or not the father had already died makes little difference. The basic trouble was expressed in the contradictory words: **"Lord . . . me first."** He put self ahead of

Christ. While it is perfectly proper to provide a decent burial for one's father, it becomes wrong when such a worthy act takes precedence over the Savior's call.

8:22 Jesus answered him, in effect: "Your first duty is to **follow Me. Let the** spiritually **dead bury** the physically **dead**. An unsaved person can do that kind of work. But there is a work which you alone can do. Give the best of your life to what really lasts. Don't waste it on trivia." We are not told how these two disciples responded. But the strong implication is that they left Christ to make a comfortable place for themselves in the world and to spend their lives hugging the subordinate. Before we condemn them, we should test ourselves on the two terms of discipleship enunciated by Jesus in this passage.

F. Power Over the Elements (8:23–27)

The Sea of Galilee is noted for sudden, violent storms that whip it into a churning froth. Winds sweep down the valley of the Jordan from the north, picking up speed in the narrow gorge. When they hit the Sea, it becomes extremely unsafe for navigation.

On this occasion, Jesus was crossing from the west side to the east. When the storm broke, **He was asleep** in the boat. The terrified disciples awoke Him with frantic pleas for help. It is to their credit that they went to the right Person. After rebuking them for their puny faith, He **rebuked the winds and the** waves. When **a great calm** descended, the men **marveled** that even the elements obeyed their humble Passenger. How little they comprehended that the Creator and Sustainer of the universe was in the ship that day!

All disciples encounter storms sooner or later. At times it seems we are going to be swamped by the waves. What a comfort to know that Jesus is in the boat with us. "No water can swallow the ship where lies the Master of ocean and earth and skies." No one can quell life's storms like the Lord Jesus.

G. Jesus Heals Two Demon-Possessed Men (8:28–34)

8:28 On the east **side** of the Sea of Galilee was **the country of the Ger-**

gesenes.[13] When Jesus arrived, He met **two** unusually violent cases of demon possession. These demoniacs lived in cave-like **tombs** and were so **fierce** they made travel in that area unsafe.

8:29–31 As Jesus approached, the demons **cried out, "What have we to do with You, Jesus, You Son of God? Have You come here to torment us before the time?"** They knew who Jesus was, and that He would finally destroy them. In these respects their theology was more accurate than that of many modern liberals. Sensing that Jesus was going to cast them out of the men, they asked that they might be transfered to **a herd of many swine feeding** nearby.

8:32 Strangely enough Jesus granted their request. But why should the Sovereign Lord accede to the request of demons? To understand His action, we must remember two facts. First, demons shun the disembodied state; they want to indwell human beings, or, if that is not possible, animals or other creatures. Secondly, the purpose of demons is without exception to destroy. If Jesus had simply cast them out of the maniacs, the demons would have been a menace to the other people of the area. By allowing them to go into the swine, He prevented their entering men and women and confined their destructive power to animals. It was not yet time for their final destruction by the Lord. As soon as the transfer took place, the **swine ran violently down the steep place into the sea** and drowned.

This incident demonstrates that the ultimate aim of demons is to destroy, and underlines the terrifying possibility that two men can be indwelt by the number of demons it takes to destroy two thousand swine (Mark 5:13).

8:33, 34 The herdsmen ran back with news of what had happened. The result was that an aroused citizenry came out to Jesus and **begged Him to** leave the area. Ever since then Jesus has been criticized for the needless slaughter of pigs and has been asked to leave because He values human life above animals. If these Gergesenes were Jews, it was unlawful for them to raise pigs. But whether or not they were Jews, their condemnation is that they valued a herd of pigs more than the healing of two demoniacs.

H. Power to Forgive Sins (9:1–8)

9:1 Rejected by the Gergesenes, the Savior recrossed the Sea of Galilee and came to Capernaum, which had become **His own city** after the people of Nazareth attempted to destroy Him (Luke 4:29–31). It was here that He performed some of His mightiest miracles.

9:2 Four men came to Him, carrying **a paralytic** on a crude bed or mat. Mark's account tells us that because of the crowd, they had to tear up the roof and lower the man into Jesus' presence (2:1–12). When **Jesus** saw **their faith,** He **said to the paralytic, "Son, be of good cheer; your sins are forgiven you."** Notice that He saw *their* faith. Faith prompted the men to bring the invalid to Jesus, and the invalid's faith went out to Jesus for healing. Our Lord first rewarded this faith by pronouncing his **sins forgiven**. The Great Physician removed the cause before treating the symptoms; He gave the greater blessing first. This raises the question whether Christ ever healed a person without also imparting salvation.

9:3–5 When **some of the scribes** heard Jesus declare the man's sins forgiven, they accused Him of blasphemy **within themselves**. After all, only God can forgive sins — and they were certainly not about to receive Him as God! The omniscient Lord Jesus read their thoughts, rebuked them for the **evil in** their **hearts** of unbelief, then asked them whether it was **easier to say, "Your sins are forgiven you," or to say, "Arise and walk."** Actually it's as easy to *say* one as the other, but which is easier to *do*? Both are humanly impossible, but the results of the first command are not visible whereas the effects of the second are immediately discernible.

9:6, 7 In order to show the scribes that He had authority **on earth to forgive sins** (and should therefore be honored as God), Jesus condescended to give them a miracle they could *see*. Turning **to the paralytic**, He said, **"Arise, take up your bed and go to your house."**

9:8 When the multitudes saw him walking home with his pallet, they registered two emotions — fear and wonder. They were afraid in the presence of an obviously supernatural visitation. They **glorified God** for giving **such power to men**. But they completely missed the significance of the miracle. The *visible* healing of the paralytic was designed to confirm that the man's sins had been forgiven, an *invisible* miracle. From this they should have realized that what they had witnessed was not a demonstration of God giving authority to men but of God's presence among them in the Person of the Lord Jesus Christ. But they didn't understand.

As for the scribes, we know from later events that they only became more hardened in their unbelief and hatred.

I. Jesus Calls Matthew the Tax-Collector (9:9–13)

9:9 The tense atmosphere building up around the Savior is temporarily relieved by Matthew's simple and humble account of his own call. A tax-collector or custom house officer, he and his fellow officials were hated intensely by the Jews because of their crookedness, because of the oppressive taxes they exacted, and most of all, because they served the interests of the Roman Empire, Israel's overlord. As **Jesus passed** the tax office, **He said to** Matthew, **"Follow Me."** The response was instantaneous; he **arose and followed**; leaving a traditionally dishonest job to become an instant disciple of Jesus. As someone has said, "He lost a comfortable job, but he found a destiny. He lost a good income but he found honor. He lost a comfortable security, but he found an adventure the like of which he had never dreamed." Not the least among his rewards were that he became one of the twelve and was honored to write the Gospel which bears his name.

9:10 The meal described here was arranged by Matthew in honor of Jesus (Luke 5:29). It was his way of confessing Christ publicly and of introducing his associates to the Savior. Necessarily, therefore, the guests were **tax-collectors** and others generally known to be **sinners**!

9:11 It was the practice in those days to eat reclining on couches and facing the table. **When the Pharisees saw** Jesus associating in this way with the social riff-raff, they went to His disciples and charged Him with "guilt by association"; surely no true prophet would eat with **sinners**!

9:12 Jesus overheard and answered,

"Those who are well have no need of a physician, but those who are sick." The Pharisees considered themselves healthy and were unwilling to confess their need for Jesus. (Actually they were extremely ill spiritually and desperately needed healing.) The tax collectors and sinners, by contrast, were more willing to acknowledge their true condition and to seek Christ's saving grace. So the charge was true! Jesus *did* eat with sinners. If He had eaten with the Pharisees, the charge would still have been true — perhaps even more so! If Jesus hadn't eaten with sinners in a world like ours, He would always have eaten alone. But it is important to remember that when He ate with sinners, He never indulged in their evil ways or compromised His testimony. He used the occasion to call men to truth and holiness.

9:13 The Pharisees' trouble was that although they followed the rituals of Judaism with great precision, their hearts were hard, cold, and merciless. So Jesus dismissed them with a challenge to **learn** the meaning of Jehovah's words, **"I desire mercy, and not sacrifice"** (quoted from Hosea 6:6). Although God had instituted the sacrificial system, He did not want the rituals to become a substitute for inward righteousness. God is not a Ritualist, and He is not pleased with rituals divorced from personal godliness — precisely what the Pharisees had done. They observed the letter of the law but had no compassion for those who needed spiritual help. They associated only with self-righteous people like themselves.

In contrast, the Lord Jesus pointedly told them, **"I did not come to call the righteous, but sinners."** He perfectly fulfilled God's desire for mercy as well as sacrifice. In one sense, there are no righteous people in the world, so He came to call all men **to repentance.** But here the thought is that His call is only effective for those who acknowledge themselves to be sinners. He can dispense no healing to those who are proud, self-righteous, and unrepentant — like the Pharisees.

J. Jesus Is Questioned About Fasting (9:14–17)

9:14 By this time **John** the Baptist was probably in prison. His disciples came to Jesus with a problem. They themselves fasted **often, but** Jesus' **disciples** did **not.** Why not?

9:15 The Lord answered with an illustration. He was **the bridegroom** and His disciples the wedding guests. **As long as** He was **with them**, there was no reason to fast as a sign of mourning. But He would be taken **from them; then** His disciples would **fast.** He *was* taken from them — in death and burial, and since His ascension He has been bodily absent from His disciples. While Jesus' words do not *command* fasting, they certainly *approve* it as an appropriate exercise for those who await the Bridegroom's return.

9:16 The question raised by John's disciples further prompted Jesus to point out that John marked the end of one dispensation, announcing the new Age of Grace, and He shows that their respective principles cannot be mixed. To try to mix law and grace would be like using a **piece of** new, **unshrunk cloth** to patch **an old garment.** When washed, the patch would shrink, ripping itself away from the old cloth. The disrepair would be worse than ever. Gaebelein complains rightly:

> A judaistic Christianity which, with a profession of Grace and the Gospel, attempts to keep the law and fosters legal righteousness is a greater abomination in the eyes of God than professing Israel in the past, worshipping idols.[14]

9:17 Or the mixture would be like putting **new wine into old wineskins.** The pressure caused by the fermentation of the new wine would burst the old skins because they had lost their elasticity. The life and liberty of the Gospel ruins the wineskins of ritualism.

The introduction of the Christian era would inevitably result in tension. The joy which Christ brought could not be contained within the forms and rituals of the OT. There must be an entirely new order of things. Pettingill makes this clear:

> Thus does the King warn His disciples against the admixture of the old . . . and the new. . . . And yet this is what has been done throughout Christendom. Judaism has been patched up and adapted everywhere among the churches and the old garment is labelled "Christianity."

The result is a confusing mixture, which is neither Judaism nor Christianity, but a ritualistic substitution of dead works for a trust in the living God. The new wine of free salvation has been poured into the old wineskins of legalism, and with what result? Why, the skins are burst and ruined and the wine is spilled and most of the precious life-giving draught is lost. The law has lost its terror, because it is mixed with grace, and grace has lost its beauty and character as grace, for it is mixed with law-works.[15]

K. Power to Heal the Incurable and Raise the Dead (9:18–26)

9:18, 19 Jesus' discourse on the change of dispensations was interrupted by a distraught **ruler** of the synagogue whose **daughter** had **just died**. He knelt before the Lord, requesting Him to come and restore her to life. It was exceptional that this ruler should seek help from Jesus; most of the Jewish leaders would have feared the scorn and contempt of their associates for doing so. **Jesus** honored his faith by starting out with His disciples toward the ruler's home.

9:20 Another interruption! This time it was **a woman** who had suffered from a hemorrhage **for twelve years**. Jesus was never annoyed by such interruptions; He was always poised, accessible, and approachable.

9:21, 22 Medical science had been unable to help this woman; in fact, her condition was deteriorating (Mark 5:26). In her extremity she met Jesus — or at least she saw Him surrounded by a crowd. Believing that He was able and willing to heal her, she edged through the crowd **and touched the** fringe **of His garment**. True faith never goes unnoticed by Him. He turned and pronounced her healed; instantly **the woman was made well** for the first time in twelve years.

9:23, 24 The narrative now returns to the ruler whose daughter had died. **When Jesus** reached the **house**, the professional mourners were wailing with what someone has called "synthetic grief." He ordered the room cleared of visitors, at the same time announcing that **the girl** was **not dead but sleeping**. Most Bible students believe the Lord was

using *sleep* here in a figurative sense for death. Some believe, however, that the girl was in a coma. This interpretation does not deny that Jesus could have raised her had she been dead, but it emphasizes that Jesus was too honest to take credit for raising the dead when actually the girl had not died. Sir Robert Anderson held this view. He pointed out that the father and all the others said she had died, but **Jesus** said she had **not**.

9:25, 26 In any case, the Lord **took** the girl **by the hand** and the miracle occurred — she got up. It didn't take long for the news of the miracle to spread throughout the district.

L. Power to Give Sight (9:27–31)

9:27, 28 As **Jesus departed from** the ruler's neighborhood, **two blind men followed Him**, pleading for sight. Though dispossessed of natural vision, these men had acute spiritual discernment. In addressing Jesus as **Son of David**, they recognized Him as the long-awaited Messiah and rightful King of Israel. And they knew that when the Messiah came, one of His credentials would be that He would give sight to the blind (Isa. 61:1, RSV margin). When Jesus tested their faith by asking if they believed He was **able to do this** (give them sight), they unhesitatingly responded, **"Yes, Lord."**

9:29, 30 Then the Great Physician **touched their eyes** and assured them that because they believed, they would see. Immediately their eyes became completely normal.

Man says, "Seeing is believing." God says, "Believing is seeing." Jesus said to Martha, "Did I not say to you that if you would believe you would see?" (John 11:40). The writer to the Hebrews noted, "By faith we understand . . . " (11:3). The Apostle John wrote, "I have written to you who believe . . . that you may know . . . " (1 Jn. 5:13). God is not pleased with the kind of faith that demands a prior miracle. He wants us to believe Him simply because He is God.

Why did **Jesus sternly** warn the healed men to tell no one? In the notes on 8:4, we suggested that probably He did not want to foment a premature movement to enthrone Him as King. The people were as yet unrepentant; He could not reign over them until they were born again. Also, a revolutionary uprising in favor of Jesus would bring terrible reprisals from the Roman government on the Jews. Besides all this, the Lord Jesus had to go to the cross before He could reign as King; anything that blocked His pathway to Calvary was at variance with the predetermined plan of God.

9:31 In their delirious gratitude for eyesight, the two men **spread the news** of their miraculous cure. While we might be tempted to sympathize, and even to admire their exuberant testimony, the hard fact is that they were crassly disobedient and inevitably did more harm than good, probably by stirring up shallow curiosity rather than Spirit-inspired interest. Not even gratitude is a valid excuse for disobedience.

M. Power to Give Speech (9:32–34)

9:32 First Jesus gave life to the dead; then sight to the blind; now speech to the dumb. There seems to be a spiritual sequence in the miracles here — life first, then understanding, and then testimony.

An evil spirit had stricken this man with dumbness. Someone was concerned enough to bring the demoniac to Jesus. God bless the noble band of the anonymous who have been His instruments in bringing others to Jesus!

9:33 As soon as **the demon was cast out, the mute spoke**. Surely we may assume that he used his restored power of speech in worship and witness for the One who had so graciously healed him. The common people acknowledged that **Israel** was witnessing unprecedented miracles.

9:34 But the Pharisees answered by saying that Jesus cast **out demons by the ruler of demons**. This is what Jesus later labeled the unpardonable sin (12:32). To attribute the miracles which He performed by the Holy Spirit to the power of Satan was blasphemy against the Holy Spirit. While others were being blessed by the healing touch of Christ, the Pharisees remained spiritually dead, blind, and dumb.

VI. APOSTLES OF THE MESSIAH-KING SENT FORTH TO ISRAEL (9:35–10:42)

A. The Need for Harvest Workers (9:35–38)

9:35 This verse begins what is known as the Third Galilean Circuit. **Jesus** traveled throughout **the cities and villages**, preaching the good news of **the kingdom**, namely, that He was the King of Israel, and that if the nation repented and acknowledged Him, He would reign over them. A bona fide offer of the kingdom was made to Israel at this time. What would have happened if Israel had responded? The Bible does not answer the question. We do know that Christ would still have had to die to provide a righteous basis by which God could justify sinners of all ages.

As Christ taught and preached, He healed all kinds of sicknesses. Just as miracles characterized the First Advent of the Messiah, in lowly grace, so they will mark His Second Advent, in power and great glory (cf. Heb. 6:5: "the powers of the age to come").

9:36 As He gazed on Israel's **multitudes**, harassed and helpless, He saw them as **sheep** without a **shepherd**. His great heart of **compassion** went out to **them**. Oh, that we might know more of that yearning for the spiritual welfare of the lost and dying. How we need to pray constantly:

> Let me look on the crowd, as my Savior did,
> Till my eyes with tears grow dim;
> Let me view with pity the wandering sheep,
> And love them for love of Him.

9:37 A great work of spiritual harvest needed to be done, **but the laborers** were **few**. The problem has persisted to this day, it seems; the need is always greater than the work-force.

9:38 The Lord Jesus told the disciples to ask **the Lord of the harvest to send out laborers into His harvest**. Notice here that the need does not constitute a call. Workers should not *go* until they are *sent*.

Christ, the Son of God has sent me
To the midnight lands;
Mine the mighty ordination
Of the pierced hands.
                              — *Frances Bevan*

Jesus did not identify **the Lord of the harvest**. Some think it is the Holy Spirit. In 10:5, Jesus Himself sends out the disciples, so it seems clear that He Himself is the One to whom we should pray in this matter of world evangelization.

B. Twelve Disciples Called (10:1–4)

10:1 In the last verse of chapter 9, the Lord instructed His disciples to pray for more laborers. To make that request sincerely, believers must be willing to go themselves. So here we find the Lord calling **His twelve disciples**. He had previously chosen them, but now He calls them to a special evangelistic mission to the nation of Israel. With the call went authority to cast out unclean spirits and to heal all kinds of diseases. The uniqueness of Jesus is seen here. Other men had performed miracles, but no other man ever conferred the power on others.

10:2–4 The **twelve apostles** were:

1. **Simon, who is called Peter**. Impetuous, generous-hearted, affectionate man that he was, he was a born leader.
2. **Andrew, his brother**. He was introduced to Jesus by John the Baptist (John 1:36, 40), then brought his brother Peter to Him. He made it his business thereafter to bring men to Jesus.
3. **James, the son of Zebedee**, who was later killed by Herod (Acts 12:2) — the first of the twelve to die as a martyr.
4. **John, his brother**. Also a son of Zebedee, he was the disciple whom Jesus loved. We are indebted to him for the Fourth Gospel, three Epistles, and Revelation.
5. **Philip**. A citizen of Bethsaida, he brought Nathanael to Jesus. He is not to be confused with Philip the Evangelist, in the book of Acts.
6. **Bartholomew**. Believed to be the same as Nathanael, the Israelite in whom Jesus found no guile (John 1:47).
7. **Thomas**, also called Didymus, meaning "twin." Commonly known as "Doubting Thomas," his doubts gave

way to a magnificent confession of Christ (John 20:28).

8. **Matthew**. The former tax-collector who wrote this Gospel.
9. **James, the son of Alphaeus**. Little else is definitely known about him.
10. **Lebbaeus, whose surname was Thaddaeus**. He is also known as Judas the son of James (Luke 6:16). His only recorded utterance is found in John 14:22.
11. **Simon, the Canaanite**, whom Luke calls the Zealot (6:15).
12. **Judas Iscariot**, the betrayer of our Lord.

The disciples were probably in their twenties at this time. Taken from varied walks of life and probably young men of average ability, their true greatness lay in their association with Jesus.

C. The Mission to Israel (10:5–33)

10:5, 6 The remainder of the chapter contains Jesus' instructions concerning a special preaching tour to the **house of Israel**. This is not to be confused with the later sending of the seventy (Luke 10:1) or with the Great Commission (Matt. 28:19, 20). This was a temporary mission with the specific purpose of announcing that **the kingdom of heaven** was near. While some of the principles are of lasting value for God's people in all ages, the fact that some were later revoked by the Lord Jesus proves they were not intended to be permanent (Luke 22:35, 36).

First the *route* is given. They were **not** to go to **the Gentiles** or to **the Samaritans**, a mixed race detested by the Jews. Their ministry was limited at this time **to the lost sheep of the house of Israel.**

10:7 The *message* was the proclamation that **the kingdom of heaven** was **at hand**. If Israel refused, there would be no excuse because an official announcement was to be made exclusively to them. The kingdom had drawn near in the Person of the King. Israel must decide whether to accept or reject Him.

10:8 The disciples were given *credentials* to confirm their message. They were to **heal the sick, cleanse the lepers, raise the dead,**[16] and **cast out demons**. The Jews demanded signs (1 Cor. 1:22) so God graciously condescended to give them signs.

As to *remuneration*, the Lord's representatives were to make no charge for their services. They had received their blessings without cost and were to dispense them on the same basis.

10:9, 10 They would not be required to make advance *provision* for the journey. After all, they were Israelites preaching to Israelites, and it was a recognized principle among the Jews that the laborer deserves his food. So it would not be necessary for them to take **gold, silver, copper**, food **bag, two tunics, sandals**, or **staffs**. Probably the meaning is *extra* sandals or an *extra* staff; if they already had a staff, they were permitted to take it (Mark 6:8). The idea is that their needs would be supplied on a day by day basis.

10:11 What arrangements were they to make for *housing*? When they entered a **city**, they were to look for a **worthy** host — one who would receive them as disciples of the Lord and who would be open to their message. Once they found such a host, they were to stay with him as long as they were in the city, rather than moving if they found more favorable living conditions.

10:12–14 If a **household** received them, the disciples were to **greet** the family, showing courtesy and gratitude in accepting such hospitality. If, on the other hand, a house refused to host the Lord's messengers, they were not obligated to pray for God's **peace** on it, that is, they would not pronounce a benediction on the family. Not only so, they were to dramatize God's displeasure by shaking **the dust** off their **feet**. In rejecting Christ's disciples, a family was rejecting Him.

10:15 He warned that such rejection would bring severer punishment **in the day of judgment** than the perversion of **Sodom and Gomorrah**. This proves that there will be degrees of punishment in hell; otherwise how could it be **more tolerable** for some than for others?

10:16 In this section Jesus counsels the twelve concerning their *behavior in the face of persecution*. They would be like **sheep in the midst of wolves**, surrounded by vicious men bent on destroying them. They should **be wise as serpents**, avoiding giving needless offense or being tricked into compromising situations. And they should be **harmless as doves**, protected by the armor of a righteous character and faith unfeigned.

10:17 They should be on guard against unbelieving Jews who would hale them into criminal courts and flog them **in their synagogues**. The attack against them would be both civil and religious.

10:18 They would be dragged **before governors and kings** for Christ's sake. But God's cause would triumph over man's evil. "Man has his wickedness but God has His way." In their hour of seeming defeat the disciples would have the incomparable privilege of testifying before rulers and **Gentiles**. God would be working all things together for good. Christianity has suffered much from civil authorities, yet "no doctrine was ever so helpful to those appointed to govern."

10:19, 20 They need not rehearse what they would say when on trial. When the time came, **the Spirit** of God would give them divine wisdom to answer in such a way as to glorify Christ and utterly confuse and frustrate their accusers. Two extremes should be avoided in interpreting verse 19. The first is the naive assumption that a Christian never needs to prepare a message in advance. The second is the view that the verse has no relevance for us today. It is proper and desirable for a preacher to prayerfully wait before God for the appropriate word for a specific occasion. But it is also true that in crises, all believers can claim God's promise to give them wisdom to speak with divine intuition. They become mouthpieces for the Spirit of their Father.

10:21 Jesus forewarned His disciples that they would have to face treachery and betrayal. **Brother** would accuse **brother. Father** would betray **his child. Children** would become informers against their **parents**, resulting in the execution of the parents.

J. C. Macaulay put it well:

We are in good company in enduring the world's hatred. . . . The servant may not expect better treatment at the hands of the enemy than the Lord Himself received. If the world had nothing better than a cross for Jesus, it will not have a royal carriage for His followers: if only thorns for Him, there will not be garlands for us. . . . Only let us see that the world's hatred of us is really "for Christ's sake," and not on account of anything hateful in us and unworthy of the gracious Lord whom we represent.[17]

10:22, 23 The disciples would **be hated by all** — not by all without exception, but by all cultures, nationalities, classes, etc., of men. **"But he who endures to the end will be saved."** Taken by itself, this could seem to imply that salvation can be earned by steadfast endurance. We know it cannot mean this because throughout the Scriptures salvation is presented as a free gift of God's grace through faith (Eph. 2:8, 9). Neither can the verse mean that those who remain faithful to Christ will be saved from physical death; the previous verse predicts the death of some faithful disciples. The simplest explanation is that endurance is the hallmark of the genuinely saved. Those who endure to the end in times of persecution show by their perseverance that they are true believers. This same statement is found in Matthew 24:13 where it refers to a faithful remnant of Jews during the Tribulation who refuse to compromise their loyalty to the Lord Jesus. Their endurance manifests them as genuine disciples.

In Bible passages dealing with the future, the Spirit of God often shifts from the immediate future to the distant future. A prophecy may have a partial and immediate significance and also a complete and more distant fulfillment. For instance, the two Advents of Christ may be merged in a single passage without explanation (Isa. 52:14, 15; Mic. 5:2–4). In verses 22 and 23 the Lord Jesus makes this kind of prophetic transition. He warns the twelve disciples of the sufferings they will undergo for His sake, then He seems to see them as a type of His devoted Jewish followers during the Great Tribulation. He leaps forward from the trials of the first Christians to those of believers prior to His Second Advent.

The first part of verse 23 could refer to the twelve disciples: But **"when they persecute you in this city, flee to another . . ."** They were not obligated to remain under the tyranny of their enemies if there was an honorable way to escape. "It is not wrong to escape from danger — only from duty."

The latter part of verse 23 carries us forward to the days preceding Christ's coming to reign: **". . . you will not have gone through the cities of Israel before the Son of Man comes."** This could not refer to the mission of the twelve because the Son of Man had already come. Some Bible teachers understand this as a reference to the destruction of Jerusalem in A.D. 70. However, it is difficult to see how this holocaust can be spoken of as "the coming of the Son of Man." It seems far more plausible to find here a reference to His Second Coming. During the Great Tribulation, Christ's faithful Jewish brethren will go forth with the gospel of the kingdom. They will be persecuted and pursued. Before they can reach all the cities of Israel, the Lord Jesus will return to judge His foes and set up His kingdom.

There might seem to be a contradiction between verse 23 and Matthew 24:14. Here it is stated that **not** all **the cities of Israel** will be reached **before the Son of Man comes**. There it says that the gospel of the kingdom will be preached in all the world before His Second Advent. However, there is no contradiction. The gospel will be preached in all nations though not necessarily to every individual. But this message will meet stiff resistance, and the messengers will be severely persecuted and hindered in Israel. Thus, not all the cities of Israel will be reached.

10:24, 25 The disciples of the Lord would often have occasion to wonder why they should have to endure ill treatment. If Jesus was the Messiah, why were His followers suffering instead of reigning? In verses 24 and 25, He anticipates their perplexity and answers it by reminding them of their relationship to Him. They were the disciples; He was their Teacher. They were servants; He was their Master. They were members of the household; He was the Master of the house. Discipleship means following the Teacher, not being superior to Him. The servant should not expect to be treated better than his Master. If men call the worthy Master of the house **"Beelzebub"** ("lord of flies," an Ekronite god whose name was used by Jews for Satan), they will hurl even greater insults at the members of His **household**. Discipleship involves sharing the Master's rejection.

10:26, 27 Three times the Lord told His followers not to fear (vv. 26, 28, 31). First, they should **not fear** the seeming victory of their foes; His cause would be gloriously vindicated in a coming day. Up to now the gospel had been relatively **covered** and His teachings had been comparatively **hidden**. But soon the disciples must boldly proclaim the Christian message which up to this point had been told them in secret, that is privately.

10:28 Second, the disciples should **not fear** the murderous rage of men. The worst that men can do is **kill the body**. Physical death is not the supreme tragedy for the Christian. To die is to be with Christ and thus far better. It is deliverance from sin, sorrow, sickness, suffering, and death; and it is translation into eternal glory. So the worst men can do is, in a real sense, the best thing that can happen to the child of God.

The disciples should not fear men but should have a reverential **fear** of **Him who is able to destroy both soul and body in hell**. This is the greatest loss — eternal separation from God, from Christ, and from hope. Spiritual death is the loss that cannot be measured and the doom that should be avoided at all cost.

The words of Jesus in verse 28 evoke memories of the saintly John Knox, whose epitaph reads, "Here lies one who feared God so much that he never feared the face of any man."

10:29 In the midst of fiery trials, the disciples could be confident of God's care. The Lord Jesus teaches this from the ubiquitous sparrow. Two of these insignificant birds were **sold for a copper coin**. Yet **not one of them** dies outside the **Father's will**, without His knowledge or His presence. As someone has said, "God attends the funeral of every sparrow."

10:30, 31 The same God who takes a personal interest in the tiny sparrow keeps an accurate count of the **hairs of the head** of each of His children. A strand of hair is of considerably less value than a sparrow. This shows that His people are **of more value** to Him **than many sparrows**, so why should they fear?

10:32 In view of the foregoing considerations, what is more reasonable than that the disciples of Christ should fearlessly **confess** Him **before men**? Any shame or reproach they might bear will be abundantly rewarded in heaven when the Lord Jesus confesses them **before** His **Father**. Confession of Christ here involves commitment to Him as Lord and Savior and the resulting acknowledgment of Him by life and by lips. In the case of most of the twelve, this led to the ultimate confession of the Lord in martyrdom.

10:33 Denial of Christ on earth will be repaid with denial **before** God **in heaven**. To deny Christ in this sense means to refuse to recognize His claims over one's life. Those whose lives say, in effect, "I never knew You" will hear Him say at last, "I never knew you." The Lord is not referring to a temporary denial of Him under pressure, as in Peter's case, but to that kind of denial that is habitual and final.

D. Not Peace But a Sword (10:34–39)

10:34 Our Lord's words must be understood as a figure of speech in which the visible results of His coming are stated as the apparent purpose of His coming. He says He **did not come to bring peace but a sword**. Actually He did come to make peace (Eph. 2:14–17); He came that the world might be saved through Him (John 3:17).

10:35–37 But the point here is that whenever individuals became His followers, their families would turn against them. A converted father would be opposed by his unbelieving son, a Christian mother by her unsaved daughter. A born again mother-in-law would be hated by her unregenerate daughter-in-law. So a choice must often be made between Christ and family. No ties of nature can be allowed to deflect a disciple from utter allegiance to the Lord. The Savior must take precedence over father, mother, son or daughter. One of the costs of discipleship is to experience tension, strife, and alienation from one's own family. This hostility is often more bitter than is encountered in other areas of life.

10:38 But there is something even

more apt to rob Christ of His rightful place than family — that is, the love of one's own life. So Jesus added, **"And he who does not take his cross and follow after Me is not worthy of Me."** The cross, of course, was a means of execution. To take the cross and follow Christ means to live in such devoted abandonment to Him that even death itself is not too high a price to pay. Not all disciples are required to lay down their lives for the Lord, but all are called on to value Him so highly that they do not count their lives precious to themselves.

10:39 Love of Christ must overmaster the instinct of self-preservation. **He who finds his life will lose it, and he who loses his life for** Christ's **sake will find it**. The temptation is to hug one's life by trying to avoid the pain and loss of a life of total commitment. But this is the greatest waste of a life — to spend it in the gratification of self. The greatest use of a life is to spend it in the service of Christ. The person **who loses his life** in devotedness to Him **will find it** in its true fullness.

E. A Cup of Cold Water (10:40–42)

10:40 Not everyone would refuse the disciples' message. Some would recognize them as representatives of the Messiah and receive them graciously. The disciples would have limited ability to reward such kindness, but they need not fret; anything done for them would be reckoned as being done for the Lord Himself and would be rewarded accordingly.

To receive Christ's disciple would be tantamount to receiving Christ Himself, and to receive Him was the same as receiving the Father **who sent** Him, since the one sent represents the sender. To receive an ambassador, who stands in the place of the government that commissions him, is to enjoy diplomatic relations with his country.

10:41 Anyone **who receives a prophet** because he is a **prophet shall receive a prophet's reward**. A. T. Pierson comments:

> The Jews regarded the reward of the prophet as the greatest; because, while kings bore rule in the name of the Lord, and priests ministered in the name of the Lord, the prophet came from the Lord to instruct both priest and king. Christ says

that if you do no more than receive a prophet in the capacity of prophet, the same reward that is given to the prophet will be given to you, if you help the prophet along. Think of that if you are inclined to criticize a speaker! If you help him to speak for God, and encourage him you will get part of his reward; but if you make it difficult for him to discharge his office, you will lose your reward. It is a great thing to help a man who is seeking to do good. You should not regard his dress, his attitude, his manners or his voice; but you should look beyond these things and say, "Is this message of God for me? Is this man a prophet of God to my soul?" If he is, receive him, magnify his word and work, and get part of his reward.[18]

The one **who receives a righteous man** because he is **a righteous man shall receive a righteous man's reward**. Those who judge others by physical attractiveness or material affluence fail to realize that true moral worth is often cloaked in very humble guise. The way a man treats the most homespun disciple is the way he treats the Lord Himself.

10:42 No kindness shown to a follower of Jesus will go unnoticed. Even **a cup of cold water** will be grandly rewarded if it is given to **a disciple** because he is a follower of the Lord.

Thus the Lord closes His special charge to the twelve by investing them with regal dignity. It is true that they would be opposed, rejected, arrested, tried, imprisoned, and perhaps even killed. But let them never forget that they were representatives of the King and that their glorious privilege was to speak and act for Him.

VII. INCREASING OPPOSITION AND REJECTION (Chaps. 11, 12)

A. John the Baptist Imprisoned (11:1–19)

11:1 Having sent the twelve on the special temporary mission to the house of Israel, Jesus **departed from there to teach and to preach in** the **cities** of Galilee where the disciples had previously lived.

11:2, 3 By now **John** had been imprisoned by Herod. Discouraged and lonely, he began to wonder. If Jesus were truly the Messiah, why did He allow His forerunner to languish in prison? Like many great men of God, John suffered a temporary lapse of faith. So **he sent two of his disciples** to ask if Jesus really was the One the prophets had promised, or if they should still be looking for the Anointed One.

11:4, 5 Jesus answered by reminding John that He was performing the miracles predicted of the Messiah: **The blind see** (Isa. 35:5); **the lame walk** (Isa. 35:6); **lepers are cleansed** (Isa. 53:4, cf. Matt. 8:16, 17); **the deaf hear** (Isa. 35:5); **the dead are raised up** (not prophesied of the Messiah; it was greater than the predicted miracles). Jesus also reminded John that **the gospel** was being **preached** to **the poor** in fulfillment of the Messianic prophecy in Isaiah 61:1. Ordinary religious leaders often concentrate their attention on the wealthy and aristocratic. The Messiah brought good news to **the poor**.

11:6 Then the Savior added, **"And blessed is he who is not offended because of Me."** On other lips this would be the boast of a supreme egotist. On Jesus' lips, it is the valid expression of His personal perfection. Instead of appearing as a colorful military general, the Messiah had come as a humble Carpenter. His gentleness, lowliness, and humiliation were out of character with the prevailing image of the militant Messiah. Men who were guided by fleshly desires might doubt His claim to kingship. But God's blessing would rest on those who, by spiritual insight, recognized Jesus of Nazareth as the promised Messiah.

Verse 6 should not be interpreted as a rebuke to John the Baptist. Everyone's faith needs to be confirmed and strengthened at times. It is one thing to have a temporary lapse of faith and quite another to be permanently stumbled as to the true identity of the Lord Jesus. No single chapter is the story of a man's life. Taking John's life in its totality, we find a record of faithfulness and perseverance.

11:7, 8 As soon as John's disciples **departed** with Jesus' words of reassurance, the Lord turned **to the multitudes** with words of glowing praise for the Baptist. This same crowd had flocked to the desert when John was preaching

there. Why? **To see** some weak, vacillating **reed** of a man, **shaken** by every passing **wind** of human opinion? Certainly not! John was a fearless preacher, an embodied conscience, who would rather suffer than be silent, and rather die than lie. Had they gone **out to see** a well-dressed palace courtier, luxuriating in comfort? Certainly not! John was a simple man of God whose austere life was a rebuke to the enormous worldliness of the people.

11:9 Had they gone out to see **a prophet**? Well, John was a prophet — in fact, the greatest of the prophets. The Lord did not imply here that he was greater as to his personal character, eloquence, or persuasiveness; he was greater because of his position as forerunner of the Messiah-King.

11:10 This is made clear in verse 10; John was the fulfillment of Malachi's prophecy (3:1) — the **messenger** who would precede the Lord and **prepare** the people for His coming. Other men had prophesied the Coming of Christ, but John was the one chosen to announce His actual arrival. It has been well said, "John *opened the way* for Christ and then he got *out of the way* for Christ."

11:11 The statement that **"he who is least in the kingdom of heaven is greater than he"** proves that Jesus was speaking of John's privilege, not his character. A person **who is least in the kingdom of heaven** does not necessarily have a better character than John, but he does have **greater** privilege. To be a citizen of the kingdom is greater than to announce its arrival. John's privilege was great in preparing the way for the Lord, but he did not live to enjoy the blessings of the kingdom.

11:12 From the opening of John's ministry to his present imprisonment **the kingdom of heaven** had suffered **violence**. The Pharisees and scribes had vigorously opposed it. Herod the king had done his part to buffet the kingdom by seizing its herald.

"... And the violent take it by force." This statement is capable of two interpretations. First, the foes of the kingdom did their best to take the kingdom in order to destroy it. Their rejection of John foreshadowed the rejection of the King Himself and thus of the kingdom. But it may also mean that those who were ready for the King's advent responded vigorously to the announcement and strained every muscle to enter. This is the meaning in Luke 16:16: "The law and the prophets were until John. Since that time the kingdom of God has been preached, and every one is pressing into it." Here the kingdom is pictured as a besieged city, with all classes of men hammering at it from the outside, trying to get in. A certain spiritual violence is necessary.

Whichever meaning one adopts, the thought is that John's preaching touched off a violent reaction, with widespread and deep effects.

11:13† **"For all the prophets and the law prophesied until John."** The entire volume from Genesis to Malachi predicted the coming of the Messiah. When John stepped out on the stage of history, his unique role was not just prophecy; it was announcing the fulfillment of all the prophecies concerning Christ's First Advent.

11:14 Malachi had predicted that before Messiah's appearance, Elijah would come as a forerunner (Mal. 4:5, 6). If the people had been **willing to receive** Jesus as Messiah, John would have filled the role of **Elijah**. John was not Elijah reincarnated — he disclaimed being Elijah in John 1:21. But he went before Christ in the spirit and power of Elijah (Luke 1:17).

11:15 Not all appreciated John the Baptist or understood the deep significance of his ministry. Therefore the Lord added, **"He who has ears to hear, let him hear!"** In other words, pay heed. Don't miss the significance of what you are hearing. If John fulfilled the prophecy concerning Elijah, then Jesus was the promised Messiah! In thus accrediting John the Baptist, Jesus was reaffirming His claim to be the Christ of God. To accept one would lead to acceptance of the other.

11:16, 17 But the **generation** to whom Jesus was speaking was not interested in accepting either. The Jews who were privileged to see the Advent of their Messiah-King had no relish for Him or His forerunner. They were a conundrum. Jesus compared them to peevish **children sitting in the marketplaces** who refused to be satisfied with any overtures. If their friends wanted to pipe

so they could **dance**, they refused. If their friends wanted to play-act a funeral, they refused to **lament**.

11:18, 19 **John came** as an ascetic, and the Jews accused him of being demon-possessed. **The Son of Man**, on the other hand, ate and drank in a normal manner. If John's asceticism made them uncomfortable, then surely they would be pleased with Jesus' more ordinary eating habits. But no! They called Him **a glutton**, a drunkard, **a friend of tax-collectors and sinners**. Of course, Jesus never ate or drank to excess; their charge was a total fabrication. It is true that He was **a friend of tax-collectors and sinners**, but not in the way they meant. He befriended sinners in order to save them from their sins, but He never shared or approved their sins.

"But wisdom is justified by her children." The Lord Jesus, of course, is Wisdom personified (1 Cor. 1:30). Though unbelieving men might slander Him, He is vindicated in His works and in the lives of His followers. Though the mass of the Jews might refuse to acknowledge Him as Messiah-King, His claims were completely verified by His miracles and by the spiritual transformation of His devoted disciples.

B. Woes on the Unrepentant Cities of Galilee (11:20–24)

11:20 Great privilege brings great responsibility. No cities were ever more privileged than Chorazin, Bethsaida, and Capernaum. The incarnate Son of God had walked their dusty lanes, taught their favored people, and performed most of His **mighty works** within their walls. In the face of this overwhelming evidence, they had stubbornly refused to **repent**. Little wonder, then, that the Lord should pronounce the most solemn doom upon them.

11:21 He began with **Chorazin** and **Bethsaida**. These cities had heard the gracious entreaties of their Savior-God, yet willfully turned Him away. His mind reverted to the cities of **Tyre and Sidon** which had fallen under the judgment of God because of their idolatry and wickedness. If they had been privileged to see the miracles of Jesus, they would have humbled themselves in deepest repentance. **In the day of judgment**, therefore, **Tyre and Sidon** would fare better

†See p. xx.

than Chorazin and Bethsaida.

11:22 The words **"it will be more tolerable in the day of judgment"** indicate that there will be degrees of punishment in hell, just as there will be degrees of reward in heaven (1 Cor. 3:12–15). The single sin that consigns men to hell is refusal to submit to Jesus Christ (John 3:36b). But the depth of suffering in hell is conditional on the privileges spurned and the sins indulged.

11:23, 24 Few cities had been as favored as **Capernaum**. It became Jesus' home town after His rejection at Nazareth (9:1, cf. Mark 2:1–12), and some of His most extraordinary miracles — irrefutable evidences of His Messiahship — were performed there. Had vile Sodom, the capital of homosexuality, been so privileged, it would have repented and been spared. But Capernaum's privilege was greater. Its people should have repented and gladly acknowledged the Lord. But Capernaum missed its day of opportunity. Sodom's sin of perversion was great. But no sin is greater than Capernaum's rejection of the holy Son of God. Therefore, Sodom will not be punished as severely as Capernaum in the day of judgment. Lifted up **to heaven** in privilege, Capernaum **will be brought down to Hades** in judgment. If this is true of Capernaum, how much truer of places where Bibles abound, where the gospel is broadcast, and where few, if any, are without excuse.

In the days of our Lord, there were four prominent cities in Galilee: Chorazin, Bethsaida, Capernaum, and Tiberias. He pronounced woes against the first three but not Tiberias. What has been the result? The destruction of Chorazin and Bethsaida is so complete that their exact sites are unknown. The location of Capernaum is not positive. Tiberias still stands. This remarkable fulfillment of prophecy is one more evidence of the Savior's omniscience and the Bible's inspiration.

C. The Savior's Reaction to Rejection (11:25–30)

11:25, 26 The three cities of Galilee had neither eyes to see nor heart to love the Christ of God. He knew their attitude was but a foretaste of rejection on a wider scale. How did He react to their impenitance? Not with bitterness, cynicism, or vindictiveness. Rather He lifted His voice in thanks to God that nothing could frustrate His sovereign purposes. **"I thank You, Father, Lord of heaven and earth, because You have hidden these things from the wise and prudent and have revealed them to babes."**

We should avoid two possible misunderstandings. First, Jesus was not expressing pleasure in the inevitable judgment of the Galilean cities. Secondly, He did not imply that God had highhandedly withheld the light from the wise and prudent.

The cities had every chance to welcome the Lord Jesus. They deliberately refused to submit to Him. When they refused the light, God withheld the light from them. But God's plans will not fail. If the intelligentsia will not believe, then God will reveal Him to humble hearts. He fills the hungry with good things and sends the rich away empty (Luke 1:53).

Those who consider themselves too wise and understanding to need Christ become afflicted with judicial blindness. But those who admit their lack of wisdom receive a revelation of Him "in whom are hidden all the treasures of wisdom and knowledge" (Col. 2:3). Jesus thanked the Father for ordaining that if some would not have Him, others would. In the face of titanic unbelief He found consolation in the overruling plan and purpose of God.

11:27 All things had **been delivered to** Christ **by** His **Father**. This would be a presumptuous claim from anyone else, but from the Lord Jesus it is a simple statement of truth. At that moment, with opposition mounting, it did not appear that He was in control; nonetheless it was true. The program of His life was moving irresistibly toward eventual glorious triumph. **"No one knows the Son except the Father."** There is incomprehensible mystery about the Person of Christ. The union of deity and humanity in one Person raises problems that boggle the human mind. For instance, there is the problem of death. God cannot die. Yet Jesus is God and Jesus died. And yet His divine and human natures are inseparable. So although we can know Him and love Him and trust Him, there is a sense in which only the Father can truly understand Him.

But the high myst'ries of Thy Name
The creature's grasp transcend;
The Father only (glorious claim!)
The Son can comprehend.
Worthy, O Lamb of God, art Thou,
That every knee to Thee should bow!
                    – *Josiah Conder*

"Nor does anyone know the Father except the Son and he to whom the Son wills to reveal Him." The Father, too, is inscrutable. Ultimately, only God is great enough to understand God. Man cannot know Him by his own strength or intellect. But the Lord Jesus can and does reveal the Father to those whom He chooses. Whoever comes to know the Son comes to know the Father also (John 14:7).

Yet, after saying all this, we must confess that in seeking to explain verse 27, we are dealing with truths too high for us. We see in a mirror dimly. Not even in eternity will our finite minds be able to fully appreciate the greatness of God or understand the mystery of the Incarnation. When we read that the Father is revealed only to those whom the Son chooses, we might be tempted to think of an arbitrary selection of a favored few. The following verse guards against such an interpretation. The Lord Jesus issues a universal invitation to all who are weary and heavy laden to come to Him for rest. In other words, the ones to whom He chooses to reveal the Father are those who trust Him as Lord and Savior. As we examine this invitation of infinite tenderness, let us remember that it was issued after the blatant rejection of Jesus by the favored cities of Galilee. Man's hate and obstinacy could not extinguish His love and grace. A. J. McClain said:

Although the nation of Israel is moving toward the ordeal of divine judgment, the King in His final word throws open wide the door of personal salvation. And thus He proves that He is a God of grace, even on the threshold of judgment.[19]

11:28 Come. To come means to believe (Acts 16:31); to receive (John 1:12); to eat (John 6:35); to drink (John 7:37); to look (Isa. 45:22); to confess (1 Jn. 4:2); to hear (John 5:24, 25); to enter a door (John 10:9); to open a door (Rev. 3:20); to touch the hem of His garment (Matt. 9:20, 21); and to accept the gift of eternal life through Christ our Lord (Rom. 6:23).

to Me. The object of faith is not a church, a creed, or a clergyman, but the living Christ. Salvation is in a Person. Those who have Jesus are as saved as God can make them.

all you who labor and are heavy laden. In order to truly come to Jesus, a person must admit that he is burdened with the weight of sin. Only those who acknowledge they are lost can be saved. Faith in the Lord Jesus Christ is preceded by repentance toward God.

and I will give you rest. Notice that **rest** here is a gift; it is unearned and unmerited. This is the *rest of salvation* that comes from realizing that Christ finished the work of redemption on Calvary's cross. It is the *rest of conscience* that follows the realization that the penalty of one's sins has been paid once for all and that God will not demand payment twice.

11:29 In verses 29 and 30, the invitation changes from salvation to service.

Take My yoke upon you. This means to enter into submission to His will, to turn over control of one's life to Him (Rom. 12:1, 2).

and learn from Me. As we acknowledge His lordship in every area of our lives, He trains us in His ways.

for I am gentle and lowly in heart. In contrast to the Pharisees who were harsh and proud, the true Teacher is meek **and lowly**. Those who take His yoke will learn to take the lowest place.

and you will find rest for your souls. Here it is not the rest of conscience but the rest of heart that is found by taking the lowest place before God and man. It is also the rest that one experiences in the service of Christ when he stops trying to be great.

11:30 "For My yoke is easy and My burden is light." Again there is a striking contrast with the Pharisees. Jesus said of them, "For they bind heavy burdens, hard to bear, and lay them on men's shoulders; but they themselves will not move them with one of their fingers" (Matt. 23:4). Jesus' yoke is easy; it does not chafe. Someone has suggested that if Jesus had had a sign outside His carpenter's shop, it would have read, "My yokes fit well."

His **burden is light**. This does not

mean that there are no problems, trials, labor, or heartaches in the Christian life. But it does mean that we do not have to bear them alone. We are yoked with One who gives sufficient grace for every time of need. To serve Him is not bondage but perfect freedom. J. H. Jowett says:

> The fatal mistake for the believer is to seek to bear life's load in a single collar. God never intended a man to carry his burden alone. *Christ therefore deals only in yokes!* A yoke is a neck harness for two, and the Lord himself pleads to be One of the two. He wants to share the labor of any galling task. The secret of peace and victory in the Christian life is found in putting off the taxing collar of "self" and accepting the Master's relaxing "yoke."[20]

D. Jesus Is Lord of the Sabbath (12:1–8)

12:1 This chapter records the mounting crisis of rejection. The rising malice and animosity of the Pharisees are now ready to spill over. The issue that opens the floodgates is the Sabbath question.

On this particular Sabbath, **Jesus** and His disciples were passing **through the grainfields. His disciples began to pluck heads of grain and to eat** them. The law permitted them to help themselves to grain from their neighbor's field as long as they did not use a sickle (Deut. 23:25).

12:2 But **the Pharisees**, legal nitpickers, charged that the **Sabbath** had been broken. Though their specific charges are not stated it is likely that they accused the disciples of: (1) harvesting (picking the grain); (2) threshing (rubbing it in their hands); (3) winnowing (separating the grain from the chaff).

12:3, 4 Jesus answered their ridiculous complaint by reminding them of an incident in the life of **David**. Once, when in exile, he and his men went into the wilderness **and ate the showbread**, twelve memorial loaves forbidden as food to any but the priests. Neither David nor his men were priests, yet God never found fault with them for doing this. Why not?

The reason is that God's law was never intended to inflict hardship on His faithful people. It was not David's fault that he was in exile. A sinful nation had rejected him. If he had been given his rightful place, he and his followers would not have had to eat the showbread. Because there was sin in Israel, God permitted an otherwise forbidden act.

The analogy is clear. The Lord Jesus was the rightful King of Israel, but the nation would not acknowledge Him as Sovereign. If He had been given His proper place, His followers would not have been reduced to eating in this way on the Sabbath or on any other day of the week. History was repeating itself. The Lord did not reprove His disciples, because they had done no wrong.

12:5 Jesus reminded the Pharisees that the **priests profane the Sabbath** by killing and sacrificing animals and by performing many other servile duties (Num. 28:9, 10), yet are **blameless** because they are engaged in the service of God.

12:6 The Pharisees knew that the priests worked every Sabbath in the temple without desecrating it. Why then should they criticize the disciples for acting as they did in the presence of *One* who is **greater than the temple**? The italicized word *One* can perhaps better read: "*something* greater than the temple is here." The "something" is the kingdom of God, present in the Person of the King.

12:7 The Pharisees had never understood the heart of God. In Hosea 6:6 He had said, **"I desire mercy and not sacrifice."** God puts compassion before ritual. He would rather see His people picking grain on the Sabbath to satisfy their hunger than observing the day so strictly as to inflict physical distress. If the Pharisees had only realized this, they would not have condemned the disciples. But they valued outward punctiliousness above human welfare.

12:8 Then the Savior added, **"For the Son of Man is Lord even of the Sabbath."** It was He who had instituted the law in the first place, and therefore He was the One most qualified to interpret its true meaning. E. W. Rogers says:

> It seems as if Matthew, here taught by the Spirit, passes in quick review the many names and offices of the Lord Jesus: He

is Son of Man; Lord of the Sabbath; My servant; My beloved; Son of David; greater than the temple; greater than Jonas; greater than Solomon. He does so in order to show the enormity of the sin of refusing to accept Him and accord Him His rights.[21]

Before proceeding with the next incident — Jesus healing the withered hand on the Sabbath — we pause to give a short review of the scriptural teaching concerning the Sabbath.

EXCURSUS ON THE SABBATH

The Sabbath day was, and always will be, the seventh day of the week (Saturday).

God rested on the seventh day, after the six days of creation (Gen. 2:2). He did not command man to keep the Sabbath day at that time, although He may have intended the principle — one day of rest in every seven — to be followed.

The nation of Israel was commanded to keep the Sabbath when the Ten Commandments were given (Ex. 20:8–11). The law of the Sabbath was different from the other nine commandments; it was a ceremonial law while the others were moral. The only reason it was wrong to work on the Sabbath was because God said so. The other commandments had to do with things that were intrinsically wrong.

The prohibition against work on the Sabbath was never intended to apply to: the service of God (Matt. 12:5), deeds of necessity (Matt. 12:3, 4), or deeds of mercy (Matt. 12:11, 12). Nine of the Ten Commandments are repeated in the NT, not as law but as instructions for Christians living under grace. The only commandment Christians are never told to keep is that of the Sabbath. Rather, Paul teaches that the Christian cannot be condemned for failing to keep it (Col. 2:16).

The distinctive day of Christianity is the first day of the week. The Lord Jesus rose from the dead on that day (John 20:1), a proof that the work of redemption had been completed and divinely approved. On the next two Lord's Days, He met with His disciples (John 20:19, 26). The Holy Spirit was given on the first day of the week (Acts 2:1; cf. Lev. 23:15, 16). The early disciples met on that day to break bread, showing forth

the Lord's death (Acts 20:7). It is the day appointed by God on which Christians should set aside funds for the work of the Lord (1 Cor. 16:1, 2).

The Sabbath or seventh day came at the end of a week of toil; the Lord's Day, or Sunday, begins a week with the restful knowledge that the work of redemption has been completed. The Sabbath commemorated the first creation; the Lord's Day is linked with the new creation. The Sabbath day was a day of responsibility; the Lord's Day is a day of privilege.

Christians do not "keep" the Lord's Day as a means of earning salvation or achieving holiness, nor from fear of punishment. They set it apart because of loving devotion to the One who gave Himself for them. Because we are released from the routine, secular affairs of life on this day, we can set it apart in a special way for the worship and service of Christ.

It is not right to say that the Sabbath was changed to the Lord's Day. The Sabbath is Saturday and the Lord's Day is Sunday. The Sabbath was a shadow; the substance is Christ (Col. 2:16, 17). The resurrection of Christ marked a new beginning, and the Lord's day signifies that beginning.

As a faithful Jew living under the law, Jesus kept the Sabbath (in spite of the accusations of the Pharisees to the contrary). As the Lord of the Sabbath, He freed it from the false rules and regulations with which it had become encrusted. ‡

E. Jesus Heals on the Sabbath (12:9–14)

12:9 From the grainfields Jesus **went into** the **synagogue**. Luke tells us that the scribes and Pharisees were there to watch Him so that they might find some charge against Him (Luke 6:6, 7).

12:10 Inside the synagogue **was a man who had a withered hand** — mute testimony to the powerlessness of the Pharisees to help him. Up to now they had treated him with cool disregard. But suddenly he became valuable to them as a means to trap Jesus. They knew that the Savior was always predisposed to alleviate human misery. If He would heal on the Sabbath, then they would catch Him in a punishable offense, they thought. So they began by raising a legal quibble: **"Is it lawful to heal on the Sabbath?"**

12:11 The Savior answered by asking if they would pull one of their **sheep** out of **a pit on the Sabbath**. Of course they would! But why? Perhaps their pretext was that it was a work of mercy — but another consideration might be that the sheep was worth money and they would not want to incur financial loss, even on the Sabbath.

12:12 Our Lord reminded them that a man is of greater **value than a sheep**. If it is right to show mercy to an animal, how much more justified is it **to do good** to a man **on the Sabbath**!

12:13, 14 Having caught the Jewish leaders in the pit of their own greed, Jesus healed the withered hand. In telling **the man** to **stretch out** his **hand**, faith and human will were called into action. Obedience was then rewarded with healing. The hand **was restored as whole as the other** by the wonderful Creator. You would think that the Pharisees would have been happy that the man, whom they had neither the power nor inclination to help, was healed. Instead they went into a white rage against Jesus **and plotted** to kill **Him**. If they had had a withered hand, they would have been glad to be healed on any day of the week.

F. Healing for All (12:15–21)

12:15, 16 When Jesus knew the thoughts of His enemies, **He withdrew**. Yet wherever He went, the crowds gathered; and wherever the sick gathered, **He healed them all**. But He charged them not to publicize His miraculous cures, not to shield Himself from danger, but to avoid any fickle movement to make Him a popular revolutionary Hero. The divine schedule must be kept. His revolution would come, not by the shedding of Roman blood, but by the shedding of His own blood.

12:17, 18 His gracious ministry was in fulfillment of the prophecy of **Isaiah** 41:9; 42:1–4. **The prophet** foresaw the Messiah as a gentle Conqueror. He pictures Jesus as the **Servant whom** Jehovah had **chosen**, the **Beloved** One **in whom** God's **soul** was **well pleased**. God would **put** His **Spirit upon Him** — a prophecy

fulfilled at the baptism of Jesus. And His ministry would reach beyond the confines of Israel; **He** would **declare justice to the Gentiles**. This latter note becomes more dominant as Israel's "NO" grows louder.

12:19 Isaiah further predicted that the Messiah would not wrangle or **cry out** and **His voice** would not be heard **in the streets**. In other words, He would not be a political rabble-rouser, stirring up the populace. McClain writes:

> This King who is God's 'servant' will not reach His rightful place of eminence by any of the usual means of carnal force or political demagoguery; nor yet by means of the supernatural forces at His command.[22]

12:20 He would not break **a bruised reed** or **quench** a **smoking flax**. He would not trample on the dispossessed or underprivileged in order to reach His goals. He would encourage and strengthen the broken-hearted, oppressed person. He would fan even a spark of faith into a flame. His ministry would continue till He would bring **justice to victory**. His humble, loving care for others would not be extinguished by the hate and ingratitude of men.

12:21 And in His name Gentiles will trust. In Isaiah this expression is worded "And the coastlands shall wait for His law," but the meaning is the same. The coastlands refer to the Gentile nations. They are pictured as waiting for His reign so that they might be His loyal subjects. Kleist and Lilly praise this quotation from Isaiah as:

> . . . one of the gems of the Gospel, a picture of Christ of great beauty . . . Isaiah pictures Christ's union with the Father, His mission to instruct the nations, His gentleness in dealing with suffering humanity and His final victory: there is no hope for the world except in His Name. Christ — the Savior of the world — not expressed in dry, scholastic terms, but clothed in rich, oriental imagery.[23]

G. The Unpardonable Sin (12:22–32)

12:22–24 When Jesus healed a **blind and mute** demoniac, the common people began to think seriously that He might be **the Son of David**, the Messiah of Israel. This enraged **the Pharisees**.

Unable to tolerate any suggestion of sympathy with Jesus, they exploded with the charge that the miracle had been performed by the power of **Beelzebub, the ruler of the demons**. This ominous indictment was the first open accusation that the Lord Jesus was demon-empowered.

12:25, 26 When He had read **their thoughts, Jesus** proceeded to expose their folly. He pointed out that no **kingdom, city**, or **house divided against itself** can continue successfully. If He was casting out Satan's demons by the power of Satan, then Satan was working **against himself**. This would be absurd.

12:27 Our Lord had a second devastating answer for the Pharisees. Some of their Jewish associates, known as exorcists, claimed to have the power to cast out demons. Jesus neither admitted nor denied their claim, but used it to point out that **if** He **cast out demons by Beelzebub**, then the Pharisees' **sons** (i.e. these exorcists) did also. The Pharisees would never admit this, but could not escape the logic of the argument. Their own associates would condemn them for implying that they exorcised as agents of Satan. Scofield said:

> The Pharisees were quick enough to resent any implication of Satanic power as far as they and their sons were concerned, but on the ground they were taking, i.e., that Christ cast out demons by Beelzebub, their own sons would judge them inconsistent; for if the power to cast out demons is Satanic, then whoever exercises that power is in league with the source of that power.[24]

They were not being logical in attributing similar effects to different causes.

12:28 The truth, of course, was that Jesus **cast out demons by the Spirit of God**. His entire life as a Man on earth was lived by the power of the Holy Spirit. He was the Spirit-filled Messiah whom Isaiah had foretold (Isa. 11:2; 42:1; 61:1–3). Therefore He said to the Pharisees, "... if I cast out demons by the **Spirit of God, surely the kingdom of God has come upon you**." This announcement must have been a crushing blow. They prided themselves on their theological knowledge, yet **the kingdom of God** had **come upon them** because the King was among them and they

hadn't even realized that He was there!

12:29 Far from being in league with Satan, the Lord Jesus was Satan's Conqueror. This He illustrates by the story of **the strong man. The strong man** is Satan. His **house** is the sphere in which he holds sway. **His goods** are his demons. Jesus is the One who **binds the strong man**, enters his **house**, and plunders **his goods**. Actually the binding of Satan takes place in stages. It began during Jesus' public ministry. It was decisively guaranteed by the death and resurrection of Christ. It will be true to a more marked degree during the King's thousand-year reign (Rev. 20:2). Finally, it will be eternally true when he is cast into the lake of fire (Rev. 20:10). At the present time the devil does not seem to be bound; he still exercises considerable power. But his doom is determined and his time is short.

12:30 Then Jesus said, **"He who is not with Me is against Me, and he who does not gather with Me scatters abroad."** Their blasphemous attitude showed that the Pharisees were not **with** the Lord; therefore, they were **against** Him. By refusing to harvest with Him, they were scattering the grain. They had accused Jesus of casting out demons by the power of Satan while actually they themselves were the servants of Satan, seeking to frustrate the work of God.

In Mark 9:40, Jesus said, "... he who is not against us is on our side." This seems a flat reversal of His words here in Matthew 12:30. The difficulty is resolved when we see that in Matthew, it is a matter of *salvation*. A man is either for Christ or against Him; there is no neutrality. In Mark, the subject is *service*. There are wide differences among the disciples of Jesus — differences in local church fellowship, methods, and interpretation of doctrines. But here the rule is that if a man is not against the Lord, he is for Him and should be respected accordingly.

12:31, 32 These verses mark a crisis in Christ's dealings with the leaders of Israel. He accuses them of committing the unpardonable sin by blaspheming against the Holy Spirit, that is, by charging that Jesus performed His miracles by the power of Satan rather than by the power of the Holy Spirit. In effect, this was calling the Holy Spirit Beelzebub, the ruler of demons.

There is forgiveness for other forms of **sin and blasphemy**. A man may even speak **against the Son of Man** and be forgiven. But to blaspheme the Holy Spirit is a sin for which there is no forgiveness **in this age or in the** millennial **age to come**. When Jesus said **in this age**, He was speaking of the days of His public ministry on earth. There is reasonable doubt whether the unpardonable sin can be committed today, because He is not bodily present performing miracles.

The unpardonable sin is not the same as rejecting the gospel; a man may spurn the Savior for years, then repent, believe, and be saved. (Of course, if he dies in unbelief, he remains unforgiven.) Nor is the unforgivable sin the same as backsliding; a believer may wander far from the Lord, yet be restored to fellowship in God's family.

Many people worry that they have committed the unpardonable sin. Even if this sin could be committed today, the fact that a person is concerned is evidence that he is not guilty of it. Those who committed it were hard and unrelenting in their opposition to Christ. They had no qualms about insulting the Spirit and no hesitancy in plotting the death of the Son. They showed neither remorse nor repentance.

H. A Tree Is Known by Its Fruit (12:33–37)

12:33 Even the Pharisees should have admitted that the Lord had done good by casting out demons. Yet they accused Him of being evil. Here He exposes their inconsistency and says, in effect, "Make up your minds. If a **tree** is **good**, its **fruit** is **good** and vice versa." Fruit reflects the quality of the tree that produced it. The fruit of His ministry had been good. He had healed the sick, the blind, the deaf, and the dumb, had cast out demons and raised the dead. Could a corrupt tree have produced such good fruit? Utterly impossible! Why then did they so stubbornly refuse to acknowledge Him?

12:34, 35 The reason was that they were a **brood of vipers**. Their malice against the Son of Man, evidenced by their venomous words, was the outflow of their evil hearts.[25] A heart filled with goodness will be evidenced by words of grace and righteousness. A wicked heart expresses itself in blasphemy, bitterness, and abuse.

12:36 Jesus solemnly warned them (and us) that people **will give account** for **every idle word** they utter. Because the words people have spoken are an accurate gauge of their lives, they will form a suitable basis for condemnation or acquittal. How great will be the condemnation of the Pharisees for the vile and contemptuous words which they spoke against God's Holy Son!

12:37 "**For by your words you will be justified, and by your words you will be condemned.**" In the case of believers, the penalty for careless speech has been paid through the death of Christ; however, our careless speech, unconfessed and unforgiven, will result in loss of reward at Christ's Judgment Seat.

I. The Sign of the Prophet Jonah (12:38–42)

12:38 Despite all the miracles Jesus had performed, **the scribes and Pharisees** had the temerity to ask Him for **a sign**, implying that they *would* believe if He would prove Himself to be the Messiah! But their hypocrisy was transparent. If they had not believed as a result of so many wonders, why would they be convinced by one more? The attitude that demands miraculous signs as a condition for belief does not please God. As Jesus said to Thomas, "Blessed are those who have not seen and yet have believed" (John 20:29). In God's economy, seeing follows believing.

12:39 The Lord addressed them as **an evil and adulterous generation**; **evil** because they were willfully blind to their own Messiah, **adulterous** because they were spiritually unfaithful to their God. Their Creator-God, a unique Person combining absolute deity and perfect humanity, stood in their midst speaking to them, yet they dared to ask Him for a sign.

12:40 He told them summarily that **no sign** would be **given to** them **except the sign of the prophet Jonah**, referring to His own death, burial, and resurrection. Jonah's experience of being swallowed by the fish and then disgorged

(Jon. 1:17; 2:10) prefigured the Lord's passion and resurrection. His rising from among the dead would be the final, climactic sign of His ministry to the nation of Israel.

Just **as Jonah was three days and three nights in the belly of the great fish, so** our Lord predicted that He would **be three days and three nights in the heart of the earth**. This raises a problem. If, as generally believed, Jesus was buried on Friday afternoon and rose again on Sunday morning, how can it be said that He was three days and nights in the tomb? The answer is that, in Jewish reckoning, any part of a day and night counts as a complete period. "A day and a night make an *onah*, and a part of an *onah* is as the whole" (Jewish saying).

12:41 Jesus depicted the guilt of the Jewish leaders by two contrasts. First, the Gentiles **of Nineveh** were far less privileged, yet when they heard the **preaching of** the errant prophet **Jonah, they repented** with deep grief. They **will rise up in the judgment** to condemn the men of Jesus' day for failing to receive Someone **greater than Jonah** — the incarnate Son of God.

12:42 Second, **the queen of** Sheba, a Gentile outside the pale of Jewish privilege, traveled from **the South**, at great effort and expense, for an interview with Solomon. The Jews of Jesus' day did not have to travel at all to see Him; He had traveled from heaven to their little neighborhood to be their Messiah-King. Yet they had no room in their lives for Him — One infinitely **greater than Solomon**. A Gentile queen will condemn them in the judgment for such wanton carelessness.

In this chapter our Lord has been presented as greater than *the temple* (v. 6); greater than *Jonah* (v. 41); and greater than *Solomon* (v. 42). He is "greater than the greatest and far better than the best."

J. An Unclean Spirit Returns (12:43–45)

12:43, 44 Now Jesus gives, in parabolic form, a summary of the past, present, and future of unbelieving Israel.

The **man** represents the Jewish nation, the **unclean spirit** the idolatry which characterized the nation from the time of its servitude in Egypt to the Babylonian captivity (which temporarily cured Israel of its idolatry). It was as if the unclean spirit had gone **out of the man**. From the end of the captivity to the present day, the Jewish people have not been idol-worshipers. They are like a house that is **empty, swept, and put in order**.

Over nineteen hundred years ago, the Savior sought admittance to that empty house. He was the rightful Occupant, the Master of the house, but the people steadfastly refused to let Him in. Though they no longer worshiped idols, they would not worship the true God either.

The **empty** house speaks of spiritual vacuum — a dangerous condition, as the sequel shows. Reformation is not enough. There must be the positive acceptance of the Savior.

12:45 In a coming day, the spirit of idolatry will decide to return to the house, accompanied by **seven spirits more wicked than himself**. Since seven is the number of perfection or completeness, this probably refers to idolatry in its fully developed form. This looks forward to the Tribulation when the apostate nation will worship the Antichrist. To bow down to the man of sin and to worship him as God is a more terrible form of idolatry than the nation has ever been guilty of in the past. And so **the last state of that man** becomes **worse than the first**. Unbelieving Israel will suffer the awful judgments of the Great Tribulation, and their suffering will far exceed that of the Babylonian Captivity. The idolatrous portion of the nation will be utterly destroyed at Christ's Second Advent.

"So shall it also be with this wicked generation." The same apostate, Christ-rejecting race that spurned the Son of God at His First Advent will suffer severe judgment at His Second Coming.

K. The Mother and Brothers of Jesus (12:46–50)

These verses describe a seemingly commonplace incident in which Jesus' family comes to speak to Him. Why had they come? Mark may give us a clue. Some of Jesus' friends decided He was out of His mind (Mark 3:21, 31–35), and perhaps His family came to take Him away quietly (see also John 7:5). When told that His **mother and brothers** were waiting **outside to speak with Him**, the Lord responded by asking, **"Who is My mother and who are My brothers?"** Then, pointing to **His disciples**, He said **"Whoever does the will of My Father in heaven is My brother and sister and mother."**

This startling announcement is pregnant with spiritual significance; it marks a distinct turning point in Jesus' dealing with Israel. Mary and her sons represented the nation of Israel, Jesus' blood relations. Up to now He had limited His ministry largely to the lost sheep of the house of Israel. But it was becoming clear that His own people would not have Him. Instead of bowing to their Messiah, the Pharisees had accused Him of being controlled by Satan.

So now Jesus announces a new order of things. Henceforth, His ties with Israel would not be the controlling factor in His outreach. Though His compassionate heart would continue to plead with His countrymen according to the flesh, chapter 12 signals an unmistakable break with Israel. The outcome is now clear. Israel will not have Him, so He will turn to those who will. Blood relationships will be superseded by spiritual considerations. Obedience to God will bring men and women, whether Jews or Gentiles, into vital relationship with Him.

Before leaving this incident, we should mention two points concerning the mother of Jesus. First, it is evident that Mary did not occupy any place of special privilege as far as access into His presence was concerned.

Second, the mention of Jesus' brothers strikes a blow at the teaching that Mary was a perpetual virgin. The implication is strong that these were actual sons of Mary and therefore half-brothers of our Lord. This view is strengthened by such other Scriptures as Psalm 69:8; Matt. 13:55; Mark 3:31, 32; 6:3; John 7:3, 5; Acts 1:14; 1 Cor. 9:5; Gal. 1:19.

VIII. THE KING ANNOUNCES A NEW INTERIM FORM OF THE KINGDOM DUE TO ISRAEL'S REJECTION (Chap. 13)

Parables of the Kingdom

We have come to a crisis point in the Gospel by Matthew. The Lord has indicated that earthly relationships are now to be superseded by spiritual ties, that it is no longer a question of Jewish birth but of obedience to God, the Father. In rejecting the King, the scribes and Pharisees have necessarily rejected the kingdom. Now by a series of parables, the Lord Jesus gives a preview of the new form which the kingdom would take during the period between His rejection and His eventual manifestation as King of kings and Lord of lords. Six of these parables begin with the words, "The kingdom of heaven is like. . . . "

In order to see these parables in proper perspective, let us review the kingdom as discussed in chapter 3. The kingdom of heaven is the sphere in which God's rule is acknowledged. It has two aspects: (1) *outward profession*, including all who claim to recognize God's rule; and (2) *inner reality*, including only those who enter the kingdom by conversion. The kingdom is found in five phases: (1) the OT phase in which it was prophesied; (2) the phase in which it was "at hand" or present in the Person of the King; (3) the interim phase, consisting of those on earth who profess to be His subjects following the King's rejection and return to Heaven; (4) the manifestation of the kingdom during the Millennium; and (5) the final, everlasting, kingdom. Every Bible reference to the kingdom fits into one of these phases. It is the third, interim phase which chapter 13 discusses. During this phase the kingdom in its inner reality (true believers) is composed, from Pentecost to the Rapture, of the same people as the church. This is the only identity between the kingdom and the church; they are not otherwise one and the same.

With this background in mind, let us look at the parables.

A. The Parable of the Sower (13:1–9)

13:1 Jesus went out of the house where He had healed the demoniac **and sat by the sea** of Galilee. Many Bible students see the house as picturing the nation of Israel and the sea, the Gentiles. Thus the Lord's movement symbolizes a break with Israel; during its interim form, the kingdom will be preached to the nations.

13:2 As **great multitudes gathered** on the beach, **He got into a boat** and began to teach the people by **parables**. A parable is a story with an underlying spiritual or moral teaching which is not always apparent immediately. The seven parables that follow tell us what the kingdom will be like during the time between His First and Second Advents.

The first four were spoken to the multitude; the last three were given only to the disciples. The Lord explained the first two and the seventh to the disciples, leaving them (and us) to interpret the others with the keys He had already given.

13:3 The first parable concerns a **sower** who planted his seed in four different types of soil. As might be expected, the results were different in each case.

13:4–8

SOIL	RESULTS
1. Hard-packed **pathway.**	1. Seeds eaten by the birds.
2. Thin layer of soil over rock deposit.	2. Seed sprouted quickly, but no root; **scorched by the sun** and **withered away.**
3. Ground infested with **thorns.**	3. The seed sprouted, but growth was impossible because of the **thorns.**
4. **Good ground.**	4. The seed sprouted, grew, **and yielded a crop:** some stalks bore **a hundredfold, some sixty, some thirty.**

13:9 Jesus closed the parable with the cryptic admonition, **"He who has ears to hear, let him hear!"** In the parable He was conveying an important message to the multitude, and a different message to the disciples. None should miss the significance of His words.

Since the Lord Himself interpets the parable in verses 18– 23, we will restrain our curiosity until we reach that paragraph.

B. The Purpose of the Parables (13:10–17)

13:10 The disciples were puzzled that the Lord should **speak to** the people in the veiled language of **parables**. So they asked Him to explain His method.

13:11 In His reply, Jesus distinguished between the unbelieving crowd and the believing disciples. The crowd, a cross-section of the nation, was obviously rejecting Him, though their rejection would not be complete until the cross. They would not be permitted to know **the mysteries** (secrets) **of the kingdom of heaven**, whereas His true followers would be helped to understand.

A mystery in the NT is a fact never previously known by man, which man could never learn apart from divine revelation, but which has now been revealed. **The mysteries of the kingdom** are hitherto unknown truths concerning the kingdom in its interim form. The very fact that the kingdom would *have* an interim form had been a secret up to now. The parables describe some of the features of the kingdom during the time when the King would be absent. Some people therefore call this "the mystery form of the kingdom" — not that there is anything mysterious about it but simply that it was never known before that time.

13:12 It may seem arbitrary that these secrets should be withheld from the multitude and revealed to the disciples. But the Lord gives the reason: **"For whoever has, to him more will be given, and he will have abundance; but whoever does not have, even what he has will be taken away."** The disciples had faith in the Lord Jesus; therefore, they would be given the capacity for more. They had accepted the light; therefore, they would receive more light. The Jewish nation, on the other hand, had rejected the Light of the world; therefore they were not only prevented from receiving more light, they would lose what little light they had. Light rejected is light denied.

13:13 Matthew Henry compares the

parables to the pillar of cloud and fire which enlightened Israel while confusing the Egyptians. The parables would be revealed to those who were sincerely interested but would prove "only an irritation to those who were hostile to Jesus."

So it was not a matter of whim on the Lord's part, but simply the outworking of a principle which is built into all of life — willful blindness is followed by judicial blindness. That is why He spoke to the Jews in parables. H. C. Woodring put it so: "Because they did not have the love of the truth, they would not get the light of the truth."[26] They professed to see, that is, to be familiar with divine truth, but Truth incarnate stood before them and they resolutely refused to see Him. They professed to hear God's Word, but the living Word of God was in their midst and they would not obey Him. They were unwilling to understand the wonderful fact of the Incarnation; therefore, the capacity to understand was taken from them.

13:14, 15 They were a living fulfillment of the prophecy of Isaiah 6:9, 10. Israel's heart had **grown dull** and their **ears** were insensitive to the voice of God. They deliberately refused to **see with their eyes**. They knew that if they saw, heard, understood, and repented, God would heal them. But in their sickness and need, they refused His help. Therefore, their punishment was that they would **hear** but **not understand**, and **see** but **not perceive**.

13:16, 17 The disciples were tremendously privileged, because they were seeing what no one had seen before. The prophets and righteous men of the OT had longed to be living when the Messiah arrived, but their desire had not been fulfilled. The disciples were favored to live at that crisis moment in history, to see the Messiah, to witness His miracles, and to hear the incomparable teaching which came from His lips.

C. Explanation of the Parable of the Sower (13:18–23)

13:18 Having explained why He used parables, the Lord now proceeds to expound the parable of the four soils. He does not identify **the sower** but we can

be sure that it refers either to Himself (v. 37) or to those who preach the message of the kingdom. He defines the seed as the word of the kingdom (v. 19). The soils represent those who hear the message.

13:19 The hard-packed pathway speaks of people who refuse to receive the message. They hear the gospel but do **not understand** it — not because they can't but because they won't. The birds are a picture of Satan; he **snatches away** the seed from the hearts of these hearers. He cooperates with them in their self-chosen barrenness. The Pharisees were hard-soil hearers.

13:20, 21 When Jesus spoke of rocky ground, He had in mind a thin layer of earth covering a ledge of rock. This represents people who hear the word and respond **with joy**. At first the sower might be elated that his preaching is so successful. But soon he learns the deeper lesson, that it is not good when the message is received with smiles and cheers. First there must be conviction of sin, contrition, and repentance. It is far more promising to see an inquirer weeping his way to Calvary than to see him walking down the aisle light-heartedly and exuberantly. The shallow earth yields a shallow profession; there is no depth to the root. But when his profession is tested by the scorching sun of **tribulation or persecution**, he decides it isn't worth it and abandons any profession of subjection to Christ.

13:22 The thorn-infested ground represents another class who hear the word in a superficial way. They appear outwardly to be genuine subjects of the kingdom but in time their interest is choked out by **the cares of this world** and by their delight in **riches**. There is no fruit for God in their lives. Lang illustrates this by a son of a money-loving father with a huge business. This son heard the Word in his youth but became engrossed in the business.

He had soon to choose between pleasing his Lord or his father. Thus the thorns were in the soil when the seed was sown and germinated; the cares of this age and the deceitfulness of riches were already at hand. He fell in with his father's wishes, devoted himself fully to business, rose to be head of the concern, and when well on in life had to acknowledge that he had neglected things heavenly. He was about to retire and he expressed his intention to be more diligent in matters spiritual. But God is not to be mocked. The man retired and died suddenly in only a few months. He left £90,000 and a spiritually wasted life. The thorns had choked the word and it was unfruitful.[27]

13:23 **The good ground** represents a true believer. **He . . . hears the word** receptively and **understands it** through obeying what he hears. Although these believers do not all produce the same amount of fruit, they all show by their fruit that they have divine life. **Fruit** here is probably the manifestation of Christian character rather than souls won to Christ. When the word *fruit* is used in the NT, it generally refers to the fruit of the Spirit (Gal. 5:22, 23).

What was the parable meant to say to the crowds? Obviously it warned against the peril of hearing without obeying. It was calculated also to encourage individuals to receive the Word sincerely, then to prove their reality by bringing forth fruit for God. As for the disciples, the parable prepared them and future followers of Jesus for the otherwise discouraging fact that relatively few of those who hear the message are genuinely saved. It saves Christ's loyal subjects from the delusion that all the world will be converted through the spread of the gospel. The disciples are also warned in this parable against the three great antagonists of the gospel: (1) the devil (the birds — the evil one); (2) the flesh (the scorching sun — tribulation or persecution); and (3) the world (the thorns — cares of the world and the delight in riches).

Finally the disciples are given a vision as to the tremendous returns from investing in human personality. Thirtyfold is 3,000 percent return, sixtyfold is 6,000 percent return, and one hundredfold is 10,000 percent return on the investment. There is actually no way of measuring the results of a single case of genuine conversion. An obscure Sunday school teacher invested in Dwight L. Moody. Moody won others. They in turn won others. The Sunday school teacher started a chain reaction that will never stop.

D. The Parable of the Wheat and Tares (13:24–30)

The preceding parable was a vivid illustration of the fact that the kingdom of heaven includes those who give only lip service to the King as well as those who are His genuine disciples. The first three soils typify the kingdom in its widest circle — outward profession. The fourth soil represents the kingdom as a smaller circle — those who have been truly converted.

13:24–26 The second **parable** — the wheat and the tares — also sets forth the kingdom in these two aspects. The wheat depicts true believers, the tares are mere professors. Jesus compares **the kingdom** to **a man who sowed good seed in his field; but while men slept, his enemy came and sowed tares among the wheat.** Unger says that the most common tare found in grainfields in the Holy Land is bearded darnel, "a poisonous grass, almost indistinguishable from wheat while the two are growing into blade. But when they come into ear, they can be separated without difficulty."[28]

13:27, 28 When **the servants** saw the tares mixed in with the grain, they asked the householder how this happened. He immediately recognized it as the work of **an enemy. The servants** were ready to pull the weeds immediately.

13:29, 30 But the farmer ordered them to wait **until the harvest**. Then reapers would separate the two. The grain would be gathered into barns and the darnel would be burned.

Why did the farmer order this delay in separation? In nature the roots of the grain and darnel are so intertwined that it is virtually impossible to pull up one without the other.

This parable is explained by our Lord in verses 37–43, so we will forego further comment till then.

E. The Parable of the Mustard Seed (13:31, 32)

Next the Savior likens **the kingdom** to **a mustard seed** which He called the smallest of **seeds**, that is, smallest in the experience of His listeners. When a man planted one of these seeds, it grew into **a tree**, a growth that is phenomenal. The normal mustard plant is more like a bush than a tree. The **tree** was large enough for **birds** to **nest in its branches**

The seed represents the humble beginning of the kingdom. At first the kingdom was kept relatively small and pure as a result of persecution. But with the patronage and protection of the state, it suffered abnormal growth. Then the birds came and roosted in it. The same word for birds is used here as in verse 4; Jesus explained the birds as meaning the evil one (v. 19). The kingdom became a nesting place for Satan and his agents. Today the umbrella of Christendom covers such Christ-denying systems as Unitarianism, Christian Science, Mormonism, Jehovah's Witnesses, and the Unification Church (Moonies).

So here the Lord forewarned the disciples that during His absence the kingdom would experience a phenomenal growth. They should not be deceived nor equate growth with success. It would be unhealthy growth. Though the tiny seed would become an abnormal tree, its largeness would become "a dwelling place of demons, a prison for every foul spirit, and a cage for every unclean and hated bird" (Rev. 18:2).

F. The Parable of the Leaven (13:33)

Next the Lord Jesus compared **the kingdom** to **leaven which a woman hid in three measures of meal**. Eventually **all** the meal became **leavened**. A common interpretation is that the meal is the world and the leaven is the gospel which will be preached throughout the world until everyone becomes saved. This view, however, is contradicted by Scripture, by history, and by current events.

Leaven is always a type of evil in the Bible. When God commanded His people to rid their houses of leaven (Ex. 12:15), they understood this. If anyone ate what was leavened from the first till the seventh day of this Feast of Unleavened Bread, he would be cut off from Israel. Jesus warned against the leaven of the Pharisees and Sadducees (Matt. 16:6, 12) and the leaven of Herod (Mark 8:15).

In 1 Corinthians 5:6–8 leaven is defined as malice and evil, and the context of Galatians 5:9 shows that *there* it means false teaching. In general, leaven means either evil doctrine or evil behavior.

So in this parable the Lord warns against the permeating power of evil working in **the kingdom of heaven**. The parable of the mustard seed shows evil in the external character of the kingdom; this parable shows the inward corruption that would take place.

We believe that in this parable the **meal** represents the food of God's people as it is found in the Bible. The **leaven** is evil doctrine. **The woman** is a false prophetess who teaches and beguiles (Rev. 2:20). Is it not significant that women have been the founders of several false cults? Forbidden by the Bible to teach in the church (1 Cor. 14:34; 1 Tim. 2:12), some have defiantly taken the place of doctrinal authorities and have adulterated the food of God's people with destructive heresies.

J. H. Brookes says:

> If the objection is raised that Christ would not liken the kingdom of heaven to that which is evil, it is sufficient to reply that He likens the kingdom to that which includes both tares and wheat, which encloses both good and bad fish, which extends over a wicked servant (Matt. xviii 23–32), which admits into it a man who had not on a wedding garment, and who was lost (Matt. xxii 1–13).[29]

G. The Use of Parables Fulfills Prophecy (13:34, 35)[†]

Jesus spoke the first four parables **to the multitude**. The use of this teaching method by the Lord fulfilled Asaph's prophecy in Psalm 78:2 that the Messiah would speak **in parables**, uttering **things kept secret from the foundation of the world**. These features of the kingdom of heaven in its interim form, hidden until this time, were now being made known.

H. Explanation of the Parable of the Tares (13:36–43)

13:36 The remainder of the Lord's discourse was spoken to the disciples, inside **the house**. Here **the disciples** may represent the believing remnant of the nation of Israel. The renewed mention of

†*See p. xx.*

the house reminds us that God has not rejected forever His people whom He foreknew (Rom. 11:2).

13:37 In His interpretation of the wheat and tares parable, Jesus identified Himself as the sower. He sowed directly during His earthly ministry, and has been sowing through His servants in succeeding ages.

13:38 The field is the world. It is important to emphasize that the field is the world, *not the church*. The **good seeds** mean **the sons of the kingdom**. It might seem bizarre and incongruous to think of living human beings being planted into the ground. But the point is that these sons of the kingdom were sown in the world. During His years of public ministry, Jesus sowed the world with disciples who were loyal subjects of the kingdom. **The tares are the sons of the wicked one**. Satan has a counterfeit for every divine reality. He sows the world with those who look like, talk like, and, to some extent, walk like disciples. But they are not genuine followers of the King.

13:39 The enemy is Satan, the enemy of God and all the people of God. **The harvest is the end of the age**, the end of the kingdom age in its interim form, which will be when Jesus Christ returns in power and glory to reign as King. The Lord is not referring to the end of the church age; it leads only to confusion to introduce the church here.

13:40–42 The reapers are the angels (see Rev. 14:14–20). During the present phase of the kingdom, no forcible separation is made of the wheat and the darnel. They are allowed to grow together. But at the Second Advent of Christ, the angels will round up all causes of sin and all evildoers and throw **them into the furnace of fire**, where they will weep and gnash their teeth.

13:43 The righteous subjects of the kingdom who are on earth during the Tribulation will enter **the kingdom of their Father** to enjoy the Millennial Reign of Christ. There they **will shine forth as the sun**; that is, they will be resplendent in glory.

Again Jesus adds the cryptic admonition, **"He who has ears to hear, let him hear!"**

This parable does not justify, as some mistakenly suppose, the toleration of ungodly people in a local Christian church. Remember that the field is the world, not the church. Local churches are explicitly commanded to put out of their fellowship all who are guilty of certain forms of wickedness (1 Cor. 5:9–13). The parable simply teaches that in its mystery form, the kingdom of heaven will include the real and the imitation, the genuine and the counterfeit, and that this condition will continue until the end of the age. Then God's messengers will separate the false, who will be taken away in judgment, from the true, who will enjoy the glorious reign of Christ on earth.

I. The Parable of the Hidden Treasure (13:44)

All the parables so far have taught that there will be good and evil in the kingdom, righteous and unrighteous subjects. The next two parables show that there will be two classes of the righteous subjects: (1) believing Jews during the periods before and after the Church Age; (2) believing Jews and Gentiles during the present age.

In the parable of the **treasure**, Jesus compares **the kingdom** to **treasure hidden in a field. A man** finds it, covers it up, then gladly **sells all he has and buys that field**.

We would suggest that the **man** is the Lord Jesus Himself. (He was the man in the parable of the wheat and tares, v. 37.) The **treasure** represents a godly remnant of believing Jews such as existed during Jesus' earthly ministry and will exist again after the church is raptured (see Psalm 135:4 where Israel is called God's peculiar treasure). They are hidden in the field in that they are dispersed throughout the world and in a real sense unknown to any but God. Jesus is pictured as discovering this treasure, then going to the cross and giving all that He had in order to buy the world (2 Cor. 5:19; 1 Jn. 2:2) where the treasure was hidden. Redeemed Israel will be brought out of hiding when her Deliverer comes out of Zion and sets up the long-awaited Messianic Kingdom.

The parable is sometimes applied to a sinner, giving up all in order to find Christ, the greatest Treasure. But this interpretation violates the doctrine of grace which insists that salvation is without price (Isa. 55:1; Eph. 2:8, 9).

J. The Parable of the Pearl of Great Price (13:45, 46)

The kingdom is also likened to **a merchant seeking beautiful pearls**. When he finds a pearl of unusually **great** value, he sacrifices all he has to buy it.

In a hymn that says, "I've found the Pearl of greatest price," the finder is the sinner and the Pearl is the Savior. But again we protest that the sinner does not have to sell all and does not have to buy Christ.

We rather believe that the **merchant** is the Lord Jesus. The **pearl of great price** is the church. At Calvary He sold all that He had to buy this pearl. Just as a pearl is formed inside an oyster through suffering caused by irritation, so the church was formed through the piercing and wounding of the body of the Savior.

It is interesting that in the parable of the treasure, the kingdom is likened to the treasure itself. Here the kingdom is not likened to the pearl but to the merchantman. Why this difference?

In the preceding parable, the emphasis is on the treasure — redeemed Israel. The kingdom is closely linked with the nation of Israel. It was originally offered to that nation and, in its future form, the Jewish people will be its principal subjects.

As we have mentioned, the church is not the same as the kingdom. All who are in the church are in the kingdom in its interim form, but not all who are in the kingdom are in the church. *The church will not be in the kingdom in its future form but will reign with Christ over the renewed earth.* The emphasis in the second parable is on the King Himself and the tremendous price He paid to woo and win a bride that would share His glory in the day of His manifestation.

As the pearl comes out of the sea, so the church, sometimes called the Gentile bride of Christ, comes largely from the nations. This does not overlook the fact that there are converted Israelites in it, but merely states that the dominant feature of the church is that it is a people called out from the nations for His Name. In Acts 15:14 James confirmed this as being the grand purpose of God at the present time.

K. The Parable of the Dragnet (13:47–50)

13:47, 48 The final parable in the series likens **the kingdom** to a sieve or **dragnet that was cast into the sea and gathered** fish **of every kind**. The fishermen sorted out the fish, keeping **the good** in containers and discarding **the bad**.

13:49, 50 Our Lord interprets the parable. The time is **the end of the age;** that is, the end of the Tribulation period. It is the time of the Second Advent of Christ. The fishermen are **the angels**. The good fish are the righteous; that is, saved people, both Jews and Gentiles. The bad fish are the unrighteous; namely, unbelieving people of all races. A separation takes place, as we also saw in the parable of the wheat and tares (vv. 30, 39–43). The righteous enter the kingdom of their Father, whereas the unrighteous are consigned to a place of fire where there is **wailing and gnashing of teeth**. This is not the final judgment, however; this judgment takes place at the outset of the Millennium; the final judgment occurs after the thousand years are finished (Rev. 20:7–15).

Gaebelein comments on this parable as follows:

> The dragnet is let into the sea, which, as we have seen before, represents the nations. The parable refers to the preaching of the everlasting gospel as it will take place during the great tribulation (Rev. 14:6, 7). The separating of the good and bad is done by angels. All this cannot refer to the present time nor to the church, but to the time when the kingdom is about to be set up. The angels will be used, as is so clearly seen in the book of Revelation. The wicked will be cast into the furnace of fire and the righteous will remain in the earth for the millennial kingdom.[30]

L. The Treasury of Truth (13:51, 52)

13:51 When He had finished the parables, the Master Teacher asked His disciples if they **understood**. They replied, **"Yes."** This may surprise us, or even make us slightly jealous of them.

Perhaps we cannot answer "yes" so confidently.

13:52 Because they understood, they were obligated to share with others. Disciples are to be channels, not terminals of blessings. The twelve were now scribes trained for the **kingdom of heaven**; that is, teachers and interpreters of the truth. They were **like a householder who brings out of his treasure things new and old**. In the OT they had a rich deposit of what we might call **old** truth. In the parabolic teaching of Christ, they had just received what was completely **new**. From this vast storehouse of knowledge they should now impart the glorious truth to others.

M. Jesus Is Rejected at Nazareth (13:53–58)

13:53–56 Having **finished these parables**, Jesus left the shores of Galilee and went to Nazareth for His last visit there. As **He taught them in their synagogue**, the people **were astonished** at His **wisdom** and His reported miracles. To them He was only **the carpenter's son**. They knew **His mother** was **Mary . . . and His brothers James, Joses, Simon, and Judas . . . and His sisters** — they were still living there in Nazareth! How could one of their own hometown boys say and do the things for which He had become so well known? This puzzled them, and they found it easier to cling to their ignorance than to acknowledge the truth.

13:57, 58 They were offended at Him. This prompted **Jesus** to point out that a genuine **prophet is** generally more appreciated away from home. His own district and His own relatives allowed their familiarity to breed contempt. Unbelief largely hindered the Savior's work in Nazareth. He healed only a few sick folk there (cf. Mark 6:5). It was not because He *could* not do the works; man's wickedness cannot restrain God's power. But He would have been blessing people where there was no desire for blessing, filling needs where there was no consciousness of need, healing people who would have resented being told they were sick.

IX. THE MESSIAH'S UNWEARIED GRACE MET BY MOUNTING HOSTILITY (14:1–16:12)

A. John the Baptist Beheaded (14:1–12)

14:1, 2 News of Jesus' ministry flowed back to **Herod the tetrarch**. This infamous son of Herod the Great was also known as Herod Antipas. It was he who had ordered the execution of John the Baptist. When he heard of Christ's miracles, his conscience began to stab him. The memory of the prophet whom he had beheaded kept coming before him. He told his servants, "It's **John**. He has come back **from the dead**. That explains these miracles."

14:3 In verses 3–12 we have what is known as a literary flashback. Matthew interrupts the narrative to review the circumstances surrounding the death of John.

14:4, 5 Herod had abandoned his wife and had been living in an adulterous, incestuous relationship with **Herodias, his brother Philip's wife**. As a prophet of God, John could not let this pass without rebuke. Indignantly and fearlessly, he pointed his finger at Herod and denounced him for his immorality.

The king was angry enough to kill him but it was not politically expedient. The people acclaimed John **as a prophet**, and would have reacted, perhaps violently, against John's execution. So the tyrant satisfied his rage momentarily by having the Baptizer imprisoned. "The ungodly like religion in the same way that they like lions, either dead or behind bars; they fear religion when it breaks loose and begins to challenge their consciences."[31]

14:6–11 On **Herod's birthday, the daughter of Herodias** so pleased the king by her dancing that he impetuously offered her anything she wanted. Prompted by her wanton mother, she brazenly asked for **John the Baptist's head . . . on a platter!** By now the king's wrath against John had somewhat subsided; perhaps he even admired the prophet for his courage and integrity. But although he was sorry, he felt he had to fulfill his promise. The order was given. John was **beheaded** and the gruesome request of the dancing girl was granted.

14:12 John's **disciples** gave their master's **body** a respectful burial, then **went and told Jesus**. They could not have gone to anyone better to pour out their grief and indignation. Nor could they have left us a better example. In times of persecution, oppression, suffering, and sorrow, we too should go and *tell it to Jesus*.

As for Herod, his crime was finished but the memory lingered on. When he heard of Jesus' activites, the entire episode returned to haunt him.

B. Feeding of the Five Thousand (14:13–21)

14:13, 14 **When Jesus heard** that Herod was troubled by reports of His miracles, He withdrew **by boat to a** secluded area by the Sea of Galilee. We can be sure He did not go because of fear; He knew that nothing could happen to Him before His time had come. We do not know the main reason for His move, but a lesser reason was that His disciples had just returned from their preaching mission (Mark 6:30; Luke 9:10) and needed a time of rest and quietness.

However, the crowds flocked from the towns and **followed Him on foot**. As He went ashore, they were waiting for Him. Far from being irritated by this intrusion, our compassionate Lord set to work immediately **and healed their sick**.

14:15 When **evening** came, that is, after 3:00 p.m., **His disciples** felt that a crisis was brewing. So many people, and nothing for them to eat! They asked Jesus to send the people **into the villages** where they could get **food**. How little they understood the heart of Christ or discerned His power!

14:16–18 The Lord assured them that there was no **need**. Why should the people leave the One who opens His hand and supplies the desire of every living thing? Then He caught the disciples off guard by saying, **"You give them something to eat."** They were staggered. "Give them something to eat? We have nothing but **five loaves and two fish**." They had forgotten that they also had Jesus. Patiently the Savior said, **"Bring**

them here to Me." That was their part.

14:19–21 We can picture the Lord directing **the multitudes to sit down on the grass**. Taking **the five loaves and the two fish**, He gave thanks, **broke** the loaves, and **gave** them **to the disciples** for distribution. There was plenty for all. When **all** were satisfied, the disciples gathered **twelve baskets** of leftovers. There was more left over when Jesus finished than when He began. Ironically enough there was a basket for each unbelieving disciple. And a multitude of perhaps 10,000 to 15,000 had been fed (5,000 men plus women and children).

The miracle is a spiritual lesson for disciples of every generation. The hungry multitude is always present. There is always a little band of disciples with seemingly pitiful resources. And always there is the compassionate Savior. When disciples are willing to give Him their little all, He multiplies it to feed thousands. The notable difference is that the **five thousand men** who were fed by Galilee had their hunger satisfied only for a short time; those today who feed upon the living Christ are satisfied forever (see John 6:35).

C. Jesus Walks on the Sea (14:22–33)

The previous miracle assured the disciples that they were following One who could abundantly provide for their needs. Now they learn that this One can protect and empower them as well.

14:22, 23 While He was dismissing the multitude, **Jesus** told the **disciples** to **get into the boat** and start back **to the other side** of the lake. Then He went up on a hillside **to pray. When evening came**, i.e., after sunset, **He was alone there**. (In Jewish reckoning there were two "evenings," see Ex. 12:6 RSV margin. One, referred to in v. 15, began in mid-afternoon, and the other, referred to here, at sunset.)

14:24–27 Meanwhile, **the boat was now far** from land and battling a **contrary** wind. As the waves battered the boat, Jesus saw the disciples' plight. **In the fourth watch of the night** (between 3:00 and 6:00 a.m.), He **went to them walking on the sea**. Thinking it was **a ghost** the disciples panicked. But immediately they heard the reassuring voice of their Master and Friend, **"Be of good cheer! It is I; do not be afraid."**

How true to our own experience! We are often storm-tossed, perplexed, in despair. The Savior seems far away. But all the time He is praying for us. When the night seems darkest, He is near at hand. We often mistake Him even then and push the panic button. Then we hear His comforting voice and remember that the waves that caused us to fear are under His feet.

14:28 When **Peter** heard the well-known, well-loved voice, his affection and enthusiasm bubbled over. **"Lord, if it is You, command me to come to You on the water."** Rather than magnify Peter's "if" as a sign of small faith, we should see his bold request as a mark of great trust. Peter sensed that Jesus' commands are His enablements, that He gives strength for whatever He orders.

14:29–33 As soon as Jesus **said, "Come,"**. . . **Peter** jumped out of the boat and began walking toward Him. As long as he kept his eyes on Jesus, he was able to do the impossible; but the minute he became occupied with **the** strong **wind**, he began to sink. Frantically he cried, **"Lord, save me!"** The Lord took him by the hand, gently rebuked his **little faith**, and brought him to the boat. As soon as Jesus went on board, **the wind ceased**. A worship meeting took place in the boat with the disciples saying to Jesus, **"Truly You are the Son of God."**

The Christian life, like walking on water, is humanly impossible. It can only be lived by the power of the Holy Spirit. As long as we look away from every other object to Jesus only (Heb. 12:2), we can experience a supernatural life. But the minute we become occupied with ourselves or our circumstances, we begin to sink. Then we must cry to Christ for restoration and divine enablement.

D. Jesus Heals in Gennesaret (14:34–36)

The boat docked at **Gennesaret**, on the northwest shore of the Sea of Galilee. As soon as the men spotted Jesus, they scoured the area for **all who were sick** and **brought** them **to Him** that the sick **might only touch the hem of His garment; as many** who did **were made perfectly well**. And so the doctors in that area had a holiday. For a while, at least, there were no sick people. The district experienced health and healing through a visit by the Great Physician.

E. Defilement Is From Within (15:1–20)

It is often pointed out that Matthew does not follow a chronological order during the early chapters. But from the beginning of chapter 14 to the end, events are largely given in the sequence in which they occurred.

In chapter 15 a dispensational order also emerges. First, the continued haggling and bickering of the Pharisees and scribes (vv. 1–20) anticipates Israel's rejection of the Messiah. Second, the faith of the Canaanite woman (vv. 21–28) pictures the gospel going out to the Gentiles in this present age. And finally the healing of great crowds (vv. 29–31) and the feeding of 4,000 (vv. 32–39) point to the future millennial age with its worldwide health and prosperity.

15:1, 2 The **scribes and Pharisees** were unrelenting in their efforts to trap the Savior. A delegation of them came **from Jerusalem**, charging His **disciples** with uncleanness for eating with **their hands** unwashed, therefore violating **the tradition of the elders**.

In order to appreciate this incident, we must understand the references to clean and unclean, and must know what the Pharisees meant by washing. The whole conception of clean and unclean goes back to the OT. The uncleanness with which the disciples were charged was entirely a ceremonial matter. If a person touched a dead body, for instance, or if he ate certain things, he contracted ceremonial defilement — he was not ritually fit to worship God. Before he could approach God, the law of God required him to go through a cleansing ritual.

But the elders had added tradition to the cleansing rituals. They insisted, for instance, that before a Jew ate, he should put his hands through an elaborate cleansing process, washing not just the hands, but also the arms up to the elbows. If he had been in the marketplace, he was supposed to take a ceremonial bath. Thus, the Pharisees criticized the disciples for failing to observe the intricacies of the washings prescribed by Jewish tradition.

15:3–6 The Lord Jesus reminded His critics that *they* transgressed **the commandment of God**, not simply **the tradition** of the elders. The law commanded men to **honor** their parents, including supporting them financially if necessary. But the scribes and Pharisees (and many others) did not want to spend money for the support of their aged parents. So they devised a tradition by which to avoid their responsibility. When asked for help by **father or mother**, all they had to do was recite such words as these: "Any money which I have and which could be used to support you has been dedicated **to God**, and therefore I cannot give it to you," and having recited this formula, they were free from financial responsibility to their parents. Following this devious tradition they had thus nullified the Word **of God** which commanded them to care for their parents.

15:7–9 By their crafty twisting of words they fulfilled the prophecy of **Isaiah** 29:13. They professed to **honor** God **with their lips, but their heart** was **far from** Him. Their worship was worthless because they were giving higher priority to the traditions of men than to the Word of God.

15:10, 11 Turning to **the multitude,** Jesus made a pronouncement of tremendous significance. He declared that **not what goes into the mouth defiles a man, but** rather **what comes out**. We can scarcely appreciate the revolutionary character of this statement. Under the Levitical code, what went into the mouth *did* defile a man. The Jews were forbidden to eat the meat of any animal which did not chew the cud and have cloven hooves. They were not allowed to eat a fish unless it had scales and fins. Minute instructions were given by God as to foods that were clean or unclean.

Now the Law-giver paved the way for the abrogation of the whole system of ceremonial defilement. He said that the food which His disciples ate with unwashed hands did not defile them. But the hypocrisy of the scribes and Pharisees — that was truly defiling.

15:12–14 When **His disciples** brought word **that the Pharisees were offended** by this denunciation, Jesus answered by comparing them to plants which had not been divinely planted. They were tares rather than wheat. They and their teachings would eventually be rooted up; that is, destroyed. Then He added, **"Let them alone. They are blind leaders of the blind."** Though professing to be authorities in spiritual matters, they were **blind** to spiritual realities as were the people they were leading. It was inevitable that **both** leaders and followers would **fall into a ditch**.

15:15 The disciples were undoubtedly shaken by this complete reversal of all they had been taught about clean and unclean foods. It was like a **parable** to them, i.e., an obscure, veiled narrative. **Peter** verbalized their unsettlement when he asked for an explanation.

15:16, 17 The Lord first expressed wonder that they were so slow to understand, then explained that true defilement is moral, not physical. Edible foods are not intrinsically clean or unclean. In fact, no material thing is evil in itself; it is the abuse of a thing that is wrong. The food man eats **enters the mouth, goes into the stomach** for digestion, then the unassimilated residue **is eliminated**. His moral being is not affected — only his body. Today we know that "every creature of God is good, and nothing is to be refused if it is received with thanksgiving; for it is sanctified by the word of God and prayer" (1 Tim. 4:4, 5). The passage is not speaking of poisonous plants, of course, but of foods designed by God for human consumption. All are good and should be eaten thankfully. If a person is allergic to some, or cannot tolerate others, he shouldn't eat them, but in general we can eat with the assurance that God uses food to nourish us physically.

15:18 If food doesn't defile, then *what does*? Jesus answered, **". . . those things which proceed out of the mouth come from the heart, and they defile a man."** Here **the heart** is not the organ that pumps blood, but the corrupt source of human motives and desires. This part of man's moral nature manifests itself by impure thoughts, then by depraved words, then by evil acts.

15:19, 20 Some of the things that

defile a man are **evil thoughts, murders, adulteries, fornications, thefts, false witness**, and **blasphemies,** (this Greek word includes slander of others).

The Pharisees and scribes were extremely careful concerning the ostentatious, punctilious observance of hand-washing ceremonies. But their inner lives were polluted. They majored in minors and overlooked the matters of real importance. They could criticize the disciples' failure to keep uninspired traditions, yet plot to kill the Son of God and be guilty of the whole catalog of sin listed in verse 19.

F. A Gentile Is Blessed For Her Faith (15:21–28)

15:21, 22 **Jesus** withdrew **to the region of Tyre and Sidon**, on the Mediterranean coast. As far as we know, this was the only time during His public ministry that He was outside Jewish territory. Here in Phoenicia, a Canaanite woman asked Him to heal her **daughter** who was **demon-possessed**.

It is important to realize that this woman was not a Jewess, but a Gentile. She was descended from the Canaanites, an immoral race which God had marked for extinction. Through Israel's disobedience, some had survived the invasion of Canaan under Joshua, and this woman was a descendant of the survivors. As a Gentile, she did not enjoy the privileges of God's chosen earthly people. She was an alien, having no hope. Positionally she had no claim on God or the Messiah.

Speaking to Jesus, she addressed Him as the **Lord**, the **Son of David**, a title which the Jews used in speaking of the Messiah. Although Jesus *was* the **Son of David**, a Gentile had no right to approach Him on that basis. That is why He did not answer her at first.

15:23 **His disciples came and urged Him** to **send her away**; to them she was a nuisance. To Him she was a welcome example of faith and a vessel in whom His grace would shine. But first He must prove and educate her faith!

15:24, 25 He reminded her that His mission was to **the lost sheep of the house of Israel**, not to Gentiles, and certainly not to Canaanites. She was undismayed by this apparent refusal. Dropping the title, *Son of David*, she worshiped Him, saying, **"Lord, help me!"** If she couldn't come to Him as a Jew to her Messiah, she would come as a creature to her Creator.

15:26 To further probe the reality of her faith, Jesus told her that it was **not good** for Him to turn aside from feeding the Jewish children in order to give bread to Gentile **dogs**. If this sounds harsh to us, we should remember that, like the surgeon's scalpel, it was not intended to hurt but to heal. She *was* a Gentile. The Jews looked upon the Gentiles as scavenging dogs, prowling the streets for scraps of food. However, Jesus here used the word for **little** pet **dogs**. The question was, "Would she acknowledge her unworthiness to receive the least of His mercies?"

15:27 Her reply was magnificent. She agreed with His description completely. Taking the place of an unworthy Gentile, she cast herself on His mercy, love, and grace. She said, in effect, "You are right! I am only one of the **little dogs** under the table. But I notice that **crumbs** sometimes **fall from** the **table** to the floor. Won't You let me have some crumbs? I am not worthy that You should heal my daughter, but I beseech You to do it for one of Your undeserving creatures."

15:28 Jesus commended her for her **great faith**. While the unbelieving children had no hunger for the bread, here was a self-confessed "doggie" crying out for it. Faith was rewarded; her daughter was **healed** instantly. The fact that our Lord healed this Gentile daughter at a distance suggests His present ministry at God's right hand, bestowing spiritual healing on Gentiles during this age when His ancient people are set aside nationally.

G. Jesus Heals Great Multitudes (15:29–31)

In Mark 7:31 we learn that the Lord left Tyre, traveled north to Sidon, then eastward across the Jordan, south through the region of the Decapolis. There, near the Sea of Galilee,[†] He healed **the lame, the blind**, the **mute**, the **maimed**, and many others. The astonished crowd **glorified the God of Israel**. The presumption is strong that this was a Gentile neighborhood. The people, associating

†*See n. xiv.*

Jesus and His disciples with Israel, correctly deduced that **the God of Israel** was working in their midst.

H. Feeding of the Four Thousand (15:32–39)

15:32 Careless (or critical) readers, confusing this incident with the feeding of the 5,000, have accused the Bible of duplication, contradiction, and miscalculation. The fact is that the two incidents are quite distinct, and supplement rather than contradict each other.

After three days with the Lord, **the multitude** had run out of food. He would not let them go away hungry; they might collapse **on the way.**

15:33, 34 Again **His disciples** became frustrated at the impossible task of feeding such a mob; this time they had only **seven** loaves **and a few little fish.**

15:35, 36 As in the case of the 5,000, Jesus seated the people, **gave thanks, broke** the loaves and fish **and gave them to His disciples** for distribution. He expects His disciples to do what they can; then He steps in and does what they can't.

15:37–39 After the people **were filled**, there were **seven large baskets** of surplus food. The number fed was **four thousand men, besides women and children.**

In the next chapter, we shall see that the statistics relating to the two feeding miracles are significant (16:8–12). Every detail of the Bible narrative is charged with meaning. After dismissing the crowd, our Lord went by **boat** to **Magdala**, on the west shore of the Sea of Galilee.

I. The Leaven of the Pharisees and Sadducees (16:1–12)

16:1 The Pharisees and Sadducees, traditional antagonists in theological matters, represented two doctrinal extremes. But their hostility gave way to cooperation as they united in a common aim to trip up the Savior. To test Him they **asked** Him to demonstrate **a sign from heaven.** In some way not clear to us, they were trying to inveigle Him into a compromising position. In asking for **a sign from heaven,** perhaps they were implying an opposite source for His previous miracles. Or perhaps they wanted some supernatural sign in the sky. All Jesus' miracles had been performed on the earth. Could He do celestial miracles as well?

16:2, 3 He answered by continuing the theme of **the sky.** When they saw a **red** sky in the **evening**, they forecast **fair weather** for the next day. They also knew that a **red, threatening** sky **in the morning** meant storms for that day.[32] They had expertise in interpreting the appearance of the sky, but they could not interpret **the signs of the times.**

What were these **signs**? The prophet who heralded the advent of the Messiah had appeared in the person of John the Baptist. The miracles prophesied of the Messiah — things no other man had ever done — had been performed in their presence. Another sign of the times was the obvious rejection of the Messiah by the Jews and the movement of the gospel to the Gentiles, all in fulfillment of prophecy. Yet in spite of this incontrovertible evidence, they had no sense of history being made or of prophecy being fulfilled.

16:4 In seeking for a sign when He Himself stood in their midst, the Pharisees and Sadducees exposed themselves as an evil, spiritually **adulterous generation. No sign** would now **be given to** them **except the sign of the prophet Jonah**. As explained in the notes on 12:39, this would be the resurrection of Christ on the third day. **A wicked and adulterous generation** would crucify its Messiah, but God would raise Him from the dead. This would be a sign of the doom of all who refuse to bow to Him as rightful Ruler.

The paragraph closes with the ominous words, **"And He left them and departed."** The spiritual implications of the words should be obvious to all.

16:5, 6 When **His disciples** rejoined the Lord on **the** east **side** of the lake, **they had forgotten to take** food with them. Therefore when Jesus greeted them with a warning to **beware of the leaven of the Pharisees and the Sadducees**, they thought He was saying, "Don't go to those Jewish leaders for food supplies!" Their preoccupation with food caused them to look for a literal, natural explanation where a spiritual lesson was intended.

16:7–10 They were still worrying about a food shortage in spite of the fact that He who fed the 5,000 and the 4,000 was with them. So He reviewed the two miraculous feedings with them. The lesson that emerged concerned divine arithmetic and divine resourcefulness, for *the less Jesus had to work with, the more He fed, and the more food there was left over*. When there were only five loaves and two fish, He fed 5,000 plus and had twelve baskets of food left. With more loaves and fish, He fed only 4,000 plus and had left over only seven basketfuls. If we put our limited resources at His disposal, He can multiply them in inverse proportion to their amount. "Little is much if God is in it."

A different word is used for **baskets**[33] here than in the feeding of the 5,000. The seven baskets in this incident are considered to have been larger than the twelve on the previous occasion. But the underlying lesson remains: Why worry about hunger and want when we are linked with One who has infinite power and resources?

16:11, 12 In speaking of **the leaven of the Pharisees and Sadducees**, the Lord had not referred to bread but to evil doctrine and conduct. In Luke 12:1 the leaven of the Pharisees is defined as hypocrisy. They professed to adhere to the Word of God in minutest details, yet their obedience was external and shallow. Inwardly they were evil and corrupt.

The leaven of **the Sadducees** was rationalism. The freethinkers of their day, they, like the liberals of today, had built a system of doubts and denials. They denied the existence of angels and spirits, the resurrection of the body, the immortality of the soul, and eternal punishment. This leaven of skepticism, if tolerated, will spread and permeate like yeast in meal.

X. THE KING PREPARES HIS DISCIPLES (16:13–17:27)

A. Peter's Great Confession (16:13–20)

16:13, 14 Caesarea Philippi was about twenty-five miles north of the Sea of Galilee and five miles east of the Jordan. When Jesus came to the surrounding villages (Mark 8:27), an incident generally recognized as the apex of His teaching ministry occurred. Up to this time He had been leading His disciples to a true apprehension of His Person. Having succeeded in this, He now turns His face resolutely to go to the cross.

He began by asking **His disciples** what men were saying as to His identity. The replies ran the gamut from **John the Baptist**, to **Elijah**, to **Jeremiah**, to **one of the** other **prophets**. To the average person He was one among many. Good but not the Best. Great but not the Greatest. A prophet but not *the* Prophet. This view would never do. It condemned Him with faint praise. If He were only another man He was a fraud because He claimed to be equal with God the Father.

16:15, 16 So He asked the disciples **who** they believed He was. This brought from **Simon Peter** the historic confession, **"You are the Christ, the Son of the living God."** In other words, He was Israel's Messiah and God the Son.

16:17, 18 Our Lord pronounced a blessing on **Simon**, son of **Jonah**. The fisherman had not arrived at this concept of the Lord Jesus through intellect or native wisdom; it had been supernaturally **revealed** to him by God the **Father**. But the Son had something important to say to Peter also. So Jesus added, **"And I also say to you that you are Peter, and on this rock I will build My church, and the gates of Hades shall not prevail against it."** We all know that more controversy has swirled around this verse than almost any other verse in the Gospel. The question is, "Who or what is the **rock**?" Part of the problem arises from the fact that the Greek words for Peter and for rock are similar, but the meanings are different. The first, *petros*, means a stone or loose rock; the second, *petra*, means rock, such as a rocky ledge. So what Jesus really said was **". . . you are Peter** (stone), **and on this rock I will build My church."** He did not say He would build His church on a stone but on a rock.

If Peter is not the rock, then what is? If we stick to the context, the obvious answer is that the rock is Peter's confession that Christ is the Son of the living God, the truth on which the church is founded. Ephesians 2:20 teaches that the church is built on Jesus Christ, the chief cornerstone. Its statement that we are built upon the foundation of the apostles and prophets refers not to them, but to the foundation laid in their teachings concerning the Lord Jesus Christ.

Christ is spoken of as a Rock in 1 Corinthians 10:4. In this connection, Morgan gives a helpful reminder:

> Remember, He was talking to Jews. If we trace the figurative use of the word rock through Hebrew Scriptures, we find that it is never used symbolically of man, but always of God. So here at Caesarea Philippi, it is not upon Peter that the Church is built. Jesus did not trifle with figures of speech. He took up their old Hebrew illustration — rock, always the symbol of Deity — and said, "Upon God Himself —Christ, the Son of the living God — I will build my church."[34]

Peter never spoke of himself as the foundation of the church. Twice he referred to Christ as a Stone (Acts 4:11, 12; 1 Pet. 2:4–8), but then the figure is different; the stone is the head of the corner, not the foundation.

"I will build My church." Here we have the first mention of the **church** in the Bible. It did not exist in the OT. The church, still future when Jesus spoke these words, was formed on the Day of Pentecost and is composed of all true believers in Christ, both Jew and Gentile. A distinct society known as the body and bride of Christ, it has a unique heavenly calling and destiny.

We would scarcely expect the church to be introduced in Matthew's Gospel where Israel and the kingdom are the prominent themes. However, consequent to Israel's rejection of Christ, a parenthetical period — the church age — follows and will continue to the Rapture. Then God will resume His dealings with Israel nationally. So it is fitting that God should introduce the church here as the next step in His dispensational program after Israel's rejection.

"The gates of Hades shall not prevail against it" may be understood in two ways. First **the gates of Hades** are pictured in an unsuccessful offensive against the church — the church will survive all attacks upon it. Or the church itself may be pictured as taking the offensive and coming off the victor. In ei-

ther case, the powers of death will be defeated by the translation of living believers and by the resurrection of the dead in Christ.

16:19 **"I will give you the keys of the kingdom of heaven"** does not mean that Peter was given authority to admit men to heaven. This has to do with the **kingdom of heaven** *on earth* — the sphere containing all who profess allegiance to the King, all who claim to be Christians. **Keys** speak of access or entrance. The keys which open the door to the sphere of profession are suggested in the Great Commission (Matt. 28:19) — discipling, baptizing, and teaching. (Baptism is not necessary for salvation but is the initiatory rite by which men publicly profess allegiance to the King.) Peter first used the keys on the Day of Pentecost. They were not given to him exclusively, but as a representative of all the disciples. (See Matt. 18:18 where the same promise is given to them all.)

"Whatever you bind on earth will be bound in heaven, and whatever you loose on earth will be loosed in heaven." This and a companion passage in John 20:23 are sometimes used to teach that Peter and his supposed successors were given the authority to forgive sins. We know that this cannot be so; only God can forgive sins.

There are two ways of understanding the verse. First, it may mean that the apostles had power to bind and to loose that we do not have today. For example, Peter bound their sins on Ananias and Sapphira so that they were punished with instant death (Acts 5:1–10), while Paul loosed the disciplined man in Corinth from the consequences of his sin because the man had repented (2 Cor. 2:10).

Or the verse may mean that whatever the apostles bound or loosed on earth must have *already* been bound or loosed in heaven (see NKJV margin). Thus Ryrie says, "Heaven, not the apostles, initiates all binding and loosing, while the apostles announce these things."[35]

The only way in which the verse is true today is in a *declarative* sense. When a sinner truly repents of his sins and receives Jesus Christ as Lord and Savior, a Christian can *declare* that person's sins to be forgiven. When a sinner rejects the

Savior, a Christian worker can *declare* his
sins to be retained. William Kelly writes,
"Whenever the Church acts in the name
of the Lord and really does His will, the
stamp of God is upon their deeds."

16:20   Again we find the Lord Jesus
commanding **His disciples** to **tell no one**
that He was the Messiah. Because of
Israel's unbelief, no good could come
from such a disclosure. And positive
harm might come from a popular movement to crown Him King; such an ill-
timed move would be ruthlessly crushed
by the Romans.

Stewart, who calls this section the
turning point of Jesus' ministry, writes:

> The day at Caesarea Philippi marks the
> watershed of the Gospels. From this point
> onward the streams begin to flow in an-
> other direction. The current of popularity
> which seemed likely in the earlier days of
> Jesus' ministry to carry him to a throne
> has now been left behind. The tide sets
> toward the Cross. . . . At Caesarea, Jesus
> stood, as it were on a dividing line. It was
> like a hilltop from which he could see be-
> hind him all the road he had traveled and
> in front of him the dark, forbidding way
> awaiting him. One look he cast back to
> where the afterglow of happy days still
> lingered and then faced round and
> marched forward toward the shadows.
> His course was now set to Calvary.[36]

B. Preparing the Disciples for His
Death and Resurrection
(16:21–23)

16:21   Now that the disciples had realized that Jesus is the Messiah, the Son
of the living God, they were ready to
hear His first direct prediction of His
death and resurrection. They now knew
that His cause could never fail; that they
were on the winning side; that no matter
what happened, triumph was assured.
So the Lord broke the news to prepared
hearts. **He must go to Jerusalem**, must
suffer many things from the religious
leaders, must **be killed, and be raised
the third day**. The news was enough to
spell the doom of any movement — all
except that last imperative — **must . . .
be raised the third day**. That made the
difference!

16:22   Peter was indignant at the
thought of his Master's enduring such
treatment. Catching hold of Him as if to
block His path, he protested, **"Far be it**

**from You, Lord; this shall not happen
to You!"**

16:23   This drew a rebuke from the
Lord Jesus. He had come into the world
to die for sinners. Anything or anyone
who hindered Him from this purpose
was out of tune with God's will. So He
said to Peter, **"Get behind Me, Satan!
You are an offense to Me, for you are
not mindful of the things of God, but
the things of men."** In calling Peter
Satan, Jesus did not imply that the apostle was demon-possessed or Satan-
controlled. He simply meant that Peter's
actions and words were what could be
expected of Satan (whose name means
adversary). By protesting against Calvary,
Peter became a hindrance to the Savior.

Every Christian is called to take up
his cross and follow the Lord Jesus, but
when the cross looms in the pathway
ahead, a voice within says, "Far be it
from you! Save yourself." Or perhaps
the voices of loved ones seek to deflect
us from the path of obedience. At such
times, we too must say, "Get behind me,
Satan! You are a hindrance to me."

C. Preparation for True Discipleship
(16:24–28)

16:24   Now the Lord Jesus plainly
states what is involved in being His disciple: denial of self, cross-bearing, and
following Him. To **deny** self is not the
same as self-denial; it means to yield to
His control so completely that self has no
rights whatever. To **take up** the **cross**
means the willingness to endure shame,
suffering, and perhaps martyrdom for
His sake; to die to sin, self, and the
world. To **follow** Him means to live as
He lived with all that involves of humility, poverty, compassion, love, grace,
and every other godly virtue.

16:25   The Lord anticipates two hindrances to discipleship. The first is the
natural temptation **to save** oneself from
discomfort, pain, loneliness, or loss. The
other is to become wealthy. As to the
first, Jesus warned that those who hug
their lives for selfish purposes would
never find fulfillment; those who recklessly abandon their lives to Him, not
counting the cost, would find the reason
for their existence.

16:26   The second temptation —
that of getting rich — is irrational. "Sup-

pose," said Jesus, "that **a man** became so successful in business that he owned **the whole world**. This mad quest would absorb so much of his time and energy that he would miss the central purpose of his life. What good would it do to make all that money, then die, leave it all behind, and spend eternity empty-handed?" Man is here for bigger business than to make money. He is called to represent the interests of his King. If he misses that, he misses everything.

In verse 24, Jesus told them the worst. That is characteristic of Christianity; you know the worst at the outset. But you never cease discovering the treasures and the blessings. Barnhouse put it well:

> When one has seen all that is forbidding in the Scriptures, there is nothing left hidden that can come as a surprise. Every new thing which we shall ever learn in this life or the next will come as a delight.[37]

16:27 Now the Lord reminds His own of **the glory** that follows the suffering. He points forward to His Second Advent when He will return to earth **with His angels** in the transcendent **glory of His Father. Then He will reward** those who live for Him. The only way to have a successful life is to project oneself forward to that glorious time, decide what will really be important then, and then go after that with all one's strength.

16:28 He next made the startling statement that **there** were **some standing** there with Him **who** would **not taste death** before they saw Him **coming in His kingdom**. The problem, of course, is that those disciples have all died, yet Christ has not come in power and glory to set up His kingdom. The problem is solved if we disregard the chapter break and consider the first eight verses of the next chapter as an explanation of His enigmatic statement. These verses describe the incident on the Mount of Transfiguration. There Peter, James, and John saw Christ transfigured. They were actually privileged to have a preview of Christ in the glory of His kingdom.

We are justified in viewing Christ's transfiguration as a prepicture of His coming kingdom. Peter describes the event as "the power and coming of our Lord Jesus Christ" (2 Pet. 1:16). The power and coming of the Lord Jesus refer to His Second Advent. And John speaks of the Mount experience as the time when " . . . we beheld His glory, the glory as of the only begotten of the Father" (John 1:14). Christ's First Coming was in humiliation; it is His Second Coming that will be in glory. Thus, the prediction of verse 28 was fulfilled on the Mount; Peter, James, and John saw the Son of Man, no longer as the humble Nazarene, but as the glorified King.

D. Preparing the Disciples for Glory: The Transfiguration (17:1–8)

17:1, 2 Six days after the incident at Caesarea Philippi, **Jesus took Peter, James, and John** up to **a high mountain**, somewhere in Galilee. Many commentators attach significance to the six days. Gaebelein, for instance, says: "Six is a man's number, the number signifying the days of work. After six days — after work and man's day is run out then the day of the Lord, the Kingdom."

When Luke says that the Transfiguration occurred "about eight days" later (9:28), he obviously includes the terminal days as well as the intervening days. Since eight is the number of resurrection and of a new beginning, it is fitting that Luke should identify the kingdom with a new beginning.

Peter, James, and John, who seem to have occupied a place of special nearness to the Savior, were privileged to see Him transfigured. Up to now His glory had been veiled in a body of flesh. But now **His face** and **clothes** became radiant **like the sun** and dazzling bright, a visible manifestation of His deity, just as the glory cloud or Shekinah in the OT symbolized the presence of God. The scene was a preview of what the Lord Jesus will be like when He comes back to set up His kingdom. He will no longer appear as the sacrificial Lamb but as the Lion of the tribe of Judah. All who see Him will recognize Him immediately as God the Son, the King of kings and Lord of lords.

17:3 Moses and Elijah appeared on the Mount and discussed His approaching death at Jerusalem (Luke 9:30, 31). Moses and Elijah may represent OT saints. Or, if we take Moses as representing the Law, and Elijah representing the Prophets, then here we see both sections of the OT pointing forward to the sufferings of Christ and the glories that should follow. A third possibility is that Moses, who went to heaven by way of death, depicts all who will be raised from the dead to enter the Millennium, while Elijah, who was translated to heaven, pictures those who will reach the kingdom by the route of translation.

The disciples Peter, James, and John may represent NT saints in general. They could also foreshadow the faithful Jewish remnant who will be alive at the Second Advent and will enter the kingdom with Christ.

The multitude at the base of the mountain (v. 14, compare Luke 9:37) has been likened to the Gentile nations which will also share in the blessings of Christ's thousand-year reign.

17:4, 5 **Peter** was deeply moved by the occasion; he had a real sense of history. Wanting to capture the splendor, he rashly suggested erecting **three** memorial **tabernacles** or booths — **one for** Jesus, **one for Moses, and one for Elijah**. He was right in putting Jesus first, but wrong in not giving Him the preeminence. Jesus is not one among equals but Lord over all. In order to teach this lesson, God the Father covered them all with a brightly glowing **cloud**, then announced, **"This is My beloved Son, in whom I am well pleased. Hear Him!"** In the Kingdom, Christ will be the peerless One, the supreme Monarch whose word will be the final authority. Thus it should be in the hearts of His followers at the present time.

17:6–8 Stunned by the glory cloud and by the voice of God, **the disciples fell on their faces**. But Jesus told them to get up and **not** to **be afraid**. As they rose, **they saw no one but Jesus only**. So it will be in the Kingdom — the Lord Jesus will be "all the glory in Immanuel's land."

E. Concerning the Forerunner (17:9–13)

17:9 Descending **from the mountain, Jesus commanded** the disciples to be silent about what they had seen until He had **risen from the dead**. The Jews, overanxious for anyone who might liberate them from the Roman yoke, would have welcomed Him to save them from *Rome*, but did not want Him as a Savior from *sin*. For all practical purposes, Israel had rejected her Messiah, and it was useless to tell the Jews of this vision of Messianic glory. After the resurrection, the message would be proclaimed worldwide.

17:10–13 The disciples had just seen a preview of Christ's coming in power and glory. But His forerunner had not appeared. Malachi had prophesied that **Elijah must come** prior to Messiah's advent (Mal. 4:5, 6), so **His disciples asked** Jesus about this. The Lord agreed that **indeed Elijah** had to come **first** as a reformer, but explained **that Elijah** had **already come**. Obviously He was referring to **John the Baptist** (see v. 13). John was not Elijah (John 1:21), but had come "in the spirit and power of Elijah" (Luke 1:17). Had Israel accepted John and his message, he would have fulfilled the role prophesied of Elijah (Matt. 11:14). But the nation did not recognize the significance of John's mission, and treated him as it pleased. John's death was an advance token of what they would do to the Son of Man. They rejected the forerunner; they would also reject the King. When Jesus explained this, the disciples realized He was referring to **John the Baptist**.

There is every reason to believe that before Christ's Second Advent, a prophet will arise to prepare Israel for the coming King. Whether it will be Elijah personally or someone with a similar ministry is almost impossible to say.

F. Preparation for Service through Prayer and Fasting (17:14–21)

Life is not all a mountain-top experience. After moments of spiritual exhilaration come hours and days of toil and expenditure. The time comes when we must leave the mountain to minister in the valley of human need.

17:14, 15 At the base of the mountain, a distraught father was waiting for the Savior. **Kneeling down** before **Him**, he poured out his impassioned plea that his demon-possessed son might be healed. The son suffered from violent **epileptic** seizures which sometimes caused him to fall **into the fire and often into the water**, so his misery was compounded by burns and near-drownings. He was a classic example of the suffering caused by Satan, the cruelest of all task-masters.

17:16 The father had gone to the **disciples** for help, only to learn that "vain is the help of man." They had been powerless to cure.

17:17 **"O faithless and perverse generation, how long shall I be with you? How long shall I bear with you?"** is addressed to the disciples. They did not have the faith to heal the epileptic, but in that respect, were a cross section of the Jewish people of that day — faithless and perverse.

17:18 As soon as the epileptic was brought to Him, **Jesus rebuked the demon**, and the sufferer **was** instantly **cured.**

17:19, 20 Puzzled by their power-lessness, **the disciples** privately asked the Lord for an explanation. His answer was straightforward: **unbelief**. If they had **faith the** size of **a mustard seed** (the smallest of seeds), they could command a **mountain** to be cast into the sea and it would happen. Of course, it should be understood that true faith must be based upon some command or promise of God. Expecting to perform some spectac-ular stunt in order to gratify a personal whim is not faith but presumption. But if God guides a believer in a certain di-rection or issues a command, the Chris-tian can have utmost confidence that mountainous difficulties will be miracu-lously removed. Nothing is impossible to those who believe.

17:21 **"This kind does not go out except by prayer and fasting"** is omitted in the RSV and most modern Bibles, be-cause it is lacking in many early manu-scripts. However, it is found in the ma-jority of the manuscripts and fits the context of an especially difficult problem.

G. Preparing the Disciples for His Betrayal (17:22, 23)

Again, without drama or fanfare, the Lord Jesus forewarned His disciples that He would be put to death. But again there was that word of vindication and victory — He would **be raised up** on **the third day**. If He had not told them of His death in advance, they would doubt-less have been completely disillusioned when it happened. A death of shame and suffering was not consistent with their expectations of the Messiah.

As it was, they were greatly dis-tressed that He was going to leave them and that He would be slain. They heard His passion prediction but seemed to have missed His resurrection promise.

H. Peter and His Master Pay Their Taxes (17:24–27)

17:24, 25 In **Capernaum** the collec-tors of the **temple tax asked** Peter if his **Teacher** paid the half-shekel used for carrying on the costly temple service. Peter answered, **"Yes."** Perhaps the mis-guided disciple wanted to save Christ from embarrassment.

The omniscience of the Lord is seen in what followed. When Peter came home, Jesus spoke to him first — before Peter had a chance to tell what had hap-pened. **"What do you think, Simon? From whom do the kings of the earth take customs and taxes, from their sons or from strangers?"** The question must be understood in the light of those days. A ruler taxed his subjects for the support of his kingdom and his family, but he didn't tax his own family. Under our form of government, everyone is taxed, including the ruler and his household.

17:26 Peter correctly answered that rulers collected tribute **from strangers**. Jesus then pointed out that **the sons are free**. The point was that the temple was God's house. For Jesus, the Son of God, to pay tribute for the support of this tem-ple would be equivalent to paying tribute to Himself.

17:27 However, rather than cause needless offense, the Lord agreed to pay the tax. But what would He do for money? It is never recorded that Jesus personally carried money. He sent Peter **to the Sea** of Galilee and told him to bring up the first fish he caught. In the mouth of that fish was **a piece of money** or *stater* which Peter used to pay the tribute — one-half for the Lord Jesus and one-half for himself.

This astounding miracle, narrated with utmost restraint, clearly demon-strates Christ's omniscience. He knew which one of all the fish in the Sea of Galilee had a stater in its mouth. He knew the location of that one fish. And he knew it would be the first fish Peter would catch.

If any divine principle had been involved, Jesus would not have made the payment. It was a matter of moral indifference to Him, and He was willing to pay rather than offend. We as believers are free from the law. Yet, in nonmoral matters, we should respect the consciences of others, and not do anything that would cause offense.

XI. THE KING INSTRUCTS HIS DISCIPLES (Chaps. 18–20)

A. Concerning Humility (18:1–6)

Chapter 18 has been called the discourse on greatness and forgiveness. It outlines principles of conduct that are suitable for those who claim to be subjects of Christ the King.

18:1 The disciples had always thought of the kingdom of heaven as the golden age of peace and prosperity. Now they began to covet positions of preferment in it. Their self-seeking spirit found expression in the question, **"Who is greatest in the kingdom of heaven?"**

18:2, 3 Jesus answered with a living object lesson. Placing **a little child** in their midst, He said that men must be **converted and become as little children** to **enter the kingdom of heaven**. He was speaking of the kingdom in its inward reality; in order to be a genuine believer a man must abandon thoughts of personal greatness and take the lowly position of a little child. This begins when he acknowledges his sinfulness and unworthiness and receives Jesus Christ as his only hope. This attitude should continue throughout his Christian life. Jesus was not implying that His disciples were not saved. All except Judas had true faith in Him, and were therefore justified. But they had not yet received the Holy Spirit as an indwelling Person, and therefore lacked the power for true *humility* that we have today (but do not use as we should). Also they needed to be converted in the sense of having all their false thinking changed to conform to the kingdom.

18:4 The greatest person in the kingdom of heaven is the one **who humbles himself as** a **little child**. Obviously the standards and values in the kingdom are exactly opposite those in the world. Our whole mode of thinking must be reversed; we must think Christ's thoughts after Him (see Phil. 2:5–8).

18:5 Here the Lord Jesus glides almost imperceptibly from the subject of a natural child to a spiritual **child**. Whoever receives one of His humble followers **in** His **name** will be rewarded as if he had received the Lord Himself. What is done for the disciple is reckoned as done for the Master.

18:6 On the other hand, anyone who seduces a believer to sin incurs enormous condemnation; **it would be better for him** to have a great **millstone** tied **around his neck and** be **drowned** in the ocean's depths. (The great millstone referred to here required an animal to turn it; a smaller one could be turned by hand.) It is bad enough to sin against oneself, but to cause a believer to sin is to destroy his innocence, corrupt his mind, and stain his reputation. Better to die a violent death than to trifle with another's purity!

B. Concerning Offenses (18:7–14)

18:7 Jesus went on to explain that it is inevitable that **offenses** should arise. The **world**, the flesh, and the devil are leagued to seduce and pervert. But if a person becomes an agent for the forces of evil, his guilt will be great. So the Savior warned men to take drastic action in disciplining themselves rather than to tempt a child of God.

18:8, 9 Whether the sinning member is the **hand or foot** or the **eye**, better to sacrifice it to the surgeon's knife than to let it destroy the work of God in another person's life. **Better to enter into life** without limbs or sight than to be consigned to hell with every member intact. Our Lord does not imply that some bodies will lack limbs in heaven, but merely describes the physical condition at the time a believer leaves this life for the next. There can be no question that the resurrection body will be complete and perfect.

18:10 Next the Son of God warned against despising **one of** His **little ones**, whether children or any who belong to the kingdom. To emphasize their importance, He added that **their angels** are constantly in the presence of God, beholding His **face. Angels** here probably means guardian angels (see also Heb. 1:14).

18:11 While omitted in RSV and most other modern Bibles, this verse about our Savior's mission is a fitting climax to this section, and it has wide manuscript support.[38]

18:12, 13 These little ones are also the object of the tender Shepherd's saving ministry. Even if one out of **a hundred sheep** goes astray, He leaves **the ninety-nine** and searches for the lost one till He finds it. The Shepherd's joy over finding a straying sheep should teach us to value and respect His little ones.

18:14 They are important not only to the angels and to the Shepherd, but also to God the **Father. It is not** His **will that one of** them **should perish**. If they are important enought to engage angels, the Lord Jesus, and God the Father, then clearly we should never despise them, no matter how unlovely or lowly they might appear.

C. Concerning Discipline of Offenders (18:15–20)

The rest of the chapter deals with the settlement of differences among church members, and with the need for exercising unlimited forgiveness.

18:15 Explicit instructions are given concerning the Christian's responsibility when wronged by another believer. First, the matter should be handled privately between the two parties. If the offender acknowledges his guilt, reconciliation is achieved. The trouble is that we don't do this. We gossip to everyone else about it. Then the matter spreads like wildfire and strife is multiplied. Let us remember that step number one is to **"go and tell him his fault between you and him alone."**

18:16 If the guilty brother does not listen, then the wronged one should take **one or two** others with him, seeking his restoration. This emphasizes the mounting seriousness of his continued unbrokenness. But more, it provides competent testimony, as required by the Scripture: **"that 'by the mouth of two or three witnesses every word may be established' "** (Deut. 19:15). No one can

measure the trouble that has plagued the church through failure to obey the simple rule that a charge against another person must be supported by the testimony of two or three others. In this respect, worldly courts often act more righteously than Christian churches or assemblies.

18:17 If the accused still **refuses** to confess and apologize, the matter should be taken before **the** local **church**. It is important to notice that the local assembly is the body responsible to hear the case, not a civil court. The Christian is forbidden to go to law against another believer (1 Cor. 6:1–8).

If the defendant refuses to admit his wrong before the church, then he is to be considered **a heathen and a tax collector**. The most obvious meaning of this expression is that he should be looked upon as being outside the sphere of the church. Though he may be a true believer, he is not living as one, and should therefore be treated accordingly. Though still in the universal church, he should be barred from the privileges of the local church. Such discipline is a serious action; it temporarily delivers a believer to the power of Satan "for the destruction of the flesh, that his spirit may be saved in the day of the Lord Jesus" (1 Cor. 5:5). The purpose of this is to bring him to his senses and cause him to confess his sin. Until that point is reached, believers should treat him courteously but should also show by their attitude that they do not condone his sin and cannot have fellowship with him as a fellow believer. The assembly should be prompt to receive him back as soon as there is evidence of godly repentance.

18:18 Verse 18 is linked with what precedes. When an assembly, prayerfully and in obedience to the Word, binds disciplinary action upon a person, that action is honored **in heaven**. When the disciplined person has repented and confessed his sin, and the assembly restores him to fellowship, that loosing action, too, is ratified by God (see John 20:23).

18:19 The question arises, "How large must an assembly be before it can bind and loose, as described above?" The answer is that **two** believers may bring such matters to God in prayer with the assurance of being heard. While verse 19 may be used as a general promise of answers to prayer, in the *context* it refers to prayer concerning church discipline. When used in connection with collective prayer in general, it must be taken in light of all other teaching on prayer. For instance, our prayers must be:

1. In conformity to the revealed will of God (1 Jn. 5:14, 15).
2. In faith (Jas. 1:6–8).
3. In sincerity (Heb. 10:22a), etc.

18:20 Verse 20 should be interpreted in light of its context. It does not refer primarily to the composition of a NT church in its simplest form, nor to a general prayer meeting, but to a meeting where the church seeks the reconciliation of two Christians separated by some sin. It may legitimately be applied to all meetings of believers where Christ is the Center, but a specific type of meeting is in view here.

To meet "in His name" means by His authority, in acknowledgment of all that He is, and in obedience to His Word. No group can claim to be the only ones who meet in His name; if that were so, His presence would be limited to a small segment of His body on earth. Wherever **two or three are gathered in** recognition of Him as Lord and Savior, he is **there in the midst.**

D. Concerning Unlimited Forgiveness (18:21–35)

18:21, 22   At this point **Peter** raised the question of **how often** he should **forgive** a **brother** who sinned against him. He probably thought he was showing unusual grace by suggesting **seven** as an outside limit. **Jesus** answered **"not . . . seven times but up to seventy times seven."** He did not intend us to understand a literal 490 times; this was a figurative way of saying "Indefinitely."

Someone might then ask, "Why bother to go through the steps outlined above? Why go to an offender alone, then with one or two others, then take him to church? Why not just forgive, and let that be the end of it?"

The answer is that there are stages in the administration of forgiveness, as follows:

1. When a brother wrongs me or sins against me, I should forgive him immediately *in my heart* (Eph. 4:32). That frees me from a bitter, unforgiving spirit, and leaves the matter on *his* shoulders.
2. While I have forgiven him in my heart, I do not yet tell him that he is forgiven. It would not be righteous to administer forgiveness publicly until he has repented. So I am obligated to go to him and rebuke him in love, hoping to lead him to confession (Luke 17:3).
3. As soon as he apologizes and confesses his sin, I tell him that he is forgiven (Luke 17:4).

18:23   Jesus then gives a parable of **the kingdom of heaven** to warn against the consequences of an unforgiving spirit by subjects who have been freely forgiven.

18:24-27   The story concerns **a certain king who wanted to** clear his bad debts off his books. One servant, who **owed him ten thousand talents,** was insolvent, so his lord ordered that he and his family be sold into slavery in payment of the debt. The distraught servant begged for time, promising to **pay** him **all** if given the chance.

> Like many debtors, he was incredibly optimistic about what he could do if only he had time (v. 26). Galilee's total revenue only amounted to 300 talents and this man owed 10,000! The detail about the vast amount is intentional. It is to shock the listeners and so capture their attention, and also to emphasize an immense debt to God. Martin Luther used to say that we are all beggars before Him. We cannot hope to pay (Daily Notes of the Scripture Union).

When the **master** saw the contrite attitude of his **servant,** he forgave him the entire 10,000 talents. It was an epic display of grace, not justice.

18:28–30   Now that servant had a fellow servant who owed him one **hundred denarii** (a few hundred dollars). Rather than forgive him, he grabbed **him by the throat** and demanded payment in full. The hapless debtor pled for an extension, but it was no use. He was thrown **into prison till he** paid **the debt** — a difficult business at best, since his chance of earning money was gone as long as he was imprisoned.

18:31–34 The other **servants**, outraged by this inconsistent behavior, **told their master**. He was furious with the merciless lender. Having been forgiven a big debt, he was unwilling to forgive a pittance. So he was returned to the jailers' custody till his debt was paid.

18:35 The application is clear. God is the King. All His servants had contracted a great debt of sin which they were unable to pay. In wonderful grace and compassion, the Lord paid the debt and granted full and free forgiveness. Now suppose some Christian wrongs another. When rebuked, he apologizes and asks forgiveness. But the offended believer refuses. He himself has been forgiven millions of dollars, but won't forgive a few hundred. Will the King allow such behavior to go unpunished? Certainly not! The culprit will be chastened in this life and will suffer loss at the Judgment Seat of Christ.

E. Concerning Marriage, Divorce and Celibacy (19:1–12)

19:1, 2 After completing His ministry in **Galilee**, the Lord turned southward to Jerusalem. Though His exact route is unknown, it seems clear that He traveled through Perea, on the east side of the Jordan. Matthew speaks of the area loosely as **the region of Judea beyond the Jordan**. The Perean ministry extends from 19:1 to 20:16 or 20:28; it is not clearly stated when He crossed the Jordan into Judea.

19:3 Probably it was the multitudes that followed Him for healing that alerted **the Pharisees** to the Lord's whereabouts. Like a pack of wild dogs, they began to close in, hoping to trap Him by His words. They asked if **divorce** was legal on any and every ground. No matter how He answered, He would infuriate some segment of the Jews. One school took a very liberal attitude toward divorce; another was extremely strict.

19:4–6 Our Lord explained that God's original intention was that a man have only one living wife. The God who created **male and female** decreed that the marriage relationship should supersede the parental relationship. He also

said that marriage is a union of persons. God's ideal is that this divinely ordained union should not be broken by human act or decree.

19:7 The Pharisees thought they had caught the Lord in a flagrant contradiction of the OT. Hadn't **Moses** made provision for **divorce**? A man could simply give his wife a written statement, then put her out of the house (Deut. 24:1–4).

19:8 Jesus agreed that **Moses** had **permitted** divorce, not as God's best for mankind, but because of Israel's backslidden condition: **"Moses because of the hardness of your hearts permitted you to divorce your wives, but from the beginning it was not so."** God's ideal was that there be no divorce. But God often tolerates conditions that are not His directive will.

19:9 Then the Lord stated with absolute authority that the past leniency on divorce was henceforth discontinued. Hereafter there would be only one valid ground for divorce — unchastity. If a person was divorced for any other reason and remarried, he was guilty of **adultery.**

Although not directly stated, it would seem from the words of our Lord that where a divorce has been obtained on the grounds of adultery, the innocent party is free to remarry. Otherwise divorce would serve no purpose not equally achieved by separation.

Sexual immorality, or fornication, is generally taken to mean adultery. However, many capable Bible students think it refers only to pre-marital immorality which is discovered after marriage (see Deut. 22:13–21). Others believe it refers to Jewish marriage customs only and that is why the "exception clause" is only here in Matthew, the Jewish Gospel.

For a fuller discussion of divorce, see notes on 5:31, 32.

19:10 When the **disciples** heard the Lord's teaching on divorce, they proved themselves creatures of extremes by adopting the absurd position that if divorce is obtainable on only one ground, then to avoid sinning in the married state **it** would be **better not to marry** at all. But that would not save them from sinning in the single state.

19:11 So the Savior reminded them that the ability to remain celibate was not the general rule; only those to whom special grace was given could forego marriage. The dictum, **"All cannot accept this saying, but only those to whom it has been given,"** does not mean that all cannot understand what follows, but that they cannot live a continent life unless they are called to it.

19:12 The Lord Jesus explained that there are three types of **eunuchs**. Some men are **eunuchs** because they were **born** without the power of reproduction. Others are so because they were castrated by men; oriental rulers often subjected the harem attendants to surgery to make them eunuchs. But Jesus especially had in mind those **who have made themselves eunuchs for the kingdom of heaven's sake**. These men could be married, and they have no physical impairment. Yet in dedication to the King and His kingdom, they willingly forego marriage in order to give themselves to the cause of Christ without distraction. As Paul wrote later, "He who is unmarried cares for the things of the Lord — how he may please the Lord" (1 Cor. 7:32). Their celibacy is not physical but a matter of voluntary abstinence.

Not all men can live such a life; only those divinely empowered: "But each one has his own gift from God, one in this manner and another in that" (1 Cor. 7:7).

F. Concerning Children (19:13–15)

It is interesting that children are introduced shortly after the discourse on divorce (see also Mark 10:1–16); often they are the ones who suffer most severely from broken homes.

Parents brought their **little children** to Jesus to be blessed by the Teacher-Shepherd. **The disciples** saw this as an intrusion and annoyance, and **rebuked** the parents. **But Jesus** intervened with those words that have since endeared Him to children of every age, **"Let the little children come to Me, and do not forbid them, for of such is the kingdom of heaven."**

Several important lessons emerge from those words. First, they should impress the servant of the Lord with the importance of reaching children, whose minds are most receptive, with the Word

of God. Second, children who wish to confess their faith in the Lord Jesus should be encouraged, not held back. No one knows the age of the youngest person in hell. If a child truly wishes to be saved, he should not be told that he is too young. At the same time, children should not be pressured into making a false profession. Susceptible as they are to emotional appeals, they should be protected from high-pressure methods of evangelism. Children do not have to become adults to be saved, but adults have to become like children (18:3, 4; Mark 10:15).

Thirdly, these words of our Lord answer the question, "What happens to children who die before they reach the age of accountability?" Jesus said, **" . . . of such is the kingdom of heaven."** That should be adequate assurance to parents who have suffered the loss of little ones.

Sometimes this passage is used to support the baptism of young children in order to make them members of Christ and inheritors of the kingdom. Closer reading will show that the parents brought the children to Jesus, not to the baptistry. It will show that the children were already possessors of the kingdom. And it will show that there is not a drop of water in the passage.

G. Concerning Riches: The Rich Young Ruler (19:16–26)

19:16 This incident provides a study in contrasts. Having just seen that the kingdom of heaven belongs to little children, we will now see how difficult it is for adults to enter.

A rich man intercepted the Lord with an apparently sincere inquiry. Addressing Jesus as **"Good Teacher"** he asked **what** he had to **do** to **have eternal life**. The question revealed his ignorance of the true identity of Jesus and of the way of salvation. He called Jesus **"Teacher,"** putting Him on the same level as other great men. And he spoke of gaining **eternal life** as a debt rather than as a gift.

19:17 Our Lord probed him on these two points. In asking, **"Why do you call Me good? There is no one good but One, that is, God,"** Jesus was not denying His own deity, but was providing the man with an opportunity to say,

"That's why I call You good — You are God."

To test him on the way of salvation Jesus said, **"But if you want to enter into life, keep the commandments."** The Savior was not implying that man can be saved by keeping the commandments. Rather, He was using the law to produce conviction of sin in the man's heart. The man was still under the delusion that he could inherit the kingdom on the principle of *doing*. Therefore, let him obey the law which told him what to *do*.

19:18–20 Our Lord quoted the five commandments dealing primarily with our fellow man, climaxing them by saying, **"You shall love your neighbor as yourself."** Blind to his own selfishness, the man boasted that he had always **kept** these commandments.

19:21 Our Lord then exposed the man's failure to love his neighbor as himself by telling him to **sell** all his possessions **and give** the money **to the poor**. Then he should **come** to Jesus and **follow** Him.

The Lord did not mean that this man could have been saved by selling his possessions and giving the proceeds to charity. There is only one way of salvation — faith in the Lord.

But in order to be saved, a man must acknowledge that he has sinned and fallen short of God's holy requirements. The rich man's unwillingness to share his possessions showed that he did not love his neighbor as himself. He should have said, "Lord, if that's what is required, then I'm a sinner. I cannot save myself by my own efforts. Therefore, I ask You to save me by Your grace." If he had responded to the Savior's instruction he would have been given the way of salvation.

19:22 Instead, **he went away sorrowful**.

19:23, 24 The rich man's response prompted **Jesus** to observe **that it is hard for a rich man to enter the kingdom of heaven**. Riches tend to become an idol. It is hard to have them without trusting in them. Our Lord declared that **"it is easier for a camel to go through the eye of a needle than for a rich man to enter the kingdom of God."** He was using a figure of speech known as hyperbole — a statement made in intensified form to produce a vivid, unforgettable effect.

It is clearly impossible for a camel to go through the eye of a needle! The "needle's eye" has often been explained as the small door in a city gate. A camel could get through it by kneeling down, but only with great difficulty. However, the word used for "needle" in the parallel passage in Luke is the same word used to describe the needle used by surgeons. It seems clear from the context that the Lord was not speaking of difficulty, but of impossibility. Humanly speaking, a rich man simply *cannot* be saved.

19:25 The **disciples** were **astonished** by these remarks. As Jews living under the Mosaic code, by which God promised prosperity to those who obeyed Him, they correctly viewed riches as indicative of God's blessing. If those who thus enjoyed God's blessing couldn't be saved, who *could*?

19:26 The Lord replied, **"With men this is impossible, but with God all things are possible."** Humanly speaking, it is **impossible** for anyone to be saved; only God can save a soul. But it is more difficult for a wealthy man to surrender his will to Christ than for a poor man, as evidenced by the fact that few rich men are converted. They find it almost impossible to replace trust in visible means of support for faith in an unseen Savior. Only God can effect such a change.

Commentators and preachers invariably inject here that it is perfectly all right for Christians to be rich. It is strange that they use a passage in which the Lord denounces wealth as a hindrance to man's eternal welfare, to justify the accumulation of earthly treasures! And it is difficult to see how a Christian can cling to riches in view of the appalling need everywhere, the imminence of Christ's Return, and the Lord's clear prohibition against laying up treasures on earth. Hoarded wealth condemns us as not loving our neighbors as ourselves.

H. Concerning Rewards for Sacrificial Living (19:27–30)

19:27 **Peter** caught the drift of the Savior's teaching. Realizing that Jesus was saying, "Forsake all and follow Me," Peter gloated that he and the other disciples had done exactly that; then he added, **"What shall we have?"** Peter's self-life was showing, the old nature reasserting itself. It was a spirit each of us must guard against. He was bargaining with the Lord.

19:28, 29 The Lord assured Peter that everything done for Him would be rewarded handsomely. As to the twelve specifically, they would have places of authority in the Millennium. **The regeneration** refers to Christ's future reign on earth; it is explained by the expression, **"when the Son of Man sits on the throne of His glory."** We have previously referred to this phase of the kingdom as the kingdom in *manifestation*. At that time the twelve will **sit on twelve thrones, judging the twelve tribes of Israel**. Rewards in the NT are closely linked with positions of administration in the Millennium (see Luke 19:17, 19). They are *awarded* at the Judgment Seat of Christ, but *manifested* when the Lord returns to earth to reign.

As to believers in general, Jesus added that all who have **left houses or brothers or sisters or father or mother or wife or children or lands for** His **sake shall receive a hundredfold, and inherit eternal life**. In this life, they enjoy a world-wide fellowship of believers that more than compensates for severed earthly ties. For the one house they leave, they receive a hundred Christian homes where they are warmly welcomed. For lands or other forms of wealth forsaken, they receive spiritual riches beyond reckoning.

The future reward for all believers is **eternal life**. This does not mean that we earn eternal life by forsaking all and sacrificing. Eternal life is a gift and cannot be earned or merited. Here the thought is that those who forsake all are rewarded with a greater capacity for enjoying eternal life in heaven. All believers will have that life but not all will enjoy it to the same extent.

19:30 The Lord closed His remarks with a warning against a bargaining spirit. He said to Peter, in effect, "Anything you do for My sake will be rewarded, but be careful that you are not guided by selfish considerations; because in that case, **many who are first will be last, and the last first.** This is illustrated by a parable in the next chap-

ter. This statement may also have been a warning that it isn't enough to start out well on the path of discipleship. It's how we finish that counts.

Before leaving this section we should notice that the expressions "kingdom of heaven" and "kingdom of God" are used interchangeably in verses 23 and 24; therefore, the two terms are synonymous.

I. Concerning Rewards for Labor in the Vineyard (20:1–16)

20:1, 2 This parable, a continuation of the discourse on rewards at the end of chapter 19, illustrates the truth that while all true disciples will be rewarded, the order of rewards will be determined by the spirit in which the disciple served.

The parable describes **a landowner who went out early in the morning to hire laborers** to work in **his vineyard**. These men contracted to work for **a denarius a day**, a reasonable wage at that time. Let us say they began to work at 6:00 a.m.

20:3, 4 At 9:00 a.m. the farmer found some other unemployed laborers **in the market place**. In this case there was no labor-management agreement. They went to work with only his word that he would give them **whatever was right**.

20:5–7 At noon and at 3:00 p.m. the farmer hired more men on the basis that he would give them a fair wage. At 5:00 p.m. he found more unemployed men. They were not lazy; they wanted work but hadn't been able to find it. So he sent them **into the vineyard** without any discussion of pay.

It is important to notice that the first men were hired as a result of a bargaining agreement; all the others left the matter of pay to the landowner.

20:8 At the end of the day, the farmer instructed his paymaster to pay the men, **beginning with the last** hired and working back **to the first**. (In this way the earliest men hired saw what the others received.)

20:9–12 It was the same pay for all — one **denarius**. The 6:00 a.m. men thought they would receive more, but no — they too got one denarius. They were bitterly resentful; after all, they had worked longer and through **the heat of the day**.

20:13, 14 In the farmer's reply to one of them we find the abiding lessons from the parable. First he **said, "Friend, I am doing you no wrong. Did you not agree with me for a denarius? Take what is yours, and go your way. I wish to give to this last man the same as to you."** The first bargained for a denarius a day and got the wage agreed on. The others cast themselves on the farmer's grace and got grace. Grace is better than justice. It is better to leave our rewards up to the Lord than to strike a bargain with Him.

20:15 Then the farmer said, **"Is it not lawful for me to do what I wish with my own things?"** The lesson, of course, is that God is sovereign. He can do as He pleases. And what He pleases will always be right, just, and fair. The farmer added, **"Or is your eye evil because I am good?"** This question exposes the selfish streak in human nature. The 6:00 a.m. men got exactly what they deserved, yet were jealous because the others got the same pay for working fewer hours. Many of us have to admit that it seems a bit unfair to us, too. This only proves that in the kingdom of heaven we must adopt an entirely new kind of thinking. We must abandon our greedy, competitive spirit, and think like the Lord.

The farmer knew that all these men needed money, so he paid them according to need rather than greed. No one received less than he deserved, but all received what they needed for themselves and their families. The lesson, according to James Stewart, is that the person "who thinks to bargain about final reward will always be wrong, and God's loving-kindness will always have the last unchallengeable word."[39] The more we study the parable in this light, the more we realize that it is not only fair but eminently beautiful. Those who were hired at 6:00 a.m. should have counted it an added recompense to serve such a wonderful master all day.

20:16 Jesus closed the parable with the words, **"So the last will be first, and the first last"** (see 19:30). There will be surprises in the matter of rewards. Some who *thought* they would be first will be last because their service was inspired by pride and selfish ambition. Others who served out of love and gratitude will be highly honored.

> Deeds of merit as we thought them,
> He will show us were but sin;
> Little acts we had forgotten,
> He will show us were for Him.
> *– Anon*

J. Concerning His Death and Resurrection (20:17–19)

It is apparent that the Lord was leaving Perea for the trip **to Jerusalem** via Jericho (see v. 29). Once again He **took the twelve disciples aside** to explain what would happen after they reached the Holy City. He would **be betrayed to the chief priests and to the scribes** — an obvious reference to the perfidy of Judas. He would be condemned **to death** by the leaders of Jewry. Lacking authority to inflict capital punishment, they would turn **Him** over **to the Gentiles** (the Romans). He would be mocked, scourged, and crucified. But death would not keep its prey — **He** would **rise again** on **the third day.**

K. Concerning Position in the Kingdom (20:20–28)

It is a sad commentary on human nature that, immediately after the third prediction of His passion, His followers were thinking more of their own glory than of His sufferings.

> Christ's first prediction of suffering gave rise to Peter's demur (16:22); the second was soon followed by the disciples' questions, "Who is the greatest . . . ?" So here, we find the third capped with the ambitious request of James and John. They persistently closed their eyes to warnings of trouble, and opened them only to the promise of glory — so getting a wrong, materialistic view of the Kingdom (Daily Notes of the Scripture Union).

20:20, 21 **The mother of** James and John came to the Lord **asking** that her boys might sit on either side of Him **in His kingdom**. It is to her credit that she wanted her sons near Jesus, and that she had not despaired of His coming reign.

But she did not understand the principles upon which honors would be bestowed in the kingdom.

Mark says that the sons made the request themselves (Mark 10:35); perhaps they did it at her direction, or perhaps the three of them approached the Lord together. No contradiction is involved.

20:22 Jesus answered frankly that they did not understand what they were asking. They wanted a crown without a cross, a throne without the altar of sacrifice, the glory without the suffering that leads to it. So He asked them pointedly, **"Are you able to drink the cup that I am about to drink?"** We are not left to wonder what He meant by **the cup**; He had just described it in verses 18 and 19. He must suffer and die.

James and John expressed ability to share in His sufferings, though perhaps their confidence was based more on zeal than knowledge.

20:23 Jesus assured them that they would **indeed drink** of His **cup**. James would be martyred and John persecuted and exiled to the Isle of Patmos. Robert Little said, "James died a martyr's death; John lived a martyr's life."

Then Jesus explained that He could not arbitrarily grant places of honor in the kingdom; the **Father** had determined a special basis on which these positions would be assigned. They thought it was a matter of political patronage, that because they were so close to Christ, they had a special claim to places of preferment. But it was not a question of personal favoritism. In the counsels of God, the places on His right hand and left hand would be given on the basis of suffering for Him. This means that the chief honors in the kingdom are not limited to first century Christians; some living today might win them — by suffering.

20:24 The other **ten** disciples **were greatly displeased** that the sons of Zebedee had made such a request. They were probably indignant because they themselves wanted to be greatest and resented any prior claims being made by James and John!

20:25–27 This gave our Lord the opportunity to make a revolutionary statement concerning greatness in His kingdom. **The Gentiles** think of greatness in terms of mastery and rule. In Christ's kingdom, greatness is manifested by service. Whoever aspires to greatness must become a **servant, and whoever desires to be first** must become a **slave**.

20:28 The Son of Man is the perfect example of lowly service. He came into the world not **to be served, but to serve, and to give His life a ransom for many.** The whole purpose of the Incarnation can be summed up in two words — **serve** and **give**. It is amazing to think that the exalted Lord humbled Himself to the manger and to the cross. His greatness was manifested in the depth of His humiliation. And so it must be for us.

He gave His life **a ransom for many**. His death satisfied all God's righteous demands against sin. It was sufficient to put away all the sins of all the world. But it is effective only for those who accept Him as Lord and Savior. Have you ever done this?

L. Healing of Two Blind Men (20:29–34)

20:29, 30 By now Jesus had crossed the Jordan from Perea and had reached **Jericho**. As He was leaving the city, **two blind men** cried out to Him, **"Have mercy on us, O Lord, Son of David!"** Their use of the title **"Son of David"** means that, though physically blind, their spiritual vision was so acute as to recognize Jesus as the Messiah. They may represent the believing remnant of blinded Israel who will acknowledge Him as the Christ when He returns to reign (Isa. 35:5; 42:7; Rom. 11:25, 26; 2 Cor. 3:16; Rev. 1:7).

20:31–34 The crowd tried to hush them, **but they cried** after Him more insistently. When Jesus asked what they wanted, they didn't indulge in generalities, as we often do when we pray. They came right to the point: **"Lord, that our eyes may be opened."** Their specific request received a specific response. **Jesus had compassion and touched their eyes. And immediately** they **received** their **sight, and they followed Him**.

With regard to His touching them, Gaebelein makes a helpful observation:

We have learned before the typical meaning of healing by touch in this Gospel. Whenever the Lord heals by touch it has reference, dispensationally, to His personal presence on the earth and His merciful dealing with Israel. When He heals by His Word, absent in person, . . . or if He is touched in faith, it refers to the time when He is absent from the earth, and Gentiles approaching Him in faith are healed by Him.[40]

There are difficulties in reconciling Matthew's account of this incident with Mark 10:46–52 and Luke 18:35–43; 19:1. Here are *two* blind men; in Mark and Luke, only *one* is mentioned. It has been suggested that Mark and Luke mention the well-known one, Bartimaeus, and Matthew, writing his Gospel especially for Jews, mentions *two* as the minimum number for a valid testimony (2 Cor. 13:1). In Matthew and Mark, the incident is said to have occurred as Jesus left Jericho; in Luke, it is said to have happened as He drew near the city. In fact there were two Jerichos, an old Jericho and a new one, and the miracle of healing probably took place as Jesus was leaving one and entering the other.

XII. PRESENTATION AND REJECTION OF THE KING (Chaps. 21–23)

A. The Triumphal Entry (21:1–11)

21:1–3 On the way up from Jericho, Jesus came to the east side of **the Mount of Olives** where Bethany and **Bethphage** were located. From there the road skirted the south end of Olivet, dipped into the Valley of Jehoshaphat, crossed the Brook Kidron and climbed up to **Jerusalem.**[†]

He **sent two disciples** to Bethany with the foreknowledge that they would **find a** tethered **donkey, and a colt with her**. They were to untie the animals and **bring them to** Jesus. If challenged, they were to explain that **the Lord** needed the beasts. Then the owner would consent. Perhaps the owner knew Jesus and had previously offered to help Him. Or this incident may demonstrate the omniscience and supreme authority of the Lord. Everything happened just as Jesus had predicted.

†See p. xxiv.

21:4, 5 The requisitioning of the animals fulfilled predictions by Isaiah and Zechariah:

"Tell the daughter of Zion,
'Behold, your King is coming to you,
Lowly, and sitting on a donkey,
A colt, the foal of a donkey.' "

21:6 After **the disciples** had spread their garments on the animals, Jesus mounted the colt (Mark 11:7) and rode onward to Jerusalem. It was a historic moment. Sixty-nine weeks of Daniel's prophecy had now run out, according to Sir Robert Anderson (see his computations in the book *The Coming Prince*). Next the Messiah would be cut off (Dan. 9:26).

In riding into Jerusalem in this manner, the Lord Jesus made a deliberate, unveiled claim to being the Messiah. Lange notes:

He fulfills intentionally a prophecy which at His time was unanimously interpreted of the Messiah. If He has previously considered the declaration of His dignity as dangerous, He now counts silence inconceivable. . . . It was hereafter never possible to say that He had never declared Himself in a wholly unequivocal manner. When Jerusalem was afterwards accused of the murder of the Messiah, it should not be able to say that the Messiah had omitted to give a sign intelligible for all alike.[41]

21:7, 8 The Lord rode to the city on a carpet of **clothes** and palm **branches**, with the acclamation of the people ringing in His ears. For a moment, at least, He was acknowledged as King.

21:9 The multitudes shouted, **"Hosanna to the Son of David! Blessed is He who comes in the name of the LORD."** This quotation from Psalm 118:25, 26 obviously applies to the Messiah's advent. **Hosanna** originally meant "save now"; perhaps the people meant, "Save us from our Roman oppressors." Later the term became an exclamation of praise. The phrases, **"Son of David"** and, **"Blessed is He who comes in the name of the LORD,"** both clearly indicate that Jesus was being recognized as the Messiah. He is the Blessed One who comes by Jehovah's authority to do His will.

Mark's account records as part of the

crowd's shouts the phrase, "Blessed is the kingdom of our father David that comes in the name of the Lord" (Mark 11:10). This indicates that the people thought the kingdom was about to be set up with Christ sitting on the throne of David. In shouting, **"Hosanna in the highest,"** the crowd was calling on the heavens to join the earth in praising the Messiah, and perhaps calling on Him to save from the highest heavens.

Mark 11:11 records that, once in Jerusalem, Jesus went to the temple — not inside the temple but into the courtyard. Presumably it was the house of God, but He was not at home in this temple because the priests and people refused to give Him His rightful place. After looking around briefly, the Savior withdrew to Bethany with the twelve. It was Sunday evening.

21:10, 11 Meanwhile, inside **the city** there was bewilderment as to His identity. Those who asked were told only that He was **Jesus the prophet from Nazareth of Galilee.** From this it seems that few really understood He was the Messiah. In less than a week, the fickle crowd would be crying, "Crucify Him! Crucify Him!"

B. Cleansing the Temple (21:12, 13)

21:12 At the outset of His public ministry, Jesus had driven commercialism out of the temple environs (John 2:13–16). But profiteering for an excessive fee had again sprung up in the outer court of the temple. Sacrificial animals and birds were being bought and sold at exorbitant rates. **Moneychangers** converted other currencies into the half-shekel which Jewish men had to pay as temple tribute (tax) — for an excessive fee. Now, as His ministry drew to a close, **Jesus** again **drove out** those who were profiteering from sacred activities.

21:13 Combining quotations from Isaiah and Jeremiah, He condemned desecration, commercialism, and exclusivism. Quoting from Isaiah 56:7, He reminded them that God intended the temple to be **a house of prayer**. They had made it a hangout of **thieves** (Jer. 7:11).

This cleansing of the temple was His first official act after entering Jerusalem.

By it He unmistakably asserted His lordship over the temple.

This incident has a twofold message for today. In our church life, we need His cleansing power to drive out bazaars, suppers, and a host of other money-making gimmicks. In our personal lives, there is constant need for the purging ministry of the Lord in our bodies, the temples of the Holy Spirit.

C. Indignation of the Priests and Scribes (21:14–17)

21:14 The next scene finds our Lord healing **the blind and the lame** in the temple yard. He attracted the needy wherever He went, and never sent them away without meeting their need.

21:15, 16† But hostile eyes were watching. And when these **chief priests and scribes** heard children hailing Jesus as **the Son of David**, they were enraged.

They said, **"Do You hear what these are saying?"** — as if they expected Him to forbid the children from addressing Him as the Messiah! If Jesus had not been the Messiah, this would have been an appropriate time to say so once for all. But His answer indicated that the children were right. He quoted Psalm 8:2 from the Septuagint: **"Out of the mouth of babes and nursing infants You have perfected praise."** If the supposedly knowledgeable priests and scribes would not praise Him as the Anointed, then the Lord would be worshiped by little children. Children often have spiritual insight beyond their years, and their words of faith and love bring unusual glory to the name of the Lord.

21:17 Leaving the religious leaders to ponder this truth, Jesus returned **to Bethany** and spent the night there.

D. The Barren Fig Tree (21:18–22)

21:18, 19 Returning to Jerusalem **in the morning**, the Lord **came to a fig tree**, hoping to find fruit on it to satisfy His hunger. Finding **nothing on it but leaves**, He said, **"Let no fruit grow on you ever again."** Immediately the fig tree withered away.

In Mark's account (11:12–14) the comment is made that it was not the season for figs. Therefore, His condemning the tree because it had no fruit would seem

†See p. xxi.

to picture the Savior as unreasonable and petulant. Knowing this cannot be true, how is this difficulty explained?

Fig trees in Bible lands produced an early, edible fruit before the leaves appeared. This was a harbinger of the regular crop. If no early figs appeared, as in the case of this fig tree, it indicated that there would be no regular figs later on.

This is the only miracle in which Christ cursed rather than blessed — destroyed rather than restored life. This has been raised as a difficulty. Such criticism betrays an ignorance of the Person of Christ. He is God, the Sovereign of the universe. Some of His dealings are mysterious to us, but we must begin with the premise that they are always right. In this case, the Lord knew that the fig tree would never bear figs and He acted as a farmer would in removing a barren tree from his orchard.

Even those who criticize our Lord for cursing the fig tree admit it was a symbolic action. This incident is the Savior's interpretation of the tumultuous welcome He had just received in Jerusalem. Like the vine and the olive tree, the fig tree represents the nation of Israel. When Jesus came to the nation there were leaves, which speak of profession, but no fruit for God. Jesus was hungry for fruit from the nation.

Because there was no early fruit, He knew there would be no later fruit from that unbelieving people, and so He cursed the fig tree. This prepictured the judgment which would fall on the nation in A.D. 70.

We must remember that while *unbelieving* Israel will be fruitless forever, a *remnant* of the nation will return to the Messiah after the Rapture. They will bring forth fruit for Him during the Tribulation and during His Millennial Reign.

Although the primary interpretation of this passage relates to the nation of Israel, it has application to people of all ages who combine high talk and low walk.

21:20–22 When **the disciples** expressed amazement at the sudden withering of the tree, the Lord told them that they could do greater miracles than this if they had **faith**. For instance, they

could say to a mountain, **"Be removed and be cast into the sea,"** and it would happen. **"And whatever things you ask in prayer, believing, you will receive."**

Again we must explain that these seemingly unqualified promises concerning prayer must be understood in light of all that the Bible teaches on the subject. Verse 22 does not mean that any Christian can ask anything he wants and expect to get it. He must pray in accordance with the conditions laid down in the Bible.

E. Jesus' Authority Questioned (21:23–27)

21:23 When Jesus **came into** the court outside **the temple** proper, **the chief priests and the elders** interrupted His teaching to ask who gave Him the **authority** to teach, to perform miracles, and to cleanse the temple. They hoped to trap Him, no matter how He answered. If He claimed to have authority in Himself as the Son of God, they would accuse Him of blasphemy. If He claimed authority from men, they would discredit Him. If He claimed authority from God, they would challenge Him. They considered themselves the guardians of the faith, professionals who by formal training and human appointment were authorized to direct the religious life of the people. Jesus had no formal schooling and certainly no credentials from Israel's rulers. Their challenge reflected the age-old resentment felt by professional religionists against men with the power of divine anointing.

21:24, 25 The Lord offered to explain His authority if they would answer a question, "Was John's baptism **from heaven or from men?"** John's **baptism** should be understood as meaning John's ministry. Therefore the question was, "Who authorized John to carry on his ministry? Was his ordination human or divine? What credentials did he hold from Israel's leaders?" The answer was obvious: John was a man sent from God. His power came from *divine enduement*, not from *human endorsement*.

The priests and elders were in a dilemma. If they admitted that John was sent by God, they were trapped. John had pointed men to Jesus as the Messiah. If John's authority was divine, why hadn't they repented and **believed on Christ**?

21:26 On the other hand, if they said that John was not commissioned by God, they adopted a position that would be ridiculed by the people, most of whom agreed that **John** was **a prophet** from God. If they had correctly answered that John was divinely sent, they would have had the answer to their own question: Jesus was the Messiah of whom John had been the forerunner.

21:27 But they refused to face the facts, so they pleaded ignorance. They could not tell the source of John's power. Then Jesus said, **"Neither will I tell you by what authority I do these things."** Why should He tell them what they already knew but were unwilling to admit?

F. Parable of the Two Sons (21:28–32)

21:28–30 This parable is a stinging rebuke to the chief priests and elders for their failure to obey John's call to repentance and faith. It concerns **a man** whose **two sons** were asked to **work in** the **vineyard**. One refused, then changed his mind and went. The other agreed to go, but never did.

21:31, 32 When asked **which** son **did the will of his father**, the religious leaders unwittingly condemned themselves by saying, **"The first."**

The Lord interpreted the parable. **Tax collectors and harlots** were like the first son. They made no immediate pretense of obeying John the Baptist, but eventually many of them did repent and believe in Jesus. The religious leaders were like the second son. They professed to approve the preaching of John, but never confessed their sins or trusted the Savior. Therefore the out-and-out sinners entered the kingdom of God while the self-satisfied religious leaders remained outside. It is the same today. Avowed sinners receive the gospel more readily than those with a veneer of false piety.

The expression **"John came to you in the way of righteousness"** means that he came preaching the necessity of righteousness through repentance and faith.

G. Parable of the Wicked Vinedressers (21:33–46)

21:33–39 Further answering the question about authority, Jesus told the **parable** of **a certain landowner who planted a vineyard and set a hedge around it**, installed **a wine press in it, ... built a tower**, rented **it to vinedressers**, and **went** away to a distant **country**. At **vintage-time ... he sent his servants to the vinedressers** to get his share of the crop, but the **vinedressers beat one, killed one, and stoned another**. When **he sent other servants**, they received the same treatment. The third time **he sent his son**, thinking **they** would **respect** him. Knowing full well that he was **the heir**, they **killed him** with the idea of seizing **his inheritance**.

21:40, 41 At this point the Lord asked the priests and elders **what** the owner would **do to those vinedressers**. They answered, **"He will destroy those wicked men miserably, and lease his vineyard to other vinedressers who will render to him the fruits in their seasons."**

The parable is not difficult to interpret. God is the landowner, Israel the vineyard (Ps. 80:8; Isa. 5:1–7; Jer. 2:21). The hedge is the Law of Moses which separated Israel from the Gentiles and preserved them as a distinct people for the Lord. The wine-press, by metonymy, signifies the fruit which Israel should have produced for God. The tower suggests Jehovah's watchful care for His people. The vinedressers are the chief priests and scribes.

Repeatedly God sent His servants, the prophets, to the people of Israel seeking from the vineyard the fruits of fellowship, holiness, and love. But the people persecuted the prophets and killed some of them. Finally, God sent His Son, saying, "They will respect My Son" (v. 37). The chief priests and scribes said, "This is the heir" — a fatal admission. They privately agreed that Jesus was the Son of God (though publicly denying it) and thus answered their own question concerning His authority. His authority came from the fact that He was God the Son.

In the parable they are quoted as saying, "This is the heir. Come, let us kill him and seize his inheritance" (v. 38). In real life they said, "If we let Him alone like this, everyone will believe in Him, and the Romans will come and take

away both our place and our nation"
(John 11:48). And so they rejected Him,
threw Him out, and crucified Him.

21:42   When the Savior asked what
the owner of the vineyard would do,
their answer condemned them, as He
shows in verses 42 and 43. He quoted
the words of Psalm 118:22: **"The stone
which the builders rejected has become
the chief cornerstone. This was the
LORD'S doing, and it is marvelous in our
eyes."** When Christ, the Stone, presented Himself to the builders — the
leaders of Israel, they had no place for
Him in their building plans. They threw
Him aside as useless. But following His
death He was raised from the dead and
given the place of preeminence by God.
He has been made the topmost stone in
God's building: "God also has highly exalted Him and given Him the name
which is above every name . . . " (Phil.
2:9).

21:43   Jesus then bluntly announced
that **the kingdom of God** would **be taken
from** Israel **and given to a nation bearing
the fruits of it**. And so it happened. Israel has been set aside as God's chosen
people and has been judicially blinded.
A hardening has come upon the race
that rejected its Messiah. The prophecy
that **the kingdom of God** would **be given
to a nation bearing the fruits of it** has
been understood as referring to: (1) the
church, composed of believing Jews and
Gentiles — "a holy nation, God's own
people" (1 Pet. 2:9); or (2) the believing
portion of Israel that will be living at the
Second Advent. Redeemed Israel will
bring forth fruit for God.

21:44 **"Whoever falls on this stone
will be broken; but on whomever it
falls, it will grind him to powder."** In
the first part of the verse, the **stone** is
on the ground; in the second part, it is
descending from above. This suggests
the two Advents of Christ. When He
came the first time, the Jewish leaders
stumbled over Him and were broken to
pieces. When He comes again, He will
descend in judgment, scattering His enemies like dust.

21:45, 46   The chief priests and
Pharisees realized these **parables** were
aimed directly at them, in answer to
their question concerning Christ's authority. They would like to have seized
Him then and there, but **they feared the
multitudes**, who still **took** Jesus **for a
prophet**.

H. Parable of the Wedding Dinner (22:1–14)

22:1–6   Jesus was not through with
the chief priests and Pharisees. In a parable of a wedding **dinner** He again pictured favored Israel as set aside and the
despised Gentiles as guests at the table.
He likened **the kingdom of heaven** to **a
certain king who arranged a marriage**
feast **for his son**. The invitation was in
two stages. First, an advance invitation,
personally conveyed by servants, which
met a flat refusal. The second invitation
announced that the feast was spread. It
was treated contemptuously by some,
who were too busy with their farms and
businesses, and violently by others, who
seized, abused, and **killed** the servants.

22:7–10   The king was so **furious**
that he **destroyed those murderers and
burned their city**. Scrapping the first
guest list, he issued a general invitation
to all who would come. This time there
wasn't an empty seat in **the wedding
hall**.

22:11–13   Among **the guests**, however, was one **who did not have a wedding garment**. Challenged on his unfitness to attend, **he was speechless**. The
king ordered him to be cast out into the
night, where there would be **weeping
and gnashing of teeth**. The attendants in
verse 13 are not the same as the servants
in verse 3.

22:14   Our Lord concluded the parable with the words, **"For many are
called, but few are chosen."**

As to the meaning of the parable, the
king is God and His Son is the Lord
Jesus. The wedding feast is an appropriate description of the festive joy which
characterizes the kingdom of heaven. Introducing the church as the bride of
Christ in this parable unnecessarily com-
plicates the picture. The main thought is
the setting aside of Israel — not the distinctive call and destiny of the church.

The first stage of the invitation pictures John the Baptist and the twelve disciples graciously inviting Israel to the
wedding feast. But the nation refused to
accept. The words, "they were not will-

ing to come" (v. 3), were climactically dramatized in the crucifixion.

The second stage of the invitation suggests the proclamation of the gospel to the Jews in the book of Acts. Some treated the message with contempt. Some treated the messengers with violence; most of the apostles were martyred.

The King, justifiably angry with Israel, sent "his armies," that is, Titus and his Roman legions, to destroy Jerusalem and most of its people in A.D. 70. They were "his armies" in the sense that He used them as His instruments to punish Israel. They were His officially even if they did not know Him personally.

Now Israel is set aside nationally and the gospel goes out to the Gentiles, both bad and good, that is, of all degrees of respectability (Acts 13:45, 46; 28:28). But the reality of each individual who comes is tested. The man without a wedding garment is one who professes to be ready for the kingdom but who has never been clothed in the righteousness of God through the Lord Jesus Christ (2 Cor. 5:21). Actually there was (and is) no excuse for the man without the wedding garment. As Ryrie notes, it was the custom in those days to provide the guests with a garment if they had none. The man obviously did not take advantage of the offered provision. Without Christ, he is speechless when challenged as to his right to enter the kingdom (Rom. 3:19). His doom is outer darkness where there is weeping and gnashing of teeth. The weeping suggests the suffering of hell. Some suggest that the gnashing of teeth signifies continued hatred and rebellion against God. If so, it disproves the notion that the fires of hell exert a purifying effect.

Verse 14 refers to the whole parable and not just to the incident of the man without the wedding garment. **Many are called**, that is, the gospel invitation goes out to many. But **few are chosen**. Some refuse the invitation, and even of those who respond favorably, some are exposed as false professors. All who respond to the good news are chosen. The only way a person can tell whether he is chosen is by what he does with the Lord Jesus Christ. As Jennings put it,

"All are called to enjoy the feast, but not all are willing to trust the Giver to provide the robe that fits for the feast."

I. Rendering to Caesar and to God (22:15–22)

Chapter 22 is a chapter of questions, recording attempts by three different deputations sent to trap the Son of God.

22:15, 16 Here we have an attempt by **the Pharisees** and **Herodians**. These two parties were bitter foes temporarily brought together by a common hatred of the Savior. Their goal was to lure Christ into making a political statement with dangerous implications. They took advantage of the Jews' division over allegiance to Caesar. Some passionately opposed submitting to the Gentile emperor. Others, like the Herodians, adopted a more tolerant view.

22:17 First they insincerely complimented His purity of character, His truthfulness, and His fearlessness. Then they dropped the loaded question, **"Is it lawful to pay taxes to Caesar, or not?"**

If Jesus answered, "No," He would not only antagonize the Herodians, but would be accused of rebellion against the Roman government. The Pharisees would have hustled Him off and pressed charges against Him. If He said, "Yes," He would run afoul of the Jews' intense nationalistic spirit. He would lose much support among the common people — support which so far hindered the leaders in their efforts to dispose of Him.

22:18, 19 Jesus bluntly denounced them as **hypocrites**, trying to trap Him. Then He asked them to show Him a **denarius**, the coin used to pay taxes to the Roman government. Every time the Jews saw the likeness and title of Caesar on the coin it was an annoying reminder that they were under Gentile authority and taxation. The denarius should have reminded them that their bondage to Rome was a result of their sin. Had they been true to Jehovah, the question of paying taxes to Caesar would never have arisen.

22:20, 21 Jesus   asked   them, **"Whose image and inscription is this?"** They were forced to answer, **"Caesar's."** Then the Lord told them, **"Render therefore to Caesar the things that are**

Caesar's, and to God the things that are God's."

Their question had boomeranged. They had hoped to trap Jesus on the question of tribute to Caesar. He exposed their failure to give tribute to God. Galling as it was, they did give Caesar his due, but they had disregarded the claims of God on their lives. And One stood before them who is the express image of God's Person (Heb. 1:3) and they failed to give Him His rightful place.

Jesus' reply shows that the believer has dual citizenship. He is responsible to obey and financially support human government. He is not to speak evil of his rulers nor work to overthrow his government. He is to pray for those in authority. As a citizen of heaven, he is responsible to obey God. If there is ever a conflict between the two, his first loyalty is to God (Acts 5:29).

In quoting verse 21, most of us emphasize the part about Caesar and skip lightly over the part about God — exactly the fault for which Jesus reprehended the Pharisees!

22:22 When the Pharisees **heard** His answer, they knew they were outdone. All they could do was marvel, then leave.

J. The Sadducees and Their Resurrection Riddle (22:23–33)

22:23, 24 As mentioned previously, the Sadducees were the liberal theologians of that day, denying the resurrection of the body, the existence of angels, and miracles. In fact, their denials were more numerous than their affirmations.

A group of them **came to** Jesus with a story designed to make the idea of resurrection look ridiculous. They reminded Him of the law concerning levirate marriage (Deut. 25:5). Under that law, if an Israelite died without leaving **children, his brother** was supposed to **marry** the widow to preserve the family name in Israel and keep the inheritance within the family.

22:25–28 Their riddle concerned a woman who lost her husband, then married one of his brothers. The second brother died, so she married the third — and so on, down to the seventh. Finally, **the woman died**. Then came the question designed to humiliate Him who is the resurrection (John 11:25): **"Therefore, in the resurrection, whose wife of the seven will she be? For they all had her."**

22:29 Basically, they argued that the idea of resurrection posed insuperable difficulties, hence it was not reasonable, therefore it was not true. Jesus answered that the difficulty was not in the doctrine but in their minds; they were ignorant of **the Scriptures** and **the power of God**.

First of all, they were ignorant **of the Scriptures**. The Bible never says the husband-wife relationship will be continued in heaven. While men will be recognizable as men, and women as women, they will all be like angels in the sense that they neither marry nor are given in marriage.

Secondly, they were ignorant of **the power of God**. If He could create men from dust, could He not as easily raise the dust of those who had died and refashion it into bodies of glory?

22:30–32 Then the Lord Jesus brought forth an argument from Scripture to show that resurrection is an absolute necessity. In Exodus 3:6 God spoke of Himself as **the God of Abraham, . . . Isaac, and . . . Jacob**. Yet Jesus pointed out, **"God is not the God of the dead, but of the living."** God made covenants with these men, but they died before the covenants were completely fulfilled. How can God speak of Himself as the God of three men whose bodies are in the grave? How can He who cannot fail to keep His promises fulfill those made to men who have already died? There is only one answer — resurrection.

22:33 No wonder **the multitudes** were **astonished at His teaching**; we are too!

K. The Great Commandment (22:34–40)

22:34–36 When the Pharisees heard that Jesus **had silenced** their antagonists the Sadducees, they came to Him for an interview. Their spokesman, **a lawyer**, asked Jesus to single out **the great commandment in the law**.

22:37, 38 In a masterful way the Lord Jesus summarized man's obligation

to God as the **first and great commandment: "'You shall love the LORD your
God with all your heart, with all your
soul, and with all your mind.'"** Mark's
account adds the phrase, "and with all
your strength" (Mark 12:30). This means
that man's first obligation is to love God
with the totality of his being. As has
been pointed out: the heart speaks of the
emotional nature, the soul of the volitional nature, the mind of the intellectual
nature, and strength of the physical nature.

22:39, 40 Then Jesus added that
man's second responsibility is to **love** his
neighbor as himself. Barnes says, "Love
to God and man comprehends the whole
of religion: and to produce this has been
the design of Moses, the prophets, the
Savior, and the apostles." We should frequently ponder the words, **"love your
neighbor as yourself."** We should think
of how very much we do love ourselves,
of how much of our activity centers
around the care and comfort of self.
Then we should try to imagine what it
would be like if we showered that love
on our neighbors. Then we should do it.
Such behavior is not natural; it is supernatural. Only those who have been born
again can do it, and then only by allowing Christ to do it through them.

L. David's Son Is David's Lord (22:41–46)

22:41, 42 While the Pharisees were
still awed by Jesus' answer to the lawyer,
He faced them with a provocative problem. **"What** did they **think about the
Christ? Whose Son is He?"**

Most Pharisees did not believe that
Jesus was the Christ; they were still waiting for the Messiah. So Jesus was not
asking them, "What do you think of
Me?" (though that, of course, was involved). He was asking in a general way
whose Son the Messiah would be when
He appeared.

They answered correctly that the
Messiah would be a descendant **of
David**.

22:43, 44 Then the Lord Jesus
quoted Psalm 110:1 where David said,
**"The LORD said to my Lord, 'Sit at My
right hand, till I make Your enemies
Your footstool.'"** The first use of the

word "LORD" refers to God the Father,
and the second to the Messiah. So David
spoke of the Messiah as his Lord.

22:45 Now Jesus posed the question, **"If David then calls Him 'Lord,'
how is He his Son?"** The answer is that
the Messiah is both David's Lord and
David's Son — both God and Man. As
God, He is David's Lord; as Man, He is
David's Son.

Had the Pharisees only been teachable, they would have realized that Jesus
was the Messiah — the Son of David
through the line of Mary, and the Son
of God as revealed by His words, works,
and ways.

22:46 But they refused to see. Completely baffled by His wisdom, they
ceased trying to trick Him with questions. Hereafter they would use another
method — *violence.*

M. Warning Against High Talk, Low Walk (23:1–12)

23:1–4 In the opening verses of this
chapter, the Savior warns the crowds
and **His disciples** against **the scribes
and the Pharisees**. These leaders sat **in
Moses' seat**, or taught the Law of Moses.
Generally, their teachings were dependable, but their practice was not. Their
creed was better than their conduct. It
was a case of high talk and low walk.
So Jesus said, **"... whatever they tell
you to observe, *that* observe and do, but
do not do according to their works; for
they say, and do not do."**

They made heavy demands (probably
extreme interpretations of the letter of
the law) on the people, but would not
assist anyone in lifting these intolerable
loads.

23:5 They went through religious
observances to be seen by men, not from
inward sincerity. Their use of phylacteries was an example. In commanding Israel to bind His words as a sign upon
their hands and as frontlets between
their eyes (Ex. 13:9, 16; Deut. 6:8; 11:18),
God meant that the law should continually be before them, guiding their activities. They reduced this spiritual
command to a literal, physical sense. En-
closing portions of Scripture in leather
capsules, they bound them to their foreheads or arms. They weren't concerned

about obeying the law as long as, by wearing ridiculously large phylacteries, they appeared super-spiritual. The law also commanded the Jews to wear tassels with blue cords on the corners of their garments, (Num. 15:37–41; Deut. 22:12). These distinctive trimmings were intended to remind them that they were a distinct people, and that they should walk in separation from the nations. The Pharisees overlooked the spiritual lesson and satisfied themselves with making longer fringes.

23:6–8 They showed their self-importance by scrambling for the places of honor **at feasts** and **in the synagogues**. They nourished their ego on **greetings in the marketplaces** and especially enjoyed being called **rabbi** (meaning "my great one," or "teacher").

23:9, 10 Here the Lord warned His disciples against using distinctive titles which should be reserved for the Godhead. We are not to be called rabbi as a distinctive title because there is one **Teacher — the Christ**. We should call no man **father**; God is our **Father**. Weston writes insightfully:

> It is a declaration of the essential relations of man to God. Three things constitute a Christian — what he is, what he believes, what he does; doctrine, experience, practice. Man needs for his spiritual being three things — life, instruction, guidance; just what our Lord declares in the ten words of the Gospel — "I am the way, and the truth, and the life". . . . Acknowledge no man as Father, for no man can impart or sustain spiritual life; install no man as an infallible teacher; allow no one to assume the office of spiritual director; your relation to God and to Christ is as close as that of any other person.[42]

The obvious meaning of the Savior's words is that in the kingdom of heaven all believers form an equal brotherhood with no place for distinctive titles setting one above another. Yet think of the pompous titles found in Christendom today: Reverend, Right Reverend, Father, and a host of others. Even the seemingly harmless "Doctor" means teacher in Latin. (This warning clearly applies to *spiritual*, rather than natural, professional or academic relationships. For in-

stance, it does not prohibit a child's calling his parent "Father," nor a patient's addressing his physician as "Doctor.") As far as earthly relationships are concerned, the rule is "respect to whom respect is due, honor to whom honor is due" (Rom. 13:7).

23:11, 12 Once again the revolutionary character of the kingdom of heaven is seen in the fact that true greatness is exactly opposite to what people suppose. Jesus said, **"He who is greatest among you shall be your servant. And whoever exalts himself will be humbled, and he who humbles himself will be exalted."** True greatness stoops to serve. Pharisees who exalt themselves will be brought low. True disciples who humble themselves will be exalted in due time.

N. Woes against the Scribes and Pharisees (23:13–36)

The Lord Jesus next pronounces eight woes on the proud religious hypocrites of His day. These are not "curses," but rather expressions of sorrow at their fate, not unlike the expression, "Alas for you!"

23:13 The first **woe** is directed against their obduracy and obstructionism. They refused to enter **the kingdom** themselves, and aggressively hindered others from **entering**. Strangely, religious leaders are often the most active opponents of the gospel of grace. They can be sweetly tolerant of everything but the good news of salvation. Natural man doesn't want to be the object of God's grace and doesn't want God to show grace to others.

23:14 The second woe[43] lambastes their appropriating of **widow's houses** and covering it up by making **long prayers**. Some modern cults use a similar technique by getting elderly widows, sometimes undiscerning believers, to sign over their property to the "church." Such pretenders to piety **will receive greater condemnation**.

23:15 The third charge against them is misdirected zeal. They went to unimaginable lengths to make one convert, but after he was **won** they made him **twice as** wicked as themselves. A modern analogy is the zeal of false cults. One group is willing to knock on 700 doors to reach one person for their cause; but the final result is evil. As someone has said, "The most converted often become the most perverted."

23:16–22 Fourthly, the Lord denounced them for their casuistry, or deliberate dishonest reasoning. They had built up a false system of reasoning to evade the payment of vows. For instance, they taught that if you swore by **the temple**, you were not obligated to pay, but if you swore **by the gold of the temple**, then you must perform the vow. They said that swearing by the gift on the altar was binding, whereas swearing by the empty altar was not. Thus they valued gold above God (the temple was the house of God), and the gift on the altar (wealth of some form) above the altar itself. They were more interested in the material than the spiritual. They were more interested in getting (the gift) than in giving (the altar was the place of giving).

Addressing them as **blind guides**, Jesus exposed their sophistry. The gold of the temple took on special value only because it was associated with God's abode. It was the altar that gave value to the gift upon it. People who think that gold has intrinsic value are blind; it becomes valuable only as it is used for God's glory. Gifts given for carnal motives are valueless; those given to the Lord or in the Lord's Name have eternal value.

The fact is that whatever these Pharisees swore by, God was involved and they were obligated to fulfill the vow. Man cannot escape his obligations by specious reasonings. Vows are binding and promises must be kept. It is useless to appeal to technicalities to evade obligations.

23:23, 24 The fifth **woe** is against ritualism without reality. The **scribes and Pharisees** were meticulous in giving the Lord a tenth of the most insignificant herbs they raised. Jesus did not condemn them for this care about small details of obedience, but He excoriated them for being utterly unscrupulous when it came to showing **justice, mercy,** and faithfulness to others. Using a figure of speech unsurpassed for expressive-

ness, Jesus described them as straining **out a gnat** and swallowing **a camel**. The gnat, a tiny insect that often fell into a cup of sweet wine, was strained out by sucking the wine through the teeth. How ludicrous to take such care with the insignificant, then bolt down the largest unclean animal in Palestine! The Pharisees were infinitely concerned with minutiae, but grossly blind to enormous sins like hypocrisy, dishonesty, cruelty, and greed. They had lost their sense of proportion.

23:25, 26 The sixth **woe** concerns externalism. The Pharisees, careful to maintain an outward show of religiousness and morality, had hearts filled with **extortion and self–indulgence**.[44] They should **first cleanse the inside of the cup and dish**, that is, make sure their hearts were cleansed through repentance and faith. Then, and only then, would their outward behavior be acceptable. There is a difference between our person and our personality. We tend to emphasize the personality — what we want others to think we are. God emphasizes the person — what we really are. He desires truth in the inward being (Ps. 51:6).

23:27, 28 The seventh **woe** also strikes out against externalism. The difference is that the sixth woe castigates the concealment of avarice, whereas the seventh condemns the concealment of **hypocrisy and lawlessness**.

Tombs were whitewashed so that Jewish people would not inadvertently touch them and thus be ceremonially defiled. Jesus likened the scribes and Pharisees to **whitewashed tombs**, which looked clean on the outside but were full of corruption inside. Men thought that contact with these religious leaders would be sanctifying, but actually it was a defiling experience because they were full of hypocrisy and iniquity.

23:29, 30 The final **woe** was against what we might label outward homage, inward homicide. The **scribes and Pharisees** pretended to honor the OT **prophets** by building and/or repairing their **tombs** and putting wreaths on their monuments. In memorial speeches, they said they **would not have** joined their ancestors in killing **the prophets**.

23:31 Jesus said to them, **"There-**

fore you are witnesses against yourselves that you are sons of those who
murdered the prophets." But how did
they witness this? It almost seems from
the preceding verse that they dissociated
themselves from their fathers who killed
the prophets. First, they admitted that
their fathers, of whom they were physical sons, shed the blood of the prophets.
But Jesus used the word **sons** in the
sense of meaning people with the same
characteristics. He knew that even as
they were decorating the prophets'
graves, they were plotting His death.
Second, in showing such respect for the
dead prophets, they were saying, "The
only prophets we like are dead ones."
In this sense also they were sons of their
fathers.

23:32 Then our Lord added, **"Fill
up, then, the measure of your fathers'
guilt."** The fathers had filled the cup of
murder part way by killing the prophets.
The scribes and Pharisees would soon fill
it to the brim by killing the Lord Jesus
and His followers, thus bringing to a terrible climax what their fathers had
begun.

23:33 At this point the Christ of
God utters those thunderous words,
**"Serpents, brood of vipers! How can
you escape the condemnation of hell?"**
Can Incarnate Love speak such scathing
words? Yes, because true love must also
be righteous and holy. The popular conception of Jesus as an innocuous reformer, capable of no emotion but love,
is unbiblical. Love can be firm, and must
always be just.

It is solemn to remember that these
words of condemnation were hurled at
religious leaders, not at drunkards and
reprobates. In an ecumenical age when
some evangelical Christians are joining
forces with avowed enemies of the cross
of Christ, it is good to ponder the example of Jesus, and to remember the
words of Jehu to Jehoshaphat, "Should
you help the wicked and love those who
hate the LORD?" (2 Chron. 19:2).

23:34, 35 Jesus not only foresaw
His own death; He plainly told the
scribes and Pharisees that they would
murder some of the messengers whom
He would send — **prophets, wise men,
and scribes.** Some who escaped martyr-

dom would be scourged in the **synagogues** and persecuted **from city to city.**
Thus the religious leaders of Israel
would heap to themselves the accumulated guilt of the history of martyrdom.
Upon them would **come all the righteous blood shed on the earth from . . .
Abel . . . to . . . Zechariah,** whose murder is recorded in 2 Chronicles 24:20, 21,
the last book in the Hebrew arrangement
of the Bible. (This is not Zechariah, author of the OT book.)

23:36 The guilt of all the past would
come on the **generation** or race to which
Christ was speaking, as if all previous
shedding of innocent blood somehow
combined and climaxed in the death of
the sinless Savior. A torrent of punishment would be poured out on the nation
that hated its Messiah without a cause
and nailed Him to a criminal's cross.

O. Jesus Laments Over Jerusalem (23:37–39)

23:37 It is highly significant that the
chapter which, more than almost any
other, contains the woes of the Lord
Jesus, closes with His tears! After His bitter denunciation of the Pharisees, He utters a poignant lament over the city of
lost opportunity. The repetition of the
name — **"O Jerusalem, Jerusalem"** — is
charged with unutterable emotion. She
had killed **the prophets** and stoned
God's messengers, yet the Lord loved
her, and would often have protectingly
and lovingly gathered her children
to Himself — **as a hen gathers her
chicks — but** she was **not willing.**

23:38 In closing His lament, the
Lord Jesus said, **"See! Your house is left
to you desolate."** Primarily the house
here is the temple, but may also include
the city of Jerusalem and the nation itself. There would be an interval between
His death and Second Coming during
which unbelieving Israel would not see
Him (after His resurrection He was seen
only by believers).

23:39 Verse 39 looks forward to the
Second Advent when a believing portion
of Israel will accept Him as their
Messiah-King. This acceptance is implicit
in the words, **"Blessed is He who comes
in the name of the LORD."**

There is no suggestion that those

who murdered Christ will have a second chance. He was speaking of Jerusalem and thus, by metonymy, of its inhabitants and of Israel in general. The next time the inhabitants of Jerusalem would see Him after His death would be when they would look on Him whom they pierced and mourn for Him as one mourns for an only son (Zech. 12:10). In Jewish reckoning there is no mourning as bitter as that for an only son.

XIII. THE KING'S OLIVET DISCOURSE (Chaps. 24, 25)

Chapters 24 and 25 form what is known as the Olivet Discourse, so named because this important pronouncement was given on the Mount of Olives. The discourse is entirely prophetic; it points forward to the Tribulation Period and the Lord's Second Coming. It primarily, though not exclusively, concerns the nation of Israel. Its locale is obviously Palestine; for example, "let those who are in Judea flee to the mountains" (24:16). Its setting is distinctly Jewish; for example, "Pray that your flight may not be . . . on the Sabbath" (24:20). The reference to the elect (24:22) should be understood as God's *Jewish elect*, not the church. The church is not found in either the prophecies or parables of the discourse, as we shall seek to demonstrate.

A. Jesus Predicts the Destruction of the Temple (24:1, 2)

The discourse is introduced by the significant statement that **Jesus went out and departed from the temple** This movement is especially significant in view of the words He had just uttered, " . . . your house is left to you desolate" (23:38). It reminds us of Ezekiel's description of the glory departing from the temple (Ezek. 9:3; 10:4; 11:23).

The disciples wanted the Lord to admire the architectural beauty of the temple with them. They were occupied with the transient instead of the eternal, concerned with shadows rather than substance. Jesus warned that the building would be so completely destroyed that **not one stone** would **be left on** top of **another**. Titus tried unsuccessfully to

save the temple, but his soldiers put it to the torch, thus fulfilling Christ's prophecy. When the fire melted the gold trim, the molten metal ran down between the stones. To get at it, the soldiers had to remove the stones one by one, just as our Lord predicted. This judgment was executed in A.D. 70 when the Romans under Titus sacked Jerusalem.

B. The First Half of the Tribulation (24:3–14)

24:3 After Jesus had crossed over to **the Mount of Olives, the disciples came to Him privately** and asked Him three questions:

1. **When** would **these things** happen; that is, when would the temple be destroyed?
2. **What** would **be the sign of** His **coming**; that is, what supernatural event would precede His return to the earth to set up His kingdom?
3. What would be the sign **of the end of the age**; that is, what would announce the end of the age immediately prior to His glorious reign? (The second and third questions are essentially the same.)

We must remember that these Jewish disciples' thinking revolved around the glorious age of the Messiah on earth. They were not thinking about Christ's coming for the church; they knew little if anything about this phase of His coming. Their expectation was His coming in power and glory to destroy His enemies and rule over the world.

Also we should be clear that they were not talking about the end of the *world* (as in the KJV), but the end of the **age** (Gk., *aiōn*).

Their first question is not answered directly. Rather the Savior seems to merge the siege of Jerusalem in A.D. 70 (see Luke 21:20–24) with a similar siege that will occur in the latter days. In the study of prophecy, we often see the Lord moving almost imperceptibly from an early, partial fulfillment to a later, final fulfillment.

The second and third questions are answered in verses 4–44 of chapter 24. These verses describe the seven year Tribulation Period which will precede

Christ's glorious Advent. The first three and one-half years are described in verses 4–14. The final three and one-half years, known as the Great Tribulation and the Time of Jacob's Trouble (Jer. 30:7), will be a time of unprecedented suffering for those on earth.

Many of the conditions characterizing the first half of the Tribulation have existed to an extent throughout human history, but will appear in greatly intensified form during the period under discussion. Those in the church have been promised tribulation (John 16:33), but this is far different from *the* Tribulation which will be poured out on a world that has rejected God's Son.

We believe that the church will be taken out of the world (1 Thess. 4:13–18) before the day of God's wrath begins (1 Thess. 1:10; 5:9; 2 Thess. 2:1–12; Rev. 3:10).

24:4, 5 During the first half of the Tribulation, many false messiahs will appear who will succeed in deceiving multitudes. The current rise of many false cults may be a prelude to this, but it is not a fulfillment. These false religious leaders will be Jews claiming to be **the Christ**.

24:6, 7 There will be **wars and rumors of wars. Nation will rise against nation, and kingdom against kingdom**. It would be easy to think that we are seeing this fulfilled today, but what we see is mild compared to what will be. Actually the next event in God's time schedule is the Rapture of the church (John 14:1–6; 1 Cor. 15:51–57). There is no prophecy to be fulfilled before then. After the church is removed, God's prophetic clock will begin and these conditions will quickly manifest themselves. **Famines, pestilences, and earthquakes** will occur **in various** parts of the earth. Even today world leaders are alarmed by the specter of famine due to the population explosion. But this will be accentuated by the shortages caused by wars.

Earthquakes are attracting increasing attention — not only those now occurring but also those that are expected. Once again, these are straws in the wind, and not the actual fulfillment of our Savior's words.

24:8 Verse 8 clearly identifies this period as **the beginning of sorrows** — the onset of birth-pangs which will bring forth a new order under Israel's Messiah-King.

24:9, 10 Faithful believers will experience great personal testing during the Tribulation. The nations will conduct a bitter hate campaign against all who are true to Him. Not only will they be tried in religious and civil courts (Mark 13:9), but many will be martyred because they refuse to recant. While such testings have occured during all periods of Christian testimony, this seems to have particular reference to the 144,000 Jewish believers who will have a special ministry during this period.

Many will apostatize rather than suffer and die. Family members will inform against their own relatives and **betray** them into the hands of bestial persecutors.

24:11 Many false prophets will appear **and deceive** hordes of people. These are not to be confused with the false messiahs of verse 5. **False prophets** claim to be spokesmen for God. They can be detected in two ways: their prophecies do not always come to pass, and their teachings always lead men away from the true God. The mention of false *prophets* adds confirmation to our statement that the Tribulation is primarily Jewish in character. **False prophets** are associated with the nation of Israel; in the church the danger comes from false *teachers* (2 Pet. 2:1).

24:12 With wickedness rampaging, human affections will be less and less evident. Acts of unlove will be commonplace.

24:13 **"But he who endures to the end shall be saved."** This obviously does not mean that men's souls will be saved at that time by their enduring; salvation is always presented in the Bible as a gift of God's grace, received by faith in Christ's substitutionary death and resurrection. Neither can it mean that all who endure will escape physical harm; we have already learned that many believers will be martyred (v. 9). It is a general statement that those who stand fast, enduring persecution without apostatizing, will be delivered at Christ's Second Advent. No one should imagine that apostasy will be a means of escape or safety. Only those who have true faith **shall be saved**. Although saving faith may have lapses, it always has the quality of permanence.

24:14 During this period, the **gospel of the kingdom** will be proclaimed worldwide, **as a witness to all nations**. As explained in the notes on 4:23, the **gospel of the kingdom** is the good news that Christ is coming to set up His **kingdom** on earth, and that those who receive Him by faith during the Tribulation will enjoy the blessings of His Millennial Reign.

Verse 14 is often misused to show that Christ could not return for His church at any moment because so many tribes have not yet heard the gospel. The difficulty is removed when we realize that this refers to His coming *with* His saints, rather than *for* His saints. And this refers to the gospel of the *kingdom*, not the gospel of the *grace of God* (see notes on 4:23).

There is a striking parallel between the events listed in verses 3–14 and those of Revelation 6:1–11. The rider on the *white* horse — **false messiah**; the rider of the *red* horse — **war**; the rider of the *black* horse — **famine**; the rider of the *pale* horse — **pestilence** or **death**. The souls under the altar are martyrs. The events described in Revelation 6:12–17 are linked with those in Matthew 24:19–31.

C. The Great Tribulation (24:15–28)

24:15 At this point we have come to the middle of the Tribulation. We know this by comparing verse 15 with Daniel 9:27. Daniel predicted that in the middle of the seventieth week, that is, at the end of three and a half years, an idolatrous image would be set up in the holy place, i.e., the temple in Jerusalem. All men will be ordered to worship this abominable idol. Failure to comply will be punishable by death (Rev. 13:15).

"**Therefore when you see the 'abomination of desolation,' spoken of by Daniel the prophet, standing in the holy place**" (whoever reads, let him understand). . . . The erection of the idol will be the signal to those who know the

Word of God that the Great Tribulation has begun. Note that the Lord wants the one who **reads** the prophecy to **understand** it.

24:16 Those who are in Judea should **flee to the mountains**; in the vicinity of Jerusalem their refusal to bow to the image would be quickly detected.

24:17–19 Utmost haste will be necessary. If a man is sitting **on the housetop**, he should leave all his possessions behind. Time spent in gathering belongings might mean the difference between life and death. The man working **in the field** should not return for **his clothes**, wherever he may have left them. **Pregnant** women and **nursing** mothers will be at a distinct disadvantage — it will be hard for them to make a speedy escape.

24:20 Believers should **pray** that the crisis will not come **in winter** with its added travel hazards, and that it will not come **on the Sabbath**, when the distance they could travel would be limited by law (Ex. 16:29). A Sabbath day's journey would not be enough to take them out of the danger area.

24:21 "**For then there will be great tribulation, such as has not been from the beginning of the world until this time, no, nor ever shall be.**" This description isolates the period from all the inquisitions, pogroms, purges, massacres, and genocides of history. This prophecy could not have been fulfilled by any previous persecutions because it is clearly stated that it will be ended by the Second Advent of Christ.

24:22 The tribulation will be so intense that **unless those days were shortened**, nobody would survive. This cannot mean that the Great Tribulation, so often specified as lasting three and a half years, will be shortened. It probably means that God will miraculously shorten the daylight hours — during which most fighting and slaughter occur. **For the elect's sake**, (those who have received Jesus) the Lord will grant the respite of earlier darkness.

24:23–26 Verses 23 and 24 contain renewed warnings against **false** messiahs **and false prophets**. In an atmosphere of crisis, reports will circulate that the Messiah is in some secret location. Such reports could be used to trap those who sincerely and lovingly look for Christ. So the Lord warns all disciples not to believe reports of a local, secret Advent. Even those who perform miracles are not necessarily from God; miracles can be satanic in origin. The Man of Sin will be given satanic power to perform miracles (2 Thess. 2:9, 10).

24:27 Christ's Advent will be unmistakable — it will be sudden, public, universal, and glorious. Like **the lightning**, it will be instantly and clearly visible to all.

24:28 And no moral corruption will escape its fury and judgment. **"For wherever the carcass is, there the eagles will be gathered together."** The carcass pictures apostate Judaism, Christendom, and the whole world system that is leagued against God and His Christ. **The eagles** or vultures typify the judgments of God which will be unleashed in connection with the Messiah's appearing.

D. The Second Advent (24:29–31)

24:29 At the close of the Great Tribulation there will be terrifying disturbances in the heavens. **The sun will be darkened**, and since the moon's light is only a reflection of the sun's, **the moon** will also withhold **its light**. The stars will plunge from heaven and planets will be moved out of their orbits. Needless to say, such vast cosmic upheavals will affect the weather, tides, and seasons on earth.

A faint idea of what it will be like is given in Velikovsky's description of what would happen if a heavenly body came close to the earth and caused it to tilt on its axis:

At that moment an earthquake would make the earth shudder. Air and water would continue to move through inertia; hurricanes would sweep the earth and the seas would rush over continents, carrying gravel and sand and marine animals, and casting them on the land. Heat would be developed, rocks would melt, volcanoes would erupt, lava would flow from fissures in the ruptured ground and cover vast areas. Mountains would spring up from the plains and would travel and climb on the shoulders of other mountains, causing faults and rifts. Lakes would be tilted and emptied, rivers would change their beds; large land areas with all their inhabitants would slip under the sea. Forests would burn and the hurricane and wild seas would wrest them from the ground on which they grew and pile them, branch and root, in huge heaps. Seas would turn into deserts, their waters flowing away.[45]

24:30 **"Then the sign of the Son of Man will appear in heaven."** We are not told what this **sign** will be. His First Advent was accompanied by a sign in heaven — the star. Perhaps a miracle star will also announce His Second Coming. Some believe **the Son of Man** is Himself **the sign**. Whatever is meant, it will be clear to all when it appears. **All the tribes of the earth will mourn** — no doubt because of their rejection of Him. But primarily the tribes of the *land*[46] will mourn — the twelve tribes of Israel. ". . . then they will look on Me whom they pierced. Yes, they will mourn for Him as one mourns for his only son, and grieve for Him as one grieves for a firstborn" (Zech. 12:10).

Then **"they will see the Son of Man coming on the clouds of heaven with power and great glory."** What a wonderful moment! The One who was spit upon and crucified will be vindicated as the Lord of life and glory. The meek and lowly Jesus will appear as Jehovah Himself. The sacrificial Lamb will descend as the conquering Lion. The despised Carpenter of Nazareth will come as King of kings and Lord of lords. His chariots will be the clouds of heaven. He will come in regal power and splendor — the moment for which creation has groaned for thousands of years.

24:31 When He descends, **He will send His angels** throughout the earth to **gather together His elect** people, believing Israel, to the land of Palestine. From all the earth they will gather to greet their Messiah and to enjoy His glorious reign.

E. The Parable of the Fig Tree (24:32–35)

24:32 **"Now learn this parable from the fig tree."** Again our Lord draws a spiritual lesson from nature. When the branches of the fig tree become green and **tender, you know that summer is near**. We have seen that the fig tree pictures the nation of Israel (21:18–22). For hundreds of years Israel has been dormant, with no government of its own, no land, no temple, no priesthood — no sign of national life. The people have been scattered throughout the world.

Then, in 1948, Israel became a nation with its own land, government, currency, stamps, etc. Spiritually, the nation is still barren and cold; there is no fruit for God. But nationally, we might say that its branches are green and **tender**.

24:33 **"So you also, when you see all these things, know that it is near, at the very doors!"** Israel's emergence as a nation means not only that the beginning of the Tribulation is near, but that the Lord Himself is near, **at the very doors!**

If Christ's coming to reign is so near, how much more imminent is the Rapture of the church? If we already see shadows of events that must precede His appearing in glory, how much closer are we to the first phase of His *Parousia*, or Advent (1 Thess. 4:13–18)?

24:34 After referring to the fig tree, Jesus added, **"Assuredly, I say to you, this generation will by no means pass away till all these things take place."** **"This generation"** could not mean the people living when Christ was on earth; they have all passed away, yet the events of chapter 24 have not taken place. What then did our Lord mean by **"this generation"**? There are two plausible explanations.

F. W. Grant and others believe the thought is: "the very generation that sees the beginning of these things will see the end."[47] The same people who see the rise of Israel as a nation (or who see the beginning of the Tribulation), will see the Lord Jesus coming in the clouds of heaven to reign.

The other explanation is that **"generation"** should be understood as *race*. This is a legitimate translation of the Greek word; it means men of the same stock, breed, or family (Matt. 12:45; 23:35, 36). So Jesus was predicting that the Jewish race would survive to see all these things accomplished. Their continued survival, despite atrocious persecution, is a miracle of history.

But I think there is an added thought.

In Jesus' day, "this generation" was a race that steadfastly refused to acknowledge Him as Messiah. I think He was predicting that national Israel would continue in its Christ-rejecting condition till His Second Coming. Then all rebellion will be crushed, and only those who willingly submit to His rule will be spared to enter the Millennium.

24:35 To emphasize the unfailing character of His predictions, Jesus added that **heaven and earth** would **pass away but His words** would **by no means pass away**. In speaking of **heaven** passing away, He was referring to the stellar and atmospheric heavens — the blue firmament above us — not to that heaven which is the dwelling place of God (2 Cor. 12:2–4). The dissolution of the heaven and the earth is described in 2 Peter 3:10–13 and mentioned again in Revelation 20:11.

F. The Day and Hour Unknown (24:36–44)

24:36 As to the exact **day and hour** of His Second Advent, **"no one knows, not even the angels of heaven,**[48] **but My Father only."** This should warn against the temptation to set dates or to believe those who do. We are not surprised that angels do not know; they are finite creatures with limited knowledge.

While those living prior to Christ's return will not know its *day* or *hour*, it seems that those familiar with the prophecy may be able to know the *year*. They will know, for instance, that it will be approximately three and one-half years after the idol image is set up in the temple (Dan. 9:27; see also Dan. 7:25; 12:7, 11; Rev. 11:2, 3; 12:14; 13:5).

24:37–39 In those days, however, most people will be indifferent, just **as in the days of Noah**. Although the days before the flood were terribly wicked, that is not the feature emphasized here. The people ate, drank, married, gave **in marriage**; in other words, they went through the routines of life as if they were going to live forever. Though warned that a flood was coming, they lived as if they were flood-proof. When it came, they were unprepared, outside the only place of safety. That is just the way it will be when Christ returns. Only those who are in Christ, the ark of safety, will be delivered.

24:40, 41 **Two men will be in the field; one will be taken** away in judgment, **the other** will be **left** to enter the Millennium. **Two women will be grinding at the mill**; they will be instantly separated. One will be swept away by the flood of judgment; the other left to enjoy the blessings of Christ's reign. (Vv. 40 and 41 are often used as a warning to the unsaved, in reference to the Rapture — the first phase of Christ's coming when He takes all believers to heaven and leaves all unbelievers behind for judgment. While that might be a valid *application* of the passage, the context makes it clear that the *interpretation* has to do with Christ's coming to reign.)

24:42–44 In view of the uncertainty as to the day and the hour, men ought to **watch**. If someone knows his house is going to be broken into, he will be ready, even if he doesn't know the exact time. The Son of Man will come when least expected by the masses. Therefore, His people should be on the tiptoes of expectancy.

G. Parable of the Wise and the Evil Servants (24:45–51)

24:45–47 In the closing section of this chapter, the Lord Jesus shows that a **servant** manifests his true character by how he behaves in view of his Master's return. All servants are supposed to feed the household at the proper time. But not all who profess to be Christ's servants are genuine.

The **wise servant** is the one who is found caring for God's people. Such a one will be honored with vast responsibility in the kingdom. The master **will make him ruler over all his goods.**

24:48–51 The **evil servant** represents a nominal believer whose behavior is not affected by the prospect of his Master's soon return. He **begins to beat his fellow servants, and to eat and drink with the drunkards.** Such behavior demonstrates that he is not ready for the kingdom. When the King comes, He will punish him and **appoint him his portion with the hypocrites,** where people weep and gnash their teeth.

This parable refers to Christ's visible return to earth as Messiah-King. But the principle equally applies to the Rapture. Many who profess to be Christians show by their hostility toward God's people and their fraternization with the ungodly that they are not looking for Christ's Return. For them it will mean judgment and not blessing.

H. Parable of the Ten Virgins (25:1–13)

25:1–5 The first word, **Then**, referring back to chapter 24, clearly places this parable in the time preceding and during the King's return to earth. Jesus likens **the kingdom of heaven** at that time **to ten virgins who took their lamps and went to meet the bridegroom. Five of them were wise** and had **oil** for their **lamps**; the others had none. While waiting, all fell asleep.

The five **wise** virgins represent true disciples of Christ in the Tribulation. The **lamps** speak of profession, and **oil** is generally acknowledged to be a type of the Holy Spirit. The **foolish** virgins represent those who profess to hold the Messianic hope but who have never been converted and thus do not have the Holy Spirit. **The bridegroom** is Christ, the King; His delay symbolizes the period between His two Advents. The fact that all ten virgins **slept** shows that outwardly there was not much to differentiate them.

25:6 At midnight the announcement rang out that **the bridegroom** was **coming**. In the previous chapter we learned that His arrival will be heralded by awesome signs.

25:7–9 The **virgins arose and trimmed their lamps** — all wanted to appear ready. The foolish ones, lacking oil, asked the others for some, but were sent to **buy** some. The wise ones' refusal seems selfish, but in the spiritual realm, no one can dispense the Spirit to another. Of course, the Holy Spirit cannot be purchased, but the Bible does use the literary figure of buying salvation without money and without price.

25:10–12 While they were gone **the bridegroom came**. The Syriac and Vulgate versions say that he came *with his bride*. This fits the prophetic picture perfectly. The Lord Jesus will return from the wedding with His bride, the church

(1 Thess. 3:13). (The wedding takes place in heaven [Eph. 5:27] after the Rapture.) The faithful remnant of Tribulation saints will go in with Him to the marriage feast. The marriage feast is a fitting designation of the joy and blessing of Christ's earthly kingdom. The wise virgins **went in with him to the wedding** (or wedding feast, JND); **and the door was closed**. It was too late for anyone else to get into the kingdom. When the **other virgins came** seeking admittance, the bridegroom disavowed knowing them — a clear proof that they had never been born again.

25:13 The lesson, Jesus said, was to **watch**, because **the day** and **hour** of His coming are unknown. Believers should live as if the Lord might come at any moment. Are our lamps trimmed and filled with oil?

I. Parable of the Talents (25:14–30)

25:14–18 This parable also teaches that when the Lord returns, there will be true and false servants. The story revolves around **a man** who, before going on a long journey, assembled **his own servants** and **gave to each** varying amounts of money, **according to his own ability**. **One** got **five talents, another** got **two**, and the last, **one**. They were to use this money to bring income to the master. The man with **five** earned **another five talents**. The man with **two** doubled his also. But the man with **one** **went and dug** a hole and buried it.

It is not difficult to see that Christ is the master and the long journey is the inter-advent period. The three servants are Israelites living during the Tribulation, responsible to represent the interests of the absent Lord. They are given responsibility according to their individual abilities.

25:19–23 After a long time the lord **. . . came back and settled accounts with them**. This depicts the Second Advent. The first two received exactly the same commendation: **"Well done, good and faithful servant; you were faithful over a few things, I will make you ruler over many things. Enter into the joy of your lord."** The test of their service was not how much they earned, but how hard they tried. Each used his ability fully and

earned one hundred percent. These represent true believers whose reward is to enjoy the blessings of the Messianic kingdom.

25:24, 25 The third servant had nothing but insults and excuses for his master. He accused him of being **hard** and unreasonable, **reaping where** he had **not sown, and gathering where** he had **not scattered seed**. He excused himself on the basis that, paralyzed with fear, he buried his **talent**. This servant was doubtless an unbeliever; no genuine servant would entertain such thoughts of his master.

25:26, 27 His lord rebuked him as **wicked and lazy**. Having such thoughts of his master, why hadn't he **deposited his money with the bankers** to earn interest? Incidentally, in verse 26, the master is not agreeing with the charges against him. Rather he is saying, "If that's the kind of master you thought I am, all the more reason to have put the talent to work. Your words condemn, not excuse you."

25:28, 29 If this man had earned one talent with his talent, he would have received the same commendation as the others. Instead, all he had to show for his life was a hole in the ground! His **talent** was **taken** and given to the man with **ten talents**. This follows a fixed law in the spiritual realm: **"To everyone who has, more will be given, and he will have abundance; but from him who does not have, even what he has will be taken away."** Those who desire to be used for God's glory are given the means. The more they do, the more they are enabled to do for Him. Conversely, we lose what we don't use. Atrophy is the reward of indolence.

The mention of **the bankers** in verse 27 suggests that if we cannot use our possessions for the Lord, we should turn them over to others who *can*. The bankers in this case may be missionaries, Bible societies, Christian publishing houses, gospel radio programs, etc. In a world like ours, there is no excuse for leaving money idle. Pierson helpfully recommends:

> Timid souls, unfitted for bold and independent service in behalf of the kingdom, may link their incapacity to the capacity

and sagacity of others who will make their gifts and possessions of use to the Master and His Church. . . . The steward has money, or it may be other gifts, that can be made of use, but he lacks faith and foresight, practical energy and wisdom. The Lord's "exchangers" can show him how to get gain for the Master. . . .The Church partly exists that the strength of one member may help the weakness of another, and that by cooperation of all, the power of the least and weakest may be increased.[49]

25:30   The unprofitable servant was cast out — excluded from the kingdom. He shared the anguished fate of the wicked. It was not his failure to invest the talent that condemned him; rather his lack of good works showed that he lacked saving faith.

J. The King Judges the Nations (25:31–46)

25:31   This section describes the Judgment of the Nations, which is to be distinguished from the Judgment Seat of Christ and the Judgment of the Great White Throne.

The Judgment Seat of Christ, a time of review and reward for believers only, takes place after the Rapture (Rom. 14:10; 1 Cor. 3:11–15; 2 Cor. 5:9, 10). The Judgment of the Great White Throne takes place in eternity, after the Millennium. The wicked dead will be judged and consigned to the Lake of Fire (Rev. 20:11–15).

The Judgment of the Nations, or Gentiles (the Greek word can mean either), takes place on earth after Christ comes to reign, as verse 31 clearly states: **"When the Son of Man comes in His glory, and all the holy angels with Him."** If we are right in identifying it with Joel 3, the location is the Valley of Jehoshaphat, outside Jerusalem (3:2). The nations will be judged according to their treatment of Christ's Jewish brethren during the Tribulation (Joel 3:1, 2, 12–14; Matt. 25:31–46).

25:32   It is important to notice that three classes are mentioned — **sheep, goats**, and Christ's brethren. The first two classes, over whom Christ sits in judgment, are Gentiles living during the Tribulation. The third class is Christ's faithful Jewish brethren who refuse to

deny His Name during the Tribulation in spite of towering persecution.

25:33–40   The King places **the sheep on His right hand, but the goats on the left**. He then invites the sheep to enter His glorious **kingdom, prepared for** them **from the foundation of the world**. The reason given is that they fed Him when **hungry, gave** Him **drink** when **thirsty**, welcomed Him when **a stranger, clothed** Him when ill-clad, visited Him in sickness, and went to Him **in prison. The righteous** sheep profess ignorance of ever showing such kindnesses to the King; He had not even been on earth in their generation. He explains that in befriending **one of the least of** His **brethren**, they befriended Him. Whatever is done for one of His disciples is rewarded as being done to Himself.

25:41–45   The unrighteous goats are told to **depart from** Him **into the everlasting fire prepared for the devil and his angels** because they failed to care for Him during the terrible Time of Jacob's Trouble. When they excuse themselves by saying they had never seen Him, He reminds them that their neglect of His followers constituted neglect of Himself.

25:46   Thus the goats **go away into everlasting punishment, but** the sheep **into eternal life**. But this raises two problems. First, the passage seems to teach that nations are saved or lost *en masse*. Second, the narrative creates the impression that the sheep are saved by good works, and the goats are condemned through failure to do good. As to the first difficulty, it must be remembered that God *does* deal with nations as such. OT history abounds with instances of nations punished because of their sin (Isa. 10:12–19; 47:5–15; Ezek. 25:6, 7; Amos 1:3, 6, 9, 11, 13; 2:1, 4, 6; Obad. 10; Zech. 14:1–5). It is not unreasonable to believe that nations will continue to experience divine retribution. This does not mean that every single individual in the nation will be involved in the outcome, but that the principles of divine justice will be applied on a national, as well as an individual basis.

The word *ethnē*, translated "nations" in this passage, can equally well be translated "Gentiles." Some believe the passage describes the judgment of individual Gentiles. Whether nations or individuals, there is the problem of how such a vast horde could be gathered before the Lord in Palestine. Perhaps it is best to think of representatives of the nations or individual classes assembled for judgment.

As to the second problem, the passage cannot be used to teach salvation by works. The uniform testimony of the Bible is that salvation is by faith and not by works (Eph. 2:8, 9). But the Bible is just as emphatic in teaching that true faith produces good works. If there are no good works, it is an indication that the person was never saved. So we must understand that the Gentiles are not saved by befriending the Jewish remnant, but that this kindness reflects their love for the Lord.

Three other points should be mentioned. First, the kingdom is said to have been prepared for the righteous from the foundation of the world (v. 34), whereas hell was prepared for the devil and his angels (v. 41). God's desire is that men should be blessed; hell was not originally intended for the human race. But if people willfully refuse life, they necessarily choose death.

The second point is that the Lord Jesus spoke of eternal (same word as "everlasting") fire (v. 41), eternal punishment (v. 46), and eternal life (v. 46). The same One who taught eternal life taught eternal punishment. Since the same word for *eternal* is used to describe each, it is inconsistent to accept one without the other. If the word translated *eternal* does not mean everlasting, there is no word in the Greek language to convey the meaning. But we know that it *does* mean everlasting because it is used to describe the eternality of God (1 Tim. 1:17).

Finally the Judgment of the Gentiles reminds us forcefully that Christ and His people are one; what affects them affects Him. We have vast potential for showing kindness to Him by showing kindness to those who love Him.

XIV. THE KING'S PASSION AND DEATH (Chaps. 26, 27)

A. The Plot to Kill Jesus (26:1–5)

26:1, 2 For the fourth and last time in this Gospel our Lord forewarned His

disciples that He must die (16:21; 17:23; 20:18). His announcement implied a close time relationship between the Passover and His crucifixion: **"You know that after two days is the Passover, and the Son of Man will be delivered up to be crucified."** This year the Passover would find its true meaning. The Paschal Lamb had at last arrived and would soon be slain.

26:3–5 Even as He was uttering the words, **the chief priests, the scribes, and the elders** were gathering in the **palace** of **Caiaphas**, the **high priest**, to map out their strategy. They wanted to arrest Him furtively and have Him killed, but did not think it prudent to do it **during the feast; the people** might react violently against His execution. It is incredible that Israel's religious leaders took the lead in plotting the death of their Messiah. They should have been the first to recognize and to enthrone Him. Instead, they formed the vanguard of His enemies.

B. Jesus Anointed at Bethany (26:6–13)

26:6, 7 This incident provides a welcome relief, coming amid the treachery of the priests, the pettiness of the disciples, and the perfidy of Judas. **When Jesus was at the house of Simon the leper in Bethany, a woman came** in and poured out **a flask** of very expensive perfume **on His head**. The costliness of her sacrifice expressed the depth of her devotion for the Lord Jesus, saying, in effect, that there was nothing too good for Him.

26:8, 9 His disciples, and Judas in particular (John 12:4, 5), looked upon the act as an enormous **waste**. They thought the money might better have been **given to the poor**.

26:10–12 Jesus corrected their distorted thinking. Her act was not wasteful, but beautiful. Not only so, it was perfectly timed. The poor can be helped at any time. But only once in the world's history could the Savior be anointed for burial. That moment had struck and one lone **woman** with spiritual discernment had seized it. Believing the Lord's predictions concerning His death, she must have realized it was now or never. As it turned out, she was right. Those women who planned to anoint His body after His burial were thwarted by the resurrection (Mark 16:1–6).

26:13 The Lord Jesus immortalized her simple act of love: **"Assuredly, I say to you, wherever this gospel is preached in the whole world, what this woman has done will also be told as a memorial to her."** Any act of true worship fills the courts of heaven with fragrance and is indelibly recorded in the Lord's memory.

C. The Treachery of Judas (26:14–16)

26:14, 15† **Then one of the twelve—** one of the disciples who had lived with the Lord Jesus, traveled with Him, seen His miracles, heard His incomparable teaching, and witnessed the miracle of a sinless life — one whom Jesus could call "my familiar friend . . . who ate my bread" (Ps. 41:9) — it was that one who lifted up his heel against the Son of God. **Judas Iscariot went to the chief priests and** agreed to sell his Master for **thirty pieces of silver**. The priests paid him on the spot — the contemptible total of about fifteen dollars.

It is striking to note the contrast between the woman who anointed Jesus at Simon's home and Judas. She valued the Savior highly. Judas valued Him lightly.

26:16 And so the one who had received nothing but kindness from Jesus went out to arrange his part of the dreadful bargain.

D. The Last Passover (26:17–25)

26:17 It was **the first day of the Feast of the Unleavened Bread** — a time when all leaven was removed from Jewish homes. What thoughts must have flooded the mind of the Lord as He sent **the disciples** into Jerusalem **to prepare for . . . the Passover**. Every detail of the meal would have poignant significance.

26:18–20 Jesus sent the disciples to look for **a certain** unnamed **man** who would lead them to the appointed **house**. Perhaps the vagueness of the instructions was designed to foil the conspirators. At any rate, we note Jesus' full knowledge of individuals, their whereabouts, and their willingness to cooperate. Note His words, **"The Teacher says, 'My time is at hand; I will keep the Passover at your house with My disciples.' "** He faced His approaching death

with poise. With perfect grace, He arranged the meal. What a privilege for this anonymous man to lend his house for this final Passover!

26:21–24 As they were eating, Jesus made the shocking announcement that **one of** the twelve would **betray** Him. The disciples were filled with sorrow, chagrin, and self-distrust. One by one they asked, **"Lord, is it I?"** When all but Judas had inquired, Jesus told them that it was the one **who dipped** with Him **in the dish**. The Lord then took a piece of bread, dipped it in the meat juice, and handed it to Judas (John 13:26) — a token of special affection and friendship. He reminded them that there was a certain irresistibility in what was going to happen to Him. But that did not free the traitor from responsibility; **it would** be better for him **if he had** never **been born**. Judas deliberately chose to sell the Savior and is thus held personally responsible.

26:25 When Judas finally asked point-blank if he were the one, Jesus answered, "Yes."

E. The First Lord's Supper (26:26–29)

In John 13:30 we learn that as soon as Judas received the piece of bread, he went out, and it was night. We therefore conclude that he was not present when the Lord's Supper was instituted (although there is considerable disagreement on this point).

26:26 After observing His last Passover, the Savior instituted what we know as the Lord's Supper. The essential elements — bread and wine — were already on the table as part of the Paschal meal; Jesus clothed them with new meaning. First He **took bread, blessed and broke it**. As He **gave it to the disciples** He **said, "Take, eat, this is My body."** Since His body had not yet been given on the cross, it is clear that He was speaking figuratively, using the bread to symbolize His body.

26:27, 28 The same is true of **the cup**; the container is used to express the thing contained. The cup contained the fruit of the vine, which in turn was a symbol of the **blood of the new covenant**. The **new**, unconditional covenant of grace would be ratified by His precious **blood** shed for many for the forgiveness of sins. His blood was *sufficient* to provide forgiveness for all. But here it was **shed for many** in that it was only *effective* in removing the sins of those who believe.

26:29 The Savior then reminded His disciples that He would **not drink** from the **fruit of the vine** with them again **until** He returned to earth to reign. Then the wine would have a new significance; it would speak of the joy and blessedness of His **Father's kingdom**.

The question is often raised whether we should use leavened or unleavened bread, fermented or unfermented wine for the Lord's Supper. There is little doubt that the Lord used unleavened bread and fermented wine (*all* wine in those days was fermented). Those who argue that leavened bread spoils the type (leaven is a picture of sin) should realize that the same is true of fermentation. It is a tragedy when we become so occupied with the *elements* that we fail to see the Lord *Himself*. Paul emphasized that it is the spiritual meaning of the bread, not the bread itself that counts. "For indeed Christ, our Passover, was sacrificed for us. Therefore, let us keep the feast, not with old leaven, nor with the leaven of malice and wickedness, but with the unleavened bread of sincerity and truth" (1 Cor. 5:7, 8). It is not the leaven in the *bread* that matters, but the leaven in our *lives*!

F. The Self-Confident Disciples (26:30–35)

26:30 Following the Lord's Supper, the little band sang **a hymn**, probably taken from Psalms 113–118 — "the Great Hallel." Then they left Jerusalem, crossed the Brook Kidron, and climbed the western slope of Olivet to the Garden of Gethsemane.

26:31 Throughout His earthly ministry the Lord Jesus had faithfully warned His disciples concerning the pathway ahead. Now He told them that they would all dissociate themselves from Him that **night**. Fear would overwhelm them when they saw the fury of the storm breaking. To save their own skins, they would forsake their Master. Zechariah's prophecy would be fulfilled: "Strike the Shepherd, and the sheep will be scattered" (13:7).

26:32 But He did not leave them without hope. Though they would be ashamed of their association with Him, He would never forsake them. After rising from the dead, He would meet them in **Galilee**. Wonderful, never-failing Friend!

26:33, 34 Peter rashly interrupted to assure the Lord that although the others might desert Him, he would **never** do such a thing. Jesus corrected the *"never"* to **"this night . . . three times."** Before **the rooster** crowed, the impetuous disciple would deny his Master **three times**.

26:35 Still protesting his loyalty, **Peter** insisted that he would **die** with Christ rather than **deny** Him. **All the disciples** chimed in their agreement. They were sincere; they meant what they said. It was just that they didn't know their own hearts.

G. The Agony in Gethsemane (26:36–46)

No one can approach this account of the Garden of Gethsemane without realizing that he is walking on holy ground. Anyone who attempts to comment on it feels a tremendous sense of awe and reticence. As Guy King wrote, "The supernal character of the event causes one to fear lest one should in any way spoil it by touching it."

26:36–38 After entering **Gethsemane** (meaning olive vat or olive press), **Jesus** told eight of the eleven **disciples** with Him to **sit** and wait, then took **Peter and the two sons of Zebedee** deeper into the garden. Might this suggest that different disciples have different capacities for empathizing with the Savior in His agony?

He began to be sorrowful and deeply distressed. He frankly told Peter, James, and John that His soul was **exceedingly sorrowful, even to death**. This was doubtless the unspeakable revulsion of His holy soul as He anticipated becoming a sin-offering for us. We who are sinful cannot conceive what it meant to Him, the Sinless One, to be made sin for us (2 Cor. 5:21).

26:39 It is not surprising that He left the three and **went a little farther** into the garden. No one else could share His suffering or pray His prayer: **"O My**

Father, if it is possible, let this cup pass from Me; nevertheless, not as I will, but as You will."

Lest we think this prayer expressed reluctance or a desire to turn back, we should remember His words in John 12:27, 28: "Now My soul is troubled, and what shall I say? Father, save Me from this hour'? But for this purpose I came to this hour. Father, glorify Your name." Therefore, in praying that the **cup** might **pass from** Him, He was *not* asking to be delivered from going to the cross. That was the very purpose of His coming into the world!

The prayer was rhetorical, that is, it was not intended to elicit an answer but to teach us a lesson. Jesus was saying in effect, "My Father, if there is any other way by which ungodly sinners can be saved than by My going to the cross, reveal that way now! But in all of this, I want it known that I desire nothing contrary to Your will."

What was the answer? There was none; the heavens were silent. By this eloquent silence we know that there was no other way for God to justify guilty sinners than for Christ, the sinless Savior, to die as our Substitute.

26:40, 41 Returning to **the disciples, He found them sleeping**. Their spirits were **willing**; their **flesh** was **weak**. We dare not condemn them when we think of our own prayer lives; we sleep better than we pray, and our minds wander when they should be watching. How often the Lord has to say to us as He said to Peter, **"Could you not watch with Me one hour? Watch and pray, lest you enter into temptation."**

26:42 Again, a second time, He went away and prayed, expressing submission to the Father's will. He would drink the cup of suffering and death to the dregs.

He was necessarily alone in His prayer life. He taught the disciples to pray, and He prayed in their presence, but He never prayed *with* them. The uniqueness of His Person and work precluded others from sharing in His prayer life.

26:43–45 When He came to the disciples the second time, they were **asleep again**. Likewise the third time: He prayed, they slept. It was then He said

to them, **"Are you still sleeping and resting? Behold, the hour is at hand, and the Son of Man is being betrayed into the hands of sinners."**

26:46 The opportunity of watching with Him in His vigil was gone. The footsteps of the traitor were already audible. Jesus said, **"Rise, let us be going"** — not in retreat but to face the foe.

Before we leave the garden, let us pause once more to hear His sobs, to ponder His sorrow, and to thank Him with all our hearts.

H. Jesus Betrayed and Arrested in Gethsemane (26:47–56)

The betrayal of the sinless Savior by one of His own creatures presents one of the most amazing anomalies of history. Apart from human depravity we would be at a loss to explain the base, inexcusable treachery of Judas.

26:47 While Jesus **was still speaking** to the eleven, **Judas** arrived with a gang armed **with swords and clubs**. Surely the weapons were not Judas's idea; he had never seen the Savior resist or fight back. Perhaps the weapons symbolized the determination of the chief priests and elders to capture Him without any possibility of escape.

26:48 Judas would use a kiss as the sign to help the mob distinguish Jesus from His disciples. The universal symbol of love was to be prostituted to its lowest use.

26:49 As he approached the Lord, Judas said, **"Greetings, Rabbi!"** then **kissed Him** profusely. Two different words for *kiss* are used in this passage. The first, in verse 48, is the usual word for kiss. But in verse 49 a stronger word is used, expressing repeated or demonstrative kissing.

26:50 With poise and convicting penetration, **Jesus** asked, **"Friend, why have you come?"** No doubt the question came with scalding power to Judas, but events were moving fast now. The mob surged in and seized the Lord Jesus without delay.

26:51 One of the disciples — we know from John 18:10 that it was Peter — **drew his sword** and **cut off** the **ear** of the high priest's **servant**. It is unlikely that Peter had aimed for the ear; he had doubtless planned a mortal blow. That his aim was as poor as his judgment must be attributed to divine Providence.

26:52 The moral glory of the Lord Jesus shines radiantly here. First He rebuked Peter: **"Put your sword in its place, for all who take the sword will perish by the sword."** In Christ's kingdom, victories are not won by carnal means. To resort to armed force in spiritual warfare is to invite disaster. Let the enemies of the kingdom use the sword; they will eventually meet defeat. Let the soldier of Christ resort to prayer, the Word of God, and the power of a Spirit-filled life.

We learn from Dr. Luke that Jesus then healed the ear of Malchus — for that was the victim's name (Luke 22:51; John 18:10). Is this not a wonderful display of grace? He loved those who hated Him and showed kindness to those who were after His life.

26:53, 54 If Jesus had desired to resist the mob, He would not have been limited to Peter's puny sword. In an instant He could have asked for and been sent **more than twelve legions of angels** (from 36,000 to 72,000). But that would only have frustrated the divine program. **The Scriptures** predicting His betrayal, suffering, crucifixion, and resurrection had to **be fulfilled**.

26:55 Then **Jesus** reminded the crowds how incongruous it was for them to **come out** after Him with weapons. They had never seen Him resort to violence or engage in plunder. Rather, He had been a quiet Teacher, **daily** sitting **in the temple**. They could easily have captured Him then, but didn't. Why come now **with swords and clubs**? Humanly speaking, their behavior was irrational.

26:56 Yet the Savior realized that man's wickedness was succeeding only in accomplishing the definite plan of God. **"All this was done that the Scriptures of the prophets might be fulfilled."** Realizing there would be no deliverance for their Master, **all the disciples forsook Him and fled** in panic. If their cowardice was inexcusable, ours is more so. They had not yet been indwelt by the Holy Spirit; we have.

I. Jesus Before Caiaphas (26:57–68)†

26:57 There were two main trials of the Lord Jesus: a religious trial before the Jewish leaders, and a civil trial before the Roman authorities. Combining the accounts from all four Gospels shows that each trial had three stages. John's account of the Jewish trial shows that Jesus was first brought before Caiaphas' father-in-law, Annas. Matthew's account begins with the second stage at the home of **Caiaphas, the high priest**. The Sanhedrin **were assembled** there. Ordinarily, accused men were given an opportunity to prepare their defense. But the desperate religious leaders hurried Jesus away from prison and justice (Isa. 53:8), in every way denying Him a fair trial.

On this particular night, the Pharisees, Sadducees, **scribes,** and **elders** who comprised the Sanhedrin showed an utter disregard for the rules under which they were supposed to operate. They were not supposed to meet at night nor during any of the Jewish feasts. They were not supposed to bribe witnesses to commit perjury. A death verdict was not to be carried out until a night had elapsed. And, unless they met in the Hall of Hewn Stone, in the temple area, their verdicts were not binding. In their eagerness to get rid of Jesus, the Jewish establishment did not hesitate to stoop to breaking their own laws.

26:58 Caiaphas was the presiding judge. The Sanhedrin apparently served as both jury and prosecution, an irregular combination, to say the least. Jesus was the Defendant. And **Peter** was a spectator — from a safe distance; he **sat with the** guards **to see the end**.

26:59–61 The Jewish leaders had a difficult time finding **false testimony against Jesus**. They would have been more successful had they fulfilled their prior obligation in the judicial process and sought evidence of His innocence. Finally, **two false witnesses** produced a garbled account of Jesus' words: "Destroy this temple, and in three days I will raise it up" (John 2:19–21). According to the witnesses, He had threatened **to destroy the temple** in Jerusalem and then rebuild it. In fact, He had been predicting His own death and subsequent resurrection. The Jews now used that prediction as an excuse for killing Him.

26:62–63 During these accusations the Lord Jesus said nothing: "as a sheep before its shearers is silent, so He opened not His mouth" (Isa. 53:7). The high priest, irritated by His silence, pressed Him for a statement; still the Savior refrained from answering. The high priest then **said to Him, "I put You under oath by the living God: Tell us if You are the Christ, the Son of God!"** The Law of Moses required that a Jew testify when put under oath by the high priest (Lev. 5:1).

26:64 Being an obedient Jew under the law, Jesus answered: **"It is as you said."** He then asserted His Messiahship and deity even more strongly: **"Nevertheless, I say to you, hereafter you will see the Son of Man sitting at the right hand of the Power, and coming on the clouds of heaven."** In essence He was saying, "I am the Christ, the Son of God, as you have said. My glory is presently veiled in a human body; I appear to be just another man. You see Me in the days of My humiliation. But the day is coming when you Jews will see Me as the glorified One, equal in all respects with God, sitting at His right hand and coming on the clouds of heaven."

In verse 64 the first **you**[50] is singular, referring to Caiaphas. The second you is plural (also the third), referring to the Jews as representative of those Israelites living at the time of Christ's glorious appearing, who will clearly see that He is the Son of God.

"The assertion is sometimes made," writes Lenski, "that Jesus never called Himself 'The Son of God.' Here (in v. 64) He *swears* that He is no less."[51]

26:65–67[†] Caiaphas did not miss the point. Jesus had alluded to a Messianic prophecy of Daniel: "I was watching in the night visions, and behold, One like the Son of Man, coming with the clouds of heaven! He came to the Ancient of Days, and they brought Him near before Him." The high priest's reaction proves that he understood Jesus was claiming equality with God (see John 5:18). He **tore his** priestly **clothes**, a sign that the witness had blasphemed. His inflamma-

tory words to the Sanhedrin assumed Jesus was guilty. When asked their verdict, the Council answered, **"He is deserving of death."**

26:68 The second stage of the trial ended with the jurists striking and spitting upon the Accused, then taunting Him to use His power as **Christ** to identify His assailants. The entire proceeding was not only unjuridical, but scandalous.

J. Peter Denies Jesus and Weeps Bitterly (26:69–75)

26:69–72 Peter's darkest hour had now arrived. As he **sat outside in the courtyard**, a young woman came by and accused him of being an associate of Jesus. His denial was vigorous and prompt, **"I do not know what you are saying."** He went **out to the gateway**, perhaps to escape further notice. But there **another girl** publicly identified him as one who had been **with Jesus of Nazareth**. This time he swore that he did not know **the Man**. "The Man" was his Master.

26:73, 74 A little later several bystanders came saying, **"Surely you also are one of them, for your speech betrays you."** A simple denial was no longer sufficient; this time he confirmed it with oaths and curses. **"I do not know the Man!"** With disquieting timing, **a rooster crowed**.

26:75 The familiar sound pierced not only the quiet of the early hours but Peter's heart as well. The deflated disciple, remembering what the Lord had said, **went out and wept bitterly**.

There is a seeming contradiction in the Gospels concerning the number and timing of the denials. In Matthew, Luke, and John, Jesus is reported as saying, "Before the rooster crows, you will deny Me three times" (Matt. 26:34; see also Luke 22:34; John 13:38). In Mark, the prediction is, ". . . before the rooster crows twice, you will deny Me three times" (Mark 14:30).

Possibly there was more than one rooster crowing, one during the night and another at dawn. Also it is possible that the Gospels record at least six different denials by Peter. He denied Christ before: (1) a young woman (Matt. 26:69,

70; Mark 14:66–68); (2) another young woman (Matt. 26:71, 72; Mark 14:69, 70); (3) the crowd that stood by (Matt. 26:73, 74; Mark 14:70, 71); (4) a man (Luke 22:58); (5) another man (Luke 22:59, 60); (6) a servant of the high priest (John 18:26, 27). We believe this last man is different from the others because he said, "Did I not see you in the garden with Him?" The others are not described as saying this.

K. Morning Trial Before the Sanhedrin (27:1, 2)

The third stage of the religious trial took place before the Sanhedrin in the **morning**. No case was to be completed on the same day it was begun unless the defendant was acquitted. A night was supposed to elapse before the verdict was pronounced "so that feelings of mercy might have time to arise." In this case the religious leaders seemed intent on stifling any feelings of mercy. However, since night trials were irregular, they convened a morning session to give legal validity to their verdict.

Under Roman rule the Jewish leaders had no authority to inflict capital punishment. Therefore we now see them hurrying Jesus **to Pontius Pilate, the** Roman **governor**. Though their hatred of everything Roman was intense, they were willing to "use" this power to satisfy a *greater* hatred. Opposition to Jesus unites the bitterest foes.

L. Judas' Remorse and Death (27:3–10)

27:3, 4 Realizing his sin in **betraying innocent blood, Judas** offered the money back to **the chief priests and elders**. These arch conspirators who had cooperated so eagerly a few hours ago now refused to have any further part in the matter. This is one of the rewards of treachery. Judas **was remorseful**, but this was not a godly repentance that leads to salvation. Sorry for the effects which his crime brought on himself, he was yet unwilling to acknowledge Jesus Christ as Lord and Savior.

27:5 In desperation Judas **threw down the pieces of silver in the temple** where only the priests could go, then went out and committed suicide. Comparing this narrative with Acts 1:18, we conclude that he hanged himself on a tree, that the rope or branch broke, and that his body was hurled over a precipice, causing it to be disemboweled.

27:6 The chief priests, too "spiritual" to put the money **into the** temple **treasury** because it was **the price of blood**, were the guilty ones who paid that money to have the Messiah turned over to them. This didn't seem to bother them. As the Lord had said, they made the outside of the cup clean, but inside it was full of deceit, treachery, and murder.

27:7–10 They used the money to buy **a potter's field** where unclean Gentile strangers might be buried, little realizing how many Gentile hordes would invade their land and splatter their streets with blood. It has been a **Field of Blood** for that guilty nation ever since.

The chief priests unwittingly fulfilled Zechariah's prophecy that the burial money would be used to make a purchase from a potter (Zech. 11:12, 13). Strangely enough, the Zechariah passage has an alternative reading — "treasury" for "potter" (see RSV).

> The priests had scruples about putting blood money into the treasury so they fulfilled the prophecy of the other reading by giving it to the potter in exchange for his field. (Daily Notes of the Scripture Union).

Matthew assigns this prophecy to **Jeremiah**, whereas it obviously comes from the book of Zechariah. He probably labels the citation from Jeremiah because that prophet stood at the head of the prophetic roll he used, according to the ancient order preserved in numerous Hebrew manuscripts and familiar from Talmudic tradition. A similar usage occurs in Luke 24:44 where the book of Psalms gives its name to the entire third section of the Hebrew canon.

M. Jesus' First Appearance Before Pilate (27:11–14)

The Jews' real grievances against Jesus were *religious*, and they tried Him on that basis. But religious charges carried no weight in the court of Rome. Knowing that, when they brought Him before Pilate they pressed three *political* charges against Him (Luke 23:2): (1) He was a revolutionary who posed a threat to the empire; (2) He urged people not to pay taxes, therefore undermining the prosperity of the empire; (3) He claimed to be a King, therefore threatening the power and position of the emperor.

In Matthew's Gospel we hear Pilate interrogating Him on the third charge. Asked if He was **the King of the Jews**, Jesus answered that He was. This brought forth a torrent of abuse and slander from the Jewish leaders. Pilate **marveled greatly** at the Defendant's silence; He would not dignify even one of their charges with an answer. Probably never before had the governor seen anyone remain silent under such attack.

N. Jesus or Barabbas? (27:15–26)

27:15–18 It was customary for the Roman authorities to placate the Jews by **releasing** a Jewish **prisoner** at Passover time. One such eligible convict was **Barabbas**, a Jew guilty of insurrection and murder (Mark 15:7). As a rebel against Roman rule, he was probably popular with his countrymen. So when Pilate gave them a choice between **Jesus** and **Barabbas**, they clamored for the latter. The governor was not surprised; he knew that public opinion had been molded in part by the chief priests, who were envious of Jesus.

27:19 The proceedings were momentarily interrupted by a messenger from Pilate's **wife**. She urged her husband to adopt a hands-off policy with regard to Jesus; she had had a very disturbing **dream** about **Him**.

27:20–23 Behind the scenes **the chief priests and elders** were passing the word for the release of **Barabbas** and the death of Jesus. So when **Pilate** asked the people again which one they wanted freed, they cried for the murderer. Snared in the web of his own indecisiveness, Pilate asked, **"What then shall I do with Jesus who is called Christ?"** They unanimously demanded His crucifixion, an attitude incomprehensible to the governor. Why crucify Him? What crime had He committed? But it was too late to plead for calm deliberation; mob hysteria had taken over. The cry rang out, **"Let Him be crucified!"**

27:24 It was obvious to **Pilate** that the people were implacable and that a riot was beginning. So he **washed his hands** in sight of the mob, declaring his innocence **of the blood** of the Accused. But water will never absolve Pilate's guilt in history's gravest miscarriage of justice.

27:25 The crowd, too frenzied to worry about guilt, was willing to bear the blame: **"His blood be on us and on our children!"** Since then the people of Israel have staggered from ghetto to pogrom, from concentration camp to gas chamber, suffering the awful guilt of the blood of their rejected Messiah. They still face the fearsome Time of Jacob's Trouble — those seven years of tribulation described in Matthew 24 and Revelation 6–19. The curse will remain until they acknowledge the rejected Jesus as their Messiah-King.

27:26 Pilate **released Barabbas to** the crowd, and the spirit of Barabbas has dominated the world ever since. The murderer is still enthroned; the righteous King is rejected. Then, as was customary, the condemned One was **scourged**. A large leather whip with bits of sharp metal embedded in it was brought down across His back, each lash opening up the flesh and releasing streams of blood. Now there was nothing for the spineless governor to do but to turn Jesus over to the soldiers **to be crucified**.

O. The Soldiers Mock Jesus (27:27–31)

27:27, 28 The soldiers of the governor took Jesus into the governor's palace and gathered the whole garrison around Him — probably several hundred men. What followed is hard to imagine! The Creator and Sustainer of the universe suffered unspeakable indignities from cruel, vulgar soldiers — His unworthy, sinful creatures. **They stripped Him and put a scarlet robe on Him**, in imitation of a king's robe. But that robe has a message for us. Since scarlet is associated with sin (Isa. 1:18), I like to think that the robe pictures my sins being placed on Jesus so that God's robe of righteousness might be placed on me (2 Cor. 5:21).

27:29, 30 They **twisted a crown of thorns** and pressed it down **on His head**. But beyond their crude jest, we understand that He wore *a crown of* *thorns* that we might wear *a crown of glory*. They mocked Him as the King of Sin; we worship Him as the Savior of sinners.

They also gave Him **a reed** — a mock scepter. They didn't know that the hand that held that reed is the hand that rules the world. That nail-scarred hand of Jesus now holds the scepter of universal dominion.

They knelt **before Him** and addressed Him as **King of the Jews**. Not content with that, **they spat on** the face of the only perfect Man who ever lived, then **took the reed and struck Him on the head** with it.

Jesus bore it all patiently; He didn't say a word. "For consider Him who endured such hostility from sinners against Himself, lest you become weary and discouraged in your souls" (Heb. 12:3).

27:31 Finally they **put His own clothes** back **on Him, and led Him away to be crucified.**

P. The Crucifixion of the King (27:32–44)

27:32 Our Lord carried His **cross** part of the way (John 19:17). Then the soldiers **compelled** a man named **Simon** (from **Cyrene**, in northern Africa) to carry it for Him. Some think he was a Jew; others that he was a black man. The important thing is that he had the wonderful privilege of bearing the cross.

27:33 Golgotha is Aramaic for "skull." Calvary is the anglicized Latin translation of the Greek *kranion.* Perhaps the area was shaped like a skull or received the name because it was a place of execution. The site is uncertain.

27:34 Prior to His being impaled, the soldiers offered Jesus the **sour wine** and **gall** given to condemned criminals as an opiate. Jesus refused to take it. For Him it was necessary to bear the full load of man's sins with no impairment of His senses, no alleviation of His pain.

27:35† Matthew describes the crucifixion simply and unemotionally. He does not indulge in dramatics, resort to sensational journalism, or dwell on sordid details. He simply states the fact: **Then they crucified Him**. Yet eternity itself will not exhaust the depths of those words.

As prophesied in Psalm 22:18, the

soldiers **divided His garments . . . and . . . cast lots** for the seamless robe. This was His entire earthly estate. Denney said, "The one perfect life that has been lived in this world is the life of Him who owned nothing, and who left nothing but the clothes He wore."

27:36 These soldiers were representatives of a world of little men. They apparently had no sense of history being made. If only they had known, they would not have *sat* down and **kept watch**; they would have *knelt* down and worshiped.

27:37 Over Christ's **head** they had put the title, **THIS IS JESUS THE KING OF THE JEWS.** The exact wording of the superscription varies somewhat in the four Gospels.[52] Mark says, "The King of the Jews" (15:26); Luke: "This is the King of the Jews" (23:38); and John: "Jesus of Nazareth, the King of the Jews" (19:19). The chief priests protested that the title should not be a statement of fact, but the mere claim of the Accused. However, Pilate overruled them; the truth was there for all to see — in Hebrew, Latin, and Greek (John 19:19–22).

27:38 The sinless Son of God was flanked by **two robbers**, because hadn't Isaiah predicted 700 years previously that He would be numbered with the transgressors (53:12)? At first, both robbers hurled insult and invective at Him (v. 44). But one repented and was saved in the nick of time; in just a few hours he was with Christ in Paradise (Luke 23:42, 43).

27:39, 40 If the cross reveals God's love, it also reveals man's depravity. Passers-by paused long enough to jeer at the Shepherd as He was dying for the sheep: **"You who destroy the temple and build it in three days, save Yourself! If You are the Son of God, come down from the cross."** This is the language of rationalistic unbelief. "Let us see and we will believe." It is also the language of liberalism. "Come down from the cross — in other words, remove the offense of the cross and we will believe." William Booth said, "They claimed they would have believed if He had come down; we believe because He stayed up."

27:41–44 The **chief priests, scribes,**

and elders joined the chorus. With unintentional insight they cried, **"He saved others; Himself He cannot save."** They meant it as a taunt; we adapt it as a hymn of praise:

> Himself He could not save,
> He on the cross must die,
> Or mercy cannot come
> To ruined sinners nigh;
> Yes, Christ the Son of God must bleed,
> That sinners might from sin be freed.
> *– Albert Midlane*

It was true in the Lord's life and in ours, too. We can't save others while seeking to save ourselves.

The religious leaders mocked His claim to be the Savior, His claim to be **the King of Israel**, His claim to be **the Son of God. Even the robbers** joined in their cursing. The religious leaders united with criminals in vilifying their God.

Q. Three Hours of Darkness (27:45–50)

27:45 All the sufferings and indignities which He bore at the hands of men were minor compared to what He now faced. **From the sixth hour** (noon) **until the ninth hour** (3:00 p.m.), **there was darkness** not **only over all the land** of Palestine but in His holy soul as well. It was during that time that He bore the indescribable curse of our sins. In those three hours were compressed the hell which we deserved, the wrath of God against all our transgressions. We see it only dimly; we simply cannot know what it meant for Him to satisfy all God's righteous claims against sin. We only know that in those three hours He paid the price, settled the debt, and finished the work necessary for man's redemption.

27:46† At about 3:00 p.m., He **cried out with a loud voice, saying, "My God, My God, why have You forsaken Me?"** The answer is found in Psalm 22:3, " . . .You are holy, enthroned in the praises of Israel." Because God is holy, He cannot overlook sin. On the contrary, He must punish it. The Lord Jesus had no sin of His own, but He took the guilt of our sins upon Himself. When God, as Judge, looked down and saw our sins upon the sinless Substitute, He withdrew from the Son of His love. It was

this separation that wrung from the heart of Jesus what Mrs. Browning so beautifully called "Immanuel's orphaned cry":

> Deserted! God could separate from His
>   own essence rather;
> And Adam's sins have swept between the
>   righteous Son and Father:
> Yea, once, Immanuel's orphaned cry
>   His universe hath shaken —
> It went up single, echoless,
>   "My God, I am forsaken!"
> *– Elizabeth Barrett Browning*

27:47, 48 When Jesus cried, **"Eli, Eli . . . ," some of those who stood** by **said** He was **calling for Elijah.** Whether they actually confused the names or were simply mocking is not clear. One used a long **reed** to lift a **sponge** soaked with **sour wine** to His lips. Judging from Psalm 69:21, this was not intended as an act of mercy but as an added form of suffering.

27:49 The general attitude was to wait and **see if Elijah** would fulfill the role Jewish tradition assigned to him — coming to the aid of the righteous. But it was not time for Elijah to come (Mal. 4:5); it was time for Jesus to die.

27:50 When He had **cried out again with a loud voice,** He **yielded up His spirit.** The **loud** cry demonstrates that He died in strength, not in weakness. The fact that He **yielded up His spirit** distinguished His death from all others. We die because we have to; He died because He chose to. Had He not said, "I lay down My life that I may take it again. No one takes it from Me, but I lay it down of Myself. I have power to lay it down, and I have power to take it again" (John 10:17, 18)?

> The Maker of the Universe
> As man for man was made a curse;
> The claims of laws which He had made,
> Unto the uttermost He paid.
> His holy fingers made the bough
> Which grew the thorns that crowned His
>   brow.
> The nails that pierced his hands were
>   mined
> In secret places He designed;
> He made the forests whence there sprung
> The tree on which His body hung.
> He died upon a cross of wood,
> Yet made the hill on which it stood.
> The sky that darkened o'er His head
> By Him above the earth was spread;

†*See p. xxii.*

The sun that hid from Him its face
By His decree was poised in space;
The spear that spilled His precious blood
Was tempered in the fires of God.
The grave in which His form was laid
Was hewn in rock His hands had made;
The throne on which He now appears
Was His from everlasting years;
But a new glory crowns His brow,
And every knee to Him shall bow.
                              – F. W. Pitt

R. The Torn Veil (27:51–54)

27:51 At the time He expired, the heavy, woven curtain separating the two main rooms of the temple was torn by an Unseen Hand **from top to bottom**. Up to then that **veil** had kept everyone except the high priest from the Holiest Place where God dwelt. Only one man could enter the inner sanctuary, and he could enter on only one day of the year.

In the book of Hebrews we learn that the veil represented the body of Jesus. Its rending pictured the giving of His body in death. Through His death, we have "boldness to enter the Holiest by the blood of Jesus, by a new and living way which He consecrated for us, through the veil, that is, His flesh" (Heb. 10:19, 20). Now the humblest believer can enter God's presence in prayer and praise at any time. But let us never forget that the privilege was purchased for us at tremendous cost — the blood of Jesus.

The death of God's Son also produced tremendous upheavals in nature — as if there was an empathy between inanimate creation and its Creator. There was an earthquake which **split** great **rocks** and **opened** many **graves**.

27:52, 53 But notice that it was not until **after** the **resurrection** of Jesus that the occupants of these tombs **were raised** and **went into** Jerusalem where they **appeared to many**. The Bible does not say whether these risen saints died again or went to heaven with the Lord Jesus.

27:54 The strange convulsions of nature convinced **the** Roman **centurion** and his men that Jesus **was the Son of God** (while there is no definite article in the Greek before Son of God, the word order does make it definite[53]). What did **the centurion** mean? Was this a full con-

fession of Jesus Christ as Lord and Savior, or an acknowledgment that Jesus was more than man? We cannot be sure. It does indicate a sense of awe, and a realization that the disturbances of nature were somehow connected with the death of Jesus, and not with the death of those who were crucified with Him.

S. The Faithful Women (27:55, 56)

Special mention is made of the **women** who had faithfully ministered to the Lord, and who had **followed** Him all the way **from Galilee** to Jerusalem. **Mary Magdalene, Mary the mother of James and Joses**, and Salome, the wife of Zebedee, were there. The fearless devotion of these women stands out with special luster. They remained with Christ when the male disciples ran for their lives!

T. The Burial in Joseph's Tomb (27:57–61)[†]

27:57, 58[††] **Joseph** of **Arimathea, a rich man** and member of the Sanhedrin, had not concurred in the Council's decision to deliver Jesus to Pilate (Luke 23:51). If up to this point he had been a secret **disciple**, he now threw caution to the wind. Boldly he **went to Pilate** and requested permission to bury his Lord. We must try to imagine the surprise to Pilate, and the provocation to the Jews, that a member of the Sanhedrin would publicly take his stand for the Crucified. In a real sense Joseph buried himself economically, socially, and religiously when he buried the body of Jesus. This act separated him forever from the establishment that killed the Lord Jesus.

27:59, 60 Pilate granted permission and **Joseph** lovingly embalmed **the body** by **wrapping it in a clean linen cloth**, placing spices between the wrappings. Then he placed **it in his** own **new tomb**, carved out of solid **rock**. The mouth of the tomb was closed by **a large stone**, shaped like a millstone and standing on its edge in a channel also carved out of stone.

Centuries before, Isaiah had predicted, "And they made His grave with the wicked — but with the rich at His death" (53:9). His enemies had doubtless planned to throw His body into the Val-

†See p. xvi.
††See p. xxiii.

ley of Hinnom to be consumed by dump-fires or eaten by foxes. But God overruled their plans and used Joseph to insure that He was buried *with the rich*.

27:61 After Joseph had departed, **Mary Magdalene** and the mother of James and Joses stayed to keep vigil **opposite the tomb**.

U. The Guarded Tomb (27:62–66)

27:62–64 The first day of the Passover, called the **Day of Preparation**, was the day of the crucifixion. **The next day the chief priests and Pharisees** were uneasy. Remembering what Jesus had said about rising again, they went to Pilate and asked for a special guard to be placed at the tomb. This was allegedly to prevent **His disciples** from stealing the body, thus creating the impression that He had risen. Should this happen, they feared, **the last deception** would **be worse than the first**; that is, the report concerning His resurrection would be worse than His claim to be the Messiah and the Son of God.

27:65, 66 Pilate answered, **"You have a guard; go your way, make it as secure as you know how."** This may mean that a Roman guard had already been assigned to them. Or it may mean "Your request is granted. I now assign a guard to you." Was there irony in Pilate's voice as he said **"as secure as you know how?"** They did their best. They sealed the stone and stationed guards, but their best security measures were just not good enough. Unger says:

> The precautions His enemies took to "make the sepulchre sure, sealing it and stationing a guard," 62-64, only resulted in God's overruling the plans of the wicked and offering indisputable proof of the King's resurrection.[54]

XV. THE KING'S TRIUMPH (Chap. 28)[†]

A. The Empty Tomb and the Risen Lord (28:1–10)

28:1–4 Before dawn on Sunday morning the two Marys **came to see the tomb**. As they arrived there **was a great earthquake. An angel . . . descended from heaven, rolled back the stone from** the mouth of the tomb, **and sat on it**. The Roman **guards**, terrified by this radiant being clothed in glistening white, fainted.

28:5, 6 The angel reassured **the women** that there was nothing for them to fear. The One they sought had **risen, as He** had promised. **"Come, see the place where the Lord lay."** The stone had been rolled away, not to let the Lord out, but to let the women see that He had risen.

28:7–10 The angel then deputized the women to **go quickly** to announce the glorious news to **His disciples**. The Lord was alive again and would meet them in **Galilee**. After delivering the message, they returned to the empty tomb. It was then that Jesus Himself appeared to them, greeting them with a single word, **"Rejoice!"**[55] They responded by falling at His **feet** and worshiping Him. He then personally commissioned them to notify the disciples that they would see Him in **Galilee**.

B. The Soldiers Bribed to Lie (28:11–15)

28:11 As soon as they regained consciousness, **some of the** soldiers sheepishly went **to the chief priests** to break the news. They had failed in their mission! The tomb was empty!

28:12, 13 It is easy to imagine the consternation of the religious leaders. The priests held a conclave with the elders to map out their strategy. In desperation, they bribed **the soldiers** to tell the fantastic yarn that while the soldiers **slept**, the **disciples stole** the body of Jesus.

This explanation raises more questions than it answers. Why were the soldiers sleeping when they should have been on guard? How could the disciples have rolled the stone away without waking them? How could all the soldiers have fallen asleep at the same time? If they were asleep, how did they know that the disciples stole the body? If the story was true, why did the soldiers have to be bribed to tell it? If the disciples had stolen the body, why had they taken time to remove the graveclothes and fold the napkin? (Luke 24:12; John 20:6, 7).

28:14 Actually the soldiers were paid to tell a story incriminating themselves; sleeping on duty was punishable by death under Roman law. So the Jewish leaders had to promise to intervene for them if the story ever got back **to the governor's ears**.

The Sanhedrin was learning that while truth is self-verifying, a lie has to be supported by countless other lies.

28:15 Yet the myth persists **among** many **Jews until this day**, and among Gentiles as well. And there are other myths. Wilbur Smith summarizes two of them:

1. First of all it has been suggested that the women went to the wrong tomb. Think about this for a moment. Would you miss the tomb of your dearest loved one between Friday afternoon and Sunday morning? Furthermore, this was not a cemetery of Joseph of Arimathea. This was his private garden. No other tombs were there.

Now, let's say there were other tombs, which there weren't, and suppose the women with their tear-filled eyes stumbled around and got to the wrong tomb. Well, let's grant that for the women. But hard-fisted Simon Peter and John, two fishermen who were not crying, also went to the tomb and found it empty. Do you think they went to the wrong tomb? But more than that, when they got to the tomb and found that it was empty, there was an angel who said, "He is not here. He is risen. Come, see the place where the Lord lay." Do you think the angel went to the wrong tomb too? Yet, don't forget, brainy men have advanced these theories. This is a nonsensical one!

2. Others have suggested that Jesus did not die, but swooned away, and that he was resuscitated somehow in this damp tomb and then came forth. They had a great big stone rolled against this tomb and this was sealed with seals of the Roman government. No man on the inside of that tomb could ever roll back the stone which came down an incline and fitted into a groove. He did not come out of that tomb as an anemic invalid.

The simple truth is that the resurrection of the Lord Jesus is a well-attested fact of history. He presented Himself alive to His disciples after His passion by many infallible proofs. Think of these specific instances when He appeared to His own:
1. To Mary Magdalene (Mark 16:9–11).
2. To the women (Matt. 28:8–10).
3. To Peter (Luke 24:34).
4. To the two disciples on the road to Emmaus (Luke 24:13–32).
5. To the disciples, except Thomas (John 20:19–25).
6. To the disciples, including Thomas (John 20:26–31).
7. To the seven disciples by the Sea of Galilee (John 21).
8. To over 500 believers (1 Cor. 15:7).
9. To James (1 Cor. 15:7).
10. To the disciples on the Mount of Olives (Acts 1:3–12).

One of the great foundation stones, unshakable and unmovable, of our Christian faith, is the historic evidence for the resurrection of the Lord Jesus Christ. Here you and I can stand and do battle for the faith because we have a situation which cannot be contradicted. It can be denied, but it cannot be disproved.[56]

C. The Great Commission (28:16–20)

28:16, 17 In **Galilee** the risen Lord Jesus appeared to His **disciples** at an unnamed mountain. This is the same appearance recorded in Mark 16:15–18 and 1 Corinthians 15:6. What a wonderful reunion! His sufferings were passed forever. Because He lived, they too would live. He stood before them in His glorified body. They worshiped the living, loving Lord — though doubts still lurked in the minds of some.

28:18 Then the Lord explained that **all authority** had **been given to** Him **in heaven and on earth**. In one sense, of course, He always had all authority. But here He was speaking of authority as Head of the new creation. Since His death and resurrection, He had authority to give eternal life to all whom God had given to Him (John 17:2). He had always had power as the firstborn of all creation. But now that He had completed the work of redemption, He had authority as the first-born from the dead — "that in all things He may have the preeminence" (Col. 1:15, 18).

28:19, 20 As Head of the new creation, He then issued the Great Commission, containing "standing orders" for all believers during the present phase of the kingdom — the time between the rejection of the King and His Second Advent.

The Commission contains three commands, not suggestions:

1. **"Go therefore and make disciples of all the nations."** This does not presuppose world conversion. By preaching the gospel, the disciples were to

see others become learners or followers of the Savior — from every nation, tribe, people, and tongue.

2. Baptize **"them in the name of the Father and of the Son and of the Holy Spirit."** The responsibility rests on Christ's messengers to teach baptism and to press it as a command to be obeyed. In believer's baptism, Christians publicly identify themselves with the Triune Godhead. They acknowledge that God is their Father, that Jesus Christ is their Lord and Savior, and that the Holy Spirit is the One who indwells, empowers, and teaches them. **Name** in verse 19 is singular. One **name** or essence, yet three Persons — **Father, Son,** and **Holy Spirit**.

3. Teach **"them to observe all things that I have commanded you."** The Commission goes beyond evangelism; it is not enough to simply make converts and let them fend for themselves. They must be taught to *obey* the commandments of Christ as found in the NT. The essence of discipleship is becoming like the Master, and this is brought about by systematic teaching of, and submission to, the Word.

Then the Savior added a promise of His presence with His disciples until the consummation **of the age**. They would not go forth alone or unaided. In all their service and travel, they would know the companionship of the Son of God.

Notice the four "alls" connected with the Great Commission: **all authority**; **all nations**; **all things**; **always**.

Thus the Gospel closes with commission and comfort from our glorious Lord. Nearly twenty centuries later His words have the same cogency, the same relevance, the same application. The task is still uncompleted.

What are we doing to carry out His last command?

ENDNOTES

[1](1:1) *Jehovah* is the anglicized form of the Hebrew name *Yahweh*, traditionally translated "LORD." Compare the similar situation with *Jesus*, the anglicized form of Hebrew *Yeshua*.

[2](4:2, 3) First class condition, using *ei* with the indicative. It may be paraphrased, "If, and I grant it, You are the Son of God" or "Since You are the Son of God."

[3](Excursus) A "dispensation" is an administration or stewardship. It describes the methods God uses in dealing with the human race at any particular time in history. The word does *not* mean a time period *per se*, but rather the divine program *during* any age. A similar use is seen when we speak of the Reagan administration, indicating the policies President Reagan followed during his years in office.

[4](5:13) Albert Barnes, *Notes on the New Testament, Matthew and Mark*, p. 47.

[5](5:22) The critical text (labeled "NU" in NKJV footnotes) omits *without a cause*, which would rule out even righteous indignation.

[6](5:44–47) The critical (NU) text reads *Gentiles* for *tax collectors*.

[7](5:44–47) The majority text (based on the majority of manuscripts) reads *friends* for *brethren*.

[8](6:13) Some scholars teach that the doxology is adapted from 1 Chronicles 29:11 for liturgical purposes. This is merely a guess. The traditional Protestant (KJV) form of the prayer is completely defensible.

[9](7:13, 14) Both the critical and majority texts have an exclamatory reading here: "How narrow is the gate and difficult is the way which leads to life, and there are few who find it!" When the oldest manuscripts (usually NU) and the vast bulk of manuscripts (M) agree against the traditional text (TR) they are almost certainly correct. In such cases the KJ tradition has weak textual support.

[10](7:28, 29) Jamieson, Fausset & Brown, *Critical and Explanatory Commentary on the New Testament*, V:50.

[11](8:2) Certain forms of leprosy mentioned in the Bible are not the same as the malady we call Hansen's disease. For example, in Leviticus, it includes conditions that can infect a house or a garment.

[12](8:16, 17) Arno C. Gaebelein, *The of Matthew*, p. 193.

[13](8:28) The NU text reads *Gadarenes*. The names of the town and of the region may overlap somewhat.

[14](9:16) Gaebelein, *Matthew*, p. 193.

[15](9:17) W. L. Pettingill, *Simple Studies in Matthew*, pp. 111, 112.

[16](10:8) The majority of mss. omit "raise the dead" here.

[17](10:21) J. C. Macaulay, *Obedient Unto Death: Devotional Studies in John's Gospel*, II:59.

[18](10:41) Arthur T. Pierson, "The Work of Christ for the Believer," *The Ministry of Keswick, First Series*, p. 114.

[19](11:27) Alva J. Gospel McClain, *The Greatness of the Kingdom*, p. 311.

[20](11:30) J. H. Jowett, Quoted in *Our Daily Bread*.

[21](12:8) E. W. Rogers, *Jesus the Christ*, pp. 65, 66.

[22](12:19) McClain, *Kingdom*, p. 283.

[23](12:21) Kleist and Lilly, further documentation unavailable.

[24](12:27) Ella E. Pohle, *C. I. Scofield's Question Box*, p. 97.

[25](12:34,35) Although both critical and majority texts omit "of his heart," it would nevertheless be understood.

[26](13:13) H. Chester Woodring, Unpublished class notes on Matthew, Emmaus Bible School, 1961.

[27](13:22) G. H. Lang, *The Parabolic Teaching of Scripture*, p. 68.

[28](13:24–26) Merrill F. Unger, *Unger's Bible Dictionary*, p. 1145.

[29](13:33) J. H. Brookes, *I Am Coming*, p. 65.

[30](13:49,50) Gaebelein, *Matthew*, p. 302.

[31](14:4,5) Source unknown.

[32](16:2,3) Of course, these weather indications are valid for Israel, not North America or Great Britain!

[33](16:7–10) The twelve *kophinoi* of the 5,000 may have held less than the seven *spurides* of the 4,000.

[34](16:17,18) G. Campbell Morgan, *The Gospel According to Matthew*, p. 211.

[35](16:19) Charles C. Ryrie, ed., *The Ryrie Study Bible, New King James Version*, p. 1506.

[36](16:20) James S. Stewart, *The Life and Teaching of Jesus Christ*, p. 106.

[37](16:26) Donald G. Barnhouse, further documentation unavailable.

[38](18:11) It is omitted by the NU text, but contained in the majority of mss. (M).

[39](20:15) James S. Stewart, *A Man in Christ*, p. 252.

[40](20:31–34) Gaebelein, *Matthew*, p. 420.

[41](21:6) J. P. Lange, *A Commentary on the Holy Scriptures*, 25 Vols., pagination unknown.

[42](23:9, 10) H. G. Weston, *Matthew, the Genesis of the New Testament*, p. 110.

[43](23:14) The critical (NU) text omits the second woe.

[44](23:25, 26) The majority text reads *unrighteousness* (*adikia*) for *self-indulgence* (*akrasia*).

[45](24:29) I. Velikovsky, *Earth in Upheaval*, p. 136.

[46](24:30) The same Greek word (*gē*, compare English prefix "geo") means both "land" and "earth."

[47](24:34) F. W. Grant, "Matthew," *Numerical Bible, The Gospels*, p. 230.

[48](24:36) The NU text adds "nor the Son."

[49](25:28, 29) *Our Lord's Teachings About Money* (tract), pp. 3, 4.

[50](26:64) The Greek singular pronoun *su* is spelled out for emphasis. The second *you* is *humin* (plural) and the third renders the ending on the verb *opsesthe*.

[51](26:64) R. C. H. Lenski, *The Interpretation of St. Matthew's Gospel*, p. 1064.

[52](27:37) If all the quoted parts are put together, it reads "This is Jesus of Nazareth, the King of the Jews." Another possibility is that each evangelist is complete but quotes different languages, which could have varied.

[53](27:54) In Greek the definite predicate nouns which precede the verb usually lack the article (part of "Colwell's Rule").

[54](27:65, 66) Merrill F. Unger, *Unger's Bible Handbook*, p. 491.

[55](28:8) "Rejoice" was the standard Greek greeting; here on Resurrection Morning the literal translation of the NKJV seems most appropriate.

[56](28:15) Wilbur Smith, "In the Study," *Moody Monthly*, April, 1969.

BIBLIOGRAPHY

Gaebelein, A. C. *The Gospel of Matthew*. New York: Loizeaux Bros., 1910.

Kelly, William. *Lectures on Matthew*. New York: Loizeaux Bros., 1911.

Lenski, R. C. H. *The Interpretation of Saint Matthew's Gospel*. Minneapolis: Augsburg Publishing House, 1933.

Macaulay, J. C. *Behold Your King*. Chicago: The Moody Bible Institute, 1982.

Morgan, G. Campbell. *The Gospel According to Matthew*. New York: Fleming H. Revell Company, 1929.

Pettingill, W. L. *Simple Studies in Matthew*. Harrisburg: Fred Kelker, 1910.

Tasker, R. V. G. *The Gospel According to St. Matthew, TBC*. Grand Rapids: Wm. B. Eerdmans Publishing Company, 1961.

Thomas, W. H. Griffith. *Outline Studies in Matthew*. Grand Rapids: Wm. B. Eerdmans Publishing Company, 1961.

Weston, H. G. *Matthew, the Genesis of the New Testament*. Philadelphia: American Baptist Publication Society, n.d.

Periodicals and Unpublished Material

Smith, Wilbur. "In the Study," *Moody Monthly*, April, 1969.

Woodring, H. Chester. Class Notes on Matthew, 1961, Emmaus Bible School, Oak Park, IL (now Emmaus Bible College).

THE GOSPEL
ACCORDING TO MARK†

Introduction

"There is a freshness and vigor about Mark that grips the Christian reader, and makes him long to serve somewhat after the example of his blessed Lord."
— August Van Ryn

I. Unique Place in the Canon

Since Mark's is the shortest Gospel and about ninety percent of his material also occurs in Matthew, Luke, or both, what contribution does he make that we could not do without?

First of all, Mark's brevity and journalistic simplicity make his Gospel an ideal introduction to the Christian faith. On new mission fields Mark is often the first book translated into a new language.

But it is not merely the direct, active *style* — especially suitable for the Romans and their modern counter-parts — but also the *content* that make Mark's Gospel special.

While Mark handles largely the same events as Matthew and Luke — with a few unique ones — he has colorful details that the others do not. For example, he mentions the way Jesus looked at the disciples, how He was angry, and how He walked ahead on the road to Jerusalem. He no doubt got these touches from Peter, with whom he was associated at the end of Peter's life. Tradition says, and probably correctly, that Mark's Gospel is essentially Peter's reminiscences, which would account for the personal details, the action, and the eyewitness effect of the book.

A common belief is that Mark is the young man who ran away naked (14:51), and that this is his modest signature to the book. (The titles on the Gospels were not originally part of the books themselves.) Since John Mark lived in Jerusa-

lem, and there is no reason to tell this little story if the young man is not related to the Gospel in some way, the tradition is likely correct.

II. Authorship††

Most authors accept the early and unanimous opinion of the church that the Second Gospel was written by John Mark. He was the son of Mary of Jerusalem, who owned a house there which the Christians used as a meeting place.

The *external evidence* for this is early, strong, and from various parts of the empire. Papias (about A.D. 110) quotes John the Elder (probably the Apostle John, though conceivably another early disciple) as saying that Mark, the associate of Peter, wrote it. Justin Martyr, Irenaeus, Tertullian, Clement of Alexandria, Origen, and the *Anti–Marcionite Prologue* to Mark all concur.

The *internal evidence* for Marcan authorship, while not extensive, does dovetail with this universal tradition of early Christianity.

The writer obviously knew Palestine well, especially Jerusalem. (The accounts regarding the upper room are more detailed than in the other Gospels — not surprising if it was in his boyhood home!) The Gospel shows some Aramaic background (the language of Palestine), Jewish customs are understood, and the vividness of the narrative suggests close ties with an eyewitness. The outline of the book's contents parallels Peter's sermon in Acts 10.

The tradition that Mark wrote in Rome is illustrated by the greater number of Latin words in his Gospel than the others (such as *centurion, census, denarius, legion,* and *praetorium*).

Ten times in the NT our author is mentioned by his Gentile (Latin) name, Mark, and three times by his combined Jewish and Gentile name, John Mark. Mark, the "servant" or attendant, first of Paul, then of his uncle Barnabas, and according to reliable tradition, of Peter before his death, was an ideal person to write the Gospel of the Perfect Servant.

III. Date

The date of Mark is debated even by conservative, Bible–believing scholars. While no date can be fixed with certainty, one prior to the destruction of Jerusalem is indicated.

Tradition is divided as to whether Mark penned Peter's preaching on the life of our Lord *before* the death of the apostle (before 64-68) or *after* his passing.

Especially if Mark is the First Gospel written, as most now teach, an early date is necessary in order for Luke to have used Mark's material. Some scholars date Mark in the early 50's, but a date from 57–60 seems quite likely.

IV. Background and Theme

In this Gospel we have the wonderful story of God's Perfect Servant, our Lord Jesus Christ. It is the story of One who laid aside the outward display of His glory in heaven and assumed the form of a Servant on earth (Phil. 2:7). It is the matchless story of One who "did not come to be served, but to serve, and to give His life a ransom for many" (Mark 10:45).

If we remember that this Perfect Servant was none other than God the Son, and that He willingly girded Himself with the apron of a slave, becoming a Servant of men, the Gospel will glow with constant splendor. Here we see the incarnate Son of God living as a dependent Man on earth. Everything He did was in perfect obedience to His Father's will, and His mighty works were all performed in the power of the Holy Spirit.

The author, John Mark, was a servant of the Lord who started well, went into eclipse for a while (Acts 15:38), and was finally restored to usefulness (2 Tim. 4:11).

Mark's style is rapid, energetic, and concise. He emphasizes the deeds of the Lord more than His words, evidenced by the fact that he records nineteen miracles, but only four parables.

As we study the Gospel, we shall seek to discover three things: (1) What does it say? (2) What does it mean? (3) What lesson is there in it for me? For all who wish to be true and faithful *servants of the Lord*, this Gospel should prove a valuable manual of service.

OUTLINE

Commentary†

I. THE SERVANT'S PREPARATION (1:1–13)

A. The Servant's Forerunner Prepares the Way (1:1–8)

1:1 Mark's theme is the good news about **Jesus Christ, the Son of God**. Because his purpose is to emphasize the servant role of the Lord Jesus, he begins not with a genealogy, but with the public ministry of the Savior. This was announced by John the Baptist, the herald of the good news.

1:2, 3 Both Malachi and Isaiah[1] predicted that a **messenger** would precede the Messiah, calling the people to be morally and spiritually prepared for His coming (Mal. 3:1; Isa. 40:3). John the Baptist fulfilled these prophecies. He was the "**messenger, . . . the voice of one crying in the wilderness.**"

1:4 His message was that the people should repent (change their minds and forsake their sins) in order to receive **the remission of sins**. Otherwise they would be in no position to receive the Lord. Only holy people are able to appreciate the Holy Son of God.

1:5 When his hearers did repent, John baptized them as an outward expression of their about-face. Baptism separated them publicly from the mass of the nation of Israel who had forsaken the Lord. It united them with a remnant who were ready to receive the Christ. It might seem from verse 5 that the response to John's preaching was universal. This was not the case. There may have been an initial burst of enthusiasm, with multitudes surging out to the desert to hear the fiery preacher, but the majority did not genuinely confess and forsake their sins. This will be seen as the narrative advances.

1:6 What kind of man was **John**? Today he would be called a fanatic and an ascetic. His home was the desert. His clothing, like Elijah's was the coarsest and the simplest. His food was sufficient to maintain life and strength, but was scarcely luxurious. He was a man who subordinated all these things to the glorious task of making Christ known. Perhaps he could have been rich, but he chose to be poor. He thus became a fitting herald of Him who had nowhere to lay His head. We learn here that simplicity should characterize all who are servants of the Lord.

1:7 His message was the superiority of the Lord Jesus. He said that Jesus was greater in power, personal excellence, and in ministry. John did not consider himself worthy to **loose** the Savior's **sandal strap** — a menial duty of a slave. Spirit-filled preaching always exalts the Lord Jesus and dethrones self.

1:8 John's baptism was **with water**. It was an external symbol, but produced no change in a person's life. Jesus would **baptize** them **with the Holy Spirit**; this baptism would produce a great inflow of spiritual power (Acts 1:8). Also it would incorporate all believers into the church, the body of Christ (1 Cor. 12:13).

B. The Forerunner Baptizes the Servant (1:9–11)

1:9 The so-called thirty silent years in Nazareth were now at an end. The Lord Jesus was ready to enter upon His public ministry. First He traveled the sixty odd miles **from Nazareth** to the **Jordan** near Jericho. There He was **baptized by John**. In His case, of course, there was no repentance because there were no sins to confess. Baptism for the Lord was a symbolic action picturing His eventual baptism into death at Calvary and His rising from the dead. Thus at the very outset of His public ministry, there was this vivid foreshadow of a cross and an empty tomb.

1:10, 11 As soon as He came **up from the water, He saw the heavens parting and the Spirit descending upon Him like a dove**. The **voice** of God the Father was heard, acknowledging Jesus as His **beloved Son**.

There never was a time in the life of our Lord when He was not filled with the Holy **Spirit**. But now the Holy Spirit came **upon Him**, anointing Him for service and enduing Him with power. It was a special ministry of the Spirit, preparatory to the three years of service that

†See p. ix.

lay ahead. The power of the Holy Spirit is indispensable. A person may be educated, talented, and fluent, yet without that mysterious quality which we call "unction," his service is lifeless and ineffective. The question is basic, "Have I had an experience of the Holy Spirit, empowering me for the service of the Lord?"

C. The Servant Tempted by Satan (1:12, 13)

The Servant of Jehovah was tempted by Satan in **the wilderness** for **forty days**. **The Spirit** of God led Him to this rendezvous — not to see if He would sin, but to prove that He could not sin. If Jesus could have sinned as a Man on earth, what assurance do we have that He cannot now sin as a Man in heaven?

Why does Mark say that He was **with the wild beasts**? Were these animals energized by Satan to seek to destroy the Lord? Or were they docile in the presence of their Creator? We can only ask the questions.

The angels ministered to Him at the end of the forty days (cf. Matt. 4:11); during the temptation He ate nothing (Luke 4:2).

Testings are inevitable for the believer. The closer one follows the Lord, the more intense they will be. Satan does not waste his gunpowder on nominal Christians, but opens his big guns on those who are winning territory in the spiritual warfare. It is not a sin to be tempted. The sin lies in *yielding* to temptation. In our own strength we cannot resist. But the indwelling Holy Spirit is the believer's power to subdue dark passions.

II. THE SERVANT'S EARLY GALILEAN MINISTRY (1:14—3:12)†

A. The Servant Begins His Ministry (1:14, 15)

Mark skips over the Lord's Judean ministry (see John 1:1–4:54) and begins with the great Galilean ministry, a period of one year and nine months (1:14–9:50). Then he deals briefly with the latter part of the Perean ministry (10:1–10:45) before moving on to the last week in Jerusalem.

†See p. xii.

Jesus came to Galilee, preaching the good news **of the kingdom²of God**. His specific message was that:

1. **The time** was **fulfilled**. According to the prophetic time-table, a date had been fixed for the public appearing of the King. It had now arrived.
2. **The kingdom of God** was **at hand**; the King was present and was making a bona fide offer of the kingdom to the nation of Israel. **The kingdom** was **at hand** in the sense that the King had appeared on the scene.
3. Men were called on to **repent and believe in the gospel**. In order to be eligible to enter the kingdom, they had to do an about-face regarding sin, and believe the good news concerning the Lord Jesus.

B. Four Fishermen Called (1:16–20)

1:16–18 As He walked along the shore of **the Sea of Galilee,**†† Jesus saw **Simon and Andrew** fishing. He had met them before; in fact, they had become disciples of His at the outset of His ministry (John 1:40, 41). Now He called them to be with Him, promising to make them **fishers of men**. Immediately they gave up their lucrative fishing business to follow Him. Their obedience was prompt, sacrificial, and complete.

Fishing is an art, and so is soul-winning.

1. It requires *patience*. Often there are lonely hours of waiting.
2. It requires *skill* in the use of bait, lures or nets.
3. It requires *discernment* and common sense in going where the fish are running.
4. It requires *persistence*. A good fisherman is not easily discouraged.
5. It requires *quietness*. The best policy is to avoid disturbances and to keep self in the background.

We become **fishers of men** by following Christ. The more like Him we are, the more successful we will be in winning others to Him. Our responsibility is to **follow** Him; He will take care of the rest.

1:19, 20 A little farther on, the Lord Jesus met **James** and **John**, the sons of **Zebedee**, as they were **mending their**

††See p. xiv.

MIRACLE	DELIVERANCE FROM:
1. Healing of man with unclean spirit (1:23–26).	1. The uncleanness of sin.
2. Healing of Simon's mother-in-law (1:29–31).	2. The feverishness and restlessness of sin.
3. Healing of the leper (1:40–45).	3. The loathesomeness of sin.
4. Healing of the paralytic (2:1–12).	4. The helplessness caused by sin.
5. Healing of the man with a withered hand (3:1–5).	5. The uselessness caused by sin.
6. Deliverance of the demoniac (5:1–20).	6. The misery, violence, and terror of sin.
7. The woman with the flow of blood (5:25–34).	7. Sin's power to sap life's vitality.
8. The raising of Jairus' daughter (5:21–24; 35–43).	8. Spiritual death caused by sin.
9. Healing of the Syro-Phoenician's daughter (7:24–30).	9. The thralldom of sin and Satan.
10. Healing of the deaf man with a speech impediment (7:31–37).	10. Inability to hear God's Word and to speak of spiritual things.
11. Healing of blind man (8:22–26).	11. Blindness to the light of the gospel.
12. Healing of the demoniac boy (9:14–29).	12. The cruelty of Satan's dominion.
13. Healing of blind Bartimaeus (10:46–52).	13. The blind and beggarly state to which sin reduces.

nets. As soon as **He called them**, they said goodbye to **their father** and **went after** the Lord.

Christ still calls men to forsake all and follow Him (Luke 14:33). Neither possessions nor parents must be allowed to hinder obedience.

C. An Unclean Spirit Cast Out (1:21–28)

Verses 21–34 describe a typical day in the life of the Lord. Miracle followed miracle as the Great Physician healed the demon-possessed and diseased.

The Savior's healing miracles illustrate how He liberates men from the dread results of sin. This is illustrated in the chart above.

Though the preacher of the gospel is not called upon to perform these acts of physical healing today, he is constantly called upon to deal with their spiritual counterparts. Are these not the greater miracles the Lord Jesus mentioned in John 14:12: "He who believes in Me, the works that I do he will do also; and greater *works* than these he will do?"

1:21, 22 But now let us return to Mark's narrative. At **Capernaum**, Jesus had **entered the synagogue** and had begun to teach **on the Sabbath**. The people realized that here was no ordinary teacher. There was undeniable power connected with His words, unlike **scribes** who droned on mechanically. His sentences were arrows from the Almighty. His lessons were arresting, convicting, challenging. The scribes peddled a second-hand religion. There was no unreality in the teaching of the Lord Jesus. He had the right to say what He did, because He lived what He taught.

Everyone who teaches the Word of God should speak with authority or not speak at all. The Psalmist said, "I believed, therefore I spoke" (Psalm 116:10). Paul echoed the words in 2 Corinthians 4:13. Their message was born of deep conviction.

1:23 **In their synagogue** there was

a man possessed, or inhabited, by a demon. The demon is described as **an unclean spirit**. This probably means that the spirit manifested its presence by making the man physically or morally unclean. Let no one confuse demon-possession with various forms of insanity. The two are separate and distinct. A demon-possessed person is actually indwelt and controlled by an evil spirit. The person is often able to perform supernatural feats and often becomes violent or blasphemous when confronted with the Person and work of the Lord Jesus Christ.

1:24 Notice that the evil spirit recognized **Jesus** and spoke of Him as the Nazarene and **the Holy One of God**. Notice too the change of pronouns from plural to singular: **"What have we to do with You?... Did you come to destroy us?... I know You...."** At first the demon speaks as joined to the man; then he speaks for himself alone.

1:25, 26 Jesus would not accept the witness of a demon, even if it was true. So He told the evil spirit to **be quiet**, then commanded him to **come out of** the man. It must have been strange to see the **convulsed** man and to hear the eerie cry of the demon as he left his victim.

1:27, 28 The miracle caused amazement. It was new and startling to the people that with a mere command, a Man could drive out a demon. Was this the beginning of a new school of religious teaching, they wondered? News of the miracle **immediately spread throughout ... Galilee**. Before leaving this portion, let us note three things:

1. The First Advent of Christ apparently aroused a great outburst of demonic activity on the earth.
2. Christ's power over these evil spirits foreshadows His eventual triumph over Satan and all his agents.
3. Wherever God works, Satan opposes. All who set out to serve the Lord can expect to be opposed every step of the way. "For we do not wrestle against flesh and blood, but against principalities, against powers, against the rulers of the darkness of this age, against spiritual hosts of wickedness in the heavenly places" (Eph. 6:12).

D. Peter's Mother-in-Law Healed (1:29–31)

"Immediately" is one of the characteristic words of this Gospel, and is especially suitable for the Gospel which stresses the servant character of the Lord Jesus.

1:29, 30 From **the synagogue** our Lord went to Simon's house. **As soon as** He arrived, he learned that **Simon's mother-in-law lay sick with a fever**. Verse 30 states that **they told Him about her at once**. They wasted no time in bringing her need to the Physician's attention.

1:31 Without a word, Jesus **took her by the hand** and helped her to her feet. She was cured **immediately**. Ordinarily a fever leaves a person in a weakened condition. In this case, the Lord not only cured the fever but gave immediate strength to serve. **And she served them**. J. R. Miller says:

> Every sick person who is restored, whether in an ordinary or extraordinary way, should hasten to consecrate to the service of God the life that is given back. ... A great many persons are always sighing for opportunities to minister to Christ, imagining some fine and splendid service which they would like to render. Meantime they let slip past their hands the very things in which Christ wants them to serve Him. True ministry to Christ is doing first of all and well one's daily duties.[3]

It is noticeable that in each of the healing miracles, the Savior's procedure is different. This reminds us that no two conversions are exactly alike. Everyone must be dealt with on an individual basis.

That Peter had a mother-in-law shows that the idea of a celibate priesthood was foreign to that day. It is a tradition of men which finds no support in the Word of God and which breeds a host of evils.

E. Healing At Sunset (1:32–34)

News of the Savior's presence had spread during the day. As long as it was the Sabbath, the people dared not bring the needy to Him. But **when the sun had set** and the Sabbath had ended, there was a rush to the door of Peter's house. There **the sick and** the **demon-possessed** experienced the power that delivers from every phase and form of sin.

F. Preaching Throughout Galilee (1:35–39)

1:35 Jesus rose **a long while before daylight** and **went out** to a **place** where He would be free from distraction and spend time in prayer. The Servant of Jehovah opened His ear each morning to receive instructions for the day from God the Father (Isa. 50:4, 5). If the Lord Jesus felt the need of this early morning quiet time, how much more should we! Notice too that **He prayed** when it cost Him something; He rose and went out **a long while before daylight**. Prayer should not be a matter of personal convenience but of self-discipline and sacrifice. Does this explain why so much of our service is ineffective?

1:36, 37 By the time **Simon** and the others got up, the crowd was gathered outside the house again. The disciples went to tell the Lord of the rising popular sentiment.

1:38 Surprisingly, He did not go back to the city, but took the disciples into the surrounding **towns**, explaining that He must **preach there also**. Why did He not return to Capernaum?

1. First of all, He had just been in prayer and had learned what God wanted Him to do that day.
2. Secondly, He realized that the popular movement in Capernaum was shallow. The Savior was never attracted by large crowds. He looked below the surface to see what was in their hearts.
3. He knew the peril of popularity and taught the disciples by His example to beware when all men spoke well of them.
4. He consistently avoided any superficial, emotional demonstration that would have put the crown before the cross.
5. His great emphasis was on preaching the Word. The healing miracles, while intended to relieve human misery, were also designed to gain attention for the preaching.

1:39 Thus to the **synagogues throughout all Galilee** Jesus went **preaching** and **casting out demons**. He combined preaching and practicing, saying and doing. It is interesting to see how often He cast out demons in synagogues. Would liberal churches today correspond to the synagogues?

G. A Leper Cleansed (1:40–45)

The account of the **leper** gives us an instructive example of the prayer that God answers:

1. It was earnest and desperate — **imploring Him**.
2. It was reverent — **kneeling down to Him**.
3. It was humble and submissive — **"If You are willing."**
4. It was believing — **"You can."**
5. It acknowledged need — **"make me clean."**
6. It was specific — not "bless me" but **"make me clean."**
7. It was personal — **"make *me* clean."**
8. It was brief — five words in the original.

Notice what happened!

Jesus was **moved with compassion**. Let us never read these words without a sense of exultation and gratitude.

He stretched out His hand. Think of it! The hand of God stretched forth in answer to humble, believing prayer.

He **touched him**. Under the law, a person became ceremonially unclean when he touched a leper. Also, there was of course the danger of contracting the disease. But the Holy Son of Man identified Himself with the miseries of mankind, dispelling the ravages of sin without being tainted by them.

He said, **"I am willing."** He is more willing to heal than we are to be healed. Then **"Be cleansed."** In an instant the skin of the leper was smooth and clear.

He forbade publicizing the miracle until first the man had appeared before **the priest** and had made the required offering (Lev. 14:2ff). This was a test, first of all, of the man's obedience. Would he do as he was told? He did not; he publicized his case, and as a result, he hindered the work of the Lord (v. 45). It was also a test of the priest's discernment. Would he perceive that the long-awaited Messiah had come, performing wonderful miracles of healing? If he was typical of the nation of Israel, he would not.

Again we find that Jesus withdrew from the crowds and ministered **in deserted places**. He did not measure success by numbers.

H. A Paralytic Healed (2:1–12)

2:1–4 Soon after the Lord **entered Capernaum . . . many gathered** around **the house** where He was. Word had spread quickly, and people were anxious to see the Miracle-Worker in action. Whenever God moves in power, people are attracted. The Savior faithfully **preached the word to them** as they clustered round the door. At the rear of the crowd was **a paralytic, carried by four** others on an improvised stretcher. The crowd hindered his getting near the Lord Jesus. There usually are hindrances in bringing others to Jesus. But faith is ingenious. The four carriers climbed the outside stairs to the roof, **uncovered** a portion of **the roof**, and lowered **the paralytic** to the ground floor — perhaps to a courtyard in the middle — bringing him near the Son of God. Someone has nicknamed these good friends Sympathy, Cooperation, Originality, and Persistence. We should each strive to be a friend who displays these qualities.

2:5 Jesus, impressed by **their faith, . . . said to the paralytic, "Son, your sins are forgiven."** Now this seemed to be a strange thing to say. It was a question of paralysis, not sin, wasn't it? Yes, but Jesus went beyond the symptoms to the cause. He would not heal the body and neglect the soul. He would not remedy a temporal condition, and leave an eternal condition untouched. So He said, **"Your sins are forgiven."** It was a wonderful announcement. Now — on this earth — in this life — the man's **sins** were **forgiven**. He didn't have to wait till the Day of Judgment. He had the present assurance of forgiveness. So do all who put their faith in the Lord Jesus.

2:6, 7 The scribes quickly caught on to the significance of the statement. They were well enough trained in Bible doctrine to know that only **God can forgive sins**. Anyone who professed to forgive sins was therefore claiming to be God. Up to this point, their logic was correct. But instead of acknowledging

the Lord Jesus to be God, they accused Him in their hearts of speaking **blasphemies**.

2:8, 9 Jesus read their thoughts, a proof in itself of His supernatural power. He asked them this provocative question: **"Is it easier** to pronounce a man's sins forgiven or his paralysis cured?" Actually it is just as easy to *say* one as the other. But it is equally impossible, humanly speaking, to *do* the one as it is to *do* the other.

2:10–12 The Lord had already pronounced the man's sins forgiven. Yes, but had it really taken place? The scribes could not *see* the man's sins forgiven, therefore they would not believe. In order to demonstrate that the man's sins had really been forgiven, the Savior gave the scribes something they could see. He told the paralytic man to get up, to carry his straw pad, **and walk**. The man responded instantly. The people were **amazed**. They had **never** seen **anything like this** before. But the scribes did not believe, in spite of the most overwhelming evidence. Belief involves the will, and they did not want to believe.

I. The Call of Levi (2:13–17)

2:13, 14 It was while He was teaching **by the sea** that Jesus saw **Levi** collecting taxes. We know Levi as Matthew, who later wrote the first Gospel. He was a Jew, but his occupation was very un-Jewish, considering he collected taxes for the despised Roman government! Such men were not always noted for their honesty — in fact, they were looked down upon, like harlots, as the scum of society. Yet it is to Levi's eternal credit that when he heard the call of Christ, he dropped everything **and followed Him**. May each of us be like him in instant and unquestioning obedience. It might seem like a great sacrifice at the time, but in eternity it will be seen as no sacrifice at all. As the missionary martyr Jim Elliot said, "He is no fool who gives what he cannot keep, to gain what he cannot lose."

2:15 A banquet was arranged at **Levi's house** so he could introduce his friends to the Lord Jesus. Most of his friends were like himself — **tax-collectors and sinners**. Jesus accepted the invitation to be present with them.

2:16 The scribes and Pharisees thought they had caught Him in a serious fault. Instead of going directly to Him, they went **to His disciples** and tried to undermine their confidence and loyalty. **How** was it **that** their Master ate and drank **with tax-collectors and sinners?**

2:17 **Jesus heard it** and reminded them that healthy people don't need a doctor — only those who are ill. The scribes thought they were **well**, therefore they did not recognize their need of the Great Physician. The tax-collectors and sinners admitted their guilt and their need of help. Jesus came to call sinners like them — not self-righteous people.

There is a lesson in this for us. We should not shut ourselves up in Christianized communities. Rather we should seek to befriend the ungodly in order to introduce them to our Lord and Savior. In befriending sinners, we should not do anything that would compromise our testimony, nor allow the unsaved to drag us down to their level. We should take the initiative in guiding the friendship into positive channels of spiritual helpfulness. It would be easier to isolate oneself from the wicked world, but Jesus didn't do it, and neither should His followers.

The scribes thought they would ruin the Lord's reputation by calling Him a friend of sinners. But their intended insult has become an endearing tribute. All the redeemed gladly acknowledge Him as the friend of sinners, and will love Him eternally for it.

J. Controversy about Fasting (2:18–22)

2:18 **The disciples of John the Baptist and of the Pharisees** practiced **fasting** as a religious exercise. In the OT, it was instituted as an expression of deep sorrow. But it had lost much of its meaning and had become a routine ritual. They noticed that Jesus' **disciples** did **not fast**, and perhaps there was a twinge of envy and self-pity in their hearts when they asked the Lord for an explanation.

2:19, 20 In reply, He compared His disciples to companions of a **bridegroom**. He Himself was the Bridegroom. **As long as** He was with them, there was no occasion for an outward demonstration of sorrow. **But the days** were coming when He would **be taken away; then they** would have occasion to **fast**.

2:21 Immediately the Lord added two illustrations to announce the arrival of a New Era which was incompatible with the previous one. The first illustration involved a new patch made of **cloth** that has not been shrunk. If used to repair **an old garment**, it will inevitably shrink and something will have to give. The garment, made of older cloth, will be weaker than the patch and will tear again wherever the patch is sewed to it. Jesus was comparing the Old Dispensation to the old garment. God never intended Christianity to patch up Judaism; it was a new departure. The sorrow of the Old Era, expressed in fasting, must give way to the joy of the New.

2:22 The second illustration involved **new wine** in **old wineskins**. The leather wineskins lost their power to stretch. If **new wine** was put into them, the pressure built up by the fermentation would burst the skins. The **new wine** typifies the joy and power of the Christian faith. The **old wineskins** depict the forms and rituals of Judaism. New wine needs new skins. It was no use for John's disciples and the Pharisees to put the Lord's followers under the bondage of sorrowful fasting, as it had been practiced. The joy and effervescence of the new life must be allowed to express themselves. Christianity has always suffered from man's attempt to mix it with legalism. The Lord Jesus taught that the two are incompatible. Law and grace are opposing principles.

K. Controversy about the Sabbath (2:23–28)

2:23, 24 This incident illustrates the conflict Jesus had just taught between the traditions of Judaism and the liberty of the gospel.

As **He went through the grainfields on the Sabbath,** ... **His disciples** picked some **grain** to eat. This didn't violate any law of God. But according to the hair-splitting traditions of the elders, the disciples had broken the Sabbath by "reaping" and perhaps even by "threshing" (rubbing the grain in their hands to remove the husks)!

2:25, 26 The Lord answered them

using an incident in the OT. **David**, though anointed as king, had been rejected, and instead of reigning, was being hunted like a partridge. One day when his provisions were gone, **he went to the house of God and** used **the showbread** to feed his men and himself. Ordinarily this showbread was forbidden to any but the priests, yet David was not rebuked by God for doing this. Why? Because things were not right in Israel. As long as David was not given his rightful place as king, God allowed him to do what ordinarily would be illegal.

This was the case with the Lord Jesus. Though anointed, He was not reigning. The very fact that His disciples had to pick grain as they traveled showed that things were not right in Israel. The Pharisees themselves should have been extending hospitality to Jesus and His disciples instead of criticizing them.

If David had actually broken the law by eating the showbread, yet was not rebuked by God, how much more blameless were the disciples who, under similar circumstances, had broken nothing but the traditions of the elders.

Verse 26 says that David **ate the showbread** when **Abiathar** was **high priest**. According to 1 Samuel 21:1, Ahimelech was priest at the time. Abiathar was his father. It may be that the high priest's loyalty to David influenced him to permit this unusual departure from the law.

2:27, 28 Our Lord closed His discourse by reminding the Pharisees that **the Sabbath** was instituted by God for man's benefit, not for his bondage. He added that **the Son of Man is also Lord of the Sabbath** — He had given the Sabbath in the first place. Therefore He had authority to decide what was permissible and what was forbidden on that day. Certainly the Sabbath was never intended to prohibit works of necessity or deeds of mercy. Christians are not obligated to keep the Sabbath. That day was given to the nation of Israel. The distinctive day of Christianity is the Lord's Day, the first day of the week. However, it is not a day encrusted with legalistic do's and don't's. Rather it is a day of privilege when, free from secular employments, believers may worship, serve, and attend to the culture of their

souls. For us it is not a question, "Is it wrong to do this on the Lord's Day?" but rather "How may I best use this day to the glory of God, to the blessing of my neighbor, and to my spiritual good?"

L. The Servant Heals on the Sabbath (3:1–6)

3:1, 2 Another test case arose on the Sabbath. As Jesus **entered the synagogue again**, He met **a man** with **a withered hand**. This raised the question, "**Would** Jesus **heal him on the Sabbath?**" If He did, the Pharisees would have a case against Him — or so they thought. Imagine their hypocrisy and insincerity. They couldn't do anything to help this man, and they resented anyone who could. They sought some ground on which to condemn the Lord of life. If He healed **on the Sabbath**, they would rush in to the kill like a pack of wolves.

3:3, 4 The Lord told **the man** to **step forward**. The atmosphere was charged with expectancy. **Then He said to** the Pharisees, **"Is it lawful on the Sabbath to do good or to do evil, to save life or to kill?"** His question revealed the Pharisees' wickedness. They thought it was wrong for Him to perform a miracle of healing on the Sabbath, but not wrong for them to plan His destruction on the Sabbath!

3:5 No wonder they didn't answer! After an embarrassed silence, the Savior ordered the man to **stretch out** his **hand**. As he did so, full strength returned, the flesh filled out to normal size, and the wrinkles disappeared.

3:6 That was more than **the Pharisees** could take. They **went out**, contacted **the Herodians**, their traditional enemies, and **plotted with** them to **destroy** Jesus. It was still the Sabbath. Herod had brought about the death of John the Baptist. Perhaps his party would be equally successful in killing Jesus. This was the Pharisees' hope.

M. Great Multitudes Throng the Servant (3:7–12)

3:7–10 Leaving the synagogue, **Jesus withdrew to the Sea** of Galilee. The sea in the Bible often symbolizes the Gentiles. Therefore His action may have depicted His turning from the Jews to the Gentiles. **A great multitude** gathered, not only **from Galilee** but from distant parts as well. The crowd was so great that Jesus asked for **a small boat** so that He could push off from shore to avoid being crushed by those who came for healing.

3:11, 12 When **unclean spirits** in the crowd cried out that He was **the Son of God**, He **sternly warned them** to stop saying this. As already noted, He would not receive the witness of evil spirits. He did not deny that He was the Son of God, but chose to control the time and manner of being revealed as such. Jesus had the power to heal, but His miracles were performed only on those who came for help. So it is with salvation. His power to save is sufficient for all, but efficient only for those who trust Him.

We learn from the Savior's ministry that need does *not* constitute a call. There was need everywhere. Jesus depended on instructions from God the Father as to where and when to serve. So must we.

III. THE SERVANT'S CALL AND TRAINING OF HIS DISCIPLES (3:13–8:38)

A. Twelve Disciples Chosen (3:13–19)

3:13–18 Faced with the task of world evangelization, Jesus appointed **twelve** disciples. There was nothing wonderful about the men themselves; it was their connection with Jesus that made them great.

They were young men. James E. Stewart has this splendid commentary on the youth of the disciples:

Christianity began as a young people's movement. . . . Unfortunately, it is a fact which Christian art and Christian preaching have too often obscured. But it is quite certain that the original disciple band was a young men's group. It is not surprising then, that Christianity entered the world as a young people's movement. Most of the apostles were probably still in their twenties when they went out after Jesus. . . Jesus himself, we should never forget, went out to his earthly ministry with the "dew of [his] youth" upon him (Ps. 110:3 — this psalm was applied to Jesus first by himself and then by the apostolic Church). It was a true instinct that led the Christians of a later day, when they drew the likeness of their master on the walls of the Catacombs, to portray Him, not old and weary and broken with pain, but as a young shepherd out on the hills of the morning. The original version of Isaac Watts' great hymn was true to fact:

> When I survey the wondrous cross
> Where *the young Prince* of Glory died.

And no one has ever understood the heart of youth in its gaiety and gallantry and generosity and hope, its sudden loneliness and haunting dreams and hidden conflicts and stong temptations, no one has understood it nearly so well as Jesus. And no one ever realized more clearly than Jesus did that the adolescent years of life, when strange dormant thoughts are stirring and the whole world begins to unfold, are God's best chance with the soul. . . . When we study the story of the first Twelve, it is a young men's adventure we are studying. We see them following their leader out into the unknown, not knowing very clearly who he is or why they are doing it or where he is likely to lead them; but just magnetized by him, fascinated and gripped and held by something irresistible in the soul of him, laughed at by friends, plotted against by foes, with doubts sometimes growing clamorous in their own hearts, until they almost wished they were well out of the whole business; but still clinging to him, coming through the ruin of their hopes to a better loyalty and earning triumphantly at last the great name the *Te Deum* gives them, "The glorious company of the apostles." It is worth watching them, for we too may catch the infection of their spirit and fall into step with Jesus.[4]

There was a threefold purpose behind the call of the twelve: (1) **that they might be with Him**; (2) **that He might send them out to preach**; and (3) that they **might have power to heal sicknesses and to cast out demons**.

First there was to be a time of training — preparation in private before preaching in public. Here is a basic principle of service. We must spend time **with Him** before we move out as God's representatives.

Secondly, they were sent out **to preach**. Proclamation of the Word of God, their basic method of evangelism, must always be central. Nothing must be allowed to subordinate it.

Finally, they were given supernatural **power**. Casting out **demons** would attest to men that God was speaking through the apostles. The Bible had not yet been completed. Miracles were the credentials of God's messengers. Today men have access to the complete Word of God; they are responsible to believe it *without* the proof of miracles.

3:19 The name of **Judas Iscariot** stands out among the apostles. There is mystery connected with one chosen as an apostle turning out to be the betrayer of our Lord. One of the greatest heartaches in Christian service is to see one who was bright, earnest, and apparently devoted, later turning his back on the Savior and going back to the world which crucified Him.

Eleven proved true to the Lord, and through them He turned the world upside down. They reproduced themselves in ever-widening circles of outreach, and in one sense, we today are the continuing fruit of their service. There is no way of telling how far-reaching our influence for Christ may be.

B. The Unpardonable Sin (3:20–30)

3:20, 21 Jesus returned from the mountain where He had called His disciples to a Galilean home. Such a **multitude** gathered that He and His apostles were kept too busy to eat. Hearing of His activities, **His own people** felt that **He** was **out of His mind**, and sought to take Him away. Doubtless they were embarrassed by the zeal of this religious fanatic in the family.

J. R. Miller comments:

They could account for His unconquerable zeal only by concluding that He was insane. We hear much of the same kind of talk in modern days when some devoted follower of Christ utterly forgets self in love for his Master. People say, "He must be insane!" They think every man is crazy whose religion kindles into any sort of unusual fervour, or who grows more earnest than the average Christian in work for the Master. . . .

That is a good sort of insanity. It is a sad pity that it is so rare. If there were more of it there would not be so many unsaved souls dying under the very shadow of our churches; it would not be so hard to get missionaries and money to send the gospel to the dark continents; there would not be so many empty pews in our churches; so many long pauses in our prayer-meetings; so few to teach in our Sunday schools. It would be a glorious thing if all Christians were beside

themselves as the Master was, or as Paul was. It is a far worse insanity which in this world never gives a thought to any other world; which, moving continually among lost men, never pities them, nor thinks of their lost condition, nor puts forth any effort to save them. It is easier to keep a cool head and a colder heart, and to give ourselves no concern about perishing souls; but we are our brothers' keepers, and no malfeasance in duty can be worse than that which pays no heed to their eternal salvation.[5]

It is always true that a man who is on fire for God seems deranged to his contemporaries. The more like Christ we are, the more we too will experience the sorrow of being misunderstood by relatives and friends. If we set out to make a fortune, men will cheer us. If we are fanatics for Jesus Christ, they will jeer us.

3:22 **The scribes** did not think He was insane. They accused Him of casting out demons by the power of **Beelzebub, the ruler of the demons**. The name **Beelzebub** means "lord of dung flies" or "lord of filth." This was a serious, vile, and blasphemous charge!

3:23 First Jesus refuted it, then pronounced the doom of those who made it. If He were casting out demons by Beelzebub, then Satan would be working against himself, frustrating his own purposes. His aim is to control men through demons, not to free them from demons.

3:24–26 A **kingdom**, a **house**, or a person **divided against** himself cannot endure. Continued survival depends upon internal cooperation, not antagonism.

3:27 The scribes' accusation was therefore preposterous. In fact, the Lord Jesus was doing the very opposite of what they said. His miracles signified the downfall of Satan rather than his prowess. That is what the Savior meant when He said, "**No one can enter a strong man's house, and plunder his goods, unless he first binds the strong man. And then he will plunder his house.**"

Satan is the **strong man**. The **house** is his dominion; he is the god of this age. **His goods** are the people over whom he holds sway. Jesus is the One who binds Satan and plunders **his house**. At Christ's Second Advent, Satan will be bound and cast into the bottomless pit for one thousand years. The Savior's casting out of demons during His ministry on earth was a forecast of His eventual complete binding of the devil.

3:28–30 In verses 28–30, the Lord pronounced the doom of the scribes who were guilty of the unpardonable sin. In accusing Jesus of casting out demons by demonic power, when it was actually by the power of the Holy Spirit that He did it, they in effect called the Holy Spirit a demon. This is blasphemy **against the Holy Spirit. All** kinds of sin can **be forgiven**, but this particular sin has no forgiveness. It is an **eternal** sin.

Can people commit this sin today? Probably not. It was a sin committed when Jesus was on earth performing miracles. Since He is not physically on earth today, casting out demons, the same possibility of blaspheming the Holy Spirit does not exist. People who worry that they have committed the unpardonable sin have not done so. The very fact that they are concerned indicates that they are not guilty of blasphemy against the Holy Spirit.

C. The Servant's True Mother and Brothers (3:31–35)

Mary, the **mother** of Jesus, came with **His brothers** to talk with Him. The crowd prevented their getting to Him, so they sent word that they were waiting **outside** for Him. When the messenger told Him that His **mother and** His **brothers**[6] wanted Him, **He looked around** and announced that His **mother** and **brother** was **whoever does the will of God.**

Several lessons emerge from this for us:

1. First of all, the words of the Lord Jesus were a rebuke to mariolatry (the worship of Mary). He did not dishonor her as His natural mother, but He did say that spiritual relationships take precedence over natural ones. It was more to Mary's credit to do the will of God than to be His mother.
2. Secondly, it disproves the dogma that Mary was a perpetual virgin. Jesus had brothers. He was Mary's firstborn, but other sons and daughters were born to her afterward (see Matt. 13:55; Mark 6:3; John 2:12; 7:3, 5, 10; Acts 1:14; 1 Cor. 9:5;

Gal. 1:19. See also Psalm 69:8).

3. Jesus put God's interests above natural ties. To His followers, He still says today: "If anyone comes to Me and does not hate his father and mother, wife and children, brothers and sisters, yes, and his own life also, he cannot be My disciple" (Luke 14:26).
4. The passage reminds us that believers are bound by stronger cords to fellow-Christians than they are to blood-relations when those relatives are unsaved.
5. Finally, it emphasizes the importance Jesus places on doing the will of God. Do I meet the standard? Am I His mother or brother?

D. The Parable of the Sower (4:1–20)

4:1, 2 **Again** Jesus **began to teach by the sea.** Again the crowd made it necessary for Him to use **a boat** as His pulpit, just a short way from the beach. And again **He taught** spiritual lessons from the world of nature about Him. He could see spiritual truth in the natural realm. It is there for all of us to see.

4:3, 4 This parable has to do with the **sower,** the **seed,** and the soil. The **wayside** soil was too hard for the seed to penetrate. **Birds...came and** ate the seed.

4:5, 6 The **stony ground** had a thin layer of dirt covering a bed of rock. Shallowness of earth prevented the seed from taking deep root.

4:7 The thorny ground had thorn bushes that cut the seed off from nourishment and sunlight, thus choking it.

4:8, 9 The **good ground** was deep and fertile with conditions favorable to the seed. **Some** seeds produced **thirtyfold, some sixty, and some a hundred.**

4:10-12 **When** the disciples were with Him **alone,** they **asked Him** why He spoke in parables. He explained to them that only those with receptive hearts were permitted **to know the mystery of the kingdom of God.** A **mystery** in the NT is a truth hitherto unknown that can only be known through special revelation. **The mystery of the kingdom of God** is that:

1. The Lord Jesus was rejected when He offered Himself as King to Israel.

2. A period of time would intervene before the kingdom would be literally set up on earth.

3. During the interim, it would exist in spiritual form. All who acknowledge Christ as King would be in the kingdom, even though the King Himself was absent.

4. The Word of God would be sown during the interim period with varying degrees of success. Some people would actually be converted, but others would be only nominal believers. All professing Christians would be in the kingdom in its outward form, but only the genuine ones would enter the kingdom in its inner reality.

Verses 11 and 12 explain why this truth was presented in parables. God reveals His family secrets to those whose hearts are open, receptive and obedient, while deliberately hiding truth from those who reject the light given to them. These are the people Jesus referred to as **"those who are outside."** The words of verse 12 may seem harsh and unfair to the casual reader: **"That seeing they may see and not perceive; and hearing, they may hear and not understand; lest they should turn and their sins be forgiven them."**

But we must remember the tremendous privilege which these people had enjoyed. The Son of God had taught in their midst and performed many mighty miracles before them. Instead of acknowledging Him as the true Messiah, they were even now rejecting Him. Because they had spurned the Light of the world, they would be denied the light of His teachings. Henceforth they would see His miracles, yet not understand the spiritual significance; hear His words, yet not appreciate the deep lessons in them.

There is such a thing as hearing the gospel for the last time. It is possible to sin away the day of grace. Men do drift beyond redemption point. There are men and women who have refused the Savior and who will never again have the opportunity to repent and be forgiven. They may hear the gospel but it falls on hardened ears and an insensible heart. We say, "Where there's life, there's hope," but the Bible speaks of some who are alive, yet beyond hope of repentance (Heb. 6:4–6, for example).

4:13 Going back to the parable of the sower, the Lord Jesus asked the disciples how they could expect to **understand** more involved **parables** if they could not understand this simple one.

4:14 The Savior did not identify **the sower**. It could be Himself or those who preach as His representatives. The seed, He said, is **the Word**.

4:15–20 The various types of soil represent human hearts and their receptivity to the Word, as follows:

The **wayside** soil (v. 15). This heart is hard. The person, stubborn and unbroken, says a determined "No" to the Savior. **Satan**, pictured by the birds, snatches away the Word. The sinner is unmoved and untroubled by the message. He is indifferent and insensible to it thereafter.

The **stony ground** (vv. 16, 17). This person makes a superficial response to **the Word**. Perhaps in the emotion of a fervent gospel appeal, he makes a profession of faith in Christ. But it is just a mental assent. There is no real commitment of the person to Christ. He receives the Word **with gladness**; it would be better if he received it with deep repentance and contrition. He seems to go on brightly for a while, but **when tribulation or persecution arises** because of his profession, he decides that the cost is too great and he abandons the whole thing. He claims to be a Christian as long as it is popular to do so, but persecution exposes his unreality.

The thorny ground (vv. 18, 19). These people also make a promising start. To all outward appearances, they seem to be true believers. But then they become preoccupied with business, with worldly worries, with the lust to become rich. They lose interest in spiritual things, until finally they abandon any claim to be Christians at all.

The **good ground** (v. 20). Here there is a definite acceptance of **the Word**, cost what it may. These people are truly born again. They are loyal subjects of Christ, the King. Neither the world, the flesh, nor the devil can shake their confidence in Him.

Even among the good ground hearers, there are varying degrees of fruitfulness. **Some** bear **thirtyfold, some sixty, and some a hundred**. What determines the degree of productivity? The life that is most productive is the one that obeys the Word promptly, unquestioningly, and joyfully.

E. The Responsibility of Those Who Hear (4:21-25)

4:21 The **lamp** here represents the truths which the Lord imparted to His disciples. These truths were not to be put **under a basket or under a bed**, but out in the open for men to see. The bushel **basket** may represent business, which if allowed, will steal time that should be given to the things of the Lord. The **bed** may speak of comfort or laziness, both enemies of evangelism.

4:22 Jesus spoke to the multitudes in parables. The underlying truth was **hidden**. But the divine intention was that the disciples explain those hidden truths to willing hearts. Verse 22 might also mean, however, that the disciples should serve in constant remembrance of a coming day of manifestation when it will be seen if business or self-indulgence were allowed to take precedence over testimony for the Savior.

4:23 The seriousness of these words is indicated by Jesus' admonition: **"If anyone has ears to hear, let him hear."**

4:24 Then the Savior added another serious warning: **"Take heed what you hear."** If I hear some command from the Word of God, but fail to obey it, I cannot pass it on to others. What gives power and scope to teaching is when people see the truth in the preacher's life.

Whatever we measure out in sharing the truth with others comes back to us with compound interest. The teacher usually learns more in preparing a lesson than the pupils. And the future reward will be greater than our puny expenditure.

4:25 Every time we acquire fresh truth and allow it to become real in our lives, we are sure to be given **more** truth. On the other hand, failure to respond to truth results in a loss of what was previously acquired.

F. Parable of the Growing Seed (4:26–29)

This parable is found only in Mark. It can be interpreted in at least two ways.

The **man** may picture the Lord Jesus casting **seed** on the earth during His public ministry, then returning to heaven. The seed begins to grow — mysteriously, imperceptively but invincibly. From a small beginning, a harvest of true believers develops. **When the grain ripens . . . the harvest** will be taken to the heavenly garner.

Or, the parable may be intended to encourage the disciples. Their responsibility is to sow **the seed**. They may **sleep by night and rise by day**, knowing that God's Word will not return to Him void, but will accomplish what He has intended it to do. By a mysterious and miraculous process, quite apart from man's strength and skill, the Word works in human hearts, producing fruit for God. Man plants and waters but God gives the increase. The difficulty with this interpretation lies in verse 29. Only God can put forth **the sickle** at **harvest** time. But in the parable, the same man who sows the seed **puts in the sickle** when the grain is ripe.

G. Parable of the Mustard Seed (4:30–34)

4:30–32 This parable pictures the growth of **the kingdom** from a beginning as small as **a mustard seed** to a tree or bush big enough for **the birds** to roost in. The kingdom began with a small, persecuted minority. Then it became more popular and was embraced by governments as the state religion. This growth was spectacular but unhealthy, much of it representing people who paid lip service to the King but were not truly converted.

As Vance Havner said:

> As long as the church wore scars, they made headway. When they began to wear medals, the cause languished. It was a greater day for the church when Christians were fed to the lions than when they bought season tickets and sat in the grandstand.[7]

The mustard bush therefore pictures professed Christendom, which has become a roosting place for all kinds of false teachers. It is the outward form of the kingdom as it exists today.

4:33, 34 Verses 33 and 34 introduce us to an important principle in teaching. Jesus taught the people **as they were able to hear it**. He built upon their previous knowledge, permitting time for them to assimilate one lesson before giving them the next. Conscious of His hearers' capacity, He did not glut them with more instruction than they could absorb (see also John 16:12; 1 Cor. 3:2; Heb. 5:12). The method of some preachers might make us think Christ had said, "Feed my giraffes" instead of "Feed my sheep"!

Although His general teaching was in parables, He **explained** them **to His disciples** in private. He gives light to those who sincerely desire it.

H. Wind and Wave Serve the Servant (4:35–41)

4:35–37 At **evening** of the **same day**, Jesus and His disciples started across the Sea of Galilee toward the eastern shore. They had not made any advance preparations. **Other little boats** followed. Then suddenly a violent **windstorm arose**. Huge **waves** threatened to swamp **the boat**.

4:38–41 Jesus was sleeping **in the stern** of the boat. The frantic disciples **awoke Him**, rebuking Him for His seeming lack of concern for their safety. The Lord **arose and rebuked the wind** and the waves. The **calm** was immediate and complete. Then Jesus briefly chided His followers for fearing and not trusting. They were stunned by the miracle. Even though they knew who Jesus was, they were impressed afresh by the power of One who could control the elements.

The incident reveals the humanity and the deity of the Lord Jesus. He slept in the stern of the boat; that's His humanity. He spoke and the sea was calm; that's His deity.

It demonstrates His power over nature, as previous miracles showed His power over diseases and demons.

Finally, it encourages us to go to Jesus in all the storms of life, knowing that the boat can never sink when He is in it.

> Thou art the Lord who slept upon the
>   pillow,
> Thou art the Lord who soothed the
>   furious sea,
> What matter beating wind and tossing
>   billow,
> If only we are in the boat with Thee?
>   – *Amy Carmichael*

I. The Gadarene Demoniac Healed (5:1–20)

5:1–5 The country of the Gadarenes[8] was on the east side of the Sea of Galilee. There Jesus met an unusually violent, demon-possessed man, a terror to society. Every effort to restrain him had failed. He lived among **the tombs** and on the mountains, yelling continually and gashing **himself with sharp stones**.

5:6–13 When the demoniac **saw Jesus**, he first acted respectfully, then complained bitterly. "How true and terrible a picture is this — a man bowed in adoration, petition and faith, and yet hating, defiant and fearing; a double personality, longing for liberty and yet clinging to passion" (Scripture Union Notes).

The exact order of events is unclear, but may have been as follows:

1. The demoniac performed an act of reverence to the Lord Jesus (v. 6).
2. Jesus ordered the **unclean spirit** to **come out** of him (v. 8).
3. The spirit, speaking through the man, acknowledged who Jesus was, challenged His right to interfere, and begged Jesus with an oath to stop tormenting him (v. 7).
4. Jesus **asked** the man's **name**. It was **Legion**, signifying he was indwelt by many demons (v. 9). This apparently does not contradict verse 2 where it says he had an unclean spirit (singular).
5. Perhaps it was the spokesman for the demons who begged permission to **enter** a **herd of swine** (vv. 10–12).
6. Permission was granted with the result that **two thousand** pigs raced down the mountainside **and drowned in the sea** (v. 13).

The Lord has often been criticized for causing the destruction of these pigs. Several points should be noted:

1. He did not cause this destruction; He permitted it. It was Satan's destructive power that destroyed the pigs.
2. There is no record of the owners finding fault. Perhaps they were Jews for whom the raising of pigs was forbidden.
3. The soul of the man was worth more

than all the pigs in the world.

4. If we knew as much as Jesus knew, we would have acted exactly the same way He did.

5:14–17 Those who witnessed the swine's destruction ran back to **the city** with the news. A crowd returned to find the ex-demoniac **sitting** at Jesus' feet **clothed and in his right mind**. The people **were afraid**. Someone has said, "They were afraid when He stilled the tempest on the sea, and now in a human soul." The witnesses recounted the whole story to the newcomers. It was too much for the populace; they pleaded with Jesus **to depart from the region**. This and not the destruction of the pigs is the shocking part of the incident. Christ was too costly a guest!

"Countless multitudes still wish Christ far from them for fear His fellowship may occasion some social or financial or personal loss. Seeking to save their possessions, they lose their souls" (Selected).

5:18–20 As Jesus was about to leave by **boat**, the healed man **begged** to accompany Him. It was a worthy request, evidencing his new life, but Jesus sent him **home** as a living witness of God's great power and mercy. The man obeyed, carrying the good news to **Decapolis**, an area embracing ten cities.

This is a standing order for all who have experienced the saving grace of God: **"Go home to your friends, and tell them what great things the Lord has done for you, and how He has had compassion on you."** Evangelism begins at home!

J. Curing the Incurable and Raising the Dead (5:21–43)

5:21–23 Back on the western shore of blue Galilee, the Lord Jesus was soon in the center of **a great multitude**. A frenzied father came running up to Him. It was **Jairus, one of the rulers of the synagogue**. His **little daughter** was dying. Would Jesus please go and **lay His hands on her** so **that she** might be **healed**?

5:24 The Lord responded and started for the home. A crowd **followed**, thronging **Him**. It is interesting that immediately following the statement of the crowd's *thronging* Him, we have an account of faith *touching* Him for healing.

5:25–29 A distracted **woman** intercepted Jesus on the way to Jairus' home. Our Lord was neither annoyed nor ruffled by this seeming interruption. How do *we* react to interruptions?

I think I find most help in trying to look on all interruptions and hindrances to work that one has planned out for oneself as discipline, trials sent by God to help one against getting selfish over one's work. . . . It is not waste of time, as one is tempted to think, it is the most important part of the work of the day — the part one can best offer to God. (Choice Gleanings Calendar)

This woman had suffered with chronic bleeding **for twelve years**. The **many physicians** she went to had apparently used some drastic forms of treatment, drained her finances, and left her **worse** rather than better. When hope of recovery was all but gone, someone told her about Jesus. She lost no time in finding Him. Easing her way through the crowd, she **touched** the border of **His garment**. Immediately the bleeding stopped and she felt completely well.

5:30 Her plan was to slip away quietly, but the Lord would not let her miss the blessing of publicly acknowledging her Savior. He had been aware of an outflow of divine **power** when she touched Him; it cost Him something to heal her. So He asked, **"Who touched My clothes?"** He knew the answer, but asked in order to bring her forward in the crowd.

5:31 His disciples thought the question was silly. Many people were jostling Him continually. Why ask **"Who touched Me?"** But there is a difference between the touch of physical nearness, and the touch of desperate faith. It is possible to be ever so near Him without trusting Him, but impossible to touch Him by faith without His knowing it and without being healed.

5:32, 33 The woman came forward, **fearing and trembling**; she **fell down before Him** and made her first public confession of Jesus.

5:34 Then He spoke words of assurance to her soul. Open confession of Christ is of tremendous importance. Without it there can be little growth in the Christian life. As we take our stand boldly for Him, He floods our souls with full assurance of faith. The words of the Lord Jesus not only confirmed her physical healing, but also no doubt included the great blessing of soul salvation as well.

5:35–38 By this time, messengers had arrived with the news that Jairus' **daughter** had died. There was no need to bring **the Teacher**. The Lord graciously reassured Jairus, then took **Peter, James, and John** to **the house**. They were met by the unrestrained weeping characteristic of eastern homes in times of sorrow, some of it done by hired mourners.

5:39–42 When Jesus assured them that **the child** was **not dead but sleeping**, their tears turned to scorn. Undaunted, He took the immediate family to the motionless child, and taking her **by the hand, said** in Aramaic, **"Little girl, I say to you, arise."** Immediately the twelve-year-old **girl** got up **and walked**. The relatives were stunned, and doubtless delirious with joy.

5:43 The Lord forbade their publicizing the miracle. He was not interested in the popular acclaim of the masses. He must resolutely press on to the cross.

If the girl had actually died, then this chapter illustrates the power of Jesus over demons, disease, and death. Not all Bible scholars agree that she was dead. Jesus said she was not dead but sleeping. Perhaps she was in a deep coma. He could just as easily have raised her from the dead, but He would not take credit for doing so if she were only unconscious.

We should not overlook the closing words of the chapter: **"He . . . said that something should be given her to eat."** In spiritual ministry, this would be known as "follow-up work." Souls that have known the throb of new life need to be fed. One way a disciple can manifest his love for the Savior is by feeding His sheep.

K. The Servant Rejected at Nazareth (6:1–6)

6:1–3 Jesus returned to Nazareth with **His disciples**. This was **His own country**, where He had worked as a Carpenter. On **the Sabbath** He taught **in the synagogue**. The people, **astonished**, could not deny the wisdom of His teaching or the wonder of His miracles. But there was a deep unwillingness to acknowledge Him as the Son of God. They thought of Him as **the carpenter, the Son of Mary**, whose brothers and **sisters** were still there. Had He returned to Nazareth as a mighty conquering Hero, they might have accepted Him more readily. But He came in lowly grace and humility. This **offended** them.

6:4–6 It was then that **Jesus** observed that **a prophet** is generally given a better reception away from home. His relatives and friends are too close to him to appreciate his person or ministry. "No place harder to serve the Lord than at home." The Nazarenes themselves were a despised people. A popular attitude was: "Can anything good come out of Nazareth?" Yet these social outcasts looked down on the Lord Jesus. What a commentary on the pride and unbelief of the human heart! Unbelief largely hindered the work of the Savior in Nazareth. He healed **a few sick people**, but that was all. The unbelief of the people amazed Him. J. G. Miller warns:

> Such unbelief as this has immense consequences for evil. It closes the channels of grace and mercy, so that only a trickle gets through to human lives in need.[9]

Again Jesus tasted the loneliness of being misunderstood and slighted. Many of His followers have shared this sorrow. Often the servants of the Lord appear in a very humble guise. Are we able to look beyond outward appearances and recognize true spiritual worth? Undaunted by His rejection in Nazareth, the Lord **went about the** surrounding **villages, teaching** the Word.

L. The Servant Sends Forth His Disciples (6:7–13)

6:7 The time had come for **the twelve** to launch out. They had been under the matchless tutelage of the Savior; now they would go forth as heralds of a glorious message. He sent **them out two by two**. The preaching would thus be confirmed in the mouths of two witnesses. Also there would be strength and mutual help in traveling together. Finally, the presence of two might be helpful in cultures where moral conditions were low. Next He **gave them power over unclean spirits**. This is worth noting. It is one thing to cast out demons; only God can confer this power on others.

6:8 If our Lord's kingdom were of this world, He would never have given the instructions which follow in verses 8–11. They are the very opposite of what the average worldly leader would give. The disciples were to go forth without provisions — **no bag, no bread, no copper in their money belts**. They were to trust Him to supply these needs.

6:9 They were allowed to take **sandals** and a staff, the latter perhaps for protection against animals, and only one tunic. Certainly no one would envy the disciples' possessions, nor be attracted to Christianity by the prospect of becoming wealthy! And whatever power the disciples would have must come from God; they were totally cast upon Him. They were sent out in the most frugal circumstances, yet representatives of the Son of God, invested with His power.

6:10 They were to accept hospitality wherever it was offered them, and were to **stay there till** they left the area. This instruction prevented their shopping around for more comfortable lodgings. Their mission was to preach the message of One who did not please Himself, who was not self-seeking. They were not to compromise the message by seeking luxury, comfort or ease.

6:11 If a place rejected the disciples and their message, they were not obligated to remain. To do so would be casting pearls before swine. In leaving, the disciples were to **shake off the dust under** their **feet**, symbolizing God's rejection of those who reject His beloved Son.

Although some of the instructions were of a temporary nature and were later withdrawn by the Lord Jesus (Luke 22:35, 36), yet they embody lasting principles for the servant of Christ in every age.

6:12, 13 The disciples **went out and preached** repentance, **cast out many demons, anointed with oil many who were sick, and healed them**. The anointing with **oil**, we believe, was a symbolic gesture, picturing the soothing, alleviating power of the Holy Spirit.

M. The Servant's Forerunner Beheaded (6:14–29)

6:14–16 When news reached **King Herod** that a miracle-worker was traveling through the land, he immediately concluded that it was **John the Baptist . . . risen from the dead**. Others said it was **Elijah** or **one of the** other **prophets**, but Herod was convinced that the man **whom** he had **beheaded** had risen. John the Baptist had been a voice from God. Herod had silenced that voice. Now the terrible pangs of conscience were stabbing Herod for what he had done. He would learn that the way of the transgressor is hard.

6:17–20 The narrative now switches back to the time of John's execution. The Baptizer had reproved Herod for entering into an unlawful marriage with **his brother Philip's wife**. Herodias, now Herod's wife, became furious and vowed to take revenge. But Herod respected John as a **holy man** and thwarted her efforts.

6:21–25 Finally her chance came. At Herod's **birthday** party, with local celebrities attending, **Herodias** arranged for her **daughter** to dance. This so **pleased Herod** that he promised to give the girl anything **up to half** his **kingdom**. Prompted by her mother, she asked for **the head of John the Baptist on a platter**.

6:26–28 **The king** was trapped. Against his own desires and better judgment, he granted the request. Sin had woven its web around him, and the vassal king was victimized by an evil woman and by a sensual dance.

6:29 When John's faithful **disciples heard** what had happened, they claimed **his corpse** and buried it, then went and told Jesus.

N. Feeding of the Five Thousand (6:30–44)

6:30 This miracle, found in all four Gospels, took place at the beginning of the third year of His public ministry. **The apostles** had just returned to Capernaum from their first preaching mission (see vv. 7–13). Perhaps they were flushed with success, perhaps weary and footsore. Recognizing their need for rest and quiet, the Lord took them by boat to a secluded area on the shore of the Sea of Galilee.

6:31, 32 We often hear, "**Come aside by yourselves to a deserted place and rest a while**" used to justify luxurious vacations for Christians. Kelly wrote:

> It would be well for us if we needed thus to rest more; that is to say, if our labors were so abundant, our self-denying efforts for the blessing of others were so continual, that we could be sure that this was the Lord's word for us.[10]

6:33, 34 A crowd followed the Lord and His disciples by taking the land route along the shore of the lake. **Jesus** had **compassion** on the people. They were wandering around without a spiritual guide, hungry and defenseless. **So He began to teach them.**

6:35, 36 As **the day** wore on, **His disciples** became restless about the crowd — so many people and **nothing to eat**. They urged the Lord to **send them away**. The same crowd that drew out the compassion of the Savior annoyed the disciples. Are people an intrusion to us, or the objects of our love?

6:37, 38 Jesus turned to the disciples and said, **"You give them something to eat."** The whole thing seemed preposterous — five thousand men, plus women and children, and nothing but five loaves and two fish — and God.

6:39–44 In the miracle that followed, the disciples saw a picture of how the Savior would give Himself to be the bread of life for a starving world. His body would be broken that others might have eternal life. In fact, the words used are highly suggestive of the Lord's Supper which commemorates His death: **He had taken**; He **blessed**; He **broke**; He **gave**.

The disciples also learned precious lessons about their service for Him:

1. Disciples of the Lord Jesus should never doubt His power to supply their needs. If He can feed **five thousand men** with **five** loaves **and two fish**, He can provide for His trusting servants under any circumstances. They can labor for Him without worry as to where their food is coming from. If they seek first the kingdom of God and His righteousness, every need will be supplied.

2. How can the perishing world ever be evangelized? Jesus says, **"You give them something to eat!"** If we give Him what we have, however trivial it may seem, He can multiply it in blessing to multitudes.

3. He handled the work in a systematic way by seating the crowd **in** groups of **hundreds and fifties**.

4. He **blessed** and **broke** the loaves and fish. Unblessed by Him, they would never have availed. Unbroken, they would have been utterly insufficient. "The reason we are not more freely given to men is that we are not yet properly broken" (Selected).

5. Jesus did not distribute the food Himself. He allowed **His disciples** to do this. His plan is to feed the world through His people.

6. There was enough for **all**. If believers today would put everything above current necessities into the work of the Lord, the whole world could hear the gospel in this generation.

7. The **fragments** that were left over (**twelve baskets full**) were more than He started with. God is a bountiful Giver. Yet notice that nothing was wasted. The surplus was gathered up. Waste is a sin.

8. One of the greatest miracles would never have happened if the disciples had stuck to their plan to rest. How often that is true with us!

O. Jesus Walks on the Sea (6:45–52)

6:45–50 The Savior can provide not only for His servants' sustenance, but for their safety as well.

After sending the disciples back to the west shore of the lake by **boat**, Jesus went up into a **mountain to pray**. In the darkness of the night, He saw them **rowing** hard against a contrary **wind**. He went to their assistance, **walking on the sea**. At first, they were terrified, thinking **it was a ghost**. Then He spoke reassuringly to them and boarded the boat. **The wind ceased** immediately.

6:51, 52 The account closes with the comment: **"They were greatly amazed in themselves beyond measure, and marveled. For they had not understood about the loaves, because their heart was hardened."** The thought seems to be that even after seeing the power of the Lord in the miracle of the loaves, they still did not realize that nothing was impossible for Him. They shouldn't have been surprised to see Him walking on the water. It was no greater a miracle than the one they had just witnessed.

Lack of faith produced hardness of heart and dullness of spiritual perception.

The church has seen in this miracle a picture of the present age and its close. Jesus on the mountain represents Christ in His present ministry in heaven, interceding for His people. The disciples represent His servants, buffeted by the storms and trials of life. Soon the Savior will return to His own, deliver them from danger and distress and guide them safe to the heavenly shore.

P. The Servant Healing at Gennesaret (6:53–56)

Back on the west side of the lake, the Lord was besieged with **sick** people. **Wherever He** went, people carried needy cases to Him on mats. **Marketplaces** became improvised hospitals. They wanted only to get close enough to Him to **touch the hem of His garment**. All who **touched Him were made well**.

Q. Tradition Versus the Word of God (7:1–23)

7:1 The Pharisees and . . . scribes were Jewish religious leaders who had built up a vast system of rigidly enforced traditions so interwoven with the law of God that they had acquired almost equal authority with the Scriptures. In some cases they actually contradicted the Scriptures or weakened the law of God. The religious leaders delighted in imposing the rules and the people accepted them meekly, satisfied with a system of rituals without reality.

7:2–4 Here we find the Pharisees and scribes criticizing Jesus because **His disciples** ate **with unwashed hands**. This doesn't mean that the disciples didn't wash their hands before they ate, but that they didn't go through the elaborate ritual prescribed by tradition. Unless, for instance, they washed up to the elbows, they were considered ceremonially **defiled**. If they had been in the market place, they were supposed to take a ceremonial bath. This complex system of washing extended even to the dipping of pots and pans. Regarding the Pharisees, E. Stanley Jones writes:

They came all the way from Jerusalem to meet Him, and their life attitudes were so negative and faultfinding that all they saw was unwashed hands. They couldn't see the greatest movement of redemption that had ever touched our planet — a movement that was cleansing the minds and souls and bodies of men. . . . Their big eyes were opened wide to the little and marginal, and blind to the big. So history forgets them, the negative — forgets them except as a background for this impact of the positive Christ. They left a criticism; He left a conversion. They picked flaws, He picked followers.[11]

7:5–8 Jesus quickly pointed out the hypocrisy of such behavior. The people were just what **Isaiah** had predicted. They professed great devotion to the Lord, but were inwardly corrupt. By elaborate rituals, they pretended to worship God, but they had substituted their traditions for the doctrines of the Bible. Instead of recognizing the Word of God as the sole authority in all matters of faith and morals, they evaded or explained away the clear demands of the Scripture by their **tradition**.

7:9, 10 Jesus singled out an example of how **tradition** had made void the law **of God**. One of the Ten Commandments demanded that children **honor** their parents (which included caring for them in their need). The **death** penalty was decreed for anyone who spoke evil of his **father or mother**.

7:11–13 But a Jewish **tradition** had arisen known as **Corban**, which meant "given" or "dedicated." Suppose that certain Jewish parents were in great need. Their son had money to care for them, but didn't want to do it. All he had to do was say "Corban," implying that his money was dedicated **to God** or the temple. This relieved him of any further responsibility to support his parents. He might keep the money indefinitely and use it in business. Whether it ever was turned over to the temple was not important. Kelly remarks:

The leaders had devised the scheme to secure property for religious purposes and to quiet persons from all trouble of conscience about the Word of God. . . . It was God Who called on man to honour his parents, and Who denounced all slight done to them. Yet here were men violating, under cloak of religion, both these commandments of God! This tradition of saying 'Corban,' the Lord treats not only as a wrong done to the parents, but as a rebellious act against the express commandment of God.[12]

7:14–16 Beginning at verse 14, the Lord made the revolutionary pronouncement that it was not what goes into a man's mouth that defiles him (such as food eaten with unwashed hands) but what comes out of man (such as traditions that set aside God's Word).

7:17–19 Even the **disciples** were mystified by this. Brought up under the teachings of the OT, they had always considered that certain foods like pork, rabbit, and shrimp were unclean and would defile them. Jesus now plainly stated that man was not defiled by what went into him. In a sense, this signaled the end of the legal dispensation.

7:20–23 It's what **comes out of** one's heart that defiles a person: **evil thoughts, adulteries, fornications, murders, thefts, covetousness, wickedness, deceit, lewdness, an evil eye, blasphemy, pride, foolishness**. In the context, the thought is that human tradition should be listed here too. The tradition of Corban was tantamount to murder. Parents could die of starvation before this wicked vow could be broken.

One of the great lessons in this passage is that we must constantly test all teaching and all tradition by the Word of God, obeying what is of God and rejecting what is of men. At first a man may teach and preach a clear, scriptural message, gaining acceptance among Bible-believing people. Having gained this acceptance, he begins to add some human teaching. His devoted followers who have come to feel that he can do no wrong follow him blindly, even if his message blunts the sharp edge of the Word or waters down its clear meaning.

It was thus that the scribes and Pharisees had gained authority as teachers of the Word. But they were now nullifying the intent of the Word. The Lord Jesus had to warn the people that it is the Word that accredits men, not men who accredit the Word. The great touchstone must always be, "What does the Word say?"

R. A Gentile Blessed for Her Faith (7:24–30)

7:24, 25 In the preceding incident Jesus showed that all foods are clean. Here He demonstrates that Gentiles are no longer common or unclean. Jesus now traveled northwest **to the region of Tyre and Sidon**, also known as Syro-Phoenecia. He tried to enter **a house** incognito, but His fame had preceded Him and His presence was soon known. A Gentile **woman** came to Him, asking for help for her demon-possessed **daughter**.

7:26 We emphasize the fact that she was **a Greek**, not a Jew. The Jews, God's chosen people, occupied a place of distinct privilege with God. He had made wonderful covenants with them, committed the Scriptures to them, and dwelt with them in the tabernacle, and later in the temple. By contrast, the Gentiles were aliens from the commonwealth of Israel, strangers from the covenants of promise, without Christ, without hope, without God in the world (Eph. 2:11, 12). The Lord Jesus came primarily to the nation of Israel. He presented Himself as King to that nation. The gospel was first preached to the house of Israel. It is important to see this in order to understand His dealings with the **Syro-Phoenician** woman. When she asked **Him to cast the demon out of her daughter**, He seemed to rebuff her.

7:27 **Jesus said** that **the children** (Israelites) should **be filled first**, and that it was not proper **to take the children's bread and throw it to the little dogs** (Gentiles). His answer was not a refusal. He said, **"Let the children be filled first."** This might sound harsh. Actually it was a test of her repentance and faith. His ministry at that time was directed primarily to the Jews. As a Gentile, she had no claim on Him or His benefits. Would she acknowledge this truth?

7:28 She did, saying in effect, **"Yes, Lord**. I am only a little Gentile dog. But I notice that puppies have a way of eating **crumbs** that children drop **under the table**. That's all I ask for — some crumbs left over from your ministry to the Jews!"

7:29, 30 This faith was remarkable. The Lord rewarded it instantly by healing the girl at a distance. When the woman went home, her **daughter** was fully recovered.

S. A Deaf Mute Healed (7:31–37)

7:31, 32 From the Mediterranean coast, our Lord returned to the east coast of **the Sea of Galilee** — the area known as **Decapolis**. There an incident took

THE FIVE THOUSAND	THE FOUR THOUSAND
1. The people were Jews (see John 6:14, 15).	1. The people were probably Gentiles (they lived in Decapolis).
2. The multitude had been with Jesus one day (6:35).	2. This crowd had been with Him three days (8:2).
3. Jesus used five loaves and two fish (Matt. 14:17).	3. He used seven loaves and a few small fish (8:5, 7).
4. Five thousand men, plus women and children were fed (Matt. 14:21).	4. Four thousand men, plus women and children were fed (Matt. 15:38).
5. The surplus filled twelve hand baskets (Matt. 14:20).	5. The surplus filled seven wicker baskets or hampers (8:8).

place that is recorded only in Mark's Gospel. Interested friends **brought to Him one who was deaf and had an impediment in his speech**. Maybe this **impediment** was caused by a physical deformity or by the fact that, never hearing sounds clearly, he could not reproduce them correctly. At any rate, he pictures the sinner, deaf to the voice of God and therefore unable to speak to others about Him.

7:33, 34 Jesus first **took** the man **aside** privately. He **put His fingers in his ears, and He spat and touched his** tongue, thus by a sort of sign language telling the man that He was about to open his ears and unloose his tongue. Next Jesus looked **up to heaven**, indicating that His power was from God. His sigh expressed His grief over the suffering which sin has brought on mankind. Finally He said **"Ephphatha,"** the Aramaic word for **"Be opened."**

7:35, 36 The man obtained normal hearing and speech **immediately**. The Lord asked the people not to publicize the miracle, but they disregarded His instructions. Disobedience can never be justified, no matter how well-meaning the persons might be.

7:37 The spectators **were astonished** by His wonderful works. They said, **"He has done all things well. He makes both the deaf to hear and the mute to speak."** They did not know the truth of what they said. Had they lived on this side of Calvary, they would have said it with even deeper conviction and feeling.

And since our souls have learned His love,
What mercies has He made us prove,
Mercies which all our praise excel;
Our Jesus hath done all things well.
– Samuel Medley

T. Feeding of the Four Thousand (8:1–10)

8:1–9 This miracle resembles the feeding of the five thousand, yet notice the differences in the chart above:

The less Jesus had to work with, the more He accomplished and the more He had left over. In chapter 7, we saw crumbs falling from the table to a Gentile woman. Here a multitude of Gentiles is fed abundantly. Erdman comments:

The first miracle in this period intimated that crumbs of bread might fall from the table for the needy Gentiles; here they may be an intimation that Jesus, rejected by His own people, is to give His life for the world, and is to be the living Bread for all nations.[13]

There is a danger in treating incidents like the feeding of the four thousand as insignificant repetition. We should approach Bible study with the conviction that every word of Scripture is filled with spiritual truth, even if we can't see it at our present state of understanding.

8:10 From Decapolis, Jesus and **His disciples** crossed the Sea of Galilee to the west side, to a place called **Dalmanutha** (Magdala in Matt. 15:39).

U. The Pharisees Seek a Sign From Heaven (8:11–13)

8:11 The **Pharisees** were awaiting Him, demanding **a sign from heaven**. Their blindness and boldness were enormous. Standing in front of them was the greatest Sign of all — the Lord Jesus Himself. He was truly a Sign who had come from heaven, but they had no appreciation for Him. They heard His matchless words, saw His wonderful miracles, came in contact with an absolutely sinless Man — God manifest in the flesh — yet in their blindness asked for **a sign from heaven**!

8:12, 13 No wonder the Savior **sighed deeply**! If any generation in the history of the world was privileged, it was the Jewish **generation** of which those Pharisees were a part. Yet, blind to the clearest evidence that the Messiah had appeared, they asked for a miracle in the heavens rather than on earth. Jesus was saying, "There won't be any more signs. You've had your chance." **Getting into the boat again**, they sailed eastward.

V. The Leaven of the Pharisees and Herod (8:14–21)

8:14, 15 During the journey **the disciples had forgotten to take bread** along. Jesus was still thinking of His encounter with the Pharisees, however, when He warned them against **the leaven of the Pharisees and the leaven of Herod**. Leaven in the Bible is a consistent type of evil, spreading slowly and quietly and affecting everything it touches. **The leaven of the Pharisees** includes hypocrisy, ritualism, self-righteousness and bigotry. The Pharisees made great outward pretensions of sanctity but were inwardly corrupt and unholy. **The leaven of Herod** may include skepticism, immorality and worldliness. The Herodians were conspicuous for these sins.

8:16–21 The disciples completely missed the point. All they could think of was food. So He directed nine rapid questions to them. The first five reproved them for their obtuseness. The last four rebuked them for worrying about the supply of their needs as long as He was with them. Had He not fed **five thousand** with **five** loaves, leaving **twelve baskets** over? Yes! Had He not fed **four thousand** with **seven** loaves, leaving **seven** hampersful over? Yes, He had. Then why did they not understand that He was abundantly able to supply the needs of a handful of disciples in a

boat? Didn't they realize that the Creator and Sustainer of the universe was in the boat with them?

W. Healing of the Blind Man at Bethsaida (8:22–26)

This miracle, found only in Mark, raises several interesting questions. First, why did Jesus lead the man **out of the town** before healing him? Why didn't He heal by simply touching the man? Why use such an unconventional means as saliva? Why didn't the man receive perfect sight immediately?[14] (This is the only cure in the Gospels which took place in stages.) Finally, why did Jesus forbid the man to tell about the miracle **in the town**? Our Lord is sovereign and is not obligated to account to us for His actions. There was a valid reason for everything He did, even though we might not perceive it. Every case of healing is different, as is every case of conversion. Some gain remarkable spiritual sight as soon as they are converted. Others see dimly at first, then later enter into full assurance of salvation.

X. Peter's Great Confession (8:27–30)

The last two paragraphs of this chapter bring us to the high water mark of the training of the twelve. The disciples needed to have a deep, personal appreciation of who Jesus is before He could share with them the pathway ahead and invite them to follow Him in a life of devotion and sacrifice. This passage brings us to the heart of discipleship. It is perhaps the most neglected area in Christian thought and practice today.

8:27, 28 Jesus and His disciples sought solitude in the far north. On the way to **Caesarea Philippi**, He opened the subject by asking what public opinion said of Him. In general, men were acknowledging Him to be a great man — equal to **John the Baptist, Elijah** or other **prophets**. But man's honor is actually dishonor. If Jesus is not God, then He is a deceiver, a madman, or a legend. There is no other possibility.

8:29, 30 Then the Lord pointedly asked the disciples for their evaluation of Him. **Peter** promptly declared Him to be **the Christ**, that is, the Messiah, or the Anointed One. Intellectually, Peter had known this. But something had happened in his life so that now there was a profound, personal conviction. Life could never be the same again. Peter could never be satisfied with a self-centered existence. If Christ was the Messiah, then Peter must live for Him in total abandonment.

Y. The Servant Predicts His Death and Resurrection (8:31–38)

Thus far we have watched the Servant of Jehovah in a life of incessant service for others. We have seen Him hated by His enemies and misunderstood by His friends. We have seen a life of dynamic power, of moral perfection, of utter love and humility.

8:31 But the path of service to God leads on to suffering and death. So the Savior now told the disciples plainly that He **must** (1) **suffer**; (2) **be rejected**; (3) **be killed**; (4) **rise again**. For Him the path to glory would lead first to the cross and the grave. "The heart of service would be revealed in sacrifice," as F. W. Grant put it.

8:32, 33 Peter could not accept the idea that Jesus would have to suffer and die; that was contrary to his image of the Messiah. Neither did he want to think that his Lord and Master would be slain by His foes. He rebuked the Savior for suggesting such a thing. It was then that Jesus said to Peter, **"Get behind Me, Satan! For you are not mindful of the things of God, but the things of men."** Not that Jesus was accusing Peter of being Satan, or of being indwelt by Satan. He meant, "You are talking like Satan would. He always tries to discourage us from wholly obeying God. He tempts us to take an easy path to the Throne." Peter's words were Satanic in origin and content, and this caused the Lord's indignation. Kelly comments:

> What was it that so roused our Lord? The very snare to which we are all so exposed: the desire of saving self; the preference of an easy path to the cross. Is it not true that we naturally like to escape trial, shame, and rejection; that we shrink from the suffering which doing God's will, in such a world as this, must ever entail; that we prefer to have a quiet, respectable path in the earth — in short, the best of both worlds? How easily one may be ensnared into this! Peter could not understand why the Messiah should go

through all this path of sorrow. Had we been there, we might have said or thought yet worse. Peter's remonstrance was not without strong human affection. He heartily loved the Savior too. But, unknown to himself, there was the unjudged spirit of the world.[15]

Note that Jesus first **looked at His disciples**, then **rebuked Peter**, as if to say, "If I do not go to the cross, how can these, My disciples, be saved?"

8:34 Then Jesus **said to them** in effect, "I am going to suffer and die so that men might be saved. If you desire to **come after Me**, you must deny every selfish impulse, deliberately choose a pathway of reproach, suffering and death, **and follow Me**. You may have to forsake personal comforts, social enjoyments, earthly ties, grand ambitions, material riches, and even life itself." Words like these make us wonder how we can really believe that it is all right for us to live in luxury and ease. How can we justify the materialism, selfishness, and coldness of our hearts? His words call us to lives of self-denial, surrender, suffering, and sacrifice.

8:35 There is always the temptation to **save** our **life** — to live comfortably, to provide for the future, to make one's own choices, with self as the center of everything. There is no surer way of losing one's life. Christ calls us to pour out our lives for His sake and the gospel's, dedicating ourselves to Him spirit, soul, and body. He asks us to spend and be spent in His holy service, laying down our lives, if necessary, for the evangelization of the world. That is what is meant by losing our lives. There is no surer way of saving them.

8:36, 37 Even if a believer could gain all the world's wealth during his lifetime, what good would it do him? He would have missed the opportunity of using his life for the glory of God and the salvation of the lost. It would be a bad bargain. Our lives are worth more than all the world has to offer. Shall we use them for Christ or for self?

8:38 Our Lord realized that some of His young disciples might be stumbled in the path of discipleship by the fear of shame. So He reminded them that those who seek to avoid reproach because of Him will suffer a greater shame when

He returns to earth in power. What a thought! Soon our Lord is coming back to earth, this time not in humiliation, but in His own personal glory and in the glory of His Father, with the holy angels. It will be a scene of dazzling splendor. He will then be ashamed of those who are ashamed of Him now. May His words **"ashamed of Me . . . in this adulterous and sinful generation"** speak to our hearts. How incongruous to be ashamed of the sinless Savior in a world that is characterized by unfaithfulness and sinfulness!

IV. THE SERVANT'S JOURNEY TO JERUSALEM (Chaps. 9, 10)

A. The Servant Transfigured (9:1–13)

Having laid before the disciples the pathway of reproach, suffering, and death which He was to take, and having invited them to follow Him in lives of sacrifice and self-renunciation, the Lord now gives the other side of the picture. Though discipleship would cost them dearly in this life, it would be rewarded with glory by and by.

9:1–7 The Lord began by saying that **some** of the disciples would **not taste death till they** saw **the kingdom of God present with power**. He was referring to **Peter, James, and John**. On the Mount of Transfiguration they saw **the kingdom of God** in **power**. The argument of the passage is that anything we suffer for Christ's sake now will be abundantly repaid when He returns and His servants appear with Him in glory. The conditions which prevailed on the Mount foreshadow the Millennial Reign of Christ.

1. Jesus **was transfigured** — dazzling splendor radiated from His Person. Even **His clothes** were **shining**, whiter than any bleach could make them.

   During His First Advent, the glory of Christ was veiled. He came in humiliation, a Man of Sorrows, and acquainted with grief. But He will return in glory. No one will mistake Him then. He will be visibly the King of kings and Lord of lords.

2. **Elijah** and **Moses** were there. They represent: (a) OT saints, or (b) the law (Moses) and the prophets (Elijah), or (c) saints who have died, and those who have been translated.

3. **Peter, James and John** were there. They may represent NT saints in general, or those who will be alive when the kingdom is set up.

4. **Jesus** was the central Person. Peter's suggestion of making **three tabernacles** was rebuked by the **cloud** and the **voice** from heaven. In all things Christ must have the preeminence. He will be the glory of Immanuel's land.

5. The **cloud** may have been the shekinah or glory cloud which stayed in the Holy of Holies in the tabernacle and temple in OT times. It was the visible expression of God's presence.

6. The **voice** was the voice of God the Father, acknowledging Christ as His **beloved Son**.

9:8 When the cloud was lifted the disciples **saw no one anymore, but only Jesus**. It was a picture of the unique, glorious and pre–eminent place He will have when the kingdom comes in power, and which He should have in the hearts of His followers at the present time.

9:9, 10 As they came down from the mountain, He commanded them not to discuss what **they had seen till** after He **had risen from the dead**. This latter point puzzled them. Perhaps they still did not grasp that He was to be slain and rise again. They wondered about the expression **rising from the dead**. As Jews they knew the truth that all would be raised. But Jesus was speaking of a selective resurrection. He would be raised from among the dead ones — not all would be raised when He arose. This is a truth found only in the NT.

9:11 The disciples had another problem. They had just had a preview of the kingdom. But hadn't Malachi predicted **that Elijah must come** as a forerunner of the Messiah, beginning the restitution of all things, and paving the way for setting up His universal reign (Mal. 4:5)? Where was Elijah? Would he **come first**, as **the scribes** said he would?

9:12, 13 Jesus answered in effect,

"**Indeed**, it is true that **Elijah** must come **first**. But a more important and immediate question is this: 'Don't the OT Scriptures predict that **the Son of Man** is to endure great sufferings and be treated with **contempt**?' As far as Elijah is concerned, **Elijah** did **come** (in the person and ministry of John the Baptist), but men treated him exactly as they wanted to — just as men treated Elijah. The death of John the Baptist was an advance token of what they would do to the Son of Man. They rejected the forerunner; they will reject the King."

B. A Demon-Possessed Boy Healed (9:14–29)

9:14–16 The disciples were not permitted to remain on the mountain-top of glory. In the valley below was groaning, sobbing mankind. A world of need lay at their feet. When Jesus and the three disciples reached the base of the mountain, an animated discussion was going on among **the scribes**, the crowd, and **the** other **disciples**. As soon as the Lord appeared, the conversation broke up and the crowd rushed to Him. "**What are you discussing with** My disciples?" He inquired.

9:17, 18 A distraught father excitedly told the Lord about his **son**, possessed with **a mute spirit**. The demon dashed the child to the ground, made him grind **his teeth** and foam **at the mouth**. These violent convulsions were causing the child to waste away. The father had asked the **disciples** to help, **but they could not**.

9:19 Jesus chided the disciples for their unbelief. Had He not given them power to cast out demons? **How long** would He have to **be with** them before they would use the authority He had given them? **How long** would He have to put up with lives of powerlessness and defeat?

9:20–23 As **they brought** the child to the Lord, the demon induced a particularly serious fit. The Lord **asked his father how long** this had been going on. It was **from childhood**, he explained. These spasms **often** had **thrown** the child **into the fire and into the water**. There had been narrow escapes from death. Then the father asked the Lord to please do something **if** He could — a

heart-rending cry, wrung from years of desperation. **Jesus** told **him** that it was not a question of His ability to heal, but of the father's ability to **believe**. Faith in the living God is always rewarded. No case is too difficult for Him.

9:24 The father expressed the paradox of faith and unbelief experienced by God's people in all ages. "**Lord, I believe; help my unbelief!**" We want to believe, yet find ourselves filled with doubt. We hate this inward, unreasonable contradiction, yet seem to fight it in vain.

9:25–27 When **Jesus** ordered **the unclean spirit** to leave the child, there was another terrible spasm, then the little body relaxed **as** if **dead**. The Savior raised him up and restored him to his father.

9:28, 29 Later when our Lord was alone with **His disciples** in **the house**, they **asked Him privately** why they hadn't been able to do it. He replied that certain miracles require **prayer and fasting**. Which of us is not faced at times in our Christian service with a sense of defeat and frustration? We have labored tirelessly and conscientiously, yet there has been no evidence of the Spirit of God working in power. We too hear the Savior's words reminding us, "**This kind . . .**" etc.

C. Jesus Again Predicts His Death and Resurrection (9:30–32)

9:30 Our Lord's visit to Caesarea Philippi had ended. Now He **passed through Galilee** — a trip that would lead Him to Jerusalem and the cross. He desired to travel unnoticed. For the most part, His public ministry was over. Now He wanted to spend time with the disciples, instructing and preparing them for what lay ahead.

9:31, 32 He told them plainly that He was going to be arrested and killed, and that **He** would **rise** again **the third day**. They somehow didn't take it in, **and were afraid to ask Him**. We are often afraid to ask too, and thus lose a blessing.

D. Greatness in the Kingdom (9:33–37)

9:33, 34 When they reached the house in **Capernaum** where they would stay, Jesus **asked them what** they had been arguing about along the way. They were ashamed to admit that they had been disputing which of them **would be the greatest**. Perhaps the Transfiguration had revived their hopes for an imminent kingdom, and they were grooming themselves for places of honor in it. It is heartbreaking to realize that at the very time Jesus had been telling them about His impending death, they were esteeming themselves better than others. The heart of man is deceitful and desperately wicked above all things, as Jeremiah said.

9:35–37 Jesus, knowing what they had argued about, gave them a lesson in humility. He said that the way to be first was to voluntarily take the lowest place of service and live for others instead of self. **A little child** was set before them and embraced by the Lord Jesus. He emphasized that a kindness shown **in** His **name** to the least esteemed, the least renowned, was an act of greatness. It was as if the kindness were shown to the Lord Himself, yes, even to God the Father. "O blessed Lord Jesus, Your teachings probe and expose this carnal heart of mine. Break me of self and let Your life be lived through me."

E. The Servant Forbids Sectarianism (9:38–42)

This chapter seems to be full of failures. Peter spoke clumsily on the Mount of Transfiguration (vv. 5, 6). The disciples failed to cast out the mute demon (v. 18). They argued over who was greatest (v. 34). In vv. 38–40, we find them demonstrating a sectarian spirit.

9:38 It was **John** the beloved who reported to Jesus that they had found a man **casting out demons in** His **name**. The disciples told him to stop because he didn't identify himself with them. The man wasn't teaching false doctrine or living in sin. He simply did not join up with the disciples.

> They drew a circle that shut me out –
> Rebel, heretic, thing to flout;
> But love and I had the wit to win –
> We drew a circle that took them in.

9:39 **Jesus said**, "Don't stop him. If he has enough faith in Me to use My name in casting out demons, he is on My side and is working against Satan. He isn't apt to turn around quickly and **speak evil of Me** or be My enemy."

9:40 Verse 40 seems to contradict Matthew 12:30 where Jesus said: "He who is not with Me is against Me; and he who does not gather with Me scatters abroad." But there is no real conflict. In Matthew, the issue was whether Christ was the Son of God or demon-empowered. On such a fundamental question, anyone who is not with Him is working against Him.

Here in Mark, the question was not the Person or work of Christ, but the matter of one's associates in the service of the Lord. Here there must be tolerance and love. Whoever **is not against** Him in service must be against Satan and therefore **on** Christ's **side**.

9:41 Even the smallest kindness done **in** Christ's **name** will be rewarded. **A cup of water** given to a disciple **because** he belongs **to Christ** will not go unnoticed. Casting out a demon in His name is rather spectacular. Giving a glass **of water** is commonplace. But both are precious to Him when done for His glory. **"Because you belong to Christ"** is the cord that should bind believers together. These words, if kept before us, would deliver us from party spirit, petty bickerings and jealousy in Christian service.

9:42 Constantly the Lord's servant must consider what effect his words and actions will have on others. It is possible to stumble a fellow believer, causing lifelong spiritual damage. **It would be better** to be drowned with a **millstone around** one's **neck** than to cause a **little** one to stray from the path of holiness and truth.

F. Ruthless Self-Discipline (9:43–50)

9:43 The remaining verses of the chapter emphasize the necessity of discipline and renunciation. Those who set out on the path of true discipleship must constantly battle with natural desires and appetites. To cater to them spells ruin. To control them insures spiritual victory.

The Lord spoke of the **hand**, the **foot**, and the **eye**, explaining that it would be better to lose one of these than to be stumbled by it into **hell**. Reaching the goal is worth any sacrifice.

The **hand** might suggest our deeds, the **foot** our walk, and the **eye** the things we crave. These are potential danger spots. Unless they are dealt with severely, they can lead to eternal ruin.

Does this passage teach that true believers can finally be lost and spend eternity in hell? Taken by itself it might suggest that. But taken with the consistent teaching of the NT, we must conclude that anyone who goes to hell was never a genuine Christian at all. A person might *profess* to be born again and appear to go on well for some time. But if that person consistently indulges the flesh, it is clear he was never saved.

9:44–48 The Lord repeatedly[16] speaks of hell as a place **where their worm does not die and the fire is not quenched**. It is tremendously solemn. If we really believed it, we would not live for things but for never-dying souls. "Give me a passion for souls, O Lord!"

Fortunately it is never morally necessary to amputate a hand or foot or to cut out an eye. Jesus did not suggest that we should practice such extremes. All He said was it would be *better* to sacrifice the use of these organs than to be dragged down to **hell** by their abuse.

9:49 Verses 49 and 50 are especially difficult. Therefore we will examine them clause by clause.

"For everyone will be seasoned with fire." The three main problems are: (1) Which **fire** is referred to? (2) What is meant by **seasoned**? (3) Does **everyone** refer to saved, to unsaved, or to both?

Fire may mean hell (as in vv. 44, 46, 48) or judgment of any kind, including divine judgment of a believer's works, and self-judgment.

Salt typifies that which preserves, purifies, and seasons. In eastern lands, it is also a pledge of loyalty, friendship, or faithfulness to a promise.

If **everyone** means the unsaved, then the thought is that they will be preserved in the fires of hell, that is, that they will suffer eternal punishment.

If **everyone** refers to believers, the passage teaches that they must: (1) be purified through the fires of God's chas-

tening in this life; or (2) preserve themselves from corruption by practicing self-discipline and self-renunciation; or (3) be tested at the Judgment Seat of Christ.

"And every sacrifice will be seasoned with salt." This clause[17] is quoted from Lev. 2:13 (see also Num. 18:19; 2 Chron. 13:5). Salt, an emblem of the covenant between God and His people, was intended to remind the people that the covenant was a solemn treaty to be kept inviolate. In presenting our bodies as a living sacrifice to God (Rom. 12:1, 2), we should season the sacrifice with salt by making it an irrevocable commitment.

9:50 "Salt is good." Christians are the salt of the earth (Matt. 5:13). God expects them to exert a healthful, purifying influence. As long as they fulfill their discipleship, they are a blessing to all.

"But if the salt loses its flavor, how will you season it?" Salt without saltiness is valueless. A Christian who is not carrying out his duties as a true disciple is barren and ineffective. It is not enough to make a good start in the Christian life. Unless there is constant and radical self-judgment, the child of God is failing to achieve the purpose for which God saved him.

"Have salt in yourselves." Be a power for God in the world. Exert a beneficial influence for the glory of Christ. Be intolerant of anything in your life that might lessen your effectiveness for Him.

"And have peace with one another." This apparently refers back to verses 33 and 34, where the disciples had argued over which of them was the greatest. Pride must be put away and replaced by humble service for all.

To summarize, verses 49 and 50 seem to picture the believer's life as a sacrifice to God. It is salted with fire, that is, mixed with self-judgment and self-renunciation. It is salted with salt, that is, offered with a pledge of unalterable devotedness. If the believer goes back on his vows, or fails to deal drastically with sinful desires, then his life will be savorless, worthless, and pointless. Therefore he should eradicate anything from his life that would interfere with his divinely-appointed mission, and he should maintain peaceful relations with other believers.

G. Marriage and Divorce (10:1–12)

10:1 From Galilee our Lord traveled southeastward to Perea, the district on the east **side of the Jordan**. His Perean ministry extends through 10:45.

10:2 The Pharisees soon found Him. They were moving in for the kill, like a pack of wolves. In an effort to trap Him, they asked Him if **divorce** was **lawful**. He referred them back to the Pentateuch. **What did Moses command?**

10:3–9 They avoided His question by stating what **Moses permitted**. He **permitted** a man to divorce his wife, provided he gave her a written **certificate of divorce**. But that was not God's ideal; it was permitted only **because of the hardness** of the people's hearts. The divine plan joined a man and woman in marriage as long as they live. This goes back to God's creation of the sexes. A man is to **leave his** parents and be so united in marriage that he and his wife are **one flesh**. Thus **joined** by **God**, they should not be separated by human decree.

10:10 Apparently this was difficult for even **His disciples** to accept. At that time, women did not have a place of honor or security. They were often treated with little more than contempt. A man could divorce his wife if he was displeased with her. She had no recourse. In many cases, she was treated as a piece of property.

10:11, 12 When the disciples questioned the Lord further, He said pointedly that remarriage after divorce was **adultery**, whether the man or the **woman** got the divorce. Taken by itself, this verse would indicate that divorce is forbidden under all circumstances. But in Matt. 19:9, He made an exception. Where one partner has been guilty of immorality, the other is permitted to get a divorce and is presumably free to remarry. It is also possible that 1 Cor. 7:15 permits divorce when an unbelieving partner deserts a Christian spouse.

Assuredly there are difficulties connected with the whole subject of divorce and remarriage. People create marital tangles so involved that it takes the wisdom of a Solomon to extricate them. The best way to avoid these tangles is to avoid divorce. Divorce places a cloud and a question mark over the lives of those involved. When divorced persons seek fellowship in a local church, the elders must review the case in the fear of God. Every case is different and must be considered individually.

This paragraph shows Christ's concern not only for the sanctity of marriage, but also for the rights of women. Christianity gives to women a standing in honor not found in other religions.

H. Blessing the Little Children (10:13–16)

10:13 Now we see the solicitude of the Lord Jesus for **little children**. Parents who **brought** their **children** to be blessed by the Teacher Shepherd were shooed away by the disciples.

10:14–16 The Lord was **greatly displeased and** explained that **the kingdom of God** belongs **to little children**, and to those who have childlike faith and humility. Adults have to become like small children in order to **enter** the kingdom.

George MacDonald used to say that he did not believe in a man's Christianity if boys and girls were never to be found playing around his door. Certainly these verses should impress the servant of the Lord with the importance of reaching little ones with the Word of God. The minds of children are most plastic and most receptive. W. Graham Scroggie said, "Be your best and give your best to the children."

I. The Rich Young Ruler (10:17–31)

10:17 A rich man intercepted the Lord with an apparently sincere inquiry. Addressing Jesus as **"Good Teacher,"** he asked **what** he had to **do** to **inherit eternal life.**

10:18 Jesus seized on the words **"Good Teacher"**. He did not refuse the title but used it to test the man's faith. Only **God** is good. Was the rich man willing to confess the Lord Jesus as God? Apparently not.

10:19, 20 Next the Savior used the law to produce the knowledge of sin. The man was still under the delusion that he could inherit the kingdom on the principle of *doing*. Then let him obey the law, which told him what to *do*. Our Lord quoted the five commandments which deal primarily with our relations to our fellow man. These five commandments say, in effect, "You shall love your neighbor as yourself." The man professed to have **kept** them from his **youth**.

10:21, 22 But did he really love his neighbor as himself? If so, let him prove it by selling all his property and giving the money **to the poor**. Oh, that was another story. He **went away sorrowful, for he had great possessions**.

The Lord Jesus did not mean that this man could have been saved by selling his possessions and giving the proceeds to charity. There is only one way of salvation — that is faith in the Lord. But in order to be saved a man must acknowledge that he is a sinner, falling short of God's holy requirements. The Lord took the man back to the Ten Commandments to produce conviction of sin. The rich man's unwillingness to share his possessions showed that he did not love his neighbor as himself. He should have said, "Lord, if that's what is required, then I'm a sinner. I cannot save myself by my own efforts. Therefore I ask You to save me by Your grace." But he loved his property too much. He was unwilling to give it up. He refused to break.

When Jesus told the man to sell all, He was *not* giving this as the way of salvation. He was showing the man that he had broken the law of God and therefore needed to be saved. If he had responded to the Savior's instruction, he would have been given the way of salvation.

But there is a problem here. Are we who are believers supposed to love our neighbor as ourselves? Does Jesus say to us, **"Sell whatever you have and give to the poor, and you will have treasure in heaven; and come, take up the cross, and follow Me"**? Each one must answer for himself, but before doing so, he should consider the following inescapable facts:

1. Thousands of people die daily of starvation.
2. More than half the world has never heard the good news.
3. Our material possessions can be used now to alleviate spiritual and physical human need.
4. The example of Christ teaches us that we should become poor that others might be made rich (2 Cor. 8:9).
5. The shortness of life and the imminence of the Lord's coming teach us

to put our money to work for Him now. After He comes it will be too late.

10:23–25 As He saw the rich man fade into the crowd, Jesus remarked on the difficulty of rich people entering **the kingdom of God**. The disciples were amazed by this remark; they linked riches with the blessing of God. So Jesus repeated, **"Children, how hard it is for those who trust in riches**[18] **to enter the kingdom of God!"** "In fact," He continued, **"It is easier for a camel to go through the eye of a needle than for a rich man to enter the kingdom of God."**

10:26, 27 This made the disciples wonder **who then can be saved**. As Jews living under the law, they correctly looked on riches as an indication of God's blessing. Under the Mosaic code, God promised prosperity to those who obeyed Him. The disciples reasoned that if a rich person couldn't enter the kingdom, then no one else could either. Jesus answered that what is humanly **impossible** is divinely **possible**.

What are we to conclude from the teaching of this passage?

First of all, it is especially difficult for rich people to be saved (v. 23) since these people tend to love their wealth more than God. They would rather give up God than give up their money. They put their trust in riches rather than in the Lord. As long as these conditions exist, they cannot be saved.

It was true in the OT that riches were a sign of God's favor. That is now changed. Instead of a mark of the Lord's blessing, riches are a test of a man's devotedness.

A camel can go through a needle's eye more easily than a rich man can go through the door of the kingdom. Humanly speaking, a rich man simply cannot be saved. Someone may object here that humanly speaking, *no one* can be saved. That is true. But it is even more true in the case of a rich man. He faces obstacles that the poor man isn't aware of. The god of mammon must be torn from the throne of his heart, and he must stand before God as a pauper. To effect this change is humanly impossible. Only God can do it.

Christians who lay up treasures on earth generally pay for their disobedience in the lives of their children. Very few children from such families go on well for the Lord.

10:28–30 Peter caught the drift of the Savior's teaching. He realized that Jesus was saying, "Forsake all and follow Me." Jesus confirmed this by promising present and eternal reward to those who forsake all for His sake and the gospel's.

1. The present reward is 10,000 per cent return, not in money, but in:
   a. **houses** — homes of other people where he is given accomodations as a servant of the Lord.
   b. **brothers and sisters and mothers and children** — Christian friends whose fellowship enriches all of life.
   c. **lands** — countries of the world which he has claimed for the King.
   d. **persecutions** — these are a part of the present reward. It is a cause of rejoicing when one is found worthy to suffer for Jesus' sake.
2. The future reward is **eternal life**. This does not mean that we earn eternal life through forsaking all. Eternal life is a gift. Here the thought is that those who forsake all are rewarded with a greater capacity for enjoying eternal life in heaven. All believers will have that life but not all will enjoy it to the same extent.

10:31 Then our Lord added a word of warning, **"Many who are first will be last; and the last first."** It isn't enough to start out well on the path of discipleship. It's how we finish that counts. Ironside said:

Not everyone who gave promise of being a faithful and devoted follower would continue in the path of self-denial for Christ's Name's sake, and some who seemed backward and whose devotedness was questionable would prove real and self-effacing in the hour of trial.[19]

J. Third Prediction of the Servant's Passion (10:32–34)

10:32 The time had now come to go **up to Jerusalem**. For the Lord Jesus this meant the sorrow and suffering of Gethsemane, the shame and agony of the cross.

What were His emotions at such a time? Can we not read them in the words **"Jesus was going before them"**? There was determination to do God's will, knowing fully what the cost would be. There was loneliness — He was out ahead of the disciples, walking alone. And there was joy — a deep, settled joy of being in the Father's will, a joyful prospect of coming glory, the joy of redeeming a bride to Himself. For the joy that was set before Him, He endured the cross, despising the shame.

As we gaze upon Him, striding in the vanguard, we too are **amazed**. Our intrepid Leader, the Author and Finisher of our faith, our glorious Master, Prince divine. Erdman writes:

Let us pause to gaze on that face and form, the Son of God, going with unfaltering step toward the Cross! Does it not awaken us to new heroism, as we follow; does it not awaken new love as we see how voluntary was His death for us; yet do we not wonder at the meaning and the mystery of that death?[20]

Those who followed **were afraid**. They knew that the religious leaders in Jerusalem were bent on His death.

10:33, 34 For the third time Jesus gave His disciples a detailed account of coming events. This prophetic outline shows Him to be more than a mere man:

1. **"Behold, we are going up to Jerusalem"** (11:1–13:37).
2. **"The Son of Man will be betrayed to the chief priests and scribes"** (14:1, 2, 43–53).
3. **"They will condemn Him to death"** (14:55–65).
4. **"And deliver Him to the Gentiles"** (15:1).
5. **"They will mock Him, and scourge Him, and spit on Him, and kill Him"** (15:2–38).
6. **"And the third day He will rise again"** (16:1–11).

K. Greatness Is Serving (10:35–45)

10:35–37 Following this poignant prediction of His approaching crucifixion, **James and John came** with a request that was at once noble and ill-timed. It was noble that they wanted to be near Christ, but it was a poor time to be seeking great things for themselves. They exhibited faith that Jesus would set up His kingdom, but they should have been thinking of His impending passion.

10:38, 39 **Jesus** asked them if they were **able to drink** His **cup**, referring to His suffering, and share His **baptism**, referring to His death. They professed to be **able**, and He said they were right. They would suffer because of their loyalty to Him, and James at least would be martyred (Acts 12:2).

10:40 But then He explained that positions of honor in the kingdom were not bestowed arbitrarily. They would be earned. It is good to remember here that *admission* to the kingdom is by grace through faith, but *position* in the kingdom will be determined by faithfulness to Christ.

10:41–44 The other **ten** disciples were **greatly displeased** that **James and John** would try to get ahead of them. But their indignation betrayed the fact that they had the same spirit. This provided the occasion for the Lord Jesus to give a beautiful and revolutionary lesson on greatness. Among the unconverted, great men are those who rule with arbitrary power, who are overbearing and domineering. But greatness in Christ's kingdom is marked by service. **Whoever . . . desires to be first** should become a **slave** to everyone.

10:45 The Supreme Example is **the Son of Man** Himself. **He did not come to be served, but to serve, and to give His life a ransom for many**. Think of it! He came at His miraculous birth. He ministered throughout His life. And in His vicarious death He gave His life.

As mentioned before, verse 45 is the key verse of the entire Gospel. It is a theology in miniature, a vignette of the greatest Life the world has ever known.

L. The Healing of Blind Bartimaeus (10:46–52)

10:46 The scene now shifts from Perea to Judea. The Lord and His disciples had crossed the Jordan and come **to Jericho**. There He met **blind Bartimaeus**, a man with a desperate need, a knowledge of the need, and a determination to have it met.

10:47 Bartimaeus recognized and addressed our Lord as the **Son of David**. It was ironical that while the nation of Israel was blind to the presence of the Messiah, a blind Jew had true spiritual sight!

10:48–52 His persistent pleas for **mercy** did not go unanswered. His specific prayer for sight brought a specific answer. His gratitude was expressed in faithful discipleship, following **Jesus** on His last trip to Jerusalem. It must have cheered the heart of the Lord to find faith like this in Jericho as He moved on toward the cross. It was a good thing that Bartimaeus sought the Lord that day because the Savior never passed that way again.

V. THE SERVANT'S MINISTRY IN JERUSALEM (Chaps. 11, 12)[†]

A. The Triumphal Entry (11:1–11)

11:1–3 The record of the last week begins here. Jesus had paused on the east slope of the **Mount of Olives**, near **Bethphage** (house of unripe figs) and **Bethany** (house of the poor, humble, oppressed).

The time had arrived to present Himself openly to the Jewish people as their Messiah-King. He would do this in fulfillment of the prophecy of Zechariah (9:9), riding on **a colt**. So He sent **two of His disciples** from Bethany into Bethphage. With perfect knowledge and complete authority, He told them to bring an unbroken **colt** which they would find tethered. If anyone challenged them, they were to say, **"The Lord has need of it."** The omniscience of the Lord, as seen here, has prompted someone to say, "This is not the Christ of modernism, but of history and of Heaven."

11:4–6 Everything happened as Jesus had predicted. They **found the colt** tied at a main intersection in the village. When challenged, the disciples replied as Jesus had told them. Then the people **let them go**.

11:7, 8[††] Though the colt had never been ridden before, it did not balk at carrying its Creator into Jerusalem. The Lord rode to the city on a carpet of **clothes** and palm **branches**, with the acclamation of the people ringing in His ears. For a moment, at least, He was acknowledged as King.

11:9, 10 The people cried:

1. **"Hosanna"** — which meant originally "Save, we pray" but which later became an exclamation of

praise. Perhaps the people meant "Save, we pray from our Roman oppressors!"

2. **"Blessed is He who comes in the name of the LORD"** — a clear recognition that Jesus was the promised Messiah (Psalm 118:26).

3. **"Blessed is the kingdom of our father David that comes in the name of the Lord!"** — they thought that **the kingdom** was about to be set up, with Christ sitting on the throne of **David**.

4. **"Hosanna in the highest!"** — a call to *praise* the Lord in the **highest** heavens, or for Him to *save* from the **highest** heavens.

11:11 Once in **Jerusalem**, Jesus went **into the temple** — not inside the sanctuary but into the temple courts. Presumably it was the house of God, but He was not at home in this temple because the priests and people refused to give Him His rightful place. **So when He had looked around** briefly, the Savior withdrew **to Bethany with the twelve** disciples. It was Sunday evening.

B. The Barren Fig Tree (11:12–14)

This incident is the Savior's interpretation of the tumultuous welcome He had just received in Jerusalem. He saw the nation of Israel as a barren **fig tree** — it had leaves of profession but no fruit. The cry of Hosanna would soon turn into the blood-curdling cry, "Crucify Him!"

There is an apparent difficulty in that He condemned the fig tree because it had no fruit, although the record distinctly says that **it was not the season for figs**. This seems to picture the Savior as unreasonable and petulant. We know this is not true; yet how can we explain this curious circumstance?

Fig trees in Bible lands produced an early edible fruit before the leaves appeared. It was a harbinger of the regular crop, here described as the **season for figs**. If no early figs appeared, it was a sign that there would be no regular crop later on. When Jesus came to the nation of Israel, there were leaves, which speak of profession, but there was no fruit for God. There was promise without fulfillment, profession without reality. Jesus was hungry for fruit from the nation. Be-

cause there was no early fruit, He knew that there would be no later fruit from that unbelieving people, and so He cursed the fig tree. This prepictured the judgment which was to fall on Israel in A.D. 70.

However, the incident does *not* teach that Israel was cursed to perpetual barrenness. The Jewish people have been set aside *temporarily*, but when Christ returns to reign, the nation will be reborn and restored to a position of favor with God.

This is the only miracle in which Christ cursed rather than blessed, destroyed life rather than restoring it. This has been raised as a difficulty. However, the objection is not valid. The Creator has the sovereign right to destroy an inanimate object in order to teach an important spiritual lesson and thus save men from eternal doom.

Although the primary interpretation of this passage relates to the nation of Israel, it has application to people of all ages who combine high talk and low walk.

C. The Servant Cleanses the Temple (11:15–19)

11:15, 16 At the outset of His public ministry, Jesus had driven commercialism out of the temple environs (John 2:13–22). Now as His ministry drew to a close, He again entered the court of the **temple** and drove out those who were profiteering from sacred activities. He even stopped the carrying of ordinary **wares through the temple area**.

11:17 Combining quotations from Isaiah and Jeremiah, He condemned desecration, exclusivism, and commercialism. God had intended the temple to be **a house of prayer for all nations** (Isa. 56:7), not just for Israel. They had made it a religious market, a hang-out for shysters and racketeers (Jer. 7:11).

11:18 **The scribes and chief priests** were cut deeply by His accusations. They wanted to **destroy Him**, but could not do it brazenly because the common people still looked on Him with a great deal of awe.

11:19 In the **evening . . . He went out of the city**. The tense of the original verb suggests it was His custom, perhaps for safety's sake. He was not afraid for Himself. We must keep in mind that part of His ministry was to preserve the sheep, that is, His own disciples (John 17:6–19) . Furthermore, it would be ludicrous for Him to surrender to His enemies' wishes before the proper time.

D. The Lesson of the Barren Fig Tree (11:20–26)

11:20–23 On the **morning** following the cursing of the fig tree, the disciples passed it on their way to Jerusalem. It had **withered away** from the roots up. When **Peter** mentioned this to the Lord, He simply said, **"Have faith in God."** But what do these words have to do with the fig tree? The following verses show that Jesus was encouraging faith as the means to remove difficulties. If disciples have **faith in God**, they can deal with the problem of fruitlessness, and remove mountainous obstacles.

However, these verses do not give a person authority to pray for miraculous powers for his own convenience or acclaim. Every act of faith must rest on the promise of God. If we know that it is God's will to remove a certain difficulty, then we can pray with utter confidence that it will be done. In fact, we can pray with confidence on any subject as long as we are confident it is according to God's will as revealed in the Bible or by the inner witness of the Spirit.

11:24 When we are really living in touch with the Lord and praying in the Spirit, we can have the assurance of answered prayer before the answer actually comes.

11:25, 26 But one of the basic requirements for answered prayer is a forgiving spirit. If we nurse a harsh, vindictive attitude toward others, we cannot expect God to hear and answer us. We must **forgive** if we are to be forgiven. This does not refer to the judicial forgiveness of sins at the time of conversion; that is strictly a matter of grace through faith. This refers to God's parental dealings with His children. An unforgiving spirit in a believer breaks fellowship with the **Father in heaven** and hinders the flow of blessing.

E. The Servant's Authority Questioned (11:27–33)

11:27, 28 As soon as He reached the temple area, the religious leaders accosted Jesus and challenged His authority by asking two questions: (1) **"By what authority are You doing these things?"** (2) **"And who gave You this authority to do these things?"** (that is, to cleanse the temple, to curse the fig tree, and to ride triumphantly into Jerusalem). They hoped to trap Him, no matter how He answered. If He claimed to have authority in Himself as the Son of God, they would accuse Him of blasphemy. If He claimed authority from men, they would discredit Him. If He claimed to have received authority from God, they would challenge the claim; they considered themselves the God-appointed religious leaders of the people.

11:29–32 **But Jesus** answered by asking a question. Was John the Baptist divinely commissioned or not? (**The baptism of John** refers to his entire ministry.) They couldn't answer without embarrassment. If John's ministry was divinely appointed, they should have obeyed his call to repent. If they disparaged John's ministry, they would risk the anger of the common people, who still considered **John** a spokesman for God.

11:33 When they refused to answer, professing ignorance, the Lord refused to discuss His authority. As long as they were unwilling to acknowledge the credentials of the forerunner, they would hardly acknowledge the higher credentials of the King Himself!

F. Parable of the Wicked Vinedressers (12:1–12)

12:1 The Lord Jesus was not through with the Jewish authorities, even if He had refused to answer their question. He now delivered, in the form of **parables**, a stinging indictment of them for their rejection of God's Son. The **man** who **planted a vineyard** was God Himself. The **vineyard** was the place of privilege then occupied by Israel. The **hedge** was the Law of Moses, which separated Israel from the Gentiles and preserved them as a distinct people for the Lord. The **vinedressers** were the religious leaders, such as the Pharisees, the scribes and the elders.

12:2–5 Repeatedly, God sent His servants, the prophets, to the people of

Israel, seeking fellowship, holiness, and love. But the people persecuted the prophets and **killed** some of them.

12:6–8 Finally God sent His beloved **Son**. Surely they would **respect** Him. But they didn't. They plotted against Him and finally **killed Him**. Thus the Lord predicted His own death and exposed His guilty murderers.

12:9 What would God **do** with such wicked men? He would **destroy** them and give the place of privilege **to others**. The **others** here may refer to the Gentiles, or to the repentant remnant of Israel in the last days.

12:10, 11 All this was in fulfillment of the OT Scriptures. In Psalm 118:22, 23, for example, it was prophesied that the Messiah would be **rejected** by the Jewish leaders in their building plans. They would have no place for this **Stone**. But following His death, He would be raised from the dead and given the place of preeminence by God. He would be made **the chief cornerstone** in God's building.

12:12 The Jewish leaders got the point. They believed that Psalm 118 spoke of the Messiah. Now they heard the Lord Jesus applying it to Himself. **They sought to lay hands on Him**, but His time had not come. **The multitude** would have taken sides with Jesus. **So** the religious leaders **left Him** for the time being.

G. Rendering to Caesar and to God (12:13–17)

Chapter 12 contains attacks on the Lord by the Pharisees and Herodians and by the Sadducees. It is a chapter of questions. (See vv. 9, 10, 14, 15, 16, 23, 24, 26, 28, 35, 37.)

12:13, 14 The Pharisees and the Herodians, bitter foes, were now brought together by a common hatred of the Savior. They desperately tried to inveigle Him into saying something which they could use as a charge against Him. So they asked Him if it was **lawful to pay taxes** to the Roman government.

No Jews particularly *enjoyed* living under Gentile rule. The Pharisees hated it with a passion, whereas the Herodians adopted a more tolerant view. If Jesus openly endorsed paying tribute to **Caesar**, He would alienate many of the Jews. If He spoke against Caesar, they would

hustle Him to the Roman authorities for arrest and trial as a traitor.

12:15, 16 Jesus asked someone to **bring** Him **a denarius**. (Apparently He Himself did not have one.) The coin bore the image of Tiberius Caesar, a reminder to the Jews that they were a conquered, subject people. Why were they in this condition? Because of their unfaithfulness and sin. They should have been humbled at having to admit that the coins they used bore the image of a Gentile dictator.

12:17 Jesus said to them, **"Render to Caesar the things that are Caesar's and to God the things that are God's."** Their great failure had not been in the first area but in the second. They had paid their Roman taxes, though reluctantly, but had disregarded the claims of God on their lives. The coin had Caesar's image on it, and therefore belonged to Caesar. Man has God's image on him — God created man in His own image (Gen. 1:26, 27) — and therefore belongs to God.

The believer is to obey and support the government under which he lives. He is not to speak evil of his rulers or work to overthrow the government. He is to pay taxes and pray for those in authority. If called on to do anything that would violate his higher loyalty to Christ, he is to refuse and to bear the punishment. The claims of God must come first. In upholding those claims, the Christian should always maintain a good testimony before the world.

H. The Sadducees and Their Resurrection Riddle (12:18–27)

12:18 The **Sadducees** were the liberals or rationalists of that day. They scoffed at the idea of bodily **resurrection**. So they came to the Lord with a preposterous story, trying to ridicule the whole idea.

12:19 They reminded Jesus that the Law of **Moses** made special provision for widows in Israel. In order to preserve the family name and to keep the property in the family, the Law stipulated that if a man died childless, **his brother** should marry the widow (Deut. 25:5–10).

12:20–23 Here was a fantastic case in which a woman married **seven brothers**, one after the other. Then **last of all** she **died**. Now for their clever question!

"**Whose wife will she be** in the resurrection?"

12:24 They thought they were smart; the Savior told them they were abysmally ignorant of both **the Scriptures** which teach resurrection and **the power of God** which raises the dead.

12:25 First they should know that the **marriage** relationship does not continue in heaven. Believers will recognize one another in heaven and will not lose their distinctions as men and women, but they will **neither marry nor** give in **marriage**. In that respect, they will resemble the **angels in heaven**.

12:26, 27 Then our Lord took the Sadducees, who valued the books of Moses above the rest of the OT, back to the account of **Moses** at **the burning bush** (Ex. 3:6). There God spoke of Himself as **the God of Abraham, the God of Isaac, and the God of Jacob**. The Savior used this to show that God was **the God of the living, not** of **the dead**.

But how so? Weren't Abraham, Isaac and Jacob dead when God appeared to Moses? Yes, their bodies were in the Cave of Machpelah in Hebron. How then is God the God of the living?

The argument seems to be this:

1. God had made promises to the patriarchs concerning the land and concerning the Messiah.
2. These promises were not fulfilled during their lifetimes.
3. When God spoke to Moses at the burning bush, the bodies of the patriarchs were in the grave.
4. Yet God spoke of Himself as the God of the living.
5. He must fulfill His promises to Abraham, Isaac, and Jacob.
6. Therefore, resurrection is an absolute necessity from what we know of the character of God.

And so the Lord's parting word to the Sadducees was, **"You are therefore greatly mistaken."**

I. The Great Commandment (12:28–34)

12:28 One of the scribes, impressed by our Lord's adroit handling of His critic's questions, **asked** Jesus **which is** the most important **commandment**. It was an honest question, and, in some ways, life's most basic question. He was really asking for a concise statement of the chief aim of man's existence.

12:29 Jesus began by quoting from the *Shema*, a Jewish statement of faith taken from Deuteronomy 6:4: **"Hear, O Israel: The LORD our God, the LORD is one."**

12:30 Then He summed up man's responsibility to God: **Love** Him with the entirety of one's **heart, soul, mind** and **strength**. God is to have the supreme place in man's life. No other love can be allowed to rival love for God.

12:31 The other half of the Ten Commandments teaches us to **love** our **neighbor as** ourselves. We are to love God *more* than ourselves, and our neighbor *as* ourselves. Thus, the life that really counts is concerned first with God, then with others. Material things are not mentioned. God is important and people are important.

12:32, 33 The scribe agreed heartily, stating with commendable clarity that **love** to God and to **one's neighbor** were far more important than rituals. He realized that people could go through religious ceremonies and put on a public display of piety without inward, personal holiness. He acknowledged that God is concerned with what a man is inwardly as well as outwardly.

12:34 When Jesus heard this remarkable observation, He told the scribe that he was **not far from the kingdom of God**. True subjects of the kingdom do not try to deceive God, their fellow-men, or themselves with external religion. Realizing that God looks on the heart, they go to Him for cleansing from sin and for power to live in a manner pleasing to Him.

After this, **no one dared** to trap the Lord Jesus by asking Him leading questions.

J. David's Son Is David's Lord (12:35–37)

The scribes had always taught that the Messiah would be a lineal descendant **of David**. Though true, this was not the whole truth. So the Lord Jesus now posed a problem to those gathered around Him in the temple court. In Psalm 110:1, David spoke of the coming Messiah as his **Lord**. How could thi[s] How could the Messiah be Davi[d] and his *Lord* at the same time? [The] answer is clear. The Messia[h was] both Man and God. As Davi[d's] would be human. As David's **Lord**, He would be divine.

The common people heard Him gladly. Apparently they were willing to accept the fact, even if they might not have understood it fully. But nothing is said of the Pharisees and scribes. Their silence is ominous.

K. Warning against the Scribes (12:38—40)

12:38, 39 **The scribes** were outwardly religious. They loved to parade **in long robes**. This distinguished them from the common herd and gave them a sanctimonious appearance. They loved to be greeted with high sounding titles in public places. It did something for their ego! They sought the places of honor **in the synagogues**, as if physical location had something to do with godliness. They not only wanted religious prominence, but social distinction as well. They wanted **the best places at feasts**.

12:40 Inwardly they were greedy and insincere. They robbed **widows** of property and livelihood in order to enrich themselves, pretending the money was for the Lord! They recited **long prayers** — great swelling words of vanity — prayers of words alone. In short, they loved *peculiarity* (long robes); *popularity* (greetings); *prominence* (best seats); *priority* (best places); *possessions* (widows' houses); *mock piety* (long prayers).

L. The Widow's Two Mites (12:41—44)

In vivid contrast to the scribes' avarice was this widow's devotion. They devoured widows' houses; she gave **all that she had** to the Lord. The incident shows the omniscience of the Lord. Watching the **rich** people dropping sizable gifts into the chest for the temple **treasury**, He knew that their giving did not represent a sacrifice. They **gave out of their abundance**. Knowing also that the two mites she gave was **her livelihood**, He announced that she gave **more than all** the rest put together. As regards monetary value, she gave very little. But the Lord estimates giving by our motive, our means, and by how much we have left. This is a great encouragement to those who have few material possessions, but a great desire to give to Him.

Amazing how we can approve the widow's action and agree with the Savior's verdict without imitating her example! If we really believed what we say we believe, we would do exactly what she did. Her gift expressed her conviction that all belonged to the Lord, that He was worthy of all, that He must have all. Many Christians today would criticize her for not providing for her future. Did this show a lack of foresight and prudence? So men would argue. But this is the life of faith — plunging all into the work of God now and trusting Him for the future. Did He not promise to provide for those who seek first the kingdom of God and His righteousness (Matt. 6:33)?

Radical? Revolutionary? Unless we see that the teachings of Christ are radical and revolutionary, we have missed the emphasis of His ministry.

VI. THE SERVANT'S OLIVET DISCOURSE (Chap. 13)

A. Jesus Predicts the Destruction of the Temple (13:1, 2)

13:1 As the Lord Jesus was leaving **the temple** area for the last time before His death, **one of His disciples** tried to arouse His enthusiasm concerning the magnificence of the temple and the surrounding architecture. The disciples were occupied with the architectural triumphs involved in erecting the enormous stones.

13:2 The Savior pointed out that these things were soon to be destroyed. **Not one stone** would **be left upon another** when the Roman armies would invade Jerusalem in A.D. 70. Why be occupied with things that are only passing shadows?

B. The Beginning of Sorrows (13:3—8)

In His discourse **on the Mount of Olives**, the Lord diverted the disciples' attention to events of greater importance. Some of the prophecies seem to depict the destruction of Jerusalem, A.D. 70; most of them obviously go beyond that date to the Tribulation Period and to the personal Return of Christ in power and glory. The *watchwords* of the discourse, which apply to believers in every dispensation, are: (1) *take heed* (vv. 5, 23, 33); (2) *do not be troubled* (v. 7); (3) *endure* (v. 13); (4) *pray* (vv. 18, 33); (5) *watch* (vv. 9, 33, 35, 37).

13:3, 4 The discourse was introduced by a question from **Peter, James, John, and Andrew**. **When** would the temple be destroyed, and **what** would **be the sign** preceding the prophesied event? The Lord's answer included the destruction of a later temple, which would take place during the Great Tribulation, prior to His Second Advent.

13:5, 6 First, they were to **take heed that no one** deceived them by claiming to be the Messiah. **Many** false Christs would appear, as seen in the rise of so many cults, each with its own anti-Christ.

13:7, 8 Secondly, they should not interpret **wars and rumors of wars** as a sign of the end times. All through the intervening period there would be international strife. In addition, there would be great cataclysms of nature — **earthquakes, famines, and troubles**. These would be but preliminary birth pangs, ushering in a period of unparalleled travail.

C. Persecution of Disciples (13:9–13)

13:9 Thirdly, the Lord predicted great personal testing for those who would be unflinching in their testimony for Him. They would be put on trial before religious and civil courts.

While this section is applicable to all periods of Christian testimony, it seems to have special reference to the ministry of the 144,000 Jewish believers who will carry the gospel of the kingdom to all nations of the earth prior to Christ's coming to reign.

13:10 Verse 10 should *not* be used to teach that **the gospel must . . . be preached to all the nations** *before the Rapture*. It *should be* proclaimed world-wide and perhaps it *will be*, but to say that it *must be* is to state something the Bible doesn't state. No prophecy needs to be fulfilled before Christ's Coming for His saints; He may come at any moment!

13:11 The Lord promised that persecuted believers on trial for His sake would be given divine help in making their defense. They would not need to prepare their case in advance; perhaps there would not be time. **The Holy Spirit** would give them exactly the right words. This promise should not be used as an excuse for not preparing sermons or gospel messages today, but is a guarantee of supernatural help for crisis times. It is a promise for martyrs, not ministers!

13:12, 13 Another feature of tribulation days will be widespread betrayal of those who are loyal to the Savior. Family members will serve as informers against believers. A great wave of anti-Christian sentiment will sweep the world. It will take courage to remain true to the Lord Jesus, **but he who endures to the end shall be saved**. This cannot mean that they will receive eternal salvation because of their endurance; that would be a false gospel. Neither can it mean that faithful believers will be saved from physical death during the Tribulation, because we read elsewhere that many will seal their testimony with their blood. What it probably means is that endurance to the end will evidence reality, that is, it will *characterize* those who are genuinely *saved*.

D. The Great Tribulation (13:14–23)

13:14–18 Verse 14 marks the middle of the Tribulation Period, the beginning of the *Great* Tribulation. We know this by comparing this passage with **Daniel** 9:27. At that time, a great abominable idol will be set up in the temple in Jerusalem. Men will be compelled to worship it or be slain. True believers will, of course, refuse.

The setting up of this idolatrous image will signal the beginning of great persecution. Those who read and believe the Bible will know that the time has come to flee from **Judea**. There will not be time to gather up personal belongings. **Pregnant** women and **nursing** mothers will be at a distinct disadvantage. If it happens **in winter**, that will add further hazards.

13:19 It will be a time of **tribulation** greater than anything in the past or the future. It is the *Great Tribulation*. The Lord Jesus is not speaking here about the general type of tribulation which believers in every age have encountered. This is a period of trouble unique in its intensity.

Notice that the **tribulation** is primarily Jewish in character. We read of the temple (v. 14, cf. Matt. 24:15) and of Judea (v. 14). It is the time of Jacob's trouble (Jer. 30:7). The church is not in view here. It will have already been taken to heaven before the Day of the Lord begins (1 Thess. 4:13–18; cf. 1 Thess. 5:1–3).

13:20 The bowls of God's wrath will be poured out on the world in those days. It will be a time of calamity, chaos, and bloodshed. In fact, the slaughter will be so great that God will supernaturally shorten the period of daylight; otherwise *no one* would survive.

13:21, 22 The Great Tribulation will again witness the rise of **false** messiahs. People will be so desperate they will turn to anyone who promises them safety. But believers will know that Christ will not appear quietly or unheralded. Even if these **false christs** perform supernatural wonders (as they will), **the elect** will not be deceived. They will realize that these miracles are satanically inspired.

Miracles are not necessarily divine. They represent superhuman departures from the known laws of nature but may represent the work of Satan, angels, or demons. The Man of Sin will be given satanic power to perform miracles (2 Thess. 2:9).

13:23 So believers should **take heed** and be forewarned.

E. The Second Advent (13:24–27)

13:24, 25 **After that tribulation**, there will be startling disturbances in the heavens. Darkness will shroud the earth both by day and by night. **The stars of heaven will fall and the powers in the heavens** (the forces that keep stellar bodies in orbit) **will be shaken**.

13:26, 27 Then the awe-struck world **will see the Son of Man** returning to the earth, not now as the lowly Nazarene but as the glorious Conqueror. He will come **in the clouds**, escorted by myriads of angelic beings and of glorified saints. It will be a scene of overwhelming power and dazzling splendor. He will dispatch His angels to **gather together His elect**, that is, all who have acknowledged Him as Lord and Savior during the Tribulation Period. From one

end of the earth to the other — from China to Colombia — they will come to enjoy the benefits of His wonderful thousand-year reign on earth. His enemies, however, will be destroyed at the same time.

F. Parable of the Fig Tree (13:28–31)

13:28 **The fig tree** is a symbol (or type) of the nation of Israel. Jesus taught here that prior to His Second Advent, the fig tree would put **forth leaves**. In 1948, the independent nation of Israel was formed. Today that nation exerts an influence in world affairs that is out of all proportion to its size. Israel can be said to be "putting forth its leaves." There is no fruit as yet; in fact, there will be no fruit until the Messiah returns to a people who are willing to receive Him.

13:29 The formation and growth of the nation of Israel tell us that the King[21] **is near — at the doors**. If His coming to reign is that near, how much nearer is His coming for the church!

13:30 Verse 30 is often understood to mean that all the things prophesied in this chapter would take place while the men of Christ's day were still living. But it cannot mean that because many of the events, especially verses 24-27, simply did not take place at that time. Others understand it to mean that the **generation** living when the fig tree put forth its leaves, that is, when the nation of Israel was formed in 1948, would be the generation that would see the Second Advent. We prefer a third view. **This generation** may mean "this race." We believe it means "this Jewish race characterized by unbelief and rejection of the Messiah." The testimony of history is that "this generation" has *not* passed away. The nation as a whole has not only survived as a distinct people, but has continued in its deep-seated animosity toward the Lord Jesus. Jesus predicted that the nation and its national characteristic would continue until His Second Advent.

13:31 Our Lord emphasized the absolute certainty of every one of His predictions. The atmospheric **heaven** and the stellar **heaven will pass away. The earth** itself will be dissolved. But every word He spoke will come to pass.

G. The Day and Hour Unknown (13:32–37)

13:32 Jesus said, **"But of that day and hour no one knows, not even the angels in heaven, nor the Son, but only the Father."** It is well known that this verse has been used by enemies of the gospel to prove that Jesus was nothing more than a man with limited knowledge like ourselves. It has also been used by sincere but misguided believers to demonstrate that Jesus emptied Himself of the attributes of deity when He came into the world as a man.

Neither of these interpretations is true. Jesus was and is both God and Man. He had all the attributes of deity and all the characteristics of perfect manhood. It is true that His deity was veiled in a body of flesh, but it was there nonetheless. There was never a time when He was not fully God.

How then can it be said of Him that He does not know the time of His Second Advent? We believe the key to the answer is found in John 15:15: " . . . a servant does not know what his master is doing. . . ." As a perfect Servant, it was not given to the Lord Jesus to know the time of His Coming. As God, of course, He does know it. But as Servant, it was not given to Him to know it for the purpose of revealing to others. James H. Brookes explains it thus:

> It is not a denial of our Lord's divine omniscience, but simply an assertion that in the economy of human redemption, it was not for Him "to know the times or seasons, which the Father hath appointed by His own authority," Acts 1:7. Jesus knew that He will come again, and often spoke of His second advent, but it did not fall to His office as Son to determine the date of His return, and hence He could hold it up before His followers as the object of constant expectation and desire.[22]

13:33–37 The chapter closes with an exhortation to watchfulness and prayer in view of the Lord's Return. The fact that we **do not know** the appointed time should keep us on the alert.

A similar situation is common in everyday life. A man goes away from home on a long trip. He leaves instructions with his servant and tells the watchman also to be on the lookout for his return. Jesus likened Himself to the traveling man. He may come back at any hour of the night. His people, serving as night watchmen, should not be found **sleeping**. So He left this word for all His people: **"Watch!"**

VII. THE SERVANT'S PASSION AND DEATH (Chaps. 14, 15)

A. The Plot to Kill Jesus (14:1, 2)

It was now Wednesday of that fateful week. In **two days** it would be **Passover**, ushering in the seven day **Feast of Unleavened Bread**. The religious leaders were determined to destroy the Lord Jesus, but didn't want to do it during the religious holidays because many of the people still considered Jesus a prophet.

Though **the chief priests and the scribes** determined **not** to kill Him **during the feast**, divine Providence overruled them, and the Paschal Lamb of God was killed at that very time (see Matt. 26:2).

B. Jesus Anointed at Bethany (14:3–9)

As a jeweler places a diamond against black velvet, the Holy Spirit and His human writer Mark skillfully highlight the radiance of a woman's love for our Lord between the dark plotting of the religious hierarchy and that of Judas.

14:3 **Simon the leper** held a feast in honor of the Savior, perhaps in gratitude for being healed. An unnamed woman (probably Mary of Bethany, John 12:3) lavishly anointed Jesus' **head** with some **very costly** perfume. Her love for Him was great.

14:4, 5 **Some** of the guests thought this was a tremendous waste. She was reckless, prodigal. Why hadn't she **sold** the perfume and **given** the money **to the poor**? (**Three hundred denarii** was the equivalent of a year's wages.) People still think it a waste to give a year of one's life to the Lord. How much more a waste would they consider it to give one's whole life to the Lord!

14:6–8 **Jesus** rebuked their murmuring. She had recognized her golden opportunity to pay this tribute to the Savior. If they were so solicitous for the poor, they would always be able to help them, because **the poor** are **always** present. But the Lord would soon die and be buried. This woman wanted to show this kindness while she could. She might not be able to care for His **body** in death, so she would show her love while He was still alive.

14:9 The fragrance of that perfume reaches down to our generation. Jesus said that she would be memorialized worldwide. She has been — through the Gospel records.

C. The Treachery of Judas (14:10, 11)

The woman prized the Savior highly. **Judas**, by contrast, valued Him very lightly. Though he had lived with the Lord Jesus for at least a year, and had received nothing but kindness from Him, Judas now sneaked off to the chief priests with a guarantee **to betray** the Son of God into their hands. They seized the offer gladly, offering to pay him for his treachery. All he had to do now was work out the details.

D. Preparations for the Passover (14:12–16)

Although the exact chronology is not certain, we have probably now come to Thursday of Passover Week. The disciples little realized that this would be the fulfillment and climax of all the Passovers that had ever been held. They asked the Lord for directions as to where to hold **the Passover. He sent** them to Jerusalem with instructions to look for a **man . . . carrying a pitcher of water** — a rarity since women usually carried waterpots. This man would lead them to the proper house. They would then ask the owner to show them to a room where **the Teacher** could **eat the Passover with** His **disciples**.

It is wonderful to see the Lord choosing and commanding in this way. He acts as the Sovereign Ruler of men and property. It is also wonderful to see responsive hearts putting themselves and their possessions at His disposal. It is good for us when He has instant, ready access to every room in our lives!

E. Jesus Predicts His Betrayal (14:17–21)

That same **evening He came with the twelve** to the upper room which had been prepared. As they reclined **and ate, Jesus** announced that **one of** the disciples would **betray** Him. They all recognized the evil propensities of their own natures. With a healthy distrust of self, each asked if he were the culprit. Jesus then disclosed the traitor as the one who dipped the bread with Him in the meat-juice, that is, the one to whom He gave the piece of bread. **The Son of Man** was going forward to His death as predicted, He said, but the doom of His betrayer would be great. In fact, **it would have been good . . . if he had never been born.**

F. The First Lord's Supper (14:22–26)

14:22–25 After taking **the bread**, Judas went out into the night (John 13:30). Jesus then instituted what we know as the Lord's Supper. Its meaning is beautifully outlined in the three words: (1) He **took** — humanity upon Himself; (2) He **broke** — He was about to be broken on the cross; (3) He **gave** — He gave Himself for us.

The bread signified His **body** given, **the cup** His **blood** shed. By His **blood** He ratified **the New Covenant**. For Him there would be no more festive joy until He returned to earth to set up His **kingdom**.

14:26 At that point, they sang **a hymn** — probably a portion of the Great Hallel — Psalms 113–118. Then **they went out** from Jerusalem, across the Kidron, **to the Mount of Olives**.

G. Peter's Self-Confidence (14:27–31)

14:27, 28 On the way, the Savior warned the disciples that they would **all** be ashamed and afraid to be known as His followers in the hours ahead. It would be as Zechariah had predicted; **the Shepherd** would be struck and His **sheep** would **be scattered** (Zech. 13:7). But He graciously assured them that He would not disown them; after rising from the dead, He would be waiting for them in **Galilee**.

14:29, 30 **Peter** was indignant at the thought of denying the Lord. The others might, but he? — Never! Jesus corrected that "Never!" to "Soon." **Before the rooster** crowed **twice**, Peter would have disowned the Savior **three times**.

14:31 "It's preposterous," shouted Peter, "I'll die before I **deny You!**" Peter wasn't the only one to make that noisy boast. **They all** engaged in brash, self-confident assertions. Let us never forget that, for we are no different. We must all learn the cowardice and weakness of our hearts.

H. The Agony in Gethsemane (14:32–42)

14:32 Darkness had settled over the land. It was Thursday night running into Friday morning. When **they came to** an enclosed piece of ground **named Gethsemane**, the Lord Jesus left eight of the disciples near the entrance.

14:33, 34 He took Peter, James, and John with Him deeper into the garden. There He experienced an overpowering burden on His holy soul as He anticipated becoming a sin-offering for us. We cannot conceive what it meant to Him, the Sinless One, to be made sin for us. He left the three disciples with instructions to **stay** there and stay awake. **He went a little farther** into the garden — alone. Thus would He go to the cross alone, bearing the awful judgment of God against our sins.

14:35 With wonder and amazement, we see the Lord Jesus prostrate on the ground, praying to God. Was He asking to be excused from going to the cross? Not at all; this was the purpose of His coming into the world. First, **He prayed that if it were possible, the hour might pass from Him**. If there was any other way by which sinners could be saved than by His death, burial, and resurrection, let God reveal that way. The heavens were silent. There was no other way in which we could be redeemed.

14:36 Again, He prayed, **"Abba, Father, all things are possible for You. Take this cup away from Me; nevertheless, not what I will, but what You will."** Notice that He addressed God as His beloved **Father** with whom **all things are possible**. Here it was not so much a matter of physical possibility as of moral. Could the Almighty Father find any other righteous basis upon which He could save ungodly sinners? The silent heavens indicated that there was no other way. The Holy Son of God must bleed that sinners might be freed from sin!

14:37–40 Returning to the three disciples, He **found them sleeping** — a sad commentary on fallen human nature. Jesus warned Peter against **sleeping** in that crucial **hour**. Only recently, Peter had boasted of his undying steadfast-

ness. Now he couldn't even stay awake. If a man cannot pray for **one hour**, it is unlikely that he will be able to resist temptation in the moment of extreme pressure. No matter how enthusiastic his spirit may be, he must reckon with the frailty of his flesh.

14:41, 42 Three times the Lord Jesus returned to find the disciples asleep. Then He said, **"Are you still sleeping and resting? It is enough! The hour has come; behold, the Son of Man is being betrayed into the hands of sinners."** With that, they got up as if to go forth. But they didn't have to go far.

I. Jesus Betrayed and Arrested (14:43–52)

14:43 Judas had already entered the garden with a posse. His cohorts were carrying **swords and clubs**, as if they were going to capture a dangerous felon.

14:44, 45 The **betrayer** had a prearranged signal. He would **kiss** the One whom they should **seize**. So he strode up to Jesus, addressed Him as **Rabbi, and kissed Him** effusively. (The emphatic form in the original suggests repeated or demonstrative kissing.) Why did Judas betray the Lord? Was he disappointed that Jesus had not seized the reins of government? Were his hopes dashed for a place of prominence in the kingdom? Was he overcome by greed? All of these might have contributed to his infamous deed.

14:46–50 The armed henchmen of the betrayer stepped forward and arrested the Lord. Peter quickly **drew his sword** and sliced **off** the **ear** of **the servant of the high priest**. It was a natural reaction, not a spiritual one. Peter was using carnal weapons to fight a spiritual warfare. The Lord rebuked Peter and miraculously restored the ear, as we read in Luke 22:51 and John 18:11. Jesus then reminded His captors how incongruous it was for them to take Him by force! He had been **daily with** them **in the temple teaching**. Why hadn't they seized Him then? He knew the answer. **The Scriptures must be fulfilled** which prophesied that He would be betrayed (Ps. 41:9), arrested (Isa. 53:7), manhandled (Ps. 22:12) and forsaken (Zech. 13:7).

14:51, 52 Mark is the only evangelist who records this incident. It is widely believed that Mark himself was the **young man** who, in his frenzy to escape, left his covering in the grasp of the armed men. The **linen cloth** was not a regular garment but a piece of **cloth** which he had picked up quickly for an improvised covering.

Erdman comments: "Probably this picturesque incident is added to show how completely Jesus was forsaken in the hours of His peril and pain. He surely knew what it was to suffer alone."

J. Jesus Before the High Priest (14:53, 54)†

The record of the ecclesiastical trial extends from verse 53 to 15:1 and is divided into three parts: (1) Trial before the high priest (vv. 53, 54); (2) Midnight meeting of the Sanhedrin (vv. 55–65); (3) Meeting of the Sanhedrin in the morning (15:1).

14:53 It is generally agreed that Mark here records the trial before Caiaphas. The trial before Annas is found in John 18:13, 19–24.

14:54 **Peter** trailed the Lord Jesus to the **courtyard of the high priest**, following at what he thought would be a safe distance. Someone has outlined his downfall as follows:

1. He first fought — misdirected enthusiasm.
2. He then fled — cowardly withdrawal.
3. Finally he followed afar off — half-hearted discipleship by night.

He sat by **the fire** with the officers, warming **himself** with the enemies of his Lord.

K. Jesus Before the Sanhedrin (14:55–65)

14:55–59†† Although it is not specifically stated, v. 55 seems to begin the account of a midnight meeting of the Sanhedrin. The body of seventy-one religious leaders was presided over by the high priest. On this particular night, the Pharisees, Sadducees, scribes and elders who comprised the Sanhedrin showed an utter disregard for the rules under which they operated. They were not supposed to meet at night or during any of the Jewish feasts. They were not supposed to bribe witnesses to commit per-

jury. A death verdict was not to be carried out until a night had elapsed. Unless they met in the Hall of Hewn Stone, in the temple area, their verdicts were not binding.

In their eagerness to do away with the Lord Jesus, the religious authorities did not hesitate to stoop to breaking their own laws. Their determined efforts produced a group of **false** witnesses but they failed to produce united testimony. Some misquoted the Lord as threatening to **destroy** the temple **made with hands, and within three days**, to rebuild **another, made without hands**. What Jesus actually said is found in John 2:19. They purposely confused the temple in Jerusalem with the temple of His body.

14:60–62 When **the high priest** first questioned Him, Jesus did not reply. But when asked under oath (Matt. 26:63) whether He was the Messiah, **the Son of the Blessed**, the Savior replied that He was, thus acting in obedience to Leviticus 5:1. Then, as if to remove any doubt as to who He claimed to be, the Lord Jesus told the high priest that he would yet **see the Son of Man sitting at the right hand of the Power, and coming** back to earth **with the clouds of heaven**. By this He meant that the high priest would yet see Him openly manifested as God. During His First Advent, the glory of His deity was veiled in a human body. But when He comes again in power and great glory, the veil will be removed and everyone will know exactly who He is.

14:63, 64 **The high priest** understood what Jesus meant. He **tore his clothes** as a sign of his righteous indignation against this supposed **blasphemy**. The one Israelite who should have been most ready to recognize and receive the Messiah was loudest in his condemnation. But not he alone; the entire Sanhedrin[23] agreed that Jesus had blasphemed, and **condemned Him to be deserving of death**.

14:65 The scene that followed was grotesque in the extreme. Some members of the Sanhedrin **began to spit on** the Son of God, **to blindfold Him**, and to challenge Him to name His assailants. It is almost incredible that the worthy Savior should have to endure such contradiction of sinners against Himself. **The officers** (temple police) joined in the scandal by hitting **Him with the palms of their hands**.

L. Peter Denies Jesus and Weeps Bitterly (14:66–72)

14:66–68 **Peter was** waiting **below in the courtyard** of the building. **One of the servant girls of the high priest** passed by. She peered intently at him, then charged him with being a follower of the Nazarene, **Jesus**. The pathetic disciple pretended complete ignorance of her charge, then moved to the porch in time to hear **a rooster** crow. It was a ghastly moment. Sin was taking its terrible toll.

14:69, 70 The **girl saw him again** and pointed him out as a disciple of Jesus. Peter made another cold denial, and probably wondered why people didn't leave him alone. Then the crowd said to Peter, **"Surely you are one of them; for you are a Galilean, and your speech shows it."**

14:71, 72 Cursing and swearing, Peter defiantly stated that he did **not know this Man**. No sooner were the words out of his mouth than the **rooster crowed**. The world of nature seemed thus to protest the cowardly lie. In a flash Peter realized that the Lord's prediction had come to pass. **He broke down and wept**. It is significant that all four Gospels record Peter's denials. We must all learn the lesson that self confidence leads to humiliation. We must learn to distrust self and to lean completely on the power of God.

M. Morning Trial Before the Sanhedrin (15:1)

This verse describes a **morning** meeting of the Sanhedrin, perhaps convened to validate the illegal action of the night before. As a result, Jesus was **bound** and taken **to Pilate**, the Roman Governor of Palestine.

N. Jesus Before Pilate (15:2–5)

15:2 Up to now, Jesus had been on trial before the religious leaders on a charge of *blasphemy*. Now He was taken before the civil court on a charge of *treason*. The civil trial took place in three stages — first before Pilate, then before Herod, and finally before Pilate again.

Pilate asked the Lord Jesus if He were **the King of the Jews**. If He were, He was presumably dedicated to the overthrow of Caesar, and thus guilty of treason.

15:3–5† **The chief priests** poured out a torrent of charges against Jesus. Pilate couldn't get over His poise in the face of such overwhelming accusations. He asked Him why He didn't defend Himself, **but Jesus** refused to answer His critics.

O. Jesus or Barabbas? (15:6–15)

15:6–8 It was the custom for the Roman Governor to release **one** Jewish **prisoner** at this feast time — sort of a political sop to the unhappy people. One such eligible prisoner was **Barabbas**, guilty of **rebellion** and **murder**. When Pilate offered to **release** Jesus, taunting the envious chief priests, the people were primed to ask for Barabbas. The very ones who were charging Jesus with treason against Caesar were asking the release of a man who was *actually* guilty of that crime! The position of the chief priests was irrational and ludicrous — but sin is like that. Basically they were jealous of His popularity.

15:9–14 Pilate asked what he should do with the One whom they called **the King of the Jews**. The people chanted savagely, **"Crucify Him!"** Pilate demanded a reason, but there was none. Mob hysteria was rising. All they would shout was, **"Crucify Him!"**

15:15 And so the spineless **Pilate** did what they wanted — **he released Barabbas**, flogged Jesus and **delivered** Him over to the soldiers for crucifixion. It was a monstrous verdict of unrighteousness. And yet it was a parable of our redemption — the guiltless One delivered to die in order that the guilty might go free.

P. The Soldiers Mock God's Servant (15:16–21)

15:16–19 **The soldiers led** Jesus **away into the hall** of the Governor's residence. After assembling **the whole garrison**, they staged a mock coronation for the King of the Jews. If they had only known! It was God the Son they **clothed with purple**. It was their own Creator they crowned with **thorns**. It was the Sustainer of the universe they mocked as

†*See p. xxi.*

King of the Jews. It was the Lord of life and glory they **struck on the head**. They **spat on** the Prince of peace. They mockingly bowed their knees to the King of kings and Lord of lords.

15:20, 21 When their crude jests were over, **they put His own clothes back on Him, and led Him out to crucify Him**. Mark mentions here that the soldiers ordered a passerby, **Simon** of Cyrene (in North Africa), to carry **His cross**. He may have been black but was more probably a Hellenistic Jew. He had two sons, **Alexander and Rufus**, who were probably believers (if **Rufus** is the same one mentioned in Rom. 16:13). In bearing the cross after Jesus, he gave us a picture of what should characterize *us* as disciples of the Savior.

Q. The Crucifixion (15:22–32)

The Spirit of God describes the crucifixion simply and unemotionally. He does not dwell on the extreme cruelty of this mode of execution, or the terrible suffering it entailed.

The exact location is unknown today. Though the traditional site, at the Church of the Holy Sepulcher, is inside the walls of the city, its advocates contend that it was outside the walls at the time of Christ. Another supposed site is Gordon's Calvary, north of the city walls and adjoining a garden area.

15:22 Golgotha is the Aramaic name meaning **skull**. Calvary is the Latin name. Perhaps the area was shaped like a skull or received the name because it was a place of execution.

15:23 The soldiers offered Jesus **wine mingled with myrrh**. This would have acted as a drug, dulling His senses. Determined to bear man's sins in His full consciousness, **He** would **not take it**.

15:24 The soldiers gambled for the clothes of those who were crucified. When they took the Savior's **garments**, they took just about everything material that He owned.

15:25–28† It was 9:00 a.m. when they **crucified Him**. Over His head they had put the title **THE KING OF THE JEWS**. (Mark does not give the full inscription but contents himself with the substance of it; see Matt. 27:37; Luke 23:38; John 19:19.) **Two robbers** were crucified with Him, **one** on each side — just as Isaiah had predicted that He

would be associated with criminals in His death (Isa. 53:12).[24]

15:29, 30 The Lord Jesus was mocked by the passers-by (vv. 29, 30), the **chief priests** and **scribes** (vv. 31, 32a), and the two robbers (v. 32b).

The passers-by were probably Jews who were ready to keep the Passover inside the city. Outside they paused long enough to hurl an insult at the Paschal Lamb. They misquoted Him as threatening to **destroy** their beloved **temple** and to rebuild it **in three days**. If He was so great, let Him **save** Himself by coming **down from the cross**.

15:31 The **chief priests** and **the scribes** scorned His claim to save **others**. **"He saved others; Himself He cannot save."** It was viciously cruel, yet unintentionally true. It was true in the Lord's life and in ours, too. We can't save *others* while seeking to save *ourselves*.

15:32 The religious leaders also challenged Him to come down **from the cross** if He were the Messiah, **the King of Israel**. Then they would **believe**, they said. Let us **see** and we will **believe**.[25] But God's order is, "Believe and then you will see."

Even the criminals reproached Him!

R. Three Hours of Darkness (15:33–41)

15:33 Between noon and three o'clock **the whole land** was shrouded in **darkness**. Jesus was then bearing the full judgment of God against our sins. He suffered spiritual desolation and separation from God. No mortal mind can ever understand the agony He endured when His soul was made a sacrifice for sin.

15:34 At the close of His agony, Jesus **cried out with a loud voice** (in Aramaic), **"My God, My God, why have You forsaken Me?"** God had **forsaken** Him because in His holiness He must dissociate Himself from sin. The Lord Jesus had identified Himself with our sins and was paying the penalty in full.

15:35, 36 Some of the cruel mob suggested He was **calling for Elijah** when He said, "Eloi, Eloi." As a final indignity, one of them soaked a **sponge** in **sour wine** and **offered it to Him** on the end of **a reed**.

15:37 Jesus **cried out** with strength and triumph — then **breathed His last**. His death was an act of His will, not an involuntary collapse.

†*See p. xxii.*

15:38 At that moment, **the veil of the temple was torn in two from top to bottom**. This was an act of God indicating that by Christ's death, access into the sanctuary of God was henceforth the privilege of all believers (see Heb. 10:19–22). A great new era had been ushered in. It would be an era of nearness to God, not of distance from Him.

15:39 The Roman officer's confession, while noble, did not necessarily acknowledge Jesus as equal with God. **The Gentile centurion** recognized Him as **the Son of God**. No doubt he had a sense of history being made. But whether his faith was genuine is not clear.

15:40, 41 Mark mentions that certain **women** remained at the cross. It deserves mention that the women shine brightly in the Gospel narratives. Considerations of personal safety drove the men into hiding. The devotion of the women put love to Christ above their own welfare. They were last at the cross and first at the tomb.

S. The Burial in Joseph's Tomb (15:42–47)[†]

15:42 The Sabbath began at sunset on Friday. **The day before the Sabbath** or other festival was known as **the Preparation**.[26]

15:43 The necessity for prompt action probably emboldened **Joseph of Arimathea** to ask Pilate for permission to bury **the body of Jesus**. Joseph was a devout Jew, perhaps a member of the Sanhedrin (Luke 23:50, 51; see also Matt. 27:57; John 19:38).

15:44, 45 Pilate could hardly believe that Jesus **was already dead**. When **the centurion** confirmed the fact, the Governor **granted the body to Joseph**. (Two different words are used for the body of Jesus in this section. Joseph asked for the *body* of the Lord Jesus and Pilate granted the *corpse* to him.)

15:46 With loving care, Joseph (and Nicodemus — John 19:38, 39) embalmed the body, **wrapped Him in the linen**, then put Him **in a** new **tomb** belonging to himself. The tomb was a small room carved **out of the rock**. The door was sealed with a coin-shaped stone which could be rolled into a groove carved out of stone.

15:47 Again the women, that is, the two Marys, are mentioned as being pres-

ent. We admire them for their unflagging and fearless affection. We are told that the preponderance of missionaries today are women. Where are the men?

VIII. THE SERVANT'S TRIUMPH (16:1–20)[††]

A. The Women at the Empty Tomb (16:1–8)

16:1–4 On Saturday evening the two Marys **and Salome** came to the tomb to embalm the body of Jesus with spices. They knew it would not be easy. They knew a huge **stone** had been rolled across the mouth of the tomb. They knew about the Roman seal and the guard of soldiers. But love leaps over mountains of difficulties to reach the object of its affection.

Very early on Sunday morning, they were wondering out loud **who** would **roll away the stone from the door of the tomb. They looked up** and saw that it was already done! How often it happens when we are intent on honoring the Savior that difficulties are removed before we get to them.

16:5, 6[†††] **Entering the tomb, they saw an angel with the appearance of a young man in white.** He quickly dispelled their fears with the announcement that Jesus had **risen**. The tomb was empty.

16:7 The angel then commissioned them as heralds of the resurrection. They were to **tell His disciples — and Peter** — that Jesus would meet them in **Galilee**. Notice that **Peter**, the disciple who had denied His Lord, was singled out for special mention. The risen Redeemer had not disowned him but still loved him and longed to see him again. A special work of restoration needed to be done. The wandering sheep must be brought back into fellowship with the Shepherd. The backslider must return to the Father's house.

16:8 The women **fled from the tomb** with mingled shock and panic. They were too afraid to tell anyone what had happened. This is not surprising. The wonder is that they had been so brave and loyal and devoted up to now.

Because two major ancient manuscripts of Mark lack verses 9–20, many modern scholars believe they are not authentic. However, there are strong arguments for their inclusion in the text:

1. Virtually all other Greek manuscripts and many church fathers *do* contain this passage.
2. Verse 8 is a most strange conclusion, especially in the Greek where the last word is (*gar*, for). This word is scarcely ever near the end of a sentence, much less of a book.
3. If, as some teach, Mark's original ending is *lost*, and this is a later summary, then our Lord's words about preservation (Matt. 24:35) apparently have failed.
4. The contents of the passage *are* orthodox.
5. The style, and especially the vocabulary, closely parallel the first chapter of the book.[27] This would illustrate the structure called *chiasm*, in which the beginning and the end of a work are parallel (abcd dcba).

B. The Appearance to Mary Magdalene (16:9–11)

16:9 The Savior's first appearance was **to Mary Magdalene**. The first time she had met Jesus, He had **cast seven demons** out of her. From then on she served Him lovingly with her possessions. She witnessed the crucifixion, and saw where His body was laid.

From the other Gospels we learn that after finding the tomb empty, she ran and told Peter and John. Coming back with her they found the sepulcher empty, as she had told them. They returned to their home but she stayed at the empty tomb. It was then that Jesus appeared to her.

16:10, 11 Again **she went** back to the city to share the good news with the sorrowing disciples. For them it was *too* good to be true. **They did not believe** it.

C. The Appearance to Two Disciples (16:12, 13)

16:12 The full account of this appearance is found in Luke 24:13–31. Here we read that **He appeared in another form to two** disciples on the road to Emmaus. To Mary He had appeared as a gardener. Now He seemed like a fellow-traveler. But it was the same Jesus in His glorified body.

16:13 When the two disciples returned to Jerusalem and reported their fellowship with the risen Savior, they met the same disbelief that Mary had encountered.

D. The Appearance to the Eleven (16:14–18)

16:14 This appearance **to the eleven** took place that same Sunday evening (Luke 24:36; John 20:19–24; 1 Cor. 15:5). Although the disciples are referred to as **the eleven**, only ten were present. Thomas was absent on this occasion. Jesus rebuked His own for their refusal to accept the reports of His resurrection from Mary and the others.

16:15 Verse 15 records the commission that was given by the Lord on the eve of His Ascension. There is thus an interval between verses 14 and 15. The disciples were commanded to **preach the gospel to** the whole creation. The Savior's goal was world evangelization. He purposed to accomplish it with eleven disciples who would literally forsake all to follow Him.

16:16 There would be two results of the preaching. Some would believe, be **baptized** and **be saved**; some would disbelieve and **be condemned**.

Verse 16 is used by some to teach the necessity of water baptism for salvation. We know it cannot mean that for the following reasons:

1. The thief on the cross was not baptized; yet he was assured of being in Paradise with Christ (Luke 23:43).
2. The Gentiles in Caesarea were baptized *after* they were saved (Acts 10:44–48).
3. Jesus Himself did not baptize (John 4:1, 2) — a strange omission if baptism were necessary for salvation.
4. Paul thanked God that he baptized very few of the Corinthians (1 Cor. 1:14–16) — an impossible thanksgiving if baptism were essential for salvation.
5. Approximately 150 passages in the NT state that salvation is by faith alone. No verse or few verses could contradict this overwhelming testimony.
6. Baptism is connected with death and burial in the NT, not with spiritual birth.

What then *does* verse 16 mean? We

believe it mentions baptism as the expected outward expression of belief. Baptism is not *a condition* of salvation, but an outward *proclamation* that the person has been saved.

16:17, 18 Jesus here describes certain miracles that would accompany those who believe the gospel. As we read the verses, the obvious question is, "Do these signs exist today?" We believe that **these signs** were intended primarily for the apostolic age, before the complete Bible was available in written form. Most of these signs are found in the Book of Acts:

1. **Cast out demons** (Acts 8:7; 16:18; 19:11–16).
2. **New tongues** (Acts 2:4–11; 10:46; 19:6).
3. Handle **serpents** (Acts 28:5).
4. **Drink** poison without harmful effects — not recorded in Acts but attributed to John and Barnabas by the church historian Eusebius.
5. **Lay hands on the sick** for healing (Acts 3:7; 19:11; 28:8, 9).

What was the purpose of these miracles? We believe the answer is found in Hebrews 2:3, 4. Before the NT was available in completed form, men would ask the apostles and others for proof that the gospel was divine. To confirm the preaching, God bore witness with signs and wonders and various gifts of the Holy Spirit.

The need for these signs is gone today. We have the complete Bible. If men won't believe that, they wouldn't believe anyway. Mark *did not say* that the miracles would continue. The words "to the end of the age" *are not found here* as they are in Matthew 28:18–20.

However, Martin Luther suggested that "the signs here spoken of are to be used according to need. When the need arises, and the Gospel is hard pressed, then we must definitely do these signs, before we allow the Gospel to be maligned and knocked down."

E. The Servant's Ascension to God's Right Hand (16:19, 20)

16:19[†] Forty days after His resurrection, our **Lord** Jesus Christ **was received up into heaven, and sat down at the right hand of God**. This is the place of honor and of power.

†See p. xxiii.

16:20 In obedience to His command, the disciples **went** forth like flaming fires, preaching the gospel and winning men to the Savior. The power of **the Lord** was **with them**. The promised **signs** accompanied their preaching, **confirming the word** they spoke.

Here the narrative ends — with Christ in heaven, with a few committed disciples on earth burdened for world evangelization and giving themselves entirely to it, and with results of eternal consequences.

We are entrusted with the Great Commission in our generation. Our task is to reach every person with the gospel. One-third of all the people who have ever lived are living today. By the year 2000, one-half of all the people who have ever lived will be living then. As the population explodes, the task increases. But the method is always the same — devoted disciples with unlimited love for Christ who count no sacrifice too great for Him.

The will of God is the evangelization of the world. What are we doing about it?

ENDNOTES

[1](1:2, 3) The critical (NU) text reads "Isaiah the prophet," but the first quote is from Malachi; the traditional reading, "the Prophets," supported by a majority of the mss., is more accurate.

[2](1:14, 15) The NU text omits "of the kingdom."

[3](1:31) J. R. Miller, *Come Ye Apart*, Reading for March 28.

[4](3:13–18) James E. Stewart, *The Life and Teaching of Jesus Christ*, pp. 55, 56.

[5](3:20, 21) Miller, *Come*, Reading for June 6.

[6](3:31–35) Both NU (oldest) and M (majority) of mss. add "and Your sisters." This is no doubt the correct reading.

[7](4:30–32) Vance Havner, further documentation unavailable.

[8](5:1–5) The NU text reads Gerasenes.

[9](6:4–6) J. G. Miller, further documentation unavailable.

[10](6:31, 32) William Kelly, *An Exposition of the Gospel of Mark*, p.85.

[11](7:2–4) E. Stanley Jones, *Growing Spiritually*, p. 109.

[12](7:11–13) Kelly, *Mark*, p. 105.

[13](8:1–9) Charles R. Erdman, *The Gospel of Mark*, p. 116.

[14](8:22–26) It is possible that the man *did* receive perfect sight in the same way that a baby born with perfect eyes still *has to learn to focus them.*

[15](8:32, 33) Kelly, *Mark*, p. 136.

[16](9:44–48) Three times (vv. 44, 46 and 48) our Lord quotes Isaiah 66:24 to warn of the dangers of hell. This emphatic parallelism of form (found in TR and majority text) is softened, we believe, by the critical (NU) text, which omits the text twice.

[17](9:49) NU text omits this clause.

[18](10:23–25) NU omits "for those who trust in riches," but this is the main emphasis of the passage.

[19](10:31) Harry A. Ironside, *Expository Notes on the Gospel of Mark*, p. 157.

[20](10:32) Erdman, *Mark*, p. 147.

[21](13:29) The subject here in Greek is merely the ending of the verb "is" (*estin*), which in context could be "He" (Christ) or "it" (summer — the events predicted). The resultant meanings are similar.

[22](13:32) James H. Brookes, *"I Am Coming,"* p. 40.

[23](14:63, 64) Joseph of Arimathea and Nicodemus are believed to have been absent from this illegal meeting.

[24](15:25–28) The critical (NU) text omits this quotation in Mark.

[25](15:32) The majority of mss. add "Him," personalizing the leaders' (probably false) promise.

[26](15:42) In modern Greek this word "Preparation" means "Friday."

[27](16:8) See further, George Salmon's *Historical Introduction to the Study of the Books of the New Testament*, pp. 144-151.

BIBLIOGRAPHY

Alexander, Joseph Addison. *The Gospel According to Mark*. Edinburgh: The Banner of Truth Trust, 1960.

Coates, C. A. *An Outline of Mark's Gospel and other Ministry*. Kingston-on-Thames: Stow Hill Bible and Tract Depot, 1964.

Cole, Alan. *The Gospel According to St. Mark*. Grand Rapids: Wm. B. Eerdmans Publishing Company, 1961.

Erdman, Charles R. *The Gospel of Mark*. Philadelphia: The Westminster Press, 1917.

Ironside, Harry A. *Expository Notes on the Gospel of Mark*. Neptune, N.J.: Loizeaux Brothers Publishers, 1948.

Kelly, William. *An Exposition of the Gospel of Mark*. London: C. A. Hammond, 1934.

Lenski, R. C. H. *The Interpretation of St. Mark's Gospel*. Minneapolis: Augsburg Publishing House, 1946.

Swete, Henry Barclay. *The Gospel According to St Mark*. London: MacMillan and Company, Limited, 1902.

THE GOSPEL
ACCORDING TO LUKE†

Introduction

"Le plus beau livre qu'il y ait"   – Ernest Renan.

I. Unique Place in the Canon

"The most beautiful book that exists" is high praise indeed, especially from a skeptic. Yet such was French critic Renan's evaluation of Luke's Gospel. And what sensitive *believer* reading the evangelist's inspired masterpiece would want to contest his words? Luke is probably the only Gentile writer chosen by God to pen His Scriptures, and this may partly explain his special appeal to us Western inheritors of the Greco-Roman culture.

Spiritually we would be much the poorer in our appreciation of the Lord Jesus and His ministry without the unique emphasis of Dr. Luke. Our Lord's love for and offer of salvation to all people, not just to the Jews, His special interest in individuals, yes, and even the poor and the outcasts, are highlighted. Luke also has strong emphasis on praise (giving us examples of the earliest Christian "hymns" in Luke 1 and 2), prayer, and the Holy Spirit.

II. Authorship††

Luke, who was by race an Antiochan and a physician by profession, was long a companion of Paul, and had careful conversation with the other apostles, and in two books left us examples of the medicine for souls which he had gained from them.

This *external evidence* by Eusebius in his *Historia Ecclesiastica*, as to the authorship of the Third Gospel (iii, 4), agrees with universal early Christian tradition. Irenaeus widely quotes the Third Gospel as by Luke. Other early supporters of

Lucan authorship include Justin Martyr, Hegesippus, Clement of Alexandria, and Tertullian. In Marcion's carefully slanted and condensed edition, Luke is the only Gospel accepted by that noted heretic. The fragmentary Muratorian Canon calls this Third Gospel "Luke."

Luke is the only evangelist to write a sequel to his Gospel, and it is from that book, the Acts, that the Lucan authorship is most clearly shown. The so-called "we" sections of Acts are passages in which the writer was personally involved (16:10; 20:5, 6; 21:15; 27:1; 28:16; cf. 2 Tim. 4:11). By the process of elimination, only Luke fits all these periods. It is quite clear from the dedications to Theophilus and the style of writing that Luke and Acts are by the same author.

Paul calls Luke "the beloved physician" and lists him separately from Jewish Christians (Col. 4:14), which would make him the only Gentile writer in the NT. In size, Luke-Acts is larger than all of Paul's epistles combined.

The *internal evidence* strengthens the external documentation and church tradition. The vocabulary (often more precise in medical terms than the other NT writers), along with the educated Greek style, support authorship by a cultured Gentile Christian doctor, but one thoroughly conversant with Jewish themes. Luke's fondness for dates and exact research (1:1–4; 3:1, e.g.) make him the very first church historian.

III. Date

The most likely date for Luke is very early in the 60's of the first century. While some put Luke between 75-85 (or even the second century), this is usually due at least partly to a denial that Christ could accurately predict the destruction of Jerusalem. The city was destroyed in A.D. 70, so the Lord's prophecy had to be recorded before that date.

Since nearly all agree that Luke must precede Acts in time, and Acts ends about A.D. 63 with Paul in Rome, a date before that is called for. The great fire of Rome and the resultant persecution of Christians as Nero's scapegoats (A.D. 64) and the martyrdoms of Peter and Paul could scarcely have been ignored by the first church historian if they had occurred already. Hence a date of about A.D. 61–62 is most likely.

IV. Background and Theme

The Greeks were looking for a perfectly divine human being — one with the best characteristics of both men and women but none of their shortcomings. Such is Luke's presentation of Christ as Son of Man — strong, yet compassionate. His humanity is prominent.

His prayer life, for example, is referred to more than in any of the other Gospels. His sympathy and compassion are mentioned frequently. Perhaps this is why women and children occupy such a prominent place. The Gospel of Luke is also known as the missionary Gospel. Here the gospel goes out to the Gentiles, and the Lord Jesus is presented as the Savior of the world. Finally, this Gospel is a discipleship manual. We trace the pathway of discipleship in the life of our Lord, and hear it expounded in His training of His followers. It is this feature we shall follow particularly in our exposition. In the life of the Perfect Man, we shall find the elements that make up the ideal life for all men. In His incomparable words we shall also find the way of the cross to which He calls us.

As we turn to studying Luke's Gospel, may we hear the Savior's call, forsake all, and follow Him. Obedience is the organ of spiritual knowledge. The meaning of the Scriptures becomes clearer and dearer to us as we enter into the experiences described.

OUTLINE

Commentary†

I. PREFACE: LUKE'S PURPOSE AND METHOD (1:1–4)

In his preface, Luke reveals himself as a historian. He describes the source materials to which he had access and the method he followed. Then he explains his purpose in writ-

ing. From the human standpoint he had two types of source materials — written accounts of the life of Christ and oral reports by those who were eye-witnesses of the events in His life.

1:1 The written accounts are described in verse 1: **Inasmuch as many**

†*See p. ix.*

have taken in hand to set in order a narrative of those things which have been fulfilled among us. . . . We do not know who these writers were. Matthew and Mark may have been among them but any others were obviously not inspired. (John wrote at a later date.)

1:2 Luke also depended on oral reports from **those who from the beginning were eyewitnesses and ministers of the word delivered . . . to us.** Luke himself does not claim to be an eyewitness but he had interviews with those who were. He describes these associates of our Lord as **eyewitnesses and ministers of the word**. Here he uses **the word** as a name of Christ, just as John does in his Gospel. **The "beginning"** here means the beginning of the Christian era heralded by John the Baptist. The fact that Luke used written and oral accounts does not deny the verbal inspiration of what he wrote. It simply means that the Holy Spirit guided him in the choice and arrangement of his materials.

James S. Stewart comments:

> Luke makes it perfectly clear that the inspired writers were not miraculously freed from the necessity of hard historical research. . . . Inspiration was not God magically transcending human minds and faculties; it was God expressing His will through the dedication of human minds and faculties. It does not supersede the sacred writer's own personality and make him God's machine; it reinforces his personality and makes him God's living witness.[1]

1:3 Luke gives a brief statement of his motivation and of the method he used: **it seemed good to me also, having had perfect understanding of all things from the very first, to write to you an orderly account, most excellent Theophilus**. As to his motivation he simply says, **it seemed good to me also**. On the human level, there was the quiet conviction that he should write the Gospel. We know, of course, that divine constraint was curiously mingled with this human decision.

As to his method, he first traced the course **of all things** accurately **from the** beginning, then he wrote them down in order. His task involved a careful, scientific investigation of the course of events in our Savior's life. Luke checked on the accuracy of his sources, eliminated all that was not historically true and spiritually relevant, then compiled his materials in order as we have them today. When Luke says that he wrote **an orderly account** he does not necessarily mean in chronological order. The events in this Gospel are not always arranged in the order in which they occurred. Rather they are in a moral or spiritual order, that is, they are connected by subject matter and moral instruction rather than by time. Although this Gospel and the book of Acts were addressed to **Theophilus**, we know surprisingly little about him. His title **most excellent** suggests that he was a government official. His name means *a friend of God*. Probably he was a Christian who held a position of honor and responsibility in the foreign service of the Roman Empire.

1:4 Luke's purpose was to give Theophilus a written account that would confirm the trustworthiness of all that he had been taught concerning the life and ministry of the Lord Jesus. The written message would afford fixity by preserving it from the inaccuracies of continued oral transmission.

And so verses 1–4 give us a brief but enlightening background into the human circumstances under which this book of the Bible was written. We know that Luke wrote by inspiration. He does not mention that here, unless he implies it in the words *from the first* (v. 3) which can also be translated *from above*.[2]

II. ADVENT OF THE SON OF MAN AND HIS FORERUNNER (1:5 – 2:52)

A. Annunciation of the Forerunner's Birth (1:5–25)

1:5, 6 Luke begins his narrative by introducing us to the parents of John the Baptist. They lived at a time when the wicked **Herod** the Great was **king of Judea**. He was an Idumean, that is, a descendant of Esau.

Zacharias (means *the Lord remembers*) was a **priest** belonging to the **division of Abijah**, one of the twenty-four shifts into which the Jewish priesthood had been divided by David (1 Chron. 24:10).

Each shift was called on to serve at the temple in Jerusalem twice a year from Sabbath to Sabbath. There were so many priests at this time that the privilege of burning incense in the Holy Place came only once in a lifetime, if at all.

Elizabeth (means *the oath of God*) was also descended from the priestly family **of Aaron**. She and her husband were devout Jews, scrupulously careful in observing the OT Scriptures, both moral and ceremonial. Of course, they were not sinless, but when they did sin, they made sure to offer a sacrifice or otherwise to obey the ritualistic requirement.

1:7 This couple had *no children*, a reproachful condition for any Jew. Doctor Luke notes that the cause of this was Elizabeth's barrenness. The problem was aggravated by the fact that **they were both well advanced in years**.

1:8–10 One day Zacharias was performing his priestly duties in **the temple**. This was a great day in his life because he had been chosen by lot **to burn incense** in the Holy Place. **The people** had gathered **outside** the temple and were **praying**. No one seems to know definitely the time signified by **the hour of incense**.

It is inspiring to notice that the Gospel opens with **people praying** at the temple and it closes with people praising God at the temple. The intervening chapters tell how their prayers were answered in the Person and work of the Lord Jesus.

1:11–14 With priest and people engaged in prayer, it was an appropriate time and setting for a divine revelation. **An angel of the Lord appeared on the right side of the altar** — the place of favor. At first **Zacharias** was terrified; none of his contemporaries had ever seen an angel. But the angel reassured him with wonderful news. **A son** would be born to **Elizabeth**, to be named **John** (*the favor* or *grace of Jehovah*). In addition to bringing **joy and gladness** to his parents, he would be a blessing to **many**.

1:15 This child would **be great in the sight of the Lord** (the only kind of greatness that really matters). First of all, he would be great in his personal separation to God; he would **drink neither wine** (made from grapes) **nor strong drink** (made from grain).

Secondly, he would be great in his spiritual endowment; he would **be filled with the Holy Spirit, even from his mother's womb**. (This cannot mean that John was saved or converted from birth, but only that God's Spirit was in him from the outset to prepare him for his special mission as Christ's forerunner.)

1:16, 17 Thirdly, he would be great in his role as herald of the Messiah. He would **turn many** of the Jewish people **to the Lord**. His ministry would be like that of **Elijah**, the prophet — seeking to bring the people into right relationship with God through repentance. As G. Coleman Luck points out:

> His preaching would turn the hearts of careless parents to a real spiritual concern for their children. Also he would bring back the hearts of disobedient, rebellious children to the "wisdom of the just."[3]

In other words, he would strive to gather out of the world a company of believers who would be ready to meet the Lord when He appeared. This is a worthy ministry for each of us.

Notice how the deity of Christ is implied in verses 16 and 17. In verse 16, it says that John would **turn many of the children of Israel to the Lord their God**. Then in verse 17 it says that John would **go before Him**. To whom does the word *Him* refer? Obviously to the *Lord their God* in the preceding verse. And yet we know that John was the forerunner of *Jesus*. The inference then is clear. Jesus is God.

1:18 The aged **Zacharias** was struck by the sheer impossibility of the promise. Both he and his **wife** were too **old** to become the parents of a child. His plaintive question expressed all the pent-up doubt of his heart.

1:19 The angel answered first by introducing himself as **Gabriel** (*strong one of God*). Though commonly described as an archangel, he is mentioned in the Scripture only as one **who stands in the presence of God** and who brings messages from God to man (Dan. 8:16; 9:21).

1:20 Because Zacharias had doubted, he would lose the power of speech **until** the child was born. Whenever a believer entertains doubts concerning God's word, he loses his testimony and his song. Unbelief seals the lips, and they remain sealed until faith returns and bursts forth in praise and witness.

1:21, 22 Outside, **the people** were waiting impatiently; ordinarily the priest who was burning incense would have appeared much sooner. When **Zacharias** finally **came out, he** had to communicate with them by making signs. Then **they** realized **that he had seen a vision in the temple**.

1:23 After his tour of duty at the temple was **completed**, the priest went back home, still unable to speak, as the angel had predicted.

1:24, 25 When **Elizabeth** became pregnant she went into seclusion in her home for **five months**, rejoicing within herself that **the Lord** had seen fit to free her from the **reproach** of being childless.

B. Annunciation of the Son of Man's Birth (1:26–38)

1:26, 27† **In the sixth month** after his appearance to Zacharias (or after Elizabeth became pregnant), **Gabriel** reappeared — this time **to a virgin** named **Mary** who lived in the **city** of **Nazareth**, in the district **of Galilee**. Mary was **betrothed to a man** named **Joseph**, a lineal descendant **of David**, who inherited legal rights to the throne of David, even though he himself was a carpenter. Betrothal was considered a much more binding contract than engagement is today. In fact, it could be broken only by a legal decree similar to divorce.

•1:28 **The angel** addressed Mary as one who was **highly favored**, one whom the Lord was visiting with special privilege. Two points should be noted here: (1) The angel did *not* worship Mary or pray to her; he simply greeted her. (2) He did *not* say that she was "full of grace," but **highly favored**.[4]

1:29, 30 Mary was understandably **troubled** by this greeting; she wondered what it meant. **The angel** calmed her fears, then told her that **God** was choosing her to be the mother of the long-awaited Messiah.

1:31–33†† Notice the important truths which are enshrined in the annunciation:

The real humanity of the Messiah — **you will conceive in your womb and bring forth a Son**.

His deity and His mission as Savior — **and shall call His name JESUS**

(meaning *Jehovah is the Savior*).

His essential greatness — **He will be great**, both as to His Person and His work.

His identity as the Son of God — **and will be called the Son of the Highest**.

His title to the throne of David — **the Lord God will give Him the throne of His father David**. This establishes Him as the Messiah.

His everlasting and universal kingdom — **He will reign over the house of Jacob forever, and of His kingdom there will be no end.**

Verses 31 and 32a obviously refer to Christ's First Advent, whereas verses 32b and 33 describe His Second Coming as King of kings and Lord of lords.

1:34, 35 Mary's question, **"How can this be?"** was one of wonder but not of doubt. How could she bear a child when she had never had relations with **a man**? Although the angel did not say so in so many words, the answer was *virgin birth*. It would be a miracle of **the Holy Spirit**. He would **come upon** her, **and the power of** God would **overshadow** her. To Mary's problem of "How?" — it seemed impossible to human reckoning — God's answer is "the Holy Spirit":

"Therefore, also, that Holy One who is to be born will be called the Son of God." Here then we have a sublime statement of the incarnation. Mary's Son would be God manifest in the flesh. Language cannot exhaust the mystery that is shrouded here.

1:36, 37 The angel then broke the news to Mary that **Elizabeth** her **relative**, was in her **sixth month** of pregnancy — she who had been **barren**. This miracle should reassure Mary that **with God nothing will be impossible.**

1:38 In beautiful submission, **Mary** yielded herself to the Lord for the accomplishment of His wondrous purposes. Then **the angel departed from her**.

C. Mary Visits Elizabeth (1:39–45)

1:39, 40 We are not told why **Mary** went to visit **Elizabeth** at this time. It may have been to avoid the scandal which would inevitably arise in Nazareth when her condition became known. If

†See p. xvix
††See p. xviii.

this is so, then the welcome given by Elizabeth and the kindness shown would have been doubly sweet.

1:41 As soon as **Elizabeth heard** Mary's voice, **the babe leaped in her womb** — a mysterious, involuntary response of the unborn forerunner to the arrival of the unborn Messiah. **Elizabeth was filled with the Holy Spirit**, that is, He took control of her, guiding her speech and actions.

Three persons in chapter 1 are said to be filled with the Holy Spirit: John the Baptist (v. 15); Elizabeth (v. 41); and Zacharias (v. 67).

One of the marks of a Spirit-filled life is speaking in psalms and hymns and spiritual songs (Eph. 5:18, 19). We are not surprised therefore to find three songs in this chapter, as well as two in the next. Four of these songs are generally known by Latin titles, which are taken from the first lines: (1) Elizabeth's Salutation [1:42–45]; (2) The *Magnificat* (it magnifies) [1:46–55]; (3) *Benedictus* (blessed) [1:68–79]; (4) *Gloria in Excelsis Deo* (glory to God in the highest) [2:14]; and (5) *Nunc Dimittis* (now You let depart) [2:29–32].

1:42–45 Speaking by special inspiration, Elizabeth saluted Mary as **"the mother of my Lord."** There was not a trace of jealousy in her heart; only joy and delight that the unborn baby would be her **Lord**. Mary was **blessed among women** in that she was given the privilege of bearing the Messiah. **The fruit of** her **womb** is **blessed** in that He is Lord and Savior. The Bible *never* speaks of Mary as "the mother of God." While it is true that she was the mother of Jesus, and that Jesus is God, it is nevertheless a doctrinal absurdity to speak of God as having a mother. Jesus existed from all eternity whereas Mary was a finite creature with a definite date when she began to exist. She was the mother of Jesus only in His Incarnation.

Elizabeth recounted the seemingly intuitive excitement of her unborn child when Mary first spoke. Then she assured Mary that her faith would be abundantly rewarded. Her expectation would be fulfilled. She had not believed in vain. Her Baby would be born as promised.

D. Mary Magnifies the Lord (1:46–56)

1:46–49 The Magnificat resembles Hannah's song (1 Sam. 2:1–10). First, **Mary** praised **the Lord** for what **He** had done for her (vv. 46b–49). Notice that she said (v. 48) **"all generations will call me blessed."** She would not be one who conferred blessings but one who would *be* blessed. She speaks of **God** as her **Savior**, disproving the idea that Mary was sinless.

1:50–53 Secondly, she praised the Lord for **His mercy on those who fear Him** in every **generation. He** puts **down the proud** and **mighty**, and exalts **the lowly** and **hungry**.

1:54, 55 Finally, she magnified the Lord for His faithfulness to **Israel** in keeping the promises He had made **to Abraham and to his seed**.

1:56 After staying with Elizabeth **about three months**, Mary **returned to her** own **house** in Nazareth. She was not yet married. No doubt she became the object of suspicion and slander in the neighborhood. But God would vindicate her; she could afford to wait.

E. Birth of the Forerunner (1:57–66)

1:57–61 At **Elizabeth's** appointed **time**, she gave birth to **a son**. Her **relatives** and friends were delighted. **On the eighth day**, when **the child** was circumcised, they thought it was a foregone conclusion that he would be named **Zacharias**, after **his father**. When **his mother** told them the child's name would be **John**, they were surprised, because none of his **relatives** had **this name**.

1:62, 63 To get the final decision, they **made signs to** Zacharias. (This indicates that he was not only dumb, but deaf as well.) Calling for **a writing tablet**, he settled the matter — the baby's **name** was **John**. The people **all marveled**.

1:64–66 But it was even more of a surprise when they noticed that the power of speech had returned to Zacharias as soon as he wrote "John." The news spread quickly **throughout all the hill country of Judea**, and people wondered about the future work of this unusual baby. They knew that the special favor **of the Lord was with him**.

F. Zacharias' Prophecy Concerning John (1:67–80)

1:67 Freed now from the fetters of unbelief and **filled with the Holy Spirit, Zacharias** was inspired to utter an eloquent hymn of praise, rich in quotations from the OT.

1:68, 69 *Praise to God for what He had done.* Zacharias realized that the birth of his son, John, indicated the imminence of the coming of the Messiah. He spoke of Christ's advent as an accomplished fact before it happened. Faith enabled him to say **God** had already **visited and redeemed His people** by sending the Redeemer. Jehovah had **raised up a horn of salvation** in the royal **house of . . . David**. (A horn was used to hold the oil for anointing kings; therefore it might mean here a *King* of salvation from the kingly line of David. Or it might be a symbol of power and thus mean "a powerful Savior.")

1:70, 71 *Praise to God for fulfilling prophecy.* The coming of the Messiah had been predicted by the **holy prophets . . . since the world began**. It would mean salvation **from** one's **enemies** and safety from foes.

1:72–75 *Praise to God for His faithfulness to His promises.* The Lord had made an unconditional **covenant** of salvation with **Abraham**. This promise was fulfilled by the coming of Abraham's seed, namely, the Lord Jesus Christ. The salvation He brought was both external and internal. Externally, it meant deliverance **from the hand of** their **enemies**. Internally, it meant serving **Him without fear, in holiness and righteousness**.

G. Campbell Morgan brings out two striking thoughts on this passage.[5] First, he points out the arresting connection between the name of John and the theme of the song — both are the grace of God. Then he finds allusions to the names of John, Zacharias and Elizabeth in verses 72 and 73.

John — the mercy promised (v. 72).

Zacharias — to remember (v. 72).

Elizabeth — the oath (v. 73).

God's favor, as announced by John, results from His remembering **the oath** of **His holy covenant**.

1:76, 77 *The mission of John, the Sav-*ior's *herald*. John would be **the prophet of the** Most High, preparing the hearts of the people for the coming of **the Lord**, and proclaiming **salvation to His people** through the forgiveness **of their sins**. Here again we see that references to Jehovah in the OT are applied to Jesus in the New. Malachi predicted a messenger to prepare the way before Jehovah (3:1). Zacharias identifies John as the messenger. We know that John came **to prepare** the way before Jesus. The obvious conclusion is that Jesus is Jehovah.

1:78, 79 *Christ's coming is likened to the sunrise.* For centuries, the world had lain **in darkness**. Now **through the tender mercy of our God**, dawn was about to break. It would come in the Person of Christ, shining on the Gentiles **who** were **in darkness and the shadow of death**, and guiding Israel's feet **into the way of peace** (see Mal. 4:2).

1:80 The chapter closes with a simple statement that **the child grew** physically and spiritually, remaining **in the deserts till the day** of his public appearance **to the nation of Israel**.

G. Birth of the Son of Man (2:1–7)

2:1–3[†] **Caesar Augustus made a decree that all the world should be registered**, that is, that **a census** should be taken throughout his empire. **This census was first** taken **while Quirinius was governing Syria**. For many years the accuracy of Luke's Gospel was called into question because of this reference to Quirinius. Later archaeological discoveries, however, tend to confirm the record. From his standpoint, **Caesar Augustus** was demonstrating his supremacy over the Greco-Roman world. But from God's standpoint, this Gentile emperor was merely a puppet to further the divine program (see Prov. 21:1).

2:4–7[††] The decree of Augustus brought **Joseph** and **Mary** to **Bethlehem**[†††] at exactly the right time in order that the Messiah might be born there in fulfillment of prophecy (Mic. 5:2). Bethlehem was crowded when they arrived **from Galilee**. The only place they could find to stay was the stable of an **inn**. That was an omen, a preview of how men would receive their Savior. It was while the couple from **Nazareth** was there that

†*See p. xvix.*
††*See p. xvix.*
†††*See pp. x–xi.*

Mary **brought forth her firstborn Son**. Wrapping **Him in swaddling cloths**, she lovingly **laid Him in a manger**.

Thus did God visit our planet in the Person of a helpless Baby, and in the poverty of an ill-smelling stable. The wonder of it! Darby expressed it nicely:

> He began in a manger, and ended on the cross, and along the way had not where to lay His head.[6]

H. The Angels and the Shepherds (2:8–20)

2:8 The first intimation of this unique birth was not given to the religious leaders in Jerusalem, but to contemplative **shepherds** on Judean hillsides, humble men who were faithful at their regular work. James S. Stewart observes:

> And is there not a world of meaning in the fact that it was very ordinary people, busy about very ordinary tasks, whose eyes first saw the glory of the coming of the Lord? It means, first, that the place of duty, however humble, is the place of vision. And it means, second, that it is the men who have kept to the deep, simple pieties of life and have not lost the child heart to whom the gates of the Kingdom most readily open.[7]

2:9–11 **An angel of the Lord** came to the shepherds, and a bright, glorious light **shone** all **around them**. As they recoiled in terror, the angel comforted them and broke the news. It was **good tidings of great joy** for **all** the **people**. That very **day, in** nearby Bethlehem, a Baby had been **born**. This Baby was **a Savior, who is Christ the Lord**! Here we have a theology in miniature. First, He is **a Savior**, which is expressed in His name, Jesus. Then He is **Christ**, the Anointed of God, the Messiah of Israel. Finally, He is **the Lord**, God manifest in the flesh.

2:12 How would the shepherds recognize Him? The angels gave them a twofold **sign**. First the Baby would be **wrapped in swaddling cloths**. They had seen babies in swaddling cloths before. But the angels had just announced that this Baby was the Lord. No one had ever seen the Lord as a little **Babe wrapped in swaddling cloths**. The second part of the sign was that He would be **lying in a manger**. It is doubtful that the shepherds had ever seen a baby in such an unlikely place. This indignity was reserved for the Lord of life and glory when He came into our world. It makes our minds dizzy to think of the Creator and Sustainer of the universe entering human history not as a conquering military hero, but as a little **Babe**. Yet this is the truth of the Incarnation.

2:13, 14 **Suddenly** heaven's pent-up ecstasy broke forth. **A multitude of the heavenly host** appeared, **praising God**. Their song, known generally today by the title, *Gloria in Excelsis Deo*, catches up the full significance of the birth of the Baby. His life and ministry would bring **glory to God in the highest** heaven, and **peace on earth, good will toward men**, or perhaps to men in whom He is well-pleased.[8] The men in whom God is well-pleased are those who repent of their sins and receive Jesus Christ as Lord and Savior.

2:15–19 As soon as **the angels** departed, **the shepherds** hurried **to Bethlehem** and **found Mary and Joseph, and** Jesus **lying in a manger**. They gave a complete report of the angel's visit, causing considerable surprise among those who had gathered in the stable. **But Mary** had a deeper understanding of what was going on; she treasured **all these things, and** knowingly **pondered them in her heart**.

2:20 **The shepherds returned** to their flocks, overjoyed at all **they had heard and seen**, and overflowing in their worship of **God**.

I. The Circumcision and Dedication of Jesus (2:21–24)

At least three different rituals are described in this passage:

1. First there was **the circumcision of** Jesus. This took place when He was **eight days** old. It was a token of the covenant that God made with Abraham. On this same day, **the Child** was named, according to Jewish custom. The angel had previously instructed Mary and Joseph to call Him **JESUS**.

2. The second ceremony was concerned with **the purification** of Mary. It took place forty days after the birth of Jesus (see Lev. 12:1–4). Ordinarily

parents were supposed to bring a lamb for a burnt offering and a young pigeon or turtledove for a sin offering.

But in the case of the poor, they were permitted to bring **"a pair of turtledoves or two young pigeons"** (Lev. 12:6–8). The fact that Mary brought no lamb, but only **two young pigeons** is a reflection of the poverty into which Jesus was born.

3. The third ritual was the presentation of Jesus at the temple in **Jerusalem**. Originally, God had decreed that the firstborn sons belonged to Him; they were to form the priestly class (Ex. 13:2). Later, He set aside the tribe of Levi to serve as priests (Ex. 28:1, 2). Then the parents were permitted to "buy back" or "redeem" their firstborn son by the payment of five shekels. This they did when they dedicated him **to the Lord**.

J. Simeon Lives to See the Messiah (2:25–35)

2:25, 26 **Simeon** was one of the godly remnant of Jews who was **waiting for** the coming of the Messiah. It was **revealed to him by the Holy Spirit that he would not** die **before** seeing **the Lord's Christ** or Anointed One. "The secret of the Lord is with those who fear Him" (Ps. 25:14). There is a mysterious communication of divine knowledge to those who walk in quiet, contemplative fellowship with God.

2:27, 28 It so happened that he entered **the temple** area on the very day that Jesus' **parents** were presenting Him to God. Simeon was supernaturally instructed that this Child was the promised Messiah. Taking Jesus **in his arms**, he uttered the memorable song now known as The Nunc Dimittis (*Now you are letting . . . depart*).

2:29–32 The burden of the song is as follows: **Lord, now You are letting** me **depart in peace**. **I have seen Your salvation** in the Person of this Baby, the promised Redeemer, as You promised me. You ordained Him to provide salvation for all classes of people. He will be **a light to bring revelation to the Gentiles** (His First Advent) and to shine in **glory** on **Your people Israel** (His Second Advent). Simeon was prepared to die

after he had met the Lord Jesus. The sting of death was gone.

2:33 Luke carefully guards the doctrine of the Virgin Birth with his precisely worded **Joseph and His mother**, as read by the King James tradition, following the majority of manuscripts.[9]

2:34, 35 After this initial outburst of praise to God for the Messiah, **Simeon blessed** the parents, then spoke prophetically **to Mary**. The prophecy consisted of four parts:

1. **This Child** was **destined for the fall and rising of many in Israel**. Those who were arrogant, unrepentant, and unbelieving would **fall** and be punished. Those who humbled themselves, repented of their sins, and received the Lord Jesus would rise and be blessed.

2. The **Child** was **destined . . . for a sign which will be spoken against**. There was a special significance connected with the Person of Christ. His very presence on earth proved a tremendous rebuke to sin and unholiness, and thus brought out the bitter animosity of the human heart.

3. **Yes, a sword will pierce through your own soul also.** Simeon was here predicting the grief which would flood Mary's heart when she would witness the crucifixion of her Son (John 19:25).

4. **. . . that the thoughts of many hearts may be revealed.** The way in which a person reacts to the Savior is a test of his inward motives and affections.

Thus Simeon's song includes the ideas of touchstone, stumblingstone, stepping-stone, and sword.

K. The Prophetess Anna (2:36–39)

2:36, 37 **Anna** the **prophetess**, was, like Simeon, a member of the faithful remnant of Israel who was waiting for the advent of the Messiah. She was **of the tribe of Asher** (meaning *happy, blessed*), one of the ten tribes carried into captivity by the Assyrians in 721 B.C. Anna must have been over one hundred years old, having been married for **seven years**, then widowed for **eighty-four years**. As **a prophetess**, she undoubtedly received divine revelations and **served** as a mouthpiece for **God**. She was faithful in her attendance at public services at **the temple**, worshiping **with fastings and** supplications **night and day**. Her **great age** did not deter her from serving the Lord.

2:38 Just as Jesus was being presented to the Lord, and as Simeon was speaking to Mary, Anna came up to this little cluster of people. **She gave thanks to the Lord** for the promised Redeemer, then **spoke** about Jesus **to** the faithful ones **in Jerusalem** who were expecting **redemption**.

2:39 After Joseph and Mary **had performed** the rites of purification and dedication, **they returned to Galilee, to their** home town, **Nazareth**. Luke omits any mention of the visit of the wise men or of the flight into Egypt.

L. The Boyhood of Jesus (2:40–52)

2:40 The normal growth of **the Child** Jesus is set forth as follows: *Physically* He **grew and became strong in spirit**.[10] He passed through the usual stages of physical development, learning to walk, talk, play, and work. Because of this He can sympathize with us in every stage of our growth. *Mentally* He was **filled with wisdom**. He not only learned His ABC's, His numbers, and all the common knowledge of that day, but He grew in **wisdom**, that is, in the practical application of this knowledge to the problems of life. *Spiritually* **the** favor **of God was upon Him**. He walked in fellowship with God and in dependence on the Holy Spirit. He studied the Bible, spent time in prayer, and delighted to do His Father's will.

2:41–44 A Jewish boy becomes a son of the law at the age of twelve. **When** our Lord **was twelve years old**, His family made their annual pilgrimage **up to Jerusalem** for **the Passover**. But when they left to return to Galilee, they didn't notice that **Jesus** was not in the entourage. This may seem strange to us unless we realize that the family probably traveled with a fairly large caravan. They no doubt assumed that Jesus was walking with others of His own age.

Before condemning Joseph and Mary, we should remember how easy it is for us to travel **a day's journey, supposing** Jesus to be **in the company**, when actually we have lost contact with Him

through unconfessed sin in our lives. In order to re-establish contact with Him, we must go back to the place where fellowship was broken, then confess and forsake our sin.

2:45–47 Returning **to Jerusalem**, the distraught parents **found** Jesus **in the temple, sitting** among **the teachers, both listening to them and asking them questions**. There is no suggestion of His acting as a precocious child, disputing with His elders. Rather He took the place of a normal child, learning in humility and quietness from His teachers. And yet in the course of the proceedings, He must have been asked some questions, because the people **were astonished at His understanding and answers**.

2:48 Even His parents **were amazed** when they found Jesus participating so intelligently in a discussion with those who were so many years older than He. Yet **His mother** expressed her accumulated anxiety and irritation by reproving Him. Didn't He know that they had been worried about Him?

2:49 The Lord's answer, His first recorded words, show that He was fully aware of His identity as the Son of God, and of His divine mission as well. **"Why did you seek Me? Did you not know that I must be about My Father's business?"** *She* said, "Your father and I." *He* said, **"My Father's business."**

2:50 At the time, **they did not understand** what He meant by His cryptic remark. It was an unusual thing for a twelve-year old Boy to say!

2:51 At any rate, they were reunited, so they could return **to Nazareth**. The moral excellence of Jesus is seen in the words **"He . . . was subject to them."** Though Creator of the universe, yet He took His place as an obedient Child in this humble Jewish family. **But** all the time, **His mother kept all these things in her heart**.

2:52 Again we have the true humanity and normal growth of our Lord depicted:

1. His mental growth — **increased in wisdom**.
2. His physical growth — **and stature**.
3. His spiritual growth — **in favor with God**.
4. His social growth — in favor with **men**.

He was absolutely perfect in every aspect of His growth. Here Luke's narrative skips silently over eighteen years which the Lord Jesus spent in Nazareth as the Son of a carpenter. These years teach us the importance of preparation and training, the need for patience, and the value of common work. They warn against the temptation to jump from spiritual birth to public ministry. Those who do not have a normal spiritual childhood and adolescence court disaster in their later life and testimony.

III. PREPARATION OF THE SON OF MAN TO MINISTER (3:1–4:30)

A. Preparation by His Forerunner (3:1–20)

3:1, 2 As a historian, Luke identifies the **year** that John began to preach by naming the political and religious leaders who were then in power — one emperor (**Caesar**), one **governor**, three with the title of **tetrarch** and two **high priests**. The political rulers mentioned imply the iron grip with which the nation of Israel was held in subjugation. The fact that there were two high priests in Israel indicate that the nation was in disorder religiously as well as politically. Though these were great men in the world's estimation, they were wicked, unscrupulous men in God's eyes. Therefore when He wanted to speak to men, He by-passed the palace and the synagogue and sent His message **to John the son of Zacharias**, out **in the wilderness**.

3:3† John immediately traveled to **all the region around the Jordan** River, probably near Jericho. There he called upon the nation of Israel to repent of its **sins** in order to receive forgiveness, and thus be prepared for the coming of the Messiah. He also called upon the people to be baptized as an outward sign that they had truly repented. John was a true prophet, an embodied conscience, crying out against sin, and calling for spiritual renewal.

3:4 His ministry was thus in fulfillment of the prophecy in **Isaiah** 40:3–5. He was a **voice of one crying in the wilderness**. Spiritually speaking, Israel was a **wilderness** at this time. As a nation,

it was arid and cheerless, bringing forth no fruit for God. In order to be ready for the coming of the Lord, the people had to undergo a moral change. When a king was going to make a royal visit in those days, elaborate preparations were made to smooth the highways and to make his approach as direct as possible. This is what John called upon the people to do, only it was not a matter of repairing literal roads but of preparing their own hearts to receive Him.

3:5 The effects of Christ's coming are described as follows:

Every valley shall be filled — those who are truly repentant and humble would be saved and satisfied.

Every mountain and hill shall be **brought low** — people like the scribes and Pharisees, who were haughty and arrogant, would be humbled.

The crooked places shall be made straight — those who were dishonest, like the tax collectors, would have their characters straightened out.

The rough ways shall be made **smooth** — soldiers and others with rough, crude temperaments would be tamed and refined.

3:6 A final result would be that **all flesh** — both Jews and Gentiles — would **see the salvation of God**. In His First Advent the offer of salvation went out to all men, though not all received Him. When He comes back to reign, this verse will have its complete fulfillment. Then all Israel will be saved, and the Gentiles too will share in the blessings of His glorious kingdom.

3:7 When **the multitudes came out** to John for baptism, he realized that they were not all sincere. Some were mere pretenders, with no hunger or thirst for righteousness. It was these whom John addressed as offspring **of vipers**. The question, **"Who warned you to flee from the wrath to come?"** implies that John had not done so; his message was addressed to those who were willing to confess their sins.

3:8 If they really meant business with God, they should show that they had truly repented by manifesting a transformed life. Genuine repentance produces **fruits**. They should not start thinking that their descent from **Abraham** was sufficient; relationship to godly people does not make men godly. **God** was not limited to the physical descendants of Abraham to carry out His purposes; He could take the **stones** by the river Jordan and **raise up children to Abraham**. *Stones* here are probably a picture of Gentiles whom God could transform by a miracle of divine grace into believers with faith like that of Abraham. This is exactly what happened. The physical seed of Abraham, as a nation, rejected the Christ of God. But many Gentiles received Him as Lord and Savior and thus became the spiritual seed of Abraham.

3:9 **The ax laid to the root of the trees** is a figurative expression, meaning that Christ's coming would test the reality of man's repentance. Those individuals who did not manifest the fruits of repentance would be condemned.

> John's words and phrases went from his mouth like swords: "generation of vipers," "wrath to come," "axe," "hewn down," "cast into the fire." The Lord's prophets were never mealy-mouthed: they were great moralists, and often their words came crashing upon the people as the battle-axes of our forefathers upon the helmets of their foes (Daily Notes of the Scripture Union).

3:10 Stung with conviction, **the people asked** John for some practical suggestions as to how to demonstrate the reality of their repentance.

3:11–14 In verses 11–14, he gave them specific ways in which they could prove their sincerity. In general, they should love their neighbors as themselves by sharing their clothing and **food** with the poor.

As for **tax collectors**, they should be strictly honest in all their dealings. Since as a class they were notoriously crooked, this would be a very definite evidence of reality.

Finally, **soldiers** on active duty were told to avoid three sins common to men in the military — extortion, slander, and discontent. It is important to realize that men were not saved by doing these things; rather these were the outward evidences that their hearts were truly right before God.

3:15, 16a John's self-effacement was remarkable. For a time, at least, he could have posed as the Messiah and attracted a great following. But instead he compared himself most unfavorably with Christ. He explained that his baptism was outward and physical, whereas Christ's would be inward and spiritual. He stated that he was **not worthy to** untie the Messiah's **sandal strap**.

3:16b, 17 Christ's baptism would be **with the Holy Spirit and fire**. His would be a two-fold ministry. First of all, **He** would **baptize** believers **with the Holy Spirit** — a promise of what would take place on the Day of Pentecost when believers were baptized into the body of Christ. But secondly, He would baptize **with fire**.

From verse 17, it seems clear that the baptism of **fire** is a baptism of judgment. There the Lord is pictured as a winnower of grain. As He shovels the grain into the air, **the chaff** is blown to the sides of the threshing floor. Then it is swept up and burned.

When John was speaking to a mixed multitude — believers and unbelievers — he mentioned both the baptism of *the Spirit* and the baptism of *fire* (Matt. 3:11 and here). When, however, he was speaking to believers only (Mark 1:5), he omitted the baptism of fire (Mark 1:8). No true believer will ever experience the baptism of fire.

3:18–20 Luke is now ready to turn the spotlight from John to Jesus. Therefore, in these verses, he summarizes the remainder of John's ministry and carries us forward to the time of his imprisonment by **Herod**. The imprisonment of John actually took place about eighteen months later. He had **rebuked** Herod for living in an adulterous relationship with his sister-in-law. **Herod** then crowned all his other evil deeds by shutting **John up in prison**.

B. Preparation by Baptism (3:21, 22)

As John recedes from our attention, the Lord Jesus moves out into the position of prominence. He opens His public ministry, at about the age of thirty, by being **baptized** in the Jordan River.

There are several points of interest in this account of His baptism:

1. All three Persons of the Trinity are found here: **Jesus** (v. 21); the **Holy Spirit** (v. 22a); the Father (v. 22b).

2. Luke alone records the fact that Jesus **prayed** at His baptism (v. 21). This is in keeping with Luke's aim to

present Christ as the Son of Man, ever dependent on God the Father. The prayer life of our Lord is a dominant theme in this Gospel. He prayed here, at the outset of His public ministry. He prayed when He was becoming well known and crowds were following Him (5:16). He spent a whole night in prayer before choosing the twelve disciples (6:12). He prayed prior to the incident at Caesarea Philippi, the highwater mark of His teaching ministry (9:18). He prayed on the Mount of Transfiguration (9:28). He prayed in the presence of His disciples, and this called forth a discourse on prayer (11:1). He prayed for backsliding Peter (22:32). He prayed in the garden of Gethsemane (22:41, 44).

3. The baptism of Jesus is one of three times when God spoke **from heaven** in connection with the ministry of His own dear **Son**. For thirty years the eye of God had examined that flawless Life in Nazareth; here His verdict was, **"I am well pleased."** The other two times when the Father publicly spoke from heaven were: When Peter suggested building three tabernacles on the Mount of Transfiguration (Luke 9:35), and when the Greeks came to Philip, desiring to see Jesus (John 12:20–28).

C. Preparation by Partaking of Humanity (3:23-28)†

Before taking up the public **ministry** of our Lord, Luke pauses to give His genealogy. If Jesus is truly human, then He must be descended from **Adam**. This genealogy demonstrates that He was. It is widely believed that this gives the genealogy of Jesus through the line of Mary. Note that verse 23 does not say that Jesus was the son of Joseph, but **"(as was supposed) the son of Joseph."** If this view is correct, then **Heli** (v. 23) was the father-in-law of Joseph and the father of Mary.

Scholars widely believe that this is the Lord's genealogy through Mary for the following reasons:

1. The most obvious is that Joseph's family line is traced in Matthew's Gospel (1:2–16).
2. In the early chapters of Luke's Gos-

pel, Mary is more prominent than Joseph, whereas it is the reverse in Matthew.
3. Women's names were not commonly used among the Jews as genealogical links. This would account for the omission of Mary's name.
4. In Matthew 1:16, it distinctly states that Jacob begot Joseph. Here in Luke, it does not say that Heli begot Joseph; it says Joseph was the son of Heli. *Son* may mean *son-in-law*.
5. In the original language, the definite article (*tou*) in the genitive form (*of the*) appears before every name in the genealogy *except one*. That one name is Joseph. This singular exception strongly suggests that Joseph was included only because of his marriage to Mary.

Although it is not necessary to examine the genealogy in detail, it is helpful to note several important points:

1. This list shows that Mary was descended from **David** through his son **Nathan** (v. 31). In Matthew's Gospel, Jesus inherited the *legal* right to the throne of David through Solomon.

As legal Son of Joseph, the Lord fulfilled that part of God's covenant with David which promised him that his throne would continue forever. But Jesus could not have been the real son of Joseph without coming under God's curse on Jechoniah, which decreed that no descendant of that wicked king would prosper (Jer. 22:30).

As the real Son of Mary, Jesus fulfilled that part of the covenant of God with David which promised him that his *seed* would sit upon his throne forever. And by being descended from David through Nathan, He did not come under the curse which was pronounced on Jechoniah.

2. **Adam** is described as **the son of God** (v. 38). This means simply that he was created by God.

3. It seems obvious that the Messianic line ended with the Lord Jesus. *No one else* can ever present valid legal claim to the throne of David.

D. Preparation by Testing (4:1–13)

4:1 There was never a time in our Lord's life when He was not full of the

†See p. xviii.

Holy Spirit, but it is specifically mentioned here in connection with His temptation. To be **filled with the Holy Spirit** means to be completely yielded to Him and to be completely obedient to every word of God. A person who is filled with the Spirit is emptied of known sin and of self and is richly indwelt by the Word of God. As Jesus was returning **from the Jordan**, where He had been baptized, He **was led by the Spirit into the wilderness** — probably the Wilderness of Judea, along the west coast of the Dead Sea.

4:2, 3 There He was **tempted for forty days by the devil** — **days** in which our Lord **ate nothing**. At the end of the forty days came the threefold temptation with which we are more familiar. Actually they took place in three different places — the wilderness, a mountain, and the temple in Jerusalem. The true humanity of Jesus is reflected by the words **He was hungry**. This was the target of the first temptation. Satan suggested that the Lord should use His divine power to satisfy bodily hunger. The subtlety of the temptation was that the act in itself was perfectly legitimate. But it would have been wrong for Jesus to do it in obedience to Satan; He must act in accordance with the will of His Father.

4:4 Jesus resisted the temptation by quoting Scripture (Deut. 8:3). More important than the satisfaction of physical appetite is obedience to God's word. He did not argue. Darby said, "A single text silences when used in the power of the Spirit. The whole secret of strength in conflict is using the word of God in the right way."

4:5–7 In the second temptation, **the devil . . . showed** Jesus **all the kingdoms of the world in a moment of time**. It doesn't take long for Satan to show all he has to offer. It was not the world itself but **the kingdoms of** this **world** he offered. There is a sense in which he *does* have **authority** over the **kingdoms of** this world. Because of man's sin, Satan has become "the ruler of this world" (John 12:31; 14:30; 16:11), "the god of this age" (2 Cor. 4:4), and "the prince of the power of the air" (Eph. 2:2). God has purposed that "the kingdoms of this world" will one day "become the kingdoms of our Lord, and of His Christ" (Rev. 11:15). So Satan was offering to Christ what would eventually be His anyway.

But there could be no short cut to the throne. The cross had to come first. In the counsels of God, the Lord Jesus had to suffer before He could enter into His glory. He could not achieve a legitimate end by a wrong means. Under no circumstances would He **worship** the devil, no matter what the prize might be.

4:8 Therefore, the Lord quoted Deuteronomy 6:13 to show that as a Man He should **worship** and **serve** God alone.

4:9–11 In the third temptation, Satan took Jesus **to Jerusalem**, to **the pinnacle of the temple**, and suggested that He **throw** Himself **down**. Had not God promised in Psalm 91:11,12 that He would preserve the Messiah? Perhaps Satan was tempting Jesus to present Himself as Messiah by performing a sensational stunt. Malachi had predicted that the Messiah would suddenly come to His temple (Mal. 3:1). Here then was Jesus' opportunity to obtain fame and notoriety as the promised Deliverer without going to Calvary.

4:12 For the third time, Jesus resisted temptation by quoting from the Bible. Deuteronomy 6:16 forbade putting **God** to the test.

4:13 Repulsed by the sword of the Spirit, **the devil** left Jesus **until an opportune time**. Temptations usually come in spasms rather than in streams.

Several additional points should be mentioned in connection with the temptation:

1. The order in Luke differs from that in Matthew. The second and third temptations are reversed; the reason for this is not clear.

2. In all three cases, the end held out was right enough, but the means of obtaining it was wrong. It is always wrong to obey Satan, to worship him or any other created being. It is wrong to tempt God.

3. The first temptation concerned the body, the second the soul, the third the spirit. They appealed respectively to the lust of the flesh, the lust of the eyes, and the pride of life.

4. The three temptations revolve around three of the strongest drives of human existence — physical appetite, desire for power and possessions, and desire for public recognition. How often disciples are tempted to choose a pathway of comfort and ease, to seek a prominent place in the world, and to gain a high position in the church.

5. In all three temptations, Satan used religious language and thus clothed the temptations with a garb of outward respectability. He even quoted Scripture (vv. 10, 11).

As James Stewart so aptly points out:

The study of the temptation narrative illuminates two important points. On the one hand, it proves that temptation is not necessarily sin. On the other hand, the narrative illuminates the great saying of a later disciple: "In that He Himself hath suffered being tempted, He is able to succour them that are tempted" (Hebrews 2:18).[11]

It is sometimes suggested that the temptation would have been meaningless if Jesus was not able to sin. The fact is that Jesus is God, and God cannot sin. The Lord Jesus never relinquished any of the attributes of deity. His deity was veiled during His life on earth but it was not and could not be laid aside. Some say that as God He could not sin but as Man He could sin. But He is still both God and Man, and it is unthinkable that He could sin today. The purpose of the temptation was not to see if He *would* sin but to prove that He could *not* sin. Only a holy, sinless Man could be our Redeemer.

E. Preparation by Teaching (4:14–30)

4:14, 15 Between verses 13 and 14 there is a gap of about one year. During this time the Lord ministered in Judea. The only record of this ministry is in John 2–5.

When **Jesus returned in the power of the Spirit to Galilee** to begin the second year of His public ministry,† His fame spread **through all the surrounding region**. As **He taught in** the Jewish **synagogues**, He was widely acclaimed.

4:16–21†† In **Nazareth**, His boyhood town, Jesus regularly went to **the synagogue on the Sabbath day**, that is, Satur-

day. There were two other things which we read that He did regularly. He prayed regularly (Luke 22:39), and He made it a habit to teach others (Mark 10:1). On one visit **to the synagogue**, He rose **to read** from the OT Scriptures. The attendant handed Him the scroll on which Isaiah's prophecy was written. The Lord unrolled the scroll to what we now know as Isaiah 61, and read verse 1 and the first half of verse 2. This passage has always been acknowledged as a description of the ministry of the Messiah. When Jesus said, **"Today this Scripture is fulfilled in your hearing,"** He was saying in the clearest possible manner that He was the Messiah of Israel.

Notice the revolutionary implications of the Messiah's mission. He came to deal with the enormous problems that have afflicted mankind throughout history:

Poverty. **To preach the gospel to the poor**.

Sorrow. **To heal the brokenhearted**.

Bondage. **To proclaim liberty to the captives**.

Suffering. **And recovery of sight to the blind**.

Oppression. **To set at liberty those who are oppressed**.

In short, He came to proclaim the acceptable year of the LORD — the dawning of a new era for this world's sighing, sobbing multitudes. He presented Himself as the answer to all the ills that torment us. And it is true, whether you think of these ills in a physical sense or in a spiritual sense. Christ is the answer.

It is significant that he stopped reading with the words " . . . **to proclaim the acceptable year of the Lord.**" He did not add the rest of the words from Isaiah " . . . and the day of vengeance of our God." The purpose of His First Coming was to preach **the acceptable year of the Lord**. This present age of grace is the accepted time and the day of salvation. When He returns to earth the second time, it will be to proclaim the day of vengeance of our God. Note that **the acceptable** time is spoken of as a **year**, the vengeance time as *a day*.

4:22 The people were obviously impressed. They spoke well of Him, having been attracted to Him by His **gracious words**. It was a mystery to them how **Joseph's son**, the Carpenter, had developed so well.

4:23 The Lord knew that this popularity was shallow. There was no real appreciation of His true identity or worth. To them, He was just one of their own home-town boys who had made good in Capernaum. He anticipated that they would **say** to Him, **"Physician, heal yourself!"** Ordinarily this parable would mean, "Do for yourself what you have done for others. Cure your own condition, since you claim to cure others." But here the meaning is slightly different. It is explained in the words that follow: **"Whatever we have heard done in Capernaum, do also here in Your country,"** that is, Nazareth. It was a scornful challenge for Him to perform miracles in Nazareth as He had done elsewhere, and thus save Himself from ridicule.

4:24–27 The Lord replied by stating a deep-rooted principle in human affairs: great men are not appreciated in their **own** neighborhood. He then cited two pointed incidents in the OT where prophets of God were not appreciated by the people of Israel and so were sent to Gentiles. When **there was a great famine** in Israel, **Elijah** was not sent to any Jewish widows — though there were plenty of them — but he **was sent** to a Gentile **widow** in **Sidon**. And although **many lepers were in Israel** when **Elisha** was ministering, he was not sent to any of them. Instead he was sent to the Gentile **Naaman**, captain of the Syrian army. Imagine the impact of Jesus' words on Jewish minds. They placed women, Gentiles, and lepers at the bottom of the social scale. But here the Lord pointedly placed all three *above* unbelieving Jews! What He was saying was that OT history was about to repeat itself. In spite of His miracles, He would be rejected not only by the city of Nazareth but by the nation of Israel. He would then turn to the Gentiles, just as Elijah and Elisha had done.

4:28 The people of Nazareth understood exactly what He meant. They were infuriated by the mere suggestion of favor being shown to Gentiles. Bishop Ryle comments:

Man bitterly hates the doctrine of the sovereignty of God which Christ had just declared. God was under no obligation to work miracles among them.[12]

4:29, 30 The people **thrust Him out of the city . . . to the brow of the hill**, intending to **throw Him down over the cliff**. Doubtless this was instigated by Satan as another attempt to destroy the royal Heir. But Jesus miraculously walked through the crowd and left the city. His foes were powerless to stop Him. As far as we know, He never returned to Nazareth.

IV. THE SON OF MAN PROVES HIS POWER (4:31–5:26)

A. Power Over An Unclean Spirit (4:31–37)

4:31–34 Nazareth's loss was Capernaum's gain. The people in the latter city recognized that His teaching was authoritative. His words were convicting and impelling. Verses 31–41 describe a typical Sabbath day in the life of the Lord. They reveal Him as Master over demons and disease. First He went to **the synagogue** and there met **a man** with **an unclean demon**. The adjective **unclean** is often used to describe evil spirits; it means that they themselves are impure and that they produce impurity in the lives of their victims. The reality of demon possession is seen in this passage. First there was a cry of terror — **"Let us alone!"** Then the spirit showed clear knowledge that Jesus was **the Holy One of God** who would eventually destroy the hosts of Satan.

4:35 **Jesus** issued a twofold command to the demon, **"Be quiet, and come out of him!"** The demon did so, after throwing the man to the ground but leaving him unharmed.

4:36, 37 The people were *amazed!* What was different about the words of Jesus that **unclean spirits** obeyed Him? What was that indefinable **authority and power** with which He spoke? No wonder **the reports about Him** spread throughout **the surrounding region**!

All the physical miracles of Jesus are pictures of similar miracles He performs in the spiritual realm. For instance, the following miracles in Luke convey these spiritual lessons:

Casting out unclean spirits (4:31–37) — deliverance from the filth and defilement of sin.

Healing Peter's mother-in-law of fever (4:38, 39) — relief from the restlessness and debility caused by sin.

Healing of the leper (5:12–16) — restoration from the loathesomeness and hopelessness of sin (see also 17:11–19).

The paralyzed man (5:17–26) — freedom from the paralysis of sin and enablement to serve God.

The widow's son raised to life (7:11–17) — sinners are dead in trespasses and sins, and need life (see also 8:49–56).

The stilling of the storm (8:22–25) — Christ can control the storms that rage in the lives of His disciples.

Legion, the demoniac (8:26–39) — sin produces violence and insanity and ostracizes men from civilized society. The Lord brings decency and sanity and fellowship with Himself.

The woman who touched the hem of His garment (8:43–48) — the impoverishment and depression brought on by sin.

Feeding of the 5,000 (9:10–17) — a sinful world starving for the bread of God. Christ satisfies the need through His disciples.

The demon-possessed son (9:37–43a) — the cruelty and violence of sin, and the healing power of Christ.

The woman with the spirit of infirmity (13:10–17) — sin deforms and cripples, but the touch of Jesus brings perfect restoration.

The man with dropsy (14:1–6) — sin produces discomfort, distress, and danger.

Blind beggar (18:35–43) — sin blinds men to eternal realities. The new birth results in opened eyes.

B. Power Over Fever (4:38, 39)

Next Jesus made a sick-call at **Simon's house**, where **Simon's wife's mother was sick with a high fever**. As soon as the Lord **rebuked the fever**, **it left her**. The cure was not only immediate but complete, since she was able to get up and serve the household. Usually a great fever leaves a person weak and listless. (Advocates of a celibate priesthood find little comfort in this passage. Peter was a married man!)

C. Power Over Diseases and Demons (4:40, 41)

4:40 As the Sabbath drew to a close, the people were freed from enforced inactivity; they **brought** a great number of invalids and demoniacs **to Him**. None came in vain. He **healed** every one of those who were diseased, and cast out the demons. Many of those who profess to be faith healers today confine their miracles to pre-chosen candidates. Jesus healed *every one* of them.

4:41 The expelled **demons** knew that Jesus was **the Christ, the Son of God**. But He would not accept the testimony of demons. They must be silenced. **They knew that He was the** Messiah, but God had other and better instruments to announce the fact.

D. Power Through Itinerant Preaching (4:42–44)

The next **day**, Jesus retired to **a deserted place** near Capernaum. **The crowd sought** till they found **Him**. They urged Him not to leave. **But He** reminded **them** that He had work to do in **the other cities . . . of Galilee**. So from synagogue to synagogue, He went **preaching** the good news about **the kingdom of God**. Jesus Himself was the King. He desired to reign over them. But first they must repent. He would not reign over a people who clung to their sins. This was the obstacle. They wanted to be saved from political problems but not from their sins.

E. Power Through Training Others: Disciples Called (5:1–11)

Several important lessons emerge from this simple account of the call of Peter.

1. The Lord used Peter's **boat** as a pulpit from which to teach the multitude. If we yield all our property and possessions to the Savior, it is wonderful how He uses them, and rewards us too.

2. He told Peter exactly where to find

plenty of fish — after Peter and the others had toiled **all night** without success. The omniscient Lord knows where the fish are running. Service carried on by our own wisdom and strength is futile. The secret of success in Christian work is to be guided by Him.

3. Though an experienced fisherman himself, Peter accepted advice from a Carpenter, and as a result, the nets were filled. **" . . . at Your word I will let down the net."** This shows the value of humility, of teachability, and of implicit obedience.

4. It was in **deep** waters that **the nets** were filled to the **breaking** point. So we must quit hugging the shore and launch out on full surrender's tide. Faith has its deep waters, and so do suffering, sorrow, and loss. It is these that fill the nets with fruitfulness.

5. **Their net** began to break and the ships **began to sink** (vv. 6, 7). Christ-directed service produces problems — but what delightful problems they are. They are the kind of problems that thrill the heart of a true fisherman.

6. This vision of the glory of the Lord Jesus produced in **Peter** an overpowering sense of his own unworthiness. It was so with Isaiah (6:5); it is so with all who see the King in His beauty.

7. It was while Peter was engaged in his ordinary employment that Christ called him to be a fisher of **men**. While you are waiting for guidance, do whatever your hand finds to do. Do it with all your might. Do it heartily as to the Lord. Just as a rudder guides a ship only when it is in motion, so God guides men when they too are in motion.

8. Christ called Peter from catching fish to catching **men**, or more literally, "taking men alive." What are all the fish in the ocean compared to the incomparable privilege of seeing one soul won for Christ and for eternity!

9. Peter, **James, and John** pulled their boats up on the beach and **forsook all and followed** Jesus on one of the best business days of their lives. And how much hung on their decision! We would probably never have heard of them if they had chosen to stay by their ships.

F. Power Over Leprosy (5:12–16)

5:12 Doctor Luke makes special mention of the fact that this **man** was **full of leprosy**. It was an advanced case and quite hopeless, humanly speaking. The faith of the leper was remarkable. He said, **"You can make me clean."** He could not have said that to any other man in the world. Yet he had absolute confidence in the power of the **Lord**. When he said, **"If You are willing"** he was not expressing doubt as to Christ's willingness. Rather he was coming as a suppliant, with no inherent right to be healed, but casting himself on the mercy and grace of the Lord.

5:13 To touch a leper was dangerous medically, defiling religiously, and degrading socially. But the Savior contracted no defilement. Instead there surged into the body of the leper a cascade of healing and health. It was not a gradual cure: **Immediately the leprosy left him**. Think what it must have meant to that hopeless, helpless leper to be made completely whole in a moment of time!

5:14 Jesus **charged him to tell no one** about the cure. The Savior did not want to attract a crowd of curiosity-seekers, or to stir up a popular movement to make Him King. Instead the Lord commanded the leper to **go . . . to the priest** and present the **offering** prescribed by **Moses** (Lev. 14:4). Every detail of the offering spoke of Christ. It was the function of **the priest** to examine the leper and to determine if he had actually been healed. The priest could not *heal*; all he could do was *pronounce* a man healed. This priest had never seen a cleansed leper before. The sight was unique; it should have made him realize that the Messiah had at last appeared. It should have been **a testimony to** all the priests. But their hearts were blinded by unbelief.

5:15, 16 In spite of the Lord's instructions not to publicize the miracle, the news traveled quickly, **and great multitudes came** to Him for healing. Jesus **often withdrew into the wilderness** for a time of prayer. Our Savior was a Man of prayer. It is fitting that this Gospel, which presents Him as Son of Man, should have more to say about His prayer life than any other.

G. Power Over Paralysis (5:17–26)

5:17 As the news of Jesus' ministry spread, **the Pharisees and teachers of the law** became increasingly hostile. Here we see them assembling in **Galilee** with the obvious purpose of finding some accusation against Him. **The power of the Lord was present to heal** the sick. Actually Jesus always had the power to heal, but the circumstances were not always favorable. In Nazareth, for instance, He could not do many mighty works because of the unbelief of the people (Matt. 13:58).

5:18, 19 Four **men brought** a paralytic **on a bed** to the house where Jesus was teaching. **They could not** get to Him **because of the crowd**, so they climbed the outside stairs to the roof. Then they lowered the man through an opening that they made by removing some tiles in the roof.

5:20, 21 Jesus took notice of the **faith** that would go to such lengths to bring a needy case to His attention. **When He saw their faith**, that is, the **faith** of the four plus the invalid, **He said to the** paralyzed man, **"Man, your sins are forgiven you."** This unprecedented statement aroused **the scribes and the Pharisees**. They knew that no one but **God** could **forgive sins**. Unwilling to admit that Jesus was God, they raised the cry of blasphemy.

5:22, 23 The Lord then proceeded to prove to them that He had actually forgiven the man's sins. First **He** asked them if it was **easier to say, "Your sins are forgiven you," or to say, "Rise up and walk"?** In one sense it is just as easy to *say* one as the other, but it is another thing to *do* either, since both are humanly impossible. The point here seems to be that it is easier to say **"Your sins are forgiven you,"** because there is no way of telling if it has happened. If you say, **"Rise up and walk,"** then it is easy to see if the patient has been healed.

The Pharisees could not *see* that the man's sins had been forgiven, so they would not believe. Therefore, Jesus performed a miracle which they could *see* to prove to them that He had truly forgiven the man's sins. He gave the paralytic the power to walk.

5:24 **"But that you may know that the Son of Man has power on earth to forgive sins"** — The title, **the Son of Man**, emphasizes the Lord's perfect humanity. In one sense, we are all sons of man, but this title *"the* Son of Man" sets Jesus off from every other man who ever lived. It describes Him as a Man according to God, One who is morally perfect, One who would suffer, bleed, and die, and One to whom universal headship has been given.

5:25 In obedience to His word, the paralyzed man got up, carried his small sleeping pad, and went home, **glorifying God**.

5:26 The crowd was literally **amazed, and they** too **glorified God**, acknowledging that they had **seen** incredible **things** that day, namely the pronouncing of forgiveness and the miracle that proved it.

V. THE SON OF MAN EXPLAINS HIS MINISTRY (5:27–6:49)

A. The Call of Levi (5:27, 28)

Levi was a Jewish **tax collector** for the Roman government. Such men were hated by their fellow-Jews, not only because of this collaboration with Rome, but because of their dishonest practices. One day while Levi was at work, Jesus passed by and invited him to become His follower. With amazing promptness, Levi **left all, rose up, and followed Him**. Think of the tremendous consequences that flowed from that simple decision. Levi, or Matthew, became the writer of the First Gospel. It pays to hear His call and follow Him.

B. Why the Son of Man Calls Sinners (5:29–32)

5:29, 30 It has been suggested that **Levi** had three purposes in arranging this **great feast**. He wanted to honor the Lord, to witness publicly to his new allegiance, and he wanted to introduce his friends to Jesus. Most Jews would not have eaten with a group of **tax collectors**. Jesus ate **with tax collectors and sinners**. He did not, of course, fraternize with them in their sins, or do anything that would compromise His testimony, but He used these occasions to teach, to rebuke, and to bless.

Their scribes and the Pharisees[13] criticized Jesus for associating with these despised people, the dregs of society.

5:31 Jesus answered that His action was in perfect accord with His purpose in coming into the world. Healthy people do not need a doctor; only **those who are sick** do.

5:32 The Pharisees considered themselves to be **righteous**. They had no deep sense of sin or of need. Therefore, they could not benefit from the ministry of the Great Physician. But these tax collectors and sinners realized that they were **sinners** and that they needed to be saved from their sins. It was for people like them that the Savior came. Actually, the Pharisees were *not* righteous. They needed to be saved as much as the tax collectors. But they were unwilling to confess their sins and acknowledge their guilt. And so they criticized the Doctor for going to people who were seriously ill.

C. The Non-Fasting of Jesus' Disciples Explained (5:33–35)

5:33 The next tactic of the Pharisees was to interrogate Jesus on the custom of fasting. After all, **the disciples of John** the Baptist had followed the ascetic life of their master. And the followers of the **Pharisees** observed various ceremonial fasts. But Jesus' disciples did not. Why not?

5:34, 35 The Lord answered in effect that there was no reason for His disciples to fast while He was still **with them**. Here He associates fasting with sorrow and mourning. When He would be **taken away from them**, that is, violently, in death, they would **fast** as an expression of their grief.

D. Three Parables on the New Dispensation (5:36–39)

5:36 Three parables follow which teach that a new dispensation had begun, and there could be no mixing of the new and the old.

In the *first* **parable**, the **old** garment speaks of the legal system or dispensation, while the **new garment** pictures the era of grace. They are incompatible. An attempt to mix law and grace results in a spoiling of both. A patch taken from a new garment spoils the new one, and it **does not match the old** one, either in appearance or strength. J. N. Darby states it well: "Jesus would do no such

thing as tack on Christianity to Judaism. Flesh and law go together, but grace and law, God's righteousness and man's, will never mix."

5:37, 38 The *second* parable teaches the folly of putting **new wine into old wineskins**. The fermenting action of the **new wine** causes pressure on the skins which they are no longer pliable or elastic enough to bear. The skins **burst** and the wine is **spilled**. The outmoded forms, ordinances, traditions, and rituals of Judaism were too rigid to hold the joy, the exuberance, and the energy of the new dispensation. The **new wine** is seen in this chapter in the unconventional methods of the four men who brought the paralytic to Jesus. It is seen in the freshness and zeal of Levi. **The old wineskins** picture the stodginess and cold formalism of the Pharisees.

5:39 The *third* parable states that **no one, having drunk old wine**, prefers **new. He says, "The old is better."** This pictures the natural reluctance of men to abandon the old for the new, Judaism for Christianity, law for grace, shadows for substance! As Darby says, "A man accustomed to forms, human arrangements, father's religion, etc., never likes the new principle and power of the kingdom."

E. The Son of Man Is Lord of the Sabbath (6:1–11)

6:1, 2 Two incidents concerning the Sabbath are now brought before us to show that the mounting opposition of the religious leaders was reaching a climax. The first occurred on "the second-first Sabbath" (literal translation). This is explained as follows: the first Sabbath was the first one after the Passover. The second was the next after that. **On the second Sabbath after the first**, the Lord and His disciples walked **through** some **grainfields**. The disciples **plucked** some **grain**, rubbed the kernels **in their hands**, and **ate them. The Pharisees** could not quarrel about the fact of the grain being taken; this was permitted by the law (Deut. 23:25). Their criticism was that it was done **on the Sabbath**. They sometimes called the plucking of grain a harvesting operation, and the **rubbing** of the grain a threshing operation.

6:3–5 The Lord's answer, using an incident from the life of David, was that the law of the Sabbath was never intended to forbid a work of necessity. Rejected and pursued, **David** and his men were **hungry**. They **went into the house of God** and **ate the showbread**, which ordinarily was reserved for **the priests**. God made an exception in David's case. There was sin in Israel. The king was rejected. The law concerning the showbread was never intended to be so slavishly followed as to permit God's king to starve.

Here was a similar situation. Christ and His disciples were hungry. The Pharisees would rather see them starve than pick wheat on the Sabbath. But **The Son of Man is also Lord of the Sabbath**. He gave the law in the first place, and no one was better qualified than He to interpret its true spiritual meaning and to save it from misunderstanding.

6:6–8 A second incident that **happened on another Sabbath** concerned a miraculous cure. **The scribes and Pharisees watched** Jesus **closely** and maliciously to see **whether He would heal** a **man** with a **withered hand . . . on the Sabbath**. From past experience and from their knowledge of Him, they had good reason to believe that He would. The Lord did not disappoint them. He first asked **the man** to **stand** in the middle of the crowd in the synagogue. This dramatic action riveted the attention of all on what was about to happen.

6:9 Then Jesus asked His critics if it was **lawful on the Sabbath to do good or to do evil**. If they answered correctly, they would have to say that it was right to do good on the Sabbath, and wrong to do harm. If it was right to do good, then He was doing good by healing the man. If it was wrong to do **evil** on the Sabbath, than they were breaking the Sabbath by plotting to kill the Lord Jesus.

6:10 There was no answer from the adversaries. Jesus then directed the man to **stretch out** his withered right **hand**. (Only Dr. Luke mentions that it was the right hand.) With the command went the necessary power. As the man obeyed, **his hand was restored** to normal.

6:11 The Pharisees and scribes **were filled with rage**. They wanted to condemn Jesus for breaking the Sabbath. All He had done was speak a few words and

the man was healed. No servile work was involved. Yet they plotted together how they might "get" Him.

The Sabbath was intended by God for man's good. When rightly understood, it did not prohibit a work of necessity or a work of mercy.

F. Twelve Disciples Chosen (6:12–19)

6:12 Jesus spent **all night in prayer** before choosing the twelve. What a rebuke this is to our impulsiveness and independence of God! Luke is the only evangelist who mentions this **night** of **prayer**.

6:13–16 The **twelve** whom **He chose** from among the wider circle of **disciples** were:

1. **Simon, whom He also named Peter**, son of Jonah, and one of the most prominent of the apostles.
2. **Andrew his brother**. It was Andrew who introduced Peter to the Lord.
3. **James** the son of Zebedee. He was privileged to go with Peter and John to the Mt. of Transfiguration. He was killed by Herod Agrippa I.
4. **John** the son of Zebedee. Jesus called James and John "Sons of Thunder." It was this John who wrote the Gospel and the Epistles bearing his name, and the book of Revelation.
5. **Philip**, a native of Bethsaida, who introduced Nathanael to Jesus. Not to be confused with Philip, the evangelist, in the book of Acts.
6. **Bartholomew**, generally understood to be another name for Nathanael. He is mentioned only in the listings of the twelve.
7. **Matthew**, the tax collector, also named Levi. He wrote the First Gospel.
8. **Thomas**, also called Twin. He said he would not believe that the Lord had risen until he saw conclusive evidence.
9. **James the son of Alphaeus**. He may have been the one who held a place of responsibility in the church at Jerusalem after James, the son of Zebedee, had been killed by Herod.
10. **Simon called the Zealot**. Little is known of him, as far as the sacred record is concerned.

11. **Judas the son of James**. Possibly the same as Jude, the author of the Epistle, and commonly believed to be Lebbaeus, whose surname was Thaddaeus (Matt. 10:3; Mark 3:18).

12. **Judas Iscariot**, presumed to be from Kerioth in Judah, and thus the only one of the apostles who was not from Galilee. The betrayer of our Lord, he was called by Jesus "the son of perdition."

The disciples were not all men of outstanding intellect or ability. They represented a cross-section of humanity. The thing that made them great was their relationship to Jesus and their commitment to Him. They were probably young men in their twenties when the Savior chose them. Youth is the time when men are most zealous and teachable and best able to endure hardship. He selected only twelve disciples. He was more interested in quality than quantity. Given the right caliber of men, He could send them out and by the process of spiritual reproduction could evangelize the world.

Once the disciples were chosen, it was important that they should be thoroughly trained in the principles of the kingdom of God. The rest of this chapter is devoted to a summary of the type of character and behavior that should be found in disciples of the Lord Jesus.

6:17–19 The following discourse is not identical with the Sermon on the Mount (Matt. 5–7). That was delivered on a mountain; this was delivered **on a level place**. That had blessings but no woes; this has both. There are other differences — in words, in length, in emphasis.[14]

Notice that this message of stern discipleship was given to the **multitude** as well as to the twelve. It seems that whenever a great multitude followed Jesus, He tested their sincerity by speaking quite bluntly to them. As someone said, "Christ first woos, then winnows."

People had come **from all Judea and Jerusalem** in the south, from **Tyre and Sidon** in the northwest, Gentiles as well as Jews. Diseased people and demoniacs pressed close to touch Jesus; they knew that healing **power** flowed **out from Him**.

It is very important to realize how revolutionary the teachings of the Savior are. Remember that He was going to the cross. He would die, be buried, rise again the third day, and return to heaven. The good news of free salvation must go out to the world. The redemption of men depended on their hearing the message. How could the world be evangelized? Astute leaders of this world would organize a vast army, provide liberal finances, generous food supplies, entertainment for the morale of the men, and good public relations.

G. Beatitudes and Woes (6:20–26)

6:20 Jesus chose twelve **disciples** and sent them out poor, hungry, and persecuted. Can the world be evangelized that way? Yes, and in no other way! The Savior began with four blessings and four woes. **"Blessed are you poor."** Not blessed are *the* poor but blessed are *you* poor. Poverty in itself is not a blessing; it is more often a curse. Here Jesus was speaking about a self-imposed poverty for His sake. He was not speaking of people who are poor because of laziness, tragedy, or reasons beyond their control. Rather He was referring to those who purposely choose to be poor in order to share their Savior with others. And when you think of it, it is the only sensible, reasonable approach. Suppose the disciples had gone forth as wealthy men. People would have flocked to the banner of Christ with the hope of becoming rich. As it was, the disciples could not promise them silver and gold. If they came at all, it would be in quest of spiritual blessing. Also if the disciples had been rich, they would have missed the blessing of constant dependence on the Lord, and of proving His faithfulness. The kingdom of God belongs to those who are satisfied with the supply of their current needs so that everything above that can go into the work of the Lord.

6:21 **"Blessed are you who hunger now."** Once again this does not mean the vast hordes of humanity who are suffering from malnutrition. Rather it refers to disciples of Jesus Christ who deliberately adopt a life of self-denial in order to help alleviate human need, both spiritual and physical. It is people who are willing to get along on a plain, inexpensive diet rather than deprive others of the gospel by their indulgence. All such self-denial will be rewarded in a future day.

"Blessed are you who weep now." Not that sorrow is in itself a blessing; the weeping of unsaved people has no lasting benefit connected with it. Here Jesus is speaking about tears that are shed for His sake. Tears for lost, perishing mankind. Tears over the divided, impotent state of the church. All sorrow endured in serving the Lord Jesus Christ. Those who sow in tears will reap in joy.

6:22 **"Blessed are you when men hate you . . . exclude you . . . revile you, and cast out your name as evil."** This blessing is not for those who suffer for their own sins or stupidity. It is for those who are despised, excommunicated, reproached, and slandered because of their *loyalty to Christ.*

The key to the understanding of these four beatitudes is found in the phrase **"for the Son of Man's sake."** Things that in themselves would be a curse become a blessing when willingly endured for Him. But the motive must be love for Christ; otherwise the most heroic sacrifices are worthless.

6:23 Persecution for Christ is cause for great rejoicing. First it will bring a **great reward in heaven**. Second it associates the sufferer with His faithful witnesses of past ages.

The four blessings describe the ideal person in the kingdom of God — the one who lives sacrificially, austerely, soberly, and enduringly.

6:24 **But**, on the other hand, the four woes present those who are least esteemed in Christ's new society. Tragically, these are the very ones who are counted great in the world today! **"Woe to you who are rich."** There are serious and moral problems connected with hoarding wealth in a world where several thousand die daily of starvation and where every other person is deprived of the good news of salvation through faith in Christ. These words of the Lord Jesus should be pondered carefully by Christians who are tempted to lay up treasures on earth, to hoard and scrimp for a rainy day. To do this is to live for the wrong world. Incidentally, this **woe** on the rich proves quite conclusively that when the Lord said "Blessed are you

poor" in v. 20, He did not mean poor in spirit. Otherwise v. 24 would have to mean "woe to you who are rich in spirit" and such a meaning is out of the question. Those who have wealth and who fail to use it for the eternal enrichment of others **have** already **received** the only reward they will ever get — the selfish, present gratification of their desires.

6:25 **"Woe to you who are full."** These are believers who eat in expensive restaurants, who live on the finest gourmet foods, who spare no expense when it comes to their groceries. Their motto is "Nothing is too good for the people of God!" The Lord says that they will **hunger** in a coming day, that is, when rewards are given out for faithful, sacrificial discipleship.

"Woe to you who laugh now." This **woe** is aimed at those whose lives are a continuous cycle of amusement, entertainment, and pleasure. They act as if life was made for fun and frolic and seem oblivious of the desperate condition of men outside of Jesus Christ. Those who **laugh now** will **mourn and weep** when they look back over wasted opportunities, selfish indulgence, and their own spiritual impoverishment.

6:26 **"Woe to you when all**[15] **men speak well of you."** Why? Because it is a sure sign you are not living the life or faithfully proclaiming the message. It is in the very nature of the gospel to offend the ungodly. Those who receive their plaudits from the world are fellow-travelers with **the false prophets** of the OT who tickled the people'e ears, telling them what they wanted to hear. They were more interested in the favor of men than in the praise of God.

H. The Son of Man's Secret Weapon: Love (6:27–38)

6:27–29a Now the Lord Jesus unveils to His disciples a secret weapon from the arsenal of God — the weapon of **love**. This will be one of their most effective weapons in evangelizing the world. However, when He speaks of **love**, He is not referring to the human emotion of that name. This is *supernatural* love. Only those who are born again can know it or display it. It is utterly impossible for anyone who does not have the indwelling Holy Spirit. A murderer may love his own children, but that is not love as Jesus intended. The one is human affection; the other is divine love. The first requires only physical life; the second requires divine life. The first is largely a matter of the emotions; the second is largely a matter of the will. Anyone can love his friends, but it takes supernatural power to love one's enemies. And *that* is the love (Gk. — *agapē*) of the NT. It means to **do good to those who hate you,** to **bless those who curse you**, to **pray for those who** are nasty to **you**, and ever and always to turn the other **cheek**.

F. B. Meyer explains:

> In its deepest sense love is the perquisite of Christianity. To feel toward enemies what others feel toward friends; to descend as rain and sunbeams on the unjust as well as the just; to minister to those who are unprepossessing and repellent as others minister to the attractive and winsome; to be always the same, not subject to moods or fancies or whims; to suffer long; to take no account of evil; to rejoice with the truth; to bear, believe, hope, and endure all things, never to fail — this is love, and such love is the achievement of the Holy Spirit. We cannot achieve it ourselves.[16]

Love like this is unbeatable. The world can usually conquer the man who fights back. It is used to jungle warfare and to the principle of retaliation. But it does not know how to deal with the person who repays every wrong with a kindness. It is utterly confused and disorganized by such other-worldly behavior.

6:29b–31 When robbed of its overcoat, love offers its suit-coat as well. It never turns away from any genuine case of need. When unjustly deprived of its property, it does not ask that it be returned. Its golden rule is to treat others with the same kindness and consideration as it would like to receive.

6:32–34 Unsaved men can **love those who love them**. This is natural behavior, and so common that it makes no impact on the world of unsaved men. Banks and loan companies will *lend* money with the hope of collecting interest. This does not require divine life.

6:35 Therefore Jesus repeated that we should **love** our **enemies, do good, and lend, hoping for nothing in return**. Such behavior is distinctly Christian and marks out those who are the **sons of the Most High**. Of course, this is not the way men *become* sons of the Most High; that can only happen through receiving Jesus Christ as Lord and Savior (John 1:12). But this is the way true believers *manifest* themselves to the world as sons of God. God treated us in the way described in verses 27–35. **He is kind to the unthankful and** the **evil**. When we act like that, we manifest the family likeness. We show that we have been born of God.

6:36 To be **merciful** means to forgive when it is in our power to avenge. The **Father** showed us mercy by not giving us the punishment we deserved. He wants us to show mercy to others.

6:37 There are two things that love doesn't do — it doesn't **judge** and it doesn't **condemn**. Jesus said, **"Judge not and you shall not be judged."** First of all, we must not judge people's motives. We cannot read the heart and so cannot know why a person acts as he does. Then we must not judge another Christian's stewardship or service (1 Cor. 4:1–5); God is the Judge in all such cases. And in general we must not be censorious. A critical, fault-finding spirit violates the law of love.

There are certain areas, however, in which Christians *must* judge. We must often judge whether other people are true Christians; otherwise we could never recognize an unequal yoke (2 Cor. 6:14). Sin must be judged in the home and in the assembly. In short, we must judge between good and evil, but we must not impugn motives or assassinate character.

"Forgive and you will be forgiven." This makes our forgiveness dependent on our willingness to forgive. But other Scriptures seem to teach that when we receive Christ by faith, we are freely and unconditionally forgiven. How can we reconcile this seeming contradiction? The explanation is that we are speaking of two different types of forgiveness — *judicial* and *parental*. *Judicial forgiveness* is that which is granted by God the Judge to everyone who believes on the Lord Jesus Christ. It means that the penalty of sins has been met by Christ and the believing sinner will not have to pay it. It is unconditional.

Parental forgiveness is that which is granted by God the Father to His erring child when he confesses and forsakes his sin. It results in the restoration of fellowship in the family of God, and has nothing to do with the penalty of sin. As Father, God cannot forgive us when we are unwilling to forgive one another. He doesn't act that way, and cannot walk in fellowship with those who do. It is parental forgiveness that Jesus refers to in the words **"and you will be forgiven."**

6:38 Love manifests itself in giving (see John 3:16; Eph. 5:25). The Christian ministry is a ministry of expenditure. Those who **give** generously are rewarded generously. The picture is of a man with a large apron-like fold in the front of his garment. He uses it for carrying seed. The more widely he broadcasts the seed, the greater his harvest. He is rewarded with **good measure, pressed down, shaken together, and running over**. He receives it **into** his **bosom**, that is, into the fold of his garment. It is a fixed principle in life that we reap according to our sowing, that our actions react upon us, that **the same measure** we **use** to others is **measured back** to us. If we sow material things we reap spiritual treasures of inestimable value. It is also true that what we keep we lose, and what we give we have.

I. Parable of the Blind Hypocrite (6:39–45)

6:39 In the previous section the Lord Jesus taught that the disciples were to have a ministry of giving. Now He warns that the extent to which they can be a blessing to others is limited by their own spiritual condition. **The blind** cannot **lead the blind; both** would **fall into the ditch**. We cannot give what we do not have ourselves. If we are blind to certain truths of God's Word, we cannot help someone else in those areas. If there are blind-spots in our spiritual life, we can be sure that there will be blind-spots in the lives of our understudies.

6:40 **"A disciple is not above his teacher, but everyone who is perfectly trained will be like his teacher."** A person cannot teach what he does not know. He cannot lead his students to a level higher than he himself has attained. The more he teaches them, the more they become like him. But his own stage of growth forms the upper limit to which he can bring them. A student is **perfectly trained** as a disciple when he becomes like his master. Deficiencies in the doctrine or life of the teacher will be carried over into the lives of his pupils, and when the instruction has been completed, the disciples cannot be expected to be above the master.

6:41–42 This important truth is still more strikingly brought out in the illustration of **the speck** and **the plank**. One day a man is walking past a threshing floor where the grain is being beaten out. A sudden gust of wind lifts a tiny **speck** of chaff and lands it squarely in his eye. He rubs the eye to get rid of the irritant, but the more he rubs it, the more irritated it becomes. Just then another man comes along, sees the distress of the first, and offers to help. But this man has a **plank** sticking out of **his own eye**! He can scarcely help because he cannot see what he is doing. The obvious lesson is that a teacher cannot speak to his disciples about blemishes in their lives if he has the same blemishes to an exaggerated degree in his own life, yet cannot see them. If we are to be a help to others, our own lives must be exemplary. Otherwise they will say to us, "Physician, heal yourself!"

6:43–45 The fourth illustration the Lord uses is the **tree** and its **fruit**. A tree bears fruit, **good** or **bad**, depending on what it is in itself. We judge a tree by the kind and quality of fruit it bears. So it is in the area of discipleship. A man who is morally pure and spiritually healthy can bring forth blessing for others **out of the good treasure of his heart**. On the other hand, a man who is basically impure only **brings forth evil**.

Thus in verses 39–45, the Lord is telling the disciples that their ministry is to be a ministry of character. What they are is more important than anything they will ever say or do. The final result of their service will be determined by what they are in themselves.

J. The Lord Demands Obedience (6:46–49)

6:46 **"But why do you call Me**

'Lord, Lord,' and do not do the things which I say?" The word *Lord* means *Master;* it means He has complete authority over our lives, that we belong to Him, and that we are obligated to do whatever He says. To call Him **Lord** and then to fail to obey Him is absurdly contradictory. A mere professed acknowledgment of His lordship is not enough. True love and faith involve obedience. We don't really love Him and we don't really believe on Him if we don't do what He says.

> Ye call me the "Way" and walk me not,
> Ye call me the "Life" and live me not,
> Ye call me "Master" and obey me not,
> If I condemn thee, blame me not.
> Ye call me "Bread" and eat me not,
> Ye call me "Truth" and believe me not,
> Ye call me "Lord" and serve me not,
> If I condemn thee, blame me not.
>   – *Geoffrey O'Hara*

6:47–49   To further enforce this important truth, the Lord gives the story of two builders. We commonly apply this story to the gospel; we say the wise man is descriptive of the one who believes and is saved; the foolish man is the one who rejects Christ and is lost. This is, of course, a valid *application.* But if we interpret the story in its context, we find that there is a deeper meaning.

The wise man is the one who **comes to** Christ (salvation), who **hears** His **sayings** (instruction), and who **does them** (obedience). He is the one who builds his life on such principles of Christian discipleship as are laid down in this chapter. This is the right way to build a life. When the house is battered by floods and streams, it stands firm because **it** is **founded on the rock**, Christ and His teachings.[17]

The foolish man is one who hears (instruction) but who fails to follow the teaching (disobedience). He builds his life on what he thinks to be best, following the carnal principles of this world. When the storms of life rage, his **house**, which is **without a foundation**, is swept away. His soul may be saved but his life is lost.

The wise man is the man who is poor, who is hungry, who mourns, and who is persecuted — all for the Son of Man's sake. The world would call such

a person foolish. Jesus calls him wise.

The foolish man is the one who is rich, who feasts luxuriously, who lives hilariously, and who is popular with everyone. The world calls him a wise man. Jesus calls him foolish.

VI. THE SON OF MAN EXPANDS HIS MINISTRY (7:1–9:50)[†]

A. Healing of the Centurion's Servant (7:1–10)

7:1–3   At the conclusion of His discourse, Jesus left the multitude and **entered Capernaum**. There He was besieged by the **elders of the Jews**, who had come to ask help for a Gentile **centurion's servant**. It seems that this centurion was especially kind to the Jewish people, even going so far as to build a synagogue for them. Like all the other centurions in the NT, he is presented in a good light (Luke 23:47; Acts 10:1–48).

It is is rather unusual for a master to be so kindly disposed toward a slave as this centurion was. When the **servant** took **sick**, the centurion asked the **elders of the Jews** to implore Jesus to heal him. This Roman officer is the only one who sought blessing from Jesus for **a servant**, as far as we know.

7:4–7   It was a strange position for the elders of the people to be in. They did not believe in Jesus, yet their friendship for the centurion forced them to go to Jesus in a time of need. They said concerning the centurion **that he was worthy**. But when the centurion met Jesus, he said, **"I am not worthy,"** meaning "I am not important enough."

According to Matthew, the centurion went directly to Jesus. Here in Luke, he sent the elders. Both are correct. First, he sent the elders, then he himself went out to Jesus.

The humility and faith of the centurion are remarkable. He did **not** consider himself **worthy** that Jesus **should enter** his house. Neither did he consider himself **worthy to come to** Jesus in person. But he had faith to believe that Jesus could heal without being bodily present. A **word** from Him would drive out the sickness.

7:8   The centurion went on to explain that he knew something about **authority** and responsibility. He had considerable experience in this realm. He himself was **under** the **authority** of the Roman government and was responsible to carry out its orders. In addition, he had **soldiers under** him who were instantly obedient to his orders. He recognized that Jesus had the same kind of authority over diseases that the Roman government had over him, and that he had over his subordinates.

7:9, 10 No wonder that **Jesus marveled at** the faith of this Gentile centurion. No one **in Israel** had made such a bold confession of Jesus' absolute authority. **Such great faith** could never go unrewarded. When they got back to the centurion's **house**, they found that **the servant** was completely **well**.

This is one of two times in the Gospels when we read that Jesus **marveled**. He marveled at the faith of this Gentile centurion, and He marveled at the unbelief of Israel (Mark 6:6).

B. Raising of the Widow's Son (7:11–17)

7:11–15 Nain was a little town southwest of Capernaum. As Jesus approached, He saw a funeral procession leaving **the city**. It was for **the only son of a widow**. The Lord **had compassion on** the bereft mother. Touching the frame on which the body was **carried** — apparently to stop the procession — Jesus ordered the **young man** to **arise**. Immediately life returned to the corpse, and the lad **sat up**. Thus the One who is Lord over death as well as over disease restored the boy **to his mother**.

7:16, 17 Fear seized the people. They had witnessed a mighty miracle. The dead was raised to life. They believed the Lord Jesus was **a great prophet** sent by God. But when they said **"God has visited His people,"** they probably did not understand that Jesus *Himself* was God. Rather they felt that the miracle was evidence that God was working in their midst in an impersonal sort of way. Their **report** of the miracle spread throughout **all the surrounding region**.

Dr. Luke's casebook records the restoration by Jesus of three "only children": the widow's son; Jairus' daughter (8:42); and the child possessed by demons (9:38).

C. The Son of Man Reassures His Forerunner (7:18–23)

7:18–20 News of the miracles of Jesus filtered back to **John** the Baptist in prison in the castle of Machaerus, on the eastern shore of the Dead Sea. If Jesus was truly the Messiah, why didn't He exercise His power in freeing John from Herod's hands? So John sent **two of his disciples** to ask Jesus if He were really the Messiah, or if the Christ was still to come. It may seem strange to us that John should ever question Jesus' Messiahship. But we must remember that the best of men suffer brief lapses of faith. Also, physical distress can lead to severe mental depression.

7:21–23 Jesus answered John's question by reminding him that He was performing miracles such as the prophets predicted would be performed by the Messiah (Isa. 35:5, 6; 61:1). Then He added, as a postscript to John, **"Blessed is he who is not offended because of Me."** This may be understood as a rebuke; John had been **offended** by the failure of Jesus to seize the reins of authority and to manifest Himself in the way people expected. But it may also be interpreted as an exhortation to John not to abandon his faith.

C. G. Moore says:

> I know of no hours more trying to faith than those in which Jesus multiplies evidences of His power and *does not use it* . . . There is need of much grace when the messengers come back saying: "Yes, He has all the power, and is all that you have thought; but He said not a word about taking you out of prison. . . ." No explanation; faith nourished; prison doors left closed; and then the message, "Blessed is he whosoever shall not be offended in me." That is all![18]

D. The Son of Man Praises His Forerunner (7:24–29)

7:24† Whatever Jesus might say to John in private, He had nothing but praise for him in public. When the people had flocked out to the desert near Jordan, what had they expected to find? A fickle, spineless, wavering opportun-

†See p. xx.

ist? No one could ever accuse John of being **a reed shaken by the wind**.

7:25 Had they then expected to find a Hollywood-style playboy, fashionably dressed, and wallowing in luxury and ease? No, that is the type of person who hangs around **king's courts**, seeking to enjoy all the pleasures of the palace and to make endless contacts for his own profit and gratification.

7:26 It was **a prophet** they went **out to see** — an embodied conscience who declared the word of the living God no matter what the cost to him might be. Indeed, he was **more than a prophet**.

7:27 He himself was the subject of prophecy, and he had the unique privilege of introducing the King. Jesus quoted from Malachi 3:1 to show that John had been promised in the OT, but in so doing, He made a very interesting change in the pronouns. In Malachi 3:1, we read, "Behold, I send My messenger, and he will prepare the way before Me." But Jesus quoted it, **"Behold, I send My messenger before Your face, who will prepare Your way before You."** The pronoun *Me* is changed to **You**.

Godet explains this change as follows:

In the prophet's view, He who was sending, and He before whom the way was to be prepared, were one and the same person, Jehovah. Hence the *before me* in Malachi. But for Jesus, who, in speaking of Himself, never confounds Himself with the Father, a distinction became necessary. It is not Jehovah who speaks of Himself, but Jehovah speaking to Jesus; hence the form *before Thee*. From which evidence, does it not follow from this quotation that, in the prophet's idea, as well as in that of Jesus, Messiah's appearing is the appearing of Jehovah?[19]

7:28 Jesus continued to praise John by asserting that **among those born of women, there** was **not a greater prophet than John**. This superiority did not refer to his personal character but to his position as forerunner of the Messiah. There were other men who were as great as he in zeal, honor, and devotion. But no one else had the privilege of announcing the coming of the King. In this, John was unique. Yet, the Lord added, the **least** one **in the kingdom of God** is **greater**

than John. To enjoy the blessings of **the kingdom is greater** than to be the forerunner of the King.

7:29 Jesus is probably still speaking in verse 29, and thus the (supplied) word *Him* should be *him*. He is recalling the reception given to John's preaching. The common **people** and the avowed sinners, like **the tax collectors**, repented and were **baptized** in the Jordan. In believing John's message and acting upon it, they **justified God**, that is, they reckoned God to be righteous in demanding that the people of Israel should first repent before Christ could reign over them. This use of the word *justify* clearly shows that it cannot mean *to make righteous*; no one could *make* God righteous. Rather it means to account God as being right in His decrees and requirements.

E. The Son of Man Criticizes His Own Generation (7:30–35)

7:30–34 **The Pharisees** and teachers of the law refused to submit to John's baptism, and thus **rejected** God's program for their welfare. In fact, it was impossible to please **the generation** of which they were the leaders. Jesus likened them to **children** playing **in the marketplace**. They didn't want to play either wedding or funeral. They were perverse, wayward, unpredictable, and refractory. No matter what ministry God used among them, they took exception to it. **John the Baptist** gave them an example of austerity, asceticism, and self-denial. They didn't like it, but criticized him as demon-possessed. **The Son of Man** ate and drank with **tax collectors and sinners**, that is, He identified Himself with those whom He came to bless. But still the Pharisees were unhappy; they called Him **a glutton** and a tippler. Fast or feast, funeral or wedding, John or Jesus — nothing and no one pleased them!

Ryle admonishes:

We must give up the idea of trying to please everyone. The thing is impossible, and the attempt is mere waste of time. We must be content to walk in Christ's steps, and let the world say what it likes. Do what we will, we shall never satisfy it, or silence its ill-natured remarks. It first found fault with John the Baptist and then with his blessed Master. And it will go on cavilling and finding fault with that Master's disciples so long as one of them is left upon earth.[20]

7:35 **"But wisdom is justified by all her children."** **Wisdom** here represents the Savior Himself. The small minority of disciples who honor Him are wisdom's **children**. Even though the mass of the people reject Him, yet His true followers will vindicate His claims by lives of love, holiness, and devotedness.

F. A Sinner Anoints the Savior (7:36–39)

7:36 In the incident which follows, we have an illustration of wisdom being justified by one of her children, namely the sinful woman. As Dr. H. C. Woodring said so pointedly, "When God cannot get religious leaders to appreciate Christ, He will get harlots to do so." Simon, **the** Pharisee, had **asked** Jesus home **to eat with him**, perhaps through curiosity or perhaps through hostility.

7:37, 38 A sinful **woman** appeared in the room at the same time. We do not know who she was; the tradition that she was Mary Magdalene lacks scriptural support. This woman **brought** a white translucent **flask** of perfume. As Jesus reclined on a couch while eating, with His head near **the table**, she **stood at His feet**. She washed **His feet with her tears, wiped them with** her **hair, and kissed** them repeatedly. Then **she anointed them** with the costly perfume. Such worship and sacrifice revealed her conviction that there was nothing too good for Jesus.

7:39 Simon's attitude was quite different. He felt that prophets, like Pharisees, should be separate from sinners. **If** Jesus **were** truly **a prophet**, he concluded, He would not let **a sinner** bestow such affection on Him.

G. Parable of the Two Debtors (7:40–50)

7:40–43 Jesus read his mind, and courteously asked **Simon** permission to say **something** to him. With consummate skill, the Lord told the story of the **creditor** and the **two debtors. One owed** fifty dollars, the other five. **When** neither

of them could **repay** at all, he cancelled both debts. At this point Jesus asked Simon **which** borrower would **love** the lender **more**. The Pharisee correctly answered, **"I suppose the one whom he forgave more."** In admitting this, he condemned himself, as Jesus proceeded to show him.

7:44–47 From the time the Lord had **entered** the **house**, the woman had lavished affection upon Him. The Pharisee, by contrast, had given Him a very cool reception, not even attending to the usual courtesies, such as washing the guest's feet, kissing His cheek and giving Him oil for His head. Why was this? The reason was that the woman had the consciousness of having been forgiven much, whereas Simon did not feel he had been a great sinner at all. **"But to whom little is forgiven, the same loves little."**

Jesus did not suggest that the Pharisee was not a great sinner. Rather He emphasized that Simon had never truly acknowledged his vast guilt and been forgiven. If he had, he would have loved the Lord as deeply as the harlot. We are all great sinners. We can all know great forgiveness. We can all love the Lord greatly.

7:48 Jesus then publicly announced to the woman that her **sins** had been **forgiven**. She had not been forgiven *because of* her love to Christ, but her love was *a result of* her forgiveness. She loved much because she had been forgiven much. Jesus took this occasion to announce publicly the forgiveness of her sins.

7:49, 50 The other guests inwardly questioned Jesus' right to forgive **sins**. The natural heart hates grace. But Jesus again assured **the woman** that her **faith** had **saved** her and that she should **go in peace**. This is something psychiatrists cannot do. They may try to explain away guilt complexes, but they can never give the joy and peace that Jesus gives.

Our Lord's conduct in eating at this Pharisee's table is misused by some Christians in defense of the practice of keeping up intimacy with unconverted people, going to their amusements, and indulging in their pleasures. Ryle gives this warning:

Those who use such an argument would do well to remember our Lord's behavior on this occasion. He carried His "Father's business" with Him to the Pharisee's table. He testified against the Pharisee's besetting sin. He explained to the Pharisee the nature of free forgiveness of sins, and the secret of true love to Himself. He declared the saving nature of faith. If Christians who argue in favor of intimacy with unconverted people will visit their houses in the spirit of our Lord, and speak and behave as He did, let them by all means continue the practice. But do they speak and behave at the tables of their unconverted acquaintances as Jesus did at Simon's table? This is a question they would do well to answer.[21]

H. Certain Women Minister to Jesus (8:1–3)

It is good to remember that the Gospels contain only a few incidents from the life and ministry of our Lord. The Holy Spirit selected those subjects which He chose to include, but passed over many others. Here we have a simple statement that Jesus ministered with His disciples in **every city and village** of Galilee. As He preached and announced the good news **of the kingdom of God**, He was ministered to, probably in the way of food and lodging, by **women** who had been blessed by Him. For instance there was **Mary called Magdalene**. Some think she was a titled lady from Magdala (Migdol). At any rate, she had been wonderfully delivered from **seven demons**. There was **Joanna**, whose husband was **Herod's steward. Susanna** was another, and there were **many others**. Their kindness to our Lord did not go unnoticed or unrecorded. Little did they think as they shared their possessions with Jesus that Christians of all subsequent ages would read of their generosity and hospitality.

The subject of the Lord's ministry was the good news of **the kingdom of God. The kingdom of God** means the realm, visible or invisible, where God's rule is acknowledged. Matthew uses the term "the kingdom of heaven," but the thought is basically the same; it simply means that "the Most High rules in the kingdom of men" (Dan. 4:17) or that "Heaven rules" (Dan. 4:26).

There are various stages of development of the kingdom in the NT:

1. First of all, the kingdom was announced by John the Baptist as being at hand (Matt. 3:1, 2).

2. Then the kingdom was actually present in the Person of the King ("the kingdom of God is in the midst of you," Luke 17:21, JND). This was the good news of the kingdom which Jesus announced. He offered Himself as Israel's King (Luke 23:3).

3. Next we see the kingdom of God rejected by the nation of Israel (Luke 19:14; John 19:15).

4. Today the kingdom is in mystery form (Matt. 13:11). Christ, the King, is temporarily absent but His rule is acknowledged in the hearts of some people on earth. In one sense the kingdom today embraces all who even profess to accept the rule of God, even if they are not truly converted. This sphere of outward profession is seen in the parable of the sower and seed (Luke 8:4–15), the wheat and the tares (Matt. 13:24–30), and the fish in the dragnet (Matt. 13:47–50). But in its deeper, truer sense, the kingdom includes only those who have been converted (Matt. 18:3) or born again (John 3:3). This is the sphere of inward reality. (See diagram in Matthew 3:1, 2.)

5. The kingdom will one day be set up in a literal sense here on earth and the Lord Jesus will reign for one thousand years as King of kings and Lord of lords (Rev. 11:15; 19:16; 20:4).

6. The final phase is what is known as the everlasting kingdom of our Lord and Savior Jesus Christ (2 Pet. 1:11). This is the kingdom in eternity.

I. Parable of the Sower (8:4–15)

8:4–8 The **parable** of the **sower** describes the kingdom in its present aspect. It teaches us that the kingdom of God includes profession as well as reality. And it forms the basis for a very solemn warning as to how we **hear** the word of God. It is no light thing to hear the Scriptures preached and taught. Those who hear are made more responsible than they ever were before. If they shrug off the message, or consider obedience an optional matter, they do so to their own loss. But if they hear and obey, they put themselves in a position to receive more light from God. The **parable** was spoken here to **a great multitude**, then explained to the disciples.

The parable told of **a sower, his seed**, four kinds of soil that received the **seed**, and four results.

KIND OF SOIL	RESULT
1. **Wayside**	**Trampled** by men and **devoured** by birds.
2. **Rock**	**Withered away** for lack of **moisture**.
3. **Thorns**	Growth **choked** by **thorns**.
4. **Good ground**	**Yielded** one hundred grains for each seed.

The Lord ended the parable with the words, **"He who has ears to hear, let him hear!"** In other words, when you hear the word of God, be careful what kind of reception you give to it. The seed must fall into **good ground** in order to become fruitful.

8:9, 10 When **His disciples** inquired concerning the meaning of **this parable**, the Lord Jesus explained that **the mysteries of the kingdom of God** would not be understood by everyone. Because the disciples were willing to trust and obey, they would be **given** the ability to understand the teachings of Christ. But Jesus purposely presented many truths **in** the form of **parables** so **that** those who had no real love for Him would **not understand**; so that **seeing, they** might **not see, and hearing they** might **not understand**. In one sense, they saw and heard. For instance, they knew that Jesus had talked about a sower and his seed. But they did **not understand** the deeper meaning of the illustration. They did not realize that their hearts were hard, impenitent, and thorny soil, and that they did not benefit from the word which they had heard.

8:11–15 Only to the disciples did the Lord expound **the parable**. They had already accepted the teaching they had received, and so they would be given more. Jesus explained that **the seed is the word of God**, i.e. the truth of God — His own teaching.

The **wayside** hearers heard the word but only in a shallow, superficial way. It remained on the surface of their lives. This made it easy for **the devil** (the birds of the air) to snatch it away.

The **rock**-hearers heard the word too, but they did not let the word break them. They remained unrepentant. No

encouragement (moisture) was given to the seed, so it withered away and died. Perhaps they made a bright profession of faith at first, but there was no reality. There seemed to be life, but there was **no root** beneath the surface. When trouble came, they abandoned their Christian profession.

The thorny gound hearers seemed to get along nicely for a while, but they proved that they were not genuine believers by their failure to go on steadfastly. The **cares, riches, and pleasures of life** took control, and the word was stifled and smothered.

The good ground represented true believers whose hearts were **noble and good**. They not only received the word but allowed it to mold their lives. They were teachable and obedient, developing true Christian character and producing **fruit** for God.

Darby summarized the message of this section as follows:

> If, on hearing, I possess that which I hear, not merely have joy in receiving it, but possess it as my own, then it becomes a part of the substance of my soul, and I shall get more; for when the truth has become a substance in my soul, there is a capacity for receiving more.[22]

J. The Responsibility of Those Who Hear (8:16–18)

8:16 At first glance there does not seem to be much connection between this section and what has gone before. Actually, however, there is a continuous flow of thought. The Savior is still emphasizing the importance of what His disciples do with His teachings. He likens Himself to a man who **has lit a lamp**, not to be put under **a vessel or under a bed**, but **on a lampstand** for all to **see the light**. In teaching the disciples the principles of the kingdom of God, He was lighting a lamp. What should they do with it?

First of all, they should not cover it **with a vessel**. In Matthew 5:15, Mark 4:21, and Luke 11:33 (KJV), the vessel is spoken of as a bushel. This of course is a unit of measure used in the world of commerce. So hiding the lamp under a bushel could speak of allowing one's testimony to be obscured or crowded out in the rush of business life. It would be better to put the lamp on top of the bushel, that is, practice Christianity in the marketplace and use one's business as a pulpit for propagating the gospel.

Secondly, the disciple should not hide the lamp **under a bed**. The bed speaks of rest, comfort, sloth, and indulgence. How these can hinder the light from shining! The disciple should put the lamp on a stand. In other words, he should live and preach the truth so that all can see.

8:17   Verse 17 seems to suggest that if we allow the message to be confined because of business or laziness, our neglect and failure will be exposed. Hiding of the truth will **be revealed**, and keeping it a secret will **come to light**.

8:18   Therefore we should be careful **how** we **hear**. If we are faithful in sharing the truth with others, then God will reveal new and deeper truths to us. If, on the other hand, we do not have this spirit of evangelistic zeal, God will deprive us of the truth we think we possess. What we don't use, we lose. G. H. Lang comments:

> The disciples listened with a mind eager to understand and ready to believe and obey: the rest heard with either listlessness, or curiosity, or resolute opposition. To the former more knowledge would be granted; the latter would be deprived of what knowledge they seemed to have.[23]

> For we must share if we would keep
> That good thing from above:
> Ceasing to give, we cease to have;
> Such is the law of love.
> – R. C. Trench

K. Jesus' True Mother and Brothers (8:19–21)

At this point in His discourse, Jesus was told that **His mother and brothers** were waiting to see Him. **Because of the crowd**, they **could not** get near **Him**. The answer of the Lord was that real relationship with Him does not depend on natural ties, but on obedience to the **word of God**. He recognizes as members of His family all who tremble at the word, who receive it with meekness, and who obey it implicitly. No crowd can prevent His *spiritual* family from having audience with Him.

L. The Son of Man Stills the Storm (8:22–25)

8:22   In the remainder of this chapter Jesus is seen exercising His lordship over the elements, over demons, over disease, and even over death. All these obey His word; only man refuses.

Violent storms do rise quickly on the Sea of Galilee, making navigation perilous. Yet perhaps this particular storm was of satanic origin; it might have been an attempt to destroy the Savior of the world.

8:23   Jesus was **asleep** when the storm broke; the fact that *He* slept attests His true humanity. The *storm* went to sleep when Jesus spoke; this fact attests His absolute deity.

8:24   The disciples **awoke** the Savior, expressing anguished fears for their own safety. With perfect poise, He **rebuked the wind** and waves; and all was **calm**. What He did to the Sea of Galilee, He can do to the troubled, storm-tossed disciple today.

8:25   He asked the disciples, **"Where is your faith?"** They should not have worried. They did not need to awaken Him. "No water can swallow the ship where lies the Master of ocean and earth and skies." To be with Christ in the boat is to be absolutely safe and secure.

The disciples did not fully appreciate the extent of the power of their Master. Their understanding of Him was defective. **They marveled** that the elements obeyed Him. They were no different from us. In the storms of life, we often despair. Then when the Lord comes to our aid, we are astonished at the display of His power. And we wonder that we did not trust Him more fully.

M. The Gadarene Demoniac Healed (8:26–39)

8:26, 27   When Jesus and His disciples reached shore, they were in the district **of the Gadarenes**.[24] There they met **a certain man** possessed with **demons**. Matthew mentions two demoniacs, while Mark and Luke speak of only one. Such seeming discrepancies might indicate that they were actually two different occasions, or that one writer gave a fuller account than the others. This particular case of demon-possession caused the victim to discard his **clothes**, shun society, and live **in the tombs**.

8:28, 29 When he saw Jesus, he begged Him to let him alone. Of course, it was **the unclean spirit** who spoke through the pitiful man.

Demon-possession is real. These demons were not mere influences. They were supernatural beings who indwelt the man, controlling his thoughts, speech, and behavior. These particular demons caused the man to be extremely violent — so much so that when he had one of these violent convulsions, **he broke the** chains that were intended to restrain him and ran off **into the wilderness**. This is not surprising when we realize that cooped up within this one man were enough demons to destroy about two thousand pigs (see Mark 5:13).

8:30, 31 The man's **name** was **Legion** because he was possessed by a legion of **demons**. These demons recognized Jesus as the Son of the Most High God. They knew too that their doom was inevitable, and that He would bring it to pass. But they sought a reprieve, begging **Him that He would not command them to** depart at once **into the abyss**.

8:32, 33 They sought permission, when cast out of the man, to enter **a herd of many swine** nearby **on the mountain**. This permission was granted, with the result that the pigs **ran** headlong **down the steep place into the lake and drowned**. The Lord is criticized today for destruction of someone else's property. However, if the swine keepers were Jews, they were engaged in an unclean and illegal business. And whether they were Jews or Gentiles, they should have valued one man more than two thousand pigs.

8:34–39 The news quickly spread throughout that region. When a great crowd gathered, they saw the former demoniac completely restored to normal sanity and to decency. **The Gadarenes** became so upset that they **asked** Jesus **to depart**. They thought more of their swine than of the Savior; more of their sows than of their souls. Darby observes:

The world beseeches Jesus to depart, desiring their own ease, which is more disturbed by the presence and power of God than by a legion of devils. He goes away. The man who was healed . . . would fain be with Him; but the Lord sends him back . . . to be a witness of the grace and power of which he had been the subject.[25]

Later when Jesus visited Decapolis, a sympathetic crowd met Him (Mark 7:31–37). Could this have been the result of the faithful witness of the healed demoniac?

N. Curing the Incurable and Raising the Dead (8:40–56)

8:40–42 Jesus went back across the Sea of Galilee to its western shore. There another crowd was **waiting for Him. Jairus, a ruler of the synagogue**, was especially anxious to see Him because he had a **twelve** year old **daughter who was dying**. He urgently **begged** Jesus to go with him quickly. But **the multitudes thronged Him**, hindering His progress.

8:43 In the crowd was a timid, yet desperate **woman**, who had been afflicted with **a flow of blood for twelve years**. Luke the physician admits that she had **spent all her** life-savings and her income **on physicians** without getting any help. (Mark adds the unprofessional touch that she actually got worse!)

8:44, 45 She sensed that there was power in Jesus to heal her, so she eased her way through the crowd to where He was. Stooping down, she **touched the border of His garment,** the hem or fringe that formed the lower border of a Jew's robe (Num. 15:38, 39; Deut. 22:12). **Immediately** the **blood stopped** flowing and she was completely cured. She tried to steal away quietly, but her escape was blocked by a question from Jesus, **"Who touched Me?" Peter** and the other disciples thought that this was a silly question; all kinds of people were shoving, pushing, and touching Him!

8:46 But Jesus recognized a touch that was different. As someone has said, "The flesh throngs, but faith touches." He knew that faith had **touched** Him, because He sensed an outflow of **power** — the power to heal the woman. He **perceived** that **power** had gone forth **from** Him. Not, of course, that He was any less powerful than He had been before, but simply that it *cost* Him something to heal. There was expenditure.

8:47, 48 The woman . . . came trembling . . . before Him and gave an apologetic explanation of why **she had touched Him**, and a grateful testimony of what had happened. Her public confession was rewarded with a public commendation of her **faith** by Jesus, and a public pronouncement of His **peace** upon her. No one ever touches Jesus by faith without His knowing it, and without receiving a blessing. No one ever confesses Him openly without being strengthened in assurance of salvation.

8:49 The healing of the woman with the issue of blood probably did not delay Jesus very long, but it was long enough for a messenger to arrive with the news that Jairus' **daughter** was **dead**, and that therefore the Teacher's services would no longer be needed. There was faith that He could heal, but none that He could raise the dead.

8:50 Jesus, however, would not be dismissed so easily. He **answered** with words of comfort, encouragement, and promise. **"Do not be afraid; only believe, and she will be made well."**

8:51–53 As soon as He arrived at the home, He went to the room, taking with Him only **Peter, James, and John,** along with the parents. Everyone was wailing in despair, but Jesus told them to stop because the girl was **not dead, but sleeping.** This caused them to ridicule Him, because they were positive **that she was dead**.

Was she really dead, or was she in a deep sleep, like a coma? Most commentators say she was dead. They point out that Jesus referred to Lazarus as being asleep, meaning that he was dead. Sir Robert Anderson says that the girl was not really dead.[26] His arguments are as follows:

1. Jesus said that the girl would "be made well." The word He used is the same word used in verse 48 of this chapter, where it refers to healing, not resurrection. The word is never used in the NT of raising the dead.

2. Jesus used a different word for sleeping in the case of Lazarus.

3. The people thought she was dead, but Jesus would not take credit for raising her from the dead when actually He knew she was sleeping.

Anderson says it is simply a matter of whom you want to believe. Jesus said that she was sleeping. The others thought they knew she was dead.

8:54–56 In any case, Jesus said to her, **"Little girl, arise." She arose immediately.** After restoring her to her parents, Jesus told them not to publicize the miracle. He was not interested in notoriety, in fickle public enthusiasm, in idle curiosity.

Thus ends the second year of Jesus' public ministry. Chapter 9 opens the third year with the sending forth of the twelve.

O. The Son of Man Sends Forth His Disciples (9:1–11)

9:1–2 This incident closely resembles the sending of the **twelve** in Matthew 10:1–15, but there are notable differences. For instance, in Matthew, the disciples were told to go only to the Jews, and they were told to raise the dead, as well as **to cure diseases**. There is obviously a reason for the condensed version in Luke, but the reason is not obvious. The Lord not only *had* power and authority to perform miracles, but He *conferred* this **power and authority** on others. **Power** means strength or ability. **Authority** means the right to use it. The message of the disciples was confirmed by signs and wonders (Heb. 2:3, 4) in the absence of the complete Bible in written form. God can heal miraculously, but whether healing should still accompany the preaching of the gospel is certainly questionable.

9:3–5 Now the disciples would have an opportunity to practice the principles which the Lord had taught them. They were to trust Him for the supply of their material needs — no **bag**, food, or **money**. They were to live very simply — no extra staff or extra tunic. They were to **stay** in the first **house** where they were made welcome — no moving around in hopes of obtaining more comfortable lodging. They were not to prolong their stay or exert pressure on those who rejected the message, but were instructed to **shake off the very dust from** their **feet as a testimony against them**.

9:6 It was presumably in **the towns** of Galilee that the disciples preached **the gospel** and healed the sick. It should be mentioned that their message had to do with the kingdom — the announcement of the King's presence in their midst and His willingness to reign over a repentant people.

9:7 **Herod** Antipas was **tetrarch** in Galilee and Perea at this time. He reigned over one-fourth of the territory included in his father, Herod the Great's, kingdom. Word reached him that Someone was performing mighty miracles in his territory. Immediately his conscience began raising questions. The memory of **John** the Baptist still troubled him. Herod had silenced that fearless voice by beheading John, but he was still haunted by the power of that life. Who was this who made Herod think continually of John? **It was** rumored **by some that John had risen from the dead**.

9:8, 9 Others guessed that it was **Elijah** or **one of the** other **prophets** of the OT. **Herod** tried to quell his anxiety by reminding others that he had **beheaded** the Baptizer. But the fear remained. **Who** was **this** anyway? He **sought to see Him** but he never did until just before the Savior's crucifixion.

The power of a Spirit-filled life! The Lord Jesus, the obscure Carpenter of Nazareth, caused Herod to tremble without ever having met Him. Never underestimate the influence of a person full of the Holy Spirit!

9:10 When **the apostles . . . had returned**, they reported the results of their mission directly to the Lord Jesus. Perhaps this would be a good policy for all Christian workers. Too often the publicizing of work leads to jealousy and division. And G. Campbell Morgan comments that "our passion for statistics is self-centered, and of the flesh, and not of the Spirit." Our Lord **took** the disciples **to a deserted place** adjoining **Bethsaida** (*house of fishing*). It seems that there were two Bethsaidas at this time, one on the west side of the Sea of Galilee and this one on the east. The exact location is unknown.

9:11 Any hopes of a quiet time together were soon shattered. A crowd of people quickly gathered. The Lord Jesus was always accessible. He did not consider this an annoying interruption. He was never too busy to bless. In fact it specifically states that **He received** (or welcomed) **them**, teaching **them about the kingdom of God** and healing **those who** needed it.

P. Feeding of the Five Thousand (9:12-17)

9:12 As evening drew on, **the twelve** became restless. So many people needing food! An impossible situation. So they asked the Lord to **send the multitude away**. How like our own hearts! In matters concerning ourselves, we say, like Peter, "Command me to come to You. . . ." But how easy it is to say concerning others, **"Send** them **away."**

9:13 Jesus would not send them away to the surrounding villages to get food. Why should the disciples go off on tours to minister to people, and neglect those who were at their own doorstep? Let the disciples feed the crowd. They protested that they had only **five loaves and two fish**, forgetting that they also had the unlimited resources of the Lord Jesus to draw on.

9:14–17 He simply asked the disciples to seat the crowd of **five thousand men** plus women and children. Then after giving thanks, He **broke** the bread and kept on giving it **to the disciples**. They in turn distributed it to the people. There was plenty of food for everyone. In fact, when the meal was over there was more food left than there had been at the outset. The left-overs filled **twelve baskets**, one for each of the disciples. Those who try to explain away the miracle merely fill pages with confusion.

This incident is filled with significance for disciples who are charged with the evangelization of the world. The **five thousand** represent lost humanity, starving for the bread of God. The disciples picture helpless Christians, with seemingly limited resources, but unwilling to share what they have. The Lord's command, "You give them something to eat" is simply a restatement of the great commission. The lesson is that if we give Jesus what we have, He can multiply it to feed the spiritually hungry multitude. That diamond ring, that insurance policy, that bank account, that sports equipment! These can be converted into gospel literature, for instance, which in turn can result in the salvation of souls, who in turn will be worshipers of the Lamb of God throughout eternity.

The world could be evangelized in this generation if Christians would surrender to Christ all that they are and have. That is the enduring lesson of the feeding of the five thousand.

Q. Peter's Great Confession (9:18–22)

9:18 Immediately following the miraculous feeding of the multitude we have Peter's great confession of Christ at Caesarea Philippi. Did the miracle of the loaves and fishes open the eyes of the disciples to see the glory of the Lord Jesus as God's Anointed One? This incident at Caesarea Philippi is commonly acknowledged to be the watershed of the Savior's teaching ministry with the twelve. Up to this point He has been patiently leading them to an appreciation of who He is and what He could do in and through them. Now He has reached that goal, and so He henceforth moves on determinedly to the cross. Jesus prayed **alone**. It is not recorded that the Lord Jesus ever prayed with the disciples. He prayed for them, He prayed in their presence, and He taught them to pray, but His own prayer life was separate from theirs. Following one of His seasons of prayer, He questioned the disciples as to who **the crowds** said **that** He was.

9:19, 20 They reported a difference of opinion: Some said **John the Baptist**; others said **Elijah**; still **others** said **one of the** OT **prophets** in resurrection. But when He asked the disciples, **Peter** confidently confessed Him as **the Christ** (or Messiah) **of God**.

James Stewart's comments concerning this incident at Caesarea Philippi are so excellent that we quote them at length:

He began with the impersonal question — "Whom do men say that I am?" That, at any rate, was not difficult to answer. For on every side men were saying things about Jesus. A dozen verdicts were abroad. All kinds of rumors and opinions

were in the air. Jesus was on every tongue. And men were not only saying things about Jesus; they were saying *great* things about Him. Some thought He was John the Baptist back from the dead. Others said He reminded them of Elijah. Others spoke of Jeremiah or another of the prophets. In other words, while current opinions were by no means unanimous as to Jesus' identity, they were unanimous that he was someone great. His place was among the heroes of his race.

It is worth remarking that history here is repeating itself. Once again Jesus is on every tongue. He is being discussed today far beyond the circle of the Christian Church. And great is the diversity of verdicts about Him. Papini, looking at Jesus, sees the Poet. Bruce Barton sees the Man of Action. Middleton Murry sees the Mystic. Men with no brief for orthodoxy are ready to extol Jesus as the paragon of saints and captain of all moral leaders forever. "Even now," said John Stuart Mill, "it would not be easy even for an unbeliever to find a better translation of the rule of virtue from the abstract into the concrete than to endeavor so to live that Christ would approve our life." Like the men of his own day who called him John, Elijah, Jeremiah, so the men of today are agreed that among the heroes and saints of all time Jesus stands supreme.

But Jesus was not content with that recognition. People were saying that he was John, Elijah, Jeremiah. But that meant that he was one in a series. It meant that there were precedents and parallels, and that even if he stood first in rank, he was still only *primus inter pares*, first among his equals. But quite certainly that is not what the Christ of the New Testament claimed. Men may agree with Christ's claim, or they may dissent from it; but as to the fact of the claim itself there is not the shadow of a doubt. Christ claimed to be something and someone unprecedented, unparalleled, unrivaled, unique (for example Matt. 10:37; 11:27; 24:35; John 10:30; 14:6).[27]

9:21, 22 Following Peter's historic confession, the Lord **commanded them** not **to tell** others; nothing must interrupt His pathway to the cross. Then the Savior unveiled His own immediate future to them. He **must suffer**, must **be rejected by the** religious leaders of Israel, must **be killed** and must **be raised the third day**. This was an astounding announcement. Let us not forget that these words were spoken by the only sinless, righteous Man who ever lived on this earth. They were spoken by the true Messiah of Israel. They were the words of God manifest in the flesh. They tell us that the life of fulfillment, the perfect life, the life of obedience to the will of God involves suffering, rejection, death in one form or another, and a resurrection to life that is deathless. It is a life poured out for others.

This of course was the very *opposite* of the popular conception of Messiah's role. Men looked for a saber-rattling, enemy-destroying leader. It must have been a shock to the disciples. But if, as they confessed, Jesus was indeed the Christ of God, then they had no reason for disillusionment or discouragement. If He is the Anointed of God, then His cause can never fail. No matter what might happen to Him or to them, they were on the winning side. Victory and vindication were inevitable.

R. Invitation to Take Up the Cross (9:23–27)

9:23 Having outlined His own future, the Lord invited the disciples to **follow** Him. This would mean denying themselves and taking up their **cross**. To **deny** self means willingly to renounce any so-called right to plan or choose, and to recognize His lordship in every area of life. To **take up** the **cross** means to deliberately choose the kind of life He lived. This involves:

- The opposition of loved ones.
- The reproach of the world.
- Forsaking family and house and lands and the comforts of this life.
- Complete dependence on God.
- Obedience to the leading of the Holy Spirit.
- Proclamation of an unpopular message.
- A pathway of loneliness.
- Organized attacks from established religious leaders.
- Suffering for righteousness' sake.
- Slander and shame.
- Pouring out one's life for others.
- Death to self and to the world.

But it *also* involves laying hold of life that is life indeed! It means finding at last the reason for our existence. And it means eternal reward. We instinctively recoil from a life of cross-bearing. Our minds are reluctant to believe that this could be God's will for us. Yet the words of Christ **"If anyone desires to come after Me"** mean that nobody is excused and nobody is excepted.

9:24 The natural tendency is to **save** our lives by selfish, complacent, routine, petty existences. We may indulge our pleasures and appetites by basking in comfort, luxury, and ease, by living for the present, by trading our finest talents to the world in exchange for a few years of mock security. But in the very act, we **lose** our lives, that is, we miss the true purpose of **life** and the profound spiritual pleasure that should go with it! On the other hand, we may **lose** our lives for the Savior's sake. Men think us mad if we fling our own selfish ambitions to the wind, if we seek first the kingdom of God and His righteousness, if we yield ourselves unreservedly to Him. But this life of abandonment is genuine living. It has a joy, a holy carefreeness, and a deep inward satisfaction that defies description.

9:25 As the Savior talked with the twelve, He realized that the desire for material riches might be a powerful deterrent against full surrender. And so He said, in effect, "Suppose you could stockpile all the gold and silver in **the whole world**, could own all the real estate and property, all the stocks and bonds — everything of material value — and suppose that in your frantic effort to acquire all this you missed the true purpose of life, what good would it do you? You would have it for only a short while; then you would leave it forever. It would be an insane bargain to sell that one, short life for a few toys of dust."

9:26 Another deterrent against total commitment to Christ is the fear of shame. It is completely irrational for a creature to be ashamed of his Creator, for a sinner to be **ashamed** of his Savior. And yet which of us is blameless? The Lord recognized the possibility of shame and solemnly warned against it. If we avoid the shame by leading nominal Christian lives, by conforming to the herd, **the Son of Man will be ashamed** of us **when He comes in His own glory, and in His Father's** glory, and in the glory **of the holy angels**. He emphasizes the triple-splendored glory of His Second Advent as if to say that any shame or reproach we may endure for Him now will seem trifling when He appears in glory compared to the shame of those who now deny Him.

9:27 This mention of His glory forms the link with what follows. He now predicts that **some** of the disciples who were **standing** there would **see the kingdom of God** before they died. His words find their fulfillment in verses 28–36, the incident on the Mount of Transfiguration. The disciples were Peter, James, and John. On the Mount they saw a foreview of what it will be like when the Lord Jesus sets up His kingdom on earth. Peter says this in effect in his Second Epistle:

For we did not follow cunningly devised fables when we made known to you the power and coming of our Lord Jesus Christ, but were eyewitnesses of His majesty. For He received from God the Father honor and glory when such a voice came to Him from the Excellent Glory: "This is My beloved Son, in whom I am well pleased." And we heard this voice which came from heaven when we were with Him on the holy mountain (1:16–18).

Notice the continuity of the Lord's teaching in this passage. He had just announced His own impending rejection, suffering, and death. He had called His disciples to follow Him in a life of self-denial, suffering, and sacrifice. Now He says in effect, "But just remember! If you suffer with Me, you will reign with Me. Beyond the cross is the glory. The reward is all out of proportion to the cost."

S. The Son of Man Transfigured (9:28–36)

9:28, 29 It was **about eight days** later that Jesus **took Peter, John, and James and went up on the mountain to pray**. The location of this **mountain** is unknown, although high, snow-capped Mt. Hermon is a likely choice. As the Lord was praying, His outward **appearance** began to change. An intriguing truth — that among the things that prayer changes is a man's countenance. **His face** glowed with a bright radiance **and His robe** gleamed with dazzling whiteness. As mentioned above, this prefigured the glory which would be His during His coming kingdom. While He was here on earth, His glory was ordi-

narily veiled in His body of flesh. He was here in humiliation, as a Bondslave. But during the Millennium, His glory will be fully revealed. All will see Him in all His splendor and majesty.

Professor W. H. Rogers puts it well:

In the transfiguration, we have in miniature form all salient features of the future kingdom in manifestation. We see the Lord clothed in glory and not in the rags of humiliation. We behold Moses in a glorified state, the representative of the regenerated who have passed through death into the kingdom. We observe Elijah shrouded in glory, the representative of the redeemed who have entered the kingdom by translation. There are three disciples, Peter, James and John, who are not glorified, the representatives of Israel in the flesh during the millennium. Then there is the multitude at the foot of the mountain, representative of the nations who will be brought into the kingdom after it has been inaugurated.[28]

9:30, 31 Moses and Elijah talked with Jesus about **His decease** (lit., *exodus*) **which He was about to accomplish at Jerusalem**. Note that His death is here spoken of as an accomplishment. Also note that death is simply an *exodus* — not cessation of existence but departure from one place to another one.

9:32, 33 The disciples were sleepy while all this was going on. Bishop Ryle says:

Let it be noted that the very same disciples who here slept during a vision of glory were also found sleeping during the agony in the garden of Gethsemane. Flesh and blood does indeed need to be changed before it can enter heaven. Our poor weak bodies can neither watch with Christ in His time of trial nor keep awake with Him in His glorification. Our physical constitution must be greatly altered before we could enjoy heaven.[29]

When they were fully awake, they saw the bright outshining of Christ's **glory**. In an effort to preserve the sacred character of the occasion, **Peter** proposed erecting **three tabernacles** or tents, **one** in honor of Jesus, **one** of **Moses**, and **one** of **Elijah**. But his idea was based upon zeal without knowledge.

9:34–36 God's **voice came out of the cloud** that enveloped them, acknowledging Jesus as His **beloved Son**, and telling them to **hear** or obey **Him**. As soon as **the voice** was past, Moses and Elijah had disappeared. Jesus **alone** was standing there. It will be like this in the kingdom; He will have the pre-eminence in all things. He will not share His glory.

The disciples left with a sense of awe so profound that they did not discuss the event with others.

T. A Demon-Possessed Boy Healed (9:37–43a)

9:37–39 From the mount of glory, Jesus and the disciples returned **the next day** to the valley of human need. Life has its moments of spiritual exaltation but God balances them with the daily round of toil and expenditure. Out **from the multitude** that **met Him** came a distraught father, pleading for Jesus to help his demon-possessed **son**. It was his **only child** and therefore his heart's delight. What an unspeakable sorrow then it was for that father to see his boy seized with demonic convulsions. These fits came on without warning. The lad would cry out and then foam **at the mouth**. Only after a fearful struggle would the demon depart, leaving him thoroughly bruised.

9:40 The distraught father had previously gone to the **disciples** for help but they were powerless. Why were the disciples unable to help the boy? Perhaps they had become professional in their ministry. Perhaps they thought they could count on a Spirit-filled ministry without constant spiritual exercise. Perhaps they were taking things too much for granted.

9:41 The Lord **Jesus** was grieved by the entire spectacle. Without naming anyone in particular, He said, **"O faithless and perverse generation. . . ."** This may have been addressed to the disciples, the people, the father, or all of them combined. They were all so helpless in the face of human need in spite of the fact that they could draw on His infinite resources of power. **How long** would He have to **be with** them and put up with them? Then He said to the father, **"Bring your son here."**

9:42, 43a As the lad **was still coming** to Jesus, he was seized by **the demon** and thrown to the ground violently. But Jesus was not overawed by this display of the power of an evil spirit; it was the unbelief of men that hindered Him rather than the power of demonism. He cast out the **unclean spirit, healed the child, and gave him back to his father**. The people **were all amazed**. They recognized that God had worked a miracle. They saw in the miracle a display of **the majesty of God**.

U. The Son of Man Predicts His Death and Resurrection (9:43b–45)

9:43b, 44 The **disciples** might be inclined to think that their Master would continue to perform miracles until at last the whole nation would acclaim Him as King. To disabuse their minds of such a notion, the Lord again reminded them that **the Son of Man** must be **betrayed into the hands of men**, that is, to be killed.

9:45 Why did they **not understand this** prediction? Simply because they lapsed back into thinking of the Messiah as a popular hero. His death would mean defeat for the cause, according to their thinking. Their own hopes were so strong that they were unable to entertain any contrary view. It was not God who concealed the truth from them, but their own determined refusal to believe. **They were** even **afraid to ask** for clarification — almost as if they were afraid to have their fears confirmed!

V. True Greatness in the Kingdom (9:46–48)

9:46 The disciples not only expected the glorious kingdom to be ushered in shortly, but they also aspired to positions of greatness in the kingdom. Already they were arguing among themselves as to who **would be greatest**.

9:47, 48 Knowing the question that was agitating them, **Jesus** brought **a little child** beside Him and explained that anyone who received a **little child in** His **name** received Him. At first glance, this does not seem to have any connection with the question of who was greatest among the disciples. But though not obvious, the connection seems to be this: true greatness is seen in a loving care for the little ones, for those who are helpless, for those whom the world passes by. Thus when Jesus said that the **"least among you all will be great,"** He was referring to the one who humbled himself to associate with believers who are non-descript, insignificant, and despised.

In Matthew 18:4, the Lord said that the greatest in the kingdom of heaven is the one who humbles himself like a little child. Here in Luke, it is a matter of identifying oneself with the lowliest among God's children. In both cases, it involves taking a place of humility, as the Savior Himself did.

W. The Son of Man Forbids Sectarianism (9:49, 50)

9:49 This incident seems to illustrate the behavior which the Lord had just told the disciples to avoid. They had found **someone casting out demons in** Jesus' **name**. They **forbade him** for no better reason than that he was **not** one of their followers. In other words, they had refused to receive a child of the Lord in His name. They were sectarian and narrow. They should have been glad that the demon had been cast out of the man. They should never be jealous of any man or group that might cast out more demons than they did. But then every disciple has to guard against this desire for exclusiveness — for a monopoly of spiritual power and prestige.

9:50 **Jesus said to him, "Do not forbid him, for he who is not against us is on our side."** As far as the Person and work of Christ are concerned, there can be no neutrality. If men are not *for* Christ, they are *against* Him. But when it comes to Christian service, A. L. Williams says:

Earnest Christians need to remember that when outsiders do anything in Christ's Name, it must, on the whole, forward His cause. . . . The Master's reply contained a broad and far-reaching truth. No earthly society, however holy, would be able exclusively to claim the Divine powers inseparably connected with a true and faithful use of His Name.[30]

VII. INCREASING OPPOSITION TO THE SON OF MAN (9:51–11:54)

A. Samaria Rejects the Son of Man (9:51–56)

9:51 **The time** of Jesus' Ascension

into heaven was now drawing near. He knew this well. He also knew that the cross lay between, so **He** resolutely moved toward **Jerusalem** and all that awaited Him there.

9:52, 53 A Samaritan **village** that lay on His route proved inhospitable to the Son of God. The people knew He was going **to Jerusalem**, and that was enough reason to bar Him, as far as they were concerned. After all, there was intense hatred between the Samaritans and the Jews. Their sectarian, bigoted spirit, their segregationist attitude, their racial pride made them unwilling to **receive** the Lord of Glory.

9:54–56 **James and John** were so angered by this discourtesy that they offered to call **fire . . . down from heaven** to destroy the offenders. Jesus promptly **rebuked them**. He had **not come to destroy men's lives but to save them**. This was the acceptable year of the Lord, and not the day of vengeance of our God. They should have been characterized by grace and not by vindictiveness.

B. Hindrances to Discipleship (9:57–62)

9:57 In these verses, we meet three would-be disciples who illustrate three of the main hindrances to whole-hearted discipleship. The first man was quite sure he wanted to **follow** Jesus anywhere and everywhere. He did not wait to be called, but impetuously offered himself. He was self-confident, unduly eager, and unmindful of the cost. He did not know the meaning of what he said.

9:58 At first, the answer of Jesus does not seem to be related to the man's offer. Actually, however, there was a very close connection. **Jesus** was saying, in effect, "Do you know what it really means to follow me? It means the forsaking of the comforts and conveniences of life. I do not have a home to call my own. This earth affords no rest to me. **Foxes** and **birds** have more in the way of natural comfort and security than I. Are you willing to follow Me, even if it means forsaking those things which most men consider to be their inalienable rights?" When we read **the Son of Man has nowhere to lay His head** we are apt to pity Him. One commentator remarks: "He does not need your pity. Pity yourself rather if you have a home that holds you back when Christ wants you out upon the high places of the world." We hear no more of the man, and can only assume that he was unwilling to give up the common comforts of life to follow the Son of God.

9:59 The second man heard Christ's call to **follow** Him. He was willing, in a way, but there was something he wanted to do **first**. He wanted to **go and bury** his **father**. Notice what he said. **"Lord, let me first go. . . ."** In other words, **"Lord . . . me first."** He called Jesus by the name of **Lord**, but actually he puts his own desires and interests **first**. The words "Lord" and "me first" are totally opposed to each other; we must choose one or the other. Whether the **father** was already dead or whether the son planned to wait at home until he died, the issue was the same — he was allowing something else to take precedence over Christ's call. It is perfectly legitimate and proper to show respect for a dead or dying father, but when anyone or anything is allowed to rival Christ, it becomes positively sinful. This man had something else to do — we might say, a job or an occupation — and this lured him away from a pathway of unreserved discipleship.

9:60 The Lord rebuked his doublemindedness with the words, **"Let the dead bury their own dead, but you go and preach the kingdom of God."** The *spiritually* dead can bury the *physically* dead, but they can't preach the gospel. Disciples should not give priority to tasks that the unsaved can do just as well as Christians. The believer should make sure that he is indispensable as far as the main thrust of his life is concerned. His principal occupation should be to advance the cause of Christ on earth.

9:61 The third would-be disciple resembled the first in that he volunteered to **follow** Christ. He was like the second in that he uttered the contradiction, **"Lord . . . me first."** He wanted **first** to say goodbye to his family. In itself, the request was reasonable and proper, but even the common civilities of life are wrong if they are placed ahead of prompt and complete obedience.

9:62 **Jesus** told him that once he put **his hand to the plow** of discipleship, he must not look[31] **back**; otherwise he was not **fit for the kingdom of God**. Christ's followers are not made of half-hearted stuff or dreamy sentimentality. No considerations of family or friends, though lawful in themselves, must be allowed to turn them aside from utter and complete abandonment to Him. The expression not **"fit for the kingdom"** does not refer to salvation but to service. It is not at all a question of *entrance* into the kingdom but of *service* in the kingdom after entering it. Our fitness for entering into the kingdom is in the Person and work of the Lord Jesus. It becomes ours through faith in Him.

And so we have three cardinal hindrances to discipleship illustrated in the experience of these men:

1. Material comforts.
2. A job or an occupation.
3. Family and friends.

Christ must reign in the heart without a rival. All other loves and all other loyalties must be secondary.

C. The Seventy Sent Forth (10:1–16)

10:1–12 This is the only account in the Gospels of the Lord's sending out the **seventy**[32] disciples. It closely resembles the commissioning of the twelve in Matthew 10. However, there the disciples were sent into the northern areas, whereas the seventy are now being sent to the south along the route the Lord was following to Jerusalem. This mission was seemingly intended to prepare the way for the Lord in His journey from Caesarea Philippi in the north, through Galilee and Samaria, across the Jordan, south through Perea, then back across the Jordan to Jerusalem.

While the ministry and office of the seventy was only temporary, nevertheless our Lord's instructions to these men suggest many life principles which apply to Christians in every age.

Some of these principles may be summarized as follows:

1. He sent them out **two by two** (v. 1). This suggests competent testimony. "In the mouth of two or three witnesses every word shall be established" (2 Cor. 13:1).

2. The Lord's servant should constantly **pray** that He will **send out la-**

borers into His harvest field (v. 2).
The need is always greater than the
supply of workers. In praying for **laborers**, we must be willing to go ourselves, obviously. Notice **pray** (v. 2),
go (v. 3).

3. The disciples of Jesus are sent
forth into a hostile environment (v. 3).
They are, to outward appearances, like
defenseless **lambs among wolves**. They
cannot expect to be treated royally by
the world, but rather to be persecuted
and even killed.

4. Considerations of personal comfort are not to be permitted (v. 4a).
**"Carry neither money bag, knapsack,
nor sandals."** The **money bag** speaks
of financial reserves. The **knapsack**
suggests food reserves. The **sandals**
may refer either to an extra pair, or to
footgear affording extra comfort. All
three speak of the poverty which,
though having nothing, yet possesses
all things and makes many rich (2 Cor.
6:10).

5. **"Greet no one along the road"** (v.
4b). Christ's servants are not to waste
time on long, ceremonious greetings,
such as were common in the East.
While they should be courteous and
civil, they must ultilize their time in
the glorious proclamation of the gospel
rather than in profitless talk. There is
not time for needless delays.

6. They should accept hospitality
wherever it is offered to them (vv. 5,
6). If their initial greeting is favorably
received, then the host is **a son of
peace**. He is a man characterized by
peace, and one who receives the message of peace. If the disciples are refused, they should not be discouraged;
their peace **will return to** them again,
that is, there has been no waste or
loss, and others will receive it.

7. The disciples should **remain in
the same house** that first offers lodging
(v. 7). To move **from house to house**
might characterize them as those who
are shopping for the most luxurious
accomodations, whereas they should
live simply and gratefully.

8. They should not hesitate to eat
whatever food and drink are offered to
them (v. 7). As servants of the Lord,
they are entitled to their upkeep.

9. Cities and towns take a position

either for or against the Lord, just as
individuals do (vv. 8, 9). If an area is
receptive to the message, the disciples
should preach there, accept its hospitality, and bring the blessings of the
gospel to it. Christ's servants should
eat such things as are set before them,
not being fastidious about their food or
causing inconvenience in the home.
After all, food is not the main thing in
their lives. Towns which receive the
Lord's messengers still have their sin-
sick inhabitants healed. Also the King
draws very **near to** them (v. 9).

10. A town may reject the gospel and
then be denied the privilege of hearing
it again (vv. 10–12). There comes a
time in God's dealings when the message is heard for the last time. Men
should not trifle with the gospel, because it may be withdrawn forever.
Light rejected is light denied. Towns
and villages which are privileged to
hear the good news and which refuse
it will be judged more severely than
the city of **Sodom**. The greater the
privilege, the greater the responsibility.

10:13, 14 As Jesus spoke these
words, He was reminded of three cities
of Galilee which had been more highly
privileged than any others. They had
seen Him perform His mighty miracles
in their streets. They had heard His gracious teaching. Yet they utterly refused
Him. If the miracles He had done in
Chorazin and **Bethsaida . . . had been
done in** ancient **Tyre and Sidon**, those
sea-coast cities would have plunged
themselves into the deepest repentance.
Because the cities of Galilee were unmoved by Jesus' works, their judgment
would be more severe than that of **Tyre
and Sidon**. As a matter of historical fact,
Chorazin and Bethsaida have been so
thoroughly destroyed that their exact location is not definitely known today.

10:15 Capernaum became the
home town of Jesus after He moved from
Nazareth. The city was **exalted to
heaven** in privilege. But it despised its
most notable Citizen and missed its day
of opportunity. So it **will be brought
down to Hades** in judgment.

10:16 Jesus closed His instructions
to the seventy with a statement that they
were His ambassadors. To reject them

was to reject Him, and to refuse Him was to refuse God, the Father.

Ryle comments:

> There is probably no stronger language than this in the New Testament about the dignity of a faithful minister's office, and the guilt incurred by those who refuse to hear his message. It is language, we must remember, which is not addressed to the twelve apostles, but to seventy disciples, of whose name and subsequent history we know nothing. Scott remarks, "To reject an ambassador, or to treat him with contempt, is an affront to the prince who commissioned and sent him, and whom he represents. The apostles and seventy disciples were the ambassadors and representatives of Christ; and they who rejected and despised them in fact rejected and despised Him."[33]

D. The Seventy Return (10:17–24)

10:17, 18 As they **returned** from their mission, **the seventy** were elated that **even the demons** had been **subject to** them. Jesus' reply may be understood in two ways. First it may mean that He saw in their success an earnest of the eventual fall of **Satan . . . from heaven**. Jamieson, Fausset, and Brown paraphrase His words:

> I followed you on your mission, and watched its triumphs; while you were wondering at the subjection to you of demons in My Name, a grander spectacle was opening to My view; sudden as the darting of lightning from heaven to earth, lo! Satan was beheld falling from heaven.

This fall of Satan is still future. He will be cast out of heaven by Michael and his angels (Rev. 12:7–9). This will take place during the Tribulation Period, and prior to Christ's Glorious Reign on earth.

A second possible interpretation of Jesus' words is as a warning against pride. It is as if He were saying: "Yes, you are quite heady because even the demons have been subject to you. But just remember — pride is the parent sin. It was pride that resulted in the fall of Lucifer, and in his being cast out of heaven. See that you avoid this peril."

10:19 The Lord had given His disciples **authority** against the forces of evil. They were granted immunity from harm during their mission. It is true of all God's servants; they are protected.

10:20 Yet they were **not** to **rejoice** in their power over **spirits, but rather in** their own salvation. This is the only recorded instance when the Lord told His disciples not to rejoice. There are subtle dangers connected with success in Christian service, whereas the fact that our **names are written in heaven** reminds us of our infinite debt to God and His Son. It is safe to rejoice in salvation by grace.

10:21 Rejected by the mass of the people, **Jesus** looked upon His humble followers and **rejoiced in the Spirit**, thanking the **Father** for His matchless wisdom. The seventy were not **the wise and prudent** men of this world. They were not the intellectuals or the scholars. They were mere **babes**! But they were babes with faith, devotion, and unquestioning obedience. The intellectuals were too wise, too knowing, too clever for their own good. Their pride blinded them to the true worth of God's beloved Son. It is through babes that God can work most effectively. Our Lord was happy for all those whom the Father had given to Him, and for this initial success of the seventy, which foretold the eventual downfall of Satan.

10:22 All things were delivered to the Son by His Father, whether things in heaven, on earth, or under the earth. God put the entire universe under the authority of His Son. **No one knows who the Son is except the Father**. There is mystery connected with the Incarnation that no one but **the Father** can fathom. How God could become Man and dwell in a human body is beyond the comprehension of the creature. No one knows **who the Father is except the Son, and the one to whom the Son wills to reveal Him**. God too is above human understanding. The Son knows Him perfectly, and the Son has revealed Him to the weak, the base, and the despised people who have faith in Him (1 Cor. 1:26–29). Those who have seen the Son have seen the Father. The only begotten Son who is in the bosom of the Father has fully told forth the Father (John 1:18).

Kelly says, "The Son does reveal the Father; but man's mind always breaks itself to pieces when he attempts to unravel the insoluble enigma of Christ's personal glory."

10:23, 24 Privately, the Lord told **His disciples** that they were living in a day of unprecedented privilege. Old Testament **prophets and kings** had **desired to see** the days of the Messiah, but had **not seen** them. The Lord Jesus here claims to be the One to whom the OT prophets looked forward — the Messiah. The disciples were privileged to **see** the miracles and **hear** the teaching of the Hope of Israel.

E. The Lawyer and the Good Samaritan (10:25–37)

10:25 The **lawyer**, an expert in the teachings of the Law of Moses, was probably not sincere in his question. He was trying to trick the Savior, to put Him thoroughly to the test. Perhaps he thought that the Lord would repudiate the law. To him, Jesus was only a **Teacher**, and **eternal life** was something he could earn or merit.

10:26–28 The Lord took all this into consideration when He answered him. If the lawyer had been humble and penitent, the Savior would have answered him more directly. Under the circumstances, Jesus directed his attention to **the law**. What did **the law** demand? It demanded that man **love the LORD** supremely, and his **neighbor as** himself. Jesus told him that if he did **this**, he would **live**.

At first, it might appear that the Lord was teaching salvation by law-keeping. Such was not the case. God never intended that anyone should ever be saved by keeping the law. The Ten Commandments were given to people who were already sinners. The purpose of the law is not to save from sin, but to produce the knowledge of sin. The function of the law is to show man what a guilty sinner he is.

It is impossible for sinful man to love God **with all** his **heart**, and his **neighbor as** himself. If he could do this from birth to death, he would not need salvation. He would not be lost. But even then, his reward would only be long life on earth, not eternal life in heaven. As long as he lived sinlessly, he would go on living. Eternal life is only for sinners who acknowledge their lost condition and who are saved by God's grace.

Thus Jesus' statement, **"Do this and you will live,"** was purely hypothetical. If His reference to the law had had its desired effect on the lawyer, he would have said, "If that's what God requires, then I'm lost, helpless, and hopeless. I cast myself on Your love and mercy. Save me by Your grace!"

10:29 Instead of that, he sought to **justify himself**. Why should he? No one had accused him. There was a consciousness of fault and his heart rose up in pride to resist. He asked, **"Who is my neighbor?"** It was an evasive tactic on his part.

10:30–35 It was in answer to that question that the Lord **Jesus** told the story of the good Samaritan. The details of the story are familiar. The robbery-victim (almost certainly a Jew) lay **half dead** on the road **to Jericho**. The Jewish **priest** and **Levite** refused to help; perhaps they feared it was a plot, or were afraid that they too might be robbed if they tarried. It was a hated **Samaritan** who came to the rescue, who applied first aid, who took the victim to **an inn**, and who made provision for his **care**. To the Samaritan, a Jew in need was his neighbor.

10:36, 37 Then the Savior asked the inescapable question. **Which** of the **three** proved **neighbor** to the helpless man? The one **who showed mercy**, of course. Yes, of course. Then the lawyer should **go and do likewise**. "If a Samaritan could prove himself a true neighbor to a Jew by showing mercy to him, then all men are neighbors."[34]

It is not difficult for us to see in the priest and Levite a picture of the powerlessness of the law to help the dead sinner; the law commanded "Love your neighbor as yourself" but it did not give the power to obey. Neither is it difficult to identify the good Samaritan with the Lord Jesus who came to where we were, saved us from our sins, and made full provision for us from earth to heaven and through all eternity. Priests and Levites may disappoint us but the Good Samaritan never does.

The story of the good Samaritan had an unexpected twist to it. It started off to answer the question "Who is my neighbor?" But it ended by posing the question "To whom do you prove yourself a neighbor?"

F. Mary and Martha (10:38–42)

10:38–41 The Lord now centers His attention on the word of God and prayer as the two great means of blessing (10:38–11:13).

Mary sat at Jesus' feet and heard His word, while **Martha was distracted** by her preparations for the Royal Guest. Martha wanted the **Lord** to rebuke her **sister** for failing to help, but Jesus tenderly rebuked **Martha** for her fretfulness!

10:42 Our Lord prizes our affection above our service. Service may be tainted with pride and self-importance. Occupation with Himself is the **one thing** needful, **that good part which will not be taken away**. "The Lord wants to convert us from Marthas into Marys," comments C. A. Coates, "just as He wants to convert us from lawyers into neighbors."[35]

Charles R. Erdman writes:

> While the Master does appreciate all that we undertake for Him, He knows that our first need is to sit at His feet and learn His will; then in our tasks we shall be calm and peaceful and kindly, and at last our service may attain the perfectness of that of Mary when in a later scene she poured upon the feet of Jesus the ointment, the perfume of which still fills the world.[36]

G. The Disciples' Prayer (11:1–4)

Between chapters 10 and 11, there is a time interval which is covered in John 9:1–10:21.

11:1 This is another of the frequent references by Luke to the prayer life of our Lord. It fits in with Luke's purpose in presenting Christ as the Son of Man, ever dependent upon God His Father. The disciples sensed that prayer was a real and vital force in the life of Jesus. As they heard Him pray, it made them want to pray too. And so **one of His disciples** asked that He would **teach** them **to pray**. He did not say, "Teach us *how* to pray," but **"Teach us to pray."** However, the request certainly includes both the fact and the method.

11:2 The model prayer which the Lord Jesus gave to them at this time is somewhat different from the so-called Lord's prayer in Matthew's Gospel. These differences all have a purpose and meaning. None of them is without significance.

First of all, the Lord taught the disciples to address God as **Our Father**. This intimate family relationship was unknown to believers in the OT. It simply means that believers are now to speak to God as to a loving heavenly **Father**. Next, we are taught to pray that God's **name** should be **hallowed**. This expresses the longing of the believer's heart that He should be reverenced, magnified, and adored. In the petition, **"Your kingdom come,"** we have a prayer that the day will soon arrive when God will put down the forces of evil and, in the Person of Christ, reign supreme over the **earth**, where His **will** shall **be done as it is in heaven**.

11:3 Having thus sought first the kingdom of God and His righteousness, the petitioner is taught to make known his personal needs and desires. The ever-recurring need for food, both physical and spiritual, is introduced. We are to live in **daily** dependence upon Him, acknowledging Him as the source of every good.

11:4 Next there is the prayer for the forgiveness of **sins**, based on the fact that we have shown a forgiving spirit to others. Obviously this does not refer to forgiveness from the penalty of sin. That forgiveness is based upon the finished work of Christ on Calvary, and is received through faith alone. But here we are dealing with parental or governmental forgiveness. After we are saved, God deals with us as with children. If He finds a hard and unforgiving spirit in our hearts, He will chastise us until we are broken and brought back into fellowship with Himself. This forgiveness has to do with fellowship with God, rather than with relationship.

The plea **"And do not lead us into temptation"** presents difficulties to some. We know that God never tempts anyone to sin. But He does allow us to experience trials and testings in life, and these are designed for our good. Here the thought seems to be that we should constantly be aware of our own proneness to wander and fall into sin. We should ask the Lord to keep us from falling into sin, even if we ourselves might want to do it. We should pray that the opportunity to sin and the desire to do so should never coincide. The prayer expresses a healthy distrust of our own ability to resist temptation. The prayer ends with a plea for deliverance **from the evil one.**[37]

H. Two Parables on Prayer (11:5–13)

11:5–8 Continuing with the subject of prayer, the Lord gave an illustration designed to show God's willingness to hear and answer the petitions of His children. The story has to do with a man who had a guest arrive at his home **at midnight.** Unfortunately he did not have enough food on hand. So he went to a neighbor, knocked on his door, and asked for **three loaves** of bread. At first the neighbor was annoyed by the interruption to his sleep and didn't bother to get up. Yet because of the prolonged banging and shouting of the worried host, he finally did get up **and give him** what he needed.

In applying this illustration we must be careful to avoid certain conclusions. It doesn't mean that God is annoyed by our persistent requests. And it doesn't suggest that the only way to get our prayers answered is to be persistent.

It *does* teach that if a man is willing to help a friend because of his importunity, God is much *more* willing to hear the cries of His children.

11:9 It teaches that we should not grow weary or discouraged in our prayer life. "Keep on asking . . . keep on seeking . . . keep on knocking. . . ."[38] Sometimes God answers our prayers the first time we ask. But in other cases He answers only after prolonged asking.

> God answers prayers:
> Sometimes, when hearts are weak,
> He gives the very gifts believers seek;
> But often faith must learn a deeper rest,
> And trust God's silence when He does not speak;
> For He whose name is love will send the best,
> Stars may burn out, nor mountain walls endure,
> But God is true; His promises are sure.
> He is our strength.   – M.G.P.

The parable seems to teach increasing degrees of importunity — asking to seeking to knocking.

11:10 It teaches that **everyone who asks receives,** everyone **who seeks finds, and** everyone **who knocks** has it **opened** to him. This is a promise that when we pray, God always gives us what we ask or He gives us something better. A "no" answer means that He knows our request would not be the best for us; His denial is then better than our petition.

11:11, 12 It teaches that God will never deceive us by giving us **a stone** when we ask **bread.** Bread in those days was shaped in a round flat cake, resembling a stone. God will never mock us by giving us something inedible when we ask for food. If we ask **for a fish,** He will not give us **a serpent,** that is, something that might destroy us. And if we ask **for an egg,** He will not give us **a scorpion,** that is, something that would cause excruciating pain.

11:13 A human father would not give bad gifts; even though he has a sinful nature, he knows **how to give good gifts to** his **children. How much more** is our **heavenly Father** willing to **give the Holy Spirit to those who ask Him.** J. G. Bellet says, "It is significant that the gift He selects as the one we most need, and the one He most desires to give, is the Holy Spirit." When Jesus spoke these words, the Holy Spirit had not yet been given (John 7:39). We should not pray today for the Holy Spirit to be *given* to us as an indwelling Person, because He comes to indwell us at the time of our conversion (Rom. 8:9b; Eph. 1:13, 14).

But it is certainly proper and necessary for us to pray for the Holy Spirit in other ways. We should pray that we will be teachable by the Holy Spirit, that we will be guided by the Spirit, and that His power will be poured out on us in all our service for Christ.

It is quite possible that when Jesus taught the disciples to ask for **the Holy Spirit,** He was referring to the *power* of the Spirit enabling them to live the other-worldly type of discipleship which He had been teaching in the preceding chapters. By this time, they were probably feeling how utterly impossible it was for them to meet the tests of discipleship in their own strength. This is, of course, true. **The Holy Spirit** is the power that enables one to live the Christian life. So Jesus pictured God as anxious to give this power to those who ask.

In the original Greek, verse 13 does not say that God will give *the* Holy Spirit, but rather He will "give Holy Spirit" (without the article). Professor H. B. Swete pointed out that when the article is present, it refers to the Person Himself, but when the article is absent, it refers to His gifts or operations on our behalf. So in this passage, it is not so much a prayer for the *Person* of the Holy Spirit, but rather for His ministries in our lives. This is further borne out by the parallel passage in Matthew 7:11 which reads, " . . . how much more will your Father who is in heaven give *good things* to those who ask Him!"

I. Jesus Answers His Critics (11:14–26)

11:14–16 Casting out a demon that had caused its victim to be **mute**, Jesus created quite a stir among the people. While **the multitudes marveled**, others became more openly opposed to the Lord. The opposition took two principal forms. **Some** accused Him of casting **out demons by** the power of **Beelzebub, the ruler of the demons. Others** suggested that He should perform a **sign from heaven**; perhaps their idea was that this might disprove the charge that had been made against Him.

11:17, 18 The accusation that He cast out demons because He was indwelt by Beelzebub is answered in verses 17–26. The request for a sign is answered in v. 29. First of all, the Lord Jesus reminded them that **every kingdom divided against itself is** destroyed, **and a house divided against** itself **falls**. If He was a tool of Satan in casting out demons, then **Satan** was fighting against his own underlings. It is ridiculous to think that the devil would thus oppose himself and obstruct his own purposes.

11:19 Secondly, the Lord reminded His critics that some of their own countrymen were at that very time casting out evil spirits. If He did it by the power of Satan, then it necessarily follows that they must be doing it by the same power. Of course, the Jews would never be willing to admit this. And yet how could they deny the force of the argu-

ment? The power to cast out demons came either from God or from Satan. It had to be one or the other; it could not be both. If Jesus acted by the power of Satan, then the Jewish exorcists depended upon the same power. To condemn Him was to condemn them also.

11:20 The true explanation is that Jesus **cast out demons with the finger of God**. What did He mean by **the finger of God**? In the account in Matthew's Gospel (12:28), we read: "But if I cast out demons by the Spirit of God, surely the kingdom of God has come upon you." So we conclude that **the finger of God** is the same as the Spirit of God. The fact that Jesus was casting out demons by the Spirit of God was evidence indeed that **the kingdom of God** had **come upon** the people of that generation. The kingdom had come in the Person of the King Himself. The very fact that the Lord Jesus was there, performing such miracles, was proof positive that God's anointed Ruler had appeared upon the stage of history.

11:21, 22 Up until now, Satan was **a strong man, fully armed**, who held undisputed sway over his court. Those who were possessed by demons were kept in his grip, and there was no one to challenge him. **His goods** were **in peace**, that is, no one had the power to dispute his sway. The Lord Jesus was **stronger than** Satan, came **upon him**, overcame **him**, took **all his armor** from him, and divided **his spoils**.

Not even His critics denied that evil spirits were being cast out by Jesus. This could only mean that Satan had been conquered and that his victims were being liberated. That is the point of these verses.

11:23 Then Jesus added that anyone **who is not with** Him **is against** Him, and anyone **who does not gather with** Him **scatters** abroad. As someone has said, "A man is either on the way or in the way." We have already mentioned the seeming contradiction between this verse and 9:50. If the issue is the Person and work of Christ, there can be no neutrality. A man who is not for Christ is against Him. But when it is a matter of Christian service, those who are not against Christ's servants are for them. In the first verse, it is a matter of salvation; in the second a matter of service.

11:24–26 It seems that the Lord is turning the tables on His critics. They had accused Him of being demon-possessed. He now likens their nation to a man who had been temporarily cured of demon possession. This was true in their history. Prior to the captivity, the nation of Israel had been possessed with the demon of idolatry. But the captivity rid them of that evil **spirit**, and since then the Jews have never been given over to idolatry. Their house has been **swept and put in order**, but they have refused to let the Lord Jesus come in and take possession. Therefore He predicted that in a coming day, the **unclean spirit** would gather **seven other spirits more wicked than himself, and they** would **enter** the house **and dwell there**. This refers to the terrible form of idolatry which the Jewish nation will adopt during the Tribulation Period; they will acknowledge the Antichrist to be God (John 5:43) and the punishment for this sin will be greater than the nation has ever endured before.

While this illustration refers primarily to Israel's *national* history, it also points up the insufficiency of mere repentance or reformation in an *individual's* life. It is not enough to turn over a new leaf. The Lord Jesus Christ must be welcomed into the heart and life. Otherwise the life is open to entrance by more vile forms of sin than ever indulged in before.

J. More Blessed Than Mary (11:27, 28)

A certain woman came **from the crowd** to hail Jesus with the words, **"Blessed is the womb that bore You, and the breasts which nursed You!"** The reply of our Lord was most significant. He did not deny that Mary, His mother, was blessed, but He went beyond this and said that it was even *more* important to **hear the word of God and keep it**. In other words, even the Virgin Mary was more blessed in believing on Christ and following Him than she was in being His mother. Natural relationship is not as important as spiritual. This should be sufficient to silence those who would make Mary an object of adoration.

K. The Sign of Jonah (11:29–32)

11:29 In verse 16, some had tempted the Lord Jesus, asking Him for **a sign** from heaven. He now answers that request by ascribing it to **an evil generation**. He was speaking primarily concerning the Jewish **generation** which was living at that time. The people had been privileged with the presence of the Son of God. They had heard His words and had witnessed His miracles. But they were not satisfied with this. They now pretended that if they could only see a mighty, supernatural work in the heavens, they would believe on Him. The Lord's answer was that **no** further **sign** would **be given to** them **except the sign of Jonah the prophet**.

11:30 He was referring to His own resurrection from the dead. Just **as Jonah** was delivered from the sea, after being in the whale's belly for three days and three nights, so the Lord Jesus would rise from the dead after being in the grave for three days and three nights. In other words, the last and conclusive miracle in the earthly ministry of the Lord Jesus would be His resurrection. **Jonah became a sign to the Ninevites**. When he went to preach to this Gentile metropolis, he went as one who figuratively, at least, had risen from the dead.

11:31, 32 The queen of the South, the Gentile Queen of Sheba, traveled a great distance **to hear the wisdom of Solomon**. She did not see a single miracle. If she had been privileged to live in the days of the Lord, how readily she would have received Him! Therefore she **will rise up in the judgment** against those wicked men who were privileged to see the supernatural works of the Lord Jesus and who nonetheless rejected Him. **A greater than Jonah**, and **a greater than Solomon** had stepped on the stage of human history. Whereas **the men of Ninevah repented at the preaching of Jonah**, the men of Israel refused to repent at the preaching of **a greater than Jonah**.

Unbelief today scoffs at the story of Jonah, assigning it to Hebrew legend. Jesus spoke of Jonah as an actual person of history, just as He spoke of Solomon. People who say they would believe if they could see a miracle are mistaken.

Faith is not based on the evidences of the senses but on the living word of God. If a man will not believe the word of God, he will not believe though one should rise from the dead. The attitude that demands a sign is not pleasing to God. That is not faith but sight. Unbelief says, "Let me see and then I will believe." God says, "Believe and then you will see."

L. Parable of the Lighted Lamp (11:33–36)

11:33 At first we might think that there is no connection between these verses and the preceding ones. But on closer examination, we find a very vital link. Jesus reminded His hearers that **no one** puts a lighted **lamp** in the cellar or **under a basket**. He puts it **on a lampstand** where it will be seen and where it will provide light for all who enter.

The application is this: God is the One who has **lit** the **lamp**. In the Person and work of the Lord Jesus, He provided a blaze of illumination for the world. If anyone doesn't see the Light, it isn't God's fault. In chapter 8, Jesus was speaking of the responsibility of those who were already His disciples to propagate the faith and not to hide it under a vessel. Here in 11:33 He is exposing the unbelief of His sign-seeking critics as caused by their covetousness and fear of shame.

11:34 Their unbelief was a result of their impure motives. In the physical realm, **the eye** is that which gives **light** to the **whole body**. If the eye is healthy, then the person can see the light. But if the eye is diseased, that is, blind, then the light cannot get in.

It is the same in the spiritual realm. If a person is sincere in his desire to know whether Jesus is the Christ of God, then God will reveal it to him. But if his motives are not pure, if he wants to cling to his greed, if he continues to fear what others will say, then he is blinded to the true worth of the Savior.

11:35 The men Jesus was addressing thought themselves to be very wise. They supposed that they had a great deal of light. But the Lord Jesus warned them to consider the fact that **the light** that was **in** them was actually **darkness**. Their own pretended wisdom and superiority kept them from Him.

11:36 The person whose motives are pure, who opens His complete being to Jesus, the Light of the world, is flooded with spiritual illumination. His inward life is enlightened by Christ just as his body is illuminated when he sits in the direct rays of a lamp.

M. Outward and Inward Cleanliness (11:37–41)

11:37–40 When Jesus accepted the invitation of **a certain Pharisee** to dinner, His host was shocked **that He had not first washed before dinner**. Jesus read his thoughts and thoroughly rebuked him for such hypocrisy and externalism. Jesus reminded him that what really counts is not the cleanliness of **the outside of the cup** but **the inside**. Outwardly, the Pharisees appeared quite righteous, but inwardly they were crooked and wicked. The same God **who made the outside** of man made the **inside** as well, and He is interested that our inward lives should be pure. "Man looks at the outward appearance, but the LORD looks at the heart" (1 Sam. 16:7).

11:41 The Lord realized how covetous and selfish these Pharisees were, so He told His host first to **give alms of such things as** he had. If he could pass this basic test of love to others, **then indeed all things** would be **clean to** him. H. A. Ironside comments:

> When the love of God fills the heart so that one will be concerned about the needs of others, then only will these outward observances have any real value. He who is constantly gathering up for himself, in utter indifference to the poor and needy about him, gives evidence that the love of God does not dwell in him.[39]

An unknown writer summarizes:

> The severe things said in verses 39–52 against Pharisees and lawyers were said at a Pharisee's dinner table (verse 37). What we call "good taste" is often made a substitute for loyalty to truth; we smile when we should frown; and we are silent when we should speak. Better break up a dinner party than break faith with God.

N. The Pharisees Rebuked (11:42–44)

11:42 The **Pharisees** were externalists. They were punctilious about the smallest details of the ceremonial law, such as tithing tiny **herbs**. But they were careless in their relations with God and with man. They oppressed the poor and failed to love God. The Lord did not rebuke them for tithing **mint and rue** and every herb, but simply pointed out that they should not be so zealous in this particular and neglect the basic duties of life, such as **justice and the love of God**. They emphasized the subordinate but overlooked the primary. They excelled in what could be seen by others but were careless about what only God could see.

11:43 They loved to parade themselves, to occupy positions of prominence **in the synagogues**, and to attract as much attention as possible **in the marketplaces**. They were thus guilty not only of externalism but of pride as well.

11:44 Finally the Lord compared them to unmarked **graves**. Under the Law of Moses, whoever touched a grave was unclean for seven days (Num. 19:16), even if he didn't know at the time that it was a grave. The **Pharisees** outwardly gave the appearance of being devout religious leaders. But they should have worn a sign warning people that it was defiling to come in touch with them. They were **like** unmarked **graves**, full of corruption and uncleanness, and infecting others with their externalism and pride.

O. The Lawyers Denounced (11:45–52)

11:45 **The lawyers** were the scribes — experts in explaining and interpreting the Law of Moses. However, their skill was limited to telling others what to do. They did not practice it themselves. One of the lawyers had felt the cutting edge of Jesus' words, and reminded Him that in criticizing the Pharisees, He was **also** insulting the legal experts.

11:46 The Lord used this as an occasion to lash out at some of the sins of the lawyers. First of all they oppressed the people with all kinds of legal **burdens**, but did nothing to help them bear **the burdens**. As Kelly remarks, "They were notorious for their contempt of the very people from whom they derived their importance."[40] Many of their rules were man-made and were connected with matters of no real importance.

11:47, 48 The lawyers were hypocritical murderers. They pretended to admire the prophets of God. They went so far as to erect monuments over **the tombs of the** OT **prophets**. This certainly seemed to be a proof of their deep respect. But the Lord Jesus knew differently. While outwardly dissociating themselves from their Jewish ancestors who **killed** the prophets, they were actually following in their footsteps. At the very time they were building **tombs** for the prophets, they were plotting the death of God's greatest Prophet, the Lord Himself. And they would continue to murder God's faithful prophets and apostles.

11:49 By comparing verse 49 with Matthew 23:34, it will be seen that Jesus Himself is **the wisdom of God**. Here He quotes **the wisdom of God** as saying, **"I will send them prophets."** In Matthew He does not give this as a quotation from the OT or from any other source, but simply presents it as His own statement. (See also 1 Cor. 1:30 where Christ is spoken of as wisdom.) The Lord Jesus promised that He would **send . . . prophets and apostles** to the men of His generation, and that the latter would **kill and persecute** them.

11:50, 51 He would require **of** that **generation the blood** of all God's spokesmen, beginning with the first recorded case in the OT, that **of Abel**, down to the last instance, that **of Zechariah, who perished between the altar and the temple** (2 Chron. 24:21). Second Chronicles was the last book in the Jewish order of the OT books. Therefore the Lord Jesus ran the entire gamut of martyrs when He mentioned **Abel** and **Zechariah**. As He uttered these words, He well knew that the generation then living would put Him to death on the cross, and thus bring to an awful climax all their previous persecution of men of God. It was because they would murder Him **that the blood of all** previous dispensations would fall upon them.

11:52 Finally the Lord Jesus denounced the **lawyers** for having **taken away the key of knowledge**, that is, for withholding God's Word from the people. Though outwardly they professed loyalty to the Scriptures, yet they stubbornly refused to receive the One of whom the Scriptures spoke. And they hindered others from coming to Christ. They didn't want Him themselves, and they didn't want others to receive Him.

P. Response of the Scribes and Pharisees (11:53, 54)

The scribes and the Pharisees were obviously angered by the Lord's straightforward accusations. They **began to assail Him vehemently**, and stepped up their efforts to trap Him in His words. By every possible device, they sought to trick Him into saying **something** for which they could condemn Him to death. In doing so, they only proved how accurately He had read their characters.

VIII. TEACHING AND HEALING ON THE WAY TO JERUSALEM (Chaps. 12–16)

A. Warnings and Encouragements (12:1–12)

12:1 An **innumerable multitude ... had gathered together** while Jesus was condemning the Pharisees and lawyers. A dispute or a debate will generally attract a throng, but this crowd was also drawn, no doubt, by Jesus' fearless denunciation of these hypocritical religious leaders. Although an uncompromising attitude toward sin is not always popular, yet it does commend itself to the heart of man as being righteous. Truth is always self-verifying. Turning **to His disciples**, Jesus warned, **"Beware of the leaven of the Pharisees."** He explained that leaven is a symbol or picture of **hypocrisy**. A hypocrite is one who wears a mask, one whose outward appearance is utterly different from what he is inwardly. The Pharisees posed as paragons of virtue but actually they were masters of masquerade.

12:2, 3 Their day of exposure would come. All that they had **covered** up would be **revealed**, and all that they had done **in the dark** would be dragged out into **the light**.

Just as inevitable as the unmasking of hypocrisy is the triumph of truth. Up to then, the message proclaimed by the disciples had been spoken in relative obscurity and to limited audiences. But following the rejection of the Messiah by Israel, and the coming of the Holy Spirit, the disciples would go forth fearlessly in the name of the Lord Jesus and proclaim the good news far and wide. Then it would **be proclaimed on the housetops**, comparatively speaking. Godet remarks, "Those whose voice cannot now find a hearing, save within limited and obscure circles, shall become the teachers of the world."[41]

12:4, 5 With the encouraging and warm-hearted words **"My friends,"** Jesus warns His disciples not to be ashamed of this priceless friendship under any trials. The worldwide proclamation of the Christian message would bring persecution and death to the loyal disciples. But there was a limit to what men like the Pharisees could do to them. Physical death was that limit. This they should not fear. God would visit their persecutors with a far worse punishment, namely eternal death in **hell**. And so the disciples were to **fear** God rather than man.

12:6, 7 To emphasize God's protective interest in the disciples, the Lord Jesus mentioned the Father's care for **sparrows**. In Matthew 10:29 we read that two sparrows are sold for a copper coin. Here we learn that **five sparrows** are **sold for two copper coins**. In other words, an extra sparrow is thrown in free when four are purchased. And yet not even this odd sparrow with no commercial value is forgotten in the sight of **God**. If God cares for that odd sparrow, how much more does He watch over those who go forth with the gospel of His Son! He numbers **the very hairs of** their **head**.

12:8 The Savior told the disciples that **whoever confesses** Him now will be confessed by Him **before the angels of God**. Here He is speaking of all true believers. To confess Him is to receive Him as only Lord and Savior.

12:9 Those who deny Him **before men will be denied before the angels of God**. The primary reference here seems to be to the Pharisees, but of course the verse includes all who refuse Christ and are ashamed to acknowledge Him. In that day, He will say, "I never knew you."

12:10 Next the Savior explained to the disciples that there is a difference between criticism of Him and blasphemy **against the Holy Spirit**. Those who speak **against the Son of Man** can **be forgiven** if they repent and believe. But blasphemy **against the Holy Spirit** is the unpardonable sin. This is the sin of which the Pharisees were guilty (see Matt. 12:22–32). What is this sin? It is the sin of attributing the miracles of the Lord Jesus to the devil. It is blasphemy **against the Holy Spirit** because Jesus performed all His miracles in the power of the Holy Spirit. Therefore, it was, in effect, saying that the Holy Spirit of God is the devil. There is no forgiveness for this sin in this age or in the age to come.

This sin cannot be committed by a true believer, though some are tortured by fears that they have committed it by backsliding. Backsliding is not the unpardonable sin. A backslider can be restored to fellowship with the Lord. The very fact that a person is concerned is evidence he has *not* committed the unpardonable sin.

Neither is rejection of Christ by an unbeliever the unforgivable sin. A person may spurn the Savior repeatedly, yet he may later turn to the Lord and be converted. Of course, if he dies in unbelief, he can no longer be converted. His sin then, in fact, does become unpardonable. But the sin which our Lord described as unpardonable is the sin which the Pharisees committed by saying that He performed His miracles by the power of Beelzebub, the prince of demons.

12:11, 12 It was inevitable that the disciples would be brought before governmental **authorities** for trial. The Lord Jesus told them that it was unnecessary for them to rehearse in advance **what** they **should say. The Holy Spirit** would put the proper words in their mouths whenever it was necessary. This does *not* mean that servants of the Lord should not spend time in prayer and study before preaching the gospel or teaching the Word of God. It should not be used as an excuse for laziness! However, it is a definite promise from the Lord that those who are placed on trial for their witness for Christ will be given special help from **the Holy Spirit**. And it is a general promise to all God's people that if they walk in the Spirit, they will be given the suitable words to speak in the crisis moments of life.

B. Warning Against Greed (12:13–21)

12:13 At this point, a man stepped out **from the crowd** and asked the Lord to settle a dispute between his **brother** and himself over an **inheritance**. It has often been said that where there's a will, there are a lot of relatives. This seems to be a case in point. We are not told whether the man was being deprived of his rightful portion, or whether he was greedy for more than his share.

12:14 The Savior quickly reminded him that He had not come into the world to handle such trivial matters. The purpose of His coming involved the salvation of sinful men and women. He would not be deflected from this grand and glorious mission to divide a pitiful inheritance. (In addition, He did not have legal authority to judge matters involving estates. His decisions would not have been binding.)

12:15 But the Lord *did* use this incident to warn His hearers against one of the most insidious evils in the human heart, namely **covetousness**. The insatiable lust for material possessions is one of the strongest drives in all of life. And yet it completely misses the purpose of human existence. **"One's life does not consist in the abundance of the things he possesses."** As J. R. Miller points out:

This is one of the red flags our Lord hung out which most people nowadays do not seem much to regard. Christ said a great deal about the danger of riches; but not many persons are afraid of riches. Covetousness is not practically considered a sin in these times. If a man breaks the sixth or eighth commandment, he is branded as a criminal and covered with shame; but he may break the tenth, and he is only enterprising. The Bible says the love of money is a root of all evil; but every man who quotes the saying puts a terrific emphasis on the word "love," explaining that it is not money, but only the love of it, that is such a prolific root.

To look about, one would think a man's life *did* consist in the abundance of the things he possesses. Men think they become great just in proportion as they gather wealth. So it seems, too; for the world measures men by their bank-account. Yet there never was a more fatal error. A man is really measured by what he *is*, and not by what he *has*.[42]

12:16–18 The **parable** of the **rich** fool illustrates the fact that possessions are *not* the principal thing in life. Because of an exceptionally good crop, this wealthy farmer was faced with what seemed to him a very distressing problem. He did not know what to do with all the grain. All his barns and silos were crammed to capacity. Then he had a brainstorm. His problem was solved. He decided to **pull down** his **barns and build** bigger ones. He could have saved himself the expense and bother of this tremendous construction project if he had just looked on the needy world about him, and used these possessions to satisfy hunger, both spiritual and physical. "The bosoms of the poor, the houses of widows, the mouths of children are the barns which last forever," said Ambrose.

12:19 As soon as his new barns were built, he planned to retire. Notice his spirit of independence: my barns, my fruits, my goods, my soul. He had the future all planned. He was going to **take** his **ease, eat, drink, and be merry**.

12:20, 21 "But when he began to think of time as his, he crashed into God to his eternal ruin." **God** told **him** that he would die that very **night**. Then he would lose ownership of all his material possessions. They would fall to someone else. Someone has defined a fool as one whose plans end at the grave. This man surely was a fool.

"Then whose will those things be?" God asked. We might well ask ourselves the question, "If Christ should come today, whose would all my possessions be?" How much better to use them for God today than to let them fall into the devil's hands tomorrow! We can lay **up treasure** in heaven with them now, and thus be **rich toward God**. Or we can squander them on our flesh, and from the flesh reap corruption.

C. Anxiety Versus Faith (12:22–34)

12:22, 23 One of the great dangers in the Christian life is that the acquisition of food and clothing becomes the first and foremost aim of our existence. We become so occupied with earning money for these things that the work of the Lord is relegated to a secondary place. The emphasis of the NT is that the cause of Christ should have first place in our lives. **Food** and **clothing** should be subordinate. We should work hard for the supply of our current necessities, then trust God for the future as we plunge ourselves into His service. This is the life of faith.

When the Lord Jesus said that we should **not worry about** food and clothing, He did not mean that we were to sit idly and wait for these things to be provided. Christianity does *not* encourage laziness! But He certainly did mean that in the process of earning money for the necessities of life, we were not to let them assume undue importance. After all, there is something more important in life than what we **eat** and what we wear. We are here as ambassadors of the King, and all considerations of personal comfort and appearance must be subordinated to the one glorious task of making Him known.

12:24 Jesus used **the ravens** as an example of how **God** cares for His creatures. They do not spend their lives in a frantic quest for food and in providing for future needs. They live in hourly dependence on God. The fact that **they neither sow nor reap** should not be stretched to teach that men should refrain from secular occupations. All it means is that God knows the needs of those whom He has created, and He will supply them if we walk in dependence on Himself. If **God feeds** the ravens, how much more will He feed those whom He has created, whom He has saved by His grace, and whom He has called to be His servants. The ravens have no barns or storehouses, yet God provides for them on a daily basis. Why then should we spend our lives building bigger barns and storage bins?

12:25, 26 **"Which of you by worrying,"** Jesus asked, **"can add one cubit to his stature?"** This indicates the folly of worrying over things (such as the future) over which we have no control. No one **by worrying can add** to his height, or to the length of his life. (The expression "his stature" can also be translated "the length of his life".) If that is so, why worry about the future? Rather, let us use all our strength and time serving Christ, and leave the future to Him.

12:27, 28 **The lilies** are next introduced to show the folly of spending one's finest talents in the obtaining of

clothes. The lilies are probably wild scarlet anemones. **They neither toil nor spin, yet** they have a natural beauty which rivals **Solomon in all his glory. If God** lavishes such beauty on flowers which bloom **today** and are burned tomorrow, will He be unmindful of the needs of His children? We prove ourselves to be of **little faith** when we worry, fret, and rush around in a ceaseless struggle to get more and more material possessions. We waste our lives doing what God would have done for us, if we had only devoted our time and talents more to Him.

12:29–31 Actually, our daily needs are small. It is wonderful how simply we can live. Why then give food and clothing such a prominent place in our lives? And why **have an anxious mind**, worrying about the future? This is the way unsaved people live. **The nations of the world** who do not know God as their Father concentrate on food, clothing, and pleasure. These things form the very center and circumference of their existence. But God never intended that His children should spend their time in the mad rush for creature comforts. He has a work to be done on earth, and He has promised to care for those who give themselves wholeheartedly to Him. If we **seek** His **kingdom**, He will never let us starve or be naked. How sad it would be to come to the end of life and realize that most of our time was spent in slaving for what was already included in the ticket home to heaven!

12:32 The disciples formed a **little flock** of defenseless sheep, sent out into the midst of an unfriendly world. They had, it is true, no visible means of support or defense. Yet this bedraggled group of young men was destined to inherit **the kingdom** with Christ. They would one day reign with Him over all the earth. In view of this, the Lord encouraged them **not** to **fear**, because if the **Father** had such glorious honors in store for them, then they need not worry about the pathway that lay between.

12:33, 34 Instead of accumulating material possessions and planning for time, they can put these possessions to work for the Lord. In this way they would be investing for heaven and for eternity. The ravages of age could not af-

fect their possessions. Heavenly treasures are fully insured against theft and spoilage. The trouble with material wealth is that ordinarily you can't have it without trusting it. That is why the Lord Jesus said, **"Where your treasure is, there your heart will be also."** If we send our money on ahead, then our affections will be weaned from the perishing things of this world.

D. Parable of the Watchful Servant (12:35–40)

12:35 Not only were the disciples to trust the Lord for their needs; they were to live in constant expectancy of His coming again. Their **waist** was to be **girded**, and their **lamps burning**. In eastern lands, a belt was drawn around the **waist** to hold up the long, flowing garments when a person was about to walk quickly or run. The girded waist speaks of a mission to be accomplished and the burning lamp suggests a testimony to be maintained.

12:36 The disciples were to live in moment-by-moment expectation of the Lord's return, as if He were a man returning **from** a **wedding**. Kelly comments:

> They should be free from all earthly encumbrances, so that the moment the Lord knocks, according to the figure, they may open to Him immediately — without distraction or having to get ready. Their hearts are waiting for Him, for their Lord; they love Him, they are waiting for Him. He knocks and they open to Him immediately.[43]

The details of the story concerning the man returning **from the wedding** should not be pressed as far as the prophetic future is concerned. We should not identify the wedding here with the Marriage Supper of the Lamb, or the man's return with the Rapture. The Lord's story was designed to teach one simple truth, namely, watchfulness for His return; it was not intended to set forth the order of events at His coming.

12:37 When the man comes back from the wedding, his **servants** are eagerly **watching** for him, ready to swing into action at his command. He is so pleased with their watchful attitude that he turns the tables, as it were. **He** girds **himself** with a servant's apron, seats them at the table, and serves them a meal. This is a very touching suggestion that He who once came into this world in the form of a bondslave will graciously condescend to serve His people again in their heavenly home. The devout German Bible scholar Bengel regarded verse 37 as the greatest promise in all God's word.

12:38 **The second watch** of the night was from 9:00 p.m. to midnight. **The third** was from midnight to 3:00 a.m. No matter what watch it was when the Master returned, his **servants** were waiting for him.

12:39, 40 The Lord changes the picture by alluding to a home owner whose house was **broken into** in an unguarded moment. The coming of **the thief** was entirely unexpected. **If the master of the house had known**, he would **not** have **allowed his house to be broken into**. The lesson is that the time of Christ's coming is uncertain; no one knows the day or the hour when He will appear. When He does come, those believers who have laid up treasures on earth will lose them all, because as someone has said, "A Christian either leaves his wealth or goes to it." If we are really watching for Christ's return, we will sell all that we have and lay up treasures in heaven where no thief can reach them.

E. Faithful and Unfaithful Servants (12:41–48)

12:41, 42 At this point **Peter** asked if Christ's **parable** on watchfulness was intended **only** for the disciples or for **all people**. The Lord's answer was that it was for all who profess to be stewards of God. The **faithful and wise steward** is the one who is set over the Master's household and who gives **food** to His people. The steward's main responsibility here concerns people, not material things. This is in keeping with the entire context, warning the disciples against materialism and covetousness. It is people who are important, not things.

12:43, 44 **When** the Lord **comes** and finds His bondslave taking a genuine interest in the spiritual welfare of men and women, He will reward him liberally. The reward probably has to do with governmental rule with Christ during the Millennium (1 Pet. 5:1–4).

12:45 The **servant** professes to be working for Christ, but actually he is an unbeliever. Instead of feeding the people of God, he abuses them, robs them, and lives in self-indulgence. (This may be a reference to the Pharisees.)

12:46 The coming of the Lord will expose his unreality, and he will be punished **with** all other **unbelievers**. The expression **"cut him in two"** may also be translated "severely scourge him" (AV margin).

12:47, 48 Verses 47 and 48 set forth a fundamental principle in regard to all service. The principle is that the greater the privilege, the greater the responsibility. For believers, it means that there will be degrees of reward in heaven. For unbelievers, it means that there will be degrees of punishment in hell. Those who have come to know God's **will** as it is revealed in the Scriptures are under great responsibility to obey it. **Much** has been **given** to them; **much will be required** of them. Those who have not been so highly privileged will also be punished for their misdeeds, but their punishment will be less severe.

F. The Effect of Christ's First Advent (12:49–53)

12:49 The Lord Jesus knew that His coming to **the earth** would not bring peace at the outset. First it must cause division, strife, persecution, bloodshed. He did not come with the avowed purpose of casting this kind of **fire on the earth**, but that was the result or effect of His coming. Although afflictions and dissensions broke out during His earthly ministry, it was not until the cross that the heart of man was truly exposed. The Lord knew that all of this must take place, and He was willing that the **fire** of persecution should burst forth as soon as necessary against Himself.

12:50 He had **a baptism to be baptized with**. This refers to His **baptism** to the point of death on Calvary. He was under tremendous constraint to go to the cross to accomplish redemption for lost mankind. The shame, suffering, and death were the Father's will for Him, and He was anxious to obey.

12:51–53 He knew very well that His coming would not give **peace on earth** at that time. And so He warned the disciples that when men came to Him, their families would persecute them and drive them out. The introduction of Christianity into an average home of **five** would split the family. It is a curious mark of man's perverted nature that ungodly relatives would often rather have their son a drunkard and dissolute person than have him take a public stand as a disciple of the Lord Jesus Christ! This paragraph disproves the theory that Jesus came to unite all humanity (godly and ungodly) into a single "universal brotherhood of man." Rather, He divided them as they have never been divided before!

G. The Signs of the Times (12:54–59)

12:54, 55 The previous verses were addressed to the disciples. Now the Savior turns **to the multitudes**. He reminds them of their skill in predicting the weather. They knew that when they saw **a cloud** to **the west** (over the Mediterranean), they were in for **a shower**. On the other hand, a **south wind** would bring scorching heat and drought. The people had the intelligence to know this. But there was more than intelligence. There was the will to know.

12:56 In spiritual matters, it was a different story. Though they had normal human intelligence, they did not realize the important **time** which had arrived in human history. The Son of God had come to this earth, and was standing in their very midst. Heaven had never come so near before. But they did not know the time of their visitation. They had the intellectual capacity to know, but they did not have the will to know, and thus they were self-deluded.

12:57–59 If they realized the significance of the day in which they lived, they would be in a hurry to make peace **with** their **adversary**. Four legal terms are used here — **adversary, magistrate, judge, officer** — and they all may refer to God. At that time God was walking in and out among them, pleading with them, giving them an opportunity to be saved. They should repent and put their faith in Him. If they refused, they would have to stand before God as their Judge. The case would be sure to go against them. They would be found guilty and condemned for their unbelief. They would be thrown **into prison**, that is,

eternal punishment. They would not come out **till** they had **paid the very last mite** — which means that they would *never* come out, because they would never be able to pay such a tremendous debt.

So Jesus was saying that they should discern the time in which they lived. Then they should get right with God by repenting of their sins and by committing themselves to Him in full surrender.

H. The Importance of Repentance (13:1–5)

13:1–3 Chapter 12 closed with the failure of the Jewish nation to discern the time in which they lived, and with the Lord's warning to repent quickly or perish forever. Chapter 13 continues this general subject, and is largely addressed to Israel as a nation, although the principles apply to individual people. Two national calamities form the basis of the resulting conversation. The first was the massacre of some **Galileans** who had come to Jerusalem to worship. **Pilate**, the governor of Judea, had ordered them to be slain while they were offering **sacrifices**. Nothing else is known concerning this atrocity. We assume the victims were Jews who had been living in Galilee. The Jews in Jerusalem might have been laboring under the delusion **that these Galileans** must have committed terrible sins, and that their death was an evidence of God's disfavor. However, the Lord Jesus corrected this by warning the Jewish people that **unless** they repented, they would **all likewise perish**.

13:4, 5 The other tragedy concerned the collapse of a **tower in Siloam** which caused the death of **eighteen** persons. Nothing else is known about this accident except what is recorded here. Fortunately, it is not necessary to know any further details. The point emphasized by the Lord was that this catastrophe should not be interpreted as a special judgment for gross wickedness. Rather, it should be seen as a warning to all the nation of Israel that **unless** they repented, a similar doom would come upon them. This doom came to pass in A.D. 70 when Titus invaded Jerusalem.

I. Parable of the Fruitless Fig Tree (13:6–9)

In close connection with the preceding, the Lord Jesus told the **parable** of the **fig tree**. It is not difficult to identify the **fig tree** as Israel, **planted** in God's **vineyard**, that is, the world. God looked for **fruit on** the tree but He **found none**. So He said to the vinedresser (the Lord Jesus) that He had sought in vain for **fruit** from the tree **for three years**. The simplest interpretation of this refers it to the first three years of our Lord's public ministry. The thought of the passage is that the fig tree had been given sufficient time to produce fruit, if it was ever going to do so. If no fruit appeared in three years, then it was reasonable to conclude that none would ever appear. Because of its fruitlessness, God ordered to **cut it down**. It was only occupying **ground** that could be used more productively. The vinedresser interceded for the fig tree, asking that it be given one more year. If at the end of that time, it was still fruitless, then He could **cut it down**. And that is what happened. It was after the fourth year had begun that Israel rejected and crucified the Lord Jesus. As a result, its capital was destroyed and the people scattered.

G. H. Lang expressed it thus:

> The Son of God knew the mind of His Father, the Owner of the vineyard, and that the dread order "Cut it down" had been issued; Israel had again exhausted the Divine forbearance. Neither a nation nor a person has reason to enjoy the care of God if not bringing forth the fruits of righteousness unto the glory and praise of God. Man exists for the honour and pleasure of the Creator: when he does not serve this just end why should not the sentence of death follow his sinful failure, and he be removed from his place of privilege?[44]

J. Healing of the Bent-Over Woman (13:10–17)

13:10–13 The real attitude of Israel toward the Lord Jesus is seen in the ruler of the synagogue. This official objected that the Savior had healed a woman on the Sabbath. The **woman** had suffered from severe curvature of the spine for **eighteen years**. Her deformity was great; she could not straighten **herself up** at all. Without even being asked, the Lord **Jesus** had spoken the healing word, had **laid His hands on her**, and had straightened her spine.

13:14 **The ruler of the synagogue** indignantly told the people that they should come for healing on the first **six days** of the week, but not on the seventh. He was a professional religionist, with no deep concern for the problems of the people. Even if they had come on the first six days of the week, he could not have helped them. He was a stickler about the technical points of the law, but there was no love or mercy in his heart. If he had had curvature of the spine for eighteen years, he would not have minded on which day he was straightened out!

13:15, 16 **The Lord** reproved his hypocrisy and that of the other leaders. He reminded them that they didn't hesitate to **loose** an **ox or donkey from the stall on the Sabbath** in order to let it drink water. If they showed such consideration for dumb animals on the Sabbath, was it wrong for Jesus to perform an act of healing on **this woman** who was **a daughter of Abraham**? The expression "a daughter of Abraham" indicates not only that she was Jewish but also a true believer, a woman of faith. The curvature of the spine was caused by **Satan**. We know from other parts of the Bible that some sicknesses are the result of Satanic activity. Job's boils were inflicted by Satan. Paul's thorn in the flesh was a messenger of Satan to buffet him. The devil is not allowed to do this on a believer, however, without the Lord's permission. And God overrules any such sickness or suffering for His own glory.

13:17 The critics of our Lord were thoroughly **put to shame** by His words. The common people **rejoiced** because a **glorious** miracle had been performed, and they knew it.

K. Parables of the Kingdom (13:18–21)

13:18, 19 After seeing this wonderful miracle of healing, the people might have been tempted to think that the kingdom would be set up immediately. The Lord Jesus disabused their minds by setting forth two parables of **the kingdom of God** which describe it as it would exist between the time of the King's rejection and His return to the earth to reign. They picture the growth of Christendom, and include mere profession as well as reality (see notes on 8:1–3).

First of all He likened **the kingdom of God** to **a mustard seed**, one of the tiniest of seeds. When cast into the ground, it produces a shrub, but not a tree. Therefore when Jesus said that this seed produced **a large tree**, He indicated that the growth was highly abnormal. It was big enough for **birds of the air** to lodge **in its branches**. The thought here is that Christianity had a humble beginning, small as a grain of **mustard seed**. But as it grew, it became popularized, and Christendom as we know it today developed. Christendom is composed of all who profess allegiance to the Lord, whether or not they have ever been born again. **The birds of the air** are vultures or birds of prey. They are symbols of evil, and picture the fact that Christendom has become the resting place for various forms of corruption.

13:20, 21 The second parable likened **the kingdom of God** to **leaven which a woman** placed **in three measures of meal**. We believe that leaven in the Scripture is always a symbol of evil. Here the thought is that evil doctrine has been introduced into the pure food of the people of God. This evil doctrine is not static; it has an insidious power to spread.

L. The Narrow Gate into the Kingdom (13:22–30)

13:22, 23 As Jesus moved **toward Jerusalem**, someone stepped out from the crowd to ask **Him** if only a **few** would be **saved**. It may have been an idle question, provoked by mere curiosity.

13:24 The Lord answered a speculative question with a direct command. He told the questioner to make sure that he himself would **enter through the narrow gate**. When Jesus said **to strive to enter through the narrow gate**, He did not mean that salvation requires effort on our part. **The narrow gate** here is new birth — salvation by grace through faith. Jesus was warning the man to make sure that he entered by this door. **"Many . . . will seek to enter and will not be able"** when once the door is shut. This does not mean that they will seek to enter in by the door of conversion, but rather that in the day of Christ's power and glory, they will want admission to His

kingdom, but it will be too late. The day of grace in which we live will have come to an end.

13:25–27 The Master of the house will rise **up and shut the door**. The Jewish nation is pictured then as knocking **at the door** and asking the **Lord** to **open**. He will refuse on the ground that He never knew them. They will protest at this point, pretending that they had lived on intimate terms with Him. But He will not be moved by these pretensions. They were **workers of iniquity**, and will not be allowed to enter in.

13:28–30 His refusal will cause **weeping and gnashing of teeth**. The **weeping** indicates remorse and the **gnashing of teeth** speaks of violent hatred of God. This shows that the sufferings of hell do not change the heart of man. Unbelieving Israelites will **see Abraham and Isaac and Jacob and all the prophets in the kingdom of God**. They themselves expected to be there, simply because they were related to Abraham, Isaac, and Jacob, but they will be **thrust out**. Gentiles will travel to the brightness of Christ's kingdom from all corners of the earth and enjoy its wonderful blessings. Thus many Jews who were first in God's plan for blessing will be rejected, while the Gentiles who were looked down upon as dogs will enjoy the blessings of Christ's Millennial Reign.

M. Prophets Perish in Jerusalem (13:31–35)

13:31 At this time, the Lord Jesus was apparently in Herod's territory. **Some Pharisees came** and warned Him to **get out** because **Herod** was trying **to kill** Him. The Pharisees seem completely out of character in professing an interest in the welfare and safety of Jesus. Perhaps they had joined in a plot with Herod to frighten Him into going to Jerusalem, where He would most certainly be apprehended.

13:32 Our Lord was not moved by the threat of physical violence. He recognized it as a plot on Herod's part and told the Pharisees to **go** back to **that fox** with a message. Some people have difficulty with the fact that the Lord Jesus spoke of Herod as a she-fox (the form is feminine in the original). They feel that it was in violation of the Scripture which forbids speaking evil of a ruler of the people (Ex. 22:28). However, this was not evil; it was the absolute truth. The gist of the message sent by Jesus was that He still had work to do for a short time. He would **cast out demons and perform** healing miracles during the few remaining days allotted to Him. Then on **the third day**, that is, the final day, He would have finished the work connected with His earthly ministry. Nothing would hinder Him in the performance of His duties. No power on earth could harm Him until the appointed time.

13:33 Further, He could not be slain in Galilee. This prerogative was reserved for the city of **Jerusalem**. It was that city which characteristically had murdered the servants of the Most High God. Jerusalem had more or less a monopoly on the death of God's spokesmen. That is what the Lord Jesus meant when He said that **"it cannot be that a prophet should perish outside of Jerusalem."**

13:34, 35 Having thus spoken the truth concerning this wicked city, Jesus turned in pathos and wept over it. This city that **kills the prophets and stones** God's messengers was the object of His tender love. **How often** He had **wanted to gather** the people of the city **together, as a hen gathers her brood . . . , but** they **were not willing**. The difficulty lay in their stubborn will. As a result, their city, their temple, and their land would be **left desolate**. They would pass through a long period of exile. In fact, they would **not see** the Lord until they changed their attitude toward Him. Verse 35b refers to the Second Advent of Christ. A remnant of the nation of Israel will repent at that **time** and will **say, "Blessed is He who comes in the name of the LORD!"** His people will then be willing in the day of His power.

N. Healing of a Man with Dropsy (14:1-6)

14:1-3 One **Sabbath** day, a ruler **of the Pharisees** invited the Lord to his house for a meal. It was not a sincere gesture of hospitality, but rather an attempt on the part of the religious leaders to find fault with the Son of God. Jesus saw **a certain man** there who was afflicted with **dropsy**, that is, swelling caused by the accumulation of water in the tissues. The Savior read the minds of His critics by asking them pointedly whether **it** was **lawful to heal on the Sabbath**.

14:4-6 Much as they would like to have said that it was not, they could not support their answer, and so **they kept silent**. Jesus therefore **healed** the man **and let him go**. To Him it was a work of mercy, and divine love never ceases its activities, even on the Sabbath (John 5:17). Then turning to the Jews, He reminded them that if one of their animals fell **into a pit**, they would certainly **pull him out on the Sabbath day**. It was in their own interests to do so. The animal was worth money to them. In the case of a suffering fellow man, they didn't care, and they would have condemned the Lord Jesus for helping him. Although **they could not answer** the reasoning of the Savior, we can be sure that they were all the more incensed at Him.

O. Parable of the Ambitious Guest (14:7-11)

As the Lord Jesus entered the Pharisee's house, He perhaps had seen the guests maneuvering for **the best places** around the table. They sought the positions of eminence and honor. The fact that He too was a guest did not prevent Him from speaking out in frankness and righteousness. He warned them against this form of self-seeking. **When** they were **invited** to a meal, they should take the lower **place** rather than the higher. When we seek a high place for ourselves, there is always the possible **shame** of being demoted. If we are truly humble before God, there is only one direction we can possibly move and that is **up**. Jesus taught that it is better to be advanced to a place of honor than to grasp that place and later have to relinquish it. He Himself is the living example of self-renunciation (Phil. 2:5-8). He humbled Himself and God exalted Him. **Whoever exalts himself will be humbled** by God.

P. The Guest List God Honors (14:12-14)

The ruler of the Pharisees had undoubtedly invited the local celebrities to this meal. Jesus perceived this at once.

He saw that the underprivileged people in the community were not included. He therefore took occasion to enunciate one of the great principles of Christianity — that we should love those who are unlovely, and who cannot repay us. The usual way for people to act is to invite their **friends, relatives**, and **rich neighbors**, always with the hope of being **repaid** in kind. It does not require divine life to act in this way. But it is positively supernatural to show kindness to **the poor, the maimed, the lame,** and **the blind**. God reserves a special reward for those who show charity to these classes. Although such guests **cannot repay** us, yet God Himself promises to reward **at the resurrection of the just**. This is also known in the Scripture as the first resurrection, and includes the resurrection of all true believers. It takes place at the Rapture, and also, we believe, at the end of the Tribulation Period. That is, the first resurrection is not one single event, but takes place in stages.

Q. Parable of the Excuses (14:15–24)

14:15–18 **One of** the guests who reclined with Jesus at the meal remarked how wonderful it would be to participate in the blessings of **the kingdom of God**. Perhaps he was impressed by the principles of conduct which the Lord Jesus had just taught. Or perhaps it was just a general remark which he made without too much thought. At any rate, the Lord replied that wonderful as it may be to **eat bread in the kingdom of God**, the sad fact is that many of those who are invited make all kinds of foolish excuses for their failure to accept. He pictured God as **a certain man** who **gave a great supper and invited many** guests. When the meal was ready, he asked **his servant** to notify the **invited** guests that everything was **now ready**. This reminds us of the great fact that the Lord Jesus finished the work of redemption on Calvary, and the gospel invitation goes out on the basis of that completed work. One person who had been invited excused himself because he had **bought a** field and he wanted to **go and see it**. Normally he should have gone and seen it before purchasing it. But even then, he was putting the love of material things ahead of the gracious invitation.

14:19, 20 The next one had **bought**

five yoke of oxen, and was **going to test them**. He pictures those who put jobs, occupations, or business ahead of the call of God. The third one said he had **married a wife, and therefore** could not **come**. Family ties and social relationships often hinder men from accepting the gospel invitation.

14:21–23 When **that servant** notified **his master** that the invitation was being rejected right and left, **the master** sent him **out** to **the city** to invite **the poor and the maimed and the lame and the blind**. "Both nature and grace abhor a vacuum," said Bengel. Perhaps the first ones invited picture the leaders of the Jewish people. When they rejected the gospel, God sent it out to the common people **of the city** of Jerusalem. Many of these responded to the call, but **still there** was **room** in the master's house. And so the lord said to the servant to **go out into the highways and** byways, **and compel** people **to come in**. This doubtless pictures the gospel going out to the Gentile people. They were not to be compelled by *force of arms* (as has been done in the history of Christendom), but rather by *force of argument*. Loving persuasion was to be used in an effort to bring them in so **that** the master's **house** might **be filled**.

14:24 Thus the original guest list was no longer useful when the meal was held, because those **who were** originally **invited** did not come.

R. The Cost of True Discipleship (14:25–35)

14:25 **Now great multitudes** followed the Lord Jesus. Most leaders would be elated by such widespread interest. But the Lord was not looking for people who would follow Him out of curiosity, with no real heart interest. He was looking for those who were willing to live devotedly and passionately for Him, and even die for Him if necessary. And so He now began to sift the crowd by presenting to them the stringent terms of discipleship. At times the Lord Jesus *wooed* men to Himself, but after they began to follow Him, He *winnowed* them. That is what is taking place here.

14:26 First of all He told those who followed Him that in order to be true disciples, they must love Him supremely. He did not ever suggest that men should have bitter hatred in their hearts toward **father, mother, wife, children, brothers and sisters**. Rather He was emphasizing that love for Christ must be so great that all other loves are hatred *by comparison* (cf. Matt. 10:37). No consideration of family ties must ever be allowed to deflect a disciple from a pathway of full obedience to the Lord.

Actually, the most difficult part of this first term of discipleship is found in the words **"and his own life also."** It is not only that we must love our relatives less; we must **hate** our **own** lives **also**! Instead of living self-centered lives, we must live Christ-centered lives. Instead of asking how every action will affect ourselves, we must be careful to assess how it will affect Christ and His glory. Considerations of personal comfort and safety must be subordinated to the great task of glorifying Christ and making Him known. The Savior's words are absolute. He said that if we did not love Him supremely, more than our family and more than our own lives, we could not be His disciples. There is no halfway measure.

14:27 Secondly, He taught that a true disciple must **bear his** own **cross and** follow Him. The cross is *not* some physical infirmity or mental anguish, but is a pathway of reproach, suffering, loneliness, and even death which a person voluntarily chooses for Christ's sake. Not all believers **bear** the **cross**. It is possible to avoid it by living a nominal Christian life. But if we determine to be all out for Christ, we will experience the same kind of satanic opposition which the Son of God knew when He was here on earth. *This is the cross.* The disciple must **come after** Christ. This means that he must live the type of life which Christ lived when He was here on earth — a life of self-renunciation, humiliation, persecution, reproach, temptation, and contradiction of sinners against Himself.

14:28–30 Then the Lord Jesus used two illustrations to emphasize the necessity of counting **the cost** before setting out to follow Him. He likened the Christian life to a building project and then to warfare. A man **intending to build a tower** sits **down first** and counts **the cost**. If he doesn't have **enough to finish it**, he doesn't proceed. Otherwise when

the foundation is laid, and the work must stop, the onlookers **begin to mock him, saying, "This man began to build and was not able to finish."** So it is with disciples. They should first count the cost, whether they really mean to abandon their lives wholeheartedly to Christ. Otherwise they might start off in a blaze of glory, and then fizzle out. If so, the onlookers will mock them for beginning well and ending ingloriously. The world has nothing but contempt for half-hearted Christians.

14:31, 32 A **king going to make war against** forces that are numerically superior must consider carefully **whether** his smaller forces have the capacity to defeat the enemy. He realizes full well that it is either absolute committal or abject surrender. And so it is in the life of Christian discipleship. There can be no half-way measures.

14:33 Verse 33 is probably one of the most unpopular verses in the entire Bible. It explicitly states that **"Whoever of you does not forsake all that he has cannot be My disciple."** There is no evading the meaning of the words. They do not say that a person must be *willing* to forsake all. Rather they say that he *must* forsake all. We must give the Lord Jesus credit for knowing what He was saying. He realized that the job would never be done in any other way. He wants men and women who esteem Him more than everything else in the world. Ryle observes:

> The man who does well for himself is the man who gives up everything for Christ's sake. He makes the best of bargains; he carries the cross for a few years in this world, and in the world to come has everlasting life. He obtains the best of possessions; he carries his riches with him beyond the grave. He is rich in grace here, and he is rich in glory hereafter. And, best of all, what he obtains by faith in Christ he never loses. It is "that good part which is never taken away."[45]

14:34, 35 **Salt** is a picture of a disciple. There is something wholesome and commendable about a person who is living devotedly and sacrificially for the Lord. But then we read of **salt** that **has lost its flavor**. Modern table salt cannot lose its savor because it is pure salt. But in Bible lands, the salt was often mixed with various forms of impurity. Therefore it was possible for salt to be wasted away and for a residue to remain in the container. But this residue was worthless. It could not even be used for fertilizing the land. It had to be discarded.

The picture is of a disciple who starts off brilliantly, and then goes back on his vows. The disciple has one basic reason for existence; if he fails to fulfill that reason, then he is a pitiable object. We read concerning the salt that **"men throw it out."** It does *not* say that *God* casts it out; that could never happen. But **men throw it out**, that is, they trample underfoot the testimony of one who began to build and was not able to finish. Kelly notes:

> There is shown the danger of what begins well turning out ill. What is there in the world so useless as salt when it has lost the one property for which it is valued? It is worse than useless for any other purpose. So with the disciple who ceases to be Christ's disciple. He is not suited for the world's purposes, and he has forsaken God's. He has too much light or knowledge for entering into the vanities and sins of the world, and he has no enjoyment of grace and truth to keep him in the path of Christ. . . . Savourless salt becomes an object of contempt and judgment.[46]

The Lord Jesus closed the message on discipleship with the words **"He who has ears to hear, let him hear!"** These words imply that not everyone will have the willingness to listen to the stringent terms of discipleship. But if a person is willing to follow the Lord Jesus, no matter what the cost may be, then he should hear and follow.

John Calvin once said, "I gave up all for Christ, and what have I found? I have found everything in Christ." Henry Drummond commented, "The entrance fee into the kingdom of heaven is nothing: the annual subscription is everything."

S. Parable of the Lost Sheep (15:1–7)

15:1, 2   The teaching ministry of our Lord in chapter 14 seemed to attract the despised **tax collectors**, and others who were outwardly **sinners**. Although Jesus reproved their sins, yet many of them acknowledged that He was right. They took sides with Christ against themselves. In true repentance, they acknowledged Him as Lord. Wherever Jesus found people who were willing to acknowledge their sin, He gravitated toward them, and bestowed spiritual help and blessing upon them.

The Pharisees and scribes resented the fact that Jesus fraternized with people who were avowedly **sinners**. They did not show grace to these social and moral lepers, and they resented Jesus' doing so. And so they hurled a charge at Him, **"This Man receives sinners and eats with them."** The charge was true, of course. They thought it was blameworthy, but actually it was in fulfillment of the very purpose for which the Lord Jesus came into the world!

It was in answer to their charge that the Lord Jesus recounted the parables of the lost sheep, the lost coin, and the lost son. These stories were aimed directly at the scribes and Pharisees, who were never broken before God to admit their lost condition. As a matter of fact, they were as lost as the publicans and sinners, but they steadfastly refused to admit it. The point of the three stories is that God receives real joy and satisfaction when He sees sinners repenting, whereas He obtains no gratification from self-righteous hypocrites who are too proud to admit their wretched sinfulness.

15:3, 4   Here the Lord Jesus is pictured under the symbol of a shepherd. The **ninety-nine** sheep represent the scribes and the Pharisees. The **lost** sheep typifies a tax collector or an acknowledged sinner. When the shepherd realizes that **one** of his sheep **is lost**, he leaves **the ninety-nine in the wilderness** (not in the fold) and goes out **after** it **until he finds it**. As far as our Lord was concerned, this journey included His descent to earth, His years of public ministry, His rejection, suffering, and death. How true are the lines from the hymn "The Ninety and Nine":

> But none of the ransomed ever knew
> How deep were the waters crossed,
> Nor how dark was the night that
>   the Lord passed through
> Ere He found His sheep that was lost.
>   – *Elizabeth C. Clephane*

15:5   Having **found** the sheep, **he**

laid **it on his shoulders** and took it to his home. This suggests that the saved sheep enjoyed a place of privilege and intimacy that it never knew as long as it was numbered with the others.

15:6 The shepherd summoned **his friends and neighbors** to **rejoice with** him over the salvation of the lost **sheep**. This speaks of the Savior's joy in seeing a sinner repent.

15:7 The lesson is clear: **There** is **joy in heaven over one sinner who repents**, but there is no joy over the ninety-nine sinners who have never been convicted of their lost condition. Verse 7 does not actually mean that there are some persons who need no repentance. All men are sinners, and all must repent in order to be saved. The verse describes those **who**, as far as they see themselves, **need no repentance**.

T. Parable of the Lost Coin (15:8–10)

The **woman** in this story may represent the Holy Spirit, seeking the lost with the **lamp** of the Word of God. The nine **silver coins** speak of the unrepentant, whereas the **one** lost **coin** suggests the man who is willing to confess that he is out of touch with God. In the previous account the sheep wandered away by its own volition. A coin is an inanimate object and might suggest the lifeless condition of a **sinner**. He is dead in sins.

The woman continues to **search carefully** for the coin **until she finds it**. Then **she calls her friends and neighbors** to celebrate with her. The lost coin which she had found brought her more true pleasure than the nine which had never been lost. So it is with God. The **sinner** who humbles himself and confesses his lost condition brings joy to the heart of God. He obtains no such joy from those who never feel their need for repentance.

U. Parable of the Lost Son (15:11–32)

15:11–16 God the Father is here depicted as **a certain man** who **had two sons. The younger son** typifies the repentant sinner, whereas the older son illustrates the scribes and the Pharisees. The latter are sons of God by creation though not by redemption. The younger son is also known as the prodigal son.

A **prodigal** is one who is recklessly extravagant, who spends money wastefully. This son became weary of his father's house and decided he wanted to leave. He could not wait for his father to die, and so asked for his **portion** of the inheritance ahead of time. The father distributed to his sons their proper share. Shortly afterward, the younger son set out **to a far country** and spent his money freely in sinful pleasures. As soon as his funds were gone a severe depression gripped the land, and he found himself destitute. The only employment he could get was as a feeder of **swine** — a job that would have been most distasteful to the average Jew. As he watched the pigs eating their bean **pods**, he envied them. They had more to eat than he had, and **no one** seemed disposed to help **him**. The friends he had when he was spending money freely had all disappeared.

15:17–19 The famine proved to be a blessing in disguise. It made him think. He remembered that his **father's hired servants** were living far more comfortably than he. They had plenty of food to eat, while he was wasting away **with hunger**. As he thought of this, he decided to do something about it. He determined to **go to** his **father** in repentance, acknowledging his sin, and seeking pardon. He realized that he was **no longer worthy to be called** his father's **son**, and planned to ask for a job as a **hired** servant.

15:20 Long before he reached his home, **his father saw him and had compassion**. He **ran and fell on his neck and kissed him**. This is probably the only time in the Bible where haste is used of God in a good sense. Stewart aptly illustrates:

> Daringly Jesus pictured God, not waiting for his shamed child to slink home, nor standing on his dignity when he came, but running out to gather him, shamed and ragged and muddied as he was, to his welcoming arms. The same name "Father" has at once darkened the color of sin and heightened the splendid glory of forgiveness.[47]

15:21–24 **The son** made his confession up to the point where he was going to ask for employment. **But the father** interrupted by ordering the slaves to put the best robe on his son, **put a ring on his hand and sandals on his feet**. He also ordered a great feast to celebrate the return of his **son** who had been **lost and was now found**. As far as the father was concerned, he had been **dead** but now was **alive again**. Someone has said, "The young man was looking for a good time, but he did not find it in the far country. He found it only when he had the good sense to come back to his father's house." It has been pointed out that **they began to be merry**, but it is never recorded that their joy ended. So it is with the salvation of the sinner.

15:25–27 When the **older son** returned from **the field** and heard all the merrymaking, he **asked** a servant **what** was going on. He told him that his younger **brother** had returned home and that his **father** was delirious with joy.

15:28-30 The older son was consumed with a jealous rage. He refused to participate in his father's joy. J. N. Darby put it well: "Where God's happiness is, there self-righteousness cannot come. If God is good to the sinner, what avails my righteousness?" When **his father** urged him to participate in the festivities, he refused, whimpering that the father had **never** rewarded him for his faithful service and obedience. He had **never** been given as much as a **young goat**, to say nothing of a fatted calf. He complained that when the prodigal son returned, after spending his father's money on **harlots**, the father did not hesitate to make a great feast. Note that he said **"this son of yours,"** not "my brother."

15:31, 32 The father's answer indicated that there is joy connected with the restoration of a **lost** one, whereas an obstinate, ungrateful, unreconciled son produces no cause for celebration.

The older son is an eloquent picture of the scribes and Pharisees. They resented God's showing mercy to outrageous sinners. To their way of thinking, if not to God's, they had served Him faithfully, had never transgressed His commandments, and yet had never been properly rewarded for all of this. The truth of the matter was that they were religious hypocrites and guilty sinners. Their pride blinded them to their distance from God, and to the fact that He

had lavished blessing after blessing upon them. If they had only been willing to repent and to acknowledge their sins, then the Father's heart would have been gladdened and they too would have been the cause of great celebration.

V. Parable of the Unjust Steward (16:1–13)

16:1, 2 The Lord Jesus now turns from the Pharisees and scribes **to His disciples** with a lesson on stewardship. This paragraph is admittedly one of the most difficult in Luke. The reason for the difficulty is that the story of the unjust steward seems to commend dishonesty. We shall see that this is not the case, however, as we proceed. The **rich man** in this story pictures God Himself. A **steward** is one who is entrusted with the management of another person's property. As far as this story is concerned, any disciple of the Lord is also a steward. This particular **steward** was accused of embezzling his employer's funds. He was called to **account**, and notified that he was being dismissed.

16:3-6 The **steward** did some fast thinking. He realized that he must provide for his future. Yet he was too old to engage in hard physical labor, and he was too proud **to beg** (though not too proud to steal). How then could he provide for his social security? He hit upon a scheme by which he could win friends who would show kindness to him when he was in need. The scheme was this: He went to one of his employer's customers and asked **how much** he owed. When the customer said **a hundred measures of oil**, the steward told him to pay for **fifty** and the account would be considered closed.

16:7 Another customer owed **a hundred measures of wheat**. The steward told him to pay for **eighty**, and he would mark the invoice "Paid."

16:8 The shocking part of the story occurs when **the master commended the unjust steward** for acting **shrewdly**. Why would anyone approve of such dishonesty? What the steward did was unjust. The following verses show that the steward was not at all commended for his crookedness, but rather for his foresight. He had acted prudently. He looked to the future, and made provision for it. He sacrificed present gain for future reward. In applying this to our own lives, we must be very clear on this point, however; the future of the child of God is not on this earth but in heaven. Just as the steward took steps to insure that he would have friends during his retirement here below, so the Christian should use his Master's goods in such a way as to insure a welcoming party when he gets to heaven.

The Lord said, **"The sons of this world are more shrewd in their generation than the sons of light."** This means that ungodly, unregenerate men show more wisdom in providing for their future in this world than true believers show in laying up treasures in heaven.

16:9 We should **make friends for** ourselves **by** *means of* **unrighteous mammon.** That is, we should use money and other material things in such a way as to win souls for Christ and thus form friendships that will endure throughout eternity. Pierson stated it clearly:

> Money can be used to buy Bibles, books, tracts and thus, indirectly, the souls of men. Thus what was material and temporal becomes immortal, becomes nonmaterial, spiritual and eternal. Here is a man who has $100. He may spend it all on a banquet or an evening party, in which case the next day there is nothing to show for it. On the other hand, he invests in Bibles at $1.00 each. It buys a hundred copies of the Word of God. These he judiciously sows as seed of the kingdom, and that seed springs up into a harvest, not of Bibles but of souls. Out of the unrighteous, he has made immortal friends, who when he fails, receive him into everlasting habitations.[48]

This then is the teaching of our Lord. By the wise investment of material possessions, we can have part in the eternal blessing of men and women. We can make sure that when we arrive at the gates of heaven, there will be a welcoming committee of those who were saved through our sacrificial giving and prayers. These people will thank us saying, "It was you who invited me here."

Darby comments:

> Man generally is God's steward; and in another sense and in another way Israel was God's steward, put into God's vineyard, and entrusted with law, promises, covenants, worship. But in all, Israel was

found to have wasted His goods. Man looked at as a steward has been found to be entirely unfaithful. Now, what is to be done? God appears, and in the sovereignty of His grace turns that which man has abused on the earth into a means of heavenly fruit. The things of this world being in the hands of man, he is not to be using them for the present enjoyment of this world, which is altogether apart from God, but with a view to the future. We are not to seek to possess the things now, but by the right use of these things to make a provision for other times. It is better to turn all into a friend for another day than to have money now. Man here is gone to destruction. Therefore now, man is a steward out of place.[49]

16:10 If we are **faithful in** our stewardship of **what is least** (money), then we will be **faithful** in handling **what is much** (spiritual treasures). On the other hand, a man who is unrighteous in using the money which God has entrusted to him is unrighteous when bigger considerations are at stake. The relative unimportance of money is emphasized by the expression **what is least.**

16:11 Anyone who is **not** honest in using **unrighteous mammon** for the Lord can scarcely expect Him to entrust **true riches** to him. Money is called **unrighteous mammon**. It is not basically evil in itself. But there probably wouldn't be any need for money if sin had not come into the world. And money is **unrighteous** because it is characteristically used for purposes other than the glory of God. It is contrasted here with **true riches**. The value of money is uncertain and temporary; the value of spiritual realities is fixed and eternal.

16:12 Verse 12 distinguishes between **what is** another's and **what is your own**. All that we have, our money, our time, our talents — belong to the Lord, and we are to use them for Him. That which is **our own** refers to rewards which we reap in this life and in the life to come as a result of our faithful service for Christ. If we have not been faithful in what is His, how can He give us **what is** our **own**?

16:13 It is utterly impossible to live for things and for **God** at the same time. If we are mastered by money, we cannot really be serving the Lord. In order to accumulate wealth, we must devote our finest efforts to the task. In the very act of doing this we rob God of what is rightfully His. It is a matter of divided loyalty. Motives are mixed. Decisions are not impartial. Where our treasure is, there our heart is also. In the effort to gain wealth, we are serving **mammon**. It is quite impossible to **serve God** at the same time. Mammon cries out for all that we have and are — our evenings, our weekends, the time we should be giving to the Lord.

W. The Greedy Pharisees (16:14–18)

16:14   **The Pharisees** were not only proud and hypocritical; they were greedy as well. They thought that godliness was a way of gain. They chose religion as one would choose a lucrative profession. Their service was not geared to glorify God and help their neighbors, but rather to enrich themselves. As they **heard** the Lord Jesus teach that they should forego wealth in this world and lay up their treasures in heaven, **they derided Him**. To them, money was more real than the promises of God. Nothing would hinder them from hoarding wealth.

16:15   Outwardly the Pharisees appeared to be pious and spiritual. They reckoned themselves to be righteous in the sight of **men**. But beneath this deceptive exterior, **God** saw the greed of their **hearts**. He was not deceived by their pretension. The type of life which they displayed, and which others approved (Psalm 49:18), was **an abomination in the sight of God**. They esteemed themselves successful because they combined a religious profession with financial affluence. But as far as God was concerned, they were spiritual adulterers. They professed love for Jehovah, but actually mammon was their god.

16:16   The continuity of verses 16–18 is very difficult to understand. On first reading, they seem to be quite unrelated to what has gone before, and to what follows. However, we feel they can be best understood by remembering that the subject of chapter 16 is the covetousness and unfaithfulness of the Pharisees. The very ones who prided themselves on the careful observance of the law are exposed as avaricious hypocrites. The spirit of the law is in sharp contrast to the spirit of the Pharisees.

The law and the prophets were until John. With these words, the Lord described the legal dispensation which began with Moses and ended with **John** the Baptist. But now a new dispensation was being inaugurated. From the time of John, the gospel of **the kingdom of God** was being **preached**. The Baptist went forth announcing the arrival of Israel's rightful King. He told the people that if they would repent, the Lord Jesus would reign over them. As a result of his preaching and the later preaching of the Lord Himself and of the disciples, there was an eager response on the part of many.

"Everyone is pressing into it" means that those who did respond to the message literally stormed into the kingdom. The tax collectors and sinners, for instance, had to jump over the roadblocks set up by the Pharisees. Others had to deal violently with the love of money in their own hearts. Prejudice had to be overcome.

16:17, 18   But the new dispensation did not mean that basic moral truths were being discarded. It would be **easier for heaven and earth to pass away than for one tittle of the law to fail**. A **tittle of the law** could be compared to the crossing of a "t" or the dotting of an "i".

The Pharisees thought they were in the kingdom of God, but the Lord was saying in effect, "You cannot disregard the great moral laws of God and still claim a place in the kingdom." Perhaps they would ask, "What great moral precept are we disregarding?" The Lord then pointed them to the law of marriage as a law that would never pass away. Any man who **divorces his wife and marries another commits adultery, and whoever marries** a **divorced** woman **commits adultery** also. This is exactly what the Pharisees were doing spiritually. The Jewish people had been brought into a covenant position with God. But these Pharisees were now turning their backs on God in a mad quest for material wealth. And perhaps the verse suggests that they were guilty of literal adultery as well as spiritual.

X. The Rich Man and Lazarus (16:19–31)

16:19–21   The Lord concludes His discourse on stewardship of material things by this account of two lives, two deaths, and two hereafters. It should be noted that this is *not* spoken of as a parable. We mention this because some critics seem to explain away the solemn implications of the story by waving it off as a parable.

At the outset, it should be made clear that the unnamed **rich man** was not condemned to Hades because of his wealth. The basis of salvation is faith in the Lord, and men are condemned for refusing to believe on Him. But this particular rich man showed that he did not have true saving faith by his careless disregard of the **beggar who was laid at his gate**. If he had had the love of God in him, he could not have lived in luxury, comfort, and ease when a fellow man was outside his front door, begging for a few **crumbs** of bread. He would have entered violently into the kingdom by abandoning his love of money.

It is likewise true that **Lazarus** was not saved because he was poor. He had trusted the Lord for the salvation of his soul.

Now notice the portrait of the rich man, sometimes called Dives (Latin for *rich*). He wore only the most expensive, custom-made clothing, and his table was filled with the choicest gourmet foods. He lived for self, catering to bodily pleasures and appetites. He had no genuine love for God, and no care for his fellow man.

Lazarus presents a striking contrast. He was a wretched **beggar**, dropped off every day in front of the rich man's house, **full of sores**, emaciated with hunger, and plagued by unclean **dogs** that **came and licked his sores**.

16:22 When **the beggar died**, he **was carried by the angels to Abraham's bosom**. Many question whether **angels** actually participate in conveying the souls of believers to heaven. We see no reason, however, for doubting the plain force of the words. Angels minister to believers in this life, and there seems no reason why they should not do so at the time of death. **Abraham's bosom** is a symbolic expression to denote the place of bliss. To any Jew, the thought of enjoying fellowship with Abraham would suggest inexpressible bliss. We take it that **Abraham's bosom** is the same as heaven. When **the rich man died**, his body **was buried** — the body that he had catered to, and for which he had spent so much.

16:23, 24 But that was not all. His soul, or conscious self, went to **Hades**. **Hades** is the Greek for the OT word *Sheol*, the state of departed spirits. In the OT period, it was spoken of as the abode of both saved and unsaved. Here it is spoken of as the abode of the unsaved, because we read that the rich man was **in torments**.

It must have come as a shock to the disciples when Jesus said that this rich Jew went to **Hades**. They had always been taught from the OT that riches were a sign of God's blessing and favor. An Israelite who obeyed the Lord was promised material prosperity. How then could a wealthy Jew go to Hades? The Lord Jesus had just announced that a new order of things began with the preaching of John. Henceforth, riches are not a sign of blessing. They are a *test* of a man's faithfulness in stewardship. To whom much is given, of him will much be required.

Verse 23 disproves the idea of "soul sleep," the theory that the soul is not conscious between death and resurrection. It proves that there is conscious existence beyond the grave. In fact, we are struck by the extent of knowledge which the rich man had. **He . . . saw Abraham afar off, and Lazarus in his bosom**. He was even able to communicate with Abraham. Calling him **Father Abraham**, he begged for **mercy**, pleading that **Lazarus** might bring a drop of **water and cool** his **tongue**. There is, of course, a question as to how a disembodied soul can experience thirst and anguish from **flame**. We can only conclude that the language is figurative, but that does not mean that the suffering was not real.

16:25 **Abraham** addressed him as **son**, suggesting that he was a descendant physically, though obviously not spiritually. The patriarch reminded him of his **lifetime** of luxury, ease, and indulgence. He also rehearsed the poverty and suffering of **Lazarus**. Now, beyond the grave, the tables were turned. The inequalities of earth were reversed.

16:26 We learn here that the choices of this life determine our eternal destiny, and once death has taken place, that destiny is **fixed**. There is no passage from the abode of the saved to that of the damned, or vice versa.

16:27–31 In death, the rich man suddenly became evangelistic. He wanted someone to go to his **five brothers** and warn them against coming **to** that **place of torment**. Abraham's reply was that these five brothers, being Jews, had the OT Scriptures, and these should be sufficient to warn them. The rich man contradicted **Abraham**, stating that **if one** should go **to them from the dead**, they would surely **repent**. However, Abraham had the last word. He stated that failure to listen to the Word of God is final. If people will not heed the Bible, they would not believe if a person rose **from the dead**. This is conclusively proved in the case of the Lord Jesus Himself. He arose from the dead, and men still do not believe.

From the NT, we know that when a believer dies, his body goes to the grave, but his soul goes to be with Christ in heaven (2 Cor. 5:8; Phil. 1:23). When an unbeliever dies, his body likewise goes to the grave, but his soul goes to Hades. For him, Hades is a place of suffering and remorse.

At the time of the Rapture, the bodies of believers will be raised from the grave and reunited with their spirits and souls (1 Thess. 4:13–18). They will then dwell with Christ eternally. At the Judgment of the Great White Throne, the bodies, spirits, and souls of unbelievers will be reunited (Rev. 20:12, 13). They will then be cast into the lake of fire, a place of eternal punishment.

And so chapter 16 closes with a most solemn warning to the Pharisees, and to all who would live for money. They do so at the peril of their souls. It is better to beg bread on earth than to beg water in Hades.

IX. THE SON OF MAN IN-STRUCTS HIS DISCIPLES (17:1–19:27)

A. Concerning the Peril of Offending (17:1, 2)

The continuity or flow of thought in this chapter is obscure. It almost seems as if Luke pieces together several disconnected subjects. However, Christ's open-ing remarks on the peril of offending may be linked with the story of the rich man at the close of chapter 16. To live in luxury, complacency, and ease could very well prove to be a stumblingblock to others who are young in the faith. Especially if a man has the reputation of being a Christian, his example will be followed by others. How serious it is to thus lead promising followers of the Lord Jesus Christ into lives of materialism and the worship of mammon.

Of course, the principle applies in a very general way. **Little ones** can be stumbled by being encouraged in worldliness. They can be stumbled by being involved in sexual sin. They can be stumbled by any teaching that waters down the plain meaning of the Scriptures. Anything that leads them away from a pathway of simple faith, of devotedness, and of holiness is a stumbling block.

Knowing human nature and conditions in the world, the Lord said that it was inevitable that **offenses should come**. But this does not diminish the guilt of those who cause the offenses. **It would be better for** such that **a millstone were hung around** their **neck**, and that they were drowned in the depths of **the sea**. It seems clear that language as strong as this is intended to picture not only physical death but eternal condemnation as well.

When the Lord Jesus speaks of offending **one of these little ones**, He probably included more than children. The reference also seems to be to disciples who are young in the faith.

B. Concerning the Need for a Forgiving Spirit (17:3, 4)

In the Christian life there is not only the peril of offending others. There is also the danger of harboring grudges, of refusing to forgive when an offending person apologizes. That is what the Lord deals with here. The NT teaches the following procedure in connection with this subject:

1. If a Christian is wronged by another Christian, he should first of all forgive the offender in his heart (Eph. 4:32). This keeps his own soul free from resentment and malice.
2. Then he should go to the offender pri-

vately and **rebuke him** (v. 3; also Matt. 18:15). **If he repents**, then he should be told that he is forgiven. Even if he sins repeatedly, then says that he repents, he should be forgiven (v. 4).

3. If a private rebuke does not prove effective, then the person who has been wronged should take one or two witnesses (Matt. 18:16). If he will not listen to these, then the matter should be taken before the church. Failure to hear the church should result in excommunication (Matt. 18:17).

The purpose of rebukes and other disciplinary action is not to get even or to humiliate the offender, but to restore him to fellowship with the Lord and with his brothers. All rebukes should be delivered in a spirit of love. We have no way of judging whether an offender's repentance is genuine. We must accept his own word that he has repented. That is why Jesus says: **"And if he sins against you seven times in a day, and seven times in a day returns to you saying, 'I repent,' you shall forgive him."** This is the gracious way our Father treats us. No matter how often we fail Him, we still have the assurance that "If we confess our sins, He is faithful and just to forgive us our sins, and to cleanse us from all unrighteousness" (1 Jn. 1:9).

C. Concerning Faith (17:5, 6)

17:5 The thought of forgiving seven times in a single day presented a difficulty, if not an impossibility to **the apostles**. They felt they were not sufficient for such a display of grace. And so they asked **the Lord** to **increase** their **faith**.

17:6 The reply of **the Lord** indicated that it was not so much a matter of the quantity of faith but of its quality. Also it was not a question of getting more faith but of using the faith they had. It is our own pride and self-importance that prevent us from forgiving our brothers. That pride needs to be rooted up and cast out. If **faith** the size of **a mustard seed** can root up a **mulberry tree** and plant it **in the sea**, it can more easily give us victory over the hardness and unbrokenness which keep us from forgiving a brother indefinitely.

D. Concerning Profitable Servants (17:7–10)

17:7–9 The true bondslave of Christ has no reason for pride. Self-importance must be plucked out by the roots and in its place there must be a true sense of unworthiness. This is the lesson we find in the story of the bondslave. This **servant** has been **plowing or tending sheep** all day. **When he has come in from the field** at the end of a day of hard work, the master does not tell him to **sit down** for supper. **Rather** he orders **him** to put on his apron and **serve supper**. Only after that is done is the slave allowed to **eat** his own meal. The master does not **thank** him for doing these things. It is expected of a slave. After all, a slave belongs to his master and his primary duty is to obey.

17:10 So disciples are bondslaves of the Lord Jesus Christ. They belong to Him — spirit, soul, and body. In the light of Calvary, nothing they can ever do for the Savior is sufficient to recompense Him for what He has done. So after the disciple has **done** everything that he has been **commanded** in the NT, he must still admit that he is an **unprofitable** servant who has only **done what was** his **duty to do.**

According to Roy Hession, the five marks of a bondservant are:

1. He must be willing to have one thing on top of another put upon him, without any consideration being given him.
2. In doing this, he must be willing not to be thanked for it.
3. Having done all this, he must not charge the master with selfishness.
4. He must confess that he is an unprofitable servant.
5. He must admit that doing and bearing what he has in the way of meekness and humility, he has not done one stitch more than it was his duty to do.[50]

E. Jesus Cleanses Ten Lepers (17:11–19)

17:11 The sin of unthankfulness is another peril in the life of the disciple. This is illustrated in the story of the ten lepers. We read that the Lord Jesus was traveling toward **Jerusalem** along the borders of **Samaria and Galilee.**

17:12–14 As He entered a certain village, . . . ten men who were lepers saw Him. Because of their diseased condition, they did not come near to Him, but they did cry out from a distance, pleading for Him to heal them. He rewarded their faith by telling them to **go** and **show** themselves **to the priests.** This meant that when they reached the priest, they would have been healed from the leprosy. The priest had no power to heal them, but he was designated as the one to *pronounce* them clean. Obedient to the word of the Lord, the lepers started out toward the priests' dwelling, and **as they went, they were** miraculously **cleansed** from the disease.

17:15–18 They all had faith to be healed but only **one** out of the ten turned back to thank the Lord. This **one,** interestingly enough, **was a Samaritan,** one of the despised neighbors of the Jewish people with whom they had no dealings. He **fell down on his face** — the true posture of worship — and **at the feet** of Jesus — the true place of worship. **Jesus** asked if it were **not** true that **ten** had been **cleansed**, but that only one, **"this foreigner,"** had returned to give thanks. **Where** were **the** other **nine?** None of them came back **to give glory to God.**

17:19 Turning to the Samaritan, the Lord Jesus said, **"Arise, go your way. Your faith has made you well."** Only the grateful ten percent inherit Christ's true riches. Jesus meets our turning back (v. 15) and our giving thanks (v. 16) with fresh blessings. **"Your faith has made you well"** suggests that whereas the nine were cleansed from leprosy, the tenth was also saved from sin!

F. Concerning the Coming of the Kingdom (17:20–37)

17:20, 21 It is hard to know whether **the Pharisees** were sincere in the question about **the kingdom**, or just mocking. But we do know that, as Jews, they entertained hopes of a kingdom which would be ushered in with great power and glory. They looked for outward signs and great political upheavals. The Savior told them, **"The kingdom of God does not come with observation,"** that is, in its present form at least, God's realm did **not come with** outward show. It was not a visible, earthly, temporal kingdom which could be pointed out as being **here** or **there.** Rather, the Savior said, **the kingdom of God** was **within** them, or better, *among* them. The Lord Jesus could not have meant that the kingdom was actually inside the hearts of the Pharisees, because these hardened religious hypocrites had no room in their hearts for Christ the King. But He meant that **the kingdom of God** was in their midst. He was the rightful King of Israel and had performed His miracles, and presented His credentials for all to see. But the Pharisees had no desire to receive Him. And so for them, the kingdom of God had presented itself and was completely unnoticed by them.

17:22 Speaking to the Pharisees, the Lord described the kingdom as something that had already come. When He turned **to the disciples**, He spoke about the kingdom as a future event which would be set up at His Second Coming. But first He described the period that would intervene between His First and Second Advents. **The days** would **come when** the disciples would **desire to see one of the days of the Son of Man,** but would **not see it.** In other words, they would long for **one of the days** when He was with them on earth and they enjoyed sweet fellowship with Him. Those days were, in a sense, foretastes of the time He would return in power and great glory.

17:23, 24 Many false christs would arise, and rulers would announce that the Messiah had come. But His followers were not to be deceived by any such false alarms. Christ's Second Advent would be as visible and unmistakable **as the lightning** which streaks from one part of the sky to the other.

17:25 Again the Lord Jesus told the disciples that before any of this could come to pass, **He** Himself would **suffer many things and be rejected by** that **generation.**

17:26, 27 Turning back to the subject of His coming to reign, the Lord taught that **the days** immediately preceding that glorious event would be like **the days of Noah.** People **ate, they drank, they married,** and **were given in mar-**

riage. These things are not wrong; they are normal, legitimate human activities. The evil was that men lived for these things and had no thought or time for God. After **Noah** and his family **entered the ark, the flood came and destroyed** the rest of the population. So the Second Coming of Christ would mean judgment for those who reject His offer of mercy.

17:28–30 Again, the Lord said that the days preceding His Second Advent would be similar to those **of Lot**. Civilization had advanced somewhat by that time; men not only **ate** and **drank**, but **they bought, they sold, they planted, they built**. It was man's effort to bring in a golden era of peace and prosperity without God. **On the** very **day that Lot**, his wife and daughters **went out of Sodom, it rained fire and brimstone from heaven and destroyed** the wicked city. **So will it be in the day when the Son of Man is revealed**. Those who concentrate on pleasure, self-gratification, and commerce will be destroyed.

17:31 It will be a **day** when attachment to earthly things will imperil a man's life. If he is **on the housetop**, he should **not** try to salvage any possessions from his **house**. If he is out **in the field**, he should **not turn back** to his house. He should flee from those places where judgment is about to fall.

17:32 Although **Lot's wife** was taken almost by force out of Sodom, her heart remained in the city. This was indicated by the fact that she turned back. She was out of Sodom, but Sodom was not out of her. As a result, God destroyed her by turning her into a pillar of salt.

17:33 **Whoever seeks to save his life** by caring only for physical safety, but not caring for his soul, **will lose it**. On the other hand anyone who **loses his life** during this period of tribulation because of faithfulness to the Lord **will** actually **preserve it** for all eternity.

17:34–36[51] The Lord's coming will be a time of separation. **Two men** will be sleeping **in one bed**. **One will be taken** away in judgment. **The other**, a believer, **will be** spared to enter Christ's kingdom. **Two women will be grinding together; the one**, an unbeliever, **will be taken** away in the storm of God's wrath; **the other**, a child of God, will be spared

to enjoy millennial blessings with Christ.

Incidentally, verses 34 and 35 accord with the rotundity of the earth. The fact that it will be night in one part of the earth and day in another, as indicated by the activities mentioned, displays scientific knowledge not discovered till many years later.

17:37 The disciples fully understood from the Savior's words that His Second Advent would be catastrophic judgment from heaven on an apostate world. So they asked the **Lord where** this judgment would fall. His answer was that **wherever the** carcass **is, there the eagles will be gathered together**. **The eagles** or vultures symbolize impending judgments. The answer therefore is that judgments would swoop down on every form of unbelief and rebellion against God, no matter where found.

In chapter 17, the Lord Jesus had warned the disciples that afflictions and persecutions lay ahead. Before the time of His glorious appearing, they would be required to go through deep trials. By way of preparation, the Savior gives further instruction concerning prayer. In the following verses, we find a praying widow, a praying Pharisee, a praying tax-collector, and a praying beggar.

G. The Parable of the Persistent Widow (18:1–8)

18:1 The **parable** of the praying widow teaches **that men always ought to pray and not lose heart**. This is true in a general sense of all men, and of all kinds of prayer. But the special sense in which it is used here is prayer for God's deliverance in times of testing. It is praying without losing **heart** during the long, weary interval between Christ's First and Second Comings.

18:2, 3 The parable pictures an unrighteous **judge** who was ordinarily quite unmoved by fear of **God** or **regard** for his fellow **man. There was** also **a widow** who was being oppressed by some unnamed **adversary**. This **widow came to** the judge persistently, asking him for **justice**, so that she might be delivered from his inhumane treatment.

18:4, 5 The judge was unmoved by the validity of her case; the fact that she was being treated unjustly did not move him to action in her behalf. However, the regularity with which she came before him prompted him to act. Her importunity and persistence brought a decision in her favor.

18:6, 7 **Then the Lord** explained to the disciples that if an **unjust judge** would act in behalf of a poor widow because of her importunity, how much more will the just **God** intervene in behalf of **His own elect**. The **elect** here might refer in a special sense to the Jewish remnant during the Tribulation Period, but it is also true of all oppressed believers in every age. The reason God has not intervened long ago is because He is longsuffering with men, not willing that any should perish.

18:8 But the day is coming when His spirit will no longer strive with men, and then **He will** punish those who persecute His followers. The Lord Jesus closed the parable with the question, **"Nevertheless, when the Son of Man comes, will He really find faith on the earth?"** This probably means the *kind* of faith that the poor widow had. But it may also indicate that when the Lord returns, there will only be a remnant who are true to Him. In the meantime, each of us should be stimulated to the kind of faith that cries to God night and day.

H. Parable of the Pharisee and the Tax Collector (18:9–14)

18:9–12 The next **parable** is addressed to people who pride **themselves** on being **righteous**, and who despise all **others** as inferior. By labeling the first man as **a Pharisee**, the Savior did not leave any doubt as to the particular class of people He was addressing. Although the Pharisee went through the motions of prayer, he was really not speaking to **God**. He was rather boasting of his own moral and religious attainments. Instead of comparing himself with God's perfect standard and seeing how sinful he really was, he compared himself with others in the community and prided himself on being better. His frequent repetition of the personal pronoun **I** reveals the true state of his heart as conceited and self-sufficient.

18:13 **The tax collector** was a striking contrast. **Standing** before God, he sensed his own utter unworthiness. He

was humbled to the dust. He **would not so much as raise his eyes to heaven, but beat his breast** and cried to **God** for mercy: **"God be merciful to me a** (literally "the") **sinner!"** He did not think of himself as one sinner among many, but as *the* sinner who was unworthy of anything from God.

18:14 The Lord Jesus reminded His hearers that it is this spirit of self-humiliation and repentance that is acceptable to God. Contrary to what human appearances might indicate, it was the tax collector who **went down to his house justified**. God exalts the humble, but He humbles those who exalt themselves.

I. Jesus and the Little Children (18:15–17)

This incident reinforces what we have just had before us, namely, that the humility of a little child is necessary for entrance into **the kingdom of God**. Mothers crowded around the Lord Jesus with their **infants** in order that they might receive blessing from Him. **His disciples** were annoyed by this intrusion into the Savior's time. But Jesus **rebuked them**, and tenderly **called . . . the little children** to Himself, saying, **"Of such is the kingdom of God."** Verse 16 answers the question, "What happens to little children when they die?" The answer is that they go to heaven. The Lord clearly said **"of such is the kingdom of God."**

Children can be saved at a very tender age. That age probably varies in the case of individual children, but the fact remains that any child, no matter how young, who wishes to come to Jesus should be permitted to do so, and encouraged in his faith.

Little children do not need to become adults in order to be saved, but adults do need the simple faith and humility of **a little child** in order to **enter** God's **kingdom**.

J. The Rich Young Ruler (18:18–30)

18:18, 19 This section illustrates the case of a man who would **not** receive the kingdom of God as a little child. One day **a certain ruler** came to the Lord Jesus, addressing Him as **Good Teacher**, and asking **what** he must **do** in order to **inherit eternal life**. The Savior first of all questioned him on the use of the title *good Teacher*. Jesus reminded him that only **God** is **good**. Our Lord was not denying that He was God, but He was trying to lead the ruler to confess that fact. If He was good, then He must be God, since only God is essentially good.

18:20 Then Jesus dealt with the question, what must I do to inherit eternal life? We know that eternal life is not inherited, and is not gained by doing good works. Eternal life is the gift of God through Jesus Christ. In taking the ruler back to **the** ten **commandments**, the Lord Jesus was not implying that he could ever be saved by keeping the law. Rather He was using the law in an effort to convict the man of sin. The Lord Jesus recited **the** five **commandments** which have to do with our duty to our fellowman, the second table of the law.

18:21–23 It is apparent that the law did not have its convicting effect in the life of the man, because he arrogantly claimed to **have kept** these commandments **from** his **youth**. Jesus told him that he lacked **one thing** — love for his neighbor. If he had really kept these commandments, then he would have sold **all** his possessions and distributed them **to the poor**. But the fact of the matter was that he did not love his neighbor as himself. He was living a selfish life, with no real love for others. This is proved by the fact that **when he heard** these things, **he became very sorrowful**, because **he was very rich.**

18:24 As the Lord **Jesus** looked upon him, He commented on the difficulty of **those who have riches** entering **the kingdom of God**. The difficulty is in having riches without loving and trusting them.

This whole section raises disturbing questions for Christians as well as unbelievers. How can we be said truly to love our neighbors when we live in wealth and comfort when others are perishing for want of the gospel of Christ?

18:25 Jesus said that **it is easier for a camel to go through the eye of a needle than for a rich man to enter the kingdom of God**. Many explanations have been given of this statement. Some have suggested that the needle's eye is a small inner gate in the wall of a city, and that a camel could enter only by kneeling down. However, Dr. Luke uses a word that specifically means a surgeon's needle and the meaning of the Lord's statement seems to lie on the surface. In other words, just as it is *impossible* **for a camel to go through the eye of a needle**, so it is *impossible* **for a rich man to enter the kingdom of God**. It is not enough to explain this as meaning that a rich man cannot, by his own efforts, enter the kingdom; that is true of rich and poor alike. The meaning is that it is *impossible* for a man to **enter the kingdom of God** *as a rich man*; as long as he makes a god of his wealth, lets it stand between himself and his soul's salvation, he cannot be converted. The simple fact of the matter is that not many rich people are saved, and those who are must first be broken before God.

18:26, 27 As the disciples thought about all of this, they began to wonder **who then** could **be saved**. To them, riches had always been a sign of God's blessing (Deut. 28:1–8). If rich Jews aren't saved, then who can be? The Lord answered that **God** could do what man cannot do. In other words, God can take a greedy, grasping, ruthless materialist, remove his love for gold, and substitute for it a true love for the Lord. It is a miracle of divine grace.

Again, this whole section raises disturbing questions for the child of God. The servant is not above his Master; the Lord Jesus abandoned His heavenly riches in order to save our guilty souls. It is not fitting for us to be rich in a world where He was poor. The value of souls, the imminence of Christ's return, the constraining love of Christ should lead us to invest every possible material asset in the work of the Lord.

18:28–30 When **Peter** reminded the Lord that the disciples had **left** their homes and families to follow Him, the Lord replied that such a life of sacrifice is rewarded liberally in this life, and will be further rewarded in the eternal state. The latter part of verse 30 (**and in the age to come eternal life**) does not mean that eternal life is gained by forsaking all; rather it refers to increased capacity for enjoying the glories of heaven, plus increased rewards in the heavenly kingdom. It means "the full realization of the life that had been received at the time of conversion, i.e., life in its fulness.''

K. Jesus Again Predicts His Death and Resurrection (18:31–34)

18:31–33 For the third time the Lord **took the twelve** and warned them in detail what awaited Him (see 9:22, 44). He predicted His passion as being in fulfillment of what **the prophets** of the OT had **written**. With divine foresight, He calmly prophesied that **He** would **be delivered to the Gentiles**. "It was more probable that He would be privately slain, or stoned to death in a tumult."[52] But the prophets had foretold His betrayal, His being **mocked and insulted and spit upon**, and so it must be. He would be scourged and killed, but **the third day He** would **rise again**.

The remaining chapters unfold the drama which He so wonderfully foreknew and foretold:

We are going up to Jerusalem (18:35–19:45).

The Son of Man **will be delivered to the Gentiles** (19:47-23:1).

He **will be mocked and insulted** (23:1–32).

They **will kill Him** (23:33–56).

The third day He will rise again (24:1–12).

18:34 Amazingly enough, the disciples **understood none of these things**. The meaning of His words **was hidden from them**. It seems hard for us to understand why they were so dull in this matter, but the reason is probably this: Their minds were so filled with thoughts of a temporal deliverer who would rescue them from the yoke of Rome, and set up the kingdom immediately, that they refused to entertain any other program. We often believe what we *want* to believe, and resist the truth if it does not fit into our *preconceived* notions.

L. The Healing of a Blind Beggar (18:35–43)

18:35–37 The Lord Jesus had now left Perea by crossing the Jordan. Luke says the incident that follows **happened as He was coming near Jericho**. Matthew and Mark say that it is when He was *leaving* Jericho (Matt. 20:29; Mark 10:46). Also Matthew says that there were two blind men; Mark and Luke both say there was one. It is possible that Luke is speaking of the new city whereas Matthew and Mark are referring to the old city. It is also possible that there was more than one miracle of the blind receiving their sight at this place. Whatever the true explanation might be, we are confident that if our knowledge were greater, the seeming contradictions would disappear.

18:38 The blind beggar somehow recognized **Jesus** as the Messiah, because he addressed Him as the **Son of David**. He asked the Lord to **have mercy on** him, that is, to restore his sight.

18:39 In spite of the attempts of some to silence the beggar, he insistently **cried out** to the Lord Jesus. The people were not interested in a beggar. Jesus was.

18:40, 41 So Jesus stood still. Darby comments insightfully, "Joshua once bade the sun stand still in the heavens, but here the *Lord* of the sun, and the moon, and the heavens, stands still at the bidding of a blind beggar." At Jesus' command the beggar was **brought to Him**. Jesus **asked** him what he wanted. Without hesitation or generalization, the beggar replied that he wanted his **sight**. His prayer was short, specific, and full of faith.

18:42, 43 Jesus then granted the request **and immediately** the man **received his sight**. Not only so, he **followed** the Lord, **glorifying God**. We may learn from this incident that we should dare to believe God for the impossible. Great faith greatly honors Him. As the poet has written:

> Thou art coming to a King,
> 　Large petitions with thee bring;
> For His grace and power are such,
> 　None can ever ask too much.
> 　　　　　　　　– *John Newton*

M. The Conversion of Zacchaeus (19:1–10)

The conversion of Zacchaeus illustrates the truth of Luke 18:27 "The things which are impossible with men are possible with God." Zacchaeus was a rich man, and ordinarily it is impossible for a rich man to enter the kingdom of God. But Zacchaeus humbled himself before the Savior, and did not let his wealth come between his soul and God.

19:1–5 It was when the Lord

passed through Jericho on His third and final trip to Jerusalem that **Zacchaeus sought to see** Him; this was undoubtedly the seeking of curiosity. Although he **was a chief tax collector**, he was not ashamed to do something unconventional in order to see the Savior. Because he was **short**, he knew he would be hindered from getting a good view of Jesus. **So he ran ahead and climbed up into a sycamore tree** alongside the route the Lord was taking. This act of faith did not go unnoticed. As **Jesus** came near, **He looked up and saw** Zacchaeus. He ordered him to **come down** quickly, and invited Himself to the tax collector's **house**. This is the only case on record where the Savior invited Himself to a home.

19:6 Zacchaeus did as he was told, **and received** the Lord **joyfully**. We can almost certainly date his conversion from this time.

19:7 The Savior's critics **all complained** against Him because He went **to be a guest with a man who** was **a** known **sinner**. They overlooked the fact that, coming into a world like ours, He was limited exclusively to such homes!

19:8 Salvation had brought a radical change in the life of the tax gatherer. He informed the Savior that he now intended to **give half** his **goods to the poor**. (Up to this time, he had been gouging as much as possible from the poor.) He also planned to make **fourfold** restitution for any money he had gained dishonestly. This was more than the law demanded (Ex. 22:4, 7; Lev. 6:5; Num. 5:7). It showed that Zacchaeus was now controlled by love whereas formerly he was mastered by greed.

There was little doubt that Zacchaeus had taken things dishonestly. Wuest translates v. 8b: "And since I have wrongfully exacted . . ." No "if" about it.

It almost sounds as if Zacchaeus were boasting of his philanthropy and trusting in this for his salvation. That is not the point at all. He was saying that his new life in Christ made him desire to make restitution for the past, and that in gratitude to God for salvation, he now wanted to use his money for the glory of God and for the blessing of his neighbors.

Verse 8 is one of the strongest in the Bible on restitution. Salvation does not relieve a person from righting the wrongs of the past. Debts contracted during one's unconverted days are not canceled by the new birth. And if money was stolen before salvation, then a true sense of the grace of God requires that this money be repaid after a person has become a child of God.

19:9 **Jesus** plainly announced that **salvation** had **come to** the **house** of Zacchaeus, because he was **a son of Abraham**. Salvation did not come because Zacchaeus was a Jew by birth. Here the expression, "a son of Abraham" indicates more than natural descent; it means that Zacchaeus exercised the same kind of faith in the Lord that Abraham did. Also, salvation did not come to Zacchaeus's home because of his charity and restitution (v. 8). These things are the effect of salvation, not the cause.

19:10 In answer to those who criticized Him for lodging with a sinner, Jesus said, **"The Son of Man has come to seek and to save that which was lost."** In other words, the conversion of Zacchaeus was a fulfillment of the very purpose of Christ's coming into the world.

N. Parable of the Ten Minas (19:11–27)

19:11 As the Savior neared **Jerusalem** from Jericho, many of His followers **thought the kingdom of God would appear immediately**. In the **parable** of the ten minas,[53] He disabused them of such hopes. He showed that there would be an interval between His First and Second Advents during which His disciples were to be busy for Him.

19:12, 13 The parable of the **nobleman** had an actual parallel in the history of Archelaus. He was chosen by Herod to be his successor but was rejected by the people. He went away to Rome to have his appointment confirmed, then returned, rewarded his servants, and destroyed his enemies.

In the parable, the Lord Jesus Himself is the **certain nobleman** who **went** to heaven to await the time when He would **return** and set up His **kingdom** on earth. The **ten servants** typify His disciples. He gave each one a mina and told them to **do business** with this mina until He came again. While there are differences in the talents and abilities of the servants of the Lord (see the parable of the talents, Matt. 25:14–30), there are some things which they have in common, such as the privileges of sharing the gospel, and representing Christ to the world, and the privilege of prayer. Doubtless the mina speaks of these.

19:14 The **citizens** represent the Jewish nation. They not only rejected Him, but even after His departure, they **sent a delegation after him, saying, "We will not have this man to reign over us."** The embassage might represent their treatment of Christ's servants such as Stephen and other martyrs.

19:15 Here the Lord is seen, in type, returning to set up His **kingdom**. Then He will reckon with those **to whom** He gave **the money**.

Believers in this present age will be reviewed as far as their service is concerned at the Judgment Seat of Christ. This takes place in heaven, following the Rapture.

The faithful Jewish remnant who will witness for Christ during the Tribulation Period will be reviewed at Christ's Second Advent. This is the judgment that seems to be primarily in view in this passage.

19:16 **The first** servant had **earned ten minas** with the one **mina** that had been entrusted to him. He had an awareness that the money was not his own (**"your mina"**) and he used it as best he could in the advancement of his master's interests.

19:17 The master praised him as being **faithful in a very little** — a reminder that after we have done our best we are unprofitable servants. His reward was to **have authority over ten cities**. Rewards for faithful service apparently are linked with rule in Christ's kingdom. The extent to which a disciple will rule is determined by the measure of his devotion and self-expenditure.

19:18, 19 **The second** servant had **earned five minas** with his original **mina**. His reward was to **be over five cities**.

19:20, 21 The third **came** with nothing but excuses. He returned the **mina**, carefully **kept . . . in a handkerchief**. He had earned nothing with it. Why not?

He as much as blamed the nobleman for it. He said the nobleman was **an austere man** who expected returns without expenditure. But his own words condemned him. If he thought the nobleman was like that, the least he could have done was to turn the mina over to a bank that it might earn some interest.

19:22 In quoting the words of the nobleman, Jesus did not admit that they were true. It was simply the sinful heart of the servant that blamed the master for his own laziness. But if he really believed them he should have acted accordingly.

19:23 Verse 23 seems to suggest that we should either put everything we have to work for the Lord, or turn it over to someone else who will use it for Him.

19:24–26 The nobleman's verdict on the third servant was to **take the mina from him, and give it to** the first **who** had earned the **ten minas**. If we don't use our opportunities for the Lord, they will be taken from us. On the other hand, if we are faithful in a very little, God will see that we will never lack the means to serve Him even more. It may seem unfair to some that the **mina** was given to the man who already had **ten**, but it is a fixed principle in the spiritual life that those who love Him and serve Him passionately are given ever-widening areas of opportunity. Failure to buy up the opportunities results in a loss of all.

The third servant suffered a loss of reward, but no other punishment is specified. There is apparently no question as to his salvation.

19:27 The citizens who would not have the nobleman as their ruler are denounced as **enemies** and doomed to death. This was a sad prediction of the fate of the nation that rejected the Messiah.

X. THE SON OF MAN IN JERUSALEM (19:28–21:38)†

A. The Triumphal Entry (19:28–40)

19:28–34 It was now the Sunday before His crucifixion. Jesus had drawn near to the eastern slope of the Mt. of Olives en route **to Jerusalem. When He drew near to Bethphage and Bethany**

†See p. xxiv.

... **He sent two of His disciples** into a **village** to get **a colt** for His entrance into Jerusalem. He told them exactly where they would find the animal and what **the owners** would say. After the disciples had explained their mission, the owners seemed quite willing to release their colt for use by Jesus. Perhaps they had been blessed previously by the ministry of the Lord and had offered to be of assistance to Him any time He needed it.

19:35–38 The disciples made a cushion or saddle for the Lord with **their own clothes. Many spread their clothes on the road** before Him as He ascended from the western base of the Mt. of Olives to Jerusalem. Then with one accord the followers of Jesus burst out in **praise for all the mighty works they had seen** Him do. They hailed Him as God's **King**, and chanted that the effect of His coming **was peace in heaven and glory in the highest**. It is significant that they cried "**Peace in heaven**" rather than "Peace on earth." There could not be peace on earth because the Prince of Peace had been rejected and was soon to be slain. But there would be **peace in heaven** as a result of the impending death of Christ on Calvary's cross and His ascension to heaven.

19:39, 40 **The Pharisees** were indignant that Jesus should be publicly honored in this way. They suggested that He should **rebuke** His **disciples**. But Jesus **answered** that such acclamation was inevitable. **If** the disciples wouldn't do it, **the stones would!** He thus rebuked the Pharisees for being more hard and unresponsive than the inanimate stones.

B. The Son of Man Weeps Over Jerusalem (19:41–44)

19:41, 42 As Jesus **drew near** to Jerusalem, He uttered a lamentation over **the city** that had missed its golden opportunity. If the people had only received Him as Messiah, it would have meant **peace** for them. But they didn't recognize that He was the source of **peace**. Now it was too late. They had already determined what they would do with the Son of God. Because of their rejection of Him, their **eyes** were blinded. Because they *would* not see Him, they *could* no longer see Him.

Pause here to reflect on the wonder of the Savior's tears. As W. H. Griffith Thomas has said, "Let us sit at Christ's feet until we learn the secret of His tears, and beholding the sins and sorrows of city and countryside, weep over them too."[54]

19:43, 44 Jesus gave a solemn preview of the siege of Titus — how that Roman general would **surround** the city, trap the inhabitants, massacre both young and old, and **level** the walls and buildings. **Not one stone** would be left **upon another**. And it was all **because** Jerusalem **did not know the time of** its **visitation**. The Lord had visited the city with the offer of salvation. But the people did not want Him. They had no room for Him in their scheme of things.

C. Second Cleansing of the Temple (19:45, 46)

Jesus had cleansed **the temple** at the outset of His public ministry (John 2:14–17). Now as His ministry rapidly drew to a close, He entered the sacred precincts and cast **out those who** were making **a house of prayer** into **a den of thieves**. The danger of introducing commercialism into the things of God is always present. Christendom today is leavened by this evil: Church bazaars and socials, organized financial drives, preaching for profit — and all in the Name of Christ.

Christ quoted Scripture (Isa. 56:7 and Jer. 7:11) to support His action. Every reformation of abuses in the church is to be built on God's Word.

D. Teaching Daily in the Temple (19:47, 48)

Jesus **was teaching daily in the temple** area — not inside the temple, but in the courts where the public was allowed. The religious leaders longed for some excuse **to destroy Him**, but **the** common **people were** still captivated by the miracle-working Nazarene. His time had not yet come. **But** soon the hour would strike, and then the **chief priests, scribes, and** Pharisees would close in for the kill.

It is now Monday. The next day, Tuesday, which was the last day of His public teaching, is described in 20:1–22:6.

E. The Son of Man's Authority Questioned (20:1–8)

20:1, 2 What a picture! The Master Teacher tirelessly proclaiming the good news **in** the shadow of **the temple**, and the leaders of Israel insolently challenging His right to teach. To them Jesus was a rude carpenter of Nazareth. He had little formal education, no academic degrees, no accreditation by an ecclesiastical body. What were His credentials? **Who gave** Him **this authority** to teach and preach to others and to cleanse the temple? They wanted to know!

20:3–8 Jesus **answered** by asking them a question; if they had answered correctly, they would have answered their own question. Was **the baptism of John** approved by God, or was it merely of human authority? They were caught. If they acknowledged that John preached with divine unction, then why didn't they obey his message by repenting and receiving the Messiah he proclaimed? But if they said John was just another professional preacher, they would stir up the anger of the masses, who still acknowledged **John** to be **a prophet** of God. **So they** said, "We do **not know where** John got his authority." Jesus said, "*Well, in that case, I won't tell you by whose authority I teach.*" If they couldn't tell that much about John, why did they question the authority of One who was greater than John? This passage shows that the great essential in teaching God's word is to be filled with the Holy Spirit. One who has that enduement can triumph over those whose power is wrapped up in degrees, human titles, and honors.

"Where did you get your diploma? Who ordained you?" The old questions, possibly begotten of jealousy, are still being asked. The successful gospel preacher who has not trodden the theological halls of some distinguished university or elsewhere is challenged on the points of his fitness and the validity of his ordination.

F. Parable of the Wicked Vinedressers (20:9–18)

20:9–12 The insistent yearning of the heart of God over the nation of Israel is recounted once again in this **parable** of the **vineyard**. God is the **certain man** who **leased** the **vineyard** (Israel) to **vinedressers** (the leaders of the nation — see Isa. 5: 1–7). He sent servants **to the vinedressers** to get **some of the fruit** for Himself; these servants were the prophets of God, like Isaiah and John the Baptist, who sought to call Israel to repentance and faith. But Israel's rulers invariably persecuted the prophets.

20:13 Finally God sent His **beloved son**, with the express thought that **they** would **respect** Him (although God knew, of course, that Christ would be rejected). Notice that Christ distinguishes Himself from all others. They were servants; He is the Son.

20:14 True to their past history, **the vinedressers** determined to get rid of **the heir**. They wanted exclusive rights as leaders and teachers of the people — **"that the inheritance may be ours."** They would not surrender their religious position to Jesus. If they killed Him, their power in Israel would be unchallenged — or so they thought.

20:15–17 So they cast him out of the vineyard and killed him. At this point Jesus asked His Jewish hearers what **the owner of the vineyard** would **do to** such wicked **vinedressers**. In Matthew, the chief priests and elders condemned themselves by answering that he would kill them (Matt. 21:41). Here the Lord Himself supplied the answer, **"He will come and destroy those vinedressers and give the vineyard to others."** This meant that the Christ-rejecting Jews would be destroyed, and that God would take **others** into the place of privilege. The "others" may refer to the Gentiles or to regenerated Israel of the last days. The Jews recoiled at such a suggestion. **"Certainly not!" they said.** The Lord confirmed the prediction by quoting Psalm 118:22. The Jewish **builders** had **rejected** Christ, **the Stone**. They had no place in their plans for Him. But God was determined that He would have the place of preeminence, by making Him **the chief cornerstone**, a stone which is indispensable and in the place of greatest honor.

20:18 The two comings of Christ are indicated in verse 18.[55] His First Advent is depicted as a **stone** on the ground; men stumbled at His humiliation and lowliness, and they were **broken** to pieces for rejecting Him. In the second part of the verse, the stone is seen falling from heaven and grinding unbelievers **to powder.**

G. Rendering to Caesar and to God (20:19–26)

20:19, 20 **The chief priests and the scribes** realized that Jesus had been speaking **against them**, so they became more intent **to lay hands on Him**. They **sent spies** to trick Him into saying something for which He could be arrested and tried by **the** Roman **governor**. These spies first praised Him as one who would be faithful to God at any cost and fearless of man — hoping that He would speak against Caesar.

20:21, 22 **Then they asked Him** if it was right for a Jew **to pay taxes to Caesar.** If Jesus said no, then they would accuse Him of treason and turn Him over to the Romans for trial. If He said yes, He would alienate the Herodians (and the great mass of the Jews, for that matter).

20:23, 24 Jesus realized the plot against Himself. He asked them for **a denarius**; perhaps He did not own one Himself. The fact that they possessed and used these coins showed their bondage to a Gentile power. **"Whose image and inscription does it have?"** Jesus asked. They admitted it was **Caesar's**.

20:25, 26 Then Jesus silenced them with the command, **"Render therefore to Caesar the things that are Caesar's, and to God the things that are God's."** They were seemingly so concerned about Caesar's interests but they were not nearly so concerned about God's interests. "The money belongs to Caesar, and you belong to God. Let the world have its coins, but let God have His creatures." It is so easy to quibble over minor matters while neglecting the principal things in life. And so easy to discharge our debts to our fellow-men while robbing God of His rightful dues.

H. The Sadducees and Their Resurrection Riddle (20:27–44)

20:27 Since the attempt to trap Jesus in a political question failed, **some of the Sadducees** next **came to Him** with a theological quibble. They denied the possibility of the bodies of the dead ever being raised again, so they sought by an extreme illustration to make the doctrine **of resurrection** appear ridiculous.

20:28–33 They reminded Jesus that in the Law of **Moses** a single man was supposed to marry his brother's widow in order to carry on the family name and preserve the family property (Deut. 25:5). A woman married **seven brothers** in succession, according to their story. When the seventh died, she was still **childless**. Then she **died also. "In the resurrection, whose wife does she become?"** is what they wanted to know. They thought they were so clever in propounding such an unanswerable problem.

20:34 **Jesus answered** that the marriage relationship was for **this** life only; it would not be continued in heaven. He did not say that husbands and wives would not recognize each other in heaven, but their relationship there would be on a completely different basis.

20:35 The expression **"those who are counted worthy to attain that age"** does not suggest that any people are personally worthy of heaven: the only worthiness sinners can have is the worthiness of the Lord Jesus Christ. "Those are counted worthy who judge themselves, who vindicate Christ, and who own that all worthiness belongs to Him."[56] The phrase **resurrection from the dead** refers to a resurrection of believers only. It literally means **resurrection** out from (Greek *ek*) **the dead** ones. The idea of a general resurrection in which all the dead, both saved and unsaved, are raised at one time is not found in the Bible.

20:36 The superiority of the celestial state is further indicated in verse 36. There is no more death; in that respect, men will be **equal to the angels**. Also they will be manifested as **sons of God**. Believers are sons of God already, but not to outward observance. In heaven, they will be visibly *manifested* as sons of God. The fact that they participated in the First Resurrection insures this. "We know that when He is revealed, we shall be like Him, for we shall see Him as He is" (1 Jn. 3:2). "When Christ who is our life appears, then you also will appear with Him in glory" (Col. 3:4).

20:37, 38 To prove the resurrection,

Jesus referred to Exodus 3:6 where **Moses** quoted **the Lord** as calling Himself **the God of Abraham, . . . Isaac, and . . . Jacob**. Now if the Sadducees would just stop to think, they would realize that: (1) God **is not the God of the dead but of the living**. (2) **Abraham, Isaac,** and **Jacob** were all dead. The necessary conclusion is that God must raise them from the dead. The Lord did not say "I *was* the God of Abraham . . . ," but "I *am*. . . ." The character of God, as the God of the living, demands the resurrection.

20:39–44 Some of the scribes had to admit the force of the argument. But Jesus was not finished; once again He appealed to God's word. In Psalm 110:1 **David** called the Messiah his **Lord**. The Jews generally agreed that the Messiah would be the **Son** of **David**. How could He be David's **Lord** and David's **Son** at the same time? The Lord Jesus Himself was the answer to the question. He was descended from David as Son of Man; yet He was David's Creator. But they were too blind to see.

I. Warning against the Scribes (20:45–47)

Then Jesus publicly warned the crowd against **the scribes**. They wore **long robes**, affecting piety. They loved to be called by distinguished titles as they walked through the **marketplaces**. They maneuvered to get **places** of prominence **in the synagogues** and at banquets. But they robbed defenseless widows of their life savings, covering up their wickedness by **long prayers**. Such hypocrisy would be punished all the more severely.

J. The Widow's Two Mites (21:1–4)

As Jesus watched **the rich putting their gifts into the treasury** of the temple, He was struck by the contrast between **the rich** and **a certain poor widow**. They gave some, but she gave **all**. In God's estimation, she gave **more than all** of them put together. They gave **out of their abundance; she** gave **out of her poverty**. They gave what cost them little or nothing; **she** gave **all the livelihood that she had**. "The gold of affluence which is given because it is not needed, God hurls to the bottomless pit;

but the copper tinged with blood He lifts and kisses into the gold of eternity."[57]

K. Outline of Future Events (21:5–11)

Verses 5–33 constitute a great prophetic discourse. Though it resembles the Olivet Discourse in Matthew 24 and 25, it is not identical. Once again we should remind ourselves that the differences in the Gospels have a deep significance.

In this discourse, we find the Lord speaking alternately of the destruction of Jerusalem in A.D. 70 and then of the conditions that will precede His Second Advent. It is an illustration of the law of double reference — His predictions soon were to have a *partial fulfillment* in the siege of Titus, but they will have a further and *complete fulfillment* at the end of the Tribulation Period.

The outline of the discourse seems to be as follows:

1. Jesus foretold the destruction of Jerusalem (vv. 5, 6).
2. The disciples asked when this would happen (v. 7).
3. Jesus first gave a general picture of events preceding His own Second Advent (vv. 8–11).
4. He then gave a picture of the fall of Jerusalem and the age that would follow (vv. 12–24).
5. Finally, He told of the signs that would precede His Second Coming, and urged His followers to live in expectation of His return (vv. 25-26).

21:5, 6 As some of the people were admiring the magnificence of Herod's **temple**, Jesus warned them not to be preoccupied with material **things** that would soon pass away. **The days** were coming when the temple would be completely leveled.

21:7 The disciples immediately became curious to know **when** this would happen **and what sign** would indicate its imminence. Their question undoubtedly referred exclusively to the destruction of Jerusalem.

21:8–11 The Savior's answer first seemed to take them ahead to the end of the age when the temple would again be destroyed prior to the setting up of the kingdom. There would be false messiahs and false rumors, **wars** and uprisings. There would not only be conflict among nations, but great catastrophes of nature — **earthquakes, . . . famines and pestilences**, terrors, **and great signs from heaven.**

L. The Period Before the End (21:12–19)

21:12–15 In the preceding section, Jesus had described events immediately preceding the end of the age. Verse 12 is introduced by the expression **"But before all these things. . . ."** So we believe that verses 12–24 describe the period between the time of the discourse and the future Tribulation Period. His disciples would be arrested, persecuted, tried before religious and civil powers, and imprisoned. It might seem like failure and tragedy to them, but actually the Lord would overrule it to make it a **testimony** for His glory. They were not to prepare their defense in advance. In the crisis hour, God would give them special **wisdom** to say things that would completely confound their **adversaries**.

21:16–18 There would be treachery within families; unsaved **relatives** would betray Christians, and **some** would even be killed because of their stand for Christ. There is a seeming contradiction between verse 16, **"and they will put some of you to death,"** and verse 18, **"But not a hair of your head shall be lost."** It can only mean that though some would die as martyrs for Christ, their spiritual preservation would be complete. They would die but they would not perish.

21:19 Verse 19 indicates that those who patiently endure for Christ rather than renouncing Him will thus prove the reality of their faith. Those who are genuinely saved will stand true and loyal at any cost. The RSV reads, "By your endurance you will gain your lives."

M. The Doom of Jerusalem (21:20–24)

Now the Lord clearly takes up the subject of the destruction of **Jerusalem** in A.D. 70. This event would be signaled by the city's being **surrounded by** the Roman **armie**s.

The Christian of an early day — the year A.D. 70 — had a specific sign to introduce the destruction of Jerusalem and the

razing of the beautiful marble temple: "When ye shall see Jerusalem compassed with armies, then know that the desolation thereof is nigh." This was to be a positive sign of the destruction of Jerusalem, and at that sign they were to flee. Unbelief might have argued that with a besieging army outside the walls, escape would be impossible; but God's Word never fails. The Roman general withdrew his armies for a short season, thus giving the believing Jews the opportunity to escape. This they did, and went out to a place called Pella, where they were preserved.[58]

Any attempt to re-enter the city would be fatal. The city was about to be punished for its rejection of the Son of God. **Pregnant** women and **nursing** mothers would be at a distinct disadvantage; they would be hindered in escaping from the judgment of God on **the land** of Israel and the Jewish **people**. Many would be slain, and the survivors would be carried off as captives in other lands.

The latter part of verse 24 is a remarkable prophecy that the ancient city of **Jerusalem** would be subject to Gentile rule from that time **until the times of the Gentiles are fulfilled.** It does not mean that the Jews might not control it for brief periods; the thought is that it would be continually subject to Gentile invasion and interference **until the times of the Gentiles are fulfilled.**

The NT distinguishes between the riches of the Gentiles, the fullness of the Gentiles, and the times of the Gentiles.

1. The *riches* of the Gentiles (Rom. 11:12) refers to the place of privilege which the Gentiles enjoy at the present time while Israel is temporarily set aside by God.
2. The *fullness* of the Gentiles (Rom. 11:25) is the time of the Rapture, when Christ's Gentile bride will be completed and taken from the earth and when God will resume His dealings with Israel.
3. The *times* of the Gentiles (Luke 21:24) really began with the Babylonian captivity, 521 B.C., and will extend to the time when Gentile nations will no longer assert control over the city of Jerusalem.

Down through the centuries from the time of the Savior's words, Jerusalem has been largely controlled by Gentile powers. Emperor Julian the Apostate (A.D. 331–363) sought to discredit Christianity by disproving this prophecy of the Lord. He therefore encouraged the Jews to rebuild the temple. They went to the work eagerly, even using silver shovels in their extravagance, and carrying the dirt in purple veils. But while they were working, they were interrupted by an earthquake and by balls of fire coming from the ground. They had to abandon the project.[59]

N. The Second Advent (21:25–28)

These verses describe the convulsions of nature and the cataclysms **on the earth** that will precede Christ's Second Advent. There will be disturbances involving **the sun . . . moon,** and **stars** that will be clearly visible on earth. Heavenly bodies will be moved out of their orbits. This might cause the earth to be tilted off its axis. There will be great tidal waves sweeping over land areas. Panic will seize mankind because of heavenly bodies on a near-collision course with the earth. But there is hope for the godly:

Then they will see the Son of Man coming in a cloud with power and great glory. Now when these things begin to happen, look up and lift up your heads, because your redemption draws near.

O. The Fig Tree and All the Trees (21:29–33)

21:29–31 Another sign indicating the nearness of His return is the **budding** of **the fig tree and all the trees. The fig tree** is an apt picture of the nation of Israel; it would begin to evidence new life in the last days. Surely it is not without significance that after centuries of dispersal and obscurity, the nation of Israel was re-established in 1948, and is now recognized as a member of the family of nations.

The shooting forth of the other trees may symbolize the phenomenal growth of nationalism and the emergence of many new governments in newly developed countries of the world. These signs would mean that Christ's glorious kingdom would soon be set up.

21:32 Jesus said that **this generation** would not **pass away till all things take place**. But what did He mean by "this generation"?

1. Some feel He referred to the generation living at the time He spoke these words, and that all things were fulfilled at the destruction of Jerusalem. But this cannot be so because Christ did not return in a cloud with power and great glory.

2. Others believe that "this generation" refers to the people living when these signs begin to take place, and that those who live to see the beginning of the signs would live to see the return of Christ. All the events predicted would happen within one generation. This is a possible explanation.

3. Another possibility is that "this generation" refers to the Jewish people in their attitude of hostility to Christ. The Lord was saying that the Jewish race would survive, scattered yet indestructible, and that its attitude toward Him would not change through the centuries. Perhaps both numbers 2 and 3 are correct.

21:33 The atmospheric and stellar heavens would **pass away**. So would the **earth** in its present form. But these predictions of the Lord Jesus would not go unfulfilled.

P. Warning to Watch and Pray (21:34–38)

21:34, 35 In the meantime, His disciples should guard against becoming so occupied with eating, drinking, and mundane **cares** that His coming might happen **unexpectedly**. That is the way **it will come on all those who** think of the **earth** as their permanent dwelling place.

21:36 True disciples should **watch** and **pray** at all times, thus separating themselves from the ungodly world which is doomed to experience the wrath of God, and identifying themselves with those who will **stand** in acceptance **before the Son of Man**.

21:37, 38 Each day the Lord taught **in the temple** area, **but at night He** slept **on the** Mt. of Olives, homeless in the world He had made. **Then early in the morning all the people** crowded around **Him** afresh **to hear Him.**

XI. THE SON OF MAN'S PASSION AND DEATH (Chaps. 22, 23)

A. The Plot to Kill Jesus (22:1, 2)

22:1 The Feast of Unleavened Bread here refers to the period beginning with the **Passover** and extending for seven more days during which no leavened bread was eaten. The Passover was held on the fourteenth of the month Nisan, the first month of the Jewish year. The seven days from the fifteenth of the month to the twenty-first were known as **the Feast of Unleavened Bread**, but in verse 1, that name takes in the entire feast. If Luke had been writing primarily to Jews, it would not have been necessary for him to mention the connection between **the Feast of Unleavened Bread** and the **Passover**.

22:2 The chief priests and scribes were ceaselessly plotting **how they might kill** the Lord Jesus, but they realized that they must do it without causing a tumult, because **they feared the people**, and knew that many still held Jesus in high esteem.

B. The Treachery of Judas (22:3–6)

22:3 Satan entered Judas, surnamed Iscariot, one of **the twelve** disciples. In John 13:27, this action is said to have taken place after Jesus had handed him the piece of bread during the Passover meal. We conclude either that this took place in successive stages, or that Luke is emphasizing the fact rather than the exact time when it took place.

22:4–6 At any rate, Judas made a bargain **with the chief priests and captains**, that is, the commanders of the Jewish temple guard. He had carefully worked out a plan by which he could **betray** Jesus into their hands without causing a riot. The plan was entirely acceptable, and they **agreed to give him money** — thirty pieces of silver, as we learn elsewhere. So Judas left to work out the details of his treacherous scheme.

C. Preparations for the Passover (22:7–13)

22:7 There are definite problems in connection with the various time periods mentioned in these verses. **The Day of Unleavened Bread** would normally be thought of as the thirteenth of Nisan when all leavened bread had to be put away from a Jewish home. But here it says it was the day on which **the Passover must be** sacrificed, and that would make it the fourteenth of Nisan. Leon Morris, along with other scholars, suggests that two calendars were used for the Passover, an official one and one followed by Jesus and others.[60] We believe that the events of the final Thursday begin here and continue through verse 53.

22:8–10 The Lord **sent Peter and John** into Jerusalem to make preparations for the celebration of **the Passover** meal. He showed His complete knowledge of all things in His instructions to them. Once inside **the city, a man** would **meet** them **carrying a pitcher of water**. This was an unusual sight in an eastern city; it was ordinarily the women who carried the pitchers of water. The man here makes a good picture of the Holy Spirit, who leads seeking souls to the place of communion with the Lord.

22:11–13 The Lord not only foreknew the location and route of this man, but He also knew that a certain homeowner would be willing to make his **large, furnished upper room** available to Him and His **disciples**. Perhaps this man knew the Lord and had made a total commitment of his person and possessions to Him. There is a difference between the **guest room** and **the large, furnished upper room**. The generous host provided better facilities than the disciples expected. When Jesus was born in Bethlehem, there was no room for Him in the inn (Gk: *kataluma*). Here He told His disciples to ask for **a guest room** (Gk: *kataluma*), but they were given something better — **a large, furnished upper room**.

Everything was as He had predicted, so the disciples **prepared the Passover**.

D. The Last Passover (22:14–18)

22:14 For centuries, the Jews had celebrated the Passover feast, commemorating their glorious deliverance from Egypt and from death through the blood of the spotless lamb. How vividly this

must all have come before the mind of
the Savior as **He sat down** with His
apostles to keep the feast for the last
time. He was the true Passover Lamb
whose blood would soon be shed for the
salvation of all who would trust in Him.

22:15, 16 **This** particular **Passover**
held inexpressible meaning for Him, and
He had ardently **desired** it **before** He
was to **suffer**. He would not keep the
Passover again till He returned to earth
and set up His glorious **kingdom**. The
construction **"With fervent desire I have
desired"** carries the sense of ardent, passionate longing. These revealing words
invite all believers of every time and
place to consider how passionately Jesus
longs for communion with us at His
table.

22:17, 18 When **He took the cup** of
wine as part of the Passover ritual, He
gave thanks for it and passed it to the
disciples, reminding them once again
that He would **not drink of the fruit of
the vine** again **until** His Millennial
Reign. The description of the Passover
meal ends with verse 18.

E. The First Lord's Supper (22:19–23)

22:19, 20 The last Passover was immediately followed by the Lord's Supper. The Lord Jesus instituted this sacred
memorial so that His followers down
through the centuries would thus remember Him in His death. He first of
all gave them **bread**, a symbol of His
body which would shortly be **given for**
them. Then **the cup** spoke eloquently of
His precious **blood** which would be shed
on the cross of Calvary. He spoke of it
as **the cup** of **the new covenant in** His
blood, which was **shed for** His own.
This means that **the new covenant**,
which He made primarily with the nation of Israel, was ratified by His **blood**.
The complete fulfillment of the New
Covenant will take place during the
kingdom of our Lord Jesus Christ on
earth, but we as believers enter into the
good of it at the present time.

It should go without saying that the
bread and wine were typical or *representative of* His body and blood. His body
had not yet been given, neither had His
blood been shed. Therefore it is absurd
to suggest that the symbols were miraculously changed into the realities. The

Jewish people were forbidden to eat
blood, and the disciples knew therefore
that He was not speaking of literal
blood, but of that which *typified* His
blood.

22:21 It seems clear that Judas was
actually present at the last supper. However, in John 13, it appears equally clear
that the betrayer left the room after Jesus
had handed the piece of bread dipped
in the gravy to him. Since this took place
before the institution of the Lord's Supper, many believe that Judas was not actually present when the bread and the
wine were passed.

22:22 The sufferings and death of
the Lord Jesus were **determined**, but
Judas betrayed Him with the full consent
of his will. That is why Jesus said, **"Woe
to that man by whom He is betrayed."**
Though Judas was one of the twelve, he
was not a true believer.

22:23 Verse 23 reveals something of
the surprise and self-distrust of the disciples. They did not know **which of them**
would be guilty of **this** dastardly **thing**.

F. True Greatness Is Serving (22:24–30)

22:24, 25 It is a terrible indictment
of the human heart that immediately
after the Lord's Supper, the disciples
should argue **among** themselves **as to
which of them** was **the greatest**! The
Lord Jesus reminded **them** that in His
economy, greatness was the very opposite of man's idea. **The kings** who
ruled over **the Gentiles** were commonly
thought of as great persons; in fact they
were **called "benefactors"**. But it was
only a title; actually they were cruel tyrants. They had the name of goodness,
but no personal characteristics to match
it.

22:26 It was **not** to be **so** of the followers of the Savior. Those who would
be great should take the place of **the
younger**. And those who would be chief
should stoop in lowly service to others.
These revolutionary dicta completely reversed the accepted traditions of the
younger being inferior to the elder, and
the chief manifesting greatness by mastery.

22:27 In men's estimation, it was
greater to be a guest at a meal than to
serve the meal. But the Lord Jesus came
as a servant of men, and all who would

follow Him must imitate Him in this.

22:28–30 It was gracious of the Lord to commend the disciples for having **continued with** Him **in** His **trials**. They had just been quarreling among themselves. Very soon they would all forsake Him and flee. And yet He knew that in their hearts, they loved Him and had endured reproach for His name's sake. Their reward would be to **sit on thrones judging the twelve tribes of Israel** when Christ returns to take the throne of David and rule over the earth. Just as surely as the Father had promised this kingdom to Christ, so surely would they reign with Him over renewed Israel.

G. Jesus Predicts Peter's Denial (22:31–34)

Now comes the last in a series of three dark chapters in the history of human faithlessness. The first was the treachery of Judas. The second was the selfish ambition of the disciples. Now we have the cowardice of Peter.

22:31, 32 The repetition **Simon, Simon**, speaks of the love and tenderness of the heart of Christ for His vacillating disciple. **Satan** had **asked** to have all the disciples that he might **sift** them **as wheat**. Jesus addressed Peter as representative of all. **But** the Lord had **prayed for** Simon **that** his **faith** might not suffer an eclipse. (**"I have prayed for you"** are tremendous words.) After he had **returned** to Him, he should **strengthen** his **brethren**. This turning back does not refer to salvation but rather to restoration from backsliding.

22:33, 34 With unbecoming self-confidence, Peter expressed readiness to accompany Jesus **to prison and to death**. But he had to be told that **before** the morning light had fully dawned, he would **deny three times that** he even knew the Lord!

In Mark 14:30, the Lord is quoted as saying that before the rooster crows twice, Peter would deny Him three times. In Matthew 26:34; Luke 22:34; John 13:38, the Lord said that before the rooster crows, Peter would deny Him three times. It is admittedly difficult to reconcile this seeming contradiction. It is possible that there was more than one cock-crowing, one during the night and

another at dawn. Also it should be noticed that the Gospels record at least six different denials by Peter. He denied Christ before:

1. A young woman (Matt. 26:69, 70; Mark 14:66–68).
2. Another young woman (Matt. 26:71, 72).
3. The crowd that stood by (Matt. 26:73, 74; Mark 14:70, 71).
4. A man (Luke 22:58).
5. Another man (Luke 22:59, 60).
6. A servant of the high priest (John 18:26, 27). This man is probably different from the others because of what he said — "Did I not see you in the garden with him?" (v. 26).

H. New Marching Orders (22:35–38)

22:35 Earlier in His ministry, the Lord **sent** the disciples out **without money bag, knapsack, and sandals** — the minimum. Bare essentials would be sufficient for them. And so it had proved. They had to confess that they had lacked **nothing.**

22:36 But now He was about to leave them, and they were to enter into a new phase of service for Him. They would be exposed to poverty, hunger, and danger, and it would be necessary for them to make provision for their current needs. They should now take **a money bag**, a **knapsack** or lunch box, and in the absence of a **sword**, they should **sell** their **garment and buy one**. What did the Savior mean when He told the disciples to **buy** a **sword**? It seems clear that He could not have intended them to use the sword as an offensive weapon against other people. This would be in violation of His teaching in such passages as:

"My kingdom is not of this world. If My kingdom were of this world, My servants would fight" (John 18:36).

"All who take the sword will perish by the sword" (Matt. 26:52).

"Love your enemies . . . " (Matt. 5:44).

"Whoever slaps you on your right cheek, turn the other to him also" (Matt. 5:39; see also 2 Cor. 10:4.)

What then did Jesus mean by the sword?

1. Some suggest that He was referring

to the sword of the Spirit which is the Word of God (Eph. 6:17). This is possible, but then the money bag, the knapsack, and the garment should be spiritualized also.

2. Williams says that the sword means the protection of an ordered government, pointing out that in Romans 13:4, it refers to the power of the magistrate.

3. Lange says the sword is for defense against human enemies, but not for offense. But Matthew 5:39 seems to rule out the use of the sword, even for defensive purposes.

4. Some think that the sword was for defense against wild animals only. This is possible.

22:37 Verse 37 explains why it was necessary for the disciples to take money bag, knapsack, and sword now. The Lord had been with them up to this point, providing for their temporal needs. Soon He would be departing from them in accordance with the prophecy of Isaiah 53:12. The things concerning Him had **an end**, that is, His earthly life and ministry would come to a close by His being **numbered with the transgressors**.

22:38 The disciples completely misunderstood the Lord. They brought forth **two swords**, implying that these would surely be enough for any problems that lay ahead. The Lord Jesus ended the conversation by saying **"It is enough."** They apparently thought that they could foil the attempt of His enemies to slay Him by using the swords. This was the farthest thought from His mind!

I. The Agony in Gethsemane (22:39–46)

22:39 The Garden of Gethsemane was situated on the western slope of **the Mount of Olives**. Jesus often went there to pray, and the **disciples**, including the betrayer, of course, knew this.

22:40 At the conclusion of the Lord's Supper, Jesus and the disciples left the upper room and went to the garden. Once they were there, He warned them to **pray that** they should **not enter into temptation**. Perhaps the particular **temptation** which He had in mind was the pressure to abandon God and His Christ when the enemies closed in.

22:41, 42 Then Jesus left the disciples and went further into the garden where He **prayed** alone. His prayer was that **if** the **Father** were willing, **this cup** might pass from Him; **nevertheless** He wanted the **will** of God to be done, **not** His own. We understand this prayer to mean: If there is any other way by which sinners can be saved than by My going to the cross, reveal that way now. The heavens were silent, because there *was* no other way.

We do not believe that Christ's sufferings in the garden were part of His atoning work. The work of redemption was accomplished during the three hours of darkness on the cross. But Gethsemane was in anticipation of Calvary. There the very thought of contact with our sins caused the Lord Jesus the keenest suffering.

22:43, 44 His perfect humanity is seen in the **agony** which accompanied His travail. **An angel appeared to Him from heaven, strengthening Him**. Only Luke records this, as well as the fact that **His sweat became like great drops of blood**. This latter detail caught the interest of the careful physician.

22:45, 46 When Jesus returned **to His disciples**, they were **sleeping**, not from indifference, but rather from sorrowful exhaustion. Once again He urged them to **rise and pray**, because the crisis hour was drawing near, and they would be tempted to deny Him before the authorities.

J. Jesus Betrayed and Arrested (22:47–53)

22:47, 48[†] By now, **Judas** had arrived with a group of the chief priests, elders, and captains of the temple to arrest the Lord. By prearrangement, the traitor was to mark out Jesus by kissing Him. Stewart comments:

It was the crowning touch of horror, the last point of infamy beyond which human infamy could not go, when out in the garden Judas betrayed his master, not with a shout or a blow or a stab, but with a kiss.[61]

With infinite pathos, **Jesus** asked, **"Judas, are you betraying the Son of Man with a kiss?"**

22:49–51 The disciples realized

†See p. xxi.

what was going to happen, and were ready to take the offensive. In fact one of them, Peter to be specific, took a sword and cut off the right ear of the servant of the high priest. Jesus rebuked him for using carnal means to fight a spiritual warfare. His hour had come, and God's predetermined purposes must come to pass. Graciously, Jesus touched the ear of the victim and healed him.

22:52, 53 Turning to the Jewish leaders and officers, Jesus asked them why they had come out after Him as if He were a fugitive robber. Had He not taught daily in the temple area, yet they had not tried to take Him then? But He knew the answer, This was their hour, and the power of darkness. It was now about midnight on Thursday.

It seems that the religious trial of our Lord had three stages. First, He appeared before Annas. Then He appeared before Caiaphas. Finally He was arraigned before the Sanhedrin. The events from this point through verse 65 probably took place between 1:00 a.m. and 5:00 a.m. on Friday.

K. Peter Denies Jesus and Weeps Bitterly (22:54–62)

22:54–57 When the Lord was brought into the high priest's house, Peter followed at a distance. Inside, he took his place with those who were warming themselves at a fire in the center of the courtyard. A servant girl looked across at Peter and exclaimed that he was one of the followers of Jesus. Pathetically Peter denied that he knew Him.

22:58–62 Shortly afterwards, someone else pointed the accusing finger at Peter as one of the followers of Jesus of Nazareth. Again Peter denied the charge. After about an hour, someone else recognized Peter as a Galilean, and also as a disciple of the Lord. Peter denied any knowledge of what the man was talking about. But this time his denial was punctuated by the crowing of the rooster. In that dark moment, the Lord turned and looked at Peter, and Peter remembered the prediction that before the rooster crows, he would deny Him three times. The look from the Son of God sent Peter out into the night to weep bitterly.

L. The Soldiers Mock the Son of Man (22:63–65)

It was the officers assigned to the sacred temple in Jerusalem who had apprehended Jesus. Now these supposed guardians of God's holy house began to mock Jesus and to beat Him. After blindfolding Him, they struck Him on the face, then asked Him to identify the one who did it. This is not all they did, but He patiently endured this contradiction of sinners against Himself.

M. Morning Trial Before the Sanhedrin (22:66–71)†

22:66–69 At daybreak (5:00–6:00 a.m.), the elders . . . led Jesus away to their council, or Sanhedrin. The members of the Sanhedrin asked Him outright if He was the Messiah. Jesus said, in effect, that it was useless to discuss the matter with them. They were not open to receive the truth. But He warned them that the One who stood before them in humiliation would one day sit on the right hand of the power of God (see Psalm 110:1).

22:70, 71 Then they asked Him plainly if He was the Son of God. There is no question what they meant. To them, the Son of God was One who was equal with God. The Lord Jesus answered "You rightly say that I am" (see Mark 14:62). That was all they needed. Had they not heard Him speak blasphemy, claiming equality with God? There was no need for further testimony. But there was a problem. In their law, the penalty for blasphemy was death. Yet the Jews were under Roman power and they did not have authority to put prisoners to death. So they had to take Jesus to Pilate, and he would not be the least bit interested in a religious charge such as blasphemy. So they had to prefer political charges against Him.

N. Jesus Before Pilate (23:1–7)

23:1, 2 Following His appearance before the Sanhedrin (the whole multitude of them), Jesus was hurried away to be put on civil trial before Pilate, the Roman governor. Three political charges were now brought against Him by the religious leaders. First of all, they accused Him of perverting the nation, that

†See p. xv.

is, of turning the loyalty of the people away from Rome. Secondly, they said that He forbade Jews **to pay taxes to Caesar**. Finally, they accused Him of making Himself **a King**.

23:3–7 When **Pilate asked** Jesus if He was **the King of the Jews, He answered** that He was. **Pilate** did not interpret His claim as any threat to the Roman Emperor. After a private interview with Jesus (John 18:33–38a), he turned **to the chief priests and** to the crowd saying that he could **find no fault** with Him. The mob became more insistent, accusing Jesus of stirring up disloyalty, **beginning** in despised **Galilee** even to Jerusalem. **When Pilate heard** the word **Galilee**, he thought he had found an escape route for himself. Galilee was **Herod's jurisdiction**, and so Pilate tried to avoid any further involvement in this case by turning Jesus over **to Herod**. It so happened that Herod was visiting **in Jerusalem at that** very **time**.

Herod Antipas was the son of Herod the Great, who massacred the infants of Bethlehem. It was Antipas who murdered John the Baptist for condemning his illicit relationship with his brother's wife. This was the Herod whom Jesus called "that fox" in Luke 13:32.

O. Herod's Contemptuous Questioning (23:8–12)

23:8 **Herod** was quite **glad** to have **Jesus** appear before him. **He had heard many things about Him**, and **for a long time** had **hoped to see some miracle** performed **by Him**.

23:9–11 No matter how much Herod **questioned** the Savior, he received no answer. The Jews became more violent in their accusations, but Jesus did not open His mouth. All **Herod** could do, he thought, was to allow his soldiers to manhandle Jesus, and to mock **Him** by clothing **Him in a gorgeous robe** and sending **Him back to Pilate**.

23:12 **Previously, Herod** and **Pilate had been at enmity** between themselves, but now the enmity was changed to friendship. They were both on the same side *against* the Lord Jesus, and this united them. Theophylact mourns in this regard: "It is a matter of shame to Christians that while the devil can persuade

wicked men to lay aside their enmities in order to do harm, Christians cannot even keep up friendship in order to do good."

P. Pilate's Verdict: Innocent but Condemned (23:13–25)

23:13–17 Because he had failed to act righteously in acquitting his royal prisoner, **Pilate** now found himself trapped. He called a hurried meeting of the Jewish leaders and explained to them that **neither . . . Herod** nor he had been able to find any evidence of disloyalty on the part of Jesus. **"Nothing deserving of death has been done by Him."** So he proposed to whip the Lord and then to let Him go. As Stewart points out:

> This sorry compromise was, of course, totally unjustifiable and illogical. It was the poor, fear-driven soul's attempt to do his duty by Jesus and to please the crowd at the same time. But it did neither, and it is no wonder that the angry priests would not accept that verdict at any price.[62]

23:18–23[†] The chief priests and rulers were enraged. They demanded the death of Jesus and the release of **Barabbas**, a notorious criminal **who had been thrown into prison** because of **rebellion** and **murder**. Again Pilate feebly attempted to exonerate the Lord, but the vicious demands of the mob drowned him out. No matter what he said, they persisted in **demanding** the death of the Son of God.

23:24, 25 And although he had already pronounced Jesus innocent, **Pilate** now condemned Him to death in order to please the people. At the same time **he released** Barabbas **to** the multitude.

Q. The Son of Man Led to Calvary (23:26–32)

23:26 It was now approximately 9:00 a.m. on Friday. On the way to the scene of crucifixion, the soldiers commanded a **man** named **Simon, a Cyrenian** to carry **the cross**. Not much is known of this man, but it appears that his two sons afterwards became well-known Christians (Mark 15:21).

23:27–30 A crowd of sympathetic followers wept for Jesus as He was led away. Addressing the **women** in the crowd as **daughters of Jerusalem**, He

†See p. xx.

told them that they should not pity Him but should pity themselves. He was referring to the terrible destruction that would descend on Jerusalem in A.D. 70. The suffering and sorrow of those **days** would be so great that **barren** women, hitherto an object of reproach, would be considered especially fortunate. The horrors of the siege of Titus would be such that men would wish for **the mountains** to **fall on** them, and for **the hills** to **cover** them.

23:31 Then the Lord Jesus added the words, **"For if they do these things in the green wood, what will be done in the dry?"** He Himself was the **green** tree, and unbelieving Israel was the **dry**. If the Romans heaped such shame and suffering on the sinless, innocent Son of God, what dreadful punishment would fall on the guilty murderers of God's beloved Son?

23:32 In the procession with Jesus **there were also two others, criminals**, scheduled for execution.

R. The Crucifixion (23:33–38)

23:33 The place of execution was **called Calvary**[63] (from the Latin for "Skull"). Perhaps the configuration of the land resembled a skull, or perhaps it was so named because it was the place of death, and a skull is often used as a symbol of death. The restraint of Scripture in describing the crucifixion is noteworthy. There is no lingering over the terrible details. There is just the simple statement, **"there they crucified Him."** Once again Stewart's remarks are to the point:

That the Messiah should die was hard enough to credit, but that He should die *such* a death was utterly beyond belief. Yet so it was. Everything which Christ ever touched — the cross included — he adorned and transfigured and haloed with splendor and beauty; but let us never forget out of what appalling depths he has set the cross on high.[64]

O teach me what it meaneth
That cross uplifted high
With One, the Man of Sorrows,
Condemned to bleed and die.
– *Lucy A. Bennett*

There were three crosses at Calvary that day, the cross of Jesus in the middle, and a criminal's cross on each side of Him. This fulfilled Isaiah 53:12 — "He was numbered with the transgressors."

23:34† With infinite love and mercy, **Jesus** cried from the cross, **"Father, forgive them, for they do not know what they do."** Who knows what a Niagara of divine wrath was averted by this prayer! Morgan comments on the Savior's love:

In the soul of Jesus there was no resentment; no anger, no lurking desire for punishment upon the men who were maltreating Him. Men have spoken in admiration of the mailed fist. When I hear Jesus thus pray, I know that the only place for the mailed fist is in hell.[65]

Then followed the dividing of **His garments** among the soldiers, and the casting of **lots** for His seamless robe.

23:35–38† **The rulers** stood before the cross, mocking Him, and challenging Him to **save Himself if He** really was the Messiah, **the chosen of God. The soldiers** also mocked Him . . . offering Him sour wine and challenging His ability to **save** Himself. Also they put a title at the head of the cross:

THIS IS THE KING OF THE JEWS.

Once again we quote Stewart:

We cannot miss the significance of the fact that the inscription was written in three languages, Greek and Latin and Hebrew. No doubt that was done in order to make sure that everyone in the crowd might read it; but Christ's Church has always seen in it — and rightly — a symbol of the universal lordship of her master. For these were the three great world languages, each of them the servant of one dominant idea. Greek was the language of culture and knowledge; in that realm, said the inscription, Jesus was king! Latin was the language of law and government; Jesus was king there! Hebrew was the language of revealed religion; Jesus was King there! Hence even as he hung dying, it was true that "on his head were many crowns" (Rev. 19:12).[66]

S. The Two Robbers (23:39–43)

23:39–41 We learn from the other Gospel narratives that both robbers reviled Jesus at the outset. If He was **the Christ**, why did He not **save** them all? But then one of them had a change of heart. Turning to his companion, he **rebuked him** for his irreverence. After all they were both suffering for crimes that they had committed. Their punishment was deserved. **But this Man** on the middle cross had **done nothing wrong**.

23:42 Turning **to Jesus**, the thief asked the **Lord**[67] to **remember** him **when** He came back and set up His **kingdom** on earth. Such faith was remarkable. The dying thief believed that Jesus would rise from the dead and would eventually reign over the world.

23:43 **Jesus** rewarded his faith with the promise that that very day, they would **be** together **in Paradise. Paradise** is the same as the third heaven (2 Cor. 12:2, 4), and means the dwelling place of God. **Today** — what speed! **With Me** — what company! **In Paradise** — what happiness! Charles R. Erdman writes:

This story reveals the truth to us that salvation is conditioned upon repentance and faith. However, it contains other important messages also. It declares that salvation is independent of sacraments. The thief had never been baptized, nor had he partaken of the Lord's Supper. . . . He did in fact boldly profess his faith in the presence of a hostile crowd and amid the taunts and jeers of rulers and soldiers, yet he was saved without any formal rites. It is further evident that salvation is independent of good works. . . . It is also seen that there is no "sleep of the soul." The body may sleep, but consciousness exists after death. Again it is evident that there is no "purgatory." Out of a life of sin and shame, the penitent robber passed immediately into a state of blessedness. Again it may be remarked that salvation is not universal. There were two robbers; only one was saved. Last of all it may be noted that the very essence of the joy which lies beyond death consists in personal communion with Christ. The heart of the promise to the dying thief was this: "Thou shalt be with me." This is our blessed assurance, that to depart is "to be with Christ" which is "very far better."[68]

From Jesus Christ's side one person may go to heaven and another to hell. Which side of the cross are you on?

T. Three Hours of Darkness (23:44–49)

23:44 **Darkness** covered the whole land (or *earth*, the Greek can mean either) from **the sixth hour until the ninth hour**, that is, from noon to 3:00 p.m. This was a sign to the nation of Israel. They had rejected the light, and now

they would be judicially blinded by God.

23:45 **The veil of the temple was torn in two** from the top to the bottom. This pictured the fact that through the death of the Lord Jesus Christ, a way of approach to God was opened to all who would come by faith (Heb. 10:20–22).

23:46, 47 It was during these three hours of darkness that Jesus bore the penalty of our sins in His body on the tree. At the close of that time, He committed His **spirit** into the **hands** of God, His **Father**, and voluntarily yielded up His life. A Roman **centurion** was so overwhelmed by the scene that **he glorified God, saying, "Certainly this was a righteous Man!"**

23:48, 49 **The whole crowd** was overcome by an awful sense of sorrow and foreboding. Some of Jesus' faithful followers, including **women who followed Him from Galilee, stood . . . watching** this most crucial scene in the history of the world.

U. The Burial in Joseph's Tomb (23:50–56)[†]

23:50–54 Up to this time, **Joseph** had been a secret disciple of the Lord Jesus. Although a **member** of the Sanhedrin, he did not agree with their verdict in the case of Jesus. Joseph now went boldly **to Pilate and asked** if he might have the privilege of removing **the body of Jesus** from the cross and giving it a proper burial. (It was between 3:00 and 6:00 p.m.) Permission was granted, and Joseph promptly **wrapped it in linen, and laid it in a tomb that was hewn out of the rock**, and which had never been used up to this time. This happened on Friday, the **day** of the **Preparation**. When it says that **the Sabbath drew near**, we must remember that the Jewish Sabbath begins on Friday at sunset.

23:55, 56 The faithful **women . . . from Galilee followed** Joseph as he took the **body** to the **tomb** and put it inside. **Then they returned and prepared spices and fragrant oils** so that they could come back and embalm the body of the One they loved. In burying the body of Jesus, Joseph also buried himself, in a sense. That act separated him forever from the nation that crucified the Lord of life and glory. He would never be a

†See p. xvi.

part of Judaism again, but would live in moral separation from it and testify against it.

On Saturday the women rested, in obedience to the commandment concerning the Sabbath.

XII. THE SON OF MAN'S TRIUMPH (Chap. 24)†

A. The Women at the Empty Tomb (24:1–12)

24:1 Then on Sunday at **early** dawn they made their way **to the tomb**, carrying **the spices which they had prepared** for the body of Jesus. But how did they expect to get to His body? Did they not know that a huge stone had been rolled against the mouth of the tomb? We are not told the answer. All we know is that they loved Him dearly, and love is often forgetful of difficulties in order to reach its object.

"Their love was early astir (v. 1) and was richly rewarded (v. 6). There is still a risen Lord for the early riser (Prov. 8:17)."

24:2–10 When they arrived **they found the stone** had been **rolled away from** the mouth of **the tomb**. As soon as **they went in**, they saw that **the body of the Lord Jesus** was missing. It is not difficult to imagine their perplexity. While they were still trying to reason it out, **two** angels (see John 20:12), **in shining garments**, appeared and assured them that Jesus was **living**; it was futile to search for Him in the tomb. He had **risen** as He had promised **when He was still** with them **in Galilee**. Had He not foretold them that **the Son of Man** had to be turned over to **sinful men and be crucified, and** that on **the third day** He would **rise again**? (Luke 9:22; 18:33). Then it all came back to them. **They returned** hurriedly to the city **and told** the news **to the eleven** disciples. Among those first heralds of the resurrection were **Mary Magdalene, Joanna,** and **Mary the mother of James**.

24:11, 12 The disciples **did not believe them** at all. It was just an old wive's tale. Incredible! Fantastic! That is what they thought — until **Peter** made a personal visit **to the tomb** and **saw the linen cloths lying** there **by themselves**.

These were the cloths that had been tightly wound around the body. We are not told whether they were unwound, or still in the shape of the body, but we are safe in presuming the latter. It appears that the Lord may have left the grave-clothes as if they had been a cocoon. The fact that the grave-clothes were left behind shows that the body was not stolen; thieves would not take time to remove the coverings. Peter returned to his house, still trying to solve the mystery. What did it all mean?

B. The Walk to Emmaus (24:13–35)

24:13 One of the **two** Emmaus disciples was a man named Cleopas; we do not know the identity of the other. It may have been his wife. One tradition is that it was Luke himself. All we can be sure of is that it was not one of the original eleven disciples (see v. 33). At any rate, the two were sadly[69] rehearsing the death and burial of the Lord as they returned **from Jerusalem** to **Emmaus**, a journey of about **seven miles**.

24:14–18 As they proceeded, a stranger came alongside them; it was the risen Lord but **they did not** recognize **Him**. He asked them what they had been talking about. At first they stopped short, a picture of abject misery. Then **Cleopas** expressed surprise that even a **stranger in Jerusalem** could have been unaware of what had **happened.**

24:19–24 Jesus drew them out further with the question, "Why, **what** did happen?" They answered by first paying tribute to **Jesus**, then reviewing His trial and crucifixion. They told of their dashed hopes, then of reports that **His body** was no longer in the tomb. Indeed some **angels** had given assurance that **He was alive.**

24:25–27 Jesus then lovingly chided them for not realizing that this was exactly the pathway which **the prophets** of the OT had foretold for the Messiah. First, He must suffer, then he would be glorified. **Beginning at** Genesis and continuing through **all the** books of the **Prophets** the Lord reviewed **all the Scriptures** which referred to **Himself,** the Messiah. It was a wonderful Bible study, and how we would love to have been with Him then! But we have the same OT, and we have the Holy Spirit

†See p. xvii.

to teach us, so we too can discover **in all the Scriptures the things concerning Himself**.

24:28, 29 By now the disciples were nearing their home. They invited their fellow-traveler to spend the night with them. At first, He courteously acted as if He were going to continue His journey; He would not force an entry. But they prevailed on Him to stay with them, and how richly they were rewarded!

24:30, 31 When they sat down for the evening meal, the Guest took the place of Host.

> The frugal meal became a sacrament, and the home became a House of God. That's what Christ does wherever He goes. They who entertain Him will be well entertained. The two had opened to Him their home, and now He opens their eyes (Daily Notes of the Scripture Union).

As He **broke** the **bread** and passed it **to them, they knew Him** for the first time. Had they seen the print of the nails in His hands? We only know that **their eyes** had been miraculously **opened** to recognize Him. As soon as this happened, **He vanished**.

24:32 Then they retraced the day's journey. No wonder their hearts had burned **within** them **while He talked with** them and **opened the Scriptures**. Their Teacher and Companion had been the risen Lord Jesus Christ.

24:33 Instead of spending the night at Emmaus, they raced back **to Jerusalem** where they **found the eleven** and others assembled **together**. "The eleven" here is a general term to indicate the original band of the disciples, excluding Judas. Actually not all eleven were present, as we learn from John 20:24, but the term is used in a collective sense.

24:34 Before the Emmaus disciples could share their joyful news, the Jerusalem disciples jubilantly announced that **the Lord** had really **risen** and had **appeared to Simon** Peter.

24:35 Then it was the turn of the two from Emmaus to say, "Yes, we know, because He walked with us, came into our home, and revealed Himself to us **in the breaking of bread**."

C. The Appearance to the Eleven (24:36–43)

24:36–41 The resurrection body of the Lord Jesus was a literal, tangible body of **flesh and bones**. It was the same body which had been buried, yet it was changed in that it was no longer subject to death. With this glorified body, Jesus could enter a room when the doors were closed (John 20:19).

This is what He did on that first Sunday night. The disciples looked up and saw Him, then heard Him say, **"Peace to you."** They were seized with panic, thinking it was a ghost. Only when He showed them the marks of His passion in **His hands and His feet** did they begin to understand. Even then, it was almost too good to be true.

24:42, 43 Then in order to show them it was really Jesus Himself, He **ate** some **broiled fish** and a piece of **honeycomb**.

D. The Opened Understanding (24:44–49)

24:44–47 These verses may be a summary of the Savior's teaching between His resurrection and His ascension. He explained that His resurrection was the fulfillment of His own **words** to them. Had He not told them that all the OT prophecies **concerning** Him had to **be fulfilled? The Law of Moses and the Prophets and the Psalms** were the three main divisions of the OT. Taken together, they signify the entire OT. What was the burden of the OT prophecies concerning Christ? They were:

1. That He must **suffer** (Psalm 22:1–21; Isa. 53:1–9).
2. That He must **rise** again **from the dead** the third day (Ps. 16:10; Jonah 1:17; Hos. 6:2).
3. **That repentance and remission of sins should be preached in His name to all nations, beginning at Jerusalem.**

Jesus **opened their understanding** to **comprehend** all these **Scriptures**. In fact, this is a chapter full of opened things: opened *tomb* (v. 12), opened *home* (v. 29), opened *eyes* (v. 31), opened *Scriptures* (v. 32), opened *lips* (v. 35), opened *understanding* (v. 45), and opened *heavens* (v. 51).

24:48, 49 The disciples were **witnesses** of the resurrection. They must go forth as heralds of the glorious message.

But first they must wait for **the Promise of** the **Father**, i.e., for the coming of the Holy Spirit at Pentecost. Then they would be **endued with** divine **power** to bear witness to the risen Christ. The Holy Spirit was promised by the Father in such OT passages as Isaiah 44:3; Ezekiel 36:27; Joel 2:28.

E. The Son of Man's Ascension (24:50–53)

24:50, 51 The Ascension of Christ took place forty days after His resurrection. **He** took His disciples **as far as Bethany**, on the eastern side of the Mt. of Olives, **and He lifted up His hands and blessed them**. While doing so, **He was** taken **up into heaven**.

24:52, 53 They worshiped Him, then **returned to Jerusalem with great joy**. For the next ten days, they spent much time **in the temple praising and blessing God**.

Luke's Gospel **opened** with devout believers at the temple, praying for the long-expected Messiah. It closes at the same place with devout believers **praising and**[70] **blessing God** for answered prayer and for accomplished redemption. It is a lovely climax to what Renan called the most beautiful book in the world. **Amen**.

ENDNOTES

[1](1:2) James S. Stewart, *The Life and Teaching of Jesus Christ*, p. 9.

[2](1:4) The same word (*anōthen*) occurs in John 3:7: "You must be born again" (or "from above").

[3](1:16, 17) G. Coleman Luck, *Luke*, p. 17.

[4](1:28) The Greek word is a *passive* participle, showing she *received* the favor. The Latin *gratia plena* ("full of grace") has been misused to teach that Mary is a *source* of grace. This points up the importance of precisely accurate translation.

[5](1:72–75) G. Campbell Morgan, *The Gospel According to Luke*. pp. 30, 31.

[6](2:7) J. N. Darby, *Synopsis of the Books of the Bible*, III:293.

[7](2:8) Stewart, *Life and Teaching*, p. 24.

[8](2:13, 14) The critical (NU) text reads "to men of good will," which seems to contradict the Bible doctrine of man's depravity. Evangelicals who accept the critical reading generally paraphrase. The KJ tradition is probably best.

[9](2:33) The NU reading "His father and mother" does not *deny* the Virgin Birth, but is less clear. Compare also v. 43 in the traditional and majority texts vs. the NU text.

[10](2:40) The NU text omits "in spirit."

[11](4:13) Stewart, *Life and Teaching*, p. 45.

[12](4:28) John Charles Ryle, *Expository Thoughts on the Gospels, St. Luke*, I:121.

[13](5:30) The NU text reads "the Pharisees and their scribes," meaning those scribes who held the Pharisaic position.

[14](6:17–19) Many scholars, however, believe the "plain" (KJ) was a *flat place* on the mountain side and the differences are merely from condensation, choice of emphasis by Matthew and Luke, and editorial arrangement (inspired by God).

[15](6:26) The majority of mss. omit "all," suggesting that only some would praise compromisers.

[16](6:27–29a) F. B. Meyer, *The Heavenlies*, p. 26.

[17](6:47–49) The critical reading ("well-built") followed in most modern Bibles, misses the point. It is not *how* but on *whom* (Christ) one builds one's life!

[18](7:21–23) C. G. Moore, quoted by W. H. Griffith Thomas, *Outline Studies in the Gospel of Luke*, p. 129.

[19](7:27) F. L. Godet, *Commentary on the Gospel of Luke*, I:350.

[20](7:30–34) Ryle, *St. Luke*, I:230.

[21](7:49, 50) *Ibid.*, p. 239.

[22](8:11–15) J. N. Darby, *The Gospel of Luke*, p. 61.

[23](8:18) G. H. Lang, *The Parabolic Teaching of the Scripture*, p. 60.

[24](8:26, 27) Here and in verse 37 the NU text reads *Gerasenes*.

[25](8:34–39) Darby, *Synopsis*, III:340.

[26](8:51–53) Sir Robert Anderson, *Misunderstood Texts of the New Testament*, p. 51.

[27](9:19, 20) Stewart, *Life and Teaching*, pp. 109, 110.

[28](9:28, 29) W. H. Rogers, further documentation unavailable.

[29](9:32, 33) Ryle, *Gospels, St. Luke*, I:320.

[30](9:50) A. L. Williams, further documentation unavailable.

[31](9:62) This probably does not mean a momentary glance back, but the "back to Egypt" mentality of the Israelites in the wilderness.

[32](10:1–12) Here and in v. 17 the NU text reads "seventy-two."

[33](10:16) Ryle, *St. Luke*, I:357, 358.

[34](10:36, 37) F. Davidson, ed., *The New Bible Commentary*, p. 851.

[35](10:42) C. A. Coates, *An Outline of Luke's Gospel*, p. 129.

[36](10:42) Charles R. Erdman, *The Gospel of Luke*, p. 112.

[37](11:4) Luke gives a shorter version of the "Disciple's Prayer," which perhaps suggests it is not to be recited word-for-word. The omissions in the critical (NU) text (see NKJV footnotes) are generally considered interpolations from Matthew by the editors of that text.

[38](11:9) The Greek *present imperative* suggests continuous action.

[39](11:41) Harry A. Ironside, *Addresses on the Gospel of Luke*, p. 390.

[40](11:46) William Kelly, *An Exposition of the Gospel of Luke*, p. 199.

[41](12:2,3) Godet, *Luke*, II:89.

[42](12:15) J. R. Miller, *Come Ye Apart*, reading for June 10.

[43](12:36) Kelly, *Luke*, p. 214.

[44](13:6–9) Lang, *Parabolic Teaching*, p. 230.

[45](14:33) Ryle, *Gospels, St. Luke*, II:86.

[46](14:34,35) Kelly, *Luke*, p. 249.

[47](15:20) Stewart, *Life and Teaching*, pp. 77, 78.

[48](16:9) *Our Lord's Teachings About Money* (tract), pp. 10, 11.

[49](16:9) J. N. Darby, *The Man of Sorrows*, p. 178.

[50](17:10) Roy Hession, *The Calvary Road*, p. 49.

[51](17:34–36) Both the oldest and the majority of mss. lack v. 36, which means it is most likely not authentic.

[52](18:31–33) Ryle, *Gospels, St. Luke*, II:282.

[53](19:11) A mina (Heb. *minah*, Gk. *mna*) was worth a great deal more than a British "pound," hence the change here from KJV.

[54](19:41,42) Griffith Thomas, *Luke*, p. 303.

[55](20:18) Others take the stone to refer to the repentant sinner falling in contrition on Jesus in true brokenness and being saved vs. the Christ-rejecter being smashed to powder at the future judgment.

[56](20:35) Coates, *Luke's Gospel*, p. 252.

[57](21:1–4) Dr. Joseph Parker, further documentation unavailable.

[58](21:20–24) *Christian Truth Magazine*, November 1962, p. 303.

[59](21:20–24) Edward Gibbon, *The Decline and Fall of the Roman Empire*, II:95-101.

[60](22:7) Leon Morris, *The Gospel According to Luke*, pp. 302-304.

[61](22:47,48) Stewart, *Life and Teaching*, p. 154.

[62](23:13–17) *Ibid.*, p. 161.

[63](23:33) This is the only place in the English Bible (KJ tradition) where this beloved name occurs. Even though there are thousands of congregations named "Calvary _____Church," most modern Bibles have scrapped this traditional rendering.

[64](23:33) Stewart, *Life and Teaching*, p. 166.

[65](23:34) Morgan, *Luke*, p. 269.

[66](23:35–38) Stewart, *Life and Teaching*, p. 168.

[67](23:42) The traditional and majority text reading, "*Lord*, remember me," is much more impressive than the critical (NU) text "*Jesus*, remember me." The title of respect "Lord" (can also mean "Sir") shows deeper faith than the use of a (then common) personal name.

[68](23:43) Erdman, *Luke*, pp. 217, 218.

[69](24:13) The NU text reads, " 'What kind of conversation is this that you have with one another?' And they stood still, looking sad."

[70](24:52, 53) The critical (NU) text omits "praising and" as well as the final "Amen"

BIBLIOGRAPHY

Coates, C. A. *An Outline of Luke's Gospel.* Kingston on Thames: Stow Hill Bible and Tract Depot, n.d.

Darby, J. N. *The Gospel of Luke.* London: James Carter, n.d.

_____. *The Man of Sorrows.* Glasgow: Pickering and Inglis, n.d.

_____. *Notes of Addresses on the Gospel of Luke.* London: C. A. Hammond, n.d.

Erdman, Charles R. *The Gospel of Luke.* Philadelphia: The Westminster Press, 1921.

Geldenhuys, Norval. *Commentary on the Gospel of Luke*, 2 vols. Grand Rapids: Zondervan Publishing House, 1977.

Ironside, H. A. *Addresses on the Gospel of Luke*. New York: Loizeaux Brothers, 1947.

Kelly, William. *An Exposition of the Gospel of Luke*. London: Pickering and Inglis, n.d.

Luck, G. Coleman. *Luke*. Chicago: Moody Press, 1960.

Morgan, G. Campbell. *The Gospel According to Luke*. New York: Fleming H. Revell Co., 1931.

Morris, Leon. *The Gospel According to St. Luke, TBC*. Grand Rapids: Wm. B. Eerdmans Publishing Company, 1974.

Thomas, W. H. Griffith. *Outline Studies in the Gospel of Luke*. Grand Rapids: Kregel Publications, 1984.

THE GOSPEL ACCORDING TO JOHN†

Introduction

"The profoundest book in the world" — A. T. Robertson.

I. Unique Place in the Canon

John specifically tells us that his book is evangelistic — "that you may believe" (20:31). For once the church has followed apostolic precedent: the millions of little pocket Gospels of John given out in the last century witness to that fact.

But John is also one of the favorite Bible books — if not the *very* favorite — of mature and devout Christians. John does not merely give the facts of the life of our Lord, but long discourses and mature reflections of an apostle who has walked with Christ from (probably) late teenage years in Galilee to extreme old age in the Province of Asia. His Gospel contains the best known verse in the NT, what Martin Luther called "the Gospel in a nutshell," John 3:16.

If John's Gospel were the *only* book in the NT, it would still afford enough meat (and milk) of the Word for a lifetime of study and meditation.

II. Authorship††

The authorship of the Fourth Gospel has been widely disputed in the past 150 years. This is undoubtedly because it gives such clear testimony to the deity of our Lord Jesus Christ. The assault has sought to prove that the Gospel was not the work of an eyewitness but the work of an unknown "religious genius" who lived fifty to one hundred years later. Thus it is supposed to reflect the thinking of the church about Christ and not what He Himself actually was, said, or did.

The Gospel itself is anonymous as to authorship, but there are many good reasons for believing that it was written by the Apostle John, one of the twelve.

Clement of Alexandria recounts that late in John's long life, the Apostle was asked by close friends who came to him at Ephesus, to write a Gospel that would supplement the Synoptic Gospels. Under the influence of the Spirit of God, John thus composed a *spiritual* Gospel. It was not that the others were considered *unspiritual*, but John's emphasis on Christ's words and the deeper meaning of the *signs* do explain why his Gospel especially could be called "spiritual."

External Evidence

Theophilus of Antioch (about A.D. 170) is the first known writer to specifically name John as the author. However, there are earlier allusions to and quotations from the Fourth Gospel in Ignatius, Justin Martyr (probably), Tatian, the Muratorian Canon, and the heretics Basilides and Valentinus.

Irenaeus completes a chain of unbroken discipleship from the Lord Jesus Himself to John, from John to Polycarp, and from Polycarp to himself. This takes us from the dawn of Christianity to near the end of the second century. Irenaeus widely quotes the Gospel as by the apostle, and as already firmly established in the church. From Irenaeus on, the Gospel is very widely attested, including such witnesses as Clement of Alexandria and Tertullian.

Until early in the nineteenth century only an obscure cult called the Alogi rejected Johannine authorship.

The very end of John 21 was probably

†See pp. iii–viii.
††See p. i.

written by the church leaders in Ephesus late in the first century, encouraging the faithful to accept John's Gospel. Verse 24 points back to "the disciple whom Jesus loved" in verse 20 and in chapter 13. This has always been taken as referring to the Apostle John.

It used to be commonly taught by liberals that the Fourth Gospel was written even in the *late* second century. In 1920, however, a fragment of John 18 (Papyrus 52, dated by objective methods as from the *first* half of the second century, and, probably about A.D. 125) was discovered in Egypt. The fact that it was found in a provincial town (not Alexandria, e.g.) confirms that the traditional date of writing in the latter part of the first century is sound, since it would take some time to reach from Ephesus to Upper (southern) Egypt. A similar fragment from John 5, Egerton Papyrus 2, also from the early second century, further confirms a date within John's lifetime.

Internal Evidence

In the late nineteenth century the noted Anglican scholar, Bishop Westcott, argued for Johannine authorship in ever-narrowing concentric circles. This may be condensed as follows: (1) The author was *a Jew* — the style of writing, the vocabulary, the familiarity with Jewish customs and characteristics, and the background of the OT reflected in this Gospel all strongly support this. (2) He was *a Jew who lived in Palestine* (1:28; 2:1, 11; 4:46; 11:18, 54; 21:1, 2). He knew Jerusalem and the temple intimately (5:2; 9:7; 18:1; 19:13, 17, 20, 41; also see 2:14–16; 8:20; 10:22). (3) *He was an eyewitness* of what he narrates. There are numerous details of places, persons, time, manner (4:46; 5:14; 6:59; 12:21; 13:1; 14:5, 8; 18:6; 19:31). (4) *He was an apostle* and shows intimate knowledge of the inner circle of the disciples and of the Lord Himself (6:19, 60, 61; 12:16; 13:22, 28; 16:19). (5) Since the author is precise in naming the other disciples and does *not* name himself, it is presumed that the unnamed person of 13:23; 19:26; 20:2; 21:7, 20 *is the Apostle John*. Three important passages for further consideration of the eyewitness character of the author are 1:14; 19:35 and 21:24.

III. Date

Irenaeus definitely states that John wrote his Gospel from Ephesus, so if he is correct, the earliest possible date would be A.D. 69 or 70, when the apostle arrived there. Since John does not mention the destruction of Jerusalem, it is possible that it had not yet happened, which would give a date before that terrible event.

Some quite liberal scholars choose a date for John as early as 45–66 because of possible links with the Dead Sea Scrolls. This is unusual, since it is generally the conservatives who prefer early dates, and nonconservatives the late dates. In this case early church traditions are on the side of the later date.

The arguments for a date late in the first century are quite strong. Most scholars agree with Irenaeus, Clement of Alexandria, and Jerome that John is the last of the four Gospels to be written, partly because he seems to build on and supplement the Synoptics. The fact that the destruction of Jerusalem is not mentioned in John may be because the book was written fifteen to twenty years *later*, when the shock had worn off. Irenaeus writes that John lived until the reign of Emperor Trajan (who started his reign in 98), and a date not too long before that reign is likely. The references to "the Jews" in this Gospel also suggest the later period, when Jewish opposition to the Christian faith had hardened into persecution.

While no precise dating is possible, the decade between A.D. 85 and 95 is the likeliest time frame.

IV. Background and Themes

John builds his Gospel around seven public miracles, or "signs." Each is designed to show that Jesus is God: (1) Turning the water into wine at the wedding in Cana of Galilee (2:9). (2) Healing the nobleman's son (4:46–54). (3) Healing the crippled man at the pool of Bethesda (5:2–9). (4) Feeding the five thousand (6:1–14). (5) Jesus' walking on the Sea of Galilee to rescue His disciples from the storm (6:16–21). (6) Healing the man blind from birth (9:1–7). (7) Raising Lazarus from the dead (11:1–44). In addition to these seven performed in public, there is an eighth sign performed only for His disciples after the resurrection — the miraculous catch of fish (21:1–14).

Charles R. Erdman says that the Fourth Gospel "has induced more persons to follow Christ, it has inspired more believers to loyal service, it has presented to scholars more difficult problems, than any other book that could be named."

The *chronology* of our Lord's earthly ministry is constructed from this Gospel. From the other three Gospels, the ministry of Christ might appear to have lasted only one year. The references to the annual feasts in John give us a duration of approximately three years for His public ministry. Note these references: The first Feast of Passover (2:12, 13); "a feast" (5:1), possibly the Passover or Purim; second (or third) Feast of Passover (6:4); the Feast of Tabernacles (7:2); the Feast of Dedication (10:22); and the last Feast of Passover (12:1).

John is also precise in his references to time. While the other three writers are often content with approximate references, John mentions such specifics as the seventh hour (4:52); the third day (2:1); two days (11:6); and six days (12:1).

The *style* and *vocabulary* of this Gospel are unique except for the Epistles of John. The sentences are short and simple. They are Hebrew in thought although Greek in language. Often the shorter the sentence the weightier the truth! The vocabulary is the most limited of all the Gospels but the most profound in meaning. Note these important words and how often they occur: Father (118), believe (100), world (78), love (45), witness, testify, etc. (47), life (37), light (24).

One marked feature of John is the occurrence of the number seven and its multiples. The ideas of perfection and completion attach to this number throughout Scripture (see Genesis 2:1–3). In this Gospel the Spirit of God perfects and completes the revelation of God in the Person of Jesus Christ, hence patterns based on the number seven are frequent.

The seven "I am's" in John are familiar: "The Bread of Life" (6:35, 41, 48, 51); "The Light of the World" (8:12; 9:5); "The Door" (10:7, 9); "The Good Shepherd" (10:11, 14); "The Resurrection and the Life" (11:25); "The Way, the Truth, and the Life" (14:6); and "The Vine" (15:1, 5). Not so familiar are the seven occurrences of "I am" without a predicate, that is, the simple statement: 4:26; 6:20; 8:24, 28, 58; 13:19; 18:5, 8. The last one is a double one.

In the sixth chapter, which has to do with the Bread of Life, the Greek word translated "bread" and "loaves" occurs twenty-one times, a multiple of seven. Also in the Bread of Life discourse the expression "bread from heaven" occurs precisely seven times; a similar expression "comes down from heaven" occurs seven times as well.

John's purpose in writing, as we have seen, was that his readers might believe "that Jesus is the Christ, the Son of God, and that believing, [they] may have life in His name" (20:31).

OUTLINE

Commentary†

I. PROLOGUE: THE SON OF GOD'S FIRST ADVENT (1:1–18)

John begins his Gospel by speaking about *the Word* — but he does not explain at first who or what the Word is. A word is a unit of speech by which we express ourselves to others. But John is not writing about *speech* but rather about a *Person*. That Person is the Lord Jesus Christ, the Son of God. God has fully expressed Himself to mankind in the Person of the Lord Jesus. By coming into the world, Christ has perfectly revealed to us what God is like. By dying for us on the cross, He has told us how much God loves us. Thus Christ is God's living Word to man, the expression of God's thoughts.

A. The Word in Eternity and Time (1:1–5)

1:1 In the beginning was the Word. He did not have a beginning Himself, but existed from all eternity. As far as the human mind can go back, the Lord Jesus was there. He never was created. He had no beginning. (A genealogy would be out of place in this Gospel of the Son of God.) **The Word was with God.** He had a separate and distinct personality. He was not just an idea, a thought, or some vague kind of example, but a real Person who lived **with God. The Word was God.** He not only dwelt **with God**, but He Himself **was God**.

The Bible teaches that there is one God and that there are three Persons in the Godhead — the Father, the Son, and the Holy Spirit. All three of these Persons are God. In this verse, two of the Persons of the Godhead are mentioned — God the Father and God the Son. It is the first of many clear statements in this Gospel that *Jesus Christ is God*. It is not enough to say that He is "a god," that He is godlike, or that He is divine. The Bible teaches that He *is* **God**.

1:2 Verse 2 would appear to be a mere repetition of what has been said, but actually it is not. This verse teaches that Christ's personality and deity were without **beginning**. He did not become a person for the first time as the Babe of Bethlehem. Nor did He somehow become a god after His resurrection, as some teach today. He is God from all eternity.

1:3 All things were made through Him. He Himself was not a created being; rather He was the Creator of **all things**. This includes mankind, the animals, the heavenly planets, the angels — **all things** visible and invisible. **Without Him nothing was made that was made.** There can be no possible exception. If a thing was made, He made it. As Creator, He is, of course, superior to anything He has created. All three Persons of the Godhead were involved in the work of creation: "God created the heavens and the earth" (Gen. 1:1). "The Spirit of God was hovering over the face of the waters" (Gen. 1:2). "All things were created through Him (Christ) and for Him" (Col. 1:16b).

1:4 In Him was life. This does not simply mean that He possessed life, but that He was and is the *source* of **life**. The word here includes both physical and spiritual life. When we were born, we received physical life. When we are born again, we receive spiritual life. Both come from Him.

The life was the light of men. The same One who supplied us with life is also **the light of men**. He provides the guidance and direction necessary for man. It is one thing to exist, but quite another to know how to live, to know the true purpose of life, and to know the way to heaven. The same One who gave us **life** is the One who provides us with **light** for the pathway we travel.

There are seven wonderful titles of our Lord Jesus Christ in this opening chapter of the Gospel. He is called (1) the Word (vv. 1, 14); (2) the Light (vv. 5, 7); (3) the Lamb of God (vv. 29, 36); (4) the Son of God (vv. 34, 49); (5) the Christ (Messiah) (v. 41); (6) the King of Israel (v. 49); and (7) the Son of Man (v. 51). The first four titles, each of which is mentioned at least twice, seem to be universal in application. The last three titles, each of which is mentioned only once, had their first application to Israel, God's ancient people.

1:5 The light shines in the darkness. The entrance of sin brought **darkness** to the minds of men. It plunged the world into **darkness** in the sense that men in general neither knew God nor wanted to know Him. Into this **darkness** the Lord Jesus came — a **light** shining in a dark place.

The darkness did not comprehend it. This may mean that the darkness did not understand the Lord Jesus when He came into the world. Men did not realize who He really was, or why He had come. Another meaning, however, is given in the NKJV margin: **the darkness did not** *overcome* **it**. Then the thought would be that man's rejection and enmity did not prevent the true **light** from shining.

B. The Ministry of John the Baptist (1:6–8)

1:6 Verse 6 refers to John the Baptist, not the John who wrote this Gospel. **John** the Baptist was **sent from God** as a forerunner of the Lord Jesus. His mission was to announce the coming of Christ and to tell the people to get ready to receive Him.

1:7 This man came to testify to the fact that Jesus was truly the **Light** of the world, so **that all** people **might** put their trust in Him.

1:8 If John had tried to attract attention to himself, he would have been unfaithful to his appointed task. He pointed men to Jesus and not to himself.

C. The Son of God's First Advent (1:9–18)

1:9 That was the true Light. Other persons down through the ages have claimed to be guides and saviors, but the One to whom John witnessed was the genuine **Light**, the best and the truest **Light**. Another translation of this verse is, "The true Light, which, coming into the world, gives light to every man." In other words, the expression **coming into the world** may describe **the true Light** rather than **every man**. It was by the coming of the **true Light . . . into the world** that every man was given light. This does not mean that every man has received some inward knowledge con-

cerning Christ. Neither does it mean that all men have heard about the Lord Jesus at one time or another. Rather, it means that the **Light** shines on all people, without regard to nationality, race, or color. It also means that by shining on all men, the Lord Jesus has revealed men in their true character. By His coming into the world as the perfect Man, He has shown how imperfect other men are. When a room is in darkness, you do not see the dust on the furniture. But when the light goes on, the room is seen as it actually is. In that same sense, the shining of **the true Light** reveals man as he actually is.

1:10 From the time of His birth in Bethlehem until the day He went back to heaven, **He was in the** very same **world** in which we now live. He had brought the whole world into being and was its rightful Owner. Instead of recognizing Him as the Creator, men thought that He was just another man like themselves. They treated Him like a stranger and an outcast.

1:11[†] **He came to His own** (things or domain, NKJV margin). He was not trespassing on someone else's property. Rather, He was living on a planet which He Himself had made. **His own** (people) **did not receive Him**. In a general sense, this might refer to all mankind, and it is true that most of mankind rejected Him. But in a special sense, the Jewish nation was His chosen, earthly people. When He came into the world, He presented Himself to the Jews as their Messiah, but they would **not receive Him**.

1:12 So now He offers Himself to all mankind again and to those who receive **Him**, He gives **the right** or authority **to become children of God**.

This verse tells us clearly how we can **become children of God**. It is not by good works, not by church membership, not by doing one's best — but by receiving **Him**, by believing **in His Name**.

1:13 To become a child in a physical sense, one must be **born**. So, also, to become a child of God, one must have a second birth. This is known as the new birth, or conversion, or being saved. This verse tells us *three ways* by which the new birth does *not* take place, and the *one way* by which it *does*. First, the three ways by which we are not born again. **Not of blood**. This means that a person does not become a Christian through having Christian parents. Salvation is not passed down from parent to child through the **blood** stream. It is not **of the will of the flesh**. In other words, a person does not have the power in his own **flesh** to produce the new birth. Although he must be willing in order to be saved, yet his own **will** is not enough to save him. Not **of the will of man**. No other man can save a person. A preacher, for instance, may be very anxious to see a certain person born again, but he does not have the power to produce this marvelous birth. How, then, does this birth take place? The answer is found in the words **but of God**. This means simply that the power to produce the new birth does not rest with anything or anyone but **God**.

1:14   The Word became flesh when Jesus was born as a Baby in the manger at Bethlehem. He had always existed as the Son of God with the Father in heaven, but now chose to come into the world in a human body. He **dwelt among us**. It was not just a short appearance, about which there might be some mistake or misunderstanding. God actually came to this earth and lived here as a Man among men. The word "**dwelt**" means "tabernacled" or "pitched His tent." His body was the tent in which He lived among men for thirty-three years.

And we beheld His glory. In the Bible, "glory" often means the bright, shining light which was seen when God was present. It also means the perfection and excellence of God. When the Lord Jesus was here on earth, He veiled His glory in a body of flesh. But there were two ways in which His glory *was* revealed. First, there was His *moral* **glory**. By this, we mean the radiance of His perfect life and character. There was no flaw or blemish in Him. He was perfect in all His ways. Every virtue was manifested in His life in exquisite balance. Then there was the visible outshining of His **glory** which took place on the Mount of Transfiguration (Matt. 17:1, 2). At that time, Peter, James, and John saw His face shining like the sun, and His garments gleaming like bright light. These three disciples were given a preview of the splendor which the Lord Jesus will have when He comes back to the earth

and reigns for a thousand years.

When John said, "**We beheld His glory**", he was referring primarily, no doubt, to the *moral* **glory** of the Lord Jesus. He and the other disciples beheld the wonder of an absolutely perfect life lived on this earth. But it is likely that John also included the incident on the Mount of Transfiguration as well. The **glory** which the disciples saw indicated to them that He was truly the Son of God. Jesus is **the only begotten of the Father**, that is, Christ is God's unique Son. God did not have any other Son like Him. In one sense, all true believers are sons of God. But Jesus is *the* Son of God — in a class all by Himself. As the Son of God, He is equal to God.

The Savior was **full of grace and truth**. On the one hand, full of undeserved kindness for others, He was also completely honest and upright, and He never excused sin or approved evil. To be completely gracious and at the same time completely righteous is something that only God can be.

1:15   John the Baptist **bore witness** that Jesus was the Son of God. Before the Lord entered upon His public ministry, John had been telling men about Him. When Jesus arrived on the scene, John said, in effect, "This is the One I have been describing to you." Jesus came **after** John as far as His birth and ministry were concerned. He was born six months after John and presented Himself to the people of Israel some time after John had been preaching and baptizing. But Jesus was **preferred before** John. He was greater than John; He was worthy of more honor, the simple reason being that **He was before** John. He existed from all eternity — the Son of God.

1:16   All who believe on the Lord Jesus receive supplies of spiritual strength out **of His fullness. His fullness** is so great that He can provide for all Christians in all countries and in all ages. The expression **grace for grace** probably means "grace upon grace" or "abundant grace." Here **grace** means God's gracious favor which He showers on His beloved children.

1:17   John contrasts the OT period and the NT era. **The law** that was **given through Moses** was not a display of grace. It commanded men to obey and condemned them to death if they failed to do so. It told men what was right but did not give them the power to do it. It was given to show men that they were sinners, but it could not save them from their sins. **But grace and truth came through Jesus Christ**. He did not come to judge the world but to save those who were unworthy, who could not save themselves, and who were His enemies. That is **grace** — heaven's Best for earth's worst.

Not only did **grace** come **through Jesus Christ**, but **truth** came by Him as well. He said of Himself, "I am . . . the truth." He was absolutely honest and faithful in all His words and works. He did not show grace at the expense of **truth**. Although He loved sinners, He did not love their sins. He realized that the wages of sin is death. And so He Himself died to pay the penalty of death that we deserved, in order that He might show undeserved kindness to us in saving our souls and giving us a home in heaven.

1:18 No one has seen God at any time. God is Spirit and therefore invisible. He does not have a body. Although He did appear to men in the OT in visible form as an Angel or as a Man, these appearances did not reveal what God is really like. They were merely temporary appearances by which He chose to speak to His people. The Lord Jesus is God's **only begotten Son**;[1] He is God's unique Son; there is no other son like Him. He always occupies a place of special nearness to God the Father. Even when He was here on earth, Jesus was still **in the bosom of the Father**. He was one with God and equal with God. This blessed One has fully revealed to men what God is like. When men saw Jesus, they saw God. They heard God speak. They felt God's love and tenderness. God's thoughts and attitudes toward mankind have been fully **declared** by Christ.

II. THE SON OF GOD'S FIRST YEAR OF MINISTRY (1:19 – 4:54)[†]

A. The Testimony of John the Baptist (1:19–34)

1:19 When news reached **Jerusalem** that a man named **John** was telling the nation to repent because the Messiah was coming, **the Jews sent** a committee of **priests and Levites** to find out who this was. The **priests** were those who carried on the important services in the temple, while the **Levites** were servants who attended to common duties there. **"Who are you?"** they asked. "Are you the long-awaited Messiah?"

1:20 Other men might have seized this opportunity for fame by claiming to be the Christ. But John was a faithful witness. His testimony was that he was **not the Christ** (the Messiah).

1:21, 22 The Jews expected Elijah to return to the earth prior to the coming of Christ (Mal. 4:5). So they reasoned that if John was not the Messiah, then perhaps he was **Elijah**. But John assured them that he was not. In Deuteronomy 18:15, Moses had said, "The LORD your God will raise up for you a Prophet like me from your midst, from your brethren. Him you shall hear." The Jews remembered this prediction and thought that John might be **the Prophet** mentioned by Moses. But again John said that it was not so. The delegation would have been embarrassed to go back to Jerusalem without a definite **answer**, and so they asked John for a statement as to who he was.

1:23 He said, "I am 'The voice of one crying in the wilderness.' " In answer to their query, the Baptist quoted from Isaiah 40:3, where it was prophesied that a forerunner would appear to announce the coming of Christ. In other words, John stated that he was the forerunner who was predicted. He was **the voice**, and Israel was **the wilderness**. Because of their sin and departure from God, the people had become dry and barren, like a desert. John spoke of himself simply as a **voice**. He did not pose as a great man to be praised and admired, but as a **voice** — not to be seen, but only to be heard. John was **the voice** but Christ was the Word. The word needs a voice to make it known and the voice is of no value without a word. The Word is infinitely greater than the voice but it can be our privilege, too, to be a voice for Him.

John's message was, **"Make straight the way of the LORD."** In other words, "The Messiah is coming. Remove everything in your life that would hinder you from receiving Him. Repent of your sins, so that He can come and reign over you as the King of Israel."

1:24, 25   The Pharisees formed a strict sect of the Jews who prided themselves on their superior knowledge of the law and on their efforts to carry out the most minute details of the instructions of the OT. Actually, many of them were hypocrites who tried to appear religious but who lived very sinful lives. They wanted to know what authority John had for baptizing if he was not one of the important persons they named.

1:26, 27   "I baptize with water," said **John**. He did not want anyone to think that *he* was important. His task was simply to prepare men for Christ. Whenever his hearers repented of their sins, he baptized them in water as an outward symbol of their inward change. **"There stands One among you, whom you do not know,"** John continued, referring, of course, to Jesus. The Pharisees did not recognize Him as the long looked-for Messiah. In effect John was saying to the Pharisees, "Do not think of me as a great man. The **One** you should be paying attention to is the Lord Jesus; yet **you do not know** who He really is." He is the One who is worthy. He came after John the Baptist, yet He deserves all the praise and preeminence. It was the duty of a slave or servant to untie his master's sandals. But John did **not** consider himself **worthy** to perform such a humble, lowly service for Christ.

1:28   The exact location of **Bethabara** (or **Bethany**, NKJV margin), is not known. But we do know that it was a place on the east side of **the Jordan** River. If we accept the reading *Bethany*, it cannot be the Bethany near Jerusalem.

1:29   The next day after the visit of the Pharisees from Jerusalem, **John** looked up and **saw Jesus coming toward him**. In the thrill and excitement of that moment, he cried out, **"Behold! The Lamb of God** who bears **the sin of the world!"** The lamb was a sacrificial animal among the Jews. God had taught His chosen people to slay a lamb and to sprinkle its blood as a sacrifice. The lamb was killed as a substitute and its blood shed so that sins might be forgiven.

However, the blood of the lambs slain during the OT period did not put away sin. Those lambs were pictures or types, pointing forward to the fact that God would one day provide a **Lamb** who would actually *take away* the sin. All down through the years, godly Jews had waited for the coming of this **Lamb**. Now at last the time had come, and John the Baptist triumphantly announced the arrival of the true **Lamb of God**.

When he said that Jesus bears **the sin of the world**, he did not mean that everyone's sins are therefore forgiven. The death of Christ was great enough in value to pay for the sins of the whole **world**, but only those sinners who receive the Lord Jesus as Savior are forgiven.

J. C. Jones points out that this verse sets forth the excellency of the Christian atonement:

1. It excels in the NATURE of the victim. Whereas the sacrifices of Judaism were irrational lambs, the sacrifice of Christianity is the Lamb of God.

2. It excels in the EFFICACY of the work. Whereas the sacrifices of Judaism only brought sin to remembrance every year, the sacrifice of Christianity took sin away. "He put away sin by the sacrifice of Himself."

3. It excels in the SCOPE of its operation. Whereas the Jewish sacrifices were intended for the benefit of one nation only, the sacrifice of Christianity is intended for all nations; "it takes away the sin of the world."[2]

1:30, 31   John never grew weary of reminding people that he was only preparing the way for Someone greater than himself who was coming. Jesus was greater than John to the same extent that God is greater than man. John was born a few months before Jesus, but Jesus had existed from all eternity. When John said, **"I did not know Him,"** he did not necessarily mean that he had never seen Him before.

Since they were cousins, it is probable that John and Jesus were well acquainted. But John had not recognized his Cousin as being the Messiah until the time of His baptism. John's mission was to prepare the way of the Lord, and then to point Him out **to** the people of **Israel** when He appeared. It was for this reason that John baptized people in water — to prepare them for the coming of Christ. It was not for the purpose of attracting disciples to himself.

1:32 The reference here was to the time John baptized Jesus in the Jordan. After the Lord went up out of the water, **the Spirit** of God descended **like a dove** and **remained upon Him** (cf. Matt. 3:16). The writer goes on to explain the meaning of this.

1:33 God had revealed to John that the Messiah was coming and that when He came, **the Spirit** would descend **upon** Him and stay **on Him**. Therefore, when this happened to Jesus, John realized that this was the One who would baptize **with the Holy Spirit. The Holy Spirit** is a Person, one of the three Persons in the Godhead. He is equal with God the Father and God the Son.

Whereas John baptized **with water**, Jesus would baptize **with the Holy Spirit**. The baptism **with the Holy Spirit** took place on the day of Pentecost (Acts 1:5; 2:4, 38). At that time, **the Holy Spirit** came down from heaven to dwell in the body of every believer and also to make each believer a member of the church, the Body of Christ (1 Cor. 12:13).

1:34 On the basis of what he saw at the baptism of Jesus, John **testified** positively to the fact that Jesus of Nazareth was **the Son of God** who was foretold as coming into the world. When John said that Christ was **the Son of God**, he meant that He was God the Son.

B. The Call of Andrew, John, and Peter (1:35–42)

1:35, 36 **The next day** referred to here is the third day that has been mentioned. **John** was **with two of his** own **disciples**. These men had heard John preach and believed what he said. But as yet they had not met the Lord Jesus. Now John bore public witness to the Lord. On the previous day, he had spoken of His Person (the Lamb of God) and His work (who takes away the sin of the world). Now he simply draws attention to His Person. His message was short, simple, selfless, and all about the Savior.

1:37 By his faithful preaching, John lost **two disciples**, but he was glad to see them following **Jesus**. So we should be more anxious for our friends to follow

the Lord than for them to think highly of us.

1:38 The Savior is always interested in those who follow Him. Here He showed His interest by turning to the two disciples and asking, **"What do you seek?"** He knew the answer to the question; He knew all things. But He wanted them to express their desire in words. Their answer, **"Rabbi, where are You staying?"** showed that they wanted to be with the Lord and to get to know Him better. They were not satisfied merely to meet Him. They longed to have fellowship with Him. **Rabbi** is the Hebrew word for **Teacher** (literally "my great one").

1:39 **He said to them, "Come and see."** No one with a genuine desire to learn more of the Savior is ever turned away. Jesus invited the two to the place where He was staying at the time — probably a very poor dwelling, compared to modern homes.

They came and saw where He was staying, and remained with Him that day (now it was about the tenth hour). Never had these men been so honored. They spent that night in the same home as the Creator of the universe. They were among the very first members of the Jewish nation to recognize the Messiah.

The tenth hour is either 10 a.m. or 4 p.m. The earlier time (Roman) is generally preferred.

1:40 **One of the two** disciples **was Andrew. Andrew** is not as well known today as his **brother, Simon Peter**, but it is interesting to notice that he was the first of the two to meet Jesus.

The name of the other was not given to us, but almost all Bible scholars assume that it was John — the one who wrote this Gospel. They reason that humility kept him from mentioning his own name.

1:41 When a person finds Jesus, he usually wants his relatives to meet Him too. Salvation is too good to keep to oneself. So Andrew went quickly **to his own brother Simon** with the thrilling news, **"We have found the Messiah!"** What an astounding announcement this was! For at least four thousand years, men had waited for the promised Christ, God's Anointed One. Now **Simon** hears from the lips of his own brother the startling news that **the Messiah** was nearby. Truly they were living where history was being made. How simple Andrew's message was. It was only five words — **"We have found the Messiah"** — yet God used it to win Peter. This teaches us that we do not have to be great preachers or clever speakers. We need only to tell men about the Lord Jesus in simple words, and God will take care of the rest.

1:42 Andrew **brought** his brother to the right place and to the right Person. He did not bring him to the church, the creed, or the clergyman. **He brought him to Jesus.** What an important act that was! Because of Andrew's interest, Simon later became a great fisher of men, and one of the leading apostles of the Lord. Simon has received more publicity than his brother, but Andrew will doubtless share Peter's reward because it was Andrew who brought him to Jesus. The Lord knew Simon's name without being told. He also knew that Simon had an unstable character. And finally, He knew that Simon's character would be changed, so that he would be firm as a rock. How did Jesus know all this? Because He was and is God.

Simon's name did change to **Cephas** (Aramaic for **stone**), and he did become a man of strong character, especially after the Ascension of the Lord and the Descent of the Holy Spirit.

C. The Call of Philip and Nathanael (1:43–51)

1:43 This is now the fourth **day** we have read about in this chapter. Bosch points out that on the first day we see *John only* (vv.15–28); on the second we see *John and Jesus* (vv. 29–34); on the third we see *Jesus and John* (vv. 35–42); and on the fourth day we see *Jesus only* (vv. 43–51). The Lord walked northward into the region known as **Galilee**. There **He found Philip** and invited him to be a follower. **"Follow Me!"** These are great words because of the One who spoke them and great because of the privilege they offered. The Savior is still issuing this simple, yet sublime, invitation to all men everywhere.

1:44 **Bethsaida** was a **city** on the shores of the Sea of Galilee. Few cities in the world have ever been so honored. The Lord performed some of His mighty miracles there (Luke 10:13). It was the home of **Philip, Andrew, and Peter**. Yet it rejected the Savior, and as a result it was destroyed so completely that now we cannot tell the exact spot where it was located.

1:45 **Philip** wanted to share his new-found joy with someone else, so he went and **found Nathanael**. New converts are the best soul-winners. His message was simple and to the point. He told Nathanael that he had **found** the Messiah who had been foretold by **Moses** and **the prophets — Jesus of Nazareth**. Actually his message was not entirely accurate. He described Jesus as being **the son of Joseph**. Jesus, of course, was born of the Virgin Mary and had no human father. **Joseph** adopted Jesus and thus became his legal father, though not His real father. James S. Stewart comments:

> It never was Christ's way to demand a full-fledged faith for a beginning. It never was his way to hold men back from discipleship on the ground of an incomplete creed. And quite certainly that is not his way today. He puts himself alongside his brethren. He bids them attach themselves to him at any point they can. He takes them with the faith that they can offer him. He is content with that as a beginning; and from that he leads his friends on, as he led the first group on, step by step, to the inmost secret of who he is and to the full glory of discipleship.[3]

1:46 **Nathanael** had problems. **Nazareth** was a despised city of Galilee. It seemed impossible to him that the Messiah would live in such a poor neighborhood. And so he voiced the question that was in his mind. **Philip** did not argue. He felt that the best way to meet objections was to introduce men directly to the Lord Jesus — a valuable lesson for all who are seeking to win others to Christ. Don't argue. Don't engage in prolonged discussions. Just bid men to **come and see**.

1:47 Verse 47 shows that **Jesus** knew all things. Without any previous acquaintance with **Nathanael**, He declared him to be **an Israelite indeed, in whom** there was **no** trickery or **deceit**. Jacob had gained a reputation for using business methods that were not entirely honest, but Nathanael was an "Israel"-ite in whom there was no "Jacob."

1:48 **Nathanael** was obviously surprised that a total Stranger should speak to him as if He had known him previously. Apparently he had been completely concealed when he was sitting **under the fig tree**. Doubtless the overhanging branches of the trees and the surrounding foliage hid him from view. But Jesus **saw** him, even though he was so hidden.

1:49 Perhaps it was the power of the Lord Jesus to see him when he was shut off from human view that convinced **Nathanael**, or this knowledge was perhaps given to him in a supernatural way. In any event, he now knew that Jesus was **the Son of God** and **the King of Israel**.

1:50 The Lord had given Nathanael two proofs that He was the Messiah. He had described his character, and He had seen Nathanael when no other eyes could have seen him. These two proofs were sufficient for Nathanael, and he believed. But now the Lord Jesus promised that he would **see greater** proofs **than these**.

1:51 Whenever Jesus introduced a saying with the words **Most assuredly** (literally "Amen, amen"[4]), He was always about to say something very important. Here He gave Nathanael a picture of the time in the future when He would come back to reign over all the earth. The world will then know that the carpenter's Son who lived in despised Nazareth was truly the Son of God and Israel's King. In that day, **heaven** will **open**. The favor of God will rest upon the King as He reigns, with Jerusalem as His capital.

It is likely that Nathanael had been meditating on the story of Jacob's ladder (Gen. 28:12). That ladder, with its ascending and descending angels, is a picture of the Lord Jesus Christ Himself, the only access to heaven. **The angels of God** will ascend and descend **upon the Son of Man. Angels** are servants **of God**, traveling like flames of fire on His errands. When Jesus reigns as King, these **angels** will travel back and forth between heaven and earth, fulfilling His will.

Jesus was saying to Nathanael that he

had seen only very minor demonstrations of His Messiahship. In the future Reign of Christ, he would see the Lord Jesus fully revealed as God's anointed Son. Then all mankind would know that Someone good did come out of Nazareth.

D. The First Sign: Water Changed to Wine (2:1–11)

2:1 **The third day** doubtless refers to **the third day** of the Lord's stay in **Galilee**. In 1:43 the Savior went into that area. We do not know exactly where **Cana** was situated, but we infer from verse 12 of this chapter that it was near Capernaum and on higher ground.

There was a wedding in Cana on this particular day, **and the mother of Jesus was there**. It is interesting to notice that Mary is spoken of as **the mother of Jesus**. The Savior was not famous because He was the Son of the Virgin Mary, but she was well-known because she was the mother of our Lord. The Scriptures always give the pre-eminent place to Christ and not to Mary.

2:2 **Jesus and His disciples were invited to the wedding**. It was a wise decision on the part of those who arranged the marriage to invite Christ. So it is still a wise decision when people today invite the Lord to their marriage. In order to do this, of course, both bride and groom must be true believers in the Lord Jesus. Then, too, they must give their lives to the Savior and determine that their home will be a place where He loves to be.

2:3 The supply of **wine** had failed. When **the mother of Jesus** realized what had happened, she presented the problem to her Son. She knew that He could perform a miracle in order to provide wine, and perhaps she wanted her Son to reveal Himself to the assembled guests as the Son of God. Wine in the Scriptures often speaks of joy. When Mary said, **"They have no wine,"** she gave a very accurate description of men and women who have never been saved. There is no real, lasting joy for the unbeliever.

2:4 The reply of the Lord to His mother seems cold and distant. But it is not as strong a rebuke as would seem to us. The word **woman** used here is a title of respect, similar to our word "lady." When the Lord asked, **"Woman, what does your concern have to do with Me?"** He indicated that in the performance of His divine mission, He was not subject to instructions from His mother, but acted entirely in obedience to the will of His Father in heaven. Mary had wanted to see Jesus glorified, but He must remind her that the time for this had **not yet come**. Before He would appear to the world as the all-conquering Christ, He must first ascend the altar of sacrifice, and this He did at the cross of Calvary.

Williams points out the following:

The expression "what does your concern have to do with me" occurs several times in the Bible. It means, "What have we in common?" The answer is, "Nothing." David uses it twice with respect to his cousins, the sons of Zeruiah. How impossible it was for them to have anything in common with him in the spiritual life! Elisha uses it in 2 Kings 3 to express how deep was the gulf between him and Jehoram the son of Ahab. Three times the demons, by using the same expression, reveal how Satan has nothing in common with Christ, or Christ with Satan. And lastly the Lord used it to the Virgin Mary to show how impassable is the gulf between His sinless Deity and her sinful humanity, and that only One Voice had authority for His ear.[5]

2:5 Mary understood the meaning of His words, and so she instructed the servants to do **whatever He** commanded them. Her words are important ones for every one of us. Notice that she did not direct men to obey *her*, or any other human being. She pointed them to the Lord Jesus and told them that He was the One who should be obeyed. The teachings of the Lord Jesus are given to us in the pages of the NT. As we read this precious book, we should remember the last recorded words of Mary, **"Whatever He says to you, do it."**

2:6 In the place where the wedding was being held, there were **six** large **stone** vessels, **containing twenty or thirty gallons** of water **apiece**. This water was used by the Jewish people for cleansing themselves from defilement. For instance, if a Jew touched a dead body, he was considered unclean until

he went through a certain ceremony of cleansing.

2:7 **Jesus** gave instructions to **fill the waterpots with water**. This the servants did immediately. The Lord used the facilities that were available when He was about to perform a miracle. He allowed men to provide **the waterpots**, and to **fill** them **with water**, but then He did what no man could ever do — changed the water into wine! It was the servants and not the disciples who **filled** the vessels with water. In this way, the Lord avoided the possibility of any charge of trickery. Also, the waterpots were filled **to the brim**, so that no one could say that wine had been added to the water.

2:8 The miracle had now taken place. The Lord instructed the servants to **draw some out** from the vessels **and take** the contents **to the master of the feast**. From this it is clear that the miracle had been instantaneous. The water did not become wine over a period of time, but in a second or so. As someone put it poetically, "The unconscious waters saw their God and blushed."

2:9 **The master of the feast** was the one who had charge of arranging the tables and the food. **When** he **had tasted** it, he realized that something unusual had happened. He **did not know where** the wine **came from**, but he knew that it was of very high quality so he immediately **called the bridegroom**.

What should be the attitude of Christians toward wine today? Wine is sometimes prescribed for medicinal purposes, and this is entirely in accordance with the teaching of the NT (1 Tim. 5:23). However, because of the terrible abuses which have come about in connection with the intemperate use of wine, most Christians will want to avoid it altogether. Anyone can become addicted to strong drink. The way to avert this danger is to leave alcoholic beverages alone. Again, one must always consider the effect of his actions on others. In our culture it would be a bad testimony on the part of a Christian if an unsaved person should see him drinking wine, and for this reason he should abstain.

2:10 The ruler of the feast draws attention to the very marked difference between the way the Lord Jesus acts and the way men commonly act. The usual practice at a wedding was to serve the best **wine** first when men could best detect and enjoy its flavor. Later on, having eaten and drunk, they would not be as aware of the quality of their beverage. At this particular wedding, the best wine came last. There is a spiritual meaning in this for us. The world commonly offers people the best it has to offer at the outset. It holds out its most attractive offers to young people. Then when they have wasted their lives in empty pleasure, the world has nothing but dregs for a person's old age. The Christian life is the very opposite. It gets better all the time. Christ keeps the best wine until the last. The feast follows the fast.

This portion of Scripture has a very direct application to the Jewish nation. There was no true joy in Judaism at this time. The people were going through a dreary round of rituals and ceremonies, but life for them was tasteless. They were strangers to divine joy. The Lord Jesus was seeking to teach them to put their faith in Him. He would turn their drab existence into fullness of joy. The water of Jewish ritual and ceremony could be turned into the wine of joyful reality in Christ.

2:11 The statement that **this** was the **beginning of signs** rules out the silly miracles attributed to our Lord in His childhood. These are found in such pseudo-gospels as "The Gospel of Peter." They attribute to our Lord miracles performed allegedly when He was a child and are a little short of blasphemous in character. Foreseeing this, the Holy Spirit safeguarded this period of our Lord's life and His character by this little additional note.

Changing water into wine was a sign, that is, a miracle with a meaning. It was a superhuman act with a spiritual meaning. These miracles also were designed to show that Jesus was indeed the Christ of God. By performing this sign, He **manifested His glory**. He revealed to men that He was indeed God — manifest in the flesh. **His disciples believed in Him**. Of course, in one sense they had believed in Him previously, but now their faith was strengthened, and they

trusted Him more fully. Cynddylan Jones points out:

> Moses' first miracle was to turn water into blood; there was a severe destructive element in it. But Christ's first miracle was to turn water into wine; there was a soothing, solacing element in it.[6]

E. The Son of God Cleanses His Father's House (2:12–17)

2:12 The Savior now left Cana and **went down to Capernaum** with **His mother, His brothers, and His disciples**. They only stayed in Capernaum a few **days**. Soon after, the Lord went up to Jerusalem.

2:13 Beginning at this point, we have the Lord's first witness to the city of **Jerusalem**. This phase of His ministry continues to chapter 3, verse 21. He both began and ended His public ministry by cleansing the temple at **Passover** time (cf. Matt. 21:12, 13; Mark 11:15–18; Luke 19:405, 46). The Passover was an annual feast commemorating the time when the children of Israel were delivered from slavery in Egypt and were led through the Red Sea to the wilderness, and then to the promised land. The first celebration of the Passover is recorded in Exodus 12. Being a devout Jew, the Lord Jesus **went up to Jerusalem** for this important day on the Jewish calendar.

2:14 Coming to **the temple, He found** that it had become a market place. **Oxen and sheep and doves** were sold there, and **the moneychangers** were carrying on their **business** as well. The animals and birds were sold to the worshipers for use as sacrifices. **The moneychangers** took the money of those who came from foreign countries and changed it into the money of Jerusalem so that the pilgrims could pay the tax to the temple. It is known that these moneychangers often took unfair advantage of those who traveled from great distances.

2:15 The **whip** which the Lord made was probably a small lash made **of cords**. It is not recorded that He actually used it on anyone. Instead, it is probable that it was merely a symbol of authority which He held in His hand. Waving the whip before Him, He **drove** the merchants **out of the temple** and **overturned the tables** of the moneychangers.

2:16 The law permitted the poor to offer a pair of doves, since they could not afford the more expensive animals. To **those who sold doves**, the Lord issued a command **to take these things away**. It was not fitting that they should **make** His **Father's house a house of merchandise**. In all ages, God has warned His people against using religious services as a means of getting rich. There was nothing cruel or unjust in any of these actions. Rather, they were simply an indication of His holiness and righteousness.

2:17 When **His disciples** saw what was happening, they were reminded of Psalm 69:9 where it was predicted that when the Messiah came, He would be utterly consumed with a **zeal for** the things of God. Now they saw Jesus manifesting an intense determination that the worship of God should be pure, and they realized that this was the One of whom the Psalmist had spoken.

We should remember that the Christian's body is the temple of the Holy Spirit. Just as the Lord Jesus was anxious that the temple in Jerusalem be kept pure, so we must be careful that our bodies be turned over to the Lord for continual cleansing.

F. Jesus Predicts His Death and Resurrection (2:18–22)

2:18 It seems that the Jewish people were always seeking some sign or miracle. They said in effect, "If You perform some great, mighty work for us, then we will believe." However, the Lord Jesus performed one miracle after another, and yet their hearts were closed to Him. In verse 18 they questioned His authority to cast businessmen out of the temple. They demanded that He should perform some **sign** to support His claim of being the Messiah.

2:19 In answer, the Lord Jesus made an amazing statement concerning His death and resurrection. He told them that they would **destroy** His sanctuary, but **in three days** He would **raise it up**. The deity of Christ is again seen in this verse. Only God could say, **"In three days I will raise it up."**

2:20 **The Jews** did not understand Him. They were more interested in material things than in spiritual truth. The only temple they could think about was Herod's temple which was then standing in Jerusalem. **It** had **taken forty-six years to build this temple**, and they could not see how any man could possibly rebuild it **in three days**.

2:21 The Lord Jesus, however, **was speaking** about **His** own **body**, which was the sanctuary in which all the fullness of the Godhead dwelt. Just as these Jews had defiled the temple in Jerusalem, so they would put Him to death in a few short years.

2:22 Later on, after the Lord Jesus had been crucified and **had risen from the dead, His disciples remembered that He had** promised to rise again in three days. With such a marvelous fulfillment of prophecy before their eyes, **they believed the Scripture, and the word which Jesus had said**.

We often come across truths which are difficult to understand. But we learn here that we should treasure the Word of God in our hearts. Some day later the Lord will make it plain to us, even though we do not understand it now. When it says that **they believed the Scripture**, it means that they believed the OT predictions concerning the resurrection of the Messiah.

G. Many Profess to Believe in Christ (2:23–25)

2:23 As a result **of the signs** which Jesus performed **in Jerusalem at the Passover, many believed in His name**. This does not necessarily mean that they actually committed their lives to Him in simple trust; rather, they professed to accept Him. There was no reality to their action; it was merely an outward display of following Jesus. It was similar to the condition which we have in the world where many people claim to be Christians who have never truly been born again through faith in the Lord Jesus Christ.

2:24 Although many believed in Him, yet **Jesus did not** believe (same word in Greek) in **them**. That is, He **did not commit Himself to them**. He realized that they were coming to Him out of curiosity. They were looking for something sensational and spectacular. **He**

knew all men — their thoughts and their motives. He knew why they acted the way they did. He knew whether their faith was real or only an imitation.

2:25 No one knew the heart of man better than the Lord Himself. **He had no need that anyone should** teach or enlighten Him on this subject. He had full knowledge of **what was in man** and why man behaved as he did.

H. Jesus Teaches Nicodemus About the New Birth (3:1–21)

3:1 The story of **Nicodemus** contrasts with what had just gone before. Many of the Jews in Jerusalem professed to believe on the Lord, but He knew their faith was not genuine. Nicodemus was an exception. The Lord recognized in him an earnest desire to know the truth. Verse 1 should begin with a connective: *"But*[7] **there was a man of the Pharisees, named Nicodemus, a ruler of the Jews."**

Nicodemus was recognized as a teacher among his people. Perhaps he came to the Lord for instruction, so that he might return to the Jews with this additional learning.

3:2 The Bible does not say *why* Nicodemus **came to Jesus by night**. The most obvious explanation is that he would have been embarrassed to be seen going to Jesus, since the Lord had by no means been accepted by the majority of the Jewish people. However, he did come to Jesus. Nicodemus acknowledged the Lord to be **a teacher** sent by **God**, since no one could perform such miracles without the direct help of **God**. In spite of all his learning, Nicodemus did not recognize the Lord as God manifest in the flesh. He was like so many today who say that Jesus was a great man, a wonderful teacher, an outstanding example. All of these statements fall very far short of the full truth. Jesus *was* and *is* God.

3:3 At first sight, the answer of the Lord Jesus does not seem to be connected with what Nicodemus had just said. Our Lord is saying, "Nicodemus, you have come to Me for teaching, but what you really need is to be **born again**. That is where you must begin. You must be born from above. Otherwise, you can never **see the kingdom of God**."

The Lord introduced these wonderful words with the expression: **"Most assuredly"** (literally *Amen, amen*). These words alert us to the fact that important truth is being given.

As a Jew, Nicodemus had been looking for a Messiah to come and free Israel from the bondage of Rome. The Roman Empire was then in control of the world, and the Jews were subject to its laws and government. Nicodemus longed for the time when the Messiah would set up His kingdom on earth, when the Jewish people would be chief among the nations, and when all their enemies would be destroyed. Now the Lord informed Nicodemus that in order to enter this kingdom, a man must be **born again**. Just as the first birth is necessary for physical life, so a second birth is necessary for divine life. (The expression **born again** may also mean "born from above.") In other words, Christ's kingdom can only be entered by those whose lives have been changed. Since His reign will be a righteous one, His subjects must be righteous also. He could not reign over people who were going on in their sins.

3:4 Here again we see how difficult it was for men to understand the words of the Lord Jesus. **Nicodemus** insisted on taking everything literally. He could not understand how a grown-up could be **born** again. He pondered the physical impossibility of a man entering **his mother's womb** again in order to **be born**.

Nicodemus illustrates that "the natural man does not receive the things of the Spirit of God, for they are foolishness to him; nor can he know them, because they are spiritually discerned" (1 Cor. 2:14).

3:5 In further explanation, Jesus told Nicodemus that he must be **born of water and the Spirit**. Otherwise, he could never **enter the kingdom of God**.

What did Jesus mean? Many insist that *literal* water is intended, and that the Lord Jesus spoke of the necessity of baptism for salvation. However, such a teaching is contrary to the rest of the Bible. Throughout the Word of God we read that salvation is by faith in the Lord Jesus Christ alone. Baptism is intended for those who have already been saved, but not as a means of salvation.

Some suggest that **water** in this verse refers to the Word of God. In Ephesians 5:25, 26 water is closely associated with the Word of God. Also, in 1 Peter 1:23 and James 1:18, the new birth is said to take place through the Word of God. It is quite possible, therefore, that water in this verse does refer to the Bible. We know that there can be no salvation apart from the Scriptures. It is the message contained in the Word of God that must be appropriated by the sinner before there can ever be the new birth.

But **water** may also refer to the Holy Spirit. In John 7:38, 39 the Lord Jesus spoke of rivers of living water, and we are distinctly told that when He used the word *water* He was speaking of the Holy Spirit. If water means the Spirit in chapter 7, why can it not have the same meaning in chapter 3?

However, there seems to be a difficulty if this interpretation is accepted. Jesus says, **"Unless one is born of water and the Spirit, he cannot enter the kingdom of God."** If **water** is taken to *mean* **the Spirit**, then it would appear that the Spirit is mentioned twice in this verse. But the word translated "and" could just as correctly have been translated "even." Thus, the verse would read: **Unless one is born of water,** *even* **the Spirit, he cannot enter the kingdom of God.** We believe that this is the correct meaning of the verse. Physical birth is not enough.[8] There must also be a spiritual birth if one is to **enter the kingdom of God**. This spiritual birth is produced by the Holy Spirit of God when a person believes on the Lord Jesus Christ. This interpretation is supported by the fact that the expression "born of the Spirit" is found twice in the verses to follow (vv. 6, 8).

3:6 Even if Nicodemus could in some way have entered his mother's womb a second time and been born a second time, that would not have corrected the evil nature in him. The expression **that which is born of the flesh is flesh** means that children born of human parents are born in sin and are hopeless and helpless as far as saving themselves is concerned. On the other hand, **that which is born of the Spirit is spirit**. A spiritual birth takes place when a person trusts in the Lord Jesus.

When a person is born again through the Spirit, he receives a new nature, and is made fit for the kingdom of God.

3:7 Nicodemus was **not** to **marvel** at the teachings of the Lord Jesus. He must realize that one **must be born again** and understand the complete inability of human nature to remedy its own fallen condition. He must realize that in order to be a subject of God's kingdom, a man must be holy, pure, and spiritual.

3:8 As He so often did, the Lord Jesus used nature to illustrate spiritual truth. He reminded Nicodemus that **the wind blows where it wishes**, and a person can **hear the sound of it, but cannot tell where it comes from and where it goes**. The new birth is very much like **the wind**. First of all, it takes place according to the will of God. It is not a power which man holds in his own control. Secondly, the new birth is invisible. You cannot see it taking place, but you can see the results of it in a person's life. When a man has been saved, a change comes over him. The evil things which he formerly loved, he now hates. The things of God which he formerly despised, these things are now the very things which he loves. Just as no one can fully understand the wind, so the new birth is a miraculous work of the Spirit of God which man is not able to comprehend fully. Moreover, the new birth, like **the wind**, is unpredictable. It is not possible to state just when and **where** it will take place.

3:9 Again, **Nicodemus** illustrated the inability of the natural mind to enter into divine things. Doubtless he was still trying to think of the new birth as a natural or physical event, rather than as a spiritual one. And so he asked the Lord Jesus: **"How can these things be?"**

3:10 Jesus **answered** that as **the teacher of Israel**, Nicodemus should have understood **these things**. The OT Scriptures clearly taught that when the Messiah came back to the earth to set up His kingdom, He would first judge His enemies and destroy all things that offend. Only those who had confessed and forsaken their sins would enter the kingdom.

3:11 The Lord Jesus then underlined the infallibility of His teaching, and yet man's unbelief concerning it. From all eternity, He had known the truthfulness of this and had only taught **what** He knew and had **seen**. But Nicodemus and most of the Jews of his day refused to believe His testimony.

3:12 What were the **earthly things** to which the Lord referred in this verse? It was His **earthly** kingdom. As a student of the OT, Nicodemus knew that one day the Messiah would come and set up a literal kingdom here on earth with Jerusalem as His capital. What Nicodemus failed to understand was that in order to enter this kingdom, there must be a new birth. What then were the **heavenly things** to which the Lord referred? They are the truths which are explained in the following verses — the wonderful way by which a person receives this new birth.

3:13 Only one person was qualified to speak about heavenly things, since He was the only One **who** was **in heaven**. The Lord Jesus was not merely a human teacher sent from God, but He was One who lived with God the Father from all eternity, and **came down** into the world. When He said that **no one has ascended to heaven**, He did not mean that OT saints such as Enoch and Elijah had not gone to heaven, but that they had been *taken up* whereas He **ascended to heaven** by His own power. Another explanation is that no human being had access to the presence of God continually in the way which He had. He could ascend to God's dwelling place in a unique way because He had descended out of heaven to this earth. Even as the Lord Jesus stood on earth, speaking with Nicodemus, He said that He was **in heaven**. How could this be? Here is a statement of the fact that, as God, the Lord was in all places at one and the same time. This is what we mean when we say that He is omnipresent. While some modern translations omit the words **who is in heaven**, they are widely supported in the manuscripts and belong to the text.

3:14 The Lord Jesus was now about to unfold heavenly truth to Nicodemus. How can the new birth take place? The penalty of man's sins must be met. People cannot go to heaven in their sins. Just **as Moses lifted up the serpent** of brass on a pole **in the wilderness** when all the children of Israel had been bitten by snakes, **so must the Son of Man be lifted up**. (Read Numbers 21:4–9.) As they wandered through the wilderness to the promised land, the children of Israel became discouraged and impatient. They complained against the Lord. To punish them, the Lord sent fiery serpents among them, and many people died. When the survivors cried to the Lord in repentance, the Lord told Moses to make **a serpent** of brass and put it on a pole. The bitten Israelite who looked to the serpent was miraculously healed.

Jesus quoted this OT incident to illustrate how the new birth takes place. Men and women have been bitten by the viper of sin and are condemned to eternal death. The serpent of brass was a type or picture of the Lord Jesus. Brass, in the Bible, speaks of judgment. The Lord Jesus was sinless and should never have been punished, but He took our place and bore the judgment which we deserved. The pole speaks of the cross of Calvary on which the Lord Jesus was lifted up. We are saved by looking to Him in faith.

3:15 The Savior was made sin for us, He who knew no sin, that we might be made the righteousness of God in Him. **Whoever believes in** the Lord Jesus Christ receives **eternal life** as a free gift.

3:16 This is one of the best known verses in all the Bible, doubtless because it states the gospel so clearly and simply. It summarizes what the Lord Jesus had been teaching Nicodemus concerning the manner by which the new birth is received. **God**, we read, **so loved the world**. **The world** here includes all mankind. God does not love men's sins or the wicked world system, but He loves people and is not willing that any should perish.

The extent of His love is shown by the fact **that He gave His only begotten Son**. God has no other Son like the Lord Jesus. It was an expression of His infinite love that He would be willing to give **His** unique **Son** for a race of rebel sinners. This does *not* mean that everyone is saved. A person must receive what Christ has done for him before God will give him eternal life. Therefore, the words are added, **"that whoever believes in Him should not perish."** There is no need for anyone to perish. A way has been provided by which all might be saved, but a person must acknowledge the Lord Jesus Christ as personal Savior. When he does this, he has eternal **life** as a present possession. Boreham says:

> When the church comes to understand the love with which God loved the world, she will be restless and ill at ease, until all the great empires have been captured, until every coral island has been won.[9]

3:17 God is not a harsh, cruel ruler anxious to pour out His anger on mankind. His heart is filled with tenderness toward man and He has gone to the utmost cost in order to save men. He could have sent **His Son into the world to condemn the world**, but He did **not** do so. On the contrary, He sent Him here to suffer, bleed, and die in order **that the world through Him might be saved**. The work of the Lord Jesus on the cross was of such tremendous value that all sinners everywhere could be saved if they would receive Him.

3:18 Now all mankind is divided into two classes: either believers or unbelievers. Our eternal destiny is determined by the attitude we take toward the Son of God. The one who trusts the Savior **is not condemned, but** the one **who does not** trust Him **is condemned already**. The Lord Jesus has finished the work of salvation, and now it is up to each individual to decide whether he will accept Him or reject Him. It is a terrible thing to reject such a gift of love. If a man will not believe on the Lord Jesus, God can do nothing else but condemn him.

Believing in His **name** is the same as believing in *Him*. In the Bible, the name stands for the person. If you trust His **name**, you trust Him.

3:19 Jesus is **the light** who came **into the world**. He was the sinless, spotless Lamb of God. He died for the sins of all the world. But do men love Him for this? No — they resent Him. They prefer their sins to having Jesus as Savior, and so they reject Him. Just as some creeping things scurry away from the light, so wicked men flee from the presence of Christ.

3:20 Those who love sin hate **the light**, because the light exposes their sinfulness. When Jesus was here in the world, sinful men were made uncomfortable by His presence because He revealed their awful condition by His own holiness. The best way to reveal the crookedness of one stick is to place a straight stick beside it. Coming into the world as a Perfect Man, the Lord Jesus revealed the crookedness of all other men, by comparison.

3:21 If a man is truly honest before God, he will come **to the light**, that is, the Lord Jesus, and realize his own utter worthlessness and sinfulness. Then he will trust the Savior for himself, and thus be born again through faith in Christ.

I. The Ministry of John the Baptist in Judea (3:22–36)

3:22 The first portion of this chapter described the Lord Jesus' witness in the city of Jerusalem. From this verse to the end of the chapter, John describes Christ's ministry in **Judea**, where doubtless He continued to proclaim the good news of salvation. As men came to the light, they were **baptized**. It would appear from this verse that Jesus Himself did the baptizing, but we learn in John 4:2 that it was done by His disciples.

3:23 The **John** referred to in this verse is John the Baptist. He was still preaching his message of repentance in the region of Judea and baptizing those Jews who were willing to repent in preparation for the coming of the Messiah. **John also was baptizing in Aenon . . . because there was much water there**. This does not prove conclusively that he baptized by immersion, but it certainly implies as much. If he baptized by sprinkling or pouring, there would have been no necessity of having **much water**.

3:24 This verse is given in explanation of John's continued ministry and of the continued response of devout Jews to it. In the near future, **John** would be **thrown into prison** and beheaded for his faithful testimony. But in the meantime, he was still diligently carrying out his commission.

3:25 It is clear from this verse that **some of John's disciples** became engaged in **a dispute** with **the Jews about**

purification. What does this mean? **Purification** here probably refers to baptism. The argument was whether the baptism of John was better than that of Jesus. Which baptism had the greater power? Which was of greater value? Perhaps **some of John's disciples** unwisely contended that no baptism could be better than that of their master. Perhaps the Pharisees tried to make John's disciples jealous of Jesus and His current popularity.

3:26 **They came to John** for a decision. They seemed to be saying to him, "If your baptism is the better, why is it that so many men are leaving you and going to Jesus?" (The expression **"He who was with you beyond the Jordan"** refers to Christ.) John bore witness to the Lord Jesus, and as a result of this witness, many of John's own disciples left him and began to follow Jesus.

3:27 If John's reply was referring to the Lord Jesus, it means that any success the Savior received was an indication of God's approval on Him. If John was referring to himself, he was saying that he had never pretended to be anyone great or important. He had never claimed that his baptism was superior to that of Jesus. He simply said here that he did not have anything but what he had received **from heaven**. That is true of all of us, and there is no reason in the world why we should be proud or seek to build up ourselves in men's esteem.

3:28 John reminded his disciples that he had pointed out time and again that he was **not the Christ, but** was simply **sent** to prepare the way for the Messiah. Why should they argue over him? Why should they seek to form a party around him? He was not the important one, but was simply trying to point men to the Lord Jesus.

3:29 The Lord Jesus Christ was **the bridegroom**. John the Baptist was merely **the friend of the bridegroom**, the "best man." **The bride** does not belong to the friend of the bridegroom, but rather to **the bridegroom** himself. Therefore, it was fitting that the people follow Jesus rather than John. **The bride** was used here to refer in a general way to all who would become disciples of the Lord Jesus. In the OT, Israel was spoken of as the wife of Jehovah. Later on in the

NT, those who are members of Christ's church are described under the figure of a bride. But here in John's Gospel, the word was used in a general sense to include those who left John the Baptist when the Messiah appeared. It did not mean either Israel or the church. John was not unhappy to lose followers. It was his great joy to listen to **the bridegroom's voice**. He was satisfied that Jesus receive all the attention. His **joy** was **fulfilled** when Christ was praised and honored by men.

3:30 The entire object of John's ministry is summarized in this verse. He labored ceaselessly to point men and women to the Lord, and to make them realize His true worth. In doing this, John realized that he must keep himself in the background. For a servant of Christ to seek to attract attention to himself is really a form of disloyalty.

Note the three "musts" in this chapter: for the *Sinner* (3:7); for the *Savior* (3:14); and for the *Saint* (3:30).

3:31 Jesus is the One **who comes from above and is above all**. This statement was designed to show His heavenly origin and supreme position. To prove his own inferiority, John the Baptist said that **he** himself was **of the earth** and was **earthly and speaks of the earth**. This simply meant that, as to his birth, he was born a man of human parents. He had not heavenly rank and could not speak with the same authority as the Son of God. He was inferior to the Lord Jesus because **He who comes from above is above all.** Christ is the supreme Sovereign of the universe. It is only proper, therefore, that men should follow Him rather than His messenger.

3:32 But when the Lord Jesus spoke, He spoke with authority. He told men **what** He had **seen and heard**. There was no possibility of error or deceit. Yet strange to say, **no one receives His testimony**. The expression **no one** is not to be taken in an absolute sense. There are individuals who accept the words of the Lord Jesus. However, John was looking at mankind in general and simply stating that the Savior's teachings were rejected by the majority. Jesus was the One who came down from heaven, but comparatively few were willing to listen to Him.

3:33 Verse 33 describes the few who

did accept the words of the Lord as being the very words of God. By their acceptance, they **certified that God is true**. So it is today. When people accept the message of the gospel, they take sides with God against themselves and against the rest of mankind. They realize that if **God** has said something, it must be **true**. Notice how clearly verse 33 teaches the deity of Christ. It says that whoever believes the **testimony** of Christ acknowledges **that God is true**. This is just another way of saying that the testimony of Christ is the testimony of *God*, and to receive the one is to receive the other also.

3:34 Jesus was the One **God has sent**. He spoke **the words of God**. To support this statement, John stated that **God does not give the Spirit by measure**. Christ was anointed by the Holy Spirit of God in a way that was not true of any other person. Others have been conscious of the help of the Holy Spirit in their ministry, but no one else ever had such a Spirit-filled ministry as the Son of God. The prophets received a partial revelation from God but "the Spirit revealed in and by Christ the very wisdom, the very heart of God to man with all its infinitude of love."

3:35 This is one of the seven times in John's Gospel where we are told that **the Father loves the Son**. Here that love is manifested in giving Him control over **all things**. Among these things over which the Savior has complete charge are the destinies of men, as explained in verse 36.

3:36 God has given Christ the power to grant **everlasting life** to all who believe on Him. This is one of the clearest verses in all the Bible on how a person can be saved. It is *simply by believing in the Son*. As we read this verse, we should realize that God is speaking. He is making a promise that can never be broken. He says, clearly and distinctly, that anyone **who believes in** His **Son has everlasting life**. To accept this promise is not a leap in the dark. It is simply believing what could not possibly be false. Those who do **not** obey **the Son** of God **shall not see life, but the wrath of God abides on** them already. From this verse we learn that our eternal destiny depends on what we do with the **Son** of

God. If we receive Him, God gives us eternal **life** as a free gift. If we reject Him, we will never enjoy everlasting **life**, and not only so, but God's **wrath** already hangs over us, ready to fall at any moment.

Notice that there is nothing in this verse about keeping the law, obeying the Golden Rule, going to church, doing the best we can, or working our way to heaven.

J. The Conversion of a Woman of Samaria (4:1–30)

4:1, 2 The **Pharisees had heard that Jesus** was baptizing **more disciples than John** and that John's popularity was evidently declining. Perhaps they had attempted to use this fact to stir up jealousy and contention between the disciples of John and those of the Lord Jesus. Actually, **Jesus Himself did not** perform the act of baptism. This was done by **His disciples**. However, the people were baptized as followers or disciples of the Lord.

4:3 By leaving **Judea** and journeying **to Galilee**, Jesus would prevent the Pharisees from being successful in their efforts to cause divisions. But there is something else of significance in this verse. **Judea** was the headquarters of the Jewish religious establishment, whereas **Galilee** was known as a heavily Gentile region. The Lord Jesus realized that the Jewish leaders were already rejecting Him and His testimony, and so here He turns to the Gentile people with the message of salvation.

4:4 **Samaria** was on the direct route from Judea to Galilee. But few Jews ever took this direct route. The region of Samaria was so despised by the Jewish people that they often took a very roundabout route through Perea to get north into Galilee. Thus, when it says that Jesus **needed to go through Samaria**, the thought is not so much that He was compelled to do so by geographical considerations, but rather by the fact that there was a needy soul in **Samaria** He could help.

4:5 Traveling into **Samaria**, the Lord Jesus came to a little village **called Sychar**. Not far from that village was a **plot of ground that Jacob** had given **to his son Joseph** (Gen. 48:22). As Jesus journeyed over this territory, all the scenes of its past history were constantly before His mind.

4:6 A spring known as **Jacob's well was there**. This ancient well can still be seen by visitors, being one of the few Biblical sites which can be identified quite positively today.

It was about noon (Jewish time) or 6 p.m. (Roman time) when **Jesus** reached the well. He was **weary** as a result of the long walk He had had, and so He **sat** down **by the well**. Although Jesus is God the Son, He is also a Man. As God, He could never become weary, but as Man, He did. We find difficulty in understanding these things. But the Person of the Lord Jesus Christ can never be fully understood by any mortal mind. The truth that God could come down into the world and live as a Man among men is a mystery which passes our understanding.

4:7 As the Lord Jesus was sitting by the well, **a woman came** out from the village **to draw water**. If, as some scholars say, it was noon, it was a very unusual time for women to go to the well for water; it was the hottest part of the day. But this woman was an immoral sinner, and she may have chosen this time out of a sense of shame because she knew that there would be no other women there to see her. Of course, the Lord Jesus knew all along that she would be at the well at this time. He knew that she was a soul in need, and so He determined to meet her and rescue her from her sinful life.

In this passage, we find the master Soul Winner at work, and we do well to study the methods He used to bring this woman to a sense of her need and to offer her the solution to her problem. Our Lord spoke to the woman just seven times. The woman spoke seven times also — six times to the Lord and once to the men of the city. Perhaps if we spoke to the Lord as much as she did, we might have the success in testimony that she had when she spoke to the men of the city. Jesus opened the conversation by asking a favor. Wearied with His journey, He **said to her, "Give me a drink."**

4:8 Verse 8 explains why, from a human standpoint, the Lord should ask her for a drink. **His disciples had gone away into** Sychar **to buy** some **food**. They ordinarily carried buckets with which to draw water, but they had taken these with them. Thus to all outward appearance, the Lord had no means for getting water from the well.

4:9 The woman recognized Jesus as **a Jew** and was amazed that He would speak to her, **a Samaritan**. The Samaritans claimed descent from Jacob, and looked on themselves as true Israelites. Actually, they were of mixed Jewish and heathen descent. Mount Gerizim had been adopted as their official place of worship. This was a mountain in Samaria, clearly visible to the Lord and to this woman as they talked together. The Jews had a deep dislike for the Samaritans. They considered them half-breeds. That is why this woman said to the Lord Jesus, **"How is it that You, being a Jew, ask a drink from me, a Samaritan woman?"** Little did she realize that she was speaking with her own Creator, and that His love rose above all the petty distinctions of men.

4:10, 11 By asking a favor, the Lord had stirred her interest and curiosity. He now arouses them still further by speaking of Himself as being both God and Man. He was first of all **the gift of God** — the One **God** gave to be the Savior of the world, His only begotten Son. But He was also a Man — the One who, wearied with His journey, asked her for **a drink**. In other words, if she had realized that the One to whom she was talking was God manifest in the flesh, she **would have asked Him** for a blessing, **and He would have given** her **living water**. The woman could only think of *literal* water and of the impossibility of His getting it without the necessary equipment. She completely failed to recognize the Lord, or to understand His words.

4:12 Her confusion deepened when she thought of the patriarch **Jacob, who** had given this **well**. He had used it **himself, as well as his sons and his livestock**. Now here was a weary traveler, centuries later, who asked for a drink from Jacob's well and yet who claimed to be able to give something better than the water which Jacob had given. If He had something better, why should He ask for water from Jacob's well?

4:13 So the Lord began to explain the difference between the literal water of Jacob's well and the water which He would give. **Whoever** drank **of this water** would **thirst again**. Surely the Samaritan woman could understand this. She had been coming out day after day to draw from the well; yet the need was never completely met. And so it is with all the wells of this world. Men seek their pleasure and satisfaction in earthly things, but these things are not able to quench the thirst of the heart of man. As Augustine said in his *Confessions*, "O Lord, You have made us for Yourself, and our hearts are restless till they rest in You."

4:14 **The water** which Jesus gives truly satisfies. **Whoever drinks** of Christ's blessings and mercies **will never thirst** again. Not only do His benefits fill the heart, but they overflow it as well. They are like a bubbling **fountain**, constantly overflowing, not only in this life but in eternity as well. The expression **springing up into everlasting life** means that the benefits of **the water** which Christ gives are not limited to earth, but will go on forever. The contrast is very vivid. All that earth can provide is not sufficient to fill the human heart. But the blessings which Christ provides not only fill the heart, but they are too great for any heart to contain.

> The whole wide world is not enough
> To fill the heart's three corners,
> But yet it craveth still;
> Only the Trinity that made it can
> Suffice the vast, triangled heart of man.
> – *George Herbert*

The pleasures of this world are for a few short years, but the pleasures which Christ provides go on **into everlasting life.**

4:15 When **the woman** heard of this marvelous water, she immediately wanted to have it. But she was still thinking of *literal* water. She did not want to have **to come** out to the well every day **to draw** the water and to carry it home on her head in a heavy waterpot. She did not realize that the water of which the Lord Jesus had been speaking was spiritual, that He was referring to all the blessings which come to a human soul through faith in Him.

4:16 There is an abrupt change in the conversation here. She had just asked for the water, and the Lord Jesus told her to **go** and **call** her **husband**. Why? Before this woman could be saved, she must acknowledge herself a sinner. She must come to Christ in true repentance, confessing her guilt and shame. The Lord Jesus knew all about the sinful life she had lived, and He was going to lead her, step by step, to see it for herself.

Only those who know themselves to be lost can be saved. All men are lost, but not all are willing to admit it. In seeking to win people for Christ, we must never avoid the sin question. They must be brought face to face with the fact that they are dead in trespasses and sins, need a Savior, cannot save themselves, that Jesus is the Savior they need, and, He will save them if they repent of their sin and trust in Him.

4:17 At first **the woman** tried to withhold the truth without telling a lie. She **said, "I have no husband."** Perhaps in a strictly legal sense, her statement was true. But it was designed to hide the hideous fact that she was then living in sin with a man who was not her husband:

> She chats about religion, discusses theology, uses a little irony, pretends to be shocked — anything to keep Christ from seeing the fugitive soul in full flight from itself (Daily Notes of the Scripture Union).

The Lord Jesus, as God, knew all about this. And so He **said to her, "You have well said, 'I have no husband.' "** Although she might be able to fool her fellow men, she was not able to fool this Man. He knew all about her.

4:18 The Lord never used His complete knowledge of all things to needlessly expose or shame a person. But He did use it, as here, in order to deliver a person from the bondage of sin. How startled she must have been when He recited her past history! She had **had five husbands**, and the man with whom she was now living was **not** her **husband**.

There is some difference of opinion about this verse. Some teach that the woman's five previous husbands had either died or deserted her, and that there was nothing sinful in her relationships with them. Whether or not this is so, it is clear from the latter part of this verse that this woman was an adulteress. **"The one whom you now have is not your husband."** This is the important point. The woman was a sinner, and until she was willing to acknowledge this, the Lord could not bless her with living water.

4:19 When her life was thus laid open before her, **the woman** realized that the One speaking to her was not an ordinary person. However, she did not yet realize that He was God. The highest estimation she could form of Him was that He was **a prophet**, that is, a spokesman for God.

4:20 It seems now that the woman had become convicted of her sins, and so she tried to change the subject by introducing a question concerning the proper place of worship. Doubtless as she said, **"Our fathers worshiped on this mountain,"** she pointed to Mount Gerizim nearby. Then she reminded the Lord (unnecessarily) that **Jews** claimed **Jerusalem** as the proper **place where one ought to worship.**

4:21 **Jesus** did not avoid her comment but used it to impart further spiritual truth. He told her that the time was **coming** when **neither on** Mt. Gerizim **nor in Jerusalem** would be the place of **worship.** In the OT, Jerusalem was appointed by God as *the* city where worship should be offered to Him. The temple in Jerusalem was the dwelling place of God, and devout Jews came to Jerusalem with their sacrifices and offerings. Of course, in the gospel age, this is no longer so. God does not have any certain place on earth where men must go to worship. The Lord explained this more fully in the verses to follow.

4:22 When the Lord said, **"You worship what you do not know,"** He condemned the Samaritan mode of worship. This is in marked contrast to those religious teachers today who say that all religions are good and that they all lead to heaven at last. The Lord Jesus informed this woman that the worship of the Samaritans was not authorized by God, neither was it approved by Him. It had been invented by man and carried on without the sanction of the Word of God. This was not so with the worship of the Jews. God had set apart the Jewish people as His chosen earthly people. He had given them complete instructions on the way to worship Him.

In saying that **"salvation is of the Jews,"** the Lord was teaching that the Jewish people were appointed by God to be His messengers, and it was to them that the Scriptures had been given. Also, it was through the Jewish nation that the Messiah was given. He was born of a Jewish mother.

4:23 Next Jesus informed the woman that, with His coming, God no longer had a certain place on earth for worship. Now those who believe on the Lord Jesus can worship God at any time and in any place. True worship means that a believer enters the presence of God by faith and *there* praises and worships Him. His body may be in a den, prison, or field, but his spirit can draw near to God in the heavenly sanctuary by faith. Jesus announced to the woman that from now on worship of the Father would be **in spirit and truth**. The Jewish people had reduced worship to outward forms and ceremonies. They thought that by religiously adhering to the letter of the law, and going through certain rituals, they were worshiping the Father. But theirs was not a worship of the spirit. It was outward, not inward. Their bodies might be bowed down on the ground but their hearts were not right before God. Perhaps they were oppressing the poor, or using deceitful business methods.

The Samaritans, on the other hand, had a form of worship, but it was false. It had no scriptural authority. They had started their own religion and were carrying out ordinances of their own invention. Thus, when the Lord said that worship must be **in spirit and truth**, He was rebuking both Jews and Samaritans. But He was also informing them that, now that He had come, it was possible for men to draw near to God through Him in true and sincere worship. Ponder this! **The Father is seeking such to worship Him**. God is interested in the adoration of His people. Does He receive this from me?

4:24 **God is Spirit** is a definition of God's being. He is not a mere man, subject to all the errors and limitations of humanity. Neither is He confined to any one place at any time. He is an invisible Person who is present in all places at one and the same time, who is all-knowing, and who is all-powerful. He is perfect in all His ways. Therefore, **those who worship Him must worship in spirit and truth**. There must be no sham or hypocrisy. There must be no pretense to being religious, when inwardly one's life is corrupt. There must be no idea that in going through a series of rituals, God is thereby pleased. Even if God instituted those rituals Himself, He still insists that man approach Him with a broken and a contrite heart. Two more "musts" are found in this chapter — "must" for the winner of souls (4:4) and "must" for the worshiper (4:24).

4:25 As the woman of Samaria had listened to the Lord, she had been made to think of the coming **Messiah**. The Holy Spirit of God had stirred up within her a desire that the **Messiah** should come. She expressed the confidence that when He did come, He would teach **all things**. In this statement, she showed a very clear understanding of one of the great purposes of Christ's coming.

The expression **"Messiah . . . who is called Christ"** is simply an explanation of the fact that these two words mean the same. **Messiah** is the Hebrew word for God's Anointed One; **Christ** is the Greek equivalent.

4:26 What **Jesus said to her** was literally, **"I who speak to you am."** The word **He** is not a part of the original text. Although the sentence is clearer with the word **He** included, yet there is a deep significance to the actual words of the Lord Jesus. In using the words **"I am"** He used one of the names which God applied to Himself in the OT. He said, "I AM is speaking to you," or, in other words, "Jehovah is the one who is speaking to you." He was announcing to her the startling truth that the One who was speaking to her was the Messiah for whom she had been looking and that He was also God Himself. The Jehovah of the OT is the Jesus of the NT.

4:27 When the **disciples** returned from Sychar they found Jesus talking with this **woman**. They were surprised that He would speak with her, for she was a Samaritan. Also, they could possi-

bly discern that she was a sinful woman. **Yet no one** asked the Lord what he was seeking from the woman or **why** He was **talking with her**. It has been well said, "The disciples marvel that He talks with the woman; they would have been better employed wondering that He talked with them!"

4:28 The woman then left her waterpot! It symbolized the various things in life which she had used in an effort to satisfy her deepest longings. They had all failed. Now that she had found the Lord Jesus, she had no more need for the things which had formerly been so prominent in her life.

> I tried the broken cisterns, Lord,
> But ah! the waters failed!
> E'en as I stooped to drink, they fled,
> And mocked me as I wailed.
>
> Now none but Christ can satisfy,
> None other name for me;
> There's love, and life, and lasting joy,
> Lord Jesus, found in Thee.
> – B. E.

She not only **left her waterpot** but she **went her way into the city**. Whenever a person is saved, he or she immediately begins to think of others who are in need of the water of life. J. Hudson Taylor said, "Some are jealous to be successors of the Apostles; I would rather be a successor of the Samaritan woman, who, while they went for food, forgot her waterpot in her zeal for souls."

4:29, 30 Her witness was simple but effective. She invited all the townspeople to **come** and **see a Man who told her all things that** she **ever did**. Also, she aroused within their hearts the possibility that this Man might indeed be the Messiah. In her own mind, there could be little doubt because He had already announced Himself to her as **the Christ**. But she raised the question in their minds so that they might go to Jesus and find out for themselves. Doubtless this woman was well known in the village for her sin and shame. How startling it must have been for the people to see her standing in the public places now, bearing public witness to the Lord Jesus Christ! The testimony of the woman was effective. The people of the village left their homes and their work and began to go out to find Jesus.

K. The Son's Delight in Doing His Father's Will (4:31–38)

4:31 Now that the **disciples** were back with the food, they encouraged the Lord to **eat**. Apparently they were not aware of the momentous events that were taking place. At this historic moment when a Samaritan city was being introduced to the Lord of Glory, their thoughts could rise no higher than food for their bodies.

4:32 The Lord Jesus had found **food** and support in winning worshipers to His Father. Compared to this joy, physical nourishment was of little importance to Him. We get what we go after in life. The disciples were interested in food. They went into the village to get food. They came back with it. The Lord was interested in souls. He was interested in saving men and women from sin, and giving them the water of everlasting life. He, too, found what He went after. What are we interested in?

4:33 Because of their earthly outlook, **the disciples** failed to understand the meaning of the Lord's words. They did not appreciate the fact that "the joy and happiness of spiritual success can for the time lift men above all bodily wants, and supply the place of material meat and drink." And so they concluded that someone must have come along and **brought** food to the Lord Jesus.

4:34 Again **Jesus** tried to turn their attention from the material to the spiritual. His **food** was **to do the will of** God, **and to finish** the **work** which God had given Him to do. This does not mean that the Lord Jesus refrained from eating actual food, but rather it means that the great aim and object of His life was not to cater to the body, but rather to do the will of God.

4:35 Perhaps the disciples had been talking together about the coming harvest. Or perhaps it was a common proverb among the Jews, **"Four months** between seed time and **harvest."** At any rate, the Lord Jesus again used the physical fact of **harvest** to teach a spiritual lesson. The disciples should not think that harvest time was still in the distance. They could not afford to spend their lives in quest of food and clothing, with the thought that God's work could be done later on. They must realize that **the fields** were **already white for harvest. The fields** here, of course, refer to the world. At the very moment when the Lord spoke these words, He was in the midst of a harvest field containing the souls of Samaritan men and women. He was telling the disciples that a great work of in-gathering lay before them, and that they should give themselves to it immediately and diligently.

So today, the Lord says to those of us who are believers, **"Lift up your eyes, and look at the fields."** As we spend time contemplating the great needs of the world, the Lord will lay on our hearts a burden for the lost souls around us. Then it will be up to us to go forth for Him, seeking to bring in the sheaves of ripened grain.

4:36 The Lord Jesus was now instructing the disciples concerning the work to which they were called. He had chosen them to be reapers. They would not only earn **wages** in this life, but they would gather **fruit** for eternity as well. Service for Christ has many rewards at the present time. But in a coming day, reapers will have the additional joy of seeing souls in heaven because of their faithfulness in proclaiming the gospel message.

Verse 36 does *not* teach that a person earns life eternal through faithful reaping, but rather that the **fruit** of that work continues on into eternal life.

In heaven, both the sower and the reaper will **rejoice together**. In natural life, the field must first be prepared for the seed, and then the seed must be sown in it. Later on, the grain is harvested. Thus it is in the spiritual life also. First of all, the message must be preached, then it must be watered with prayer. But when the harvest season comes, all who have had a part in the work **rejoice together**.

4:37 **In this**, the Lord saw a fulfillment of **the saying** that was common in that day, **"One sows, and another reaps."** Some Christians are called on to preach the gospel for many years without seeing very much fruit for their labor. Others step in at the end of those years, and many souls turn to the Lord.

4:38 Jesus was sending His disciples into areas that had already been prepared by others. Throughout the OT period, the prophets had foretold the coming of the gospel era and of the Messiah. Then, too, John the Baptist came as a forerunner of the Lord, seeking to prepare the hearts of the people to receive Him. The Lord Himself had sown the seed in Samaria, and prepared a harvest for the reapers. Now the disciples were about to step into the harvest field, and the Lord wanted them to know that, although they would have the joy of seeing many turning to Christ, they should understand that they were entering **into** other men's **labors**.

Very few souls are ever saved through the ministry of a single person. Most people have heard the gospel many times before they ever accept the Savior. Therefore, the one who finally leads a person to Christ should not exalt himself as if he were the only instrument God used in this marvelous work.

L. Many Samaritans Believe in Jesus (4:39–42)

4:39 As a result of the simple and forthright testimony of the woman of Samaria, **many** of her people **believed** on the Lord Jesus. All she said was, **"He told me all that I ever did,"** and yet that was sufficient to bring others to the Savior. This should be an encouragement to each of us to be simple, courageous, and direct in our witness for Christ.

4:40 The reception given to the Lord Jesus by the Samaritans was in marked contrast to that of the Jews. **The Samaritans** seemed to have some real appreciation of this wonderful Person, and **they urged Him to stay with them**. As a result of their invitation, the Lord **stayed there two days**. Just think how privileged this city of Sychar was, that it should entertain the Lord of life and glory during this period of time!

4:41, 42 No two conversions are exactly alike. Some believed because of the testimony of the woman. **Many more believed because of** the words of the Lord Jesus Himself. God uses various means in bringing sinners to Himself. The great essential is that there should be faith in the Lord Jesus Christ. It is wonderful to hear these Samaritans bearing such clear testimony to the Savior. There was no doubt in their minds at all. They had

complete assurance of salvation based not on the word of a woman, but on the words of the Lord Jesus Himself. Having **heard Him** and believed His words, the Samaritans had come to know **that this** was **indeed the Christ,**[10] **the Savior of the world**. Only the Holy Spirit could have given them this insight. The Jewish people apparently thought that the Messiah would be for them alone. But the Samaritans realized that the benefits of Christ's mission would extend to all **the world**.

M. The Second Sign: Healing of the Nobleman's Son (4:43–54)

4:43, 44 **After the two days** which He spent among the Samaritans, the Lord turned His footsteps northward **to Galilee**. Verse 44 seems to present a difficulty. It states that the reason for the Savior's moving from Samaria to Galilee was **that a prophet has no honor in his own country**. And yet Galilee *was* His own country, since Nazareth was a city located in that region. Perhaps what the verse means is that Jesus went into some part of Galilee other than Nazareth. In any case, the statement is certainly true that a person is not usually appreciated as much in his own home town as he is in other places. One's relatives and friends think of him as a mere youngster and one of themselves. Certainly the Lord Jesus was not appreciated by His own people as He should have been.

4:45 When the Lord returned **to Galilee**, He was given a favorable reception because the people had **seen all the things He** had done **in Jerusalem at the feast**. Obviously **the Galileans** referred to here were Jews. They had gone down to **Jerusalem** to worship. There they had seen the Lord and had witnessed some of His mighty works. Now they were willing to have Him in their midst in Galilee, not because they acknowledged Him to be the Son of God, but because they were curiously interested in One who was arousing so much comment everywhere He went.

4:46 Again the village of **Cana** was honored by a visit from the Lord Himself. On the first visit, some of the people had seen Him turn water into wine. Now they were to witness another mighty miracle by Him, the effect of which would extend to **Capernaum**. The **son** of **a certain nobleman . . . was sick at Capernaum**. This man was undoubtedly a Jew employed by Herod, the king.

4:47 He had **heard that Jesus had** been in **Judea** and had now returned to **Galilee**. He must have had some faith in the ability of Christ to heal because he came directly **to Him and implored Him to come down and heal his** dying **son**. In this sense, he seems to have a greater trust in the Lord than most of his fellow countrymen.

4:48 Speaking not only to the nobleman, but to the Jewish **people** in general,[11] the Lord reminded them of a national characteristic, that they desired to see miracles before they would **believe**. In general, we find that the Lord Jesus was not as pleased with a faith that was based on miracles as He was with that which was based on His Word alone. It is more honoring to Him to believe a thing simply because He said it than because He gives some visible proof. It is characteristic of man that he wants to see before he believes. But the Lord Jesus teaches us that we should first believe, and then we will see.

Signs and **wonders** both refer to miracles. **Signs** are miracles that have a deep meaning or significance. **Wonders** are miracles that cause men to be amazed by their supernatural qualities.

4:49 **The nobleman**, with the persistence of true faith, believed that the Lord Jesus could do his son good, and he wanted a visit from the Lord more than anything else. In one sense, his faith was defective. He thought that Jesus would have to be at the boy's bedside before He could heal him. However, the Savior did not rebuke him for this but rewarded him for the measure of faith which he *did* exhibit.

4:50 Here we see the man's faith growing. He exercised what faith he had, and the Lord gave him more. Jesus sent him home with the promise, **"Your son lives."** The son had been healed! Without any miracle or visible proof, **the man believed the word** of the Lord **Jesus** and started for home. That is faith in action!

4:51, 52 **As he was now** nearing home, **his servants** came out to meet him with the happy news that his **son**

was well. The man was not at all shocked by this announcement. He had believed the promise of the Lord Jesus, and having believed, he would now see the evidence. The father **inquired of** the servants as to the time **when** his son **got better**. Their answer revealed that the healing was not gradual; it had taken place instantly.

4:53 There could now be not the slightest doubt about this wonderful miracle. At the seventh hour of the previous day, **Jesus** had **said to** the nobleman in Cana, **"Your son lives." At the** very **same hour** in Capernaum, the son had been healed, and the fever had left him. From this the nobleman learned that it was not necessary for the Lord Jesus to be physically present to work a miracle or answer prayer. This should encourage all Christians in their prayer life. We have a mighty God who hears our requests and who is able to work out His purposes in any part of the world at any time.

The nobleman **himself believed, and his whole household**. It is apparent from this and similar verses in the NT that God loves to see families united in Christ. It is not His will that there should be divided families in heaven. He takes care to record the fact that the **whole household** believed in His Son.

4:54 The healing of the nobleman's son was not the second miracle in the Lord's entire ministry up to this point. It was **the second sign Jesus** performed in **Galilee** after **He had come** from **Judea**.

III. THE SON OF GOD'S SECOND YEAR OF MINISTRY (Chap. 5)[†]

A. The Third Sign: Healing of the Impotent Man (5:1–9)

5:1 As chapter 5 opens, the time had come for one of the Jewish feasts. Many believe this was Passover, but it is impossible to be sure. Born into the world as a Jew, and obedient to the laws which God had made for the Jewish people, **Jesus went up to Jerusalem** for the **feast**. As Jehovah of the OT, the Lord Jesus had been the One who instituted the Passover in the first place. Now as a

Man, obedient to His Father, He obeyed the very laws which He had made.

5:2 In Jerusalem, there was **a pool** named **Bethesda**,[12] meaning "house of mercy" or "house of pity." This **pool** was located **by the Sheep Gate**. The exact location is now known and excavated (near the Crusader Church of St. Anne). Around the pool there were **five porches** or large open spaces capable of holding a number of people. Some Bible teachers think that these five porches represent the Law of Moses and speak of its inability to help man out of his deep troubles.

5:3 Apparently the pool of Bethesda was known as a place where miracles of healing occurred. Whether these miracles took place throughout the year, or only at certain times, such as on feast days, we do not know. Surrounding the pool were a large number of **sick people** who had come with the hope of being cured. Some were **blind**, others **lame**, and still others were **paralyzed**. These various types of infirmity picture sinful man in his helplessness, blindness, lameness, and uselessness.

These people, suffering from the effect of sin in their bodies, were **waiting for the moving of the water**. Their hearts were filled with longing to be freed from their sicknesses, and they earnestly desired to find healing. Says J. G. Bellett:

> They lingered round that uncertain, disappointing water, though the Son of God was present. . . . Surely there is a lesson for us in this. The pool thickly populated, and Jesus passing by unheeded! What a witness of man's religion! Ordinances, with all their complicated machinery, sought after, and the grace of God slighted.[13]

5:4 The narrative here is not sufficient to satisfy our curiosity. We are simply told that **an angel went down at a certain time** and **stirred up the water**. The **first** one who was able to get into the water at that time was healed of his sickness. You can imagine what a pathetic sight it was to see so many people in need of help, struggling to get into the water, and yet only one being able to receive healing power.

While in many versions of the Bible, the latter part of verse 3 (beginning with the words "waiting for the moving of the water") and all of verse 4 are missing, these words are in the majority of manuscripts. Also, the story makes little sense without an explanation of why these sick people were there.

5:5, 6 One of the men who was waiting by the pool had been an invalid for **thirty-eight years**. This means that he had been in this condition even before the Savior was born. The Lord Jesus had complete knowledge of everything. He had never met this man before. Yet He knew that he had been an invalid **a long time**.

In loving compassion, **He said to him, "Do you want to be made well?"** Jesus knew that this was the greatest longing of the man's heart. But He also wanted to draw out from the man an admission of his own helplessness and of his desperate need for healing. It is much the same with salvation. The Lord knows that we desperately need to be saved, but He waits to hear the confession from our own lips that we are lost, that we need Him and accept Him as our Savior. We are not saved by our own will, yet the human will must be exercised before God saves a soul.

5:7 The answer of **the sick man** was rather pathetic. For years he had lain by the pool, waiting to get in, but every time **the water was stirred up**, there was no one to help him. Every time he would try to get in, someone else got there ahead of him. This reminds us how disappointed we are if we depend on our fellow men to save us from our sins.

5:8 The man's **bed** was a pad or light mattress. Jesus told him to **rise**, carry his pad, **and walk**. The lesson here is that when we are saved, we are not only told to rise, but also to walk. The Lord Jesus gives us healing from the plague of sin, and then He expects us to walk in a manner worthy of Him.

5:9 The Savior never tells anyone to do a thing without giving the power to do it. Even as He spoke, new life and power flowed into the body of the invalid. He was healed immediately. It was not a gradual recovery. Limbs that had been useless or weak for years now throbbed with strength. Then there was immediate obedience to the word of the Lord. He **took up his bed and walked**.

What a thrill it must have been for him to do this after thirty-eight years of sickness!

This miracle took place on **the Sabbath**, the seventh day of the week —our Saturday. The Jewish people were forbidden to do any work on the Sabbath. This man was a Jew, and yet at the instruction of the Lord Jesus, he did not hesitate to carry his mattress despite Jewish traditions regarding the day.

B. The Opposition of the Jews (5:10–18)

5:10 When **the Jews** saw the man carrying his mattress on **the Sabbath**, they challenged him. These people were very strict and even cruel in carrying out their religious observances and clung rigidly to the letter of the law, but they themselves often did not show mercy and compassion to others.

5:11 The healed man gave a very simple answer. He said that the One who cured him told him to **take up** his **bed and walk**. Anyone who had the power to heal a man who had been sick for thirty-eight years ought to be obeyed, even if he instructed a person to carry his bed on the Sabbath! The healed man did not really know who the Lord Jesus was at this time. He spoke of Him in a very general way, and yet with real gratitude.

5:12 The Jews were anxious to find out who dared tell this man to break their Sabbath tradition, and so they asked him to identify the culprit. The Law of Moses decreed that one who broke the Sabbath should be stoned to death. The Jews cared little that a paralytic had been healed.

5:13 The **healed** man did not know who had cured him. And it was impossible to point Him out, because **Jesus had** slipped away from the crowd that had gathered.

This incident marks one of the great turning points in the public ministry of the Lord Jesus Christ. Because He performed this miracle on the Sabbath, He stirred up the anger and hatred of the Jewish leaders. They began to pursue Him and to seek His life.

5:14 Some time later **Jesus found** the healed man **in the temple**, where doubtless he was thanking God for the wonderful miracle that had taken place in his life. The Lord reminded him that because he had been so highly favored, he was therefore under solemn obligation. Privilege always brings with it responsibility. **"See, you have been made well. Sin no more, lest a worse thing come upon you."** It seems clear that the man's sickness had originally come to him as a result of some sin in his life. This is not true of all sickness. Many times illness in a person's life has no direct connection with any sin he has committed. Infants, for instance, may be sick before they are old enough to sin knowingly.

"Sin no more," said Jesus, expressing God's standard of holiness. If He had said, "Sin as little as possible," He would not have been God. God cannot condone sin in any degree. Then the warning was added, **"lest a worse thing come upon you."** The Lord did not indicate what He meant by a worse thing. However, He doubtless intended the man to understand that sin has far more terrible results than physical sickness. Those who die in their sins are condemned to eternal wrath and anguish.

It is a more serious thing to sin against grace than against law. Jesus had shown wonderful love and mercy to this man. Now it would be a poor response if he would go out and carry on in the same kind of sinful life which had originally led to his illness.

5:15 Like the woman of Samaria, this **man** desired to bear public witness to His Savior. He **told the Jews that it was Jesus who had made him well**. He wanted to pay tribute to Jesus, though the Jews were not interested in such tribute. Their chief desire was to apprehend Jesus and punish Him.

5:16 Here is a terrible exposure of the wicked heart of man. The Savior had come and performed a great act of healing and these **Jews** were infuriated. They resented the fact that the miracle took place **on the Sabbath**. They were cold-blooded religionists, more interested in ceremonial observances than they were in the blessing and welfare of their fellow men. They did not realize that it was the very One who set apart the Sabbath in the first place who now performed an act of mercy on this day. The Lord Jesus had not broken the Sabbath. The law forbade menial work on that day, but it did not prohibit the performance of acts of necessity or of mercy.

5:17 Having finished the work of creation in six days, God had rested on the seventh day. This was the Sabbath. However, when sin entered the world, God's rest was disturbed. He would now work ceaselessly to bring men and women back into fellowship with Himself. He would provide a means of redemption. He would send out the gospel message to every generation. Thus, from the time of Adam's fall up to the present time, God **has been working** ceaselessly, and He is still working. The same was true of the Lord Jesus. He was engaged in His Father's business, and His love and grace could not be confined to only six days of the week.

5:18 This verse is very important. It tells us that **the Jews** became more determined than ever **to kill** the Lord Jesus **because He not only** had broken **the Sabbath, but** had claimed equality **with God**! To their narrow minds, it seemed that the Lord had broken the Sabbath although it was not true. They did not realize that God never intended the Sabbath to impose a hardship on man. If a man could be cured of a disease on the Sabbath, God would not require that he should suffer one day longer.

When Jesus spoke of **God** as **His Father**, they realized that He was claiming to be **equal with God**. To them, this was terrible blasphemy. Actually, of course, it was only the truth.

Did the Lord Jesus really claim to be equal with God? If He had not intended this, then He would have explained it to the Jews. Instead of that, He stated in even more positive terms, in the verses that follow, that He was indeed one with the Father. As J. Sidlow Baxter puts it:

He claims equality in seven particulars: (1) Equal in working: "What things soever he (the Father) doeth, these also doeth the Son likewise" (v. 19). (2) Equal in knowing: "For the Father loveth the Son, and showeth him all things that himself doeth" (v. 20). (3) Equal in resurrecting: "For as the Father raiseth up the dead . . . so the Son quickeneth whom he will" (v. 21 with vv. 28, 29). (4) Equal in judging: "For the Father judgeth no man, but hath committed all judgment unto the Son" (v. 22 with v. 27). (5) Equal in honour: "That all men should honour the Son even as they honour the Father" (v. 23). (6) Equal in regenerating: "He that heareth my word, and believeth on him that sent me . . . is passed from death unto life" (vv. 24, 25). (7) Equal in self-existence: "For as the Father hath life in himself; so hath he given to the Son to have life in himself" (v. 26).[14]

C. Jesus Defends His Claim to Be Equal with God (5:19–29)

5:19 The Savior was so vitally linked with God the Father that He could not act independently. He does not mean that He did not have the power to do anything by Himself, but that He was so closely united with God that He could only do the very things which He saw His **Father** doing. For while the Lord claimed equality with the Father, He did not claim independency too. He is not independent of although He is fully equal with Him.

The Lord Jesus clearly intended the Jews to think of Him as equal with God. It would be absurd for a mere man to claim to do the very things which God Himself **does**. Jesus claims to see what the Father is doing. In order to make such a claim, He must have continual access to the Father and complete knowledge of what is going on in heaven. Not only so, but Jesus claims to do the very things which **He sees the Father do**. This is certainly an assertion of His equality with God. He is omnipotent.

5:20 It is a special mark of the Father's love for His **Son** that He **shows Him all things that He Himself does**. These **things** Jesus not only saw; He had the power to perform them as well. Then the Savior went on to say that God would **show Him greater works than these**, so **that** the people might **marvel**. Already they had seen the Lord Jesus performing miracles. They had just seen Him heal a man who had been crippled for thirty-eight years. But they would see **greater** marvels than this. The first such marvel would be the raising of the dead (v. 21). The second was the work of judging mankind (v. 22).

5:21 Here is another clear statement as to the equality of the Son with the Father. The Jews accused Jesus of making Himself equal with God. He did not deny the charge, but rather set forth these tremendous proofs of the fact that He and the Father are one. Just **as the Father raises the dead and gives life to them, even so the Son gives life to whom He will**. Could this ever be said of Him if He were a mere man? To ask the question is to answer it.

5:22 The NT teaches that God **the Father . . . has committed all** the work of **judgment to the Son**. In order for the Lord Jesus to do this work, He must, of course, have absolute knowledge and perfect righteousness. He must be able to discern the thoughts and motives of men's hearts. How strange it was that the Judge of all the earth should stand before these Jews, asserting His authority, and yet they did not recognize Him!

5:23 Here we have the reason God has given authority to His Son to raise the dead and to judge the world. The reason is so **that all should honor the Son just as they honor the Father**. This is a most important statement, and one of the clearest proofs in the Bible of the deity of the Lord Jesus Christ. Throughout the Bible we are taught that God alone is to be worshiped. In the Ten Commandments, the people were forbidden to have any god but the one true God. Now we are taught **that all should honor the Son just as they honor the Father**. The only conclusion we can come to from this verse is that Jesus Christ is God.

Many people claim to worship God, but deny that Jesus Christ is God. They say that He was a good man or more godlike than any other man who ever lived. But this verse puts Him on an absolute equality with God, and requires that men should give Him the *same honor* which they give to *God the Father*. If a person **does not honor the Son**, then he **does not honor the Father**. It is useless to claim a love for God if one does not have the same love for the Lord Jesus Christ. If you have never realized before who Jesus Christ is, then ponder this verse carefully. Remember that it is the Word of God, and accept the glorious truth that Jesus Christ is God manifest in the flesh.

5:24 In the preceding verses, we learned that the Lord Jesus had the power to give life and that, also, the work of judgment had been committed to Him. Now we learn how one may receive spiritual life from Him and escape **judgment**.

This is one of the favorite gospel verses in the Bible. Multitudes have become possessors of eternal life through its message. Doubtless the reason for its being so greatly loved is the manner in which it sets forth the way of salvation so clearly. The Lord Jesus began the verse with the words **"Most assuredly,"** drawing attention to the importance of what He was about to say. Then He added the very personal announcement, **"I say to you."** The Son of God is speaking to us in a very personal and intimate way.

"He who hears My word." To hear the word of Jesus means not only to listen to it, but also to receive it, to believe it, and to obey it. Many people hear the gospel preached, but do nothing about it. The Lord is saying here that a man must accept His teaching as divine, and believe that He is indeed the Savior of the world.

"And believes in Him who sent Me." It is a matter of believing God. But does that mean that a person is saved simply by believing God? Many profess to believe in God, yet they have never been converted. No, the thought here is that one must believe God, who sent the Lord Jesus Christ into the world. What must he believe? He must believe that God **sent** the Lord Jesus to be our Savior. He must believe what God says about the Lord Jesus, namely, that He is the only Savior and that sins can only be put away through His work on Calvary.

"Has everlasting life." Notice it does not say that he will have eternal life, but that he **has** it right now. **Everlasting life** is the life of the Lord Jesus Christ. It is not only life that will go on forever, but it is a (higher) quality of life. It is the life of the Savior imparted to us who believe in Him. It is the spiritual life received when a man is born again, in contrast to the natural life which he received at his physical birth.

"And shall not come into judgment." The thought here is that he is not condemned now and will never be condemned in the future. The one who believes on the Lord Jesus is free from **judgment** because Christ has paid the penalty for his sins on Calvary. God will not demand the payment of this penalty twice. Christ has paid it as our Substitute, and that is sufficient. He has finished the work, and nothing can be added to a finished work. The Christian will never be punished for his sins.[15]

"But has passed from death into life." The one who has trusted Christ **has passed** out of a state of spiritual **death into** one of spiritual **life**. Before conversion, he was dead in trespasses and in sins. He was dead as far as love for God or fellowship with the Lord was concerned. When he put his faith in Jesus Christ, he was indwelt by the Spirit of God and became a possessor of divine life.

5:25 This is the third time the Lord has used the expression **most assuredly** in chapter 5, and the seventh time so far in this Gospel. When the Lord said that **the hour** was **coming and now is**, He did not refer to a period of sixty minutes, but rather He was saying that the time was coming, and had already arrived. The time referred to was His coming onto the stage of history.

Who are **the dead** spoken of in this verse? Who are they who would **hear the voice of the Son of God** and **live**? This may refer of course to those people who were raised from the dead by the Lord during His public ministry. But the verse has a wider meaning than this. **The dead** referred to are those who are dead in trespasses in sins. They **hear the voice of the Son of God** when the gospel is preached. When they accept the message and receive the Savior, then they pass from death into life.

Supporting the idea that verse 25 refers to spiritual matters and not physical, we list the comparisons and contrasts between it and verses 28, 29:

V. 25 — Life from Death	Vv. 28, 29 — Life after Death
"The hour is coming, and now is"	"the hour is coming"
"the dead"	"all who are in the graves"
"will hear the voice"	"will hear His voice"
"those who hear will live"	"and come forth"

5:26 This verse explains how a person can receive life from the Lord Jesus. Just **as the Father** is the Source and Giver of **life, so He has** decreed that **the Son**, too, should **have life in Himself** and should be able to give it to others. This again is a distinct statement as to the deity of Christ and as to His equality with the Father. It cannot be said of any man that he has life in himself. Life was given to each one of us, but it was never given to the Father or to the Lord Jesus. From all eternity, They have had life dwelling in Them. That life never had a beginning. It never had a source apart from Them.

5:27 Not only has God decreed that the Son should have life in Himself, but He also **has given Him authority** to be Judge of the world. The power to judge has been given to Jesus **because He is the Son of Man**. The Lord is called both Son of God and **Son of Man**. The title *Son of God* is a reminder to us that the Lord Jesus is one of the Members of the holy Trinity, one of the Persons of the Godhead. As Son of God, He is equal with the Father and with the Holy Spirit, and as Son of God, He gives life. But He is also **the Son of Man**. He came into this world as a Man, lived here among men, and died on the cross as a Substitute for men and women. He was rejected and crucified when He came into the world as a Man. When He comes again, He will come to judge His enemies and to be honored in this same world where He was once so cruelly treated. Because He is both God and Man, He is perfectly qualified to be Judge.

5:28 Doubtless as Christ was making these strong claims as to His equality with God the Father, the Jews who were listening were amazed. He realized, of course, the thoughts that were going through their minds, and so He here told them that they should **not marvel at** these things. Then He went on to reveal to them some even more startling truth. In a time yet future, all of those whose bodies **are** lying **in the graves will hear His voice**. How foolish it would be for anyone who was not God to predict that bodies lying in the grave would one day hear His voice! Only God could ever support such a statement.

5:29 All the dead will one day be raised. Some will be raised to **life**, and others to **condemnation**. What a solemn truth it is that every person who has ever lived or will ever live falls into one of these two classes![16]

Verse 29 does *not* teach that people who have done good will be saved because of their good deeds, and those who have done evil will be condemned because of their wicked lives. A person is not saved by doing good, but he does good because he has been saved. Good works are not the root of salvation but rather the fruit. They are not the cause, but the effect. The expression **those who have done evil** describes those who have never put their faith and trust in the Lord Jesus, and consequently whose lives have been **evil** in the sight of God. These will be raised to stand before God and to be sentenced to eternal doom.

D. Four Witnesses to Jesus as the Son of God (5:30–47)

5:30 At first, **"I can of Myself do nothing"** seems to say that the Lord Jesus did not have the power to do anything by Himself. However, that was not the case. The thought is that He is so closely united with God the Father that He could not act by Himself. He could not do anything on His own authority. There was no trace of willfulness in the Savior. He acted in perfect obedience to His Father and always in fullest fellowship and harmony with Him.

This verse has often been used by false teachers to support their claim that Jesus Christ was not God. They say that because He could not do anything of His own self, therefore He was just a man. But the verse proves the very opposite. Men can do the things they want, whether they are in accordance with the will of God or not. But because of who He was, the Lord Jesus could not so act. It was not a *physical* impossibility, but a *moral* impossibility. He had the physical power to do all things, but He could not do anything that was wrong: and it would have been wrong for Him to have done anything that was not the will of God the Father for Him. This statement sets the Lord Jesus apart from every other man who ever lived.

As the Lord Jesus listened to His Father and daily received instructions from Him, so He thought, taught, and acted. The word **judge** does not here have the sense of deciding on legal matters but rather of deciding what was proper for Him to do and say.

Because the Savior had no selfish motives, He could decide matters fairly and impartially. His one ambition was to please His Father and to do His will. Nothing was allowed to stand in the way of this. Therefore, His judgment of matters was not influenced by what would be for His own best advantage. Our opinions and teachings are generally affected by what we want to do and what we want to believe. But it was not so with the Son of God. His opinions or judgments were not biased in His own favor. He was without prejudice.

5:31 In the remaining verses of this chapter, the Lord Jesus Christ described the various witnesses to His deity. There was the witness of John the Baptist (vv. 32–35); the witness of His works (v. 36); the witness of the Father (vv. 37, 38); and the witness of the OT Scriptures (vv. 39–47).

First, Jesus made a general statement on the subject of witnessing. He said, **"If I bear witness of Myself, My witness is not true."** This did not mean for a moment that the Lord Jesus could ever say anything that was not true. Rather, He was simply stating a general fact that the witness of a single person was not considered sufficient evidence in a court of law. God's divine decree was that at least two or three witnesses were required before a valid judgment could be formed. And so the Lord Jesus was about to give not two or three, but four witnesses to His deity.

5:32 There is a question as to whether this verse refers to John the Baptist, God the Father, or the Holy Spirit. Some believe that the word **another** describes John the Baptist and that this verse is linked with the three that follow. Others believe that the Lord here was speaking about the **witness** which the Holy Spirit bears concerning Him. We believe that He was referring to the **witness** of the Father (the capitalized **He** shows the NKJV translators see a reference to Deity).

5:33 Having introduced the greatest of all witnesses, His Father, the Lord then turned to the testimony of **John**. He reminded the unbelieving Jews that they **sent** men **to John** to hear what he had to say, and John's testimony was all about the Lord Jesus Christ. Instead of pointing men to himself, he pointed them to the Savior. He bore **witness to the One who is the truth**.

5:34 The Lord Jesus reminded His listeners that His claim to be equal with God was not based simply on the **testimony** of human beings. If that was all He had, then His case would indeed be a weak one. But He introduced the testimony of John the Baptist since he was a man sent from God and since he testified that the Lord Jesus was indeed the Messiah and the Lamb of God who takes away the sin of the world.

Then He added, **"But I say these things that you may be saved."** Why was the Lord Jesus speaking to the Jews at such great length? Was He simply trying to show that He was right and that they were wrong? On the contrary, He was bringing before them these wonderful truths in order that they might realize who He was and accept Him as the promised Savior. This verse gives us a clear view of the loving and tender heart of the Lord Jesus. He spoke to those who hated Him and who would soon be seeking in every possible way to take His life. But there was no hatred in His heart toward them. He could only love them.

5:35 Here the Lord paid tribute to John the Baptist as **a burning and shining lamp**. This meant that he was a very zealous man, one who had a ministry that brought **light** to others, and one who was consumed in the process of pointing people to Jesus. At first, the Jewish people had flocked to John the Baptist. He was something of a novelty, a strange figure who had come into their lives, and they went out to listen to him. **For a time**, they accepted him as a popular religious teacher.

Why then, after accepting John so warmly, would they not accept the One of whom John preached? They rejoiced temporarily, but there was no repentance. They were inconsistent. They received the forerunner, but would not receive the King! Jesus paid high tribute to John. For any servant of Christ to be called **a burning and shining lamp** is true praise from the Son of God. May each of us who loves the Lord Jesus desire that we, too, may be flames of fire for Him, burning ourselves out but bringing light to the world in the process.

5:36 The testimony **of John** was not Christ's greatest proof of His deity. The miracles which the Father gave Him to do bore **witness of** Him, that **the Father** had truly **sent** Him. Miracles in themselves are not a proof of deity. In the Bible, we read of men who were given the power to perform miracles, and we even read of evil beings with the power to do supernatural wonders. But the miracles of the Lord Jesus were different from all others. First of all, He had the power *in Himself* to do these mighty works, whereas others were *given* the power. Other men have performed miracles, but they could not confer the power to perform miracles on others. The Lord Jesus not only performed miracles Himself, but He gave His apostles the authority to do likewise. Furthermore, **the works** performed by the Savior were the very ones which were prophesied in the OT concerning the Messiah. Finally, the miracles that the Lord Jesus performed were unique in character, scope, and number.

5:37, 38 Again the Lord spoke of the witness which **the Father** had borne to Him. Perhaps this referred to the time when the Lord Jesus was baptized. Then the voice of God the Father was heard from heaven stating that Jesus was His beloved Son, in whom He was well pleased. But it should be added that in the life, ministry, and miracles of the Lord Jesus, the Father also bore witness to the fact that He was the very Son of God.

The unbelieving Jews had **neither heard** the **voice** of God **at any time, nor seen His form**. This was because they did **not have His word abiding in** them. God speaks to men through His Word, the Bible. These Jews had the OT Scriptures, but they did not allow God to speak to them through the Scriptures. Their hearts were hardened, and their ears were dull of hearing.

They had never seen God's Form or Person because they did **not believe** on the One whom God had **sent**. God the Father does not have a Form or Shape that is visible to mortal eyes. He is Spirit and therefore invisible. But God has revealed Himself to men in the Person of the Lord Jesus Christ. In a very real way, those who believed on Christ saw the Form of God. Unbelievers merely looked upon Him as another man like themselves.

5:39 The first part of this verse may be understood[17] in two ways. First of all, the Lord Jesus may be telling the Jews to **search the Scriptures**. Or He may be simply stating the fact that they did **search the Scriptures** because they thought that in the mere possession of the Scriptures, they had **eternal life**. Either interpretation of the verse is possible. Probably the Lord Jesus was simply stating the fact that the Jews searched **the Scriptures** and thought that in doing so they were receiving **eternal life**. They did not realize that the OT Scriptures telling of the coming Messiah were actually telling about Jesus. It is terrible to think that men with the Scriptures in their hands could be so blind. But it was even more inexcusable that after the Lord Jesus spoke to them in this way, they still refused to accept Him. Notice the latter part of this verse carefully. **"These are they which testify of Me."** This simply means that the main subject of the OT was the coming of Christ. If anyone misses that in studying the OT, he misses the most important part of it.

5:40 The Jews were **not willing to come to** Christ **that** they might **have life**. The real reason people do not accept the Savior is not because they cannot understand the gospel, or find it impossible to believe on Jesus. There is nothing about the Lord Jesus that makes it impossible for them to trust Him. The real fault lies in man's own will. He loves his sins more than he loves the Savior. He does not want to give up his wicked ways.

5:41 In condemning the Jews for their failure to receive Him, the Lord did not want them to think that He was hurt because they had not given Him **honor**. He did not come into the world for the purpose of being praised by the **men** of this world. He was not dependent on their praise, but rather sought the praise of His Father. Even if men rejected Him, that did not detract from His glory.

5:42 Man's failure to receive the Son of God is here traced back to its cause. These men did **not have the love of God in** them, that is, they loved themselves rather than God. If they had loved God, they would have received the One whom God had sent. By their rejection of the Lord Jesus, they showed their utter lack of **love** for His Father.

5:43 The Lord Jesus came **in His Father's name**, that is, He came to do His Father's will, to bring glory to His Father, and to obey His Father in all things. If men had really loved God, they would have loved the One who sought to please God in all He said and did.

Jesus now predicted that **another** would **come in his own name** and that the Jews *would* **receive him**. Perhaps in one sense He was referring to many false teachers who arose after Him and sought to be honored by the nation. Perhaps He was referring to leaders of false cults down through the centuries who have claimed to be the Christ. But more probably He was referring here to the Antichrist. In a coming day, a self-appointed ruler will rise among the Jewish people and demand to be worshiped as God (2 Thess. 2:8–10). The majority of the Jewish nation will accept this Antichrist as their ruler, and as a result they will come under severe judgment from God (1 Jn. 2:18).

5:44 Here the Lord gave another reason for the failure of the Jewish people to accept Him. They were more interested in the approval of their fellow men than they were in God's approval. They were afraid of what their friends would say if they left Judaism. They were not willing to endure the reproach and suffering which would be heaped upon them if they became followers of the Lord Jesus. As long as a person is afraid of what others will say or do, he cannot be saved. In order to believe on the Lord Jesus, one must desire God's approval more than anyone else's. He must **seek the honor that comes from the only God**.

5:45 The Lord would **not** need to **accuse** these Jews **to the Father**. Of course, there were many charges He could bring against them. But there would be no need for Him to do it, because the writings of **Moses** would be sufficient to accuse them. These Jews took great pride in the OT and especially in the five books written by **Moses**, the

Torah. They were proud that these Scriptures were given to Israel. But the trouble was that they did not obey the words of Moses, as verse 46 shows.

5:46 The Lord Jesus put the writings of Moses on the same level of authority as His own words. We are reminded that "all Scripture is given by inspiration of God." Whether we read the OT or the New, we are reading the very Word of God. If the Jews had **believed** the words of **Moses**, they would have believed the Lord Jesus Christ also, because Moses **wrote about** the coming of Christ. An example of this is found in Deuteronomy 18:15, 18:

> The Lord Your God will raise up for you a Prophet like me from your midst, from your brethren. Him you shall hear. . . . I will raise up for them a Prophet like you from among their brethren, and will put My words in His mouth, and He shall speak to them all I command Him.

In these verses Moses predicted the coming of Christ, and told the Jewish people to listen to Him and obey Him when He came. Now the Lord Jesus had come, but the Jews failed to receive Him. Thus He said that Moses would accuse them to the Father because they pretended to believe in Moses and yet they did not do what Moses commanded. The words **he wrote about Me** are a clear statement by our Lord that the OT Scriptures contain prophecies about Him. Augustine stated this concisely: "The New is in the Old concealed; the Old is in the New revealed."

5:47 If the Jews would **not believe** the **writings** of Moses, it was not likely that they would believe the **words** of Jesus. There is a very close connection between the OT and the New. If a man doubts the inspiration of the OT Scriptures, it is not likely that he will accept the words of the Lord Jesus as being inspired. If people attack certain parts of the Bible, it won't be long before they cast doubt on the rest of the Book as well. King states:

> The Lord's allusion is, of course, to the Pentateuch, the Five Books of Moses — the portion of the Bible that has been more savagely attacked than any other; and, strangely enough, the portion which, so far as our records go, the Master quoted more than any other. As if,

long before the attacks began, He would set His own imprimatur upon them.[18]

IV. THE SON OF GOD'S THIRD YEAR OF MINISTRY: GALILEE (Chap. 6)

A. The Fourth Sign: Feeding of the Five Thousand (6:1–15)

6:1 The expression **after these things** means that a period of time had elapsed since the events in chapter 5 took place. Just how much time we do not know, but we do know that **Jesus** had traveled from the area around Jerusalem up to the Sea of Galilee. When it says that He crossed the sea, it probably means that He went from the northwestern shore to the northeastern side. **The Sea of Galilee** was also known as **the Sea of Tiberias**, because the city of Tiberias was located on its western bank. This city, the capital of the province of Galilee, was named after the Roman Emperor Tiberius.

6:2, 3 **A great** crowd of people **followed Him**, not necessarily because they believed on Him as the Son of God, but rather **because they saw** the miracles which He had done for **those who were diseased**. A faith founded on miracles is never as pleasing to God as that which is founded on His Word alone. God's Word should not require miracles to verify it. Anything that God says is true. It cannot possibly be false. That should be enough for anyone. The literal translation of verse 3 is **"And Jesus went up on** *the* **mountain"**, but this may merely mean the mountainous (or hilly) region around the Sea.

6:4 It is not clear why John mentioned that the **Passover was near**. Some suggest that the Lord Jesus was probably thinking about the Passover when He gave His wonderful message in this chapter on the true Bread of Life. He had not gone to Jerusalem for the Passover. John spoke of **the Passover** as **a feast of the Jews**. Actually, of course, it had been instituted by God in the OT. He had given it to the Jewish people, and in that sense it was **a feast of the Jews**. But the expression **a feast of the Jews** might also mean that God no longer recognized it as one of His own feasts because the Jewish nation celebrated it as a mere ritual, without any real heart interest. It had lost its real meaning, and was no longer a feast of Jehovah.

6:5 **Jesus** was not annoyed when He saw the **great multitude**, thinking they would disturb His rest or His time with the disciples. His first thought was to provide something for them to **eat**. And so He turned to **Philip** and asked where **bread** could be purchased to feed the multitude. When Jesus asked a question, it was never for the purpose of adding to His own knowledge, but to teach others. He knew the answer, but Philip didn't.

6:6 The Lord was going to teach Philip a very valuable lesson and **test** his faith. Jesus **Himself knew** that He would perform a miracle to feed this great crowd of people. But did Philip realize that He was able to do this? Was Philip's faith great or was it small?

6:7 Apparently Philip's faith did not rise to very great heights. He made some quick calculations and decided that even **two hundred denarii worth of bread** would not be enough to provide even **a little** meal for everyone. We do not know exactly how much bread could be purchased for **two hundred denarii** in that day, but it must have been a very great amount. A denarius was a worker's daily wage.

6:8, 9 **Andrew** was **Simon Peter's brother**. They lived in the vicinity of Bethsaida, along the shore of the Sea of Galilee. Andrew also decided that it would be difficult to feed such a throng. He noticed a little boy with **five barley loaves and two small fish**, but he felt that these would be almost useless in attempting to satisfy the hunger of **so many**. This **lad** did not have very much, but he was willing to put it at the disposal of the Lord Jesus. As a result of his kindness, this story was recorded in each of the four Gospels. He did not do very much, but "little is much if God is in it," and he has become famous throughout the world.

6:10 In making the people **sit down** (literally, recline), the Lord Jesus provided for their comfort. Notice He chose a place where there **was much grass**. It was unusual to find such a place in that region, but the Lord took care that the crowd would eat in a clean, pleasant place.

It is recorded that there were thousands of **men** (Greek: "males"), so this means that there were women and children in addition. The mention of the number **five thousand** is made to indicate what a mighty miracle was about to take place.

6:11 **Jesus took the loaves** and gave **thanks** for them. If He did this before partaking of food or serving it, how much more should we pause to thank God before eating our meals. Next **He distributed** the food **to the disciples**. There is a real lesson for us in this. The Lord Jesus did not do it all Himself. He enlisted the service of others. It has been well said, "You do what you can do; I'll do what I can do; and the Lord will do what we cannot do."

By the time the Lord **distributed** the bread **to the disciples**, it had been wonderfully multiplied. The exact moment when this miracle took place is not recorded, but we know that in a miraculous way those five loaves and two small fish became enough in the Lord's hands to feed this great throng. The disciples went about serving the bread and **the fish to those sitting down**. There was no scarcity because it is distinctly stated that they gave them of the fish **as much as they wanted**.

Griffith Thomas has reminded us that in this story we have a beautiful picture of:

> (a) the perishing world; (b) the powerless disciples; (c) the perfect Savior. This miracle involved a true act of creation. No mere man could take five loaves and two small fish and expand them in such a way as to feed so many people as this. It has been well said, "'Twas springtime when He blessed the bread, 'twas harvest when He brake." And it is also true, "Loaves unblessed are loaves unmultiplied."[19]

6:12 This is a very beautiful touch. If Jesus had been a mere man He would never have bothered to think about the remaining **fragments**. Any man who can feed five thousand does not worry about a few leftover crumbs! But Jesus is God, and with God there must be no wasting of His bounties. He does not want us to squander the precious things He has given to us, and so He takes care to instruct that the broken pieces which remained should be gathered up **so that nothing** might be **lost**.

Many people try to explain away this miracle. The crowd, they say, saw the little boy give his five loaves and two fish to Jesus. This made them realize how selfish they were, so they decided to take out their lunches and share them with each other. In this way, there was food for everyone. But no such explanation will fit the facts, as we shall see in the next verse.

6:13 Twelve baskets of bread were gathered up after the people had finished eating. It would be a sheer impossibility to gather up as much bread as this if it had just been a matter of each person having his own lunch with him. Man's explanations prove ridiculous. There can be only one conclusion, and that is that a mighty miracle had been performed.

6:14 The people themselves recognized that it was a miracle. They would not have done so if they had simply eaten their own lunches. In fact, they were so convinced that it was a miracle that they were willing to acknowledge that Jesus was **the Prophet who** would **come into the world**. They knew from the OT that a prophet was coming, and they looked for him to deliver them from the control of the Roman Empire. They were waiting for an earthly monarch. But their faith was not genuine. They were not willing to admit that Jesus was the Son of God or to confess their sins and accept Him as Savior.

6:15 As a result of Jesus' miracle, the people wanted **to make Him king**. Again, if Jesus were only a man, He doubtless would have submitted readily to their request. Men are only too anxious to be exalted and to be given a place of prominence. But Jesus was not moved by such appeals to vanity and pride. He realized that He had come into the world to die as a Substitute for sinners on the cross. He would do nothing to interfere with that objective. He would not ascend the throne until first He had ascended the altar of sacrifice. He must suffer, bleed, and die before He would be exalted.

F. B. Meyer writes:

As St. Bernard said, He always fled when they wanted to make Him King, and presented Himself when they wanted to crucify Him. With this clearly in mind let us not hesitate to adopt the noble works of Ittai the Gittite: "As the Lord liveth, and as my lord the king liveth, surely in what place my lord the king shall be, whether in death or life, even there also will thy servant be" (II Samuel 15:21). And He will surely answer, as that same David did to another fugitive who came to identify himself with his cause: "Abide with me, fear not; for he that seeketh my life seeketh thy life, but with me thou shalt be in safeguard."[20]

B. The Fifth Sign: Jesus Walks on the Water and Rescues His Disciples (6:16–21)

6:16, 17 It was **evening**. Jesus had gone to the mountain by Himself. The crowd doubtless returned to their homes, leaving the disciples by themselves. And so the disciples decided to go **down to the sea** and prepare for their trip back across the Sea of Galilee.

As they **went over the sea toward Capernaum, it was already dark**. **Jesus** was **not** with **them**. Where was He? He was up on the mountain praying. What a picture of Christ's followers today. They are on the stormy sea of life. It is **dark**. The Lord Jesus is nowhere to be seen. But that does not mean that He is unaware of what is going on. He is in heaven praying for those He loves.

6:18 The Sea of Galilee is subject to sudden and violent storms. Winds travel down the valley of the Jordan River at a great speed. When they hit the Sea of Galilee, they cause the waves to rise very high. It is not safe for small boats to be out on **the sea** at such a time.

6:19 The disciples **had rowed about three or four miles**. From a human standpoint, they were in great danger. At the right moment, they looked up and **saw Jesus walking on the sea, and drawing near the boat**. Here is another marvelous miracle. The Son of God was walking on the waters of the Sea of Galilee. The disciples **were afraid** because they did not fully realize who this wonderful Person was.

Notice how simply the story is told. The most amazing facts are being told to us, but John did not use big words to impress us with the greatness of what was taking place. He used great restraint in setting forth the facts.

6:20 Then the Lord Jesus spoke wonderful words of comfort. **"It is I; do not be afraid."** If He were only a man, they might well be afraid. But He is the mighty Creator and the Sustainer of the universe. With such a One close at hand, there was no reason to fear. He who made the Sea of Galilee in the first place could cause its waters to be calm in the second place, and could bring His fearful disciples safely to shore. The words **"It is I"** are literally "I AM." So far this is the second time in John's Gospel where Jesus used this name of Jehovah as applying to Himself.

6:21 When they realized that it was the Lord Jesus, they welcomed **Him into the boat. Immediately** they found themselves at their destination. Here another miracle is stated but not explained. They did not have to row any farther. The Lord Jesus brought them to dry **land** instantly. What a wonderful Person He is!

C. The People Seek a Sign (6:22–34)

6:22 It is now the **day** after the one in which the five thousand were fed. The multitude of **people** are still in the area northeast of the Sea of Galilee. They had watched the disciples get into the small **boat** the previous evening, and they knew that **Jesus had not** gone with them. Only one boat had been available at that time, and **the disciples** had taken it.

6:23 The following day, **boats** had come **from Tiberias, near the place where** the Lord Jesus had fed the multitude. But the Lord could not have departed in one of these because they had just arrived. But perhaps it was in these small boats that the multitude crossed over to Capernaum, as recorded in the following verses.

6:24 **The people** had watched Jesus very carefully. They knew that He had gone up into the mountain to pray. They knew that He had not gone in the boat with the disciples across the lake. Yet on the following day He was nowhere to be found. They decided to cross the sea **to Capernaum,** where the disciples were most likely to be. They could not understand how **Jesus** could be there, but they decided to go and seek Him anyway.

6:25, 26 Arriving at Capernaum, **they found Him** there. They could not conceal their curiosity, and asked Him **when** He had arrived.

Jesus answered their question indirectly. He realized that they did not seek Him because of who He was but rather because of the food which He gave them. They had seen Him perform a mighty miracle on the day before. This should have convinced them that He was indeed the Creator and the Messiah. But their interest was simply in food. They had eaten of **the** miracle **loaves,** and their hunger had been satisfied.

6:27 So Jesus first advised them **not** to **labor for the food which perishes.** The Lord did not mean that they should not work for their daily living, but He did mean that this should not be the supreme aim in their lives. Satisfying one's physical appetite is not the most important thing in life. Man consists not only of body, but of spirit and soul as well. We should labor **for the food which endures to everlasting life.** Man should not live as if his body were all. He should not devote all his strength and talents to the feeding of his body, which in a few short years will be eaten by worms. Rather, he should make sure that his soul is fed day by day with the Word of God. "Man shall not live by bread alone, but by every word that proceeds out of the mouth of God." We should work tirelessly to acquire a better knowledge of the Word of God.

When the Lord Jesus said that **God the Father** had **set His seal on Him,** He meant that **God** had sent Him and approved Him. When we set our seal to something, it means that we promise that it is true. God sealed the Son of Man in the sense that He endorsed Him as One who spoke the truth.

6:28 The people now asked the Lord what they must do in order to **work the works of God.** Man is always trying to earn his way to heaven. He likes to feel that there is something he can do to merit salvation. If he can somehow contribute to the saving of his soul, then he can find a ground for boasting; and this is very pleasing to him.

6:29 Jesus saw through their hypocrisy. They pretended that they wanted to work for God, and yet they did not want to have anything to do with the Son of God. **Jesus** told them that the first thing they must do is accept the One whom God had **sent**. So it is today. Many are seeking to earn their way to heaven by good works. But before they can do good works for God, they must first **believe** on the Lord Jesus Christ. Good works do not precede salvation; they follow it. The only good **work** a sinner can do is to confess his sins and receive Christ as Lord and Savior.

6:30 This verse was a further proof of the wickedness of the hearts of the people. One day previously, they had seen the Lord Jesus feed five thousand men with five loaves and two fish. On the very next day, they came to Him and asked Him for some **sign** that would prove His claims to be the Son of God. Like most unbelievers, they wanted to see first, and then they would believe. **"That we may see it, and believe You."** But this is not God's order. God says to sinners, "If you believe, then you will see." Faith must always come first.

6:31 Going back to the OT, the Jews reminded Jesus of the miracle of the manna[21] in the wilderness. They seemed to be saying that Jesus had never done anything as wonderful as that. They quoted from Psalm 78:24, 25, where it is written: **"He gave them bread from heaven to eat."** They implied that Moses called down food from heaven; the Lord was not as great as Moses, because He had only multiplied *existing* food!

6:32 The Lord's answer conveys at least two thoughts. First of all, it was *not* **Moses** who gave them the manna, but God. Moreover, the manna was not the true spiritual **bread from heaven**. The manna was literal food, designed for the physical body, but it had no value beyond this life. The Lord Jesus was here speaking about **the true**, ideal, and genuine **bread** which God gives out of heaven. It is bread for the soul and not for the body. The words **My Father** are a claim by Christ to deity.

6:33 The Lord Jesus revealed Himself as **the bread of God** which came **down from heaven and** gives **life**. He was showing the superiority of **the bread of God** to the manna in the wilderness. The manna did not impart life but only

sustained physical life. *It* was not intended for the whole world but only for Israel. The **true bread comes down from heaven and gives life** to men — not just to one nation but **to all the world**.

6:34 The Jews still did not realize that the Lord Jesus was speaking about Himself as the true bread, and so they asked Him for the **bread**. They were still thinking in terms of a literal loaf. Unfortunately, there was no real faith in their hearts.

D. Jesus, the Bread of Life (6:35–65)

6:35 Now **Jesus** stated the truth simply and clearly. He is **the bread of life**. Those who come to Him find enough in Him to satisfy their spiritual hunger forever. Those who believe on Him find their thirst forever quenched. Notice the words **I am** in this verse and recognize that the Lord was making a claim to equality with Jehovah. It would be folly for a sinful man to utter the words of verse 35. No mere man can satisfy his own hunger or thirst, much less satisfy the spiritual appetite of the whole world!

6:36 In verse 30, the unbelieving Jews had asked the Lord for a sign in order that they might see and believe. Here Jesus said that He had already told them that they had **seen** Him — the greatest sign of all — **and yet** they did **not believe**. If the Son of God could stand before them in perfect manhood and not be recognized by them, then it was doubtful that any sign He would perform would convince them.

6:37 The Lord was not discouraged by the unbelief of the Jews. He knew that all the Father's purposes and plans would be fulfilled. Even if the Jews to whom He was speaking would not accept Him, then He knew that all of those who were chosen by God would come to Him. As Pink puts it, "The realization of the invincibility of the eternal counsels of God gives a calmness, a poise, a courage, a perseverance which nothing else can."

This verse is very important because it states in a few words two of the most important teachings in the Bible. The first is that God has given certain ones to Christ and that **all** those whom He has given will be saved. The other is the teaching of man's responsibility. In order to be saved, a man must come to the Lord Jesus and accept Him by faith. God does choose some people to be saved, but the Bible never teaches that He chooses some to be damned. If anyone is saved, it is because of the free grace of God. But if anyone perishes forever, it is his own fault. All men are condemned by their own sinfulness and wickedness. If all men went to hell, they would be receiving only what they deserve. In grace, God stoops down and saves individual people out of the great mass of humanity. Does He have the right to do this? He certainly does. God can do as He chooses, and no man can deny Him this right. We know that God will never do anything that is wrong or unjust.

But just as the Bible teaches that God has elected certain persons to salvation, it also teaches that man is responsible to accept the gospel. God makes a universal offer — that if a man will believe on the Lord Jesus Christ, he will be saved. God does not save men against their will. A person must come to Him in repentance and faith. Then God will save him. No one who comes to God through Christ will be **cast out**.

The human mind cannot reconcile these two teachings. However, we should believe them even if we cannot understand them. They are Biblical teachings and are clearly stated here.

6:38 In verse 37, the Lord Jesus said that all of God's plans would eventually be fulfilled with regard to the salvation of those who were given to Him. Since this was the Father's will, the Lord would personally undertake to bring it to pass, as His mission was to do the will of God. **"I have come down from heaven"** said Christ, clearly teaching that He did not begin His life in the manger at Bethlehem. Rather, He existed from all eternity with God the Father in heaven. Coming into the world, He was the obedient Son of God. He voluntarily took the place of a servant in order to carry out **the will** of His Father. This does not mean that He did not have a will of His own, but rather that His **own will** was in perfect agreement with the will of God.

6:39 **The will of the Father** was

that everyone who was given to Christ would be saved and kept until the resurrection of the just, when they would be raised and taken home to heaven. The words **nothing** and **it** refer to believers. Here He was thinking not of individual believers but of the entire body of Christians who would be saved down through the years. The Lord Jesus was responsible to see that not one member of the body would be lost but that the whole body would be raised **up at the last day**.

As far as *Christians* are concerned, **the last day** refers to the **day** when the Lord Jesus will come in the air, when the dead in Christ will rise first, when the living believers will be changed, and when all will be caught up to meet the Lord in the air, to be forever with the Lord. To the *Jews*, it meant the coming of the Messiah in glory.

6:40 The Lord now went on to explain how a person became a member of the family of the redeemed. God's **will** is **that everyone who sees the Son and believes in Him may have everlasting life**. To *see* the Son here means not to see Him with the physical eyes but rather with the eyes of faith. One must see or recognize that Jesus Christ is the Son of God and the Savior of the world. Then, too, he must believe on Him. This means that by a definite act of faith, he must receive the Lord Jesus as his own personal Savior. All who do this receive **everlasting life** as a present possession and also receive the assurance that they will be raised **at the last day**.

6:41 The people were quite unprepared to accept the Lord Jesus, and they showed this by murmuring **against Him**. He had claimed to be **the bread which came down from heaven**. They realized that this was a claim of great importance. To come **down from heaven**, one could not be a mere man or even a great prophet. And **so they complained** about **Him** because they were not willing to believe His words.

6:42 They assumed that **Jesus** was **the son of Joseph**. Here, of course, they were wrong. Jesus was born of the Virgin Mary. Joseph was not His father. Rather, our Lord was conceived of the Holy Spirit. Their failure to believe in the virgin birth led to their darkness and unbelief. So it is today. Those who refuse to accept the Lord Jesus as the Son of God who came into the world through the womb of the virgin find themselves compelled to deny all the great truths concerning the Person and work of Christ.

6:43 Although they had not been speaking directly to Him, yet He knew what they were saying, and here **Jesus** told them **not** to **murmur among** themselves. The following verses explain why their murmuring was useless and profitless. The more the Jews rejected the testimony of the Lord Jesus, the more difficult His teachings became. "Light rejected is light denied." The more they spurned the gospel, the harder it became for them to accept the gospel. If the Lord told them simple things and they would not believe, then He would expound to them more difficult things and they would be thoroughly ignorant of what He was saying.

6:44 Man in himself is utterly hopeless and helpless. He does not even have the strength to come to Jesus by himself. Unless the Father first begins to work in his heart and life, he will never realize his terrible guilt and his need of a Savior. Many people have difficulty with this verse. They suppose that it teaches that a man may desire to be saved and yet might find it impossible. This is not so. But the verse does teach in the strongest possible way that God is the One who first acted in our lives and sought to win us to Himself. We have the choice of accepting the Lord Jesus or refusing Him. But we never would have had the desire in the first place if God had not spoken to our hearts. Again the Lord added the promise that He will **raise** every true believer **up at the last day**. As we have seen before, this refers to the coming of Christ for His saints, when the dead will be raised and the living will be changed. It is a resurrection of believers only.

6:45 Having stated in strong terms that no man could come to Him unless the Father drew him, the Lord goes on to explain how the Father draws men. First of all, He quotes from Isaiah 54:13, **"And they shall all be taught by God."** God not only simply chooses individuals. He does something about it. He

speaks to their hearts through the teaching of His precious Word.

Then man's own will is involved. Those who respond to the teaching of God's Word and learn **from the Father** are the ones who come to Christ. Here again we see the two great truths of God's sovereignty and man's choice placed side by side in Scripture. They show us that salvation has a divine side and a human side as well.

When Jesus said, **"It is written in the prophets,"** He meant, of course, the books of the prophets. He meant Isaiah in particular, but the thought He expressed here is found throughout all the prophets. It is by the teachings of God's Word and God's Spirit that men are drawn to God.

6:46 The fact that people are taught by God does **not** mean that they have **seen** Him. The only One who **has seen the Father** is the One who came from God, namely the Lord Jesus Himself.

All those who are taught by God are taught about the Lord Jesus Christ because God's teaching has Christ Himself as its grand Subject.

6:47 Verse 47 is one of the clearest and briefest statements in all the Word of God concerning the way of salvation. The Lord Jesus stated in words that could hardly be misunderstood — that whoever **believes in** Him **has everlasting life**. Notice He introduced these momentous words with His emphatic **"most assuredly."** This is one of many verses in the NT that teaches that salvation is not by works, not by law-keeping, not by church membership, not by obeying the Golden Rule, but simply by believing in the Lord Jesus Christ.

6:48, 49 Now the Lord Jesus states that *He* is the **bread of life** of which He had been speaking. The **bread of life** means, of course, **the bread** which gives **life** to those who eat it. The Jews had previously brought up the subject of the **manna in the wilderness** and challenged the Lord Jesus to produce some food as wonderful as that. Here the Lord reminded them that their **fathers** had eaten the **manna in the wilderness** and were **dead**. In other words, **manna** was for this life only. It did not have any power to give eternal life to those who ate it. By the expression, **"Your fathers,"**

the Lord dissociated Himself from fallen humanity and implied His unique deity.

6:50 In contrast to the manna, the Lord Jesus spoke of Himself as **the bread which comes down from heaven**. If anyone ate this bread, he would **not die**. This did not mean that he would not die physically, but that he would have eternal life in heaven. Even if he did die physically, his body would be raised at the last day, and he would spend eternity with the Lord.

In this and in the following verses, the Lord Jesus spoke repeatedly of men *eating of Him*. What does He mean by this? Does He mean that men must eat of Him in a physical, literal way? Obviously that idea is impossible and repulsive. Some think, however, that He meant to teach that we must eat of Him in the communion service; that in some miraculous way the bread and wine are changed into the body and blood of Christ and that in order to be saved we must partake of those elements. But this is not what Jesus said. The context makes it quite clear that to **eat** of Him means to believe on Him. When we trust the Lord Jesus Christ as our Savior, we appropriate Him by faith. We partake of the benefits of His Person and of His work. Augustine said, "Believe and you have eaten."

6:51 Jesus is **the living bread**. He not only lives in Himself, but is life-giving. Those who eat **this bread . . . will live forever**. But how can this be? How can the Lord give eternal life to guilty sinners? The answer is found in the latter part of this verse: **"The bread that I shall give is My flesh, which I shall give for the life of the world."** Here the Lord Jesus was pointing forward to His death on the cross. He would give His **life** as a ransom for sinners. His body would be broken, and His blood would be poured out as a sacrifice for sins. He would die as a Substitute. He would pay the penalty that our sins demanded. And why would He do this? He did it **for the life of the world**. He would not die just for the Jewish nation, or even just for the elect. But His death would be of sufficient value for the whole world. This does not, of course, mean that the whole world will be saved, but rather that the work of the

Lord Jesus at Calvary would be sufficient in its value to save the whole world, if all men came to Jesus.

6:52 **The Jews** were still thinking in terms of literal, physical bread and **flesh**. Their thoughts were unable to rise above the things of this life. They did not realize that the Lord Jesus was using physical things to teach spiritual truths. And so they asked among themselves how **this** mere **Man** could possibly give **His flesh** to be eaten by others. A parachute opens only after you jump out of the plane. Faith precedes sight and prepares your soul to understand, your heart to believe, your will to obey. All your questions of "How?" are answered by yielding to the authority of Christ, as Paul did when he cried, "Lord, what do You want me to do?"

6:53 Once again **Jesus**, knowing all things, realized exactly what they were thinking and saying. And so He warned them solemnly that if they did not **eat His flesh** and **drink His blood**, they would **have no life in** them. This could not refer to the bread and the wine used at the Lord's Supper. When the Lord instituted His Supper, on the night in which He was betrayed, his body had not yet been broken and His blood had not yet been shed. The disciples partook of the bread and the wine, but they did not literally eat His flesh and drink His blood. The Lord Jesus was simply stating that unless we appropriate to ourselves by faith the value of His death for us on Calvary, we can never be saved. We must believe on Him, receive Him, trust Him, and make Him our very own.

6:54 By comparing this verse with verse 47, it can be definitely shown that to eat His flesh and to drink His blood means to believe on Him. In verse 47 we read that "He who believes in Me has everlasting life." In verse 54, we learn that **whoever eats** His **flesh** and **drinks** His **blood has eternal life**. Now things equal to the same thing are equal to each other. To eat His **flesh** and to drink His **blood** is to believe on Him. All who believe on Him will be raised up **at the last day**. This refers, of course, to the bodies of those who have died trusting in the Lord Jesus.

6:55 The **flesh** of the Lord Jesus is **food indeed**, and His **blood is drink in-**

deed.[22] This is in contrast to the food and drink of this world which is only of temporary value. The value of the death of the Lord Jesus is never-ending. Those who partake of Him by faith receive life that goes on forever.

6:56 A very close union exists between Himself and those who are believers in Him. Whoever **eats** His **flesh and drinks** His **blood abides in** Him, **and** He abides in that person. Nothing could be closer or more intimate than this. When we eat literal food, we take it into our very being; and it becomes a part of us. When we accept the Lord Jesus as our Redeemer, He comes into our lives to abide, and we, too, abide (continually dwell) in Him.

6:57 Now the Lord gave another illustration of the close bond that existed between Himself and His people. The illustration was His own connection with God the Father. **The living Father** had **sent** the Lord Jesus into the world. (The expression **living Father** means the Father who is the Source of life). As a Man here in the world, Jesus lived **because of the Father**, that is, by reason of the Father. His life was lived in closest union and harmony with God the Father. God was the center and circumference of His life. His purpose was to be occupied with God the Father. He was here as a Man in the world, and the world did not realize that He was God manifest in the flesh. Although He was misunderstood by the world, yet He and His Father were one. They lived in closest intimacy. That is exactly the way it is with believers in the Lord Jesus. They are here in the world, misunderstood by the world, hated and often persecuted. But because they have put their faith and trust in the Lord Jesus, they **live because of** Him. Their lives are closely bound up with His life, and this life shall endure forever.

6:58 This verse seems to summarize all that the Lord has said in the previous verses. He **is the bread which came down from heaven**. He is superior to **the manna** which the **fathers ate** in the wilderness. That bread was only of temporary value. It was only for this life. But Christ is the Bread of God who gives eternal life to all who feed on Him.

6:59 The crowd had followed Jesus and His disciples to **Capernaum** from the northeast side of the Sea of Galilee. Apparently the multitude had found Jesus **in the synagogue**[23] and it was there that He delivered the message on the Bread of Life to them.

6:60 By this time, the Lord Jesus had **many** more **disciples** than the original twelve. Anyone who followed Him and professed to accept His teachings was known as a disciple. However, not all who were known as His disciples were real believers. Now **many** of those who professed to be **His disciples** said, **"This is a hard saying."** They meant that His teaching was offensive. It was not so much that it was hard for them to understand, as that it was distasteful for them to receive. When they said, **"Who can understand it"** (literally "hear"), they meant, "Who can stand and listen to such offensive doctrine?"

6:61 Here again we find evidence that the Lord had complete knowledge. **Jesus knew** exactly what the **disciples** were saying. He knew that they were complaining at His claim to have come down from heaven and that they did not like it when He said that men must eat His flesh and drink His blood to have everlasting life. And so He asked them, **"Does this offend you?"**

6:62 They took offense because He said that He had come down from heaven. Now He asked them **what** will they think if they **should see** Him **ascend** back into heaven, which He knew He would do after His resurrection. They were also offended by His saying that men must eat His flesh. What would they think, then, if they should see that body of flesh **ascend where He was before**? How would men be able to eat His literal flesh and drink His literal blood after He had gone back to the Father?

6:63 These people had been thinking in terms of Christ's literal flesh, but here He told them that eternal life was not gained by eating flesh but by the work of the Holy Spirit of God. Flesh cannot give life; only **the Spirit** can do this. They had taken His words literally and had not realized that they were to be understood spiritually. And so here the Lord Jesus explained that **the words that** He spoke were **spirit and they** were **life**; when His sayings about eating His flesh and drinking His blood were understood in a spiritual way, as meaning *belief* in Him, then those who accepted the message would receive eternal life.

6:64 Even as He said these things, the Lord realized that some of His listeners did not understand Him because they would **not believe**. The difficulty lay not so much in their inability as in their unwillingness. **Jesus knew from the beginning** that some of His professed followers would **not believe** on Him and that one of His disciples **would betray Him**. Of course, **Jesus knew** all this from eternity, but here it probably means that He was aware of it from the very start of His ministry on earth.

6:65 Now He explained that it was because of their unbelief that He had previously told them **that no one** could **come to** Him **unless** it were **granted to him** by His **Father**. Such words are an attack on the pride of man, who thinks that he can earn or merit salvation. The Lord Jesus told men that even the power to **come** to Him can only be received from God the **Father**.

E. Mixed Reactions to the Savior's Words (6:66–71)

6:66 These sayings of the Lord Jesus proved so distasteful to **many** who had followed Him that they now left Him and were no longer willing to associate with Him. These disciples were never true believers. They followed the Lord for various reasons, but not out of genuine love for Him or appreciation of who He was.

6:67 At this point **Jesus** turned **to the twelve** disciples and challenged them with the question as to whether they, too, would leave Him.

6:68 Peter's answer is worthy of note. He said in effect, "**Lord**, how could we leave You? **You** teach the doctrines which lead to **eternal life**. If we leave You, there is no one else to whom we could go. To leave You would be to seal our doom."

6:69 Speaking for the twelve, Peter further said that they had **come to believe and know that** the Lord Jesus was the *Messiah*, **the Son of the living God**.[24] Notice again the order of the words "**believe and know.**" First of all, they had put their faith in the Lord Jesus Christ, and then they came to **know** that He was

indeed all that He professed to be.

6:70 In verses 68 and 69, Peter had used the word "we" as meaning all twelve of the disciples. Here in verse 70, the Lord Jesus corrected him. He should not say so confidently that all twelve were true believers. It is true that the Lord had **chosen** the **twelve** disciples, but **one of** them was **a devil**. There was one in the company who did not share Peter's views concerning the Lord Jesus Christ.

6:71 The Lord Jesus knew that **Judas Iscariot** was going to **betray Him**. He knew that Judas never really accepted Him as Lord and Savior. Here again we have the all-knowledge of the Lord. Also, we have an evidence of the fact that Peter was not infallible when speaking for the disciples!

In the bread of life discourse, our Lord began with fairly simple teaching. But as He progressed, it was apparent that the Jews were rejecting His words. The more they closed their hearts and minds to the truth, the more difficult His teaching became. Finally He talked about eating His flesh and drinking His blood. That was too much! They said, "This is a hard saying; who can understand it" and they quit following Him. Rejection of the truth results in judicial blindness. Because they *would* not see, they came to the place where they *could* not see.

V. THE SON OF GOD'S THIRD YEAR OF MINISTRY: JERUSALEM (7:1–10:39)[†]

A. Jesus Rebukes His Brothers (7:1–9)

7:1 There was a lapse of some months between chapters 6 and 7. **Jesus** remained **in Galilee. He did not want** to stay **in Judea**, which was headquarters for **the Jews**, because they **sought to kill Him**. It is generally agreed that **the Jews**[25] referred to in this verse were the leaders or rulers. They were the ones who hated the Lord Jesus most bitterly, and who sought opportunities **to kill Him**.

7:2 The **Feast of Tabernacles** was one of the important events in the Jewish calendar. It came at the time of harvest, and celebrated the fact that the Jews

†*See p. xxiv.*

lived in temporary shelters or booths after they came out of Egypt. It was a festive, joyous holiday, looking *forward* to the coming day when the Messiah would reign and the saved Jewish nation would dwell in the land in peace and prosperity.

7:3 The Lord's **brothers** mentioned in verse 3 were likely sons born to Mary after the birth of Jesus, (some say cousins or other distant relatives). But no matter how close the relationship to the Lord Jesus was, they were not thereby saved. They did not truly believe on the Lord Jesus. They told Him that He should go to the Feast of Tabernacles in Jerusalem and perform some of His miracles there so **that** His **disciples** might **see** what He was doing. The **disciples** spoken of here were not the twelve, but rather those who professed to be followers of the Lord Jesus in Judea.

Although they did not believe on Him, they wanted Him to manifest Himself openly. Perhaps they wanted the attention that would come to them as relatives of a famous person. Or more probably, they were envious of His fame and were urging Him to go to Judea in hopes that He might be killed.

7:4 Perhaps these words were spoken in sarcasm. His relatives seemed to imply that the Lord was looking for publicity. Why else was He performing all these miracles in Galilee if He did not want to become famous? "Now is Your big opportunity," they say in effect. "You have been seeking to become famous. You should go to Jerusalem for the feast. Hundreds of people will be there, and You will have an opportunity to perform miracles for them. Galilee is a quiet place, and You are practically performing Your miracles in secret here. Why do You do this when we know that You want to become well-known?" Then they added, **"If You do these things, show Yourself to the world."** The thought here seems to be, "If You are really the Messiah, and if You are doing these miracles to prove it, why don't You offer these proofs where they will really count, namely, in Judea?"

7:5 **His brothers** had no sincere desire to see Him glorified. They **did not** really **believe** Him to be the Messiah. Neither were they willing to trust themselves to Him. What they said was said in sarcasm. Their hearts were not right before the Lord. It must have been especially bitter for the Lord Jesus to have His own brothers doubt His words and His works. Yet how often it is that those who are faithful to God find their bitterest opposition from those who are nearest and dearest to them.

7:6 The Lord's life was ordered from the beginning to the end. Each day and every movement was in accordance with a pre-arranged schedule. The opportune **time** for manifesting Himself openly to the world had **not yet come**. He knew exactly what lay before Him, and it was not the will of God that He should go to Jerusalem at this time in order to make a public presentation of Himself. But He reminded His brothers that their **time** was **always ready** or opportune. Their lives were lived according to their own desires and not in obedience to the will of God. They could make their own plans and travel as they pleased, because they were only intent on doing their own will.

7:7 **The world** could **not hate** the Lord's brothers because they belonged to the world. They took sides with the world against Jesus. Their whole lives were in harmony with the world. **The world** here refers to the system which man has built up and in which there is no room for God or for His Christ: the world of culture, art, education, or religion. In fact, in Judea it was particularly the religious world, since it was the rulers of the Jews who hated Christ the most.

The world hated Christ **because** He testified concerning it **that its works** were **evil**. It is a sad commentary on man's depraved nature that when a sinless, spotless Man came into the world, the world sought to kill Him. The perfection of Christ's life showed how imperfect everyone else's life was. Just as a straight line reveals the crookedness of a zigzag line when they are placed side by side, so the Lord's coming into the world served to reveal man in all his sinfulness. Man resented this exposure of himself. Instead of repenting and crying to God for mercy, he sought to destroy the One who revealed His sin.

F. B. Meyer comments:

Ah, it is one of the most terrible rebukes that Incarnate Love can administer, when it says of any now, as it did of some in the days of his flesh: "The world cannot hate you." Not to be hated by the world; to be loved and flattered and caressed by the world — is one of the most terrible positions in which a Christian can find himself. "What bad thing have I done," asked the ancient sage, "that he should speak well of me?" The absence of the world's hate proves that we do not testify against it that its works are evil. The warmth of the world's love proves that we are of its own. The friendship of the world is enmity with God. Whosoever therefore will be a friend of the world is the enemy of God (John vii. 7; xv. 19; James iv. 4).[26]

7:8 The Lord told His brothers to **go up to this feast**. There was something very sad about this. They pretended to be religious men. They were going to keep the Feast of Tabernacles. Yet the Christ of God was standing in their midst, and they had no real love for Him. Man loves religious rituals because he can observe them without any real heart interest. But bring him face to face with the Person of Christ and he is ill at ease. Jesus said that He was **not yet**[27] **going up to this feast** because His **time** had **not yet fully come**. He did not mean that He would not go to the feast at all, because we learn in verse 10 that He did go. Rather, He meant that He would not go with His brothers and have a great and public manifestation. It was not time for that. When He would go, He would go quietly and with a minimum of publicity.

7:9 So the Lord **remained in Galilee** after His brothers had gone up to the feast. They had left behind the One who could ever impart to them the joy and rejoicing of which the Feast of Tabernacles spoke.

B. Jesus Teaches in the Temple (7:10–31)

7:10 Sometime after **His brothers had gone up** to Jerusalem, the Lord Jesus made a quiet trip there. As a devout Jew, He desired to attend **the feast**. But as the obedient Son of God, He could **not** do so **openly, but as it were in secret**.

7:11 **The Jews** who **sought Him at the feast** were doubtless the rulers who sought to kill Him. When they asked,

"**Where is He?**" they were not interested in worshiping Him, but rather in destroying Him.

7:12 It is clear that the presence of the Lord was creating quite a stir **among the people**. More and more, the miracles which He performed were compelling men to make up their minds as to who He really was. There was an undercurrent of conversation at the feast as to whether He was genuine or a false prophet. **Some said, "He is good"; others said, "No . . . He deceives the people."**

7:13 The opposition of the Jewish rulers to Jesus had become so intense that no one dared to speak **openly** in favor **of Him**. Doubtless many of the common people recognized that He was truly the Messiah of Israel, but they did not dare to come out and say it because they feared the leaders would persecute them.

7:14 **The Feast** of Tabernacles lasted for several days. After it was about half over, **Jesus went up into the** outside area of the **temple** (known as the porch where the people were allowed to gather) **and taught**.

7:15 Those who heard the Savior **marveled**. Doubtless it was His knowledge of the OT that impressed them most. But also the breadth of His learning and His ability to teach attracted their attention. They knew that Jesus had never been to any of the great religious schools of that day, and they could not understand how He could have such an education as He did. The world still expresses amazement and often complains when it finds believers with no formal religious training who are able to preach and teach the Word of God.

7:16 Once again it is beautiful to see how the Lord refused to take any credit for Himself, but simply tried to glorify His Father. **Jesus answered** simply that His teaching was **not** His own, **but** that it came from the One **who sent** Him. Whatever the Lord Jesus spoke and whatever He taught were the things which His Father told Him to speak and to teach. He did not act independently of the Father.

7:17 If the Jews really wanted to know whether His message was true or not, it would be easy for them to find out. If **anyone** really **wills to do** God's **will**, then God will reveal to him whether the teachings of Christ are divine or whether the Lord was simply teaching what He Himself wanted to teach. There is a wonderful promise here for everyone earnestly seeking the truth. If a person is sincere, and truly wants to know what is the truth, God will reveal it to him. "Obedience is the organ of spiritual knowledge."

7:18 Anyone **who speaks from himself**, that is, according to his own will, **seeks his own glory**. But it was not so with the Lord Jesus. He sought **the glory of** the Father **who sent Him**. Because His motives were absolutely pure, His message was absolutely **true. No unrighteousness** was **in Him**.

Jesus was the only One of whom such words could be spoken. Every other teacher has had some selfishness mixed in his service. It should be the ambition of every servant of the Lord to glorify God rather than self.

7:19 The Lord then made a direct accusation against the Jews. He reminded them that **Moses** gave them **the law**. They gloried in the fact that they possessed the law. They forgot that there was no virtue in merely possessing the law. The law demanded obedience to its precepts or commandments. Although they gloried in the law, evidently none of them kept it, for even then they were plotting to kill the Lord Jesus. The law expressly forbade murder. They were breaking the law in their intentions concerning the Lord Jesus Christ.

7:20 **The people** felt the sharp edge of Jesus' accusation but, rather than admitting He was right, they began to abuse Him. They said that He had **a demon**. They challenged His statement that any of them was **seeking to kill** Him.

7:21 **Jesus** now went back to the healing of the impotent man at the pool of Bethesda. It was this miracle that stirred up the hatred of the Jewish leaders against Him, and it was at this point that they began their vicious plot to kill Him. The Lord reminded them that He **did one work**, and they **all** marveled at it. Not that they marveled at it with admiration, but rather they were shocked

that He should do such a thing on the Sabbath.

7:22 The Law of **Moses** commanded that a male child should be circumcised eight days after birth. (Actually, circumcision had **not** originated with **Moses**, but had been practiced by **the 'fathers'**, that is, by Abraham, Isaac, Jacob, etc.) Even if the eighth day fell **on the Sabbath**, the Jews did not consider it wrong to **circumcise** the baby boy. They felt that it was a work of necessity and that the Lord allowed for such a work.

7:23 If they circumcised a child **on the Sabbath**, in order to obey **the law of Moses** regarding circumcision, why should they find fault with the Lord Jesus for making **a man completely well on the Sabbath**? If the law allowed for a work of necessity, would it not also allow for a work of mercy?

Circumcision is a minor surgical operation performed on the male child. Needless to say, it causes pain, and its physical benefits are minor. In contrast with this, the Lord Jesus made a man completely well on the Sabbath. And the Jews found fault with Him.

7:24 The trouble with the Jews was that they judged things **according to** outward **appearance** and not according to inward reality. Their judgment was not righteous. Works which seemed perfectly legitimate when performed by themselves seemed absolutely wrong when performed by the Lord. Human nature always tends to judge according to sight rather than according to reality. The Lord Jesus had not broken the Law of Moses; it was they who were breaking it by their senseless hatred of Him.

7:25 By this time, it had become well-known in **Jerusalem** that the Jewish leaders were plotting against the Savior. Here some of the common people asked if this was not the One whom their rulers were pursuing.

7:26 They could not understand that the Lord Jesus was allowed to speak so openly and **boldly**. If the rulers hated Him as much as the people had been led to believe, why did they allow Him to continue? Is it possible that they had come to find out that He was **truly** the Messiah after all, as He claimed to be?

7:27 The people who did not believe Jesus to be the Messiah thought they knew where He came from. They believed He came from Nazareth. They knew His mother, Mary, and supposed that Joseph was His father. It was commonly believed by the Jews of that day that when the Messiah came, He would come suddenly and mysteriously. They had no idea that He would be born as a Baby and grow up as a Man. They should have known from the OT that He would be born in Bethlehem, but it seemed that they were quite ignorant of the details concerning the coming of the Messiah. That is why they said, **"When Christ comes, no one knows where He is from."**

7:28 At this point **Jesus cried out** to the people who had gathered and were listening to the conversation. They did indeed **know** Him, He said, and knew **where** He came **from**. Here, of course, He was saying that they knew Him simply as a Man. They knew Him as Jesus of Nazareth. But what they did not know was that He was also God. This was what He went on to explain in the rest of the verse.

As to His humanity, He lived in Nazareth. But they should realize, too, that He did **not come** from Himself but that He had been sent from God the Father, whom these people did **not know**. In these words, the Lord Jesus made a direct claim to equality with God. He **did not come of** Himself, that is, of His own authority and to do His own will. Rather, He had been sent into the world by the **true** God, and this God they did **not know**.

7:29 But He knew Him. He dwelt with God from all eternity and was equal in all respects with God the Father. For when the Lord said that He was **from** God, He did not simply mean that He was **sent** from God, but that He always lived with God and was equal with Him in all respects. In the expression **"He sent Me,"** the Lord stated in the clearest possible way that He was the Christ of God, the Anointed One, whom God had sent into the world to accomplish the work of redemption.

7:30 The Jews understood the significance of Jesus' words and realized He was claiming to be the Messiah. They considered this to be sheer blasphemy, and attempted to arrest Him, but were not able to lay **hands on Him because His hour had not yet come**. The power of God preserved the Lord Jesus from the wicked schemes of men until the time came when He should be offered up as a sacrifice for sin.

7:31 Actually **many of the people believed on** the Lord Jesus. We would like to think that their belief was genuine. Their reasoning was this. What more could Jesus do to prove He was the Messiah? When **the Christ** came, if Jesus was not the Messiah, would He be able to **do more** numerous or more wonderful **signs** than Jesus had done? Obviously from their question they believed the miracles of Jesus proved Him to be the real Messiah.

C. The Enmity of the Pharisees (7:32–36)

7:32 As **the Pharisees** moved in and out among the people, they **heard** this undercurrent of conversation. **The crowd was murmuring** about the Savior, not in the sense of complaining against Him, but secretly revealing their admiration for Him. The Pharisees were afraid that this might enlarge into a great movement to accept Jesus, and so they **sent officers to** arrest **Him**.

7:33 The words of verse 33 were undoubtedly spoken to the officers who came to arrest Him, as well as to the Pharisees and to the people in general.

The Lord Jesus did not weaken His previous claims at all. If anything, He only strengthened them. He reminded them that He would only be with them **a little while longer**, and then He would go back to God the Father **who sent** Him. Undoubtedly this only made the Pharisees the more angry.

7:34 In a coming day, the Pharisees would **seek** Him and would **not** be able to **find** Him. There would come in their lives a time when they would need a Savior, but it would be too late. He would have gone back to heaven, and because of their unbelief and wickedness, they would not be able to meet Him there. The words of this verse are especially solemn. They remind us that there is such a thing as the passing of opportunity. Men may have the opportunity to be saved today; if they reject it, they may never have the opportunity again.

7:35 **The Jews** failed to understand the meaning of the Lord's words. They did not realize He was going back to heaven. They thought that perhaps He was going on a preaching tour, ministering to the Jewish people scattered **among the Greeks**, and also perhaps even teaching the Greeks themselves.

7:36 Again they expressed their wonder at His words. **What did** He mean when **He said** that they would **seek** Him **and** would **not** be able to **find** Him? Where could He go without their being able to follow Him? The Jews here illustrate the blindness of unbelief. There is no heart as dark as the heart that refuses to accept the Lord Jesus. In our own day, we have the expression "there are none so blind as those who will not see." This was exactly the case here. They did not *want* to accept the Lord Jesus, and therefore they *could* not.

D. The Promise of the Holy Spirit (7:37–39)

7:37 Though not mentioned in the OT, the Jews had a ceremony of carrying water from the Pool of Siloam and pouring it into a silver basin by the altar of burnt offering for each of the first seven days of the Feast of Tabernacles. On the eighth day, this was not done, which made Christ's offer of the water of eternal life even more startling. The Jewish people had gone through this religious observance, and yet their hearts were not satisfied because they had not truly understood the deep meaning of the feast. Just before they departed for their homes, **on the last day, that great day of the feast Jesus stood and cried** out to them. He invited them to **come** to Him for spiritual satisfaction. Pay particular attention to the words. His invitation was extended to **anyone**. His gospel was a universal gospel. There was no one who could not be saved if he would simply come to Christ.

But notice the condition. The Scripture says, **"If anyone thirsts."** "Thirst" here speaks of spiritual need. Unless a person knows he is a sinner, he will never want to be saved. Unless he realizes he is lost, he will never desire to be found. Unless one is conscious of a great spiritual lack in his life, he will never want to go to the Lord to have that need supplied. The Savior invited the thirsting soul to come to Him — not to the church, the preacher, the waters of baptism, or the Lord's Table. Jesus said, **"Let him come to Me."** No one or nothing else will do. **"Let him come to Me and drink."** To **"drink"** here means to appropriate Christ for oneself. It means to trust Him as Lord and Savior. It means to take Him into our lives as we would take a glass of water into our bodies.

7:38 Verse 38 proves that to come to Christ and drink is the same as to *believe* on Him. All who believe on Him will have their own needs supplied and will receive **rivers** of spiritual blessing that will **flow** out from them to others. All through the OT it was taught that those who accepted the Messiah would be helped themselves and would be channels of blessing to others (e.g. Isa. 55:1). The expression **"out of his heart will flow rivers of living water"** means out of the person's inward parts or inner life would flow streams of help to others. Stott points out that we drink in small gulps or sips, but these are multiplied into a mighty confluence of flowing streams. Temple warns: "No one can be indwelt by the Spirit of God and keep that Spirit to himself. Where the Spirit is, He flows forth; if there is no flowing forth, He is not there."

7:39 It is clearly stated that the expression "living water" refers to **the Holy Spirit**. Verse 39 is very important because it teaches that all who receive the Lord Jesus Christ also receive the Spirit of God. In other words, it is not true, as some claim, that the Holy Spirit comes to indwell people sometime after their conversion. This verse clearly and distinctly states that all who believe on Christ receive the Spirit. At the time the Lord Jesus spoke these words, **the Holy Spirit** had **not yet** been **given**. It was not until the Lord **Jesus** went back to heaven and **was glorified** that the Holy Spirit descended on the day of Pentecost. From

that moment on, every true believer in
the Lord Jesus Christ has been indwelt
by the Holy Spirit.

E. Divided Opinion Concerning Jesus (7:40–53)

7:40, 41 Many who listened were
now convinced that the Lord Jesus was
the Prophet of whom Moses spoke in
Deuteronomy 18:15, 18. **Others** were
even willing to acknowledge that Jesus
was **the Christ**, the Messiah. But some
thought this was impossible. They believed that Jesus came from Nazareth in
Galilee, and there was no prophecy in
the OT that **the Christ** would **come out
of Galilee**.

7:42 These Jews were right in believing that **the Christ** would come **from
the town of Bethlehem** and be descended from **David**. If they had just
taken the trouble to inquire, they would
have found that Jesus *was* born in Bethlehem, and that He *was a direct descendant
of* David through Mary.

7:43 Because of these differing
opinions and because of their general ignorance, **there was a division among the
people because of** Christ. It is still the
same. Men and women are divided on
the subject of Jesus Christ. Some say He
was simply a Man like the rest of us.
Others are willing to admit that He was
the greatest Man who ever lived. But
those who believe the Word of God
know that "Christ . . . is over all, the
eternally blessed God" (Rom. 9:5).

7:44 Efforts were still being made to
arrest the Lord Jesus, but no one was
successful in taking Him. As long as a
person is walking in the will of God,
there is no power on earth that can hinder him. "We are immortal until our
work is done." The Lord's time had not
yet come, and so men were unable to
harm Him in any way.

7:45 Now the **Pharisees** and **chief
priests** had sent **officers** to take Jesus.
The officers had returned, but did not
have the Lord with them. **The chief
priests and Pharisees** were annoyed and
asked the officers **why** they had **not
brought Him**.

7:46 Here was an instance where
sinful men were compelled to speak well
of the Savior, even if they did not them-

selves accept Him. Their memorable
words were, **"No man ever spoke like
this Man!"** Doubtless these officers had
listened to a good many men in their
day, but they had never heard anyone
speak with such authority, grace, and
wisdom.

7:47, 48 In an effort to intimidate
the officers, **the Pharisees** accused them
of being **deceived** by Jesus. They reminded them that none of **the rulers** of
the Jewish nation **believed in Him**. What
a terrible argument this was! It was very
much to their shame that leading men
in the Jewish nation had failed to recognize the Messiah when He came.

These Pharisees were not only unwilling to believe on the Lord Jesus
themselves, but it is clear that they did
not want others to believe on Him either. So it is today. Many who do not
want to be saved themselves do everything in their power to prevent their relatives and friends from being saved also.

7:49 Here the Pharisees spoke of
the mass of the Jewish people as ignorant **and accursed**. Their argument was
that if the common people knew anything at all about the Scriptures, they
would know that Jesus was not the Messiah. The Pharisees could not have been
more wrong!

7:50 At this point **Nicodemus**
spoke **to them**. It was **he who came to
Jesus by night** and who learned that he
must be born again. It would appear that
Nicodemus had actually trusted the Lord
Jesus Christ and been saved. Here he
stepped forward, among the rulers of
the Jews, to say a word for his Lord.

7:51 Nicodemus' point was that the
Jews had not given Jesus a fair chance.
The Jewish **law** did not **judge a man before it** heard his case. And yet that was
what the Jewish leaders were doing at
this very point. Were they afraid of the
facts? The answer was obviously that
they were.

7:52 Now the rulers turn on one of
their own company, that is, on Nicodemus. They asked him with a sneer if he
was **also** one of Jesus' followers **from
Galilee?** Did he not know that the OT
spoke of **no prophet** as coming **out of
Galilee**? Here, of course, the rulers
showed their own ignorance. Had they

never read of the prophet Jonah? He had come from Galilee.

7:53 The Feast of Tabernacles was now over. The men returned to their own homes. Some had met the Savior face to face and trusted in Him. But the majority had rejected Him, and the leaders of the Jewish people were more determined than ever to do away with Him. They considered Him a threat to their religion and way of life.

F. The Woman Taken in Adultery (8:1–11)

8:1 This verse is closely linked with the last verse of chapter 7. The connection is better seen by putting the two verses together as follows: "And everyone went to his own house, **but Jesus went to the mount of Olives.**" The Lord had truly said, "Foxes have holes and birds of the air have nests, but the Son of Man has nowhere to lay His head."

8:2 The Mount of Olives was not far away from the temple. **Early in the morning**, the Lord Jesus walked down the side of Olivet, crossed the Kidron Valley, and climbed back up into the city, where **the temple** was located. **All the people came to Him, and He sat down and taught them**.

8:3 **The scribes** (a group of men who copied and taught the Scriptures) **and** the **Pharisees** were anxious to trick the Lord Jesus into saying something wrong so that they would have some charge to bring against Him. They had just **brought . . . a woman caught** in the very act of **adultery**, and they made her stand in the middle of the crowd, probably facing Jesus.

8:4 The accusation of adultery was made against **this woman**, and it was doubtless true. There is no reason to question that she was **caught** while committing this terrible sin. But where was the man? Too often in life women have been punished when men who were also guilty have gone free.

8:5 The trick was now clear. They wanted the Lord to contradict **the Law of Moses**. If they could succeed in doing that, then they could turn the common people against Jesus. They reminded the Lord that **Moses, in the law commanded** that a person taken in the act of adultery **should be stoned** to death. For their own wicked purposes, the Pharisees hoped the Lord would disagree, and so they asked Him what He had to say on the subject. They thought that justice and the Law of Moses demanded that she should be made an example. As Darby says:

> It comforts and quiets the depraved heart of man if he can only find a person worse than himself: he thinks the greater sin of another excuses himself; and while accusing and vehemently blaming another, he forgets his own evil. He thus rejoices in iniquity.[28]

8:6 They had no real charge against the Lord and were trying to manufacture one. They knew that if He let the woman go free, He would be opposing the Law of Moses and they would **accuse Him** of being unjust. If, on the other hand, He condemned the woman to death, then they might use this to show that He was an enemy of the Roman government, and they might also say that He was not merciful. **Jesus stooped down and wrote on the ground with His finger**. There is absolutely no way of knowing what He wrote. Many people are quite confident that they know, but the simple fact of the matter is that the Bible does not tell us.

8:7 Dissatisfied, the Jews kept insisting that He make some reply. So Jesus simply stated that the penalty of the law should be carried out, but that it should be done by those who had committed no sin. Thus the Lord upheld the Law of Moses. He did not say that the woman should be free from the penalty of the law. But what He did do was to accuse every one of these men of having sinned themselves. Those who wish to judge others should be pure themselves. This verse is often used to excuse sin. The attitude is that we are free from blame because everyone else has done things that are wrong. But this verse does not excuse sin. Rather, it condemns those who are guilty even though they have never been caught.

8:8 Once **again** the Savior **stooped down and wrote on the ground**. These are the only recorded instances of the Lord Jesus writing anything, and what He wrote has long since been erased from the earth.

8:9 **Those who** accused the woman were **convicted by their conscience**.

They had nothing else to say. They began to go away, **one by one**. They were all guilty, from **the oldest** to the youngest. **Jesus was left alone**, with **the woman standing** nearby.

8:10 In wonderful grace, the Lord Jesus pointed out to the woman that all her **accusers** had vanished. They were nowhere to be found. There was not a single person in the entire crowd who dared to condemn her.

8:11 The word **Lord** here probably means "Sir." When the woman **said, "No one,** Sir," the Lord uttered those wonderful words, **"Neither do I condemn you; go and sin no more."** The Lord did not claim to have civil authority in such a matter. This power was vested in the Roman government, and He left it there. He neither condemned nor pardoned her. That was not His function at this time. But He did issue a warning to her that she should refrain from sinning.

In the first chapter of John, we learned that "grace and truth came through Jesus Christ." Here was an example of that. In the words **"neither do I condemn you,"** we have an example of grace; the words **"go, and sin no more"** are words of truth. The Lord did not say, "Go, and sin as little as possible." Jesus Christ is God, and His standard is absolute perfection. He cannot approve of sin in any degree. And so He sets before her the perfect standard of God Himself.[29]

G. Jesus the Light of the World (8:12–20)

8:12 The scene now shifts to the treasury of the temple (see v. 20). A multitude was still following Him. He turned to them and made one of the many grand statements as to His Messiahship. He said, **"I am the light of the world."** Naturally speaking, **the world** is in the darkness of sin, ignorance, and aimlessness. **The light of the world** is Jesus. Apart from Him, there is no deliverance from the blackness of sin. Apart from Him, there is no guidance along the way of life, no knowledge as to the real meaning of life and the issues of eternity. Jesus promised that anyone following Him would **not walk in darkness, but have the light of life**.

To follow Jesus means to believe on Him. Many people have the mistaken idea that they can live as Jesus lived without ever being born again. To follow Jesus means to come to Him in repentance, to trust Him as Lord and Savior, and then to commit one's whole life to Him. Those who do this have guidance in life and clear and bright hope beyond the grave.

8:13 **The Pharisees** now challenged Jesus on a legal point. They reminded Him that He was testifying concerning Himself. A person's own testimony was not considered sufficient because the average human being is biased. The Pharisees did not mind casting doubt on the words of Jesus. In fact they doubted that they were **true** at all.

8:14 The Lord recognized that usually it was necessary to have two or three witnesses. But in His case, His **witness** was absolutely **true** because He is God. He knew that He had come from heaven and was going back to heaven. But they did **not know where** He had **come from and where** He was **going**. They thought He was just another man like themselves and would not believe that He was the eternal Son, equal with the Father.

8:15 The Pharisees judged others by outward appearances and according to merely human standards. They looked upon Jesus as the Carpenter of Nazareth and never stopped to think that He was different from any other man who ever lived. The Lord Jesus said that He judged **no one**. This may mean that He did not judge men according to worldly standards, like the Pharisees did. Or more probably it means that His purpose in coming into the world was not to *judge* people but to *save* them.

8:16 **If** the Lord were to **judge**, His **judgment** would be righteous and **true**. He is God and everything He does is done in partnership **with the Father who sent** Him. Over and over again, the Lord Jesus emphasized to the Pharisees His unity with God **the Father**. It was this that stirred up in their hearts the bitterest antagonism toward Him.

8:17, 18 The Lord acknowledged that **the testimony of two** witnesses was required by the **Law** of Moses. Nothing He had said was intended to deny that fact.

If they insisted on having two witnesses, it was not difficult for Him to produce them. First of all, He bore **wit-**

ness of Himself by His sinless life and by the words that came out of His mouth. Secondly, **the Father** bore **witness** to the Lord Jesus by His public statements from heaven and by the miracles which He gave the Lord to do. Christ fulfilled the prophecies of the OT concerning the Messiah, and yet in face of this strong evidence, the Jewish leaders were unwilling to believe.

8:19 The Pharisees' next question was doubtless spoken in scorn. Perhaps they looked around the crowd as they said, **"Where is Your Father?" Jesus answered** by telling them that they **neither** recognized who He truly was nor did they know His **Father**. Of course, they would have denied vigorously any such ignorance of God. But it was true nonetheless. If they had received the Lord Jesus, they **would have known** His **Father also**. But no one can know God the Father except through Jesus Christ. Thus, their rejection of the Savior made it impossible for them to honestly claim that they knew and loved God.

8:20 Here we learn that the scene of the previous verses was **in the treasury** of **the temple**. Again the Lord is surrounded by divine protection, **and no one** is able to lay **hands on Him** to arrest Him or kill Him. **His hour had not yet come**. **His hour** refers to the time when He would be crucified at Calvary to die for the sins of the world.

H. The Jews' Debate with Jesus (8:21–59)

8:21 Again **Jesus** showed perfect knowledge of the future. He told His critics He was **going away** — referring not only to His death and burial, but to His resurrection and ascension back into heaven. The Jewish people would continue to **seek** for the Messiah, not realizing that He had already visited them and that they had rejected Him. Because of their rejection, they would **die in** their **sin** ("sin" is singular in Greek and in NKJV). This would mean that they would be forever prevented from entering heaven, where the Lord was going. It is a solemn truth! Those who refuse to accept the Lord Jesus have no hope of heaven. How dreadful to die in one's sins, without God, without Christ, without hope forever!

8:22 **The Jews** did not understand that the Lord spoke of going back to heaven. What did He mean by "going away"? Did He mean that He would escape from their plot to kill Him by committing suicide? It was strange that they should think this. If He were to **kill Himself**, there would be nothing to prevent them from doing the same and following Him in death. But it was just another example of the darkness of unbelief. It seems amazing that they could be so dull and ignorant of what the Savior was saying!

8:23 Doubtless thinking of their foolish reference to suicide, the Lord told them that they were **from beneath**. This meant that they had a very low outlook on things. They could not rise above the literal things of time and sense. They had no spiritual understanding. In contrast, Christ was **from above**. His thoughts, words, and deeds were heavenly. All that they did savored of **this world**, whereas His whole life told that He came from a purer land than this world.

8:24 Jesus often used repetition for emphasis. Here He solemnly warned them again that they would **die in** their **sins**. If they steadfastly refused to believe on Him, there was no alternative. Apart from the Lord Jesus, there is no way to obtain forgiveness of sins, and those who **die** with **sins** unforgiven cannot possibly enter heaven at last. The word **He** is not found in this verse in the original, though it may be implied. It reads literally: **"If you do not believe that I am, you will die in your sins."** We see in the words *I am* another claim to deity by the Lord Jesus.

8:25 The Jews were completely perplexed by the teachings of the Lord Jesus. They asked Him pointedly **who** He was. Perhaps they meant this in sarcasm, as if to say, "Who do You think You are, that You should speak to us in this way?" Or perhaps they were really anxious to hear what He would say concerning Himself. His answer is worthy of note: **"Just what I have been saying to you from the beginning."** He was the promised Messiah. The Jews had heard Him say so frequently, but their stubborn hearts refused to bow to the truth. But His answer can have another meaning — the Lord Jesus was exactly what He preached. He did not say one thing and do another. He was the living embodiment of all that He taught. His life agreed with His teaching.

8:26 The meaning of verse 26 is not clear. It seems the Lord was saying that there were **many** additional **things** He could **say** and **judge concerning** these unbelieving Jews. He could expose the wicked thoughts and motives of their hearts. However, He was obediently speaking only those things which the Father had given Him to speak. And since the Father **is true**, He is worthy to be believed and listened to.

8:27 The Jews **did not understand** at this point **that He** was speaking **to them of** God **the Father**. It seems that their minds were becoming more clouded all the time. Previously when the Lord Jesus claimed to be the Son of God, they had realized He was claiming equality with God the Father. But not so anymore.

8:28 Again **Jesus** prophesied what was going to happen. First of all, the Jews would lift up **the Son of Man**. This refers to His death by crucifixion. After they had done that, they would **know that** He was the Messiah. They would know it by the earthquake and by the darkness, but, most of all, by His bodily resurrection from the dead. Notice carefully the words of the Lord, **"Then you will know that** I am." Here, again, the word **He** is not in the original. The deeper meaning is, "Then **you will know that I am** God." Then they would understand He did nothing from Himself, that is, by His own authority. Rather, He came into the world as the dependent One, speaking only those things which the **Father** had **taught** Him to say.

8:29, 30 The Lord's relationship with God the Father was very intimate. Each of these expressions was a claim to equality with God. Throughout all of His earthly ministry, the Father was **with** Him. At no time was Jesus left **alone**. At all times He did the things that were pleasing to God. These words could only be spoken by a sinless Being. No one born of human parents could ever truthfully utter those words, **"I always do those things that please Him."** Too often we do the things that please ourselves.

Sometimes we are prompted to please our fellow men. Only the Lord Jesus was completely taken up with the desire to do the things that were well-pleasing to God.

As He spoke these wonderful **words**, Jesus found that **many** professed to believe on Him. Doubtless some were genuine in their faith. Others might only have been prompted to give lip service to the Lord.

8:31 Then **Jesus** made a distinction between those who are disciples and those who are **disciples indeed**. A disciple is anyone who professes to be a learner, but a **disciple indeed** is one who has definitely committed himself to the Lord Jesus Christ. Those who are true believers have this characteristic — they **abide in** His **Word**. This means that they continue in the teachings of Christ. They do not turn aside from Him. True faith always has the quality of permanence. They are not saved by abiding in His Word, but they abide in His Word because they are saved.

8:32 The promise is made to every true disciple that he **shall know the truth, and the truth shall make** him **free**. The Jews did not know the truth, and they were in a terrible form of bondage. They were in the bondage of ignorance, error, sin, law, and superstition. Those who truly know the Lord Jesus are delivered from sin, they walk in the light, and are led by the Holy Spirit of God.

8:33 Some of the Jews who were standing by heard the Lord's reference to being made free. They resented it immediately. They boasted of their descent from Abraham and said that they had **never been in bondage**. But this was not true. Israel had been in bondage to Egypt, Assyria, Babylon, Persia, Greece, and now Rome. But even more than that, even while they still spoke with the Lord Jesus they were in bondage to sin and to Satan.

8:34 It is evident that the Lord was speaking about the bondage **of sin**. He reminded His Jewish listeners that **whoever** practices **sin is a slave of sin**. These Jews pretended to be very religious, but the truth of the matter was that they were dishonest, irreverent, and soon to be murderers — for even now they were plotting the death of the Son of God.

8:35 Jesus next compared the relative positions **in the house** of **a slave** and **a son**. The **slave** did not have any assurance that he would live there forever; whereas the **son** was at home in the house. Whether the word "Son" applies to the Son of God or whether it applies to those who become children of God by faith in Christ, it is clear that the Lord Jesus was telling these Jews that they were not sons, but slaves who could be put out at any time.

8:36 There is no question that the word **Son** in this verse refers to Christ Himself. Those who are made **free** by Him are made **free indeed**. This means that when a person comes to the Savior and receives eternal life from Him, that person is freed from the slavery of sin, legalism, superstition, and demonism.

8:37 The Lord acknowledged that, as far as physical lineage was concerned, these Jews were **Abraham's descendants** (literally "seed"). But it was evident they were not of the *spiritual* seed of Abraham. They were not godly men like Abraham was. They sought **to kill** the Lord Jesus because His teachings had **no place** in them. This means that they did not allow the words of Christ to take effect in their lives. They resisted His doctrines and would not yield to Him.

8:38 The things Jesus taught them were things He had been commissioned by His **Father** to speak. He and His Father were so completely one that the words He spoke were the words of God the Father. The Lord Jesus perfectly represented His Father while here on the earth. In contrast, the Jews did those things which they had learned from *their father*. The Lord Jesus did not mean their literal, earthly father, but rather *the devil*.

8:39 Once again the Jews claimed kinship to **Abraham**. They boasted in the fact that **Abraham** was their **father**. However, the Lord Jesus pointed out that although they were Abraham's descendants [seed] (v. 37), they were not his **children**. Usually children look, walk, and talk like their parents. But not so with these Jews. Their lives were the opposite of Abraham's. Though descendants of Abraham according to the flesh, yet morally they were children of the devil.

8:40 The Lord proceeded to give a very clear example of the difference between them and Abraham. Jesus had come into the world, speaking to them nothing but **the truth**. They were offended and stumbled over His teaching, and so tried **to kill** Him. **Abraham did not do this**. He took his place on the side of truth and righteousness.

8:41 It was very clear who their father was because they acted just like him. They did **the deeds of** their **father**, that is, the devil. The Jews may well have been accusing the Lord of being **born of fornication**. But many Bible students see in the word **fornication** a reference to idolatry. The Jews were saying that they had never committed spiritual adultery. They had always been true to **God**. He is the only One they ever acknowledged as their **Father**.

8:42 The Lord showed the falseness of their claim by reminding them that if they loved God, they **would love** Him whom God had **sent**. It is foolish for anyone to claim to love God and at the same time to hate the Lord Jesus Christ. Jesus said He **proceeded forth . . . from God**. This meant that He was the eternally begotten Son of God. There was no particular time at which He was born the Son of God, but this relationship of Son to the Father existed from all eternity. He also reminded them that He **came from God**. Obviously, He was here stating His pre-existence. He dwelt in heaven with the Father long before He ever appeared on this earth. But the Father **sent** Him into the world to be the Savior of the world, and so He came as the obedient One.

8:43 There is a difference in verse 43 between **speech** and **word**. Christ's **word** referred to the things He taught. His **speech** referred to the words with which He expressed His truths. They could **not** even **understand** His **speech**. When He spoke of bread, they thought only of literal bread. When He spoke of water, they never connected it with spiritual water. Why was it that they could not understand His speech? It was because they were unwilling to tolerate His teachings.

8:44 Now the Lord Jesus came out openly and told them that **the devil** was their **father**. This did not mean that they had been born of the devil in the way believers are born of God. Rather, it meant, as Augustine said, that they were children of the devil *by imitation*. They showed their relationship to the devil by living the way he lived. **"The desires of your father you want to do"** expresses the intention or tendency of their hearts.

The devil was **a murderer from the beginning**. He brought death to Adam and the whole human race. Not only was he **a murderer**, but was **a liar** as well. He did **not stand in the truth, because there is no truth in him. When he** told **a lie, he** was merely speaking **from his own resources**. Lies formed a part of his very existence. **He is a liar and the father** of lies. The Jews imitated the devil in these two ways. They were murderers because the intention of their hearts was to kill the Son of God. They were liars because they said that God was their Father. They pretended to be godly, spiritual men, but their lives were wicked.

8:45 Those who give themselves over to lying seem to lose the capacity for discerning the truth. Here stood the Lord Jesus before these men, and he had always spoken **the truth**. Yet they would **not believe** Him. This showed that their real character was wicked. Lenski puts it well:

> When it meets the truth, the corrupted mind seeks only objections; when it meets what differs from this truth, it sees and seeks reasons for accepting this difference.[30]

8:46 Only Christ, the sinless Son of God, could ever truly utter words like these. There was not a person in the world who could convict Him of a single **sin**. There was no defect in His character. He was perfect in all His ways. He spoke only words of truth, and yet they would **not believe** Him.

8:47 If a man really loves God, he will hear and obey **God's words**. The Jews showed by their rejection of the Savior's message that they did not really belong to **God**. It is clear from verse 47 that the Lord Jesus claimed to speak the very words of God. There could be no misunderstanding of this.

8:48 Once again **the Jews** resorted to abusive language, because they could not answer the words of the Lord Jesus in any other way. In calling Him **a Samaritan**, they senselessly used an ethnic slur. It was as if they said that He was not a pure Jew, but was an enemy of Israel. Also, they accused Him of having **a demon**. By this they doubtless meant that He was insane. To them, only a man out of his mind would ever make the claims which Jesus had been making.

8:49 Notice the even-tempered way in which **Jesus answered** His enemies. His teachings were not the words of one who had **a demon**, but rather of One who sought to **honor** God the **Father**. It was for this they were dishonoring Him, not because He was crazy, but because He was completely taken up with the interests of His Father in heaven.

8:50 They should have known that at no time did he **seek** His **own glory**. All He did was calculated to bring glory to His Father. Even though He accused them of dishonoring Him, that did not mean that He was seeking His **own glory**. Then the Lord added the words, **"There is One who seeks and judges."** This One referred, of course, to God. God the Father would seek glory for His beloved Son, and would judge all of those who failed to give Him this glory.

8:51 Again we have one of those majestic sayings of the Lord Jesus, words which could only be uttered by One who was God Himself. The words are introduced by the familiar emphatic expression **"Most assuredly, I say to you."** Jesus promised that **if anyone keeps** His **Word**, that person **shall never see death**. This cannot refer to *physical death* because many believers in the Lord Jesus die each day. The reference is to *spiritual death*. The Lord was saying that those who believe on Him are delivered from eternal **death** and shall never suffer the pangs of hell.

8:52 **The Jews** were now more convinced than ever that Jesus was "mad." They reminded Him that **Abraham** and **the prophets** were all **dead**. Yet He had said that **if anyone** kept His **Word he** would **never taste death**. How can these things be reconciled?

8:53 They realized the Lord was actually claiming to be **greater than** their **father Abraham** and **the prophets**. Abraham never delivered anyone from death, and he could not deliver himself from death. Neither could the prophets. Yet here was One who claimed to be able to deliver His fellow men from death. He must consider Himself greater than the fathers.

8:54 The Jews thought Jesus was seeking to attract attention to Himself. **Jesus** reminded them that this was not the case. It was the **Father** who was honoring Him, the very **God** they professed to love and serve.

8:55 The Jews said that God was their Father, but actually they did not know Him. Yet here they were speaking with One who *did* **know** God the Father, One who was equal with Him. They wanted Jesus to deny His equality with the Father, but He said that if He did this, He would be **a liar**. He knew God the Father and obeyed **His word**.

8:56 Since the Jews insisted on bringing Abraham into the argument, the Lord reminded them that **Abraham** had looked forward to the **day** of the Messiah, and he had actually **seen it** by faith, **and was glad**. The Lord Jesus was saying that *He* was the One to whom Abraham looked forward. Abraham's faith rested in the coming of Christ.

When did Abraham see Christ's day? Perhaps it was when he took Isaac to Mount Moriah to offer him as a burnt offering to God. The whole drama of the Messiah's death and resurrection was acted out at that time, and it is possible that Abraham saw it by faith. Thus the Lord Jesus claimed to be the fulfillment of all the prophecies in the OT concerning the Messiah.

8:57 Once again **the Jews** revealed their inability to understand divine truth. Jesus had said, "Abraham rejoiced to see My day," but they answered as though He had said that He had seen Abraham. There is a great difference here. The Lord Jesus claimed for Himself a position greater than Abraham. He was the Object of Abraham's thoughts and hopes. Abraham looked forward by faith to Christ's day.

The Jews could not understand this. They reasoned that Jesus was **not yet fifty years old**. (Actually He was only about thirty-three years of age at this time.) How could He have **seen Abraham**?

8:58 The Lord Jesus here made another clear claim to be God. He did not say, **"Before Abraham was, I** *was*.**"** That might simply mean that He came into

existence before Abraham. Rather, He used the Name of God: **I AM**. The Lord Jesus had dwelt with God the Father from all eternity. There was never a time when He came into being, or when He did not exist. Therefore He said, **"Before Abraham was, I AM."**

8:59 At once the Jews attempted to put Jesus to death, **but He hid Himself and went out of the temple**. The Jews understood exactly what Jesus meant when He said, "Before Abraham was, I AM." He was claiming to be Jehovah! It was for this reason they sought to stone Him, because to them this was blasphemy. They were unwilling to accept the fact that the Messiah was standing in their midst. They would not have Him to reign over them!

I. The Sixth Sign: Healing of the Man Born Blind (9:1–12)

9:1 This incident may have taken place **as Jesus** was leaving the temple area, or it may have occurred some time after the events of chapter 8. It is recorded that the man had been **blind from birth** to show the hopelessness of his condition and the wonder of the miracle that gave him sight.

9:2 The **disciples asked** a rather strange question. They wondered if the blindness had been caused by the man's own sin or by his parents' sin. How could the blindness have been caused by his own sin, when he had been *born* **blind**? Did they believe in some form of reincarnation, the belief that the soul of the dead returned to earth in a new body? Or did they suggest that he might have been born blind because of sins which God knew he would commit after his birth? It is clear that they thought the blindness was directly connected with sin in the family. We know that this was not necessarily so. Although all sickness, suffering, and death came into the world ultimately as a result of sin, it is *not* true that in any particular case a person suffers because of sins which he has committed.

9:3 Jesus did not mean that the man had not sinned, or that his parents had not sinned. Rather, He meant that the blindness was not a direct result of sin in their lives. God had allowed this man to be born blind in order that the man might become a means of displaying the mighty **works of God**. Before the man was born, the Lord Jesus knew He would give sight to those blind eyes.

9:4 The Savior realized that He had about three years of public ministry before He would be crucified. Every moment of that time must be spent in working for God. Here was a man who had been blind from his birth. The Lord Jesus must perform a miracle of healing on him, even though it was the Sabbath. The time of His public ministry would soon be over, and He would no longer be here on earth. This is a solemn reminder to everyone who is a Christian that life's day is swiftly passing, and **the night is coming** when our service on earth will be forever over. Therefore, we should use the time that is given to us to serve the Lord acceptably.

9:5 When Jesus was **in the world** as a Man, He was **the light of the world** in a very direct and special way. As He went about performing miracles and teaching the people, they saw **the light of the world** before their very eyes. The Lord Jesus is *still* the Light of the world, and all who come to Him are promised that they will not walk in darkness. However, in this verse the Lord was speaking particularly of His public ministry on earth.

9:6 We are not told why Jesus mixed **clay** and **saliva** and put it on **the eyes of the blind man**. Some have suggested that the man had no eyeballs and that the Lord Jesus simply created them, giving him eyeballs. Others suggest that in giving sight to the blind, the Lord Jesus commonly used methods that were despised in the eyes of the world. He used weak and insignificant things in working out His purposes. Even today, in giving sight to the spiritually blind, God uses men and women who are made of the dust of the earth.

9:7 The Lord called the faith of the blind man into operation by telling him to **go** and **wash in the pool of Siloam**. Though he was blind, yet he probably knew the location of the pool and was able to do as he was told. The Scripture notes that the word **Siloam** means **Sent**. Perhaps this is a reference to the Messiah (the "Sent" One). The One who was performing this miracle was the One

who had been sent into the world by God the Father. The blind man **went and washed** in the pool, and received his sight. It is not a case that his sight was restored, because he had never seen before at all. The miracle was instantaneous and the man was able to use his eyes immediately. What a delightful surprise it must have been for him to look for the first time upon the world in which he had lived!

9:8, 9 **The neighbors** of the man were startled. They could hardly believe that this was the same man who had **sat and begged** for so long. (It should be this way also when a person is saved. Our neighbors should be able to notice the difference in us.) **Some** insisted it was the same man. **Others**, not quite so sure, were only willing to admit that there was a resemblance. But the man removed all doubt by stating that he was the one who had been born blind.

9:10 Whenever Jesus performed a miracle, it provoked all kinds of questions in the hearts of men. Often these questions gave the believer an opportunity to witness for the Lord. Here people asked the man **how** it all happened.

9:11 His testimony was simple, yet convincing. He recited the facts of his healing, giving credit to the One who had performed the miracle. At this time, the man did not realize who the Lord Jesus was. He simply referred to Him as **"a Man called Jesus."** But later on the man's understanding grew and he came to know who Jesus is.

9:12 When we witness concerning the Lord Jesus Christ, we often create a desire in the hearts of others to come to know Him, too.

J. Increasing Opposition from the Jews (9:13–41)

9:13 Apparently in earnest enthusiasm over the miracle, some of the Jewish people **brought** the **blind** man **to the Pharisees**. They probably did not realize how the religious leaders would resent the fact that this man had been healed.

9:14 Jesus had performed the miracle on **a Sabbath**. The critical Pharisees did not realize that God never intended the Sabbath to prevent an act of mercy or of kindness.

9:15 The man had another opportunity to witness for Jesus. When **the Pharisees also asked him again how he had received his sight**, they heard the simple story once again. The man did not mention the name of Jesus here, probably not because he was afraid to do so, but because he realized that everyone knew who had done this mighty work. By this time, the Lord Jesus was well known in Jerusalem.

9:16 Now another **division** arose over who Jesus was. **Some of the Pharisees** announced boldly that Jesus could not be a godly Man because He had broken **the Sabbath. Others** reasoned that a sinful man could not perform such a wonderful miracle. Jesus often caused divisions among people. Men were forced to take sides and be either for Him or against Him.

9:17 The Pharisees asked **the man** who had been **blind** what he thought of Jesus. As yet, he did not realize that Jesus was God. But his faith had grown to such an extent that he was willing to admit that Jesus was **a prophet**. He believed that the One who had given him sight had been sent by God, and had a divine message.

9:18, 19 Many of **the Jews** were still unwilling to **believe** that a miracle had been performed. And so **they called the parents** of the man to see what they would say.

Who would know better than parents if a child had been born without sight? Surely their testimony would be conclusive. So the Pharisees **asked them** whether this was their **son** and also **how** he received his sight.

9:20, 21 The testimony of **his parents** was very positive. **This** was their **son**, and they knew through years of heartache **that** he had always been **blind**.

Beyond that, they were unwilling to go. They did **not know** how his sight was restored, they said, **or who** the person was who restored it. They directed the Pharisees back to the son himself. He could **speak for himself**.

9:22, 23 Verse 22 explains the timidity of the **parents**. They had heard that any man confessing that Jesus was the Messiah **would be put out of the synagogue**. This excommunication was a very serious matter for any Jew. They

were not willing to pay such a price. It would mean the loss of a means of livelihood, as well as a loss of all the privileges of the Jewish religion.

It was for fear of the Jewish rulers, **therefore**, that **the parents** shifted the testimony back to their son.

9:24 **"Give God the glory!"** may have two meanings. First of all, it may be a form of oath. Perhaps the Pharisees were saying, "Now tell the truth. **We know that this Man is a sinner"**. Or it may mean that the Pharisees were demanding that God be given the glory for the miracle, and that no credit be given to Jesus because the Pharisees considered Him to be a sinful man.

9:25 The Pharisees met failure at every turn. Every time they tried to discredit the Lord Jesus, it resulted in bringing more honor to Him. The man's testimony here was beautiful. He did **not know** too much about the Person of Jesus, but he did **know** that **though** once he **was blind**, **now** he saw. This was a testimony that no one could deny.

So it is in the case of those who have been born again. The world may doubt, scoff, and sneer, but no one can deny our testimony when we say that once we were lost, and now we have been saved by the grace of God.

9:26, 27 **Again** they reopened the questioning, asking him to repeat the details. By now the man who had been blind was obviously annoyed. He reminded them that he had **told** them the facts **already**, and they did **not listen. Why** did they **want to hear it again**? Were they interested in becoming **disciples** of Jesus? Obviously, this was asked in sarcasm. He knew very well that they hated Jesus, and had no desire to follow Him.

9:28 It has been said, "When you have no case, abuse the plaintiff." That is what happened here. The Pharisees had utterly failed to shake the testimony of this man, so they began to abuse him. They accused him of being a **disciple** of Jesus, as if that were the worst thing in the world! Then they professed to be **Moses' disciples**, as if that were the greatest thing possible.

9:29 The Pharisees said **that God spoke to Moses**, but they spoke slightingly of Jesus. If they had believed the writings of Moses, they would have accepted Jesus as their Lord and Savior. Also, if they had thought a little, they would have realized that Moses never gave sight to a man who had been born blind. A greater than Moses was in their midst, and they did not realize it.

9:30 The man's sarcasm now became biting. It was something that the Pharisees didn't expect. The man said to them in effect, "You men are the rulers in Israel. You are the teachers of the Jewish people. And yet here is a Man in your midst who has the power to give sight to blind eyes, and **you do not know where He is from**. Shame on you!"

9:31 The man was now becoming bolder in his witness. His faith was growing. He reminded them that as a general principle, **God does not hear sinners** or work miracles through them. God does not approve of men who are evil, and does not give power to such men to perform mighty works. Worshipers **of God**, on the other hand, receive God's commendation and are assured of God's approval.

9:32, 33 This man realized that he was the first man in all of human history who had been **born blind** and who had received his sight. He could not understand that the Pharisees should witness such a miracle and find fault with the Person who performed it.

If the Lord Jesus **were not from God, He could** never **do** a miracle of this nature.

9:34 Again the Pharisees turned to abuse. They insinuated that this man's blindness was the direct result of **sins**. What right had he to be **teaching** them? The truth is that he had every right in the world, for, as Ryle has said, "The teaching of the Holy Ghost is more frequently to be seen among men of low degree than among men of rank and education." When it says **they cast him out**, this probably refers to more than his being cast out of the temple. It probably means that he was excommunicated from the Jewish religion. And yet what was the ground for the excommunication? A man born blind had been given his sight on the Sabbath. Because he would not speak evil of the One who had performed the miracle, he was excommunicated.

9:35 **Jesus** now sought out this man. It is as if Jesus had said, "If they do not want you, I will take you." Those who are cast out for Jesus' sake lose nothing, but gain a great blessing in His personal welcome and fellowship. See how the Lord Jesus led the man to personal faith in Himself as the Son of God! He simply asked the question, **"Do you believe in the Son of God?"**[31]

9:36 Although he had received his physical sight, the man was still in need of spiritual vision. He asked the Lord **who** the Son of God was, that he might **believe in Him**. In using the word **"Lord"** here, the man was simply saying "Sir."

9:37 **Jesus** now introduced Himself to the man as the Son of God. It was not a mere man who had given him sight and performed the impossible in his life. It was the Son of God, the One whom he had seen and who was now **talking with** him.

9:38 At this the man simply and sweetly placed his faith in the Lord Jesus and fell down and **worshiped Him**. He was now a saved soul as well as a healed man. What a great day this had been in his life! He had received both physical and spiritual sight.

Notice that the blind man did not worship the Lord until he knew that Jesus was the Son of God. Being an intelligent Jew, he would not worship a mere man. But as soon as he learned that the One who healed him was God the Son, **he worshiped Him** — not for what He had done but for who He was.

9:39 At first glance this verse seems to contradict John 3:17, "For God did not send His Son into the world to condemn the world . . ." But there is no real conflict. The purpose of Christ's coming into the world was not to judge but to save. However, judgment is the inevitable result for all who fail to receive Him.

The preaching of the gospel has two effects. **Those who** admit that they **do not see** are given sight. But **those who** insist that they can **see** perfectly, without the Lord Jesus, are confirmed in their blindness.

9:40 **Some of the Pharisees** realized that the Lord Jesus was speaking of them and of their blindness. So they came to Him and brazenly asked if He meant to insinuate that they were **blind also**. Their question expected a negative answer.

9:41   The Lord's answer may be paraphrased as follows: **"If** you admit that you are **blind** and sinful, and that you need a Savior, then your sins can be forgiven you, and you can be saved. But you profess that you are in need of nothing. You claim that you are righteous and that you have no sin. **Therefore**, there is no forgiveness of sins for you." When **Jesus said, " . . . you would have no sin,"** He did not mean that they would be absolutely sinless. But He meant that comparatively speaking, they would be sinless. If they had only acknowledged their blindness in failing to recognize Him as Messiah, their sin would have been as nothing compared to the enormous sin of professing to see, yet failing to recognize Him as the Son of God.

K.   Jesus, the Door of the Sheep (10:1–10)

10:1   These verses are closely linked with the latter part of chapter 9. There the Lord Jesus had been speaking to the Pharisees, who claimed to be rightful shepherds of the people of Israel. It was to them, in particular, that the Lord Jesus referred here. The solemn character of what He was about to say is indicated by the expression **"Most assuredly, I say to you."**

A **sheepfold** was an enclosure in which sheep were sheltered at night. It was an area surrounded by a fence and having one opening that was used as a door. Here **the sheepfold** refers to the Jewish nation.

Many came to the Jewish people, professing to be their spiritual rulers and guides. They were self-appointed messiahs for the nation. But they did not come by the way which the OT predicted the Messiah would come. They climbed up **some other way**. They presented themselves to Israel in a manner of their own choosing. These men were not true shepherds, but thieves and robbers. Thieves are those who take what does not belong to them, and robbers are those who use violence in doing so. The Pharisees were thieves and robbers. They sought to rule over the Jews, and yet did everything in their power to hinder them from accepting the true Messiah. They persecuted those who followed Jesus, and eventually they would put Jesus to death.

10:2   Verse 2 refers to Jesus Himself. He came to the lost sheep of the house of Israel. He was the true **shepherd of the sheep**. He entered **by the door**, that is, He came in exact fulfillment of the OT prophecies concerning the Messiah. He was not a self-appointed Savior, but came in perfect obedience to the will of His Father. He met all the conditions.

10:3   There is considerable disagreement as to the identity of **the doorkeeper** in this verse. Some think this expression refers to the prophets of the OT who foretold the coming of the Christ. Others believe it refers to John the Baptist, since he was the forerunner of the true Shepherd. Still others are equally sure that **the doorkeeper** in this verse is the Holy Spirit who opens the door for the entrance of the Lord Jesus into hearts and lives.

The sheep heard the shepherd's **voice**. They recognized his voice as that of the true shepherd. Just as literal sheep recognize the voice of their own shepherd, so there were those among the Jewish people who recognized the Messiah when He appeared. Throughout the Gospel, we have heard the Shepherd calling **His own sheep by name**. He called to several disciples in chapter 1, and they all heard His voice and responded. He called the blind man in chapter 9. The Lord Jesus still calls those who will receive Him as Savior, and the call is personal and individual.

The expression **and leads them out** may refer to the fact that the Lord Jesus led those who heard His voice out of the sheepfold of Israel. There they were shut up and enclosed. There was no liberty under the law. The Lord **leads** His sheep into the freedom of His grace. In the last chapter, the Jews had cast the man out of the synagogue. In doing so, they had been assisting the work of the Lord without knowing it.

10:4   When the true shepherd **brings out His own sheep**, he does not drive them, but He leads **them**. He does not ask them to go anywhere that He

Himself has not first gone. He is ever out in front of the sheep as their Savior, their Guide, and Example. Those who are true **sheep** of Christ **follow Him**. They do not *become* sheep by following His example, but by being born again. Then when they are saved, they have a desire to go where He leads.

10:5 The same instinct that enables a sheep to recognize the voice of the true shepherd also prompts it to **flee from a stranger**. The strangers were the Pharisees and other leaders of the Jewish people who were only interested in the sheep for their own personal advantage. The man who received his sight illustrates this. He recognized the voice of the Lord Jesus but knew that the Pharisees were strangers. Therefore, he refused to obey them, even though it meant being excommunicated.

10:6 It is distinctly stated now that **Jesus used this illustration** on the Pharisees, **but they did not understand** — the reason being they were not true sheep. If they had been, they would have heard His voice and followed Him.

10:7 Then Jesus used a new illustration. He was no longer speaking about the door of the sheepfold, as in verse 2. Now He was presenting Himself as **the door of the sheep**. It was no longer a question of entering the sheepfold of Israel, but rather the picture was of the elect sheep of Israel passing out of Judaism and coming to Christ, **the door**.

10:8 Others had come **before** Christ, claiming authority and position. But the elect sheep of Israel did not hear them because they knew they were claiming what did not rightfully belong to them.

10:9 Verse 9 is one of those delightful verses which is simple enough for the Sunday School pupil to understand, and yet which can never be exhausted by the most learned scholars. Christ is **the door**. Christianity is not a creed, or a church. Rather it is a Person, and that Person is the Lord Jesus Christ. **"If anyone enters by Me."** Salvation can only be received through Christ. Baptism will not do; neither will the Lord's Supper. We must enter in by Christ, and by the power which He gives. The invitation is for anyone. Christ is the Savior of Jew and Gentile alike. But to be saved, a person must enter in. He must receive Christ by faith. It is a personal act, and without it there is no salvation. Those who do enter in are **saved** from the penalty, the power, and eventually from the very presence of sin.

After salvation, they **go in and out**. Perhaps the thought is that they go into the presence of God by faith to worship, and then they go out into the world to witness for the Lord. At any rate, it is a picture of perfect security and liberty in the service of the Lord. Those who enter **find pasture**. Christ is not only the Savior, and the One who gives freedom, but He is also the Sustainer and Satisfier. His sheep **find pasture** in the Word of God.

10:10 The purpose of **the thief** is **to steal, and to kill, and to destroy**. He comes for purely selfish motives. In order to gain his own desires, he would even **kill** the sheep. But the Lord Jesus does not come to the human heart for any selfish reason. He comes to give, not to get. He comes that people **may have life, and that they may have it more abundantly**. We receive life the moment we accept Him as our Savior. After we are saved, however, we find that there are various degrees of enjoyment of this life. The more we turn ourselves over to the Holy Spirit, the more we enjoy the life which has been given to us. We not only have **life** then, but we **have it more abundantly**.

L. Jesus, the Good Shepherd (10:11–18)

10:11 Many times the Lord Jesus used the expression **"I am,"** one of the titles of Deity. Each time He was making a claim to equality with God the Father. Here he presented Himself as **the good shepherd who** laid down **His life for the sheep**. Ordinarily, the sheep were called upon to lay down their lives for the shepherd. But the Lord Jesus died for the flock.

> When blood from a victim must flow,
> This Shepherd by pity was led,
> To stand between us and the foe,
> And willingly died in our stead.
>   *– Thomas Kelly*

10:12   **A hireling** is one who serves for money. For instance, a shepherd might pay someone else to take care of his sheep. The Pharisees were hirelings. Their interest in the people was prompted by the money they received in return. The **hireling** did **not own the sheep**. When danger came, he ran away and left the sheep to the mercy of **the wolf**.

10:13   We do what we do because we are what we are. The hireling served for pay. He did **not care about the sheep**. He was more interested in his own welfare than in their good. There are many hirelings in the church today — men who choose the ministry as a comfortable occupation, without true love for God's sheep.

10:14   Again the Lord speaks of Himself as **the good shepherd. Good** (Gk., *kalos*) here means "ideal, worthy, choice, excellent." He is all of these. Then He speaks of the very intimate relationship that exists between Himself and His **sheep**. He knows His own, and His **own** know Him. This is a very wonderful truth.

10:15   It is unfortunate that this verse is punctuated as a new sentence. Actually, it is better read as follows: ". . . and I know My sheep, and am known by My own, just **as the Father knows Me**, and **I know the Father.**" This is truly a thrilling truth! The Lord compared His relationship with the sheep with the relationship that existed between Himself and His Father. The same union, communion, intimacy, and knowledge that there is between the Father and the Son also exists between the Shepherd and the sheep. **"And I lay down My life for the sheep,"** He said. Again we have one of the many statements of the Lord Jesus in which He looked forward to the time when He would die on the cross as a Substitute for sinners.

10:16   Verse 16 is the key to the entire chapter. The **other sheep** to whom the Lord referred here were the Gentiles. His coming into the world was especially in connection with the sheep of Israel, but He also had in mind the salvation of Gentiles. The Gentile sheep were **not** of the Jewish **fold**. But the great heart of compassion of the Lord Jesus went out to these sheep as well, and He was under divine compulsion to **bring** them to Himself. He knew that they would be more ready than the Jewish people to **hear** His **voice**.

In the latter part of the verse there is the very important change from the **fold** of Judaism to the **flock** of Christianity. This verse gives a little preview of the fact that in Christ, Jew and Gentile would be made one, and that the former distinctions between these peoples would disappear.

10:17   In verses 17 and 18, the Lord Jesus explained what He would do in order to bring both elect Jews and Gentiles to Himself. He looked forward to the time of His death, burial, and resurrection. These words would be utterly out of place were the Lord Jesus a mere man. He spoke of laying **down** His **life** and taking **it again** by His own power. He could only do this because He is God. The **Father** loved the Lord Jesus **because** of His willingness to die and rise again, in order that lost sheep might be saved.

10:18   **No one** could take the Lord's life **from** Him. He is God, and is thus greater than all the murderous plots of His creatures. He had **power** in Himself **to lay down** His life, **and** He also had **power to take it again**. But did not men kill the Lord Jesus? They did. This is clearly stated in Acts 2:23 and in 1 Thessalonians 2:15. The Lord Jesus allowed them to do it, and this was an exhibition of His **power to lay down** His life. Furthermore, He "gave up His Spirit" (John 19:30) as an act of His own strength and will.

"This command I have received from My Father," He said. The Father had commissioned or instructed the Lord to lay down His life and to rise again from among the dead. His death and resurrection were essential acts in fulfillment of the Father's will. Therefore, He became obedient unto death, and rose again the third day, according to the Scriptures.

**M. Division Among the Jews
   (10:19–21)**

10:19   The words of the Lord Jesus

caused **a division again among the Jews**. Christ's entrance into the world, and into homes, and into hearts, produces a sword, rather than peace. Only when men receive Him as Lord and Savior do they know the peace of God.

10:20, 21 The Lord Jesus was the only perfect Man who ever lived. He never said a wrong word or committed an evil deed. Yet such was the depravity of the heart of man that when He came, speaking words of love and wisdom, men said that **He** had **a demon and** was **mad**, and was not worthy to be listened to. This was certainly a dark spot on the record of the human race. **Others** thought differently. They recognized **the words** and works of the Lord Jesus as those of a good Person and not of **a demon**.

N. Jesus Proved to Be the Christ by His Works (10:22–39)

10:22 At this point there is a break in the narrative. The Lord Jesus was no longer speaking to the Pharisees, but to the Jews in general. We do not know what time elapsed between verse 21 and verse 22. Incidentally, this is the only mention in the Bible of **the Feast of Dedication**, or in Hebrew, Hanukkah. It is generally believed that this feast was instituted by Judas Maccabeus when the temple was rededicated after being defiled by Antiochus Epiphanes, 165 B.C. It was a yearly feast, instituted by the Jewish people, and not one of the feasts of the Lord. **It was** not only **winter** according to the calendar, but also spiritually.

10:23, 24 The Lord's public ministry was almost over, and He was about to demonstrate His complete dedication to God the Father by His death on the cross. **Solomon's porch** was a covered area, adjoining Herod's temple. As the Lord walked there, there would have been plenty of room for the Jews to gather around Him.

The Jews surrounded Him and said, "How long do You keep us in doubt (or suspense)? **If You are the Christ, tell us plainly."**

10:25, 26 **Jesus** again reminded them of His words and His **works**. He had often told them that He was the

Messiah, and the miracles He performed proved that His claim was true. Again He reminded the Jews that He performed His miracles by authority of His Father and for His Father's glory. In doing so, He showed that He was indeed the One whom the Father had sent into the world.

Their unwillingness to receive the Messiah proved that they were **not of** His **sheep**. If they had been set apart to belong to Him, they would have shown a willingness to believe Him.

10:27 These next few verses teach in unmistakable terms that no true sheep of Christ will ever perish. The eternal security of the believer is a glorious fact. Those who are true **sheep** of Christ **hear** His **voice**. They **hear** it when the gospel is preached, and they respond by believing on Him. Thereafter, they **hear** His voice day by day and obey His Word. The Lord Jesus knows His sheep. He knows each one by name. Not even one will escape His attention. No one could be lost through an oversight or carelessness on His part. Christ's sheep **follow** Him, first by exercising saving faith in Him, then by walking with Him in obedience.

10:28 Christ gives **eternal life** to His sheep. This means life that will last forever. It is *not* life that is *conditional* on their behavior. It is **eternal life**, and that means everlasting. But **eternal life** is also a quality of life. It is the life of the Lord Jesus Himself. It is a life that is capable of enjoying the things of God down here, and a life that will be equally suitable to our heavenly home. Note these next words carefully. **"They shall never[32] perish."** If any sheep of Christ ever perished, then the Lord Jesus would have been guilty of failing to keep a promise, and this is not possible. Jesus Christ is God, and He cannot fail. He has promised in this verse that no sheep of His will ever spend eternity in hell.

Does this mean then that a person may be saved and then live the way he pleases? Can he be saved and then carry on in the sinful pleasures of this world? No, he no longer desires to do these things. He wants to follow the Shepherd. We do not live the Christian life in order to become a Christian or in order to retain our salvation. We live a Christian life because *we are* Christians. We desire to live a holy life, not out of fear of losing our salvation, but out of gratitude to the One who died for us. The doctrine of eternal security does not encourage careless living, but rather is a strong motive for holy living.

No one is able to **snatch** a believer out of Christ's **hand**. His hand is almighty. It created the world; and it even now sustains the world. There is no power that can **snatch** a sheep from His grasp.

10:29 Not only is the believer in the hand of Christ; he is in the **Father's hand** as well. This is a twofold guarantee of safety. God the Father **is greater than all; and no one is able to snatch** a believer **out of** the **Father's hand**.

10:30 Now the Lord Jesus added a further claim to equality with God: **"I and My Father are one."** Here the thought probably is that Christ and the **Father are one** *in power*. Jesus had just been speaking about the power that protects Christ's sheep. Therefore, He added the explanation that His power is the same as the power of God the Father. Of course the same is true of all the other attributes of Deity. The Lord Jesus Christ is God in the fullest sense and is equal with the Father in every way.

10:31 There was no question in the minds of **the Jews** as to what the Savior meant. They realized that He was setting forth His deity in the plainest way. Therefore they **took up stones** in order **to stone Him**.

10:32 Before they had a chance to hurl the stones, **Jesus** reminded them of the **many good works** He had performed by commandment **from** His **Father**. He then asked them **which of those** works so infuriated them that they wanted to **stone** Him.

10:33 **The Jews** denied that it was for any of His miracles that they sought to kill Him. Rather, they wanted to stone Him because they felt He had spoken **blasphemy** by claiming to be equal with **God** the Father. They refused to admit that He was anything more than a man. Yet it was very evident to them that He made Himself **God**, as far as His claims were concerned. They would not tolerate this.

10:34 Here the Lord Jesus quoted to the Jews from Psalm 82:6. He called this a part of their **law**. In other words, it was taken from the OT which they acknowledged to be the inspired Word of God. The complete verse is as follows: "I said, 'You are gods, and all of you are children of the Most High.' " The Psalm was addressed to the judges of Israel. They were called **"gods"** not because they were actually divine, but because they represented God when they judged the people. The Hebrew word for "gods" (*elohim*) is literally "mighty ones" and may be applied to important figures such as judges. (It is clear from the rest of the Psalm that they were only men and not deities because they judged unjustly, showed respect of persons, and otherwise perverted justice.)

10:35 The Lord used this verse from the Psalms to show that God used the word **gods** to describe men **to whom the word of God came**. In other words, these men were spokesmen for God. God spoke to the nation of Israel through them. "They manifested God in His place of authority and judgment, and were the powers whom God had ordained." **"And the Scripture cannot be broken,"** said the Lord, expressing His belief in the inspiration of the OT Scriptures. He speaks of them as infallible writings which must be fulfilled, and which cannot be denied. In fact, the very words of Scripture are inspired, not just its thoughts or ideas. His whole argument is based on the single word **gods**.

10:36 The Lord was arguing from the lesser to the greater. If unjust judges were called "gods" in the OT, how much more right did He have to say He was the Son of God. The word of God *came* to them; He *was* and *is* the Word of God. They were *called* gods; He *was* and *is* God. It could never have been said of them that the **Father** had **sanctified** them **and sent** them **into the world**. They were born into the world like all other sons of fallen Adam. But Jesus was sanctified by God **the Father** from all eternity to be the Savior of the world, and He was **sent into the world** from heaven where He had always dwelt with His Father. Thus Jesus had every right to claim equality with God. He was not blaspheming when He claimed to be **the Son**

of God, equal with the Father. The Jews themselves used the term "gods" to apply to corrupt men who were mere spokesmen or judges for God. How much more could He claim the title because He actually *was* and *is* God. Samuel Green states it well:

> The Jews accused Him of making Himself God. He does not deny that in so speaking He made Himself God. But He does deny that He blasphemed, and this on a ground that might fully justify Him even in claiming the honors of deity; namely, that He was the Messiah, the Son of God, Immanuel. That the Jews did not consider Him as in the least withdrawing His lofty claims, is evident from the continued enmity that was manifested. See verse 39.[33]

10:37 Again the Savior appealed to the miracles which He performed as proof of His divine commission. However, note the expression **"the works of My Father."** Miracles, in themselves, are not a proof of deity. We read in the Bible of evil beings having the power at times to perform miracles. But the miracles of the Lord were **the works of** His **Father**. They proved Him to be the Messiah in a twofold way. First, they were the miracles which the OT predicted would be performed by the Messiah. Second, they were miracles of mercy and compassion, works that benefited mankind and which would not be performed by an evil person.

10:38 Verse 38 has been helpfully paraphrased by Ryle as follows:

> If I do the works of my Father, then, though ye may not be convinced by what I say, be convinced by what I do. Though ye resist the evidence of my words, yield to the evidence of my works. In this way learn to know and believe that I and my Father are indeed one, He in me and I in Him, and that in claiming to be His Son, I speak no blasphemy.

10:39 Again the Jews realized that instead of denying His previous claims, the Lord Jesus had only strengthened them. Thus they made another attempt to arrest Him, but He eluded them once more. The time was not far distant now when He would permit Himself to be taken by them, but as yet, His hour had not come.

VI. THE SON OF GOD'S THIRD YEAR OF MINISTRY: PEREA (10:40–11:57)

A. Jesus' Withdrawal Across the Jordan (10:40–42)

10:40 The Lord **went away again beyond the Jordan to the** very **place where** He began His public ministry. His three years of wondrous words and works were drawing to a close. He ended them where He began them — outside the established order of Judaism, in a place of rejection and loneliness.

10:41 Those who **came to Him** were probably sincere believers. They were willing to bear His reproach, to take their place with Him outside the camp of Israel. These followers paid a glowing tribute to **John** the Baptist. They remembered that John's ministry was not spectacular or sensational, but it was **true**. Everything he said about the Lord Jesus was fulfilled in the ministry of the Savior. This should encourage each one who is a Christian. We may not be able to do mighty miracles or gain public attention, but at least we can bear a true testimony to our Lord and Savior Jesus Christ. This is of great value in God's sight.

10:42 It is lovely to notice that in spite of His rejection by the nation of Israel, the Lord Jesus did find some lowly, receptive hearts. **Many**, we are told, **believed in Him there**. Thus it is in every age. There is always a remnant of the people who are willing to take their place with the Lord Jesus, cast out by the world, hated and scorned, but enjoying the sweet fellowship of the Son of God.

B. The Illness of Lazarus (11:1–4)

11:1 We now come to the last great miracle in the *public* ministry of the Lord Jesus. In some senses, it was the greatest of all — the raising of a dead man. **Lazarus** lived in the little village of **Bethany**, about two miles east of Jerusalem. **Bethany** was also known as the home **of Mary and her sister Martha**. Pink quotes Bishop Ryle:

> Let it be noticed that the presence of God's elect children is the one thing which makes towns and countries famous

in God's sight. The village of Martha and Mary is noticed, while Memphis and Thebes are not named in the New Testament.[34]

11:2 John explains that **it was that Mary** of Bethany **who** had **anointed the Lord with fragrant oil and wiped His feet with her hair**. This singular act of devotion was emphasized by the Holy Spirit. The Lord loves the willing affection of His people.

11:3 When Lazarus took sick, the Lord Jesus was apparently on the east side of the Jordan River. The **sisters sent** word **to Him** immediately that Lazarus, **whom** He loved, was **sick**. There was something very touching in the way these sisters presented their case to the Lord. They appealed to His love for their brother as a special argument why He should come and help.

11:4 When Jesus ... said, "This sickness is not unto death," He did mean that Lazarus would not die, but that **death** would not be the final outcome of **this sickness**. Lazarus would die, but he would be raised again from the dead. The real purpose of the sickness was **the glory of God, that the Son of God may be glorified through it**. God allowed this to happen so that Jesus would come and raise Lazarus from the dead, and thus be manifested again as the true Messiah. Men would glorify **God** for this mighty miracle.

There is absolutely no suggestion that Lazarus' sickness was a result of some special sin in his life. Rather, he is presented as a devoted disciple and a special object of the Savior's love.

C. Jesus' Journey to Bethany (11:5–16)

11:5 When sickness enters our homes, we are not to conclude that God is displeased with us. Here sickness was directly linked with His love rather than His anger. "Whom He loves He chastens."

11:6, 7 We would be apt to reason that if the Lord really loved these three believers, then He would drop everything and hurry to their home. Instead, **when He heard** the news, **He stayed two more days ... where He was**. God's delays are not God's denials. If our prayers are not answered immediately, perhaps He is teaching us to wait, and if we wait

patiently, we will find that He will answer our prayers in a much more marvelous way than we ever anticipated. Not even His love for Martha, Mary, and Lazarus could force Christ to act ahead of the proper time. Everything He did was in obedience to His Father's will for Him, and in keeping with the divine timetable.

After two days that might have seemed to be lost time, the Lord Jesus proposed to **the disciples** that they should all **go to Judea again**.

11:8 **The disciples** were still painfully aware of how **the Jews sought to stone** Christ after He had given sight to the blind man. They expressed surprise that He would even think of going into Judea in the face of such personal danger.

11:9 **Jesus answered** them as follows: In the ordinary course of events, there are **twelve hours** of light **in the day**, when men can work. As long as a man works during this allotted time, there is no danger of his stumbling or falling **because he sees** where he is going and what he is doing. **The light of this world**, or daylight, keeps him from accidental death through stumbling.

The spiritual meaning of the Lord's words is as follows: The Lord Jesus was walking in perfect obedience to the will of God. There was thus no danger of His being killed before the appointed time. He would be preserved until His work was done.

In a sense this is true of every believer. If we are walking in fellowship with the Lord and doing His will, there is no power on earth that can kill us before God's appointed time.

11:10 The person who **walks in the night** is one who is not faithful to God, but is living in self-will. This man **stumbles** easily **because** he does not have divine guidance to illuminate his pathway.

11:11 The Lord spoke of Lazarus' death as *sleep*. However, it should be noticed that in the NT sleep is *never* applied to the soul but only to the body. There is no teaching in the Scripture that at the time of death, the soul is in a state of sleep. Rather, the believer's soul goes to be with Christ, which is far better. The Lord Jesus revealed His omniscience in this statement. He knew Lazarus had already died, although the report He had heard was that Lazarus was sick. He knew because He is God. While anybody may awaken another out of physical sleep, only the Lord could awaken Lazarus out of death. Here Jesus expressed His intention of doing that very thing.

11:12 **His disciples** did not understand the Lord's reference to sleep. They did not realize that He was speaking of death. Perhaps they believed that sleeping was a symptom of recovery, and they concluded that if Lazarus was able to sleep soundly, then **he** had passed the crisis and would **get well**. The verse might also mean that if physical sleep were the only thing wrong with Lazarus, then there was no need to go to Bethany to help him. It is possible that the disciples were fearful for their own safety and that they seized upon this excuse for not going to the home of Mary and Martha.

11:13, 14 Here it is clearly stated that when **Jesus spoke** of sleep, He was referring to **death** but that His disciples had not understood this. There can be no misunderstanding. **Jesus** notified His disciples **plainly, "Lazarus is dead."** How calmly the disciples received the news! They did not ask the Lord, "How do you know?" He spoke with complete authority, and they did not question His knowledge.

11:15 The Lord Jesus was not glad that Lazarus had died, but He was **glad** He **was not** at Bethany at the time. If He had been there, Lazarus would not have died. Nowhere is it recorded in the NT that a person died in the presence of the Lord. The disciples would see a greater miracle than the prevention of death. They would see a man raised from the dead. In this way, their faith would be strengthened. Therefore, the Lord Jesus said that He was **glad** for their sakes that He had not been at Bethany.

He added, **"that you may believe."** The Lord was not implying that the disciples had not already believed on Him. Of course they had! But the miracle they were about to see at Bethany would greatly strengthen their faith in Him. Therefore, He urged them to **go** with Him.

11:16 **Thomas** reasoned that if the Lord Jesus went into that area, He would be killed by the Jews. If the disciples went with Jesus, he was sure that they too would be killed. And so in a spirit of pessimism and gloom, he urged them all to accompany Jesus. His words are not an example of great faith or courage, but rather of discouragement.

D. Jesus: The Resurrection and The Life (11:17–27)

11:17, 18 The fact of Lazarus' being in the grave for **four days** was added as proof that he was dead. Notice how the Holy Spirit takes every precaution to show that the resurrection of Lazarus was really a miracle. Lazarus must have died shortly after the messengers left to find Jesus. It was a day's journey from Bethany to Bethabara, where Jesus was. After hearing of Lazarus' illness, Jesus stayed two days. Then it was a day's journey to Bethany. This explains the four days Lazarus was in the grave.

As noted previously, **Bethany** was **about two miles** (fifteen stadia) east of **Jerusalem**.

11:19 The nearness of Bethany to Jerusalem made it possible for **many of the Jews** to join **the women around Martha and Mary, to comfort them**. Little did they realize that in a short time their comfort would be entirely unnecessary and that this house of mourning would be turned into a house of great joy.

11:20 **Then Martha, as soon as she heard that Jesus was coming, went** out to meet **Him**. The meeting took place just outside the village. We are not told why **Mary** remained **in the house**. Perhaps she had not received the report of Jesus' arrival. Maybe she was paralyzed with grief, or was simply waiting in a spirit of prayer and trust. Did she sense what was about to happen because of her closeness to the Lord? We do not know.

11:21 It was real faith that enabled **Martha** to believe that Jesus could have prevented Lazarus from dying. Still, her faith was imperfect. She thought He could only do this if He were bodily present. She did not realize that He could heal a man from a distance, still less that He could raise the dead. Often in times of sorrow, we talk like Martha. We think that if such and such a drug or medicine had been discovered, then this loved one would not have died. But all these things are in the hands of the Lord, and nothing happens to one of His own without His permission.

11:22 Again the faith of this devoted sister shone out. She did not know *how* the Lord Jesus would help, but she believed that He would. She had confidence that **God** would grant Him His request and that He would bring good out of this seeming tragedy. However, even now, she did not dare to believe that her brother would be raised from the dead. The word which Martha used for "ask" is the word normally used to describe a creature supplicating or praying to the Creator. It seems clear from this that Martha did not yet recognize the deity of the Lord Jesus. She realized that He was a great and unusual Man, but probably no greater than the prophets of old.

11:23 In order to draw out her faith to greater heights, the Lord Jesus made the startling announcement that Lazarus would **rise again**. It is wonderful to see how the Lord deals with this sorrowing woman and seeks to lead her step by step to faith in Himself as the Son of God.

11:24 **Martha** realized that Lazarus would **rise** from the dead some day, but she had no thought that it could happen that very day. She believed in **the resurrection** of the dead and understood that it would happen in what she called **"the last day."**

11:25 It is as if the Lord had said, "You do not understand Me, Martha. I do not mean that Lazarus will rise again at the last day. I am God, and I have the power of **resurrection** and of **life** in My hand. I can raise Lazarus from the dead right now, and will do it."

Then the Lord looked forward to the time when all true believers would be raised. This will take place when the Lord Jesus comes back again to take His people home to heaven.

At that time there will be two classes of believers. There will be those who have died in faith, and there will be those who are living at His Return. He comes to the first class as the *Resurrection* and to the second as the *Life*. The first class is described in the latter part of verse 25 — **"He who believes in Me,**

though he may die, he shall live." This means that those believers who have died before Christ's coming will be raised from the dead.

Burkitt remarks:

O love, stronger than death! The grave cannot separate Christ and His friends. Other friends accompany us to the brink of the grave, and then they leave us. Neither life nor death can separate from the love of Christ.[35]

Bengel comments, "It is beautifully consonant with divine propriety, that no one is ever read of as having died while the Prince of Life was present."

11:26 The second class is described in verse 26. Those who are alive at the time of the Savior's coming and who believe on Him **shall never die**. They will be changed, in a moment, in a twinkling of an eye, and taken home to heaven with those who have been raised from the dead. What precious truths have come to us as a result of Lazarus' death! God brings sweetness out of bitterness and gives beauty for ashes. Then the Lord pointedly asked Martha, to test her faith, **"Do you believe this?"**

11:27 Martha's faith blazed out in noontime splendor. She confessed Jesus to be **the Christ, the Son of God**, whom the prophets had predicted was **to come into the world**. And we should notice that she made this confession *before* Jesus had raised her brother from the dead and not afterwards!

E. Jesus Weeps at Lazarus' Tomb (11:28–37)

11:28, 29 Immediately after this confession, Martha rushed back into the village and greeted **Mary** with the breathless announcement, **"The Teacher has come, and is calling for you."** The Creator of the universe and the Savior of the world had come to Bethany and was **calling for** her. And it is still the same today. This same wonderful Person stands and calls people in the words of the gospel. Each one is invited to open the door of his heart and let the Savior in. Mary's response was immediate. She wasted no time, but **rose quickly** and went to Jesus.

11:30, 31 **Now Jesus** met Martha

and Mary outside the village of Bethany.

The Jews did not know He was near, since Martha's announcement of the fact to Mary had been a secret one. It was not unnatural that they should conclude that **Mary** had gone out **to the tomb to weep there**.

11:32 **Mary . . . fell down** at the Savior's **feet**. It may have been an act of worship, or it may have been that she was simply overcome with grief. Like Martha, she uttered the regret that Jesus had not been present in Bethany, for in that case, their **brother would not have died**.

11:33 To see Mary and her friends in sorrow caused Jesus to groan and to be **troubled**. Doubtless He thought of all the sadness, suffering, and death which had come into the world as a result of man's sin. This caused Him inward grief.

11:34 The Lord of course knew **where** Lazarus was buried, but He asked the question in order to awaken expectation, to encourage faith, and to call forth man's cooperation. Doubtless it was with deep earnestness and sincere desire that the mourners led the Lord to the grave.

11:35 Verse 35 is the shortest in the English Bible.[36] It is one of the three instances in the NT where the Lord is said to have **wept**. (He wept in sorrow over the city of Jerusalem and also in the garden of Gethsemane.) The fact that **Jesus wept** was an evidence of His true humanity. He shed real tears of grief when He witnessed the terrible effects of sin on the human race. The fact that **Jesus wept** in the presence of death shows it is not improper for Christians to weep when their loved ones are taken. However, Christians do not sorrow as others who have no hope.

11:36 **The Jews** saw in the tears of the Son of Man an evidence of His love for Lazarus. Of course, they were correct in this. But He also loved *them* with a deep and undying love, and many of them failed to understand this.

11:37 Again the presence of the Lord Jesus caused questionings among the people. Some of them recognized Him as the same One who had given sight to **the blind** man. They wondered why He could not **also have kept** Lazarus **from dying**. Of course, He could have done so, but instead He was going to perform a mightier miracle, which brought greater hope to believing souls.

F. The Seventh Sign: The Raising of Lazarus (11:38–44)

11:38 It would seem that Lazarus' **tomb** was **a cave** under the earth, into which one would have to descend by means of a ladder or a flight of stairs. **A stone** was placed on top of the mouth of the cave. It was unlike the tomb of the Lord Jesus in that the latter was carved out of rock and a person could doubtless walk into it, as into the side of a hill, without climbing or descending.

11:39 Jesus commanded the onlookers to **take away the stone** from the mouth of the grave. He could have done this Himself by merely speaking the word. However, God does not ordinarily do for men what they can do for themselves.

Martha expressed horror at the thought of opening the grave. She realized that her brother's body had been there for **four days** and feared that it had begun to decompose. Apparently, no attempt had been made to embalm the body of Lazarus. He would have been buried the same day on which he died, as was the custom then. The fact that Lazarus was in the grave for **four days** was important. There was no possibility of his being asleep or in a swoon. All the Jews knew that he was **dead**. His resurrection can only be explained as a miracle.

11:40 It is not clear when **Jesus** had spoken the words of verse 40. In verse 23, He had told her that her brother would rise again. But doubtless what He here said was the substance of what He had previously told her. Notice the order in this verse, **"Believe . . . see."** It is as if the Lord Jesus had said, "If you will just believe, you will see Me perform a miracle that only God could perform. You will **see the glory of God** revealed in Me. But first you must **believe**, and then you will **see**."

11:41 **The stone** was then removed from the grave. Before performing the miracle, **Jesus** thanked His **Father** for having **heard** His prayer. No previous prayer of the Lord Jesus is recorded in this chapter. But doubtless He had been speaking to His Father continually during this entire period and had prayed that God's Name might be glorified in the resurrection of Lazarus. Here He thanked the Father in anticipation of the event.

11:42 Jesus prayed audibly so that **the people** might **believe that** the Father had **sent** Him, that the Father told Him what to do and what to say, and that He always acted in perfect dependence on God the Father. Here again we have the essential union of God the Father and the Lord Jesus Christ emphasized.

11:43 This is one of the few instances in the NT where the Lord Jesus is said to have **cried with a loud voice**. Some have suggested that if He had not mentioned **Lazarus** by name, then all the dead in the graves would have come forth!

11:44 How did Lazarus come **out**? Some think he hobbled out of the grave; others think that he crawled out on hands and knees; still others point out that his body would have been wrapped tightly in graveclothes and that it would have been impossible for him to have come out by his own power. They suggest that his body came out of the tomb through the air until his feet touched the ground in front of the Lord Jesus. The fact that his **face was wrapped with a cloth** is added as a further proof that he had been dead. No one could have lived for four days with **his face** bound by such **a cloth**. Again the Lord enlisted the participation of the people by commanding them to **loose** Lazarus **and let him go**. Only Christ can raise the dead, but He gives us the task of removing stones of stumbling, and of unwinding the graveclothes of prejudice and superstition.

G. Believing and Unbelieving Jews (11:45–57)

11:45, 46 To **many** of the onlookers, this miracle unmistakably proclaimed the deity of the Lord Jesus Christ, and they **believed in Him**. Who else but God could call forth a body from the grave

after it had been dead for four days?

But the effect of a miracle on a person's life depends on his moral condition. If one's heart is evil, rebellious, and unbelieving, he will not believe even though he were to see one raised from the dead. That was the case here. **Some** of the Jews who witnessed the miracle were unwilling to accept the Lord Jesus as their Messiah in spite of such undeniable proof. And so they **went away to the Pharisees** to report what had happened in Bethany. Was it that they might come and believe on Jesus? Rather, it was probably in order that the Pharisees might be further stirred up against the Lord and seek to put Him to death.

11:47 Then the chief priests and the Pharisees gathered their official **council** to discuss what action should be taken. The question **"What shall we do?"** means "What are we going to do about this? Why are we so slow in acting? **This Man** is performing many miracles, and we are doing nothing to stop Him." The Jewish leaders spoke these words to their own condemnation. They admitted that the Lord Jesus was performing **many signs**. Why then did they not believe on Him? They did not *want* to believe because they preferred their sins to the Savior.

Ryle well says:

This is a marvellous admission. Even our Lord's worst enemies confess that our Lord did miracles, and many miracles. Can we doubt that they would have denied the truth of His miracles, if they could? But they do not seem to have attempted it. They were too many, too public, and too thoroughly witnessed for them to dare to deny them. How, in the face of this fact, modern infidels and skeptics can talk of our Lord's miracles as being impostures and delusions, they would do well to explain! If the Pharisees who lived in our Lord's time, and who moved heaven and earth to oppose His progress, never dared to dispute the fact that He worked miracles, it is absurd to begin denying His miracles now, after eighteen centuries have passed away.[37]

11:48 The leaders felt they could no longer remain inactive. If they did not intervene, the mass of the people would be persuaded by the miracles of Jesus. If the people thus acknowledged Jesus to be their King, it would mean trouble with Rome. The Romans would think that Jesus had come to overthrow their empire; they would then move in and punish the Jews. The expression **"take away both our place and nation"** means that the Romans would destroy the temple and scatter the Jewish people. These very things took place in A.D. 70 — not, however, because the Jews *accepted* the Lord, but rather because they *rejected* Him.

F. B. Meyer put it well:

> Christianity endangers businesses, undermines profitable but wicked trades, steals away customers from the devil's shrines, attacks vested interests, and turns the world upside down. It is a tiresome, annoying, profit-destroying thing.[38]

11:49, 50 **Caiaphas** was **high priest** from A.D. 26 to 36. He presided at the religious trial of the Lord and was present when Peter and John were brought before the Sanhedrin in Acts 4:6. He was not a believer in the Lord Jesus, in spite of the words which he here uttered.

According to Caiaphas, the chief priests and Pharisees were wrong in thinking that the Jews would die on account of Jesus. Rather, he predicted that Jesus would die for the Jewish nation. He said that it was better that Jesus would **die for the people**, rather than that **the whole nation** should have trouble with the Romans. It almost sounds as if Caiaphas really understood the reason for Jesus' coming into the world. We would almost think that Caiaphas had accepted Jesus as the Substitute for sinners — the central doctrine of Christianity. But unfortunately, that is not the case. What he said was true, but he himself did not believe on Jesus to the saving of his soul.

11:51, 52 This explains why Caiaphas said what he did. **He did not** speak **on his own authority**, that is, he did not make these things up by himself. He did not speak this of his own will. Rather, the message that he uttered was given to him by God, with a deeper message than he intended. It was a divine prophecy **that Jesus would die for the nation** of Israel. It was given to Caiaphas because he was **high priest that year**. God spoke through him because of the office he held and not because of his own personal righteousness, for he was a sinful man.

The prophecy of Caiaphas was **not that** the Lord would die for the **nation** of Israel **only, but also that He would gather together** His elect among the Gentiles of the earth. Some think that Caiaphas was referring to Jewish people dispersed throughout the earth, but more probably he was referring to Gentiles who would believe on Christ through the preaching of the gospel.

11:53, 54 The Pharisees were not convinced by the miracle at Bethany. Rather, they were even more hostile toward the Son of God. **From that day on they plotted** His **death** with a new intensity.

Realizing the mounting hostility of the Jews, the Lord Jesus went off **to a city called Ephraim**. We do not know today where Ephraim was except that it was in a quiet, secluded area **near the wilderness**.

11:55 The announcement that **the Passover of the Jews was near** reminds us we are coming to the close of the Lord's public ministry. It was at this *very Passover* that He was to be crucified. The people were required to **go up to Jerusalem before the Passover to purify themselves**. For instance, if a Jew had touched a dead body, it was necessary for him to go through a certain ritual in order to be cleansed from ceremonial defilement. This purifying was done through various types of washings and offerings. The sad thing is that the Jewish people were thus seeking to purify themselves, while at the same time planning the death of the Passover Lamb. What a terrible exposure of the wickedness of the heart of man!

11:56, 57 As the people gathered **in the temple**, they began to think about the miracle worker named **Jesus** who had been in their country. A discussion arose as to whether He would **come to the feast**. The reason some thought He would not come is given in verse 57.

Official orders had gone out from **the chief priests and the Pharisees** for the arrest of Jesus. Anyone who knew of His whereabouts was commanded to notify the authorities so that **they might seize Him** and put Him to death.

VII. THE SON OF GOD'S MINISTRY TO HIS OWN
(Chaps. 12–17)

A. Jesus Anointed at Bethany (12:1–8)

12:1 The home in **Bethany** was a place where **Jesus** loved to be. There He enjoyed sweet fellowship with **Lazarus**, Mary, and Martha. In coming **to Bethany** at this time, He was, humanly speaking, exposing Himself to danger because nearby Jerusalem was headquarters for all the forces that were arrayed against Him.

12:2 In spite of the many who were opposed to Jesus, there were still a few hearts which beat true to Him. **Lazarus was one of those who sat at the table with** the Lord, **and Martha served**. The Scripture does not say anything about what Lazarus saw or heard from the time he died until he was raised again. Perhaps he had been forbidden by God to divulge any such information.

12:3 Several instances are recorded in the Gospels where the Lord Jesus was anointed by a woman. No two incidents are exactly alike, but this incident is generally thought to parallel Mark 14:3–9. Mary's devotion to Christ caused her to take this **pound of very costly oil of spikenard** and anoint His **feet**. She was saying in effect that there was nothing too valuable to give to Christ. He is worthy of everything that we have and are.

Each time we meet Mary, she is at the feet of Jesus. Here she is wiping **His feet with her hair**. Since a woman's hair is her glory, she was laying her glory, as it were, at His feet. Needless to say, Mary herself would have carried the fragrance of the perfume for some time after this. Thus when Christ is worshiped, the worshipers themselves carry away something of the fragrance of that moment. No house is so filled with pleasant aroma as the house where Jesus is given His rightful place.

12:4, 5 Here the flesh is seen intruding into this most sacred of occasions. The **one** who was about to **betray** his Lord could not stand to see precious **oil** used in this way.

Judas did not consider Jesus to be worth **three hundred denarii**. He felt that the perfume should have been **sold** and **given to the poor**. But this was sheer hypocrisy. He cared no more for the poor than he did for the Lord. He was about to betray Him, not for **three hundred denarii**, but for a tenth of that amount. Ryle well says:

> That anyone could follow Christ as a disciple for three years, see all His miracles, hear all His teaching, receive at His hand repeated kindnesses, be counted an apostle, and yet prove rotten at heart in the end, all this at first sight appears incredible and impossible! Yet the case of Judas shows plainly that the thing can be. Few things, perhaps, are so little realized as the extent of the fall of man.[39]

12:6 John was quick to add that Judas did **not** say **this** because **he** had any real love **for the poor, but because he was a thief** and was greedy. Judas **had the money box; and he used to take what was put in it.**

12:7 The Lord answered in effect, "Do not prevent her from doing this. **She has kept this** oil **for the day of My burial.**[40] Now she wants to lavish it on Me in an act of affection and worship. She should be permitted to do so."

12:8 There would never be a time when there would not be **poor** people on whom others might lavish their kindness. But the Lord's ministry on earth was swiftly drawing to a close. Mary would *not* **always** have the opportunity to use this oil upon Him. This should remind us that spiritual opportunities are passing. We should never delay doing what we can for the Savior.

B. The Plot Against Lazarus (12:9–11)

12:9 The word quickly spread that Jesus was near Jerusalem. It was no longer possible to keep His presence secret. **Many of the Jews** came to Bethany to see Him, and others came to **see Lazarus, whom He had raised from the dead**.

12:10, 11 The insane hatred of the human heart is again pictured in this verse. **The chief priests plotted to put Lazarus to death also**. One would think that he had committed high treason by being raised from the dead! It was nothing over which he had control, and yet they considered him worthy of death.

Because of Lazarus, **many of the Jews . . . believed in Jesus**. Lazarus was therefore an enemy to the Jewish "establishment", and he must be put out of the way. Those who bring others to the Lord are always made the target for persecution and even martyrdom.

Some commentators suggest that because the chief priests were Sadducees, who denied the resurrection, they wanted to get rid of the evidence by destroying Lazarus.

C. The Triumphal Entry (12:12–19)

12:12, 13 We now come to the triumphal entry of **Jesus** into **Jerusalem**. It was the Sunday before His crucifixion.

It is difficult to know exactly what this **multitude** thought about Jesus. Did they really understand that He was the Son of God and the Messiah of Israel? Or did they merely look upon Him as a King who would deliver them from Roman oppression? Were they carried away with the emotion of the hour? Doubtless some in the group were true believers, but the general impression is that most of the people had no real heart interest in the Lord.

Palm branches are a token of rest and peace after sorrow (Rev. 7:9). The word **"Hosanna"** means "Save now, we pray you." Putting these thoughts together, it would seem as if the people were acknowledging Jesus to be the One sent from God to save them from Roman cruelty and to give them rest and peace after the sorrow of their long years of Gentile oppression.

12:14, 15 Jesus rode into the city on **a young donkey**, a common mode of transportation. More than that, however, the Lord was fulfilling prophecy in riding in this manner.

This quotation was taken from Zechariah 9:9. There the prophet predicted that when the **King** came to Israel, He would be **sitting on a donkey's colt**. The **daughter of Zion** is a figurative expression referring to the Jewish people, **Zion** being a hill in the city of Jerusalem.

12:16 The **disciples did not** realize that what was happening was in exact fulfillment of Zechariah's prophecy, that Jesus was actually entering Jerusalem as the rightful King of Israel. **But** after the Lord had gone back to heaven to be **glorified** at the right hand of the Father, it dawned on the disciples that these events were in fulfillment of the Scriptures.

12:17, 18 In the crowd that watched Jesus entering Jerusalem were **people** who had seen Him raise **Lazarus . . . from the dead**. These told the others around them that this One riding on the colt was the same One who had brought Lazarus back to life again. As the report of this notable **sign** spread, a great throng of **people** came out to meet Jesus. Unfortunately, their motive was curiosity rather than true faith.

12:19 As the crowd grew in size, and interest in the Savior mounted, **the Pharisees** were beside themselves. Nothing they could say or do had the slightest effect. With frenzied exaggeration, they cried out that **the** whole **world** had **gone after** Jesus. They did not realize that the interest of the crowd was but a passing thing, and that those who really were willing to worship Jesus as the Son of God were very few.

D. Certain Greeks Wish to See Jesus (12:20–26)

12:20 The **Greeks** who came to Jesus were Gentiles who had become converts to Judaism. The fact that they **came up to worship at the feast** shows that they were no longer carrying on the religious practices of their ancestors. Their coming to the Lord Jesus at this occasion pictures the fact that when the Jews rejected the Lord Jesus, the Gentiles would hear the gospel and many of them would believe.

12:21 No reason is given why **they came to Philip**. Perhaps his Greek name and the fact that he **was from Bethsaida of Galilee** made him attractive to those Gentile proselytes. Their request was a noble one indeed. **"Sir, we wish to see Jesus."** No one who has this sincere desire in his heart is ever turned away unrewarded.

12:22 Perhaps Philip was not too sure as to whether the Lord would see these Greeks. Christ had previously told the disciples not to go to the Gentiles with the gospel, so **Philip** went to **Andrew**, and together they **told Jesus**.

12:23 Why did the Greeks want to see Jesus? If we read between the lines, we can surmise that the wisdom of Jesus appealed to them and that they wanted to exalt Him as their popular philosopher. They knew that He was on a collision course with the Jewish leaders and wanted Him to save His life, perhaps by going to Greece with them. Their philosophy was "Spare yourself," but **Jesus** told **them** that this philosophy was directly opposed to the law of harvest. He would be **glorified** in His sacrificial death and not by a comfortable life.

12:24 Seed never produces grain until first it **falls into the ground and dies**. The Lord Jesus here referred to Himself as **a grain** (or kernel) **of wheat**. If He did not die, He would abide **alone**. He would enjoy the glories of heaven by Himself; there would be no saved sinners there to share His glory. But if He died, He would provide a way of salvation by which many might be saved.

The same applies to us, as T. G. Ragland says:

> If we refuse to be corns of wheat — falling into the ground, and dying; if we will neither sacrifice prospects, nor risk character, and property, and health; nor, when we are called, relinquish home, and break family ties, for Christ's sake; *then we shall abide alone*. But if we wish to be fruitful, we must follow our Blessed Lord Himself, by becoming a corn of wheat, and dying, *then we shall bring forth much fruit*.[41]

12:25 Many people think that the important things in life are food, clothing, and pleasure. They live for these things. But in thus loving their lives, they fail to realize that the soul is more important than the body. By neglecting their soul's welfare, they lose their lives. On the other hand, there are those who count all things loss for Christ. To serve Him, they forego things highly prized among men. These are the people who **will keep** their lives **for eternal life**. To hate one's life means to love Christ more than one loves his own interests.

12:26 To serve Christ, one must **follow** Him. He would have His servants obey His teachings and resemble Him morally. They must apply the example of His death to themselves. All servants are promised the constant presence and protection of their Master, and this applies not only to the present life but to eternity as well. Service now will receive God's approval in a coming day. Whatever one suffers of shame or reproach here will be small indeed compared to the glory of being publicly commended by God the **Father** in heaven!

E. Jesus Faces Imminent Death (12:27–36)

12:27 Increasingly, the Lord's thoughts were upon the events that lay immediately before Him. He was thinking of the cross, and contemplating the time when He would become the Sin Bearer, and endure the wrath of God against our sins. In thinking of His "hour of heartbreak" (JBP), His **soul** was **troubled**. How should He pray in such a moment? Should He ask His **Father** to **save** Him **from** the **hour**? He could not pray for this because the **purpose** of His coming into the world was to go to the cross. He was born to die.

12:28 Instead of praying that He might be saved from the cross, the Lord Jesus rather prayed that the **name** of His Father might be glorified. He was more interested that honor should come to God than in His own comfort or safety. God now spoke from heaven, saying that He *had* **glorified** His Name and would **glorify it again**. The Name of God was glorified during the earthly ministry of Jesus. The thirty silent years in Nazareth, the three years of public ministry, the wonderful words and works of the Savior — all of these greatly glorified the Name of the Father. But still greater glory would be brought to God through the death, burial, resurrection, and Ascension of Christ.

12:29 Some of those standing by mistook the voice of God for thunder. Such people are always trying to put a natural explanation on spiritual things. Men who are unwilling to accept the fact of miracles try to explain the miracles away by some natural law. Others knew it was not thunder, and yet they did not recognize it as the voice of God. Realizing it must have been superhuman, they could only conclude that it was the voice of **an angel**. God's voice can only be heard and understood by those who are helped by the Holy Spirit. People can listen to the gospel over and over, and yet it might be ever so meaningless to them unless the Holy Spirit speaks to them through it.

12:30 The Lord explained to the listeners that **this voice did not** need to be audible in order for *Him* to hear it. Rather, it was made audible for the sake of those who were standing by.

12:31 **"Now is the judgment of this world,"** He said. The world was about to crucify the Lord of life and glory. In doing so, it would condemn itself. Sentence would be passed upon it for its awful rejection of Christ. That is what the Savior meant here. Condemnation was about to be passed on guilty mankind. **The ruler of this world** is Satan. In a very real sense, Satan was utterly defeated at Calvary. He thought he had succeeded in doing away with the Lord Jesus once for all. Instead, the Savior had provided a way of salvation for men, and at the same time had defeated Satan and all his hosts. The sentence has not yet been carried out on the devil, but his doom has been sealed. He is still going through the world carrying on his evil business, but it is just a matter of time before he will be **cast** into the lake of fire.

12:32 The first part of this verse refers to Christ's death on the cross. He was nailed to a cross of wood and **lifted up from the earth**. The Lord said that if He were thus crucified, He would **draw all peoples to** Himself. Several explanations have been given for this. Some think that Christ draws all people either to salvation or to judgment. Others think that if Christ is lifted up in the preaching of the gospel, then there will be a great power in the message, and souls will be drawn to Him. But probably the correct explanation is that the crucifixion of the Lord Jesus resulted in **all** *kinds* of people being drawn to Him. It does not mean all people without exception, but people from every nation, tribe, and language.

12:33 When the Lord Jesus spoke of being lifted up, He signified the kind of **death He would die**, that is, by crucifixion. Here again we have evidence of the all–knowledge of the Lord. He knew in advance that He would not die in bed or by accident, but that He would be nailed to a cross.

12:34 **The people** were puzzled by this statement of the Lord about being **lifted up**. They knew that He claimed to be the Messiah, and yet they knew from the OT that the Messiah would live forever (see Isa. 9:7; Ps. 110:4; Dan. 7:14; Mic. 4:7). Notice that the people quoted Jesus as saying, **"The Son of Man must be lifted up."** Actually, He had said, "I, if I be lifted up from the earth." Of course, the Lord Jesus had referred to Himself many times as the Son of Man, and perhaps He had even spoken previously of the Son of Man being lifted up, so it was not difficult for the people to put the two thoughts together.

12:35 When the people asked Jesus who the Son of Man was, He spoke of Himself again as **the light** of the world. He reminded them that **the light** would only be with them for a short while. They should come to the Light and walk in the Light; otherwise **darkness** would soon **overtake** them, and they would stumble around in ignorance.

The Lord seemed to liken Himself to the sun and to the daylight it offers. The sun rises in the morning, reaches its peak at noon, and descends over the horizon in the evening. It is only with us for a limited number of hours. We should avail ourselves of it while it is here, because when the night comes, we do not have the benefit of it. Spiritually, the one who believes on the Lord Jesus is the one who walks in the light. The one who rejects Him **walks in darkness** and **does not know where he is going**. He lacks divine guidance, and stumbles through life.

12:36 Again the Lord Jesus warned His listeners to **believe** on Him **while** there was still opportunity. By doing so, they would **become sons of light**. They would be assured of direction through life and into eternity. After speaking these words, the Lord **departed** from the people and remained in obscurity for a while.

F. Failure of Most Jews to Believe (12:37–43)

12:37[†] John paused at this time to express amazement that **although** the Lord Jesus **had done so many** mighty **signs**, yet the people **did not believe in Him**. As we have mentioned before, their unbelief was not caused by any lack of evidence. The Lord had given the most convincing proofs of His deity, but the people did not want to believe. They wanted a king to rule over them, but they did not want to repent.

12:38 The unbelief of the Jews was in fulfillment of the prophecy in Isaiah 53:1. The question, **"Lord, who has believed our report?"** calls for the answer, "Not very many!" Since the arm in Scripture speaks of power or strength, **the arm of the LORD** speaks of the mighty power of God. God's power is only **revealed** to those who believe the report concerning the Lord Jesus Christ. Therefore, because not many accepted the announcement concerning the Messiah, the power of God was not revealed to many.

12:39 When the Lord Jesus presented Himself to the nation of Israel, they rejected Him. Over and over again, He came back to them with the offer of salvation, but they kept saying "no" to Him. The more men reject the gospel, the harder it becomes for them to receive it. When men close their eyes to the Light, God makes it more difficult for them to see the Light. God causes them to be struck with what is known as judicial blindness, that is, a blindness which is God's judgment on them for refusing His Son.

12:40 This quotation was from Isaiah 6:9, 10. God **blinded** the **eyes** of the people of Israel **and hardened their hearts**. He did not do this at first, but only after they had closed their eyes and hardened their own hearts. As a result of Israel's stubborn and willful rejection of the Messiah, they cut themselves off from sight, understanding, conversion, and healing.

12:41 In Isaiah 6 the prophet was described as seeing the **glory** of God. John now added the explanation that it was *Christ's* **glory** which Isaiah **saw**, and it was of Christ that he **spoke**. Thus, this verse is another important link in the chain of evidence that proves Jesus Christ to be God.

12:42 **Many** of **the rulers** of the Jews became convinced that Jesus was the Messiah. However, they did not dare to share their conviction with the others lest they be excommunicated. We would like to think that these men were genuine believers in the Lord Jesus, but it is doubtful. Where there is true faith, there will be confession of Christ, sooner or later. When Christ is really accepted as Savior, one does not hesitate to make it known, regardless of the consequences.

12:43 It was obvious that these men were more interested in **the praise of** their fellow **men** than they were in **the praise of God**. They thought more of man's approval than of God's. Can a person like this really be a genuine believer in Christ? See chapter 5, verse 44, for the answer.

G. The Peril of Unbelief (12:44–50)

12:44 A paraphrase of verse 44 is as follows: "The one **who believes in Me** actually **believes** not only in Me, **but** also in My Father **who sent Me**". Here again the Lord taught His absolute union with God the Father. It was impossible to believe in One without believing in the Other. To believe in Christ is to believe in God the Father. One cannot believe in the Father unless he gives equal honor to the Son.

12:45 In one sense, nobody can see God the Father. He is Spirit, and therefore invisible. But the Lord Jesus had come into the world to let us know what God is like. By this we do not mean that He lets us know what God is like physically, but morally. He has revealed the character of God to us. Therefore, whoever has seen Christ has seen God the Father.

12:46 The illustration of **light** was apparently one of our Lord's favorites. Again He referred to Himself **as a light** coming **into the world** in order that those who believe in Him **should not abide in darkness**. Apart from Christ, men are in deepest darkness. They do not have a right understanding of life, death, or eternity. But those who come to Christ in faith no longer grope about for the truth, because they have found the truth in Him.

12:47 The purpose of Christ's First Coming was **not to judge the world but to save**. He did not sit in judgment on those who refused to hear His words or believe on Him. This does not mean that He will not condemn these unbelievers in a coming day, but that judgment was not the object of His First Advent.

12:48 The Lord now looked forward to a coming day when those who rejected His words will stand before the judgment bar of God. At that time, the **words** or teaching of the Lord Jesus will be sufficient to condemn them.

12:49 The things He taught were not things He had made up Himself or learned in the schools of men. Rather, as the obedient Servant and Son, He had only spoken those things which the Father commissioned Him to **speak**. This is the fact that will condemn men at the last day. The word that Jesus spoke was the Word of God, and men refused to hear it. The Father had told Him not only **what** to **say** but **what** He should **speak**. There is a difference between the two. The expression **"what I should say"** refers to the substance of the message; **"what I should speak"** means the very words which the Lord should use in teaching the truth of God.

12:50 Jesus knew the Father had commissioned Him to give **everlasting life** to those who would believe on Him. **Therefore**, Christ delivered the message as it was given to Him by **the Father**.

We now come to a distinct break in the narrative. Up to this point the Lord has presented Himself to Israel. Seven distinct signs or miracles are recorded, each one illustrating an experience which will result when a sinner puts his faith in Christ. The signs are:

1. Changing the water into wine at the wedding in Cana of Galilee (2:1–12). This pictures the sinner who is a stranger to divine joy being transformed by the power of Christ.
2. Healing the nobleman's son (4:46–54). This pictures the sinner as being sick and in need of spiritual health.
3. Healing the cripple at the pool of Bethesda (chap. 5). The poor sinner is without strength, helpless, and unable to do a thing to remedy his own condition. Jesus cures him of his infirmity.
4. Feeding the five thousand (chap. 6). The sinner is without food, hungry, and in need of that which imparts strength. The Lord provides food for his soul so that he never needs to hunger.
5. Calming the Sea of Galilee (6:16–21).

The sinner is seen in a place of danger. The Lord rescues him from the storm.
6. Healing a man blind from birth (chap. 9). This man pictures the blindness of the human heart until it is touched by the power of Christ. Man cannot see his own sinfulness, or the beauties of the Savior, until enlightened by the Holy Spirit.
7. Raising Lazarus from the dead (chap. 11). This, of course, reminds us that the sinner is dead in trespasses and in sins and needs life from above.

All these signs are intended to prove that Jesus is the Christ, the Son of God.

H. Jesus Washes His Disciples' Feet (13:1–11)

In chapter 13, the Upper Room Discourse begins. Jesus was no longer walking among the hostile Jews. He had retired with His disciples to an upper room in Jerusalem for a final time of fellowship with them before going forth to His trial and crucifixion. John 13 through 17 is one of the best-loved sections in the entire NT.

13:1 The day before the crucifixion, the Lord **Jesus knew that** the time **had come** for Him to die, to rise again, and to go back to heaven. He had **loved His own**, that is, those who were true believers. **He loved them to the end** of His earthly ministry, and will continue to love them throughout eternity. But **He** also **loved them to** an infinite degree, as He was about to demonstrate.

13:2 John does not say which **supper** is referred to here — whether the Passover, the Lord's Supper, or an ordinary meal. **The devil** sowed the thought in **the heart of Judas** that the time was now ripe to **betray Jesus**. Judas had plotted evil against the Lord long before this, but he was now given the signal for carrying out his foul plans.

13:3 Verse 3 emphasizes *who* was performing a slave's task — not just a rabbi or teacher, but **Jesus**, who was conscious of His deity. He knew the work that had been committed to Him; He knew **that He had come from God** and that He was already on His journey back **to God**.

13:4 It was the consciousness of

who He was, and of His mission and destiny, that enabled Him to stoop down and wash the disciples' feet. Rising **from supper**, the Lord **laid aside His** long outer **garments**. Then He put a **towel** around Himself as an apron, taking the place of a slave. We might have expected this incident to be in the Gospel of Mark, the Gospel of the Perfect Servant. But the fact that it is in the Gospel of the Son of God makes it all the more remarkable.

This symbolic act reminds us of how the Lord left the ivory palaces above, came down into this world as a Servant, and ministered to those He had created.

13:5 In eastern lands, the use of open sandals made it necessary **to wash** one's **feet** frequently. It was common courtesy for a host to arrange to have a slave wash the feet of his guests. Here the divine Host became the slave and performed this lowly service. "Jesus at the feet of the traitor — what a picture! What lessons for us!"

13:6 **Peter** was shocked to think of the Lord's **washing** his **feet**, and he expressed his disapproval that One so great as the Lord should condescend to one so unworthy as he. "The sight of God in the role of a servant is disturbing."

13:7 **Jesus** now taught Peter that there was a spiritual meaning to what He was doing. Foot-washing was a picture of a certain type of spiritual washing. Peter knew that the Lord was performing the physical act, but he did **not** **understand** the spiritual *significance*. He would **know** it soon, however, because the Lord explained it. And he would **know** it by experience when later he was restored to the Lord after having denied Him.

13:8 **Peter** illustrates the extremes of human nature. He vowed that the Lord would **never wash** his **feet** — and here "never" literally means "not for eternity." The Lord answered Peter that apart from His washing, there could be no fellowship with Him. The meaning of foot-washing is now unfolded. As Christians walk through this world, they contract a certain amount of defilement. Listening to vile talk, looking at unholy things, working with ungodly men inevitably soil the believer. He needs to be constantly cleansed.

This cleansing takes place by the water of the Word. As we read and study the Bible, as we hear it preached, and as we discuss it with one another, we find that it cleanses us from the evil influences about us. On the other hand, the more we neglect the Bible, the more these wicked influences can remain in our minds and lives without causing us any great concern. When Jesus said **"you have no part with Me,"** He did not mean that Peter could not be saved unless He washed him, but rather that fellowship with the Lord can be maintained only by the continual cleansing action of the Scriptures in his life.

13:9, 10 Now **Peter** shifted to the other extreme. A minute ago, he was saying, "Never." Now he said, "Wash me all over."

On the way back from the public bath, a person's feet would get dirty again. He didn't need another bath but did need to have his feet washed. **"He who is bathed needs only to wash his feet, but is completely clean."** There is a difference between the bath and the basin. The *bath* speaks of the cleansing received at the time of one's salvation. Cleansing from the *penalty* of sin through the blood of Christ takes place only once. The *basin* speaks of cleansing from the *pollution* of sin and must take place continually through the Word of God. There is one bath but many foot-washings. **"You are clean, but not all of you"** means that the disciples had received the bath of regeneration — that is, all the disciples but Judas. He had never been saved.

13:11 With full knowledge of all things, the Lord **knew** that Judas **would betray Him**, and so He singled out one as never having had the bath of redemption.

I. Jesus Teaches His Disciples to Follow His Example (13:12–20)

13:12 It would seem that Christ **washed** the **feet** of *all* the disciples. Then He put on **His** outer **garments and sat down again** to explain to them the spiritual meaning of what He had done. He opened the conversation by asking a question. The questions of the Savior make an interesting study. They form one of His most effective methods of teaching.

13:13, 14 The disciples had acknowledged Jesus to be their **Teacher and Lord**, and they were right in doing so. But His example showed that the highest rank in the power structure of the kingdom is that of servant.

If the **Lord and Teacher** had **washed** the disciples' **feet**, what excuse could they have for not washing **one another's feet**? Did the Lord mean that they should *literally* wash each other's feet with water?[42] Was He here instituting an ordinance for the church? No, the meaning here was spiritual. He was telling them that they should keep each other clean by constant fellowship over the Word. If one sees his brother growing cold or worldly, he should lovingly exhort him from the Bible.

13:15, 16 The Lord had **given** them **an example**, an object lesson of what they **should do** to one another spiritually.

If pride or personal animosities prevent us from stooping to serve our brethren, we should remember that we are **not greater than** our **Master**. He humbled Himself to wash those who were unworthy and unthankful, and He knew that one of them would betray Him. Would you minister in a lowly way to a man if you knew he was about to betray you for money? Those who were **sent** (the disciples) should not consider themselves too lofty to do anything that the One **who sent** them (the Lord Jesus) had done.

13:17 To **know these** truths concerning humility and unselfishness and service is one thing, but one can know them and never practice them. The real value and blessedness lie *in doing* them!

13:18 What the Lord had just been teaching about service did **not** apply to Judas. He was not one of those whom the Lord would send into all the world with the gospel. Jesus knew the Scriptures concerning His betrayal must **be fulfilled** — such Scriptures as Psalm 41:9. Judas was one who had eaten his meals with the Lord for three years, and yet he **lifted up his heel against** Him — an expression indicating that he betrayed the Lord. In Psalm 41 the betrayer is described by the Lord as "my own familiar friend."

13:19 The Lord revealed His betrayal to the disciples in advance so **that when it** came **to pass**, the disciples would know that Jesus was true deity. The italicized word **He** can be omitted from the end of this verse. **"You may believe that I AM."** The Jesus of the NT is the Jehovah of the Old. Thus, fulfilled prophecy is one of the great proofs of the deity of Christ and also, we might add, of the inspiration of Scriptures.

13:20 Our Lord knew that His betrayal might cause the other disciples to stumble or doubt. So He added this word of encouragement. They should remember that they were being sent on a divine mission. They were to be so closely identified with Him that to receive *them* was the same as receiving *Him*. Also, those who received Christ received God the Father. They were thus to be comforted by their close link with God the Son and God the Father.

J. Jesus Predicts His Betrayal (13:21–30)

13:21, 22 The knowledge that one of His disciples would betray Him caused the Lord to be deeply **troubled**. It seems that Jesus was here giving the betrayer a final opportunity to abandon his evil plan. Without exposing him directly, the Lord revealed His knowledge that **one of** the twelve would **betray** Him. Yet even this did not change the traitor's mind.

The rest of the disciples did not suspect Judas. They were surprised that one of their number would do such a thing and puzzled as to who he could be.

13:23 In those days, people did not sit up at a table for a meal but reclined on low couches. The disciple **whom Jesus loved** was John, the writer of this Gospel. He omitted mentioning his own name, but did not hesitate to mention the fact that he held a place of special affection in the Savior's heart. The Lord loved all the disciples, but John enjoyed a special sense of closeness to Him.

13:24, 25 **Peter therefore motioned** rather than speaking audibly. Perhaps by nodding his head, he asked John to find out the name of the betrayer.

Leaning back on Jesus' breast John asked the fateful question in a whisper and was probably answered in a low voice also.

13:26 Jesus answered that He would **give a piece of bread . . . dipped** in wine or meat juice to the traitor. Some say that an Eastern host gave the bread to the honored guest at a meal. By making **Judas** the honored guest, the Lord thus tried to win him to repentance by His grace and love. Others suggest that the bread was commonly passed in this way in connection with the Passover supper. If that is true, then Judas left during the Passover supper and before the Lord's Supper was instituted.

13:27 The devil had already put it into Judas' heart to betray the Lord. Now **Satan entered him**. At first, it was merely a suggestion. But Judas entertained it, liked it, and agreed to it. Now the devil took control of him. Knowing the betrayer was now fully determined, the Lord told him to **do** it **quickly**. Obviously, He was not encouraging him to do evil but simply expressing sorrowful resignation.

13:28, 29 This verse confirms that the previous conversation between Jesus and John about the bread was not heard by the other disciples. They still did not know that Judas was about to betray their Lord.

Some thought that Jesus had simply told Judas to go quickly and **buy** something **for the feast**, or because Judas was the treasurer, that the Savior had instructed him to make a donation **to the poor**.

13:30 Judas **received the piece of bread** as a token of special favor, and then left the company of the Lord and of the other disciples. The Scriptures add the meaningful words **and it was night.** It **was** not only **night** in a literal sense, but **it was night** spiritually for Judas — a night of gloom and remorse that would never end. It is always night when men turn their backs on the Savior.

K. The New Commandment Given (13:31–35)

13:31 As soon as Judas left, **Jesus** began to speak with the disciples more freely and intimately. The tension was gone. **"Now the Son of Man is glorified,"** He said. The Lord was anticipating the work of redemption which He was about to accomplish. His death might have seemed like defeat, yet it was the means by which lost sinners could be saved. It was followed by His resurrection and ascension, and He was

greatly honored in it all. **And God is glorified in** the work of the Savior. It proclaimed Him to be a *holy* God who could not pass over sin, but also a *loving* God who did not desire the death of the sinner; it proclaimed how He could be a *just* God, yet be able to *justify* sinners. Every attribute of deity was superlatively magnified at Calvary.

13:32 **"If God is glorified in Him,"** and He is,[43] **"God will also glorify Him in Himself."** God will see that appropriate honor is given to His beloved Son. **"And glorify Him immediately"** — without delay. God the Father fulfilled this prediction of the Lord Jesus by raising Him from the dead and seating Him at His own right hand in heaven. God would not wait until the kingdom was ushered in. He would **glorify** His Son **immediately**.

13:33 For the first time the Lord Jesus addressed His disciples as **little children** — a term of endearment. And He used it only after Judas had departed. He was only to **be with** them **a little while longer**. Then He would die on the cross. They would **seek** Him then, but would not be able to follow Him, for He would return to heaven. The Lord had told the same thing **to the Jews**, but He meant it in a different sense. For the disciples, His departure would only be temporary. He would come again for them (chap. 14). But for **the Jews**, His leaving them would be final. He was returning to heaven, and they could not follow Him because of their unbelief.

13:34 During His absence, they were to be governed by the **commandment** of **love**. This commandment was not new in point of time because the Ten Commandments taught love to God and to one's neighbor. But this **commandment** was **new** in other ways. It was **new** because the Holy Spirit would empower believers to obey it. It was **new** in that it was *superior* to the old. The old said, "Love your *neighbor*," but the new said, "Love your *enemies*."

It has been well said that the law of love to others is now explained with new clarity, enforced by new motives and obligations, illustrated by a new example, and obeyed in a new way.

Also it was new, as explained in the

verse, because it called for a *higher degree* of love: **"As I have loved you, that you also love one another."**

13:35 The badge of Christian discipleship is not a cross worn around the neck or on the lapel, or some distinctive type of clothing. Anyone could profess discipleship by these means. The true mark of a Christian is **love** for his fellow Christians. This requires divine power, and this power is only given to those indwelt by the Spirit.

L. Jesus Predicts Peter's Denial (13:36–38)

13:36 **Simon Peter** did not understand that Jesus had spoken of His death. He thought He was going on some earthly journey and did not understand why he could not go along. The Lord explained that Peter *would* **follow** Him later, that is, when he died, but could not do so now.

13:37 With typical devotion and enthusiasm, **Peter** expressed willingness to die for the Lord. He thought he could endure martyrdom by his own strength. Later he actually did die for the Lord, but it was because he had been given special strength and courage by God.

13:38 **Jesus** checks his "zeal without knowledge" by telling Peter something he himself did not know — that before the night was ended, he would deny the Lord **three times**. Thus Peter was reminded of his weakness, cowardice, and inability to follow the Lord for even a few hours by his own power.

M. Jesus: the Way, the Truth, and the Life (14:1–14)

14:1 Some link verse 1 to the last verse of chapter 13 and think it was spoken to Peter. Although he would deny the Lord, yet there was a word of comfort for him. But the plural forms in Greek ("ye" in old English) show it was spoken to *all* the disciples, hence we should pause after chapter 13. The thought seems to be: "I am going away, and you will not be able to see Me. But **let not your heart be troubled; you believe in God**, and yet you do not see Him. Now **believe in Me** in the same way." Here is another important claim to equality with God.

14:2 The **Father's house** refers to heaven, where there are many dwelling places. There is room there for all the redeemed. **If it were not so**, the Lord **would have told** them; He would not have them build on false hopes. **"I go to prepare a place for you"** may have two meanings. The Lord Jesus went to Calvary to prepare a place for His own. It is through His atoning death that believers are assured a place there. But also the Lord went back to heaven to prepare a place. We do not know very much about this place, but we know that provision is being made for every child of God — "a prepared place for a prepared people!"

14:3 Verse 3 refers to the time when the Lord **will come** back **again** into the air, when those who have died in faith will be raised, when the living will be changed, and when all the blood-bought throng will be taken home to heaven (1 Thess. 4:13–18; 1 Cor. 15:51–58). This is a personal, literal coming of Christ. As surely as He went away, He **will come again**. His desire is to have His own with Him for all eternity.

14:4, 5 He was going to heaven, and they knew **the way** to heaven, for He had told them many times.

Apparently **Thomas** did not understand the meaning of the Lord's words. Like Peter, he may have been thinking of a journey to some place on the earth.

14:6 This lovely verse makes it clear that the Lord Jesus Christ is Himself **the way** to heaven. He does not merely show the way; He *is* **the way**. Salvation is in a Person. Accept that Person as your own, and you have salvation. Christianity is Christ. The Lord Jesus is not just one of many ways. He is the *only* Way. **No one comes to the Father except through** Him. The way to God is not by the Ten Commandments, the Golden Rule, ordinances, church membership — it is through Christ and Christ alone. Today many say that it does not matter what you believe as long as you are sincere. They say that all religions have some good in them and that they all lead to heaven at last. But Jesus said, **"No one comes to the Father except through Me."**

Then the Lord is **the truth**. He is not just One who teaches the truth; He *is* **the truth**. He is the embodiment of Truth.

Those who have Christ have the Truth. It is not found anywhere else.

Christ Jesus is **the life**. He is the source of life, both spiritual and eternal. Those who receive Him have eternal life because He *is* the Life.

14:7 Once more the Lord taught the mysterious union that exists between the Father and Himself. If the disciples had recognized who Jesus really was, they **would have known** the **Father also**, because the Lord revealed the Father to men. **From now on**, and especially after Christ's resurrection, the disciples would understand that Jesus was God the Son. Then they would realize that to know Christ was **to know** the Father, and to see the Lord Jesus was to see God. This verse does not teach that God and the Lord Jesus are the same Person. There are three distinct *Persons* in the Godhead, but there is only *one God*.

14:8 Philip wanted the **Lord** to give some special revelation of **the Father**, and that would be all he would ask. He did not understand that everything the Lord was, and did, and said, was a revelation of the Father.

14:9 Jesus patiently corrected him. Philip had been with the Lord for a **long** time. He was one of the first disciples to be called (John 1:43). Yet the full truth of Christ's deity and of His unity with the Father had not yet dawned on him. He did not know that when he looked at Jesus, he was looking at One who perfectly displayed **the Father.**

14:10, 11 The words **"I am in the Father, and the Father in Me"** describe the closeness of the union between **the Father** and the Son. They are separate Persons, yet They are one as to attributes and will. We should not be discouraged if we cannot understand this. No mortal mind will ever understand the Godhead. We must give God credit for knowing things that we can never know. If we fully understood Him, we would be as great as He! Jesus had power to speak the words and to do the miracles, but He came into the world as the Servant of Jehovah and He spoke and acted in perfect obedience to the Father.

The disciples should **believe** that He was one with **the Father** because of His own testimony to that fact. But if not, then they should certainly **believe** because of **the works** He performed.

14:12 The Lord predicted that those who believed on Him would perform miracles like He did, and even **greater works**. In the book of Acts, we read of the apostles performing miracles of bodily healing, similar to those of the Savior. But we also read of greater miracles — such as the conversion of three thousand on the day of Pentecost. Doubtless it was to the world-wide proclamation of the gospel, the salvation of so many souls, and the building of the church that the Lord referred to by the expression **greater works**. It is **greater** to save souls than to heal bodies. When the Lord returned to heaven, He was glorified, and the Holy Spirit was sent to earth. It was through the Spirit's power that the apostles performed these greater miracles.

14:13 What a comfort it must have been to the disciples to know that, even though the Lord was leaving them, they could pray to the Father in His Name and receive their requests. This verse does not mean that a believer can get anything he wants from God. The key to understanding the promise is in the words **in My name — whatever you ask in My name**. To ask in Jesus Name is not simply to insert His Name at the end of the prayer. It is to ask in accordance with His mind and will. It is to ask for those things which will glorify God, bless mankind, and be for our own spiritual good.

In order to ask in Christ's Name, we must live in close fellowship with Him. Otherwise we would not know His attitude. The closer we are to Him, the more our desires will be the same as His are. **The Father** is **glorified in the Son** because the Son only desires those things that are pleasing in God's sight. As prayers of this nature are presented and granted, it causes great glory to be brought to God.

14:14 The promise is repeated for emphasis and as a strong encouragement to God's people. Live in the center of His will, walk in fellowship with the Lord, **ask** for **anything** that the Lord would desire, and your prayers will be answered.

N. The Promise of Another Helper (14:15–26)

14:15 The Lord Jesus was about to leave His disciples, and they would be filled with sorrow. How would they be able to express their **love** to Him? The answer was by keeping His commandments. Not by tears, but by obedience. The **commandments** of the Lord are the instructions which He has given us in the Gospels, as well as the rest of the NT.

14:16 The word translated **pray** that is used here of our Lord is not the same word used to describe an inferior praying to a superior, but of one making request of his equal. The Lord would **pray the Father** to send **another Helper**. The word **Helper** (*Paraclete*) means one called to the side of another to help. It is also translated Advocate (1 Jn. 2:1). The Lord Jesus is our Advocate or Helper, and the Holy Spirit is **another Helper** — not another of a different kind, but another of similar nature. The Holy Spirit would **abide** with believers **forever**. In the OT, the Holy Spirit came upon men at various times, but often left them. Now He would come to remain **forever**.

14:17 The Holy Spirit is called **the Spirit of truth** because His teaching is true and He glorifies Christ who is the truth. **The world cannot receive** the Holy Spirit because it cannot see Him. Unbelievers want to see before they will believe — although they believe in wind and electricity, and yet they cannot see them. The unsaved do not know or understand the Holy Spirit. He may convict them of sin, and yet they do not know that it is He. The disciples knew the Holy Spirit. They had known Him to work in their own lives and had seen Him working through the Lord Jesus.

"He dwells with you, and will be in you." Before Pentecost, the Holy Spirit came upon men and dwelt **with** them. But since Pentecost, when a man believes on the Lord Jesus, the Holy Spirit takes up His abode in that man's life forever. The prayer of David, "Do not take Your Holy Spirit from me," would not be suitable today. The Holy Spirit is never taken from a believer, although He may be grieved, or quenched, or hindered.

14:18 The Lord would **not leave** His disciples as **orphans**, or desolate. He would **come to** them again. In one sense, He came to them after His resurrection, but it is doubtful if that is what is meant. In another sense, He came to them in the Person of the Holy Spirit on the day

of Pentecost. This spiritual coming is the true meaning here. "There was something about Pentecost which made it a coming of Jesus." In a third sense, He will literally come to them again at the end of this age, when He will take His chosen ones home to heaven.

14:19 No unbeliever saw the Lord Jesus after His burial. After He was raised, He was seen only by those who loved Him. But even after His Ascension, His disciples continued to see Him by faith. This is doubtless meant by the words **"but you will see Me."** After the world could no longer see Him, His disciples would continue to see Him. **"Because I live, you will live also."** Here He was looking forward to His resurrection life. It would be the pledge of life for all who trusted Him. Even if they should die, they would be raised again to die no more.

14:20 **"At that day"** probably refers again to the descent of the Holy Spirit. He would instruct believers in the truth that just as there was a vital link between the Son and the Father, so there would be a marvelous union of life and interests between Christ and His saints. It is difficult to explain how Christ is **in** the believer, and the believer is **in** Christ at the same time. The usual illustration is of a poker in the fire. Not only is the poker in the fire, but the fire is in the poker.[44] But this does not tell the full story. Christ is in the believer in the sense that His life is communicated to him. He actually dwells in the believer through the Holy Spirit. The believer is in Christ in the sense that he stands before God in all the merit of the Person and work of Christ.

14:21 The real proof of one's love to the Lord is obedience to His **commandments**. It is useless to talk about loving Him if we do not want to obey Him. In one sense, the Father loves all the world. But He has a special love for those who love His Son. Those are also loved by Christ, and He makes Himself known to them in a special way. The more we love the Savior, the better we shall know Him.

14:22 The **Judas** mentioned here had the misfortune to have the same name as the traitor. But the Spirit of God kindly distinguished him from **Iscariot**. He could not understand how the Lord

touch with Christ moment by moment.

15:5   Christ Himself is **the vine**; believers are vine **branches**. It is not a question of the branch living its life for the Vine, but simply of letting the life of the Vine flow out through the branches. Sometimes we pray, "Lord, help me to live my life for You." It would be better to pray, "Lord Jesus, live out Your life through me." **Without** Christ, we **can do nothing**. A vine branch has one great purpose — to bear fruit. It is useless for making furniture or for building homes. It does not even make good firewood. But it *is* good for fruitbearing — as long as it abides in the vine.

15:6   Verse 6 has caused much difference of opinion. Some believe that the person described is a believer who falls into sin and is subsequently lost. Such an interpretation is in direct contradiction to the many verses of Scripture which teach that no true child of God will ever perish. Others believe that this person is a professor — one who pretends to be a Christian but who was never born again. Judas is often used as an illustration.

We believe that this person is a true believer because it is with true Christians that this section is concerned. The subject is not salvation but abiding and *fruitbearing*. But through carelessness and prayerlessness this believer gets out of touch with the Lord. As a result, he commits some sin, and his testimony is ruined. Through failure to abide in Christ, he is thrown **out as a branch** — not by Christ, but by other people. The branches are gathered and thrown **into the fire, and they are burned**. It is not God who does it, but people. What does this mean? It means that people scoff at this backslidden Christian. They drag his name in the mud. They throw his testimony as a Christian into the fire. This is well illustrated in the life of David. He was a true believer, but he became careless toward the Lord and committed the sins of adultery and murder. He caused the enemies of the Lord to blaspheme. Even today, atheists ridicule the name of David (and of David's God). They cast him, as it were, into the fire.

15:7   Abiding is the secret of a successful prayer life. The closer we get to the Lord, the more we will learn to think His thoughts after Him. The more we get to know Him through His Word, the more we will understand His will. The more our will agrees with His, the more we can be sure of having our prayers answered.

15:8   As the children of God exhibit the likeness of Christ to the world, the **Father is glorified**. People are forced to confess that He must be a great God when He can transform such wicked sinners into such godly saints. Notice the progression in this chapter: fruit (v. 2), more fruit (v. 2), **much fruit** (v. 8).

"So you will be My disciples." This means that we *prove to be* His **disciples** when we abide in Him. Others can then see that we are true disciples, that we resemble our Lord.

15:9   The love which the Savior has for us is the same as the love of **the Father** for the Son. Our hearts are made to bow in worship when we read such words. It is the same in quality and degree. It is "a vast, wide, deep, unmeasurable love, that passeth knowledge, and can never be fully comprehended by man." It is "a deep where all our thoughts are drowned." **"Abide in My love,"** said our Lord. This means we should continue to realize His love and to enjoy it in our lives.

15:10   The first part of verse 10 tells us how we can abide in His love; it is by keeping His **commandments**. "There is no other way to be happy in Jesus, but to trust and obey." The second half of the verse sets before us our Perfect Example. The Lord Jesus **kept** His **Father's commandments**. Everything He did was in obedience to the will of God. He remained in the constant enjoyment of the Father's **love**. Nothing ever came in to mar that sweet sense of loving fellowship.

15:11   Jesus found His own deep **joy** in communion with God His Father. He wanted His disciples to have that joy that comes from dependence upon Him. He wanted *His* **joy** to be theirs. Man's idea of joy is to be as happy as he can by leaving God out of his life. The Lord taught that real joy comes by taking God into one's life as much as possible. **"That your joy may be full,"** or "fulfilled." Their joy would be fulfilled in abiding in

Christ and in keeping His commandments. Many have used John 15 to teach doubts concerning the security of the believer. They have used the earlier verses to show that a sheep of Christ might eventually perish. But the Lord's purpose was not "that your doubts may be full," but **that your joy may be full**.

Q. The Command to Love One Another (15:12–17)

15:12 The Lord would soon leave His disciples. They would be left in a hostile world. As tensions increased, there would be the danger of the disciples' contending with one another. And so the Lord leaves this standing order, **"Love one another, as I have loved you."**

15:13 Their love should be of such a nature that they should be willing to die for one another. People who are willing to do this do not fight with each other. The greatest example of human self-sacrifice was for a man to die **for his friends**. The disciples of Christ are called to this type of devotion. Some lay down their lives in a literal sense; others spend their whole lives in untiring service for the people of God. The Lord Jesus is the Example. He laid down His life for His friends. Of course, they were enemies when He died for them, but when they are saved, they become His friends. So it is correct to say that He died for His friends as well as for His enemies.

15:14 We show that we are His **friends** by doing **whatever** He commands us. This is not the way we become His friends, but rather the way we exhibit it to the world.

15:15 The Lord here emphasized the difference between **servants** and **friends**. **Servants** are simply expected to do the work marked out for them, but **friends** are taken into one's confidence. To the friend we reveal our plans for the future. Confidential information is shared with him. In one sense the disciples would always continue to be servants of the Lord, but they would be more than this — they would be friends. The Lord was even now revealing to them the things which He had **heard from** His **Father**. He was telling them of His own departure, the coming of the Holy Spirit, His own coming again, and their responsibility to Him in the meantime. Someone has pointed out that as branches, we *receive* (v. 5); as disciples, we *follow* (v. 8); and as friends, we *commune* (v. 15).

15:16 Lest there be any tendency for them to become discouraged and give up, Jesus reminded them that He was the One who **chose** them. This may mean that He **chose** them to eternal salvation, to discipleship, or to fruitfulness. He had appointed the disciples to the work which lay before them. We **should go and bear fruit. Fruit** may mean the graces of the Christian life, such as love, joy, peace, etc. Or it may mean souls won for the Lord Jesus Christ. There is a close link between the two. It is only as we are manifesting the first kind of fruit that we will ever be able to bring forth the second.

The expression **"that your fruit should remain"** leads us to think that fruit here means the salvation of souls. The Lord chose the disciples to go and bring forth *lasting* **fruit**. He was not interested in mere professions of faith in Himself, but in genuine cases of salvation. L. S. Chafer notes that in this chapter we have prayer effectual (v. 7), joy celestial (v. 11), and fruit perpetual (v. 16). **"That whatever you ask . . . ."** The secret of effective service is prayer. The disciples were sent forth with the guarantee that **the Father** would grant them **whatever** they asked in Christ's **name**.

15:17 The Lord was about to warn the disciples about the enmity of the world. He began by telling them to **love one another**, to stick together, and to stand unitedly against the foe.

R. Jesus Predicts the World's Hatred (15:18–16:4)

15:18, 19 The disciples were not to be surprised or disheartened **if the world hates** them. (The **if** does not express any doubt that this would happen; it was certain.) The world **hated** the Lord, and it will hate all who resemble Him.

Men of the world love those who live as they do — those who use vile language and indulge in the lusts of the flesh, or people who are cultured but live only for themselves. Christians condemn them by their holy lives, **therefore the world hates** them.

15:20 Here **servant** literally means "slave." A disciple should not expect any better treatment from the world than **his Master** received. He will be persecuted just as Christ was. His word will be refused just as the Savior's was.

15:21 This hatred and persecution is **"for My name's sake."** It is because the believer is linked to Christ; because he has been separated from the world by Christ; and because he bears Christ's name and likeness. The world is ignorant of God. **They do not know** that the Father **sent** the Lord into the world to be the Savior. But ignorance is no excuse.

15:22 The Lord was not teaching here that if He had not come, then men would not have been sinners. From the time of Adam, all men had been sinners. But their sin would not have been nearly so great as it now was. These men had seen the Son of God and heard His wonderful words. They could find no fault in Him whatever. Yet they rejected Him. It was this that made their sin so great. And so it was a matter of comparison. Compared with their terrible sin of rejecting the Lord of glory, their other sins were as nothing. Now they had **no excuse for their sin**. They had rejected the Light of the world!

15:23 In hating Christ, they hated His **Father also**. The Two are One. They could not say that they loved God, for if they had, they would have loved the One God sent.

15:24 They were not only responsible for having heard the teaching of Christ; they also saw His miracles. This added to their condemnation. They saw **works which no one else** had ever performed. To reject Christ in face of this evidence was inexcusable. The Lord compared all their other sins to this one sin, and said that the former were as nothing when placed alongside the latter. Because they **hated** the Son, they hated His **Father**, and this was their terrible condemnation.

15:25 The Lord realized that man's attitude toward Him was in exact fulfillment of prophecy. It was predicted in Psalm 69:4 that Christ would be **hated ... without a cause**. Now that it had happened, the Lord commented that the very OT which these men prized had predicted their senseless hatred of Him. The fact that it was prophesied did not mean that these men *had to* hate Christ. They hated Him by *their own deliberate choice*, but God foresaw that it would happen, and He caused David to write it down in Psalm 69.

15:26 In spite of man's rejection, there would be a continued testimony to Christ. It would be carried on by **the Helper** — the Holy Spirit. Here the Lord said that *He* would **send** the Spirit **from the Father**. In John 14:16, the *Father* was the One who sent the Spirit. Is this not another proof of the equality of the Son and the Father? Who but God could send One who is God? **The Spirit of truth ... proceeds from the Father**. This means that He is constantly being sent forth by God, and His coming at the day of Pentecost was a special instance of this. The Spirit testifies concerning Christ. This is His great mission. He does not seek to occupy men with Himself, though He is one of the members of the Trinity. But He directs the attention of both sinner and saint to the Lord of glory.

15:27 The Spirit would testify directly through the disciples. They had **been with** the Lord **from the beginning** of His public ministry and were especially qualified to tell of His Person and work. If anyone could have found any imperfection in the Lord, those who had been with Him the most could have. But they never knew Him to commit a sin of any kind. They could testify to the fact that He was the sinless Son of God and the Savior of the world.

16:1 The disciples probably cherished the hope of the Jewish people generally — that the Messiah would set up His kingdom and that the power of Rome would be broken. Instead of that, the Lord told them that He was going to die, rise again, and go back to heaven. The Holy Spirit would come, and the disciples would go out as witnesses for Christ. They would be hated and persecuted. The Lord told them all this in advance so that they would not be disillusioned, **made to stumble**, or shocked.

16:2, 3 Excommunication from **the synagogues** was considered by most Jews to be one of the worst things that could happen. Yet this would happen to these Jews who were disciples of Jesus. The Christian faith would be so hated that those who sought to stamp it out would **think** they were pleasing **God**. This shows how a person may be very sincere, very zealous, and yet very *wrong*.

Failure to recognize the deity of Christ lay at the root of the matter. The Jews would not receive Him, and in so doing, they refused to receive **the Father**.

16:4   Again the Lord warned the disciples in advance so they would not be moved by these afflictions when they happened. They would **remember** that the Lord had predicted persecution; they would know that it was all a part of His plan for their lives. The Lord had not told them much about this earlier because He was with them. There was no need to trouble them or to cause their minds to wander from the other things He had to teach them. But now that He was leaving them, He must tell them of the path that lay ahead for them.

S. The Coming of the Spirit of Truth (16:5–15)

16:5   Verse 5 seems to express disappointment that the disciples were not more interested in what was ahead for the Lord. Although they had asked in a general way **where** He was **going**, they had not seemed too involved.

16:6   They were more concerned with their own future than with His. Before Him lay the cross and the grave. Before them lay persecution in their service for Christ. They were **filled** with **sorrow** over their own troubles rather than over His.

16:7   **Nevertheless**, they would not be left without help and comfort. Christ would send the Holy Spirit to be their **Helper**. It was **to** the **advantage** of the disciples that the **Helper** should come. He would empower them, give them courage, teach them, and make Christ more real to them than He had ever been before. **The Helper** would not come until the Lord Jesus went back to heaven and was glorified. Of course, the Holy Spirit had been in the world before this, but He was coming in a new way — to convict the world and to minister to the redeemed.

16:8   The Holy Spirit would **convict the world** in respect **of sin, and of righteousness, and of judgment**. This is generally taken to mean that He creates an inward awareness of these things in the life of the individual sinner. While this is true, it is not exactly the teaching in this portion. The Holy Spirit condemns **the world** by the very fact that He is here. He should not be here, because the Lord Jesus should be here, reigning over the world. But the world rejected Him, and He went back to heaven. The Holy Spirit is here in place of a rejected Christ, and this demonstrates the world's guilt.

16:9   The Spirit convicts the world **of** the **sin** of failing to **believe** on Christ. He was worthy of belief. There was nothing about Him that made it impossible for men to believe on Him. But they refused. And the Holy Spirit's presence in the world is witness to their crime.

16:10   The Savior claimed to be righteous, but men said He had a demon. God spoke the final word. He said, in effect, "My Son is righteous, and I will prove it by raising Him from the dead and taking Him back to heaven." The Holy Spirit witnesses to the fact that Christ was right and the world was wrong.

16:11   The presence of the Holy Spirit also convicts the world **of** coming **judgment**. The fact that He is here means that the devil has already been condemned at the cross and that all who refuse the Savior will share his awful judgment in a day yet future.

16:12   There were **still . . . many** other **things** the Lord had to tell the disciples, but they could not take them in. This is an important principle of teaching. There must be a certain progress in learning before advanced truths can be received. The Lord never overwhelmed His disciples with teaching. He gave it to them "line upon line, precept upon precept."

16:13   The work which the Lord began was to be continued by the **Spirit of truth**. **He** would **guide** them **into all truth**. There is a sense in which **all truth** was committed to the apostles in their lifetime. They, in turn, committed it to writing, and we have it today in our NT.

This, added to the OT, completed God's written revelation to man. But it is, of course, true in all ages that the Spirit guides God's people into all the truth. He does it through the Scriptures. **He will** only **speak** the things that are given to Him to say by the Father and the Son. **"He will tell you things to come."** This, of course, is done in the NT, and particularly in the book of Revelation where the future is unveiled.

16:14 His principal work will be to **glorify** Christ. By this we can test all teaching and preaching. If it has the effect of magnifying the Savior, then it is of the Holy Spirit. **"He will take of what is Mine"** means that He will receive of the great truths that concern Christ. These are the things He reveals to believers. The subject can never be exhausted!

16:15 All the attributes of **the Father** belong to the Son as well. It is these perfections that Christ was speaking of in verse 14. The Spirit unveiled to the apostles the glorious perfections, ministries, offices, graces, and fullness of the Lord Jesus.

T. Sorrow Turned to Joy (16:16–22)

16:16 The precise time-frame of verse 16 is uncertain. It may mean the Lord would be away from them for three days, and then He would reappear to them after His resurrection. It may mean He would go back to His Father in heaven, and then after **a little while** (the present Age), He would come back to them (His Second Coming). Or it may mean that for **a little while** they would **not see** Him with their physical eyes, but after the Holy Spirit was given on the day of Pentecost, they would perceive Him by faith in a way they had never seen Him before.

16:17 His disciples were confused. The reason for the confusion was that in verse 10, the Savior had said, "I go to My Father and you see Me no more." Now He said, **"A little while, and you will not see Me; and again a little while, and you will see Me."** They could not reconcile these statements.

16:18 They asked each other the meaning of the words **"a little while."** Strangely enough, we have the same problem today. We do not know whether it refers to the three days before His

resurrection, the forty days before Pentecost, or the more than 1900 years prior to His Coming again!

16:19, 20 Being God, the Lord Jesus was able to read their thoughts. By His questions, He revealed His full knowledge of their perplexity.

He did not answer their problem directly but gave further information concerning the "little while." **The world** would **rejoice** because they had succeeded in crucifying the Lord Jesus, but the disciples would **weep and lament**. But it would only be for a short while. Their **sorrow** would be **turned into joy**, and it was — first by the resurrection, and secondly by the coming of the Spirit. Then, for all disciples of all ages, grief will be turned to rejoicing when the Lord Jesus comes back again.

16:21 Nothing is more remarkable than the speed with which a mother forgets the **labor** pains after her **child** is born. So it would be with the disciples. The sorrow connected with the absence of their Lord would be quickly forgotten when they would see Him again.

16:22 Again we must express ignorance as to the time indicated by the Lord's words, **"I will see you again."** Does this refer to His resurrection, His sending of the Spirit at Pentecost, or His Second Advent? In all three cases, the result is rejoicing, and a **joy** that cannot be taken away.

U. Praying to the Father in Jesus' Name (16:23–28)

16:23 Up to now, the disciples had come to the Lord with all their questions and requests. **In that day** (the age ushered in by the descent of the Spirit at Pentecost), He would no longer be with them bodily, so they would no longer be asking Him questions. But did that mean that they would have no one to whom to go? No, **in that day** it would be their privilege to **ask the Father**. He would grant their requests for Jesus' sake. Requests will be granted, not because we are worthy, but because the Lord Jesus is worthy.

16:24 Prior to this, the disciples had never prayed to God the Father in the Lord's **name**. Now they were invited to **ask**. Through answered prayer, their **joy** would **be** fulfilled.

16:25 The meaning of much of the Lord's teaching was not always apparent on the surface. He used parables and **figurative language**. Even in this chapter we cannot always be sure of the precise meaning. With the coming of the Holy Spirit, the teaching **about the Father** became more plain. In Acts and the Epistles the truth is no longer revealed through parables but through direct statements.

16:26 "That day" again is the Age of the Holy Spirit, in which we now live. Our privilege is to pray to the Father in the **name** of the Lord Jesus. **"I do not say to you that I shall pray the Father for you,"** that is, the Father does not need to be urged to answer our prayers. The Lord will not have to entreat Him. But we should still remember that the Lord Jesus is the Mediator between God and man, and He does intercede on behalf of His people before the throne of God.

16:27 **The Father** loved the disciples because they had received Christ and **loved** Him and **believed** in His deity. This is the reason why the Lord did not have to plead with the Father. With the coming of the Holy Spirit, they would enjoy a new sense of intimacy with the Father. They would be able to approach Him with confidence, and all because they **loved** His Son.

16:28 Here the Lord repeated His claim to equality with God the Father. He did not say "I came forth from *God*" as if He were just a Prophet sent by God, but **"I came forth from the Father."** This means He is the eternal Son of the eternal Father, equal with God the Father. He came **into the world** as One who had lived elsewhere before His Coming. At His Ascension, He left the world and returned **to the Father**. This is a brief biographical account of the Lord of glory.

V. Tribulation and Peace (16:29–33)

16:29, 30 Jesus' **disciples** thought that they were now able to understand Him for the first time. He was no longer using figurative language, they **said**.

They thought that they **now** entered into the mystery of His Person. **Now** they were **sure that** He had all-knowledge and **that** He **came forth from** *God*. But He had said that He came forth

from the *Father*. Did they understand the meaning of this? Did they understand that Jesus was one of the Persons of the Godhead?

16:31 **Jesus** suggested by this question that their belief was still imperfect. He knew they loved and trusted Him, but did they really know that He was God manifest in the flesh?

16:32 In a short while He would be arrested, tried, and crucified. The disciples would all forsake Him and flee to their homes. But He would not be deserted because **the Father** would be **with** Him. It was this union with God the Father that they did not understand. This was the thing that would support Him when they had all escaped for their lives.

16:33 The purpose of this discourse with the disciples was **that** they might **have peace**. When they would be hated, pursued, persecuted, falsely condemned, and even tortured, they could have **peace** *in Him*. He overcame **the world** at the cross of Calvary. In spite of their tribulations, they could rest assured that they were on the winning side.

Also, with the coming of the Holy Spirit, they would have new powers of endurance and new courage to face the foe.

W. Jesus Prays for His Ministry (17:1–5)

We now come to what is known as the High-Priestly prayer of the Lord Jesus. In this prayer, He made intercession for His own. It is a picture of His present ministry in heaven where He prays for His people. Marcus Rainsford puts it well:

The whole prayer is a beautiful illustration of our blessed Lord's intercession at the right hand of God. Not a word against His people; no reference to their failings, or their shortcomings. . . . No. He speaks of them only as they were in the Father's purpose, as in association with Himself, and as the recipients of the fulness He came down from heaven to bestow upon them. . . . All the Lord's particular petitions for His people relate to spiritual things; all have reference to heavenly blessings. The Lord does not ask riches for them, or honours, or worldly influence, or great preferments, but He does most earnestly pray that they may be kept from evil, separated from the world, qualified for duty, and brought home safely to heaven. Soul prosperity is the best prosperity; it is the index of true prosperity.[45]

17:1 The hour had **come**. Many times His enemies had been unable to take Him because His hour had *not* come. But now the time had arrived for the Lord to be put to death. "**Glorify Your Son**," the Savior prayed. He was looking ahead to His death on the cross. If He were to remain in the grave, the world would know that He was just another man. But if God glorified Him by raising Him from the dead, that would be proof He was God's Son and the world's Savior. God answered this request by raising the Lord Jesus on the third day and then later by taking Him back to heaven and crowning Him with glory and honor.

"**That Your Son also may glorify You**," the Lord continued. The meaning of this is explained in the next two verses. Jesus glorifies the Father by giving eternal life to those who believe on Him. It brings great glory to God when ungodly men and women are converted and manifest the life of the Lord Jesus on this earth.

17:2 As a result of His work of redemption at the cross, God has given His Son **authority over all** mankind. This **authority** entitled Him to **give eternal life to** those whom the Father had **given Him**. Here again we are reminded that before the foundation of the world, God marked out certain ones as belonging to Christ. Remember, though, that God offers salvation to anyone who will receive Jesus Christ. There is no one who cannot be saved by trusting the Savior.

17:3 Here is a simple explanation of how **eternal life** is obtained. It is by knowing **God and Jesus Christ. The only true God** is in contrast to idols, which are not genuine gods at all. This verse does not mean that Jesus Christ is not the true God. The fact that His Name is mentioned together with God the Father's as being the joint source of eternal life means that They are equal. Here the Lord called Himself **Jesus Christ. Christ** was the same as Messiah. This verse disproves the charge that Jesus never claimed to be the Messiah.

17:4 As the Lord uttered these words, He was speaking as if He had already died, been buried, and risen again. He had **glorified** the Father by His sinless life, by His miracles, by His suffering and death, and by His resurrection. He had **finished the work** of salvation the Father had **given** Him **to do**. As Ryle puts it:

> The crucifixion brought glory to the Father. It glorified His wisdom, faithfulness, holiness, and love. It showed Him wise, in providing a plan whereby He could be just, and yet the justifier of the ungodly. — It showed Him faithful in keeping His promise, that the seed of the woman should bruise the serpent's head. — It showed Him holy, in requiring His law's demands to be satisfied by our great Substitute. — It showed Him loving, in providing such a Mediator, such a Redeemer, and such a Friend for sinful man as His co-eternal Son.
>
> The crucifixion brought glory to the Son. It glorified His compassion, His patience, and His power. It showed Him most compassionate, in dying for us, suffering in our stead, allowing Himself to be counted sin and a curse for us, and buying our redemption with the price of His own blood. — It showed Him most patient, in not dying the common death of most men, but in willingly submitting to such pains and unknown agonies as no mind can conceive, when with a word He could have summoned His Father's angels, and been set free. — It showed Him most powerful, in bearing the weight of all transgressions of the world, and vanquishing Satan, and despoiling him of his prey.[46]

17:5 Before Christ came into the world, He dwelt in heaven with the Father. When the angels looked upon the Lord, they saw all the glory of Deity. To every eye, He was obviously God. But when He came among men, the glory of Deity was veiled. Though He was still God, it was not apparent to most onlookers. They saw Him merely as the carpenter's Son. Here, the Savior is praying that the visible manifestation of His glory in heaven might be restored. The words "**glorify Me together with Yourself**" mean "glorify Me in Your presence in heaven. Let the original glory which I shared with You before My Incarnation be resumed." This clearly teaches the pre-existence of Christ.

X. Jesus Prays for His Disciples (17:6–19)

17:6 Jesus had **manifested** the Father's **name to the** disciples. The "name" in Scripture means the Person, His attributes, and character. Christ had fully declared the Father's true nature. The disciples had been **given** to the Son **out of the world**. They were separated from the unbelieving mass of mankind and set apart to belong to Christ. "They were the Father's *by election* before the world was, and became Christ's by the gift of the Father, and by purchase of blood," wrote J. G. Bellett.

"They have kept Your word," said the Lord. In spite of all their failures and shortcomings, He credits them with having believed and obeyed His teaching. "Not a word against His people," Rainsford writes, "no allusion to what they had done or were about to do — forsake Him."

17:7, 8 The Savior had perfectly represented His Father. He explained to the disciples that He did not speak or act by His own authority, but only as the Father instructed Him. So they **believed that** the Father had **sent** the Son.

Moreover, Christ did not *originate* His own mission. He came in obedience to the Father's will. He was the perfect Servant of Jehovah.

17:9 As High Priest, He prayed for the disciples; He did **not pray for the world**. This should not be taken to mean that Christ never prayed for the world. On the cross, He prayed, "Father, forgive them; for they do not know what they do."

But here He was praying as the One who represented believers before the throne of God. There His prayer can only be for His own.

17:10 The perfect union between the Father and the Son is shown here. No mere man could truthfully say these words. We might be able to say to God, **"All Mine are Yours,"** but we could not say, **"All Yours are Mine."** It is because the Son is equal with the Father that He could say it. In these verses (6–19), Jesus presents His poor and backward flock, and, robing each lamb in a coat of many colors, declares, **"I am glorified in them."**

17:11 Again the Lord Jesus anticipated His return to heaven. He prayed as if He had already gone. Notice the title **Holy Father. Holy** speaks of One who is *infinitely high*. **Father** speaks of One who is *intimately nigh*.

Jesus' prayer **"that they all may be one"** refers to unity of Christian character. As the Father and Son are One in moral likeness, so believers should be united in this respect — that they are like the Lord Jesus.

17:12 **While** He **was with** the disciples, the Savior **kept them in** the Father's **name**, that is, by His power and authority, and true to Him. **"None of them is lost,"** said Jesus, **"except the son of perdition,"** that is, Judas. But this did not mean that Judas was one of those given to the Son by the Father or that he was ever a genuine believer. The sentence means this: "Those that You gave Me I have kept, and none of them is lost, but the son of perdition is lost, that the Scripture might be fulfilled." The title **"the son of perdition"** means Judas was consigned to eternal ruin or damnation. Judas was not compelled to betray Christ in order to fulfill prophecy, but he chose to betray the Savior and in so doing **the Scripture** was **fulfilled**.

17:13 The Lord explained why He was praying in the presence of His disciples. It was as if He said to them: "These are intercessions which I shall never cease to make in heaven before God. But now I make them **in the world**, in your hearing, so you may more distinctly understand how I am there to be employed in promoting your welfare, so that you may be made in large measure partakers of **My joy**."

17:14 The Lord gave God's **word** to the disciples, and they received it. As a result, **the world** turned on them and **hated them**. They had the characteristics of the Lord Jesus, and so **the world** despised them. They did not fit in with the world's scheme of things.

17:15 The Lord did **not pray that** the Father **should take** believers home to heaven immediately. They must be left here to grow in grace and to witness for Christ. **But** Christ's prayer was that they might be kept **from the evil one**. Not escape, but preservation.

17:16 Christians **are not of the**

world, just as Christ was **not of the world**. We should remember this when tempted to engage in some worldly pastime or enter into worldly associations where the name of Jesus is unwelcome.

17:17 To **sanctify** means to set apart. The Word of God has a sanctifying effect on believers. As they read it and obey it, they are set apart as vessels suitable for the Master's use. That is exactly what the Lord Jesus was praying for here. He wanted a people who were set apart to God from the world, and usable by God. **"Your word is truth,"** Jesus said. He did not say, as so many do today, "Your word *contains* truth," but **"Your word IS truth."**

17:18 The Father **sent** the Lord Jesus **into the world** to reveal the character of God to men. As the Lord prayed, He realized that He would soon be going back to heaven. But future generations would still need some witness concerning God. This work must be done by believers, through the power of the Holy Spirit. Of course, Christians can never represent God as perfectly as Christ did because they can never be equal with God. But believers are here just the same to represent God to the world. It is for this reason Jesus **sent them into the world**.

17:19 *To sanctify* does not necessarily mean to *make* holy. He *is* holy as to His personal character. The thought is that the Lord *set Himself apart* for the work His Father sent Him to do — that is, His sacrificial death. It may also mean that He set Himself apart by taking His place outside the world and entering into the glory. "His sanctification is the pattern of, and the power for, ours," says Vine. We should be set apart from the world and find our portion with Him.

Y. Jesus Prays for All Believers (17:20–26)

17:20 Now the High Priest extended His prayer beyond the disciples. He prayed for generations yet unborn. In fact, every believer reading this verse can say, "Jesus prayed for me over 1900 years ago."

17:21 The prayer was for unity among believers, but this time it was with the salvation of sinners in view.

The unity for which Christ prayed was not a matter of external church union. Rather it was a unity based on common moral likeness. He was praying that believers might **be one** in exhibiting the character of God and of Christ. This is what would cause **the world** to **believe that** God had **sent** Him. This is the unity which makes the world say, "I see Christ in those Christians as the Father was seen in Christ."

17:22 In verse 11, the Lord prayed for unity in fellowship. In verse 21, it was unity in witness-bearing. Now it is unity in **glory**. This looks forward to the time when saints will receive their glorified bodies. **"The glory which You gave Me"** is the glory of resurrection and ascension.

We do not have this glory yet. It has been **given** to us as far as the purposes of God are concerned, but we will not receive it until the Savior returns to take us to heaven. It will be manifested to the world when Christ returns to set up His kingdom on earth. At that time, the world will realize the vital unity between the Father and the Son, and the Son and His people, and will believe (too late) that Jesus was the Sent One from God.

17:23 **The world** will not only realize that Jesus was God the Son, but it will also know that believers were loved by God just as Christ was loved by God. That we should be so loved seems almost incredible, but there it is!

17:24 The Son desires to have His people with Himself in glory. Every time a believer dies, it is, in a sense, an answer to this prayer. If we realized this, it would be a comfort to us in our sorrow. To die is to go to be with Christ and to **behold** His **glory**. This **glory** is not only the glory of deity which He had with God before the world began. It is also the glory He acquired as Savior and Redeemer. This **glory** is a proof that God **loved** Christ **before the foundation of the world**.

17:25 **The world** failed to see God revealed in Jesus. But a few disciples did, and they believed **that** God had **sent** Jesus. On the eve of His crucifixion, there were only a few faithful hearts in the whole of mankind — and even those were about to forsake Him!

17:26 The Lord Jesus had **declared** the Father's **name** to His disciples when He was with them. This meant that He revealed the Father to them. His words and works were the words and works of the Father. They saw in Christ a perfect expression of the Father. Jesus has continued to **declare** the Father's Name through the ministry of the Holy Spirit. Ever since the day of Pentecost, the Spirit has been teaching believers about God the Father. Especially through the Word of God, we can know what God is like. When men accept the Father as He is revealed by the Lord Jesus, they become special objects of the Father's **love**. Since the Lord Jesus indwells all believers, the Father can look upon them and treat them as He does His only Son. Reuss remarks:

> The love of God which, before the creation of the physical world, had its adequate object in the person of the Son (v. 24), finds it, since the creation of the new spiritual world, in all those who are united with the Son.[47]

And Godet adds:

> What God desired in sending His Son here on earth was precisely that He might form for Himself in the midst of humanity a family of children like Him.[47]

It is because the Lord Jesus is in the believer that God can love him as He loves Christ.

> So dear, so very dear to God,
> I cannot dearer be;
> The love wherewith He loves the Son,
> Such is His love for me!
>
> *– Catesby Paget*

The petitions made by Christ for His people, as Rainsford notes,

> . . . refer to spiritual things, to heavenly blessings. Not for riches, or honor, or worldly influence, but deliverance from evil, separation from the world, qualification for duty, and a safe arrival in heaven.[48]

VIII. THE SON OF GOD'S PASSION AND DEATH (Chaps. 18, 19)

A. Judas Betrays the Lord (18:1–11)

18:1 The words of chapters 13–17 were spoken in Jerusalem. Now **Jesus** left the city and walked eastward toward the Mount of Olives. In doing so, He crossed **the Brook Kidron** and came to the Garden of Gethsemane, which was on the western slope of Olivet.

18:2, 3 **Judas** knew that the Lord spent a great deal of time praying in the garden. He **knew** that the most likely **place** to find the Lord was in the place of prayer.

The **detachment of troops** was probably Roman soldiers; whereas the **officers** were Jewish officials, representing **the chief priests and Pharisees**. They **came with lanterns, torches, and weapons**. "They came to seek the Light of the world with lanterns."

18:4 The Lord **went forward** to meet them, without waiting for them to find Him. This demonstrated His willingness to go to the cross. The soldiers could have left their weapons at home; the Savior would not resist. The question **"Whom are you seeking?"** was designed to draw forth from their own lips the nature of their mission.

18:5 They sought **Jesus of Nazareth**, little realizing that He was their Creator and their Sustainer — the best Friend they ever had. Jesus said, **"I am."** (The **"He"** is not found in the original, but needed in English.) He meant not only that He was Jesus of Nazareth but that He was Jehovah as well. As mentioned previously, I AM is one of the Names of Jehovah in the OT. Did this cause **Judas** to wonder afresh, as he **stood with** the others in the crowd?

18:6 For a brief moment, the Lord Jesus had revealed Himself to them as the I AM, the Almighty God. The revelation was so overpowering that **they drew back and fell to the ground**.

18:7 **Again** the Lord **asked them** to tell Him **whom** they were **seeking**. And again the answer was the same — in spite of the effect which two words of Christ had just had upon them.

18:8, 9 Again **Jesus answered** that He was the One, and that He was Jehovah. **"I have told you that I AM."** Since they sought Him, He told them that they should **let** the disciples **go their way**. It is wonderful to see His unselfish interest in others at a time when His own life was in peril. Thus, too, the words of John 17:12 were fulfilled.

18:10 **Simon Peter** thought the time

had come to use violence in an effort to save his Master from the crowd. Acting without instructions from the Lord, he **drew** his **sword** and **struck the high priest's servant**. Undoubtedly he intended to kill him, but the sword was deflected by an Unseen Hand, so that it **cut off** only **his right ear**.

18:11 **Jesus** rebuked the ill-advised zeal of **Peter**. **The cup** of suffering and death had been **given** to Him by His **Father**, and He intended to **drink** it. Luke, the physician, recorded how the Lord touched and healed Malchus' ear at this point (22:51).

B. Jesus Arrested and Bound (18:12–14)

18:12, 13 This was the first time that wicked men had been able to lay hold of **Jesus** and to tie up His arms.

Annas had been high priest previously. It is not clear why Jesus should have been brought to him **first**, rather than to **Caiaphas**, his son-in-law, **who was high priest** at the time. What is important to see is that Jesus was first put on trial before the Jews in an attempt to prove Him guilty of blasphemy and heresy. That was what we might call a *religious* trial. Then He was taken to be tried before the Roman authorities, and here the attempt was made to prove that He was an enemy of Caesar. That was the *civil* trial. Since the Jews were under Roman rule, they had to work through the Roman courts. They could not carry out the death penalty, for instance. This must be done by Pilate.

18:14 John explained that the high priest was the same **Caiaphas** who had prophesied **that one man should die for the** nation (see John 11:50). He was now about to have part in the fulfillment of the prophecy. James Stewart writes:

> This was the man who was the accredited guardian of the nation's soul. He had been set apart to be the supreme interpreter and representative of the Most High. To him was committed the glorious privilege of entering once every year into the holy of holies. Yet this was the man who condemned the Son of God. History provides no more startling illustration of the truth that the best religious opportunities in the world and the most promising environment will not guarantee a man's salvation or of themselves ennoble his

soul. "Then I saw," says John Bunyan, closing his book, "that there was a way to hell, even from the gates of heaven."[49]

C. Peter Denies His Lord (18:15–18)

18:15 Most Bible scholars believe that **the other disciple** mentioned here was John, but that humility prevented him from mentioning his own name, especially in view of Peter's shameful failure. We are not told how John had become so well **known to the high priest**, but it is a fact that gained him admittance **into the courtyard**.

18:16, 17 **Peter** was not able to get in until John went out and spoke to the woman who was the doorkeeper. Looking back, we wonder if it was a kindness for John to use his influence in this way. It is significant that Peter's first denial of the Lord was not before a powerful, terrifying soldier, but before a simple **servant girl who kept the door**. He denied that he was a disciple of Jesus.

18:18 Peter now mingled with the enemies of his Lord and tried to conceal his identity. Like many another disciple, he **warmed himself** at this world's **fire**.

D. Jesus Before the High Priest (18:19–24)†

18:19 It is not clear whether **the high priest** here is Annas or Caiaphas. If it was Annas, as seems most likely, he was probably called high priest out of courtesy because he once held this office. **The high priest then asked Jesus about His disciples and His** teachings, as if these posed a threat to the Mosaic Law and the Roman government. It is obvious that these people had no real case against the Lord, and so they were trying to make one up.

18:20 **Jesus answered him** that His ministry had been carried on **openly**. He had nothing to hide. He had **taught** in the presence of **the Jews**, both in **synagogues and in the temple**. There was no secrecy.

18:21 This was a challenge to bring forth some of the Jews who had listened to Him. Let them bring charges against Him. If He had done or said something wrong, let the witnesses be produced.

18:22 The challenge obviously irritated the Jews. It left them without a

†See p. xv.

case. And so they resorted to abuse. **One of the officers** slapped **Jesus** for speaking to **the high priest like that**.

18:23 With perfect poise and unanswerable logic, the Savior showed the unfairness of their position. They could not accuse Him of speaking evil; yet they struck Him for telling the truth.

18:24 The preceding verses describe the questioning before Annas. The trial before Caiaphas is not described by John. It fits in between 18:24 and 18:28.

E. Peter's Second and Third Denials (18:25–27)

18:25 The narrative now turns back to **Simon Peter**. In the cold of the early morning hours, he **warmed himself** by the fire. Doubtless his clothing and accent indicated that he was a Galilean fisherman. The one standing with him asked if he was a disciple of this Jesus. But **he denied** the Lord again.

18:26 Now it was **a relative** of Malchus who spoke to Peter. He had seen **Peter cut off** his relative's **ear**. "**Did I not see you in the garden with** this Jesus?"

18:27 **Peter** for the third time **denied** the Lord. **Immediately**, he heard the crowing of **a rooster** and was reminded of the words of the Lord, "The rooster shall not crow till you have denied Me three times." From the other Gospels we know that Peter went out at this point and wept bitterly.

F. Jesus Before Pilate (18:28–40)

18:28 The religious trial was ended, and the civil trial is about to begin. The scene is the hall of judgment or the palace of the governor. The Jews did not want to go into the palace of a Gentile. They felt that they would have been **defiled** and would thus be prevented from eating **the Passover**. It did not seem to bother them that they were plotting the death of the Son of God. It would have been a tragedy for them to enter a Gentile house, but murder was a mere trifle. Augustine remarks:

> O impious blindness! They would be defiled, forsooth, by a dwelling which was another's, and not be defiled by a crime which was their own. They feared to be defiled by the praetorium of an alien

judge, and feared not to be defiled by the blood of an innocent brother.[50]

Hall comments:

> Woe unto you priests, scribes, elders, hypocrites! Can there be any roof so unclean as that of your own breasts? Not Pilate's walls, but your own hearts, are impure. Is murder your errand, and do you stop at a local infection? God shall smite you, ye white walls! Do you long to be stained with blood — with the blood of God? And do ye fear to be defiled with the touch of Pilate's pavement? Doth so small a gnat stick in your throats, while ye swallow such a camel of flagitious wickedness? Go out of Jerusalem, ye false disbelievers, if ye would not be unclean! Pilate hath more cause to fear, lest his walls should be defiled with the presence of such prodigious monsters of iniquity.[51]

Poole remarks, "Nothing is more common than for persons overzealous about rituals to be remiss about morals."[52] The expression "**that they might eat the Passover**" probably means the feast which *followed* the Passover. The Passover itself had been held on the previous night.

18:29 **Pilate**, the Roman Governor, gave in to the religious scruples of the Jews by going **out** to where they were. He began the trial by asking them to state the charge **against this** Prisoner.

18:30 Their answer was bold and rude. They said, in effect, that they had already tried the case and found Him guilty. All they wanted Pilate to do was to pronounce the sentence.

18:31 **Pilate** tried to evade responsibility and throw it back on the Jews. If they had already tried Jesus and found Him guilty, then why did they not sentence **Him according to** their **law**? The answer of the Jews was very significant. They said, in so many words: "We are not an independent nation. We have been taken over by the Roman power. Civil government has been taken from our hands, and we no longer have the authority **to put anyone to death**." Their answer was evidence of their bondage and subjection to a Gentile power. Furthermore, they wanted to shift the odium of Christ's death onto Pilate.

18:32 Verse 32 may have two different meanings: (1) In Matthew 20:19, Jesus had predicted that He would be delivered up to the Gentiles to be killed. Here the Jews were doing that very thing to Him. (2) In many places, the Lord said that He would be "lifted up" (John 3:14; 8:28; 12:32, 34). This referred to death by crucifixion. The Jews used stoning in cases of capital punishment; whereas crucifixion was the Roman method. Thus, by their refusal to carry out the death penalty, the Jews unknowingly fulfilled these two prophecies concerning the Messiah (see also Psalm 22:16).

18:33　**Pilate** now took Jesus into **the Praetorium** for a private interview and asked Him point blank — **"Are You the King of the Jews?"**

18:34　**Jesus answered him**, in effect, "As governor, have you ever heard that I tried to overthrow the Roman power? Has it ever been reported to you that I proclaimed myself a King who would undermine Caesar's empire? Is this a charge which you know by personal experience, or is it just what you have heard these Jews saying?"

18:35　There was real contempt in Pilate's question, **"Am I a Jew?"** He implied that he was too important to be troubled with such a local Jewish problem. But his answer was also an admission that he knew of no real charge against Jesus. He only knew what the rulers of the Jews had said.

18:36　The Lord then confessed He *was* a King. But not the kind of king the Jews accused Him of being. And not the kind that would threaten Rome. Christ's **kingdom** is not advanced by human weapons. Otherwise His disciples **would fight** to prevent His capture by the Jews. Christ's **kingdom is not from here**, that is, not of this world. It does not receive its power or authority from the world; its aims and objectives are not carnal.

18:37　When **Pilate** asked Him if He was **a king, . . . Jesus answered, "You say rightly that I am a king."** But His kingdom is concerned with **truth**, not with swords and shields. It was to **bear witness to the truth** that He came **into the world. The truth** here means the truth about God, Christ Himself, the Holy Spirit, man, sin, salvation, and all the other great doctrines of Christianity. **Everyone who loves the truth hears** His **voice**, and that is how His empire grows.

18:38　It is difficult to say what **Pilate** meant when he **said to Him, "What is truth?"** Was he puzzled, or sarcastic, or interested? All we know is that the Truth Incarnate stood before him, and he did not recognize Him. Pilate now hurried to the Jews with the admission that he could find **no fault in** Jesus **at all**.

18:39　It was the **custom** among the Jews **at the Passover** to request the release of some Jewish prisoner from the Romans. Pilate seized upon this custom in an effort to please the Jews and at the same time **release** Jesus.

18:40　The scheme failed. The Jews did not want Jesus; they wanted **Barabbas. Barabbas was a robber**. The wicked heart of man preferred a bandit to the Creator.

G. Pilate's Verdict: Innocent but Condemned (19:1–16)

19:1　It was most unjust for **Pilate** to scourge an innocent Person. Perhaps he hoped that this punishment would satisfy the Jews and that they would not demand the *death* of Jesus. Scourging was a Roman form of punishment. The prisoner was beaten with a whip or a rod. The whip had pieces of metal or bone in it, and these cut deep gashes in the flesh.

19:2, 3　**The soldiers** mocked Jesus' claim to be King. A crown for the King! But it was **a crown of thorns**. This would have caused extreme pain as it was pressed onto His brow. Thorns are a symbol of the curse which sin brought to mankind. Here we have a picture of the Lord Jesus bearing the curse of our sins, so that we might wear a crown of glory. The **purple robe** was also used in mockery. **Purple** was the color of royalty. But again it reminds us of how our sins were placed on Jesus in order that we might be clothed with the robe of God's righteousness.

How solemn it is to think of the eternal Son of God being slapped by the **hands** of His creatures! Mouths which He formed are now being used to mock Him!

19:4　**Pilate then went out again** to the mob and announced that he was about to bring Jesus **out to** them, but that He was innocent. Thus Pilate condemned himself by his own words. He found no fault in Christ; yet he would not let Him go.

19:5 As **Jesus came out** with **the crown of thorns and the purple robe,** Pilate announced Him as **"the Man."** It is difficult to know whether he said this in mockery, in sympathy, or without any particular emotion.

19:6 **The chief priests** noticed that Pilate was wavering, so they cried out fiercely that Jesus should be crucified. It was *religious* men who were leaders in the death of the Savior. Often, down through the centuries, it has been church officials who have persecuted true believers most bitterly. **Pilate** seemed to be disgusted with them and with their unreasonable hatred of Jesus. He said, in effect: "If that is the way you feel, why don't **you take Him and crucify Him**? As far as I am concerned, He is innocent." Yet Pilate knew that the Jews could not put Him to death because that power could only be exercised by the Romans at that time.

19:7 When they saw that they had failed to prove that Jesus was a threat to Caesar's government, they brought forth their religious charge against Him. Christ claimed equality with God by saying that He was **the Son of God**. To the Jews, this was blasphemy and should be punished by death.

19:8, 9 The possibility of Jesus' being the Son of God troubled **Pilate**. He was already uneasy about the whole affair, but this made him **more afraid**. Pilate took Jesus **into the Praetorium** or judgment hall and asked Him **where** He came **from**. In all of this, Pilate presented a most tragic figure. He confessed with his own lips that Jesus had done no wrong; yet he did not have the moral courage to let Him go because he feared the Jews. Why did **Jesus** give **him no answer**? Probably because He knew that Pilate was unwilling to act in accordance with the light he had. Pilate had sinned away his day of opportunity. He would not be given more light when he had not responded to the light he had.

19:10 **Pilate** tried to force the Lord to answer by threatening Him. He reminded Jesus that, as Roman governor, he had **power** or authority **to release** Him or to **crucify** Him.

19:11 The self-control of the Lord Jesus was remarkable. He was more calm than Pilate. He answered quietly that whatever **power** Pilate possessed **had been given** to him by God. All governments are ordained by God, and all authority, whether civil or spiritual, is from God.

"The one who delivered Me to you" may refer to: (1) *Caiaphas,* the high priest; (2) *Judas,* the betrayer; or (3) the Jewish *people* in general. The thought is that these Jews should have known better. They had the Scriptures which predicted the coming of the Messiah. They should have recognized Him when He came. But they rejected Him and were even now crying out for His life. This verse teaches us that there are degrees of guilt. Pilate was guilty, but Caiaphas, and Judas, and all the wicked Jews were *more* guilty.

19:12 Just as **Pilate** became determined **to release** Jesus, the Jews used their last and most telling argument. **"If you let this Man go, you are not Caesar's friend."** (Caesar was the official title of the Roman Emperor.) As if they cared for Caesar! They hated him. They would like to destroy him, and free themselves from his control. Yet here they were pretending to protect Caesar's empire from the threat of this Jesus who claimed to be a king! They reaped the punishment of this terrible hypocrisy when the Romans marched into Jerusalem in A.D. 70 and utterly destroyed the city and slaughtered its inhabitants.

19:13 **Pilate** could not afford to have the Jews accuse him of disloyalty to Caesar, and so he weakly submitted to the mob. He now **brought Jesus out** to a public area **called the Pavement,** where such matters were often handled.

19:14 Actually, the Passover feast had been held on the previous evening. The **Preparation Day of the Passover** means the preparation for the feast that followed it. **"About the sixth hour"** was probably 6 a.m. but there are unresolved problems concerning the methods of reckoning time in the Gospels. **"Behold your King!"** Almost certainly, Pilate said this to annoy and provoke the Jews. He doubtless blamed them for trapping him into condemning Jesus.

19:15 The Jews were insistent that Jesus must be crucified. Pilate taunted them with the question, "You mean you want to **crucify your** own **King?"** Then the Jews stooped very low by saying, **"We have no king but Caesar!"** Faithless nation! Refusing your God for a wicked, heathen monarch.

19:16 Pilate was willing to please the Jews, and so he turned Jesus over to the soldiers **to be crucified**. He loved the praise of men more than the praise of God.

H. The Crucifixion (19:17–24)

19:17 The word translated **cross** may refer to a single piece of wood (a stake), or it may have been two cross pieces. At any rate, it was of such size that a man could normally carry it. Jesus carried **His cross** for some distance. Then, according to the other Gospels, it was given to a man named Simon of Cyrene to carry. **The Place of a Skull** may have received this name in one of two ways: (1) The land itself may have resembled a skull, especially if it was a hill with caves in the side of it. Such a site is "Gordon's Calvary" in Israel today. (2) It was the place where criminals were executed; perhaps skulls and bones were found in the area, though in light of the Mosaic Law on burial this is most unlikely.

19:18 The Lord Jesus was nailed to the cross, hands and feet. The cross was then lifted up and dropped into a hole in the ground. The only perfect Man who ever lived, and this was the reception He received from His own! If you have never before trusted Him as your Lord and Savior, will you not do it now, as you read this simple account of how He died for you? Two thieves were crucified with Him, **one on either side**. This was in fulfillment of the prophecy of Isaiah 53:12: "He was numbered with the transgressors."

19:19 It was the custom to put **a title** above the head of the crucified, and to indicate the crime. Pilate ordered that the title **JESUS OF NAZARETH, THE KING OF THE JEWS**, should be placed on the center cross.

19:20 Alexander expresses it eloquently:

In Hebrew, the sacred tongue of patriarchs and seers. In Greek, the musical and golden tongue which gave a soul to the objects of sense and a body to the abstractions of philosophy. In Latin, the dialect of a people originally the strongest of all the sons of men. The three languages represent the three races and their ideas — revelation, art, literature; progress, war, and jurisprudence. Wherever these three desires of the human race exist, wherever annunciation can be made in human language, wherever there is a heart to sin, a tongue to speak, an eye to read, the Cross has a message.[53]

The place . . . was near the city. The Lord Jesus was crucified outside the city limits. The exact location is no longer known for certain.

19:21 **The chief priests** did not like the wording. They wanted it to read as a *claim* made by Jesus, but not as a *fact* (which it was).

19:22 **Pilate** would not change the writing. He had become impatient with the Jews and would not give in to them any more. But he should have shown this determination sooner!

19:23 At such executions, **the soldiers** were allowed to share the personal effects of those who died. Here we find them dividing Christ's **garments** among themselves. Apparently there were five pieces altogether. They divided four, but there was still **the tunic**, which **was without seam** and could not be cut up without making it worthless.

19:24 They **cast lots** for the tunic, and it was handed over to the unnamed winner. Little did they know that in doing this, they were fulfilling a remarkable prophecy written a thousand years previously (Ps. 22:18)! These fulfilled prophecies remind us afresh that this Book is the inspired Word of God, and that Jesus Christ is indeed the promised Messiah.

I. Jesus Commends His Mother to John (19:25–27)

19:25 Many Bible students think that there are four women named in this verse, as follows: (1) Mary, the **mother** of Jesus; (2) Mary's **sister**, Salome, the mother of John; (3) **Mary, the wife of Clopas**; (4) **Mary Magdalene**.

19:26, 27 In spite of His own suffering, the Lord had tender regard for others. Seeing **His mother**, and John, **the disciple**, He introduced John to her as the one who would hereafter take the place of son to her. In calling His mother **"Woman,"** the Lord did not show any lack of respect. But it is noticeable that He did not call her "Mother." Does this have any lesson for those who might be tempted to exalt Mary to the place where she is adored? Jesus here instructed John to care for Mary as if she were his own **mother**. John obeyed and took Mary **to his own home**.

J. The Work of Christ Finished (19:28–30)

19:28   Between verse 27 and 28, we have, no doubt, the three hours of darkness — from noon to 3:00 p.m. It was during this time that Jesus was forsaken by God as He suffered the penalty of our sins. His cry, **"I thirst!"** indicated real, physical thirst, which was intensified by crucifixion. But it also reminds us that, greater than His physical thirst was His spiritual thirst for the salvation of the souls of men.

19:29   The soldiers gave Him **sour wine** to drink. They probably tied **a sponge** to the end of a rod with **hyssop** and pressed it to His lips. (**Hyssop** is a plant, also used at the Passover — Ex. 12:22.) This is not to be confused with the vinegar mixed with gall, which had been offered to Him earlier (Matt. 27:34). He did not drink that because it would have acted as a pain reliever. He must bear our sins in full consciousness.

19:30   **"It is finished!"** The work His Father had given him to do! The pouring out of His soul as an offering for sin! The work of redemption and of atonement! It is true that He had not yet died, but His death, burial, and ascension were as certain as if already accomplished. So the Lord Jesus could announce that the way had been provided whereby sinners could be saved. Thank God today for the finished work of the Lord Jesus on the cross of Calvary!

Some Bible scholars tells us that **bowing His head** may mean that He leaned His head backward. Vine says, "Not the helpless dropping of the head after death, but the deliberate putting of His head into a position of rest."

That **He gave up His spirit** emphasizes the fact that His death was voluntary. He determined the time of His death. In full control of His faculties, He *dismissed* **His spirit** — an act no mere man could accomplish.

K. Piercing of the Savior's Side (19:31–37)

19:31   Again we see how careful these religious **Jews** were about details when they were committing cold-blooded murder. They "strained out a gnat and swallowed a camel." They thought it would **not** be proper to allow the bodies to **remain on the cross on the Sabbath** (Saturday). There would be a religious feast in the city. So they requested Pilate to have the **legs** of the three **broken** to hasten death.

19:32[†]   The Scripture does not describe how the legs were broken. However, they must have been broken in many different places, since a single break would not bring on death.

19:33   These soldiers were well experienced in such matters. They knew that **Jesus . . . was already dead.** There was no possibility of His being in a faint or swoon. **They did not break His legs.**

19:34[††]   We are not told why **one of the soldiers pierced His side.** Perhaps it was a final outburst of the wickedness of his heart. "It was the sullen shot of the defeated foe after the battle, telling out the deep-seated hatred in man's heart toward God and His Christ." There is no agreement on the significance of the **blood and water.** Some take it as an indication that Jesus died of a ruptured heart — but we have already read that His death was a voluntary act. Others think it speaks of baptism and the Lord's Supper, but this seems farfetched. **Blood** speaks of cleansing from the guilt of sin; whereas **water** typifies cleansing from the defilement of sin through the Word. This is expressed in the verse:

> Let the water and the blood,
>   From Thy riven side which flowed
>   Be of sin the double cure,
>   Save me from its *guilt* and *power.*
>   – *Augustus Toplady*

19:35   Verse 35 may refer to the fact that Jesus' legs were not broken, the piercing of Jesus' side, or to the entire crucifixion scene. **He who has seen** undoubtedly refers to John, who wrote the account.

19:36   This verse obviously looks

back to verse 33 as a fulfillment of Exodus 12:46: "Nor shall you break one of its bones." That verse refers to the Passover lamb. God's decree was that the bones were to be maintained unbroken. Christ is the true Passover Lamb, fulfilling the type with great exactness.

19:37 Verse 37 looks back to verse 34. Although the soldier did not realize it, his action was another wonderful fulfillment of **Scripture** (Zech. 12:10). "Man has his wickedness, but God has His way." Zechariah's prophecy refers to a future day when believing Jews will see the Lord coming back to the earth. "They will look on Me whom they pierced. Yes, they will mourn for Him as one mourns for his only son."

L. The Burial in Joseph's Tomb (19:38–42)†

19:38 This begins the account of the burial of Jesus. Up to now, **Joseph of Arimathea** had been a secret believer. **Fear of the Jews** had kept him from confessing Christ openly. Now he boldly stepped forward to claim **the body of Jesus** for burial. In doing this, he exposed himself to excommunication, persecution, and violence. It is only regrettable that he was not willing to take his stand for a rejected Master while Jesus was still ministering to the masses.

19:39, 40 John's readers are by now familiar with **Nicodemus**, having met him previously when he **came to Jesus by night** (chap. 3) and when he urged that Jesus be given a fair hearing before the Sanhedrin (John 7:50, 51). He now joins Joseph, bringing with him a **hundred pounds** of **myrrh and aloes**. These **spices** were probably in powdered form and were spread on the body. Then **the body** was **bound** with **strips of linen.**

19:41 Almost every detail in this passage was a fulfillment of prophecy. Isaiah had predicted that men would plan to bury the Messiah with the wicked but that He would be with the rich in His death (Isa. 53:9). **A new tomb** in a **garden** would obviously belong to a rich man. In Matthew we learn that it belonged to Joseph of Arimathea.

19:42 The body of **Jesus** was put in the tomb. The Jews were anxious to have the body out of the way because of their feast that began at sunset. But it was all

a part of God's determination that the body should be in the heart of the earth for three days and three nights. In that connection, it should be noted that in Jewish reckoning, any part of a day was counted as a day. So the fact that the Lord was in the tomb for a *part* of three days was still a fulfillment of His prediction in Matthew 12:40.

IX. THE SON OF GOD'S TRIUMPH (Chap. 20)††

A. The Empty Tomb (20:1–10)

20:1 **The first day of the week** was Sunday. **Mary Magdalene went to the tomb** before dawn. It is probable that the tomb was a small room carved in the side of a hill or cliff. **The stone** was no doubt shaped like a coin — round and flat. It would fit into a groove or gutter along the front of the tomb and could be rolled across the door to close it. When Mary got there, **the stone had been** removed already. This, incidentally, had taken place *after* Christ's resurrection, as we learn in Matthew 28.

20:2 Mary immediately **ran** to **Peter** and John with the breathless announcement that someone had removed the Lord's body **out of the tomb**. She did not say who had done it, but just said **they** to indicate that this was all she knew. The faithfulness and devotion of women at the crucifixion and resurrection of our Lord should be noticed. The disciples had forsaken the Lord and fled. The women stood by without regard for their personal safety. These things are not without meaning.

20:3, 4 It is difficult to imagine what **Peter** and John were thinking as they hurried **out** of the city to the garden near Calvary. John was probably younger than Peter and reached the **tomb first**.

20:5 It is likely that there was a low opening to the tomb, requiring one to stoop to enter or to look in. John **saw the linen cloths lying there**. Had they been unwound from the body, or were they still in the general shape in which they had been wrapped around the body? We suspect that the latter was the case. **Yet he did not go in** the tomb.

20:6, 7 By now **Peter** had caught up and he **went into** the tomb without hesitation. There is something about his impulsive manner that makes us feel a kinship to him. **He too saw the linen cloths lying there**, but the body of the Savior was not there.

The detail about **the handkerchief** was added to show that the Lord's departure was orderly and unhurried. If someone had stolen the body, he would not have carefully **folded** the cloth!

20:8 John entered the tomb and **saw** the orderly arrangement of the linen and the handkerchief. But when it says that **he saw and believed**, it means more than physical sight. It means that he comprehended. Before him were the evidences of Christ's resurrection. They showed him what had happened, **and he ... believed.**

20:9 Up until now, the disciples did not really understand the OT **Scripture** which stated that the Messiah **must rise again from the dead.** The Lord Himself had told them repeatedly, but they did not take it in. John was the first to understand.

20:10 Then the disciples returned to wherever they were staying — probably in Jerusalem. They doubtless concluded that there was no use waiting by the tomb. It would be better to go and tell the other disciples what they had found.

B. The Appearance to Mary Magdalene (20:11-18)

20:11 The first two words are striking — **But Mary**. The other two disciples went home, *but Mary.* . . . Here again we have the love and devotion of a woman. She had been forgiven much; therefore, she loved much. She kept a lonely vigil outside the tomb, weeping because, as she thought, the body had been stolen, probably by the Lord's enemies.

20:12 This time, as she looked inside, **she saw two angels**, stationed **where the body of Jesus had lain**. It is remarkable how these tremendous facts are stated quietly and without emotion.

20:13 Mary did not seem to have any fear or surprise. She answered their question as if this were quite a normal experience. It is obvious from her answer that she still did not realize that Jesus had risen and was alive again.

20:14 At this point, something caused her to look in back of her. It was **Jesus** Himself, but she did not recognize Him. It was still early in the morning, and perhaps light had not yet dawned. She had been weeping continually, and doubtless her vision was clouded. Also, possibly God prevented her from recognizing the Lord until the proper time had come.

20:15 The Lord knew the answers to these questions; but He wanted to hear them from her own lips. **She** supposed **Him to be the gardener**. The Savior of the world may be very near to men, and yet not recognized. He usually comes in lowly guise, however, and not as one of the great ones of the earth. In her answer, Mary did not name the Lord. Three times she referred to Jesus as **Him**. There was only one Person with whom she was concerned, and she felt it quite unnecessary to identify Him further.

20:16 Mary now heard a familiar voice calling her by name. There was no mistaking the fact — it was **Jesus**! She called Him **Rabboni**, which means "my Great **Teacher**." Actually, she was still thinking of Him as the Great Teacher she had known. She did not realize that He was now more than her Teacher — He was her Lord and Savior. So the Lord prepared to explain to her the newer and fuller way in which she would hereafter know Him.

20:17 Mary had known Jesus personally as a Man. She had seen miracles happen when He was bodily present. So she concluded that if He was not with her in a visible way, then she could have no hope of blessing. The Lord must correct her thinking. He said, **"Do not cling to Me** simply as a Man in the flesh. **I have not yet ascended to My Father**. When I do return to heaven, the Holy Spirit will be sent down to the earth. When He comes, He will reveal Me to your heart in a way you have never known Me before. I will be nearer and dearer to you than was possible during My life here."

Then He told her to **go to His brethren** and tell them of the new order that had been ushered in. For the first time, the Lord referred to the disciples as **"My brethren."** They were to know that His

Father was their Father, and His God was their God. Not until now were believers made "sons" and "heirs of God."

The Lord Jesus did not say, "Our Father," but **"My Father and your Father."** The reason is that God is His Father in a different sense than He is ours. God is the **Father** of the Lord Jesus from all eternity. Christ is the Son by eternal generation. The Son is equal with the Father. We are sons of God by adoption. It is a relationship that begins when we are saved and will never end. As sons of God, we are not equal with God and never shall be.

20:18 **Mary Magdalene** obeyed her commission and became what someone has called "the apostle to the apostles." Can we doubt that this great privilege was given to her as a reward for her devotion to Christ?

C. The Appearance to His Disciples (20:19–23)

20:19 It was now Sunday **evening. The disciples were assembled** together, perhaps in the upper room where they had met three nights ago. **The doors were** locked **for fear of the Jews**. Suddenly they saw **Jesus** standing **in the midst**, and they heard His voice saying, **"Peace."** It seems clear that the Lord entered the room without opening the doors. This was a miracle. It should be remembered that His resurrection body was a real body of flesh and bones. Yet He had the power to pass through barriers and otherwise act independently of natural laws. The words **"Peace be with you"** now have new meaning because Christ has made peace by the blood of His cross. Those who are justified by faith have peace with God.

20:20 After announcing peace to them, **He showed them** the marks of His passion, by which peace had been obtained. They saw the print of the nails and the wound cause by the spear. Joy filled their hearts to realize it was truly **the Lord**. He had done as He said He would. He had risen from the dead. The risen Lord is the source of the Christian's joy.

20:21 Verse 21 is very beautiful. Believers are not meant to enjoy His peace selfishly. They are to share it with oth-

ers. So He sends them into the world, **as the Father** had **sent** Him:

> Christ came into the world as a poor Person.
> He came as a Servant.
> He emptied Himself.
> He delighted to do the Father's will.
> He identified Himself with man.
> He went about doing good.
> He did everything by the power of the Holy Spirit.
> His goal was the cross.

Now He said to the disciples, **"I also send you."**

20:22 This is one of the most difficult verses in the entire Gospel. We read that Jesus **breathed on** the disciples and said, **"Receive the Holy Spirit."** The difficulty is that the Holy Spirit was not given until later, on the day of Pentecost. Yet how could the Lord speak these words without the event taking place immediately?

Several explanations have been offered: (1) Some suggest that the Lord was simply making a promise of what they would receive on the day of Pentecost. This is hardly an adequate explanation. (2) Some point out that what the Savior actually said was, "Receive Holy Spirit," rather than, "Receive *the* Holy Spirit." They conclude from this that the disciples did not receive *the* Holy Spirit in all His fullness at this time, but only some ministry of the Spirit, such as a greater knowledge of the truth, or power and guidance for their mission. They say that the disciples received a guarantee or a foretaste of the Holy Spirit. (3) Others state that there was a full outpouring of the Holy Spirit upon the disciples at this time. This seems unlikely in view of such statements as Luke 24:49 and Acts 1:4, 5, 8, where the coming of the Holy Spirit was still spoken of as future. It is clear from John 7:39 that the Spirit could not come in His fullness until Jesus was glorified, that is, until He had gone back to heaven.

20:23 This is another difficult verse, about which there has been a great deal of controversy. (1) One view is that Jesus actually gave His apostles (and their supposed successors) the *power* to forgive sins or to retain sins. This is in direct contradiction of the Bible teaching that only God can forgive sins (Luke 5:21). (2) Gaebelein quotes a second view: "The power promised and authority given is in connection with the preaching of the Gospel, announcing on what terms sins would be forgiven, and if these terms are not accepted, sins would be retained." (3) A third view (which is similar to the second), and the one that we accept, is that the disciples were given the right to *declare* sins forgiven.

Let us illustrate this third view. The disciples go out preaching the gospel. Some people repent of their sins and receive the Lord Jesus. The disciples are authorized to tell them that their **sins** have been **forgiven**. Others refuse to repent and will not believe on Christ. The disciples tell them that they are still in their sins, and that if they die, they will perish eternally.

In addition to this explanation, we should also note that the disciples were given special authority by the Lord in dealing with certain sins. For instance, in Acts 5:1–11, Peter used this power, and it resulted in the death of Ananias and Sapphira. Paul is seen retaining the sin of an evil-doer in 1 Corinthians 5:3–5, 12, 13, and remitting sin in 2 Corinthians 2:4–8. In these cases, it is forgiveness from the punishment of these sins in this life.

D. Doubt Turned to Faith (20:24–29)

20:24 We should not jump to the conclusion that **Thomas** should be blamed for not being present. Nothing is said to indicate the reason for his absence.

20:25 Thomas *is* to be blamed for his unbelieving attitude. He must have visible, tangible proof of the Lord's resurrection; otherwise he **will not believe**. This is the attitude of many today, but it is not reasonable. Even scientists believe many things that they can neither see nor touch.

20:26 One week later the Lord appeared to **His disciples** again. This time **Thomas** was **with them**. Again the Lord Jesus entered the room in a miraculous way and again greeted them with **"Peace to you!"**

20:27† The Lord dealt gently and patiently with His faithless follower. He invited him to prove the reality of His resurrection by putting his **hand** into the spear wound in His **side**.

20:28 Thomas was convinced. Whether he ever did put his hand into the Lord's side, we do not know. But he knew at last that Jesus was risen and that He was both **Lord** and **God**. John Boys puts it nicely: "He acknowledged the divinity he did not see by the wounds he did see."

20:29 The important thing to notice is that **Jesus** accepted worship as God. If He were only a man, He should have refused it. But Thomas' faith was not the kind that was most pleasing to the Lord. It was belief based on sight. More **blessed are those who have not seen and yet have believed**.

The surest evidence is the Word of God. If God says a thing, we honor Him by believing it; but we dishonor Him by demanding additional evidence. We should believe simply because He said it and because He cannot lie or be mistaken.

E. The Purpose of John's Gospel (20:30, 31)

Not all the miracles performed by Jesus are recorded in John's Gospel. The Holy Spirit selected those signs which would best serve His purpose.

Here we have John's object in writing the book. It was so that his readers **may believe that Jesus is the** true Messiah and **the Son of God. Believing**, they will **have** eternal **life in His name**.

Have you believed?

X. EPILOGUE: THE RISEN SON WITH HIS OWN (Chap. 21)

A. Christ Appears to His Disciples in Galilee (21:1–14)

21:1 The scene now changes to the **Sea of Tiberias** (Galilee).†† The disciples had journeyed north to their homes in Galilee. The Lord Jesus met them there. The phrase **in this way He showed Himself** means John is about to describe the manner in which Christ appeared to them.

21:2 Seven of the disciples **were together** at the time — **Peter, Thomas, Na-**

---

thanael, James and John (**the sons of Zebedee**), **and two others** whose names we do not know.

21:3   Simon Peter decided to go **fishing** on the lake, and the others agreed to go with him. This seemed to be a most natural decision, though some Bible students feel that the trip was not in the will of God and that they went without first praying. **That night they caught nothing.** They were not the first fishermen to spend a night fishing without success! They illustrate the uselessness of human efforts apart from divine help, especially in the matter of fishing for souls.

21:4   Jesus was waiting for them as they rowed toward **the shore** in **the morning**, although they **did not** recognize Him. Perhaps it was still quite dark, or perhaps they were prevented from knowing Him by God's power.

21:5 It is the same as if the Lord asked, "Young men, have you anything to eat?" Disappointedly **they answered Him, "No."**

21:6 As far as they knew, He was just a stranger, walking along the shore. Yet, in response to His advice, they **cast the net on the right side of the boat**, and lo and behold! A great load **of fish**. So many that they could not pull in the net! This shows that the Lord Jesus had perfect knowledge as to the location of the fish in the lake. It also teaches us that when the Lord directs our service, there are no more empty nets. He knows where there are souls ready to be saved, and He is willing to direct us to them — if we will let Him.

21:7 John was the first to recognize **the Lord** and promptly told **Peter**. The latter **put on his outer garment** and went to the shore. We are not told whether he swam or waded, or walked on the water (as some suggest).

21:8   The other disciples transferred from the large fishing boat to a **little** rowboat and dragged **the net** the remaining three hundred feet to land.

21:9 The Savior had their breakfast all ready — broiled **fish** and **bread**. We do not know whether the Lord caught these **fish** or whether He obtained them miraculously. But we do learn that He is not dependent on our poor efforts.

Doubtless in heaven we shall learn that while many people were saved through preaching and personal witness, many others were saved by the Lord Himself without any human help.

21:10 He now instructed them to pull in the net with **the fish** — not to cook them, but to count them. In doing so, they would be reminded that "the secret of success is to work at His command and to act with implicit obedience to His Word."

21:11 The Bible gives the exact number of fish in the net — **one hundred and fifty-three**. Many interesting explanations have been offered as to the meaning of this number: (1) The number of languages in the world at that time. (2) The number of races or tribes in the world, toward which the gospel net would be spread out. (3) The number of different kinds of fish in the sea of Galilee, or in the world. There is no doubt that it speaks of the variety of those who would be saved through the preaching of the gospel — some from every tribe and nation. The fishermen knew that it was remarkable that **the net** had **not broken**. This is further evidence that "God's work carried on in God's way will never lack God's resources." He will see that the net does not break.

21:12 The invitation to **breakfast** is heard, and the disciples gather around the fire of coals to partake of the good things the Lord had provided. Peter must have had his own thoughts as he saw the fire of coals. Was he reminded of the fire at which he warmed himself when he denied the Lord? The disciples felt a strange sense of awe and solemnity in the presence of the Lord. There He stood in His resurrection body. There were many questions they would like to have asked Him. But they did not dare. They knew **it was the Lord** — even if they felt a certain sense of mystery shrouded His Person.

21:13   Jesus now served breakfast to them. And they were probably reminded of a similar occasion when He fed the five thousand with a few loaves and fishes.

21:14 This was **the third time** mentioned by John that Jesus appeared **to His disciples**. That there were other times is clear from the other Gospels. In this Gospel, He appeared to the disciples on the evening of the day of the resurrection, then one week later, and now by the shore of blue Lake Galilee.

B. The Restoration of Peter (21:15–17)

21:15 The Lord first took care of their physical needs. Then when they were warm and had eaten, He turned to **Peter** and dealt with spiritual matters. Peter had publicly denied the Lord three times. Since then, he had repented and had been restored to fellowship with the Lord. In these verses, Peter's restoration is publicly acknowledged by the Lord.

It has often been pointed out that two different words for **love** are used in these verses. We might paraphrase verse 15 as follows: **"Simon, son of Jonah,**[54] **do you love Me more than these** other disciples love Me?" **He said to Him, "Yes, Lord, you know that I** *am fond of* **You."** Peter would no longer boast that he would never forsake the Lord, even if all the other disciples did. He had learned his lesson.

"Feed My lambs," Jesus said. A very practical way of demonstrating love for Christ is by feeding the young ones in His flock. It is interesting to note that the conversation had changed from fishing to shepherding. The former speaks of the works of evangelism; while the latter suggests teaching and pastoral care.

21:16 For the **second time**, the Lord asked Peter if he loved Him. Peter replied the second time, with genuine distrust of himself, **"You know that I** *am fond of* **You."** This time **He said to him, "Tend My sheep."** There are lambs and sheep in Christ's flock, and they need the loving care of one who loves the Shepherd.

21:17 Just as Peter had denied the Lord thrice, so he was given three opportunities to confess Him.

This time, Peter appealed to the fact that Jesus was God and therefore knew **all things**. He said **the third time, "You know that I** *am fond of* **You."** And for the last time, he was told that he could demonstrate this by feeding Christ's **sheep**. In this passage, the underlying lesson is that love for Christ is the only acceptable motive for serving Him.

C. Jesus Predicts Peter's Death (21:18–23)

21:18 **When** Peter was **younger**, he had great freedom of movement. He went **where** he **wished**. But the Lord here told him that at the end of his life, he would be arrested, bound, and carried off to execution.

21:19 This explains verse 18. Peter **would glorify God** by dying as a martyr. He who had denied the Lord would be given courage to lay down his life for Him. The verse reminds us that we can glorify God in death as well as in life. Then Jesus exclaimed, **"Follow Me!"** As He said it, He must have started to leave.

21:20 It seems that **Peter** began to follow the Lord, and then **turning around, saw** John **following** too. Here John paused to identify himself as the one **who also had leaned on** Jesus' **breast at the** Passover **Supper**, and had asked the name of the betrayer.

21:21 As **Peter** saw John, the thought probably crossed his mind, **"What about** John? Is he going to die as a martyr too? Or will he still be alive when the Lord comes back again?" He asked the Lord concerning John's future.

21:22 The Lord's answer was that Peter should not be concerned about John's latter days. Even if he were to survive until the Second Coming of Christ, this should not make any difference to Peter. Many failures in Christian service arise from disciples' being more occupied with one another than with the Lord Himself.

21:23 The Lord's words were misquoted. He **did not say** that John would still be alive when He came back again. He only said that even if that were the case, why should that affect Peter? Many see significance in the fact that Jesus here linked John with His Second Advent, and that John was the one who was privileged to write the Revelation of Jesus Christ, describing the end times in great detail.

D. John's Closing Witness to Jesus (21:24, 25)

21:24 John added a word of personal testimony to the accuracy of the things which he had written. Others take this as the attestation of the elders of the church in Ephesus to John's Gospel.

21:25 We have no fear in taking verse 25 literally! Jesus is God and is therefore infinite. There is no limit to the meaning of His words or to the number of His works. While He was here on earth, He was still the Upholder of all things — the sun, moon, and stars. Who could ever describe all that is involved in keeping the universe in motion? Even in His miracles on earth, we have only the barest description. In a simple act of healing, think of the nerves, muscles, blood corpuscles, and other members that He controlled. Think of His direction of germs, fishes, animal life. Think of His guidance in the affairs of men. Think of His control over the atomic structure of every bit of matter in the universe. Could **the world itself** possibly **contain the books** to describe such infinite details? The answer is an emphatic "No."

And so we come to the end of our commentary on John's Gospel. Perhaps we realize a little better why it has come to be one of the best loved parts of the Bible. Certainly one can scarcely read it thoughtfully and prayerfully without falling in love afresh with the blessed Person whom it presents.

ENDNOTES

[1](1:18) The critical text (NU in NKJV margin) reads *only begotten God*. The traditional *only begotten Son* is found in most manuscripts and also in 3:16.

[2](1:29) J. Cynddylan Jones, *Studies in the Gospel According to St. John*, p. 103.

[3](1:45) James S. Stewart, *The Life and Teaching of Jesus Christ*, pp. 66, 67.

[4](1:51) Only John reports the "double amen" (NKJV, *most assuredly*). The other Gospels, apparently *condensing* our Lord's expression, read "amen" (NKJV, *assuredly*).

[5](2:4) George Williams, *The Student's Commentary on the Holy Scriptures*, p. 194.

[6](2:11) Jones, *Studies*, p. 148.

[7](3:1) The little Greek connective *de* can mean *and*, *now*, *but*, etc. Modern English Bibles tend to delete these frequently. This is one of the few places

where the KJV did so, and the NKJV followed suit.

[8](3:5) Another valid interpretation that fits the context of contrasting spiritual and physical birth is that the water refers to physical birth and the Spirit refers to the Holy Spirit. The rabbis used "water" for the male seed, and water could also refer to the sack of watery liquid which breaks when a baby is born.

[9](3:16) F. W. Boreham, further documentation unavailable.

[10](4:41, 42) The critical text (NU) omits *the Christ*.

[11](4:48) In Greek there are separate forms for addressing one person (cf. Old English *thou*, *thee*) and more than one (cf. *ye*, *you*). The plural is used here.

[12](5:2) The critical text reads *Bethzatha*, but archaeology has confirmed the traditional name used in the majority of manuscripts and the KJV tradition.

[13](5:3) James Gifford Bellett, *The Evangelists*, p. 50.

[14](5:18) J. Sidlow Baxter, *Explore the Book*, V:309.

[15](5:24) There are other verses which teach that a believer will one day stand before the Judgment Seat of Christ (Rom. 14:10; 2 Cor. 5:10). However, the question of his sins will not be brought up at that time for punishment. That question was settled at Calvary. At the Judgment Seat of Christ, the believer's life and service will be reviewed, and he will either receive rewards or suffer loss. It will not be then a question of his soul's salvation, but of his life's fruitfulness.

[16](5:29) If this were the only verse in the Bible on the subject of resurrection, one would think that all the dead will be raised at the same time. However, we know from other portions of Scripture, particularly Revelation 20, that a period of at least one thousand years elapses between the two resurrections. The First Resurrection is the resurrection of those who have been saved through faith in Christ. The Second Resurrection includes all who have died as unbelievers.

[17](5:39) The Greek verb form for *search* is ambiguous. It may be *imperative* ("Search," KJV) or *indicative* ("you search," NKJV). The context favors the NKJV translation.

[18](5:47) Guy King, *To My Son*, p. 104.

[19](6:11) W. H. Griffith Thomas, *The*

Apostle John: His Life and Writings, pp. 173, 74.

²⁰(6:15) Frederick Brotherton Meyer, Tried By Fire, p. 152.

²¹(6:31) The manna was a small, round, white food which God miraculously provided for Israel in the wilderness. They had to gather the manna from the ground each morning of the first six days of every week.

²²(6:55) NU text reads "true food . . . true drink," but the meaning is virtually the same (reality).

²³(6:59) A synagogue is a local Jewish religious meeting place, but is not the same as the temple in Jerusalem where alone animal sacrifices could be made.

²⁴(6:69) The critical text (NU) reads "You are the Holy One of God."

²⁵(7:1) It is helpful to know that the Greek word for "Jew" (Ioudaios) can mean (1) a Judean (as opposed to a Galilean); (2) a Jewish person of any sort (including one who accepts Christ); (3) or an opponent of Christianity, especially a religious leader. John uses it mostly in the last sense, though he himself was a Jew in the second sense.

²⁶(7:7) Meyer, Tried, p. 129.

²⁷(7:8) The critical (NU) text's omission of "yet" is unfortunate. It seems to imply deception on our Lord's part.

²⁸(8:5) J. N. Darby, further documentation unavailable.

²⁹(8:11) 7:53 through 8:11 does not appear in the most ancient mss. of John, but is found in over 900 Greek mss. (the vast majority). There is some question as to whether these verses form a part of the original text. We believe that it is proper to accept them as part of the inspired text. All that they teach is in perfect agreement with the rest of the Bible. Augustine writes that some excluded this passage for fear it would promote loose views on morality.

³⁰(8:45) R. C. H. Lenski, The Interpretation of Colossians, Thessalonians, Timothy, Titus, Philemon, pp. 701, 02.

³¹(9:35) The NU text reads "Son of Man" here, which does not fit the context of worship nearly as well as the majority reading.

³²(10:28) The Greek has a double negative for emphasis (not permitted in standard English).

³³(10:36) Samuel Green, "Scripture Testimony to the Deity of Christ," p. 7.

³⁴(11:1) Arthur W. Pink, Exposition of the Gospel of John, III:12.

³⁵(11:25) Burkitt, further documentation unavailable.

³⁶(11:35) The shortest verse in the Greek NT is on the opposite side of the emotional spectrum, "Rejoice always" (Pantote chairete, 1 Thess. 5:16).

³⁷(11:47) J. C. Ryle, Expository Thoughts on the Gospels, St. John, II:295.

³⁸(11:48) Meyer, Tried, p. 112.

³⁹(12:5) Ryle, John, II:309, 10.

⁴⁰(12:7) The critical text's reading "that she may keep" instead of "she has kept" seems to contradict both this context and Mary's absence at the tomb on Easter morning. NIV solves the problem by paraphrasing.

⁴¹(12:24) T. G. Ragland, further documentation unavailable.

⁴²(13:13, 14) Of course, there are times, especially in Eastern lands, when one would literally wash someone else's feet, but this is only one example of humble service.

⁴³(13:32) The Greek grammar (first class condition plus ei with the indicative) assumes it to be true.

⁴⁴(14:20) Other popular illustrations include the bird in the air with the air in the bird, and the fish in water with the water in the fish.

⁴⁵(17:1) Marcus Rainsford, Our Lord Prays for His Own, p. 173.

⁴⁶(17:4) Ryle, John, III:40, 41.

⁴⁷(17:26) F. L. Godet, Commentary on the Gospel of John, II:345.

⁴⁸(17:26) Rainsford, Our Lord Prays, p. 173.

⁴⁹(18:14) Stewart, Life and Teaching, p. 157.

⁵⁰(18:28) Augustine, Quoted by Ryle, John, III:248.

⁵¹(18:28) Bishop Hall, Ibid.

⁵²(18:28) Poole, Ibid.

⁵³(19:20) Alexander, further documentation unavailable.

⁵⁴(21:15) The critical (NU) text names Peter's father John instead of Jonah (also vv. 16, 17).

BIBLIOGRAPHY

Godet, F. L. Commentary on the Gospel of John. Grand Rapids: Zondervan Publishing House, 1969 (Reprint of 1893 ed., 2 vols. in one).

Hole, F. B. *The Gospel of John Briefly Expounded*. London: The Central Bible Truth Depot, n.d.

Ironside, H. A. *Addresses on the Gospel of John*. New York: Loizeaux Bros., 1956.

Jones, J. Cynddylan. *Studies in the Gospel according to St. John*. Toronto: William Briggs, 1885.

Kelly, William. *An Exposition of the Gospel of John*. London: C. A. Hammond Trust Bible Depot, 1966.

Lenski, R. C. H. *The Interpretation of St. John's Gospel*. Minneapolis: Augsburg Publishing House, 1942.

Macaulay, J. C. *Obedience Unto Death: Devotional Studies in John's Gospel*. Grand Rapids: Wm. B. Eerdmans Publishing Co., 1942.

Pink, Arthur W. *Exposition of the Gospel of John*. Vol. III. Swengel, Pennsylvania: Bible Truth Depot, 1945.

Rainsford, Marcus. *Our Lord Prays for His Own*. Chicago: Moody Press, 1955.

Ryle, J. C. *Expository Thoughts on the Gospels: St. John*. London: James Clarke and Co., Ltd., 1957.

Tasker, R. V. G. *The Gospel According to St. John*. Grand Rapids: Wm. B. Eerdmans Publishing Company, 1968.

Tenney, Merrill C. *JOHN: The Gospel of Belief*. Grand Rapids: Wm. B. Eerdmans Publishing Company, 1948.

Thomas, W. H. Griffith. *The Apostle John: Studies in His Life and Writings*. Grand Rapids: Wm. B. Eerdmans Publishing Company, 1968.

Van Ryn, A. *Meditations in John*. Chicago: Moody Press, 1949.

Vine, W. E. *John, His Record of Christ*. London: Oliphants, 1957.

Westcott, B. F. *The Gospel According to St. John*. Grand Rapids: Wm. B. Eerdmans Publishing Co., 1954.

THE ACTS OF THE APOSTLES

Introduction

"Christ is the theme, the church is the means, and the Spirit is the power."
— W. Graham Scroggie

I. Unique Place in the Canon

The Acts of the Apostles is the only *inspired* church history; it is also the *first* church history, and the only primary church history to cover the earliest days of the faith. All others merely draw on Luke's work with a few traditions (and many conjectures!) added. We would be at a total loss without this book. To go from the life of our Lord in the Gospels right into the Epistles would be a tremendous leap. Who were the congregations being addressed and how did they come to be? Acts answers these and many other questions. It is a bridge not only between the life of Christ and the Christ-life taught in the Epistles, but it is also a transitional link between Judaism and Christianity, between Law and Grace. This constitutes one of the main difficulties in interpreting Acts, that is, the gradual widening of horizons from a small Jewish movement centered in Jerusalem to a worldwide faith that has made inroads in the imperial capital itself.

II. Authorship[†]

The authorship of Luke and Acts is the same, as nearly all agree. If the Third Gospel is by Luke, so is Acts, and vice versa (see Introduction to Luke).

The *external evidence* that Luke wrote Acts is early, strong, and widespread. The anti-Marcionite Prologue to Luke (c. 160–180), the Muratorian Canon (c. 170–200), and the early church fathers Irenaeus, Clement of Alexandria, Tertullian, and Origen all concur on Lucan authorship of Acts. So do nearly all who follow them in church history, including such authorities as Eusebius and Jerome.

The *internal evidence* in Acts itself that Luke wrote it is threefold. In the beginning of Acts, the writer specifically refers to an earlier work, also dedicated to Theophilus. Luke 1:1–4 shows that the Third Gospel is the account that is meant. The style, compassionate outlook, vocabulary, apologetic emphasis, and many small details tie the two works together. Were it not for a desire to have Luke with the other three Gospels, no doubt the two would have been together like 1 and 2 Corinthians.

Second, from the text of Acts it is clear that the author was a travel companion of Paul. This appears in the famous "we" passages (16:10–17; 20:5–21:18; 27:1–28:16), where the author is actually present at the events recorded. Skeptical attempts to explain these as a "fictional" touch are not convincing. If they were just added to make the work look more authentic, why so *seldom* and *subtly* introduced — and why is no *name* given to the "I" implied in the "we"?

Finally, when other companions of Paul who are mentioned by the author in the third person are eliminated, as well as companions known *not* to have been with Paul during the "we" sections, Luke is the only viable person left.

III. Date

While the date of some NT books is not crucial, it is more important in Acts, which is specifically a church *history*, and the very first one at that.

Three dates have been proposed for Acts, two accepting Lucan authorship and one denying it:

1. A second century date, of course,

rules out Luke as author; he could hardly have lived beyond A.D. 80 or 85 at the latest. While some (liberal) scholars feel that the author used Josephus' *Antiquities* (c. A.D. 93), the parallels that they allege regarding Theudas (Acts 5:36) do not agree, and the similarities are not strong in any event.

2. A commonly held view is that Luke wrote Luke-Acts between 70–80. This would allow for Luke to have used Mark in his Gospel (probably from the 60's).

3. A strong case can be made that Luke ended Acts where he did soon after the time the book's history ends — during Paul's first imprisonment in Rome.

It is *possible* that *Luke* was planning a third volume (but it was apparently not in God's will), and so Luke did not yet mention the devastating events (to Christians) between A.D. 63 and 70. However, the following omissions suggest the early date: Nero's ferocious persecution of Christians in Italy after the burning of Rome (64); the Jewish war with Rome (66–70); the martyrdom of Peter and Paul (later 60's); and most traumatic for Jews and Hebrew Christians, the destruction of Jerusalem. It is most likely, therefore, that Luke wrote Acts while Paul was in prison in Rome, about A.D. 62 or 63.

IV. Background and Themes

The Acts of the Apostles throbs with life and action. In it we see the Holy Spirit at work, forming the church, empowering the church, and expanding her outreach. It is the magnificent record of the Sovereign Spirit using most unlikely instruments, overcoming most formidable obstacles, employing most unconventional methods, and achieving most remarkable results.

Acts takes up the narrative where the Gospels leave off, then carries us by swift, dramatic descriptions over the early, turbulent years of the infant church. It is the record of the great transition period when the NT church was throwing off the graveclothes of Judaism, and displaying its distinctive character as a new fellowship in which Jews and Gentiles are one in Christ. For this reason, Acts has been aptly called the story of "the weaning time of Isaac."

As we read, we feel something of the spiritual exhilaration that is present when God is at work. At the same time, we sense the tension that arises when sin and Satan oppose and obstruct.

In the first twelve chapters the Apostle Peter occupies a key role, as he courageously preaches to the nation of Israel. From chapter 13 on, the Apostle Paul comes to the forefront as the zealous, inspired, and tireless apostle to the Gentiles.

Acts covers a period of about thirty-three years. J. B. Phillips has pointed out that in no comparable period of human history has "any small body of ordinary people so moved the world that their enemies could say, with tears of rage in their eyes, that these men 'have turned the world upside down!' "[1]

OUTLINE

III. THE CHURCH TO THE END OF THE EARTH (9:32–28:31)
- A. Peter's Preaching of the Gospel to the Gentiles (9:32–11:18)
- B. The Planting of the Church at Antioch (11:19–30)
- C. The Persecution by Herod and His Death (12:1–23)
- D. Paul's First Missionary Journey: Galatia (12:24–14:28)
- E. The Council at Jerusalem (15:1–35)
- F. Paul's Second Missionary Journey: Asia Minor and Greece (15:36–18:22)
- G. Paul's Third Missionary Journey: Asia Minor and Greece (18:23–21:26)
- H. Paul's Arrest and Trials (21:27–26:32)
- I. Paul's Voyage to Rome and Shipwreck (27:1–28:16)
- J. Paul's House-Arrest and Witness to the Jews in Rome (28:17–31)

Commentary†

I. THE CHURCH IN JERUSALEM (Chaps. 1–7)††

A. The Risen Lord's Promise of the Spirit (1:1–5)

1:1 The Book of Acts opens with a reminder. Luke, the beloved physician, had written to **Theophilus** previously — a writing which we now know as The Gospel According to Luke (see Luke 1:1–4). In the last verses of that Gospel, he had told Theophilus that immediately prior to His Ascension, the Lord Jesus had promised His disciples that they would be baptized with the Holy Spirit (Luke 24:48–53).

Now Luke is going to continue the narrative, so he goes back to this thrilling promise as a starting point. And it is fitting that he should do so, because in that promise of the Spirit lay concealed in germ form all the spiritual triumphs unfolded in the Book of the Acts. Luke describes his Gospel as **the former account**, or the first book. In it he had recorded the things **that Jesus** *began* **both to do and teach**. In Acts he carries on the record by recounting the things that Jesus *continued* to do and teach through the Holy Spirit after His Ascension.

Notice that the Lord's ministry was one of both *doing* and *teaching*. It was not doctrine without duty, or creed without conduct. The Savior was the living embodiment of what He taught. He practiced what He preached.

1:2 Theophilus would remember that Luke's previous book ended with the account of the Savior's Ascension, here described as His being **taken up**.

He would also remember the tender last instructions the Lord had given the eleven **apostles** before He left.

1:3 For the **forty days** between His resurrection and Ascension, the Lord had appeared to His disciples, offering the strongest possible **proofs** of His bodily resurrection (see John 20:19, 26; 21:1, 14).†††

During this time, He had also discussed with them the affairs of **the kingdom of God**. His primary concern was not with the kingdoms of this world, but with the realm or sphere where God is acknowledged as King.

The kingdom is not to be confused with the church. The Lord Jesus offered Himself to the nation of Israel as King but was rejected (Matt. 23:37). His literal kingdom on earth was therefore postponed until Israel repents and receives Him as Messiah (Acts 3:19–21).

At the present time, the King is absent. However, He does have an invisible kingdom on earth (Col. 1:13). It is made up of all who profess allegiance to Him (Matt. 25:1–12). In one sense it consists of everyone who claims to be a Christian; that is its outward aspect (Matt. 13:1–52). But in its inward reality it includes only those who have been born again (John 3:3, 5). **The kingdom** in its present condition is described in the parables of Matthew 13.

The church is something entirely new. It was not the subject of OT prophecy (Eph. 3:5). It is composed of all believers from Pentecost to the Rapture. As the Bride of Christ, the church will reign with Him in the Millennium and share

His glory forever. Christ will return as King at the end of the Great Tribulation, destroy His foes, and set up His reign of righteousness over all the earth (Ps. 72:8).

Although His reign from Jerusalem lasts for only one thousand years (Rev. 20:4), yet **the kingdom** is everlasting in the sense that all of God's foes will have been finally destroyed, and He will reign eternally in heaven without opposition or hindrances (2 Pet. 1:11).

1:4 Luke now relates a meeting of the Lord with His disciples as they **assembled together** in a room in **Jerusalem**. The risen Redeemer **commanded them** to remain in **Jerusalem**. But why in **Jerusalem**, they might well wonder! To them it was a city of hatred, violence, and persecution!

Yes, **the** fulfillment of that **Promise of the Father** would occur in **Jerusalem**. The coming of the Spirit would take place in the very city where the Savior had been crucified. The presence of the Spirit there would bear testimony to man's rejection of the Son of God. The Spirit of truth would reprove the world of sin, righteousness, and judgment — and this would take place first in **Jerusalem**. And the disciples would receive the Holy Spirit in the city where they themselves had forsaken the Lord and had fled to save their own skins. They would be made strong and fearless in the place where they had shown themselves to be weak and cowardly.

This was not the first time the disciples had heard of **the Promise of the Father** from the Savior's lips. Throughout His earthly ministry, and especially in His Upper Room Discourse, He had told them of the Helper who would come (see Luke 24:49; John 14:16, 26; 15:26; 16:7, 13).

1:5 Now, in His last meeting with them, He repeats the promise. Some, if not all of them had already been **baptized** by **John with water**. But John's baptism was outward and physical. Before many days would pass,[2] they would be **baptized with the Holy Spirit**, and this baptism would be inward and spiritual. The first baptism identified them outwardly with the repentant portion of the nation of Israel. The second would incorporate them into the church, the

Body of Christ, and would empower them for service.

Jesus promised that they would **be baptized with the Holy Spirit not many days from now**, but there is no mention of the baptism in fire (Matt. 3:11, 12; Luke 3:16, 17). The latter is a baptism of judgment for unbelievers only and is still future.

B. The Ascending Lord's Mandate to the Apostles (1:6–11)

1:6 Perhaps the incident recorded here took place on the Mount of Olives, over against Bethany. This was the spot from which the Lord Jesus went back to heaven (Luke 24:50, 51).

The disciples had been thinking about the coming of the Spirit. They remembered that the prophet Joel spoke of the outpouring of the Spirit in connection with the Messiah's glorious reign (Joel 2:28). They therefore concluded that the Lord would set up His **kingdom** soon, since He had first said that the Spirit would be given "not many days from now." Their question revealed that they still expected Christ to set up His literal earthly **kingdom** immediately.

1:7 The Lord did *not* correct them for expecting His literal reign on earth. Such a hope was and is justified. He simply told them they could not **know** when His kingdom would come. The date had been fixed by the Father's sole **authority**, but He had not chosen to reveal it. It was information that belonged exclusively to Himself.

The expression **times or seasons** is used in the Bible to refer to various events foretold by God that are yet to come to pass in connection with the nation of Israel. Being of Jewish background, the disciples would understand the expression here to refer to the crucial days prior to and including the establishment of Christ's thousand-year reign on earth.

1:8 Having suppressed their curiosity as to the future date of this kingdom, the Lord Jesus directed their attention to what was more immediate — the nature and sphere of their mission. As to its nature, they were to **be witnesses**; as to its sphere, they were to witness **in Jerusalem, and in all Judea and Samaria, and to the end of the earth.**

But first they must **receive power** — the **power** of **the Holy Spirit**. This **power** is the grand indispensable of Christian witness. A man may be highly talented, intensively trained, and widely experienced, but without spiritual **power** he is ineffective. On the other hand, a man may be uneducated, unattractive, and unrefined, yet let him be endued with the **power** of **the Holy Spirit** and the world will turn out to see him burn for God. The fearful disciples needed **power** for witnessing, holy boldness for preaching the gospel. They would receive this **power** when **the Holy Spirit** came **upon** them.

Their witness was to begin **in Jerusalem**, a meaningful prearrangement of the grace of God. The very city where our Lord was crucified was first to receive the call to repentance and faith in Him.

Then **Judea**, the southern section of Palestine with its strong Jewish population, and with **Jerusalem** as its chief city.

Then **Samaria**, the region in the center of Palestine, with its hated, half-breed population with whom the Jews had no dealings.

Then **the end** of the then-known world — the Gentile countries which had hitherto been outside the pale as far as religious privilege was concerned. In this ever widening circle of witness, we have a general outline of the flow of history in Acts.

1. The *witness* in **Jerusalem** (Chaps. 1–7)
2. The *witness* in **Judea** and **Samaria** (8:1–9:31)
3. The *witness* to **the end of the earth** (9:32–28:31)

1:9 As soon as the Savior had commissioned His disciples, **He was taken up** into heaven. This is all the Scripture says — **He was taken up, and a cloud received Him out of their sight**. Such a spectacular event, yet it is described so simply and quietly! The restraint which the writers of the Bible used in telling their story points to the inspiration of the Word; it is not customary for men to handle such unusual events with such reserve.

1:10 Again without any expression of shocked surprise, Luke narrates the appearance of **two men . . . in white apparel**. These were obviously angelic beings who were enabled to appear on earth in the form of **men**. Perhaps these were the same angels who appeared at the tomb following the resurrection (Luke 24:4).

1:11 The angels first addressed the disciples as **men of Galilee**. As far as we know, all the disciples except Judas Iscariot came from the region west of the Sea of Galilee.

Then the angels awoke them from their reverie, as they looked into heaven. Why were they **gazing up into heaven**? Was it sorrow, or worship, or wonder? Doubtless it was a mixture of all three, though primarily sorrow. So a word of comfort was given. The ascended Christ would come again.

Here we have a clear promise of the Lord's Second Advent to set up His kingdom on the earth. It is not the Rapture, but the coming to reign that is in view.

1. He ascended from the Mount of Olives (v.12).	1. He will return to the Mount of Olives (Zech. 14:4.)
2. He ascended personally.	2. He will return personally (Mal. 3:1).
3. He ascended visibly.	3. He will return visibly (Matt. 24:30).
4. He was received up in a cloud. (v. 9)	4. He will come on the clouds of heaven (Matt. 24:30).
5. He ascended gloriously.	5. He will return with power and great glory (Matt. 24:30).

C. The Prayerful Disciples Waiting in Jerusalem (1:12–26)

1:12 In Luke 24:52 the disciples returned to Jerusalem *with great joy.* "Light from the love of God kindled these men's hearts and made their faces shine in spite of the sea of troubles that surrounded them."

It was a short trip of about three quarters of a mile **from the mount called Olivet**, down through the Kidron Valley, and up to the city. This was the greatest distance a Jew might travel on the **Sabbath** in NT times.

1:13 Once inside the city, **they went up into the upper room where they were staying**.

The Spirit of God here lists the names

of the disciples for the fourth and last time (Matt. 10:2–4; Mark 3:16–19; Luke 6:14–16). But now there is a notable omission: the name of Judas Iscariot is absent from the roll call. The traitor had gone to his deserved doom.

1:14 As the disciples gathered together, it was **with one accord**. This expression, occurring eleven times in Acts, is one of the keys that unlocks the secret of blessing. Where brethren dwell together in unity, God commands the blessing — life for evermore (Ps. 133).

A second key is given in the words, **continued . . . in prayer**. Now, as then, God works when people pray. Ordinarily we would rather do anything than pray. But it is only when we wait before God in desperate, believing, fervent, unhurried, united **prayer** that the reviving, energizing power of the Spirit of God is poured out.

It cannot be emphasized too strongly that *unity and prayer were the prelude to Pentecost.*

Gathered **with** the disciples were certain unnamed **women** (probably those who had followed Jesus), also **Mary the mother of Jesus, and . . . His brothers**. There are several points of interest here.

1. This is the last mention of **Mary** by name in the NT — doubtless "a silent protest against Mariolatry." The disciples were not praying *to* her, but **with** her. She was waiting with them to receive the gift of the Holy Spirit.

2. **Mary** is called **the mother of Jesus** but not "the mother of God." Jesus is the name of our Lord in His humanity. Since, as man, He was born of **Mary**, it is proper that she should be called **the mother of Jesus**. But never in the Bible is she called "the mother of God." Although Jesus Christ is truly God, it is doctrinally inaccurate and absurd to speak of God as having a human mother. As God, He existed from all eternity.

3. The mention of the **brothers** of Jesus, coming after the reference to **Mary**, makes it likely that these were actual sons of **Mary** and half-brothers of Jesus. Several other verses in addition to this refute the idea, held by some, that **Mary** was a perpetual virgin and never bore any children after the birth of Jesus (see, for instance, Matt. 12:46; Mark 6:3; John 7:3, 5;

1 Cor. 9:5; Gal. 1:19. See also Psa. 69:8).

1:15 One day, when **about a hundred and twenty disciples** were gathered together, **Peter** was led to remind them of OT Scriptures which dealt with the one who would betray the Messiah.

1:16, 17 At the outset, Peter mentioned that a certain prophecy written by **David concerning Judas . . . had to be fulfilled**. But before quoting **this Scripture** he reminded them that although Judas had been one of the twelve and had shared in their apostolic ministry, yet he served as **guide to those who arrested Jesus**. Notice the moderation Peter uses in describing this dastardly act. Judas became a traitor by his own deliberate choice, and thus he fulfilled the prophecies that someone would sell the Lord to His enemies.

1:18, 19 These two verses are treated as a parenthesis written by Luke and not a part of Peter's message. They complete the historical facts concerning Judas through the time of his death and thus pave the way for the appointment of his successor.

There is no contradiction between the mode of Judas' death as given here, and that which is found in Matthew 27:3–10. Matthew states that after he had given the thirty pieces of silver to the chief priests and elders, he went out and hanged himself. The chief priests then took the money and bought a burial ground.

Here in Acts, Luke says that Judas **purchased a field with the** money, that he fell **headlong . . . and all his entrails gushed out**.

Putting the two accounts together, it appears that the actual purchase transaction concerning the field was arranged by the chief priests. However, Judas bought the **field** in the sense that it was his money and they merely acted as his agents. He hanged himself on a tree in the cemetery, but the rope probably broke, pitching his body forward and causing it to **burst open**.

As this incident became known **in Jerusalem**, the potter's field came to be called **Akel Dama, that is, Field of Blood** or "bloody field" in Aramaic.

1:20 Peter's message now continues, after Luke's explanatory parenthesis. First, he explains that David was referring to the betrayer of Jesus in Psalm

69:25: **"Let his dwelling place be desolate, and let no one live in it."**[3]

Then he comes to the particular prophecy which must now be fulfilled: **"Let another take his office"** (Ps. 109:8). The Apostle Peter understood this to mean that after Judas' defection, a replacement must be appointed to fill **his office**. It is good to see his desire to obey the word of God.

1:21, 22 Whoever was to be chosen had to fulfill two requirements:

1. He had to be one who had **accompanied** the disciples during the three years of Christ's public ministry — **from** His **baptism** by **John** to is Ascension.
2. He had to be able to bear responsible **witness** to the **resurrection** of the Lord.

1:23–26 The names of two men were put forward as possessing the necessary qualifications, **Joseph . . . surnamed Justus**, and **Matthias**. But which one was to be chosen? The apostles committed the matter to the Lord, asking for a revelation of His choice. Then **they cast lots** and **Matthias** was indicated as the proper successor to Judas, who had gone **to his own place**, i.e., eternal doom.

Two questions invariably arise here:

1. Were the disciples acting properly when they named **Matthias**? Should they have waited until God raised up the Apostle Paul to fill the vacancy?
2. Was it proper for them to **cast lots** in order to discern the mind of the Lord?

With regard to the first question, there is nothing in the record to indicate the disciples acted wrongly. They had been spending much time in prayer; they were seeking to obey the Scriptures; and they seemed to be of one mind in selecting a successor to Judas. Furthermore, the ministry of Paul was quite distinct from that of the twelve, and there is no suggestion that he was ever intended to replace Judas. The twelve were commissioned by Jesus on earth to preach to Israel, whereas Paul was called to the ministry by Christ in glory and sent to the Gentiles.

As far as casting lots was concerned, this method of discerning the divine will was recognized by the OT: "The lot is cast into the lap, but its every decision is from the LORD" (Prov. 16:33).

Apparently the choice of Matthias by lot was sanctioned by the Lord, because the apostles are thereafter called "*the twelve*" (see Acts 6:2).

PRAYER IN THE BOOK OF ACTS

Acts is a study in successful prayer. Already in chapter 1 we have seen the disciples praying on two different occasions. Their prayer in the upper room following the Ascension was answered by Pentecost. Their prayer for guidance in choosing a successor to Judas was answered by the lot's falling on Matthias. And so it is throughout the book.

Those who were converted on the day of Pentecost continued steadfastly in prayer (2:42). The succeeding verses (43–47) describe the ideal conditions which prevailed in this prayerful fellowship.

Following the release of Peter and John, the believers prayed for boldness (4:29). As a result, the place was shaken, they were all filled with the Holy Spirit, and they spoke the word of God with boldness (4:31).

The twelve suggested that seven men be chosen to handle financial matters so they themselves might devote their time more fully to prayer and the ministry of the Word (6:3, 4). The apostles then prayed and laid hands on the seven (6:6). The next verses record thrilling new triumphs for the gospel (6:7, 8).

Stephen prayed as he was about to be martyred (7:60). Chapter 9 records an answer to that prayer — the conversion of an onlooker, Saul of Tarsus.

Peter and John prayed for the Samaritans who believed, with the result that they received the Holy Spirit (8:15–17).

Following his conversion, Saul of Tarsus prayed in the house of Judas; God answered the prayer by sending Ananias to him (9:11–17).

Peter prayed at Joppa, and Dorcas was raised to life (9:40). As a result, many believed on the Lord (9:42).

The Gentile centurion Cornelius prayed (10:2); his prayers went up as a memorial before God (10:4). An angel appeared to him in a vision, instructing him to send for a man named Simon Peter (10:5). The next day Peter prayed

(10:9). His prayer was answered by a heavenly vision that prepared him to open the doors of the kingdom to Cornelius and other Gentiles (10:10–48).

When Peter was imprisoned, the Christians prayed for him earnestly (12:5). God answered by miraculously delivering him from jail — much to the astonishment of those who were praying (12:6–17).

The prophets and teachers at Antioch fasted and prayed (13:3). This launched the first missionary journey of Paul and Barnabas. It has been said that "this was the mightiest outreach of prayer ever seen; for it touched the ends of the earth, even to us, through Paul and Barnabas, the missionaries."

On a return trip to Lystra and Iconium and Antioch, Paul and Barnabas prayed for those who had believed (14:23). One of these was Timothy. Was it an answer to these prayers that Timothy joined Paul and Silas on their second missionary journey?

In prison at Philippi, the midnight prayers of Paul and Silas were answered by an earthquake and by the conversion of the jailer and his family (16:25–34).

Paul prayed with the Ephesian elders at Miletus (20:36); this brought a touching demonstration of their affection for him and of their grief that they would not see him again in this life.

The Christians at Tyre prayed with Paul on the beach (21:5), and these prayers doubtless followed him to Rome and to the executioner's block.

Prior to his shipwreck, Paul publicly prayed, giving thanks to God for the food. This brought cheer to the forlorn crew and passengers (27:35, 36).

On the island of Malta, Paul prayed for the governor's sick father. The result was that the patient was miraculously healed (28:8).

So it seems clear that prayer was the atmosphere in which the early church lived. And when Christians prayed, God worked! ‡

D. The Day of Pentecost and the Birth of the Church (2:1–47)

2:1 The Feast of **Pentecost**, typifying the pouring out of the Holy Spirit, was fifty days after the Feast of Firstfruits, which spoke of the resurrection of Christ. On this particular **Day of Pentecost** the disciples **were all with one accord in one place**. A fitting subject for their conversation might have been the OT passages dealing with the Feast of Pentecost (see Lev. 23:15, 16, for example). Or perhaps they were singing Psalm 133, "Behold, how good and how pleasant it is for brethren to dwell together in unity!"[4]

2:2 The coming of the Spirit involved a sound to hear, a sight to see, and a miracle to experience. The **sound**, which was **from heaven** and **filled the whole house**, was like **a rushing mighty wind**. **Wind** is one of several fluid types of the Holy Spirit (oil, fire, water), speaking of His sovereign, unpredictable movements.

2:3 The sight to see was **divided tongues, as of fire**, resting **upon each of** the disciples. It does not say they were tongues of fire, but **tongues as of fire**.

This phenomenon is not to be confused with the baptism of fire. Although the baptism of the Spirit and the baptism of fire are spoken of together (Matt. 3:11, 12; Luke 3:16, 17), they are two separate and distinct events. The first is a baptism of blessing, the second of judgment. The first affected believers, the second will affect unbelievers. By the first, believers were indwelt and empowered, and the church was formed. By the second, unbelievers will be destroyed.

When John the Baptist was addressing a mixed group (repentant and unrepentant, see Matt. 3:6, 7) he said Christ would baptize them with the Holy Spirit and fire (Matt. 3:11). When he was speaking only to those who were truly repentant (Mark 1:5), he said Christ would baptize them with the Holy Spirit (Mark 1:8).

What then is the meaning, in Acts 2:3, of the **divided tongues, as of fire**? The **tongues** doubtless refer to speech, and probably to the miraculous gift of speaking in other languages which the apostles were to receive at this time. The **fire** may refer to the Holy Spirit as the source of this gift, and may also describe the bold, burning, enthusiastic preaching which would follow.

The thought of enthusiastic utterance seems especially fitting, because enthusiasm is the normal condition of a Spirit-filled life, and witness is its inevitable outcome.

2:4 The miracle to experience, connected with Pentecost, was the filling of **the Holy Spirit**, followed by the speaking **with other tongues**.

Up to now, the Spirit of God had been *with* the disciples, but now He took up His residence *in* them (John 14:17). Thus the verse marks an important turning point in the Spirit's dealings with men. In the OT, the Spirit came upon men, but not as an abiding Resident (Ps. 51:11). Beginning with the Day of Pentecost, the Spirit of God indwelt people permanently: He came to stay (John 14:16).

On the Day of Pentecost, the believers were not only indwelt by the Holy Spirit, but they were filled with Him as well. We are indwelt by God's Spirit the moment we are saved, but to be filled with the Spirit we must study the Word, spend time in meditation and prayer, and live in obedience to the Lord.⁵ If the filling of the Spirit were automatically guaranteed today, we would not be exhorted, "Be filled with the Spirit" (Eph. 5:18).

The coming of the Holy Spirit on the Day of Pentecost also formed believers into the church, the Body of Christ.

For by one Spirit we were all baptized into one body — whether Jews or Greeks, whether slaves or free — and have all been made to drink into one Spirit (1 Cor. 12:13). Henceforth, believing Jews and Gentiles would become one new man in Christ Jesus and members of the same Body (Eph. 2:11–22).

The disciples who were **filled with the Holy Spirit began to speak with other tongues, as the Spirit gave them utterance**. From the following verses, it is clear they were given the miraculous power to speak *actual foreign languages* which they had never studied. It was not gibberish or ecstatic utterances but definite languages then in use in other parts of the world. This gift of **tongues** was one of the signs or wonders which God used to bear witness to the truth of the message which the apostles preached (Heb. 2:3, 4). At that time, the NT had not been written. Since the complete word of God is now available in written form, the need for the sign gifts

has largely passed (though, of course, the sovereign Spirit of God could still use them if He so desired).

The occurrence of **tongues** on the Day of Pentecost should not be used to prove that **tongues** are the invariable accompaniment of the gift of the Spirit. If that were the case, why is there no mention of tongues in connection with:

1. The conversion of the 3,000 (Acts 2:41)?
2. The conversion of the 5,000 (Acts 4:4)?
3. The reception of the Holy Spirit by the Samaritans (Acts 8:17)?

In fact, the only other occurrences of the gift of **tongues** in the Book of Acts are:

1. At the conversion of the Gentiles in the house of Cornelius (Acts 10:46).
2. At the rebaptism of John's disciples in Ephesus (Acts 19:6).

Before leaving verse 4, we should mention that there is considerable difference among Bible students concerning the whole subject of the baptism of the Holy Spirit, both as to the number of times it has taken place, and the results flowing from it.

As to its frequency, some believe that:

1. It took place only once — at Pentecost. The Body of Christ was formed at that time, and all believers since then have entered into the good of the baptism.
2. It took place in three or four stages — at Pentecost (chap. 2); at Samaria (chap. 8); at the house of Cornelius (chap. 10); at Ephesus (chap. 19).
3. It takes place every time a person is saved.

As to its effect in the lives of individuals, some hold that it is a "second work of grace," commonly taking place after conversion, and resulting in a more or less complete sanctification. This view lacks scriptural support. As has already been mentioned, the baptism of the Holy Spirit is that operation by which believers were:

1. Incorporated into the church (1 Cor. 12:13).
2. Endued with power (Acts 1:8).

2:5–13 **Jews, devout men** had gathered **in Jerusalem** from all over the then-known world to observe the Feast of

Pentecost. When they heard the rumor of what had happened, they assembled at the house occupied by the apostles. Then, as now, men were attracted when the Spirit of God was at work.

By the time **the multitude** reached the house, the apostles were already speaking in tongues. Much to their amazement, the visitors heard these Galilean disciples speaking in a great variety of foreign languages. The miracle, however, was with those who spoke, not with those who heard. Whether those in the audience were Jews by birth or converts to Judaism, whether they were from east or west, north or south, each one heard **the** mighty **works of God** described **in his own language.** The word, **language**, used in verses 6 and 8 is the one from which we get our word, "dialect."

It is widely believed that one purpose of the gift of tongues at Pentecost was to proclaim the gospel to people of different languages simultaneously. For instance, one writer says, "God gave His law in one language to one nation, but He gave His gospel in all languages to all nations."

But the text does not bear this out. Those who spoke in tongues were declaring **the wonderful works of God** (2:11). This was a sign to the people of Israel (1 Cor. 14:21, 22), intended to excite amazement and marvel. Peter, by contrast, preached the gospel in a language that most, if not all, of his audience could understand.

The response to the tongues among the visitors was varied. Some seemed deeply interested, whereas others accused the apostles of being **full of new wine**. The disciples were indeed under an influence outside their own power, but it was the influence of the Holy Spirit, not of **wine**!

Unregenerate men are always ready to offer a natural explanation for spiritual phenomena. Once when God's voice was heard from heaven, some said it thundered (John 12:28, 29). Now unbelievers mockingly explained the exhilaration caused by the coming of the Spirit in terms of **new wine**. "The world," said Schiller, "likes to tarnish shining objects, and to drag those that are exalted down to the dust."

2:14 The disciple who had denied his Lord with oaths and curses now steps forward to address the throng. No longer the timid and vacillating follower, he has become lion-like and forceful. Pentecost has made the difference. **Peter** is now filled with the Spirit.

At Caesarea Philippi, the Lord had promised to give Peter the keys of the kingdom of heaven (Matt. 16:19). Here in Acts 2 we see him using the keys to open the door to the Jews (v. 14) as later, in chapter 10, he will open it to the Gentiles.

2:15 First the apostle explains that the unusual events of the day were not the result of new wine. After all, **it** was **only** 9:00 a.m., and it would be virtually unheard of for so many to be **drunk** at that early hour. Also, Jews engaged in the exercises of the synagogue on a feast day abstained from eating and drinking until 10:00 a.m., or even noon, depending on when the daily sacrifice was offered.

2:16–19 The true explanation was that the Spirit of God had been poured out, as **spoken by the prophet Joel** (Joel 2:28ff).

Actually, the events of Pentecost were not a complete fulfillment of Joel's prophecy. Most of the phenomena described in verses 17–20 did not take place at this time. But what did happen at Pentecost was a foretaste of what would happen **in the last days**, prior to **the great and awesome day of the LORD**. If Pentecost fulfilled Joel's prophecy, why is a promise given later (3:19) that if there was national repentance and Israel received the One they had crucified, He would come back and bring in the day of the Lord?

The quotation from Joel is an example of the Law of Double Reference, by which a Bible prophecy has a partial fulfillment at one time and a complete fulfillment at a later time.

The Spirit of God *was* poured out at Pentecost but not literally on *all* flesh. The final fulfillment of the prophecy will take place at the end of the Tribulation Period. Prior to the glorious return of Christ, there will be **wonders** in the heavens, and **signs** on the earth (Matt. 24:29, 30). The Lord Jesus Christ will then appear on the earth to put down

His enemies and to establish His kingdom. At the beginning of His thousand-year reign, the Spirit of God will be poured out **on all flesh**, Gentiles as well as Jews, and this condition will prevail, for the most part, throughout the Millennium. Various manifestations of the Spirit will be given without regard to sex, age, or social status. There will be **visions** and **dreams**, which suggest the reception of knowledge; and prophecy, which suggests its impartation to others. Thus, the gifts of revelation and communication will be in evidence. All this will occur in what Joel described as **the last days** (v. 17). This, of course, refers to the last days of Israel and not of the church.

2:20 The supernatural signs in the heavens are distinctly said to occur **before the coming of the . . . day of the LORD**. In this context, **the day of the LORD** refers to His personal return to the earth to destroy His foes and to reign in power and great glory.

2:21 Peter closes the quotation from Joel with the promise that **whoever calls on the name of the LORD shall be saved**. This is the good news for all ages, that salvation is offered to all people on the principle of faith in the Lord. **The name of the LORD** is an expression that includes all that the Lord is. Thus, to **call on His name** is to **call on** Himself as the true object of faith and as the only way of salvation.

2:22–24 But who is the Lord? Peter will next announce the startling news that this Jesus whom they had crucified is both Lord and Christ. He does so first by speaking of the life of Jesus, then His death, resurrection, ascension, and finally His glorification at **the right hand of God** the Father. If they had any illusions that **Jesus** was still in a Judean tomb, Peter will soon disabuse their minds! They must be told that the One they had murdered is in heaven, and they must still reckon with Him.

Here then is the flow of the apostle's argument: **Jesus of Nazareth** was demonstrated to be **a Man** from **God by** the many **miracles** He performed in the power of **God** (v. 22). In His **determined purpose and foreknowledge, God delivered Him** into the hands of the Jewish people. They, in turn, turned Him over to the Gentiles (men without the law) to

be **crucified and put to death** (v. 23). However, **God raised** Him **up** from among the dead, **having loosed the pains⁶ of death. It was not possible** for death to hold Him a prisoner **because**:

1. The character of God demanded His resurrection. He had died, the Sinless for the sinful. God must raise Him as proof of His complete satisfaction with the redemptive work of Christ.

2. The prophecies of the OT demanded His resurrection. This is the particular point which Peter presses in the following verses.

2:25–27 In Psalm 16 David had written prophetically concerning the Lord's life, death, resurrection, and glorification.

As to His life, **David** described the unbounded confidence and assurance of One who lived in uninterrupted fellowship with His Father. **Heart**, **tongue**, and **flesh** — His whole being was filled with joy and **hope**.

As to His death, David **foresaw** that God **would not leave** His **soul in Hades, nor** would He allow His **Holy One to see corruption**. In other words, the **soul** of the Lord Jesus would not be left in the disembodied state, neither would His body be permitted to disintegrate. (This verse should not be used to prove that the Lord Jesus went to some prison house of departed spirits in the lowest parts of the earth at the time of His death. His soul went to heaven⁷ — Luke 23:43 — and His body was placed in the tomb.)

2:28 As to the resurrection of the Lord, David expressed confidence that God would show Him the path of life. In Psalm 16:11a, David wrote, "You will show me the path of life." In Acts 2:28a, Peter quoted it, **You have made known to me the ways of life**. Peter changed the future tense to the past tense. The Holy Spirit obviously directed him to do this since the resurrection was now past.

The present glorification of the Savior was predicted by David in the words, **You will make me full of joy in Your presence**, or as Psalm 16:11 puts it, "In Your presence is fullness of joy; at Your right hand are pleasures forevermore."

2:29 Peter argues that **David** could not have been saying these things about himself, because *his* body *had seen corrup-*

tion. **His tomb** was well known to the Jews of that day. They knew he had not been raised.

2:30, 31 When he wrote the Psalm, **David** was speaking as **a prophet**. He remembered that **God** had promised to **raise up** One of his descendants **to sit on his throne** forever. **David** realized that this One would be the Messiah, and that though He would die, His **soul** would not be **left in** the disembodied condition, and His body would not decay.

2:32, 33 Now Peter repeats an announcement that must have shocked his Jewish audience. The Messiah of whom **David** prophesied was **Jesus** of Nazareth. **God** had **raised** Him from among the dead, as the apostles could all testify because they were eyewitnesses to His resurrection. Following His resurrection, the Lord Jesus was **exalted to the right hand of God**, and now **the Holy Spirit** had been sent as promised by **the Father**. This was the explanation of what had happened in Jerusalem earlier in the day.

2:34, 35 Had not **David** also predicted the exaltation of the Messiah? He was not speaking of himself in Psalm 110:1. Instead he was quoting Jehovah as saying to the Messiah, **"Sit at My right hand, till I make Your enemies Your footstool."** (Note carefully that verses 33–35 predict a waiting time between the glorification of Christ and His return to punish His enemies and set up His kingdom.)

2:36 Now, once again, the announcement comes crashing down upon the Jewish people. GOD HAS MADE BOTH LORD AND CHRIST — THIS JESUS WHOM YOU CRUCIFIED (Gk. word order). As Bengel said, "The sting of the speech is put at the end" — **THIS JESUS, whom you crucified**. They had **crucified** God's Anointed One, and the coming of the Holy Spirit was evidence that Jesus had been exalted in heaven (see John 7:39).

2:37 So mighty was the convicting power of the Holy Spirit that there was an immediate response from the audience. Without any invitation or appeal from Peter, they cried out, **"What shall we do?"** The question was prompted by

a deep sense of guilt. They now realized that the Jesus whom they had slain was God's beloved Son! This Jesus had been raised from the dead and was now exalted in heaven. This being so, how could these guilty murderers possibly escape judgment?

2:38 Peter's answer was that they should **repent and be baptized in the name of Jesus Christ for the remission of sins**. First, they were to **repent**, acknowledging their guilt, and taking sides with God against themselves.

Then they were to **be baptized for** (or unto) **the remission of** their **sins**. At first glance, this verse seems to teach salvation by baptism, and many people insist that this is precisely what it *does* mean. Such an interpretation is impossible for the following reasons:

1. In dozens of NT passages, salvation is said to be by faith in the Lord Jesus Christ (John 1:12; 3:16, 36; 6:47; Acts 16:31; Rom. 10:9, for example). No verse or two could conceivably contradict such overwhelming testimony.
2. The thief on the cross had the assurance of salvation apart from baptism (Luke 23:43).
3. The Savior is not stated to have baptized anyone, a strange omission if baptism is essential to salvation.
4. The Apostle Paul was thankful that he baptized only a few of the Corinthians — a strange cause for thankfulness if baptism has saving merit (1 Cor. 1:14–16).

It is important to notice that only Jews were ever told to be baptized for the forgiveness of sins (see Acts 22:16). In this fact, we believe, is the secret to the understanding of this passage. The nation of Israel had crucified the Lord of glory. The Jewish people had cried out, "His blood be on us and on our children" (Matt. 27:25). The guilt of the Messiah's death was thus claimed by the people of Israel.

Now, some of these Jews had come to realize their mistake. By repentance they acknowledged their sin to God. By trusting the Lord Jesus as their Savior they were regenerated and received eternal forgiveness of sins. By public water baptism they dissociated themselves

from *the nation* that crucified the Lord
and identified themselves with *Him*.
Baptism thus became the outward sign
that their sin in connection with the rejection of Christ (as well as all their sins)
had been washed away. It took them off
Jewish ground and placed them on
Christian ground. But baptism did not
save them. Only faith in Christ could do
that. To teach otherwise is to teach another gospel and thus be accursed (Gal.
1:8, 9).

An alternative interpretation of baptism **for the remission of sins** is given
by Ryrie:

> This does not mean in order that sins
> might be remitted, for everywhere in the
> New Testament sins are forgiven as a re-
> sult of faith in Christ, not as a result of
> baptism. It means be baptized because of
> the remission of sins. The Greek preposi-
> tion *eis*, for, has this meaning "because
> of" not only here but also in such a pas-
> sage as Matthew 12:41 where the meaning
> can only be "they repented because of
> [not in order to] the preaching of Jonah."
> Repentance brought the remission of sins
> for this Pentecostal crowd, and because of
> the remission of sins they were asked to
> be baptized.[8]

Peter assured them that if they repented and were **baptized**, they would
receive the gift of the Holy Spirit. To insist that this order applies to us today
is to misunderstand God's administrative dealings in the early days of the
church. As H. P. Barker has so ably
pointed out in *The Vicar of Christ*, there
are four communities of believers in the
Book of Acts, and the order of events in
connection with the reception of the
Holy Spirit is different in each case.

Here in Acts 2:38 we read about *Jewish* Christians. For them, the order was:
1. Repentance.
2. Water baptism.
3. Reception of the Holy Spirit.

The conversion of *Samaritans* is recorded in Acts 8:14–17. There we read
that the following events occurred:
1. They believed.
2. They were baptized in water.
3. The apostles prayed for them.
4. The apostles laid their hands on
   them.
5. They received the Holy Spirit.

In Acts 10:44–48 the conversion of
Gentiles is in view. Notice the order here:
1. Faith.
2. Reception of the Holy Spirit.
3. Water baptism.

A final community of believers is
made up of *disciples of John the Baptist*,
Acts 19:1–7:
1. They believed.
2. They were rebaptized.
3. The Apostle Paul laid his hands on
   them.
4. They received the Holy Spirit.

Does this mean there were four ways
of salvation in the Book of Acts? Of
course not. Salvation was, is, and always
will be on the basis of faith in the Lord.
But during the transition period recorded in Acts, God chose to vary the
events connected with the reception of
the Holy Spirit for reasons which He
knew but did not choose to reveal to us.

Then which of these patterns applies
to us today? Since Israel nationally has
rejected the Messiah, the Jewish people
have forfeited any special privileges they
might have had. Today God is calling out
of the Gentiles a people for His Name
(Acts 15:14). Therefore, the order for
today is that which is found in Acts 10:
     Faith.
     Reception of the Holy Spirit.
     Water baptism.

We believe this order applies to all
today, to Jews as well as to Gentiles. This
may sound arbitrary at first. It might be
asked, "When did the order in Acts 2:38
cease to apply to Jews and the order in
Acts 10:44–48 begin?" No definite date
can be given, of course. But the Book of
Acts traces a gradual transition from the
gospel's going out primarily to Jews, to
its being repeatedly rejected by the Jews,
to its going out to the Gentiles. By the
end of the Book of Acts the nation of Israel had been largely set aside. By unbelief it had forfeited any special claim
as God's chosen people. During the
Church Age it would be reckoned with
the Gentile nations, and God's order for
the Gentiles, outlined in Acts 10:44–48,
would apply.

2:39 Peter next reminds them that
the promise of the Holy Spirit **is to** them
and to their **children** (the Jewish people)
and to all who are afar off (the Gen-

tiles), even **as many as** . . . **God** would **call**.

The very people who had said, "His blood be on us and on our children," are now assured of grace for themselves and their children if they will trust the Lord.

This verse has often been used mistakenly to teach that children of believing parents are thereby assured of covenant privileges, or that they are saved. Spurgeon answers this effectively:

> Will not the Church of God know that "that which is born of the flesh is flesh, and that which is born of the Spirit is Spirit?" "Who can bring a clean thing out of an unclean?" The natural birth communicates nature's filthiness, but it cannot convey peace. Under the new covenant, we are expressly told that the sons of God are "born, not of blood, nor of the will of the flesh, nor of the will of man, but of God."[9]

The important thing to notice is that **the promise** is not only **to you and to your children** but **to all who are afar off, as many as the Lord our God will call.** It is as inclusive as the "whosoever" of the gospel invitation.

2:40   Not all of Peter's message is recorded in this chapter, but the gist of the remainder was that the Jewish hearers should save themselves from the crooked, **perverse generation** that rejected and murdered the Lord Jesus. They could do this by receiving Jesus as their Messiah and Savior and by publicly disclaiming any further connection with the guilty nation of Israel through Christian baptism.

2:41   There was a great forward surge of people, desiring to be baptized as outward evidence that they had **gladly**[10] **received** Peter's **word** as the word of the Lord.

There **were added** to the company of believers that day **about three thousand souls.** If the best proof of a Holy Spirit ministry is the conversion of souls, then surely Peter's was that kind of ministry. Doubtless this Galilean fisherman was reminded of the words of the Lord Jesus, "I will make you fishers of men" (Matt. 4:19). And perhaps of the Savior's saying, "Most assuredly, I say to you, he who believes in Me, the works that I do he will do also; and greater works than

these he will do; because I go to My Father" (John 14:12).

It is instructive to notice the care with which the number of converts is recorded — *about* **three thousand souls.** All servants of the Lord might exercise similar caution in tabulating so-called decisions for Christ.

2:42   The proof of reality is in continuance. These converts proved the reality of their profession by continuing **steadfastly in**:

1. **The apostles' doctrine.** This means the inspired teachings of the apostles, delivered orally at first, and now preserved in the NT.

2. **Fellowship.** Another evidence of new life was the desire of the new believers to be with the people of God and share things in common with them. There was a sense of being separated to God from the world, and a community of interests with other Christians.

3. **The breaking of bread.** This expression is used in the NT to refer both to the Lord's Supper and to eating a common meal. The meaning in any particular case must be determined by the sense of the passage. Here it obviously refers to the Lord's Supper, since it would be quite unnecessary to say that they continued steadfastly eating their meals. From Acts 20:7 we learn that the practice of the early Christians was to break bread on the first day of the week. During the early days of the church, a love feast was held in connection with the Lord's Supper as an expression of the love of the saints for one another. However, abuses crept in, and the "agape" or love feast was discontinued.

4. **Prayers.** This was the fourth principal practice of the early church, and expressed complete dependence on the Lord for worship, guidance, preservation, and service.

2:43   A sense of reverential awe came over the people. The mighty power of the Holy Spirit was so evident that hearts were hushed and subdued. Astonishment filled their souls as they saw **the apostles** performing **many wonders and signs. Wonders** were miracles which excited wonder and amazement. **Signs**

were miracles designed to convey instruction. A miracle could be both a *wonder* and a *sign*.

2:44, 45 The believers continually assembled together and held **all things in common** trust. So mightily was the love of God shed abroad in their hearts that they did not look upon **their** material **possessions** as their own (4:32). Whenever there was a genuine case of **need** in the fellowship, they sold personal property and distributed the proceeds. Thus there was an equality.

> Among those who believed was manifested a unity of heart and interest, in which the natural selfishness of the fallen condition was swallowed up in the fulness of a love which the sense of the divine love had begotten. They were together in such sort that all they had was held in common; not by any law or outward constraint, which would have spoiled it all, but in the consciousness of what they were all to Christ, and what Christ was to each and all of them. Enriched by Him with a blessing which nothing could diminish, but the more they ministered it, the more they had it, "they sold their possessions and goods, and distributed them to all, as any one had need."[11]

Many argue today that we need not follow the early believers in this practice. One might just as well contend that we should not love our neighbors as ourselves. This sharing of all one's real estate and personal property was the inevitable fruit of lives that were filled with the Holy Spirit. It has been said, "A real Christian could not bear to have too much when others have too little."

2:46 This verse gives the effect of Pentecost on religious life and home life.

As to *religious life*, we must remember that these early converts were of Jewish background. Although the church was now in existence, the ties with the Jewish temple were not severed immediately. The process of throwing off the graveclothes of Judaism continued throughout the period of the Acts. And so the believers continued to attend the services **in the temple**,[12] where they heard the OT read and expounded. In addition, of course, they met together in homes for the functions listed in verse 42.

As to their *home life*, we read that they broke **bread**, taking **their food with gladness and simplicity of heart**. Here it seems clear that the **breaking** of **bread** refers to the eating of regular meals. The joy of their salvation overflowed into every detail of life, gilding the mundane with an aura of glory.

2:47 Life became an anthem of praise and a psalm of thanksgiving for those who had been delivered from the power of darkness and translated into the Kingdom of the Son of God's love.

At the outset, the believers had **favor with all the people**. But this was not to last. The nature of the Christian faith is such that it inevitably stirs up the hatred and opposition of the human heart. The Savior warned His disciples to beware of popularity (Luke 6:26), and promised them persecution and tribulation (Matt. 10:22, 23). So this **favor** was a momentary phase, soon to be replaced by unrelenting opposition.

And the Lord added to the church daily those who were being saved. The Christian fellowship grew by conversions each day. Those who heard the gospel were responsible to accept Jesus Christ by a definite act of the will. The Lord's electing and adding does not rule out human responsibility.

In this chapter, then, we have had the account of the outpouring of the Holy Spirit, Peter's memorable address to the assembled Jews, the conversion of a great multitude, and a brief description of life among the early believers. An excellent resume of the latter was given in the *Encyclopaedia Brittanica*, 13th edition, in the article on "Church History":

> The most notable thing about the life of the early Christians was their vivid sense of being a people of God, called and set apart. The Christian Church in their thought was a divine, not a human, institution. It was founded and controlled by God, and even the world was created for its sake. This conception . . . controlled all the life of the early Christians, both individual and social. They regarded themselves as separate from the rest of the world and bound together by peculiar ties. Their citizenship was in heaven, not on earth, and the principles and laws by which they strove to govern themselves were from above. The present world was but temporary, and their true life was in

the future. Christ was soon to return, and the employments and labors and pleasures of this age were of small concern. . . . In the everyday life of Christians the Holy Spirit was present, and all the Christian graces were the fruits. A result of this belief was to give their lives a peculiarly enthusiastic or inspirational character. Theirs were not the everyday experiences of ordinary men, but of men lifted out of themselves and transported into a higher sphere.

Just to read this article is to realize in some measure how far the church has drifted from its original vigor and solidarity!

THE HOUSE CHURCH AND PARACHURCH ORGANIZATIONS

Since the first use of the word *church* (Gk. *ekklēsia*) in Acts is found here[13] (2:47), we pause to consider the centrality of the church in the thinking of the early Christians.

The church in the Book of Acts and in the rest of the NT was what is often called a house church. The early Christians met in houses rather than in special ecclesiastical buildings. It has been said that religion was loosed from specially sacred places and centered in that universal place of living, the home. Unger says that homes continued to serve as places of Christian assembly for two centuries.[14]

It might be easy for us to think that the use of private homes was forced by economic necessity rather than being the result of spiritual considerations. We have become so accustomed to church buildings and chapels that we think they are God's ideal.

However, there is strong reason to believe that the first century believers might have been wiser than we are.

First, it is inconsistent with the Christian faith and its emphasis on love to spend thousands of dollars on luxurious buildings when there is such appalling need throughout the world. In that connection, E. Stanley Jones wrote:

> I looked on the Bambino, the child Christ in the Cathedral at Rome, laden with expensive jewels, and then walked out and looked upon the countenance of hungry children and wondered whether Christ, in view of this hunger, was enjoying His jewels. And the thought persisted that if He was, then I could no longer enjoy the thought of Christ. That bejeweled Bambino and the hungry children are a symbol of what we have done in putting around Christ the expensive livery of stately cathedrals and churches while leaving untouched the fundamental wrongs in human society whereby Christ is left hungry in the unemployed and the dispossessed.[15]

Not only is it inhumane; it is also uneconomical to spend money on expensive buildings that are used for no more than three, four, or five hours during the week. How have we ever allowed ourselves to drift into this unthinking dream world where we are willing to spend so much in order to get so little usage in return?

Our modern building programs have been one of the biggest hindrances to the expansion of the church. Heavy payments on principal and interest cause church leaders to resist any efforts to hive off and form new churches. Any loss of members would jeopardize the income needed to pay for the building and its upkeep. An unborn generation is saddled with debt, and any hope of church reproduction is stifled.

It is often argued that we must have impressive buildings in order to attract the unchurched to our services. Aside from being a carnal way of thinking, this completely overlooks the NT pattern. The meetings of the early church were largely for believers. The Christians assembled for the apostles' teaching, fellowship, breaking of bread, and prayer (Acts 2:42). They did not do their evangelizing by inviting people to meetings on Sunday but by witnessing to those with whom they came in contact throughout the week. When people did get converted, they were then brought into the fellowship and warmth of the house church to be fed and encouraged.

It is sometimes difficult to get people to attend services in dignified church buildings. There is a strong reaction against formalism. Also there is a fear of being solicited for funds. "All the church wants is your money," is a common complaint. Yet many of these same people are willing to attend a conversational Bible class in a home. There they do not have to be style-conscious, and they enjoy the informal, unprofessional atmosphere.

Actually the house church is ideal for every culture and every country. And probably if we could look over the entire world, we would see more churches meeting in homes than in any other way.

In contrast to today's imposing cathedrals, churches, and chapels — as well as a whole host of highly organized denominations, mission boards, and *parachurch* organizations, the apostles in the Book of Acts made no attempt to form an organization of any kind for carrying on the work of the Lord. The local church was God's unit on earth for propagating the faith and the disciples were content to work within that context.

In recent years there has been an organizational explosion in Christendom of such proportions as to make one dizzy. Every time a believer gets a new idea for advancing the cause of Christ, he forms a new mission board, corporation, or institution!

One result is that capable teachers and preachers have been called away from their primary ministries in order to become administrators. If all mission board administrators were serving on the mission field, it would greatly reduce the need for personnel there.

Another result of the proliferation of organizations is that vast sums of money are needed for overhead, and thus diverted from direct gospel outreach. The greater part of every dollar given to many Christian organizations is devoted to the expense of maintaining the organization rather than to the primary purpose for which it was founded.

Organizations often hinder the fulfillment of the Great Commission. Jesus told His disciples to teach all the things He had commanded. Many who work for Christian organizations find they are not permitted to teach all the truth of God. They must not teach certain controversial matters for fear they will alienate the constituency to whom they look for financial support.

The multiplication of Christian institutions has too often resulted in factions, jealousy, and rivalry that have done great harm to the testimony of Christ.

Consider the overlapping multiplicity of Christian organizations at work, at home, and abroad. Each competes for limited personnel and for shrinking financial resources. And consider how many of these organizations really owe their origin to purely human rivalry, though public statements usually refer to God's will (Daily Notes of the Scripture Union).

And it is often true that organizations have a way of perpetuating themselves long after they have outlived their usefulness. The wheels grind on heavily even though the vision of the founders has been lost, and the glory of a once dynamic movement has departed. It was spiritual wisdom, not primitive naivete, that saved the early Christians from setting up human organizations to carry on the work of the Lord. G. H. Lang writes:

> An acute writer, contrasting the apostolic work with the more usual modern missionary methods, has said that "we found missions, the apostles founded churches." The distinction is sound and pregnant. The apostles founded churches, *and they founded nothing else*, because for the ends in view nothing else was required or could have been so suitable. In each place where they laboured they formed the converts into a local assembly, with elders — always elders, never an elder (Acts 14:23; 15:6, 23; 20:17; Phil. 1:1) — to guide, to rule, to shepherd, men qualified by the Lord and recognized by the saints (1 Cor. 16:15; 1 Thess. 5:12, 13; 1 Tim. 5:17–19); and with deacons, appointed by the assembly (Acts 6:1–6; Phil. 1:1) — in this contrasted with the elders — to attend to the few but very important temporal affairs, and in particular to the distribution of the funds of the assembly. . . . All they (the apostles) did in the way of organizing was to form the disciples gathered into other such assemblies. No other organization than the local assembly appears in the New Testament, nor do we find even the germ of anything further.[16]

To the early Christians and their apostolic leadership, the congregation was the divinely ordained unit on earth through which God chose to work, and the *only* such unit to which He promised perpetuity was *the church*. ‡

E. The Healing of a Lame Man, and Peter's Charge to Israel (3:1–26)

3:1 It was 3:00 p.m. when **Peter and John went up together to the temple** in

Jerusalem. As mentioned previously, the early Jewish Christians continued to attend the temple services for some time after the church was formed. This was a period of adjustment and transition, and the break with Judaism was not made instantaneously. Believers today would not be justified in following their example in this, since we have the full revelation of the NT and are told to "go forth to Him, outside the camp, bearing His reproach" (Heb. 13:13. See also 2 Cor. 6:17, 18).

3:2 As they approached the temple, they saw men carrying a crippled beggar to his customary spot at the **gate . . . called Beautiful**. The helpless condition of this man, **lame** since birth, is in marked contrast to the beauty of the architecture of the temple. It reminds us of the poverty and ignorance which abound in the very shadow of great cathedrals, and of the helplessness of mighty ecclesiastical systems to assist those who are physical and spiritual cripples.

3:3 The lame man had obviously given up hope of ever being cured, so he contented himself to ask for a handout.

3:4 Instead of looking on this man as a helpless wretch, **Peter** saw him as one in whom the mighty power of God might be demonstrated! "If we are led by the Spirit, we will fix our eyes on those whom God intends to bless, instead of firing blank cartridges and beating the air" (Selected).

Peter's command, **"Look at us,"** was not intended to attract publicity to John and himself, but merely to insure the undivided attention of the beggar.

3:5, 6 Still **expecting** nothing more than financial help, the cripple **gave them his attention**. Then he heard an announcement that was both disappointing and thrilling to him. As far as a handout was concerned, Peter had nothing to give. But he had something better to give. By the authority **of Jesus Christ of Nazareth**, he commanded the lame man to **rise up and walk**. A witty old preacher said, "The crippled beggar asked for *alms* and he got *legs*."

It is said that Thomas Aquinas visited the pope at a time when large sums of money were being counted. The pope boasted, "We need no longer say with Peter, 'Silver and gold I do not have!' " Aquinas replied, "Neither can you say with Peter, 'Rise up and walk!' "

3:7 As Peter helped the man to his feet, **strength** flowed into the hitherto useless **feet and ankle bones**. Here we are reminded again that in the spiritual life, there is a curious mingling of the divine and the human. Peter helps the man to his feet; then God performs the cure. We must do what we can do; then God will do what we cannot do.

3:8 The miracle of healing was immediate, not gradual. Notice how the Spirit of God multiplies words of action and movement: **leaping up, stood . . . walked and entered . . . walking, leaping**.

When we remember the slow, painful process an infant goes through in learning to walk, we realize how wonderful it was for this man to walk and leap right away, for the first time in his life.

This miracle, performed in the Name of Jesus, was a further testimony to the people of Israel that the One they had crucified was alive and was willing to be their Healer and Savior.

3:9, 10 The fact that the beggar had lain daily at the door of the temple made him a familiar sight. Now that he was healed, the miracle was necessarily generally known. **The people** could not deny that a mighty miracle had taken place, but what was the meaning of it all?

3:11 As the **healed** man **held on to Peter and John**, as to his physicians, **all the people ran together** at **Solomon's porch**, a portion of the temple area. Their amazement and wonder provided the opportunity for Peter to preach to them.

3:12 **Peter** first diverts the attention of the people from the cured man, and from the apostles. The explanation of the miracle was not to be found in any of them.

3:13–16 Quickly he brings them to the true Author of the miracle. It was Jesus, the One they had rejected, denied, and **killed**. **God raised** Him **from the dead** and **glorified** Him in heaven. Now, **through faith in** Him, **this man**

had been cured of his helplessness.

Peter's holy boldness in accusing the men of Israel is remarkable. His charges against them are:

1. They **delivered up** Jesus (to the Gentiles for trial).
2. They **denied** Him **in the presence of Pilate, when he was determined to** release **Him**.
3. They **denied the Holy One and the Just, and asked for** the release of **a murderer** (Barabbas).
4. They **killed the Prince** (or Author) **of life**.

Notice, by contrast, God's treatment of Jesus:

1. He **raised** Him **from the dead** (v. 15).
2. He **glorified His Servant Jesus** — not His Son Jesus, as in the 1611 Version (v. 13).

Notice finally the emphasis on **faith** in Christ as the explanation of the miracle of healing (v. 16). In this verse, as elsewhere, the **name** stands for the person. Thus, **faith in His name** means **faith in** Christ.

3:17 There is a distinct change in Peter's tone in this verse. Having charged the men of Israel with the death of the Lord Jesus, he now addresses them as his Jewish **brethren**, graciously allowing that they **did it in ignorance**, and urging them to repent and be converted.

It almost seems contradictory to hear Peter say that the Jews crucified the Lord Jesus in ignorance. Did He not come with the full credentials of the Messiah? Did He not perform wondrous miracles in their midst? Did He not infuriate them by claiming to be equal with God? Yes, this is all true. And yet they were ignorant of the fact that Jesus Christ was God incarnate. They expected the Messiah to come, not in lowly grace, but rather as a mighty military deliverer. They looked upon Jesus as an impostor.

They did not know He was truly the Son of God. They probably thought they were doing God a service in killing Him. Thus the Savior Himself said at the time of the crucifixion, "They do not know what they do" (Luke 23:34), and Paul later wrote, "Had they [the princes of this age] known, they would not have crucified the Lord of glory" (1 Cor. 2:8).

All this was designed to assure the men of Israel that their sin, however great, was still subject to the forgiving grace of God.

3:18 Without excusing their sin, Peter shows that **God** overruled it to fulfill His own purposes. The **prophets** of the OT had predicted that the Messiah **would suffer**. The Jewish people were the ones who inflicted the suffering on Him. But now He offered Himself to them as Lord and Savior. Through Him they could receive forgiveness of their sins.

3:19 The people of Israel should **repent** and make an about-face. When they would do this, their **sins** would **be blotted out, so that times of refreshing may come**.

It must be remembered that this message is addressed to the men of Israel (v. 12). It emphasizes that national repentance must precede national restoration and blessing. The **times of refreshing . . . from the presence of the Lord** refer to the blessings of Christ's future kingdom on earth, as mentioned in the next verse.

3:20[†] Following Israel's repentance, God will **send** the Messiah, **Jesus**. As mentioned previously, this refers to the Second Advent of Christ to set up His thousand-year reign on the earth.

3:21 The question inevitably arises at this point, "If Israel had repented when Peter was speaking, would the Lord Jesus have returned to earth?" Great and godly men have differed on this subject. Some insist He would have returned; otherwise, they say the promise was not a bona fide one. Others take the passage as being prophetic, as showing the order of events that would actually take place. The question is a purely hypothetical one. The facts are that Israel did not repent, and the Lord Jesus has not returned.

It is clear from verse 21 that **God** foresaw that the nation of Israel would reject Christ, and that the present age of grace would intervene before His Second Coming. **Heaven must receive** Christ **until the times of restoration of all things. The times of restoration of all things** point forward to the Millennium.

†*See p. xx.*

They do not indicate universal salvation, as some have suggested; such a teaching is foreign to the Bible. Rather they point to the time when creation will be delivered from the bondage of corruption and Christ will reign in righteousness as King over all the earth.

These **times of restoration** had been foretold by the **prophets** of the OT period.

Verse 21 has been used in an effort to disprove the pretribulation Rapture. The argument is that if the heavens must receive Jesus until the beginning of the Millennium, then He cannot come before then to take the church home to heaven. The answer, of course, is that Peter is speaking here to the men of Israel (v. 12). He is discussing God's dealings with Israel nationally. *As far as the nation of Israel is concerned*, the Lord Jesus will remain in heaven until He comes to reign at the end of the Tribulation. But individual Jews who believe on Him during this Church Age will share with believing Gentiles in the Rapture of the church, which could take place at any moment. Also, in the Rapture, the Lord does not leave the heavens; we go to Him in the air.

3:22 As an example of an OT prophecy looking forward to Christ's glorious reign, Peter quotes Deuteronomy 18:15, 18, 19. The passage pictures the Lord Jesus as God's **Prophet** in Israel's golden age, announcing God's will and law.

When Moses said, **"The Lord your God will raise up for you a Prophet like me,"** he did not mean likeness as to character or ability, but likeness in the sense that both were *raised up by God*. "He will raise Him up as He raised me up."

3:23 During Christ's reign on earth, those who refuse to **hear** and obey Him will **be utterly destroyed**. Of course, those who reject Him today suffer eternal judgment also, but the primary thought of this passage is that Christ will yet rule with a rod of iron and that those who disobey Him and rebel against Him will be promptly executed.

3:24 To further emphasize that the times of restoration were well predicted, Peter adds that **all the prophets from**

Samuel and his successors spoke of **these days**.

3:25 Peter now reminds his Jewish hearers that the promise of these times of blessing was made to them as **sons of the prophets** and descendants of Abraham. After all, **God** had **made** a **covenant** with **Abraham** to bless **all the families of the earth** in his **seed**. All the promises of millennial blessing center in the **Seed**, i.e., in Christ. They should therefore accept the Lord Jesus as Messiah.

3:26 **God** had already **raised up His Servant** (3:13), and had **sent Him** first to the nation of Israel. This refers to the Incarnation and life of our Lord rather than to His resurrection. If they would receive Him, He would turn **away every one of** them **from** their **iniquities**.

In this sermon by Peter, delivered to the people of Israel, we notice that it is *the kingdom* that is in view rather than *the church*. Also the emphasis is national rather than individual. The Spirit of God is lingering over Israel in longsuffering mercy, pleading with God's ancient people to receive the glorified Lord Jesus as Messiah and thus hasten the advent of Christ's kingdom on earth.

But Israel would not hear.

F. The Persecution and Growth of the Church (4:1–7:60)

4:1–4 The first persecution of the infant church was about to break out. True to pattern, it arose from the religious leaders. **The priests, the captain of the temple, and the Sadducees** rose up against the apostles.

Scroggie suggests that **the priests** represent religious intolerance; **the captain of the temple**, political enmity; and **the Sadducees**, rationalistic unbelief. **The Sadducees** denied the doctrine of resurrection. This brought them into open conflict with the apostles, since **the resurrection** was the keynote of apostolic preaching! Spurgeon sees a parallel:

The Sadducees, as you know, were the Broad School, the liberals, the advanced thinkers, the modern-thought people of the day. If you want a bitter sneer, a biting sarcasm, or a cruel action, I commend you to these large-hearted gentlemen. They are liberal to everybody, except to those who hold the truth; and for those they have a reserve of concentrated bitterness which far excels wormwood and gall. They are so liberal to their brother errorists that they have no tolerance to spare for evangelicals.[17]

These leaders resented the fact that the apostles were teaching the people; they felt this was their sole prerogative. Then, too, they were angered by the proclamation **in Jesus** of **the resurrection** *from* **the dead**. If **Jesus** had risen **from** among **the dead**, then the Sadducees were discredited.

In verse 2, the expression **resurrection** *from* **the dead** is important because it disproves the popular idea of a general resurrection at the end of the world. This passage and others speak of resurrection *out from among* dead ones. In other words, some will be raised while others (unbelievers) will remain in the grave until a later time.

The leaders decided to hold the apostles under a sort of house arrest until the next day, since it was getting late. (The miracle of healing in chapter 3 had been performed around 3:00 p.m.)

In spite of official opposition, many people turned to the Lord. About **five thousand** men (Gk. *andres*, "males") are mentioned as entering the Christian fellowship. Commentators are disagreed whether this included the three thousand saved at Pentecost. It does not include women and children.

4:5, 6 **The next day**, the religious council, known as the Sanhedrin, sat as a court of inquiry, intending to put a stop to the activities of these public nuisances. All they succeeded in doing was to give the apostles another chance to witness for Christ!

Together with **their rulers, elders, and scribes** were:

1. **Annas the high priest,** before whom the Lord had been first taken. He formerly was high priest but perhaps was allowed to retain the title as a courtesy.
2. **Caiaphas**, the son-in-law of Annas, who presided at the trial of the Lord.
3. **John and Alexander**, about whom nothing else is known.
4. All who **were of the family of the high priest,** men of high-priestly descent.

4:7 The trial opened by their asking the apostles **by what power or by what name** they had performed the miracle. **Peter** stepped forward to deliver his third successive public confession of Christ in Jerusalem. It was a priceless opportunity to preach the gospel to the religious establishment, and he seized it eagerly and fearlessly.

4:8–12 First he reminded them that they were unhappy because the apostles had performed **a good deed . . . to a helpless man**. Though **Peter** didn't say it, the healed man had begged at the gate of the temple, and the rulers had never been able to heal him. Then the apostle delivered a thunderbolt by announcing **that** it was in **the name of Jesus . . . whom** they had **crucified** that the man was cured. **God** had **raised** Jesus **from the dead**, and it was by His power that the miracle had been performed. The Jews did not have any place for **Jesus** in their building scheme, so they **rejected** and **crucified** Him. But **God raised** Him **from the dead** and exalted Him in heaven. The **rejected stone** thus became **the chief cornerstone**, the indispensable stone that completes the structure. And He *is* indispensable. There is no **salvation** without Him. He is the exclusive Savior. **No other name under heaven** has been **given among men** for **salvation**, and it is by this **name** alone that **we must be saved**.

As we read verses 8–12, let us remember that these words were spoken by the same man who had denied the Lord three times with oaths and curses.

4:13 Dry, formal religion is ever intolerant of enthusiastic, vital evangelism that produces results in hearts and lives. Its leaders are nonplussed to see **uneducated and untrained men** making an impact on the community while they with all their wisdom "fail to rise above flesh and blood."

In the New Testament there is no distinction between clergy and laity. This distinction is a relic brought over from Romanism. John Huss fought and died in Czechoslovakia for the doctrine of the priesthood of all believers, and the Hussite symbol to this present day is the communion cup standing upon the open Bible. It was this truth of a royal priesthood and every believer a witness that was the dynamic force in the early Church. Without the aid of any modern equipment, or transportation, or translation and publication of the Word, the Gospel of God's grace shook the whole Empire until there were saints even in Caesar's household. God is calling us back to primitive Christianity.[18]

The Sanhedrin was struck by **the boldness of Peter and John**. They would like to have brushed them aside as **uneducated and** ignorant fishermen from Galilee. But there was something about their self-control, their empowered lives, their fearlessness that made them think of Jesus when he was on trial. They attributed the boldness of the apostles to the fact **that they had been with Jesus** in the past, but the real explanation was that they were filled with the Holy Spirit *now*.

4:14–18 Then, too, it was embarrassing to have the healed cripple there in the courtroom. There was no denying that a miracle had taken place.

J. H. Jowett writes:

Men may more than match you in subtlety of argument. In intellectual argument you may suffer an easy defeat. But the argument of a redeemed life is unassailable. "Seeing the man that was healed standing with them, they could say nothing against it."[19]

In order to discuss their strategy, they sent Peter and John outside the room temporarily. Their dilemma was this: they could not punish the apostles for performing an act of kindness; yet if they did not stop these fanatics, their own religion would be seriously threatened by loss of members. So they decided to forbid Peter and John to talk to the people about **Jesus** in private conversation, or to preach Him publicly.

4:19, 20 **Peter and John** could not agree to such a restriction. Their first loyalty and responsibility was **to God**, not to man. If they were honest, the rulers would have to admit this. The apostles had witnessed the resurrection and ascension of Christ. They had sat under His teaching day after day. They were responsible to bear witness to their Lord and Savior, Jesus Christ.

4:21, 22 The weakness of the rulers' position is seen in the fact that they could not punish the apostles; all **the people** knew that a gracious miracle had taken place. The healed man, **over forty years old**, was well known, because his sad plight had been displayed publicly for a long time. So all the Sanhedrin could do was to dismiss the accused apostles with further threats.

4:23 With an instinct of freeborn sons of God, the apostles **went** directly **to their** fellow believers as soon as they were **let go** by the authorities. They sought and found their fellowship with "the panting, huddled flock whose only crime was Christ." So in all ages one test of a Christian's character is where he finds fellowship and companionship.

4:24–26 As soon as the saints **heard** what had happened, they cried to the Lord in prayer. Addressing **God** with a word meaning "Absolute Master," a word seldom used in the NT, they praised Him first as the Creator of **all** things (and therefore superior to the creatures who were now opposing His truth). Then they adopted the words of **David** in Psalm 2, which he spoke by the Holy Spirit in connection with the opposition of governmental powers **against His Christ**. Actually, the Psalm points forward to the time when Christ will come to set up His kingdom and when **kings** and **rulers** will seek to thwart that purpose. But the early Christians realized that the situation in their day was similar, so they applied the words to their own circumstances. As has been said, they showed true spirituality by the divine skill with which they wove Holy Scripture into the body of their prayers.

4:27, 28 Their application of the quotation from the Psalm is given next. Right there in Jerusalem the Romans and the Jews had leagued **together** against *God's* **holy Servant,**[20] **Jesus. Herod** represented the Jews, and **Pilate** acted for the Gentiles. But there is a surprise ending in verse 28. One would expect it to say that these rulers had gathered together to do whatever their wicked hearts had planned. Instead, it says that they had **gathered together to do whatever** *God's* **hand and purpose** had **determined before**.

Matheson explains:

The idea is that their effort of opposition to the divine will proved to be a stroke of alliance with it. . . . They met together in a council of war against Christ; unconsciously to themselves they signed a treaty for the promotion of Christ's glory. . . . Our God does not beat down the storms that rise against Him; He rides upon them; He works through them.[21]

4:29, 30 Having expressed confidence in God's overruling power, the Christians made three specific requests:

1. **Look on their threats**. They did not presume to dictate to God how to punish these wicked men, but simply left the matter with Him.

2. **Grant to Your servants . . . all boldness**. Their own personal safety was not the important thing. Fearlessness in preaching the word was paramount.

3. **Stretching out Your hand to heal**. The early preaching of the gospel was attested by God through **signs and wonders** performed **through the name of . . . Jesus**. Here God is petitioned to continue confirming the ministry of the apostles in this way.

4:31 When they had prayed, the place . . . was shaken — a physical expression of the spiritual power that was present. **They were all filled with the Holy Spirit**, indicating their obedience to the Lord, their walking in the light, their yieldedness to Him. They continued to speak **the word of God with boldness**, a clear answer to their prayer in verse 29.

There are seven times in the Book of Acts when men are said to be filled with or full of the Holy Spirit. Notice the purposes or the results:

1. For speaking (2:4; 4:8; and here).
2. For serving (6:3).
3. For shepherding (11:24).
4. For rebuking (13:9).
5. For dying (7:55).

4:32–35 When hearts are aflame with love for Christ, they are also kindled with love for one another. This love manifests itself in giving. Thus the early believers expressed the reality of their common life in Christ by practicing a community of goods. Instead of selfishly holding on to personal possessions, they looked upon their property as belonging to all the fellowship. Whenever there was a **need**, they would sell **lands or houses** and bring **the proceeds** to the apostles for distribution. It is important to see that **they distributed** whenever a **need** arose; it was not an arbitrary equal division at one particular time.

F. W. Grant explains:

There was therefore no general renunciation of personal title but a love that knew no holding back from the need of another. It was the instinct of hearts that had found their real possessions in that sphere into which Christ had risen.[22]

Somewhat sarcastic but sadly too often true is F. E. Marsh's modern parallel:

One has said, in contrasting the early Church with the Christianity of today, "Is it not a solemn thought, that if the evangelist Luke were describing modern instead of primitive Christianity, he would have to vary the phraseology of Acts 4:32–35 somewhat as follows: . . . "And the multitude of them that professed were of hard heart and stony soul, and every one said that all the things which he possessed were his own: and they had all things in the fashion. And with great power gave they witness to the attractions of this world, and great selfishness was upon them all. And there were many among them that lacked love, for as many as were possessors of lands bought more, and sometimes gave a small part thereof for a public good, so their names were heralded in the newspapers, and distribution of praise was made to every one according as he desired."[23]

There is mysterious power connected with lives that are utterly dedicated to the Lord. Thus it is not a coincidence that we read in verse 33, **And with great power the apostles gave witness to the resurrection of the Lord Jesus. And great grace was upon them all**. It seems that when God finds people who are willing to turn their possessions over to Him, He gives their testimony a remarkable attractiveness and force.

Many argue that this sharing of goods was a temporary phase of life in the early church and was not intended to be an example to us. Such reasoning only exposes our own spiritual poverty. If we had the power of Pentecost in our hearts, we would have the fruits of Pentecost in our lives.

Ryrie points out:

This is not "Christian communism." The sale of property was quite voluntary (v.

34). The right of possession was not abolished. The community did not control the money until it had voluntarily been given to the Apostles. The distribution was not made equally but according to need. These are not communistic principles. This is Christian charity in its finest display.[24]

Note two marks of a great church in verse 33 — **great power** and **great grace**. Vance Havner lists four other marks, as follows: great fear (5:5, 11); great persecution (8:1); great joy (8:8; 15:3); a great number who believed (11:21).

4:36, 37 These verses are an introductory link with chapter 5. The generosity of **Barnabas** is set forth in striking contrast to the hypocrisy of Ananias. As a **Levite, Joses . . . named Barnabas** would not ordinarily have owned land. The Lord was to be the portion of the Levites. How or why he obtained the land, we do not know. But we do know that the law of love worked so powerfully in the life of this **Son of Encouragement** that he **sold** the **land** and **laid** the money **at the apostles' feet.**

5:1–4 When God is working in power, **Satan** is on hand to counterfeit, corrupt, and contend. But where there is real spiritual power, deceit and hypocrisy will be readily exposed.

Ananias and **Sapphira** were apparently moved by the generosity of Barnabas and others. Perhaps they desired to receive the praise of men for some similar act of kindness, so **they sold a possession** and gave a portion of the proceeds to the apostles. Their sin was in professing to give all, while only giving some. No one had asked them to sell the property. **After it was sold**, they were not obligated to give all. But they *pretended* a total dedication, while actually they held some back.

Peter charged **Ananias** with lying **to the Holy Spirit** and **not** just **to men.** In lying **to the Holy Spirit**, he **lied to God**, since **the Holy Spirit** *is* **God.**

5:5, 6 At this point, **Ananias fell down** dead, and was carried out by **the young men** to be buried. This was a solemn act of God's chastening hand on the early church. It does not at all affect the question of Ananias' salvation, of his eternal security. Rather, it was a case of

God showing His displeasure at this first eruption of sin in His church. "As one commentator put it," quotes Richard Bewes, " 'Either Ananias or the Spirit must go.' " Such was the white-hot purity of that early Christian fellowship that a lie of that kind couldn't live within it."

5:7–11 About three hours later, when Sapphira appeared, **Peter** charged her with collaborating with her husband in putting **the Spirit of the Lord** to the test. He told her of her husband's fate and predicted the same for her. **Immediately she** collapsed and died, and was carried out for burial.

Peter's ability to pronounce judgment on this couple is an example of the special miraculous powers given to the apostles. Perhaps it was a fulfillment of the Lord's promise, "If you retain the sins of any, they are retained" (John 20:23). It is further seen by Paul's ability to deliver an offending Christian to Satan for the destruction of the flesh (1 Cor. 5:5). There is no reason to believe that this power continued after the time of the apostles.

One can imagine the sense of awe that swept over the church, indeed over all who heard the news of these two deaths.

5:12–16 After the death of Ananias and Sapphira, the **apostles** continued to perform miracles as the people gathered around them **in Solomon's Porch.** So vivid was the sense of God's presence and power that men did not lightly associate with them or make glib professions of faith. And yet the common **people esteemed them highly**, many taking their place as **believers** in the Lord Jesus. The **people** carried their **sick out into the streets on beds** and mattresses so that Peter's **shadow might fall on some of them** as he passed by. Anyone could see that there was reality and power in the lives of the apostles, and that they were channels through whom God was blessing others. From the suburbs came the **sick** and the demon-possessed, **and they were all healed.**

It is clear from Hebrews 2:4 that miracles like these were God's method of bearing witness to the ministry of the apostles. With the completion of the NT in written form, the need for such **signs** largely passed away. As far as modern "healing campaigns" are concerned, it should be enough to note that *of those brought to the apostles,* **they were all healed**. This is not true of so-called faith healers.

5:17–20 True Holy Spirit ministry invariably leads to conversion on the one hand and bitter opposition on the other. So it was here. **The high priest** (probably Caiaphas) and his Sadducean friends were furious that these fanatical disciples of Jesus were wielding such influence among the people. They resented any threat to their exclusive role as religious leaders, and especially despised preaching concerning bodily resurrection, which they, of course, utterly denied.

Unable to cope with **the apostles** other than by force, they had them arrested and imprisoned. That **night an angel of the Lord** led the apostles out of **the prison** and told them to return to **the temple and speak to the people all the words of this life**. Luke records the miraculous intervention of the **angel** without any expression of surprise or wonder. If the apostles themselves were shocked, there is no indication in the narrative.

The **angel** aptly referred to the Christian faith as **this life**. It is not just a creed or set of doctrines, but a *Life* — the resurrection **life** of the Lord Jesus imparted to all who trust Him.

5:21 At daybreak the apostles were teaching at **the temple**. In the meantime, **the high priest** met in solemn conclave with **the council** (the Sanhedrin) and the senate (**all the elders**), and waited for the prisoners to be **brought** before them.

5:22–25 The bewildered **officers** had to report to the court that everything at **the prison** was in good order — except that the prisoners were gone! **The doors** were properly locked, **and the guards** were all at their stations, but the occupants were missing. A distressing report indeed! "Where will it all end?" mused **the captain of the temple and the chief priests**. "How far will this popular movement go?" Then their questions were interrupted by a messenger announcing that the escaped prisoners were back at their old stand **in the temple — teaching the people**! We must

admire their courage, and we must regain the capacity of the early church to suffer for our convictions at any cost.

5:26 **The officers** used no **violence** in bringing the apostles to the council. **They feared the people** would stone them if they were openly rough to these followers of Jesus, now held in high regard by many of **the** common **people**.

5:27, 28 **The high priest** served as spokesman. **"Did we not strictly command you not to teach in this name?"** He purposely avoided using the name of the Lord Jesus Christ. **"You have filled Jerusalem with your doctrine."** This was an unintentional compliment to the effectiveness of the apostles' ministry. "You **intend to bring this Man's blood on us.**" But the Jewish leaders had already done this when they cried, "His blood be on us and on our children" (Matt. 27:25).

5:29–32 Previously the apostles had prayed for boldness to speak the word. Now with courage from above, they insist that their obligation is **to obey God rather than men**. They flatly declare that **Jesus** had been **raised up** by **God**, that Israel had **murdered** Him **by hanging** Him **on a tree**, but that **God** had **exalted** Him **to His right hand** — a **Prince and Savior**. As such He was willing **to give repentance to Israel and forgiveness of sins**. As a final thrust, the apostles add that they **are His witnesses to these things, and so also is the Holy Spirit whom God** gives **to those who obey Him** by believing on His Son.

God raising **up Jesus** (v. 30) may refer to His Incarnation or His resurrection. The probable meaning here is that **God raised** Him **up**, in Incarnation, to be the **Savior**.

5:33–37 Deep conviction accompanied the words of these embodied consciences — so deep that the rulers of the Jews **plotted to kill them**. At this juncture Gamaliel intervened. He was one of the most distinguished of Israel's rabbis, and the **teacher** of Saul of Tarsus. His advice does not indicate that he was a Christian or that he was even pro-Christian. It was simply worldly wisdom.

After having **the apostles** taken from the room, he first reminded the Sanhedrin that if this movement were not **of God**, it would soon collapse. Two illustrations of this principle were offered: (1) **Theudas**, a self-styled leader with **about four hundred** revolutionaries, who **was slain** and whose men **were scattered**; (2) **Judas of Galilee**, another fanatic, who stirred up an abortive sedition among the Jews, but who **also perished**, and whose followers **were dispersed**.

5:38, 39 **If** this Christian religion were not **of God**, the best thing would be to leave it **alone**, and it would soon fade out. To combat it would only make it more determined to survive. (This argument is not altogether true. Many godless institutions have flourished for centuries. In fact, they have gained more adherents than the truth. But the argument is true in God's time, if not in man's.)

On the other hand, Gamaliel continued, **if** the movement were **of God**, they would not be able to **overthrow it**, and they would **be found** in the awkward position of fighting **against God**.

5:40 This logic appealed to the rulers, so **they called for the apostles**, ordered them to be **beaten**, forbade them to **speak in the name of Jesus, and let them go**. The beating was senseless and unrighteous, the unreasonable reaction of bigoted hearts to the truth of God.[25] The command that accompanied the beating was foolish and futile; they might as well have ordered the sun not to shine as to command the disciples to keep silent concerning **the name of Jesus**!

5:41, 42 The beating inflicted on the apostles had two unexpected results. First, it caused them deep joy **that they were counted worthy to suffer shame for** the **name**[26] they loved. Second, it sent them forth with renewed zeal and persistence, **daily in the temple** and in homes, **teaching and preaching Jesus as the** Messiah.

So once again Satan outwitted himself.

THE CHRISTIAN AND GOVERNMENT

As the early Christians moved forward with the gospel, it was inevitable that they would run into opposition from governmental authorities, especially from the religious leaders who at that time had considerable jurisdiction in civil affairs. The believers were prepared for this and reacted with poise and dignity.

In general their policy was to respect and obey their rulers, since the latter are ordained by God and are servants of God to promote the common good. Thus, when Paul unknowingly rebuked the high priest, and was called to account, he immediately apologized, quoting Exodus 22:28: "You shall not speak evil of a ruler of your people" (Acts 23:5).

However, when men's laws ran afoul of the commandments of God, then the Christians' policy was to disobey the government and suffer the consequences, whatever they might be. For instance, when Peter and John were forbidden to preach the gospel, they answered, "Whether it is right in the sight of God to listen to you more than to God, you judge. For we cannot but speak the things which we have seen and heard" (4:19, 20). And when Peter and the apostles were arraigned for continuing to teach in Christ's Name, Peter replied, "We ought to obey God rather than men" (5:29).

There is no suggestion that they ever did or would join in any attempt to overthrow the government. In spite of persecution and oppression, they wished only good for their rulers (26:29).

It goes without saying that they would never stoop to any form of dishonesty to gain favors from the government. The governor, Felix, for instance, waited in vain to receive a bribe from Paul (24:26).

They did not consider it inconsistent with their Christian calling to use their rights of citizenship (16:37; 21:39; 22:25–28; 23:17–21; 25:10, 11).

Yet they themselves did not engage in the politics of this world. Why? No explanation is given. But this much is clear: they were people of one purpose — to preach the gospel of Christ. They gave themselves to this task without distraction. They must have believed that the gospel is the answer to man's problems. This conviction was so strong that they could not be satisfied with subordinate approaches, such as politics.‡

6:1 If the devil cannot destroy by attacks from without, he will seek to overthrow by dissension within. This is illustrated in these verses.

In the early days of the church, it was customary to make daily disbursements to the poor widows of the church who had no other means of support. Some of the believers who had been Greek-speaking Jews complained **because their widows** were not receiving the same treatment as the widows of **Hebrews** (those from Jerusalem and Judea).

6:2, 3 **The twelve** apostles realized that with the increasing growth of the church, some provision would have to be made for handling these business matters. They themselves did not want to forsake the ministry of **the word of God** in order to handle financial matters, so they counseled that the church should designate **seven** spiritual **men** to handle the temporal affairs of the church.

Although these men are not designated deacons in the Bible, it is not unreasonable to think of them as such. In the expression, **serve tables**, the word **serve** is the verb form of the noun from which we get the English word *deacon*, so their function literally was to "deacon" tables.

Their qualifications here are threefold:

1. **Of good reputation**   Reputable
2. **Full of the Holy**   Spiritual
   Spirit
3. Full of **wisdom**   Practical

More detailed qualifications are given in 1 Timothy 3:8–13.

6:4 The apostles would **give** themselves **continually to prayer and to the ministry of the word**. The order here is significant — first **prayer**, then **the ministry of the word**. They made it a point to speak to God about men before speaking to men about God.

6:5, 6 Judging from the names of the seven men who were chosen, most of them were Greek-speaking Jews before their conversion. This was certainly a most gracious concession to the very group that had made the complaint. Hereafter there could be no charge of favoritism from that quarter. When the love of God fills men's hearts, it triumphs over pettiness and selfishness.

Only two of the deacons are well-known to us — **Stephen**, who became the first martyr of the church; and **Philip**, the evangelist who later carried the gospel to Samaria, won the Ethiopian eunuch to Christ, and entertained Paul at Caesarea.

After praying, the apostles expressed their fellowship with the choice of the church by laying **hands on** the seven.

6:7 If verse 7 is read with the preceding verses, it seems to indicate that the provision of deacons to care for business affairs resulted in a great forward thrust for the gospel. As **the word of God spread**, many **disciples** were added to the fellowship **in Jerusalem, and a great many of the** Jewish **priests** became followers of the Lord Jesus.

6:8 The narrative now centers on one of the deacons, **Stephen**,[27] who was mightily used by God in performing miracles and in preaching the word. He is the first man other than an apostle who is said to have performed miracles in the Book of Acts. Was this promotion to higher service a result of his faithfulness as a deacon? Or was it simply an additional ministry which he carried on at the same time? It is impossible to decide from the text.

6:9 Opposition to Stephen's powerful ministry arose from the synagogue. These were places where Jews gathered together on the Sabbath for instruction in the law. The synagogues were named according to the people who met there. The **Freedmen** were perhaps Jews who had been freed from slavery by the Romans. Cyrene was a city in Africa, some of whose Jews had apparently settled in Jerusalem. The Alexandrian Jews had come from the seaport of Egypt by that name. **Cilicia** was the southeastern province of Asia Minor, and **Asia** was a province of Asia Minor made up of three territories. Apparently communities of Jews from all of these places had synagogues in or near Jerusalem.

6:10–14 These zealous Jews proved no match for Stephen as they disputed with him. The words which he spoke and the power with which he spoke them were irresistible. In a desperate move to silence them, **they secretly induced** false witnesses to accuse Stephen of blasphemy **against Moses and God**.[28]

Soon he was standing before the Sanhedrin, charged with speaking **against** the temple **and the law**. They falsely quoted him as saying that **Jesus** would **destroy** the temple and **change** the whole system **which Moses delivered** to Israel.

6:15 The Sanhedrin heard the charges, but as they looked at Stephen, they **saw** not the face of a demon, but **the face of an angel**. They saw the mysterious beauty of a life that is fully surrendered to the Lord, determined to proclaim the Truth, and more concerned with what God thinks than with what men may say. They saw something of the glory of Christ reflected in the radiant face of His devoted follower.

In chapter 7 we have Stephen's masterful defense. It begins quietly with what seems to be a review of Jewish history. As it progresses, it concentrates on two individuals, Joseph and Moses, who were raised up by God, rejected by Israel, then exalted as deliverers and saviors. Though Stephen does not compare their experiences directly with Christ's, the analogy is unmistakable. Then at length, Stephen launches into a scathing attack on Israel's leaders, charging them with resisting the Holy Spirit, murdering the Righteous One, and failing to keep the law of God.

Stephen must have known that his life was at stake. To spare himself, all he had to do was deliver a compromising, placating speech. But he would rather die than betray his sacred trust. Admire his courage!

7:1–8 This first section of the message takes us back to the beginning of the Hebrew nation. It is not exactly clear why Abraham's history is dealt with at such length, unless it is:

1. To show Stephen's familiarity with and love for the nation of Israel.

2. To lead up to the story of Joseph and Moses, both types of the rejection of Christ.

3. To show that Abraham worshiped God acceptably even though his worship was not confined to a specific locality. (Stephen had been accused of speaking against the temple — "this holy place.")

The salient points in Abraham's biography are:

1. His call by God **in Mesopotamia** (vv. 2, 3).

2. His journey to **Haran**, then to Canaan (v. 4).

3. God's promise of the land to Abraham, though the patriarch himself was not given any of it — as was proved by his purchase of the cave of Machpelah as a burial place (v. 5). The fulfillment of that promise is still future (Heb. 11:13–40).

4. God's prediction of Israel's bondage in Egypt and of eventual deliverance (vv. 6, 7). Both parts of this prediction were accomplished by men who had been rejected by the nation: Joseph (vv. 9–19); Moses (vv. 20–36). The **four hundred years** mentioned in verse 6 and in Genesis 15:13 refer to the time when the Jewish people were afflicted in Egypt. The four hundred and thirty years cited in Exodus 12:40 and Galatians 3:17 cover the period from the arrival of Jacob and his family in Egypt to the Exodus and the giving of the law. The Israelites were not persecuted during their first thirty years in Egypt; in fact, they were treated quite royally.

5. **The covenant of circumcision** (v. 8a).

6. The birth of **Isaac**, then **Jacob**, then **the twelve patriarchs** (v. 8b). This, of course, brings the history up to Joseph, one of Jacob's twelve sons.

7:9–19 Of all the types of Christ in the OT, **Joseph** is one of the clearest and most precious, although he is never specifically stated to be. Surely the Jews of Stephen's day must have felt the sharp arrows of conviction as they heard Stephen review the steps of Joseph's career, then remembered what they had done to Jesus of Nazareth!

1. **Joseph sold into Egypt** by his brothers (v. 9).

2. The rejected one raised to power and glory in **Egypt** (v. 10).

3. Joseph's brothers driven to **Egypt** by **famine**, but failed to recognize their brother (vv. 11, 12).

4. **The second time Joseph was made known to** them. Then the rejected one became the savior of his family (vv. 13, 14). Note: There seems to be a contradiction between the

seventy–five souls given in verse 14 and the seventy mentioned in Genesis 46:27. Stephen followed the Greek translation of Genesis 46:27 and Exodus 1:5, which has seventy-five. The Hebrew text has seventy, indicating nothing more serious than a different way of numbering Jacob's family.[29]

5. The death of the patriarchs, and their burial in the land of Canaan (vv. 15, 16). Another difficulty appears in this verse. Here it says that **Abraham bought** a burial place from **Hamor**. Genesis 23:16, 17 says that *Abraham* bought the cave of Machpelah in Hebron from the sons of Heth. *Jacob* bought land in Shechem from the children of Hamor (Gen. 33:19). There are several possibilities: (1) Abraham may have bought land in Shechem as well as in Hebron. Later Jacob could have repurchased the plot in Shechem. (2) Stephen could have used Abraham's name for Abraham's descendant, Jacob. (3) Stephen may have condensed the purchases by Abraham and Jacob into one for brevity.[30]

6. The growth of Jacob's family **in Egypt** and their slavery after Joseph's death (vv. 17–19). This, of course, prepares us for the next step in Stephen's argument — the treatment which Moses received at the hands of his people.

7:20–43 Stephen is showing with incisive boldness that the Jewish people were guilty on at least two previous occasions of rejecting saviors whom God had raised up to deliver them. His second proof is **Moses**.

Stephen had been charged with speaking blasphemous words against Moses (6:11). He proves that the nation of Israel is the guilty party — guilty of refusing this man of God's choice.

Stephen reviews the life of Moses, as follows:

1. Birth, early life, and education in Egypt (vv. 20–22). The phrase, **mighty in words**, may refer to his writings, since he disclaimed being eloquent (Ex. 4:10).

2. His first rejection by **his brethren** when he defended one of them against an **Egyptian** (vv. 23–28). Note verse 25! How it reminds us of Christ's rejection by His own!

3. His exile **in the land of Midian** (v. 29).

4. God's appearance **to him in** the burning **bush**, sending him back **to Egypt to deliver** his people (vv. 30–35).

5. He became the savior of the nation (v. 36).

6. His prophecy concerning the coming Messiah (v. 37). (**Like me** means "as He raised me.")

7. His role as law-giver to **the congregation in the wilderness** (v. 38).

8. Moses rejected a second time by the people, as they worshiped the golden **calf** (vv. 39–41). The idolatry of Israel is elaborated in verses 42 and 43. While professing **to offer . . . sacrifices** to the Lord, the people **took up the tabernacle of Moloch**, one of the most loathsome of all ancient forms of idolatry, and bowed to **Remphan**, a stellar deity. For this sin God warned that they would be carried off into Babylonian captivity. In verses 42 and 43 Stephen quotes from the Septuagint version of Amos 5:25–27. That is why the captivity is said to be **beyond Babylon** instead of "beyond Damascus." Both are, of course, true.

History repeats itself. In every generation we can find the same pattern. *People are the same.* When confronted with God's message, they do not understand (25). When urged to live at peace, they refuse to listen (27). When given a God-sent deliverer, they reject him (39). When rescued from an evil situation, they prefer useless idols to the merciful God (41). Such is human nature — rebellious, ungrateful, foolish. *God is the same.* The God who spoke to Moses was the same God who had spoken to his ancestors (32). This God hears when people are troubled (34). He comes to deliver (34). He leads His people from death to life (36). He surrenders to their own desires those who willfully reject Him (42). Such is our great God — merciful, powerful, holy. He is always the same, whatever happens (Mal. 3:6). For Stephen's hearers it was a warning not to trifle with God. It is also an assurance that every promise of God stands firm forever.[31]

7:44–46 Stephen had been charged with speaking against the temple. He replies by going back to the days when Israel had **the tabernacle** (tent) **of witness**

in the wilderness. It was during this same time that the people were also worshiping the host of heaven. When Joshua led the Israelites into the land of Canaan, and the heathen inhabitants were expelled, the tabernacle was brought into the land and continued until the days of David. The fathers had asked to find a dwelling for the God of Jacob and had thus found favor before God.

7:47–50 David's desire to build the temple was not granted, but Solomon built Him a house.

Although the temple was the dwelling place of God among His people, God was not confined to that building. Solomon stated this clearly when the temple was dedicated (1 Kgs. 8:27). Also Isaiah had warned the people that buildings are not what really count with God but rather the moral and spiritual condition of men's lives (Isa. 66:1, 2). He looks for a broken and contrite heart, for a man who trembles at His word.

7:51–53 The Jewish leaders had charged Stephen with speaking against the law. He now answers the accusation with a brief, finely worded denunciation.

It was *they* who were stiff-necked and uncircumcised in heart and ears. "He rebukes them, not as the Israel of God, but as stubborn and uncircumcised Gentiles in heart and ears." They were sons of their fathers in habitually resisting the Holy Spirit. Their fathers had persecuted the prophets who foretold the coming of Christ. Now they had betrayed and murdered this Just One. They were the people who had failed to keep the law — the very people to whom it was given by the direction of angels.

Nothing more needed to be said! Indeed, nothing more could be said! They had sought to put Stephen on the defensive. But he became the prosecutor and they the guilty defendants. His message was one of God's final words to the Jewish nation before the gospel started moving out to the Gentiles.

7:54–60 As soon as Stephen bore public testimony to seeing the heavens opened, the mob refused to listen to him further; they cried fiercely, charged upon him, dragged him outside the city walls and stoned him.

As if incidentally, the Spirit records the name of a young man who stood guard over the clothes of the perspiring executioners. The name was Saul. It is as if the Spirit would say to us, "Remember that name. You will hear it again!"

Stephen's death resembled that of our Lord:

1. He prayed, "Lord Jesus, receive my spirit" (v. 59). Jesus had prayed, "Father, into Your hands I commit My spirit" (Luke 23:46).

2. He prayed, "Lord, do not charge them with this sin" (v. 60). Jesus had prayed, "Father, forgive them, for they do not know what they do" (Luke 23:34).

Does it not suggest that through occupation with the Lord, Stephen had been "transformed into the same image from glory to glory, just as by the Spirit of the Lord" (2 Cor. 3:18)?

Then, having prayed, he fell asleep. When the word "sleep" is used in connection with death in the NT, it refers to the body, not the soul. The believer's soul goes to be with Christ at the time of death (2 Cor. 5:8); the *body* is pictured as sleeping.

Ordinarily the Jews were not allowed to carry out the death penalty; this was reserved for their Roman overlords (John 18:31b). But the Romans seem to have made an exception when the temple was threatened. Stephen had been accused of speaking against the temple, and though the charge was unfounded, he was executed by the Jews. The Lord Jesus had been accused of threatening to destroy the temple (Mark 14:58), but the testimony of the witnesses conflicted.

II. THE CHURCH IN JUDEA AND SAMARIA (8:1–9:31)

A. The Ministry of Philip in Samaria (8:1–25)

8:1 Again the Spirit of God introduces the name of Saul. Great strivings of soul were being born within him. Outwardly his reign of terror would continue, but his days as a foe of Christianity were numbered. Saul was consenting to Stephen's death, but in so doing he was paving the way for his own undoing as an arch-persecutor.

A new era begins with the words, "At that time". Stephen's death seemed to trigger a widespread assault **against the church**. Believers **were scattered throughout . . . Judea and Samaria**.

The Lord had instructed His followers to begin their witness in Jerusalem, but then to branch out to Judea, Samaria, and the end of the earth. Up to this time their witness had been confined entirely to **Jerusalem**. Perhaps they had been timid about branching out. Now they are forced to do it by persecution.

The apostles themselves remained in the city. As Kelly dryly observed, "Those who stayed would naturally be the most obnoxious of all."

From the human standpoint, it was a dark day for the believers. The life of a member of their fellowship had been laid down. They themselves were being chased like rabbits. But from the divine standpoint, it was not dark at all. A grain of wheat had been planted in the ground, and much fruit would inevitably result. The winds of affliction were scattering the seeds of the gospel to distant places, and who could estimate the extent of the harvest?

8:2 The **devout men** who buried Stephen are not identified. Perhaps they were Christians who had not yet been driven out of Jerusalem. Or perhaps they were pious Jews who saw something in the martyr which made them esteem him worthy of a decent burial.

8:3 Again the name of **Saul**! With unbounded energy he is harassing **the church**, **dragging** his hapless victims from their homes, and **committing them to prison**. If only he could forget Stephen — such poise — such unshakable conviction — the face of an angel! He must drown out the memory, and he seeks to do it by stepping up his attacks on Stephen's fellow-believers.

8:4–8 The dispersal of the Christians did not silence their testimony. **Everywhere** they **went** they carried the good news of salvation. **Philip**, the "deacon" of chapter six, headed north to **the city of Samaria**.[32] He not only proclaimed Christ but performed many **miracles**. **Unclean spirits** were driven out and the **paralyzed and lame were healed**. The people gave heed to the gospel, and, as might be expected, **great joy** resulted.

The primitive church obeyed the explicit commands of Jesus Christ:

It went out as Christ had gone (John 20:21; cf. Acts 8:1–4).

It sold its goods and gave to the poor (Luke 12:33; 18:22; cf. Acts 2:45; 4:34).

It left father, mother, houses, and lands to go everywhere preaching the Word (Matt. 10:37; cf. Acts 8:1–4).

It made disciples and taught them to work and obey (Matt. 28:18, 19; cf. 1 Thess. 1:6).

It took up its cross and followed Christ (Acts 4; 1 Thess. 2).

It rejoiced in tribulation and persecution (Matt. 5:11, 12; cf. Acts 16; 1 Thess. 1:6–8).

It left the dead to bury their dead and went and preached the gospel (Luke 9:59, 60).

It shook the dust from off its feet and moved on when men refused to hear (Luke 9:5; cf. Acts 13:51).

It healed, exorcised, raised the dead, and bore lasting fruit (Mark 16:18; Acts 3–16).[33]

8:9–11 Among the most notable of those who heard Philip was a sorcerer **called Simon**. He himself had **previously** made a big impression on **Samaria** by his amazing feats of **sorcery**. He pretended to be very important, and some of the people were actually convinced that he was **"the great power of God."**

8:12, 13 When many of the people **believed** the preaching of **Philip** and **were baptized**, **Simon also** professed to be a believer,[34] **was baptized**, and followed **Philip**, fascinated by **the miracles** he performed.

From what follows it seems that Simon had not been born again. He was a professor but not a possessor. Those who teach salvation by baptism are faced with a dilemma here. Simon had been baptized, but he was still in his sins.

Notice that **Philip preached** good news **concerning the kingdom of God and the name of Jesus Christ. The kingdom of God** is the sphere where the rule of God is acknowledged. At the present time, the King is absent. Instead of a literal, earthly kingdom, we have a spiritual, invisible kingdom in the lives of all who are loyal to Him. In the future the King will return to the earth to set up a literal kingdom with Jerusalem as His capital. In order to truly enter the kingdom, in any of its forms, a person must be born again. Faith in **the name of Jesus Christ** is the means of experiencing the new birth. This, then, was doubtless the gist of Philip's preaching.

8:14–17 **When** news **that Samaria had** avidly **received the word** reached **the apostles . . . at Jerusalem, they sent Peter and John to them**. By the time they arrived, the believers **had been baptized in the name of the Lord Jesus**, but they had not received **the Holy Spirit**. Obviously acting in accordance with divine guidance, the apostles **prayed** that these believers **might receive the Holy Spirit** and **laid** their **hands on them**. As soon as this was done, **they received the Holy Spirit**.

This immediately raises the question, "Why the difference between the order of events here and on the day of Pentecost?" At Pentecost the Jewish people:

1. Repented.
2. Were baptized.
3. Received the Holy Spirit.
   Here the Samaritans:
1. Believed.
2. Were baptized.
3. Had the apostles pray for them and lay their hands on them.
4. Received the Holy Spirit.

Of one thing we can be sure: they were all saved in the same way — by faith in the Lord Jesus Christ. He is the only Way of Salvation. However, during this transitional time, bridging Judaism and Christianity, God chose to act sovereignly in connection with various communities of believers. Jewish believers were asked to dissociate themselves from the nation of Israel by baptism before they received the Spirit. Now the Samaritans must have special prayer and the apostles' hands laid on them. But why?

Perhaps the best answer is that it was intended to give expression to the unity of the church, whether made up of Jews or Samaritans. There was a real danger that the church in Jerusalem might retain ideas of Jewish superiority, and that they might continue to have no dealings with their Samaritan brethren. To avoid the possibility of schism, or the thought of two churches (one Jewish and one Samaritan), God sent the apostles to lay their hands on the Samaritans. This expressed full fellowship with them as believers in the Lord Jesus. They were all members of one body, all one in Christ Jesus.

When verse 16 says that **they had only been baptized in** (or into) **the name of the Lord Jesus** (see also 10:48 and 19:5), this does not mean that it was different from being baptized "in the name of the Father and of the Son and of the Holy Spirit" (Matt. 28:19). "Luke is not recording a formula used," writes W. E. Vine, "but is simply stating an historical fact." Both expressions signify allegiance and identification, and all true believers gladly acknowledge their loyalty to a union with the Trinity and the Lord Jesus.

8:18–21 **Simon** the sorcerer was deeply impressed by the fact that **the Holy Spirit was given** when the apostles laid their **hands** on the Samaritans. He had no deep sense of the spiritual implications of this, but rather looked on it as a supernatural power which would serve him well in his trade. So he offered money to the apostles in an effort to buy the power.

Peter's answer indicates that **Simon** was not a truly converted man:

1. **"Your money perish with you."** No believer will ever *perish* (John 3:16).
2. **"You have neither part nor portion in this matter"**; in other words, he was not in the fellowship.
3. **"Your heart is not right in the sight of God."** This is a fitting description of an unsaved person.
4. **"You are poisoned by bitterness and bound by iniquity."** Could these words be true of a regenerate person?

8:22–24 Peter urged **Simon** to **repent** of his great sin, and **pray** that his wicked plan might be forgiven. Simon's reply was to ask Peter to serve as a mediator between God and himself. He was the forerunner of those who would rather go to a human mediator than to the Lord Himself. That there was no true repentance on Simon's part is indicated by the words, **"Pray to the Lord for me, that none of these things which you have spoken may come upon me."** He was not sorry for his sin, but only for the consequences which it might bring on him.

It is from this man, **Simon**, that we

get the modern word, "simony" — making a business out of that which is sacred. It includes the sale of indulgences and other supposed spiritual benefits, and all forms of commercialism in divine matters.

8:25 After Peter and John **had testified and preached the word of the Lord, they returned to Jerusalem**. But now that a beachhead had been established, they continued to preach **in many villages of the Samaritans**.

B. Philip and the Ethiopian Eunuch (8:26–40)

8:26 It was during this great spiritual awakening in Samaria that **an angel of the Lord** directed **Philip** to a new field of labor. He was to leave the place where many were being blessed, and minister to one man. An angel could direct **Philip** but could not do Philip's work of preaching the gospel. That privilege was given to men, not to angels.

In unquestioning obedience, **Philip** journeyed south from Samaria to **Jerusalem**, and then to one of the routes that led **to Gaza**.[35] It is not clear whether the words, **"This is desert"** refer to the route or to Gaza itself. However, the effect is the same: **Philip** left a place of habitation and spiritual fertility for a barren area.

8:27–29 Somewhere along the route he caught up with a caravan. In the main chariot was the treasurer of **Candace**[36] **the queen of the Ethiopians, a eunuch**[37] **of great authority**. (Ethiopia was the southern part of Egypt and the Sudan.) This man had apparently become a convert to Judaism, since he had been **to Jerusalem to worship** and was now returning home. As the chariot rolled along, **he was reading Isaiah the prophet**. With split-second timing, **the Spirit** directed **Philip** to **overtake this chariot**.

8:30, 31 **Philip** opens the conversation with a friendly question, **"Do you understand what you are reading?"** The eunuch readily admits his need of someone to guide him, and invites **Philip** to **sit with him** in the **chariot**. The utter lack of racial prejudice here is refreshing.

8:32, 33 How wonderful it was that the eunuch "happened" to be reading Isaiah 53, with its unsurpassed description of the suffering Messiah! Why did

Philip approach at that particular time in his reading?

The passage in Isaiah pictures One who was meek and **silent** before His enemies; One who was hurried away from **justice** and a fair trial; and One who had no hope of posterity because He was killed in the prime of manhood and while unmarried.

8:34, 35 **The eunuch** wondered whether Isaiah was speaking **of himself or of some other man**. This, of course, gave **Philip** the desired opportunity to tell how these Scriptures were perfectly fulfilled in the life and death of Jesus of Nazareth. No doubt while he was in Jerusalem the Ethiopian had heard reports about a man named **Jesus**, but these reports would, of course, have cast Him in an unfavorable light. Now **the eunuch** learns that **Jesus** of Nazareth is the suffering Servant of Jehovah, of whom Isaiah wrote.

8:36 It seems probable that Philip had explained to the Ethiopian the privilege of Christian baptism, identifying oneself with Christ in His death, burial, and resurrection. Now as they near a body of **water**, **the eunuch** signifies his desire to be **baptized**.

8:37 Verse 37 of the KJV and NKJV is omitted from most Greek manuscripts of the NT. Not that its teaching is at all inconsistent with the rest of Scripture; belief in **Jesus Christ** is certainly prerequisite to baptism. But the verse is simply not supported by the major NT documents.[38]

8:38 **The chariot** is stopped, and **Philip** baptizes **the eunuch**. That the baptism was by immersion is evident by the expressions, they **went down into the water** and they **came up out of the water**.[39]

One is impressed by the simplicity of the ceremony. Out on a desert route a believer baptized a new convert. The church was not present. None of the apostles was there. Doubtless only the retinue of servants in the caravan witnessed the baptism of their master; they would understand that he was now a follower of Jesus of Nazareth.

8:39 As soon as the baptism was over, **the Spirit of the Lord caught Philip away**. This suggests more than mere guidance to another location. Rather, it speaks of miraculous and sudden removal. Its purpose was **that the eunuch** would not become occupied with the human instrument of his conversion, but with the Lord Himself.

> May His beauty rest upon me,
> As I seek the lost to win,
> And may they forget the channel,
> Seeing only Him.
>   – Kate B. Wilkinson

The eunuch **went on his way rejoicing**. There is a joy that comes from obedience to the Lord that surpasses all other pleasurable emotions.

8:40 Philip, in the meantime, resumes his evangelistic ministry **at Azotus** (OT Ashdod), north of Gaza and west of Jerusalem, near the coast. From there he works his way north along the coast **to Caesarea**.

And what of the eunuch? There was no opportunity for what we call "follow-up work" by Philip. All the evangelist could do was to commit him to God and to the OT Scriptures. Yet with the power of the Holy Spirit this new disciple doubtless returned to Ethiopia[40] witnessing to all of the saving grace of the Lord Jesus Christ.

EXCURSUS ON BELIEVER'S BAPTISM

The baptism of the eunuch which we have just considered is one of many indications that Christian baptism was taught and practiced by the early church (2:38; 22:16). It was not the same as John's baptism, which was a baptism indicating repentance (13:24; 19:4). Rather, it was a public confession of identification with Christ.

It invariably followed conversion (2:41; 8:12; 18:8) and was for women as well as men (8:12) and Gentiles as well as Jews (10:48). Households are said to have been baptized (10:47, 48; 16:15; 16:33), but in at least two of these cases it is implied that all the members of the household had *believed*. It is *never* stated that infants were baptized.

Believers were baptized very soon after their conversion (8:36; 9:18; 16:33). Apparently it was on the basis of their profession of faith in Christ. No probationary period was required to manifest the reality of their profession. Of course,

the threat of persecution probably restrained people from making professions lightly.

That baptism did not have saving value is seen in the case of Simon (8:13). Even after professing faith and being baptized, he was "poisoned by bitterness and bound by iniquity" (8:23). His "heart" was "not right in the sight of God" (8:21).

As has been mentioned, the mode of baptism was immersion (8:38, 39) — "both Philip and the eunuch went down into the water . . . when they came up out of the water. . . ." Even many present-day advocates of sprinkling and pouring admit that immersion was the practice of the first century disciples.

Twice baptism seems to be linked with the forgiveness of sins. On the day of Pentecost Peter said, "Repent, and let every one of you be baptized in the name of Jesus Christ for the remission of sins . . ." (2:38). And later Ananias said to Saul, "Arise and be baptized, and wash away your sins, calling on the name of the Lord . . ." (22:16). In both instances the instructions were given to Jews; no Gentile was ever told to be baptized for the remission of sins. In believer's baptism a Jew publicly repudiated his connection with the nation that rejected and crucified its Messiah. The basis of his forgiveness was faith in the Lord Jesus. The purchase price of his forgiveness was the precious blood of the Lord. The way in which his forgiveness was administered was through water baptism, because his baptism publicly removed him from Jewish ground and put him on Christian ground.

The baptismal formula, "in the name of the Father and of the Son and of the Holy Spirit" (Matt. 28:19), does not appear in the Book of Acts. The Samaritans were baptized in the name of the Lord Jesus (8:16), and the same was true of John's disciples (19:5). However, this does not necessarily mean that the triune formula was not used. The phrase, "in the name of the Lord Jesus," may mean "by the authority of the Lord Jesus."

John's disciples were baptized twice — first with John's baptism unto repentance, then at the time of their conversion, with believer's baptism (19:3, 5).

This provides a precedent for the "rebaptism" of those who were christened or baptized before they were saved. ‡

C. The Conversion of Saul of Tarsus (9:1–31)

9:1, 2 Chapter 9 marks a distinct turning point in Acts. Up to now, Peter has held a position of prominence as he preached to the nation of Israel. From now on, the Apostle Paul will gradually become the foremost figure, and the gospel will increasingly go out to the Gentiles.

Saul of Tarsus was perhaps in his early thirties at this time. He was generally regarded by the rabbis as one of the most promising young men in Judaism. As to zeal, he outstripped all of his fellows.

As he watched the growth of the Christian faith, known as **the Way**,[41] he saw in it a threat to his own religion. Therefore, with seemingly unbounded vigor, he set out to destroy this pernicious sect. For instance, he had obtained official authorization from **the high priest** to search **Damascus** in Syria for disciples of Jesus to **bring them bound to Jerusalem** for trial and punishment.

9:3–6 His traveling party drew **near Damascus. Suddenly a** great **light shone around him from heaven,** causing Saul to fall **to the ground.** He **heard a voice saying to him, "Saul, Saul, why are you persecuting Me?"** When Saul inquired, **"Who are You, Lord?"** he was told, **"I am Jesus, whom you are persecuting."**

In order to appreciate Saul's emotions at this time, it is necessary to remember that he was convinced that **Jesus** of Nazareth was dead and buried in a Judean grave. Since the leader of the sect had been destroyed, all that was now necessary was to destroy his followers. Then the earth would be free of this scourge.

Now with crushing force, Saul learns that Jesus is not dead at all, but that He has been raised from the dead and has been glorified at the right hand of God in heaven! It was this sight of the glorified Savior that changed the entire direction of his life.

Saul also learned that day that when he had been persecuting the disciples of **Jesus**, he had been **persecuting** the Lord Himself. Pain inflicted on the members of the Body on earth was felt by the Head of the Body in heaven.

For Saul it was first doctrine, then duty. First, he was properly instructed as to the Person of Jesus. Then he was sent into Damascus where he would receive his marching orders.

9:7–9 The men who journeyed with him were in a thorough daze by this time. They had heard a sound from heaven, but not the articulate words which **Saul** had heard (22:9). They had not seen the Lord; only **Saul** had seen Him and had been called to apostleship at this time.

The proud Pharisee was now **led by the hand . . . into Damascus** where he remained **three days without sight.** During that time he **neither ate nor drank.**

9:10–14 One can picture the effect of the news on the Christians in **Damascus.** They knew that Saul had been on his way to capture them. They had prayed for divine intervention. Perhaps they had even dared to pray for Saul's conversion. Now they hear that the archenemy of the Faith has become a Christian. They can hardly believe their ears.

When the Lord instructed **Ananias,** one of the **Damascus** believers, to visit **Saul, Ananias** poured out all the forebodings of his heart concerning this man. But when assured that **Saul** was now **praying** instead of persecuting, **Ananias** went to **the house of Judas** on **Straight** Street.

9:15, 16 The Lord had wonderful plans for Saul: **". . . he is a chosen vessel of Mine to bear My name before Gentiles, kings, and the children of Israel. For I will show him how many things he must suffer for My name's sake."** Primarily Saul was to be the apostle to the **Gentiles**, and this commission would bring him before **kings**. But he would also preach to his countrymen according to the flesh, and here he would experience the keenest persecution.

9:17, 18 In a touching display of Christian grace and love, **Ananias** expresses full fellowship with the new convert by **laying his hands on him,** calling him **"Brother Saul,"** and explaining the purpose of his visit. It was that **Saul** might **receive** his **sight and** that he might **be filled with the Holy Spirit**.

It should be noted here that **the Holy Spirit** was given to **Saul** through the laying on of hands of a simple disciple. **Ananias** was what the commentators call a "layman." That the Lord should use one who was not an apostle should certainly be a rebuke to those who seek to confine spiritual prerogatives to the "clergy."

When a person is truly converted, certain things always happen. There are certain marks which show the reality of that conversion. This was true of Saul of Tarsus. What were these marks? Francis W. Dixon lists a few of them:

1. He met the Lord and heard His voice (Acts 9:4–6). He received a divine revelation, and only that could have convinced him and made him the humble inquirer and devoted follower that he became.
2. He was filled with a longing to obey the Lord and to do His will (Acts 9:6).
3. He began to pray (Acts 9:11).
4. He was baptized (Acts 9:18).
5. He united in fellowship with God's people (Acts 9:19).
6. He began to testify powerfully (Acts 9:20).
7. He grew in grace (Acts 9:22).

"LAY" MINISTRY

One of the most important lessons we can learn from Acts is that Christianity is a lay movement, and that the work of witnessing was not committed to a special class, such as priests or clergymen, but to all believers.

Harnack claimed that

when the church won its greatest victories in the early days in the Roman Empire, it did so not by teachers or preachers or apostles, but by informal missionaries.[42]

Dean Inge wrote:

Christianity began as a lay prophetic religion. . . . It is on the laity the future of Christianity depends. . . .[43]

Bryan Green says:

The future of Christianity and the evangelization of the world rest in the hands of ordinary men and women and not primarily in those of professional Christian ministers.[44]

Leighton Ford says:

A church which bottlenecks its specialists . . . to do its witnessing is living in violation of both the intention of its Head and the consistent pattern of the early Christians. . . .Evangelism was the task of the whole church, not just the "name characters."[45]

And finally, J. A. Stewart writes:

Each member of the local assembly went out to win souls for Christ by personal contact and then brought these newborn babes back into these local churches where they were indoctrinated and strengthened in the faith of the Redeemer. They, in turn, went out to do likewise.[46]

The simple fact is that in the apostolic church there was no such person as a clergyman or minister who presided over a local congregation. The normal local church consisted of saints, bishops, and deacons (Phil. 1:1). *The saints were all ministers*, in the NT sense. The bishops were the elders, overseers, or spiritual guides. The deacons were servants who carried on duties in connection with the finances of the local church, etc.

No one bishop or elder occupied a place as clergyman. There was a body of elders working together as shepherds of the assembly.

But someone may ask, "What about the apostles, prophets, evangelists, pastors, and teachers? Weren't they the clergymen of the early churches?" This is answered in Ephesians 4:12. These gifts were given to build up the saints in order that they (the saints) might carry on the ministry and, thus, build up the body of Christ. Their goal was not to settle themselves as permanent officials over a local congregation, but to work toward the day when the local church could carry on by itself. Then they could move on to establish and strengthen *other* assemblies.

According to church historians, the clerical system arose in the second century. It was not known in the Acts period. It has served as a hindrance to world evangelization and the expansion of the church, because it makes *too much* depend on *too few*.

Believers in the NT are not only ministers; they are priests as well. As holy priests, they have constant access by faith into the presence of God to worship

Him (1 Pet. 2:5). As royal priests, they are privileged to tell about the One who called them out of darkness into His marvelous light (1 Pet. 2:9). The priesthood of all believers does not mean that everyone is qualified to preach or teach publicly; it deals primarily with worship and witness. But it does mean that in the church there is no longer a special class of priests who have control of worship and service. ‡

9:19–25 The disciples in **Damascus** opened their hearts and homes to **Saul**. He soon made his way to **the synagogues**, proclaiming boldly that Jesus **is the Son of God**. Consternation resulted among his Jewish hearers. They had understood that he hated the name of Jesus. Now he was teaching that Jesus is God! How could it be?

How long he stayed **in Damascus** on this first visit we do not know. From Galatians 1:17 we do, however, learn that he left Damascus, went to Arabia for an unspecified length of time, then returned to Damascus. Where does the trip to Arabia fit into the record in Acts 9? Possibly between verses 21 and 22.

Many of God's most used servants have had an Arabian or wilderness experience before being sent out to preach.

In Arabia **Saul** had opportunity to meditate on the great events that had taken place in his life, and especially on the gospel of the grace of God, which had been committed to him. When he returned to **Damascus** (v. 22), he was able to confound **the Jews** in the synagogues, **proving that this Jesus is the** Messiah of Israel. This so infuriated them that they **plotted** against the life of this one who had once been their champion but who was now an "apostate," a "renegade," a "turncoat." **Saul** escaped by being lowered **by night . . . through** a hole in **the city wall in a large basket**. It was an ignominious exit, but **Saul** was now a broken man anyway, and broken men can endure reproach for Christ's sake that others would shun.

9:26–30 From the human standpoint, **Jerusalem** was the most dangerous place **Saul** could visit. However, assurance that one is in the will of God permits him to make proper allowance for his personal safety.

Whether this was Saul's first visit to **Jerusalem** as a Christian, the same one that took place three years after his conversion (Gal. 1:18), is debated. On his first visit to **Jerusalem** he met Peter and James, but none of the other apostles. Here, in verse 27, it says that **Barnabas . . . brought him to the apostles**. This could, of course, mean Peter and James, or it could mean all of the apostles. If the latter is intended, then this is a second visit to **Jerusalem**, not mentioned elsewhere.

At first **the disciples** in **Jerusalem were afraid** to receive **Saul**, doubting the sincerity of his profession as a believer. **Barnabas** proved true to his name as a *son of consolation* by befriending **Saul**, recounting his conversion, and telling of his fearless testimony for Christ **at Damascus**. The believers soon realized that **Saul** was genuine when they saw him preaching **boldly in the name of the Lord Jesus** in **Jerusalem**. He provoked the strongest opposition among **the Hellenists**. When **the brethren** saw that his life was in danger from these Jews, they escorted **Saul** to the seaport of **Caesarea**. From there he went to his home town of **Tarsus**, near the southeast coast of Asia Minor.

9:31 Then followed a breathing spell for **the churches** in Palestine. It was a time of consolidating the gains they had made, and of seeing the fellowship grow numerically and spiritually.

III. THE CHURCH TO THE END OF THE EARTH (9:32–28:31)

A. Peter's Preaching of the Gospel to the Gentiles (9:32–11:18)

9:32–34 As the narrative now reverts to **Peter**, we find him visiting believers in various parts of Judea. At length he comes to **Lydda** (Lod), northwest of Jerusalem, on the road to Joppa (modern Jaffa, or Yafo). There he finds a paralytic **who had been bedridden eight years**. Calling him by name, **Peter** announces that **Jesus the Christ** is his Healer. Aeneas **immediately** arises and carries his pallet. It is highly probable that Aeneas received spiritual life and physical healing at the same time.

9:35 The healed paralytic proved to

be a testimony for the Lord in the city of **Lydda and** in the entire coastal Plain of **Sharon**. Many **turned to the Lord** as a result.

9:36–38 **Joppa** was the major seaport of Palestine, located on the Mediterranean about thirty miles northwest of Jerusalem. Among the Christians there was a kindhearted lady named **Dorcas**,[47] who was well-known for making clothes for the poor. When **she** suddenly **died**, the disciples **sent** an urgent message to **Lydda**, asking **Peter** to come without **delay**.

9:39–41 Upon his arrival, he found **all the widows . . . weeping** pathetically as they showed the **garments which Dorcas had made** for them. He asked them to leave, then **knelt down and prayed**, and commanded **Tabitha** to **arise**. Immediately she was restored to life, and rejoined her Christian friends.

9:42 This miracle of resurrection **became** widely **known**, so that **many believed on the Lord**. However, comparing verse 42 with verse 35, it seems that more were converted through the healing of Aeneas than through the raising of Dorcas.

9:43 Peter **stayed many days in Joppa**, staying in the house of **Simon, a tanner**. The mention of Simon's trade here is significant. The Jews considered tanning a disreputable business. Constant contact with the bodies of dead animals caused ceremonial defilement. The fact that Peter lived with **Simon** showed he was no longer bound by this particular Jewish scruple.

It has often been pointed out that in three successive chapters we have the conversion of a descendant of one of Noah's sons. The Ethiopian eunuch (chap. 8) was undoubtedly of the line of Ham. Saul of Tarsus (chap. 9) was a descendant of Shem. Now here in chapter 10, in Cornelius, we see one of Japheth's posterity. It is a striking witness to the fact that the gospel is for all races and all cultures, and that in Christ all these natural distinctions are abolished. As Peter used the keys of the kingdom in opening the door of faith to the Jews in chapter 2, he is seen doing the same to the Gentiles in chapter 10.

10:1, 2 The chapter opens **in Caesarea**, about thirty miles north of Joppa. **Cornelius** was a Roman military officer. As **a centurion** he commanded about one hundred men. He was attached to **the Italian Regiment**. Even more remarkable than his military prominence was his piety. He was a **devout**, God-fearing **man, who gave alms generously** to impoverished Jewish **people, and prayed** consistently. Ryrie suggests he was probably "a proselyte of the gate; that is, he believed in the God of Judaism and His government, but had not yet taken any of the steps to become a full-fledged proselyte."[48]

Whether he was a saved man is open to question. Those who say he was refer to verse 2 and 35, where Peter says with obvious reference to **Cornelius**, that "whoever fears Him (God), and works righteousness is accepted by Him." Those who teach **Cornelius** was not saved point to 11:14, where the angel is quoted as promising him that Peter would tell him words whereby he might be saved.

Our view is that **Cornelius** is an example of a man who lived up to the light which God gave him. While this light was not sufficient to save him, God insured that he was given the additional light of the gospel. Before Peter's visit, he did not have the assurance of salvation, but he did feel a kinship with those who worshiped the true God.

10:3–8 At **about** 3:00 p.m. one day **Cornelius** had **a** clear **vision** in which **an angel of God** appeared to him and addressed him by name. Being a Gentile, he was not as aware of the ministry of angels as a Jew would be, and so he was afraid and mistook the angel for the Lord. The angel spoke reassuringly of God's appreciation of his **prayers** and **alms**, then told him to **send** south **to Joppa** for a man named **Simon Peter**, then **lodging with Simon, a tanner . . . by the sea**.[49] With unquestioning obedience, the centurion **sent** off **two of his household servants** and a military attaché who was also a God-fearing man.

10:9–14 **The next day**, at **about** noon, **Peter went up on** the flat roof of Simon's house in Joppa **to pray. He** was **hungry** at the time and would like to have eaten, but the meal was still being prepared down below. His hunger, of course, provided a fitting preparation for what was to follow. Falling **into a trance**, he **saw** a **sheet . . . let down** from **heaven** by its **four corners**, with **all kinds of four-footed animals . . . , birds**, and reptiles in it, clean and **unclean**. A **voice** from heaven directed the **hungry** apostle to **"Rise, . . . kill and eat!"** Remembering the Law of Moses which forbade a Jew to eat any **unclean** creature, **Peter** uttered the historic contradiction, **"Not so, Lord!"** Scroggie comments, "Whoever says 'not so' should never add 'Lord,' and whoever truly says 'Lord' will never say 'Not so.' "

10:15, 16   When Peter explained his past unbroken record in the matter of eating only kosher food, the **voice** from heaven said, **"What God has cleansed you must not call common." Three times** this dialogue took place, then the sheet returned to **heaven**.

It is clear that the vision had deeper significance than the mere matter of eating foods, clean and unclean. True, with the coming of the Christian faith, these regulations concerning foods were no longer in effect. But the real significance of the vision was this: God was about to open the door of faith to the Gentiles. As a Jew, Peter had always looked upon the Gentiles as unclean, as aliens, as strangers, as far off, as godless. But now God was going to do a new thing. Gentiles (represented by the unclean beasts and birds) were going to receive the Holy Spirit the same as the Jews (clean beasts and birds) had already received Him. National and religious distinctions were to be dissolved, and all true believers in the Lord Jesus would be on the same level in the Christian fellowship.

10:17–23a   While **Peter** was pondering **this vision** in his heart, the servants of **Cornelius** arrived at **the gate** and inquired for him. Directed by **the Spirit**, he went down from the housetop to greet them. When he learned the purpose of their visit, he **invited them in** and gave them accommodations for the night. The servants paid high tribute to their master as **"a just man, one who fears God and has a good reputation among all the nation of the Jews."**

10:23b–29   On the next day Peter set out for **Caesarea with** the three servants of Cornelius **and some brethren from Joppa**. They apparently journeyed all day, because it was on **the following day** that **they** reached **Caesarea**.

In anticipation of their arrival **Cornelius . . . had called together his relatives and close friends**. When **Peter** arrived, the centurion **fell down at his feet** as an act of reverence. The apostle refused such worship, protesting that he was only **a man** himself. It would be fitting if all self-appointed "successors" of **Peter** would imitate his humility by forbidding people to kneel before *them*!

Finding a crowd assembled inside the house, **Peter** explained that as a Jew he would not ordinarily have come into a Gentile house like this one, but that **God** had revealed to him that he should no longer think of the Gentiles as being untouchables. Then he asked **for what reason** they had **sent for** him.

10:30–33   Cornelius readily described the vision he had seen **four days** before when an angel assured him that his **prayer** had **been heard** and directed him to **send** for **Peter**. The hunger of the Gentile heart for the word of God is praiseworthy. He said, **"Now therefore, we are all present before God, to hear all the things commanded you by God."** Such an open and teachable spirit is sure to be rewarded with divine instruction.

10:34, 35   Peter prefaced his message with a frank admission. Up to now he had believed that God's favor was limited to the nation of Israel. Now he realized that **God** did not respect a man's person because of his nationality, but was interested in an honest, contrite heart, whether in a Jew or a Gentile. **"In every nation whoever fears Him and works righteousness is accepted by Him."**

There are two principal interpretations of verse 35:

1. Some think that if one truly repents and seeks after God, he is saved even if he has never heard about the Lord Jesus. The argument is that although the man himself might not know about Christ's substitutionary sacrifice, yet God knows about it and saves the man on the basis of that sacrifice. He reckons the value of the work

of Christ to the man whenever He finds true faith.

2. The other view is that even if a man fears God and works righteousness, he is not thereby saved. Salvation is only by faith in the Lord Jesus Christ. But when God finds a man who has lived up to the light he has received about the Lord, He makes sure that the man hears the gospel and thus has the opportunity to be saved.

We believe that the second view is the proper interpretation.

10:36–38 Peter next reminds his hearers that although the gospel message was sent to the Jews first, yet **Jesus Christ . . . is Lord of all** — Gentile as well as Jew. His audience must have heard the story of **Jesus of Nazareth**; it had begun in **Galilee**, at the time **John** was baptizing, and had spread **throughout all Judea**. This **Jesus**, **anointed** by the **Spirit**, had lived a life of selfless service for others, **doing good and healing all who were oppressed by the devil**.

10:39–41 The apostles were **witnesses** to the truth **of all** Jesus **did**. They traveled with Him in all Judea **and in Jerusalem**. In spite of His perfect life, men **killed** Him **by hanging** Him **on a** stake. **God raised** Him from among the dead **on the third day**, and He was seen by **witnesses chosen before by God**. As far as we know, the Lord Jesus was not seen by any unbelievers after His resurrection. But the apostles not only saw Him; they **ate and drank with Him**. This, of course, shows that the Savior's resurrection body was tangible, material, and physical.

10:42 In resurrection, the Lord commissioned the apostles to proclaim Him as **Judge of the living and the dead**. This agrees with many other Scriptures which teach that the Father has committed all judgment to the Son (John 5:22). This means, of course, that as Son of Man He will judge Jews and Gentiles alike.

10:43 But Peter does not linger on a note of judgment. Instead he introduces a grand statement of evangelical truth, explaining how the judgment can be avoided. As **all the prophets** of the OT had taught, **whoever believes** in the name of the Messiah **will receive remission of sins**. It is not an offer to Israel alone, but takes in all the world. Would you like to know the forgiveness of sins? Then believe in Him!

10:44–48 **While Peter was still speaking . . . , the Holy Spirit** was **poured out on the Gentiles**. They all spoke **with tongues**, praising **God**. This was a sign to those present that Cornelius and his household had indeed **received the Holy Spirit**. The Jewish-born visitors from Joppa **were astonished** to think that **Gentiles** could receive **the Holy Spirit** as such, without becoming Jewish proselytes. But **Peter** was not bound to the same extent by Jewish prejudices. He sensed immediately that God was making no distinction between Jew and Gentile, so he proposed that the household of Cornelius should **be baptized**.

Notice the expression, **who have received the Holy Spirit just as we have**. These Gentiles had been saved in the same way as the Jews — simple faith. There was no suggestion of law-keeping, circumcision, or any other ordinance or ritual.

Notice, too, the order of events in connection with the reception of the Holy Spirit by the Gentiles:

1. They **heard the word**, that is, they believed (v. 44).
2. They **received the Holy Spirit** (v. 44, 47).
3. They were **baptized** (v. 48).

This is the order of events that prevails for Jew and Gentile alike in this dispensation, when God is calling out of the nations a people for His Name.

It is not surprising that after this gracious work of God's Spirit in Caesarea, the believers prevailed on Peter **to stay** with them **a few days**.

11:1–3 Word quickly got back to **Judea** that Peter had preached to **the Gentiles** and that they had been saved. Therefore, **when Peter** returned **to Jerusalem**, he was challenged by **those of the circumcision** for eating with Gentiles. **The circumcision** here refers to Christians of Jewish birth who were still bound by their former ways of thinking. For instance, they believed that a Gentile must be circumcised in order to obtain full blessing from the Lord. They still thought it was wrong for Peter to eat with Gentiles.

11:4–14 In defending his action, **Peter** gave a simple recital of all that had happened — his **vision** of the **sheet let down from heaven**, the appearance of **an angel** to Cornelius, the arrival of the messengers from Cornelius, the Spirit's command to accompany them, and the pouring out of **the Holy Spirit** on the Gentiles. Since **God** had worked in so many definite and yet distinct ways, to resist or oppose would obviously have been to oppose the Lord.

In his message, **Peter** added several interesting details not given in the previous chapter:

1. He said that the **sheet . . . from heaven . . . came** right down to where he was (v. 5).
2. He spoke of observing it **intently** (v. 6).
3. Peter adds the detail that **six brethren** accompanied him from Joppa to Caesarea (v. 12).
4. In verse 14 we are informed that the angel promised Cornelius that Peter would **tell** him **words by which** he **and all** his **household** would be **saved**. This verse is one of the principal evidences that Cornelius was not a saved man before Peter's arrival.

11:15 According to Peter's account, **the Holy Spirit fell upon** the Gentiles **as** he **began to speak**. In Acts 10:44 it appears that he had already been speaking some time. Apparently he had begun to speak but was interrupted before he had proceeded very far.

11:16 When **the Holy Spirit** fell on the Gentiles, Peter thought immediately of Pentecost. Then his mind went back further to the Lord's promise that His disciples would **"be baptized with the Holy Spirit."** He realized that the promise had been fulfilled in part at Pentecost and was now being fulfilled again.

11:17 Then Peter faced the circumcision party with this question: **If therefore God** chose to pour out the Spirit on the Gentiles, **as** He had done previously on the Jews who **believed . . . , who was** Peter that he should **withstand God**?

11:18 It is to the credit of these Hebrew Christians that when they had heard Peter's account, they recognized the hand of **God** in it all and did a complete about-face. All their objections were gone. In their place was praise to **God** for granting **to the Gentiles repentance to life.**

B. The Planting of the Church at Antioch (11:19–30)

11:19 The narrative now goes back to the time of **the persecution** following the martyrdom of **Stephen**. In other words, the events described in the next verses took place *before* the conversion of Cornelius.

Those who were scattered after the persecution carried the gospel to:

1. **Phoenicia**, the narrow coastland along the northeast Mediterranean, and including the ports of Tyre and Sidon (modern Lebanon).
2. **Cyprus**, a large island in the northeast Mediterranean.
3. **Cyrene**, a port city on the north coast of Africa (modern Libya).

However, they preached the gospel **to no one but the Jews.**

11:20, 21 But there were certain of the believers **from Cyprus and Cyrene** who went **to Antioch** and there proclaimed the good news to **the Hellenists.**[50] Blessing accompanied their preaching **and a great number believed and turned to the Lord**. F. W. Grant says: "It is remarkable how officialism is discredited in all this. We do not know the name of a single person used in the work."

The introduction of Christianity to Antioch was an important step in the forward march of the church. Antioch was located on the river Orontes in Syria, north of Palestine. It was considered the third city of the Roman Empire, and has been dubbed "the Paris of the ancient world." From here, Paul and his companions later went forth on their missionary journeys, taking the good news to the Gentiles.

11:22–24 When **news** of great spiritual awakening reached **the church in Jerusalem**, it was decided to send warmhearted, kindly **Barnabas** to **Antioch**. This dear man saw at a glance that the Lord was working mightily among these

Gentiles, so he **encouraged them** to **continue with the Lord** with great determination. How good it was that this infant church should be visited by such **a good man, full of the Holy Spirit and of faith**! While he was there, **a great many people** came **to the Lord**. Also, unity with the church at Jerusalem was preserved.

11:25, 26 Then **Barnabas** remembered **Saul** of **Tarsus**! It was he who had introduced **Saul** to the apostles at Jerusalem. Then **Saul** had been whisked out of the city to rescue him from the plots of the Jews. Since then he had been in his home town, **Tarsus**. Anxious to encourage **Saul** in the ministry and to give the church in **Antioch** the benefit of his teaching, **Barnabas departed for Tarsus** and **brought** Saul **to Antioch**. For a **whole year** this splendid team worked with the church there, teaching **a great many people**.

It was **in Antioch** that **the disciples were first called Christians**. Doubtless it was a term of reproach at that time, but since then it has been welcomed by all who love the Savior.

J. A. Stewart comments:

> Saintly F. B. Meyer has said: "Antioch will ever be famous in Christian annals, because a number of unordained and unnamed disciples, fleeing from Jerusalem in the face of Saul's persecution, dared to preach the Gospel to Greeks and to gather the converts into a church in entire disregard of the initial rite of Judaism."
>
> If these believers had gone from a modern congregation in which the ministry was designated to the sole responsibility of one man, this triumphant period of the Church's history could never have been written. How tragic that in the average church the ministry gifts of the Holy Spirit lie dormant and latent, because the average believer has no opportunity to minister. *As long as every little group of believers has a paid pastor to take care of them, there is one thing certain, and that is, the world will never be evangelized.* Thank God for all the voluntary Sunday school superintendents, Sunday school and Bible class teachers and so-called laymen. If they all had to be paid for their services very few churches would be able to function financially.[51]

11:27–30 Although **Antioch** became the center from which the gospel went out to the *Gentiles*, it always maintained full and hearty fellowship with the church in **Jerusalem**, which was the center for *Jewish* evangelism. The following incident illustrates this fact.

Certain **prophets came from Jerusalem to Antioch** at about this time. These **prophets** were believers who had been gifted by the Holy Spirit to speak as mouthpieces of God. They received revelations from the Lord and delivered them to the people. **One of them, named Agabus**, predicted that **a great famine** would sweep over the inhabited earth. The **famine** did come **in the days of Claudius Caesar**. **The disciples** at **Antioch** promptly decided **to send relief to** their Christian **brethren dwelling in Judea**. This was certainly a touching testimony that the middle wall of partition between Jew and Gentile was tumbling down, and that ancient antagonisms were obliterated by the cross of Christ. The grace of God was manifest in these **disciples** who gave unanimously, spontaneously, and proportionately. They gave, **each according to his ability**. F. W. Grant sadly noted, "Today it seems to be 'every one a little of his superfluity, and the richest in proportion least of all.'"

The money was **sent to the elders by the hands of Barnabas and Saul**. This is the first mention of **elders** in connection with the church. The idea of **elders** was familiar to Jews, however, since there were elders in the synagogue. No information is given as to how these men in Jerusalem became **elders**. In the Gentile churches, **elders** were appointed by apostles or their representatives (14:23; Titus 1:5). The qualifications of elders are given in 1 Timothy 3:1–7 and Titus 1:6–9.

C. The Persecution by Herod and His Death (12:1–23)

12:1, 2 Satan's relentless attacks on the church continued. This time the persecution came from **Herod the king**. This was Herod Agrippa I, a grandson of Herod the Great. He was appointed king over Judea by the Roman Emperor, Claudius. An observer of the Law of Moses, he went to great lengths to please the Jews. It was in pursuance of this policy that **he** harassed **some from**

the church and **killed James the brother of John with the sword**.

It was this **James** who had been with Peter and John on the Mount of Transfiguration with our Lord; and it was his mother who had requested that her two sons might sit beside Christ in His kingdom.

This chapter affords an interesting study of God's ways in connection with His people. **James** was put to death by the enemy, yet Peter was miraculously delivered. Human reason would ask why such preference should be shown to Peter. Faith rests on the love and wisdom of God, knowing that:

> Ill that God blesses is our good,
>   And unblest good is ill,
> And all is right that seems most wrong,
>   If it be His good will.
>   – *Frederick W. Faber*

12:3, 4 **The Jews** responded so enthusiastically to the execution of James that Herod was encouraged to do the same with **Peter**. However, it was by then **the Days of Unleavened Bread**, and executions were not exactly appropriate during religious holidays. Also the Jews would be too busy with their ceremonies to appreciate the favor, so Herod ordered **Peter** to jail during the interim. The apostle was guarded by sixteen soldiers in **four squads** of four soldiers each.

12:5 **The church** in Jerusalem prayed earnestly for **Peter**, especially as the death of James was so vivid in their minds. G. C. Morgan comments, "That force of earnest, halting prayer was mightier than Herod, and mightier than hell."

12:6–11 **That night . . . when Herod** planned **to bring him out**, **Peter was sleeping** soundly, manacled **between two soldiers**. Someone has called his slumber a triumph of faith. He probably remembered the Lord's promise that he would live to be an old man (John 21:18), and so he knew that Herod could not kill him prematurely. Suddenly **an angel of the Lord** appeared, and the cell was flooded with **light**. Tapping **Peter on the side**, **the angel** ordered him to get up **quickly**.

Immediately the handcuffs **fell off**.

Then with short, crisp sentences, **the angel** told **Peter** to dress, to **tie on** his **sandals**, to throw his cloak around him, and to **follow**. Though in a daze, **Peter followed** the angel **past the first and second guard posts** of the prison. When **they came to the iron gate**, it **opened** automatically, as if by an electric eye. It was only after they had passed through **one street** of the city, and **the angel** had vanished, that **Peter** came **to himself** and realized it was not a dream, but **that the Lord** had miraculously **delivered** him **from the hand of Herod** and of the Jews.

12:12 When he stopped long enough to consider, Peter realized that the disciples would be **praying** at **the house of Mary, the mother of John . . . Mark**. It must have been an all-night prayer meeting, since Peter's escape from prison probably took place during the early morning hours.

12:13–15 **Peter knocked at the door of the gate** and waited. **A girl named Rhoda** (Gk., "Rose") **came to answer**, but was so excited when she heard **Peter** that she failed to **open the gate**! She **ran** back to announce the good news to those who were praying. They thought she was crazy, and did not hesitate to tell her so, **yet she kept insisting that** the apostle was really at **the gate**. They said, "It must be **his** guardian **angel**," but she stated positively that it was Peter.

These believers have often been chided for their unbelieving prayers; they were actually surprised when their prayers were answered. But any such criticism is probably influenced by our own nervous self–consciousness. Instead of chiding others, we should be greatly comforted that God answers such faithless prayers. We all tend to be unbelieving believers.

12:16, 17 **Peter**, in the meantime, had been standing on the doorstep, **knocking**. **When they** finally **opened the door** and he stepped in, all their doubts vanished, and they broke out into great expressions of joy. He quickly quieted them down, gave a brief account of his miraculous deliverance, asked them to convey the news **to James** (probably the son of Alphaeus) **and to the brethren, and** then **departed**. It is impossible to know where he went at this time.

12:18, 19 When morning came and **Peter** was missing, **the** hapless **soldiers** were thrown into a state of panic. For **Herod**, too, it was a traumatic experience to be so outwitted. Nothing that **the soldiers** could say sounded at all convincing. In fact, the lameness of their testimony probably infuriated the king all the more. So he ordered them to be executed. He then left for **Caesarea** to nurse his wounded pride.

12:20 For some unknown reason, **Herod had** become **very angry with the people of Tyre and Sidon**, two commercial ports on the Mediterranean. **The people** of these cities took advantage of his holiday in Caesarea to ingratiate themselves with him, because they depended on importing grain from Judea. So they befriended **Blastus the king's personal aide**, and through him requested restoration of diplomatic relations.

12:21–23 One day **Herod** came forth in all his **royal** finery to address the people. They shouted deliriously, **"The voice of a god and not of a man!"** He made no effort to refuse such divine honors, or to **give glory to God**. Therefore, **an angel of the Lord struck Him** with a fearful disease **and he died**. This was in A.D. 44.

Thus, the one who had executed James to please the Jews is himself slain at the hands of Him who is able to destroy both body and soul in hell. **Herod** reaped what he sowed.

D. Paul's First Missionary Journey: Galatia (12:24–14:28)†

12:24 Meanwhile, the gospel expands its outreach continually. God makes the wrath of man praise Him, and the remainder of wrath He restrains (Ps. 76:10). He makes the devices of the people of no effect, but the counsel of the Lord stands forever (Ps. 33;10, 11).

12:25 After they had **fulfilled** their mission in **Jerusalem** by delivering the gift from Antioch, **Barnabas and Saul returned** to Antioch,[52] taking **with them Mark**, who was a nephew of **Barnabas**, and later wrote the Second Gospel.

It is impossible to know whether **Barnabas and Saul** were in **Jerusalem** at the time of the death of James, the imprisonment of Peter, or the death of Herod.

Many Bible commentators feel that chapter 13 marks a distinct break in the Book of Acts. Some even go so far as to call it Volume II of Acts. The Apostle Paul has now definitely come into the place of prominence, and Antioch in Syria becomes the center from which the gospel radiates to the Gentiles.

13:1 A **church** had been formed in **Antioch**, as we learned in chapter 11. Instead of having one man designated as the minister or pastor, this assembly had a plurality of gifts. Specifically, there were at least five **prophets and teachers**. As mentioned previously, a prophet was a man specially gifted by the Holy Spirit to receive revelations directly from God and to preach them to others. In a real sense, the **prophets** were mouthpieces for the Lord, and could often foretell coming events. **Teachers** were men to whom the Holy Spirit had given the ability to expound or explain the Word of God to others in a simple and understandable manner.

The names of the **prophets and teachers** are given as follows:

1. **Barnabas**. We have already been introduced to this splendid servant of Christ and Paul's faithful co–worker. Here he is mentioned first, perhaps because he was the oldest in the faith, or in service for Christ.

2. **Simeon who was called Niger** (nye-jer). We judge from his name that he was a Jew by birth, perhaps from an African Jewish community. Or perhaps he adopted the name **Niger** (black or swarthy) for convenience in working with Gentiles. Of course, he may have been black, as the name would suggest. Nothing else is known of him.

3. **Lucius of Cyrene**. He was probably one of the men of **Cyrene** who came to **Antioch** first, preaching the Lord Jesus (11:20).

4. **Manaen** (same as the OT name Menahem). He is listed as one **brought up with Herod the tetrarch**. It is interesting to think of one who had lived in such close relationship with the wicked **Herod** Antipas being one of the earliest converts to the Christian faith. The title, **tetrarch**, indicates that **Herod** ruled over a fourth part of his father's kingdom.

†See p. xxviii.

5. **Saul**. Although mentioned last in this list, **Saul** was to become a living embodiment of the truth, "The last shall be first."

These five men illustrate that the early church was integrated and color-blind as far as man's skin is concerned. "A new measuring stick has been brought into being: it is not *who* you are but *whose*."

13:2 These prophets and teachers had gathered together for a time of prayer and fasting, probably with the entire church. From the context, it appears clear that the expression, **they ministered to the Lord**, means they spent time in prayer and intercession. By fasting, they denied the legitimate claims of the body so as to give themselves more undistractedly to spiritual exercises.

Why had they come together to pray? Is it unreasonable to believe that they convened this meeting because of a deep burden for the evangelization of the world? The record does not indicate that it was an all–night prayer meeting, but the implication certainly is that it was of more serious and prolonged nature than the usual "prayer meeting" of today.

As they prayed, **the Holy Spirit** definitely instructed them to **separate** . . . **Barnabas and Saul for the** specific **work** which He had in mind. This, incidentally, is a very definite proof of the personality of **the Holy Spirit**. If He were nothing but an influence, it would be inconceivable that such language as this could be used. How did **the Holy Spirit** convey this message to the prophets and teachers? Although no definite answer is given, it is likely that He spoke through one of these men who were prophets — either Simeon, Lucius, or Manaen.

Barnabas is mentioned first here, then **Saul**. But when they returned to Antioch, the order was reversed.

This verse is of tremendous practical importance in emphasizing the role of **the Holy Spirit** in the guidance of the early church, and the sensitivity of the disciples to His leading.

13:3 After the Holy Spirit had thus revealed His will, the men continued to fast and pray. Then the three (Simeon, Lucius, and Manaen) **laid hands on** Barnabas and Saul. This was not an official act of "ordination" such as is practiced in Christendom today where a church official confers ecclesiastical status on a subordinate. It was simply an expression of their fellowship with these two men in the work to which the Holy Spirit had called them. The idea of ordination as a rite which confers exclusive authority to administer the "sacraments" and perform other ecclesiastical duties is unknown in the NT. Barnhouse comments:

> A great error in our modern way of doing things is to expect one man to possess all the necessary gifts for leadership. Thus, a church may have several hundred members but only one pastor. He is supposed to be able to preach, comfort and so on. In fact, of the eight gifts mentioned in our text (Romans 12:6–8) seven are usually considered to be the functions of the ordained minister, while the eighth is the function of the congregation. And what one gift is left to the congregation? It is that of paying the bills. Something is out of order here.
>
> Someone may ask if I am suggesting that laymen should preach. Without question, when a layman has a grasp of the Scriptures he should exercise his gift and preach at every opportunity. The growth of laymen's movements is significant and is a step in the right direction — back to the New Testament way of doing things.[53]

It should be remembered that Barnabas and Saul had already been in the work of the Lord for about eight years before this time. They were not novices in the service of Christ. They had already experienced the "ordination of the Pierced Hands." Now their fellow-servants at Antioch were simply expressing their identification with them in this special commission to take the gospel to the Gentiles.

The words, **they sent them away**, are more literally, "they let them go" or "set them free" for the work.

13:4 With this verse begins what has commonly been known as Paul's First Missionary Journey. The record of this journey extends to 14:26. It was concerned chiefly with evangelizing Asia Minor. The Second Missionary Journey carried the gospel to Greece. The Third Missionary Journey included return visits to the churches of Asia Minor and Greece, but it was chiefly concerned with the Province of Asia and the city of Ephesus. Paul's missionary labors covered a period of about fifteen years.

(In tracing Paul's journeys, we shall indicate the places visited by printing the entire name in capital letters the first time it is mentioned on any particular journey.)

From Antioch in Syria the two intrepid servants of Christ first **went down to SELEUCIA** (pronounced sel-you'-shi-a), a seaport about sixteen miles from Antioch. From there **they sailed to** the island of **CYPRUS.**

13:5 After landing at **SALAMIS** (sal'-a-mis), on the east coast of Cyprus, they visited various **synagogues** and **preached the word** there. It was a custom in the synagogues for any Jewish man to be given the opportunity to read or expound the Scriptures. **John** Mark, at this time, was serving **as their assistant** (not "minister," as in the KJV). In going to the synagogue first, Barnabas and Saul were fulfilling the divine injunction that the gospel should go to the Jew first, then to the Gentiles.

13:6 From Salamis they worked their way across the entire length of **the island to PAPHOS** on the west coast. Salamis was the chief commercial city of the island. **Paphos** was the capital.

13:7, 8 There they met a Jewish **false prophet** and **sorcerer** named **Bar-Jesus** (meaning *Son of Jesus* or *of Joshua*). Somehow this **sorcerer** had become closely associated with **Sergius Paulus,** the Roman **proconsul**[54] or administrative officer of the island. The latter is described as **an intelligent man.** When **this man . . . called for Barnabas and Saul** to come to him so he could be instructed in **the word of God**, the **sorcerer** tried to interfere; he was probably satanically inspired to hinder the gospel.

In verse 8 his name is given as **Elymas**, meaning "wise man." It was, of course, a dreadful misnomer.

13:9, 10 Realizing that Sergius Paulus was an earnest seeker after truth, and that the sorcerer was an enemy of the truth, **Saul** openly rebuked him in unsparing terms. Lest anyone might suspect that **Saul** was speaking in the energy of the flesh, it is explicitly stated that he was **filled with the Holy Spirit** at the time. Fixing his eyes **intently** on the sorcerer, **Saul** accused him of being **full of all** guile **and all fraud.** Nor was

Saul deceived by the name Bar-Jesus; he tore away that mask and labeled Elymas as a **son of the devil.** The magician was an **enemy of all righteousness**, working ceaselessly to distort the truth of God.

13:11 Then, speaking with the special disciplinary authority vested in him as an apostle, Saul announced that Elymas would be stricken with blindness **for a time.** Because he had tried to keep others, such as the proconsul, in spiritual darkness, he himself would be punished with physical blindness. **Immediately a dark mist fell on him**, and he groped his way around, trying to find **someone** willing **to lead him by the hand.**

Elymas might be taken as a picture of the nation of Israel, not only unwilling to accept the Lord Jesus, but seeking to prevent others from doing so as well. As a result, Israel has been judicially blinded by God, but only **for a time.** Eventually a repentant remnant of the nation will turn to Jesus as Messiah and be converted.

13:12 The proconsul was obviously impressed by the miraculous stroke from God, but he was even more impressed by **the teaching** which had been given to him by Barnabas and Saul. He became a true believer in the Lord Jesus, the first trophy of grace on the first missionary journey.

Note that in this narrative (v. 9) Luke begins using Saul's Gentile name, Paul, rather than his Jewish name, Saul. The use of the name, *Paul*, signals the increasing outflow of the gospel to the Gentiles.

13:13 The fact that **Paul** has now taken the place of prominence is indicated by the words, **Paul and his party. From Paphos** they sailed northwest to **PERGA in PAMPHYLIA** (pam-fil'-i-a). **Pamphylia** was a Roman province on the southern coast of Asia Minor. **Perga** was its capital, and was located seven miles inland on the River Cestrus (Kestros).

It was when they reached **Perga** that **John** Mark left them and **returned to Jerusalem.** Maybe he didn't relish the thought of taking the gospel to the Gentiles. **Paul** considered his withdrawal such a defect in service that he refused to allow Mark to accompany him on the second journey. This caused a sharp cleavage between **Paul** and Barnabas, resulting in their taking separate paths as far as future Christian service was concerned (cf. 15:36–39). Eventually, Mark regained the confidence of the Apostle **Paul** (2 Tim. 4:11).

No further details are given as to the visit to **Perga.**

13:14, 15 The next stop was **ANTI-OCH in PISIDIA** (pi-sid'-i-a). This was approximately one hundred miles north of **Perga**. Once again the two heralds of the cross made their way to **the synagogue on the Sabbath**. After the Scriptures had been read, **the rulers of the synagogue** recognized these visitors as Jewish and invited them to speak, **if** they had **any word of exhortation for the people**. This liberty of proclaiming the truth of the gospel in synagogues was not to continue long.

13:16 Never being one to miss an opportunity to preach the gospel, **Paul stood up** and addressed the synagogue. His general plan of attack was to lay a foundation of Jewish history, then to bring his hearers up to the events connected with the life and ministry of Christ, then to proclaim the resurrection of Christ with considerable emphasis, announce remission of sins through the Savior, and warn of the peril of rejecting Him.

13:17 The message begins with God's choice of the nation of **Israel** as His earthly people. It moves quickly on to the time when they were **strangers in the land of Egypt**, and magnifies His grace in delivering them from the oppression of Pharaoh **with** His **uplifted arm.**

13:18 **Forty years** God **put up with** the **ways** of the people of Israel **in the wilderness**. The verb translated **put up with**, while it means just that by usage, is derived from a word that may suggest a more positive note, namely, taking care of somebody's needs. This the Lord certainly did for Israel in spite of all their complaining.

13:19–22 **The four hundred and fifty years** that Paul mentions is probably meant to go back to the time of the patriarchs and so would be inclusive of that period up to the judges.[55]

Following their entrance into Canaan, God **gave** the people **judges . . . until** the time of **Samuel the prophet**. When **they asked for a king** like the other nations, **God gave them Saul the son of Kish, a man of the tribe of Benjamin**; he ruled over them **for forty years**. Because of his disobedience, **Saul** was **removed** from the throne, and **David** was **raised up** to replace him. God paid high tribute to **David** as **a man after** His **own heart, who** would **do all** His **will**. Verse 22 combines quotations from Psalm 89:20 and 1 Samuel 13:14.

13:23 From the subject of David, Paul made an easy and swift transition to **Jesus**, David's **seed**. As someone has well said, "All roads in Paul's preaching led to Christ." It is perhaps difficult for us to appreciate the courage involved in announcing to the people of **Israel** that **Jesus** was a **Savior** whom **God** according to promise had brought to them. This was not exactly the light in which they had been accustomed to view **Jesus**!

13:24 After this brief introduction, Paul went back to the ministry of **John** the Baptist. Prior to Christ's **coming** (that is His public ministry), **John** had **preached . . . the baptism of repentance to all the people of Israel**. This means he had announced the **coming** of the Messiah, and told **the people** to repent in preparation for that **coming**. They were to signify their **repentance** by being baptized in the Jordan River.

13:25 Not for one minute did **John** permit the suggestion that he might be the promised Messiah. Up to the time when he **was finishing his** ministry, he kept insisting he was **not** the **One** of whom the prophets had spoken. In fact, he was **not worthy to loose** the **sandals** of the **One** whose coming he announced.

13:26 Addressing his audience as **brethren** and **sons of the family of Abraham**, Paul reminded them that **the word of this salvation** was **sent** first to the nation of Israel. It was to the lost sheep of the house of Israel that Jesus came. It was to them that the disciples were instructed to first preach the message.

13:27, 28 But the people **in Jerusalem, and their rulers** did not recognize Jesus as the long-sought Messiah. They did not realize He was the One of whom **the Prophets** had written. When they heard predictions concerning the Messiah from the Scriptures each **Sabbath**, they did not link them with Jesus of Nazareth. Instead, they themselves were the means of fulfilling those very Scriptures by **condemning Him. And though they found no cause of death in Him**, they turned Him over to **Pilate** to **be put to death**.

13:29 In the first part of the verse, **they** refers to the Jewish people who fulfilled the Scriptures by rejecting the Messiah. In the latter part of the verse, **they** refers to Joseph of Arimathea and Nicodemus, who lovingly buried the body of the Lord Jesus.

13:30, 31 The fact that Jesus rose **from the dead** was well attested. **Those who came up with** Jesus **from Galilee to Jerusalem** were still alive, and their witness could not be denied.

13:32–33 The apostle next announced that **the promise** of the Messiah **which was made to the fathers** in the OT had been **fulfilled** in Jesus. It was **fulfilled** first in His birth in Bethlehem. Paul saw the birth of Christ as a fulfillment of Psalm 2:7, where God says, **"You are My Son, today I have begotten You."** This verse does not mean that Christ began to be the Son of God when He was born in Bethlehem. He was God's Son from all eternity, but He was manifested to the world as the Son of God through His Incarnation. Psalm 2:7 should not be used to deny the eternal Sonship of Christ.

13:34 The resurrection of the Lord Jesus comes into view in verse 34. God **raised Him from the dead, no more to return to corruption**. Paul then quoted Isaiah 55:3: **"I will give you the sure mercies of David."** This quotation presents a difficulty to the average reader. What connection can there possibly be between this verse in Isaiah and the resurrection of Christ? How is the resurrection of the Savior linked with God's covenant with **David**?

God promised **David** an everlasting throne and kingdom, and a seed to sit upon that throne forever. In the meantime **David** had died, and his body had returned to dust. The kingdom had continued for some years after David, but then for over four hundred years Israel had been without a king. The line of **David** continued down through the

years to Jesus of Nazareth. He inherited legal right to the throne of **David** through Joseph. Joseph was His legal father, though not His real father. The Lord Jesus was a lineal descendant of **David** through Mary.

Paul is emphasizing that the **sure** blessings promised to **David** find their fulfillment in Christ. He is the seed of **David** who will yet sit on the throne of **David**. Since He has risen **from the dead**, and lives in the power of an endless life, the eternal aspects of God's covenant with **David** are made certain in Christ.

13:35 This is further emphasized in verse 35, where the apostle quotes Psalm 16:10, **"You will not allow Your Holy One to see corruption."** In other words, since the Lord Jesus has risen from the dead, death has no more power over Him. He will never die again, nor will His body ever **see corruption**.

13:36, 37 Although **David** uttered the words of Psalm 16:10, he could not have been speaking about himself. **After he had served his own generation by the will of God**, he died, **was buried**, and his body returned to dust. But the Lord Jesus was **raised** from the dead the third day, before his body could experience **corruption**.

13:38 On the basis of the work of Christ, of which His resurrection was the divine seal of approval, Paul was now able to announce remission **of sins** as a present reality. Notice his words: **"Through this Man is preached to you the forgiveness of sins."**

13:39 But there was more to it than that. Paul could also now announce full and free justification from all things. This was something **the law of Moses** could never offer.

Justification is the act of God by which He reckons or declares to be righteous those ungodly sinners who receive His Son as Lord and Savior. It is a legal act which takes place in the mind of God, and by which the sinner is cleared of every charge against him. God can righteously acquit the guilty sinner, because the penalty for his sins has been fully met by the substitutionary work of the Lord Jesus Christ on the cross.

On first reading, it might appear that **the law of Moses** could justify from some things, but through Christ a person can receive justification from many other things. But that is not the teaching at all. **The law** could never justify anyone; it could only condemn. What Paul is saying here is that through faith in Christ a man can **be justified from** every charge of guilt that might be brought against him — a clearance that could never be obtained under **the law of Moses.**

13:40, 41 The apostle then closes his message with a solemn warning to those who might be tempted to refuse God's great offer of present salvation. He quotes from Habakkuk 1:5 (and perhaps segments of Isa. 29:14 and Prov. 1:24–31), where God warned those **despisers** of His word that He would bring wrath upon them of such magnitude that they wouldn't even **believe** it if He told them in advance. In Paul's day this might have applied to the destruction of Jerusalem in A.D. 70, but it would also include God's eternal judgment of those who reject His Son.

13:42, 43 When the service in **the synagogue** was over, **many of the Jews and devout** converts to Judaism **followed Paul and Barnabas** with deepest interest. These two servants of the Lord gave them a hearty word of encouragement **to continue in the grace of God**.

13:44 One week later Paul and Barnabas returned to the synagogue to continue where they had left off. **Almost the whole city** gathered **to hear the word of God**. The ministry of these two devoted preachers had made a deep impression on many of the people.

13:45 However, the popularity of this "alien message" **filled the Jews with envy** and rage. They openly contradicted Paul's message and used strong, intemperate language against him.

13:46, 47 **Paul and Barnabas** were not easily intimidated. They explained that they were under obligation to declare the message first of all to the Jewish people. However, since they had rejected the message, and had thus condemned themselves as **unworthy of everlasting life**, the preachers announced they were turning **to the Gentiles** with the gospel. If any authorization were needed for such a break with Jewish tradition, then the words of Isaiah

49:6 would do. Actually, in this verse God is speaking to the Messiah when He says, **"I have set you as a light to the Gentiles, that you should be for salvation to the ends of the earth."** But the Spirit of God permits the servants of the Messiah to apply these words to themselves, since they were His instruments in bringing **light** and **salvation** to the Gentile nations.

13:48 If this announcement of salvation for **the Gentiles** infuriated the Jews, it caused great rejoicing among **the Gentiles** who were present. **They glorified the word of the Lord** which they had heard. All who were **appointed to eternal life believed**. This verse is a simple statement of the sovereign election of God. It should be taken at its face value and believed. The Bible teaches definitely that God chose some before the foundation of the world to be in Christ. It teaches with equal emphasis that man is a free moral agent and that if he will accept Jesus Christ as Lord and Savior, he will be saved. Divine election and human responsibility are both scriptural truths, and neither should be emphasized at the expense of the other. While there seems to be a conflict between the two, this conflict exists only in the human mind, and not in the mind of God.

Men are damned by their own choice and not by any act of God. If all mankind received what is its just due, then all would be lost. But God in grace stoops down and saves some. Does He have a right to do this? Of course He does. The doctrine of the sovereign election of God is a teaching that gives God His proper place as the Ruler of the universe who can do as He chooses and who will never choose to do anything unrighteous or unkind. Many of our difficulties with this subject would be solved if we would remember the words of Erdman:

> The sovereignty of God is absolute; yet it is never exercised in condemning men who ought to be saved, but rather has resulted in the salvation of men who deserved to be lost.[56]

13:49, 50 In spite of the opposition of the Jews, **the word of the Lord was being spread throughout all the sur-**

rounding **region**. This further aroused the opposition party to hinder and obstruct. **The Jews stirred up** some **devout . . . women** who had become converts to Judaism and were **prominent** in the community to agitate against the missionaries. Also they used **the chief men of the city** to further their wicked purposes. Such a storm of **persecution** was **stirred up** that **Paul and Barnabas** were forcibly evicted from the area.

13:51, 52 In accordance with the instructions of the Lord (Luke 9:5; 10:11), **they shook off the dust from their feet** and moved on **to ICONIUM**. However, the incident was not interpreted by the Christians as a defeat or a retreat, for we read that they **were filled with joy and with the Holy Spirit**. Iconium, located east and south of Antioch in Asia Minor, today is called Konya.

14:1, 2 In **Iconium**, as in other places where there was a **synagogue**, Paul and Barnabas were permitted to preach, in accordance with the custom prevailing among the Jews at that time. The Spirit of God accompanied the word with such power that a **great** number of **Jews and** Gentile proselytes accepted the Lord Jesus. This aroused the ire of those **Jews** who refused to obey the gospel, and they in turn **stirred up the Gentiles . . . against the brethren**. In the Book of Acts the unbelieving Jews were the instigators of much of the persecution of the apostles, though they themselves did not necessarily administer the punishment. They were masters at persuading the *Gentiles* to carry out their wicked purposes.

14:3 Although they knew trouble was brewing, the preachers continued to speak **boldly in** the name of **the Lord**, who confirmed the divine nature of the message by empowering them to perform **signs and wonders**. **Signs and wonders** are two different words for miracles. The word "sign" simply means that the miracle conveys a lesson, whereas the word "wonder" suggests that the miracle creates a sense of awe.

14:4–7 As tension built up in the city, sides were naturally formed. Some **sided with the Jews, and** some **with the apostles**. Finally the unbelieving **Gentiles and Jews** made a determined rush

to assault **the apostles**.[57] To escape stoning, they fled **to LYSTRA** (lis'-tra) **and DERBE**, both **cities of LYCAONIA** (lye-kay-own'-ia), a district in the center of Asia Minor. With no lessening of ardor, they continued **preaching the gospel** in that entire region.

When Paul and Barnabas were threatened with stoning, **they fled** to **Lycaonia**. At other times in their missionary labors, they seemed to remain in a place in spite of danger. Why did they escape at some junctures and stand their ground at others? There does not seem to be any neat explanation. The great controlling principle in Acts is the guidance of the Holy Spirit. These men lived in close, intimate communion with the Lord. Abiding in Him, they received marvelous communications of the divine mind and will. To them, this was the important thing, rather than a well-arranged set of rules of conduct.

14:8, 9 In **Lystra** the missionaries came in touch with a man who had been **a cripple** from birth. As he listened to **Paul speaking**, he evidenced an unusual interest. **Paul** somehow realized that this man **had faith to be healed**. Although we are not told how **Paul** knew this, we do believe that a true evangelist is given the ability to discern the state of souls with whom he deals. He is able to tell whether they are only mildly curious, or whether they are in actual soul trouble because of conviction of sin.

14:10–12 As soon as **Paul** commanded the man to get **up on** his **feet, . . . he leaped and walked**. Since the miracle had been performed openly, and since Paul had undoubtedly attracted considerable attention by speaking **with a loud voice**, **the people** were greatly impressed. In fact a popular movement began with the purpose of worshiping **Barnabas** as **Zeus**, and **Paul** as **Hermes**.[58] **The people** actually believed that their **gods** had paid them a visit in the person of the two missionaries. For some reason not stated, they looked on **Barnabas** as being the chief god. Because **Paul** had done the speaking, they designated him as **Hermes**, the messenger of **Zeus**.

14:13 Even **the priest of Zeus** became convinced that a divine visitation had taken place; he rushed out of the temple that **was** at the gateway **of their city** with **oxen and garlands** for a great sacrifice. This entire movement was a more subtle form of danger to the Christian faith than all the other forms of opposition recorded. For a successful Christian worker a greater peril than persecution is the tendency for people to center their spiritual attention, not on Christ, but on His servant.

14:14, 15a At first **Barnabas and Paul** did not realize what the crowd was up to, because they didn't understand the Lycaonian vernacular. As soon as it became clear to the missionaries that the people were about to worship them as gods, **they tore their clothes** as a public expression of protest and sorrow. Then they **ran in among the multitude**, and with impassioned words they warned them against such folly. Instead of being gods, they were **men with the same nature as** the Lycaonians. Their object was simply to bring the good news that the people **should turn from** lifeless idols **to the living God**.

14:15b–17 It is noticeable that Paul and Barnabas did not quote the OT to these Gentiles, as they did to the Jews. Rather, they began with the story of creation, a subject of immediate interest to Gentile peoples in all countries and in all ages. The missionaries explained that **in bygone generations** God **allowed all nations to walk in their own ways**. Even then, however, they had evidence of the existence of God in creation and in providence. It was **He** who lovingly provided **rain . . . and fruitful seasons** for them, **filling** their **hearts with food and gladness**. This latter expression is a figurative way of saying that in providing **food** for their bodily means, **God** filled their **hearts with** the **gladness** that comes from the enjoyment of **food.**

14:18 The message had its desired result. The people reluctantly desisted from their intention of **sacrificing to** these servants of the Lord.

14:19, 20 Jews from Pisidian **Antioch and Iconium** caught up with **Paul** and Barnabas in Lystra. They succeeded in turning the Gentile populace against the missionaries. The same crowd that wanted to reverence them as gods now **stoned Paul and dragged him out of the** city, **supposing** that they had killed him.

Kelly's comments on this section are most apropos:

> And why? That very refusal of homage, which the Lystrans were ready to pay, is most offensive to man, and disposes him to believe the most odious misrepresentations of those he was about to worship. Men exalt themselves by human adoration; and to be balked of it soon turns to the hatred and perhaps death of those who seek the honour of the only God. So it was here. Instead of changing their minds like the Maltese (who from a murderer regarded Paul as a god, Acts 28:6), they listen to Jewish calumny though ordinarily despised, and stone as a false prophet him to whom they had been so lately wishing to sacrifice, leaving him dragged without the city as a dead man.[59]

Was Paul actually **dead** as a result of the stoning? If this is the incident referred to in 2 Corinthians 12:2, he himself did not know. The best we can say is that his restoration was miraculous. As **the disciples gathered around him, he rose up and went** back **into the city** with them. **The next day he departed with Barnabas to DERBE**.

14:21 Considerations of personal safety were not uppermost in the minds of the missionaries. This is seen in the fact that **when they had preached the gospel** at Derbe, **they returned to LYSTRA**, the scene of Paul's stoning. This illustrates what has been called "the power of comeback and quick recovery."

Although Timothy is not mentioned here, he may have been saved at this time through the preaching of Paul. When the apostle next visited **Lystra**, Timothy was already a disciple, and was highly regarded by the brethren (Acts 16:1, 2). However, the fact that Paul later spoke of him as his true child in the faith (1 Tim. 1:2) does not *necessarily* mean that Paul had won him to Christ. He may have been a "true child" by following the example of Paul's life and service.

When their work at **Lystra** was completed, the missionaries revisited **ICONIUM** and PISIDIAN **ANTIOCH**, where churches had already been established. Their purpose at this time was what we call "follow-up work." They were never satisfied merely to preach the gospel and see souls won to the Savior. For them, this was only the beginning. They then sought to build up the believers in their most holy faith, especially by teaching them the truth of the church and its importance in God's program.

Erdman points out:

A proper missionary program has as its aim the establishing on the field of self-governing, self-sustaining, self-propagating churches. This was ever the purpose and the practice of Paul.[60]

14:22 The exact nature of their follow-up work was **strengthening the souls of the disciples** and establishing the Christians **in the faith** by instructing them from the word of God. Paul described the process in Colossians 1:28, 29: "We warn everyone we meet, and we teach everyone we can, all that we know about him, so that, if possible, we may bring every man up to his full maturity in Christ Jesus. This is what I am working at all the time, with all the strength that God gives me" (JBP).

Second, they exhorted **them to continue in the faith**, an exhortation especially timely in view of the widespread persecution then prevalent. With this exhortation went a reminder that **we must through many tribulations enter the kingdom of God**. This refers to **the kingdom of God** in its future aspect, when believers will share Christ's glory. A person enters **the kingdom of God** in the first place through the new birth. Persecutions and **tribulations** do not have any saving value. However, those who **enter the kingdom of God** by faith at the present time are promised that the pathway to future glory is filled with **tribulations**. "If indeed we suffer with Him, that we may also be glorified together" (Rom. 8:17b).

14:23 At this time, the missionaries also **appointed elders in every church**. In this connection, several observations should be made:

1. New Testament elders (presbyters) were godly, mature men who exercised spiritual leadership in the local church. They are also spoken of as bishops and overseers.

2. In the Book of Acts, elders were not appointed when a church was first founded. Rather, it was when the apostle *revisited* the churches that this was done. In other words, during the intervening time there was opportunity for those who had been made elders by the Holy Spirit to become manifest.

3. Elders were appointed by the apostles and by their delegates. At this time the NT was not yet written to give explicit instructions concerning the qualifications of elders. The apostles knew what these qualifications were, however, and they were able to single out the men who met the scriptural requirements.

4. We do not have apostles today to appoint elders. However, we do have the qualifications of elders in 1 Timothy 3 and Titus 1. Therefore each local assembly should be able to recognize those men in it who meet God's requirements as undershepherds of the sheep.

After Paul and Barnabas had **prayed with fasting, they commended** the believers **to the Lord**. It seems extraordinary to us that assemblies could be started in such a short time, that they should receive such brief periods of instruction from the missionaries, and yet that they should go on brightly for the Lord, functioning as autonomous churches. The answer ultimately lies in the mighty power of the Holy Spirit of God. However, the power was manifest in the lives of men like Paul and Barnabas. Everywhere they went they exerted a mighty influence for God. People detected reality in their lives. Their public preaching was backed up by the example of their own lives, and the influence of this twofold testimony was incalculable.

Verses 21 to 23 give the apostolic pattern — preaching the gospel, teaching the converts, and establishing and strengthening churches.

14:24–26 After they had **passed through** the district of **Pisidia, they** traveled south **to PAMPHYLIA**. There they revisited **PERGA**, then **they went down to** the seaport city of **ATTALIA** where they boarded a ship and **sailed to ANTIOCH** in SYRIA. This brought them to the end of their first missionary journey. It was from **Antioch** that **they had been**

commended to the grace of God for the work which they had just completed.

14:27 What a joyful time it must have been when **they gathered the church** at Antioch **together** to hear an account of the missionary labors of these two great men of God. With becoming Christian modesty, **they reported all that God had done with them, and that He had opened the door of faith to the Gentiles**. It was not what they had done for **God**, but what **He** had been pleased to accomplish through them.

14:28 They stayed in Antioch **a long time with the disciples**. Estimates vary between one and two years.

MISSIONARY STRATEGY

It is thrilling to see how a small group of nondescript disciples living in an obscure corner of the world were imbued with a glorious vision for the evangelization of the world and how they carried it out. Each one felt directly involved in this task and gave himself or herself to it without reserve.

Much of the evangelism was carried on by local believers in connection with their everyday duties. They "gossiped" the gospel in their own neighborhoods.

In addition, the apostles and others traveled from country to country, preaching the gospel and planting churches. They went out by twos or in larger companies. Sometimes a younger man went out with an older; for instance, Timothy with Paul.

Basically there were two methods — personal evangelism and mass evangelism. In connection with the latter, it is interesting to notice that most of the preaching was impromptu, and arose from some local situation or crisis.

Nearly all the preachings that took place as recorded there (in Acts) were under circumstances which precluded any possibility of the preacher preparing his discourse; every one of these occasions was unexpected.[61]

As E. M. Bounds has said, their preaching was not the performance of an hour but rather the overflow of a life.

The apostles and their associates were guided by the Holy Spirit, but this guidance was often confirmed by their local church. Thus we read that the prophets and teachers at Antioch laid their hands on Barnabas and Paul and sent them off on the First Missionary Journey (13:2). Again we read that Timothy had the confidence of the brethren at Lystra and Iconium before he set out with Paul (16:2). And Paul and Silas were recommended to the grace of God by the church at Antioch prior to the Second Missionary Journey (15:40).

It is commonly taught that their geographical strategy was to go into large cities and plant churches so that those churches would then evangelize the surrounding territory. This is perhaps an oversimplification. Basically their strategy was to follow the guidance of the Holy Spirit, whether to a large city or a small one. The Holy Spirit led Philip from revival in Samaria to a single man on the road to Gaza (8:26–40). And He led Paul to Berea (17:10), which Cicero called an "out-of-the-way city." Frankly, we do not see a fixed, inflexible geographical strategy in the Book of Acts. Rather we see the sovereign Spirit moving in accordance with His own will.

Local churches were established wherever people responded to the gospel. These assemblies gave permanence and stability to the work. They were self-governing, self-financing, and self-propagating. The apostles revisited the congregations to strengthen and encourage the believers (14:21, 22; 15:41; 20:1, 2) and to appoint elders (14:23).

In their missionary travels the apostles and their associates were sometimes self-supporting (18:3; 20:34); sometimes they were supported by gifts from churches and individuals (Phil. 4:10, 15-18). Paul worked to provide not only for himself but for those who were with him (20:34).

Though they were *commended* to the grace of God by their local church, and *supported* by local churches, yet they were not *controlled* by local churches. They were the Lord's free agents in declaring all the counsel of God and in holding back nothing that was profitable (20:20).

At the conclusion of their missionary journeys, they returned to their home church and gave a report of how the Lord had worked through them (14:26-28; 18:22, 23). This is a good pattern for all missionaries to follow in every age of the church.‡

E. The Council at Jerusalem (15:1–35)

15:1 The dispute which arose over circumcision in the church at Antioch is also described in Galatians 2:1–10. Taking the two accounts together, we get the following picture: **Certain** false brethren **from** the church in **Jerusalem** traveled to Antioch and began preaching in the assembly there. The substance of their message was that Gentiles must be **circumcised** in order to **be saved**. It was not enough that they should believe on the Lord Jesus Christ; they must also put themselves under the Law **of Moses**. This, of course, was a frontal attack on the gospel of the grace of God. The true gospel of grace teaches that Christ finished the work necessary for salvation on the cross. All a sinner needs to do is receive Him by faith. The moment human merit or works are introduced, then it is no longer of grace. Under grace, all depends on God and not on men. If conditions are attached, then it is no longer a gift but a debt. And salvation *is* a gift; it is not earned or merited.

15:2, 3 **Paul and Barnabas** vigorously opposed these Judaizers, knowing that they had come to rob the Gentile believers of their liberty in Christ Jesus.

Here in Acts 15 we learn that the brethren in Antioch decided to send **Paul and Barnabas and certain others . . . to Jerusalem, to the apostles and elders** there. In Galatians 2:2 Paul says that he went to Jerusalem by revelation. There is no contradiction, of course. The Spirit of God revealed to Paul that he should go, and also revealed to the church in Antioch that the brethren should send him. En route **to Jerusalem** the group stopped at various points in **Phoenicia and Samaria**, giving an account of **the conversion of the Gentiles**, and causing **great joy** wherever the story was told.

15:4 **When** he first arrived in **Jerusalem**, Paul went to **the apostles and the elders** privately and gave them a full account of the gospel which he had been preaching to the Gentiles. They had to admit that it was the same gospel which they had been preaching to the Jews.

15:5 Apparently it was in an open meeting of the entire church that certain **of the Pharisees who** were believers **rose up** and contended that Gentiles must be circumcised and must **keep the law of Moses** in order to be disciples in the truest sense.

15:6 From verse 6 it might appear that only **the apostles and elders** were present when the final decision was made. However, verse 12 seems to indicate that the entire church was there as well.

15:7–10 As **Peter rose** to his feet, perhaps the opposition felt he would support their position. After all, **Peter** was the apostle to the circumcision. However, their hopes were doomed to disappointment. **Peter** reminded the audience that some years previously **God** had ordained that **the Gentiles should** first **hear . . . the gospel** from his lips. This took place in the house of Cornelius. When **God** saw that the hearts of those **Gentiles** were reaching out to Him in faith, He gave **them the Holy Spirit, just as He did** to the Jews on the Day of Pentecost. At that time, **God** did not require these **Gentiles** to be circumcised. The fact that they were **Gentiles** made no difference; He cleansed **their hearts by faith**. Since **God** had accepted **the Gentiles** on the principle of **faith** and not of law-keeping, **Peter** asked the assembly why they should now think of **putting** the Gentiles under the **yoke** of the law — **a yoke . . . which neither** their **fathers nor** they had been **able to bear**. The law never saved anyone. Its ministry was condemnation, not justification. By the law is the knowledge of sin, not salvation from sin.

15:11 Peter's final decision is worthy of special notice. He expressed the deep conviction that **through the grace of the Lord Jesus** (and not through law-keeping) **we** (the Jews) **shall be saved in the same manner as they** (the Gentiles). One would have expected Peter, as a Jew, to say that the Gentiles would be saved the same as the Jews. But **grace** is here seen triumphing over ethnic distinctions.

15:12 After Peter had finished, **Bar-**

nabas and Paul gave an account of how God had visited **the Gentiles**, and had accompanied the preaching of the gospel with **miracles and wonders**.

15:13, 14 Peter had told how the Lord had opened the door of faith to **the Gentiles at the first** through him. Paul and Barnabas added their testimony as to how the Lord had worked through them in evangelizing **the Gentiles**. **James** now stated authoritatively that God's present purpose for this age is to call out of **the Gentiles . . . a people for His name**. This was, in substance, what **Simon** (Peter) had just related.

15:15–19 Then James quoted from Amos 9:11, 12. Notice that he did not say that the calling out of **the Gentiles** was in fulfillment of the prophecy of Amos, but rather that it *agreed* with **the words of the prophets**. The assembly should not think it a strange thing that **God** should visit **the Gentiles** with salvation, because this had been clearly predicted in the OT. **God** had foretold that **Gentiles** would be blessed as such, and not as believing Jews.

The quotation from Amos looks forward to the Millennium, when Christ will sit upon the throne of **David** and when the **Gentiles** will **seek** after **the LORD**. James did *not* intimate that this prophecy was being fulfilled at the time he spoke. Rather, he said that the salvation of **Gentiles** which was then taking place was *in harmony* or agreement with what Amos said would take place later.

James' argument was this: First **God** would visit **the Gentiles to take out of them a people for His name**. This is what was then happening (and is still happening). Converted **Gentiles** were included in the church with converted Jews. What was then happening on a small scale (the salvation of **the Gentiles**) would later happen on a larger scale. Christ would return, restore Israel nationally, and save **all the Gentiles who** would be **called by** His **name**.

James looked on contemporary events as God's first visitation of **the Gentiles**. He felt this first visitation was in perfect harmony with what Amos predicted — the future visitation of **the Gentiles** when Christ returns as King. The two events *agree* though they are not identical.

Notice, then, the order of events:

1. The taking out of **the Gentiles a people for His name** (v. 14) during this present Age of Grace.
2. The restoration of the believing portion of the nation of Israel at Christ's second advent (v. 16).
3. The salvation of Gentile nations following the restoration of Israel (v. 17). These **Gentiles** are referred to as **all the Gentiles who are called by My name**.

James' quotation of Amos 9:11, 12 is quite different from the rendering in the OT. Part of this difference is explained by the fact that James apparently quoted in Greek. However, the quotation is quite different even from the Septuagint. One explanation is that the same Holy Spirit who originally inspired the words now permitted them to be changed in order to meet the problem at hand. Another is that the Hebrew manuscripts have several readings in Amos 9. Alford believes James must have quoted from a translation close to a received Hebrew text, otherwise the Pharisees would never have accepted the quotation as proof.

After this I will return (v. 16). James had already stated that God's program for this present age was to open the door of faith to **the Gentiles**. Not all of them would be saved, but He would **take out of them a people for His name**. Now James added that **after this**, that is, after the church has been called out from the nations, God would **return** and **rebuild the tabernacle of David, which** is **fallen** and in **ruins. The tabernacle of David** is a figurative expression describing his house or family. Its restoration is a type of the future restoration of the royal family and the re-establishment of the throne of **David** with Christ sitting upon it as King. Israel will then become the channel of blessing to the world. **The rest of mankind** will **seek the LORD, even all the Gentiles who are called by** His **name**.

The quotation from Amos closes with the statement that these are the words of **the LORD who does all these things**.

Therefore, because God's present purpose is to call out from **the Gentiles a people for** Himself, James cautioned against troubling **the Gentiles** by putting them under the Law of Moses. As far as salvation is concerned, all that was needed was faith.

15:20 However, he suggested that in writing to the church at Antioch the saints there be advised **to abstain from things polluted by idols, from sexual immorality, from things strangled, and from blood**. It might seem at first that James was here reversing himself. Was this not a form of legalism? Was he not now putting them back under the law? The answer is that this advice did not have to do with the subject of salvation at all. That issue had already been settled. But this advice had to do with *fellowship* between Jewish and Gentile believers. While obedience to these instructions was not a condition of salvation, it was certainly of great importance in avoiding sharp cleavages in the early church.

The things prohibited were:

1. **Things polluted by idols**. In verse 29 this is explained as foods offered to idols. If Gentile believers went on eating these foods, then their Jewish brethren might seriously wonder whether they had given up idolatry. Although Gentile Christians might have liberty to eat such foods, it might prove a stumbling block to weak Jewish brethren, and would therefore be wrong.

2. **Sexual immorality**.[62] This was the cardinal sin of the Gentiles. It was therefore especially important for James to include this with the other subjects mentioned. Nowhere in the Bible is the command to abstain from **sexual immorality** ever revoked. It is of standing application for all ages.

3. **Things strangled**. This prohibition goes back to the covenant which God made with Noah after the flood (Gen. 9:4). Thus it is a standing order for the human race and not just for the nation of Israel.

4. **Blood**. This too goes back to Genesis 9:4 and thus precedes the Law of Moses. Since the Covenant with Noah was never abrogated, we take it that these regulations are still in effect today.

15:21 This explains why the advice of verse 20 was given. There were Jews **in every city** who had always been taught that it was wrong to do these things that James warned against. It was wrong not only to commit immorality but also to eat food offered to idols, meat from strangled animals, and blood. Why then should the Gentiles offend God by committing immorality, or offend man by doing the other things?

15:22 It was thus definitely decided that Gentiles did not need to be circumcised in order to be saved. The next step was **to send** official notice of this in writing **to** the church at **Antioch. The apostles and elders** in Jerusalem, **with the whole church**, designated **Judas**, called **Barsabas, and Silas**, both **leading men among the brethren**, to go back **to Antioch with Paul and Barnabas**. This **Silas** is the one who later became a traveling companion of **Paul**, and who is referred to as Silvanus in the Epistles.

15:23–29 The substance of the letter is given here. Notice that the false brethren who went from Jerusalem to Antioch originally had never received the authorization or approval of the church in Jerusalem (v. 24).

The moment by moment reliance of the disciples on **the Holy Spirit** is suggested in verse 28: **For it seemed good to the Holy Spirit, and to us . . . .** Someone has spoken of this as "the senior partnership of the Holy Spirit."

15:30, 31 When **the letter** from Jerusalem was **read** in the church at **Antioch**, it proved to be a great **encouragement**. The disciples there now knew that God saved them as Gentiles, and not by their becoming Jews.

15:32, 33 **Judas and Silas** remained for some ministry meetings, in which they **exhorted and** built up **the brethren** in the faith. After a prolonged time of happy fellowship and service in Antioch, they went back to Jerusalem.

15:34 Verse 34 in the King James tradition does not appear in either the oldest or majority of manuscripts (see NKJV footnote). Apparently some copyists thought it would be helpful to supply this information in order to explain the apparent contradiction between verses 33 and 40. In verse 33 Silas is pictured as returning to Jerusalem. But then in verse 40 he is seen accompanying Paul on his Second Missionary Journey. The obvious solution is that Silas did return to Jerusalem, but was then contacted by

Paul with an invitation to accompany him on his travels.

15:35 Paul and Barnabas stayed **in Antioch** at this time, **teaching and preaching the word of the Lord**. There were **many** other servants of the Lord who ministered to the assembly. The events described in Galatians 2:11–14 probably occurred at this time.

F. Paul's Second Missionary Journey: Asia Minor and Greece (15:36–18:22)†

15:36–41 The time had come to begin the Second Missionary Journey. **Paul** broached the subject **to Barnabas**, suggesting that they revisit the cities where they had previously **preached the word**. When **Barnabas** insisted that his nephew, **Mark**, accompany them, **Paul** strongly opposed the plan. He remembered vividly how Mark **had departed from them in Pamphylia**, and doubtless feared he would do it again. **The contention** between **Barnabas** and **Paul became so sharp** that these two honored servants of the Lord **parted from one another**. **Barnabas took Mark and sailed to Cyprus**, the place of his birth, and also the first stop on the First Missionary Journey. **Paul chose Silas** and **went through SYRIA and CILICIA, strengthening the churches**.

Verses 36 and 41 give us additional insight into the true pastoral spirit of **Paul**. His loving care for the people of God was once mirrored by an eminent teacher who said he would rather perfect one saint to the work of ministering than call hundreds of people to the beginnings of Christian life.

At this point the question inevitably arises, "Who was right, **Paul** or **Barnabas**?" There was probably fault on both sides. Perhaps **Barnabas** allowed his judgment to be swayed by his natural affection for **Mark**. Verse 39 indicates that there was **sharp contention** between **Paul** and **Barnabas**. "By pride comes nothing but strife" (Prov. 13:10). Therefore they were both guilty of pride in the matter. Those who think **Paul** was right point out that **Barnabas** disappears from the story at this point. Also, **Paul** and **Silas** were **commended by the brethren to the grace of God**, but this is *not* said in the case of Barnabas and John Mark. In any event, it is heartening to remember that Mark finally did win his colors, and was completely restored to the confidence of Paul (2 Tim. 4:11).

THE AUTONOMY OF THE LOCAL CHURCH

The council at Jerusalem might appear at first sight to be a sort of denominational supreme court. But the facts are otherwise.

Every local assembly in the early days of Christianity was autonomous — that is, self-governing. There was no federation of churches with a centralized authority over them. There were no denominations and therefore no denominational headquarters. Each local church was directly responsible to the Lord. This is pictured in Revelation 1:13 where the Lord is seen standing in the middle of the seven golden lampstands. These represent the seven churches of Asia. The point is that there was no governing agency between the individual churches and the great Head of the church Himself. Each one was governed *directly* by Him.

Why is this so important? First, it hinders the spread of error. When churches are linked together under a common control, the forces of liberalism, rationalism, and apostasy can capture the entire ground simply by seizing the central headquarters and denominational schools. Where churches are independent, the struggle must be waged by the enemy against a host of separate units.

Second, the autonomy of the local church is an important protection when a hostile government is in power. When churches are federated, a totalitarian government can control them all by controlling the few leaders at headquarters. When churches refuse to recognize any centralized authority, they can more readily go underground in times of oppression.

Many governments today, whether democratic or dictatorial, try to bring about the union of small, independent churches. They say they do not want to deal with a large number of local units but with a central committee representing them all. Free governments try to bring about this union by the offer of certain favors and benefits. Other governments try to force the union by edict,

†*See p. xxix.*

as Hitler did during the Third Reich. In either case, the churches which yield to the pressure lose their scriptural character as well as their ability to resist modernism and to carry on secretly in time of persecution.

Some may object that the churches in Acts did have a central authority, namely, the council in Jerusalem which we have just considered. However, a careful study of the passage will show that this was not an official body with regulatory powers. It was simply a gathering of apostles and elders acting in an advisory capacity.

The council did not summon the men to come from Antioch; the latter decided to consult the men in Jerusalem. The decision of the council was not binding on the churches; it was simply offered as the combined judgment of the group.

The history of the church speaks for itself. Wherever there has been federation of churches under a central organization, there has been an acceleration of decline. The purest testimony for God has been maintained by churches which are free from outside human domination. ‡

16:1, 2 Memories must have come back to Paul like swallows to a barn when **he** returned **to DERBE and LYSTRA**. The memory of his stoning at **Lystra** might conceivably have raised misgivings about ever returning. But the apostle knew that God had people in this area, and no consideration of personal safety could deter him.

As suggested previously, **Timothy** may have been converted through Paul's ministry during the apostle's first visit to **Lystra** (apparently Timothy's home town. Timothy's mother, Eunice, and grandmother, Lois, were both **Jewish** believers (2 Tim. 1:5). **His father was Greek** and may have died by this time.

It rejoiced Paul's heart to learn from **the brethren . . . at Lystra and Iconium** that **Timothy** was progressing well in the Christian faith. **Paul** invited him to go along on this missionary trip. We do well to notice that the early apostles not only worked in pairs, but also took along younger brethren (Mark and Timothy) for training in practical aspects of the Christian ministry. What a privilege it

was for these young men to be yoked together with seasoned veterans in Christian missionary enterprise.

16:3 Before **Paul** departed, he **circumcised** Timothy. Why did he do this, when he had steadfastly refused to have Titus circumcised some time previously (Gal. 2:1–5)? The answer is simply this: in the case of Titus it was a question of fundamental Christian doctrine, whereas here it was not. The false teachers were insisting that a full-blooded Gentile, like Titus, had to be circumcised in order to be saved. Paul recognized this as a denial of the sufficiency of Christ's atoning work, and would not allow it. Here the case was entirely different. The people of the area knew that Timothy was Jewish from his mother. **Paul**, Silas, and Timothy were going forth on evangelistic work. Their first contacts would frequently be with the Jews. If these **Jews** knew that Timothy was not circumcised, they might refuse to listen; whereas if he were, there would be no possibility of offense on this score. Since it was entirely a matter of moral indifference and not of doctrinal importance, **Paul** submitted Timothy to this Jewish ordinance. He was made all things to all men that he might by all means save some (1 Cor. 9:19–23).

The interpretation that Paul's circumcising of Timothy was in order to gain an audience for the gospel with the Jews seems to be strongly implied by the words, **and circumcised him because of the Jews . . . for they all knew that his father was Greek.**

16:4–5 As the three missionaries traveled **through the cities** of Lycaonia, **they delivered to** the churches **the decrees** which had been drawn up **by the apostles and elders at Jerusalem**. These **decrees** were, in brief, as follows:

1. As far as salvation is concerned, faith alone is necessary. Circumcision or law-keeping should not be added to faith as a condition for being saved.

2. Sexual immorality was forbidden for all believers and for all time, but this reminder was probably addressed primarily to converted Gentiles, since this was (and is) their besetting sin.

3. Meats offered to idols, meat from animals that had been strangled, and blood were forbidden as food, not as

matters essential to salvation, but to facilitate fellowship between Jewish and Gentile believers. Some of these instructions were subsequently revised (see 1 Cor. 8–10; 1 Tim. 4:4, 5).

As a result of the ministry of these men, **the churches were strengthened in the** Christian **faith, and increased in number daily.**

16:6–8 These verses are of vital importance because they show the superintendence and guidance of **the Holy Spirit** in the missionary strategy of the apostles. After revisiting the churches in **PHRYGIA** and **GALATIA**, they had thought of going into the province of **Asia**, in western Asia Minor, but **the Holy Spirit** forbade them. We are not told why; some have suggested that perhaps in the divine counsels this region was allocated to Peter (see 1 Pet. 1:1). At any rate they traveled northwest into the district of **MYSIA**. This was actually included in the province of **Asia**, but apparently they did not preach there. When they attempted next **to go** northeast **into Bithynia**, along the coast of the Euxine (Black) Sea, **the Spirit did not permit them**. So they went directly west to the coastal city of **TROAS**. From there the missionaries could look across the Aegean Sea toward Greece, the threshold of Europe. Ryrie writes:

> Asia needed the Gospel, but this was not God's time. Need did not constitute their call. They had just come from the east; they had been forbidden to go south or north, but they did not presume that the Lord was leading them to the west — they waited His specific directions. Logic alone is not the basis for a call.[63]

16:9 During a night **vision** Paul saw **a man of MACEDONIA** calling to him to **come over** and **help**. **Macedonia** was the northern part of Greece, due west of Troas. Whether consciously or not, **Macedonia** (and all Europe!) needed the gospel of redeeming grace. The Lord had been closing doors in Asia so His servants would carry the good news to Europe. Stalker paints the picture:

> [The man of Macedonia] represented Europe, and his cry for help Europe's need of Christ. Paul recognized in the vision a divine summons; and the very next sunset which bathed the Hellespont in its gold light shone upon his figure seated on

the deck of a ship, the prow of which was moving toward the shore of Macedonia.[64]

16:10 There is a significant change here in the personal pronoun from *he* to *we*. It is generally believed that Luke, the writer of Acts, joined Paul, Silas, and Timothy at this time. From here on he records the events as an eyewitness.

DIVINE GUIDANCE

In order to function effectively on earth, the early church depended on the guidance of its Head in heaven. But how did the Lord Jesus make known His will to His servants?

He had left His *general strategy* with them before He ascended, when He said, "You shall be witnesses to Me in Jerusalem, and in all Judea and Samaria, and to the end of the earth" (Acts 1:8).

After His Ascension, He made known His will to them in several ways.

Peter and the other disciples were guided by the OT *Scriptures* (Ps. 69:25) to choose a successor for Judas (1:15–26).

On at least five occasions the Lord guided men through *visions* — Ananias (9:10–16); Cornelius (10:3); Peter (10:10, 11, 17); Paul (twice — 16:9, 10; 18:9).

Twice He guided through *prophets* (11:27–30; 21:10–12).

At other times the Christians were guided by *circumstances*. For instance, they were scattered or driven by persecution (8:1–4; 11:19; 13:50, 51; 14:5, 6). Civil authorities asked Paul and Silas to leave Philippi (16:39, 40). Later Paul was taken from Jerusalem to Caesarea by the authorities (23:33). The circumstance of Paul's appeal to Caesar determined his trip to Rome (25:11), and the later shipwreck affected the timing and sequence of moves (27:41; 28:1).

Sometimes guidance came through the *counsel and initiative of other Christians*. The church in Jerusalem sent Barnabas to Antioch (11:22). Agabus prophesied a famine, and this moved the church in Antioch to send relief to the saints in Judea (11:27–30). The brethren at Antioch sent Paul and Barnabas to Jerusalem (15:2). Judas and Silas were sent out by the church at Jerusalem with Barnabas and Paul (15:25–27). Paul and Silas were commended by the brethren to the grace of God as they set out on the Second Missionary Journey (15:40). Paul took Timothy with him when he left Lystra (16:3). The brethren in Thessalonica sent Paul and Silas to Berea because of the threat of violence (17:10). The brethren in Berea, in turn, sent Paul away for the same reason (17:14, 15). Finally, Paul sent Timothy and Erastus to Macedonia (19:22).

In addition to the above methods of guidance, there are several instances where men seem to have received communications of the divine will *directly*. An angel of the Lord guided Philip to the Ethiopian eunuch (8:26). The Holy Spirit spoke to the prophets and teachers at Antioch as they fasted and prayed (13:1, 2). Paul and Timothy were forbidden by the Holy Spirit to preach the word in Asia (16:6). Later they tried to go to Bithynia, but the Spirit did not permit them to go (16:7).

To summarize then, the early Christians received guidance:

1. Through the Scriptures.
2. Through visions and prophecies.
3. Through circumstances.
4. Through the advice and initiative of other Christians.
5. Through direct communication, possibly in an inward, subjective manner. ‡

16:11, 12 **Sailing** northwest **from Troas**, the tireless ambassadors of Christ first anchored for a night off the island of **SAMOTHRACE**. They **next** reached the mainland at the port of **NEAPOLIS**, over 120 miles from **Troas**, then journeyed inland a few miles **to PHILIPPI, which** was **the foremost city of that part of Macedonia, a colony.**

16:13–15 Apparently there was no synagogue in Philippi, but Paul and his companions heard that some Jewish people gathered **on the Sabbath** outside **the city** by **the riverside**. Reaching the spot, they found a group of **women** praying, including one **named Lydia**. She was probably a convert to Judaism. Originally **from the city of Thyatira**, in the district of Lydia, in western Asia Minor, she had moved to Philippi, where **she was a seller of purple**-dyed cloth. **Thyatira** was famous for its dyes.

Not only was her ear open to the gospel; **her heart** was open as well. After receiving the Lord Jesus, **she and her household were baptized.** The members of **her household** had, of course, been converted also before they **were baptized**. There is no mention of Lydia's being married; **her household** could have consisted of servants.

Lydia was not saved by good works, but she was saved in order to do them. She proved the reality of her faith by opening her home to Paul, Silas, Luke, and Timothy.

16:16–18 Another day, when **Paul** and his companions were going to the place of **prayer**, they met **a slave girl** who had **a spirit of divination**. Possessed by a demon, she was able to foretell the future and to make other astounding revelations. In this way she **brought** considerable income to **her masters**.

When she **met** the Christian missionaries, and **for many days** thereafter, she **followed** them, crying out, **"These men are the servants of the Most High God, who proclaim to us the way of salvation."** What she said was *true*, but **Paul** knew better than to accept testimony from demons. Also he was grieved because of the wretched condition of this enslaved girl. So, **in the** all-powerful **name of Jesus Christ**, he commanded the demon **to come out of her**. Immediately she was freed from this dreadful bondage, and became a sane, rational person.

MIRACLES

Miracles are woven throughout the narrative of the Book of Acts. The following are some of the more prominent ones:

The miraculous gift of tongues (2:4; 10:46; 19:6).

The healing of the lame man at the gate of the temple (3:7).

The sudden judgmental death of Ananias and Sapphira (5:5, 10).

The deliverance of the apostles from prison (5:19).

Saul's encounter with the glorified Christ (9:3–6).

The healing of Aeneas by Peter (9:34).

The restoration to life of Dorcas (9:40).

Peter's vision of the sheet let down from heaven (10:11).

Peter's deliverance from prison (12:7–10).

The slaying of Herod by an angel (12:23).

The judgment of blindness on Elymas, the sorcerer (13:11).

The healing of the crippled man at Lystra by Paul (14:10).

Paul's restoration after being stoned at Lystra (14:19, 20).

Paul's vision of the man of Macedonia calling for help (16:9).

Paul's casting out the evil spirit from the girl in Philippi (16:18).

The deliverance of Paul and Silas from prison in Philippi (16:26).

Paul's raising Eutychus to life (20:10, 11).

The prophecy of Agabus (21:10, 11).

Paul's deliverance from a viper at Malta (28:3–6).

The healing of Publius' father of fever (28:8).

The healing of others' diseases (28:9).

In addition to these, it is said that the apostles worked wonders and signs (2:43); Stephen performed great wonders and signs among the people (6:8); Philip worked miracles and signs (8:6, 13); Barnabas and Paul worked signs and wonders (15:12); and God worked miracles by the hands of Paul (19:11).

In studying Acts, the question naturally arises, "Should we expect these same miracles today?" There are two extremes to be avoided in answering the question. The first is the position that since Jesus Christ is the same yesterday, today, and forever, we should be seeing the same miracles that were found in the early church.

The opposite extreme is that miracles were only for the early days of the church and that we have no right to look for them today.

It is true that Jesus Christ is the same yesterday, today, and forever (Heb. 13:8). But that does not mean that the divine methods never change. The plagues God used in Egypt, for instance, have never been repeated. His power is the same. He can still perform any kind of miracles. But that does not mean He *must* perform the same miracles in every

age. He is a God of infinite variety.

On the other hand, we should not wave miracles aside as not being for the Church Age. It is all too easy to assign miracles to dispensational pigeonholes and content ourselves with lives that never rise above flesh and blood.

Our lives should be charged with supernatural power. We should be constantly seeing God's hand in the marvelous converging of circumstances. We should be experiencing His guidance in a miraculous, mysterious way. We should experience events in our lives that lie beyond the laws of probability. We should be aware that God is arranging contacts, opening doors, overruling opposition. Our service should crackle with the supernatural.

We should be seeing direct answers to prayer. When our lives touch other lives, we should see something happening for God. We should see His hand in breakdowns, delays, accidents, losses, and seeming tragedies. We should experience extraordinary deliverances and be aware of strength, courage, peace, and wisdom beyond our natural limits.

If our lives are lived only on the natural level, how are we any different from non-Christians? God's will is that our lives should be supernatural, that the life of Jesus Christ should flow out through us. When this takes place, impossibilities will melt, closed doors will open, and power will surge. Then we will be supercharged with the Holy Spirit, and when people get near us, they will feel the sparks of the Spirit.‡

16:19–24 Instead of being grateful that this young woman was no longer demon-possessed, **her masters** bitterly resented the resulting loss **of profit. They** therefore **dragged . . . Paul and Silas** before **the magistrates** (praetors), and trumped up charges against them. Basically, they accused them of being troublemaking **Jews** who were trying to upset the Roman way of life. The mob reacted violently, **and the magistrates tore off** the **clothes** of Paul and Silas **and commanded them to be beaten.** After a thorough beating, the missionaries were sent to jail, with special instructions to **the jailer to keep them securely.** He responded by putting **them into the inner**

prison and fastening **their feet in the stocks**.

In this passage we see two of Satan's chief methods. First, he tried false friendship — the testimony of the demon-possessed girl. When this failed, he resorted to open persecution. Grant says: "Alliance or persecution — these are the alternatives: false friendship or open war." A. J. Pollock comments:

How the Devil must have triumphed as he thought he had brought the career of these devoted servants of Christ to an abrupt close. His triumphing was premature as it ever must be. In this case it turned out to his utter discomfiture, and to the furtherance of the work of the Lord.[65]

16:25 The **midnight** hour found **Paul and Silas . . . praying and singing**. Their joy was completely independent of earthly circumstances. The source of all their **singing** was high in heaven above. Morgan admits:

Any man can sing when the prison doors are open, and he is set free. The Christian soul sings in prison. I think that Paul would probably have sung a solo had I been Silas: but I nevertheless see the glory and grandeur of the Spirit that rises superior to all the things of difficulty and limitation.[66]

16:26 As the other prisoners were listening to their prayers and hymns of praise to God, the prison was rocked by an unusual **earthquake**. It **opened . . . all the doors** and unloosed the stocks and **chains**, but it did not demolish the building.

16:27, 28 When the jailer awoke and saw the **prison** wide **open**, he assumed that **the prisoners had** made their escape. Aware that his own life would be forfeited, he **drew his sword** to commit suicide. **But Paul** assured him there was no need for him to do that, because **all** the prisoners were still present and accounted for.

16:29, 30 Now a new emotion swept over the jailer. His fears of losing his job and perhaps his life gave way to deep conviction of sin. He was now afraid to meet God in his sins. He cried, **"Sirs, what must I do to be saved?"**

This question must precede every genuine case of conversion. A man must know he is *lost* before he can be *saved*. It is premature to tell a man how to be saved until first he can say from his heart, "I truly deserve to go to hell."

16:31 The only people in the NT who were ever told to believe on the Lord Jesus Christ were convicted sinners. Now that the jailer was thoroughly broken up over his sins, he was told: **"Believe on the Lord Jesus Christ, and you will be saved, you and your household."**

There is no suggestion here that his family would be saved automatically if *he* trusted Christ. The meaning is that if he believed **on the Lord Jesus Christ**, he would **be saved**, and his **household** would **be saved** in the same way. "Believe . . . and you will be saved, and let your household do the same."

Many people today seem to have difficulty knowing what it means to believe. However, when a sinner realizes he is lost, helpless, hopeless, hellbound, and when he is told to believe on Christ as Lord and Savior, he knows exactly what it means. It is the only thing left that he *can* do!

16:32–34 After Paul and Silas had a teaching session with the household, the jailer demonstrated the genuineness of his conversion by washing their wounds, and by being **baptized** without delay. Also he **brought them into his house** and fed them, rejoicing all the time **with all his household** that they had all come to know the Lord.

Again we would mention that there is no support for believing there were infants or very young children in the household who were baptized. They were all old enough to believe **in God**.

16:35 Apparently **the magistrates** had a change of heart during the night, because in the morning they **sent the officers** (lictors) with instructions to release the two prisoners.

16:36, 37 When the jailer announced the good news **to Paul**, the apostle refused to leave under such circumstances. After all, Silas and he, though Jews by birth, were citizens of Rome. They had been tried and **beaten** unfairly. Now did the magistrates think they would slink away as if guilty and in disgrace? **No indeed!** Let the magistrates **come** and release the prisoners.

16:38–40 **The magistrates** did come, and rather apologetically at that! They urged Paul and Silas **to depart from the city** without further disturbance. With the dignity of sons of the King, the Lord's servants **went out of the prison**, but they did not leave the city immediately. First they went to Lydia's **house**, conferred with **the brethren**, and **encouraged them**. How wonderful! The ones who should have been comforted were encouraging others.

When their mission in Philippi was accomplished, they **departed** with full colors flying.

17:1 After leaving Philippi, Paul and Silas traveled thirty-three miles southwest to **AMPHIPOLIS** (am-fip'-o-lis). Their next stop was **APOLLONIA** (ap-o-lo'-ni-a), another thirty miles southwest. From there they moved in a westward direction thirty-seven miles to **THESSALONICA** (thes-a-lo-nye'-ka). This city was strategically located on trade routes, and was thus an excellent center of commerce. The Holy Spirit chose it as a base from which the gospel would radiate in many directions. In our day, the city is known as Saloniki.

Luke may have remained at Philippi when Paul and Silas left there to claim new territory for the Lord. This is suggested by the narrative changing from the first person plural (we) to the third person (**they**).

17:2, 3 As **was** their **custom**, the missionaries located a Jewish synagogue and preached the gospel there. **For three Sabbaths**[67] Paul opened the OT and showed convincingly that it was predicted **that the** Messiah **had to suffer and rise again from the dead**. Having established this **from the Scriptures**, Paul went on to declare that **Jesus** of Nazareth was the long awaited Messiah. Had He not suffered, and died, and risen from the dead? Did this not prove that He was **the Christ** of God?

17:4–7 **Some** of the Jews **were persuaded**, and took their place with **Paul and Silas** as Christian believers. Also many of the Greek proselytes **and not a few of the leading women** of the city were converted. This provoked the unbe-

lieving **Jews** to decisive action. They rounded up some of the hoodlums **from the marketplace**, incited a riot, and besieged **the house of Jason** where **Paul and Silas** had been guests. **When they did not find** Paul and Silas in the house, **they dragged Jason and some** of his fellow believers before **the rulers of the city** (politarchs). Without meaning to, they paid a genuine tribute to Paul and Silas when they described them as men who had **turned the world upside down**. Then they charged them with plotting to overthrow the government **of Caesar** by preaching about **another king — Jesus**. It was, to say the least, a strange thing for **Jews** to be so zealous in safeguarding the government **of Caesar**, because they had little or no love for the Roman Empire.

But was their charge true? Doubtless they had heard Paul proclaim the Second Coming of Jesus to reign as king over all the earth. But this did not pose an immediate threat to Caesar, since Christ would not return to reign until Israel had repented nationally.

17:8, 9 The politarchs were **troubled** by these reports. They required **Jason** and those with him to post bail, probably adding instructions for his guests to leave the city. Then **they let them go**.

17:10–12 **The brethren** in Thessalonica decided it would be well for the preachers to leave, so they **sent** them **away by night to BEREA**. These indomitable and irrepressible evangelists **went** straight to **the synagogue of the Jews**. As they preached the gospel there, the Jews showed their open-mindedness by searching, checking, and comparing **the** OT **Scriptures**. They had a simple and teachable attitude and a determination to test all teaching by **the** Sacred **Scriptures**. **Many of** these Jews **believed**. And there were also a good number of converts from **prominent** Gentile **women as well as men**.

17:13, 14 **When** word trickled back to **Thessalonica** that **Paul and Silas** were carrying on their ministry in **Berea**, **the** Thessalonian **Jews** made a special trip to **Berea and stirred up the crowds** against the apostle. **The brethren** thereupon **sent Paul** toward the seacoast, accompanied by an escort of believers. They probably went as far as DIUM and sailed from there to PIRAEUS, the port city of ATHENS. **Silas and Timothy remained** in Berea.

17:15 It was a long journey from Berea **to Athens**. It showed the true devotion of the Christians there that some of the brethren were willing to accompany **Paul** all the way. When it came time for them to leave **Paul** in **Athens**, he sent word by them **for Silas and Timothy to** join **him with all speed**.

17:16 While waiting for **them at Athens**, **Paul** was deeply burdened by the idolatry of **the city**. Although **Athens** was the center of culture, education, and fine arts, **Paul** was interested in none of these things. He did not occupy his time with sightseeing trips. Arnot comments:

It was not that he valued marble statues less, but living men more. . . . He is not the weak but the strong man who regards immortal souls as transcendently more important than fine arts. . . . Paul did not consider idolatry picturesque and harmless, but grievous.[68]

17:17, 18 He reasoned in the synagogue with the Jews and with the Gentile worshipers, whereas **in the marketplace** he preached to all who would listen. It was in this way that he came in touch with some **Epicurean and Stoic philosophers**. The Epicureans were followers of a philosopher named Epicurus, who taught that pleasure and not the pursuit of knowledge is the chief end of life. The Stoics were pantheists who believed that wisdom lay in being free from intense emotion, unmoved by joy or grief, willingly submissive to natural law. When these two schools of philosophy heard Paul, they considered him a **babbler** (Greek, "seed-picker") and **a proclaimer of foreign gods, because he preached to them Jesus and the resurrection.**

17:19–21 They took him and brought him to the Areopagus, a judicial body like a supreme court that met on the hill of Mars. In this particular case, it was not exactly a trial, but simply a hearing in which Paul would be given an opportunity to set forth his teaching before the members of the court and the multitude. This is somewhat explained in verse 21. **The Athenians** loved to stand around and talk, and to listen to others. They seemed to have an unlimited amount of time for this.

17:22 Standing **in the midst** of the court, **Paul** delivered what has come to be known as the Mars Hill Address. It must be remembered in studying this address that he was speaking to Gentiles, not Jews. They did not have a background in the OT, so he had to find some subject of common interest with which to begin. He began with the observation that the Athenians were **very religious**. That Athens was indeed a **religious** city was well attested by the fact that it was reputed to have more idols in it than men!

17:23 When he thought of the idols he had seen, **Paul** was reminded of **an altar with this inscription: TO THE UNKNOWN GOD**. He found in that **inscription** a point of departure for his message. The apostle saw in the **inscription** the recognition of two important facts. First, the fact of the existence of **God**, and second, the fact that the Athenians were ignorant of **Him**. It was then a very normal and natural transition for **Paul** to enlighten them concerning **the** true **God**. As someone has said, he turned the wandering stream of their piety into the right channel.

17:24, 25 Missionaries tell us that the best place to begin in teaching pagans about God is the account of creation. This is exactly where Paul began with the people of Athens. He introduced **God** as the One **who made the world and everything in it**. As he looked around on the numerous idol temples nearby, the apostle reminded his hearers that the true **God does not dwell in temples made with hands. Nor is He** dependent on the service of **men's hands**. In idol temples, the priests often bring food and other "necessities" to their gods. But the true **God** does not need anything from man, because **He** is the source of **life, breath, and all things**.

17:26–28a Paul next discussed the origin of the human race. All nations came from the common ancestor, Adam. Not only were the nations brought forth by God, but **He** also arranged the years, and **determined** the countries in which the various peoples would dwell. **He** showered innumerable mercies on them in order that they might **seek** Him. **He** wanted them to **grope for Him and find Him**, even though in actuality **He is not far from each one**. It is **in** the true God that **we live and move and have our being. He** is not only our Creator but our environment as well.

17:28b To further emphasize the relationship of the creature to the Creator, Paul quoted from **some of** their Greek **poets**, who **said, "For we are also His offspring."** This is not to be interpreted as teaching the brotherhood of man and the fatherhood of God. We are the **offspring** of God in the sense that He created us, but we only become *sons* of God through faith in the Lord Jesus Christ.

17:29 But Paul's argument continues. If men **are the offspring of God**, then it is impossible to think of God as a **gold or silver or stone** idol. These are **shaped by art and man's devising**, and therefore are not as great as men. These idols are, in a sense, the offspring of human beings, whereas the truth is that human beings are the creation of God.

17:30 Having exposed the folly of idolatry, Paul goes on to state that for many centuries **God overlooked** the **ignorance** of the Gentiles. But now that the revelation of the gospel has come, He **commands all men everywhere to repent**, that is, to do an about-face.

17:31 This is an urgent message, **because** God **has appointed a day on which He will judge the world in righteousness by** the Lord Jesus Christ, **the Man whom He has ordained**. The judgment referred to here will take place when Christ returns to earth to put down His enemies and begin His Millennial Reign. The positive assurance that this will take place is found in the fact that God raised the Lord Jesus **from the dead**. Thus Paul leads up to his favorite theme, the resurrection of Christ.

17:32, 33 Perhaps Paul did not finish his message. It may be that he was interrupted by the scorn of those who **mocked** at the idea of a **resurrection of the dead. Others** did not mock, but hesitated. They delayed taking any action by saying, **"We will hear you again on this matter."** "They counted the time of closing with Christ an evil day. They couldn't say 'Never' but 'Not Now.' "

17:34 However, it would not be right to say that Paul's message was a failure. After all, **Dionysius** believed, and he was an **Areopagite**, a member of the court. **A woman named Damaris** also believed **and others** whose names are not given.

So Paul departed from among them. "We hear no more of Athens. To centers of persecution Paul returned again, but to intellectual flippancy, there was nothing more to be said" (Selected).

Some people criticize this sermon because it seems to praise the Athenians for their religiosity when actually they were gross idolaters; it supposes a recognition of the true God from an inscription that might have been intended for an idol; it seems to accommodate itself too much to the manners and customs of the Athenians; and it does not present the gospel as clearly and forcibly as some other messages by the apostle. These criticisms are unjustified. We have already sought to explain that Paul first sought a point of contact, then by easy steps he led his hearers first to the knowledge of the true God, then to the necessity of repentance in view of Christ's coming as judge. It is sufficient vindication of Paul's preaching that souls were genuinely converted through it.

UNCONVENTIONAL PULPITS

Paul's preaching on Mars Hill is an illustration of the *unconventional places* in which the early believers preached the word.

The *open air* was a favorite. At Pentecost the message may have been preached out of doors, judging from the number who heard and were saved[69] (Acts 2:6, 41). Other general instances of open-air preaching are found in 8:5, 25, 40; 13:44; 14:8–18.

The environs of *the temple* echoed with the message on at least three occasions (3:1–11; 5:21, 42). Paul and his associates spoke the Word *by the riverside* in Philippi (16:13). Here in Athens he preached *in the marketplace* (17:17) before the address on Mars Hill.[†] In Jerusalem

†*See p. xxvi.*

he addressed an angry mob *from the stairs* of the fortress of Antonia (21:40–22:21).

At least four times the message was declared before the Jewish *Sanhedrin*: by Peter and John (4:8, 19); by Peter and the other apostles (5:27–32); by Stephen (7:2–53); and by Paul (22:30–23:10).

Paul and his associates habitually preached the gospel *in the synagogues* (9:20; 13:5, 14; 14:1; 17:1, 2, 10, 17; 18:4, 19, 26; 19:8).

Private homes were used repeatedly. Peter preached in Cornelius' house (10:22, 24). Paul and Silas witnessed in the home of the Philippian jailer (16:31, 32). In Corinth Paul preached in the house of Crispus, the ruler of the synagogue (18:7, 8). He preached till midnight in a private house in Troas (20:7). He taught from house to house in Ephesus (20:20) and in his own hired house in Rome (28:30, 31).

Philip preached to an Ethiopian eunuch *in a chariot* (8:31–35), and Paul preached on *board a ship* (27:21–26). At Ephesus he reasoned daily *in a schoolroom* (19:9).

Paul preached *in civil courts* before Felix (24:10), Festus (25:8), and Agrippa (26:1–29).

In 8:4 we read that the persecuted believers went *everywhere* preaching the word.

It shows that they did not think the proclamation of the message should be confined to some specially "consecrated" building. Wherever there were people, there was both reason and opportunity for making Christ known. A. B. Simpson agrees:

The early Christians regarded every situation as an opportunity to witness for Christ. Even when brought before kings and governors, it never occurred to them that they might evade the issue and avoid identifying themselves with Christ because of being fearful of the consequences. It was simply an occasion to preach to kings and rulers whom otherwise they could not reach. It is probable that God allows every human being to cross our path in order that we may have the opportunity to leave some blessing in his path, and drop into his heart and life some influence that will draw him nearer to God.[70]

The Lord Jesus had commissioned them to "Go into all the world and preach the gospel to every creature" (Mark 16:15). The Book of Acts shows them carrying out the command.

We might add that most of the preaching in Acts was spontaneous and extemporaneous. Usually there wasn't time to prepare a message. "It was not the performance of an hour but the preparation of a lifetime." It was the preachers who were prepared, not the sermons.‡

18:1 Some believe **Paul departed from Athens** because of the meager results of his preaching there. We prefer to believe that he was led by the Holy Spirit to journey westward **to CORINTH**, the capital of ACHAIA. Here, in this city noted for immorality, the gospel must be preached and a church established.

18:2, 3 At Corinth, Paul formed a friendship with a couple named **Aquila** and **Priscilla** which was to continue through his life. **Aquila** was **a Jew** from **Pontus**, the northeastern province of Asia Minor. He and his wife had been living in **Rome**, but they had been driven out by an anti-semitic decree of **Claudius** Caesar. Since Corinth was located on the main route from **Rome** to the East, they had stopped here and set up shop as **tentmakers**. Paul was also a tentmaker by trade, and he became acquainted with them.

Life's best revelations flash upon us while we abide in the fields of duty. Keep to your daily breadwinning and amid your toils you shall receive great benedictions and see glad visions. . . . The shop or office or warehouse may become as the house of God. Do thy work and do it diligently: In it, thou mayest find rare soul fellowships, as did Aquila and Priscilla.[71]

It is not clear from the narrative whether **Aquila** and **Priscilla** were already Christians when Paul met them, or whether they were saved through his ministry. Perhaps the burden of evidence is on the side of their being believers when they came to Corinth.

18:4 Paul **reasoned in the synagogue every Sabbath, and persuaded both Jews and** Gentile proselytes that

Jesus was indeed the Christ of God.

18:5 Paul had left **Silas and Timothy** in Berea when he moved on to Athens. At Athens he had sent word for them to join him. They caught up with him in Corinth.

After their arrival, **Paul was compelled by the Spirit**. This may mean that the burden of the Lord was upon him to preach the message with great diligence, testifying **to the Jews that Jesus is the Christ**. There might be a suggestion that the apostle no longer spent time making tents here, but gave himself entirely to preaching the gospel.

It was at approximately this time in his history that Paul wrote 1 Thessalonians (about A.D. 52).

18:6 The unbelieving Jews **opposed** Paul **and blasphemed** or railed. To reject the gospel is ultimately to oppose *oneself*. The unbeliever harms no one so much as himself.

Paul **shook** out **his garments and said to them, "Your blood be upon your own heads; I am clean. From now on I will go to the Gentiles."** The shaking of his clothing was an expressive act, signifying his dissociation from them. However, this did not prevent his going to the synagogue in another city, namely, Ephesus (19:8).

The apostle's words are a solemn reminder to every believer that there is such a thing as blood-guiltiness. The Christian is a debtor to all men. If he fails to discharge that debt by proclaiming the gospel, God will hold him responsible. If, on the other hand, he faithfully witnesses for Christ and meets with stubborn refusal, then he himself is free from guilt, and the responsibility rests with the Christ-rejecter.

This verse represents another step in the setting aside of the nation of Israel, and the proclamation of the gospel to the Gentiles. God had decreed that the good news should go to the Jews first, but throughout Acts, as the nation of Israel rejects the message, the Spirit of God sorrowfully turns aside from that people.

18:7, 8 Following the outburst of the Jews, the apostle went to the home of **Justus**, a Gentile convert to Judaism who lived **next door to the synagogue**. As he carried on his ministry from this base, the Apostle Paul had the joy of seeing **Crispus, the ruler of the synagogue, . . . with all his household** come to the Lord. **Many** other Corinthians trusted in the Savior **and were baptized**. Paul baptized Crispus and a few others (1 Cor. 1:14–16), but his usual practice was to have some other believer do the baptizing. Paul feared that people would form a party around himself, instead of being undistracted in their love and loyalty to the Lord Jesus.

18:9, 10 The Lord graciously **spoke to Paul in the night by a vision**, assuring him that there was nothing to **be afraid** of. The apostle should continue to preach the word, assured of God's presence and protection. There were **many people in** the **city** who belonged to the Lord in the sense that He was working in their lives and they would ultimately be saved.

18:11 Paul stayed in Corinth eighteen months, **teaching the word of God**. Valuable background material concerning this period is found in 1 and 2 Corinthians.

18:12–16 It was probably toward the end of Paul's stay in Corinth that **Gallio** was appointed **proconsul of Achaia** (approximately A.D. 51). Thinking the new **proconsul** would be friendly to them, **the Jews brought Paul** before him at **the judgment seat** (*bēma*) in the marketplace at Corinth. The accusation was that **Paul** was persuading them **to worship God contrary to the** Jewish **law**. Before the apostle had an opportunity to testify, **Gallio** dismissed the matter with utter contempt. He told the Jews that this was strictly a matter of their **own law** and not one that came under his jurisdiction. **If it were a matter of wrongdoing or wicked crimes**, then it would be reasonable for **Gallio** to **bear** patiently **with** the Jews, but actually it was only **a question of words and names and** the Jewish **law**. The **proconsul** had no intention of becoming **a judge of such matters**, so he dismissed the case.

18:17 Some think that **the Greeks** punished **Sosthenes** for bringing Paul before **Gallio** on such an empty charge. When it says that **Gallio took no notice of these things**, it does not mean he was uninterested in the gospel, although that was probably true. He evidently did not want to become involved in Jewish laws and customs.

18:18 After these incidents, **Paul remained** in Corinth **a good while**. Perhaps it was during this time that he wrote 2 Thessalonians.

When he finally **took leave of** Corinth with **Priscilla and Aquila**, he sailed for Syria, his object being to return to Antioch. Commentators are divided as to whether it was **Paul** or **Aquila** who **had his hair cut off at Cenchrea**, the eastern harbor of Corinth.[72]

Some feel that the manner of the **vow** was strongly Jewish, and not fitting for a man of Paul's spiritual maturity. There is probably no way to decide the matter finally.

18:19, 20 When the ship landed at **EPHESUS**, Priscilla and Aquila disembarked with the intention of staying there. Paul took advantage of the vessel's brief stay to go to **the synagogue and** reason **with the Jews**. Surprisingly enough, they wanted him to remain longer, but he could not do so.

18:21 The ship was leaving. But he promised to **return** to **Ephesus**, **God willing**, after keeping the **coming feast in Jerusalem.**

18:22 The ship's next stop was **CAESAREA**. From there, the apostle went **up and greeted the church** in Jerusalem. Then **he went down to ANTIOCH** for what was to be his final visit.

Thus ends Paul's Second Missionary Journey.

G. Paul's Third Missionary Journey: Asia Minor and Greece (18:23–21:26)[†]

18:23 **After** a fairly lengthy visit at Antioch, Paul was ready to set out on another extended missionary itinerary. The record of this journey extends from verse 23 through 21:16.

The first regions to be visited were **GALATIA and PHRYGIA**. The apostle went to the churches there, one by one, **strengthening all the disciples.**

18:24–26 The scene now shifts back to **Ephesus** where we left **Aquila and Priscilla**. **An eloquent** preacher **named Apollos** arrived there, one who was **mighty in the** OT **Scriptures**. He was **a Jew** by birth, and came from **Alexandria**, the capital of northern Egypt. Al-

though his preaching was accompanied by much power, and although he was very zealous, yet he was somewhat deficient in his knowledge of the Christian faith. He had apparently been well schooled in the ministry of **John** the Baptist, and knew how **John** had called the nation of Israel to repentance in preparation for the coming of the Messiah. Apparently he did not know about Christian baptism or some other matters of Christian doctrine. **When Aquila and Priscilla heard him speak . . . in the synagogue**, they recognized that he needed further instruction, so **they** lovingly **took him aside and explained to him the way of God more accurately**. It is to the credit of this **eloquent** preacher that he was willing to be taught by a tentmaker and his wife.

18:27, 28 As a result of his teachable spirit, **the brethren** at Ephesus encouraged him in his desire to go to Corinth in order to preach the word. In fact they **wrote** a letter of commendation for him. As a result **he** was a great help to the believers in Corinth and **vigorously refuted the Jews** there **publicly, showing that Jesus is** indeed **the Christ** of God.

19:1 When Paul originally visited **Ephesus**, he promised the Jews in the synagogue that he would return, in the will of God. In fulfillment of that promise, he journeyed from the regions of Galatia and Phrygia along the inland route, over mountainous terrain **to EPHESUS** on the western coast of proconsular Asia. Arriving there he met about twelve men who professed to be **disciples**. As he talked with them, he realized that their knowledge of the Christian faith was very imperfect and defective. He wondered if they had ever really received the Holy Spirit.

19:2 Therefore he asked them, **"Did you receive the Holy Spirit when you believed?"** In the KJV Paul's question reads, "Have ye received the Holy Ghost since ye believed?" This wrongly implies that the reception of the Holy Spirit takes place *subsequent* to salvation.

The thought of this verse is not that the reception of the Holy Spirit is a work of grace which follows salvation. As soon as a sinner trusts the Savior, he receives the Holy Spirit.

The reply of the disciples was, **"We have not so much as heard whether**

†See p. xxx.

there is a Holy Spirit," or as it is rendered in the ASV, "We did not so much as hear whether the Holy Spirit was given." Since these men were disciples of John the Baptist, as we learn in the next verse, they should have known about the existence of **the Holy Spirit** from the OT. Not only so, but John had taught his disciples that the One who came after him would baptize them with the Holy Spirit. What these disciples did not know was that **the Holy Spirit** had already been given on the Day of Pentecost.

19:3, 4 When the apostle raised the question of baptism, he found out that these men knew only about **John's baptism**. In other words, the extent of their knowledge was that the Messiah was at hand, and they had signified their **repentance** by **baptism** as a necessary preparation for receiving Him as King. They did not know that **Christ** had died, had been buried, and had risen from the dead and ascended back to heaven, and that He had sent the Holy Spirit. **Paul** explained all this to them. He reminded them that when **John** baptized with the **baptism of repentance**, he urged them to **believe** . . . **on Christ Jesus**.

19:5 When they heard this, they were baptized in the name of the Lord Jesus. Throughout the Book of Acts the emphasis is distinctly on the lordship of Jesus. Therefore, the disciples of John here **were baptized** by the authority **of the Lord Jesus** and as a public acknowledgment that in their lives they accepted Jesus Christ as Lord (Jehovah).

19:6, 7 Paul then **laid** his **hands on them**, and they received **the Holy Spirit**. This is the fourth distinct time in Acts when **the Holy Spirit** was given. The first was in chapter 2, on the Day of Pentecost, and involved the Jews primarily. The second was in Acts 8, when the Spirit was given to the Samaritans through the laying on of the hands of Peter and John. The third time was in Acts 10, at the household of the Gentile, Cornelius, in Joppa. We have previously pointed out that the order of events leading up to the reception of **the Holy Spirit** is different in each case.

Here in Acts 19 the order is:
Faith.
Re-baptism.

Laying on of the apostle's **hands**.
Reception of **the Holy Spirit**.

By giving **the Holy Spirit** to John's disciples through the laying on of Paul's **hands**, the Lord forestalled the possibility of a charge being made later that Paul was inferior to Peter, John, or the other apostles.

When the disciples of John received **the Holy Spirit they spoke with tongues and prophesied**. Such supernatural powers were God's method of working in the days before the NT was given. Today we know that we receive **the Holy Spirit** at the time of conversion, not by signs and wonders, or even by feelings, but by the testimony of the NT Scriptures.

The moment a person believes on the Lord Jesus Christ, he is indwelt by the Holy Spirit; he is sealed by the Holy Spirit; he receives the earnest of the Spirit; he receives the anointing of the Spirit; and he is baptized by the Spirit into the Body of Christ. However, this does not deny that in a believer's life there are subsequent *crises* of the Spirit. There is no denying that the Holy Spirit often comes on individuals in a sovereign manner, empowering them for special ministries, giving them great boldness in the faith, and pouring out upon them a passion for souls.

19:8 For three months Paul visited **the synagogue** in Ephesus,† **reasoning and persuading concerning the things of the kingdom of God**. By **reasoning**, we understand that he spoke to the intellects of the people. By **persuading**, he sought to influence their wills, especially with regard to faith in Jesus as the Christ. The subject of his discourses was **"The Things of the Kingdom of God."**

C. E. Stuart clarifies:

Not, be it observed, that he preached the *Gospel* of the Kingdom: that would have been dispensationally out of place. The Lord preached that. It, however, fell into abeyance on His death, to be revived in a coming day (Matthew 24:14; Revelation 14:6, 7). But Paul reasoned about the Kingdom of God, for that now exists on earth.[73]

19:9, 10 When some of the Jews were **hardened** (as to their intellects) and disobedient (as to their wills), when they began to agitate **the multitude** against **the Way**, Paul left the synagogue and

withdrew his **disciples** from the Jews there. He took them to **the school of Tyrannus**, where he had freedom to teach them **daily**. It is generally thought that **Tyrannus** was a Greek who conducted classes in philosophy or rhetoric. **For two years** the apostle made disciples and then sent them out to teach others also. As a result the whole province of **Asia heard the word of the Lord Jesus, both Jews and Greeks**. Thus a great door and effectual was opened to Paul, even though there were many adversaries (1 Cor. 16:9).

19:11, 12 As an apostle of Jesus Christ, **Paul** had the power to perform signs and wonders. These were proofs of his apostleship, and authenticated the message he preached. So great was the power that flowed through him **that even handkerchiefs or aprons** which he touched would be carried away to **the sick** or demon-possessed, and healing would result. The question arises whether these **miracles** can be duplicated today. The Holy Spirit of God is sovereign, and He can do as He pleases. However, it must be admitted that the apostles and their delegates had supernatural powers conferred upon them. Since we do not have apostles today in the full sense of the word, it is futile to insist that their miracles have been perpetuated.

19:13, 14 Whenever God works in power, Satan is invariably on hand to obstruct and oppose. While Paul was preaching and performing miracles, there were certain wandering Jews in Ephesus who were **exorcists**. These men commanded **evil spirits** (using **the name of the Lord Jesus** as a magic formula) to come out of **those who** were possessed. That certain of the Jews actually had the power to expel demons was acknowledged by the Lord Jesus (Luke 11:19).

Among the Jewish magicians practicing this were seven sons of Sceva (pronounced see'-vah). This man was made **chief priest**, or the priest in charge of the twenty-four courses. One day his sons were trying to expel an evil spirit from a demoniac. They said to the demon, **"We adjure you by the Jesus whom Paul preaches."**

19:15, 16 They uttered the words, but they did not have the power, and the demon did not obey. In fact, the reply of **the evil spirit** was most illuminating. He said, **"Jesus I know, and Paul I know; but who are you?"**

F. B. Meyer has an amusing comment on this, which is worth quoting:

> When the sons of Sceva started on the demon, he turned on them, and said, "You little dwarfs, you lilliputians, who are you? I know Paul! I don't know you, I have never heard about you before; your name has never been talked about down in Hell. No one knows you, nor about you outside of this little bit of a place called Ephesus."
>
> Yes, and there is the question that was put to me today: "Does anyone know of me down in Hell?" Do the devils know about us? Are they scared about us? Are they frightened by us? Or do they turn upon us? When we preach on Sunday, or when we visit in the streets, or take our Sunday School Class, the devil says, "I don't know you, you are not worth my powder and shot; you can go on doing your work. I am not going to upset Hell to stop you."[74]

It is interesting how the Scripture distinguishes between **the evil spirit** (v. 15) and **the man in whom the evil spirit** dwelt (v. 16). In verse 15 the demon spoke. But in verse 16 the demoniac himself **leaped on** the sons of Sceva, **overpowered them**, stripped them, and wounded them.

19:17 When news of this defeat of the forces of Satan became known in the surrounding area, a deep sense of awe **fell on** the people, **and the name of the Lord Jesus was magnified**. It was not Paul's name that received the glory, but **the name of** Paul's Savior.

19:18, 19 So mightily did the Spirit of God work among those who had practiced various forms of magical art that a great number turned to Christ, **confessing . . . their deeds**. After doing so, they made a public demonstration of their faith by gathering up **their books** that dealt with magic and burning them in a great bonfire. The original cost of the books would have been **fifty thousand pieces of silver**. It is difficult to determine exactly how much that would be in our currency — perhaps between eight and ten thousand dollars.

19:20 This well-publicized renunciation of pagan practices caused **the word of the Lord** to grow **mightily** and to prevail. Perhaps if modern Christians would burn their trashy books and magazines, the word would prevail much more.

19:21 As Paul's time at Ephesus began to draw to a close, he determined **to go** back **to Jerusalem** via **Macedonia and Achaia**, and after that he would **also see Rome**. His great heart of love and compassion was always reaching out to centers where the gospel could be planted, and from which it could spread.

19:22 **He sent Timothy and Erastus** on ahead to **Macedonia**, but **he lingered in Asia for a time**. It was probably at this time that he wrote 1 Corinthians (about A.D. 56).

19:23–27 As a result of Paul's ministry, many Ephesians turned to the Lord from their idols. The spiritual awakening in the city was so widespread that it caused a business recession among the idol-makers. **Demetrius, a silversmith**, was one of those seriously affected. He **made silver shrines of Diana**.[75] Serving as a spokesman for the **trade**, **Demetrius** gathered together all his fellow craftsmen and sought to stir them up to take some resolute action. He reminded them how **Paul** had been so successful in persuading **many people** that there are no **gods which are made with** human **hands**. He revealed his real motive when he said that their **trade** was **in danger**, but he sought to give it a religious coloring by pretending great reverence for **Diana** and her **temple**.

19:28–31 The meeting of silversmiths soon developed into a mob scene in which **the whole city** became involved. Chanting **"Great is Diana of the Ephesians!"**, the crowd **rushed into the theater** (arena or coliseum), and **seized Gaius and Aristarchus**, two of **Paul's traveling companions**, doubtless with the purpose of killing them. **Paul** himself **wanted** to step in and speak to the mob, but he was prevented by **the disciples**, and also by the Asiarchs (officers elected by the cities who at their own expense furnished festivals in honor of the gods). These civic benefactors who had be-friended **Paul** told him that it would be most unwise for him to enter the arena.

19:32 By this time the mob was completely out of control. Many did not know why they were there. Conflicting voices were heard on every hand.

19:33, 34 A Jew named **Alexander** sought to step forward and address the mob. Doubtless his purpose was to defend the Jews as being completely innocent in the matter. **But when** the crowd **found out that he was a Jew**, they put up a tremendous protesting roar. **For about two hours** they chanted, **"Great is Diana of the Ephesians!"**

19:35 At this crucial moment, **the city clerk** succeeded in quieting **the crowd**. His speech was as successful as it was lame. He said in effect that the Ephesians had nothing to fear. After all, everyone knew that Ephesus had been appointed **the city** to serve as **temple guardian of the great goddess Diana**. Although thirteen cities in Asia had an interest in the temple, yet that sacred building was the solemn charge of the Ephesians. Also to them fell the privilege of guarding an **image** of **Diana** which was supposed to have fallen from heaven.

19:36–40 Implying that their religious foundations were secure, and that nothing could ever topple the worship of Diana, he told the people that they were foolish to make such a fuss. After all, the men against whom they were crying out had not been **robbers of temples** or **blasphemers of** Diana. **If Demetrius and his fellow craftsmen** had a just complaint, the regular **courts** of law were **open** to them, with **proconsuls** ready to hear their **charges**. If they had anything else to say, there was always the possibility of gathering together **in the lawful assembly**. But they had been gathering as a **disorderly** mob. The Roman Empire took a very dim view of any such proceedings. If they were ever **called . . . to account for this** mob scene, they would not be able to justify themselves. Also the city clerk knew that his job and possibly his life would be in danger if news of a riot got back to Rome.

19:41 By this time the mob had been quieted, and they now hastened away to their homes.

Strange to say, it was the action of the town clerk in the interests of civil order, and not the uproar, that ended Paul's ministry there. As long as there was healthy opposition, Paul felt the door of opportunity was widely open in Ephesus (1 Cor. 16:8, 9). But it appears that when municipal protection was extended to him, he moved on (Selected).

The word, **assembly** (vv. 32, 39, 41), translates the Greek word, *ekklēsia*, meaning a called out company of people. It is the same word translated *church* in other parts of the NT. Whether the word refers to a heathen mob, as here, or the congregation of Israel, as in Acts 7:38, or the NT church, must be determined from the context. The word, *assembly*, is a better translation of *ekklēsia* than the word, *church*. The word, *church*, comes from a Greek word meaning "belonging to the Lord" (*kuriakē*, cf. Scottish "kirk"). In modern usage, it commonly refers to a religious building. That is why many Christians prefer the word *assembly*; it expresses the fact that the church is a called out group of people, not a building or even a denomination.

20:1 From verse 1 it would appear that the apostle traveled directly from Ephesus to **Macedonia**. However, from 2 Corinthians we learn that he first went to TROAS. There he found an open door to preach the gospel but was anxious to see Titus and to learn from him how the Corinthians had received his First Epistle. When he did not find Titus in Troas, he crossed over the northeastern corner of the Aegean Sea **to MACEDONIA**. Undoubtedly he landed at NEAPOLIS, then traveled inland to PHILIPPI. While in **Macedonia**, probably at Philippi, he met Titus and was greatly encouraged by the news from Corinth. It was probably at this time that he wrote 2 Corinthians (A.D. 56?). (See 2 Cor. 1:8, 9; 2:12–14; 7:5–7.)

20:2, 3a After ministering for some time in Macedonia, he journeyed south **to GREECE** or ACHAIA. Most of the **three months** there were undoubtedly spent in CORINTH, and it was during this period that he wrote Romans. Some also believe that Galatians was written at this time.

20:3b Originally, Paul had planned to travel straight from Corinth across the Aegean **to Syria**. However, when he learned that **the Jews** were plotting to destroy him somewhere along that route, he changed his plans and went northward again **through MACEDONIA**.

20:4 At this time we are introduced to some of Paul's traveling companions. It is stated that they **accompanied him** as far as **Asia**, but we know that certain of them even went with him to Rome:

Sopater of Berea was possibly the same as Sosipater, a relative of Paul mentioned in Romans 16:21.

Aristarchus of Thessalonica nearly lost his life in the riot at Ephesus (Acts 19:29). We later read of him as being a fellow prisoner with Paul in Rome (Phmn. 24; Col. 4:10).

Secundus, also a native of Thessalonica, accompanied Paul as far as Asia, probably Troas or Miletus.

Gaius of Derbe is not to be confused with the Macedonian who was seized by the mob at Ephesus (Acts 19:29). Another Gaius is mentioned as being an inhabitant of Corinth and Paul's host while there (Rom. 16:23). John's Third Epistle is addressed to a man named Gaius, probably living in some city near Ephesus. Gaius was a very common name.

Timothy not only **accompanied** Paul **to Asia** but was with him in Rome during his first imprisonment. Subsequently he traveled with Paul through proconsular Asia. In his Second Letter to Timothy, Paul expressed the desire to see him again, but we do not know whether this wish was ever fulfilled.

Tychicus, a native **of Asia** Minor, probably journeyed as far as Miletus with the apostle. Later he rejoined Paul in Rome and is mentioned as laboring with him up to and during the time of his second imprisonment.

Trophimus was apparently a Gentile whose home was in Ephesus, in **Asia** Minor. He went with Paul to Jerusalem and unwittingly was the cause of the apostle's arrest. He is also mentioned in 2 Timothy 4:20.

20:5, 6 It appears that the above seven brethren traveled on ahead to **Troas**, while Paul and Luke visited **PHILIPPI**. (We believe that Luke was with the apostle because of the use of the first person pronoun, **us** in verse 5, **we** in verse 6, etc.) **After the Days of Unleavened Bread**, or the Passover, Paul and Luke sailed from Macedonia to **TROAS**. The journey would not ordinarily have taken **five days**. No explanation is given here for the delay.

20:7–9 Comparing verses 6 and 7, it appears that the apostle purposely waited in Troas for seven days so he could be there for the breaking of **bread** on the Lord's Day. It is certainly clear from verse 7 that it was the practice of the early Christians to gather together **on the first day of the week** in order to observe the Lord's Supper.

That **Paul** should have spoken **until midnight** should cause us no shocked surprise. When the spiritual temperature of a church is high, the Spirit of God is free to work without being fettered by the bondage of timepieces. As the night wore on, it became hot and stuffy **in the upper room**. Perhaps the **many lamps** contributed to this, as well as the number of people present. **A certain young man named Eutychus**, sitting in an open **window**, fell asleep and plummeted to the ground below. It was a fall of three stories, and he was killed by it.

20:10 But Paul went down and stretched himself over the body of the young man, as the prophets did of old. He then announced to the people that they should not make any more fuss about the matter since Eutychus was now alive. It might seem from Paul's words that their concern was unnecessary because the young man had not died; **his life** was still **in him**. But it is clear from verse 9 that he was actually dead. Acting with the power of an apostle, **Paul** had miraculously restored him to life.

20:11, 12 When Paul returned upstairs, they broke **bread** (v. 11), i.e., they observed the Lord's Supper, for which they had come together (v. 7). Then they ate a common meal, perhaps the *agapē* or love feast. This fellowship meal was held in conjunction with the Lord's Supper in the early days of the church, but abuses crept in (1 Cor. 11:20–22), and it was gradually discontinued.

After an all-night meeting, never to be forgotten, the apostle bade farewell to the believers in Troas.

20:13–15 Paul left Troas **on foot**, and walked twenty miles across the neck of a promontory of land **to ASSOS**. His traveling companions went by **ship** around the promontory, then picked him up on the southern side. Perhaps he wanted time to be alone and to meditate on the word of God.

Sailing south along the western coast of Asia Minor, they first came **to MITYLENE** (pronounced mit-i-le'-ne), the chief city of the island of LESBOS. The following night they apparently anchored off the island of **CHIOS** (pronounced key'-os). Another day's journey brought them to the island of **SAMOS**, **and** they **stayed at TROGYLLIUM**. Finally the travelers put in at **MILETUS**, a port on the southwest coast of Asia Minor, thirty-six miles south of Ephesus.

20:16 Paul intentionally bypassed **Ephesus**, because he feared that a visit there would occupy too much time, and **he was hurrying to** get to **Jerusalem** for **the Day of Pentecost**.

20:17 Upon landing at **Miletus**, Paul sent word to **the elders in Ephesus**,[†] asking them to come for a meeting. Undoubtedly it took considerable time for the message to reach them, and for them to make the journey south. However, they were well rewarded by the magnificent message they heard from the lips of the great apostle. In it we have a valuable portrait of an ideal servant of the Lord Jesus Christ. We see a man who was fanatically devoted to the Savior. He labored in season, out of season. He was tireless, indomitable, indefatigable. He was marked by true humility. No cost was too great for him to pay. His ministry was the result of deep exercise of soul. He had a holy boldness and fearlessness. Whether he lived or died was not important; but it was important that the will of God should be carried out and that men should hear the gospel. He was unselfish in all that he did. He would rather give than receive. He was undaunted by difficulties. He practiced what he preached.

20:18, 19 The apostle reminded the elders of Ephesus of his **manner** of life when he **lived among** them. **From the first day that** he set foot in **Asia**, and all the time he was there, he served **the Lord with** true **humility** and self-denial.

†See p. xxvii.

In connection with his ministry, there was a constant strain on his emotional system; there were **tears** of sorrow and **trials**. Constantly he suffered persecution as a result of **the plotting of the Jews**. Yet in spite of all the adverse circumstances, his ministry was bold and fearless.

20:20, 21 **Paul** held **back nothing** from the Ephesians that would be for their spiritual welfare. He **taught** them **publicly and from house to house**, constrained by the love of Christ. To him, it was not a matter of holding meetings at stated intervals, but rather of buying up every opportunity to encourage growth among the believers. Without discrimination as to nationality or religious background, he preached the necessity of **repentance toward God and faith toward our Lord Jesus Christ**. These are two fundamental elements of the gospel. In every genuine case of conversion, there are both **repentance** and **faith**. They are the two sides of the gospel coin. Unless a person were duly repentant, saving **faith** would be impossible. On the other hand, **repentance** would be of no avail unless it was followed by **faith** in the Son of God. **Repentance** is an about-face by which the sinner acknowledges his lost condition and bows to God's judgment as to his guilt. **Faith** is commitment of one's self to Jesus Christ as Lord and Savior.

In many NT passages, **faith** alone is stated to be the condition of salvation. However, **faith** presupposes **repentance**. How could a person truly accept Jesus Christ as Savior unless he realized that he needed a Savior? This realization, brought about by the convicting ministry of the Holy Spirit, is **repentance**.

20:22, 23 Having reviewed his past conduct among the Ephesians, the apostle now looks ahead to the sufferings that await him. He was constrained **in his spirit to go to Jerusalem**. It was an inner compulsion, which he was apparently unable to throw off. Although he did not know exactly what the turn of events would be in Jerusalem, he did know **that chains and tribulations** would be a regular part of his life. **The Holy Spirit** had been making this fact known to him **in every city**, perhaps through

the ministry of prophets, or perhaps by the mysterious, inner communication of divine intelligence.

20:24 As the apostle weighed this outlook in his mind, he did not think that his own **life** was the great consideration. His ambition was to obey God and to please Him. If in doing this, he would be called upon to offer up his **life**, he was willing to do so. No sacrifice he could make would be too great for the One who died for him. All that mattered was that he **finish** his **race** and complete **the ministry which** he **received from the Lord Jesus, to testify to the gospel of the grace of God**. No title could better express the good news which Paul preached — **the gospel of the grace of God**. It is the thrilling message of God's undeserved favor to guilty, ungodly sinners who deserve nothing but everlasting hell. It tells how the Son of God's love came from heaven's highest glory to suffer, bleed, and die on Calvary in order that those who believe on Him might receive forgiveness of sins and everlasting life.

20:25–27 Paul was sure he would never see his beloved Ephesian brethren again, but his conscience was clear in leaving them, because he knew he had not held back from declaring to them **the whole counsel of God**. He had instructed them not only in the fundamentals of the gospel, but in all the truths that were vital for godly living.

20:28 Since he would never again meet them on earth, he delivered a solemn charge to the elders that they should first of all **take heed** to their own spiritual condition. Unless they were living in fellowship with the Lord, they could not expect to be spiritual guides in **the church**.

Their function as elders was to **take heed . . . to all the flock, among which the Holy Spirit** had **made** them **overseers**. As mentioned previously, **overseers** in the NT are also called bishops, elders, and presbyters. This verse emphasizes that elders are not appointed or elected by the local assembly. They are **made overseers** by **the Holy Spirit**, and should be recognized by the believers among whom they labor.

Among other things they were responsible **to shepherd the church of God**. The importance of such a charge is seen in the words which follow: **which He purchased with His own blood**. This latter expression has been the cause of considerable discussion and disagreement among Bible scholars. The difficulty is that **God** is here pictured as shedding **His blood**, whereas **God** is Spirit. It was the Lord Jesus who shed His blood, and although Jesus is God, yet nowhere else does the Bible speak of **God** bleeding or dying.

The majority of manuscripts read "the church of the Lord and God which He purchased with His own blood," apparently suggesting that Person of the Godhead (the Lord) who actually shed His blood.

Perhaps J. N. Darby comes closest to the correct sense of the passage in his New Translation: "The assembly of God, which He has purchased with the blood of His own." Here God is the One who purchased the church, but He did it with the blood of His own Son, the blessed Lord Jesus.

20:29, 30 Paul was well aware **that after** his **departure**, the church would be attacked from without and from within. False teachers, **wolves** in sheep's clothing, would prey upon the flock, showing no mercy. From within the fellowship, men would aspire to places of prominence, speaking perversions of the truth, and trying **to draw away the disciples after themselves**.

20:31 In view of these imminent perils, the elders should be on their guard, and constantly **remember** how **for three years** the apostle had warned them **night and day with tears**.

20:32 Paul's great resource now was to **commend** them **to God and to the word of His grace**. Notice that he did not **commend** them to other human leaders, or to supposed successors of the apostles. Rather he entrusted them **to God and** the Bible. This is an eloquent testimony to the sufficiency of the inspired Scriptures. It is they which are **able to build up** the believers and to **give** them **an inheritance among all those who are sanctified**.

20:33–35 In closing his message, the Apostle Paul once again set before

the elders the example of his own life and ministry. He could say in all honesty that he had **coveted no one's silver or gold or apparel**. It was not the hope of financial gain that motivated him in the work of the Lord. He was essentially a poor man, as far as material things were concerned, but he was rich toward God. Holding out his hands before them, he could remind them that those **hands** had labored in order to provide for the **necessities** of life, both for himself **and for those who were with** him. But he went beyond that also. He labored as a tentmaker in order that he might have means to help **the weak** — those physically ill, or **weak** as far as moral scruples are concerned, or **weak** in spiritual matters. The elders should remember this, and seek in all things the good of others, remembering **the words of the Lord Jesus, ". . . It is more blessed to give than to receive."** Interestingly enough, these words of our Lord are not found in any of the Gospels. They do represent the sum of much of His teaching, but here they are given as an inspired addition to His words in the Gospels.

20:36–38 At the conclusion of his message, Paul **knelt** on the ground **and prayed with** the elders. For them it was a time of deep sorrow. They showed their affection for the beloved apostle by falling **on** his **neck** and kissing **him**. The thing that particularly grieved them was his statement **that they would see his face no more**. Heavyhearted, they **accompanied him to the ship** for the voyage to Jerusalem.

21:1–4a After the tender and affectionate farewell at Miletus, Paul and his companions sailed to the island of **COS**, where they spent the night. **The following day** they continued southeast **to the island of RHODES**. Leaving the northern tip of the island, they sailed eastward **to PATARA**, a seaport of Lycia on the southern coast of Asia Minor. At **Patara** they transferred to **a ship** that was **sailing over to Phoenicia**, the coastal strip of **Syria**, of which **Tyre** was one of the principal cities. As they sailed southeast across the Mediterranean, they skirted south of the island of **Cyprus**, leaving **it on the left** hand. The first port of call on the mainland of Palestine was **TYRE**. Since **the ship was to unload her cargo** there, Paul and the others looked up the Christian believers and **stayed** with them **seven days**.

21:4b It was during this time that these disciples **told Paul through the Spirit** that he should not set foot in **Jerusalem**. This raises the age-old question as to whether **Paul** was deliberately disobedient in going **to Jerusalem**, whether he unwittingly failed to discern the mind of the Lord, or whether he was actually in the will of God in going. A casual reading of verse 4b might seem to indicate that the apostle was willful and headstrong, acting in deliberate defiance of the Spirit. However, a more careful reading might indicate that **Paul** did not actually know that these warnings were given **through the Spirit**. Luke, the historian, tells his readers that the advice of the Tyrian disciples was Spirit-inspired, but he does not say that the apostle knew this as a definite fact. It seems far more probable that **Paul** interpreted the advice of his friends as calculated to save him from physical suffering or even death. In his love for his Jewish countrymen, he did not feel that his physical well-being was the important consideration.

21:5, 6 **When** the seven **days** had expired, the believers of Tyre turned out *en masse* to accompany the missionaries to the beach in an eloquent demonstration of their Christian love. After a time of prayer and affectionate goodbys, **the ship** pulled out and those left on shore **returned home**.

21:7 The next stop was **PTOLEMAIS** (pronounced tol-e-may'-is), a seaport approximately twenty-five miles south of Tyre, and now known as Akko (Acre), near Haifa. It was named after Ptolemy. A stopover of one day permitted the Lord's servants to visit the local **brethren**.

21:8 **On the next day** they took the final portion of their voyage — a thirty-mile sail south **to CAESAREA**, on the Plain of Sharon. There they stayed **in the house of Philip the evangelist** (not to be confused with the apostle by that name). It was this **Philip** who was chosen to be a deacon by the church in Jerusalem and who carried the gospel to Samaria.

Through his instruction, the Ethiopian eunuch had been saved.

21:9 Philip **had four virgin daughters who prophesied**. This means they were gifted by the Holy Spirit to receive messages directly from the Lord and to convey them to others. Some have inferred from this verse that it is permissible for women to preach and teach in the church. However, since it is *expressly forbidden* for women to teach, speak, or have authority over the men in the assembly (1 Cor. 14:34, 35; 1 Tim. 2:11, 12), it can only be concluded that the prophetic ministry of these **four virgin daughters** was carried on in the home or in other non-church gatherings.

21:10, 11 During Paul's stay in Caesarea, **a certain prophet named Agabus came down from Judea**. It was the same **prophet** who came to Antioch from Jerusalem and predicted the famine which took place during the reign of Claudius (Acts 11:28). Now **he took Paul's belt** and **bound his own hands and feet with it**. By this dramatic action, like many of the prophets before him, he was acting out his message. Then he gave the meaning of the object lesson. Just as he had **bound** himself, **hands and feet**, **so** would **the Jews** of **Jerusalem bind** the hands and feet of Paul **and deliver him** over to the Gentile authorities. Paul's service for the Jews (symbolized by the **belt**) would result in his being captured by them.

21:12–14 **When** the apostle's companions and the Christians in Caesarea heard this, they **pleaded with him not to go up to Jerusalem**. But he could not sympathize with their concern. Their tears only served to break his **heart**. Should the fear of chains and imprisonment restrain him from doing what he considered to be God's will? He would have them know that he was **ready not only to be bound, but also to die at Jerusalem for the name of the Lord Jesus**. All their arguments proved of no value. He was determined to go, and so they simply said, **"The will of the Lord be done."**

It is difficult to believe that Paul's parting words were spoken by a man who was knowingly disobeying the guidance of the Holy Spirit. We know that the disciples in Tyre told him through the Spirit that he should not go to Jerusalem (v. 4). But did Paul *know* they spoke through the Spirit? And did not the Lord later seem to approve his trip to Jerusalem when He said, "Be of good cheer, Paul; for as you have testified for Me in Jerusalem, so you must also bear witness at Rome" (23:11)? Two things are clear: First, *Paul* did not think his personal safety was the main consideration in serving the Lord. Second, the Lord overruled all these events for His glory.

21:15, 16 From Caesarea **to Jerusalem** was an overland journey of more than fifty miles, a long trip in those days of slow transportation. The apostle's traveling party had been increased by the addition of **some of the disciples from Caesarea** and also by a Christian brother named **Mnason** (pronounced nay'-son). Originally from **Cyprus**, he had been one of the earliest disciples there. Now he was living in **Jerusalem**, and was privileged to be host to the apostle and those who journeyed with him during Paul's last visit to **Jerusalem**.

Paul's missionary journeys really end with his arrival in **Jerusalem**. The remainder of the Book of Acts is occupied with his arrest, trial, journey to Rome, trial, and imprisonment there.

21:17, 18 Upon arrival in **Jerusalem**, the apostle and his friends were cordially received by **the brethren**. The next day a meeting was arranged with **James and all the elders**. There is no way of knowing for sure which **James** is referred to here. It could be James, the brother of our Lord, James, the son of Alphaeus, or some other person with that name. The first is the most likely.

21:19, 20a Paul took the lead by telling **in detail** what **God had done among the Gentiles through his ministry**. This caused considerable rejoicing.

21:20b–22 However, the Jewish brethren were apprehensive. Word had traveled around that the Apostle Paul had preached and taught against Moses and the law. This could mean trouble in Jerusalem.

The specific charge being made against Paul was that he taught **all the Jews** in foreign lands **to forsake Moses**, by telling them **not to circumcise their children nor to walk according to the** Jewish **customs**. Did Paul actually teach this or did he not?

He did teach that Christ was the end of the law for righteousness to those who believe. He did teach that once the Christian faith had come, believing Jews were no longer under the law. He taught that if a man received circumcision as a means of obtaining justification, then such a man cut himself off from salvation in Christ Jesus. He taught that to return to the types and shadows of the law, after Christ had come, was dishonoring to Christ. In view of this, it is not hard to see why the Jews should think of him as they did.

21:23, 24 But the Jewish brethren in Jerusalem had a scheme which they thought would placate their countrymen, both saved and unsaved. They suggested that Paul should take upon himself a Jewish **vow**. **Four men** were already in the process of doing this. Paul should join them, purify himself with them, **and pay their expenses**. F. W. Grant explains:

> Let him take these four men, who being believers like himself could yet bind themselves with the Nazirite vow, and presenting himself with them in the Temple purified, take upon him the expenses necessary for the completion of it, and that publicly, that all might recognize clearly his own relation to the law.[76]

We do not know much about what this **vow** involved. The details are veiled in obscurity. But all we need to know is that it was a *Jewish* **vow**, and that if the Jews saw the apostle going through the ritual connected with it, they would **know** assuredly that he was not turning others away from **the law** of Moses. It would be an indication to the Jews that the apostle himself kept **the law**.

The action of the apostle in taking on himself this Jewish **vow** has been defended and criticized. In *defense* of Paul it has been argued that he was acting according to his own principle to be all things to all men, if by any means he might save some (1 Cor. 9:19–23). On the other hand, Paul has been *criticized* for going too far in an effort to conciliate the Jews, and thus creating the impression that he was under the law. In other words, Paul has been charged with being inconsistent with his view that the believer is not under the law, either for justification or as a rule of life (Gal. 1 and 2). We tend to agree with this criticism, but we also feel that one should be careful in judging the apostle's motives.

21:25 The Jerusalem brethren advised Paul that no rules need be imposed on Gentile believers other than those proposed by the council in Jerusalem, namely, **the Gentiles . . . should** abstain **from things offered to idols, from blood, from things strangled, and from sexual immorality**.

21:26 The steps taken by **Paul** are not clear to us today. Many commentators think this was the Nazirite vow. But even if this were the case, we still do not understand the various steps in the ceremony as described in this section.

H. Paul's Arrest and Trials (21:27–26:32)

21:27–29 **When the seven days** of the vow **were almost ended**, Paul's attempt to pacify **the Jews** proved futile. When some of **the** unbelieving **Jews from** proconsular **Asia** saw him **in the temple**, they incited a riot against him. Not only did they charge him with teachings that were contrary to **the** Jewish **people** and to **the law**, but they also accused him of defiling **the temple** by taking Gentiles into the inner courts. What actually happened was this: **they had previously seen Paul** with **Trophimus in the city** of Jerusalem. **Trophimus** was a Gentile convert from Ephesus. Because they saw them together, **they supposed that Paul had** taken his Gentile friend **into the** inner courts of **the temple**.

21:30–35 Although the charge was obviously false, it served its purpose. **All the city was** thrown into an uproar. The mob **seized Paul, and dragged him out of the temple** area, closing the gates of the inner courts behind them. As they proceeded **to kill him**, word reached the chiliarch, a military **commander** in charge **of the garrison** of Antonia. He came in a hurry with some of his **soldiers** and **took** Paul from the infuriated mob, **bound** him **with two chains**, and **asked who he was and what he had done**. The mob was, of course, incoherent and confused. **Some . . . cried one thing and some another**. The frustrated

officer **commanded** the soldiers to bring the prisoner **into the barracks** so he could find out more definitely what was going on. Even in the attempt to do this, **the mob** surged forward with such determination that Paul **had to be carried by the soldiers** up the stairs.

21:36 As they did so, they heard words ringing out from **the multitude** — words that perhaps some of them had heard before — **"Away with him!"**

21:37–39 Just as they were about to take **Paul into the barracks**, he asked the officer if he could say something. The officer was startled to hear **Paul** speaking **Greek**. He apparently thought he had arrested an **Egyptian** who had **stirred up a rebellion and led four thousand** men called **assassins out into the wilderness**. **Paul** quickly assured him that he was **a Jew from** the city of **Tarsus, in Cilicia**. As such, he was **a citizen of no mean city**; it was famous as a place of culture, education, and commerce, and had been declared a "free city" by Augustus. With characteristic fearlessness, the apostle requested permission **to speak to the people.**

21:40 **Permission** was granted, and as **Paul stood** there, flanked by Roman soldiers, he quieted the crowd by motioning **with his hand**. The **silence** was as **great** as the tumult had been. He was now ready to give his testimony to the Jerusalem Jews.

The Hebrew language here probably means Aramaic (a closely related tongue) as spoken by the Hebrews at that time.

22:1, 2 In addressing the Jewish mob, the apostle wisely used Aramaic rather than Greek. As soon as **they heard** their mother tongue, they were pleasantly surprised, and their shouts subsided, at least for the moment.

22:3–5 Paul began with his roots as **a Jew, born in Tarsus of Cilicia**; his education **at the feet of** the well-known Jewish teacher, **Gamaliel**; and his instruction in Judaism. He then gave special emphasis to his zeal as a Jew. He had **persecuted** the Christian faith, filling the **prisons** with those who believed in Jesus. The **high priest** and the Sanhedrin could bear **witness** to the thoroughness of his methods. It was **from** them that he **received letters** authorizing him to go **to Damascus** and **bring** back Christians from **there to Jerusalem to be punished**.

22:6–8 Up to this point in Paul's message the Jews could understand perfectly, and, if they were honest, they would have to agree that what had been said was true. Now the apostle is going to tell them of an event which changed the entire direction of his life. It will be up to them to decide whether this event was of God.

As Paul **journeyed** to **Damascus . . . a great light from heaven shone around** him. The fact that it happened **about noon**, here recorded for the first time, indicates that the **light** was more brilliant and glorious than the sun at its height. Struck to the ground by the intensity of the **light**, the persecutor heard **a voice** from heaven **saying, "Saul, Saul, why are you persecuting Me?"** Upon inquiry, he learned that it was **Jesus of Nazareth** who was speaking to him from heaven. The Nazarene had risen from the dead and was glorified above.

22:9 The men who traveled with him **saw the light**, and heard the sound of **the voice** (9:7), but they did **not hear** the actual words that were spoken. In other words, they were conscious of noise, but not of articulate speech.

22:10, 11 Having had this private audience with the Lord of Life and Glory, Paul made a complete commitment of his spirit, soul, and body to the Savior. This is indicated by his question, **"What shall I do, Lord?"** The Lord Jesus directed him to **go into Damascus, and there** he would receive his instructions. Blinded by the **light** of Christ's **glory**, he was **led by the hand** into the city.

22:12 In Damascus he was visited by **Ananias**. Paul describes him to his Jewish audience as **a devout man according to the law, having a good testimony with all the Jews who dwelt there**. The **testimony** of such a man was important in corroborating the account of Paul's conversion.

22:13 Addressing Paul as **"Brother Saul,"** Ananias commanded him to **receive** his **sight**. It was then that Paul first **looked up at him**.

22:14–16 In verses 14–16 we learn for the first time that Ananias said to Paul,

"The God of our fathers has chosen you that you should know His will, and see the Just One, and hear the voice of His mouth. For you will be His witness to all men of what you have seen and heard. And now why are you waiting? Arise and be baptized, and wash away your sins, calling on the name of the Lord."

Several points of interest and importance should be noted in these verses. First, Ananias stated that it was **the God of our fathers** who had ordered the events on the road to Damascus. If the Jews were to oppose and resist what had happened, they were really fighting against **God**. Second, Ananias told Paul that he would be a **witness** for the Lord to *all* men. This should have prepared the Jewish crowd for Paul's announcement that he had been sent to the Gentiles. Finally, Paul was told to **arise and be baptized, and wash away** his **sins**.

Verse 16 has been misused to teach baptismal regeneration. It *is* possible that the verse only applies to Paul as a Jew who needed to dissociate himself from his Christ-rejecting nation by water baptism (see comments on 2:38).

A simpler solution, based on the grammatical construction of the original is as follows: Unlike the KJV, which punctuates as if there are four items in a row on the same level, the NKJV, following the original, pairs the first two items and the second two items. In the Greek there is a finite verb modified by a participle in each half of the verse. A literal rendering would be: "Having arisen be baptized, and have your sins washed off (by) calling on the name of the Lord."[77] This last clause is supported by general biblical teaching (cf. Joel 2:32; Acts 2:21; Rom. 10:13).

22:17–21 Now, for the first time, we learn of an experience Paul had toward the close of his first visit **to Jerusalem** after conversion. While he **was praying in the temple**, he fell into **a trance** and heard the Lord commanding him to **get out of Jerusalem quickly**, because the people would **not receive** his **testimony concerning** Christ. It seemed incredible to the apostle that his own people would refuse to listen to him. After all, they knew what a zealous Jew he had been, how he had **imprisoned** and beaten the disciples of Jesus, and how he had even been an accomplice to the murder of **Stephen**. But the Lord repeated

His command, "Depart, for I will send you far from here to the Gentiles."

22:22, 23 Up to this point, the Jews had been listening to Paul quietly. But his mention of going to the Gentiles with the gospel aroused insane jealousy and hatred. Chanting furiously in wild disorder, they cried out for Paul's life.

22:24, 25 When **the commander** saw them in their mad frenzy, he concluded that Paul must have been guilty of some very serious crime. Apparently he could not understand Paul's message since it was given in Aramaic, so he determined to extract a confession from the apostle by torturing him. He therefore **ordered** his prisoner **to be brought into the barracks** and bound with thongs in order to be scourged. As these preparations for the **scourging** were moving ahead deliberately, **Paul** quietly asked the centurion if it was legal **to scourge a Roman** citizen when he was **uncondemned**. As a matter of fact, it was unlawful even to tie up **a Roman** citizen before his guilt had been proved! To scourge him was a very serious offense.

22:26 The centurion quickly **went and told the commander** to **take care what** he did to Paul, because **this man** was **a Roman** citizen.

22:27, 28 This brought **the commander** to **Paul** in a hurry. On inquiry, he learned that the apostle was indeed **a Roman** citizen. There were three ways to become **a Roman** in those days. *First*, citizenship was sometimes granted by imperial decree as a reward for services rendered, etc. *Second*, it was possible to become **a Roman** by birth. This was the case with **Paul**; he **was born** in Tarsus, a free city of the Roman Empire, and his father was **a Roman** citizen. *Finally*, it was possible to purchase **citizenship**, often at a very high price. Thus **the commander** had **obtained** his **citizenship** by paying **a large sum**.

22:29 Disclosure of Paul's **Roman** citizenship cancelled all plans to scourge him, and caused fear among the authorities.

22:30 The commander was obviously anxious **to know for certain why Paul** had been **accused by the Jews**. At the same time he was determined to carry out the proceedings in a legal and orderly manner. Therefore, on the day after the mob scene in Jerusalem, he had

Paul taken out of prison and brought before **the chief priests and** the Sanhedrin.

23:1, 2 Standing before the Sanhedrin, **Paul** prefaced his remarks with a statement that throughout his life he had **lived in all good conscience. The high priest, Ananias**, was infuriated by this statement. He doubtless looked on **Paul** as an apostate from the Jewish religion, a renegade, a turncoat. How could one who had turned from Judaism to Christianity claim such innocence? Accordingly **the high priest** ordered that the prisoner be slapped **on the mouth**. This order was extremely unjust, since the case had hardly gotten underway.

23:3 Paul snapped back to Ananias that **God** would **strike** him for being such a **whitewashed wall**! Outwardly the high priest seemed righteous and just; inwardly he was corrupt. Professing to **judge** others **according to the law**, here he commanded **Paul to be struck contrary to the law**.

23:4 The attendants were shocked by the apostle's scathing rebuke. Did he not know that he was speaking to the **high priest**?

23:5 For some reason unknown to us, **Paul** had not actually realized **that** Ananias **was the high priest**. The Sanhedrin had been assembled on short notice, and perhaps Ananias was not wearing his official robes. It may even be that he was not occupying the seat customarily assigned to **the high priest**. Or perhaps Paul's weak eyesight was the cause. Whatever the reason, **Paul** had not intentionally spoken **evil** of the duly constituted **ruler**. He quickly apologized for his words, quoting Exodus 22:28: **"You shall not speak evil of a ruler of your people."**

23:6 Sensing from the conversation in the courtroom that there was lack of agreement between **the Sadducees** and **Pharisees**, the apostle decided to widen the rift by declaring himself to be **a Pharisee** who was on trial because he believed in the **resurrection of the dead**. **The Sadducees**, of course, denied the **resurrection**, as well as the existence of spirits or angels. The **Pharisees**, being very orthodox, believed in both (see 23:8).

Paul has been criticized here for using what might seem to be a carnal expedient to divide his audience. "We cannot avoid feeling," writes A. J. Pollock, "that Paul was wrong in claiming to be a Pharisee, and thus snatch a strategical advantage by setting the rival Sadducees and Pharisees at variance."

23:7–9 Whether or not he was justified, his words did provoke **a dissension . . . between the Pharisees and the Sadducees**, and caused **a loud outcry**. Some of **the scribes of the Pharisees** defended Paul's innocence, and said in effect, "What does it matter anyway, **if a spirit or an angel has spoken to him?**"

23:10 The controversy between the opposing factions became so heated that **the commander** ordered **the soldiers** to escort the prisoner out of the hall and back to **the barracks**.

23:11 The following night the Lord Jesus made a personal appearance to **Paul** in the prison, and said, **"Be of good cheer, Paul; for as you have testified for Me in Jerusalem, so you must also bear witness at Rome."** It is remarkable that in a passage where the apostle's actions have been subject to considerable criticism, **the Lord** should personally praise him for having borne faithful witness **in Jerusalem**. There was not a word of criticism or reproach from the Savior. Rather, it was a message of sheer praise and promise. Paul's service was not over yet. As he had been faithful in his ministry **in Jerusalem**, so he would **also bear witness** for Christ **at Rome.**

23:12–15 The next **day, some of the Jews banded together** to kill the Apostle Paul. In fact, **more than forty of** them **bound themselves under an oath that** they would **eat nothing until** they had **killed** "this imposter." Their scheme was as follows: they went **to the chief priests and elders**, suggesting that a meeting of the Sanhedrin be announced in order to hear Paul's case more thoroughly. The Sanhedrin would ask **the commander** to bring the prisoner to them. But the **forty** assassins would lie in ambush somewhere between the prison and the council hall. When **Paul** came near them, they would pounce on him and **kill him.**

23:16–19 In the providence of God, a nephew of the apostle overheard the plot and reported it to **Paul**. The latter believed in availing himself of legitimate means to insure his safety; therefore, he reported the matter to **one of the centurions**. The centurion personally escorted the **young man to the commander.**

23:20, 21 Paul's nephew not only gave a complete account of the plot, but made a fervent plea to the commander not to **yield to** the demand of **the Jews** that **Paul** be brought to them.

23:22 When **the commander** had heard the story, he dismissed **the young man** with instructions not to tell anyone else of their meeting together. He now realized that he had to take prompt and decisive action to deliver his prisoner from the burning wrath of the Jews.

23:23–25 The commander quickly **called for two centurions** and arranged for a military escort to take the apostle **to Caesarea**. The guard was made up of **two hundred soldiers, seventy horsemen, and two hundred spearmen**. The trip was to be made under cover of darkness — at nine o'clock at **night**.

The great size of the military escort was not intended to be a tribute to this faithful messenger of Christ. Rather, it was an expression of the determination of the commander to maintain his reputation with his Roman superiors; if the Jews succeeded in killing Paul, a Roman citizen, then the officer in charge would be required to answer for his laxness.

23:26–28 The commander identifies himself as **Claudius Lysias** in the letter which he wrote to the Roman **governor Felix**. The purpose of the letter was, of course, to explain the situation with regard to Paul. It is rather amusing to see how **Lysias** sought to portray himself as a hero and a defender of public righteousness. He probably was extremely fearful lest it be reported to **Felix** that he had tied up an uncondemned **Roman** citizen. Fortunately for **Claudius Lysias**, Paul did not tattle.

23:29, 30 The commander explained that his investigation showed Paul to be innocent of any charge **deserving of death or chains**. Rather, the tumult seemed to be concerned with **questions of** Jewish **law**. Because of a plot against Paul, he felt it advisable to send Paul to Caesarea so that **his accusers** could come there also, and the whole matter could be aired in Felix's presence.

23:31–35 The trip **to Caesarea** was broken briefly at **Antipatris**, a city about thirty-nine miles from Jerusalem and twenty-four miles from **Caesarea**. Since there was little or no more danger of ambush from the Jews from this point on, **the soldiers** returned to Jerusalem, leaving **the horsemen** to escort **Paul to Caesarea**. Upon arrival, they delivered **Paul** to Felix, together with **the letter** from Lysias. When preliminary inquiry satisfied Felix as to the apostle's Roman citizenship, he promised to hear his case **when** his **accusers** had **come** down from Jerusalem. In the meantime **Paul** was **commanded to be kept in Herod's** palace or **Praetorium**.

The Roman governor, Felix, had enjoyed a meteoric rise from slavery to a position of political prominence in the Roman Empire. As to his personal life, he was grossly immoral. At the time of his appointment to be governor of the province of Judea, he was husband of three royal ladies. While in office, he fell in love with Drusilla, who was married to Azizus, king of Emesa. According to Josephus, a marriage was arranged through Simon, sorcerer from Cyprus.

He was a cruel despot, as is evidenced by the fact that he arranged the assassination of a high priest named Jonathan, who criticized him for his misrule.

It was this Felix before whom Paul had to appear.

24:1   Five days after **Paul** had left Jerusalem for Caesarea, **Ananias the high priest** arrived with certain members of the Sanhedrin. They hired a Roman named **Tertullus** to be their prosecuting attorney. His duty was to stand before Felix and press the charges **against Paul**.

24:2–4 **Tertullus** opened the case for the prosecution by showering the governor with flattery. Of course, there was a measure of truth to what he said. **Felix** had maintained rule and order by suppressing riots and insurrections. But Tertullus' words went beyond a mere acknowledgment of that fact, in an obvious effort to ingratiate his cause with the governor.

24:5–8 He then proceeded to specify four distinct charges against the Apostle Paul:

1. He was **a plague**, that is, a pest or a nuisance.

2. He was **a creator** of revolt **among all the Jews**.
3. He was **a ringleader of the sect of the Nazarenes**.
4. He **tried to profane the temple.**

24:9 After Tertullus had expressed confidence in Felix's ability to determine the accuracy of the charges against Paul, **the Jews** who were present added their voice in support of Tertullus' charges.

24:10 **Paul**, in response to a nod from **the governor**, rose to his own defense. First he expressed satisfaction at being permitted to appear before a man who, because of **many years** of experience, had familiarity with the customs and manners of the Jewish people. This might sound like flattery, but actually it was merely a courteous statement of the truth.

The apostle then answered the charges that were made against him, one by one.

24:11 As to his being a public nuisance, he replied that only **twelve days** had passed since he **went up to Jerusalem**, and that his purpose in going was **to worship**, not to cause a disturbance.

24:12, 13 Next he denied the charge that he incited the Jews to rebel. At no time, either **in the temple**, . . . **the synagogues or in the city**, had he disputed with the people or attempted to stir them up. These were the facts, and no one could disprove them.

24:14–17 Paul did not deny the third charge, namely, that he was a ringleader of the **sect** of the Nazarenes. But what he did say was that in this capacity he served **the God of** the Jews, **believing all things which are written in the** OT. He shared the expectation of all orthodox Jews, especially the Pharisees, **that there** would **be a resurrection of the dead, both of the just and the unjust**. In the light of that coming **resurrection**, he sought to preserve an unclouded relationship with the Lord and with his fellow men at all times. Far from stirring the Jews up to insurrection, Paul had come to Jerusalem **to bring alms** to the Jewish people. He was referring, of course, to the collection from the churches of Macedonia and Achaia, earmarked for the needy Hebrew Christian saints in Jerusalem.

24:18, 19 With regard to the fourth charge, namely, that he had profaned **the temple**, Paul made this reply: While he was in the act of bringing offerings to **the temple**, in the performance of a Jewish vow, certain **Jews from Asia found** him and accused him of taking unclean Gentiles into **the temple**. This, of course, was not true. The apostle was alone at the time, and had been **purified** from ceremonial defilement. These accusing **Jews from Asia** who caused the riot against him in Jerusalem **ought to have** come to Caesarea to accuse him, **if they had anything against** him.

24:20, 21 Paul then challenged **those** Jews **who** were present to state clearly what crimes he had been proved guilty of when he **stood before the council** in Jerusalem. They could not do it. All they would be able to say was that Paul **cried out, "Concerning the resurrection of the dead I am being judged by you this day."** In other words, those things in the accusation that were criminal were not true, and those things that were true were not criminal.

24:22 When Felix heard the case, he was faced with a dilemma. He knew enough about the Christian faith to realize who was right. The prisoner before him was obviously innocent of any crime against Roman law. Yet if he were to acquit Paul, he would incur the wrath of the Jewish people. From a political standpoint, it was important that he should curry their favor. So he adopted the expedient of continuing the case. He announced he would wait until **Lysias the commander** could come to Caesarea. Actually this was just a delaying tactic. We have no record that **the commander** ever did arrive.

24:23 In concluding the case, Felix **commanded** that although **Paul** should be retained in custody, he should be permitted reasonable **liberty**, and that **his friends** should be allowed to **visit him** and **provide** him food and clothing. This certainly indicates that the governor did not consider **Paul** a desperate criminal.

24:24, 25a Some days after the public trial, **Felix** and **his wife Drusilla** arranged a private interview with the apostle in order that they might hear more **concerning the** Christian **faith**.

With consummate fearlessness, **Paul reasoned** with this profligate governor and his adulterous wife **about righteousness, self-control, and the judgment to come**. They knew little of personal **righteousness**, either in their public or personal life. They were strangers to **self-control**, as was witnessed by their present evil marriage. They needed to be warned concerning **the judgment to come**, because unless their sins were pardoned through the blood of Christ, they would perish in the lake of fire.

24:25b, 26 Felix seemed to be more moved than Drusilla. Although he **was afraid**, he did not trust the Savior. He deferred making a decision for Christ with the words, **"Go away for now; when I have a convenient time I will call for you."** Sadly enough, this **convenient time** never came, as far as the Bible record is concerned. Yet this was not Paul's last testimony to **Felix**. The governor called him repeatedly during the next two years, while the apostle was a prisoner in Caesarea. Actually, **Felix** hoped that some of Paul's friends would pay him a handsome bribe in order to have him released.

24:27 After two years, in A.D. 60, **Porcius Festus succeeded Felix. Felix, wanting to do the Jews a favor, left Paul** as a manacled prisoner in Caesarea.

25:1 Porcius **Festus** was appointed Roman governor of Judea by the Emperor Nero in the autumn of A.D. 60. **Caesarea** was the political center for the Roman province of Syria, of which Judea was a part. **After three days** Festus **went up from Caesarea to Jerusalem**, the religious capital of his jurisdiction.

25:2, 3 Although it was now two years since **Paul** was imprisoned in Caesarea, **the Jews** had not forgotten him, neither had their murderous hatred subsided. Thinking that they might be able to obtain a political **favor** from the new governor, **the high priest and** principal **men of the Jews** filled his ear with charges **against Paul** and asked for him to be sent **to Jerusalem** for trial. Probably they meant that he should be tried before the Sanhedrin, but their real plan was to waylay him on the journey and **kill him**.

25:4, 5 But Festus had doubtless

been informed of their previous plan to kill **Paul**, and of the elaborate preparations taken by the commander in Jerusalem to spirit him away to Caesarea. He therefore refused their request, but promised them that he would permit them an opportunity to state their case against **Paul** if they could come to **Caesarea.**

25:6–8 After a stay of **more than ten days** in Jerusalem, Festus returned **to Caesarea** and convened the court **the next day**. The Jews hastened to the attack, bringing **many serious** charges **against Paul**, but failing to **prove** any of them. Sensing the poverty of their case, the apostle contented himself with a simple denial of any crime **against the law**, **against the temple**, or **Caesar.**

25:9–11 For a moment it seemed as if **Festus** was willing to accede to the request of **the Jews** that **Paul** be sent **to Jerusalem** for trial before the Sanhedrin. However, he would not do this without the prisoner's permission. **Paul** obviously realized that if he agreed, he would never reach **Jerusalem** alive. He therefore refused by stating that the court in Caesarea was the proper place for a trial. If he had **committed** a crime against the Roman Empire, he was not unwilling to die for it. But if he was not guilty of such a sin, then on what legal ground could he be handed over to **the Jews**? Taking full advantage of his rights as a Roman citizen, the Apostle Paul then uttered the memorable words, **"I appeal to Caesar."**

Was **Paul** justified in appealing **to Caesar**? Should he not have committed his cause entirely to God, and refused to stoop to dependence on his earthly citizenship? Was this one of the "mistakes of Paul?" We cannot say with finality. All we know is that his appeal **to Caesar** hindered his being set free at this time, and that even if he hadn't appealed, he would have reached Rome some other way.

25:12 **Festus** briefly **conferred** with his legal advisors concerning the procedure in such matters. He then said to Paul, perhaps in a defiant tone, **"You have appealed to Caesar? To Caesar you shall go!"**

25:13 Some time **after** this, **King** Herod **Agrippa II** and his sister **Bernice**

came **to Caesarea** to congratulate **Festus** on his new appointment. **Agrippa** was the son of Herod Agrippa I, who murdered James and imprisoned Peter (Acts 12). His sister was a woman of unusual beauty. While historians ascribe an unsavory reputation to her, including her relations with her brother, the NT is silent as to her personal character.

25:14–16 During their rather long stay in Caesarea, **Festus** decided to tell Agrippa about a problem he was facing with a prisoner named Paul. First he recounted the crude demand **of the Jews** that sentence be passed against Paul without a formal trial. Portraying himself as the upholder and protector of proper judicial processes, he told how he had insisted on a trial at which the defendant could meet his **accusers face to face** and be given the opportunity to defend himself.

25:17–19 When the case came to trial, Festus found that the prisoner was not guilty of any crime against the empire. Rather, the case revolved around **"some questions about their own religion and about a certain Jesus, who had died, whom Paul affirmed to be alive."**

25:20–22 Festus then reviewed his offer to **Paul to go to Jerusalem**, and of Paul's appeal to the **Augustus** (a *title* for Caesar here, not a *name*). This, of course, raised a problem. In sending his prisoner to Rome, what charge would he make against him? Since **Agrippa** was a Jew, and therefore conversant with matters involving Judaism, Festus hoped he would get some help in drawing up a suitable charge.

In speaking of the Savior of the world, Festus used the expression, **a certain Jesus**. Bengel's comment on this is worth repeating: "Thus speaks this miserable Festus of Him to Whom every knee shall bow."

25:23 **The next day** a formal hearing was arranged. **Agrippa and Bernice** arrived **with great pomp**. They were accompanied by **the commanders and the prominent men of the city**. Then **Paul was brought in.**

25:24–27 Once again, **Festus** set forth the history of the case — the insistent demands **of the Jews** for Paul's death, the inability of **Festus** to find the apostle guilty of any crime **deserving of**

death, and then Paul's appeal to Caesar. Festus' dilemma, of course, was this: he was forced by Paul's appeal to send him to Nero, yet there was no adequate *legal basis* for a trial. **Festus** plainly stated that he hoped **Agrippa** would be able to help him; after all, it did seem rather **unreasonable to send a prisoner and not to specify the charges against him**. These proceedings were more in the nature of a hearing than a trial. The Jews were not present to accuse the apostle, and **Agrippa** was not expected to render a binding decision.

26:1–3 The scene before us has been well described as "an enslaved king and an enthroned prisoner." From the spiritual standpoint, **Agrippa** was a pitiable figure, whereas the apostle soared on wings of faith, superior to his circumstances.

When given his cue by **Agrippa**, **Paul stretched out his hand and** began a stirring recital of his Christian experience. First, he expressed gratitude that he was permitted to present his case before one who, being a Jew, was conversant with the **customs and questions which** prevailed among the Jewish people. His introduction was not mere flattery; it was a statement of Christian courtesy and simple truth.

26:4, 5 As to his early **life**, the apostle was an exemplary Jew. **The Jews** would have to admit, if only they **were willing to testify**, that Paul had followed a pathway of **the strictest** orthodoxy, being a consistent **Pharisee.**

26:6 **Now** he was on trial for no greater crime than the fact that he clung to **the hope of the promise made by God** to the Jewish **fathers** in the OT. The flow of Paul's argument here seems to be as follows: In the OT God made various covenants with the leaders of Israel, such as Abraham, Isaac, Jacob, David, and Solomon. The principal covenant had to do with the promise of the Messiah, His coming to deliver the nation of Israel and to reign over the earth. The patriarchs of the OT died without seeing the fulfillment of this promise. Does this mean that God would not carry out the terms of the covenants? He would most assuredly do so! But how could He do it when the fathers were already dead? The answer is, "By raising them from

the dead." Thus, in a very direct way, the apostle links the promises made to the OT saints with the resurrection of the dead.

26:7 The apostle pictured the **twelve tribes** of Israel as **earnestly** and ceaselessly **serving God**, hoping to see the **promise** fulfilled. This reference to the **twelve tribes** is important in view of the current teaching that ten of the tribes of Israel have been "lost" since the captivity. Though they were scattered among the Gentile nations, the Apostle Paul saw them as a distinct people, **serving God** and looking for the promised Deliverer.

26:8 This then was Paul's crime! He believed **that God** would fulfill His promise to the fathers by raising them from **the dead**. What was so **incredible** about this? Paul asked Agrippa and all those who were with him.

26:9–11 Reverting to the story of his life, Paul recounted the savage and unremitting campaign he waged against the followers of the Christian faith. With all his strength he opposed **the name of Jesus of Nazareth**. With **authority from the chief priests**, he imprisoned **many of** the Christians in Jerusalem. When they stood trial before the Sanhedrin, he cast his vote against them consistently. Over and over again he arranged punishment for those whom he found **in every synagogue**, and he did all he could to force them to deny their Lord. (When it says that he **compelled**[78] them to **blaspheme**, it does not mean he was successful, but *he tried to* do it.) Paul's hate campaign against the disciples of **Jesus** had overflowed from Jerusalem and Judea **to foreign cities**.

26:12–14 It was while he was on one of these foreign expeditions that a great transforming experience occurred in his life. He was en route **to Damascus**, equipped with official papers authorizing him to arrest the Christians and bring them back to Jerusalem for punishment. **At midday** he was overcome by a vision of glory. **A light from heaven** shone upon him, **brighter than the** midday **sun**. After he **had fallen to the ground**, he **heard a voice** asking this probing question: **"Saul, Saul, why are you persecuting Me?"** The **voice** also added the revealing words, **"It is hard**

for you to kick against the goads."
Goads were sharply pointed instruments
used to force stubborn animals to move
ahead. Paul had been kicking **against** the
goad of his own conscience, but even
more important, **against** the convicting
voice of the Holy Spirit. He had never
been able to forget the poise and grace
with which Stephen had died. He had
been fighting **against** God Himself.

26:15 Paul asked, **"Who are You,
Lord?"** The voice replied, **"I am Jesus
whom you are persecuting."** *Jesus*? How
could that be? Hadn't Jesus been crucified and buried? Hadn't His disciples
stolen His body and laid it away in some
secret place? How then could Jesus be
speaking to him now? The truth quickly
dawned on Paul's soul. Jesus had indeed
been buried, but He had *risen* from the
dead! He had ascended back to heaven,
from where He was now speaking to
Paul. In persecuting the Christians, Paul
had been **persecuting** their Master. And
in **persecuting** Him, he had been **persecuting** the Messiah of Israel, the very
Son of God.

26:16 Next Paul gives a condensed
summary of the commission which was
given him by the risen Lord Jesus Christ.
He was told by the Lord to **rise and
stand on** his **feet.** He had had this special revelation of Christ in glory because
he was appointed to be a servant of the
Lord **and a witness** of all he had **seen**
that day, and of all the great truths of
the Christian faith which would yet be
made known to him.

26:17 The promise that Paul would
be delivered **from the Jewish people** and
the Gentiles must be understood as
meaning deliverance in general until his
work was done.

26:18 Paul would be sent especially
to the Gentiles **to open their eyes, in
order to turn them from darkness to
light, and from the power of Satan to
God.** Through faith in the Lord Jesus,
they would **receive forgiveness of sins
and an inheritance among those who are
sanctified.** H. K. Downie shows how
verse 18 is an excellent summary of what
the gospel does:

1. It relieves from darkness.
2. It releases from the power of Satan.
3. It remits sins.
4. It restores a lost inheritance.

26:19–23 Having been thus commissioned, Paul explains to **Agrippa** that
he **was not disobedient to the heavenly
vision.** Both **in Damascus and in Jerusalem, and throughout all . . . Judea, and
then to the Gentiles** he preached to men
that they should repent and **turn to
God,** doing **works** that prove the reality
of their **repentance.** This is what he was
doing when **the Jews seized** him **in the
temple and tried to kill** him. But **God**
had given him protection and **help,** and
he continued to testify to all with whom
he came in contact, preaching the message **which the prophets and Moses**
preached in the OT. The message was
that the Messiah **would suffer, that He
would be the first to rise from the dead,**
and that He **would** show **light** both **to
the Jewish people and to the Gentiles.**

26:24–26 Being a Gentile, **Festus**
had probably failed completely to follow
the flow of the apostle's argument. Thoroughly unable to appreciate a man who
was filled with the Holy Spirit, he impetuously accused **Paul** of being crazy as
the result of his **much learning.** With no
trace of irritation or temper, the apostle
quietly denied the charge and emphasized that his **words** were those **of truth
and reason.** He then expressed confidence that **the king** knew the truth of
what he had been saying. Paul's life and
testimony had not been a secret. The
Jews knew all about it, and doubtless the
reports had reached Agrippa.

26:27 Addressing the king directly,
Paul asked, **"King Agrippa, do you believe the prophets?"** Then Paul answered his own question, **"I know that
you do believe."** The force of the argument is unmistakable. Paul was saying
in effect, "I believe all that the prophets
said in the OT. **You,** too, **believe** their
testimony, don't you, **Agrippa?** How
then can the Jews accuse me of a crime
deserving of death? Or how could you
condemn me for believing what you
yourself believe?"

26:28 That **Agrippa** felt the force of
the argument is indicated by his words,
**"You almost persuade me to become a
Christian."** However, there is consider-
able disagreement as to exactly what
Agrippa meant. Those who follow the
King James tradition feel that the king
had actually been brought to the thresh-

old of decision for Christ. They feel that Paul's answer in verse 29 substantiates this. Others think that **Agrippa** was using irony, asking Paul, as it were, "Do you think that with a little persuasion you can make me a Christian?" In other words, he was evading the pressure of the apostle's words with a joke.

26:29 Whether Agrippa was speaking in sincerity or in jest, **Paul** answered with deadly earnestness. He expressed the fervent wish that, whether with little persuasion or with much, both Agrippa and **all** the others present might enter into the joys and blessings of the Christian life, that they might share all Paul's privileges, that they **might become** like him, **except for** the **chains**. Morgan writes:

> He would die to save Agrippa, but he would not put his chains upon Agrippa. That is Christianity. Magnify it, multiply it, apply it. The sincerity that persecutes is not Christian. The sincerity that dies to deliver, but will not impose a chain, is Christianity.[79]

26:30–32 **The king**, the **governor**, **Bernice**, and the other officials left the room to confer privately. They were all forced to admit that Paul had **done nothing deserving of death or chains**. Perhaps with a tinge of regret, **Agrippa said to Festus** that **if** Paul **had not appealed to Caesar**, he **might have been set free**.

We naturally wonder why the appeal **to Caesar** could not be cancelled. Whether or not such an appeal was unalterable, we do know that it was God's purpose that the apostle to the Gentiles should go to Rome for trial before the Emperor (23:11), and there find the fulfillment of his desire to be made conformable to the death of his Lord.

I. Paul's Voyage to Rome and Shipwreck (27:1–28:16)[†]

This chapter presents the thrilling saga of the apostle's voyage from Caesarea to Malta, en route to Rome. If Paul had not been a passenger, we would never have heard of the trip, or of the shipwreck. The passage is full of nautical terms, and is therefore not always easy to follow.

27:1 The journey began at Caesarea. **Paul** was placed in the custody of an officer **named Julius**. This **centurion** was attached to the **Augustan Regiment**, a distinguished legion of the Roman army. Like all the other centurions mentioned in the NT, he was a man of superior character in kindness, justice, and consideration for others.

27:2 There were other prisoners on board, who, like Paul, were being taken to Rome for trial. Also on the passenger list were the names of **Aristarchus** and Luke, both traveling companions of the apostle on earlier journeys. The **ship** on which they embarked was from **Adramyttium**, a city of Mysia in the northwest corner of Asia Minor. It was scheduled **to sail** north and west, making stops at ports **along the coasts of** proconsular **Asia**, the western province of Asia Minor.

27:3 The ship sailed north along the coast of Palestine, putting in **at Sidon**, seventy miles from Caesarea. **Julius**, the centurion, **kindly** permitted **Paul to go** ashore and visit **his friends and receive care.**

27:4, 5 From Sidon, the route cut across the northeast corner of the Mediterranean, passing **Cyprus** on the left, and thus taking advantage of the side of the island sheltered from the wind. In spite of **the winds** being **contrary**, the ship crossed over to the southern coast of Asia Minor, then **sailed** westward past **Cilicia and Pamphylia** till it arrived at **Myra, a** port **city of Lycia**.

27:6 **There the centurion** transferred his prisoners to another **ship**, since the first one would not take them any closer **to Italy**; it would rather sail up the western coast of Asia Minor to its home port.

The second **ship** was from Alexandria, on the northern coast of Africa. It carried 276 people, both crew and passengers, and a cargo of wheat. From Alexandria it had sailed due north across the Mediterranean to Myra, and was now heading west for **Italy**.

27:7, 8 For **many days** travel was slow, due to adverse winds. It was **with difficulty** that the crew brought the ship over against the harbor of **Cnidus** (pronounced nigh'-dus), a port on the extreme southwest corner of Asia Minor. Since **the wind** was against them, they headed south and sailed along the sheltered east side of the island of **Crete**. Rounding Cape **Salmone**, they turned westward and bucked heavy winds until they came to **Fair Havens**, a harbor **near the city of Lasea**, on the south central coast of **Crete.**

27:9, 10 By **now** considerable **time** had been lost due to unfavorable **sailing** conditions. The approach of winter weather made further travel **dangerous**. It must have been late September or early October, since **the Fast** (the Day of Atonement) **was already over**. **Paul** warned the crew that navigation was unsafe and that if **this voyage** were continued, there would be the danger of losing **the cargo and ship,** and even the **lives** of some on board.

27:11, 12 However, **the helmsman and the owner of the ship** wanted to proceed. **The centurion** accepted their judgment, and most of the others agreed with them too. It was felt that **the harbor was not** as **suitable** as **Phoenix** would be as a place to spend the **winter**. **Phoenix** was located forty miles west of Fair Havens, at the southwest tip of **Crete**. Its **harbor** opened **toward the southwest and northwest**.

27:13–17 **When the south wind blew softly**, the mariners thought they could make the extra distance to Phoenix. They weighed anchor, and sailed westward, hugging the shore. Then a violent northeaster (**Euroclydon**[80]) beat down upon them from the cliffs along the coast. Unable to steer the desired course, the crew was forced to let **the ship** be driven by the gale. They were driven southwest to a small **island called Clauda**,[81] twenty to thirty miles from **Crete**. When they reached the protected side of the **island**, they had **difficulty** securing **the skiff** which they had been towing. But finally they were able to hoist **it on board**. Then they tied **cables** around the hull of **the ship** to keep it from being torn apart by the heavy seas. They greatly feared they would be driven south to **Syrtis**, a gulf on the coast of Africa noted for its dangerous shoals. To prevent this, **they struck sail and so were driven.**

27:18, 19 After a day of drifting at the mercy of the storm, they began to throw the cargo overboard. On the third day they threw **the ship's tackle overboard**. Doubtless **the ship** had been taking a lot of water, and it was therefore necessary to lighten its load to prevent it from sinking.

27:20 For many days they were tossed about helplessly without sight of **sun** or **stars**, and thus without the ability to take bearings and find out where they were. **Hope** of survival **was finally given up**.

27:21–26 Despair was accentuated by hunger. The men had not eaten for many days. Doubtless they spent their time working for the preservation of the ship and bailing out water. Perhaps there were no facilities for cooking. Sickness, fear, and discouragement probably robbed them of appetite. There was no shortage of food, but neither was there an inclination to eat.

Then Paul stood in the midst of them with a message of hope. First he gently reminded them that they **should . . . not have sailed from Crete**. Then he assured them that though **the ship** would be lost, there would be **no loss of life**. How did he know? **An angel** of the Lord had appeared to him that **night**, assuring him that he would yet stand **before Caesar** in Rome. **God** had **granted** the apostle **all those who** sailed **with** him, in the sense that they, too, would be preserved. Therefore they should cheer up. **Paul** believed that all would be well, even though they would be shipwrecked **on a certain island**.

A. W. Tozer writes insightfully:

> When the "south wind blew softly," the ship that carried Paul sailed smoothly enough and no one on board knew who Paul was or how much strength of character lay hidden behind that rather plain exterior. But when the mighty tempest, Euroclydon, burst upon them, Paul's greatness was soon the talk of everyone on the ship. The apostle, though himself a prisoner, quite literally took command of the vessel, made decisions and issued orders that meant life or death to the people. And I think the crisis brought to a head something in Paul that had not been clear even to him. Beautiful theory was quickly crystallized into hard fact when the tempest struck.[82]

27:27–29 Fourteen days had elapsed since they left Fair Havens. They were now drifting helplessly in a part of the Mediterranean known as **the Adriatic**, the **sea** between Greece, Italy, and Africa. **About midnight the sailors**

sensed that they were drawing near some land; perhaps they could hear the breakers dashing against the shore. When they first measured the depth, they **found it** was **twenty fathoms** (120 feet), then a little later it was **fifteen fathoms**. To prevent running the ship aground, **they dropped four anchors from the stern, and prayed for** daylight.

27:30–32 Fearing for their lives, some of **the sailors** plotted to get ashore in the small boat. They were in the process of lowering **the skiff** from the bow of **the ship** — pretending they were **putting out** more **anchors** — when **Paul** reported their plot **to the centurion. Paul** warned that **unless** the sailors remained on board, the rest would not **be saved. Then the soldiers cut away the ropes** attached to **the skiff and let it fall off. The sailors** were thus compelled to try to save their own lives on board **the ship,** as well as the lives of the others.

27:33, 34 Phillips titles verses 33–37 "Paul's sturdy common sense." To appreciate the drama of the moment, we should really know something of the terror of a violent storm at sea. Then too, we should remember that Paul was not the captain of the ship but only a captive passenger.

Shortly before daybreak **Paul implored** the people to eat, reminding them that they had gone two weeks **without food**. The time had come to eat; their well-being depended on it. The apostle assured them that **not a hair** of anyone's head would be lost.

27:35 Then he set the example for them by taking **bread**, giving **thanks to God** publicly for it, and eating. How often we shrink from praying in front of others! Yet how often such prayer speaks louder than our preaching.

27:36, 37 Thus **encouraged,** they **took food themselves.** There **were two hundred and seventy-six persons on the ship**.

27:38–41 After eating, **they lightened the ship** by throwing **out the wheat into the sea. Land** was nearby, **but they** could **not recognize it.** The decision was made to beach **the ship,** as far on shore as **possible. They let go the anchors,** leaving **them in the sea.** Then they untied the rudders that had previously been raised, and lowered them into position. Hoisting **the mainsail,** they **made**

for shore and drove the ship aground at **a place where two seas met** — probably in a channel between two islands. The bow **stuck fast** in the sand, **but the stern** soon began to break apart **by the violence of the waves.**

27:42–44 The soldiers' plan was to **kill the prisoners** to prevent **escape, but the centurion, wanting to save Paul,** overruled. He ordered all **who could swim** to make for shore. **The rest** were told to float in **on boards** or other **parts of the ship.** In this way, every one of the crew and passengers **escaped safely to land**.

28:1, 2 As soon as the crew and passengers reached shore, they learned that they were on the **island** of **Malta.** Some of **the natives** of the island saw the shipwreck and witnessed the victims struggling through the water to get to shore. They very graciously built **a fire** for the new arrivals, who were thoroughly drenched and **cold,** both from the sea and from **the rain.**

28:3 While **Paul** was helping with **the fire,** he was bitten by a poisonous snake. Apparently the snake had lain dormant among some of the driftwood. When the wood was placed **on the fire,** the **viper** quickly revived and struck out against the apostle. It **fastened on his hand,** not just in the sense of coiling on it, but actually biting it.

28:4–6 At first the local citizens concluded the apostle must be **a murderer.** Although he had **escaped** from the shipwreck, **yet justice** was tracking him down and he would soon **swell up or suddenly fall down dead.** However, when Paul showed no ill effects from the snake bite, **they changed their minds** and decided **he was a god!** This is another vivid illustration of the fickleness and changeableness of the human heart and mind.

28:7 The leading citizen of the island of Malta at that time **was Publius.** He owned considerable land in the vicinity of the beach where the shipwrecked party landed. This wealthy Roman official **received** Paul and his friends **courteously,** and provided accommodations for them **for three days,** that is, until permanent quarters could be arranged in which they would spend the winter.

28:8 The kindness of this Gentile did not go unrewarded. At about that time, his **father** took **sick** with **fever and dysentery**. **Paul went in to him and prayed, and he laid his hands on him and healed him.**

28:9, 10 News of this healing miracle spread quickly throughout **the island**. During the next three months the sick were brought to Paul and were all cured. The people of Malta showed their appreciation to the apostle and to Luke[83] when they left by showering them with many honors, and bringing many gifts that would be helpful on the trip to Rome.

28:11 **After** the **three months** of winter had passed, and navigation was safe again, the centurion, with his prisoners, embarked on **an Alexandrian ship . . . which had wintered at the island**. The **figurehead** of this **ship was the Twin Brothers**, that is, Castor and Pollux. These were supposed, by heathen sailors, to be the patron gods of mariners.

28:12–14 From Malta they sailed about eighty miles to **Syracuse**, the capital of Sicily, located on its east coast. The ship stopped there for **three days**, then proceeded to **Rhegium**, on the southwest corner of Italy, at the toe. **After one day** a favorable **south wind blew**, enabling the crew to sail 180 miles northward along the west coast of Italy **to Puteoli**, on the northern shore of the Bay of Naples. **Puteoli** was about 150 miles southeast of **Rome**. There the apostle **found** Christian **brethren**, with whom he was permitted to enjoy fellowship for **seven days.**

28:15 We are not told how news reached Rome of the arrival of Paul in Puteoli. However, two different groups **of brethren** set out **to meet** him. One group traveled forty-three miles southeast of Rome to The Market of Appius. The other group traveled thirty-three miles southeast to the **Three Inns**. **Paul** was greatly cheered and encouraged by this touching demonstration of the love of the saints in Rome.

28:16 Upon arrival in **Rome**, he **was permitted to dwell** in a private home, **with the soldier who guarded him.**

J. Paul's House-Arrest and Witness to the Jews in Rome (28:17–31)[†]

28:17–19 In accordance with his policy of witnessing to **the Jews** first, **Paul** sent an invitation to their religious leaders. **When they had come together** in his rented house, he explained his case **to them**. He told them that although he had **done nothing against** the Jewish **people, or** their **customs**, yet **the Jews of Jerusalem** had **delivered** him **into the hands of the Romans** for trial. The Gentile authorities could find no fault in him, and wanted to free him, **but when the Jews** cried out **against it**, the apostle **was compelled to appeal to Caesar**. In making this appeal, it was not for the purpose of bringing any charge against the Jewish **nation**. Rather, it was that he might defend himself.

28:20 It was because he was innocent of any crime against the Jewish people that he had **called** the chief Roman Jews together. Actually it was **because** of **the hope of Israel** that he **was bound with** a **chain. The hope of Israel**, as explained previously, refers to the fulfillment of the promises made to the Jewish patriarchs, especially the promise of the Messiah. Inherent in the fulfillment of these promises was the resurrection of the dead.

28:21, 22 The Jewish leaders professed to know nothing about the Apostle Paul. They had not **received** any **letters from Judea concerning** him, and none of their fellow Jews had brought reports to them against him. However, they did want to hear more from Paul, because they knew that the Christian faith with which he was associated was **spoken against everywhere.**

28:23 Some time later a great number of these Jews came to Paul's **lodging** to hear more from him. He availed himself of the opportunity to testify to them concerning **the kingdom of God**, and to persuade them **concerning Jesus**. In so doing he quoted to them from **the Law of Moses and the Prophets, from morning till evening.**

28:24 Some believed the message he brought, **and some disbelieved**. (Disbelieving is stronger than a simple failure to accept the message. It indicates a positive rejection.)

28:25–28 When **Paul** saw that once again the gospel was being, on the whole, rejected by the Jewish nation, he quoted Isaiah 6:9 and 10, where the

[†]*See p. xxxi.*

prophet was commissioned to preach the word to a **people** whose **hearts** were **dull**, whose **ears** were deaf, and whose **eyes** were blinded. The apostle felt again the heartbreak of preaching good news to those who did not want to hear it. In view of this rejection by the Jews, **Paul** announced that he was taking the gospel **to the Gentiles**, and he expressed the assurance that **they** would **hear it.**

28:29 The unbelieving **Jews departed**, arguing **among themselves**. As Calvin points out, Paul's quoting a prophecy against them irritated the ungodly element who rejected the Messiah. It whipped them into a fury against those Jews who accepted Him. The reformer makes a helpful application:

> Finally, it will be in vain for anyone to object from this that the Gospel of Christ causes contentions, when it is obvious that these spring only from the stubbornness of men. And indeed, in order to enjoy peace with God, it is necessary for us to wage war with those who treat Him with contempt.[84]

28:30 Then **Paul** remained in Rome for **two whole years**, living **in his own rented house**, and ministering to a continual line of visitors. It was probably during this time that he wrote the Epistles to the Ephesians, Philippians, Colossians, and Philemon.

28:31 He enjoyed a considerable measure of liberty, **preaching the kingdom of God and teaching the things which concern the Lord Jesus Christ with all confidence, no one forbidding him**.

Thus the Book of Acts closes. Some think it ends with a strange abruptness. However, the pattern outlined at the outset had now been fulfilled. The gospel had reached out to Jerusalem, Judea, Samaria, and now the Gentile world.

The events in the life of Paul after the close of Acts can only be inferred from his later writings.

It is generally believed that after his two years in Rome, his case came before Nero and the verdict was acquittal.

He then embarked on what has come to be known as his Fourth Missionary Journey. Places which he probably visited on this trip, though not necessarily in this order were:

1. COLOSSE and EPHESUS (Phmn. 22).
2. MACEDONIA (1 Tim. 1:3; Phil. 1:25; 2:24).
3. EPHESUS (1 Tim. 3:14).
4. SPAIN (Rom. 15:24).
5. CRETE (Titus 1:5).
6. CORINTH (2 Tim. 4:20).
7. MILETUS (2 Tim. 4:20).
8. Winter spent in NICOPOLIS (Titus 3:12).
9. TROAS (2 Tim. 4:13).

We have no information as to why, when, or where he was arrested, but we do know he was brought to Rome as a prisoner a second time. This imprisonment was much more harsh than the first (2 Tim. 2:9). He was deserted by most of his friends (2 Tim. 4:9–11), and knew that the time of his death was at hand (2 Tim. 4:6–8).

Tradition says he was beheaded outside Rome in A.D. 67 or 68. For Paul's eulogy, read his own words in 2 Cor. 4:8–10, 6:4–10, and 11:23–28 along with our commentary on these inspiring summaries.

THE MESSAGE OF ACTS

After reading the Book of Acts, it is good to review the principles and practices of the early Christians. *What characterized the individual believers and the local churches of which they were members?*

First, it is obvious that the first century Christians lived first and foremost for the interests of the Lord Jesus. Their whole outlook was Christ-centered. The primary reason for their existence was to witness for the Savior, and they gave themselves to this task with vigor. In a world which was engaged in a mad struggle for survival, there was a hard core of zealous Christian disciples who sought first the kingdom of God and His righteousness. To them, everything else was subordinated to this glorious calling.

Jowett notes with admiration:

> The disciples had been baptized with . . .the holy, glowing enthusiasm caught from the altar of God. They had this central fire, from which every other purpose and faculty in life gets its strength. This fire in the apostles' soul was like a furnace fire in a great liner, which drives her through the tempests and through the en-

vious and engulfing deep. Nothing could stop these men! Nothing could hinder their going . . . A strong imperative rings throughout all their doings and all their speech. They have heat and they have light because they were baptized by the power of the Holy Ghost.[85]

The message they preached centered around the resurrection and glory of the Lord Jesus Christ. They were witnesses to a risen Savior. Men had slain the Messiah, but God had raised Him from among the dead and given Him the place of highest honor in heaven. Every knee must bow to Him — the glorified Man at God's right hand. There is no other way of salvation.

In an environment of hate, bitterness, and greed, the disciples manifested love to all. They repaid persecution with kindness, and prayed for their assailants. Their love toward other Christians forced their enemies to exclaim, "See how these Christians love one another!"

We get the distinct impression that they lived sacrificially for the spread of the gospel. They did not look upon material possessions as their own, but as a stewardship from God. Wherever there was genuine need, there was a prompt flow of funds to meet the need.

The weapons of their warfare were not carnal, but mighty through God to the pulling down of strongholds. They realized that they were not fighting against religious or political leaders, but rather against evil powers in heavenly places. So they went forth armed with faith, prayer, and the word of God. Unlike Islam, Christianity did not grow through the use of force.

These early Christians lived in separation from the world. They were in it but not of it. They maintained active contact with unbelievers as far as their witness was concerned, but never compromised their loyalty to Christ by engaging in the world's sinful pleasures. As pilgrims and strangers, they traveled through a foreign land seeking to be a blessing to all without partaking of its defilement.

Did they engage in politics or seek to remedy the social evils of the day? Their outlook was that all the ills and abuses in the world arise from man's sinful nature. In order to remedy the evils, one must get at the cause. Political and social reforms treat the symptoms without affecting the disease itself. Only the gospel can get at the heart of the matter, changing man's evil nature. And so they were not distracted by second-best remedies. They preached the gospel in season, out of season. Everywhere the gospel went, the festering sores were eliminated or reduced.

They were not surprised when they ran into persecution. They had been taught to expect it. Instead of retaliating or even vindicating themselves, they committed their cause to God, who judges righteously. Instead of seeking escape from trials, they prayed for boldness to proclaim Christ to all with whom they came in contact.

The goal before the disciples was world evangelization. To them there was no distinction between home and foreign missions. The field was the world. Their evangelistic activity was not an end in itself, that is, they were not content to lead souls to Christ and then let them flounder on by themselves. Rather, the converts were gathered into local Christian assemblies. Here they were taught the word, nurtured in prayer, and otherwise strengthened in the faith. Then they were challenged to go out with the message to others.

It was the establishment of local churches that gave permanence to the work and provided for evangelical outreach in the surrounding areas. These congregations were indigenous, that is, they were self-governing, self-propagating, and self-financing. Each assembly was independent of other churches, yet there was the fellowship of the Spirit between them. Each assembly sought to reproduce other assemblies in adjacent territory. And each one was financed from within. There was no central treasury or parent organization.

The assemblies were primarily spiritual havens for believers rather than centers for reaching the unsaved. Church activities included the breaking of bread, worship, prayer, Bible study, and fellowship. Gospel meetings were not held in the assemblies as such but rather wherever there was opportunity to address the unsaved — in synagogues, in marketplaces, on the streets, in prisons, and from house to house.

The churches did not meet in special

buildings erected for the purpose but in the homes of believers. This gave great mobility to the church in times of persecution, permitting it to "go underground" quickly and easily.

At the outset, there were certainly no denominations. All believers were recognized as members of the body of Christ and every local church as an expression of the church universal.

Neither was there a distinction between clergy and laity. No one man had exclusive rights in an assembly with regard to teaching, preaching, baptizing, or administering the Lord's Supper. There was a recognition of the fact that every believer had some gift, and there was liberty for the exercise of that gift.

Those who were gifted as apostles, prophets, evangelists, pastors, and teachers did not seek to establish themselves as indispensable officials in a church. Their function was to build up the saints in the faith so that they, too, might be able to serve the Lord daily. The gifted men of the NT period were equipped for their work by a special anointing of the Holy Spirit. This accounts for the way in which unlearned and homespun men exercised such an influence on their age. They were not "professional" in the sense we think of the term today, but lay preachers with unction from on high.

The proclamation of the message in the Book of Acts was often accompanied by miracles — signs and wonders and various gifts of the Holy Spirit. While these miracles seem more prominent in the early chapters, they continue to the end of the book.

After a local church was in operation, the apostles or their representatives appointed elders — men who were spiritual overseers. These men shepherded the flock. There were several elders in each church.

The noun, "deacon," is not specifically applied to a church officer in the Book of Acts. However, the verb form of the word is used to describe service carried on for the Lord, whether spiritual or temporal.

The early believers practiced baptism by immersion. The general impression is that believers were baptized soon after their conversion. On the first day of the week the disciples gathered together to remember the Lord in the breaking of bread. This service was probably not as formal as it is today. It seems to have been observed in connection with a common meal or a love feast.

The early church was addicted to prayer. It was the lifeline with God. The prayers were earnest, believing, and fervent. The disciples also fasted in order that all their powers might be concentrated on spiritual matters without distraction or drowsiness.

It was after prayer and fasting that the prophets and teachers at Antioch commended Barnabas and Saul to a special missionary program. Both of these men had been serving the Lord for some time prior to this. The commendation was not an official ordination, therefore, but an acknowledgment by the leaders at Antioch that the Holy Spirit had really called them. It was also an expression of the whole-hearted fellowship of the assembly in the work which Barnabas and Saul were undertaking.

Those who went out in evangelistic service were not controlled by their home assembly in this service. They were apparently free to serve as the Holy Spirit guided them. But they did report back to their home church as to the blessing of God on their labors.

In this connection, the church was not a highly organized complex, but a living organism which moved in constant obedience to the leading of the Lord. The Head of the church, Christ in heaven, directed the members, and they sought to keep themselves teachable, mobile, and responsive. Thus instead of finding an inflexible pattern of service in the Book of Acts, we find a fluidity, a refreshing absence of rigidity. For instance, there was no hard and fast rule as to how long an apostle spent in one place. In Thessalonica Paul may have stayed three months, but in Ephesus he remained three years. It all depended on how long it took to build up the saints so that they could carry on the Christian ministry by themselves.

There are some who feel that the apostles concentrated their attention on the large cities, depending on the churches established there to fan out into the suburbs. But is this true? Did the apostles have any such fixed and finalized strategy? Or did they follow orders from the Lord from day to day — whether to important centers or to trivial hamlets?

Certainly one of the outstanding impressions we get from the Book of Acts is that the early believers expected and depended on the guidance of the Lord. They had forsaken all for Christ's sake. They had nothing and no one but the Lord Himself. So they looked to Him for daily directions and were not disappointed.

It seems to have been the practice for itinerant Christian workers to travel in pairs. The partner would often be a younger worker who would thus serve his apprenticeship. The apostles were constantly looking for faithful younger men whom they could disciple.

At times the Lord's servants were self-supporting, e.g., Paul working as a tentmaker. At other times they were supported by love gifts from individuals or churches.

Another notable impression is that those who were spiritual leaders were recognized as such by the saints who worked with them. It was the Holy Spirit who empowered them to speak with authority. And it was the same Holy Spirit who gave other believers the true spiritual instinct to submit to this authority.

The disciples obeyed human governments up to a point. That point was reached when they were forbidden to preach the gospel. Then they obeyed God rather than man. When punished by civil authorities, they bore it unresistingly, without ever conspiring against the government.

The gospel was preached first to the Jews, then after Israel's national refusal of the message, the good news went out to the Gentiles. The command, "to the Jew first," was fulfilled historically in the Book of Acts. Jews today are on the same basis as Gentiles before God — there is no difference, "for all have sinned and fall short of the glory of God."

There was tremendous power in connection with the ministry of the early church. Through fear of God's displeasure, people did not lightly make professions of being Christians. Sin in the church came to light quickly and was severely punished by God in some cases, e.g., Ananias and Sapphira.

A final and lasting conviction that flows from studying Acts is this: If *we* were to follow the example of the early church in faith, sacrifice, devotedness, and tireless service, the world could be evangelized in our generation. ‡

ENDNOTES

[1](Intro) J. B. Phillips, *The Young Church in Action*, p. vii.

[2](1:5) Between Christ's resurrection and ascension were forty days. Ten additional days elapsed before Pentecost. But the Lord did not say exactly how many days, perhaps to keep the disciples in a state of expectation.

[3](1:20) This is not an exact quotation from the Psalm as we have it in our Bible. There are two possible reasons for this. (1) The writers of the NT often quoted OT Scriptures from the Septuagint Version (LXX) while our translations were made from the original Hebrew text; this would make for some variation in the words. (2) As is often the case, the Holy Spirit, who inspired the OT, exercises the liberty of adapting it somewhat when quoting it in a NT context.

[4](2:1) The same words are used for "dwell together" in the Greek Version of Psalm 133:1 (132:1 in the LXX) as are used here in Acts for "in one place" (*epi to auto*).

[5](2:4) Other ministries of the Holy Spirit which become ours at *conversion* are: the anointing (1 John 2:27), the sealing (Eph. 1:13), and the guarantee (Eph. 1:14). Other ministries of the Spirit which are *conditional* upon our obedience and surrender are: guidance (Acts 8:29), joy (1 Thess. 1:6), and power (Rom. 15:13).

[6](2:22–24) The word translated *pains* usually refers to labor pangs. The resurrection of Christ is likened to a birth from death to life. The sufferings connected with the entire process were intense but temporary. In Psalm 18:5 the same expression is rendered "the sorrows of Sheol."

[7](2:25–27) Paradise is the same as the third heaven (2 Cor. 12:2, 4).

[8](2:38) Charles C. Ryrie, *The Acts of the Apostles*, p. 24.

[9](2:39) Charles H. Spurgeon, *The Treasury of the New Testament*, I:530.

[10](2:41) The critical (NU) text omits "gladly."

[11](2:44, 45) F. W. Grant, "Acts," *The Numerical Bible: Acts to 2 Corinthians*, VI:25, 26.

[12](2:46) Whenever we read of Paul and others going into the temple, it means into the temple *courts*, not into the sanctuary. Only the priests could enter there. Gentiles were permitted to go only into the outer court; to venture further was punishable by death.

[13](Excursus) In the critical text "church" doesn't occur till 5:11.

[14](Excursus) Merrill F. Unger, *Unger's Bible Handbook*, p. 586.

[15](Excursus) E. Stanley Jones, *Christ's Alternative to Communism*, p. 78.

[16](Excursus) G. H. Lang, *The Churches of God*, p. 11.

[17](4:1–4) Charles Haddon Spurgeon, further documentation unavailable.

[18](4:13) James A. Stewart, *Evangelism*, p. 95.

[19](4:14–18) J. H. Jowett, *The Redeemed Family of God*, p. 137.

[20](4:27, 28) Here "Servant" is the preferred translation of *pais*, rather than "child," as in 3:13, 26; 4:30.

[21](4:27, 28) George Matheson, *Rest By the River*, pp. 75-77.

[22](4:32–35) Grant, "Acts," p. 34.

[23](4:32–35) F. E. Marsh, *Fully Furnished*, p. 74.

[24](4:32–35) Ryrie, *Acts*, p. 36.

[25](5:40) Ryrie suggests that the beating might have been for their disobedience to the previous command of the Sanhedrin (cf. Deut. 25:2,3).

[26](5:41) There are three intriguing variations in the ms. traditions here: TR: "His name"; NU: "the name"; M: "the name of Jesus".

[27](6:8) Stephen (Gk., *Stephanos*) means "garland" or "victory wreath."

[28](6:10–14) The word order may indicate that they were more jealous of Moses' honor than of God's!

[29](7:9–19) "The original and the Greek version might both be true; the latter reckoning in five sons of Manasseh and Ephraim born in Egypt (1 Chron. vii. 14–27), according to a latitude of various forms, by no means uncommon in such lists." Kelly, *Acts*, p. 84.

[30](7:9–19) For further reverent treatment of this and the previous problem,

see Kelly, *Acts*, pp. 84, 85.

[31](7:20–43) Daily Notes of the Scripture Union, May 31, 1969.

[32](8:4–8) It is *down* from Jerusalem in altitude.

[33](8:4–8) Homer L. Payne, "What Is A Missionary Church?" *The Sunday School Times*, February 22, 1964, p. 129.

[34](8:12, 13) Since the text says Simon "believed" and he asks Peter to pray for him (v. 24), an argument has been made that he was saved but very carnal.

[35](8:26) An ancient Philistine city on the Mediterranean coast southwest of Jerusalem, en route from Palestine to Egypt.

[36](8:27–29) *Candace* (or *Kandake*) is probably a title, like Pharaoh, rather than a personal name.

[37](8:27–29) Male servants of female dignitaries were sometimes castrated. Eunuchs were barred from first class citizenship in Judaism (Deut. 23:1). They were limited to the status of "proselytes of the gate." But here a eunuch becomes a full-fledged member of the Christian church.

[38](8:37) Both the oldest (NU) and the majority (M) of manuscripts lack this verse. It is thought to be a baptismal formula used in Rome in the early second century, being found in Western mss., including the Latin translation. Those who teach baptismal regeneration obviously do not want to lose this verse.

[39](8:38) That the ancient mode of baptism was immersion is admitted by most Roman Catholic scholars, Calvin, and many who practice pouring or sprinkling. In all fairness, however, it should be mentioned that "into" and "out of" can also be translated "to" and "from," though the NKJV is quite literal and accurate.

[40](8:40) Ethiopia is the only country in Africa with a continuous Christian tradition from earliest times to today. Philip's faithfulness was perhaps the key that unlocked the door for the church there.

[41](9:1, 2) See also 19:9, 23; 22:4; 24:14, 22.

[42](Excursus) Harnack, Quoted by Leighton Ford, *The Christian Persuader*, p. 46.

[43](Excursus) Dean Inge, Quoted by E. Stanley Jones, *Conversion*, p. 219.

[44](Excursus) Bryan Green, *Ibid.*

45(Excursus) Leighton Ford, Quoted by Jones, *Conversion*, p. 46.

46(Excursus) James A. Stewart, *Pastures of Tender Grass*, p. 70.

47(9:36–38) Tabitha is Aramaic and Dorcas is Greek for *gazelle*.

48(10:1, 2) Ryrie, *Acts*, p. 61.

49(10:3–8) It was expedient for a tanner to operate outside the city limits. To be close to the sea was ideal for sanitary disposal of animal carcasses.

50(11:20, 21) In the NT, "Hellenists" usually means Grecian Jews, but here it can only mean Greeks, i.e., Gentiles. Note the context: Verse 19, "preaching the word to no one but the Jews only." Verse 20, "to Greeks also" (in contrast to Jews).

51(11:25, 26) James A. Stewart, *Evangelism*, pp. 100, 101.

52(12:25) Both Alexandrian (NU) and Majority (M) texts read *"to* Jerusalem." Since Barnabas and Saul are again at Antioch in 13:1, it is possible that copyists "corrected" the reading to "from."

53(13:3) Donald Grey Barnhouse, *The Measure of Your Faith*, Book 69, p. 21.

54(13:7, 8) In the KJV of verse 7, Sergius Paulus is called a "deputy," but more accurately his title was "proconsul" (NKJV). Luke showed exact knowledge of the names of offices which were then common in the Roman Empire. Thus, in Greek he called the magistrates at Philippi *stratēgoi*, Latin, *praetors* (16:20), and identified the officers as *rhabdouchoi*, Latin, *lictors* (16:35). He correctly named the rulers of Thessalonica as *politarchs* (17:6), whereas in Ephesus he correctly distinguished them as *asiarchs* (19:31).

"All these were the local authorities in the different cities, the Roman governor, or proconsul, being over them as ruling in each province. Luke then, by giving each his correct title in these different cities, shows that he knew well what he was about and this mark of accuracy should increase confidence in him as a faithful historian" — C. E. Stuart, *Tracings from the Acts of the Apostles*, p. 272.

55(13:19–22) See Kelly, *Acts*, pp. 185, 186 for a discussion of the chronological and textual problem.

56(13:48) Charles R. Erdman, *The Epistle of Paul to the Romans* p. 109.

57(14:4–7) Here the word practically equals "missionaries."

58(14:10–12) These Greek names are used in the original text. The 1611 text uses Jupiter and Mercury, the more common Latin names of these gods.

59(14:19, 20) Kelly, *Acts*, p. 202.

60(14:21) Erdman, *Acts*, p. 109.

61(Excursus) C. A. Coates, *An Outline of Luke's Gospel*, p. 254.

62(15:20) Some think that the four forbidden practices refer back to Leviticus 17 and 18, as follows: things polluted by idols (17:8, 9); sexual immorality — not only adultery and polygamy (18:20), homosexuality (18:22), and bestiality (18:23), but also marrying blood relatives (18:6–14) and even relatives by marriage, that is, in-law relatives (18:15, 16); eating things strangled or improperly butchered (17:15); eating blood (Lev. 17:10–12). Jewish believers would be offended if they saw Gentile believers violating these codes (Acts 15:21).

63(16:6–8) Ryrie, *Acts*, pp. 88, 89.

64(16:9) James Stalker, *Life of St. Paul*, p. 78.

65(16:19–24) A. J. Pollock, *The Apostle Paul and His Missionary Labors*, p. 56.

66(16:25) G. Campbell Morgan, *The Acts of the Apostles*, pp. 389,390.

67(17:2, 3) Some believe Paul spent about three months in Thessalonica, though he taught in the synagogue for only three Sabbaths.

68(17:16) William Arnot, *The Church in the House: A Series of Lessons on the Acts of the Apostles*, pp. 379ff.

69(Excursus) Some scholars believe the preaching took place in the temple courts.

70(Excursus) A. B. Simpson, further documentation unavailable.

71(18:2, 3) Dinsdale T. Young, *Neglected People of the Bible*, pp. 232, 233.

72(18:18) The participle for cutting of the hair is right after "Aquila," and far removed from "Paul" in the original (v. 18 is all one sentence in Greek).

73(19:8) Stuart, *Tracings*, p. 285.

74(19:15, 16) F. B. Meyer, quoted by W. H. Aldis, *The Keswick Convention 1934*, p. 60.

75(19:23–37) *Diana* is the Latin for the Greek *Artemis*, a many-breasted fertility goddess.

[76](21:23, 24) Grant, "Acts," p. 147.

[77](22:14–16) The supplied "by" is commonly understood in such a construction (participle of means). Paraphrased: "Get up (*anastas*) and get baptized (*baptisai*); get your sins washed away (*apolousai*) by means of calling on (*epikalesamenos*) the name of the Lord."

[78](26:9–11) The Greek tense here is no doubt a *conative* imperfect: "I tried to compel them . . ."

[79](26:29) Morgan, *Acts*, p. 528.

[80](27:13–17) The NU text reads *Euraquilon*.

[81](27:13–17) The NU text reads *Cauda*.

[82](27:21–26) A. W. Tozer, *That Incredible Christian*, p. 134.

[83](28:9, 10) It is at least possible that Luke used his medical skills alongside Paul's gift of healing. If God disapproved of the medical profession He would hardly have chosen a physician to write 28% of the NT (Luke-Acts)!

[84](28:29) John Calvin, *The Acts of the Apostles*, II:314. The NU text omits verse 29.

[85](Excursus) J. H. Jowett, *Things that Matter Most*, p. 248.

BIBLIOGRAPHY

Arnot, William. *The Church in the House: A Series of Lessons on the Acts of the Apostles*. New York: Robert Carter & Brothers, 1873.

Blaiklock, E. M. *The Acts of the Apostles, TBC*. Grand Rapids: Wm. B. Eerdmans Publishing Company, 1959.

Calvin, John. *The Acts of the Apostles*, 2 vols. Grand Rapids: Wm. B. Eerdmans Publishing Company, 1977.

Erdman, Charles R. *The Acts*. Philadelphia: The Westminster Press, 1919.

Kelly, William. *An Exposition of the Acts of the Apostles*. London: C. A. Hammond, 1952.

Martin, Ralph. *Understanding the New Testament: Acts*. Philadelphia: A. J. Holman Company, 1978.

Morgan, G. Campbell. *The Acts of the Apostles*. New York: Fleming H. Revell Co., 1924.

Rackham, R. B. *The Acts of the Apostles*. London: Methuen, 1901.

Ryrie, Charles Caldwell. *Acts of the Apostles*. Chicago: Moody Press, 1961.

Stuart, C. E. *Tracings from the Acts of the Apostles*. London: E. Marlborough and Company, n.d.

THE EPISTLE TO THE ROMANS

Introduction

"The cathedral of the Christian faith." — Frédéric Godet

I. Unique place in the Canon

Romans has always stood at the head of Paul's letters, and rightly so. Since Acts ends with Paul's arrival in Rome, it is logical to have the Epistle section of the NT begin with the apostle's letter to the Roman church, written before he visited the Christians there. More decisively, Romans is the most important book theologically in the whole NT, being as close to a systematic presentation of Christian theology as will be found in God's word.

Historically, Romans is the most influential of Bible books. Augustine was converted through reading Romans 13:13 and 14 (A.D. 380). The Protestant Reformation was launched when Martin Luther finally understood the meaning of God's righteousness, and that "the just shall live by faith" (1517).

John Wesley received assurance of salvation through hearing the preface to Luther's commentary on Romans read in a Moravian house church on Aldersgate Street in London (1738). John Calvin wrote, "When anyone understands this Epistle, he has a passage opened to him to the understanding of the whole Scripture."

II. Authorship[†]

Heretics and even radical negative critics for once accept a universal orthodox position — that the author of Romans was the apostle to the Gentiles. In fact, the heretic Marcion is the first known writer to *specifically* name Paul as author. The book is quoted by such orthodox Christians as Clement of Rome, Ignatius, Justin Martyr, Polycarp, Hippolytus, and Irenaeus. The Muratorian Canon also lists the letter as Pauline.

The *internal evidence* for Pauline authorship is very strong as well. The theology, vocabulary, and spirit are all distinctively Paul's. Of course, the fact that the letter *says* it is from Paul (1:1) is not enough to convince skeptics, but this is further borne out by other references, such as 15:15–20. What is most convincing, perhaps, is the large number of casual coincidences with the book of Acts that have no appearance of being contrived. For example, references to the collection for the saints, to Gaius, Erastus, and a long-planned trip to Rome, all point to Paul as the author. Tertius was his amanuensis (16:22).

III. Date

Romans was written after 1 and 2 Corinthians, because the collection being formed when those letters were written is now ready and about to be taken to the poor saints at Jerusalem. References to Cenchrea, the port city for Corinth (16:1), and other details make most scholars opt for Corinth as the city of origin. Since Paul was there only three months (at the close of his Third Missionary Journey) before he was chased away due to plots against him, it must be during this short period that the Epistle was penned. This makes the date about A.D. 56.

IV. Background and Themes[††]

How did Christianity first reach Rome? We cannot be positive, but it may be that Jews from Rome who were converted in Jerusalem on the Day of Pentecost (see Acts 2:10) carried back the good news. That was in A.D. 30.

[†]See p. ii.
[††]See p. i.

Paul had never been in Rome when he wrote this letter from Corinth about twenty-six years later. But he knew quite a few of the Christians there, as is seen in chapter 16. Christians in those days were people on the move, whether as a result of persecution or as heralds of the gospel or in the ordinary course of their work. These Christians in Rome were from both Jewish and Gentile backgrounds.

Paul finally did reach Rome around A.D. 60, but not in the way he expected. He came as a prisoner for Christ Jesus.

Romans is a classic. To the unsaved it offers a clear exposition of their sinful, lost condition and God's righteous plan for saving them. New believers learn of their identification with Christ and of victory through the power of the Holy Spirit. Mature believers find never-ending delight in its wide spectrum of Christian truth: doctrinal, prophetical, and practical.

An excellent way to understand the Epistle to the Romans is as a dialogue between Paul and some unnamed objector. As Paul sets forth the gospel, he seems to hear this objector raising all kinds of arguments against it. The apostle replies to his opponent's questions one by one. By the time he is finished, Paul has answered every major attitude that man can take regarding the gospel of the grace of God.

Sometimes the objections are clearly stated; sometimes they are only implied. But whether stated or implied, they all revolve around the gospel — the good news of salvation by grace through faith in the Lord Jesus Christ, apart from the works of the law.

We will think of Romans as dealing with eleven main questions: (1) What is the subject of the Letter? (1:1, 9, 15, 16);

(2) What is the gospel? (1:1–17); (3) Why do men need the gospel? (1:18–3:20); (4) According to the gospel, how can ungodly sinners be justified by a holy God? (3:21–31); (5) Does the gospel agree with the OT Scripture? (4:1–25); (6) What are the benefits of justification in the believer's life? (5:1–21); (7) Does the teaching of salvation by grace through faith permit or even encourage sinful living? (6:1–23); (8) What is the relationship of the Christian to the law? (7:1–25); (9) How is the Christian enabled to live a holy life? (8:1–39); (10) Does the gospel, by promising salvation to both Jews and Gentiles, mean that God has broken His promises to His earthly people, the Jews? (9:1–11:36); (11) How should those who have been justified by grace respond in their everyday lives? (12:1–16:27).

An acquaintance with these eleven questions and their answers will give a working knowledge of this important Epistle. The answer to the first question, "What is the subject of Romans?" is, of course, "the gospel." Paul wastes no time in getting to the point. Four times in the first sixteen verses he mentions it (vv.1, 9, 15, 16).

This gives rise to the second question, "What is the gospel?" The word itself means *good news*. But in vv. 1–17 the apostle tells us six important facts about the good news: (1) Its source is God (v. 1); (2) It was promised by the prophetic OT Scriptures (v. 2); (3) It is the good news concerning God's Son, the Lord Jesus Christ (v. 3); (4) It is God's power for salvation (v. 16); (5) It is for all men, Gentiles as well as Jews (v. 16); (6) It is by faith alone (v. 17). With that as an introduction, let us take a more detailed look at these verses.

OUTLINE

I. DOCTRINAL: THE GOSPEL OF GOD (Chaps. 1–8)

    A. Introduction to the Gospel (1:1–15)

    B. The Gospel Defined (1:16, 17)

    C. The Universal Need for the Gospel (1:18–3:20)

    D. The Basis and Terms of the Gospel (3:21–31)

    E. The Harmony of the Gospel with the Old Testament (Chap. 4)

    F. The Practical Benefits of the Gospel (5:1–11)

    G. The Triumph of Christ's Work over Adam's Sin (5:12–21)

Commentary

I. DOCTRINAL: THE GOSPEL OF GOD (Chaps. 1–8)

A. Introduction to the Gospel (1:1-15)

1:1 **Paul** introduces himself as one who was *purchased* (implied in the designation **a bondservant of Jesus Christ**), *called* (on the road to Damascus he was **called to be an apostle**, a special emissary of the Savior), and **separated** (set apart **to** take **the gospel** to the Gentiles [see Acts 9:15; 13:2]). We too have been purchased by the precious blood of Christ, called to be witnesses to His saving power, and set apart to tell the good news wherever we go.

1:2 Lest any of Paul's Jewish readers think the gospel is completely new and unrelated to their spiritual heritage, he mentions that the OT **prophets** had **promised** it, both in clear-cut statements (Deut. 18:15; Isa. 7:14; Hab. 2:4) and in types and symbols (e.g., Noah's ark, the serpent of brass, and the sacrificial system).

1:3 The gospel is the good news concerning God's **Son, Jesus Christ our Lord, who** is a descendant **of David according to the flesh** (that is, as far as His humanity is concerned). The expression **according to the flesh** implies that our Lord is more than a man. The words mean as to His *humanity*. If Christ were only a man, it would be unnecessary to single out this feature of His being, since there would be no other. But He is more than a man, as the next verse shows.

1:4 The Lord Jesus is marked out as **the Son of God with power**. The Holy Spirit, here called **the Spirit of holiness**, marked Jesus out at His baptism and throughout His miracle-working ministry. The Savior's mighty miracles, performed in the power of the Holy Spirit,[1] bore witness to the fact that He is the Son of God. When we read that He is **declared to be the Son of God with power . . . by the resurrection from the dead**, we naturally think of His own resurrection. But a literal reading here is "by resurrection of dead persons," so the apostle may also be thinking of Christ's raising of Jairus' daughter, the widow of Nain's son, and Lazarus. However, there is little question that it is the Lord's own resurrection that is primarily in view.

When we say that Jesus is **the Son of God**, we mean that He is a Son like no one else is. God has many sons. All believers are His sons (Gal. 4:5–7). Even angels are spoken of as sons (Job 1:6; 2:1). But Jesus is God's Son in a *unique* sense. When our Lord spoke of God as His Father, the Jews rightly understood Him to be claiming equality with God (John 5:18).

1:5 It was **through** Jesus Christ our Lord that Paul **received grace** (the undeserved favor that saved him) **and apostleship**. When Paul says **we have received grace and apostleship**, he is almost certainly using the editorial *we*, referring to himself alone. His linking of **apostleship** with the **nations** or Gentiles points to him and not to the other apostles. Paul was commissioned to call men of all nations to obedience of faith — that is, to obey the message of the gospel by repenting and believing on the Lord Jesus Christ (Acts 20:21). The goal of this worldwide proclamation of the message was for His name, to please and to bring glory to Him.

1:6 **Among** those who had responded to the gospel were those Paul dignified with the title **the called of Jesus Christ**, emphasizing that it was God who took the initiative in their salvation.

1:7 The Letter is addressed **to all** believers **in Rome**, and not (as in other Epistles) to a single church. The final chapter of the letter indicates that there were several gatherings of believers in the city, and this salutation embraces them all.

Beloved of God, called to be saints. These two lovely names are true of all who have been redeemed by the precious blood of Christ. These favored ones are objects of divine love in a special way, and are also called to be set apart to God from the world, for that is the meaning of **saints**.

Paul's characteristic greeting combines **grace** and **peace**. **Grace** (*charis*) is a Greek emphasis, and **peace** (*shalom*) is the traditional Jewish greeting. The combination is especially appropriate because Paul's message tells how believing Jews and Gentiles are now one new man in Christ.

The **grace** mentioned here is not the grace that saves (Paul's readers were already saved) but the **grace** that equips and empowers for Christian life and service. **Peace** is not so much peace with God (the saints already had that because they were justified by faith) but rather the **peace** of God reigning in their hearts while they were in the midst of a turbulent society. **Grace** and **peace** came **from God our Father and the Lord Jesus Christ**, strongly implying the equality of the Son with the Father. If Jesus were only a man, it would be absurd to list Him as equal with the Father in bestowing **grace** and **peace**. It would be like saying, "Grace and peace from God the Father and from Abraham Lincoln."

1:8 Whenever possible, the apostle began his letters by expressing appreciation for whatever was commendable in his readers. (A good example for all of us!) Here he thanks **God through Jesus Christ**, the Mediator, that the **faith** of the Roman Christians was proclaimed **throughout the whole world**. Their testimony as Christians was talked about throughout the Roman Empire, which then constituted the **whole world** from the perspective of those living in the Mediterranean area.

1:9 Because the Roman Christians let their light shine before men, Paul was constrained to pray for them **without ceasing**. He calls **God** as his **witness** to the constancy of his **prayers**, because no one else could know this. But **God** knows — the God whom the apostle served with his **spirit in the gospel of His Son**. Paul's service was with his **spirit**. It was not that of a religious drudge, going through endless rituals and reciting prayers and liturgies by rote. It was service bathed in fervent, believing prayers. It was willing, devoted, tireless service, fired by a spirit that loved the Lord Jesus supremely. It was a flaming passion to make known the good news about God's Son.

1:10 Coupled with Paul's thanksgiving to God for the Roman saints was his prayer that he might visit them in the not-too-distant future. As with everything else, he wanted his journey to be according to **the will of God**.

1:11 The apostle's impelling desire was to help the saints spiritually so that they might be further **established** in the faith. There is no thought here of his conferring some "second blessing" on them, nor did he intend to impart some spiritual gift by the laying on of his hands (though he did this for Timothy in 2 Tim. 1:6). It was a matter of helping their **spiritual** growth through the ministry of the word.

1:12 He goes on to explain that there would be **mutual** blessing. He would **be encouraged** by their **faith**, and they by his. In all edifying society, there is spiritual enrichment. "As iron sharpens iron, so a man sharpens the countenance of his friend" (Prov. 27:17). Note Paul's humility and graciousness — he was not above being helped by other saints.

1:13 He had **often planned to** visit Rome **but** had been **hindered**, perhaps by pressing needs in other areas, perhaps by the direct restraint of the Holy Spirit, perhaps by the opposition of Satan. He desired to **have some fruit among** the Gentiles in Rome **as** he had **among the other Gentiles**. Here he is speaking of **fruit** in the gospel, as the next two verses show. In verses 11 and 12 his aim was to see the Roman Christians built up in their faith. Here he desires to see souls won for Christ in the capital of the Roman Empire.

1:14 Anyone who has Christ has the answer to the world's deepest need. He has the cure to the disease of sin, the way to escape the eternal horrors of hell, and the guarantee of everlasting happiness with God. This puts him under solemn obligation to share the good news with people of all cultures — **barbarians** — and people of all degrees of learning — **wise and unwise**. Paul felt the obligation keenly. He said **"I am a debtor"**.

1:15 To discharge that debt, he was **ready to preach the gospel to** those **in Rome** with all the power God gave him. It was surely not to the believers in Rome, as this verse might seem to suggest, for they had already responded to the glad tidings. But he was ready to preach to the unconverted Gentiles in the metropolis.

B. The Gospel Defined (1:16, 17)

1:16 Paul was **not ashamed** to take God's good news to sophisticated Rome, even though the message had proved to be a stumbling block to the Jews and foolishness to the Greeks, for he knew that **it is the power of God to salvation** — that is, it tells how God by His power saves everyone who believes on His Son. This power is extended equally to Jews and Greeks.

The order **for the Jew first and also for the Greek** was fulfilled historically during the Acts period. While we have an enduring obligation to God's ancient people, the Jews, we are not required to evangelize them before going to the Gentiles. Today God deals with Jews and Gentiles on the same basis, and the message and timing are the same to all.

1:17 Since the word **righteousness** occurs here for the first time in the Letter, we will pause to consider its meaning. The word is used in several different ways in the NT, but we shall consider only three uses.

First, it is used to describe that characteristic of God by which He always does what is right, just, proper, and consistent with all His other attributes. When we say that God is righteous, we mean that there is no wrong, dishonesty, or unfairness in Him.

Secondly, the righteousness of God can refer to His method of justifying ungodly sinners. He can do this and still be righteous because Jesus as the sinless Substitute has satisfied all the claims of divine justice.

Finally, the righteousness of God refers to the perfect standing which God provides for those who believe on His Son (2 Cor. 5:21). Those who are not in themselves righteous are treated as if they were righteous because God sees them in all the perfection of Christ. Righteousness is imputed to their account.

Which is the meaning in verse 17? While it could be any of the three, the righteousness of God seems to refer especially to His way of justifying sinners by faith.

The righteousness of God is revealed in the gospel. First the gospel tells us that God's righteousness demands that sins be punished, and the penalty is eternal death. But then we hear that God's love provided what His righteousness demanded. He sent His Son to die as a Substitute for sinners, paying the penalty in full. Now because His righteous claims have been fully satisfied, God can righteously save all those who avail themselves of the work of Christ.

God's righteousness **is revealed from faith to faith**. The expression **from faith to faith** may mean: (1) from God's faithfulness to our faith; (2) from one degree of faith to another; or (3) by faith from start to finish. The last is the probable meaning. God's righteousness is not imputed on the basis of works or made available to those who seek to earn or deserve it. It is revealed on the principle of faith alone. This is in perfect agreement with the divine decree in Habakkuk 2:4, **"The just shall live by faith,"** which may also be understood to mean "The justified-by-faith ones shall live."

In the first seventeen verses of Romans, Paul has introduced his subject and stated briefly some of the principal points. He now addresses the third main question, "Why do men need the gospel?" The answer, in brief, is because they are lost without it. But this raises four subsidiary questions: (1) Are the heathen who have never heard the gospel lost? (1:18–32); (2) Are the self-righteous moralists, whether Jews or Gentiles, lost? (2:1–16)· (3) Are God's ancient earthly people, the Jews, lost? (2:17–3:8); (4) Are all men lost? (3:9–20).

C. The Universal Need for the Gospel (1:18–3:20)

1:18 Here we have the answer to the question "Why do men need the gospel?" The answer is that they are lost without it, and that **the wrath of God is revealed from heaven against** the wickedness **of men who suppress the truth** in an unrighteous manner and by their unrighteous lives. But how is God's wrath **revealed**? One answer is given in the context. God gives men over to uncleanness (1:24), to vile affections (1:26), and to a reprobate mind (1:28). But it is also true that God occasionally breaks through into human history to show His extreme displeasure at man's sin — for example, the flood (Gen. 7); the destruction of Sodom and Gomorrah (Gen. 19); and the punishment of Korah, Dathan, and Abiram (Num. 16:32).

1:19 "Are the heathen who have never heard the gospel lost?" Paul shows that they are, not because of knowledge they don't have, but **because** of the light which they do have, yet refuse! Those things which **may be known of God** in creation have been revealed **to them**. God has not left them without a revelation of Himself.

1:20 Ever **since the creation of the world**, two **invisible** characteristics of God have been on display for all to see: **His eternal power and** His divinity or **Godhead**. The word Paul uses here means *divinity* or *godhood*. It suggests the character of God rather than His essential being, His glorious attributes rather than His inherent deity. His deity is assumed.

The argument here is clear: Creation demands a Creator. Design demands a Designer. By looking up at the sun, moon, and stars, anyone can know there is a God.

The answer to the question "What about the heathen?" is this: **they are without excuse**. God has revealed Himself to them in creation, but they have not responded to this revelation. So people are not condemned for rejecting a Savior they have never heard of, but for being unfaithful to what they could know about God.

1:21 Although they knew God by His works, **they did not glorify Him** for who He is or thank Him for all He has done. Rather, they gave themselves over to **futile** philosophies and speculations about other gods, and as a result lost the capacity to see and think clearly. "Light rejected is light denied." Those who don't want to see lose the capacity to see.

1:22 As men grew more conceited over their self-styled knowledge, they plunged deeper into ignorance and nonsense. These two things always characterize those who reject the knowledge of God — they become insufferably conceited and abysmally ignorant at the same time.

1:23 Instead of evolving from lower forms, "early man" was of a high moral order. By refusing to acknowledge the true, infinite, **incorruptible God**, he *de*volved to the stupidity and depravity that go with idol worship. This whole passage gives the lie to evolution.

Man is instinctively religious. He must have some object to worship. When he refused to worship the living God, he made his own gods of wood and stone representing **man, birds, animals, and creeping things**, or reptiles. Notice the downward progression — **man, birds, animals, creeping things**. And remember that man becomes like what he worships. As his concept of deity degenerates, his morals degenerate also. If his god is a reptile, then he feels free to live as he pleases. Remember too that a worshiper generally considers himself inferior to the object of worship. Created in the image and after the likeness of God, man here takes a place lower than that of serpents!

When man worships idols, he worships demons. Paul states clearly that the things which the Gentiles sacrifice to idols they sacrifice to demons and not to God (1 Cor. 10:20).

1:24 Three times it is said that **God gave** man **up**. He **gave them up to uncleanness** (1:24), to vile passions (1:26), and to a reprobate mind (1:28). In other words, God's wrath was directed against man's entire personality.

In response to the evil lusts of their hearts, God abandoned them to heterosexual uncleanness — adultery, fornication, lewdness, prostitution, harlotry, etc. Life became for them a round of sex orgies in which **to dishonor their bodies among themselves**.

1:25 This abandonment by God was because they first abandoned **the truth** about Him **for** the **lie** of idolatry. An idol is a lie, a false representation of God. An idolater worships the image of a **creature**, and thus insults and dishonors **the Creator, who is** eternally worthy of honor and glory, not of insult.

1:26 For this same reason **God gave** people **up to** erotic activity with members of their own sex. **Women** became lesbians, practicing unnatural sex and knowing no shame.

1:27 Men became sodomites, in total perversion of their natural functions. Turning away from the marriage relationship ordained by God, they **burned** with **lust for** other **men** and practiced homosexuality. But their sin took its toll in their bodies and souls. Disease, guilt, and personality deformities struck at them like the sting of a scorpion. This disproves the notion that anyone can commit this sin and get away with it.

Homosexuality is being passed off today by some as a sickness and by others as a legitimate alternative lifestyle. Christians must be careful not to accept the world's moral judgments but to be guided by God's word. In the OT, this sin was punishable by death (Lev. 18:29; 20:13), and here in the NT those who practice it are said to be worthy of death (Rom. 1:32). The Bible speaks of homosexuality as a very serious sin, as evidenced by God's obliteration of Sodom and Gomorrah, where militant "gays" ran riot (Gen. 19:4–25).

The gospel offers pardon and forgiveness to homosexuals, as it does to all sinners who repent and believe in the Lord Jesus Christ. Christians who have fallen into this heinous sin can find forgiveness and restoration through confessing and forsaking the sin. There is complete deliverance from homosexuality to all who are willing to obey God's word. Ongoing counseling assistance is very important in most cases.

It is true that some people seem to have a natural tendency toward homosexuality. This should not be surprising, since fallen human nature is capable of just about any form of iniquity and perversion. The gross sin does not consist in the inclination toward it but in yielding to and practicing it. The Holy Spirit gives the power to resist the temptation and to have lasting victory (l Cor. 10:13). Some of the Christians in Corinth were living proofs that homosexuals need not be irrevocably bound to that lifestyle (1 Cor. 6:9–11).

1:28 Because of men's refusal to retain God in their knowledge, either as Creator, Sustainer, or Deliverer, **God gave them over to a debased mind to** commit a catalog of other forms of wickedness. This verse gives deep insight into why evolution has such enormous appeal for natural men. The reason lies not in their intellects but in their wills. They do not want **to retain God in their knowledge**. It is not that the evidence for evolution is so overwhelming that they are compelled to accept it; rather, it is because they want some explanation for origins that will eliminate God completely. They know that if there is a God, then they are morally responsible to Him.

1:29 Here, then, is the dark list of additional sins which characterize man in his alienation from God. Notice that he is *full* of them, not just an occasional dabbler in them. He is trained in sins which are not fitting for a human being: **unrighteousness** (injustice); **sexual immorality**[2] (fornication, adultery, and other forms of illicit sex); **wickedness** (active evil); **covetousness** (greed, the incessant desire for more); **maliciousness** (the desire for harm on others; venomous hatred); **full of envy** (jealousy of others); *full of* **murder** (premeditated and unlawful killing of another, either in anger or in the commission of some other crime); *full of* **strife** (wrangling, quarreling, contentiousness); *full of* **deceit** (trickery, treachery, intrigue); *full of* **evil-mindedness** (ill-will, spite, hostility, bitterness); **whisperers** (secret slanderers, gossips);

1:30 **backbiters** (open slanderers, those who bad-mouth others); **haters of God** (or hateful to God); **violent** (despiteful, insulting); **proud** (haughty, arrogant); **boasters** (braggarts, self-paraders); **inventors of evil things** (devisers of mischief and new forms of wickedness); **disobedient to parents** (rebellious to parental authority);

1:31 **undiscerning** (lacking moral and spiritual discernment, without conscience); **untrustworthy** (breaking promises, treaties, agreements, and contracts whenever it serves their purposes); **unloving** (acting in total disregard of natural ties and the obligations that go with them); **unforgiving**[3] (irreconcilable or implacable); **unmerciful** (cruel, vindictive, without pity).

1:32 Those who abuse sex (1:24), who pervert sex (1:26, 27), and who practice the other sins listed (1:29–31) have an innate knowledge not only that these things are wrong but also that they themselves are **deserving of death**. They know this is God's verdict, however much they seek to rationalize or legalize these sins. But this does not deter them from indulging in these forms of ungodliness. In fact they unite with others to promote them, and feel a sense of camaraderie with their partners-in-sin.

THE UNREACHED HEATHEN

What then, is God's answer to the question "Are the heathen who have never heard the gospel lost?" The condemnation of the heathen is that they did not live up to the light which God gave them in creation. Instead they become idolaters, and as a result abandoned themselves to lives of depravity and vileness.

But suppose an individual heathen *does* live up to the light God gives him. Suppose he burns his idols and seeks the true God. What then?

There are two schools of thought among evangelical believers on this subject.

Some believe that if a pagan lives up to the light of God in creation, God will send him the gospel light. Cornelius is cited as an example. He sought God. His prayers and alms came up as a memorial before God. Then God sent Peter to tell him how to be saved (Acts 11:14).

Others believe that if a man trusts the one true and living God as He is revealed in creation, but dies before he hears the gospel, God will save him on the basis of the work of Christ at Calvary. Though the man himself knew nothing about the work of Christ, God reckons the value of that work to his account when he trusts God on the basis of the light he has received. Those who hold this view point out that this is how God saved people before Calvary and how He still saves morons, imbeciles, and also children who die before they reach the age of accountability.

The first view can be supported by the case of Cornelius. The second view lacks scriptural support for the era following the death and resurrection of Christ (our present era), and it also weakens the necessity for aggressive missionary activity. ‡

Paul has shown that the pagans are lost and need the gospel. Now he turns to a second class of people, whose exact identity is somewhat in dispute. We believe that the apostle is talking here to self-righteous moralists, whether Jews or Gentiles. The first verse shows that they are self-righteous moralists by the way they condemn the behavior of others (yet commit the same sins themselves). Verses 9, 10, 12, 14, and 15 show that Paul is speaking to both Jews and Gentiles. So the question before the court is: *Are the self-righteous moralists, whether Jews or Gentiles, also lost?* And the answer, as we shall see, is, "Yes, they are lost too!"

2:1 This second class consists of those who look down their noses at the heathen, considering themselves more civilized, educated, and refined. They condemn the pagans for their gross behavior, yet are equally guilty themselves though perhaps in a more sophisticated way. Fallen man can see faults in others more readily than in himself. Things hideous and repulsive in the lives of others seem quite respectable in his own. But the fact that he can **judge** sins in others shows that he knows the difference between right and wrong. If he knows that it is wrong for someone to steal his wife, then he knows that it is wrong for him to steal someone else's wife. Therefore, when someone commits the very sins he condemns in others, he leaves himself without excuse.

The sins of cultured people are essentially the same as those of the heathen. Although a moralist may argue that he has not committed every sin in the book, he should remember the following facts:

1. he is capable of committing them all.
2. by breaking one commandment, he is guilty of all (Jas. 2:10).
3. he has committed sins of thought which he may never have committed in actual deed, and these are forbidden by the word. Jesus taught that the lustful look, for instance, is tantamount to adultery (Matt. 5:28).

2:2 What the smug moralist needs is a lesson on **the judgment of God**. The apostle proceeds to give that lesson in verses 2–16. The first point is that **the judgment of God is according to truth**. It is not based on incomplete, inaccurate, or circumstantial evidence. Rather, it is based on the truth, the whole truth, and nothing but the truth.

2:3 Secondly, **the judgment of God** *is inescapable* on those who condemn others for the very sins they practice themselves. Their capacity to **judge** others does not absolve them from guilt. In fact, it increases their own condemnation.

The judgment of God is inescapable unless we *repent and are forgiven.*

2:4 Next we learn that *the judgment of God is sometimes delayed.* This delay is an evidence of **His goodness, forbearance, and longsuffering. His goodness** means that He is kindly disposed to sinners, though not to their sins. His **forbearance** describes His holding back punishment on man's wickedness and rebellion. His **longsuffering** is His amazing self-restraint in spite of man's ceaseless provocation.

The goodness of God, as seen in His providence, protection, and preservation, is aimed at leading men **to repentance**. He is "not willing that any should perish but that all should come to repentance" (2 Pet. 3:9).

Repentance means an about-face, turning one's back on sin and heading in the opposite direction. "It is a change of mind which produces a change of attitude, and results in a change of action."[4] It signifies a man's taking sides with God against himself and his sins. It is more than an intellectual assent to the fact of one's sins; it involves the conscience too, as John Newton wrote: "My conscience felt and owned my guilt."

2:5 The fourth thing we learn about the judgment of God is that *it is graduated according to the accumulation of guilt.* Paul pictures hardened and unrepentant sinners **treasuring up** judgment **for** themselves, as if they were building up a fortune of gold and silver. But what a fortune that will be in the day when God's **wrath** is finally revealed at the **judgment** of the Great White Throne (Rev. 20:11–15)! In that day **the judgment of God** *will be seen to be absolutely* **righteous**, without prejudice or injustice of any kind.

2:6 In the next five verses Paul reminds us that *the judgment of God will be* **according to** *one's* **deeds**. A man may boast of great personal goodness. He may rely heavily on his racial or national origin. He may plead the fact that there were men of God in his ancestry. But he will be judged by *his own conduct*, and not by any of these other things. His works will be the determining factor.

If we took verses 6–11 by themselves, it would be easy to conclude that they teach salvation by works. They *seem* to say that those who do good works will thereby earn eternal life.

But it should be clear that the passage

cannot mean that, because then it would flatly contradict the consistent testimony of the rest of Scripture to the effect that salvation is by faith apart from works. Chafer points out that about 150 passages in the NT condition salvation solely on faith or believing.[5] No one passage, when rightly understood, can contradict such overwhelming testimony.

How then are we to understand this passage? First we must understand that good works do not begin until a person has been born again. When the people asked Jesus, "What shall we do, that we may work the works of God?" He replied, "This is the work of God, that you believe in Him whom He sent" (John 6:28, 29). So the first good work that anyone can do is to believe on the Lord Jesus Christ, and we must constantly remember that *faith is not a meritorious work* by which a person earns salvation. So if the unsaved are judged by their works, they will have nothing of value to present as evidence. All their supposed righteousness will be seen as filthy rags (Isa. 64:6). Their condemning sin will be that they have not believed on Jesus as Lord (John 3:18). Beyond that, their works will determine the degree of their punishment (Luke 12:47, 48).

If *believers* are judged according to their works, what will be the outcome? Certainly they cannot present any good works by which they might earn or deserve salvation. All their works before salvation were sinful. But the blood of Christ has wiped out the past. Now God Himself cannot find any charge against them for which to sentence them to hell. Once they are saved, they begin to practice good works — not necessarily good works in the world's eyes, but good works as God sees them. Their good works are the result of salvation, not the meritorious cause. At the Judgment Seat of Christ, their works will be reviewed and they will be rewarded for all faithful service.

But we must constantly remember that this passage does not deal with believers — only with the ungodly.

2:7 In explaining that judgment will be according to works, Paul says that God will render **eternal life to those who by patient continuance in doing good seek for glory, honor, and immortality**. As already explained, this does *not* mean that these people are saved **by patient continuance in doing good**. That would be another gospel. No one would naturally live that kind of life, and no one could live it without divine power. Anyone who really fits this description has already been saved by grace through faith. The fact that he seeks **for glory, honor, and immortality** shows that he has already been born again. The whole tenor of his life shows that he has been converted.

He seeks for the **glory** of heaven; the **honor** that comes only from God (John 5:44); the **immortality** that characterizes the resurrection body (1 Cor. 15:53, 54); the heavenly inheritance, which is imperishable, undefiled, and unfading (1 Pet. 1:4).

God will award **eternal life** to all who manifest this evidence of a conversion experience. **Eternal life** is spoken of in several ways in the NT. It is a present possession which we receive the moment we are converted (John 5:24). It is a future possession which will be ours when we receive our glorified bodies (here and in Rom. 6:22). Although it is a gift received by faith, it is sometimes associated with rewards for a life of faithfulness (Mark 10:30). All believers will have **eternal life**, but some will have a greater capacity for enjoying it than others. It means more than endless existence; it is a quality of **life**, the more abundant **life** which the Savior promised in John 10:10. It is the very **life** of Christ Himself (Col. 1:27).

2:8 Those who are self-seeking and do not obey the truth, but rather obey unrighteousness, will be awarded indignation and wrath. They do not obey the truth; they have never answered the gospel call. Rather, they have chosen to obey unrighteousness as their master. Their lives are characterized by strife, wrangling, and disobedience — sure proof that they were never saved.

2:9 Now the apostle repeats God's verdict concerning the two kinds of workers and works, except that this time He does it in inverse order.

The verdict will be **tribulation and anguish** to everyone **who does evil**. Here again we must stress that these evil works betray an evil heart of unbelief. The works are the outward expression of a person's attitude toward the Lord.

The expression **of the Jew first, and also of the Greek** shows that *the judgment of God will be according to privilege or light received*. The Jews were **first** in privilege as God's earthly chosen people; therefore, they will be **first** in responsibility. This aspect of God's judgment will be developed further in verses 12–16.

2:10 The verdict will be **glory, honor, and peace to everyone**, Jew or Gentile, **who works what is good**. And let us not forget that no one can work good, as far as God is concerned, unless he has first placed his faith and trust in the Lord Jesus Christ.

The expression **to the Jew first, and also to the Greek** cannot indicate favoritism, because the next verse points out that God's judgment is impartial. So the expression must indicate the historical order in which the gospel went out, as in 1:16. It was proclaimed first to Jews, and the first believers were Jews.

2:11 Another truth concerning the judgment of God is that *it is without respect of persons*. In human courts of law, preference is shown to the good-looking, wealthy, and influential; but **God** is strictly impartial. No considerations of race, place, or face will ever influence Him.

2:12 As mentioned above, verses 12–16 expand the point that the judgment of God will be according to the measure of light received. Two classes are in view: those who do not have the law (the Gentiles) and those who are under the law (the Jews). This includes everyone except those who are in the church of God (see 1 Cor. 10:32, where the human race is divided into these three classes).

Those who **have sinned without law will also perish without law**. It does not say "will be *judged* without law" but **will also perish without law**. They will be judged according to whatever revelation the Lord gave them, and, failing to live up to that revelation, they will **perish**.

Those who **have sinned** under **the law will be judged by the law**, and if they have not obeyed it, they too will

perish. The law demands total obedience.

2:13 Mere possession of the law is not enough. The law demands perfect and continuous obedience. No one is accounted righteous simply because he knows what the law says. The only conceivable way of obtaining justification under the law would be to keep it in its entirety. But since all men are sinners, it is impossible for them to do this. So this verse is really setting forth an ideal condition rather than something that is capable of human attainment.

The NT teaches emphatically that it is impossible for man to be justified by law-keeping (see Acts 13:39; Rom. 3:20; Gal. 2:16, 21; 3:11). It was never God's intention that anyone be saved by the law. Even if a person could keep it perfectly from this day forward, he still would not be justified, because God requires that which is past. So when verse 13 says that **doers of the law** will be **justified**, we must understand it as meaning that the law demands obedience, and if anyone could produce perfect obedience from the day he was born, he would be justified. But the cold, hard fact is that no one can produce this.

2:14 Verses 14 and 15 are a parenthesis, looking back to verse 12a, where we learned that Gentiles who sin without the law shall perish without the law. Now Paul explains that although the law was not given to the Gentiles, yet they have an innate knowledge of right and wrong. They know instinctively that it is wrong to lie, steal, commit adultery, and murder. The only commandment they would not know intuitively is the one concerning the Sabbath; that one is more ceremonial than moral.

So what it boils down to is that the **Gentiles, who do not have the law, . . . are a law to themselves**. They form their own code of right and wrong behavior from their moral instincts.

2:15 They **show the work of the law written in their hearts**. It is not the *law itself* which is written in their hearts, but **the work of the law**. The work which the law was designed to do in the lives of the Israelites is seen in some measure in the lives of Gentiles. The fact that they know that it is right to respect their parents, for example, shows **the work of the law written in their hearts**. They also know that certain acts are basically wrong. **Their conscience**, serving as a monitor, confirms this instinctive knowledge. And their thoughts are constantly deciding the rightness or wrongness of their actions, **accusing or excusing**, forbidding or allowing.

2:16 This verse is a continuation of the thought in verse 12. It tells *when* those without law and those under the law will be judged. And in doing so it teaches one final truth about the judgment of God — namely, that *it will take into account* **the secrets of men**, *not just their public sin*. Sin which is secret at the present time will be open scandal at the Judgment of the Great White Throne. The Judge at that solemn time will be **Jesus Christ**, since the Father has committed all judgment to Him (John 5:22). When Paul adds, **according to my gospel**, he means "so my gospel teaches." **My gospel** means the gospel Paul preached, which was the same one which the other apostles preached.

2:17 The apostle has a third class to deal with, so now he turns to the question: *Are the Jews, to whom the law was given, also lost?* And of course the answer is, "Yes, they are lost too!"

There is no doubt that many Jews felt they were immune from God's judgment. God would never send **a Jew** to hell, they thought. The Gentiles, on the other hand, were fuel for the flames of hell. Paul must now destroy this pretension by showing that under certain circumstances Gentiles may be closer to God than Jews.

First he reviews those things which a Jew prized as giving him an inside track with God. He bore the name of **a Jew** and thus was a member of God's chosen earthly people. He rested **on the law**, which was never designed to give rest but rather to awaken the conscience to a sense of sinfulness. He gloried **in God**, the only true God, who had entered into a unique covenant relationship with the nation of Israel.

2:18 He knew God's **will**, because a general outline of that will is given in the Scriptures. He approved the **things that are excellent**, because the **law**

taught him how to assess moral values.

2:19 He prided himself on being **a guide to the** morally and spiritually **blind, a light to those who** were in the **darkness** of ignorance.

2:20 He felt qualified to correct the **foolish** or untaught and to teach **babes**, because the **law** gave him an outline of **knowledge** and of the **truth.**

2:21 But these things in which the Jew boasted had never changed his life. It was simply pride of race, religion, and knowledge without any corresponding moral transformation. He taught others but did not take the lessons to heart himself. He preached against stealing but did not practice what he preached.

2:22 When he forbade **adultery**, it was a case of "Do as I say, not as I do." While he did loathe and **abhor idols**, he didn't hesitate to **rob temples**, perhaps by actually looting heathen shrines.

2:23 He gloried in the possession of **the law**, but dishonored the **God** who gave it by **breaking** its sacred precepts.

2:24 This combination of high talk and low walk caused **the Gentiles** to blaspheme **the name of God**. They judged the Lord, as men always do, by those who professed to be His followers. It was true in Isaiah's day (Isa. 52:5) and it is still true today. Each of us should ask:

> If of Jesus Christ their only view
> May be what they see of Him in you,
> (Insert your name), what do they see?

2:25 In addition to the law, the Jew prided himself on the rite of **circumcision**. This is a minor surgical operation performed on the foreskin of the Jewish male. It was instituted by God as a sign of His covenant with Abraham (Gen. 17:9–14). It expressed the separation of a people to God from the world. After a while the Jews so prided themselves on having had the operation that they contemptuously called the Gentiles "the uncircumcision."

Here Paul links **circumcision** with the **Law** of Moses and points out that it was only valid as a sign when it was combined with a life of obedience. God is not a mere ritualist; He is not satisfied with external ceremonies unless they are accompanied by inward holiness. So a circumcised Jew who transgresses the law might just as well be uncircumcised.

When the apostle speaks about keepers or doers of the law in this passage, we must not take the words in an absolute sense.

2:26 Thus, if a Gentile adheres to the morality prescribed by **the law**, even if he isn't under the law, **his uncircumcision** is more acceptable than the circumcision of a Jewish transgressor. In such a case the Gentile's heart is circumcised, and that is what counts.

2:27 The superior behavior of the Gentile condemns the Jew, who, **with** his **written code and circumcision** does not keep the **law** or live the circumcised life, the life of separation and sanctification.

2:28 In God's reckoning, **a true Jew** is not simply a man who has Abraham's blood flowing in his veins or who has the mark of circumcision in his body. A person may have both these things and be the scum of the earth morally. The Lord is not swayed by external considerations of race or religion; He looks for inward sincerity and purity.

2:29 A real **Jew** is the one who is not only a descendant of Abraham but who also manifests a godly life. This passage does not teach that all believers are Jews, or that the church is the Israel of God. Paul is talking about those who are born of Jewish parentage and is insisting that the mere fact of birth and the ordinance of circumcision are not enough. There must also be inward reality.

True **circumcision is** a matter **of the heart** — not just a literal cutting of the body but the spiritual reality of surgery on the old, unregenerate nature.

Those who thus combine the outward sign and the inward grace receive God's praise, if not man's. There is a play on words in this last verse that is not apparent in the English. The word "Jew" comes from "Judah," meaning **praise. A** real **Jew** is one whose character is such as to receive **praise from God**.

3:1 Paul continues the subject of the guilt of the Jews in the first eight verses of this chapter. Here a Jewish objector appears and begins to cross-examine the apostle. The questioning proceeds as follows:

OBJECTOR: If all you have said in 2:17–29 is true, then **what** is the **advantage** of being a **Jew** and what **profit** is there from **circumcision?**

3:2 *PAUL:* The Jews have had many special privileges. The most important is that they were entrusted with **the oracles of God**. The OT Scriptures were given to Jews to write and to preserve, but how have the people of Israel responded to this tremendous privilege? On the whole, they have demonstrated an appalling lack of faith.

3:3 *OBJECTOR:* Well, granted that not all Jews have believed, but does this mean that God will go back on His promises? After all, He did choose Israel as His people and He made definite covenants with them. Can the **unbelief** of some cause **God** to break His word?

3:4 *PAUL:* **Certainly not!** Whenever there is a question whether God or man is right, always proceed on the basis that **God** is right and **every man** is **a liar**. This is what David said, in effect, in Psalm 51:4: "The complete truthfulness of all You say must be defended, and You must be vindicated every time You are called into question by sinful man." Our sins only serve to confirm the truthfulness of God's words.

3:5 *OBJECTOR:* If that's the case, why does God condemn us? **If our unrighteousness** causes **the righteousness of God** to shine more gloriously, how can **God** visit us with **wrath?** (Paul notes here that in quoting these words, he is using a typically human argument.)

3:6 *PAUL:* Such an argument is unworthy of serious consideration. If there were any possibility of God's being unrighteous, then how could He be fit to **judge the world?** Yet we all admit that He *will* judge the world.

3:7 *OBJECTOR:* But if my sin brings glory to God, if **my lie** vindicates His **truth**, if He causes man's wrath to praise Him, then how can He consistently find fault with me **as a sinner?**

3:8 Why wouldn't it be logical to say —

PAUL: Let me interrupt to say that **some** people actually accuse us Christians of using this argument, but it is a slander.

OBJECTOR: Why wouldn't it be logical to say, **"Let us do evil, that good may come"?**

PAUL: All I can say is that the **condemnation** of people who talk like that is well-deserved.

(Actually this last argument, stupid as it seems, is constantly leveled against the gospel of the grace of God. People say, "If you could be saved just by faith in Christ, then you could go out and live in sin. Since God's grace superabounds over man's sin, then the more you sin, the more His grace abounds." The apostle answers this objection in chapter 6.)

3:9 OBJECTOR: Are you saying, **then**, that **we** Jews are **better than** those sinful Gentiles? Or the question may be, according to some versions, "Are we Jews worse than the Gentiles?" The answer in either case is that the Jews are no better and no worse. All are sinners.

That leads up to and parallels the next question in Paul's presentation. He has shown that the heathen are lost; the self-righteous moralists, whether Jews or Gentiles, are lost; the Jews are lost. Now he turns to the question: *Are all men lost?*

The answer is, "Yes, **we have** already **charged** that **all** people **are under** the power of **sin**." This means that Jews are no different from Gentiles in this respect.

3:10 If further proof is needed, that proof is found in the OT. First we see that sin has affected everyone born of human parents (3:10–12) and then we see that sin has affected every part of a man (3:13–18). We might paraphrase it as follows: "There is **not** a single **righteous** person" (Ps. 14:1).

3:11 "There is no one who has a right understanding of God. **There is** no one **who seeks after God**" (Ps. 14:2). If left to himself, fallen man would never seek God. It is only through the work of the Holy Spirit that anyone ever does.

3:12 "**All** have gone astray from God. All mankind has become corrupt. There is not one who lives a good life, **no, not one**" (Ps. 14:3).

3:13 "Men's throats are like **an open tomb**. Their speech has been consistently deceitful" (Ps. 5:9). "Their conversation flows from poisonous lips" (Ps. 140:3).

3:14 "Their mouths are **full of cursing** and hatred" (Ps. 10:7).

3:15 "Their feet are swift to** carry them on missions of murder" (Isa. 59:7).

3:16 "They leave a trail of ruin **and misery**" (Isa. 59:7).

3:17 "They have never **known** how to make **peace**" (Isa. 59:8).

3:18 "They have no respect for **God**" (Ps. 36:1).

This, then, is God's X-ray of the human race. It reveals universal unrighteousness (3:10); ignorance and independence toward God (3:11); waywardness, unprofitableness, and lack of any goodness (3:12). Man's throat is full of rottenness, his tongue is deceitful, his lips are venomous (3:13); his mouth is full of swearing (3:14); his feet are bent on murder (3:15); he leaves behind trouble and destruction (3:16); he doesn't know how to make peace (3:17); and he has no regard for God (3:18). Here we see the total depravity of man, by which we mean that sin has affected all of mankind and that it has affected every part of his being. Obviously every man has not committed every sin, but he has a nature which is *capable* of committing them all.

If Paul had wanted to give a more complete catalog of sins, he could have mentioned *the sins of sex*: adultery, homosexuality, lesbianism, perversion, bestiality, prostitution, rape, lewdness, pornography, and smut. He could have mentioned *the sins associated with war*: destruction of innocents, atrocities, gas chambers, ovens, concentration camps, torture devices, sadism. He could have mentioned *sins of the home*: unfaithfulness, divorce, wifebeating, mental cruelty, child abuse. Add to these the crimes of murder, mutilation, theft, burglary, embezzlement, vandalism, graft, corruption. Also *the sins of speech*: profanity, suggestive jokes, sensual language, cursing, blasphemy, lies, backbiting, gossip, character assassination, grumbling, and complaining. *Other personal sins* are: drunkenness, drug addiction, pride, envy, covetousness, ingratitude, filthy thought-life, hatred, and bitterness. The list is seemingly endless — pollution, littering, racism, exploitation, deceit, betrayal, broken promises, and on and on. What further proof of human depravity is needed?

3:19 When God gave the law to Israel, He was using Israel as a sample of the human race. He found that Israel was a failure, and He correctly applied this finding to all of humanity. It is the same as when a health inspector takes a test-tube of water from a well, tests the sample, finds it polluted, and then pronounces the entire well polluted.

So Paul explains that when **the law** speaks, it speaks **to those who are under the law** — the people of Israel — in order **that every mouth**, *Jew and Gentile*, **may be stopped, and all the world** be brought in **guilty before God**.

3:20 **No** one can **be justified by** keeping **the law**. The law was not given to justify people but to produce **the knowledge of sin** — not the knowledge of *salvation*, but **the knowledge of sin**.

We could never know what a crooked line is unless we also knew a straight line. The law is like a straight line. When men test themselves by it, they see how crooked they are.

We can use a mirror to see that our face is dirty, but the mirror is not designed to wash the dirty face. A thermometer will tell if a person has a fever, but swallowing the thermometer will not cure the fever.

The law is good when it is used to produce conviction of sin, but it is worthless as a savior from sin. As Luther said, its function is not to justify but to terrify.

D. The Basis and Terms of the Gospel (3:21–31)

3:21 We now come to the heart of the Letter to the Romans, when Paul answers the question: *According to the gospel, how can ungodly sinners be justified by a holy God?*

He begins by saying that **the righteousness of God** has been revealed **apart from the law**. This means that a plan or program has been **revealed** by which God can righteously save unrighteous sinners, and that it is not by requiring men to keep the law. Because God is holy, He cannot condone sin or overlook it or wink at it. He must punish it. And the punishment for sin is death. Yet God loves the sinner and wants to save him; there is the dilemma. God's righteousness demands the sinner's death, but His love desires the sinner's eternal happiness. The gospel reveals how God can save sinners without compromising His righteousness.

This righteous plan is **witnessed by the Law and the Prophets**. It was foretold in the types and shadows of the sacrificial system that required the shedding of blood for atonement. And it was foretold by direct prophecies (see, e.g., Isa. 51:5, 6, 8; 56:1; Dan. 9:24).

3:22 Verse 21 told us that this righteous salvation is *not* obtained on the basis of law-keeping. Now the apostle tells us how it *is* obtained — **through faith in Jesus Christ**. Faith here means utter reliance on the living Lord Jesus Christ as one's only Savior from sin and one's only hope for heaven. It is based on the revelation of the Person and work of Christ as found in the Bible.

Faith is not a leap in the dark. It demands the surest evidence, and finds it in the infallible word of God. Faith is not illogical or unreasonable. What is more reasonable than that the creature should trust his Creator?

Faith is not a meritorious work by which a man earns or deserves salvation. A man cannot boast because he has believed the Lord; he would be a fool *not* to believe Him. Faith is not an attempt to earn salvation, but is the simple acceptance of the salvation which God offers as a free gift.

Paul goes on to tell us that this salvation is **to all and on all**[6] **who believe**. It is **to all** in the sense that it is available to all, offered to all, and sufficient for all. But it is only **on** those **who believe**; that is, it is effective only in the lives of those who accept the Lord Jesus by a definite act of faith. The pardon is for all, but it becomes valid in an individual's life only when he accepts it.

When Paul says that salvation is available to all, he includes Gentiles as well as Jews, because now **there is no difference**. The Jew has no special privilege and the Gentile is at no disadvantage.

3:23 The availability of the gospel is as universal as the need. And the need is universal because **all have sinned**[7] **and fall short of the glory of God**. Everybody **sinned** in Adam; when he sinned, he acted as the representative for all his descendants. But men are not only sinners by nature; they are also sinners by *practice*. They **fall short**, in themselves, **of the glory of God.**

EXCURSUS ON SIN

Sin is any thought, word, or deed that falls short of God's standard of holiness and perfection. It is a missing of the mark, a coming short of the target. An Indian whose arrow fell short of its target was heard to say, "Oh, I sinned." In his language,[8] the same word was used to express sinning and falling short of the target.

Sin is lawlessness (1 Jn. 3:4), the rebellion of the creature's will against the will of God. Sin is not only doing what is wrong but the failure to do what one knows to be right (Jas. 4:17). Whatever is not of faith is sin (Rom. 14:23). This means that it is wrong for a man to do anything about which he has a reasonable doubt. If he does not have a clear conscience about it, and yet goes ahead and does it, he is sinning.

"All unrighteousness is sin" (1 Jn. 5:17). And the thought of foolishness is sin (Prov. 24:9). Sin begins in the mind. When encouraged and entertained, it breaks forth into an act, and the act leads on to death. Sin is often attractive when first contemplated, but hideous in retrospect.

Sometimes Paul distinguishes between sins and sin. Sins refer to wrong things that we have done. Sin refers to our evil nature — that is, to what we are. What we *are* is a lot worse than anything we have ever done. But Christ died for our evil nature as well as for our evil deeds. God forgives our sins, but the Bible never speaks of His forgiving our sin. Instead, He *condemns* or *judges* sin in the flesh (Rom. 8:3).

There is also a difference between sin and transgression. Transgression is a violation of a known law. Stealing is basically sinful; it is wrong in itself. But stealing is also a transgression when there is a law that forbids it. "Where there is no law there is no transgression" (Rom. 4:15).

Paul has shown that all men have sinned and continually come short of God's glory. Now he goes on to present the remedy. ‡

3:24 Being justified freely by His grace. The gospel tells how God justifies sinners as a free gift and by an act of unmerited favor. But what do we mean when we speak of the act of justifying?

The word *justify* means to reckon or declare to be righteous. For example, God pronounces a sinner to be righteous when that sinner believes on the Lord Jesus Christ. This is the way the word is most often used in the NT.

However, a man can justify God (see Luke 7:29) by believing and obeying God's word. In other words, he declares God to be righteous in all that God says and does.

And, of course, a man can justify himself; that is, he can protest his own righteousness (see Luke 10:29). But this is nothing but a form of self-deception.

To justify does not mean to actually *make* a person righteous. We cannot *make* God righteous; He already *is* righteous. But we can *declare* Him to be righteous. God does not *make* the believer sinless or righteous in himself. Rather, God puts righteousness to his account. As A. T. Pierson put it, "God in justifying sinners actually calls them righteous when they are not — does not impute sin where sin actually exists, and does impute righteousness where it does not exist."[9]

A popular definition of justification is *just as if I'd never sinned*. But this does not go far enough. When God justifies the believing sinner, He not only acquits him from guilt but clothes him in His own righteousness and thus makes him absolutely fit for heaven. "Justification goes beyond acquittal to approval; beyond pardon to promotion."[10] Acquittal means only that a person is set free from a charge. Justification means that positive righteousness is imputed.

The reason God can declare ungodly sinners to be righteous is because the Lord Jesus Christ has fully paid the debt of their sins by His death and resurrection. When sinners accept Christ by faith, they are justified.

When James teaches that justification is by works (Jas. 2:24), he does not mean that we are saved by good works, or by faith plus good works, but rather by the kind of faith that results in good works.

It is important to realize that justification is a reckoning that takes place in the mind of God. It is not something a believer feels; he knows it has taken place because the Bible says so. C. I. Scofield expressed it this way: "Justification is that act of God whereby He declares righteous all who believe in Jesus. It is something which takes place in the mind of God, not in the nervous system or emotional nature of the believer."

Here in Romans 3:24 the apostle teaches that we are **justified freely**. It is not something we can earn or purchase, but rather something that is offered as a gift.

Next we learn that we are **justified . . . by** God's **grace**. This simply means that it is wholly apart from any merit in ourselves. As far as we are concerned, it is undeserved, unsought, and unbought.

In order to avoid confusion later on, we should pause here to explain that there are six different aspects of justification in the NT. We are said to be justified by grace, by faith, by blood, by power, by God, and by works; yet there is no contradiction or conflict.

We are justified by grace — that means we do not deserve it.

We are justified by faith (Rom. 5:1) — that means that we have to receive it by believing on the Lord Jesus Christ.

We are justified by blood (Rom. 5:9) — that refers to the price the Savior paid in order that we might be justified.

We are justified by power (Rom. 4:24, 25) — the same power that raised the Lord Jesus from the dead.

We are justified by God (Rom. 8:33) — He is the One who reckons us righteous.

We are justified by works (Jas. 2:24) — not meaning that good works earn justification, but that they are the evidence that we have been justified.

Returning to 3:24, we read that we are justified **through the redemption that is in Christ Jesus. Redemption** means buying back by payment of a ransom price. The Lord Jesus bought us back from the slave market of sin. His precious blood was the ransom price which was paid to satisfy the claims of a holy and righteous God. If someone asks, "To whom was the ransom paid?" he misses the point. The Scriptures nowhere suggest that a specific payment was made either to God or to Satan. The ransom was not paid to anyone but was an abstract settlement that provided a righteous basis by which God could save the ungodly.

3:25   God set forth Christ Jesus **as a propitiation. A propitiation** is a means by which justice is satisfied, God's wrath is averted, and mercy can be shown on the basis of an acceptable sacrifice.

Three times in the NT Christ is spoken of as **a propitiation**. Here in Romans 3:25 we learn that those who put their faith in Christ find mercy by virtue of His shed blood. In 1 John 2:2 Christ is described as the propitiation for our sins, and for those of the whole world. His work is sufficient for the whole world but is only effective for those who put their trust in Him. Finally, in 1 John 4:10, God's love was manifested in sending His Son to be the propitiation for our sins.

The prayer of the publican in Luke 18:13 was literally "God be propitious to me, the sinner." He was asking God to show mercy to him by not requiring him to pay the penalty of his aggravated guilt.

The word **propitiation** also occurs in Hebrews 2:17: "Therefore, in all things He had to be made like His brethren, that He might be a merciful and faithful High Priest in things *pertaining* to God, to make propitiation for the sins of the people." Here the expression "to make propitiation" means to put away by paying the penalty.

The OT equivalent of the word *propitiation* is *mercy-seat*. The mercy-seat was the lid of the ark. On the Day of Atonement the high priest sprinkled the mercy-seat with the blood of a sacrificial victim. By this means errors of the high priest and of the people were atoned for or covered.

When Christ made propitiation for our sins, He went much further. He not only *covered them* but *did away with them completely*.

Now Paul tells us in 3:25 that **God set** Christ **forth as a propitiation by His blood, through faith**. We are not told to put our faith in His blood; *Christ Himself* is the object of our faith. It is only a resurrected and living Christ Jesus who can save. He is the propitiation. **Faith** in Him is the condition by which we avail ourselves of the **propitiation**. **His blood** is the price that was paid.

The finished work of Christ declares God's **righteousness** for the remission of **sins** that are past. This refers to sins committed before the death of Christ. From Adam to Christ, God saved those who put their faith in Him on the basis of whatever revelation He gave them. Abraham, for example, believed God, and it was reckoned to him for righteousness (Gen. 15:6). But how could God do this righteously? A sinless Substitute had not been slain. The blood of a perfect Sacrifice had not been shed. In a word, Christ had not died. The debt had not been paid. God's righteous claims had not been met. How then could God save believing sinners in the OT period?

The answer is that although Christ had not yet died, God knew that He *would* die, and He saved men on the basis of the still-future work of Christ. Even if OT saints didn't know about Calvary, *God* knew about it, and He put all the value of Christ's work to their account when they believed God. In a very real sense, OT believers were saved on credit. They were saved on the basis of a price still to be paid. They looked forward to Calvary; we look back to it.

That is what Paul means when he says that the propitiation of Christ declares God's **righteousness because He had passed over the sins that were previously committed**. He is not speaking, as some wrongly think, of sins which an individual person has committed before his conversion. This might suggest that the work of Christ took care of sins before the new birth, but that a man is on his own after that. No, he is dealing with the seeming leniency of God in apparently overlooking the sins of those who were saved before the cross. It might seem that God excused those sins or pretended not to see them. Not so, says Paul. The Lord knew that Christ would make full expiation, and so He saved men on that basis.

So the OT period was a time of the **forbearance** of God. For at least 4000 years He held back His judgment on sin. Then in the fullness of time He sent His Son to be the Sin-bearer. When the Lord Jesus took our sins upon Himself, God unleashed the full fury of His righteous, holy wrath on the Son of His love.

3:26 Now the death of Christ declares God's **righteousness**. God is **just** because He has required the full payment of the penalty of sin. And He can justify the ungodly without condoning their sin or compromising His own righteousness because a perfect Substitute has died and risen again. Albert Midlane has stated the truth in poetry:

> The perfect righteousness of God
> Is witnessed in the Savior's blood;
> 'Tis in the cross of Christ we trace
> His righteousness, yet wondrous grace.
>   God could not pass the sinner by,
> His sin demands that he must die;
> But in the cross of Christ we see
> How God can save, yet righteous be.
>   The sin is on the Savior laid,
> 'Tis in His blood sin's debt is paid;
> Stern justice can demand no more,
> And mercy can dispense her store.
>   The sinner who believes is free,
> Can say, "The Savior died for me";
> Can point to the atoning blood,
> And say, "That made my peace
>   with God."

3:27 **Where is boasting then** in this wonderful plan of salvation? **It is excluded**, shut out, banned. **By what** principle is boasting **excluded**? By the principle **of works**? **No**. If salvation were by works, that would allow room for all kinds of self-congratulation. But when salvation is on the principle **of faith**, there is no room for **boasting**. The justified person says, "I did all the sinning; Jesus did all the saving." True faith disavows any possibility of self-help, self-improvement, or self-salvation, looking only to Christ as Savior. Its language is:

> In my hand no price I bring,
> Simply to Thy cross I cling;
> Naked, come to Thee for dress,
> Helpless, look to Thee for grace.
> Foul, I to the fountain fly;
> Wash me, Savior, or I die.
>   — *Augustus M. Toplady*

3:28 As the reason why boasting is

excluded, Paul reiterates **that a man is justified by faith apart from the deeds of the law**.

3:29 How does the gospel present God? Is He the exclusive **God of the Jews**? No, He is **also the God of the Gentiles**. The Lord Jesus Christ did not die for one race of mankind but for the whole world of sinners. And the offer of full and free salvation goes out to whosoever will, Jew or Gentile.

3:30 There aren't two Gods — one for the Jews and one for the Gentiles. There is only **one God** and only one way of salvation for all mankind. He justifies **the circumcised by faith and the uncircumcised through faith**. Whatever the reason for the use of different prepositions here (**by** and **through**[11]), there is no difference in the instrumental cause of justification; it is **faith** in both cases.

3:31 An important question remains. When we say that salvation is by faith and not by law-keeping, do we imply that the law is worthless and should be disregarded? Does the gospel wave the law aside as if it had no place? **On the contrary**, the gospel establishes **the law**, and this is how:

The law demands perfect obedience. The penalty for breaking the law must be paid. That penalty is DEATH. If a lawbreaker pays the penalty, he will be lost eternally. The gospel tells how Christ died to pay the penalty of the broken law. He did not treat it as a thing to be ignored. He paid the debt in full. Now anyone who has broken the law can avail himself of the fact that Christ paid the penalty on his behalf. Thus the gospel of salvation by faith upholds the law by insisting that its utmost demands must be and have been fully met.

E. The Harmony of the Gospel with the Old Testament (Chap. 4)

The fifth main question that Paul takes up is: *Does the gospel agree with the teachings of the OT?* The answer to this question would be of special importance to the Jewish people. Therefore the apostle now shows that there is complete harmony between the gospel in the NT and in the Old. Justification has always been by faith.

4:1 Paul proves his point by refer-

ring to two of the greatest figures in Israel's history: Abraham and David. God made great covenants with both these men. One lived centuries before the law was given, and the other lived many years afterward. One was justified before he was circumcised, and the other after.

Let us first consider **Abraham**, whom all Jews could call their forefather. What was his experience **according to the flesh?**[12] What did he find concerning the way in which a person is justified?

4:2 If Abraham was justified by works, then he would have reason for boasting. He could pat himself on the back for earning a righteous standing **before God**. But this is utterly impossible. No one will ever be able to boast before God (Eph. 2:9). There is nothing in the Scriptures to indicate that Abraham had any grounds for boasting that he was justified by his works.

But someone may argue, "Doesn't it say in James 2:21 that Abraham was justified by works?" Yes it does, but there the meaning is quite different. Abraham was justified by faith in Genesis 15:6 when he believed God's promise concerning a numberless posterity. It was thirty or more years later that he was justified (vindicated) by works when he started to offer Isaac as a burnt offering to God (Gen. 22). This act of obedience proved the reality of his faith. It was an outward demonstration that he had been truly justified by faith.

4:3 What does the Scripture say concerning Abraham's justification? It says "he believed in the Lord, and He accounted it to him for righteousness" (Gen. 15:6). God revealed Himself to Abraham and promised that he would have a numberless posterity. The patriarch believed in the Lord, and God put **righteousness** to his account. In other words, Abraham was justified by faith. It was just as simple as that. Works had nothing to do with it. They aren't even mentioned.

4:4 All of this brings us to one of the sublimest statements in the Bible concerning the contrast between works and faith in reference to the plan of salvation.

Think of it this way: when a man

works for a living and gets his paycheck at the end of the week, he is entitled to his **wages**. He has earned them. He does not bow and scrape before his employer, thanking him for such a display of kindness and protesting that he doesn't deserve the money. Not at all! He puts the money in his pocket and goes home with the feeling that he has only been reimbursed for his time and labor.

But that's not the way it is in the matter of justification.

4:5 Shocking as it may seem, the justified man is the one **who**, first of all, **does not work**. He renounces any possibility of earning his salvation. He disavows any personal merit or goodness. He acknowledges that all his best labors could never fulfill God's righteous demands.

Instead, he **believes on Him who justifies** *the ungodly*. He puts his faith and trust in the Lord. He takes God at His word. As we have seen, this is not a meritorious action. The merit is not in his faith, but in *the Object of his faith*.

Notice that he **believes on Him who justifies** *the ungodly*. He doesn't come with the plea that he has tried his best, that he has lived by the Golden Rule, that he has not been as bad as others. No, he comes as an **ungodly**, guilty sinner and throws himself on the mercy of God.

And what is the result? **His faith is accounted** to him **for righteousness**. Because he has come believing instead of working, God puts **righteousness** to his account. Through the merits of the risen Savior, God clothes him with **righteousness** and thus makes him fit for heaven. Henceforth God sees him in Christ and accepts him on that basis.

To summarize, then, justification is for the ungodly — not for good people. It is a matter of grace — not of debt. And it is received by faith — not by works.

4:6 Next Paul turns to **David** to prove his thesis. The words **just as** at the beginning of this verse indicate that David's experience was the same as Abraham's. The sweet singer of Israel said that the happy man is the sinner whom God reckons righteous **apart from works**. Although David never said this

in so many words, the Apostle derives it from Psalm 32:1, 2, which he quotes in the next two verses.

4:7 Blessed are those whose lawless deeds are forgiven,
And whose sins are covered;
4:8 Blessed is the man to whom the LORD shall not impute sin.

What did Paul see in these verses? First of all, he noticed that David said nothing about works; forgiveness is a matter of God's grace, not of man's efforts. Second, he saw that if God doesn't **impute sin** to a person, then that person must have a righteous standing before Him. Finally, he saw that God justifies the ungodly; David had been guilty of adultery and murder, yet in these verses he is tasting the sweetness of full and free pardon.

4:9 But the idea may still lurk in some Jewish minds that the chosen people had a corner on God's justification, that only those who were circumcised could be justified. The apostle turns again to the experience of **Abraham** to show that this is not so. He poses the question, "Is righteousness imputed to believing Jews only, or to believing Gentiles as well?" The fact that Abraham was used as an example might seem to suggest that it was only to Jews.

4:10 Here Paul seizes on a historical fact that most of us would never have noticed. He shows that Abraham was justified (Gen. 15:6) before he was ever **circumcised** (Gen. 17:24). If the father of the nation of Israel could be justified **while he was** still **uncircumcised**, then the question arises, "Why can't other uncircumcised people be justified?" In a very real sense, Abraham was justified while still on Gentile ground, and this leaves the door wide open for other Gentiles to be justified, entirely apart from circumcision.

4:11 Circumcision, then, was not the instrumental cause of Abraham's justification. It was merely an outward **sign** in his flesh that he had been justified by faith. Basically, circumcision was the external token of the covenant between God and the people of Israel; but here its meaning is expanded to indicate the righteousness which God imputed to Abraham through faith.

In addition to being a sign, circumcision was a seal — **a seal of righteousness of the faith which he had while still uncircumcised**. A **sign** points to the existence of that which it signifies. A **seal** authenticates, confirms, certifies, or guarantees the genuineness of that which is signified. Circumcision confirmed to Abraham that he was regarded and treated by God as righteous through faith.

Circumcision was **a seal of the righteousness of** Abraham's **faith**. This may mean that his **faith** was righteous or it may mean that he obtained righteousness through **faith**. The latter is almost certainly the correct meaning; **circumcision** was **a seal of the righteousness** which belonged to his **faith** or which he obtained on the basis of **faith**.

Because Abraham was justified before he was circumcised, **he** can **be the father of** other **uncircumcised** people — that is, of believing Gentiles. They can be justified the same way he was — by faith.

When it says that Abraham is **the father** of believing Gentiles, there is no thought of physical descent, of course. It simply means that these believers are his children because they imitate his faith. They are not his children by birth but by following him as their pattern and example. Neither does the passage teach that believing Gentiles become the Israel of God. The Israel of God is composed of those *Jews* who accept Jesus, the Messiah, as their Lord and Savior.

4:12 Abraham received the sign of **circumcision** for another reason also — namely, that he might be **the father of** those Jews who are not only circumcised **but who also** follow his footsteps in a path of **faith**, the kind of **faith which** he **had while still uncircumcised**.

There is a difference between being Abraham's descendants and Abraham's children. Jesus said to the Pharisees, "I know that you are Abraham's descendants" (John 8:37). But then He went on to say, "If you were Abraham's children, you would do the works of Abraham" (John 8:39). So here Paul insists that physical circumcision is not what counts. There must be **faith** in the living God. Those **of the circumcision** who believe in the Lord Jesus Christ are the true Israel of God.

To summarize, then, there was a time in Abraham's life when he had **faith** and was **still uncircumcised**, and another time when he had faith and was circumcised. Paul's eagle eye sees in this fact that both believing Gentiles and believing Jews can claim Abraham as their father and can identify with him as his children.

4:13 "The argument continues relentlessly on as Paul chases every possible objector down every possible alleyway of logic and Scripture."[13] The apostle now must deal with the objection that blessing came through the law and that therefore the Gentiles who did not know the law were cursed (see John 7:49).

When God promised **Abraham** and **his seed** that he would be **heir of the world**, He did not make the promise conditional on adherence to some legal code. (The law itself wasn't given until 430 years later — Gal. 3:17.) It was an unconditional **promise** of grace, to be received by **faith** — the same kind **of faith** by which we obtain God's **righteousness** today.

The expression **heir of the world** means that he would be the father of believing Gentiles as well as of Jews (4:11, 12), that he would be the father of many nations (4:17, 18) and not just of the Jewish nation. In its fullest sense the promise will be fulfilled when the Lord Jesus, Abraham's seed, takes the scepter of universal empire and reigns as King of kings and Lord of lords.

4:14 If those who seek God's blessing, and particularly the blessing of justification, are able to inherit it on the basis of lawkeeping, then **faith is made void and the promise made of no effect**. Faith is set aside because it is a principle that is completely opposite to law: **faith** is a matter of *believing*, while **law** is a matter of *doing*. The promise would then be worthless because it would be based on conditions that no one would be able to meet.

4:15 The law brings about God's **wrath**, not His blessing. It condemns those who fail to keep its commandments perfectly and continuously. And since none can do that, all who are under the law are condemned to death. It is impossible to be under the law without being under the curse.

But **where there is no law there is no transgression. Transgression** means the violation of a known **law**. Paul does not say that where there is no law, there is no *sin*. An act can be inherently wrong even if there is no law against it. But it becomes **transgression** when a sign goes up saying "Speed Limit 20 MPH."

The Jews thought they inherited blessing through having the law, but all they inherited was **transgression**. God gave the law so that sin might be seen as **transgression**, or to put it another way, so that sin might be seen in all its sinfulness. He never intended it to be the way of salvation for sinful transgressors!

4:16 Because law produces God's wrath and not His justification, God determined that He would save men by **grace** through **faith**. He would give eternal life as a free, undeserved gift to ungodly sinners who receive it by a simple act of **faith**.

In this way **the promise** of life is **sure to all the seed**. We should mention two words here — *sure* and *all*. First, God wants **the promise** to be *sure*. If justification depended on man's law-works, he could never be sure because he could not know if he had done enough good works or the right kind. No one who seeks to *earn* salvation enjoys full assurance. But when salvation is presented as a gift to be received by believing, then a man can be sure that he is saved on the authority of the word of God.

Second, God wants **the promise** to be **sure to** *all* **the seed** — not just to the Jews, to whom **the law** was given, **but also to** Gentiles who put their trust in the Lord in the same way that **Abraham** did. **Abraham is the father of us all** — that is, of **all** believing Jews and Gentiles.

4:17 To confirm Abraham's fatherhood over all true believers, Paul injects Genesis 17:5 as a parenthesis: **"I have made you a father of many nations."** God's choice of Israel as His chosen, earthly people did not mean that His grace and mercy would be *confined* to them. The apostle ingeniously quotes verse after verse from the OT to show that it always was God's intention to honor faith wherever He found it.

The phrase **in the presence of Him whom he believed** continues the thought from 4:16: ". . . Abraham, who is the father of us all." The connection is this: Abraham is the father of us all in the sight of Him (God) whom he (Abraham) believed, even **God who gives life to the dead** and speaks of **things** that **do not** yet **exist as** already existing. To understand this description of God, we have only to look at the verses that follow. **God gives life to the dead** — that is, to Abraham and Sarah, for although they were not dead physically, they were childless and beyond the age when they could have children (see 4:19). God **calls those things which do not yet exist as** already existing — that is, a numberless posterity involving many nations (see 4:18).

4:18 In the preceding verses Paul has emphasized that the promise came to Abraham by faith and not by law that it might be by grace and that it might be sure to all the seed. That leads quite naturally to a consideration of Abraham's faith in the God of resurrection. God promised Abraham posterity as numberless as the stars and the sand. Humanly speaking, the chances were all but hopeless. But **contrary to** human **hope**, Abraham **believed, in hope** that he would **become the father of many nations**, just as God had promised in Genesis 15:5: **"So shall your descendants be."**

4:19 When the promise of a great posterity was first made to Abraham, he was seventy-five years old (Gen. 12:2–4). At that time he was still physically able to become a father, because after that he begot Ishmael (Gen. 16:1–11). But in this verse Paul is speaking of the time when Abraham was about 100 years old and the promise was renewed (Gen. 17:15–21). By now the possibility of creating new life apart from the miraculous power of God had vanished. However, God had promised him a son, and Abraham believed God's promise.

Without **being weak in faith**, he **did not**[14] **consider his own body**, which was **already dead**, nor **the deadness of Sarah's womb**. Humanly speaking, it was utterly hopeless, but Abraham had faith.

4:20 The apparent impossibility that **the promise** would ever be fulfilled didn't stagger him. God had *said* it; Abraham *believed* it; that *settled* it. As far as the patriarch was concerned there was only one impossibility, and that was for God to lie. Abraham's faith was strong and vibrant. He gave **glory to God**, honoring Him as the One who could be depended on to fulfill His promise in defiance of all the laws of chance or probability.

4:21 Abraham did not know *how* God would fulfill His word, but that was incidental. He knew God and had every confidence that God **was** fully **able** to do **what He had promised**. In one way it was wonderful faith, but in another way it was the most reasonable thing to do, because God's word is the surest thing in the universe, and for Abraham there was no risk in believing it!

4:22 God was pleased to find a man who took Him at His word; He always is. And so He credited **righteousness** to Abraham's account. Where once there had been a balance of sin and guilt, now there was nothing but a righteous standing before God. Abraham had been delivered from condemnation and was justified by a holy God through faith.

4:23 The historical narrative of his justification by faith **was not written for his sake alone**. There was a sense, of course, in which it *was* written for his sake — a permanent record of his acquittal and his now-perfect standing before God.

4:24 But it was written **also for us**. Our faith is likewise reckoned for righteousness when we **believe** on God, **who raised up Jesus our Lord from the dead**. The only difference is this: Abraham believed that God *would* give life to the dead (that is, to his weak body and Sarah's barren womb). We believe that God *has* given life to the dead by raising the Lord Jesus Christ. C. H. Mackintosh explains:

> Abraham was called to believe in a promise, whereas we are privileged to believe in an accomplished fact. He was called to look forward to something which was to be done; we look back on something that

is done, even an accomplished redemption, attested by the fact of a risen and glorified Savior at the right hand of the majesty in the heavens.[15]

4:25 The Lord Jesus **was delivered up because of our offenses, and was raised because of our justification**. Although the preposition **because of** (Gk. *dia*) is used here in connection with both our offenses and our justification, the context demands a different shade of meaning in each case. He **was delivered up** not only **because of our offenses** but in order to put them away. **He was raised up because of our justification** — that is, in order to demonstrate God's complete satisfaction with the work of Christ by which we are justified. In the first instance, **our offenses** were the problem that needed to be dealt with. In the second instance, **our justification** is the result that is assured by Christ's resurrection. There could have been no justification if Christ had remained in the tomb. But the fact that He rose tells us that the work is finished, the price has been paid, and God is infinitely satisfied with the sin-atoning work of the Savior.

F. The Practical Benefits of the Gospel (5:1–11)

The apostle carries his case for justification forward another step by taking up the question: *What are the benefits of justification in the believer's life?* In other words, does it really work? His answer is a resounding *yes*, as he enumerates seven major blessings that every believer possesses. These blessings flow to the believer through Christ. He is the Mediator between God and man, and all God's gifts are channeled through Him.

5:1 The first great benefit enjoyed by those of us who have **been justified by faith** is **peace with God through our Lord Jesus Christ**. The war is over. Hostilities have ceased. Through the work of Christ all causes of enmity between our souls and God have been removed. We have been changed from foes to friends by a miracle of grace.

5:2 **Also we** enjoy **access** *into an indescribable position of favor with God*. We are accepted in the Beloved One; therefore we are as near and dear to God as

His own Beloved Son. The Father extends the golden scepter to us and welcomes us as sons, not strangers. **This grace**, or standing in favor, embraces every aspect of our position before God, a position that is as perfect and permanent as Christ's because we are in Him.

As if that were not enough, *we also* **rejoice in hope of the glory of God**. This means that we joyfully look forward to the time when we will not only gaze on the splendor of God, but will ourselves be manifested in glory (see John 17:22; Col. 3:4). We cannot comprehend the full significance of that hope here on earth, nor will we get over the wonder of it through all eternity.

5:3 The fourth blessing that flows from justification is that **we also glory in tribulations** — not so much in their present discomforts as in their eventual results (see Heb. 12:11). It is one of the delightful paradoxes of the Christian faith that joy can coexist with affliction. The opposite of joy is sin, not suffering. One of the by-products of **tribulation** is that it produces **perseverance** or steadfastness. We could never develop **perseverance** if our lives were trouble-free.

5:4 Paul now goes on to explain that **perseverance** works **character**. When God sees us bearing up under our trials and looking to Him to work out His purposes through them, He awards us His Good Endurance Seal of Approval. We have been tested and approved. And this sense of His approval fills us with **hope**. We know He is working in our lives, developing our character. This gives us confidence that, having begun a good work in us, He will see it through to completion (Phil. 1:6).

5:5 **Hope does not disappoint**. If we were to hope for something but then later find that we were never going to get it, our hope would be put to shame or disappointed. But the hope of our salvation will never be put to shame. We will never be disappointed or find that we have rested on a false confidence. How can we be so sure? **Because the love of God has been poured out in our hearts. The love of God** could mean either our love for God or His love for us. Here it means the latter because verses 6–20 rehearse some of the great proofs

of God's love for us. **The Holy Spirit, given to us** the moment we believe, floods our hearts with these expressions of God's eternal love, and by these we are assured that He will see us safely home to heaven. After you receive the Spirit, you will sense that God loves you. This is not a vague, mystical feeling that "Somebody up there" cares about humanity, but the deep-seated conviction that a personal God really loves *you* as an individual.

5:6[†] In verses 6–20, Paul argues from the lesser to the greater. His logic is that if God's love went out to us when we were His ungodly enemies, will He not much more preserve us now that we belong to Him? This brings us to the fifth benefit of our justification; *we are eternally secure in Christ*. In developing this theme, the apostle introduces five "much mores."

The "much more" of deliverance from wrath (5:9).

The "much more" of preservation by His resurrection life (5:10).

The "much more" of the gift of grace (5:15).

The "much more" of the believer's reign in life (5:17).

The "much more" of abounding grace (5:20).

In verses 6, 7, and 8 Paul emphasizes what **we were** (**without strength, ungodly,** sinners) when **Christ died for** us. In verses 9 and 10 he emphasizes what we are now (justified by Christ's blood, reconciled by His death) and the resulting certainty of what the Savior will do for us (deliver us from wrath, preserve us by His life).

First we are reminded that we were weak, helpless, **without strength**, and unable to save ourselves. But at the predetermined time the Lord Jesus Christ visited our planet and died for men. And He did not die for good men, as some might suppose, but **for the ungodly**. There was no virtue, no excellence in us to commend us to God. We were utterly unworthy, but **Christ died for** us anyway.

5:7 This act of divine love was unique and unparalleled by anything in human experience. The average man's life is precious to him, and he would not

†*See p. xxii.*

think of throwing it away for an unworthy person. For example, he would not die for a murderer, an adulterer, or a mobster. In fact, he would be reluctant to **die** even **for a "righteous" man**, one who is honest and dependable but not especially warmhearted. It is possible, in an extreme case, that he would die for a **"good" man**, meaning one who is kind, friendly, loving, and lovable.

5:8 The **love** of **God** is completely supernatural and otherworldly. He demonstrated **His** marvelous **love toward us** by sending His beloved Son to die **for us while we were still sinners**. If we ask why He did it, we must look for the answer in the sovereign will of God Himself. There was no good in us to call forth such love.

5:9 Now a new set of conditions exists. We are no longer reckoned as guilty sinners. At the enormous cost of the Savior's **blood**, shed for us at Calvary, we have been counted righteous by God. Since He went to such tremendous cost to justify us when we were sinners, will He not **much more** save us **from wrath through** Christ? If He has already paid the greatest price to bring us into His favor, is it likely that He would allow us to perish in the end?

Saved from wrath could mean either "saved out of wrath" or "delivered from any contact with wrath." Here we believe the preposition (Gk. *apo*) means the latter — saved away from any contact with the wrath of God, either in time or in eternity.

5:10 Going back to what we were and what we now are, think of it this way. It was **when we were enemies** that **we were reconciled to God through the death of His Son**. We were hostile toward the Lord and quite content to have it so. Left to ourselves, we felt no need of being reconciled to Him. Think of it — **enemies** of God!

God did not share our attitude in the matter. He intervened in a display of pure grace. The substitutionary death of Christ removed the cause of our hostility toward God — namely, our sins. By faith in Christ we have been **reconciled to God.**

If God purchased our reconciliation so dearly, will He ever let us go? If **we were reconciled through the death of His Son**, which is a symbol of utter weakness, shall we not be preserved to the end by the present life of Christ at the right hand of God, a life of infinite power? If His **death** had such power to save us, how much more will **His life** have power to keep us!

5:11 And now we come to the sixth benefit of justification: **we also rejoice in God through our Lord Jesus Christ**. We not only rejoice in His gifts but in the Giver Himself. Before we were saved we found our joys elsewhere. Now we exult whenever we *remember* Him, and are sad only when we *forget* Him. What has produced this marvelous change, so that we can now be glad in God? It is the work of the **Lord Jesus Christ**. Like all our other blessings, this joy comes to us **through** Him.

The seventh benefit enjoyed by the justified is found in the words **We have now received the reconciliation.**[16] **Reconciliation** refers to the establishment of harmony between God and man through the sacrificial work of the Savior. The entrance of sin had brought estrangement, alienation, and enmity between man and God. By putting away sin, which had caused the alienation, the Lord Jesus restored those who believe on Him to a state of harmony with God. We should note, in passing, that *God* did not need to be reconciled. It was *man* who needed it, because he was at enmity with God.

G. The Triumph of Christ's Work over Adam's Sin (5:12–21)

5:12 The rest of chapter 5 serves as a bridge between the first part of the letter and the next three chapters. It is linked with the first part by picking up the subjects of condemnation through Adam and justification through Christ, and by showing that the work of Christ far outweighs in blessing what the work of Adam did in misery and loss. It is linked with chapters 6–8 by moving from justification to sanctification, and from acts of sin to the sin in human nature.

Adam is portrayed in these verses as the federal head or representative of all those who are in the old creation. Christ is presented as the Federal Head of all those who are in the new creation. A federal head acts for all those who are under him. For example, when the President of a country signs a bill into law, he is acting for all the citizens of that country.

That is what happened in Adam's case. As a result of his **sin**, human **death** entered **the world**. Death became the common lot of all Adam's descendants because they had **all sinned** in him. It is true that they all committed individual acts of sin as well, but that is not the thought here. Paul's point is that Adam's sin was a *representative act*, and all his posterity are reckoned as having **sinned** in him.

Someone might object that it was Eve and not Adam who committed the first sin on earth. That is true, but since Adam was the first to be created, *headship* was given to him. So he is seen as acting for all his descendants.

When the Apostle Paul says here that **death spread to all men**, he is referring to *physical* **death**, even though Adam's sin brought spiritual death as well. (Vv. 13 and 14 show that physical death is in view.)

When we come to this passage of Scripture, certain questions inevitably arise. Is it fair that Adam's posterity should be constituted sinners just because he sinned? Does God condemn men for being born sinners, or only for those sins which they have actually committed? If men are born with a sinful nature, and if they therefore sin because they are born sinners, how can God hold them responsible for what they do?

Bible scholars have wrestled with these and a host of similar problems and have come up with a surprising variety of conclusions. However, there are certain *facts* that we can be *sure* of.

First, the Bible does teach that all men are sinners, both by nature and by practice. Everyone born of human parents inherits Adam's sin, and also sins by his own deliberate choice.

Second, we know that the wages of sin is death — both physical death and eternal separation from God.

But no one has to pay the penalty of sin unless he wants to. This is the important point. At enormous cost, God sent His Son to die as a Substitute for sinners.

Salvation from sin and its wages is offered as a free gift through faith in the Lord Jesus Christ.

Man is condemned on three grounds: He has a *sinful nature*, Adam's *sin is imputed* to him, and he is a *sinner by practice*. But his crowning guilt is his rejection of the provision which God has made for his salvation (John 3:18, 19, 36).

But someone will ask, "What about those who have never heard the gospel?" This question is answered in part, at least, in chapter 1. Beyond that we can rest in the assurance that the Judge of all the earth will do right (Gen. 18:25). He will never act unjustly or unfairly. All His decisions are based on equity and righteousness. Although certain situations pose problems to our dim sight, they are not problems to Him. When the last case has been heard and the doors of the courtroom swing shut, no one will have a legitimate basis for appealing the verdict.

5:13 Paul will now demonstrate that Adam's sin affected the whole race. He first points out that **sin was in the world** during the period from Adam to the giving of the **law** at Mount Sinai. But during that time there was no clearly revealed law of God. Adam had received a clear oral commandment from the Lord, and many centuries later the Ten Commandments were a distinct written revelation of divine law. But in the intervening period men did not have a legal code from God. Therefore, although there was **sin** during that time, there was *no transgression*, because transgression is the violation of a known law. **But sin is not imputed** *as transgression* **when there is no law** forbidding it.

5:14 Yet **death** did not take a holiday during the age when there was no law. With the single exception of Enoch, **death** held sway over all mankind. You could not say that these people died because they had transgressed a clear command of God, as Adam did. Why then did they die? The answer is implied: they died because they had sinned in Adam. If this seems unfair, remember that this has nothing to do with salvation. All those who put their faith in the Lord were saved eternally. But they died *physically* just the same, and the reason they died was because of the sin of their federal head, Adam. In his role as federal head, Adam was **a type** (symbol) **of Him who was to come** — that is, the Lord Jesus Christ. In the succeeding verses Paul will develop the subject of these two federal heads, but more by contrast than by similarities. He will show that:

> In Christ the sons of Adam boast
> More blessings than their father lost.

5:15 The first contrast is between **the offense** of Adam and **the free gift** of Christ. By the trespass of the first man, the **many died**. The **many** here refers, of course, to Adam's descendants. Death here may include spiritual as well as physical death.

The free gift abounds much more **to the many**. The free gift is the marvelous manifestation of **the grace of God** abounding to a race of sinners. It is made possible **by the grace of the one Man, Jesus Christ**. It was amazing grace on His part to die for His rebellious creatures. Through His sacrificial death, the gift of eternal life is offered **to the many**.

The two *manys* in this verse do not refer to the same people. The first **many** includes all who became subject to death as a result of Adam's trespass. The second **many** means all who become members of the new creation, of which Christ is the Federal Head. It includes only those to whom God's grace has **abounded** — that is, true believers. While God's mercy is showered on all, His grace is appropriated only by those who trust the Savior.

5:16 There is another important contrast between Adam's sin and Christ's **gift**. The **one offense** of Adam brought inevitable **judgment**, and the verdict was "Condemned." The **free gift** of Christ, on the other hand, dealt effectively with **many offenses**, not just one, and resulted in the verdict "Acquitted." Paul highlights the differences between Adam's sin and Christ's gift, between the terrible havoc wrought by one sin and the tremendous deliverance wrought from many sins, and finally between the verdict of **condemnation** and the verdict of **justification**.

5:17 By the one man's offense, death reigned as a cruel tyrant. But by the gracious **gift of righteousness**, a gift of overflowing grace, all believers **reign in life through the One, Jesus Christ**.

What grace this is! We are not only delivered from death's reign as a tyrant over us, but we reign as kings, enjoying life now and eternally. Do we really understand and appreciate this? Do we live as the royalty of heaven, or do we grovel among the muckheaps of this world?

5:18 The **offense** of Adam brought **condemnation** to all men, but the **righteous act** of Christ brought **justification of life** to all. **The righteous act** was not the Savior's life or His keeping of the law, but rather His substitutionary death on Calvary. This is what brought **justification of life** — that is, the **justification** that results in **life** — and brought it **to all men**.

The two *alls* in this verse do not refer to the same people. The first **all** means **all** who are in Adam. The second **all** means **all** who are in Christ. This is clear from the words in the preceding verse "those who *receive* abundance of grace and of the gift of righteousness. . . ." *The gift must be received by faith.* Only those who trust the Lord receive **justification of life**.

5:19 Just **as by** Adam's **disobedience** to God's command **many were made sinners, so also by** Christ's **obedience** to the Father many who trust Him are declared **righteous**. Christ's obedience led Him to the cross as our Sin-bearer.

It is futile for universalists to use these verses to try to prove that all men will eventually be saved. The passage deals with two federal headships, and it is clear that just as Adam's sin affects those who are "in him," so Christ's righteous act benefits only those who are "in Him."

5:20 What Paul has been saying would come as a jolt to the Jewish objector who felt that everything revolved around the law. Now this objector learns that sin and salvation center not in the law but in two federal heads. That being the case, he might be tempted to ask, "Why then was the law given?" The apostle answers, **The law entered that**

the offense might abound. It did not originate sin, but it revealed sin as an **offense** against God. It did not save from sin but revealed sin in all its awful character.

But God's grace proves to be greater than all man's sin. **Where sin abounded**, God's **grace** at Calvary **abounded much more!**

5:21 Now that the reign of sin, inflicting death on all men, has been ended, **grace** reigns **through righteousness**, giving **eternal life through Jesus Christ our Lord**. Notice that grace reigns **through righteousness**. All the demands of God's holiness have been met, and the penalty of the law has been paid, so God can now grant eternal life to all who come pleading the merits **of Christ**, their Substitute.

Perhaps we have in these verses a partial answer to the familiar question, "Why did God allow sin to enter the world?" The answer is that God has received more glory and man has received more blessings through Christ's sacrifice than if sin had never entered. We are better off in Christ than we ever could have been in an unfallen Adam. If Adam had never sinned, he would have enjoyed continued life on earth in the Garden of Eden. But he had no prospect of becoming a redeemed child of God, an heir of God, or a joint-heir with Jesus Christ. He had no promise of a home in heaven or of being with Christ and like Him forever. These blessings come only **through** the redemptive work of **Jesus Christ our Lord.**

H. The Gospel's Way to Holy Living (Chap. 6)

What Paul had said at the close of chapter 5 — that grace superabounded over all man's sin — raises another question, and a very important one. *Does the teaching of the gospel (salvation by grace through faith) permit or even encourage sinful living?*

The answer, an emphatic denial, extends over chapters 6–8. Here in chapter 6 the answer centers around three key words: *know* (vv. 3, 6), *reckon* or *consider* (v. 11), and *present* (v. 13).

It will help us to follow Paul's argument in this chapter if we understand the difference between the believer's position and his practice. His position is his standing in Christ. His practice is what he is or should be in everyday life.

Grace puts us into the position, then teaches us to walk worthy of it. Our position is absolutely perfect because we are *in Christ*. Our practice should increasingly correspond to our position. It never will correspond perfectly until we see the Savior in heaven, but we should be becoming more and more conformed to His image in the meantime.

The apostle first sets forth the truth of our identification with Christ in death and resurrection, and then exhorts us to live in the light of this great truth.

6:1 The Jewish objector comes forward with what he thinks is a clinching argument. If the gospel of grace teaches that man's sin provides for an even greater display of God's grace, then doesn't it suggest that **we** should **continue in sin that grace may** be all the more abundant?

A modern version of this argument is as follows: "You say that men are saved by grace through faith, apart from the law. But if all you have to do to be saved is believe, then you could go out and live in sin." According to this argument, grace is not a sufficient motivation for holy living. You must put people under the restraints of the law.

It has been helpfully suggested that there are four answers in the chapter to the initial question, **Shall we continue in sin?**

1. You *cannot*, because you are united to Christ. Reasoning (vv. 1–11).
2. You *need not*, because sin's dominion has been broken by grace. Appealing (vv. 12–14).
3. You *must not*, because it would bring sin in again as your master. Commanding (vv. 15–19).
4. You *had better not*, for it would end in disaster. Warning (vv. 20–23).[17]

6:2 Paul's first answer, then, is that we cannot continue in sin because we have **died to sin**. This is a positional truth. When Jesus died to sin, He died as our Representative. He died not only as our *Substitute* — that is, *for us* or *in our place* — but He also died as our *Representative* — that is, *as us*. Therefore, when He died, we died. He died to the whole question of sin, settling it once and for all. All those who are in Christ are seen by God as having died to sin.

This does not mean that the believer is sinless. It means that he is identified with Christ in His death, and in all that His death means.

6:3 The first key word in Paul's presentation is **KNOW**. Here he introduces the subject of baptism to show that it is morally incongruous for believers to go on in sin. But the question immediately arises, "To which baptism is he referring?" So an introductory word of explanation is necessary.

When a person is saved, he is **baptized into Christ Jesus** in the sense that he is identified with Christ in **His death** and resurrection. This is not the same as the baptism in (or of) the Spirit, though both occur simultaneously. The latter baptism places the believer in the body of Christ (1 Cor. 12:13); it is not a baptism **into** death. The baptism **into Christ** means that in the reckoning of God, the believer has died with Christ and has risen with Him.

When Paul speaks of baptism here, he is thinking both of our spiritual identification with Christ and of its portrayal in water baptism. But as the argument advances, he seems to shift his emphasis in a special way to water baptism as he reminds his readers how they were "buried" and "planted together" in the "likeness" of Christ's death.

The NT never contemplates the abnormal situation of an unbaptized believer. It assumes that those who are converted submit to baptism right away. Thus our Lord could speak of faith and baptism in the same breath: "he who believes and is baptized will be saved" (Mark 16:16). Though baptism is not a requirement for salvation, it should be the invariable public sign of it.

6:4 Water **baptism** gives a visual demonstration of **baptism** into Christ. It pictures the believer being immersed in death's dark waters (in the person of the Lord Jesus), and it pictures the new man in Christ rising to walk in newness of life. There is a sense in which a believer attends the funeral of his old self when he is baptized. As he goes under the water he is saying, "All that I was as a sinful son of Adam was put to death at the cross." As he comes up out of the water he is saying, "It is no longer I who live, but Christ lives in me" (see Gal. 2:20).

Conybeare and Howson state that "this passage cannot be understood unless it be borne in mind that the primitive baptism was by immersion."

The apostle moves on to state that the resurrection of Christ makes it possible for us to **walk in newness of life**. He states that **Christ was raised from the dead by the glory of the Father**. This simply means that all the divine perfections of God — His righteousness, love, justice, etc. — demanded that He raise the Lord. In view of the excellence of the Person of the Savior, it would not have been consistent with God's character to leave the Savior in the tomb. God *did* raise Him, and because we are identified with Christ in His resurrection, **we** can and **should walk in newness of life.**

6:5 Just as **we have been united together** with Christ **in the likeness of His death, certainly we also shall be** united with Him **in the likeness of His resurrection**. The words **the likeness of His death** refer to the believer's being put under the water in baptism. The actual union with Christ in His death took place nearly 2000 years ago, but baptism is a "likeness" of what happened then.

We not only go under the water; we come up out of the water, a **likeness of His resurrection**. While it is true that the phrase **in the likeness** is not part of the original text in the second part of this verse, it must be supplied to complete the meaning.

Just as we **have been united** with Christ **in the likeness of His death** (immersion in water), so **we** are united with Him **in the likeness of His resurrection** (being raised out of the water). The clause **we shall be** does not necessarily indicate futurity. Hodge says:

> The reference is not to what is to happen hereafter, but to the certainty of sequence, or causal connection. If the one thing happens, the other shall surely follow.[18]

6:6 We confess in baptism **that our old man was crucified with** Christ. **Our old man** refers to all that we were as children of Adam — our old, evil, unregenerate selves, with all our old habits and appetites. At conversion we put off the **old man** and put on the new man, as if exchanging filthy rags for spotless clothing (Col. 3:9, 10).

The crucifixion of **the old man** at Calvary means **that the body of sin** has been put out of commission. **The body of sin** does not refer to the physical body. Rather, it means indwelling sin which is personified as a tyrant, ruling the person. This body of sin **is done away with**, that is, *annulled* or *rendered inoperative as a controlling power*. The last clause shows that this is the meaning: **that we should no longer be slaves of sin**. The tyranny of sin over us has been broken.

6:7 For he who has died has been freed from sin. Here is a man, for example, who is sentenced to die in the electric chair for murdering a police officer. As soon as he dies, **he** is **freed** (literally "justified") **from** that sin. The penalty has been paid and the case is closed.

Now we have died with Christ on the cross of Calvary. Not only has our penalty been paid, but sin's stranglehold on our lives has been broken. We are no longer the helpless captives of sin.

6:8 Our death **with Christ** is one side of the truth. The other side is **that we shall also live with Him**. We **died** to sin; we live to righteousness. Sin's dominion over us has been shattered; we share Christ's resurrection life here and now. And we shall share it for all eternity, praise His name!

6:9 Our confidence is based on the fact that the risen Christ will never die again. **Death no longer has dominion over Him**. Death did have dominion over Him for three days and nights, but that dominion is forever passed. Christ can never die again!

6:10 When the Lord Jesus **died, He died to** the whole subject of **sin once for all. He died** to sin's claims, its wages, its demands, its penalty. He finished the work and settled the account so perfectly that it never needs to be repeated. Now that **He lives, He lives to God**. In one sense, of course, He always lived to God. But now **He lives to God** in a new relationship, as the Risen One, and in a new sphere, where sin can never enter.

Before going on, let us review the first ten verses. The general subject is *sanctification* — God's method for holy living. As to our standing before God, we are seen as having died with Christ and having risen with Him. This is pictured in baptism. Our death with Christ ends our history as men and women in Adam. God's sentence on our old man was not reformation but death. And that sentence was carried out when we died with Christ. Now we are risen with Christ to walk in newness of life. Sin's tyranny over us has been broken, because sin has nothing to say to a dead person. Now we are free to live for God.

6:11 Paul has described what is true of us *positionally*. Now he turns to the *practical outworking* of this truth in our lives. We are to **RECKON** ourselves **to be dead to sin, but alive to God in Christ Jesus our Lord**.

To **reckon** here means to accept what God says about us as true and to live in the light of it. Ruth Paxson writes:

> [It means] believing what God says in Romans 6:6 and knowing it as a fact in one's own personal salvation. This demands a definite act of faith, which results in a fixed attitude toward "the old man." We will see him where God sees him — on the Cross, put to death with Christ. Faith will operate continuously to keep him where grace placed him. This involves us very deeply, for it means that our hearty consent has been given to God's condemnation of and judgment upon that old "I" as altogether unworthy to live and as wholly stripped of any further claims upon us. The first step in a walk of practical holiness is this reckoning upon the crucifixion of "the old man."[19]

We **reckon** ourselves **dead to sin** when we respond to temptation as a dead man would. One day Augustine was accosted by a woman who had been his mistress before his conversion. When he turned and walked away quickly, she called after him, "Augustine, it's me! it's me!" Quickening his pace, he called back over his shoulder, "Yes, I know, but it's no longer me!"[20] What he meant was that he was **dead to sin** and **alive to God**. A dead man has nothing to do with immorality, lying, cheating, gossiping, or any other sin.

Now we are **alive to God in Christ Jesus**. This means that we are called to holiness, worship, prayer, service, and fruitbearing.

6:12 We saw in 6:6 that our old man

was crucified so that sin as a reigning tyrant might be knocked out, so that we would no longer be the helpless captives of sin. Now the practical exhortation is based on what is true positionally. We should **not let sin reign in** our **mortal** bodies by obeying its evil desires. At Calvary the reign of sin was ended by death. Now we must make it so practically. Our cooperation is needed. Only God can make us holy, but He will not do it without our willing involvement.

6:13 That brings us to the third key word in this chapter — **PRESENT**. We must **not present** the **members** of our body **to sin**, to be used as weapons or tools of wickedness. Our obligation is to turn control of our members **to God**, to be used in the cause of **righteousness**. After all, we have been raised to life from death; and, as we are reminded in 6:4, we should walk in newness of life.

6:14 Now another reason is given why **sin shall not have dominion over** us as believers. The first reason was that our old man was crucified with Christ (6:6). The second reason is that we **are not under law but under grace**.

Sin does have the upper hand over a person who is under law. Why? Because the law tells him what to do but doesn't give him the power to do it. And the law stirs up dormant desires in fallen human nature to do what is forbidden. It's the old story that "forbidden fruit is sweet."

Sin does **not have dominion over** the person who is under grace. The believer has died to sin. He has received the indwelling Holy Spirit as the power for holy living. And he is motivated by love for the Savior, not by fear of punishment. **Grace** is the only thing that really produces holiness. As Denney says, "It is not restraint but inspiration that liberates from sin; not Mount Sinai but Mount Calvary which makes saints."[21]

6:15 Those who are afraid of **grace** insist that it gives license for sinning. Paul meets this error head-on by asking the question, then flatly denying it. We are free from the law but not lawless. **Grace** means freedom to serve the Lord, not to sin against Him.

In 6:1 the question was, "Shall we continue in sin?" Here the question is, **"Shall we sin** just a little?" The answer in both cases is a horrified **"Certainly**

not!"** God cannot condone any sin at all.

6:16 It is a simple fact of life that when we submit ourselves to someone as our master we become that person's slave. Likewise, if we sell out to sin, we become **slaves** of sin, and eternal **death** lies waiting at the end of that road. If, on the other hand, we choose to obey God, the result is a holy life. Sin's slaves are bound by guilt, fear, and misery, but God's servants are free to do what the new nature loves. So why be a slave when you can be free?

6:17 "Thank God that you, who were at one time the servants of sin, honestly responded to the impact of Christ's teaching when you came under its influence" (JBP). The Roman Christians had given wholehearted obedience to the gospel of grace to which they had been committed, including all the **doctrine** Paul teaches in this Letter.

6:18 Correct doctrine should lead to correct duty. Responding to the truth that they had **been set free from sin** as master, they **became slaves of righteousness**. The phrase **free from sin** does not mean that they no longer had a sinful nature. Neither does it mean that they no longer committed acts of sin. The context shows that it is referring to freedom from sin as the dominating power in life.

6:19 In verse 18 the apostle spoke of slaves of righteousness, but he realizes that those who live righteously are not actually in bondage. "Practical righteousness is not slavery, except when we speak after the manner of men."[22] Those who practice sin are slaves of sin, but those whom the Son sets free are free indeed (John 8:34, 36).

Paul explains that, in using the simile of **slaves** and master, he is speaking **in human terms**; that is, he is using a familiar illustration from everyday life. He does this **because of the weakness of** their **flesh** — in other words, because of their intellectual and spiritual difficulty in understanding truth when it is stated in general terms. Truth often needs to be illustrated in order to become intelligible.

Before their conversion the believers had surrendered their bodies **as slaves of** all kinds of **uncleanness** and to one kind of wickedness after another. Now they should dedicate those same bodies **as**

slaves of righteousness, so that their lives would be truly holy.

6:20 **When** they **were slaves of sin**, the only freedom they knew was freedom from **righteousness**. It was a desperate condition to be in — bound by every evil and **free** from every good!

6:21 Paul challenges them (and us) to inventory the fruits of an unsaved life, fruits in those activities **of which** believers **are now ashamed**. Marcus Rainsford has drawn up such an inventory, as follows:

1. Faculties abused. 2. Affections prostrated. 3. Time squandered. 4. Influence misused. 5. Best friends wronged. 6. Our best interests violated. 7. Love outraged — especially the love of God. Or to sum it up in one word — SHAME.[23]

The end of those things is death. "Every sin," writes A. T. Pierson, "tends to death, and, if persisted in, ends in death as its goal and fruit."[24]

6:22 Conversion changes a man's position completely. Now he is **free from sin** as his master, and he becomes a willing slave to **God**. The result is a holy life now and **everlasting life** at the **end** of the journey. Of course the believer has eternal **life** now too, but this verse refers to that **life** in its fullness, including the glorified resurrection body.

6:23 The apostle summarizes the subject by presenting these vivid contrasts:

Two masters — **sin** and **God**.
Two methods — **wages** and free **gift**.
Two aftermaths — **death** and **eternal life**.

Notice that eternal life is in a Person, and that Person is **Christ Jesus our Lord**. All who are **in Christ** have **eternal life**. It's as simple as that!

I. The Place of the Law in the Believer's Life (Chap. 7)

The apostle now anticipates a question that will inevitably arise: *What is the relationship of the Christian to the law?* Perhaps Paul had Jewish believers especially in mind in answering this question, since the law was given to Israel, but the principles apply just as much to Gentile believers who foolishly want to put themselves under the law as a rule of life after they have been justified.

In chapter 6 we saw that death ended the tyranny of the sin nature in the life of the child of God. Now we will see that death likewise ends the dominion of the law over those who were under it.

7:1 This verse is connected with 6:14: "You are not under law but under grace." The connection is, "You should know that you are not under law — or are you ignorant of the fact **that the law has dominion over a man** only when **he** is alive?" Paul is speaking to those who are familiar with fundamental principles of law, and who therefore should know that the **law** has nothing to say to a dead man.

7:2 To illustrate this, Paul shows how death breaks the marriage contract. A **woman** is bound **by the** marriage **law to her husband as long as he lives. But if** he **dies, she is released** from that **law**.

7:3 If a woman **marries another man while her husband** is living, she is guilty of adultery. **If**, however, **her husband dies, she is free** to marry again without any cloud or guilt of wrongdoing.

7:4 In applying the illustration, we must not press each detail with exact literalness. For example, *neither* the husband *nor* the wife represents the law. The point of the illustration is that just as death breaks the marriage relationship, so the death of the believer with Christ breaks the jurisdiction of the law over him.

Notice that Paul does *not* say that the law is dead. The law still has a valid ministry in producing conviction of sin. And remember that when he says "we" in this passage, he is thinking of those who were Jews before they came to Christ.

We have been made **dead to the law through the body of Christ, the body** here referring to the giving up of His **body** in death. We are no longer joined **to the law**; we are now joined to the risen Christ. One marriage has been broken by death, and a new one has been formed. And now that we are free from **the law, we** can **bear fruit to God**.

7:5 This mention of fruit brings to mind the kind of **fruit** we bore **when we were in the flesh**. The expression **in the flesh** obviously doesn't mean "in the body." **In the flesh** here is descriptive of our standing before we were saved. Then the flesh was the basis of our standing before God. We depended on what we were or what we could do to win acceptance with God. **In the flesh** is the opposite of "in Christ."

Prior to our conversion we were ruled by **sinful passions which were aroused by the law**. It is not that the law *originated* them, but only that by naming and then forbidding them it stirred up the strong desire to *do* them!

These **sinful passions** found expression in our physical members, and when we yielded to temptation we produced poison fruit that results in **death**. Elsewhere the apostle speaks of this fruit as the works of the flesh: "adultery, fornication, uncleanness, lewdness, idolatry, sorcery, hatred, contentions, jealousies, outbursts of wrath, selfish ambitions, dissensions, heresies, envy, murders, drunkenness, revelries" (Gal. 5:19–21).

7:6 Among the many wonderful things that happen when we are converted is that we are **delivered from the law**. This is a result of our having died with Christ. Since He died as our Representative, we **died** with Him. In His death He fulfilled all the claims of the law by paying its awful penalty. Therefore we are free from the law and from its inevitable curse. There can be no double jeopardy.

> Payment God will not twice demand —
> First at my bleeding Surety's hand
> And then again at mine.
> – *Augustus M. Toplady*

We are now set free to **serve in the newness of the Spirit and not in the oldness of the letter**. Our service is motivated by love, not fear; it is a service of freedom, not bondage. It is no longer a question of slavishly adhering to minute details of forms and ceremonies but of the joyful outpouring of ourselves for the glory of God and the blessing of others.

7:7 It might seem from all this that Paul is *critical* of the law. He had said that believers are dead to sin and dead to the law, and this might have created the impression that the law is evil. But this is far from the case.

In 7:7–13 he goes on to describe the important role which the law played in his own life before he was saved. He emphasizes that the law itself is not sinful, but that it *reveals sin in man*. It was the law that convicted him of the terrible depravity of his heart. As long as he compared himself with other people, he felt fairly respectable. But as soon as the demands of God's law came home to him in convicting power, he stood speechless and condemned.

The one particular commandment that revealed sin to him was the tenth: **You shall not covet**. Coveting takes place in the mind. Although Paul may not have committed any of the grosser, more revolting sins, he now realized that his thought life was corrupt. He understood that evil thoughts are sinful as well as evil deeds. He had a polluted thought life. His outward life may have been relatively blameless, but his inward life was a chamber of horrors.

7:8 **Sin, taking opportunity by the commandment, produced in me all manner of evil desire**. **Evil desire** here means coveting. When the law forbids all kinds of evil coveting, man's corrupt nature is inflamed all the more to do it. For example, the law says, in effect, "You must not conjure up all sorts of pleasurable sexual encounters in your mind. You must not live in a world of lustful fantasies." The law forbids a dirty, vile, suggestive thought-life. But unfortunately it doesn't give the power to overcome. So the result is that people under law become more involved in a dream-world of sexual uncleanness than ever before. They come to realize that whenever an act is forbidden, the fallen nature wants to do it all the more. "Stolen water is sweet, and bread eaten in secret is pleasant" (Prov. 9:17).

Apart from the law sin is **dead**, relatively speaking. The sinful nature is like a sleeping dog. When the law comes and says "Don't," the dog wakes up and goes on a rampage, doing excessively whatever is forbidden.

7:9 Before being convicted by the law Paul was **alive**; that is, his sinful nature was *comparatively* dormant and he was blissfully ignorant of the pit of iniquity in his heart.

But when the commandment came — that is, when it came with crushing conviction — his sinful nature became thoroughly inflamed. The more he tried to obey, the worse he failed. He **died** as far as any hope of achieving salvation by his own character or efforts was concerned. He **died** to any thought of his own inherent goodness. He **died** to any dream of being justified by law-keeping.

7:10 He found that **the commandment, which was to bring life** actually turned out to **bring death** for him. But what does he mean that the commandment **was to bring life**? This probably looks back to Leviticus 18:5, where God said, "You shall therefore keep My statutes and My judgments, which if a man does, he shall live by them: I *am* the Lord." *Ideally* the law promised life to those who kept it. The sign outside a lion's cage says, "Stay back of the railing." If obeyed, the commandment brings life. But for the child who disobeys and reaches in to pet the lion, it brings death.

7:11 Again Paul emphasizes that the law was not to blame. It was indwelling **sin** that incited him to do what the law prohibited. Sin tricked him into thinking that the forbidden fruit wasn't so bad after all, that it would bring happiness, and that he could get away with it. It suggested that God was withholding pleasures from him that were for his good. Thus sin **killed** him in the sense that it spelled death to his best hopes of deserving or earning salvation.

7:12 **The law** itself **is holy, and** each **commandment is holy and just and good**. In our thinking we must constantly remember that there is nothing wrong with the law. It was given by God and therefore is perfect as an expression of His will for His people. The weakness of the law lay in the "raw materials" it had to work with: it was given to people who were already sinners. They needed the law to give them the knowledge of sin, but beyond that they needed a Savior to deliver them from the penalty and power of sin.

7:13 **What is good** refers to the law, as is specifically stated in the preceding verse. Paul raises the question "Did the law **become death to me?**" which means "Is the law the culprit, dooming Paul (and all the rest of us) to death?" The answer, of course, is **"Certainly not!"**

Sin is the culprit. The law didn't originate sin, but it showed sin in all its exceeding sinfulness. "By the law *is* the knowledge of sin" (3:20b). But that is not all! How does man's sinful nature respond when God's holy law forbids it to do something? The answer is well-known. What may have been dormant desire now becomes a burning passion! Thus **sin through the commandment** becomes **exceedingly sinful**.

There might seem to be a contradiction between what Paul says here and in 7:10. There he said he found the law to bring death. Here he denies that the law became death to him. The solution is this: The law by itself can neither improve the old nature on the one hand nor cause it to sin on the other. It can reveal sin, just as a thermometer reveals the temperature. But it cannot *control* sin like a thermostat controls the temperature.

But what happens is this. Man's fallen human nature instinctively wants to do whatever is forbidden. So it uses the law to awaken otherwise-dormant lusts in the sinner's life. The more man tries, the worse it gets, till at last he is brought to despair of all hope. Thus sin uses the law to cause any hope of improvement to die in him. And he sees the exceeding sinfulness of his old nature as he never saw it before.

7:14 Up to this point the apostle has been describing a past experience in his life — namely, the traumatic crisis when he underwent deep conviction of sin through the law's ministry.

Now he changes to the present tense to describe an experience he had since he was born again — namely, the conflict between the two natures and the impossibility of finding deliverance from the power of indwelling sin through his own strength. Paul acknowledges **that the law is spiritual** — that is, holy in itself and adapted to man's spiritual benefit. But he realizes that he is **carnal** because he is not experiencing victory over the power of indwelling sin in his life. He is **sold under sin**. He feels as if he is sold as a slave with sin as his master.

7:15 Now the apostle describes the struggle that goes on in a believer who does not know the truth of his identification with Christ in death and resurrection. It is the conflict between the two natures in the person who climbs Mount Sinai in search of holiness. Harry Foster explains:

> Here was a man trying to achieve holiness by personal effort, struggling with all his might to fulfill God's "holy and righteous and good" commandments (v.12), only to discover that the more he struggled, the worse his condition became. It was a losing battle, and no wonder, for it is not in the power of fallen human nature to conquer sin and live in holiness.[25]

Notice the prominence of the first-person pronouns — I, me, my, myself; they occur over forty times in verses 9–25! People who go through this Romans 7 experience have taken an overdose of "Vitamin I." They are introspective to the core, searching for victory in self, where it cannot be found.

Sadly, most modern Christian psychological counseling focuses the counselee's attention on himself and thus adds to the problem instead of relieving it. People need to know that they have died with Christ and have risen with Him to walk in newness of life. Then, instead of trying to improve the flesh, they will relegate it to the grave of Jesus.

In describing the struggle between the two natures, Paul says, **what I am doing, I do not understand**. He is a split personality, a Dr. Jekyll and Mr. Hyde. He finds himself indulging in things that he doesn't want to do, and practicing things that he hates.

7:16 In thus committing acts which his better judgment condemns, he is taking sides **with the law** against himself, because the law condemns them too. So he gives inward assent that the law is **good**.

7:17 This leads to the conclusion that the culprit is not the new man in Christ, but the sinful, corrupt nature that dwells in him. But we must be careful here. We must not excuse our sinning by passing it off to indwelling **sin**. *We* are responsible for what we do, and we must not use this verse to "pass the buck." All Paul is doing here is tracking down the source of his sinful behavior, not excusing it.

7:18 There can be no progress in holiness until we learn what Paul learned here — **that in me (that is, in my flesh) nothing good dwells**. The **flesh** here means the evil, corrupt nature which is inherited from Adam and which is still in every believer. It is the source of every evil action which a person performs. There is nothing good in it.

When we learn this, it delivers us from ever looking for any good in the old nature. It delivers us from being disappointed when we don't find any good there. And it delivers us from occupation with ourselves. There is no victory in introspection. As the saintly Scot, Robert Murray McCheyne said, for every look we take at ourselves, we should take ten looks at Christ.

To confirm the hopelessness of the flesh, the apostle mourns that although he has the desire to do what is right, he doesn't have the resources in himself to translate his desire into action. The trouble, of course, is that he is casting his anchor inside the boat.

7:19 Thus the conflict between the two natures rages on. He finds himself failing to do **the good** he wants to do, and instead doing **the evil** that he despises. He is just one great mass of contradictions and paradoxes.

7:20 We might paraphrase this verse as follows: **"Now if I** (the old nature) **do what I** (the new nature) **don't want to do, it is no longer I** (the person) **who do it, but sin that dwells** within **me."** Again let it be clear that Paul is not excusing himself or disclaiming responsibility. He is simply stating that he has not found deliverance from the power of indwelling sin, and that when he sins, it is not with the desire of the new man.

7:21 He finds a principle or **law** at work in his life causing all his good intentions to end in failure. When he wants to do what is right, he ends up by sinning.

7:22 As far as his new nature is concerned, he delights **in the law of God**. He knows that the law is holy, and that it is an expression of the will of God. He wants to do God's will.

7:23 But he sees a contrary principle at work in his life, striving against the new nature, and making him a captive **of** indwelling **sin**. George Cutting writes:

> The law, though he delights in it after the inward man, gives him no power. In other words, he is trying to accomplish what God has declared to be an utter impossibility — namely, making the flesh subject to God's holy law. He finds that the flesh minds the things of the flesh, and is very enmity itself to the law of God, and even to God Himself.[26]

7:24 Now Paul lets out his famous, eloquent groan. He feels as if he has a decomposing body strapped to his back. That **body**, of course, is the old nature in all its corruption. In his wretchedness he acknowledges that he is unable to deliver himself from this offensive, repulsive bondage. He must have help from some outside source.

7:25 The burst of thanksgiving which opens this verse may be understood in at least two ways. It may mean **"I thank God** that deliverance comes **through Jesus Christ our Lord"** or it may be an aside in which Paul thanks God **through** the Lord **Jesus** that he is no longer the wretched man of the preceding verse.

The rest of the verse summarizes the conflict between the two natures before deliverance is realized. **With the** renewed **mind**, or the new nature, the believer serves **the law of God, but with the flesh** (or old nature) **the law of sin.** Not till we reach the next chapter do we find the way of deliverance explained.

J. The Holy Spirit as the Power for Holy Living (Chap. 8)

The subject of holy living continues. In chapter 6 Paul had answered the question, "Does the teaching of the gospel (salvation by faith alone) permit or even encourage sinful living?" In chapter 7 he faced up to the question, "Does the gospel tell Christians to keep the law in order to lead a holy life?" Now the question is: *How is the Christian enabled to live a holy life?*

We notice right away that the personal pronouns that were so prominent in chapter 7 largely disappear, and that the Holy Spirit becomes the dominant Person. This is an important key to understanding the passage. Victory is not in ourselves but in the Holy Spirit, who indwells us. A. J. Gordon lists seven helps of the Spirit: freedom in service (v. 2); strength for service (v. 11); victory over sin (v. 13); guidance in service (v. 14); the witness of sonship (v. 16); assistance in service (v. 26); assistance in prayer (v. 26).

8:1 From the valley of despair and defeat, the apostle now climbs the heights with the triumphant shout, **There is therefore now no condemnation to those who are in Christ Jesus**! This may be understood in two ways.

First, there is **no** divine **condemnation** as far as our sin is concerned, because we are in Christ. There was condemnation as long as we were in our first federal head, Adam. But now we are in Christ and therefore are as free from condemnation as He is. So we can hurl out the challenge:

> Reach my blest Savior first,
>   Take Him from God's esteem;
> Prove Jesus bears one spot of sin,
>   Then tell me I'm unclean.
>   – *W. N. Tomkins*

But it may also mean that there is no need for the kind of self-condemnation which Paul described in chapter 7. We may pass through a Romans 7 experience, unable to fulfill the law's requirements by our own effort, but we don't have to stay there. Verse 2 explains why there is **no condemnation**.[27]

8:2 The Spirit's law of **life in Christ Jesus has made us free from the law of sin and death**. These are two opposite laws or principles. The characteristic principle of the Holy Spirit is to empower believers for holy living. The characteristic principle of indwelling sin is to drag a person down to death. It is like the law of gravity. When you throw a ball into the air, it comes back down because it is heavier than the air it displaces. A living bird is also heavier than the air it displaces, but when you toss it up in the air, it flies away. The law of *life* in the bird overcomes the law of gravity. So the Holy Spirit supplies the risen life of the Lord Jesus, making the believer **free from the law of sin and death.**

8:3 The law could never get people

to fulfill its sacred requirements, but grace has succeeded where law failed. Let us see how!

The law could not produce holy living because **it was weak through the flesh**. The trouble was not with the law but with fallen human nature. The law spoke to men who were already sinners and who were without strength to obey. But God intervened **by sending His own Son in the likeness of sinful flesh**. Take careful notice that the Lord Jesus did not come in sinful flesh itself but **in "the likeness of" sinful flesh**. He did no sin (1 Pet. 2:22), He knew no sin (2 Cor. 5:21), and there was no sin in Him (1 Jn. 3:5). But by coming into the world in human form, He resembled sinful humanity. As a sacrifice for sin, Christ **condemned sin in the flesh**. He died not only for the sins which we commit (1 Pet. 3:18) but also for our sin nature. In other words, He died for what we *are* just as much as for what we have *done*. In so doing, **He condemned sin in the flesh**. Our sin nature is never said to be forgiven; it is **condemned**. It is the sins that we have *committed* that are forgiven.

8:4 Now **the righteous requirement of the law** is **fulfilled in us who do not walk according to the flesh but according to the Spirit**. As we turn over the control of our lives to the Holy Spirit, He empowers us to love God and to love our neighbor, and that, after all, is what the law requires.

In these first four verses the apostle has gathered together the threads of his argument from 5:12 to 7:25. In 5:12–21 he had discussed the federal headships of Adam and of Christ. Now in 8:1 he shows that the condemnation which we inherited from our identification with Adam is removed by our identification with Christ. In chapters 6 and 7 he discussed the horrendous problem of sin in the nature. Now he announces triumphantly that the Spirit's law of life in Christ Jesus has made us free from the law of sin and death. In chapter 7 the whole subject of the law was brought up. Now we learn that the law's requirements are met by the Spirit-controlled life.

8:5 Those who live according to the flesh — that is, those who are unconverted — are concerned with **the things of the flesh**. They obey the impulses of the flesh. They live to gratify the desires of the corrupt nature. They cater to the body, which in a few short years will return to dust.

But those who live according to the Spirit — that is, true believers — rise above flesh and blood and live for those things that are eternal. They are occupied with the word of God, prayer, worship, and Christian service.

8:6 To be carnally minded — that is, the mental inclination of the fallen nature — **is death**. It is death as far as both present enjoyment and ultimate destiny are concerned. It has all the potential of death in it, just like an overdose of poison.

But **to be spiritually minded is life and peace**. The Spirit of God is the guarantee of life that is life indeed, of peace with God, and of a life of tranquility.

8:7 The mind-set of the flesh is death because it **is enmity against God**. The sinner is a rebel against God and in active hostility to Him. If any proof were needed, it is seen most clearly in the crucifixion of the Lord Jesus Christ. The mind of the flesh **is not subject to the law of God**. It wants its own will, not God's will. It wants to be its own master, not to bow to His rule. Its nature is such that it cannot be subject to God's law. It is not only the *inclination* that is missing but the *power* as well. The flesh is dead toward God.

8:8 It is no surprise, therefore, that **those who are in the flesh cannot please God**. Think of that! There is nothing an unsaved person can do to **please God** — no good works, no religious observances, no sacrificial services, absolutely nothing. First he must take the guilty sinner's place and receive Christ by a definite act of faith. Only then can He win God's smile of approval.

8:9 When a person is born again, he is no longer **in the flesh but in the Spirit**. He lives in a different sphere. Just as a fish lives in water and a man lives in the air, so a believer lives in the Spirit. He not only lives in the Spirit, but the Spirit lives in him. In fact, if he is not indwelt by the Spirit of Christ, he does not belong to Christ. Though there is a question whether **the Spirit of Christ** here is the same as the Holy Spirit, the assumption that they are the same seems to fit best in the context.

8:10 Through the ministry of the Spirit, **Christ is** actually **in** the believer. It is amazing to think of the Lord of life and glory dwelling in our bodies, especially when we remember that these bodies are subject to death **because of sin**. Someone may argue that they are not dead yet, as the verse seems to say. No, but the forces of death are already working in them, and they will inevitably die if the Lord doesn't return in the meantime.

In contrast to the body, **the spirit**[28] **is life because of righteousness**. Though once dead toward God, it has been made alive through the righteous work of the Lord Jesus Christ in His death and resurrection, and because the righteousness of God has been credited to our account.

8:11 But the reminder that the body is still subject to death need cause no alarm or despair. The fact that **the** Holy **Spirit** indwells our bodies is a guarantee that, just as He **raised Christ from the dead**, so He **will also give life to** our **mortal bodies**. This will be the final act of our redemption — when our bodies are glorified like the Savior's body of glory.

8:12 Now when we see the stark contrast between the flesh and the Spirit, what conclusion do we draw? We owe nothing **to the flesh, to live according to** *its* dictates. The old, evil, corrupt nature has been nothing but a drag. It has never done us a bit of good. If Christ had not saved us, **the flesh** would have dragged us down to the deepest, darkest, hottest places in hell. Why should we feel obligated to such an enemy?

8:13 Those who **live according to the flesh** must **die**, not only physically but eternally. To **live according to the flesh** is to be unsaved. This is made clear in 8:4, 5. But why does Paul address this to those who were already Christians? Does he imply that some of them might eventually be lost? No, but the apostle often includes words of warning and self-examination in his Letters, realizing that in every congregation there may be some people who have never been genuinely born again.

The rest of the verse describes what is characteristically true of genuine believers. By the enablement of **the** Holy **Spirit** they **put to death the deeds of the body**. They enjoy eternal life now, and will enter into life in its fullness when they leave this earth.

8:14 Another way of describing true believers is to say that they **are led by the Spirit of God**. Paul is not referring here to spectacular instances of divine guidance in the lives of eminent Christians. Rather, he is speaking of what is true of all **sons of God** — namely, that they **are led by the Spirit of God**. It is not a question of the degree in which they are yielded to the Holy Spirit, but of a relationship which takes place at the time of conversion.

Sonship implies reception into God's family, with all the privileges and responsibilities of adult sons. A new convert does not have to wait a certain time before he enters into his spiritual inheritance; it is his the moment he is saved, and it applies to all believers, men and women, boys and girls.

8:15 Those living under law are like minor children, bossed around as if they were servants, and shadowed by the fear of punishment. But when a person is born again, he is not born into a position of servitude. He is not brought into God's household as a slave. Rather, he receives **the spirit of adoption**; that is, he is placed in God's family as a mature son. By a true spiritual instinct he looks up to God and calls Him **"Abba, Father."** **Abba** is an Aramaic word which suffers in translation. It is an intimate form of the word *father* — such as "papa" or "daddy." While we may hesitate to use such familiar English words in addressing God, the truth remains that He who is infinitely high is also intimately nigh.

The phrase **the Spirit**[29] **of adoption** may be a reference to the Holy Spirit as the One who makes the believer aware of his special dignity as a son. Or it may mean the realization or attitude of adoption in contrast to **the spirit of bondage**.

Adoption is used in three different ways in Romans. Here it refers to the consciousness of sonship which the Holy Spirit produces in the life of the believer. In 8:23 it *looks forward* to that time when the believer's body will be redeemed or glorified. In 9:4 it *looks back* to that time when God designated Israel as His son (Ex. 4:22).

In Galatians 4:5 and Ephesians 1:5, the word means "son-placing" — that is, the act of placing all believers as mature, adult sons with all the privileges and responsibilities of sonship. Every believer is a child of God in that he is born into a family of which God is the Father. But every believer is also a son — a special relationship carrying the privileges of one who has reached the maturity of manhood.

In the NT **adoption** *never* means what it means in our society — to take a child of other parents as one's own.

8:16 There is a spiritual instinct in the newborn believer that he is a son of God. The Holy **Spirit** tells him that it is so. **The Spirit Himself bears witness with** the believer's **spirit that** he is a member of God's family. He does it primarily through the word of God. As a Christian reads the Bible, the Spirit confirms the truth that, because he has trusted the Savior, he is now a child of God.

8:17 Membership in God's family brings privileges that boggle the mind. All God's **children** are **heirs of God**. An heir, of course, eventually inherits his father's estate. That is just what is meant here. All that the Father has is ours. We have not yet come into the possession and enjoyment of all of it, but nothing can prevent our doing so in the future. **And** we are **joint heirs with Christ**. When He returns to take the scepter of universal government, we will share with Him the title deeds to all the Father's wealth.

When Paul adds, **if indeed we suffer with Him, that we may also be glorified together**, he is not making heroic suffering a condition for salvation. Neither is he describing some elite inner circle of overcomers who have endured great afflictions. Rather, he sees all Christians as being co-sufferers and all Christians as **glorified** with Christ. The **if** is equivalent to "since." Of course, there are some who suffer more than others in the cause of Christ, and this will result in differing degrees of reward and glory. But all who acknowledge Jesus as Lord and Savior are seen here as incurring the hostility of the world, with all its shame and reproach.

8:18 The greatest shame we may endure for Christ here on earth will be a mere trifle when He calls us forth and publicly acknowledges us before the hosts of heaven. Even the excruciating pain of the martyrs will seem like pinpricks when the Savior graces their brows with the crown of life. Elsewhere Paul speaks of our present sufferings as light afflictions which are only for a moment, but he describes the glory as an exceeding and eternal weight (2 Cor. 4:17). Whenever he describes the coming glory, his words seem to bend under the weight of the idea.[30] If we could only appreciate **the glory** that is to be ours, we could count **the sufferings** along the way as trivia!

8:19 Now in a bold literary figure Paul personifies the whole **creation** as **eagerly** looking forward to the time when we will be revealed to a wondering world as **the sons of God**. This will be when the Lord Jesus returns to reign and we return with Him.

We are already **the sons of God**, but the world neither recognizes nor appreciates us as such. And yet the world is looking forward to a better day, and that day cannot come until the King returns to reign with all His saints. "The whole creation is on tiptoe to see the wonderful sight of the sons of God coming into their own" (JBP).

8:20 When Adam sinned, his transgression affected not only mankind, but all **creation**, both animate and inanimate. The ground is cursed. Many wild animals die violent deaths. Disease afflicts birds and animals as well as fish and serpents. The results of man's sin have rippled like shockwaves throughout all creation.

Thus, as Paul explains, **the creation was subjected to futility**, frustration, and disorder, **not** by its own choice, **but** by the decree of God because of the disobedience of man's first federal head.

The words **in hope** at the end of verse 20 may also be connected with the following verse: "in hope that the creation itself also will be set free" (NASB).

8:21 Creation looks back to the ideal conditions that existed in Eden. Then it surveys the havoc that was caused by the entrance of sin. Always there has been the hope of a return to an idyllic state, when **creation itself also will be delivered from the bondage of corruption** to enjoy the freedom of that golden era when we as God's **children** will be revealed in glory.

8:22 We live in a sighing, sobbing, suffering world. **The whole creation groans** and suffers pain like that of childbirth. Nature's music is in the minor key. The earth is racked by cataclysm. The blight of death is on every living thing.

8:23 Believers are not exempt. Although they **have the firstfruits of the Spirit**, guaranteeing their eventual deliverance, they still **groan** for that day of glory. **The** Holy **Spirit** Himself is **the firstfruits**. Just as the first handful of ripened grain is a pledge of the entire harvest to follow, so the Holy Spirit is the pledge or guarantee that the full inheritance will be ours.

Specifically, He is the guarantee of the coming **adoption, the redemption of** the **body** (Eph. 1:14). In one sense we have already been adopted, which means that we have been placed into God's family as sons. But in a fuller sense our **adoption** will be complete when we receive our glorified bodies. That is spoken of as **the redemption of our body**. Our spirits and souls have already been redeemed, and our bodies will be redeemed at the time of the Rapture (1 Thess. 4:13–18).

8:24 We were saved in this attitude of **hope**. We did not receive all the benefits of our salvation at the moment of conversion. From the outset we looked forward to full and final deliverance from sin, suffering, disease, and death. If we had already received these blessings, we wouldn't be hoping for them. We only hope for what is in the future.

8:25 Our hope for deliverance from the presence of sin and all its baneful results is based on the promise of God, and is therefore as certain as if we had already received it. So **we eagerly wait for it with perseverance**.

8:26 Just as we are sustained by this glorious hope, so **the Spirit** sustains us **in our weaknesses**. We are often perplexed in our prayer life. **We do not know** how to **pray as we** should. We

pray selfishly, ignorantly, narrowly. But once again the Spirit comes alongside to assist us in our weakness, interceding **for us with groanings which cannot** find expression. In this verse it is the Spirit who groans and not we who groan, though that is also true.

There is mystery here. We are peering into the unseen, spiritual realm where a great Person and great forces are at work on our behalf. And although we cannot understand it all, we can take infinite encouragement from the fact that a groan may sometimes be the most spiritual prayer.

8:27 If God **searches the hearts** of men, He can also interpret **the mind of the Spirit**, even though that mind finds expression only in groans. The important thing is that the Holy Spirit's prayers for us are always **according to the will of God**. And because they are always in accordance with God's will, they are always for our good. That explains a lot, as the next verse reveals.

8:28 God is working **all things together for good to those who love** Him, **to those who are called according to His purpose**. It may not always seem so! Sometimes when we are suffering heartbreak, tragedy, disappointment, frustration, and bereavement, we wonder what good can come out of it. But the following verse gives the answer: whatever God permits to come into our lives is designed to conform us to the image of His Son. When we see this, it takes the question mark out of our prayers. Our lives are not controlled by impersonal forces such as chance, luck, or fate, but by our wonderful, personal Lord, who is "too loving to be unkind and too wise to err."

8:29 Now Paul traces the majestic sweep of the divine program designed to bring many sons to glory.

First of all, God **foreknew** us in eternity past. This was not a mere intellectual knowledge. As far as knowledge is concerned, He knew *everyone* who would ever be born. But His foreknowledge embraced only those whom He foreordained or **predestined to be conformed . . . to the image of His Son**. So it was knowledge with a purpose that could never be frustrated. It is not enough to say that God **foreknew** those whom He realized would one day repent and believe. Actually it is His foreknowledge that insures eventual repentance and belief.

That ungodly sinners should one day be transformed into the image of Christ by a miracle of grace is one of the most astounding truths of divine revelation. The point is not, of course, that we will ever have the attributes of deity, or even that we will have Christ's facial resemblance, but that we will be *morally* like Him, absolutely free from sin, and will have glorified bodies like His.

In that day of glory **He** will **be the firstborn among many brethren**. **Firstborn** here means first in rank or honor. He will not be One among equals, but the One who has the supreme place of honor among His brothers and sisters.

8:30 Everyone who was **predestined** in eternity is **also called** in time. This means that he not only hears the gospel but that he responds to it as well. It is therefore an effectual call. All are called; that is the general (yet also valid) call of God. But only a few respond; that is the effectual (conversion-producing) call of God.

All who respond are **also justified** or given an absolutely righteous standing before God. They are clothed with the righteousness of God through the merits of Christ and are thereby fit for the presence of the Lord.

Those who are **justified** are **also glorified**. Actually we are *not* glorified as *yet*, but it is so sure that God can use the past tense in describing it. We are as certain of the glorified state as if we had already received it!

This is one of the strongest passages in the NT on the eternal security of the believer. For every million people who are foreknown and **predestined** by God, *every one* of that million will be **called**, **justified**, and **glorified**. Not one will be missing! (Compare the "all" in John 6:37.)

8:31 When we consider these unbreakable links in the golden chain of redemption, the conclusion is inevitable! **If God is for us**, in the sense that He has marked us out for Himself, then no one **can be** successful **against us**.[31] If Omnipotence is working on our behalf, no lesser power can defeat His program.

8:32 **He who did not spare His own Son, but delivered Him up for us all**. What marvelous words! We must never allow our familiarity with them to dull their luster or lessen their power to inspire worship. When a world of lost mankind needed to be saved by a sinless Substitute, the great God of the universe did not hold back His heart's best Treasure, but gave Him over to a death of shame and loss on our behalf.

The logic that flows from this is irresistible. If God has already given us the greatest gift, is there any lesser gift that He will not give? If He has already paid the highest price, will He hesitate to pay any lower price? If He has gone to such lengths to procure our salvation, will He ever let us go? **How shall He not with Him also freely give us all things?**

"The language of unbelief," Mackintosh said, "is, 'How shall He?' The language of faith is 'How shall He not?' "[32]

8:33 We are still in a courtroom setting, but now a remarkable change has taken place. While the justified sinner stands before the bench, the call goes out for any accusers to step forward. But there is none! How could there be? If God has already justified His elect, **who** can **bring a charge**?

It greatly clarifies the argument of this verse and the following one if we supply the words "No one, because . . ." before each answer. Thus this verse would read, **Who shall bring a charge against God's elect?** *No one, because* **it is God who justifies**. If we do not supply these words, it might sound as if God is going to bring a charge against His elect, the very thing that Paul is denying!

8:34 Another challenge rings out! Is there anyone here to condemn? *No one, because* **Christ** has **died** for the defendant, has been raised from the dead, is now **at the right hand of God** interceding for him. If the Lord Jesus, to whom all judgment has been committed, does not pass sentence on the defendant but rather prays for him, then there is no one else who could have a valid reason for condemning him.

8:35 Now faith flings its final challenge: is there anyone here who can banish the justified **from the love of Christ**? A search is made for every adverse circumstance that has been effective in causing separations in other areas of human life. But none can be found. Not the threshing flail of **tribulation** with its steady pounding of **distress** and affliction, nor the monster of anguish, bringing extreme pain to mind and body, nor the brutality of **persecution**, inflicting suffering and death on those who dare to differ. Nor can the gaunt specter of **famine** — gnawing, racking, and wasting down to the skeleton. Nor can **nakedness**, with all it means in the way of privation, exposure, and defenselessness. Nor can **peril** — the threat of imminent and awful danger. Nor can the **sword** — cold, hard, and death-dealing.

8:36 If any of these things could separate the believer from the love of Christ, then the fatal severance would have taken place long ago, because the career of the Christian is a living death. That is what the psalmist meant when he said that, because of our identification with the Lord, **we are killed all day long**, and are like **sheep** that are doomed to **slaughter** (Ps. 44:22).

8:37 Instead of separating us from Christ's love, these things only succeed in drawing us closer to Him. We are not only **conquerors**, but **more than conquerors**.[33] It is not simply that we triumph over these formidable forces, but that in doing so we bring glory to God, blessing to others, and good to ourselves. We make slaves out of our enemies and stepping stones out of our roadblocks.

But all of this is not through our own strength, but only **through Him who loved us**. Only the power of Christ can bring sweetness out of bitterness, strength out of weakness, triumph out of tragedy, and blessing out of heartbreak.

8:38 The apostle has not finished his search. He ransacks the universe for something that might conceivably separate us from God's love, then dismisses the possibilities one by one —

death with all its terrors;

life with all its allurements;

angels nor principalities, supernatural in power and knowledge;

powers, whether human tyrants or angelic adversaries;

things present, crashing in upon us;

things to come, arousing fearful forebodings;

8:39 height nor depth, those things that are in the realm of dimension or space, including occult forces.[34] Then, to make sure that he is not missing anything, Paul adds:

nor any other created thing.

The outcome of Paul's search is that he can find nothing that can **separate us from the love of God which is in Christ Jesus our Lord**.

No wonder these words of triumph have been the song of those who have died martyr's deaths and the rhapsody of those who have lived martyr's lives!

II. DISPENSATIONAL: THE GOSPEL AND ISRAEL (Chaps. 9–11)

A. Israel's Past (Chap. 9)

In chapters 9–11 we hear Paul's answer to the Jewish objector who asks: *Does the gospel, by promising salvation to Gentiles as well as Jews, mean that God has broken His promises to His earthly people, the Jews?* Paul's answer covers Israel's past (chap. 9), its present (chap. 10), and its future (chap. 11).

This section contains a great emphasis on divine sovereignty and human responsibility. Romans 9 is one of the key passages in the Bible on the sovereign election of God. The next chapter sets forth the balancing truth — the responsibility of man — with equal vigor.

DIVINE SOVEREIGNTY AND HUMAN RESPONSIBILITY

When we say that God is sovereign, we mean that He is in charge of the universe and that He can do as He pleases. In saying that, however, we know that, because He is God, He will never do anything wrong, unjust, or unrighteous. Therefore, to say that God is sovereign is merely to allow God to be God. We should not be afraid of this truth or apologize for it. It is a glorious truth and should cause us to worship.

In His sovereignty, God has elected or chosen certain individuals to belong to Himself. But the same Bible that teaches God's sovereign election also teaches human responsibility. While it is true that God elects people to salvation, it is also true they must choose to be saved by a definite act of the will. The divine side of salvation is seen in the words, "All that the Father gives Me will come to Me." The human side is found in the words that follow: "and the one who comes to Me I will by no means cast out" (John 6:37). We rejoice, as believers, that God chose us in Christ before the foundation of the world (Eph. 1:4). But we believe just as surely that whoever will may take of the water of life freely (Rev. 22:17). D. L. Moody illustrated the two truths this way: When we come to the door of salvation, we see the invitation overhead, "Whosoever will may come." When we pass through, we look back and see the words "Elect according to the foreknowledge of God" above the door. Thus the truth of man's responsibility faces people as they come to the door of salvation. The truth of sovereign election is a family truth for those who have already entered.

How can God choose individuals to belong to Himself and at the same time make a *bona fide* offer of salvation to all people everywhere? How can we reconcile these two truths? The fact is that we cannot. To the human mind they are in conflict. But the Bible teaches both doctrines, and so we should believe them, content to know that the difficulty lies in our minds and not in God's. These twin truths are like two parallel lines that meet only in infinity.

Some have tried to reconcile sovereign election and human responsibility by saying that God foreknew who would trust the Savior and that those are the ones whom He elected to be saved. They base this on Romans 8:29 ("whom He foreknew He also predestined") and 1 Peter 1:2 ("elect according to the foreknowledge of God"). But this overlooks the fact that God's foreknowledge is *determinative*. It is not just that He *knows* in advance who will trust the Savior, but that He *predetermines* this result by drawing certain individuals to Himself.

Although God chooses some men to be saved, He never chooses anyone to be damned. To put it another way, though the Bible teaches election, it never teaches divine reprobation. But someone may object, "If God elects

some to blessing, then He necessarily elects others to destruction." But that is not true! The whole human race was doomed to destruction by its own sin and not by any arbitrary decree of God. If God allowed everyone to go to hell — and He could justly have done that — people would be getting exactly what they deserved. The question is, "Does the sovereign Lord have a right to stoop down and select a handful of otherwise-doomed people to be a bride for His Son?" The answer, of course, is that He does. So what it boils down to is this: if people are lost, it is because of their own sin and rebellion; if people are saved, it is because of the sovereign, electing grace of God.

To the man who is saved, the subject of God's sovereign choice should be the cause of unceasing wonder. The believer looks around and sees people with better characters, better personalities, and better dispositions than his own, and asks, "Why did the Lord choose me?"

Why was I made to hear Thy voice,
And enter while there's room,
When thousands make a wretched choice,
And rather starve than come?
— *Isaac Watts*

The truth of election should not be used by the unsaved for excusing their unbelief. They must not say, "If I'm not elect, there's nothing I can do about it." The only way they can ever know they are elect is by repenting of their sins and receiving the Lord Jesus Christ as Savior (1 Thess. 1:4–7).

Neither should the truth of election be used by Christians to excuse a lack of evangelistic zeal. We must not say, "If they're elect, they'll be saved anyway." Only God knows who the elect are. We are commanded to preach the gospel to all the world, for God's offer of salvation is a genuine invitation to all people. People reject the gospel because of the hardness of their hearts, and not because God's universal invitation is insincere.

There are two dangers to be avoided in connection with this subject. The first is to hold only one side of the truth — for example, to believe in God's sovereign election and to deny that man has any responsible choice in connection with his salvation. The other danger is to overemphasize one truth at the expense of the other. The scriptural approach is to believe in God's sovereign election and to believe with equal force in human responsibility. Only in this way can a person hold these doctrines in their proper biblical balance. ‡

Now let us turn to Romans 9 and follow the beloved apostle as he unfolds this subject.

9:1 In insisting that salvation is for Gentiles as well as for Jews, Paul gave the appearance of being a traitor, a turncoat, a renegade as far as Israel was concerned. So he here protests his deep devotion to the Jewish people by using a solemn oath. He speaks **the truth**. He is **not lying**. His **conscience**, in fellowship with **the Holy Spirit**, attests the truth of what he is saying.

9:2 When he thinks first of Israel's glorious calling, and now of its rejection by God because it rejected the Messiah, his **heart** is filled with **great sorrow and continual grief**.

9:3 He **could** even **wish** himself **accursed** or cut off from Christ if through the forfeiting of his own salvation his Jewish brothers might be saved. In this strong statement of self-abnegation, we sense the highest form of human love — that which constrains a man to lay down his life for his friends (John 15:13). And we feel the enormous burden which a converted Jew experiences for the conversion of his **countrymen**. It reminds us of Moses' prayer for his people: "Yet now, if You will forgive their sin — but if not, I pray, blot me out of Your book which You have written" (Ex. 32:32).

9:4 As Paul weeps over his people, their glorious privileges pass in review. They **are Israelites**, members of God's ancient chosen people.

God had *adopted* that nation to be His son (Ex. 4:22) and delivered His people out of Egypt (Hos. 11:1). He was a father to Israel (Deut. 14:1), and Ephraim was His firstborn (Jer. 31:9). (*Ephraim* is used here as another name for the nation of Israel.)

The Shekinah or **glory** cloud symbolized God's presence in their midst, guiding and protecting them.

It was with Israel, not with the Gentiles, that God made the **covenants**. It was with Israel, for example, that He made the Palestinian Covenant, promising them the land from the River of Egypt to the Euphrates (Gen. 15:18). And it is with Israel that He will yet ratify the New Covenant, promising "the perpetuity, future conversion, and blessing of a repentant Israel (Jer. 31: 31–40)."[35]

It was to Israel that **the law** was given. They and they alone were its recipients.

The elaborate rituals and **service of God** connected with the tabernacle and the temple were given to Israel, as well as the priesthood.

In addition to the covenants mentioned above, God made innumerable **promises** to Israel of protection, peace, and prosperity.

9:5 The Jewish people rightfully claim the patriarchs as their own — Abraham, Isaac, Jacob, and the twelve sons of Jacob. These were the forefathers of the nation. And they had the greatest privilege of all — the Messiah is an Israelite, as far as His human descent is concerned, though He is also the Sovereign of the universe, **the eternally blessed God**. Here we have a positive statement of the deity and humanity of the Savior. (Some Bible versions weaken the force of this verse. For example, the RSV reads, ". . . and of their race, according to the flesh, is the Christ. God who is over all be blessed for ever. Amen." The Greek does not rule out the RSV here from a strictly grammatical viewpoint, but spiritual discernment in comparing Scripture with Scripture favors the reading in the KJV, NKJV, and other conservative translations.)[36]

9:6 The apostle now faces up to a serious theological problem. If God made promises to Israel as His chosen earthly people, how can this be squared with Israel's present rejection and with the Gentiles being brought into the place of blessing? Paul insists that this does not indicate any breach of promise on God's part. He goes on to show that God has always had a sovereign election process based upon promise and not just on lineal descent. Just because a person is born into the nation **of Israel** does not mean that he is an heir to the promises.

Within the nation **of Israel**, God has a true, believing remnant.

9:7 Not **all** Abraham's offspring are counted as his **children**. Ishmael, for example, was of **the seed of Abraham**. But the line of promise came through Isaac, not through Ishmael. The promise of God was, **"In Isaac your seed shall be called"** (Gen. 21:12). As we pointed out in the notes on 4:12, the Lord Jesus made this same interesting distinction when talking with the unbelieving Jews in John 8:33–39. They said to Him, "We are Abraham's descendants . . . " (v. 33). Jesus admitted this, saying, "I know you are Abraham's descendants" (v. 37). But when they said, "Abraham is our father," the Lord replied, "If you were Abraham's children, you would do the works of Abraham" (v. 39). In other words, they were descended from Abraham, but they didn't have Abraham's faith and therefore they were not his spiritual children.

9:8 It is not physical descent that counts. The true Israel consists of those Jews who were selected by God and to whom He made some specific **promise**, marking them out as His **children**. We see this principle of sovereign election in the cases of Isaac and Jacob.

9:9 God appeared to Abraham, promising that He would return **at the** appointed **time** and that **Sarah** would **have a son**. That **son**, of course, was Isaac. He was truly a child of **promise** and a child of supernatural birth.

9:10 Another case of sovereign election is found in the case of Jacob. **Isaac** and **Rebecca** were the parents, of course. But **Rebecca** was carrying *two* babies, not one.

9:11 A pronouncement was made before **the children** were ever **born**. This pronouncement could not, therefore, have had anything to do with works of merit by either child. It was entirely a matter of God's choice, based on His own will and not on the character or attainments of the subjects. **The purpose of God according to election** means His determination to distribute His favors according to His sovereign will and good pleasure.

This verse, incidentally, disproves the idea that God's choice of Jacob was based on His foreknowledge of what Jacob would do. It specifically says that it was **not** made on the basis **of works!**

9:12 God's decision was that **the older** would **serve the younger**. Esau would have a subservient place to Jacob. The latter was chosen to *earthly glory and privilege*. Esau was the firstborn of the twin brothers and ordinarily would have had the honors and privileges associated with that position. But God's selection passed him by and rested on Jacob.

9:13 To further enforce God's sovereignty in choosing, Paul quotes Malachi 1:2, 3: **"Jacob I have loved, but Esau I have hated."** Here God is speaking of the two nations, Israel and Edom, of which **Jacob** and **Esau** were heads. God marked out Israel as the nation to which He promised the Messiah and the messianic kingdom. Edom received no such promise. Instead, its mountains and heritage were laid waste for the jackals of the wilderness (Mal. 1:3; see also Jer. 49:17, 18; Ezek. 35:7–9).

Although it is true that the quotation from Malachi 1:2, 3 describes God's dealings with nations rather than individuals, it is used to support His sovereign right to choose individuals as well.

The words **Jacob I have loved, but Esau I have hated** must be understood in the light of the sovereign decree of God that stated, **The older shall serve the younger**. The preference for Jacob is interpreted as an act of love, whereas bypassing Esau is seen as hatred *by comparison*. It is not that God hated Esau with a harsh, vindictive animosity, but only that He loved Esau less than Jacob, as seen by His sovereign selection of Jacob.

This passage refers to *earthly blessings*, and not to eternal life. God's hatred of Edom doesn't mean that individual Edomites *can't* be saved, any more than His love of Israel means that individual Jews *don't* need to be saved. (Note also that Esau *did* receive some earthly blessings, as he himself testified in Gen. 33:9.)

9:14 The apostle correctly anticipated that his teaching on sovereign election would stir up all kinds of objections. People still accuse God of unfairness. They say that if He chooses some, then He thereby necessarily damns the rest. They argue that if God has settled everything in advance, then there's nothing anyone can do about it, and God is unrighteous for condemning people.

Paul hotly denies any possibility of **unrighteousness** on God's part. But instead of watering down God's sovereignty in order to make it more palatable to these objectors, he proceeds to restate it more vigorously and without apology.

9:15 He first quotes God's word to Moses, **"I will have mercy on whomever I will have mercy, and I will have compassion on whomever I will have compassion"** (see Ex. 33:19). Who can say that the Most High, the Lord of heaven and earth, does not have the right to show **mercy** and **compassion**?

All people are condemned by their own sin and unbelief. If left to themselves, they would *all* perish. In addition to extending a genuine gospel invitation to all people, God chooses some of these condemned people to be special objects of His grace. But this does not mean that He arbitrarily chooses the others to be condemned. They are already condemned because they are lifelong sinners and have rejected the gospel. Those who are chosen can thank God for His grace. Those who are lost have no one to blame but themselves.

9:16 The conclusion, then, is that the ultimate destiny of men or of nations does not rest in the strength of their will or in the power of their exertions, but rather in the **mercy** of **God**.

When Paul says that **it is not of him who wills**, he does not mean that a person's will is not involved in his salvation. The gospel invitation is clearly directed to a person's will, as shown in Revelation 22:17: "Whoever desires, let him take the water of life freely." Jesus exposed the unbelieving Jews as being *unwilling* to come to Him (John 5:40). When Paul says, **nor of him who runs**, he does not deny that we must strive to enter the narrow gate (Luke 13:24). A certain amount of spiritual earnestness and willingness are necessary. But man's will and man's running are not the primary, determining factors: salvation is of the Lord. Morgan says:

> No willing on our part, no running on our own, can procure for us the salvation we need, or enable us to enter into the blessings it provides. . . . Of ourselves we shall have no will for salvation, and shall

make no effort toward it. Everything of human salvation begins in God.[37]

9:17 God's sovereignty is seen not only in showing mercy to some but in hardening others. **Pharaoh** is cited as an example.

There is no suggestion here that the Egyptian monarch was doomed from the time of his birth. What happened was this. In adult life he proved to be wicked, cruel, and extremely stubborn. In spite of the most solemn warnings he kept hardening his heart. God could have destroyed him instantly, but He didn't. Instead, God preserved him alive in order that He might display His **power** in him, and that through him God's name might be known worldwide.

9:18 Pharaoh repeatedly hardened his own heart, and *after* each of these times God *additionally* hardened Pharaoh's heart as a judgment upon him. The same sun that melts ice hardens clay. The same sun that bleaches cloth tans the skin. The same God who shows mercy to the brokenhearted also hardens the impenitent. Grace rejected is grace denied.

God has the right to show **mercy** to whomever He wishes, and to harden whomever He wishes. But because He is God, He never acts unjustly.

9:19 Paul's insistence on God's right to do what He pleases raises the objection that, if that is so, **He** shouldn't **find fault** with anyone, since no one **has** successfully **resisted His will**. To the objector, man is a helpless pawn on the divine chessboard. Nothing he can do or say will change his fate.

9:20 The apostle first rebukes the insolence of any creature who dares to find fault with his Creator. Finite **man**, loaded down with sin, ignorance, and weakness, is in no position to talk back to **God** or question the wisdom or justice of His ways.

9:21 Then Paul uses the illustration of **the potter** and **the clay** to vindicate the sovereignty of God. **The potter** comes into his shop one day and sees a pile of formless clay on the floor. He picks up a handful of clay, puts it on his wheel, and fashions a beautiful **vessel**. Does he have a right to do that?

The potter, of course, is God. **The**

clay is sinful, lost humanity. If the potter left it alone, it would all be sent to hell. He would be absolutely just and fair if He left it alone. But instead He sovereignly selects a handful of sinners, saves them by His grace, and conforms them to the image of His Son. Does He have the right to do that? Remember, He is not arbitrarily dooming others to hell. They are already doomed by their own willfulness and unbelief.

God has the absolute power and authority to make a vessel for honor with some of the clay and another for dishonor with some. In a situation where everyone is unworthy, He can bestow His blessings where He chooses and withhold them whenever He wishes. "Where all are undeserving," Barnes writes, "the utmost that can be demanded is that He should not treat any with injustice."[38]

9:22 Paul pictures God, the great Potter, as facing a seeming conflict of interests. On the one hand, He wishes to show His wrath and exhibit His power in punishing sin. But on the other hand He desires to bear patiently with vessels of wrath prepared for destruction. It is the contrast between the righteous severity of God in the first place, and His merciful longsuffering in the second. And the argument is, "If God would be justified in punishing the wicked immediately but, instead of that, shows great patience with them, who can find fault with Him?"

Notice carefully the phrase vessels of wrath prepared for destruction. Vessels of wrath are those whose sins make them subject to God's wrath. They are prepared for destruction by their own sin, disobedience, and rebellion, and not by some arbitrary decree of God.

9:23 Who can object if God wishes to make known the riches of His glory to people to whom He desires to show mercy — people whom He had selected beforehand for eternal glory? Here C. R. Erdman's comment seems especially helpful:

> God's sovereignty is never exercised in condemning men who ought to be saved, but rather it has resulted in the salvation of men who ought to be lost.[39]

God does not prepare vessels of wrath for destruction, but He does prepare vessels of mercy for glory.

9:24 Paul identifies the vessels of mercy as those of us who are Christians, whom God called from both Jewish and Gentile worlds. This lays the foundation for much that is to follow — the setting aside of all but a remnant of the nation of Israel and the call of the Gentiles to a place of privilege.

9:25 The apostle quotes two verses from Hosea to show that the call of the Gentiles should not have come as a surprise to the Jews. The first is Hosea 2:23: "I will call them My people, who were not My people, and her beloved, who was not beloved." Now actually in Hosea these words refer to Israel and not to the Gentiles. They look forward to the time when Israel will be restored as God's people and as His beloved. But when Paul quotes them here in Romans he applies them to the call of the Gentiles. What right does Paul have to make such a radical change? The answer is that the Holy Spirit who inspired the words in the first place has the right to reinterpret or reapply them later.

9:26 The second verse is Hosea 1:10: "And it shall come to pass in the place where it was said to them, 'You are not My people,' There they shall be called sons of the living God." Once again, in its OT setting this verse is not speaking about the Gentiles but describing Israel's future restoration to God's favor. Yet Paul applies it to God's acknowledgment of the Gentiles as His sons. This is another illustration of the fact that when the Holy Spirit quotes verses from the OT in the NT, He can rightfully apply them as He wishes.

9:27 The rejection of all but a remnant of Israel is discussed in 9:27–29. Isaiah predicted that only a minority of the children of Israel would be saved, even though the nation itself might grow to tremendous numbers (Isa. 10:22).

9:28 When Isaiah said, "He will finish the work and cut it short in righteousness because the LORD will make a short work upon the earth" (Isa. 10:23), he was referring to the Babylonian invasion of Palestine and Israel's subsequent exile. The work was God's work of judgment. In quoting these words Paul is saying that what had happened to Israel in the past could and would happen again in his day.

9:29   As Isaiah said before (in an earlier part of his prophecy): **Unless the LORD of** the armies of heaven **had left** some survivors, Israel would have been wiped out **like Sodom** and **Gomorrah** (Isa. 1:9).

9:30   What, Paul asks, is the conclusion of all this as far as this present Church Age is concerned? The first conclusion is **that Gentiles, who** characteristically **did not pursue righteousness** but rather wickedness, and who certainly didn't pursue a righteousness of their own making, **have** found **righteousness** through **faith** in the Lord Jesus Christ. Not all Gentiles, of course, but only those who believed in Christ were justified.

9:31 Israel, on the other hand, which sought justification on the basis of law-keeping, never found a **law** by which they might obtain **righteousness.**

9:32   The reason is clear. They refused to believe that justification is **by faith** in Christ, **but** went on stubbornly trying to work out their own righteousness by personal merit. **They stumbled** over the **stumbling stone**, Christ Jesus the Lord.

9:33   This is exactly what the Lord foretold through Isaiah. The Messiah's coming to Jerusalem would have a twofold effect. To some people He would prove to be **a stumbling stone and rock of offense** (Isa. 8:14). Others would believe **on Him** and find no reason for **shame**, offense, or disappointment (Isa. 28:16).

B. Israel's Present (Chap. 10)

10:1   Paul's teachings were most distasteful to the unconverted Jews. They considered him a traitor and an enemy of Israel. But here he assures his Christian **brethren** to whom he was writing that the thing that would bring the greatest delight to his heart and the thing for which he prays **to God** most earnestly **for Israel is that they may be saved**.

10:2   Far from condemning them as godless and irreligious, the apostle gives his testimony **that they have a zeal for God**. This was apparent from their careful observance of the rituals and ceremonies of Judaism, and from their intolerance of every contrary doctrine. But **zeal** is not enough; it must be combined with truth. Otherwise it can do more harm than good.

10:3   This is where they failed. They were **ignorant of God's righteousness**, **ignorant** of the fact that God imputes **righteousness** on the principle of faith and not of works. They went about trying to produce a **righteousness** of **their own** by law-keeping. They tried to win God's favor by their own efforts, their own character, their own good works. They steadfastly refused to submit to God's plan for reckoning righteous those ungodly sinners who believe on His Son.

10:4   If they had only believed on **Christ**, they would have seen that He **is the end of the law for righteousness**. The purpose of the law is to reveal sin, to convict and condemn transgressors. It can never impart righteousness. The penalty of the broken law is death. In His death, Christ paid the penalty of the law which men had broken. When a sinner receives the Lord Jesus Christ as his Savior, the law has nothing more to say to him. Through the death of his Substitute, he has died to the law. He is through with the law and with the futile attempt to achieve righteousness through it.

10:5   In the language of the OT, we can hear the difference between the words of the law and the words of faith. In Leviticus 18:5, for example, **Moses writes that** the man who achieves the **righteousness** which the **law** demands **shall live by** doing so. The emphasis is on his achieving, his doing.

Of course, this statement presents an ideal which no sinful man can meet. All it is saying is that if a man could keep the law perfectly and perpetually, he would not be condemned to death. But the law was given to people who were *already* sinners and who were *already* condemned to death. Even if they could keep the law perfectly from that day forward, they still would be lost because God requires payment for those sins which are past. Any hopes that men may have for obtaining righteousness by the law are doomed to failure from the outset.

10:6   In order to show that the language of faith is quite different from that of the law, Paul first quotes from Deuteronomy 30:12, 13, which reads:

> It is not in heaven, that you should say,
> "Who will ascend into heaven for us and bring it to us, that we may hear and do it?"
> Nor is it beyond the sea, that you should say,
> "Who will go over the sea for us and bring it to us, that we may hear it and do it?"

The interesting thing is that, in their setting in Deuteronomy, these verses are not referring to faith and the gospel at all. They are speaking about the law, and specifically the commandment to "turn to the LORD your God with all your heart and with all your soul" (Deut. 30:10b). God is saying that the law is not hidden, distant, or inaccessible. A man doesn't have to go up to **heaven** or cross the sea to find it. It is near at hand and waiting to be obeyed.

But the Apostle Paul takes these words and reapplies them to the gospel. He says that the language of **faith** doesn't ask a man to climb to **heaven to bring Christ down**. For one thing, that would be utterly impossible; but it would also be quite *unnecessary*, because Christ has already come down to earth in His Incarnation!

10:7 When the apostle quotes Deuteronomy 30:13, he changes it from "Who will go over the sea" to **Who will descend into the abyss**. His point is that the gospel does not ask men to **descend into** the grave **to bring Christ up from** among **the dead**. This would be impossible, but it would also be unnecessary, because Christ has already risen from the dead. Notice that in 10:6, 7 we have the two doctrines concerning Christ which were hardest for a Jew to accept — His Incarnation and His Resurrection. Yet he must accept these if he is to be saved. We will see these two doctrines again in 10:9, 10.

10:8 If the gospel doesn't tell men to do the humanly impossible, or to do what has already been done by the Lord, **what** then **does it say?**

Again Paul adapts a verse from Deuteronomy 30 to say that the gospel is **near**, accessible, intelligible, and easily obtained; it can be expressed in familiar conversation (**in your mouth**); and it can be readily understood in the mind (**in your heart**) (Deut. 30:14). It is the good news of salvation by faith which Paul and the other apostles preached.

10:9 Here it is in a nutshell: First you must accept the truth of the Incarnation, that the Babe of Bethlehem's manger is the Lord of life and glory, that the **Jesus** of the NT is the **Lord** (Jehovah) of the OT.

Second, you must accept the truth of His resurrection, with all that it involves. **God has raised Him from the dead** as proof that Christ had completed the work necessary for our salvation, and that God is satisfied with that work. Believing this with the **heart** means believing with one's mental, emotional, and volitional powers.

So **you confess with your mouth the Lord Jesus and believe in your heart that God has raised Him from the dead**. It is a personal appropriation of the Person and work of the Lord Jesus Christ. That is saving faith.

The question often arises, "Can a person be saved by accepting Jesus as Savior without also acknowledging Him as Lord?" The Bible gives no encouragement to anyone who believes with mental reservations: "I'll take Jesus as my Savior but I don't want to crown Him Lord of all." On the other hand, those who make submission to Jesus as Lord a *condition of salvation* face the problem, "To what degree must He be acknowledged as Lord?" Few Christians would claim to have made an absolute and complete surrender to Him in this way. When we present the gospel, we must maintain that *faith is the sole condition of justification*. But we must also remind sinners and saints constantly that Jesus Christ *is* Lord (Jehovah-God), and should be acknowledged as such.

10:10 In further explanation, Paul writes that **with the heart one believes unto righteousness**. It is not a mere intellectual assent but a genuine acceptance with one's whole inward being. When a person does that, he is instantly justified.

Then **with the mouth confession is made unto salvation**; that is, the believer publicly confesses the salvation he has already received. Confession is *not a condition* of salvation but the inevitable outward expression of what has happened: "If on Jesus Christ you trust, speak for Him you surely must." When a person really believes something, he wants to share it with others. So when a person is genuinely born again, it is too good to keep secret. He confesses Christ.

The Scriptures assume that when a person is saved he will make a public confession of that salvation. The two go together. Thus Kelly said, "If there be no confession of Christ the Lord with the mouth, we cannot speak of salvation; as our Lord said, 'He that believeth and is baptized shall be saved.' "[40] And Denney comments,

"A heart believing unto righteousness, and a mouth making confession unto salvation, are not really two things, but two sides of the same thing."[41]

The question arises why confession comes first in 10:9, then belief, whereas in 10:10 belief comes first, then confession. The answer is not hard to find. In verse 9 the emphasis is on the Incarnation and the resurrection, and these doctrines are mentioned in their chronological order. The Incarnation comes first — Jesus is Lord. Then the resurrection — God raised Him from the dead. In verse 10 the emphasis is on the order of events in the salvation of a sinner. First he **believes**, then he makes a public **confession** of his **salvation.**

10:11 The apostle now quotes Isaiah 28:16 to emphasize that **whoever believes on Him will not be put to shame**. The thought of public confession of Christ might arouse fears of shame, but the opposite is true. Our confession of Him *on earth* leads to His confession of us *in heaven*. Ours is a hope that will never be disappointed.

The word **whoever** forms a link with what is to follow — namely, that God's glorious salvation is for all, Gentiles as well as Jews.

10:12 In Romans 3:23 we learned that there is no difference between Jew and Gentile as far as the need for salvation is concerned, for all are sinners. Now we learn that there is **no distinction** as far as the availability of salvation is concerned. The Lord is not an exclusive God, but is **Lord over all** mankind. He

is rich in grace and mercy **to all who call upon Him**.

10:13 Joel 2:32 is quoted to prove the universality of the gospel. One could scarcely wish for a simpler statement of the way of salvation than is found in these words: **"Whoever calls on the name of the LORD shall be saved." The name of the LORD** stands for the LORD Himself.

10:14 But such a gospel presupposes a universal proclamation. Of what use is a salvation offered to Jews and Gentiles if they never hear about it? Here we have the heartbeat of Christian missions!

In a series of three "how's" (**how shall they call . . . believe . . . hear without a preacher**), the apostle goes back over the steps that lead to the salvation of Jews and Gentiles. Perhaps it will be clearer if we reverse the order, as follows:

God sends out His servants.

They preach the good news of salvation.

Sinners hear God's offer of life in Christ.

Some of those who hear believe the message.

Those who believe call on the Lord.

Those who call on Him are saved.

Hodge points out that this is an argument founded on the principle that if God wills the end, He also wills the means to reach that end.[42] This, as we have said, is the basis of the Christian missionary movement. Paul is here vindicating his preaching the gospel to the Gentiles, a policy which the unbelieving Jews considered inexcusable.

10:15 God is the One who sends. We are the ones who **are sent**. What are we doing about it? Do we have **the beautiful feet** which Isaiah ascribed to Him **who** brought **glad tidings of good things** (Isa. 52:7)? Isaiah writes of **the beautiful feet** of *Him* — that is, the Messiah. Here in Romans 10:15 the "him" becomes "them." *He* came with **beautiful feet** 1900 years ago. Now it is *our* privilege and responsibility to go with **beautiful feet** to a lost and dying world.

10:16 **But** Paul's ever-present grief is that the people of Israel did **not all** listen to **the gospel**. Isaiah had prophesied as much when he asked, **"Lord, who has believed our report?"** (Isa. 53:1). The question calls for the answer, "Not many." When the announcement of the Messiah's First Advent was heralded, not many responded.

10:17 In this quotation from Isaiah, Paul notices that the belief spoken of by the prophet springs from the message that is heard, and that the message comes through the **word** about the Messiah. So he lays down the conclusion that **faith comes by hearing, and hearing by the word of God. Faith** comes to men when they hear our preaching concerning the Lord Jesus Christ, which is based, of course, on the written **word of God**.

But hearing with the ears is not enough. A person must hear with an open heart and mind, willing to be shown the truth of God. If he does, he will find that the word has the ring of truth, and that the truth is self-authenticating. He will then believe. It should be clear, of course, that the **hearing** alluded to in this verse does not involve the ears exclusively. The message might be *read*, for example. So "to hear" means to receive the word by whatever means.

10:18 What then has been the problem? Haven't both Jews and Gentiles **heard** the gospel preached? Yes. Paul borrows the words of Psalm 19:4 to show that they have. He says, **Yes, indeed:**

"Their sound has gone out to all the earth,
And their words to the ends of the world."

But the surprising thing is that these words from Psalm 19 are not speaking of the gospel. Rather, they describe the universal witness of the sun, moon, and stars to the glory of God. But as we said, Paul borrows them and says, in effect, that they are equally true of the worldwide proclamation of the gospel in his own day. By inspiration of the Spirit of God, the apostle often takes an OT passage and applies it in quite a different way. The same Spirit who originally gave the words surely has the right to reapply them later on.

10:19 The call of the Gentiles and the rejection of the gospel by the *majority*

of Jews should not have come as a surprise to the nation of **Israel**. Their own Scriptures foretold exactly what would happen. For example God warned that He would **provoke** Israel **to jealousy** by a non-nation (the Gentiles), and **anger** Israel **by a foolish**, idolatrous **nation** (Deut. 32:21).

10:20 In even bolder language, **Isaiah** quotes the Lord as being **found by** the Gentiles, who weren't really looking for Him, and being **made manifest to those who** weren't inquiring for Him (Isa. 65:1). Taken as a whole, the Gentiles didn't seek after God. They were satisfied with their pagan religions. But many of them *did respond* when they heard the gospel. Relatively speaking, the Gentiles responded more than the Jews.

10:21 Against this picture of the Gentiles flocking to Jehovah, Isaiah portrays the Lord standing all day long with outstretched, beckoning **hands to** the nation of **Israel**, and being met with disobedience and stubborn refusal.

C. Israel's Future (Chap. 11)

11:1 What about the future of Israel? Is it true, as some teach, that God is through with Israel, that the church is now the Israel of God, and that all the promises to Israel now apply to the church?[43] Romans 11 is one of the strongest refutations of that view in all the Bible.

Paul's opening question means, **"Has God cast away His people** *completely*? That is, has every single Israelite been cast off?" **Certainly not!** The point is that although God **has cast** off **His people**, as is distinctly stated in 11:15, this does not mean that He has rejected *all* of them. Paul himself is a proof that the casting away has not been complete. After all, he was an **Israelite, of the seed of Abraham**, and **of the tribe of Benjamin**. His credentials as a Jew were impeccable.

11:2 So we must understand the first part of this verse as saying, **"God has not** *completely* **cast away His people whom He foreknew,"** The situation was similar to that which existed in the time of **Elijah**. The mass of the nation had turned away from God to idols. Conditions were so bad that Elijah prayed **against Israel** instead of for it!

11:3 He reminded the LORD how the people had silenced the voice of the **prophets** in death. They had **torn down** God's **altars**. It seemed to him that his was the only faithful voice for God that was left, and his **life** was in imminent danger.

11:4 But the picture wasn't as dark and hopeless as Elijah feared. God reminded the prophet that He had **reserved** for Himself **seven thousand men** who had steadfastly refused to follow the nation in worshiping **Baal**.

11:5 What was true **then** is true now: God never leaves Himself without a witness. He always has a faithful **remnant** chosen by Himself as special objects of His **grace**.

11:6 God doesn't choose this remnant on the basis **of their works**, but **by** His sovereign, electing **grace**. These two principles — **grace** and **works** — are mutually exclusive. A gift cannot be earned. What is free cannot be bought. What is unmerited cannot be deserved. Fortunately, God's choice was based on **grace**, not on **works**; otherwise no one could ever have been chosen.

11:7 The conclusion, then, is that **Israel** failed to obtain righteousness because they sought it through self-effort instead of through the finished work of Christ. The remnant, chosen by God, succeeded in obtaining righteousness through faith in the Lord Jesus. The nation suffered what might be called judicial blindness. Refusal to receive the Messiah resulted in a decreased capacity and inclination to receive Him.

11:8 This is exactly what the OT predicted would happen (Isa. 29:10; Deut. 29:4). **God** abandoned them to a state of **stupor** in which they became insensitive to spiritual realities. Because they refused to see the Lord Jesus as Messiah and Savior, now they lost the power to **see** Him. Because they would not hear the pleading voice of God, now they were smitten with spiritual deafness. That terrible judgment continues **to this very day**.

11:9 **David**, too, anticipated the judgment of God on Israel. In Psalm 69:22, 23 he described the rejected Savior as calling on God to turn **their table** into **a snare and a trap**. The **table** here means the sum total of the privileges and blessings which flowed through Christ. What should have been a blessing was turned into a curse.

11:10 In the Psalms passage, the suffering Savior also called on God to **let their eyes be darkened** and their bodies bent over as by toil or in old age (or, their loins made to shake continually).

11:11 Paul now raises another question. **Have they stumbled that they should fall?** Here we must supply the word *finally* or *forever*. Did they stumble that they might fall and never be restored? The apostle denies such a suggestion emphatically. God's purpose is restorative. His purpose is that as a result of their fall, **salvation** might **come to the Gentiles**, thus provoking Israel **to jealousy**. This **jealousy** is designed to bring Israel back to God eventually.

Paul does not deny the fall of Israel. In fact, he admits it in this very verse — **Through their fall, . . . salvation has come to the Gentiles** — and in the next verse — "If their *fall* is riches for the world." But he vigorously opposes the idea that God is through with Israel forever.

11:12 As a result of Israel's rejection of the gospel, the nation was set aside and the gospel went out to **the Gentiles**. In this sense the **fall** of the Jews has meant **riches for the world**, and Israel's loss has been the Gentiles' gain.

But if that is true, **how much more** will Israel's restoration result in rich blessing for all the world! When Israel turns to the Lord at the close of the Great Tribulation, she will become the channel of blessing to the nations.

11:13 The apostle here addresses the **Gentiles** (11:13–24). Some think he is speaking to the Gentile Christians in Rome, but the passage demands a different audience — that is, the Gentile nations as such. It will greatly assist one to understand this passage if he sees Paul as speaking of Israel nationally and of **the Gentiles** as such. He is not speaking of the church of God; otherwise we face the possibility of the church's being cut off (11:22), and this is unscriptural.

Since Paul was **an apostle to the Gentiles**, it was quite natural for him to speak to them very candidly. In doing so, he was only fulfilling his **ministry**.

11:14 He sought by every **means** to **provoke to jealousy those who** were his countrymen, so that he might be used to **save some of them**. He knew and we know that he himself couldn't save anyone. But the God of salvation identifies Himself so closely with His servants that He permits them to speak of their doing what only He can do.

11:15 This verse repeats the argument of 11:12 in different language. When Israel was set aside as God's chosen, earthly people, the Gentiles were brought into a position of privilege with God and thus in a figurative sense were reconciled. When Israel is restored during the Millennial Reign of Christ, it will be like worldwide regeneration or resurrection.

This may be illustrated in the experience of Jonah, who was a figure of the nation of Israel. When Jonah was cast out of the boat during the storm, this resulted in deliverance or salvation for a boatload of Gentiles. But when Jonah was restored and preached to Nineveh, it resulted in salvation for a city full of Gentiles. So Israel's temporary rejection by God has resulted in the gospel going out to a handful of Gentiles, comparatively speaking. But when Israel is restored, vast hordes of Gentiles will be ushered into the kingdom of God.

11:16 Now Paul employs two metaphors. The first has to do with **the firstfruit** and **the lump**, the second with **the root** and **the branches**. **The firstfruit** and **the lump** speak of dough, not of fruit. In Numbers 15:19–21 we read that a piece of dough was consecrated to the Lord as a heave offering. The argument is that if the piece of dough is set apart to the Lord, so is all the dough that might be made from it.

As for the application, the **firstfruit** is Abraham. He was **holy** in the sense that he was set apart by God. If this was true of him, it is true of his chosen posterity. They are set apart to a position of external privilege before God.

The second metaphor is **the root** and **the branches**. **If the root is** set apart, **so are the branches**. Abraham is **the root** in the sense that he was the first to be set apart by God to form a new society, distinct from the nations. If Abraham

was set apart, so are those who are descended from him in the chosen line.

11:17 The apostle continues the metaphor of **the root** and **the branches**.

The branches that **were broken off** picture the unbelieving portion of the twelve tribes of Israel. Because of their rejection of the Messiah, they were removed from their place of privilege as God's chosen people. But only **some of the branches were** removed. A remnant of the nation, including Paul himself, had received the Lord.

The **wild olive tree** refers to the Gentiles, viewed as one people. They were **grafted in** to the olive tree.

With them the Gentiles partook of the root and fatness of **the olive tree**. The Gentiles share the position of favor that had originally been given to Israel and is still held by the believing remnant of Israel.

In this illustration it is important to see that the main trunk of **the olive tree** is *not Israel*, but rather God's line of *privilege* down through the centuries. If the trunk were Israel, then you would have the bizarre picture of Israel being broken off from Israel and then grafted back into Israel again.

It is also important to remember that **the wild olive** branch is *not the church* but the Gentiles viewed collectively. Otherwise you face the possibility of true believers being cut off from God's favor. Paul has already shown that this is impossible (Rom. 8:38, 39).

When we say that the trunk of the tree is the line of privilege down through the centuries, what do we mean by "line of privilege"? God decided to set apart a certain people to occupy a special place of nearness to Himself. They would be set apart from the rest of the world and would have special privileges. They would enjoy what we today might call the "favored-nation status." In the different ages of history, He would have a special inner circle.

The nation of Israel was the first to be in this line of privilege. They were God's ancient, chosen, earthly people. Because of their rejection of the Messiah, **some of** these **branches were broken off** and thus lost their position of "favorite son." The Gentiles **were grafted** into the olive tree and became partakers with believing Jews **of the root and fatness**. The **root** points back to Abraham, with whom the line of privilege began. The **fatness** of an olive tree refers to its productivity — that is, to its rich crop of olives and oil derived from them. Here the **fatness** signifies the privileges that flowed from union with **the olive tree**.

11:18 But the Gentiles should **not** take a holier-than-thou attitude toward the Jews, or **boast** of any superiority. Any such boasting overlooks the fact that they didn't originate the line of privilege. Rather, it is the line of privilege that put them where they are, in a place of special favor.

11:19 Paul anticipates that the imaginary Gentile with whom he has been conversing **will say**, "Jewish **branches were broken off** so **that I** and other Gentile branches **might be grafted in.**"

11:20 The apostle admits that the statement is partially true. Jewish branches **were broken off**, and the Gentiles were grafted **in**. But it was because of the **unbelief** of Israel and not because the Gentiles had any special claim on God. The Gentiles were grafted in because, as a people, they stood **by faith**. This expression, **you stand by faith**, seems to indicate that Paul is speaking about true believers. But that is not necessarily the meaning. The only way in which the Gentiles stood **by faith** was that, comparatively speaking, they demonstrated more faith than the Jews did. Thus Jesus said to a Gentile centurion, "I have not found such great faith, not even in Israel" (Luke 7:9). And Paul later said to the Jews at Rome, "Therefore let it be known to you that the salvation of God has been sent to the Gentiles, and they will hear it!" (Acts 28:28). Notice, "they will hear it." As a people they are more receptive to the gospel today than Israel. To **stand** here is the opposite of to *fall*. Israel had fallen from its place of privilege. The Gentiles had been grafted into that place.

But let him who stands beware lest he fall. Gentiles should not be puffed up with pride **but** should rather **fear.**

11:21 **If God did not** hesitate to cut off **the natural branches** from the line of privilege, there is no reason to believe that **He** would **spare** the wild olive branches under similar circumstances.

11:22 So in the parable of the olive tree, we see two great contrasting facets of God's character — His **goodness and** His **severity**. His **severity** is manifest in the removal of Israel from the favored-nation status. His **goodness** is seen in His turning to the Gentiles with the gospel (see Acts 13:46; 18:6). But that **goodness** must not be taken for granted. The Gentiles too could **be cut off** if they do not maintain that relative openness which the Savior found during His earthly ministry (Matt. 8:10; Luke 7:9).

It must be constantly borne in mind that Paul is not speaking of the church or of individual believers. He is speaking about the Gentiles as such. Nothing can ever separate the Body of Christ from the Head, and nothing can separate a believer from the love of God, but the Gentile peoples can be removed from their present position of special privilege.

11:23 And Israel's severance need not be final. **If they** abandon their national **unbelief**, there is no reason why God cannot put them back into their original place of privilege. It would not be impossible for God to do this.

11:24 In fact, it would be a much less violent process for God to reinstate Israel as His privileged people than it was to put the Gentiles into that place. The people of Israel were the original branches in the tree of God's favor, and so they are called **natural branches**. The Gentile branches came from a **wild** olive tree. To graft a **wild** olive branch **into a cultivated olive tree** is an unnatural graft, or, as Paul says, it is **contrary to nature**. To graft natural branches **into** their original **cultivated olive tree** is a very natural process.

11:25 Now the apostle reveals that the future restoration of Israel is not only a possibility but is an assured fact. What Paul now reveals is a **mystery** — a truth hitherto unknown, a truth that could not be known by man's unaided intellect, but a truth that has now been made known. Paul sets it forth so that Gentile believers will not be **wise in** their **own opinion**, looking down their nationalistic noses at the Jews. **This mystery** is as follows:

Blindness in part has happened to Israel. It has not affected all the nation, but only the unbelieving segment.

That **blindness** is temporary. It will continue only **until the fullness of the Gentiles** arrives. **The fullness of the Gentiles** refers to the time when the last member will be added to the church, and when the completed Body of Christ will be raptured home to heaven. **The fullness of the Gentiles** must be distinguished from the *times* of the Gentiles (Luke 21:24). **The fullness of the Gentiles** coincides with the Rapture. The phrase "times of the Gentiles" refers to the entire period of Gentile domination over the Jews, beginning with the Babylonian captivity (2 Chron. 36:1–21) and ending with Christ's return to earth to reign.

11:26 While Israel's judicial blindness is removed at the time of the Rapture, that does not mean that all Israel will be saved right away. Jews will be converted throughout the Tribulation Period, but the entire elect remnant will not be saved until Christ returns to earth as King of kings and Lord of lords.

When Paul says that **all Israel will be saved**, he means **all** *believing* **Israel**. The unbelieving portion of the nation will be destroyed at the Second Advent of Christ (Zech. 13:8, 9). Only those who say "Blessed is He who comes in the name of the Lord" will be spared to enter the kingdom.

This is what Isaiah referred to when he spoke of the Redeemer coming to **Zion** and turning transgression away **from Jacob** (Isa. 59:20). Notice that it is not Christ's coming to Bethlehem, but His coming to **Zion** — that is, His Second Coming.

11:27 It is the same time referred to in Isaiah 27:9 and Jeremiah 31:33, 34, when God shall take away their sins under the terms of the New **Covenant.**

11:28 So we might summarize Israel's present status by saying first that **concerning the gospel they are enemies for your sake**. **They are enemies** in the sense of being cast off, set aside, alienated from God's favor so that the gospel might go forth to the Gentiles.

But that is only half the picture. **Concerning the election they are beloved for the sake of the fathers** — that is, Abraham, Isaac, and Jacob.

11:29 The reason they are still beloved is that God's **gifts** and **calling** are never rescinded. God does not take back His gifts. Once He has made an unconditional promise, He never goes back on it. He gave Israel the special privileges listed in 9:4, 5. He called Israel to be His earthly people (Isa. 48:12), separate from the rest of the nations. Nothing can change His purposes.

11:30 The Gentiles were **once** an untamed, **disobedient** people, but when Israel spurned the Messiah and the gospel of salvation, God turned to the Gentiles in **mercy**.

11:31 A somewhat similar sequence of events will occur in the future. Israel's disobedience will be followed by **mercy**, when they are provoked to jealousy **through the mercy shown** to the Gentiles. Some teach that it is through the Gentiles' showing mercy to the Jews that they will be restored, but we know that this is not so. Israel's restoration will be brought about by the Second Advent of the Lord Jesus (see 11:26, 27).

11:32 When we first read this verse, we might get the idea that God arbitrarily condemned both Jews and Gentiles to unbelief, and that there was nothing they could do about it. But that is not the thought. The unbelief was their own doing. What the verse is saying is this: having found both Jews and Gentiles disobedient, God is pictured as imprisoning them both in that condition, so that there would be no way out for them except on His terms.

This **disobedience** provided scope for God to **have mercy on all**, both Jews and Gentiles. There is no suggestion here of universal salvation. God has shown **mercy** to the Gentiles and will yet show **mercy** to the Jews also, but this does not insure the salvation of everyone. Here it is **mercy** shown along national lines. George Williams says:

> God having tested both the Hebrew and the Gentile nations, and both having broken down under the test, He shut them up in unbelief so that, being manifestly without merit, and having by demonstration forfeited all claims and all rights to divine favor, He might, in the unsearchable riches of His grace, have mercy upon them all.[44]

11:33 This concluding doxology looks back over the entire Epistle and the divine wonders that have been unfolded.

Paul has expounded the marvelous plan of salvation by which a just God can save ungodly sinners and still be just in doing so. He has shown how Christ's work brought more glory to God and more blessing to men than Adam lost through his sin. He has explained how grace produces holy living in a way that law could never do. He has traced the unbreakable chain of God's purpose from foreknowledge to eventual glorification. He has set forth the doctrine of sovereign election and the companion doctrine of human responsibility. And he has traced the justice and harmony of God's dispensational dealings with Israel and the nations. Now nothing could be more appropriate than to burst forth in a hymn of praise and worship.

Oh, the depth of the riches both of the wisdom and knowledge of God!

The **riches** of God! He is rich in mercy, love, grace, faithfulness, power, and goodness.

The **wisdom** of God! His **wisdom** is infinite, unsearchable, incomparable, and invincible.

The **knowledge of God!** "God is omniscient," writes Arthur W. Pink, "He knows everything: everything possible, everything actual; all events, all creatures, of the past, the present, and the future."[45]

His decisions are **unsearchable**: they are too deep for mortal minds to fully understand. The **ways** in which He arranges creation, history, redemption, and providence are beyond our limited comprehension.

11:34 No created being can know **the mind of the LORD,** except to the extent that He chooses to reveal it. And even then we see in a mirror, dimly (1 Cor. 13:12). No one is qualified to advise God. He doesn't need our counsel, and wouldn't profit by it anyway (see Isa. 40:13).

11:35 No one has ever made God obligated to him (see Job 41:11). What gift of ours would ever put the Eternal in a position where He had to repay?

11:36 The Almighty is self-contained. He is the source of every good, He is the active Agent in sustaining and controlling the universe, and He is the Object for which everything has been created. Everything is designed to bring **glory** to Him.

Let it be so! **To** Him **be glory forever. Amen.**

III. DUTIFUL: THE GOSPEL LIVED OUT (Chaps. 12–16)

The rest of Romans answers the question: *How should those who have been justified by grace respond in their everyday lives?* Paul takes up our duties toward other believers, toward the community, toward our enemies, toward the government, and toward our weaker brothers.

A. In Personal Consecration (12:1, 2)

12:1 Serious and devout consideration of **the mercies of God**, as they have been set forth in chapters 1–11, leads to only one conclusion — we should **present** our **bodies** as **a living sacrifice, holy, acceptable to God**. Our **bodies** stand for all our members and, by extension, our entire lives.

Total commitment is our **reasonable service**. It is our **reasonable service** in this sense: if the Son of God has died for me, then the least I can do is live for Him. "If Jesus Christ be God and died for me," said the great British athlete C. T. Studd, "then no sacrifice can be too great for me to make for him."[46] Isaac Watts' great hymn says the same thing: "Love so amazing, so divine, demands my heart, my life, my all."

Reasonable service may also be translated "spiritual worship." As believer-priests, we do not come to God with the bodies of slain animals but with the spiritual sacrifice of yielded lives. We also offer to Him our service (Rom. 15:16), our praise (Heb. 13:15), and our possessions (Heb. 13:16).

12:2 Secondly, Paul urges us **not** to **be conformed to this world**, or as Phillips paraphrases it: "Don't let the world around you squeeze you into its own mold." When we come to the kingdom of God, we should abandon the thought-patterns and lifestyles of the world.

The **world** (literally *age*) as used here means the society or system that man has built in order to make himself happy without God. It is a kingdom that is antagonistic to God. The god and prince of this world is Satan (2 Cor. 4:4; John 12:31; 14:30; 16:11). All unconverted people are his subjects. He seeks to attract and hold people through the lust of the eyes, the lust of the flesh, and the pride of life (1 Jn. 2:16). The world has its own politics, art, music, religion, amusements, thought-patterns, and lifestyles, and it seeks to get everyone to conform to its culture and customs. It hates nonconformists — like Christ and His followers.

Christ died to deliver us from **this world**. The world is crucified to us, and we are crucified to the world. It would be absolute disloyalty to the Lord for believers to love the world. Anyone who loves the world is an enemy of God.

Believers are not of the world any more than Christ is of the world. However, they are sent into the world to testify that its works are evil and that salvation is available to all who put their faith in the Lord Jesus Christ. We should not only be separated from the world; we should **be transformed by the renewing of** our **mind**, which means that we should think the way God thinks, as revealed in the Bible. Then we can experience the direct guidance of God in our lives. And we will find that, instead of being distasteful and hard, His **will** is **good and acceptable and perfect**.

Here, then, are three keys for knowing God's will. The *first* is a yielded body, the *second* a separated life, and the *third* a transformed mind.

B. In Serving through Spiritual Gifts (12:3–8)

12:3 Paul speaks here **through the grace** that was **given to** him as an apostle of the Lord Jesus. He is going to deal with various forms of straight and crooked thinking.

First he says that there is nothing in the gospel that would encourage anyone to have a superiority complex. He urges us to be humble in exercising our gifts. We should never have exaggerated ideas of our own importance. Neither should we be envious of others. Rather, we should realize that each person is unique and that we all have an important function to perform for our Lord. We should be happy with the place **God has dealt**

to us in the Body, and we should seek to exercise our gifts with all the strength that God supplies.

12:4 The human **body** has **many members**, yet each one has a unique role to play. The health and welfare of the body depend on the proper functioning of each member.

12:5 That is how it is in the **body of Christ**. There is unity (**one body**), diversity (**many**), and interdependency (**members of one another**). Any gifts we have are not for selfish use or display but for the good of the **body**. No gift is self-sufficient and none is unnecessary. When we realize all this, we are thinking soberly (12:3).

12:6 Paul now gives instructions for the use of certain **gifts**. The list does not cover all the **gifts**; it is meant to be suggestive rather than exhaustive.

Our **gifts** differ **according to the grace that is given to us**. In other words, God's **grace** deals out differing **gifts** to different people. And God gives the necessary strength or ability to use whatever **gifts** we have. So we are responsible to use these God-given abilities as good stewards.

Those who have the gift of **prophecy** should **prophesy in proportion to** their **faith**. A prophet is a spokesman for God, declaring the word of the Lord. Prediction may be involved, but it is not a necessary element of prophecy. In the early church, writes Hodge, the prophets were "men who spoke under the immediate influence of the Spirit of God, and delivered some divine communication relative to doctrinal truths, to present duty, to future events, as the case may be."[47] Their ministry is preserved for us in the NT. There can be no inspired, prophetic additions to the body of Christian doctrine today since the faith has been once for all delivered to the saints (see Jude 3). Thus a prophet today is simply one who declares the mind of God as it has been revealed in the Bible. Strong says:

All modern prophecy that is true is but the republication of Christ's message — the proclamation and expounding of truth already revealed in Scripture.[48]

Those of us who have the gift of

prophecy should **prophesy in proportion to our faith.** This may mean "according to the rule or norm of the faith" — that is, in accordance with the doctrines of the Christian faith as they are found in the Scriptures. Or it may mean "according to the proportion of our faith" — that is, to the extent that God gives us faith. Most versions supply the word "our" here, but it is not found in the original.[49]

12:7 Ministry is a very broad term meaning service for the Lord. It does not mean the office, duties, or functions of a clergyman (as commonly used today). The person who has the gift of **ministry** has a servant-heart. He sees opportunities to be of service and seizes them.

A *teacher* is one who is able to explain the word of God and apply it to the hearts of his hearers. Whatever our gift is, we should give ourselves to it wholeheartedly.

12:8 Exhortation is the gift of stirring up the saints to desist from every form of evil and to press on to new achievements for Christ in holiness and in service.

Giving is the divine endowment which inclines and empowers a person to be aware of needs and to help meet them. He should do so **with liberality**.

The gift of *leading* is almost certainly connected with the work of elders (and perhaps also deacons) in a local church. The elder is an undershepherd who stands out in front of the flock and leads **with** care and **diligence**.

The gift of **mercy** is the supernatural capacity and talent of aiding those who are in distress. Those who have this gift should exercise it **with cheerfulness**. Of course, we should all show mercy and do it cheerfully.

A Christian lady once said, "When my mother became old and needed someone to care for her, my husband and I invited her to come and live with us. I did all I could to make her comfortable. I cooked for her, did her washing, took her out in the car, and generally cared for all her needs. But while I was going through the motions outwardly, I was unhappy inside. Subconsciously I resented the interruption of our usual schedule. Sometimes my mother would say to me, 'You never smile anymore.

Why don't you ever smile?' You see, I was showing mercy, but I wasn't doing it with cheerfulness."

C. In Relation to Society (12:9–21)

12:9 Next Paul lists some characteristics that every believer should develop in his dealings with other Christians and with the unconverted.

Love should **be without hypocrisy**. It should not wear a mask, but should be genuine, sincere, and unaffected.

We should **abhor** all forms of **evil** and **cling to** everything **good**. In this setting **evil** probably means all attitudes and acts of unlove, malice, and hatred. **Good**, by contrast, means every manifestation of supernatural love.

12:10 In our relations with those who are in the household of faith, we should demonstrate our love by tender affection, not by cool indifference or routine acceptance.

We should prefer to see others honored rather than ourselves. Once a beloved servant of Christ was in a side room with other notables before a meeting. Several had already moved onto the platform before it was his turn. When he appeared at the door, thunderous applause broke out for him. He quickly stepped aside and applauded so that he would not share the honor that he sincerely thought was intended for others.

12:11 Moffatt's colorful translation of this verse is: "Never let your zeal flag, maintain the spiritual glow, serve the Lord." Here we are reminded of the words of Jeremiah 48:10: "A curse on him who is slack in doing the LORD'S work!" (NEB).

> 'Tis not for man to trifle; life is brief
>   And sin is here.
> Our age is but the falling of a leaf,
>   A dropping tear.
> We have not time to sport away
>   the hours;
> All must be earnest in a world like
>   ours.
>
> – *Horatius Bonar*

12:12 No matter what our present circumstances may be, we can and should rejoice **in** our **hope** — the coming of our Savior, the redemption of our bodies, and our eternal glory. We are exhorted to be **patient in tribulation** — that is, to bear up bravely under it. Such all-conquering endurance is the one thing which can turn such misery into glory. We should continue **steadfastly in prayer**. It is **in prayer** that the work is done and victories are won. **Prayer** brings power in our lives and peace to our hearts. When we pray in the Name of the Lord Jesus, we come the closest to omnipotence that it is possible for mortal man to come. Therefore we do ourselves a great disservice when we neglect to pray.

12:13 Needy **saints** are everywhere — the unemployed, those who have been drained by medical bills, forgotten preachers and missionaries in obscure places, and senior citizens whose resources have dwindled. True Body-life means sharing with those who are in need.

"Never grudging a meal or a bed to those who need them" (JBP). **Hospitality** is a lost art. Small homes and apartments are used as excuses for not receiving Christians who are passing through. Perhaps we do not want to face the added work and inconvenience. But we forget that when we entertain God's children, it is the same as if we were entertaining the Lord Himself. Our homes should be like the home in Bethany, where Jesus loved to be.

12:14 We are called to show kindness toward our persecutors instead of trying to repay them in kind. It requires divine life to repay unkindness and injury with a courtesy. The natural response is to curse and retaliate.

12:15 Empathy is the capacity for sharing vicariously the feelings and emotions of others. Our tendency is to be jealous when others rejoice, and to pass by when they mourn. God's way is to enter into the joys and sorrows of those around us.

12:16 To **be of the same mind toward one another** does not mean that we must see alike on nonessential matters. It is not so much uniformity of mind as harmony of relationships.

We should avoid any trace of snobbishness and should be as outgoing toward **humble**, lowly folk as toward those of wealth and position. When an illustrious Christian arrived at the terminal he was met by leaders from the church where he was to speak. The limousine

pulled up to take him to a plush hotel. "Who usually entertains visiting preachers here?" he asked. They mentioned an elderly couple in a modest home nearby. "That's where I would prefer to stay," he said.

Again, the apostle warns against a believer being **wise in** his **own opinion**. The realization that we have nothing that we did not receive should keep us from an inflated ego.

12:17 Repaying **evil for evil** is common practice in the world. Men speak of giving tit for tat, of repaying in kind, or of giving someone what he deserves. But this delight in vengeance should have no place in the lives of those who have been redeemed. Instead, they should act honorably in the face of abuse and injury, as in all the circumstances of life. To **have regard** means to *take thought for* or *be careful to do*.

12:18 Christians should not be needlessly provocative or contentious. The righteousness of God is not worked out by belligerence and wrath. We should love peace, make peace, and be at peace. When we have offended others, or when someone has offended us, we should work tirelessly for a peaceful resolution of the matter.

12:19 We must resist the tendency to avenge wrongs that are done to us. The expression **give place to wrath** may mean to allow *God* to take care of it for you, or it may mean to submit passively in a spirit of nonresistance. The rest of the verse favors the first interpretation — to stand back and let the **wrath** of God take care of it. **Vengeance is** God's prerogative. We should not interfere with what is His right. He will repay at the proper time and in the proper manner. Lenski writes:

> God has long ago settled the whole matter about exacting justice from wrongdoers. Not one of them will escape. Perfect justice will be done in every case and will be done perfectly. If any of us interfered, it would be the height of presumption.[50]

12:20 Christianity goes beyond non-resistance to active benevolence. It does not destroy its enemies by violence but converts them by love. It feeds the **enemy** when he **is hungry** and satisfies his thirst, thus heaping live **coals of fire**

on his head. If the live **coal** treatment seems cruel, it is because this idiomatic expression is not properly understood. To heap live **coals** on a person's head means to make him ashamed of his hostility by surprising him with unconventional kindness.

12:21 Darby explains the first part of this verse as follows: "If my bad temper puts you in a bad temper, you have been overcome of evil."[51]

The great black scientist, George Washington Carver, once said, "I will never let another man ruin my life by making me hate him."[52] As a believer he would not allow evil to conquer him.

But overcome evil with good. It is characteristic of Christian teaching that it does not stop with the negative prohibition but goes on to the positive exhortation. **Evil** can be overpowered **with good**. This is a weapon we should use more frequently.

Stanton treated Lincoln with venomous hatred. He said that it was foolish to go to Africa in search of a gorilla when the original gorilla could be found in Springfield, Illinois. Lincoln took it all in stride. Later Lincoln appointed Stanton as war minister, feeling that he was the most qualified for the office. After Lincoln was shot, Stanton called him the greatest leader of men. Love had conquered![53]

D. In Relation to Government (13:1–7)

13:1 Those who have been justified by faith are obligated to **be subject** to human government. Actually the obligation applies to everyone, but the apostle here is concerned especially with believers. God established human government after the flood when He decreed, "Whoever sheds man's blood, by man his blood shall be shed" (Gen. 9:6). That decree gave authority to men to judge criminal matters and to punish offenders.

In every ordered society there must be authority and submission to that authority. Otherwise you have a state of anarchy, and you cannot survive indefinitely under anarchy. Any government is better than no government. So God has instituted human government, and no government exists apart from His

will. This does not mean that He approves of all that human rulers do. He certainly does not approve of corruption, brutality, and tyranny! But the fact remains that **the authorities that exist are appointed by God**.

Believers can live victoriously in a democracy, a constitutional monarchy, or even a totalitarian regime. No earthly government is any better than the men who comprise it. That is why none of our governments is perfect. The only ideal government is a beneficent monarchy with the Lord Jesus Christ as King. It is helpful to remember that Paul wrote this section on subjection to human government when the infamous Nero was Emperor. Those were dark days for Christians. Nero blamed them for a fire which destroyed half the city of Rome (and which he himself may have ordered). He caused some believers to be immersed in tar, then ignited as living torches to provide illumination for his orgies. Others were sewn up in animal skins, then thrown to ferocious dogs to be torn to pieces.

13:2 And yet it still holds that anyone who disobeys or rebels against the government is disobeying and rebelling against what God has ordained. **Whoever resists** lawful **authority** earns and deserves punishment.

There is an exception, of course. A Christian is not required to obey if the government orders him to sin or to compromise his loyalty to Jesus Christ (Acts 5:29). No government has a right to command a person's conscience. So there are times when a believer must, by obeying God, incur the wrath of man. In such cases he must be prepared to pay the penalty without undue complaint. Under no circumstances should he rebel against the government or join in an attempt to overthrow it.

13:3 As a rule, people who do what is right need not fear the authorities. It is only those who break the law who have to fear punishment. So if anyone wants to enjoy a life free from tickets, fines, trials, and imprisonments, the thing to do is to be a law-abiding citizen. Then he will win the approval of the authorities, not their censure.

13:4 The ruler, whether president,

governor, mayor, or judge, is a **minister** of God in the sense that he is a servant and representative of the Lord. He may not know God personally, but he is still the Lord's man officially. Thus David repeatedly referred to the wicked King Saul as the Lord's anointed (1 Sam. 24:6, 10; 26:9, 11, 16, 23). In spite of Saul's repeated attempts on David's life, the latter would not allow his men to harm the king. Why? Because Saul was the king, and as such he was the Lord's appointee.

As servants of God, rulers are expected to promote the **good** of the people — their security, tranquility, and general welfare. If any man insists on breaking the law, he can expect to pay for it, because the government has the authority to bring him to trial and punish him. In the expression **he does not bear the sword in vain** we have a strong statement concerning the power which God vests in the government. **The sword** is not just an innocuous symbol of power; a scepter would have served that purpose. **The sword** seems to speak of the ultimate power of the ruler — that is, to inflict capital punishment. So it will not do to say that capital punishment was for the OT era only and not for the New. Here is a statement in the NT that implies that the government has the authority to take the life of a capital offender. People argue against this by quoting Exodus 20:13 in the KJV: "Thou shalt not kill." But that commandment refers to murder, and capital punishment is not murder. The Hebrew word translated "kill" in the KJV specifically means "murder" and is so translated in the NKJV: "You shall not murder."[54] Capital punishment was prescribed in the OT law as the required punishment for certain serious offenses.

Again the apostle reminds us that the ruler is **God's minister**, but this time he adds, **an avenger to execute wrath on him who practices evil**. In other words, in addition to being a **minister** of God to us **for good**, he also serves God by dispensing punishment to those who break the law.

13:5 What this means is that we should be obedient subjects of the government for two reasons — the fear of punishment and the desire to maintain a good **conscience**.

13:6 We owe the government not only obedience but financial support by paying **taxes**. It is to our advantage to live in a society of law and order, with police and fire protection, so we must be willing to bear our share of the cost. Government officials are giving their time and talents in carrying out God's will for the maintenance of a stable society, so they are entitled to support.

13:7 The fact that believers are citizens of heaven (Phil. 3:20) does not exempt them from responsibility to human government. They must pay whatever **taxes** are levied on their income, their real estate, and their personal property. They must pay required **customs** on merchandise being transported from one country to another. They must demonstrate a respectful **fear** of displeasing those who are charged with enforcing the laws. And they must show **honor** for the *names and offices* of all civil servants (even if they can't always respect their *personal* lives).

In this connection, Christians should never join in speaking in a derogatory way of the President or the Prime Minister. Even in the heat of a political campaign they should refuse to join in the verbal abuse that is heaped upon the head of state. It is written, "You shall not speak evil of a ruler of your people" (Acts 23:5).

E. In Relation to the Future (13:8–14)

13:8 Basically, the first part of this verse means "Pay your bills on time." It is not a prohibition against any form of debt. Some kinds of debt are inevitable in our society: most of us face monthly bills for telephone, gas, light, water, etc. And it is impossible to manage a business without contracting some debts. The admonition here is not to get into arrears (overdue accounts).

But in addition there are certain principles which should guide us in this area. We should not contract debts for nonessentials. We should not go into debt when there is no hope of repaying. We should avoid buying on the installment plan, incurring exorbitant interest charges. We should avoid borrowing to buy a product that depreciates in value. In general, we should practice financial responsibility by living modestly and within our means, always remembering that the borrower is slave to the lender (see Prov. 22:7).

The one debt that is always outstanding is the obligation to **love**. The word used for *love* in Romans, with only one exception (12:10), is *agapē*, which signifies a deep, unselfish, superhuman affection which one person has for another. This otherworldly **love** is not activated by any virtue in the person loved; rather, it is completely undeserved. It is unlike any other love in that it goes out not only to the lovable but to one's enemies as well.

This love manifests itself in giving, and generally in sacrificial giving. Thus, God so loved the world that He gave His only begotten Son. Christ loved the church and gave Himself for it.

It is primarily a matter of *the will* rather than the emotions. The fact that we are *commanded* **to love** indicates that it is something we can choose to do. If it were an uncontrollable emotion that swept over us at unexpected moments, we could scarcely be held accountable. This does not deny, however, that the emotions can be involved.

It is impossible for an unconverted person to manifest this divine love. In fact, it is impossible even for a believer to demonstrate it in his own strength. It can only be exhibited by the power of the indwelling Holy Spirit.

Love found its perfect expression on earth in the Person of the Lord Jesus Christ.

Our love to God manifests itself in obedience to His commandments.

The man **who loves** his neighbor **has fulfilled the law**, or at least that section of the law which teaches love for our fellowmen.

13:9 The apostle singles out those **commandments** which forbid acts of unlove against one's neighbor. They are **the commandments** against **adultery**, **murder**, theft, perjury, and coveting. Love doesn't exploit another person's body; immorality does. Love doesn't take another person's life; **murder** does. Love doesn't **steal** another person's property; theft does. Love doesn't deny justice to others; **false witness** does.[55]

Love doesn't even entertain wrong desires for another person's possessions; coveting does.

And if there is any other commandment. Paul could have mentioned one other: "Honor your father and your mother." They all boil down to the same dictum: **Love your neighbor as yourself**. Treat him with the same affection, consideration, and kindness that you treat yourself.

13:10 **Love** never seeks to **harm** another. Rather, it actively seeks the welfare and honor of all. Therefore the man who acts in love is really fulfilling the requirements of the second table of the **law**.

13:11 The rest of the chapter encourages a life of spiritual alertness and moral purity. The **time** is short. The Dispensation of Grace is drawing to a close. The lateness of the hour demands that all lethargy and inactivity be put away. **Our salvation is nearer than** ever. The Savior is coming to take us to the Father's house.

13:12 The present age is like a **night** of sin that has just about run its course. The **day** of eternal glory is about to dawn for believers. This means that we should **cast off** all the filthy garments of worldliness — that is, everything associated with unrighteousness and evil. And we should **put on the armor of light**, which means the protective covering of a holy life. The pieces of armor are detailed in Ephesians 6:14–18. They describe the elements of true Christian character.

13:13 Notice that the emphasis is on our practical Christian walk. Since we are children of the **day**, we should **walk** as sons of light. What does a Christian have to do with wild parties, drunken brawls, sex orgies, vile excesses, or even with bickering and envy? Nothing at all.

13:14 The best policy we can follow is, first of all, **to put on the Lord Jesus Christ**. This means that we should adopt His whole lifestyle, live as He lived, accept Him as our Guide and Example.

Secondly, we should **make no provision for the flesh, to fulfill its lusts. The flesh** here is the old, corrupt nature. It incessantly cries to be pampered with comfort, luxury, illicit sexual indulgence, empty amusements, worldly pleasures, dissipation, materialism, etc. We **make**

provision for the flesh when we buy things that are associated with temptation, when we make it easy for ourselves to sin, when we give a higher priority to the physical than to the spiritual. We should not indulge the flesh even a little. Rather, we should "give no chances to the flesh to have its fling" (JBP).

This was the very passage that God used in converting the brilliant but carnal Augustine to Christ and purity. When he reached verse 14 he surrendered to the Lord. He has been known in history ever since as "Saint" Augustine.

F. In Relation to Other Believers (14:1–15:13)

14:1 Romans 14:1–15:13 deals with important principles to guide God's people in dealing with matters of secondary importance. These are the things that so often cause conflict among believers, but such conflict is quite unnecessary, as we shall see.

A **weak** Christian is one who has unfounded scruples over matters of secondary importance. In this context, he was often a converted Jew who still had scruples about eating nonkosher foods or working on Saturday.

The first principle is this: a **weak** Christian should be received into the local fellowship, but **not** with the idea of engaging him in **disputes** about his ultra-scrupulousness. Christians can have happy fellowship without agreeing on nonessentials.

14:2 A believer who walks in full enjoyment of Christian liberty has faith, based on the teachings of the NT, that **all** foods are clean. They are sanctified by the word of God and prayer (1 Tim. 4:4, 5). A believer with a weak conscience may have qualms about eating pork, or any other meat, for that matter. He may be a vegetarian.

14:3 So *the second principle* is that there must be mutual forbearance. The mature Christian must not **despise** his weak brother. Neither should the weak brother **judge** as a sinner someone who enjoys ham, shrimp, or lobster. **God has received him** into His family, a member in good standing.

14:4 *The third principle* is that each believer is a **servant** of the Lord, and we have no right to sit in judgment, as if we were the master. It is before **his own Master** that each one stands approved or disapproved. One may look down on someone else with icy condescension, sure that he will make shipwreck of the faith because of his views on these matters. But such an attitude is wrong. **God** will sustain those on both sides of the question. His power to do so is adequate.

14:5 Some Jewish Christians still looked on the Sabbath as a day of obligation. They had a conscience about doing any work on Saturday. In that sense, they esteemed **one day above another**.

Other believers did not share these Judaistic scruples. They looked on **every day alike**. They did not look upon six days as secular and one as sacred. To them all days were sacred.

But what about the Lord's Day, the first day of the week? Does it not have a special place in the lives of Christians? We see in the NT that it was the day of our Lord's resurrection (Luke 24:1–9). On the next two Lord's days, Christ met with His disciples (John 20:19, 26). The Holy Spirit was given on the Day of Pentecost, which was on the first day of the week; Pentecost occurred seven Sundays after the Feast of Firstfruits (Lev. 23:15, 16; Acts 2:1), which symbolizes Christ's resurrection (1 Cor. 15:20, 23). The disciples gathered to break bread on the first day of the week (Acts 20:7). Paul instructed the Corinthians to take a collection on the first day of the week. So the Lord's Day does stand out in the NT in a special way. But rather than being a day of *obligation*, like the Sabbath, it is a day of *privilege*. Released from our ordinary employment, we can set it apart in a special way for worshiping and serving our Lord.

Nowhere in the NT are Christians ever told to keep the Sabbath. And yet at the same time we recognize the principle of one day in seven, one day of rest after six days of work.

Whatever view one holds on this subject, the principle is this: **let each be fully convinced in his own mind**. Now it should be clear that such a principle applies only to matters that are morally *neutral*. When it comes to *fundamental* doctrines of the Christian faith, there is no room for individual opinions. But in this area where things are neither right nor wrong in themselves, there is room for differing views. They should not be allowed to become tests of fellowship.

14:6 The one **who observes the day**, in this verse, is a Jewish believer who still has a bad conscience about doing any work on Saturday. It is not that he looks upon Sabbath-keeping as a means of obtaining or retaining salvation; it is simply a matter of doing what he thinks will please **the Lord**. Likewise, a person **who does not observe the day** does so to honor Christ, the substance, rather than the mere shadow of the faith (Col. 2:16, 17).

One who has liberty to eat nonkosher foods bows his head and **gives God thanks** for them. So does the believer with the weak conscience, who eats only kosher foods. Both ask the blessing from God.

In both cases **God** is honored and thanked, so why should this be made the occasion of strife and conflict?

14:7 The lordship of Christ enters into every aspect of a believer's life. We don't live to ourselves but to the Lord. We don't die to ourselves but to the Lord. It is true that what we do and say affects others, but that is not the thought here. Paul is emphasizing that the Lord should be the goal and object of the lives of His people.

14:8 Everything we do in life is subject to Christ's scrutiny and approval. We test things by how they appear in His presence. Even in death we aspire to glorify the Lord as we go to be with Him. Both in life and in death we belong to Him.

14:9 One of the reasons for which **Christ died and rose and lived again** is **that He might be** our **Lord**, and that we might be His willing subjects, gladly rendering to Him the devotion of our grateful hearts. His lordship continues even in death, when our bodies lie in the grave and our spirits and souls are in His presence.

14:10 Because this is true, it is folly for an overscrupulous Jewish Christian to condemn the **brother** who doesn't keep the Jewish calendar and who doesn't limit himself to kosher foods. Likewise, it is wrong for the strong brother to **show contempt** to the weak **brother**. The fact is that every one of us

is going to **stand before the judgment seat of Christ**,[56] and that will be the only evaluation that really counts.

This judgment has to do with a believer's service, not his sins (1 Cor. 3:11–15). It is a time of review and reward, and is not to be confused with the Judgment of the Gentile nations (Matt. 25:31–46) or the Judgment of the Great White Throne (Rev. 20:11–15). The latter is the final judgment of all the wicked dead.

14:11 The certainty of our appearance before the *bēma* of Christ is reinforced by a quotation from Isaiah 45:23, where Jehovah Himself makes a strong affirmation that **every knee shall bow** before Him in acknowledgement of His supreme authority.

14:12 **So then** it is clear that we will all **give** an **account of** *ourselves*, not of our brothers, **to God**. We judge one another too much, and without the proper authority or knowledge.

14:13 Instead of sitting in judgment on our fellow Christians in these matters of moral indifference, we should **resolve** that we will never do anything to hinder a brother in his spiritual progress. None of these nonessential matters is important enough for us to cause a brother to stumble or **to fall.**

14:14 Paul knew, and we know, that no foods are ceremonially **unclean** any longer, as they were for a Jew living under the law. The food we eat is sanctified by the word of God and prayer (1 Tim. 4:5). It is sanctified by the word in the sense that the Bible distinctly sets it apart as being good. It is sanctified by prayer when we ask God to bless it for His glory and for the strengthening of our bodies in His service. But if a weak brother thinks it is wrong for him to eat pork, for example, then it is wrong. To eat it would be to violate his God-given conscience.

When Paul says here **that there is nothing unclean of itself**, we must realize that he is speaking *only* of these *indifferent* matters. There are plenty of things in life that are unclean, such as pornographic literature, suggestive jokes, dirty movies, and every form of immorality. Paul's statement must be understood in the light of the context. Christians do not contact ceremonial defilement by eating foods which the Law of Moses branded unclean.

14:15 When I sit down to eat with a weak **brother**, should I insist on my legitimate right to eat Crab Louis or Lobster Thermidor, even if I know he thinks it is wrong? If I do, I am not acting **in love**, because love thinks of others, not of self. Love foregoes its legitimate rights in order to promote the welfare of a brother. A dish of food isn't as important as the spiritual well-being of **one for whom Christ died**. And yet if I selfishly parade my rights in these matters, I can do irreparable damage in the life of a weak brother. It isn't worth it when you remember that his soul was redeemed at such a towering cost — the precious blood of the Lamb.

14:16 So the principle here is that we should not allow these secondary things, which are perfectly permissible in themselves, to give occasion to others to condemn us for our "looseness" or "lovelessness." It would be like sacrificing our good name for a mess of pottage.

14:17 What really counts in **the kingdom of God** is not dietary regulations but spiritual realities. **The kingdom of God** is the sphere where God is acknowledged as Supreme Ruler. In its widest sense, it includes all who even *profess* allegiance to God. But in its inward reality it includes only those who are born again. That is its usage here.

The subjects of the kingdom are not intended to be food faddists, gourmets, or wine connoisseurs. They should be characterized by lives of practical **righteousness**, by dispositions of **peace** and harmony, and by mind-sets of **joy in the Holy Spirit**.

14:18 It isn't what a man eats or doesn't eat that matters. It is a holy life that wins God's honor and man's approval. Those who put the emphasis on righteousness, peace, and joy serve **Christ** by obeying His teachings.

14:19 Thus *another principle* emerges. Instead of bickering over inconsequential matters, we should make every effort to maintain **peace** and harmony in the Christian fellowship. Instead of stumbling others by insisting on our rights, we should strive to build up others in their most holy faith.

14:20 **God** is doing a **work** in the life of each one of His children. It is frightening to think of hindering that work in the life of a weak brother over such secondary matters as **food**, drink, or days. For the child of God, all foods are now clean. But it would be wrong for him to eat any specific food if, in doing so, he would offend a brother or stumble him in his Christian walk.

14:21 It is a thousand times better to refrain from **meat** or **wine** or **anything** else than to offend a **brother** or cause him to decline spiritually. Giving up our legitimate rights is a small price to pay for the care of one who is **weak**.

14:22 I may have complete liberty to partake of every kind of food, knowing that God gave it to be received with thanksgiving. But I should not needlessly flaunt that liberty before those who are weak. It is better to exercise that liberty in private, when no one could possibly be offended.

It is good to walk in the full enjoyment of one's Christian liberty, not being fettered by unwarranted scruples. But it is better to forego one's legitimate rights than have to condemn oneself for offending others. One who avoids stumbling others is the **happy** person.

14:23 As far as the weak brother is concerned, it is wrong for him to eat anything about which he has conscientious scruples. His eating is not an act of **faith**; that is, he has a bad conscience about it. And it is a **sin** to violate one's conscience.

It is true that a person's conscience is not an infallible guide; it must be educated by the word of God. But, writes Merrill Unger, "Paul lays down the law that a man should follow his conscience, even though it be weak; otherwise moral personality would be destroyed."[57]

15:1 The first thirteen verses of chapter 15 continue the subject of the previous chapter, dealing with matters of moral indifference. Tensions had arisen between the converts from Judaism and those from paganism, so Paul here pleads for harmonious relations between these Jewish and Gentile Christians.

Those **who are strong** (that is, with full liberty regarding things that are morally indifferent) are **not to please** themselves by selfishly asserting their rights.

Rather, they should treat their **weak** brothers with kindness and consideration, making full allowance for their excessive **scruples**.

15:2 Here the principle is this: don't live to please self. Live to **please** your **neighbor**, to do him **good**, to build him up. This is the Christian approach.

15:3[†] **Christ** has given us the example. He lived to please His Father, not Himself. He said, **"The reproaches of those who reproached You fell on Me"** (Ps. 69:9). This means that He was so completely taken up with God's honor that when men insulted God He took it as a personal insult to Himself.

15:4 This quotation from the Psalms reminds us that the OT Scriptures **were written for our learning**. While they were not written directly *to* us, they contain invaluable lessons **for** us. As we encounter problems, conflicts, tribulations, and troubles, the Scriptures teach us to be steadfast, and they impart **comfort**. Thus, instead of sinking under the waves, we are sustained by the **hope** that the Lord will see us through.

15:5 This consideration leads Paul to express the wish that **the God** who gives steadfastness and **comfort** will enable the strong and the weak, Gentile and Jewish Christians, to live harmoniously **according to** the teaching and example of **Christ Jesus**.

15:6 The result will be that the saints will be united in the worship of **the God and Father of our Lord Jesus Christ**. What a picture! Saved Jews and saved Gentiles worshiping the Lord with **one mouth**!

There are four mentions of the **mouth** in Romans, forming a biographical outline of a "well-saved soul." At the beginning, his mouth was full of cursing and bitterness (3:14). Then his mouth was stopped, and he was brought in guilty before the Judge (3:19). Next he confesses with his mouth Jesus as Lord (10:9). And finally his **mouth** is actively praising and worshiping the Lord (15:6).

15:7 One more principle emerges from all this. In spite of any differences that might exist concerning secondary matters, we should **receive one another, just as Christ also received us**. Here is the true basis for reception in the local assembly. We do not receive on the basis

of denominational affiliation, spiritual maturity, or social status. We should **receive** those whom **Christ** has **received**, in order to promote the **glory of God**.

15:8 In the next six verses the apostle reminds his readers that the ministry of **Jesus Christ** includes Jews and Gentiles, and the implication is that our hearts should also be big enough to include both. Certainly Christ came to serve **the circumcision** — that is, the Jewish people. God had repeatedly promised that He would send the Messiah to Israel, and Christ's coming confirmed the truth of those **promises**.

15:9 But Christ brings blessings to **the Gentiles** also. God purposed that the nations should hear the gospel, and that those people who believe should **glorify God for His** great **mercy**. This should not come as a surprise to Jewish believers, because it is frequently foretold in their Scriptures. In Psalm 18:49, for example, David anticipates the day when the Messiah will **sing** praise to God in the midst of a host of Gentile believers.

15:10 In Deuteronomy 32:43 the Gentiles are pictured as rejoicing in the blessings of salvation **with His people** Israel.

15:11 In Psalm 117:1 we hear Israel calling on the **Gentiles** to **praise the LORD** in the Millennial Reign of the Messiah.

15:12 Finally **Isaiah** adds his testimony to the inclusion of **the Gentiles** in the dominion of the Messiah (Isa. 11:1, 10). The particular point here is that **the Gentiles** would share in the privileges of the Messiah and His gospel.

The Lord Jesus is **a root of Jesse** in the sense that He is Jesse's Creator, not that He sprang from Jesse (though that *also* is true). In Revelation 22:16 Jesus speaks of Himself as the Root and Offspring of David. As to His deity, He is David's Creator; as to His humanity, He is David's descendant.

15:13 So Paul closes this section with a gracious benediction, praying that **the God** who gives good **hope** through grace will fill the saints **with all joy and peace** as they believe on Him. Perhaps he is thinking especially of Gentile believers here, but the prayer is suitable for all. And it is true that those who **abound in hope by the power of the Holy Spirit**

†See p. xxii.

have no time to quarrel over nonessentials. Our common hope is a powerful unifying force in the Christian life.

G. In Paul's Plans (15:14–33)

15:14 In the rest of chapter 15 Paul states his reason for writing to the Romans and his great desire to visit them.

Though he has never met the Roman Christians, he is **confident** that they will welcome his admonitions. This confidence is based on what he has heard of their **goodness**. In addition, he is assured of their **knowledge** of Christian doctrine, which qualifies them **to admonish** others (NKJV mg.).

15:15 In spite of his confidence in their spiritual progress, and in spite of the fact that he was a stranger to them, Paul didn't hesitate to remind them of some of their privileges and responsibilities. His frankness in writing as he did arose from **the grace given to** him **by God** — that is, **the grace** that appointed him as an apostle.

15:16 He was appointed by God to be a sort of serving-priest **of Jesus Christ to the Gentiles**. He looked upon his work of **ministering the gospel of God** as a priestly function in which he presented saved **Gentiles** as an **acceptable offering** to God because they had been set apart **by the Holy Spirit** to God through the new birth. G. Campbell Morgan exults:

> What a radiant light this sheds on all our evangelistic and pastoral effort! Every soul won by the preaching of the gospel is not only brought into a place of safety and of blessing; he is an offering to God, a gift which gives Him satisfaction, the very offering He is seeking. Every soul carefully and patiently instructed in the things of Christ, and so made conformable to His likeness, is a soul in whom the Father takes pleasure. Thus we labor, not only for the saving of men, but for the satisfying of the heart of God. This is the most powerful motive.[58]

15:17 If Paul engages in boasting, it is not in his own person that he glories, but **in Christ Jesus**. And it is not in his own accomplishments but in what **God** has been pleased to do through him. A humble servant of Christ does not engage in unseemly boasting, but rather he is conscious of the fact that God is using

him to accomplish His purposes. Any temptation to pride is tempered by the realization that he is nothing in himself, that he has nothing except what he has received, and that he can do nothing for Christ except by the power of the Holy Spirit.

15:18 Paul does **not** presume **to speak of** what **Christ** had done through the ministry of others. He confines himself to the way the Lord had used *him* to win **the Gentiles** to obedience, both by what he said and by what he did — that is, by the message he preached and by the miracles he performed.

15:19 The Lord confirmed the apostle's message by miracles that taught spiritual lessons and that inspired amazement, and by various manifestations of the Spirit's power. The result was that he had **fully preached the gospel**, beginning at **Jerusalem** and extending in a circle **to Illyricum** (north of Macedonia, on the Adriatic Sea). **From Jerusalem . . . to Illyricum** describes the *geographical* extent of his ministry and not the chronological order.

15:20 In following this route, Paul's **aim** was **to preach the gospel** in virgin territory. His audiences were composed primarily of Gentiles who had never heard of **Christ** before. Thus he was not building on anyone else's **foundation**. Paul's example in pioneering in new areas does not necessarily bind other servants of the Lord to this exact activity. Some are called to move in and teach, for example, after new churches have been planted.

15:21 This foundational work among the Gentiles was a fulfillment of Isaiah's prophecy (52:15) that the Gentiles who had never previously been evangelized would **see**, and that those who had never previously **heard** the good news would **understand** and respond in true faith.

15:22, 23 In his desire to plow untilled territory, Paul had been too occupied to get to Rome in the past. **But now** the foundation had been laid in the region described in 15:19. Others could build on the foundation. Paul was therefore free to fulfill his long-standing **desire** to visit Rome.

15:24 His plan was to stop off at Rome en route **to Spain**. He would not be able to stay long enough to enjoy all the fellowship with them that he would like, but his desire to **enjoy** their **company** would be partially satisfied at least. Then he knew that they would give whatever help was needed to complete his trip to Spain.

15:25 **But** in the meantime he was **going to Jerusalem** to deliver the funds which had been collected among Gentile churches for **the** needy **saints** in Judea. This is the collection that we read about in 1 Corinthians 16:1 and 2 Corinthians 8 and 9.

15:26, 27 The believers in **Macedonia and Achaia** had gladly contributed to a fund to relieve the distress among the **poor** Christians. This collection was completely voluntary on the part of the donors, and also quite appropriate for them to give. After all, they had benefited spiritually by the coming of the gospel to them through Jewish believers. So it was not too much to expect that they would share with their Jewish brethren **in material things**.

15:28, 29 As soon as Paul had **performed this** mission, delivering the funds as promised, he would visit Rome on his way **to Spain**. He had every confidence that his visit to Rome would be accompanied by **the fullness of the blessing of the gospel** which **Christ** always pours out when God's word is preached in the power of the Holy Spirit.

15:30 The apostle closes this section with a fervent appeal for their **prayers**. The basis on which he appeals is their mutual union with **the Lord Jesus Christ** and their **love** which came from **the** Holy **Spirit**. He asks them to agonize **in prayers to God for** him. As Lenski says, "This calls for prayers into which one puts his whole heart and soul as do the contestants in the arena."[59]

15:31 Four specific prayer requests are given. *First*, Paul asks for prayer that he will **be delivered from** zealots **in Judea who** were fanatically opposed to the gospel, just as he himself had once been.

Second, he wants the Romans to pray that the Jewish **saints** will accept the relief funds in good grace. Strong religious prejudices remained against Gentile believers and against those who preached to the Gentiles. Then there is always the possibility of people being offended at the idea of receiving "charity." It often takes more grace to be on the receiving end than on the giving end!

15:32 The *third* request was that the Lord might see fit to make the visit to Rome a joyful one. The words **by the will of God** express Paul's desire to be led by the Lord in all things.

Last of all, he asks that his visit might be one in which he **may be refreshed** in the midst of a tumultuous and fatiguing ministry.

15:33 And now Paul closes the chapter with the prayer that **the God** who is the source **of peace** might be their portion. In chapter 15 the Lord has been named *the God of patience* and *consolation* (v. 5), *the God of hope* (v. 13), and now **the God of peace**. He is the source of everything good and of everything a poor sinner needs now and eternally. **Amen.**

H. In Appreciative Recognition of Others (Chap. 16)

At first glance the closing chapter of Romans seems to be an uninteresting catalog of names that have little or no meaning for us today. However, upon closer study this neglected chapter yields many important lessons for the believer.

16:1 **Phoebe** is introduced as **a servant**[60] **of the church in Cenchrea**. We need not think of her as belonging to some special religious order. Any sister who serves in connection with a local assembly can be a "deaconess."

16:2 Whenever the early Christians traveled from one church to another, they carried letters of introduction. This was a real courtesy to the church being visited and a help to the visitor.

So the apostle here introduces Phoebe and asks that she be welcomed as a true believer **in a manner worthy of** fellow-believers. He further asks that she be assisted in every way possible. Her commendation is that she has given herself to the ministry of helping others, including Paul himself. Perhaps she was the tireless sister who was forever showing hospitality to preachers and other believers in Cenchrea.

16:3 Next Paul sends greetings to **Priscilla and Aquila**, who had been such valiant **fellow workers** of his **in** the service of **Christ Jesus**. How we can thank God for Christian couples who pour themselves out in sacrificial labor for the cause of Christ!

16:4 On one occasion Priscilla and Aquila actually **risked their** lives **for** Paul — a heroic act of which no details are given. But the apostle is grateful, and so are the **churches of** converted **Gentiles** to whom he ministered.

16:5 **Greet the church that is in their house**. This means that an actual congregation of believers met in their house. Church buildings were unknown until the late second century. Earlier, when Priscilla and Aquila lived in Corinth, they had a church in their house also.

Epaenetus means "praiseworthy." No doubt this first convert in the province of Achaia[61] was true to his name. Paul speaks of him as **my beloved.**

16:6 The prominence of women's names in this chapter emphasizes their wide sphere of usefulness (vv. 1, 3, 6, 12, etc.). **Mary** worked like a Trojan for the saints.

16:7 We do not know when **Adronicus and Junia** were **fellow prisoners** with Paul. We cannot be sure whether the word **countrymen** means that they were close relatives of the apostle or simply fellow Jews. Again, we do not know whether the expression **of note among the apostles** means that they were respected *by* the **apostles** or that they themselves were outstanding **apostles**. All we can know for certain is that they became Christians **before** Paul.

16:8 Next we meet **Amplias, beloved** by the apostle. We would never have heard of any of these people except for their connection with Calvary. That is the only greatness about any of us.

16:9 **Urbanus** wins the title **fellow worker**, and **Stachys** is called **my beloved**. Romans 16 is like a miniature of the Judgment Seat of Christ, where there will be praise for every instance of faithfulness to Christ.

16:10 **Apelles** had come through some great trial with flying colors and had won the seal of **approved in Christ**.

Paul greets **the household of Aristobulus**, probably meaning Christian slaves belonging to this grandson of Herod the Great.

16:11 **Herodion** was probably a slave also. A **countryman** of Paul, he may have been the only *Jewish* slave belonging to the household of Aristobulus.

Then some of the slaves belonging to **Narcissus** were also believers, and Paul includes them in his greetings. Even those who are lowest on the social ladder are not excluded from the choicest blessings of Christianity. The inclusion of slaves in this list of names is a lovely reminder that in Christ all social distinctions are obliterated because we are all one in Him.

16:12 **Tryphena** and **Tryphosa** had names that meant "dainty" and "luxurious," but they were veritable workhorses in their service for the Lord. **The beloved Persis** was another of those women workers that are so needed in local churches but seldom appreciated until they are gone.

16:13 **Rufus** may be the son of Simon, who carried the cross for Jesus (Matt. 27:32). He was **chosen in the Lord** not only as to his salvation but also as to his Christian character; that is, he was a choice saint. The **mother** of Rufus had shown maternal kindness to Paul, and this earned his affectionate title "my mother."

16:14, 15 Perhaps **Asyncritus, Phlegon, Hermas, Patrobas**, and **Hermes** were active in a house church, like the one in the house of Priscilla and Aquila (16:3, 5). **Philologus and Julia, Nereus and his sister, and Olympas** may have been the nucleus of another house church.

16:16 The **holy kiss** was the common mode of affectionate greeting among the saints then and is still practiced in some countries today. It is designated as a **holy kiss** to guard against impropriety. In our culture, the **kiss** is generally replaced by the handshake.

The churches in Achaia, where Paul was writing, joined in sending their greetings.

16:17 The apostle cannot close the letter without a warning against ungodly teachers who might worm their way into the church. The Christians should be on their guard against any such who form parties around themselves and set traps to destroy the faith of the unwary. They should be on the lookout for any whose teaching is **contrary to the** sound **doctrine** which the Christians had **learned**, and should **avoid them** completely.

16:18 These false teachers are not

obedient to **our Lord Jesus Christ**. They obey **their own** appetites. And they are all too successful in hoodwinking the unsuspecting by their winsome and **flattering speech.**

16:19 Paul was **glad** that his readers' **obedience** to the Lord was well-known. But still he wanted them to be able to discern and obey **good** teaching and to be unresponsive to **evil**.

16:20 In this way, **the God** who is the source **of peace** would give them a swift victory over **Satan**.

The apostle's characteristic benediction wishes all needed enablement for the saints as they journey toward glory.

16:21 We know **Timothy**, Paul's son in the faith and faithful co-worker. We know nothing of **Lucius** except that he, like Paul, was of Jewish parentage. We may have previously met **Jason** (Acts 17:5) and **Sosipater** (Acts 20:4), also Jews.

16:22 **Tertius** was the one to whom Paul had dictated **this epistle**. He takes the liberty of adding his personal well-wishes to the readers.

16:23 There are at least four men by the name of **Gaius** in the NT. This is probably the same one spoken of in 1 Corinthians 1:14. He was noted for his hospitality, not only to Paul but to any Christians who needed it. **Erastus** was **treasurer of the city** of Corinth. But was he the same person mentioned in Acts 19:22 and/or 2 Timothy 4:20? We cannot be sure. **Quartus** is mentioned simply as **a brother**, but after all, what an honor, what a dignity!

16:24 **The grace of our Lord Jesus Christ be with you all** is Paul's typical closing benediction. It is the same as v. 20b with the addition of **all**. As a matter of fact, in most manuscripts of Romans, this is the last verse, and the doxology in vv. 25-27 comes *after chapter 14*. The Alexandrian (NU) text omits v. 20. Both the benediction and the doxology are beautiful ways to end the book. And both end with **Amen**.

16:25 The Epistle closes with a doxology. It is addressed to the God **who is able** to make His people stand firm in accordance with the **gospel** which Paul preached and which he calls **my gospel**. There is only one way of salvation, of course; but it was entrusted to him as "the Apostle to the Gentiles", whereas Peter, for example, preached it to the Jews. It is the public heralding of the message about **Jesus Christ** concerning **the revelation** of a marvelous truth **kept secret since the world began**. A **mystery**, in the NT is a truth never previously known, and a truth which human intellect could never discover, but one which has now been made known.

16:26 The particular mystery spoken of here is the truth that believing Jews and believing Gentiles are made fellow heirs, fellow members of the Body of Christ, and fellow partakers of His promise in Christ by the gospel (Eph. 3:6).

It **now has been made manifest** by the writing of the prophets — not the prophets of the OT but those of the NT period. It was unknown in the OT Scriptures but has been revealed in **the prophetic Scriptures** of the NT (see Eph. 2:20; 3:5).

It is the gospel message which God **has** commanded to be **made known to all nations** in order that people might obey **the faith** and be saved.

16:27 **God alone** is the source and display of pure wisdom, and to Him belongs **glory through Jesus Christ**, our Mediator, **forever**.

And so ends Paul's magnificent Epistle. How indebted we are to the Lord for it! And how poor we would be without it! **Amen.**

ENDNOTES

[1](1:4) Some commentators take "the Spirit of holiness" to refer to Christ's own holy being, i.e., His own human spirit.

[2](1:29) It is easy to see how some mss. copyists could delete *sexual immorality* by mistake: in the Greek the word *porneia* looks so much like the next word *ponēria* (evil).

[3](1:31) Verse 31 contains five negative words beginning with "alpha-privative" (cf. a-theist, "no God"), similar in word structure to our English words beginning with "un-". NU omits *unforgiving* (*aspondous*) which looks much like *unloving* (*astorgous*).

[4](2:4) A. P. Gibbs, *Preach and Teach the Word*, p. 12/4.

[5](2:6) Lewis S. Chafer, *Systematic Theology*, III:376.

[6](3:22) NU text omits "and on all."

[7](3:23) Literally "sinned" (aorist, not perfect).

[8](Excursus) The same is true in Hebrew and Greek.

[9](3:24) Arthur T. Pierson, *Shall We Continue in Sin?* p. 23.

[10](3:24) Paul Van Gorder, in *Our Daily Bread*.

[11](3:30) Cranfield points out (*Romans*, I: 222) that attempts to find a very subtle difference are not convincing. Augustine was probably correct in ascribing the change to rhetorical variety.

[12](4:1) Or the experience of "Abraham our (fore)father according to the flesh."

[13](4:13) *Daily Notes of the Scripture Union*, (further documentation unavailable).

[14](4:19) While some manuscripts omit "not," the resultant meaning is much the same.

[15](4:24) C. H. Mackintosh, *The Mackintosh Treasury: Miscellaneous Writings by C. H. Mackintosh*, p. 66.

[16](5:11) The KJV rendering "atonement" was correct in 1611, when it meant "at-one-ment" or reconciliation.

[17](6:1) J. Oswald Sanders, *Spiritual Problems*, p. 112.

[18](6:5) Charles Hodge, *The Epistle to the Romans*, p. 196.

[19](6:11) Ruth Paxson, *The Wealth, Walk, and Warfare of the Christian*, p. 108.

[20](6:11) C. E. Macartney, *Macartney's Illustrations*, pp. 378, 379.

[21](6:14) James Denney, "St. Paul's Epistle to the Romans," *The Expositor's Greek Testament*, II:635.

[22](6:19) Charles Gahan, *Gleanings in Romans, in loco.*

[23](6:21) Marcus Rainsford, *Lectures on Romans VI*, p. 172.

[24](6:21) Pierson, *Shall We Continue in Sin?* p. 45.

[25](7:15) Harry Foster, article in *Toward the Mark*, p. 110.

[26](7:23) George Cutting, "The Old Nature and the New Birth" (booklet), p. 33.

[27](8:1) The words "who do not walk according to the flesh, but according to the Spirit" are widely thought to be miscopied from v. 4. However, they do occur in most mss., and may simply give further description of those in Christ.

[28](8:10) The NKJV translators took *pneuma* to refer to the *Holy* Spirit, hence the capital "S". The original mss. were in all "capitals" (uncials), so it is a matter of interpretation. We take it as referring to the believer's (human) spirit.

[29](8:15) See note 28. Here the alternative meaning of Spirit is not the *human* spirit, but an attitude that is the opposite of slavery.

[30](8:18) In Hebrew, the word for *glory* is derived from the verb *to be heavy*, hence the Jews would see a play on words, even though veiled by the Greek.

[31](8:31) This was John Calvin's life verse.

[32](8:32) C. H. Mackintosh (further documentation unavailable).

[33](8:37) A very literal rendering is "we super-conquer" (*hupernikōmen*).

[34](8:39) These words were used in astrology, for example.

[35](9:4) *The New Scofield Reference Bible*, p. 1317.

[36](9:5) See Hodge, *Romans*, pp. 299–301 for a detailed exposition of this question.

[37](9:16) G. Campbell Morgan, *Searchlights from the Word*, pp. 335, 336.

[38](9:21) Albert Barnes, *Barnes's Notes on the New Testament*, p. 617.

[39](9:23) Charles R. Erdman, *The Epistle of Paul to the Romans*, p. 109.

[40](10:10) William Kelly, *Notes on the Epistle to the Romans*, p. 206.

[41](10:10) James Denney, quoted by Kenneth Wuest in *Romans in the Greek New Testament*, p. 178.

[42](10:14) Hodge, *Romans*, p. 545.

[43](11:1) It is sad to note that many who appropriate Israel's blessings for the church are quite satisfied to leave them the predicted curses!

[44](11:32) George Williams, *The Student's Commentary on the Holy Scriptures*, p. 871.

[45](11:33) Arthur W. Pink, *The Attributes of God*, p. 13.

[46](12:1) Norman Grubb, *C. T. Studd, Cricketer and Pioneer*, p. 141.

[47](12:6) Hodge, *Romans*, p. 613.

[48](12:6) A. H. Strong, *Systematic Theology*, p. 12.

[49](12:6) However, the definite article, used here in the original, practically

equals a pronoun in some contexts.

[50](12:19) R. C. H. Lenski, *St. Paul's Epistle to the Romans*, p. 780.

[51](12:21) J. N. Darby, from footnote on Romans 12:21 in his *New Translation*.

[52](12:21) George Washington Carver (further documentation unavailable).

[53](12:21) Quoted by Charles Swindoll in *Growing Strong in the Seasons of Life*, pp. 69, 70.

[54](13:4) The usual Hebrew verbs for "kill" and "slay" are *qātal* and *hārag*. The specific verb "murder" (*rāhats*) is used in the Ten Commandments, and the Greek translation is equally clear.

[55](13:9) NU text omits this commandment here.

[56](14:10) Some ancient mss. (NU) read "judgment seat of God" rather than "of Christ" (TR and M texts). But we know that *Christ* will be the Judge, since the Father has committed all judgment to Him (John 5:22).

[57](14:23) Merrill F. Unger, *Unger's Bible Dictionary*, p. 219.

[58](15:16) Morgan, *Searchlights*, p. 337.

[59](15:30) Lenski, *Romans*, p. 895.

[60](16:1) The feminine form of *diakonos* ("servant," "deacon") would probably have been used if a specific office for women had been meant.

[61](16:5) NU text reads *Asia* here (but Corinth, from which Paul was probably writing, was in *Achaia*).

BIBLIOGRAPHY

Cranfield, C. E. B. *The Epistle to the Romans, Vol. I (ICC)*, Edinburgh: T. & T. Clark Ltd., 1975.

Denney, James. "St. Paul's Epistle to the Romans," *The Expositor's Greek Testament, Vol. II.* Grand Rapids: Wm. B. Eerdmans Publishing Company, 1961.

Erdman, C. R. *The Epistle of Paul to the Romans.* Philadelphia: The Westminster Press, 1925.

Gahan, Charles. *Gleanings in Romans.* Published by author.

Hodge, Charles. *Commentary on the Epistle to the Romans.* New York: George H. Doran Company, 1886.

Kelly, William. *Notes on the Epistle to the Romans.* London: G. Morrish, 1873.

Lenski, R. C. H. *St. Paul's Epistle to the Romans.* Minneapolis: Augsburg Publishing House, 1961.

Newell, William R. *Romans Verse by Verse.* Chicago: Moody Press, 1938.

Rainsford, Marcus. *Lectures on Romans VI.* London: Charles J. Thynne, 1898.

Shedd, William G. T. *A Critical and Doctrinal Commentary on the Epistle of St. Paul to the Romans.* Grand Rapids: Zondervan, 1967.

Stifler, James M. *The Epistle to the Romans: A Commentary Logical and Historical.* Chicago: Moody Press, 1960.

Wuest, Kenneth S. *Romans in the Greek New Testament.* Grand Rapids: Wm. B. Eerdmans Publishing Company, 1964.

THE FIRST EPISTLE TO
THE CORINTHIANS

Introduction

"A fragment of ecclesiastical history like no other." — Weizäcker

I. Unique Place in the Canon

First Corinthians is the "problem book" in the sense that Paul handles the problems ("Now concerning . . .") that faced the congregation in the wicked city of Corinth. As such it is most needed by today's problem-racked churches. The divisions, hero-worship of leaders, immorality, legal battles, marital problems, doubtful practices, and regulation of spiritual gifts, are all handled here.

It would be wrong, however, to think it was all problems! This is the Epistle that contains 1 Corinthians 13, the most beautiful essay on love, not just in the Bible, but in *all* literature. The remarkable teaching on the resurrection — both Christ's and ours (chap. 15), the regulation of the Lord's Supper (chap. 11), the command to take part in the collection (chap. 16), are all here.

We would be very much the poorer without 1 Corinthians. It is a treasure trove of practical Christian teaching.

II. Authorship[†]

All scholars agree that what we call 1 Corinthians is an authentic product of Paul's pen. Some (chiefly liberal) writers think they see some "interpolations" in the letter, but these are subjective conjectures with no supporting manuscript evidence. 1 Corinthians 5:9 apparently implies a previous (uncanonical) letter from Paul that the Corinthians misunderstood.

The *external evidence* for 1 Corinthians is very early, the book being specifically referred to by Clement of Rome (c. A.D. 95) as "the Epistle of the blessed Apostle Paul." Other early church writers quoting the book are Polycarp, Justin Martyr, Athenagoras, Irenaeus, Clement of Alexandria, and Tertullian. It is listed in the Muratorian Canon and comes after Galatians in the heretic Marcion's own "canon," the *Apostolicon*.

The *internal evidence* is very strong as well. Besides the author's references to himself as Paul in 1:1 and 16:21, the argument in 1:12–17; 3:4, 6, 22 also supports Pauline authorship. Coincidences with Acts and with other letters of Paul, plus the strong flavor of genuine apostolic concern rule out a forgery and make the arguments for authenticity overwhelming.

III. Date

Paul tells us he is writing from Ephesus (16:8, 9, cf. v. 19). Since he ministered there for three years, 1 Corinthians was most likely written in the latter half of that extended ministry, or about A.D. 55 or 56. Some scholars date it even earlier.

IV. Background and Theme[††]

Ancient Corinth was (and is) in southern Greece, west of Athens, strategically situated on the trade routes in Paul's day. It became a great center for international commerce, and immense quantities of traffic came to this city. Because of the depraved religion of the people, it soon became the center also for the grossest forms of immorality, so that the name Corinth was a byword for

†See p. i.
††See p. ii.

all that was impure and sensual. So lewd was the city's reputation, there was even a verb coined, *korinthiazomai*, which meant *to lead a debased life*.

The Apostle Paul first visited Corinth on his Second Missionary Journey (Acts 18). At first he labored among the Jewish people, together with Priscilla and Aquila, his fellow tentmakers. When most Jews rejected his message, he turned to the Gentiles in Corinth. Souls were saved through the preaching of the gospel, and a church was formed.

About three years later, when Paul was preaching in Ephesus, he received a letter from Corinth, telling of serious difficulties in the assembly there and also asking various questions as to matters of Christian practice. It was in answer to this letter that the First Epistle to the Corinthians was written.

The theme of the Epistle is how to set right a worldly and carnal church that regards lightly the attitudes, errors, and actions that the Apostle Paul viewed with such alarm. As Moffatt put it so succinctly, "The Church was in the world, as it had to be, but the world was in the Church, as it ought not to be."

Since such a situation is still common in many congregations, the relevance of 1 Corinthians is lasting.

OUTLINE

Commentary

I. INTRODUCTION (1:1–9)

A. Salutation (1:1–3)

1:1 **Paul** was **called to be an apostle of Jesus Christ** on the Damascus road. This call did not come from or through men, but directly from the Lord Jesus. **An apostle** is literally "a sent one." The first apostles were witnesses of Christ in resurrection. They also could perform miracles to confirm that the message they preached was divine. Paul could truly say in the language of Gerhard Tersteegen:

> Christ the Son of God has sent me
> To the midnight lands;
> Mine the mighty ordination
> Of the piercèd hands.

When Paul wrote, a **brother** named **Sosthenes** was with him, so Paul includes his name in the salutation. It cannot be known for sure whether this is the same Sosthenes as in Acts 18:17, the ruler of the synagogue who was publicly beaten by the Greeks. Possibly this leader had been saved through Paul's preaching and was now helping him in the work of the gospel.

1:2 The letter is addressed first of all **to the church of God which is at Corinth**. It is encouraging that there is no place on earth too immoral for an assembly belonging to God to be established. The Corinthian congregation is further described as **those who are sanctified in Christ Jesus, called . . . saints. Sanctified** here means set apart to God from the world, and describes the *position* of all who belong to Christ. As to their *practical condition*, they should set themselves apart day by day in holy living.

Some people contend that sanctification is a distinct work of grace whereby a person obtains the eradication of the sin nature. Such a teaching is contradicted in this verse. The Corinthian Christians were far from what they should have been in practical holiness, but the fact remains that they were positionally **sanctified** by God.

As saints they were members of a great fellowship: **called to be saints, with all who in every place call on the name of Jesus Christ our Lord, both theirs and ours**. Although the teachings of this Epistle were first addressed to the saints in Corinth, they are also intended for all those of the worldwide fellowship who acknowledge the lordship of Christ.

1:3 First Corinthians is in a very special way the letter of His lordship. In discussing the many problems of assembly and personal life, the apostle constantly reminds his readers that Jesus Christ is Lord and that all we do should be done in acknowledgment of this great truth.

Paul's characteristic greeting is given in verse 3. **Grace and peace** summarize his entire gospel. **Grace** is the source of every blessing, and **peace** is the result in the life of a man who accepts the grace of God. These great blessings come **from God our Father and the Lord Jesus Christ**. Paul does not hesitate to mention **the Lord Jesus** in the same breath with **God our Father**. This is one of hundreds of similar expressions in the NT implying the equality of the Lord Jesus with God the Father.

B. Thanksgiving (1:4–9)

1:4 Having concluded his salutation, the apostle now turns to thanksgiving for the Corinthians and for the wonderful work of God in their lives (vv. 4–9). It was a noble trait in Paul's life that always sought to find something thankworthy in the lives of his fellow believers. If their practical lives were not very commendable, then he would at least **thank** his **God** for what He had done for them. This is exactly the case here. The Corinthians were not what we would call spiritual Christians. But Paul can at least give thanks **for the grace of God which was given to** them **by Christ Jesus.**

1:5 The particular way in which God's grace was manifested to the Corinthians was in their being richly endowed with gifts of the Holy Spirit. Paul specifies gifts of **utterance and all knowledge**, presumably meaning that the Corinthians had been given the gifts of tongues, interpretation of tongues, and knowledge to an extraordinary degree. **Utterance** has to do with outward expression and **knowledge** with inward comprehension.

1:6 The fact that they had these gifts was a confirmation of God's work in their lives, and that is what Paul means when he says, **even as the testimony of Christ was confirmed in you**. They heard **the testimony of Christ**, they received it by faith, and God testified that they were truly saved by giving them these miraculous powers.

1:7 As far as the possession of gifts was concerned, the Corinthian church was not inferior to any other. But the mere possession of these gifts was not in itself a mark of true spirituality. Paul was really thanking the Lord for something for which the Corinthians themselves were not directly responsible. Gifts are given by the ascended Lord without regard to a person's own merit. If a person has some gift, he should not be proud of it but use it humbly for the Lord.

The fruit of the Spirit is another matter entirely. This involves the believer's own surrender to the control of the Holy Spirit. The apostle could not commend the Corinthians for evidence of the fruit of the Spirit in their lives, but only for what the Lord had sovereignly bestowed on them — something over which they had no control.

Later in the Epistle the apostle will have to reprove the saints for their abuse of these gifts, but here he is content to express thanks that they had received these gifts in such unusual measure.

The Corinthians were **eagerly waiting for the revelation of our Lord Jesus Christ**. Bible students are not agreed as to whether this refers to Christ's coming for His saints (1 Thess. 4:13–18), or the Lord's coming with His saints (2 Thess. 1:6–10), or both. In the first case it would be a revelation of Christ only to believers, whereas in the second it would be His Revelation to the whole world. Both the Rapture and the glorious appearing of Christ are **eagerly** awaited by the believer.

1:8 Now Paul expresses the confidence that the Lord **will also confirm** the saints **to the end, that** they might **be blameless in the day of our Lord Jesus Christ**. Once again it is striking that Paul's thanksgiving is concerned with what God will do rather than with what the Corinthians have done. Because they have trusted Christ, and because God confirmed this fact by giving the gifts of the Spirit to them, Paul was confident that God would keep them for Himself until Christ's coming for His people.

1:9 Paul's optimism concerning the Corinthians is based on the faithfulness of **God** who called them **into the fellowship of His Son**. He knows that since God had gone to such tremendous cost

to make them sharers of the life of **our Lord**, He would never let them slip out of His hands.

II. DISORDERS IN THE CHURCH (1:10–6:20)

A. Divisions among Believers (1:10–4:21)

1:10 The apostle is now ready to take up the problem of **divisions** in the church (1:10–4:21). He begins with a loving exhortation to unity. Instead of commanding with the authority of an apostle, he pleads with the tenderness of a brother. The appeal for unity is based on **the name of our Lord Jesus Christ**, and since the name stands for the Person, it is based on all that the Lord Jesus is and has done. The Corinthians were exalting the name of men; that could only lead to divisions. Paul will exalt the name of the Lord Jesus, knowing that only in this way will unity be produced among the people of God. To **speak the same thing** means to be of **the same mind and** of one accord. It means to be united as to loyalty and allegiance. This unity is produced when Christians have the mind of Christ, and in the verses to follow, Paul will tell them in a practical manner how they can think Christ's thoughts after Him.

1:11 News concerning the **contentions** in Corinth had come to Paul from **Chloe's household**. In naming his informers, Paul lays down an important principle of Christian conduct. We should not pass on news about our fellow believers unless we are willing to be quoted in the matter. If this example were followed today, it would prevent most of the idle gossip which now plagues the church.

1:12 Sects or parties were being formed within the local church, each one claiming its distinctive leader. Some acknowledged preference for **Paul**, some for **Apollos**, some for **Cephas** (Peter). Some even claimed to belong to **Christ**, probably meaning that they *alone* belonged to Him, to the exclusion of others!

1:13 Paul's indignant rebuke of sectarianism is found in verses 13–17. To form such parties in the church was to deny the unity of the body of **Christ**. To follow human leaders was to slight the One who had been crucified for them. To take the name of a man was to forget that in baptism, they had acknowledged their allegiance to the Lord Jesus.

1:14 The rise of parties in Corinth made Paul thankful **that** he **had baptized** only a few in the assembly there. He mentions **Crispus and Gaius** as among those whom he had baptized.

1:15, 16 He would never want anyone to **say that** he **had baptized in** his **own name**. In other words, he was not trying to win converts to himself or to make a name for himself. His sole aim was to point men and women to the Lord Jesus Christ.

On further reflection Paul remembered that he had **also baptized the household of Stephanas**, but he could **not** think of **any other**.

1:17 He explains that **Christ did not send** him primarily **to baptize, but to preach the gospel**. This does not mean for a moment that Paul did not believe in baptism. He has already mentioned the names of some whom he *did* baptize. Rather, it means that his main business was not to baptize; he probably entrusted this work to others, perhaps to some of the Christians in the local church. This verse, however, does lend its testimony against any idea that baptism is essential to salvation. If that were true, then Paul would be saying here that he was thankful that he saved none of them except Crispus and Gaius! Such an idea is untenable.

In the latter part of verse 17, Paul is making an easy transition to the verses that follow. He did not **preach the gospel** by using **wisdom of words, lest the cross of Christ should be made of no effect**. He knew that if men were impressed by his oratory or rhetoric, then to that extent he had defeated himself in his efforts to set forth the true meaning of **the cross of Christ**.

It will help us to understand the section that follows if we remember that the Corinthians, being Greeks, were great lovers of human wisdom. They regarded their philosophers as national heroes. Some of this spirit had apparently crept into the assembly at Corinth. There were those who desired to make the gospel more acceptable to the intelligentsia. They did not feel that it had status among scholars, and so they wanted to intellectualize the message. This worship of intellectualism was apparently one of the issues that was causing the people to form parties around human leaders. Efforts to make the gospel more acceptable are completely misguided. There is a vast difference between God's wisdom and man's, and there is no use trying to reconcile them.

Paul now shows the folly of exalting men, and emphasizes that to do this is inconsistent with the true nature of the gospel (1:18–3:4). His first point is that the message of the cross is the opposite of all that men consider to be true wisdom (1:18–25).

1:18 **The message of the cross is foolishness to those who are perishing**. As Barnes so aptly stated:

> The death on the cross was associated with the idea of all that is shameful and dishonorable; and to speak of salvation only by the sufferings and death of a crucified man was fitted to excite in their bosoms only unmingled scorn.[1]

The Greeks were lovers of wisdom (the literal meaning of the word "philosophers"). But there was nothing in the gospel message to appeal to their pride of knowledge.

To those **who are being saved**, the gospel **is the power of God**. They hear the message, they accept it by faith, and the miracle of regeneration takes place in their lives. Notice the solemn fact in this verse that there are only two classes of people, those who perish and those who are saved. There is no in-between class. Men may love their human wisdom but only the gospel leads to salvation.

1:19 The fact that the gospel would be offensive to human wisdom was prophesied by Isaiah (29:14):

"I will destroy the wisdom of the wise, and bring to nothing the understanding of the prudent."

S. Lewis Johnson in *The Wycliffe Bible Commentary* notes that in context these "words are God's denouncement of the policy of the 'wise' in Judah in seeking an alliance with Egypt when threatened by Sennacherib."[2] How true it is that God delights to accomplish His purposes in ways that seem foolish to men. How often He uses methods that the wise of this world would ridicule, yet they achieve the desired results with wonderful accuracy and efficiency. For example, man's wisdom assures him that he can earn or merit his own salvation. The gospel sets aside all man's efforts to save himself and presents Christ as the only way to God.

1:20 Paul next hurls out a defiant challenge: **"Where is the wise? Where is the scribe? Where is the disputer of this age?"** Did God consult them when He devised His plan of salvation? Could they ever have worked out such a plan of redemption if left to their own wisdom? Can they rise to disprove anything that God ever said? The answer is an emphatic "No!" **God** has **made foolish the wisdom of this world.**

1:21 Man cannot by his own **wisdom** come to the knowledge of God. For centuries God gave the human race this opportunity, and the result was failure. Then **it pleased God** by the preaching of the cross, a **message** that seems foolish to men, **to save those who believe**. The foolishness of the thing preached refers to the cross. Of course, we know that it is not foolishness, but it seems foolish to the unenlightened mind of man. Godet says that verse 21 contains a whole philosophy of history, the substance of entire volumes. We should not hurry over it quickly, but ponder deeply its tremendous truths.

1:22 It was characteristic of the **Jews** to **request a sign**. Their attitude was that they would believe if some miracle were shown to them. The **Greeks** on the other hand searched for **wisdom**. They were interested in human reasonings, in arguments, in logic.

1:23 But Paul did not cater to their desires. He says, **"We preach Christ crucified."** As someone has said, "He was not a sign-loving Jew, nor a wisdom-loving Greek, but a Savior-loving Christian."

To the Jews, Christ crucified was **a stumbling block**. They looked for a mighty military leader to deliver them from the oppression of Rome. Instead of that, the gospel offered them a Savior nailed to a cross of shame. **To the Greeks**, Christ crucified was **foolishness**. They could not understand how One who died in such seeming weakness and failure could ever solve their problems.

1:24 But strangely enough, the very things that the Jews and the Gentiles sought are found in a wonderful way in the Lord Jesus. To those who hear His call and trust in Him, **both Jews and Greeks, Christ** becomes **the power of God and the wisdom of God**.

1:25 Actually there is neither foolishness nor weakness with God. But the apostle is saying in verse 25 that what seems to be **foolishness** on God's part, in the eyes of men, is actually **wiser than men** at their very best. Also, what seems to be **weakness** on God's part, in the eyes of men, turns out to be **stronger than** anything that **men** can produce.

1:26 Having spoken of the gospel itself, the apostle now turns to the people whom God calls by the gospel (vv. 26–29). He reminds the Corinthians that **not many wise according to the flesh, not many mighty, not many noble are called**. It has often been pointed out that the text does not say "not any" but **not many**. Because of this slight difference, one English lady of noble blood used to testify that she was saved by the letter "m."

The Corinthians themselves had not come from the upper intellectual crust of society. They had not been reached by high-sounding philosophies but by the simple gospel. Why, then, were they putting such a premium on human wisdom and exalting preachers who sought to make the message palatable to the worldly-wise?

If men were to build a church, they would want to enroll the most prominent members of the community. But verse 26 teaches us that the people men esteem so highly, God passes by. The ones He calls are not generally the ones the world considers great.

1:27 **God has chosen the foolish things of the world to put to shame the wise, and God has chosen the weak things of the world to put to shame the things which are mighty.** As Erich Sauer says:

The more primitive the material, the greater — if the same standard of art can be reached — the honor of the Master; the smaller the army, the mightier — if the same great victory can be won — the praise of the conqueror.[3]

God used trumpets to bring down the walls of Jericho. He reduced Gideon's army from 32,000 to 300 to rout the armies of Midian. He used an oxgoad in the hand of Shamgar to defeat the Philistines. With the jawbone of a donkey He enabled Samson to defeat a whole army. And our Lord fed over 5,000 with nothing more than a few loaves and fishes.

1:28 To make up what someone has called "God's five-ranked army of fools," Paul adds **the base things of the world and the things which are despised** and **the things which are not**. Using such unlikely materials, God brings **to nothing the things that are**. In other words, He loves to take up people who are of no esteem in the eyes of the world and use them to glorify Himself. These verses should serve as a rebuke to Christians who curry the favor of prominent and well-known personages and show little or no regard for the more humble saints of God.

1:29 God's purpose in choosing those of no account in the eyes of the world is that all the glory should accrue to Himself and not to man. Since salvation is entirely of Him, He alone is worthy to be praised.

1:30 Verse 30 emphasizes even further that all we are and have comes from Him — not from philosophy, and that there is therefore no room for human glory. First of all, Christ **became for us wisdom**. He is the wisdom of God (v. 24), the One whom God's wisdom chose as the way of salvation. When we have Him we have a positional wisdom that guarantees our full salvation. Secondly, He is our **righteousness**. Through faith in Him we are reckoned righteous by a holy God. Thirdly, He is our **sanctification**. In ourselves we have nothing in the way of personal holiness, but in Him we are positionally sanctified, and by His power we are transformed from one degree of sanctification to another. Finally, He is our **redemption**, and this doubtless speaks of redemption in its final aspect when the Lord will come and take

us home to be with Himself, and when we shall be redeemed — spirit, soul, and body.

Traill delineated the truth sharply:

> Wisdom out[side] of Christ is damning folly — righteousness out[side] of Christ is guilt and condemnation — sanctification out[side] of Christ is filth and sin — redemption out[side] of Christ is bondage and slavery.[4]

A. T. Pierson relates verse 30 to the life and ministry of our Lord:

> His deeds and His words and His practices, these show Him as the wisdom of God. Then come His death, burial, and resurrection: these have to do with our righteousness. Then His forty days' walk among men, His ascension up on high, the gift of the Spirit, and His session at the right hand of God, have to do with our sanctification. Then His coming again, which has to do with our redemption.[5]

1:31 God has so arranged it that all these blessings should come to us **in the LORD**. Paul's argument therefore is, "Why glory in men? They cannot do any one of these things for you."

2:1 The apostle now reminds the saints of his ministry among them and how he sought to glorify God and not himself. He came to them proclaiming **the testimony of God**, not **with excellence of speech or of wisdom**. He was not at all interested in showing himself off as an orator or philosopher. This shows that the Apostle Paul recognized the difference between ministry that is soulish and that which is spiritual. By soulish ministry, we mean that which amuses, entertains, or generally appeals to man's emotions. Spiritual ministry, on the other hand, presents the truth of God's word in such a way as to glorify Christ and to reach the heart and conscience of the hearers.

2:2 The content of Paul's message was **Jesus Christ and Him crucified. Jesus Christ** refers to His Person, while **Him crucified** refers to His work. The Person and work of the Lord Jesus form the substance of the Christian evangel.

2:3 Paul further emphasizes that his personal demeanor was neither impressive nor attractive. He was with the Corinthians **in weakness, in fear, and in much trembling**. The treasure of the gospel was contained in an earthen vessel that the excellence of the power might be of God and not of Paul. He himself was an example of how God uses weak things to confound the mighty.

2:4 Neither Paul's **speech** nor his **preaching** were in **persuasive words of human wisdom, but in demonstration of the Spirit and of power**. Some suggest that his **speech** refers to the material he presented and his **preaching** to the manner of its presentation. Others define his **speech** as his witness to individuals and his **preaching** as his messages to groups. According to the standards of this world, the apostle might never have won an oratorical contest. In spite of this, **the Spirit** of God used the message to produce conviction of sin and conversion to God.

2:5 Paul knew that there was the utmost danger that his hearers might be interested in himself or in his own personality rather than in the living Lord. Conscious of his own inability to bless or to save, he determined that he would lead men to trust in **God** alone rather than **in the wisdom of men**. All who proclaim the gospel message or teach the word of God should make this their constant aim.

2:6 First of all, the **wisdom** shown in the gospel is divine in its origin (vv. 6, 7). **We speak wisdom among those who are mature** or full-grown. **Yet** it is **not the wisdom of this age**, nor would it be wisdom in the eyes of **the rulers of this age**. Their wisdom is a perishable thing which, like themselves, is born for one brief day.

2:7 **We speak the wisdom of God in a mystery**. **A mystery** is a NT truth not previously revealed, but now made known to believers by the apostles and prophets of the early Church Age. This mystery is the **hidden wisdom which God ordained before the ages for our glory**. The mystery of the gospel includes such wonderful truths as the fact that *now* Jews and Gentiles are made one in Christ; that the Lord Jesus will come and take His waiting people home to be with Himself; and that not all believers will die but all will be changed.

2:8 **The rulers of this age** may refer to demonic spirit beings in the heavenlies or to their human agents on earth.

They didn't understand the hidden wisdom of God (Christ on a cross) or realize that their murder of the Holy Son of God would result in their own destruction. **Had they known** the ways of God, **they would not have crucified the Lord of glory**.

2:9 The processes of revelation, inspiration, and illumination are described in verses 9–16. They tell us how these wonderful truths were made known to the apostles by the Holy Spirit, how they in turn passed on these truths to us by inspiration of the Holy Spirit, and how we understand them by the illumination of the Holy Spirit.

The quotation in verse 9 from Isaiah 64:4 is a prophecy that God had treasured up wonderful truths which could not be discovered by the natural senses but which in due time He would reveal to **those who love Him**. Three faculties (**eye** and **ear** and **heart**, or mind) by which we learn earthly things, are listed, but these are not sufficient for the reception of divine truths, for there the Spirit of God is necessary.

This verse is commonly interpreted to refer to the glories of heaven, and once we get that meaning in our minds, it is difficult to dislodge it and accept any other meaning. But Paul is really speaking here about the truths that have been revealed for the first time in the NT. Men could never have arrived at these truths through scientific investigations or philosophical inquiries. The human mind, left to itself, could never discover the wonderful mysteries which were made known at the beginning of the gospel era. Human reason is totally inadequate to find the truth of God.

2:10 That verse 9 does not refer to heaven is proven by the statement that **God has revealed them to us through His Spirit**. In other words, these truths foretold in the *OT* were made known to the apostles of the *NT* era. The **us** refers to the writers of the NT. It was by the **Spirit** of God that the apostles and prophets were enlightened, because **the Spirit searches all things, yes, the deep things of God**. In other words, the Spirit of God, one of the members of the Godhead, is infinite in wisdom and understands all the truths of God and is able to impart them to others.

2:11 Even in human affairs no one

knows what a **man** is thinking but he himself. No one else can possibly find out unless the man himself chooses to make it known. Even then, in order to understand a man, a person must have **the spirit of** a **man**. An animal could not fully understand our thinking. So it is with God. The only one who can understand the things of God is **the Spirit of God.**

2:12 The **we** of verse 12 refers to the writers of the NT, although it is equally true of all the Bible writers. Since the apostles and prophets had received the Holy Spirit, He was able to share with them the deep truths of God. That is what the apostle means when he says in this verse: **"Now we have received, not the spirit of the world, but the Spirit who is from God, that we might know the things that have been freely given to us by God."** Apart from **the Spirit who is from God**, the apostles could never have received the divine truths of which Paul is speaking and which are preserved for us in the NT.

2:13 Having described the process of revelation by which the writers of Sacred Scripture received truth from God, Paul now goes on to describe the process of inspiration, by which that truth was communicated to us. Verse 13 is one of the strongest passages in the word of God on the subject of verbal inspiration. The Apostle Paul clearly states that in conveying these truths to us, the apostles did **not** use **words** of their own choosing or words dictated by **man's wisdom**. Rather, they used the very words **which the Holy Spirit** taught them to use. And so we believe that the actual words of Scripture, as found in the original autographs, were the very words of God (and that the Bible in its present form is entirely trustworthy).

A howl of objection arises at this point since to some people what we have said implies *mechanical dictation*, as if God did not allow the writers to use their own style. Yet we know that Paul's writing style is quite different from Luke's, for example. How, then, can we reconcile verbal inspiration with the obvious individual style of the writers? In some way which we do not understand, God gave the very words of Scripture, and yet He clothed those words with the individual style of the writers, letting their human personality be part of His perfect word.

The expression **comparing spiritual things with spiritual** can be explained in several ways. It may mean (1) teaching spiritual truths with Spirit-given words; (2) communicating spiritual truths to spiritual men; or (3) comparing spiritual truths in one section of the Bible with those in another. We believe that the first explanation fits the context best. Paul is saying that the process of inspiration involves the conveying of divine truth with words that are especially chosen for that purpose by the Holy Spirit. Thus we could paraphrase: "presenting spiritual truths in spiritual words."

It is sometimes objected that this passage cannot refer to inspiration because Paul says we **speak**, not "we write." But it is not uncommon to find the verb "to speak" used of inspired writings (e.g., John 12:38, 41; Acts 28:25; 2 Pet. 1:21).

2:14 Not only is the gospel divine in its revelation and divine in its inspiration, but now we learn that it can only be received by the power of **the Spirit of God**. Unaided, **the natural man does not receive the things of the Spirit of God. They are foolishness to him.** He cannot possibly understand them **because they** can only be **spiritually** understood.

The colorful Vance Havner advises:

> The wise Christian wastes no time trying to explain God's program to unregenerate men; it would be casting pearls before swine. He might as well try to describe a sunset to a blind man or discuss nuclear physics with a monument in the city park. The natural man cannot receive such things. One might as well try to catch sunbeams with a fishhook as to lay hold of God's revelation unassisted by the Holy Spirit. Unless one is born of the Spirit and taught by Him, all this is utterly foreign to him. Being a Ph. D. does not help, for in this realm it could mean 'Phenomenal Dud!'[6]

2:15 On the other hand, the man who is illuminated by the Spirit of God can discern these wonderful truths even though **he himself** cannot be **rightly judged** by the unconverted. Perhaps he is a carpenter, or plumber, or fisherman; yet he is an able student of the Holy Scriptures. "The Spirit-controlled Christian investigates, inquires into, and scrutinizes the Bible and comes to an appreciation and understanding of its contents" (KSW). To the world he is an enigma. He may never have been to college or seminary, yet he can understand the deep mysteries of the word of God and perhaps even teach them to others.

2:16 The apostle now asks with Isaiah the rhetorical question: **"Who has known the mind of the LORD that he may instruct Him?"** To ask the question is to answer it. God cannot be known through the wisdom or power of men. He is known only as He chooses to make Himself known. However, those who have **the mind of Christ** are able to understand the deep truths of God.

To review then, first there is *revelation* (vv. 9–12). This means that God revealed previously unknown truths to men by the Holy Spirit. These truths were made known supernaturally by the Spirit of God.

Secondly, there is *inspiration* (v. 13). In transmitting these truths to others, the apostles (and all other writers of the Bible) used the very words which the Holy Spirit taught them to use.

Finally, there is *illumination* (vv. 14–16). Not only must these truths be miraculously *revealed* and miraculously *inspired*, but they can only be *understood* by the supernatural power of the Holy Spirit.

3:1 When Paul first visited Corinth, he had fed the believers with the elementary milk of the word because they were weak and young in the faith. The teaching which had been given to them was suitable to their condition. They could not receive deeply spiritual instruction because they were new believers. They were mere **babes in Christ**.

3:2 Paul had taught them only the elementary truths concerning Christ, which he speaks of as **milk**. They were not able to take **solid food** because of their immaturity. In the same vein, the Lord Jesus said to His disciples, "I still have many things to say to you, but you cannot bear them now" (John 16:12). With regard to the Corinthians, the tragic thing was that they still had not improved sufficiently to receive deeper truth from the apostle.

3:3 The believers were **still** in a **carnal** or fleshly state of soul. This was evidenced by the fact that there was **envy** and **strife** among them. Such behavior is characteristic of the men of this world, but not of those who are led by the Spirit of God.

3:4 In forming parties around human leaders, such as **Paul** and **Apollos**, they were acting on a purely human level. That is what Paul means when he asks, "Are you not . . . behaving like mere men?"

Up to this point, the Apostle Paul has been showing the folly of exalting men by a consideration of the true nature of the gospel message. He now turns to the subject of the Christian ministry and shows from this standpoint also, it is sheer foolishness to exalt religious leaders by building parties around them.

3:5 **Apollos** and **Paul** were *servants* (*minister* is Latin for "servant") **through whom** the Corinthians had come to believe in the Lord Jesus. They were simply agents and not the heads of rival schools. How unwise then of the Corinthians to raise servants to the rank of master. Ironside quaintly comments at this point, "Imagine a household divided over servants!"

3:6 Using a figure from agriculture, Paul shows that the servant is after all very limited in what he can do. **Paul** himself could plant and **Apollos** could water, but only **God** could give **the increase**. So today, some of us can preach the word and all of us can pray for unsaved relatives and friends, but the actual work of salvation can only be done by the Lord.

3:7 Looking at it from this point, we can readily see that the planter and the waterer are really not very important, relatively speaking. They have not the power in themselves to bring forth life. Why then should there be any envy or rivalry among Christian workers? Each should do the work that has been allotted to him, and rejoice when the Lord shows His hand in blessing.

3:8 **He who plants and he who waters are one** in the sense that they both have the same object and aim. There should be no jealousy between them. As far as service is concerned, they are on the same level. In a coming day, **each one will receive his own reward according to his own labor**. That day is the Judgment Seat of Christ.

3:9 God is the One to whom all are

responsible. All His servants are **fellow workers**, laboring together in **God's** tilled harvest **field**, or, to change the picture, working together on the same **building**. Erdman renders the thought as follows: "We are fellow-workers who belong to God and are working with one another."[7]

3:10 Continuing with the idea of building, the apostle first of all acknowledges that anything he has been able to accomplish has been due to **the grace of God**. By this he means the undeserved ability from God to do the work of an apostle. Then he goes on to describe his part in the beginning of this assembly at Corinth: **"As a wise master builder, I have laid the foundation."** He came to Corinth preaching Christ and Him crucified. Souls were saved and a local church was planted. Then he adds: **"And another builds on it."** By this, he doubtless refers to other teachers who subsequently visited Corinth and built on the foundation which had already been established there. However, the apostle cautions: **"But let each one take heed how he builds on it."** He means that it is a solemn thing to exercise a teaching ministry in the local church. Some had come to Corinth with divisive doctrines and with teachings contrary to the word of God. Paul was doubtless conscious of these teachers as he penned the words.

3:11 Only one foundation is required for a building. Once it is laid, it never needs to be repeated. The Apostle Paul had laid the foundation of the church at Corinth. That **foundation** was **Jesus Christ**, His Person and Work.

3:12 Subsequent teaching in a local church may be of varying degrees of value. For instance, some teaching is of lasting worth, and might be likened to **gold, silver**, or **precious stones**. Here **precious stones** probably do not refer to diamonds, rubies, or other gems but rather to the granite, marble, or alabaster used in the construction of costly temples. On the other hand, teaching in the local church might be of passing value or of no value at all. Such teaching is likened to **wood, hay**, and **straw**.

This passage of Scripture is commonly used in a general way to refer to the lives of all Christian believers. It is true that we are all building, day by day, and the results of our work will be manifested in a coming day. However, a careful student of the Bible will want to note that the passage does not refer primarily to all believers but rather to preachers and teachers.

3:13 In a coming day, **each one's work will become clear. Day** refers to the Judgment Seat of Christ when all service for the Lord will be reviewed. The process of review is likened to the action of **fire**. Service that has brought glory to God and blessing to man, like gold, silver, and precious stones, will not be affected by the fire. On the other hand, that which has caused trouble among the people of God or failed to edify them will be consumed. **The fire will test each one's work, of what sort it is.**

3:14 Work in connection with the church may be of three types. In verse 14 we have the first type — service that has been of a profitable nature. In such a case, the servant's life work **endures** the test of the Judgment Seat of Christ and the worker **will receive a reward**.

3:15 The second type of work is that which is useless. In this case, the servant **will suffer loss**, although **he himself will be saved, yet so as through fire**. E. W. Rogers points out: "Loss does not imply the forfeiture of something once possessed."[8] It should be clear from this verse that the Judgment Seat of Christ is not concerned with the subject of a believer's sins and their penalty. The penalty of a believer's sins was borne by the Lord Jesus Christ on the cross of Calvary, and that matter has been settled once for all. Thus the believer's salvation is not at all in question at the Judgment Seat of Christ; rather it is a matter of his service.

Through failure to distinguish between salvation and rewards, the Roman Catholic Church has used this verse to try to support its teaching of purgatory. However, a careful examination of the verse reveals no hint as to purgatory. There is no thought that the fire purifies the character of a man. Rather, the fire tests a man's work or service, of what sort it is. The man is saved despite the fact that his works are consumed by the fire.

An interesting thought in connection with this verse is that the word of God is sometimes likened to fire (see Isa. 5:24 and Jer. 23:29). The same word of God which will test our service at the Judgment Seat of Christ is available to us now. If we are building in accordance with the teachings of the Bible, then our work will stand the test in that coming day.

3:16 Paul reminds the believers **that they are the temple** (Gk., the inner shrine or sanctuary) **of God and that the Spirit of God dwells in** them. It is true that every individual believer is also a temple of God indwelt by the Holy Spirit, but that is not the thought here. The apostle is looking at the church as a collective company, and wishes them to realize the holy dignity of such a calling.

3:17 A third class of work in the local church is that which may be spoken of as destructive. Apparently there were false teachers who had come into the church at Corinth and whose instruction tended more to sin than to holiness. They did not think it a serious matter to thus cause havoc in a temple of God, so Paul thunders out this solemn declaration: **"If anyone defiles the temple of God, God will destroy him."** Viewed in its local setting, this means that if any man enters a local church and wrecks its testimony, **God will destroy him**. The passage is speaking of false teachers who are not true believers in the Lord Jesus. The seriousness of such an offense is indicated by the closing words of verse 17: **"For the temple of God is holy, which temple you are."**

3:18 In Christian service, as in all of Christian life, there is always the danger of self-deception. Perhaps some of those who came to Corinth as teachers posed as men of extreme wisdom. Any who have an exalted view of their own worldly wisdom must learn that they must become fools in the eyes of the world in order to **become wise** in God's estimation. Godet helpfully paraphrases at this point:

If any individual whatever, Corinthian or other, while preaching the gospel *in your assemblies* assumes the part of a wise man and reputation of a profound thinker, let him assure himself that he will not attain true wisdom until he has passed through a crisis in which that wisdom of his with which he is puffed up will perish and after which only he will receive the wisdom which is from above.[9]

3:19 **The wisdom of this world is foolishness with God.** Man by searching could never find out God, neither would human wisdom ever have devised a plan of salvation by which God would become Man in order to die for guilty, vile, rebel sinners. Job 5:13 is quoted in verse 19 to show that God triumphs over the supposed wisdom of men to work out His own purposes. Man with all his learning cannot thwart the plans of the Lord; instead, God often shows them that in spite of their worldly wisdom, they are utterly poor and powerless.

3:20 Psalm 94:11 is quoted here to emphasize that **the Lord knows** all the reasonings **of the wise** men of this world, and He further knows **that they are futile**, empty, and fruitless. But why is Paul going to such pains to discredit worldly wisdom? Simply for this reason — the Corinthians were placing a great premium on such wisdom and were following those leaders who seemed to exhibit it in a remarkable degree.

3:21 In view of all that had been said, **no one** should **boast in men**. And as far as true servants of the Lord are concerned, we should not boast that we belong to them but rather realize that they all belong to us. **All things are yours.**

3:22 Someone has called verse 22 "an inventory of the possessions of the child of God." Christian workers belong to us, whether **Paul** the evangelist, or **Apollos** the teacher, or **Cephas** the pastor. Since they all belong to us, it is folly for us to claim that we belong to any *one* of them. Then **the world** is ours. As joint heirs with Christ, we will one day come into possession of it, but in the meantime it is ours by divine promise. Those who tend its affairs do not realize that they are doing so for us. **Life** is ours. By this we do not mean merely existence on earth but life in its truest, fullest sense. And **death** is ours. For us it is no longer a dread foe that consigns the soul to the dark unknown; rather it is now the messenger of God that brings the soul to heaven. **Things present** and **things to come — all are** likewise ours. It has been truly said that all things serve the man who serves Christ. A. T. Robertson once said: "The stars in their courses fight for the man who is partner with God in the world's redemption."

3:23 All Christians belong to Christ. Some in Corinth were claiming to belong to Him to the exclusion of all others. They formed the "Christ-party." But Paul refutes any such contention. We are all **Christ's, and Christ is God's**. By thus showing the saints their true and proper dignity, Paul reveals in bold relief the folly of forming parties and divisions in the church.

4:1 In order that they might properly appraise Paul and the other apostles, he says that the saints should look upon them **as servants** or assistants **of Christ and stewards of the mysteries of God**. A steward is a servant who cares for the person or property of another. **The mysteries of God** were the previously hidden secrets which God revealed to the apostles and prophets of the NT period.

4:2 A major requirement **in stewards** is to **be found faithful**. Man values cleverness, wisdom, wealth, and success; but God is looking for those who will be faithful to Jesus in all things.

4:3 The faithfulness that is required in stewards is a difficult thing for people to evaluate. That is why Paul says here that **with** him **it is a very small thing that** he **should be judged by** the Corinthians **or by a human court**. Paul realizes how utterly unable man is to form a competent judgment of true faithfulness to God. He adds: **"In fact, I do not even judge myself."** He realized that he was born into the human family with a judgment that was constantly biased in his own favor.

4:4 When the apostle says **"I know of nothing against myself,"** he means that in the matter of Christian service, he is not conscious of any charge of unfaithfulness that might be brought against him. He does not mean for a moment that he does not know of any sin in his life or any way in which he falls short of perfection! The passage should be read in the light of the context, and the subject here is Christian service and faithfulness in it. But even if he did not know anything against himself, **yet** he was **not justified by this**. He simply was not competent to judge in the matter. After all, the Lord is the Judge.

4:5 In view of this, we should be ex-tremely careful in our appraisal of Christian service. We tend to exalt the spectacular and sensational, and depreciate that which is menial or inconspicuous. The safe policy is to **judge nothing before the time**, but to wait **until the Lord comes**. He will be able to judge, not only what is seen by the eye, but also the motives of the hearts — not only what was done, but *why* it was done. He will **reveal the counsels of the hearts**, and, needless to say, anything that was done for self-display or self-glory will fail to receive a reward.

That **each one's praise will come from God** is not to be taken as a flat promise that every believer's service will show up in a favorable way in that day. The meaning is that everyone who *deserves* praise will receive praise **from God** and not from men.

In the next eight verses, the apostle states quite clearly that pride is the cause of the divisions that have come into the church at Corinth.

4:6 He first explains that in speaking about the Christian ministry and the tendency to follow human leaders (3:5–4:5), he used himself and **Apollos** as the examples. The Corinthians were not forming parties around Paul and Apollos alone, but also around other men who were then in their church. However, out of a sense of Christian courtesy and delicacy, Paul **transferred** the entire matter **to** himself **and Apollos** so that by their example the saints would learn not to have exaggerated opinions of their leaders or to gratify their pride by the formation of parties. He wanted the saints to evaluate everything and everyone by the Scriptures.

4:7 If one Christian teacher is more gifted than another, it is because God made him so. Everything he has, he received from the Lord. In fact it is true of all of us that everything we have has been given to us by God. That being the case, why should we be proud or puffed up? Our talents and gifts are not the result of our own cleverness.

4:8 The Corinthians had become self-sufficient; they were **already full**. They prided themselves on the abundance of spiritual gifts in their midst; they were **already rich**. They were living in luxury, comfort, and ease. There was no sense of need. They acted as if they were already reigning, but they were doing so without the apostles. Paul states that he **could wish** that the time to reign had already come so that he **might reign with** them! But in the meantime, "lifetime is training time for reigning time," as someone has said. Christians will reign with the Lord Jesus Christ when He comes back and sets up His kingdom on earth. In the meantime, their privilege is to share the reproach of a rejected Savior. H. P. Barker warns:

> It is positive disloyalty to seek our crown before the King gets his. Yet this is what some of the Christians at Corinth were doing. The apostles themselves were bearing the reproach of Christ. But the Corinthian Christians were "rich" and "honorable." They were seeking a good time where their Lord and Master had such a hard time.[10]

At coronations, peers and peeresses never put on their coronets until the sovereign has been crowned. The Corinthians were reversing this; they were already reigning while the Lord was still in rejection!

4:9 In contrast to the self-satisfaction of the Corinthians, Paul describes the lot of **the apostles**. He pictures them as thrown into the arena with wild beasts while **men** and **angels** look on. As Godet has said: "It was not time for the Corinthians to be self-complacent and boasting, while the church was on the throne and the apostles were under the sword."

4:10 While the apostles were treated as **fools for Christ's sake**, the saints enjoyed prestige in the community as **wise** Christians. The apostles were **weak, but** the Corinthians suffered no infirmity. In contrast to the dishonor of the apostles was the eminence of the saints.

4:11 It did not seem to the apostles that the hour of triumph or of reigning had come. They were suffering from **hunger and thirst** and nakedness and persecution. They were hunted, pursued, and **homeless.**

4:12 They supported themselves by **working with** their **own hands**. For reviling, they returned blessing. When they were **persecuted**, they did not fight back, but patiently endured.

4:13 When **defamed**, they entreated

men to accept the Lord Jesus. In short, they were **made as the filth of the world, the** scum **of all things**. This description of suffering for the sake of Christ should speak to all our hearts. If the Apostle Paul were living today, could he say to us, as he said to the Corinthians, "You have reigned as kings without us"?

4:14 In verses 14–21, Paul gives a final admonition to the believers on the subject of divisions. Conscious of the fact that he has been using irony, he explains that he has **not** done so **to shame** the Christians, **but** rather to **warn** them **as** his **beloved children**. He was not inspired by bitterness to speak as he had done, but rather by a sincere interest in their spiritual welfare.

4:15 The apostle reminds them that **though** they **might have ten thousand instructors in Christ, yet** they have only one father in the faith. Paul himself had led them to the Lord; he was their spiritual father. Many others might come along to teach them, but no others could have the same tender regard for them as the one who pointed them to the Lamb. Paul does not at all intend to depreciate the ministry of teaching, but is simply stating what we all know to be true, namely, that many can be engaged in Christian service without the personal interest in the saints that is characteristic of one who has pointed them to Christ.

4:16 Paul **therefore** urges them to be imitators of himself, that is, in his unselfish devotion to Christ and in his tireless love and service for his fellow believers, such as he has described in verses 9–13.

4:17 In order to help them reach this goal, Paul **sent Timothy to** them, his **beloved and faithful son in the Lord**. Timothy was instructed to **remind** them **of** Paul's **ways in Christ**, ways which he taught in all the churches. Paul is saying that he practiced what he preached, and this should be true of everyone who engages in Christian service.

4:18 When Paul explained that he was sending Timothy to them, perhaps some of his detractors in Corinth would rise quickly to suggest that Paul was afraid to come himself. These men were **puffed up** in suggesting that Paul was **not coming** personally.

4:19 But he promises that he **will**

come in the near future, **if the Lord wills**. When he does, he will expose the pride of those who can talk so freely, but have no spiritual **power**.

4:20 After all, it is **power** that counts, **for the kingdom of God is not** concerned principally with words but with action. It does not consist of profession, but of reality.

4:21 The manner in which Paul comes to them will depend on themselves. If they show a rebellious spirit, he will **come to** them **with a rod**. If, on the other hand, they are humble and submissive, he will come **in love and a spirit of gentleness**.

B. Immorality among Believers (Chap. 5)

Chapter 5 deals with the necessity for disciplinary action in a church when one of the members has committed serious sin of a public nature. Discipline is necessary for the church to retain its holy character in the eyes of the world and also so that the Holy Spirit may work ungrieved in its midst.

5:1 Apparently it had become widely **reported** that one of the men in the fellowship at Corinth had committed **sexual immorality**. Here it was a very extreme form of sin, one that was **not even** practiced **among the** ungodly **Gentiles**. Specifically, the sin was **that** this **man** had had illicit intercourse with **his father's wife**. The man's own mother had no doubt died and the father had married again. So his father's wife, in this case, would then refer to his stepmother. She was probably an unbeliever, because nothing is said about taking action against her. The church did not have jurisdiction in her case.

5:2 How had the Corinthian Christians reacted to all this? Instead of plunging into deep mourning, they were proud and haughty. Perhaps they were proud of their tolerance in not disciplining the offender. Or perhaps they were so proud of the abundance of spiritual gifts in the church that they did not give serious thought to what had taken place. Or perhaps they were more interested in numbers than in holiness. They were not sufficiently shocked by sin.

You are puffed up, and have not rather mourned, that he who has done

this deed might be taken away from among you. This implies that if the believers had taken the proper attitude of humiliation before the Lord, He Himself would have acted in the matter, taking some form of disciplinary action on the offender. Erdman says:

> They should have understood that the true glory of the Christian church consists not in the eloquence and gifts of its great teachers, but in the moral purity and the exemplary lives of its members.[11]

5:3 In contrast to their indifference, the apostle states that even though he was **absent**, yet he had **already judged** the matter as if he were present.

5:4 He pictures the church being assembled to take action against the offender. Although he is not present bodily, yet he is there in **spirit** as they meet **in the name of our Lord Jesus Christ**. The Lord Jesus had given authority to the church and to the apostles to exercise discipline in all such cases. Thus Paul says he would act with the **power** (or authority) **of our Lord Jesus**.

5:5 The action he would take would be to **deliver such a one to Satan for the destruction of the flesh, that his spirit may be saved in the day of the Lord Jesus**. Commentators disagree on the meaning of this expression. Some feel that it describes the act of excommunication from the local church. Outside the church is the sphere of Satan's dominion (1 Jn. 5:19). Therefore, "to deliver to Satan" would be simply to excommunicate from the church. Others feel that the power to deliver to Satan was a special power granted to apostles but no longer in existence today.

Again, there is disagreement as to the meaning of the expression **the destruction of the flesh**. Many feel that it describes physical suffering that would be used by God to break the power of sinful lusts and habits in the man's life. Others feel that **the destruction of the flesh** is a description of slow death, which would give a man time to repent and be spared.

In any case, we should remember that the discipline of believers is always calculated to bring about their restoration to fellowship with the Lord. Excommunication in never an end in itself, but always a means toward an end. The ultimate purpose is **that his spirit may be saved in the day of the Lord Jesus**. In other words, there is no thought of the man's eternal damnation. He is disciplined by the Lord in this life because of the sin he has committed, but he is **saved in the day of the Lord Jesus.**

5:6 Paul now reproves the Corinthians for their **glorying** or boasting. Maybe they excused themselves by saying that it happened only once. They should have known **that a little leaven leavens the whole lump. Leaven** here is a picture of moral sin. The apostle is saying that if they tolerate a little moral sin in the church, it will soon grow and expand until the whole fellowship is seriously affected. Righteous, godly discipline is necessary in order to maintain the character of the church.

5:7 Thus they are commanded to **purge out the old leaven**. In other words, they should take stern action against evil so that they might be a **new**, in the sense of a pure **lump**. Then Paul adds: **Since you truly are unleavened**. God sees them in Christ as holy, righteous, and pure. Now the apostle is saying that their state should correspond with their standing. As to *position* they were unleavened. Now as to their *practice* they should also be unleavened. Their natures should correspond with their name, and their conduct with their creed.

For indeed Christ, our Passover, was sacrificed for us. In thinking about the unleavened bread, Paul's mind goes back to the Passover Feast where, on the eve of the first day of the Feast, the Jew was required to remove all leaven from his house. He went to the kneading trough and scraped it clean. He scrubbed the place where the leaven was kept till not a trace remained. He searched the house with a lamp to make sure that none had been overlooked. Then he lifted up his hands to God and said, "Oh God, I have cast out all the leaven from my house, and if there is any leaven that I do not know of, with all my heart I cast it out too." That pictures the kind of separation from evil to which the Christian is called in this day.

The slaying of the Passover lamb was a type or picture of the death of our Lord Jesus Christ on the cross. This verse is one of many in the NT that establishes the principle of *typical* teaching. By this we mean that persons and events of the OT were *types* or shadows of things that were to come. Many of them pointed forward directly to the coming of the Lord Jesus to put away our sins by the sacrifice of Himself.

5:8 **The feast** here does not refer to the Passover or to the Lord's Supper but rather is used in a general way to describe the whole life of the believer. Our entire existence is to be a festival of joy, and it is to be celebrated **not with** the **old leaven** of sin **nor with the leaven of malice and wickedness**. As we rejoice in Christ, we must have no evil thoughts in our hearts toward others. From this we see that the Apostle Paul was not speaking about literal leaven, such as the yeast that is used in making bread, but rather he was using leaven in a spiritual sense to describe the manner in which sin defiles that with which it comes into contact. We are to live our lives **with the unleavened bread of sincerity and truth.**

5:9 Now Paul explains to them that he had previously written in a letter that they were **not to keep company with sexually immoral people**. The fact that such an epistle is lost does not affect the inspiration of the Bible at all. Not every letter Paul wrote was inspired, but only those which God has seen fit to include in the Holy Bible.

5:10 The apostle now goes on to explain that in warning them to have no company with **sexually immoral people**, he did not mean to imply that they should separate themselves from any contact at all with ungodly men. As long as we are in the world, it is necessary for us to do business with unsaved people and we have no way of knowing the depths of sin to which they have descended. In order to live a life of complete isolation from sinners, **you would need to go out of the world**.

So Paul says that he did not at all mean complete separation from **the sexually immoral people of this world, or** the **covetous, or extortioners, or idolaters. Covetous** people are those who are convicted of dishonesty in business or financial affairs. For instance, anyone who is found guilty of tax fraud is subject to excommunication for covetousness. **Extortioners** are those who enrich themselves by using violent means, such as threats of harm or death. **Idolaters** are those who are given over to the worship of anyone or anything other than the true God, and who practice the terrible sins of immorality that are almost always connected with idolatry.

5:11 What Paul really wants to warn them against is having fellowship with a professing **brother** who engages in any of these terrible sins. We might paraphrase his words as follows:

> What I meant to say and what I now repeat is that you should not even eat a common meal with any professing Christian who is sexually immoral, or a covetous man, or an idolater, or a reviler, or a drunkard, or an extortioner.

It is often necessary for us to have contact with the unsaved, and we can often use these contacts in order to witness to them. Such contact is not as dangerous to the believer as having fellowship with those who profess to be Christians and yet live in sin. We should never do anything that such a person might interpret as condoning his sin.

To the list of sinners mentioned in verse 10, Paul adds revilers and drunkards in verse 11. **A reviler** is a man who uses strong, intemperate language against another. But we would add a word of caution here. Should a man be excommunicated from the church if on one occasion only he should lose his temper and use unguarded words? We would think not, but would suggest that this expression refers to habitual practice. In other words, **a reviler** would be one who is known as being characteristically abusive toward others. At any rate, this should be a warning to us to exercise control of our language. As Dr. Ironside has mentioned, many people say that they are just *careless* with their tongue, but he points out that they might just as well say that they are careless with a machine gun.

A drunkard is one given to excess in the use of alcoholic beverages.

Does the Apostle Paul mean that we are **not even to eat with such a** Christian who engages in these practices? That is exactly what the verse teaches! We are not to eat with him at the Lord's Supper,

nor are we to enjoy a social meal with him. There may be exceptional cases. A Christian wife, for instance, would still be obligated to eat with her husband who had been disfellowshiped. But the general rule is that professing believers who are guilty of the sins listed should be subjected to social ostracism in order to impress on them the enormity of their transgression and to bring them to repentance. If it is objected that the Lord ate with publicans and sinners, we would point out that these men did not profess to be His followers, and in eating with them He did not recognize them as His disciples. What this passage teaches is that we should not fellowship with *Christians* who are living wicked lives.

5:12 Paul's two questions in verse 12 mean that Christians are not responsible for the judgment of the unsaved. Wicked men in the world about us will be brought into judgment by the Lord Himself in a coming day. But we do have a responsibility as far as judging **those who are inside** the confines of the church. It is the duty of the local church to exercise godly discipline.

Again, if it is objected that the Lord taught, "Judge not that you be not judged," we would reply that there He is speaking about motives. We are not to judge men's motives because we are not competent for that type of judgment. But the word of God is equally clear that we are to judge known sin in the assembly of God so as to maintain its reputation for holiness and so as to restore the offending brother to fellowship with the Lord.

5:13 Paul explains that **God** will take care of the judgment of **those who are outside**, that is, of the unsaved. In the meantime, the Corinthians should exercise the judgment which God has committed to them by putting away **the evil person** from among themselves. This calls for a public announcement in the church that this brother is no longer in fellowship. The announcement should be made in genuine sorrow and humiliation and should be followed by continual prayer for the spiritual restoration of the wanderer.

C. Lawsuits among Believers (6:1–11)

The first eleven verses of chapter 6 have to do with lawsuits among believers. News had come to Paul that some Christians were going to law against their fellow believers — before the judges of this world. So he lays down these instructions of lasting value for the church. Note the repetition of the expression "Do you not know" (vv. 2, 3, 9, 15, 16, 19).

6:1 The opening question expresses shocked surprise that any of them would think of taking a brother **to law before the unrighteous**, that is, before unsaved judges or magistrates. He finds it rather inconsistent that those who know true righteousness should go before men who are not characterized by righteousness. Imagine Christians looking for justice from those who have none to give!

6:2 A second glaring inconsistency is that those who one day **will judge the world** should be incapable of judging trivial matters that come up among themselves. The Scriptures teach that believers will reign with Christ over the earth when He returns in power and glory, and that matters of judgment will be committed to them. If Christians are going to **judge the world**, should they not be able to handle petty differences that plague them now?

6:3 Paul reminds the Corinthians that they will **judge angels**. It is almost astounding to consider the manner in which the apostle injects such a momentous statement into the discussion. Without fanfare or build-up, he states the tremendous fact that Christians will one day **judge angels**. We know from Jude v. 6 and 2 Peter 2:4, 9 that angels will be judged. We also know that Christ will be the Judge (John 5:22). It is because of our union with Him that we can be spoken of as judging angels in a coming day. If we are considered qualified to judge angels, we should be able to handle the everyday problems that arise in **this life.**

6:4 **If then you have judgments concerning things pertaining to this life, do you appoint those who are least esteemed by the church to judge?** Unsaved judges are not given places of honor or esteem by the local church. They are, of course, respected for the work they are doing in the world, but as far as church matters are concerned they do not have any jurisdiction. Thus

Paul is asking the Corinthians:

> When matters arise between you requiring the impartial judgment of some third party, do you go outside the confines of the church and set men to judge you who are not recognized by the church for spiritual discernment?

6:5 Paul asks this question to move them to **shame**. Is it true that in an assembly that boasted of its wisdom and of the rich bestowment of gifts on its members, **not** one **wise man** could be found to settle these quarrels **between his brethren?**

6:6 Apparently not one such wise man was available, since a Christian **brother** was going **to law against** his own **brother** in Christ, taking family matters before the unbelieving world. Truly a deplorable situation!

6:7 The expression **"Now therefore, it is already an utter failure for you"** shows they were entirely wrong in this thing. They shouldn't even think of going to law against one another. But perhaps one of the Christians would object at this point: "Paul, you don't understand. Brother so-and-so cheated me in business dealings." Paul's answer is: **"Why do you not rather accept wrong? Why do you not rather let yourselves be cheated?"** This would be the truly Christian attitude to take. It is much better to receive a wrong than to commit one.

6:8 But this was not the attitude among the Corinthians. Instead of being willing to accept wrong and be cheated, they were actually committing **wrong** against others, even their own brothers in Christ.

6:9 Had they forgotten that people whose lives are characteristically **unrighteous will not inherit the kingdom of God**? If they have forgotten, then he will remind them of a list of sinners who will have no part in God's **kingdom**. He does not mean to imply that Christians can practice such sins and be lost, but rather he is saying that people who practice such sins are not Christians.[12]

In this list, **fornicators** are distinct from **adulterers**. Here fornication means illicit sexual intercourse on the part of an unmarried person, whereas adultery would mean such conduct on the part of a married person. **Idolaters** are mentioned again, as in the two previous lists in chapter 5. **Homosexuals** here means those who allow their bodies to be used in a perverted way, while **sodomites** are those who practice sodomy on others.

6:10 To the list are added **thieves, covetous, drunkards, revilers,** and **extortioners. Thieves** are those who take what does not belong to them. Notice that the sin of covetousness is always listed among the most wicked vices. Though men might excuse it and think lightly of it, God condemns it vigorously. A **covetous** man is one with an inordinate desire for possessions that often drives him to use unjust means of acquiring the same. **Drunkards,** as has been said, are primarily those who are addicted to the use of alcohol. **Revilers** are those who use abusive speech against others. **Extortioners** are those who take advantage of others' poverty or necessities to secure exorbitant gain.

6:11 Paul does not imply that these sins were practiced by the Corinthian believers, but he is warning them that such things characterized them before they were saved — **such were some of you. But** they had been **washed** and **sanctified** and **justified.** They had been **washed** from their sin and impurity through the precious blood of Christ, and they were being continually washed from defilement through the word of God. They were **sanctified** by the operation of the Spirit of God, being set apart to God from the world. They had been **justified in the name of the Lord Jesus Christ and by the Spirit of God;** that is, they had been reckoned righteous before God on the basis of the work of the Lord Jesus on the cross for them. What is Paul's argument here? It is simply this, as so aptly expressed by Godet: "Such a fathomless depth of grace is not to be recrossed."

D. Moral Laxness among Believers (6:12–20)

6:12 In the concluding verses of this chapter, the apostle lays down some principles for judging between right and wrong. The first principle is that a thing may be lawful and yet not helpful. When Paul says, **"All things are lawful for me,"** he does not mean all things in an absolute sense. For instance, it would not be lawful for him to commit any of the sins mentioned above. He is here speaking only about those things that are morally indifferent. For example, the question as to whether a Christian should eat pork was a very real issue among believers in Paul's time. Actually, it was a matter of moral indifference. It did not really matter to God whether a man ate pork. Paul is simply saying that certain things might be legitimate and yet not profitable. There might be certain things which would be permissible for me to do and yet if someone else saw me doing them, he might be stumbled by my action. In such a case, it would not be at all suitable for me.

The second principle is that some things might be **be lawful** and yet they might be enslaving. Paul states: **"I will not be brought under the power of any."** This would have a very direct message today with regard to the subjects of liquor, tobacco, and drugs. These things, as well as many others, are enslaving and the Christian should not allow himself to be thus put in bondage.

6:13 A third principle is that some things are perfectly lawful for the believer and yet their value is temporary. Paul says: **"Foods for the stomach, and the stomach for foods, but God will destroy both it and them."** This means that the human **stomach** has been so constructed that it can receive **foods** and digest them. Likewise, God has wonderfully designed **foods** so they can be received by the human **stomach.** And yet we should not live for foods, because they are only of temporary value. They should not be given an undue place in the life of the believer. Don't live as if the greatest thing in life is to gratify your appetites.

Although the body is wonderfully designed by God for the reception and assimilation of food, there is one thing that is certain; **the body is not for sexual immorality** but **for the Lord, and the Lord for the body.** In planning the human body, God never intended that it should be used for vile or impure purposes. Rather He planned that it should be used for the glory of the Lord and in His blessed service.

There is something amazing in this verse which should not escape notice.

Not only is **the body for the Lord**, but even more wonderful is the thought that **the Lord is for the body**. This means that the Lord is interested in our bodies, their welfare, and their proper use. God wants our bodies to be presented to Him a living sacrifice, holy, and acceptable (Rom. 12:1). As Erdman says: "Without the Lord, the body can never attain its true dignity and its immortal destiny."[13]

6:14 The fact that the Lord is for the body is further explained in this verse. **God** has not only **raised up the Lord** Jesus from among the dead, but He **will also raise us up by His power**. His interest in our body does not end at the time of death. He is going to **raise** the body of every believer to fashion it like the glorious body of the Lord Jesus. We will not be disembodied spirits in eternity. Rather, our spirit and soul will be reunited with our glorified body, thus to enjoy the glories of heaven forever.

6:15 To further emphasize the need for personal purity in our lives and for guarding our bodies from impurity, the apostle reminds us that our **bodies are members of Christ**. Every believer is a member of the body of Christ. Would it be proper, then, to **take the members of Christ and make them members of a harlot?** To ask the question is to answer it, as Paul does with an indignant **Certainly not!**

6:16 In the act of sexual union, two bodies become **one**. It was so stated at the dawn of creation: **For "the two," He says, "shall become one flesh"** (Gen. 2:24). This being so, if a believer should be **joined to a harlot**, it would be the same as making a member of Christ a member of a harlot. The two would become **one body.**

6:17 Just as in the physical act there is a union of two into one, so when a person believes on the Lord Jesus Christ and is **joined to** Him, the believer and Christ become so united that they can henceforth be spoken of as **one spirit**. This is the most perfect merging of two persons that is possible. It is the closest type of a union. Paul's argument, therefore, is that those who are thus **joined to the Lord** should never tolerate any type of union that would be in conflict with this spiritual wedlock.

A. T. Pierson writes:

> The sheep may wander from the shepherd, and the branch be cut off from the vine; the member be severed from the body, the child alienated from the father, and even the wife from the husband; but when two spirits blend in one, what shall part them? No outward connection or union, even of wedlock is so emphatically expressive of perfect merging of two lives in one.[14]

6:18 And so the apostle warns the Corinthians to **flee sexual immorality**. They are not to dabble with it, trifle with it, study it, even talk about it. They are to **flee** from it! A beautiful Bible illustration of this is found in the account of Joseph when he was tempted to sin by Potiphar's wife (Gen. 39). While there may be safety in numbers, sometimes there is more safety in flight!

Then Paul adds: **"Every sin that a man does is outside the body; but he who commits sexual immorality sins against his own body."** Most sins have no direct effect on one's **body**, but **sexual immorality** is unique in the sense that it does *directly* affect one's body: a person reaps the consequences of this sin in his own body. The difficulty is that the verse says that *every* sin that a man commits is outside the body. But we believe that the apostle is speaking here in a comparative sense. While it is true that gluttony and drunkenness, for example, affect a person's body, most sins do not. And not even gluttony or drunkenness affect the body as directly, as extensively, or as destructively as immorality. Sex outside marriage inevitably and irresistibly works havoc on the offender.

6:19 Again Paul reminds the Corinthians that theirs was a holy and dignified calling. Had they forgotten that their bodies were a **temple of the Holy Spirit**? That is the solemn truth of Scripture, that every believer is indwelt by the Spirit of God. How could we ever think of taking a body in which the *Holy* Spirit dwells and using it for *vile* purposes? Not only is our body the shrine of the Holy Spirit, but in addition, **we are not our own**. It is not for us to take our bodies and use them the way we desire. In the final analysis, they do not belong to us; they belong to the Lord.

6:20 We are the Lord's both by creation and redemption. Here the latter is particularly in view. His ownership of us dates back to Calvary. We **were bought at a price**. At the cross, we see the price tag which the Lord Jesus put on us. He thought us to be of such value that He was willing to pay for us with the price of His own precious blood. How greatly Jesus must have loved us to bear our sins in His body on the cross!

That being the case, I can no longer think of my body as my own. If I am to take it and use it in the way I desire, then I am acting as a thief, taking that which does not belong to me. Rather I must use my **body** to **glorify God**, the One to whom it belongs.

Bates exclaimed:

> Head! Think of Him whose brow was thorn-girt. Hands! Toil for Him whose hands were nailed to the cross. Feet! Speed to do His behests whose feet were pierced. Body of mine! Be His temple whose body was wrung with pains unspeakable.[15]

We should also glorify God **in our spirit**, since both material and immaterial parts of man **are God's.**[16]

III. APOSTOLIC ANSWERS TO CHURCH QUESTIONS (Chaps. 7–14)

A. Concerning Marriage and Celibacy (Chap. 7)

7:1 Up to this point, Paul has been dealing with various abuses in the church at Corinth which he had heard of by direct report. Now he is about to answer questions which the saints at Corinth sent to him. The first has to do with marriage and the single state. He therefore first lays down the broad principle that it **is good for a man not to touch a woman. "To touch"** a woman, in this case, means to have a physical relationship. The apostle does *not* imply that the unmarried state is holier than marriage, but simply that it is better to be unmarried if one desires to give oneself to the service of the Lord without distraction. This will be explained in later verses.

7:2 Paul recognizes, however, that the single state carries with it tremendous temptations to impurity. Thus he qualifies the first statement by saying: **"Because of sexual immorality, let each man have his own wife, and let each woman have her own husband."** For **each man** to **have his own wife** means monogamous marriage. Verse 2 establishes the principle that God's order for His own people continues to be what it always was, namely, that a person should have only one spouse.

7:3 In the married state, each one should **render to** his partner the obligations of married life, since there is a mutual dependence. When it says: **"Let the husband render to his wife the affection due her,"** it means, "Let him carry out his obligations to her as a husband." She should, of course, **do likewise** to him. Note the delicacy Paul uses on this topic. There is no coarseness or vulgarity. How different from the world!

7:4 In marital union there is a dependence of **the wife** upon the **husband** and vice versa. In order to carry out God's order in this holy union, both husband and wife must recognize their interdependence.

7:5 Christenson writes:

> In plain language this means that if one partner desires the sexual relationship, the other should respond to that desire. The husband and wife who adopt this down-to-earth approach to sex will find it a wonderfully satisfying aspect of their marriage — for the simple reason that the relationship is rooted in reality, and not in some artificial or impossible ideal.[17]

Perhaps when some of these Corinthians were first saved, they began to think that the intimacies of married life were not consistent with Christian holiness. Paul will disabuse their minds of any such idea. Here he firmly tells them that Christian couples are **not** to **deprive one another**, that is, to deny one's partner's rights as far as the other partner's body is concerned. There are only two exceptions. First of all, such an abstinence should only be by mutual **consent** so that the husband and wife **may give** themselves to **fasting and prayer**. The second condition is that such abstinence should only be temporary. Husband and wife should **come together again**, lest Satan tempt them for their **lack of self-control**.

7:6 Verse 6 has given rise to a great deal of speculation and controversy. Paul says: **"But I say this as a concession, not as a commandment."** Some have taken this to mean that the apostle did not consider the foregoing words to be inspired by God. Such an interpretation is untenable, since he claims in 1 Corinthians 14:37 that the things which he was writing to the Corinthians were the commandments of the Lord. We feel rather that the apostle was saying that under certain circumstances, it was all right for a married couple to abstain from the marriage act, but that this abstinence is a permission, **not a commandment**. Christian people do not have to refrain from this act in order to give themselves undividedly to prayer. Others feel that verse 6 refers to the whole idea of marriage, that is, that Christians are permitted to marry but are not commanded to do so.

7:7 Paul now begins advice to the unmarried. It is clear, first of all, that he considered the unmarried state preferable, but he recognized that it could be followed only as God enabled. When he says: **"For I wish that all men were even as I myself,"** it is obvious from the context that he means "unmarried." There is much diversity of opinion as to whether Paul had always been a bachelor, or whether he was a widower at the time he wrote this. However, for present purposes, it is not necessary to settle the debate, even if we could. Where Paul says: **"But each one has his own gift from God, one in this manner, and another in that,"** he means that God gives grace to some to remain unmarried whereas He definitely calls others to the married state. It is an individual matter, and no general legislation can be adopted which can be applicable to all.

7:8 Therefore he advises **the unmarried and the widows** to **remain even as** he is himself.

7:9 However, if they lack the power of **self-control** in the unmarried state, then they are permitted to **marry. For it is better to marry than to burn with passion.** This passionate burning involves the very grave danger of falling into sin.

7:10 The next two verses are addressed to **married** couples, where both partners are believers. **Now to the mar-**ried I command, yet not I, but the Lord** simply means that what Paul was teaching here had already been taught by **the Lord** Jesus *when He was on earth*. Christ had already given an explicit command on this subject. For instance, He had forbidden divorce except on the ground of unfaithfulness (Matt. 5:32; 19:9). The overall instruction that Paul gives is that **a wife is not to depart from her husband.**

7:11 However, he recognizes that there are extreme cases where it might be necessary for a wife to leave her husband. In such a case, she is obligated to **remain unmarried, or be reconciled to her husband**. Separation does not break the marriage tie; rather it gives opportunity for the Lord to heal the differences that have come between and to restore both parties to fellowship with Him and with one another. The **husband** is commanded **not to divorce his wife**. No exception is made in his case.

7:12 Verses 12–24 deal with the problem of a marriage where only one party is a believer. Paul prefaces his remarks with the statement: **"But to the rest I, not the Lord, say."** Again, we strongly emphasize that this does not mean that what Paul is saying represents his own viewpoints and not the Lord's. He is simply explaining that what he is about to say had **not** previously taught by **the Lord** Jesus when He was here on earth. There is no instruction in the Gospels similar to this. The Lord Jesus simply did not take up the case of a marriage where only one member was a believer. But now Christ has instructed His apostle in this matter and so what Paul says here is the inspired word of God.

But to the rest means to those whose partners are not believers. This passage does *not* condone a Christian's marrying an unsaved person. It probably has in view the situation where one of the partners was saved after marriage.

"If any brother has a wife who does not believe, and she is willing to live with him, let him not divorce her." In order to appreciate this passage of Scripture properly, it is helpful to remind ourselves of God's commandment to His people in the OT. When Jews married heathen wives and had children by them, they were commanded to put both the wives and the children away. This is clearly seen in Ezra 10:2, 3 and Nehemiah 13:23–25.

Now the question has arisen in Corinth as to what a wife who had been converted should do about her husband and children, or what a man who has an unbelieving wife should do with her. Should he put her away? The answer is obviously negative. The OT commandment no longer applies to the people of God under grace. If a Christian has a non-Christian wife, **and she is willing to live with him**, he should not leave her. This does not mean that it is all right for a man to marry a non-believer, but simply that being married to her when he was converted, he should not leave her.

7:13 Likewise, **a woman who has a** non-Christian **husband** who **is willing to live with her** should stay with her husband. Perhaps by her meek and godly testimony before him, she will win him to the Lord.

7:14 Actually the presence of a believer in a non-Christian home has a sanctifying influence. As mentioned before, to *sanctify* means to set apart. Here it does not mean that the unbelieving husband is saved by his wife, neither does it mean that he is made holy. Rather it means that he is set apart in a position of external privilege. He is fortunate to have a Christian wife who prays for him. Her life and testimony are an influence for God in the home. Speaking from a human point of view, the likelihood of that man being saved is greater when he has a godly, Christian wife than if he had an unbelieving wife. As Vine puts it: "He receives a spiritual influence holding the possibility of actual conversion."[18] The same would hold true, of course, in the case of an **unbelieving wife** and a Christian **husband. The unbelieving wife** would be **sanctified** in such a case.

Then the apostle adds: **"otherwise your children would be unclean; but now they are holy."** We have already mentioned that in the OT the children were to be put away as well as the heathen wife. Now Paul explains that in the dispensation of grace, children born of a marriage where one partner is a believer and the other is not **are holy**. The word **holy** comes from the same root word translated **sanctified** in this verse. It does not at all mean that the children are made holy in themselves, that is, that they necessarily live clean and pure lives. Rather it means that they are set apart in a place of privilege. They have at least one parent who loves the Lord, and who tells them the gospel story. There is a strong possibility of their being saved. They are privileged to live in a home where one of the parents is indwelt by the Spirit of God. In this sense, they are sanctified. This verse also includes the assurance that it is not wrong to have children when one parent is a Christian and the other is not. God recognizes the marriage, and the children are not illegitimate.

7:15 But what should be the attitude of a Christian if the unsaved partner desires to leave? The answer is that he or she should be allowed to **depart**. The expression **"a brother or a sister is not under bondage in such cases"** is very difficult to explain with finality. Some believe that it means that if the unbeliever deserts the believer, and there is every reason to believe that the desertion is final, then the believer is free to obtain a divorce. Those who hold this view teach that verse 15 is a parenthesis, and that verse 16 is connected with verse 14 as follows:

1. Verse 14 states that the ideal situation is for a believer to remain with an unbelieving partner because of the sanctifying influence of a Christian in the home.
2. Verse 16 suggests that through staying in the home, the believer may win the unbeliever to Christ.
3. Verse 15 is a parenthesis, allowing the believer to be divorced (and possibly to remarry) if he or she is deserted by the unbeliever.

The hope of eventual salvation is connected with continued union rather than with the unbeliever's leaving the home.

But other Bible students insist that verse 15 deals only with the subject of separation and not with divorce and remarriage. To them, it simply means that if the unbeliever departs, he should be allowed to do so peacefully. The wife is not under any obligation to keep the marriage together beyond what she has already done. **God has called us to peace**, and we are not required to use emotional displays or legal processes to prevent the unbeliever from departing.

Which is the right interpretation? We find it impossible to decide definitely. It does seem to us that the Lord taught in Matthew 19:9 that divorce is permitted where one party has been guilty of unfaithfulness (adultery). We believe that in such a case, the innocent party is free to remarry. As far as 1 Corinthians 7:15 is concerned, we cannot be positive that it permits divorce and remarriage where an unbeliever has deserted his Christian partner. However, anyone who is guilty of this form of desertion will almost inevitably enter into a new relationship very soon, and thus the original union will be broken anyway. J. M. Davies writes:

> The unbeliever who departs would very soon be married to another, which would automatically break the marriage bond. To insist that the deserted party remain unmarried would put a yoke upon him/her which in the majority of cases, they would not be able to bear.[19]

7:16 One's understanding of verse 16 varies somewhat depending on the interpretation of verse 15.

If a person believes that verse 15 does not sanction divorce, he points to this verse as proof. He argues that the believer should permit separation but should not divorce the unbeliever because that would prevent the possibility of the restoration of the marriage union and the likelihood of the unbeliever's being saved. If, on the other hand, a person believes that divorce is permitted when a believer has been deserted, then this verse is linked with verse 14, and verse 15 is considered as a parenthesis.

7:17 There is sometimes a feeling among new converts that they must make a complete break with every phase of their former life, including institutions such as marriage which are not in themselves sinful. In the newfound joy of salvation, there is the danger of using forcible revolution to overthrow all that one has previously known. Christianity does not use forcible revolution in order to accomplish its purposes. Rather, its changes are made by peaceful means. In verses 17–24, the apostle lays down the general rule that becoming a Christian need not involve violent revolution against existing ties. Doubtless he has marriage ties primarily in view, but he also applies the principle to racial and social ties.

Each believer is to walk in accordance with the calling of the Lord. If He has called one to married life, then he should follow this in the fear of the Lord. If God has given grace to live a celibate life, then a man should follow that calling. In addition, if at the time of a person's conversion, he is married to an unsaved wife, then he need not overturn this relationship, but should continue to the best of his ability to seek the salvation of his wife. What Paul is stating to the Corinthians is not for them alone; this is what he taught **in all the churches**. Vine writes:

> When Paul says, "and so ordain I in all the churches," he is not issuing decrees from a given center, but is simply informing the Church at Corinth that the instructions he was giving them were what he gave in every church.[20]

7:18 Paul deals with the subject of racial ties in verses 18 and 19. If a man was a Jew at the time of his conversion, and bore in his body the mark of circumcision, he need not take a violent revulsion at this and seek to obliterate all physical marks of his former way of life. Likewise, if a man were a heathen at the time of his new birth, he does not have to seek to hide his heathen background by taking on the marks of a Jew.

We might also interpret this verse to mean that if a Jew were converted, he should not be afraid to live on with his Jewish wife, or if a Gentile were converted he should not try to flee from that background. These external differences are not what really count.

7:19 As far as the essence of Christianity is concerned, **circumcision is nothing and uncircumcision is nothing**. What really counts is **keeping the commandments of God**. In other words, God is concerned with what is inward, not with what is outward. The relationships of life need not be violently forsaken by the entrance of Christianity. "Rather," Kelly says, "by the Christian faith, the believer is raised to a position where he is superior to all circumstances."[21]

7:20 The general rule is that **each one** should **remain** with God in that state **in which he was called**. This, of course, only refers to callings that are not in themselves sinful. If a person were engaged in some wicked business at the time of conversion, he would be expected to leave it! But the apostle here is dealing with things not wrong in themselves. This is proved in the following verses where the subject of slaves is discussed.

7:21 What should **a slave** do when he is saved? Should he rebel against his owner and demand his freedom? Does Christianity insist that we go around seeking our "rights"? Paul gives the answer here: **"Were you called while a slave? Do not be concerned about it."** In other words, "Were you a slave at the time of your conversion? Do not be needlessly concerned about that. You can be a slave and still enjoy the highest blessings of Christianity."

But if you can be made free, rather use it. There are two interpretations of this passage. Some feel that Paul is saying, "If you can become free, by all means avail yourself of this opportunity." Others feel that the apostle is saying that even if a slave could become free, Christianity does not require him to avail himself of that freedom. Rather he should use his bondage as a testimony to the Lord Jesus. Most people will prefer the first interpretation (and it is probably correct), but they should not overlook the fact that the second would be more nearly in accord with the example left to us by the Lord Jesus Christ Himself.

7:22 **He who is called in the Lord while a slave is the Lord's freedman.** This does not mean a man who was freeborn but rather one who was made free, that is, a slave who obtained his freedom. In other words, if a man was a slave at the time of his conversion, he should not let that worry him, because he **is the Lord's freedman**. He has been set free from his sins and from the bondage of Satan. On the other hand, if a man were **free** at the time of his conversion, he should realize that from now on

he is a **slave**, bound hand and foot to the Savior.

7:23 Every Christian has been **bought at a price**. He henceforth belongs to the One who bought him, the Lord Jesus. We are to be Christ's bondslaves and **not become slaves of men.**

7:24 Therefore, no matter what one's social state was, he can consistently **remain with God** in that state. These two words *with God* are the key which unlocks the whole truth. If a man is **with God**, then even slavery can be made true freedom. "It is that which ennobles and sanctifies any position in life."

7:25 In verses 25–38, the apostle is addressing himself to the unmarried, whether male or female. The word **virgins** can be used to apply to either. Verse 25 is another verse that some have used to teach that the contents of this chapter are not necessarily inspired. They even go to such extremes as to say that Paul, being a bachelor, was a male chauvinist and that his personal prejudices are reflected in what he says here! To adopt such an attitude, of course, is to deal a vicious attack on the inspiration of Scriptures. When Paul says he has **no commandment from the Lord** about **virgins**, he simply means that during the Lord's earthly ministry He did not leave any explicit instruction on this subject. Therefore Paul gives his own **judgment, as one whom the Lord in His mercy has made trustworthy**, and this judgment is inspired of God.

7:26 In general, it **is good** to be unmarried, **because of the present distress. The present distress** refers to the sufferings of this earthly life in general. Perhaps there was a special time of distress at the time Paul wrote this letter. However, distress has continued to exist and will last until the Lord comes.

7:27 Paul's advice is that those who are already married should **not seek** to be separated. On the other hand, if a man **is loosed from a wife**, he should **not seek a wife**. The expression **loosed from a wife** here does not only mean widowed or divorced. It simply means free from the marriage bond, and could include those who never married.

7:28 Nothing Paul says should be

If a woman's **husband dies, she is at liberty to be married to** another man. This same truth is enunciated in Romans 7:1–3, namely, that death breaks the marriage relationship. However, the apostle adds the qualification that she is free to marry **whom she wishes, only in the Lord**. This means, first of all, that the person she marries must be a Christian, but it means more than this. **In the Lord** means "in the will of the Lord." In other words, she might marry a Christian and still be out of the will of the Lord. She must seek the guidance of the Lord in this important matter and marry the believer whom the Lord would have for her.

7:40   Paul's frank judgment is that a widow **is happier if she remains** unmarried. This does not contradict 1 Timothy 5:14 where Paul expresses his judgment that younger widows should marry. Here he is stating his general idea — in 1 Timothy a specific exception.

Then he adds, **"I think I also have the Spirit of God."** Some misunderstand these words to mean that Paul was not sure of himself in stating these things! Again we protest vigorously against any such interpretation. There can be no question as to the inspiration of what Paul wrote in this portion. He is using irony here. His apostleship and his teaching had been under attack by some at Corinth. They professed to have the mind of the Lord in what they were saying. Paul is saying in effect, "Whatever else others may say of me, I think that I also have the Spirit of God. They profess to have Him but surely they do not think that they have a monopoly on the Holy Spirit."

We know that Paul did indeed **have the Spirit** in all that he wrote to us, and that the path of happiness for us is to follow his instructions.

B. Concerning Eating Meats Offered to Idols (8:1–11:1)

The question of eating meat offered to idols is taken up in 8:1–11:1, a real problem to those recently converted to Christ from heathenism. Perhaps they would be invited to a social event at a temple where a great feast would be spread with meat previously offered to idols. Or perhaps they would go to the market to buy meat and find that the butcher was selling meat that had been offered to idols. This would not affect the quality of the meat, of course, but should a Christian buy it? In another scenario, a believer might be invited to a home and be served food that had been offered up to some idol deity. If he knew that this had been the case, should he partake of the food? Paul addresses himself to these questions.

8:1 The apostle begins by stating that **concerning things offered to idols**, both the Corinthians and he himself had **knowledge**. It was not a subject about which they were completely ignorant. They **all** knew, for instance, that the mere act of offering a piece of meat to an idol had not changed it in any sense. Its flavor and nutritional value remained the same. However, Paul points out that **knowledge puffs up, but love edifies**. By this he means that knowledge in itself is not a sufficient guide in these matters. If knowledge were the only principle that were applied, then it might lead to pride. Actually in all such matters the Christian must use not only knowledge but also love. He must not only consider what is lawful for himself, but what would be best for others.

8:2, 3 Vine paraphrases verse 2 as follows: "If a man imagines he has fully acquired knowledge, he has not even begun to know how it ought to be gained." Without love there can be no true knowledge. On the other hand, **if anyone loves God, this one is known by Him** in the sense that God approves him. In one sense, of course, God knows everybody, and in another sense He knows especially those who are believers. But here the word "know" is used to denote favor or approval. If anyone makes his decisions in such matters as meats offered to idols out of love to God and man and not out of mere knowledge, that person wins the smile of God's approval.

8:4 As far as things **offered to idols** are concerned, believers understand that **an idol is** not a real god with power, knowledge, and love. Paul was not denying the existence of idols themselves; he knew that there were such things as images carved out of wood or stone. Later on he acknowledges that behind these idols there are demon-powers. But what he emphasizes here is that the gods which these idols purport to represent do not exist. **There is no other God but one**, that is, the God and Father of our Lord Jesus Christ.

8:5 Paul admits that there were many **so-called gods** in heathen mythology, such as Jupiter, Juno, and Mercury. Some of these gods were supposed to live **in heaven**, and others, such as Ceres and Neptune, here **on earth**. In this sense **there are many gods and many lords**, that is, mythological beings which people worshiped and were in bondage to.

8:6 Believers know that **there is one** true **God, the Father, of whom are all things, and we for Him**. This means that God, our Father, is the Source or Creator of **all things** and that **we** were created **for Him**. In other words, He is the purpose or goal of our existence. We also know that there is **one Lord**, namely **Jesus Christ, through whom are all things, and through whom we live**. The expression **through whom are all things** describes the Lord Jesus as the Mediator or Agent of God, whereas the expression **through whom we live** indicates that it is through Him that we have been created and redeemed.

When Paul says that **there is one God, the Father**, and **one Lord Jesus Christ**, he does not mean that the Lord Jesus Christ is not God. Rather he simply indicates the respective roles which these two Persons of the Godhead fulfilled in creation and in redemption.

8:7 **However**, not all Christians, especially new converts, understand the liberty which they have in Christ Jesus. Having come from backgrounds of idolatry and being used to idols, they think they are committing idolatry when they eat meat that has been **offered to an idol**. They think that the idol is a reality **and** therefore **their conscience, being weak, is defiled**.

The expression **weak** here does not mean physically weak or even spiritually weak. It is a term describing those who are unduly scrupulous in matters of moral indifference. For instance, as far as God is concerned, it is not wrong for a believer to eat pork. It would have been wrong for a Jew to do so in the OT, but a Christian is at perfect liberty to partake of such food. However, a Jew converted to Christianity might still have scruples about this. He might feel that it is wrong to eat a roast pork dinner. He is what the Bible calls a weak brother. It means that he is not living in the full enjoyment of his Christian liberty. Actually, as long as he thinks that it is wrong to eat pork, he would sin if he went ahead and did it. That is what is meant by the expression **their conscience, being weak, is defiled**. If my conscience condemns a certain act and I go ahead and commit it, then I have sinned. "Whatever is not from faith is sin" (Rom. 14:23).

8:8 **Food** in itself is not a matter of great consequence **to God**. Refraining from certain foods does not give us favor with God, nor does partaking of such foods make us better Christians.

8:9 But although there is nothing to gain by eating these foods, there might be much to lose if in so doing I cause a **weak** Christian to stumble. This is where the principle of love must come in. A Christian has liberty to eat meat that has been previously offered in sacrifice to idols, but it would be utterly wrong for him to eat if in so doing he offends a **weak** brother or sister.

8:10 The danger is that the weak brother might be encouraged to do what his conscience condemns, if he **sees** another doing something which to him is questionable. In this verse, the apostle condemns **eating in an idol's temple** because of the effect it would have on others. Of course, when Paul speaks here of **eating in an idol's temple**, he is referring to some social event or some general celebration, such as a wedding. It would never be right to eat in such a temple if the meal involved participation in idol-worship in any way. Paul later condemns that (10:15–26). The expression **for if anyone sees you who have knowledge** means if anybody sees you, who have a full measure of Christian liberty, who know that meat offered to idols is not unclean or impure, etc. The important principle here is that we must not only consider what effect such an action would have on ourselves, but even more important, what effect it would have on others.

8:11 A man may so parade his

knowledge of what is legitimate for a Christian as to cause a brother in Christ to stumble. The word **perish** does not mean that he would lose his eternal salvation. It means not the loss of *being* but the loss of *well-being.* This weak brother's testimony would be hurt and his life would be adversely affected as far as usefulness for God is concerned. The tremendous seriousness of so offending a weak brother in Christ is indicated by the words **for whom Christ died**. Paul's argument is that if the Lord Jesus Christ loved this man so much that He was willing to die for him, we should not dare to hinder his spiritual progress by doing anything that would stumble him. A few slices of meat are not worth it!

8:12 It is not just a matter of sinning against a brother in Christ, or of wounding his **weak conscience**. It constitutes sin **against Christ** Himself. Whatever we do to the least of His brethren we do to Him. What hurts one of the members of the Body hurts the Head as well. Vine points out that in dealing with each subject, the apostle leads his readers to view it in the light of the atoning death of Christ. Barnes says, "It is an appeal drawn from the deep and tender love, the sufferings, and the dying groans of the Son of God."[27] **Sin against Christ** is what Godet calls "the highest of crimes." Realizing this, we should be very careful to examine all our actions in the light of their effect on others, and to refrain from doing anything that would cause a brother to be offended.

8:13 Because it is sin against Christ to make one's **brother stumble**, Paul states that he **will never again eat meat** if in so doing he makes his **brother stumble**. The work of God in the life of another person is far more important than a tender roast! Although the subject of meats offered to idols is not a problem for most Christians today, the *principles* which the Spirit of God gives us in this section are of abiding value. There are many things today in the Christian life, which, while not forbidden in the word of God, would yet cause needless offense to weaker Christians. While we might have the right to participate in them, a greater right is to forego that right for the spiritual welfare of those we

love in Christ, our fellow-believers.

At first glance, chapter 9 might seem to indicate a new subject. However, the question of meats offered to idols continues for two more chapters. Paul is merely turning aside here to give *his own example* of self-denial for the good of others. He was willing to forego his right to financial support as an apostle in accordance with the principle set forth in 8:13. Thus this chapter is closely linked with chapter 8.

9:1 As we know, there were those in Corinth who questioned Paul's authority. They said that he was not one of the twelve, and therefore not a genuine apostle. Paul protests that he was free from human authority, a genuine **apostle** of the Lord Jesus. He bases his claim on two facts. First of all, he had **seen Jesus Christ our Lord** in resurrection. This took place on the road to Damascus. He also points to the Corinthians themselves as proof of his apostleship by asking the question, **"Are you not my work in the Lord?"** If they had any doubt as to his apostleship, they should examine themselves. Were they saved? Of course they would say they were. Well, who pointed them to Christ? The Apostle Paul did! Therefore, they themselves were proof of the fact that he was a genuine apostle of the Lord.

9:2 **Others** may not recognize him as **an apostle**, but surely the Corinthians themselves should. They were **the seal of** his **apostleship in the Lord.**

9:3 Verse 3 probably refers to what has gone before (and not to what follows, as the NKJV punctuates it). Paul is saying that what he has just said is his **defense to those who examine** him, or who question his authority as an apostle.

9:4 In verses 4–14, the apostle discusses his **right** to financial support as an apostle. As one who had been sent by the Lord Jesus, Paul was entitled to financial remuneration from the believers. However, he had not always insisted on this right. He had often worked with his hands, making tents, in order that he might be able to preach the gospel freely to men and women. No doubt his critics took advantage of this, suggesting that the reason that he did not take support was that he knew he was not a real apostle. He introduces the subject by asking a question: **"Do we have no right to eat and drink?** — that is — without having to work for it? Are we not entitled to be supported by the church?"

9:5 Do we have no right to take along a believing wife, as do also the other apostles, and **the brothers of the Lord, and Cephas?** Perhaps some of Paul's critics suggested that Paul did not marry because he knew that he and his wife would not be entitled to the support of the churches. Peter and the other apostles were married, as were also **the brothers of the Lord.** Here the apostle is stating that he would have just as much right to be married and enjoy the support of the Christians for both his wife and himself. The expression **"to take along a believing wife"** refers not only to the right to marry, but also to the right of support for both husband and wife. **The brothers of the Lord** probably means His actual half-brothers, or possibly His cousins. This text alone does not solve the problem, although other Scriptures indicate that Mary did have other children after Jesus, her Firstborn (Luke 2:7; see Matt. 1:25; 12:46; 13:55; Mark 6:3; John 2:12; Gal. 1:19).

9:6 It appears that **Barnabas,** like Paul, had worked to provide for his material needs while preaching the gospel. Paul asked if they both did not have the **right to refrain from working** and to be cared for by the people of God.

9:7 The apostle based his first claim to financial support on the example of the other apostles. He now turns to an argument from human affairs. A soldier is not sent to war **at his own expense.** Whoever **plants a vineyard** is never expected to do so without receiving some recompense from **its fruit.** Finally, a shepherd is not expected to keep **a flock** without being given a right to partake **of the milk.** Christian service is like warfare, agriculture, and pastoral life. It involves fighting against the enemy, caring for God's fruit trees, and serving as an under-shepherd for His sheep. If the right of support is recognized in these earthly occupations, how much more should it be in the service of the Lord!

9:8 Paul next turns to the OT for further proof of his point. Does he have

to base his argument merely on these mundane things of life, such as warfare, agriculture, and shepherding? **Does not the** Scripture **say the same** thing?

9:9 It is clearly stated in Deuteronomy 25:4 that **an ox** should **not** be muzzled **while it treads out the grain.** That is, when an animal is used in a harvesting operation, it should be allowed to partake of some of the harvest. **Is it oxen God is concerned about?** God does care for oxen, but He didn't cause these things to be written in the OT merely for the sake of dumb animals. There was a spiritual principle involved to be applied to our life and service.

9:10 Or does He say it altogether for our sakes? The answer is "yes," our welfare was in His mind when these words were **written.** When a man **plows,** he **should plow** with the expectation of some remuneration. So likewise, when a man **threshes,** he should be able to look forward to some of the harvest in recompense. Christian service resembles plowing and threshing, and God has decreed that those who engage in these aspects of His service should not do so at their own expense.

9:11 Paul speaks of himself as having **sown spiritual things for** the Christians at Corinth. In other words, he came to Corinth preaching the gospel to them and teaching them precious spiritual truths. That being so, is it asking too much if in return they should minister to him of their finances or other **material things**? The argument is that "the wages of the preacher are greatly inferior in value to what he has given. Material benefits are small compared with spiritual blessings."

9:12 Paul was aware that the church at Corinth was supporting **others** who were preaching or teaching there. They recognized this obligation to other men but not to the Apostle Paul, and so he asks: **"If others are partakers of this right over you, are we not even more?"** If they recognized the right of others to financial support, why should they not then recognize that he, their father in the faith, had this right? Doubtless some of those who were being supported were the Judaizing teachers. Paul adds that, although he had **this right,** he did not use it with the Corinthians but endured

all things lest he **hinder the gospel of Christ**. Rather than insist on his right to receive support from them, he bore all sorts of privations and hardships so that the gospel would not be hindered.

9:13 Paul next introduces the argument from the support of those who served in the Jewish temple. Those who had official duties in connection with the temple service were supported from the income the temple received. In this sense they lived off **the things of the temple**. Also, the priests themselves **who** served **at the altar** were given a certain portion **of the offerings** that were brought to **the altar**. In other words, both the Levites, who had the ordinary duties around the temple, and the priests, to whom were entrusted the more sacred duties, were alike supported for their service.

9:14 Finally, Paul introduces the definite command of **the Lord** Himself. He **commanded that those who preach the gospel should live from the gospel**. This would be conclusive proof alone of Paul's right to support from the Corinthians. But this raises the question of why he did not insist on being supported by them. The answer is given in verses 15–18.

9:15 He explains that he **used none of these things**, that is, he did not insist on his rights. Neither was he writing **these things** at the present time in order that they might send money to him. He would rather **die than that anyone should** be able to rob him of his **boasting**.

9:16 Paul is saying that he cannot **boast** in the fact that he preaches the gospel. A divine compulsion **is laid upon** him. It is not a vocation that he chose for himself. He received the "tap on the shoulder" and he would have been a most miserable man if he had not obeyed the divine commission. This does not mean the apostle was not willing to preach the gospel, but rather that the decision to preach did not come from himself, but from the Lord.

9:17 If the Apostle Paul preached the gospel **willingly**, he would **have** the **reward** that goes with such service, namely, the right of maintenance. Throughout the Old and New Testaments, it is clearly taught that those who serve the Lord are entitled to support from the Lord's people. In this passage, Paul does not mean that he was an unwilling servant of the Lord, but is simply stating that there was a divine compulsion in his apostleship. He goes on to emphasize this in the latter part of the verse. **If** he preached **against** his **will**, that is, if he preached because there was a fire burning within him and he could not refrain from preaching, then he had **been entrusted with a stewardship** of the gospel. He was a man acting under orders, and therefore he could not boast in that.

Verse 17 is admittedly difficult, and yet the meaning seems to be that Paul would not claim his right of maintenance from the Corinthians because the ministry was not an occupation which he chose by himself. He was placed in it by the hand of God. The false teachers in Corinth might claim their right to be supported by the saints, but the Apostle Paul would seek his reward elsewhere.

Knox's translation of this verse is as follows: "I can claim a reward for what I do of my own choice; but when I act under constraint, I am only executing a commission."

Ryrie comments:

> Paul could not escape his responsibility to preach the gospel, because a stewardship (responsibility) had been committed to him and he was under orders to preach even though he was never paid (cf. Luke 17:10).[28]

9:18 If then he could not boast in the fact that he preached the gospel, of what would he boast? Of something that was a matter of his own choice, namely, that he presented **the gospel of Christ without charge**. This is something he could determine to do. He would preach the gospel to the Corinthians, at the same time earning his own living, so as not to use to the full his right for maintenance **in the gospel**.

To summarize the apostle's argument here, he is making a distinction between what was obligatory and what was optional. There is no thought of any reluctance in his preaching the gospel. He did that cheerfully. But in a very real sense, it was a solemn obligation that rested upon him. Therefore in the discharge of that obligation there was no reason for his boasting. In preaching the gospel, he could have insisted on his right to financial support, but he did not do this; rather he decided to give the gospel **without charge** to the Corinthians. Since this was a matter of his own will, he would glory in this. As we have suggested, Paul's critics claimed that his working as a tentmaker indicated that he did not consider himself to be a true apostle. Here he turns his self-support in such a way as to prove that his apostleship was nonetheless real; in fact, it was of a very high and noble character.

In verses 19–22, Paul cites his example of the waiving of legitimate rights for the gospel's sake. In studying this section, it is important to remember that Paul does not mean that he ever sacrificed important principles of the Scripture. He did not believe that the end justified the means. In these verses he is speaking about matters of moral indifference. He accommodated himself to the customs and habits of the people with whom he worked in order that he might gain a ready ear for the gospel. But never did he do anything which might compromise the truth of the gospel.

9:19 In one sense he was **free from all men**. No one could exercise jurisdiction or compulsion over him. Yet he brought himself under bondage **to all** people in order **that** he **might win the more**. If he could make a concession without sacrificing divine truth he would do it in order to win souls to Christ.

9:20 **To the Jews** he **became as a Jew, that** he **might win Jews**. This cannot mean that he put himself back under the Law of Moses in order to see Jews saved. What it does mean might be illustrated in the action which Paul took in connection with the circumcision of Timothy and Titus. In the case of Titus, there were those who insisted that unless he was circumcised, he couldn't be saved. Realizing that this was a frontal attack on the gospel of the grace of God, Paul stoutly refused to have Titus circumcised (Gal. 2:3). However, in the case of Timothy it seems that no such issue was involved. Therefore, the apostle was willing that Timothy should be circumcised if this would result in a wider hearing of the gospel (Acts 16:3).

To those who are under the law, as under the law,[29] **that I might win those who are under the law. Those who are under the law** refers to the Jewish people. But Paul had already spoken of his dealings with the Jews in the first part of the verse. Why does he then repeat the subject here? The explanation that has often been offered is that when he speaks of Jews in the first part of the verse, he is referring to their national customs, whereas here he is referring to their religious life.

At this point a brief word of explanation is necessary. As a Jew, Paul had been born under the law. He sought to obtain favor with God by keeping the law, but found that he was unable to do so. The law only showed him what a wretched sinner he was, and utterly condemned him. Eventually he learned that the law was not a way of salvation, but only God's method of revealing to man his sinfulness and his need of a Savior. Paul then trusted in the Lord Jesus Christ, and in so doing he became free from the condemning voice of the law. The penalty of the law which he had broken was paid by the Lord Jesus on the cross of Calvary.

After his conversion, the apostle learned that the law was not the way of salvation, nor was it the rule of life for one who had been saved. The believer is not under law but under grace. This does not mean that he can go out and do as he pleases. Rather, it means that a true sense of the grace of God will prevent him from even wanting to do these things. Indwelt by the Spirit of God, the Christian is raised to a new level of behavior. He now desires to live a holy life, not out of fear of punishment for having broken the law, but out of love for Christ, who died for him and rose again. Under law the motive was fear, but under grace the motive is love. Love is a far higher motive than fear. Men will do out of love what they would never do from terror.

Arnot says:

God's method of binding souls to obedience is similar to His method of keeping the planets in their orbits — that is, by flinging them out free. You see no chain keeping back these shining worlds to prevent them from bursting away from their center. They are held in the grip of an invisible principle. . . . And it is by the invisible bond of love — love to the Lord who bought them — that ransomed men are constrained to live soberly and righteously and godly.[30]

With that brief background in mind, let us now get back to the latter half of verse 20. **To those who are under the law, as under the law, that I might win those who are under the law.** When he was with Jewish people, Paul behaved as a Jew in matters of moral indifference. For instance, he ate the foods which the Jewish people ate and refrained from eating such things as pork which were forbidden to them. Perhaps Paul also refrained from working on the Sabbath day, realizing that if he did this, the gospel might gain a more ready hearing from the people.

As a born-again believer in the Lord Jesus, the Apostle Paul was not under the law as a rule of life. He merely adapted himself to the customs, habits, and prejudices of the people in order that he might win them to the Lord.

9:21 Ryrie writes:

Paul is not demonstrating two-facedness or multi-facedness, but rather he is testifying of a constant, restrictive self-discipline in order to be able to serve all sorts of men. Just as a narrowly channeled stream is more powerful than an unbounded marshy swamp, so restricted liberty results in more powerful testimony for Christ.[31]

To **those who are without law**, Paul acted **as** one **without law** (although he himself was **not without law toward God, but under law toward Christ**). **Those who are without law** does not refer to rebels or outlaws who do not recognize any law, but is a general description of Gentiles. The law, as such, was given to the Jewish nation and not to the Gentiles. Thus when Paul was with the Gentiles he complied with their habits and feelings as far as he could possibly do so and still be loyal to the Savior. The apostle explained that even while he thus acted as **without law**, he was nevertheless **not without law toward God**. He did not consider that he was free to do as he pleased, **but** he was **under law toward Christ**. In other words, he was bound to love, honor, serve, and please the Lord Jesus, not now by the Law of Moses, but by the law of love. He was "enlawed" to Christ. We have an expression "When in Rome, do as the Romans do." Paul is saying here that when he was with the Gentiles, he adapted himself to their manner of living as far as he could consistently do so and still be loyal to Christ. But we must keep in mind that this passage deals only with cultural things and not with doctrinal or moral matters.

9:22 Verse 22 speaks of those who are **weak** or overscrupulous. They were excessively sensitive about matters that were really not of fundamental importance. **To the weak**, Paul **became as**[32] **weak, that** he **might win** them. He would be a vegetarian if necessary rather than offend them by eating meat. In short, Paul became **all things to all men, that** he **might by all means save some**. These verses should never be used to justify a sacrifice of scriptural principle. They merely describe a readiness to accommodate to the customs and habits of the people in order to win a hearing for the good news of salvation. When Paul says **that I might by all means save some**, he does not think for a moment that he could save another person, for he realized that the Lord Jesus was the only Person who could save. At the same time it is wonderful to notice that those who serve Christ in the gospel are so closely identified with Him that He even allows them to use the word **save** to describe a work in which they are involved. How this exalts and ennobles and dignifies the gospel ministry!

Verses 23–27 describe the peril of losing one's reward through lack of self-discipline. To Paul the refusal of financial help from the Corinthians was a form of rigid discipline.

9:23 **Now this I do for the gospel's sake, that I may be partaker of it with you.** In the preceding verses Paul had been describing how he submerged his own rights and desires in the work of the Lord. Why did he do this? He did it **for the gospel's sake**, in order **that** he might share in the triumphs of the gospel in a coming day.

9:24 Doubtless as the apostle wrote the words found in verse 24, he was reminded of the Isthmian games that were held not far from Corinth. The Corinthian believers would be well-acquainted with those athletic contests. Paul reminds them that while many **run in a race**, not all receive **the prize**. The Christian life is like a race. It requires self-discipline. It calls for strenuous effort. It demands definiteness of purpose. The verse does not, however, suggest that in the Christian race only one can win the prize. It simply teaches that we should all run as winners. We should all practice the same kind of self-denial that the Apostle Paul himself practiced. Here, of course, the prize is not salvation, but a reward for faithful service. Salvation is nowhere stated to be the result of our faithfulness in running the race. Salvation is the free gift of God through faith in the Lord Jesus Christ.

9:25 Now Paul changes the figure from running to wrestling. He reminds his readers that **everyone who competes** in the games, that is, wrestles, exercises self-control **in all things**. A wrestler once asked his coach, "Can't I smoke and drink and have a good time and still wrestle?" The coach replied, "Yes, you can, but you can't win!" As Paul thinks of the contestants at the games, he sees the winner stepping up to receive his prize. What is it? It is **a perishable crown**, a garland of flowers or a wreath of leaves that will soon wither away. But in comparison he mentions **an imperishable crown** which will be awarded to all those who have been faithful in their service to Christ.

> We thank Thee for the crown
>   Of glory and of life;
> 'Tis no poor withering wreath of earth,
>   Man's prize in mortal strife;
> 'Tis incorruptible as is the Throne,
>   The kingdom of our God and
>   His Incarnate Son.
> – *Horatius Bonar*

9:26 In view of this imperishable crown, Paul states that he therefore runs **not with uncertainty**, and fights **not as one who beats the air**. His service was neither purposeless nor ineffectual. He had a definite aim before his eyes, and his intention was that his every action should count. There must be no wasted time or energy. The apostle was not interested in wild misses.

9:27 Instead, he disciplined his **body, and** brought **it into subjection, lest when** he had **preached to others**, he

himself might be rejected or **disqualified**. In the Christian life, there is a necessity for self-control, for temperance, for discipline. We must practice self-mastery.

The Apostle Paul realized the dread possibility that after he had **preached to others**, he himself might be **disqualified**. Considerable debate has centered on the meaning of this verse. Some hold that it teaches that a person can be saved and then subsequently lost. This, of course, is in conflict with the general body of teaching in the NT to the effect that no true sheep of Christ will ever perish.

Others say that the word translated **disqualified**[33] is a strong word and refers to eternal damnation. However, they interpret the verse to mean that Paul is not teaching that a person who was ever saved could be disqualified, but simply that one who failed to exercise self-discipline had never been really saved in the first place. Thinking of the false teachers and how they indulged every passion and appetite, Paul sets forth the general principle that if a person does not keep his body in subjection, this is proof that he never really was born again; and although he might preach to others, he himself will be disqualified.

A third explanation is that Paul is not speaking here of salvation at all but of service. He is not suggesting that he might ever be lost, but that he might not stand the test as far as his service was concerned and might be rejected for the prize. This interpretation exactly fits the meaning of the word *disqualified* and the athletic context. Paul recognizes the awful possibility that, having **preached to others**, he himself might be *put on the shelf* by the Lord as no longer usable by Him.

In any event, the passage is an extremely serious one and should cause deep heart-searching on the part of everyone who seeks to serve the Lord Christ. Each one should determine that by the grace of God he will never have to learn the meaning of the word by experience.

As Paul has been thinking of the necessity for self-control, the example of the Israelites comes before his mind. In chapter 10, he remembers how they became self-indulgent and careless in the discipline of their bodies, and thus became disqualified and disapproved.

First of all, he speaks of the privileges of Israel (vv. 1–4); then the punishment of Israel (v. 5); and finally the causes of Israel's downfall (vv. 6–10). Then he explains how these things apply to us (vv. 11–13).

10:1 The apostle reminds the Corinthians **that all** the Jewish **fathers were under the cloud** and **all passed through the sea**. The emphasis is on the word **all**. He is thinking back to the time of their deliverance from Egypt and how they were miraculously guided by a pillar of **cloud** by day and pillar of fire by night. He is thinking back to the time when they passed through the Red Sea and escaped into the wilderness. As far as privilege was concerned, they all enjoyed divine guidance and divine deliverance.

10:2 Not only that, but **all were baptized into Moses in the cloud and in the sea.** To be **baptized into Moses** means to be identified with him and to acknowledge his leadership. As Moses led the children of Israel out of Egypt toward the Promised Land, all the nation of Israel pledged allegiance to Moses at first and recognized him as the divinely appointed savior. It has been suggested that the expression "under the cloud" refers to that which identified them with God, and the expression "through the sea" describes that which separated them from Egypt.

10:3 They **all ate the same spiritual food**. This refers to the manna which was miraculously provided for the people of Israel as they journeyed through the wilderness. The expression **spiritual food** does not mean that it was nonmaterial. It does not mean that it was invisible or unreal. Rather, **spiritual** simply means that the material food was a type or picture of spiritual nourishment, and that the spiritual reality is what the writer had primarily in mind. It may also include the idea that the food was supernaturally given.

10:4 All through their journeyings, God wonderfully provided water for them to drink. It was real water, but again it is called **spiritual drink** in the sense that it was typical of spiritual refreshment, and miraculously provided.

They would have died from thirst many times had not the Lord given them this water in a miraculous way. The expression **they drank of that spiritual Rock that followed them** does not mean that a literal, material rock journeyed behind them as they traveled. The Rock signifies the river that flowed from it and followed the Israelites. **That Rock was Christ** in the sense that He was the One who provided it and the One it represents, providing living water to His people.

10:5 After enumerating all these marvelous privileges that were theirs, the apostle must now remind the Corinthians that **with most of** the Israelites **God was not well pleased, for their bodies were scattered in the wilderness**. Although all Israel left Egypt and all professed to be one in heart and soul with their leader, Moses, yet the sad truth is that although their bodies were in the wilderness, yet their hearts were still back in Egypt. They enjoyed a physical deliverance from the bondage of Pharaoh, but they still lusted after the sinful pleasures of that country. Of all the warriors over twenty years of age who left Egypt, only two, Caleb and Joshua, ever won the prize — they reached the Promised Land. The carcasses of the rest of them fell **in the wilderness** as an evidence of God's displeasure.

Note the contrast between the word "all" in the first four verses and the word **most** in verse 5. They were all privileged, but **most of them** perished. Godet marvels:

> What a spectacle is that which is called up by the apostle before the eyes of the self-satisfied Corinthians: all those bodies, sated with miraculous food and drink, strewing the soil of the desert![34]

10:6 In the events that happened in the time of the Exodus, we see teaching that applies to us. The children of Israel were actually **examples** for us, showing us what will happen to us if we also **lust after evil things as they** did. As we read the OT, we should not read it merely as history, but as containing lessons of practical importance for our lives today.

In the verses to follow, the apostle is going to list some of the specific sins into which they fell. It is worth noticing that many of these sins are concerned with the gratification of bodily appetites.

10:7 Verse 7 refers to the worship of the golden calf and the feast that followed it, as recorded in Exodus 32. When Moses came down from Mount Sinai, he found that the people had made a golden calf and were worshiping it. We read in Exodus 32:6 how **the people sat down to eat and drink, and rose up to play**, that is, to dance.

10:8 The sin mentioned in verse 8 refers to the time when the sons of Israel intermarried with the daughters of Moab (Num. 25). Seduced by Balaam the prophet, they disobeyed the word of the Lord and fell into immorality. We read in verse 8 that **in one day twenty-three thousand fell**. In the OT, it says that twenty-four thousand died in the plague (Num. 25:9). Critics of the Bible have often used this to try to show a contradiction in the Sacred Scriptures. If they would read the text more carefully, they would see that there is no contradiction. Here it simply states that *twenty-three thousand* fell *in one day*. In the OT, the figure of *twenty-four thousand* describes the entire number that died *in the plague.*

10:9 Paul next alludes to the time when the Israelites complained about the food and expressed doubt as to the goodness of the Lord. At that time God sent **serpents** among them and many perished (Num. 21:5, 6). Here again it is noticeable how food gratification was their downfall.

10:10 The sin of Korah, Dathan, and Abiram is referred to here (Num. 16:14–47). Again there was complaining against the Lord because of the food situation (Num. 16:14). The Israelites did not practice self-control with regard to their bodies. They did not discipline their bodies or put them in a place of subjection. Rather, they made provision for the lusts of the flesh, and this proved to be their downfall.

10:11 The next three verses give the practical application of the events. First of all, Paul explains that the meaning of these events is not limited to their historical value. They have a significance for us today. **They were written** as a warning to us who are living after the close

of the Jewish age and during the gospel age, "to us to whom the revenues of the past ages have descended," as Rendall Harris put it so well.

10:12 They constitute a warning to the self-confident: **Let him who thinks he stands take heed lest he fall**. Perhaps this refers especially to the strong believer who thinks he can dabble with self-gratification and not be affected by it. Such a person is in greatest danger of falling under the disciplinary hand of God.

10:13 But then Paul adds a marvelous word of encouragement for those who are tempted. He teaches that the testings, trials, and temptations which face us are **common** to all. However, **God is faithful, who will not allow** us **to be** tested **beyond what** we **are able**. He does not promise to deliver us from temptation or testing, but He does promise to limit its intensity. He further promises to provide **the way of escape, that** we **may be able to bear it**. Reading this verse, one cannot help but be struck by the tremendous comfort it has afforded to tested saints of God through the centuries. Young believers have clung to it as to a life-line and older believers have reposed on it as upon a pillow. Perhaps some of Paul's readers were being fiercely tempted at the time to go into idolatry. Paul would comfort them with the thought that God would not allow any unbearable temptation to come their way. At the same time they should be warned that they should not expose themselves to temptation.

10:14 The section from 10:14 through 11:1 returns to deal more specifically with the subject of meat offered to idols. First of all, Paul takes up the question as to whether believers should participate in feasts in idol temples (vv. 14–22).

Therefore, my beloved, flee from idolatry. Perhaps it was a real test for the believers at Corinth to be invited to participate in an idol feast at one of the temples. Some might feel that they were above temptation. Perhaps they would say that surely it would not hurt to go just once. The apostle's inspired advice is to **flee from idolatry**. He does not say to study about it, to become better acquainted with it, or to trifle with it in any way. They should run in the opposite direction.

10:15, 16   Paul knows that he is addressing himself to intelligent people who can understand what he is saying. In verse 16 he makes reference to the Lord's Supper. He says first of all: **"The cup of blessing which we bless, is it not the communion of the blood of Christ?"** **The cup of blessing** refers to the **cup** of wine which is used at the Lord's Supper. It is a **cup** which speaks of the tremendous **blessing** which has come to us through the death of Christ; therefore it is called **the cup of blessing**. The clause **which we bless** means "for which we give thanks." When we take that cup and press it to our lips, we are saying in effect that we are participants in all the benefits that flow from the blood of Christ. Therefore we might paraphrase this verse as follows:

> The cup which speaks of the tremendous blessings which have come to us through the blood of the Lord Jesus, and the same cup for which we give thanks, what is it but a testimony to the fact that all believers are partakers of the benefits of the blood of Christ?

The same thing is true of **the bread which we break**, the communion loaf. As we eat the bread, we say, in effect, that we have all been saved through the offering of His body on the cross of Calvary and that we are therefore members of His body. In short, the cup and the loaf speak of fellowship with Christ, of participating in His glorious ministry for us.

The question has been raised as to why the blood should be mentioned first in this verse whereas in the institution of the Lord's Supper, the bread is mentioned first. A possible answer is that Paul is speaking here of the order of events when we come into the Christian fellowship. Usually a new convert understands the value of the blood of Christ before he recognizes the truth of the one body. Thus this verse might give the order in which we understand salvation.

10:17   All believers, **though many, are one body in Christ**, represented by **that one** loaf of **bread. All partake of that one bread** in the sense that all have fellowship in the benefits that flow from the giving of the body of Christ.

10:18   What Paul is saying in these verses is that eating at the Lord's Table signifies fellowship with Him. The same was true of those Israelites who ate **of the sacrifices**. It meant that they had fellowship with **the altar**. The reference, no doubt, is to the peace offering. The people brought their sacrifices to the temple. A portion of the offering was burnt on the altar with fire; another portion was reserved for the priests; but the third part was set aside for the offerer and his friends. They ate of the offering on the same day. Paul is emphasizing that all who ate of the offering identified themselves with God and with the nation of Israel and, in short, with all of which **the altar** spoke.

But how does this fit in with the portion of the Scripture that we are studying? The answer is quite simple. Just as partaking of the Lord's Supper speaks of fellowship with the Lord, and just as the Israelites, partaking of the peace offering, spoke of fellowship with the altar of Jehovah, so eating at an idol feast in the temple speaks of fellowship with the idols.

10:19   **What am I saying then? That an idol is anything, or that what is offered to idols is anything?** Does Paul mean to imply by all this that meat offered to idols changes its character or quality? Or does he mean to say that an idol is real, that it hears, sees, and has power? Obviously the answer to both of these questions is "No."

10:20   What Paul does want to emphasize is that **the things which the Gentiles sacrifice** are offered **to demons**. In some strange and mysterious way, idol worship is linked with demons. Using the idols, the demons control the hearts and minds of those who worship them. There is one devil, Satan, but there are many demons which are his messengers and agents. Paul adds: **"I do not want you to have fellowship with demons."**

10:21   **You cannot drink the cup of the Lord and the cup of demons; you cannot partake of the Lord's table and of the table of demons.** In this verse the cup of the Lord is a figurative expression to describe the benefits which come to us through Christ. It is a figure of speech known as metonymy, where the container is used to denote the thing contained. The expression **the Lord's table** is likewise a figurative expression. It is not the same as the Lord's Supper, although it might include the latter. A table is an article of furniture where food is set out and where fellowship is enjoyed. Here the **table** of the Lord means the sum total of the blessings which we enjoy in Christ.

When Paul says that **you cannot drink the cup of the Lord and the cup of demons**, that **you cannot partake of the Lord's table and of the table of demons**, he does not mean that it is a physical impossibility. It would be a physical possibility, for instance, for a believer to go to an idol temple and to participate in a feast there. But what Paul means here is that it would be morally inconsistent. It would be an act of treachery and disloyalty to the Lord Jesus to profess adherence or allegiance to Him, on the one hand, and then to go and have fellowship with those who sacrifice to idols. It would be morally improper and utterly wrong.

10:22 Not only that, it would not be possible to do this without provoking **the Lord to jealousy**. As William Kelly said, "Love cannot but be jealous of wandering affections, it would not be love if it did not resent unfaithfulness."[35] The Christian should fear to thus displease the Lord, or to provoke His righteous indignation. Do we think that we are **stronger than He**? That is, do we dare to grieve Him and risk an exhibition of His disciplinary judgment upon us?

10:23 The apostle turns from the subject of participation in idol feasts and takes up some general principles that should govern Christians in their daily life. When he says **all things are lawful**, he does not mean all things in an absolute sense. For instance, he is not implying for a moment that it would be lawful for him to commit murder or to get drunk! Here again we must understand the expression as referring only to matters of moral indifference. There is a great area in Christian life where things are perfectly legitimate in themselves and yet where for other reasons it would

not be wise for a Christian to participate. Thus Paul says: **"All things are lawful for me, but all things are not helpful."** For instance, a thing might be quite lawful for a believer and yet might be equally unwise in view of the national customs of the people where he dwells. Also, things that are lawful in themselves might not be edifying. That is, a thing might not result in building up a brother in his most holy faith. Should I then be high-handed in demanding my own rights or should I consider what would help my brother in Christ?

10:24 In all the decisions we make, we should not be selfishly thinking of what will benefit ourselves, but we should rather think of what would be for our neighbor's **well-being**. The principles we are studying in this section could very well be applied to matters of dress, food and drink, standards of living, and the entertainments in which we participate.

10:25 If a believer went to **the meat market** to buy some meat, he was not required to ask the merchant whether that meat had been previously offered to idols. The meat itself would not be affected in one way or another, and there would be no question of loyalty to Christ involved.

10:26 In explanation of this advice, Paul quotes from Psalm 24:1: **"The earth is the LORD'S, and all its fullness."** The thought here is that the food that we eat has been graciously provided by the Lord for us and is specifically intended for our use. Heinrici tells us that these words from Psalm 24 are commonly used among the Jews as a thanksgiving at the table.

10:27 Now Paul takes up another situation which might cause the believers to ask questions. Suppose an unbeliever **invites** a believer to his home for **dinner**. Would a Christian be free to accept such an invitation? Yes. If you are invited to a meal in an unbeliever's home and you are disposed to go, you are at liberty to **eat whatever is set before you, asking no question for conscience' sake**.

10:28 If, during the course of the meal, another Christian should be present who has a weak conscience and informs you that the meat you are eating has been **offered to idols**, should you eat it? No. You should not indulge, because in so doing you might be stumbling him and hurting his conscience. Neither should you eat if an unbeliever would be hindered from accepting the Lord through this action. At the end of verse 28, Psalm 24:1 is once again quoted : **"The earth is the LORD'S, and all its fullness."**[36]

10:29 In the case just cited you would not refrain from eating because of *your own* conscience. You would have perfect liberty, as a believer, to eat the meat. But the weak brother sitting by has a **conscience** about it, and so you refrain from eating out of respect to his conscience.

The question, **"For why is my liberty judged by another man's conscience?"** could perhaps be paraphrased as follows:

Why should I selfishly display my freedom to eat the meat and in so doing be condemned by the other man's conscience? Why should I expose my freedom to the condemnation of his conscience? Why should I let my good be evil spoken of? (see Rom. 14:16).

Is a piece of meat so important that I should cause such an offense to a fellow-believer in the Lord Jesus Christ? (However, many commentators believe that here Paul is quoting the objection of the Corinthians, or asking a rhetorical question, before answering it in the following verses.)

10:30 What the apostle seems to be saying is that to him it seems very contradictory to give **thanks** to God on the one hand, when by so doing he is wounding a brother. It is better to deny oneself a legitimate right than to give thanks to God for something which will cause others to speak **evil** of you. William Kelly comments that it is "better to deny one's self and not allow one's liberty to be condemned by another or incur evil speaking for that for which one gives thanks." Why make such a use of freedom as to give offense? Why let my giving of thanks be exposed to misconstruction or be called sacrilege or scandal?

10:31 There are two great rules to guide us in all our Christian lives. The first is **the glory of God**, and the second is the welfare of our fellow men. Paul gives the first of these here: **"Therefore, whether you eat or drink, or whatever you do, do all to the glory of God."** Christian young people are often faced with decisions as to whether a certain course of action would be right or wrong for them. Here is a good rule to apply: Is there any **glory** for **God** in it? Can you bow your head before you participate in it and ask the Lord that He will be magnified by what you are about to do?

10:32 The second rule is the welfare of our fellow men. We should **give no offense** or occasion for stumbling, **either to the Jews or to the Greeks or to the church of God**. Here Paul divides all mankind into three classes. **The Jews**, of course, are the nation of Israel. **The Greeks** are the unconverted Gentiles, whereas **the church of God** includes all true believers in the Lord Jesus Christ, whether of Jewish or Gentile stock. In one sense we are bound to offend others and excite their wrath if we faithfully witness to them. However, that is not what is spoken of here. Rather, the apostle is thinking of *needless* **offense**. He is cautioning us against using our legitimate rights in such a way as to stumble others.

10:33 Paul can honestly say that he seeks to **please all men in all things, not seeking** his **own profit, but the profit of many**. Probably few men have ever lived so unselfishly for others as the great Apostle Paul.

11:1 Verse 1 of chapter 11 probably goes better with chapter 10. Paul had just been speaking of how he tried to gauge all his actions in the light of their effect on others. Now he tells the Corinthians to **imitate** him, **just as** he **also** copied **Christ**. He renounced personal advantages and rights in order to help those about him. The Corinthians should do likewise, and not selfishly parade their freedoms in such a way as to hinder the gospel of Christ or offend the weak brother.

C. Concerning Women's Head-Coverings (11:2–16)

Verses 2–16 of chapter 11 are devoted to the subject of women's head-coverings. The remaining verses deal with abuses in connection with the Lord's Supper (vv. 17–34). The first section of the chapter has been much disputed. Some think that the instruction given here was applicable only to Paul's day. Some even go so far as to contend that these verses reflect Paul's prejudice against women, since he was a bachelor! Still others simply *accept* the teaching of this portion, seeking to *obey* its precepts even if they do not understand them all.

11:2 The apostle first of all commends the Corinthians for the way in which they remembered him **in all things**, and held fast **the traditions just as** he had **delivered them. Traditions** refer not to habits and practices that have arisen in the church down through the years, but rather, in this case, to the inspired instructions of the Apostle Paul.

11:3 Paul now introduces the subject of women's head coverings. Behind his instruction is the fact that every ordered society is built on two pillars — authority and subjection to that authority. It is impossible to have a well-functioning community where these two principles are not observed. Paul mentions three great relationships involving authority and subjection. First, **the head of every man is Christ**; Christ is Lord and man is subject to Him. Secondly, **the head of woman is man**; the place of headship was given to the man, and the woman is under his authority. Third, **the head of Christ is God**; even in the Godhead, One Person has the place of rule and Another takes the place of willing subordination. These examples of headship and submission were designed by God Himself and are fundamental in His arrangement of the universe.

At the outset it should be emphasized that subjection does *not* mean inferiority. Christ is subject to God the Father but He is not inferior to Him. Neither is woman inferior to man, though she is subordinate to him.

11:4 **Every man** who prays or prophesies with **his head covered dishonors his head**, that is, Christ. It is saying, in effect, that the man does not acknowledge Christ as **his head**. Thus it is an act of gross disrespect.

11:5 **Every woman who prays or prophesies with her head uncovered dishonors her head**, that is, the man. She is saying, in effect, that she does not recognize man's God-given headship and will not submit to it.[37]

If this were the only verse in the Bible on the subject, then it would imply that it is all right for a woman to pray or prophesy in the assembly as long as she has a veil or other covering on her head. But Paul teaches elsewhere that women should be silent in the assembly (1 Cor. 14:34), that they are not permitted to teach or to have authority over the man but to be in silence (1 Tim. 2:12).

Actually meetings of the assembly do not come into view until verse 17, so the instructions concerning the head-covering in verses 2–16 cannot be confined to church meetings. They apply to whenever a woman prays or prophesies. She prays silently in the assembly, since 1 Timothy 2:8 limits public prayer to the men (lit., males). She prays audibly or silently at other times. She prophesies when she teaches other women (Titus 2:3–5) or children in the Sunday school.

11:6 **If a woman is not covered**, she might as well **be shorn. But if it is shameful for a woman to be shorn or shaved**, then she should be **covered**. The unveiled head of a woman is as shameful as if her hair were cut off. The apostle is *not* commanding a barber's operation but rather telling what moral consistency would require!

11:7 In verses 7–10, Paul teaches the subordination of the woman to the man by going back to creation. This should forever lay to rest any idea that his teaching about women's covering was what was *culturally* suitable in his day but not applicable to us today. The headship of man and the subjection of woman have been God's order from the very beginning.

First of all, man **is the image and glory of God** whereas **woman is the glory of man**. This means that man was placed on earth as God's representative, to exercise dominion over it. Man's uncovered head is a silent witness to this fact. The woman was never given this place of headship; instead she **is the glory of man** in the sense that she "renders conspicuous the authority of man," as W. E. Vine expresses it.[38]

Man indeed ought not to cover his head in prayer; it would be tantamount to veiling the **glory of God**, and this would be an insult to the Divine Majesty.

11:8 Paul next reminds us that **man was not** created **from woman but woman** was created **from man**. The man was first, then the woman was taken from his side. This priority of the man strengthens the apostle's case for man's headship.

11:9 The purpose of creation is next alluded to in order to press home the point. **Nor was man created** primarily **for the woman, but** rather **woman for the man**. The Lord distinctly stated in Genesis 2:18, "It is not good that man should be alone; I will make him a helper comparable to him."

11:10 Because of her position of subordination to man, **the woman ought to have a symbol of authority on her head. The symbol of authority** is the head-covering and here it indicates *not* her own authority but subjection to the authority of her husband.

Why does Paul add **because of the angels**? We would suggest that **the angels** are spectators of the things that are happening on earth today, as they were of the things that happened at creation. In the first creation, they saw how woman usurped the place of headship over the man. She made the decision that Adam should have made. As a result of this, sin entered the human race with its unspeakable aftermath of misery and woe. God does not want what happened in the first creation to be repeated in the new creation. When the angels look down, He wants them to see the woman acting in subjection to the man, and indicating this outwardly by a covering on her head.

We might pause here to state that the head-covering is simply an outward sign and it is of value only when it is the outward sign of an inward grace. In other words, a woman might have a covering on her head and yet not truly be submissive to her husband. In such a case, to wear a head-covering would be of no value at all. The most important thing is to be sure that the heart is truly subordinate; then a covering on a woman's head becomes truly meaningful.

11:11 Paul is not implying that man is at all independent of the woman, so he adds: **"Nevertheless, neither is man independent of woman, nor woman independent of man, in the Lord."** In other words, man and woman are mutually dependent. They need one another and the idea of subordination is not at all in conflict with the idea of mutual interdependence.

11:12 Woman came from man by creation, that is, she was created from Adam's side. But Paul points out that **man also comes through woman**. Here he is referring to the process of birth. The woman gives birth to the man child. Thus God has created this perfect balance to indicate that the one cannot exist without the other.

All things are from God means that He has divinely appointed **all** these **things**, so there is no just cause for complaint. Not only were these relationships created by **God**, but the purpose of them all is to glorify Him. All of this should make the man humble and the woman content.

11:13 The apostle now challenges the Corinthians to **judge among** themselves if it is **proper for a woman to pray to God with her head uncovered**. He appeals to their instinctive sense. The suggestion is that it is not reverent or decorous for a woman to enter into the presence of God unveiled.

11:14 Just how does **nature itself teach** us that it is a shame for **a man** to have **long hair** is not made clear. Some have suggested that a man's hair will not naturally grow into as long tresses as a woman's. For a man to have long hair makes him appear effeminate. In most cultures, the male wears his hair shorter than the female.

11:15 Verse 15 has been greatly misunderstood by many. Some have suggested that since a woman's **hair is given to her for a covering**, it is not necessary for her to have any other covering. But such a teaching does grave violence to this portion of Scripture. Unless one sees that *two* coverings are mentioned in this chapter, the passage becomes hopelessly confusing. This may be demonstrated by referring back to verse 6. There we read: "For if a woman is not covered, let her also be shorn." According to the interpretation just mentioned, this would mean that if a woman "does not have her hair on," then she might just as well be shorn. But this is ridiculous. If she does not "have her hair on," she could not possibly be shorn!

The actual argument in verse 15 is that there is a real analogy between the spiritual and the natural. God gave woman a natural covering of **glory** in a way He did not give to man. There is a spiritual significance to this. It teaches that when a woman prays to God, she should wear a covering on her head. What is true in the natural sphere should be true in the spiritual.

11:16 The apostle closes this section with the statement: **"But if anyone seems to be contentious, we have no such custom, nor do the churches of God."** Does Paul mean, as has been suggested, that the things he has just been saying are not important enough to contend about? Does he mean that there was no such custom of women veiling their heads in the churches? Does he mean that these teachings are optional and not to be pressed upon women as the commandments of the Lord? It seems strange that any such interpretations would ever be offered, yet they are commonly heard today. This would mean that Paul considered these instructions as of no real consequence, and he had just been wasting over half a chapter of Holy Scripture in setting them forth!

There are at least two possible explanations of this verse which fit in with the rest of the Scripture. First of all, the apostle may be saying that he anticipates that certain ones will **be contentious** about these matters, but he adds that **we have no such custom**, that is, the custom of contending about this. We do not argue about such matters, but accept them as the teaching of the Lord. Another interpretation, favored by William Kelly, is that Paul was saying that **the churches of God** did not have any such custom as that of women praying or prophesying without being covered.

D. Concerning the Lord's Supper (11:17–34)

11:17 The apostle rebukes the Corinthians for the fact that there were divisions among them as they gathered together (vv. 17–19). Note the repetition of the expression "when you come together" or related words (11:17, 18, 20, 33, 34; 14:23, 26). In 11:2 Paul had had occasion to praise them for keeping the traditions which he had delivered to them, but there was one matter in which he could **not praise** them, and that is the matter about which he is to speak. When

they gathered together for public meetings, they came **together not for the better but for the worse**. This is a solemn reminder to us all that it is possible to go away from meetings of the church and to have been harmed rather than benefited.

11:18 The **first** cause of rebuke was the existence of **divisions** or schisms. This does not mean that parties had broken away from the church and formed separate fellowships, but rather that there were cliques and factions within the congregation. A schism is a party inside, whereas a sect is a different party outside. Paul could **believe** these reports of divisions because he knew that the Corinthians were in a carnal state, and he had previous occasion in this Epistle to rebuke them because of their divisions.

F. B. Hole writes:

> Paul was prepared to give at least partial credence to the reports of the divisions at Corinth, since he knew that, owing to their carnal state, there were bound to be these opinionated factions in their midst. Here Paul reasons forward from their state to their actions. Knowing them to be carnal and walking as men, he knew that they would certainly fall victims to the inveterate tendency of the human mind to form its strong opinions, and the factions founded in those opinions, ending in the schisms and divisions. He knew, too, that God could overrule their folly and take occasion to make manifest those that were approved of Him, walking according to the Spirit and not as man; and consequently eschewing the whole of this divisive business.[39]

11:19 Paul foresaw that the schisms already begun in Corinth would increase until they became more serious. Although in general this would be detrimental to the church, yet one good thing would come out of it, that is, that those who were truly spiritual and who were **approved** of God would **be recognized among** the Corinthians. When Paul says in this verse: **"there must also be factions[40] among you,"** this does not mean that it is a *moral*[41] necessity. God is not condoning splits in the church here. Rather, Paul means that because of the carnal conditions of the Corinthians, it was inevitable that **factions** would result. Divisions are proof that some have failed to discern the mind of the Lord.

11:20 Paul now directs his second rebuke against abuses in connection with the Lord's Supper. When the Christians gathered together, ostensibly to celebrate **the Lord's Supper**, their conduct was so deplorable that Paul says they could not possibly remember the Lord in the way in which He appointed. They might go through the outward motions, but their entire deportment would preclude any true remembrance of the Lord.

11:21 In the early days of the church, Christians celebrated the "agapē," or love feast along with the Lord's Supper. The love feast was something like a common meal, shared in a spirit of love and fellowship. At the end of the love feast, the Christians often had the remembrance of the Lord with the bread and wine. But before very long, abuses crept in. For instance, in this verse it is implied that the love feast lost its real meaning. Not only did the Christians not wait for one another, but the rich ones shamed their poorer brethren by having lavish meals and not sharing them. Some went away **hungry**, whereas others were actually **drunk**! Since the Lord's Supper often followed the love feast, they would still be drunk when they sat down to partake of the Lord's Supper.

11:22 The apostle indignantly rebukes such disgraceful conduct. If they insist on carrying on in such a way, then they should at least have the reverence not to do it in a **church** meeting. To practice intemperance at such a time and to **shame** one's poorer brethren is most inconsistent with the Christian faith. Paul cannot but withhold **praise** from the saints for acting in this way; and in withholding **praise**, he thereby condemns them strongly.

11:23 To show the contrast between their conduct and the real meaning of the Lord's Supper, he goes back to its original institution. He shows that it was not a common meal or a feast, but a solemn ordinance of the Lord. Paul **received** his knowledge concerning this directly **from the Lord** and he mentions this to show that any violation would be actual disobedience. What he is teaching, then, he received by revelation.

First of all, he mentions how **the Lord Jesus on the** very **night in which He was betrayed took bread**. The literal rendering is "while He was being betrayed." While the foul plot to deliver Him up was going on outside, **the Lord Jesus** gathered in the upper room with His disciples and **took** the **bread**.

The fact that this occurred at **night** does not necessarily mean that the Lord's Supper must thereafter be observed only at night. At that time, sundown was the beginning of the Jewish day. Our day begins at sunrise. Also it has been remarked that there is a difference between apostolic *example* and apostolic *precepts*. We are not obligated to do all that the apostles *did*, but we are most certainly obligated to obey all that they *taught*.

11:24 The Lord Jesus took the bread, first of all, and gave **thanks** for it. Since the bread was typical of His body, He was, in effect, thanking God that He had been given a human body in which He might come and die for the sins of the world.

When the Savior said, **"This is My body,"** did He mean that the bread actually *became* His body in some real sense? The Roman Catholic dogma of *transubstantiation* insists that the bread and the wine are literally changed into the body and the blood of Christ. The Lutheran doctrine of *consubstantiation* teaches that the true body and blood of Christ are in, with, and under the bread and wine on the table.

In answer to these views, it should be sufficient to remember that when the Lord Jesus instituted this memorial, His body had not yet been given, nor had His blood been shed. When the Lord Jesus said, **"This is My body,"** He meant, "This is symbolic of My body" or "This is a picture of My body which is broken for you." To eat the bread is to remember Him in His atoning death for us. There is inexpressible tenderness in our Lord's expression "in remembrance of Me."

11:25 **In the same manner** the Lord Jesus **also took the cup after** the Passover **supper, saying, "This cup is the new covenant in My blood. This do, as**

often as you drink it, in remembrance of Me." The Lord's Supper was instituted immediately after the Passover Feast. That is why it says that the Lord Jesus **took the cup after supper**. In connection with **the cup**, He said that it was **the new covenant in** His **blood**. This refers to the covenant that God promised to the nation of Israel in Jeremiah 31:31–34. It is an unconditional promise by which He agreed to be merciful to their unrighteousness and to remember their sins and iniquities no more. The terms of the new covenant are also given in Hebrews 8:10–12. The covenant is in force at the present time, but unbelief keeps the nation of Israel from enjoying it. All who do trust the Lord Jesus receive the benefits that were promised. When the people of Israel turn to the Lord, they will enjoy the blessings of the new covenant; that will be during Christ's thousand-year reign on earth. The **new covenant** was ratified by the **blood** of Christ, and that is why He speaks of **the cup** as being **the new covenant in** His **blood**. The foundation of the new covenant was laid through the cross.

11:26 Verse 26 touches on the question as to how frequently the Lord's Supper should be observed. **For as often as you eat . . . and drink. . . .** No legalistic rule is laid down; neither is any fixed date given. It seems clear from Acts 20:7 that the practice of the disciples was to meet on the first day of the week to remember the Lord. That this ordinance was not intended simply for the early days of the church is abundantly proved by the expression **till He comes**. Godet beautifully points out that the Lord's Supper is "the link between His two comings, the monument of the one, the pledge of the other."[42]

In all this instruction concerning the Lord's Supper it is notable that there is not a word about a minister or priest officiating. It is a simple memorial service left for all the people of God. Christians gather together simply as believer-priests to thus proclaim the Lord's death **till He comes.**

11:27 Having discussed the origin and purpose of the Lord's Supper, the apostle now turns to the consequences of participating in it wrongly. Whoever **eats this bread or drinks this cup of the Lord in an unworthy manner will be guilty of the body and blood of the Lord**. We are all unworthy to partake of this solemn Supper. In that sense, we are unworthy of any of the Lord's mercy or kindness to us. But that is not the subject here. The apostle is not speaking of our own personal unworthiness. Cleansed by the blood of Christ, we can approach God in all the worthiness of His own beloved Son. But Paul is speaking here of the disgraceful conduct which characterized the Corinthians as they gathered together for the Lord's Supper. They were **guilty** of careless, irreverent behavior. To act thus is to **be guilty of the body and blood of the Lord.**

11:28 As we come to the Lord's Supper, we should do so in a judged condition. Sin should be confessed and forsaken; restitution should be made; apologies should be offered to those we have offended. In general we should make sure that we are in a proper state of soul.

11:29 To eat and to drink **in an** inconsistent **manner** is to eat and drink **judgment to** oneself, **not discerning the Lord's body**. We should realize that the Lord's body was given in order that our sins might be put away. If we go on living in sin, while at the same time partaking of the Lord's Supper, we are living a lie. F. G. Patterson writes, "If we eat the Lord's Supper with unjudged sin upon us, we do not discern the Lord's body which was broken to put it away."

11:30 Failure to exercise self-judgment resulted in God's disciplinary judgment upon some in the church at Corinth. **Many** were **weak and sick**, and not a few slept. In other words, physical illness had come upon some, and some were taken home to heaven. Because they did not judge sin in their lives, the Lord was required to take disciplinary action against them.

11:31 On the other hand, **if we** exercise this self-judgment, it will not be necessary to so chasten us.

11:32 God is dealing with us as with His own children. He loves us too dearly to allow us to go on in sin. Thus we soon feel the shepherd's crook on our necks pulling us back to Himself. As someone has said, "It is possible for the saints to be fit for heaven (in Christ) but not fitted to remain on the earth in testimony."

11:33 **When** the believers **come together** for the love feast, or agapē, they should **wait for one another**, and not selfishly proceed without regard for the other saints. "Waiting for one another" is in contrast to verse 21, "each one takes his own supper ahead of others."

11:34 **But if anyone is hungry, let him eat at home.** In other words, the love feast, linked as it was with the Lord's Supper, was not to be mistaken for a common meal. To disregard its sacred character would be to **come together for judgment.**

And the rest I will set in order when I come. Undoubtedly there were other minor matters which had been mentioned to the apostle in the letter from the Corinthians. Here he assures them that he will deal with these matters personally when he visits them.

E. Concerning the Gifts of the Spirit and Their Use in the Church (Chaps. 12–14)

Chapters 12–14 deal with the gifts of the Spirit. There had been abuses in the assembly in Corinth, especially in connection with the gift of tongues, and Paul writes in order to correct those abuses.

There were believers in Corinth who had received the gift of tongues, which means that they were given the power to speak foreign languages without ever having studied those languages.[43] But instead of using this gift to magnify God and edify other believers, they were using it to show off. They stood up in the meetings and spoke in languages which no one else understood, hoping that others would be impressed by their linguistic proficiency. They exalted the sign-gifts above the others, and claimed superior spirituality for those who spoke in tongues. This led to pride on the one hand, and to feelings of envy, inferiority, and worthlessness on the other. It was therefore necessary for the apostle to correct these erroneous attitudes and to establish controls in the exercise of the gifts, especially tongues and prophecy.

12:1 He does **not want** the saints at Corinth **to be ignorant** in the matter of **spiritual** manifestations or **gifts.** The literal reading here is **"Now concerning** 'spirituals,' **brethren, I do not want you to be ignorant."** Most versions supply the word *gifts* to complete the sense. However, the next verse suggests that Paul might have been thinking not only of manifestations of the Holy Spirit but of evil spirits as well.

12:2 Before conversion the Corinthians had been idolaters, enslaved by evil spirits. They lived in fear of the spirits and were **led** about by these diabolical influences. They witnessed supernatural manifestations of the spirit world and heard spirit-inspired utterances. Under the influence of evil spirits, they sometimes surrendered self-control, and said and did things beyond their own conscious powers.

12:3 Now that they are saved, the believers must know how to judge all spirit-manifestations, that is, how to discern between the voice of evil spirits and the authentic voice of the Holy Spirit. The crucial test is the testimony that is given concerning the Lord Jesus. If a man says, **"Jesus is accursed,"** you can be sure that he is demon-inspired, because evil spirits characteristically blaspheme and curse the name of Jesus. **The Spirit of God** would never lead anyone to speak of the Savior in this way; His ministry is to exalt the Lord Jesus. He leads people to **say that Jesus is Lord**, not just with their lips, but with the warm, full confession of their hearts and lives.

Notice that the three Persons of the Trinity are mentioned in verse 3 and also in verses 4–6.

12:4 Paul next shows that while there is a variety **of gifts** of the Holy Spirit in the church, there is a basic, threefold unity, involving the three Persons of the Godhead.

First of all, **there are diversities of gifts, but the same Spirit**. The Corinthians were acting as if there was only one gift — tongues. Paul says, "No, your unity is not found in the possession of one *common* gift, but rather in possession of the Holy Spirit who is the Source of *all* the gifts."

12:5 Next the apostle points out that **there are differences of ministries**

or services in the church. We don't all have the same work. But what we have in common is that whatever we do is done for **the same Lord** and with a view to serving others (not self).

12:6 Then again, though **there are diversities of activities** as far as spiritual gifts are concerned, **it is the same God who** empowers each believer. If one gift seems more successful or spectacular or powerful than another, it is not because of any superiority in the person possessing it. It is God who supplies the power.

12:7 The **Spirit** manifests Himself in the life of **each** believer by imparting some gift. There is no believer who does not have a function to perform. And the gifts are given **for the profit of** the entire body. They are not given for self-display or even for self-gratification but in order to help others. This is a pivotal point in the entire discussion.

That leads quite naturally to a list of some of the gifts of the Spirit.

12:8 **The word of wisdom** is the supernatural power to speak with divine insight, whether in solving difficult problems, defending the faith, resolving conflicts, giving practical advice, or pleading one's case before hostile authorities. Stephen so demonstrated the word of wisdom that his adversaries "were not able to resist the wisdom and the Spirit by which he spoke" (Acts 6:10).

The word of knowledge is the power to communicate information that has been divinely revealed. This is illustrated in Paul's use of such expressions as "Behold, I tell you a mystery" (1 Cor. 15:51) and "For this we say to you by the word of the Lord" (1 Thess. 4:15). In that primary sense of conveying new truth, the word of knowledge has ceased, because the Christian faith has been once for all delivered to the saints (Jude 3). The body of Christian doctrine is complete. In a secondary sense, however, **the word of knowledge** may still be with us. There is still a mysterious communication of divine knowledge to those who live in close fellowship with the Lord (see Psalm 25:14). The sharing of that knowledge with others is **the word of knowledge**.

12:9 The gift of **faith** is the divine ability to remove mountains of difficulty in pursuing the will of God (13:2) and to do great exploits for God in response to some command or promise of God as found in His word or as communicated privately. George Müller is a classic example of a man with the gift of faith. Without ever making his needs known to anyone but God, he cared for 10,000 orphans over a period of sixty years.

The **gifts of healings** have to do with the miraculous power to heal diseases.

12:10 **Working of miracles** could include casting out demons, changing matter from one form to another, raising the dead, and exercising power over the elements. Philip worked miracles in Samaria, and thereby gained a hearing for the gospel (Acts 8:6, 7).

The gift of **prophecy**, in its primary sense, signified that a person received direct revelations from God and transmitted them to others. Sometimes the prophets predicted future events (Acts 11:27, 28; 21:11); more often they simply expressed the mind of God. Like the apostles, they were concerned with the foundation of the church (Eph. 2:20). They themselves were not the foundation, but they laid the foundation in what they taught concerning the Lord Jesus. Once the foundation was laid, the need for the prophets ceased. Their ministry is preserved for us in the pages of the NT. Since the Bible is complete, we reject any so-called prophet who claims to have additional truth from God.[44]

In a weaker sense, we use the word "prophet" to describe any preacher who declares the word of God authoritatively, incisively, and effectively. Prophecy can also include the ascription of praise to God (Luke 1:67, 68) and the encouragement and strengthening of His people (Acts 15:32).

Discerning of spirits describes the power to detect whether a prophet or other person is speaking by the Holy Spirit or by Satan. A person with this gift has special ability to discern if a man is an imposter and an opportunist, for instance. Thus Peter was able to expose Simon as one who was poisoned by bitterness and in the bond of iniquity (Acts 8:20–23).

The gift of **tongues**, as has been mentioned, is the ability to speak a foreign language without ever having learned it.

Tongues were given for a sign, especially to Israel.

The interpretation of tongues is the miraculous power to understand a language which the person has never known before and to convey the message in the local language.

It is perhaps significant that this list of gifts begins with those that are connected primarily with the intellect and closes with those dealing primarily with the emotions. The Corinthians had reversed this in their thinking. They exalted the gift of tongues above the other gifts. They somehow thought that the more a man had of the Holy Spirit, the more he was carried off by a power beyond himself. They confused power with spirituality.

12:11 All the gifts mentioned in verses 8–10 are produced and controlled by **the same Spirit**. Here again we see that He does not give the same gift to everyone. He distributes **to each one individually as He wills**. This is another important point — the Spirit sovereignly apportions the gifts. If we really grasp this, it will eliminate pride on the one hand, because we don't have anything that we didn't receive. And it will eliminate discontent on the other hand, because Infinite Wisdom and Love decided what gift we should have, and His choice is perfect. It is wrong for everyone to desire the same gift. If everyone played the same instrument, you could never have a symphony orchestra. And if a body consisted only of tongue, it would be a monstrosity.

12:12 **The** human **body** is an illustration of unity and diversity. **The body is one**, yet **has many members**. Although all the believers are different and perform different functions, yet they all combine to make one functioning unit — the **body**.

So also is Christ is more precisely translated: "So also is *the* Christ." "The Christ" here refers not only to the glorified Lord Jesus Christ in heaven, but to the Head in heaven and to His members here on earth. All believers are members of the Body of Christ. Just as the human body is a vehicle by which a person expresses himself to others, so the Body of Christ is the vehicle on earth by which He chooses to make Himself known to the world. It is an evidence of wonderful grace that the Lord would ever allow the expression "the Christ" to be used to include those of us who are members of His body.

12:13 Paul goes on to explain how we became members of the Body of Christ. **By** (or in) **one Spirit we were all baptized into one body**. The more literal translation here is "*in*[45] one Spirit." This may mean that the Spirit is the element in which we were baptized, just as water is the element in which we are immersed in believer's baptism. Or it may mean that the Spirit is the Agent who does the baptizing, thus **by one Spirit**. This is the more probable and understandable meaning.

The baptism of the Holy Spirit took place on the Day of Pentecost. The church was born at that time. We partake of the benefits of that baptism when we are born again. We become members of the **Body** of Christ.

Several important points should be noted here: First, the baptism of the Holy Spirit is that divine operation which places believers in the Body of Christ. It is not the same as water baptism. This is clear from Matthew 3:11; John 1:33; Acts 1:5. It is not a work of grace subsequent to salvation whereby believers become more spiritual. **All** the Corinthians had been **baptized** in the Spirit, yet Paul rebukes them for being carnal — not spiritual (3:1). It is *not* true that speaking in tongues is the invariable sign of being baptized by the Spirit. **All** the Corinthians had been **baptized**, but not all spoke in tongues (12:30). There *are* crisis experiences of the Holy Spirit when a believer surrenders to the Spirit's control and is then empowered from on high. But such an experience is *not* the same as the baptism of the Spirit, and should not be confused with it.

The verse goes on to say that believers **have all been made to drink into one Spirit**. This means that they partake of the **Spirit** of God in the sense that they receive Him as an indwelling Person and receive the benefits of His ministry in their lives.

12:14 Without a variety of members you could not have a human **body**. There must be **many** members, each one different from the others, working in obedience to the head and in cooperation with the others.

12:15 When we see that diversity is essential to a normal, healthy body, it will save us from two dangers — from belittling ourselves (vv. 15–20) and from belittling others (vv. 21–25). It would be absurd for **the foot** to feel unimportant because it can't do the work of **a hand**. After all, the foot can stand, walk, run, climb, dance — and kick, as well as a host of other things.

12:16 **The ear** shouldn't try to become a dropout because it is **not an eye**. We take our ears for granted till deafness overtakes us. Then we realize what a tremendously useful function they perform.

12:17 **If the whole body were an eye**, you would have a deaf oddity fit only for a circus sideshow. Or if the body had only ears, it wouldn't have a nose to detect when the gas was escaping and soon wouldn't even be able to hear because it would be unconscious or dead.

The point that Paul is driving at is that if the body were all tongue, it would be a freak, and a monstrosity. And yet the Corinthians were so overemphasizing the gift of tongues that they were, in effect, creating a local fellowship that would be *all tongue*. It could talk, but that was all it could do!

12:18 **God** has not been guilty of such folly. In His matchless wisdom, He has arranged the different **members . . . in the body just as He pleased**. We should give Him credit for knowing what He is doing! We should be profoundly grateful for whatever gift He has given us and joyfully use it for His glory and for building up others. To be envious of someone else's gift is sin. It is rebellion against God's perfect plan for our lives.

12:19 It is impossible to think of a body with only **one member**. So the Corinthians should remember that if they all had the gift of tongues, then they would not have a functioning **body**. Other gifts, though less spectacular and less sensational, are nonetheless necessary.

12:20 As God has ordained, there are **many members, yet one body**. These facts are obvious to us in connection with the human body, and they should be equally obvious to us in connection with our service in the church.

12:21 Just as it is folly for one person to envy another's gift, so it is equally foolish for anyone to depreciate another's gift or feel that he doesn't need the others. **The eye cannot say to the hand, "I have no need of you"; nor again the head to the feet, "I have no need of you."** The eye can see things to be done, but it can't do them. It depends on the hand for that. Again, the head might know that it is necessary to go to a certain place, but it depends on the feet to take it there.

12:22 Some **members of the body . . . seem to be weaker** than others. The kidneys, for instance, don't seem to be as strong as the arms. But the kidneys are indispensable whereas the arms are not. We can live without arms and legs, or even without a tongue, but we cannot live without heart, lungs, liver, or brain. Yet these vital organs never put themselves on public display. They just carry on their functions unostentatiously.

12:23 Some **members** of the body are attractive while others are not so elegant. We compensate by putting clothes over those that are not so beautiful. Thus there is a certain mutual care among the members, minimizing the differences.

12:24 Those **parts** of the body that are **presentable** don't need extra attention. **But God** has combined all the differing members of **the body** into an organic structure. Some members are comely, some homely. Some do well in public, some not so well. Yet God has given us the instinct to appreciate all the members, to realize that they are all interdependent, and to counterbalance the deficiencies of those that are not so handsome.

12:25 The mutual care of the members prevents division or **schism in the body**. One gives to another what is needed, and receives in return the help which only that other member can give. This is the way it must be in the church. Overemphasis on any one gift of the Spirit will result in conflict and schism.

12:26 What affects **one member** affects **all**. This is a well-known fact in the human body. Fever, for instance, is not confined to one part of the body, but affects the whole system. So it is with other types of sickness and pain. An eye doctor often can detect brain tumor, kidney disease, or liver infection by looking into the eye. The reason is that, although all these members are distinct and separate, yet they all form part of the one body, and they are so vitally linked together that what affects one member affects all. Therefore, instead of being discontent with our lot, or, on the other hand, instead of feeling a sense of independence from others, we should have a real sense of solidarity in the Body of Christ. Anything that hurts another Christian should cause us the keenest sorrow. Likewise, if we see another Christian **honored**, we should not feel jealous, but we should **rejoice with** him.

12:27 Paul reminds the Corinthians that they **are the body of Christ**. This cannot mean *the* Body of Christ in its totality. Neither can it mean *a* Body of Christ, since there is only one Body. It can only mean that they collectively formed a microcosm or miniature of the Body of Christ. **Individually** each one is a member of that great cooperative society. As such he should fulfill his function without any feeling of pride, independence, envy, or worthlessness.

12:28 The apostle now gives us another list of gifts. None of these lists is to be considered as complete. **And God has appointed these in the church: first apostles.** The word **first** indicates that not all are apostles. The twelve were men who had been commissioned by the Lord as His messengers. They were with Him during His earthly ministry (Acts 1:21, 22) and, with the exception of Judas, saw Him after His resurrection (Acts 1:2, 3, 22). But others besides the twelve were apostles. The most notable was Paul. There were also Barnabas (Acts 14:4, 14); James, the Lord's brother (Gal. 1:19); Silas and Timothy (1 Thess. 1:1; 2:6). Together with the NT prophets, the apostles laid the doctrinal foundation of the church in what they taught about the Lord Jesus Christ (Eph. 2:20). In the strict meaning of the word, we no longer have apostles. In a wider sense, we still have messengers and church-planters sent forth by the Lord. By calling them *missionaries* instead of apostles, we avoid creating the impression that they have the extraordinary authority and power of the early apostles.

Next are the **prophets**. We have already mentioned that prophets were spokesmen of God, men who uttered the very word of God in the day before it was given in complete written form. **Teachers** are those who take the word of God and explain it to the people in an understandable way. **Miracles** might refer to raising the dead, casting out demons, etc. **Healings** have to do with the instantaneous cure of bodily diseases, as mentioned previously. **Helps** are commonly associated with the work of deacons, those entrusted with the material affairs of the church. The gift of **administrations**, on the other hand, is usually applied to elders or bishops. These are the men who have the godly, spiritual care of the local church. Last is the gift of **tongues**. We believe that there is a significance in the order. Paul mentions apostles first and tongues last. The Corinthians were putting tongues *first* and disparaging the apostle!

12:29, 30 When the apostle asks if every believer has the same gift — whether apostle, prophet, teacher, miracles, healings, helps, governments, tongues, interpretations of tongues — the grammar in the original shows that he expects and requires a "No" answer.[46] Therefore any suggestion, expressed or implied, that *everyone* should have the gift of tongues, is contrary to the word of God and is foreign to the whole concept of the body with its many different members, each with its own function.

If, as stated here, not everyone has the gift of tongues, then it is wrong to teach that tongues are the sign of the baptism of the Spirit. For, in that case, not everyone could expect that baptism. But the truth is that *every* believer has already been baptized by the Spirit (v. 13).

12:31 When Paul says: **"But earnestly desire the best gifts,"** he is speaking to the Corinthians as a local church, not as individuals. We know this because the verb is plural in the original. He is saying that as an assembly they should desire to have in their midst a good selection of gifts that edify. The best gifts are those that are most useful rather than those that are spectacular. All gifts are given by the Holy Spirit and none should be despised. Yet the fact is that some are of greater benefit to the body than others. These are the ones that every local fellowship should ask the Lord to raise up in the assembly.

And yet I show you a more excellent way. With these words Paul introduces the Love Chapter (1 Cor. 13). What he is saying is that the mere possession of gifts is not as important as the exercise of these gifts in love. Love thinks of others, not of self. It is wonderful to see a man who is unusually gifted by the Holy Spirit, but it is still more wonderful when that man uses that gift to build up others in the faith rather than to attract attention to himself.

People tend to divorce chapter 13 from its context. They think it is a parenthesis, designed to relieve the tension over tongues in chapters 12 and 14. But that is not the case. It is a vital and continuing part of Paul's argument.

The abuse of tongues had apparently caused strife in the assembly. Using their gifts for self-display, self-edification, and self-gratification, the "charismatics" were not acting in love. They received satisfaction out of speaking publicly in a language they had never learned, but it was a real hardship on others to have to sit and listen to something they did not understand. Paul insists that all gifts must be exercised in a spirit of love. The aim of love is to help others and not to please self.

And perhaps the "non-charismatics" had overreacted in acts of unlove. They might even have gone so far as to say that all tongues are of the devil. Their Greek tongues might have been worse than the "charismatic" tongues! Their lovelessness might have been worse than the abuse of tongues itself.

So Paul wisely reminds them all that love is needed on both sides. If they would act in love toward one another, the problem would be largely solved. It is not a problem that calls for excommunication or division; it calls for love.

13:1 Even if a person could **speak** in all languages, human and angelic, but didn't use this ability for the good of others, it would be no more profitable or pleasant than the **clanging**, jangling sound of metals crashing against each other. Where the spoken word is not understood, there is no profit. It is just a nerve-racking din contributing nothing to the common good. For tongues to be beneficial, they must be interpreted. Even then, what is said must be edifying. **The tongues of angels** may be figurative for exalted speech, but it does not mean an unknown language, because whenever angels spoke to men in the Bible, it was in the common speech, easily understood.

13:2 Likewise one might receive marvelous revelations from God. He might **understand** the great **mysteries** of God, tremendous truths hitherto unrevealed but now made known to him. He might receive a great inflow of divine **knowledge**, supernaturally imparted. He might be given that heroic **faith** which is able to **remove mountains**. Yet if these wonderful gifts are used only for his own benefit and not for the edifying of other members of the Body of Christ, they are of no value, and the holder is **nothing**, that is, he is of no help to others.

13:3 If the apostle gave all his **goods to feed the poor**, or even gave his **body to be burned**, these valiant acts would not profit him unless they were done in a spirit of **love**. If he were merely trying to attract attention to himself and seek a name for himself, then his display of virtue would be valueless.

13:4 Someone has said: "This did not start out to be a treatise on love, but like most literary gems of the NT, it was introduced in connection with some local situation." Hodge has pointed out that the Corinthians were impatient, discontented, envious, inflated, selfish, indecorous, unmindful of the feelings and interests of others, suspicious, resentful, and censorious.

And so the apostle now contrasts the characteristics of true love. First of all, **love suffers long and is kind**. Longsuffering is patient endurance under provocation. Kindness is active goodness, going forth in the interests of others. **Love does not envy** others; rather it is pleased that others should be honored and exalted. **Love does not parade itself, is not puffed up**. It realizes that whatever it has is the gift of God, and that there is nothing in man of which to be proud. Even gifts of the Holy Spirit are sovereignly bestowed by God and should not make a person proud or haughty, no matter how spectacular the gift might be.

13:5 Love **does not behave rudely**. If a person is truly acting in love, he will be courteous and considerate. Love **does not** selfishly **seek its own**, but is interested in what will assist others. Love **is not provoked**, but is willing to endure slights and insults. Love **thinks no evil**, that is, it does not attribute bad motives to others. It does not suspect their actions. It is guileless.

13:6 Love **does not rejoice in iniquity, but rejoices in the truth.** There is a certain mean streak in human nature which takes pleasure in what is unrighteous, especially if an unrighteous act seems to benefit one's self. This is not the spirit of love. Love **rejoices** with every triumph of **the truth**.

13:7 The expression **bears all things** may mean that love patiently endures **all things**, or that it hides or conceals the faults of others. The word **bears** may also be translated "covers." Love does not needlessly publicize the failures of others, though it must be firm in giving

godly discipline when necessary.

Love **believes all things**, that is, it tries to put the best possible construction on actions and events. Love **hopes all things** in the sense that it earnestly desires that all things work out for the best. Love **endures all things** in the way of persecution or ill treatment.

13:8 Having described the qualities that characterize those who exercise their gift in love, the apostle now takes up the permanence of love, as contrasted with the temporary character of gifts. **Love never fails.** Throughout eternity, love will go on in the sense that we will still love the Lord and love one another. These gifts, on the other hand, are of temporary duration.

There are two principal interpretations of verses 8–13. One traditional view is that the gifts of prophecy, tongues, and knowledge will cease when believers enter the eternal state. The other view is that these gifts have already ceased, and that this occurred when the Canon of Scripture was completed. In order to present both views, we will paraphrase verses 8 through 12 under the labels ETERNAL STATE and COMPLETED CANON.

ETERNAL STATE

Love will never cease. In contrast, the prophecies which exist at the present time will be ended when God's people are home in heaven. While there is the gift of knowledge just now, this will be stopped when we reach the final consummation in glory. (When Paul says knowledge. . . will vanish away, he cannot mean that there will be no knowledge in heaven. He must be referring to the gift of knowledge whereby divine truth was supernaturally imparted.)

13:9 In this life our knowledge is partial at best, and so are our prophecies. There are many things we do not understand in the Bible, and many mysteries in the providence of God.

COMPLETED CANON

Love will never cease. While there are prophecies (at the time of Paul), the need for such direct revelations would end when the last book of the NT was completed. Tongues were still in use in Paul's day, but they would cease in and of themselves when the sixty-six books of the Bible were finished, because they would no longer be necessary to confirm the preaching of the apostles and prophets (Heb. 2:3, 4). Knowledge of divine truth was being given by God to the apostles and prophets, but this would also stop when the complete body of Christian doctrine was once for all delivered.

We, i.e., the apostles, know in part (in the sense that we are still receiving inspired knowledge by direct revelation from God), and we prophesy in part (because we can only express the partial revelations we are receiving).

13:10 But when that which is perfect has come, i.e., when we reach the perfect state in the eternal world, then the gifts of partial knowledge and partial prophecy will be done away.

But when that which is perfect has come, i.e., when the Canon is completed by the last book's being added to the NT, then periodic or piecemeal revelations of divine truth will be stopped, and the telling forth of this truth will be done away. There will be no more need for partial revelations since the complete word of God will be here.

13:11 This life may be compared to childhood, when our speech, understanding, and thoughts are very limited and immature. The heavenly state is comparable to full adulthood. Then our childish condition will be a thing of the past.

The sign gifts were connected with the childhood of the church. The gifts were not childish; they were necessary gifts of the Holy Spirit. But once the full revelation of God was available in the Bible, the miracle gifts were no longer needed and were put aside. The word child[47] here means a baby without the full power of speech.

13:12 As long as we are on earth, we see things dimly and indistinctly, as if we were looking in a blurry mirror. Heaven, by contrast will be like seeing things face to face, i.e., without anything between to obscure the vision. Now our knowledge is partial, but then we shall know just as we also are known — which means more fully. We will never have perfect knowledge, even in heaven. Only God is omniscient. But our knowledge will be vastly greater than it is now.

Now (during the apostolic age) we see in a mirror, dimly. No single one of us (apostles) has received God's full revelation. It is being given to us in portions, like parts of a puzzle. When the Canon of Scripture is completed, the obscurity will be removed and we will see the picture in its entirety. Our knowledge (as apostles and prophets) is partial at present. But when the last book has been added to the NT, we will know more fully and intimately than ever before.

13:13 Faith, hope, and **love** are what Kelly calls "the main moral principles characteristic of Christianity." These graces of the Spirit are superior to the gifts of the Spirit, and they are more lasting, too. In short, the *fruit* of the Spirit is more important than the *gifts* of the Spirit.

And **love** is **the greatest** of the graces because it is most useful to others. It is not self-centered but others-centered.

Now before leaving this chapter, there are a few observations to be made. As mentioned above, a widely accepted interpretation of verses 8–12 is that they contrast conditions in this life with those in the eternal state.

But many devout Christians hold to the COMPLETED CANON view, believing that the purpose of the sign gifts was to confirm the preaching of the apostles before the word of God was given in final written form, and that the need for these miracle gifts passed when the NT was completed. While this second view merits serious consideration, it can hardly be proved decisively. Even if we believe that the sign gifts largely passed away at the end of the apostolic era, we cannot say with finality that God could not, if He wished, use these gifts today. Whichever view we hold, the abiding lesson is that while the gifts of the Spirit are partial and temporary, the fruit of the Spirit is eternal and is more excellent. If we practice love, it will save us from the misuse of gifts and from the strife and divisions that have arisen as a result of their abuse.

14:1 The connection with the previous chapter is apparent. Christians should **pursue love**, and this will mean that they will always be trying to serve others. They should also earnestly **desire**

spiritual gifts for their assembly. While it is true that gifts are distributed by the Spirit as He wishes, it is also true that we can ask for gifts that will be of greatest value in the local fellowship. That is why Paul suggests that the gift of prophecy is eminently desirable. He goes on to explain why prophecy, for instance, is of greater benefit than tongues.

14:2　He who speaks in a tongue without interpretation is not speaking for the benefit of the congregation. **God** understands what he is saying but the people don't because it is a foreign language to them. He might be setting forth marvelous truths, hitherto unknown, but it does no good because it is all unintelligible.

14:3 The man **who prophesies**, on the other hand, builds people up, encourages them, and comforts them. The reason for this is that he is speaking in the language of the people; that is what makes the difference. When Paul says that the prophet builds up, stirs up, and binds up, he is not giving a definition. He is simply saying that these results follow when the message is given in a language the people know.

14:4 Verse 4 is commonly used to justify the private use of tongues for self-edification. But the fact that the word "church" is found nine times in this chapter (vv. 4, 5, 12, 19, 23, 28, 33, 34, 35) offers rather convincing evidence that Paul is not dealing with a believer's devotional life in the privacy of his room, but with the use of tongues in the local assembly. The context shows that, far from advocating the use of tongues for self-edification, the apostle is condemning any use of the gift in the church that does not result in helping *others*. Love thinks of others and not of self. If the gift of tongues is used in love, it will benefit others and not only oneself.

He who prophesies edifies the church. He is not parading his gift for personal advantage, but speaking constructively in a language the congregation can understand.

14:5 Paul does not despise the gift of tongues; he realizes that it is a gift of the Holy Spirit. He could not and would not despise anything that comes from the Spirit. When he says **"I wish you all spoke with tongues,"** he is renouncing any selfish desire to limit the gift to himself and a favored few. His desire is similar to one expressed by Moses: "O, that all the Lord's people were prophets, and that the Lord would put His Spirit upon them" (Num. 11:29b). But in saying this, Paul knew that it was not God's will that all believers should have any one gift (see 12:29, 30).

He would *rather* that the Corinthians **prophesied**, because in so doing they would be building up one another, whereas when they spoke in tongues without interpretation, their listeners would not understand and therefore would not be benefited. Paul preferred **edification** to display. "What astonishes is far less important for the spiritual mind than what edifies," as Kelly expresses it.[48]

The expression **unless indeed he interprets** could mean "unless the one speaking in tongues interprets" or "unless someone interprets."

14:6 Even if Paul himself came to Corinth **speaking with tongues**, it would not **profit** them unless they could understand what he said. They would have to be able to recognize what he was saying as **revelation** and **knowledge**, or **prophesying** and **teaching**. Commentators agree that **revelation** and **knowledge** have to do with inward reception, whereas **prophesying** and **teaching** have to do with the giving out of the same. Paul's point in this verse is that in order to profit the church, a message must be understood. He goes on to prove this in the following verses.

14:7 First of all, he uses the illustration of musical instruments. Unless a **flute or harp** makes a **distinction in the** notes, no one will know what is being **piped or played**. The very idea of enjoyable music includes the thought of distinction in notes, a definite rhythm, and a certain amount of clarity.

14:8 The same is true of a **trumpet**. The call to arms must be clear and distinct, otherwise no one **will prepare for battle**. If the trumpeter merely stands up and blows one long blast in a monotone, no one will stir.

14:9 So it is with the human tongue. Unless the speech we utter is intelligible, no one will know what is being said. It would be as profitless as **speaking into the air**. (In verse 9, "tongue" means the organ of speech, not a foreign language.) There is a practical application in all of this, namely, that ministry or teaching should be clear and simple. If it is "deep" and over the heads of the people, then it will not profit them. It might result in bringing a certain measure of gratification to the speaker, but it will not help the people of God.

14:10 Paul passes to another illustration of the truth he has been setting forth. He speaks of the **many** different **kinds of languages in the world**. Here the subject is broader than human languages; it includes the communications of other creatures. Perhaps Paul is thinking of the various birdcalls and the squeals and grunts used by animals. We know, for instance, that there are certain mating, migratory, and feeding calls used by birds. Also there are certain sounds used by animals to warn of danger. Paul is simply stating here that all of these voices have a definite meaning. **None of them is without significance.** Each one is used to convey some definite message.

14:11 It is true also with human speech. Unless a person speaks with articulate sounds, no one can understand him. He might as well be repeating meaningless gibberish. Few experiences can be more trying than the attempt to communicate with one who does not understand your language.

14:12 In view of this, the Corinthians should mingle their zeal **for spiritual gifts** with the desire to edify **the church**. "Make the edification of the church your aim in this desire to excel," Moffatt translates it. Notice that Paul never discourages them in their zeal for spiritual gifts, but seeks to guide and instruct them so that in the use of these gifts they will reach the highest goal.

14:13 If a man **speaks in a tongue**, he should **pray that he may interpret**. Or the meaning might be to pray that *someone* may interpret.[49] It is possible that a man who has the gift of tongues might also have the gift of interpretation, but

that would be the exception rather than the rule. The analogy of the human body suggests different functions for different members.

14:14 If a man, for instance, prays **in a tongue** at a meeting of the church, his **spirit prays** in the sense that his feelings find utterance, though not in the commonly used language. But his **understanding is unfruitful** in the sense that it doesn't benefit anyone else. The congregation doesn't know what he is saying. As we will explain in the notes on 14:19, we take the phrase **my understanding** to mean "other people's understanding of me."

14:15 What is the conclusion then? It is simply this: Paul **will** not only **pray with the spirit, but** he **will also pray** in such a manner as to be understood. This is what is meant by the expression: **"I will also pray with the understanding."** It does not mean that he will pray with his *own* understanding, but rather that he will pray so as to help others to understand. Likewise he **will sing with the spirit**, and **also sing** so as to be understood.

14:16 That this is the correct meaning of the passage is made abundantly clear by verse 16. If Paul gave thanks with his own spirit, but not in such a way as to be understood by others, how could one who did not understand the language he was using **say "Amen"** at the close?

He who occupies the place of the uninformed means a person who is sitting in the audience and does not know the language that is being used by the speaker. This verse incidentally authorizes the intelligent use of the **"Amen"** in public gatherings of the church.

14:17 Speaking in a foreign language, one might indeed really be giving **thanks** to God, but others are **not edified** if they do not know what is being said.

14:18 The apostle apparently had the ability to speak **more** foreign languages than **all** of them. We know that Paul had learned some languages, but here the reference is undoubtedly to his gift of tongues.

14:19 In spite of this superior language ability, Paul says that he **would rather speak five words with** his **under-**

standing, that is, so as to be understood, **than ten thousand words in a** foreign **tongue**. He was not at all interested in using this gift for self-display. His chief aim was to help the people of God. Therefore he determined that when he spoke he would do so in such a way that others would understand him.

The expression **my understanding** is what is known as an "objective genitive."[50] It does not mean what I myself understand, but what others understand when I speak.

Hodge demonstrates that the context here has to do, not with Paul's own understanding of what he spoke in tongues, but of other people's understanding him:

> That Paul should give thanks to God that he was more abundantly endowed with the gift of tongues, if that gift consisted in the ability to speak in languages which he himself did not understand, and the use of which, on that assumption, could according to his principle benefit neither himself nor others, is not to be believed. Equally clear is it from this verse that to speak with tongues was not to speak in a state of mental unconsciousness. The common doctrine as to the nature of the gift is the only one consistent with this passage. Paul says that although he could speak in foreign languages more than the Corinthians, he would rather speak five words *with his understanding*, i.e., so as to be intelligible, than ten thousand words in an unknown tongue. *In the church*, that is, in the assembly, that I might teach others also (katēcheō) to instruct orally, Gal. 6:6. This shows what is meant by speaking *with the understanding*. It is speaking in such a way as to convey instruction.[51]

14:20 Paul next exhorts the Corinthians against immaturity in their thinking. Children prefer amusement to usefulness, flashy things to stable ones. Paul is saying, "Don't take a childish delight in these spectacular gifts which you use for self-display. There is one sense in which you should be childlike, and that is in the matter of **malice** or evil. But in other matters, you should think with the maturity of men."

14:21 Next the apostle quotes from Isaiah to show that tongues are a sign to *unbelievers* rather than to believers. God said that because the children of Israel had rejected His message and had mocked it, He would speak to them through a foreign language (Isa. 28:11). The fulfillment of this took place when the Assyrian invaders came into the land of Israel, and the Israelites heard the Assyrian language being spoken in their midst. This was a sign to them of their rejection of God's word.

14:22 The argument here is that since God intended **tongues** as **a sign** to **unbelievers**, the Corinthians should not insist on using them so freely in gatherings of believers. It would be better if they prophesied, since prophesying was a sign for believers and **not for unbelievers**.

14:23 **If the whole church comes together in one place, and all** the Christians **speak with tongues** without interpretation, what would strangers coming in think about it all? It would not be a testimony to them; rather they would think that the saints were mental cases.

There is an *apparent* contradiction between verse 22 and verses 23–25. In verse 22, we are told that tongues are a sign to unbelievers whereas prophecy is for believers. But in verses 23–25, Paul says that tongues used in the church might only confuse and stumble unbelievers whereas prophecy might help them.

The explanation of the seeming contradiction is this: The unbelievers in verse 22 are those who have rejected the word of God and closed their hearts to the truth. Tongues are a sign of God's judgment on them, as they were on Israel in the Isaiah passage (v. 21). The unbelievers in verses 23–25 are those who are willing to be taught. They are open to hear the word of God, as is evidenced by their presence in a Christian assembly. If they hear Christians speaking in foreign languages without interpretation, they will be hindered, not helped.

14:24 If strangers enter a meeting where the Christians are prophesying rather than speaking in tongues, the visitors hear and understand what is being said and they are **convinced by all** and **convicted by all**. What the apostle is emphasizing here is that no real conviction of sin is produced unless the listeners understand what is being said. When tongues are being used with no interpretation, then obviously visitors are not helped at all. Those who prophesy would, of course, do it in the language in current use in that area, and as a result listeners would be impressed by what they heard.

14:25 The secrets of a man's **heart are revealed** by prophecy. He feels that the speaker is addressing him directly. The Spirit of God works conviction in his soul. **And so, falling down on his face, he will worship God and report that God is truly among** these people.

And so Paul's point in verses 22–25 is that tongues without interpretation produce no conviction among unbelievers, whereas prophecy does.

14:26 Because of the abuses that had entered the church in connection with the gift of tongues, it was necessary for the Spirit of God to set forth certain regulations to control the use of this gift. In verses 26–28, we have such controls.

What happened when the early church came **together**? It appears from verse 26 that the meetings were very informal and free. There was liberty for the Spirit of God to use the various gifts which He had given to the church. One man, for instance, would read **a psalm**, and then another would set forth some **teaching**. Another would speak in **a** foreign **tongue**. Another would present **a revelation** which he had received directly from the Lord. Another would interpret the tongue that had already been given. Paul gives tacit approval to this "open meeting" where there was liberty for the Spirit of God to speak through different brothers. But having stated this, he sets forth the first control in the exercise of these gifts. Everything must **be done** with a view to **edification**. Just because a thing is sensational or spectacular does not mean that it has any place in the church. In order to be acceptable, ministry must have the effect of building up the people of God. That is what is meant by **edification** – spiritual growth.

14:27 The second control is that in any one meeting no more than **three** may speak in tongues. **If anyone speaks in a tongue, let there be two or at the most three.** There was to be no such thing as a meeting where a multitude of people would arise to show their proficiency in foreign languages.

Next we learn that the two or three who were permitted to speak in tongues in any one meeting must do so **in turn**. That means that they must not speak at the same time, but one after the other. This would avoid the bedlam and disorder of several speaking at once.

The fourth rule is that there must be an **interpreter. Let one interpret.** If a man got up to speak in a foreign language, he must first determine that there was someone present to interpret what he was about to say.

14:28 If there was **no interpreter** present, then he must **keep silent in church**. He could sit there and **speak** inaudibly **to himself and to God** in this foreign language, but he was not permitted to do so publicly.

14:29 Rules for governing the prophetic gift are set forth in verses 29-33a. First of all, **two or three prophets** were to speak and **the others** were to **judge**. No more than **three** were to take part in any one meeting, and the Christians who listened were to determine whether this was truly a divine utterance or whether the man might be a false prophet.

14:30 As we have mentioned previously, a prophet received direct communications from the Lord and revealed them to the church. But it is possible that after giving this revelation, he might go on to preach to the people. So the apostle lays down the rule that if a prophet is speaking and **anything is revealed to another** prophet sitting in the audience, then **the first** is required to stop speaking to make way for the one who has received the latest revelation. The reason, as suggested, is that the longer the first man talks, the more apt he is to speak by his own power rather than by inspiration. In continued speech there is always the danger of shifting from God's words to one's own words. Revelation is superior to anything else.

14:31 The prophets should be given the opportunity to speak **one by one**. No one prophet should take all the time. In that way, the greatest benefit would result to the church — **all** would be able to **learn** and **all** would **be** exhorted or **encouraged**.

14:32 A very important principle is set forth in verse 32. Reading between the lines, we suspect that the Corinthians had the false idea that the more a man was possessed by the Spirit of God, the less self-control he had. They felt that he was carried away in a state of ecstasy and they contended, according to Godet, that the more spirit, the less intelligence or self-consciousness there would be. To them, a man under the control of the Spirit was in a state of passivity, and could not control his speech, the length of time he spoke, or his actions in general. Such an idea is thoroughly refuted by the passage of Scripture before us. **The spirits of the prophets are subject to the prophets.** That means that he is not carried away without his consent, or against his will. He cannot evade the instructions of this chapter on the pretense that he just couldn't help it. He himself can determine when or how long he should speak.

14:33   **For God is not the author of confusion but of peace.** In other words, if a meeting is the scene of pandemonium and disorder, then you can be *sure* that the Spirit of God is not in control!

14:34   As is well-known, the verse divisions and even the punctuation of the NT were added centuries after the original manuscripts were written. The last clause of verse 33 makes much greater sense modifying the church practice in verse 34 than a universal truth about the omnipresent God (some Greek Testaments and English translations use this punctuation). For instance, the ASV reads: "As in all the churches of the saints, let the women keep silent in the churches: for it is not permitted unto them to speak; but let them be in subjection, as also saith the law." The instructions which Paul is giving to the Corinthian saints do not apply to them alone. These are the same instructions that have been addressed to **all the churches of the saints**. The uniform testimony of the NT is that while women have many valuable ministries, it is not given to them to have a public ministry to the whole church. They are entrusted with the unspeakably important work of the home and of raising children. But they are not allowed to speak publicly in the assembly. Theirs is to be a place of submission to the man.

We believe that the expression **as the law also says** has reference to the woman's being submissive to the man. This is clearly taught in the law, which here probably means the Pentateuch primarily. Genesis 3:16, for instance, says "your desire shall be for your husband. And he shall rule over you."

It is often contended that what Paul is forbidding in this verse is for the women to chatter or gossip while the service is going on. However, such an interpretation is untenable. The word here translated speak (*laleō*) did not mean to chatter in Koinē Greek. The same word is used of God in verse 21 of this chapter, and in Hebrews 1:1. It means to speak authoritatively.

14:35   Indeed, women are not permitted to ask questions publicly in the church. **If they want to learn something**, they should **ask their own husbands at home**. Some women might try to evade the previous prohibition against speaking by asking questions. It is possible to teach by the simple act of questioning others. So this verse closes any such loophole or objection.

If it is asked how this applies to an unmarried woman or a widow, the answer is that the Scriptures do not try to take up each individual case, but merely set forth general principles. If a woman does not have a husband, she could ask her father, her brother, or one of the elders of the church. Actually, this may be translated, "Let them ask their menfolks[52] at home." The basic rule to be remembered is that **it is shameful for women to speak in church**.

14:36   Apparently the Apostle Paul realized that his teaching here would cause considerable contention. How right he was! To meet any arguments, he uses irony in verse 36 by asking: **Or did the word of God come originally from you? Or was it you only that it reached?** In other words, if the Corinthians professed to know more about these matters than the apostle, he would ask them if they, as a church, produced **the word of God**, or if they were the **only** ones who had received it. By their attitude they seemed to set themselves up as an official authority on these matters. But the facts are that no church originated the word of God, and no church has exclusive rights to it.

14:37 In connection with all the foregoing instructions, the apostle here emphasizes that they are not his own ideas or interpretations, but that they **are the commandments of the Lord**, and any man who is **a prophet** of the Lord or who is truly **spiritual** will **acknowledge** that that is the case. This verse is a sufficient answer to those who insist that some of Paul's teachings, especially those concerning women, reflected his own prejudices. These matters are not Paul's private view; they are **the commandments of the Lord**.

14:38 Of course, some would not be willing to accept them as such, and so the apostle adds that **if anyone is ignorant, let him be ignorant**. If a person refuses to acknowledge the inspiration of these writings and to bow to them obediently, then there is no alternative but for him to continue in his ignorance.

14:39 To sum up the preceding instructions on the exercise of gifts, Paul now tells the **brethren** to **desire earnestly to prophesy**, but **not** to **forbid** men **to speak with tongues**. This verse shows the relative importance of these two gifts — one they were to **desire earnestly**, while the other they were **not** to ban. Prophecy was more valuable than tongues because sinners were convicted through it and saints edified. Tongues without interpretation served no other purpose than to speak to God and to one's self, and to display one's own proficiency with a foreign language, a proficiency that had been given to them by God.

14:40 Paul's final word of admonition is that **all things** must **be done decently and in order**. It is significant that this control should be placed in this chapter. Down through the years, those who have professed to have the ability to speak in tongues have not been noted for the orderliness of their meetings. Rather, many of their meetings have been scenes of uncontrolled emotion and general confusion.

To summarize, then, the Apostle Paul sets forth the following controls for the use of tongues in the local church:

1. We must not forbid the use of tongues (v. 39).
2. If a man speaks in a tongue, there must be an interpreter (vv. 27c, 28).
3. Not more than three may speak in tongues in any one meeting (v. 27a).
4. They must speak one at a time (v. 27b).
5. What they say must be edifying (v. 26b).
6. The women must be silent (v. 34).
7. Everything must **be done decently and in order** (v. 40).

These are the abiding controls which apply to the church in our day.

IV. PAUL'S ANSWER TO DENIERS OF THE RESURRECTION (Chap. 15)

This is the great resurrection chapter. Some teachers had entered the church at Corinth, denying the possibility of bodily resurrection. They did not deny the fact of life after death, but probably suggested that we would simply be spirit beings and not have literal bodies. The apostle here gives his classic answer to these denials.

A. Certainty of the Resurrection (15:1–34)

15:1, 2 Paul reminds them of the good news which he had **preached** to them, which they had **received**, and in **which** they now stood. This was not a new doctrine for the Corinthians, but it was necessary that they should be reminded of it at this critical time. It was this **gospel** by which the Corinthians had been **saved**. Then Paul adds the words **if you hold fast that word which I preached to you — unless you believed in vain**. It was by the gospel of the resurrection that they had been saved — unless, of course, there was no such thing as resurrection, in which case they could not have been saved at all. The **if** in this passage does not express any doubt as to their salvation, nor does it teach that they were saved by holding fast. Rather, Paul is simply stating that if there is no such thing as resurrection, then they weren't saved at all. In other words, those who denied bodily resurrection were launching a frontal attack on the whole truth of the gospel. To Paul, the resurrection was fundamental. Without it there was no Christianity. Thus this verse is a challenge to the Corinthians to hold fast the gospel which they had received in the face of the attacks which were currently being made against it.

15:3　Paul had **delivered to** the Corinthians the message **which** he had **also received** by divine revelation. The first cardinal doctrine of that message was **that Christ died for our sins according to the Scriptures**. This emphasizes the substitutionary character of the death of Christ. He did not die for His own sins, or as a martyr; He **died for our sins**. He **died** to pay the penalty that **our sins** deserved. This was all **according to the Scriptures. The Scriptures** here refer to the OT Scriptures, since the NT was not yet in written form. Did the OT Scriptures actually predict that Christ would die for the sins of the people? The answer is an emphatic "Yes!" Isaiah 53, verses 5 and 6, are sufficient proof of this.

15:4[†]　The burial of Christ was prophesied in Isaiah 53:9, and His resurrection in Psalm 16:9, 10. It is important to notice how Paul emphasizes the testimony of **the Scriptures**. This should always be the test in all matters relating to our faith: "What do the Scriptures say?"

15:5　In verses 5–7, we have a list of those who were eyewitnesses of the resurrection. First of all, the Lord appeared to **Cephas** (Peter). This is very touching indeed. The same faithless disciple who had denied his Lord three times is graciously privileged to have a private appearance of that same Lord in resurrection. Truly, how great is the grace of the Lord Jesus Christ! **Then** the Lord also appeared to **the twelve** disciples. Actually the twelve were not all together at this time, but the expression **the twelve** was used to denote the body of disciples, even though not complete at any one particular moment. It should be stated that not all the appearances which are recorded in the Gospels are mentioned in this list. The Spirit of God selects those resurrection appearances of Christ which are most pertinent for His use.

15:6　The Lord's appearance to **over five hundred brethren** is commonly believed to have taken place in Galilee. At the time Paul wrote, most of these brethren were still living, although some had gone home to be with the Lord. In other words, should anyone wish to contest the truthfulness of what Paul was saying, the witnesses were still alive and could be questioned.

15:7　There is no way of knowing which **James** is referred to here, although most commentators assume him to be the Lord's half-brother. Verse 7 also tells us that the Lord appeared to **all the apostles**.

15:8　Paul next speaks of his own personal acquaintance with the risen Christ. This took place on the road to Damascus, when he saw a great light from heaven and met the glorified Christ face to face. **One born out of due time** means an abortion or an untimely birth. Vine explains it as meaning that in point of time, Paul speaks of himself as inferior to the rest of the apostles, just as an immature birth comes short of a mature one. He uses it as a term of self-reproach in view of his past life as a persecutor of the church.

15:9　As the apostle thinks of the privilege he had of meeting the Savior face to face, he is filled with a spirit of unworthiness. He thinks of how he **persecuted the church of God** and how, in spite of that, the Lord called him to be an apostle. Therefore he bows himself in the dust as **the least of the apostles**, and **not worthy to be called an apostle**.

15:10　He hastens to acknowledge that whatever he now is, he is **by the grace of God**. And he did not accept this grace as a matter of fact. Rather it put him under the deepest obligation, and he labored tirelessly to serve the Christ who saved him. Yet in a very real sense it was not Paul himself, **but the grace of God which was** working **with** him.

15:11　Now Paul joins himself with the other apostles and states that no matter which of them it was who preached, they were all united in their testimony as to the gospel, and particularly as to the resurrection of Christ.

15:12　In verses 12–19, Paul lists the consequences of the denial of bodily resurrection. First of all, it would mean that Christ Himself has not risen. Paul's logic here is unanswerable. Some were saying that there is no such thing as bodily resurrection. All right, Paul says, if that is the case, then Christ has not risen. Are you Corinthians willing to admit this? Of course they were not. In order to prove the possibility of any fact, all you have to do is to demonstrate that it has already taken place once. To prove the fact of bodily resurrection, Paul is willing to base his case upon the simple fact that **Christ** has already **been raised from the dead.**

15:13 But if there is no resurrection of the dead, then obviously **Christ is not risen**. Such a conclusion would involve the Corinthians in hopeless gloom and despair.

15:14 If Christ is not risen, then the **preaching** of the apostles was **empty**, or having no substance. Why was it **empty**? First of all, because the Lord Jesus had promised that He would rise from the dead on the third day. If He did *not* rise at that time, then He was either an imposter or mistaken. In either case, He would not be worthy of trust. Secondly, apart from the resurrection of Christ, there could be no salvation. If the Lord Jesus did not rise from the dead, then there would be no way of knowing that His death had been of any greater value than any other person's. But in raising Him from the dead, God testified to the fact that He was completely satisfied with the redemptive work of Christ.

Obviously, if the apostolic message was false, then **faith** would be **empty** too. There would be no value in trusting a message that was false or empty.

15:15 It would not simply be a matter that the apostles were preaching a false message; actually it would mean that they had been testifying against **God**. They **testified of God that He raised up Christ** from the dead. If God didn't do this, then the apostles had been bringing **false** witness against Him.

15:16 If resurrection is an utter impossibility, then there can be no exception to it. On the other hand, if resurrection had taken place once, for instance in the case of Christ, then it can no longer be thought of as an impossibility.

15:17 If Christ has not been raised, the **faith** of believers **is futile** and devoid of power. And there is no forgiveness of **sins**. Thus to reject the resurrection is to reject the value of the work of Christ.

15:18 As for those who had died believing **in Christ**, their case would be absolutely hopeless. If Christ did not rise, then their faith was just a worthless thing. The expression **fallen asleep** refers to the bodies of believers. Sleep is never used of the soul in the NT. The soul of the believer departs to be with Christ at the time of death, while the body is spoken of as sleeping in the grave.

We should also say a word concerning the word **perished**. This word *never* means annihilation or cessation of being. As Vine has pointed out, it is not loss of *being*, but rather loss of *well-being*. It speaks of ruin as far as the purpose for which a person or thing was created.

15:19 If Christ is not risen, then living believers are in as wretched a condition as those who have died. They, too, have been deceived. They **are of all men the most pitiable**. Paul is here doubtless thinking of the sorrows, sufferings, trials, and persecutions to which Christians are exposed. To undergo such afflictions for a false cause would be pathetic indeed.

15:20 The tension is relieved as Paul triumphantly announces the fact of the resurrection of Christ and of the blessed consequences that follow. **But now Christ is risen from the dead, . . . the firstfruits of those who have fallen asleep**. There is a difference in the Scripture between the resurrection *of* the dead and the resurrection *from* the dead. The previous verses have been dealing with the resurrection of the dead. In other words, Paul has been arguing in a general way that the dead do indeed rise. But Christ rose *from* the dead. This means that when He rose, not all the dead rose. In this sense it was a limited resurrection. Every resurrection is a resurrection of the dead, but only that of Christ and of believers is a resurrection *from among* dead people.

15:21 It was **by man** that **death** first **came** into the world. That **man** was Adam. Through his sin, death came upon all men. God sent His Son into the world as a **Man** in order to undo the work of the first man and to raise believers to a state of blessedness such as they could never have known in Adam. Thus it was by the **Man** Christ Jesus that there **came the resurrection of the dead**.

15:22 Adam and **Christ** are presented as federal heads. This means that they acted for other people. And all who are related to them are affected by their actions. **All** who are descended from **Adam die. So in Christ all shall be made alive**. This verse has sometimes been taken to teach universal salvation. It is argued that the same ones who die in Adam will be made alive in Christ, and that all will eventually be saved. But that is not what the verse says. The key expressions are **in Adam** and **in Christ. All** who are **in Adam die. All** who are **in Christ shall be made alive**, that is, only believers in the Lord Jesus Christ will be raised from the dead to dwell eternally with Him. The **all** who **shall be made alive** is defined in verse 23 as those who are Christ's at His Coming. It does not include Christ's enemies, for they shall be put under His feet (v. 25), which, as someone has said, is a strange name for heaven.

15:23 Next we have the groups or classes involved in the first resurrection. First is the resurrection of **Christ** Himself. He is spoken of here as **the firstfruits**. Firstfruits were a handful of ripened grain from the harvest field before the actual harvest started. They were a pledge, a guarantee, a foretaste of what was to follow. The expression does not necessarily mean that Christ was the first one to rise. We have instances of resurrection in the OT, and the cases of Lazarus, the widow's son, and Jairus' daughter in the NT. But Christ's resurrection was different from all of these in that, whereas they rose to die again, Christ rose to die no more. He rose to live in the power of an endless life. He rose with a glorified body.

The second class in the first resurrection is described as **those who are Christ's at His coming**. This includes those who will be raised at the time of the Rapture, and also those believers who will die during the Tribulation and will be raised at the end of that time of trouble, when Christ comes back to reign. Just as there are stages in the coming of Christ, so there will be stages in the resurrection of His saints. The first resurrection does not include all who have ever died, but only those who have died with faith in Christ.

Some teach that only those Christians who have been faithful to Christ, or who have been overcomers will be raised at this time, but the Scriptures are very clear in refuting this. All **who are Christ's** will be raised at His coming.

15:24 The expression **then comes the end** refers, we believe, to **the end** *of the resurrection*. At the close of Christ's Millennial Reign, when He shall have put down all His enemies, there will be the resurrection of the wicked dead. This is the last resurrection ever to take place. All who have ever died in unbelief will stand before the Judgment of the Great White Throne to hear their doom.

After the Millennium and the destruction of Satan (Rev. 20:7–10), the Lord Jesus will deliver **the kingdom to God the Father**. By that time He will have abolished **all rule and all authority and power**. Up to this time the Lord Jesus Christ has been reigning *as the Son of Man*, serving as God's Mediator. At the end of the thousand-year reign, God's purposes on earth will have been perfectly accomplished. All opposition will have been put down and all enemies destroyed. The reign of Christ *as Son of Man* will then give way to the eternal kingdom in heaven. His reign *as Son of God* in heaven will continue forever.

15:25 Verse 25 emphasizes what has just been said, namely, that Christ's reign will continue until every trace of rebellion and enmity has been put down.

15:26 Even during Christ's Millennial Reign, people will continue to die, especially those who openly rebel against the Lord. But at the Judgment of the Great White Throne, **death** and Hades will be cast into the Lake of Fire.

15:27 God has decreed that **all things** shall be **put** under the **feet** of the Lord Jesus. Of course, in putting **all things under Him**, God necessarily excepted Himself. Verse 27 is rather hard to follow because it is not clear to whom each pronoun is referring. We might paraphrase it as follows: "For God has put all things under Christ's feet. But when God says, all things are put under Christ, it is obvious that God is excluded, who put all things under Christ."

15:28 Even after **all things** have been put in subjection to the Son, He

Himself will continue to be **subject** to **God** forever.

> God has made Christ ruler, administrator of all His plans and counsels. All authority and power is put in His hands. There is a time coming when He will render His account of the administration committed to Him. After He has brought everything into subjection, He will hand the kingdom back to the Father. Creation will be brought back to God in a perfect condition. Having accomplished the work of redemption and restoration for which He became Man, He will retain the subordinate place that He took in Incarnation. If He should cease to be man after having brought to pass all that God purposed and designated, the very link that brings God and man together would be gone. (Selected)

15:29 Verse 29 is perhaps one of the most difficult and obscure verses in all the Bible. Many explanations have been offered as to its meaning. For instance, it is contended by some that living believers may be baptized for those who have died without having undergone this rite. Such a meaning is quite foreign to the Scriptures. It is based on a single verse and must be rejected, not having the collective support of other Scripture. Others believe that baptism for the dead means that in baptism we reckon ourselves to have died. This is a possible meaning, but it does not fit in too well with the context.

The interpretation which seems to suit the context best is this: At the time Paul wrote, there was fierce persecution against those who took a public stand for Christ. This persecution was especially vicious at the time of their baptism. It often happened that those who publicly proclaimed their faith in Christ in the waters of baptism were martyred shortly thereafter. But did this stop others from being saved and from taking their place in baptism? Not at all. It seemed as though there were always new replacements coming along to fill up the ranks of those who had been martyred. As they stepped into the waters of baptism, in a very real sense **they** were being **baptized for**, or *in the place of* (Gk. *huper*) the dead. Hence **the dead** here refers to those who died as a result of their bold witness for Christ. Now the apostle's argument here is that it would be foolish to be thus baptized to fill up the ranks of those who had died if there is no such thing as resurrection from the dead. It would be like sending replacement troops to fill up the ranks of an army that is fighting a lost cause. It would be like fighting on in a hopeless situation. **If the dead do not rise at all, why then are they baptized for the dead?**

15:30 And why do we stand in jeopardy every hour? The Apostle Paul was constantly exposed to danger. Because of his fearlessness in preaching Christ, he made enemies wherever he went. Secret plots were hatched against him in an effort to take his life. He could have avoided all this by abandoning his profession of Christ. In fact, it would have been wise for him to abandon it if there was no such thing as resurrection from the dead.

15:31 I affirm, by the boasting in you which I have in Christ Jesus our Lord, I die daily might be paraphrased: "As surely as I rejoice over you as my children in Christ Jesus, every day of my life I am exposed to death."

15:32 The apostle now recalls the fierce persecution which he encountered **at Ephesus**. We do not believe that he was actually thrown into the arena with wild beasts, but rather that he is speaking here of wicked men as wild **beasts**. Actually, as a Roman citizen, Paul could not have been forced to fight with wild animals. We do not know to what incident he refers. However, the argument is clear that the apostle would have been foolish to engage in such dangerous warfare as he had if he were not assured of resurrection from the dead. Indeed it would have been much wiser for him to adopt the philosophy: **"If the dead do not rise, 'Let us eat and drink, for tomorrow we die!' "**

We sometimes hear Christians say that if this life were all, then they would still rather be Christians. But Paul disagrees with such an idea. If there were no resurrection, we would be better off to make the most of *this* life. We would live for food, clothing, and pleasure. This would be the only heaven we could look forward to. But since there *is* a resurrection, we dare not spend our lives for these things of passing interest. We must live for "then" and not for "now."

15:33 The Corinthians should **not be deceived** on this score. **Evil company corrupts good habits.** Paul is referring to the false teachers who had come into the church at Corinth, denying the resurrection. The Christians should realize that it is impossible to associate with **evil** people or evil teachings without being corrupted by them. Evil doctrine inevitably has an effect on one's life. False teachings do not lead to holiness.

15:34 The Corinthians should **awake to righteousness** and **not sin.** They should not be deluded by these evil teachings. **Some do not have the knowledge of God. I speak this to your shame.** This verse is commonly interpreted to mean that there are still men and women who have never heard the gospel story, and that Christians should be ashamed of their failure to evangelize the world. However, while this may be true, we believe that the primary meaning of the passage is that there were men in the fellowship at Corinth who did **not have the knowledge of God**. They were not true believers, but wolves in sheep's clothing, false teachers who had crept in unawares. It was to the **shame** of the Corinthians that these men were allowed to take their place with the Christians and to teach these wicked doctrines. The carelessness which let ungodly people enter the assembly resulted in lowering the congregation's whole moral tone, thus preparing an opening for the intrusion of all kinds of error.

B. Consideration of Objections to the Resurrection (15:35–57)

15:35 In verses 35–49, the apostle goes into greater detail concerning the actual mode of the resurrection. He anticipates two questions which would inevitably arise in the minds of those who questioned the fact of bodily resurrection. The first is: **"How are the dead raised up?"** The second is: **"And with what body do they come?"**

15:36 The first question is answered in verse 36. A common illustration from nature is used to illustrate the possibility of resurrection. A seed must fall into the ground and die before the plant can come forth. It is wonderful indeed to think of the mystery of life that is hidden in every tiny seed. We may dissect the seed and study it under the microscope, but the secret of the life principle remains an unfathomable mystery. All we know is that the seed falls into the ground and from that unlikely beginning there springs forth life from the dead.

15:37 The second question is taken up next. Paul explains that when you **sow** a seed, **you do not sow the** plant **that shall** eventually result, **but** you sow a bare **grain — perhaps wheat or some other grain**. What do we conclude from this? Is the plant the same as the seed? No, the plant is not the same as the seed; however, there is a very vital connection between the two. Without the seed there would have been no plant. Also, the plant derives its features from the seed. So it is in resurrection.

> The resurrection body has identity of kind and continuity of substance with that which is sown, but it is purified from corruption, dishonor, and weakness, and made incorrupt, glorious, powerful, and spiritual. It is the same body, but it is sown in one form and raised in another. (Selected)

15:38 **God** produces **a body** according to the seed that was sown, and **each seed** has its own type of plant as a result. All the factors which determine the size, color, leaf, and flower of the plant are somehow contained in the seed that is sown.

15:39 To illustrate the fact that the glory of the resurrection body will be different from the glory of our present bodies, the Apostle Paul points out that **all flesh is not the same** kind. For instance, there is human **flesh, flesh of animals**, flesh **of fish**, and flesh **of birds**. These are distinctly different, and yet they are all flesh. There is similarity without exact duplication.

15:40 And just as there is a difference between the splendor of heavenly **bodies** (the stars, etc.) and bodies which are associated with this earth, so there is a difference between the body of the believer now and the one which he will have after death.

15:41 Even among the celestial bodies themselves, there is a difference of **glory.** For instance, **the sun** is brighter than **the moon, and one star differs from another in** brightness.

Most commentators agree that Paul is still emphasizing that the glory of the resurrection body will be different from the glory of the body which we have on earth at the present time. They do not think that verse 41, for instance, indicates that in heaven there will be differences of glory among believers themselves. However, we tend to agree with Holsten that "the way in which Paul emphasizes the diversities of the heavenly bodies implies the supposition of an analogous difference of glory between the risen." It is clear from other passages of Scripture that we shall not all be identical in heaven. Although all will resemble the Lord Jesus morally, that is, in freedom from sin, it does not follow that we shall all *look* like the Lord Jesus physically. He will be distinctly recognizable as such throughout all eternity. Likewise, we believe that each individual Christian will be a distinct personality recognizable as such. But there will be differences of reward granted at the Judgment Seat of Christ according to one's faithfulness in service. While all will be supremely happy in heaven, some will have greater *capacity* for enjoying heaven. Just as there will be differences of suffering in hell, according to the sins that a man has committed, so there will be differences of enjoyment in heaven, according to what we have done as believers.

15:42 Verses 42–49 show the contrast between what the believer's body is now and what it will be in its eternal state. **The body is sown in corruption, it is raised in incorruption.** At the present time, our bodies are subject to disease and death. When they are placed in the grave, they decompose and return to dust. But it will not be so with the resurrection body. It will no longer be subject to sickness or decay.

15:43 The present body **is sown in dishonor**. There is nothing very majestic or glorious about a dead body. However, this same body will be **raised in glory**. It will be free from wrinkles, scars, the marks of age, overweight, and the traces of sin.

It is sown in weakness, it is raised in power. With the coming of old age, **weakness** increases until death itself strips a man of all strength whatever. In eternity, the body will not be subject to these sad limitations, but will be possessed of powers that it does not have at the present time. For instance, the Lord Jesus Christ in resurrection was able to enter a room where the doors were locked.

15:44 **It is sown a natural body, it is raised a spiritual body.** Here we must be very careful to emphasize that spiritual does *not* mean nonmaterial. Some people have the idea that in resurrection we will be disembodied spirits. That is not at all the meaning of this passage, nor is it true. We know that the resurrection body of the Lord Jesus was composed of flesh and bones because He said, "A spirit does not have flesh and bones as you see I have" (Luke 24:39). The difference between **a natural body** and **a spiritual body** is that the former is suited to life here on earth whereas the latter will be suited to life in heaven. The former is usually soul-controlled whereas the latter is spirit-controlled. **A spiritual body** is one that will be truly the servant of the spirit.

God created man spirit, soul, and body. He always mentions the spirit first, because His intention was that the spirit should be in the place of preeminence or dominance. With the entrance of sin, something very strange happened. God's order seems to have been upset, and the result is that man always says "body, soul, and spirit." He has given the body the place which the spirit should have had. In resurrection it will not be so; the spirit will be in the place of control which God originally intended.

15:45 **And so it is written, "The first man Adam became a living being." The last Adam became a life-giving spirit.** Here again **the first man Adam** is contrasted with the Lord Jesus Christ. God breathed into Adam's nostrils the breath of life and he became a living being (Gen. 2:7). All who are descended from him bear his characteristics. **The last Adam**, the Savior, **became a life-giving spirit** (John 5:21, 26). The difference is that in the first case, Adam *was given* physical life, whereas in the second case Christ *gives* eternal life to others. Erdman explains:

As the descendants of Adam, we are made like him, living souls inhabiting mortal bodies, and bearing the image of an earthly parent. But as the followers of Christ, we are yet to be clothed with immortal bodies and to bear the image of our heavenly Lord.[53]

15:46 The apostle now sets forth a fundamental law in God's universe, namely, **the spiritual is not first, but the natural, and afterward the spiritual**. This can be understood in several ways. Adam, **the natural** man, came first on the stage of human history; then Jesus, **the spiritual** Man. Second, we are born into the world as **natural** beings; then when we are born again, we become **spiritual** beings. Finally, we first receive **natural** bodies, then in resurrection we will receive **spiritual** bodies.

15:47 The first man was of the earth, made of dust. This means that his origin was **of the earth** and that his characteristics were earthly. He was **made of** the **dust** of the ground in the first place, and in his life he seemed in a very real sense to be earth-bound. **The second Man is the Lord**[54] **from heaven.**

15:48 Of the two men mentioned in verse 45, Jesus was the second. He existed from all eternity, but as Man, he came after Adam. He came from heaven, and everything He did and said was **heavenly** and spiritual rather than earthly and soulish.

As it is with these two federal heads, so it is with their followers. Those who are born of Adam inherit his characteristics. Also those who are born of Christ are a **heavenly** people.

15:49 As we have borne the characteristics of Adam as to our natural birth, **we shall**[55] **also bear the image of** Christ in our resurrection bodies.

15:50 Now the apostle turns to the subject of the transformation that will take place in the bodies of believers, both living and dead, at the time of the Lord's Return. He prefaces his remarks with the statement **that flesh and blood cannot inherit the kingdom of God**. By this he means that the present body which we have is not suited to **the kingdom of God** in its eternal aspect, that is, our heavenly home. It is also true that **corruption** cannot **inherit incorruption**.

In other words, our present bodies which are subject to disease, decay, and decomposition, would not be suited for life in a state where there is no corruption. This raises the problem, then, of how the bodies of living believers can be suited for life in heaven.

15:51 The answer is in the form of **a mystery**. As previously stated, **a mystery** is a truth previously unknown, but now revealed by God to the apostles and made known through them to us.

We shall not all sleep, that is, not all believers will experience death. Some will be alive when the Lord returns. But whether we have died or are still alive, **we shall all be changed**. The truth of resurrection itself is not a mystery, since it appears in the OT, but the fact that not all will die and also the change of living saints at the Lord's Return is something that had never been known before.

15:52 The change will take place instantly, **in the twinkling of an eye, at the last trumpet. The last trumpet** here does not mean the end of the world, or even the last trumpet mentioned in Revelation. Rather, it refers to the **trumpet** of God which will sound when Christ comes into the air for His saints (1 Thess. 4:16). When the **trumpet** sounds, **the dead will be raised incorruptible, and we shall be changed**. What a tremendous moment that will be, when the earth and the sea will yield up the dust of all those who have died trusting in Christ down through the centuries! It is almost impossible for the human mind to take in the magnitude of such an event; yet the humble believer can accept it by faith.

15:53 We believe that verse 53 refers to the two classes of believers at the time of Christ's Return. **This corruptible** refers to those whose bodies have returned to the dust. They will **put on incorruption. This mortal**, on the other hand, refers to those who are still alive in body but are subject to death. Such bodies will **put on immortality.**

15:54 When the dead in Christ are raised and the living changed with them, **then shall be brought to pass the saying that is written, "Death is swallowed up in victory"** (Isa. 25:8). How magnificent!

C. H. Mackintosh exclaims:

> What are death, the grave, and decomposition in the presence of such power as this? Talk of being dead four days as a difficulty! Millions that have been mouldering in the dust for thousands of years shall spring up in a moment into life, immortality and eternal glory, at the voice of that blessed One.[56]

15:55 This verse may well be a taunt song which believers sing as they rise to meet the Lord in the air. It is as if they mock **Death** because for them it has lost its **sting**. They also mock **Hades** because for them *it* has lost the battle to keep them as its own. **Death** holds no terror for them because they know their sins have been forgiven and they stand before God in all the acceptability of His beloved Son.

15:56 **Death** would have no **sting** for anyone if it were not for **sin**. It is the consciousness of sins unconfessed and unforgiven that makes men afraid to die. If we know our sins are forgiven, we can face death with confidence. If, on the other hand, sin is on the conscience, death is terrible — the beginning of eternal punishment.

The strength of sin is the law, that is, **the law** condemns the sinner. It pronounces the doom of all who have failed to obey God's holy precepts. It has been well said that if there were no sin, there would be no death. And if there were no law, there would be no condemnation.

> The throne of death rests on two bases: sin, which calls for condemnation, and the law which pronounces it. Consequently, it is on these two powers that the work of the Deliverer bore.[57]

15:57 Through faith in Him, we have **victory** over death and the grave. Death is robbed of its sting. It is a known fact that when certain insects sting a person, they leave their stinger imbedded in the person's flesh, and being thus robbed of their "sting," they die. In a very real sense death stung itself to death at the cross of **our Lord Jesus Christ**, and now the King of Terrors is robbed of his terror as far as the believer is concerned.

C. Concluding Appeal in Light of the Resurrection (15:58)

In view, then, of the certainty of the resurrection and the fact that faith in Christ is not in vain, the Apostle Paul exhorts his **beloved brethren** to **be steadfast, immovable, always abounding in the work of the Lord, knowing that** their **labor is not in vain in the Lord**. The truth of resurrection changes everything. It provides hope and steadfastness, and enables us to go on in the face of overwhelming and difficult circumstances.

V. PAUL'S FINAL COUNSEL (Chap. 16)

A. Concerning the Collection (16:1–4)

16:1 The first verse of chapter 16 concerns a **collection** which was to be taken up by the church in Corinth and sent to needy **saints** in Jerusalem. The exact cause of their poverty is not known. Some have suggested that it was a result of famine (Acts 11:28–30). Possibly another reason is that those Jews who professed faith in Christ were ostracized and boycotted by their unbelieving relatives, friends, and fellow countrymen. They doubtlessly lost their jobs and in countless ways were subjected to economic pressures designed to force them to give up their profession of faith in Christ. Paul had already **given orders to the churches of Galatia** in connection with this very matter, and he now instructs the Corinthians to respond in the same manner that the Galatian saints had been exhorted to do.

16:2 Although the instructions given in verse 2 were for a specific collection, yet the principles involved are of abiding value. First of all, the laying by of funds was to be done **on the first day of the week**. Here we have a very strong indication that the early Christians no longer regarded the Sabbath or seventh day as an obligatory observance. The Lord had risen on the first day of the week, the Day of Pentecost was on the first day of the week, and the disciples gathered together on the first day of the week to break bread (Acts 20:7). Now they are to **lay something aside** for the saints **on the first day of the week**.

The second important principle is that the instructions concerning the collections were for **each one**. Rich and poor, slave and free, all were to have a part in the sacrifice of giving of their possessions.

Further, this was to be done systematically. **On the first day of the week** they were to **lay something aside, storing up.** It was not to be haphazard, or reserved for special occasions. The gift was to be set aside from other money and devoted to special use as occasion demanded. Their giving was also to be proportionate. This is indicated by the expression **as he may prosper**.

That there be no collections when I come. The Apostle Paul did not want this to be a matter of last-minute arrangement. He realized the serious possibility of giving without due preparation of heart or pocketbook.

16:3 Verses 3 and 4 give us very valuable insight into the care that should be taken with funds that are gathered in a Christian assembly. It is noticeable, first, that the funds were not to be entrusted to any one person. Even Paul himself was not to be the sole recipient. Secondly, we notice that the arrangements as to who would carry the money were not made arbitrarily by the Apostle Paul. Rather, this decision was left to the local assembly. When they selected the messengers, Paul would **send** them **to Jerusalem**.

16:4 If it was decided that it would be well for the apostle to **go** to Jerusalem **also**, then the local brethren would accompany him there. Notice that he says "they will go with me" rather than "I will go with them." Perhaps this is an allusion to Paul's authority as an apostle. Some commentators suggest that the factor that would determine whether or not Paul went would be the size of the gift, but we hardly believe that the great apostle would be guided by such a principle.

B. Concerning His Personal Plans (16:5–9)

16:5 Paul discusses his personal plans in verses 5–9. From Ephesus, where he wrote this letter, he planned to **pass through Macedonia**. Then he hoped to move south to Corinth.

16:6–8 Possibly Paul would **spend the winter with** the saints in Corinth and then they would speed him on his way, **wherever** he would **go** from there. For the present, then, he would not see them en route to Macedonia, but he did look forward to staying with them later for a while, **if the Lord** would so permit. Before leaving Macedonia, Paul expected to **tarry in Ephesus until Pentecost**. It is from verse 8 that we learn that the Epistle was written from Ephesus.

16:9 Paul realized that there was a golden opportunity for serving Christ at that time at Ephesus. At the same time he realized that **there** were **many adversaries**. What an unchanging picture this verse gives us of Christian service: On the one hand, there are the fields white already to harvest; on the other, there is a sleepless foe who seeks to obstruct, divide, and oppose in every conceivable way!

C. Closing Exhortations and Greetings (16:10–24)

16:10 The apostle adds a word concerning **Timothy**. If this devoted young servant of the Lord came to Corinth, they should receive him **without fear**. Perhaps this means that Timothy was naturally of a timid disposition, and that they should not do anything to intensify this tendency. Perhaps, on the other hand, it means that he should be able to come to them **without** any **fear** of not being accepted as a servant of the Lord. That the latter is probably the proper meaning is indicated by Paul's words: **"For he does the work of the Lord, as I also do."**

16:11 Because of Timothy's faithful service for Christ, **no one** should **despise him**. Instead, an earnest effort should be made to **send him on his journey in peace, that he** might return to Paul in due time. The apostle was looking forward to a reunion with Timothy and **with the brethren.**

16:12 Now **concerning . . . brother Apollos,** Paul had **strongly urged him to** visit Corinth **with the brethren**. Apollos did not feel that this was God's will for him **at the time**, but he indicated that he would go to Corinth **when he** had the opportunity. Verse 12 is valuable to us in showing the loving spirit that prevailed among the servants of the Lord. Someone has called it a beautiful picture of "unjealous love and respect." It also shows the liberty that prevailed for each servant of the Lord to be guided by the Lord without dictation from any other source. Even the Apostle Paul himself was not authorized to tell Apollos what to do. In this connection Ironside commented: "I would not like to tear this chapter out of my Bible. It helps me to understand God's way of guiding His servants in their ministry for Him."[58]

16:13, 14 Now Paul delivers some pithy exhortations to the saints. They are to **watch** constantly, to **stand fast in the faith**, to **be brave** and to **be strong**. Perhaps Paul is thinking again of the danger of false teachers. The saints are to be on guard all the time. They are not to give up an inch of vital territory. They are to behave with true courage. Finally, they are to **be strong** in the Lord. In **all that** they **do**, they are to manifest **love**. This will mean lives of devotion to God and to others. It will mean a giving of themselves.

16:15 Next follows an exhortation concerning **the household of Stephanas**. These dear Christians were **the firstfruits of Achaia**, that is, the earliest converts in **Achaia**. Apparently from the time of their conversion, they had addicted **themselves to the ministry** (service) **of the saints.** They set themselves to serve the people of God. **The household of Stephanas** was mentioned previously in 1:16. There Paul states that he baptized that household. Many have insisted that **the household of Stephanas** included infants, and have sought thereby to justify the baptism of babies. However, it seems rather clear from this verse that there were no infants in this household, since it is distinctly stated that they **devoted themselves to the ministry of the saints.**

16:16 The apostle exhorts the Christians to **submit to such, and to everyone who** helps in the work **and labors**. We learn from the general teaching of the NT that those who set themselves apart for the service of Christ should be shown the loving respect of all the people of God. If this were done more generally, it would prevent a great deal of division and jealousy.

16:17 **The coming of Stephanas, Fortunatus, and Achaicus** had brought joy to Paul's heart. They **supplied what was lacking on** the **part** of the Corinthians. This may mean that they showed kindness to the apostle which the Corinthians had neglected to do. Or more probably it means that what the Corinthians were *unable* to do because of their distance from Paul, these men had accomplished.

16:18 They brought news from Corinth to Paul, and conversely they brought back news from the apostle to their home assembly. Again Paul commends them to the loving respect of the local church.

16:19 **The churches of Asia** refers to the congregations in the *province* of Asia (*Asia Minor* today), of which Ephesus was the capital. **Aquila and Priscilla** were apparently living in Ephesus at this time. At one time they had lived in Corinth, and thus were known to the saints there. **Aquila** was a tentmaker by trade, and had worked with Paul in this occupation. The expression **the church that is in their house** gives us a view of the simplicity of assembly life at that time. Christians would gather together in their homes for worship, prayer, and fellowship. Then they would go out to preach the gospel at their work, in the market place, in the local prison, and wherever their lot was cast.

16:20 **All the brethren** in the assembly join in sending their loving greetings to their fellow believers in Corinth. The apostle enjoins his readers to **greet one another with a holy kiss**. At that time, the **kiss** was a common mode of greeting, even among men. **A holy kiss** means a greeting without sham or impurity. In our sex-obsessed society, where perversion is so prevalent, the widespread use of the kiss as a mode of greeting might present serious temptations and lead to gross moral failures. For that reason, the handshake has largely taken the place of the kiss among Christians in English-speaking cultures. Ordinarily we should not allow cultural considerations to excuse us from strict adherence to the words of Scripture. But in a case like this, where literal obedience might lead to sin or even the appearance of evil because of local cultural conditions, we are probably justified in substituting the handshake for the kiss.

16:21 Paul's usual habit was to dictate his letters to one of his co-workers. However, at the end he would take pen in hand, add a few words in his own writing, and then give his characteristic **salutation**. That is what he does at this point.

16:22 Accursed translates the Greek word *anathema*. Those who do **not love the Lord Jesus** are condemned already, but their doom will be manifest at the coming of the Lord Jesus Christ. A Christian is one who loves the Savior. He loves the Lord Jesus more than anyone or anything in the world. Failure to love God's Son is a crime against God Himself. Ryle comments:

> St. Paul allows no way of escape to the man who does not love Christ. He leaves no loophole or excuse. A man may lack clear head-knowledge and yet be saved. He may fail in courage, and be overcome by the fear of man, like Peter. He may fall tremendously, like David, and yet rise again. But if a person does not love Christ he is not in the way of life. The curse is yet upon him. He is on the broad road that leadeth to destruction.[59]

O Lord, come! translates *maranatha*, an Aramaic expression used by the early Christians. If spaced "maran atha" it means "Our Lord has come," and if spaced "marana tha" it means Our **Lord, come!**

16:23 Grace was Paul's favorite theme. He loved to open and end his Letters on this exalted note. It is one of the true marks of his authorship.

16:24 Throughout the entire Epistle we have listened to the heartbeat of this devoted apostle of Christ. We have listened to him as he sought to edify, comfort, exhort, and admonish his children in the faith. There was no doubt of his **love** for them. When they read these closing words, perhaps they would feel ashamed that they had allowed false teachers to come in, questioned Paul's apostleship, and turned away from their original love for him.

ENDNOTES

[1](1:18) Albert Barnes, *Notes on the New Testament, 1 Corinthians*, p. 14.

[2](1:19) S. Lewis Johnson, "First Corinthians," *The Wycliffe Bible Commentary*, p. 1232.

[3](1:27) Erich Sauer, *The Dawn of World Redemption*, p. 91.

[4](1:30) Traill, further documentation unavailable.

[5](1:30) Arthur T. Pierson, *The Ministry of Keswick, First Series*, p. 104.

[6](2:14) Vance Havner, further documentation unavailable.

[7](3:9) Charles R. Erdman, *The First Epistle of Paul to the Corinthians*, p. 40.

[8](3:15) E. W. Rogers, *Concerning the Future*, p. 77.

[9](3:18) Frédéric L. Godet, *Commentary on First Corinthians*, p. 195.

[10](4:8) H. P. Barker, *Coming Twice*, p. 80.

[11](5:2) Erdman, *First Corinthians*, p. 55.

[12](6:9) Some differentiate between "entering" the kingdom and "inheriting" the kingdom. They teach that a believer could conceivably not conquer a major sin in his life and yet be saved. He would "enter" the kingdom but have little or no inheritance (reward) in it. However, this passage deals with the unrighteous, i.e., the unregenerate.

[13](6:13) Erdman, *First Corinthians*, p. 63.

[14](6:17) A. T. Pierson, *Knowing the Scriptures*, p. 147.

[15](6:20) Bates, further documentation unavailable.

[16](6:20) The NU text omits the reference to the spirit here.

[17](7:5) Larry Christenson, *The Christian Family*, p. 24.

[18](7:14) W. E. Vine, *First Corinthians*, p. 97.

[19](7:15) J. M. Davies, further documentation unavailable.

[20](7:17) W. E. Vine, *The Divine Plan of Missions*, p. 63.

[21](7:19) William Kelly, *Notes on the First Epistle to the Corinthians*, p. 123.

[22](7:29) Harry A. Ironside, *First Epistle to the Corinthians*, p. 223.

[23](7:29) Vine, *First Corinthians*, p. 104.

[24](7:33) *Ibid.*, p. 105.

[25](7:36) However, the standard Greek word for *virginity* is the abstract noun *parthenia*, and if Paul meant this, one wonders why he used the simple word for "virgin," as in Matthew 1:23.

[26](7:38) The "himself" has been supplied; it is not in the Greek.

[27](8:12) Barnes, *1 Corinthians*, p. 147.

[28](9:17) Charles C. Ryrie, *The Ryrie Study Bible, New King James Version*, p. 1771.

[29](9:20) The NU text adds the explanatory words here, "though not being myself under the law."

[30](9:20) William Arnot, *The Church in the House*, pp. 467, 468.

[31](9:21) Charles C. Ryrie, *The Grace of God*, p. 83.

[32](9:22) NU omits "as," but it seems important to Paul's argument — he didn't *actually* become weak.

[33](9:27) Much of the problem stems from the KJV translation "castaway." The word *a-dokimos* simply means "not-approved." As an athletic term, it translates very well by our English "disqualified."

[34](10:5) Godet, *First Corinthians*, pp. 59, 60.

[35](10:22) Kelly, *First Corinthians*, p. 166.

[36](10:28) NU omits the repetition.

[37](11:5) It is clear from verses 4 and 5 that in situations involving prayer and prophesying, a woman should be *covered* whenever it is proper for a man to be *uncovered*. Women who have difficulty knowing what to do and when to do it should observe the man's example and do the opposite.

[38](11:7) Vine, *Expository Dictionary, under Glory*, , p. 154.

[39](11:18) F. B. Hole, "The Administration of the Mystery" (booklet), p. 5.

[40](11:19) The Greek word is *haireseis*, but here it does not have the *later* meaning "heresies." See note on Titus 3:10.

[41](11:19) Greek usually uses *opheilō* for *moral* necessity. Here Paul uses the regular word for *logical* necessity, *dei*.

[42](11:26) Godet, *First Corinthians*, p. 163.

[43](12:Intro) *Glōssa* ("tongue") is the ordinary Greek word for "language." Similarly, formal English still occasionally says, e.g., "the French tongue."

[44](12:10) Much of what some people call "prophecy" today is either merely a re-wording of Bible texts or actual error that does not come true. Both are often in a poor imitation of King James English, as though God could not communicate in today's language!

[45](12:13) The Greek word *en* can be translated *in, with* or *by* with equal accuracy (context permitting), but we consider "in" the most "literal" because it is related to Greek *en*.

[46](12:29, 30) These questions start with *mē* in Greek, suggesting a paraphrase such as, "Surely, all don't speak in tongues?" — and so forth.

[47](13:11) The word is *nēpios* (cf. Heb. 5:13).

[48](14:5) Kelly, *First Corinthians*, p. 229.

[49](14:13) However, there is no indication in the original that the subject of "may interpret" is different from that of "speaks."

[50](14:19) The literal rendering is "understanding of me." The "of me" is in the genitive and is the *object* of the action suggested by the noun. The same *form* can be a *subjective* genitive. The context determines which is best.

[51](14:19) Charles Hodge, *First Corinthians*, p. 292.

[52](14:35) The same Greek word *andres* can mean "husbands," "males" or "men-(folks)."

[53](15:45) Erdman, *First Corinthians*, p. 148.

[54](15:47) NU text omits "the Lord."

[55](15:49) The majority of Greek mss. have an exhortation here: "Let us bear . . . ."

[56](15:54) C. H. Mackintosh, *The Mackintosh Treasury: Miscellaneous Writings by C. H. Mackintosh*, p. 125.

[57](15:56) Godet, *First Corinthians*, p. 446.

[58](16:12) Ironside, *First Corinthians*, p. 542.

[59](16:22) J. C. Ryle, *Holiness*, p. 235.

BIBLIOGRAPHY

Barnes, Albert. *Notes on the New Testament.* (Vol. V, 1 Corinthians). London: Blackie & Son, n.d.

Davies, J. M. *The Epistles to the Corinthians.* Bombay: Gospel Literature Service, 1975.

The apostle knows that the same God who **delivered** him in the past is able to **deliver** him day by day, and **will** continue to **deliver** him until that final, grand moment when he will be completely released from the tribulations and persecutions of this world.

1:11 Here Paul generously assumes that the Corinthian Christians had been praying for him while he was going through this time of deep testing. Actually, many of the believers had become critical of the great apostle, and there could have been a serious question whether they were remembering him before the throne of grace at all. However, he is willing to give them the benefit of the doubt. The expression **the gift granted to us through many** refers to **the gift** of Paul's deliverance which was brought about through the prayers of **many persons**. He sees his escape as a direct result of the intercession of the saints. He says that because many had prayed, **many persons** can now give **thanks** because their prayers were answered.

C. Explanation of Paul's Change of Plans (1:12—2:17)

1:12 The reason Paul feels he can depend on the prayers of the believers is that he has always been straightforward in his dealings with them. He can boast of his integrity toward them, and his conscience bears witness to the fact that his conduct was characterized by **simplicity and godly sincerity**, that is, the transparent genuineness that comes from God. He did not stoop to the methods of **fleshly** men, **but** acted openly before all with the undeserved strength (**grace**) which **God** supplied. This should have been apparent in a special way to the Corinthians.

1:13 The integrity which characterized his past dealings with the Corinthians is true also of this letter. He is **writing** exactly what he means. There is no need for them to read between the lines. The meaning is on the surface, simple and obvious. It is exactly **what** they **read or understand**, and he hopes that they will continue to acknowledge it **even to the end**, that is, as long as they live.

1:14 The assembly in Corinth had acknowledged Paul **in part**, that is, some of the believers had acknowledged him but not all. The loyal ones understood these two facts — that they would be proud of him and that he would be proud of them **in the day of the Lord Jesus. The day of the Lord Jesus** looks forward particularly to the Judgment Seat of Christ when the service of the redeemed will be evaluated and rewarded. When Paul looked forward to that tribunal, he invariably saw the faces of those who had been saved through his ministry. They would be his joy and crown of rejoicing, and they, in turn, would rejoice that he had been God's instrument to lead them to Christ.

1:15 The expression **in this confidence** mean with the **confidence** that they rejoiced in him as a true apostle of Jesus Christ, and as one whose sincerity was above question. He wanted **to come to** them with the assurance of their trust, esteem, and affection. He **intended to come** first to them **before** he went into Macedonia, and then again on the return from Macedonia. They would thus have had a **second benefit** in the sense of two visits rather than one.

1:16 The "second benefit" is further explained by verse 16. As mentioned, the plan was that when Paul left Ephesus he would cross over into Achaia, where Corinth was located, and then travel north into **Macedonia**. After having preached there, he would retrace his steps south to Corinth. He hoped that the Corinthian believers would then help him **on** his **way to Judea** —probably by their hospitality and prayers, but not by their money, since he later states his determination not to accept funds from them (11:7–10).

1:17 Paul's original plan never came to pass. He journeyed from Ephesus to Troas, and when he did not find Titus, he went directly to Macedonia, omitting Corinth from his itinerary. So here he asks, **"Therefore when I was planning this, did I do it lightly?"** This is probably exactly what his detractors were saying. "Fickle, changeable Paul! He says one thing and does another! Could such a man be a true apostle?" The apostle challenges the Corinthians as to whether he is undependable. When he plans, does he **plan according to** fleshly motives with the result that it is **Yes** one minute and **No** the next? Is he guided simply by considerations of comfort and expediency? Phillips catches the spirit of this verse in his paraphrase: "Because we had to change this plan, does it mean that we are fickle? Do you think I plan with my tongue in my cheek, saying 'Yes' and meaning 'No'?"

1:18 Paul seems to pass from his **word** concerning his travel plans to his preaching. Perhaps his critics were saying that if he was undependable in his ordinary conversation, then his preaching could not be trusted.

1:19 Paul argues that his actions were not untrustworthy because the Savior he preached was the divine, unchangeable One in whom there was no vacillation or changeableness. When he first visited Corinth with **Silvanus and Timothy** (Acts 18:5), they had preached the trustworthy **Son of God**. "The message was not unstable because it concerned **the Son of God** who was not vacillating." The argument is that no one who preaches the Lord Jesus in the Spirit could possibly act the way his critics had accused him. Denney says, "Paul's argument here could have been used by a hypocrite, but no critic could ever have invented it." How could he preach a faithful God and himself be unfaithful to his own word?

1:20 **All the promises of God**, no matter how many they are, find their fulfillment *in Christ*. All who find **in Him** the fulfillment of God's promises add their **Amen**:

We open our Bibles at a promise, we look up to God, and God says, "You can have all that through Christ." Trusting Christ, we say, "Amen" to God. God speaks through Christ, and we believe in Christ; Christ reaches down and faith stretches up, and every promise of God is fulfilled in Jesus Christ. In and through Him we appropriate and take them to ourselves and say, "Yes, Lord; I trust You." This is the believing yes.[3]

All of this is **to the glory of God through us**. Denney writes: "He is glorified when it dawns on human souls that He has spoken good concerning them beyond their utmost imaginings, and when that good is seen to be indubitably safe and sure in His Son."

The two words **through us**, remind the Corinthians that it was **through** the preaching of men like Silvanus, Timothy, and Paul that they had ever come to claim the promises of God in Christ. If the apostle was a fraud, as his enemies charged, then could it be that God had used a cheat and a liar to effect such marvelous results? The answer, of course, is no.

1:21 Paul next shows that the Corinthians and he were all bound in the same bundle of life. **God** had established them in the faith, confirming them **in Christ** by the ministry of the word of God. He had also **anointed** them with **the Spirit**, qualifying, empowering, and teaching them.

1:22 He **also** had **sealed** them and **given** them **the Spirit in** their **hearts as a guarantee**. Here we have two more ministries of the Holy Spirit. The seal is the mark of ownership and security. **The Spirit** indwelling the believer is the mark that the believer now belongs to God and that he is eternally secure. The seal, of course, is invisible. People do not know that we are Christians by some badge we wear, but only by the evidences of a Spirit-filled life. God has also **given** them **the Spirit in** their **hearts as a guarantee** or downpayment in pledge that the entire inheritance will follow. When God saves a man, He gives him the indwelling Holy **Spirit**. Just as surely as a man receives **the Spirit**, so surely will he enter into the full inheritance of God. The same kind of blessings which the Holy Spirit makes real in our lives today will be ours in full measure in a day yet future.

1:23 From verse 23 through verse 4 of chapter 2, Paul returns to the charge of vacillation that had been made against him and gives a straightforward explanation of why he did not visit Corinth as planned. Since no man could discern the real inward motives of Paul's action, he calls **God** to **witness** to this fact. If the apostle had visited **Corinth** at the time planned, he would have had to deal very firmly with the situation there. He would have had to deliver a personal rebuke to the saints because of their carelessness in tolerating sin in the assembly. It was **to spare** them pain and sadness that Paul delayed his trip **to Corinth**.

1:24 But having said that, the Apostle Paul would not want anyone to think that he was acting as a dictator over the Corinthians. And so he adds here, **"Not that we have dominion over your faith, but are fellow workers for your joy; for by faith you stand."** It was not that the apostle wanted to lord it **over** their Christian **faith**. He did not want them to think of him as a tyrant. Rather, he and his co-workers were merely helpers of their **joy**, that is, he only wanted to do what would assist them in their Christian pathway and thus add to their enjoyment.

The latter part of verse 24 may also be rendered "for *in* faith you stand *fast.*" That is, there was no need for them to be corrected as to their faith, for in that sphere they stood firm enough. The matters he sought to correct were not matters of doctrine as much as of practical behavior in the church.

2:1 This verse continues the thought from the last two verses of chapter 1. Paul further explains that the reason he did not go to Corinth as planned was that he did not want to cause them the **sorrow** that would inevitably follow a rebuke from him. The words **I determined . . . I would not come again to you in sorrow** seems to imply that he had made a sorrowful or painful visit subsequent to the first visit recorded in Acts 18:1–17. Such an interim visit may also be implied in 2 Corinthians 12:14; 13:1.

2:2 If the apostle came to Corinth with a personal rebuke to the Christians, he would of course sadden them. In that case, he too would be saddened because they were the very people to whom he was looking for joy. As Ryrie puts it, "If I hurt you, who will be left to make me glad but sad people? That wouldn't be any comfort."

2:3 Rather than cause this mutual **sorrow** through a personal visit, the Apostle Paul decided to write a letter. His hope was that the Letter would accomplish the desired result, that the Corinthians would exercise discipline in connection with the offending brother, and that Paul's next visit would not be clouded by strained relations between this people he so dearly loved and himself.

Does the letter referred to in the first part of verse 3 refer to the First Epistle of Paul to the Corinthians, or to some other letter which no longer exists today? Many believe that it could not be 1 Corinthians because of the description in verse 4, that it was written out of much affliction and anguish of heart, and with many tears. Other scholars feel that the description here fits the First Epistle very well. It is possible that Paul wrote a stern letter to Corinth that is no longer available. Presumably he wrote it after the sorrowful visit (2 Cor. 2:1) and appointed Titus to deliver it. Such a letter may be referred to in 2:4, 9; 7:8, 12.

Whichever view is correct, the thought in verse 3 is that Paul **wrote** them as he did so that when he visited them, he would not **have sorrow over** the sadness of those who should give him **joy**. He had confidence that the same things that brought **joy** to him would bring **joy** to them also. In the context, this means that the godly handling of the discipline problem would result in mutual rejoicing.

2:4 In this verse we have keen insight into the heart of a great pastor. Paul was deeply pained by the fact that sin had been tolerated in the assembly at Corinth. It caused him **much affliction and anguish of heart**, and hot **tears** of sorrow flowed down his cheeks. It is obvious that the apostle was more affected by sin in Corinth than the Corinthians themselves were. They should not interpret this letter as an attempt to hurt their feelings, but rather as a proof of his **love** for them. He hoped that, by his writing, they would have sufficient time to remedy the situation, so that his subsequent visit to them would be a joyful one. "Faithful are the wounds of a friend." We should not resent it if we are counseled or warned in a godly manner. Rather, we should realize that any person who would do this really has an interest in us. Righteous rebuke should be taken as from the Lord, and we should be grateful for it.

2:5 From verse 5 through verse 11, the apostle refers more directly to the incident that had caused the difficulty. Notice the extreme grace and Christian consideration which he shows. Not once does he name the offense or the offender. The expression **"if anyone has**

caused grief" may refer to the incestuous man of 1 Corinthians 5:1, or to someone else who had caused trouble in the assembly. We will assume that it refers to the former. Paul did not regard it as a personal offence against himself. It had caused **grief** to **all** the believers **to some extent**.

2:6 The believers at Corinth had agreed on disciplinary action for the offender. Apparently they had excommunicated him from the church. As a result of this action, he had become truly repentant and had been restored to the Lord. Now Paul tells the Corinthians that the man's **punishment** has been **sufficient**. They should not needlessly prolong it. In the latter part of the verse, we find the expression **which was inflicted by** "the many" (lit.). Some believe that "the many" means **the majority**. Others insist that it means *all* the members *except* the one disciplined. The latter deny that a **majority** decision is sufficient in church matters. They say that where the Spirit of God is allowed to lead, there should be unanimous action.

2:7, 8 Now that the man has become thoroughly repentant, the Corinthians should **forgive and** seek to strengthen **him** by receiving him back into their fellowship. If they do not do this, there is the danger that he might be **swallowed up with too much sorrow**, that is, he might despair of the reality of his forgiveness and go on in constant gloom and discouragement.

The Corinthians could **reaffirm** their **love to him** by opening wide their arms and receiving him back with joy and tenderness.

2:9 In writing the First Epistle to the Corinthians, Paul had **put** the saints **to the test**. Here was an opportunity for them to show whether they were **obedient** to the word of the Lord, as ministered to them by the Apostle Paul. He had suggested at that time that they should put the man out of the fellowship of the church. That is exactly what they did, thus proving themselves to be truly **obedient**. Now Paul would have them go one step further, that is, to receive the man back.

2:10 Phillips paraphrases verse 10, "If you will forgive a certain person, rest assured that I forgive him too. Insofar as I had anything personally to forgive, I do forgive him, as before Christ." Paul wants the saints to know that he is thoroughly in fellowship with them as they forgive the repentant offender. If he had had **anything** to forgive, he does **forgive** it for the sake of the Corinthians, and as **in the presence of Christ**.

The emphasis in this letter on church discipline is an index of its importance. Yet it is a subject that is all but neglected in many evangelical churches today. It is another instance where we can profess to believe in the inspiration of the Scriptures, yet refuse to obey them when it suits our purposes.

2:11 Just as there is danger for an assembly if it does not take disciplinary action when called for, so there is a danger of not exercising forgiveness when true repentance has taken place. **Satan** is always ready to step into a situation such as this with his cunning devices. In the first case, he will wreck the testimony of an assembly through tolerated sin, and in the second, he will overwhelm the repentant person with overmuch sorrow, if the assembly does not restore him. If Satan can't destroy by immorality, he will try by the unmeasured sorrow following repentance.

Commenting on the expression **"we are not ignorant of his devices"**, J. Sidlow Baxter says:

> Satan uses all manner of stratagems to turn souls from the truth: a sieve to "sift" them (Luke 22:31), "devices" to trick (as in our text), "weeds" to "choke" (Matt. 13:22), "wiles" to intrigue (Eph. 6:11), the roaring of a lion to terrify (1 Pet. 5:8), the disguise of an angel to deceive (2 Cor. 11:14) and "snares" to entangle them (2 Tim. 2:26).[4]

2:12 Paul now resumes the subject of his change in plans where he left off in verse 4. He had not gone to Corinth as he previously announced he would. The previous verses explained that his failure to visit Corinth was to avoid doing so in a harsh spirit of rebuke. In verses 12 through 17, Paul tells exactly what did happen to him at this important point in his ministry. As mentioned before, Paul left Ephesus and journeyed **to Troas** in hopes of meeting Titus there and receiving news from Corinth. When he got to Troas, some wonderful **door** of opportunity **opened** out before him **by the Lord** for preaching **Christ's gospel.**

2:13 In spite of this golden opportunity, Paul's **spirit** was troubled. **Titus** was not there to meet him. The burden of the Corinthian church lay heavily on the apostle's heart. Should he stay in Troas and preach the gospel of Christ? Or should he press on into Macedonia? His decision was made; he would cross over into **Macedonia**. One wonders what the reaction of the Corinthians was when they read these words. Did they realize, perhaps with a trifle of shame, that it was *their* behavior which caused such restlessness in the life of the apostle, and which resulted in his having to refuse a wonderful gospel opportunity in order to learn of their spiritual welfare?

2:14 Paul was not defeated. No matter where he went in the service of Christ there was victory. And so he bursts out in thanksgiving: **But thanks be to God who always leads us in triumph in Christ**. A.T. Robertson says:

> Without a word of explanation, Paul leaps out of the Slough of Despond and sprints like a bird to the heights of joy. He soars aloft like an eagle, with proud scorn of the valley beneath him.[5]

Paul here borrows a figure from the triumphal processions of Roman conquerors. Returning home after glorious victories, they would lead their captives along the streets of the capital. Incense bearers would march along both sides, and the **fragrance** of the incense would permeate the scene. So Paul pictures the Lord marching as a conqueror from Troas to Macedonia, and leading the apostle in His train. Wherever the Lord goes, through His servants, there is victory. **The fragrance of** the **knowledge of** Christ is diffused through the apostle in every place. F. B. Meyer writes:

> Wherever they went men knew Jesus better; the loveliness of the Master's character became more apparent. Men became aware of a subtle fragrance, poured upon the air, which attracted them to the Man of Nazareth.[6]

Thus Paul does not feel that he has suffered a defeat in his warfare with Satan, but the Lord has won a victory and Paul shares it.

2:15 In the triumphal processions to which Paul refers, the fragrance of the incense meant glorious victory to the conquerors, but it spoke of doom for the captives. Thus the apostle notes that the preaching of the gospel has a twofold effect. It signifies one thing **among those who are being saved**, and something altogether different **among those who are perishing**. To those who accept it, it is a pledge of a glorious future; to others it is an omen of doom. But **God** is glorified in either case, for to Him it is **the fragrance** of grace in the one case and of justice in the other. F. B. Meyer states it well:

> When, therefore, we are told that we may be to God a sweet savour of Christ, it must be meant that we may so live as to recall to the mind of God what Jesus was in His mortal career. It is as though, as God watches us from day to day, He should see Jesus in us, and be reminded (speaking after the manner of men) of that blessed life which was offered as an offering and a sacrifice to God for a sweet smelling savour.[7]

2:16 To the saved, Christians **are the aroma of life leading to life**, but to the perishing, **the aroma of death leading to death**. We are what Phillips calls "the refreshing fragrance of life itself," bringing life to those who believe, but the "deathly smell of doom" to those who refuse to believe. This twofold effect is beautifully illustrated in an incident in the OT. When the ark of God was captured by the Philistines, it caused death and destruction as long as it was among them (1 Sam. 5). But when it was brought back to the house of Obed-Edom, it brought blessing and prosperity for him and for his household (2 Sam. 6:11). As Paul contemplates the tremendous responsibility of preaching the message that has such far-reaching consequences, he cries out, **"And who is sufficient for these things?"**

2:17 The connection between verse 17 and verse 16 is better seen if we supply the words "We are." "Who is sufficient for these things? We are, because we **are not . . . peddling the word of God"**, etc. (But this still must be understood in conjunction with 3:5 where Paul says that his sufficiency is from God.) The **so many**[8] refers to the Judaizing teachers who sought to turn the Corinthians away from the apostle. What were these men like? Paul says they peddled, huckstered, or made merchandise of **the word of God**. They had mercenary motives. They tried to turn the ministry into a profitable profession. This same word for **peddling** was also used of those who adulterated wine, often by adding to it. And so these false teachers sought to adulterate the word of God by adding their own doctrines to it. They sought, for instance, to mix law and grace.

Paul was not one of those who adulterated or merchandised the word of God. Rather, he could describe his ministry by four significant expressions. The *first* is **as of sincerity**. This means "as of transparency." His ministry was an honest one. There was no trickery or subterfuge in connection with it. Everything was out in the open. Robertson humorously explains the meaning of this expression: "Paul's berries were as good at the bottom as at the top."[9]

Secondly, he describes his service **as from God**. In other words, everything he spoke was **from God**. God was the source of his message, and it was **from God** he derived the strength to carry on. *Then* he adds **in the sight of God.** This means that the apostle served the Lord, conscious of the fact that **God** was always looking down upon him. He had a real sense of responsibility to God and realized that nothing could be hidden from the eye of God. *Then finally* he adds, **we speak . . . in Christ**. This means that he spoke in the name of **Christ**, with the authority of **Christ**, and as a spokesman for **Christ.**

D. Paul's Credentials for the Ministry (3:1–5)

3:1 In the latter part of 2:17, the apostle had used four distinct expressions to describe his ministry. He realized that this might sound to some, especially his critics, as if he were commending himself. And so he begins this chapter with the question, **Do we begin again to commend ourselves?** The **again** does not imply that he had commended himself previously. Rather, it simply means that he had been *accused* of doing so, and now he anticipates the repetition of such a charge against him.

Or do we need, as some others, epistles of commendation to you or letters of commendation from you? The **some others** to whom Paul is here referring are the false teachers of 2:17. They came to Corinth with **epistles of commendation**, perhaps from Jerusalem. And possibly when they left Corinth, they carried with them **letters of commendation from** the assembly there. Letters of commendation *were* used in the early church by Christians traveling from one place to the other. The apostle does not at all seek to discourage such a practice in this verse. Instead he is stating rather subtly that the *only* thing these false teachers had to commend them was the letter they carried! Otherwise they had no credentials to offer.

3:2 The Judaizers who had come to Corinth raised questions as to Paul's apostolic authority. They denied that he was a true servant of Christ. Perhaps they raised such doubts in the Corinthians' minds in order that the latter might demand a letter of recommendation from the Apostle Paul the next time he visited them. He has already asked them if he needs such a letter. Had he not come to Corinth when they were heathen idolaters? Had he not led them to Christ? Had not the Lord set His seal upon the ministry of the apostle by giving him precious souls in Corinth? That is the answer. The Corinthians themselves were Paul's **epistle, written in** his heart but **known and read by all men**. In his case there was no need of a letter written with pen and ink. They were the fruit of his ministry, and they were enshrined in his affections. Not only that, but they were **known and read by all men** in the sense that their conversion was a well-known fact in the whole area. People realized that a change had come over these people, that they had turned to God from idols, and that they were now living separated lives. They were the evidence of Paul's divine ministry.

3:3 At first glance, verse 3 seems to contradict verse 2. Paul had said that the Corinthians were his epistle; here he says that they are **an epistle of Christ**. In verse 2, he says that the epistle is written in his heart; in the latter part of verse 3, it seems clear that Christ has written the epistle on the hearts of the

Corinthians themselves. How can these differences be reconciled? The answer is that in verse 2 Paul is stating that the Corinthians were his letter of recommendation. Verse 3 gives the explanation. Perhaps we might get the connection by joining the two verses as follows: "You are our epistle . . . because **you are clearly** declared to be **an epistle of Christ**." In other words, the Corinthians were Paul's letter of recommendation because it was clear to all that the Lord had done a work of grace in their lives. They were obviously Christians. Since Paul had been the human instrument in bringing them to the Lord, they were his credentials. This is the thought in the expression **ministered by us**. The Lord Jesus is the One who had done the work in their lives, but He did it through the ministry of Paul.

Whereas the letters of recommendation used by Paul's enemies were written **with ink**, Paul's epistle was written **by the Spirit of the living God** and was therefore divine. **Ink**, of course, is subject to fading, erasure, and destruction, but when **the Spirit of . . . God** writes in human hearts, it is forever. Then Paul adds that the epistle of Christ has been written **not on tablets of stone but on tablets** that are hearts **of flesh**. People visiting Corinth did not see Christ's epistle engraved on some great monument in the middle of the market place, but rather the letter was written in the hearts and lives of the Christians there.

As Paul contrasted **tablets of stone** and **tablets** that are hearts **of flesh**, there is little doubt that he also had in mind the difference between the law and the gospel. The law had, of course, been inscribed on tablets of stone on Mount Sinai, but under the gospel, God secures obedience through the message of grace and love that is written in human hearts. Paul will take up this subject in greater detail shortly, so he merely alludes to it here.

3:4 As we have listened to Paul speak with such confidence about his apostleship and the ministry the Lord had committed to him, we might well ask, "How can you dare to speak with such assurance in the matter, Paul?" The answer is given here in verse 4. Defense of his apostleship might seem like self-commendation, but here he denies that. He says that his confidence is **toward God**, i.e., confidence that can withstand God's scrutiny. He does not have any confidence in himself or in his own ability, but **through Christ**, and in the work which Christ had done in the lives of the Corinthians, he finds proof of the reality of his ministry. The remarkable change in the lives of the Corinthians commended the apostle.

3:5 Here, again, Paul disclaims any adequacy in or of himself that would enable him to reckon himself to be an apostle of Jesus Christ. The power for his ministry did **not** come **from** within, **but** from above. The apostle was not anxious to take credit for himself. He realized that if **God** had not made him sufficient for the ministry, then nothing would have been accomplished.

E. The Old and New Covenants Contrasted (3:6–18)

3:6 Having discussed *his own* credentials, and his qualification for the ministry, Paul now launches into an extended account of the ministry itself. In the verses to follow, he contrasts the Old Covenant (the law) and **the new covenant** (the gospel). There is a good reason why he should do so at this point. Those who were criticizing him so severely in Corinth were the Judaizers. These were the men who sought to mix law and grace. They taught Christians that they must observe certain portions of the Law of Moses in order to be fully accepted by God. And so the apostle is here going to demonstrate the superiority of the New Covenant to the Old. He prefaces his remarks by saying that God has made him competent as a servant of **the new covenant**. A covenant, of course, is a promise, an agreement, or a testament. The Old Covenant was the legal system delivered by God to Moses. Under it, blessing was conditioned upon obedience. It was a covenant of works. It was an agreement between God and man, that if man did his part, God would do His also. But because it depended on man, it could not produce righteousness. **The new covenant** is the gospel. Under it, God covenants to bless man freely by His grace through the redemption that is in Christ Jesus. Everything under the

New Covenant depends on God and not on man. Therefore, the New Covenant is able to accomplish what the Old could never do.

Paul gives several striking contrasts between the law and the gospel. He begins here in verse 6 with the first by saying, **Not of the letter, but of the Spirit; for the letter kills, but the Spirit**, or **spirit** (NKJV mg.) **gives life**. This is widely interpreted to mean that if you just take the outward, literal words of Scripture and try to be obedient to the letter without desiring to be obedient to the full spirit of the passage, then it harms you rather than helps you. The Pharisees were an illustration of this. They were scrupulous in their tithing to the very minutest extent, but they did not show mercy and love to others (Matt. 23:23). While this is a valid *application* of this passage, it is not the *interpretation*. In verse 6 the *letter* refers to the Law of Moses, and the *spirit* refers to the gospel of the grace of God. When Paul says that **the letter kills**, he is speaking of the ministry of the law. The law condemns all who fail to keep its holy precepts. "By the law is the knowledge of sin" (Rom. 3:20). "Cursed is everyone who does not continue in all things which are written in the book of the law, to do them" (Gal. 3:10). God never intended the law to be the means of giving life. Rather it was designed to bring the knowledge of sin and to convict of sin. The New Covenant is here called *spirit*. It represents the spiritual fulfillment of the types and shadows of the Old Covenant. What the law demanded but could never produce is now effected by the gospel.

J. M. Davies summarizes:

This ministry of the "letter" that killeth is illustrated in the 3000 killed at Sinai, at the inauguration of the Old Covenant; and the ministry of the Spirit, the life-giving ministry, is illustrated in the 3000 saved on the day of Pentecost.[10]

3:7 Verses 7 and 8 continue the contrast between the two covenants. Here the apostle is particularly contrasting the **glory** which attended the giving of the law with the glory which is connected with the gospel. The words **glory** and **glorious** are found in chapters 3 and 4

seventeen times. The Old Covenant is called **the ministry of death, written and engraved on stones**. This can only refer to the Ten Commandments. They threatened death to all who did not keep them (Ex. 19:13). Paul does *not* say that there was no glory connected with the giving of the law. That certainly was not the case. When God gave the Ten Commandments to Moses on Mount Sinai, there were great manifestations of the divine presence and power (Ex. 19). In fact, as Moses stood there communing with God, his own face began to shine, a reflection of the splendor of God. Thus **the children of Israel could not look steadily at the face of Moses because of the glory of his countenance**. It was too dazzling for them to view constantly. But then Paul adds the significant words **which glory was passing away**. This means that the bright shining which appeared on the face of Moses was not permanent. It was a temporary, passing glory. The spiritual meaning of this is that the **glory** of the Old Covenant was temporary. The law had a very definite function. It was given to reveal sin. It was a display of the holy requirements of God, and in that sense was glorious. But it was given until the time of Christ, who is the fulfillment of the law for righteousness to those who believe (Rom. 10:4). It was a *shadow*; He is the *substance*. It was a picture of better things to come, and those things find their reality in the Savior of the world.

3:8 Now if the law did have this glorious character, how much **more glorious** is the **ministry of the Spirit**? The expression **"the ministry of the Spirit"** refers to the gospel. The Spirit of God works through the preaching of the gospel, and in turn the Spirit of God is ministered to those who receive the good news of salvation. The **will** in **"how will the ministry of the Spirit"** does not express future time but the inevitable consequence. If one fact or condition exists, then another **will** certainly follow.

3:9 Here the Old Covenant is called **the ministry of condemnation**. That was its result. It brought **condemnation** to all men, because no one could perfectly keep the law. Yet there was a certain **glory** connected with it. It had a real purpose and a real usefulness for that time. But **the ministry of righteousness exceeds much more in glory**. Hodge says, "The ministration of righteousness is that ministration which reveals a righteousness by which men are justified, and thus freed from the condemnation pronounced upon them by the law."[11] The glories of the gospel are not the kind that appeal to physical sight but those deep and lasting excellencies that appeal to the spirit. The glories of Calvary far eclipse the glories of Sinai.

3:10 Although in one sense the law **was made glorious**, yet when you compare it with the *New* Covenant it really **had no glory** at all. The verse expresses to us a strong comparison and says that when the two covenants are placed side by side, one completely outshines the other, that is, the New Covenant surpasses the Old. A. T. Robertson states, "The greater glory dims the less. In one point at least, the old seems to have no glory at all, because of the superabundant glory of the new covenant."[12] Denney comments: "When the Sun shines in His strength, there is no other glory in the sky."[13]

3:11 For if what is passing away was glorious (literally, with glory), what remains is much more glorious (literally, glorious in glory). We should notice the two prepositions, *with* and *in*. The thought is that glory accompanied the giving of the law, but it is the very element of the New Covenant. Glory was in attendance when the Old Covenant was delivered, but the gospel of God's grace is **glorious** *in itself*.

This verse also contrasts the transient, temporary character of the law and the permanent character of the gospel. **What is passing away** can only refer to the Ten Commandments — "the ministry of death, written and engraved on stones" (v. 7). Thus this verse refutes the claims of Seventh Day Adventists, who say that the ceremonial law has been done away but not the Ten Commandments.

3:12 The **hope** which Paul refers to here is the sharp conviction that the glory of the gospel will never fade or become dim. Because of this strong assurance, he speaks the word with **great boldness**. He had nothing to hide. There is no reason to use a veil. In many religions of the world today, there are supposed mysteries. New converts must be initiated into these deep secrets. They pass from one order to the next. But with the gospel it is not so. Everything is clear and open. The gospel speaks plainly and with full assurance on such subjects as salvation, the Trinity, heaven, and hell.

3:13 **Unlike Moses, who put a veil over his face so that the children of Israel could not look steadily at the end of what was passing away**. The background to verse 13 is found in Exodus 34:29–35. There we learn that when Moses came down from Mount Sinai, after having been in the presence of the Lord, he did not know that his face was shining. The children of Israel were afraid to come near him because of the glory of his face. But he beckoned them to come near, and they did so. Then he gave them as commandments all that the Lord had told him. In Exodus 34:33 we read: "When Moses had finished speaking with them, he put a veil on his face." In 2 Corinthians 3:13, the apostle explains why Moses did this. He did it **so that the children of Israel could not look steadily at the end of what was passing away**. The glory on his face was a fading glory. In other words, the law which God had given to him had a transient glory. It was fading even then, and Moses did not want them to see **the end** of it. It was not that Moses wanted to hide the glory itself, but rather the *passing* of the glory. F. W. Grant has beautifully stated, "The glory on the face of Moses must give way to the glory in Another Face."[14] That has taken place with the coming of the Lord Jesus Christ. The result is that the minister of the New Covenant does not have to hide his face. The glory of the gospel will never grow dim or fade away.

3:14 **But their minds were blinded**. The children of Israel did not realize the true significance of what Moses was doing. And down through the centuries it has been so with the Jewish people. Even at the time of Paul's writing they still clung to the law as a means of salvation and would not accept the Lord Jesus Christ.

For until this day the same veil remains unlifted in the reading of the Old

Testament. In other words, at the time the apostle wrote, when the Jews read **the Old Testament**, they did not discover the secret which Moses hid from their forefathers beneath the **veil**. They did not realize that the glory of the law was a passing glory, and that the law had found its fulfillment in the Lord Jesus Christ.

The veil is taken away in Christ. The word *veil* here is in italics (supplied by translators), and some suggest that it is *not* the veil but *the Old Covenant* which is done away in Christ. An even more likely meaning is that *the difficulty in understanding* **the Old Testament** vanishes when a person comes to Christ. Hodge puts it well:

> The Old Testament Scriptures are intelligible only when understood as predicting and prefiguring Christ. The knowledge of Christ . . . removes the veil from the Old Testament.[15]

3:15 Here the figure changes slightly. In the OT illustration, the veil was over the *face* of Moses, but now **a veil lies on** the *hearts* of the Jewish people. They are still trying to obtain righteousness on the principle of *doing*, never realizing that the work has already been *done* by the Savior on the cross of Calvary. They are seeking to gain salvation by their own merit, not realizing that the law utterly condemns them and that they should flee to the arms of the Lord for mercy and grace.

3:16 The **one** in verse 16 may refer to the heart of an *individual* Jew, or it may refer to Israel *nationally*. When either **turns to the Lord** and accepts Jesus as Messiah, then **the veil is taken away**, the obscurity is gone. Then the truth dawns that all the types and shadows of the law find their fulfillment in God's beloved Son, the Messiah of Israel. If the *nation* of Israel is in view, then the verse points forward to a day yet future when a believing remnant will turn **to the Lord**, as prophesied in Romans 11:25, 26, 32.

3:17 Paul has been emphasizing that Christ is the key to the OT. Here he re-emphasizes that truth by saying, **Now the Lord is the Spirit**. Most versions, including NKJV, capitalize **Spirit**, interpreting it as the Holy Spirit. But the context suggests that the Lord is the spirit of the OT just as "the testimony of Jesus is the spirit of prophecy" (Rev. 19:10). All the types and shadows of the OT find their fulfillment in Christ. **Where the Spirit**[16] **of the Lord is, there is liberty** means that wherever Jesus Christ is recognized as Lord or Jehovah, **there is liberty**, that is, freedom from the bondage of the law, freedom from obscurity in reading the Scriptures, and freedom to gaze upon His face without a veil between.

3:18 In the Old Covenant, Moses alone was allowed to see the glory of the Lord. Under the New Covenant, **we all** have the privilege **of beholding . . . the glory of the Lord**. Moses' face had to be veiled after he had finished speaking with the people, but we can have an **unveiled face**. We can keep our face **unveiled** by confessing and forsaking sin, by being completely honest with God and ourselves. As a veteran missionary to India once said, we must "drop the veils of sin, of make-believe, all playacting, all putting up of unreal fronts, all attempts at compromises, all halfway measures, all Yes and No."

The next step is **beholding as in a mirror the glory of the Lord. The mirror** is the word of God. As we go to the Bible, we see the Lord Jesus revealed in all His splendor. We do not yet see Him face to face, but only as mirrored in the word.

And note that it is **the glory of the Lord** that we behold. Here Paul is not thinking so much of the moral beauty of Jesus as a Man here on earth, but rather of His present glory, exalted at the right hand of God. The glory of Christ, as Denney points out, is that:

> He shares the Father's throne, that He is the Head of the Church, possessor and bestower of all the fulness of divine grace, the coming Judge of the world, conqueror of every hostile power, intercessor for His own, and, in short, bearer of all the majesty which belongs to His kingly office.[17]

As we are occupied with the glory of the risen, ascended, exalted Lord Jesus Christ, **we are being transformed into the same image**. Here, in a word, is the secret of Christian holiness — occupation with Christ. Not by occupation with

self; that brings only defeat. Not by occupation with others; that brings disappointment. But by occupation with **the
glory of the Lord**, we become more and
more like Him.

This marvelous, transforming process
takes place **from glory to glory**, that is,
from one degree of **glory** to another. It
is not a matter of instant change. There
is *no experience* in the Christian life that
will reproduce His image in a moment.
It is a process, not a crisis. It is not like
the fading glory of the law, but an ever-
increasing glory.

The power for this wonderful process
is the Holy Spirit of God — **just as by
the Spirit of the Lord**. As we behold the
Lord of glory, study Him, contemplate
Him, gaze on Him adoringly, **the Spirit
of the Lord** works in our life the marvelous miracle of increasing conformity to
Christ.

Darby points out how Stephen was
changed by beholding:

> We see it in Stephen when he is stoned,
> and he looks up and sees the glory of God
> and Jesus. Christ had said, "Father, for-
> give them; for they know not what they
> do"; and the view of Jesus in the glory
> of God draws from Stephen the prayer,
> "Lord, lay not this sin to their charge."
> And again on the cross, Christ says, "Fa-
> ther, into Thy hands I commend my
> spirit"; and Stephen says, "Lord Jesus, re-
> ceive my spirit." He is changed into
> Christ's image.[18]

Consider then the transcendent glory
of the New Covenant. Whereas only *one*
man had the glory on his face in the Old
Covenant, today it is the blood-bought
privilege of *every* child of God. Also, instead of merely reflecting the glory of
God in our faces, **we all** in the New Covenant **are** actually **being transformed**
(lit., *metamorphosed*) **into the same image
from glory to glory, just as by the Spirit
of the Lord**. Whereas Moses' face reflected glory, our faces radiate glory
from inside.

Thus Paul brings to a close his rather
mystical and deeply spiritual exposition
of the New Covenant and of how it compares with the Old.

F. Obligation to Preach a Clear Gospel (4:1–6)

4:1   In the first six verses of chapter
4, Paul emphasizes the solemn responsibility of every servant of Christ to make
the message of the gospel plain. There
can be no veil. Nothing must be hidden
or mysterious. All must be clear, honest,
and sincere.

Paul has been speaking of the marvelous way in which God had qualified
him to be an able servant of the New
Covenant. He now takes up the thread
of thought from that point. Realization
of the tremendous dignity of the Christian **ministry** prevents such a man as
Paul from losing **heart**. Of course, there
is much to discourage and depress in
Christian service, but the Lord gives
mercy and grace to help in every time
of need. Thus, no matter what the discouragements may be, the encouragements are always greater.

Paul did **not lose heart**. He did not
act cowardly, but rather courageously, in
the face of seemingly insurmountable
barriers.

4:2   Phillips gives a colorful paraphrase of verse 2:

> We use no hocus-pocus, no clever tricks,
> no dishonest manipulation of the Word of
> God. We speak the plain truth and so
> commend ourselves to every man's con-
> science in the sight of God.

Here doubtless the apostle is thinking
once again of the false teachers who had
come into the Corinthian church. Their
methods were the same as are always
used by forces of evil, namely, shameful
enticements to sin, crafty juggling of the
truth, use of tricky arguments, and adul-
teration of the word of God. With regard
to the latter expression, **nor handling
the word of God deceitfully**, Paul doubtless alludes to the favorite pastime of
these men — of seeking to mix law and
grace.

The apostle's method was very different. It is expressed in the words, **but by
manifestation of the truth commending
ourselves to every man's conscience in
the sight of God. Manifestation of the
truth** may take two forms. We manifest
the truth when we tell it out in a plain,
understandable manner. But we also
manifest it when we live it in our lives
before others so that they can see it by
our example. Paul used both of these
methods. He preached the gospel, and
he obeyed the gospel in his own life. In
doing so, he sought to commend himself

to every man's conscience in the sight of God.

4:3 The apostle has been speaking of the tremendous care he used in seeking to make the truth of God clear to men, both by precept and by practice. If the **gospel is veiled** or hidden to some, it certainly is not God's fault, and Paul does not want it to be his fault either. And yet even as he writes the words, he is aware that there are those who simply cannot seem to take it in. Who are they? It is **those who are perishing**. Why are they thus blinded? The answer is given in the following verse.

4:4 Satan is the culprit. He is here called **the god of this age**. He has succeeded in putting a veil over the minds of the unbelieving ones. He would keep them in perpetual darkness, **lest the light of the gospel of the glory of Christ ... should shine on them** that they might be saved.

In our physical universe, the sun is always shining. We do not always see it, but the reason for that is that something has come between the sun and us. So it is with the gospel. **The light of the gospel** is always shining. God is always seeking to shine into the hearts of men. But Satan puts various barriers between unbelievers and God. It may be the cloud of pride, or of rebellion, or of self-righteousness, or any one of a hundred other things. But all of these serve effectively to hinder **the light of the gospel** from shining in. Satan simply does not want men to be saved.

The gospel has to do with **Christ in glory**. It is not the Carpenter of Nazareth who is presented to the believer's view. It is not simply Christ outstretched on the cross of shame. But it is the Lord Jesus Christ who has died, been buried, who has risen again, and who is even now at the right hand of God in heaven. He is the object of the believer's faith — the glorified Son of God in heaven.

4:5 In this one verse we have both the poorest theme for a preacher, and the best theme. The poorest theme is **ourselves**, while the best theme is *Christ Jesus the Lord*.

Apparently the Judaizers had a great habit of preaching about themselves. Paul separates himself from such a company. He would not waste the people's time by preaching on such an unworthy subject. His theme was **Christ Jesus the Lord**. He sought to bring men and women to the place where they were willing to bow the knee to Jesus Christ and to pay their homage to Him as Lord of their lives.

The apostle introduced his team as **your bondservants for Jesus' sake**. In so doing, he effectively hid himself and his co-workers in the background. They were only slaves, ready to help in any way that would bring men to the Lord Jesus.

4:6 Paul here compares the conversion of a sinner to the entrance of light at the dawn of creation.

Originally **God commanded light to shine out of darkness**. He said, " 'Let there be light,' and there was light" (Gen. 1:3).

Now Paul is saying here that **the same God** who originally **commanded light to shine out of darkness has shone in our hearts**. This is very beautiful. In the first creation God *commanded* the light to shine. But in the new creation, **God** Himself shines into **our hearts**. How much more personal this is!

The events in the early part of Genesis 1 are a picture of what takes place in the new creation. God originally created man as an innocent being. But sin came in, and with it came gross darkness.

As the gospel is preached, the Spirit of God moves on the heart of a person, just as He moved on the face of the deep after the original creation.

Then God shines into the heart of this person, showing him that he is a guilty sinner and needs a Savior. "The material creation in Genesis began with light and so also does the spiritual creation. God 'shines in our hearts' by the Holy Ghost, and then spiritual life begins" (Selected).

The verse goes on to explain to us why **God has shone in our hearts**. In the KJV and NKJV it reads, **to give the light of the knowledge of the glory of God in the face of Jesus Christ**. It sounds from this that His purpose is just *to give us* **the light of the knowledge of the glory of God**. But J. N. Darby suggests a significant change in this verse in his New Translation: "*For the shining forth* of the knowledge of the glory of God in the face of Jesus Christ." In other words,

God does not shine in our hearts simply **to give** us this **knowledge**, but rather that through us the knowledge might *shine to others.* "We are not the terminals of our blessings or exercises, but the channels." (Selected)

A Scriptural illustration of this is found in the life of Paul himself. On the road to Damascus, God shone in his heart. He realized that the One whom he had hated and who he thought was buried in a Judean tomb was the Lord of glory. From that day he went out to spread **the light of the knowledge of the glory of God** as it is found **in the face of Jesus Christ.**

G. An Earthen Vessel with a Heavenly Destiny (4:7–18)

4:7 Having spoken of the obligation to make the message plain, the Apostle Paul now thinks of the human instrument to which the wonderful gospel treasure had been committed. The **treasure** is the glorious message of the gospel. The **earthen vessel**, on the other hand, is the frail human body. The contrast between the two is tremendous. The gospel is like a precious diamond that scintillates brilliantly every way in which it is turned. To think that such a precious diamond has been entrusted to such a frail, fragile earthenware vessel!

> Earthen vessels, marred, unsightly,
> Bearing Wealth no thought can know;
> Heav'nly Treasure, gleaming brightly —
> Christ revealed in saints below!
>
> Vessels, broken, frail, yet bearing
> Through the hungry ages on,
> Riches giv'n with hand unsparing,
> God's great Gift, His precious Son!
>
> O to be but emptier, lowlier,
> Mean, unnoticed and unknown,
> And to God a vessel holier,
> Filled with Christ, and Christ alone!
>
> Naught of earth to cloud the Glory!
> Naught of self the light to dim!
> Telling forth Christ's wondrous story,
> Broken, empty — filled with Him!
> – *Tr. Frances Bevan*

Why has God ordained that **this treasure** should be **in earthen vessels**? The answer is so **that the excellence of the power may be of God and not of us**. God does not want men to be occupied with the human instrument, but rather with His own power and greatness. And so He deliberately commits the gospel message to weak, often uncomely human beings. All the praise and glory must go to the Creator and not the creature.

> It is a secret joy to find
> The task assigned beyond our powers;
> For thus, if ought of good be wrought,
> Clearly the praise is His, not ours.
> – *Houghton*

Jowett says:

> There is something wrong when the vessel robs the treasure of its glory, when the casket attracts more attention than the jewel which it bears. There is a very perverse emphasis when the picture takes second place to the frame, and when the ware which is used at the feast becomes a substitute for the meal. There is something deadly in Christian service when "the excellency of the power" is of us and not of God. Such excellency is of a very fleeting kind, and it will speedily wither as the green herb and pass into oblivion.[19]

As Paul penned verse 7, it is almost certain he was thinking of an incident in Judges 7. There it is recorded that Gideon equipped his army with trumpets, empty pitchers, and lamps within the pitchers. At the appointed signal, his men were to blow their trumpets and break the pitchers. When the pitchers were broken, the lamps shone out in brilliance. This terrified the enemy. They thought there was a vast host after them, instead of just three hundred men. The lesson is that, just as in Gideon's case the light only shone forth when the pitchers were broken, so it is in connection with the gospel. Only when human instruments are broken and yielded to the Lord can the gospel shine forth through us in all its magnificence.

4:8 The apostle now goes on to explain that because the treasure has been committed to earthen vessels, there is seeming defeat on the one hand, yet perpetual victory on the other. There is weakness to all outward appearance, but in reality incomparable strength. When he says, **We are hard pressed on every side, yet not crushed**, he means that he is constantly **pressed** by adversaries and difficulties, yet not completely hindered from uttering the message freely.

Perplexed, but not in despair. From the human standpoint, Paul often did not know there could possibly be a solution to his difficulties, and yet the Lord never allowed him to reach the place of **despair**. He was never brought into a narrow place from which there was no escape.

4:9 Persecuted, but not forsaken. At times, he could feel the hot breath of the enemy on the back of his neck, yet the Lord never abandoned him to his foes. **Struck down, but not destroyed** means that Paul was many times seriously "wounded in action," yet the Lord raised him up again to go with the glorious news of the gospel.

The *New Bible Commentary* paraphrases verses 8 and 9: "Hemmed in, but not hamstrung; not knowing what to do, but never bereft of all hope; hunted by men, but never abandoned by God; often felled, but never finished."

We may wonder why the Lord allowed His servant to go through such testings and trials. We would think that he could have served the Lord more efficiently if He had allowed his pathway to be free from troubles. But this Scripture teaches the very opposite. God, in His marvelous wisdom, sees fit to allow His servants to be touched by sickness, sorrow, affliction, persecution, difficulties, and distresses. All are designed to break the earthen pitchers so that the light of the gospel might shine out more clearly.

4:10 The life of the servant of God is one of constant **dying**. Just as **the Lord Jesus** Himself, in His lifetime, was constantly exposed to violence and persecution, so those who follow in His steps will meet the same treatment. But it does not mean defeat. This is the way of victory. Blessing comes to others as we thus die daily.

It is only in this way that the life of Jesus can be apparent in our bodies. **The life of Jesus** does not here mean primarily His life as a Man on earth, but His present **life** as the exalted Son of God in heaven. How can the world see the life of Christ when He is not personally or physically present in the world today? The answer is that as we Christians suffer in the service of the Lord, His life is **manifested in our body.**

4:11 This thought of **life** from **death** is continued in verse 11. It is one of the deepest principles of our existence. The meat we eat and by which we live comes through the death of animals. It is so in the spiritual realm. "The blood of the martyrs is the seed of the church." The more the church is persecuted and afflicted and hunted and pursued, the more Christianity spreads.

And yet it is difficult for us to accept this truth. When violence comes to a servant of the Lord, we normally think of it as a tragedy. Actually, this is God's normal way of dealing. It is not the exception. Constant exposure **to death for Jesus' sake** is the divine manner in which **the life of Jesus** is **manifested in our mortal** bodies.

4:12 Here the apostle sums up all that he has said by reminding the Corinthians that it was through his constant suffering that **life** came to them. In order for Paul ever to go to Corinth with the gospel, he had to suffer untold hardships. But it was worth it all, because they had trusted in the Lord Jesus and now had eternal life. Paul's physical suffering and loss meant spiritual gain to others. Robertson says, "His dying was working out for the good of those who were benefited by his ministry."[20]

Oftentimes we have the tendency to cry out to the Lord in sickness, asking Him to deliver us from it, so that we might serve Him better. Perhaps we should sometimes thank God for such afflictions in our lives, and glory in our infirmities that the power of Christ might rest upon us.

4:13 The apostle has been speaking of the constant frailty and weakness of the human vessel to which the gospel is entrusted. What then is his attitude toward all this? Is he defeated and discouraged and dismayed? The answer is no. Faith enables him to go on preaching the gospel, because he knows that beyond the sufferings of this life lie unspeakable glories.

In Psalm 116:10 the psalmist says, **"I believed and therefore I spoke."** He trusted in the Lord, and therefore what he said was the result of that deep-seated faith. Paul is here saying that the same is true in his case. He had the same spirit of faith which the Psalmist had when he uttered those words. Paul says, **"We also believe and therefore speak."**

The afflictions and persecutions of Paul's life did not seal his lips. Wherever there is true faith, there must be the expression of it. It cannot be silent.

> If on Jesus Christ you trust,
>   Speak for Him you surely must;
> Though it humble to the dust,
>   If you love Him, say so.
>
> If on Jesus you believe
>   And the Saviour you receive
> Lest you should the Spirit grieve,
>   Don't delay, but say so.

4:14 If it seems strange to us that Paul was not shaken by the constant danger of death, we find the answer in verse 14. This is the secret of his fearlessness in uttering the Christian message. He knew that this life was not all. He knew that for the believer there was the certainty of resurrection. The same God **who raised up the Lord Jesus** would **also raise up** the Apostle Paul **with Jesus and** would **present** him **with** the Corinthians.

4:15 With the certain and sure hope of resurrection before him, the apostle was willing to undergo terrible hardships. He knew that all such sufferings had a twofold result. They abounded in blessing for the Corinthians, and thus caused **thanksgiving to abound to the glory of God**. These two motives actuated Paul in all he said and did. He was concerned with **the glory of God** and the blessing of his fellow men.

Paul realized that the more he suffered, the more the **grace** of God was made available to others. The more people who were saved, the more **thanksgiving** ascended to **God**. And the more **thanksgiving** ascended to **God**, the more **God** was glorified.

The *Living Bible* seems to capture the spirit of the verse in this paraphrase:

> These sufferings of ours are for your benefit. And the more of you who are won to Christ, the more there are to thank him for his great kindness, and the more the Lord is glorified.

4:16 Paul had been explaining his willingness to undergo all kinds of suffering and danger because he had before him the certain hope of resurrection. **Therefore** he did **not lose heart**. Although on the one hand, the process of physical decay was going on constantly, yet on the other hand there was a spiritual renewal which enabled him to go on in spite of every adverse circumstance.

The fact that the **outward man is perishing** needs little explanation or comment. It is all too evident in our bodies! But Paul is here rejoicing in the fact that God sends daily supplies of power for Christian service. Thus it is true, as Michelangelo said, "The more the marble wastes, the more the statue grows."

Ironside comments:

> We are told that our material bodies are completely changed every seven years. . . Yet we have a consciousness of being the same persons. Our personality is unchanged from year to year, and so with regard to the greater change as yet to come. The same life is in the butterfly that was in the grub.[21]

4:17 After reading the terrible afflictions which the Apostle Paul endured, it may seem hard for us to understand how he could speak of them as **light affliction**. In one sense, they were not at all light. They were bitter and cruel.

But the explanation lies in the *comparison* which Paul makes. The afflictions viewed by themselves might be ever so heavy, but when compared with the **eternal weight of glory**[22] that lies ahead, then they are **light**. Also the **light affliction is but for a moment**, whereas the glory is **eternal.** The lessons we learn through afflictions in this world will yield richest fruit for us in the world to come.

Moorehead observes: "A little joy enters into us while we are in the world; we shall enter into joy when there. A few drops here; a whole ocean there."[23]

There is a pyramid in this verse which, as F. E. Marsh has pointed out, does not tire the weary climber but brings unspeakable rest and comfort to his soul.

Glory
Weight of glory
Eternal weight of glory
Exceeding and eternal weight of glory
More exceeding and eternal weight of glory
Far more exceeding and eternal
weight of glory[24]

4:18 In this verse **look** does not merely describe human vision; rather it conveys the idea of regarding a thing as important. As far as **the things which are seen** are concerned, they are not the goal of one's existence. Here they refer primarily to the hardships, trials, and sufferings which Paul endured. These were incidental to his ministry; the great object of his ministry was what is **not seen**. This might include the glory of Christ, the blessing of one's fellow men, and the reward that awaits the faithful servant of Christ at the Judgment Seat.

Jowett comments:

> To be able to see the first is sight; to be able to see the second is insight. The first mode of vision is natural, the second mode is spiritual. The primary organ in the first discernment is intellect; the primary organ in the second discernment is faith. . . . All through the Scriptures this contrast between sight and insight is being continually presented to us, and everywhere we are taught to measure the meagerness and stinginess of the one, and set it over the fulness and expansiveness of the other.[25]

H. Living in the Light of Christ's Judgment Seat (5:1–10)

The verses to follow are closely linked with what has gone before. Paul has been speaking of his present sufferings and distresses, and the future glory which lay before him. This brings him face to face with the subject of death. In this section we have one of the greatest unfoldings of death in all the word of God, and the Christian's relationship to it.

5:1 In verse 1, the apostle speaks of our present mortal body as **our earthly house, this tent**. A **tent** is not a permanent dwelling, but a portable one for pilgrims and travelers.

Death is spoken of as the dissolving of **this tent**. The **tent** is taken down at the time of death. The body goes into the grave, whereas the spirit and soul of the believer go to be with the Lord.

Paul opens the chapter with the assurance that if his **earthly house** should be **destroyed** (as a result of the sufferings mentioned in the preceding chapter) he knows he has **a building from God, a house not made with hands, eternal in the heavens**. Notice the distinction between **tent** and **building**. The temporary **tent** is taken down, but a new, permanent **house** awaits the be-

liever in the land beyond the skies. This is **a building from God**, in the sense that God is the One who gives it to us.

Furthermore, it is **a house not made with hands**. Why should Paul say this? Our present bodies are not made with hands; so why should he emphasize that our future, glorified bodies will not be made with hands? The answer is that the expression **not made with hands** means "not of this creation." This is made clear in Hebrews 9:11, where we read, "But Christ came as High Priest of the good things to come, with the greater and more perfect tabernacle *not made with hands, that is, not of this creation.*" What Paul is saying in 2 Corinthians 5:1 is that whereas our present bodies are suited to life on this earth, our future, glorified bodies will not be of this creation. They will be especially designed for life in heaven.

The believer's future body is also described as **eternal in the heavens**. It is a body that will no longer be subject to disease, decay, and death, but one that will endure forever in our heavenly home.

It might sound from this verse as if a believer receives this building from God the moment he dies, but that is not the case. He does not get his glorified body until Christ comes back for His church (1 Thess. 4:13–18). What happens to the believer is this. At the time of death, his spirit and soul go to be with Christ where he is consciously enjoying the glories of heaven. His body is placed in the grave. At the time of the Lord's return, the dust will be raised from the grave, God will fashion it into a new, glorified body, and it will then be reunited with the spirit and the soul. Between death and Christ's coming for His saints, the believer might be said to be in a disembodied condition. However, this does not mean that he is not fully conscious of all the joy and bliss of heaven. He is!

Before leaving verse 1 we should mention that there are three principal interpretations of the **house not made with hands, eternal in the heavens**:

1. Heaven itself.
2. An intermediate body between death and resurrection.
3. The glorified body.

The house can scarcely be heaven itself, because it is said to be **eternal** *in* the heavens and *"from* heaven" (5:2). As far as an intermediate body is concerned, the Scriptures never mention such a body. Moreover, the house not made with hands is described as *eternal* in the heavens, which would not be true of an intermediate body. The third view — that the house is the resurrection body of glory — seems to be the correct one.

5:2 In this present mortal body, we are often forced to **groan** because of the way it limits us and impedes us in our spiritual lives. What we greatly desire is to **be clothed with our habitation which is from heaven**.

In this verse, the apostle seems to change his figure from a tent to clothing. A suggested explanation of this is that Paul was a tentmaker and realized that similar material used for tents was also used for clothing. At any rate, the meaning is clear that he longed to receive his glorified body.

5:3 What does **naked** mean in this verse? Does it mean that the person is unsaved and therefore without any covering of righteousness before God? Does it mean that the person, though saved, will be without reward at the Judgment Seat of Christ? Or does it mean that the saved person does not have a body between the time of death and resurrection, and is naked in the sense that he is a disembodied spirit?

This writer understands it to mean disembodied or unclothed. Paul is saying that his earnest desire is not for death, and for the disembodied state that goes with it, but rather for the coming of the Lord Jesus Christ when all those who have died will receive their glorified bodies.

5:4 That our interpretation of verse 3 is valid seems to be borne out by verse 4. The apostle says that **we who are in this** present earthly **tent groan, being burdened, not because we want to be unclothed, but further clothed, that mortality may be swallowed up by life**. In other words, he did not look forward to the state *between* death and the Rapture as the ideal hope of the believer, but to what will take place *at* the Rapture when believers will receive a body that will no longer be subject to death.

5:5 It is **God ... who has prepared us for this very** purpose, namely, the redemption of the body. This will be the climax of His glorious purposes for us. At the present time we are redeemed as to our spirit and soul, but then redemption will include the body as well. Just think of it — God made us with this goal in view — the glorified state — a house not made with hands, eternal in the heavens!

And how can we be sure that we will have a glorified body? The answer is that **God ... has given us the Spirit as a guarantee**. As explained previously, the fact that every believer possesses the indwelling **Spirit** of God is a pledge that *all* God's promises to the believer will be fulfilled. He is a token of what is to come. **The Spirit** of God is Himself **a guarantee** that what God has already given to us in part will one day be ours in full.

5:6 It was the deep assurance of these precious realities that enabled Paul to be always of good courage. He knew that as long as he was **at home in the body**, he was **absent from the Lord**. This was certainly not the ideal state for Paul, but he was willing that it should be so if he could serve Christ down here and be a help to the people of God.

5:7 The fact that **we walk by faith, not by sight** is abundant proof that we are absent from the Lord. We have never gazed upon the Lord with our physical eyes. Only through faith have we ever seen Him. As long as we are at home in the body, we have a life that is less close and intimate than the life of actual sight.

5:8 Verse 8 resumes the thought of verse 6 and completes it. Paul is of good courage in view of the blessed hope that lies before him, and he can say that he is **well pleased rather to be absent from the body and to be present with the Lord**. He has what Bernard calls a case of "heavenly homesickness."

This verse might seem to contradict what the apostle has just been saying. In the preceding verses he has been longing for the glorified body. But here he says that he is willing **rather to be absent from the body and to be present with the Lord**, that is, willing rather to be in the disembodied state that exists between death and the Rapture.

But there is no contradiction. There are three possibilities for the Christian, and it is simply a matter of which is most to be preferred. There is the present life on earth in this mortal body. There is the state between death and the coming of Christ, a disembodied state, but one in which the spirit and soul are consciously enjoying Christ's presence. Finally, there is the consummation of our salvation when we receive our glorified bodies at the coming again of the Lord Jesus. Paul is simply teaching in this passage that the first state is good, the second is better, and the third is best of all.

5:9 The believer should **make it** his **aim to be well pleasing to** the Lord. While his salvation is not dependent on works, his reward in a coming day will be directly proportionate to his faithfulness to the Lord. A believer should always remember that *faith* is linked with *salvation*, and *works* are linked with *reward*. He is saved by grace through faith, not of works; but once he is saved, he should be ambitious to perform good works, and for so doing he will receive rewards.

Notice that Paul wanted to **be well pleasing to Him, whether present or absent**. This means that his service on earth was designed to bring pleasure to the heart of his Lord, whether Paul was still here on earth or whether he was standing before the Judgment Seat of Christ.

5:10 One motive for being well pleasing to Christ is that **we must all appear before** His **judgment seat**. Actually it is not just a matter of *appearing* there, but of being *made manifest*. The NEB correctly says, "We must all have our lives laid open before the tribunal of Christ." It is one thing to appear in a doctor's office and quite another thing to be X-rayed by him there. **The judgment seat of Christ** will reveal our lives of service for Christ exactly as they have been. Not only the *amount* of our service, but also its *quality*, and even the very *motives* that prompted it will be brought into review.

Although sins after conversion will have an effect on our service, a believer's sins, as such, will not be brought into review for judgment at this solemn time.

That judgment took place over 1900 years ago, when the Lord Jesus bore our sins in His body on the tree. He fully paid the debt that our sins deserved, and God will never bring those sins into judgment again (John 5:24). **The judgment seat of Christ** has to do with our service for the Lord. It will not be a matter of whether we are saved or not; that is already an assured fact. But it is a matter of reward and loss at that time.

I. Paul's Good Conscience in the Ministry (5:11–6:2)

5:11 This verse is commonly taken to mean that since Paul was aware of God's terrible judgment on sin and the horrors of hell, he went everywhere seeking to persuade men to accept the gospel. While true, we believe this is not the primary meaning in this particular passage.

Paul is not here speaking so much of the terror of the Lord for the unsaved as of the *reverential awe* in which he sought to serve **the Lord** and to please Him. As far as God is concerned, the apostle knows that his life is an open book. But he would like the Corinthians also to be persuaded of his integrity and faithfulness in the ministry of the gospel. And so he says, in effect:

Since we know the fear **of the Lord, we** try to **persuade men** as to our integrity and sincerity as ministers of Christ. But whether we succeed in persuading men or not, **we are** well-known **to God**. And we hope that this will be the case in the **consciences** of you Corinthians as well!

This explanation seems to fit best with the context.

5:12 Immediately Paul realizes that what he has just said might be misinterpreted as self-praise. He does not want anyone to think that he is indulging in *that*! And so he adds, **we do not commend ourselves again to you**. This does not mean that he ever *had* commended himself to them, but he had been *accused* of doing so time and again, and he here seeks to disabuse their minds of any such idea.

Why then has he been giving such a prolonged defense of his ministry? Paul's answer is "We . . . give you opportunity to boast on our behalf, that you may have an answer for those who boast in appearance and not in heart." He was not interested in commending himself. Rather he realized that he was being sharply criticized by the false teachers in the presence of the Corinthian saints. He wanted the believers to know how to answer these attacks on him, and so he was giving them this information that they might be able to defend him when he was condemned in their presence.

He describes his critics as **those who boast in appearance and not in heart** (compare 1 Sam. 16:7). In other words, they were interested in outward show, but not in inward reality, integrity, and honesty. Physical appearance or eloquence or seeming zeal meant everything to them. "To the externalists, superficial appearances were everything and sincerity of heart counted for nothing" (Selected).

5:13 It would seem from this verse that the apostle had even been accused of insanity, of fanaticism, of various forms of mental disturbances. He does not deny that he lived in what Denney has called a state of "spiritual tension." He simply says that **if** he is **beside** himself, **it is for God**. Anything that might seem like insanity to his critics was really his deep-hearted devotion for the Lord. He was consumed with a passion for the things of God. **If**, on the other hand, he was **of sound mind**, it was for the sake of the Corinthians. What the verse says, in short, is that all of Paul's behavior could be explained in one of two ways: either it was zeal for God, or it was for the welfare of his fellow believers. In both cases, his motives were entirely unselfish. Could his critics say that of themselves?

5:14 No one who studies the life of the apostle can fail to wonder what made him serve so tirelessly and unselfishly. Here, in one of the greatest sections of all his letters, he gives the answer — **the love of Christ**.

Does **the love of Christ** here refer to His love for us or to our love for Him? There can be no question that it is His love for us. The only reason that we love at all is because He first loved us. It is His love that **compels** us, moves us along, as a person is moved along in a crowd of Christmas shoppers. As Paul contemplated the marvelous **love** which **Christ** had shown to him, he could not help but be moved along in service for his wonderful Lord.

In dying for all, Jesus acted as our Representative. When He died we **all died** — in Him. Just as Adam's sin became the sin of his posterity, so Christ's death became the death of those who believe on Him (Rom. 5:12–21; 1 Cor. 15:21, 22).

5:15 The apostle's argument is irresistible. Christ **died for all**. Why did He die **for all**? So that those who **live** through faith in Him **should live no longer for themselves, but for Him**. The Savior did not die for us so that we might go on living our own petty, selfish lives the way we want to live them. Rather He died for us so that we might henceforth turn over our lives to Him in willing, glad devotion. Denney explains:

> In dying our death, Christ has done for us something so immense in love, that we ought to be His, and only His for ever. To make us His is the very object of His death.[26]

5:16 Perhaps Paul is here referring back to verse 12, where he described his critics as those who boast in appearance, and not in heart. Now he takes up that subject again by teaching that when we come to Christ, there is a new creation. **From now on** we do not judge men in a carnal, earthly way, according to appearances, human credentials, or national origin. We see them as precious souls for whom Christ died. He added that even though he had **known Christ according to the flesh**, that is, as merely another man, yet he did not know Him in that way any more. In other words, it was one thing to know Jesus as a next-door neighbor in the village of Nazareth, or even as an earthly messiah, and quite another thing to know the glorified Christ who is at the right hand of God at this present time. We know the Lord Jesus more intimately and more truly today as He is revealed to us through the word by the Spirit, than those knew Him who judged Him simply according to human appearances when He was on earth.

David Smith comments:

Though the Apostle had once shared that Jewish ideal of a secular Messiah, he had now attained to a loftier conception. Christ was for him the risen and glorified Savior, truly not known according to the flesh, but according to the spirit; not by historic tradition, but by immediate and vital fellowship.[27]

5:17 **If anyone is in Christ**, that is, saved, **he is a new creation**. Before conversion, one might have judged others according to human standards. But now all that is changed. **Old** methods of judging **have passed away; behold, all things have become new**.

This verse is a favorite with those who have recently been born again, and is often quoted in personal testimonies. Sometimes in being thus quoted, it gives quite a false impression. Listeners are apt to think that when a man is saved, old habits, evil thoughts, and lustful looks are forever done away, and everything becomes literally new in a person's life. We know that this is not true. The verse does not describe a believer's practice but rather his position. Notice it says that if anyone is **in Christ**. The words **in Christ** are the key to the passage. **In Christ, old things have passed away** and **all things have become new**. Unfortunately, "in me" not all this is true as yet! But as I progress in the Christian life, I desire that my practice may increasingly correspond to my position. One day, when the Lord Jesus returns, the two will be in perfect agreement.

5:18 **All things are of God**. He is the Source and Author of them **all**. There is no ground for human boasting. It is this same **God who has reconciled us to Himself through Jesus Christ, and has given us the ministry of reconciliation**.

This splendid statement of the scriptural doctrine of reconciliation is found in *A New and Concise Bible Dictionary*:

> By the death of the Lord Jesus on the cross, God annulled in grace the distance which sin had brought in between Himself and man, in order that all things might, through Christ, be presented agreeably to himself. Believers are already reconciled, through Christ's death, to be presented holy, unblamable, and unreprovable (a new creation). God was in Christ, when Christ was on earth, reconciling the world unto Himself, not imput-

ing unto them their trespasses; but now that the love of God has been fully revealed in the cross, the testimony has gone out world-wide, beseeching men to be reconciled to God. The end is that God may have His pleasure in man.[28]

5:19 The ministry of reconciliation is here explained as the message **that God was in Christ reconciling the world to Himself**. There are two possible understandings of this statement, both of which are scripturally correct. First of all, we may think of it as saying **that God was in Christ**, in the sense that the Lord Jesus Christ is Deity. This is certainly true. But then we could also understand it as meaning **that God was, in Christ, reconciling the world to Himself**. In other words, He was **reconciling the world**, but He was doing it **in** the person of the Lord Jesus **Christ**.

Whichever interpretation we accept, the truth remains clear that God was actively removing the cause of the estrangement that had come between Himself and man by dealing with sin. God does not need to be reconciled, but man *does* need to be reconciled to Him.

Not imputing their trespasses to them. At first reading, it might seem that this verse teaches universal salvation, that all men are saved through the work of Christ. But such a teaching would be completely in disagreement with the rest of the word of God. God has provided a way by which men's trespasses might not be imputed to them, but while that way is available to all, it is effective only in those who are in Christ. The trespasses of unsaved men are definitely reckoned to them, but the moment these men trust the Lord Jesus as Savior, they are reckoned righteous in Him, and their sins are blotted out.

In addition to His reconciling work, God **has** also **committed to** His servants **the word of reconciliation**. In other words, He has entrusted them with the marvelous privilege of going forth and preaching this glorious message to all men everywhere. Not to angels did He give such a sacred charge, but to poor, feeble man.

5:20 In the previous verse the apostle said he has been given the message of reconciliation. He has been sent forth to preach this message to mankind. We would like to suggest that from 5:20 through 6:2 we have a *summary* of the word of reconciliation. In other words, Paul lets us listen to the message which he preached to the unsaved as he went from country to country and continent to continent. It is important to see this. Paul is not here telling the Corinthians to be reconciled to God. They are already believers in the Lord Jesus. But he is telling the Corinthians that this is the message which he preaches to the unsaved wherever he goes.

An ambassador is a minister of state, representing his own ruler in a foreign land. Paul always speaks of the Christian ministry as an exalted and dignified calling. Here he likens himself to an envoy sent by **Christ** to the world in which we live. He was a spokesman for God, and **God** was **pleading through** him. This seems rather strange language to apply to an ambassador. Usually we do not think of an ambassador as **pleading**, but that is the glory of the gospel, that, in it, God is actually on bended knee and with tear-dimmed eye begging men and women to **be reconciled to** Himself. If any enmity exists, it exists on man's part. God has removed any barriers to complete fellowship between Himself and man. The Lord has done all he can possibly do. Now man must lay down his arms of rebellion, must cease his stubborn revolt, and must **be reconciled to God**.

5:21 This verse gives us the doctrinal foundation for our reconciliation. How has God made reconciliation possible? How can He receive guilty sinners who come to Him in repentance and faith? The answer is that the Lord Jesus has effectively dealt with the whole problem of our sins, so now we can be reconciled to God.

In other words, God **made** Christ **to be sin for us** — Christ **who knew no sin** — **that we might become the righteousness of God in Him**.

We must beware of any idea that on the cross of Calvary the Lord Jesus Christ actually became *sinful* in Himself. Such an idea is false. Our sins were placed *on* Him, but they were not *in* Him. What happened is that God made Him to be a sin-offering on our behalf. Trusting in Him, we are reckoned righteous by God. The claims of the law have

been fully satisfied by our Substitute.

What a blessed truth it is that the One **who knew no sin** was **made sin for us, that we** who knew no righteousness **might become the righteousness of God in Him**. No mortal tongue will ever be able to thank God sufficiently for such boundless grace.

6:1 Some understand that in this verse Paul is addressing the Corinthians and encouraging them to make full use of **the grace** that had been shown to them.

We rather think that Paul is still giving an account of the message which he preached to the unsaved. He has already told unbelievers of the marvelous grace which has been offered to them by God. Now he further begs them **not to receive** such **grace in vain**. They should not allow the seed of the gospel to fall in barren soil. Rather they should respond to such a marvelous message by receiving the Savior of whom it tells.

6:2 Paul now quotes from Isaiah 49:8. If we go back and study that chapter, we find that God is in controversy with His people because of their rejection of the Messiah. In verse 7 you see the Lord Jesus rejected by the nation, and we know that His rejection led to His death. But then in verse 8 we have the words of Jehovah, assuring the Lord Jesus that His prayer has been heard and that God would help and preserve Him.

In the day of salvation I have helped you. This refers to the resurrection of the Lord Jesus Christ. The **acceptable time** and **the day of salvation** would be ushered in by Christ's resurrection from among the dead.

In his preaching of the gospel, Paul seizes upon this marvelous truth and announces to his unsaved listeners, **Behold, now is the accepted time; behold, now is the day of salvation**. In other words, the era of which Isaiah had prophesied as **the day of salvation** has already come, so Paul urges men to trust the Savior while it is still **the day of salvation**.

J. Paul's Behavior in the Ministry (6:3–10)

6:3 Here Paul switches from the message which he preached to his own behavior in the Christian **ministry**. He realized that there are always people who are looking for an excuse not to listen to the message of salvation, and if they can find that excuse in the inconsistent life of the preacher, so much the better. So he reminds the Corinthians that he gave **no offense in anything, that** the **ministry** might **not be blamed**. As we pointed out previously, the ministry here does not refer to some dignified, ecclesiastical office, but rather to the service of Christ. The idea of human ordination is not involved. The **ministry** belongs to all who are Christ's.

6:4   In verses 4 through 10 the apostle describes the way he sought to carry out his ministry — a manner that was above reproach. Conscious that he was a servant of the Most High, he always sought to behave in a manner worthy of such a calling. On this section Denney finely comments:

> The fountains of the great deep are broken up with him as he thinks of what is at issue; he is in all straits, as he begins, and can speak only in disconnected words, one at a time; but before he stops, he has won his liberty, and pours out his soul without restraint.[29]

Verses 4 and 5 describe the physical sufferings which Paul endured and which attested him as a sincere, faithful servant of the Lord. The next two verses have to do with the Christian graces which he exhibited. Then in verses 8 through 10 he lists the contrasting experiences which are so typical of the Christian ministry.

In much patience doubtless describes Paul's longsuffering toward individuals, local churches, and all the afflictions which were calculated to move him from his pathway of steadfastness.

Tribulations might refer to actual persecutions which he endured for the name of Christ.

Needs convey the idea of the privations he suffered, probably of food, clothing, and lodging.

Distresses might well include the unfavorable circumstances in which he often found himself.

6:5   Paul suffered many **stripes** as stated in Acts 16:23. His **imprisonments** are later referred to in 2 Corinthians 11:23, and doubtless the **tumults** refer to the riots and uproars which often fol-

lowed his preaching of the gospel. (The message that Gentiles could be saved in the same way as Jews caused some of the most violent outbursts.) Paul's **labors** might include his tent-making but also doubtless other forms of manual labor, to say nothing of his travels. **Sleeplessness** describes his constant need for being on the alert against the wiles of the devil and the efforts of his enemies to harm him. **Fastings** might include voluntary abstinence from food, but here it more probably means hunger that was forced by poverty.

6:6   Paul's ministry was conducted **by purity**, that is, in chastity and holiness. He could never be justly accused of immorality.

It was also conducted **by knowledge**, and this perhaps refers to the fact that it was not a ministry of ignorance but of divinely imparted **knowledge**. This is wonderfully shown by the breadth of divine truth revealed in Paul's Epistles.

The Corinthians should not need any proof of his **longsuffering**! The patient way in which he had put up with their sins and failings should have been proof enough! Paul's **kindness** was shown in his unselfish giving of himself for others, in his loving attitude toward the people of God, and in his sympathetic demeanor.

The expression **by the Holy Spirit** doubtless means that all Paul did was done in the Spirit's power and in subjection to Him.

By sincere love suggests that the **love** which was so obvious in the life of the Apostle Paul toward others was not pretended or hypocritical, but genuine. It characterized all his actions.

6:7   **By the word of truth** may indicate that all of Paul's ministry was carried out in obedience to **the word of truth**, or it may mean that it was an honest ministry, consistent with the type of message which he preached, namely, **the word of truth**.

By the power of God doubtless signifies that the apostle did not carry on his work in his own power, but in simple dependence on the strength which **God** provides. Some have also suggested that this may be a reference to the miracles which the apostle was empowered to perform because he was an apostle.

The armor of righteousness is described in Ephesians 6:14–18. It pictures an upright, consistent character. Someone has said, "When a man is clothed in practical righteousness, he is impregnable." If our conscience is void of offense toward God and man, the devil has little to shoot at.

There is some doubt as to the exact meaning of the expression **on the right hand and on the left**. One of the more probable explanations is that in ancient warfare the sword was held in the right hand and the shield in the left. The sword spoke of offensive combat and the shield of defensive. In that case, Paul would here be saying that a good Christian character is the best offense and defense.

6:8 Here and in verses 9 and 10 Paul describes some of the sharp contrasts that are found in service for the Lord Jesus. The true disciple experiences the mountain tops and the valleys, as well as all the territory that lies between. It is a life of **honor and dishonor**, of victory and seeming defeat, of commendation and criticism. The true servant of God is the object of **evil report and good report**. Some speak well of his zeal and courage, whereas others have only condemnation for him. He is treated as a deceiver or impostor, **and yet** he is **true** for all that. He is no impostor, but a genuine servant of the Most High God.

6:9 In one sense Paul was **unknown**, unappreciated, and misunderstood as far as the world was concerned, and yet he was **well known** to God and to his fellow believers.[30]

His life was one of daily **dying, and** yet **behold** he lived! Threatened, hunted, pursued, persecuted, and imprisoned, he won his freedom only to preach the gospel with greater zeal. This is further emphasized in the expression **as chastened, and yet not killed. Chastened** here has to do with the punishment which he endured at the hands of men. Many times, perhaps, they thought they had brought his tumultuous life to a close — only to hear of his exploits for Christ in other cities!

6:10 There was sorrow in connection with the ministry, and **yet** Paul was **always rejoicing**. Needless to say, he sorrowed over rejection of the gospel message, over the failures of God's people, and over his own shortcomings. Yet, when he thought of the Lord, and of the promises of God, there was always great cause to look up and rejoice.

Paul was a **poor** man as far as this world's goods are concerned. We do not read of his having property and wealth. Yet think of the lives that have been enriched through his ministry! Though he possessed **nothing**, yet in a sense he had **all things** that really counted.

"In these climacteric sentences," writes A. T. Robertson, "Paul lets his imagination loose and it plays like lightning on the clouds."[31]

K. Paul's Appeal for Openness and Affection (6:11–13)

6:11 And now the apostle bursts into an impassioned appeal for the **Corinthians** to open their hearts to him. He had **spoken openly** and frankly to them of his love. Since the mouth speaks out of the abundance of the heart, Paul's opened mouth spoke of a heart that was wide with affection for these people. That this is the general meaning of the verse is indicated by the following words: **our heart is wide open**, that is, ready to receive them in love.

As Tozer expressed it: "Paul was a little man with a vast interior life; his great heart was often wounded by the narrowness of his disciples. The sight of their shrunken souls hurt him much."[32]

6:12 Any restriction in **affections** between the Corinthians and Paul is not in himself but in them. They might have limited love toward him, so that they were not sure whether they should receive him or not, but he was not at all limited in his love toward them. The lack of love was on their side, not Paul's.

6:13 If they want to recompense his love to them (he is speaking to those who were his **children** in the faith), they should allow their affections toward him to **be** more **open**. Paul felt toward them as a father. They should love him as their father in the faith. Only God could bring this about, but they should allow Him to do it in their lives.

The Moffatt translation catches the idea of verses 11 through 13 nicely:

O Corinthians, I am keeping nothing back from you; my heart is wide open for you.

"Restraint?" — that lies with you, not me. A fair exchange now, as the children say! Open your hearts wide to me.

L. Paul's Appeal for Scriptural Separation (6:14–7:1)

6:14 The connection between verses 13 and 14 is this: Paul has told the saints to be open in their affections toward him. Now he explains that one way to do this is to separate from all forms of sin and unrighteousness. Doubtless he is thinking, in part, of false teachers who had invaded the assembly at Corinth.

Mention of the unequal yoke suggests Deuteronomy 22:10: "You shall not plow with an ox and a donkey together." The ox was a clean animal and the donkey unclean, and their step and pull are unequal. By way of contrast, when believers are yoked with the Lord Jesus, they find that His yoke is easy and His burden is light (Matt. 11:29, 30).

This section of 2 Corinthians is one of the key passages in all the word of God on the subject of separation. It is clear instruction that the believer should separate himself from **unbelievers**, iniquity, darkness, Belial, idols.

It certainly refers to the marriage relationship. A Christian should not marry an unsaved person. However, in cases where a believer is *already* married to an unbeliever, this passage does not justify separation or divorce. God's will in such a case is that the marriage relationship should be maintained with a view to the eventual salvation of the unsaved member (1 Cor. 7:12–16).

In addition to this, it refers to business. A Christian should not go into partnership with one who does not know the Lord. It applies clearly to secret orders or fraternities: How could one who is faithful to Christ consistently go on in an association where the name of the Lord Jesus is unwelcome? Its application to social life would be as follows: A Christian should maintain contact with the unsaved in an effort to win them to Christ, but he should never engage in their sinful pleasures or in any of their activities in such a way as to lead them to think he is no different than they. Then this section would also apply to religious matters: A faithful follower of Christ would not want to hold membership in a church where unbelievers were knowingly admitted as members.

Verses 14 through 16 cover all the important relationships of life:

Righteousness and *lawlessness* describe the whole sphere of moral behavior.

Light and *darkness* have to do with intelligence as to the things of God.

Christ and *Belial* have to do with the realm of authority, in other words, the person or thing whom one acknowledges as master in his life.

Believer and *unbeliever* have to do with the realm of faith.

The temple of God and *idols* take in the whole subject of a person's worship. **Righteousness** and **lawlessness** can have no fellowship together: they are moral opposites. Neither can **light** have **communion with darkness**. When **light** enters a room, the **darkness** is dispelled. Both cannot exist together at the same time.

6:15 The name **Belial** means "worthlessness" or "wickedness." Here it is a name for the evil one. Can there ever be peace between **Christ** and Satan? Obviously not! Neither can there be fellowship between **a believer** and **an unbeliever**. To attempt it is treason against the Lord.

6:16 **Idols** have nothing to do with **the temple of God**. That being the case, how can believers traffic with idols, since they are **the temple of the living God**. Idols here, of course, mean not only carved images but any objects which come between the soul and Christ. They could be money or pleasure or fame or material things.

The apostle finds abundant proof that we are **the temple of the living God** in such passages as Exodus 29:45, Leviticus 26:12 and Ezekiel 37:27. Denney says:

> [Paul] expects Christians to be as much in earnest as Jews to keep the sanctity of God's house inviolate; and now, he says, that house are we: it is ourselves we have to keep unspotted from the world.[33]

6:17 That being so, Paul issues a challenging call to **come out**. He quotes from Isaiah 52:11. These are God's plain instructions to His people concerning separation from evil. Christians are not to stay in the midst of it, as part of it, in order to remedy it. God's program is **come out**. The **unclean** thing in this verse is primarily the heathen world, no doubt, but it also applies to any form of evil, whether commercial, social, or religious.

The verse should *not* be used to teach separation from other believers. Christians are exhorted to endeavor "to keep the unity of the Spirit in the bond of peace."

6:18 It is often very hard for Christians to sever ties that have existed for years in order to be obedient to the word of God. It would seem that God anticipates such a difficulty in verse 18. He has already said in verse 17, "I will receive you," and now He adds, **"I will be a Father to you, and you shall be My sons and daughters, says the LORD Almighty."** The recompense for standing with Christ outside the camp of evil is to know fellowship with the **Father** in a new and more intimate way. It does not mean that we become sons and daughters by obedience to His word, but that we are *manifestly* His **sons and daughters** when we behave in this way, and we will experience the joys and delights of sonship in a way we never have before.

"The blessedness of true separation is nothing less than the glorious companionship of the great God Himself" (Selected).

The problem abounds on every hand today among evangelical Christians in liberal and neo-orthodox churches. They are continually asking, "What shall I do?" God's answer is found here. They should leave a fellowship where the Lord Jesus is not honored and exalted as God's well-beloved Son and the Savior of the world. They can do more for God outside such a fellowship than they will ever accomplish inside it.

7:1 This verse is closely linked with what has gone before. It does not begin a new paragraph but closes the paragraph that began with 6:14.

The **promises** referred to in this verse are those quoted in verses 17 and 18 of the previous chapter. "I will receive you . . . will be a Father to you . . . you shall be My sons and daughters." In view of these marvelous **promises** of God, we should **cleanse ourselves from all filthiness of the flesh and spirit**. Defilement of **the flesh** includes all forms

of physical impurity, whereas filthiness of the **spirit** covers one's inward life, motives, and thoughts.

But God not only gives the negative side, there is also the positive. **Perfecting holiness in the fear of God**. We are not only to put aside that which is defiling, but we are to become increasingly conformed to the Lord Jesus Christ in our daily lives. This verse does not suggest that it is ever possible to become perfectly holy while still here on earth. Practical sanctification is a process that goes on through our lifetime. We grow in likeness to the Lord Jesus Christ until the day when we see Him face to face, and then we shall be like Him throughout all eternity. It is as we have a reverential fear or awe of God that we have a desire in our hearts to become holy. May we all learn to say with the godly McCheyne, "Lord, make me as holy as it is possible for a man to be on this side of heaven."

M. Paul's Joy at the Good News from Corinth (7:2–16)

7:2 **Open your hearts to us.** There was no reason why the Corinthians should not do this, Paul goes on to say, because he had **wronged no one**, he had **corrupted no one**, he had **cheated no one**. Whatever his critics might be saying against him, the Apostle Paul had not injured anyone, he had not taken advantage of anyone financially.

7:3 Nothing Paul has said or is saying is intended **to condemn** the Corinthians in any way. He had repeatedly assured them that his deep affection for them would continue in life and in death.

7:4 Because he felt so intimately attached to the saints at Corinth, the apostle felt at liberty to use **great boldness of speech** when addressing them directly. But if his frankness to them was great, so also was his **boasting** about them in the presence of others. Thus they should not misinterpret his bluntness as indicating any lack of love; rather they should realize that he was truly proud of them and that he spoke highly of them wherever he went. Probably the particular aspect of their Christian life which evoked sincere commendation from Paul was their willing attitude in connection with the collection for the poor saints in Jerusalem. The apostle will come to that subject directly, but here he only makes a passing allusion to it.

I am filled with comfort. I am exceedingly joyful in all our tribulation. These expressions are explained in the verses to follow. Why was Paul so **joyful** in spite of **all** his **tribulation**? The answer is that Titus brought him a good report concerning the Corinthians, and this proved to be a source of tremendous cheer and encouragement to him.

7:5 We have previously mentioned how Paul left Ephesus and journeyed to Troas in search of Titus. Not finding him there, he crossed over **to Macedonia**. Now he explains that even his arrival in Macedonia did not give him the **rest** he sought. He was still disquieted, still **troubled**, still persecuted. On the **outside**, the enemy was hammering away mercilessly, while on the **inside** there were **fears** and anxieties — connected, no doubt, with the fact that he had not yet made contact with Titus.

7:6 Then **God** stepped in and **comforted** Paul **by the coming of Titus**. At this time the apostle experienced the truth of Proverbs 27:17, "As iron sharpens iron, so a man sharpens the countenance of his friend." Picture the joyful meeting between these two devoted servants of Christ, Paul's questions tumbling out one on top of the other, and Titus trying to answer them as quickly as possible! (See also Prov. 25:25.)

7:7 But it was **not only** the joyful reunion with his friend that made Paul so glad; rather it was the report of how **comforted** Titus had been with the response of the Corinthians to Paul's letter.

It was good news to hear that the Corinthians longed to see the Apostle Paul. This was in spite of the determined efforts on the part of the false teachers to alienate the affections of the saints from Paul. Not only were they anxious to see him, but they evidenced real **mourning**. This **mourning** may have been over the careless attitude they had taken by tolerating sin in the assembly, or it may have been over the distress and anxiety they had caused the apostle. In addition to this **mourning**, Titus reported their genuine regard for Paul and their **earnest desire** to please him.

Thus the apostle's rejoicing was **not** just in the **coming** of Titus, but in these evidences of the fact that the Corinthians had been obedient to Paul's instructions and that they still felt kindly toward him.

7:8 For even if I made you sorry with my letter, I do not regret it; though I did regret it. For I perceive the same epistle made you sorry, though only for a while.

The **letter** Paul refers to may be what we know as 1 Corinthians, or it may be a second letter, now lost to us, which dealt with the saints rather severely.

With regard to Paul's **regret** over having written the **letter**, this point should be made clear. Assuming he refers to 1 Corinthians, it does not at all affect the subject of inspiration. The things which the apostle wrote were the very commandments of the Lord; yet Paul himself was still a man, prone to the discouragements and anxieties of other men. Williams comments:

> The distinction between the writer and inspiration appears in verse 8. He knew that his first letter was inspired. Its words were "the commandments of the Lord," but as a feeble, anxious, and affectionate man, he trembled lest the effect of the communications should estrange the Corinthians from him, and should cause them pain. This is an interesting instance of the difference between the individuality of the Prophet and the message of the Holy Spirit given to him.[34]

To summarize, Paul is saying this: When the Corinthians first read his letter, it came as a rebuke to them, and they were pained. After sending the letter, the apostle anticipated their reaction to it, and this made him sorry. Not that he was conscious of having done any wrong; that is not the thought here at all. Rather he was sorry that in carrying out his work for the Lord, it was necessary that others should at times be cast into unhappiness temporarily in order that God's purposes might be worked out in their lives.

In the latter part of verse 8, Paul emphasizes that though the letter had **made** them **sorry**, yet it was **only for a while**. The first effect of the letter was to cause pain. But the sorrow did not last.

The whole process which the apostle is describing here may be likened to the work of a surgeon. In order for him to remove a dangerously infected part from the human body, it is necessary for him to cut deep into the flesh. He does not rejoice in thus causing pain to the patient, though he knows it must be done if the patient is to regain his health. Especially if the patient is a close friend, the surgeon is keenly aware of the suffering that will be necessary. But he realizes that this suffering is only temporary, and he is willing that it should be so in order that the final outcome might be favorable.

7:9 Paul did **not rejoice** in having inflicted pain on the Corinthians **but that** their temporary **sorrow** led them **to** the place of **repentance**. In other words, their sorrow led them to a change of mind resulting in a change of life. **Repentance**, says Hodge, "is not merely a change of purpose, but includes a change of heart which leads to a turning from sin with grief and hatred thereof unto God."[35]

The sorrow of the Corinthians was according to the will of God; it was the kind of sorrow that God likes to see. Because their sorrow and repentance were of a genuine, **godly** nature, they suffered no permanent ill effects from the rebuke delivered to them by the Apostle Paul.

7:10 This verse contrasts **godly sorrow** and **the sorrow of the world. Godly sorrow** means grief which comes into a man's life after he has committed a sin and which leads to his repentance. He realizes that God is speaking to him, and so he takes sides with God against himself and against his sin.

When Paul says that **godly sorrow produces repentance leading to salvation**, he is not necessarily thinking of the salvation of the soul (although that could be true also). After all, the Corinthians were already saved. But here **salvation** is used to describe *deliverance* from any type of sin, bondage, or affliction in a person's life.

There is a question whether the expression **not to be regretted** refers to repentance or salvation. Since it is equally true that no one ever regrets **repentance** *or* **salvation**, we can leave the question open.

The sorrow of the world is not true repentance but mere remorse. It **produces** bitterness, hardness, despair, and eventually **death**. It is illustrated in the life of Judas. He was not sorry for the results which his sin brought to the Lord Jesus, but only remorseful because of the terrible harvest which he himself reaped from it.

7:11 The apostle points to the experience of the Corinthians as an example of what he said in the first part of verse 10. The **very thing** which he had spoken concerning godly sorrow was manifest in their own lives. We would say today, "As evidence of this very fact **that you sorrowed in a godly manner.**" Then he goes on to state various results of their godly sorrow.

First of all, it produced **diligence**, or earnest care, in them. If this passage refers to the case of discipline described in the First Epistle, then this expression means that although at first they had been indifferent, they subsequently became very concerned about the whole matter.

Secondly he says, **what clearing of yourselves**. This does not mean that they tried to *justify* or excuse themselves, but rather that by taking resolute action, they tried to clear themselves of any further guilt or blame in the matter. Their change in attitude led to this change in action.

What indignation may refer to their attitude toward the sinner because of the reproach he brought on the name of Christ. But more probably it refers to their attitude toward themselves for ever having allowed such a thing to go on for so long without taking action on it.

What fear doubtless means they acted in the **fear** of the Lord, but it may also include the thought that they feared a visit from the apostle, if he had to come with a rod.

What vehement desire literally means "what longing." Most commentators agree that this refers to a genuine longing which had been awakened in their souls for a visit from Paul. However, it could also mean a strong **desire** to see the wrong righted and the evil corrected.

What zeal has been variously explained as meaning **zeal** for the glory of God, for the restoration of the sinner, for their own cleansing from defilement in the matter, or for taking sides with the apostle.

What vindication means "what punishment or what avenging." The thought simply is that they took corrective action against the offender in the assembly. They were determined that sin must be punished.

Paul then adds: **In all things you proved yourselves to be clear in the matter.** Of course, we are not to understand by this that they were never to blame, but simply that they had done everything they could to take the proper action and to act as they should have acted in the first place.

7:12 There are four major problems in this verse. First, which letter does Paul refer to in this expression, **I wrote to you**? Second, who is the man **who had done the wrong**? Third, who is the man **who suffered wrong**? Finally, should the last part of the verse be translated **our care for you**, or "your care for us"?

The letter could be the one we know as 1 Corinthians, or it could be a subsequent letter which was not preserved for us. The wrongdoer could be the incestuous man of 1 Corinthians 5, or it could be some rebel in the church. If Paul is speaking of the incestuous man, then the injured person was the man's own father. On the other hand, if the wrongdoer was a rebel, then the injured person was Paul himself or some unidentified victim.

In the KJV and NKJV, the latter part of the verse reads: **but that our care for you in the sight of God might appear to you**. But most modern versions are similar to the NASB: "that your earnestness on our behalf might be made known to you in the sight of God."

7:13 Because his letter had had the desired effect, Paul was **comforted**. The Corinthians had repented and taken sides with him. In addition, he was encouraged by the enthusiasm **Titus** showed concerning the saints; he had **been refreshed by** his contact with them.

7:14 Apparently before the apostle sent Titus to Corinth, he had spoken to him glowingly about the believers there. Now he is saying his **boasting** did not prove to be untrue. All that he had said about the Corinthians was verified by the experience of **Titus** in their midst. Just as everything the apostle had ever said to the Corinthians was true, **so** his

boasting to Titus had been **found true** also.

7:15 Obviously Titus did not know what kind of a reception he would get when he reached southern Greece. Perhaps he had anticipated the worst. But when he did arrive, the Corinthians gave him a cordial welcome, and not only so, they endeared themselves to him all the more by being obedient to the instructions which he carried from the Apostle Paul.

When the apostle says that they received Titus **with fear and trembling**, he does not mean abject terror or cowardly fear, but rather a sense of reverence before the Lord in the matter and a scrupulous desire to please.

7:16 When Paul says he had **confidence in** the saints **in everything**, we must not make his words say more than he intended. They certainly do not mean that he considered the Corinthians to be beyond the possibility of sin or failure. But rather they mean that the **confidence** which he had placed in them, and of which he had boasted to Titus, had not been in vain. They had proved themselves *worthy* of his trust. It doubtless includes the idea also that since they had taken a proper attitude in reference to the matter discussed in the First Epistle, he feels justified in having full **confidence in** them.

This verse completes the first section of 2 Corinthians, a section which, as we have seen, has been devoted to a description of the apostle's ministry and a determined effort on Paul's part to strengthen the bonds which existed between the Corinthians and himself. The next two chapters handle "the grace of giving."

II. PAUL'S EXHORTATION TO COMPLETE THE COLLECTION FOR THE JERUSALEM SAINTS (Chaps. 8, 9)

A. Good Examples of Generous Giving (8:1–9)

8:1 Paul wanted the believers to know the very unusual way in which **the grace of God** had manifested itself among the Christians in **the churches of Macedonia** (northern Greece). Philippi and Thessalonica were two of the cities where churches had been planted.

The particular way in which these Macedonians showed that they had received **the grace of God** was by their *generosity*.

8:2 These Christians had been going through **a great trial of affliction**. Ordinarily, people thus tested would seek to save their money to provide for their future. And especially so if they were not very prosperous, as was the case with the Macedonians. They did not have very much money at all. Yet their Christian **joy** was so overflowing that when the need of the saints in Jerusalem was presented to them, they reversed all ordinary behavior and gave in a most liberal manner. They were able to combine **affliction, joy, poverty,** and **liberality**.

8:3 There were other unique features about their generosity. Their giving not only equaled **their ability**; it went **beyond their ability**. Also **they were freely willing**, that is, they gave spontaneously, without having to be pressured, coaxed, or cajoled.

8:4 So urgent were they in the matter that they begged Paul for the privilege of sharing in the relief of the Jerusalem saints. Perhaps the apostle hesitated to accept their kindness, knowing how poor they were themselves at the time. But they would not take "no" for an answer. They wanted to be allowed to give.

8:5 Probably Paul had **only** expected or **hoped** that they would act as most other mortals do: they give grudgingly at first, then increase the amount of the gift as greater pressure is brought to bear upon them. But not so the Macedonians! These beloved Christians **first gave** the greatest gift — **themselves**. Then afterwards it was an easy thing for them to give their money. When Paul says **they gave themselves to the Lord, and then to us by the will of God**, he simply means that first there was the complete committal of their lives to Christ, then they willingly gave themselves to Paul in the sense that they wanted to help in the collection for Jerusalem. They said to Paul, in effect, "We have given ourselves to the Lord, and now we give ourselves to you as His administrator. You tell us what to do, since you are an apostle of Christ, our Lord."

"Contributions to the work of the Lord," says G. Campbell Morgan, "are only valuable as they are the gifts of those who are themselves yielded to God."

8:6 The apostle was so elated over the example of the Macedonians that he now wanted the Corinthians to imitate them. And so he says that he **urged Titus** to **complete** the work which he had begun at Corinth. In other words, when Titus had first visited the Corinthians, he had brought up this whole matter of the collection with them. Now when he goes back, he is instructed to see that good intentions are translated into *action*.

8:7 Since the Corinthians were so outstanding in many ways (and they were), Paul now wants them to excel in the matter of giving. He gives them credit for abounding **in faith, in speech, in knowledge, in all diligence** (earnestness), **and in** their **love for** him. In the First Epistle, Paul had commended them for their knowledge and speech. Here he adds several other virtues, doubtless as a result of Titus' visit.

The expression **in faith** may describe strong faith in God, the *gift* of faith, or *faithfulness* in their dealings with their fellow men.

In speech doubtless refers to their proficiency in the use of tongues, a subject which occupied considerable place in the First Epistle.

In knowledge may refer to the charismatic gift or to the breadth of their grasp of divine truths.

In all diligence describes their zeal and earnestness in the things of God.

Finally, their **love for** Paul is mentioned as being praiseworthy. Now Paul would like to add another expression to the list, namely, "in all generosity." Denney warns of:

> . . . the man who abounds in spiritual interests, who is fervent, prayerful, affectionate, able to speak in the Church, but unable to part with his money.[36]

8:8 Paul is not commanding this in a harsh, legalistic manner. Rather, he would like to put the **sincerity of** their **love** to the test, and especially so in the light of the eagerness or earnestness of the Macedonian Christians in this matter. When Paul states that he did **not** say this **by commandment**, he does not mean that it is not inspired. He simply means that the giving should come from a willing heart, because "God loves a cheerful giver."

8:9 It is at this point that the Apostle Paul introduces one of the greatest verses in this grand letter. Against a background of the petty circumstances of life in Macedonia and in Corinth he paints a lovely portrait of the most generous Person who ever lived.

The word **grace** is used in a variety of ways in the NT, but here the meaning is unmistakably that of generosity. How generous was the Lord Jesus? He was so generous that He gave *all He had* for our sakes **that** we **through His poverty might become** eternally **rich**.

Moorehead comments:

> He was rich in possessions, power, homage, fellowship, happiness. He became poor in station, circumstances, in His relations with men. We are urged to give a little money, clothing, food. He gave Himself.[37]

This verse teaches the pre-existence of the Lord Jesus. When was He **rich**? Certainly not when He came into the world as the Babe of Bethlehem! And certainly not during His thirty-three years of wandering "as a homeless stranger in the world His hands had made." He was rich in a bygone eternity, dwelling with the Father in the courts of heaven. But **He became poor**. This refers not only to Bethlehem but to Nazareth, Gethsemane, Gabbatha, and Golgotha. And it was all for our sakes, **that** we **through His poverty might become rich**.

If this is true, and it certainly is, then it should be our greatest joy to give all that we are and have to Him. No argument could be more forceful than this in the midst of Paul's discussion of Christian giving.

B. Good Advice to Complete the Collection (8:10, 11)

8:10 Now the apostle returns to the Corinthians. They had thought of making a collection for the poor saints before the Macedonians had decided to do it.

The Corinthians had actually begun to do it before the Macedonians started their fund. To be consistent, they should finish what they began **a year ago**. It would be to their advantage, because it would prove their sincerity and consistency.

8:11 Whatever their reason for delay, Paul tells them that they should disregard it and **complete** the thing which they had shown **a readiness** to do. They should do it according to the ability which they then had and not according to what they might like to do in the future if their wealth increased.

C. Three Good Principles for Generous Giving (8:12–15)

8:12 It seems the Corinthians had delayed in making a collection for the needy saints at Jerusalem hoping that they would be able to send more at a later date. They are here reminded, however, that it is not a question of how much they send at all. If there is a real desire in their heart to have fellowship in this good matter, then God accepts their gift, however small it may be. It's the heart attitude that counts.

8:13 Paul's purpose is not to put the Corinthians under financial strain. His thought is **not that** the Jerusalem church **should be eased** and the Corinthian church **burdened** or impoverished.

8:14 This verse describes God's program for the relief of want in the church of the Lord Jesus Christ. The Lord's purpose is that whenever a need exists in one area among Christians, then there should be a flow of funds from other areas to that needy spot. This constant flow and interflow of funds would result in an **equality** among the churches world-wide.

Thus, at the time Paul was writing, there would be a flow of funds from Corinth, Macedonia, and other places to Jerusalem. But perhaps in the future the saints at Jerusalem might be well cared for, whereas there might be definite **lack** in Corinth. In such an instance the flow of funds would be reversed. That is what Paul means by this verse. Now the need was in Jerusalem, but sometime in the future it might be in Corinth, and in that case others would help them.

8:15 This principle of equality is

emphasized by a quotation from Exodus 16:18. When the children of Israel went out to gather the manna, some were able to gather more than others. But it didn't matter. When the manna was distributed, each man received the same amount — one omer, or about five pints. So **"He who gathered much had nothing left over, and he who gathered little had no lack."** If anyone tried to *hoard* manna, it bred worms!

The equalization didn't happen by miracle or magic. It happened because those who had too much *shared* with those who didn't have enough. Hodge observes:

> The lesson . . . taught in Exodus and by Paul is that, among the people of God, the superabundance of one should be employed in relieving the necessities of others; and that any attempt to countervail this law will result in shame and loss. Property is like manna; it will not bear hoarding.[38]

Along the same lines is this selection from an unknown source:

> God intends each man to have a share of the good things of life. Some gather more, however, and some less. Those who have more should share with those who have less. God permits the unequal distribution of property, not so that the rich shall selfishly enjoy it, but share it with the poor.

D. Three Good Brethren to Prepare the Collection (8:16–24)

8:16 In these next two verses **Titus** is commended for the excellent attitude he has taken in the matter. First, **God** is thanked for putting **the same earnest care for** the Corinthians **into the heart of Titus**. Paul had found a kindred spirit in his fellow worker. The **same** burden which the apostle had for the Corinthians, he found to be shared by **Titus.**

8:17 Paul had exhorted Titus to go to Corinth with this Letter, but the exhortation was not necessary. He wanted to go **of his own accord**.

The clause **he went to you** probably means "he is going to you." It illustrates the epistolary aorist tense, which views the action not at the time when Paul wrote the Letter but when the Corinthians read it. Titus was unquestionably the one who carried this Letter to Corinth.

He didn't leave for Corinth until Paul finished the Letter.

8:18 Verses 18 through 22 describe two other Christian brethren who would accompany Titus on his mission. The first one is described in verses 18 through 21, and the second in verse 22. Both are unnamed.

This section of Scripture is valuable in showing the precautions which the Apostle Paul took in handling funds lest there be any basis for accusing him of mishandling the money.

The first **brother** referred to was one who was worthy of **praise** because of his work **in the gospel**. There is a great difference of opinion as to who is meant. Some say Luke, others Silas, some Trophimus. But perhaps by trying to guess we miss the whole spirit of the passage. Is it not intentional that he is unnamed? True discipleship often involves obscurity. This was so with the little maid who was used so greatly in the life of Naaman, the leper. It was also true with the little boy who put his lunch at the disposal of the Lord Jesus.

8:19 This unnamed brother **was also chosen by the churches** to make the journey necessitated by **this gift**. In other words, he was appointed to be one of the messengers to carry this freely-given contribution. The apostle looked upon himself and the others as servants or administrators of this gracious work. They did it for **the glory of the Lord Himself**. And they wanted it to demonstrate their willingness and eagerness to serve the poor saints in Jerusalem.

8:20 The apostle was too wise a man to handle this money alone, or to commit it to any one other man. He insisted on its being handled by a group of two or three or more. That is what he means here in verse 20. To avoid any possibility of misrepresentation or scandal, he ensured that the handling of **this lavish gift** might be done in such a way that no evil speaking could result.

8:21 **Providing honorable things** means making sure that things are done honestly. Paul was anxious that his actions should not only be honest **in the sight of the Lord**, but that they should also be above reproach **in the sight of men**. Morgan notes: "It is the business of the Christian community to do its business in such a way that men of the world will have no cause to suspect anything contrary to righteousness in its affairs."[39]

This verse, incidentally, is nearly the same as Proverbs 3:3, 4 in the Septuagint.

8:22 Here we have another unknown **brother** whom Paul had appointed to help in this important matter. He had **often proved diligent** in many matters, and now he showed special diligence with regard to this particular errand, **because of the great confidence** he had **in** the Corinthians.

At this point the NKJV says, **because of the great confidence which** *we have* in you. The words **we have** are supplied (italics), and many prefer that *he has* be understood instead. Then Paul would be commending him not only for his past faithfulness, but because of his keen interest on this particular occasion by reason of *his* **confidence** in the Corinthians.

8:23 Therefore, Paul says that **if anyone inquires about** these three men, the Corinthians could tell them that **Titus** is Paul's **partner and fellow worker** for the Corinthians, and that these other two **brethren** are **messengers of the churches** and **the glory of Christ**. The expression **the glory of Christ** is certainly an exalted description of these men. It is because they are deputies **of the churches** that they are so called. They make the work of the Lord shine before the eyes of men. They are a credit to the Lord and reflect His glory.

8:24 In view of all this, the Corinthians should give them a good reception and should justify Paul's **boasting** about them by entrusting to them the generous gift for the saints at Jerusalem. This would be **proof** to the surrounding **churches** of their Christian **love**. Phillips translates the verse, "So do let them, and all the Churches, see how genuine is your love, and justify all the nice things we have said about you!"

E. Appeal to the Corinthians to Justify Paul's Boasting of Them (9:1–5)

9:1 It was quite unnecessary for Paul **to write to** the Corinthians **concerning** the subject of sending financial help

to needy **saints** — yet he proceeded to do so anyway. Perhaps there is a trace of irony in this verse. Actually, in some respects it was not necessary for him to write to them. They had shown a willingness from the outset to participate in the collection for Jerusalem. As far as willingness was concerned, they were to be commended. But they simply had not carried out their original intentions. That is why he feels it necessary to enlarge on the **superfluous.**

9:2 There was no question about their **willingness**. From the time the subject was first broached they had shown **zeal** and earnestness. In fact, Paul had boasted about them to the Christians in Macedonia. He told them **that Achaia was ready a year ago. Achaia**, the southern part of Greece, is here used to refer to Corinth, since Corinth was located there. When **the Macedonians** heard that the Christians in Corinth had been ready for a year, many of them (the Macedonians) were **stirred up**; they caught the contagion of Christian giving and decided to give themselves to it wholeheartedly.

9:3 When Paul says here that he has **sent the brethren**, he really means he is sending them. The past tense views it from the perspective of the readers rather than the writer. **The brethren** are the three mentioned in the previous chapter: Titus and two unnamed Christians. They were being sent so that Paul's boasting concerning the Corinthians would not be in vain with regard to the collection. The mission of the three brethren would be to ensure that the collection was prepared by the time that Paul got there.

9:4 When the apostle would make the trip from Macedonia south to Corinth, it was not unlikely that one of the Macedonian believers would accompany him on the trip. How embarrassing it would be to the Apostle Paul **if**, after boasting of the Corinthians, he should bring one of those **Macedonians** and **find** that the Corinthians had actually done nothing about the gift for Jerusalem! In such an event Paul's confidence in the Corinthians would have been put to shame, **not to mention** that the Corinthians themselves would then have real cause to be ashamed for their neglect.

Phillips' translation of this verse is colorful:

> For, between ourselves, it would never do if some of the Macedonians were to accompany me on my visit to you and find you unprepared for this act of generosity! We (not to speak of you) should be horribly ashamed, just because we had been so proud and confident of you.

9:5 This then is why Paul **thought it necessary to exhort** these three **brethren to go to** Corinth before he himself went. They would **prepare** their **generous gift beforehand, which** they **had previously promised** for the Jerusalem saints.

That it may be ready as a matter of generosity and not as a grudging obligation. There was no thought that these funds should be wrung out of the saints as by extortion but that it should be a manifestation of their **generosity**, given through their own free will.

F. The Good Rewards of Generous Giving (9:6–15)

9:6 In verses 6 through 15 the Apostle Paul lists some of the wonderful rewards and benefits of Christian giving. First, he sets forth the law of the harvest. It is a well-known fact in agriculture that a generous sowing of seed is necessary if there is to be a generous harvest. Perhaps the farmer is ready to put the seed in the ground. Shall he sow liberally or shall he take some of the grain and use it as food during the months ahead? The thought here is that if **he sows** it liberally, he **will also reap** out of all proportion to what he **sows**.

We should remember this with regard to agriculture — the farmer does not reap the exact amount of grain he sows, but much more proportionately. So it is in Christian giving: it is not a question of receiving back exactly what one has given but receiving back far out of proportion to the amount of the gift. Of course, the return is not so much in money as in spiritual blessings.

9:7 **Each one** is to **give as he purposes in his heart**. It will be necessary for him to consider what is necessary for his own immediate needs. He will have

to think of just obligations which he will incur in the course of normal life. But then above that, he should think of the needs of his fellow Christians, and of the claims of Christ upon him. Taking all these considerations into view, he should give **not grudgingly or of necessity**. It is possible to give and yet not be happy about it. It is also possible to give under the pressure of emotional appeals or public embarrassment. None of these things will do. **God loves a cheerful giver.** It has often been pointed out that our word *hilarious* comes from the word translated **cheerful** (*hilaron*).

Does God really need our money? No, the cattle on a thousand hills belong to Him, and if He needed anything, He would not tell us (Psalm 50:10–12). But our heart's attitude is what is important to Him. He loves to see a Christian who is so filled with the joy of the Lord that he wants to share what he has with others.

God loves a cheerful giver because, as Jowett says:

> Cheerful giving is born of love, and therefore it is a lover loving a lover and rejoicing in the communion. Giving is the language of loving; indeed, it has no other speech. "God so *loved* that He *gave!*" Love finds its very life in giving itself away. Its only pride in possession is the joy of surrender. If love has all things, it yet possesses nothing.[40]

9:8 Here we have a promise that, if a person really wants to be generous, God will see that he is given the opportunity. **Grace** is here used as a synonym for resources. **God is able** to supply us with resources so that we will not only have a **sufficiency** ourselves, but so that we will be able to share what we have with others and thus **have an abundance for every good work**.

Notice the *alls* of this verse. **All grace**, **always** (that is, *at all times*), **all sufficiency, all things, every good work**.

9:9 Now the apostle quotes from Psalm 112:9. The expression **He has dispersed abroad** refers to the act of sowing seed. The verse describes a man who has been generous in his sowing of the seed, or more particularly in his deeds of kindness. The specific kindness in which he engaged was giving **to the poor**. Is he the loser by such action? No! **His righteousness endures forever.** This means that if we disperse kindness as a sower scatters his seed, we will be laying up for ourselves treasures in heaven. The results of our kindness will endure **forever.**

9:10 The illustration of **the sower** continues. The same God **who supplies seed to the sower and bread for food** is careful to make sure that those who show kindness to others will reap certain rewards. Some of those rewards are now listed. First, He will **multiply the seed you have sown.** That is, He will give greater opportunity and more abundant results from showing kindness to His people. Furthermore, He will **increase the fruits of your righteousness.** The Corinthians were righteous in giving to the saints at Jerusalem. As a result of that giving they would receive fruit by way of eternal reward. As God increased their ability to give, and they increased in generosity, the rewards would **increase** accordingly.

9:11 It is certainly clear from this section that a person never impoverishes himself by giving to the Lord. Rather, every act of kindness has a reflex action, and the reward is all out of proportion to the gift given. Thus Paul says here that the Christians, by their giving, would be **enriched in everything for** further displays of great **liberality.** As the apostles looked on and saw the Corinthians growing in the grace of giving, they (the apostles) would give thanks **to God.**

9:12 When the gift from the Corinthians was put to work in Jerusalem, it would not only supply **the needs of the saints** there but would also result in many people giving thanks **to God.** We have noticed, time and again, the emphasis Paul puts on **thanksgivings.** Anything which resulted in the Lord being thanked assumed great importance in Paul's eyes.

9:13 There are still other benefits that would result from the Corinthians' gift. It would be a definite **proof** to the Judean Christians that there really had been a work of **Christ** in the lives of these Gentile converts. At one time the Jewish Christians had real doubts about such converts as the Corinthians. Perhaps they did not consider them to be full-fledged Christians. But this kindness would be to them a great **proof** of the reality of the faith of the Corinthians, and **they** would **glorify God for** what **the gospel of Christ** had done in Achaia, as well as for the **liberal** contribution which had been made to them.

9:14 And that is not all! Two more benefits follow. Because of the gift from Corinth to Jerusalem, the Jewish Christians would henceforth be careful to pray for the saints in Corinth, and there would be strong ties of affection. The saints in Jerusalem would **long for** the Corinthians because of **the exceeding grace of God** which the latter had shown.

9:15 At this point Paul simply bursts out into an exclamation! This verse has been a puzzle to many Bible scholars. They cannot see that it is closely connected with what has gone before. And they wonder what is meant by **His indescribable gift.**

But it seems to us that as the Apostle Paul reaches the end of his section on Christian giving, he is forced to think of the greatest Giver of all — **God** Himself. He thinks, too, of the greatest **gift** of all — the Lord Jesus Christ. And so he would leave his Corinthian brethren on this high note. They are children of God and followers of Christ. Then let them follow such worthy examples!

III. PAUL'S VINDICATION OF HIS APOSTLESHIP (Chaps. 10–13)

The last four chapters of this Epistle deal primarily with Paul's defense of his apostleship. The words of the Apostle Peter seem especially appropriate in describing this particular portion of Paul's writings: "In which are some things hard to understand." Paul is obviously answering charges made against him by his critics, but we are forced to form our own conclusions as to what the charges were by studying the text of Paul's answers. Throughout this section the apostle uses a great deal of irony. The difficulty is in knowing just *when* he is doing so!

However, it is a most rewarding portion of God's precious word, and we would certainly be much poorer without it.

A. Paul's Reply to His Accusers (10:1–12)

10:1 In verses 1–6 we have the apostle's answer to those who accused him of acting in accordance with the methods of worldly men.

First, he introduces himself simply as **I, Paul, myself**. Second, he pleads with the saints instead of acting in a dictatorial manner. Third, he bases his appeal on **the meekness and gentleness of Christ**. He is, of course, thinking of the pathway of the Lord Jesus when He was on earth as a Man. This, incidentally, is one of Paul's few references to the Savior's life on earth. Ordinarily, the apostle refers to Christ as the ascended, glorified One at the right hand of God.

In further description of himself, Paul says, **I who in presence am lowly among you, but being absent am bold toward you**. This obviously is spoken in irony. What his critics said was that Paul was cowardly when he was present with the people, but when he was **absent** he was **bold** as a lion. His boldness, they said, was evident in the overbearing attitude which he took in his letters.

10:2 This verse is connected with the *first part* of verse 1. There Paul started to say that he pleaded with the Corinthians, but he did not tell what was the content of his entreaty. Here he explains: **"I beg you that when I am present I may not be bold with that confidence by which I intend to be bold against some, who think of us as if we walked according to the flesh."** He did not want **to be bold** toward them as he intended **to be bold** toward those who accused him of acting in a carnal manner.

10:3 Here the thought is that **although** the apostles were living in bodies of **flesh**, they did not wage the Christian warfare **according to** fleshly methods or motives.

10:4 **The weapons of** the Christian **warfare are not carnal**. The Christian, for instance, does not use swords, guns, or the strategy of modern warfare in spreading the Christian gospel from shore to shore. But those are not the only carnal weapons of which the apostle is speaking. The Christian does not use wealth, glory, power, fluency, or cleverness to accomplish his aims.

Rather, he uses methods that are **mighty in God for pulling down strongholds**. Faith in the living God, prayer, and obedience to the word of God are the effective weapons of every true soldier of Jesus Christ. It is by these that **strongholds** are razed.

10:5 This verse tells us what is meant by "strongholds" in verse 4.

Paul saw himself as a soldier warring against the proud reasonings of man, **arguments** which oppose the truth. The true character of these **arguments** is described in the expression **against the knowledge of God**. It could be applied today to the reasonings of scientists, evolutionists, philosophers, and religionists who have no room for God in their scheme of things. The apostle was in no mood to sign a truce with these. Rather he felt committed to bring **every thought into captivity to the obedience of Christ**. All men's teachings and speculations must be judged in the light of the teachings of the Lord Jesus Christ. Paul would not condemn human reasoning as such, but would warn that we must not allow our intellects to be exercised in defiance of the Lord and in disobedience to Him.

10:6 As a soldier of Christ, the apostle was also **ready to punish all disobedience, when** the Corinthians had shown their **obedience** first of all. He was not going to act against the false teachers at Corinth until he was, first, sure of the **obedience** of the believers in all things.

10:7 The first sentence may be a question: **"Do you look at things according to the outward appearance?"** (NKJV). It may be a statement of fact: "You are looking only on the surface of things" (NIV). Or it may be an imperative: "Look at what is before your eyes" (RSV), that is, "Face the facts."

If we take it as a statement, it means that the Corinthians were prone to judge a man by whether or not he had a commanding presence, impressive eloquence, or great powers of logic. They were swayed by external appearance rather than by inward reality.

If anyone is convinced in himself

that he is Christ's, let him again consider this in himself, that just as he is Christ's, even so we are Christ's. Here Paul may be referring to those who said, "I am of Christ" (1 Cor. 1:12), probably meaning to the exclusion of others. He answers that no one has an exclusive claim on Christ. He belongs to the Lord Jesus as truly as they.

Whoever the exclusive Christians were, Paul does not deny they belonged to Christ. Therefore, in this passage he can hardly be referring to the false apostles and deceitful workers who transformed themselves into apostles of Christ (11:14). It seems that in this Letter Paul is dealing with different adversaries, some saved and some unsaved.

10:8 As an apostle of the Lord Jesus Christ, Paul had been given **authority** in connection with the churches he established. The aim of this authority was to build up the saints in their most holy faith. The false teachers, on the other hand, were exercising an authority among the Corinthians which they had never received from the Lord. Not only so, but they were exercising this authority in a manner to tear down the saints rather than build them up. So Paul says that even if he boasted more abundantly in the **authority, which the Lord gave** him, he would not be put to shame for it. His claims would eventually prove to be true.

10:9 He has said this in order that he might not **seem to terrify** the Christians **by** his **letters**. In other words, if the apostle should boast of his God-given authority, he does not want the Christians to think he is trying to scare them. That would be playing into the hands of his critics. Rather the Corinthians should remember that his authority was given to him for building them up, and that is how he used it.

10:10 Here we are permitted to listen to the very charge which was made against the Apostle Paul. His opponents charged him with writing threatening **letters**, but they said **his bodily presence is weak, and his speech contemptible**.

10:11 All who made such charges should **consider** that **when** Paul was going to be **present** with them, he would be the same as they said he was in his **letters**. This does not mean that Paul ad-mitted to being overbearing in his letters. That was what they *said* about him. But he is saying that he would deal severely with them when he met them face to face. There would be no cowardliness about him.

10:12 It is obvious that the false teachers were in the habit of comparing themselves with others. They would hold up Paul before the gaze of the Corinthians in such a way as to make him a laughingstock. They considered themselves to be the inner circle. They were the elite ones. According to them, no one could stand by them and be seen in a favorable light. So Paul says in obvious satire, **"For we dare not class ourselves or compare ourselves with those who commend themselves. But they, measuring themselves by themselves, and comparing themselves among themselves, are not wise."** Bold as they accused Paul to be in his Letter, he here says he is not bold enough to number himself **with those who commend themselves**, or with those whose only standard of measurement is their own life.

It should be obvious that if a person's only standard is himself, then he is always right! There is no room for improvement. Those who do this **are not wise**. As has been well said, "It is the bane of all cliques and coteries to ignore all excellence out of their own party."

B. Paul's Principle: To Break New Ground for Christ (10:13–16)

10:13 In verses 13–16 Paul states his intention of boasting only in **the sphere** of ministry **which God** had given to him. He made it a practice not to intrude into someone else's work when he wanted to boast. This is an obvious reference to the Judaizers. It was *their* practice to work their way into churches already established by the Apostle Paul or some other Christian, and there build upon another man's foundation. When they boasted, they were actually boasting in something that was the work of another.

Paul says he **will not boast** concerning matters which lie outside **the sphere** of his own service for Christ. Rather, he will make his boast in the places and persons where God had honored his ministry. That would include Corinth, since he had gone there with the gospel and a church had been formed as a result.

Arthur S. Way aptly translates:

> But I — *I* do not vaunt of prerogatives beyond my legitimate province. I confine myself within the limits of the sphere of operations allotted to me by God — and that province certainly included my mission to you.

Actually, Paul had been commissioned by the Lord to take the gospel to the Gentiles. This commission would, of course, include Corinth. The apostles in Jerusalem had agreed to this, but now false teachers were coming from Jerusalem and invading the provinces which God had given to the Apostle Paul.

10:14 The apostle is not indulging in excessive boasting. God had appointed a sphere of service to him. That sphere included Corinth. He had come to Corinth, preached the gospel, and planted a church. If he had not come as far as Corinth, he could be accused of boasting beyond his proper limit.

He had undergone trial, testing, affliction, and difficulties in order that he might reach the Corinthians. Now others were invading the sphere which he had pioneered, and they were probably boasting loudly about their achievements.

The NIV translates this difficult verse: "We are not going too far in our boasting, as would be the case if we had not come to you, for we did get as far as you with the gospel of Christ."

10:15 The apostle is determined that he will **not** boast of matters which were not directly the result of his own service for Christ. That is the very thing of which the Judaizers were guilty: they boasted in other men's labors. They tried to steal Paul's sheep, assassinated his character, contradicted his teaching, and assumed a false authority.

Paul's hope was that when the Corinthians' **faith increased**, and he could move on, their **faith** would express itself in practical help that would enable him to go into still further regions as God's apostle. As he thus extended his ministry, he would follow his rule consistently.

The troubles at Corinth were so occupying his time that he was hindered from fulfilling his mission to the regions beyond.

10:16 The rule was **to preach the gospel in the regions beyond** the Corinthians (probably meaning Western Greece, Italy, and Spain) **and not to boast in another man's sphere of accomplishment**. The Apostle Paul did not intend to trespass on others' fields of labor or to glory in what other men had done before he got to a certain place.

C. Paul's Supreme Goal: The Commendation of the Lord (10:17, 18)

10:17 If anyone **glories**, he should **glory in the LORD**. Doubtless this means he should **glory** only **in** what **the LORD** has been pleased to do through him. This seems to be the general direction of the apostle's argument.

10:18 After all, self-commendation is not what wins God's approval. The question that Paul's critics should face is this: Has the Lord commended you by so blessing your ministry that souls have been saved, that saints have been established in the faith, and that churches have been planted? Can you demonstrate the approval of the Lord by pointing to those who have been converted through your preaching? This is what counts. Paul was willing and able to show such proof of the Lord's commendation of his ministry.

In this chapter and the next, Paul indulges in what he calls folly. He is going to engage in the foolish business of speaking well of himself. It is not that he wants to do this at all. It was positively distasteful to him. But he asks the Corinthians to bear with him as he thus makes a fool of himself.

Apparently the false teachers had engaged in a great deal of boasting. They doubtless gave glowing accounts of their service and of their spectacular successes. Paul had never done this. He had preached Christ and not himself.

The Corinthians seemed to prefer the boasting type of ministry, and so Paul asks them to let him engage in it for a while.

D. Paul's Assertion of His Apostleship (11:1–15)

11:1 Oh, that you would bear with me in a little folly — and indeed you do bear with me. Paul wishes they would put up with him as he indulges in boasting. But then he senses that they are already doing it, so the request is unnecessary.

11:2 Three reasons are then given why he should make this request of them. The first reason is that he was **jealous for** the Corinthians **with godly jealousy**. He had **betrothed** them **to one husband, that** he might **present** them **as a chaste virgin to Christ**. Paul felt a personal responsibility for the spiritual welfare of the Corinthian saints. His desire was that in a coming day, i.e., at the Rapture, he could present them to the Lord Jesus, uncorrupted by the false teachings that were then prevalent. It was because he was thus jealous over them that he was willing to indulge in what seemed to be folly.

11:3 The second reason for Paul's playing the fool was his **fear** that the saints might be deceived and their **minds** might **be corrupted from the simplicity** and purity of devotion to **Christ**. Here **simplicity** means singleheartedness. He wanted them to be devoted to the Lord Jesus alone, and not to allow their hearts' affections to be drawn away by anyone else. Then, too, he wanted them to be unspotted in their devotedness to the Lord.

The apostle remembers how **the serpent deceived Eve by his craftiness**. He did it with an appeal to her mind or intellect. That is exactly what the false teachers were doing in Corinth. Paul would have the heart of the Corinthian virgin to be undivided and unspotted.

Note that Paul treats the account of Eve and the serpent as fact, not myth.

11:4 The third reason why the apostle was willing to indulge in a little folly was that the Corinthians had shown a readiness to listen to false teachers.

When anyone came to Corinth actually preaching **another Jesus**, and professing to dispense **a different spirit** than the Holy Spirit, and proclaiming a **different gospel**, the Corinthians put up with such a one quite willingly. They showed a lovely toleration of these views. Paul is saying sarcastically, "If you do that with others, why don't you do it with me?"

The final words, **"you may well put up with it!"** must be understood as

irony. The apostle is not endorsing their acceptance of heresy, but chiding them for their gullibility and lack of discernment.

11:5 The reason they should be willing to put up with Paul is that he is **not at all inferior to the most eminent apostles**. The expression, **most eminent**, is used in sarcasm. The literal (and modern-sounding!) rendering is "the super-apostles."

The Reformers quoted this verse to refute the papal notion that Peter was the chief apostle and that the popes inherited this primacy.

11:6 Though Paul might have been **untrained in speech**, he certainly was **not** deficient **in knowledge**. This should have been obvious to the Corinthians, because it was from the apostle that they had received their **knowledge** of the Christian faith. Whatever Paul's deficiencies might have been as far as eloquence was concerned, he apparently had made himself intelligible to the saints at Corinth. They themselves would have to bear witness to this.

11:7 If his unpolished speech was not the reason the Corinthians had taken such a negative attitude toward him, perhaps it was because he had committed an offense **in humbling** himself **that** they **might be exalted**. The rest of the verse explains what he means here. When the apostle was with the Corinthians he did not receive any financial assistance from them. Perhaps they felt he had committed a sin in taking such a humble place that they might have a high one.

11:8 The expression, **"I robbed other churches,"** is a figure of speech known as hyperbole. It is an exaggerated statement designed to produce a real effect on the mind. Paul does not mean he literally robbed other churches, of course, but it simply means that while he was serving the Lord at Corinth he received financial assistance from **other churches** so that he might serve the Corinthians without any remuneration at all from them.

11:9 There were times during his stay at Corinth when the Apostle Paul was actually **in need**. Did he make known that **need** to the Corinthians and insist on help from them? He certainly did not. Some **brethren who came from**

Macedonia supplied what he **lacked** in material things.

In every way possible the apostle **kept** himself **from being burdensome to** the Corinthians, and he intended to continue so doing. With regard to the Corinthians, he would not insist on his right as an apostle to be cared for by them.

11:10 Paul is determined that **no one** will rob him of his ground of **boasting in the regions of Achaia**, where Corinth is located. He is doubtless referring here to his critics who used his abstinence as an argument against him. They said he realized he was not a true apostle, and that is why he did not insist on being supported by the Christians (1 Cor. 9). In spite of the charges of his critics, he will continue to boast that he served the Corinthians without taking any money from them.

11:11 **Why** will he boast like this? **Because** he does **not love** the Corinthians? **God knows** this is not so! His heart was full of the deepest affection for them. It seemed that no matter what the apostle did, he was criticized. If he had taken money from the Corinthians, his opponents would have said he was just preaching for what he got out of it. By not taking money from them he subjected himself to the charge that he did not really **love** them. But **God knows** the truth of the matter, and Paul is content to leave it with Him.

11:12 It seems clear that the Judaizers expected, demanded, and received money from the Corinthians. Like most cultists, they would not have served unless it paid them financially. Paul was determined to **continue** his policy of not receiving money from the believers in Corinth. If the false teachers wanted to engage in a boasting match with him, let them follow his policy. But he knew they would never be able to boast of serving without monetary reward. Thus he cut out this ground of boasting from under them.

11:13 Paul's real estimate of these men, pent up so far in the Letter, at last bursts forth. He can contain himself no longer! He must call them what they are. **Such are false apostles** in the sense that they never were commissioned by the Lord Jesus Christ. They either assumed the office themselves or had it conferred

on them by other men. They are **deceitful workers**, and this describes the methods by which they went about from church to church seeking to gain adherents to their false teachings. **Transforming themselves into apostles of Christ**, they pretended to represent Him. Paul has no desire to be on the same level as **such** men.

The things which the apostle says of these Judaizing teachers are true of false teachers in the present day. "Evil, we all know, could never tempt us if we saw it simply as it is; disguise is essential to its power; it appeals to man through ideas and hopes which he cannot but regard as good" (Selected).

11:14 The apostle has just said that his critics in Corinth posed falsely as apostles of Christ. But he is not surprised at this when he thinks of the tactics of their master: **And no wonder! For Satan himself transforms himself into an angel of light.**

Satan is commonly pictured today as a horned, evil-looking red creature with a tail. But such, of course, is far removed from the manner in which he presents himself to men.

Others think of Satan in connection with a poor drunkard, wallowing in the gutter on Skid Row. But this, too, is a false impression of what Satan is really like.

This verse tells us that he masquerades as **an angel of light**. Perhaps by way of illustration we might say he poses as a minister of the gospel, wearing religious clothing, and standing in the pulpit of a fashionable church. He uses religious words such as *God, Jesus,* and *the Bible*. But he deludes his hearers, teaching that salvation is by good works or by human merit. He does not preach redemption through the blood of Christ.

11:15 J. N. Darby once stated that Satan is never more satanic than when he carries a Bible. This is the thought in verse 15. If Satan himself poses falsely, it is not surprising if his agents do the same. How do they pose? As false teachers? As atheists? As infidels? The answer is no. They pose as **ministers of righteousness**. They profess to be **ministers** of religion. They profess to lead people in the way of truth and **righteousness**, but they are agents of the evil one.

Their **end will be according to their works**. They destroy — they **will** be destroyed. Their deeds lead men to their doom; they themselves will be led to final perdition.

E. Paul's Sufferings for Christ Support His Apostleship (11:16–33)

11:16 In saying all this, Paul hopes that **no one** will **think** of him as a boasting **fool**. But if they insist on doing so, yet let them **receive** him **as a fool** so **that** he **also** might **boast a little**.

Notice the **also** in the latter part of this verse: **that I also may boast a little**. This word has real significance. The false teachers were doing plenty of boasting. Paul says, in effect, "Even **if** you have to look on me as **a fool**, which I am not, even then **receive me** so that I may do a little boasting like these other men do."

11:17 This verse has two possible interpretations. Some suggest that what Paul is saying here, though it was truly inspired, was **not** given to him by commandment of **the Lord**.

The other interpretation is that what Paul is doing here, that is, boasting, is **not according to the Lord** in the sense that it did not follow the Lord's example. The Lord Jesus never boasted.

Phillips apparently adopts the first view by translating: "I am not now speaking as the Lord commands me but as a fool who must be 'in on' this business of boasting."

But we prefer the second view —that **boasting** was **not according to the Lord**, and that Paul was acting in seeming foolishness by thus engaging in self-glory. Ryrie comments: "He had to indulge in it [boasting], he says, against his natural instincts, so that he could call some significant facts to their attention."[41]

11:18 The Corinthians had recently heard a great deal from men who were engaging in self-glory according to corrupt human nature. If the Corinthians thought that the false teachers had sufficient cause for glorying, let them consider his boasts and see if they were not well-grounded.

11:19 Paul again resorts to satire. What he was asking them to do with himself, they were doing with others

daily. They considered themselves too **wise** to be taken in by foolishness. But that was exactly what was happening, as he goes on to explain.

11:20 They were willing to **put up with** the type of man described.

Who was the man described? It is obvious from what follows that he was the Judaizing teacher, the false apostle who was preying on the Corinthians. First, he brought them **into bondage**. This speaks undoubtedly of the slavery of the law (Acts 15:10). He taught that faith in Christ was not sufficient for salvation, but that people must also obey the Law of Moses.

Second, he devoured the saints, in the sense that he made heavy financial demands on them. He did not serve them for the sake of love, but was interested in the monetary return.

The expression, **one takes from you**, is a metaphor for fishing or hunting. The false teacher tried to make these people his prey, leading them about as he desired.

It was characteristic of these men that they exalted themselves by pride and boastfulness. By criticizing others, they always tried to make themselves appear greater in the sight of men.

Finally, they struck the believers **on the face**, a great indignity. We need not hesitate to understand this literally, because arrogant churchmen down through the years have actually struck their parishioners as a way of asserting their authority.

The apostle marvels that the Corinthians were willing to **put up with** such abusive treatment from these false teachers, and yet they were not willing to bear with him in his loving warnings and admonitions to them.

Darby states: "It is wonderful what people will suffer from what is false — very much more than they will endure from what is true."[42]

11:21 In this verse some have suggested that Paul is saying: "I speak thus, by way of disparaging myself, as though when I was with you in person, I had been weak and afraid to assert my authority in the way which these men do."

Another suggestion is that the meaning is: "In saying this, I disparage myself, because if that is strength, then I have been weak." Phillips' translation agrees with this latter view: "I am almost ashamed to say that I never did brave strong things like that to you."

Paul says that if the way the false teachers acted is real strength, then he has to say to his shame that he never showed that kind of strength, but rather weakness. Yet he quickly adds that in whatever aspect these other men had reason to be bold, he certainly had the same right to be bold as they. Moffatt states it well with these words: "but let them vaunt as they please, I am equal to them (mind, this is the role of a fool!)." With that introduction the Apostle Paul launches into one of the most magnificent sections in this Epistle, showing his right to the claim as a true servant of the Lord Jesus Christ.

You will remember that the question had been raised in the church at Corinth as to whether Paul was a true apostle. What credentials could he show that he had received a divine call? How could he prove to anyone's satisfaction that he was equal to the twelve apostles, for instance?

He is ready with his answer, but perhaps it is not exactly what we would expect. He does not bring forth a diploma to show he had graduated from some seminary. Neither does he bring an official letter, signed by the brethren in Jerusalem, stating that they had ordained him to the work. He does not present his personal accomplishments or skills. Rather, he brings before us a moving record of sufferings he had endured in the work of the gospel. Do not miss the drama and the pathos of this portion of 2 Corinthians. Picture the intrepid Paul as he hastens ceaselessly over land and sea on his missionary journeys, constrained by the love of Christ, and willing to endure untold hardships if only men might not perish for want of the gospel of Christ. Rarely can we read these verses without being deeply moved and greatly shamed.

11:22 The false teachers made much of their Jewish ancestry. They claimed to be full-blooded **Hebrews**, descended from Israel, and of **the seed of Abraham**. They still labored under the delusion that this family tree gave them

favor in the sight of God. They did not realize that God's ancient people, Israel, had now been set aside by God because of their rejection of the Messiah. They did not realize that as far as God was concerned, there was now no difference between Jew and Gentile: all were sinners, and all needed to be saved through faith in Christ alone.

It is useless for them to boast in this regard. Their lineage did not give them any superiority over Paul, since he, too, was a Hebrew, an Israelite, and of **the seed of Abraham**. But these were not the things which proved him to be an apostle of Christ. And so he hurries on to the main portion of his argument: in one respect they could not excel him — in hardships and sufferings.

11:23 They were **ministers of Christ** by profession; he was a servant "in devotion, labor and suffering." The Apostle Paul could never forget he was a follower of the *suffering* Savior. He realized that the servant is not above his master, and that an apostle could not expect better treatment in the world than his Master had received. Paul reckoned that the more faithfully he served Christ and reproduced the Savior, the more abundantly he would suffer at the hands of men. To him, suffering was the mark or badge of Christ's servants. Though he felt like **a fool** in thus boasting, necessity demanded that he speak the truth, and the truth was that these false teachers were not noted for their suffering. They chose the easy path. They avoided reproach, persecution, and dishonor. For this reason Paul felt they were in a poor position to attack him as a servant of Christ.

Let us now look at the catalog of hardships which Paul enumerates as supporting his claim to be a true apostle.

In labors more abundant. He thinks of the scope of his missionary journeys, how he had traveled widely throughout the Mediterranean area to make Christ known.

In stripes above measure. Here we have a description of the beatings which he received at the hands of the enemies of Christ, both heathen and Jewish.

In prisons more frequently. The only one of these imprisonments recorded in the Scripture, up to this time in Paul's career, is that of Acts 16:23, where he and Silas were thrown into the jail at Philippi. Now we learn that this was only one of many imprisonments, that Paul was no stranger to the dungeon.

In deaths often. Undoubtedly, as the apostle wrote this, he thought of his close escape from death at Lystra (Acts 14:19). But he could also look back on other similar times when life was all but gone as a result of his persecutions.

11:24 The Law of Moses forbade the Jews to inflict more than forty stripes at one time (Deut. 25:3). In order to make sure that they did not break this law, it was common for the Jews to inflict only thirty-nine stripes. These would be inflicted, of course, only in what they considered to be cases of deep guilt. The Apostle Paul here informs us that his own people according to the flesh had given him the full measure of punishment on **five** different occasions.

11:25 Three times I was beaten with rods. The only case mentioned in the NT is that which occurred at Philippi (Acts 16:22). But there were two other times when Paul suffered this painful and humiliating treatment.

Once I was stoned. This is no doubt the occasion at Lystra, to which we have already referred (Acts 14:19). This stoning was so severe that Paul's body was dragged out of the city, supposedly dead.

Three times I was shipwrecked. Not all Paul's trials were directly from the hands of men. At times he was tossed about by the convulsions of nature. None of the shipwrecks mentioned here is recorded for us. (The shipwreck in Acts 27 on the way to Rome occurred later in Paul's history.)

A night and a day I have been in the deep. Again, no experience recorded in Acts seems to answer to this. There is a question whether the deep here refers to a dungeon, or the sea. If it means the sea, was Paul on a raft or in an open boat? If not, he could only have survived such an experience in the water by direct, miraculous intervention by the Lord.

11:26 In journeys often. If you turn to the maps at the back of most Bibles, you will usually find one labeled "The Missionary Journeys of St. Paul." As you

follow the lines showing the general routes he traveled, and realize how primitive transportation facilities were in those days, you will realize a little more the depth of meaning of this expression!

Then Paul goes on to list eight different types of dangers which he encountered. There were **perils of waters**, referring to swollen rivers and streams. There were **perils of robbers**, since many of the routes which he traveled were infested with outlaws. He faced **perils from his own countrymen**, the Jews, as well as from **the Gentiles** to whom he sought to bring the gospel. There were **perils in the city**, such as Lystra, Philippi, Corinth, and Ephesus. Also he faced **perils in the wilderness**, probably referring to the thinly populated areas in Asia Minor and Europe. He met **perils in the sea** — from storms, hidden rocks, and perhaps pirates. Finally, there were **perils among false brethren**, no doubt referring to those Jewish legalists who posed as Christian teachers.

11:27 Weariness refers to Paul's incessant work, while **toil** carries with it the thought of the exhaustion and suffering connected with work.

In sleeplessness often. On many of his trips it would doubtless be necessary for him to sleep out in the open. But with dangers besetting him on every hand, it would be necessary for him to pass many a sleepless night, watching for the approach of danger.

In hunger and thirst, in fastings often. The great apostle was often forced to go hungry and thirsty as he went about serving the Lord. **Fastings** here may mean those of a voluntary nature, but more probably they were forced on him through food shortages.

In cold and nakedness. Sudden changes in weather, combined with the fact that he was often poorly shod and inadequately clothed, added these extreme forms of discomfort to his life. Hodge comments:

> The greatest of the apostles here appears before us, his back lacerated by frequent scourgings, his body worn by hunger, thirst, and exposure; cold and naked, persecuted by Jews and Gentiles, driven from place to place without any certain dwelling. This passage, more than any other, makes even the most laborious of the

modern ministers of Christ hide their face in shame. What have they ever done or suffered to compare with what this apostle did? It is a consolation to know that Paul is now as pre-eminent in glory, as he was here in suffering.[43]

11:28 Besides the other things, that is, those that were out of course or exceptional, Paul **daily** carried the steady burden of **all the** Christian **churches** on his heart. How significant it is that this climaxes all the other trials! Paul was a true pastor. He loved and cared for the Lord's people. He was not a hireling shepherd, but a true undershepherd of the Lord Jesus. That is exactly what he is seeking to prove in this portion of Scripture, and from the standpoint of every reasonable person, he certainly has won his point. His burden for the churches reminds us of the saying, "Church making is heartbreaking. Church mending is never ending."

11:29 This verse is closely linked with the previous verse. In verse 28 the apostle was saying he carried about daily the care of all the churches. Here he explains what he means. If he hears of some Christian who **is weak**, he feels that weakness himself. He endures the sufferings of others sympathetically. If he learns that some brother in Christ has been offended, he burns **with indignation**. What affects the people of God affects him. He sorrows in their tragedies and rejoices in their triumphs. And all this exhausts the nervous energy of a servant of Christ. How well Paul knew it!

11:30 Not his successes, not his gifts or abilities, but his weaknesses, his reproaches, the indignities he endured — these form the subject of his boasting. These are not the things that men usually boast about, or that make them famous.

11:31 In thinking of his sufferings and indignities, Paul's mind instinctively goes back to the most humiliating moment in his entire career. If he is going to glory in the things that concern his weakness, then he cannot fail to mention the experience he had at Damascus. For any man to boast of such a humiliating experience is so contrary to human nature that Paul here calls on **God** to attest the truthfulness of what he says.

11:32 Fuller details of this episode are given in Acts 9:19–25. After his conversion near **Damascus**, Paul began to preach the gospel in the synagogues there. At first his preaching aroused curious interest, but after a while the Jews plotted to kill him. They set a watch at the gates day and night, **desiring to arrest** him.

11:33 One night the disciples took the apostle, placed him **in a basket**, and lowered him **through a window in the wall** of the city to the ground outside. He was then able to escape.

But why does Paul mention this incident? J. B. Watson suggests:

> He takes hold of what men made an occasion of shame and ridicule and sets it in the light of being another proof that the paramount interest in his life was to serve the Lord Christ, for whose sake he was prepared to sacrifice his personal pride and appear as a coward in the eyes of men.[44]

F. Paul's Revelations Support His Apostleship (12:1–10)

12:1 The apostle wishes he didn't have **to boast** at all. It is not becoming or **profitable**, but under the circumstances it is necessary. So he will pass on from the lowest, most humiliating event in his ministry to the highest, most exalted. He will tell about a personal audience with the **Lord** Himself.

12:2 Paul knew **a man** who had this experience **fourteen years ago**. Although Paul does not identify him, there is no question but that he himself is the person referred to. In speaking of such an exalted experience, he will not mention himself personally, but will simply speak in a general way. The **man** referred to was **in Christ**, that is, a Christian.

12:3 Paul does not know **whether** he was **in the body or out of the body** at the time. Some have conjectured that this might have happened during one of Paul's persecutions, such as the one at Lystra. They say that he might have actually died and gone to heaven. But the text certainly does not demand such an interpretation. In fact, if Paul did not know whether he was **in the body or out of the body**, that is, alive or dead, at the time, it would be strange if any modern commentators could throw additional light on the subject!

The important thing is that this man **was caught up to the third heaven**. Scripture implies the existence of three heavens. The first is the atmosphere above us, that is, the blue sky. The second is the stellar heaven. The third is the highest heaven where the throne of God is.

It is clear from what follows that Paul was actually in the same place of bliss as that to which the Lord Jesus took the repentant thief after his death, that is, to God's dwelling place.

12:4 Paul **heard** the language of **Paradise** and understood what was spoken, but he was not allowed to repeat any of it when he came back to the earth. The **words** were **inexpressible** in the sense that they were too sacred to be uttered and therefore not for publication. G. Campbell Morgan writes:

> There are some who seem eager to talk of visions and revelations which they have had. The question is as to whether such eagerness is not proof that the visions and revelations are not "of the Lord." When they are granted (and they certainly are granted to the servants of God under certain circumstances), they produce a reverent reticence. They are too solemn, too overwhelming, to be lightly described or discussed, but the effect of them will be apparent in all life and service.[45]

12:5 When boasting of weakness, the apostle didn't mind mentioning himself. But when boasting of visions and revelations of the Lord, he would not apply them directly to himself, but would rather speak of the experience impersonally as having occurred to some man he knew. He was not denying that he was the one who had the experience, but was simply refusing to involve himself directly and personally.

12:6 There are many other great experiences of which the apostle could **boast**. If he should **desire** to engage in this boasting, he would **not be a fool** in doing so. Anything he would say would be **the truth**. But he is not going to do it, because he does not want **anyone** to **think** more highly of him than they actually find him **to be or** than they hear **from** him.

12:7 This whole section is a most accurate description of the life of a servant of Christ. It has its moments of deep humiliation, such as the event at Damascus. Then it has its mountain top experiences, such as Paul's exhilarating revelation. But normally after a servant of the Lord has enjoyed one of these experiences, the Lord allows him to suffer some **thorn in the flesh**. That is what we have here.

We learn many priceless lessons from this verse. First, it is proof that even divine revelations of the Lord do not correct **the flesh** in us. Even after the apostle had listened to the language of Paradise, he still had the old nature, and was in danger of falling into the snare of pride. As R. J. Reid has said:

> "A man in Christ" is safe in the presence of God as he listens to the untranslatable things spoken in paradise, but he needs "a thorn in the flesh" upon his return to earth, for the flesh in him would boast of his paradise experience.[46]

What was Paul's **thorn in the flesh**? All we can say for sure is that it was some bodily trial which God allowed to come into his life. No doubt the Lord purposely failed to specify exactly what the **thorn** was so that tried and tested saints down through the years might feel a closer kinship with the apostle as *they* suffer. Perhaps it was some form of eye disease,[47] perhaps an earache, perhaps malaria, perhaps migraine headaches, perhaps something connected with Paul's speech. Moorehead states: "The precise nature of it has been concealed perhaps that all afflicted ones may be encouraged and helped by Paul's unnamed yet painful experience."[48] Our trials may be very different from Paul's, but they should produce the same exercise and fruits.

The apostle describes the **thorn in the flesh** as **a messenger of Satan to buffet** him. In one sense it represented an effort on Satan's part to hinder Paul in the work of the Lord. But God is greater than Satan, and He used the **thorn** to further the work of the Lord by keeping Paul humble. Successful service for Christ depends on a weak servant. The weaker he is, the more the power of Christ accompanies his preaching.

12:8 **Three times** Paul **pleaded with the Lord** that the thorn in the flesh **might depart from** him.

12:9 Paul's prayer was answered,

but not in the way he had hoped. In effect, God said to Paul, "I will not remove the thorn, but I will do something better: I will give you grace to bear it. And just remember, Paul, that although I have not given you what you asked for, yet I am giving you what you need most deeply. You want my power and strength to accompany your preaching, don't you? Well, the best way to have that happen is for you to be kept in a place of weakness."

This was God's repeated answer to Paul's thrice repeated prayer. And it continues to be God's answer to his suffering people throughout the world. Better than the removal of trials and sufferings is the companionship of the Son of God in them, and the assurance of His strength and enabling grace.

Notice that God says, **My grace IS sufficient for you**. We don't have to ask Him to make His grace sufficient. It already **IS**!

The apostle is completely satisfied with the Lord's answer, so he says, **"Therefore most gladly I will rather boast in my infirmities, that the power of Christ may rest upon me."**

When the Lord explained the wisdom of His actions, Paul said in effect that that was the only way he would want it to be. So instead of complaining and grumbling about the thorn, he would **rather boast in** his **infirmities**. He would get down on his knees and thank the Lord for them. He would gladly endure them if only the power of Christ might rest upon him. J. Oswald Sanders puts it well:

> The world's philosophy is, "What can't be cured must be endured." But Paul radiantly testifies, "What can't be cured can be enjoyed. I enjoy weakness, sufferings, privations, and difficulties." So wonderful did he prove God's grace to be, that he even welcomed fresh occasions of drawing upon its fullness. "I gladly glory . . . I even enjoy" — my thorn."[49]

Emma Piechynska, the wife of a Polish nobleman, led a long life of frustration and disappointment. Yet her biographer paid a remarkable tribute to her triumphant faith: "She made magnificent bouquets out of the refusals of God!"

12:10 Naturally speaking, it is quite impossible for us to **take pleasure** in the type of experiences listed here. But the key to the understanding of the verse is found in the expression, **for Christ's sake**. We should be willing to endure in His cause, and in the furtherance of His gospel, things which we would not ordinarily endure for ourselves or for the sake of some loved one.

It is when we are conscious of our own weakness and nothingness that we most depend on the power of God. And it is when we are thus cast on Him in complete dependence that His power is manifested to us, and we are truly **strong**.

William Wilberforce, who led the fight to abolish slavery in the British Empire, was physically weak and frail, but he had deep faith in God. Boswell said of him, "I saw what seemed to me a shrimp become a whale."

In this verse Paul is obeying the word of the Lord in Matthew 5:11, 12. He is rejoicing when men reviled and persecuted him.

G. Paul's Signs Support His Apostleship (12:11–13)

12:11 At this point Paul seems to be weary of his seeming boastfulness. He feels he has **become a fool in boasting** as he has done. He should not have done it, but the Corinthians really **compelled** him. They should have been the ones to commend him when his critics leveled their cruel attacks against him. Though he was **nothing** in himself, yet he was certainly not behind **the most eminent apostles** in whom they gloried.

12:12 He reminds them that when he went to Corinth and preached the gospel, God attested the preaching with **the signs of an apostle**. These signs were miracle powers given to the apostles by God so that their hearers might know that they were indeed sent by the Lord.

The words **signs and wonders and mighty deeds** do not describe three different types of miracles, but rather miracles viewed in three different aspects. **Signs** were miracles that conveyed a definite meaning to human intelligence. **Wonders**, on the other hand, were so remarkable that they stirred up human emotions. **Mighty deeds** were performances that were obviously of superhuman power.

It is nice to notice that Paul says that **the signs of an apostle** *were accomplished* among them. He uses the passive voice. He does not claim credit for them himself, but says God did them through him.

12:13 As far as the display of miracles was concerned, the Corinthians were not a bit **inferior to other churches**. They witnessed as many of these, at the hands of the Apostle Paul, as the **other churches** which he visited. In what sense then were they **inferior to** any of **the other churches**? The only difference Paul can see is that he had not been **burdensome** to the Corinthians. That is, he had not insisted on financial assistance from them. If this made them **inferior**, then Paul asks them to **forgive** him **this wrong**. This was the only "sign" of an apostle he did not insist on!

H. Paul's Pending Visit to Corinth (12:14–13:1)

12:14 **Now for the third time I am ready to come to you.** This can be understood to mean the apostle had been *ready* to visit Corinth three times, but that he had only *been there* once. He did not go the second time, because he did not want to deal harshly with the believers. Now he is **ready** to go **the third time**, and this will be his second visit.

Or it may mean he was about to make his **third** visit. The first is recorded in Acts 18:1. The second was the sorrowful visit (2 Cor. 2:1; 13:1). This will be **the third**.

When he does come, Paul is determined that **he will not be burdensome to** them. He means, of course, he will not accept any financial return from them. He will be independent of them as far as his support is concerned. The reason for this is that he was not after their material wealth but after themselves. Paul was more interested in people than he was in things.

He wants to play the part of a parent, as far as the Corinthians are concerned. **Children ought not to lay up for the parents, but the parents for the children.** This is simply a statement of life as we know it. In the normal course of events,

it is **the parents** who work hard and diligently to see that the **children** have food and clothing. The **children** ordinarily do not take this care for **the parents**. So Paul is saying he would like to be permitted to act as a parent to them.

One should be careful not to read too much into this sentence. It does *not* mean that parents ought to lay up wealth for the future of their children. This has nothing to do with future needs, but only with present necessities. Paul was thinking only of the supply of his immediate needs as he was serving the Lord in Corinth. He was determined that he would not depend on the saints there. There was no thought in his mind that they ought to be laying up a nest egg for his old age or that he should be doing that for them.

12:15 Here we have a beautiful glimpse into the unquenchable love of the Apostle Paul for the people of God in Corinth. He was willing **gladly** to give himself in tireless service and sacrifice for their souls, that is, for their spiritual welfare. He loved them more abundantly than the false teachers who were in their midst did, yet he was **loved less** by them. But that did not make any difference. Even if he had no hope of return of love from them, he would keep on loving them. In this he was truly following the Lord.

12:16 The apostle takes up the very words which his critics were using against him. They were saying, in effect, "Well, granted that Paul himself did not take money from you directly. However, he used trickery to get it. He sent delegates to you, and they took money back to him."

12:17 If I did not sponge off you directly, **did I** send others who did? The apostle asks the Corinthians directly if these charges against him were true.

12:18 He answers his own question. The expression, **I urged Titus,** probably means **I urged Titus** *to visit you.* But Paul did not send him alone. He **sent** another **brother** along **with him** lest there might be a breath of suspicion about Paul's motives. What happened when Titus reached Corinth? Did he insist on his rights? Did he ask the Corinthians to support him? Did he try to make a gain of them? No, it appears from this passage that Titus worked for his living by engaging in some secular occupation. That is suggested by the questions, **"Did we not walk in the same spirit? Did we not walk in the same steps?"** In other words, both Titus and Paul followed the same policy of working so that they would not have to be supported by the Corinthians.

12:19 The Corinthians would think, from all that Paul had said, that his aim was simply to **excuse** himself **to** them as if they were his judges. On the contrary, what he really was doing was writing these things to them as in the presence of **God**, in order that they might be built up. He wanted to strengthen them in the Christian life and warn them against the perils that were facing them. He was more interested in helping them than in defending his own reputation.

The supplied words (italics) in the expression, *we do* all things, might perhaps better read *we write* all these things (cf. 2 Cor. 13:10).

12:20 Paul desired that when he visited Corinth, he might find the Christians going along happily one with another, having renounced the false teachers, and having acknowledged the authority of the apostles.

Also when he visited them, he wanted to come with joy and not with heaviness. He would be greatly grieved if he should find **contentions, jealousies, outbursts of wrath, selfish ambitions**, and other forms of carnal conflict.

12:21 After all, these Corinthians were Paul's joy and crown of rejoicing. They were his glorying. He certainly did not want to come to them and have to be ashamed of them. Neither did he want to have to **mourn** over **many who** had **sinned** and had **not repented of** their **uncleanness, fornication, and lewdness**.

To whom does Paul refer as the **many** who had **practiced** these sins? It is only reasonable to assume they were in the church in Corinth; otherwise he would not be discussing them in this way in a Letter to the church. But it cannot be assumed that they were true believers. It specifically says they **practiced** these sins, and Paul elsewhere makes it clear

that anyone whose life is characterized by such behavior cannot inherit the kingdom of God (1 Cor. 6:9, 10). The apostle would **mourn** over them because they had not repented and would therefore have to be excommunicated.

Darby points out that this chapter opens with the third heaven and closes with vile sins on earth. Between the two, he notes that there is the remedy — the power of Christ resting on the Apostle Paul.[50]

13:1 Paul was about to visit Corinth. When he did, the cases of sin among the believers would be investigated. Such investigations would proceed according to the divine principle laid down in Deuteronomy 19:15: **"By the mouth of two or three witnesses every word shall be established."** Paul did not mean he would be conducting the trial. This would be done by the local church, and he would act as a counselor in the matter.

I. Paul's Apostleship Supported by the Corinthians Themselves (13:2–6)

13:2 On his second visit, otherwise unrecorded, Paul had warned them he would deal severely with the offenders. **Now** although **absent**, he foretells them all that when he comes **again** he **will not spare those who have** been sinning.

13:3 The Corinthians had been deceived by the false teachers into doubting that Paul was a true apostle. In fact, they actually challenged him to give them some **proof** that he was an authentic spokesman for God. What were his credentials that **Christ** was really **speaking** through him? The apostle begins his reply by quoting their impertinent request: **"since you seek a proof of Christ speaking in me . . ."**

Then in a parenthesis, he reminds them that Christ had revealed Himself to them through him in a **mighty** way. There had been nothing **weak** about the tremendous revolution in their lives when they believed the gospel message.

13:4 Mention of the words "weak" and "mighty" reminded Paul of the paradox of strength out of weakness which was seen in the Savior's life and is seen in the lives of His servants. Our Lord **was crucified in weakness, yet He lives**

by the power of God. So His followers are feeble in themselves, yet the Lord demonstrates His **power** through them. When Paul says, **we shall live with Him by the power of God toward you**, he is not speaking of the resurrection. Rather he means that when he visits them, he will demonstrate the mighty **power of God** in dealing with those who were sinning. They said he was weak and contemptible; he will show them he can be strong in exercising discipline!

13:5 This verse connects with the first part of verse 3 as follows: "Since you seek a proof of Christ speaking in me . . . **examine yourselves as to whether you are in the faith.**" They themselves were the proof of his apostleship. It was through him that they were led to the Savior. If they wanted to see his credentials, they should look at themselves.

Verse 5 is often misused to teach that we should look *within ourselves* for assurance of salvation, but this could lead to discouragement and doubt. Assurance of salvation comes first and foremost through the word of God. The moment we trust Christ we can know on the authority of the Bible that we have been born again. As time goes on, we do find other evidences of the new life — a new love for holiness, a new hatred of sin, love of the brethren, practical righteousness, obedience, and separation from the world.

But Paul is not telling the Corinthians to engage in self-examination as a proof of their salvation. Rather he is asking them to find in their salvation a proof of his apostleship.

There were only two possibilities: either **Jesus Christ** was **in** them, or they were **disqualified**, spurious. The word translated **disqualified** was used to describe metals which, when tested, were found to be false. So the Corinthians were either true believers, or they were **disqualified** by failure to pass the test.

13:6 If they concluded that they were genuinely saved, then it must follow that the Apostle Paul was genuine and **not disqualified**. The wonderful transformation that took place in the lives of the Corinthians could scarcely have come through a false teacher.

J. Paul's Desire to Do the Corinthians Good (13:7–10)

13:7 Paul now continues the subject of the discipline of sinning members of the church at Corinth. He states he is praying **to God that** the Corinthians would **do no evil** by countenancing sin in their midst, but that they would work ceaselessly toward the discipline and restoration of the sinning members. He does not pray this in order that he himself might **appear approved**, or might be seen in a better light. He does not want them to do it simply because he could then point to their obedience as an evidence of his authority. That is not the thought at all. He wants them to do it because it is *right* and *honest*. And he would rather have them do that, even **though** it meant that he might **seem disqualified**.

Here again we have an evidence of the unselfishness of Paul. In his prayer life his thoughts were constantly on what was for the good of others and not for his own recognition. If Paul went to Corinth with a rod, asserted his authority, and succeeded in gaining obedience to his instructions concerning discipline, then he could use this as an argument against the false teachers. He could say this was evidence of his lawful authority. But he would rather that the Corinthians take the necessary action themselves, in his absence, even if that might put him in an unfavorable light as far as the legalists were concerned.

13:8 The **we** of this verse probably refers to the apostles. Paul is saying that all they do must be done with a view to the furtherance of **the truth** of God, and not with any selfish motives in view. Even in the matter of discipline, no thought of personal vindictiveness must enter. All must be carried out with a view to the glory of God and the good of one's fellow Christians.

13:9 Here again the apostle expresses his utter unselfishness as far as the Corinthians were concerned. If his weakness, humiliation, and reproach resulted in their being strengthened in the things of God, then he was **glad**. While he thus rejoiced, he also prayed **that** they might **be made complete**. With regard to the subject of dealing with sinful offenders in their midst, Paul prayed that they might become **complete** and entire. That the whole will of God might be worked out in their lives was his fervent desire. As Hodge puts it, "Paul prayed that they might be perfectly restored from the state of confusion, contention and evil into which they had fallen."[51]

13:10 It was with their perfecting in view that he wrote this Letter to them. He would rather write while **absent** from them that these results might be secured, than that **being present** he **should** have to **use sharpness**, as authorized by **the Lord**. But even if he were **present** and dealt severely with them, it would still be **for** their **edification and not for** their **destruction**.

K. Paul's Gracious Trinitarian Farewell (13:11–14)

13:11 The apostle now draws this rather stormy Epistle to an abrupt close. After bidding them **farewell** (the Greek greeting literally means "rejoice"), he delivers four exhortations. First, they should **become complete**. The verb is the same as the one used of mending nets in Matthew 4:21, and can also mean "mend your ways." The Corinthians were to stop quarreling and sinning, and live in harmony with each other.

Be of good comfort may also be understood as "be encouraged" or "be exhorted." They had been given strong admonitions by the Apostle Paul. Here he tells them to receive these admonitions in a good spirit and to act on them.

Be of one mind. The only way, of course, in which Christians can **be of one mind** is to have *the mind of Christ*. It is to think as He thinks, to bring all their thoughts and reasonings in subjection to Himself.

Live in peace. It is evident from 12:20 that there had been disputes and wranglings among them. This is always the case when legalism is allowed to enter. So Paul here told them first to discipline the offenders and to get along with their fellow Christians in peace.

If they do this, **the God of love and peace will be with them**. Of course, in one sense the Lord is *always* with His people. But this means He will manifest Himself to them in a special nearness and dearness if they are obedient in these regards.

13:12 The **holy kiss** was a characteristic greeting among Christians in the days of the apostles. It is designated as a *holy* kiss, meaning it was not just a symbol of artificial affection, but that it was sincere and pure. It is still practiced by Christians in many countries today. However, in some countries, kissing among men could be misinterpreted as a sign of homosexuality. Practicing such a tradition would not be obligatory if it brought serious reproach on the Christian testimony. In such cases a holy handshake would be preferable. Hodge says:

> It is not a command of perpetual obligation, as the spirit of the command is that Christians should express their mutual love in the way sanctioned by the age and community in which they live.[52]

13:13 The greetings from **all the saints** would remind the Corinthians of the breadth of the fellowship into which they had been brought, and would also tell them that other churches were looking on to see their progress and obedience to the Lord.

13:14 Here we have one of the lovely benedictions of the NT, and the only one that embraces all three members of the Trinity.

Lenski concludes:

> With the picture of the great apostle spreading his hands over the Corinthians with this profound New Testament benediction his voice sinks into silence. But the benediction remains upon our hearts.[53]

ENDNOTES

[1](1:2) James Denney, *The Second Epistle to the Corinthians*, p. 11.

[2](1:10) The critical (NU) text has one past and two future tenses.

[3](1:20) H. W. Cragg, *The Keswick Week*, p. 126.

[4](2:11) J. Sidlow Baxter, *Awake My Heart*, taken from the Nov. 10 reading, "Intoxication with Error."

[5](2:14) A. T. Robertson, *The Glory of the Ministry*, p. 32.

⁶(2:14) Frederick Brotherton Meyer, *Paul*, p. 77.

⁷(2:15) *Ibid.*, p. 78.

⁸(2:17) The majority text is worded very strongly: "as the rest"; no doubt this is hyperbole, as so often is the case in 2 Corinthians.

⁹(2:17) Robertson, *Ministry*, p. 47.

¹⁰(3:6) J. M. Davies, *The Epistles to the Corinthians*, pp. 168, 169.

¹¹(3:9) Charles Hodge, *A Commentary on the Second Epistle to the Corinthians*, p. 61.

¹²(3:10) Robertson, *Ministry*, p. 70.

¹³(3:10) Denney, *Second Corinthians*, p. 123.

¹⁴(3:13) F. W. Grant, "2 Corinthians," *The Numerical Bible*, VI:547.

¹⁵(3:14) Hodge, *Second Corinthians*, p. 71.

¹⁶(3:17) The NKJV translators took this as a reference to the Holy Spirit, and so capitalized it. The original was in *all* capitals (uncials), hence either is possible.

¹⁷(3:18) Denney, *Second Corinthians*, pp. 139, 140.

¹⁸(3:18) J. N. Darby, *Notes on I and II Corinthians*, pp. 189, 190.

¹⁹(4:7) J. H. Jowett, *Life in the Heights*, p. 65.

²⁰(4:12) Robertson, *Ministry*, p. 157.

²¹(4:16) H. A. Ironside, further documentation unavailable.

²²(4:17) In Hebrew the word for "glory" is derived from the root "to be heavy," which probably suggested Paul's wording.

²³(4:17) William C. Moorehead, *Outline Studies in the New Testament: Acts to Ephesians*, p. 191.

²⁴(4:17) F. E. Marsh, *Fully Furnished*, p. 103.

²⁵(4:18) Jowett, *Life in the Heights*, pp. 68, 69.

²⁶(5:15) Denney, *Second Corinthians*, p. 199.

²⁷(5:16) David Smith, further documentation unavailable.

²⁸(5:18) *A New and Concise Bible Dictionary*, p. 652.

²⁹(6:4) Denney, *Second Corinthians*, p. 230.

³⁰(6:9) "As unknown and yet well known" is fittingly inscribed on the tombstone of John Nelson Darby (1800-1882), who had a worldwide ministry not unlike that of Paul.

³¹(6:10) Robertson, *Ministry*, p. 238.

³²(6:11) A. W. Tozer, *The Root of the Righteous*, 1955.

³³(6:16) Denney, *Second Corinthians*, p. 246.

³⁴(7:8) George Williams, *Student's Commentary on the Holy Scriptures*, p. 904.

³⁵(7:9) Hodge, *Second Corinthians*, p. 182.

³⁶(8:7) Denney, *Second Corinthians*, p. 267.

³⁷(8:9) Moorehead, *Acts to Ephesians*, pp. 179, 180.

³⁸(8:15) Hodge, *Second Corinthians*, p. 206.

³⁹(8:21) G. Campbell Morgan, *Searchlights from the Word*, p. 345.

⁴⁰(9:7) Jowett, *Life in the Heights*, p. 78.

⁴¹(11:17) Charles C. Ryrie, *The Ryrie Study Bible, New King James Version*, p. 1797.

⁴²(11:20) J. N. Darby, *Notes on I and II Corinthians*, p. 236.

⁴³(11:27) Hodge, *Second Corinthians*, p. 275.

⁴⁴(11:33) J. B. Watson, further documentation unavailable.

⁴⁵(12:4) Morgan, *Searchlights*, p. 346.

⁴⁶(12:7) R. J. Reid, *How Job Learned His Lesson*, p. 69.

⁴⁷(12:7) See Galatians 4:15 and 6:11.

⁴⁸(12:7) Moorehead, *Acts to Ephesians*, p. 197.

⁴⁹(12:9) J. Oswald Sanders, *A Spiritual Clinic*, pp. 32, 33.

⁵⁰(12:21) Darby, *I and II Corinthians*, p. 253.

⁵¹(13:9) Hodge, *Second Corinthians*, p. 309.

⁵²(13:12) *Ibid.*, p. 312.

⁵³(13:14) R. C. H. Lenski, *The Interpretation of St. Paul's First and Second Epistles to the Corinthians*, p. 1341.

BIBLIOGRAPHY

Darby, J. N. *Notes on I and II Corinthians.* London: G. Morrish, n.d.

Davies, J. M. *The Epistles to the Corinthians.* Bombay: Gospel Literature Service, 1975.

Denney, James. *The Second Epistle to the Corinthians.* London: Hodder & Stoughton, 1894.

Erdman, C. R. *Second Epistle of Paul to the*

Corinthians. London: Philadelphia: Westminster Press, 1929.

Grant, F. W. "2 Corinthians," *The Numerical Bible*. Vol. 6, Acts – 2 Corinthians. New York: Loizeaux Brothers, 1901.

Hodge, Charles. *The Second Epistle to the Corinthians*. London: The Banner of Truth Trust, 1959.

Hughes, Philip E. *Commentary on the Second Epistle to the Corinthians*. Grand Rapids: Wm. B. Eerdmans Publishing Co., 1962.

Kelly, William. *Notes on the Second Epistle to the Corinthians*. London: G. Morrish, 1882.

Lenski, R. C. H. *The Interpretation of St. Paul's First and Second Epistles to the Corinthians*. Columbus: Wartburg Press, 1937.

Luck, G. Coleman. *Second Corinthians*. Chicago: Moody Press, 1959.

Robertson, A. T. *The Glory of the Ministry*. New York: Fleming H. Revell Co., 1911.

Wilson, Geoffrey B. *2 Corinthians: A Digest of Reformed Comment*. London: The Banner of Truth Trust, 1973.

THE EPISTLE TO THE GALATIANS

Introduction

"The 'Magna Charta' of spiritual freedom for the whole world and for all time." — Charles R. Erdman

I. Unique Place in the Canon

A large percentage of English-speaking peoples, as well as many French people, are of Celtic origin — that is, Scottish, Irish, Welsh, or Breton. These ethnic groups especially will be fascinated to know that one of Paul's earliest letters was written to their ancestors ("Galatia," "Celt," and "Gaul" are all related words).

About 278 B.C. a large number of these European Gauls migrated to what is today Turkey. Their boundaries became fixed and their state was named "Galatia." Many people think they can see "Celtic" traits in such things as the changeableness of the Galatians (in Acts 13 and Galatians 3:1, e.g.).

Be that as it may, the Epistle to the Galatians fulfills a crucial role in early Christianity. Though often seen as a "first draft" of Romans (since it covers the gospel of grace, Abraham, the law, etc., in a similar manner), Galatians is a stern, impassioned effort to save Christianity from becoming just a messianic sect of legalistic Judaism. How the Galatians themselves reacted we do not know, but the gospel of grace, apart from the works of the law, *did* triumph, and Christianity went on to become a global faith.

During the Reformation, Galatians became so important to Luther that he referred to the book as "my Kaethe" (his affectionate name for his wife). His *Commentary on Galatians* influenced not merely scholars, but the common folk, and is still in print and studied.

II. Authorship†

The genuineness of Galatians as a Pauline Epistle has never seriously been in question. It is quoted as Paul's by Polycarp, Ignatius, Justin Martyr, Origen, Irenaeus, Tertullian, and Clement of Alexandria. It is listed in the Muratorian Canon as Paul's and, probably due to its strong anti-Judaizing language, receives first place in Marcion's *Apostolicon*. The *external evidence* is thus very strong.

The *internal evidence* for Paul's authorship starts with the personal references in 1:1 and 5:2, and the remark near the end (6:11) that he wrote it in "large letters." This is widely taken to refer to a possible eye disease of the apostle. Supporting evidence includes the fact that the Galatians once would have been willing to pluck their *eyes* out for Paul. Many historical notes dovetail with Acts. The dispute over circumcision and whether Paul was a real apostle were flaming issues in the 50's and 60's but dead issues soon afterward.

III. Date

The date of the Epistle depends on the precise meaning of the expressions "the churches of Galatia" and "Galatians." If it refers to the southern part of Asia Minor, an earlier date, even before the Jerusalem Council, is likely. If the northern part is meant, a later date is called for.

Geographically the term "Galatia" was used for the north and *politically* it was used for the south — the Roman province of Galatia.

The North Galatian theory was standard until the 1800's and is largely held by German scholars still. There is no evidence that Paul ever ministered to the

"Galatians" of that area, but this certainly does not rule it out.

Especially since Sir William Ramsay made it popular, the South Galatian theory has been widely held in Great Britain and North America. Since Luke gives much space in Acts to Paul's missionary work in this area (Antioch in Pisidia, Iconium, Lystra, and Derbe), it would seem likely that the apostle would have written to his converts there. Since Paul evangelized southern Galatia on his First Missionary Journey and revisited it on his Second, an early date is possible for Galatians. If the letter was penned *before* the Jerusalem Council of Acts 15 (A.D. 49), this would explain why the question of circumcision was still a very live issue. Theodor Zahn, a leading conservative German scholar, dates Galatians during Paul's Second Missionary Journey, from Corinth. This would make it his very earliest Epistle.

If the northern theory is correct, Galatians was probably written in the 50's, perhaps as early as 53, but probably later.

If, as we believe, the southern theory is correct, and especially if Galatians was written before Paul attended the Jerusalem Council, which decided the issue of circumcision for Gentile Christians, the book can be dated A.D. 48.

IV. Background and Theme†

During his early missionary journeys, the Apostle Paul visited Asia Minor, preaching the glorious message that salvation is by faith in Christ alone. Many

†*See p. ii.*

of his hearers were saved, and churches were formed, several of them in Galatia. The inhabitants of Galatia were known to be restless, warlike, and changeable.

After Paul had left this area, false teachers entered the churches and introduced wrong doctrine. They taught that salvation was by faith in Christ *plus* keeping the law. Their message was a mixture of Christianity and Judaism, of grace and law, of Christ and Moses. They also tried to turn the Galatians away from Paul by saying he was not a genuine apostle of the Lord and, therefore, his message was not reliable. They sought to destroy confidence in the message by undermining confidence in the messenger. Many of the Galatian Christians were affected by their evil suggestions.

What sorrow and disappointment must have filled Paul's heart when such news from Galatia reached him! Had his labors among these people been in vain? Could the Christians still be rescued from these Judaistic, legalistic teachings? Paul was stirred to swift and decisive action. He took up his pen and wrote this indignant letter to his beloved children in the faith. In it, he sets forth the true character of salvation as being given by grace from beginning to end, not earned by law-keeping either in whole or in part. Good works are not a condition of salvation, but a fruit of it. The Christian has died to the law; he leads a life of holiness, not by his own efforts, but by the power of the indwelling Holy Spirit of God.

OUTLINE

III. PRACTICAL: PAUL DEFENDS CHRISTIAN FREEDOM IN
THE SPIRIT (5:2–6:18)
   A. The Peril of Legalism (5:2–15)
   B. Power for Holiness (5:16–25)
   C. Practical Exhortations (5:26–6:10)
   D. Conclusion (6:11–18)

Commentary

I. PERSONAL: PAUL DEFENDS HIS AUTHORITY (Chaps. 1, 2)

A. Paul's Purpose in Writing (1:1–10)

1:1 At the outset, **Paul** insists that his call as **an apostle** was divine. It did **not** originate with **men, nor** was it communicated from God **through** some **man.** It came directly **through Jesus Christ and God the Father who raised Him from the dead.** A man who is thus called by God alone and is responsible to God alone has freedom to preach God's message without fear of man. So the apostle was independent of the twelve apostles and of everybody else, both as to his message and his ministry.

In this verse, the deity of Christ is both stated and implied. It is stated in the expression **nor through man, but through Jesus Christ.** It is implied by the way in which Paul links together **Jesus Christ and God the Father**, putting them on equality with one another. Then **God the Father** is mentioned as the One **who raised** Jesus **from the dead.** Paul had good reason to remind the Galatians of this. The resurrection was proof of God's complete satisfaction with the work of Christ for our salvation. Apparently, the Galatians were not wholly satisfied with the Savior's work, because they were trying to improve on it by adding their own efforts at law-keeping.

Paul was called by the *risen* Christ, in contrast to the twelve apostles, who were called by the Lord Jesus during His earthly ministry. Ever afterward, the resurrection formed an important part of his message.

1:2 The apostle associates himself with **all the brethren who** were **with** him. These **brethren** joined in appealing to the Galatians to hold on to the truth of the gospel. This Letter **to the churches of Galatia** shows a deliberate lack of warmth. Ordinarily Paul addressed believers as "the church of God," "saints," or "the faithful in Christ Jesus." He often expressed thanks for the Christians, or praise for their virtues. Frequently he mentioned individuals by name. But there is none of that here. The seriousness of the error in the Galatian churches caused him to be stern and cool toward them.

1:3 **Grace and peace** are two of the great words of the gospel. **Grace** is God's undeserved kindness toward ungodly sinners. Instead of asking man to *do*, it tells what God has *done*, and invites men to receive salvation as a free gift. Scofield says, "Instead of looking for good men whom it may approve, grace is looking for condemned, guilty, speechless, and helpless men whom it may save, sanctify, and glorify."

Peace is the result of grace. When a sinner receives the Savior, he has **peace** with God. He rests in the knowledge that the penalty for his sins has been paid, that all his sins have been forgiven, and that he will never be condemned. But grace not only *saves*; it *keeps* as well. And we need not only the blessing of *peace with God* but *the peace of God* also. These are the blessings which Paul wishes for the Galatians as he opens his Letter. Surely the Galatians realized that these blessings could never come by the law. The law brought a curse on all who broke its precepts. It never brought peace to a single soul.

1:4 Paul next reminds his readers of the tremendous cost of their salvation. Note the words: our Lord Jesus Christ, **who gave Himself for our sins.** If He **gave Himself** to settle the sin question, then it is both unnecessary and impossible for us to add to such a work, or to help atone for our sins by law-keeping.

Christ is the sole and sufficient Savior. Christ died to **deliver us from this present evil age**. This includes not only the moral and political corruption of this age, but also the religious world which mixes rituals and ceremonies with faith in Christ. It was especially timely, therefore, for the Galatians to be reminded that they were going back into the very system from which Christ had died to rescue them! Christ's redemption was **according to the will of our God and Father**. This places the credit where it belongs — not in man's puny efforts, but rather in the sovereign will of God. It emphasizes that Christ is God's way of salvation and that there is no other.

Verse 4 should be a reminder that God is not interested in improving the world, or making men comfortable in it, but in delivering men from it. Our priorities should coincide with His.

1:5 According to the gospel of grace, all the **glory** for man's salvation goes to God the Father and to the Lord Jesus Christ. Man cannot share this glory as a co-savior by keeping the law.

Each phrase in these five verses is meaningful, much truth being expressed in a few words. Paul has stated in embryo the two main subjects which will occupy the rest of the Epistle — *his own authority as an apostle* and *his gospel of the grace of God*. He is now ready to speak directly to the Galatians concerning the problem at hand.

1:6, 7 Paul confronts the Galatians at once on their readiness to accept error. He is amazed that they should so suddenly surrender the truth of the gospel, and he solemnly labels their action as deserting God for a false gospel. God had **called** them into **the grace of Christ**; now they were putting themselves under the curse of the law. They had accepted the true gospel; now they were abandoning it for **a different gospel** which was not good news at all. It was just a perverted message, a mixture of grace and law.

1:8, 9 Paul twice pronounces the solemn curse of God on anyone who preaches **any other gospel**. God has only one message for doomed sinners: He offers salvation by grace through faith, entirely apart from law-keeping. Those who proclaim any other way of salvation

must necessarily be doomed. How very serious it is to preach a message that results in the eternal destruction of souls! Paul was not tolerant of such false teachers and neither should we be. John Stott warns:

> We are not to be dazzled, as many people are, by the person, gifts or office of teachers in the church. They may come to us with great dignity, authority and scholarship. They may be bishops or archbishops, university professors or even the pope himself. But if they bring a gospel other than the gospel preached by the apostles and recorded in the New Testament, they are to be rejected. We judge them by the gospel; we do not judge the gospel by them. As Dr. Alan Cole expresses it, "The outward person of the messenger does not validate his message; rather, the nature of the message validates the messenger."[1]

Notice that the apostle says **an angel from heaven**, not "an angel from God." **An angel from heaven** could conceivably bring a false message, but an angel from God could not. Language could not express more clearly the uniqueness of the gospel. It is the *only* way of salvation. Self-effort or human merit have no part. The gospel alone offers salvation without money or price. Whereas the law has a curse for those who fail to *keep* it, the gospel has a curse for those who seek to *change* it.

1:10 Paul is probably reminded at this point that his enemies accused him of changing the message to suit his audience, so he asks, in effect, "In insisting that there is only one gospel, am I trying to please **men, or God**?" Obviously he is not trying to **please men**, because they hate the suggestion that there is only one way to heaven. If Paul changed his message to suit **men**, he **would not be a bondservant of Christ**; in fact, he would be inviting the wrath of God to fall upon himself.

B. Paul's Defense of His Message and Ministry (1:11–2:10)

1:11, 12 The apostle now presents six arguments in defense of his message and ministry. First, the gospel was received by divine revelation and independently of man. It was **not according to man** in the sense that man did not originate it. A moment's reflection will confirm this. Paul's gospel makes everything of God and nothing of man. This is not the kind of salvation that men would devise! Paul **neither received it from** some other person, **nor was** he **taught it** through books. **It came** to him by direct **revelation** from **Jesus Christ** Himself.

1:13, 14 Secondly, Paul's failure to include Jewish law in his gospel could not be laid to any ignorance of **Judaism** on his part. By birth and training, he was steeped in the law. By personal choice, he became a notorious persecutor of **the church**. In passionate zeal **for the traditions of** his **fathers**, he surpassed many other Jews of his own age. Therefore, his gospel of salvation by faith apart from the law could certainly not be attributed to any ignorance of the law. Why then did he omit it from his preaching? Why did his gospel run counter to his background, his natural inclinations, and his whole religious development? Simply because it was not the result of his own thinking, but was given to him directly by God.

1:15–17 Thirdly, the first few years of his ministry were carried on independently of the other **apostles**. Paul now demonstrates his independence of other men in connection with his gospel. After his conversion, he **did not immediately confer with** human leaders, **nor did** he **go up to Jerusalem** where the other **apostles** were. Instead, he **went to Arabia**, then **returned again to Damascus**. His determination to avoid Jerusalem was not out of disrespect for his fellow-apostles; it was rather because he had been commissioned by the risen Lord Himself and given a unique ministry to the Gentiles (2:8). Hence his gospel and his service needed no human authorization. He was independent of man altogether.

Several expressions in these verses deserve careful consideration. Note the expression in verse 15: **God . . . separated me from my mother's womb**. Paul realized that even before his birth, he had been set apart by God for a special work. He adds that God **called me through His grace**, referring to his conversion on the road to Damascus. If he had received what he deserved at that

moment, he would have been cast into hell. But Christ, in wonderful grace, saved him and sent him out to preach the faith he had sought to destroy. In verse 16 he shows that God intended **to reveal His Son in** him. This gives us a wonderful view of God's purpose in calling us — to reveal His Son in *us*, so that we may represent the Lord Jesus to the world. He reveals Christ to our hearts (v. 16) in order that He may display Christ through us (vv. 16–23) in order that God may be glorified in this display (v. 24). Paul's special assignment was to preach Christ among the Gentiles.

In verse 17 he says, **"I went to Arabia."** Every servant of the Lord needs a time of seclusion and meditation. Moses had his forty years on the backside of the desert. David was alone with God while he tended sheep on the hillsides of Judea.

1:18–20 Fourthly, when Paul finally visited Jerusalem, he met only **Peter** and **James**. Apart from that, he was relatively unknown to the churches in Judea (1:21–24). To demonstrate further his independence of the other apostles, Paul recounts that he did not visit Jerusalem until at least **three years** after his conversion. He went up to make the acquaintance of **Peter**[2] — a personal, not an official visit (Acts 9:26–29). While there, he also met **James, the Lord's brother**. His stay with Peter lasted only **fifteen days** — scarcely long enough for a training course! Moreover, the text indicates he was on perfect equality with these servants of the Lord.

1:21–24 After that, he spent much of his time in **the regions of Syria and Cilicia** — so much so that **the churches of Judea** did not know him personally. All they knew was that this one who had treated the Christians so cruelly was now a Christian himself and was preaching Christ to others. Because of this **they glorified God** for what He had done in the life of Paul. (Do others glorify God because of the change in our lives?)

2:1 Fifthly, during Paul's later visit to Jerusalem, the apostles there agreed that his gospel was divine (2:1–10). Because the church began at Jerusalem, and the apostles more or less made that city their headquarters, certain Christians felt that the church there was "the mother church." Thus Paul had to contend with the charge that he was somewhat inferior because he was not one of the Jerusalem apostles. He replies with a detailed account of his later trip **to Jerusalem**. Whether this was **fourteen years** after his conversion, or after his first trip, we do not know. We do know that he received a revelation from Christ to go, together **with Barnabas**, his co-worker, and **Titus**, a Gentile converted through Paul's ministry. The Judaizers had insisted that Titus be circumcised for full salvation. The Apostle Paul was adamantly opposed because he realized that the truth of the gospel was at stake. (Later when Paul himself circumcised Timothy, no important principle was involved — Acts 16:3.)

E. F. Kevan says:

> Paul saw that circumcision for justification was not the innocent little rite that the unthinking man might assume it to be. To undergo circumcision was to seek to be justified by a legalistic method of law-keeping, and thus to deny the very foundations of grace.[3]

2:2 When Paul reached Jerusalem he **communicated to them that gospel which** he preached **among the Gentiles, but privately to those who were of reputation, lest by any means** he **might run, or had run, in vain**. Why did Paul speak **privately** to the spiritual leaders rather than to the entire assembly? Did he want them to approve his gospel, in case he had been preaching something false? Obviously not! This is contrary to all that the apostle has been saying. He has insisted that his message was divinely revealed to him. He had no doubts that the doctrine he preached was the truth. The real explanation must be sought elsewhere. It was a matter of common courtesy to speak to the leaders first. It was also desirable that the leaders should be thoroughly convinced as to the genuineness of Paul's gospel. If they had any questions or difficulties, Paul wanted to answer them at the outset. Then he could go before the church with the full support of the other apostles. In dealing with a large number of people, there is always the danger that emotional appeals will sway the group. Therefore, Paul desired to present his

gospel **privately** at first, in an atmosphere free from possible mass hysteria. Had Paul acted otherwise, a serious dispute might have arisen, dividing the church into a Jewish wing and a Gentile one. Then the purpose of Paul's trip to Jerusalem would have been defeated. This is what he means by **lest by any means I might run, or had run, in vain.**

2:3 The whole question of legalism was brought to a head in the case of **Titus**. Would the Jerusalem church receive this Gentile convert into fellowship, or would it insist that he first **be circumcised**?[4] After considerable discussion and debate, the apostles decided that circumcision was not necessary for salvation. Paul had won a resounding victory.[5]

2:4 The underlying reason why Paul was led to go to Jerusalem is made clear by linking the beginning of verse 2 with the beginning of verse 4: "I went up by revelation . . . **and this occurred because of false brethren secretly brought in.**" This refers to what had previously taken place in Antioch (Acts 15:1, 2). Some Jewish teachers from Jerusalem, posing as Christians, had somehow been **secretly** brought into the church at Antioch and were teaching that circumcision was essential for salvation.

2:5 Paul and Barnabas opposed them vigorously. To settle the matter, Paul, Barnabas, and others went to Jerusalem to obtain an opinion from the apostles and elders there.

2:6 Those who were esteemed as leaders in Jerusalem **added nothing** to him, either to his message or to himself as an apostle. This was remarkable. In the previous chapter, he had emphasized that his contact with the other apostles had been minimal. Now when he finally did confer with them, they agreed that he had been preaching the same gospel as they. What an important point this is! These Jewish leaders agreed that his gospel was not defective in any way. Though Paul had been independent of them, and had not been taught by them, yet the gospel they preached was exactly the same as his own. (Paul does not intend to belittle the other apostles, he simply states that **whatever they were**, namely, companions of the

Lord Jesus when He was on earth, did not give them any superior authority in his estimation. God does not accept man's person as far as such external distinctions are concerned.)

2:7, 8 The apostles in Jerusalem recognized that Paul had, by undeserved favor, been commissioned to take the gospel to **the uncircumcised** (the Gentiles) just as **Peter** had been sent to the Jews. Both men preached the same gospel, but primarily to different nationalities.

2:9, 10 Even **James, Cephas** (Peter), and **John**, apparently **pillars** of the church, **perceived** that God was working through Paul, and **gave** him **and Barnabas the right hand of fellowship** in taking the gospel **to the Gentiles**. This was not an official ordination, but an expression of their loving interest in Paul's work. The only suggestion they made was that Paul and Barnabas should **remember the poor, the very thing which** Paul states he **was eager to do.**

C. Paul Rebukes Peter (2:11–21)

2:11 As Paul's sixth and final answer to the attacks on his apostleship, he tells how it was necessary for him to rebuke the Apostle **Peter**[6] — considered by many Jewish Christians as the chief of the apostles. (This passage effectively refutes the notion that Peter was the infallible leader of the church.)

2:12 When Peter first came to Antioch, **he would eat with the Gentiles** in the full enjoyment of his Christian liberty. By Jewish tradition, he could not have done this. Some time later, a group **came** down **from James** in Jerusalem to Antioch for a visit. They claimed to represent James, but he later denied this (Acts 15:24). They were probably Jewish Christians who were still clinging to certain legal observances. When they arrived, Peter stopped having fellowship with the Gentiles, **fearing** that the news of his behavior would get back to the legalist faction in Jerusalem. In doing this, he was denying one of the great truths of the gospel — that all believers are one in Christ Jesus, and that national differences do not affect fellowship. Findlay says: "By refusing to eat with uncircumcised men, he affirmed implicitly that, though believers in Christ, they were still to him 'common and unclean,' that the Mosaic rites imparted a higher sanctity than the righteousness of faith."

2:13 Others followed Peter's example, including **Barnabas**, Paul's valued co-laborer. Recognizing the seriousness of this action, Paul boldly accused Peter of **hypocrisy**. Paul's rebuke is given in verses 14–21.[7]

2:14 As a Christian, Peter knew that God no longer recognized national differences; he had lived as a Gentile, eating their foods, etc. By his recent refusal to eat with Gentiles, Peter was implying that observances of Jewish laws and customs was necessary for holiness, and that the Gentile believers would have to **live as Jews**.

2:15 Paul seems to be using irony here. Did not Peter's conduct betray a lingering conviction concerning the superiority of the **Jews**, and the despised position of the **Gentiles**? Peter should have known better, because God had taught him before the conversion of the Gentile Cornelius to call no man common or unclean (Acts 10 and 11:1–18).

2:16 Jews who had been saved knew that there was no salvation in **the law**. The law condemned to death those who failed to obey it perfectly. This brought the curse on all, because all have broken its sacred precepts. The Savior is here presented as the only true object of faith. Paul reminds Peter that "**even we** Jews" came to the conclusion that salvation is **by faith in Christ and not by** law-keeping. What was the sense now of Peter's putting Gentiles under the law? The law told people what to do but gave them no power to do it. It was given to reveal sin, not to be a savior.

2:17 Paul and Peter and others had sought justification in **Christ** and in Christ alone. Peter's actions at Antioch, however, seemed to indicate that he was not completely justified, but had to go back under the law to complete his salvation. If this is so, then Christ is not a perfect and sufficient Savior. If we go to Him to have our sins forgiven, but then have to go elsewhere in addition, is not Christ **a minister of sin** in failing to fulfill His promises? If, while we are professedly depending on Christ for justification, we then go back to the law (which can only condemn us as sinners), do we act as Christians? Can we hope for Christ's approval on such a course of action that in effect makes Him **a minister of sin**? Paul's answer is an indignant **Certainly not!**

2:18 Peter had abandoned the whole legal system for faith in Christ. He had repudiated any difference between Jew and Gentile when it came to finding favor with God. Now, by refusing to eat with Gentiles, he is building up **again** what he once **destroyed**. In so doing, he proves himself to be **a transgressor**. Either he was wrong in leaving the law for Christ, or he is wrong now in leaving Christ for the law!

2:19 The penalty for breaking the law is death. As a sinner, I had broken the law. Therefore, it condemned me to die. But Christ paid the penalty of the broken law for me by dying in my place. Thus when Christ died, I died. He died to the law in the sense that He met all its righteous demands; therefore, in Christ, I too have **died to the law.**

The Christian has **died to the law**; he has nothing more to do with it. Does this mean that the believer is at liberty to break the Ten Commandments all he wants? No, he lives a holy life, not through fear of the law, but out of love to the One who died for him. Christians who desire to be under the law as a pattern of behavior do not realize that this places them under its curse. Moreover, they cannot touch the law in one point without being responsible to keep it completely. The only way we can **live to God** is by being dead to the law. The law could never produce a holy life; God never intended that it should. His way of holiness is explained in verse 20.

2:20 The believer is identified **with Christ** in His death. Not only was *He* crucified on Calvary, *I* was **crucified** there as well — in Him. This means the end of me as a sinner in God's sight. It means the end of me as a person seeking to merit or earn salvation by my own efforts. It means the end of me as a child of Adam, as a man under the condemnation of the law, as my old, unregenerate self. The old, evil "I" has been crucified; it has no more claims on my daily life. This *is* true as to my standing before God; it *should* be true as to my behavior.

The believer does not cease to live as a personality or as an individual. But the one who is seen by God as having died is not the same one who lives. **It is no longer I who live, but Christ** who **lives in me.** The Savior did not die for me in order that I might go on living my life as I choose. He died for me so that from now on He might be able to live His life in me. **The life which I now live in** this human body, **I live by faith in the Son of God.** Faith means reliance or dependence. The Christian lives by continual dependence on Christ, by yielding to Him, by allowing Christ to live His life in him.

Thus the believer's rule of life is Christ and not the law. It is not a matter of striving, but of trusting. He lives a holy life, not out of fear of punishment, but out of love to **the Son of God, who loved** him **and gave Himself for** him.

Have you ever turned your life over to the Lord Jesus with the prayer that His life might be manifest in your body?

2:21 **The grace of God** is seen in His unconditional gift of salvation. When man tries to earn it, he is making it void. It is no longer by grace if man deserves it or earns it. Paul's final thrust at Peter is effective. If Peter could obtain favor with God by Jewish observances, **then Christ died** for nothing; He literally threw His life away. Christ died because man could obtain **righteousness** in no other way — not even by law-keeping.

Clow says:

> The deepest heresy of all, which corrupts churches, leavens creeds with folly, and swells our human hearts with pride, is salvation by works. "I believe," writes John Ruskin, "that the root of every schism and heresy from which the Christian Church has suffered, has been the effort to earn salvation rather than to receive it; and that one reason why preaching is so ineffective is that it calls on men oftener to work for God than to behold God working for them."[8]

II. DOCTRINAL: PAUL DEFENDS JUSTIFICATION BY FAITH (3:1–5:1)

A. The Great Truth of the Gospel (3:1–9)

3:1 Their actions exhibited a lack of

understanding and reason. To turn to law from grace is to be **bewitched**. It is to be lulled as by a magic spell and unwarily to accept falsehood for truth. When Paul asks: **"Who has bewitched you?"**, the *who* is singular (Gk., *tis*),[9] not plural, perhaps suggesting that the devil was the author of this false teaching. Paul himself had preached **Jesus Christ** to the Galatians **as crucified**, emphasizing that the cross was to separate them forever from the curse and bondage of the law. How could they return to the law and thus disregard the cross? Had not the truth laid hold of them practically?

3:2 One question should be sufficient to settle the whole matter. Let them go back to the time of their conversion — the time when the Holy Spirit came to dwell in their bodies. How **did** they **receive the Spirit**? By doing, or by believing? Obviously it was by believing. No one ever received the Spirit by keeping **the law.**

3:3 If they could not *obtain* salvation by works, could they expect to grow in holiness or Christian maturity by the law? If the power of **the Spirit** was necessary to save them, could they complete the process by fleshly efforts?

3:4 When the Galatians first trusted in Christ, they exposed themselves to bitter persecution, perhaps partly at the hands of Jewish zealots who hated the gospel of grace. Was all that suffering **in vain**? In going back to the law were they not saying that the persecutors were right after all? **If indeed it was in vain**. Paul expresses continued hope that they will return to the gospel for which they once **suffered**.

3:5 There is a question whether **He** (or *he*)[10] in verse 5 refers to God, to Paul, or to someone else who was ministering to the Galatians at the time he was writing the Letter. Ultimately, it must apply to God, since only **He** can supply **the** Holy **Spirit**. However, in a secondary sense, it could apply to a Christian worker as the instrument through whom God performs His will. This would give a very exalted view of the Christian ministry. Someone has said: "Real Christian work of any sort is conveying the Holy Spirit to others; it is actually the dispensing of the Spirit."

If the apostle is speaking of himself, he is probably thinking of the miracles which accompanied his preaching and their reception of Christ (Heb. 2:4). However, the tense of the verb indicates not something that happened in the past, but something going on at the time of writing. Paul is probably referring to the miraculous gifts bestowed by the Holy Spirit on believers after their conversion, as described in 1 Corinthians 12:8–11.

Does He do it by the works of the law, or by the hearing of faith? The answer is: **By the hearing of faith**. The indwelling of the Holy Spirit and His subsequent work in the believer are never earned nor merited, but are always given by grace and received by **faith**. Thus the Galatians should have realized from their own experiences that blessing comes by faith and not by law-keeping.

For his second proof, Paul now turns to the very Scriptures which the false teachers were using to show the necessity of circumcision! What did the OT really say?

3:6 Paul had demonstrated that God's dealings with the Galatians were entirely on the basis of faith. Now he shows that men were saved in the same way even in OT times. The question in verse 5 was: "Does He do it by the works of the law, or by the hearing of faith?" The answer was: "By the hearing of faith." With that answer in mind, verse 6 opens, **just as Abraham. . . .** He was justified in the same way — by the hearing of faith.

Perhaps the Jewish teachers were using Abraham as their hero and example, basing their argument for the necessity of circumcision on his experience (Gen. 17:24, 26). If so, Paul will fight them on their own ground. How then was Abraham saved? **Abraham believed God.** It was not by any meritorious act at all. He simply **believed God**. There is no merit attached to that; in fact, a man is a fool not to believe God. Believing God is the only thing man can do in connection with salvation, which leaves him no ground for boasting. It is not a "good work," involving human effort. It gives no place to the flesh. What is more right than for a creature to trust his Creator or a child his Father?

Justification is an act of God by which He declares righteous all who believe on

Him. God can properly deal with sinners in this way because Christ died as a substitute for sinners on Calvary's cross, paying the debt of their sins. Justification does not mean that God makes the believer righteous and sinless in himself. He reckons him to be righteous on the basis of the work of the Savior. God gives the trusting sinner a righteous standing which makes him fit for heaven, then expects him to live righteously in gratitude for what He has done for him. The important thing to note here is that justification has nothing to do with law-keeping. It is entirely on the principle of faith.

3:7 Doubtless the Jewish teachers were maintaining that in order to be real sons of Abraham, the Galatians had to be circumcised. Paul refutes this. The real **sons of Abraham** are not those who are born Jews, or those who become Jewish converts, but those who are saved by faith. In Romans 4:10, 11, Paul shows that Abraham was reckoned righteous *before* he was circumcised. In other words, he was justified while he was still on *Gentile* ground.

3:8 The OT is depicted as a prophet, looking down the centuries and **foreseeing that God would justify the Gentiles** as well as Jews on the principle of **faith**. The blessing of **the Gentiles by faith** was not only foreseen by the OT, but was actually announced to Abraham in Genesis 12:3 — "In you all the families of the earth shall be blessed."

When we first read this quotation from Genesis, we find it difficult to see how Paul found such a meaning in it. Yet the Holy Spirit, who wrote that verse in the OT, knew that it contained the gospel of salvation by faith to all nations. Since Paul was writing by inspiration of the same Holy Spirit, he was enabled to explain to us the underlying meaning: **In you** — that is, along with Abraham, in the same way as Abraham. **All the nations** — the Gentiles as well as the Jews. **Shall be blessed** — be saved. How was Abraham saved? **By faith.** How will the nations be saved? In the same way as Abraham — by faith. Moreover, they will be saved as Gentiles, not by becoming Jews.

3:9 All **those who** exercise **faith** in God **are** justified **with believing Abraham**, according to the testimony of the Jewish Scriptures.

B. Law Versus Promise (3:10–18)

3:10 Paul shows from the Sacred Writings that, far from conferring a blessing, the law can only **curse**. This verse does not say "As many as have broken the law," but: **As many as are of the works of the law**, that is, all who seek to obtain favor with God on the basis of obeying the law. They **are under the curse**, that is, condemned to death. **For it is written** (in Deut. 27:26) **"Cursed is everyone who does not continue...."** It is not enough to keep the law for a day, or a month, or a year. One must **continue** to keep it. Obedience must be complete. It is not enough to keep just the Ten Commandments. All six hundred and some laws in the five books of Moses must be obeyed!

3:11 The false teachers are once again refuted from the OT. Paul quotes the prophet Habakkuk to show that God has always justified men **by faith** and not by law. The quotation in the original Greek word order reads: "The just (or righteous) by faith shall live." In other words, those who have been reckoned righteous by faith, not by works, shall have eternal life. The justified-by-faith-ones **shall live.**

3:12 The law does not ask men to believe. It does not even ask men to *try* to keep the commandments. It calls for strict, complete, and perfect obedience, as was so clearly taught in Leviticus. It is a contrary principle to faith. The law says: "Do and live." Faith says: "Believe and live." Paul's argument then is this: The just person shall live by faith. A person under **law** does **not** live by **faith**. Therefore, he is not *just* before God. When Paul says: **"The man who does them shall live by them,"** he is stating a theoretical axiom or ideal but one that is impossible to attain.

3:13 To redeem is to buy back, or to deliver by paying the price. **The curse of the law** is death — the penalty for breaking its commandments. Christ has delivered those under law from paying the penalty of death demanded by the law. (Paul is undoubtedly speaking primarily of believing Jews when he uses the pronoun **us**, although the Jews were representatives of the entire human race.)

Cynddylan Jones says:

The Galatians imagined that Christ only half purchased them, and that they had to purchase the rest by their submission to circumcision and other Jewish rites and ceremonies. Hence their readiness to be led away by false teachers and to mix up Christianity and Judaism. Paul says here: (according to the Welsh translation) "Christ hath *wholly* purchased us from the curse of the law."[11]

Christ redeemed men by dying in their place, enduring the dreadful wrath of God against sins. The **curse** of God fell on Him as man's Substitute. He did not become sinful in Himself, but man's sins were placed upon Him.

Christ did not redeem men **from the curse of the law** by keeping the Ten Commandments perfectly during His lifetime. Scripture does not teach that His perfect obedience to the law is reckoned to us. Rather He delivered men from the law by bearing its dreadful curse in death. Apart from His death there could be no salvation. The law taught that when condemned criminals were hanged on a tree, it was a sign of their being under the curse of God (Deut. 21:23). Here the Holy Spirit sees in that passage a prophecy of the manner in which the Savior would die to bear the curse for His creatures. He was hung between heaven and earth as though unworthy of either. In His death by crucifixion, He is said to have been hanged **on a tree** (Acts 5:30; 1 Pet. 2:24).

3:14 God had promised to bless Abraham and to bless all the world through him. **The blessing of Abraham** is really salvation by grace through faith. The penalty of death required by God must first be paid. So the Lord Jesus was made a curse in order that God might reach out to both Jews and Gentiles in grace. Now in Christ (a descendant of Abraham), the nations are blessed.

God's promise to Abraham in Genesis 12:3 does not mention the Holy Spirit. But Paul tells us here, by inspiration of God, that the gift of the Holy **Spirit** was included in God's uncondi-

tional covenant of salvation with Abraham. It was there in embryo. The Holy Spirit could not come as long as the law was in the way. Christ had to die and be glorified before the Spirit could be given (John 16:7).

The apostle has demonstrated that salvation is by faith, not law, by (1) the experience of the Galatians, and (2) the witness of the OT Scriptures. He now turns to an illustration from everyday life.

Paul's argument in this section may be summarized as follows: In Genesis 12:3, God promised to bless all families of the earth in Abram. This promise of salvation included Gentiles as well as Jews. In Genesis 22:18, God also promised: "In your seed all the nations of the earth shall be blessed." He said *seed* (singular), not "seeds" (plural). God was referring to One Person, the Lord Jesus Christ, who was a direct descendant of Abraham (Luke 3:34). In other words, God promised to bless all nations, Gentile as well as Jewish, through Christ. The promise was unconditional; it required neither good works nor legal obedience. It was a simple promise meant to be received in simple faith.

Now the law, given to Israel 430 years later, could not add conditions to the promise nor alter it in any way. In human affairs this would be unrighteous; in divine matters it would be unthinkable. The conclusion therefore is that God's promise of blessing to the Gentiles is through Christ, by faith and not by law-keeping.

3:15 In human affairs, when a **covenant** or will is signed and sealed, no one would think of changing the document or adding to it. If human testaments cannot be broken, how much less can God's!

3:16 No doubt the Judaizers had argued that although the promises were originally made to Abraham and to his seed (the people of Israel) by faith, yet these same people of Israel were subsequently put under the law. Therefore, the Galatians, though originally saved by faith, must now observe the Ten Commandments. Paul answers: **The promises** were made to **Abraham and his Seed** (singular). "Seed" may sometimes denote a multitude, yet here it denotes one Person, namely Christ. (We ourselves would probably never see this in reading the OT, but the Spirit of God enlightens us.)

3:17 God's promise to Abraham was unconditional; it did not depend on works at all. God simply agreed to give Abraham a Seed (Christ). Though he had no child, Abraham believed God, thus believing also in the Christ to come, and he was justified. The coming of the **law — four hundred and thirty years later** could not affect **the promise** of salvation in any way. It could neither revoke the promise nor add conditions to it.

Perhaps the Judaizers were suggesting that the law, coming 430 years after the promise, had the effect of annulling it. "Not at all!" Paul says, in effect: "The promise was like a will, and had been ratified by a death (the covenant sacrifice, Gen. 15:7–11; see also Heb. 9:15–22). It could not be revoked."

The 430 years are reckoned from the time that God confirmed the Abrahamic Covenant to Jacob, just as Jacob was preparing to enter Egypt (Gen. 46:1–4), and they extend to the giving of the law about three months after the exodus.

3:18 **The inheritance** must be either by faith or by works. It cannot be by both. Scripture makes it clear that it was given **to Abraham by** unconditional **promise**. So it is with salvation. It is offered as an unconditional gift. Any thought of working for it is excluded.

C. The Purpose of the Law (3:19–29)

3:19 **What purpose then does the law serve?** If, as Paul contended, the law did not annul or add conditions to the promise God made to Abraham, **what** *was* the **purpose** of **the law**? The law was intended to reveal sin in its true character as transgression. Sin existed before the law, but man did not recognize it as transgression until the law came. Transgression is the violation of a known law.

The law was given to a nation of sinners. They could never obtain righteousness by keeping it because they did not have the power to obey it. The law was meant to show men what hopeless sinners they were, so they would cry out to God to save them by His grace. God's covenant with Abraham was an uncon-

ditional promise of blessing; the law resulted only in cursing. The law demonstrated the unworthiness of man to receive free and unconditional blessing. If man is to be blessed, it must be by the grace of God.

The Seed is Christ. Therefore, the law was given as a temporary measure until the coming of Christ. The promised Abrahamic blessing was to come through Him. A contract between two parties involves **a mediator**, a go-between. The law involved two contracting parties — God and Israel. Moses served as go-between (Deut. 5:5). The angels were God's messengers in delivering the law to Moses (Deut. 33:2; Ps. 68:17; Acts 7:53; Heb. 2:2). The participation of Moses and the angels spoke of distance between God and His people, of a people unfit for His presence.

3:20 If there was only one contracting party, and he made an unconditional promise, requiring nothing from the other party, there would be no need of **a mediator**. The fact that the law required a mediator implied that man must keep his part of the agreement. This was the weakness of the law; it called for obedience from those who did not have the power to give it. When **God** made His promise to Abraham, He was the sole contracting Party. This was the strength of the promise: everything depended on God and nothing on man. No mediator was involved, because none was needed.[12]

3:21 Did **the law** set aside **the promises** or take their place? **Certainly not!** If it were possible to give **a law** by which sinners could achieve the perfection required by God, then certainly salvation would have been by law-keeping. God would not have sent the Son of His love to die for sinners if He could have achieved the same result in some less costly way. But the law had plenty of both *time* and *people* to demonstrate that it could not save sinners. In this sense it was "weak through the flesh" (Rom. 8:3). All the law could do was show men their hopelessness and impress on them that salvation could only be by the free grace of God.

3:22 The OT showed that all men are sinners, including those under the law. It was necessary that man should be thus thoroughly convinced of sin, in order **that the promise** of salvation **by faith in Jesus Christ might be given to those who believe**. The key words in verse 22 are **faith, given**, and **believe**. There is no mention of "doing" or "law-keeping."

3:23 **Faith** here is the Christian faith. It refers to the era ushered in by the death, burial, resurrection, and ascension of the Lord Jesus, and the preaching of the gospel at Pentecost. Before that time, the Jews **were kept under guard** as if in a prison or in custody. They were fenced in by the law's requirements, and since they could not fulfill these, they were restricted to the way of **faith** for salvation. The people under law were thus confined until the glorious news of deliverance from the bondage of the law was announced in the gospel.

3:24 **The law** is pictured as a guardian and guide of children, or as a **tutor**.[13] This emphasizes the thought of teaching; the law taught lessons concerning the holiness of God, the sinfulness of man, and the need for atonement. Here the word is used to describe one who exercises discipline and general supervision over minors, or the immature.

The words **to bring us** are not in the original, but were supplied by the translators of the King James tradition. If we leave them out, the verse teaches that the law was a Jewish guardian up **to Christ**, that is, until the coming of Christ, or with the coming of Christ in view. There is a sense in which the law preserved the people of Israel as a distinct nation by regulations concerning marriage, property, foods, etc. When "the faith" came, it was first announced to this nation that had been so miraculously kept in ward through the centuries. Justification **by faith** was promised on the basis of the finished work of Christ, the Redeemer.

3:25 The law is the **tutor**, but once the Christian **faith** has been received, believing Jews **are no longer under** the law. How much less Gentiles, such as the Galatians, who were *never* under the tutor! Verse 24 teaches that man is *not justified by law*; verse 25 teaches that the *law is not the rule of life* for one who is justified.

3:26 Notice the change in pronouns from "we" to **you**. In speaking of the Jews as "we", Paul showed that they were kept under law until the coming of Christ. The law maintained them as a separate people to whom justification by faith might be preached. When they were justified, they ceased to be under law, and their distinctive character as Jews ceased. The pronoun **"you"** from here to the end of the chapter includes both saved Jews and saved Gentiles. Such people **are all sons of God through faith in Christ Jesus**.

3:27 Union with **Christ**, which takes place at the time of conversion, is confessed in water baptism. This baptism does not make a person a member of Christ or an inheritor of the kingdom of God. It is a public identification with Christ, which Paul speaks of as a "putting on" of **Christ**. Just as a soldier proclaims himself a member of the army by "putting on" his uniform, so a believer identifies himself as one who belongs to Christ by being **baptized** in water. By this act he publicly expresses submission to Christ's leadership and authority. He portrays visibly that he is a son of God.

It is certain that the apostle is *not* suggesting that water baptism unites a person to Christ. That would be a blatant repudiation of his basic thesis that salvation is by faith alone.

Nor is Paul likely referring here to Spirit baptism, which places a believer in the body of Christ (1 Cor. 12:13). The baptism of the Holy Spirit is invisible. There is nothing about it that corresponds to a public "putting on" of Christ.

This is a baptism that is *unto* Christ (JND). Just as the Israelites were baptized *unto* Moses, identifying themselves with him as their leader, so believers today are baptized *unto* Christ, signifying their recognition of Him as rightful Lord.

By baptism the believer signifies also the burial of the flesh and its efforts to obtain righteousness. He signifies the end of the old way of life and the beginning of the new one. In water baptism the Galatians confessed that they had died with Christ and had been buried with Him. Just as Christ died to the law, so they were dead to the law, and should not therefore desire to be under it as a rule of life. Just as Christ has, by His death, broken down the distinction between Jew and Gentile, so they have died to such national differences. They **have put on Christ** in the sense that they now live a completely new life — the life of Christ.

3:28 The law made distinctions between these classes. For instance, the distinction between Jew and Gentile is insisted on in Deuteronomy 7:6; 14:1, 2. In his morning prayer, a Jewish man thanked God that He had not made him a Gentile, a slave, or a woman. **In Christ Jesus** these differences disappear, that is, as far as acceptance with God is concerned. A Jew is not preferred over a Gentile, a free man is not more favored than a slave, nor is a man more privileged than a woman. All are on the same level because they are **in Christ Jesus**.

This verse must not be pressed into meaning something it does not say. As far as everyday life is concerned (not to mention public ministry in the church), God *does* recognize the distinction between male and female. The NT contains instructions addressed to each; it also speaks separately to slaves and masters. But in obtaining blessing from God, these things do not matter. The great thing is to be **in Christ Jesus**. (This refers to our heavenly position, not to our earthly condition.) Before God the believing Jew is not a bit superior to the converted pagan! Govett says: "All the distinctions which the law made are swallowed up in the common grave which God has provided." Therefore, how foolish it is for Christians to seek further holiness by setting up differences which Christ has abolished.

3:29 The Galatians were deluded into thinking that they could become Abraham's seed by keeping the law. Paul shows otherwise. Christ is the seed of Abraham; the inheritance promised to Abraham was fulfilled in Christ. When sinners believe on Him, they become one with Him. Thus they become **Abraham's seed** and, in Christ, they inherit all of God's blessings.

D. Children and Sons (4:1–16)

4:1, 2 The picture is of a wealthy father who intends to turn over control of his wealth to the son when he reaches maturity. However, **as long as he is** still **a child**, the heir's status is like that of **a slave**. He is continually told to do this and not to do that. He has **stewards** who manage his property and **guardians** in charge of his person. Thus, although the inheritance is surely his, he does not enter into it until he has grown up.

4:3 This was the condition of the Jews under law. They **were children**, being ordered around by the law just like slaves. They **were in bondage** under the **elements of the world**, meaning the elementary principles of the Jewish religion. The ceremonies and rituals of Judaism were designed for those who did not know God the Father as He is revealed in Christ. An illustration might be found in a child learning the rudiments of spelling by using blocks, or learning to identify objects by means of pictures. The law was full of shadows and pictures, appealing to the spiritual senses by means of the physical and external. Circumcision is an example of this. Judaism was physical, external, and temporal; Christianity is spiritual, internal, and permanent. These externals were a form of **bondage** to the **children.**

4:4[†] **The fullness of the time** refers to the time appointed by the Heavenly Father when the heirs would become of age (see v. 2).

In this verse we have, in a few words, a marvelous statement as to the deity and humanity of the Savior. He is the eternal Son of God; yet He **was born of a woman**. If Jesus had been only a man, it would be gratuitous to say that He **was born of a woman**. How else could a mere man be born? The expression, in our Lord's case, witnesses to His unique Person and the unique mode of His birth.

Born into the world as an Israelite, He was therefore **born under the law**. As Son of God, the Lord Jesus would never have been under the law; He was the One who gave it. But, in condescending grace, He put Himself **under the law** that He had made, in order that He might magnify it in His life, and bear its curse in His death.

4:5 The law demanded a price from those who failed to keep it — the price of death. Before God could bring men

†*See p. xviii.*

into the wonderful position of sonship, this price had to be paid. So the Lord Jesus, coming into the world as a member of the human race and of the Jewish nation, paid the price which the law demanded. Because He is God, His death was infinite in value, that is, it was sufficient to pay for any number of sinners. Because He was Man, He could die as a substitute for man. Govett says: "Christ, by nature Son of God, became Son of man, that we, by nature sons of man, might become sons of God. Wonderful exchange!"

As long as men were slaves, they could not be **sons**. Christ delivered them from the bondage of the law in order that they might be adopted **as sons**. Notice here the distinction between becoming a *child* of God and a *son* of God (compare Rom. 8:14, 16). The believer is born into the family of God as a *child* (see John 1:12). The emphasis here is on the fact of divine birth, not on the privileges and responsibilities of sonship. The believer is adopted into the family as a *son*. Every Christian is a son immediately and is brought into the inheritance of which he is an heir. Thus the instructions to Christians in the NT assume no infancy among the saints. All are treated as mature sons.

Adoption in Roman culture differed from that in modern life. We think of adoption as taking someone else's child to be one's own. But in the NT, **adoption** means putting believers into the position of mature sons with all the privileges and responsibilities of that position.

4:6 In order that those who **are sons** of God might realize the dignity of this position, **God sent** the Holy **Spirit** at Pentecost to indwell them. The Spirit creates an awareness of sonship, causing the saint to address God as **Father. "Abba, Father"** is a familiar form of address, combining the Aramaic and Greek words for "father." No slave could address the head of a family in this fashion; it was reserved for members of the family, and expresses love and confidence. Note the Trinity in this verse — **Spirit, Son** and **Father** — in that order.

4:7 The believer is **no longer a slave**; he is not under the law. Now he is **a son** of God. Since Christ, as God's

Son, is the heir of all God's riches, the Christian is **an heir of God through Christ**.[14] All that God has is his by faith.

In rabbinical schools in Israel today a student is not allowed to read the Song of Solomon or Ezekiel 1 until he is forty years old. The Song of Solomon is considered too sexually explicit for a younger mind, and Ezekiel 1 contains a description of the glory of the ineffable God. The Talmud tells that when a certain person under forty began to read Ezekiel 1, fire came out from the page and consumed him. What this shows is that a person under law is not considered a *man* until he is forty. (The well-known *bar mitzvah* at age thirteen only makes a Jewish boy a "son of the covenant" — the meaning of the term — and thus responsible to keep the law.) Up to the age of forty the Orthodox man is considered a minor.

Not so with believers under grace. The moment they are saved the whole inheritance is theirs. They are treated as adult, mature sons and daughters, and the whole Bible is theirs to read, enjoy, and obey.

In light of these truths Harrison's exhortation is very appropriate:

Child of His love, all things are yours —
He tells you this in 1 Corinthians 3:22, 23
to arouse you to a realization of riches beyond your utmost powers of imagination to comprehend. Consider the universe. Whose is it, but His and yours? Then live royally.[15]

4:8 The Galatians had once been under bondage to idols. Before their conversion, they had been heathens who worshiped idols of wood and stone — false **gods**. Now they were turning to another type of bondage — bondage to the law.

4:9 **How** could they excuse their conduct? They had come to know **God**, or, if they didn't know Him in a deep experiential way, at least they were **known by** Him, that is, they were saved. Yet they were turning from His power and riches (of which they were heirs) **to weak and** poor things, the things connected with the law, such as circumcision, holy days, and rules of diet. They were again putting themselves **in bondage** to things that could neither save nor enrich but could only impoverish them.

Paul labels the law and all its ceremonies as **weak and beggarly**. God's laws were beautiful in their time and place, but they are positive hindrances when substituted for the Lord Jesus. It is idolatry to turn from Christ to law.

4:10, 11 The Galatians were observing the Jewish calendar with its Sabbaths, its festivals, **and seasons**. Paul expresses fear for those who profess to be Christians, yet seek to find favor with God by legal observances. Even unregenerate people can observe **days and months and years.** It gives some people intense satisfaction to feel there is something they can do in their own strength to win God's smile. But this implies that man has some strength, and hence, to that extent, he does not need the Savior.

If Paul could write in this manner to the Galatians, what would he write to professing Christians today who are seeking to attain holiness by legal observances? Would he not condemn the traditions brought into Christianity from Judaism — a humanly ordained priesthood, distinctive vestments for the priest, Sabbath-keeping, holy places, candles, holy water, and so forth?

4:12 Apparently the Galatians had forgotten their gratitude to Paul when he first preached the gospel to them. But he addresses them as **"Brethren"** in spite of their failures and his fears for them. Paul had been a Jew under law. Now, in Christ, he was free from the law. So he says, **"Become like me** —delivered from the law and no longer living under it." The Gentile Galatians had never been under law, and were not under it now. Thus the apostle says: **"I became like you.** I, who was a Jew, now enjoy the freedom from law which you Gentiles always had."

You have not injured me at all. It is not exactly clear what Paul had in mind here. Perhaps he is saying that he had no feeling of personal injury as a result of their treatment of him. That they should have turned away from him to the false teachers was not so much a blow at him personally as a blow at the truth of God and thus an injury to their own selves.

4:13 The **gospel** was **first . . . preached** to them in **physical infirmity.**[16]

God often uses weak, despised, poor instruments to accomplish His work in order that the glory will be His and not man's.

4:14 Paul's illness was a **trial** to himself and to those who listened to him. However, the Galatians did not reject him because of his physical appearance or because of his speech. Instead, they **received** him **as an angel of God**, that is, a messenger sent by God, and **even as Christ Jesus** Himself. Since he represented the Lord, they received him as they would receive the Lord (Matt. 10:40). They accepted Paul's message as the very word of God. This should be a lesson to all Christians concerning their treatment of the Lord's messengers. When we receive them cordially, we receive Him in the same way (Luke 10:16).

4:15 When they first heard the gospel, they acknowledged what a rich **blessing** it was to their souls. So great was their appreciation that they would have given their **own eyes** to Paul, if it were possible. (This might be an indication that Paul's "thorn in the flesh" was an eye disease.) But where is this sense of gratitude now? Unfortunately, it has vanished like the morning dew.

4:16 What accounted for their changed attitude toward Paul? He was still preaching the same message, earnestly contending for **the truth** of the gospel. If this made him their **enemy**, then their position was dangerous indeed.

E. Bondage or Freedom (4:17–5:1)

4:17 The motives of the false teachers differed from Paul's: they wanted a following, whereas he was interested in the spiritual welfare of the Galatians (4:17–20). The false teachers were zealous in their efforts to win the affections of the Galatians, but their motives were not sincere. **They want to exclude you.** The Judaizers wanted to cut the Galatians off from the Apostle Paul and from other teachers. They wanted a following, and sought to form a sect in order to get it. Stott warns: "When Christianity is turned into a bondage to rules and regulations, its victims are inevitably in subjection, tied to the apron strings of their teachers, as in the Middle Ages."[17]

4:18 Paul says, in effect, "I do not

mind others fussing over you, even when I am absent from you, as long as they are doing so with pure motives and for a **good** cause."

4:19 By calling the Galatians his **little children**, Paul would remind them that it was he who had pointed them to Christ. He is undergoing birth-pangs again for them, not this time seeking their salvation, but rather that **Christ** might be **formed in** them. Christlikeness is God's full objective for His people (Eph. 4:13; Col. 1:28).

4:20 This verse might mean that Paul was puzzled as to the true status of the Galatians. Their defection from the truth had left him with **doubts**. He would like to be able **to change** his **tone** and speak with certainty and conviction about them. Or perhaps he was perplexed as to their reaction to his Letter. He would rather be speaking with them in person. Then he could better express himself by changing the **tone** of his voice. If they were receptive to his rebukes, he could be tender. If, however, they were haughty and rebellious, he could be stern. As it was, he was perplexed about them; he could not tell what their reaction to his message would be.

Since the Jewish teachers made so much of Abraham and insisted that believers must follow his example by being circumcised, Paul turns to Abraham's domestic history to show that legalism is slavery and cannot be mixed with grace.

God had promised that Abraham would have a son, even though he and Sarah were too old, naturally speaking, to have children. Abraham believed God and thus was justified (Gen. 15:1–6). Sometime afterward, Sarah became discouraged, waiting for the promised son, and suggested that Abraham should have a child by her slave-girl, Hagar. Abraham followed her advice, and Ishmael was born. This was not the heir promised by God, but the son of Abraham's impatience, carnality, and lack of trust (Gen. 16).

Then, when Abraham was one hundred years old, the child of promise, Isaac, was born. Obviously this birth was miraculous; it was made possible only by the mighty power of God (Gen. 21:1–5). At the customary feast in obser-

vance of the weaning of Isaac, Sarah saw Ishmael mocking her son. She thereupon ordered Abraham to expel Ishmael and his mother from the home, saying, "The son of this bondwoman shall not be heir with my son, namely, with Isaac" (Gen. 21:8–11). This is the background for the argument which the apostle now takes up.

4:21 **Law** in this verse is used in two different senses. The first refers to law as a means of attaining holiness, and the second to the OT books of the law (Genesis through Deuteronomy), particularly Genesis. Paul is saying, **"Tell me, you who desire to** obtain favor with God by law-keeping, **do you not** listen to the message of the book of **the law?"**

4:22, 23 The **two sons** were Ishmael and Isaac. The **bondwoman** was Hagar, and the **freewoman** was Sarah. Ishmael was born as a result of Abraham's scheming intervention. Isaac, on the other hand, was given to Abraham by **promise** of God.

4:24 The story is **symbolic**; it has a deeper meaning than at first appears. The real significance of the events is not expressly stated, but is implied. Thus, the true story of Isaac and Ishmael represents deep spiritual truth, which Paul now proceeds to explain.

The two women represent **two covenants: Hagar** the covenant of law, and Sarah the covenant of grace. The law was given at **Mount Sinai**. Strangely enough, the word "Hagar" in the Arabic language means "Rock," and the Arabs called Mt. Sinai "the Rock."

4:25 The covenant given at **Sinai** produced slavery; thus **Hagar**, a slavegirl, was a fitting type of the law. **Hagar** represents **Jerusalem**, the capital of the Jewish nation, and the center for the unsaved Israelites who were still seeking to obtain righteousness by keeping the law. These, together **with** their **children**, their followers, are **in bondage**. For Paul to link unbelieving Israelites with Hagar rather than with Sarah, with Ishmael rather than with Isaac, was a stinging characterization.

4:26 The capital city of those who are justified by faith is the heavenly **Jerusalem**. It **is the mother of** all believers, both Jew and Gentile.

4:27 This quotation from Isaiah 54:1

is a prediction that the children of the heavenly city will be more numerous than those of earthly Jerusalem. Sarah was the woman who for so long was **barren**. Hagar was the woman **who has a husband**. In what way are we to understand the eventual triumph of Sarah, or the heavenly Jerusalem? The answer is that the **children** of promise include all those, Gentiles as well as Jews, who come to God by faith — **many more** than the children of Hagar who abide under the law.

4:28 True believers are born not of the will of man nor of the will of the flesh, but of God. It is not natural descent that counts, but divine miraculous birth by faith in the Lord Jesus.

4:29 Ishmael mocked Isaac, and it has always been true that those born of the flesh have **persecuted** those **born** of **the Spirit**. Consider the sufferings of our Lord and of the Apostle Paul at the hands of unsaved men. It may seem to us a trivial offense that Ishmael should mock Isaac, but Scripture records it, and Paul sees in it a principle that still abides — the enmity between **the flesh** and **the Spirit.**

4:30 Let the Galatians then appeal to **Scripture**, and they will hear this verdict. Law and grace cannot be mixed; it is impossible to inherit God's blessings on the basis of human merit or fleshly effort.

4:31 Those who have trusted Christ have no connection with the law as a means of obtaining divine favor. They are children of the freewoman, and they follow the social condition of their mother.

5:1 The last verse of chapter 4 describes the believer's position — he is free. This first verse of chapter 5 refers to his practice — he should live as a **free** man. Here we have a very good illustration of the difference between law and grace. The law would say: "If you earn your freedom, you will become free." But grace says: "You have been made free at the tremendous cost of the death of Christ. In gratitude to Him, you should **stand fast therefore in the liberty with which Christ has made** you **free**." Law commands but does not enable. Grace provides what law demands, then enables man to live a life consistent with his position by the power of the Holy

Spirit and rewards him for doing it.

As C. H. Mackintosh says, "The law demands strength from one who has none, and curses him if he cannot display it. The gospel gives strength to one who has none, and blesses him in the exhibition of it."[18]

> "Run, John, and live," the law commands,
> But gives me neither legs nor hands;
> Far better news the Gospel brings,
> It bids me fly and gives me wings.

III. PRACTICAL: PAUL DEFENDS CHRISTIAN FREEDOM IN THE SPIRIT (5:2–6:18)

A. The Peril of Legalism (5:2–15)

5:2 Legalism makes Christ of no value. The Judaizers insisted on the necessity of Gentile believers being **circumcised** for salvation. Paul, speaking with the authority of an apostle, insists that to depend on circumcision is to make **Christ** of no benefit. Says Jack Hunter:

> In the Galatian situation, circumcision to Paul was not a surgical operation, nor merely a religious observance. It represented a system of salvation by good works. It declared a gospel of human effort apart from divine grace. It was law supplanting grace; Moses supplanting Christ; for to add to Christ was to take from Christ. Christ supplemented was Christ supplanted; Christ is the only Savior — solitary and exclusive. Circumcision would mean excision from Christ.[19]

5:3 Legalism requires men **to keep the whole law**. People under law cannot accept the easy commandments and reject the others. If a person attempts to please God by being circumcised, then he is under obligation **to keep the whole law**. Thus a man is entirely under law, or not under law at all. Obviously, if he is entirely under law, Christ is valueless to him. The Lord Jesus is not only a *complete* Savior, but also an *exclusive* one. Paul is not referring in this verse to any who might have been circumcised in the past, but only to those who might undergo this rite as a necessity for complete justification, to those who assert the obligations of law-keeping for their acceptance with God.

5:4 Legalism means the abandonment of **Christ** as one's only hope of righteousness. This verse has given rise to considerable discussion. Many different interpretations have been offered, but these may be grouped broadly in three classes, as follows:

1. Many hold that Paul here teaches that it is possible for a person to be truly saved, then to fall into sin, and therefore to fall from grace and be forever lost. This has come to be known as "the falling away doctrine."

We believe such an interpretation to be unsound for two compelling reasons: First, the verse does not describe saved persons who fall into sin. In fact, there is no mention of falling into sin. Rather, the verse is speaking of those who are living moral, respectable, upright lives and hope to be saved thereby. Thus the passage acts as a boomerang on those who use it to support the falling away doctrine. They teach that a Christian must keep the law, live a perfect life and otherwise refrain from sinning in order to remain saved. However, this Scripture insists that all who seek to be justified by works of law or self-effort **have fallen from grace.**

Secondly, this interpretation contradicts the over-all, consistent testimony of the NT to the effect that every true believer in the Lord Jesus Christ is eternally saved, that no sheep of Christ will ever perish, and that salvation depends entirely on the finished work of the Savior, and not on man's feeble efforts (John 3:16, 36; 5:24; 6:47; 10:28).

2. A second interpretation of the verse is that it refers to those who were originally saved by faith in the Lord Jesus, but who subsequently put themselves under the law to retain their salvation or to achieve holiness. In other words, they were saved by grace, but now seek to be kept by law. In this case, to fall from grace is, as Philip Mauro put it, "to turn from God's way of perfecting His saints by the work of the Spirit in them, and to seek that end through the observance of external rites and ceremonies, which men of the flesh can observe as well as saints of God."

This view is unscriptural, first because the verse does not describe Christians who seek holiness or sanctification, but rather unsaved persons who seek *justification* by law-keeping. Note the wording — **you who attempt to be justified by law.** And second, this explanation of the verse implies the possibility of saved people being subsequently severed from Christ, and this is inconsistent with right views of the grace of God.

3. The third interpretation is that Paul is speaking of people who might profess to be Christians but who are not truly saved. They are seeking to be justified by keeping the law. The apostle is telling them that they cannot have two saviors; they must choose either Christ or the law. If they choose the law, then they are severed from Christ as their only possible hope of righteousness; they **have fallen from grace.** Hogg and Vine express it clearly:

> Christ must be everything or nothing to a man; no limited trust or divided allegiance is acceptable to Him. The man who is justified by the grace of the Lord Jesus Christ is a Christian; the man who seeks to be justified by the works of the law is not.[20]

5:5 The apostle shows that the hope of the true believer is far different from that of the legalist. The Christian waits **for the hope of righteousness.** He hopes for the time when the Lord will come, when he will receive a glorified body, and when he will sin no more. Notice that it does not say that the Christian hopes for righteousness; he already has a right standing before God through the Lord Jesus Christ (2 Cor. 5:21). But he waits for the moment when he will be completely righteous in himself. He does not hope to achieve this by anything that he can do, but rather **through the Spirit** and **by faith.** The Holy Spirit is going to do it all, and the believer simply looks to God in faith to bring it to pass. The legalist, on the other hand, hopes to earn righteousness by his own works, law-keeping, or religious observances. It is a vain hope, because righteousness cannot be achieved in this way.

Notice that Paul uses the pronoun **we** in this verse, referring to true Christians, whereas in verse 4 he uses the pronoun "you" when speaking to those who seek justification by works of law.

5:6 Legalism **avails** nothing. As far

as a person who is **in Christ Jesus** (that is, a Christian) is concerned, **circumcision** does not make him any better, and **uncircumcision** does not make him any worse. What God looks for in the believer is **faith working through love.** **Faith** is complete dependence on God. **Faith** is not idle; it manifests itself in unselfish service to God and man. The motive of all such service is **love.** Thus **faith** works **through love**; it is prompted by **love,** not by law. This is a truth found many times in the Scriptures — that God is not interested in rituals, but in the reality of a godly life.

5:7 Legalism is disobedience to **the truth**. The Galatians had made a good start in the Christian life, but someone had **hindered** them. It was the Judaizers, the legalists, the false apostles. By accepting their erroneous teachings, the saints were disobeying **the truth** of God.

5:8 Legalism is not a divine teaching. **Persuasion** here means belief or doctrine. **Him who calls you** refers to God. Thus the belief that circumcision and law-keeping should be added to faith in Christ does not come from God but from the devil.

5:9 Legalism leads to more and more evil. **Leaven** in the Scripture is a common symbol of evil. Here it refers to the evil doctrine of the Judaizers. The natural tendency of **leaven**, or yeast, to affect all the meal with which it comes in contact is used here to show that **a little** error must inevitably lead to more. Evil is never static. It must defend its lies by adding more lies. Legalism is like garlic; there is no such thing as a little of it. If a few people in a church hold false doctrine, they will get more and more followers, unless sternly dealt with.

5:10 Legalism brings judgment on its teachers. Paul was confident that the Galatians would reject the false teachings. His **confidence** was **in the Lord**, which may mean that the Lord had given assurance to Paul on this matter. Or, knowing the Lord as he did, he was sure that the Great Shepherd would restore His wandering sheep, perhaps even through the Letter which Paul was then writing to them.

As for the false teachers themselves, they would be punished by God. It is a serious thing to teach error and thereby to wreck a church (1 Cor. 3:17). It is much worse, for instance, to teach that drunkenness is permissible than to be a drunkard yourself, for the false teacher makes scores of others like himself.

5:11 Legalism does away with **the offense of the cross**. Paul now answers the absurd charge that even he at times preached the necessity of circumcision. He is still suffering **persecution** at the hands of the Jews. This **persecution** would stop instantly if he preached **circumcision**, because that would mean he had abandoned preaching **the cross**. The cross is an **offense** to man. It offends him or stumbles him because it tells him that there is nothing he can do to earn salvation. It gives no place to the flesh and its efforts. It spells an end to human works. If Paul were to introduce works by preaching circumcision, then he would be setting aside the whole meaning of the cross.

5:12 The apostle's wish that the troublemakers **would . . . cut themselves off** may be understood literally; he wishes that they were castrated. They were zealous in using the knife to circumcise others; now let the knife be used to make them eunuchs. It is probably preferable to take the words figuratively; in other words, Paul wishes that the false teachers were cut off from the Galatians altogether.

The gospel of grace has always been accused of permitting men to live as they like. People say: "If salvation is by faith alone, then there is no control over a person's conduct afterwards." But the apostle is quick to point out that Christian liberty does not mean license to sin. The believer's standard is the life of the Lord Jesus, and love for Christ impels him to hate sin and love holiness.

Perhaps it was especially necessary for Paul to warn his readers against license here. When men have been under the restraints of law for some time and are then granted their freedom, there is always the danger of going from the extreme of bondage to that of carelessness. The proper balance is that liberty which lies between law and license. The Christian is free from the law, but not lawless.

5:13 Christian **liberty** does not permit sin; it rather encourages loving service. **Love** is seen as the motive of all

Christian behavior, whereas under law, the motive is fear of punishment. Findlay says: "Love's slaves are the true freemen."

The Christian's freedom is *in Christ Jesus* (2:4), and this excludes any possible thought that it might ever mean freedom to sin. We must never turn our freedom into a base of operations **for the flesh**. Just as an invading army will seek to gain a beachhead and use it as a base of operations for further conquest, so the flesh will utilize a little license to expand its territory.

A proper outlet for our freedom is this: "Make it a habit to be slaves one to another."

A. T. Pierson says:

> True freedom is found only in obedience to proper restraint. A river finds liberty to flow, only between banks: without these it would only spread out into a slimy, stagnant pool. Planets, uncontrolled by law, would only bring wreck to themselves and to the universe. The same law which fences us in, fences others out; the restraints which regulate our liberty also insure and protect it. It is not control, but the right kind of control, and a cheerful obedience which make the free man.[21]

5:14 At first, it seems strange that Paul should introduce the **law** here after emphasizing all through the Epistle that believers are not under it. He is not urging his readers to go back to the law; he is showing that what the law demanded but could not produce is the very thing that results from the exercise of Christian liberty.

5:15 Legalism invariably leads to quarreling, and apparently it had done so in Galatia. How strange! Here were people who wanted to be under the law. The law requires them to love their neighbors. Yet the very reverse has happened. They have been backbiting and devouring one another. This behavior springs from the flesh, to which the law gives a place, and on which it acts.

B. Power for Holiness (5:16–25)

5:16 The believer should **walk in the Spirit**, not in the flesh. To **walk in** (or by) **the Spirit** is to allow Him to have His way. It is to remain in communion with Him. It is to make decisions in the light of His holiness. It is to be occupied with Christ, because the Spirit's ministry is to engage the believer with the Lord Jesus. When we thus **walk in the Spirit, the flesh**, or self-life, is treated as dead. We cannot be occupied at the same time with Christ and with sin.

Scofield says:

> The problem of the Christian life is based on the fact that so long as the Christian lives in this world he is, so to speak, two trees — the old tree of the flesh, and the new tree of the divine nature implanted by the new birth; and the problem itself is, how to keep barren the old tree and to make fruitful the new tree. The problem is solved by walking in the Spirit.[22]

This verse and those that follow show that **the flesh** is still present with the Christian; the idea of the eradication of the sinful nature is thus refuted.

5:17 **The Spirit** and **the flesh** are in constant conflict. God could have removed the fleshly nature from believers at the time of their conversion, but He did not choose to do so. Why? He wanted to keep them continually reminded of their own weakness; to keep them continually dependent on Christ, their Priest and Advocate; and to cause them to praise unceasingly the One who saved such worms. Instead of removing the old nature, God gave us His own Holy Spirit to indwell us. God's Spirit and our flesh are perpetually at war, and will continue to be at war until we are taken home to heaven. The believer's part in the conflict is to yield to the Spirit.

5:18 Those who are Spirit-led **are not under the law**. This verse might be understood in two ways: **Led by the Spirit** is a description of all Christians. Therefore, no Christians are **under the law**; they are not depending on self-effort. It is the **Spirit** who is resisting the motions of evil within them, not they themselves. Also, to be **led by the Spirit** means to be lifted above the flesh and to be occupied with the Lord. When one is so occupied, he is not thinking of the law or the flesh. The Spirit of God does not lead people to look to the law as a means of justification. Rather, He points them to the risen Christ as the only ground of acceptance before God.

5:19–21 We have mentioned before that the law appeals to the energy of the flesh. What kind of **works** does fallen human nature produce? There is no difficulty in identifying **the works of the flesh**. They are **evident** to all. **Adultery**[23] is unfaithfulness in the marriage relationship. **Fornication** is unlawful sexual intercourse. **Uncleanness** is moral evil, sensuality. **Lewdness** is shameless conduct involving absence of restraint. **Idolatry** is not only the worship of idols, but also the immorality that accompanies demon worship. **Sorcery** is witchcraft, the Greek word being related to drugs (*pharmakeia*). Because drugs were used in sorcery, the word came to mean intercourse with evil spirits, or the use of magic spells. It may also include superstitions, "bad luck," etc. **Hatred** means strong feelings of malice directed toward individuals. **Contentions** are discord, variance, quarrels. **Jealousies** are distrust, suspicions. **Wrath** is **outbursts** of hot anger or passions. **Selfish ambitions** are self-centered strivings to be "number one," even at others' expense. **Dissensions** are separations caused by disagreements. **Heresies** are sects formed by men with self-willed opinions. **Envy** is displeasure at the success or prosperity of others. **Murders**[24] are unlawful killing of others. **Drunkenness** refers to intoxication caused by strong drink. **Revelries** are riotous gatherings for entertainment, accompanied by drunkenness.

Paul warns his readers, as he had told them before, **that those who practice such things will not inherit the kingdom of God**. The passage does not teach that a drunkard cannot be saved, but it does say that those whose lives are *characterized* by the above catalog of fleshly works are not saved.[25]

Why should Paul write in this manner to churches of Christians? The reason is that not all who profess to be saved are true children of God. Thus throughout the NT the Holy Spirit often follows the presentation of wonderful spiritual truths with the most solemn warnings to all who profess the name of Christ.

5:22, 23 It is significant that the apostle distinguishes between the *works* of the flesh, and the **fruit of the Spirit**. Works are produced by human energy. **Fruit** is grown as a branch abides in the vine (John 15:5). They differ as a factory and a garden differ. Note that **fruit** is singular, not plural. The Holy Spirit produces one kind of **fruit**, that is, Christlikeness. All the virtues now listed describe the life of the child of God. Dr. C. I. Scofield has pointed out that every one of them is foreign to the soil of the human heart.

Love is what God is, and what we ought to be. It is beautifully described in 1 Corinthians 13, and told out in all its fullness at the cross of Calvary. **Joy** is contentment and satisfaction with God and with His dealings. Christ displayed it in John 4:34. **Peace** could include the peace of God as well as harmonious relations among Christians. For peace in the life of the Redeemer, see Luke 8:22–25. **Longsuffering** is patience in afflictions, annoyances, and persecutions. Its supreme example is found in Luke 23:34. **Kindness** is gentleness, perhaps best explained in the attitude of the Lord toward little children (Mark 10:14). **Goodness** is kindness shown to others. To see goodness in action, we have but to read Luke 10:30–35. **Faithfulness** may mean trust in God, confidence in our fellow Christians, fidelity, or reliability. This latter is probably the meaning here. **Gentleness** is taking the lowly place as Jesus did when He washed His disciples' feet (John 13:1–17). **Self-control** means literally holding oneself in, especially regarding sex. Our lives should be disciplined. Lust, passions, appetites, and temper should be ruled. We should practice moderation. As Samuel Chadwick points out:

In newspaper English the passage reads something like this: the fruit of the Spirit is an affectionate, lovable disposition; a radiant spirit and a cheerful temper; a tranquil mind and a quiet manner; a forbearing patience in provoking circumstances and with trying people; a sympathetic insight and tactful helpfulness; generous judgment and a big-souled charity; loyalty and reliableness under all circumstances; humility that forgets self in the joy of others; in all things self-mastered and self-controlled, which is the final mark of perfection. How striking this is in relation to 1 Cor. 13![26]

Paul closes this list with the cryptic comment: **"Against such there is no law."** Of course not! These virtues are pleasing to God, beneficial to others, and good for ourselves. But how is this fruit produced? Is it by man's effort? Not at all. It is produced as Christians live in communion with the Lord. As they gaze upon the Savior in loving devotion, and obey Him in daily life, the Holy Spirit works a wonderful miracle. He transforms them into the likeness of Christ. They become like Him by beholding Him (2 Cor. 3:18). Just as the branch derives all its life and nourishment from the vine, so the believer in Christ derives his strength from the True Vine, and is thus able to live a fruitful life for God.

5:24 Those who are Christ's have crucified the flesh. The verb tense[27] here indicates something that happened decisively in the past. It actually occurred at the time of our conversion. When we repented, there was a sense in which we nailed the old, evil, corrupt nature to the cross with all its affections and lusts. We determined that we would no longer live to cater to our fallen nature, that it would no longer dominate it. Of course, this decision has to be renewed continually in our lives. We must constantly keep the flesh in the place of death.

5:25 If here carries the thought of "since." Since we have eternal life by the work of **the** Holy **Spirit** in us, let us live out the new life by the power of **the** same **Spirit**. The law never could give life, and was never intended to be the Christian's rule of life.

C. Practical Exhortations (5:26–6:10)

5:26 In this verse there are three attitudes to be avoided:

1. Conceit — **Let us not become conceited**, literally holding of false or empty opinion (of ourselves). God does not want Christians to be boastful or conceited braggarts; it does not fit in with being a sinner saved by grace. Men living under law often become proud of their miserable achievements, and taunt those who do not come up to their standards, and legalistic Christians will often run down other Christians who don't have the same lists of borderline things that they condemn.

2. Provocation — **Provoking one another**. It is a denial of the Spirit-filled life to provoke or challenge other people to measure up to one's own private

viewpoints. One never knows the problems and temptations of another person's heart, never having walked in his shoes.

3. Envy — **Envying one another**. Envy is specifically the sin of wanting something that belongs to someone else to which one has no right or claim. Envy begrudges another person's superior success, talents, possessions, or good looks. Persons of few talents or weak character are apt to envy those who seem to be more successful lawkeepers. All such attributes are foreign to grace. A true believer should esteem others better than himself. Lawkeepers desire false glory. True greatness is to serve unnoticed, to labor unseen.

6:1 Here is a lovely statement on how a sinning believer is to be treated by other Christians. It is in sharp contrast to the law, of course, which called down judgment on offenders. To be **overtaken in any trespass** describes a man who has committed an act of sin rather than one who is habitually sinful. Such a person is to be dealt with by **spiritual** Christians. A carnal Christian might, by a hard, cold attitude, do more harm than good. Then, too, the offender will not be likely to receive the admonition of one who is himself out of touch with the Lord.

This verse raises an interesting question. If a man is truly spiritual, would he admit it? Are not spiritual people most conscious of their shortcomings? Who then would do the work of restoration, if doing so marked him as a spiritual man? Would it not betray a lack of modesty? The answer is this: A truly spiritual man will never boast of his condition, but he will have the tender heart of a shepherd, making him want to restore the transgressor. He will not act in a spirit of pride or superiority, but **in a spirit of gentleness**, remembering that he **also** might **be tempted.**

6:2 Burdens refers to failures, temptations, testings, and trials. Instead of standing off at a distance and criticizing, we should fly to the side of a brother in trouble or distress and help him in every possible way.

The law of Christ includes all the commandments of the Lord Jesus for His people found in the NT. It may be summarized by the commandment, "that you love one another" (John 13:34; 15:12). We fulfill this when we **bear one another's burdens**. **The law of Christ** is far different from that of Moses. Moses' Law promised life for obedience, but gave no power to obey, and could only encourage obedience by the fear of punishment. **The law of Christ**, on the other hand, is loving instruction for those who already have life. Believers are enabled to keep its precepts by the power of the Holy Spirit, and their motivation is love to Christ.

6:3 We are all made out of the same dust. When we see a brother sin, we should remember that it might have been ourselves. For a Christian to have a superiority complex is a form of self-deception. Certainly we should never think that bearing others' burdens is beneath our dignity.

6:4 This seems to be a warning against the habit of comparing ourselves with others, and finding cause for satisfaction. The apostle points out that we will be examined individually and not in comparison with others at the Judgment Seat of Christ. Therefore, we should take heed to ourselves, so that we might be able to rejoice in *our* **work** rather than in *others'* failures.

6:5 In verse 2, Paul teaches that we should share one another's sorrows, sufferings, and problems in this present life. In verse 5, the thought is that every one of us will have to **bear his own load** of responsibility at the Judgment Seat of Christ.

6:6 Believers are responsible to support their Christian teachers. To **share in all good things** means **to share** with them the material **things** of life, and also to sustain them with prayer and godly interest.

6:7 Although others may not notice our neglect of God's servants, He sees it, and gives a harvest accordingly. We **reap** what we sow, and we reap in greater quantities than we sow. When the farmer **sows** wheat, he reaps wheat, sometimes thirtyfold, sixtyfold, or a hundredfold. Scofield remarks that "the Spirit is not speaking here to sinners about their sins, but to saints about their meanness."

Of course, it is true in a wider sense that "those who plow iniquity and sow trouble reap the same" (Job 4:8) and that those who "sow the wind . . . reap the whirlwind" (Hos. 8:7). J. A. Froude, the historian, said, "One lesson, and only one, history may be said to repeat with distinctness, that the world is built somehow on moral foundations, that in the long run, it is well with the good, and in the long run it is ill with the wicked."[28]

6:8 Although it is true in a general sense that we reap whatever we sow, it should be noticed that this reminder follows an exhortation on Christian giving. Viewed in that light, we see that sowing **to the flesh** means spending one's money on oneself, one's own pleasures and comforts. Sowing **to the Spirit** is using one's money for the furtherance of God's interests.

Those who do the former reap a harvest of disappointment and loss right here on earth because they learn as they grow older that the flesh they lived to please is decaying and dying. Then in the age to come they lose eternal rewards. Those who sow **to the Spirit will of the Spirit reap everlasting life**. There are two ways in which eternal life (same word translated **everlasting**) is used in the Bible: (1) It is the present possession of every believer (John 3:36). (2) It is that which the believer receives at the end of his life here on earth (Rom. 6:22). Those **who sow to the Spirit** enjoy eternal life here and now in a way which other Christians do not. Then, too, they will reap the rewards which accompany faithfulness when they reach their heavenly home.

6:9 Lest any should become discouraged, Paul reminds his readers that the rewards are certain, even if not immediate. You do not harvest a field of wheat the day after you sow the seed. So in the spiritual realm, the rewards surely follow faithful sowing **in due season**.

6:10 **The household of faith** includes all who are saved, without regard to denominations or divisions. Our kindness is not to be limited to believers, but is to be shown to them in a special way. It is not *negative* — how little harm, but *positive* — how much **good** we can do that is to be our objective. John Wesley said it so succinctly: "Do all the good you can, in all the ways you can, to all the people you can, as long as ever you can."

D. Conclusion (6:11–18)

6:11 See with what large letters I have written to you with my own hand! Instead of dictating it to an assistant, as he usually did, Paul had written the letter himself. The **large letters** with which he wrote might have indicated his deep feeling in seeking to combat the legalists and how serious he considered the Judaizing error to be, or that Paul's eyesight was poor, as many have suggested from this and other passages. We feel that the latter view is correct.

6:12 The Judaizers wanted to make a **good showing in the flesh** by building up a large group of followers. They could do this by insisting on circumcision. People are often quite willing to observe rites and ceremonies as long as they are not required to change their habits. It is common today to build up a large church membership by lowering the standards. Paul sees through the insincerity of these false teachers and accuses them of seeking to avoid **persecution for the cross of Christ**. The cross signifies the condemnation of the flesh and its efforts to please God. The cross spells death for the fleshly nature and its noblest efforts. The cross means separation from evil. Therefore, men hate the glorious message of the cross, and persecute those who preach it.

6:13 The legalists were not really interested in keeping **the law**. What they wanted was an easy way to obtain converts, so that they could **boast** of a long list of followers. Boice says: "It was an attempt to win others to that which was itself bankrupt; for not even those who were circumcised were able to keep the law."

6:14 Paul's ground for boasting is not in the flesh of men, but **in the cross of our Lord Jesus Christ**. On that **cross** the world died to Paul and Paul to the world. When a man is saved, the world says goodbye to him, and he says goodbye **to the world**. He is spoiled as far as **the world** is concerned because he is no longer interested in its fleeting pleasures; **the world** has lost its attraction for him, because he has found One who completely satisfies. Findlay says: "He can never believe in it, never take pride in it, nor do homage to it any more. It is stripped of its glory and robbed of its power to charm or govern him." Thus **the cross** is a great barrier or dividing line between the world and the child of God.

6:15 Although at first sight it might not seem so, this verse is one of the most important statements of Christian truth in the entire Epistle.

Circumcision was an external observance, a ritual. The Jewish teachers made everything depend on the observance of this ceremony. **Circumcision** was the foundation of Judaism. Paul sweeps it aside with a flourish — "**circumcision** is nothing." Neither ritual nor Judaism nor legalism counts. Then Paul adds — **nor uncircumcision**. There are those who pride themselves on their absence of ritual. Their whole church service is a revolt against ceremony. This is of no value either.

What really counts with God is **a new creation**. He wants to see the transformed life. Findlay writes: "The true Christianity is that which turns bad men into good, which transforms the slaves of sin into sons of God." All men are in one of two creations. As born into the world, they are sinful, helpless, and condemned. All their efforts to save themselves, or to assist God in their salvation by good character or good works, are futile, and leave them unchanged. The **new creation** is headed by the risen Christ, and includes all who have been redeemed from sin and given new life in Him. Because the **new creation** is all of Christ from start to finish, it excludes any thought of gaining God's favor through character or works. A life of holiness is produced, not by the observance of ritual, but by yielding to Christ and permitting Him to live His life in the believer. The **new creation** is not an improvement of or addition to the old, but something entirely different.

6:16 Of what **rule** is Paul speaking here? It is the **rule** of the new creation. He pronounces the double blessing of **peace and mercy** on all those who judge teaching by the question — "Is it of the new creation?" — and who reject all that is not.

And upon the Israel of God. Many have taken this to mean the church. However, **the Israel of God** refers to those Jews by natural birth who accept the Lord Jesus as Messiah. There was neither peace nor mercy for those who walked under the law, but both are the portion of those in the new creation.

6:17   Paul, once the slave of the law, had been delivered from that bondage by the Lord Jesus. Now he belonged to the Lord as a willing slave. Just as slaves were branded with the mark of their master, so Paul had the ownership **marks of the Lord Jesus** on his **body**. What were they? They were the scars which he received at the hands of his persecutors. Now he says: "Don't let anyone try to reclaim me. Don't talk to me about the brand-mark of circumcision, indicating bondage to the law. I wear the brand of my new Master, Jesus Christ."

6:18   The apostle is now about to lay down his pen. But he must close with an added word. What will it be? **GRACE** — the word which so characterizes his gospel. **Grace**, not law. It was the theme on which he began (1:3); it is the theme with which he closes. **The grace of our Lord Jesus Christ be with your spirit. Amen.**

LEGALISM

On completing a study of Galatians, one might conclude that Paul defeated the teachers of legalism so effectively that the issue would never trouble the church again. History and experience prove otherwise! Legalism has become so important a part of Christendom that most people believe that it actually belongs.

Yes, the legalists are still with us. What else shall we call those professed ministers of Christ who teach, for instance, that confirmation, baptism, or church membership are necessary for salvation; that the law is the believer's rule of life; that we are saved by faith but kept by works? What is it but Judaism brought over into Christianity when we are asked to accept a humanly ordained priesthood with its distinctive clothing, buildings patterned after the temple with their carved altars and elaborate rituals, and a church calendar with its Lenten season, its feasts, and its fasts?

And what is it but the Galatian heresy when believers are warned that they must keep the Sabbath if they are to be saved at last? Modern preachers of legalism are making tremendous inroads among those who profess faith in Christ, and for this reason every believer should be warned of their teaching and instructed how to answer them.

The prophets of the Sabbath usually begin by preaching the gospel of salvation by faith in Christ. They use beloved evangelical hymns to lure the unwary, and appear to place much emphasis on the Scriptures. But before long, they put their followers under the Law of Moses, especially the commandment concerning the Sabbath. (The Sabbath is the seventh day of the week, or Saturday.)

How do they dare to do this in the light of Paul's clear teaching that the Christian is dead to the law? How do they get around the plain statements of Galatians? The answer is that they make a sharp distinction between the moral law and the ceremonial law. The moral law is the Ten Commandments. The ceremonial law covers the other regulations given by God, such as rules concerning unclean foods, leprosy, offerings to God, and so forth.

The moral law, they say, has never been revoked. It is an expression of God's eternal truth. To commit idolatry, murder, or adultery will always be contrary to God's law. The ceremonial law, however, has been done away in Christ. Therefore, they conclude, when Paul teaches that the Christian is dead to the law, he is speaking about the ceremonial law and not the Ten Commandments.

Since the moral law is still in effect, Christians are bound to keep it, they insist. This means that they must keep the Sabbath, that they must do no work on that day. They assert that one of the popes of the Roman Catholic Church ordered the change from Sabbath-observance to observance of Sunday, in utter violation of Scriptures.

This reasoning sounds very logical and appealing. However, its great condemning feature is that it is entirely contrary to God's word! Note the following points:

1. In 2 Corinthians 3:7–11, the Ten Commandments are definitely stated to be "done away" for the believer in Christ. In verse 7, the law is described as "the ministry of death, written and engraved on stones." This could only mean the moral law, not the ceremonial law. Only the Ten Commandments were engraved in stones by the finger of God (Ex. 31:18). In verse 11, we read that the ministry of death, though glorious, is *done away*. Nothing could be more decisive than this. The Sabbath has no claim on the Christian.

2. No Gentile was ever commanded to keep the Sabbath. The law was given to the Jewish nation only (Ex. 31:13). Although God Himself rested on the seventh day, He did not command anyone else to do so until He gave the law to the children of Israel.

3. Christians did not switch from the Sabbath to the first day of the week because of the decree of any pope. We set aside the Lord's Day in a special way for worship and for service because the Lord Jesus rose from the dead on that day, a proof that the work of redemption was completed (John 20:1). Also, on that day the early disciples met to break bread, showing forth the Lord's death (Acts 20:7), and it was the day appointed by God for the Christians to set apart their offerings as the Lord had prospered them (1 Cor. 16:1, 2). Furthermore, the Holy Spirit was sent down from heaven on the first day of the week.

Christians do not "observe" the Lord's Day as a means of achieving holiness, or from fear of punishment; they set it apart because of loving devotion to the One who gave Himself for them.

4. Paul does not distinguish between the moral law and the ceremonial law. Rather, he insists that the law is a complete unit, and that a curse rests on those who seek to attain righteousness by it, yet fail to keep it all.

5. Nine of the Ten Commandments are repeated in the NT as moral instruction for the children of God. They deal with things that are inherently right or wrong. The one command-

ment which is omitted is the law of the Sabbath. The keeping of a day is not inherently right or wrong. There is no instruction to Christians to keep the Sabbath. Rather the Scripture distinctly states that the Christian *cannot be condemned* for failing to keep it! (Col. 2:16).

6. The penalty for breaking the Sabbath in the OT was death (Ex. 35:2). But those who insist on believers keeping the Sabbath today do not carry out the penalty on offenders. They thus dishonor the law and destroy its authority by failing to insist that its demands be met. They are saying, in effect, "This is God's law and you must keep it, but nothing will happen if you break it."

7. Christ, and not the law, is the believer's rule of life. We should walk as He walked. This is an even higher standard than was set by the law (Matt. 5:17–48). We are empowered to live holy lives by the Holy Spirit. We want to live holy lives because of our love for Christ. The righteousness demanded by the law is fulfilled by those who do not walk according to the flesh but according to the Spirit (Rom. 8:4).

Thus, the teaching that believers must keep the Sabbath is directly contrary to Scripture (Col. 2:16), and is simply a "different gospel" upon which God's word pronounces a curse (Gal. 1:7, 9).

May each one be given wisdom from God to discern the evil doctrine of legalism in whatever form it may appear! May we never seek justification or sanctification through ceremonies or human effort, but depend completely and only on the Lord Jesus Christ for every need. May we always remember that legalism is an insult to God because it substitutes the shadow for the Reality — ceremonialism for Christ. ‡

ENDNOTES

[1](1:8, 9) John Stott, *Only One Way: The Message of Galatians*, pp. 27, 28.

[2](1:18–20) The critical text reads *Cephas* (Aramaic form of *Peter*).

[3](2:1) E. F. Kevan, *The Keswick Week 1955*, p. 29.

[4](2:3) Circumcision is a minor surgical operation performed on the male. When

God ordained it for Abraham and his descendants, He intended it as a sign of His covenant with them, namely, that He would be their God and they would be His people (Gen. 17:1–11). It was not only a physical mark, but also a spiritual symbol. Abraham was circumcised as a sign that he had trusted in God (Rom. 4:11). The Jews soon forgot the *spiritual* meaning of circumcision, and carried it out simply as a ceremony. Thus the rite became valueless as far as God was concerned.

In the NT, circumcision is no longer commanded since God is now dealing in grace with Gentiles and Jews alike. In the early days of the church, a group of Jewish believers insisted that circumcision was necessary for salvation. Hence this party was known as "the circumcision" (Gal. 2:12).

⁵(2:3) A fairly full account of this meeting at Jerusalem is given in Acts 15. It should be studied carefully.

⁶(2:11) See note 2.

⁷(2:13) The punctuation, including quotation marks, is editorial. Some interpreters end the quotation here and view vv. 15–21 as Paul's *later explanation* of what he said to Peter.

⁸(2:21) W. M. Clow, *The Cross in the Christian Experience*, p. 114.

⁹(3:1) While Greek has separate singular and plural forms for *who*, an answer in the plural could not be ruled out here.

¹⁰(3:5) The most ancient manuscripts were all in "capitals." (Lower case letters evolved later.) Hence, while capitalization is editorial, the capital **H** for *He* is well taken in context.

¹¹(3:13) J. Cynddylan Jones, *Studies in the Gospel According to St. John*, p. 113.

¹²(3:20) Though there seems to be a contradiction between the argument here and the fact that Christ is later spoken of as the Mediator of the New Covenant (Heb. 9:15), the word *mediator* is used in two different senses in these two places. Moses served as a mediator simply by receiving the law from God and delivering it to the people of Israel. He was the go-between, or the people's representative. Christ is Mediator of the New Covenant in a far higher sense. Before God could righteously dispense the blessings of this covenant, the Lord Jesus

had to die. Just as death alone puts a person's last will and testament into force, so the New Covenant had to be sealed with His blood. He had to give Himself a ransom for all (1 Tim. 2:6). Christ not only insures the blessings of the covenant for His people, but also maintains His covenant people in a world that is antagonistic toward them. This He does as High Priest and Advocate, and this is also a part of His mediatorial work.

¹³(3:24) The Greek word *paidagōgos* (whence the English *pedagogy*) literally means a "child-leader." Such a person, usually a slave, was to see that the child got to and from school. Sometimes he taught as well.

¹⁴(4:7) The critical text reads simply *an heir through God.*

¹⁵(4:7) Norman B. Harrison, *His Side Versus Our Side*, p. 71.

¹⁶(4:13) Several theories have been advanced as to Paul's "infirmity." Some eye disease, among several that are common in the Middle East, is a likely candidate. Malaria, migraine, epilepsy, and other problems have also been suggested.

¹⁷(4:17) Stott, *Galatians*, p. 116.

¹⁸(5:1) C. H. Mackintosh, further documentation unavailable.

¹⁹(5:2) Jack Hunter, *What the Bible Teaches, Galatians – Philemon*, p. 78.

²⁰(5:4) C. F. Hogg and W. E. Vine, *Epistle of Paul the Apostle to the Galatians*, p. 241.

²¹(5:13) Arthur T. Pierson, further documentation unavailable.

²²(5:16) C. I. Scofield, further documentation unavailable.

²³(5:19–21) The critical text (NU) omits *adultery*. The word *fornication* (*porneia*) is often translated *sexual immorality*, which would include adultery. However, it is unlikely Paul would fail to specifically mention this rampant sin of marital infidelity in a catalogue of the flesh's vices.

²⁴(5:19–21) The critical text omits *murders* (*phonoi*). Since this word looks so much like the previous word (*phthonoi*, "envy"), it would be easy to delete it in copying.

²⁵(5:19–21) See note on 1 Corinthians 6:9.

²⁶(5:22, 23) Samuel Chadwick, quoted by James A. Stewart, *Pastures of Tender Grass*, p. 253.

[27](5:24) English usage demands that the aorist *estaurōsan* be translated as a present perfect, but the aorist indicative stresses the deed, *not* lasting results.

[28](6:7) J. A. Froude, further documentation unavailable.

BIBLIOGRAPHY

Cole, Alan. *The Epistle of Paul to the Galatians*. Grand Rapids: Wm. B. Eerdmans Publishing Company, 1965.

Eadie, John. *Commentary on the Epistle of Paul to the Galatians*. Edinburgh: T. and T. Clark, 1884.

Harrison, Norman B. *His Side Versus Our Side*. Minneapolis: The Harrison Service, 1940.

Hogg, C. F., and W. E. Vine. *Epistle to the Galatians*. Glasgow: Pickering and Inglis, 1922.

Ironside, Harry A. *Expository Messages on the Epistle to the Galatians*. New York: Loizeaux Brothers, 1941.

Kelly, William. *Lectures on the Epistle of Paul the Apostle to the Galatians*. London: G. Morrish, n.d.

Lightfoot, J. B. *The Epistle of St. Paul to the Galatians*. Grand Rapids: Zondervan Publishing House, 1962.

Stott, John. R. *Only One Way: The Message of Galatians*. Downers Grove, IL: Inter-Varsity Press, 1968.

Introduction

"The crown of St. Paul's writings."   – J. Armitage Robinson
"Paul's third heaven epistle."   – A. T. Pierson

I. Unique Place in the Canon

In some ways Ephesians is a typical Pauline Epistle: the salutation, the thanksgiving, the development of doctrine followed by the application of that doctrine as our duty, and the closing greetings. Yet Ephesians, while a genuine letter, is almost like a sermon or even a Christian service with prayers and a doxology. In this letter, as Moorehead writes, "We pass into the stillness and hush of the sanctuary. . . .Here prevails the atmosphere of repose, of meditation, of worship and peace."[1]

In spite of the fact that so many commentators agree with Robinson's evaluation quoted above, some modern scholars, abandoning eighteen or nineteen centuries of Christian teaching, claim Paul could not have written Ephesians. But is this a valid viewpoint in light of the facts?

II. Authorship††

As far as the *external evidence* that Ephesians is an authentic Pauline Epistle, the case is solid and strong. No other Pauline Epistle has such an early and continuous stream of witnesses, starting with Clement of Rome, Ignatius, Polycarp, and Hermas, and going on with Clement of Alexandria, Irenaeus, and Hippolytus. Marcion included it in his "canon," though calling it "Laodiceans." The Muratorian Canon also lists Ephesians as by Paul.

Internal evidence includes the fact that the author twice *says* he is Paul (1:1 and 3:1), and the contents of the letter are so similar (in *some* respects) to Colossians that they must have been written close to one another in time. The structure of Ephesians, as was mentioned, is typically Pauline. Granted, Paul does introduce some new thoughts in this book, but if a writer cannot do so without being accused of being a forger, the opportunities for biblical writers helping to mature the saints will prove difficult indeed!

The German liberal Schleiermacher was probably the first to reject Pauline authorship. Many moderns have followed suit, such as Moffatt and Goodspeed. Vocabulary, style, "advanced" doctrine, and other subjective arguments are mustered to deny this book to the apostle. However, every one of these theories can be answered satisfactorily. In light of the overwhelming external evidence and the large number of scholarly commentators who see Ephesians as not merely in the spirit of Paul, but, as Coleridge expressed it, his very "divinest writing," the letter should be accepted as genuine.

III. Date

Along with Colossians, Philippians, and Philemon, Ephesians is one of the so-called "Prison Epistles." *Which* imprisonment is involved (3:1; 4:1) has been debated. While some believe it was Paul's two-year stay in Caesarea, or even an unproven Ephesian imprisonment, the weight of evidence seems to come down on the first Roman imprisonment (soon after A.D. 60). Like Colossians (4:7–9), this letter was carried to the province of Asia by Tychicus (6:21, 22). This explains the similarity of doctrinal content, the same ideas being fresh in the apostle's mind as he wrote these letters.

†See p. xxvii.
††See p. i.

719

IV. Background and Theme[†]

The main subject of Ephesians is what Paul calls "the mystery." By that he does not mean something that cannot be explained, but rather a wonderful truth never revealed before but now made known.

This sublime truth, which forms the theme of the book, is the announcement that believing Jews and believing Gentiles are now one in Christ Jesus. They are fellow members of the church, the Body of Christ. At the present time they are seated in Christ in heavenly places. In the future they will share His glory as Head over all things.

The mystery is found in each of Ephesians' six chapters.

In chapter 1 it is called the mystery of God's will, and looks forward to the time when all things in heaven and on earth will be headed up in Christ (vv. 9, 10). Believing Jews (v. 11, "we") and believing Gentiles (v. 13, "you") will have their share in the glory of that day. They will reign with Him over the whole universe as His Body and His fullness (vv. 22, 23).

Chapter 2 describes the process by which Jews and Gentiles are saved by the grace of God; how they are reconciled to God and to one another; how, in union with Christ, they become one new man; and how they form a holy temple in which God dwells by His Spirit.

Chapter 3 gives the most complete explanation of the mystery. There it is spoken of as the mystery of "the Christ" (v. 4, JND), meaning Christ, the Head, and all believers, His Body. In this Body,

[†]See p. ii.

believing Gentiles are fellow heirs, fellow members, and fellow partakers of God's promise (v. 6).

Chapter 4 emphasizes the unity of the Body and God's plan for its growth to maturity (vv. 1–16).

In chapter 5, the mystery is called Christ and the church (v. 32). The relationship between Christ and the church is the pattern for the relationship between a believing husband and wife.

Finally, in chapter 6, Paul speaks of the mystery of the gospel, for which he was an ambassador in chains (vv. 19, 20).

Try to imagine the impact of this news on the Gentile believers to whom it was sent. Not only were they saved by grace through faith, the same as the Jews, but for the first time they occupied a place of equal privilege with them. They were in no way inferior as far as their standing before God was concerned. And they were destined to be enthroned with Christ as His Body and His Bride, sharing the glory of His universal reign.

Another important theme of Ephesians is *love* (Greek, *agapē*, the love expressed through the will). Paul starts and ends his Epistle with this concept (1:4; 6:24), and uses the verb and noun more in Ephesians than anywhere else in his Letters. This may show the Holy Spirit's foreknowledge, because while thirty years in the future the large and active congregation would still be obeying the command to fight false doctrine, our Lord tells them in His Letter to Ephesus that He held it against them that they had left their first *love* (Rev. 2:4).

OUTLINE

II. THE BELIEVER'S PRACTICE IN THE LORD (Chaps. 4–6)

  A. Appeal for Unity in the Christian Fellowship (4:1–6)

  B. Program for Proper Functioning of the Members of the Body (4:7–16)

  C. Appeal for a New Morality (4:17–5:21)

  D. Appeal for Personal Piety in the Christian Household (5:22–6:9)

  E. Exhortations Concerning the Christian Warfare (6:10–20)

  F. Paul's Personal Greetings (6:21–24)

Commentary

I. THE BELIEVER'S POSITION IN CHRIST (Chaps. 1–3)

A. Salutation (1:1, 2)

1:1 The name **Paul** means "small." Although physically he may have fitted this description, spiritually his influence was enormous. He introduces himself as **an apostle of Jesus Christ**. This means he was commissioned by the ascended Lord to perform a special mission. That mission was to preach *the gospel* to the Gentiles and to teach the great truth concerning *the church* (3:8, 9). Since Ephesians deals with the church, and since this truth was first revealed to the apostles and prophets (3:5), it is fitting that Paul should introduce himself as **an apostle**. It was not a mark of pride to do so; rather it was an explanation of how he could speak with authority on the subject. The source of his authority is expressed in the words, **by the will of God**. Paul did not choose his work as an occupation. And no men appointed him to it. It was a divine call from beginning to end (Gal. 1:1).

The letter is addressed **to the saints who are in Ephesus, and faithful in Christ Jesus**. **Saints** are people who have been separated to God from the world. It is a name which is applied in the NT to all born-again believers. Basically the word refers to a believer's position **in Christ** rather than to what he is in himself. **In Christ** all believers are **saints**, even though in themselves they are not always saintly. For instance, Paul addressed the Corinthians as saints (1 Cor. 1:2), even though it is clear from what follows that they were not all living holy lives. Yet God's will is that our practice should correspond to our position: **saints** should be saintly.

And faithful in Christ Jesus. The word, **faithful**, means "believing ones" and is thus a description of all true Christians. Of course, believers should also be **faithful** in the sense that they are reliable and trustworthy. But the primary thought here is that they had acknowledged **Christ Jesus** to be their only Lord and Savior.

Two of the oldest manuscripts omit the words, **in Ephesus**, although they stand in most manuscripts. Many scholars think this was a circular letter, written to be read by local gatherings of Christians in several places, of which the church at Ephesus was the most prominent. Fortunately the question affects neither the authenticity of the letter nor its value for us.

1:2 Next comes the apostle's greeting to the saints. Every word is loaded with spiritual significance — unlike many of the empty greetings we use today.

Grace means divine assistance for daily living. Paul's readers had already been saved by the grace of God, His undeserved favor to the lost. But now they needed strength **from God** to face the problems, trials, and sorrows of life. That is what the apostle wishes for them here.

Peace means a spirit at rest in all the changing circumstances of life. The saints had already experienced peace *with* God when they were converted. But day by day they needed the **peace** *of* God, that is, the calm, settled repose that is independent of circumstances and that results from taking everything to God in prayer (Phil. 4:6, 7).

It is worth noticing that **grace** comes first, then **peace**. This is always the order. Only after **grace** has dealt with the sin question can **peace** be known. And only through the undeserved strength which God gives from day to day can the believer experience **peace**, perfect **peace**, in all the changing moods of life.

Grace (*charis*) was a characteristically Greek word. The Jews use the word **peace** (Hebrew: *shâlōm*) as a greeting. Put them together and we have, in miniature, the gospel for the whole world. When we unite them we also have the truth of the NT church which Paul expounds so fully in Ephesians — Jew and Gentile formed into one Body in Christ.

Grace . . . and peace come **from God our Father and the Lord Jesus Christ**. Paul did not hesitate to put the **Lord Jesus** on the same level as **God** the Father: he honored the Son just as he honored the **Father**. So should we (John 5:23).

Let us not overlook the marvelous conjunction of the words **God our Father**. The word, **God**, taken by itself might convey the impression of One who is infinitely high and unapproachable. The name, **Father**, on the other hand, speaks of One who is intimately near and accessible. Join the two by the pronoun, **our**, and we have the staggering truth that the high and lofty **God**, who inhabits eternity, is the loving **Father** of everyone who has been born again through faith in the **Lord Jesus.**

The full title of our Savior is **Lord Jesus Christ**. As **Lord** He is our absolute Master, with full rights to all we are and have. As **Jesus** He is our Savior from sin. As **Christ** He is our divinely anointed Prophet, Priest, and King. How much His name unfolds to every listening ear!

B. Paul's Praise to God for the Blessings of Grace (1:3–14)

1:3 Following his brief salutation, the apostle lifts his voice in a magnificent hymn of praise, soaring into some of the sublimest heights of NT worship. Here we have the overflow of a heart that adores God for the blessings of grace. In these verses (3–14) Paul traces God's activity in salvation from eternity past through time and on into eternity future. And this necessarily involves a discussion of the mystery of God's will — believing Jews and Gentiles as co-sharers of the glorious inheritance.

He begins by calling on all who know

God to bless Him, that is, to bring joy to His heart by praise and worshiping love. The **blessed** One is **the God and Father of our Lord Jesus Christ**. At certain times Jesus addressed God as God (Matt. 27:46). At other times He spoke of Him as Father (John 10:30). The **blessed** One is also the Blesser. We bless Him by praising Him. He blesses us and makes us glad by showering us with the riches of His grace.

He **has blessed us with every spiritual blessing in the heavenly places in Christ**. Here is a pyramid of grace:

> blessing
> spiritual blessing
> every spiritual blessing
> every spiritual blessing in the
> heavenly places
> every spiritual blessing in the heavenly
> places in Christ

Notice first how unstinted are His heart and hand — **every spiritual blessing**. Notice, too, that these are *spiritual* blessings. The simplest way to explain this is to contrast them with the blessings of Israel under the law. In the OT, a faithful, obedient Jew was rewarded with long life, a large family, abundant crops, and protection from his enemies (Deut. 28:2–8). The blessings of Christianity, in contrast, are **spiritual**, that is, they deal with treasures that are nonmaterial, invisible, and imperishable. It is true that the OT saints also enjoyed some spiritual blessings, but as we shall see, the Christian today enjoys blessings that were unknown in previous times.

Our blessings are *in the heavenly places*, literally "*in the heavenlies.*" Instead of being material blessings in earthly places, they are **spiritual** blessings *in the heavenly places*. The expression, **in the heavenly places**, is used five times in Ephesians:

1:3 The sphere of our **spiritual** blessing
1:20 The scene of Christ's present enthronement
2:6 The scene of our present enthronement in Christ
3:10 The locale from which angels witness God's wisdom exhibited in the church
6:12 The region which is the source of our present conflict with evil spirits

When we put these passages together,

we have a truly scriptural definition of **the heavenly places**. As Unger put it, they are "the realm of the believer's position and experience as a result of his being united to Christ by the baptism of the Spirit." All **spiritual** blessings are *in Christ*. It was He who procured them for us through His finished work at Calvary. Now they are available through Him. Everything that God has for the believer is in the Lord Jesus. In order to receive the blessings, we must be united to Christ by faith. The moment a man is *in Christ*, he becomes the possessor of them all. Chafer writes, "To be in Christ, which is the portion of all who are saved, is to partake of all that Christ has done, all that He is, and all that He ever will be."[2]

In Christ is one of the key expressions of Ephesians. There are two closely related lines of truth in the NT — the truth of the believer's position and the truth of his practice.

First, the believer's position. Everyone in the world is either "in Adam" or "in Christ." Those who are "in Adam" are in their sins and therefore condemned before God. There is nothing they can do in themselves to please God or gain His favor. They have no claim on God, and if they were to receive what they deserve, they would perish eternally.

When a person is converted, God no longer looks upon him as a condemned child of Adam. Rather He sees him as being **in Christ**, and He accepts him on that basis. It is important to see this. The believing sinner is not accepted because of what he is in himself, but because he is **in Christ**. When he is **in Christ**, he stands before God clothed in all the acceptability of Christ Himself. And he will enjoy God's favor and acceptance as long as Christ does, namely, forever.

The believer's position, then, is what he is **in Christ**. But there is another side to the picture — the believer's practice. This is what he is in himself. His position is perfect, but his practice is imperfect. Now God's will is that his practice should increasingly correspond to his position. It never will do so perfectly until he is in heaven. But the process of sanctification, growth, and increasing Christlikeness should be going on con-

tinually while he is here on earth.

When we understand the difference between the believer's standing and his state, it enables us to reconcile such seemingly opposite verses as the following:

Believers are perfect (Heb. 10:14)	Believers should be perfect (Matt. 5:48)
Believers are dead to sin (Rom. 6:2)	Believers should reckon themselves dead to sin (Rom. 6:11)
Believers are a holy nation (1 Pet. 2:9)	Believers should be holy (1 Pet. 1:15)

The first column deals with position, the second with practice.

Paul's Letter to the Ephesians itself is divided into two halves that parallel this truth: (Chaps. 1–3): Our position — what we are in Christ; (Chaps. 4–6): Our practice — what we should be in ourselves. The first half has to do with doctrine, the second half with duty. In the first three chapters our position is often described by such phrases as "in Christ," "in Christ Jesus," "in Him," "in whom." In the last three chapters the phrase, "in the Lord," is often used to express the believer's responsibility to Christ as Lord. Someone has well said that the first part of the letter pictures the believer in the heavenlies in Christ, whereas the last part views him in the kitchen.

Now we are ready to consider some of the **spiritual** blessings **in the heavenly places** which are ours **in Christ**.

1:4 The first is what is commonly known as election. **Just as He chose us in Him before the foundation of the world, that we should be holy and without blame before Him in love.**

Notice first the positive fact of election in the words, **He chose us**. Then there is the positional aspect of the truth, **in Him**: it is in the Person and work of the Lord Jesus that all God's purposes for His people are brought to pass. The time of God's election is indicated by the expression, **before the foundation of the world**. And the purpose is **that we should be holy and without blame before Him in love**. This purpose will not be completely realized until we are with Him in heaven (1 John 3:2), but the process should be going on continually in our lives down here.

Prayer: "Lord, make me holy now,
since this is Your eventual
purpose for me.   Amen."

DIVINE ELECTION

The doctrine of election raises serious problems in the human mind, so we must consider more fully what the Bible does (and does not) teach on this subject.

First, it teaches that God does choose men to salvation (2 Thess. 2:13). It addresses believers as those who are "elect according to the foreknowledge of God" (1 Pet. 1:2). It teaches that people can know whether they are elect by their response to the gospel: those who hear and believe it are elect (1 Thess. 1:4–7).

On the other hand, the Bible never teaches that God chooses men to be lost. The fact that He chooses some to be saved does not imply that He arbitrarily condemns all the rest. He never condemns men who deserve to be saved (there are none), but He does save some who ought to be condemned. When Paul describes the elect, he speaks of them as "vessels of mercy which He had prepared beforehand for glory" (Rom. 9:23); but when he turns to the lost, he simply says, "vessels of wrath prepared for destruction" (Rom. 9:22). God prepares vessels of mercy to glory, but He does not prepare men for destruction: they do this for themselves by their own unbelief.

The doctrine of election lets God be God. He is sovereign, that is, He can do as He pleases, though He never pleases to do anything unjust. If left alone, all men would be lost. Does God have the right to show mercy to some?

But there is another side to the story. The same Bible that teaches sovereign election also teaches human responsibility. No one can use the doctrine of election as an excuse for not being saved. God makes a bona fide offer of salvation to all people everywhere (John 3:16; 3:36; 5:24; Rom. 10:9, 13). Anyone can be saved by repenting of his sins and believing on the Lord Jesus Christ. Therefore, if a person is lost, it is because he chooses to be lost, not because God desires it.

The fact is that the same Bible teaches election and free salvation to all who will receive it. Both doctrines are found in a single verse: "All that the Father gives Me will come to Me, and the one who comes to Me I will by no means cast out" (John 6:37). The first half of the verse speaks of God's sovereign choice; the last half extends the offer of mercy to all.

This poses a difficulty for the human mind. How can God choose some and yet offer salvation freely to all men? Frankly, this is a mystery. But the mystery is on our side, not on God's. The best policy for us is to believe both doctrines because the Bible teaches both. The truth is not found somewhere between election and man's free will, but in both extremes. W. G. Blaikie summarizes:

> Divine sovereignty, human responsibility and the free and universal offer of mercy are all found in Scripture, and though we are unable to harmonize them by our logic, they all ought to have a place in our minds.[3] ‡

1:5 The second spiritual blessing from the treasury of God's grace is predestination, or foreordination. Though somewhat related to election, it is not the same. Election pictures God's choice of people to salvation. But predestination is an advance on this: it means that God determined ahead of time that all who would be saved would also be adopted into His family **as sons**. He could have saved us without making us His sons, but He chose to do both.

Many translations link the last two words of verse 4 with verse 5 as follows: **in love having predestined us**.

This reminds us of the unique affection that prompted God to deal with us so graciously.

We have the fact of our glorious **adoption** in the phrase, **having predestined us to adoption as sons**. In the NT, **adoption** means placing a believer in the family of God as a mature, adult son with all the privileges and responsibilities of sonship (Gal. 4:4–7). The Spirit of adoption plants within the believer the instinct to address God as Father (Rom. 8:15).

Our **adoption as sons** is **by Jesus**

Christ. God could never have brought us into this position of nearness and dearness **to Himself** as long as we were in our sins. So the Lord Jesus came to earth, and by His death, burial, and resurrection He settled the sin question to God's satisfaction. It is the infinite value of His sacrifice on Calvary that provides a righteous basis on which God can adopt us **as sons**.

And it is all **according to the good pleasure of His will**. This is the sovereign motivation behind our predestination. It answers the question, "Why did He do it?" Simply because it was His **good pleasure**. He could not be satisfied until He had surrounded Himself with sons, conformed to the image of His only begotten Son, with Him and like Him forever.

1:6 To the praise of the glory of His grace, by which He has made us accepted in the Beloved. As Paul has contemplated the grace of God first in electing us and then in predestining us to be His sons, he punctuates his meditation with this refrain that is at once an exclamation, an explanation, and an exhortation. It is an *exclamation* — a holy gasp at the transcendent glories of such grace. It is an *explanation* that the object and the result of all God's gracious dealings with us is His own **glory**. Eternal adoration is due to Him for such matchless favor. Notice the terms of His **grace** — **He** (freely) **made us accepted**. The recipients of His **grace** — **us**. The channel of His **grace** — **in the Beloved**. Finally, it is an *exhortation*. Paul is saying, "Let us **praise** Him for His glorious **grace**". Before we go any farther, let us do it!

> Great God of wonders! All Thy ways
> Display Thine attributes divine;
> But the bright glories of Thy grace
> Above Thine other wonders shine:
> Who is a pard'ning God like Thee?
> Or who has grace so rich and free?
> — *Samuel Davies*

1:7 As we trace the sublime sweep of God's eternal plan for His people, we come next to the fact of **redemption**. This describes that aspect of the work of Christ by which we are freed from the bondage and guilt of sin and introduced into a life of liberty. The Lord Jesus is the Redeemer (**In Him we have redemp-**

tion). We are the redeemed. **His blood** is the ransom price; nothing less would do.

One of the results of redemption is **the forgiveness of sins. Forgiveness** is not the same as **redemption**; it is one of its fruits. Christ had to make full satisfaction for our sins before they could be forgiven. This was done at the cross. And now —

> Stern justice can demand no more
> And mercy can dispense her store.

The measure of our **forgiveness** is given in the words, **according to the riches of His grace**. If we can measure **the riches of** God's **grace**, then we can measure how fully He has forgiven us. His **grace** is infinite! So is His **forgiveness**!

1:8 It was in grace that He chose us, predestined us, and redeemed us. But that is not all. God has superabounded that same grace **toward us in all wisdom and prudence**. This means He has graciously shared His plans and purposes with us. His desire is that we should have intelligence and insight into His plans for the church and for the universe. And so He has taken us into His confidence, as it were, and has revealed to us the great goal toward which all history is moving.

1:9 Paul now explains the particular way in which God has abounded toward us in all wisdom and prudence, namely, by making **known to us the mystery of His will**. This is the dominant theme of the Epistle — the glorious truth concerning Christ and the church. It is a **mystery**, not in the sense that it is mysterious, but that it is a sacred secret previously unknown but now revealed to the saints. This glorious plan originated in the sovereign will of God, quite apart from any outside influences: it was **according to His good pleasure**. And the grand subject of the plan is the Lord Jesus Christ; this is indicated by the clause, **which He purposed in Himself.**

1:10 Now Paul begins a more detailed explanation of the secret of God's plan, and in this chapter he is thinking particularly of the future aspect of the mystery. Chapters 2 and 3 will add further light on the present aspect of the mystery.

The time which Paul has in view is indicated by the expression, **the dispensation** (administration, Gk., *oikonomia*) **of the fullness of the times**. We understand this to refer to the Millennium, when Christ will return to the earth to reign as King of kings and Lord of lords. God has a special economy or plan of administration for the final era of human history on this earth.

The plan is "to head up all things in the Christ" (JND). During the Millennial Reign, **all things in heaven** and **on earth** will be summed up **in Christ**. The Savior who is now rejected and disowned will then be the preeminent One, the Lord of all, the object of universal worship. This is God's goal — to set up **Christ** as Head over **all things**, heavenly and earthly, in the kingdom.

The extent of the dominion of Christ is found in the words, "the things in the heavens and the things upon the earth" (JND). Bellett writes:

This is a secret never made known before. In the prophet Isaiah, we get a beautiful picture of the millennial earth; but do we ever get the millennial heavens with Christ at their head? Was it ever said by Isaiah that all things in heaven and earth should be headed up in the glorified Man?[4]

Verse 10 is sometimes used to support the false doctrine of universal salvation. It is twisted to suggest that eventually everything and everyone will be restored and reconciled in Christ. But that is quite foreign to the passage. Paul is speaking about universal *dominion*, not universal salvation!

1:11 One vital feature of the mystery is that believing Jews and believing Gentiles have their share in this grand program of God. The apostle speaks of the mystery in relation to Jewish believers in verses 11 and 12; in relation to Gentile believers in verse 13; then he combines them both in verse 14.

As for the Christians of Jewish ancestry, Paul writes, **In Him also we have obtained an inheritance**. Their right to a share is not based on their former national privileges, but solely on their union with Christ. The **inheritance** here looks forward to the time when they and all true believers will be manifested to an amazed world as the Body of Christ, the Bride of the Lamb.

From all eternity these Jewish Christians were marked out for this place of privilege by the sovereign will of God, **being predestined according to the purpose of Him who works all things according to the counsel of His will.**

1:12 The purpose of this predestination was **that** they **should be to the praise of His glory**. In other words, they are trophies of the grace of God, exhibiting what He can do with such unlikely raw materials, and thus bringing **glory** to Him.

The apostle speaks of himself and other believing Jews as **we who first trusted in Christ**. He is thinking of the godly remnant of Jews who responded to the gospel in the early days of Christianity. The good news was first preached to the Jews. Most of the nation of Israel flatly rejected it. But the godly remnant believed on the Lord Jesus. Paul was one of that number.

It will be different when the Savior returns to the earth the second time. Then the nation will look on Him whom they pierced and will mourn for Him as for an only Son (Zech. 12:10). "And so all Israel will be saved, as it is written: 'The Deliverer will come out of Zion, and He will turn away ungodliness from Jacob' " (Rom. 11:26).

Paul and his Christian contemporaries of Jewish background trusted in the Messiah before the rest of the nation. That is why he uses the description, "we . . . who have trusted beforehand in Christ" (FWG).

Those who "fore-hoped" in Messiah will reign with Him over the earth. The rest of the nation will be the earthly subjects of His kingdom.

1:13 Now Paul switches from believers who had been born Jews to those who had been born Gentiles; he indicates this by changing from "we" to **you**. Those who have been saved from paganism have a share in the mystery of God's will, as well as converted Jews. And so the apostle here traces the steps by which the Ephesians and other Gentiles had been brought into union with Christ.

They **heard** the gospel.

They **believed** in Christ.

They **were sealed with the Holy Spirit of promise.**

First they **heard the word of truth, the gospel of** their **salvation**. Basically, this refers to the good news of **salvation** through faith in the Lord Jesus. But in a wider sense it includes all the teachings of Christ and the apostles.

Having heard this message, they made a commitment of themselves to Christ by a decisive act of faith. The Lord Jesus is the true object of faith. **Salvation** is found in Him alone.

As soon as they **believed,** they **were sealed with the Holy Spirit of promise**. This means that every true believer receives the **Spirit** of God as a sign that he belongs to God and that he will be kept safe by God until the time he receives his glorified body. Just as in legal matters a seal indicates ownership and security, so it does in divine affairs. The indwelling Spirit brands us as God's property (1 Cor. 6:19, 20), and guarantees our preservation until the day of redemption (Eph. 4:30).

Our seal is called **the Holy Spirit of promise**. First, He is the *Holy* Spirit; this is what He is in Himself. Then, He is the Spirit of *promise*. He was promised by the Father (Joel 2:28; Acts 1:4), and by the Lord Jesus (John 16:7). In addition, He is the guarantee that all God's promises to the believer will be fulfilled.

Verse 13 rounds out the first of many mentions of the Trinity in this Letter:

God the Father (v. 3)

God the Son (v. 7)

God the Spirit (v. 13)

1:14 Again Paul changes his pronouns. He merges the "we" of verses 11 and 12 with the "you" of verse 13 to form the **our** of verse 14. By this deft literary device, he drops a hint of what he will more fully explain in chapters 2 and 3 — the union of believing Jews and believing Gentiles to form a new organism, the church.

The Holy Spirit is **the guarantee of our inheritance**. This is a downpayment, pledging that the full amount will be paid. It is the same in kind as the full payment, but not the same in amount.

As soon as we are saved, the Holy Spirit begins to reveal to us some of the riches that are ours in Christ. He gives us foretastes of the coming glory. But how can we be sure that we will get the full inheritance some day? The Holy Spirit Himself is the earnest or **guarantee.**

As the seal, He guarantees that we ourselves will be kept safely for the inheritance. As the earnest, He guarantees the **inheritance** will be kept securely for us.

The Spirit is the **guarantee until the redemption of the purchased possession**. The **guarantee** looks forward to the full **redemption**, just as the firstfruits look forward to the complete harvest. The Spirit's role as earnest will cease when **the purchased possession** is redeemed. But what does Paul mean by **the purchased possession?**

1. He may mean **our inheritance**. All that God possesses is ours through the Lord Jesus: we are heirs of God and joint heirs with Jesus Christ (Rom. 8:17; 1 Cor. 3:21–23). The universe itself has been defiled through the entrance of sin, and needs to be reconciled and purified (Col. 1:20; Heb. 9:23). When Christ returns to the earth to reign, this groaning creation will be delivered from the bondage of corruption into the glorious liberty of the children of God (Rom. 8:19–22).

2. The expression, **the purchased possession**, may mean the believer's body. Our spirits and souls were redeemed when we first believed, but the redemption of our bodies is still future. The fact that we suffer, grow old, and die proves that our bodies have not yet been redeemed. When Christ returns for us (1 Thess. 4:13–18), our bodies will be fashioned anew so they can be conformed to the body of His glory (Phil. 3:21). Then they will be fully and forever redeemed (Rom. 8:23).

3. Finally, **the purchased possession** may refer to the church (1 Pet. 2:9: "His own special people"). In this case, its redemption also looks forward to the Rapture, when Christ will present the church to Himself a glorious church without spot or wrinkle or any such thing (Eph. 5:27). Some believe that in this view, God's own **possession** may also include the OT saints.

Whichever view we hold, the ultimate result is the same — **to the praise of His glory**. God's marvelous plan for His people will then have reached a glorious consummation, and He will be the object of continual praise. Three times in this chapter Paul has reminded us that the intended goal and inevitable result of all God's actions is that He should be magnified and glorified.

To the praise of the glory of His grace (v. 6)

That we should be to the praise of His glory (v. 12)

To the praise of His glory (v. 14)

C. Paul's Thanksgiving and Prayers for the Saints (1:15–23)

1:15 In the preceding passage, extending from verse 3 through verse 14 (a single sentence in Greek!), the apostle has traced the thrilling sweep of God's program from eternity past to eternity future. He has ranged over some of the most awe-inspiring thoughts that can occupy our minds, thoughts so exalted that Paul now shares with his readers his deep prayer burden for their spiritual enlightenment in such concepts. His great desire for them is that they might appreciate their glorious privileges in Christ and the tremendous power which was required to give Christ to the church as Head over all creation.

The introductory **Therefore** looks back to all that God has done and will yet do for those who are members of the body of Christ, as described in verses 3–14.

After I heard of your faith in the Lord Jesus and your love for all the saints. It was when he received this information that Paul was assured his readers were possessors of the spiritual blessings just described, and was driven to prayer for them. Their **faith in the Lord Jesus** brought the miracle of salvation to their lives. Their **love for all the saints** demonstrated the transforming reality of their conversion.

Those Bible scholars who do not think this Letter was written exclusively to the Ephesians point to this verse as evidence. Paul speaks here of having heard of the faith of his readers — as if he had never met them. But he had spent at least three years in Ephesus

(Acts 20:31). They therefore conclude the Letter was sent to several local congregations, of which Ephesus was only one.

Fortunately the question does not affect the lessons we can learn from the verse. For instance, we see that the **Lord** is presented as the true object of faith: **your faith in the Lord Jesus**. We are not told to believe in a creed, in the church, or in Christians. Saving faith is in the risen, exalted Christ at God's right hand.

Another lesson for us is the expression, **your love for all the saints**. Our love should not be limited to those of our own area of fellowship, but should flow out to all who have been cleansed by the blood of Christ, to all the household of faith.

A third lesson is found in the combination of **faith** and **love**. Some people say they have faith, but it is hard to find any love in their lives. Others profess great love but are quite indifferent to the necessity of faith in Christ. True Christianity combines sound doctrine and sound living.

1:16 The faith and love of the believers impelled Paul to praise the Lord for them and to pray for them unceasingly. Scroggie puts it nicely:

Thanksgiving is for the foundation already laid, but intercession is for the superstructure going up. Thanksgiving is for past attainments, but intercession is for future advancements. Thanksgiving is for the actual in their experience, but intercession is for the possible in God's purpose for them.

1:17 What a privilege it is to have this glimpse into the prayer life of a man of God. In fact, there are two such glimpses in this Letter — here and in 3:14–21. Here the prayer is for spiritual illumination; there it is for spiritual strength. Here the prayer is addressed to **God**; there to the Father. But in every case Paul's prayers were unceasing, specific, and appropriate to the current needs of the people. Here the prayer is addressed to **the God of our Lord Jesus Christ, the Father of glory**. The expression, **the Father of glory**, may mean that God is either:

1. the Source or Originator of all glory,
2. the One to whom all glory belongs, or

3. the Father of the Lord Jesus, who is the manifestation of God's glory.

The prayer continues that He **may give to you the spirit of wisdom and revelation in the knowledge of Him**. The Holy Spirit is the Spirit **of wisdom** (Isa. 11:2), and of **revelation** (1 Cor. 2:10). But since every believer is indwelt by Him, Paul cannot be praying that his readers might receive the Person of the Holy Spirit but rather that they might receive a special measure of illumination from Him.

Revelation deals with the imparting of knowledge; **wisdom** has to do with the proper use of it in our lives. The apostle is not thinking of knowledge in general but of the specific **knowledge** (Gk., *epignōsis*) **of Him**. He wants the believers to have a deep, spiritual, and experimental **knowledge** of God — a **knowledge** that cannot be gained by intellectual ability, but only by the gracious ministry of the Spirit.

Dale explains:

These Ephesian Christians had already Divine illumination, or they would not have been Christians at all; but Paul prayed that the Divine Spirit who dwelt in them would make their vision clearer, keener, stronger, that the Divine power and love and greatness might be revealed to them far more fully. And perhaps in these days in which men are making such rapid discoveries in inferior provinces of thought, discoveries so fascinating and so exciting as to rival in interest, even for Christian men, the manifestation of God in Christ, there is exceptional need for the church to pray that God would grant it a *"spirit of wisdom and revelation"*; if He were to answer that prayer we should no longer be dazzled by the knowledge which relates to "things seen and temporal," it would be outshone by the transcendent glory of "things unseen and eternal."[5]

1:18 We have seen that the source of spiritual illumination is God; the channel is the Holy Spirit; and the supreme subject is the full knowledge of God. Now we come to the organs of enlightenment: **the eyes of your hearts** (NKJV margin[6]) **being enlightened**.

This figurative expression teaches us that proper understanding of divine realities is not dependent on our having keen intellects but rather tender **hearts**.

It is a matter of the affections as well as of the mind. God's revelations are given to those who love Him. This opens up wonderful possibilities for every believer, because though we may not all have high I.Q.'s, we can all have loving **hearts**.

Next Paul specifies the three particular areas of divine knowledge which he desires for the saints:

1. **the hope of His calling**
2. **the riches of the glory of His inheritance in the saints**
3. the exceeding greatness of His power toward us who believe

The hope of His calling points forward to the future; it means that eventual destiny which He had in mind for us when He called us. It includes the fact that we shall be with Christ and like Him forever. We shall be manifested to the universe as sons of God and reign with Him as His spotless Bride. We hope for this, not in the sense that there is any doubt about it, but rather because it is that aspect of our salvation which is still future and to which we look forward.

The riches of the glory of his inheritance in the saints is the second tremendous vastness for believers to explore. Notice the way in which Paul stacks words upon words in order to produce the effect of immensity and grandeur:

His inheritance
His inheritance in the saints
The glory of His inheritance in the saints
The riches of the glory of His inheritance
in the saints

There are two possible ways of understanding this, and both are so meaningful that we present both. According to the first, **the saints are His inheritance**, and He looks on them as a treasure of incomparable worth. In Titus 2:14 and 1 Peter 2:9, believers are described as "His own special people." It is certainly an exhibition of unspeakable grace that vile, unworthy sinners, saved through Christ, could ever occupy such a place in the heart of God that He would speak of them as **His inheritance**.

The other view is that the **inheritance** means all that *we* will inherit. In brief, it means the whole universe put under the reign of Christ, and we, His Bride, reigning with Him over it. If we really appreciate the wealth of the glory of all He has in store for us, it will spoil us for the attractions and pleasures of this world.

1:19 Paul's third petition for the saints is that they might have a deep appreciation of the **power** which God engages to bring all this to pass: **the exceeding greatness of His power toward us who believe**.

F. B. Meyer says, "It is *power*. It is *His* power. It is *great* power; nothing less would suffice. It is *exceeding* great power, beyond the furthest cast of thought."[7]

This is the power which God used in our redemption, which He uses in our preservation, and which He will yet use in our glorification. Lewis Sperry Chafer writes:

Paul wants to impress the believer with the greatness of the power which is engaged to accomplish for him everything that God has purposed according to His work of election, predestination and sovereign adoption.[8]

1:20 To further emphasize the magnitude of this power, the apostle next describes the greatest exhibition of divine **power** the world has ever known, namely, the power that **raised** Christ out **from** among **the dead** and enthroned Him at God's **right hand**. Perhaps we would think that the creation of the universe was the greatest display of God's might. Or God's miraculous deliverance of His people through the Red Sea. But no! The NT teaches that Christ's resurrection and ascension required the greatest outflow of divine energy.

Why was this? It seems that all the hosts of hell were massed to frustrate God's purposes by keeping Christ in the tomb, or by preventing His ascension once He was raised. But God triumphed over every form of opposition. Christ's resurrection and glorification were a shattering defeat for Satan and his hosts, and a glorious spectacle of victorious power.

No one is sufficient to describe such power. So Paul borrows several words from the vocabulary of dynamics in his description of the power which is employed on our behalf: **"according to** that *working* **of** the *strength* **of His** *might* **which He** *energized* **in Christ when He**

raised Him from the dead.'' The words seem to bend under the weight of the idea. It is hardly necessary for us to distinguish between the different words; it is enough to marvel at the immensity of the power and to worship our God for His omnipotence!

Meyer exclaims:

A marvelous lift was there! From the grave of mortality to the throne of the eternal God, who only has immortality. From the darkness of the tomb to the insufferable light. From this small world to the center and metropolis of the universe. Open the compasses of your faith to measure this measureless abyss. Then marvel at the power which bore your Lord across it.[9]

As far as the Scriptures are concerned, the resurrection of Christ was the first such event in human history (1 Cor. 15:23). Others had been raised from the dead, but they died again. The Lord Jesus was the first to rise in the power of an endless life. Following Christ's resurrection and ascension, God **seated Him at His right hand in the heavenly places**. The **right hand** of God signifies the place of privilege (Heb. 1:13), power (Matt. 26:64), distinction (Heb. 1:3), delight (Ps. 16:11), and dominion (1 Pet. 3:22).

The location is further described as **in the heavenly places**. This indicates that the phrase includes the dwelling place of God. That is where the Lord Jesus is today in a literal body of flesh and bones, a glorified body no longer capable of dying. Where He is, we soon shall be.

1:21 The glorification of our Savior is further described as **far above all principality and power and might and dominion, and every name that is named, not only in this age but also in that which is to come**. The Lord Jesus is superior to every ruler or authority, human or angelic, now and forever.

In the heavenlies there are different ranks of angelic beings, some evil and some good. They have different degrees of power. Some, for instance, might correspond to our human offices of president, governor, mayor, or ward alderman. No matter how great their rule, authority, **power**, and **dominion** might be, Christ is **far above** them.

And this is true **not only in** the **age**

in which we live **but also in** the coming **age**, that is, the literal Thousand-Year Reign of Christ on earth. He will then be King over all kings and Lord over all lords. He will be exalted above all created beings; no exception can be named.

1:22 In addition, God has **put all** created **things under His feet**. This signifies universal dominion, not only over men and angels, but over all the rest of His creation, animate and inanimate. The writer of Hebrews reminds us that at the present time we do not see all things put under Him (Heb. 2:8). That is true. Though universal dominion belongs to Christ, He does not exercise it as yet. Men, for instance, still rebel against Him and deny Him or resist Him. But God has decreed that His Son will yet wield the scepter of universal dominion, and it is as certain as if it were a present reality.

What follows is almost incredible. This One whose nail-scarred hand will exercise sovereign authority over all the universe — God has given this glorious One **to the church**! Here Paul makes a startling revelation concerning the mystery of God's will; step by step he has been leading up to this climactic announcement. With graphic skill he has been describing the resurrection, glorification, and dominion of Christ. While our hearts are still awestruck at the contemplation of this all-glorious Lord, the apostle says, "It is in His capacity as **head over all things** that Christ has been given **to the church**."

If we read this verse carelessly, we might understand it to say that Christ is the Head of **the church**. While that is true enough, the verse says a lot more. It says that **the church** is closely associated with Him who has been given universal sway.

In verse 21 we learned that Christ is far above every *creature* in heaven and on earth, in this age and in the coming age. In the first part of verse 22 we learned that **all things** as well as all created beings are in subjection **under His feet**. Now we learn that the unique calling of **the church** is to be associated with Him in His boundless dominion. **The church** will share His rule. All the rest of creation will be under His rule.

1:23 In this final verse of chapter 1, we learn how close is the relationship between Christ and the church. Two figures are given: (1) The church **is His body**; (2) It is **the fullness of Him who fills all in all**.

No relationship could be closer than that of the head and the **body**. They are one in vital union and indwelt by one Spirit. The church is a company of people called out from the world between Pentecost and the Rapture, saved by marvelous grace, and given the unique privilege of being the **body** of Christ. No other group of believers in any age ever has had or will have this distinction.

The second description of the church is **the fullness of Him who fills all in all**. This simply means that the church is the complement of Christ, who is everywhere at one and the same time. A complement is that which fills up or completes. It implies two things which when brought together constitute a whole. Just as a body is the complement of the head, so the church is the complement of Christ.

But lest anyone should think this implies any imperfection or incompleteness in Christ, Paul quickly adds, **the fullness of Him who fills all in all**. Far from His needing anything to fill up any lack of completeness, the Lord Jesus is Himself the One **who fills all in all**, who permeates the universe and supplies it with all that it needs.

Admittedly, this is too much for us to understand. We can only admire the infinite mind and plan of God while admitting our own inability to comprehend it.

D. God's Power Manifest in the Salvation of Gentiles and Jews (2:1–10)

2:1 The chapter break should not obscure the vital connection between the latter part of chapter 1 and the verses that follow. There we watched the mighty power of God as it raised Christ from the grave and crowned Him with glory and honor. Now we see how that same power has worked in our own lives, raising us from spiritual death and seating us in Christ in the heavenlies.

This passage resembles the first chapter of Genesis. In each we have: (1) a scene of desolation, chaos, and ruin (Gen. 1:2a; Eph. 2:1–3); (2) the introduction of divine power (Gen. 1:2b; Eph. 2:4); (3) the creation of new life (Gen. 1:3–31; Eph. 2:5–22).

When Ephesians 2 opens, we are spiritual corpses in death valley. When it closes, we are not only seated in Christ in the heavenlies; we form a habitation of God through the Spirit. In between we have the mighty miracle that brought about this remarkable transformation.

The first ten verses describe God's power in the salvation of Gentiles and Jews. No Cinderella ever advanced from such rags to such riches!

In verses 1 and 2 Paul reminds his Gentile readers that before their conversion they **were dead**, depraved, diabolical, and disobedient. They **were** spiritually **dead** as a result of their **trespasses and sins**. This means they were lifeless toward God. They had no vital contact with Him. They lived as if He did not exist. The cause of death was **trespasses and sins**. **Sins** are any form of wrongdoing, whether consciously committed or not, and thoughts, words, or deeds which fall short of God's perfection. **Trespasses** are sins which are committed in open violation of a known law. In a wider sense they may also include any form of false steps or blunders.

2:2 The Ephesians had been depraved as well as dead. They **walked according to the course of this world**. They conformed to the spirit of this age. They indulged in the sins of the times. The world has a mold into which it pours its devotees. It is a mold of deceit, immorality, ungodliness, selfishness, violence, and rebellion. In a word, it is a mold of depravity. That is what the Ephesians had been like.

Not only so, their behavior was diabolical. They followed the example of the devil, **the prince of the power of the air**. They were led around by the chief ruler of evil spirits, whose realm is the atmosphere. They were willingly obedient to the god of this age. This explains why the unconverted often stoop to vile forms of behavior lower than that of animals.

Finally, they were disobedient, walking according to **the spirit who now works in the sons of disobedience**. All unsaved people are **sons of disobedience** in the sense that they are character-ized by **disobedience** to God. They are energized by Satan and are therefore disposed to defy, dishonor, and disobey the Lord.

2:3 Paul's switch of the personal pronoun from *you* to *we* indicates he is now speaking primarily of Jewish believers (although what he says is also true of everyone before conversion). Three words describe their status: carnal, corrupt, and condemned.

Among whom also we all once conducted ourselves in the lusts of our flesh. It was among the sons of disobedience that Paul and his fellow Christians also walked prior to their new birth. Their life was *carnal*, concerned only with the gratification of fleshly desires and appetites. Paul himself had lived an outwardly moral life on the whole, but now he realized how self-centered it was. And what he was in himself was a lot worse than anything he had ever done.

The unconverted Jews were also *corrupt*, **fulfilling the desires of the flesh and of the mind**. This indicates an abandonment to every natural desire. **Desires of the flesh and of the mind** may range all the way from legitimate appetites to various forms of immorality and perversion; here the emphasis is probably on the grosser sins. And notice, Paul refers to sins of thought as well as to sinful acts.

F. B. Meyer warns:

> It is as ruinous to indulge the desires of the *mind* as those of the *flesh*. By the marvelous gift of imagination we may indulge unholy fancies, and throw the reins on the neck of the steeds of passion — always stopping short of the act. No human eye follows the soul when it goes forth to dance with satyrs or to thread the labyrinthine maze of the islands of desire. It goes and returns unsuspected by the nearest. Its credit for snow-white purity is not forfeited. It is still permitted to watch among the virgins for the Bridegroom's advent. But if this practice is unjudged and unconfessed, it marks the offender a son of disobedience and a child of wrath.[10]

This is Paul's final description of the unsaved Jews: they were **by nature children of wrath, just as the others**. This means they had a natural predisposition to anger, malice, bitterness, and hot temper. They shared this with the rest of mankind. Of course, it is also true that they are under the **wrath** of God. They are appointed to death and judgment. Notice that man's three enemies are mentioned in verses 2 and 3: the world (v. 2), the devil (v. 2), and the flesh (v. 3).

2:4 The words, **But God**, form one of the most significant, eloquent, and inspiring transitions in all literature. They indicate that a stupendous change has taken place. It is a change from the doom and despair of the valley of death to the unspeakable delights of the kingdom of the Son of God's love.

The Author of the change is **God** Himself. No one else *could* have done it, and no one else *would* have done it.

One characteristic of this blessed One is that He **is rich in mercy**. He shows **mercy** to us by not treating us the way we deserve to be treated (Ps. 103:10). "Though it has been expended by Him for six millennia, and myriads and myriads have been partakers of it, it is still an unexhausted mine of wealth," as Eadie remarks.[11]

The reason for His intervention is given in the words, **because of His great love with which He loved us**. His love is great because He is its source. Just as the greatness of a giver casts an aura of greatness on his gift, so the surpassing excellence of God adds superlative luster to His love. It is greater to be loved by the mighty Sovereign of the universe, for instance, than by a fellow human being. God's love is great because of the price He paid. Love sent the Lord Jesus, God's only begotten Son, to die for us in agony at Calvary. God's love is great because of the unsearchable riches it showers on its objects.

2:5 And God's love is great because of the extreme unworthiness and unloveliness of the persons loved. **We were dead in trespasses**. We were enemies of God. We were destitute and degraded. He loved us in spite of it all.

As a result of God's love for us, and as a result of the redeeming work of Christ, we have been: (1) **made alive together with Christ**; (2) raised up with Him; (3) seated in Him.

These expressions describe our spiritual position as a result of our union

with Him. He acted as our Representative — not only *for* us, but *as* us. Therefore when He died, we died. When He was buried, we were buried.

When *He* was **made alive**, raised, and seated in the heavenlies, so were *we*. All the benefits of His sacrificial work are enjoyed by us because of our link with Him. To be **made alive together with Him** means that converted Jews and converted Gentiles are now associated with Him in newness of life. The same power that gave Him resurrection life has given it to us also.

The marvel of this causes Paul to interrupt his train of thought and exclaim, **By grace you have been saved**. He is overwhelmed by the fathomless favor which God has shown to those who deserved the very opposite. That is **grace**!

We have already mentioned that mercy means we do not get the punishment we deserve. **Grace** means we *do* get the salvation we do *not* deserve. We get it as a gift, not as something we earn. And it comes from One who was not compelled to give it. A. T. Pierson says:

> It is a voluntary exercise of love for which He is under no obligation. What constituted the glory of grace is that it is an utterly unfettered, unconstrained exercise of the love of God toward poor sinners.[12]

2:6 Not only have we been made alive with Christ; we have also been **raised up** with Him. Just as death and judgment are behind Him, they are behind us also. We stand on the resurrection side of the tomb. This is our glorious position as a result of our union with Him. And because it is true of us positionally, we should live as those who are alive from the dead.

Another aspect of our position is that we are seated in Him **in the heavenly places in Christ**. By our union with Him we are seen as already delivered from this present evil world and seated **in Christ** in glory. This is how God sees us. If we appropriate it by faith, it will change the character of our lives. We will no longer be earthbound, occupied with the trivial and the transient. We will seek those things which are above, where Christ is seated at the right hand of God (Col. 3:1).

The key to verses 5 and 6 is the

phrase, **in Christ Jesus**. It is in Him that we have been made alive, raised, and seated. He is our Representative; therefore His triumphs and His position are ours. George Williams exclaims, "Amazing thought! That a Mary Magdalene and a crucified thief should be the companions in glory of the Son of God."

2:7 This miracle of transforming grace will be the subject of eternal revelation. Throughout the endless ages God will be unveiling to the heavenly throng what it cost Him to send His Son to this jungle of sin, and what it cost the Lord Jesus to bear our sins at the cross. It is a subject that will never be exhausted. Again Paul builds words upon words to suggest something of its immensity:

> His kindness toward us
> His grace in His kindness toward us
> The riches of His grace in His kindness
> toward us
> The exceeding riches of His grace in His
> kindness toward us

Now it follows that if God will be disclosing this throughout eternity, then we will be learning forever and ever. Heaven will be our school. God will be the Teacher. **His grace** will be the subject. We will be the students. And the school term will be eternity.

This should deliver us from the idea that we will know everything when we get to heaven. Only God knows everything, and we will never be equal with Him.[13]

It also raises the interesting question: How much will we know when we get to heaven? And it suggests the possibility that we can prepare for the heavenly university by majoring in the Bible right now.

2:8 The next three verses present as clear a statement of the simple plan of salvation as we can find in the Bible.

It all originates with the **grace** of God: He takes the initiative in providing it. Salvation is given to those who are utterly unworthy of it, on the basis of the Person and work of the Lord Jesus Christ.

It is given as a present possession. Those who are saved can know it. Writing to the Ephesians, Paul said, **You have been saved**. He knew it, and they knew it.

The way we receive the gift of eternal life is **through faith**. **Faith** means that man takes his place as a lost, guilty sinner, and receives the Lord Jesus as his only hope of salvation. True saving faith is the commitment of a person to a Person.

Any idea that man can earn or deserve salvation is forever exploded by the words, **and that not of yourselves**. Dead people can *do* nothing, and sinners *deserve* nothing but punishment.

It is the gift of God. A gift, of course, is a free and unconditional present. That is the only basis on which God offers salvation. **The gift of God** is *salvation* **by grace** and **through faith**. It is offered to all people everywhere.

2:9 It is **not of works**, that is, it is not something a person can earn through supposedly meritorious deeds. It cannot be earned, for instance, by:

1. Confirmation
2. Baptism
3. Church membership
4. Church attendance
5. Holy Communion
6. Trying to keep the Ten Commandments
7. Living by the Sermon on the Mount
8. Giving to charity
9. Being a good neighbor
10. Living a moral, respectable life

People are not saved by **works**. And they are *not* saved by faith *plus* **works**. They are **saved through faith** *alone*. The minute you add works of any kind or in any amount as a means of gaining eternal life, salvation is no longer by grace (Rom. 11:6). One reason that **works** are positively excluded is to prevent human boasting. If anyone could be saved by his **works**, then he would have reason to **boast** before God. This is impossible (Rom. 3:27).

If anyone could be saved by his own good works, then the death of Christ was unnecessary (Gal. 2:21). But we know that the reason He died was because there was no other way by which guilty sinners could be saved.

If anyone could be saved by his own good works, then he would be his own savior, and could worship himself. But this would be idolatry, and God forbids it (Ex. 20:3).

Even if someone could be saved through faith in Christ plus his own good works, you would have the impossible situation of two saviors — Jesus and the sinner. Christ would then have to share the glory of saviorhood with another, and this He will not do (Isa. 42:8).

Finally, if anyone could contribute to his salvation by works, then God would owe it to him. This, too, is impossible. God cannot be indebted to anyone (Rom. 11:35).

In contrast to works, faith excludes boasting (Rom. 3:27), because it is non-meritorious. A man has no reason to be proud that he has trusted the Lord. Faith in Him is the most sane, rational, sensible thing a person can do. To trust one's Creator and Redeemer is only logical and reasonable. If we cannot trust Him, whom can we trust?

2:10 The result of salvation is that **we are His workmanship** — the handiwork of God, not of ourselves. A born-again believer is a masterpiece of God. When we think of the raw materials He has to work with, His achievement is all the more remarkable. Indeed, this masterpiece is nothing less than a new creation through union with Christ, for "if anyone is in Christ, he is a new creation; old things have passed away; behold, all things have become new" (2 Cor. 5:17).

And the object of this new creation is found in the phrase, **for good works**. While it is true that we are not saved *by* **good works**, it is equally true that we are saved **for** good works. **Good works** are not the *root* but the *fruit*. We do not work *in order to be saved*, but *because we are saved*.

This is the aspect of the truth that is emphasized in James 2:14–26. When James says that "faith without works is dead," he does not mean we are saved by faith plus works, but by the kind of faith that results in a life of **good works**. **Works** prove the reality of our faith. Paul heartily agrees: **we are His workmanship, created in Christ Jesus for good works**.

God's order then is this:

Faith –› Salvation –› Good Works –› Reward

Faith leads to salvation. Salvation results in **good works**. Good works will be rewarded by Him.

But the question arises: What kind of **good works** am I expected to do? Paul answers, **Good works, which God prepared beforehand that we should walk in them**. In other words, God has a blue-print for every life. Before our conversion He mapped out a spiritual career for us. Our responsibility is to find His will for us and then obey it. We do not have to work out a plan for our lives, but only accept the plan which He has drawn up for us. This delivers us from fret and frenzy, and insures that our lives will be of maximum glory to Him, of most blessing to others, and of greatest reward to ourselves.

In order to find out the **good works** He has planned for our individual lives, we should: (1) confess and forsake sin as soon as we are conscious of it in our lives; (2) be continually and unconditionally yielded to Him; (3) study the word of God to discern His will, and then do whatever He tells us to do; (4) spend time in prayer each day; (5) seize opportunities of service as they arise; (6) cultivate the fellowship and counsel of other Christians. God prepares us **for good works**. He prepares **good works** for us to perform. Then He rewards us when we perform them. Such is His grace!

E. The Union of Believing Jews and Gentiles in Christ (2:11–22)

In the first half of chapter 2 Paul traced the salvation of individual Gentiles and Jews. Now he advances to the abolition of their former national differences, to their union in Christ, and to their formation into the church, a holy temple in the Lord.

2:11 In verses 11 and 12 the apostle reminds his readers that prior to their conversion they were **Gentiles** by birth and therefore outcasts as far as the Jews were concerned. First, they were despised. This is indicated by the fact that the Jews called them **Uncircumcision**. This meant the Gentiles did not have the surgical sign in their flesh that marked the Israelites as God's covenant people. The name "uncircumcised" was an ethnic slur, similar to the names that people use today for despised nationalities. We can feel something of its sting when we hear David say concerning the Gentile Goliath, "Who is this uncircumcised Philistine, that he should defy the armies of the living God?" (1 Sam. 17:26).

The Jews, by contrast, spoke of themselves as **the Circumcision**. This was a name of which they were proud. It identified them as God's chosen earthly people, set apart from all the other nations of the earth. Paul seems to take exception to some of their boasting by saying their circumcision was only **made in the flesh by hands**. It was merely physical. Though they had the outward sign of God's covenant people, they did not have the inward reality of true faith in the Lord. "For he is not a Jew who is one outwardly, nor is circumcision that which is outward in the flesh; but he is a Jew who is one inwardly; and circumcision is that of the heart, in the Spirit, not in the letter; whose praise is not from men but from God" (Rom. 2:28, 29).

But whether or not the Jews were circumcised in heart, the point in verse 11 is that in their own eyes they were *the* people and the Gentiles were despised. This enmity between Jews and Gentiles was the greatest racial and religious difference the world has ever known. The Jew enjoyed a position of great privilege before God (Rom. 9:4, 5). The Gentile was a foreigner. If he wanted to worship the true God in the appointed way, he actually had to become a Jewish convert (cf. Rahab and Ruth). The Jewish temple in Jerusalem was the only place on earth where God had placed His name and where men could approach Him. Gentiles were forbidden to enter the inner temple courts on pain of death.

In His interview with a Gentile woman from the region of Tyre and Sidon, the Lord Jesus tested her faith by picturing the Jews as children in the house and the Gentiles as little dogs under the table. She acknowledged she was only a little dog, but asked for some crumbs the children might drop. Needless to say, her faith was rewarded (Mark 7:24–30). Here in Ephesians 2:11 the apostle is reminding his readers that they were formerly Gentiles and therefore despised.

2:12 The Gentiles were also **without Christ**: they had no Messiah. It was to the nation of Israel that He was promised. Although it was predicted that blessing would flow to the nations through the ministry of the Messiah (Isa. 11:10; 60:3), yet He was to be born a Jew and to minister primarily "to the lost sheep of the house of Israel" (Matt. 15:24). In addition to being without the

Messiah, the Gentiles were **aliens from the commonwealth of Israel**. An alien is one who does not "belong." He is a stranger and foreigner, without the rights and privileges of citizenship. As far as the community of **Israel** was concerned, the Gentiles were on the outside, looking in. And they were **strangers from the covenants of promise**. God had made **covenants** with the nation of **Israel** through such men as Abraham, Isaac, Jacob, Moses, David, and Solomon. These **covenants** promised blessings to the Jews. For all practical purposes, the Gentiles were outside the pale. They were without **hope**, both nationally and individually. Nationally, they had no assurance that their land, their government, or their people would survive. And individually their outlook was bleak: they had **no hope** beyond the grave. Someone has said that their future was a night without a star. Finally, they were **without God in the world**. This does not mean they were atheists. They had their own gods of wood and stone, and worshiped them. But they did not know the one and only true God. They were God–less in a godless, hostile world.

2:13 The words, **But now**, signal another abrupt transition (cf. 2:4). The Ephesian Gentiles had been rescued from that place of distance and alienation, and had been elevated to a position of nearness to God. This was brought about at the time of their conversion. When they trusted the Savior, God placed them **in Christ Jesus** and accepted them in the beloved One. From then on they were as **near** to God as Christ is, because they were **in Christ Jesus**. The cost of effecting this marvelous change was **the blood of Christ**. Before these Gentile sinners could enjoy the privilege of nearness to God, they had to be cleansed from their sins. Only **the blood of Christ** shed at Calvary could do this. When they received the Lord Jesus by a definite act of faith, all the cleansing value of His precious blood was credited to their account.

Jesus not only **brought** them **near**; He also created a new society in which the ancient enmity between Jew and Gentile was forever abolished. Up to NT times, all the world was divided into two classes — Jew and Gentile. Our Savior has introduced a third — the church of God (1 Cor. 10:32). In the verses that follow, we see how believing Jews and believing Gentiles are now made one in Christ, and are introduced into this new society, where there is neither Jew nor Gentile.

2:14 For He Himself is our peace. Notice it does not say, "He made peace." That, of course, is true too, as we will see in the next verse. Here the fact is that **He Himself** *is* our peace. But how can a person *be* peace?

This is how: When a Jew believes on the Lord Jesus, he loses his national identity; from then on he is "in Christ." Likewise, when a Gentile receives the Savior, he is no longer a Gentile; henceforth he is "in Christ." In other words, believing Jew and believing Gentile, once divided by enmity, are now **both one** in Christ. Their union with Christ necessarily unites them with one another. Therefore a Man **is** the **peace**, just as Micah predicted (Mic. 5:5).

The scope of His work as **our peace** is detailed in verses 14–18.

First is the work of union which we have just described. He **has made both one** — that is, both believing Jews and Gentiles. They are no longer Jews or Gentiles, but Christians. Strictly speaking, it is not accurate even to speak of them as Jewish Christians or Gentile Christians. All fleshly distinctions, such as nationality, were nailed to the cross.

The second phase of Christ's work might be called demolition: **He . . . has broken down the middle wall of separation**. Not a literal wall, of course, but the invisible barrier set up by the Mosaic Law of commandments contained in ordinances which separated the people of Israel from the nations. This has often been illustrated by the wall which restricted non-Jews to the Court of the Gentiles in the temple area. On the wall were No Trespassing signs which read: "Let no one of any other nation come within the fence and barrier around the Holy Place. Whoever is caught doing so will himself be responsible for the fact that his death will ensue."

2:15 A third aspect of Christ's work

was abolition of **the enmity** that smoldered between Jew and Gentile and also between man and God. Paul identifies the law as the innocent cause of the enmity, that is, **the law of commandments contained in ordinances**. The Law of Moses was a single legislative code; yet it was made up of separate, formal commandments; these in turn consisted of dogmas or decrees covering many, if not most, areas of life. The law itself was holy, just, and good (Rom. 7:12), but man's sinful nature used the law as an occasion for hatred. Because the law actually did set up Israel as God's chosen earthly people, many Jews became arrogant and treated the Gentiles with contempt. The Gentiles struck back with deep hostility, which we have come to know all too well as anti-Semitism. But how did Christ remove the law as the cause of **enmity**? First, He died to pay the penalty of the law that had been broken. He thus completely satisfied the righteous claims of God. Now the law has nothing more to say to those who are "in Christ"; the penalty has been paid for them in full. Believers are not under law but under grace. However, this does not mean they can live as they please; it means they are now enlawed to Christ, and should live as *He* pleases.

As a result of abolishing the hostility stirred up by the law, the Lord has been able to usher in a new creation. He has made in Himself **from the two**, that is, from believing Jew and believing Gentile, **one new man** — the church. Through union with Him, the former combatants are united with one another in this **new** fellowship. The church is **new** in the sense that it is a kind of organism that never existed before. It is important to see this. The NT church is not a continuation of the Israel of the OT. It is something entirely distinct from anything that has preceded it or that will ever follow it. This should be apparent from the following:

1. It is **new** that a Gentile should have equal rights and privileges with a Jew.
2. It is **new** that both Jews and Gentiles should lose their national identities by becoming Christians.
3. It is **new** that Jews and Gentiles

should be fellow members of the Body of Christ.

4. It is **new** that a Jew should have the hope of reigning with Christ instead of being a subject in His kingdom.

5. It is **new** that a Jew should no longer be under the law.

The church is clearly a **new** creation, with a distinct calling and a distinct destiny, occupying a unique place in the purposes of God. But the scope of Christ's work does not stop there. He has also made **peace** between Jew and Gentile. He did this by removing the cause of hostility, by imparting a new nature, and by creating a new union. The cross is God's answer to racial discrimination, segregation, anti-Semitism, bigotry, and every form of strife between men.

2:16 In addition to reconciling Jew and Gentile to one another, Christ has reconciled **them both to God**. Though Israel and the nations were normally bitterly opposed to each other, there was one sense in which they were united — in their hostility to God. The cause of this hostility was sin. By His death on the cross, the Lord Jesus removed **the enmity** by removing the cause. Those who receive Him are reckoned righteous, forgiven, redeemed, pardoned, and delivered from the power of sin. The enmity is gone; now they have peace with **God**. The Lord Jesus unites believing Jew and Gentile **in one body**, the church, and presents this Body to **God** with all trace of antagonism gone.

God never needed to be reconciled to us; He never hated us. But we needed to be reconciled to Him. The work of our Lord on the cross provided a righteous basis on which we could be brought into His presence as friends, not as foes.

2:17 In verse 14 Christ *is* our peace. In verse 15 He *made* peace. Now we find that **He came and** *preached* **peace**. When and how did He come? First, He came personally in resurrection. Second, He came representatively by the Holy Spirit. He **preached peace** in resurrection; in fact, **peace** was one of the first words He spoke after rising from the dead (Luke 24:36; John 20:19, 21, 26). Then He sent out the apostles in the power of the Holy Spirit and **preached peace** through them

(Acts 10:36). The good news of **peace** was presented to **you who were afar off** (Gentiles) **and to those who were near** (Jews), a gracious fulfillment of God's promise in Isaiah 57:19.

2:18 The practical proof that a state of peace now exists between members of the one Body and God is that they **have access** at any time into the presence of God. This is in sharp contrast to the OT economy, in which only the high priest could go into the Holy of Holies, the place of God's presence. And he could enter there on only one day of the year. Eadie points up the contrast:

> But now the most distant Gentile who is in Christ really and continuously enjoys that august spiritual privilege, which the one man of the one tribe of the one nation on the one day of the year, only typically and periodically possessed.[14]

Through prayer any believer can enter the throne room of heaven, kneel before the Sovereign of the universe, and address Him as **Father**.

The normal order to be followed in prayer is given here. First, it is **through Him** (the Lord Jesus). He is the one Mediator between God and man. His death, burial, and resurrection removed every legal obstacle to our admission to God's presence. Now as Mediator he lives on high to maintain us in a condition of fellowship with the Father. We approach God in His name; we have no worthiness of our own, so we plead His worthiness. The participants in prayer are **we both** — believing Jews and believing Gentiles. The privilege is that we **have access**. Our Helper in prayer is the Holy Spirit — **by one Spirit**. "The Spirit helps in our weaknesses. For we do not know what we should pray for as we ought, but the Spirit Himself makes intercession for us with groanings which cannot be uttered" (Rom. 8:26).

The One we approach is **the Father**. No OT saint ever knew God as Father. Before the resurrection of Christ, men stood before God as creatures before the Creator. It was after He rose that He said, "Go to my brethren and say to them, 'I am ascending to My Father and your Father, and to My God and your God'" (John 20:17). As a result of His redemptive work, believers were then able for the first time to address God as **Father**. In verse 18 all three Persons of the Trinity are directly involved in the prayers of the humblest believer: he prays to God the **Father**, approaching Him **through** the Lord Jesus Christ, in the power of the Holy **Spirit**.

2:19 In the last four verses of this chapter, the Apostle Paul lists some of the overwhelming new privileges of believing Gentiles. They **are no longer strangers and foreigners**. Never again will they be aliens, dogs, uncircumcision, outsiders. Now they are **fellow citizens with** all **the saints** of the NT period. Believers of Jewish ancestry have no advantage over them. All Christians are first-class citizens of heaven (Phil. 3:20, 21). They are also **members of the household of God**. Not only have they been "super-naturalized" into the divine kingdom; they have been adopted into the divine family.

2:20 Finally, they have been made members of the church, or as Paul pictures it here, they have become stones in the construction of a holy temple. With great detail the apostle describes this temple — its **foundation**, its **chief cornerstone**, its cohesive agent, its unity and symmetry, its growth, and its other unique features.

This temple is *built on the foundation of the apostles and prophets*. This refers to **the apostles and prophets** of the NT era; it could not possibly refer to OT prophets, because they knew nothing about the church. It does not mean that **the apostles and prophets** *were* the foundation of the church. Christ is **the foundation** (1 Cor. 3:11). But they laid the foundation in what they taught about the Person and work of the Lord Jesus. The church is founded on Christ as He was revealed by the confession and teaching of **the apostles and prophets**. When Peter confessed Him as the Christ, the Son of the living God, Jesus announced that His church would be built on that rock, namely, on the solid truth that He is the anointed of God and God's unique Son (Matt. 16:18). In Revelation 21:14 the apostles are associated with the twelve foundations of the holy Jerusalem. They are not the foundation

but are linked with it, because they first taught the great truth concerning Christ and the church. The **foundation** of a building needs to be laid only once. **The apostles and prophets** did this work once for all. **The foundation** they laid is preserved for us in the writings of the NT, though they themselves are with us no longer. In a secondary sense, there are men in all ages whose ministry is apostolic or prophetic. Missionaries and church planters are apostles in a lower sense, and those who preach the word for edification are prophets. But they are not apostles and prophets in the primary sense.

Jesus Christ is not only **the foundation** of the temple; He is its **chief cornerstone** as well. No one picture or type can adequately portray Him in His manifold glories or in His varied ministries. There are at least three possible explanations of **the chief cornerstone**, all of which point to the Lord Jesus Christ as the unique, preeminent, and indispensable Head of the church.

1. We generally think of **the cornerstone** as one that lies at a lower front corner of a building. Since the rest of the structure seems to be supported by it, it has come to signify something of fundamental importance. In that sense it is a true type of the Lord. Also, since it joins two walls together, there may be a suggestion of the union of believing Jews and Gentiles in the church through Him.

2. Some Bible scholars believe that the word translated **the chief cornerstone** refers to the keystone of an arch. This stone occupies the highest place in the arch and provides support for the other stones. So Christ is the preeminent One in the church. He is also the indispensable One: remove Him and the rest will collapse.

3. A third possible understanding of the term is that it is the capstone of a pyramid. This stone occupies the highest place in the structure. It is the only stone of that size and shape. And its angles and lines determine the shape of the whole pyramid. So Christ is the Head of the church. He is unique as to His Person and ministry. And He is the One who gives the church its

unique features. First, its **foundation**:

2:21 The words, **in whom**, refer to Christ: He is the source of the church's life and growth. Blaikie says:

> In him we are added to it; in him we grow in it; in him the whole temple grows towards the final consummation, when the *topstone* shall be brought out with shouts of 'Grace, grace unto it.'[15]

The unity and symmetry of the **temple** are indicated by the expression, **the whole building, being fitted together**. It is a unity made up of many individual members. Each member has a specific place in the **building** for which he or she is exactly suited. Stones excavated from the valley of death by the grace of God are found to fit together perfectly. The unique feature of this building is that it **grows**. However, this feature is not the same as the growth of a building through the addition of bricks and cement. Think of it rather as the growth of a living organism, such as the human body. After all, the church is not an inanimate building. Neither is it an organization. It is a living entity with Christ as its Head and all believers forming the Body. It was born on the day of Pentecost, has been growing ever since, and will continue to grow until the Rapture.

This growing building of living materials is described as **a holy temple in the Lord**. The word Paul used for **temple** referred not to the outer courts but to the inner shrine (Gk., *naos*), not the suburbs but the sanctuary. He was thinking of the main building of the temple complex, which housed the Most Holy Place. There God dwelt and there He manifested Himself in a bright, shining cloud of glory.

There are several lessons for us here: (1) God indwells the church. Saved Jews and Gentiles form a living sanctuary in which He dwells and where He reveals His glory. (2) This **temple** is **holy**. It is set apart from the world and dedicated to Him for sacred purposes. (3) As **a holy temple**, the church is a center from which praise, worship, and adoration ascend to God through the Lord Jesus Christ.

Paul further describes this **holy temple** as being **in the Lord**. In other words, the Lord Jesus is its source of holiness. Its members are **holy** positionally through union with Him, and they should be **holy** practically out of love for Him.

2:22 In this wonderful temple, believing Gentiles have an equal place with believing Jews. It should thrill us to read this, as it must have thrilled the Ephesians and others when they heard it for the first time. The tremendous dignity of the believers' position is that they form **a dwelling place of God in the Spirit**. This is the purpose of the temple — to provide a place where **God** can live in fellowship with His people. The church is that place. Compare this with the position of the Gentiles in the OT. At that time they could not get near God's dwelling. Now they themselves *form* a good part of it!

And notice the ministry of each of the Persons of the Godhead in connection with the church: (1) **In whom**, that is, in Christ. It is through union with Him that we are built into the temple. (2) **A dwelling place of God**. This temple is the home of God the Father on earth. (3) **In the Spirit**. It is in the Person of the Holy **Spirit** that **God** indwells the church (1 Cor. 3:16).

And so the chapter that began with a description of Gentiles who were dead, depraved, diabolical, and disobedient, closes with those same Gentiles cleansed from all guilt and defilement, and forming **a dwelling place of God in the Spirit!**

F. A Parenthesis on the Mystery (3:1–13)

3:1 Paul begins a statement in verse 1 that is interrupted in verse 2 and not resumed till verse 14. The intervening verses form a parenthesis, the theme of which is the mystery — Christ and the church.

What makes this of special interest is that this present Church Age is itself a parenthesis in God's dealings. This can be explained as follows: During most of the period of history recorded in the OT, God was dealing primarily with the Jewish people. In fact, from Genesis 12 through Malachi 4 the narrative centers almost exclusively on Abraham and his descendants. When the Lord Jesus came to earth, He was rejected by Israel. As a result, God set aside that nation temporarily as His chosen, earthly people. We are now living in the Church Age, when Jews and Gentiles are on the same level before God. After the church has been completed and is taken home to heaven, God will resume His program with Israel nationally. The hands on the prophetic clock will begin to move once more. So the present age is sort of a parenthesis between God's past and future dealings with Israel. It is a new administration in the divine program — unique and separate from anything before or after it.

In verses 2–13 Paul gives a fairly detailed explanation of this parenthesis. Is it an undesigned coincidence that in doing so he uses a literary parenthesis to explain a dispensational parenthesis?

The apostle opens the section, **For this reason I, Paul, the prisoner of Christ Jesus for you Gentiles**. The phrase, **For this reason**, looks back to what he had just been saying about the place of privilege into which believing Gentiles are brought as a result of their union with Christ.

It is generally believed that this Letter was written during Paul's first Roman imprisonment. But he does not speak of himself as a prisoner of Rome. That might have indicated a sense of defeat, a feeling of self-pity, or a craving for sympathy. Paul calls himself **the prisoner of Christ Jesus**; this speaks of acceptance and dignity and triumph. Ruth Paxson puts it well:

There is no smell of prison in Ephesians, for Paul is not bound in spirit. He is there as the prisoner of Rome, but this he will not admit, and claims to be the prisoner of Jesus Christ. What is the secret of such victorious other-worldliness? Paul's spirit is with Christ in the heavenlies, though his body languishes in prison.[16]

His imprisonment was definitely on behalf of **the Gentiles**. Throughout his ministry he ran into bitter opposition for teaching that believing Gentiles now enjoyed equal rights and privileges with believing Jews in the Christian church. What finally triggered his arrest and trial before Caesar was a false charge that he had taken Trophimus, an Ephesian, into the temple area that was out of bounds

for Gentiles (Acts 21:29). But behind the charge was the already fierce hostility of the religious leaders.

3:2 Now Paul breaks his train of thought and launches into a discourse on the mystery, in what we have already referred to as a literary parenthesis dealing with a dispensational parenthesis.

The **if** in verse 2 (**if indeed you have heard ...**) might create the impression that the apostle's readers did not know of his special mission to the Gentiles. In fact, this verse is sometimes used to prove that Paul did not know the persons to whom he wrote and that therefore the Letter could not have been written to the beloved Ephesians. But "if" often carries the meaning of "since." Thus Phillips paraphrases it, "For you must have heard. . . ." They had surely known that this special ministry had been committed to him. He describes that ministry as a **dispensation of the grace of God**. Here **dispensation** refers to a stewardship. A steward is one who is appointed to administer the affairs of someone else. Paul was God's steward, charged with setting forth the great truth regarding the NT church. It was a stewardship of God's **grace** in at least three senses:

1. As to the one chosen. It was undeserved favor to Paul that selected him for such a high privilege.
2. As to the contents of the message. It was the message of God's free and unmerited kindness.
3. As to its recipients. The Gentiles were quite unworthy people to be so favored.

Yet this stewardship of **grace** was given to Paul in order that he in turn might impart it to the Gentiles.

3:3 He had not learned **the mystery** from anyone else, nor had he discovered it through his own intelligence. It was **made known to** him by direct **revelation** from God. We are not told where this happened, or how; all we know is that in some miraculous way God showed Paul His plan for a church composed of converted Jews and converted Gentiles. We have already mentioned that a **mystery** is a sacred secret hitherto unknown, humanly unknowable, and now divinely revealed. The apostle had alluded to **the mystery** briefly in 1:9–14, 22, 23; 2:11–22.

3:4 What he had already written on the subject was sufficient to demonstrate to his readers that he had a God-given insight into **the mystery of** the **Christ**. Blaikie paraphrases this passage as follows:

With reference to which, *i.e.,* to what I wrote afore: to make that more intelligible I write on the subject more fully now, so that you shall see that your instructor is thoroughly informed in this matter of the mystery. . . .[17]

Darby's translation, "the mystery of *the* Christ," suggests that it is the mystical Christ that is in view here, that is, the Head *and* the Body. (For another instance of the name **Christ** including both the Lord Jesus and His people, see 1 Cor. 12:12.)

3:5 Verses 5 and 6 give us the most complete definition we have of the mystery. Paul explains what a mystery is, then he explains what the mystery of the Christ is.

First, it is a truth **which in other ages was not made known to the sons of men**. This means it is futile to look for it in the OT. There may be types and pictures of it there, but the truth itself was unknown at that time.

Second, it is a truth which **has now been revealed by the** Holy **Spirit** to God's **holy apostles and prophets**. God was the Revealer; the **apostles and prophets** were the ones set apart to receive the revelation; **the** Holy **Spirit** was the channel through whom the revelation came to them.

Unless we see that the **apostles and prophets** were those of the NT, not the OT period, this verse is contradictory. The first part says this truth was not revealed in other ages; therefore it was unknown to the OT prophets. How then could it be made known in Paul's day by men who had been dead for centuries? The obvious meaning is that the great truth of Christ and the church was made known to men of the Church Age like Paul who were specially commissioned by the risen Lord to serve as His spokesmen or mouthpieces. (Paul does not claim to be the *only* one to whom this sacred secret was disclosed; he was one among many, though he was the foremost in transmitting the truth to Gen-

tiles of his day, and to succeeding generations through his Epistles.)

It is only fair to mention that many Christians take quite a different view from that given above. They say the church actually did exist in the OT; that Israel was then the church; but that the truth of the church has now been more fully revealed. They say, "The mystery was not known in other ages *as* it is now revealed. It was known *but not to the same extent as now*. We have a *fuller revelation*, but we are still the Israel of God, that is, a continuation of God's people." To support their argument, they point to Acts 7:38 in the 1611 KJV, where the nation of Israel is called "the church (NKJV, NASB,: *congregation*) in the wilderness." It is true that God's chosen people are spoken of as the congregation in the wilderness, but this does not mean they have any connection with the *Christian* church. After all, the Greek word *ekklēsia* is a general term which can mean any assembly, congregation, or called-out group. It is not only applied to Israel in Acts 7:38; the same word, translated *assembly*, is used in Acts 19:32, 41 of a heathen mob. We have to determine from the context *which* "church" or assembly is meant.

But what about the argument that verse 5 means the church existed in the OT though it was not as fully revealed then as now? This is answered in Colossians 1:26, which states flatly that the mystery was "hidden from ages and from generations, but now has been revealed to His saints." It is not a question of the degree of revelation but of the fact of it.

3:6 Now we come to the central truth of the mystery, namely, that in the church of the Lord Jesus Christ, believing **Gentiles** are **fellow heirs**, fellow members, and fellow **partakers of His promise in Christ through the gospel**. In other words, converted **Gentiles** now enjoy equal title and privileges with converted Jews.

First, they are **fellow heirs**. As far as the inheritance is concerned, they share equally with saved Jews. They are heirs of God, joint heirs with Jesus Christ, and **fellow heirs** with all the redeemed.

Then they are fellow members **of the same body**. They are at no distance or disadvantage now, but share a position of equality with saved Jews in the church.

Finally, they are fellow **partakers** of the **promise in Christ through the gospel**. The **promise** here may mean the Holy Spirit (Acts 15:8; Gal. 3:14), or it may take in all that is promised in **the gospel** to those who are **in Christ** Jesus. **Gentiles** are copartners with Jews in all of this.

None of this was true in the OT dispensation, nor will it be true in the coming kingdom of Christ.

In the OT, Israel held a distinct place of privilege before God. A Jew would have laughed at any suggestion that a Gentile held an equal share with him in the promises of God. It simply was not true. The prophets of Israel did predict the call of the Gentiles (Isa. 49:6; 56:6, 7), but they nowhere hinted that Gentiles would be fellow members of a body in which Jews did not have any priority.

In the coming kingdom of our Lord, Israel will be the head of the nations (Isa. 60:12); Gentiles will be blessed, but it will be through Israel (Isa. 60:3; 61:6; Zech. 8:23).

The calling of Israel was primarily, though not exclusively, to temporal blessings in earthly places (Deut. 28; Amos 9:13–15). The calling of the church is primarily to spiritual blessings in heavenly places (Eph. 1:3). Israel was called to be God's chosen earthly people. The church is called to be the heavenly Bride of Christ (Rev. 21:2, 9). Israel will be blessed under the rule of Christ in the Millennium (Hos. 3:5); the church will reign with Him over the entire universe, sharing His glory (Eph. 1:22, 23).

Therefore it should be clear that the church is not the same as Israel or the kingdom. It is a new society, a unique fellowship, and the most privileged body of believers we read about in the Bible. The church came into being after Christ ascended and the Holy Spirit was given (Acts 2). It was formed by the baptism of the Holy Spirit (1 Cor. 12:13). And it will be completed at the Rapture, when all who belong to Christ will be taken home to heaven (1 Thess. 4:13–18; 1 Cor. 15:23, 51–58).

3:7 Having emphasized the equal partnership of Gentiles and Jews in the church, Paul now moves on to discuss his own ministry in connection with it (vv. 7–9).

First, he **became a minister** of the gospel. Wuest writes, "The word 'minister' is misleading, since it is the technical word used today to designate the pastor of a church." It never means that in the NT. The basic meaning of the word is *servant*; Paul simply meant he served the Lord in connection with the mystery.

The ministry was in the nature of an undeserved gift: **according to the gift of the grace of God given to me**. And it was not only a display of **grace**; it also demonstrated God's **power** in effectually reaching the proud, self-righteous Pharisee, saving his soul, commissioning him as an apostle, empowering him to receive revelations, and strengthening him for the work. So Paul says **the gift** was given to him **by the effective working of His power.**

3:8 The apostle speaks of himself as **less than the least of all the saints**. This might seem like mock humility to some. Actually it is the true self-estimate of one who is filled by the Holy Spirit. Anyone who sees Christ in His glory realizes his own sinfulness and uselessness. In Paul's case there was the added memory that he had persecuted the Lord Jesus (Acts 9:4) by persecuting the church of God (Gal. 1:13; Phil. 3:6). In spite of this, the Lord had commissioned him in a special way to take the gospel to **the Gentiles** (Acts 9:15; 13:47; 22:21; Gal. 2:2, 8). Paul was the apostle to **the Gentiles** as Peter was to the Jews. His ministry was twofold: it concerned the gospel, and it concerned the church. First, he told men how to be saved, then he led them on into the truth of the NT church. For him evangelism was not an end in itself but a step toward establishing and strengthening indigenous NT churches.

The first function of his ministry was to **preach among the Gentiles the unsearchable riches of Christ**. Blaikie expresses it well:

> Two attractive words, *riches* and *unsearchable*, conveying the idea of the things that are most precious being infinitely abundant. Usually precious things are rare; their very rarity increases their price; but here that which is most precious is also boundless — riches of compassion and

love, of merit, of sanctifying, comforting
and transforming power, all without limit,
and capable of satisfying every want,
craving, and yearning of the heart, now
and evermore.[18]

When a person trusts the Lord Jesus, he
immediately becomes a spiritual billion-
aire; in Christ he possesses inexhaustible
treasures.

3:9 The second part of Paul's ministry was **to make all see what is** "the administration of the mystery" (JND), in
other words, to enlighten them as to
how **the mystery** is being worked out in
practice. God's plan for this present age
is to call out of the Gentiles a people for
His name (Acts 15:14), a Bride for His
Son. All that is involved in this plan is
the administration (*stewardship*, NKJV
margin[19]) **of the mystery. All** here must
mean **all** *believers*. Unsaved people could
not be expected to understand the deep
truths of **the mystery** (1 Cor. 2:14). Paul
therefore is referring to **all** in the sense
of saved people of **all** *kinds* — Jews and
Gentiles, slave and free.

This **mystery** had **from the beginning
of the ages been hidden in God**. The
plan was itself in the mind of God eternally, but here the thought is that He
kept it a secret throughout **the ages** of
human history. Once again we notice
the care the Holy Spirit takes to impress
us with the fact that the assembly,
or church universal is something new,
unique, unprecedented. It was not
known before to anyone but God. The
secret was **hidden in God who created
all things**. He **created** the material universe, He **created the ages**, and He **created** the church — but in His wisdom
He decided to withhold any knowledge
of this new creation until the First Advent of Christ.

3:10 One of God's present purposes
in connection with the mystery is to reveal His **manifold wisdom** to the angelic
hosts of heaven. Paul again uses the
metaphor of a school. God is the
Teacher. The universe is the classroom.
Angelic dignitaries are the students. The
lesson is on "The multi-faceted **wisdom
of God**." **The church** is the object lesson. From heaven the angels are compelled to admire His unsearchable judgments and marvel at His ways past

finding out. They see how God has triumphed over sin to His own glory. They
see how He has sent heaven's Best for
earth's worst. They see how He has redeemed His enemies at enormous cost,
conquered them by love, and prepared
them as a Bride for His Son. They see
how He has blessed them with all spiritual blessings in the heavenlies. And
they see that through the work of the
Lord Jesus on the cross, more glory has
come to God and more blessing has
come to believing Jews and Gentiles than
if sin had never been allowed to enter.
God has been vindicated; Christ has
been exalted; Satan has been defeated;
and the church has been enthroned in
Christ to share His glory.

3:11 The mystery itself, its concealment, its eventual disclosure, and the
manner in which it exhibits the wisdom
of God are all **according to the eternal
purpose which He accomplished in
Christ Jesus our Lord**. Before the world
was made, God knew Satan would fall
and man would follow him in sin. And
He had already prepared a counter-
strategy, a master plan. This plan has
been worked out in the incarnation,
death, resurrection, ascension, and glorification of Christ. The whole program
centered in Christ and has been realized
through Him. Now God can save ungodly Jews and Gentiles, make them
members of the Body of Christ, conform
them to the image of His Son, and honor
them in a unique way as the Bride of the
Lamb throughout eternity.

3:12 As a result of Christ's work
and our union with Him, we now have
the unspeakable privilege of entering
into God's presence at any time, in full
confidence of being heard, and without
any fear of being scolded (Jas 1:5). Our
boldness is the respectful attitude and
absence of fear we have as children addressing their Father. Our **access** is our
liberty to speak to God in prayer. Our
confidence is the assurance of a welcome, a hearing, and a wise and loving
answer. And it is all **through faith in
Him,** that is, our **faith in** the Lord Jesus
Christ.

3:13 In view of the dignity of his
ministry and the wonderful results that
flowed from it, Paul encouraged the

saints not to be disheartened when they thought of his sufferings. He was glad to endure **tribulations** in carrying out his mission to the Gentiles. Rather than being discouraged by his troubles, he says, in effect, they should be proud he was counted worthy to suffer for the Lord Jesus. They should rejoice to think of the benefit of his **tribulations** to them and to other Gentiles. They should see his current imprisonment as **glory**, not disgrace.

G. Paul's Prayer for the Saints (3:14–19)

3:14 Now the apostle picks up the thought he had begun in verse 1 and had interrupted with a parenthetical section on the mystery. Therefore, the words, **For this reason**, refer back to chapter 2 with its description of what the Gentiles had been by nature and what they had become through union with Christ. Their astonishing rise from poverty and death to riches and glory drives Paul to pray they will always live in the practical enjoyment of their exalted position.

His posture in prayer is indicated: **I bow my knees**. This does not mean kneeling must always be the posture of the body, though it should always be the posture of the soul. We may pray as we walk, sit, or recline, but our spirits should be bowed in humility and reverence.

The prayer is addressed **to the Father**. In a general sense, God is the Father of all mankind, meaning He is their Creator (Acts 17:28, 29). In a more restricted sense, He is the Father of all believers, meaning He has begotten them into His spiritual family (Gal. 4:6). In a unique sense He is **the Father of our Lord Jesus Christ**, meaning They are equal (John 5:18).

3:15 The particular role of the Father which Paul has in view is as the One **from whom the whole family in heaven and earth is named**. This may mean:

1. All the redeemed in heaven and on earth look to Him as Head of the family.

2. All created beings, angelic and human, owe their existence to Him not only as individuals but as families as well. Families in heaven include the various grades of angelic creatures. Families on earth are the different races springing from Noah and now divided into various nations.

3. All fatherhood in the universe derives its name from Him. The Fatherhood of God is the original and the ideal; it is the prototype of every other paternal relationship. Phillips translates the verse, "from whom all fatherhood, earthly or heavenly, derives its name."

3:16 We cannot help but be struck by the vastness of Paul's request: **That He would grant you,** *according to the riches of His glory*. He is going to ask that the saints might **be** spiritually **strengthened**. But to what extent? Jamieson, Fausset, and Brown answer: "in abundance, consonant to the riches of His glory; not 'according to' the narrowness of our hearts."[20] Preachers often point out that there is a difference between the expressions "out of the riches" and **according to the riches**. A wealthy person might give a trifling amount; it would be *out of* his riches, but *not in proportion* to them! Paul asks that God will give strength **according to** the riches of His perfections. Since the Lord is infinitely rich in glory, let the saints get ready for a deluge! Why should we ask so little of so great a King? When someone asked a tremendous favor of Napoleon it was immediately granted because, said Napoleon, "He honored me by the magnitude of his request."

> Thou art coming to a King,
> Large petitions with thee bring;
> For His grace and power are such,
> None can ever ask too much.
> — *John Newton*

Now we come to Paul's specific prayer requests. Instead of a series of disconnected petitions, we should think of them as a progression in which each petition lays the groundwork for the next. Picture them as a pyramid: the first request is the bottom layer of stones. As the prayer advances, Paul builds toward a glorious climax.

The first request is that they would **be strengthened with might through His**

Spirit in the inner man. The blessing sought is *spiritual* power. Not the power to perform spectacular miracles, but the spiritual vigor needed to be mature, stable, intelligent Christians. The One who imparts this power is the Holy **Spirit**. Of course, He can give us strength only as we feed on the word of God, as we breathe the pure air of prayer, and as we get exercise in daily service for the Lord.

This power is experienced **in the inner man**, that is, the spiritual part of our nature. It is **the inner man** that delights in the law of God (Rom. 7:22). It is **the inner man** that is renewed day by day, even though the outward man is perishing (2 Cor. 4:16). Though it is of God, our **inner man** needs strength, growth, and development.

3:17 The second step is **that Christ may dwell in your hearts through faith**. This is the result of the Spirit's invigoration: we are strengthened in order **that Christ may dwell in** our **hearts**. Actually, the Lord Jesus takes up His personal residence in a believer at the time of conversion (John 14:23; Rev. 3:20). But that is not the subject of this prayer. Here it is not a question of His being *in* the believer, but rather of His feeling *at home* there! He is a permanent Resident in every saved person, but this is a request that He might have full access to every room and closet; that He might not be grieved by sinful words, thoughts, motives, and deeds; that He might enjoy unbroken fellowship with the believer. The Christian heart thus becomes the home of Christ, the place where He loves to be — like the home of Mary, Martha, and Lazarus in Bethany. The heart, of course, means the center of the spiritual life; it controls every aspect of behavior. In effect, the apostle prays that the lordship of Christ might extend to the books we read, the work we do, the food we eat, the money we spend, the words we speak — in short, the minutest details of our lives.

The more we are strengthened by the Holy Spirit, the more we will be like the Lord Jesus Himself. And the more we are like Him, the more He will "settle down and feel completely at home in our hearts" (KSW).

We enter into the enjoyment of His indwelling **through faith**. This involves constant dependence on Him, constant surrender to Him, and constant recognition of His "at home-ness." It is **through faith** that we "practice His presence," as Brother Lawrence quaintly put it.

Up to this point Paul's prayer has involved each member of the Trinity. The Father is asked (v. 14) to strengthen the believers through His Spirit (v. 16) **that Christ** might be completely at home in their **hearts** (v. 17). One of the great privileges of prayer is that we can engage the eternal Godhead to work in behalf of others and ourselves.

The result of Christ's unrestricted access is that the Christian becomes **rooted and grounded in love**. Here Paul borrows words from the worlds of botany and building. The root of a plant provides nourishment and support. The groundwork of a building is the foundation on which it rests. As Scroggie says, "Love is the soil in which our life must have its roots; and it is the rock upon which our faith must ever rest."[21] To be **rooted and grounded in love** is to be established **in love** as a way of life. The life of **love** is a life of kindness, selflessness, brokenness, and meekness. It is the life of Christ finding expression in the believer (see 1 Cor. 13:4–7).

3:18 The preceding requests have outlined a program of spiritual growth and development which prepares the child of God to be fully able to grasp **with all the saints what is the width and length and depth and height**.

Before we consider the dimensions themselves, let us notice the expression, **with all the saints**. The subject is so great that no one believer can possibly grasp more than a small fraction of it. So there is need to study, discuss, and share with others. The Holy Spirit can use the combined meditations of a group of exercised believers to throw a flood of additional light on the Scriptures.

The dimensions are generally taken to refer to the love of Christ, although the text does not say this. In fact, the love of Christ is mentioned separately in the following clause. If the love of Christ is intended, then the connection might be shown as follows:

Width   — The world (John 3:16)
Length   — Forever (1 Cor. 13:8)
Depth   — Even the death of the
            cross (Phil. 2:8)
Height   — Heaven (1 John 3:1–2)

F. B. Meyer expresses it well:

There will always be as much horizon before us as behind us. And when we have been gazing on the face of Jesus for millenniums, its beauty will be as fresh and fascinating and fathomless as when we first saw it from the gate of Paradise.[22]

But these dimensions may also refer to the mystery which holds such an important place in Ephesians. In fact, it is easy to find these dimensions in the text itself:

1. The **width** is described in 2:11–18. It refers to the wideness of God's grace in saving Jews and Gentiles, and then incorporating them into the church. The mystery embraces both these segments of humanity.

2. The **length** extends from eternity to eternity. As to the past, believers were chosen in Christ before the foundation of the world (1:4). As to the future, eternity will be a perpetual unfolding of the exceeding riches of His grace in His kindness toward us through Christ Jesus (2:7).

3. The **depth** is vividly portrayed in 2:1–3. We were sunk in a pit of unspeakable sin and degradation. Christ came to this jungle of filth and corruption in order to die in our behalf.

4. The **height** is seen in 2:6, where we have not only been raised up with Christ, but enthroned in Him in the heavenlies to share His glory.

These are the dimensions, then, of immensity and, indeed, infinity. As we think of them, "all we can do," Scroggie says, "is to mark the order in this tumult of holy words."

3:19 The apostle's next request is that the saints might **know** by experience **the** knowledge-surpassing **love of Christ**. They could never explore it fully, because it is an ocean without shores, but they could learn more and more about it from day to day. And so he prays for a deep, experimental knowledge and enjoyment of the wonderful **love** of our wonderful Lord.

The climax in this magnificent prayer is reached when Paul prays **that you may be filled with** (lit. *unto*, Gk. *eis*) **all the fullness of God**. **All the fullness** of the Godhead dwells in the Lord Jesus (Col. 2:9). The more He dwells in our hearts by faith, the more we are **filled** unto all

the fullness of God. We could never be filled *with* all the fullness of God. But it is a goal toward which we move.

And yet having explained this, we must say there are depths of meaning here we have not reached. As we handle the Scriptures, we are aware that we are dealing with truths that are greater than our ability to understand or explain. We can use illustrations to throw light on this verse, for example, the thimble dipped in the ocean is filled with water, but how little of the ocean is in the thimble! Yet when we have said all this, the mystery remains, and we can only stand in awe at God's word and marvel at its infinity.

H. Paul's Doxology (3:20, 21)

3:20 The prayer closes with a soul-inspiring doxology. The preceding requests have been vast, bold, and seemingly impossible. But God **is able to do** more in this connection than **we** can **ask or think**. The extent of His ability is seen in the manner in which Paul pyramids words to describe superabundant blessings:

Able
Able to do
Able to do what **we ask**
Able to do what **we think**
Able to do what **we ask or think**
Able to do all that **we ask or think**
Able to do above all that **we ask or think**
Able to do abundantly above all that **we ask or think**
Able to do exceedingly abundantly above all that **we ask or think**

The means by which God answers prayer is given in the expression, **according to the power that works in us**. This refers to the Holy Spirit, who is constantly at work in our lives, seeking to produce the fruit of a Christlike character, rebuking us because of sin, guiding us in prayer, inspiring us in worship, directing us in service. The more we are yielded to Him, the greater will be His effectiveness in conforming us to Christ.

3:21 **To Him be glory in the church by Christ Jesus to all generations, forever and ever. Amen**. God is the worthy object of eternal praise. His wisdom and power are displayed in the angelic hosts; in sun, moon, and stars; in animals, birds, and fish; in fire, hail, snow, and mist; in wind; in mountains, hills, trees;

in kings and people, old men and young; in Israel and the nations. All these are intended to praise the name of the Lord (Ps. 148).

But there is another group from which endless **glory** will be given to God, that is, **the church** — Christ the Head and believers, the Body. This redeemed community will be an eternal witness to His matchless, marvelous grace. Williams writes:

> The eternal glory of God as God and Father will be made visible throughout all ages in the Church and in Christ Jesus. Amazing statement! Christ and the Church as One Body will be the vehicle of that eternal demonstration.[23]

Even now the church should be giving glory to His name "in the services of praise, in the pure lives of its members, in its world-wide proclamation of the Gospel, and in its ministries to human distress and need" (Erdman).

The duration of this praise is **to all generations, forever and ever**. As we hear Paul call for eternal praise to God in the church and in Christ Jesus, the response of our hearts is a hearty **Amen!**

II. THE BELIEVER'S PRACTICE IN THE LORD (Chaps. 4—6)

A. Appeal for Unity in the Christian Fellowship (4:1–6)

4:1 There is a major break at this point in Ephesians. The previous chapters have dealt with the Christian's calling. In the last three chapters, he is urged to **walk worthy of** his **calling**. The position into which grace has lifted us was the dominant theme up to now. From here on it will be the practical outworking of that position. Our exalted standing in Christ calls for corresponding godly conduct. So it is true that Ephesians moves from the heavenlies in chapters 1–3, to the local church, to the home, and to general society in chapters 4–6. As Stott has pointed out, these closing chapters teach that "we must cultivate unity in the church, purity in our personal lives, harmony in our homes and stability in our combat with the powers of evil."

For the second time Paul refers to himself as a **prisoner** — this time as a **prisoner of the Lord**. Theodoret comments: "What the world counted ignominy, he counts the highest honor, and he glories in his bonds for Christ, more than a king in his diadem."

As one who was imprisoned as a result of faithfulness and obedience to the Lord, Paul exhorts his readers **to walk worthy of** their **calling**. He does not command or direct. With tenderness and gentleness he appeals to them in the language of grace.

The word, **walk**, is found seven times in this Letter (2:2, 10; 4:1, 17; 5:2, 8, 15); it describes a person's entire lifestyle. A **worthy** walk is one that is consistent with a Christian's dignified position as a member of the Body of Christ.

4:2 In every sphere of life, it is important to show a Christlike spirit. This consists of:

Lowliness — a genuine humility that comes from association with the Lord Jesus. **Lowliness** makes us conscious of our own nothingness and enables us to esteem others better than ourselves. It is the opposite of conceit and arrogance.

Gentleness — the attitude that submits to God's dealings without rebellion, and to man's unkindness without retaliation. It is best seen in the life of Him who said, "I am gentle and lowly in heart." Wright comments:

> What an astonishingly wonderful statement! The One who made the worlds, who flung the stars into space and calls them by name, who preserves the innumerable constellations in their courses, who weighs the mountains in scales and the hills in a balance, who takes up the isles as a very little thing, who holds the waters of the ocean in the hollow of His hand, before whom the inhabitants of the earth are as grasshoppers, when He comes into human life finds Himself as essentially meek and lowly in heart. It is not that He erected a perfect human ideal and accommodated Himself to it; He *was* that.[24]

Longsuffering — an even disposition and a spirit of patience under prolonged provocation. This has been illustrated as follows: Imagine a puppy and a big dog together. As the puppy barks at the big dog, worrying and attacking him, the big dog, who could snap up the puppy with one bite, patiently puts up with the puppy's impertinence.

Bearing with one another in love — that is, making allowance for the faults and failures of others, or differing personalities, abilities, and temperaments. And it is not a question of maintaining a façade of courtesy while inwardly seething with resentment. It means positive love to those who irritate, disturb, or embarrass.

4:3 Endeavoring to keep the unity of the Spirit in the bond of peace. In forming the church, God had eliminated the greatest division that had ever existed among human beings — the rift between Jews and Gentiles. In Christ Jesus these distinctions were abolished. But how would it work out in their life together? Would there still be lingering antagonisms? Would there be a tendency to form a "Jewish Church of Christ" and a "Church for the Nations?" To guard against any divisions or smoldering animosities, Paul now pleads for unity among Christians.

They should give diligence **to keep the unity of the Spirit**. The Holy **Spirit** has made all true believers one in Christ; the Body is indwelt by one **Spirit**. This is a basic **unity** that nothing can destroy. But by quarreling and bickering, believers can act as if it were not so. **To keep the unity of the Spirit** means to live at peace with one another. **Peace** is the ligament which binds the members of the Body together in spite of their wide natural differences. A common reaction when differences arise is to divide and start another party. The spiritual reaction is this: "In essentials, unity. In doubtful questions, liberty. In all things, charity." There is enough of the flesh in every one of us to wreck any local church or any other work of God. Therefore, we must submerge our own petty, personal whims and attitudes, and work together in **peace** for the glory of God and for common blessing.

4:4 Instead of magnifying differences, we should think of the seven positive realities which form the basis of true Christian unity.

One body. In spite of differences in race, color, nationality, culture, language, and temperament, there is only **one body**, made up of all true believers from Pentecost to the Rapture. Denominations, sects, and parties hinder the outworking of this truth. All such man-made divisions will be swept away when the Savior returns. Therefore, our watchword at the present time should be, "Let names and sects and parties fall, and Jesus Christ be all in all."

One Spirit. The same Holy **Spirit** who indwells each believer individually (1 Cor. 6:19) also indwells the Body of Christ (1 Cor. 3:16).

One hope. Every member of the church is called to one destiny — to be with Christ, to be like Him, and to share His glory endlessly. The **one hope** includes all that awaits the saints at the Return of the Lord Jesus and thereafter.

4:5 One Lord. "For even if there are so-called gods, whether in heaven or on earth (as there are many gods and many lords), yet for us there is one God, . . . and one Lord Jesus Christ, through whom are all things, and through whom we live" (1 Cor. 8:5, 6; see also 1 Cor. 1:2.)

One faith. This is the Christian **faith**, the body of doctrine "once for all delivered to the saints" (Jude 3), and preserved for us in the NT.

One baptism. There is a twofold sense in which this is true. First, there is **one baptism** by the Spirit, by which those who trust Christ are placed in the body (1 Cor. 12:13). Then there is **one baptism** by which converts confess their identification with Christ in death, burial, and resurrection. Though there are different modes of baptism today, the NT recognizes one believers' baptism, in the name of the Father and of the Son and of the Holy Spirit. By being baptized, disciples express allegiance to Christ, the burial of their old self, and a determination to walk in newness of life.

4:6 One God. Every child of God recognizes **one God and Father of all** the redeemed, who is:

Above all — He is the supreme Sovereign of the universe.

Through all — He acts through all, using everything to accomplish His purposes.

In you all — He dwells in all believers, and is present in all places at one and the same time.

B. Program for Proper Functioning of the Members of the Body (4:7–16)

4:7 The doctrine of the unity of the Body of Christ has a twin truth, namely, the diversity of its members. Each member has a particular role assigned. No two members are alike, and no two have exactly the same function. The part to be played by each one is assigned **according to the measure of Christ's gift**, that is, He does it as He sees fit. If **Christ's gift** here means the Holy Spirit (John 14:16, 17; Acts 2:38, 39), then the thought is that the Holy Spirit is the One who assigns some gift to every saint, and who also gives the ability to exercise that gift. As each member fulfills his appointed work, the Body of Christ grows both spiritually and numerically.

4:8† In order to assist each child of God to find and fulfill his function, the Lord has given some special **gifts** of ministry, or service to the church. These should not be confused with the gifts mentioned in the previous verse. Every believer has some gift (v. 7), but not everyone is one of the **gifts** named in verse 11: these are special **gifts** designed for the growth of the body.

First, we find that the Giver of those special **gifts** is the risen, ascended, glorified Lord Jesus Christ. Paul quotes Psalm 68:18 as a prophecy that the Messiah would ascend to heaven, would conquer His foes and lead them **captive**, and, as a reward for His victory, would receive **gifts** for **men**.

4:9 But this raises a problem! How could the Messiah ascend to heaven? Had He not lived in heaven with God the Father from all eternity? Obviously, if He was to ascend to heaven, He must first come down from heaven. The prophecy of His Ascension in Psalm 68:18 implies a prior descent. So we might paraphrase verse 9 as follows: **"Now** when it says in Psalm 68 **'He ascended'** — what does it mean but that **He also first descended into the lower parts of the earth."** We know that this is exactly what happened. The Lord Jesus **descended** to Bethlehem's manger, to the death of the cross, and to the grave. **The lower parts of the earth** have sometimes been taken to refer to hades

†*See p. xxiii.*

or hell. But that would not fit in with the argument here: His Ascension necessitated a previous descent to earth but not to hell. In addition, the Scriptures indicate that Christ's spirit went to heaven, not hell, when He died (Luke 23:43, 46).

The New English Bible translates this verse: "Now the word 'ascended' implies that he also descended to the lowest level, down to the very earth."

4:10 The prophecy of Psalm 68:18 and the descent implied in the prophecy were exactly fulfilled by the Incarnation, death, and burial of the Lord Jesus. The One **who descended** from heaven **is also the One who** conquered sin, Satan, demons, and death, and **who ascended far above** the atmosphere and stellar **heavens, that He might fill all things**.

He does **fill all things** in the sense that He is the source of all blessing, the sum of all virtues, and the supreme Sovereign over all. "There is not a place between the depth of the cross and the height of the glory which He has not occupied," writes F. W. Grant.[25]

The central thought in verses 8–10 is that the Giver of the gifts is the ascended Christ. There were no such gifts before He went back to heaven. This lends further support to the contention that the church did not exist in the OT; for if it did, it was a church without gifts.

4:11 The names of the gifts are now given. To our surprise we find they are men, not natural endowments or talents. **He Himself gave some to be apostles, some prophets, some evangelists, and some pastors and teachers**.

Apostles were men who were directly commissioned by the Lord to preach the word and to plant churches. They were men who had seen Christ in resurrection (Acts 1:22). They had power to perform miracles (2 Cor. 12:12) as a means of confirming the message they preached (Heb. 2:4). Together with NT prophets, their ministry was primarily concerned with the foundation of the church (Eph. 2:20). The apostles referred to in this passage mean only those who were apostles *after* the Ascension of Christ.

Prophets were spokesmen or mouthpieces of God. They received direct revelations from the Lord and passed them on to the church. What they spoke by the Holy Spirit was the word of God.

In the primary sense we no longer have apostles and prophets. Their ministry ended when the foundation of the church was laid, and when the NT canon was completed. We have already emphasized that Paul is speaking here of NT **prophets**; they were given by Christ after His Ascension. To think of them as OT prophets introduces difficulties and absurdities into the passage.

Evangelists are those who preach the good news of salvation. They are divinely equipped to win the lost to Christ. They have special ability to diagnose a sinner's condition, probe the conscience, answer objections, encourage decisions for Christ, and help the convert find assurance through the word. Evangelists should go out from a local church, preach to the world, then lead their converts to a local church where they will be fed and encouraged.

Pastors are men who serve as undershepherds of the sheep of Christ. They guide and feed the flock. Theirs is a ministry of wise counsel, correction, encouragement, and consolation.

The work of **pastors** is closely related to that of elders in a local church, the principal difference being that a pastor is a gift whereas the elder is an office. The NT pictures a number of pastors in a local church (Acts 20:17, 28; 1 Pet. 5:1, 2) rather than one pastor or presiding elder.

Teachers are men who are divinely empowered to explain what the Bible says, interpret what it means, and apply it to the hearts and consciences of the saints. Whereas an evangelist may preach the gospel from a passage out of context, the teacher seeks to show how the passage fits into the context.

Because **pastors and teachers** are linked in this verse, some conclude only one gift is intended, that it should read "pastor-teachers." But this is not necessarily so. A man may be a teacher without having the heart of a shepherd. And a pastor may be able to use the word without having the distinctive gift of teaching. If **pastors and teachers** are the same persons here in verse 11, then, by

the same rule of grammar,[26] so are apostles and prophets in 2:20.

One final word. We should be careful to distinguish between divine gifts and natural talents. No unsaved person, however talented, could be an evangelist, pastor, or teacher in the NT sense. Neither could a Christian, for that matter, unless he has received that particular gift. The gifts of the Spirit are supernatural. They enable a man to do what would be humanly impossible for him.

4:12 We come now to the function or purpose of the gifts. It is **for the equipping of the saints for the work of the ministry, for the edifying of the body of Christ**. The process is this:

1. The gifts equip **the saints**.
2. **The saints** then serve.
3. The **body** is then built up.

The ministry is not a specialized occupation limited to men with professional training. The word simply means *service*. It includes every form of spiritual service. And what this verse teaches is that every believer should be "in the ministry."

The gifts are given to perfect or equip all Christians to serve the Lord, and thus to build up **the body of Christ**. Vance Havner explains in his inimitable way:

> Every Christian is commissioned, for every Christian is a missionary. It has been said that the Gospel is not merely something to come to church to hear but something to go from the church to tell — and we are all appointed to tell it. It has also been said, 'Christianity began as a company of lay witnesses; it has become a professional pulpitism, financed by lay spectators!' Nowadays we hire a church staff to do 'full-time Christian work,' and we sit in church on Sunday to watch them do it. Every Christian is meant to be in full-time Christian service . . . There is indeed a special ministry of pastors, teachers and evangelists — but for what? . . . For the perfecting of the saints for their ministry.[27]

These divinely given men should not serve in such a way as to make people perpetually dependent on them. Instead, they should work toward the day when the saints will be able to carry on by themselves. We might illustrate this as follows:

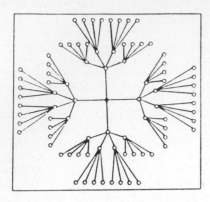

The circle in the center depicts, let us say, the gift of a teacher. He ministers to those in the circle around him so that they are equipped, that is, built up in the faith. Then they go forth and minister to others according to the gifts God has given them. In this way the church grows and expands. It is the divine method of producing growth in **the body of Christ**, both in size and spirituality.

Limitation of Christian service to a select class of men hinders the development of God's people, stifles the cause of world evangelism, and stunts the growth of the church. The distinction between clergy and laity is unscriptural and perhaps the greatest single hindrance to the spread of the gospel.

4:13 Verse 13 answers the question, "How long will this growth process continue?" The answer is **till we all come to** a state of **unity**, maturity, and conformity.

Unity. When the Lord takes His church home to heaven, we will all arrive at **the unity of the faith**. "Now we see in a mirror dimly" with regard to many matters. We have differences of opinion on a host of subjects. Then we will all be fully agreed. And we will reach **the unity of . . . the knowledge of the Son of God**. Here we have individual views of the Lord, of what He is like, of the implications of His teachings. Then we will see Him as He is, and know as we are known.

Maturity. At the Rapture we will also reach full growth or maturity. Both as individuals and as the Body of Christ, we will achieve perfection of spiritual development.

Conformity. And we will be conformed to Him. Everyone will be morally like **Christ**. And the universal church will be a full-grown Body, perfectly suited to its glorious Head. "The fulness of Christ is the Church itself, the fulness of Him that filleth all in all" (FWG). **The measure of the stature** of the church means its complete development, the fulfillment of God's plan for its growth.

4:14 When the gifts operate in their God-appointed manner, and the saints are active in service for the Lord, three dangers are avoided — immaturity, instability, and gullibility.

Immaturity. Believers who never become involved in aggressive service for Christ never emerge from being spiritual **children**. They are undeveloped through lack of exercise. It was to such that the writer to the Hebrews said, "For though by this time you ought to be teachers, you need someone to teach you again. . . ." (Heb. 5:12).

Instability. Another danger is spiritual fickleness. Immature Christians are susceptible to the grotesque novelties and fads of professional quacks. They become religious gypsies, moving **to and fro** from one appealing fantasy to another.

Gullibility. Most serious of all is the danger of deception. Those who are babes are unskillful in the word of righteousness, their senses are not exercised to discern between good and evil (Heb. 5:13, 14). They inevitably meet some false cultist who impresses them by his zeal and apparent sincerity. Because he uses religious words, they think he must be a true Christian. If they had studied the Bible for themselves, they would be able to see through his deceitful juggling of words. But now they are **carried about** by his **wind of doctrine** and led by unprincipled **cunning** into a form of systematized error.

4:15 The last two verses in the paragraph describe the proper process of growth in the Body of Christ. First, there is the necessity of doctrinal adherence: **but, speaking the truth**. . . . There can be no compromise as to the fundamentals of the faith. Second, there must be a right spirit: **but, speaking the truth in love**. If it is spoken in any other way, the result is a one-sided testimony. Blaikie admonishes:

> Truth is the element in which we are to live, move, and have our being. . . . But truth must be inseparably married to love; good tidings spoken harshly are not good tidings. The charm of the message is destroyed by the discordant spirit of the messenger.[28]

Then as the gifts equip the saints, and as the saints engage in active service, they **grow up in all things into** Christ. Christ is the aim and object of their growth, and the sphere of growth is **in all things**. In every area of their lives they become more like **Him**. As the Head has His way in the church, His Body will give an ever more accurate representation of Him to the world!

4:16 The Lord Jesus is not only the goal of growth, He is the source of growth as well. **From** Him **the whole body** is involved in the **growth** process. The marvelous integration of the members of the Body is described by the phrase, **joined and knit together**. This means that every member is exactly designed for his own place and function, and perfectly **joined** to every other member so as to make a complete, living organism. The importance, yes, the indispensability of every member is next indicated: **joined and knit together by what every joint supplies**. The human body consists primarily of bones, organs, and flesh. The bones are bound together by joints and ligaments, and the organs also are attached by ligaments. Each joint and ligament fulfills a role in the growth and usefulness of the body. So it is in **the body** of Christ. No member is superficial; even the most humble believer is necessary.

As each believer fulfills his proper role, **the body** grows as a harmonious, well-articulated unit. In a very real sense, **the body causes growth of the body**, paradoxical as it sounds. This simply means that **growth** is stimulated by **the body** itself as the members feed on the Bible, pray, worship, and witness for Christ. As Chafer said, "The Church, like the human body, is self-developing." In addition to growth in size, there is a building up **of itself in love**.

This speaks of the mutual concern of the members for one another. As Christians abide in Christ and fulfill their proper function in the church, they grow closer to one another **in love** and unity.

C. Appeal for a New Morality (4:17–5:21)

4:17 Here begins the apostle's eloquent appeal for a new morality, an appeal which extends to 5:21. Testifying **in the Lord**, that is, by authority of **the Lord** and by divine inspiration, he urges the Christians to put off every trace of their past life, as if it were a muddy coat, and to put on the virtues and excellencies of the Lord Jesus Christ. **You should no longer walk as the rest of the Gentiles walk**. They were no longer **Gentiles**; they were Christians. There should be a corresponding change in their lives. Paul saw the Christless world of the nations sunk in ignorance and degradation. Seven terrible things characterized them. They were:

Aimless. They walked **in the futility of their mind**. Their life was empty, purposeless, and fruitless. There was great activity but no progress. They chased bubbles and shadows, and neglected the great realities of life.

4:18 *Blind*. "They live blindfold in a world of illusion" (JBP). **Their understanding** was **darkened**. First, they had a native incapacity to understand spiritual truths, and then, because of their rejection of the knowledge of the true God, they suffered blindness as a judgment from the Lord.

Ungodly. They were **alienated from the life of God**, or at a great distance from Him. This was brought about by their willful, deep-seated ignorance and by the hardness of their hearts. They had rejected the light of God in creation and in conscience, and had turned to idolatry. Thereafter they had plunged farther and farther from God.

4:19 *Shameless*. They were **past feeling**. W. C. Wright explains:

> Moule translates it: "having got over the pain." How expressive! When conscience is at first denied, there is a twinge of pain; there is a protest that can be heard. But if the voice is silenced, presently the voice becomes less clear and clamant; the pro-

test is smothered; the twinge is less acute, until at last it is possible to "get over the pain."[29]

Sordid. They consciously gave **themselves over to lewdness**, that is, to vile forms of behavior. The cardinal sin of the Gentiles was and still is sexual immorality. They descended to unparalleled depths of depravity; the walls of Pompeii tell the story of shame and lost decency. The same sins characterize the Gentile world today.

Indecent. In their sexual sin, they worked **all uncleanness**. There is a suggestion here that they gave themselves up to every kind of **uncleanness** as if they were carrying on a trade or business in **lewdness**.

Insatiable. **With greediness**. They were never satisfied. They never had enough. Their sin created an enormous appetite for more of the same thing.

4:20 How different all this was from the **Christ** whom the Ephesians had come to know and love! He was the personification of purity and chastity. He knew no sin, He did no sin, there was no sin in Him.

4:21 The **if** in **if indeed you have heard Him and have been taught by Him** is not meant to cast doubt on the conversion of the Ephesians. It simply emphasizes that all those who had **heard** Christ and had **been taught by Him** had come to know Him as the essence of holiness and godliness. To have heard Christ means to have **heard Him** with the hearing of faith — to have accepted Him as Lord and Savior. The expression, **taught by Him**, refers to the instruction the Ephesians received as they walked in fellowship with Him subsequent to their conversion. Blaikie remarks: "All truth acquires a different hue and a different character when there is a personal relation to Jesus. Truth apart from the Person of Christ has little power."[30] **As the truth is in Jesus**. He not only teaches the truth; He is truth incarnate (John 14:6). The name **Jesus** takes us back to His life on earth, since that is His name in Incarnation. In that spotless life which He lived as a Man in this world, we see the very antithesis of the walk of the Gentiles which Paul has just described.

4:22 In the school of Christ we learn that at the time of conversion we put away our **old man which grows corrupt** through **deceitful lusts. The old man** means all that a person was before his conversion, all that he was as a child of Adam. It is corrupted as a result of giving in to **deceitful**, evil cravings which are pleasant and promising in anticipation but hideous and disappointing in retrospect. As far as his position in Christ is concerned, the believer's **old man** was crucified and buried with Christ. In practice, the believer should reckon it to be dead. Here Paul is emphasizing the positional side of the truth — we have **put off the old man** once for all.

4:23 A second lesson the Ephesians learned at the feet of Jesus was that they were being **renewed in the spirit of** their **mind**. This points to a complete about-face in their thinking, a change from mental impurity to holiness. The Spirit of God influences the thought processes to reason from God's standpoint, not from that of unsaved men.

4:24 The third lesson is that they had **put on the new man** once for all. **The new man** is what a believer is in Christ. It is the new creation, in which old things have passed away and all things have become new (2 Cor. 5:17). This **new** kind of **man** is **according to God**, that is, **created** in His likeness. And it manifests itself **in true righteousness and holiness. Righteousness** means right conduct toward others. **Holiness** is "piety towards God, which puts Him in His place," as F. W. Grant defines it.[31]

4:25 Paul now moves from the believer's standing to their state. Because they have put off the old man and have put on the new man through their union with Christ, they should demonstrate this startling reversal in their everyday lives.

They can do this, first, by **putting away lying** and putting on truthfulness. **Lying** here includes every form of dishonesty, whether it is shading of the truth, exaggeration, cheating, failure to keep promises, betrayal of confidence, flattery, or fudging on income taxes. The Christian's word should be absolutely trustworthy. His yes should mean yes, and his no, no. The life of a Christian becomes a libel rather than a Bible when he stoops to any form of tampering with truthfulness.

Truth is a debt we owe to all men. However, when Paul uses the word, **neighbor**, here, he is thinking particularly of our fellow believers. This is clear from the motive given: **for we are members of one another** (cf. Rom. 12:5; 1 Cor. 12:12–27). It is as unthinkable for one Christian to lie to another as it would be for a nerve in the body to deliberately send a false message to the brain, or for the eye to deceive the rest of the body when danger is approaching.

4:26 A second area for practical renewal in our lives is in connection with sinful **wrath** and righteous anger. There are times when a believer may be righteously **angry**, for instance, when the character of God is impugned. In such cases anger is commanded: **Be angry**. Anger against evil can be righteous. But there are other times when anger is sinful. When it is an emotion of malice, jealousy, resentment, vindictiveness, or hatred because of personal wrongs, it is forbidden. Aristotle said, "Anybody can become angry — that is easy; but to be angry with the right person, to the right degree, at the right time, for the right purpose, and in the right way — that is *not* easy."

If a believer gives way to unrighteous **wrath**, he should confess and forsake it quickly. Confession should be made both to God and to the victim of his anger. There should be no nursing of grudges, no harboring of resentments, no carrying over of irritations. **Do not let the sun go down on your wrath**. Anything that mars fellowship with God or with our brethren should immediately be made right.

4:27 Unconfessed sins of temper provide **the devil** with a foothold or a base of operations. He is capable of finding plenty of these without our deliberately helping him. Therefore, we must not excuse malice, wrath, envy, hatred, or passion in our lives. These sins discredit the Christian testimony, stumble the unsaved, offend believers, and harm ourselves spiritually and physically.

4:28 Now Paul turns his attention to the contrasting behavior patterns of stealing and sharing. The old man steals;

the new man shares. Put off the old; put on the new! The fact that Paul would ever address such instruction as **"Let him who stole steal no longer"** to believers disproves any notion that Christians are sinlessly perfect. They still have the old, evil, selfish nature that must be reckoned dead in daily experience. Stealing may take many forms — all the way from grand larceny to nonpayment of debts, to witnessing for Christ on the employer's time, to plagiarism, to the use of false measurements, and to falsifying expense accounts. Of course, this prohibition against stealing is not new. The Law of Moses forbade theft (Ex. 20:15). It is what follows that makes the passage distinctively Christian. Not only should we refrain from stealing, we should actually **labor** in an honorable occupation in order to be able to share with others who are less fortunate. Grace, not law, is the power of holiness. Only the positive power of grace can turn a thief into a philanthropist.

This is radical and revolutionary. The natural approach is for men to work for the supply of their own needs and desires. When their income rises, their standard of living rises. Everything in their lives revolves around self. This verse suggests a nobler, more exalted view of secular employment. It is a means of supplying a modest standard of living for one's family, but also of alleviating human **need**, spiritual and temporal, at home and abroad. And how vast that **need** is!

4:29 The apostle now turns to the subject of speech, and contrasts that which is worthless with that which edifies. **Corrupt** speech generally means conversation that is filthy and suggestive; this would include off-color jokes, profanity, and dirty stories. But here it probably has the wider sense of any form of conversation that is frivolous, empty, idle, and worthless. Paul deals with obscene and vile language in 5:4; here he is telling us to abandon profitless speech and substitute constructive conversation. The Christian's speech should be:

Edifying. It should result in building up the hearers.

Appropriate. It should be suitable to the occasion.

Gracious. It should **impart grace to the hearers**.

4:30   And do not grieve the Holy Spirit of God, by whom you were sealed for the day of redemption. If this is taken in connection with the preceding verse, it means that worthless talk grieves the Spirit. It may also be linked to verses 25–28 to indicate that lying, unrighteous anger, and stealing also hurt Him. Or in a still wider sense, it may be saying that we should abstain from anything and everything that grieves Him.

Three powerful reasons are suggested:

1. He is the *Holy* Spirit. Anything that is not holy is distasteful to Him.

2. He is the Holy Spirit of **God**, a member of the blessed Trinity.

3. We **were sealed** by Him **for the day of redemption**. As mentioned previously, a seal speaks of ownership and security. He is the seal that guarantees our preservation until Christ returns for us and our salvation is complete. Interestingly enough, Paul here uses the eternal security of the believer as one of the strongest reasons why we should *not* sin.

The fact that He can be grieved shows that the Holy Spirit is a Person, not a mere influence. It also means He loves us, because only a person who loves can be grieved. The favorite ministry of God's Spirit is to glorify Christ and to change the believer into His likeness (2 Cor. 3:18). When a Christian sins, He has to turn from this ministry to one of restoration. It grieves Him to see the believer's spiritual progress interrupted by sin. He must then lead the Christian to the place of repentance and confession of sin.

4:31 All sins of temper and tongue should be put away. The apostle lists several of them. Though it is not possible to distinguish each one precisely, the overall meaning is clear:

Bitterness — Smoldering resentment, unwillingness to forgive, harsh feeling.

Wrath — Bursts of rage, violent passion, temper tantrums.

Anger — Grouchiness, animosity, hostility.

Clamor — Loud outcries of anger, bawling, angry bickering, shouting down of opponents.

Evil speaking — Insulting language, slander, abusive speech.

Malice — Wishing evil on others, spite, meanness.

4:32 The foregoing sins of temper should be terminated, but the vacuum must be filled by the cultivation of Christlike qualities. The former are natural vices; the following are supernatural virtues:

Kindness — An unselfish concern for the welfare of others, and a desire to be helpful even at great personal sacrifice.

Tenderheartedness — A sympathetic, affectionate, and compassionate interest in others, and a willingness to bear their burden.

Forgiveness — A readiness to pardon offenses, to overlook personal wrongs against oneself, and to harbor no desire for retaliation.

The greatest example of One who forgives is God Himself. The basis of His forgiveness is the work of Christ at Calvary. And we are the unworthy objects. God could not forgive sin without proper satisfaction being made. In His love He provided the satisfaction which His righteousness demanded. **In Christ**, that is, in His Person and work, God found a righteous basis on which He could forgive us.

Since He forgave us when we were in debt "millions of dollars," we ought to forgive others when they owe us "a few dollars" (Matt. 18:23–28. JBP). Lenski counsels:

> The moment a man wrongs me I must forgive him. Then *my* soul is free. If I hold the wrong against him I sin against God and against him and jeopardize my forgiveness with God. Whether the man repents, makes amends, asks my pardon or not, makes no difference. I have instantly forgiven him. He must face God with the wrong he has done; but that is his affair and God's and not mine save that I should help him according to Matt. 18:15, etc. But whether this succeeds or not and before this even begins, I must forgive him.[32]

5:1 God's example of forgiveness in 4:32 forms the basis of Paul's exhortation here. The connection is this: God in Christ has forgiven you. Now **be imita-**

tors of God in forgiving one another. A special motive is appended in the words, **as dear children**. In natural life, children bear the family likeness and should seek to uphold the family name. In spiritual life, we should manifest our Father to the world and seek to walk worthy of our dignity as His beloved **children.**

5:2 Another way in which we should resemble the Lord is by walking **in love**. The rest of the verse explains that to **walk in love** means to give ourselves for others. This is what Christ, our perfect Example, did. Amazing fact! He loved us. The proof of His love is that He gave Himself for us in death at Calvary.

His gift is described as **an offering and a sacrifice to God**. An offering is anything given to God; **a sacrifice** here includes the additional element of death. He was the true burnt **offering**, the One who was completely devoted to do the will of God, even to the death of the cross. His **sacrifice** of unspeakable devotion is eulogized as being **for a sweet-smelling aroma**. F. B. Meyer comments, "In love so measureless, so reckless of cost, for those who were naturally so unworthy of it, there was a spectacle which filled heaven with fragrance and God's heart with joy."[33]

The Lord Jesus pleased His Father by giving Himself for others. The moral is that we too can bring joy to God by giving ourselves for others.

> Others, Lord, yes, others!
> Let this my motto be;
> Help me to live for others
> That I may live like Thee.
> – *Charles D. Meigs*

5:3 In verses 3 and 4 the apostle reverts to the topic of sexual sins and decisively calls for saintly separation from them. First, he mentions various forms of sexual immorality:

Fornication. Whenever it is mentioned in the same verse as adultery, **fornication** means illicit intercourse among *unmarried* persons. However, when, as here, the word is not distinguished from adultery, it probably refers to *any* form of sexual immorality, and the NKJV usually so translates it. (Our word "pornography," literally, "whore-writing," is related to the word translated **fornication**.)

Uncleanness. This too may mean immoral acts, but perhaps it can also include impure pictures, obscene books, and other suggestive materials that go along with lives of indecency and that feed the fires of passion.

Covetousness. While we generally think of this as meaning the lust for money, here it refers to sensual desire — the insatiable greed to satisfy one's sexual appetite outside the bounds of marriage. (See Ex. 20:17: "You shall not covet . . . your neighbor's wife. . . .")

These things should **not even be named among** Christians. It goes without saying that they should never have to be named as *having been committed* by believers. They should not even be *discussed* in any way that might lessen their sinful and shameful character. There is always the greatest danger in speaking lightly of them, making excuses for them, or even discussing them familiarly and continually. Paul accents his exhortation with the phrase, **as is fitting for saints**. Believers have been separated from the corruption that is in the world; now they should live in practical separation from dark passion, both in deed and word.

5:4 Their speech should also be free from every trace of:

Filthiness. This refers to dirty stories, suggestive jokes with a sexual coloring, and all forms of obscenity and indecency.

Foolish talking. This means empty conversation that is worthy of a moron. Here it may include gutter language.

Coarse jesting. This means jokes or talk with unsavory, hidden meanings. To talk about something, to joke about it, to make it a frequent subject of conversation is to introduce it into your mind, and to bring you closer to actually doing it.

It is always dangerous to joke about sin. Instead of using his tongue for such unworthy and unbecoming talk, the Christian should deliberately cultivate the practice of expressing **thanks** to God for all the blessings and mercies of life. This is pleasing to the Lord, a good example to others, and beneficial to one's own soul.

5:5 There is no room for doubt as to God's attitude toward immoral per-

lying in spiritual death. The light calls them to life and illumination. If they answer the invitation, **Christ will** shine on them and **give** them **light.**

5:15 In the next seven verses, Paul contrasts foolish footsteps and careful conduct by a series of negative and positive exhortations. The first is a general plea to his readers to.**walk not as fools but as wise**. As mentioned previously, **walk**, is one of the key words of the Epistle: it is mentioned seven times to describe "the whole round of the activities of the individual life." To **walk circumspectly** is to live in the light of our position as God's children. To **walk as fools** means to descend from this high plane to the conduct of worldly men.

5:16 The walk of wisdom calls us to redeem **the time** or buy up the opportunities. Every day brings its opened doors, its vast potential. **Redeeming the time** means living lives noted for holiness, deeds of mercy, and words of help. What lends special urgency to this matter is the **evil** character of **the days** in which we live. They remind us God will not always strive with man, the day of grace will soon close, the opportunities for worship, witness, and service on earth will soon be forever ended.

5:17 So we should **not be unwise, but understand what the will of the Lord is**. This is crucial. Because of the abounding evil and the shortness of the time, we might be tempted to spend our days in frantic and feverish activity of our own choosing. But this would amount to nothing but wasted energy. The important thing is to find out God's **will** for us each day and do it. This is the only way to be efficient and effective. It is all too possible to carry on Christian work according to our own ideas and in our own strength, and be completely out of **the will of the Lord**. The path of wisdom is to discern God's **will** for our individual lives, then to obey it to the hilt.

5:18 And do not be drunk with wine, in which is dissipation. In our North American culture, such a command seems almost shocking and unnecessary, since total abstinence is the rule among so many Christians. But we must remember that the Bible was written for believers in all cultures, and in many

countries wine is still a fairly common beverage on the table. The Scriptures do not condemn the use of wine, but they do condemn its abuse. The use of wine as a medicine is recommended (Prov. 31:6; 1 Tim. 5:23). The Lord Jesus made wine for use as a beverage at the wedding in Cana of Galilee (John 2:1–11).

But the use of wine becomes abuse under the following circumstances and is then forbidden:

1. When it leads to excess (Prov. 23:29–35).
2. When it becomes habit-forming (1 Cor. 6:12b).
3. When it offends the weak conscience of another believer (Rom. 14:13; 1 Cor. 8:9).
4. When it hurts a Christian's testimony in the community and is therefore not to the glory of God (1 Cor. 10:31).
5. When there is any doubt in the Christian's mind about it (Rom. 14:23).

Paul's recommended alternative to being **drunk with wine** is being **filled with the Spirit**. This connection too may startle us at first, but when we compare and contrast the two states, we see why the apostle links them in this way.

First, there are certain similarities:

1. In both conditions, the person is under a power outside himself. In one case it is the power of intoxicating liquor (sometimes called "spirits"); in the other case it is the power of **the Spirit**.
2. In both conditions, the person is fervent. On the Day of Pentecost, the fervency produced by **the Spirit** was mistaken for that produced by new wine (Acts 2:13).
3. In both conditions, the person's walk is affected — his physical walk in the case of drunkenness and his moral behavior in the other instance.

But there are two ways in which the two conditions present sharp contrasts:

1. In the case of drunkenness, there is **dissipation** and debauchery. The Spirit's filling never produces these.
2. In the case of drunkenness, there is loss of self-control. But the fruit of **the Spirit** is self-control (Gal. 5:23).

A believer who is filled **with the Spirit** is never transported outside himself where he can no longer control his actions; the spirit of a prophet is always subject to the prophet (1 Cor. 14:32).

Sometimes in the Bible, the filling **with the Spirit** seems to be presented as a sovereign gift of God. For instance, John the Baptist was **filled with the** Holy **Spirit** from his mother's womb (Luke 1:15). In such a case, the person receives it without any prior conditions to be met. It is not something for which he works or prays; the Lord gives it as He pleases. Here in Ephesians 5:18 the believer is *commanded* to **be filled with the Spirit**. It involves action on his part. He must meet certain conditions. It is not automatic but the result of obedience.

For this reason the Spirit's filling should be distinguished from certain other of His ministries. It is *not* the same as any of the following functions:

1. *The baptism* by the Holy Spirit. This is the work of the Spirit which incorporates the believer in the body of Christ (1 Cor. 12:13).
2. *The indwelling.* By this ministry the Comforter takes up His residence in the body of the Christian and empowers him for holiness, worship, and service (John 14:16).
3. *The anointing.* **The Spirit** Himself is the anointing who teaches the child of God the things of the Lord (1 John 2:27).
4. *The earnest* and *the seal.* We have already seen that the Holy Spirit as the earnest guarantees the inheritance for the saint, and as the seal He guarantees the saint for the inheritance (Eph. 1:13, 14).

These are some of the ministries of the Spirit which are realized in a person the moment he is saved. Everyone who is in Christ automatically has the baptism, the indwelling, the anointing, the earnest, and the seal.

But the filling is different. It is not a once-for-all crisis experience in the life of a disciple; rather it is a continuous process. The literal translation of the command is "Be being filled with the Spirit." It may begin as a crisis experience, but it must continue thereafter as a moment-by-moment process. Today's filling will not do for tomorrow. And certainly it is a state greatly to be desired. In fact, it is the ideal condition of the believer on earth. It means that the Holy Spirit is having His way relatively ungrieved in the life of the Christian, and that the believer is therefore fulfilling his role in the plan of God for that time.

How then can a believer **be filled with the Spirit**? The Apostle Paul does not tell us here in Ephesians; he merely commands us to **be filled**. But from other parts of the word, we know that in order to **be filled with the Spirit** we must:

1. Confess and put away all known sin in our lives (1 John 1:5–9). It is obvious that such a holy Person cannot work freely in a life where sin is condoned.
2. Yield ourselves completely to His control (Rom. 12:1, 2). This involves the surrender of our will, our intellect, our body, our time, our talents, and our treasures. Every area of life must be thrown open to His dominion.
3. Let the word of Christ dwell in us richly (Col. 3:16). This involves reading the word, studying it, and obeying it. When the word of Christ dwells in us richly, the same results follow (Col. 3:16) as follow the filling of **the Spirit** (Eph. 5:19).
4. Finally, we must be emptied of self (Gal. 2:20). To be filled with a new ingredient a cup must first be emptied of the old. To **be filled with** *Him*, we must first be emptied of *us*.

An unknown author writes:

Just as you have left the whole burden of your sin, and have rested on the finished work of Christ, so leave the whole burden of your life and service, and rest upon the present inworking of the Holy Spirit. Give yourself up, morning by morning, to be led by the Holy Spirit and go forth praising and at rest, leaving Him to manage you and your day. Cultivate the habit all through the day, of joyfully depending upon and obeying Him, expecting Him to guide, to enlighten, to reprove, to teach, to use, and to do in and with you what He wills. Count upon His working as a fact, altogether apart from sight or feeling. Only let us believe in and obey the

Holy Spirit as the Ruler of our lives, and cease from the burden of trying to manage ourselves; then shall the fruit of the Spirit appear in us as He wills to the glory of God.

Does a person know it when he is **filled with the Spirit**? Actually, the closer we are to the Lord, the more we are conscious of our own complete unworthiness and sinfulness (Isa. 6:1–5). In His presence, we find nothing in ourselves to be proud of (Luke 5:8). We are not aware of any spiritual superiority over others, any sense of "having arrived." The believer who is **filled with the Spirit** is occupied with Christ and not with self.

At the same time, he may have a realization that God is working in and through his life. He sees things happen in a supernatural way. Circumstances click miraculously. Lives are touched for God. Events move according to a divine timetable. Even forces of nature are on his side; they seem chained to the chariot wheels of the Lord. He sees all this; he realizes that God is working for and through him; and yet he feels strangely detached from it all as far as taking any credit is concerned. In his inmost being, he realizes it is all of the Lord.

5:19 Now the apostle gives four results of being filled with the Spirit. First, Spirit-filled Christians speak **to one another in psalms and hymns and spiritual songs**. The divine infilling opens the mouth to talk about the things of the Lord, and enlarges the heart to share these things with others. While some see all three categories as parts of the Book of Psalms, we understand only **psalms** to mean the inspired writings of David, Asaph, and others. **Hymns** are noninspired songs which ascribe worship and praise directly to God. **Spiritual songs** are any other lyrical compositions dealing with spiritual themes, even though not addressed directly to God.

A second evidence of the filling is inward joy and praise to God: **singing and making melody in your heart to the Lord**. The Spirit-filled life is a fountain, bubbling over with joy (Acts 13:52). Zacharias is an illustration: when he was filled with the Holy Spirit, he sang with all his heart to the Lord (Luke 1:67–79).

5:20 A third result is thanksgiving: **giving thanks always for all things to God the Father in the name of our Lord Jesus Christ**. Where the Spirit reigns, there is gratitude **to God**, a deep sense of appreciation, and a spontaneous expression of it. It is not occasional, but continual. Not only for the pleasant things, but for all things. Anyone can be thankful for sunshine; it takes the power of the Spirit to be thankful for the storms of life.

The shortest, surest way to all happiness is this:

Make it a rule to thank and praise God for everything that happens to you. For it is certain that whatever seeming calamity comes to you, if you thank and praise God for it, you turn it into a blessing. If you could work miracles, you could not do more for yourself than by this thankful spirit: for it needs not a word spoken and turns all that it touches into happiness. (Selected)

5:21 The fourth test of being Spirit-filled is **submitting to one another in the fear of God**. Erdman admonishes:

It is a phrase too often neglected. . . . It names a test of spirituality which Christians too seldom apply. . . . Many persons feel that shouts of hallelujah and exulting songs and the utterance of praise in more or less "unknown tongues" are all proofs of being "filled with the Spirit." These all may be spurious and deceitful and without meaning. Submission to our fellow Christians, modesty of demeanor, humility, unwillingness to dispute, forbearance, gentleness — these are the unmistakable proofs of the Spirit's power. . . .Such mutual submission to their fellow Christians should be rendered "in the fear of Christ," that is, in reverence to him who is recognized as the Lord and Master of all.[37]

These then are four results of the Spirit's filling — speaking, singing, thanking, and submitting. But there are at least four others:

1. Boldness in rebuking sin (Acts 13:9–12), and in testifying for the Lord (Acts 4:8–12, 31; 13:52–14:3).
2. Power for service (Acts 1:8; 6:3, 8; 11:24).
3. Generosity, not selfishness (Acts 4:31, 32).
4. Exaltation of Christ (Acts 9:17, 20) and of God (Acts 2:4, 11; 10:44, 46).

We should earnestly desire to be

filled with the Spirit, but only for the glory of God, not for our own glory.

D. Appeal for Personal Piety in the Christian Household (5:22–6:9)

5:22 Though a new section begins here, there is a close link with the preceding verse. There Paul had listed subjection to one another as one of the results of the divine infilling. In the section from 5:22 to 6:9, he cites three specific areas in the Christian household where submission is the will of God:

Wives should **submit to** their *own husbands*.

Children should submit to their *parents*.

Bondservants should submit to their *masters*.

The fact that all believers are one in Christ Jesus does not mean that earthly relationships are abolished. We must still respect the various forms of authority and government which God has instituted. Every well-ordered society rests on two supporting pillars — authority and submission. There must be some who exercise authority and some who submit to that rule. This principle is so basic that it is found even in the Godhead: "But I want you to know that . . . the head of Christ is God" (1 Cor. 11:3). God ordained human government. No matter how wicked a government may be, yet from God's standpoint it is better than no government, and we should obey it as far as we can without disobeying or denying the Lord. The absence of government is anarchy, and no society can survive under anarchy.

The same is true in the home. There must be a head, and there must be obedience to that head. God ordained that the place of headship be given to the man. He indicated this by creating man first, then creating woman for the man. Thus, both in the order and purpose of creation, He put man in the place of authority and woman in the place of submission.

Submission never implies inferiority. The Lord Jesus is submissive to God the Father, but in no way is He inferior to Him. Neither is the woman inferior to the man. In many ways she may be superior — in devotedness, in sympathy, in diligence, and in heroic endurance. But **wives** are commanded to **submit to** their **own husbands, as to the Lord**. In submitting to the authority of her husband, a wife is submitting to the Lord's authority. This in itself should remove any attitude of reluctance or rebellion.

History abounds with illustrations of the chaos resulting from disobedience to God's pattern. By usurping the place of leadership, and acting for her husband, Eve introduced sin into the human race, with all its catastrophic results. In more recent times many of the false cults were started by women who usurped a place of authority which God never intended them to have. Women who leave their God-appointed sphere can wreck a local church, break up a marriage, and destroy a home.

On the other hand, there is nothing more attractive than a woman fulfilling the role which God has assigned to her. A full-length portrait of such a woman is given in Proverbs 31 — an enduring memorial to the wife and mother who pleases the Lord.

5:23 The reason for the wife's submission is that her **husband is** her **head**. He occupies the same relation to her that Christ occupies to the church. **Christ is head of the church; and He is the Savior of the body**. (The word Savior here can have the meaning of Preserver, as it has in 1 Tim. 4:10, JND). So **the husband is head of the wife**, and he is her preserver as well. As **head** he loves, leads, and guides; as preserver he provides, protects, and cares for her.

We all know there is great revulsion against this teaching in our day. People accuse Paul of being a bigoted bachelor, a male chauvinist, a woman-hater. Or they say his views reflect the social customs of his day but are no longer applicable today. Such statements are, of course, a frontal attack on the inspiration of the Scriptures. These are not merely Paul's words; they are the words of God. To refuse them is to refuse Him and invite difficulty and disaster.

5:24 Nothing could more exalt the role of the wife than comparing it to the role of **the church** as the Bride of **Christ**. The church's submission is the pattern to be followed by the wife. She is to be subject in everything — that is, **everything** that is in accordance with the will of God. No wife would be expected to obey her husband if he required her to compromise her loyalty to the Lord Jesus. But in all the normal relationships of life, she is to obey her husband, even if he is an unbeliever.

5:25 If the foregoing instructions to **wives** stood alone, if there were no correspondingly high instructions to **husbands**, then the presentation would be one-sided, if not unfair. But notice the beautiful balance of truth in the Scriptures, and the corresponding standard they require of the **husbands**. **Husbands** are not told to keep their wives in subjection; they are told to **love** their **wives just as Christ also loved the church**. It has been well said that no wife would mind being submissive to a husband who loves her as much as **Christ** loves **the church**. Someone wrote of a man who feared he was displeasing God by loving his wife too much. A Christian worker asked him if he loved her more than Christ loved the church. He said no. "Only when you go beyond that," said the worker, "are you loving your wife too much." Christ's love for **the church** is presented here in three majestic movements extending from the past to the present to the future. In the past, He demonstrated His love for **the church** by giving **Himself for her**. This refers to His sacrificial death on the cross. There He paid the greatest price in order to purchase a Bride for Himself. Just as Eve was brought forth from the side of Adam, so, in a sense, **the church** was created from the wounded side of the Savior.

5:26 At the present time His love for the church is shown in His work of sanctification: **that He might sanctify and cleanse her with the washing of water by the word**. To **sanctify** means to set apart. Positionally the church is already sanctified; practically she is being set apart day by day. She is going through a process of moral and spiritual preparation, similar to the one-year course of beauty culture which Esther took before being presented to King Ahasuerus (Est. 2:12–16). The process of sanctification is carried on by the **washing of water by the word**. In simple terms this means that the lives of believers are cleansed as they hear the words of Christ and obey them. Thus Jesus said to the disciples, "You are already clean because of the word which I have spoken to you" (John 15:3). And He linked sanctification with the word in His high priestly prayer: "Sanctify them by Your truth. Your word is truth" (John 17:17). Just as the blood of Christ cleanses once for all from the guilt and penalty of sin, so the word of God cleanses continually from the defilement and pollution of sin. This passage teaches that the church is being bathed at the present time, not with literal water, but with the cleansing agent of the word of God.

5:27 In the past, Christ's love was manifested in our *redemption*. In the present, it is seen in our *sanctification*. In the future, it will be displayed in our *glorification*. He Himself will **present her to Himself a glorious church, not having spot or wrinkle or any such thing, but . . . holy and without blemish**. She will then reach the acme of beauty and spiritual perfection.

A. T. Pierson rightly can exclaim:

Think of it — when the omniscient eye looks upon us at the last, He will not find anything that to His immaculate holiness can be so much as a pimple or a mole on a human face. How incredible![38]

F. W. Grant concurs:

No sign of old age about it, no defect; nothing will suit Him then but the bloom and eternity of an eternal youth, the freshness of affections which will never tire, which can know no decay. The Church will be holy and blameless then. After all that we have known of her history, it would be strange to read that, if we did not know how gloriously God maintains His triumph over sin and evil.[39]

5:28 After soaring off on this magnificent rhapsody dealing with Christ's love for the church, Paul now returns to remind husbands that this is the pattern they are to imitate: **So husbands ought to love their own wives as their own bodies**. In imitation of Christ's love, they should **love their own wives** as being indeed **their own bodies**.

In the Greek, the word "own" occurs

six times in verses 22–33. This emphatic use of the word "own" reminds us that monogamy is God's will for His people. Although He permitted polygamy in the OT, He never approved it.

It is also interesting to notice the varied ways in which Paul describes the close relationship of the husband and the wife. He says that in loving his wife, a man is loving his own body (v. 28a); **himself** (vv. 28b, 33); and "his own flesh" (v. 29). Since marriage involves a true union of persons, and two become one flesh, a man **who loves his wife** is, in a very real sense, loving **himself.**

5:29 Man is born with the instinct to care for his own body. He feeds, clothes, and bathes it; he protects it from discomforts, pain, and harm. Its continued survival depends on this care. This solicitous interest is a pale shadow of the care **the Lord** has for **the church.**

5:30 For we are members of His body. The grace of God is amazing! It not only saves us from sin and hell, but incorporates us into Christ as **members of His** mystical **Body.** What volumes this speaks concerning His love for us: He cherishes us as His own Body. What care: He nourishes, sanctifies, and trains us. What security: He will not be in heaven without His **members.** We are united to Him in a common life. Whatever affects the members affects theHead also.

5:31 The apostle now quotes Genesis 2:24 as presenting God's original concept in instituting the marriage relationship. First, the man's relationship to his parents is superseded by a higher loyalty, that is, his loyalty to his wife. In order to realize the high ideal of the marital relationship, he leaves his parents **and is joined to his wife.** The second feature is that husband and wife **become one flesh**: there is a real union of two persons. If these two basic facts were kept in mind, they would eliminate in-law troubles on the one hand, and marital strife on the other.

5:32 This is a great mystery, but I speak concerning Christ and the church. Paul now climaxes his discussion of the marriage relationship by announcing this wonderful truth, hitherto unknown, namely, that as a wife is to her husband, so **the church** is to **Christ**.

When Paul says the **mystery** is **great**, he does not mean it is very mysterious. Rather he means that the implications of the truth are tremendous. The **mystery** is the wonderful purpose which was hidden in God in previous ages, but which has now been revealed. That purpose is to call out of the nations a people to become the Body and Bride of His glorious Son. The marriage relationship thus finds its perfect antitype in the relation between **Christ and the church.**

> One spirit with the Lord:
> Jesus, the glorified,
> Esteems the church for which He bled,
> His body and His bride.
> — *Mary Bowley Peters*

5:33 This final verse is a sentence summary of what the apostle has been saying to husbands and wives. To the husbands the concluding admonition is this: **let each one of you**, without exception, **love his wife as** being **himself**. Not merely as you might love yourself, but in recognition of the fact that she is one with you. To the wives the word is: **see that** you continually **respect** and obey your **husband**. Now stop and think for a moment! What would happen if these divine instructions were widely followed by Christian people today? The answer is obvious. There would be no strife, no separation, no divorce. Our homes would be more like foretastes of heaven than they often are.

6:1 In chapter 5 we learned that one of the results of being filled with the Spirit is being submissive to one another. We saw that a Spirit-filled wife, for instance, is submissive to her husband. Now we learn that Spirit-filled **children** willingly submit to the authority of their parents. The fundamental duty of all children is to **obey** their **parents in the Lord**. Whether the children are Christians or whether the parents are Christians does not make any difference. The parent-child relationship was ordained for all mankind, not just for believers. The command to **obey . . . in the Lord** means, first, that children should **obey** with the attitude that in doing so they are obeying **the Lord**: their obedience should be as if to Him. Second, it means they should **obey** in all matters which are in accordance with the will of God. If their parents ordered them to sin, they should not be expected to comply. In such a case they should courteously refuse and suffer the consequences meekly and without retaliation. However, in all other cases they must be obedient.

Four reasons are given why they should obey. First, it **is right**. It is a basic principle built into the very structure of family life that those who are immature, impulsive, and inexperienced should submit to the authority of parents, who are older and wiser.

6:2 The second reason is that it is scriptural. Here Paul quotes Exodus 20:12: **Honor your father and mother** (see also Deut. 5:16). This command to **honor** parents is the **first** of the Ten Commandments with a specific **promise** of blessing attached to it. It calls for children to respect, love, and obey their parents.

6:3 The third reason is that it is for the best interests of the children: **that it may be well with you**. Think of what would happen to a child who received no instruction and no correction from his parents! He would be personally miserable and socially intolerable.

The fourth reason is that obedience promotes a full life: **and you may live long on the earth**. In the OT, a Jewish child who obeyed his parents did enjoy a long life. In this Gospel Age, it is not a rule without exceptions. Filial obedience is not always connected with longevity. A dutiful son may die at an early age. But it is true in a general way that the life of discipline and obedience is conducive to health and longevity, whereas a life of rebellion and recklessness often ends prematurely.

6:4 The instructions to children are now balanced with advice **to fathers**. They should **not provoke** their **children** to anger with unreasonable demands, with undue harshness, with constant nagging. Rather children should be nurtured **in the training and admonition of the Lord**. **Training** means discipline and correction, and may be verbal or corporal. **Admonition** means warning, rebuke, reproof. Child-training should be "in the **Lord**," that is, carried out in accordance

with His will as revealed in the Bible by one who acts as His representative.

Susannah Wesley, the mother of seventeen children, including John and Charles, once wrote:

> The parent who studies to subdue self-will in his child, works together with God in the renewing and saving of a soul. The parent who indulges it, does the Devil's work, makes religion impractical, salvation unattainable, and does all that in him lies to damn his child, soul and body forever.[40]

6:5 The third and final sphere of submission in the Christian household is that of servants to **masters**. The word Paul uses is **bondservants** or slaves, but the principles apply to servants or employees of all types.

The first duty of employees is to **those who are** their **masters according to the flesh**. The expression, **masters according to the flesh**, reminds us that the employer has jurisdiction as far as physical or mental work is concerned, but he cannot dictate in spiritual matters or command the conscience.

Second, servants should be respectful. **Fear and trembling** do not mean cowering servility and abject terror; they mean a dutiful respect and a **fear** of offending the Lord and the employer.

Third, service should be conscientious, or **in sincerity of heart**. We should endeavor to deliver sixty minutes of work for every hour of pay.

Next, our work should be **as to Christ**. These words show that there should be no real distinction between the secular and the sacred. All that we do should be for Him — with a view to pleasing and honoring Him and to attracting others to Him. The most menial and commonplace tasks in life are ennobled and dignified when they are done for the glory of God. Even washing dishes! That is why some Christian housewives have this motto over their kitchen sink: "Divine service held here three times daily."

6:6 We should always be diligent, not only when the boss is looking, but conscious that our Master is always looking. It is a natural tendency to slack off when the employer is away, but it is a form of dishonesty. The Christian's standards of performance should not vary according to the geographical location of the foreman. A customer once urged a Christian sales clerk to give him more than he was paying for, assuring him that his employer was not looking. The sales clerk replied, "My Master is always looking!" As servants of Christ, we should be **doing the will of God from the heart**, that is, with a sincere desire to please Him. Erdman says:

> Labor is immeasurably dignified by such considerations as these. The task of the humblest slave may be ennobled by being rendered in such a way as to please Christ, with such good will, with such hearty readiness and zeal, as to merit the approval of the Lord.[41]

6:7 Then, too, we should serve **with good will**. Not with an outward display of compliance while we are inwardly seething with resentment, but cheerfully and willingly. Even if a master is overbearing, abusive, and unreasonable, our work can still be done **as to the Lord and not to men**. It is this type of supernatural behavior that speaks the loudest in the kind of world in which we live.

6:8 A great incentive to do all as if to Christ is the assurance that He will reward every such good work. **Whether a person is a slave or free** makes no difference. The Lord notes all the jobs, pleasant or disagreeable, that are done for Him, and He will reward each worker.

Before leaving this section on slaves, some comments should be made:

1. The NT does not condemn slavery as such. In fact, it likens the true believer to a slave (bondservant) of Christ (v. 6). But the abuses of slavery have disappeared wherever the gospel has gone — mainly by moral reformation.

2. The NT has more to say to slaves than it has to kings. This may be a reflection of the fact that not many wise, mighty, or noble are called (1 Cor. 1:26). Probably most Christians are found in the lower economic and social brackets. The emphasis on slaves also shows that the most menial servants are not excluded from the choicest blessings of Christianity.

3. The effectiveness of these instructions to slaves is seen in the fact that in the early days of Christianity, Christian slaves frequently brought higher prices at the auction than heathen bondservants. It should be true today that Christian employees are worth more to their employers than those who have never been touched by the grace of God.

6:9 Masters should be guided by the **same** general principles as servants. They should be fair, kind, and honest. They should be particularly careful to refrain from abusive and **threatening** language. If they exercise discipline in this area, they will never have to resort to physical abuse of their servants. And they should always remember that they have a **Master also**, the same **Master** who **is in heaven** that the slave has. Earthly distinctions are leveled in the presence of the Lord. Both master and servant will one day give an account to Him.

E. Exhortations Concerning the Christian Warfare (6:10–20)

6:10 Paul is coming to the close of his Epistle. Addressing all the family of God, he makes a stirring appeal to them as soldiers of Christ. Every true child of God soon learns that the Christian life is a warfare. The hosts of Satan are committed to hinder and obstruct the work of Christ and to knock the individual soldier out of combat. The more effective a believer is for the Lord, the more he will experience the savage attacks of the enemy: the devil does not waste his ammunition on nominal Christians. In our own strength we are no match for the devil. So the first preparatory command is that we should be continually strengthened **in the Lord and in the boundless resources of His might**. God's best soldiers are those who are conscious of their own weakness and ineffectiveness, and who rely solely on Him. "God has chosen the weak things of the world to put to shame the things which are mighty" (1 Cor. 1:27b). Our weakness commends itself to **the power of His might**.

6:11 The second command is concerned with the need for divine **armor**. The believer must **put on the whole armor of God that** he **may be able to**

stand **against the** stratagems **of the devil**. It is necessary to be completely armed; one or two pieces will not do. Nothing less than the whole panoply which God provides will keep us invulnerable. **The devil** has various stratagems — discouragement, frustration, confusion, moral failure, and doctrinal error. He knows our weakest point and aims for it. If he cannot disable us by one method, he will try for another.

6:12 This warfare is not a matter of contending against godless philosophers, crafty priests, Christ-denying cultists, or infidel rulers. The battle is against demonic forces, against battalions of fallen angels, against evil spirits who wield tremendous power. Though we cannot see them, we are constantly surrounded by wicked spirit-beings. While it is true that they cannot indwell a true believer, they can oppress and harass him. The Christian should not be morbidly occupied with the subject of demonism; neither should he live in fear of demons. In the armor of God, he has all he needs to hold his ground against their onslaughts. The apostle speaks of these fallen angels as **principalities** and **powers**, as **rulers of the darkness of this age**, and as **spiritual hosts of wickedness in the heavenly places**. We do not have sufficient knowledge to distinguish between these; perhaps they refer to spirit-rulers with differing degrees of authority, such as presidents, governors, mayors, and aldermen, on the human scale.

6:13 As Paul wrote, he was probably guarded by a Roman soldier in full armor. Always quick to see spiritual lessons in the natural realm, he makes the application: we are flanked by formidable foes; we must **take up the whole armor of God, that** we **may be able to withstand** when the conflict reaches its fiercest intensity, and still be found standing when the smoke of battle has cleared away. **The evil day** probably refers to any time when the enemy comes against us like a flood. Satanic opposition seems to occur in waves, advancing and receding. Even after our Lord's temptation in the wilderness, the devil left Him for a season (Luke 4:13).

6:14 The first piece of armor mentioned is the belt of **truth**. Certainly we must be faithful in holding the **truth** of God's word, but it is also necessary for the **truth** to hold us. We must apply it to our daily lives. As we test everything by the **truth**, we find strength and protection in the combat.

The second piece is **the breastplate of righteousness**. Every believer is clothed with the righteousness of God (2 Cor. 5:21), but he must also manifest integrity and uprightness in his personal life. Someone has said, "When a man is clothed in practical righteousness, he is impregnable. Words are no defense against accusation, but a good life is." If our conscience is void of offense toward God and man, the devil has nothing to shoot at. David put on **the breastplate of righteousness** in Psalm 7:3–5. The Lord Jesus wore it at all times (Isa. 59:17).

6:15 The soldier must have his **feet shod with the preparation of the gospel of peace**. This suggests a readiness to go out with the good news **of peace**, and therefore an invasion into enemy territory. When we relax in our tents, we are in deadly peril. Our safety is to be found in following the beautiful feet of the Savior on the mountains, bearing glad tidings and publishing peace (Isa. 52:7; Rom. 10:15).

> Take my feet and let them be
> Swift and beautiful for Thee
>   – *Frances Ridley Havergal*

6:16 In addition, the soldier must take **the shield of faith** so that when **the fiery darts of the wicked one** come zooming at him, they will hit the shield and fall harmlessly to the ground. **Faith** here is firm confidence in the Lord and in His word. When temptations burn, when circumstances are adverse, when doubts assail, when shipwreck threatens, **faith** looks up and says, "I believe God."

6:17 **The helmet** God provides is **salvation** (Isa. 59:17). No matter how hot the battle, the Christian is not daunted, since he knows that ultimate victory is sure. Assurance of eventual deliverance preserves him from retreat or surrender. "If God is for us, who can be against us?" (Rom. 8:31).

Finally, the soldier takes **the sword of the Spirit, which is the word of God**. The classic illustration of this is our Lord's use of this **sword** in His encounter with Satan. Three times He quoted the word of God — not just random verses but the appropriate verses which the Holy Spirit gave Him for that occasion (Luke 4:1–13). **The word**[42] **of God** here does not mean the whole Bible, but the particular portion of the Bible which best suits the occasion.

David Watson says:

> God gives us all the protection that we need. We must see that there is a "ring of truth" about our walk with the Lord, that our lives are right ("righteous") with God and with one another, that we seek to make peace wherever we go, that we lift up that shield of faith together to quench the flaming darts of the evil one, that we protect our minds from fears and anxieties that easily assail, and that we use God's word to good effect in the power of the Spirit. Remember it was by the repeated sword thrusts of God's word that Jesus overcame his adversary in the wilderness.[43]

6:18 **Prayer** is not mentioned as a part of the armor; but we would not be overrating its importance if we say that it is the atmosphere in which the soldier must live and breathe. It is the spirit in which he must don the armor and face the foe. **Prayer** should be continual, not sporadic; a habit, not an isolated act. Then too the soldier should use all kinds of **prayer**: public and private; deliberate and spontaneous; supplication and intercession; confession and humiliation; praise and thanksgiving.

And **prayer** should be **in the Spirit**, that is, inspired and led by Him. Formal prayers recited merely by rote (without giving thought to their meaning) — of what value are they in combat against the hosts of hell? There must be vigilance in **prayer**: **watchful to this end**. We must watch against drowsiness, mind-wandering, and preoccupation with other things. **Prayer** requires spiritual keenness, alertness, and concentration. And there must be **perseverance** in prayer. We must keep on asking, seeking, knocking (Luke 11:9). **Supplication** should be made **for all the saints**. They

are engaged in the conflict too, and need to be supported in **prayer** by their fellow soldiers.

6:19 Regarding Paul's personal request, **and for me**, Blaikie remarks:

> Mark the *unpriestly* idea! So far from Paul having a store of grace for all the Ephesians, he needed their prayers that, out of the one living store, the needful grace might be given to him.[44]

Paul was writing from prison. Yet he did not ask prayer for his early release. Rather he asked for **utterance** in opening his **mouth boldly** to declare **the mystery of the gospel**. This is Paul's final mention of **the mystery** in Ephesians. Here it is presented as the reason for his bonds. Yet he has no regrets. Quite the contrary! He wants to broadcast it more and more.

6:20 Ambassadors are generally granted diplomatic immunity from arrest and imprisonment. But men will tolerate almost anything better than they will tolerate the gospel. No other subject stirs such emotion, arouses such hostility and suspicion, and provokes such persecution. So Christ's representative was **an ambassador in chains**. Eadie states it well:

> A legate from the mightiest Sovereignty, charged with an embassy of unparalleled nobleness and urgency, and bearing with him credentials of unmistakable authenticity, is detained in captivity.[45]

The particular part of Paul's message that stirred the hostility of narrow religionists was the announcement that believing Jews and believing Gentiles are now formed into one new society, sharing equal privileges, and acknowledging Christ as Head.

F. Paul's Personal Greetings (6:21–24)

6:21, 22 Paul was sending **Tychicus** from Rome to Ephesus to let the saints know how he was getting along. He commends **Tychicus** as **a beloved brother and faithful minister** (servant) **in the Lord**. There are only five references to this man in the NT. He was one of the party that traveled with Paul from Greece to Asia (Acts 20:4). He was the apostle's messenger to the Christians at Colosse (Col. 4:7); to Ephesus (cf. 6:21

with 2 Tim. 4:12) and possibly to Titus in Crete (Titus 3:12). His twofold mission at this time was to inform the saints concerning Paul's welfare in prison, and also to encourage their **hearts**, allaying any unnecessary fears.

6:23 In the closing verses, we have Paul's characteristic greetings — *peace* and *grace*. In combining these two, he wishes for his readers the sum of all blessings. Also in combining the characteristic Jewish and Gentile words, he may be making a final veiled reference to the mystery of the gospel — Jew and Gentile now made one in Christ. In verse 23 he desires that his readers may have **peace** and **love with faith. Peace** would garrison their hearts in every circumstance of life. **Love** would enable them to worship God and work with one another. **Faith** would empower them for exploits in the Christian warfare. All these blessings come **from God the Father and the Lord Jesus Christ**, a fact that would be impossible if They were not equal.

6:24 Finally the beloved apostle wishes **grace** for **all those who love our Lord Jesus Christ** with an incorruptible, sincere love. True Christian love has the quality of permanence: its flame may flicker and grow low at times, but it is never extinguished.

The Roman prison has long since given up its noble inmate. The great apostle has entered into his reward and seen the face of his Beloved. But the Letter is still with us — as fresh and alive as the day it came from his heart and pen. In the twentieth century it still speaks to us words of instruction, inspiration, conviction, and exhortation.

In concluding our commentary on Ephesians we find ourselves in hearty agreement with the words of H. W. Webb-Peploe:

> There is perhaps no writing in the Book of God so majestic and so wonderful: and therefore, how impossible it is for any man, as a messenger even from God Himself, to do justice to it in the space allotted to us! I hope we may draw nigh to it, simply seeking for teachings upon holiness, teachings by which we may be sent forth to live a nobler and higher life than hitherto, and by which we may be enabled to glorify God.[46]

ENDNOTES

[1](Intro) William G. Moorehead, *Outline Studies in Acts and the Epistles*, p. 214.

[2](1:3) Lewis Sperry Chafer, *The Ephesian Letter*, p. 74.

[3](Excursus) W. G. Blaikie, "Ephesians," *Pulpit Commentary*, XLVI:3.

[4](1:10) John G. Bellett, *Brief Notes on the Epistle to the Ephesians*, pp. 6, 7.

[5](1:17) R. W. Dale, *The Epistle to the Ephesians; Its Doctrines and Ethics*, p. 133.

[6](1:18) Both the oldest and the vast majority of existing mss. read *hearts* (lit. *kardias*, the singular), not *understanding* (*dianoias*). The marginal reading is thus undoubtedly correct.

[7](1:19) F. B. Meyer, *Key Words of the Inner Life*, p. 92.

[8](1:19) Chafer, *Ephesian Letter*, p.57.

[9](1:20) Meyer, *Key Words*, p. 93.

[10](2:3) *Ibid*, p. 140.

[11](2:4) John Eadie, *Commentary on the Epistle to the Ephesians*, p. 141.

[12](2:5) A. T. Pierson, "The Work of Christ for the Believer," *The Ministry of Keswick, First Series*, pp. 118, 119.

[13](2:7) First Corinthians 13:12 and 1 John 3:2 are sometimes used to prove that we will be omniscient in heaven. However, the first reference deals only with recognition of one another in heaven and the second with moral and physical likeness to Christ.

[14](2:18) Eadie, *Ephesians*, p. 187.

[15](2:21) Blaikie, "Ephesians," XLVI:68.

[16](3:1) Ruth Paxson, *The Wealth, Walk and Warfare of the Christian*, p. 57.

[17](3:4) Blaikie, "Ephesians," XLVI:104.

[18](3:8) *Ibid*, XLVI:105, 106.

[19](3:9) The Greek word for *stewardship* or *dispensation*, especially in the large (uncial) letters of the earliest mss., could easily be mistaken for the similar-looking word for *fellowship* (cf. OIKONOMIA and KOINŌNIA). The margin is correct; the traditional reading has very weak support.

[20](3:16) Jamieson, Fausset, and Brown, *Commentary Practical and Explanatory on the Whole Bible*, VI:408.

[21](3:17) W. Graham Scroggie, "Paul's Prison Prayers," the Ministry of Keswick, Second Series, p. 49.

[22](3:18) Meyer, *Key Words*, pp. 53, 54.

²³(3:21) George Williams, *The Student's Commentary on the Holy Scriptures*, p. 925.

²⁴(4:2) Walter C. Wright, *Ephesians*, p. 85.

²⁵(4:10) F. W. Grant, "Ephesians," *The Numerical Bible, Acts to 2 Corinthians*, VI:341.

²⁶(4:11) "Granville Sharp's rule" states that (in Greek) two nouns of office, title, or quality joined by *kai* (*and*), with only the first having the definite article, refer to the same person. A good example of this construction is "our God and Savior Jesus Christ" in 2 Peter 1:1, where the liberal RSV translators felt constrained by grammar to be stronger for the deity of Christ than even the King James. (The grammatical rule was not clearly defined till the late 1700's.) In the plural, as here, the rule does not always apply, though the construction at least closely associates the two nouns (cf. "Scribes and Pharisees," etc.).

²⁷(4:12) Vance Havner, *Why Not Just Be Christians*, p. 63.

²⁸(4:15) Blaikie, "Ephesians," XLVI: 150.

²⁹(4:19) Wright, *Ephesians*, p. 100.

³⁰(4:21) Blaikie, "Ephesians," XLVI: 151.

³¹(4:24) Grant, "Ephesians," p. 344.

³²(4:32) R. C. H. Lenski, *The Interpretation of St. Paul's Epistles to the Galatians, to the Ephesians, and to the Philippians*, p. 588.

³³(5:2) Meyer, *The Heavenlies*, p. 25.

³⁴(5:9) The NU text reads *light* (*phōtos*) for *Spirit* (*Pneumatos*).

³⁵(5:13) Blaikie, "Ephesians," XLVI: 209.

³⁶(5:13) Bishop Ellicott and Dean Alford preferred this translation.

³⁷(5:21) Charles R. Erdman, *Ephesians*, p. 106.

³⁸(5:27) Pierson, "The Work of Christ," p. 138.

³⁹(5:27) Grant, "Ephesians," VI:350.

⁴⁰(6:4) Quoted by William W. Orr in *Bible Hints on Rearing Children*, p. 19.

⁴¹(6:6) Erdman, *Ephesians*, p. 119.

⁴²(6:17) Paul does not use the widely known word *logos* here, but *rhēma* (related to our word *rhetoric*), an expressed word or saying, here a specific "word" from God for a specific need. Sometimes *logos* and *rhēma* are virtually synonymous.

⁴³(6:17) David Watson, *Discipleship*, p. 183.

⁴⁴(6:19) Blaikie, "Ephesians," XLVI: 260.

⁴⁵(6:20) Eadie, *Ephesians*, p. 480.

⁴⁶(6:24) H. W. Webb-Peploe, "Grace and Peace in Four Pauline Epistles," *The Ministry of Keswick, First Series*, p. 69.

BIBLIOGRAPHY

Bellett, John G. *Brief Notes on the Epistle to the Ephesians*. London: G. Morrish, n.d.

Blaikie, W. G. "Ephesians," *Pulpit Commentary, Vol. XLVI*. New York: Funk & Wagnalls, n.d.

Chafer, Lewis Sperry. *The Ephesian Letter*. Findlay, Ohio: Dunham Publishing Company, 1935.

Dale, R. W. *The Epistle to the Ephesians: Its Doctrine and Ethics*. London: Hodder and Stoughton, 1893.

Eadie, John. *Commentary on the Epistle to the Ephesians*. Grand Rapids: Zondervan Publishing House, 1957.

Erdman, Charles R. *The Epistle of Paul to the Ephesians*. Philadelphia: Westminster Press, 1931.

Flint, V. Paul. *Epistle to the Ephesians: To the Praise of His Glory*. Oak Park, IL: Emmaus Bible School, n.d.

Meyer, Frederick Brotherton. *Key Words of the Inner Life: Studies in the Epistle to the Ephesians*. Fleming H. Revell Company, 1893.

———. *The Heavenlies*. Westchester, IL: Good News Publishers, n.d.

Paxson, Ruth. *The Wealth, Walk and Warfare of the Christian*. New York: Fleming H. Revell Co., 1939.

Wright, Walter C. *Ephesians*. Chicago: Moody Press, 1954.

THE EPISTLE TO THE PHILIPPIANS

Introduction

"A little volume of graciousness, bound within the covers of grace."
— J. H. Jowett

I. Unique Place in the Canon

A denomination's "First Church" in any town or city has special prestige in the eyes of its adherents. Imagine, then, the importance of the first known church — before there were any denominations — not merely in a single town, but in all of Europe! Such was the congregation at Philippi, in ancient Macedonia (northern Greece). How Christians in the West should rejoice (and even non-Christians, if they knew of the blessed by-products of Christianity they enjoy) that Paul heeded "the Macedonian call" and turned west, not east, in his evangelization of the Roman Empire! Perhaps the continent of Asia would today be sending Christian missionaries to Europe and North America instead of vice versa, had not the gospel taken hold in Europe.

The Philippian assembly was generous, sending support to Paul time and again. And that, humanly speaking, is the reason for this "thank you letter."

But Philippians is much, much more. It is truly the Epistle of joy — forms of "joy" and "rejoice" occurring over twelve times in its four chapters. Paul knew how to rejoice in good times or hard times (4:11). Also, there is little controversy or negative admonition in this "upbeat" Letter.

The key reason Christians *can* rejoice is that the Son of God was willing to come to earth as a Man — and a Bondservant at that! Not stopping at healing and teaching, He went all the way to death — even death on a cross. Philippians 2:5–11 expresses this great truth in a beautiful paragraph that many believe is an early Christian hymn, either quoted by Paul or original with him. Even this passage is included to teach unity through humility. Doctrine is never divorced from duty in the NT, as it often is among modern church people — with sad results.

This, then, is Philippians, one of the most cheerful and attractive books in the whole word of God.

II. Authorship[†]

Since most scholars regard the Pauline authorship of Philippians as indisputable, we cite the evidence largely for completeness. Some scholars think they see traces of *two* letters combined in Philippians, or at least that the Bondservant passage (2:5–11) is interpolated. No manuscript evidence exists for these theories.

The *external evidence* is strong. Those who quote the Letter early — often specifically mentioning it as by Paul — include Ignatius, Clement of Rome, Polycarp, Irenaeus, Clement of Alexandria, and Tertullian. Both Marcion's "canon" and the Muratorian Canon ascribe the book to Paul.

Besides the obvious reference to Paul in 1:1, the entire style and wording ring with Pauline tones. The arguments against Pauline authorship tend to be petty, such as maintaining that the reference to "bishops and deacons" in 1:1 demands a date later than Paul's lifetime. This would be true if we read back *later* ideas of bishops into the first century. But Paul uses *bishops* (*episkopoi*, the Greek work for overseers or superintendents) both in the Pastoral Epistles and Acts 20:28 as synonymous with *elders*. Also,

[†]See p. i.

it should be noted that the single congregation addressed had a *plurality* of bishops.

H. A. A. Kennedy beautifully sums up the *internal evidence*:

> Perhaps no Pauline epistle bears more conclusively the stamp of authenticity. There is an artlessness, a delicacy of feeling, a frank outpouring of the heart which could not be simulated.[1]

III. Date

Like Ephesians, Colossians, and Philemon, Philippians was written from prison, hence the category "Prison (or Captivity) Epistles." But while the other three were almost assuredly written and sent at nearly the same time (about A.D. 60), Philippians is clearly written a little later. Marcion specifically says that Paul wrote Philippians from Rome, and this fits well with 1:13 and 4:22, which verses suggest Rome as the place of origin. Paul spent two years under arrest in Rome; hints found in the Letter suggest that Philippians was written near the end of that time. For example, 1:12–18 would imply a certain length of time for preaching in the Eternal City since Paul arrived. That Paul's case was about to be decided (and probably in a positive way — by release) seems indicated in 1:12, 13, 19, 23–26.

These facts, plus allowing time for letters, visits, and gifts of money that are alluded to in the Epistle, give us a date of late A.D. 61.

IV. Background and Theme[†]

It was a momentous day in the history of Christian missions when the Apostle Paul came as far as Troas on his Second Missionary Journey. Troas was located on the northwest coast of Asia Minor, across the Aegean Sea from Greece. One night, in a vision, a man of Macedonia appeared to the apostle, saying, "Come over to Macedonia, and help us" (Acts 16:9). Immediately Paul arranged to sail for Macedonia with Timothy, and also with Luke and Silas. They first set foot on *European* soil at Neapolis, then journeyed inland to Philippi. The latter city was at that time a Roman colony, governed by Roman officials,

and granting the rights and privileges of Roman citizenship to its inhabitants.

On the Sabbath, the gospel preachers went down by the riverside where a group of women were in the habit of gathering for prayer (Acts 16:13). One of these was Lydia, a seller of purple from the city of Thyatira. When she accepted the gospel message, she became the first known convert to Christianity on the continent of Europe.

But Paul's stay in Philippi did not prove entirely peaceful. A young woman possessed with a spirit of divination (foretelling future events) met the servants of the Lord and for some time followed them, crying out, "These men are the servants of the Most High God, who proclaim to us the way of salvation" (Acts 16:17). Not willing to accept the testimony of one possessed by an evil spirit, the apostle commanded the demon to come out of her. When her masters, who had profited from this girl's predictions, saw what had happened, they were furious with Paul. They dragged him and Silas into the market place to face the representatives of Rome. These magistrates, in turn, commanded that they should be beaten and thrown into prison.

What happened in that Philippian jail is now well-known. At midnight, Paul and Silas were praying and singing praises to God. Suddenly there was a great earthquake, opening all the doors of the prison and causing the prisoners' chains to be loosed. The jailer, thinking that the prisoners had escaped, was about to kill himself when Paul reassured him that his inmates had not fled. Then the jailer cried out, "Sirs, what must I do to be saved?" The memorable answer came back, "Believe on the Lord Jesus Christ and you will be saved" (Acts 16:31). God's grace had won another trophy at Philippi. In the morning, the local authorities urged Paul and his companions to leave town as quickly as possible. This Paul refused to do. He reminded them that they had beaten him, a Roman citizen, and had imprisoned him without a fair trial. After continued appeals from the magistrates to leave the city, Paul and his companions first went to visit in the home of Lydia and then took their leave (Acts 16:40).

†See p. ii.

About ten years later, Paul wrote to the Philippians. He was in prison again. The Philippians had heard that Paul was in prison, so they sent a gift of money to him. Epaphroditus had been commissioned to carry this gift to Paul. After delivering it, he decided to stay there a while and help the apostle in his troubles. Epaphroditus himself became ill in carrying out these duties; in fact, he nearly died. But God had mercy on him and raised him back to health once again. He is now ready to go back to Philippi, to his home assembly, and so the apostle is sending back this Letter of acknowledgment with him.

Philippians is one of the most personal and affectionate of Paul's Epistles. It reveals clearly that this congregation held a very special place of esteem in his affection. As we read it, we detect the very tender bond that existed between the great apostle and this church which he had founded.

OUTLINE

Commentary

I. PAUL'S GREETING, PRAISE, AND PRAYER (1:1–11)

1:1 Paul and Timothy are linked together at the opening of this Epistle. This does not mean that Timothy helped to write the Letter. He had been with Paul when he first visited Philippi, so he was known to the saints there. Now **Timothy** is with **Paul** as the apostle opens this Letter.

Paul was now an older man (Phmn. 9), while Timothy was still quite young. Thus youth and age were yoked together in the service of the Best of masters. Jowett puts it nicely: "It is the union of springtime and autumn; of enthusiasm and experience; of impulse and wisdom; of tender hope and quiet and rich assurance."[2]

Both are described as **bondservants of Jesus Christ**. Both loved their Master. The ties of Calvary bound them to the service of their Savior forever.

The Letter is addressed **to all the saints in Christ Jesus who are in Philippi, with the bishops and deacons**. The word *all* recurs in this Epistle quite frequently. Paul's affectionate interest went out to **all** the Lord's people.

The saints in Christ Jesus who are in Philippi describes the dual position of the believers. As to their spiritual status, they were set apart by God **in Christ**

Jesus. As to their geographical location, they were at **Philippi**. Two places at the same time!

Then the apostle mentions **the bishops and deacons. The bishops** were the elders or overseers in the assembly — those who took a pastoral interest in the flock of God and who led the flock by their godly example. The **deacons**, on the other hand, were the servants of the church who were probably chiefly concerned with its material affairs, such as finances, etc.

There were only these three groups in the church — **saints, bishops, and deacons**. If there had been a clergyman in charge, Paul would have mentioned him also. Instead he speaks only of **bishops** (plural) and **deacons** (also plural).

Here we have a remarkable picture of the simplicity of church life in the early days. **The saints** are mentioned first, then their *spiritual guides*, and last their *temporal servants*. That is all!

1:2 In Paul's characteristic greeting, he wishes the saints **grace . . . and peace**. The former is not so much the grace which comes to a sinner at the time of his conversion as the **grace** which he must constantly obtain at the throne of grace to help in every time of need (Heb. 4:16). Likewise, the **peace** which Paul craves for them is not so much peace with God, which is theirs already, as the **peace** of God which comes through prayer and thanksgiving (4:6, 7).

Both blessings come **from God our Father and the Lord Jesus Christ**. The apostle honors the Son even as he honors the Father (John 5:23). There is no mistaking that to Paul, Jesus Christ is God.

1:3 Now Paul bursts into a song of thanksgiving. But that is nothing new for the apostle. The walls of the Philippian jail had echoed the songs of Paul and Silas on their first visit there. As he writes these words, he is probably a prisoner in Rome — but he is still singing "songs in the night." The indomitable Paul! **Every remembrance** of the Philippians awakened thanksgiving in his heart. Not only were they his children in the faith, but in many ways they had proved to be a model church.

1:4 In every prayer, he made sup-

plication for the Philippians **with joy**. To him it was a sheer delight to pray for them — not dull drudgery. From this and many similar passages in Paul's writing, we learn that he was a man of prayer. It is not necessary to search further for the reason he was so wonderfully used of God. When we remember the extent of his travels and the host of Christians he knew, we marvel that he maintained such a personal, intimate interest in them all.

1:5 The specific reason for his thanksgiving was their **fellowship** in furthering **the gospel from the first day until now. Fellowship** might include financial assistance, but it extends also to prayer support and a wholehearted devotion to the spread of the good news. When Paul mentions **the first day**, one cannot help wondering if the jailor was still alive when this Letter was publicly read to the assembly at Philippi. If so, this mention of Paul's introduction to the Philippian believers would certainly have struck a responsive chord in his heart.

1:6 As the apostle thinks of the good start the believers have made in the Christian life, he is **confident** that God will finish the **good work** He **has begun.**

The work which His goodness began,
The arm of His strength will complete;
His promise is Yea and Amen,
And never was forfeited yet.
                    – *Augustus M. Toplady*

Good work may refer to their salvation, or it may mean their active financial participation in the furtherance of the gospel. **The day of Jesus Christ** refers to the time of His coming again to take His people home to heaven and probably also includes the Judgment Seat of Christ, when service for Him will be reviewed and rewarded.

1:7 Paul feels justified in being thankful for the Philippians. In his **heart** he treasures a lasting memory of how loyally they stood with him, whether he was on trial, in prison, or traveling about **in the defense and confirmation of the gospel. The defense of the gospel** refers to the ministry of answering the critics, while the **confirmation of the gospel** relates rather to establishing the message more firmly in the hearts of those who are already believers. W. E. Vine says:

"The gospel both overthrows its foes and strengthens its friends."[3] **Grace** here means the undeserved strength from God to carry on the work of the Lord in the face of severe opposition.

1:8 The memory of their faithful co-operation makes the apostle **long** to be with them again. He calls **God** to **witness how greatly** he yearns **for** them **with the affection of Jesus Christ**. Paul's expression of love is all the more remarkable when we remember that he had been born a Jew and was writing to people of Gentile descent. The grace of God had broken down the ancient hatred, and now they were all one in Christ.

1:9 Thanksgiving now gives way to prayer. Will Paul ask wealth, comfort, or freedom from trouble for them? No, he asks that their **love** might constantly increase **in knowledge and all discernment**. The primary aim of the Christian life is to **love** God and to **love** one's fellow man. But love is not just a matter of the emotions. In effective service for the Lord, we must use our intelligence and exercise **discernment**. Otherwise, our efforts are apt to be futile. So Paul is here praying not only that the Philippians will continue in the display of Christian love, but also that their **love** will be exercised in full **knowledge and all discernment.**

1:10 Love that is thus enlightened will enable them to discern the things that are more **excellent**. In all realms of life, some things are good and others are better. The good is often the enemy of the best. For effective service, these distinctions must be made.

Love that is enlightened will also enable them to avoid what is questionable or downright wrong. Paul would have them **sincere**,[4] that is, utterly transparent, and blameless in view of **the day of Christ**. To be **without offense** does not mean to be sinless. We all commit sins, but the blameless person is the one who confesses and forsakes the sin, asking forgiveness from those who were wronged and making restitution whenever possible.

The day of Christ, as in verse 6, refers to the Rapture and the subsequent judgment of the believer's works.

1:11 The final petition of the apostle's prayer is that the Christians might be **filled with the fruits of righteousness**, that is, with **the fruits** which **righteousness** produces, or with all the Christian virtues that make up a righteous life. The source of these virtues is **Jesus Christ**, and their object is **the glory and praise of God**. This petition of Paul is exactly parallel to the words in Isaiah 61:3, "that they may be called trees of righteousness (**being filled with the fruits of righteousness**), the planting of the Lord (**which are by Jesus Christ**), that He may be glorified (**to the glory and praise of God.**)"

"The word 'fruit,' " Lehman Strauss writes, ". . . is associated closely with our relation to Christ and His expectation of us. The branches on a vine are intended to bear fruit."[5]

II. PAUL'S IMPRISONMENT, PROSPECTS, AND PLEA FOR PERSEVERANCE (1:12–30)

1:12 The prayer is ended. Paul next rehearses his blessings, that is, the benefits that have resulted from his imprisonment. Jowett calls this section "The Fortune of Misfortune."

The apostle would have the **brethren know that the things which happened** to him, that is, his trial and imprisonment, have resulted in **the furtherance of the gospel** rather than its hindrance, as might have been expected. This is another wonderful illustration of how God overrules the wicked plans of demons and men and brings triumph out of seeming tragedy and beauty from ashes. "Man has his wickedness, but God has His way."

1:13 First of all, Paul's **chains** have become **evident** as being **in Christ**. By this he means that it has become widely known that he was imprisoned as a result of his testimony for Christ and not as a criminal or evildoer.

The real reason for his **chains** became well-known throughout the **palace guard** and in all other places. **Palace guard** may mean either: (1) The whole praetorian **guard**, that is, the Roman soldiers who guarded the **palace** where the emperor dwelt, or (2) The whole praetorium itself. The praetorium was the **palace** and here would include all of its occupants. In any event, Paul is saying that his imprisonment has served as a testimony to the representatives of the Roman imperial power where he was.

T. W. Drury writes:

The very chain which Roman discipline riveted on the prisoner's arm secured to his side a hearer who would tell the story of patient suffering for Christ, among those who, the next day, might be in attendance on Nero himself.[6]

1:14 A second favorable outcome of his imprisonment was that other Christians were thereby encouraged to be more fearless in testifying for the Lord Jesus. Persecution often has the effect of transforming quiet and bashful believers into courageous witnesses.

1:15 The motive in some hearts was jealousy and rivalry. They preached **Christ** out of **envy** and contentiousness.

Others had sincere and pure motives; they preached Christ **from good will**, in an honest effort to help the apostle.

1:16 The jealous preachers thought that by doing this they might make Paul's imprisonment more bitter. Their message was good, but their temper was bad. It is sad to think that Christian service can be carried on in the energy of the flesh, motivated by greed, strife, pride, and envy. This teaches the necessity for watching our motives when we serve the Lord. We must not do it for self-display, for the advancement of a religious sect, or for the defeat of other Christians.

Here is a good example of the necessity for our love to be exercised in knowledge and discernment.

1:17 Others were preaching the gospel **out of** pure and sincere **love, knowing that** Paul was determined to defend **the gospel**. There was nothing selfish, sectarian, or cruel in their service. They knew very well that Paul had been committed to prison because of his bold stand for **the gospel**. So they determined to carry on the work while he was thus confined.

1:18 Paul refuses to be downcast by the wrong motives of some. **Christ is** being **preached** by both groups, and that is for him a great cause for rejoicing.

It is remarkable that under such difficult circumstances, Paul does not feel sorry for himself or seek the sympathy of others. Rather he is filled with the joy of the Lord and encourages his readers to rejoice also.

1:19 The outlook is encouraging. The apostle knows that the whole course of events will lead to his **deliverance. Deliverance** (KJV, "salvation") here does not mean the salvation of Paul's soul, but rather his liberation from prison. The means which God will use in effecting his release will be the **prayer** of the Philippians and the ministry or help of the **Spirit of Jesus Christ**. Marvel here at the importance which Paul puts on the prayers of a feeble band of believers. He sees them as sufficiently powerful to thwart the purposes and the mighty power of Rome. It is true; Christians can influence the destiny of nations and change the course of history through prayer.

The supply of the Spirit of Jesus Christ means the power of the Holy Spirit stretched forth in his behalf — the strength which the Spirit would supply to him. In general, it refers to "the boundless resources which the Spirit supplies to enable believers to stand fast, regardless of what the circumstances may be."

1:20 As he thought of the prayers of the Christians and the assistance of the Holy Spirit, he expressed his eager desire and **hope** that he might never **be ashamed**, but rather that he might always have a fearless and outspoken witness for Christ.

And no matter what the outcome of judicial processes might be — whether he was to be freed or put to **death** — his ambition was that **Christ** should **be magnified in** his **body**. To magnify does not mean to make Christ greater. He is already great, and nothing we can do will make Him greater. But to magnify means to cause Christ to be esteemed or praised by others. Guy King shows how Christ can **be magnified** by our bodies in **life:**

. . . magnified by lips that bear happy testimony to Him; magnified by hands employed in His happy service; magnified by feet only too happy to go on His errands; magnified by knees happily bent in prayer for His kingdom; magnified by shoulders happy to bear one another's burdens.[7]

Christ can also **be magnified** in our bodies **by death** — bodies worn out in His service; bodies pierced by savage spears; bodies torn by stones or burned at the stake.

1:21 Here, in a nutshell, is Paul's philosophy of life. He did not live for money, fame, or pleasure. The object of his life was to love, worship, and serve the Lord Jesus. He wanted his life to be like the life of **Christ**. He wanted the Savior to live out His life through him.

And to die is gain. To die is to be with Christ and to be like Him forever. It is to serve Him with unsinning heart and with feet that will never stray. We do not ordinarily think of death as one of our gains. Sad to say, the outlook today seems to be that "to live is earthly gain, and to die would be the end of gain." But, says Jowett: "To the Apostle Paul, death was not a darksome passageway, where all our treasures rot away in a swift corruption; it was a place of gracious transition, 'a covered way that leadeth into light.' "[8]

1:22 **If** it is God's will for Paul to **live on** a while longer **in the flesh**, then that will mean fruitful **labor** for him. He will be able to give further help to the Lord's people. But it was a difficult decision for him — whether to go to the Savior whom he loved, or to remain on earth in the Lord's service, to which he was also very attached. He did not know which to **choose.**

1:23 To be **hard pressed between the two** means to be required to make a difficult decision between **two** possibilities — that of going home to heaven or that of remaining on earth as an apostle of Christ Jesus.

He ardently longed **to depart and be with Christ, which is far better**. If he only considered his own interests, this is doubtless the choice he would make.

Notice that Paul did not believe in any theory of soul-sleep. He believed that the Christian goes to **be with Christ** at the time of death and that he is in the conscious enjoyment of the presence of the Lord. How ridiculous it would be for him to say, as some do today: "To live is Christ; to sleep is gain." Or, "To depart and to sleep is far better." "Sleep" is used in the NT of the believer's *body* at the time of death (1 Thess. 4:14),

never of his soul. Soul-sleep is a myth.

Notice, too, that death is not to be confused with the coming of the Savior. At the time of death, we go to **be with Him**. At the time of the Rapture, He comes to us.

1:24 **For** the sake of the Philippians, it was **more needful** for Paul to live on earth a while longer. One cannot help but be impressed with the unselfishness of this great-hearted man. He does not think of his own comfort or ease, but rather of what will best advance the cause of Christ and the welfare of His people.

1:25 **Being confident of this** — that he was still needed on earth to instruct, comfort, and encourage the saints — Paul knew that he would not be put to death at this time. How did he know? We believe that he lived so close to the Lord that the Holy Spirit was able to communicate this knowledge to him. "The secret of the Lord is with those who fear Him." (Ps. 25:14). Those who dwell deep in God, in quiet meditation, hear secrets that are drowned out by the noise, rush, and bustle of life today. You have to be near to hear. Paul was near.

By remaining in the flesh, Paul would be able to promote their spiritual **progress and** increase the **joy** that was theirs through trusting in the Lord.

1:26 Through his being spared for longer life and service on earth, the Philippians would have added cause for **rejoicing** in the Lord when he would visit them once again. Can you not imagine how they would throw their arms around him and kiss him, and praise the Lord with great joy when he would arrive at Philippi? Perhaps they would say, "Well, Paul, we prayed for you, but honestly, we never expected to see you here again. But how we praise the Lord that He has given you back to us once more!"

1:27 Now Paul adds a word of caution: **"Only let your conduct be worthy of the gospel of Christ."** Christians should be Christlike. Citizens of heaven should behave accordingly. We should be in practice what we are in position.

In addition to this plea for consistency, the apostle makes an appeal for constancy. Specifically, he desires **that** **whether** he comes to them personally, or, being **absent**, hears reports about them, he may know that they are standing **fast** with a common **spirit**, and unitedly laboring earnestly **for the faith of the gospel**, that is, the Christian faith. Christians face a common foe; they should not fight each other but should unite against the enemy.

1:28 Neither were they to be **terrified by** the enemies of the gospel. Fearlessness in the face of persecution has a twofold meaning. First, it is an omen of destruction to those who fight against God. Secondly, it is a sign **of salvation** to those who brave the wrath of the foe. **Salvation** is probably used here in its future tense, referring to the eventual deliverance of the saint from trial and the redemption of his body as well as his spirit and soul.

1:29 The Philippians should remember that it is a privilege **to suffer** for **Christ** as well as **to believe in Him.**

Dr. Griffith John wrote that once when he was surrounded by a hostile heathen crowd and was beaten, he put his hand to his face and when he withdrew it, saw that it was bathed in blood. "He was possessed by an extraordinary sense of exaltation, and he rejoiced that he had been counted worthy to suffer for His Name." Is it not remarkable that even suffering is exalted by Christianity to such a lofty plane? Truly, even "an apparent trifle burns with the fire immortal when it is in communion with the Infinite." The cross dignifies and ennobles.

1:30 The connection of this verse with the previous one is better understood if we supply the words "Since you are engaged in":

The privilege of suffering for Christ has been granted to you, since you are engaged in **the same** kind of **conflict which you saw in me** when I was in Philippi **and now hear** that I am still waging.

III. EXHORTATION TO UNITY BASED ON CHRIST'S EXAMPLE OF HUMILITY AND SACRIFICE (2:1–16)

Although the church at Philippi was exemplary in many respects, and Paul had occasion to commend the saints warmly, yet there was an undercurrent of strife. There was a difference of opinion between two women, Euodia and Syntyche (4:2). It is helpful to keep this in mind because in chapter 2 the apostle is dealing directly with the cause and cure of contentions among the people of God.

2:1 The **if** in this verse is not the "if" of doubt but of argument. The verse lists four great considerations which should draw believers together in harmony and cooperation. The apostle is saying, in effect: "*Since* there is so much encouragement **in Christ**, *since* His **love** has such a tremendous persuasiveness, *since* **the** Holy **Spirit** brings us all together in such a wonderful **fellowship**, and *since* there is so much tender **affection and mercy** in Christianity, we should all be able to get along in happy harmony with one another."

F. B. Meyer describes these four motives as:

1. The persuasiveness of Christ.
2. The tender care that love gives.
3. The sharing of the Spirit.
4. Humaneness and pity.[9]

It is clear that the apostle is making an appeal for unity based on common devotion to Christ and common possession of the Holy Spirit. With all that there is **in Christ**, the members of His Body should have unity of purpose, affection, accord, sympathy.

2:2 If these foregoing arguments carry any weight with the Philippians, then Paul begs them, on the basis of such arguments, that they should **fulfill** his **joy**. Up to this time, the Philippians had indeed given Paul much joy. He does not deny that for a moment, but now he asks that they should fill the cup of his joy to overflowing. They could do this **by being like-minded, having the same love**, and **being of one accord** and **of one mind.**

Does this mean that all Christians are expected to think and act alike? The word of God nowhere gives such a suggestion. While we are definitely expected to agree on the great fundamentals of the Christian faith, it is obvious that on many minor matters there will be a great deal of difference of opinion. *Uniformity* and *unity* are not the same thing. It is possible to have the latter without the former. Although we might not agree on minor matters, yet we can submerge our own opinions, where no real principle is involved, for the good of others.

To be **like-minded** really means to have the mind of Christ, to see things as He would see them, and to respond as He would respond. To have **the same love** means to show **the same love** to others that the Lord has shown to us, a love that did not count the cost. To be **of one accord** means to work together in harmony toward a common goal. Finally, to be **of one mind** means to act so unitedly as to show that Christ's mind is directing our activities.

2:3 **Nothing** whatever should **be done through selfish ambition or conceit**, since these are two of the greatest enemies of unity among the people of God. **Selfish ambition** is the desire to be number one, no matter what the cost. **Conceit** speaks of pride or self-display. Wherever you find people who are interested in gathering a clique around themselves or in promoting their own interests, there you will find the seeds of contention and strife. The remedy is found in the latter part of the verse. **In lowliness of mind let each esteem others better than himself.** This does not mean that we must consider criminals as having better moral characters than our own, but rather that we should live for others unselfishly, putting their interests above our own. It is easy to read an exhortation like this in the word of God, but quite another thing to appreciate what it really means, and then put it into actual practice. To **esteem others better than** ourselves is utterly foreign to the human mind, and we cannot do it in our own strength. It is only as we are indwelt and empowered by the Holy Spirit that it can ever be practiced.

2:4 The cure of troubles among the people of God is to be more concerned with the **interests of others** than with the things of our **own** lives. In a very real way the word **others** forms the key of this chapter. It is as we give our lives in devoted service for others that we rise above the selfish strife of men.

> Others, Lord, yes, others,
> Let this my motto be;
> Help me to live for others,
> That I might live like Thee.
> – *Charles D. Meigs*

2:5 **Let this mind be in you which was also in Christ Jesus.** Paul is now going to hold up before the eyes of the Philippians the example of the Lord Jesus Christ. What kind of attitude did He exhibit? What characterized His behavior toward others? Guy King has well described the mind of the Lord Jesus as: (1) The selfless mind; (2) The sacrificial mind; (3) The serving mind. The Lord Jesus consistently thought of others.[10]

> He had no tears for His own griefs,
> But sweat-drops of blood for mine.
> – *Charles H. Gabriel*

2:6 When we read that Christ Jesus was **in the form of God**, we learn that He existed from all eternity as **God**. It does not mean that He merely resembled God, but that He actually *is* God in the truest sense of the word.

Yet He **did not consider it robbery to be equal with God**. Here it is of utmost importance to distinguish between personal and positional equality with God. As to His Person, Christ always *was*, *is*, and *will be* equal with God. It would be impossible for Him to give that up. But positional equality is different. From all eternity Christ was positionally equal with His Father, enjoying the glories of heaven. But He **did not consider** this position something that He had to hold on to at all costs. When a world of lost mankind needed to be redeemed, He was willing to relinquish His positional equality **with God** — the comforts and joys of heaven. He **did not consider** them something that He had to grasp forever and under all circumstances.

Thus He was willing to come into this world to endure the contradiction of sinners against Himself. God the Father was never spit on or beaten or crucified. In this sense, the Father was greater than the Son — not greater as to His Person, but rather as to His position and the manner in which He lived. Jesus expressed this thought in John 14:28: "If you loved Me, you would rejoice because I said, 'I am going to the Father,' for My Father is greater than I." In other words, the disciples should have rejoiced to learn that He was going home to heaven. While on earth, He had been cruelly treated and rejected. He had been in lower circumstances than His Father. In that sense, His Father was greater. But when He went back to heaven, He would be equal with the Father in *His circumstances* as well as in *His Person*.

Gifford explains:

Thus it is not the nature or essence . . .but the *mode of existence* that is described in this second clause ["did not consider it robbery to be equal with God"]; and one mode of existence may be changed for another, though the essential nature is immutable. Let us take St. Paul's own illustration, 2 Cor. viii.9, "Though He was rich, yet for your sakes He became poor, that you through His poverty might become rich." Here in each case there is a change of the *mode of existence*, but not of the nature. When a poor man becomes rich, his *mode of existence* is changed, but not his nature as man. It is so with the Son of God; from the rich and glorious *mode of existence* which was the fit and adequate manifestation of His divine nature, He for our sakes descended, in respect of His human life, to the infinitely lower and poorer *mode of existence* which He assumed together with the nature of man.[11]

2:7   But made Himself of no reputation. The literal translation is: "But He emptied Himself." The question immediately arises, "Of what did the Lord Jesus empty Himself?"

In answering this question, one must use the greatest care. Human attempts to define this emptying have often ended by stripping Christ of His attributes of Deity. Some say, for instance, that when the Lord Jesus was on earth, He no longer had all-knowledge or all-power. He was no longer in all places at one and the same time. They say He voluntarily laid aside these attributes of Deity when He came into the world as a Man. Some even say He was subject to the limitations of all men, that He became liable to error, and accepted the common opinions and myths of His day!

This we utterly deny. The Lord Jesus did not lay aside any of the attributes of God when He came into the world.

He was still omniscient (all-knowing).

He was still omnipresent (present in all places at one and the same time).

He was still omnipotent (all-powerful).

What He did was to empty Himself of His

positional equality with God and to veil the glory of Deity in a body of human flesh. The glory was all there, though hidden, but it did shine forth on occasions, such as on the Mount of Transfiguration. There was no moment in His life on earth when He did not possess all the attributes of God.

Aside He threw His most divine array,
And hid His Godhead in a veil of clay,
And in that garb did wondrous love
    display,
Restoring what He never took away.

As mentioned before, one must use great care in explaining the words "He emptied Himself." The safest method is to let the succeeding expressions provide the explanation. He emptied Himself by **taking the form of a bondservant, and coming in the likeness of men**. In other words, He emptied Himself by taking upon Himself something He never had before — *humanity*. He did not lay aside His deity, only His place in heaven, and that only temporarily.

If He had been a mere man, this would not have been an act of emptying. We do not empty ourselves by being born into the world. But for God to become Man — that is the emptying of Himself. In fact, only God could do it.

Taking the form of a bondservant. The Incarnation and life of the Savior may be summarized by those lovely words of John 13:4: "Jesus . . . laid aside His garments, took a towel and girded Himself." The towel or apron is the badge of service. It was used by slaves. And it was used by the blessed Lord Jesus because He came "not to be served, but to serve, and to give His life a ransom for many" (Matt. 20:28). But let us pause to remind ourselves of the train of thought in this passage. There were contentions among the saints at Philippi. Paul exhorts them to have the mind of Christ. The argument, in brief, is that if Christians are willing to take the lowly place, to serve others, and to give their lives in sacrifice, there will be no quarrels. *People who are willing to die for others do not generally quarrel with them.*

Christ always existed, but came into the world **in the likeness of men**, meaning "as a real Man." The humanity of the Lord is as real as His deity. He is true God and true Man. But what a mystery this is! No created mind will ever be able to understand it.

2:8 Each section of this passage describes the increasing depth of the humiliation of God's beloved Son. He was not only willing to leave the glory of heaven! He emptied Himself! He took the form of a bondservant! He became Man! But now we read that **He humbled Himself**! There was no depth to which He would not stoop to save our guilty souls. Blessed be His glorious name forever!

He humbled Himself by becoming **obedient to the point of death**. This is marvelous in our eyes! He obeyed even though it cost Him His life. **Obedient to the point of death** means He obeyed to the end. Truly He was the Merchant who went and sold all that He had to buy the pearl of great price (Matt. 13:46).

Even the death of the cross. Death by crucifixion was the most shameful form of execution. It might be compared to the gallows, the electric chair, or the gas chamber — reserved only for murderers. And that was the form of **death** reserved for heaven's Best when He came into this world. He was not allowed to die a natural death in bed. His was not to be an accidental death. He must die **the** shameful **death of the cross.**

2:9 Now there is an abrupt change. The previous verses describe what the Lord Jesus did. He took the path of self-renunciation. He did not seek a name for Himself. He humbled Himself.

But now we turn to a consideration of what *God* has done. If the Savior humbled Himself, **God also has highly exalted Him**. If He did not seek a name for Himself, **God has given Him the name which is above every name**. If He bent His knees in service to others, God has decreed that **every knee** shall **bow** to Him.

And what is the lesson in this for the Philippians — and for us? The lesson is that the way up is down. We should not exalt ourselves but be the servants of others, that God may exalt us in due time.

God exalted Christ by raising Him from the dead and opening the heavens to receive Him back to His own right hand. Not only that — **God has given Him the name which is above every name.**

Scholars are divided as to what this **name** is. Some say it is the name *Jesus,* which contains the name of *Jehovah.* In Isaiah 45:22, 23, it is decreed that every knee will bow to the name of Jehovah (God).

Others feel that **the name which is above every name** is simply a figurative way of saying the highest place in the universe, a position of supremacy and dominion. Both explanations are acceptable.

2:10 God was so completely satisfied with the redemptive work of Christ that He determined that **every knee should bow** to Him — of beings **in heaven, on earth**, and **under the earth**. This does not mean that all these beings will be saved. Those who do not *willingly* bow the knee to Him now will one day be *compelled* to do so. Those who will not be reconciled in the day of His grace will be subjugated in the day of His judgment.

2:11 In matchless grace, the Lord journeyed from glory to Bethlehem, to Gethsemane, and to Calvary. God, in return, will honor Him with universal homage and the universal acknowledgment of His lordship. Those who have denied His claims will one day admit that they have played the fool, that they have greatly erred, and that Jesus of Nazareth is indeed the Lord of glory.

Before leaving this magnificent passage on the Person and work of the Lord Jesus, we should repeat that it was introduced in connection with a minor problem in the church at Philippi. Paul did not set out to write a treatise on the Lord. Rather, he was merely seeking to correct selfishness and party spirit in the saints. The cure of their condition is the mind of Christ. Paul brings the Lord into every situation. "Even in dealing with matters most delicate, distressing and distasteful," Erdman writes, "he is able to state truth in such striking beauty as to make it appear like a precious jewel embedded in a clod of earth."[12]

2:12 Having set forth the example of Christ in such brilliant luster, the apostle is now ready to press home the exhortation based on it.

The Philippians had **always obeyed** Paul when he was present with them. **Now much more in** his **absence**, they should **work out** their **own salvation with fear and trembling.**

Again we come to a passage of Scripture concerning which there has been much confusion. At the outset, we should be very clear that Paul is not teaching that salvation can be earned by works. Throughout his writings, he repeatedly emphasizes that salvation is not by works but by faith in the Lord Jesus Christ. What then does the verse mean?

1. It may mean that we are to **work out** the salvation which God has placed within us. God has given us eternal life as a free gift. We are to live it out by lives of practical holiness.

2. **Salvation** here may mean the solution of their problem at Philippi. They had been plagued with squabbles and strife. The apostle has given them the remedy. Now they are to apply the remedy by having the mind of Christ. Thus they would **work out** their **own salvation**, or the solution of their difficulty.

The salvation spoken of here is not that of the soul, but deliverance from the snares which would hinder the Christian from doing the will of God. In a similar vein, Vine describes it as the present entire experience of deliverance from evil.

Salvation has many different meanings in the NT. We have already noticed that in 1:19 it means deliverance from prison. In 1:28 it refers to the eventual salvation of our bodies from the very presence of sin. The meaning in any particular case must be determined in part, at least, by the context. We believe that in this passage **salvation** means the solution of the problem that was vexing the Philippians, that is, their contentions.

2:13 Now Paul reminds them that it is possible for them to work out their salvation because **it is God who works in** them **both to will and to do for His good pleasure**. This means that **it is God** who puts within us the wish or desire to do His will in the first place. Then He also **works in** us the power to carry out the desire.

Here again we have the wonderful merging of the divine and human. In one sense, we are called on to work out

our salvation. In another sense, it is only God who can enable us to do it. We must do our part, and God will do His. (However, this does not apply to the forgiveness of sins, or to the new birth. Redemption is wholly the work of God. We simply believe and enter in.)

2:14 As we do His good pleasure, we should do it without grumbling or questioning: "Not somehow but triumphantly." **Complaining and disputing** usually lead to graver offenses.

2:15 By refraining from complaints and disputes, we **may** be **blameless and harmless** (sincere and guileless). To be **blameless** means that no charge can be sustained against a person (see Dan. 6:4). A **blameless** person may sin, but he apologizes, confesses, and makes it right whenever possible. To be **harmless** here means to be sincere or without deceit.

Children of God should be **without fault in the midst of a crooked and perverse generation**. By lives without blemish, God's children will stand out all the more clearly against the dark background of this world.

This leads Paul to think of them **as lights** in a dark night. The darker the night, the brighter the light appears. Christians are **lights** or light-bearers. They cannot create any light, but they can reflect the glory of the Lord so that others may see Jesus in them.

2:16 **Holding fast** (KJV "forth") **the word of life**. As lights we shine, but that does not excuse us from witnessing with our voices. There should be the twofold testimony of life and lips.

If the Philippians fulfill these functions, the apostle knows he will have some ground for glorying **in the day of Christ**. He feels a responsibility not only to see souls saved but also to present every man perfect in Christ (Col. 1:28).

The day of Christ refers to the time of His return and of the judgment of the believer's service (1:6, 10). If the Philippians are faithful in their labor for the Lord, it will be evident in that day that Paul's service had **not** been **in vain.**

IV. THE CHRISTLIKE EXAMPLE OF PAUL, TIMOTHY, AND EPAPHRODITUS (2:17–30)

In the preceding section, Paul has set

forth the Lord Jesus as the prime example of the lowly mind. But some might be tempted to say, "Oh, but He is God and we are only mortals." So Paul now gives three examples of men who exhibited the mind of Christ — himself, Timothy, and Epaphroditus. If Christ is the sun, then these three are moons, reflecting the glory of the sun. They are lights in a dark world.

2:17 The apostle uses a very beautiful illustration to describe the service of the Philippians and of himself. He borrows the picture from the common practice among both Jews and pagans of pouring out **a drink offering** or libation over a **sacrifice** as it was being offered.

He speaks of the Philippians as the offerers. Their **faith** is the **sacrifice**. Paul himself is the **drink offering**. He would be happy to be **poured out** in martyrdom **on the sacrifice and service of** their **faith**.

Williams comments:

> The apostle compares the self-sacrifice and energy of the Philippians with his own, magnifying theirs and minimizing his. They were both laying down their lives for the sake of the gospel, but their action he regards as the great sacrifice, and his as only the drink offering poured out upon it. Under this beauteous figure of speech, he speaks of his possible approaching death as a martyr.[13]

If this should be his lot, he would be **glad and rejoice** that it should be so.

2:18 **For the same reason**, the Philippians should **be glad and rejoice with** Paul. They should not look on his possible martyrdom as a tragedy but congratulate him on such a glorious homegoing.

2:19 Up to this point, Paul has cited two examples of self-sacrificing love — the Lord Jesus and himself. Both were willing to pour out their lives to death. Two more examples of selflessness remain — **Timothy** and **Epaphroditus**.

The apostle hopes **to send Timothy** to Philippi in the near future so that he **may be encouraged** by news concerning them.

2:20 Among Paul's companions, Timothy was unique in his unselfish care for the spiritual condition of the Philippians. There was **no one** else whom Paul could send to them with the same confidence. This is a high commendation indeed for one as young as Timothy!

2:21 The others had become engulfed in the ocean of **their own** private interests. They had become so engrossed with the cares of this life that they had no time for **the things which are of Christ Jesus**. Does this have a message for us today in our little world of homes, refrigerators, television sets, and other *things*? (see Luke 8:14.)

2:22 Timothy was the apostle's child in the faith, and he played the part with true faithfulness. They knew **his proven character**, his real worth, **that as a son** serves with **his father**, so Timothy **served with** Paul **in** the work of preaching **the gospel**.

2:23, 24 Because Timothy had thus proved himself, Paul hoped **to send him** to the Philippians as soon as he learned the outcome of his appeal to Caesar. This is doubtless the apostle's meaning in the expression **as soon as I see how it goes with me**. He hopes that his appeal will be successful, and that he will be set free so that he might visit the Philippians once more.

2:25 Next we see the mind of Christ in **Epaphroditus**. Whether this is the same man as the Epaphras of Colossians 4:12, we cannot be sure. At any rate, he lived in Philippi and was a messenger for the assembly there.

Paul speaks of him as: (1) **my brother**; (2) my **fellow worker**; (3) my **fellow soldier**. The first title speaks of affection, the second of hard work, and the third of conflict. He was a man who could work with others, and this is certainly a great essential in Christian life and service. It is one thing for a believer to work independently, having everything his own way. It is far more difficult to work with others, to play "second fiddle," to allow for individual differences, to submerge one's own desires and opinions for the good of the group. Let us be **fellow workers** and **fellow soldiers**!

In addition, Paul speaks of him as **your messenger and the one who ministered to my need**. This gives us another valuable clue into his personality. He was willing to do common or menial work. Many today are only interested in work that is public and pleasant. How thankful we should be for those who carry on the routine work quietly and inconspicuously! By doing the hard work, Epaphroditus humbled himself. But God exalted him by recording his faithful service in Philippians 2 for all future generations to read.

2:26 The saints had sent Epaphroditus to help Paul—a journey of at least 700 miles. The faithful messenger took **sick** as a result; indeed, he came very close to death. This caused him grave concern — not the fact that he was so sick, but the fear that the saints might hear about it. If they did, they would reproach themselves for sending him on this journey and for thus endangering his life. Surely in Epaphroditus we see "a heart at leisure from itself."

Many Christians have the unfortunate habit of dwelling at great length on their illnesses or operations. Too often this is but a manifestation of the hyphenated sins of the self-life: self-pity, self-occupation, self-display.

2:27 Epaphroditus had been **sick** near to **death, but God had mercy on him**. This section is valuable to us for the light it throws on the subject of divine healing:

1. First of all, sickness is not always the result of sin. Here is a man who was sick because of the faithful discharge of his duties (see v. 30), **". . .for the work of Christ he came close to death."**

2. Secondly, we learn that it is not always God's will to heal instantly and miraculously. It appears that Epaphroditus' illness was prolonged and his recovery gradual (see also 2 Tim. 4:20; 3 Jn. 2).

3. Thirdly, we learn that healing is a mercy from God and not something we can demand from Him as being our right.

Paul adds that **God had mercy** not only on Epaphroditus **but on** himself **also, lest** he **should have sorrow upon sorrow**. The apostle already had considerable grief in connection with his imprisonment. If Epaphroditus had died, he would have had additional sorrow.

2:28 Now that Epaphroditus had recovered so well, Paul has **sent him** back home **the more eagerly**. The Philippians would **rejoice** to have their beloved brother back again, and this would lessen Paul's sorrow also.

2:29 Not only should they **receive** Epaphroditus joyfully, but they should also **esteem** this dear man of God. It is a great dignity and privilege to be engaged **in** the service of **the Lord**. The saints should recognize this, even when it concerns one with whom they are very familiar.

2:30 As mentioned previously, Epaphroditus' illness was directly connected with his tireless service for **Christ**. This is of great value in the eyes of the Lord. It is better to *burn out* for Christ than to *rust out*. It is better to die in the service of Jesus than to be counted a mere statistic among those who die from illness or accident.

Does **"to supply what was lacking in your service toward me"** suggest that the Philippians had neglected Paul and that Epaphroditus had done what they should have done? This seems unlikely, since it was the saints at Philippi who had sent Epaphroditus to Paul in the first place.

We suggest that their lack of **service** refers to their *inability* to visit Paul in person and help him directly because of their distance from Rome. Instead of rebuking them, the apostle is merely stating that Epaphroditus did, as their representative, what they were unable to do in person.

V. WARNING AGAINST FALSE TEACHERS (3:1–3)

3:1 Finally, my brethren does not mean that Paul is about to close his Epistle. The literal meaning is "As for the rest . . . ." The same word is used again in 4:8.

He exhorts them to **rejoice in the Lord**. The Christian can always find real joy in **the Lord**, no matter what his circumstances may be. "The source of all his singing is high in heaven above." Nothing can really affect his joy unless it first robs him of his Savior, and this clearly is impossible. Natural happiness is affected by pain, sorrow, sickness, poverty, and tragedy. But Christian joy rides high over all the billows of life. Proof of this is found in the fact that Paul gives this exhortation from prison. Surely we can take the advice from such a man as he!

He does not find it irksome to repeat himself to the Philippians because he knows it is for their safety. But how does he repeat himself? Does this refer to the preceding expression where he urges them to **rejoice in the Lord**? Or does it mean the verses to follow where he warns them against the Judaizers? We believe that the latter is in view. Three times in verse 2 he uses the word **beware**. To use this repetition is **not tedious** for him, but for them it is a true safeguard.

3:2 They are to **beware of dogs, . . . of evil workers**, and **of the mutilation**. All three expressions probably refer to the same group of men — false teachers who sought to put Christians under the laws of Judaism and taught that righteousness could be obtained by lawkeeping and ritual.

First of all, they were **dogs**. In the Bible, **dogs** are unclean animals. The term was used by Jews to describe Gentiles! In eastern countries, dogs were homeless creatures, running wild in the streets and scrounging food as best they could. Here Paul turns the tables and applies the term to those Jewish false teachers who were seeking to corrupt the church. They were really the ones who were living on the outside, trying to exist on rituals and ceremonies. They were "picking up the crumbs when they might sit down to a feast."

Secondly, they were **evil workers**. Professing to be true believers, they gained admission into Christian fellowships in order to spread their false teachings. The results of their work could only be evil.

Then Paul also calls them **the mutilation**. This is a sarcastic term to describe their attitude toward circumcision. Doubtless they insisted that a person must be circumcised in order to be saved. But all they meant by this was the physical, literal act of circumcision. They were not at all concerned with its spiritual meaning. Circumcision speaks of death to the flesh. It means that the claims of the fleshly nature should not be allowed. While they insisted on the literal act of circumcision, they gave full rein to the flesh. There was no heart acknowledgment that the flesh had been put to death at the cross. Paul was saying that they were mere mutilators of the flesh, who did not distinguish between the ceremony and its underlying meaning.

3:3 In contrast with these, Paul states that **we** (true believers) **are the circumcision** — not those who happen to be born of Jewish parents or who have been literally circumcised, but those who realize that the flesh profits nothing, that man can do nothing in his own strength to win God's smile of approval. Then Paul gives three characteristics of those who are the true circumcision:

1. They **worship God in** (or by) **the Spirit**. That is, theirs is a true spiritual worship, not one of mere ceremonies. In true worship, a person enters into the presence of God by faith, and pours out his love, praise, adoration and homage. Soulish worship, on the other hand, is occupied with beautiful buildings and ecclesiastical furniture, with elaborate ceremonies, with brocaded priestly garments, and with whatever appeals to the emotions.

2. Members of the true circumcision **rejoice** (or glory) **in Christ Jesus**. He alone is the ground of their boasting. They do not pride themselves in personal attainments, in cultural background, or in faithfulness to sacraments.

3. They **have no confidence in the flesh**. They do not think they can be saved through fleshly efforts in the first place or be kept by their own strength thereafter. They do not expect any good from their Adamic nature and are therefore not disappointed when they find none!

VI. PAUL'S HERITAGE AND PERSONAL ACHIEVEMENTS RENOUNCED FOR CHRIST (3:4–14)

3:4 As Paul thought of how these men boasted in their fleshly advantages and attainments, a smile doubtless formed on his lips. If they could brag, how much **more so** could he! In the next two verses, he shows how that to a preeminent degree he possessed those natural assets in which man normally glories. "He seemed to have belonged to almost every kind of aristocracy which excites the dreams and kindles the aspirations of men."

Concerning these two verses, Arnot has said: "The whole stock-in-trade of the self-righteous Pharisee is inventoried here. He delights to display the filthy rags and make a show of them openly."

You will notice that Paul speaks of: pride of ancestry (v. 5a); pride of orthodoxy (v. 5b); pride of activity (v. 6a); pride of morality (v. 6b).

3:5 Here, then, is the list of Paul's natural and fleshly advantages:

circumcised the eighth day — he was a Jew by birth, not an Ishmaelite or a convert to Judaism.

of the stock of Israel — a member of God's chosen earthly people.

of the tribe of Benjamin — a tribe that was considered an aristocratic leader (Judg. 5:14), and the one that gave Israel its first king.

a Hebrew of the Hebrews — he belonged to that segment of the nation that had held onto its original language, customs, and usages.

concerning the law, a Pharisee — the Pharisees had remained orthodox, whereas the Sadducees had abandoned the doctrine of the resurrection.

3:6 concerning zeal, persecuting the church — Paul sincerely thought that he had been doing God's service when he had attempted to wipe out the "sect" of Christians. He saw in it a threat to his own religion and therefore felt he must exterminate it.

concerning the righteousness which is in the law, blameless — this cannot mean that Paul had perfectly kept the law. He confesses in Romans 7:9, 10 that such was not the case. He speaks of himself as being **blameless**, not sinless. We can only conclude that when Paul had violated any part of the law, he was careful to bring the sacrifice required. In other words, he had been a stickler in seeking to observe the rules of Judaism to the letter.

Thus, as to birth, pedigree, orthodoxy, zeal, and personal righteousness, Saul of Tarsus was an outstanding man.

3:7 But now the apostle makes the great renunciation. Here he gives us his own "Profit and Loss Statement." On one side he lists the above-mentioned items, the things that had been **gain to** him. On the other side he writes the single word **Christ**. They all amount to nothing when compared with the treasure which he had found in Christ. He **counted** them **loss for Christ**. Guy King says, "All financial gain, all material gain, all physical gain, all intellectual gain, all moral gain, all religious gain — all these are no gains at all compared with the Great Gain."[14]

As long as he trusted in these things, he could never have been saved. Once he was saved, they no longer meant anything to him because he had seen the glory of the Lord, and all other glories seemed like nothing in comparison.

3:8 In coming to Christ for salvation, Paul had renounced **all things** and counted them worthless when compared to **the excellence of the knowledge of Christ Jesus**, his **Lord. The excellence of the knowledge** is a Hebrew way of saying "the excellent knowledge" or "the surpassing worth of knowing."

Ancestry, nationality, culture, prestige, education, religion, personal attainments — all these the apostle abandoned as grounds for boasting. Indeed, he counted **them as** dung or **rubbish** in order that he might **gain Christ.**

Although the present tense is used in this verse and in the one following, Paul is looking back primarily to the time of his conversion. In order to **gain Christ**, he had had to turn his back on the things he had always been taught to prize most highly. If he were to have Christ as his gain, he had to say "good-bye" to his mother's religion, his father's heritage, and his own personal attainments.

And so he did! He completely severed his ties with Judaism as a hope of salvation. In doing so, he was disinherited by his relatives, disowned by his former friends, and persecuted by his fellow countrymen. He literally **suffered the loss of all things** when he became a Christian.

Because the present tense is used in verse 8, it sounds as if Paul was still seeking to **gain Christ**. Actually, he had won Christ when he first acknowledged Him as Lord and Savior. But the present tense indicates that this is still his attitude — he still counts all else **as rubbish** when compared to the value of knowing the Lord Jesus. The great desire of his heart is: "That Christ may be my gain." Not gold, or silver, or religious reputation, but Christ.

3:9 And be found in Him. Here again it sounds as if Paul was still trying to be found in Christ. The fact is that he is looking back to the tremendous decision which faced him before he was saved. Was he willing to abandon his own efforts to earn salvation, and simply trust in Christ? He had made his choice. He had abandoned all else in order to be found in Christ. The moment he believed on the Lord Jesus, he stood in a new position before God. No longer was he seen as a child of sinful Adam, but now he was seen *in Christ*, enjoying all the favor which the Lord Jesus enjoys before God the Father.

Likewise he had renounced the filthy rags of his own self-righteousness, which he had sought to win by keeping the law, and had chosen the **righteousness** of **God** which is bestowed on everyone who receives the Savior. **Righteousness** is here spoken of as a garment or covering. Man needs righteousness in order to stand before God in favor. But man cannot produce it. And so, in grace, God gives *His own* **righteousness** to those who receive His Son as Lord and Savior. "He (God) made Him (Christ) who knew no sin *to be* sin for us, that we might become the righteousness of God in Him" (2 Cor. 5:21).

Again we would like to emphasize that verses 8 and 9 do not suggest that Paul had not yet received the righteousness of God. On the contrary, this became his possession when he was regenerated on the road to Damascus. But the present tense simply indicates that the results of that important event continued up to the present and that Paul still considered Christ to be worth far more than anything he had given up.

3:10 As we read this verse, we come to the supreme emotion of the apostle's life. F. B. Meyer calls it "The Soul's Quest for the Personal Christ."

The most frequent treatment of this passage is to "spiritualize" it. By this is meant that **sufferings, death,** and **resurrection** are not to be taken literally. Rather, they are used to describe certain spiritual experiences, such as mental suffering, dying to self, and living the resurrected life, etc. However, we would like to suggest that the passage should be taken literally. Paul is saying he wants to live as Christ lived. Did Jesus suffer? Paul wants to suffer too. Did Jesus die? Then Paul wants to die by martyrdom in his service for Christ. Did Jesus rise from among the dead? Then Paul wishes to do the same. He realized that the servant is not above his Master. Thus, he desired to follow Christ in **His sufferings, death,** and **resurrection**. He does not say that all must adopt this view, but for him there could be no other pathway.

That I may know Him. To **know Him** means to gain practical day-by-day acquaintance with Him in such an intimate way that the apostle himself would become more Christlike. He wants the life of Christ to be reproduced in himself.

And the power of His resurrection. The **power** that raised the Lord from the dead is set forth in Scripture as the greatest display of might which the universe has ever seen (Eph. 1:19, 20). It would seem as if all the hosts of evil were determined to keep His body in the tomb. God's mighty power defeated this infernal army by raising the Lord Jesus from the dead on the third day. This same **power** is placed at the disposal of all believers (Eph. 1:19), to be appropriated by faith. Paul is stating his ambition to experience this power in his life and testimony.

And the fellowship of His sufferings. It takes divine strength to suffer for Christ. That is why **the power of His resurrection** is put before **the fellowship of His sufferings**.

In the life of the Lord, suffering preceded glory. So then it must be in the life of Paul. He must share Christ's **sufferings**. He realized that there would be nothing of an atoning value in his own sufferings as there was in Christ's, but he knew, too, that it would be inconsistent for him to live in luxury and ease in a world where his Lord was rejected, scourged, and crucified. Jowett comments: "He was not contented to share the triumph of Olivet; he wanted to feel something of the pang and chill and loneliness of Gethsemane."[15]

Being conformed to His death. As

mentioned before, this is usually explained as meaning that Paul wanted to live the crucified life, to die practically to sin, self, and the world. But we feel that such an interpretation robs the passage of its shocking force. It does mean that, but also much more. Paul was a passionately devoted follower of the One who died on the cross of Calvary. Not only that, he was present when the first martyr of the Christian church died; in fact, he was an accomplice in murdering him! We believe Paul was actually anxious to pour out his life in the same way. Perhaps he would have felt embarrassed to meet Stephen in heaven if he had come by any more comfortable route than martyrdom. Jowett agrees:

> Many Christians are satisfied with expenditure in which there is no "shedding of blood." They give away what they can easily spare. Their gifts are detached things, and the surrender of them necessitates no bleeding. They engage in sacrifice as long as it does not involve life; when the really vital is demanded, they are not to be found. They are prominent at all triumphant entries, and they willingly spend a little money on colorful decorations — on banners and palm branches; but when "Hurrahs" and "Hosannas" change into ominous murmurs and threats, and Calvary comes into sight, they steal away into safe seclusion.
> But here is an Apostle who joyfully anticipates this supreme and critical demand. He is almost impatient at his own dribblings of blood-energy in the service of the kingdom! He is eager if need be to pour it out![16]

In a similar vein Hudson Taylor wrote:

> There is a needs-be for us to give *ourselves* for the life of the world. . . .Fruit-bearing involves cross-bearing. "Except a corn of wheat fall into the ground and die, it abideth alone." We know how the Lord Jesus became fruitful — not by bearing His cross only, but by dying on it. Do we know much of fellowship with Him in this? There are not two Christs — an easy-going Christ for easy-going Christians, and a suffering, toiling Christ for exceptional believers. There is only one Christ. Are we willing to abide in Him and so to bear fruit?[17]

Finally, C. A. Coates says:

> The knowledge of Christ in glory was the supreme desire of Paul's heart, and this desire could never exist without producing an intense longing to reach Him in the place where He is. Hence the heart that longs after Him instinctively turns to the path by which He reached that place in glory, and earnestly desires to reach Him in that place by the very path which He trod. The heart asks, "How did *He* reach that glory? Was it through resurrection? And did not sufferings and death necessarily precede resurrection?" Then the heart says, "Nothing would please me so well as to reach Him in resurrection glory by the very path which took *Him* there." It is the martyr spirit. Paul wanted to tread as a martyr the pathway of suffering and death, that he might reach resurrection and glory by the same path as the blessed One who had won his heart.[18]

3:11 Here again we are faced with a problem of interpretation. Are we to take this verse literally, or are we to spiritualize it? Various explanations have been offered, the principal of which are as follows:

1. Paul was not sure that he would be raised from the dead, so he was straining every muscle to insure his participation in the resurrection. Such a view is impossible! Paul always taught that resurrection was by grace and not by human works. In addition, he expressed the definite confidence that he would participate in the resurrection (2 Cor. 5:1–8).

2. Paul was not speaking of a physical resurrection at all, but was referring to his desire to live the resurrection life while still here on earth. Perhaps the majority of commentators hold this view.

3. Paul was talking about physical resurrection, but he was not expressing any doubt about his participation in it. Rather he was saying that he was not concerned about the sufferings that might lie before him en route to the resurrection. He was willing to undergo severe trials and persecutions, if that was what lay between the present time and the resurrection. The expression **"if, by any means"** does not necessarily express doubt (see Acts 27:12; Rom. 1:10; 11:14), but strong desire or expectation that does not count the cost.

We agree with the third interpretation. The apostle wanted to be conformed to Christ. Since Christ had suffered, died, and been raised from among the dead, Paul wanted nothing better than this for himself. We fear that our own desire for comfort, luxury, and ease often causes us to remove the sharp, cutting edges of some of these Bible verses. Would it not be safer to take them at their face value — literally — unless that sense is impossible in the light of the rest of the Bible?

Before leaving this verse, we should notice that Paul is speaking of **the resurrection from** *among* **the dead**. This is not a resurrection of all the dead. Rather, it describes a **resurrection** in which some will be raised, but others will remain in the grave. We know from 1 Thessalonians 4:13–18 and 1 Corinthians 15:51–57 that believers will be raised at the coming of Christ (some at the Rapture and some at the end of the Tribulation), but the rest of the dead will not be raised until after Christ's Thousand-Year Reign on earth; cf. Rev. 20:5.

3:12 The apostle did not consider that he was **already perfected. Perfected** refers not to the resurrection in the previous verse, but to the whole subject of conformity to Christ. He had no idea that it was possible to achieve a state of sinlessness or to arrive at a condition in life where no further progress could be achieved. He realized that "satisfaction is the grave of progress."

Thus he pressed on in order that the purpose for which the Lord Jesus had saved him might be fulfilled in him. The apostle had been apprehended by **Christ Jesus** on the road to Damascus. What was the purpose of this momentous meeting? It was that Paul might from then on be a pattern-saint, that God might show through him what Christ can do in a human life. He was not yet perfectly conformed to Christ. The process was still going on, and Paul was deeply exercised that this work of God's grace might continue and deepen.

3:13 This man who had learned to be content with whatever material things he had (4:11) never could be content with his spiritual attainments. He did **not count** himself to have "arrived," as we would say today. What then did he do?

But one thing I do. He was a man of single purpose. He had one aim and ambition. In this he resembled David, who said, "One thing have I desired of the Lord."

Forgetting those things which are behind would mean not only his sins and failures but also his natural privileges, attainments, and successes which he had described earlier in this chapter, and even his spiritual triumphs.

And reaching forward to those things which are ahead: namely, the privileges and responsibilities of the Christian life, whether worship, service, or the personal development of Christian character.

3:14 Looking at himself as a runner in a race, Paul describes himself as exerting every effort **toward the goal for the prize of the upward call of God in Christ Jesus**.

The goal is the finish line at the end of the race track. **The prize** is the award presented to the winner. Here **the goal** would be the finish of life's race, and perhaps more particularly the Judgment Seat of Christ. **The prize** would be the crown of righteousness which Paul elsewhere describes as the prize for those who have run well (2 Tim. 4:8).

The upward call of God in Christ Jesus includes all the purposes that God had in mind in saving us. It includes salvation, conformity to Christ, jointheirship with Him, a home in heaven, and numberless other spiritual blessings.

VII. EXHORTATION TO A HEAVENLY WALK, AS EXEMPLIFIED BY THE APOSTLE (3:15–21)

3:15 As many as are mature should share Paul's willingness to suffer and die for Christ and to bend every effort in the quest for likeness to the Lord Jesus. This is the mature view of the Christian faith. Some would call it extreme, radical, or fanatical. But the apostle states that those who are full-grown will see that this is the only sane, logical, reasonable response to the One who shed His lifeblood for them on Calvary.

If in anything you think otherwise, God will reveal even this to you. Paul realizes that not all will agree with him in adopting such a dangerous philosophy. But he expresses the confidence that if a person is really willing to know the truth of the matter, **God will reveal** it to him. The reason we have such an easy-going, complacent Christianity today is because we do not want to know the truth; we are not willing to obey the demands of ideal Christianity. **God** is willing to show the truth to those who are willing to follow it.

3:16 Then the apostle adds that, in the meantime, we should live up to whatever light the Lord has given us. It would not do to mark time until we came to a fuller knowledge of what is required of us as Christians. While we wait for the Lord to reveal the full implications of the cross to us, we should obey whatever **degree** of truth we have received.

3:17 Now Paul turns to exhortation, first by encouraging the Philippians to be followers, or imitators of himself. It is a tribute to his exemplary life that he could ever write such words. We often hear the expression in jest, "Do as I say, not as I do." Not so the apostle! He could hold up his own life as a model of wholehearted devotion to Christ and to His cause.

Lehman Strauss comments:

Paul considered himself the recipient of God's mercy that he might be a "pattern"; thus his whole life, subsequent to his conversion, was dedicated to presenting to others an outline sketch of what a Christian should be. God saved Paul in order that he might show by the example of his conversion that what Jesus Christ did for him He can and will do for others. Was not this the special object our Lord had in view in extending His mercy to you and me? I believe He has saved us to be a pattern to all future believers. Are we serving as examples of those who have been saved by His grace? May it be so![19]

And note those who so walk, as you have us for a pattern. This refers to any others who were living the same kind of life as Paul. It does not mean to mark them out disapprovingly, as in the next verse, but to observe them with a view to following in their steps.

3:18 Just as verse 17 describes those whom believers *should* follow, this passage tells of those we *should not* follow. The apostle does not identify these men specifically. Whether they were the Juda-

izing false teachers mentioned in verse 2, or professed Christian teachers who turned liberty into license, and used grace as a pretext for sin, he does not say.

Paul had warned the saints about these men previously, and he does so again with **weeping**. But why the tears in the midst of such a stern denunciation? Because of the harm these men did among the churches of God. Because of the lives they ruined. Because of the reproach they brought on the name of Christ. Because they were obscuring the true meaning of the cross. Yes, but also because true love weeps even when denouncing **the enemies of the cross of Christ**, just as the Lord Jesus wept over the murderous city of Jerusalem.

3:19 These men were destined to eternal perdition. This does not mean annihilation, but the judgment of God in the lake of fire forever.

Their **god** was **their belly**. All their activities, even their professed religious service, were directed toward the purchase of food (and perhaps drink) for the gratification of their bodily appetite. F. B. Meyer described these men with keen insight: "There is no chapel in their life. It is all kitchen."

Their **glory** was **in their shame**. They boasted in the very things they should have been ashamed of — their nakedness and their immoral behavior.

They were occupied with **earthly things**. For them, the important things in life were food, clothing, honor, comfort, and pleasure. Eternal issues and heavenly things did not disturb their groveling in the muck of this world. They carried on as if they were going to live on earth forever.

3:20 The apostle now contrasts the heavenly-minded attitude of the true believer.

At the time the Epistle was written, Philippi was a colony of Rome (Acts 16:12). The Philippians were citizens of Rome, enjoying its protection and privileges. But they were also citizens of their local government. Against this backdrop, the apostle reminds the believers that their **citizenship is in heaven**. Moffat translates it: "But we are a colony of heaven."

This does not mean that Christians are not *also* citizens of earthly countries.

Other Scriptures clearly teach that we are to be subject to governments because they are ordained by God (Rom. 13:1–7). Indeed, believers should be obedient to the government in all matters not expressly forbidden by the Lord. The Philippians owed allegiance to the local magistrates, and also to the Emperor in Rome. So believers have responsibilities to earthly governments, but their first loyalty is to the Lord in heaven.

Not only are we citizens of heaven, but **we also eagerly wait for the Savior** from heaven! **Eagerly wait for** is strong language (in the original) to express the earnest expectation of something believed to be imminent. It means literally to thrust forward the head and neck as in anxious expectation of hearing or seeing something.

3:21 When the Lord Jesus comes from heaven, He will change these bodies of ours. There is nothing vile or evil about the human body in itself. The evil lies in the wrong uses to which it is put.

But it is a **lowly body**, a body of humiliation. It is subject to wrinkles, scars, age, suffering, sickness, and death. It limits and cramps us!

The Lord will **transform** it into a body of glory. The full extent of the meaning of this we do not know. It will no longer be subject to decay or death, to the limitations of time or of natural barriers. It will be a real body, yet perfectly suited to conditions in heaven. It will be like the resurrection **body** of the Lord Jesus.

This does not mean that we will all have the same physical appearance! Jesus was distinctly recognizable after His resurrection, and doubtless each individual will have his or her own individual physical identity in eternity.

Also, this passage does not teach that we shall be like the Lord Jesus as far as the attributes of God are concerned. We shall never have all-knowledge or all-power; neither shall we be in all places at one and same time.

But we shall be morally like the Lord Jesus. We shall be forever free from sin. This passage does not give us enough to satisfy our curiosity, but it is enough to inspire comfort and stimulate hope.

According to the working by which He is able even to subdue all things to Himself. The transformation of our bod-

ies will be accomplished by the same divine power which the Lord will later use **to subdue all things to Himself**. He is "able to save" (Heb. 7:25). He is "able to aid" (Heb. 2:18). He is "able to keep" (Jude 24). Now in this verse we learn that He is **able to subdue**. "This is . . . our God forever and ever: He will be our guide even to death" (Ps. 48:14).

VIII. APPEAL FOR HARMONY, MUTUAL ASSISTANCE, JOY, FORBEARANCE, PRAYERFULNESS, AND A DISCIPLINED THOUGHT LIFE (4:1–9)

4:1 On the basis of the wonderful hope which the apostle had set before the minds of the believers in the previous verse, he now exhorts them to **stand fast in the Lord**. This verse is filled with endearing names for the believers. First of all, Paul calls them his **brethren**. But not only his brethren — his **beloved brethren**. Then he adds the thought that he longs for them, that is, he longs to be with them again. Further, he speaks of them as his **joy and crown**. Doubtless he means that they are his **joy** at the present time and will be his **crown** at the Judgment Seat of Christ. Finally, he closes the verse with the expression **beloved**. The apostle really loved people, and doubtless this is one of the secrets of his effectiveness in the work of the Lord.

4:2 Euodia and **Syntyche** were women in the church at Philippi who were having difficulty getting along together. We are not given details as to the cause of their disagreement (and perhaps it is just as well!).

The apostle uses the word **implore** twice to show that the exhortation is addressed just as much to one as to the other. Paul urges them **to be of the same mind in the Lord**. It is impossible for us to be united in all things in daily life, but, as far as the things of **the Lord** are concerned, it is possible for us to submerge our petty, personal differences in order that the Lord may be magnified and His work advanced.

4:3 There is considerable speculation as to the identity of the **true companion** (or yoke-fellow[20]) whom Paul addresses in this verse. Timothy and Luke have both been suggested, but Epaphroditus is probably the person spoken of. He is exhorted to **help these women who** had **labored** with Paul **in the gospel**. We take it that these women were Euodia and Syntyche, and that the Apostle Paul is giving what experience has proven to be sound advice. Often when two people have been quarreling, the quarrel can best be settled by taking it to an independent third party — someone with mature, spiritual judgment. It is not that he acts arbitrarily in the case and hands down a decision, but rather that by appealing to the word of God, he is able to show the contending persons the scriptural solution to their problem.

Care should be taken in interpreting the expression "[they] **labored with me in the gospel**." By no stretch of the imagination can this be taken to mean that they preached the gospel with the Apostle Paul. There are many ways in which women can labor in the gospel — by hospitality to the servants of Christ, by home visitation, by teaching younger women and children — without assuming a ministry of public teaching or preaching.

Another co-laborer named **Clement** is mentioned. Nothing further is known of him with certainty. Then Paul mentions **the rest of** his **fellow workers, whose names are in the Book of Life**. This is a lovely way of expressing the eternal and unspeakable blessedness that attaches to faith in Christ and service for Him.

4:4 Turning now to the entire church, Paul repeats the favorite exhortation. The secret of his exhortation is found in the words **in the Lord**. No matter how dark the circumstances of life may be, it is always possible for the Christian to **rejoice in the Lord**.

Jowett shares his experience regarding Christian joy:

Christian joy is a mood independent of our immediate circumstances. If it were dependent on our surroundings, then, indeed, it would be as uncertain as an unprotected candle burning on a gusty night. One moment the candle burns clear and steady, the next moment the blaze leaps to the very edge of the wick,

and affords little or no light. But Christian joy has no relationship to the transient setting of the life, and therefore it is not the victim of the passing day. At one time my conditions arrange themselves like a sunny day in June; a little later they rearrange themselves like a gloomy day in November. One day I am at the wedding; the next day I stand by an open grave. One day, in my ministry, I win ten converts for the Lord; and then, for a long stretch of days, I never win one. Yes, the days are as changeable as the weather, and yet the Christian joy can be persistent. Where lies the secret of its glorious persistency?

Here is the secret. "Lo! I am with you *all the days.*" In all the changing days, "He changeth not, neither is weary." He is no fairweather Companion, leaving me when the year grows dark and cold. He does not choose my days of prosperous festival, though not to be found in my days of impoverishment and defeat. He does not show Himself only when I wear a garland, and hide Himself when I wear a crown of thorns. He is with me "all the days" — the prosperous days and the days of adversity; days when the funeral bell is tolling, and days when the wedding bell is ringing. "All the days." The day of life — the day of death — the day of judgment.[21]

4:5 Now Paul urges them to **let** their **gentleness be known to all men**. This has also been translated yieldedness, sweet reasonableness, and willingness to give up one's own way. The difficulty does not lie in *understanding* what is meant, but in *obeying* the precept **"to all men."**

The Lord is at hand may mean that the Lord is now present, or that the Lord's coming is near. Both are true, though we favor the latter view.

4:6 Is it really possible for a Christian to **be anxious for nothing**? It is possible as long as we have the resource of believing prayer. The rest of the verse goes on to explain how our lives can be free from sinful fretting. Everything should be taken to the Lord in **prayer**. **Everything** means *everything*. There is nothing too great or small for His loving care!

Prayer is both an act and an atmosphere. We come to the Lord at specific times and bring specific requests before Him. But it is also possible to live in an *atmosphere* of prayer. It is possible that the mood of our life should be a prayerful mood. Perhaps the word *prayer* in this verse signifies the overall attitude of our life, whereas **supplication** signifies the specific **requests** which we bring to the Lord.

But then we should notice that our **requests** should **be made known to God with thanksgiving**. Someone has summarized the verse as saying that we should be "anxious in nothing, prayerful in everything, thankful for anything."

4:7 If these attitudes characterize our lives, **the peace of God, which surpasses all understanding, will guard our hearts and minds through Christ Jesus. The peace of God** is a sense of holy repose and complacency which floods the soul of the believer when he is leaning hard upon God.

> Stayed upon Jehovah,
> Hearts are fully blessed;
> Finding, as He promised,
> Perfect peace and rest.
>
> *– Frances Ridley Havergal*

This **peace surpasses all understanding**. People of the world cannot understand it at all, and even Christians possessing it find a wonderful element of mystery about it. They are surprised at their own lack of anxiety in the face of tragedy or adverse circumstances.

This **peace** garrisons the heart and the thought life. What a needed tonic it is, then, in this day of neuroses, nervous breakdowns, tranquilizers, and mental distress.

4:8 Now the apostle gives a closing bit of advice concerning the thought life. The Bible everywhere teaches that we can control what we think. It is useless to adopt a defeatist attitude, saying that we simply cannot help it when our minds are filled with unwelcome thoughts. The fact of the matter is that we *can* help it. The secret lies in positive thinking. It is what is now a well-known principle — the expulsive power of a new affection. A person cannot entertain evil thoughts and thoughts about the Lord Jesus at the same time. If, then, an evil thought should come to him, he should immediately get rid of it by meditating on the Person and work of Christ.

The more enlightened psychologists and psychiatrists of the day have come to agree with the Apostle Paul on this matter. They stress the dangers of negative thinking.

You do not have to look very closely to find the Lord Jesus Christ in verse 8. Everything that is **true, noble, just, pure, lovely, of good report**, virtuous, and **praiseworthy** is found in Him. Let us look at these virtues one by one: **True** means not false or unreliable, but genuine and real. **Noble** means honorable or morally attractive. **Just** means righteous, both toward God and man. **Pure** would refer to the high moral character of a person's life. **Lovely** has the idea of that which is admirable or agreeable to behold or consider. **Of good report** has also been translated "of good repute" or "fair sounding." **Virtue**, of course, speaks of moral excellence; and **praiseworthy**, something that deserves to be commended.

In verse 7, Paul had assured the saints that God would garrison their hearts and thoughts in Christ Jesus. But he is not neglectful to remind them that they, too, have a responsibility in the matter. God does not garrison the thought-life of a man who does not *want* it to be kept pure.

4:9 Again the Apostle Paul sets himself forth as a pattern saint. He urges the believers to practice **the things which** they **learned** from him and which they **saw in** his life.

The fact that this comes so closely after verse 8 is significant. Right living results from right thinking. If a person's thought-life is pure, then his life will be pure. On the other hand, if a person's mind is a fountain of corruption, then you can be sure that the stream that issues from it will be filthy also. And we should always remember that if a person thinks an evil thought long enough, he will eventually do it.

Those who are faithful in following the example of the apostle are promised that **the God of peace will be with** them. In verse 7, the peace of God is the portion of those who are prayerful; here the **God of peace** is the Companion of those who are holy. The thought here is that God will make Himself very near and dear in present experience to all whose lives are embodiments of the truth.

IX. PAUL'S THANKS FOR FINANCIAL GIFTS FROM THE SAINTS (4:10–20)

4:10 In verses 10–19, Paul speaks of the relationship which existed between the church at Philippi and himself in connection with financial assistance. No one could ever tell how meaningful these verses have been for saints of God who have been called upon to go through times of financial pressure and reverses!

Paul rejoices that **now at last**, after a period of time had elapsed, the Philippians had sent him practical assistance in the work of the Lord. He does not blame them for the period of time in which no help was received; he gives them credit that they wanted to send gifts to him but that they **lacked opportunity** to do so. Moffatt translates: "For what you lacked was never the care but the chance of showing it."

4:11 In handling the whole subject of finances, it is lovely to see the delicacy and courtesy which Paul employs. He does not want them to think that he is complaining about any shortage of funds. Rather, he would have them know that he is quite independent of such mundane circumstances. He had **learned . . . to be content**, no matter what his financial condition might be. Contentment is really greater than riches, for "if contentment does not produce riches, it achieves the same object by banishing the desire for them."

"It is a blessed secret when the believer learns how to carry a high head with an empty stomach, an upright look with an empty pocket, a happy heart with an unpaid salary, joy in God when men are faithless" (Selected).

4:12 Paul knew **how to be abased**, that is, by not having the bare necessities of life; and he also knew **how to abound**, that is, by having more given to him at a particular time than his immediate needs required. **Everywhere and in all things** he had **learned both to be full and to be hungry, both to abound and to suffer need**. How had the apostle

learned such a lesson? Simply in this way: he was confident that he was in the will of God. He knew that wherever he was, or in whatever circumstances he found himself, he was there by divine appointment. If he was **hungry**, it was because God wanted him to be hungry. If he was **full**, it was because his Lord had so planned it. Busily and faithfully engaged in the service of his King, he could say, "Even so, Father, for so it seemed good in Your sight."

4:13 Then the apostle adds the words which have been a puzzle to many: **"I can do all things through Christ who strengthens me."** Could he possibly mean this literally? Did the apostle really believe that there was nothing he could not do? The answer is this: When the Apostle Paul said that he could **do all things**, he meant **all things** which were God's will for him to do. He had learned that the Lord's commands are the Lord's enablements. He knew that God would never call on him to accomplish some task without giving the necessary grace. **All things** probably applies not so much to great feats of daring as to great privations and hungerings.

4:14 In spite of what he had said, he wants the Philippians to know that they **have done well** in having **shared in** his **distress**. This probably meant the money they sent to supply his needs during his imprisonment.

4:15 In the past, the **Philippians** had excelled in the grace of **giving**. During the early days of Paul's ministry, **when** he **departed from Macedonia, no church shared with** him financially except the Philippians.

It is remarkable how these seemingly unimportant details are recorded forever in God's precious word. This teaches us that what is given to the Lord's servants is given to the Lord. He is interested in every cent. He records all that is done as to Him, and He rewards with good measure, pressed down, shaken together, and running over.

4:16 **Even** when he was in **Thessalonica,** they **sent aid once and again for** his needs. It is apparent that the Philippians were living so close to the Lord that He was able to direct them in their giving. The Holy Spirit placed a burden on their hearts for the Apostle Paul. They responded by sending money to him **once and again**, that is, twice. When we remember that Paul was in Thessalonica only a short time, it makes their care for him there all the more remarkable.

4:17 The utter unselfishness of Paul is indicated in this verse. He was more elated by their gain than by their **gift**. Greater than his desire for financial help was his longing that **fruit** should abound **to** the **account** of the believers. This is exactly what happens when money is given to the Lord. It is all recorded in the account books and will be repaid a hundredfold in a coming day.

All that we have belongs to the Lord, and when we give to Him, we are only giving Him what is His own. Christians who argue as to whether or not they should tithe their money have missed the point. A tithe or tenth part was commanded to Israelites under the law as the minimum gift. In this age of grace, the question should not be, "How much shall I give the Lord?" but rather, "How much dare I keep for myself?" It should be the Christian's desire to live economically and sacrificially in order to give an ever-increasing portion of his income to the work of the Lord that men might not perish for want of hearing the gospel of Christ.

4:18 When Paul says **I have all** he means **I have all** *I need*, **and abound**. It seems strange in this day of twentieth-century commercialism to hear a servant of the Lord who is not begging for money, but who, on the contrary, admits having sufficient. The unrestrained begging campaigns of the present day are an abomination in the sight of God and a reproach to the name of Christ. They are completely unnecessary. Hudson Taylor once said, "God's work carried on in God's way will never lack God's resources." The trouble today is that we have failed to distinguish between working for God and the work of God. It is possible to engage in so-called Christian service which might not be the will of God at all. Where there is an abundance of money, there is always the greatest danger of embarking on ventures which might not have the divine

sanction. To quote Hudson Taylor once again: "What we greatly need to fear is not insufficient funds, but too much unconsecrated funds."

The love-gift which **Epaphroditus** brought from the Philippians to Paul is described as a **sweet-smelling aroma, an acceptable sacrifice, well pleasing to God**. The only other time these words are used, they refer to Christ Himself (Eph. 5:2). Paul dignifies the sacrificial giving of the Philippians by describing what it meant to God. It ascended as a fragrant **sacrifice** to Him. It was both **acceptable** and **well pleasing.**

Jowett exclaims:

> How vast, then, is the range of an apparently local kindness! We thought we were ministering to a pauper, and in reality we were conversing with the King. We imagined that the fragrance would be shut up in a petty neighborhood, and lo, the sweet aroma steals through the universe. We thought we were dealing only with Paul, and we find that we were ministering to Paul's Savior and Lord.[22]

4:19 Now Paul adds what is perhaps the best-known and best-loved verse in this entire chapter. We should notice that this promise follows the description of their faithful stewardship. In other words, because they had given of their material resources to God, even to the point where their own livelihood was endangered, **God** would **supply** their every **need**. How easy it is to take this verse out of context and use it as a soft pillow for Christians who are squandering their money on themselves with seldom a thought for the work of God! "That's all right. God will supply all your need."

While it is true in a general sense that **God** does **supply** the needs of His people, this is a specific promise that those who are faithful and devoted in their giving to Christ will never suffer lack.

It has often been remarked that God supplies the needs of His people — not *out of* His riches, **but according to His riches in glory by Christ Jesus**. If a millionaire gave a dime to a child, he would be giving *out of* his riches. But if he gave a hundred thousand dollars to some worthy cause, he would be giving *according to* his riches. God's supply is **accord-**

ing to His riches in glory by Christ Jesus, and nothing could be richer than that!

Williams calls verse 19 a note drawn upon the bank of faith:

My God — the name of the Banker.

Shall supply — the promise to pay.

All your need — the value of the note.

According to His riches — the capital of the bank.

In glory — the address of the bank.

By Christ Jesus — the signature at the foot, without which the note is worthless.[23]

4:20 Thinking of God's abundant provision causes the apostle to break out into praise. This is suitable language for every child of God who daily experiences God's gracious care, not only in the supply of material things, but also in providing guidance, help against temptation, and the quickening of a languishing devotional life.

X. CLOSING GREETINGS (4:21–23)

4:21 Thinking of the believers as they are gathered together and listening to the Letter which he was writing to them, Paul greets every saint in Christ Jesus and sends greetings from the brethren who are with him.

4:22 We are compelled to love this verse for its reference to Caesar's household. Our imaginations are strongly tempted to run riot. Who are the members of Nero's household referred to here? Were they some of the soldiers who had been assigned to watch the Apostle Paul, and who had been saved through his ministry? Were they slaves or freedmen who worked in the palace? Or might the expression include some officials of the Roman government? We cannot know with certainty, but here we have a lovely illustration of the truth that Christians, like spiders, find their way into king's palaces (Prov. 30:28)! The gospel knows no boundaries. It can penetrate the most forbidding walls. It can plant itself in the very midst of those who are seeking to exterminate it. Truly, the gates of Hades shall not prevail against the church of Jesus Christ!

4:23 Now Paul closes with his characteristic greeting. Grace sparkled on the first page of this Letter, and now is found again at the close. Out of the abundance of a man's heart his mouth speaks. Paul's heart was filled to overflowing with the greatest theme of all the ages — the grace of God through Christ — and it is not at all surprising that this precious truth should flood over into every channel of his life.

Paul Rees concludes for us:

The greatest of humans has written his warmest of letters. The love-task is finished. The day is done. The chain is still there upon the apostolic wrist. The soldier is still on guard. Never mind! Paul's spirit is free! His mind is clear! His heart is glowing!

And next morning Epaphroditus strides away to Philippi![24]

ENDNOTES

[1](Intro) H. A. A. Kennedy, "Philippians," *The Expositor's Greek Testament*, III:407.

[2](1:1) J. H. Jowett, *The High Calling*, p. 2.

[3](1:7) W. E. Vine, *The Epistles to the Philippians and Colossians*, p. 23.

[4](1:10) By derivation the word translated "sincere" (eilikrinēs) means "unmixed," or possibly "sun-proof." If the latter, it has the same idea as English "sincere" (lit. "without wax"). An honest sculptor would keep chipping away to remove a flaw in a white marble statue. An "insincere" one would fill the gouge up with wax. But, in the sun, a statue with a wax filling would soon expose the sculptor's cover-up.

[5](1:11) Lehman Strauss, *Devotional Studies in Philippians*, p. 63.

[6](1:13) T. W. Drury, *The Prison Ministry of St. Paul*, p. 22.

[7](1:20) Guy King, *Joy Way*, p. 33.

[8](1:21) Jowett, *Calling*, p. 34.

[9](2:1) F. B. Meyer, *Devotional Commentary on Philippians*, pp. 77-79.

[10](2:5) King, *Joy Way*, p. 51.

[11](2:6) E. H. Gifford, *The Incarnation*, pp. 44, 45.

[12](2:11) Charles R. Erdman, further documentation unavailable.

[13](2:17) George Williams, *The Student's Commentary on the Holy Scriptures*, p. 931.

[14](3:7) King, *Joy Way*, p. 81.

[15](3:10) Jowett, *Calling*, p. 217.

[16](3:10) *Ibid.*, pp. 81, 82.

[17](3:10) Hudson Taylor, quoted by Mrs. Howard Taylor in *Behind the Ranges*, p. 170.

[18](3:10) C. A. Coates, further documentation unavailable.

[19](3:17) Strauss, *Philippians*, p. 202.

[20](4:3) "Yoke-fellow" (Gk. *su(n)zugos*) may be a proper name (Synzygus). Though it has not yet been found elsewhere, it is the sort of name a slave especially might receive.

[21](4:4) Jowett, *Day by Day*, pp. 169-171.

[22](4:18) *Ibid*, p. 225.

[23](4:19) Williams, *Student's Commentary*, p. 934.

[24](4:23) Paul Rees, *The Adequate Man*, p. 127.

Bibliography

Erdman, C. R. *The Epistle of Paul to the Philippians*. Philadelphia: Westminster Press, 1928.

Gifford, E. H. *The Incarnation: A Study of Philippians*. London: Hodder & Stoughton, 1897.

Jowett, J. H. *The High Calling*. London: Andrew Melrose, 1909.

Kelly, William. *Lectures on Philippians and Colossians*. London: G. Morrish, n.d.

Kennedy, H. A. A. "Philippians," *The Expositor's Greek Testament, Vol. III*. Grand Rapids: Wm. B. Eerdmans Publishing Co., 1961.

King, Guy H. *Joy Way*. London: Marshall, Morgan & Scott, Ltd., 1954.

Meyer, F. B. *Devotional Commentary on Philippians*. Grand Rapids: Kregel Publications, 1979.

Rees, Paul. *The Adequate Man*. Westwood, N.J.: Fleming H. Revell Co., 1959.

Strauss, Lehman. *Devotional Studies in Philippians*. Neptune, N.J.: Loizeaux Bros. Publishers, 1959.

Vine, W. E. *The Epistles to the Philippians and Colossians*. London: Oliphants, 1955.

Introduction

"To go into [Colossians] itself, to rethink its inspired thought that is clothed in inspired language, to let the light and the power of this thought fill the soul and mold the life, this is enrichment for time and for eternity."
— R. C. H. Lenski

I. Unique Place in the Canon

Most of Paul's Letters were written to congregations in large or important cities: Rome, Corinth, Ephesus, Philippi. Colosse was a town that had seen better days. Even the assembly there did not become well-known in early church history. In short, were it not for this inspired Epistle to the Christians there, Colosse would today be a name known only to students of ancient history.

Although the place was insignificant, the Letter that the apostle sent there is very important. Along with John 1 and Hebrews 1, Colossians 1 presents the most marvelous exposition of the absolute deity of our Lord Jesus Christ. Since this doctrine is fundamental to all Christian truth, its value cannot be overstressed.

The Letter also has rich instruction on relationships, cultic religion, and the Christian life.

II. Authorship[†]

There is no proof that anyone questioned the Pauline authorship of Colossians until the nineteenth century, so complete is the positive evidence. The *external evidence* is especially strong. Those who quote the Letter, often naming Paul as the author, include Ignatius, Justin Martyr, Theophilus of Antioch, Irenaeus, Clement of Alexandria, Tertullian, and Origen. Both the Canons of Marcion and Muratori accept Colossians as authentic.

The *internal evidence* includes the simple fact that thrice the writer *says* he is Paul (1:1, 23; 4:18) and the contents

agree with those statements. The exposition of doctrine followed by duty is typical of the apostle. Perhaps the most persuasive proof of authenticity is the strong link with Philemon, which everyone accepts as Pauline. Five of the same men mentioned in that little Letter also show up in Colossians. Even such a critic as Renan was impressed with the Philemon parallels, and *he had doubts about Colossians*.

The arguments *against* Pauline authorship center on vocabulary, the doctrine of Christ, and apparent references to Gnosticism. Regarding the first point, new vocabulary in Colossians replaces some of Paul's favorite words. Salmon, a conservative British scholar of the past century, rather wittily counters the argument: "I cannot subscribe to the doctrine that a man writing a new composition must not, on pain of losing his identity, employ any word that he has not used in a former one."[1] Regarding the Christology of Colossians, it dovetails with that of Philippians and John, and only those who desire to transform the deity of Christ into a second century development from paganism should have any trouble with this doctrine.

As to Gnosticism, the liberal Scottish scholar Moffatt thought that the early stage of Gnosticism presented in Colossians could well have existed in the first century.[2]

Thus the Pauline authorship of Colossians rests on a firm foundation.

III. Date

As one of the "Prison Epistles," Colossians could conceivably come from

Paul's two-year incarceration in Caesarea (Acts 23:23; 24:27). However, since the evangelist Philip was his host there, it seems unlikely that the apostle would neglect to mention him, Paul being such a courteous and gracious Christian. A possible Ephesian imprisonment has also been suggested, though this is much less likely. The favored time for this Letter and Philemon is in the middle of Paul's first Roman imprisonment, about A.D. 60 (Acts 28:30, 31).

Fortunately, as is usually true, an understanding of this book does not depend on a full knowledge of the circumstances under which it was written.

IV. Background and Theme[†]

Colosse was a city in the province of Phrygia, in the area now known as Asia Minor. It was located ten miles east of Laodicea and thirteen miles southeast of Hierapolis (see 4:13). It was also located about one hundred miles east of Ephesus, at the mouth of a pass in the Cadmian mountain range (a narrow glen twelve miles long) on the military route from the Euphrates to the West. Colosse was on the Lycus (Wolf) River, which flows westward into the Maeander River shortly after it passes Laodicea. There the water from the hot springs of Hierapolis joins the cold waters from Colosse, producing a "lukewarm" condition at Laodicea. Hierapolis was both a health center and a religious center, while Laodicea was the metropolis of the valley. Colosse had been larger previous to NT times. The name is thought possibly to relate to the word "colossus," from the fantastic shapes of its limestone formations.

We do not know exactly how the gospel first reached Colosse. At the time Paul wrote this Letter, he had never met the believers there (2:1). It is generally believed that Epaphras was the one who first brought the good news of salvation to this city (1:7). Many believe that he was converted through Paul when the apostle spent the three years at Ephesus. Phrygia is a part of Proconsular Asia, and Paul was in Phrygia (Acts 16:6; 18:23), but not Colosse (2:1).

We do know from the Letter that a false teaching which in its full-blown form became known as Gnosticism was beginning to threaten the church at Colosse. The Gnostics prided themselves on their knowledge (Gk., *gnōsis*). They claimed to have information superior to that of the apostles and tried to create the impression that a person could not be truly happy unless he had been initiated into the deepest secrets of their cult.

Some of the Gnostics denied the true humanity of Christ. They taught that "the Christ" was a divine *influence* that came out from God and rested on the Man, Jesus, at His baptism. They further taught that the Christ left Jesus just before His crucifixion. The result, according to them, was that Jesus died, but the Christ did not.

Certain branches of Gnosticism taught that between God and matter there are various levels or grades of spirit beings. They adopted this view in an effort to explain the origin of evil. A. T. Robertson explains:

> The Gnostic speculation concerned itself primarily with the origin of the universe and the existence of evil. They assumed that God is good and yet there is evil in existence. Their theory was that evil is inherent in matter. And yet the good God could not create evil matter. So they postulated a series of emanations, aeons, spirits, angels that came in between God and matter. The idea was that one aeon came from God, another aeon from this aeon, and so on till there was one far enough away from God for God not to be contaminated by the creation of evil matter and yet close enough to have power to do the work.[3]

Some Gnostics, believing that the body was inherently sinful, practiced asceticism, a system of self-denial or even self-torture, in an effort to attain a higher spiritual state. Others went to the opposite extreme, living in carnal indulgence, saying that the body didn't matter or have any affect on a person's spiritual life!

It seems that traces of two other errors were found in Colosse. These were antinomianism and Judaism. Antinomianism is the teaching that under grace a person does not need to practice self-control but may give full vent to his bodily appetites and passions. Old Testament Judaism had degenerated into a

†*See p. ii.*

system of ceremonial observances by which a man hoped to achieve righteousness before God.

The errors which existed in Colosse are still with us today. Gnosticism has reappeared in Christian Science, Theosophy, Mormonism, Jehovah's Witnesses, Unity, and other systems. Antinomianism is characteristic of all who say that because we are under grace, we can live as we please. Judaism was originally a God-given revelation, whose forms and ceremonies were intended to teach spiritual truths in a typical way, as the Epistle to the Hebrews and other parts of the NT show. This lapsed into a system in which the forms themselves were considered to be meritorious, and so the spiritual meaning was often largely ignored. It has its counterpart today in the many religious systems which teach that a person can gain merit and favor with God by his own works, ignoring or denying his sinful state and need of salvation from God alone.

In Colossians, the Apostle Paul masterfully counteracts all these errors by displaying the glories of the Person and work of our Lord Jesus Christ.

This Epistle bears a striking resemblance to Paul's Letter to the Ephesians. However, it is a resemblance without repetition. Ephesians views believers as seated with Christ in heavenly places. Colossians, on the other hand, sees believers on earth, with Christ their glorified Head in heaven. The emphasis in *Ephesians* is that the *believer* is *in Christ*. *Colossians* speaks of *Christ in the believer*, the hope of glory. In Ephesians, the thrust is on the church as the "Body" of Christ, "the fullness of Him who fills all in all" (Eph. 1:23). Hence the unity of the Body of Christ is stressed. In Colossians, the headship of Christ is set forth extensively in chapter 1, with the necessity of our "holding fast to the Head" (2:18, 19), being submissive to Him. Fifty-four of the 155 verses in Ephesians are similar to verses found in Colossians.

OUTLINE

I. THE DOCTRINE OF THE PRE-EMINENCE OF CHRIST (Chaps. 1, 2)

   A. Salutation (1:1, 2)
   B. Paul's Thanksgiving and Prayer for the Believers (1:3–14)
   C. The Glories of Christ the Church's Head (1:15–23)
   D. The Ministry Committed to Paul (1:24–29)
   E. Christ's Sufficiency Against the Perils of Philosophy, Legalism, Mysticism, and Asceticism (2:1–23)

II. THE BELIEVER'S DUTY TO THE PREEMINENT CHRIST (Chaps. 3, 4)

   A. The Believer's New Life: Putting Off the Old Man and Putting on the New (3:1–17)
   B. Appropriate Behavior for Members of the Christian Household (3:18–4:1)
   C. The Believer's Prayer Life and Witness by Life and Speech (4:2–6)
   D. Glimpses of Some of Paul's Associates (4:7–14)
   E. Greetings and Instructions (4:15–18)

Commentary

I. THE DOCTRINE OF THE PRE-EMINENCE OF CHRIST (Chaps. 1, 2)

A. Salutation (1:1, 2)

1:1 In the days when the NT was written, it was customary to begin a letter with the name of the writer. Thus **Paul** introduces himself as **an apostle of Jesus Christ by the will of God. An apostle** was one who had been especially sent forth by the Lord Jesus as a messenger. In order to confirm the message that they preached, apostles were given the power to perform miracles (2 Cor. 12:12). In addition, we read that when the apostles laid their hands on believers in certain cases, the Holy Spirit was given (Acts 8:15–20; 19:6). There are no apostles in the world today in the strict sense of the word, and it is folly for men to claim to be successors of the original twelve. Ephesians 2:20 is taken by many to indicate that the work of those with the distinctive gift of apostles and prophets had to do chiefly with the founding of the church, in contrast with the work of evangelists, pastors, and teachers (Eph. 4:11), which continue throughout this dispensation.

Paul traces his apostleship to **the will of God** (see also Acts 9:15; Gal. 1:1). It was not an occupation which he had chosen for himself or for which he had been trained by men. Neither was the office given to him by human ordination. It was not "from men" (as the source), neither "through men" (as the instrument). Rather, his entire ministry was carried out under the solemn realization that God Himself had chosen him to be an apostle.

With Paul at the time this Letter was written was **Timothy our brother**. It is good to notice here a complete lack of officialism in Paul's attitude toward Timothy. Both were members of a common brotherhood and there was no thought of a hierarchy of church dignitaries with pompous titles and distinguishing clothing.

1:2 The Letter is addressed to **the saints and faithful brethren in Christ who are in Colosse**. Here are two of the lovely names that are given in the NT to all Christians. **Saints** means that they are separated to God from the world and that as a result they should lead holy lives. **Faithful brethren** indicates that they are children of a common Father through faith in the Lord Jesus; they are believing brothers and sisters. Christians are also called disciples and believers in other sections of the NT.

In Christ speaks of their *spiritual* position. When they were saved, God placed them in Christ, "accepted in the beloved." Henceforth, they had His life and nature. Henceforth, they would no longer be seen by God as children of Adam or as unregenerate men, but He would now see them in all the acceptability of His own Son. The expression **in Christ** conveys more of intimacy, acceptance, and security than any human mind can understand. The *geographical* location of these believers is indicated by the expression **who are in Colosse**. It is doubtful that we would ever have heard of this town had it not been that the gospel was preached there and souls were saved.

Paul now greets the saints with the lovely salutation: **Grace to you and peace from God our Father and the Lord Jesus Christ.** No two words could better embrace the blessings of Christianity than **grace and peace**. **Grace** was a common Greek expression, while **peace** was the common Jewish greeting; and the words were used at meeting or parting. Paul united them, and elevated their meaning and use. **Grace** pictures God stooping down to sinful, lost humanity in loving and tender compassion. **Peace** summarizes all that results in the life of a person when he accepts God's grace as a free gift. R. J. Little said: "Grace can mean many things, and is like a blank check. Peace is definitely part of the Christian's heritage, and we should not allow Satan to rob us of it." The order of the words is significant: **grace** first, then **peace**. If God had not first acted in love and mercy toward us, we would still be in our sins. But because He took the initiative and sent His Son to die for us, we now can have peace with God, peace with man, and the peace of God in our souls. Even having said all this, one despairs of ever adequately defining such tremendous words as these.

B. Paul's Thanksgiving and Prayer for the Believers (1:3–14)

1:3 Having greeted these saints in terms which have become the watchword of Christianity, the apostle does something else which is very characteristic of him — he falls to his knees in **thanks** and prayer. It seems that the apostle always began his prayer with praise to the Lord, and this is a good example for us to follow. His prayer is addressed **to the God and Father of our Lord Jesus Christ**. Prayer is the unspeakable privilege of having audience with the Sovereign of the universe. But it may be asked: "How could a mere man dare to stand in the awful presence of the infinitely high God?" The answer is found in our text. The glorious and majestic God of the universe is **the Father of our Lord Jesus Christ**. The One who is infinitely high has become intimately nigh. Because as believers in Christ we share His life, God is our Father also (John 20:17). We can draw near through Christ. **Praying always for you.** Taken by itself, this expression does not seem remarkable, but it takes on new meaning when we remember that this describes Paul's interest in people he had never met. We often find it difficult to remember our own relatives and friends before the throne of grace, but think of the prayer list the Apostle Paul must have kept! He prayed not only for those he knew but also for Christians in faraway places whose names had been mentioned to him by others. Truly Paul's untiring prayer life helps us to understand him better.

1:4 He had heard of the Colossians' **faith in Christ Jesus and of** their **love to all the saints**. He first mentions their **faith in Christ Jesus**. That is where we must always begin. There are many religious people in the world today who are constantly talking about their love for others. But if you question them, you find that they do not have any **faith in** the Lord **Jesus**. Such love is hollow and meaningless. On the other hand, there are those who profess to have **faith in Christ**, yet you look in vain for any evidence of **love** in their lives. Paul would likewise question the sincerity of their faith. There must be true **faith** in the Savior, and this faith must be evidenced by a life of **love** to God and to one's fellow man.

Paul speaks of **faith** as being **in Christ Jesus**. It is very important to notice this. The Lord Jesus Christ is always set forth in Scripture as the Object of faith. A person might have unbounded faith in a bank, but that faith is only valid as long as the bank is reliable. The faith itself will not insure the safety of one's money if the bank is poorly managed. So it is in the spiritual life. Faith in itself is not sufficient. That faith must be centered in the Lord Jesus Christ.

Since He can never fail, no one who trusts Him will ever be disappointed.

The fact that Paul had heard of their **faith** and of their **love** shows that they certainly were not secret believers. In fact, the NT gives little encouragement to anyone who seeks to go on as a secret disciple. The teaching of the Word of God is that if a person has truly received the Savior, then it is inevitable that he will make public confession of Christ.

The love of the Colossians went out to **all the saints**. There was nothing local or sectarian about their love. They did not love only those of their own fellowship, but wherever they found true believers, their love flowed out freely and warmly. This should be a lesson to us that our love should not be narrow or limited to our own local fellowship, or to missionaries from our own country. We should recognize the sheep of Christ wherever they are found, and manifest our affection to them wherever possible.

1:5 It is not entirely clear how this verse connects with what has gone before. Is it connected with verse 3: We give thanks...**because of the hope which is laid up for you in heaven**? Or is it connected with the latter part of verse 4: Your love for all the saints, **because of the hope which is laid up for you in heaven**? Either interpretation is possible. The apostle could be giving thanks, not only for their faith and their love, but also for the future inheritance which would one day be theirs. On the other hand, it is also true that faith in Christ Jesus and love to all the saints are exercised in view of that which lies before us. In any case, we can all see that Paul is here listing the three cardinal virtues of the Christian life: faith, love, and **hope**. These are also mentioned in 1 Corinthians 13:13 and 1 Thessalonians 1:3; 5:8. Lightfoot says: "Faith rests on the past; love works in the present; hope looks to the future."[4]

In this verse, **hope** does not mean the attitude of waiting or looking forward to something, but rather it refers to that for which a person hopes. Here it means the fulfillment of our salvation when we shall be taken to heaven and will enter into our eternal inheritance. The Colossians had heard about this **hope** previously, perhaps when Epaphras preached the gospel to them. What they had heard is described as the **word of the truth of the gospel**. The **gospel** is here described as a message of *true* good news. Perhaps Paul was thinking of the *false* teachings of the Gnostics when he wrote this. Someone has defined "truth" as that which God says about a thing (John 17:17). **The gospel** is true because it is God's word.

1:6 The truth of the gospel had **come to** the Colossians even **as it** had **in all the** then-known **world**. This must not be taken in an absolute sense. It could not mean that *every man and woman* in the world had heard the gospel. It may mean, in part, that some from *every nation* had heard the good news of salvation (Acts 2). It may also mean that the gospel was for all men, and was being spread abroad without purposeful limitation. Paul is also describing the inevitable results which it produced. In Colosse and **in all** the other parts of **the world** where the gospel was preached, it bore **fruit** and was **growing** (NKJV margin[5]). This is stated to show the supernatural character of the gospel. In nature, a plant does not usually bear fruit and increase at the same time. Many times, it has to be pruned in order to bear fruit, for if it is allowed to grow wild, the result is that all the life of the plant goes into leaves and branches rather than into fruit. But the gospel does both at the same time. It bears **fruit** in the salvation of souls and in the upbuilding of the saints, and it also spreads from city to city and from nation to nation.

This is precisely the effect that the gospel had in the lives of the Colossians **since the day** they **heard and knew the grace of God in truth**. There was numerical growth in the church at Colosse and, in addition, there was spiritual growth in the lives of the believers there.

It appears that great strides had been made in the first century, and that the gospel did reach Europe, Asia, and Africa, going farther than many persons have supposed. Still, there is no ground for thinking that it covered the entire earth. **The grace of God** is used here as a lovely description of the gospel message. What could more beautifully summarize the glad tidings than the wonderful truth of God's grace bestowed on

guilty men who deserve God's wrath!

1:7 The apostle clearly states that it was **from Epaphras** that the believers had heard the gospel message and had come to know it experientially in their lives. Paul commends Epaphras as a **dear fellow servant** and **a faithful minister of Christ on** their **behalf**. There was nothing of bitterness or jealousy about the Apostle Paul. It did not bother him to see another preacher receiving commendation. In fact, he was the first to express his appreciation for other servants of the Lord.

1:8 It was from Epaphras that Paul himself had heard of the Colossians' **love in the Spirit**. This was not a merely human affection, but it was that genuine **love** for the Lord and for His people which is created by the indwelling **Spirit** of God. This is the only reference to the Holy Spirit in this Epistle.

1:9 Having concluded this thanksgiving, Paul now begins to make specific intercession for the saints. We have already mentioned how broad were the apostle's prayer interests. We should further point out that his requests were always specifically suited to the need of the people of God in any particular location. He did not pray in generalities. Here he seems to make four separate requests for the Colossians: (1) spiritual insight; (2) a worthy walk; (3) abundant power; (3) a thankful spirit.

There was nothing mean or stingy about his requests. This is especially obvious in verses 9, 10, and 11 by his use of the words *all*, *fully*, and *every*. (1) **All wisdom and spiritual understanding** (v. 9). (2) "fully pleasing" (v. 10). (3) "Every good work" (v. 10). (4) "All might" (v. 11). (5) "All patience and longsuffering" (v. 11).

For this reason connects with the preceding verses. It means *because of Epaphras' report* (vv. 4, 5, 8). From the first time he had **heard** about these dear saints at Colosse and their faith, love, and hope, the apostle had made it his practice to pray for them. First, he prayed that they might **be filled with the knowledge of** God's **will in all wisdom and spiritual understanding**. He did not ask that they should be satisfied with the boasted knowledge of the Gnostics. He would have them enter into the full

knowledge of God's **will** for their lives as revealed in His word. This knowledge is not of a worldly or carnal nature; it is characterized by spiritual **wisdom and spiritual understanding** — **wisdom** to apply the knowledge in the best way, and **understanding** to see what agrees and what conflicts with God's will.

1:10 There is a very important connection between verse 10 and verse 9. Why did the Apostle Paul want the Colossians to be filled with the knowledge of God's will? Was it so they might become mighty preachers or sensational teachers? Was it so they might attract large followings to themselves, as the Gnostics sought to do? No, the true purpose of spiritual wisdom and understanding is to enable Christians to **walk worthy of the Lord, fully pleasing Him**. Here we have a very important lesson on the subject of guidance. God does not reveal His will to us in order to satisfy our curiosity. Neither is it intended to cater to our ambition or pride. Rather the Lord shows us His will for our lives in order that we might please Him in all that we do.

Being fruitful in every good work. Here is a helpful reminder that although a person is not saved *by* good works, he most certainly is saved *for* good works. Sometimes in emphasizing the utter worthlessness of good works in the salvation of souls, we may create the impression that Christians do not believe in good works. Nothing could be further from the truth! We learn in Ephesians 2:10 that "we are His workmanship, created in Christ Jesus for good works." Again, Paul wrote to Titus: "This is a faithful saying, and these things I want you to affirm constantly, that those who have believed in God should be careful to maintain good works" (Tit. 3:8).

Not only did Paul want them to bear fruit **in every good work**, but also to increase **in the knowledge of God**. How is this done? First of all, it is done through the diligent study of God's word. Then it is also found in obeying His teachings and serving Him faithfully. (The latter seems to be the prominent thought here.) As we do these things, we enter into a deeper **knowledge of** the Lord. "Then shall we know, if we follow on to know the Lord (Hos. 6:3, KJV).

Notice the repetition of words dealing with knowledge in chapter 1 and realize that there is a definite advance in thought with each use. In verse 6, they *"knew* the grace of God." In verse 9, they had "the *knowledge* of His will." In verse 10, they were "*increasing* in the *knowledge* of God." Perhaps we could say that the first refers to salvation, the second to study of the Scriptures, and the third to service and Christian living. Sound doctrine should lead to right conduct, which expresses itself in obedient service.

1:11 The apostle's third request is that the saints might be **strengthened with all might, according to His glorious power**. (Note the progression: *filled,* v. 9; *fruitful,* v. 10; *fortified,* v. 11.) The Christian life cannot be lived by mere human energy. It requires supernatural strength. Therefore Paul desires that the believers might know the power of the risen Son of God, and he furthermore desires that they should know this **according to His glorious power**. The request is not that this power might be *out of* His glorious power, but **according to** it. **His glorious power** is limitless and that is just the scope of the prayer. Peake writes: "The equipment with power is proportional not simply to the recipient's need, but to the Divine supply."[6]

Why did Paul want the Christians to have this power? Was it so they might go out and perform spectacular miracles? Was it so they might raise the dead, heal the sick, cast out demons? Once again the answer is "No." This power is needed so that the child of God may have **all patience and longsuffering with joy**. This deserves careful attention! In parts of Christendom today, great emphasis is placed upon so-called miracles, such as speaking in tongues, healing the sick, and similar sensational acts. But there is a greater miracle than all of these in the age in which we live: A child of God suffering patiently and thanking God in the midst of the trial!

In 1 Corinthians 13:4, longsuffering is connected with kindness; here with **joy**. We suffer because we cannot escape sharing the groaning of creation. To maintain **joy** within and kindness to others requires God's power, and is Christian victory. The difference between **patience** and **longsuffering** has been defined as the difference between enduring without complaint and enduring without retaliation. God's grace has achieved one of its greatest objects in the life of the believer who can suffer patiently and praise God in the midst of the fiery trial.

1:12 **Giving thanks** in this verse refers to the Colossians, not Paul (it is plural in the original). Paul is praying that they might not only be strengthened with all might but that they also might have a thankful spirit, that they might never fail to express their gratitude **to the Father**, who **qualified** them **to be partakers of the inheritance of the saints in the light**. As sons of Adam, we were not fit to enjoy the glories of heaven. In fact, if unsaved people could somehow be taken to heaven, they would not enjoy it, but would rather be in the deepest misery. Appreciation of heaven requires a fitness for it. Even as believers in the Lord Jesus, we do not have any fitness for heaven in ourselves. The only title to glory which we have is found in the Person of the Lord Jesus Christ:

> I stand upon His merit,
>   I know no other stand,
> Not e'en where glory dwelleth,
>   In Immanuel's land.
> — *Anne Ross Cousin*

When God saves someone, He instantly bestows on that person fitness for heaven. That fitness is Christ. Nothing can improve on that. Not even a long life of obedience and service here on earth makes a person more fit for heaven than he was the day he was saved. Our title to glory is found in His blood. While the inheritance is **in the light** and "reserved in heaven," we believers on earth have the Holy Spirit as the "guarantee of our inheritance." Therefore we can rejoice in what lies ahead for us, while enjoying even now the "firstfruits of the Spirit."

1:13 In making us "qualified . . . to be partakers of the inheritance of the saints in the light," God **has delivered us from the power of darkness and conveyed us into the kingdom of the Son of His love** (cf. 1 Jn. 2:11). This can be illustrated by the experience of the children of Israel, as recorded in Exodus. They had been living in Egypt, groaning under the lashes of the taskmasters there. By a marvelous act of divine intervention, God delivered them out of that fearful bondage and led them through the wilderness to the promised land. Similarly, as sinners we were in bondage to Satan, but through Christ we have been **delivered from** his clutches and now we are subjects of Christ's **kingdom**. Satan's kingdom is one of **darkness** — an absence of light, warmth, and joy; while the **kingdom** of Christ is one of **love**, which implies the presence of all three.

The kingdom of Christ is seen in Scripture in several different aspects. When He came to the earth the first time, He offered a literal kingdom to the nation of Israel. The Jews wanted deliverance from the Roman oppressor, but they did not want to repent of their sins. Christ could only reign over a people who were in proper spiritual relationship to Him. When that was made clear to them, they rejected their King and crucified Him. Since then, the Lord Jesus has gone back to heaven and we now have the kingdom in mystery form (Matt. 13). This means that the kingdom does not appear in visible form. The King is absent. But all who accept the Lord Jesus Christ during this present age acknowledge Him as their rightful Ruler, and thus they are subjects of His kingdom. In a coming day, the Lord Jesus will come back to earth, set up His kingdom with Jerusalem as capital, and reign for one thousand years. At the end of that time, Christ will put down all enemies under His feet and then deliver up the kingdom to God the Father. That will inaugurate the eternal kingdom, which will continue throughout eternity.

1:14 Having mentioned the kingdom of the Son of God's love, Paul now launches into one of the grandest passages in all the word of God on the Person and work of the Lord Jesus. It is hard for us to know whether he has finished his prayer, or whether it continues through these verses we are about to study. But it is not of great importance, because even if the following verses are not pure prayer, they certainly are pure worship.

Sturz has pointed out that "in this amazing passage which exalts Jesus Christ more than any other, His name does not appear even once in any form." While this is remarkable in one sense, yet it is not to be wondered at. For who else but our blessed Savior could ever fulfill the description which is given to us here? The passage reminds us of Mary's question to the gardener: "Sir, if You have carried Him away, tell me where You have laid Him, and I will take Him away" (John 20:15). She did not name Him. There *was* only one Person to her mind.

Christ is first presented as the One **in whom we have redemption . . . ,**[7] **the forgiveness of sins. Redemption** describes the act whereby we were bought from the slave market of sin. The Lord Jesus, as it were, put a price tag on us. How highly did He value us? He said, in effect, "I value them so highly that I am willing to shed My blood to purchase them." Since we have been purchased at such a tremendous cost, it should be clear to us that we no longer belong to ourselves; we have been bought with a price. Therefore we should not live our lives the way we choose. Borden of Yale pointed out that if we take our lives and do what we want with them, we are taking something that does not belong to us, and therefore we are thieves!

Not only has He redeemed us; He has given us **the forgiveness of sins**. This means that God has cancelled the debt which our sins incurred. The Lord Jesus Christ paid the penalty on the cross; it never needs to be paid again. The account is settled and closed, and God has not only forgiven, but He has removed our sins as far as the east is from the west (Ps. 103:12).

C. The Glories of Christ the Church's Head (1:15–23)

1:15 In the next four verses, we have the Lord Jesus described: (1) in His relationship to God (v. 15); (2) in His relationship to creation (vv. 16, 17); and (3) in His relationship to the church (v. 18).

The Lord is here described as **the image of the invisible God. Image** carries with it at least two ideas. First, it

conveys the thought that the Lord Jesus has enabled us to see what God is like. God is Spirit and is therefore invisible. But in the Person of Christ, God made Himself visible to mortal eyes. In that sense the Lord Jesus is **the image of the invisible God**. Whoever has seen Him has seen the Father (see John 14:9). But the word **image** also conveys the idea of "representative." God had originally placed Adam on the earth to represent His interests, but Adam failed. Therefore, God sent His only begotten Son into the world as His Representative to care for His interests and to reveal His heart of love to man. In that sense, He is the image of God. The same word **image** is used in 3:10, where believers are said to be the image of Christ.

Christ is also **the firstborn over all creation**, or "of every created being." What does this mean? Some false teachers suggest that the Lord Jesus is Himself a created being, that He was the first Person whom God ever made. Some of them are even willing to go so far as to admit that He is the greatest creature ever to come from the hand of God. But nothing could be more directly contrary to the teaching of the word of God.

The expression "firstborn" has at least three different meanings in Scripture. In Luke 2:7, it is used in *a literal sense*, where Mary brought forth her firstborn Son. There it means that the Lord Jesus was the first Child to whom she gave birth. In Exodus 4:22, on the other hand, it is used in *a figurative sense*. "Israel is My son, even My firstborn." In that verse there is no thought of an actual birth having taken place, but the Lord is using this word to describe the distinctive place which the nation of Israel had in His plans and purposes. Finally, in Psalm 89:27, the word "firstborn" is used to designate *a place of superiority*, of supremacy, of uniqueness. There God says that He will make David His firstborn, higher than the kings of the earth. David was actually the last-born son of Jesse according to the flesh. But God determined to give him a place of unique supremacy, primacy, and sovereignty.

Is not that exactly the thought of Colossians 1:15 — **the firstborn over all creation**? The Lord Jesus Christ is God's unique Son. In one sense all believers are sons of God, but the Lord Jesus is God's Son in a way that is not true of any other. He existed before all creation and occupies a position of supremacy over it. His is the rank of eminence and dominion. The expression **firstborn over all creation** has nothing to do with birth here. It simply means that He is God's Son by an eternal relationship. It is a title of priority of *position*, and not simply one of time.

1:16 False teachers use verse 15 (especially in the KJV) to teach that the Lord Jesus was a created being. Error can usually be refuted from the very passage of Scripture which the cultists use. That is the case here. Verse 16 states conclusively that the Lord Jesus is not a creature, but the very Creator. In this verse we learn that **all things** — the whole universe of things — **were created** not only **by Him** but **through Him and for Him**. Each of these prepositions conveys a different thought. First of all, we read that **by Him all things were created**. Here the thought is that the power to create was in His Being. He was the Architect. Later in the verse we learn that **all things were created through Him**. This speaks of Him as the Agent in creation. He was the Person of the Godhead through whom the creative act was performed. Also, all things were created **for Him**. He is the One for whom all things were created, the goal of creation.

Paul goes to great lengths to emphasize that **all things were created through** Christ, whether things **in heaven**, or things **on earth**. This leaves no loopholes for anyone to suggest that although He created some things, He Himself was created originally.

The apostle then goes on to state that the Lord's creation included things **visible and** things **invisible**. The word **visible** needs no explanation, but doubtless the Apostle Paul realized that when he said **invisible** he would arouse our curiosity. Therefore, he proceeds to give a break-down of what he means by things **invisible**. They include **thrones, dominions, principalities**, and **powers**. We believe that these terms refer to angelic beings, although we cannot distinguish between the different ranks of these intelligent beings.

The Gnostics taught that there were various ranks and classes of spirit beings between God and matter, and that Christ belonged to one of these classes. In our day the Spiritists claim that Jesus Christ is an advanced spirit of the sixth sphere. Jehovah's Witnesses teach that before our Lord came into the world, He was a created angel and none other than the archangel Michael! Here Paul vigorously refutes such absurd notions by stating in the clearest possible terms that the Lord Jesus Christ is the Creator of angels — in fact, of all beings, whether **visible** or **invisible**.

1:17 He is before all things, and in Him all things consist. Paul says, "He **is** before all things," not "He *was* before all things." The present tense is often used in the Bible to describe the timelessness of Deity. The Lord Jesus said, for instance: "Before Abraham was, I AM" (John 8:58).

Not only did the Lord Jesus exist before there was any creation, but also **in Him all things consist**. This means that He is the Sustainer of the universe and the Source of its perpetual motion. He controls the stars and the sun and the moon. Even while He was here on earth He was the One who was controlling the laws by which our universe functions in an orderly manner.

1:18 The dominion of the Lord Jesus not only covers the natural universe, but it also extends to the spiritual realm. **He is the head of the body, the church.** All believers in the Lord Jesus during this dispensation are formed into what is known as **the body** of Christ, or **the church**. Just as a human body is a vehicle by which the person expresses himself, so the Body of Christ is that vehicle which He has on earth by which He chooses to express Himself to the world. And **He is the head of** that **body**. The head speaks of guidance, dictation, control. He occupies the place of **pre-eminence** in the church.

He is **the beginning**. We understand this to mean **the beginning** of the new creation (see Rev. 3:14), the source of spiritual life. This is further explained by the use of the expression **the firstborn from the dead**. Here again we must be careful to emphasize that this does not mean that the Lord Jesus was the first to rise from the dead. There were cases of resurrection in the OT as well as in the NT. But the Lord Jesus was the first to rise from the dead *to die no more*, He was the first to rise with a glorified body, and He rose as the Head of a new creation. His resurrection is unique, and is the pledge that all who trust in Him will also rise. It proclaims Him as supreme in the spiritual creation.

Alfred Mace put it well:

> Christ cannot be second anywhere. He is "firstborn of every creature," because He has created everything (Col. 1:15, 16). He is also firstborn from the dead in connection with a redeemed and heavenly family. Thus creation and redemption hand the honors of supremacy to Him because of Who He is and of what He has done; "that in all things He might have the preeminence." He is first everywhere.[8]

The Lord Jesus has thus a double preeminence — first in creation, and then in the church. God has decreed that in *all things* **HE may have the preeminence.** What an answer this is to those who, in Paul's day (and our own), would seek to rob Christ of His deity, and to make of Him only a created being, however exalted!

As we read **that in all things He may have the preeminence**, it is only proper that we should ask ourselves, "Does He have the preeminence in my life?"

1:19 Darby translates verse 19 as follows: "For in Him all the fullness of the Godhead was pleased to dwell." The King James tradition could make it sound as if at some point in time the Father (notice italics for words not in the Greek) was pleased to make all fullness dwell in the Son. The real meaning is that **the fullness** of the Godhead always dwelt in Christ.

Gnostic heretics taught that Christ was a kind of "halfway house" to God, a necessary link in the chain. But there were other, better links on ahead. "Go on from Him," they urged, "and you will reach the fullness." "No," Paul answers, "Christ is Himself the complete fullness!"

All fullness *dwells* in Christ. The word for **dwell** here means to dwell permanently,[9] and not simply to visit temporarily.

1:20 Verse 19 is connected with verse 20 as follows: "For it pleased *the Father* **by Him** (Christ) **to reconcile all things to Himself . . . having made**

peace through the blood of His cross." In other words, it was not only the Godhead's good pleasure that all fullness should dwell in Christ (v. 19), but also that Christ should **reconcile all things to Himself**.

There are two reconciliations mentioned in this chapter: (1) The reconciliation of **things** (v. 20), and (2) the reconciliation of persons (v. 21). The first is still future, whereas the second is past for all who have believed in Christ.

RECONCILIATION

To reconcile means to restore to a right relationship or standard, or to make peace where formerly there was enmity. The Bible never speaks of God as needing to be reconciled to man, but always of man being reconciled to God. The carnal mind is enmity toward God (Rom. 8:7), and because of this, man needs to be reconciled.

When sin entered the world, man became estranged from God. He adopted an attitude of hostility toward God. Therefore, he needed to be reconciled.

But sin affected all of creation, not just the human family.

1. Certain of the angels had sinned sometime in the past. (However, there is no indication in God's word that these angels will ever be reconciled. They are "reserved in everlasting chains under darkness for the judgment of the great day," Jude 6.) In Job 4:18, Eliphaz states that God charged His angels with folly.

2. The animal creation was affected by the entrance of sin: "For the earnest expectation of the creation eagerly waits for the revealing of the sons of God. For the creation was subjected to futility. . . . For we know that the whole creation groans and labors with birth pangs together until now" (Rom. 8:19–22). The fact that animals suffer sickness, pain, and death is evidence that they are not exempt from the curse of sin.

3. The ground was cursed by God after Adam sinned (Gen. 3:17). This is evidenced by weeds, thorns, and thistles.

4. In the book of Job, Bildad tells us that even the stars are not pure in God's sight (Job 25:5), so apparently sin has affected the stellar world.

5. Hebrews 9:23 says that things in heaven itself needed to be purified. We do not know all that is meant by this, but perhaps it suggests that heavenly things have been defiled through the presence of Satan, who has access to God as the accuser of the brethren (Job 1:6, 7; Rev. 12:10). Some think this passage refers to the dwelling place of God; others to the stellar heavens. The latter suggests that it is in the stellar spaces that Satan has access to God. In any case, all agree that the throne of God is certainly not defiled by sin.

One of the purposes of the death of Christ was to make possible the reconciliation of persons and things to God. In order to do this, He had to remove the cause of enmity and alienation. This He effectively did by settling the sin question to God's entire satisfaction.

The scope of reconciliation is indicated in Colossians 1, as follows. (1) All who believe on the Lord Jesus Christ are already reconciled to God (v. 21). Although Christ's reconciling work is sufficient for all mankind, it is only effective for those who avail themselves of it. (2) Eventually all things will be reconciled, whether things on earth or things in heaven (v. 20). This refers to the animal creation, and to inanimate things that have been defiled by sin. However, it does not refer to Satan, to other fallen angels, or to unbelieving men. Their eternal doom is clearly pronounced in the Scriptures.

Reconciliation is not said to extend to "things under the earth." There is a difference between reconciliation and subjugation. The latter is described in Philippians 2:10: "That at the name of Jesus every knee should bow, of those in heaven, and of those on earth, and of those under the earth." Or, as Darby translates it, "of heavenly and earthly and infernal beings." All created beings, even fallen angels, will eventually be compelled to bow to the Lord Jesus, but this does not mean that they will be reconciled. We emphasize this because Colossians 1:20 has been used to teach the false doctrine of universal salvation — namely, that Satan himself, fallen angels, and unbelieving men will all be reconciled to God eventually. Our passage limits the extent of reconciliation by the phrase things on earth or things in heaven. "Things under the earth," or infernal things, are not included. ‡

1:21 Paul reminds the Colossians that reconciliation in their case was already an accomplished fact. Before their conversion, the Colossians had been Gentile sinners, **alienated** from God and **enemies** of His in their minds because of their **wicked works** (Eph. 4:17, 18). They desperately needed to be reconciled, and the Lord Jesus Christ, in His matchless grace, had taken the initiative.

1:22 He reconciled them **in the body of His flesh through death**. It was not by His life but by His **death**. The expression **the body of His flesh** simply means that the Lord Jesus effected reconciliation by dying on the cross in a real human **body** (not as a spirit being, which the Gnostics claimed Him to be). Compare Hebrews 2:14–16, where Christ's Incarnation is declared a necessity in order to effect redemption. The Gnostic concept denied this.

The wonderful result of this reconciliation is expressed in the words **to present you holy, and blameless, and above reproach in His sight**. What marvelous grace, that ungodly sinners can be delivered from their past evil life and conveyed into such a realm of blessing!

Well might C. R. Erdman say: "In Christ is found a God who is near, who cares, who hears, who pities and who saves."[10]

The full efficacy of Christ's reconciliation with regard to His people will be seen in a coming day when we are presented to God the Father without sin, stain, or any charge against us, and when, as worshipers, we shall gladly acknowledge Christ as the Worthy One (Rev. 5).

1:23 Now the Apostle Paul adds one of those if[11] passages which have proved very disconcerting to many children of God. On the surface, the verse seems to teach that our continued salvation depends on our continuing **in the faith**. If this is so, how can this verse be reconciled with other portions of the word of God, such as John 10:28, 29, which declare that no sheep of Christ can ever perish?

In seeking to answer this question,

we would like to state at the outset that the eternal security of the believer is a blessed truth which is set forth clearly in the pages of the NT. However, the Scriptures also teach, as in this verse, that true faith always has the quality of permanence, and that one who has really been born of God will go on faithfully to the end. Continuance is a proof of reality. Of course there is always the danger of backsliding, but a Christian falls only to rise again (Prov. 24:16). He does not forsake the faith.

The Spirit of God has seen fit to put many of these so-called "if" passages in the word of God in order to challenge all who profess the name of Christ as to the reality of their profession. We would not want to say anything that might dull the sharp edge of these passages. As someone has said: "These 'ifs' in Scripture look on professing Christians here in the world and they come as healthy tests to the soul."

Pridham comments on these challenging verses as follows:

> The reader will find, on a careful study of the Word, that it is the habit of the Spirit to accompany the fullest and most absolute statements of grace by warnings which imply a ruinous failure on the part of some who nominally stand in faith. . . . Warnings which grate harshly on the ears of insincere profession are drunk willingly as medicine by the godly soul. . . . The aim of all such teaching as we have here is to encourage faith, and condemn, by anticipation, reckless and self-confident professors.[12]

Doubtless with the Gnostics primarily in mind, the apostle is urging the Colossians **not** to be **moved away from the hope** that accompanies **the gospel**, or which the **gospel** inspires. They should **continue in the faith** which they learned from Epaphras, **grounded and steadfast.**

Again Paul speaks of the gospel as having been **preached to every creature** (or "all creation") **under heaven**. The gospel goes out to all creation, but it has not as yet reached literally every creature. Paul is arguing the worldwide proclamation of the gospel as a testimonial to its genuineness. He sees in this the evidence that it is adaptable to the needs of mankind everywhere. The verse does not mean that every person in the world at that time had heard the gospel. It was not a fact accomplished, but a process going on. Also, the gospel had reached to all the Bible world, that is, the Mediterranean world.

Paul speaks of himself as **a minister**, a Latin word that simply means "a servant." It has nothing of officialdom about it. It does not denote a lofty office so much as humble service.

D. The Ministry Committed to Paul (1:24–29)

1:24 The last six verses of chapter 1 describe Paul's ministry. First of all, it was carried out in an atmosphere of suffering. Writing from prison, Paul can say that he **now** rejoices **in** his **sufferings for** the saints, that is, on their account. As a servant of the Lord Jesus Christ, he was called upon to endure untold hardships, persecutions, and **afflictions**. These to him were a privilege — the privilege of filling up that which was left behind of **the afflictions of Christ**. What does the apostle mean by this? First of all, this cannot refer to the *atoning* sufferings of the Lord Jesus Christ on the cross. Those were finished once and for all, and no man could ever share in them. But there is a sense in which the Lord Jesus still suffers. When Saul of Tarsus was struck to the ground on the road to Damascus, he heard a voice from heaven saying, "Saul, Saul, why do you persecute Me?" Saul had not been consciously persecuting the Lord — he had only been persecuting the Christians. He learned, however, that in persecuting believers, he was persecuting their Savior. The Head in heaven feels the sufferings of His Body on earth.

Thus, the Apostle Paul looks on all the suffering that Christians are required to go through for the sake of the Lord Jesus as being part of the sufferings of Christ which still remain. They include suffering for righteousness' sake, suffering for His sake (bearing His reproach), and for the gospel's sake.

But **the afflictions of Christ** refer not only to sufferings *for* Christ. They also describe *the same kind of* sufferings that the Savior endured when He was here, though far less in degree.

The afflictions endured by the apostle

in his **flesh** were **for the sake of** Christ's **body**, namely, **the church**. The sufferings of unsaved people are, in a sense, purposeless. There is no high dignity attached to them. They are only a foretaste of the pangs of hell to be endured forever. But not so the sufferings of Christians. When they suffer for Christ, Christ in a very real way suffers with them.

1:25 Of which I became a minister. Paul had already used this expression at the close of verse 23. Now he repeats it. However, there is a difference in these two usages. The apostle had a twofold ministry: first, he was commissioned to preach the gospel (v. 23); and secondly, he was sent forth to teach the marvelous mystery of the church (v. 25). There is a real lesson in this for every true servant of Christ. We are not expected simply to lead men to Christ by the gospel and then abandon them to get along as best they can. Rather, we are expected to direct our evangelistic efforts to the formation of local NT churches where the converts can be built up in their most holy faith, including the truth of the church. The Lord wants His babes to be directed to feeding stations where they will be nourished and where they can grow.

Thus in Colossians 1 we have seen (1) Christ's twofold preeminence, (2) Christ's twofold reconciliation, and (3) Paul's twofold ministry. Here in verse 25, when Paul says, **"of which I became a minister,"** he is referring to his ministry with regard to the church and not the gospel. This is clear from the expression which follows: **According to the stewardship** (or "dispensation") **from God given to me for you**. A steward is one who cares for the interests or property of another. Paul was a steward in the sense that the great truth of the church was entrusted to him in a very special way. While the mystery of the Body of Christ was not revealed to him alone, yet he was chosen as the one who would carry this precious truth to the Gentiles. It includes the unique position of the church in its relation to Christ and the dispensations, with its constitution, its distinctive hope and destiny, and the many other truths concerning its life and order which God gave to Paul and the other apostles.

When he says, **which was given to me for you**, he is thinking of the Colossians as Gentile believers. The Apostle Peter had been sent to preach to the Jewish people, while Paul had been entrusted with a similar mission to the Gentiles.

One of the most difficult expressions in this chapter is **to fulfill the word of God**. Exactly what does Paul mean by this? First of all, we know that he does not mean that he completed the word of God by adding the last book to it. As far as we know, the book of Revelation, written by John, was the last book to be added to the NT in point of time. In what sense, then, did Paul **fulfill** or complete **the word of God**?

First of all, **to fulfill** may mean to declare fully, to make known. Thus, Paul had declared the whole counsel of God. We would suggest secondly that he fulfilled the word of God doctrinally. The great truth of the mystery forms the capstone of the NT revelation. In a very real way, it completes the circle of subjects that are covered in the NT. While other books were written later than Paul's, yet they do not contain any great mysteries of the faith that are not found in the writings of the Apostle Paul. In a very real sense the revelations concerning the mystery of the church filled up the word of God. Nothing that was added later was new truth in the same sense.

1:26 That Paul's fulfilling of the word of God had to do with **the mystery** is borne out in this verse, namely, **the mystery which has been hidden from ages and from generations, but now has been revealed to His saints**. In the NT, a mystery is a truth not previously revealed, but now made known to the sons of men through the apostles and prophets of the NT. It is a truth that man could never have arrived at by his own intelligence but which God has graciously deigned to make known.

This verse is one of the many in the NT which teach that the truth of the church was not known in the OT period. It had **been hidden from ages and from generations** (Eph. 3:2–13; Rom. 16:25–27). Thus it is wrong to speak of the church as having begun with Adam or Abraham. The church began on the Day of Pentecost, and the truth of the church was revealed by the apostles. The church in the NT is not the same as Israel in the Old. It is something that never previously existed.

Israel began with God calling Abraham out from Ur of the Chaldees, giving up the rest of the nations to their sins and idolatry. He made a nation out of Abraham's seed, distinct from all others and separate from them. The church is the reverse of this, and is a union of believers from all races and nationalities into one Body, morally and spiritually separated from all others. That the church is not the continuation of Israel can be seen from a number of things, one being the figure of the "olive tree" which Paul uses in Romans 11 to show that the nation of Israel retains its identity, though the individual Jew who believes in Christ becomes part of the church (Col. 3:10, 11).

1:27 The truth of **this mystery** may be summarized as follows: (1) The church is the Body of Christ. All true believers are members of the Body, and are destined to share Christ's glory forever. (2) The Lord Jesus is the Head of the Body, providing its life, nourishment, and direction. (3) Jews have no preference as to admission to the church; neither are Gentiles at any disadvantage. Both Jew and Gentile become members of the Body through faith and form one new man (Eph. 2:15; 3:6). That Gentiles could be saved was not a hidden truth in the OT; but that converted Gentiles would be fellow members of the Body of Christ, to be His companions in glory, and to reign with Him, was a truth never previously known.

The particular aspect of the mystery which Paul is emphasizing in verse 27 is that the Lord Jesus is willing to dwell within the Gentile heart. **Christ in you, the hope of glory.** This was spoken to the Colossians, who were Gentiles. F. B. Meyer exclaims: "That He should dwell in the heart of a child of Abraham was deemed a marvelous act of condescension, but that He should find a home in the heart of a Gentile was incredible." And yet that is exactly what was involved in the mystery — "that the Gentiles should be fellow heirs, of the same body, and partakers of His promise in Christ through the gospel" (Eph. 3:6). To

emphasize the importance of this truth, the apostle does not merely say "this mystery" or "the glory of this mystery," but **the riches of the glory of this mystery**. He piles words upon words in order to impress his readers with the fact that this is a glorious truth that deserves their closest attention.

Which is Christ in you, the hope of glory. The indwelling **Christ** is the believers' **hope of glory**. We have no other title to heaven than the Savior Himself. The fact that He indwells us makes heaven as sure as if we were already there.

1:28 The expression **Him we preach** is significant. The **Him**, of course, refers back to the Lord Jesus Christ (v. 27). Paul is saying that he preached a Person. He did not spend his time on politics or philosophy, but concentrated on the Lord Jesus Himself, because he realized that Christianity is Christ. **Warning every man and teaching every man in all wisdom, that we may present every man perfect in Christ Jesus**. Here we have further insight into the ministry of the beloved apostle. It was a man-to-man ministry. He warned the unsaved of the awful wrath to come, and he taught the saints the great truths of the Christian faith.

Then we see the emphasis which he placed on follow-up work. He felt a real sense of responsibility toward those whom he had pointed to the Savior. He was not satisfied to see souls saved and then to pass on. He wanted to **present every man perfect in Christ Jesus**. Paul pictures himself as a priest offering up sacrifices to God. The sacrifices here are men and women. In what condition does he offer them to the Lord? Are they weak or mere babes in Christ? No, he wants them to be mature, full-grown, adult Christians. He wants them to be well-grounded in the truth. Do we share a similar burden for those whom we have led to Christ?

1:29 It was toward this goal that the apostle labored, as well as all the other apostles. And yet he realized that he was not doing this in his own strength, but **according to His working which** worked **in him mightily**. In other words, he realized that it was only as he was empowered by the Lord that he was able to serve Him at all. He was conscious of the fact that the Lord was **working in** him **mightily** as he went from place to place planting churches and feeding the saints of God.

Verses 28 and 29 are especially helpful in Phillips' translation:

> So, naturally, we proclaim Christ. We warn everyone we meet, and we teach everyone we can, all that we know about Him, so that, if possible, we may bring every man up to his full maturity in Christ. This is what I am working at all the time, with all the strength that God gives me.

E. Christ's Sufficiency Against the Perils of Philosophy, Legalism, Mysticism, and Asceticism (2:1–23)

2:1 This verse is closely linked with the last two verses of chapter 1. There the Apostle Paul had been describing his strivings, by teaching and preaching, to present every believer mature in Christ. Here his strivings are of a different nature. Now they are spoken of as **great conflict** in prayer. And here this **great conflict** is in behalf of those he had never met. From the first day he had heard of the Colossians, he had prayed for them as well as for **those in** the neighboring city of **Laodicea**, and for other Christians whom he had not as yet met (see Rev. 3:14–19 for the later sad state of the church there).

Verse 1 is a comfort to those who are never privileged to engage in public ministry. It teaches that we need not be limited by what we can do in the presence of people. We can serve the Lord in the privacy of our rooms on our knees. If we do serve publicly, our effectiveness depends largely on our private devotions before God.

2:2 The exact content of Paul's prayer is given in this verse. The first part of the prayer is **that their hearts may be encouraged**. The Colossians were in danger of the teachings of the Gnostics. Therefore, **encouraged** here means confirmed or strengthened.

The second part of the prayer is that they might be **knit together in love**. If the saints went on in happy, loving fellowship with one another, they would

present a solid flank against the onslaughts of the foe. Also, if their hearts were warm in love to Christ, He would reveal to them the deeper truths of the Christian faith. It is a well-known principle of Scripture that the Lord reveals His secrets to those who are close to Him. John, for instance, was the apostle who leaned on Jesus' chest, and it was no coincidence that he was also the one to whom the great revelation of Jesus Christ was given.

Next Paul prayed that they might enter into **all** the **riches of the full assurance of understanding**. The more they entered into an **understanding** of the Christian faith, the more fully convinced they would be of its truthfulness. The more firmly grounded the Christians were in the faith, the less would be the danger of their being led away by the false teachings of the day.

The expression **full assurance** is used three times in the NT. (1) Full assurance of *faith* — we rest on God's word, His testimony to us (Heb. 10:22). (2) Full assurance of *understanding* — we know and are assured (Col. 2:2). (3) Full assurance of *hope* — we press on with confidence as to the outcome (Heb. 6:11).

The climax of Paul's prayer is found in the words **to the knowledge of the mystery of God, both of the Father and of Christ**.

What does Paul mean when he says that they may know **the mystery of God . . . and of Christ**? He is still referring to the truth of the church — Christ, the Head of the Body, and all believers members of the Body. But the particular aspect of the mystery which he has in mind is the headship of Christ. He is anxious that the saints should acknowledge this truth. He knows that if they realize the greatness of their Head, they will not be drawn away by Gnosticism or the other evil cults that threatened them.

Paul wants the saints to use Christ, to utilize His resources, to draw upon Him in every emergency. He wants them to see that Christ, who, as Alfred Mace puts it:

> . . . is *in* His people, is possessed of every attribute of deity, and of infinite, unutter-

able, measureless resources, so that they did not need to go outside of Him for anything. "To them God willed to make known what are THE RICHES of the glory of THIS MYSTERY among the Gentiles: WHICH IS CHRIST IN YOU, the hope of glory" (Col. 1:27). The truth of this, known in power, is the sure and certain antidote for Laodicean pride, rationalistic theology, traditional religion, demon-possessed spiritualistic mediums, and every other form of opposition or counterfeit.[13]

2:3   In Christ **are hidden all the treasures of wisdom and knowledge**. The Gnostics, of course, boasted of an understanding far surpassing anything found within the pages of divine revelation. Their wisdom was something in addition to what was found in Christ or Christianity. But here Paul is saying that **all the treasures of wisdom and knowledge** are hidden in Christ, the Head. Therefore, there is no need for believers to go beyond what is written in the Scriptures. **The treasures** in Christ are hidden from unbelief; and even the believer needs to know Christ intimately to enter into them.

Christ is *in* the believer as Head, center and resource. By the vastness of His unsearchable riches, by the pre-eminent wealth of His infinite greatness, by all that He is essentially as God, by all He has accomplished in creation and in redemption, by His personal, moral and official glories, He crowds out the whole army of professors, authors, mediums, critics, and all others arrayed against Him. (Selected)

There is more in this verse than meets the eye. All **knowledge** is found in Christ. He is the incarnation of truth. He said: "I am the way, the truth, and the life." Nothing that is true will ever conflict with His words or His works. The difference between **knowledge** and **wisdom** has often been explained as follows: **Knowledge** is the understanding of truth, whereas **wisdom** is the ability to apply what truth has been learned.

2:4   Because all wisdom and knowledge are in Christ, Christians should not be deluded with the **persuasive words** of false cultists. If a man does not have the truth, then he must seek to attract a following through the clever presentation of his message. That is exactly what her-

etics always do. They argue from probabilities and build a system of teaching on deductions. On the other hand, if a man is preaching the truth of God, then he does not need to depend on such things as eloquence or clever arguments. The truth is its own best argument and, like a lion, will defend itself.

2:5   This verse shows how intimately aware the Apostle Paul was of the problems and perils facing the Colossians. He pictures himself as a military officer looking over the assembled troops as they stand ready for inspection. The two words **order** and **steadfastness** are military terms. The first describes the orderly array of a company of soldiers, whereas the second pictures the solid flank which is presented by them. Paul rejoices as he sees (**in spirit** though not in body) how the Colossians were standing true to the word of God.

2:6   Now he encourages them to go on in the same way in which they had originally begun, that is, by faith. **As you therefore have received Christ Jesus the Lord, so walk in Him.** The emphasis here seems to be on the word **Lord**. In other words, they had acknowledged that in Him there was complete sufficiency. He was enough, not only for salvation, but for the whole of their Christian life. Now Paul urges the saints to go on acknowledging the lordship of Christ. They should not stray from Him by accepting the teachings of men, however convincing they may sound. The word **walk** is one that is often used of the Christian life. It speaks of action and progress. You cannot walk and remain in the same place. So it is in the Christian life; we are either going forward or backward.

2:7   Paul first uses an expression from agriculture, then one from architecture. The expression **rooted** refers to what took place at the time of our conversion. It is as if the Lord Jesus Christ is the soil and we find our roots in Him, drawing all our nourishment from Him. This emphasizes, too, the importance of having our roots deep, so that when opposing winds blow, we will not be moved (Matt. 13:5, 20, 21).

Then Paul switches to the figure of a building. **Built up in Him.** Here the

Lord Jesus is suggested as the foundation, and we are being **built** on **Him**, the Rock of Ages (Luke 6:47–49). We were **rooted** once for all, but we are being **built up**.

And established in the faith. The word **established** might also be translated "confirmed," and the thought is that this is a process that goes on continuously through the Christian life. The Colossians had been taught the fundamentals of Christianity by Epaphras. As they continued on in the Christian pathway, these precious truths would be continually confirmed in their hearts and lives. Conversely, 2 Peter 1:9 indicates that failure to progress in spiritual life results in doubt and loss of the joy and blessing of the gospel.

Paul concludes this description with the words **abounding in it with thanksgiving**. He does not want Christians to be coldly doctrinal, but he wants their hearts to be captivated by the marvelous truths of the gospel so that they in turn will overflow in praise and thankfulness to the Lord. **Thanksgiving** for the blessings of Christianity is a wonderful antidote against the poison of false doctrine.

Arthur Way translates verse 7 as follows: "Be like trees fast-rooted, like buildings steadily rising, feeling His presence about you, and even (for to this your education has led up) unshaken in your faith, and overflowing with thanksgiving."

2:8 Now Paul is ready to deal directly with the specific errors that had threatened the believers in the Lycus Valley, where Colosse was situated. **Beware lest anyone cheat you through philosophy and empty deceit.** False teachings seek to rob men of what is worthwhile, but offer nothing substantial in its place. **Philosophy** means literally "the love of wisdom." It is not evil in itself, but becomes evil when men seek wisdom apart from the Lord Jesus Christ. Here the word is used to describe man's attempt to find out by his own intellect and research those things which can only be known by divine revelation (1 Cor. 2:14). It is evil because it exalts human reason above God and worships the creature more than the Creator. It is characteristic of the liberals of our day,

with their boasted intellectualism and rationalism. **Empty deceit** refers to the false and valueless teachings of those who profess to offer secret truths to an inner circle of people. There is really nothing to it. But it gathers a following by catering to man's curiosity. Also it appeals to their vanity by making them members of the "select few."

The **philosophy and empty deceit** which Paul attacks are **according to the tradition of men, according to the basic principles of the world, and not according to Christ. The tradition of men** here means religious teachings which have been invented by men but which have no true foundation in the Scriptures. (A tradition is a fixation of a custom which began as a convenience, or which suited some particular circumstance.) **The basic principles of the world** refer to Jewish rituals, ceremonies, and ordinances by which men hoped to obtain God's favor.

> The Law of Moses had served its purpose as a type of things to come. It had been a "primary school" to prepare the heart for the coming Christ. To return to it now would be to play into the hands of the false teachers who conspired to use a discarded system to displace the Son of God. (Daily Notes of the Scripture Union)

Paul would have the Colossians test all teaching by whether or not it agreed with the doctrines of **Christ**. Phillips' translation of this verse is helpful: "Be careful that nobody spoils your faith through intellectualism or high sounding nonsense. Such stuff is at best founded on men's ideas of the nature of the world, and disregards Christ!"

2:9 It is marvelous to see how the Apostle Paul constantly brings his readers back to the Person of Christ. Here he gives one of the most sublime and unmistakable verses in the Bible on the deity of the Lord Jesus Christ. **For in Him dwells all the fullness of the Godhead bodily.** Note the intended accumulation of evidence as to the fact that Christ is God. First of all, you have His deity: "For in Him dwells . . . **the Godhead bodily.**" Secondly, you have what someone has called the amplitude of deity: "For in Him dwells *the fullness of* **the Godhead bodily.**" Finally, you have what has been called the absolute completeness of deity: "For in Him dwells *all* **the fullness of the Godhead bodily.**" (This is an effective answer to the various forms of Gnosticism that deny the deity of the Lord Jesus — Christian Science, Jehovah's Witnesses, Unity, Theosophy, Christadelphianism, etc.)

Vincent says: "The verse contains two distinct assertions: (1) That the fulness of the Godhead eternally dwells in Christ . . . ; (2) The fulness of the Godhead dwells in Him . . . as one having a human body."[14] Many of the cults mentioned above would admit that some form of divinity dwelt in Jesus. This verse is identifying **all the fullness of the Godhead** with Him, in His manhood. The argument is clear — if there is such a sufficiency in the Person of the Lord Jesus Christ, why be satisfied with teachings which slight or ignore Him?

2:10 The apostle is still trying to impress on his readers the all-sufficiency of the Lord Jesus Christ, and of the perfect standing which they have **in Him**. It is a marvelous expression of the grace of God that the truth of verse 10 should follow that of verse 9. In Christ dwells all the fullness of the Godhead bodily, and the believer is **complete in Him**. This does not mean, of course, that the believer is indwelt by all the fullness of the Godhead. The only One of whom that was ever true, or ever shall be true, is the Lord Jesus Christ. But what this verse teaches is that the believer has in Christ all that is needed for life and godliness. Spurgeon gives a good definition of our completeness. He says we are (1) Complete without the aid of Jewish ceremony. (2) Complete without the help of philosophy. (3) Complete without the inventions of superstition. (4) Complete without human merit.

This One in whom we are complete **is the head of all principality and power**. The Gnostics were greatly taken up with the subject of angels. Mention of this is made later on in this chapter. But Christ is head over all the angelic beings, and it would be ridiculous to be occupied with angels when we can have the Creator of angels as the object of our affections and enjoy communion with Him.

2:11 **Circumcision** was the typical rite of Judaism. It is a minor surgical operation in which the knife was applied to the flesh of the male child. Spiritually it signified death to the flesh, or a putting aside of the evil, corrupt, unregenerate nature of man. Unfortunately, the Jewish people became occupied with the literal ceremony but neglected its spiritual meaning. In trying to achieve favor with God through ceremonies and good works, they were saying in effect that there was something in human flesh which could please God. Nothing could be further from the truth.

In the verse before us physical circumcision is not in view, but rather that spiritual **circumcision** which is true of everyone who has put his faith and trust in the Lord Jesus. This is clear from the expression **the circumcision made without hands**. What the verse is teaching is this: Every believer is circumcised **by the circumcision of Christ. The circumcision of Christ** refers to His death on the cross of Calvary. The thought is that when the Lord Jesus died, the believer died also. He died to sin (Rom. 6:11), to the law, to self (Gal. 2:20), and to the world (Gal. 6:14). (This circumcision was "made without hands" in the sense that human hands can have no part in it by way of merit. Man cannot deserve or earn it. It is God's work.) Thus he has put off **the body of the sins of the flesh**. In other words, when a person is saved, he becomes associated with Christ in His death, and renounces any hope of earning or deserving salvation through fleshly efforts. Samuel Ridout writes: "Our Lord's death has not only put away the fruit, but condemned and set aside the very root which bore it."

2:12 Paul now turns from the subject of circumcision to that of **baptism**. Just as circumcision speaks of death to the flesh, even so **baptism** speaks of the burial of the old man. Thus we read: **Buried with Him in baptism, in which you also were raised with Him through faith in the working of God, who raised Him from the dead.** The teaching here is that we have not only died with Christ, but we have been **buried with Him**. This was typified at our baptism. It took place at the time of our conversion, but we expressed it in public confession when we went into the waters of baptism. Baptism is burial, the burial of all that we were as children of Adam. In baptism we acknowledge that nothing in ourselves could ever please God, and so we are putting the flesh out of God's sight forever. But it does not end with burial. Not only have we been crucified with Christ and buried with Him, but we have also risen with Him to walk in newness of life. All of this takes place at the time of conversion. It is **through faith in the working of God, who raised** Christ **from the dead**.

2:13 The Apostle Paul now makes the application of all this to the Colossians. Before their conversion, they had been **dead in** their **trespasses**. This means that because of their sins, they were spiritually dead toward God. It does not mean that their spirits were dead, but simply that there was no motion in their spirits toward God and there was nothing they could do to win God's favor. Not only were they **dead in** sins, but also Paul speaks of **the uncircumcision of** their **flesh. Uncircumcision** is often used in the NT to describe the Gentile peoples. The Colossians had been Gentiles. They had not been members of God's earthly people, the Jews. Therefore, they had been in a position of distance from God, and had given full rein to the flesh with its lusts. But when they heard the gospel and believed on the Lord Jesus Christ, they had been **made alive together with** Christ, and **all** their **trespasses** had been **forgiven**. In other words, what had really happened to the Colossians was that their whole lifestyle had been changed. Their history as sinners had come to an end, and now they were new creatures in Christ Jesus. They were living on the resurrection side. Therefore they should say "goodbye" to all that characterized them as men in the flesh.

2:14 Paul now goes on to describe something else that was included in the work of Christ. **Having wiped out the handwriting of requirements that was against us, which was contrary to us. And He has taken it out of the way, having nailed it to the cross. The handwriting of requirements that was against us** describes the law. In a sense, the Ten Commandments were against us, condemning us because we did not keep them perfectly. But the Apostle Paul is thinking not only about the Ten Commandments, but also about the ceremonial law that was given to Israel. In the ceremonial law, there were all kinds of commandments with regard to holy days, foods, and other religious rituals. These were all a part of the prescribed religion of the Jews. They pointed forward to the coming of the Lord Jesus. They were shadows of His Person and His work. In His death on the cross, He took all this out **of the way**, nailing it **to the cross** and canceling it as a bill is canceled when the debt is paid. As Meyer put it: "By the death of Christ on the cross, the law which condemned men lost its penal authority, inasmuch as Christ by His death endured for man the curse of the law and became the end of the law."[15] Kelly summarizes neatly: "The law is not dead, but we have died to it."

Paul's language here very likely refers to an ancient practice of nailing the written evidence of a canceled debt in a public place as a notice to all that the creditor had no more claim on the debtor.

2:15 By His death on the cross and His subsequent resurrection and ascension, the Lord Jesus also conquered evil **powers**, making **a public spectacle of them**, and **triumphing over them**. We believe that this is the same triumph that is described in Ephesians 4, where the Lord Jesus is said to have led captivity captive. His death, burial, resurrection, and ascension were a glorious triumph over all the hosts of hell and of Satan. As He passed up through the atmosphere on His way back to heaven, He passed through the very domain of the one who is the prince of the power of the air.

Perhaps this verse carries special comfort for those who have been converted from demonism but who might still be obsessed with a fear of evil spirits. There is nothing to fear if we are in Christ, because He has **disarmed principalities and powers**.

2:16 Once again the Apostle Paul is ready to make the application of what he has just been stating. We might summarize the foregoing as follows: The Colossians had died to all efforts to please God by the flesh. They had not only died, but they had been buried with Christ and had risen with Christ to a new kind of life. Therefore they should be done forever with the Judaizers and Gnostics, who were trying to draw them back to the very things to which the Colossians had died. **So let no one judge you in food or in drink, or regarding a festival or a new moon or sabbaths.** All human religions place men under bondage to ordinances, rules, regulations, and a religious calendar. This calendar usually includes annual observances (holy days), monthly festivals (new moons), or weekly holidays (sabbaths). The expression **"Therefore let no one judge you"** means that a Christian cannot be justly condemned by others if, for instance, he eats pork, or if he fails to observe religious festivals or holy days. Some false cults, such as Spiritism, insist on their members abstaining from meats. For centuries Roman Catholics were not supposed to eat meat on Friday. Many churches require abstinence from certain foods during Lent. Others, like the Mormons, say that a person cannot be a member in good standing if he drinks tea or coffee. Still others, notably the Seventh Day Adventists, insist that a person must keep the Sabbath in order to please God. The Christian is not under such ordinances. For a fuller treatment of the law, the Sabbath, and legalism, see the excurses at Matthew 5:18, 12:8, and Galatians 6:18.

2:17   The Jewish religious observances were **a shadow of things to come, but the substance** (or body) **is** Christ's. They were instituted in the OT as a pre-picture. For instance, the Sabbath was given as a type of the rest which would be the portion of all who believed on the Lord Jesus Christ. Now that the Lord Jesus has come, why should men continue to be occupied with the shadows? It is the same as being occupied with a picture when the very person pictured is present.

2:18   It is rather difficult to know the exact meaning of this verse, because we are not fully acquainted with all that the Gnostics taught. Perhaps it means that these people pretended to be so humble that they would not dare to approach God directly. Perhaps the Gnostics taught that they must approach God through angels, and so in their supposed **humility** they worshiped **angels** rather than the Lord. We have something similar to this in the world today. There are Roman Catholics who say that they would not think of praying directly to God or to the Lord Jesus, and so their motto is "To Jesus through Mary." This seems to be a **false humility** on their part and a worshiping of a created being. Christians should not allow anyone to rob them of their reward by such unscriptural practices. The word is clear that there is "one Mediator between God and men, the Man Christ Jesus" (1 Tim. 2:5).

The Apostle Paul goes on with the obscure expression: **intruding into those things which he has not[16] seen.** The Gnostics professed to have deep, secret mysteries, and in order to learn what these mysteries were, a person had to be initiated. Perhaps the secrets included many so-called visions. Supposed visions are an important element in such present-day heresies as Mormonism, Spiritism, Catholicism, and Swedenborgianism. Those who were members of the inner circle were naturally proud of their secret knowledge. Paul therefore adds: **Vainly puffed up by his fleshly mind.** They took a superior attitude toward others and created the impression that one could be happy only through entering into these deep secrets. We might pause here to say that much of this is characteristic of the secret fraternal organizations of our day. The Christian who is walking in fellowship with his Lord will have neither time nor sympathy for such organizations.

The important point to notice in this verse is that the various religious practices of these men were performed according to their own will. They had no scriptural authority. They did not act in subjection to Christ. They became **vainly puffed up by** the **mind** of their flesh because they were doing exactly what they themselves wanted to do, in independence of the Lord; yet their conduct appeared to be humble and religious.

2:19   And not holding fast to the Head. The Lord Jesus is here spoken of

having **died** with Him. Our own hearts are always ready to dispute this fact, because we feel so very much alive to sin and temptation. But the wonderful thing is that as we by faith reckon ourselves to have died with Christ, it becomes a moral reality in our lives. If we live as those who have died, then our lives will become increasingly conformed to the life of the Lord Jesus Christ. Of course, we will never reach perfection in this life, but it is a process that should be going on in every believer.

Not only have we **died**, but also our **life is hidden with Christ in God**. The things that concern and interest the worldly man are found on this planet on which we live. However, the things that are of greatest concern to the believer are all bound up in the Person of the Lord Jesus Christ. His destiny and ours are inseparable. Paul's thought is that since our **life is hidden with Christ in God**, we should not be occupying ourselves with the petty things of this world, and especially the religious world about us.

But there is another thought connected with the expression **your life is hidden with Christ in God**. The world does not see our spiritual life. Men do not understand us. They think it is strange that we do not live like they do. They do not comprehend our thoughts, our motives, or our ways. Just as it is said of the Holy Spirit that the world "neither sees Him, nor knows Him," so it is with our spiritual life; it **is hidden with Christ in God**. First John 3:1 tells us: "Therefore the world does not know us, because it did not know Him." The real separation from the world lies in the fact that the world does not understand, but rather misunderstands the believer.

3:4 To climax his description of the believer's portion in Christ, the apostle now looks on to Christ's coming again. **When Christ who is our life appears, then you also will appear with Him in glory.** At the present time we are raised with Him and enjoying a life that is not seen or understood by men. But the day is coming when the Lord Jesus will return for His saints. Then we **will appear with Him in glory**. Men will understand us then and realize why we behaved as we did.

3:5 In verse 3, we were told that we died. Here we are told to **put to death** our **members which are on the earth**. In these two verses we have a very clear illustration of the difference between a believer's standing and state. His standing is that he has died. His state should be that of reckoning himself dead to sin by putting **to death** his **members which are on the earth**. Our standing is what we are in Christ. Our state is what we are in ourselves. Our standing is the free gift of God through faith in the Lord Jesus Christ. Our state represents our response to God's grace.

Here we should also notice the difference between law and grace. God does not say, "If you live a life of freedom from sin, then I will give you a position of death with Christ." That would be law. Our position would depend on our own efforts, and needless to say, no one would ever attain that position. Instead of that, God says: "I freely give to all who believe on the Lord Jesus a position of favor in My sight. Now go out and live a life that is consistent with such a high calling." That is grace!

When the apostle says that we should **put to death** our **members which are on the earth**, he does *not* mean that we should literally destroy any of the members of our physical body! The expression is figurative, and is explained in the phrases that follows. The word **members** is used to signify the various forms of lust and hatred that are enumerated.

Fornication is generally used to describe unlawful sexual intercourse or immorality, especially between single people (Matt. 15:19; Mark 7:21). Sometimes it is broader, and is translated sexual immorality. **Uncleanness** refers to impurity of thought, word, or action. It speaks of moral filth rather than physical dirtiness here. **Passion** denotes strong and unbridled lust. **Evil desire** speaks of intense and often violent craving. **Covetousness** in general means greediness or the desire to have more, but here it may refer especially to an unholy desire to satisfy sexual appetite which **is idolatry**.

The list begins with acts and moves on to motives. The various forms of sexual sin are described, then they are traced to their lair, namely, the covetous heart of man. The word of God is clear in teaching that there is nothing inherently wrong in sex. God made man with the power for reproduction. But the sin comes when those things which God has so graciously bestowed upon His creatures are used for vile, illicit purposes. Sexual sin was the cardinal offense of the pagan world in Paul's day, and doubtless it still holds first place. Where believers are not yielded to the Holy Spirit, sexual sins often come into their lives and prove their downfall.

3:6 Men think that they can commit these outrageous sins and escape punishment. The heavens seem to be silent, and man increases in his boldness. But God is not mocked. **The wrath of God** comes down **upon the sons of disobedience** for these things. These sins have their consequences in this life; people reap in their own bodies the results of sexual immorality. In addition they will reap a terrible harvest of judgment in a day yet future.

3:7 Paul reminds the Colossians that they once indulged in these sins before their conversion. But the grace of God had come in and delivered them from impurity. That was a chapter in their life which was now covered by the blood of Christ. They now had a new life which empowered them to live for God. See Galatians 5:25: "If we live in the Spirit, let us also walk in the Spirit."

3:8 Since they had been redeemed at such a tremendous cost, they should now **put off** all these things like a dirty garment. Not only does the apostle refer to the various forms of unholy lust listed in verse 5, but also to the types of wicked hatred which he is about to enumerate.

Anger is, of course, a strong spirit of dislike or animosity, a vengeful spirit, a settled feeling of hatred. **Wrath** describes an intense form of anger, probably involving violent outbursts. **Malice** is wicked conduct toward another with the idea of harming his person or reputation. It is an unreasonable dislike that takes pleasure in seeing others suffer. **Blasphemy** here means reviling, that is, strong, intemperate language used against another person. It means scolding in a harsh, insolent manner. **Filthy language** means shameful speaking, and describes that which is lewd, indecent, or corrupt. It is disgraceful, impure language. In this catalog of sin the apostle goes from motives to acts. Bitterness starts in the human heart and then manifests itself in the various ways which have been described.

3:9 In verse 9 the apostle is saying in effect, "Let your state be consistent with your standing." **You have put off the old man**; now put him off practically by refraining from lies. Lying is one of the things that belongs to **the old man**, and it has no place in the life of the child of God. Every day in our lives we are tempted to distort the truth. It may be by withholding information on an income tax form, or by cheating on an examination, or even by exaggerating the details of a story. Lying becomes doubly serious when we injure another by a false statement, or by creating a false impression.

3:10 Not only have we put off the old man, but we **have put on the new man, who is renewed in knowledge according to the image of Him who created him**. Just as the old man refers to all that we were as sons of Adam, with an unregenerate nature, so **the new man** refers to our new position as children of God. There has been a new creation, and we are new creatures. God's purpose is that this new man should always be growing more and more like the Lord Jesus Christ. We should never be satisfied with our present attainments, but should always press on to the goal of increasing conformity to the Savior. He is our example and the rule of our lives. In a coming day, when we stand before the Judgment Seat of Christ, we will be judged not by how much better our lives were than others but rather by how our life measured up to the life of the Lord Jesus Himself.

> The image of God is not seen in the shape of our bodies, but in the beauty of the renewed mind and heart. Holiness, love, humility, meekness, kindness, and forgiveness — these make up the divine character. (Daily Notes of the Scripture Union)

3:11 In the new creation of which

the apostle has been speaking, **there is neither Greek nor Jew, circumcised nor uncircumcised, barbarian, Scythian, slave nor free, but Christ is all and in all**. Differences of nationality, religion, culture, and social level are not the things that count. As far as standing before God is concerned, all believers are on the same level, and in local church fellowship this same attitude should be adopted.

This does not mean that there are no distinctions in the church. Some have the gift of evangelist, some of pastor, and some of teacher. Some men are elders in the church and some are deacons. Thus, the verse does not disparage proper distinctions.

Neither should the verse be taken to teach that the distinctions listed have been abolished in the world. Such is not the case. There is still the **Greek** and the **Jew, Greek** here standing for the Gentile peoples in general. There are **the circumcised** and **the uncircumcised**. These two expressions are generally used in the NT to describe Jew and Gentile respectively. However, here they might refer more particularly to the ritual itself as practiced by the Jewish people, and as disregarded by the Gentiles.

There is still the **barbarian** (uncultured person) and the **Scythian**. These two expressions are not here set in contrast to one another. The **Scythians** were barbarians, but were generally considered to be the more extreme form; they were the wildest and most savage of the barbarians. The final contrast is between **slave** and **free. Free** refers to those who never had been in bondage, but were born free. For the Christian these worldly distinctions are no longer of importance. It is Christ who really counts. He is everything to the believer and in everything. He represents the center and circumference of the Christian's life.

Bishop Ryle states this truth boldly:

> The three words — Christ is all — are the essence and substance of Christianity. If our hearts can really go along with them, it is well with our souls. . . . Many give Christ a certain place in their religion but not the place which God intended Him to fill. Christ alone is not "all in all" to their souls. No! It is either Christ and the church — or Christ and the sacraments — or Christ and His ordained ministers — or Christ and their own repentance — or Christ and their own goodness — or Christ and their own prayers — or Christ and their own sincerity and charity, on which they practically rest their souls.[19]

3:12 In verse 10, Paul said that we have put on the new man. Now he gives some practical ways in which this can be done in our everyday lives. First of all, he addresses the Colossians as **the elect of God**. This refers to the fact that they had been chosen by God in Christ before the foundation of the world. God's electing grace is one of the mysteries of divine revelation. We believe the Scripture clearly teaches that God, in His sovereignty, has chosen men to belong to Christ. We do not believe that God has ever chosen anyone to be damned. Such a teaching is directly contrary to Scripture. Just as we believe in God's electing grace, we also believe in man's responsibility. God does not save men against their will. The same Bible that says "elect according to the foreknowledge of God" also says "whoever calls on the name of the Lord shall be saved."

Next Paul addresses the Colossians as **holy and beloved. Holy** means sanctified, or set apart (same word as "saints") to God from the world. We are positionally holy, and we should be practically holy in our lives as well. Because we are the objects of God's love, it gives us a desire to please Him in every way.

Now Paul describes the Christian graces which we are to **put on** as a garment. **Tender mercies** speaks of a heart of compassion. **Kindness** speaks of the unselfish spirit of doing for others. It is an attitude of affection or goodwill. **Humility** means lowliness, the willingness to be humbled and to esteem others better than oneself. **Meekness** does not speak of weakness, but rather the strength to deny oneself and to walk in grace toward all men. Vine says:

> The common assumption is that when a man is meek, it is because he cannot help himself; but the Lord was "meek" because He had the infinite resources of God at His command. Described negatively, meekness is the opposite to self-assertiveness and self-interest; it is equa-

nimity of spirit that is neither elated nor cast down, simply because it is not occupied with self at all.[20]

If **humility** is the "absence of pride," then **meekness** is "the absence of passion." **Longsuffering** speaks of patience under provocation and of the long endurance of offense. It combines joy and a kind attitude toward others, along with perseverance in suffering.

3:13 Bearing with one another describes the patience we should have with the failings and odd ways of our brethren. In living with others, it is inevitable that we will find out their failures. It often takes the grace of God for us to put up with the idiosyncrasies of others, as it must for them to put up with ours. But we must bear with one another. **Forgiving one another, if anyone has a complaint against another.** There are few disputes among the people of God which could not be solved quickly if these injunctions were heeded. Forgiveness should be exercised toward others when they have offended. We often hear the complaint: "But he was the one who offended me. . . ." That is exactly the type of situation in which we are called upon to forgive. If the other person had not offended us, there would have been no need for forgiveness. If we had been the one who had committed the offense, then we should have gone and asked for pardon. Forbearance suggests our not taking offense; forgiveness — not holding it. There could scarcely be any greater incentive to forgiveness than is found in this verse: **Even as Christ forgave you, so you also must do.** How did **Christ** forgive us? He forgave us without a cause. So should we. He forgave us freely. So should we. He forgave and He forgot. So should we. Both as to manner and extent, we should follow our blessed Lord in this wonderful attitude.

3:14 Love is here spoken of as the outer garment, or the belt, which binds all the other virtues together in order to make up **perfection**. It holds together in symmetry all parts of the Christian character. It is possible that a person might manifest some of the virtues above without really having love in his heart. And so Paul is emphasizing here that what

we do must be done in a genuine spirit of **love** for our brethren. Our actions should not be grudging but should be born out of wholehearted affection. The Gnostics thought of knowledge as **the bond of perfection**, but Paul corrects this view by insisting that **love** is **the bond of perfection.**

3:15 The peace of God should act as an umpire **in** our **hearts**. If in anything we are in doubt, we should ask ourselves the questions: "Does it make for peace?" or "Would I have peace in my heart if I went ahead and did it?"

This verse is especially helpful when seeking guidance from the Lord. If the Lord really wants you to embark upon a certain course of action, He will most assuredly give you **peace** about it. If you do not have that peace, then you should not proceed. As has been said: "Darkness about going is light about staying."

Christ called us to enjoy His peace, both as individuals and also in the church. Do not overlook the importance of the latter part of this verse: **To which also you were called in one body.** One way in which we could enjoy peace would be to live in isolation from all other Christians. But this is not God's purpose. He has set the solitary in families. God's intention is that we should gather together in local churches. Although living with other Christians may try our patience at times, yet God in this way can develop virtues in the Christian's life which He could not produce in any other manner. So we should not shirk our responsibilities in the local church, nor give them up when we are annoyed or provoked. Rather we should seek to live compatibly with our fellow believers and help them in all we do and say.

And be thankful. This refrain is repeated over and over again in Paul's writings. There must have been a good reason: The Spirit of God must consider a **thankful** spirit very important. And we believe that it is! — important not only for a person's spiritual life, but for his physical welfare as well. Doctors have found out what the Scriptures have taught through the years — that a cheerful, **thankful** attitude of mind is beneficial for the body, and that worry, depression, and a complaining spirit are definitely harmful to one's health. Usually we think of thankfulness as something that is determined by our immediate circumstances, but Paul here shows that it is a grace to be cultivated. We are responsible to be **thankful**. Of all peoples of the world, we have the most for which to give thanks (compare Deut. 33:29). The fault is not in any lack of subject matter, but only in our selfish hearts.

3:16 There is disagreement as to how verse 16 should be punctuated. There was no punctuation in the original language of the NT, and the meaning of such a verse as this is largely determined by the punctuation marks that are used. We suggest the following: **Let the word of Christ dwell in you richly in all wisdom, teaching and admonishing one another; in psalms, hymns, and spiritual songs, singing with grace in your hearts to the Lord.**

There are thus three sections to the verse. First, we are to **let the word of Christ dwell in** us **richly. The word of Christ** refers to the teachings of Christ as found in the Bible. As we saturate our hearts and minds with His holy word, and seek to walk in obedience to it, then **the word of Christ** is really at home in our hearts.

The second thought is that **in all wisdom** we should be **teaching and admonishing one another**. Every Christian has a responsibility to his brothers and sisters in Christ concerning this matter. **Teaching** has to do with doctrine, whereas **admonishing** has to do with duty. We owe it to our brethren to share our knowledge of the Scripture with them, and to seek to help by practical and godly counsel. When **teaching and admonishing** are given **in wisdom**, they are more likely to find acceptance than when we speak with force but unwisely or without love.

The third thing is that with **psalms and hymns and spiritual songs** we should sing **with grace in** our **hearts to the Lord. Psalms** describe those inspired utterances which are found in the book by that name, which were sung as part of Israel's worship. **Hymns**, on the other hand, are generally understood as songs of worship and praise addressed to God

the Father or to the Lord Jesus Christ. For example:

> Jesus! the very thought of Thee
> With sweetness fills my breast;
> But sweeter far Thy face to see,
> And in Thy presence rest.
> – Attributed to Bernard of Clairvaux

These **hymns** are not inspired in the same sense as the **psalms. Spiritual songs** refer to religious poetry describing Christian experience. An illustration of this might be found in the words:

> O what peace we often forfeit,
> O what needless pain we bear,
> All because we do not carry
> Everything to God in prayer.
> – Joseph Scriven

Using these various types of songs we should sing **with grace** or thanksgiving, **in** our **hearts to the Lord**. At this point it might be well to say that the Christian should use discernment in the type of music he uses. Much of the so-called "Christian" music of today is light and frothy. A great deal of this music is utterly contrary to Scripture, and still more is so similar to the world's "pop" and rock that it is a discredit to the name of Christ.

Verse 16 is very similar to Ephesians 5:18, 19, where we read: "And do not be drunk with wine, in which is dissipation; but be filled with the Spirit, speaking to one another in psalms, hymns, and spiritual songs, singing and making melody in your heart to the Lord." In Colossians 3:16, the main difference is that instead of saying "be filled with the Spirit," Paul says: **"Let the word of Christ dwell in you richly."** In other words, being filled with the Spirit and being filled with God's word are both requisites for living joyful, useful, fruitful lives. We shall not be filled with the Spirit unless we are saturated with God's word; and the study of God's word will not be effective unless we yield up our inmost being to the control of the Holy Spirit. Can we not therefore conclude that to be filled with the Spirit means to be filled with God's word? It is not some mysterious, emotional crisis that comes in the life, but rather day by day feeding on the Scriptures, meditating on them, obeying them, and living by them.

3:17 Verse 17 is an all-inclusive rule

by which to judge our conduct as Christians. Young people today especially have a difficult time deciding whether certain things are right or wrong. This verse, committed to memory, can prove to be the key for unlocking many of these problems. The great test should be: Can I do this **in the name of the Lord Jesus** Christ? Would this be to His glory? Could I expect His blessing to rest on it? Would I want to be doing it when He comes back again? Notice that this test should apply to the words we speak and to the deeds we do. Obedience to this command ennobles all of life. It is a precious secret when the Christian learns to do all as to the Lord and for His glory. Once again the apostle adds the word, **"Giving thanks to God the Father through Him."** Thanks! *Thanks!* **Thanks**! It is a perpetual duty for those saved by grace and destined for the courts of heaven.

B. Appropriate Behavior for Members of the Christian Household (3:18—4:1)

Paul now gives a series of exhortations to members of the Christian household. The series continues through 4:1. He has advice for wives and husbands, for children and parents, and for servants and masters. At first, it may seem like an abrupt change to turn from the subjects which have occupied Paul to such mundane matters as home life. But actually this is most significant.

THE CHRISTIAN HOME

God considers the home to be a very important force in the Christian life. The well-known statement, "The hand that rocks the cradle rules the world," has truth in it beyond what appears on the surface. The family unit was designed by God for the preservation of much that is worthwhile in life. As less and less attention is devoted to the home, even so our civilization deteriorates rapidly. Paul's first Letter to Timothy teaches in a special way that God has ordained home life as the means of developing spiritual qualities, so that one's fitness for leadership in the church grows out of his proved character in the home.

In the verses to follow we have some of the fundamental principles to guide in the establishment of a Christian home. In studying this section, we should be aware of the following "musts."

1. There must be a family altar — a time each day when the family gathers for the reading of the Holy Scriptures and for prayer.

2. The father must have his place of authority in the home, and he must exercise it in wisdom and love.

3. The wife and mother should realize that her first responsibility to God and to the family is in the home. In general, it is not wise for the wife to have an outside job. There are, of course, exceptional cases.

4. The husband and wife should present a godly example to their children. They should be united on all matters, including the disciplining of the children, when necessary.

5. The family unit should be maintained. It is all too possible to become so engrossed in business, social life, and even in Christian service that the children suffer from lack of affection, companionship, instruction, and discipline. Many parents have had to confess mournfully over a wayward son or daughter: "And while your servant was busy here and there, he was gone" (1 Kgs. 20:40).

6. With regard to the disciplining of children, three cardinal rules have been suggested. Never punish in anger. Never punish unjustly. Never punish without explaining the reason.

7. It is good for children to learn to bear the yoke in their youth (Lam. 3:27), to learn the discipline of work and of accepting responsibility, and the value of money.

8. Above all, Christian parents should avoid being ambitious for their children in a carnal, worldly way, but should constantly hold before them the service of our Lord as the most profitable way in which to spend their lives. For some, it might mean full-time service on a mission field; for others, it might mean service for the Lord in a secular occupation. But in either case, work for the Lord should be the primary consideration. Whether at home, at work, or wherever we may be, we should be conscious of the fact that we

represent our Savior, and so every word and act should be worthy of Him, and should, in fact, be governed by Him. ‡

3:18 The first injunction of the apostle is addressed to **wives**. They are enjoined to **submit to** their **own husbands, as is fitting in the Lord**. According to the divine plan, the husband is head of the house. The woman has been given the place of submission to her husband. She is not to dominate or to lead, but to follow his leadership, wherever she can do so without compromising her loyalty to Christ. There are, of course, instances in which the woman cannot obey her husband and still be faithful to Christ. In such an instance, her first loyalty is to the Lord Jesus. Where a Christian woman has a backward husband, this verse indicates that she should help him to fulfill his proper place in the home, rather than for her to usurp it because she may be more clever.

3:19 The balance which is presented to us in the word of God is beautiful. The apostle does not stop with this advice to wives; he now goes on to show that **husbands**, too, have a responsibility. They are to **love** their **wives, and not to be bitter toward them**. If these simple precepts were followed, many of the problems of married life would disappear, and homes would be happier in the Lord. Actually no wife would be likely to object to submitting to a husband who truly loves her. It has been noted that the husband is not told to make his wife obey him. If she does not, he should take it to the Lord. The submission should be her voluntary act "as is fitting in the Lord."

3:20 Children are admonished: **obey your parents in all things, for this is well pleasing in the Lord**. In all ages, families have been held together by two simple principles — authority and obedience. Here we have the latter. Notice that this obedience is to be **in all things**. This means not only in the things that are agreeable, but those which are not so naturally pleasing.

Christian children who have unsaved parents are often placed in a difficult position. They want to be true to the Lord, and yet at the same time they are faced with demands made upon them by their parents. In general, we feel that if they honor their parents, God will in turn honor them. As long as they are living in the home of their parents, they have a very definite obligation to perform. Of course, they should not do anything that would be contrary to the teachings of Christ, but ordinarily they would not be called upon to do such. Often they will be called upon to do things that might seem very distasteful to them, but as long as it is not distinctly wrong or sinful, they can determine to do it as to the Lord. In this way they can be a good testimony to their parents and seek to win them to the Lord.

3:21 Fathers should **not provoke** their **children, lest they become discouraged**. It is interesting that this advice is addressed to **fathers** and not to mothers. Does it not reveal that the danger of a father committing this fault is greater than that of a mother? Kelly suggests that mothers are probably more prone to spoil the children.

3:22 From verse 22 to the end of the chapter, the Spirit of God addresses **bondservants** or slaves. It is interesting to note the amount of space devoted in the NT to slaves. This is not without significance. It shows that no matter how low a person's social status may be, he still can attain the very highest in the Christian life through faithfulness to the word of God. Perhaps it also reflects the foreknowledge of God that most Christian people would occupy places of service rather than positions of authority. For instance, there is very little instruction in the NT that refers to rulers of nations, but there is considerable advice for those who devote their lives in the service of others. Slaves in the days of Paul usually received very little consideration, and doubtless it struck the early Christians as unusual that so much attention was given to them in these Letters. But it shows how the grace of God reaches down to men, no matter how menial their position might be. C. H. Mackintosh notes: "The slave is not shut out from the service of God. By simply doing his duty in the sight of God, he can adorn the doctrine and bring glory to God."

Bondservants are told to **obey in all things** those who are their **masters according to the flesh**. There is a gentle reminder here that these masters are only **masters according to the flesh**. They have another Master who is above all and who sees all that is done to the lowliest of His children. Slaves are not to serve **with eyeservice, as menpleasers, but in sincerity of heart, fearing God**. (For a good example of this in the OT, see Genesis 24:33.) Especially when a person is oppressed, it is a temptation to slack off in work when the master is not looking. But the Christian servant will realize that his Master is always looking, and so even though his earthly circumstances may be very bitter, he will work as to the Lord. **In sincerity of heart** means that he will have a pure motive — only to please the Lord Jesus.

It is interesting that there is no express prohibition against slavery in the NT. The gospel does not overthrow social institutions by revolution. However, wherever the gospel has gone, slavery has been uprooted and eliminated. This does not mean that these instructions are therefore without meaning for us. All that is said here may very well be applied to employees and employers.

3:23 **Whatever** is done should be done **heartily** (literally "from the soul") **as to the Lord and not to men**. In every form of Christian service as well as in every sphere of life, there are many tasks which people find obnoxious. Needless to say, we try to avoid such work. But this verse teaches us the very important lesson that the humblest service can be glorified and dignified by doing it for the Lord. In this sense, there is no difference between secular and sacred work. All is sacred. Rewards in heaven will not be for prominence or apparent successes; they will not be for talents or opportunities; but rather for faithfulness. Thus obscure persons will fare very well in that day if they have carried out their duties faithfully as to the Lord. Two mottoes which are often hung over the kitchen sink are: "Not somehow, but triumphantly," and "Divine service held here three times daily."

3:24 **The Lord** is keeping the records at the present time, and everything done as to Him will command His attention. "The kindness of God will repay the kindness of men." Those who have little of earthly inheritance **will receive the reward of the inheritance** in heaven. Let us remember this the next time we are called upon to do something that we do not like to do, whether in the church, in the home, or at work; it is a testimony for Christ to do it uncomplainingly, and to do the best possible job.

3:25 Paul does not specify just whom he has in mind in verse 25. Perhaps we would most naturally think of an unjust master, one who oppresses his servants. Maybe a Christian servant has become weary of obeying his unjust demands. "Never mind," Paul is saying, "the Lord knows all about it, and He will take care of the wrongs, too."

But although this might include masters, it is addressed primarily to servants. Slipshod service, cheating, loafing, or other forms of insincerity will not go unnoticed. **There is no partiality** with God. He is the Master of all, and the distinctions that prevail among men mean nothing to Him. If slaves rob their masters (as Onesimus apparently did), they will have to give an account to the Lord.

4:1 This verse logically goes with the closing verse of chapter 3. **Masters** should **give** their **bondservants what is just and fair**. They should not withhold from them a proper wage, but should pay them well for the work they have done. This is addressed directly to Christian employers. God hates the oppression of the poor, and the gifts of a man who has grown rich through unfair labor practices are unacceptable to the Lord. God says in effect: "You keep your money; I don't like the way you made it" (see Jas. 5:1–4). Masters should not be high-minded but should fear. They **also have a Master in heaven**, One who is just and righteous in all His ways.

Before closing this section it is interesting to note how the Apostle Paul repeatedly brings these matters of everyday life under the searchlight of the lordship of Christ as follows: (1) Wives — as is fitting in the Lord (v. 18). (2) Children — well-pleasing to the Lord (v. 20). (3) Servants — fearing the Lord (v. 22). (4) Servants — as to the Lord (v. 23).

C. The Believer's Prayer Life and Witness by Life and Speech (4:2–6)

4:2 Paul never tires of exhorting the

people of God to be diligent in their **prayer** life. Doubtless one of the regrets we all will have when we get to heaven will be that we did not spend more time in prayer, especially when we will realize the extent to which our prayers were answered. There is a great deal of mystery in connection with the whole subject of prayer, many questions which cannot be answered. But the best attitude for the Christian is not to seek to analyze, dissect, or understand prayer's deeper mysteries. The best approach is to keep praying in simple faith, leaving aside one's intellectual doubts.

Not only are we to **continue earnestly in prayer**, but we are also to be **vigilant in it**. This immediately reminds us of the Lord Jesus' request to the disciples in the Garden of Gethsemane: "Watch and pray, lest you enter into temptation." They were not vigilant, and so fell sound asleep. Not only are we to watch against sleep, but also against wandering thoughts, listlessness, and unreality. And we are to watch to see that we are not robbed of time for prayer (Eph. 6:18). Then again, our prayers are to be **with thanksgiving**. Not only are we to be thankful for past answers to prayer, but in faith we can also thank the Lord for prayers He has not answered. Guy King summarizes nicely: "His love wants the best for us; His wisdom knows the best for us; and His power gets the best for us."[21]

4:3 Paul asks that the Colossians remember to pray **also for** him, and for the servants of the Lord who are with him in Rome. It is beautiful to notice that he does not ask that he might be released from prison, but rather **that God would open a door** to him for preaching **the word**. The apostle wanted God to open doors for him. What an important lesson there is for us in this! It is all too possible for us to go around opening doors for ourselves in Christian service. But this is a peril to be avoided. If the Lord opens the doors for us, then we can confidently enter them, knowing that He is leading. On the other hand, if we open the doors for ourselves, then we cannot be sure that we are in the center of the Lord's will, and we might soon be stooping to carnal means to carry on the so-called

work of the Lord. Paul's specific request is that **a door for the word** might be opened to him **to speak the mystery of Christ, for which** he was **in chains**. The **mystery of Christ** in this verse is the truth of the church, and particularly that aspect of it which might be defined by the expression "Christ for the Gentiles." That was the special aspect of the gospel message which had been committed to Paul to preach. It was because he dared to suggest that Gentiles could be saved in the same way as Jews that the Jewish leaders finally succeeded in having him sent to Rome as a prisoner.

There are some who teach that the great mystery of the church was revealed to Paul while he was in prison. They therefore put great emphasis on the "Prison Epistles" while seeming to underestimate the importance of the Gospels and other books of the NT. But it is clear from this verse that the preaching of the mystery was the *cause* of his imprisonment and therefore must have been revealed to him some time before his arrest.

4:4 He is anxious to **make it manifest**, that is, to preach it in such a clear manner that it will be readily understood by the people. This should be the desire of every Christian who seeks to make Christ known. There is no virtue in being "deep." We should aim to reach the masses of humanity and, in order to do so, the message must be presented simply and clearly.

4:5 Christians should **walk in wisdom toward those who are outside**. In their everyday behavior, they should realize that they are being carefully watched by unbelievers. The world is more interested in our walk than in our talk. In the language of Edgar Guest: "I'd rather see a sermon, than hear one, any day." This does not mean that the Christian should not also confess Christ with his lips, but the point is that his walk should correspond with his talk. It should never be said of him, "High talk, low walk."

Redeeming the time means "buying up opportunities." Every day of our lives we face opportunities for witnessing to the saving power of the Lord Jesus Christ. As these opportunities come along, we should be ready to snap them up. The word "buying" implies that there is often a cost involved. But whatever the cost may be, we should be ready to share our precious Savior with those who do not know Him.

4:6 Our **speech** should **always be with grace, seasoned with salt, that** we **may know how** we **ought to answer each one**. If our conversation is to be always **with grace**, it must be courteous, humble, and Christlike. It should be free from gossip, frivolity, uncleanness, and bitterness. The expression **seasoned with salt** may have a number of meanings. Some commentators think that although our language should be gracious, it should be equally honest and without hypocrisy. Other think of **salt** as that which heightens flavor, and so Paul is saying that our conversation should never be dull, flat, or insipid, but should always be worthwhile and profitable. Lightfoot says that heathen writers used "salt" as a figure of speech for "wit." Paul changes wit to wisdom. Perhaps the best way to explain the expression is to study the language of the Lord Jesus. To the woman taken in the act of adultery, He said: "Neither do I condemn you: go, and sin no more." Here we have the grace and the salt. First of all, the grace, "neither do I condemn you"; then the salt, "go, and sin no more." Then again the Lord Jesus said to the woman at Jacob's well: "Give Me a drink. . . . Go, call your husband." The first speaks of grace, whereas the second reminds us more of salt.

That you may know how you ought to answer each one. Perhaps the Apostle Paul is here thinking particularly of the Gnostics who came to the Colossians with their plausible doctrines. They should be ready to **answer** these false teachers with words of wisdom and faithfulness.

D. Glimpses of Some of Paul's Associates (4:7–14)

4:7 **Tychicus** was apparently the one who was chosen by the Apostle Paul to carry this Letter from Rome to Colosse. Maclaren pictures how amazed Tychicus would have been if told that "these bits of parchment would outlast all the ostentatious pomp of the city, and that his name, because written in them, would be known to the end of time all over the world."

Paul here assures the saints that when Tychicus arrives he will **tell** them **all the news** of the apostle's affairs. Again it is nice to read the combination of titles which Paul bestows on this brother. He calls him **a beloved brother, faithful minister, and fellow servant in the Lord**. How much more to be coveted are titles such as these than high-sounding ecclesiastical names that are given to church officials in our day!

4:8 Tychicus' trip to Colosse would serve two purposes. First of all, he would give the saints a firsthand account of Paul and his companions in Rome, and also he would **comfort** the **hearts** of the Colossians. Here again, **comfort** probably has more the idea of "strengthen" or "encourage" (see 2:2) than that of consoling. His ministry to them would have the general effect of helping them to stand against the false teaching that was then prevalent.

4:9 The mention of the name **Onesimus** brings before us the lovely story unfolded in Paul's Letter to Philemon. Onesimus was the runaway slave who sought to escape from punishment by fleeing to Rome. Somehow he had come in contact with Paul, who, in turn, had pointed him to Christ. Now Onesimus is going to travel back to his former master, Philemon, in Colosse. He will carry Paul's Letter to Philemon, while Tychicus carries the Letter to the church at Colosse. Picture the excitement among the believers in Colosse when these two brethren arrived with the Letters from Paul! Doubtless they sat up late in the evening, asking questions about conditions in Rome and hearing of Paul's courage in the service of his Savior.

4:10 Not much is known about **Aristarchus** except that he had previously been arrested in connection with his service for the Lord, as recorded in Acts 19:29. Now he is Paul's **fellow prisoner** in Rome.

Mark is here spoken of as **the cousin of Barnabas**. This young man had started out with Paul and Barnabas in missionary labors. Because of his failure,

Paul decided that he should be left at home, but Barnabas insisted on taking him with him. This caused a rift between the two older workers. However, it is good to learn that Mark's failure was not final, and he is now restored to the confidence of the beloved Paul.

If Mark should visit Colosse, the saints there are told to **welcome him**. The expression **about whom you received instructions** does not necessarily mean that the Colossians had previously received instructions concerning Mark. It may refer to the instructions which Paul is now giving to them: **If he comes to you, welcome him**. The tense of the verb **received** may simply mean that by the time the Colossians read this Letter, they would have received instructions. The mention of Mark, the writer of the Second Gospel, reminds us that we are *all* writing a gospel day by day:

> We each write a gospel, a chapter a day,
> By deeds, looks and likes, the things
>   that we say,
> Our actions betray us — words faithful
>   and true —
> Say, "What is the gospel according
>   to you?"

4:11 Another co-worker of Paul is spoken of as **Jesus, who is called Justus. Jesus** was a common name then, as it still is in certain countries. It was the Greek equivalent of the Hebrew name "Joshua." No doubt this man was **called Justus** because his Christian friends would feel the incongruity of anyone having the same name as the Son of God.

The three foregoing men were all converted Jews. Indeed they were the **only** three former Jews who were **fellow workers** with Paul **for the kingdom of God**, men who had **proved to be a comfort to** him.

4:12 As Paul is bringing his Letter to a close, **Epaphras** reminds him to be sure to send his own personal greetings to the dear saints in Colosse. Epaphras, a native of Colosse, was constantly remembering the believers **in his prayers**, asking the Lord that they might **stand perfect and complete in all the will of God**.

4:13 Paul bears **witness** to the fact **that** Epaphras travailed in prayer not only for those in Colosse, but also for the Christians **in Laodicea and those in Hierapolis**. This man had a personal interest in the people of God with whom he was acquainted. Doubtless he had a very long prayer list, and it would not be at all surprising if he remembered each one in prayer every day. "He prays hard for you all the time, that you may stand fast, ripe in conviction, and wholly devoted to doing God's will" (NEB).

4:14 Now Paul sends greetings from **Luke, the beloved physician, and Demas**. Here we have a study in contrasts. **Luke** had traveled with Paul considerably and had probably ministered to him both physically and spiritually during his times of sickness, persecution, and imprisonment.

Demas, on the other hand, had gone on with the apostle for a while, but it was necessary at last for the apostle to say of him: "Demas has forsaken me, having loved this present world, and has departed for Thessalonica" (2 Tim. 4:10).

E. Greetings and Instructions (4:15–18)

4:15 Greetings are now sent to **the brethren who are in Laodicea**, to **Nymphas, and the church that** was **in his house**. We read again of the church in Laodicea in Revelation 3:14–22. The church there became lukewarm about the things of God. It became utterly materialistic and self-satisfied. Thinking that all was well, the people did not realize their own nakedness. Manuscripts differ as to whether Nymphas (a man) or Nympha (a woman) is addressed. But it is sufficient to notice that there was a church in that home in Colosse. In those days the Christians did not have elaborate edifices such as are used today. However, most of us will readily agree that the power of God in a local church is far more important than an elaborate building or fine furnishings. Power is not dependent upon the latter; luxurious church buildings often serve as a hindrance to power.

4:16 **When this epistle** had been **read** in Colosse, it was to be sent to **the church of the Laodiceans** to be read there also. Undoubtedly this was done, but from what we learn in Revelation 3, it seems that the Laodiceans did not heed the message of this Letter, at least in a lasting way.

Paul also directs that **the epistle from Laodicea** should be read in Colosse. There is no way of knowing what Letter is referred to. Some believe that Paul's so-called Letter to the Ephesians was the one in view. Some ancient manuscripts omit the words "in Ephesus" in Ephesians 1:1. This has led commentators to believe that the Letter to the Ephesians might have been a circular Letter which was supposed to be read in several different churches — for instance, Ephesus, Laodicea, then Colosse. This view is also strengthened by the fact that so few personal references are made in *Ephesians* compared to the number made in Colossians.[22]

4:17 **Archippus** is told to **take heed to the ministry which** he had **received in the Lord**, and to **fulfill it**. Here again, we do not have definite information as to what **ministry** is referred to. Many have believed that **Archippus** was a son of Philemon, and that he was active in the church at Colosse. The verse will become much more meaningful to us if we assume that our name is Archippus, and if we hear the Spirit of God saying to us: **"Take heed to the ministry which you have received in the Lord, that you may fulfill it."** Each one of us has been given some service by the Lord, and we will some day be required to give an account of what we have done with it.

4:18 At this point, the apostle took the pen in his **own hand** and signed his closing **salutation** with his Gentile name **Paul**. Doubtless as he did so the **chains** on his hands proved an inconvenience in writing, but it reminded him to say to the Colossians: **Remember my chains**. "The sound of pen and chains together is the final sign that the preacher's chains cannot bind the Word of God."[23] Then he closed the Epistle with the words **Grace be with you. Amen.** A. T. Robertson writes: "There is no richer word than the word 'grace,' for it carries in it all of God's love as seen in the gift of His Son for us."[24] **Amen.**

ENDNOTES

[1](Intro) George Salmon, *A Historical Introduction to the Study of the Books of the New Testament*, p. 384.

[2](Intro) *New Bible Commentary*, p. 1043.

[3](Intro) A. T. Robertson, *Paul and the Intellectuals*, p. 16.

[4](1:5) J. B. Lightfoot, *Saint Paul's Epistles to the Colossians and to Philemon*, p. 134.

[5](1:6) Both NU and M texts add "and growing."

[6](1:11) A. S. Peake, "Colossians," *The Expositor's Greek Testament*, III:499.

[7](1:14) The words "through His blood" definitely occur in the parallel passage in Ephesians 1:7, but here they are neither in the oldest (NU) nor in the majority (M) of Greek mss.

[8](1:18) Alfred Mace, further documentation unavailable.

[9](1:19) The strengthened form of *oikeō* used here (*katoikeō*) suggests settling down and being at home.

[10](1:22) Charles R. Erdman, *Epistle of Paul to the Colossians and Philemon*, p. 46.

[11](1:23) The Greek language has two words for "if" (*ei* and *ean*) and several grammatical constructions to note the type of condition the writer or speaker envisions. Here the *ei* with the indicative *epimenete* is a first class condition (Paul takes it for granted that they *will* continue).

[12](1:23) Pridham, further documentation unavailable.

[13](2:2) Alfred Mace, further documentation unavailable.

[14](2:9) Marvin Vincent, *Word Studies in the New Testament*, II:906.

[15](2:14) F. B. Meyer, further documentation unavailable.

[16](2:18) The word *not* is omitted in the NU text, but the resultant meaning would be much the same. Whether they actually saw anything or not, it was all carnal emptiness.

[17](3:2) Robertson, *Intellectuals*, p. 149.

[18](3:2) F. B. Hole, *Paul's Epistles, Volume Two*, p. 105.

[19](3:11) J. C. Ryle, *Holiness*, pp. 436, 455.

[20](3:12) W. E. Vine, *Expository Dictionary of New Testament Words*, p. 56.

[21](4:2) Guy King, *Crossing the Border*, p. 111.

[22](4:16) On the other hand, since Paul spent three years at Ephesus, he would have known *so many* people there that it would have been precarious to choose a handful for fear of offending the rest.

[23](4:18) *New Bible Commentary*, p. 1051.
[24](4:18) Robertson, *Intellectuals*, p. 211.

BIBLIOGRAPHY
(Colossians and Philemon)

Carson, Herbert M. *The Epistles of Paul to the Colossians and to Philemon*. Grand Rapids: Wm. B. Eerdmans Publishing Co., 1960.

English, E. Schuyler. *Studies in the Epistle to the Colossians*. New York: Our Hope Press, 1944.

Erdman, Charles R. *Epistles of Paul to the Colossians and Philemon*. Philadelphia: Westminster Press, 1933.

King, Guy. *Crossing the Border*. London: Marshall, Morgan and Scott, Ltd., 1957.

Lightfoot, J. B. *Saint Paul's Epistle to the Colossians and to Philemon*. Grand Rapids: Zondervan Publishing House, reprint of 1879 edition by MacMillan.

Maclaren, Alexander. "Colossians and Philemon," *The Expositor's Bible*. London: Hodder and Stoughton, 1888.

Nicholson, W. R. *Popular Studies in Colossians: Oneness with Christ*. Grand Rapids: Kregel Publications, 1903.

Peake, Arthur S. "Colossians," *The Expositor's Greek Testament*. Vol. 3. Grand Rapids: Wm. B. Eerdmans Publishing Co., 1961.

Robertson, A. T. *Paul and the Intellectuals*. Nashville: Sunday School Board of the Southern Baptist Convention, 1928.

Rutherfurd, John. *St. Paul's Epistles to Colossae and Laodicea*. Edinburgh: T. & T. Clark, 1908.

Sturz, Richard. *Studies in Colossians*. Chicago: Moody Press, 1955.

Thomas, W. H. Griffith. *Studies in Colossians and Philemon*. Grand Rapids: Baker Book House, 1973.

Vine, W. E. *The Epistle to the Philippians and Colossians*. London: Oliphants, 1955.

THE FIRST EPISTLE TO
THE THESSALONIANS

Introduction

*"This letter, more than any other of Paul's, is characterised by simplicity,
gentleness, and affection . . . here there is no controversy."*
— W. Graham Scroggie

I. Unique Place in the Canon

The first book by any famous author is usually highly prized as indicating earliest emphasis and gift of communication. First Thessalonians may well be Paul's first inspired Letter. The amazing amount of Christian teaching that the apostle was able to fit into his short stay at Thessalonica is clearly indicated by the many doctrines he discusses as already known by the Thessalonians.

Today the Rapture and Second Advent of our Lord are widely believed and looked for by evangelical Christians. This was not always so. The revival of interest in this doctrine, especially through the writings of the early Brethren in Great Britain (1825-1850) was largely based on 1 Thessalonians. Without this short Letter we would be terribly deprived in our understanding of the various aspects of Christ's return.

II. Authorship†

That 1 Thessalonians is an authentic Pauline Letter is denied by virtually no Bible scholars. The support for this is sufficient, as J. E. Frame says, "unless one is prepared to assert that Paul never lived or that no letter from him has survived."[1]

External evidence that Paul is the author is found in Polycarp, Ignatius, and Justin, as well as the Marcionite Canon and the Muratorian Canon (early lists of Christian Scriptures — one heretical and one orthodox).

Internal evidence is the use of Pauline vocabulary and style, and the outlook of a tender-hearted, spiritual father. The historical allusions coincide with Acts. Both in 1:1 and 2:18 the writer calls himself Paul.

III. Date

First Thessalonians was written from Corinth during Paul's eighteen-month stay there, not long after Timothy came to Paul (1 Thess. 3:6; 2:17). Since Gallio (Acts 18) is believed to have arrived as proconsul in the early summer of A.D. 51, Paul must have gone there in early 50 and written 1 Thessalonians soon after. Nearly all scholars date the book in the early 50's, and it is probably safe to date the Letter more precisely in A.D. 50 or 51, only twenty years after our Lord's Ascension.

IV. Background and Themes††

It was during Paul's Second Missionary Journey that the light of the gospel first broke in on the darkness of Thessalonica (Acts 17:1–10).

After Paul and Silas had been released from jail in Philippi, they traveled to Thessalonica via Amphipolis and Apollonia. Thessalonica at that time was a strategic city, both commercially and politically. True to form, Paul went to the Jewish synagogue and showed from the OT that the Messiah had to suffer and rise from the dead. He then went on to declare that Jesus of Nazareth was the promised Messiah. That lasted for three Saturdays. Some of the Jews were convinced, and took their place with Paul and Silas as Christian believers. Also, many of the Greek proselytes and quite a few of the leading women of the city were converted. Then the backlash started. Those Jews who did *not* believe rounded up some of the hoodlums from the marketplace, incited a riot, and besieged the house of Jason, where Paul and Silas had been staying. When they didn't find the preachers in the house, they dragged Jason and some of the other believers before the city rulers (politarchs), accusing them of having turned the world upside down. It was an unintended compliment! Then they charged the Christians with plotting to overthrow Caesar by promoting another King named Jesus. The politarchs were troubled. They required Jason and his colleagues to post bail, probably adding strict orders for his guests to get out of town. Then Jason and the others were released.

The Christian brethren in Thessalonica decided that it would be wise for the preachers to leave town, so they sent them by night to Berea.

The remarkable thing is that when Paul and Silas departed, they left behind a congregation of believers who were instructed in the doctrines of the faith and who were unmoved by the persecution they endured. It would be easy to conclude from Acts 17:2 that Paul and his companions were in Thessalonica for only three Sabbaths. However, that may have been only the duration of their teaching ministry *in the synagogue*. Paul and his team may have spent as long as three months *in the city*. The apostle's Letters to them show that the Thessalonians had a broad acquaintance with Christian doctrine, and they could scarcely have received this in three or four weeks.

From Berea, Paul went to Athens (Acts 17:15). There he heard that the believers in Thessalonica were being persecuted. He tried to visit them, but Satan hindered (1 Thess. 2:17, 18), so he sent Timothy to them (3:1, 2). Timothy brought back a report that was, on the whole, encouraging (3:6–8), and this prompted the apostle to write this Letter. In it, he defends his ministry against slanderous attacks; he calls for separation from the prevailing immorality of that culture; he corrects misapprehensions about those who had died in Christ; he rebukes those who had quit working in view of Christ's coming; and he urges the saints to respect their spiritual leaders.

One of the most important themes of 1 Thessalonians is the return of the Lord Jesus. It is mentioned at least once in each of the five chapters. G. R. Harding Wood put these references together and came up with the following excellent synopsis:

> The Christian who is expecting the return of the Lord Jesus has no room for: (1) Idols in his heart (1:9, 10); (2) Slackness in his service (2:9, 19); (3) Divisions in his fellowship (3:12, 13); (4) Depression in his mind (4:13–18); or (5) Sin in his life (5:23).[2]

OUTLINE

I. SALUTATION (1:1)

II. PAUL'S PERSONAL RELATIONS WITH THE THESSALONIANS 1:2–3:13)

    A. Paul's Commendation of the Thessalonians (1:2–10)

    B. Review of Paul's Ministry, Message, and Conduct at Thessalonica (2:1–12)

    C. Review of the Thessalonians' Response to the Gospel (2:13–16)

    D. Explanation of Paul's Failure to Return to Thessalonica (2:17–20)

    E. The Mission of Timothy to Thessalonica (3:1–10)

    F. Paul's Specific Prayer (3:11–13)

III. PRACTICAL EXHORTATIONS (4:1–5:22)

    A. The Sanctification that Fulfills God's Will (4:1–8)

    B. The Love that Thinks of Others (4:9, 10)

Commentary

I. SALUTATION (1:1)

The Letter opens with the names of three men who had been accused of turning the world upside down. The charge was intended as a slander; it was actually a tribute.

Paul was the author of the Epistle. **Silvanus and Timothy** were traveling with him at the time, so he included their names. **Silvanus** is probably the same as the Silas who sang a duet with Paul in the prison at Philippi (Acts 16:25). **Timothy** is the young brother from Lystra who had joined Paul just before the trip to Thessalonica (Acts 16:1).

The letter was written **to the church of the Thessalonians in God the Father and the Lord Jesus Christ**. The word we translate as *church* was used at that time to describe any kind of an assembly, so Paul wants to make it clear that this is not a heathen assembly but one that is related to **God** as **Father and** to **Jesus Christ** as **Lord**.

The greeting **grace . . . and peace** embraces the best blessings that anyone could enjoy this side of heaven. **Grace** is God's undeserved favor in every aspect of our lives. **Peace** is the unruffled quietness which defies the crashing, crushing circumstances of life. **Grace** is the cause and **peace**, the effect. Paul repeats the dual divine names as the co-equal source of the blessings, this time putting the possessive personal pronoun **our** in front of **Father**.[3]

II. PAUL'S PERSONAL RELATIONS WITH THE THESSALONIANS (1:2–3:13)

A. Paul's Commendation of the Thessalonians (1:2–10)

1:2, 3 Whenever Paul prayed he mentioned the Thessalonians. (Are we as faithful in remembering our Christian brothers and sisters?) And it was always with **thanks** that he prayed for them, **remembering** their **work of faith**, their **labor of love**, and their **patience of hope**.

Their **work of faith** probably refers primarily to their conversion to God. This description of **faith** as a **work** reminds us of the time some people asked Jesus, "What shall we do, that we may work the works of God?" Jesus answered them, "This is the work of God, that you believe in Him whom He sent" (John 6:28, 29). In this sense, faith is an act or deed. But it is not toil by which a man earns merit or in which he can boast. In fact, it is the only work that man can perform without robbing Christ of His glory as Savior and without denying his own status as a helpless sinner. Faith is a non-meritorious work by which the creature acknowledges his Creator and the sinner acknowledges his Savior. The expression **work of faith** also includes the *life* of faith which follows conversion.

In addition to their **work of faith**, Paul remembered their **labor of love**. This speaks of their service for God motivated by **love** to the Lord Jesus. Christianity is not a life to be endured for duty's sake, but a Person to be served for love's sake. To be His slave is perfect freedom, and "love for Him makes drudgery divine." Compared to love, the profit motive is a cheap, tawdry inducement. Love for Christ draws forth service that the dollar could never inspire. The Thessalonians were living testimonies to this fact.

Finally, Paul was thankful for their **patience of hope**. This speaks of their steadfast waiting for Jesus. They had been undergoing persecution as a result of their valiant stand for Christ. But no cracks had appeared in what Phillips calls their "sheer dogged endurance."

The place of remembrance is indicated by the phrase **in the sight of our God and Father**. As Paul entered the presence of God in prayer, he rehearsed the spiritual birth and growth of the saints and breathed out his thanksgiving for their faith, love, and hope.

1:4 The apostle was assured that these saints had been chosen **by God** before the foundation of the world. But how did he know? Did he have some supernatural insight? No, he knew they were among the elect by the way they had received the gospel.

The doctrine of **election**[4] teaches that God chose certain people in Christ before the foundation of the world (Eph. 1:4). It does *not* teach that He chose some to be damned. If men are finally lost, it is because of their own sin and unbelief.

The same Bible that teaches election also teaches human responsibility or man's free choice. God makes a *bona fide* offer of salvation to all people everywhere. Whoever comes to Christ will find a warm welcome.

These two doctrines, election and freedom of choice, create an irreconcilable conflict in the human mind. But the Bible teaches both and so we should believe both even if we can't harmonize them.

We do not know who the elect are, and so we should carry the gospel to all the world. Sinners should not use the doctrine of election as an excuse for not believing. If they will repent and believe on the Lord Jesus Christ, God will save them.

1:5 By **our gospel** Paul does not imply a different message from that of the other apostles. The contents were the same; the difference was in the messengers. The Thessalonians had not treated the message as a mere religious lecture; they had, of course, received it in word, but not **in word only**.

It was **in power, and in the Holy Spirit, and in much assurance** that it came to them: (1) **In power**. The message worked in their lives with supernatural energy, producing conviction of sin, repentance, and conversion. (2) **In the Holy Spirit**. This power was produced by the Holy Spirit. (3) **In much assurance**. Paul preached with great confidence in the message. The Thessalonians accepted it with **much assurance** as the word of God. The result in their lives was full assurance of faith.

Paul now reminds them of his own conduct while he was with them. He not only preached the gospel, but lived a consistent life. The best sermon is a holy life.

1:6 Thus Paul could say, **"You became followers of us and of the Lord."** One would have expected him to say "of the Lord and of us," mentioning the Lord first. But here he is giving the order of their experience. Their first introduction to the Lord Jesus was in the life of the apostle.

It is sobering to think that people are supposed to be able to see Christ in us. We should be able to say with Paul, "Imitate me, just as I also imitate Christ" (1 Cor. 11:1).

Notice that they received the word with **affliction** and **joy**. This is how they had imitated the Lord and the apostles. Externally there was **affliction**; internally there was **joy**. It is an unusual combination! For the man of the world, it is impossible to experience joy and affliction simultaneously; to him, sorrow is the opposite of joy. The Christian has a **joy of the Holy Spirit** that is independent of circumstances; to him, the opposite of joy is sin.

The **affliction** they endured was the persecution which followed their conversion.

1:7 The Thessalonians became model Christians. First of all, their example of joy in the midst of persecution was an example to believers **in Macedonia and Achaia**, that is, to all the Christians in Greece.

1:8 But their testimony didn't stop there. They became reproducing Christians. Like ripples in a pool, **the word of the Lord** spread out in ever-widening circles: first **in Macedonia and Achaia**, then **in every place**. Soon the news of their **faith toward God** became so widespread that Paul didn't have to speak about it; the people already knew.

We are not intended to be termini of our blessings, but channels through which they can flow to others. God shines in our hearts so that the light might shine out to others (2 Cor. 4:6, JND translation). If we have really drunk the water of salvation, then rivers of living water will flow forth to those around us (John 7:37, 38).

1:9 It was a matter of common conversation that when the apostle and his colleagues went to Thessalonica, they had received a royal welcome. Also it had become a matter of common knowledge that a startling transformation had taken place in the lives of many people. They had **turned to God from** their pagan **idols** and had yielded their will to God as bondslaves.

Notice that they **turned to God from idols**, not from idols to God. It wasn't that they had become fed up with their idols and then decided to give God a chance. No, they **turned to God** and found Him so satisfying that they dropped their idols.

> It's that look that melted Peter,
> It's that face that Stephen saw,
> It's that heart that wept with Mary,
> Can alone from idols draw.
>
> *— Ora Rowan*

Let us never lose the sense of thrill and awe that is implicit in this account. Two men go into a heathen city with the word of the Lord. They preach the gospel in the power of the Spirit. The miracle of regeneration takes place: men and women become so enraptured with the Savior that they abandon their idols. Next you have a local assembly of believers praising God, living lives of holiness, bravely enduring persecution, and winning others to Christ. Truly the Lord's service is the prince of callings!

1:10 Not only were the Thessalonians serving the living and true God (in contrast to idols which are lifeless and false), but they were waiting for the Lord Jesus. Notice the details of their expectation:

1. The Person — **His Son**
2. The Place — **from heaven**
3. The Pledge — **whom He raised from the dead**
4. The Precious Name — **even Jesus**
5. The Prospect — **who delivers us from the wrath to come**

Thus we have in verses 9 and 10 the three aspects of the Thessalonians' experience:

Turning (compare work of faith, v. 3)
Serving (compare labor of love, v. 3)
Waiting (compare patience of hope, v. 3)

G. R. Harding Wood[5] analyzes them as follows:

> Following — looking to God
> Serving — looking on the fields
> Waiting — looking for Jesus

The Thessalonians were waiting for God's **Son from heaven**. This implies the possibility of His coming during their lifetime, in fact, *at any moment* during their lifetime. The imminent return of the Lord Jesus is the Christian's hope. It is found in many passages of the NT, of which the following are a few:

Luke 12:36 — "And you yourselves be like men who wait for their master."

Romans 8:23 — ". . . waiting for the adoption, the redemption of our body."

1 Corinthians 11:26 — "For as often as you eat this bread and drink this cup, you proclaim the Lord's death till He comes."

2 Corinthians 5:2 — "For in this we groan, earnestly desiring to be clothed with our habitation which is from heaven."

Galatians 5:5 — "For we through the Spirit eagerly wait for the hope of righteousness by faith."

Philippians 3:20 — "We also eagerly wait for the Savior, the Lord Jesus Christ."

Philippians 4:5 — "The Lord is at hand."

Titus 2:13 — "Looking for the blessed hope and glorious appearing of our great God and Savior Jesus Christ."

Hebrews 9:28 — "To those who eagerly wait for Him He will appear a second time, apart from sin, for salvation."

James 5:7–9 — "Therefore, be patient, brethren, until the coming of the Lord . . . for the coming of the Lord is at hand . . . the Judge is standing at the door."

1 Peter 4:7 — "But the end of all things is at hand."

1 John 3:3 — "And everyone who has this hope in Him purifies himself, just as He is pure."

Jude 21 — ". . . looking for the mercy of our Lord Jesus Christ unto eternal life."

Revelation 3:11 — "I am coming quickly!" 22:7 — "Behold, I am coming quickly!" 22:12 — "And behold, I am coming quickly . . ." 22:20 — " 'Surely . . . quickly.' Amen. Even so, come, Lord Jesus!"

The Christian knows that he may be required to pass through death, but he also knows that the Lord may come at any moment and that, in that event, he will enter heaven without dying.

No prophecy of the Scripture needs to be fulfilled before the coming of Christ for His people. It is *the next great event* in God's program.

We cannot be looking for the Lord's return at any moment if some event or period of time has to intervene. The pretribulation Rapture position is the only one that permits the believer to look for Christ's coming today. Other views force abandonment of the imminency of His return.

The One we look for is Jesus, our Deliverer **from the wrath to come**. This description of the coming Savior may be understood in two ways:

1. He delivers us from the eternal punishment of our sins. On the cross He endured the **wrath** of God against our sins. Through faith in Him, we have the value of His work reckoned to our account. Henceforth there is no condemnation for us because we are in Christ Jesus (Rom. 8:1).

2. But He also delivers us from the coming period of judgment when the **wrath** of God will be poured out on the world that has rejected His Son. This period is known as the Tribulation and the time of Jacob's Trouble (Dan. 9:27; Matt. 24:4–28; 1 Thess. 5:1–11; 2 Thess. 2:1–12; Rev. 6:1–19:10).

B. Review of Paul's Ministry, Message, and Conduct at Thessalonica (2:1–12)

2:1 In the latter part of 1:5, Paul briefly alluded to his personal character and conduct while he was at Thessalonica. Now he launches into a more thorough review of his ministry, message, and lifestyle.

The point is that the primary ministry of a Christian is the ministry of *character*. What we are is far more important than anything we ever say. Our uncon-

scious influence speaks more loudly than our conscious influence. James Denney said:

> A Christian's character is the whole capital he has for carrying on his business. In most other callings, a man may go on, no matter what his character is, provided his balance at the bank is on the right side; but a Christian who has lost his character has lost everything.[6]

The missionary martyr Jim Elliot wrote in his journal:

> In spiritual work, if nowhere else, the character of the worker decides the quality of his work. Shelley and Byron may be moral free-lancers and still write good poetry. Wagner may be lecherous and still produce fine music, but it cannot be so in any work for God. Paul could refer to his own character and manner of living for proof of what he was saying to the Thessalonians. Nine times over in this first epistle he says, "You know," referring to the Thessalonians' firsthand observation of Paul's private as well as public life. Paul went to Thessalonica and lived a life that more than illustrated what he preached; it went beyond illustration to convincing proof. No wonder so much work in the Kingdom is shoddy; look at the moral character of the worker.[7]

Perhaps in these verses the apostle is defending himself against the false accusation of his critics. At any rate, he first reminds the Thessalonians that his ministry was successful. They themselves were living evidence that his work had been fruitful. They knew that his visit **was not in vain**. They themselves had been converted and a congregation had been established.

2:2 Then, too, his ministry was courageous. The bitter opposition and outrageous treatment **at Philippi**, including his imprisonment there with Silas, did not daunt, discourage, or intimidate him. He pressed on to Thessalonica. There, with the courage which only God can give, he preached **the gospel** in the face of **much conflict**. A less robust person could have thought of numerous theological reasons why God was calling him to more congenial audiences. But not Paul! He preached the message fearlessly despite great opposition, a direct result of the Spirit's filling.

2:3 The apostle's **exhortation** to believe the gospel was true in its source, pure in its motive, and dependable in its method. As to its source, it did not spring from false doctrine but from the truth of God. As to its motive, the apostle looked on the Thessalonians unselfishly, with their good in view, and not with any ulterior, impure desire. As to its method, there was no clever plot to deceive them. Apparently his jealous enemies were accusing him of heresy, lustful desire, and craftiness.

2:4 To Paul the ministry was a sacred stewardship. He was the steward, **approved by God**, and **the gospel** was the precious treasure that had been **entrusted** to him by God. His responsibility was to please God by the faithful proclamation of the message, no matter what man's reaction might be. It was clear to him that he couldn't please both God and man, so he chose to please **God, who tests our hearts** and then rewards accordingly.

A steward is obligated to please the one who pays him. Preachers may sometimes be tempted to hold back the full truth for fear of repercussion from those who contribute to their support. But God is the Master, and He knows when the message is watered down or suppressed.

2:5 In verses 5–12 Paul gives an account of his behavior at Thessalonica; in doing so, he has left a splendid pattern for all servants of Christ.

First of all, he never stooped to flattery or insincerity in order to achieve results. His words were honest and transparent, and his motives were free from hypocrisy.

Second, he never used the work of the Lord as **a cloak** under which he could hide a selfish desire to get rich. His service was not a false front **for covetousness**.

To disprove any charge of flattery, he appeals to the saints. But to disprove any thought of **covetousness**, he appeals to **God**, who is the only One who can read the heart.

2:6 Here we have another impressive insight into the character of this great man of God. **As apostles of Christ**, he and his colleagues were entitled to financial support (here called **glory**) from the Thessalonians. But they were deter-

mined that they would not be burdensome to them, so they worked day and night to provide for their own needs. It was a different story in Corinth. There Paul worked so as not to give his critics any ground for accusing him of preaching for money. In Thessalonica he worked because the saints were poor and persecuted, and he did not want to be an added burden to them.

2:7 Instead of lording it over God's heritage, he was **gentle among** them **as a nursing mother** caring for **her own children**. Paul realized that new converts need **nursing**, and he carried on this ministry with all the solicitude of a devoted **mother**.

2:8 So deep was his affectionate concern for them, he was anxious to share with them rather than to receive from them. His was not a cold, perfunctory dispensing of **the gospel of God** but a pouring out of his very soul. He loved them, and love is heedless of cost. Like his Master, he did not come to be served, but to serve and to give his life (Mark 10:45).

2:9 A further evidence of Paul's unselfishness is here: we see him working as a tentmaker in order to earn a living so that he could minister to the people without being **a burden to any of** them. While it is true that the gospel preacher is entitled to financial support from other Christians, it is commendable to see him foregoing this right, if necessary, from time to time. A true minister of Christ will continue to preach the gospel whether he receives money for it or has to work to finance himself. Notice the expressions **labor and toil** and **night and day**. The gospel didn't cost the Thessalonians a penny, but it cost Paul plenty.

2:10 The believers could testify to Paul's exemplary behavior toward them; and **God also** was a Witness that he was devout (or holy), just (or righteous), and blameless. Holy, that is, separated to God from sin. Righteous in character and in conduct. Blameless toward God and man. If the best sermon is a holy life, Paul was a great preacher. Not like another preacher whose eloquence was greater than his conduct: when he was in the pulpit, the people wished he would never leave it, but when he was out of it, they wished he would never enter it again!

2:11 In verse 7, he had compared himself to a nursing mother; now he changes the figure to that of a devoted **father**. If the former suggests tenderness and affection, the latter suggests wisdom and counsel. **As a father**, he **exhorted** them to live a holy life, he encouraged them to go on for the Lord in spite of persecutions, and he testified concerning the blessedness of obedience to the will and word of God.

2:12 The goal of Paul's ministry was that the saints might **walk worthy of God who calls** them **into His own kingdom and glory**.

In ourselves we are unworthy of God or of a place in heaven; the only worthiness we have is found in the Lord Jesus Christ. But as sons of God, we are expected to **walk worthy** of the high calling. We can do this by submitting ourselves to the control of the Holy Spirit and by confessing and forsaking sin in our lives continually.

All who are saved are subjects of God's **own kingdom**. At the present time that **kingdom** is invisible, and the King is absent. But the moral and ethical teachings of the kingdom apply to us today. When the Lord Jesus returns to reign, the **kingdom** will then be set up in visible form, and we will share the **glory** of the King in that day.

C. Review of the Thessalonians' Response to the Gospel (2:13–16)

2:13 Now the apostle picks up another theme which he had touched on in 1:5a — the Thessalonians' response to the preaching of the gospel. When they received the message, i.e., *heard* it, they did not receive, i.e., *accept* it as the word of men but as the word of God. The NKJV brings this out clearly:

> For this reason we also thank God without ceasing, because when you received the word of God which you heard from us, you welcomed it not as the word of men, but as it is in truth, the word of God, which also effectively works in you who believe.

Paul is deeply thankful for their re-

ception and acceptance of the message. This is another example of his selflessness. Most of us want others to believe what we say simply because *we* say it. But man's word forms a shaky foundation for faith. Only God can be fully trusted, and it is only when His word is trusted that results are produced in hearts and lives. This is what happened to the Thessalonians — the word was working **effectively** in their lives because they believed. Walter Scott wrote:

> His Word — the Bible — is inspired, or God-breathed, in all its books and parts as originally written. It is our only authority in all things, for all circumstances, and all times. There is needed a generation who shall tremble at the Word of God. It is life's chart; our guidance, our light, our moral safeguard. Thank God for the Sacred Volume.[8]

2:14 What results had the Bible produced in the lives of these believers? Not only had they been saved; they were enabled to stand firm in the face of severe persecution. This was good evidence of the reality of their conversion. By their steadfast endurance, they **became imitators of the** Christian **churches in Judea**. The only difference was that the Thessalonians **suffered** at the hands of their Gentile **countrymen**, whereas the believers in Judea were persecuted by **the Judeans**.

2:15 At this mention of the Judeans, Paul launches into an indictment of them as arch-opponents of the gospel. And who should know better than he? At one time he had been a ringleader of those Jews who attempted to liquidate the Christian faith. Then after his conversion he himself felt the sharp edge of the sword of their persecution.

The crowning sin of the Jews was killing **the Lord Jesus**. While the actual crucifixion was carried out by the Romans, it was the Jews who stirred them up to do it. This came as a climax to centuries of persecution of God's **prophets** sent to the nation of Israel (Matt. 21:33–39).

In the Christian era, they had already **persecuted** Paul and other apostles, mistakenly thinking that they were pleasing **God**. Their actions were displeasing to Him and they made themselves **contrary to all men**.

2:16 Not content to reject the gospel themselves, they were determined to prevent Paul and his associates from preaching the message **to the Gentiles**. Nothing infuriated them more than to hear that Gentiles could **be saved** in the same way as Jews.

In their opposition to the will of God, they were carrying on where their fathers had left off: **always to fill up the measure of their sins**. It was as if they were determined to keep the cup of their guilt full at all times.

But their doom is pronounced, for **wrath has come upon them to the uttermost**. Paul does not specify what he means by this **wrath**. Perhaps it is a general statement of impending judgment as a result of a full measure of guilt. We do know that within twenty years (A.D. 70) Jerusalem was destroyed and the surviving Jews were scattered throughout the earth.

From passages such as this, some have suggested that Paul was anti-semitic and that the NT is an anti-semitic book. The truth is that Paul had a deep love for his countrymen, the Jews, and was even willing to be cut off from Christ if it could have meant their salvation (Rom. 9:1–3). Though his ministry was primarily to the Gentiles, he never lost his burden for the evangelization of the Jews; at times this burden almost seems to have taken precedence over his primary mission.

What the apostle says here about the Judean leaders is historical fact and not personal invective. And we must remember that God moved him to write what he did. Anti-semitism is unchristian and cannot be justified under any circumstances. But it is not anti-semitic to say that the Jewish people are charged by God with the death of His Son (Acts 2:23), just as the Gentiles also are held responsible for their part (1 Cor. 2:8).

D. Explanation of Paul's Failure to Return to Thessalonica (2:17–20)

2:17 In the next four verses, the apostle explains his failure to return to Thessalonica. Perhaps his carping critics accused him of cowardice in not going back because of the opposition he had encountered there.

Paul first makes it clear that the separation was only physical. The expression **having been taken away from you** means that they were orphaned by the departure of their spiritual father. However, his affectionate interest in them had never waned. Notice the words that express the intensity of his love: **endeavored more eagerly . . . with great desire**.

2:18 Twice he had tried to go back to Thessalonica, but twice **Satan** had **hindered**. The exact nature of Satan's opposition is not always known.

Neither do we know how Paul could be sure it was the devil who **hindered** him and not the Lord. In Acts 16:6 we read that Paul and his party were forbidden by the Holy Spirit to preach the word in Asia. In the next verse, they tried to go to Bithynia but the Spirit would not permit them to go. How can we know when it is the Spirit and when it is the devil who is hindering? Perhaps one way is this: when we know that we are in the will of God, any hindrances that arise are not the Spirit's work but the devil's. Also, Satan can be expected to hinder whenever God is blessing. But God always overrules Satan's opposition. In this particular case, Paul's inability to go to Thessalonica resulted in the writing of this Letter. The Letter, in turn, has resulted in glory to God and blessing to us.

2:19 Why was the apostle so interested in going back to the Thessalonian believers? Because they were his children in the Lord. He had pointed them to Christ and felt responsible for their spiritual growth. He knew that he would have to give an account of them in a coming day. They were his **hope** of reward at the Judgment Seat of Christ. He wanted to be able to rejoice in them. They would be his **crown of rejoicing** before the **Lord Jesus Christ at His coming**.

It seems obvious from this verse that Paul expected to recognize the Thessalonians in heaven. And it follows that we too will know our loved ones in heaven.

In verse 19 Paul speaks of his children in the faith as being his **crown**. Elsewhere in the NT we read of other crowns: the crown of righteousness (2 Tim. 4:8); the crown of life (Jas. 1:12;

Rev. 2:10); the crown of glory (1 Pet. 5:4) — all of them incorruptible (1 Cor. 9:25).

2:20 The saints were his **glory and joy**. He had invested in human personality and his reward was spiritual sons and daughters who would worship the Lamb of God for all eternity.

THE COMING
OF THE LORD

In verse 19, we have the first use of the word **coming** in 1 Thessalonians with regard to the Lord's return. Because this is the major theme of this Epistle, we are going to pause here and give an explanation of what we believe to be the scriptural teaching on the subject.

There are three principal Greek words used in the NT with reference to Christ's return:

parousia (pa-roo-SEE-ah): coming and subsequent presence

apokalupsis (apo-KAL-yoop-sis): unveiling, revelation

epiphaneia (epi-FAHN-ee-ah): manifestation

The word most commonly used is *parousia*. It means a *presence* or a *coming alongside*. Vine says it denotes both an arrival and a consequent presence. When we think of the Lord's coming, we should think of it not only as a momentary event but as a period of time.

Even in English, the word *coming* is used in this way. For instance, "Christ's coming to Galilee brought healing to multitudes." Here we do not mean the day He arrived in Galilee but the whole period of time He spent in that area. So when we think of Christ's coming, we should think of a period of time rather than an isolated event.

Now if we take all the occurrences of *parousia* in the NT, we find that they describe a period of time with (1) a beginning, (2) a course, (3) a manifestation, and (4) a climax.

1. The *beginning* of the *parousia* is the Rapture. It is described in the following passages (the word which translates *parousia* is italicized in each case):

For as in Adam all die, even so in Christ all shall be made alive. But each one in his own order: Christ the firstfruits, afterward those who are Christ's at His *coming* (1 Cor. 15:22, 23).

But I do not want you to be ignorant, brethren, concerning those who have fallen asleep, lest you sorrow as others who have no hope. For if we believe that Jesus died and rose again, even so God will bring with Him those who sleep in Jesus. For this we say to you by the word of the Lord, that we who are alive and remain until the *coming* of the Lord will by no means precede those who are asleep. For the Lord Himself will descend from heaven with a shout, with the voice of an archangel, and with the trumpet of God. And the dead in Christ will rise first. Then we who are alive and remain shall be caught up together with them in the clouds to meet the Lord in the air. And thus we shall always be with the Lord. Therefore comfort one another with these words (1 Thess. 4:13–18).

Now, brethren, concerning the *coming* of our Lord Jesus Christ and our gathering together to him . . . (2 Thess. 2:1).

Therefore be patient, brethren, until the *coming* of the Lord. See how the farmer waits for the precious fruit of the earth, waiting patiently for it until it receives the early and latter rain. You also be patient. Establish your hearts, for the *coming* of the Lord is at hand (James 5:7, 8).

And now, little children, abide in Him, that when He appears, we may have confidence and not be ashamed before Him at His *coming* (1 John 2:28).

2. The *course* of the *parousia* includes the Judgment Seat of Christ when rewards will be given to believers for faithful service:

For what is our hope, or joy, or crown of rejoicing? Is it not even you in the presence of our Lord Jesus Christ at His *coming*? (1 Thess. 2:19).

Now may the God of peace Himself sanctify you completely; and may your whole spirit, soul, and body be preserved blameless at the *coming* of our Lord Jesus Christ (1 Thess. 5:23).

Another event which should probably be included in the *course* of the *parousia* is the Marriage Supper of the Lamb. From its location in the book of

Revelation, we know that it will take place prior to Christ's glorious reign. We include it here even though the word *coming* is not used in connection with it.

And I heard, as it were, the voice of a great multitude, as the sound of many waters and as the sound of mighty thunderings, saying, "Alleluia! For the Lord God Omnipotent reigns! Let us be glad and rejoice and give Him glory, for the marriage of the Lamb has come, and His wife has made herself ready." And to her it was granted to be arrayed in fine linen, clean and bright, for the fine linen is the righteous acts of the saints. Then he said to me, "Write: 'Blessed are those who are called to the marriage supper of the Lamb!' " (Rev. 19:6–9).

3. The *manifestation* of Christ's coming is His return to earth in power and great glory to reign as King of kings and Lord of lords. The Rapture will not be seen by the world; it takes place in a split second. But every eye will see Christ when He comes to reign. Therefore it is called the *manifestation* of His *parousia*. This is the third phase of His coming.

Now as He sat on the Mount of Olives, the disciples came to Him privately, saying, "Tell us, when will these things be? And what will be the sign of Your *coming*, and of the end of the age?" (Matt. 24:3).

For as the lightning comes from the east and flashes to the west, so also will the *coming* of the Son of Man be (Matt. 24:27).

But as the days of Noah were, so also will the *coming* of the Son of Man be (Matt. 24:37).

And [they] did not know until the flood came and took them all away, so also will the *coming* of the Son of Man be (Matt. 24:39).

So that He may establish your hearts blameless in holiness before our God and Father at the *coming* of our Lord Jesus Christ with all His saints (1 Thess. 3:13).

And then the lawless one will be revealed, whom the Lord will consume with the breath of His mouth and destroy with the brightness of His *coming* (2 Thess. 2:8).

For we did not follow cunningly de-

vised fables when we made known to you the power and *coming* of our Lord Jesus Christ, but were eyewitnesses of His majesty (2 Pet. 1:16). [Here Peter is speaking about the manifestation of Christ's *parousia* as it was pre-pictured on the Mount of Transfiguration.]

4. Finally we have the *climax* of the *parousia*. It is referred to in the following verse:

Where is the promise of His *coming*? For since the fathers fell asleep, all things continue as they were from the beginning of creation (2 Pet. 3:4).

In this latter chapter we read of scoffers who will arise in the last days, denying the probability of Christ's return. What aspect of the *parousia* do they mean?

Are they referring to the Rapture? No. They probably know nothing about the Rapture. Are they referring to Christ's coming to reign? No. It is apparent that they are not. The entire context indicates that they are ridiculing the final punishment of all evildoers by the Lord. They mean a last, climactic judgment of God on the earth, or what they call "the end of the world." Their argument is that they have nothing to worry about. God hasn't intervened in history and He won't intervene in the future. So they feel free to continue in their evil words and deeds.

Peter answers their scoffing by pointing forward to the time, *after the thousand-year reign of Christ*, when the heavens and the earth as we now know them will be utterly destroyed. This climax of Christ's *parousia* is after the Millennium and at the inauguration of the eternal state.

In addition to *parousia*, the other two words used in the original language of the NT to describe the coming of the Lord are *apokalupsis* and *epiphaneia*.

Apokalupsis means an *unveiling* or a *Revelation*. Bible students are divided whether it *always* refers to the third phase of Christ's coming — His coming to the earth in power and glory — or whether it might also refer to the Rapture when He will be revealed to the church.

In the following verses it could refer either to the Rapture or to the coming back to the earth to reign over it:

So that you come short in no gift, eagerly waiting for the *revelation* of our Lord Jesus Christ (1 Cor. 1:7).

That the genuineness of your faith, being much more precious than gold that perishes, though it is tested by fire, may be found to praise, honor, and glory at the *revelation* of Jesus Christ (1 Pet. 1:7).

Therefore gird up the loins of your mind, be sober, and rest your hope fully upon the grace that is to be brought to you at the *revelation* of Jesus Christ (1 Pet. 1:13).

But rejoice to the extent that you partake of Christ's sufferings, that when His glory is *revealed*, you may also be glad with exceeding joy (1 Pet. 4:13).

In another passage this word seems to refer quite clearly to Christ's coming to reign:

And to give you who are troubled rest with us when the Lord Jesus is *revealed* from heaven with His mighty angels (2 Thess. 1:7).

Epiphaneia means a *manifestation* or an *appearing*. Again, some think it refers both to Christ's appearing for His saints and to His appearing with His saints; others say it refers only to the latter. The word is found in the following passages:

And then the lawless one will be revealed, whom the Lord will consume with the breath of His mouth and destroy with the *brightness* (lit., *manifestation*) of His coming (2 Thess. 2:8).

That you keep this commandment without spot, blameless until our Lord Jesus Christ's *appearing* (1 Tim. 6:14).

I charge you therefore before God and the Lord Jesus Christ, who will judge the living and the dead at His *appearing* and His kingdom (2 Tim. 4:1).

Finally, there is laid up for me the crown of righteousness, which the Lord, the Righteous Judge, will give to me on that Day, and not to me only but also to all who have loved His *appearing* (2 Tim. 4:8).

Looking for the blessed hope and glorious *appearing* of our great God and Savior Jesus Christ (Tit. 2:13).

The first and third verses clearly describe the appearing of Christ to the world. The others could conceivably refer to the Rapture also. The one thing that is clear is that both the Rapture and Christ's coming to reign are held before the believer as events for which he waits with eagerness. At the time of the Rapture, he will see the Savior and will receive his glorified body. When Christ returns to earth, the believer will appear with Him in glory (Col. 3:4). It is at this time also that the believer's rewards will be manifested. These rewards are given out previously at the Judgment Seat of Christ, but they are seen by all when Christ comes to reign. What are the rewards? In Luke 19:17–19 there is a hint that they have to do with local rule in the Millennium. One person is made ruler over ten cities, another over five.

By studying the various references to the Lord's coming, we have seen that it refers to a period of time rather than to a single event, and that this period of time has various phases or stages. There is a beginning, a course, a manifestation, and a climax. It begins with the Rapture, includes the Judgment Seat of Christ, will be visibly displayed when Christ returns to earth, and will end when the heavens and earth as we now know them are destroyed by fire. ‡

E. The Mission of Timothy to Thessalonica (3:1–10)

The words *your faith* occur five times in chapter 3 (vv. 2, 5, 6, 7, 10) and are a key to understanding the passage. The Thessalonians were passing through severe persecution, and Paul was anxious to know how their faith was standing up to the test. Thus the chapter is a lesson on the importance of follow-up work. It is not enough to lead sinners to the Savior. They must be helped to grow in grace and in the knowledge of the Lord.

3:1 In chapter 3 we continue to hear the heartbeat of Paul as he expresses his undying interest in the saints at Thessalonica. While he was **in Athens** he developed an intolerable craving to know how his converts were getting on. Satan had hindered his personal return. Finally he could not stand inaction any longer; he decided to send Timothy to the Thessalonians, while he remained **in Athens alone**. (The *we* is editorial.) There is a certain sadness to think of him there **alone**. The sights of a great city held no attraction for him; he was burdened with the care of the churches.

3:2 Notice the "degrees" after Timothy's name: **our brother and minister of God, and our fellow laborer in the gospel of Christ**. The word **minister**[9] here and elsewhere in the NT simply means *servant*. The idea of a separate class known as clergymen originated in later years.

What a privilege it was for Timothy to serve his apprenticeship under the beloved brother Paul! Now that he has proved himself, he is sent on a mission to Thessalonica alone.

The purpose of the trip was **to establish** the saints **and encourage** them **concerning** their **faith**. They had been persecuted because of their confession of Christ. This was a critical time for the young converts; Satan was probably dropping subtle suggestions that maybe they were wrong after all in becoming Christians!

It would be interesting to hear Timothy as he taught them to expect opposition, to bear it bravely, and to rejoice in it. They needed encouragement not to buckle under the pressure of opposition.

3:3 In the heat of persecution, it would be easy for the Thessalonians to think it strange that they should suffer so severely, and to wonder if God was displeased with them. Timothy reminded them that it wasn't strange at all: this is normal for Christians, so they shouldn't **be shaken** or lose heart.

3:4 Paul reminds them that even when he was in Thessalonica, he used to tell them that Christians were appointed to afflictions. His prediction came true in their own lives. How well they knew it!

Trials form a necessary discipline in our lives:

1. They prove the reality of our faith, and weed out those who are mere professors (1 Pet. 1:7).

2. They enable us to comfort and encourage others who are going through trials (2 Cor. 1:4).

3. They develop certain graces, such as endurance, in our character (Rom. 5:3).

4. They make us more zealous in spreading the gospel (Acts 4:29; 5:27–29: 8:3, 4).

5. They help to remove the dross from our lives (Job 23:10).

3:5 The apostle repeats the substance of verses 1 and 2: **when** further delay proved unendurable for him, he **sent** Timothy to find out how the Christians there were weathering the storm. His great anxiety was that the devil might have tricked them into giving up their aggressive Christian testimony in exchange for relaxation of the persecution. It is the ever-present temptation to swap loyalty to Christ for personal comfort, to by-pass the cross in pursuit of a crown. Who of us does not have to pray, "Forgive me, Lord, for so often finding ways to avoid the pain and sacrifice of discipleship. Strengthen me today to walk with You no matter what the cost."

If Satan had induced the saints to recant, then Paul felt his labor there would have been for nothing.

3:6 **Timothy** came back to Corinth **from** the Thessalonians with **good news**. First of all, he reassured Paul concerning their **faith and love**. They were not only standing true to the teachings of the Christian **faith**, but they were also manifesting the distinctive virtue of **love**. This is ever the test of reality — not just an orthodox acceptance of the Christian creed, but "faith working through love" (Gal. 5:6). Not just your "faith in the Lord Jesus" but also "your love for all the saints" (Eph. 1:15).

Was it significant that Timothy mentioned their **faith and love**, but omitted any reference to their hope? Had the devil shaken their confidence in the return of Christ? Possibly. As William Lincoln said, "The devil hates that doctrine because he knows the power of it in our lives." If their hope was defective, Paul certainly seeks to repair it in this Epistle of hope.

Timothy also reported that the Thessalonians had kind memories of the apostle and his friends, and that they were as anxious for a reunion as Paul, Silas, and Timothy were.

3:7 This news was like cold water to Paul's thirsty soul (Prov. 25:25). In all his distress and affliction, he was greatly encouraged **by** their **faith**.

3:8 He exclaims, **"For now we live, if you stand fast in the Lord."** The suspense of not knowing had been a living death to him. Now life quickly returned when he heard that all was well. What a commentary this is on the unselfish devotion of this great man of God!

3:9 Words failed to express adequately **to God** the **thanks** which filled Paul's heart. His cup of **joy** was overflowing every time he remembered them **before** his **God**.

3:10 Paul's prayer life was habitual, not spasmodic: **night and day**. It was intensely fervent: **praying exceedingly**. It was specific: **that we may see your face**. And it was altruistic: **that we may . . . perfect what is lacking in your faith**.

F. Paul's Specific Prayer (3:11–13)

3:11 The chapter closes with Paul's prayer for a return trip to them, and for the development of even greater love in them. The request is addressed to **our God and Father Himself, and our Lord Jesus Christ**. Then this plural subject is followed by a singular verb. This usage indicates the deity of Christ and the unity of the Godhead.

3:12 The Thessalonians had actually been commendable in manifesting true Christian love, but there is always room for development. And so he prays for a deeper measure: **may the Lord make you increase and abound in love**. Their love should embrace their fellow believers and all men, including their enemies. Its model or pattern should be the love of the apostles: **just as we do to you**.

3:13 The result of love in this life is blamelessness in the next. If we love one another and all mankind, we will stand **blameless in holiness before our God** when **Christ** comes **with all His saints**, for love is the fulfilling of the law (Rom. 13:8; Jas. 2:8).

Someone has paraphrased the prayer as follows: "The Lord enable you more and more to spend your lives in the interests of others, in order that He may so establish you in Christian character now, that you might be vindicated from every charge that might possibly be brought against you . . . ."

In chapter 2 we saw that the coming of Christ has several stages or phases: a beginning, a course, a manifestation, and a climax. It is the third phase that is referred to in verse 13: **the coming of our Lord Jesus Christ with all His saints**. The Judgment Seat of Christ will have already taken place in heaven. The awards will already have been made. But these awards will be manifested to all when the Savior returns to earth as King of kings and Lord of lords.

Saints here probably means those believers who have been caught up to heaven at the time of the Rapture (1 Thess. 4:14). Some think that it means angels, but Vincent says it refers to *the holy and glorified people of God*. He points out that angels have nothing to do with anything in this Epistle, but that glorified believers are closely connected with the subject that was troubling the Thessalonians. He adds, "This does not exclude the attendance of angels on the Lord's coming, but when Paul speaks of such attendance, he says *with the angels of his power*, as in 2 Thessalonians 1:7."[10]

III. PRACTICAL EXHORTATIONS (4:1–5:22)

A. The Sanctification that Fulfills God's Will (4:1–8)

4:1 The word **finally** doesn't mean that Paul is about to close the Letter. It often indicates a change of subject, such as a shift to practical exhortations.

Three prominent words at the close of chapter 3 were *holiness, love,* and *coming*. These are three of the principal subjects of chapter 4: (1) Holiness (vv. 1–8), (2) Love (vv. 9, 10), and (3) Coming (vv. 13–18). The other main theme is industriousness (vv. 11, 12).

Chapter 4 opens with a plea to walk in holiness and thus to please God, and closes with the taking up of the saints. Paul was probably thinking of Enoch when he wrote this. Notice the similarity: (1) Enoch walked with God (Gen. 5:24a); (2) Enoch pleased God (Heb. 11:5b); and (3) Enoch was taken up (Gen. 5:24b; Heb. 11:5a). The apostle commends the believers for their practical holiness, but urges them to advance to new levels of accomplishment. Holiness is a process, not an achievement.

4:2 While he was with them, Paul repeatedly charged them, with the authority of **the Lord Jesus**, that they should please God by lives of practical holiness.

4:3 **The will of God** for His people **is** their **sanctification**. To sanctify means to set apart for divine use. In one sense, all believers have been set apart from the world to the service of the Lord; this is known as positional sanctification, and it is perfect and complete (1 Cor. 1:2; Heb. 10:10). However, in another sense, believers should sanctify themselves, that is, they should separate themselves from all forms of sin; this is known as practical or progressive sanctification. It is a process that will continue until the believer's death or the Lord's return. It is this latter use of the word that is found in verse 3. (See the discussion of sanctification under 5:23 below.)

The specific sin against which Paul warns is unlawful sexual activity, and in this section is probably the same as adultery. It is one of the principal sins of the heathen world. The admonition, **that you should abstain from sexual immorality**, is needed today as much as in the first century of the church.

4:4 The Christian program is for every one **to possess his own vessel in sanctification and honor**. The word **vessel** in this verse may mean a wife or it may mean the man's own body. It is used of a wife in 1 Peter 3:7 and of the body in 2 Corinthians 4:7.

The RSV understands it to mean a wife: "that each one of you know how to take a wife for himself in holiness and honor."

The NEB adopts the view that the body is meant: "every one of you must learn to gain mastery over his body, to hallow and honor it."

If we allow the context to decide, then **vessel** means the man's wife. The teaching is that each man should treat his wife honorably and decently, never stooping to any form of marital unfaithfulness. This reinforces monogamy as God's will for mankind (see also 1 Cor. 7:2).

4:5 The Christian view of marriage is in sharp contrast to that of the ungodly. As one commentator said, "When Jesus laid His hands on the

woman in Luke 13:13, she was made straight. When pagan man touches a woman, she is made crooked."

The Gentiles think of sex as a means of gratifying the **passion of lust**. To them chastity is a weakness, and marriage a means of making sin legal. By their filthy conversation and their obscene writings on public walls, they glory in their shame.

4:6 Sexual immorality is a sin against God's Holy Spirit (1 Cor. 6:19); it is a sin against one's own body (1 Cor. 6:18); but it is also a sin against other persons. So Paul adds: **that no one should take advantage of and defraud his brother in this matter**. In other words, a Christian man must not go beyond the bounds of marriage and **defraud** a **brother** by stealing the affections of the brother's wife. Though these offenses are not generally punished in criminal courts today, **the Lord is the avenger of all such**. Sexual sins bring on a terrible harvest of physical and mental disorders in this life, but these are nothing compared to their eternal consequences, if they are unconfessed and unforgiven. Paul had **forewarned** the Thessalonians of this.

One of Britain's most gifted writers of the nineteenth century fell into sexual sin and ended in prison and disgrace. He wrote:

> The gods have given me almost everything. But I let myself be lured into long spells of senseless and sensual ease. . . . Tired of being on the heights, I deliberately went to the depths in search for new sensation. . . . *I grew careless of the lives of others*. I took pleasure where it pleased me and passed on. I forgot that every little action of the common day makes or unmakes character, and that therefore what one has done in the secret chamber, one has some day to cry aloud from the housetop. I ceased to be lord over myself. I was no longer the captain of my soul, and did not know it. I allowed pleasure to dominate me. I ended in horrible disgrace.[11]

He grew careless of the lives of others, or, as Paul would say, he transgressed and wronged **his brother in this matter**.

4:7 **God did not call us** on the basis of moral **uncleanness**, but in connection with lives of **holiness** and purity. He has called us from a cesspool of degradation, and has begun in us a lifelong process designed to make us more and more like Himself.

4:8 Anyone who **rejects this** instruction isn't simply despising the teaching of a **man**, such as Paul; he is defying, disregarding, flouting, and rejecting **God** Himself — **who has also given**[12] **us His** *Holy* **Spirit.** The word *Holy* is emphatic here. How can one who is indwelt by the **Holy Spirit** indulge in sexual sin?

Notice that all members of the Trinity are mentioned in this paragraph. The Father (v. 3), the Son (v. 2), and the **Holy Spirit** (v. 8). Wonderful thought! All three Persons in the Godhead are interested and involved in the sanctification of the believer.

The subject changes now from lust (vv. 1–8) to love (vv. 9–12), and the exhortation changes from abstain to abound.

B. The Love that Thinks of Others (4:9, 10)

4:9 Not only is the believer to have a controlled body; he should also have a heart of love for his brothers in the Lord. **Love** is the key word of Christianity as sin is of heathenism.

There was **no need** to **write** to the Thessalonians about this virtue. They were **taught by God to love** their brothers, both by divine instinct (1 John 2:20, 27) and by the instruction of Christian teachers. The believers at Thessalonica distinguished themselves by loving all the Christians in all of Macedonia. By commending them for it, Paul memorialized them forever.

4:10 As has been mentioned, brotherly kindness is not an achievement; it is something that must be practiced continually, and so Paul exhorts the believers to **increase more and more** in this grace.

Why is love of **the brethren** so important? Because where there is love, there is unity; and where there is unity, there is the Lord's blessing (Ps. 133:1, 3).

C. The Life that Speaks to Outsiders (4:11, 12)

4:11 Paul encouraged the saints to **aspire** to do three things. In today's par-

lance the three commands in this verse would be:

1. Don't seek after the limelight. Be content to be "little and unknown, loved and prized by Christ alone."

2. **Mind your own business** instead of butting into other people's affairs.

3. Be self-supporting. Don't be a parasite or a "moocher", sponging off others.

4:12 The fact that we are Christians and are looking for Christ's coming does not relieve us of the practical responsibilities of life. We should remember that the world is watching us. Men judge our Savior by us. We should **walk properly toward** unbelievers and be independent of them financially.

D. The Hope that Comforts Believers (4:13–18)

4:13 Old Testament believers had an imperfect and incomplete knowledge of what happened to a person at the time of death. To them *sheol* was an all-purpose word used to describe the disembodied state, both of believers and unbelievers.

They believed that everyone would die eventually, that apparently there would be one general resurrection at the end of the world, and then a final judgment. Martha reflected these sketchy views when she said, "I know that he (Lazarus) will rise again in the resurrection at the last day" (John 11:24).

The Lord Jesus brought "life and immortality to light by the gospel" (2 Tim. 1:10). Today we know that the believer departs to be with Christ at the time of death (2 Cor. 5:8; Phil. 1:21, 23). The unbeliever is said to be in Hades (Luke 16:22, 23). We know that not all believers will die, but that all will be changed (1 Cor. 15:51). We know that there will be more than one resurrection. At the Rapture, only believers will be raised (1 Cor. 15:23; 1 Thess. 4:16); the wicked dead will be raised at the end of the thousand-year reign of Christ (Rev. 20:5).

When Paul first went to Thessalonica, he taught the Christians about Christ's coming to reign and the events that would follow. But in the meantime, problems had arisen regarding those saints who had died. Would their bodies remain in the graves until the last day?

Would they be excluded from participation in Christ's coming and in His glorious kingdom? To answer their questions and to allay their fears, Paul now describes the order of events at the time of Christ's coming for his people.

The formula, **I do not want you to be ignorant, brethren**, is used to alert readers to an important announcement. Here the announcement concerns **those who have fallen asleep**, that is, those believers who have *died*. Sleep is used to describe the *bodies* of departed Christians, never their spirits or souls. Sleep is an appropriate simile of death, because in death a person seems to be sleeping. Even our word *cemetery* comes from a Greek word meaning "sleeping place" (*koimētērion*). And sleep is a familiar simile, because every night we act out this symbol of death, and every morning is like a resurrection.

The Bible does not teach that the soul sleeps at the time of death. The rich man and Lazarus were both conscious in death (Luke 16:19–31). When the believer dies, he is "present with the Lord" (2 Cor. 5:8). To die is to "be with Christ," a position which Paul speaks of as "gain" and as being "far better" (Phil. 1:21, 23). This would scarcely be true if the soul were sleeping!

Neither does the Bible teach annihilation. There is no cessation of being in death. The believer enjoys eternal life (Mark 10:30). The unbeliever suffers eternal punishment (Mark 9:48; Rev. 14:11).

With regard to those saints who have died, the apostle says that there is no need for hopeless sorrow. He does not rule out sorrow; Jesus wept at the grave of Lazarus, though He knew He would raise him in a few minutes (John 11:35–44). But he rules out the despairing grief of those who have no hope of heaven, of reunion, of anything but judgment.

The expression **others who have no hope** invariably reminds me of a funeral I attended where the stricken relatives clustered around the casket of an unsaved relative and wailed inconsolably, "Oh, Marie, my God, my God, Marie!" It was an unforgettable scene of unrelieved hopelessness.

4:14 The basis of the believer's hope is the resurrection of Christ. Just as surely as **we believe that Jesus died and rose again**, so we believe that those who have fallen asleep in Jesus will be raised and will participate in His coming. "For as in Adam all die, even so in Christ all shall be made alive" (1 Cor. 15:22). His resurrection is the pledge and proof of ours.

Notice the expression **sleep in Jesus** or "those who through Jesus sleep." Knowing that it is merely the Lover of our souls giving sleep to the bodies of His beloved ones robs death of its terror.

Our positive assurance concerning those who have died in Christ is that **God will bring** them **with Him**. This may be understood in two ways:

1. It may mean that at the time of the Rapture, God will raise the bodies of believers and bring them back to heaven with the Lord Jesus.

2. Or it may mean that when Christ comes back to the earth to reign, God will bring back with Christ those who have died in faith. In other words, the apostle is saying, "Don't worry that those who have died will miss out in the glory of the coming kingdom. God will bring them back with Jesus when the latter returns in power and great glory." (This is the generally preferred meaning.)

But how can this be? Their bodies are now lying in the grave. How can they come back with Jesus? The answer is given in verses 15–17. Before Christ comes to set up His kingdom, He will return to take His own people home to be with Him in heaven. Then at a later date, He will come back with them.

4:15 How did Paul know this? His answer is, **this we say to you by the word of the Lord**. He received this as *a direct revelation* from **the Lord**. We are not told how he received it — whether by a vision, by an audible voice, or by the inward impression of the Holy Spirit. But it is definitely a truth unknown to men up to that time.

Then he goes on to explain that when Christ returns, the living saints will not have any precedence or advantage over sleeping saints.

In this verse Paul speaks of himself as one who would be **alive** at Christ's **coming** (see also 1 Cor. 15:51, 52). However, in 2 Corinthians 4:14 and 5:1, he speaks of the possibility of his being among those who will be raised. The obvious conclusion is that we should look for the Lord to come at any moment, yet realize that we may be called to reach heaven by way of death.

4:16 The exact order of events at Christ's coming for His saints is now given. **The Lord Himself will descend from heaven**. He will not send an angel, but will come **Himself**!

It will be **with a shout, with the voice of an archangel, and with the trumpet of God**. Several explanations have been offered as to the significance of these commanding sounds, but frankly it is almost impossible to speak with finality about them:

1. Some feel that the **shout** is the voice of the Lord Jesus Himself which raises the dead (John 5:25; 11:43, 44) and changes the living. Others, like Hogg and Vine, say that the shout is the archangel's voice.

2. **The voice of** Michael, the **archangel**, is commonly understood as an assembling command for the OT saints, since he is so closely associated with Israel (Dan. 12:1; Jude 9; Rev. 12:4–7). Others think its purpose is to revive Israel nationally. And still others suggest **the voice of an archangel** summons the angels as a military escort to accompany the Lord and His saints through enemy territory back to heaven (cf. Luke 16:22).

3. **The trumpet of God** is the some as the last trumpet of 1 Corinthians 15:52, which has to do with the resurrection of believers at the time of the Rapture. It calls the saints to eternal blessing. It is not to be confused with the seventh trumpet of Revelation 11:15–18, which signals the final outpouring of judgment on the world during the Tribulation. The last **trumpet** *here* is the last for the church. The seventh trumpet of Revelation is the last for the unbelieving world (though it is never specifically called the "last trumpet").

The bodies of **the dead in Christ will rise first**. Whether this includes the OT saints is debatable. Those who think it does point out that the archangel's voice is heard at this time, and that he is

closely linked with the destinies of Israel (Dan. 12:1). Those who think that the OT saints will not be raised at the Rapture remind us that the phrase **in Christ** (**the dead in Christ**) is never applied to believers who lived before the Church Age; these believers will probably be raised at the end of the Tribulation (Dan. 12:2). In any case it is clear that this is definitely *not* a general resurrection. Not all the dead are raised at this time, but only **the dead in Christ**.

4:17 Then the living **shall be caught up together with them in the clouds to meet the Lord in the air**. The word *Rapture*, which we use to describe this first phase of the Lord's return, is derived from the verb used here in the Latin Bible meaning *caught up.*[13] A "rapture" is a snatching away or a catching up. It is used of Philip in Acts 8:39, of Paul in 2 Corinthians 12:2, 4, and of the male Child in Revelation 12:5.

The air is Satan's sphere (Eph. 2:2), so this is a triumphal gathering in open defiance of the devil right in his own stronghold.

Think of all that is included in these verses! The earth and the sea yielding up the dust of all the dead in Christ. Then the transforming miracle by which this dust is formed into glorified bodies, free forever from sickness, pain, and death. Then the space-flight to heaven. And all of this taking place in the twinkling of an eye (1 Cor. 15:52).

Men of the world have difficulty believing the account of the creation of man in Genesis 1 and 2. If they have difficulty with creation, what will they do with the Rapture — when God will recreate millions of people from the dust that has been buried, scattered, strewn, or swept up on the beaches of the world?

Men of the world are enthusiastic about space travel. But can their greatest exploits compare with the wonder of traveling to heaven in a split second without taking our own atmosphere with us, as the space men have to do when they go on short hops to outer space?

In connection with Christ's coming there is a sound to hear, a sight to see, a miracle to feel, a meeting to enjoy, and a comfort to experience.

It is also good to notice the recurrence of the word **Lord** in these verses: the *word* of the Lord (v. 15), the *coming* of the Lord (v. 15), the Lord *Himself* (v. 16), to **meet the Lord** (v. 17), to **always be with the Lord** (v. 17).

Forever **with the Lord**! Who can tell all the joy and blessedness that is included in these words?

4:18 Therefore comfort one another with these words. Thoughts of the Lord's coming do not produce terror for the believer. It is a hope that thrills and cheers and comforts.

INDICATIONS OF THE LAST TIMES

There are many indications that the Rapture may be near. We consider the following as straws in the wind:

1. The formation of the State of Israel in 1948 (Luke 21:29). The fig tree (Israel) is shooting forth, that is, putting forth its leaves (Luke 21:29–31). For the first time in centuries, the Jews have a national existence in their own homeland. This means that the kingdom of God is near.

2. The rise of many other nations (Luke 21:29). Jesus predicted that not only the fig tree would shoot forth but all the trees as well. We have recently witnessed the demise of colonial governments and the proliferation of new nations. It is an era of new nationalism.

3. The return of Israel to the land in unbelief (Ezek. 36:24, 25). Ezekiel prophesied that it would only be after their return that they would be cleansed from their sins. Israel today is largely an agnostic nation; only a small (but very vocal) segment of the people are orthodox Jews.

4. The ecumenical movement (Rev. 17, 18). We understand Babylon the Great to be a vast religious, political, and commercial system made up of apostate religious bodies that profess to be Christian, perhaps a merger of apostate Catholicism and apostate Protestantism. Christendom is becoming increasingly apostate (1 Tim. 4:1; 2 Thess. 2:3) and is moving toward a world super-church.

5. The worldwide increase in Spiritism (1 Tim. 4:1–3). It is sweeping over vast areas of the earth at this moment.

6. The drastic decline of moral standards (2 Tim. 3:1–5). The daily newspapers offer plenty of evidence of this.

7. Violence and civil disobedience (2 Thess. 2:7, 8). A spirit of lawlessness is abounding in the home, in national life, and even in the church.

8. People with a form of godliness but denying its power (2 Tim. 3:5).

9. The rise of the anti-Christian spirit (1 Jn. 2:18), manifested in the multiplication of false cults which profess to be Christian but deny every fundamental doctrine of the faith. They deceive by imitation (2 Tim. 3:8).

10. The tendency for nations to confederate along lines that approximate the line-up of the latter day. The European Common Market, based on what is known as the Treaty of Rome, may lead to the revival of the Roman Empire — the ten toes of iron and clay (Dan. 2:32–35).

11. Denial of the impending intervention of God in the affairs of the world by way of judgment (2 Pet. 3:3, 4).

To these could be added indications such as earthquakes in many countries, the threat of worldwide famine, and the increasing hostility among nations (Matt. 24:6, 7). The failure of governments to maintain law and order and to suppress terrorism creates the climate for a world dictator. The building of nuclear arsenals gives added meaning to such questions as, "Who is able to make war with him?" i.e., the beast (Rev. 13:4). Worldwide television facilities may be the means for fulfilling Scriptures describing events that will be seen simultaneously all over the planet (Rev. 1:7).

Most of these events are foreseen as occurring before Christ returns to the earth to reign. The Bible does not say they will take place before the Rapture but before His appearing in glory. If that is so, and if we see these trends developing already, then the obvious conclusion is that the Rapture must be near at hand. ‡

E. The Day of the Lord (5:1–11)

5:1 Bible teachers often apologize

for chapter breaks, explaining that the subject should continue without interruption. But here the chapter break is appropriate. Paul begins a new subject. He leaves his discussion of the Rapture and turns to the Day of the Lord. The words translated **but concerning** (Gk., *peri de*) indicate a new line of thought, as so often in 1 Corinthians.

For true believers the Rapture is a comforting hope, but what will it mean for those who are outside of Christ? It will mean the beginning of a period referred to here as **the times and the seasons**. This period is primarily Jewish in character. During this time God will resume His dealings with the nation of Israel, and the endtime events to which the OT prophets pointed will occur. When the apostles asked Jesus when He would set up His kingdom, He answered that it was not for them to know the times and the seasons (Acts 1:7). It seems that **the times and the seasons** cover the period prior to the setting up of the kingdom as well as the kingdom period itself.

Paul felt **no need** to **write to** the Thessalonians about **the times and the seasons**. For one thing, the saints would not be affected by them; they would be taken to heaven before these epochs began.

Also, **the times and the seasons** and the Day of the Lord are subjects that are found in the OT. The Rapture is a mystery (1 Cor. 15:51), never revealed until the time of the apostles.

5:2 The saints already knew about **the day of the Lord**. They knew that the exact time was unknown, and that it would come when least expected. What does Paul mean by **the day of the Lord**? It is certainly not a day of twenty-four hours, but a period of time with certain characteristics.

In the OT this term was used to describe any time of judgment, desolation, and darkness (Isa. 2:12; 13:9–16; Joel 2:1, 2). It was a time when God marched forth against the enemies of Israel and punished them decisively (Zeph. 3:8–12; Joel 3:14–16; Obad. 15–17; Zech. 12:8, 9). But it was also any occasion on which God punished His own people for their idolatry and backsliding (Joel 1:15–20; Amos 5:18; Zeph. 1:7–18). Basically it spoke of judgment on sin, of victory for the cause of the Lord (Joel 2:31, 32), and

untold blessing for His faithful people.

In the future, **the day of the Lord** will cover approximately the same period as the times and the seasons. It will begin after the Rapture and will include:

1. The Tribulation, i.e., the time of Jacob's trouble (Dan. 9:27; Jer. 30:7; Matt. 24:4–28; 2 Thess 2:2; Rev. 6:1–19:16).
2. The coming of Christ with His saints (Mal. 4:1–3; 2 Thess 1:7–9).
3. The thousand-year reign of Christ on the earth (Joel 3:18 [cf. v. 14]; Zech 14:8, 9 [cf. v. 1]).
4. The final destruction of the heavens and earth by fire (2 Pet. 3:7, 10).

The day of the Lord is the time when Jehovah will publicly intervene in human affairs. It is characterized by judgment on the enemies of Israel and on the apostate portion of the nation of Israel, by deliverance of His people, by establishment of Christ's kingdom of peace and prosperity, and glory for Himself.

The apostle reminds his readers **that the day of the Lord** will come **as a thief in the night**. It will be completely unexpected, taking men off guard. The world will be wholly unprepared.

5:3 This Day will also come deceptively, suddenly, destructively, inevitably, and inescapably.

There will be an air of confidence and security in the world. Then God's judgment will suddenly begin to descend with vast destructive force. **Destruction** does not mean loss of being, or annihilation; it means loss of well-being, or ruin as far as the purpose of one's existence is concerned. It will be as inevitable and unavoidable as **labor pains upon a pregnant woman**. From this judgment there will be no escape for unbelievers.

5:4 It is important to notice the change in pronouns from "they" and "them" in the previous verses to **you** and we in the following verses.

The Day of the Lord will be a time of wrath for the unsaved world. But what will it mean to us? The answer is that we are not in danger because we **are not in darkness**.

This Day will come as a thief in the night (v. 2). The only way it will **overtake** anyone is **as a thief**, and the only persons it will **overtake** will be those who are in the night, that is, the unconverted. It will not **overtake** believers at all, because they **are not in darkness**.

At first reading, this verse might seem to say that the Day of the Lord *will* overtake believers but *not as a thief*. But this is not so. It *will not overtake them at all* because when the thief comes to this world's night, the saints will be dwelling in eternal light.

5:5 All Christians are **sons of light and sons of the day**. They **are not of the night nor of darkness**. It is this fact that will exempt them from the judgment that God will pour out on the world that has rejected His Son. The judgments of the Day of the Lord are aimed only at those who are in moral darkness and spiritual night, at those who are alienated from God.

When it says here that Christians are **sons of the day**, it does not mean the Day of the Lord. To be **sons of the day** means to be people who belong to the realm of moral uprightness. The Day of the Lord is a time of judgment on those who belong to the realm of moral darkness.

5:6 The next three verses call believers to a life that is consistent with their exalted position. This means watchfulness and sobriety. We are to **watch** against temptation, laziness, lethargy, and distraction. Positively, we should **watch** for the Savior's return.

Sobriety here means not only being **sober** in conversation and in general demeanor but being temperate as far as food and drink are concerned.

5:7 In the natural realm, **sleep** is associated with **night**. So in the spiritual realm, careless indifference characterizes those who are sons of darkness, that is, the unconverted.

Men prefer to carry on their drunken revelry **at night**; they love darkness rather than light because their deeds are evil (John 3:19). The very name "night club" links the ideas of drinking and carousing with the darkness of night.

5:8 Those **who are of the day** should walk in the light as He is in the light (1 Jn. 1:7). This means judging and forsaking sin, and avoiding excesses of all kinds. It also means putting on the Christian armor and keeping it on. The armor consists of **the breastplate of faith and love** and the **helmet** of **the hope of salvation**. In other words, the armor is **faith, love,** and **hope** — the three cardi-

nal elements of Christian character. It is not necessary to press the details of **the breastplate** and **helmet**. The apostle is simply saying that sons of light should wear the protective covering of a consistent, godly life. What preserves us from the corruption that is in the world through lust? **Faith**, or dependence on God. **Love** for the Lord and for one another. The **hope** of Christ's return.

Important Contrasts in Chapter Five

Unbelievers ("they")	Believers ("you")
sleeping	not sleeping
drunk	not drunk
in darkness	not in darkness
of the night and darkness	sons of light and sons of the day
overtaken unexpectedly by the Day of the Lord as a thief in the night	not overtaken unexpectedly by the Day of the Lord as a thief in the night.
sudden and inescapable destruction, as labor pains of a pregnant woman	not appointed to wrath but to obtain salvation

5:9 The Rapture has two aspects, **salvation** and **wrath**. For the believer it means the consummation of his **salvation** in heaven. For the unbeliever, it means the ushering in of a time of **wrath** on earth.

Since we are of the day, **God did not appoint us to** the **wrath** which He will pour out during the Tribulation Period, but rather to **salvation** in its fullest sense — freedom forever from the very presence of sin.

Some understand **wrath** here to refer to the punishment which unbelievers will suffer in hell. Of course it is true that God has not appointed us to that, but it is gratuitous to introduce that thought here. Paul is not talking about hell, but about future events on earth. The context deals with the Day of the Lord — the greatest period of **wrath** in the history of man on earth (Matt. 24:21). We do not have an appointment with the executioner but with the Savior.

Some say that the Tribulation is the time of Satan's wrath (Rev. 12:12), not the wrath of God. They say that the church will experience the wrath of Satan, but will be delivered from the wrath of God at the Second Coming of Christ. However, the following verses speak of the wrath of God and of the Lamb, and their setting is during the Tribulation Period: Revelation 6:16, 17; 14:9, 10, 19; 15:1, 7; 16:1, 19.

5:10 This verse emphasizes the tremendous price our Lord Jesus Christ paid to deliver us from wrath and insure our salvation. He **died for us, that whether we wake or sleep, we should live together with Him**.

There are two ways of understanding the expression **whether we wake or sleep**. Some scholars understand it to mean "living or dead" at the time of the Rapture. They point out that there will be two classes of believers at that time — those who have died in Christ, and those who are still living. So the thought would be that whether we are among the living or the dead at the time of Christ's return, **we** shall **live together with Him**. Christians who die lose nothing. The Lord explained this to Martha: "I am the resurrection and the life: he who believes in Me, though he may die [i.e., a Christian who dies before the Rapture], he shall live [he will be raised from among the dead]. And whoever lives and believes in Me [a believer who is alive at the time of the Rapture] shall never die . . ." (John 11:25, 26).

The other view held by scholars is that **wake or sleep** means "watchful or worldly." In other words, Paul is saying that whether we are spiritually alert or carnally indifferent to spiritual things, we will be caught up to meet the Lord. Our eternal salvation does not depend on our spiritual keenness during the closing moments of our time on earth. If truly converted, **we** will **live together with Him** when He comes again, whether we are on the tiptoes of expectancy or in the prone position of slumber. Our spiritual condition will determine our rewards, but our salvation depends on faith in Christ alone.

Those who hold this second viewpoint point out that the word for **wake** is the same word translated "watch" in verse 6. And the word for **sleep** is used in verses 6 and 7 to mean "insensitivity to divine things, involving conformity to the world" (Vine). But it is *not* the same

word used in 4:13, 14, 15 to mean death.[14]

5:11 In view of so great salvation, in love for so great a Savior, and in the light of His soon return, we should exhort one another by teaching, encouragement, and example, and we should build each other up with the word of God and with loving care. Because we will live together with Him then, we should live together with one another cooperatively now.

F. Varied Exhortations to the Saints (5:12-22)

5:12 Perhaps the elders of the church in Thessalonica had rebuked those who had quit working and were "mooching off" others. And no doubt the drones didn't take the rebuke too well! That may account for this exhortation to the leaders and to those led.

When Paul urges the saints **to recognize those who labor among** them, he means to respect and obey their spiritual guides. This is clear from the words **"and are over you in the Lord and admonish you."** Elders are undershepherds of God's sheep. Their responsibility is to teach, rule, and warn.

This verse is one of many in the NT that shows that there was no one-man rule in the apostolic churches. There was a group of elders in each congregation, pastoring the local flock. As Denney explains:

At Thessalonica there was not a single president, a minister in our sense, possessing to a certain extent an exclusive responsibility; the presidence was in the hands of a plurality of men.[15]

However, the absence of *one-man* rule does not justify *every-man* rule. The assembly should not be a *democracy*, but an *aristocracy*, the rule of the *best* qualified.

5:13 Elders serve as representatives of the Lord. Their work is the work of God. For that reason, they should be held in high regard and **love**.[16] The exhortation **"be at peace among yourselves"** is no incidental insertion. The number one problem among Christians everywhere is the problem of getting along with each other. Every believer has enough of the flesh in him to divide and wreck any local church. Only as empowered by the Spirit can we develop the love, brokenness, forbearance, kindness, tender-heartedness, and forgiveness that are indispensable for **peace**. A particular threat to **peace** which Paul may be warning against is the formation of cliques around human leaders.

5:14 This verse seems to be addressed to the spiritual leaders of the congregation; it tells them how to deal with problem brothers:

1. **Warn those who are unruly** — those who won't keep in step but insist on disturbing the peace of the church by their irresponsible behavior. Here the **unruly** are those who refuse to work. They are the same as those described in 2 Thessalonians 3:6-12, walking disorderly, not working, but being busybodies.

2. **Comfort the fainthearted** — those who need constant exhortation to rise above their difficulties and go on steadfastly for the Lord.

Concerning the KJV rendering, *Comfort the feeble-minded*, Ockenga remarks: "If the word meant feeble-minded we would still comfort them. They seem to gather when the gospel is preached." And isn't this a tribute to the gospel and to the Christian church? At least there is one sphere where they find sympathy, love, and consideration.

3. **Uphold the weak** — that is, help those who are spiritually, morally, or physically weak. Spiritual and moral support of those who are **weak** in the faith is probably the main idea, though we should not rule out financial help as well.

4. **Be patient with all** — show the grace of longsuffering when others tend to irritate and provoke.

5:15 Speaking now to Christians in general, Paul forbids any thought of retaliation. The natural reaction is to strike back, to return tit for tat. But the Christian should be so in fellowship with the Lord Jesus that he will react in a supernatural way. In other words, he will instinctively show kindness and love to other believers and to the unsaved as well.

5:16 Joy can be the constant experience of the Christian, even in the most adverse circumstances, because Christ is the source and subject of his joy, and Christ is in control of the circumstances. Incidentally, **"Rejoice always"** is the shortest verse in the Greek NT, even if "Jesus wept" is the shortest in the English.

5:17 Prayer should be the constant attitude of the Christian — not that he abandons his regular duties and gives himself wholly to prayer. He prays at certain regular times; he also prays extemporaneously as need arises; and he enjoys continual communion with the Lord by prayer.

5:18 Giving **thanks** to God should be the Christian's native emotion. If Romans 8:28 is true, then we should be able to praise the Lord at all times, in all circumstances, and for **everything**, just as long as in doing so we do not excuse sin.

These three good habits have been called the standing orders of the church. They represent **the will of God in Christ Jesus for** us. The words **in Christ Jesus** remind us that He taught us these things during His earthly ministry and He was the living embodiment of what He taught. By teaching and example, He revealed to us God's will concerning joy, prayer, and thanksgiving.

5:19 The next four verses seem to deal with behavior in the assembly.

To **quench the Spirit** means to stifle His work in our midst, to limit and hinder Him. Sin quenches the Spirit. Traditions quench Him. Man-made rules and regulations in public worship quench Him. Disunity quenches Him. Someone has said, "Cold looks, contemptuous words, silence, studied disregard, go a long way to quench Him. So does unsympathetic criticism." Ryrie says that the Spirit is quenched whenever His ministry is stifled in an individual or in the church.

5:20 If we link this verse with the previous one, then the thought is that we quench the Spirit when we **despise** prophesyings. For instance, a young brother may make some inelegant statement in public ministry. By criticizing him in such a way as to make him ashamed of his testimony for Christ we quench the Spirit.

In its primary NT sense, to prophesy meant to speak the word of God. The inspired utterances of the prophets are preserved for us in the Bible. In a secondary sense, to prophesy means to declare the mind of God as it has been revealed in the Bible.

5:21 We must evaluate what we hear and **hold fast what is good**, genuine, and true. The standard by which we **test** all preaching and teaching is the word of God. There will be abuses from time to time wherever the Spirit has liberty to speak through different brethren. But quenching the Spirit is not the way to remedy these abuses.

As Dr. Denney wrote:

An open meeting, a liberty of prophesying, a gathering in which any one could speak as the Spirit gave him utterance is one of the crying needs of the modern Church. [17]

5:22 Abstain from every form of evil may mean false tongues, prophecies, or teachings, or it may mean **evil** in general.

A. T. Pierson points out that there are seven distinct frames of mind for the Christian in verses 16-22:

1. The praiseful frame (16). Finding all God's dealings to be infinitely grand.

2. The prayerful frame (17). Prayer should never be unsuitable or unseemly.

3. The thankful frame (18). Even in circumstances not pleasant to the flesh.

4. The spiritual frame (19). He should have full liberty in and through us.

5. The teachable frame (20). *Any* channel which God chooses to use.

6. The judicial frame (21). Compare 1 John 4:1. Test all by the word of God.

7. The hallowed frame (22). If evil takes shape in your mind, avoid that evil. [18]

IV. FINAL GREETINGS TO THE THESSALONIANS (5:23-28)

5:23 Now Paul prays for the sanctification of the Christians. The source is **the God of peace**. The scope is found in the word **completely**, meaning "every part of your being."

This verse has been pressed into service by some to prove the "Holiness" doctrine of entire sanctification — that a believer can become *sinlessly perfect* in this life. However, that is not what Paul means when he prays, **the God of peace Himself sanctify you completely**. He is not praying for the eradication of the sin nature but rather that sanctification would extend to every part of their being — **spirit, soul, and body**.

SANCTIFICATION

There are four phases of sanctification in the NT — pre-conversion, positional, practical or progressive, and perfect.

1. Even before a person is saved, he is set apart in a position of external privilege. Thus we read in 1 Corinthians 7:14 that an unbelieving husband is sanctified by his believing wife. This is *pre-conversion sanctification*.

2. Whenever a person is born again, he is *positionally sanctified* by virtue of his union with Christ. This means that he is set apart to God from the world. It is referred to in such passages as Acts 26:18; 1 Corinthians 1:2; 6:11; 2 Thessalonians 2:13; Hebrews 10:10, 14.

3. But then there is *progressive sanctification*. This is a present setting apart of the believer to God from the world, sin, and self. It is the process by which he becomes more Christlike. This is the sanctification which Paul prays for the Thessalonians here. It is also found in 1 Thessalonians 4:3, 4; 2 Timothy 2:21. It is brought about by the Holy Spirit when we are obedient to the word of God (John 17:17; 2 Cor. 3:18). Such practical sanctification is a process that should continue as long as the believer is on earth. He will never achieve perfection or sinlessness on earth, but he should ever be pressing toward that goal.

4. *Perfect sanctification* refers to the believer's final condition in heaven. When he goes to be with the Lord, he will be morally like the Lord, completely and finally set apart from sin (1 Jn. 3:1-3). ‡

The apostle also prays for the preservation of the Thessalonians. This preservation should include the complete person — **spirit, soul, and body**. Notice the order. Man always says body, soul, and spirit. God always says **spirit, soul, and body**. In the original creation, the spirit was of first importance, the body last. Sin reversed the order; man lives for the body and neglects the spirit. When we pray for one another, we should follow the biblical order, putting spiritual welfare before physical needs.

From this verse and others, it is clear that we are tripartite beings. Our **spirit** is that part which enables us to have communion with God. Our **soul** has to do with our emotions, desires, affections, and propensities (John 12:27). Our **body** is the house in which our person dwells (2 Cor. 5:1).

All of our parts need to **be preserved** entire, that is, complete and sound. One commentator has suggested the needs for preservation as follows:

1. The spirit from (a) everything that would defile it (2 Cor. 7:1); (b) everything that would hinder the testimony of the Holy Spirit to the saints' relationship with God (Rom. 8:16); or (c) everything that would prevent the worship which He seeks (John 4:23; Phil 3:3).

2. The soul from (a) evil thoughts (Matt. 15:18, 19; Eph. 2:3); (b) fleshly appetites that war against it (1 Pet. 2:11); and (c) contention and strife (Heb. 12:15).

3. The body from (a) defilement (1 Thess. 4:3-8); and (b) evil uses (Rom. 6:19).

Some deny that the unsaved have a spirit. Perhaps they base this on the fact that they are spiritually dead (Eph. 2:1). However, the fact that the unsaved are spiritually dead does not mean that they have *no* spirit. It means that they are dead as far as fellowship with God is concerned. Their spirits may be very much alive, for example, as far as contact with the world of the *occult* is concerned, but they are dead *Godward*.

Lenski warns:

Many are satisfied with a partial Christianity, some parts of their life are still worldly. The apostolic admonitions constantly prod into all the corners of our nature so that none may escape purification.[19]

The prayer goes on to desire that God's sanctification and preservation will so extend to every part of their personalities that the believers will be **blameless at the coming of our Lord Jesus Christ**. This seems to point to the Judgment Seat of Christ, which follows the Rapture. At that time, the Christian's life, service, and testimony will be reviewed, and he will be rewarded or suffer loss.

5:24 As we learned in 4:3, our sanctification is the will of God. He has called us to eventually stand blameless before Him. Having begun this work in us, He will finish it (Phil. 1:6). **He who calls** us **is faithful** to His promise.

5:25 As Paul closes, he asks for the prayers of the saints. He never outgrew the need for prayer and neither do we. It is a sin to fail to **pray for** fellow believers.

5:26 Next he asks that **all the brethren** be greeted **with a holy kiss**. At that time, this was the accepted mode of greeting. In some countries it is still customary for men to kiss men, and women to kiss women. In still other cultures men kiss the women and vice versa. But more often than not this has led to abuses and has had to be abandoned.

The kiss was not instituted by the Lord as a prescribed form of greeting or taught by the apostles as obligatory. The Bible wisely allows for other modes of greeting in cultures where kissing might lead to sexual laxness. The Spirit of God seeks to guard against such irregularities by insisting that the **kiss** must be **holy**.

5:27 The apostle solemnly charges **that this epistle be read to all the holy**[20] **brethren**. Two points should be noted here:

1. Paul invests the Letter with the authority of the word of God. The OT was read publicly in the synagogues. Now **this epistle** will **be read** aloud in the churches.

2. The Bible is for all Christians, not for some inside circle or privileged class. All its truths are for all the saints.

Denney wisely insists:

There is no attainment in wisdom or in goodness which is barred against any man by the gospel; and there is no surer mark of faithlessness and treachery in a church than this, that it keeps its members in a perpetual pupilage or minority, discouraging the free use of Holy Scripture, and taking care that all it contains is not read to all the brethren.[21]

Notice that in verses 25-27 we have three keys to a successful Christian life: (1) prayer (v. 25); (2) love for fellow believers, which speaks of fellowship (v. 26); and (3) reading and study of the word (v. 27).

5:28 Finally we have Paul's characteristic close. He opened his First Epistle to the Thessalonians with grace, and now he closes it with the same theme. To the apostle Christianity is **grace** from beginning to end. **Amen**.

ENDNOTES

[1](Intro) James Everett Frame, *A Critical and Exegetical Commentary on the Epistles of St. Paul to the Thessalonians,* (ICC), p. 37.

[2](Intro) George Robert Harding Wood, *St. Paul's First Letter,* pp. 13, 14.

[3](1:1) The critical text omits "from God our Father and the Lord Jesus Christ," but it is found in the vast majority of mss. It would be easy to omit it in copying since it is nearly identical to the phrase used immediately preceding.

[4](1:4) See Ephesians 1 for an "Excursus on Divine Election."

[5](1:10) Wood, *First Letter,* p. 17.

[6](2:1) James Denney, further documentation unavailable.

[7](2:1) Elliot, Elisabeth, ed., *The Journals of Jim Elliot,* p. 218.

[8](2:13) Walter Scott, further documentation unavailable.

[9](3:2) *Minister* is simply a Latin word for *servant.*

[10](3:13) Marvin Vincent, *Word Studies in the New Testament,* IV:34.

[11](4:6) Oscar Wilde, who left his lovely wife to engage in homosexuality.

[12](4:8) The critical (NU) text reads "who also gives."

[13](4:17) The Latin past participle *raptus,* from the verb *rapere.* Jerome's exact wording in the Vulgate is "rapiemur cum illis" (we shall be raptured with them).

[14](5:10) The words in the original are as follows: *wake* in 5:10 and *watch* in 5:6 are *grēgoreō* (the origin of the masculine name "Gregory," or "watchful"). *Sleep* in 5:6, 7 stands for *katheudō,* which can refer to literal sleep or "spiritual laziness and indifference" (Arndt and Gingrich). In 4:13–15, *sleep* translates *koimaō.*

[15](5:12) James Denney, *The Epistles to Thessalonians,* p. 205.

[16](5:13) For a detailed exposition of elders, see comments on 1 Timothy 3:1-7 and Titus 1:5-9.

[17](5:21) Denney, *Thessalonians,* p. 244.

[18](5:22) Arthur T. Pierson, further documentation unavailable.

[19](5:23) R. C. H. Lenski, *The Interpretation of St. Paul's Epistles to the Colossians, to the Thessalonians, to Timothy, to Titus, and Philemon,* p. 364.

[20](5:27) The critical text omits "holy."

[21](5:27) Denney, *Thessalonians,* pp. 263, 264.

BIBLIOGRAPHY
(1 and 2 Thessalonians)

Buckland, A. R. *St. Paul's First Epistle to the Thessalonians.* Philadelphia: The Union Press, 1908.

———. *St. Paul's Second Epistle to the Thessalonians.* Philadelphia: The Union Press, 1909.

Denney, James. *The Epistles to the Thessalonians.* New York: George H. Doran Company, n.d.

Eadie, John. *A Commentary on the Greek Text of the Epistles of Paul to the Thessalonians.* London: MacMillan, 1877.

Frame, James E. *A Critical and Exegetical Commentary on the Epistles of Paul to the Thessalonians,* ICC. New York: Chas. Scribner's Sons, 1912.

Hogg, C. F. and W. E. Vine, *The Epistles of Paul the Apostle to the Thessalonians.* London: C. A. Hammond, 1953.

Kelly, William. *The Epistles of Paul the Apostle to the Thessalonians.* London: C. A. Hammond, 1953.

Morris, Leon. *The Epistles of Paul to the Thessalonians,* TBC. Grand Rapids: Wm. B. Eerdmans Publishing Company, 1957.

———. *The First and Second Epistles to the Thessalonians,* NIC. Grand Rapids: Wm. B. Eerdmans Publishing Company, 1959.

Wood, George Robert Harding. *St. Paul's First Letter.* London: Henry E. Walter Ltd., 1952.

THE SECOND EPISTLE TO THE THESSALONIANS

Introduction

"As in the first Epistle, the apostle does not immediately grapple with the error, but prepares the hearts of the saints gradually and on all sides so as to clench the truth and exclude the error once it is exposed. This is the way of divine grace and wisdom; the heart is set right, and not the mere point of error or evil dealt with." — William Kelly

I. Unique Place in the Canon

The important truths found in this little Letter are both doctrinal and practical. Paul further explains and corrects the Thessalonians' understanding of the Second Coming and the revelation about the man of sin. He also gives sound advice as to those who would use the Second Coming as an excuse not to work — don't let them eat, either!

II. Authorship[†]

If anything, the *external evidence* for 2 Thessalonians is even stronger than for 1 Thessalonians. Not only is it attested early by Polycarp, Ignatius, and Justin (as well as being found in the Marcionite Prologue and the Muratorian Canon), but Irenaeus quotes 2 Thessalonians by name.

Since it is so short, the Epistle does not have as much *internal evidence* as 1 Thessalonians, but it does complement and agree so well with that Epistle that few scholars hesitate to accept its Pauline authorship.

III. Date

Second Thessalonians was written in response to further problems and also the misunderstanding of parts of 1 Thessalonians. A few months or even weeks are all that are needed to pass between the writing of the two Letters. Paul, Silvanus, and Timothy were still together (1:1), and Corinth is the only city where we read of their being together (Acts 18:1, 5). Hence the date is the early 50's, probably A.D. 50 or 51.

IV. Background and Themes[†]

There were three principal reasons for another Letter, even so soon after the first. The saints were being persecuted and needed to be encouraged (chap. 1). They were being misled as to the Day of the Lord and needed to be enlightened (chap. 2). Some were living in idleness in view of the Lord's Return and needed to be corrected (chap. 3).

With regard to the Day of the Lord, the believers were fearful that they were already in it. Their fears were strengthened by false rumors to the effect that Paul himself was teaching that the Day was now present. So the apostle sets the record straight.

It should be apparent that the Day of the Lord is not the same as the coming of the Lord, that is, the Rapture. The saints were not fearful that the Lord had come; they were fearful that they were in the Tribulation, the first phase of the Day of the Lord.

Paul had never taught that any events *had to occur before the Rapture*. But now he teaches that *before the Day of the Lord* begins, there will be a great apostasy, the restrainer will be removed, and the man of sin will be revealed'.

[†]*See p. i.*
[†]*See p. ii.*

863

For the proper understanding of this Letter, nothing is more important than to see the distinction between the Rapture, the Day of the Lord, and Christ's Coming to reign. The Day of the Lord is defined in the notes on 1 Thessalonians 5:2. The distinction between the Rapture and the Revelation is made in an Excursus at 2 Thessalonians 1:7.

OUTLINE

I. SALUTATION (1:1, 2)

II. PAUL AND THE THESSALONIANS (1:3–12)
  A. Paul's Debt of Thanks (1:3–5)
  B. The Righteous Judgment of God (1:6–10)
  C. Paul's Prayer for the Saints (1:11, 12)

III. CONCERNING THE DAY OF THE LORD (2:1–12)
  A. An Appeal for Stability (2:1, 2)
  B. The Man of Sin (2:3–12)

IV. THANKSGIVING AND PRAYER (2:13–17)
  A. Paul's Thanks that the Saints Would Escape Judgment (2:13, 14)
  B. Paul's Prayer that the Saints Would Be Comforted and Established (2:15–17)

V. PRACTICAL EXHORTATIONS (3:1–15)
  A. For Mutual Prayer (3:1–5)
  B. For Dealing with the Insubordinate (3:6–15)

VI. BLESSING AND GREETING (3:16–18)

Commentary

I. SALUTATION (1:1, 2)

1:1 **Silvanus and Timothy** were with **Paul** when he wrote this Letter from Corinth. The Letter is addressed **to the church of the Thessalonians**; this reveals its human composition and geographical location. **In God our Father** distinguishes the assembly from a heathen gathering. **And in the Lord Jesus Christ** marks it out as a Christian congregation.[1]

1:2 The apostle does not wish fame, fortune, or pleasure for the saints, but **grace and peace**. **Grace** provides enablement for everything within the will of God, and **peace** gives serenity in every kind of circumstance. What more could a person desire for himself or for others?

Grace and peace are **from God our Father and the Lord Jesus Christ**. **Grace** precedes **peace**; we must know God's **grace** before we can experience His **peace**. Paul's mention **of God our Father and the Lord Jesus Christ** as co-sources of these blessings implies the equality of the Father and the Son.

II. PAUL AND THE THESSALONIANS (1:3–12)

A. Paul's Debt of Thanks (1:3–5)

1:3 The Letter begins with thanksgiving for the saints. To read this is to listen to the heartbeat of a true servant of Christ as he rejoices over his beloved spiritual children. To him thanksgiving was a continual duty to **God**, and it was an appropriate duty as well in view of the **faith** and **love** of the Christians. Their **faith** was making astonishing strides, and each one without exception was showing more and more **love** to the others. This was an answer to the apostle's prayer (1 Thess. 3:10, 12).

Notice the order: first **faith**, then

love. "Faith puts us in contact with the eternal spring of love in God Himself," writes C. H. Mackintosh, "and the necessary consequence is that our hearts are drawn out in love to all who belong to Him."

1:4 Their spiritual progress caused Paul and his associates to **boast** about them to other **churches of God**. They had remained steadfast and full of faith in spite of the **persecutions** they were enduring. **Patience** here means steadfastness or perseverance.

1:5 The fact that they were standing up so bravely under the persecutions and afflictions was an indication of the **righteous** dealings **of God**. He was supporting them, strengthening them, encouraging them. If they had not received His divine power, they would never have been able to demonstrate such patience and faith in suffering for Christ.

Their heroic endurance proved them **worthy of the kingdom of God**. It did not suggest that any personal merit entitled them to enter the kingdom; it is only through the merits of Christ that anyone will be there. But those who suffer on behalf of the kingdom here show that they are among those who will reign with Him in that coming day (Rom. 8:17; 2 Tim. 2:12).

E. W. Rogers, in commenting on the phrase **you may be counted worthy of the kingdom of God**, states:

> This has to do with human responsibility. On the side of divine sovereignty we have been made meet to be partakers of the inheritance of the saints in light, and this meetness is solely due to our association with Christ in His death and resurrection. We are graced in the Beloved, altogether independent of anything in ourselves, either before or since we were saved. But God allows His people to go through persecutions and tribulations in order to develop in them the moral excellencies which make them "worthy citizens" of that kingdom.

> Some of the apostles rejoiced that they were counted worthy to suffer for Jesus' name. Paul's prayer for the Thessalonians

that God would count them worthy of their calling most certainly had nothing to do with adding anything to the work of Christ. The Cross makes the believer worthy of his position in the kingdom, but patience and faith in tribulation manifest such an one as morally worthy of it. Among members of any earthly society there are those who are discreditable as well as others. Paul prayed that it should not be so among these saints.[2]

B. The Righteous Judgment of God (1:6–10)

1:6 The righteous action of **God** is seen in two ways — punishment for the persecutors and then rest for the persecuted.

Williams says:

> God's action in allowing His people to be persecuted, and in permitting the existence of their persecutors, had a double purpose — first, to test the fitness of His people for government (v. 5); and second, to manifest the fitness of their persecutors for judgment.[3]

1:7 Just as God will mete out punishment to the enemies of His people, so He will award **rest** to those who suffer for His sake.

We should not conclude from verse 7 that suffering saints will not obtain relief from trial until Christ comes back from heaven in flaming fire. When a believer dies, he obtains rest. Living believers will enjoy relaxation from all tensions at the time of the Rapture. What this verse is saying is that when the Lord pours out judgment on His adversaries, the saints will be seen by the world to be enjoying **rest**.

The time of God's righteous retribution is **when the Lord Jesus is revealed from heaven with His mighty angels**. Retribution for the ungodly and **rest** for believers are included in His coming. Which phase of Christ's coming is referred to here? It is clearly the third phase — the *manifestation* of His coming, when He returns with His saints to the earth.

THE RAPTURE AND REVELATION

But someone may ask, "How do you know that the Rapture and the Revelation are separate events?" The answer is that they are differentiated in the Scriptures in the following ways:

The Rapture	*The Revelation*
1. Christ comes to the air (1 Thess. 4:17).	1. He comes to the *earth* (Zech.14:4).
2. He comes *for* His saints (1 Thess. 4:16, 17).	2. He comes *with* His saints (1 Thess. 3:13; Jude 14).
3. The Rapture is a mystery, i.e., a truth unknown in OT times (1 Cor. 15:51).	3. The Revelation is not a mystery; it is the subject of many OT prophecies (Ps. 72; Isa. 11; Zech. 14).
4. Christ's coming *for* His saints is never said to be preceded by celestial portents.	4. His coming *with* His saints will be heralded by signs in the heavens (Matt. 24:29, 30).
5. The Rapture is identified with the Day of Christ (1 Cor. 1:8; 2 Cor. 1:14; Phil. 1:6, 10).	5. The Revelation is identified with the Day of the Lord (2 Thess. 2:1–12, NU Text).
6. The Rapture is presented as a time of blessing (1 Thess. 4:18).	6. The main emphasis of the Revelation is on judgment (2 Thess. 2:8–12).
7. The Rapture takes place in a moment, in the twinkling of an eye (1 Cor. 15:52). This strongly implies that it will not be witnessed by the world.	7. The Revelation will be visible worldwide (Matt. 24:27; Rev. 1:7).
8. The Rapture seems to involve the church primarily (John 14:1–4; 1 Cor. 15:51–58; 1 Thess. 4:13–18).	8. The Revelation involves Israel primarily, then also the Gentile nations (Matt. 24:1– 25:46).
9. Christ comes as the Bright and Morning Star (Rev. 22:16).	9. He comes as the Sun of Righteousness with healing in His wings (Mal. 4:2).
10. The Rapture is not mentioned in the Synoptic Gospels, but is alluded to several times in John's Gospel.	10. The Revelation is characteristic in the Synoptics but hardly mentioned in John's Gospel.
11. Those taken are taken for blessing (1 Thess. 4:13–18). Those left are left for judgment (1 Thess. 5:1–3).	11. Those taken are taken for judgment. Those left are left for blessing (Matt. 24:37–41).
12. No dating system is given for events preceding the Rapture.	12. An elaborate dating system is given for the Revelation, such as 1260 days, 42 months, 3½ years (see Dan. 7:25; 12:7, 11, 12; Rev. 11:2; 12:14; 13:5).
13. The title "Son of Man" is never used in any of the passages dealing with the Rapture.	13. The revelation is spoken of as the coming of the Son of Man (Matt. 16:28; 24:27, 30, 39; 26:64; Mark 13:26; Luke 21:27).

Granted then that these are two separate events, yet how do we know that they do not occur at approximately the same time? How do we know that they are separated by an interval? Three lines of proof can be mentioned:

1. The first is based on Daniel's prophecy of seventy weeks (Dan. 9:25–27). We are now living in the parenthetical Church Age, between the sixty-ninth and seventieth weeks. The seventieth week is the Tribulation Period of seven years. The church is taken home to heaven before the Tribulation Period (Rom. 5:9; 1 Thess. 1:10; 1 Thess. 5:9; Rev. 3:10). The coming of Christ to reign takes place after the seventieth week (Dan. 9:24; Matt. 24).

2. The second line of proof for an interval of time between the Rapture and the Manifestation is based on the structure of the book of Revelation. In the first three chapters, the church is seen on earth. Chapters 4 through 19:10 describe the Tribulation Period when God's wrath will be poured out on the world that has rejected His Son. The church is never mentioned as being on earth during this period. The church is apparently taken to heaven at the close of chapter 3. In Revelation 19:11, Christ returns to earth to subdue His foes and to set up His kingdom — at the close of the Tribulation Period.

3. There is a third consideration which necessitates a time interval between Christ's coming *for* the saints and His coming *with* the saints. At the time of the Rapture, *all* believers are taken out of the world and are given their glorified bodies. Yet when Christ returns to reign, there will be believers on earth who will not as yet have glorified bodies and who will marry and raise children during the Millennium (Isa. 11:6, 8). Where do these believers come from? There must be a period of time between the Rapture and the Revelation during which they are converted. ‡

Now to return to verse 7, we have the arrival of **the Lord Jesus** in power and great glory. He is attended by **angels** through whom His power is exerted.

1:8 The **flaming fire** may be a reference to the Shekinah, the glory cloud which symbolizes God's presence (Ex. 16:10). Or it may be a picture of the fiery judgment which is about to be unleashed (Ps. 50:3; Isa. 66:15). Probably it is the latter.

When God takes **vengeance**, it is not vindictiveness, but righteous recompense. There is no thought of "getting even" but rather of meting out the punishment which His holy, righteous character demands. He has no pleasure in the death of the wicked (Ezek. 18:32).

Paul describes two classes marked out for retribution:

1. **Those who do not know God** — those who have rejected the knowledge of the true God as revealed in creation and in conscience (Rom. 1, 2).

They may never have heard the gospel.

2. **Those who do not obey the gospel of our Lord Jesus Christ** — those who have heard the gospel and have rejected it. The gospel is not simply a statement of facts to be believed, but a Person to be obeyed. Belief in the NT sense involves obedience.

1:9 **These shall be punished**. A god who doesn't punish sin is no god at all. The idea that a God of love must not punish sin overlooks the fact that God is also holy and must do what is morally right.

The nature of the punishment is here defined as **everlasting destruction**. The word translated "everlasting" or "eternal" (*aiōnios*) is used seventy times in the NT. Three times it may mean "ages of limited duration" (Rom. 16:25; 2 Tim. 1:9; Tit. 1:2). The other times it means eternal or endless. It is used in Romans 16:26 to describe the unending existence of God.

Destruction never means annihilation. It means loss of well-being, or ruin as far as the purpose of existence is concerned. The wineskins which the Lord Jesus described in Luke 5:37 were "destroyed" (same root word as used here). They did not cease to exist, but they were ruined as far as further usefulness was concerned.

This passage is often used by post-tribulationists to confirm their position. They understand it to say that believers will not obtain rest and their persecutors will not be punished until Christ comes back to reign, and this is admittedly at the end of the Tribulation. Therefore, they conclude that the hope of believers is the post-tribulation Rapture.

What they fail to see is that the Thessalonians to whom this was written have all died and are already enjoying rest with the Lord in heaven. Likewise, their persecutors have all died and are already suffering in Hades.

Why then does Paul seem to say that these conditions will not take place until Christ returns to earth in power and great glory? The reason is that this will be the time that these conditions will be *openly manifested to the world*. Then the world will see that the Thessalonians were right and their persecutors were wrong. The saints will be seen enjoying rest when they return with Christ in glory. The **destruction** of the Lord's enemies at the end of the Tribulation will be a public demonstration of the doom of all who have afflicted God's people in all ages.

It will help us to remember that Christ's coming to reign is a time of *manifestation*. What has been true all along will be unveiled for all the world to see. This is not true of the Rapture.

The punishment of the wicked also includes banishment **from the presence of the Lord and from the glory of His power**. To perish without Him is to be without Him forever.

1:10 His coming will be a time of glory for the Lord and of amazement for the spectators.

He will **be glorified in His saints**, that is, He will be honored because of what He has done in and through them. Their salvation, sanctification, and glorification will be tributes to His matchless grace and power.

He will **be admired among all those who believe**.⁴ Amazed onlookers will gasp as they see what He has been able to do with such unpromising human beings!

And this will include the Thessalonian believers too, because they had received and believed the **testimony** of the apostles. They would share in the glory and triumph of **that Day**, namely, the Day of the Revelation of Jesus Christ.

By way of review, we might paraphrase verses 5–10 as follows: "Your patience in the midst of tribulation is very significant. In all this God is working out His righteous purposes. Your steadfast endurance of persecution shows that you are among the company of those who will share the glories of Christ's coming reign. On the one hand, God will measure out judgment to those who now trouble you. On the other hand, He will give rest to you who are now troubled, along with us also — Paul, Silvanus, and Timothy. He will judge your enemies when He comes from heaven with the angelic executors of His power in flaming fire, punishing those who are wilfully ignorant of God and those who are wilfully disobedient to the gospel. These will suffer everlasting destruction, even banishment from the Lord's face and from the display of His power, when He returns to be glorified in all believers — including you, because you did believe the gospel message we preached to you."

C. Paul's Prayer for the Saints (1:11, 12)

1:11 In the preceding verses the apostle has been describing the glorious calling of the saints. They have been called to suffer persecution, which in turn fits them for rule in the kingdom. Now he prays that their lives in the meantime will be counted **worthy of** such a high **calling**, and that God's mighty **power** will enable them to obey every impulse to do good, and to accomplish every task undertaken in **faith**.

1:12 The result would be twofold. First, **the name of our Lord Jesus Christ** would **be glorified in** them. This means that they would give an accurate representation of Him to the world, and thus bring glory to Him. Then they, too, would be glorified **in Him**. Their association with Him, their Head, would bring honor to them as members of His Body.

Chapter 1 closes with the reminder that this prayer can be answered only **according to the grace of our God and the Lord Jesus Christ**. Thus he concludes a marvelous explanation of the meaning and outcome of suffering in the believer's life. Imagine how encouraged the Thessalonians were when they read this reassuring message!

III. CONCERNING THE DAY OF THE LORD (2:1–12)

A. An Appeal for Stability (2:1, 2)

2:1 Paul now undertakes to correct a misunderstanding that had arisen in the minds of the saints **concerning the coming of our Lord Jesus Christ** and the Day of the Lord. The saints were suffering such severe persecution that it was easy for them to think that they were already in the first part of the Day of the Lord, i.e., the Tribulation Period. And rumors were floating around that the *apostle himself* believed and taught that the Day of the Lord had arrived! So he must set the record straight.

A crucial question arises in verse 1 concerning the small word which Paul uses: **concerning** (Gk. *huper*). The problem is whether he is beseeching the saints "about" **the coming of our** Lord or "by" **the coming of our Lord**. If the first is the meaning, then the passage seems to teach that the Rapture and the Day of the Lord are one and the same event, since the following verses clearly deal with the Day of the Lord. If the second is the meaning, then Paul is appealing to them *on the basis of* the prior Rapture, that they should not think they were in the Day of the Lord. The question is debatable. We agree with William Kelly when he adopts the second view:

> The comfort of the Lord's coming is employed as a motive and means for counteracting the uneasiness created by the false presentation that the day (of the Lord) was there.[5]

We understand Paul to be saying, "I appeal to you on the basis of the Rapture that you should not fear that you are in the Day of the Lord. The Rapture must take place first. You will be taken home to heaven at that time and will thus escape the horrors of the Day of the Lord."

The expression **the coming of our Lord Jesus Christ and our gathering together to Him** seems to refer unmistakably to the Rapture. That is the time when we will be gathered to meet Him in the air.

2:2 It should be clear that the Rapture is not the same as the Day of the Lord. The Thessalonians were not worried that the Lord had come; they knew that He had not. But they *were* worried that the Day of the Lord had begun. The intense persecution they were enduring made them think they were in the Tribulation, the first phase of the Day of the Lord.

Rumors had been circulating that Paul himself had said that the Day of the Lord had arrived. Like most rumors, they were very garbled. One version intimated that Paul had received the information **by spirit**, that is, by a special revelation. According to another report, the news had come **by word**, that is, the apostle had publicly taught that the Tribulation had begun. **By letter as if from us** is generally understood to refer to a forged letter, purportedly from Paul, that the Day of the Lord had started. The expression **as if from us** probably goes with **spirit**, **word**, and **letter**. None of these sources was to be trusted.

According to the KJV and NKJV (following the majority of manuscripts), the saints were afraid that **the day of Christ had come. The day of Christ** and similar expressions usually point forward to the Rapture and the Judgment Seat of Christ (1 Cor. 1:8; 5:5; 2 Cor. 1:14; Phil 1:6, 10; 2:15, 16).

But the Thessalonians were not in fear that the Day of Christ was at hand. That would have meant release from their sufferings. Most pre-tribulationists prefer the reading in the RV: "the day of the Lord is now present."[6] Paul's readers were afraid that the Day of God's *wrath* had begun.

B. The Man of Sin (2:3-12)

2:3 Now the apostle explains why they could not be in **that Day**. Certain events must take place first. After the Rapture, these events will begin to happen.

First of all there will be **the falling away**, or the apostasy.[7] What does this mean? We can only surmise that it refers to a wholesale abandonment of Christianity, a positive rejection of the Christian faith.

Then a great world figure will arise. As to his character, he is **the man of sin** or lawlessness,[8] that is, the very embodiment of sin and rebellion. As to his destiny, he is **the son of perdition**; he is doomed to eternal judgment.

The Scriptures contain many descriptions of important personages who will arise during the Tribulation, and it is difficult to know when different names apply to the same person. Some commentators believe that the man of sin will be a Jewish Antichrist. Others teach that he will be the Gentile head of the revived Roman Empire. Here are the names of some of the great rulers of the end times:

... the man of sin and son of perdition (2 Thess. 2:3)

... the Antichrist (1 Jn. 2:18)

... the little horn (Dan. 7:8, 24b–26)

... the king of fierce features (Dan. 8:23–25)

... the prince who is to come (Dan. 9:26)

... the willful king (Dan. 11:36)

... the worthless shepherd (Zech. 11:17)

... the beast out of the sea (Rev. 13:1–10)

... the beast out of the earth (Rev. 13:11–17)

... the scarlet beast with seven heads and ten horns (Rev. 17:4, 8–14)

... the king of the North (Dan. 11:6)

... the king of the South (Dan. 11:40)

... the false prophet (Rev. 19:20; 20:10)

... Gog, of the land of Magog (Ezek. 38:2–39:11) [not to be confused with the Gog of Rev. 20:8 who arises *after* the Millennium]

... the one who comes in his own name (John 5:43)

The man of sin has been given an intriguing variety of identifications down through the years. He has been equated with the Roman Catholic Church, the Pope, the Roman Empire, the final form of apostate Christendom, Judas reincarnated, Nero reincarnated, the Jewish State, Mohammed, Luther, Napoleon, Mussolini, and the embodiment of Satan.

2:4 He will violently oppose every form of divine worship and will enthrone himself **in the temple of God** in Jerusalem. This description clearly identifies him as Antichrist, the one who is *opposed to* Christ and who sets himself up *in the place of* Christ.[9]

Daniel 9:27 and Matthew 24:15 show that this blasphemous action of the Antichrist takes place in the middle of the Tribulation Period. Those who refuse to worship him will be persecuted and many will be martyred.

2:5 Paul used to tell the Thessalonians **these things** when he **was still with** them. However, with contradictory teaching being given to them which seemed to accurately describe the fierce persecutions they were then enduring, they had forgotten what the apostle had said. We all forget too easily and need to be constantly reminded of the great truths of the faith.

2:6 They knew **what** was **restraining** the full and open manifestation of

the man of sin, and what would continue to restrain him until the appointed time.

This brings us to the third great unanswered question in this chapter. The first is, "What is the apostasy?" The second is, "Who is the man of sin?" The third is, "What or who is the restrainer?"

In the first part of verse 6, the restrainer is described in an impersonal way ... **what is restraining**. But then in verse 7 it is a person — He who now restrains.[10] E. W. Rogers puts it clearly:

> It is Something and Someone who wittingly, purposefully, and designedly holds it in check *with the view* to ensuring that the Man of Lawlessness is revealed in his own proper time.[11]

Seven of the more common views as to the identity of the restrainer are: (1) the Roman Empire, (2) the Jewish State, (3) Satan, (4) the principle of law and order as found in human government, (5) God, (6) the Holy Spirit, and (7) the true church as indwelt by the Spirit.

The Holy Spirit indwelling the church and the individual believer seems to fit the description of the restrainer more completely and accurately than any of the others. Just as the restrainer is spoken of as Something and Someone in this chapter, so the Spirit is spoken of in John 14:26, 15:26, 16:8, 13, 14 as both neuter (the Holy Spirit) and masculine (He).[12] As early as Genesis 6:3, the Holy Spirit is spoken of in connection with the restraint of evil. Then later He is seen in this same role in Isaiah 59:19b, John 16:7–11, and 1 John 4:4.

It is by the indwelling Spirit that believers are the salt of the earth (Matt. 5:13) and the light of the world (Matt. 5:14). Salt is a preservative, but it also hinders the spread of corruption. Light dispels darkness, the sphere in which men love to perform their evil deeds (John 3:19). When the Holy Spirit leaves the world as the permanent Indweller of the church (1 Cor. 3:16) and of individual believers (1 Cor. 6:19), the restraint of lawlessness will be gone.

2:7 Even when Paul wrote, **the mystery of lawlessness** was **already at work**. By this we understand that a tremendous spirit of disobedience to God was already stirring beneath the surface.

It was at work in **mystery** form — not that it was mysterious but rather that it was not yet fully manifested. It was still in germ form.

What has hindered the full display of this spirit? We believe that the presence of the Holy Spirit indwelling the church and indwelling every believer has been the restraining power. He will continue to exercise this function **until He is taken out of the way**, that is, at the Rapture.

But here an objection is raised. How can the Holy Spirit be removed from the world? As one of the Persons of the Godhead, isn't He omnipresent, that is, everywhere at all times? How then can He leave the world?

Of course, the Holy Spirit is omnipresent. He is always in all places at one and the same time. And yet there was a distinct sense in which He *came* to the earth on the Day of Pentecost. Jesus had repeatedly promised that He and the Father would send the Spirit (John 14:16, 26; 15:26; 16:7). How then did the Spirit come? He came as the permanent Indweller of the church and of every believer. Until Pentecost the Spirit had been *with* believers, but since Pentecost He has dwelt *in* them (John 14:17). Until Pentecost the Spirit was known to depart from believers — hence David's prayer, "Do not take your Holy Spirit from me" (Ps. 51:11b). After Pentecost the Spirit remains forever in believers of the Church Age (John 14:16).

The Holy Spirit will, we believe, *leave* the world in the same sense in which He *came* at Pentecost — that is, as the abiding Indweller of the church and of each believer. He will still be in the world, convicting people of sin and leading them to saving faith in Christ. His removal at the Rapture does not mean that no one will be saved during the Tribulation. Of course they will. But these people will not be members of the church, but rather the subjects of Christ's glorious kingdom.

2:8 After the church has been Raptured to heaven, **the lawless one will be revealed** to the world. In this verse, the apostle skips over the career of the Antichrist and describes his ultimate doom. It almost sounds as if he will be destroyed as soon as he is revealed. But

that of course is not so. He is allowed to conduct the reign of terror described in verses 9–12 before he is brought down at Christ's coming to reign.

If we are right in believing that the man of sin is revealed after the Rapture and that he continues until Christ's Revelation, then his mad career lasts approximately seven years — the length of the Tribulation Period.

The **Lord** Jesus **will consume** him **with the breath of His mouth** (cf. Isa. 11:4; Rev. 19:15), and will bring him to nothing by the manifestation **of His coming**. A word from Christ and the bright shining (Gk., *epiphaneia*) of His appearing (*parousia*) are all that are necessary to end the regime of this raging impostor.

The manifestation of Christ's coming, as has already been explained, is when He returns to the earth to take the throne and reign for one thousand years.

2:9 **The coming of the lawless one is** in accordance with **the working of Satan**. His career resembles that **of Satan** because he is energized by Satan. He will display all kinds of miracles and **signs and lying wonders**.

Here it is important to note that not all miracles are of God. The devil and his agents can perform miracles. The man of lawlessness will also perform them (Rev. 13:13–15).

A miracle indicates *supernatural* power but not necessarily *divine* power. The miracles of our Lord proved Him to be the promised Messiah, not simply because they were supernatural, but because they fulfilled prophecy and were of such a moral nature that Satan could not have done them without harming his own cause.

2:10 The Antichrist will unscrupulously use every form of wickedness to deceive the perishing people — those who heard the gospel during the Age of Grace but who had no **love** for **the truth**. If they had believed, they would have been **saved**. But now they are deceived by the miracles of the Antichrist.

2:11 God actually will **send them** a working of error that **they should believe the lie**. **The lie**, of course, is the Antichrist's claim to be God. These people refused to receive the Lord Jesus as God manifest in the flesh. When He was on earth, He warned men, "I have come in My Father's name, and you do not receive Me: if another comes in his own name, him you will receive" (John 5:43). So now they receive the man of sin who comes in his own name and demands worship as God. "Light rejected is light denied." If a person sets up an idol in his heart, God will answer him according to his idol (Ezek. 14:4).

The Antichrist will probably be Jewish (Ezek. 28:9, 10; Dan. 11:37, 38). Jews would not be deceived by one posing as the Messiah unless he claimed to be descended from the tribe of Judah and the family of David.

2:12 From this passage it seems that those who hear the gospel in this Age of Grace but who do not trust Christ will not have another opportunity to be saved after the Rapture. If men do not believe the Lord Jesus now, they will believe the Antichrist then. It says here that they **all** will be judged because of their unbelief and their love of evil. This is reminiscent of Luke 14:24, "For I say to you that none of those men who were invited shall taste my supper."

We know that many people will be saved during the Tribulation Period. One hundred and forty-four thousand Jews, for instance, will be saved and will be God's messengers in preaching the gospel of the kingdom throughout the world. Through their ministry many others will be saved. But it seems that those who will be saved are those who never heard the gospel clearly presented during this present age and who never deliberately refused the Savior.

IV. THANKSGIVING AND PRAYER (2:13–17)

A. Paul's Thanks that the Saints Would Escape Judgment (2:13, 14)

2:13 In the first twelve verses, Paul described the doom of the Antichrist and his followers. Now he turns to the Thessalonian Christians and thinks of their calling and destiny by way of contrast. As he does so, he expresses thanks to God for these **brethren beloved by the Lord**, and proceeds to give a summary of their salvation — past, present, and future.

God . . . chose you. The Bible clearly teaches that **God** chooses men to salvation, but it never teaches that He chooses some to be damned. Men are lost through their own deliberate choice. Apart from God's intervention, all would be lost. Does God have the right to choose some to be saved? Basically His desire is for all to be saved (1 Tim. 2:4; 2 Pet. 3:9). However, the Bible does not teach "Universalism," the theory that all will eventually be saved.

From the beginning. This has two possible readings. First, it may mean that God's choice was made before the foundation of the world (Eph. 1:4). Second, the expression may also be read "as first fruits," indicating that the Thessalonians, saved so early in the Christian dispensation, were chosen by God to be among the first of a great harvest of redeemed souls.

For salvation. This should be contrasted with the preceding verses. Unbelievers are doomed by their unbelief to eternal destruction, whereas believers are chosen **for salvation**.

Through sanctification by the Spirit. Here we have the Holy Spirit's preconversion work. He sets individuals apart to God from the world, convicts them of sin, and points them to Christ. Someone has well said, "If it had not been for Christ, there would have been no *feast*; if it had not been for the Holy Spirit, there would have been no *guests!*"

And belief in the truth. First you have God's part in salvation; now you have man's. Both are necessary. Some people can see only God's election, and they imply that man can do nothing about it. Others overemphasize man's part, and neglect God's sovereign choice. The truth lies in both extremes. Election and human responsibility are *both* Bible doctrines, and it is best to believe and teach both, even if we can't understand how both can be true.

2:14 To which He called you by our gospel. God *chose* us to salvation in eternity. **He called** us to it in time. The call refers to the moment when a person believes the truth. **Our gospel** does not mean that there are other genuine gospels. There is only one gospel, but there are many different preachers of it, and many different audiences. Paul is referring to the **gospel** of God which was preached by him.

For the obtaining of the glory of our Lord Jesus Christ. Here the apostle peers into the future and sees the ultimate outcome of salvation — to be with Christ and be like Him forever. J. N. Darby captures the thought in his beautiful hymn:

> And is it so — I shall be like Thy Son?
> Is this the grace which He for me has
>   won?
> Father of glory, thought beyond all
>   thought!
> In glory, to His own blest likeness
>   brought!

Thus in verses 13 and 14 we have "a system of theology in miniature," a marvelous summary of the scope of God's purposes with His believing people. He has shown us that salvation "originates in a divine choice, is wrought out by divine power, is made effective through a divine message, and will be perfected in divine glory."

B. Paul's Prayer that the Saints Would Be Comforted and Established (2:15–17)

2:15 In view of their superlative calling, the saints are exhorted to **stand fast and hold the traditions which** they **were taught**, either by the apostles' words or by their Letters. The important thing to notice here is that the only **traditions** which are reliable and authoritative are the inspired utterances of the apostles. Jesus condemned the scribes and Pharisees for nullifying the commandments of God by *their* traditions (Matt. 15:6). And Paul warned the Colossians against *the traditions of men* (Col. 2:8). **The traditions** we should hold are the great truths which have been handed over to us in the sacred Scriptures.

This verse is sometimes used to justify the traditions of churches or of religious leaders. But any traditions which are contrary to the word of God are worthless and dangerous. If mere human traditions are accepted as equal with the Bible, who is to decide which traditions are right and which are wrong?

2:16 Having told out his message to the saints, the apostle now prays it in. He commonly follows his teaching with prayer (1 Thess. 5:23, 24; 2 Thess. 3:16). The prayer is addressed to **our Lord Jesus Christ Himself, and our God and Father**. We are accustomed to Paul's mentioning both divine Persons in the same breath, but it is unusual for him to mention the Son first. He is, of course, emphasizing their essential unity and complete equality. In the Greek, the plural subject (**Christ** and **God**) is followed by four singular verb forms (loved, gave, comfort, establish). What is this but a further indication of the unity of nature of the Son and Father in the Godhead?

God's past provision is introduced as an encouragement to trust Him for future courage and strength. He **loved us and** gave us **everlasting consolation and good hope by grace**. Doubtless this looks back to the greatest exhibition of God's love — the gift of His Son for us. Because we know that He settled the sin question at Calvary, we have eternal comfort now and the **hope** of a glorious future — and it is all through His marvelous **grace**.

2:17 The prayer itself is that God will **comfort** their **hearts and establish** them **in every good word and work**. Not just encouragement in the midst of distress, but strength to move forward in the battle. The word "retreat" wasn't in the apostle's vocabulary, and it shouldn't be in ours either.

Don't miss the expression **every good word and work**. Truth on our lips is not enough; it must be worked out in our life. So in our lives there should be the order of teaching and doing, doctrine and duty, preaching and practice.

V. PRACTICAL EXHORTATIONS (3:1–15)

A. For Mutual Prayer (3:1–5)

3:1 Paul felt the need for the prayers of the saints. This chapter opens with his request for prayer in three areas: (1) for the dissemination of the message; (2) for the triumph of the message; (3) for the preservation of the messengers.

He desires **that the word of the Lord**

may run swiftly — a graphic picture of the gospel sprinting from place to place in spite of obstacles (see Ps. 147:15).

He also desires that the word will produce the same marvelous spiritual and moral revolutions elsewhere that it did in Thessalonica.

3:2 The third request is that the apostle and his co-workers might **be delivered from unreasonable and wicked men**. He seems to be referring to some specific opposition, probably from Jews in Corinth (Acts 18:1–18). The choice of the word **unreasonable** was appropriate; there is nothing more irrational than people's opposition to the gospel and its messengers. It is something that baffles explanation. They may talk reasonably about politics, science, or a host of other subjects, but when it comes to the gospel, they lose all sense of reason.

3:3 Don't miss the beauty of the contrast between verse 2: "not all have faith" and verse 3: **But the Lord is faithful**. This teaches us to look away from faithless men to our never-failing God. He is **faithful** to confirm us to the end (1 Cor. 1:9). He is **faithful** to deliver us out of temptation (1 Cor. 10:13). He is **faithful** and just to forgive us our sins, and to cleanse us from all unrighteousness (1 John 1:9). And here He is **faithful** to **establish** and to **guard** us **from the evil one**, i.e., Satan.

3:4 Not all have faith . . . the Lord is faithful . . . **we have confidence** [faith] **in the Lord concerning you**. As Denney has remarked, "In the Lord you may depend on those who in themselves are weak, unstable, willful, foolish." Now Paul reminds the saints of their responsibility to **do the things** he commands them. Here again we have the wonderful and curious mingling of the divine and the human: God will keep you; now you keep the commandments. It is the same thought in 1 Peter 1:5: "Kept by the power of God" [His part], "through faith" [our part]. We also see it in Philippians 2:12, 13: "Work out your own salvation [our part], . . . for it is God who works in you [His part]."

3:5 In times of persecution it is easy to develop bitter thoughts toward others and to give up because of the duration and intensity of the suffering. It is for this reason that the apostle prays that the Thessalonians will love as **God** loves,

and will be steadfast as **Christ** is steadfast.

The KJV's "the patient waiting for Christ" is translated **the patience of Christ** in the NKJV. In the 1611 version it would mean steadfastness while *waiting* for Christ's Return. In the NKJV, it means showing the same **patience** or endurance which Christ showed as a Man on earth and which He still shows as Man in heaven.[13]

The Lord in this verse may refer to the Holy Spirit, and thus all three members of the Trinity would be mentioned, as they are in 2:13, 14.

B. For Dealing with the Insubordinate (3:6–15)

3:6 It seems clear that some of the saints at Thessalonica had stopped working for a living because they were so intently waiting for the Lord's return. Paul does not encourage this as a spiritual attitude, but proceeds to give definite instructions as to how to deal with such brethren.

His instructions are in the form of a command to **withdraw from every brother who walks disorderly**, that is one who does not keep in step with the others, but who refuses to work, and who sponges off others (see vv. 10, 11). Believers should show their disapproval of such a **brother** by refusing to mingle with him socially. The offense is not serious enough to warrant excommunication from the church, however.

The tradition which the Thessalonians **received from** Paul was one of tireless industry, hard work, and self-support.

3:7 He did not abandon his tent-making just because he knew the Lord Jesus was coming again. He was indeed expecting Christ to come at any moment, but he was serving and working with the realization that the Lord might not come during his lifetime.

3:8 No one could accuse him of planting himself in someone's home and eating the food which someone else's toil had earned. He earned his own living while he was preaching the gospel. This meant long days and weary nights, but Paul was determined that he would **not be a burden to any of** them.

3:9 As a preacher of the gospel, the apostle had a right to be supported by those who were converted through his ministry (1 Cor. 9:6–14; 1 Tim. 5:18). But he preferred to forego his right in order that he might be **an example** of noble independence and unwearied diligence.

3:10 The Thessalonians had already been commanded not to support shirkers. If an able-bodied Christian refused to work, **neither** should **he eat**. Does this conflict with the fact that believers should always be kind? Not at all! It is not a kindness to encourage laziness. Spurgeon says, "The truest love to those who err is not to fraternize with them in their error but to be faithful to Jesus in all things."

3:11 Now the apostle uses a delightful play on words[14] to bring out the inconsistency of the pseudo-spirituality of these disorderly brothers. His words have been paraphrased variously as follows:

1. "Some who don't attend to business but are busybodies."
2. "Some that are not busy people but are busybodies."
3. "Some that are not busy in their own business but are over-busy in other people's business."
4. "Minding everybody's business but their own."

3:12 All **such** are commanded and exhorted **through our Lord Jesus Christ** to **work** without fanfare and earn **their own** living. This is a good testimony and glorifies God.

3:13 Those who have been working faithfully are encouraged to press on. It is the end of the race that counts, not the beginning; so they should **not grow weary in doing** the right thing.

3:14 But what about a man who refuses to **obey** the apostle's instructions? The other Christians should discipline him by refusing to have social fellowship with him. The purpose of this discipline is to shame him for his behavior and constrain him to mend his ways.

3:15 However, this discipline is not as strong as excommunication. Here the offender is still looked on **as a brother**. In excommunication, he is counted as "a heathen and a tax-collector" (Matt. 18:17).

The discipline of a believer always has in view his restoration to the Lord and to the people of God. It should not be carried out in a spirit of bitterness or enmity, but rather in Christian courtesy and firmness. He should **not** be treated **as an enemy, but** rather **as a brother**.

It seems strange to us today that Christians in Thessalonica were so ardently looking for the Lord's return that they abandoned their daily duties. That does not seem to be a peril to the church today! We have gone to the opposite extreme. We are so taken up with business and money-making that we have lost the freshness and thrill of the hope of His imminent coming.

VI. BLESSING AND GREETING (3:16–18)

3:16 This verse has been called "a peaceful close to a stormy Epistle." In it Paul prays that the suffering saints at Thessalonica may know the **peace** of **the Lord of peace** at all times and **in every way**.

The Christian is not dependent on anything in this world for his serenity. It is based entirely on the Person and work of the Lord Jesus. The world cannot give it or take it away. But we must appropriate it in all the circumstances of life. "Peace is not cessation from persecution, but is the calm of heart that comes from faith in God and that is independent of circumstances."

3:17, 18 At this point **Paul** apparently took the pen from the hand of his amanuensis (secretary) and wrote the closing **salutation**. He speaks of his greeting as being the **sign in every epistle** he writes. Some have understood this to mean that Paul's own handwriting at the end of each Letter proved it to be genuinely his. Others believe that the **sign** is the characteristic Pauline benediction: **the grace of our Lord Jesus Christ be with you all** (Rom. 16:24; 1 Cor. 16:23; 2 Cor. 13:14; Gal. 6:18; Eph. 6:24; Phil. 4:23; Col. 4:18; 1 Thess. 5:28; 1 Tim. 6:21; 2 Tim. 4:22; Tit. 3:15; Phmn. 25; and, if Paul wrote Hebrews, Heb. 13:25). From these references, we see that all his Epistles end on a **grace** note.

THE RAPTURE OF THE CHURCH

The truth of the Lord's return appears in each chapter of 1 Thessalonians and in the first two chapters of the Second Epistle. It is the unifying theme, the

Answer: These words were spoken to *the men of Israel* (v. 4). *As far as the nation of Israel is concerned*, the statement is true. It agrees with the Savior's words to Jerusalem in Matthew 23:39, "You shall see Me no more till you say, 'Blessed is He who comes in the name of the Lord!' " That will take place at the end of the Tribulation Period. But the church will have been Raptured to heaven seven years earlier.

6. Psalm 110:1 says that Christ will sit at the right hand of God until all His enemies are destroyed. This will be at the end of the Tribulation.

Answer: In Revelation 20:8,9, we read of some who will be enemies of Christ at the end of the Millennium — that is 1000 years after the close of the Tribulation. The right hand of God may describe a position of honor and power as well as a geographical location.

7. In Titus 2:13, the blessed hope is the same as the glorious appearing. Therefore the Rapture takes place at the same time as the Revelation. Therefore, we do not look for a pretribulation Rapture but for Christ's coming to reign.

Answer: This argument is based on a rule of Greek syntax called Granville Sharp's rule which says: When two nouns connected by "and" (Gk. *kai*) are in the same case, and a definite article precedes the first noun but not the second, the second noun refers to the same person or thing the first noun does and is a further description of it. To give an example, Titus 2:13 says, "the glory of our great God and Savior Jesus Christ." The words "God" and "Savior" are connected by "and"; they are in the same case (objects of preposition "of"); the definite article (part of Greek for "our") precedes "God" but not "Savior." Therefore, according to Granville Sharp's rule, the word "Savior" refers to the same person as "God" and is a further description of Him. This proves, of course, that our Savior, Jesus Christ, is God.

Now in the same verse, it says in the Greek, "looking for the blessed hope and glorious appearing." Thus it is claimed that, according to Granville Sharp's rule, the blessed hope is the same as the glorious appearing, and since the glorious appearing is *generally* understood to be Christ's coming to reign, the believer's hope is not a pretribulation Rapture but Christ's coming in glory to the earth.

There are two answers to this. First of all, like all good rules, Granville Sharp's rule has exceptions. One is in Luke 14:23 where the Greek reads, "Go out into the highways and hedges." If the rule holds, then we must believe that highways are the same as hedges! A second exception is in Ephesians 2:20: "the foundation of the apostles and prophets." But no careful student would say that apostles and prophets are the same.

But even supposing that the blessed hope *is* the same as the glorious appearing, what is to prevent us from looking on the Rapture as Christ's glorious appearing to the church whereas the Revelation is His glorious appearing to the world? The words *apokalupsis* (revelation) and *epiphaneia* (shining forth or appearing) could refer to the Rapture as well as to Christ's coming to reign.

8. Other Scriptures which show that the believer's hope is Christ's coming to reign are 1 Corinthians 1:7; 1 Timothy 6:14; 2 Timothy 4:8; 1 Peter 1:7, 13; 4:13.

Answer: The words "revelation" and "appearing" used in these passages apply both to Christ's coming for His saints and to His coming with His saints. First, He reveals Himself and appears to the church, then later to the world.

But even if all the verses quoted did refer to Christ's coming to reign, it should be clear that the believer's hope embraces all the blessings of the prophetic future. We look forward to the Rapture, Christ's coming to reign, the Millennium, and the eternal state.

9. The traditional hope of the church has not been the pretribulation Rapture. This only began in the last 160 years or so through the teaching of J. N. Darby.

Answer: The NT church was waiting for God's Son from heaven. The saints did not know when He would come so they watched for Him at any time.

Arguments directed at what any person did or did not teach are called *ad hominem* (to the person) and are regarded as irrelevant to an issue. The question is "What does Scripture teach?", not "What did so-and-so teach?"

10. The last trumpet of 1 Corinthians 15:52 and the trumpet of God (1 Thess.

4:16) are connected with the Rapture and are the same as the seventh trumpet of Revelation 11:15. Since the seventh trumpet sounds at the end of the Tribulation when "the kingdoms of this world have become the kingdom of our Lord, and of His Christ," the return must be post-tribulational.

Answer: These trumpets are not all the same. The "last trumpet" is the same as the "trumpet of God." It announces the Rapture and signals the resurrection of believers and their translation to the Father's house. It is the "last trumpet" for the church. The seventh trumpet in Revelation 11:15 is the last in a series of judgments during the Tribulation. It is the last trumpet for unbelieving Israel and unbelieving Gentiles. The "last trumpet" of 1 Corinthians 15:52, also called the "trumpet of God" (1 Thess. 4:16), takes place before the Tribulation. The seventh trumpet takes place at the end of the Tribulation.

11. The first resurrection of Revelation 20:4, 5 takes place at the end of the Tribulation, and not seven years earlier, as the pretribulationists state.

Answer: The first resurrection is not an isolated event but a series. It began with the resurrection of Christ (1 Cor. 15:23). The next stage will be the resurrection of believers at the Rapture. The third stage will be the resurrection of Tribulation saints at the time of Christ's return to the earth (Rev. 20:4,5). In other words, the first resurrection includes the resurrection of Christ and of all true believers, no matter when they are raised. All unbelievers will be raised at the end of the Millennium to stand before the Great White Throne (Rev. 20:11–15).

12. In Matthew 13:24–30, the wheat and tares grow together until the end of the age, that is, until the end of the Tribulation.

Answer: True, but this parable is speaking of the kingdom of heaven and not of the church. There will be true and false people in the kingdom until the end of the Tribulation.

13. The Rapture couldn't be secret because there will be a shout, the voice of the archangel, and the trumpet of God (1 Thess. 4:16).

Answer: The teaching that the Rapture will be secret is based on the fact that it will take place in the twinkling of an eye (1 Cor. 15:52). It will be all over before the world has a chance to see anything or to know what has happened.

14. George Müller, Samuel Tregelles, Oswald Smith, and other noted men have held the post-tribulation view.

Answer: The argument proves nothing. There have been great men on both sides of the question.

15. Most references in the NT to Christ's coming refer to His coming to reign.

Answer: This does not deny the truth of the Rapture. Just because there are more references to heaven than to hell in the NT does not mean that there is no hell.

16. The church will not endure the wrath of God in the Tribulation, but it will endure the wrath of the Antichrist or the wrath of Satan.

Answer: Six times in the book of Revelation the wrath of the Tribulation Period is identified as the *wrath of God*:

"Then a third angel followed them, saying with a loud voice, 'If anyone worships the beast and his image, and receives his mark on his forehead or on his hand, he himself shall also drink of the wine of *the wrath of God*, which is poured out full strength into the cup of His indignation. He shall be tormented with fire and brimstone in the presence of the holy angels and in the presence of the Lamb' " (14:9, 10).

"So the angel thrust his sickle into the earth and gathered the vine of the earth, and threw it into the great winepress of *the wrath of God*" (14:19).

"Then I saw another sign in heaven, great and marvelous: seven angels having the seven last plagues, for in them *the wrath of God* is complete (15:1).

"Then one of the four living creatures gave to the seven angels seven golden bowls full of *the wrath of God* who lives forever and ever" (15:7).

"Then I heard a loud voice from the temple saying to the seven angels, 'Go and pour out the bowls of *the wrath of God* on the earth' " (16:1).

"Now the great city was divided into three parts, and the cities of the nations fell. And great Babylon was remembered before *God*, to give her the cup of the wine of the fierceness of *His wrath*" (16:19).

17. When Jesus says, "I am coming quickly" (Rev. 22:7,12, 20), it does not mean at any moment. Rather it means that His coming will be sudden.

Answer: It is a debated point. Even if it does mean "sudden," there are still verses like Hebrews 10:37, "For yet a little while, and He who is coming will come and will not tarry."

18. The restrainer in 2 Thessalonians 2:6–8 is not the Holy Spirit but the Roman government or the power of God.

Answer: This has been discussed in the notes on that passage.

19. Christ's coming couldn't have been imminent in the apostolic days because Peter and Paul both knew that they would die (John 21:18, 19; 2 Pet. 1:14, 15; 2 Tim. 4:6).

Answer: Paul sometimes spoke of himself as being alive when the Lord returns (1 Thess. 4:15) and sometimes as being among those believers who would die and be raised (Phil. 3:10, 11). That is the proper attitude for all of us. We expect the Lord to come in our lifetime, but we realize that we may die before the Rapture.

Peter believed that the end of all things was at hand (1 Pet. 4:7), and he condemned those scoffers who denied the Lord's coming by saying that "all things continue as they were from the beginning of creation" (2 Pet. 3:4).

20. The Lord's coming cannot be at any moment because the gospel must go out to all the world before He comes (Matt. 24:14).

Answer: This refers to *the gospel of the kingdom* (v. 14) which will go out to all the world during the Tribulation Period. The terms of this gospel are, "Believe on the Lord Jesus Christ and you will be saved, and when Christ comes, you will enter the Millennium with Him." It is the same way of salvation that we preach, but ours looks forward to the Rapture. In other words, we say, "Believe on the Lord Jesus Christ and you will be saved, and when Jesus comes, you will go to the Father's house with Him."

21. Passages like Matthew 28:19, 20 and Acts 1:8 speak of the gospel going out to "all the nations" and to "the end of the earth." This being so, it was not possible for the Lord to come during the lifetime of the apostles.

Answer: In Colossians 1:6, 23, Paul states that "all the world" and "every creature under heaven" had heard the gospel. In Romans 10:18, the gospel is said to have gone to the ends of the world. Of course, we understand that these passages refer to the known world at that time, the countries adjacent to the Mediterranean.

22. Paul's long term missionary plans, as given in Acts 18:21; 23:11; Romans 15:22–25, 30, 31, show that he did not expect the Lord to come in the immediate future.

Answer: Paul's plans were made, subject to the will of God (Acts 18:21; Rom. 1:10; 1 Cor. 4:19). He worked as if the Lord would not come back in his lifetime, but waited and watched as if He would return at any time.

23. Paul spoke of perilous times in the last days (1 Tim. 4:1–3; 2 Tim. 3:1–5). This presupposed a time lapse during which the Lord would not come.

Answer: Paul also said the mystery of iniquity was already working (2 Thess. 2:7), and John said it was "the last hour" in his day (1 Jn. 2:18). These men did not see any problem here that made the hope of Christ's imminent return impossible.

24. Parables such as Matthew 25:14–30 and Luke 19:11–27 presuppose that a long period of time would elapse before the Lord returned. Therefore the early believers could not have been looking for the Lord to come at any moment.

Answer: Apparently the early believers did not base their doctrine on parables because they *were* looking for the Rapture! (1 Thess. 1:10). But quite apart from that, the "long time" of Matthew 25:19 is too indefinite to rule out imminency. The parable in Luke teaches that the *kingdom* would not appear immediately (Luke 19:11), but this does not preclude an any-moment Rapture of the *church*.

ENDNOTES

[1](1:1) There is still (or again) a NT as-

sembly of Christians in Thessalonica (today called Saloniki).

²(1:5) E. W. Rogers, *Concerning the Future*, p. 80.

³(1:6) George Williams, *The Student's Commentary on the Holy Scriptures*, p. 948.

⁴(1:10) Both the oldest (NU) and the majority (M) of mss. have "who have believed" here, undoubtedly the correct reading.

⁵(2:1) William Kelly, further documentation unavailable.

⁶(2:2) "Lord" (*Kurios*) is the critical (NU) reading. The traditional reading *Christos* (TR) of the KJ and NKJV is not (as sometimes) weakly supported; here it is the *majority* reading. Some scholars understand the "Day of Christ" as a reference to the final period of persecution, which can only begin when the man of sin has been revealed. Some of the Thessalonians wrongly thought that this period had already begun. By connecting this period with a post-Rapture event, Paul effectively refutes this notion.

⁷(2:3) Some theologians, such as J. Dwight Pentecost, translate *apostasia* as "departure," and refer it to the Rapture itself. If this is valid it is an air-tight verse for the pretribulational Rapture.

⁸(2:3) "Sin" is the TR and majority reading; "lawlessness" is the critical reading.

⁹(2:4) The Greek preposition (here a prefix) *anti* has both the meaning "against" and "in place of." Both meanings fit the Antichrist.

¹⁰(2:6) The Greek has a *neuter* article and participle in v. 6 and a *masculine* article and participle in v. 7.

¹¹(2:6) Rogers, *Future*, p. 65.

¹²(2:6) The Holy Spirit is spoken of in the neuter for strictly grammatical reasons (the word *pneuma* is neuter). The masculine is used to stress His personality.

¹³(3:5) Both are valid translations of the genitive noun *Christou* (lit. "of Christ"). The KJ translates as an *objective* genitive (the "of-word" receiving the action suggested by the noun it modifies). The NKJV *subjective* genitive has Christ as the One showing the patience.

¹⁴(3:11) The Greek words are "not at all *ergazomenous* (working), but *periergazomenous* (working around or meddling around)." (Note the root *"erg"* — work.)

BIBLIOGRAPHY

See Bibliography at the end of *1 Thessalonians*.

THE PASTORAL EPISTLES

Introduction

"The Pastoral Epistles have played an important part in the history of the Christian Church and have amply justified their inclusion in the New Testament Canon. Their appeal lies in their blend of sound practical advice and theological statement, which has proved invaluable to Christians both personally and collectively."
— Donald Guthrie

I. The Meaning of the Term "Pastoral Epistles"

Since the 1700's, 1 and 2 Timothy and Titus have been called "the Pastoral Epistles." The description may be misleading or helpful, depending on how one understands it.

If the designation suggests that the Letters contain practical suggestions on how to care for the sheep of the Lord, then it has served its purpose well.

However, if it suggests that Timothy and Titus were settled clergymen (modern pastors) of the churches in Ephesus and Crete, respectively, then you have been misled.

Older editions of the King James Bible contain uninspired subscripts at the end of the Epistles which have lent credence to this historical error. For instance, at the end of 2 Timothy is this non-inspired addition:

> The second epistle unto Timotheus, ordained the first bishop of the church of the Ephesians, was written from Rome, when Paul was brought before Nero the second time.

And at the end of Titus is this explanation:

> It was written to Titus, ordained the first bishop of the church of the Cretians, from Nicopolis of Macedonia.

Albert Barnes, himself a clergyman, can scarcely be charged with prejudice when he comments:

> There is no evidence that Titus was the first bishop of the church there, or that he was the first one there to whom might be properly applied the term bishop in the Scriptural sense. Indeed, there is positive evidence that he was not the first, for Paul was there with him, and Titus was "left" there to complete what he had begun.
>
> There is no evidence that Titus was "bishop" there at all in the prelatical sense of the term, or even that he was a settled pastor.
>
> These subscriptions are so utterly destitute of authority, and are so full of mistakes, that it is high time they were omitted in the editions of the Bible. They are no part of the inspired writings but are of the nature of "notes and comments," and are constantly doing something, perhaps much, to perpetuate error. The opinion that Timothy and Titus were "prelatical bishops," the one of Ephesus and the other of Crete, depends far more on these worthless subscriptions than on anything in the epistles themselves. Indeed, there is no evidence of it in the epistles, and, if these subscriptions were removed, no man from the New Testament would ever suppose that they sustained that office at all.[1]

Fortunately the subscriptions finally have been removed from modern versions of the NT, but the error they promulgated dies hard.

Timothy and Titus were sent to churches on temporary missions by the Apostle Paul to instruct the believers and to warn them against false teachers.

Since virtually all Bible scholars agree that these three Letters are from the *same period* and by the *same hand*, we will handle their authorship and authenticity as a unit.

II. Authorship of These Epistles[†]

Until 1804, when Schmidt denied that Paul wrote these Epistles, the entire church and even non-believers accepted them as genuine Letters of the great apostle.

Since that time it has grown ever more common to label these books as "forgeries," though "pious" ones (as if fraud could go with true piety!). Most liberals and some otherwise conservative people have trouble accepting the books as genuinely Pauline or at least *totally* so. Since there is much important teaching on how to guide a church and other important doctrines — *including warnings against heretics and unbelief in the latter days* — we feel it is necessary to give more detail on these Epistles' authenticity than any others except 2 Peter.

III. External Evidence

The external evidence for the Pastorals is very strong. In fact, if this were the only criterion for acceptance or rejection, they would win without question.

Irenaeus is the first known author to quote these Epistles directly. Tertullian and Clement of Alexandria ascribed them to Paul, as did the Muratorian Canon. Earlier fathers who seem to have known the Letters include Polycarp and Clement of Rome.

Marcion did not include these three Books in his "canon," according to Tertullian. This is probably not really a vote against their authenticity as much as against their *contents*. Marcion was the sort of cult leader to chafe under Paul's harsh attacks against incipient Gnosticism (see Introduction to Colossians) included in the Pastoral Epistles. Passages which this anti-Semitic heretic would especially dislike include 1 Timothy 1:8; 4:3; 6:20 and 2 Timothy 3:16, 17.

IV. Internal Evidence

Nearly all the attacks against Paul's having written the Pastoral Epistles are based on supposed evidence to the contrary *within* the Letters themselves.

Three main lines of evidence are alleged: historical, ecclesiastical, and linguistic. We will briefly examine and explain each of these three problems.

The historical problem. Several events and people in these books cannot be fitted into Acts or our knowledge of Paul's ministry from the other Epistles. Paul's leaving Trophimus sick at Miletus and his cloak and parchments at Troas do not fit in with his known travels.

This is an easy argument to refute. Yes, it is true they don't fit in with Acts; they don't *need* to. Philippians 1:25 suggests Paul was expecting to be released, and Christian tradition says that he was, and ministered for some years before he was re-imprisoned and beheaded. The events, friends, and enemies mentioned in the Pastorals are thus from this period of missionary work *between* the two imprisonments.

The ecclesiastical problem. It is said that the church organization is too late for Paul — second century, in fact. While it is true that bishops, elders, and deacons are discussed in the Pastorals, there is no evidence they were the "monarchical" type of bishops of the second and following centuries. In fact, Philippians 1:1, an earlier Epistle, mentions a plurality of bishops (overseers) in one church, not one bishop over a church, or the even later system of one bishop over several churches. Also, the words *elders* and *bishops* are used interchangeably in Timothy and Titus, whereas, starting in the second century, with persistent encouragement from Ignatius, one "bishop" was singled out to be over the other men as "presbyters."

The very basic teaching on church leaders thus clearly suggests the *apostolic* age, not the second century.

The linguistic argument. The strongest attack is based on the difference in style and vocabulary between these three Letters and the other ten we accept as by Paul. Some of Paul's favorite words and expressions are not found here, and many words not used in his other Letters *are* (36% new words). Statistical methodology is made to "prove" Paul "couldn't" have written these Letters. (The same method has challenged poems by Shakespeare with similar negative results.)

It is well to acknowledge that there are *actual problems* here. For once the theories are not almost completely based on prejudice against unpalatable scriptural doctrine. (However, the latter-day apostates who are attacked in the Pastorals do sound surprisingly like some of the very scholars who insist Paul is not the author of them.)

First of all, it is important to remember that these are the Letters of an old man facing death, one who has had much broadening travel and acquired many new friends since getting out of prison (2 Timothy is written from his second imprisonment). Everyone increases his vocabulary as he ages, reads, travels, and mixes with new people.

Second, we must realize the subject matter of these Letters — church officers, ethics, and apostasy — automatically calls for new words.

These Epistles are also far too short for a fair use of the statistical method. Perhaps most significantly, 80% of the NT vocabulary occurring only in the Pastorals is found in the Greek OT (LXX), as Guthrie states in his *Introduction*. Since Paul was ministering in Greek, it is obvious he knew the OT Scriptures in that language as well as in the Hebrew original. In short, these words which Paul is alleged to have used were at least part of his "recognition vocabulary." The church fathers who used Greek as their everyday language saw no problem in Pauline authorship of the Pastorals. (The fact that some *did* so for Hebrews shows they were sensitive to a writer's style.)

Putting all the answers to the arguments together, and especially when joined with the ancient and universal acceptance by orthodox believers of these Letters as from Paul's own hand, we also can accept them as such with a good conscience. In fact, the highly *ethical* content of these Epistles rules out a forger, "pious" or otherwise. These are the inspired words of God (2 Tim. 3:16, 17) communicated through the Apostle Paul.

V. Background and Themes of the Pastoral Epistles

Frankly, we do not have too much background for the period of Paul's life covered by these Epistles. The best we can do is to piece together the biographical statements which are found in the Letters themselves, and these are very sketchy.

There are several words and themes which recur frequently in these Letters. These give us an insight into the subjects which occupied Paul's mind increasingly as his ministry was drawing to a close.

Faith is one of the characteristic words. As the peril of apostasy increased, Paul sought to emphasize the great body of Christian doctrine which had been delivered to the saints. He described various attitudes which men had taken or would take toward faith.

1. Some suffered shipwreck concerning the faith (1 Tim. 1:19).
2. Some would depart from the faith (1 Tim. 4:1).
3. Some would deny the faith (1 Tim. 5:8).
4. Some would cast off their first faith (1 Tim. 5:12).
5. Some would stray from the faith (1 Tim. 6:10).
6. Some missed the mark concerning the faith (1 Tim. 6:21).

Clearly related is the expression *sound doctrine*. "Sound" here means more than correct or orthodox. It means healthy or health-giving. It is the word from which "hygiene" comes. Here, of course, it is spiritual hygiene. Note the following:

Sound doctrine (1 Tim. 1:10; 2 Tim. 4:3; Tit. 1:9; 2:1).
Wholesome words (1 Tim. 6:3).
Sound words (2 Tim. 1:13).
Sound in the faith (Tit. 1:13; 2:2).
Sound speech (Tit. 2:8).

The word *conscience* is mentioned six times, as follows:

1 Timothy 1:5, 19; 3:9; 4:2
2 Timothy 1:3
Titus 1:15

Godliness is emphasized as the practical proof of the soundness of one's doctrine — 1 Timothy 2:2, 10; 3:16; 4:7, 8; 5:4; 6:3, 5, 6, 11; 2 Timothy 3:5 (outward form of godliness only); 3:12; Titus 1:1; 2:12.

Being *sober* or *sober-minded* are qualities which the apostle felt were worthy of cultivation by his young assistants — 1 Timothy 2:9, 15; 5:6, 8; 2 Timothy 3:2, 11; Titus 1:8; 2:2, 4, 6, 12.

We should notice, too, the many *good* things which the apostle mentions:

Good conscience (1 Tim. 1:5, 19).

The law is good (1 Tim. 1:8).

A good warfare (1 Tim. 1:18).

Prayer is good (1 Tim. 2:3).

Good works (1 Tim. 2:10; 3:1; 5:10, 25; 6:18; 2 Tim. 2:21; 3:17; Tit. 1:16; 2:7, 14; 3:1, 8, 14).

Good behavior (1 Tim. 3:2).

Good testimony (1 Tim. 3:7).

A good standing (1 Tim. 3:13).

Every creature is good (1 Tim. 4:4).

A good minister (1 Tim. 4:6).

Good doctrine (1 Tim. 4:6).

Piety is good (1 Tim. 5:4).

The good fight of faith (1 Tim. 6:12; 2 Tim. 4:7).

Good confession (1 Tim. 6:13).

Good foundation (1 Tim. 6:19).

Good thing (2 Tim. 1:14; Tit. 2:3; 3:8).

A good soldier (2 Tim. 2:3).

Good people (2 Tim. 3:3; Tit. 1:8; 2:5).

Good fidelity (Tit. 2:10).

A final interesting word study concerns the medical terms which are found in these Letters. Some think that this is a reflection of the fact that Dr. Luke was a close companion of Paul at this time.

We have already mentioned that the word "sound" means health-giving and is used to describe doctrine, words, speech, and faith.

In 1 Timothy 4:2, Paul speaks of a seared conscience. "Seared" means cauterized as with a hot instrument.

The expression "obsessed with disputes" means sick about them, and refers to mental illness (1 Tim. 6:4).

"Cancer" in 2 Timothy 2:17 is translated "gangrene" in the Revised Version (the Greek word is the origin of this latter).

"Itching ears" (2 Tim. 4:3) is a final expression used by Paul in his diagnosis of these latter-day clinical cases.

With this background, let us now turn to the First Epistle to Timothy for a verse-by-verse study of its contents.

THE FIRST EPISTLE TO TIMOTHY

Introduction

"This Epistle would give Timothy some documentary proof of his authorization to act as the apostle's representative. Accordingly much of the Epistle is directly occupied with the personal life and activities of Timothy himself."
— D. Edmond Hiebert

I. Unique Place in the Canon

Those who would rob the church of the Pastoral Epistles as authentic Letters of the great Apostle Paul do severe damage to the faith. We suspect that the main problem for them does not really lie so much in the so-called "un-Pauline vocabulary," as it does in the *very* Pauline way these words are often put together! They condemn in advance the very things some of these people are doing and teaching.

The truth, beauty, and spiritual force of 1 Timothy comes through to anyone meditating on the text as such without preconceived notions. In fact, many who deny the Pauline authorship sense this so strongly that they feel forced to suggest that fragments of *genuine* Pauline Letters were woven into the alleged forger's excellent work! For example, the French skeptic of the past century, Ernest Renan, writes: "Some passages of these letters are so beautiful that we cannot help asking if the forger had not in his hands some authentic notes of Paul, which he has incorporated into his apocryphal composition."[1]

How much simpler to accept the nearly universal teaching of the church from earliest times that these are — *in their entirety* — "authentic notes of Paul"!

Very important revelation on church order, women's ministry, and church officers is found in 1 Timothy. How the man of God should live is clearly outlined by a model *par excellence*, Paul himself.

II. Authorship

See the Introduction to the Pastoral Epistles for a discussion of 1 Timothy's authorship.

III. Date

Nearly all conservatives agree that 1 Timothy is the first of the Pastorals to be written, with Titus soon after and 2 Timothy right before Paul's death. If Paul was released from house arrest in A.D. 61, allowing for his travels, a date between 64 and 66 is indicated. The Epistle was probably written from Greece.

IV. Background and Themes[†]

The theme of 1 Timothy is set forth quite clearly in 3:14, 15:

> These things I write to you, though I hope to come to you shortly; but if I am delayed, I write so that you may know how you ought to conduct yourself in the house of God, which is the church of the living God, the pillar and ground of the truth.

Paul states here quite simply that there is a standard of behavior for the church of God and that he is writing to Timothy to enable him to know it.

It is not enough to say to a child who is misbehaving, "Behave yourself!" if the child does not know what is expected in the way of good behavior. He must be told first what good behavior *is*. 1 Timothy does this for the child of God in relation to the church of God.

A summary glance at the various chapters supports the theme as outlined above. Chapter 2 shows us what that be-havior is in relation to public prayer and to women's role in public. Chapter 3 sets forth requirements for those who will be taking places of responsibility and leadership in the assembly. Chapter 5 stresses the congregation's responsibility toward widows.

OUTLINE

I. SALUTATION (1:1, 2)

II. PAUL'S CHARGE TO TIMOTHY (1:3–20)
   A. Charge to Silence False Teachers (1:3–11)
   B. Thanksgiving for the True Grace of God (1:12–17)
   C. Restatement of the Charge to Timothy (1:18–20)

III. INSTRUCTIONS CONCERNING CHURCH LIFE (2:1–3:16)
   A. Regarding Prayer (2:1–7)
   B. Regarding Men and Women (2:8–15)
   C. Regarding Elders and Deacons (3:1–13)
   D. Regarding Conduct in the Church (3:14–16)

IV. APOSTASY IN THE CHURCH (4:1–16)
   A. Warning Against the Impending Apostasy (4:1–5)
   B. Positive Instructions in View of the Impending Apostasy (4:6–16)

V. SPECIFIC INSTRUCTIONS CONCERNING VARIOUS CLASSES OF BELIEVERS (5:1–6:2)
   A. Different Age Groups (5:1, 2)
   B. Widows (5:3–16)
   C. Elders (5:17–25)
   D. Bondservants and Masters (6:1, 2)

VI. FALSE TEACHERS AND THE LOVE OF MONEY (6:3–10)

VII. CLOSING CHARGES TO TIMOTHY (6:11–21)

Commentary

I. SALUTATION (1:1, 2)

1:1 **Paul** first of all introduces himself as **an apostle of Jesus Christ. An apostle** is a "sent one," so Paul is simply stating that he had been divinely appointed to missionary work. Paul's authorship was **by the commandment of God our Savior and the Lord Jesus Christ, our hope**. This emphasizes that Paul had not chosen the ministry by himself as a means of livelihood; neither had he been ordained to this work by men. He had a definite call from God to preach, teach, and suffer. In this verse, **God** the Father is called **our Savior**. Usually in the NT, the Lord Jesus is spoken of as the Savior. But there is no contradiction. God is the **Savior** of men in the sense that He desires their salvation, He has sent His Son to accomplish the work of redemption, and He gives eternal life to all who accept the Lord Jesus by faith. Christ is the Savior in the sense that He actually went to the cross and finished the work that was necessary in order that God might righteously save ungodly sinners.

The Lord Jesus Christ is spoken of here as **our hope**. This reminds one of Colossians 1:27: "Christ in you, the hope of glory." Our only hope of getting to heaven is found in the Person and work of the Lord Jesus. In fact, all the bright prospects which are held out before us in the Bible are ours only because of our connection with Christ Jesus.

Note further Ephesians 2:14, where Christ is our peace, and Colossians 3:4, where He is our life. Christ is our peace, dealing with the problem of our sins in the past; Christ is our life, dealing with the problem of power for the present; and Christ is our hope, dealing with the problem of deliverance in the future.

1:2 The Letter is addressed **to Timothy**, who is described as **a true son in the faith** (**in the** realm of **faith**). This may indicate that Timothy was saved through the apostle, perhaps during Paul's first visit to Lystra (Acts 14:6–20). But the general impression in Acts is that Timothy was already a disciple when Paul first met him (Acts 16:1, 2). In that case the expression **true son in the faith** means that Timothy exhibited the same spiritual and moral qualities as Paul; he was a **true** descendant of the apostle because he manifested the same character.

Stock says: "Happy is the young Christian worker who has such a leader, and happy is the Christian leader who 'hath his quiver full' of such 'true' children."

The usual salutation in NT Letters is "grace and peace." In 1 and 2 Timothy, Titus, and 2 John, this is enlarged to **grace, mercy and peace**. All of these latter Epistles were written to individuals rather than to churches, and this explains the addition of **mercy**.

Grace means all the divine resources needed for Christian life and service. **Mercy** speaks of God's compassionate care and protection for one who is needy and prone to fail. **Peace** means the inner tranquility that comes from leaning on the Lord. These three blessings come from **God our Father and Jesus Christ our Lord**. The deity of Christ is implied in this verse in that Paul speaks of Him as equal with the Father. The expression **Jesus Christ our Lord** stresses the Lordship of Christ. Whereas the word "Savior" occurs twenty-four times in the NT,

the word "Lord" occurs 522 times. We should be able to make a personal application of these important statistics.

II. PAUL'S CHARGE TO TIMOTHY (1:3–20)

A. Charge to Silence False Teachers (1:3–11)

1:3 It seems probable that after Paul's first imprisonment at Rome, he visited Ephesus with Timothy. When Paul moved on to Macedonia, he instructed Timothy to stay in Ephesus for a while to teach the word of God and to warn the believers against false teachers. From Macedonia, Paul apparently traveled south to Corinth, and it was perhaps from that city that he wrote this first Letter to Timothy. In verse 3, the apostle is saying in effect: "Just **as I** previously instructed you to stay **in Ephesus when I went into Macedonia**, so I am repeating those instructions now." It is not to be understood from this that Timothy was appointed pastor of the church at Ephesus. There is no such thought in the passage. Rather, he was there on a temporary mission, charging certain men in the assembly not to **teach** doctrines contrary to the Christian faith or supposed additions to it. The principal false doctrines in question were legalism and Gnosticism. Just in case Timothy was tempted to run away from these problems, Paul is telling him to stay on the job.

1:4 Timothy was also exhorted to charge these men not to pay attention **to fables and endless genealogies**. It is impossible for us to know definitely what these **fables** and **genealogies** were. Some connect them with legends that had arisen among some Jewish teachers. Others think they refer to the myths and generations of the Gnostics. It is interesting to notice that the false cults of today are characterized by these same things. Many fanciful stories have arisen with regard to the founders of false religions, and genealogies occupy an important place in Mormonism.

Such worthless subjects serve only to provoke questionings and doubts in people's minds. They do not produce **godly edification which is in faith**. The whole plan of redemption is designed by God, not to stir up doubts and **disputes**, but rather to induce **faith** in the hearts of men. These men in the Ephesian assembly should not be devoting their attention to such valueless themes as **fables and genealogies**, but rather should devote themselves to the great truths of the Christian faith, which will prove a blessing to men and will inspire **faith** rather than doubt.

1:5 Perhaps the most important thing to understand in this verse is that **commandment** does not refer to the Law of Moses or the Ten Commandments, but to the charge of verses 3 and 4. This is brought out clearly in the NKJV: **Now the purpose of the commandment is love.** . . . Paul is saying that the goal or aim of the charge which he has just given Timothy is to produce not just orthodoxy but **love from a pure heart, from a good conscience, and from sincere faith**. These things always follow when the gospel of the grace of God is preached.

Love doubtless includes love to God, to one's fellow believers, and to the world in general. It must spring out of **a pure heart**. If one's inner life is unclean, then true Christian love can scarcely flow from it. This love must also be the by-product of **a good conscience**, that is, a **conscience** void of offense toward God and man. Finally, this love must be the outcome of **sincere** (literally, "unhypocritical") **faith**, that is, faith that does not wear a mask.

False teachings could never produce these things which Paul lists, and certainly they are never the outcome of fables and endless genealogies! It is the teaching of the grace of God that produces **a pure heart, a good conscience, a sincere faith**, and that therefore results in **love**.

Verse 5 gives us the test of all true teaching, namely, does it produce these results?

1:6 There were some who had **strayed** from these things, that is, from a pure heart, a good conscience, and sincere faith. The expression **turned aside** may mean either they aimed improperly or missed the mark. The former is no doubt the meaning here. It was not a question of these men having tried to reach these things; they did not even aim for them. As a result, they **turned aside to idle talk**. Their preaching was aimless; it led nowhere; it failed to make men holy.

Paul frequently uses the word **some** in this Epistle. At the time he wrote 1 Timothy, these false teachers represented a minority in the church. When we come to 2 Timothy, we shall see that the word "some" is no longer prominent. The balance of power had changed. Departure had become much more general. The minority apparently had become the majority.

1:7 The false teachers referred to in the previous verses were Judaizers, who sought to mix Judaism and Christianity, law and grace. They maintained that faith in Christ was not sufficient for salvation. They insisted that a man must be circumcised or in other ways must keep the Law of Moses. They taught that the law was the believer's rule of life.

This false teaching has been present in every century of church history, and it is the plague which has been most successful in corrupting Christendom today. In its modern form, it states that although faith in Christ is necessary for salvation, a person must also be baptized, or join the church, or keep the law, or do penance, or tithe, or perform some other type of "good works." Those who teach this present-day legalism fail to realize that salvation is by faith in Christ without the deeds of the law. They do not realize that good works are the *result* of salvation and not the cause. A man does not become a Christian by doing these good works, but rather he does these good works because he is a Christian. They do not see that Christ, and not the law, is the believer's rule of life. They fail to understand that a man cannot be under the law without being under the curse. The law condemns to death all who fail to keep its sacred precepts. Since no man is able to obey the law perfectly, then all are condemned to death. But Christ has redeemed believers from the curse of the law because He was made a curse for us.

The apostle says of these self-styled **teachers of the law** that they did not understand **what they** were saying **nor the things** about which they were making confident affirmations. They could not speak intelligently about the law because they did not understand the purpose for which the law was given or the relationship of the believer to the law.

1:8 Paul makes it abundantly clear that there is nothing the matter with the law. "Therefore the law is holy, and the commandment holy and just and good" (Rom. 7:12). But the law must be used **lawfully**. It was never given as a means of salvation (Acts 13:39; Rom. 3:20; Gal. 2:16, 21; 3:11). The lawful use of **the law** is to so employ it in preaching and teaching as to produce conviction of sin. It should not be presented as a means of salvation or as a rule of life.

Guy King has pointed out that the three lessons which the law teaches are: "We ought. We haven't. We can't." When the law has done its work in the life of a sinner, then that person is ready to cry out to God, "Lord, save me by Your grace!"[2] Those who teach that the law is essential for salvation or sanctification are not consistent. They say that if a Christian breaks the law, then he need not be put to death. This is not establishing the authority of the law. Law without penalty is nothing but good advice.

1:9 The law is not made for a righteous person. If a man is righteous, he does not need a law. That is true of the Christian. When he is saved by the grace of God, he does not need to be placed under the Ten Commandments in order for him to live a holy life. It is not fear of punishment that makes a Christian live in a godly manner, but rather love for the Savior who died at Calvary.

The apostle goes on to describe the type of people for whom the law was given. Many Bible commentators have pointed out that there is a close connection between this description and the Ten Commandments themselves. The Ten Commandments are divided into two sections: the first four have to do with man's duty toward God (godliness), whereas the remaining six have to do with his duty toward his neighbor (righteousness). The following words seem to correspond to the first section of the Ten Commandments: **For the lawless and insubordinate, for the ungodly and for sinners, for the unholy and profane. . . .** The expression **for man-slayers** is linked with the sixth commandment: **You shall not murder.** Here **manslayers** refers to murderers, and not just to a person who kills another accidentally.

1:10 The words **for fornicators, for sodomites** describe immoral heterosexuals and homosexuals. Here they are linked to the seventh commandment: "You shall not commit adultery." The phrase **for kidnappers** is obviously related to the eighth commandment: "You shall not steal." **For liars, for perjurers** (or false swearers) connects with the ninth commandment: "You shall not bear false witness against your neighbor."

The final words **and if there is any other thing that is contrary to sound doctrine** are not directly related to the tenth commandment, but rather seem to sweep back over all the commandments and summarize them.

1:11 It is difficult to decide how this verse is connected with what has gone before. It may mean that the sound doctrine mentioned in verse 10 **is according to the . . . gospel**. Or it may mean that all that Paul has been saying about the law in verses 8–10 is in perfect agreement with **the gospel** which he preached. Or again, it may mean that all that Paul has been saying about false teachers in verses 3–10 is in accord with **the gospel** message. While it is true that the gospel is **glorious**, the emphasis here may be on the fact that the gospel tells of *the glory* (the literal translation of **glorious**) of **God** in a wonderful way. It tells how the same God who is holy, righteous, and just is at the same time a God of grace, mercy, and love. His love provided what His holiness demanded; now those who receive the Lord Jesus are given eternal life.

This is the **gospel . . . which was committed** to the apostle's **trust**. It centers around the glorified Lord Jesus Christ and tells men that He is not only Savior but Lord as well.

B. Thanksgiving for the True Grace of God (1:12–17)

1:12 In the preceding passage, Paul has been describing the false teachers who were seeking to impose the law on the believers in Ephesus. He is now reminded of his own conversion. It was not through law-keeping but by the grace of God. The apostle had not been a righteous man but the chief of sinners. Verses 12–17 seem to illustrate the lawful use of the law from Paul's own experience. The law was not to him a way of salvation, but rather a means of conviction of sin.

First of all he bursts out into thanksgiving to **Christ Jesus** for His enabling grace. The emphasis is not on what Saul of Tarsus did for the Lord but what the Lord did for him. The apostle could never get over the wonder that the Lord Jesus not only saved him but **counted** him **faithful**, appointing him to His service. The law could never have shown such grace. Rather, its inflexible terms would have condemned the sinner Saul to death.

1:13 That Paul had broken the Ten Commandments before his conversion is abundantly evident from this verse. He speaks of himself as **formerly a blasphemer, a persecutor, and an insolent man**. As **a blasphemer**, he spoke evil concerning the Christians and their Leader, Jesus. As **a persecutor**, he sought to put Christians to death because he felt that this new sect posed a threat to Judaism. In carrying out his evil plan, he took delight in committing **insolent**, violent, and outrageous acts against the believers. Although it is not as obvious from the English words, there is an ascending scale of wickedness in the three words **blasphemer, persecutor, and insolent**. The first sin is a matter of words only. The second describes suffering inflicted on others for their religious beliefs. The third includes the idea of cruelty and abuse.

But Paul **obtained mercy**. He did not receive the punishment he deserved **because** he **did** these things **ignorantly in unbelief**. In persecuting Christians, he thought he was doing God's service. Since his parents' religion taught the worship of the true God, he could only conclude that the Christian faith was opposed to the Jehovah of the OT. With all the zeal and energy he possessed, he sought to defend the honor of God by killing the Christians.

Many insist that zeal and earnestness and sincerity are the important things

with God. But Paul's example shows that zeal is not enough. In fact, if a man is wrong, his zeal only makes the wrong more intense. The more zeal he has, the more damage he does!

1:14 Not only did Paul escape the punishment he deserved (mercy), but he also received **abundant** kindness which he did not deserve (**grace**). Where his sin had abounded, God's grace abounded much more (Rom. 5:20).

The fact that the **grace** of the Lord was not bestowed on Paul in vain is indicated by the words **"with faith and love which are in Christ Jesus."** The grace which came to Paul was accompanied by **faith and love which are in Christ Jesus**. It could, of course, mean that just as grace came from the Lord, so faith and love found their origin in Him. But the meaning seems to be clearer if we understand that God's grace was not refused by Paul, but that he responded by trusting the Lord Jesus and by loving this Blessed One whom he formerly had hated.

1:15 This is the first of five "faithful sayings" in the Pastoral Epistles. **This is a faithful saying** because it is the word of God, who can neither lie nor be mistaken. Men can afford to believe this statement with implicit trust. Indeed, to disbelieve it is unreasonable and unwise. It is **worthy of all acceptance** because it applies to all, tells what God has done for all, and extends the gift of salvation to all.

Christ Jesus emphasizes the deity of our Lord. The One who came from heaven to earth was first of all *God* (**Christ**) and then *Man* (**Jesus**). The pre-existence of the Savior is suggested in the words He **came into the world**. Bethlehem was not the beginning of His existence. He had dwelt with God the Father from all eternity, but He came into the world as a Man on a specific errand. The calendar testifies to the fact that He came; we speak of this as A.D. 19—, the year of our Lord 19—. Why did He come? **To save sinners.** It was not to save good people (there were none!). Neither was it to save those who kept the law perfectly (none had done this either).

Here we come to the very heart of the difference between true Christianity and all other teachings. False religions tell man that there is something he can do or be in order to win favor with God. The gospel tells man that he is a sinner, that he is lost, that he cannot save himself, and that the only way he can get to heaven is through the substitutionary work of the Lord Jesus on the cross. The type of law teaching which Paul described earlier in this chapter gives a place to the flesh. It tells man exactly what he wants to hear, namely, that he can somehow contribute to his own salvation. But the gospel insists that all the glory for the work of salvation must go to Christ alone, that man does nothing but the sinning, and that the Lord Jesus does all the saving.

The Spirit of God brought Paul to the place where he realized he was the **chief** of sinners, or as some translate it: "a foremost one among sinners." If he was not the chief of sinners, then certainly he was in the front rank. Notice that the title "chief of sinners" is not given to a man steeped in idolatry or immorality, but rather to a deeply religious man, one who had been brought up in an orthodox Jewish home! His sin was doctrinal; he did not accept the word of God concerning the Person and work of the Lord Jesus Christ. Rejection of the Son of God is the greatest of sins.

Also, it should be noted that he says **of whom I am chief** — not "was" but **am**. The godliest saints are often the most conscious of their own sinfulness.

In 1 Corinthians 15:9 (written about A.D. 57), Paul called himself "the least of the apostles." Then in Ephesians 3:8 (written about A.D. 60), he called himself "less than the least of all saints." Now in 1 Timothy 1:15, written some years later, he calls himself the **chief** of **sinners**. Here we have an outline of Paul's progress in Christian humility.

Darby's translation of the expression **of whom I am chief** is "of whom I am (the) first." The thought is not so much that he was the worst sinner who ever lived but that he was first in relation to the nation of Israel. In other words, his conversion was a unique foreshadowing of the future conversion of the nation of Israel. He was "one born out of due time" (1 Cor. 15:8) in the sense that he was born again prior to the rebirth of his people Israel. Just as he was saved by a direct revelation from heaven and apart from human instrumentality, so perhaps in this same way the Jewish remnant will be saved during the coming Tribulation Period. This interpretation seems to be borne out by the words "first" and "pattern" in verse 16.

1:16 This explains why Paul obtained mercy. It was so that he might be an exhibit of the **longsuffering** of **Jesus Christ**. Just as he had been the chief of sinners, so now he would be the chief display of the untiring grace of the Lord. He would be "Exhibit A," a living example, as William Kelly said, of "divine love rising above the most active hostility, of divine longsuffering exhausting the most varied and persistent antagonism."[3]

Paul's case would be **a pattern**. In the printing trade, pattern means a first proof. It signifies a specimen or a sample. Paul's conversion would be a **pattern** of what God would do with the nation of Israel when the Deliverer comes out of Zion (Rom. 11:26).

In a more general sense the verse means that none need despair, no matter how wicked they might be. They can console themselves that since the Lord has already saved the chief of sinners, they too can find grace and mercy by coming to Him as penitents. By believing on Him, they too can find **everlasting life**.

1:17 As Paul thinks of God's marvelous dealings with him in grace, he bursts out into this lovely doxology. It is difficult to know whether it is addressed to God the Father or to the Lord Jesus. The words **the King eternal** seem to refer to the Lord Jesus because He is called the "Kings of kings, and Lord of lords" (Rev. 19:16). However, the word **invisible** seems to refer to the Father, since the Lord Jesus was obviously visible to mortal eyes. The fact that we are not able to distinguish which Person of the Godhead is intended might serve as an indication of Their absolute equality.

The King eternal is spoken of, first of all, as **immortal**. This means incorruptible or imperishable. God in His essence is also **invisible**. Men have seen appearances of God in the OT, and the Lord Jesus fully revealed God to us in visible form, but the fact remains that God Himself is invisible to human eyes. Next He is spoken of as **God who alone is wise**. In the final analysis, all wisdom comes from God (Jas. 1:5).

C. Restatement of the Charge to Timothy (1:18–20)

1:18 The **charge** mentioned here is no doubt the charge Paul had given Timothy in verses 3 and 5 to rebuke false teachers. To encourage his **son Timothy** to carry out this important commission, the apostle reminds him of the circumstances which led to his call to Christian service.

According to the prophecies previously made concerning you seems to mean that before Paul met Timothy, a prophet had arisen in church and announced that Timothy would be used by the Lord in His service. A prophet was a spokesman for God who received revelations of God's will with regard to some particular course of action, and communicated these revelations to the church. Young Timothy was singled out by prophetic utterances and his future role as a servant of Jesus Christ was thus made known. If he should ever be tempted to lose heart or become discouraged in the work of the Lord, he should remember these **prophecies** and thus be inspired and stimulated to **wage the good warfare.**

1:19 In this warfare, he should hold **faith and a good conscience**. It is not enough just to be doctrinally accurate as to the Christian faith. One might be ever so orthodox, and yet not have **a good conscience**.

Hamilton Smith writes:

> Those who are gifted, and much before the public eye, have to beware, lest amid constant engagements, constant preaching, and public work before men, they neglect the secret life of godliness before God. Does not Scripture warn us that it is possible to preach with all the eloquence of men and angels, and yet be nothing? That which bears fruit for God, and will have its bright reward in the day to come, is the life of godliness from which all true service must flow.[4]

Some of those living in Paul's day had thrust a good conscience from them

and thus had **suffered shipwreck** as far as **the faith** was concerned. They have been likened to a foolish sailor who throws his compass overboard.

Those who had made **shipwreck** of the faith were true believers, but they simply had not maintained tender consciences. Their Christian life had started out like a gallant ship putting out to sea, but instead of returning to port with banners waving and a full cargo, they had foundered on the rocks and brought shame on themselves and their testimony.

1:20 We do not know whether **Hymenaeus and Alexander** are the ones mentioned in 2 Timothy 2:17 and 4:14. Neither do we know the nature of their blasphemy. All we are told is that they abandoned a good conscience and that they blasphemed. In the NT, **blaspheme**[5] does not always mean to speak evil of God. It might also be used to describe abusive or evil speaking against one's fellow men. It might be used to describe the lives of these men as well as the words of their lips. By making shipwreck of the faith, they had undoubtedly caused others to speak evil of the way of truth, and thus their lives were living blasphemies.

Theirs is the tragedy of once bright, effective Christians being sidetracked into error through the stifling of their consciences.

The apostle says that he **delivered** these men **to Satan**. Some scholars see in these words a simple reference to the act of excommunication. They understand them to mean that Paul had put these two men out of the local church and that this action was designed to bring them to repentance and to a restoration of fellowship with the Lord and with His people. The difficulty with this view is that excommunication was a function of the local church and not of an apostle. In 1 Corinthians 5 Paul did not excommunicate the incestuous man but counseled the Corinthians to do so.

The other major interpretation of this passage is that delivering **to Satan** was a power given to the apostles which is no longer in evidence today because there are no apostles. According to this view, the apostles had authority to turn a sinning person over **to Satan** for the infliction of physical suffering or, even in extreme cases, of death, as in the case of Ananias and Sapphira (Acts 5:1–11). The discipline here was obviously for corrective purposes — **that they may learn not to blaspheme**. It was not a question of damnation but of chastisement.

III. INSTRUCTIONS CONCERNING CHURCH LIFE (2:1–3:16)

A. Regarding Prayer (2:1–7)

Paul has concluded his first charge to Timothy concerning the false teachers, and now he moves on to the subject of prayer. It is generally agreed that this passage has to do with public prayer, although there is nothing in it that would not be equally applicable to one's private devotional life.

2:1 Prayer **for all men** is both a privilege and an obligation. It is a sheer privilege for us to have audience with God in behalf of our fellow men. And it is an obligation, too, for we are debtors to all with reference to the good news of salvation.

The apostle lists four aspects of prayer — **supplications, prayers, intercessions, and giving of thanks**. It is rather difficult to distinguish between the first three. In modern usage, **supplication** has the thought of strong and earnest pleading, but here the thought is more that of specific requests for specific needs. The word here translated **prayers** is a very general term, covering all kinds of reverent approaches to God. **Intercessions** describe those forms of petition in which we address God as our Superior in behalf of others. **Giving of thanks** describes prayer in which we rehearse the grace and kindness of our Lord, and pour out our hearts in gratitude to Him.

We might summarize the verse, then, by saying that in praying **for all men**, we should be humble, worshipful, trustful, and thankful.

2:2 Special mention is made here of **kings and all who are in authority**. These must occupy a special place in our prayers. Elsewhere, Paul has reminded us that the authorities that exist are ordained of God (Rom. 13:1) and that they are ministers of God to us for good (Rom. 13:4).

This verse takes on special color when we remember that it was written in the days of Nero. The terrible persecutions which were inflicted on the Christians by this wicked ruler did not affect the fact that Christians should pray for their governmental heads. The NT teaches that a Christian is to be loyal to the government under which he lives, except when that government orders him to disobey God. In such a case his first responsibility is to God. A Christian should not engage in revolution or in violence against the government. He may simply refuse to obey any order that is contrary to the word of God and then quietly and submissively take the punishment.

The reason the apostle gives for praying for rulers is **that we may lead a quiet and peaceable life in all godliness and reverence**. It is for our own good that the government should be stable and that the country be preserved from revolution, civil war, turmoil, and anarchy.

2:3 That we should pray for all men, including kings and those in authority, **is good and acceptable in the sight of God**. It is **good** in itself and **acceptable in the sight of God our Savior**. The title which Paul gives to God here is significant. God's desire is for the salvation of all men. Therefore, to pray for all men is to promote the will of God in this regard.

2:4 This explains further what we have already pointed out in verse 3. **God desires all men to be saved** (Ezek. 33:11; John 3:16; 2 Pet. 3:9). Therefore, we should pray for **all men** everywhere.

This verse sets forth clearly the divine and the human aspects of salvation. The first half of the verse indicates that man must **be saved**. The verb here is passive; man cannot save himself but must **be saved** by God. This is the divine side of salvation.

In order to be saved, man must **come to the knowledge of the truth**. God does not save men against their will. He does not populate heaven with rebellious subjects. Man must come to Him who said:

"I am the Way, the Truth, and the Life." This is the human side.

From this, it should be clear that this verse does not teach universal salvation. Although God **desires** that **all men** should **be saved**, yet not all men will be saved. It was not initially God's will that the children of Israel should wander for thirty-eight years in the wilderness; yet they did it just the same. He permitted it, but it was not the pathway of blessing which He had planned for them.

2:5 The connection of this verse with what precedes is not entirely clear. However, the thought seems to be this: **God** is **one**; therefore, He is the God of all men, and prayer should be addressed to Him in behalf of all men. As the one God, He desires the salvation of all men. If He were one of many gods, He might be concerned only about His own worshipers.

Secondly, One is **Mediator between God and men**. This being so, no man can come to God in any other way. A **mediator** is a go-between, a middleman who can stand between two and communicate with both. Through Christ, Himself Man, God is enabled to approach men with forgiveness of sins. Consequently any poor sinner can approach Him, and will by no means be rejected.

Paul identifies the Mediator as **the Man, Christ Jesus**. This does not deny the deity of the Lord Jesus. In order to be the **Mediator between God and men**, He must be both God and Man. The Lord Jesus is God from all eternity, but He became Man in Bethlehem's manger. He represents the whole race of humanity. The fact that He is both God and Man is indicated in the name **Christ Jesus. Christ** describes Him as God's anointed One, the Messiah. **Jesus** is the name given to Him in Incarnation.

The verse effectively answers the teaching so common today that the blessed Virgin Mary or angels or saints are mediators between God and man. There is only **one Mediator**, and His name is **Christ Jesus.**

Verse 5 summarizes the messages of the OT and NT. **One God** was the message of the OT entrusted to Israel; **one Mediator** — the message of the NT entrusted to the church. As Israel failed in her responsibility by worshiping idols, so the professing church has failed in her responsibility by introducing other mediators — Mary, saints, clergy, etc.

2:6 The emphasis is on the fact that God desires the salvation of all men. Here this is further shown by the fact that Christ Jesus **gave Himself a ransom for all**. A **ransom** is a price paid to release or set another free. Notice that the **ransom** is **for all**. This means that the work of the Lord Jesus on Calvary's cross was sufficient to save **all** sinners. It does not mean that all will be saved, since man's will is also involved.

This verse is one of many which teach that the death of Christ was substitutionary. He died in behalf of **all**. Whether all will accept it is another question, but the fact remains that the redemptive work of Christ was sufficient in value **for all**.

To be testified in due time means that the testimony concerning Christ's substitutionary work was to be borne in its own time. The same God who desires the salvation of all men and provided the way of salvation for all men, has decreed that the gospel message should go out in this age in which we live. All of this is designed to demonstrate the overwhelming longing on the part of God to bless mankind.

2:7 As a final demonstration of God's desire for the salvation of all men, Paul states that he **was appointed a preacher and an apostle to the Gentiles**. Then, as now, Gentiles constituted the greater portion of the population of the world. It was not to one small segment of mankind, such as the Jews, that the apostle was sent, but rather to the Gentile nations.

He speaks of himself as **a preacher and an apostle** and **a teacher. A preacher** is literally a herald, a proclaimer of the gospel. The duties of **an apostle** may be somewhat broader — he not only preaches the gospel but plants churches, guides local churches in matters of order and discipline, and speaks with authority as one sent by the Lord Jesus Christ. **A teacher** expounds the word of God in such a manner that it will be understood by the people.

To give added emphasis to what he

is saying, Paul confirms his claim to be **a teacher of the Gentiles** by the words **"I am speaking the truth in Christ, and not lying."** The words **"in faith and truth"** may describe the faithful and honest way in which the apostle carried out his teaching ministry, but more probably they describe the contents of his teaching. In other words, he taught the Gentiles in matters pertaining to **faith** and **truth**.

B. Regarding Men and Women (2:8–15)

2:8 The subject of public prayer is now resumed, and this time our attention is directed to those who should lead the people of God in prayer. The introductory words **I desire** express Paul's active and inspired desire in this matter.

In the original language of the NT, there are two words which may be translated **men**. One word means mankind in general, whereas the other means **men** in contrast to women. It is the second word that is used here. The apostle's instruction is that public prayer should be led by **the men** rather than by the women. And it means all the men, not just the elders.

The expression **everywhere** may be taken to mean that any individual Christian may pray at any time, no matter where he may be. But since the subject here seems to be public prayer, it would be better to understand this verse as saying that wherever a mixed group of Christians is gathered together for prayer, it is **the men** and not the women who should lead in this exercise.

Three qualifications are added, applying to those who are to pray publicly. First of all, they should lift up **holy hands**. The emphasis here is not so much on the physical posture of the one praying as on his inward life. His hands should be **holy hands**. The **hands** here are figurative of the man's entire manner of life. Secondly, he should be **without wrath**. This points out the inconsistency of one who is given to displays of temper, rising in the local church to speak to God in behalf of those assembled. Finally, he should be without **doubting**. This may mean that he has faith in the ability and willingness of God to hear and answer prayer. We can summarize

these qualifications by saying that a man should exhibit holiness and purity *selfward*, love and peace *manward*, and unquestioning faith *Godward*.

2:9 Having discussed the personal requisites of the men who lead in public prayer, the apostle now turns to the things which should characterize **the women** who are in the congregation at such a time. First of all, he states that they should **adorn themselves in modest apparel, with propriety and moderation**. John Chrysostom gives a definition of **modest apparel** which can scarcely be improved upon:

> And what then is *modest apparel*? Such as covers them completely and decently, and not with superfluous ornaments; for the one is decent and the other is not. What? Do you approach God to pray with broidered hair and ornaments of gold? Are you come to a ball? a marriage-feast? a carnival? There such costly things might have been seasonable: here not one of them is wanted. You have come to pray, to ask pardon for your sins, to plead for your offences, beseeching the Lord. . . . Away with such hypocrisy![6]

Propriety means avoiding anything that would cause shame. It carries the thought of being modest and discreet. **Moderation** means that a woman will be moderate in her dress. On the one hand, she will not seek to attract attention to herself by expensive, conspicuous fashions. These might tend to provoke admiration or even jealousy from those who should be worshiping God. On the other hand, she should avoid attracting attention to herself by wearing clothes that are drab or old-fashioned. The Scriptures seem to teach a moderate, middle-of-the-road policy in regard to clothing.

Some of the excesses to be avoided are **braided hair, gold, pearls, or costly clothing. Braided hair** would not necessarily exclude simple braids, which might be very modest, but rather an elaborate adorning of the head with showy hairdos. The use of jewelry or expensive clothing as a means of self-exhibition is decidedly inappropriate at the time of prayer.

2:10 The positive side of women's adorning is brought before us in this verse. The adorning which is fitting **for**

women professing godliness is found in the performance of **good works**. Such "clothing" does not distract others from communion with God, but rather provokes such fellowship. Neither does it cause envy or jealousy in a wrong sense, but only encourages others to follow the example. **Good works** are a prominent theme in the Pastoral Epistles, forming a very necessary balance to sound doctrine.

2:11 As far as her part in public meetings of the church, **a woman** is to **learn in silence with all submission**. This is consistent with the rest of Scripture on this subject (1 Cor. 11:3–15; 14:34, 35).

2:12 When Paul says: **I do not permit a woman to teach**, he is speaking as inspired of God. This does not represent Paul's own personal prejudice, as some say. It is God who decrees that women should not have a public teaching ministry in the church. The only exceptions to this are that they are permitted to teach children (2 Tim. 3:15) and young women (Tit. 2:4). Neither is a woman **to have authority over a man**. That means that she must not have dominion over a man, **but** is **to be in silence** or quietness. Perhaps we should add that the latter part of this verse is by no means limited to the local assembly. It is a fundamental principle in God's dealings with mankind that man has been given the headship and that woman is in the place of subjection. This does not mean that she is inferior; that is certainly not true. But it does mean that it is contrary to God's will that the woman should have authority or dominion over the man.

2:13 To prove his point, Paul first of all goes to the creation of **Adam** and **Eve**. **Adam was formed first, then Eve.** The very order of the creation was significant. By creating man **first**, God intended him to be the head, the one who would exercise direction, the one who would have authority. The fact that woman was created second means that she should be in submission to her husband. By basing his argument on the order of creation, Paul rules out any thought that this is a matter of local culture.

2:14 The second proof refers to the entrance of sin into the human race. Instead of approaching **Adam** directly, the serpent went to Eve with his temptations and lies. According to God's intention, Eve should not have acted independently. She should have gone to Adam and put the matter before him. Instead of that, she allowed herself to be **deceived** by Satan and **fell into transgression**.

In this connection, it is noteworthy that false teachers today usually visit homes when the wife is most apt to be there alone, that is, when the husband will most probably be away at work.

Adam was not deceived. It appears that he sinned with his eyes open. There are those who suggest that when he saw that his wife had already fallen into sin, he wanted to maintain his unity with her, and so he himself plunged into sin. But the Scriptures do not state this. They merely state that **the woman** was **deceived**, but that **Adam was not.**

2:15 This is one of the most difficult verses in the Pastoral Epistles, and many explanations have been offered. Some think that it is a simple promise from God that a Christian mother **will be saved** from death in the physical act of **childbearing**. However, this is not always true, because some godly, devoted Christians have died in the act of bringing life into the world. Others think that **childbearing** (literally, "*the* childbearing") refers to the birth of the Messiah, and that women are saved through the One who was born of a woman. However, this scarcely seems to satisfy the sense of the passage, since men are saved in the same way. No one could reasonably suggest that the verse means that a woman receives eternal salvation by virtue of becoming a mother of children; this would be salvation by works, and works of a most unusual nature!

We would suggest the following as the most reasonable interpretation of the passage. First of all, salvation in this context does not refer to the salvation of her *soul*, but rather to the salvation of her *position* in the church. From what Paul has just said in this chapter, the impression might arise in the minds of some that the woman has no place in God's purposes and counsels; she is reduced to a nonentity. But Paul would dispute this claim.

Although it is true that no public ministry in the church is assigned to her, she does have an important ministry. God has decreed that woman's place is in the home, and more specifically in the ministry of raising children for the honor and glory of the Lord Jesus Christ. Think of the mothers of the leaders in the Christian church today! These women never mounted a public platform to preach the gospel, but in raising their children for God, they have been truly **saved** as far as position and fruitfulness for God are concerned.

Lilley writes:

> She shall be saved from the results of sin and be enabled to maintain a position of influence in the Church by accepting her natural destination as a wife and mother, provided this surrender is further ratified by bringing forth the fruit of sanctified Christian character.[7]

It may be asked at this point: "What about those women who never marry?" The answer is that in this passage God is dealing with women in general. The majority of Christian women do marry and bear children. As far as the exceptions are concerned, there are many other useful ministries committed to them and yet which do not involve public teaching or having authority over men.

Note the qualifying clause at the end of verse 15: **She will be saved in childbearing, if they continue in faith, love, and holiness, with self-control**. It is not exactly an unconditional promise. The thought is that if the husband and wife maintain a consistent Christian testimony, honor Christ in the home, and raise their children in the fear and admonition of the Lord, then the woman's position **will be saved**. But if the parents live careless, worldly lives, and neglect the training of their children, then these children may be lost to Christ and the church. In such a case, the woman does not achieve the true dignity which God has ordained for her.

Let no one think that because woman's ministry is private and in the home that it is any less important than that which is more public. It has been truly said: "The hand that rocks the cradle rules the world." In a coming day, at the Judgment Seat of Christ, it is faithfulness that will count, and this is something which can be exhibited in the home as well as in the pulpit.

C. Regarding Elders and Deacons (3:1–13)

3:1 The second **faithful saying** in 1 Timothy has to do with the work of bishops in the local church. **A bishop** is a Christian man of mature experience and understanding who assists in exercising godly care over the spiritual life of a local fellowship. He does not rule by lording it over God's heritage, but rather he leads by his spiritual example.

Today, "bishop" signifies a church official who exercises authority over many local congregations. But invariably in the NT there were several bishops in one church (Acts 14:23; 20:17; Phil. 1:1; Jas. 5:14).

A bishop is the same as an overseer. The same word translated **bishop** in this verse is translated "overseer" in Acts 20:28. A bishop, or overseer, is the same as an elder. The same men who are called elders in Acts 20:17 are called overseers in Acts 20:28 (cf. also Tit. 1:5 and 1:7). Elders are the same as presbyters, for although the latter word is not found in the NT, the English word "elder" translates the Greek word *presbuteros*. Thus, the words "bishop," "overseer," "elder," and "presbyter" all refer to the same person.

Actually, the word translated "elder" (*presbuteros*) is sometimes used to describe an older man, and not necessarily one who is a leader in the church (1 Tim. 5:1, Gk.), but at most other times "elder" describes a man recognized in a local church as one who exercises pastoral care among the people of God.

The NT envisages bishops or elders in every local church (Phil. 1:1). However, it would not be accurate to say that a church could not exist without bishops. From Titus 1:5, it seems clear that there were young churches in Crete in which elders had not as yet been recognized.

Only the Holy Spirit of God can make a man an elder. This is clear in Acts 20:28. The Holy Spirit lays a burden on a man's heart to take up this important work and also equips him for it. It is impossible to make a man a bishop by voting him into office or by ordaining him. The responsibility of the local assembly is to recognize those men in its midst who have been made elders by God the Holy Spirit (1 Thess. 5:12, 13). It is true that we find the appointment of elders in the book of Titus, but there it was simply a matter of Titus' singling out those men who had the qualifications of elders. At that time, the Christians did not have the NT in printed form, as we have it today. Therefore, they did not know what the exact qualifications for elders were. So Paul sent Titus to them with this information and instructed Titus to set apart those men who had been raised up by the Spirit of God for the work.

The recognition of elders by a local assembly might be quite informal. It often happens that Christians instinctively know who their elders are because they have acquainted themselves with the qualifications of elders in 1 Timothy 3 and Titus 1. On the other hand, the recognition of elders may be a more formal procedure. A local church might gather together for the express purpose of publicly recognizing the elders. In this case, the procedure usually is to read the pertinent Scripture passages, to have them expounded, and then to have the local Christians designate whom they consider to be the elders in that assembly. The names are then announced to the entire congregation. If a church does not have qualified elders, then its only resource is to pray that the Lord will raise up such men in days to come.

The Scripture does not specify any *number* of elders for a local church, though there *is always a plurality*. It is simply a matter of how many men respond to the leading of the Holy Spirit in this matter.

If a man desires the position of a bishop, he desires a good work. There is the tendency to think this is a dignified, ecclesiastical office, entailing little or no responsibility, whereas overseership is actually humble service among the people of God; it is **work.**

3:2 The qualifications of a bishop are given in verses 2–7. They stress four main prerequisites: personal character, the witness of the home, teaching aptitude, and a measure of experience. These are God's standards for any who would exercise spiritual leadership in the local church. Some argue today that no one can measure up to these standards. However, this is not true. Such an argument robs the Sacred Scriptures of their authority and permits men to take the place of a bishop who have never been qualified by the Holy Spirit.

A bishop, then, must be blameless. This means that no charge of serious wrong can be sustained against him. It does not mean that he is sinless, but rather that if he does commit some fault, he makes it right with both God and man. He must be irreproachable, not only having an untarnished reputation, but deserving it.

Secondly, he must be **the husband of one wife**. This requirement has been understood in several ways. Some suggest that it means that a bishop must be married. The argument is that a single man would not have the proper breadth of experience to deal with family problems as they arise. If this expression means that a bishop must be married, then it must also be argued in verse 4 than an elder must have children as well, following the same line of reasoning.

Others think that **the husband of one wife** means that if a bishop's first wife died, then he does not marry again. This is a very strict interpretation that might cast reflection on the holiness of the marriage relationship.[8]

A third interpretation is that the words mean that a bishop must not be divorced. This view has considerable merit, although it scarcely seems to be a complete explanation.

Another view is that a bishop must not have been guilty of any unfaithfulness or irregularity in his marriage. His moral life must be above question. This is certainly true, whatever else the passage might mean.

A final explanation is that this means that a bishop may not be a polygamist. This may seem a strange explanation to us, but it has considerable merit. On mission fields today, it often happens that a polygamist gets saved. Perhaps at the time of his conversion, he had four wives. He subsequently asks for baptism and reception into the local church.

What is the missionary to do? Someone answers that the man should put away three of his wives. However, this action causes grave difficulty. For one thing, he would ask which ones he should put away. He loves them all and is providing a home for them all. Also, if he should put away three wives, they would have no means of livelihood, and some of them might be plunged into prostitution in order to eke out an existence. God's solution of a problem like this would never be to remedy one sin by many worse sins. Christian missionaries in many places solve the problem by allowing the man to be baptized and to be received into the local church, but he can never be an elder in the church as long as he is a polygamist.

Temperate refers not only to matters of food and drink, but also to the avoidance of extremes in spiritual matters.

Sober-minded means that this man is not giddy or frivolous. He is serious, earnest, discerning, and discreet. He realizes that as "dead flies putrefy the perfumer's ointment, and cause it to give off a foul odor; so does a little folly to the one respected for wisdom and honor" (Eccl. 10:1).

A bishop must be **of good behavior**, that is, he must be well-ordered in his habits.

Hospitable signifies that he is a lover of strangers. His home is open to saved and unsaved alike, and he seeks to be a blessing to all who come beneath his roof.

An elder must be **able to teach**. As he visits those with spiritual problems, he must be able to turn to the Scriptures and explain the will of God in such matters. He must be able to feed the flock of God (1 Pet. 5:2) and to use the Scriptures in refuting those who bring false doctrines (Acts 20:29–31). It does not necessarily mean that a bishop must have the gift of teaching, but rather that in his house-to-house ministry, as well as in the assembly, he can set forth the doctrines of the faith and rightly divide the Word of Truth, and is ready and keen to do it.

3:3 The expression **given to wine** means addicted to alcoholic drinks. The bishop must not be a man who overindulges in **wine** and thus causes quarrels, that is, abusive brawlings.

Not violent means that this man does not use physical violence on another. For instance, if he is a master, he never hits his servant.

The words **not greedy for money** are not found in some ancient manuscripts, but are in the majority.[9] The love of money will bear evil fruit in the church as well as in the world.

An elder must be **gentle**. In his work in the church, he will need forbearance, patience, and a spirit of yieldedness.

He must **not** be **quarrelsome**, contentious, and arguing about every little thing. He does not insist on his own rights but is even-tempered and congenial.

A bishop must **not** be **covetous**, that is, a lover of money. Here the emphasis is on the word "lover." He is concerned with the spiritual life of the people of God and refuses to be distracted by a strong desire for material things.

3:4 In order to be recognized as an overseer, a man must rule **his own house well, having his children in submission** to him. This qualification would apply as long as a man's children are living in his home. After they have gone off and started to raise their own families, there would no longer be the same opportunity for demonstrating this subjection. If a man **rules his own house well**, he will avoid the extremes of undue harshness and of unrighteous leniency.

3:5 The argument here is clear. Unless **a man** shows fitness **to rule his own** home, **how will he** ever expect to **take care of the church of God**? In his own home, the number of persons is comparatively small. They are all related to him, and most of the members are very much younger than he. In the church, on the other hand, the numbers are apt to be much greater, and with this increase in numbers there goes a corresponding diversity of temperaments. It is obvious that if a man is unfit to rule in the smaller sphere, he would be clearly disqualified for the larger.

Verse 5 is important because it defines the work of an elder. It is to **take care of the church of God**. Notice it does not say "to rule" the church of God. An elder is not a despot, or even a benevolent ruler, but rather one who guides the people of God as a shepherd guides the sheep.

The only other time the expression "take care of" is used in the NT is in the story of the Good Samaritan (Luke 10:34). The same tender, compassionate care shown by the Good Samaritan to the victim of the robbers should be shown by the elder who cares for the church of God.

3:6 Not a novice. A recent convert to Christianity, or a person who is young in the faith, is not qualified to be a bishop. The work requires men of experience and understanding in the faith. The danger is that a novice might become **puffed up with pride** and then **fall into the same condemnation as the devil. Condemnation** of **the devil** does not mean the judgment which Satan brings on a man, but rather the judgment which fell on Satan himself because of his pride. He sought a high position for which he was not qualified, and as a result, he was brought low.

3:7 A bishop is a man who **must have a good** reputation in the community. **Those who are outside** refers to unsaved neighbors. Without this **good testimony**, he becomes subject to the accusations of men **and the snare of the devil**. The accusations may come from believers and unbelievers alike. **The snare of the devil** is the trap which Satan lays for those whose lives are not consistent with their profession. Once he has caught men in this trap, he holds them up to ridicule, scorn, and contempt.

3:8 The apostle now moves on from bishops to **deacons**. In the NT, a deacon is simply one who serves. It is generally understood that a deacon is one who cares for the temporal affairs of the local church, whereas bishops care for its spiritual life. This understanding of the duties of deacons is largely based on Acts 6:1–5, where men were appointed to care for the daily distribution of funds to widows in the church. Actually, the noun "deacon" is not used in this passage, but the verb form is used in verse 2: "It is not desirable that we should leave the word of God and serve (literally 'deacon') tables."

The qualifications for **deacons** are very similar to those of bishops, although not quite as strict. One notable difference is that it is not required that a deacon should be apt to teach.

Deacons must be reverent, dignified, and worthy of respect. They must **not** be **double-tongued**, that is, they must not give conflicting reports to different persons or at different times. They must be consistent.

They must **not** be **given to** excess **wine**. The NT does not forbid the use of wine for medicinal purposes, or as a beverage in those countries where the water supply is polluted. But even though the moderate use of wine is permitted, the Christian must also consider his testimony in regard to this matter. Whereas in some countries it might be perfectly all right for a Christian to drink wine without having any adverse effect on his testimony, in other countries it might cause an unbeliever to stumble, should he see a Christian indulging in wine. Thus, although the use of wine might be lawful, it might not be expedient.

Deacons must **not** be **greedy for money**. As has been mentioned, one of the functions of a deacon might be to handle the funds of the local church. This exposes him to special temptation if he has a lust for money. He might be tempted to help himself. Judas was not the last treasurer to betray his Lord for mere money!

3:9 Deacons must hold **the mystery of the faith with a pure conscience**. This means that they must be sound in doctrine and in life. They must not only know the truth; they must live it. **The mystery of the faith** is a description of the Christian **faith**. Many of the doctrines of Christianity were kept secret throughout the OT period but were then revealed by the apostles and prophets of the NT. That is why the word **mystery** is used here.

3:10 Deacons should **first be tested**, as in the case of elders. This means that they should be observed for some time and perhaps even given some minor responsibilities in the local church. As they prove themselves to be trustworthy and faithful, then they can be advanced to greater responsibilities. **Then let them serve as deacons**, or simply, "let them minister." As with bishops, the emphasis is not so much on an ecclesiastical office as it is on service for the Lord and His people.

Whenever a man has been **found blameless** in his personal life and in his public life, he may be allowed to serve as a deacon. **Blameless** here refers particularly to the qualifications that have just been mentioned.

At this point it may be well to mention a few of the men who might be considered as deacons in a local church. The treasurer certainly would be one, and also the correspondent or secretary, the Sunday School superintendent, and the ushers.

3:11 This verse apparently refers to the **wives** of deacons, or to the wives of bishops and deacons. The **wives** of those who are given responsibilities in the church should certainly be women of Christian testimony and integrity, such as will help their husbands in their important work.

However, the same word used for "wives" may also be translated "women." This translation would permit the additional interpretation of women deacons. There were such women in the early church, e.g. Rom. 16:1, where Phoebe is spoken of as a servant (same word as "deacon") of the church at Cenchrea.[10] A clue as to the type of service which these women performed in the church is given in Romans 16:2, where Paul says of Phoebe that "she has been a helper of many and of myself also."

Whichever interpretation one accepts, these women **must be reverent**, dignified, and sober. They must **not** be **slanderers**, spending their time gossiping about others, passing on false and malicious reports designed to injure the reputation of others. They must be **temperate**, exhibiting self-control and restraint.

Finally, they must be **faithful in all things**. This might not only mean true to the Christian faith, but also dependable, loyal, and worthy of confidence. They should be able to keep personal confidences and family secrets.

3:12 The apostle now reverts to the subject of **deacons**. He first specifies that they must be **husbands of one wife**. The various interpretations of this expression have been given in connection with verse 2 of this chapter. It is sufficient here to say that, like the bishops, the deacons must be above reproach in their married life.

They, too, must rule **their children and their own houses well**. The NT looks on failure to do this as a defect of Christian character. This does not mean that men must be autocratic and imperious, but it does mean that **their children** should be obedient and a testimony to the truth.

3:13 The clause **those who have served well as deacons obtain for themselves a good standing** is well illustrated in the cases of Philip and Stephen. In Acts 6:5, these two men are named among the seven deacons who were appointed. The work to which they were appointed was to handle the distribution of money to the widows in the church. As they were faithful in these duties, it seems that the Spirit of God advanced them to greater spheres of service; for, as the book of Acts continues, we find Philip serving as an evangelist and Stephen as a teacher. Having **served well as deacons**, they were promoted and given **a good standing** in the eyes of the local church. A person who faithfully discharges an assignment, even if it is a small matter, will soon come to be respected and esteemed for reliability and devotion.

In addition, Philip and Stephen were granted **great boldness in the faith which is in Christ Jesus**. This doubtless means that they were given great liberty in witnessing for Christ, in teaching, and in prayer. This was certainly true of Stephen in his remarkable address before he was martyred.

D. Regarding Conduct in the Church (3:14–16)

3:14 The apostle had written the preceding with the hope of seeing Timothy soon. **These things**, however, might refer not only to what precedes but also to what follows.

3:15 Paul recognized the possibility of being **delayed**, or even of his not getting to Ephesus at all. Actually, we do not know whether he ever was able to rejoin Timothy in Ephesus. And so if he tarried long, he wanted Timothy **to know how** believers **ought to conduct** themselves **in the house of God**.

In the preceding verses, Paul has been describing how bishops, deacons, and their wives ought to behave. Now he explains how Christians in general should behave in **the house of God**.

The house of God is here defined as **the church of the living God, the pillar and ground of the truth**. In the OT, God dwelt in the tabernacle and temple, but in the NT, He dwells in **the church**. It is spoken of as **the church of the living God**, and this contrasts it to a temple in which there are lifeless idols.

The church is spoken of as **the pillar and ground of the truth**. A pillar was not only used to support a structure, but oftentimes a pillar was set up in a public marketplace and notices were posted on it. It was thus a proclaimer. The church is the unit on earth which God has chosen to proclaim and display His **truth**. It is also the **ground of the truth**. Here **ground** carries the thought of foundation or supporting structure. This pictures the church as that which is entrusted with the defense and support of the truth of God.

3:16 This is a difficult verse. One difficulty is in discerning just how it fits in with what has preceded. One suggestion is that here we have an epitome of the truth, of which the church is the pillar and ground (v. 15). Another is that this verse gives the example and power of godliness which Paul insists is an integral part of proper behavior in the house of God. J. N. Darby said:

This is often quoted and interpreted as if it spoke of the mystery of the Godhead, or the mystery of Christ's Person. But it is the mystery of godliness, or the secret by which all real godliness is produced — the divine spring of all that can be called piety in man. . . . Godliness springs from the knowledge of the incarnation, death, resurrection and ascension of the Lord Jesus Christ. . . . This is how God is known; and from abiding in this flows godliness.[11]

When Paul says that **the mystery of godliness** is **great**, he does not mean that it is very mysterious but that the previously unknown truth concerning the Person and work of the Lord Jesus is very marvelous and wonderful.

God[12] **was manifested in the flesh** refers to the Lord Jesus, and particulary to His Incarnation. True **godliness** was manifest in the flesh for the first time when the Savior was born as a Babe in Bethlehem's manger.

Does **justified in the Spirit** mean "justified in His own human spirit"? Or does it mean "justified by the Holy Spirit"? We understand it to mean the latter. He was vindicated by the Holy **Spirit** of God at His baptism (Matt. 3:15–17), transfiguration (Matt. 17:5), resurrection (Rom. 1:3, 4), and ascension (John 16:10).

The Lord Jesus was **seen by angels** at His birth, temptation, His agony in the Garden of Gethsemane, resurrection, and ascension.

From the day of Pentecost onward, He has been **preached among the Gentiles**. The proclamation has reached not only the Jewish people but the farthest corners of the earth.

Believed on in the world describes the fact that some from almost every tribe and nation have trusted the Lord Jesus. It does not say "believed on *by* the world." Although the proclamation has been worldwide, yet its reception has been only partial.

Received up in glory is generally agreed to refer to His Ascension to heaven after the work of redemption had been completed, and to His present position there. Vincent points out that it reads *"received up in* (not *into*) glory."* It means "with attendant circumstances of pomp or majesty, as we say of a victorious general."

Some make this list of events chronological. For instance, they say that **manifested in the flesh** refers to the incarnation; **justified in the Spirit** refers to Christ's death, burial, and resurrection; **seen by angels** describes His ascension into heaven; **preached among the Gentiles** and **believed on in the world** are the events that followed His ascension; and, finally, **received up in glory** refers to a coming day when all His redeemed are gathered, raised from the dead, and received up with Him to glory. Then, and only then, will **the mystery of godliness** be complete, according to this view.

However, we see no reason that the order *must* be chronological. Some believe we have in this verse a fragment of an early Christian hymn. If so, it is rather similar to our gospel song "One Day":

> Living, He loved me; dying, He saved me;
> Buried, He carried my sins far away;
> Rising, He justified freely forever:
> One day He's coming — oh, glorious day!
> – *Charles H. Marsh*

IV. APOSTASY IN THE CHURCH (4:1–16)

A. Warning Against the Impending Apostasy (4:1–5)

4:1 There are two ways in which **the Spirit** might be thought of as speaking **expressly**. First of all, what Paul is about to say was certainly given to him by divine revelation. But it might also mean that throughout the Scriptures, and particularly in the NT, it is **expressly** taught that the **latter times** will be characterized by departure from the faith.

Latter times means "in later times," periods of time subsequent to that time when the apostle was writing.

Some will depart from the faith. The word **some** is characteristic of 1 Timothy. What was a minority in this Epistle seems to have become the majority in 2 Timothy. The fact that these people **depart** or fall away **from the faith** does not mean that they were ever saved, but simply that they had professed to be Christians. They knew about the Lord Jesus Christ and had been told that He was the only Savior. They professed for a time to follow Him, but then they apostatized from the faith.

One can scarcely read this section without thinking of the rise of cults in our own day. The way these false systems have spread is accurately described here. A great part of their membership is made up of persons who were formerly in so-called Christian churches. Perhaps at one time these churches had been sound in the faith, but then they drifted toward the social gospel. The cultist teachers came along offering a more positive message, and these professing Christians were ensnared.

They give willing **heed** or assent to **deceiving spirits and doctrines of demons. Deceiving spirits** is used here in a figurative sense to describe the false teachers, indwelt by evil spirits, who deceive the unwary. **Doctrines of demons** does not mean teachings *about* demons, but rather **doctrines** which are inspired *by* **demons** or have their source in the demon world.

4:2 The word **hypocrisy** suggests "wearing a mask." How typical this is of the false cultists! They try to hide their true identity. They do not want people to know the system with which they are identified. They masquerade by using Bible terms and singing Christian hymns. Not only are they hypocrites, but they are liars as well. Their teaching is not according to the truth of God's word; they know this, and purposely deceive the people.

Their conscience is **seared with a hot iron**. Perhaps early in their lives their conscience had been tender, but they suppressed it so often and sinned against the light so much that now their conscience has become insensitive and hardened. They no longer have any scruples about contradicting the word of God and teaching things they know are untrue.

4:3 Two of the doctrines of demons are now stated. The first is the teaching that it is wrong **to marry**. This is directly contrary to the word of God. God Himself instituted marriage, and He did this before sin ever entered the world. There is nothing unholy about marriage, and when false teachers forbid marriage, they are attacking what God ordained.

An illustration of this teaching is the law **forbidding** certain priests and nuns **to marry**. However, even more directly, this verse refers to the teaching of spiritists called spiritual affinity by which, according to A. J. Pollock, "the marriage tie is derided, and in its practical working, men and women are seduced from their lawful partners to form unholy and unlawful links with their so-called spiritual affinities." We might also mention the attitude of Christian Science toward marriage. Its founder, Mrs. Eddy, thrice married, wrote:

> Until it is learned that God is the Father of all, marriage will continue. . . . Matrimony, which was once a fixed fact among us, must lose its present adherence.[13]

The second teaching of demons is **to**

abstain from certain foods. Such teaching is found among spiritists, who claim that the eating of animal flesh hinders one in contacting the spirits. Also, among Theosophists and Hindus, there is a horror of sacrificing any kind of life because they believe that the soul of a man may come back and live in an animal or other creature.

The pronoun which may refer to marriage and to foods. Both were created by God to be shared by us with thanksgiving. He did not intend them only for the unregenerate but for those who believe and know the truth.

4:4 Every creature (or creation) of God is good. Both foods and marriage are creations of God, and are not to be refused if . . . received with thanksgiving. He instituted marriage for the propagation of human life (see Gen. 1:28), and food for the sustaining of life (Gen. 9:3).

4:5 The word of God sets apart both food and marriage for man's use. Food is thus sanctified in Genesis 9:3; Mark 7:19; Acts 10:14, 15; and 1 Corinthians 10:25, 26. Marriage is set apart in 1 Corinthians 7 and Hebrews 13:4.

They are also sanctified through prayer. Before partaking of a meal, we should bow our heads and give thanks for the food (see Matt. 14:19; Acts 27:35). By this act we are asking the Lord to sanctify the food to strengthen our bodies so that we might serve Him more acceptably. Before entering into marriage we should pray that God will bless the union for His glory, for the blessing of others, and for the good of the bride and groom.

It is a good testimony for Christians to give thanks for meals when in the presence of unsaved people. The blessing should not be showy or long, but neither should we try to conceal the fact that we are thanking God for our food.

B. Positive Instructions in View of the Impending Apostasy (4:6–16)

4:6 By instructing the brethren about these things mentioned in verses 1–5, Timothy will be a good minister of Jesus Christ. As mentioned previously, the word minister means "servant." He will be a servant, nourished in the words of faith and of the good doctrine which he has carefully followed up to this time.

4:7 In this section, Paul is thinking of Christian service as a form of athletic contest. In verse 6, he spoke of the suitable diet for one who is serving Christ — he should be nourished in the words of the faith and of the good doctrine. In verse 7, he speaks of exercise that has godliness as its aim.

The apostle advises Timothy to reject profane and old wives' fables. He is not to combat them or spend a lot of time on them. Rather, he is to disdain them, to treat them with contempt. Old wives' fables make us think of Christian Science, which was founded by a woman, seems to appeal especially to elderly women, and teaches fables instead of truth.

Instead of wasting time on myths and fables, he should exercise himself to godliness. Such exercise involves reading and studying the Bible, prayer, meditation, and witnessing to others. Stock says, "There is no such thing as drifting into godliness; the 'stream of tendency' is against us." There must be exercise and effort.

4:8 Here two kinds of exercise are contrasted. Bodily exercise has certain values for the body, but these values are limited and of short duration. Godliness, on the other hand, is good for man's spirit, soul, and body, and is not only for time but for eternity as well. As far as this life is concerned, godliness yields the greatest joy, and as far as the life which is to come is concerned, it holds promise of bright reward and of capacity to enjoy the glories of that scene.

4:9 It is generally agreed that this verse refers back to the saying about godliness. The fact that godliness is of widespread and eternal value is a faithful saying and worthy of all acceptance. This is the third faithful saying in this Epistle.

4:10 For to this end we both labor and suffer reproach.[14] The end mentioned is the life of godliness. Paul states that this is the great goal toward which he exerts his finest efforts. This would not seem a worthy aim in life to unbelievers. But the Christian sees beyond the passing things of this world and sets his hope on **the living God**. This hope can never be disappointed for the very reason that He is **the living God, who is the Savior of all men, especially of those who believe. God** is **the Savior of all men** in the sense that He preserves them in the daily providences of life. But He **is** also **the Savior of all men** in the sense pointed out previously — that He has made adequate provision for the salvation **of all men**. He is the Savior of **those who believe** in a special way because they have availed themselves of His provision. We might say that He is the potential Savior of all men and the actual Savior of those who believe.

4:11 **These things** probably refers to what Paul has been saying in verses 6–10. Timothy is to **command and teach** such precepts, continually bringing them before the people of God.

4:12 At the time of this Letter, Timothy was probably between thirty and thirty-five years of age. In contrast with some of the elders in the assembly at Ephesus, he would be a comparatively young man. That is why Paul says here, **"Let no one despise your youth."** This does not mean that Timothy is to put himself on a pedestal and consider himself immune from criticism. Rather, it means he is to give nobody occasion to condemn him. By being **an example to the believers**, he is to avoid the possibility of justified criticism.

In word refers to Timothy's conversation. His speech should always be that which should characterize a child of God. He should not only avoid such speech as is distinctly forbidden, but also such as would not be edifying for his hearers.

In conduct refers to one's entire demeanor. Nothing about his deportment should cause reproach on the name of Christ.

In love suggests that **love** should be the motive for conduct, as well as the spirit in which it is carried out and the goal toward which it strives.

In spirit is lacking in most modern versions and commentaries that follow the critical text. However, the words do occur in the traditional and majority

texts. Guy King decries the fact that *enthusiasm*, his insightful understanding of the phrase, is a:

> . . . quality strangely lacking from the make-up of many Christians. Plenty of enthusiasm for a football match, or for an election campaign, but so little of it for the service of GOD. How the magnificent enthusiasm of the Christian Scientists, the Jehovah's Witnesses, the Communists should put us to shame. Oh, for the flaming zeal again that once the church knew. This fine spirit will greatly help Timothy as he seeks to consolidate the position and to advance the line.[15]

In faith probably means "in faithfulness," and carries the idea of dependability and steadfastness.

Purity should characterize not only his acts but his motives as well.

4:13 This verse probably refers primarily to the local church, rather than to Timothy's personal life. He should **give attention** to the public **reading** of the Scriptures, **to exhortation**, and **to doctrine** or teaching. There is a definite order here. First of all, Paul emphasizes the public **reading** of the word of God. This was especially necessary at that time, since the distribution of the Scriptures was very limited. Few people had a copy of the word. After reading the Scriptures, Timothy was to exhort the believers on the basis of what had been read, and then he was to teach the great truths of the word of God. This verse reminds us of Nehemiah 8, and especially verse 8: "So they read distinctly from the book, in the Law of God; and they gave the sense, and helped them to understand the reading."

However, we should not leave out the thought of private devotions from this verse. Before Timothy could exhort and teach the word of God to others, he should first make it real in his own life.

4:14 We are not told exactly what **gift** had been given to Timothy — whether evangelist, pastor, or teacher. The general tenor of these Epistles would lead us to think that he was a pastor-teacher. However, we do know that **the gift . . . was given to** him **by prophecy with the laying on of the hands of the eldership**. First of all, it **was given** along with or **by prophecy**.

This simply means that a prophet in a local church at one time stood up and announced that the Spirit of God had imparted some **gift** to Timothy. The prophet did not confer the gift, but announced it. This was accompanied by **the laying on of the hands of the eldership**. Again we would emphasize that the presbyters, or elders, did not have the power to bestow the gift on Timothy. Rather, by laying their hands on him, they signified public recognition of what the Holy Spirit had already done.

The process is seen in Acts 13. In verse 2, the Holy Spirit singled out Barnabas and Saul for a specific work. Perhaps it was through a prophet that this word was transmitted. Then the local brethren fasted and prayed and laid their hands on Barnabas and Saul and sent them away (v. 3).

This same policy is followed by many local Christian communities today. When it becomes evident to the elders that a man has been given some gift of the Holy Spirit, they commend that man to the work of the Lord, indicating their confidence in him and their recognition of the Spirit's work in his life. Their commendation does not bestow a gift on him but merely recognizes that this has already been done by the Spirit of God.

There is a difference between what happened when the elders laid their hands on Timothy, as mentioned here, and when Paul laid his hands on Timothy, as described in 2 Timothy 1:6. In the former case, the action was in no way official, nor was it responsible for Timothy's gift. It only expressed fellowship with him in his work. In the latter case, Paul was actually the apostolic channel through whom the gift was imparted.

4:15 The words **meditate on these things** can be translated "cultivate" or "take pains with these things." This may well be the meaning here, since the next words are **give yourself entirely to them**. Paul is encouraging Timothy to give himself undividedly and undistractedly to the work of the Lord. He should be all-out in his efforts. In this way, his **progress** will **be evident to all**. Paul does not want Timothy to hit a plateau in his Christian service and then settle down into a comfortable rut. Rather, he wants

him to be always advancing in the things of the Lord.

4:16 Notice the order here. Timothy is first to **take heed to** himself **and** then **to the doctrine**. This emphasizes the importance of the personal life in any servant of Christ. If his life is wrong, he might be ever so orthodox in his doctrine, but it is of no avail. A. W. Pink has well said: "Service becomes a snare and an evil if it be allowed to crowd out worship and the cultivation of one's own spiritual life."

By continuing in the things Paul has been writing about, that is, reading, exhortation, and instruction, Timothy would **save both** himself **and those who** heard him. The word **save** here has nothing to do with the salvation of the soul. The chapter opened with a description of the false teachers who were causing havoc among the people of God. Paul is telling Timothy that by faithful adherence to a godly life and to the word of God, he **will save** himself from these false teachings and he will also rescue his hearers from them as well.

V. SPECIFIC INSTRUCTIONS CONCERNING VARIOUS CLASSES OF BELIEVERS (5:1–6:2)

A. Different Age Groups (5:1, 2)

5:1 This verse introduces a section on Timothy's behavior toward members of the Christian family among whom he would be working. Being younger and perhaps more aggressive, Timothy might be tempted to become impatient and resentful with some of the **older** men; hence, the admonition that he is **not** to **rebuke an older man** sharply, **but exhort him as a father**. It would be improper for him, as a younger man, to assault such a person with verbal blows.

There might also be the danger of this young servant of Christ manifesting an overbearing attitude toward **the younger men**. And so Paul tells him that he is to treat the younger men **as brothers**; he is to be just like one of them and not adopt a domineering attitude toward them.

5:2 Older women are to be regarded **as mothers** and treated with the dignity, love, and respect that is their due.

Purity should characterize all his dealings with **younger women**. Not only should he avoid what is positively sinful, but he should also steer clear of acts of indiscretion or any behavior which might have the appearance of evil.

B. Widows (5:3–16)

5:3   From verses 3–16, Paul takes up the subject of **widows** in the local church and the treatment which should be given to them.

First of all, the church should **honor** those **who are really widows. Honor** here not only carries the idea of respect but also includes the thought of financial help. A real widow is one who has no other means of support but is wholly cast upon the Lord for her maintenance. She has no living relatives who will care for her.

5:4, 5   A second class of **widows** is described in this verse. These are the ones who have **children or grandchildren**. In such cases, the **children** should learn to show practical godliness at home by repaying their mother (or grandmother) for all that she has done for them. The verse teaches clearly that **piety** begins **at home**. It is a poor testimony to the Christian faith to speak loudly about one's religion and then to neglect those who are linked to us by ties of nature!

It is **acceptable**[16] in the sight of **God** for Christians to take care of loved ones who are otherwise without support. In Ephesians 6:2, the Apostle Paul clearly teaches: "Honor your father and mother, which is the first commandment with promise." As mentioned previously, a real **widow** is one who is without financial resources and who must constantly look to **God** for the supply of her daily bread.

5:6, 7   In contrast to the godly widow of verse 5 is the one who gives herself to **pleasure**. There is some disagreement as to whether this woman is a true believer or a mere professor. We believe that she is a genuine Christian — but backslidden. She is **dead** as far as communion with God or usefulness for Him are concerned. Timothy is to warn such widows against living in **pleasure**

and is also to teach Christians to care for those who are related to them and are destitute.

5:8   The seriousness of failing to **provide for** one's **own** relatives, **and especially for those of** one's own immediate **household**, is emphasized here. It constitutes a denial of **the faith**. The Christian faith consistently maintains that those who are true believers should care for one another. When a Christian fails to do this, he denies by his actions the very truths which Christianity teaches. Such a person **is worse than an unbeliever** for the simple reason that many unbelievers show loving care for their own relatives. Also, a Christian can thus bring reproach on the name of the Lord in a way that an unbeliever cannot do.

5:9   It appears from this verse that a definite roll or list of names was kept in each local church, indicating those widows who were cared for by the church. Paul here specifies that no **widow** should be thus enrolled **under sixty years** of age.

The expression **the wife of one man** raises the same problem as the similar expression in connection with bishops and deacons. Similar interpretations of the expression have been given. It doubtless means that her married life must have been above reproach, without suspicion of moral wrong.

5:10   In order to be enrolled, a widow must also have a reputation for having performed such **good works** as should characterize a spiritual believer.

The words **if she has brought up children** doubtless means that she must have brought them up in such a manner as to reflect creditably on herself and her Christian home. There would be no virtue in simply rearing children, but only in bringing them up well.

Another mark of a godly widow is that she has shown hospitality to **strangers**. Over and over again in the NT, the grace of hospitality is mentioned and commended.

Washing the feet of visitors was the duty of a slave. So here the thought doubtless is that the widow has performed very menial services for her fellow Christians. But it might also mean to have **washed the saints' feet** in a spiritual way, with the washing of water by the word. This would not mean public ministry, but simply visiting in homes and using the word of God in such a way as to cleanse believers from defilement contracted in their daily walk.

Relief of **the afflicted** refers to acts of mercy performed for those who are sick, sorrowing, or otherwise in distress.

In short, in order to be enrolled on the list of a local assembly, this widow must have **diligently followed every good work**.

5:11 This is a difficult verse, but the meaning seems to be as follows: In general, it would be a mistake to make **younger widows** a charge of the local church. Being young, they would probably **desire to marry** again. This would not be wrong in itself, but the desire might become so strong at times that one of these young widows might even marry an unbeliever. The apostle speaks of this as to **grow wanton against Christ**. When it comes to a choice between marrying a pagan or remaining unmarried out of love to Christ and obedience to His word, the young widow is apt to **marry**. This would, of course, bring reproach on the local church which supported her.

5:12 Condemnation ("damnation," KJV) here does not mean eternal perdition, but simply that she has this judgment or **condemnation** for having **cast off** her **first faith**. At one time she professed the greatest loyalty and devotion to the Lord Jesus Christ, but now when the opportunity comes along to marry one who does not love Christ, she forgets her initial vows or pledges to Christ and goes off with the unbeliever, unfaithful to the Heavenly Bridegroom.

Paul is not criticizing young widows for marrying. As a matter of fact he urges them to marry (v. 14). What he finds fault with is their spiritual decline, their throwing divine principles to the wind in order to get a man.

5:13 For the local church to assume full financial responsibility for the younger widows might encourage them **to be idle**, with its associated evils. Instead of attending to their own responsibilities, they might become **gossips and busybodies**, occupying themselves with subjects that are none of their concern.

No action taken by a local church should ever encourage such behavior because, as mentioned before, it reflects unfavorably on the Christian testimony.

5:14 Paul **therefore** states that as a general principle, it is preferable that **younger widows marry, bear children**, and maintain a Christian home that is above reproach. Of course, Paul realized that it would not always be possible for every young widow to remarry. The initiative must ordinarily be taken by the man. But he is simply laying down a general principle to be followed whenever possible.

The adversary, or Satan, is always on the lookout for charges to hurl against the Christian testimony, and Paul seeks to guard against the possibility of there being any such legitimate causes **to speak reproachfully**.

5:15 What the apostle has been saying about young widows is not mere conjecture or speculation. It had **already** happened. **Some** had **turned aside after Satan**, in the sense that they had listened to the voice of **Satan** and had chosen an unbelieving partner in disobedience to the word of the Lord.

5:16 The subject now reverts to the obligation of relatives to care for their own. **If any believing man**[17] **or woman has** a widow in the family who needs support, then the believer should assume this responsibility so that **the church** will be free to care for those who are actually destitute and without near relatives.

This entire passage, verses 3–16, tells what the church *must* do under certain circumstances, not what it *may* do if it feels there are extenuating circumstances and if it is able to do so. The length of the paragraph shows that it is an important subject in the mind of the Holy Spirit, and yet it is one which is greatly neglected in most church circles today.

C. Elders (5:17–25)

5:17 The rest of this chapter deals with elders. First of all, Paul lays down the rule that **elders who rule well** should **be counted worthy of double honor**. Rule might better be translated "take the lead" (Darby). It is not a question of control, but of example. Such elders are **worthy of double honor. Honor** might mean respect, but it also includes the idea of financial reimbursement (Matt. 15:6). **Double honor** includes both ideas. First of all, he is **worthy of** respect from God's people because of his work, but also, if his time is devoted to this work fully, he is also **worthy of** financial help. **Those who labor in the word and doctrine** are probably the ones who spend so much time in preaching and teaching that they are not able to carry on regular employment.

5:18 Two Scriptures are introduced here to prove the statement that the elder is worthy of recompense. The first is Deuteronomy 25:4, and the second is taken from Luke 10:7. This verse is especially interesting in connection with the inspiration of the Scriptures. Paul takes one verse from the OT and one from the NT, places them side by side on the same level, and refers to them both as **the Scripture**. It is obvious from this that Paul considered the NT writings as of equal authority with the OT.

These Scriptures teach that **an ox** which is used in the harvesting process should not be deprived of a share of **the grain**. Also, a **laborer** is entitled to a portion of the fruit of his labor. So it is with elders. In spite of the fact that their work might not be physical, yet they are worthy of the support of God's people.

5:19 Since elders occupy a position of responsibility in the church, they become a special target of Satan's attack. For this reason the Spirit of God takes steps to guard them against false accusations. The principle is laid down that no disciplinary action should be taken **against an elder** unless the charge can be corroborated by the testimony of **two or three witnesses**. Actually, this same principle applies to disciplining any church member, but it is emphasized here because there was a special danger of elders being unjustly accused.

5:20 In the case of an elder who had been found guilty of **sinning** in such a way as to harm the testimony of the church, such a man should be publicly rebuked. This action impresses all believers with the seriousness of sin in connection with Christian service and serves as a strong deterrent in the lives of others.

Some commentators believe that verse 20 does not apply especially to elders, but to all Christians. Certainly the principle is applicable to all Christians, but the setting of the verse seems to link it directly with elders.

5:21 In dealing with matters of discipline in the local church, there are two dangers to be avoided. The first is **prejudice**, and the other is **partiality**. It is easy to be unfavorably prejudiced against a man and thus to prejudice the case. Also, it is all too easy to show **partiality** toward a man because of his wealth, position in the community, or his personality. Thus Paul solemnly charges Timothy in the sight of **God and the Lord Jesus Christ and** also in the sight of **the elect angels**, that he should obey these instructions without judging a matter before all the facts are known or without showing favor toward a man simply because he is a friend or well-known. Each case must be judged as in the sight of **God and the Lord Jesus**, and also in the sight of the **angels**. The angels are observers of the world in which we live, and they should see perfect righteousness in matters of discipline in the church. **The elect angels** are those who have not been involved in sin or rebellion against God, but kept their first estate.

5:22 When prominent men identify themselves with a local church, there is sometimes the tendency to advance them quickly to positions of responsibility. Here Timothy is warned against haste in recognizing newcomers. Neither should he identify himself with men whose characters are unknown to him, lest in so doing he **share in** their **sins**. Not only is he to **keep** himself morally clean but also **pure** in the sense of free from association with the sins of others.

5:23 It is not clear how this verse connects with the preceding. Perhaps the apostle wisely anticipated that Timothy's involvement in congregational problems and difficulties would have an adverse effect on his stomach. If so, Timothy would not be the first or the last to suffer from this affliction! More probably Timothy was the frequent victim of contaminated water that is still common in many parts of the world. The apostle's advice, **"No longer drink only water,"** means that Timothy should not use water to the exclusion of **a little wine**.

Paul advises the use of **a little wine for** his **stomach's sake** and his **frequent infirmities**. This verse is dealing only with the medicinal use of wine, and should never be stretched to condone its excessive use.

There is no doubt that it is real **wine** that is referred to here and not just grape juice. It is doubtful that grape juice even existed at this time, since grape juice is made by pasteurization, a process not yet known. The fact that it was real wine is implied in the expression **a little wine**. If it were not real wine, then there would be no sense in stipulating that only **a little** should be used.

This verse also sheds light on the subject of divine healing. Although Paul, as an apostle, doubtless had the power to heal all kinds of diseases, yet he did not always use it. Here he justifies the use of medicines in a case of stomach ailment.

5:24 In this verse the apostle seems to go back to the discussion in verse 22, where he had been warning Timothy against undue haste in laying hands on other men. Verses 24 and 25 explain this further.

Some men's sins are clearly evident and are so obvious that they may be compared to a trumpeter, blaring on in front of the man, announcing him to be a sinner, all the way **to** his **judgment**. But that is not the case with all. **Some men** who are sinners are not exposed until some time **later**.

In the first class, we might think of the drunkard who is known as such by the whole community. On the other hand, there is the husband who is carrying on a secret love affair with another woman. The community might not know about this at the time, but oftentimes the whole scandal is revealed at a **later** date.

5:25 It is somewhat similar in the case of good people. Some obviously seem to be good at once. Others are more retiring and modest, and it is only with the passing of time that their actual goodness becomes known. Even if we cannot see good, there may be some which will come to light later. The lesson to draw from all this is that we should not judge a person on first acquaintance,

but rather allow time for true character to show itself.

D. Bondservants and Masters (6:1, 2)

6:1 The conduct of slaves is now brought before us. They are spoken of as **bondservants** who **are under the yoke**, that is, **the yoke** of slavery. The apostle, first of all, speaks to slaves who have unsaved **masters**. Should slaves in such a case act insolently toward their masters? Should they rebel or run away? Should they do as little work as possible? On the contrary, they should **count their own masters worthy of all honor**. This means that they should give them due respect, work obediently and faithfully, and in general seek to be a help rather than a hindrance. The great motive for such diligent service is that the testimony for Christ is involved. If a Christian slave were to act rudely or rebelliously, then the master would blaspheme **the name of God** and the Christian faith. He would conclude that believers were a worthless lot.

The history of the early church reveals that Christian slaves generally commanded a higher price on the slave market than unbelievers. If a master knew that a certain slave on the auction block was a Christian, he would generally be willing to pay more for that slave, since he knew that the slave would serve him faithfully and well. This is high tribute to the Christian faith.

This verse reminds us that no matter how low a person's position may be on the social scale, yet he has every opportunity for witnessing for Christ and bringing glory to His name.

It has often been pointed out that the institution of slavery is not openly condemned in the NT. However, as the teachings of Christianity have spread, the abuses of slavery have been abolished.

Every true believer should realize that he is a bondslave of Jesus Christ. He has been bought with a price; he no longer belongs to himself. Jesus Christ owns him — spirit, soul, and body, and deserves the very best he has.

6:2 This verse deals with slaves **who have believing masters**. Doubtless there would be a very great temptation for such slaves to **despise** their masters. It is not at all unlikely that when the local church met together on Lord's Day evening for the breaking of bread (Acts 20:7), there would be Christian masters and Christian slaves seated around the table — all **brethren** in Christ Jesus. But the slaves were not, on this account, to think that the social distinctions of life were thereby abolished. Just because a master was a Christian did not mean that the slave did not owe him honor and service. The fact that the master was both a believer and a **beloved** brother should influence the slave to serve him faithfully.

Christian masters are here spoken of not only as faithful (**believers**) **and beloved**, but also as **those who are benefited**. This is generally taken to mean that they, too, are sharers in the blessing of salvation. However, the words might also be understood to mean that since both slaves and masters are interested in doing good, they should serve together, each trying to help the other.

The words **teach and exhort these things** doubtless refer to the preceding instructions to Christian slaves. The present-day application would be, of course, to the employer-employee relationship.

VI. FALSE TEACHERS AND THE LOVE OF MONEY (6:3–10)

6:3 Paul now turns his attention to those who might be disposed to teach new and strange doctrines in the church. These men do **not consent to wholesome words**. **Wholesome** here means health-giving words. Such were the **words** which were spoken by **our Lord Jesus Christ** when He was here on earth and which are found in the Gospels. Such also is the entire body of teaching found in the NT. This is **doctrine which accords with godliness** in the sense that it encourages and promotes godly behavior.

6:4 Such men are **proud**. They profess to have superior knowledge, but actually they know **nothing**. As Paul mentioned previously, they do not know what they are talking about.

They dote about **disputes and arguments over words**. The word **obsessed** literally means to be sick. These men are not spiritually healthy, and instead of teaching healthful words, as in the previous verse, they teach words that produce sick saints. They raise various questions that are not spiritually edifying and strive **over words**.

Since the things they talk about are not matters of Bible doctrine, there is no way of settling them decisively. As a result, their teaching stirs up **envy, strife, reviling**, and **evil suspicions**. Lenski says:

> In their questions and word battles, one envies the other because of the proficiency which he develops; there is strife as they vie with and contradict each other; blasphemies result, namely, denunciations couched in sacred words.[18]

6:5 These **wranglings** come from **men of corrupt**, that is, diseased, **minds**. Lenski comments trenchantly:

> The diseased state of the mind consists in a corruption and a disintegration — the mental faculties no longer function normally in the moral and the spiritual field. They do not react normally to the truth. All reality and its presentation in verity ought to produce the reaction of acceptance, especially the saving divine gospel realities should have this effect; all lies, falsities, perversions ought to produce rejection, most of all those in the moral and the spiritual field. . . . When it meets "the truth," the corrupted mind sees and seeks only objections; when it meets what differs from this truth, it sees and seeks reasons for accepting this difference.[19]

Also, these men are **destitute of the truth**. At one time, they had acquaintance with the truth, but because of their rejection of the light, they have been deprived of what **truth** they once had.

These men **suppose that godliness is a means of gain**. Apparently, they choose to be religious teachers as a profession in which they are well paid for a minimum of work. "They make the holiest of vocations a money-gaining craft."

This not only reminds us of the hireling shepherds who pose as Christian ministers but have no real love for the truth, but it also makes us think of the commercialism which has become so common in Christendom — the sale of indulgences, games of lottery, bazaars and sales, etc. **From such withdraw yourself.**[20] We are commanded to steer clear of such ungodly professors.

6:6 Just as the previous verse gave a false definition of gain, so this verse gives the true meaning of the word. The combination of **godliness with contentment is great gain.** Godliness without contentment would give a one-sided testimony. Contentment without godliness would not be distinctively Christian at all. But to have real **godliness** and at the same time to be satisfied with one's personal circumstances is more than money can buy.

6:7 This chapter bears a close resemblance to the teachings of the Lord Jesus in the Sermon on the Mount. Verse 7 reminds us of His instruction that we should trust our heavenly Father for the supply of our needs.

There are three times in life when we have empty hands — at birth, at the time we come to Jesus, and at death. This verse reminds us of the first and the last. **We brought nothing into the world, and it is certain that we can carry nothing out.**

Before Alexander the Great died, he said: "When I am dead, carry me forth on my bier, with my hands not wrapped in cloth, but laid outside, so that all may see that they are *empty*." Bates comments on this:

> Yes, those hands which once wielded the proudest scepter in the world; which once held the most victorious sword; which once were filled with silver and gold; which once had power to save or to sign away life, were now EMPTY.[21]

6:8 Contentment consists of satisfaction with the basic necessities of life. Our heavenly Father knows that we need **food** and covering and has promised to supply these. Most of an unbeliever's life revolves around **food and clothing**. The Christian should seek first the kingdom of God and His righteousness, and God will see that he does not lack the essentials of life.

The word translated **clothing** here means covering and can include a place to live as well as clothes to wear. We should be **content** with **food, clothing, and a place to live.**

6:9 Verses 9–16 deal directly with those who have an insatiable **desire to be rich**. Their sin lies not in being wealthy, but in coveting to be so. **Those who desire to be rich** are people who are not content with food, clothes, and lodging, but are determined to have more.

Desiring **to be rich** leads a man **into temptation**. In order to achieve his goal, he is enticed to use dishonest and often violent methods. Such methods include gambling, speculation, fraud, perjury, theft, and even murder. Such a man also falls into **a snare** or a trap. The desire becomes so strong that he cannot deliver himself from it. Perhaps he promises himself that when he reaches a certain figure in the bank account he will stop. But he cannot. When he reaches that goal, he has the desire for more. The desire for money also brings with it cares and fears, which entangle the soul. People who determine to become wealthy fall **into many foolish . . . lusts**. There is the desire to "keep up with the Joneses." In order to maintain a social level in the community, they are often driven to sacrifice some of the really worthwhile values in life.

They also fall into **harmful lusts**. Greed for wealth causes men to endanger their health and jeopardize their souls. Indeed, that is the end toward which they are drifting. They become so occupied with material things that they become drowned **in destruction and perdition**. In their ceaseless quest for gold, they neglect their never-dying souls. Barnes warns:

> The destruction is complete. There is a total ruin of happiness, of virtue, of reputation, and of the soul. The ruling desire to be rich leads on a train of follies which ruins everything here, and hereafter. How many of the human family have thus been destroyed![22]

6:10 **The love of money is a root of all kinds of evil.** Not all evil in the universe springs from the **love of money**. But it is certainly one of the great sources of many varieties of **evil**. For instance, it leads to envy, strife, theft, dishonesty, intemperance, forgetfulness of God, selfishness, embezzlement, etc.

It is not money in itself which is spoken of, but **the love of money**. Money might be used in the service of the Lord in a variety of ways where only good would result. But here it is the inordinate desire for **money** that leads to sin and shame.

One particular evil of the love of money is now mentioned, that is, a wandering **from the** Christian **faith**. In their mad striving after gold, men neglect spiritual things, and it becomes difficult to tell whether they were ever really saved at all.

Not only did they lose their grip on spiritual values, but they **pierced themselves through with many sorrows**. Think of the **sorrows** connected with the greed for riches! There is the tragedy of a wasted life. There is the sorrow of losing one's children to the world. There is the grief of seeing one's wealth vanish overnight. There is the fear of meeting God, either unsaved or at least empty-handed.

Bishop J. C. Ryle summarizes:

Money, in truth, is one of the most *unsatisfying* of possessions. It takes away some cares, no doubt; but it brings with it quite as many cares as it takes away. There is trouble in the getting of it. There is anxiety in the keeping of it. There are temptations in the use of it. There is guilt in the abuse of it. There is sorrow in the losing of it. There is perplexity in the disposing of it. Two-thirds of all the strifes, quarrels, and lawsuits in the world arise from one simple cause — *money*![23]

The richest man in the world at one time owned oil wells, refineries, tankers, and pipelines; also hotels, a life insurance company, a finance company, and aircraft companies. But he surrounded his 700-acre estate with bodyguards, vicious dogs, steel bars, searchlights, bells, and sirens. In addition to being afraid of planes, ships, and crackpots, he feared disease, old age, helplessness, and death. He was lonely and gloomy and admitted that money could not buy happiness.[24]

VII. CLOSING CHARGES TO TIMOTHY (6:11–21)

6:11 Timothy here is addressed as a **man of God**. This title was often given to prophets in the OT and described a man who was godlike in his behavior.

It may indicate that Timothy had the gift of prophecy. The opposite of **man of God** is "man of sin," as found in 2 Thessalonians 2. The man of sin will be the very embodiment of sin. Everything about him will make men think of sin. Timothy is to be a **man of God**, a man who will make men think of God and glorify God.

In his service for Christ, Timothy should **flee** from conceit (v. 4), impurity (v. 5), a discontented spirit (vv. 6–8), foolish and harmful lusts (v. 9), and the love of money (v. 10). He should cultivate Christian character — the only thing he can take with him into heaven. Here the elements of Christian character are given as **righteousness, godliness, faith, love, patience, gentleness.**

Righteousness speaks of justice and integrity in our dealings with our fellow men. **Godliness** is Godlikeness. **Faith** might also mean faithfulness, or dependability. **Love** speaks of our affection for both God and our fellow men. **Patience** has been defined as steadfastness or endurance under trial, whereas **gentleness** is a kindly and humble disposition.

6:12 Not only is Timothy to *flee* and to *follow*, but he is also to **fight**. Here the word **fight** does not mean to combat, but rather to contend. The word is not taken from the battlefield but from the athletic contest. **The good fight** spoken of here is the Christian **faith** and the race connected with it. Timothy is to run well in that race. He is to **lay hold on eternal life**. This does not mean that he is to strive for salvation. That is already his possession. But here the thought is to live out in daily practice the **eternal life** which was already his.

Timothy had been called to this **eternal life** at the time of his conversion. Also, he had **confessed the good confession in the presence of many witnesses**. Perhaps this refers to his baptism, although it might also include his whole subsequent testimony for the Lord Jesus Christ.

6:13 The apostle now delivers a solemn charge to Timothy, and he does so in the presence of the two greatest Witnesses. First of all, the charge is given **in the sight of God who gives life to all things**. Perhaps in writing to Timothy,

Paul was conscious that one day he might have to lay down his life for his confession of the Lord Jesus. If that is the case, then it is good for this young warrior to remember that God is the One **who gives life to all things**. Even if men succeed in killing Timothy, yet his faith is in the One who raises the dead.

Secondly, the charge is given in the sight of **Christ Jesus**. He is the great example of **the good confession. Before Pontius Pilate**, He **witnessed the good confession**. Though this may refer to all the Savior's words and actions before the Roman governor, it perhaps points particularly to His statement in John 18:37: "For this cause I was born, and for this cause I have come into the world, that I should bear witness to the truth. Everyone who is of the truth hears My voice." This unfaltering confession was held before Timothy as an example to be followed in bearing witness to the truth.

6:14 Timothy is charged to **keep this commandment**. Some think this refers to the command to fight the good fight mentioned above. Others suggest it might refer to the entire charge which Paul has given to Timothy in this Epistle. Others think of the **commandment** as the message of the gospel, or the revelation of God as given in the word of God. We believe it is the charge to maintain the truth of the Christian faith.

The expressions **without spot, blameless** apply to Timothy rather than to the command. In keeping the **commandment**, Timothy is to maintain a testimony that is **without spot** and that will be unrebukable.

In the NT, **our Lord Jesus Christ's appearing** is constantly held before the believer. Faithfulness to Christ in this world will be rewarded at the Judgment of Christ. These rewards, in turn, will be manifested when the Lord Jesus comes back to the earth to set up His kingdom. It is then that the results of faithfulness or unfaithfulness will be clearly revealed.

6:15 Bible scholars are not agreed as to whether the pronouns in this verse and the next refer to God the Father or to the Lord Jesus Christ. Taken by itself, verse 15 seems to refer to the Lord Jesus, because He is definitely called **King of kings and Lord of lords** in Revelation 17:14. On the other hand, verse 16 seems to refer particularly to God the Father.

In any case, the meaning of verse 15 seems to be this: When the Lord Jesus Christ comes back to reign upon the earth, men will realize **who is the blessed and only Potentate**. The appearance will manifest who is the true **King**. At the time Paul wrote to Timothy, the Lord Jesus was the rejected One, and He still is. But a day is coming when it will be clearly shown that He is **the King** over all those who reign and He is **the Lord** over all those who rule as **lords**.

Blessed means not only worthy to be praised, but One who has in Himself the fullness of all blessing.

6:16 At the appearing of the Lord Jesus, men will also realize that it is God **alone** who **has immortality** or deathlessness. This means that He is the only One who has it *inherently*. Angels have had immortality conferred upon them, and at the resurrection, believers will receive bodies that are immortal (1 Cor. 15:53, 54), but God has **immortality** in Himself.

God is next spoken of as **dwelling in unapproachable light**. This speaks of the bright, shining glory which surrounds the throne of God. Man in his natural condition would be vaporized by this splendor. Only those who are accepted in the Beloved One and complete in Christ can ever approach God without being destroyed.

In His essential being, **no man has seen** God **or can see** Him. In the OT, men saw appearances of God, known as theophanies. In the NT, God has perfectly revealed Himself in the Person of His beloved Son, the Lord Jesus Christ.

However, it is still true that God is invisible to mortal eyes.

To this One, **honor and everlasting power** are due, and Paul closes his charge to Timothy with this ascription of homage to God.

6:17 Paul spoke earlier at length about those who desired to be rich. Here he deals with **those who are** already **rich**. Timothy should **command** them **not to be haughty**. This is a temptation to the wealthy. They are apt to look down on those who do not have a great deal of money as being uncouth, uncultured, and not very clever. This, of course, is not necessarily true. Great riches are not a sign of God's blessing in the NT, as they were in the OT. Whereas wealth was a token of divine favor under the law, the great blessing of the new dispensation is affliction.

The rich should not **trust in**, literally, "the uncertainty of **riches**." Money has a way of sprouting wings and flying away. Whereas great resources give the appearance of providing security, the fact is that the only sure thing in this world is the word of God.

Therefore, the rich are exhorted to trust **in the living God, who gives us richly all things to enjoy**. One of the great snares of riches is that it is difficult to have them without trusting in them. Yet this is really a form of idolatry. It is a denial of the truth that God is the One **who gives us richly all things to enjoy**. This latter statement does not condone luxurious living, but simply states that God is the Source of true enjoyment, and material things cannot produce this.

6:18 The Christian is reminded that the money he possesses is not his own. It is given to him as to a steward. He is responsible to use it for the glory of God and for the well-being of his fellow men. He should use it in the performance of **good works** and be **willing to share** it with the needy.

John Wesley's rule of life was, "Do all the good you can, by all the means you can, in all the ways you can, in all the places you can, at all the times you can, to all the people you can, as long as ever you can."

Willing to share expresses the idea that he should be ready to use it wherever the Lord may indicate.

6:19 This verse emphasizes the truth that it is possible for us to use our material things in such a way in this life that they will reap **eternal** dividends. By using our funds in the work of the Lord at the present time, we are **storing up . . . a good foundation for the time to come**. In this way, we **lay hold on** the **life** which is life indeed.

6:20 Now we come to Paul's final exhortation to **Timothy**. He is encouraged to **guard what was committed to** him. This probably refers to the true

doctrines of the Christian faith. It is not here a question of Timothy's soul or of his salvation, but rather of the truth of the gospel of the grace of God. Like money deposited in a bank, the truth entrusted to Timothy was to be preserved "entire and whole and unharmed."

He is to avoid **the profane and idle babble and contradictions of what is falsely called knowledge. Idle babble** or chatter is empty talk about matters which are not profitable.

Paul realized that Timothy would encounter a great deal of teaching which posed as true knowledge but which was actually opposed to the Christian revelation. Bishop Moule writes:

> The Gnostics of Paul's day claimed to lead their disciples "past the common herd of mere *believers* to a superior and gifted circle who should *know* the mysteries of being, and who by such *knowing* should live emancipated from the slavery of matter, ranging at liberty in the world of spirit."[25]

From all such Timothy should turn away.

This would refer, in our day, first of all to false cults, such as "Christian Science." This system claims to be Christian in character and also claims to have true **knowledge**, but it is **falsely** so-**called**. It is neither *Christian* nor *science*!

This verse may also be applied to many forms of natural science,[26] as taught in our schools today. Actually, no true finding of science will ever contradict the Bible, because the secrets of science were placed in the universe by the same One who wrote the Bible, God Himself. But many so-called facts of science are in reality nothing but unproved theories. Any such hypotheses which contradict the Bible should be rejected.

6:21 Paul realized that some professed Christians had been taken up with these false teachings and had **strayed concerning the faith**. These closing verses bring before us the great dangers of so-called intellectualism, rationalism, modernism, liberalism, and every other "ism" which disregards or waters down Christ.

Grace be with you. This benediction is Paul's "trademark," because only

God's **grace** can keep His people on the "strait and narrow" way. **Amen**

ENDNOTES

Introduction to Pastoral Epistles

[1] Albert Barnes, *Notes on the New Testament: Thessalonians, Timothy, Titus, Philemon*, p. 289.

1 Timothy

[1] (Intro to 1 Timothy) Quoted from *L'Eglise chrétienne*, p. 95, by George Salmon in *A Historical Introduction to the Study of the Books of the New Testament*, p. 413.

[2] (1:8) Guy King, *A Leader Led*, p. 25.

[3] (1:16) William Kelly, *An Exposition of the Two Epistles to Timothy*, p. 22.

[4] (1:19) Hamilton Smith, further documentation unavailable.

[5] (1:20) The Greek word *blasphēmeō (defame, blaspheme)* is used for both God and man. Our English derivative is used almost exclusively for God and sacred things.

[6] (2:9) John Chrysostom, quoted by Alfred Plummer in *The Pastoral Epistles*, p. 101.

[7] (2:15) Lilley, further documentation unavailable.

[8] (3:2) Christians who hold this view stress the elder's loyalty to the one woman implied in the Greek construction: "a one-woman-kind-of-man."

[9] (3:3) Since deacons must not be money-lovers (3:8), it seems unlikely that Paul would have omitted this quality for the even more responsible elders.

[10] (3:11) Probably it had not yet become a church *office* for women at this early date. See note in *Ryrie Study Bible, NKJV*, p. 1850.

[11] (3:16) J. N. Darby, "Notes of a Lecture on Titus 2:11–14," *The Collected Writings of J. N. Darby*, VII:333.

[12] (3:16) The sacred names of God, Christ, the Spirit, etc., were abbreviated in ancient mss. The Greek abbreviation for *God* looks exactly like the word for "who" plus a short horizontal stroke that differentiates a *theta* from an *omicron* and another stroke above the word to show it is an abbreviation. The mss. read variously "God" (TR and majority text), "who" (NU) and "which." We accept the traditional reading of the majority of mss., followed by the KJV and NKJV.

[13] (4:3) Mary Baker Eddy, *Science and Health with Key to the Scriptures*, pp. 64, 65.

[14] (4:10) The critical (NU) text reads "we labor and strive."

[15] (4:12) King, *Leader*, p. 79.

[16] (5:4) Both the oldest and the majority of mss. lack "good and" before "acceptable." The shorter reading is no doubt original.

[17] (5:16) The omission of the believing *man* from this verse in the NU text is probably accidental. It seems highly unlikely that Paul would write only of those widows being cared for by believing *women*.

[18] (6:4) R. C. H. Lenski, *The Interpretation of St. Paul's Epistles to the Thessalonians, to Timothy, to Titus and to Philemon*, p. 700.

[19] (6:5) *Ibid*, pp. 701, 702.

[20] (6:5) The NU text omits this sentence.

[21] (6:7) Bates, further documentation unavailable.

[22] (6:9) Albert Barnes, *Notes on the New Testament: Thessalonians, Timothy, Titus, Philemon*, p. 199.

[23] (6:10) J. C. Ryle, *Practical Religion*, p. 215.

[24] (6:10) From news reports about the late Howard Hughes.

[25] (6:20) H. C. G. Moule, *Studies in II Timothy*, p. 91.

[26] (6:20) The Latin word *scientia* simply means "knowledge." The English derivative "science" (1611 text) now has a much narrower meaning, hence NKJV's change.

BIBLIOGRAPHY

(Pastoral Epistles)

Bernard, J. H. *The Pastoral Epistles*. Cambridge: University Press, 1899.

Erdman, Charles R. *The Pastoral Epistles of Paul*. Philadelphia: Westminster Press, 1923.

Fairbairn, Patrick. *Commentary on the Pastoral Epistles*. Edinburgh: T. & T. Clark, 1874.

Guthrie, Donald. *The Pastoral Epistles*,

(TBC). Grand Rapids: Wm. B. Eerdmans Publishing Co., 1957.

Hiebert, D. Edmond. *First Timothy*. Chicago: Moody Press, 1957.

_____. *Second Timothy*. Chicago: Moody Press, 1958.

_____. *Titus and Philemon*. Chicago: Moody Press, 1957.

Ironside, H. A. *Addresses, Lectures, Expositions on Timothy, Titus, and Philemon*. New York: Loizeaux Bros., 1947.

Kelly, William. *An Exposition of the Epistle of Paul to Titus*. London: Weston, 1901.

_____. *An Exposition of the Two Epistles to Timothy*, 3d Ed. Oak Park, IL: Bible Truth Publishers, n.d.

Kent, Homer A. *The Pastoral Epistles*. Chicago: Moody Press, 1958.

King, Guy H. *A Leader Led: A Devotional Study of I Timothy*. Fort Washington, Pa.: Christian Literature Crusade, 1944.

_____. *To My Son: An Expositional Study of II Timothy*. Fort Washington, Pa.: Christian Literature Crusade, 1944.

Lock, Walter. *A Critical and Exegetical Commentary on the Pastoral Epistles* (*ICC*). Edinburgh: T. & T. Clark, 1924.

Moule, H. C. G. *Studies in II Timothy*. Grand Rapids: Kregel Publications, 1977.

Plummer, Alfred. *The Pastoral Epistles*. New York: George H. Doran Company, n.d.

Smith, Hamilton. *The Second Epistle to Timothy*. Wooler, Northumberland, England: Central Bible Hammond Trust Ltd., n.d.

Stock, Eugene. *Plain Talks on the Pastoral Epistles*. London: R. Scott, 1914.

Van Oosterzee, J. J. "The Pastoral Letters." *Lange's Commentary on the Holy Scriptures*. Vol. 23. Grand Rapids: Zondervan Publishing House, n.d.

Vine, W. E. *Exposition of the Epistles to Timothy*. London: Pickering & Inglis, 1925.

Wuest, Kenneth S. *The Pastoral Epistles in the Greek New Testament*. Grand Rapids: Wm. B. Eerdmans Publishing Co., 1953.

THE SECOND EPISTLE TO TIMOTHY

Introduction

"The Second Epistle to Timothy . . . is the expression of his [Paul's] heart, who outside Palestine, had, under God, founded and built the assembly of God on earth, and it was written in sight of its failure, and its departure from the principles on which he had established it." — J. N. Darby

I. Unique Place in the Canon

The last words of famous people are generally cherished by those who loved the individuals. While 2 Timothy does not constitute literally Paul's last words, it is his last known writing to the Christians, originally sent to his beloved young lieutenant, Timothy.

Sitting in his dank dungeon in Rome, with only a hole in the ceiling for light, and awaiting execution by beheading, the spiritual, intelligent, and tenderhearted apostle, now aged and worn out from his long and arduous race for God, pens a final appeal to hold firmly to the truth and life that Timothy has been taught.

Like a number of "Second" Epistles, 2 Timothy deals with false teachers and the apostates of the last days. One cannot help but think that much of the frontal attack on the authenticity of 2 Timothy (and even more so of 2 Peter) is because the skeptical religious leaders who write these negative theories are themselves convicted of using religion as a cloak, the very crime about which Paul forewarns us (3:1-9).

No matter what some may say, 2 Timothy is much needed, and only too authentic!

II. Authorship

See the Introduction to the Pastoral Epistles for a discussion of 2 Timothy's authorship.

III. Date

Second Timothy was written from prison (traditionally the Mamertime Prison in Rome, still displayed to tourists). As a Roman citizen Paul could not be thrown to the lions or crucified, but "merited" execution with a sword by decapitation. Since he was killed under Nero, who died June 8, 68, the date for 2 Timothy is likely restricted to sometime between the autumn of 67 and the spring of 68.

IV. Theme[†]

The theme of 2 Timothy is well expressed in 2:15: "Be diligent to present yourself approved to God, a worker who does not need to be ashamed, rightly dividing the word of truth." In contrast to 1 Timothy, where collective, congregational conduct is emphasized, here individual responsibility and behavior are prominent. This theme may be stated as "Individual Responsibility in a Time of Collective Failure."

There is much collective failure in the professing church in this Letter. There has been great departure from the faith and from the truth. How does this affect the individual believer? Is he excused from seeking to hold to the truth and live a godly life? The answer of 2 Timothy is a decided *No!* "Be diligent to present yourself approved. . . ."

The situation of young Daniel in the court of Babylon (Dan. 1) illustrates this.

†*See p. ii.*

Because of the prolonged wickedness of the Israelites, he and a number of others had been taken captive to Babylon by Nebuchadnezzar. They were deprived of all the outward forms of the Jewish religion — sacrifices, priestly ministry, temple worship, etc. Indeed, these were soon to be entirely suspended when a few years later Jerusalem was destroyed and the entire nation was taken into captivity. Did Daniel, therefore, say to himself, "I might as well forget the Law and the Prophets and accommodate myself to the practices, standards, and morals here at Babylon"? History records the bright, glowing answer in his remarkable life of faith in circumstances seemingly so adverse.

Thus, too, the message of 2 Timothy speaks to the individual child of God who finds the collective church testimony of this day a far cry from the NT simplicity and holiness in which it began. He or she is still held responsible to "live godly in Christ Jesus" (2 Tim. 3:12).

OUTLINE

I. INTRODUCTORY GREETINGS TO TIMOTHY (1:1–5)

II. EXHORTATIONS TO TIMOTHY (1:6–2:13)
   A. To Fidelity (1:6–18)
   B. To Endurance (2:1–13)

III. FIDELITY VERSUS APOSTASY (2:14–4:8)
   A. Fidelity to True Christianity (2:14–26)
   B. The Coming Apostasy (3:1–13)
   C. The Man of God's Resource in View of the Apostasy (3:14–4:8)

IV. PERSONAL REQUESTS AND REMARKS (4:9–22)

Commentary

I. INTRODUCTORY GREETINGS TO TIMOTHY (1:1–5)

1:1 **Paul** introduces himself at the outset of the Letter as **an apostle of Jesus Christ**. He had been commissioned to special service by the glorified Lord. This appointment was not by men or through men, but directly through **the will of God**. Also, Paul speaks of his apostleship as being **according to the promise of life which is in Christ Jesus**. God has made **a promise** that all who believe **in Christ Jesus** will receive eternal **life**. Paul's call to be an **apostle** was in harmony with this **promise**. In fact, if there had been no such promise, there would have been no need of an apostle like Paul.

As Vine puts it: "It was according to the divine purpose that life, which was in Christ Jesus in the eternal past, should be given to us. It was consistent with this purpose that Paul should become an apostle."[1]

V. Paul Flint expounds the five references to life in this Epistle as 1:1, the *promise* of life; 1:10, the *presentation* of life; 2:11, the *participation* of life; 3:12, the *pattern* of life; and 4:1, the *purpose* of life.

1:2 **Timothy** is addressed as **a beloved son**. It cannot be definitely proved that Timothy was actually converted through the ministry of Paul. Their first recorded meeting is found in Acts 16:1 where Timothy is described as already being a disciple before Paul came to Lystra. At any rate, the apostle looked on him as **a beloved son** in the Christian faith.

As in 1 Timothy, Paul's greeting consists of **grace, mercy, and peace**. It was pointed out in the commentary on 1 Timothy that when writing to churches, Paul characteristically wishes for them grace and peace. When writing to Timothy, he adds the word **mercy**. Guy King has suggested that grace is needed for every service, mercy for every failure, and peace for every circumstance. Someone else has said, "Grace to the worthless, mercy to the helpless, and peace to the restless." Hiebert defines **mercy** as "the self-moved, spontaneous loving-kindness of God which causes Him to deal in compassion and tender affection with the miserable and distressed."[2]

These blessings flow **from God the Father and Christ Jesus our Lord**. Here is another instance where Paul honors *the Son* just as he honors the **Father**.

1:3 In his characteristic style, Paul next breaks into thanksgiving. As we read this, we should remember that he was writing from a Roman dungeon. He had been imprisoned for preaching the gospel and was now treated as a common criminal. The Christian faith was being actively suppressed by the Roman government, and many believers had already been put to death. In spite of all these adverse circumstances, Paul can begin his Letter to Timothy with the words, **"I thank God!"**

The apostle was now serving God **with a pure conscience, as** his Jewish **forefathers** had done. Although his forebears were not Christians, they were believers in the living God. They worshiped Him and sought to serve Him. They held "the hope and resurrection of the dead," as Paul pointed out in Acts 23:6. That is why he could further say, in Acts 26:6, 7a: "And now I stand and am judged for the hope of the promise made by God to our fathers. To this promise [of resurrection] our twelve tribes, earnestly serving God night and day, hope to attain."

Thus Paul could speak of his service for the Lord as being according to the example of his ancestors. The word he uses for **serve**[3] refers to loyalty and allegiance. He acknowledged the true God.

Next Paul speaks of his unceasing remembrance of Timothy **in** his **prayers, night and day**. Whenever the great apostle spoke to the Lord in prayer, he would be reminded of his beloved, young coworker and would bring his name before the Throne of Grace. Paul knew that his own time of service was rapidly drawing to a close. He knew that Timothy would be left alone, humanly speaking, to carry on his witness for Christ. He knew of the difficulties that would face him, and so he prayed continually for this young warrior of the faith.

1:4 How it must have touched Timothy's heart to read these words! The Apostle Paul had what Moule called a "home-sick yearning" **to see** him. This was certainly a mark of special love and esteem, and it speaks eloquently of the graciousness, tenderness, and humility of Paul.

Perhaps it was the last time they parted that Timothy broke down. His **tears** had made a deep impression on his elder co-worker. Hiebert suggests it was when Paul had been "torn from him" by the police or Roman soldiers.[4] Paul could not forget, and now he longs to be with Timothy again so **that** he might **be filled with joy**. He does not rebuke Timothy for those **tears**, as though they were unmanly, or as though there was no place for emotions in Christianity. J. H. Jowett used to say: "Tearless hearts can never be heralds of the passion. When our sympathy loses its pang, we can no longer be the servants of the passion."

1:5 In some way or other, Paul had been reminded of Timothy's **genuine faith**. His **faith** was sincere, true, and did not wear a mask.[5]

But Timothy was not the first in his family to be saved. Apparently, his Jewish **grandmother Lois** had heard the good news of salvation and accepted the Lord Jesus as Messiah. And her daughter **Eunice**, also a Jewess (Acts 16:1), had become a Christian. In this way, Timothy had come to learn the great truths of the Christian faith, and he represented the third generation in that family to trust the Savior. Nothing is said in the Scriptures as to whether Timothy's father was ever converted.

Although salvation cannot be inherited from believing parents, it certainly is true that there is a household principle in the Scriptures. It appears that God loves to save entire families. It is not His will that there should be a missing member.

Notice that **faith** is said to have **dwelt** in **Lois** and **Eunice**. It was not there as an occasional visitor, but as an abiding presence with them. Paul was **persuaded** that that was the case with Timothy **also**. It was a genuine faith that Timothy would maintain in spite of all the trials which he might have to face in connection with it.

II. EXHORTATIONS TO TIMOTHY (1:6—2:13)

A. To Fidelity (1:6–18)

1:6 Because of his godly family background and his own faith, Timothy is urged **to stir up the gift of God which is in** him. We are not told what **the gift of God** is. Some take it to mean the Holy Spirit. Others understand it to mean a special ability conferred by the Lord for some form of Christian service, for instance, the gift of an evangelist, pastor, or teacher. It seems clear that Timothy had been called into Christian service and had been given some special enablement. Here he is encouraged to kindle **the gift** into a living flame. He should not become discouraged by the general failure around him. Neither should he become professional in his service for the Lord and lapse into a comfortable routine. Rather, he should be concerned to use his gift more and more as the days grow darker and darker.

This **gift** was in Timothy **through the laying on of** the apostle's **hands**. This is not to be confused with the ordination service which is practiced in clerical circles today. This means exactly what it says — that **the gift** was actually given to Timothy at the moment Paul laid his **hands** upon him. The apostle was the channel by which the gift was conferred.

The question will immediately arise, "Does this take place today?" The answer is that it does not. The power to confer a gift by the laying on of hands was given to Paul as an apostle of Jesus Christ. Since we do not have apostles in that same sense today, we no longer have the power to perform apostolic miracles.

This verse should be studied in connection with 1 Timothy 1:18 and 4:14. Putting these three verses together, we find that the following is the order of events, as expressed by Vine. By prophetic utterance, Paul was guided to Timothy as one raised up for special service. By the formal act on the apostle's part, the Lord bestowed a gift on Timothy. The elders recognized what the Lord had done by laying on their hands. The latter action was not an act of ordination, conferring a gift or ecclesiastical position.[6]

Or, as Stock summarizes, "The gift came 'through' Paul's hands, but 'with' the presbyters' hands."

1:7 Facing martyrdom himself, Paul takes time out to remind Timothy that **God has not given us a spirit of fear** or cowardice. There is no time for fearfulness or timidity.

But God has given us a spirit of **power**. Unlimited strength is at our disposal. Through the enabling of the Holy Spirit, the believer can serve valiantly, endure patiently, suffer triumphantly, and, if need be, die gloriously.

God has also given us a spirit **of love**. It is our **love** for God that casts out fear and makes us willing to give ourselves for Christ, whatever the cost may be. It is our **love** for our fellow men that makes us willing to endure all kinds of persecutions and repay them with kindness.

Finally, God has given us a spirit of **a sound mind**, or discipline. The words **a sound mind** do not completely convey the thought. They might suggest that a Christian should be sane at all times, free from nervous breakdowns or other mental ailments. This verse has often been misused to teach that a Christian who is living close to the Lord could never be afflicted with any kind of mental ills. That is not a scriptural teaching. Many mental ills can be traced to *inherited* weaknesses. Many others may be the result of some *physical* condition not connected in any way with the person's spiritual life.

What this verse is teaching is that God has given us a spirit of self-control or self-mastery. We are to use discretion and not to act rashly, hastily, or foolishly. No matter how adverse our circumstances, we should maintain balanced judgment and act soberly.

1:8 Timothy is told that he should

not be ashamed. In verse 12, Paul states that he is not ashamed. Finally, in verse 16, we read that Onesiphorus was not ashamed.

It was a day when preaching the gospel was a crime. Those who sought to witness publicly for their Lord and Savior were persecuted. But this should not daunt Timothy. He should **not be ashamed** of the gospel, even though it involves suffering. Neither should he **be ashamed** of the Apostle Paul in prison. Already some of the Christians had turned their backs on him. Doubtless they feared that to identify themselves with him would invite persecution and possibly death.

Timothy was exhorted to take his **share** of **the sufferings** that accompany **the gospel** and to bear it **according to the power of God**. He should not try to avoid any disgrace that might be connected with it, but rather join with Paul in enduring such disgrace.

1:9 The apostle has been encouraging Timothy to be zealous (vv. 6, 7) and courageous (v. 8). Now Paul explains why this is the only reasonable attitude to take; it is found in God's wonderful dealings with us in grace. First of all, He **saved us**. This means that He delivered us from the penalty of sin. He constantly delivers us from the power of sin, and in a day yet future, He will deliver us from the very presence of sin. Also, He has freed us from the world and from Satan.

Again, God has **called us with a holy calling**. Not only has He delivered us from evil, but He has bestowed upon us all spiritual blessings in the heavenlies in Christ Jesus. The Christian's holy calling is described in some detail in Ephesians 1-3, especially in chapter 1. There we learn that we are chosen, predestined, adopted as sons, accepted in the Beloved, redeemed through His blood, forgiven, sealed with the Holy Spirit, and given the earnest of our inheritance. (In addition to this holy calling, we have a high calling, Phil. 3:14, and a heavenly calling, Heb. 3:1.)

This salvation and calling are **not according to our works**. In other words, they were given to us by God's grace. This means that we did not deserve them, but rather deserved the very op-

posite. We could not earn them; neither did we seek them. But God freely bestowed them upon us without condition or price.

This is further explained by the words **according to His own purpose and grace**. Why should God have so loved ungodly sinners that He was willing to send His only Son to die for them? Why should He go to such a cost to save them from hell and to bring them to heaven so that they could spend eternity with Him? The only possible answer is: **according to His own purpose and grace**. The reason for His action did not lie in us. Rather, it lay in His own great heart of love. He loved us because He loved us!

His favor **was given to us in Christ Jesus before time began**. This means that in the past eternity, God determined upon this wonderful plan of salvation. He determined to save guilty sinners through the substitutionary work of His dear Son. He decided to offer eternal life to as many as would accept Jesus Christ as Lord and Savior. The method by which we could be saved was planned not only before we were born, but even **before time began**.

1:10 The same gospel that was designed in eternity was **revealed** in time. It was **revealed by the appearing of our Savior Jesus Christ**. During the days of His flesh, He publicly proclaimed the good news of salvation. He taught men that He must die, be buried, and rise from the dead in order that God might righteously save ungodly sinners.

He **abolished death**. But how can this be, when we know that death is still very common in the world? The thought is that He annulled death, or put it out of commission. Before Christ's resurrection, death ruled as a cruel tyrant over men. It was a dreaded foe. The fear of death held men in bondage. But the resurrection of the Lord Jesus is a pledge that all who trust in Him will rise from the dead to die no more. It is in this sense that He has annulled death. He has robbed it of its sting. Death is now the messenger of God which brings the soul of the believer to heaven. It is our servant rather than our master.

Not only has the Lord Jesus annulled **death**, He has **brought life and immor-**

tality to light through the gospel. In the OT period, most men had a very vague and misty idea of life after death. They spoke of departed loved ones as in Sheol, which simply means the invisible state of departed spirits. Although they had a heavenly hope set before them, yet for the most part they did not understand it clearly.

Since the coming of Christ, we have much greater light on this subject. For instance, we know that when a believer dies, his spirit departs to be with Christ, which is far better. He is absent from the body and at home with the Lord. He enters into eternal life in all its fullness.

Christ has not only brought life to light, but also immortality. Immortality refers to the resurrection of the body. When we read in 1 Corinthians 15:53 that "this corruptible must put on incorruption," we know that even though the body is placed in the grave and returns to dust, yet at the coming of Christ that same body will be raised from the grave and fashioned into a body of glory, similar to that of the Lord Jesus Himself. The OT saints did not have this knowledge. It was brought to us through the appearing of our Savior, Jesus Christ.

1:11 It was to proclaim this glorious gospel that Paul was appointed a preacher, an apostle, and a teacher of the Gentiles. A preacher is a herald whose function is to publicly proclaim a message. An apostle is one who has been divinely sent, divinely equipped, and divinely empowered. A teacher is one whose function is to indoctrinate others; he explains the truth in an understandable manner so that others may respond by faith and obedience. Of the Gentiles[7] stresses his special ministry to the non-Jewish nations.

1:12 It was because of his faithful performance of duty that Paul was suffering imprisonment and loneliness. He had not hesitated to declare the truth of God. No fears for personal safety had sealed his lips. Now that he had been arrested and jailed, he still had no regrets. He was not ashamed, and neither should Timothy be ashamed. Although Paul could not be confident as to his personal safety, he was completely confident as to the One whom he had believed. Though Rome might succeed in

putting the apostle to death, men could not touch his Lord. Paul knew that the One whom he had trusted was able. Able to do what? Able to keep what I have committed to Him until that Day. Commentators are divided as to what Paul is referring to here. Some think that it is his soul's salvation. Others understand this to refer to the gospel. In other words, although the Apostle Paul himself might be put to death, yet the gospel could not be hindered. The more men sought to oppose it, the more it would prosper.

Perhaps it is best to take the expression in its broadest sense. Paul was persuaded that his entire case was in the best of hands. Even as he faced death, he had no misgivings. Jesus Christ was his Almighty Lord, and with Him there could be no defeat or failure. There was nothing to worry about. Paul's salvation was sure, and so was the ultimate success of his service for Christ here on earth.

That Day is a favorite expression of Paul. It refers to the coming of the Lord Jesus Christ, and particularly to the Judgment Seat of Christ when service for Him will be brought into review and when the kindness of God will reward the faithfulness of men.

1:13 This verse may be understood in two ways. First of all, Timothy is encouraged to hold fast the pattern of sound words. It is not just that he is to be loyal to the truth of God's word, but that he is to cling to the very expressions by which this truth is conveyed. Perhaps an illustration of this might help. In our day, it is sometimes suggested that we should abandon such old-fashioned expressions as "being born again" or "the blood of Jesus." People want to use more sophisticated language. But there is a subtle danger here. In abandoning the scriptural mode of expression, they often abandon the very truths which are communicated by these expressions. Therefore, Timothy should hold fast the very pattern of healthful words.

But the verse might also suggest that Paul's words were to serve as a model or pattern to Timothy. Everything that Timothy subsequently taught should harmonize with the outline that had been given to him. In carrying out his ministry, Timothy should do so **in faith and love which are in Christ Jesus. Faith** means not only trust, but dependence as well. **Love** includes not only **love** to God, but also **love** to our fellow believers and to the perishing world around us.

1:14 That good thing refers to the gospel. The message of redeeming love had been **committed** or entrusted to Timothy. He is not told to add to it or to improve on it in any way. His responsibility is to guard it through **the Holy Spirit who dwells in us**. As Paul wrote this Letter, he was conscious of the widespread departure from the faith which was menacing the church. Attacks would be made on the Christian faith from many different quarters. Timothy was admonished to stand true to the word of God. He would not have to do this in his own strength. The indwelling **Holy Spirit** would supply all that he needed for this task.

1:15 As the apostle thinks of the dark clouds gathering over the church, he is reminded of how the Christians **in Asia** had **turned away from** him. Since at the time this Letter was written Timothy was probably located in Ephesus, he knew exactly what the apostle was writing about.

It is likely that the Christians in Asia severed their connections with Paul when they learned that he had been arrested and imprisoned. They forsook him at the very time he needed them most. Probably their reason was that they feared for their own safety. The Roman government was on the lookout for all who sought to propagate the Christian faith. The Apostle Paul was one of the best-known representatives of Christianity. Any who dared to contact him publicly would be marked out at once as being sympathetic to the cause.

It is neither stated nor implied that these Christians forsook the Lord or the church. Nevertheless, it was an act of cowardice and unfaithfulness to desert Paul in this crisis hour.

Perhaps **Phygellus and Hermogenes** were leaders in the movement to dissociate themselves from Paul. At any rate, they brought upon themselves an immortality of shame and contempt for refusing to bear the reproach of Christ in

fellowship with His servant. Guy King's comment is that "they couldn't help their ugly names, but they could have helped their ugly character."

1:16 There are two schools of thought with regard to **Onesiphorus**. Some think that he too had forsaken Paul, and that is why the apostle prays that **the Lord** will **grant mercy to** him. Others feel that he is mentioned as a happy exception to those who have just been described. We believe that the latter view is correct.

Paul asks that **the Lord** will **grant mercy to the household of Onesiphorus. Mercy** is the reward for those who have been merciful, according to Matthew 5:7. We are not told exactly how Onesiphorus **refreshed** Paul. Perhaps he brought food and clothing to the damp, dark Roman dungeon. At any rate, he **was not ashamed** to go to Paul in prison. No considerations of personal safety could prevent his helping a friend in time of need.

Jowett expressed it exquisitely:

It is a beautiful lineament in the character of Onesiphorus which is given in the Apostle's phrase, "He was not ashamed of my chain." . . . A man's chain often lessens the circle of his friends. The chain of poverty keeps many people away, and so does the chain of unpopularity. When a man is in high repute he has many friends. When he begins to wear a chain, the friends are apt to fall away. But the ministers of the morning breeze love to come in the shades of night. They delight to minister in the region of despondency, and where the bonds lie heaviest upon the soul. "He was not ashamed of my chain." The chain was really an allurement. It gave speed to the feet of Onesiphorus and urgency to his ministry.[8]

This verse has sometimes been misused to support prayers for the dead. The argument is that Onesiphorus had already died when Paul wrote this and that Paul was asking God to show mercy to him. There is not the vaguest hint that Onesiphorus was dead. Proponents of this view are idle babblers clutching at a straw to shore up an unbiblical practice.

1:17 When Onesiphorus **arrived in Rome**, he had at least three choices. First, he could have avoided any contact with the Christians. Secondly, he could have met with the believers secretly. Finally, he could boldly expose himself to danger by visiting Paul in prison. This would bring him into direct contact with the Roman authorities. To his everlasting credit, he chose the last policy. **He sought** Paul **out very zealously and found** him.

1:18 The apostle prays that this faithful friend might **find mercy from the Lord in that** coming **Day. Mercy** is here used in the sense of reward. **That Day**, as previously mentioned, refers to the time when rewards will be given, namely, the Judgment Seat of Christ.

In closing this section, the Apostle Paul reminds Timothy how Onesiphorus had served Paul **at Ephesus** in many different ways.

B. To Endurance (2:1–13)

2:1 To **be strong in the grace that is in Christ Jesus** means to be courageous with the strength which His **grace** provides, to go on faithfully for the Lord with the undeserved ability that comes through union with Him.

2:2 Not only is Timothy to be strengthened himself, but he is to provide for the spiritual strengthening of **others**. He is responsible to transmit to others the inspired teachings which he had received from the apostle. Paul was soon to pass off the scene. He had faithfully taught Timothy in the presence of **many witnesses**. Timothy's own day of service would be short at best, and he, too, should so order his ministry that others would be prepared to carry on as teachers.

This verse does *not* support the notion of apostolic succession. Neither does it refer to the present day practice of ordination of ministers. Rather, it is simply the Lord's instruction to the church to ensure a succession of competent teachers.

It has often been pointed out that there are four generations of believers in this verse, as follows:

1. The Apostle Paul.
2. Timothy and many witnesses.
3. Faithful men.
4. Others.

This Scripture emphasizes the importance of every-member evangelism. If each believer truly did his part the world could be evangelized within a generation. However, this is merely hypothetical in the light of the perversity of man's will, the rival "evangelism" of world religions and the cults, and many other obstacles. Positively, however, one thing is certain: Christians could do a great deal better than the record so far!

Notice that Timothy is to **commit** the truth **to faithful men**, that is, men who are believers and who are themselves dependable. These men should be able **to teach others also**. This presupposes some competency as far as teaching ministry is concerned.

2:3 It has often been pointed out that Paul uses a wealth of similes in this chapter to describe Timothy: (1) Son (v. 1); (2) Soldier (vv. 3, 4); (3) Athlete (v. 5); (4) Farmer (v. 6); (5) Worker (v. 15); (6) Vessel (v. 21); (7) Servant (v. 24).

As a good soldier of Jesus Christ, Timothy should **endure**[9] suffering and **hardship**. (For a list of the many hardships Paul himself endured, see 2 Cor. 11:23–29.)

2:4 The soldier described in this verse is one who is on active duty. Not only so, but he is in the thick of the combat. No soldier in such grim circumstances **entangles himself with the affairs of this life**.

Does this mean that those who are in the Lord's service should never engage in secular occupations as well? Certainly not! Paul himself worked as a tentmaker while he was preaching the gospel and planting churches. He testified that his own hands ministered to his necessities.

The emphasis is on the word **entangles**. The soldier must not allow ordinary affairs of life to become the main object of existence. For instance, he must not make acquiring food and clothing the main aim of life. Rather, the service of Christ must always occupy the prominent place, while the things of this life are kept in the background. Kelly says: "To entangle oneself in the businesses of life means really to give up separation from the world by taking one's part in outward affairs as a bona fide partner in it."[10]

A soldier on duty keeps himself in readiness for orders from headquarters. His desire is to **please** the one **who enlisted him**. The believer, of course, has been enlisted by the Lord, and our love for Him should cause us to maintain a light hold on the things of this world.

2:5 The figure now changes to an athlete who **competes** in the games. In order to receive the reward, he must obey **the rules** of the game. So it is in Christian service. How many fall out before they reach the finish line, disqualified because they did not maintain an unquestioning obedience to the word of God!

What are some of the rules in connection with Christian service? (1) The Christian must practice self-discipline (1 Cor. 9:27). (2) He must not fight with carnal weapons, but with spiritual ones (2 Cor. 10:4). (3) He must keep himself pure. (4) He must not strive, but be patient.

Someone has said: "A spare-time Christian is a contradiction in terms; a man's whole life should be one strenuous endeavor to live out his Christianity in every moment and in every sphere of his life."

2:6 **The hard-working farmer must be first to partake of the crops.** According to all principles of righteousness, the one who labors to bring forth **the crops** has a prior right to participate in them.

This would serve as an encouragement to Timothy, should he ever become discouraged in his labor for the Lord. Such toil will not go unrewarded. Although many will participate in the harvest in a coming day, yet Timothy's labor of love would not go unnoticed. Indeed, he would be the **first to partake** of the fruit of his own labor.

2:7 But there is more in these three illustrations of Christian service than appears on the surface. Timothy is exhorted to consider them and to meditate on them. As he does so, Paul prays[11] that **the Lord** will **give** him **understanding in all things**. He will realize that the Christian ministry resembles warfare, athletics, and farming. Each of these occupations has its own responsibilities, and each brings its own reward.

2:8 At this point, the apostle reaches the high-water mark in his series of encouragements to young Timothy. He comes to the example of the Lord Jesus, and he can go no higher. His is an example of suffering followed by

glory. **Remember that Jesus Christ, of the seed of David, was raised from the dead according to my gospel.** The thought is not that Timothy is to remember certain things *about* the Lord Jesus, but rather that he is to remember the Person Himself, alive **from the dead**.

In one sense, this verse is a brief summary of the gospel which Paul preached. The crucial point in that gospel is the resurrection of the Savior. Hiebert writes: "Not the vision of a crucified Jesus but the vision of a risen Lord is held up before Timothy."[12]

The expression **of the seed of David** is a simple statement that Jesus is the Christ, the descendant **of David**, in whom the Messianic promises of God are fulfilled.

Constant remembrance of the Savior's Person and work is essential for all who want to serve Him. Especially for those facing suffering and possible death, there is great encouragement in remembering that even the Lord Jesus Himself reached the glory of heaven by way of the cross and the grave.

2:9 It was for proclaiming the gospel outlined in verse 8 that Paul was now chained in a Roman prison. He was looked upon **as an evildoer**, as a common criminal. There was much to discourage. Not only was the Roman government determined to put him to death, but some of his own Christian friends had turned away from him.

And yet in spite of these bitter circumstances, Paul's happy spirit soars high above the dungeon walls. He forgets his own dismal outlook when he remembers that **the word of God is not chained**. As Lenski said so well, "The apostle's living voice may be smothered in his own blood, but what his Lord speaks through him still resounds in the wide world." Not all the armies in the world can hinder the word of God from going forth. They might just as well try to stop the rain or the snow from falling (Isa. 55:10, 11). Harvey says:

With irresistible, divine energy it is advancing in its career of triumph, even while its defenders suffer imprisonment and martyrdom. Men die, but Christ and His gospel live and triumph through the ages.[13]

2:10 Because of the irresistible nature of the gospel, Paul was willing to **endure all things for the sake of the elect. The elect** here refers to all those chosen by God for eternal salvation. While the Bible does teach that God chooses people to be saved, it nowhere says that He selects some to be damned. Those who are saved are saved by the sovereign grace of God. Those who are lost are lost by their own deliberate choice.

No one should quarrel with God over the doctrine of election. This doctrine simply allows God to be God, the Sovereign of the universe, who deals in grace, justice, righteousness, and love. He never does anything unfair or unkind, but He often shows favor that is completely unmerited.

The apostle realized that through his suffering for the sake of the gospel, souls were saved and that these very souls would one day participate in **eternal glory** with **Christ Jesus**. The vision of guilty sinners, saved by the grace of God and glorified together with Christ Jesus, was sufficient to inspire Paul to bear all things. In this, we are reminded of the words attributed to the godly Rutherford:[14]

> Oh, if one soul from Anwoth
>   Meet me at God's right hand,
> My heaven shall be two heavens
>   In Immanuel's land.

2:11 Verses 11–13 are thought by some to be from an early Christian hymn. Whether that is so or not, they certainly present some inflexible principles concerning man's relationship to the Lord Jesus Christ. Hiebert writes: "The central truth of these pithy statements is that faith in Christ identifies the believer with Him in everything while unbelief just as surely separates men from Him."[15] This is the fourth **faithful saying** in Paul's Letters to Timothy.

The first principle is that **if we died with** Christ, **we shall also live with Him.** This is true of every believer. In a spiritual sense, **we died with Him** the moment we trusted Him as our Savior. We were buried with Him, and we rose again with Him from among the dead. Christ died as our Representative and Substitute. We should have died for our

sins, but Christ died in our place. God reckons us to have **died with Him,** and this means that **we shall also live with Him** in heaven.

Perhaps this verse also has an application to those who die as Christian martyrs. Those who thus follow Him in death will likewise follow Him in resurrection.

2:12 In a sense, it is also true of all Christians that they **endure** and that they **shall also reign with** Christ. True faith always has the quality of permanence, and in this sense all believers do **endure.**

However, it should also be pointed out that not all will reign with Christ to the same extent. When He comes back to reign over the earth, His saints will return with Him and share in that rule. But the extent of one's rule will be determined by his faithfulness during this present life.

Those who **deny** Christ will be denied by Him. Here the thought is not of a temporary denial of the Savior under duress, as in the case of Peter, but a permanent, habitual denial of Him. These words describe an unbeliever — one who has never embraced the Lord Jesus by faith. All such will be denied by the Lord in a coming day, no matter how pious their profession might have been.

2:13 This verse also describes unbelievers. Dinsdale Young explains: "God cannot be inconsistent with Himself. It would be inconsistent with His character to treat the faithful and the unfaithful alike. He is evermore true to righteousness, whatever we are."[16]

The words should not be interpreted to teach that God's faithfulness will be demonstrated in upholding those who are unbelieving. Such is not the case. If men are unbelieving, **He** must be **faithful** to His own character and must treat them accordingly. As Van Oosterzee says, "He is just as faithful in His threatenings as in His promises."[17]

III. FIDELITY VERSUS APOSTASY (2:14–4:8)

A. Fidelity to True Christianity (2:14–26)

2:14 Timothy is to **remind them of**

these things, that is, the things of verses 11-13. But to whom does Paul refer with the word them? He probably refers in a general sense to all of Timothy's hearers and in a special sense to those who were introducing strange doctrines. This is evident from the remaining part of the verse, where those who obviously occupied the place of teachers or preachers are warned not to strive about words. Apparently there were those in Ephesus who made great issues over the technical meaning of certain words. Instead of building up the saints in the truth of God's word, they were only undermining the faith of some who heard them.

Dinsdale Young warns:

> It is so easy to become a theological crank — so readily are we engrossed with questions that are of no supreme moment. Life is too brief and too busy for the wasting of brain and heart on what is not formative of character.
>
> When a world awaits evangelization, it ill becomes us to be forever either sauntering or hurrying along doctrinal byways. Keep to the highways. Be true to the greater verities. Emphasize essentials, not incidentals. Do not emulate the victims of panic in the days of Shamgar and of Jael, who left the highways unoccupied and walked through byways.[18]

2:15 Timothy should **be diligent to present** himself **approved to God**. His efforts should be concentrated on becoming **a worker who does not need to be ashamed**. This he could do by **rightly dividing the word of truth**. This latter expression means to handle the Scriptures correctly, to "hew the line," or as Alford put it, "to manage rightly to treat truth fully without falsifying."[19]

2:16 **Profane and idle babblings** are teachings that are irreverent, evil, and useless. It is not profitable for the people of God and should be shunned. Timothy is not instructed to combat these teachings but rather to treat them with disdain, not even dignifying them with his attention.

One serious thing about these babblers is that they are never static. They always **increase** in **ungodliness**. It is so with all forms of error. Those who teach error must be continually adding to it. This explains the new dogmas and pronouncements that are constantly being issued by false religious systems. Needless to say, the more these doctrinal errors are expanded, the **more ungodliness** results.

2:17 The way in which evil teachings **spread** is compared to **cancer**. Most of us know only too well how this dread disease spreads rapidly in the human body, destroying tissue wherever it goes.

The word *cancer* can also be rendered "gangrene."[20] Gangrene refers to the mortification of part of the body when it is cut off from its normal supply of blood and nutrition.

Elsewhere in the NT, evil doctrine is likened to leaven, which, if allowed to spread, will eventually affect the whole lump of meal.

Two men are named whose teachings were corrupting the local church. They were **Hymenaeus and Philetus**. Because they failed to handle the word of truth correctly, they take their place with others in God's hall of shame.

2:18 Their false teaching is here exposed. They told the people **that the resurrection** was **already past**. Perhaps they meant that when a person was saved and was raised to newness of life with Christ, that was the only resurrection he could expect. In other words, they spiritualized the resurrection and scoffed at the idea of a literal raising of the body from the grave. Paul recognized this as a serious threat to the truth of Christianity.

Hamilton Smith says:

> If the resurrection is past already, it is evident that the saints have reached their final condition while yet on earth, with the result that the church ceases to look for the coming of the Lord, loses the truth of its heavenly destiny, and gives up its stranger and pilgrim character. Having lost its heavenly character, the church settles down on the earth, taking a place as part of the system for the reformation and government of the world.[21]

By overthrowing **the faith of some**, these men earned for themselves an undesirable entry in God's eternal book.

2:19 As Paul thinks of Hymenaeus and Philetus and their false teaching, he realizes afresh that dark days are coming upon the church. Unbelievers have been accepted into the local church. Spiritual

life is at such a low ebb that it is often
hard to tell true Christians from mere
professors. Christendom is a mixed multitude, and the resulting confusion is
devastating.

In the midst of such a condition, Paul
finds comfort in the assurance that **the
solid foundation of God stands**. This
means that whatever has been established by **God** Himself will endure in
spite of all the declension in the professing church.

Various explanations have been given
as to what is meant by **the solid foundation of God**. Some suggest that it is the
true church. Others say it refers to the
promise of God, to the Christian faith,
or to the doctrine of election. But is it
not clear that the **foundation of God** refers to *anything that the Lord does*? If He
sends out His word, nothing can hinder
it. Hamilton Smith says: "No failure of
man can set aside the foundation that
God has laid, or prevent God from completing what He has commenced. . . .
Those who are the Lord's, though hidden in the mass, cannot be ultimately
lost."[22]

The **foundation of God** has a twofold
seal. There is a divine side to it and a
human side as well. From the divine
side, **the Lord knows those who are His**.
He **knows** them, not only in the sense
of recognition, but of approval and
appreciation. Lenski says He knows
them "with appropriating and effective
love."[23] The human side of the **seal** is
that **everyone who names the name of
Christ**[24] should **depart from iniquity**. In
other words, those professing to be
Christians can prove the reality of their
profession by lives of holiness and godliness. The true Christian should have no
dealings with unrighteousness.

A seal is a mark of ownership and
also an emblem of guarantee and security. Thus the **seal** on God's **foundation**
signifies His ownership of those who are
true believers and the guarantee that all
who have been converted will prove the
reality of their new life by departing
from unrighteousness.

2:20 In this illustration, we understand that the **great house** refers to
Christendom in general. In a broad
sense, Christendom includes believers

and professors — those who are truly
born again and those who are mere
nominal Christians.

Vessels of gold and silver would
therefore refer to genuine believers.

Vessels **of wood and clay** refer not to
unbelievers in general, but to those in
particular who were evil workers and
who taught false doctrines, such as Hymenaeus and Philetus (v. 17).

Certain things should be noticed
about these vessels. First of all, there is
an important distinction between the
materials of which the vessels are made.
Secondly, there is a difference in the
uses to which they are put. Finally, there
is the distinction as to their ultimate destiny. The vessels of wood and clay are
discarded after a while, but those of gold
and silver are retained as valuable.

The expression **some for honor and
some for dishonor** has been variously interpreted. Some suggest that **dishonor**
simply means less honor. In that case,
all the vessels would stand for true believers, but some are used for the highest purposes and some for the lowest.
Others feel that the vessels **for honor**
would refer to men like Paul and Timothy, whereas those **for dishonor** would
refer to such men as Hymenaeus and
Philetus.

2:21 The interpretation of this passage largely depends on one's understanding of the meaning of *the latter* in
**"Therefore, if anyone cleanses himself
from the latter."**

Does **latter** refer to the vessels of
wood and clay? Does it refer to the false
teachings that have been mentioned previously in this chapter? Or does it refer
in a general way to evil men?

The most natural meaning seems to
be to connect **latter** with vessels for dishonor. Timothy is instructed to separate
himself from evil men and especially
from evil teachers such as those Paul
had just mentioned — Hymenaeus and
Philetus.

Timothy is *not* instructed to leave the
church. Neither is he told to leave Christendom as such. It would be impossible
for him to do this without giving up his
Christian profession, since Christendom
includes all who profess to be believers.
Rather, it is a question of separating

from evildoers and avoiding contamination from wicked doctrine.

If a man keeps himself free from evil associations, **he will be a vessel for honor**. God can use only clean vessels in holy service. "Be clean, you who bear the vessels of the Lord" (Isa. 52:11). Such a man will also be **sanctified** in the sense that he will be set apart from evil to the service of God. He will be **useful for the Master** — a quality greatly to be desired by all who love the Lord. Finally, he will be **prepared for every good work**. He will be ready at all times to be used in whatever way his Master may dictate.

2:22 Not only is Timothy to separate himself from iniquitous men, but he is to separate himself from the **lusts** of the flesh. **Youthful lusts** may refer not only to physical appetites but also to the lust for money, fame, and pleasure. They may also include self-will, impatience, pride, and levity. As we have mentioned, Timothy was probably about thirty-five years of age at this time. Therefore, **youthful lusts** do not necessarily mean such lusts as would be particularly characteristic of a teenager but would include all the unholy desires that would present themselves to a young servant of the Lord and seek to divert him from the path of purity and righteousness.

Not only is Timothy to **flee**; he is also to follow. There is the negative and the positive.

He should **pursue righteousness**. This simply means that his dealings with his fellow men, saved and unsaved, should always be characterized by honesty, justice, and fairness.

Faith may mean faithfulness or absolute integrity. On the other hand, it may include a continual dependence on the Lord. Hiebert defines it as "sincere and dynamic confidence in God."[25]

Love cannot be limited here to love to God alone, but must also include love for one's brethren and for the world of lost sinners. Love always considers others; it is essentially unselfish.

Peace carries the idea of harmony and compatibility.

These virtues are to be followed **with those who call on the Lord out of a pure heart**. Just as in verse 21 Timothy was warned to separate himself from wicked men, so here he is taught to associate himself with Christians who are walking in purity before the Lord. He is not to follow the virtues of the Christian life in isolation, but rather he must take his place as a member in the Body and seek to work with his fellow members for the good of the Body.

2:23 In the course of his Christian ministry, Timothy would often be faced with trifling and stupid questions. Such questions would spring from an ignorant, uneducated mind and would have no real benefit connected with them. Such **disputes** should be refused because **they** only stir up **strife**. Needless to say, these are not questions connected with the great fundamentals of the Christian faith, but rather silly problems that would only succeed in wasting time and causing confusion and arguments.

2:24 **The servant of the Lord** here is literally the Lord's *bondservant*. It is fitting that this title should be used in a verse where gentleness and patience are encouraged.

Although the Lord's servant must contend for the truth, yet he must not be contentious or argumentative. Rather, he must **be gentle to all** and approach men with the purpose of instructing them rather than of winning an argument. He must be **patient** with those who are slow to understand and even with those who do not seem disposed to accept the truth of God's word.

2:25 The Lord's bondservant must exercise meekness and **humility** in dealing with **opposition**. A person wrongs his own soul by refusing to bow to the word of God. Such people need to be corrected lest they ignorantly go on with the mistaken notion that their view is in accordance with the Scriptures.

If God perhaps will grant them repentance, so that they may know the truth. At first, this might seem to suggest that there is some question as to God's willingness to grant repentance to these people. That, however, is not the case. The fact of the matter is that God is waiting to forgive them if only they will come to Him in confession and repentance. God does not withhold repentance from anyone, but men are so often unwilling to admit that they are wrong.

2:26 The servant of the Lord should so deal with erring men that **they may come to their senses and escape the snare of the devil**. They have **been taken captive by him to do his will**, and, as it were, bewitched or intoxicated by him.

B. The Coming Apostasy (3:1–13)

3:1 The apostle now gives Timothy a description of conditions that will exist in the world prior to the Lord's coming. It has often been pointed out that the list of sins that follows is very similar to the description of the ungodly heathen in Romans 1. The remarkable thing is that the very conditions that exist among the heathen in their savagery and uncivilized state will characterize professing believers **in the last days**. How solemn this is!

The last days referred to here are the days between the apostolic period and the appearing of Christ to set up His kingdom.

3:2 One cannot study these verses without being struck by the repetition of the word **lovers**. In verse 2, for instance, we find **lovers** of self and **lovers of money**. In verse 3, the expression "despisers of good" means literally "no-lovers-of good." In verse 4, we read of "lovers of pleasure rather than lovers of God."

In verses 2–5, nineteen characteristics of mankind during the last days are given. We shall simply list them and give synonyms that explain their meaning:

Lovers of themselves — self-centered, conceited, egotistical.

Lovers of money — greedy for money, avaricious.

Boasters — braggarts, full of great swelling words.

Proud — arrogant, haughty, overbearing.

Blasphemers — evil speakers, profane, abusive, foulmouthed, contemptuous, insulting.

Disobedient to parents — rebellious, undutiful, uncontrolled.

Unthankful — ungrateful, lacking in appreciation.

Unholy — impious, profane, irreverent, holding nothing sacred.

3:3 Unloving — hard-hearted, unnaturally callous, unfeeling.

Unforgiving — implacable, refusing to make peace, refusing efforts toward reconciliation.

Slanderers — spreading false and malicious reports.

Without self-control — men of uncontrolled passions, dissolute, debauched.

Brutal — savage, unprincipled.

Despisers of good — haters of whatever or whoever is good; utterly opposed to goodness in any form.

3:4 Traitors — treacherous, betrayers.

Headstrong — reckless, self-willed, rash.

Haughty — making empty pretensions, conceited.

Lovers of pleasure rather than lovers of God — those who love sensual pleasures but not God.

3:5 Outwardly these people seem religious. They make a profession of Christianity, but their actions speak louder than their words. By their ungodly behavior, they show that they are living a lie. There is no evidence of the power of God in their lives. While there might have been reformation, there never was regeneration. Weymouth translates: "They will keep up a make-believe of piety and yet exclude its power." Likewise Moffatt: "Though they keep up a form of religion, they will have nothing to do with it as a force." Phillips puts it: "They will maintain a façade of 'religion' but their conduct will deny its validity." They want to be religious and to have their sins at the same time (cf. Rev. 3:14–22). Hiebert warns: "It is the fearful portrayal of an apostate Christendom, a new paganism masquerading under the name of Christianity."[26]

From all **such people** Timothy is exhorted to **turn away**. These are the vessels described in the previous chapter from which he is to purge himself.

3:6 Among the corrupt men of the last days, Paul now singles out a particular group, namely, leaders and teachers of false cults. This detailed description of their character and methods finds its fulfillment in the cults of our present day.

First of all, we read that they **creep**

or worm their way **into households**. It is not by accident that this description reminds us of the movement of a serpent. If they revealed their true identity, they would not succeed in getting into many of these homes, but they use various subtle devices, such as speaking about God, the Bible, and Jesus (even if they do not believe what Scripture teaches about these).

Next it says that they **make captives of gullible women**. This is characteristic. They plan their visit when the husband is apt to be at work or elsewhere. History repeats itself. Satan approached Eve in the Garden of Eden and deceived her. She usurped authority over her husband, making the decision that should have been left to him. Satan's methods have not changed. He still approaches the womenfolk with his false teachings and leads them captive. These **women** are **gullible** in the sense that they are weak and unstable. They do not lack brains as much as they lack strength of character.

They are described as **loaded down with sins, led away by various lusts**. This suggests, first of all, that they are burdened under a sense of sin and feel a need in their lives. It is at this crucial time that the false cultists arrive. How sad it is that those who know the truth of God's word are not more zealous in reaching these anxious souls. Secondly, we read that they are **led away by various lusts**. Weymouth understands this to mean "led by ever-changing caprice." Moffatt calls them "wayward creatures of impulse." The thought seems to be that, conscious of their load of sin and seeking relief from it, they are willing to expose themselves to every passing wind of doctrine and to every religious novelty.

3:7 The expression **always learning** does not mean that they are continually learning more about the Lord Jesus and the word of God. Rather, it means that they are constantly delving into one cult after another, but **never able to come to the knowledge of the truth**. The Lord Jesus is Himself the Truth. These women seem to come ever so close to Him at times, but they are taken captive by the enemy of their souls and never attain the rest that is found only in the Savior.

It should be noted at this point that members of the various cults invariably say, "I am learning _____," mentioning the system by name. They can never speak with finality as to an accomplished redemption through faith in Jesus Christ.

This verse also makes us think of the vast present-day increase in knowledge in every realm of human endeavor, the tremendous emphasis on education so prevalent in modern life, and yet the abysmal failure of it all to bring men to the knowledge of the truth.

3:8 Three pairs of men are mentioned in this Epistle:

Phygellus and Hermogenes (1:15) — *ashamed* of the truth.

Hymenaeus and Philetus (2:17, 18) — *erred* concerning the truth.

Jannes and Jambres (3:8) — *resisted* the truth.

In this eighth verse, Paul returns to the leaders and teachers of false cults. He compares them to **Jannes and Jambres** who **resisted Moses**. Who were these men? Actually, their names are not mentioned in the OT, but it is generally understood that they were two of the chief Egyptian magicians who were called in by Pharaoh to imitate the miracles performed by Moses.

The question arises as to how Paul knew their names. This should present no difficulty, for if they were not passed down by Jewish tradition, it is not at all unreasonable that the names could have been given to him by divine revelation.

The important thing is that they **resisted Moses** by imitating his works, by counterfeit miracles. That is precisely the case with the false cultists. They withstand the work of God by imitating it. They have their own Bible, their own way of salvation — in short, they have a substitute for everything in Christianity. They withstand the truth of God by presenting a cheap perversion, and sometimes by resorting to magical arts.

These **men** are **of corrupt mind**. Arthur Way translates it: "their minds are rotten to the core." Their minds are distorted, debased, and depraved.

When tested concerning **the** Christian **faith**, they are found to be **disapproved** and spurious. The greatest single test that can be applied to them is to ask the simple question, "Is Jesus Christ God?" Many of them seek to hide their false doctrine by admitting that Jesus is the Son of God, but they mean that He is a son of God in the same sense that others are children of God. But when faced with the question, "Is Jesus Christ God?" they show their true colors. They not only deny the deity of Jesus Christ but usually become angry when so challenged. This is true of Christian Scientists, Spiritualists, Christadelphians, Jehovah's Witnesses, and "The Way."

3:9 Paul assures Timothy that these false teachers **will progress no further**. The difficulty here is that in every age they seem to be prospering on every hand, and nothing seems to hinder their advance in the world!

The probable meaning is that every system of error is eventually exposed. False systems come and go, one after the other. Although they might seem to prosper mightily, and even for a long time, yet the time comes when their falsity becomes evident to all. They can lead men up to a certain point, even offering a certain measure of reformation. But they fail in that they have no regeneration. They cannot offer a man freedom from the penalty and power of sin. They cannot give life.

Jannes and Jambres could imitate Moses to a certain extent by their acts of magic. However, when it came to producing life from death, they were utterly powerless. This is the very issue on which the false cults meet their defeat.

3:10 In marked contrast to these false teachers was the life and ministry of Paul. Timothy was well aware of the nine prominent features which characterized this servant of the Lord. He had followed Paul closely and could testify to the fact that here was a man who was faithful to Christ and His word.

The apostle's **doctrine** or teaching was true to the word of God and loyal to the Person of the Lord Jesus Christ. His **manner of life**, or conduct, was consistent with the message he preached. His **purpose** in life was to be separate from moral and doctrinal evil. **Faith** here may mean Paul's trust in the Lord, or his own personal fidelity. Timothy knew him as one who was utterly dependent

on the Lord, and at the same time, one who was honest and trustworthy. The apostle's **longsuffering** was seen in his attitude toward his persecutors and critics, and toward physical afflictions. As to **love**, he was selflessly devoted to the Lord and to his fellow men. The less he was loved by others, the more determined he was to love. **Perseverance** literally means "bearing up under," that is, fortitude or endurance.

3:11 Some of the **persecutions** and **afflictions**, or sufferings, of Paul are described in 2 Corinthians 11:23–28. However, he is thinking particularly of those with which Timothy would have been personally acquainted. Since Timothy's home was **Lystra**, he would know about the **persecutions** which came to Paul there and in the neighboring cities of **Antioch** and **Iconium**. The inspired record of these sufferings is given in the book of Acts — Antioch, Acts 13:45, 50; Iconium, Acts 14:3–6; Lystra, Acts 14:19, 20.

Paul exults in the fact that **the Lord** had **delivered** him **out of . . . all** of these crises. The Lord had not delivered *from* trouble, but He had delivered him **out of** the troubles. This is a reminder to us that we are not promised freedom from difficulties, but we are promised that the Lord will be with us and will see us through.

3:12 **Persecution** is an integral part of a devout Christian life. It is well that every young Timothy should be reminded of this. Otherwise, when he is called upon to go through deep waters, he might be tempted to think that he has failed the Lord or that the Lord is displeased with him for some reason. The fact is that **persecution** is inevitable for **all who desire to live** in a **godly** manner.

The reason for this **persecution** is simple. A **godly** life exposes the wickedness of others. People do not like to be thus exposed. Instead of repenting of their ungodliness and turning to Christ, they seek to destroy the one who has shown them up for what they really are. It is totally irrational behavior, of course, but that is characteristic of fallen man.

3:13 Paul had no illusions that the world would gradually become better and better, until finally all men would be converted. Rather, he knew by divine revelation that the very opposite would be the case. **Evil men and impostors will grow worse and worse**. They would become more subtle in their methods and more bold in their attacks. Not only would they deceive others, but they themselves would be ensnared by the very false teaching with which they sought to trap their hearers. After having peddled their lies for so long, they would actually come to believe them personally.

C. The Man of God's Resource in View of the Apostasy (3:14–4:8)

3:14 Time and time again, Timothy is reminded to **continue** steadfastly in the teachings of the word of God. This would be his great resource in a day when false doctrines would abound on every hand. If he knew and obeyed the Scriptures, he would not be led away by these subtle errors.

Timothy had not only **learned** the great truths of the faith, but he had become personally **assured** of them as well. Doubtless he would be told that such teachings were old-fashioned and not sufficiently cultural or intellectual. But he should not abandon truth for theories or human speculations.

The apostle further counsels him to remember **from whom** he had **learned** these truths. There is some difference of opinion as to whether the word **whom** refers to Paul himself, Timothy's mother and grandmother, or the apostles in general. In any case, the thought is that the Sacred Scriptures had been taught to him by those whose lives witnessed to the reality of their faith. They were godly people who lived with a single eye to the glory of God.

3:15 This is a most suggestive verse. The thought is that from **childhood** Timothy had known the sacred writings or letters. There is even the thought here that when his mother taught him his ABC's, she did so by using portions of the OT **Scriptures**. From infancy, he had been under the influence of the inspired writings, and under no circumstances should he forget that blessed Book which had molded his life for God and for good.

The Holy Scriptures are spoken of as being continually **able to make** men **wise**

for salvation. This means, first of all, that men learn the way of **salvation** through the Bible. It might also carry the thought that assurance of salvation comes through the word of God.

Salvation is **through faith which is in Christ Jesus**. We should mark this well. It is not through good works, baptism, church membership, confirmation, obeying the Ten Commandments, keeping the Golden Rule, or in any other way that involves human effort or merit. **Salvation** is **through faith** in the Son of God.

3:16 When Paul speaks of **all Scripture**, he is definitely referring to the complete OT, but also to those portions of the NT that were then in existence. In 1 Timothy 5:18, he quotes the Gospel of Luke (10:7) as Scripture. And Peter speaks of Paul's Epistles as Scriptures (2 Pet. 3:16). Today we are justified in applying the verse to the entire Bible.

This is one of the most important verses in the Bible on the subject of inspiration. It teaches that the Scriptures are God-breathed.[27] In a miraculous way, He communicated His word to men and led them to write it down for permanent preservation. What they wrote was the very word of God, inspired and infallible. While it is true that the individual literary style of the writer was not destroyed, it is also true that the very words he used were words given to him by the Holy Spirit. Thus we read in 1 Corinthians 2:13: "These things we also speak, not in words which man's wisdom teaches but which the Holy Spirit teaches; comparing spiritual things with spiritual." If this verse says anything at all, it says that the inspired writers used WORDS which the Holy Spirit taught. This is what is meant by *verbal* inspiration.

The writers of the Bible did not give their own private interpretation of things, but wrote the message which was given to them by God. "Knowing this first, that no prophecy of Scripture is of any private interpretation, for prophecy never came by the will of man, but holy men of God spoke as they were moved by the Holy Spirit" (2 Pet. 1:20, 21).

It is false to say that God simply gave the thoughts to the individual writers and allowed them to express these thoughts in their own words. The truth insisted on in the Scriptures is that the very words originally given by **God** to men were God-breathed.

Because the Bible is the word of God, it **is profitable**. Every portion of it **is profitable**. Although man might wonder about some of the genealogies or obscure passages, yet the Spirit-taught mind will realize that there is spiritual nourishment in every word that has proceeded from the mouth of God.

The Bible **is profitable for doctrine**, or teaching. It sets forth the mind of God with regard to such themes as the Trinity, angels, man, sin, salvation, sanctification, the church, and future events.

Again, it is profitable **for reproof**. As we read the Bible, it speaks to us pointedly concerning those things in our lives which are displeasing to God. Also, it is profitable for refuting error and for answering the tempter.

Again, the word is profitable **for correction**. It not only points out what is wrong but sets forth the way in which it can be made right. For instance, the Scriptures not only say, "Let him who stole steal no longer," but add, "Rather let him labor, working with his hands what is good, that he may have something to give to him who has need." The first part of the verse might be considered as **reproof**, whereas the second part is **correction**.

Finally, the Bible is profitable **for instruction in righteousness**. The grace of God teaches us to live godly lives, but the word of God traces out in detail the things which go to make up a godly life.

3:17 Through the word, **the man of God may be complete** or mature. He is **thoroughly equipped** with all that he needs to bring forth **every good work** which makes up the goal of his salvation (Eph. 2:8–10). This is in sharp contrast to the modern ideas of being equipped by means of academic degrees.

Lenski writes:

> The Scripture is thus absolutely incomparable; no other book, library, or anything else in the world is able to make a lost sinner wise for salvation; no other scripture, since it lacks inspiration of God, whatever profit it may otherwise afford, is profitable for these ends: teaching us

the true saving facts — refuting the lies and the delusions that deny these facts — restoring the sinner or fallen Christian to an upright position — educating, training, disciplining one in genuine righteousness.[28]

4:1 Paul now begins his final solemn charge to Timothy. He does so in the sight of **God and the Lord Jesus Christ**. All service should be carried out with the realization that it is watched by God's all-seeing eye.

In this verse, the Lord Jesus is spoken of as the One **who will judge the living and the dead at His appearing and His kingdom**. The English word **at** might suggest that when the Savior returns to earth to set up His kingdom, there will be a general resurrection and a general judgment. But in the original the Greek word *kata*[29] literally means "according to" or "in accordance with."

The Lord Jesus *is* the One **who will judge the living and the dead**, but no *time* is specified. Christ's **appearing and His kingdom** are presented by Paul as motives for faithful service.

We know from other Scriptures that the Second Coming of Christ is *not* the time when He will judge the living and the dead. *The wicked dead* will not be judged until the end of the Thousand-year Reign of Christ, according to Revelation 20:5.

The believer's service will be rewarded at the Judgment Seat of Christ, but these rewards will be manifested **at Christ's appearing and His kingdom**. It appears that rewards have to do with rule or administration during the Millennium. For instance, those who have been faithful will rule over ten cities (Luke 19:17).

4:2 In view of God's present observation of His servants and of His future reward, Timothy should herald **the word**. He should do so with a sense of urgency, availing himself of every opportunity. The message is **in season** at all times, even when some might think it to be **out of season**. As a servant of Christ, Timothy will be called upon to **convince**, that is, to prove or refute. He will have to **rebuke** what is false. He will be required to **exhort** or encourage sinners to believe and saints to go on for the Lord. In all of this, he must be unfailing in patient **longsuffering and** in the faithful **teaching** of sound doctrine.

4:3 In verses 3–6, the apostle gives two strong reasons for the charge he has just given. The first is that there will be a general turning away from wholesome **doctrine**. The second is that Paul's time of departure is at hand.

The apostle foresees a time when people will show a positive distaste for health-giving teaching. They will willfully turn away from those who teach the truth of God's word. Their **ears** will itch for doctrines that are pleasing and comfortable. To satisfy their lust for novel and gratifying doctrine, **they will** accumulate a group of **teachers** who will tell them what they want to hear.

4:4 The lust for inoffensive preaching will cause people to **turn their ears away from the truth** to myths. It is a poor exchange — to sacrifice truth for **fables** — but this is the wretched reward of those who refuse sound doctrine.

4:5 To **be watchful in all things** really means to be sober **in all things**. Timothy should be serious in his work, temperate, and well-balanced. He should not shun **afflictions** but should suffer willingly whatever hardships might come to him in his service for Christ.

There is some difference of opinion as to the expression **do the work of an evangelist.** Some think that Timothy actually *was* **an evangelist** and that here Paul was simply telling him to carry out this ministry. Others think that Timothy did not have the *gift* of evangelism, being perhaps a pastor or teacher, but that this should not prevent him from preaching the gospel as occasion arose. It seems likely that Timothy actually was **an evangelist** and that Paul's words are simply an encouragement for him to be all that evangelists should be.

In every respect, he should **fulfill** his **ministry**, devoting his finest talents to all the demands of his service.

4:6 The second reason for Paul's solemn charge to Timothy was his own approaching death. He was now about to be **poured out as a drink offering**. He likens the shedding of his blood in martyrdom to the pouring out of **a drink offering** over a sacrifice (see Ex. 29:40; Num. 15:1–10). Paul had previously likened his death to a drink offering in

Philippians 2:17. Hiebert says: "His whole life has been presented to God as a living sacrifice; now his death, comparable to the pouring out of the wine as the last act of the sacrificial ceremony, will complete the sacrifice."[30]

The time of my departure is at hand. The Greek word *analusis* (literally "up-loosing," whence English "analysis"), which Paul uses here to describe his **departure**, is a most expressive one, giving at least four different word pictures: (1) It was a seaman's word, used of the "un-loosing" of a ship from its anchorage. (2) It was a plowman's word, denoting the "unyoking" of a weary team of animals after a hard day. (3) It was a traveler's expression, suggesting the "striking" of a tent, preparatory to setting out on a march. (4) It was a philosopher's term, signifying the "solution" (analysis) of a problem. Here again we see the richness of the imagery used by the great apostle.

4:7 At first glance, it might seem as if Paul were boasting in this verse. However, such is not the case. The thought is not so much that he had fought *a* good fight, but rather that he had **fought** and was still fighting *the* **good fight**, namely, the fight of faith. He had spent his energies in the good contest. **Fight** here does not necessarily mean combat, but might just as well indicate an athletic contest.

Even as he wrote, he realized that **the** strenuous **race** was nearly over. He had been running on the course and was in sight of the goal.

Then, too, Paul had **kept the faith**. This means not only that Paul himself had continued to believe in and obey the great doctrines of **the** Christian **faith**, but also that, as a steward, he had guarded the doctrine which had been committed to him and had passed it on to others in its original purity.

4:8 The apostle here expresses confidence that the **righteousness** which he had manifested in his service would be rewarded by the righteous Lord at the Judgment Seat of Christ.

The Lord is here spoken of as **the righteous Judge**, but the thought is not that of a criminal court judge but of one at an athletic contest. Unlike earthly judges, He will have full and complete knowledge, He will not show respect of persons, He will evaluate motives as well as deeds, and His judgments will be accurate and impartial.

The crown of righteousness is the garland (here, not a diadem) which will be given to those believers who have exhibited **righteousness** in their service. Indeed, it will be given **to all** those **who have loved** Christ's **appearing**. If a man really longs with affection for the coming of Christ and lives in the light of that event, then his life will be righteous, and he will be rewarded accordingly. Here is a fresh reminder that the Second Coming of Christ, when truly believed and loved, exercises a sanctifying influence on one's life.

IV. PERSONAL REQUESTS AND REMARKS (4:9–22)

4:9 Paul, the aged, longs to have the companionship of his younger brother in the Lord. He therefore urges him to do his best **to come** to Rome in the near future. The apostle was feeling keenly the loneliness of his imprisonment in Rome.

4:10 One of the bitterest experiences in Christian service is to be forsaken by those who were formerly one's fellow laborers. **Demas** had been a friend of Paul's, a fellow believer, and a fellow worker. But now Paul was in prison, Christians were being persecuted, and the political climate was distinctly unhealthful for Christians. Instead of loving the Lord's appearing, **Demas** fell in love with **this present world**, and so left Paul and **departed for Thessalonica**. This does not necessarily mean that Demas gave up his Christian profession and became an apostate. Neither does it mean that he was not a true believer. Possibly his fears for his personal safety caused him to become a backslider.

The apostle then adds that **Crescens** had gone to **Galatia**, and **Titus** to **Dalmatia**. There is no suggestion of blame in these words; perhaps they had gone to these places on Christian service. This is the only mention of **Crescens** (whose name means "growing") in the Bible. We know nothing more about him. This should be an encouragement to all believers. No matter how humble their position in life may be, even an errand run for the Lord will not go unnoticed or unrewarded.

4:11 The beloved Doctor **Luke** was the only one who maintained contact with Paul in Rome. How much it must have meant to the apostle to have the spiritual encouragement and professional skill of this great man of God!

And how thankful we can be for the latter part of verse 11! It holds encouragement to all of us who have failed the Lord in our service that He will yet give us another opportunity to go forth for Him. **Mark** went with Paul and Barnabas on their First Missionary Journey, but then left them at Perga to return home. When it came time to go out on the Second Missionary Journey, Paul did not want to bring Mark along because of the young man's previous retreat. When Barnabas insisted that Mark should accompany them, the matter was resolved by Paul's leaving for Syria and Cilicia with Silas, while Barnabas and Mark went to Cyprus. Later on, Paul and Mark were reconciled, and here the apostle specifically asks for **Mark** as one who **is useful to** him **for ministry**.

4:12 Those who believe that Timothy was in Ephesus when Paul wrote this Letter to him suggest that the apostle sent **Tychicus to Ephesus** as a replacement during Timothy's approaching absence. They suggest that Paul's meaning here is: "But **Tychicus** I am commissioning to go **to Ephesus**."

4:13 **The cloak** mentioned here may be either an outer garment or a bag used for carrying books. It is generally understood to refer to the former here.

There is no agreement as to the difference between **the books** and **the parchments**.[31] Were they portions of Scripture? Were they some of Paul's Letters? Were they papers which he would be using at his trial? Were they blank pieces of papyrus or parchment which he wanted to use for writing? It is impossible to decide definitely. But the strong suggestion is that even in his imprisonment, the apostle wanted to keep busy with his writing and his reading.

An interesting true story is told in connection with this apparently unimportant Bible verse. F. W. Newman, Cardinal Newman's younger brother, once asked J. N. Darby how we could possibly be any the poorer if this verse were not in the Bible. Was it not of temporary value only? Would anything be lost if Paul had never written it? Darby promptly replied: "I would certainly have lost something; for this is the verse that saved me from selling my library. Every word, depend upon it, is from the Spirit, and is for eternal service."[32]

4:14 **Alexander the coppersmith** may have been the same one referred to by Paul in 1 Timothy 1:20 as having made shipwreck of the faith. In any event, he had done great **harm** to the apostle. We can only speculate as to the nature of his evil. Linking this verse with the verses that follow, it seems probable that **Alexander** testified against the apostle and brought false charges against him. Conybeare and Howson translate: "Alexander the coppersmith charged me with much evil." The apostle is confident that **the Lord** will **repay him according to his works**.

4:15 This verse anticipates Timothy's arrival in Rome. He **also must beware of** Alexander, lest he, too, suffer at the hands of this evil man. It is not unlikely that Alexander **greatly resisted** Paul's **words** by opposing his testimony at the public hearing.

4:16 Paul is probably still thinking of the events of the past few days. His **first defense** means the first opportunity which he was given to defend himself at this, his last trial.[33] It does seem sad indeed that **no one stood** up to speak a word in behalf of this valiant apostle whose writings have enriched the subsequent centuries. No one would undertake his defense, but there is no bitterness in his heart for all that. Like the Savior before him, he prays that **it** might **not be charged against them**.

4:17 He may have been forsaken by men, **but the Lord stood with** him. Not only so, but he was divinely strengthened to preach the gospel at his trial. The message went forth without hindrance, and a Gentile law court heard the message of salvation. Stock marvels:

All the Gentiles — what a throng of distinguished Romans may be included in

that simple phrase! — heard that day the message of God to mankind; all heard the Crucified and Exalted Jesus set forth as the One Savior. It is an overwhelming thought; the imagination fails to realize so tremendous a scene; it must have been one of the great moments of history; and what may not Eternity reveal to us of its results?[34]

The word **strengthened** in this verse is not a common one; it is found only eight times in the NT. It is used in Acts 9:22 at the beginning of Paul's public ministry: he "increased . . . in strength." Here it is used again, but now at the end of his public ministry — a touching reminder of the sustaining strength of the Lord throughout His servant's life.

The expression **"I was delivered out of the mouth of the lion"** is a way of saying that Paul was granted a temporary delay. The trial was continued. The danger was temporarily averted. Attempts have been made to identify the lion as Nero, the devil, and literal wild animals. But perhaps it is simpler to understand the word as meaning danger in general.

4:18 When the apostle said **the Lord** would **deliver** him **from every evil work**, he did not imply that he would be indefinitely delivered from execution. He knew that the time of his death was drawing near (v. 6). What then did he mean? Doubtless he meant that the Lord would save him from doing anything that would be a blot on the closing days of his testimony. The Lord would deliver him from recanting, from denying His name, from cowardice, or from any form of moral breakdown.

Not only so, but Paul was sure that the Lord would **preserve** him **for His heavenly kingdom**. The **heavenly kingdom** refers not to Christ's Millennial Reign on earth, but to heaven itself, where the rule of the Lord is acknowledged perfectly.

Here the apostle bursts into an ascription of **glory** to God **forever and ever**. **Forever and ever** is literally "to the ages of the ages" and the words represent the strongest expression of eternality possible in the Greek language. Technically, there are no "ages" in eternity, but since the human mind has no conception of timelessness, it is compelled to use expressions of time.

4:19 Now Paul sends greetings to a married couple who had served with him often in the gospel. **Prisca** (or Priscilla) **and Aquila** first met Paul in Corinth, and then traveled with him to Ephesus. They lived for a time in Rome (Rom. 16:3), and, like Paul, were tentmakers.

Onesiphorus was previously mentioned in 1:16 as one who had often refreshed the apostle and had not been ashamed of his imprisonment.

4:20 Perhaps **Erastus** is the same one who was treasurer of the city of **Corinth** (Rom. 16:23).

Trophimus is mentioned previously in Acts 20:4 and 21:29. Converted in Ephesus, he had accompanied Paul to Jerusalem. The Jews there thought that Paul had taken him into the temple. Here we read that Paul had **left** him **in Miletus sick**. This statement is important in showing that, although the apostle had the miraculous power of healing, he did not always use it. The miracle of healing was never employed as a matter of personal convenience, but rather as a testimony to unbelieving Jews as to the truth of the gospel.

4:21 Timothy should do his **utmost to come before winter** weather made travel difficult or impossible. His imprisoned friend in Rome needed his presence and was waiting for him. The repeated exhortations to Timothy **to come** are very touching (see 1:3, 4; 4:9).

Next we have greetings to Timothy from **Eubulus, Pudens, Linus, Claudia, and all the brethren**. These names might seem of little consequence, but they are a touching reminder, as Rodgers says, that "one of the special joys and privileges of Christian service is the way in which friendships are created and enriched."

4:22 And now Paul brings his last Epistle to a close. Speaking to Timothy in particular, he says, **"The Lord Jesus Christ[35] be with your spirit."** Then, addressing all those who were with Timothy at the time he received the Letter, the apostle adds: **"Grace be with your spirit. Amen."**

Here he lays down his pen. The Letter is finished. His ministry is ended.

But the fragrance of his life and testimony abides with us still, and we shall meet him again and talk with him about the grand themes of the gospel and the church.

ENDNOTES

[1](1:1) W. E. Vine, *Exposition of the Epistles to Timothy*, pp. 60, 61.

[2](1:2) D. Edmond Hiebert, *Second Timothy*, p. 26.

[3](1:3) The Greek word is *latreuō*, related to *latreia*, "worship" (cf. English "mariolatry," the adoration of Mary).

[4](1:4) Hiebert, *Second Timothy*, p. 31.

[5](1:5) The Greek for "genuine" is literally "unhypocritical." By derivation a hypocrite is a play-actor who answers from under (*hupo*) his mask.

[6](1:6) Vine, *Exposition*, under the verses listed.

[7](1:11) The critical (NU) text omits "of the Gentiles."

[8](1:16) J. H. Jowett, *Things that Matter Most*, p. 161.

[9](2:3) NU text reads "share."

[10](2:4) William Kelly, *An Exposition of the Two Epistles to Timothy*, p. 213.

[11](2:7) The critical (NU) text reads "the Lord will give you" (future indicative, not a prayer).

[12](2:8) Hiebert, *Second Timothy*, p. 59.

[13](2:9) Harvey, further documentation unavailable.

[14](2:10) The beloved hymn "Immanuel's Land" was written by Anne Ross Cousin, but, it is said, using phraseology from Samuel Rutherford's writings.

[15](2:11) Hiebert, *Second Timothy*, p. 62.

[16](2:13) Dinsdale T. Young, *Unfamiliar Texts*, p. 253.

[17](2:13) J. J. Van Oosterzee, "The Pastoral Letters," *Lange's Commentary on the Holy Scriptures*, XI:95.

[18](2:14) Dinsdale T. Young, *The Enthusiasm of God*, p. 154.

[19](2:15) Henry Alford, *The Greek Testament*, III:384.

[20](2:17) The Greek word here is *gangraina*, but that does not necessarily mean that our English derivative is the best *translation*.

[21](2:18) Hamilton Smith, further documentation unavailable.

[22](2:19) Hamilton Smith, *The Second Epistle to Timothy*, p. 27.

[23](2:19) R. C. H. Lenski, *The Interpre-*

tation of St. Paul's Epistles to the Colossians, to the Thessalonians, to Timothy, to Titus and to Philemon, p. 804.

²⁴(2:19) Both the NU and M texts read "Lord" for "Christ," which makes it close to Num. 16:5.

²⁵(2:22) Hiebert, *Second Timothy,* p. 76.

²⁶(3:5) Hiebert, *ibid.,* p. 86.

²⁷(3:16) The Greek word is *theopneustos.*

²⁸(3:17) Lenski, *Epistles, p. 841.*

²⁹(4:1) *The critical text reads kai ("and") for kata.*

³⁰(4:6) Hiebert, *Second Timothy,* pp. 109, 110.

³¹(4:13) Greek, *membranas.* These ex-pensive mss. were probably Bible books or perhaps commentaries.

³²(4:13) Quoted by H. A. Ironside, *Timothy, Titus and Philemon,* p. 255.

³³(4:16) Conceivably the trial at the end of Paul's *first* imprisonment is meant.

³⁴(4:17) Eugene Stock, *Plain Talks on the Pastoral Epistles,* pagination unavailable.

³⁵(4:22) NU text omits *Jesus Christ.*

BIBLIOGRAPHY

See Bibliography at the end of 1 Timothy.

THE EPISTLE TO TITUS

Introduction

"This is a short epistle, but it contains such a quintessence of Christian doctrine, and is composed in such a masterly manner, that it contains all that is needful for Christian knowledge and life."   — Martin Luther

I. Unique Place in the Canon

Three short chapters written over nineteen centuries ago to a little-known missionary on an obscure island by an aging senior missionary — what possible relevance could these have for Christians in the "enlightened" twentieth century? Granted, if they were *only* the words of Paul (and most liberals will not even grant *that!*) they could have merely an interest for church history buffs or those majoring in early Christian thought.

But these are also "words which the Holy Spirit teaches," and as such have a contribution to make that *no other book* can fill. The handling of the subject of elders strengthens and supports the very similar teaching found in 1 Timothy. The repetition is not redundant, but like so many other parallels in the Bible, especially in the OT, merely emphasizes how much God desires His people to grasp certain principles.

Probably the most prized passage in Titus is 2:11–14, which is written with a lovely balanced style that enhances the doctrine of grace.

II. Authorship

See the Introduction to the Pastoral Epistles for a discussion of the authorship of the Epistle to Titus.

III. Date

Because of the similarity of themes and wording, Titus is believed by conservative scholars to have been written about the same time or soon after 1 Timothy. At any rate it came *between* 1 and 2 Timothy in time, not after 2 Timothy. While an exact date is impossible to give, sometime between A.D. 64 and 66 is likely. The place of origin is probably Macedonia.

IV. Theme[†]

Besides the general themes that Titus shares in common with the other two Pastoral Epistles (see Introduction to the Pastoral Epistles), Titus gives a fine concise summary of how a believer should adorn the doctrine of *grace* with *godliness* and *good works*. Many today who seem pleased with the doctrine of grace apparently have little interest in displaying it in good works, or even godliness. Such an attitude is wrong and suggests a misapprehension of true grace.

Paul sums up the theme perfectly: "This is a faithful saying, and these things I want you to affirm constantly, that those who have believed in God should be careful to maintain good works" (3:8a).

[†]*See p. ii.*

OUTLINE

Commentary

I. SALUTATION (1:1–4)

1:1 **Paul** was both **a bondservant of God and an apostle of Jesus Christ**. The first pictures him as a slave of the Supreme Master, the second as an envoy of the Sovereign Lord. The first speaks of submission, the second of authority. He became a **bondservant** by personal commitment, an **apostle** by divine appointment.

The goals of his ministry were to further **the faith of God's elect and the acknowledgement of the truth**. Furthering their **faith** may mean either bringing them *to faith* or conversion in the first place, or leading them on *in the faith* after salvation. Since the phrase, the **acknowledgement of the truth** seems to cover the second meaning, we understand the apostle to mean that his two basic aims were: (1) *evangelism* —furthering **the faith of God's elect**; (2) *education* — furthering their knowledge **of the truth**. It is an echo of Matthew 28:20 — preaching the gospel to all nations and teaching them to observe all things Christ commanded. In specifying without apology that it is **the faith of God's elect** he is called to promote, the apostle confronts us with the doctrine of election. Few doctrines of Scripture have suffered more misunderstanding, provoked more debate, and strained more intellects. Briefly, it teaches that God chose certain ones in Christ before the foundation of the world with the ultimate intention that they should be holy and blameless before Him (Eph. 1:4).[1]

Having spoken of his apostleship as being involved with **the faith of God's elect** and their **acknowledgement of the truth**, Paul now adds that this **truth accords with godliness**. This means that the Christian faith is consistent with true holiness and is adapted to lead men to practical **godliness**. Soundness in faith demands purity in life. Nothing could be more incongruous than the preacher of whom it was said, "When he was in the pulpit, the people wished he would never leave it. When he was out of the pulpit, they wished he would never enter it!"

1:2 Paul's commission in connection with the gospel has a third great emphasis. It was not only concerned with: (1) *evangelism* — furthering the faith of God's elect, past tense; and (2) *education* — furthering their knowledge of the truth, present tense; but also (3) *expectation* — **in hope of eternal life**, future tense.

The NT speaks of **eternal life** as both a present possession and a future hope. The word **hope** does not imply uncertainty. The moment we trust Christ as Savior we have eternal life as a present possession (John 5:24) and become heirs to all the benefits of His redemptive work, but we will not experience the practical enjoyment of all of them until we reach our eternal home. We **hope** in the sense that we are looking forward to **eternal life** in its final form when we will receive our glorified bodies and be forever free from sin, sickness, sorrow, suffering, and death (Phil. 3:20, 21; Tit. 3:7).

The **hope** is sure because it was **promised** by God. Nothing is as sure as the word of **God, who cannot lie**, who cannot be deceived, and who would not deceive. There is no risk in believing what He says. In fact nothing is more reasonable than for the creature to believe his Creator.

God promised eternal life **before time**

began. This may be understood in two ways. First, God determined in past eternity to give eternal life to all who would believe on the Lord Jesus, and what He determined was the same as a promise. Or it may mean that all the blessings of salvation were contained in germ form in the promise of the Messiah found in Genesis 3:15. This was before the ages of time or dispensations began to unfold.

1:3   In due time God made known this glorious program of eternal life which He had decided on in past ages. He had not fully revealed it in OT times. Believers then had a very hazy idea of life after death. But the vagueness disappeared with the coming of the Savior. He "brought life and immortality to light through the gospel" (2 Tim. 1:10). And the good news was broadcast by Paul and the other apostles in fulfillment of **the commandment of God our Savior**, that is, in obedience to the Great Commission.

1:4 The Letter is addressed **to Titus**, Paul's **true son in** a **common faith**. But who is this Titus?

We have to piece together his biography from sparse references to him in three of Paul's Letters. A Greek by birth (Gal. 2:3), he was born again by faith in the Lord Jesus, possibly through Paul's ministry (Tit. 1:4). A battle was then raging over what was the true gospel. On one side were Paul and all those who taught salvation by grace through faith plus nothing. On the other side were the Judaizers who insisted that circumcision (and thus lawkeeping) was requisite for first-class citizenship in God's kingdom. Titus became a test case in the controversy. Paul and Barnabas took him to Jerusalem (Gal. 2:1) for a conference with the apostles and elders. The decision of the council was that a Gentile like Titus did not have to submit to Jewish laws and ceremonies in order to be saved (Acts 15:11). Gentiles did not have to become Jews. Jews did not have to become Gentiles. Rather, Jews and Gentiles became a new creation when they believed in Jesus.

Thereafter Titus became one of Paul's most valuable assistants, serving as a "trouble-shooter" in Corinth and Crete. The apostle first sent him from Ephesus to Corinth, presumably to cor-

rect doctrinal and ethical disorders in the assembly there. When Titus later rejoined Paul in Macedonia, Paul was overjoyed to hear that the Corinthians had responded positively to his apostolic admonitions (2 Cor. 2:12, 13; 7:5–7, 13–16). From Macedonia, Paul sent Titus to Corinth again, this time to expedite a collection for poor saints in Jerusalem (2 Cor. 8:6, 16, 17; 12:18). Paul described him as "my partner and fellow worker concerning you" (2 Cor. 8:23). We do not definitely know when Paul was with Titus in Crete, but it is generally believed to have been after the apostle's first imprisonment in Rome.

The last mention of Titus is in 2 Timothy 4:10. He was with Paul during part of his second imprisonment, but then Paul reports him as having left for Dalmatia, the Yugoslavia of today. Paul may have sent him there, though the general tone of the verse is that of a lonely and deserted man.

The apostle speaks of Titus as his **true son in** a **common faith**. This may mean that Paul was instrumental in Titus' conversion, but not necessarily. Paul also addressed Timothy as his true son in the faith (1 Tim. 1:2), yet it is possible that Timothy was already a disciple when Paul first met him (Acts 16:1). So the expression may mean that these younger men exhibited spiritual qualities similar to Paul's, and that in Christian service there was a filial bond.

For his young lieutenant Paul wishes **grace, mercy, and peace**. In this context, **grace** means the divine strength needed for life and service. **Mercy** is compassion on man's deep need. **Peace** means freedom from anxiety, panic, and distraction despite adverse circumstances. These come jointly **from God the Father and the Lord Jesus Christ our Savior**. In thus linking the Father and the Son as the sources of **grace, mercy, and peace**, the Spirit of God implies their complete equality.

II. ELDERS IN THE CONGREGATION (1:5–9)

1:5 When Paul left Crete, there were certain **things** that still needed to be **set in order**, there were false teachers to be silenced, and there was the pressing need for recognized spiritual guides in the assemblies. He left Titus to handle these matters.

We do not know how the Christian faith first came to Crete. Perhaps the best guess is that Cretans who were in Jerusalem on the Day of Pentecost (Acts 2:11) returned with the good news, and that local churches were subsequently established.

Neither can we be sure as to when Paul was in Crete with Titus. We know that he touched in at Crete on his voyage to Rome as a prisoner (Acts 27:12), but the circumstances would hardly have permitted active ministry in the churches. Since Acts makes no other reference to Paul's being in Crete, it is generally supposed that the visit took place after his first Roman imprisonment. Resorting to a little biblical detective work, we can reconstruct the following itinerary from various references in Paul's writings.

First Paul sailed from Italy to Crete on his way to Asia (Western Turkey today). Leaving Titus in Crete (Tit. 1:5), he traveled to Ephesus, the capital of Asia. At Ephesus he deputized Timothy to correct doctrinal errors that were creeping in there (1 Tim. 1:3, 4). Then he sailed across the Aegean Sea to Macedonia to fulfill his prior intention while in prison to visit Philippi as soon as he was free (Phil. 1:26). Finally, he traveled southwest across Greece to Nicopolis, where he planned to stay for the winter and where he expected Titus to join him (Tit. 3:12).

According to Homer, there were between ninety and one hundred cities in Crete as early as his time, and churches had apparently been formed in several of them. In each there was a need for responsible **elders** to be appointed.

ELDERS

Elders in the NT sense are mature Christian men of sterling character who provide spiritual leadership in a local assembly. The name elder, which refers to the spiritual maturity of the man, is translated from the Greek word *presbuteros*, (which turned into the English "presbyter"). The Greek word *episkopos*, translated "bishop," "overseer" or "guardian," is also used in reference

to elders, describing their function as undershepherds of God's flock.

The names "elders" and "bishops" are generally understood to refer to the same persons for the following reasons. In Acts 20:17, Paul called for the elders (*presbuteroi*) from Ephesus; in verse 28 he addressed them as guardians (*episkopoi*). In 1 Peter 5:1, 2, Peter similarly uses the terms interchangeably. The qualifications for bishops (*episkopoi*) in 1 Timothy 3 and those for elders (*presbuteroi*) in Titus 1 are substantially the same.

In modern usage, "bishop" has come to mean a prelate who supervises a diocese or a group of churches in a district. But the word never means this in the NT. The scriptural pattern is to have *several* bishops in *one* church rather than *one* bishop over *several* churches.

Nor should an elder be confused with the modern pastor, who is primarily responsible for preaching, teaching, and administering the sacraments in a local church. It is generally acknowledged that there was no such person in the early church. The primitive assemblies were composed of saints, bishops, and deacons (Phil. 1:1) — that is all. The clerical system did not rise until the second century.

A pastor in the NT sense is one of the special-service gifts which the risen, ascended Christ bestowed to build up the saints for the work of ministering (Eph. 4:11, 12). In many respects the work of pastors and elders is similar; both are called to tend and feed the flock of God. But the two are never equated. Conceivably, a pastor may have a traveling ministry, while an elder is usually associated with one local assembly.

The functions of elders are given in considerable detail:

1. They shepherd and care for the church of the Lord (Acts 20:28; 1 Tim. 3:5; 1 Pet. 5:2).

2. They are alert to protect the church from attacks, both from without and within (Acts 20:29–31).

3. They lead and rule, but by guiding, not driving (1 Thess. 5:12; 1 Tim. 5:17; Heb. 13:7, 17; 1 Pet. 5:3).

4. They preach the word, teach sound doctrine, and refute those who contradict it (1 Tim. 5:17; Tit. 1:9–11).

5. They moderate and arbitrate in doctrinal and ethical matters (Acts 15:5, 6; 16:4).

6. By their life they are an example to the flock (Heb. 13:7; 1 Pet. 5:3).

7. They seek to restore the believers who have been overtaken in any trespass (Gal. 6:1).

8. They keep watch over the souls of Christians in the local assembly as those who will have to give account (Heb. 13:17).

9. They exercise a ministry of prayer, especially with regard to the sick (Jas. 5:14, 15).

10. They are involved in the care of poor saints (Acts 11:30).

11. They share in the commendation of gifted men to the work to which God has called them (1 Tim. 4:14).

It is clear that in the early church, elders were appointed by the apostles and their representatives (Acts 14:23; Tit. 1:5). This does not mean, however, that the apostles and their delegates had the power to *make* a man an elder. In order to become a bishop, there must be both divine enablement and human willingness. Only the Holy Spirit can make a man a bishop or guardian (Acts 20:28), but the man must aspire to the work (1 Tim. 3:1). There must be this mingling of the divine and the human.

When local churches were first established in the apostolic days, there were no elders in them; all the believers were novices. But as time passed, the Lord prepared certain ones for this important ministry. Since the NT was not yet available in written form, Christians in general did not know the qualifications and duties of elders. Only the apostles and their assistants knew. On the basis of this knowledge, they singled out the men who met the divine standards and publicly named them as such.

Today we have the complete NT. We know what an elder is and what he is supposed to do. When we see qualified men who are actively serving as overseers, we recognize them (1 Thess. 5:12) and obey them (Heb. 13:17). It is not a question of *our* electing them but of recognizing those whom *God* has raised up for this work.

The qualifications of elders are found in 1 Timothy 3:1–7 and here in Titus.

Sometimes we hear the remark that if these are the requirements, then there are no bishops today. This idea downgrades the authority of the Scriptures by implying that they don't mean what they say. There is nothing unreasonable or unattainable in the standards given. We betray our own low spiritual state when we treat the Bible as excessively idealistic. ‡

1:6 Elders are men who are **blameless**, that is, of unquestioned integrity. No charge of false doctrine or irregular behavior can be proved against them. It does not mean that they are sinless, but that if they do minor wrongs, they are prompt to make them right by confession to God, by apology to the person(s) wronged, and by restitution, if applicable.

The second qualification, that they be **the husband of one wife**, has been understood in at least seven different ways: (1) a man must be married; (2) he must not be divorced; (3) he must not be remarried after divorce; (4) he must not be remarried after the death of his first wife; (5) he must not be a polygamist; (6) he must not have concubines or lesser wives; (7) in general, he must be a faithful husband and an example of strict morality.

If the phrase **husband of one wife** means that a man must be married, then by the same reasoning he must have children, because this same verse states that his **children** must be believers. Certainly it is preferable for an elder to have a family; he can deal more intelligently with family problems in the congregation. But it is doubtful that this verse prohibits any unmarried man from being an elder.

It probably does not mean that he must not be divorced under any circumstances, because the Savior taught that divorce is permissible in at least one instance (Matt. 5:32; 19:9).[2]

Neither can it be taken as an absolute prohibition of remarriage after divorce in all cases. For example, a believer who is entirely innocent might be divorced by an unbelieving wife who then remarries. In such a case, the Christian was not responsible. Since the first marriage was broken by the divorce and remarriage of his unbelieving partner, he is free to re-marry.

The interpretation that eligibility for the work of an elder is forfeited if a man remarries after the death of his first wife is ruled out by the principle stated in 1 Corinthians 7:39: "A wife is bound by law as long as her husband lives; but if her husband dies, she is at liberty to be married to whom she wishes, only in the Lord."

Certainly the expression **the husband of one wife** means that an elder must not be a polygamist nor have a concubine or mistress. In summary, it means that his married life must be an example of purity to the flock.

In addition he must have **faithful children not accused of dissipation or insubordination**. More than most of us care to admit, the Bible holds parents responsible for the way their children turn out (Prov. 22:6). When a family is well-governed and well-trained in the word of God, the **children** generally follow the godly example of their parents. Although a father cannot determine the salvation of his children, he can prepare the way of the Lord by positive instruction in the word, by loving discipline, and by avoiding hypocrisy and inconsistency in his own life.

If children are spendthrifts and rebels against parental authority, the Scriptures lay the responsibility at the father's door. His indulgence and permissiveness have been to blame. If he cannot rule his own family well, it is unlikely that he would be a suitable elder, since the same principles apply in each case (1 Tim. 3:5).

There is a question whether this requirement concerning **faithful children** applies only as long as children are under parental authority in the home, or whether it includes those who are away from home. We favor the first view, remembering, however, that home training is one of the principal determinants of ultimate character.

1:7 A bishop is **a steward of God**. It is not *his* congregation that he helps to oversee. He is deputized to handle God's affairs in God's assembly. For the second time it is specified that he must be **blameless** — surely this is repetition for emphasis. Let there be no doubt — he must be a man who is above reproach both doctrinally and morally. He must **not** be **self-willed**. If a man is headstrong, obstinately right with no possibility that those who differ might be, if he is unyielding and impatient of contradiction, then he is unsuited to be a spiritual leader. An elder is a moderator, not a dogmatic autocrat.

He must **not** be **quick-tempered**. If he has a volatile temperament, he has learned to bridle it. If he has a hot temper, he never lets it show.

He must **not** be **given to wine**. In our culture, this might seem so elementary as to scarcely need mentioning. But we must remember that the Bible was written for all cultures. In countries where wine is used by Christians as a common beverage, there is the danger of overindulgence and disorderly conduct. That lack of self-control is in view here.

The Bible distinguishes between the use of wine and its abuse. Its use in moderation as a beverage was allowed when Jesus turned the water into wine at the wedding in Cana (John 2:1–11). Its use for medicinal purposes is prescribed by Paul for Timothy (1 Tim. 5:23; see also Prov. 31:6). The abuse of wine and strong drink is condemned in Proverbs 20:1; 23:29–35. While total abstinence is not demanded in the word, there is one situation in which refraining is called for, namely, when drinking wine would offend a weaker brother or cause him to stumble (Rom. 14:21). This is the overriding consideration which causes great numbers of Christians in North American to abstain from alcohol entirely.

With the elder, the question is not the total prohibition of wine, but rather the excessive use of wine, which leads to brawling.

Neither should he be **violent**. He must not resort to the use of physical force by striking others. We have heard of officious clerics who gave an occasional blow to refractory members of their parish. This type of overbearing intimidation is forbidden for a bishop.

He must not be **greedy for money**, insatiably determined to get rich, but careless as to the means employed. It is true, as Samuel Johnson said, that "the lust of gold, unfeeling and remorseless, is the last corruption of degenerate man." A true elder can say with Paul:

"I have coveted no one's silver or gold or apparel" (Acts 20:33).

1:8 On the positive side, a bishop must be **hospitable**. His home should always be open to strangers, to those with personal problems, to the disheartened and the oppressed. It should be a place of happy Christian fellowship, where every guest is received as if he were the Lord Himself.

Next he must be **a lover of what is good** — good people and good things. His speech, his activities, and his associations should reveal that he is separated from all that is shady, questionable, or wrong.

He must be **sober-minded**. This means that he is prudent, discreet, and master of himself. The same word is used in Titus 2:2, 5, 6, 12, where it has the thought of being sensible, self-controlled, and sober.

In his dealings with others, the elder must be **just**. In relation to God he must be **holy**. In respect to himself he must be **self-controlled**. This is what Paul referred to in Galatians 5:22, 23: "The fruit of the Spirit is . . . self-control." It means that a person has every passion and appetite under control to obey Christ. While the power for this can only come from the Holy Spirit, there must be discipline and cooperation on the part of the believer.

1:9 The bishop must be sound in the faith. He must hold tenaciously to the spiritually healthful doctrines taught by the Lord Jesus and the apostles which have been preserved for us in the NT. Only then will he be able to give the saints a balanced diet of **sound doctrine**, and silence those who speak against the truth.

These are the qualifications of spiritual guides in the local assembly. It should be noticed that nothing is said about their physical prowess, educational attainments, social status, or business acumen. A hunchbacked street sweeper, homespun and unlettered, might be a qualified elder because of his spiritual stature. It is not true, as is sometimes suggested, that the same qualities that make a man successful in business also fit him for leadership in the church.

One other point should be men-

tioned. The picture that emerges of a godly elder is not that of a man who arranges for speakers, disburses funds, contracts for building repairs, and that's all! The true elder is deeply and vitally involved in the spiritual life of the church by his instruction, exhortation, encouragement, rebuke, and correction.

III. ERROR IN THE CONGRE-GATION (1:10–16)

1:10 In the early church there was "the liberty of the Spirit," that is, freedom for the men to participate in the meetings as led by the Holy Spirit. Paul describes such an "open" meeting in 1 Corinthians 14:26: "How is it then, brethren? Whenever you come together, each of you has a psalm, has a teaching, has a tongue, has a revelation, has an interpretation. Let all things be done for edification." It is an ideal situation when the Spirit of God is thus free to speak through various members of the congregation. But human nature being what it is, wherever such liberty exists, you almost invariably find men rushing in to abuse it with false doctrine, unedifying nit-picking, or seemingly endless rambling, devoid of the Spirit.

This had happened in the Cretan congregations. Paul realized that there must be strong spiritual leadership to control the abuses and to preserve the liberty of the Spirit. He also realized that great care was needed in appointing elders who were fully qualified. So here he rehearses the conditions which called for prompt action in appointing elders in the churches.

Many insubordinate men had risen up to defy the authority of the apostles and deny their teachings. They were **both idle talkers and deceivers**. Their talk produced no spiritual benefits. Rather, it robbed people of the truth and led them into error.

The principal troublemakers were **those of the circumcision** party, that is, Jewish teachers who professed to be Christians and yet insisted that Christians must be circumcised and observe the ceremonial law. This was a practical denial of the all-sufficiency of the work of Christ.

1:11 Men like this must be muzzled. They must learn that the assembly is not a democracy, and that freedom of speech has limits. They had been over-turning **whole households**. Does this suggest that they had been peddling their pernicious doctrines behind the scenes in private homes? It is a favorite method of the cults (2 Tim. 3:6). Their motives were suspect as well. They were out for money, using the ministry as a front for a lucrative business. Their message appealed to the legalistic streak in man, encouraging him to believe that he can gain God's favor by going through religious motions even though his life may be corrupt and defiled. They taught for **dishonest gain** what they had no right to teach.

1:12 Here Paul reminds Titus of the kind of people he is dealing with. The unusually blunt and caustic description was true of the false teachers in particular and of the **Cretans** in general. He quotes Epimenides, one of their own poetic spokesmen who lived around 600 B.C., as calling them inveterate **liars, evil beasts, lazy gluttons**. It seems that every people has national characteristics, but few could beat the Cretans in depravity. They were habitual and compulsive **liars**. They were like fierce animals, living to indulge gross and wild passions. Allergic to work and addicted to gluttony, they lived lives that were all kitchen and no chapel!

1:13 The apostle confirms the accuracy of the character sketch. Titus had unpromising raw materials to work with — enough to discourage any missionary! But Paul did not write the people off or counsel Titus to abandon them. Through the gospel there is hope for the worst of men. So Paul advises his assistant to **rebuke them sharply, that they may be sound** or healthy **in the** Christian **faith**. Some day these men might be not only exemplary believers, but also godly elders in the local churches. This passage overflows with encouragement for Christian workers in difficult fields of the world (and what field is not difficult?). Beyond the grossness, denseness, and unresponsiveness of the people, there is always the vision of their becoming gracious, pure, and fruitful saints.

1:14 In severely rebuking the false teachers, Titus was charged to warn them against **Jewish fables and commandments of men who turn from the truth**. The Judaizers lived in a world of religious fantasies and of rules centering around clean and unclean foods, the observance of days, and the avoidance of ceremonial defilement. It was of this which Paul wrote in Colossians 2:23: "These things indeed have an appearance of wisdom in self-imposed religion, false humility, and neglect of the body, but are of no value against the indulgence of the flesh."

1:15 What the apostle says next has given rise to such misinterpretation that it requires a detailed explanation. He writes: **"To the pure all things are pure, but to those who are defiled and unbelieving nothing is pure; but even their mind and conscience are defiled."**

If we take the words **to the pure all things are pure** out of context as a statement of *absolute* truth in *all* areas of life, we are in trouble! All things are *not* pure, even to those whose minds are pure. Yet people have actually used this verse to justify vile magazines, suggestive movies, and even immorality itself. This is what Peter speaks of as twisting the Scriptures "to their own destruction" (2 Pet. 3:16).

Let it be clearly understood that this verse has absolutely nothing to do with things that are sinful in themselves and condemned in the Bible. This proverbial saying must be understood in the light of the context. Paul has *not* been speaking about matters of clear-cut morality, of things that are inherently right or wrong. Rather, he has been discussing matters of moral indifference, things that were ceremonially defiling for a Jew living under the law but that are perfectly legitimate for a Christian living under grace. The obvious example is the eating of pork. It was forbidden to God's people in the OT, but the Lord Jesus changed all that when He said that nothing entering into a man can defile him (Mark 7:15). In saying this He pronounced all foods clean (Mark 7:19). Paul echoed this truth when he said: "But food does not commend us to God; for neither if we eat are we the better, nor if we do not eat are we the worse" (1 Cor. 8:8). When he says: **"To the pure all things are pure,"** he means that to the born again believer all foods are clean, **but to those who are defiled and unbelieving nothing is pure**. It is not what a person eats that defiles him but what comes out of his heart (Mark 7:20–23). If a man's inner life is impure, if he does not have faith in the Lord Jesus, then nothing is pure to him. The observance of dietary rules won't do a thing for him. More than anything else he needs to be converted, to receive salvation as a free gift rather than trying to earn it through rituals and legalism. The very minds and consciences of defiled people are corrupted. Their mental processes and their moral powers are defiled. It is not a question of external ceremonial defilement, but of inward corruption and depravity.

1:16 Obviously speaking of the false teachers, that is, the Judaizers, Paul says that **they profess to know God, but** by their **works they deny Him**. They pose as Christian believers, but their practice does not match their profession. To amplify his stinging castigation, the apostle denounces them as being **abominable, disobedient, and disqualified**. Their personal behavior was abhorrent. In God's eyes, theirs was a record of crass disobedience. As for good works toward God or man, they were worthless. Was it within the bounds of Christian love for Paul to speak about others in such strong language? The answer is an emphatic *yes*! Love never glosses over sin. These men were perverting the gospel, dishonoring the Person and work of the Lord Jesus, and deluding the souls of men. To be indulgent with such deceivers is sin.

IV. EXERCISE IN THE CONGREGATION (2:1–15)

2:1 The lives of the false teachers were a *libel* rather than a *Bible*. By their conduct they denied the great truths of the faith. Who can measure the damage to the Christian testimony by those who professed great sanctity but lived a lie? The task assigned to Titus (and to all true servants of the Lord) was to teach what **is proper for sound doctrine**. He was to close the awful chasm between the lips of God's people and their lives. Actually this is the keynote of the Epistle — the practical outliving of healthy doctrine in good works. The following verses give practical examples of what these good works should be.

2:2 First we come to **the older men** — not elders in the official sense, but men of physical age and maturity. They should be **sober**. Primarily this means moderate in the use of wine, but extends to mean careful in all areas of conduct. They should be **reverent** and dignified, yes, but please — not gloomy! Others have enough troubles of their own. The older men should be **temperate**, that is, balanced and discreet. They should be **sound in faith**. Age makes some people callous, bitter, and cynical. Those who are healthy in faith are thankful, optimistic, and good company. They should be sound **in love**. Love is not self-centered; it thinks of others and manifests itself in giving. And they should be vigorous **in patience**. Age has its infirmities and disabilities, often hard to take. Those who are sound in endurance bear up under their trials graciously and with fortitude.

2:3 Older women should also be **reverent in behavior**. Deliver us from giddy women whose thoughts are centered on frivolous matters! They should **not be slanderers**. The word Paul uses here is the Greek word for devil (*diabolos*). It is an apt word because malicious gossip is diabolical in its source and character. They should not be slaves to drink. In fact, they should not become enslaved by any food, beverage, or medicine. Although not assigned a *public* teaching ministry in the church, older women are commissioned to teach in the home. Who can measure the potential of such a ministry!

2:4 Specifically, an older woman should **admonish the young women**. Years of Bible study and practical experience enable her to pass on valuable counsel to those starting out in life. Otherwise each new generation is doomed to learn the hard way, repeating the mistakes of the past. While the responsibility for teaching is put on the **older**

women here, any wise young person will cultivate the friendship of godly older Christians and solicit their advice and correction.

A young woman should be taught to **love** her husband. But this means more than just kissing him when he leaves for work. It includes the myriad ways in which she can show that she really respects him — by acknowledging his headship in the home, by making no major decisions apart from him, by keeping an orderly home, by paying attention to personal appearance, by living within their means, by confessing promptly, by forgiving graciously, by keeping the lines of communication always open, by refraining from criticizing or contradicting her husband in front of others, and by being supportive when things go wrong.

They should be taught to **love their children** — by reading and praying with them, by being at home when they return from school or play, by disciplining firmly and fairly, and by molding them for the Lord's service rather than for the world — and hell.

2:5 Young women should be taught **to be discreet**. This means having a fine sense of what is appropriate for them as Christians and avoiding extremes. They should be **chaste**, faithful to their husbands and avoiding impurity in thought, word, or action. They should be good **homemakers**. They should realize that this is divine service which can be done for the glory of God. Older women should try to inculcate the high honor of serving the Lord in the home as a wife and mother rather than working in industry or business and neglecting the home and family. Young women should be taught how to be **good** — how to live for others, to be hospitable, to be gracious and generous, and not to be self-centered and possessive. They should be **obedient to their own husbands**, acknowledging them as head of the house. If a wife is more gifted and capable than her husband, rather than dominating him, she should encourage and aid him to be more active in home leadership and in serving the local church. If tempted to nag, she should resist the temptation and praise him instead. All of this is to keep **the word of God**

from being **blasphemed** or discredited. Throughout this Letter, Paul is conscious of the reproach brought upon the Lord's cause by the inconsistent lives of His people.

2:6 Paul did *not* urge Titus to teach the young women. For discretion's sake this ministry is left to the older women. But Titus is told to **exhort the young men**, and the particular admonition is that they should **be sober-minded** and control themselves. An appropriate word — since youth is the time of brimming zeal, restless energy, and burning drives. In every area of life, they need to learn continence and balance.

2:7 Paul has a special bit of advice for Titus too. As one charged with a public ministry in the churches, Titus has to exercise care to present a consistent **pattern of good works**. There should be a close parallel between his **doctrine** and his deportment. His teaching should be characterized by **integrity, reverence,** and **incorruptibility. Integrity** means that the teaching should correspond with the faith once-for-all delivered to the saints. By **reverence** Paul insists that the teaching should be dignified and sensible. **Incorruptibility**, a virtue unfortunately deleted here in most modern Bible versions,[3] has to do with the sincere teacher who cannot be corrupted from the way of truth.

2:8 Sound speech that cannot be condemned is free from anything to which exception might be taken. It should be free from side-issues, doctrinal novelties, fads, crudities, and the like. This type of ministry is irresistible. Those who oppose sound teaching are put to shame because they cannot find a chink in the believer's armor. There is no argument as effective as a holy life!

2:9 Special instructions are now given for slaves. We should remember that the Bible acknowledges the existence of institutions of which it does not necessarily approve. For instance, the OT records the polygamous lives of many of the patriarchs, yet polygamy was never God's will for His people. God has never approved of the injustices and cruelties of slavery; He will hold the masters responsible in a coming day. At the same time the NT does not advocate the overthrow of slavery by forcible revolution. Rather, it condemns and removes the abuses of slavery by the power of the gospel. History shows that the evils of slavery have disappeared wherever the word of God has been widely preached and taught.

But in the meantime, where slavery still exists, a slave is not excluded from the very best in Christianity. He can be a witness to the transforming power of Christ, and he can adorn the doctrine of God our Savior. More space in the NT is devoted to slaves than to rulers of nations! This may be a clue to their relative importance in the kingdom of God. Christian **bondservants** should be **obedient**, except when it would mean disobeying the Lord. In that case they would have to refuse and patiently suffer the consequences as Christians. They should give satisfaction in every respect, that is, be productive both as to quantity and quality. All such service can be done as to Christ and will be fully rewarded by Him. They should **not** talk **back** or be impudent. Many slaves had the privilege of leading their masters to the Lord Jesus in the early days of Christianity, largely because the difference between pagan slaves and themselves was so glaring.

2:10 One of the most obvious differences was that Christians did not succumb to the besetting sin of other slaves, namely, **pilfering**. The Christian ethic bound them to strict honesty. Is it any wonder that Christian slaves commanded higher prices at public auctions? In general they were taught to show complete and true **fidelity**. They were to be totally trustworthy and thus **adorn the doctrine of God our Savior** in every aspect of their lives and service. What was true of Christian bondservants then should be true of all Christian employees today.

2:11 The next four verses form a beautiful vignette of our salvation. But in admiring this literary gem, we must not divorce it from its setting. Paul has been urging consistent behavior on all members of the family of God. Now he shows that one of the great purposes of our salvation is to produce lives of unadulterated holiness.

For the grace of God . . . has appeared. Here **the grace of God** is virtually synonymous with the Son of God.

God's grace **appeared** when the Lord Jesus visited our planet and especially when He gave Himself for our sins. He appeared for the salvation of **all men**. His substitutionary work is sufficient for the redemption of **all**. A bona fide offer of pardon and forgiveness is made **to all**. But only those who truly receive Him as Lord and Savior are saved. There is no suggestion here or elsewhere in the Bible that everyone will be saved at last. Universal salvation is a lie of the devil.

2:12 The same grace that saves us also trains us in the school of holiness. There are "No-No's" in that school which we must learn to renounce. The first is **ungodliness**, which means irreligion. The second is **worldly lusts** — not just sexual sins, but also the lust for wealth, power, pleasure, fame, or anything else that is essentially worldly.

On the positive side, grace teaches us to **live soberly, righteously** toward others, and **godly** in the pure light of His presence. These are the virtues that should characterize us in this world, where everything about us is going to be dissolved. It is the place of our pilgrimage and not our final home.

2:13 While living as aliens in the world, we are inspired by a magnificent **hope** — the **appearing** of the glory **of our great God and Savior Jesus Christ**. By this are we to understand the Rapture, when Christ appears in glory to the church and conveys it to heaven (1 Thess. 4:13–18)? Or does it refer to Christ's coming to reign, when He appears in glory to the world, puts down His foes, and sets up His kingdom (Rev. 19:11–16)? Basically we believe Paul is speaking of the first — Christ's coming for His bride, the church. But whether it is His coming as Bridegroom or as King, the believer should be prepared and looking for His **glorious** arrival.

2:14 As we await His Return we never forget the purpose of His First Coming and of His self-sacrifice. He **gave Himself** not only to save us from the guilt and penalty of sin but to **redeem us from every lawless deed**. It would have been a half-way salvation if the penalty of sin had been canceled but its dominion in our lives was left unconquered.

He also gave Himself to **purify for**

Himself His own special people. The 1611 King James quaintly⁴ says "a peculiar people." Too often we *are* a peculiar people, but not in the way He intended! He didn't die to make us an odd or strange people, but a **people** who belong to Him in a **special** way — not to the world or to ourselves. And **He gave Himself for us that** we might be **zealous for good works**. We should have enthusiasm to perform acts of kindness in His name and for His glory. When we think of the zeal of men for sports, politics, and business, we should be provoked to jealousy and inspired to good deeds.

2:15 **These** are **things** that Titus was commissioned to teach — everything discussed in the foregoing verses, and particularly the purposes of the Savior's passion. He was to **exhort** or encourage the saints to lives of practical godliness and to **rebuke** any who contradicted the apostolic teachings either by word or by life. And he didn't have to be apologetic in carrying on a forceful ministry; let him do it **with all authority** and boldness of the Holy Spirit. **Let no one despise you.** Titus need have no qualms about his youth, his Gentile background, or any natural disability. He was speaking the word of God, and this made all the difference.

V. EXHORTATION IN THE CONGREGATION (3:1–11)

3:1 Titus was also to **remind** believers in the Cretan assemblies of their responsibilities toward their government. The Christian approach is that all governments are ordained of God (Rom. 13:1). A regime might be very unchristian or even anti-christian, but *any* government is better than no government at all. The absence of government is anarchy, and people cannot survive for long under anarchy. Even if a ruler does not know God personally, he is still "the anointed of the Lord" in his official position, and should be respected as such. Christians should be obedient **to rulers and authorities**. But if a government leaves its God-ordained sphere and commands a believer to disobey God, then the believer should refuse on the principle of Acts 5:29: "We ought to obey God

rather than men." If he is punished he should bear the punishment meekly as to the Lord. He should never join in rebellion against the government or seek its overthrow by violence.

THE CHRISTIAN AND THIS WORLD

Believers should obey the laws, including traffic laws, and pay their taxes and other levies. In general they should be law-abiding, respectful, obedient subjects. However, there are three areas in which Christians differ considerably as to their proper responsibility. These are the matters of voting, of seeking elected office, and of going to war with the armed forces. With regard to the first two, the following helpful guidelines are laid down in the Bible:

1. Christians are in the world but are not of it (John 17:14, 16).

2. The whole world system is in the hands of the wicked one, and has been condemned by God (1 Jn. 5:19b; 2:17; John 12:31).

3. The Christian's mission is not to improve the world, but to see men saved out of it.

4. While the believer is almost unavoidably a citizen of some earthly country, his primary citizenship is from heaven — so much so that he is to look upon himself as a pilgrim and an alien down here (Phil. 3:20; 1 Pet. 2:11).

5. No soldier on active duty should entangle himself with the affairs of this life, lest he displease the one who has enlisted him (2 Tim. 2:4).

6. The Lord Jesus said: "My kingdom is not of this world" (John 18:36). As His ambassadors, we should represent this truth to the world.

7. Politics tend to become corrupt by their very nature. Christians should separate themselves from iniquity (2 Cor. 6:17, 18).

8. In voting, a Christian would normally vote for a man thought to be upright and honest. But sometimes it is God's will to exalt the lowest of men (Dan. 4:17). How could we know and obey the will of God in such cases?

The other question is whether a believer should go to war when ordered by his country. There are strong arguments on both sides, but it seems to me that the balance of evidence is against participating. The principles listed above bear on the problem, but there are additional ones. (1) Our Lord said, "If My kingdom were of this world, My servants would fight" (John 18:36). (2) He also said, "All who take the sword will perish by the sword" (Matt. 26:52). (3) The whole idea of taking human life is opposed to the teaching of Him who said, "Love your enemies" (Matt. 5:44).

Those who are opposed to bearing arms can be grateful if they live in a country where they are allowed to register as conscientious objectors or non-combatants.

On the other hand, many Christian men *have* served in combat with honor. They have noted that the NT presents centurions (e.g. Cornelius and Julius) in a very favorable light. Also, figures of speech from military life are used to illustrate the *Christian* warfare (e.g. Eph. 6:10–17). If soldiering were inherently *wrong* it is hard to see how Paul could call on us to be "good soldiers of Jesus Christ." Whichever view a person holds, he should not judge or condemn those who disagree. There is room for differing opinions. ‡

An additional obligation of the Christian disciple is that he **be ready for every good work**. Not all jobs are honorable — much modern advertising is built on lies, and some businesses sell products that are harmful to man's spiritual, mental, and physical health. In all good conscience, these occupations should be avoided.

3:2 A Christian should **speak evil of no one**. Elsewhere the Bible specifically forbids speaking evil of a ruler (Ex. 22:28; Acts 23:5) — a command that all Christians should remember in the heat of a political campaign or in times of oppression and persecution. But here the injunction is broadened to protect everyone from ridicule, slander, insult, or verbal abuse. What oceans of grief and trouble could be avoided if Christians would obey this simple precept **to speak evil of no one**!

We should be **peaceable** and avoid quarreling. It takes two to generate a dispute. When someone tried to pick a quarrel with Dr. Ironside over a matter of minor importance which he had preached on, he would reply, "Well, dear brother, when we get to heaven, one of us is going to be wrong, and perhaps it will be me." That spirit put an end to all argument.

We should be **gentle**. It is hard to think about this quality without thinking of the Lord Jesus. He was mild-mannered and kind, peaceful and conciliatory. And we should show **all humility**, or courtesy, **to all men**. It seems so proper that courtesy should be taught as one of the Christian virtues. Essentially it means humbly thinking of others, putting others first, and saying and doing the gracious thing. Courtesy serves others before self, jumps at opportunities to assist, and expresses prompt appreciation for kindnesses received. It is never crude, vulgar, or rude.

3:3 Once again, in the midst of a strongly ethical section the apostle introduces a doctrinal classic on our salvation, with emphasis on the goal of salvation being a life of good works. The flow of thought is: (1) Our condition before salvation, verse 3; (2) the nature of our salvation, verses 4–7; (3) the practical result of salvation, verse 8. God's picture of us before our conversion is not flattering. Professing to know all the answers, **we were** actually **foolish**, unable to comprehend spiritual truths, and unwise in our choices and conduct. We were **disobedient** to God and perhaps to parents and other authorities as well. We were **deceived** by the devil and our own perverted judgment, always missing the right way and ending up on dead-end streets. We were **serving various** unclean habits, enslaved by an evil thought-life and besetting sins of all kinds. Life was a constant round of bitter **malice and envy** toward others. Unlovable and selfish, we were miserable and made others miserable. **Hateful and hating one another**: What a sad commentary on life among quarreling neighbors, warring fellow employees, cut-throat business competitors, and feuding families!

3:4 The dismal picture of man's depravity is interrupted by one of the great *buts* of Scripture. How thankful we can be for these nick-of-time conjunctions that signal God's marvelous intervention to save man from destroying himself! Someone has called them God's road-blocks on man's way to hell.

But when the kindness and love of God our Savior toward man appeared . . . This occurred when the Lord Jesus appeared to the world over nineteen hundred years ago. In another sense, God's goodness and lovingkindness **appeared** to us when we were saved. It was a manifestation of these attributes that He would send His beloved Son to die for a world of rebellious sinners. The word used for **love . . . toward men** is the Greek word from which *philanthropy* comes; it combines the thoughts of love, graciousness, and compassion. The title **God our Savior** refers to **God** the Father — **our Savior** in the sense that He sent His Son into the world as our Sacrifice for sin. The Lord Jesus is also called **God our Savior** (2:13) because He paid the necessary penalty in order that we might be pardoned and forgiven.

3:5 **He saved us** from the guilt and penalty of all our sins — past, present, and future. They were all future when the Savior died, and His death covered them all. But one of the simplest, clearest truths of the gospel is the most difficult for man to receive. It is that salvation is **not** based on good **works**; one doesn't become a Christian by living a Christian life. It is not good people who go to heaven. The consistent testimony of the Bible is that man cannot earn or merit salvation (Eph. 2:9; Rom. 3:20; 4:4, 5; 9:16; 11:6; Gal. 2:16; 3:11). Man cannot save himself by good works; all his righteous deeds are like polluted rags in God's sight (Isa. 64:6). He cannot become a Christian by living a Christian life for the simple reason that he has no power in himself to live a Christian life. It is not good people who go to heaven; it is sinners who have been saved by God's grace!

Good works do not earn salvation; they are the *result* of salvation. Wherever there is true salvation there will also be good works. So we read that God did not save us because of **works of righteousness which we have done, but according to His mercy**. Salvation is a work of **mercy** — not justice. Justice demands that the deserved punishment be administered; **mercy** provides a righteous way by which the punishment is averted.

God saved us by **the washing of regeneration**. Conversion is really a new creation (2 Cor. 5:17), and here that new creation is presented under the figure of a bath. It is the same figure used by the Lord Jesus when He taught the disciples that there is only one bath of regeneration but many necessary cleansings from defilement (John 13:10). That bath of regeneration has nothing to do with baptism. It is not a bodily cleansing by water, but a moral cleansing by the word of God (John 15:3). Baptism is not even a symbol of this bath; it rather depicts burial with Christ into death (Rom. 6:4).

Our new birth is also spoken of as a **renewing of the Holy Spirit**. The Spirit of God brings about a marvelous transformation — not putting new clothes on the old man, but putting a new man in the clothes! The Holy Spirit is the *Agent* in regeneration and the word of God is the *instrument*.

3:6 God **poured out** the Holy Spirit **on us abundantly**. Every believer is indwelt by the Spirit from the moment he is born again. The Spirit is sufficient to bring about the glorious renewal referred to. The Spirit is given **through Jesus Christ our Savior**. Just as the abundance of Pharaoh's court was mediated to Jacob's sons through Joseph, so the blessings of God, including the inexpressible blessing of His Spirit, are mediated to us through the Lord Jesus. Jesus is our "Joseph."

All three Persons of the Blessed Trinity are mentioned in connection with our salvation: God the Father, (v. 4); the Holy Spirit, (v. 5); and God the Son (v. 6).

3:7 The immediate result of our regeneration is **that having been justified by His grace we should become heirs according to the hope of eternal life**. Through the redemption that is in Christ Jesus, God reckons us righteous by an act of amazing grace. And we **become heirs** of all that God has prepared for those who love Him. Everything that is included in being with Christ and like Him for all eternity is our hope.

3:8 When Paul says **"This is a faithful saying"** are we to understand the preceding section, or the rest of the verse? The thrust of his argument seems to be that, having been saved from so much by such a great salvation, we should live in a manner worthy of our high calling.

Titus was to insist on these things (discussed in vv. 1–7) in his ministry in Crete so that believers would **be careful to maintain good works**. Although the expression **good works** may mean honorable occupations, the wider meaning — **good works** in general — is probably the right one. Teaching which calls for behavior that is consistent with one's Christian profession is excellent and **profitable**. All teaching should have a personal and practical application.

3:9 Of course, there are always traps to be avoided in the Christian ministry. In Paul's day there were stupid **disputes** over clean and unclean foods, Sabbath regulations, and observance of holy days. Arguments arose over **genealogies**, both angelic and human. There was bickering over intricate regulations that had been superimposed on the law. Paul was disgusted with them as being **unprofitable and useless**.

Servants of the Lord in our day may take Paul's advice to heart by avoiding the following tangents:

Pre-occupation with methods rather than with spiritual realities. For example, the ancient debates over whether to use fermented wine or grape juice, leavened or unleavened bread, a common cup or individual cups — as if these were important questions in the Bible!

Quibbling over words.

Majoring on one truth, or even one aspect of a truth, to the exclusion of all else.

Allegorizing the Scriptures until they become absurd.

Theological nit-picking that edifies no one.

Wandering from the word into political by-paths and into Christian crusades against this and that.

What a tragedy to spend precious time on these things while a world is perishing!

3:10 The **man** who majors on these minors is a **divisive** heretic.[5] He usually has one note on his violin and plays it to death. Soon he gathers around himself a coterie of people with a negative outlook, and the rest he drives away. He will divide an assembly rather than abandon his doctrinal hobbyhorse. No church should put up with such nonsense. If after one or two warnings, he refuses to desist, he should be expelled from the fellowship of the local church and the Christians should refrain from having social contact with him. Hopefully, this ostracism will bring him to repentance and to a more balanced handling of the word of God.

3:11 Lest anyone think that **such a person** is not a serious threat to the church, the apostle castigates him as **warped and sinning, being self-condemned**. His behavior is a perversion rather than a version of Christianity. He is **sinning** by forming a sect or party. He is **self-condemned** because he stubbornly clings to his wickedness after being warned by responsible Christians.

VI. CONCLUSION (3:12–15)

3:12 The Epistle closes with a few short directives to Titus. Paul planned to **send** either **Artemas, or Tychicus** to relieve Titus in Crete. We have met **Tychicus** before (Acts 20:4; Eph. 6:21; Col. 4:7), but **Artemas** we have not. It seems from 2 Timothy 4:12 that **Tychicus** was sent to Ephesus rather than to Crete, so **Artemas** was probably the replacement in Crete. As soon as he arrived, Titus was to go to **Nicopolis**, where Paul had determined to **spend the winter**. There were at least seven cities called Nicopolis in those days, but most commentators believe Titus chose the one in Epirus, in western Greece.

3:13 Titus was going to have visitors — **Zenas the lawyer and Apollos**. Perhaps they were the ones who brought the Letter from Paul to Titus. There were two kinds of lawyers in those days — scribes, who expounded the religious law, and advocates, who handled matters of civil law. We are left to decide which fraternity **Zenas** belonged to. I cast my vote for the former, suspecting he may have been called in to help Titus quell the interminable squabbles over the

Law of Moses (v. 9). If he was a civil lawyer, he was an honest one! The only other **Apollos** of whom we read in the NT is the one mentioned in Acts 18:24–28 and 1 Corinthians. Perhaps this is the same man. When Paul told Titus to **send** these two **on their journey with haste**, he included in his exhortation hospitality during their stay in Crete and everything necessary for their onward travel.

3:14 Titus was to teach the other Christians (**our people**) to show hospitality, to care for the sick and afflicted, and to be generous toward those who were in need. Instead of working merely to meet their own needs and wants, they should have the distinctly Christian vision of earning money in order to share with the less privileged (see Eph. 4:28b). This would save them from the misery of selfishness and the tragedy of a wasted, unfruitful life.

3:15 The closing greetings should not be thought of as trite and unimportant. In countries where Christians are few in number, despised, and persecuted, these kind words convey vast quantities of love, friendship, and encouragement. **All who** were **with** the apostle sent greetings to Titus, and Titus was asked to convey kind regards to all who loved Paul and his team **in the faith**. Finally, Paul closes the Letter on the theme that dominated his life — the **grace** of the Lord.

Grace be with you all. Amen.

ENDNOTES

[1](1:1) See Ephesians 1 and Romans 9 for fuller treatment of election.

[2](1:6) Many believe that while divorce is sometimes valid, a church *officer* should not be a divorced person.

[3](2:7) As so often (see NKJV footnotes), omissions are favored by the critical text, which is based largely on the oldest extant manuscripts, coming chiefly from Egypt. The KJV and NKJV favor the traditional text, (TR), which is usually, but by no means always, supported by the majority of manuscripts as well (majority text).

[4](2:14) It sounds quaint today because the meaning of "peculiar" has changed. The KJV is a very accurate translation; most so-called "errors" are (as here) due to nearly four centuries of changes in English.

[5](3:10) The word *heretic* (KJV) is from a Greek word meaning factious or *divisive* (NKJV). A person who splits churches usually teaches false or "heretical" doctrine, but this is a later development of the word *hairetikos* itself.

BIBLIOGRAPHY

See Bibliography at the end of 1 Timothy.

THE EPISTLE TO PHILEMON

Introduction

"A true little masterpiece in the art of letter-writing." — Ernest Renan

"We are all [the Lord's] Onesimi." — Martin Luther

I. Unique Place in the Canon

Some might suggest that we would be well able to do without this little Letter from Paul. They would be totally wrong. In the first place, it is universally recognized as an authentic personal Letter straight from the apostle's heart. As such it is a gem to start with. It has often been compared with a secular letter on the same subject — a runaway slave — by the Roman author Pliny the Younger to a friend. Except in the realm of elegant rhetoric, Paul's Letter comes out on top.

This little missive shows the courtesy, tact — with a dash of humor — and the loving heart of Paul. While it does not teach doctrine outright, it is a perfect illustration of the doctrine of "imputation" because of Paul's command to "charge that to my account." Just as Onesimus' failings were charged to Paul's "account" and Paul's ability to pay applied to Onesimus' helpless estate, so the Christian has his sins "imputed," or charged, to our Lord's account and our Lord's saving merits put on his own ledger. No wonder the great reformer, Martin Luther, wrote:

Here we see how St. Paul lays himself out for poor Onesimus, and with all his means pleads his cause with his master: and so sets himself as if he were Onesimus, and had himself done wrong to Philemon. Even as Christ did for us with God the Father, thus also St. Paul does for Onesimus with Philemon. . . . We are all His Onesimi, to my thinking.[1]

II. Authorship†

Everyone but the most negative critics accepts the Pauline authorship of Philemon. In fact, Renan was so sure of this authenticity that it made him question his own rejection of the authenticity of the closely related Colossian Epistle.

Since Philemon is so brief and so personal it is not surprising that there are not many early quotations from the Letter.

External Evidence

Philemon is quoted or alluded to in the writings of Ignatius, Tertullian, and Origen. Eusebius says it was one of the books accepted by all Christians (*homologoumena*). Marcion included it in his "canon" and it is also recognized by the Muratorian Canon.

Internal Evidence

Even in this short Letter Paul mentions himself by name three times (vv. 1, 9, 19). Verses 2, 23, 24 have close ties with Colossians 4:10-17, and so the two Epistles help support one another's authenticity. Thus the internal evidence agrees with the external.

III. Date

The Letter was sent at the same time as the Epistle to the Colossians (about A.D. 60), or about thirty years after the Ascension of our Lord.

IV. Background and Theme††

We have to piece together the story

†*See p. i.*
††*See p. ii.*

behind this Letter from the contents of the Epistle itself and from Paul's Letter to the Colossians. It appears that Philemon was a resident of Colosse (cf. Col. 4:17 with Phmn. v. 2) who had been converted through the Apostle Paul (v. 19). One of his slaves, Onesimus, had run away from him (vv. 15, 16) and there is a hint that Onesimus might have helped himself to some of his master's possessions as well (v. 18).

The fugitive reached Rome during the time that Paul was imprisoned there (v. 9). We can't be sure whether the apostle was actually behind bars at the time or whether it was within the period when he was allowed the freedom of his own rented house (Acts 28:30). By a curious chain of circumstances, Onesimus met Paul in the busy metropolis and was led to Christ through his ministry (v.

10). In the days that followed, a mutual bond of love developed (v. 12) and Onesimus proved to be a valued helper to the apostle (v. 13). But they both agreed that the proper thing would be for Onesimus to return to Philemon and make right the wrongs of the past. So Paul wrote this Letter to Philemon, interceding for Onesimus and presenting strong reasons why he should be graciously restored to his master's favor (v. 17). It was at this time that Paul also wrote the Letter to the Colossians. He assigned Tychicus to act as postman and sent Onesimus back to Colosse with him (Col. 4:7-9).

This is the most personal of all Paul's Letters. The Epistles to Timothy and Titus were also written to individuals but they deal with matters of assembly practice more than with personal affairs.

OUTLINE

Commentary

I. SALUTATION (Vv. 1–3)

V. 1 **Paul** introduces himself as **a prisoner** rather than as an apostle. He could have used his authority, but he prefers to appeal from what might seem a low place of disadvantage. Yet the apostle gilds this low place with the glory of heaven. He is **a prisoner of Christ Jesus**. Not for a minute will he grovel as a prisoner of Rome! He sees beyond the emperor to the King of kings. **Timothy** was with him as he wrote, and so he links this faithful disciple with him, though the Letter is obviously Paul's.

The main addressee is **Philemon**. His name means "affectionate," and apparently he was true to his name because Paul describes him as **our beloved friend and fellow laborer**.

V. 2 Since **Apphia** is a feminine name, most scholars assume that she

was Philemon's wife. The fact that the Letter is addressed in part to her reminds us that Christianity exalts womanhood.[2] Later we shall see how it also exalts slaves. Sanctified imagination has almost invariably identified **Archippus** as the son of Philemon. We can't be sure, but we do know that he was actively engaged in the Christian warfare. Paul honors him as a **fellow soldier**. We can picture him as a dedicated disciple of the Lord Jesus, on fire with a holy passion. In Colossians, Paul singled him out for special attention: "And say to Archippus, 'Take heed to the ministry which you have received in the Lord, that you may fulfill it' " (Col. 4:17).

If Philemon, Apphia, and Archippus give us a picture of a NT Christian family, the expression **the church in your house** calls up the image of a NT church. It seems clear from this that Philemon's **house** was the meeting place for an assembly of believers. It was there they gathered for worship, prayer, and Bible study. From there they went forth to witness for Christ in a world that would never welcome their message but would never forget it either. As they met together in Philemon's home, the Christians were all one in Christ Jesus. Rich and poor, male and female, master and slave — all were there as full-fledged members of the family of God. As soon as they returned to the work-a-day world, their social distinctions would reappear. But at the Lord's Supper, for instance, they were all on the common level of the holy priests. Philemon would have no precedence over Onesimus.

V. 3 Paul's characteristic greeting seems to embody the best he could desire for those he loved. **Grace** includes all the undeserved favor which God showers on His people. **Peace** here is the spiritual serenity and poise which stabilize the lives of those who are taught by His grace. Both blessings come **from God our Father and the Lord Jesus Christ**. This is full of significance. It means that the Lord Jesus is equal with **God** the **Father** in bestowing **grace** and **peace**. It would be blasphemy to give such honor to Christ if He were not truly and fully God.

II. PAUL'S THANKSGIVING AND PRAYER FOR PHILEMON (Vv. 4–7)

V. 4 Whenever Paul prayed for Philemon, he thanked **God** for this noble brother. We have every reason to believe that he was a choice trophy of the grace of God — the kind of man you would like to have as a friend and brother. Some commentators suggest that Paul is using diplomacy in these opening verses, that his purpose is to "soften" Philemon's heart to receive Onesimus back again. This ascribes an unworthy motive to the apostle and casts a shadow over the inspired text. Paul would not have said it if he had not sincerely meant it.

V. 5 There were two qualities in Philemon's character that gave great joy to Paul — his **love** and the **faith which** he had **toward the Lord Jesus and to-**

ward all the saints. His faith in Christ showed he had the root of divine life and his love **toward all the saints** showed that he had the fruit as well. His faith was productive.

In Ephesians 1:15, 16 and Colossians 1:3, 4 Paul expressed similar thanks for the saints to whom those Letters were addressed. However, in those places he put faith before love. Here he puts love before faith. Why the difference? Maclaren answers: "The order here is the order of analysis, digging down from manifestation to cause. The order in the parallel passages is the order of production ascending from root to flower."

There is another interesting feature of Paul's arrangement here. He divides the expression "Love toward all the saints" by inserting **faith . . . toward the Lord Jesus** after love. We might put it as follows: "love (and faith . . . toward the Lord Jesus) toward all the saints." The object of **faith** is **the Lord Jesus**. The object of **love** is the **saints**. But Paul wraps the faith clause with the love clause, as if to forewarn Philemon that he is about to have a special opportunity to manifest the reality of his faith by showing love to the slave Onesimus. Thus there is special emphasis in the word *all* — **all the saints**.

V. 6 The previous two verses expressed Paul's thanks for Philemon. This one discloses the nature of the apostle's prayer for him. The **sharing of your faith** means the practical kindness which Philemon showed to others. We can share our faith not only by preaching Christ but also by feeding the hungry, clothing the destitute, comforting the bereaved, relieving the distressed — yes, even by forgiving a runaway slave. Paul prayed then that Philemon's life of benevolence would lead many to acknowledge that all his good deeds came from **Christ Jesus**. There is tremendous power and influence in a life where the love of God is manifest. It is one thing to read about love in a book, but how compelling it is to see the Word become flesh in a human life!

V. 7 News of Philemon's overflowing generosity and self-sacrificial love traveled from Colosse to Rome, bringing **great joy**[3] (**or thanksgiving**, NKJV margin) and comfort to Christ's prisoner. It had been a great privilege for Paul to lead Philemon to the Lord, but now how rewarding it was to hear that his child in the faith was going on well for the Lord. How assuring it was to know that **the hearts of the saints** were being greatly **refreshed by** this beloved **brother**, and especially by his **love**. No one lives to himself, and no one dies to himself. Our actions affect others. We cannot measure the range of our influence. We have limitless potential for good or for evil.

III. PAUL'S PLEA FOR ONESIMUS (Vv. 8–20)

V. 8 Now Paul comes to the main purpose of the Letter. He is about to intercede for Onesimus. But how will he approach the subject? As an apostle, he could justifiably say to Philemon, "Now, my brother, it is your duty as a believer to forgive and restore this runaway, and that's exactly what I'm telling you to do." Paul could have ordered him to do it, and Philemon would no doubt have obeyed. But that would have been a hollow victory in this case.

V. 9 If the apostle did not win Philemon's heart, then Onesimus might have returned to an icy reception. Only obedience that was motivated by love would make the slave's status in the home tolerable. Perhaps as he wrote this, Paul thought of the Savior's words: "If you love Me, keep My commandments" (John 14:15). And so **for love's sake**, he preferred to **appeal** rather than to order. Would Philemon's love reach across the sea where an **aged** ambassador[4] of Christ was a prisoner for the Lord Jesus? Would he be moved by two considerations — Paul, **the aged, and now also a prisoner**? We do not know exactly how old the apostle was at this time. Estimates range from fifty-three to sixty-three. That might not seem old today, but he was probably prematurely old because of the way he had burnt himself out in the service of Christ. And now he was **a prisoner** for **Jesus Christ**. In mentioning this, he wasn't looking for sympathy, but he did hope that Philemon would weigh these factors in making his decision.

V. 10 In the original of this verse

the name *Onesimus* comes last. **"I appeal to you**, concerning a son of mine, **whom I have begotten while in my chains —** **Onesimus."** By the time Philemon reached the name of his derelict slave, he was completely disarmed. Imagine his surprise when he learned that the "scoundrel" had been converted and, even more surprising, had been led to Christ through Paul, the prisoner!

One of the hidden delights of the Christian life is to see God working in marvelous, miraculous ways, revealing Himself in converging circumstances that cannot be explained by coincidence or chance. First Paul had led Philemon to the Lord. Then the apostle had later been arrested and taken to Rome for trial. Philemon's slave had run away and made his way to Rome. Somehow or other he had met Paul and had been converted. Master and slave were both born again through the same preacher but in widely separated places and under quite different circumstances. Was it a coincidence?

V. 11 The name Onesimus means **profitable**. But when he ran away, Philemon was probably tempted to call him a worthless rascal. Paul says, *in effect*, "Yes, he was useless as far as you were concerned, but now he is useful **to you and to me."** The slave who was returning to Philemon was a better slave than the one who had run away. It has been said that in NT times Christian slaves commanded a higher price on the market than others. It should be true today that Christian employees are more valuable as workers than unbelievers.

V. 12 The attitude of the NT toward slavery comes into focus in this Epistle. We notice that Paul does not condemn slavery or prohibit it. In fact, he sends Onesimus back to his master. But the abuses connected with slavery are condemned and prohibited throughout the NT. Maclaren writes:

> The New Testament . . . meddles directly with no political or social arrangements, but lays down principles which will profoundly affect these, and leaves them to soak into the general mind.[5]

Forcible revolution is not the Bible way to correct social evils. The cause of man's inhumanity lies in his own fallen nature. The gospel attacks the *root cause*, and offers a new creation in Christ Jesus.

It is conceivable that a slave who has a kind master might be better off than if he were independent. This is true, for instance, of believers, who are bondservants of the Lord Jesus. Those who are His slaves enjoy the truest form of freedom. In **sending** Onesimus **back** to Philemon, Paul was not doing an injustice to the slave. Both master and slave were believers. Philemon would be obligated to treat him with Christian kindness. Onesimus would be expected to serve with Christian faithfulness. The deep affection which the apostle had for Onesimus is expressed in the words **sending . . . my own heart**. Paul felt as if he were losing a part of himself.

We should notice that the important principle of restitution is set forth. Now that Onesimus was saved, was it necessary for him to return to his former master? The answer is definitely "Yes." Salvation removes the penalty and power of sin, but it does *not* cancel debts. The new Christian is expected to settle all unpaid accounts and to make right all wrongs, insofar as it is humanly possible. Onesimus was obligated to return to his master's service, and to repay any money which he might have stolen.

V. 13 The apostle's personal preference would have been **to keep** Onesimus **with** *him* in Rome. There were many things that the converted slave could have done for Paul while he was imprisoned for the gospel's sake. And this would have been an opportunity for Philemon to **minister** to the apostle — by providing an assistant. But it would have the drawback of being done without Philemon's knowledge or permission.

V. 14 Paul would not force a kindness from the slave's owner by keeping Onesimus with him in Rome. He would do **nothing** in connection with Onesimus **without** Philemon's **consent**. The kindness would be robbed of its beauty if it were done **by compulsion** and not by a free and loving willingness.

V. 15 It is a mark of spiritual maturity to be able to look beyond the adverse circumstances of the moment and see God working all things together for good to those who love Him (Rom. 8:28).

When Onesimus ran away, perhaps Philemon was filled with bitterness and a sense of financial loss. Would he ever see the slave again? Now Paul traces the rainbow through the dark clouds. Onesimus was lost to the family in Colosse for a while **that** they **might** have **him** back **forever**. This should be the comfort of Christians who lose believing relatives and friends in death. The separations are for a little while; the reunion will be eternal.

V. 16 Philemon was not only getting Onesimus back — he was receiving him under better conditions than he had ever known him before. It would no longer be the customary master-slave relationship. Onesimus was now **more than a slave**; he was **a beloved brother** in the Lord. Henceforth the fear motive would be replaced by the love motive. Paul had already enjoyed his fellowship as **a beloved brother**. But now he would no longer have him there in Rome. The apostle's loss would be Philemon's gain. He would now know Onesimus as a brother **both in the flesh and in the Lord**. The former slave would justify Paul's confidence both **in the flesh**, that is, by his devoted service in a physical way, and **in the Lord**, that is, by his fellowship as a believer.

V. 17 The apostle's request is startling both in its boldness and in its tenderness. He asks Philemon to **receive** Onesimus **as** he **would** receive the apostle himself. He says: **"If then you count me as a partner, receive him as you would me."** The words are reminiscent of the Savior's statements: "He who receives you receives Me, and he who receives Me receives Him who sent Me" (Matt. 10:40), and, "Inasmuch as you did it to one of the least of these My brethren, you did it to Me" (Matt. 25:40). They also remind us that God has accepted us in the Person of His Son, that we are as near and dear to God as Christ is.

If Philemon considered Paul **as a partner**, as one with whom he was in fellowship, then the apostle asks him to receive Onesimus on the same basis. This doesn't require that Onesimus be treated as a perpetual guest in the family with no obligation to work. He would still be a servant in the home, but one who belonged to Christ and was therefore a brother in the faith.

V. 18 The apostle doesn't say that Onesimus had stolen anything from Philemon, but this verse suggests such a possibility. Certainly theft was one of the cardinal sins of slaves. Paul is willing to accept responsibility for any loss that Philemon might have sustained. He recognizes that restitution should be made. The conversion of Onesimus did not cancel his debts to man. So Paul tells Philemon to **put that on** his **account**.

We cannot read this without being reminded of the enormous debt which we had contracted as sinners, and of how it was all charged to the account of the Lord Jesus at Calvary. He paid the debt in full when He died as our Substitute. We are also reminded here of Christ's ministry as our Advocate. When Satan, the accuser of the brethren, brings charges against us for wrongs we have done, our blessed Lord says in effect, "Charge that to My account." The doctrine of reconciliation is illustrated in this book. Onesimus had been estranged from Philemon because of wrongdoing. Through the ministry of Paul (we have every reason to believe) the distance and "enmity" were removed. The slave was reconciled to his master. So we were estranged from God because of our sin. But through the death and resurrection of Christ, the cause of enmity has been removed and believers are reconciled to God.

V. 19 Ordinarily Paul dictated his Letter to someone else, writing only the closing lines with his **own hand**. We can't be sure whether he wrote this entire Letter by hand, but at this point at least he took the pen and, in his familiar scrawl, committed himself to pay any debts incurred by Onesimus. He would do this in spite of the fact that Philemon owed him a considerable debt. Paul had led him to the Lord. He owed his spiritual life to the apostle, as far as the human instrument was concerned. But Paul would not press him for payment of the debt.

V. 20 Addressing Philemon as **brother**, the aged Paul asks only for some benefit in the Lord, some refreshment in Christ. He is pleading that Onesimus be received graciously, that he be forgiven and restored to his place of service in the household — not now as a slave but as a brother in the family of God.

IV. CLOSING REMARKS (Vv. 21–25)

V. 21 The apostle had every **confidence** that Philemon would do **even more** than was requested. He himself had been freely forgiven by Christ. He would not do less, surely, for Onesimus. We have then a vivid illustration of Ephesians 4:32: "And be kind to one another, tenderhearted, forgiving one another, just as God in Christ also forgave you."

V. 22 But how would Paul know how Philemon had treated Onesimus? He hoped to visit Colosse and be a guest in Philemon's home. He expected to be released by the civil authorities in answer to the **prayers** of the Christians. And so he asks Philemon to **prepare a guest room for** him. Perhaps that would have been one of the first tasks assigned to Onesimus: "Get the guest room ready for our brother Paul." We do not know whether Paul ever reached Colosse. All we can do is assume that the **guest room** was ready for him, and that all the members of the household were eager to see him, their hearts having been knitted together in love.

V. 23 **Epaphras** may have been the one who planted the assembly in Colosse (Col. 1:7, 8; 4:12, 13). Now a **fellow prisoner** with Paul in Rome, he joins in sending greetings to Philemon.

V. 24 With Paul at this time were **Mark, Aristarchus, Demas,** and **Luke**. These names are also mentioned in Colossians 4:10, 14. Jesus, called Justus, is mentioned in Colossians 4, though omitted here for some reason. **Mark** was the writer of the Second Gospel. He had proved to be a faithful servant of the Lord after his early failure (2 Tim. 4:11, cf. Acts 13:13; 15:36–39). **Aristarchus**, a believer from Thessalonica, accompanied Paul on several journeys including the trip to Rome. In Colossians 4:10, Paul called him "my fellow prisoner." **Demas** later forsook Paul, having loved this present world (2 Tim. 4:10). **Luke**, the beloved physician, proved to be a faithful companion and helper to the end (2 Tim. 4:11).

V. 25 The Letter closes with Paul's characteristic benediction. He wishes the **grace of our Lord Jesus Christ** to **be with** Philemon's **spirit**. Life can hold no greater blessing than the unmerited favor of the Savior as one's moment-by-moment experience. To walk in the constant realization and enjoyment of His Person and work is all that heart can desire.

Paul laid down his pen and handed the Letter to Tychicus for delivery to Philemon. Little did he realize the extent to which the message of this Epistle would influence Christian behavior for centuries to follow. The Letter is a classic of love and courtesy, as applicable today as it was when it was written. **Amen**.

ENDNOTES

[1](Intro) Martin Luther, quoted by J. B. Lightfoot, *Saint Paul's Epistles to the Colossians and to Philemon*, pp. 317, 318 (translation updated by the present editor).

[2](V. 2) If one compares the status of Christian women with pagan and Muslim women, she (or he) will have to agree that the true "Liberator of women" is the Lord Jesus Christ.

[3](V. 7) The majority of mss. read *thanksgiving* (*charin*) for *joy* (*charan*).

[4](V. 9) The Greek words for "aged" (*presbutēs*) and *ambassador* (*presbeutēs*) are so similar that Bentley conjectured that Paul wrote "ambassador." The traditional mss. are totally against this conjecture, however nicely it may fit the context.

[5](V. 12) Alexander Maclaren, "Colossians and Philemon," *The Expositor's Bible*, p. 461.

BIBLIOGRAPHY

See Bibliography at the end of Colossians.

THE EPISTLE TO THE HEBREWS

Introduction

"There is no portion of Scripture whose authorship is more disputed, nor any of which the inspiration is more indisputable."

— Conybeare and Howson

I. Unique Place in the Canon

The Epistle to the Hebrews is unique in the NT on many counts. While it does not start as a letter, it does so end, and is clearly addressed either to or from Italy (13:24), to a specific group, probably Hebrew Christians. It has been suggested that it was originally addressed to a small house church and therefore had no link with a large and famous congregation to keep alive the tradition of its origin and destination. The style is the most literary in the NT. It is poetic, and full of quotations from the Septuagint. It has a large vocabulary and uses the Greek language very precisely in verb tense and other details.

Though very *Jewish* in one sense (it has been compared to Leviticus), the warnings against drifting from the reality of Christ's death to mere religious ritual are always needed in *Christendom*. Hence the book's great importance.

II. Authorship[†]

Hebrews is anonymous, even though some earlier editions of the KJV printed Paul's name as part of the heading of the book. The early Eastern Church (Dionysius and Clement, both of Alexandria) suggested Paul as author. After much doubting, this view came to prevail from Athanasius onward, so that the West finally agreed. Few today, however, would maintain Pauline authorship. Origen agreed that the *contents* were Pauline, and there are some Pauline touches in it, but the style in the original is very different from Paul's. (This does not *rule*

out Pauline authorship, because a literary genius can alter his style.)

Several possible authors have been suggested through the years: Luke, whose style is similar, and who was familiar with Paul's preaching, Barnabas, Silas, Philip, even Aquila and Priscilla.

Luther suggested Apollos, a man who fits the style and content of the book: mighty in the OT Scriptures, and very eloquent (Alexandria, his home town, was noted for rhetoric). An argument against Apollos is that no Alexandrian tradition preserves such a theory, an unlikely situation if a native Alexandrian wrote it.

For some reason the Lord has seen fit to keep the author unknown. One suggestion is that Paul *did* write it but purposely veiled his authorship due to Jewish prejudice against him. While this is possible, the ancient words of Origen have never been bettered: "But who wrote the Epistle God alone knows for certain."

III. Date

In spite of the anonymous human *authorship*, it is possible to *date* the Epistle rather closely.

External evidence demands a first-century writing, since Clement of Rome used the book (c. A.D. 95). While Polycarp and Justin Martyr quote the Letter, they do not name the author. Dionysius of Alexandria quotes Hebrews as by Paul, and Clement of Alexandria says Paul wrote it in Hebrew and Luke translated it. (The book does not, however, read like a translation.) Irenaeus and

[†]*See p. i.*

971

nation was incredible and the fact of His humiliation was shameful. To the Jews, Jesus was only a man, and therefore He belonged to a lower order than the angels. The following verses show that *even as Man*, Jesus was better than the angels.

First, it is pointed out that God did not decree that **the** habitable **world** of the future should be under the control of **angels**. **The world to come** here means the golden age of peace and prosperity which the prophets so frequently mentioned. We speak of it as the Millennium.

2:6 Psalm 8:4–6 is quoted to show that the eventual dominion over the earth has been given to man, not to angels. In a sense, man is insignificant, and yet God is **mindful of him**. In a sense, man is unimportant, yet God does **take care of him**.

2:7 In the scale of creation, man has been given a **lower** place **than the angels**. He is more limited as to knowledge, mobility, and power. And he is subject to death. Yet in the purposes of God, man is destined to be **crowned with glory and honor**. The limitations of his body and mind will be largely removed, and he will be exalted on the earth.

2:8 Everything will be put **under** man's authority in that coming day — the angelic hosts, the world of animals, birds, and fishes, the planetary system — in fact, every part of the created universe will be put **under** his control.

This was God's original intention for man. He told him, for instance, to "fill the earth and subdue it; have dominion over the fish of the sea, over the birds of the air, and over every living thing that moves on the earth" (Gen. 1:28).

Why then don't we see **all** things **in subjection under him**? The answer is that man lost his dominion because of his sin. It was Adam's sin that brought the curse on creation. Docile creatures became ferocious. The ground began to bring forth thorns and thistles. Man's control over nature was challenged and limited.

2:9 However, when the Son of Man returns to reign over the earth, man's dominion will be restored. Jesus, as Man, will restore what Adam lost, and more besides. So while we do not see

everything under man's control at the present time, **we** do **see Jesus**, and in Him we find the key to man's eventual rule over the earth.

For a little while, He was made **lower than the angels**, specifically, for the thirty-three years of His earthly ministry. His descent from heaven to Bethlehem, to Gethsemane, to Gabbatha, to Golgotha, and to the tomb, mark the stages in His humiliation. But now He is **crowned with glory and honor**. His exaltation is a result of His suffering and death; the cross led to the crown.

God's gracious purpose in it all was that Christ **might taste death for everyone**. The Savior died as our Representative and as our Substitute; that is, He died as man and He died for man. He bore in His body on the cross all God's judgment against sin so that those who believe on Him will never have to bear it.

2:10 It was entirely in keeping with the righteous character of God that man's dominion should be restored through the humiliation of the Savior. Sin had disturbed God's order. Before order could be brought out of chaos, sin must be dealt with righteously. It was consistent with the holy character of God that Christ should suffer, bleed, and die to put away sin.

The wise Planner is described as the One **for whom are all things and by whom are all things**. First He is the objective or goal of all creation; all things were made for His glory and pleasure. But He is also the Source or Originator of all creation; nothing was made apart from Him.

His great purpose was **bringing many sons to glory**. When we consider our own worthlessness, it staggers us to think that He would have even bothered with us, but it is because He is the God of all grace that He has called us to His eternal glory.

What is the cost of our glorification? The **captain** of our **salvation** had to be made **perfect through sufferings**. As far as His moral character is concerned, the Lord Jesus was always sinlessly perfect. He could never be made perfect in this respect. But He had to be made **perfect** *as our Savior*. In order to purchase eternal redemption for us, He had to suffer all the punishment that our sins deserved. We could not be saved by His spotless life; His substitutionary death was an absolute necessity.

God found a way of saving us that was worthy of Himself. He sent His only begotten Son to die in our place.

2:11 The next three verses emphasize the perfection of Jesus' humanity. If He is going to regain the dominion which Adam lost, then it must be demonstrated that He is true Man.

First, the fact is stated: **For both He who sanctifies and those who are being sanctified are all of one**, that is, they are all possessors of humanity. Or, ". . .have all one origin" (RSV), meaning that in their humanity, they all have one God and Father.

Christ is the One **who sanctifies**, that is, He sets apart or separates men to God from the world. Blessed are all those whom He thus sets apart!

A sanctified person or thing is one set apart from ordinary uses to be for God's own possession, use, and enjoyment. The opposite of sanctification is profanation.

There are four types of sanctification in the Bible: *pre-conversion sanctification, positional sanctification, practical sanctification,* and *perfect sanctification*. These types of sanctification are detailed in the Excursus at 1 Thessalonians 5:23, which should be read carefully.

The reader should be on the lookout for the various passages in Hebrews where sanctification is mentioned, and should seek to determine which type of sanctification is in view.

It is because He became a true Man that **He is not ashamed** to speak of His followers as **brethren**. Is it possible that the Eternal Sovereign of the universe should become man and identify Himself so closely with His creatures that He would call them brothers?

2:12 The answer is found in Psalm 22:22 where we hear Him say, **"I will declare Your name to My brethren."** The same verse also pictures Him as identified with His people in common worship, **"in the midst of the assembly I will sing praise to You."** In His dying agony, He looked forward to the day when He would lead the ransomed throng in **praise** to God the Father.

2:13 Two more verses are quoted from the Jewish Scriptures to prove Christ's humanity. In Isaiah 8:17 (LXX), He speaks of putting His **trust** in God. Implicit confidence in Jehovah is one of the greatest marks of true humanity. Then in Isaiah 8:18, the Lord is quoted as saying, "Here am I and the children whom the LORD has given me!" The thought is that they are members of a common family, acknowledging a common Father.

2:14 Those who consider the humiliation of the Son of Man to be shameful are now asked to consider four important blessings that flow from His passion.

The first is the destruction of Satan. How did this happen? There was a special sense in which God gave His children to Christ to sanctify, save, and emancipate. Since these children had human natures, the Lord Jesus assumed a body of flesh and blood. He set aside the outward display of His deity and veiled His Godhead in a "robe of clay."

But He did not stop at Bethlehem. "All the way to Calvary He went for me because He loved me so."

Through His **death**, He destroyed the one **who had the power of death, that is, the devil**. Destruction here means the loss of well-being rather than loss of being. It means to nullify or to bring to nothing. Satan is still actively opposing the purposes of God in the world, but he received a death wound at the cross. His time is short and his doom is sure. He is a defeated foe.

In what sense does the devil have **the power of death**? Probably the chief sense in which he has this power is in *demanding* death. It was through Satan that sin first entered the world. God's holiness decreed the death of all who sinned. So in his role as adversary, the devil can demand that the penalty be paid.

In heathen lands his power is also seen in the ability of his agents, the witch doctors, to pronounce a curse on a person and for that person to die without any natural cause.

There is no suggestion in Scripture that the devil can inflict death on a believer without the permission of God (Job 2:6), and therefore he cannot set the time of a believer's death. Through wicked men, he is sometimes permitted to kill the believer. But Jesus warned His disciples not to fear those who could destroy the body, but rather to fear God who can destroy both soul and body in hell (Matt. 10:28).

In the OT, Enoch and Elijah went to heaven without dying. No doubt this was because, as believers, they were reckoned to have died in the still-future death of Christ.

When Christ comes at the Rapture, all living believers will go to heaven without dying. But they too escape death because God's holiness was satisfied for them in the death of Christ. The risen Christ now has "the keys of Hades and of Death" (Rev. 1:18), that is, He has complete authority over them.

2:15 The second blessing traced to Christ's humiliation is emancipation from **fear**. Before the cross, the **fear of death** held men in lifelong servitude. Though there are occasional flashes of light in the OT concerning life after death, the general impression is one of uncertainty, horror, and gloom. What was hazy then is clear now because Christ brought life and immortality to light by the gospel (2 Tim. 1:10).

2:16 The third tremendous blessing is expiation of sin. In coming into the world, the Lord did **not give aid to angels, but He does give aid to the seed of Abraham**. "Give aid to" is a translation of *epilambanō*, "to take hold" (hence the KJV's "he took not on [him the nature of] angels; but he took on [him] the seed of Abraham"). While the verb might not have the idea of violent grasping which it carries elsewhere, the ideas of help and deliverance are suggested by its use here.

The seed of Abraham may mean Abraham's *physical* descendants, the Jews, or it may mean his *spiritual* seed — the believers of every age. The important point is that they are human, not angelic beings.

2:17 This being so, it was necessary that **He** should **be made like His brethren** in every respect. He assumed true and perfect humanity. He became subject to human desires, thoughts, feelings, emotions, and affections — with this important exception: He was without sin. His humanity was the ideal;

ours has been invaded by a foreign element, sin.

His perfect humanity fits Him to **be a merciful and faithful High Priest in things pertaining to God**. He can be **merciful** to man and **faithful** to God. His chief function as **High Priest** is to **make propitiation** [satisfaction] **for the sins of the people**. To accomplish this He did what no other High Priest ever did or could do — He offered *Himself* as a sinless sacrifice. He willingly died in our place.

2:18 The fourth blessing is help for the **tempted**. Because **He Himself has suffered** and has been **tempted, He is able to aid those who are** going through temptation. He can help others going through it because He has been there Himself.

Here again we must add a word of qualification. The Lord Jesus was **tempted** from without, but never from within. The temptation in the wilderness shows Him **being tempted** from without. Satan appeared to Him and sought to appeal to Him by external stimuli. But the Savior could never be tempted to sin by lusts and passions within, for there was no sin in Him and nothing to respond to sin. He **suffered, being tempted**. Whereas it pains us to resist temptation, it pained Him to be tempted.

C. Christ Superior to Moses and Joshua (3:1—4:13)

3:1 Moses was one of Israel's greatest national heroes. Therefore the third main step in the writer's strategy is to demonstrate Christ's infinite superiority to Moses.

The message is addressed to **holy brethren, partakers of the heavenly calling**. All true believers are **holy** as to their position, and they should be holy as to their practice. In Christ they are holy; in themselves they ought to be holy.

Their **heavenly calling** is in contrast to the earthly call of Israel. Old Testament saints were called to material blessings in the land of promise (though they did have a heavenly hope as well). In the Church Age, believers are called to spiritual blessings in the heavenlies now and to a heavenly inheritance in the future.

Consider Jesus. He is eminently worthy of our consideration as **the Apostle and High Priest of our confession**. In confessing Him as **Apostle**, we mean that He represents God to us. In confessing Him as **High Priest**, we mean that He represents us before God.

3:2 There is one aspect in which He was admittedly similar to Moses. He **was faithful to** God, just **as Moses also was faithful in** God's **house**. The **house** here does not mean only the tabernacle but also the entire sphere in which Moses represented God's interests. It is the **house** of Israel, God's ancient earthly people.

3:3 But there the similarity ends. In every other respect there is undisputed superiority. First the Lord Jesus is **worthy of more glory than Moses** because the builder of a **house has more honor than the house** itself. The Lord Jesus was the Builder of God's house; Moses was only a part of the house.

3:4 Second, Jesus is greater because He is God. **Every house** must have a builder. The One **who built all things is God**. From John 1:3, Colossians 1:16, and Hebrews 1:2, 10, we learn the Lord Jesus was the active Agent in creation. The conclusion is unavoidable — Jesus Christ is God.

3:5 The third point is that Christ is greater as a Son. **Moses** was a **faithful . . . servant** in all God's **house** (Num. 12:7), pointing men forward to the coming Messiah. He testified **of those things which would be spoken afterward**, that is, the good news of salvation in Christ. That is why Jesus said on one occasion, "If you believed Moses, you would believe Me; for he wrote about Me" (John 5:46). In His discourse with the disciples on the road to Emmaus, Jesus began at Moses and all the prophets, and "expounded to them in all the Scriptures the things concerning Himself" (Luke 24:27).

3:6 But Christ was faithful over God's house **as a Son**, not as a servant, and in His case, sonship means equality with God. God's house is **His own house**.

Here the writer explains what is meant by God's **house** today. It is composed of all true believers in the Lord Jesus: **whose house we are if we hold fast the confidence and the rejoicing of**

the hope firm to the end.[1] At first this might seem to imply that our salvation is dependent on our holding fast. In that case, salvation would be by our endurance rather than by Christ's finished work on the cross. The true meaning is that we prove we are God's house if we hold fast. Endurance is a proof of reality. Those who lose confidence in Christ and in His promises and return to rituals and ceremonies show that they were never born again. It is against such apostasy that the following warning is directed.

3:7 At this point the writer interjects the second warning of the Epistle — a warning against hardening the heart. It had happened to Israel in the wilderness and it could happen again. So **the Holy Spirit** is still speaking through Psalm 95:7–11, as He did when He first inspired it, **"Today, if you will hear His voice."**

3:8 Whenever God speaks, we should be swift to hear. To doubt His word is to call Him a liar and to incur His wrath.

Yet that was Israel's history **in the wilderness**. It was a dreary record of complaint, lust, idolatry, unbelief, and rebellion. At Rephidim, for instance, they complained because of lack of water and doubted God's presence in their midst (Ex. 17:1–17). At the wilderness of Paran when the unbelieving spies returned with an evil report of discouragement and doubt (Num. 13:25–29), the people decided that they should go back to Egypt, the land of their slavery (Num. 14:4).

3:9 God was so highly incensed that He decreed that the people should wander in the wilderness for forty years (Num. 14:33–34). Of all those soldiers who came out of Egypt who were twenty years old or older, only two would ever enter the land of Canaan — Caleb and Joshua (Num. 14:28–30).

It is significant that just as Israel spent **forty years** in the wilderness, so the Spirit of God dealt with the nation of Israel for approximately forty years after the death of Christ. The nation hardened its heart against the message of Christ. In A.D. 70, Jerusalem was destroyed and the people were scattered among the Gentile nations.

3:10 God's keen displeasure with

Israel in the wilderness brought forth this stern denunciation. He accused them of a perpetual proneness to wander away from Him, and of a willful ignorance of His **ways**.

3:11 In His **wrath**, He **swore** that **they** would **not enter** His **rest**, that is, the land of Canaan.

3:12 Verses 12–15 give the application which the Holy Spirit draws for us from Israel's experience. As elsewhere in Hebrews, the readers are addressed as **brethren**. This does not mean that they were all true Christians. So all who profess to be believers should be constantly on guard against a pernicious **heart of unbelief** that might cause them to fall away **from the living God**. It is a constant menace.

3:13 One antidote is mutual exhortation. Especially in days of difficulty and distress, God's people should be **daily** urging others not to forsake Christ for religions that cannot deal with sin effectively.

Notice that this exhortation is not limited to a ministerial class but is the duty of all brethren. It should continue as long as it is called **"Today,"** that is, as long as God's offer of salvation by grace through faith continues. **"Today"** is the accepted time; it is the day of salvation.

To fall away is to **be hardened through the deceitfulness of sin**. Sin often looks beautiful in anticipation. Here it offers escape from the reproach of Christ, lower standards of holiness, rituals that appeal to the aesthetic senses, and the promise of earthly gain. But it is hideous in retrospect. It leaves a man with no forgiveness of sins, no hope beyond the grave, and no possibility of repentance.

3:14 Again we are reminded that **we have become** companions **of Christ if we hold** fast our first **confidence steadfast to the end**. Verses like this are often misused to teach that a person can be saved and then lost again. However, such an interpretation is impossible because the overwhelming testimony of the Bible is that salvation is freely bestowed by God's grace, purchased by Christ's blood, received by man's faith, and evidenced by his good works. True faith always has the quality of perma-

nence. We don't hold fast in order to retain our salvation, but as proof that we have been genuinely saved. Faith is the root of salvation; endurance is the fruit. Who are Christ's companions? The answer is, "Those who by their steadfastness in the faith prove that they really belong to Him."

3:15 Now the writer concludes the personal application of Israel's sad experience by repeating the words of Psalm 95:7, 8: **"Today, if you will hear His voice, do not harden your hearts as in the rebellion."** This poignant appeal, once directed to Israel, is now directed to any who might be tempted to forsake the good news and return to the law.

3:16 The chapter closes with a historical interpretation of Israel's apostasy. In a series of three questions and answers, the writer traces Israel's rebellion, provocation, and retribution. Then he states the conclusion.

Rebellion. The rebels are identified as **all who came out of Egypt, led by Moses**. Caleb and Joshua were the lone exceptions.

3:17 *Provocation.* It was these same rebels who provoked Jehovah for **forty years**. There were about 600,000 of them, and by the time the forty years were ended, the desert was dotted with 600,000 graves.

3:18 *Retribution.* These were the same ones who were excluded from the land of Canaan because of their disobedience.

The simple recital of these questions and answers should have a profound influence on any who might be tempted to leave the despised minority of true Christians for the vast majority of people who have an outward form of religion but deny the power of godliness. Is the majority always right? In this chapter of Israel's history, only two were right and over half a million were wrong!

A. T. Pierson emphasizes the seriousness of Israel's sin as follows:

Their unbelief was a fourfold provocation:

1. It was an assault on God's truth, and made Him a liar.

2. It was an assault upon His power, for it counted Him as weak and unable to bring them in.

3. It was an attack upon His immuta-

bility; for, although they did not say so, their course implied that He was a changeable God, and could not do the wonders He had once wrought.

4. It was also an attack upon His fatherly faithfulness, as though He would encourage an expectation He had no intention of fulfilling.[2]

Caleb and Joshua, on the contrary, honored God by accounting His word absolutely true, His power infinite, His disposition unchangingly gracious, and His faithfulness such that He would never awaken any hope which He would not bring to fruition.

3:19 *Conclusion.* It was **unbelief** that kept the rebellious children out of the promised land, and it is **unbelief** that keeps man out of God's inheritance in every dispensation. The moral is clear: beware of an evil heart of **unbelief**.

The following verses form one of the most difficult passages in the entire Letter. There is little agreement among the commentators as to the exact flow of the argument, although the over-all teaching of the section is fairly clear.

The theme of 4:1–13 is God's rest and the need of diligence in reaching it. It will be helpful for us at the outset if we notice that several kinds of rest are mentioned in the Bible:

1. God rested after the sixth day of creation (Gen. 2:2). This rest did not indicate weariness as a result of toil, but rather satisfaction with the work He had completed. It was the rest of complacency (Gen. 1:31). God's rest was interrupted by the entrance of sin into the world. Since that time He has been working ceaselessly. As Jesus said, "My Father has been working until now, and I have been working" (John 5:17).

2. Canaan was intended to be a land of rest for the children of Israel. Most of them never entered the land, and those who did, failed to find the rest that God intended for them. Canaan is used here as a type or picture of God's final, eternal rest. Many of those who failed to reach Canaan (Korah, Dathan, and Abiram, for example) picture present-day apostates who fail to reach God's rest because of their unbelief.

3. Believers today enjoy rest of conscience, knowing that the penalty for

their sins has been paid through the finished work of the Lord Jesus. This is the rest which the Savior promised, "Come to Me . . . and I will give you rest" (Matt. 11:28).

4. The believer also enjoys a rest in serving the Lord. Whereas the preceding is a rest of salvation, this is a rest of service. "Take My yoke upon you and learn from Me . . . and you will find rest for your souls" (Matt. 11:29).

5. Finally there is the eternal rest which awaits the believer in the Father's house in heaven. This future rest, also called a Sabbath rest (Heb. 4:9), is the final rest of which the others are either types or foretastes. This rest is the principal subject (Heb. 4:1–13).

4:1 No one should think that the promise of **rest** is no longer valid. It has never had a complete and final fulfillment in the past; **therefore** the offer is still in effect.

But all who profess to be believers should make sure that they do not **come short of** the goal. If their profession is empty, there is always the danger of turning away from Christ and embracing some religious system that is powerless to save.

4:2 We have had good news **preached to us** — the good news of eternal life through faith in Christ. The Israelites also had good news preached to them — the good news of rest in the land of Canaan. But they did not benefit from the gospel of rest.

There are two possible explanations for their failure, depending on which manuscript reading of verse 2 we adopt. According to the NKJV, the reason for their failure was that the message was **not mixed with faith in those who heard it**. In other words, they did not believe it or act upon it.

The other reading (NKJV margin) is that "they were not united by faith with those who heeded it." The meaning here is that the majority of the Israelites were not united by faith with Caleb and Joshua, the two spies who believed the promise of God.

In either case, the prominent idea is that unbelief excluded them from the rest which God had prepared for them in the land of promise.

4:3 The continuity of thought becomes difficult in this verse. There seem to be three disjointed and unrelated clauses, yet we can see that there is a common thread in each clause — the theme of God's rest.

First we learn that **we who have believed** are the ones who **enter** God's **rest**. Faith is the key that opens the door. As has been pointed out already, believers today enjoy rest of conscience because they know that they will never be brought into judgment for their sins (John 5:24). But it is also true that those who believe are the only ones who will ever enter God's final rest in glory. It is probably this future rest that is primarily intended here.

The next clause reinforces the idea by stating it negatively: **as He has said: "So I swore in My wrath, 'They shall not enter My rest' "** (quoted from Ps. 95:11). Just as faith admits, so unbelief excludes. We who trust Christ are sure of God's rest; the unbelieving Israelites could not be sure of it because they did not believe God's word.

The third clause presents the most difficulty: it says, **although the works were finished from the foundation of the world**. Perhaps the simplest explanation is found by linking this with the preceding clause. There God had used the future tense in speaking of His rest: **They shall not enter My rest**. The future tense implies that God's rest is still a live option, even though some forfeited it through disobedience, and this rest is still available in spite of the fact that God's **works were finished from the foundation of the world**.

4:4 This verse is intended to prove from Scripture that **God rested** after the work of creation was completed. The author's vagueness in identifying the passage quoted does not indicate any ignorance on his part. It is merely a literary device in quoting a verse from a book that was not at that time divided into chapters and verses. The verse is adapted from Genesis 2:2: "And God rested on the seventh day from all His works."

Here the *past* tense is used and it might seem to indicate to some that God's rest belongs only to history and not to prophecy, that it has no relevance

for us today. But that is not the case.

4:5 To reinforce the idea that the reference to God's rest after creation does not mean that it is a closed issue, the writer again quotes with slight change from Psalm 95:11, where the *future* tense is used, **"They shall not enter My rest."** He is saying, in effect, "In your thinking, do not confine God's rest to what happened back in Genesis 2; remember that God later spoke about His rest as something that was still available."

4:6 Up to this point in the argument we have seen that, from the creation, God has been offering rest to mankind. The admission gate has been open.

The Israelites in the wilderness failed to **enter because of** their **disobedience**. But that did not mean that the promise was no longer in effect!

4:7 The next step is to show that even **in** the case of **David**, about 500 years after the Israelites were shut out from Canaan, God was still using the word **"Today"** as a day of opportunity. The writer had already quoted Psalm 95:7, 8 in Hebrews 3:7, 8, 15. He now quotes it again to prove that God's promise of rest did not cease with the Israelites in the wilderness. In David's time, He was still pleading with men to trust Him and **not** to **harden** their **hearts**.

4:8 Some Israelites did, of course, enter Canaan with **Joshua**. But even these did not enjoy the final **rest** which God has prepared for those who love Him. There was conflict in Canaan, and sin, sickness, sorrow, suffering, and death. If they had exhausted God's promise of rest, then He would not have offered it again in the time of David.

4:9 The preceding verses have been leading up to this conclusion: **There remains therefore a rest for the people of God**. Here the writer uses a different Greek word for **rest** (*sabbatismos*), which is related to the word *Sabbath*. It refers to the eternal rest which will be enjoyed by all who have been redeemed by the precious blood of Christ. It is a "Sabbath" keeping that will never end.

4:10 Whoever enters God's **rest** enjoys a cessation from labor, just **as God did** on the seventh day.

Before we were saved, we may have

tried to work for our salvation. When we realized that Christ had finished the work at Calvary, we abandoned our own worthless efforts and trusted the risen Redeemer.

After salvation, we expend ourselves in loving toil for the One who loved us and gave Himself for us. Our good works are the fruit of the indwelling Holy Spirit. We are often weary in His service, though not weary of it.

In God's eternal rest, we shall cease from our labors down here. This does not mean that we will be inactive in heaven. We shall still worship and serve Him, but there will be no fatigue, distress, persecution, or affliction.

4:11 The previous verses demonstrate that God's rest is still available. This verse says that diligence is necessary in order **to enter that rest**. We must **be diligent** to make sure that our only hope is Christ the Lord. We must diligently resist any temptation merely to profess faith in Him and then to renounce Him in the heat of suffering and persecution.

The Israelites were careless. They treated God's promises lightly. They hankered for Egypt, the land of their bondage. They were not diligent in appropriating God's promises by faith. As a result, they never reached Canaan. We should be warned by their example.

4:12 The next two verses contain a solemn warning that unbelief never goes undetected. It is detected first by **the word of God**. (The term used here for *word* is *rhēma* not *logos*, the familiar word used by John in the prologue to his Gospel. This verse refers, not to the Living Word, Jesus, but to the written word, the Bible.) This **word of God** is:

living — constantly and actively alive.

powerful — energizing.

cutting — **sharper than any two-edged sword**.

dividing — **piercing** the **soul and spirit**, the two invisible, nonmaterial parts of man. Piercing the **joints and marrow**, the **joints** permitting the outward movements and the **marrow** being the hidden but vital life of the bones.

discerning — discriminating and judging with regard to **the thoughts and intents of the heart**. It is the word that judges us, not we who judge the word.

4:13 Second, unbelief is detected by the living Lord. Here the pronoun shifts from the impersonal to the personal: **And there is no creature hidden from His sight**. Nothing escapes His notice. He is absolutely omniscient. He is constantly aware of all that is going on in the universe. Of course, the important point in the context is that He knows where there is real faith and where there is only an intellectual assent to facts.

II. CHRIST SUPERIOR IN HIS PRIESTHOOD (4:14-10:18)

A. Christ's High Priesthood Superior to Aaron's (4:14–7:28)

4:14 These verses take up again the strong current of the writer's thought which he had introduced in 3:1 — Christ as the **great High Priest** of His people. They present Him as the great resource of His needy people, able to keep them from falling. Also they change the emphasis "from the word as scrutinizer to the Lord as Sympathizer." When the word has thoroughly exposed us (vv. 12, 13), we can go to Him for mercy and grace.

Notice the excellencies of our wonderful Lord:

1. He is **a great High Priest**. There were many high priests under the Mosaic economy, but none was ever called great.

2. He **has passed through** the atmospheric heaven and the stellar heaven to the third heaven, the dwelling place of God. This speaks, of course, of His ascension and glorification at the Father's right hand.

3. He is human. **Jesus** was the name given to Him at His birth and it is the name that is particularly linked with His humanity.

4. He is divine. **The Son of God**, when used of Christ, speaks of His absolute equality with God the Father. His humanity qualified Him from our viewpoint; His deity, from God's viewpoint. No wonder He is called **a great High Priest**.

4:15 Then too we must consider His

experience. No one can truly **sympathize** with someone else unless he has been through a similar experience himself. As Man our Lord has shared our experiences and can therefore understand the testings which we endure. (He cannot sympathize with our wrongdoing because He never experienced it.)

> In every pang that rends the heart,
> The Man of Sorrows has a part.

He was **tempted** in every respect **as we are, yet without sin**. The Scriptures guard the sinless perfection of the Lord Jesus with jealous care, and we should too. He knew no sin (2 Cor. 5:21), He committed no sin (1 Pet. 2:22), and there is no sin in Him (1 Jn. 3:5).

It was impossible for Him to sin, either as God or as Man. As the perfect Man, He could do nothing of His own accord; He was absolutely obedient to the Father (John 5:19), and certainly the Father would never lead Him to sin.

To argue that His temptation was not meaningful if He could not sin is fallacious. One purpose of the temptation was to demonstrate conclusively that He could *not* sin.[3]

If you put gold to the test, the test is not less valid because the gold is pure. If there were impurity, the test would show it up. Similarly it is wrong to argue that if He could not sin, He was not perfectly human. *Sin is not an essential element in humanity*; rather it is a foreign intruder. Our humanity has been marred by sin; His is perfect humanity.

If Jesus could have sinned as a Man on earth, what is to prevent His sinning as a Man in heaven? He did not leave His humanity behind when He ascended to the Father's right hand. He was impeccable on earth and He is impeccable in heaven.

4:16 Now the gracious invitation is extended: draw near with confidence **to the throne of grace**. Our confidence is based on the knowledge that He died to save us and that He lives to keep us. We are assured of a hearty welcome because He has told us to **come**.

The people in OT days could not draw near to Him. Only the high priest could approach Him, and then only on one day of the year. We can go into His presence at any time of the day or night and **obtain mercy and find grace to help in time of need**. His **mercy** covers the things we should not have done, and His **grace** empowers us to do what we should do but do not have the power to do.

Morgan writes helpfully:

> I am never tired of pointing out that the Greek phrase translated "in time of need" is a colloquialism of which "in the nick of time" is the exact equivalent. "That we may receive mercy and find grace to help *in the nick of time*" — grace just when and where I need it. You are attacked by temptation. At the moment of assault, you look to Him, and the grace is there to help in the nick of time. There is no postponement of your petition until the evening hour of prayer. But there in the city street with the flaming temptation in front of you, turn to Christ with a cry for help, and the grace will be there in the nick of time.[4]

Up to this point, Jesus has been shown to be superior to the prophets, the angels, and Moses. We now turn to the important theme of priesthood to see that Christ's high priesthood is of a superior order to Aaron's.

When God gave the law to Moses on Mount Sinai, He instituted a human priesthood by which the people might draw near to Him. He decreed that the priests must be descended from the tribe of Levi and from the family of Aaron. This order is known as the Levitical or Aaronic priesthood.

Another divinely ordained priesthood is mentioned in the OT, that of the patriarch Melchizedek. This man lived in the days of Abraham, long before the law was given, and served both as a king and a priest. In the passage before us the author will show that the Lord Jesus Christ is a priest after the order of Melchizedek, and that this order is superior to the Aaronic priesthood.

In the first four verses we have a description of the Aaronic priest. Then in verses 5–10 Christ's fitness as a priest is detailed, mostly by way of contrast.

5:1 The first qualification of the Aaronic **priest** was that he had to be chosen **from among men**. In other words, he had to be a man himself.

He was appointed to act **for men** in relation **to God**. He belonged to a special caste of men who served as intermediaries between men and God. One of his principal functions was **to offer both gifts and sacrifices for sins**. **Gifts** refer to any offerings that were presented to God. **Sacrifices** refer to those special offerings in which blood was shed as atonement for sins.

5:2 He had to **have compassion on** human frailty and to deal gently with the ignorant and wayward. His own frail flesh equipped him to understand the problems his people were facing.

The reference in this verse to the **ignorant** and wayward is a reminder that the sacrifices in the OT were for sins not done willfully. No provision was made in the law for deliberate sin.

5:3 But while his being human was an advantage in that it identified the priest with the people, his sinful humanity was a disadvantage. He had **to offer sacrifices for himself** as well as for the **sins of the people**.

5:4 The office of priest was not something that men chose as a vocation. They had to be **called** to the work **by God, just as Aaron was**. God's call was limited to Aaron and his descendants. No one outside that family could serve in the tabernacle or the temple.

5:5† The writer now turns to **Christ** and demonstrates His fitness as a priest because of His divine appointment, His manifest humanity, and His acquired qualifications.

As to His appointment, its source was God Himself. It was a sovereign call, having nothing to do with human genealogy. It involved a better relationship than any earthly priest ever had. Our **Priest** is the unique **Son** of God, eternally **begotten**, begotten in incarnation, and begotten in resurrection.

5:6 Then Christ's priesthood is of a better order because in Psalm 110:4 God declared Him to be **a priest forever according to the order of Melchizedek**. This superiority will be explained more fully in chapter 7. The prominent thought here is that, unlike the Aaronic priesthood, this one is **forever**.

5:7 Christ is not only the sinless Son of God; He is also true Man. The writer refers to the variety of human experiences through which He passed **in the days of His flesh** to prove this. Notice the words used to describe His life and especially His experience in the Garden of Gethsemane: **prayers and supplications, with vehement cries and tears**. They all speak of His career as a dependent Man, living in obedience to God, and sharing all man's emotions that are not connected with sin.

Christ's prayer was not that He might be saved from dying; after all, to die for sinners was His very purpose in coming to the world (John 12:27). His prayer was that He might be delivered *out of* death (JND), that His soul might not be left in Hades. This prayer was answered when God raised Him from the dead. He **was heard because of His godly fear**.

5:8 Now once again we come face to face with that profound mystery of the incarnation — how God could become Man in order to die for men.

Though He was a Son, or better, Son though He was — He was not *a* Son, that is, one of many, but He was the only begotten Son of God. In spite of this tremendous fact, **He learned obedience by the things which He suffered**. His entrance into this world as a Man involved Him in experiences which He would never have known had He remained in heaven. Each morning His ear was open to receive instructions from His Father for that day (Isa. 50:4). **He learned obedience** experimentally as the Son who was always subject to His Father's will.

5:9 And having been perfected. This *cannot* refer to His personal character because the Lord Jesus was absolutely perfect. His words, His works, and His ways were absolutely flawless. In what sense then was He **perfected**? The answer is in His office as our Savior. He could never have become our perfect Savior if He had remained in heaven. But through His incarnation, death, burial, resurrection, and ascension, He completed the work that was necessary to save us from our sins, and now He has the acquired glory of being the perfect Savior of the world.

Having returned to heaven, **He became the author of eternal salvation to**

†*See p. xxi.*

all who obey Him. He is the Source of salvation for all, but only those **who obey Him** are saved.

Here **salvation** is conditional on obeying Him. In many other passages salvation is conditional on faith. How do we reconcile this seeming contradiction? First of all, it is the obedience of faith (Rom. 1:5; 16:25–27): "the obedience which God requires is faith in His word." But it is also true that saving faith is the kind that results in obedience. It is impossible to believe, in the true NT sense, without obeying.

5:10 Having gloriously accomplished the fundamental work of priesthood, the Lord Jesus was addressed **by God as High Priest "according to the order of Melchizedek."**

It should be mentioned here that though Christ's priesthood is of the Melchizedekan order, yet His priestly functions are similar to those carried on by the Aaronic priests. In fact, the ministry of the Jewish priests was a foreshadow or picture of the work that Christ would accomplish.

5:11 At this point the author must digress. He would like to continue with the subject of Christ's Melchizedekan priesthood but he cannot. He is under divine constraint to rebuke his readers for their immaturity and at the same time to warn them seriously against the danger of falling away.

It is sadly true that our apprehension of divine truth is limited by our own spiritual condition. **Dull** ears cannot receive deep truths! How often it is true of us, as of the disciples, that the Lord has many things to say to us but we cannot bear them (John 16:12).

5:12 The writer reminds the Hebrews that they had been receiving instruction long enough now so that they should be teaching others. But the tragedy was that they still needed **someone to teach** them **the** ABCs of the word **of God**.

You ought to be teachers. God's order is that every believer should mature to the point where he can teach others. Each one teach one! While it is true that certain ones have a special gift of teaching, it is also true that every believer should engage in some teaching

ministry. It was never God's intention that this work should be limited to a few.

You have come to need milk and not solid food. In the physical realm, a child who never advances from milk to solids is impaired. There is a form of stunted growth in the spiritual realm as well (1 Cor. 3:2).

5:13 Professing believers who stay on a **milk** diet are **unskilled in the word of righteousness**. They are hearers of the word but not doers. They lose what they do not use, and remain in a state of perpetual infancy.

They do not have a keen sense of discernment in spiritual matters and are "tossed to and fro and carried about with every wind of doctrine, by the trickery of men, in the cunning craftiness of deceitful plotting" (Eph. 4:14).

5:14 Solid spiritual **food** is for the full-grown, for **those who by reason of use have their senses exercised to discern both good and evil**. By obeying the light they receive from God's word, these people are able to form spiritual judgments and save themselves from moral and doctrinal dangers.

In this context the particular sense in which the readers are urged to distinguish between **good and evil** is in relation to Christianity and Judaism. Not that Judaism was evil in itself; the Levitical system was introduced by God Himself. But it was intended to point forward to Christ. He is the fulfillment of the ceremonial types and shadows. Now that Christ has come, it is sinful to return to the pictures of Him. Anything that rivals Christ in the affections and loyalties of men is evil. Spiritually mature believers are able to discern between the inferiority of the Aaronic priesthood and the superiority of Christ's.

6:1 The warning which began in 5:11 continues throughout this chapter. It is one of the most controversial passages in the entire NT. Since so many godly Christians are disagreed on its interpretation, we must not speak with dogmatism. We present the explanation which seems most consistent with the context and with the rest of the NT.

First of all, the readers are exhorted to leave **the elementary principles of**

Christ, literally, "the word of the beginning of Christ" (FWG), or "the beginning word of Christ" (KSW). We understand this to mean the basic doctrines of religion that were taught in the OT and were designed to prepare Israel for the coming of the Messiah. These doctrines are listed in the latter part of verse 1 and in verse 2. As we shall seek to show, they are not the fundamental doctrines of Christianity but rather teachings of an elementary nature which formed the foundation for later building. They fell short of Christ risen and glorified. The exhortation is to leave these basics, not in the sense of abandoning them as worthless, but rather of advancing from them to maturity. The implication is that the period of Judaism was a time of spiritual infancy. Christianity represents full growth.

Once a foundation has been laid, the next step is to build upon it. A doctrinal **foundation** was laid in the OT; it included the six fundamental teachings which are now listed. These represent a starting point. The great NT truths concerning Christ, His Person, and His work, represent the ministry of maturity.

The first OT doctrine is **repentance from dead works**. This was preached constantly by the prophets as well as by the forerunner of the Messiah. They all called on the people to turn from **works** that were **dead** in the sense that they were devoid of faith.

Dead works here may also refer to works which formerly were right, but which now are **dead** since Christ has come. For example, all the services connected with temple worship are outmoded by the finished work of Christ.

Second, the writer mentions **faith toward God**. This again is an OT emphasis. In the NT, Christ is almost invariably presented as the object of faith. Not that this displaces faith in God; but a faith in God which leaves out Christ is now inadequate.

6:2 Instruction about **baptisms** refers not to Christian baptism,[5] but to the ceremonial washings which figured so prominently in the religious lives of the priests and people of Israel (see also 9:10).

The ritual of **laying on of hands** is de-scribed in Leviticus 1:4; 3:2; 16:21. The offerer or the priest laid his hands on the head of an animal as an act of identification. In figure, the animal bore away the sins of the people who were associated with it. This ceremony typified vicarious atonement. We do not believe that there is any reference here to the laying on of hands as practiced by the apostles and others in the early church (Acts 8:17; 13:3; 19:6).

Resurrection of the dead is taught in Job 19:25–27, Psalm 17:15, and it is implied in Isaiah 53:10–12. What was seen only indistinctly in the OT is brightly revealed in the New (2 Tim. 1:10).

The final foundational truth of the OT was **eternal judgment** (Ps. 9:17; Isa. 66:24).

These first principles represented Judaism, and were preparatory to the coming of Christ. Christians should not continue to be content with these but should press on to the fuller revelation they now have in Christ. The readers are urged to pass "from shadow to substance, from type to antitype, from husk to kernel, from the dead forms of the religion of their ancestors to the living realities of Christ."

6:3 The author expresses his desire to help them **do this**,[6] **if God permits**. However, the limiting factor will be on their side and not on God's. God will enable them to advance to full spiritual manhood, but they must respond to the word positively by exercising true faith and endurance.

6:4 We come now to the heart of the warning against apostasy. It applies to a class of people whom **it is impossible** to restore again to repentance. Apparently these people had once repented (though no mention is made of their faith in Christ). Now it is clearly stated that a renewed repentance is impossible.

Who are these people? The answer is given in verses 4 and 5. In examining the great privileges which they enjoyed, it should be noticed that all these things could be true of the unsaved. It is never clearly stated that they had been born again. Neither is any mention made of such essentials as saving faith, redemption by His blood, or eternal life.

They had **once** been **enlightened**.

They had heard the gospel of the grace of God. They were not in darkness concerning the way of salvation. Judas Iscariot had been enlightened but he rejected the light.

They **tasted the heavenly gift**. The Lord Jesus is the heavenly Gift. They had tasted of Him but had never received Him by a definite act of faith. It is possible to taste without eating or drinking. When men offered wine mixed with gall to Jesus on the cross, He tasted it but He would not drink it (Matt. 27:34). It is not enough to taste Christ; unless we eat the flesh of the Son of Man and drink His blood, that is, unless we truly receive Him as Lord and Savior, we have no life in us (John 6:53).

They had **become partakers of the Holy Spirit**. Before we jump to the conclusion that this necessarily implies conversion, we should remember that the Holy Spirit carries on a preconversion ministry in men's lives. He sanctifies unbelievers (1 Cor. 7:14), putting them in a position of external privilege. He convicts unbelievers of sin, of righteousness, and of judgment (John 16:8). He leads men to repentance and points them to Christ as their only hope. Men may thus partake of the Holy Spirit's benefits without being indwelt by Him.

6:5 They had **tasted the good word of God**. As they heard the gospel preached, they were strangely moved and drawn to it. They were like the seed that fell on rocky ground; they heard the word and immediately received it with joy, but they had no root in themselves. They endured for a while, but when tribulation or persecution arose on account of the word, they promptly fell away (Matt. 13:20, 21).

They had tasted **the powers of the age to come**. **Powers** here means "miracles." **The age to come** is the Millennial Age, the coming era of peace and prosperity when Christ will reign over the earth for one thousand years. The miracles which accompanied the preaching of the gospel in the early days of the church (Heb. 2:4) were a foretaste of signs and wonders which will be performed in Christ's kingdom. These people had witnessed these miracles in the first century, in fact, they might have participated in them. Take, for instance, the miracles of the loaves and fishes. After Jesus had fed the five thousand, the people followed Him to the other side of the sea. The Savior realized that, though they had tasted a miracle, they did not really believe in Him. He said to them, "Most assuredly, I say to you, you seek Me, not because you saw the signs, but because you ate of the loaves and were filled" (John 6:26).

6:6 **If they fall away,**[7] after enjoying the privileges just enumerated, it is impossible **to renew them again to repentance**. They have committed the sin of apostasy. They have reached the place where the lights go out on the way to hell.

The enormous guilt of apostates is indicated in the words **since they crucify again for themselves the Son of God, and put Him to an open shame** (v. 6b). This signifies a deliberate, malicious spurning of Christ, not just a careless disregard of Him. It indicates a positive betrayal of Him, a joining of forces against Him, and a ridiculing of His Person and work.

APOSTASY

Apostates are people who hear the gospel, make a profession of being Christians, become identified with a Christian church, and then abandon their profession of faith, decisively repudiate Christ, desert the Christian fellowship, and take their place with enemies of the Lord Jesus Christ. Apostasy is a sin which can be committed only by unbelievers, not by those who are deceived but by those who knowingly, willfully, and maliciously turn against the Lord.

It should not be confused with the sin of the average unbeliever who hears the gospel but does nothing about it. For instance, a man may fail to respond to Christ after repeated invitations from the Holy Spirit. But he is not an apostate. He can still be saved if he will commit himself to the Savior. Of course, if he dies in unbelief, he is lost forever, but he is not hopeless as long as he is capable of exercising faith in the Lord.

Apostasy should not be confused with backsliding. A true believer may wander very far away from Christ.

Through sin his fellowship with God is shattered. He may even reach the point where he is no longer recognized as a Christian. But he can be restored to full fellowship as soon as he confesses and forsakes his sin (1 Jn. 1:9).

Apostasy is not the same as the unpardonable sin mentioned in the Gospels. That was the sin of attributing the miracles of the Lord Jesus to the prince of the demons. His miracles were actually performed in the power of the Holy Spirit. To attribute them to the devil was tantamount to blaspheming the Holy Spirit. It implied that the Holy Spirit was the devil. Jesus said that such a sin could never be forgiven, either in that age or in the age to come (Mark 3:22–30). Apostasy is similar to blasphemy against the Holy Spirit in that it is an eternal sin, but there the resemblance ends.

I believe that apostasy is the same as the sin leading to death, mentioned in 1 John 5:16b. John was writing about people who had professed to be believers and had participated in the activities of local churches. They then had imbibed the false teaching of the Gnostics and had spitefully left the Christian fellowship. Their deliberate departure indicated that they had never been truly born again (1 Jn. 2:19). By openly denying that Jesus is the Christ (1 Jn. 2:22), they had committed the sin leading to death, and it was useless to pray for their recovery (1 Jn. 5:16b).

Some earnest Christians are troubled when they read Hebrews 6 and similar passages. Satan uses these verses especially to unsettle believers who are having physical, mental, or emotional difficulties. They fear that they have fallen away from Christ and that there is no hope for restoration. They worry that they have drifted beyond redemption's point. The fact that they are even concerned about it is conclusive evidence that they are *not* apostates! An apostate would not have any such fears; he would brazenly repudiate Christ.

If the sin of apostasy does not apply to believers, to whom then does it apply in our day? It applies, for instance, to a young man who makes a profession of faith in Christ and seems to go on brightly for a while, but then something

happens in his life. Perhaps he experiences bitter persecution. Perhaps he falls into gross immorality. Or perhaps he goes off to college and is shaken by the anti-Christian arguments of atheistic teachers. With full knowledge of the truth, he deliberately turns away from it. He completely renounces Christ and viciously tramples on every sacred fundamental doctrine of the Christian faith. The Bible says it is impossible to restore such a one to repentance, and experience corroborates the Bible. We have known many who have apostatized from Christ, but we have never known one who has returned to Him.

As we approach the end of this age, we can expect a rising tide of apostasy (2 Thess. 2:3; 1 Tim. 4:1). Therefore the warning against falling away becomes more relevant with every day that passes. ‡

6:7 Now the writer turns to the world of nature to find a counterpart to the true believer (v. 7) and to the apostate (v. 8). In both cases the person is likened to the land. The privileges listed in verses 4 and 5 are compared to the invigorating **rain**. The crop of vegetation speaks of the ultimate response of the person to the privileges received. This in turn determines whether the land is blessed or cursed.

The true believer is like the land **which drinks in the rain**, brings forth useful vegetation, and is blessed by **God**.

6:8 The apostate is like land that also is well watered but it **bears** nothing but **thorns and briers**, the fruit of sin. It receives but never produces useful plants. Such land is worthless. It is condemned already. Its destiny **is to be burned**.

6:9 There are two strong indications in verses 9 and 10 that the apostates described in the preceding verses are unbelievers. First, there is the abrupt change in pronouns. In discussing apostates, the writer refers to them as "they." Now in addressing true believers, he uses the pronouns **you** and **your**.

The second indication is even clearer. Speaking to believers, he says, **"But, beloved, we are confident of better things** concerning you, yes, **things that accompany salvation.**" The inference is that the things he had described in verses 4–6 and 8 do *not* accompany salvation.

6:10 Two of the things that accompany salvation were manifest in the lives of the saints — their **work and** their **labor of love**. Their faith manifested itself in a life of good works, and they had the hallmark of true Christianity — active **love** for the household of faith. They continued to serve the Lord's people for His sake.

6:11 The next two verses seem to be written to a different class of people; namely, to those of whom the writer was not sure. These were the ones who seemed to be in danger of drifting back into Judaism.

First, he desires **that** they will **show the same** earnestness as the true believers have shown in realizing **the full assurance of hope until the end**. He wants them to go on steadfastly for Christ until the final hope of the Christian is realized in heaven. This is a proof of reality.

6:12 They should **not become sluggish**, allowing their feet to drag and their spirits to lag. They should press on, imitating all true believers **who through faith and patience inherit the promises**.

6:13 The closing section of chapter 6 is linked with the exhortation in verse 12 to press on with confidence and patience. The example of **Abraham** is given as a stimulus and the certainty of the believer's hope is affirmed.

In one sense, the Christian may seem to be at a disadvantage. He has given up all for Christ, and has nothing material to show for it. Everything is in the future. How then can he be sure that His hope is not in vain?

The answer is found in God's **promise to Abraham**, a promise that included in germ form all that He would later bestow in the Person of Christ. When God made that promise, **He swore by Himself** since **He could swear by no one greater**.

6:14 The promise is found in Genesis 22:16, 17: "By Myself I have sworn, says the LORD . . . blessing I will bless you, and multiplying I will multiply your descendants. . . ." God pledged Himself to carry out this promise, and therefore its fulfillment was assured.

6:15 Abraham believed in God; he **patiently endured**; and he received the fulfillment. Actually Abraham was not taking a chance in believing God. No risk was involved. The word of God is the surest thing in the universe. Any **promise** of God is as certain of fulfillment as if it had already taken place.

6:16 In human affairs, **men swear by** someone **greater** than themselves. In courts of law, for example, they promise to tell the truth and then add, "so help me, God." They appeal to God for confirmation that what they are going to say is true.

When men take **an oath** to confirm a promise, that normally ends all **dispute**. It is understood that the promise will be kept.

6:17 **God** wanted His believing people to be absolutely assured that what He promised would come to pass. Actually His bare promise would have been enough, but He wanted **to show** it to a greater extent than even by a promise. So He added **an oath** to the promise.

The heirs of promise are all those who by faith are children of faithful Abraham. The **promise** referred to is the promise of eternal salvation to all who believe on Him. When God made a promise of a seed to Abraham, the promise found its full and ultimate fulfillment in Christ, and all the blessings that flow from union with Christ were therefore *included* in the promise.

6:18 The believer now has **two** unchangeable **things** on which to rely — His word and His oath. It is impossible to imagine anything more secure or certain.[8] God promises to save all who believe on Christ; then He confirms it with an oath. The conclusion in inevitable: the believer is eternally secure.

In the remainder of chapter 6 the writer employs four figures to drive home the utter reliability of the Christian hope: (1) a city of refuge, (2) an anchor, (3) a forerunner, and (4) a High Priest.

First, those who are true believers are pictured as fleeing from this doomed world to the heavenly city of **refuge**. To encourage them in their flight, God has given them an unfailing **hope** based upon His word and His oath.

6:19 In the storms and trials of life this **hope** serves **as an anchor of the soul**. The knowledge that our glorification is as certain as if it had already happened keeps us from drifting on the wild waves of doubt and despair.

The **anchor** is not cast in the shifting sands of this world but takes hold in the heavenly sanctuary. Since our **hope** is the anchor, the meaning is that our hope is secured in God's very **Presence behind the veil**. Just as sure as the anchor is there, we shall be there also.

6:20 **Jesus** has gone into the inner shrine also as our **forerunner**. His presence there insures the ultimate entrance of all who belong to Him. It is no exaggeration to say that the simplest believer on earth is as certain of heaven as the saints who are already there.

D. Anderson-Berry writes:

The word translated "forerunner" is found nowhere else in the New Testament. This expresses an idea never contemplated in the Levitical economy, for the high priest entered the holiest only as a representative. He entered where none could follow. But our Forerunner is a pledge that where He is, we also shall be. As Forerunner He (1) announced our future arrival there; (2) took possession of heaven's glories on our behalf; and (3) has gone to be able to bid His people welcome when they come, and to present them before the Majesty of heaven.[9]

The fourth figure is that of **High Priest**. Our Lord has **become High Priest forever according to the order of Melchizedek**. His eternal priesthood guarantees our eternal preservation. Just as surely as we have been reconciled to God by His death, so surely are we saved by His life as our Priest at God's right hand (Rom. 5:10).

This mention of **Jesus** as **High Priest** in **the order of Melchizedek** reminds us that this subject was interrupted at 5:10 when the author digressed on the extended warning against apostasy. Now he is ready to resume his theme that Christ's high priesthood is superior to Aaron's. He has skillfully returned to the main flow of argument.

7:1 **Melchizedek** was an enigmatic figure who appeared briefly on the stage of human history (Gen. 14:18–20), then disappeared. Centuries later his name was mentioned by David (Ps. 110:4). Then, after a lapse of additional centuries, it reappears in the book of Hebrews. One thing is apparent: God arranged the details of his life so that he would be an excellent type of our Lord Jesus Christ.

In these first three verses of chapter 7 we have some historical facts concerning him. We are reminded that he combined the offices of **king** and **priest** in his person. He was **king of Salem** (later called Jerusalem), and **priest of the Most High God**. He was the political and spiritual leader of his people. That is, of course, God's ideal — that there should be no separation between the secular and the sacred. When sinful man is reigning it is necessary to separate church and state. Only when Christ reigns in righteousness will it be possible to unite the two (Isa. 32:1,17).

Melchizedek encountered **Abraham** when the latter was **returning from** a military victory **and blessed him**. The significance of this act is reserved for verse 7. If we had only the OT Scriptures, we would never realize the deep significance of these seemingly irrelevant details.

7:2 **Abraham gave a tenth part of** the spoils of war to this mysterious king-priest. Again we must wait till verses 4, 6, 8–10 to learn the hidden meaning of Abraham's tithe.

In the Scriptures, a man's name stands for what he is. We learn about Melchizedek's name and his title: his name means **"king of righteousness"** and his title (**king of Salem**) means **"king of peace."**

It is not without meaning that **righteousness** is mentioned first, then **peace**. There cannot be peace unless first there is righteousness.

We see this clearly in the work of Christ. At the cross, "Mercy and truth . . . met together; righteousness and peace . . . kissed" (Ps. 85:10). Because the Savior met all the righteous demands of God against our sins, we can have peace with God.

7:3 The puzzle concerning Melchizedek deepens when we read that he had neither **father** nor **mother**, neither **genealogy**, birth, nor death. If we divorce these statements from their context, we would have to conclude that he was a visitor from heaven or from another planet, or that he was a special creation of God.

But the key to understanding lies in taking these statements in their context. The subject is priesthood. The writer is distinguishing between the Melchizedekan priesthood and the Aaronic. In order to qualify for the Aaronic priesthood a man had to be born of the tribe of Levi and of the family of Aaron. Genealogy was all-important. Also, his qualification began at birth and ended at death.

Melchizedek's priesthood was quite different. He did not inherit the priesthood by being born into a priestly family. God simply picked him out and designated him as a priest. *As far as his priesthood was concerned*, there is no record of his **father** or **mother** or **genealogy**. In his case, this was of no importance, *and as far as the record is concerned*, no mention is made of his birth or death; therefore his priesthood continues.

We should not conclude that Melchizedek had no parents, that he was never born, and that he never died. That is not the point. The thought is that *as far as his priesthood was concerned*, there is no record of these vital statistics because his ministry as priest was not dependent on them.

He was not the Son of God, as some have mistakenly thought, but was **made like the Son of God** in this respect, that his priesthood continued without interruption.

Now the author is going to demonstrate that Melchizedek's priesthood is superior to Aaron's. There are three arguments in the proof: the argument concerning the tithes and blessing; the argument concerning a change that has taken place, replacing the Aaronic priesthood; and the argument concerning the perpetuity of the Melchizedekan priesthood.

7:4 In verses 4–10 we have the first argument. It opens with an unusual interjection, asking the readers to **consider** the greatness of Melchizedek. **Even the patriarch Abraham gave** him **a tenth of the spoils** of battle. Since Abraham was one of the greatest stars in the Hebrew firmament, it follows that Melchizedek must have been a star of even *greater* magnitude.

7:5 As far as the Levitical priests were concerned, they were authorized by **the law** to collect **tithes** from their fellow Hebrews. Both the priests and the people traced their descent from **Abra-**

ham, the father of the faithful.

7:6 **But** when Melchizedek **received tithes from Abraham**, it was an unusual and unconventional transaction. Abraham, called to be the father of the nation from which Messiah would come, was paying deference to one who was not connected with the chosen people. Melchizedek's priesthood leaped over racial barriers.

Another significant fact is that Melchizedek **blessed** Abraham. He said, "Blessed be Abram of God Most High, Possessor of heaven and earth" (Gen. 14:19, 20).

7:7 When one man blesses another man, it is understood that the superior blesses the inferior. This does not signify any personal or moral inferiority, of course, but simply an inferiority of position.

As we read these arguments based on the OT, we should try to picture the reactions of the Hebrew readers. They had always revered Abraham as one of their greatest national heroes, and rightly so. But now they learn that Abraham acknowledged a "non-Jewish" priest as his superior. Just think! This was in their Bible all the time and they had never noticed it.

7:8 In the Aaronic priesthood **tithes** were received by men who were subject to death. There was a constant succession of priests, each one serving his own generation, then passing on. In Melchizedek's case there is no mention of his having died. Therefore he can represent a priesthood which is unique in that it is perpetual.

7:9 In receiving tithes from **Abraham**, Melchizedek virtually received them from **Levi**. Since Levi was the head of the priestly tribe, it amounts to saying that the Aaronic priesthood **paid tithes** to Melchizedek and thus acknowledged the superiority of the latter.

7:10 By what chain of reckoning can it be said that Levi paid tithes to Melchizedek? Well, first of all, Abraham was actually the one who paid the tithes. He was the great-grandfather of Levi. Though Levi had not yet been born, he was **in the loins of** Abraham, that is, he was destined to be descended from the patriarch. Abraham really acted as a representative for all his posterity when he gave a tenth to Melchizedek. Therefore Levi, and the priesthood that sprang from him, took second place to Melchizedek and to his priesthood.

7:11 In verses 11–20 we find the second argument that shows Melchizedek's priesthood to be superior to Aaron's. The argument is that there has been a change in the priesthood. The priesthood of Christ has set aside the Levitical priesthood. This would not have been necessary if the latter had achieved its purpose fully and finally.

The fact is that **perfection** was not attainable **through the Levitical** system. Sins were never put away and the worshipers never obtained rest of conscience. The priesthood that was set up under the Law of Moses was not the ultimate one.

Another kind of priesthood is now in effect. The perfect Priest has now come, and His priesthood is **not** reckoned **according to the order of Aaron** but rather after **the order of Melchizedek**.

7:12 The fact that the **priesthood** has been **changed** forces the conclusion that the entire legal structure on which the priesthood was based has been changed also. This is a very radical announcement! Like a tolling bell, it rings out the old order of things and rings in the new. We are no longer under the law.

7:13 That there has been a change in the law is evident from the fact that the Lord Jesus **belongs to** a **tribe** which was barred from performing priestly function by the Levitical law.

7:14 It was **from** the tribe **of Judah** that **our Lord** was descended. The Mosaic legislation never authorized anyone from that tribe to be a priest. Yet Jesus is a Priest. How can that be? Because the law has been changed.

7:15 The author has additional evidence that there has been a vast change in the law of the priesthood. **Another** kind of **priest** has arisen **in the likeness of Melchizedek**, and His qualification for the office is quite different from that of Aaron's sons.

7:16 The Levitical priests became eligible by meeting the legal requirements concerning bodily descent. They had to be born of the tribe of Levi and of the family of Judah.

But what qualifies the Lord to be a Priest like Melchizedek is His **endless life**. It is not a question of pedigree but of personal, inherent power. He lives forever.

7:17 This is confirmed by the words of Psalm 110:4, where David points forward to the Messiah's priesthood: **"You are a priest forever according to the order of Melchizedek."** Here the emphasis is on the word **forever**. His ministry will never cease because His life will never end.

7:18 The law which set up the Aaronic priesthood has been annulled **because of its weakness and unprofitableness**. It has been canceled by the advent of Christ.

In what sense was the law weak and unprofitable? Was it not given by God Himself? Could God give anything that was impotent and useless? The answer is that God never intended this to be the ultimate law of priesthood. It was preparatory to the coming of God's *ideal* priesthood. It was a partial and temporary picture of that which would be perfect and final.

7:19 It was also weak and useless in the sense that it **made nothing perfect**. The people were never able to go into the presence of God in the Most Holy Place. This enforced distance between God and man was a constant reminder that the sin question was not settled once for all.

But now **a better hope** has been introduced **through which we draw near to God**. That **better hope** is the Lord Jesus Himself; those who have Him as their only hope have perfect access **to God** at any time.

7:20 Not only has there been a change in the order of priesthood and in the law of priesthood, but also, as we shall now see, there has been a change in the method of induction. The reasoning here revolves around the use of God's **oath** in connection with Christ's priesthood. The oath signifies the introduction of that which is unchangeable and everlasting. Rainsbury says, "Nothing less than the oath of Almighty God guarantees the efficacy and the eternity of the priesthood of our blessed Lord Jesus."[10]

7:21 The Aaronic priests were appointed **without an oath**. Therefore the implication is that their priesthood was intended to be provisional and not enduring.

But God addressed Christ **with an oath** in designating Him as a priest. The form of the oath is found in Psalm 110:4: **"The Lord has sworn and will not relent, 'You are a priest forever according to the order of Melchizedek.' "** Henderson says:

> God places behind Christ's commission the eternal verities of His throne, and the immutable attributes of His nature. If they can change, the new priesthood can change. Otherwise it cannot.[11]

7:22 It follows from this that **Jesus is the surety of a better covenant**. The Aaronic priesthood was a part of the Old Covenant. The priesthood of Christ is connected with the New **covenant**. Covenant and priesthood stand or fall together.

The *New* Covenant is an unconditional agreement of grace which God will make with the house of Israel and with the house of Judah when the Lord Jesus sets up His kingdom on earth (Jer. 31:33, 34). Believers today enjoy some of the blessings of the New Covenant but its complete fulfillment will not be realized until Israel is restored and redeemed nationally.

Jesus is the **surety of** the New **covenant** in the sense that He Himself is the Guarantee. By His death, burial, and resurrection, He provided a righteous basis on which God can fulfill the terms of the covenant. His endless priesthood is also vitally linked with the unfailing fulfillment of the terms of the covenant.

7:23 We now come to the third and final argument concerning the superiority of the Melchizedekan priesthood.

The priests of Israel were **many**. It is said that there were eighty-four high **priests** in the history of the nation, and of course, there were innumerable lesser priests. The office periodically changed hands because of the **death** of the incumbents. The ministry suffered from these inevitable interruptions.

7:24 In the case of Christ's priesthood, there is no such failure because He lives **forever**. His **priesthood** is never passed on to anyone else, and there is no interruption to its effectiveness. It is **unchangeable** and intransmissible.

7:25 Because He **lives** forever **He is also able to save to the uttermost those who come to God** by Him. We generally understand this to refer to His work in saving sinners from the penalty of sin, but actually the writer is speaking of Christ's work in saving saints from the power of sin. It is not so much His role as Savior as that of High Priest. There is no danger that any believers will be lost. Their eternal security rests on His perpetual **intercession for them. He is also able to save** them for all time because His present ministry for them at God's right hand can never be interrupted by death.

7:26 Christ's priesthood is superior to Aaron's because of His personal excellence. He is **holy** in His standing before God. He is **harmless** or guileless in His dealings with men. He is **undefiled** in His personal character. He is **separate from sinners** in His life at God's right hand. He **has become higher than the heavens** in His present and eternal splendor. It is **fitting for us** to have such a High Priest.

7:27 Unlike the Levitical priests, our High Priest **does not need** to offer sacrifices **daily; this He did once for all**. He does **not need** to offer **for His own sins** because He is absolutely sinless. A third amazing way in which He differs from the former priests is that **He offered up Himself** for the sins of the people. The Priest gave Himself as the sacrifice. Wonderful, matchless grace of Jesus!

7:28 **The law** sets up **priests** who are personally imperfect; they are characterized by **weakness** and failure; they are only ritually holy.

God's **oath**, given after the law, **appoints the Son** as a Priest **who has been perfected forever**. This oath was referred to in verse 21 of this chapter and quoted from Psalm 110:4.

There are momentous implications in the material we have just covered. Human priesthood has been superseded by a divine and eternal priesthood. How foolish, then, for men to set up priestly systems patterned after the OT and to intrude upon the functions of our great High Priest!

B. Christ's Ministry Superior to Aaron's (Chap. 8)

8:1 In the verses that follow, Christ's ministry is shown to be superior to Aaron's because He officiates in a better sanctuary (vv. 1–5) and in connection with a better covenant (vv. 7–13).

Now the writer has come to the **main point** of his argument. He is not summarizing what has been said but stating the main thesis to which he has been leading in the Epistle.

We have such a High Priest. There is a triumphant note in the words **we have**. They are an answer to those Jewish people who taunted the early Christians with the words, "We have the tabernacle; we have the priesthood; we have the offerings; we have the ceremonies; we have the temple; we have the beautiful priestly garments." The believers' confident answer is, "Yes, you have the shadows but we have the fulfillment. You have the ceremonies but we have Christ. You have the pictures but we have the Person. And our High Priest **is seated at the right hand of the throne of the Majesty in the heavens**. No other high priest ever sat down in recognition of a finished work, and none ever held such a place of honor and power."

8:2 He serves the people in **the sanctuary** of heaven. This is **the true** tent, of which the earthly tabernacle was a mere copy or representation. **The true tabernacle** was **erected** by **the Lord and not man**, as was the earthly tent.

8:3 Since one of the principal functions of a **high priest** is **to offer both gifts and sacrifices**, it follows that our High Priest must do this also.

Gifts is a general term covering all types of offerings presented to God. **Sacrifices** were gifts in which an animal was slain. What does Christ offer? The question is not answered directly until chapter 9.

8:4 This verse skips over the question of what Christ offers, and simply reminds us that **on earth He would not be** eligible to offer gifts in the tabernacle or temple. Our Lord was descended from Judah and not from the tribe of Levi or the family of Aaron. For this reason He was not qualified to serve in the earthly sanctuary. When we read in the Gospels that Jesus went into the temple (see Luke 19:45), we must understand that He went only into the area surrounding it, and not into the Holy Place or the Holy of Holies.

This of course raises the question whether Christ performed any high priestly functions when he was on earth, or was it only after He ascended that He began His priestly work? The point of verse 4 is that *He was not qualified on earth as a Levitical priest, and could not serve in the temple in Jerusalem*. But this does not mean that He could not perform the functions of *a Melchizedekan priest*. After all, His prayer in John 17 is a high priestly prayer, and His offering of Himself as the one perfect sacrifice at Calvary was certainly a priestly act (see 2:17).

8:5 The tabernacle on earth was a replica **of the heavenly** sanctuary. Its layout depicted the manner in which God's covenant people could approach Him in worship. First there was the door of the outer court, then the altar of burnt offering, then the laver. After that the priests entered the Holy Place and the high priest entered the Most Holy Place where God manifested himself.

The tabernacle was never intended to be the ultimate sanctuary. It was only a **copy and shadow**. When God called **Moses** up to Mount Sinai and told him to build the tabernacle, He gave him a definite blueprint to follow. This **pattern** was a type of a higher, **heavenly**, spiritual reality.

Why does the writer emphasize this so forcefully? Simply to impress on the minds of any who might be tempted to go back to Judaism that they were leaving the substance for the shadows when they should be going on from shadow to substance.

Verse 5 clearly teaches that the OT institutions were types of heavenly realities; therefore it justifies the teaching of typology when it is done in consonance with Scripture and without becoming fanciful.

8:6 This verse forms a transition between the subject of the superior sanctuary and the discussion of the **better covenant**.

First, there is a comparison. Christ's ministry is as superior to the ministry of the Aaronic priests as the **covenant** He mediates is superior to the old one.

Second, a reason is given: the **covenant** is **better** because it is enacted **on better promises**.

Christ's **ministry** is infinitely better. He offered Himself, not an animal. He presented the value of His own blood, not the blood of bulls and goats. He put away sins, not merely covered them. He gave believers a perfect conscience, not an annual reminder of sins. He opened the way for us to enter into the presence of God, not to stand outside at a distance.

He is also Mediator of a better covenant. As **Mediator** He stands between God and man to bridge the gap of estrangement. Griffith Thomas compares the covenants succinctly:

The covenant is "better" because it is absolute not conditional, spiritual not carnal, universal not local, eternal not temporal, individual not national, internal not external. [12]

It is a **better covenant** because it is founded **on better promises**. The covenant of law promised blessing for obedience but threatened death for disobedience. It required righteousness but did not give the ability to produce it.

The New Covenant is an unconditional covenant of grace. It imputes righteousness where there is none. It teaches men to live righteously, empowers them to do so, and rewards them when they do.

8:7 **That first covenant** was not perfect, that is, it was not successful in achieving an ideal relationship between man and God. It was never intended to be the final covenant, but was preparatory to the coming of Christ. The fact that **a second** covenant is mentioned later shows that the **first** was not the ideal.

8:8 Actually the trouble was not with the first covenant itself: "the law is holy, and the commandment holy and just and good" (Rom. 7:12). The trouble was with the people to whom it was given; the law had poor raw materials to work with. This is stated here: **Because finding fault with them, He says** . . . . He did not find fault with the covenant but with His covenant people. The first covenant was based on man's promise to obey (Ex. 19:8; 24:7), and therefore it was not destined to last very long. The New Covenant is a recital, from beginning to end, of what God agrees to do; this is its strength.

The writer now quotes Jeremiah 31:31–34 to show that in the Jewish Scriptures God had promised a New Covenant. The whole argument revolves around the word **new**. If the old was sufficient and satisfactory, why introduce a new one?

Yet God specifically promised to **make a new covenant with the house of Israel and with the house of Judah**. As mentioned previously, the **new covenant** has to do primarily with the nation of **Israel** and not with the church. It will find its complete fulfillment when Christ comes back to reign over the repentant and redeemed nation. In the meantime some of the blessings of the covenant are enjoyed by all believers. Thus when the Savior passed the cup of wine to His disciples, He said, "This is the new covenant in My blood. This do, as often as you drink it, in remembrance of Me" (1 Cor. 11:25).

Henderson quotes the following:

And so we distinguish between the primary interpretation to Israel, and the secondary, spiritual application to the Church today. We now enjoy in the power of the Holy Spirit the blessings of the new covenant, and yet there will be still further and future manifestations for Israel according to God's promise. [13]

8:9 God specifically promised that the New Covenant would not be like **the covenant that** He **made with** them **when** He **took them by the hand** out **of Egypt**. How would it be different? He does not say, but perhaps the answer is implied in the remainder of the verse, **because they did not continue in My covenant, and I disregarded them, says the LORD**. The covenant of the law failed because it was conditional; it called for obedience from a people who did not produce it.

By making the New Covenant an *unconditional* covenant of grace, God avoids any possibility of failure since fulfillment depends on Himself alone and He cannot fail.

The quotation from Jeremiah contains a radical change. The words in the Hebrew text of Jeremiah 31:32 are "though I was a husband to them." Some early translations of Jeremiah read, "so I disregarded (or turned away from) them." The Holy Spirit, who inspired the words of Jeremiah and superintended the preservation of the Bible, directed the writer to the Hebrews to select this alternate reading.

8:10 Notice the repetition of the words **I will**. The Old Covenant tells what man must do; the New Covenant tells what God will do. **After** the **days** of Israel's disobedience are past, He **will put** His **laws in their mind** so that they will know them, and **on their hearts** so that they will love them. They will want to obey, not through fear of punishment but through love for Him. The laws will no longer be written in stone but on the fleshly tables of the heart.

I will be their God, and they shall be My people. This speaks of nearness. The OT told man to stand at a distance; grace tells him to come near. It also speaks of an unbroken relationship and unconditional security. Nothing will ever interrupt this blood-bought tie.

8:11 The New Covenant also includes universal knowledge of the Lord. During Christ's Glorious Reign, it will not be necessary for a man to **teach his neighbor** or **his brother** to **know the LORD**. Everyone will have an inward consciousness of Him, **from the least . . . to the greatest**: "The earth shall be full of the knowledge of the LORD as the waters cover the sea" (Isa. 11:9).

8:12 Best of all, the New Covenant promises mercy for an unrighteous people and eternal forgetfulness of **their sins**. The law was inflexible and unbending: "Every transgression and disobedience received a just reward" (Heb. 2:2).

Furthermore, the law could not deal effectively with sins. It provided for the atonement of sins but not for their removal. (The Hebrew word for atonement comes from the verb meaning *cover*.) The sacrifices prescribed in the law made a man ceremonially clean, that is, they qualified him to engage in the religious life of the nation. But this ritual cleansing was external; it did not touch a man's inward life. It did not provide moral cleansing or give him a clear conscience.

8:13 The fact that God introduces a **New Covenant** means that the **first** is **obsolete**. Since this is so, there should be no thought of going back to the law. Yet that is exactly what some of the professing believers were tempted to do. The author warns them that the legal covenant is outmoded; a better covenant has been introduced. They should get in step with God.

C. Christ's Offering Superior to Old Testament Sacrifices (9:1–10:18)

9:1 In 8:3 the writer made passing mention of the fact that every high priest must have something to offer. He is now ready to discuss the offering of our great High Priest and to contrast it with the OT offerings. To introduce the subject he gives a rapid review of the layout of the tabernacle and of the regulations for worship.

9:2 The **tabernacle** was a tentlike structure in which God dwelt among the Israelites from the time of their encampment at Mount Sinai to the building of the temple. The area around the tabernacle was called the outer court. It was enclosed by a fence consisting of a series of bronze posts with linen cloth stretched between them. As the Israelite entered the tabernacle court through the gate at the east, he came to the altar of burnt offering, where the sacrificial animals were slain and burned; then to the laver, a large bronze stand containing water, in which the priests washed their hands and feet.

The tabernacle itself measured about 45 feet long, 15 feet wide, and 15 feet high. It was divided into two compartments. The first, the Holy Place, was 30 feet long and the second, the Most Holy Place, was 15 feet long.

The tent consisted of a wooden framework covered by goats' hair curtains and weatherproof drapes of animal skins. These coverings formed the top, back, and sides of the tent. The front of the tabernacle was an embroidered veil.

The Holy Place contained three articles of furniture:

1. The **table** of **showbread**, on which were twelve cakes of bread, representing the twelve tribes of Israel. These cakes were called "bread of the Presence" because they were set before the face or presence of God.
2. The golden **lampstand**, with seven arms reaching upward and holding oil-burning lamps.
3. The golden altar of incense, on which the holy incense was burned morning and evening.

9:3 **Behind the second veil** was **the Holiest of All** or the Holy of Holies. Here God manifested Himself in a bright shining cloud. It was the one spot on earth where He could be approached with the blood of atonement.

9:4 This second compartment of the original tabernacle contained **the ark of the covenant**, a large wooden chest **overlaid on all sides with gold**. Inside the chest were **the golden pot** holding **manna, Aaron's rod that budded, and the** two **tablets of the** law. (When the temple was erected later, there was nothing in the ark but the tablets of the law — see 1 Kgs. 8:9).

Verse 4 says that **the golden censer** was also in the Most Holy Place. The Greek word translated **censer**[14] can mean either the incense altar (mentioned in Ex. 30:6 as being in the Holy Place) or the **censer** with which the high priest carried the incense. The best explanation is the latter. The writer regarded the **censer** as belonging to the Most Holy Place because the high priest carried it in from the incense altar into the Holiest Place on the Day of Atonement.

9:5 The gold lid of the ark of the covenant was known as **the mercy seat**. On top of it were two golden figures known as **cherubim**. They faced each other, with wings overspread, and with heads bowed over the cover of the ark.

The writer stops with this brief description. It is not his purpose to go into great **detail**, but merely to outline the contents of the tabernacle and the way of approach to God which it depicted.

9:6 Since the writer is going to contrast Christ's offering with the offerings of Judaism, he must first of all describe those which were required by the law. There were many he could choose from, but he selects the most important in the whole legal system, the sacrifice which was offered on the great Day of Atonement (Lev. 16). If he can prove Christ's work to be superior to that of the high priest on the outstanding day of Israel's religious calendar, then he has won his point.

The priests had access to the outer tent, that is, the Holy Place. They went there continually in the performance of their ritual duties. The common people were not permitted in this room; they had to stay outside.

9:7 Only one man in the world could go into the Most Holy Place — **the high priest** of Israel. And that one man, out of one race, out of one tribe, out of one family, could enter on only one day of the year — the Day of Atonement. When he did enter, he was required to carry a basin of **blood, which he offered for himself and for the people's sins committed in ignorance**.

9:8 There were deep spiritual truths connected with this. **The Holy Spirit** was teaching that sin had created distance between man and God, that man must approach God through a mediator, and that the mediator could approach God only through the blood of a sacrificial victim. It was an object lesson to teach **that the way into** God's presence **was not yet** opened for worshipers.

Imperfect access continued **while the first tabernacle was still standing**. Darby's translation may be preferable here: "While as yet the first tabernacle has [its] standing." The tabernacle was displaced by the temple during the reign of Solomon, but it still had a standing until the death, burial, and resurrection of Christ. The principles it proclaimed concerning approach to God were still valid until the veil of the temple was ripped in two from the top to the bottom.

9:9 The tabernacle system **was symbolic for the present time**. A picture of something better to come, it was an imperfect representation of Christ's perfect work.

The **gifts and sacrifices** could never **make** the worshipers **perfect in regard to the conscience**. If complete remission of sins had been procured, then the offerer's **conscience** would have been free from the guilt of sin. But this never happened.

9:10 As a matter of fact, the Levitical offerings dealt **only with** ritual defilements. They were concerned with such externals as clean and unclean **foods and drinks**, and with ceremonial **washings** that would rid the people of ritual impurity, but they did not deal with moral uncleanness.

The offerings were concerned with a people who were in covenant relationship with God. They were designed to maintain the people in a position of ritual purity so that they could worship. They had nothing to do with salvation or with cleansing from sin. The people were saved by faith in the Lord, on the basis of the work of Christ still future.

Finally, the sacrifices were temporary. They were imposed **until the time of reformation**. They pointed forward to the coming of Christ and to His perfect offering. The Christian era is **the time of reformation** referred to here.

9:11 **Christ** has appeared **as High Priest of the good things to come**,[15] that is, of the tremendous blessings that He bestows on those who receive Him.

His sanctuary is a **greater and more perfect** tent. It is **not made with hands** in the sense that it is not constructed of this world's building materials. It is the sanctuary of heaven, the dwelling place of God.

> No temple made with hands,
>   His place of service is;
> In heaven itself He serves,
>   A heavenly priesthood His:
> In Him the shadows of the law
> Are all fulfilled, and now withdraw.
>   — Thomas Kelly

9:12 Our Lord **entered the Most Holy Place once for all**. At the time of His Ascension, He went into God's presence, **having** finished the work of **redemption** at Calvary. We should never cease to rejoice over those words, **once for all**. The work is completed. Praise the Lord!

He offered **His own blood**, not the blood of bulls and goats. Animal blood had no power to put away sins; it was effective only in cases of technical offenses against religious ritual. But the blood of Christ is of infinite value; its power is sufficient to cleanse all the sins of all the people who have ever lived, all the people who are now living, and all the people who will ever live. Of course, its power is applicable only to those who come to Him by faith. But its cleansing potential is unlimited.

By His sacrifice He **obtained eternal redemption**. The former priests obtained annual atonement. There is a vast difference between the two.

9:13 To illustrate the difference between the sacrifice of Christ and the ceremonies of the law, the writer now turns to the ritual of the red **heifer**. Under the law, if an Israelite touched a dead body, he became ceremonially unclean for seven days. The remedy was to mix **the ashes of a heifer** with pure spring water and to sprinkle the defiled person on the third and seventh days. He then became clean.

Mantle says:

> The ashes were regarded as a concentration of the essential properties of the sin-offering, and could be resorted to at all times with comparatively little trouble and no loss of time. One red heifer availed for centuries. Only six are said to have been required during the whole of Jewish history; for the smallest quantity of the ashes availed to impart the cleansing virtue to the pure spring water (Numbers 19:17).[16]

9:14 If the ashes of a heifer had such power to cleanse from one of the most serious forms of outward defilement, **how much more** powerful is **the blood of Christ** to **cleanse** from inward sins of the deepest dye!

His offering was **through the eternal Spirit**. There is some difference of opinion as to the meaning of this expression. Some interpret it to mean, "through an eternal spirit," meaning the willing spirit in which He made His sacrifice in contrast to the involuntary character of animal offerings. Others understand it to mean, "through His eternal spirit." We rather believe that the *Holy Spirit* is in view; He made His sacrifice in the power of the Holy **Spirit.**

It was an offering made **to God**. He

was the spotless, sinless Lamb of God whose moral perfection qualified Him to be our Sin-bearer. The animal sacrifices had to be physically spotless; He was without blemish morally.

His **blood** cleanses the **conscience from dead works to serve the living God**. It is not merely a physical purging or a ceremonial cleansing but a moral renewal that purifies the conscience. It cleanses from those dead works which unbelievers produce in an effort to earn their own cleansing. It frees men from these lifeless works **to serve the living God**.

9:15 The previous verses stressed the superiority of the blood of the New Covenant to the blood of the Old. This leads to the conclusion of verse 15 — that Christ **is the Mediator of the New Covenant**. Wuest explains:

> The word "mediator" is the translation of *mesites* which refers to one who intervenes between two, to make or restore peace and friendship, to form a compact, or to ratify a covenant. Here the Messiah acts as a go-between or mediator between a holy God and sinful man. By His death on the cross, He removes the obstacle (sin) which caused an estrangement between man and God. When the sinner accepts the merits of Messiah's sacrifice, the guilt and penalty of his sin is his no more, the power of sin in his life is broken, he becomes the recipient of the divine nature, and the estrangement between himself and God, both legal and personal, disappears.[17]

Now those who are called may receive the promised **eternal inheritance**. Through Christ's work saints of the OT as well as of the New enjoy **eternal** salvation and **eternal** redemption.

The fact that qualifies believers of the pre-Christian era for the inheritance is that a **death** has occurred, that is, the death of Christ. His death redeems them from **transgressions under** the law.

There is a sense in which God saved OT people "on credit." They were justified by faith, just as we are. But Christ had not died as yet. Then how could God save them? The answer is that He saved them on the basis of what He knew Christ would accomplish. They knew little or nothing of what Christ would do at Calvary. But God knew, and He reckoned the value of that work

to their account when they believed whatever revelation He gave them of Himself.

In a sense a great debt of transgression had accumulated under the Old Covenant. By His death, Christ redeemed believers of the former dispensation from these **transgressions**.

The manner in which God saved them through the still-future work of Christ is known as the pretermission of sins. It is discussed in Romans 3:25, 26.

9:16 The author's mention of inheritance in verse 15 reminds him that before a last will and **testament** can be probated, evidence must be submitted that the **testator** has died. Usually a death certificate is sufficient evidence.

9:17 The testator may have drawn up his will many years previously and kept it secure in his safe, but it does not take effect until he dies. As long as he is alive, his property cannot be distributed to those named in the will.

9:18 Now the subject switches from a person's last will to the Old **Covenant** given by God through Moses. (The English words "covenant" and "testament" both translate the same Greek word, *diathēkē*.) Here too a death had to take place. It was ratified by the shedding of **blood**.

In ancient times every covenant was made valid by the sacrificial death of an animal. The blood was a pledge that the terms of the covenant would be fulfilled.

9:19 After **Moses** had recited the laws to Israel, **he took the blood of calves and goats, with water, scarlet wool, and hyssop, and sprinkled both the book** of the law **itself and all the people**. In this way Moses arranged the ceremony for the solemn sealing of the covenant.

In Exodus 24:1–11, we read that Moses **sprinkled** the altar and **the people**; no mention is made of sprinkling **the book**, or of the **water, scarlet wool**, and **hyssop**. It is best to view both accounts as complementary.

God, represented by the altar, and **the people** were the contracting parties. **The book** was the covenant. The sprinkled **blood** bound both parties to keep the terms of the covenant. The people promised to obey, and the LORD promised to bless them if they did.

9:20 As Moses sprinkled the blood he said, **"This is the blood of the covenant which God has commanded you."** This action pledged the life of the people if they failed to keep the law.

9:21 In a similar manner Moses **sprinkled with blood both the tabernacle and all the vessels** used in worship. This ritual is not found in the OT. No mention is made of blood in the consecration of the tabernacle in Exodus 40. However, the symbolism is clear. Everything that has any contact with sinful man becomes defiled and needs to be cleansed.

9:22 **Almost** everything under **the law** was **purified with blood**. But there were exceptions. For instance, when a man was to be numbered in a census among the children of Israel, he could bring a half-shekel of silver as "atonement money" instead of a blood offering (Ex. 30:11–16). The coin was a token symbolizing atonement for the man's soul in order for him to be reckoned as one of God's people. Another exception is found in Leviticus 5:11, where certain forms of ritual uncleanness could be dealt with by an offering of fine flour.

These exceptions dealt with *atonement* for, or *covering* of, sin, although generally speaking a blood offering was required even for atonement. But as far as **remission** of sin is concerned, there is no exception: **blood** must be shed.

9:23 The rest of chapter 9 compares and contrasts the two covenants.

First of all, the earthly tabernacle had to **be purified with** the blood of bulls and goats. As has been pointed out this was a ceremonial purification. It was a symbolic sanctification of a symbolic sanctuary.

The **heavenly** sanctuary was the reality of which the earthly tent was a copy. It has to be cleansed **with better sacrifices than these**, that is, with the **sacrifices of** Christ. The use of the plural to describe the single offering of Christ is a figure of speech known as the plural of majesty.

It may seem surprising that the heavenly places needed to **be purified**. Perhaps a clue is found in Job 15:15, "the heavens are not pure in His sight." Doubtless this is because Satan committed the first act of sin in heaven (Isa.

14:12–14), and because he still has access to the presence of God as the accuser of the brethren (Rev. 12:10).

9:24 **Christ** did **not** enter the man-made sanctuary, which was a pattern or figure **of the true** one, **but into heaven itself**. There He appears **in the presence of God for us**.

It is difficult to understand why anyone would want to leave the reality and go back to the copy, why anyone would leave the great High Priest serving in the heavenly sanctuary to return to the priests of Israel serving in a symbolic tent.

9:25 The Lord Jesus did not make repeated offerings, **as the** Aaronic **high priest** had to do. The latter went into **the Most Holy Place** on one day of the year — that is, the Day of Atonement, and he did not offer his own blood but the **blood** of sacrificial animals.

9:26 If Christ had made repeated offerings, that would have meant repeated suffering, since His offering was His own life. It is unthinkable that He should have suffered the agonies of Calvary periodically **since the foundation of the world**! And unnecessary too!

Under the New Covenant, there is:

1. Positive finality — **He has appeared once** for all. The work never needs to be repeated.
2. A propitious time — He appeared **at the end of the ages**, that is, after the Old Covenant had conclusively demonstrated man's failure and powerlessness.
3. A perfect work — He appeared, **to put away sin**. The emphasis is on the words **put away**. It was no longer a matter of annual atonement. Now it was eternal forgiveness.
4. A personal sacrifice — He put away sin **by the sacrifice of Himself**. In His own body He bore the punishment which our sins deserved.

Bearing shame and scoffing rude,
In my place condemned He stood;
Sealed my pardon with His blood;
Hallelujah! What a Saviour!
— *Philip P. Bliss*

9:27 Verses 27 and 28 seem to present another contrast between the Old Covenant and the New. The law condemned sinners **to die once, but after this the judgment**. The law was given to a people who were already sinners and who could not keep it perfectly. Therefore it became a means of condemnation to all who were under it.

9:28 The New Covenant introduces the infinite sacrifice of **Christ**; He **was offered once to bear the sins of many**. It presents the blessed hope of His imminent Return; **to those who eagerly wait for Him He will appear a second time**. But when He returns, it will not be to deal with the problem of **sin**: He finished that work at the cross. He will come to take His people home to heaven. This will be the culmination of their **salvation**; they will receive their glorified bodies and be forever beyond the reach of sin.

The expression, **those who eagerly wait for Him**, is a description of all true believers. All the Lord's people look for Him to return, though they may not agree on the exact order of events connected with His Coming.

The Bible does not teach that only a certain group of especially spiritual Christians will be taken to heaven at the time of the Rapture. It describes the participants as "the dead in Christ" and "we who are alive and remain" (1 Thess. 4:16, 17); this means all true believers, dead or living. In 1 Corinthians 15:23 the participants are identified as "those who are Christ's."

It has often been pointed out that we have three appearances of Christ in verses 24–28. They may be summarized as follows:

Verse 26: He *has* appeared. This refers to His First Advent when He came to earth to save us from the penalty of sin (the *past* tense of salvation).

Verse 24: He *now* appears. This is a reference to His present ministry in the presence of God to save us from the power of sin (the *present* tense of salvation).

Verse 28: He *will* appear. This speaks of His imminent Return when He will save us from the presence of sin (the *future* tense of salvation).

10:1 **The law** was only **a shadow of the good things** that were **to come**. It pointed forward to the Person and work of Christ but it was a poor substitute for reality. To prefer the law to Christ is like preferring a picture to the person represented. It is an *insult* to His majesty!

The weakness of the legal system is seen in the fact that its sacrifices had to be constantly repeated. This repetition proved their total inability to meet the claims of a holy God. Notice the expressions used to capture this idea of repetitiveness: **the same sacrifices**; **offer continually**; **year by year**.

The **sacrifices** were utterly unable to perfect the worshipers, that is, they never gave the people a **perfect** conscience as far as sin was concerned. The Israelites never enjoyed the consciousness of being cleared forever from the guilt of sin. They never had complete rest of conscience.

10:2 If the offerings had completely and finally absolved them from sin, **then would they not have ceased** making the annual trek to the tabernacle or temple? The regular recurrence of the sacrifices branded them as ineffectual. Whoever has to take medicine every hour to stay alive can hardly be said to be cured.

10:3 Instead of pacifying the conscience, the Levitical system stabbed it awake each year. Behind the beautiful ritual of the Day of Atonement lurked the annual reminder that sins were only being covered, not removed.

10:4 **The blood of bulls and goats** simply did **not** have the power to **take away sins**. As mentioned previously, these sacrifices dealt with ritual errors. They gave a certain ceremonial cleansing but they were utter failures as far as providing satisfaction for man's corrupt nature or for his evil deeds.

10:5 In contrast to the weakness of the Levitical offerings, we come now to the strength of the superlative sacrifice of Christ. By way of introduction, we are permitted to hear the Savior's soliloquy at the time of His incarnation. Quoting from Psalm 40, He noted God's dissatisfaction with the sacrifices and offerings of the Old Covenant. God had instituted these sacrifices, yet they were never His ultimate intention. They were never designed to put away sins but rather to point forward to the Lamb of God who would bear away the sin of the world. Could God be pleased with rivers of animal blood or with heaps of animal carcasses?

Another reason for God's dissatisfaction is that the people thought they were pleasing Him by going through ceremonies while their inward lives were sinful and corrupt. Many of them went through the dreary round of sacrifices with no repentance or contrition. They thought that God could be appeased with their animal sacrifices whereas He was looking for the sacrifice of a broken heart. They did not realize that God is not a ritualist!

Dissatisfied with the former sacrifices, God **prepared** a human **body** for His Son which was an integral part of His human life and nature. This, of course, refers to the unfathomable wonder of the Incarnation when the eternal Word became flesh so that, as Man, He might die for men.

It is interesting that the clause **a body You have prepared for Me**, adapted from Psalm 40:6, is capable of two other meanings. In that Psalm it reads, "My ears You have opened," and in the margin it says, "ears You have dug for Me." The open ear, of course, signifies that the Messiah was always ready to receive His instructions from God and to obey them instantly. The dug ear may be an allusion to the Hebrew slave (Ex. 21:1–6), whose ear was bored with an awl to the door as a sign that he willingly indentured himself to his master forever. In His Incarnation, the Savior said, in effect, "I love My Master . . . I will not go out free."

10:6 Continuing the quotation from Psalm 40, the Messiah repeated that God took **no pleasure in burnt offerings and sacrifices for sin**. The animals were unwilling victims whose blood was powerless to cleanse. Also they never represented God's ultimate desire. They were types and shadows looking forward to the sacrifice of Christ. As an end in themselves, they were valueless.

10:7 What did bring pleasure to God was the Messiah's willingness to do the **will** of **God**, no matter what the cost might be. He proved His willing obedience by offering Himself on the altar of sacrifice. As our Lord uttered those words, He was reminded that from the beginning to the end of the OT, it is witnessed of Him that He took wholehearted delight in accomplishing God's **will**.

10:8 In verses 8–10 the writer gives the spiritual significance of the soliloquy.

He sees it as signaling the demise of the old sacrificial system and the inauguration of the one perfect, complete, and final offering of Jesus Christ.

He repeats the quotation from Psalm 40 in condensed form to emphasize God's lack of **pleasure in** the sacrifices that were **offered according to the law**.

10:9 Then the writer sees significance in the fact that immediately after declaring God's displeasure with the old, the Messiah stepped forward, as it were, to do the thing that *would* please the heart of His Father.

The conclusion: **He takes away the first that He may establish the second**, that is, He abolishes the old system of offerings that were required by law, and introduces His own great sacrifice for sin. The legal covenant retires to the wings of the stage as the New Covenant moves to the center.

10:10 **By that will** of God, to which Jesus was utterly obedient, **we have been sanctified through the offering of the body of Jesus Christ once for all**. George Landis comments:

> This is a positional sanctification, as is the case all through Hebrews with the exception of 12:14, and is true of all believers (1 Cor. 6:11) and not merely of a few "advanced Christians." It is accomplished by the will of God and the sacrifice of Christ. We are set apart **by** God, **to** God, and **for** God. It is not to be confused with the progressive work of God's Spirit in the believer through the Word (John 17:17–19; 1 Thess. 5:23).[18]

10:11 The ministry of **every** Aaronic **priest** is now contrasted sharply with that of Christ. The former stood **daily** in the performance of their duties. There was no chair in the tabernacle or temple. There could be no rest because their work was never completed. They **repeatedly** offered **the same sacrifices**. It was an unending routine which left sins untouched and the conscience unrelieved.

These **sacrifices** could **never take away sins**. "Aaron," writes A. B. Bruce, "though an important personage within the Levitical system, was after all but a sacerdotal drudge, ever performing ceremonies which had no real value."[19]

10:12 Our blessed Lord offered a single **sacrifice for sins**. None other would ever be needed!

No blood, no altar now,
The sacrifice is o'er!
No flame, no smoke ascends on high,
The lamb is slain no more.
But richer blood has flowed
From nobler veins
To purge the soul from guilt
And cleanse the reddest stains.
            — *Horatius Bonar*

Having finished the work of redemption, He "sat down in perpetuity at [the] right hand of God" (JND). This verse may correctly be punctuated to read either He "*offered one sacrifice for sins forever*," or that He "*forever sat down*." Both are true, but we tend to believe that the latter is the correct interpretation. He is seated uninterruptedly because sin's tremendous claim has been settled forever. He is seated **at the right hand of God**, the place of honor, power, and affection.

Someone may object that He cannot be seated *forever* since He will one day rise in judgment. There is no contradiction here, however. As far as making an offering for sin is concerned, He has sat down in perpetuity. As far as judgment is concerned, He is not seated forever.

10:13 He waits **till His enemies are made His footstool**, till the day when every knee will bow to Him, and every tongue acknowledge Him as Lord to the glory of God the Father (Phil. 2:10, 11). This will be the day of His public vindication on earth.

10:14 The surpassing value of His **offering** is seen in that by it **He has perfected forever** (or in perpetuity) **those who are being sanctified. Those who are being sanctified** here means all who have been set apart to God from the world, that is, all true believers. They have been **perfected** in a twofold sense. First, they have a perfect standing before God; they stand before the Father in all the acceptability of His beloved Son. Second, they have a perfect conscience as far as the guilt and penalty of sin are concerned; they know that the price has been paid in full and that God will not demand payment a second time.

10:15 **The Holy Spirit also witnesses to** the fact that under the New Covenant, sins would be effectively dealt with once and for all. He **witnesses to** it through the OT Scriptures.

10:16 In Jeremiah 31:31, **the LORD** promised to make a New **covenant** with His chosen earthly people.

10:17 **Then** in the very same passage, **He adds, "Their sins and their lawless deeds I will remember no more."** It is arresting that Jeremiah 31:34 contained this promise of full and final forgiveness of sins; yet some of those who lived in the day when the promise began to be fulfilled were disposed to return to the never-ending sacrifices of Judaism!

10:18 The promise of forgiveness under the New Covenant means that **there is no longer an offering for sin**. With these words, *no longer an offering for sin*, the author closes what we might call the doctrinal portion of the Epistle. He wants to have these words ringing in our hearts and minds as he now presses upon us our practical obligations.

III. WARNING AND EXHORTATIONS (10:19–13:17)

A. Warning Not to Despise Christ (10:19–39)

10:19 In OT times the people were kept at a distance; now in Christ we are brought near through **the blood** of His cross. Therefore we are encouraged to draw near.

This exhortation assumes that all believers are now priests because we are told to have **boldness to enter the Holiest by the blood of Jesus**. The common people during the Jewish economy were barred from the Holy Place and the Most Holy Place; only the priests could enter the first room, and only the high priest could enter the second. Now that is all changed. God has no special place where only a special caste of men may approach Him. Instead, all believers may come into His presence by faith at any time and from any place on earth.

Through the veil God bids me enter
By the new and living way;
Not in trembling hope I venture —
Boldly I His call obey;
There, with Christ my God, I meet
God upon the mercy-seat!

All the worth I have before Him
Is the value of the blood:

I present, when I adore Him
Christ, the First-fruits, unto God.
Him with joy doth God behold;
Thus is my acceptance told!
　　　　　　　— *Author unknown*

10:20 Our approach is by **a new and living way**. **New** here may have the meaning of "newly slain" or "newly made". **Living** seems to be a reference to Jesus in resurrection, therefore, to a **living** Savior. This way was opened **through the veil, that is, His flesh**. This clearly teaches that **the veil** between the two compartments of the tabernacle was a type of the body of our Lord. In order for us to have access into God's presence, the veil had to be rent, that is, His body had to be broken in death. This reminds us that we cannot draw near by Christ's sinless life, but only by His vicarious death. Only through the mortal wounds of the Lamb can we go in. Every time we enter God's presence in prayer or worship, let us remember that the privilege was bought for us at tremendous cost.

10:21 We not only have great confidence when we enter the presence of God; we also have a great **High Priest over the house of God**. Even though we are priests (1 Pet. 2:9; Rev. 1:6), yet we still need a Priest ourselves. Christ is our great **High Priest**, and His present ministry for us assures our continued welcome before God.

10:22 **Let us draw near**. This is the believer's blood-bought privilege. How wonderful beyond all words that we are invited to have audience, not with this world's celebrities, but with the Sovereign of the universe! The extent to which we value the invitation is shown by the manner in which we respond to it.

There is a fourfold description of how we should be spiritually groomed in entering the throne room.

1. **With a true heart**. The people of Israel drew near to God with their mouth, and honored Him with their lips, but their heart was often far from Him (Matt. 15:8). Our approach should be with utter sincerity.

2. **In full assurance of faith**. We draw near with utter confidence in the promises of God and with the firm conviction that we shall have a gra-

cious reception into His presence.

3. **Having our hearts sprinkled from an evil conscience**. This can be brought about only by the new birth. When we trust Christ, we appropriate the value of His blood. *Figuratively* speaking, we sprinkle our hearts with it, just as the Israelites sprinkled their doors with the blood of the Passover lamb. This delivers us from an evil conscience. Our testimony is:

Conscience now no more condemns us,
For His own most precious blood
Once for all has washed and cleansed us,
Cleansed us in the eyes of God.
　　　　　　　— *Frances Bevan*

4. **And our bodies washed with pure water**. Again this is *symbolic* language. **Our bodies** represent our lives. The **pure water** might refer either to the word (Eph 5:25, 26), to the Holy Spirit (John 7:37–39), or to the Holy Spirit using the word in cleansing our lives from daily defilement. We are cleansed once for all from the guilt of sin by the death of Christ, but cleansed repeatedly from the defilement of sin by the Spirit through the word (see John 13:10).

Thus we might summarize the four requisites for entering God's presence as sincerity, assurance, salvation, and sanctification.

10:23 The second exhortation is to **hold fast the confession of our hope**. Nothing must be allowed to turn us from the staunch **confession** that our only **hope** is in Christ.

For those who were tempted to give up the future, unseen blessings of Christianity for the present, visible things of Judaism, there is the reminder that **He who promised is faithful**. His promises can never fail; no one who trusts in Him will ever be disappointed. The Savior will come, as He has **promised**, and His people will be with Him and like Him forever.

10:24 We should also be discovering ways of encouraging fellow believers to manifest **love** and to engage in **good works**. In the NT sense, **love** is not an emotion but an act of the will. We are *commanded* to **love**, therefore it is something we can and must *do*. **Love** is the root; **good works** are the fruit. By our example and by our teaching, we should **stir up** other believers to this kind of life.

> Loving hearts are gardens,
> Loving thoughts are roots,
> Loving words are flowers,
> And good works their fruits.
> — *Adapted*

10:25 Then we should continue to meet **together** and **not** desert the local fellowship, as **some** do. This may be considered as a general exhortation for all believers to be faithful in their church attendance. Without question we find strength, comfort, nourishment, and joy in collective worship and service.

It may also be looked on as a special encouragement for Christians going through times of persecution. There is always the temptation to isolate oneself in order to avoid arrest, reproach, and suffering, and thus to be a secret disciple.

But basically the verse is a warning against apostasy. To forsake the local assembly here means to turn one's back on Christianity and revert to Judaism. Some were doing this when this Letter was written. There was need to exhort one another, especially in view of the nearness of Christ's Return. When He comes, the persecuted, ostracized, despised believers will be seen to be on the winning side. Until then, there is need for steadfastness.

10:26 Now the writer introduces his fourth grim warning. As in the previous cases, it is a warning against apostasy, here described as a deliberate **sin**.

As has been indicated, there is considerable disagreement among Christians as to the real nature of this **sin**. The problem, in brief, is whether it refers to:

1. True Christians who subsequently turn away from Christ and are lost.

2. True Christians who backslide but who are still saved.

3. Those who profess to be Christians for a while, identify themselves with a local church, but then deliberately turn away from Christ. They were never truly born again, and now they never can be.

No matter which view we hold, there are admitted difficulties. We believe that the third view is the correct one because it is most consistent with the over-all teaching of Hebrews and of the entire NT.

Here in verse 26 apostasy is defined as sinning deliberately **after** receiving **the knowledge of the truth**. Like Judas, the person has heard the gospel. He knows the way of salvation; he has even pretended to receive it; but then he deliberately repudiates it.

For such a person, **there no longer remains a sacrifice for sins**. He has decisively and conclusively rejected the once-for-all sacrifice of Christ. Therefore God has no other way of salvation to offer to him.

There is a sense in which all sin is willful, but the author here speaks of apostasy as a willful sin of extraordinary seriousness.

The fact that the author uses **we** in this passage does not necessarily mean that he includes himself. In verse 39 he definitely *excludes* himself and his fellow believers from those who draw back into perdition.

10:27 Nothing remains but a **certain fearful expectation of judgment**; there is no hope of escape. It is impossible to renew the apostate to repentance (6:4). He has knowingly and willfully cut himself off from God's grace in Christ. His fate is a **fiery indignation which will devour the adversaries**. It is pointless to haggle over whether this means literal fire. The language is obviously designed to denote punishment that is dreadfully severe.

Note that God classes apostates as **adversaries**. This indicates positive opposition to Christ, not a mild neutrality.

10:28 The doom of the lawbreaker in the OT is now introduced to form a backdrop against which to contrast the greater doom of the apostate. A man who broke **Moses' law** by becoming an idolater died **without mercy** when his guilt was proven by **the testimony of two or three witnesses** (Deut. 17:2–6).

10:29 The apostate will be counted worthy of **much worse punishment** because his privilege has been much greater. The enormity of his sin is seen in the three charges that are leveled against him:

1. He **has trampled the Son of God underfoot**. After professing to be a fol-

lower of Jesus, he now brazenly asserts that he wants nothing more to do with Him. He denies any need for Christ as Savior and positively rejects Him as Lord.

In Japan there is a crucifix which was used by the government in days of persecution. It was placed on the ground, and everybody had to tread on the face of the Crucified. The non-Christians did not hesitate to tread on His face; the real Christians refused and were killed. The story goes that the face of Jesus was worn down and marred by people trampling on it.

2. He has **counted the blood of the covenant by which he was sanctified a common thing**. He counts as useless and unholy the **blood** of Christ which ratified the New Covenant. He had been set apart by this **blood** in a place of external privilege. Through his association with Christian people, he had been sanctified, just as an unbelieving husband is sanctified by his believing wife (1 Cor. 7:14). But that does not mean that he was saved.

3. He has **insulted the Spirit of grace**. The Spirit of God had illuminated him concerning the good news, convicted him of sin, and pointed him to Christ as the only Refuge of the soul. But he had **insulted** the gracious **Spirit** by utterly despising Him and the salvation He offered.

10:30 Willful repudiation of God's beloved Son is a sin of immense magnitude. God will sit in judgment on all who are guilty of it. He has said, **"Vengeance is Mine, I will repay"** (see Deut. 32:35). **Vengeance** in this sense means full justice. When used of God it has no thought of vindictiveness or of "getting even." It is simply the meting out of what a person actually deserves. Knowing the character of God, we can be sure that He will do as He has said by repaying the apostate in just measure.

And again, "The LORD will judge His people." God will avenge and vindicate those who truly belong to Him, but here in verse 30, the obvious reference is to judgment of evil people.

If it causes difficulty to think of apostates being spoken of as **His people**, we should remember that they are His by creation and also for a while by profession. He is their Creator though not their Redeemer, and they once professed to be His people, even though they never knew Him personally.

10:31 The abiding lesson for all is this: do not be among those who **fall into** God's **hands** for judgment because **it is a fearful thing**.

Nothing in this passage of Scripture was ever intended to disturb and unsettle the minds of those who truly belong to Christ. The passage was purposely written in its sharp, searching, challenging style so that all who profess the name of Christ might be warned about the terrible consequences of turning away from Him.

10:32 In the remaining verses of chapter 10, the writer gives three strong reasons why the early Jewish Christians should continue steadfastly in their allegiance to Christ.

1. Their **former** experiences should stimulate them.

2. The nearness of the reward should strengthen them.

3. The fear of God's displeasure should deter them from going back.

First of all, then, their past experiences should stimulate them. After they professed faith in Christ, they became the targets of bitter persecution: their families disowned them, their friends forsook them, and their foes hounded them. But instead of producing cowardice and fear, these **sufferings** strengthened them in their faith. Doubtless they felt something of the exhilaration of being counted worthy to suffer dishonor for His name (Acts 5:41).

10:33 Sometimes their suffering was individual; they were taken out alone and publicly exposed to abuse and affliction. At other times, they suffered with other Christians.

10:34 They were not afraid to visit those who were prisoners for Christ, even though there was always the danger of guilt by association.

When their **goods** were confiscated by the authorities, they **accepted** it **joyfully**. They chose to be true to Jesus rather than to keep their material possessions. They knew that they had "an inheritance incorruptible and undefiled and that does not fade away" (1 Pet.

1:4). It was truly a miracle of divine grace that enabled them to value earthly wealth so lightly.

10:35 The second great consideration is this: the nearness of the **reward** should strengthen them. Having endured so much in the past, they should not capitulate now. The author says in effect, "Don't miss the harvest of your tears" (F. B. Meyer). They were now nearer to the fulfillment of God's promise than ever before. This was no time to turn back.

"Don't throw away your trust now — it carries with it a rich reward in the world to come" (JBP).

10:36 What they needed was **endurance**, the determination to remain under the persecutions rather than escape them by denying Christ. Then after having **done the will of God**, they would **receive** the promised reward.

10:37 The coming reward synchronizes with the Return of the Lord Jesus; hence the quotation from Habakkuk 2:3, **"For yet a little while, and He who is coming will come and will not tarry."** In Habakkuk the verse reads, "For the vision is yet for an appointed time; but at the end it will speak, and it will not lie. Though it tarries, wait for it; because it will surely come, it will not tarry."

Concerning this change Vincent says:

> In the Hebrew, the subject of the sentence is the vision of the extermination of the Chaldees. . . . As rendered in the Septuagint either Jehovah or Messiah must be the subject. The passage was referred to Messiah by the later Jewish theologians and is so taken by our writer.[20]

A. J. Pollock comments:

> The Old Testament passage and the altered quotation in the New Testament are alike verbally inspired and equally Scripture. The IT in Habakkuk refers to the vision — and deals with the coming of Christ to reign. IT becomes HE in Hebrews and refers to the Rapture.

Then he continues in a more general vein:

> When an inspired writer quotes from the Old Testament he uses just as much of the passage quoted as suits the purpose of the Divine Mind, though never contradicting it; altering it often in order to convey, not the exact meaning of the Old Testament passage, but the fuller meaning

intended to be conveyed by the Holy Spirit in the New Testament. . . . Now no one but God could so treat Scripture. The fact that it is done, and done largely, is another claim to inspiration. God is the Author of the Bible, and He can quote His OWN words, altering and adding to them to suit His purpose. But if any of us quote Scripture, we must do it with careful exactitude. We have no right to alter a jot or tittle. But the Author of the Book can do this. It matters little what pen He uses, whether it be Moses or Isaiah, Peter or Paul, or Matthew or John, it is all His writing.[21]

10:38 A final incentive to steadfast endurance is the fear of God's displeasure. Continuing the quotation from Habakkuk, the author shows that the life that pleases God is the life of **faith**: **Now the just**[22] **shall live by faith**. This is the life that values God's promises, that sees the unseen, and that perseveres to the end.

On the other hand the life that displeases God is that of the man who renounces the Messiah and returns to the obsolete sacrifices of the temple: **But if anyone draws back, My soul has no pleasure in him**.

10:39 The writer quickly dissociates himself and his fellow believers from **those who draw back to perdition**. This separates apostates from genuine Christians. Apostates **draw back** and are lost. True believers **believe** and thus preserve their souls from the doom of the renegade.

With this mention of faith ("believe" and "faith" are the same root word in Greek), the groundwork is laid for a fuller discussion of the life that pleases God. The illustrious eleventh chapter follows quite naturally at this point.

B. Exhortation to Faith by Old Testament Examples (Chap. 11)

11:1 This chapter deals with the vision and endurance of **faith**. It introduces us to men and women of the OT who had 20/20 spiritual vision and who endured tremendous shame and suffering rather than renounce their faith.

Verse 1 is not really a formal definition of faith; rather it is a description of what **faith** *does* for us. It makes **things hoped for** as real as if we already had them, and it provides unshakable **evi-**

dence that the unseen, spiritual blessings of Christianity are absolutely certain and real. In other words, it brings the future within the present and makes the invisible seen.

Faith is confidence in the trustworthiness of God. It is the conviction that what God says is true and that what He promises will come to pass.

Faith must have some revelation from God, some promise of God as its foundation. It is not a leap in the dark. It demands the surest evidence in the universe, and finds it in the word of God. It is not limited to possibilities but invades the realm of the impossible. Someone has said, "Faith begins where possibilities end. If it's possible, then there's no glory for God in it."

> Faith, mighty faith the promise sees,
> And looks to God alone;
> Laughs at impossibilities
> And cries, "It shall be done."
> *— Author unknown.*

There are difficulties and problems in the life of faith. God tests our faith in the crucible to see if it is genuine (1 Pet. 1:7). But, as George Müller said, "Difficulties are food for faith to feed on."

11:2 Because they walked by faith and not by sight, the OT worthies received divine approval. The rest of this chapter is an illustration of how God has borne witness to them.

11:3 Faith provides us with the only factual account of creation. God is the only One who was there; He tells us how it happened. We believe His word and thus we know. McCue states: "The conception of God pre-existent to matter and by His fiat calling it into being is beyond the domain of reason or demonstration. It is simply accepted by an act of faith."

By faith we understand. The world says, "Seeing is believing." God says, "Believing is seeing." Jesus said to Martha, "Did I not say to you that if you would believe you would see . . . " (John 11:40). The Apostle John wrote, "These things I have written to you who believe . . . that you may know" (1 Jn. 5:13). In spiritual matters faith precedes understanding.

The worlds were framed by the word of God. God spoke and matter came into being. This agrees perfectly with man's discovery that matter is essentially energy. When God spoke, there was a flow of energy in the form of sound waves. These were transformed into matter, and the world sprang into being.

The things which are seen were not made out of things which are visible. Energy is invisible; so are atoms, and molecules, and gases to the naked eye, yet in combination they become visible.

The fact of creation as set forth here in Hebrews 11:3 is unimpeachable. It has never been improved on and never will.

11:4 Adam and Eve are bypassed in the honor roll of faith. When Eve had to decide whether God or Satan was telling the truth, she decided that Satan was. However, this does not deny that they were subsequently saved by faith, as pictured by the coats of skin.

Abel must have had some revelation that sinful man can approach God only on the ground of shed blood. Perhaps he learned this from his parents who were restored to fellowship with God only after He had clothed them with the skins of animals (Gen. 3:21). At any rate, he exhibited **faith** by approaching God with the blood of a **sacrifice**. Cain's sacrifice was one of vegetables or fruit and was therefore bloodless. Abel illustrates the truth of salvation by grace through faith. Cain pictures man's futile attempt to save himself by good works.

George Cutting points out that "it was not the personal excellence of Abel that God looked at in counting him righteous, but the excellence of the sacrifice that he brought and his faith in it." And so it is with us: we are not justified because of our character or good works, but solely because of the excellence of the sacrifice of Christ and our acceptance of Him.

Abel was killed by Cain because law hates grace. Self-righteous man hates the truth that he cannot save himself and that he must cast himself on the love and mercy of God.

But Abel's testimony is perpetuated: **Through** his faith he **still speaks**. There is a sense in which faith enables a man's vocal chords to go on functioning long after his body is lying in the grave.

11:5 Sometime during his life **Enoch** must have received a promise from God that he would go to heaven without dying. Up to that time everyone had died — sooner or later. There was no record of anyone ever having been **taken away** without dying. But God promised and Enoch believed. It was the most sane, rational thing that Enoch could do; what is more reasonable than that the creature should believe his Creator?

And so it happened! Enoch walked with the invisible God for three hundred years (Gen. 5:21–24) and then he walked into eternity. **Before he was taken he had this testimony, that he pleased God**. The life of faith always pleases **God**; He loves to be trusted.

11:6 **Without faith it is impossible to please Him**. No amount of good works can compensate for lack of **faith**. After all is said and done, when a man refuses to believe God, he is calling Him a liar. "He who does not believe God has made Him a liar" (1 Jn. 5:10), and how can God be pleased by people who call Him a liar?

Faith is the only thing that gives God His proper place, and puts man in his place too. "It glorifies God exceedingly," writes C. H. Mackintosh, "because it proves that we have more confidence in His eyesight than in our own."

Faith not only believes that God exists, but it also trusts Him to reward **those who diligently seek Him**. There is nothing about God that makes it impossible for men to believe. The difficulty is with the human will.

11:7 The **faith** of **Noah** was based on God's warning that He was going to destroy the world with a flood (Gen. 6:17). There had never been a flood in human experience, in fact, there is some reason to believe that there had never been rainfall up to that time (Gen. 2:5, 6). Noah believed God and built **an ark**, even though he was probably very far from navigable waters. Doubtless he was the butt of many a joke. But Noah's faith was rewarded: **his household** was saved, **the world** was **condemned** by his life and testimony, and he **became heir of the righteousness which is** received on the basis of **faith**.

Perhaps many of the early Jewish Christians to whom this Letter was written often wondered why, if they were

right, they were such a small minority. Noah steps out from the pages of the OT to remind them that in his day only eight people were right and all the rest of the world perished!

11:8 **Abraham** was probably an idolater, living in Ur of the Chaldees, when God appeared to him and told him to move. With the obedience of **faith**, he left home and country, **not knowing** his ultimate destination. Doubtless his friends ridiculed him for such folly but his attitude was:

> I go on not knowing —
> I would not if I might,
> I'd rather walk in the dark with God
> Than walk alone in the light;
> I'd rather walk by faith with Him
> Than to walk alone by sight.
>   — *Helen Annis Casterline*

The walk of faith often gives the impression to others of being imprudent and reckless, but the man who knows God, is content to be led blindfolded, **not knowing** the route ahead.

11:9 God had promised **the land** of Canaan to Abraham. In a very real sense it belonged to him. Yet the only parcel of ground he ever bought in it was a tomb for his dead. He was content to live **in tents**, the symbol of pilgrimage, instead of in a fixed abode. For the time being, he treated Canaan **as if it were a foreign country**.

The companions of his pilgrimage were his son and grandson. His godly example left its mark on them also; even though they were **heirs with him of the same promise** that the land would be theirs.

11:10 Why did Abraham hold such a light grip on real estate? Because **he waited for** *the* **city which has foundations, whose builder and maker is God**. He did not have his heart set on present, material things, but on the eternal. In the original there is a definite article before both **city** and **foundations** — **the** city and *the* **foundations**. In the reckoning of faith there is only one **city** worthy of the name and only one with sure **foundations**.

God is the architect of this heavenly city and He is its **builder** as well. It is the model city, without slums, polluted air, polluted water, or any of the other problems that plague our metropolitan centers.

11:11 By faith Sarah was miraculously empowered **to conceive** when she was about ninety years old. The record clearly states that **she was past** the time of life when she could bear a child. But she knew that God had promised her a baby, and she knew He could not go back on His word. She had shatterproof faith that He would do what He **had promised**.

11:12 Abraham was about ninety-nine when Isaac was born. Humanly speaking it was just about impossible for him to become a father, yet God had promised a numerous posterity and so it must be.

Through Isaac, Abraham became the father of an **innumerable** earthly family, the Hebrew nation. Through Christ, he became father of an **innumerable** spiritual family, that is, true believers of every subsequent age. The **sand by the seashore** probably pictures the *earthly* progeny, while the **stars of the sky** illustrate the *heavenly* people.

11:13 The patriarchs **all died in faith**. They did not live to see the fulfillment of **the** divine **promises**. For instance, Abraham never saw his numerous progeny. The Hebrew nation never occupied all the land that had been promised to it. The OT saints never saw the fulfillment of the promise of the Messiah. But their telescopic vision brought **the promises** near, so near that they are pictured as waving at them in joyful anticipation.

They realized that this world was not their final home. They were content to be **strangers and pilgrims**, refusing the urge to nestle to make themselves comfortable. Their desire was to pass through the world without taking any of its character upon themselves. Their hearts were set on pilgrimage (Ps. 84:5, Knox).

11:14 Their lives indicated **plainly that they** were seeking **a homeland**. Faith implanted a homing instinct in them which was never satisfied by the delights of Canaan. There was always a yen for a better land which they could call home.

11:15 In saying that they were seeking a homeland, the writer wants to make it clear that he is *not* referring to the land of their birth. If Abraham had desired to go back to Mesopotamia, he could have done so, but that was no longer home to him.

11:16 The true explanation is that they were seeking **a heavenly** homeland. This is rather remarkable when we remember that most of the promises to the people of Israel had to do with material blessings on this earth. But they had a heavenly hope as well, and this hope enabled them to treat this world as a foreign country.

This spirit of pilgrimage is especially pleasing to God. Darby writes, "He is not ashamed to be called the God of those whose heart and portion are in heaven." **He has prepared a city for them**, and there they find rest and satisfaction and perfect peace.

11:17 We now come to the greatest test of Abraham's **faith**. God told him to offer up his only son, **Isaac**, upon the altar. With unhesitating obedience, Abraham set forth to offer to God the dearest treasure of his heart. Was he oblivious of the tremendous dilemma? God had promised him numberless progeny. Isaac was **his only begotten son**. Abraham was now 117 and Sarah was 108!

11:18 The promise of a great host of descendants was to be fulfilled **in Isaac**. The dilemma was this: if Abraham killed Isaac, how could the promise ever be fulfilled? Isaac was now about seventeen and unmarried.

11:19 Abraham knew what God had promised; that was all that mattered. He concluded that if God required him to slay his son, **God** would **raise him up, even from the dead** in order to fulfill the promise.

Up to this time there had been no recorded case of resurrection from the dead. Human experience had no statistics to offer. In a real sense, Abraham invented the idea of resurrection. His faith in the promise of God drove him to the conclusion that God would have to raise Isaac.

In a figurative sense, he did receive Isaac back **from the dead**. He had committed himself to the fact that Isaac must be slain. God credited him with the act. But, as Grant put it so poignantly, the

Lord "spared Abraham's heart a pang He would not spare His own." He provided a ram to take Isaac's place, and the only begotten son was returned to his father's heart and home.

Before leaving this outstanding example of faith, there are two points that should be mentioned. First, God never really intended for Abraham to slay his son. Human sacrifices were never God's will for His people. He tested Abraham's faith and found it to be genuine; then He rescinded His order.

Second, Abraham's faith in the promise of a numerous progeny was tested over a period of one hundred years. The patriarch was seventy-five when the promise of a son was first given. He waited twenty-five years before Isaac was born. Isaac was seventeen when Abraham took him up on Mount Moriah to offer him to God. Isaac was forty when he married and was married twenty years before the twins were born. Abraham died when he was 175. At that time his descendants consisted of one son (seventy-five years old) and two grandchildren (fifteen years old). Yet during his lifetime, "He did not waver at the promise of God through unbelief, but was strengthened in faith, giving glory to God, and being fully convinced that what He had promised He was also able to perform" (Rom. 4:20, 21).

11:20 It is hard for our western minds to understand what was so unusual in the faith of **Isaac**, **Jacob**, and Joseph, as recorded in the next three verses. **Isaac**, for instance, achieved a place in faith's hall of fame because he invoked future blessings on **Jacob and Esau**. What was remarkable about that?

Before the children were born, the Lord announced to Rebekah that the boys would become the source of two nations and that the older (Esau) would serve the younger (Jacob). Esau was Isaac's favorite and, as the elder son, would normally have received the best portion from his father. But Rebekah and Jacob deceived Isaac, whose sight was now poor, into giving the best blessing to *Jacob*. When the plot was exposed, Isaac trembled violently. But he remembered God's word that the older would serve the younger, and in spite of his predilection for Esau, he realized that

God's overruling of his natural weakness must stand.

11:21 There were many inglorious chapters in the life of **Jacob**, but he is honored as a hero of faith nevertheless. His character improved with age and he died in a burst of glory. When he **blessed** Ephraim and Manasseh, **the sons of Joseph**, he crossed his hands so that the older son's blessing fell on Ephraim, the younger. In spite of Joseph's protests, Jacob insisted that the blessings must stand because this was the order which the Lord had specified. Though his physical sight was dim, his spiritual sight was keen. The closing scene of Jacob's life finds him worshiping while **leaning on the top of his staff**. C. H. Mackintosh summarizes in his usual lovely style:

> The close of Jacob's career stands in most pleasing contrast with all the previous scenes of his eventful history. It reminds one of a serene evening after a tempestuous day: the sun, which during the day had been hidden from view by clouds, mists, and fogs, sets in majesty and brightness, gilding with his beams the western sky, and holding out the cheering prospect of a bright tomorrow. Thus it is with our aged patriarch. The supplanting, the bargain-making, the cunning, the management, the shifting, the shuffling, the unbelieving selfish fears, — all those dark clouds of nature and of earth seem to have passed away, and he comes forth, in all the calm elevation of faith, to bestow blessings, and impart dignities, in that holy skillfulness which communion with God can alone impart.[23]

11:22 Joseph's **faith** was also strong **when he was dying**. He believed God's promise that He would deliver **the people of Israel** out of Egypt. Faith enabled him to picture the exodus already. It was so sure to him that he instructed his sons to carry **his bones** with them for burial in Canaan. "Thus," writes William Lincoln, "while surrounded by Egypt's pomp and splendor, his heart was not there at all, but with his people in their future glory and blessing."[24]

11:23 It is really the **faith** of **his parents** and not of **Moses** himself that is in view here. As they looked on their baby, **they saw he was a beautiful child** — but it was more than *physical* beauty. They saw that he was a child of destiny, one whom God had marked out for a special work. Their faith that God's purposes would be worked out gave them courage to defy **the king's command** and to hide the child for **three months**.

11:24 By faith Moses himself was able to make several noble renunciations. Though reared in the luxury of Egypt's palace and assured of all the things that men strive for, he learned that "it is not the possession of things but the forsaking of them that brings rest" (J. Gregory Mantle).

First of all, he refused Egypt's fame. He was the adopted **son of Pharaoh's daughter** and therefore assured of a place in the social elite, perhaps even as Pharaoh's successor. But he had been born of better blood — a member of God's chosen earthly people. From this nobility he could not *step down* to Egypt's royalty. In his adult years he made his choice; he would not hide his true nationality to win a few short years of earthly fame. The result? Instead of occupying a line or two of hieroglyphics on some obscure tomb, he is memorialized in God's eternal Book. Instead of being found in a museum as an Egyptian mummy, he is famous as a man of God.

11:25 Second, he repudiated the **pleasures** of Egypt. Humble association **with the** suffering **people of God** meant more to him than the transient gratification of his appetites. The privileges of sharing ill-treatment with his own people was greater pleasure to him than dissipation in Pharaoh's court.

11:26 Third, he turned his back on **the treasures in Egypt**. Faith enabled him to see that the fabulous treasure houses of Egypt were worthless in the light of eternity. So he chose to suffer the same kind of **reproach** as the Messiah would later suffer. Loyalty to God and love for His people were valued by him more that the combined wealth of Pharaoh. He knew that these were the things that would count one minute after he died.

11:27 Then, he also renounced Egypt's *monarch*. Emboldened **by faith**, he made his exit from the land of bondage, careless of **the wrath of the king**. It was a clear break from the politics of this world. He feared Pharaoh so little because he feared God so much. He kept his eyes on "the blessed and only Potentate, the King of kings and Lord of lords, who alone has immortality, dwelling in unapproachable light, whom no man has seen or can see, to whom be honor and everlasting power. Amen" (1 Tim. 6:15, 16).

11:28 Finally, he rejected Egypt's *religion*. By instituting **the Passover** and by **sprinkling** the **blood**, he emphatically separated himself from Egyptian idolatry forever. He flung down the gauntlet in defiance of the religious establishment. For him, salvation was through the blood of the lamb, not through the waters of the Nile. As a result, the firstborn of Israel were spared while the **firstborn** of Egypt were slain by the destroyer.

11:29 At first **the Red Sea** seemed to spell disaster to the Hebrew refugees. With the enemy in hot pursuit, they seemed to be trapped. But in obedience to God's word, they moved forward and the waters parted: "The LORD caused the sea to go back by a strong east wind all that night, and made the sea into dry land, and the waters were divided" (Ex. 14:21). When **the Egyptians** tried to follow, their chariot wheels became clogged, the waters returned to their usual place, and Pharaoh's armies **were drowned**. Thus the Red Sea became a causeway of deliverance to Israel but a dead end of doom to the Egyptians.

11:30 The walled city of **Jericho** was the first military objective in the conquest of Canaan. Reason would claim that such an impregnable fortress could be taken only by superior forces. But faith's methods are different. God uses strategies that appear foolish to men in order to accomplish His purposes. He told the people to encircle the city **for seven days**. On the seventh day they were to march around it seven times. The priests were to give a loud blast on their trumpets, the people were to shout, and **the walls** would fall. Military experts would write off the method as ludicrous. But it worked! The weapons of the spiritual warfare are not worldly but have divine power to destroy strongholds (2 Cor. 10:4).

11:31 We do not know when **the harlot Rahab** became a worshiper of Jehovah, but it is clear that she did. She abandoned the false religion of Canaan to become a Jewish proselyte. Her faith received a rigorous test when the spies came to her home. Would she be loyal to her country and her fellow countrymen, or would she be true to the Lord? She decided to stand on the Lord's side, even if it meant betraying her country. By giving friendly welcome to **the spies**, she and her family were spared, while her disobedient neighbors perished.

11:32 At this point the writer asks a rhetorical question: **And what more shall I say?** He has given an imposing list of men and women who demonstrated faith and endurance in OT times. How many more must he give in order to make his point?

He has not run out of examples, but only out of time. It would take too long to go into details so he will satisfy himself to name a few and catalog some triumphs and testings of faith.

There was **Gideon** whose army was reduced from 32,000 to 300. First the timid were sent home, then those who thought too much of their own comfort. With a hard core of true disciples, Gideon routed the Midianites.

Then there was **Barak**. When called to lead Israel to battle against the Canaanites, he agreed only on the condition that Deborah would go with him. In spite of this cowardly facet in his character, God saw real trust and lists him among the men of faith.

Samson was another man of obvious weakness. Yet, in spite of that, God detected the faith that enabled him to kill a young lion with his hands, to destroy thirty Philistines in Ashkelon, to slay one thousand Philistines with the jawbone of a donkey, to carry away the gates of Gaza, and finally to pull down the temple of Dagon and slay more Philistines in his death than he had in his life.

Though an illegitimate child, **Jephthah** rose to be the deliverer of his people from the Ammonites. He illustrates the truth that faith enables a man to rise above his birth and environment and make history for God.

The faith of **David** shines out in his contest with Goliath, in his noble behavior toward Saul, in his capture of Zion, and in countless other episodes. In his psalms, we find his faith crystallized in penitence, praise, and prophecy.

Samuel was the last of Israel's judges and her first prophet. He was God's man for the nation at a time when the priesthood was marked by spiritual bankruptcy. He was one of the greatest leaders in Israel's history.

Add to this list **the prophets**, a noble band of God's spokesmen, men who were embodied consciences, who would rather die than lie, who would rather go to heaven with a good conscience than stay on earth with a bad one.

11:33 The writer now turns from naming people of faith to citing their exploits.

They **subdued kingdoms**. Here our minds turn to Joshua, to the judges (who were really military leaders), to David, and to others.

They **worked righteousness**. Kings like Solomon, Asa, Jehoshaphat, Joash, Hezekiah, and Josiah are remembered for reigns which, though not perfect, were characterized by **righteousness**.

They **obtained promises**. This may mean that God made covenants with them, as in the case of Abraham, Moses, David, and Solomon; or it may mean that they received the fulfillment of promises, thus demonstrating the truth of God's word.

They **stopped the mouths of lions**. Daniel is an outstanding example here (Dan. 6:22), but we should also remember Samson (Judg. 14:5, 6) and David (1 Sam. 17:34, 35).

11:34 They **quenched the violence of fire**. The fiery furnace succeeded only in burning the fetters of the three young Hebrews and setting them free (Dan. 3:25). Thus it proved to be a blessing in disguise.

They **escaped the edge of the sword**. David escaped Saul's malicious attacks (1 Sam. 19:9,10), Elijah escaped the murderous hatred of Jezebel (1 Kgs. 19:1–3), and Elisha escaped from the king of Syria (2 Kgs. 6:15–19).

They won strength **out of weakness**. Many symbols of **weakness** are found in the annals of faith. Ehud, for instance, was left-handed; yet he slew the king of Moab (Judg. 3:12–22). Jael, a member of "the weaker sex," killed Sisera with a tent peg (Judg. 4:21). Gideon used fragile earthen pitchers in the defeat of the

Midianites (Judg. 7:20). Samson used the jawbone of a donkey to slay one thousand Philistines (Judg. 15:15). They all illustrate the truth that God has chosen the weak things of the world to shame the strong (1 Cor. 1:27).

They **became valiant in battle**. Faith endowed men with strength beyond what was natural and enabled them to overcome in the face of insurmountable odds.

They put **to flight the armies of the aliens**. Though often under-equipped and greatly outnumbered, the armies of Israel walked off with the victory to the confusion of the foe and the amazement of everyone else.

11:35 Women received their dead by resurrection. The widow of Zarephath (1 Kgs. 17:22) and the woman of Shunem (2 Kgs. 4:34) are cases in point.

But faith has another face. In addition to those who performed dazzling feats, there were those who endured intense suffering. God values the latter as much as the former.

Because of their faith in the Lord, some were subjected to cruel torture. If they would have renounced Jehovah, they would have been released; but to them it was better to die and be raised again to heavenly glory than to continue this life as traitors to God. In the time of the Maccabees, a mother and her seven sons were put to death, one after the other, and in sight of each other, by Antiochus Epiphanes. They refused to accept release **that they might obtain a better resurrection**, that is, better than a mere continuation of life on earth. Morrison comments:

So this is also a result of faith, *not* that it brings deliverance to a man, but that sometimes, when deliverance is offered, it gives him a fine courage to refuse it. There are seasons when faith shows itself in taking. There are seasons when it is witnessed in refusing. There is a deliverance that faith embraces. There is a deliverance that faith rejects. They were tortured, not accepting deliverance — that was the sign and seal that they were faithful. There are hours when the strongest proof of faith is the swift rejection of the larger room.[25]

11:36 Others were mocked and flogged, and were bound in prison. For faithfulness to God, Jeremiah endured all these forms of punishment (Jer. 20:1–6; 37:15). Joseph too was imprisoned because he would rather suffer than sin (Gen. 39:20).

11:37 They were stoned. Jesus reminded the scribes and Pharisees that their ancestors had murdered Zechariah in this way between the sanctuary and the altar (Matt. 23:35).

They were sawn in two. Tradition says that Manasseh used this method of executing Isaiah.

They **were tempted**.[26] This clause probably describes the tremendous pressures that were brought to bear on believers to compromise, to recant, to commit acts of sin, or in any way to deny their Lord.

They **were slain with the sword**. Uriah the prophet paid this price for his faithful proclamation of God's message to King Jehoiakim (Jer. 26:23); but the expression here refers to mass slaughter such as occurred in the times of the Maccabees.

They wandered about in sheepskins and goatskins, being destitute, afflicted, tormented. Moorehead comments:

They might have rustled in silks and velvets and luxuriated in the palaces of princes had they denied God and believed the world's lie. Instead, they wandered about in sheepskins and goatskins, themselves accounted no better than goats or sheep, nay, they like these reckoned fit only for the slaughter.[27]

They suffered poverty, privation, and persecution.

11:38 The world treated them as if they were not worthy to live. But the Spirit of God burst forth here with the interjection that actually it was the other way around — **the world was not worthy** *of them*.

They wandered in deserts and mountains and **in dens and caves of the earth**. Dispossessed of homes, separated from families, pursued like animals, expelled from society, they endured heat and cold, distress and hardship, but they would not deny their Lord.

11:39 God has borne witness to the faith of these OT heroes, yet they died before receiving the fulfillment of **the promise**. They did not live to see the

Advent of the long awaited Messiah or to enjoy the blessings that would flow from His ministry.

11:40 God had reserved **something better for us**. He had arranged **that they should not be made perfect apart from us**. They never did enjoy a perfect conscience as far as sin was concerned; and they will not enjoy the full perfection of the glorified body in heaven until we are all caught up to meet the Lord in the air (1 Thess 4:13–18). The spirits of OT saints are already perfect in the presence of the Lord (Heb. 12:23), but their bodies will not be raised from among the dead until the Lord returns for His people. Then they will enjoy the perfection of resurrection glory.

To put it another way, the OT believers were not as privileged as we are. Yet think of their thrilling triumphs and tremendous trials! Think of their exploits and their endurance! They lived on the other side of the cross; we live in the full glory of the cross. Yet how do our lives compare with theirs? This is the cogent challenge of Hebrews 11.

C. Exhortation to Hope in Christ (Chap. 12)

12:1 We must bear in mind that Hebrews was written to people who were being persecuted. Because they had forsaken Judaism for Christ, they were facing bitter opposition. There was a danger that they might interpret their suffering as a sign of God's displeasure. They might become discouraged and give up. Worst of all, they might be tempted to return to the temple and its ceremonies.

They should not think that their sufferings were unique. Many of the witnesses described in chapter 11 suffered severely as a result of their loyalty to the Lord, yet they endured. If they maintained unflinching perseverance with their lesser privileges, how much more should we to whom the better things of Christianity have come.

They surround us as a **great cloud of witnesses**. This does *not* mean that they are spectators of what goes on on earth. Rather they witness to us by their lives of faith and endurance and set a high standard for us to duplicate.

This verse invariably raises the question, "Can saints in heaven see our lives on earth or know what is transpiring?" The only thing we can be sure they know is when a sinner is saved: "I say to you that likewise there will be more joy in heaven over one sinner who repents than over ninety-nine just persons who need no repentance" (Luke 15:7).

The Christian life is a race that requires discipline and endurance. We must strip ourselves of everything that would impede us. Weights are things that may be harmless in themselves and yet hinder progress; they could include material possessions, family ties, the love of comfort, lack of mobility, etc. In the Olympic races, there is no rule against carrying a supply of food and beverage, but the runner would never win the race that way.

We must also **lay aside . . . the sin which so easily ensnares us**. This may mean sin in any form, but especially the sin of unbelief. We must have complete trust in the promises of God and complete confidence that the life of faith is sure to win.

We must guard against the notion that **the race** is an easy sprint, that everything in the Christian life is rosy. We must be prepared to press on with perseverance through trials and temptations.

12:2 Throughout the race, we should look away from every other object and keep our eyes riveted on **Jesus**, the foremost Runner. A. B. Bruce comments:

> One stands out conspicuous above all the rest . . . the Man who first perfectly realised the idea of living by faith . . . , who undauntedly endured the bitter suffering of the cross, and despised the ignominy of it, sustained by a faith that so vividly realised coming joy and glory as to obliterate the consciousness of present pain and shame.[28]

He is the **author**, or pioneer, **of our faith** in the sense that He has provided us with the only perfect example of what the life of faith is like.

He is also the **finisher of our faith**. He not only began the race but finished it triumphantly. For Him the race course stretched from heaven to Bethlehem, then on to Gethsemane and Calvary, then out of the tomb and back to heaven. At no time did He falter or turn back. He kept His eyes fixed on the coming glory when all the redeemed would be gathered with Him eternally. This enabled Him to think nothing of **shame** and to endure suffering and death. Today He is seated **at the right hand of the throne of God.**

12:3 The picture now changes from a race to a fight against sin. Our undaunted Captain is the Lord Jesus; no one ever **endured such hostility from sinners** as He. Whenever we have a tendency to grow **weary and discouraged**, we should think of what He went through. Our trials will seem trifling by comparison.

12:4 We are engaged in a ceaseless **striving against sin**. Yet we **have not resisted** to the point of **bloodshed**, that is, to the point of death. *He did!*

12:5 The Christian view of suffering is now presented. Why do persecution, testings, trials, sickness, pain, sorrow, and trouble come into the life of the believer? Are they a sign of God's anger or displeasure? Do they happen by chance? How should we react to them?

These verses teach that these things are part of God's educative process for His children. Although they do not come from God, He permits them, then overrules them for His glory, for our good, and for the blessing of others.

Nothing happens by chance to the Christian. Tragedies are blessings in disguise, and disappointments are His appointments. God harnesses the adverse circumstances of life to conform us to the image of Christ.

So the early Hebrew believers were exhorted to remember Proverbs 3:11, 12, where God addresses them as **sons**. There He warns them against despising His discipline or losing courage under His rebuke. If they rebel or give up, they lose the benefit of His dealings with them and fail to learn His lessons.

12:6 When we read the word *chastening*, or *chastisement*, we tend to think of a whipping. But here the word means child training or education. It includes instruction, discipline, correction, and warning. All are designed to cultivate

Christian virtues and drive out evil. In this passage, the chastening was not punishment for wrongdoing, but training through persecution.

The passage in Proverbs distinctly states that God's discipline is a proof of His love, and no **son** of His escapes chastisement.

12:7 By remaining submissive to the **chastening** of **God**, we permit His discipline to mold us into His image. If we try to short-circuit His dealings with us, He may have to teach us over a longer period of time, using more instructive, and consequently, more difficult methods. There are grades in the school of God, and promotion comes only when we have learned our lessons.

So when testings come to us, we should realize that God is treating us as **sons**. In any normal father-son relationship, the father trains his **son** because he loves him and wants the best for him. God loves us too much to let us develop naturally.

12:8 In the spiritual realm, those who do not experience God's discipline are **illegitimate** children, not true **sons**. After all, a gardener does not prune thistles, but he does prune grapevines. As in the natural, so in the spiritual.

12:9 Most of us have experienced discipline from our **human fathers**. We did not interpret this as a sign that they hated us. We realized that they were interested in our welfare, **and we paid them respect**.

How **much more** should we respect the training of **the Father of spirits and live!** God is **the Father** (or source) of all beings that are spirit or that have a spirit. Man is a spirit dwelling in a human body. By being subject to God we enjoy life in its truest sense.

12:10 The discipline of earthly parents is not perfect. It lasts only for a time, that is, during childhood and youth. If it has not succeeded then, it can do no more. And it is **as seemed best to them**, according to what they think is right. Sometimes it may not be right.

But God's discipline is always perfect. His love is infinite and His wisdom is infallible. His chastenings are never the result of whim, but always for our profit. His objective **is that we may be**

partakers of His holiness. And godliness can never be produced outside God's school. Jowett explains:

The purpose of God's chastening is not punitive but creative. He chastens "that we may share His holiness." The phrase "that we may share" has direction in it, and the direction points toward a purified and beautified life. The fire which is kindled is not a bonfire, blazing heedlessly and unguardedly, and consuming precious things; it is a refiner's fire, and the Refiner sits by it, and He is firmly and patiently and gently bringing holiness out of carelessness and stability out of weakness. God is always creating even when He is using the darker means of grace. He is producing the fruits and flowers of the Spirit. His love is always in quest of lovely things.[29]

12:11 At the time, all discipline seems painful. But **it yields the peaceable fruit of righteousness to those who have been trained by it**. That is why we often come across such testimonies, like this by Leslie Weatherhead:

Like all men I love and prefer the sunny uplands of experience, where health, happiness, and success abound, but I have learned far more about God and life and myself in the darkness of fear and failure than I have ever learned in the sunshine. There are such things as the treasures of darkness. The darkness, thank God, passes. But what one learns in the darkness one possesses for ever. "The trying things," says Bishop Fenelon, "which you fancy come between God and you, will prove means of unity with Him, if you bear them humbly. Those things that overwhelm us and upset our pride, do more good than all that which excites and inspirits us."[30]

Or consider the following testimony by C. H. Spurgeon:

I am afraid that all the grace I have got out of my comfortable and easy times and happy hours might almost lie on a penny. But the good that I have received from my sorrows and pains and griefs is altogether incalculable. What do I not owe to the hammer and the anvil, the fire and the file? Affliction is the best bit of furniture in my house.[31]

12:12 Believers should not cave in under the adverse circumstances of life; their lapse of faith might have an unfavorable influence on others. Drooping **hands** should be reinvigorated to serve the living Christ. **Feeble knees** should be strengthened for persevering prayer.

12:13 Faltering **feet** should be guided in **straight paths** of Christian discipleship. Williams writes:

All who follow the Lord fully smooth the path of faith for feeble brethren; but those who do not follow fully, roughen the path for others' feet and create spiritual cripples.[32]

G. H. Lang gives a fine illustration:

A weary traveler, tired of the road and the buffeting of the tempest, stands dispirited and limp. With shoulders bowed, hands hanging slack, knees bent and shaking, he is ready to give up and sink to the ground. Such can God's pilgrim become, as pictured by our writer.

But one comes to him confident of mien, with kindly smile and firm voice, and says, "Cheer up, stand erect, brace your limbs, take heart of grace. You have already come far; throw not away your former toils. A noble home is at the end of the journey. See, yonder is the direct road to it; keep straight on; seek from the great Physician healing for your lameness. . . . Your Forerunner went this same hard road to the palace of God; others before you have won through; others are on the way; you are not alone; only press on! and you too shall reach the goal and win the prize."

Happy is he who knows how to sustain with words him that is weary (Isaiah 50:4). Happy is he who accepts exhortation (Hebrews 13:22). And thrice happy is he whose faith is simple and strong so that he finds no occasion of stumbling in the Lord when His discipline is severe.[33]

12:14 Christians should strive for peaceable relations **with all people** and at all times. But this exhortation is especially needful when persecution is prevalent, when some are defecting from the faith, and when nerves are frayed. At such times it is all too easy to vent one's frustration and fears on those who are nearest and dearest.

We should also strive for the **holiness without which no one will see the Lord**. What is the **holiness** referred to here? To answer the question we should remind ourselves that *holiness* is used of believers in at least three different ways in the NT.

First of all, the believer becomes *positionally* holy at the time of his conversion; he is set apart to God from the world (1 Cor. 1:2; 6:11). By virtue of his union with Christ, he is sanctified forever. This is what Martin Luther meant when he said, "My holiness is in heaven." Christ is our holiness, that is, as far as our standing before God is concerned.

Then there is a *practical* sanctification (1 Thess. 4:3; 5:23). This is what we should be day by day. We should separate ourselves from every form of evil. This holiness should be progressive, that is, we should be growing more and more like the Lord Jesus all the time.

Finally, there is *complete* or *perfect* sanctification. This takes place when a believer goes to heaven. Then he is forever free from sin. His old nature is removed, and his state perfectly corresponds to his standing.

Now which holiness are we to **pursue**? Obviously it is practical sanctification that is in view. We do not strive after positional sanctification; it is ours automatically when we are born again. And we do not strive after the perfect sanctification that will be ours when we see His face. But practical or progressive sanctification is something that involves our obedience and cooperation; we must cultivate this holiness continually. The fact that we must follow it is proof that we do not fully attain it in this life. (See notes under 2:11 for a more detailed description of the various aspects of sanctification.)

Wuest writes:

> The exhortation is to the born-again Jews who had left the Temple, to live such consistent saintly lives, and to cling so tenaciously to their new-found faith, that the unsaved Jews who had also left the Temple and had outwardly embraced the New Testament truth, would be encouraged to go on to faith in Messiah as High Priest, instead of returning to the abrogated sacrifices of the Levitical system. These truly born-again Jews are warned that a limping Christian life would cause these unsaved Jews to be turned out of the way.[34]

But a difficulty remains! Is it true that we cannot see the Lord without practical sanctification? Yes, there is a sense in which this is true; but let us understand that this does not mean that we earn the right to see God by living holy lives. Jesus Christ is our only title to heaven.

What this verse means is that there must be practical **holiness** as a proof of new life within. If a person is not growing more holy, he is not saved. When the Holy Spirit indwells a person, He manifests His presence by a separated life. It is a matter of cause and effect; if Christ has been received, the rivers of living water will flow.

12:15 The next two verses seem to present four distinct sins to avoid. But there is a strong suggestion in the context that this is another warning against the single sin of apostasy and that these four sins are all related to it.

First of all, apostasy is a failure to obtain **the grace of God**. The person looks like a Christian, talks like a Christian, professes to be a Christian, but he has never been born again. He has come so near the Savior but has never received Him; so near and yet so far.

Apostasy is a **root of bitterness**. The person turns sour against the Lord and repudiates the Christian faith. His defection is contagious. Others are **defiled** by his complaints, doubts, and denials.

12:16 Apostasy is closely linked with immorality. A professing Christian may fall into gross moral sin. Instead of acknowledging his guilt, he blames the Lord and falls away. Apostasy and sexual sin are connected in 2 Peter 2:10, 14, 18 and Jude 8, 16, 18.

Finally, apostasy is a form of irreligion, illustrated by **Esau**. He had no real appreciation for the birthright; he willingly bartered it for the momentary gratification of his appetite.

12:17 Later Esau was remorseful at the loss of the older son's double portion, but it was too late. His father could not reverse the blessing.

So it is with an apostate. He has no real regard for spiritual values. He willingly renounces Christ in order to escape reproach, suffering, or martyrdom. He cannot be renewed to repentance. There may be remorse but no godly repentance.

12:18 Those who are tempted to return to the law should remember the terrifying circumstances that attended the giving of the law and should draw spiritual lessons from them. The scene was Mount Sinai, a literal, tangible **mountain** that was all on **fire**. It was enveloped in a pall or veil that made everything seem indistinct, obscure, and nebulous. A violent storm raged around it.

12:19 In addition to these natural disorders, there were terrible supernatural phenomena. **A trumpet** blasted away, and a **voice** thundered out so ominously that the people pled for it to stop.

12:20 They were completely unnerved by the divine edict that **"If so much as a beast touches the mountain, it shall be stoned** to death."[35] They knew that if it meant death to a dumb, uncomprehending animal, how much more surely would it mean death to those who understood the warning.

12:21 The entire scene was **so terrifying** and forbidding that **Moses** himself was **trembling**. All this speaks eloquently of the nature and ministry of the law. It is a revelation of God's righteous requirements and of His wrath against sin. The purpose of the law was not to provide the knowledge of salvation but to produce the knowledge of sin. It speaks of distance between God and man because of sin. It is a ministry of condemnation, darkness, and gloom.

12:22 Believers have not come to the forbidding terrors of Sinai but to the welcome of grace:

> The burning mount and the mystic veil,
> With our terrors and guilt are gone;
> Our conscience has peace that can
>   never fail,
> 'Tis the Lamb on high on the throne.
> — *James G. Deck*

Now every blood-brought child of God can say:

> The terrors of law and of God,
> With me can have nothing to do;
> My Saviour's obedience and blood
> Hide all my transgressions from view.
> — *A. M. Toplady*

"We *have* already arrived in principle where in full reality we shall be forever. The future is already the present. In today we possess tomorrow. On earth we own Heaven" (Selected).

We do not come to a tangible mountain on earth. Our privilege is to enter the sanctuary in heaven. By faith, we approach God in confession, praise, and prayer. We are not limited to one day of the year, but may enter the holiest at any time with the knowledge that we are always welcome. God no longer says, "Stay at a distance"; He says, "Come near with confidence."

Law has its Mount Sinai but faith has its **Mount Zion**. This heavenly mountain symbolizes the combined blessings of grace — all that is ours through the redeeming work of Christ Jesus.

Law has its earthly Jerusalem but faith has its **heavenly** capital above. **The city of the living God** is in heaven, the city which has the foundations, whose Architect and Builder is God.

As we enter the presence of God, we are surrounded by an august gathering. First of all, there are myriads **of angels** who though untainted by sin cannot join with us in song because they do not know "the joy that our salvation brings."

12:23 Then we are with the **general assembly of the firstborn** ones **who are registered in heaven**. These are members of the **church**, the Body and Bride of Christ, who have died since Pentecost and are now consciously enjoying the Lord's presence. They await the Day when their bodies will be raised from the grave in glorified form and reunited with their spirits.

By faith we see **God the Judge of all**. No longer does darkness and gloom hide Him; to faith's vision His glory is transcendent.

The OT saints are there, **the spirits of just men made perfect**. Justified by faith, they stand in spotless purity because the value of Christ's work has been imputed to their account. They too await the time when the grave will yield up its ancient charges and they will receive glorified bodies.

12:24 **Jesus** is there, **the Mediator of the new covenant**. There is a difference between Moses as mediator of the Old Covenant and Jesus as **Mediator of the new**. Moses served as a mediator simply by receiving the law from God and delivering it to the people of Israel. He was the go-between, or the people's representative, offering the sacrifices by which the covenant was ratified.

Christ is **Mediator of the new covenant** in a far higher sense. Before God could righteously make this covenant, the Lord Jesus had to die. He had to seal the covenant with His own blood and give Himself a ransom for many (1 Tim. 2:6).

He secured the blessings of the New Covenant for His people by His death. He insures these blessings for them by His endless life. And He preserves His people to enjoy the blessings in a hostile world by His present ministry at God's right hand. All this is included in His mediatorial work.

Bearing the scars of Calvary, the Lord Jesus is exalted at God's right hand, a Prince and a Savior.

> We love to look up and behold Him there,
> The Lamb for His chosen slain;
> And soon shall His saints all His glories share,
> With their Head and their Lord shall reign.
>   *– James G. Deck*

Finally, there is **the blood of sprinkling that speaks better things than** the blood of Abel. When Christ ascended, He presented to God all the value of **the blood** He shed at the cross. There is no suggestion that He literally carried His blood into heaven, but the merits of His blood have been made known in the sanctuary. Again, J. G. Deck puts truth into poetry:

> His precious blood is sprinkled there,
> Before and on the throne;
> And His own wounds in Heaven declare
> The work that saves is done.

His precious **blood** is contrasted with the blood **of Abel**. Whether we understand the latter as meaning the blood of Abel's sacrifice or Abel's own blood which was shed by Cain, it is still true that Christ's blood speaks more graciously. The blood of Abel's sacrifice said, "Covered temporarily"; Christ's blood says, "Forgiven forever." Abel's own blood cried, "Vengeance"; Christ's blood cries, "Mercy, pardon, and peace."

12:25 The closing verses of chapter 12 contrast God's revelation at Sinai with His revelation in and through Christ. The incomparable privileges and glories of the Christian faith are not to be treated lightly. God is speaking, inviting, wooing. To **refuse Him** is to perish.

Those who disobeyed the voice of God as it was heard in the law were punished accordingly. When privilege is greater, responsibility is also greater. In Christ, God has given His best and final revelation. Those who reject His voice as it now **speaks from heaven** in the gospel are more responsible than those who broke the law. **Escape** is impossible.

12:26 At Sinai God's voice caused an earthquake. But when He speaks in the future His voice will also produce a "heavenquake." This was, in substance, predicted by the prophet Haggai (2:6): "Once more (it is a little while) I will shake heaven and earth, the sea and dry land."

This shaking will take place during the period from the Rapture to the end of Christ's kingdom. Prior to Christ's coming to reign there will be violent convulsions of nature both on earth and in the heavens. Planets will be moved out of orbit causing raging tides and roaring seas. Then at the close of Christ's Millennial Reign, the earth, the stellar heavens, and the atmospheric heavens will be destroyed by fervent heat (2 Pet. 3:10–12).

12:27 When God said, **"Yet once more,"** He anticipated a complete and final **removal of** the heavens and the earth. This event will explode the myth that what we can see and touch and handle is real and that unseen things are unreal. When God ends the sifting and shaking process, only that which is real will **remain**.

12:28 Those who were occupied with the tangible, visible ritualism of Judaism were clinging to things that could be shaken. True believers have **a kingdom which cannot be shaken**. This should inspire the most fervent worship and adoration. We should unceasingly praise Him **with reverence and godly fear.**

12:29 **God is a consuming fire** to all who refuse to listen to Him. But even to His own, His holiness and righteousness are so great that they should produce profoundest homage and respect.

D. Exhortation to Various Christian Graces (13:1–17)

13:1 The practical section of Hebrews continues with six exhortations concerning graces that should be developed. First is **love** of the brethren. There should be a sense of family relationship toward all true Christians and a recognition of this kinship by loving words and acts (1 Jn. 3:18).

13:2 The readers are urged to show hospitality to **strangers**. This might refer primarily to believers who were fleeing from persecution and were hard-pressed to find food and lodging; to entertain them was to expose the host and hostess to danger. The verse may also be understood as a general encouragement to show hospitality to any believers who need it.

There is always the thrilling possibility that in doing this we may **unwittingly** entertain **angels!** This of course looks back to Abraham's experience with three men who were actually angelic beings (Gen. 18:1-15).[36] Even if we never have real angels in our homes, we may have men and women whose very presence is a benediction and whose godly influence on our family may have results that reach on into eternity.

13:3 The third exhortation concerns care for imprisoned believers. This almost certainly means those who were jailed because of their testimony for Christ. They would need food, warm clothing, reading matter, and encouragement. The temptation would be for other believers to shield themselves from association with **prisoners** and thus from the danger of guilt by association. They should **remember** that in visiting **prisoners**, they were visiting Christ.

Compassion should also be shown for the **mistreated**; again this doubtless means persecuted Christians. The readers should resist any tendency to shield themselves from the danger that such compassion might involve. For ourselves, we can broaden the application of the verse to include sympathy for all suffering saints. We should remember that we **are in the body also** and therefore subject to similar afflictions.

13:4 **Marriage** should be held in honor by all. We should remember that it was instituted by God before sin entered the world and that it is His holy will for mankind. To treat it as unclean, as ascetics do, or even to make jests and puns about it, as Christians sometimes

do, are alike forbidden in the Scripture.

Those who are married should be faithful to their vows and thus keep the marriage **bed undefiled**. In spite of modern man's smug laxness in this area, the fact remains that any sexual relations outside the bounds of marriage are sin. Adultery is not sickness; it is sin. And it is a sin which **God will** inevitably **judge**. No form of immorality will escape. He judges it in this life — through bodily ailments, broken families, mental and nervous afflictions, personality deformities. Unless it is pardoned through the blood of Christ, He will judge it in eternal fire.

Reformation Bishop Latimer reminded the immoral King Henry VIII of this in a way that was as convicting as it was courageous. He presented the king with a finely wrapped Bible. On the wrapping was inscribed the words, "Fornicators and adulterers God will judge."

13:5 The sixth virtue to cultivate is contentment. Remember that the adherents of Judaism were continually saying, "We have the tabernacle. We have the priesthood. We have the offerings. We have the beautiful ritual. What do you have?" Here the writer quietly says to the Christians: **Let your conduct be without covetousness; be content with such things as you have.** I should say so! What the Christian has is so infinitely greater than the best of Judaism — why shouldn't he **be content**? He has Christ; that is enough.

The love of silver can be a tremendous hindrance to the believer. Just as a small silver coin held before the eye comes between it and the sun, so **covetousness** breaks fellowship with God and hinders spiritual progress.

The greatest riches a person can have lie in possessing Him who promises, **"I will never leave you nor forsake you."** In Greek, strong negation is expressed by using two or more negatives. (This is the opposite of English structure in which a double negative makes a positive assertion.) In this verse the construction is very emphatic: it combines *five* negatives to indicate the impossibility of Christ deserting his own!

13:6 The words of Psalm 118:6 are the confident confession of the one who has Christ: **"The LORD is my helper; I will not fear. What can man do to me?"** The fact is that in Christ we have perfect security, perfect protection, perfect peace.

13:7 The readers are instructed to **remember** their leaders, the Christian teachers **who** spoke **the word of God to** them. What was **the outcome of their conduct?** They had not turned back to the Levitical system but had maintained their confession steadfast to the end. Perhaps some of them were martyred for Christ's sake. Theirs is the **faith** to imitate, the faith that clings to Christ and to Christian doctrine, and that brings God into every move in life. We are not all called to the same forms of service, but we are all called to a life of faith.

13:8 The connection of this verse with the preceding one is not clear. Perhaps the simplest way to understand it is as a summary of the teaching, the goal, and the faith of these leaders. The gist of their teaching was this: **Jesus Christ is the same yesterday, today, and forever.** The goal of their lives was **Jesus Christ — the same yesterday, today, and forever.** The foundation of their faith was that **Jesus** is the **Christ** (Messiah), **the same yesterday, today, and forever.**

13:9 Next follows a warning against the false teachings of legalism. The Judaizers insisted that holiness was connected with externals, such as ceremonial worship and clean foods, for example. The truth is that holiness is produced **by grace,** not by law. Legislation concerning clean and unclean foods was designed to produce *ritual* cleanness. But this is not the same thing as *inward* holiness. A man might be ceremonially clean and yet be filled with hatred and hypocrisy. Only God's grace can inspire and empower believers to live holy lives. Love for the Savior who died on account of our sins motivates us to "live soberly, righteously, and godly in the present age" (Tit. 2:12). After all, endless rules concerning foods and drinks have not profited their adherents.

13:10 Let us not miss the triumph of the words, **"We have an altar."** They are the Christian's confident answer to the repeated taunts of the Judaizers. Our **altar** is Christ, and therefore it includes all the blessings that are found in Him. Those who are connected with the Levitical system **have no right to** partake of the better things of Christianity. They must first repent of their sins and believe in Jesus Christ as only Lord and Savior.

13:11 Under the sacrificial system, certain **animals** were slain and their blood was **brought into the** Most Holy Place **by the high priest** as a sacrifice **for sin. The bodies of those animals** were carried to a place away from the tabernacle environs and burned. **Outside the camp** means outside the outer fence that enclosed the tabernacle court.

13:12 The animals burned outside the camp were a type; the Lord **Jesus** was the antitype. **He** was crucified **outside the** city walls of Jerusalem. It was outside the camp of organized Judaism that He sanctified **the people with His own blood.**

13:13 The application for the early readers of the Epistle was this: they should make a clean break with Judaism. Once for all they should turn their backs on the temple sacrifices and appropriate the finished work of Christ as their sufficient sacrifice.

The application for us is similar: **the camp** today is the entire religious system that teaches salvation by works, by character, by ritual, or by ordinances. It is the modern church system with its humanly ordained priesthood, its material aids to worship, and its ceremonial trappings. It is corrupt Christendom, a church without Christ. The Lord Jesus is outside and we should **go forth to Him, . . . bearing His reproach.**

13:14 Jerusalem was dear to the hearts of those who served at the temple. It was the geographic center of their "camp." The Christian has **no** such **city** on earth; his heart is set on the heavenly city, the new Jerusalem, where the Lamb is all the glory.

13:15 In the NT all believers are priests. They are holy priests, going into the sanctuary of God to worship (1 Pet. 2:5), and they are royal priests going out into the world to witness (1 Pet. 2:9). There are at least three sacrifices which a believer-priest offers. First, there is the sacrifice of his person (Rom. 12:1). Then, here in verse 15 is the second: **the sacri-**

fice of praise. It is offered to God through the Lord Jesus. All our praise and prayer passes through Him before it reaches God the Father; our great High Priest removes all impurities and imperfections and adds His own virtue to it.

> To all our prayers and praises
> Christ adds His sweet perfume;
> And love the censer raises
> These odors to consume.
> — Mary B. Peters

The sacrifice of praise is the fruit of those lips that acknowledge His name. The only worship that God receives is that which flows from redeemed lips.

13:16   The third sacrifice is the offering of our possessions. We are to use our material resources in doing good, and in sharing with those who are in need. With such sacrificial living God is well pleased. It is the opposite of accumulating for self.

> The race of God's anointed priests
> Shall never pass away;
> Before His glorious Face they stand
> And serve Him night and day.
> Though reason raves, and unbelief
> Flows on a mighty flood,
> There are, and shall be, till the end,
> The hidden priests of God.
> His chosen souls, their earthly dross
> Consumed in sacred fire,
> To God's own heart their hearts ascend
> In flame of deep desire;
> The incense of their worship fills
> His Temple's holiest place;
> Their song with wonder fills the Heavens,
> The glad new song of grace.
> — Gerhard Tersteegen

13:17   In verses 7 and 8, the readers were instructed to remember their past leaders. Now they are taught to obey their present leaders. This probably refers primarily to the elders in the local church. These men act as representatives of God in the assembly. Authority has been given to them, and believers should be submissive to this authority. As undershepherds, the elders watch out for the souls of the flock. They will have to give account to God in a coming day. They will do it either joyfully or sadly, depending on the spiritual progress of their charges. If they have to do it sadly, that will mean loss of reward for the saints concerned. So it is to everyone's benefit to respect the lines of authority which God has laid down.

IV. CLOSING BENEDICTION (13:18–25)

13:18   As the writer comes to the close of his Letter, he adds a personal appeal for prayer. The rest of the verse suggests that he may have been under attack from critics. We can guess who the critics were — those who were coercing people to return to the worship of the Old Covenant. He protests that, in spite of any charges that were being brought against him, his conscience was clear and his desire was pure.

13:19   An added reason for prayer was that he might be restored to them the sooner. Perhaps this refers to release from prison. We can do no more than speculate on this point.

13:20   Then he adds one of the most beautiful benedictions of the Bible — one that takes its place with Numbers 6:24–26; 2 Corinthians 13:14; and Jude 24, 25. It is addressed to the God of peace. As has been mentioned, OT saints never had perfect peace of conscience. But under the New Covenant, we have peace with God (Rom. 5:1) and the peace of God (Phil. 4:7). The verse goes on to explain that this peace is the fruit of Christ's work. God raised our Lord Jesus from the dead as a sign that His work on the cross settled the sin question once for all.

Christ, as the good Shepherd, gave His life for the sheep (John 10:11). As the great Shepherd, He rose from the dead, having accomplished redemption (Heb. 13:20). As the Chief Shepherd, He is coming again to reward His servants (1 Pet. 5:4). We see Him as the good Shepherd in Psalm 22, as the great Shepherd in Psalm 23, and as the Chief Shepherd in Psalm 24.

He was brought back from the dead in accordance with the everlasting covenant. Wuest comments on this phrase:

The New Testament is called the eternal one, in contrast to the First Testament which was of a transitory nature. It was within the sphere of the eternal covenant that Messiah, having died for sinful man, was raised up from among those who are dead. He could not be a high priest after the order of Melchizedek if He was not raised from the dead. Sinful man needs a living Priest to give life to the believing sinner, not a dead priest merely to pay for his sins. Thus, it was provided within the New Testament that the priest who offered Himself for sacrifice would be raised from the dead.[37]

13:21 The prayer begun in verse 20 is that the saints might be equipped with **every good work to do** God's **will**. There is a curious mingling here of the divine and the human. God equips us with everything **good**. God works in us **what is well pleasing in His sight**. He does it **through Jesus Christ**. Then we do His will. In other words, He places the desire in us; He gives us the power to do it; then we do it; and He rewards us.

The prayer ends with the acknowledgment that Jesus Christ is worthy of **glory forever and ever**.

> Worthy of homage and of praise,
> Worthy by all to be adored;
> Exhaustless theme of heavenly lays
> Thou, Thou art worthy, Jesus Lord.
> – *Frances Ridley Havergal*

13:22 The writer now urges his readers to heed the **exhortation** of his Letter, that is, to abandon ritualistic religion and cleave to Christ with true purpose of heart.

He speaks of his Epistle as a brief one, and it is, considering how much more he could have said about the Levitical system and how it finds its fulfillment in Christ.

13:23 The mention **that our brother Timothy had been set free** here confirms many in their view that Paul wrote the Letter. There is the added touch that the writer plans to travel with Timothy, another possible sign pointing to Paul. But we cannot be sure, so it is best to leave the question open.

13:24 Greetings are sent to all the Christian leaders **and all the saints**. We should not overlook the many touches of Christian courtesy in the Epistles, and we should imitate them in our day.

Some believers **from Italy** were with the writer, and they too wanted to send their greetings. This suggests that the Letter was written to or from there.

13:25 It is especially fitting that this epistle of the New Covenant should end on a grace note: **Grace be with you all**. The New Covenant is an unconditional covenant of free grace, telling out God's

unbounded favor for unworthy sinners through the sacrificial work of the Lord Jesus Christ. **Amen**.

THE MESSAGE OF HEBREWS FOR TODAY

Does the Epistle to the Hebrews have a message for us in the twentieth century?

Although Judaism is not the dominant religion today that it was in the early days of the church, yet the legalistic spirit has permeated Christendom. In his well-known booklet, *Rightly Dividing the Word of Truth*, Dr. C. I. Scofield writes:

> It may be safely said that the *Judaizing of the Church* has done more to hinder her progress, pervert her mission, and destroy her spiritually, than all other causes combined. Instead of pursuing her appointed path of separation from the world and following the Lord in her heavenly calling, she has used Jewish Scriptures to justify herself in lowering her purpose to the civilization of the world, the acquisition of wealth, the use of an imposing ritual, the erection of magnificent churches . . . and the division of an equal brotherhood into "clergy" and "laity."[38]

The Letter calls on us to separate ourselves from all religious systems in which Christ is not honored as the only Lord and Savior and in which His work is not recognized as the once-for-all offering for sin.

Hebrews teaches us that the types and shadows of the OT system found their fulfillment in our Lord. He is our great High Priest. He is our Sacrifice. He is our Altar. He serves in the heavenly sanctuary and His priesthood will never end.

It teaches that all believers are priests, and that they have instant access into the presence of God by faith at any time. They offer the sacrifices of their person, their praise, and their possessions.

David Baron writes:

> To adopt the model of the Levitical priesthood in the Christian Church, which ritualism endeavors to do, is nothing else but an attempt, with unholy hands, to sew together again the veil which the blessed, reconciled God had Himself rent in twain;

and like saying, "stand aside, come not nigh to God" to those who are "made nigh by the blood of Christ."[39]

The book of Hebrews teaches us that we have a *better* covenant, a *better* Mediator, a *better* hope, *better* promises, a *better* homeland, a *better* priesthood, and *better* possessions — *better* than the best that Judaism could offer. It assures us that we have eternal redemption, eternal salvation, an eternal covenant, and an eternal inheritance.

It warns solemnly against the sin of apostasy. If a person professes to be a Christian, associates with a Christian church, then turns away from Christ and joins those who are enemies of the Lord, it is impossible for such a one to be renewed to repentance.

The Epistle to the Hebrews encourages true Christians to walk by faith and not by sight because this is the life that pleases Christ. It also encourages us to bear up steadfastly under sufferings, trials, and persecutions in order that we might receive the promised reward.

Hebrews teaches that because of their many privileges, Christians have a very special responsibility. The superiorities of Christ make them the most highly favored people in the world. If such privileges are neglected, they will suffer loss accordingly at the Judgment Seat of Christ. More is expected of them than of those who lived under the law; and more will be required in a coming day.

"Therefore let us go forth to Him, outside the camp, bearing His reproach" (13:13). ‡

ENDNOTES

[1](3:6) The NU text omits "firm to the end."

[2](3:18) Arthur T. Pierson, further documentation unavailable.

[3](4:15) Theologians summarize the doctrine as to whether or not Christ could sin in two Latin phrases: "non posse peccare" — *not possible to sin* and "posse non peccare" — *possible not to sin*. The true teaching is *non posse peccare*: He could not sin.

[4](4:16) G. Campbell Morgan, "Choice Gleanings Calendar."

[5](6:2) The words are not the same in the original: The usual word for "baptism" is *baptisma*; here the word is *baptismoi*, "ritual washings."

[6](6:3) The majority text reads, "And let us do this. . . ."

[7](6:6) The NKJV margin is a better translation (since the form and context are the same as the previous clauses): "and have fallen away."

[8](6:18) The majority of mss. read "we have strong consolation" (indicative), rather than "might have strong consolation" (subjunctive). The former is even more certain.

[9](6:20) D. Anderson-Berry, *Pictures in the Acts*, p. 36ff.

[10](7:20) A. W. Rainsbury, "Able to Save to the Uttermost," *The Keswick Week, 1958*, p. 78.

[11](7:21) George Henderson, *Studies in the Epistle to the Hebrews*, p. 86.

[12](8:6) W. H. Griffith Thomas, *Hebrews: A Devotional Commentary*, p. 103.

[13](8:8) Henderson, *Hebrews*, p. 92.

[14](9:4) The word *thumiatērion* is a thing or place for burning incense.

[15](9:11) The NU text reads "that have come."

[16](9:13) J. Gregory Mantle, *Better Things*, p. 109.

[17](9:15) Kenneth S. Wuest, *Hebrews in the Greek New Testament*, p. 162, 163.

[18](10:10) George M. Landis, *Epistle to the Hebrews: On to Maturity*, p. 116.

[19](10:11) Alexander Balmain Bruce, *The Epistle to the Hebrews: The First Apology for Christianity*, p. 34.

[20](10:37) Marvin Vincent, *Word Studies in the New Testament*, II:1150.

[21] (10:37) A. J. Pollock, *Modernism Versus the Bible*, p. 19.

[22](10:38) The NU text reads, "my just one."

[23](11:21) C. H. Mackintosh, *Genesis to Deuteronomy: Notes on the Pentateuch*, p. 133.

[24](11:22) William Lincoln, *Lectures on the Epistle to the Hebrews*, p. 106.

[25](11:35) G. H. Morrison, "Morrison on Luke," *The Glasgow Pulpit Series*, I:42.

[26](11:37) The critical (NU) text omits "were tempted."

[27](11:37) William G. Moorehead, *Outline Studies in the New Testament. Philippians to Hebrews*, p. 248.

[28](12:2) A. B. Bruce, *Hebrews*, pp. 415, 416.

[29](12:10) J. H. Jowett, *Life in the Heights*, pp. 247, 248.

[30](12:11) Leslie Weatherhead, *Prescription for Anxiety*, p. 32.

[31](12:11) C. H. Spurgeon, "Choice Gleanings Calendar."

[32](12:13) George Williams, *The Student's Commentary on the Holy Scriptures*, p. 989.

[33](12:13) G. H. Lang, *The Epistle to the Hebrews*, pp. 240, 241.

[34](12:14) Wuest, *Hebrews*, p. 222.

[35](12:20) The words "or shot with an arrow" are lacking in most mss., including the oldest. They are most likely a later addition.

[36](13:2) It is believed that one of these three was the Angel of the LORD, the pre-incarnate Christ.

[37](13:20) Wuest, *Hebrews*, p. 242.

[38](Excursus) C. I. Scofield, *Rightly Dividing the Word of Truth*, p. 17.

[39](Excursus) David Baron, *The New Order of Priesthood*, pp. 39, 40.

BIBLIOGRAPHY

Bruce, Alexander Balmain. *The Epistle to the Hebrews: The First Apology for Christianity*. Edinburgh: T. & T. Clark, 1908.

Govett, Robert. *Christ Superior to Angels, Moses and Aaron*. London: J. Nisbet, 1884.

Henderson, G. D. *Studies in the Epistle to the Hebrews*. Barkingside, England: G. F. Vallance, n.d.

Hewitt, Thomas. *The Epistle to the Hebrews, TBC*. Grand Rapids: Eerdmans, 1960.

Ironside, H. A. *Hebrews and Titus*. Neptune, N.J.: Loizeaux Brothers, 1932.

Kelly, William. *Introductory Lectures to the Epistle to the Hebrews and the Epistle to Philemon*. Oak Park IL: Bible Truth Publishers, n.d.

Landis, G. M. *Epistle to the Hebrews: On to Maturity*. Oak Park: Emmaus Bible School, 1964.

Lang, G. H. *The Epistle to the Hebrews*. London: Paternoster Press, 1951.

Lincoln, William. *Lectures on the Epistle to the Hebrews*. Boston: Believers' Book-Room, n.d.

Mantle, J. Gregory. *"Better Things": A Series of Bible Readings on the Epistle to the Hebrews*. New York: Christian Alliance Publishing Co., 1921.

Meyer, F. B. *The Way into the Holiest*. Grand Rapids: Zondervan Publishing House, 1950.

Moffatt, James. *A Critical and Exegetical Commentary on the Epistle to the Hebrews, ICC*. Edinburgh: T. & T. Clark, 1924.

Moule, H. C. G. *Studies in Hebrews*. Grand Rapids: Kregel Publications, 1977.

Newell, W. R. *Hebrews Verse by Verse*. Chicago: Moody Press, 1947.

Pfeiffer, Charles F. *The Epistle to the Hebrews*. Chicago: Moody Press, 1962.

Rainsbury, A. W. "Able to Save to the Uttermost," *The Keswick Week*. London: Marshall, Morgan and Scott Ltd., 1958.

Thomas, W. H. Griffith. *Hebrews: A Devotional Commentary*. Grand Rapids: Wm. B. Eerdmans Publishing Co., 1961.

Vine, W. E. *The Epistle to the Hebrews*. London: Oliphants Ltd., 1952.

Westcott, B. F. *The Epistle to the Hebrews*. London: MacMillan, 1889.

Wuest, K. S. *Hebrews in the Greek New Testament*. Grand Rapids: Eerdmans Publishing Co., 1947.

THE EPISTLE OF JAMES

Introduction

"[James is] a preacher who speaks like a prophet . . . in language which for forcibleness is without parallel in early Christian literature, excepting the discourses of Jesus."
— Theodor Zahn

I. Unique Place in the Canon

Martin Luther's low estimation of James' Epistle as a "right strawy Epistle" was dead wrong! Luther's misunderstanding of James' teaching on good works amid the Reformer's fierce battle with those who taught salvation by faith plus works caused him to err here. He is not the only one to misjudge this earliest of Christian Letters. Some have called the book "a string of pearls," suggesting there is no cohesion to the Letter, but just several well-developed paragraphs strung together!

Actually, this little book is a masterpiece of didactic writing. It has a strong Jewish flavor, even referring to the Christian assembly (2:2, Gk.) as a "synagogue" — merely the Greek word for congregation — yet soon to be used exclusively for *Jewish* congregations, as today.

James used nature to illustrate spiritual truth thirty times in five short chapters. Here one is reminded of the teaching of our Lord.

This is a very practical Epistle. It deals with some unpopular subjects, such as controlling one's tongue, the danger of kowtowing to the rich, and the need to show that our faith is real by our lives.

II. Authorship†

Many Bible names were changed in their journey from Hebrew through Greek, Latin, and French into English. None is more different from its source than "James," which translates Greek "Iakobos", taken from Hebrew Yaakov ("Jacob"). The name *Jacob* ("James") was very popular among the Jews, and there are four men so named in the NT. Each one has been suggested as the writer of this Epistle, but with varying degrees of likelihood and scholarly support.

1. James *the Apostle*, son of Zebedee and brother of John (Matt. 4:21). If the Apostle James were the author, there would not have been the reluctance to accept this Letter for so long (see below). Also, James was martyred in A.D. 44, which is probably before the book was written.

2. James *the son of Alphaeus* (Matt. 10:3). He is almost *unknown* except that he is in the lists of apostles. The fact that the author could refer to himself as "James" with no distinguishing titles shows he was *well-known* at that time.

3. James *the father of Judas* (not Iscariot, Luke 6:16). This man was even more obscure and can safely be ruled out.

4. James *the half brother of our Lord* (Matt. 13:55; Gal. 1:19). This is almost surely the author of our Epistle. He is well-known, yet modest, since he doesn't mention his physical relationship to Christ (see also Introduction to Jude). This is the man who presided at the Jerusalem Council and stayed at that city until his death. He was notable as a very *Jewish* Christian, extremely strict in lifestyle. In short, he is remembered by history (Josephus) and church tradition as just such a Christian who would have written just such an Epistle.

†See p. i.

1031

External Evidence

James has one of the weakest *external* testimonies, being only *alluded* to, not quoted, by the earliest church fathers. It is also not in the Muratorian Canon. This is probably because it was from Jerusalem, addressed to Eastern Jews and *seemed* to many people to contradict Paul on justification by faith.

However, James is quoted by Cyril of Jerusalem, Gregory of Nazianzus, Athanasius, and Jerome. Eusebius tells us that James was among books spoken against (*antilegomena*) by some Christians, but he himself quoted it as Holy Scripture.

Internal Evidence

The *internal evidence* for James is quite strong. It harmonizes with what we know of James' style from Acts and Galatians, and also with the history of the Dispersion known from other sources. There is no reason to forge such a book; it contains no major doctrinal additions (as a heretical second century forgery invariably does). Josephus tells us that James had a very good reputation for devotion to the law among Jews, but was martyred for witnessing for his Messiah when this was forbidden. This Jewish historian says that James was stoned by order of the high priest Ananias. Eusebius tells us James was thrown from the pinnacle of the temple and finally clubbed to death. Hegesippus combines both these traditions.

The argument that the Greek style of the Epistle of James is "too good" for a Palestinian Jew shows an unbecoming ignorance of the amazing intellectual talents of the chosen people.

III. Date

Josephus says James was killed in 62, so the Letter must predate that. Since the Epistle says nothing of the decisions on the law made at the Jerusalem Council (A.D. 48 or 49) over which meeting James presided (Acts 15), a date between A.D. 45 and 48 is widely accepted.

IV. Background and Themes[†]

While this may be the first book of the NT to be written, and thus has a strongly Jewish flavor, its teachings must not be relegated to another age. They are applicable to us today, and very much needed.

To achieve his goal, James draws heavily on the teachings of the Lord Jesus in the Sermon on the Mount. This will be readily seen by the following comparisons:

Subject	James	Parallel in Matthew
Adversity	1:2,12; 5:10	5:10–12
Prayer	1:5; 4:3; 5:13–18	6:6–13; 7:7–12
The Single Eye	1:8; 4:8	6:22,23
Wealth	1:10,11; 2:6,7	6:19–21, 24–34
Wrath	1:19,20; 4:1	5:22
The Law	1:25; 2:1, 12,13	5:17–44
Mere Profession	1:26,27	6:1–18
The Royal Law	2:8	7:12
Mercy	2:13	5:7
Faith and Works	2:14–26	7:15–27
Root and Fruit	3:11,12	7:16–20
True Wisdom	3:13	7:24
The Peacemaker	3:17,18	5:9
Judging Others	4:11,12	7:1–5
Rusted Treasures	5:2	6:19
Oaths	5:12	5:33–37

There are frequent references to the law in this Letter. It is called "the perfect law" (1:25), "the royal law" (2:8), and "the law of liberty" (2:12). James does not teach that his readers are under law for salvation or as a rule of life. Rather, portions of the law are cited as instruction in righteousness for those who are under grace.

There are many resemblances to the book of Proverbs in James. Like Proverbs, his style is rugged, vivid, graphic, and difficult to outline. The word *wisdom* recurs frequently.

Another key word in James is *breth-*

†See p. ii.

ren. It occurs fifteen times, and reminds us that James is writing to believers, even if at times he seems to address the unconverted also.

In some ways, the Letter of James is the most authoritarian in the NT. That is, James issues instructions more profusely than any of the other writers. In the short space of 108 verses, there are fifty-four commands (imperative forms).

OUTLINE

Commentary

I. SALUTATION (1:1)

The writer introduces himself as **James, a bondservant of God and of the Lord Jesus Christ**. If the author was the Lord's half-brother, as we believe, then a wonderful change had come into his life. At one time, he had not believed in the Lord Jesus (John 7:5). He may have shared the view that Jesus was out of His mind (Mark 3:21). But our Lord patiently sowed the seed of the word. Though unappreciated, He taught the great principles of the kingdom of God. Then the seed took root in the life of James. A mighty transformation resulted. The skeptic became a servant. And he wasn't ashamed to say so!

By calling himself **a bondservant of God and of the Lord Jesus Christ**, James correctly puts **God** and **the Lord Jesus** on the same level as equals. He honors the Son just as he honors the Father (John 5:23). James knew that "no man can serve two masters" (Matt. 6:24). Yet he spoke of himself as a servant of God and of the Lord Jesus. There is no contradiction here because God the Father and God the Son are co-equal.

The Letter is addressed **to the twelve tribes which are scattered abroad**, literally which are in the Dispersion (Gk., *Diaspora*). These people were Jews by birth, belonging to the **twelve tribes** of Israel. Because of Israel's sin, the people had been driven from their native land and were now dispersed in the countries surrounding the Mediterranean. The *original* dispersion took place when the ten tribes were carried into captivity by the Assyrians, 721 B.C. Some of these returned to the land in the days of Ezra and Nehemiah, but only a remnant. On the Day of Pentecost, devout Jews were visiting Jerusalem from every nation of the then-known world (Acts 2:4). These could properly be called Jews of the Dispersion. But a later dispersion of *Christian* Jews took place. In Acts 8:1, we read that the early Christians (mostly of Jewish ancestry) were scattered abroad throughout Judea and Samaria by the persecutions of Saul. This dispersion is referred to again where we read that believers were driven to Phoenicia, Cyprus, and Antioch. Therefore, the people to whom James wrote could have been Jews who had been dispersed in any one of these crisis times.

Since all true believers are strangers and pilgrims in this world (Phil. 3:20; 1 Pet. 2:11), we can apply this Letter to ourselves, even if it wasn't written directly to us.

A more difficult question is whether James is addressing non-Christian Jews, Jews who had been converted to Christ, or both believing and unbelieving Jews. Primarily the author seems to be writing to true, born again believers (1:18). Yet there are times when he seems to be addressing professing Christians or even the unconverted. This is one of the proofs of the very early date of the Letter: the rift between Hebrew Christians and unbelieving Jews was not yet an accomplished fact.

II. TRIALS AND TEMPTATIONS (1:2–17)

1:2 In this section James deals with the subject of temptation. He uses the word in two different senses. In verses 2–12, the temptations are what we might call *holy* **trials** or problems which are sent from God, and which test the reality of our faith and produce likeness to Christ. In verses 13–17, on the other hand, the subject is *unholy temptations*, which come from within, and which lead to sin. The Christian life is filled with problems. They come uninvited and unexpected. Sometimes they come singly and sometimes in droves. They are inevitable. James does not say *"if* **you fall into various trials"** but **when**. We can never get away from them. The question is, "What are we going to do about them?"

There are several possible attitudes we can take toward these testings and **trials** of life. We can rebel against them (Heb. 12:5) by adopting a spirit of defiance, boasting that we will battle through to victory by our own power. On the other hand, we can lose heart or give up under pressure (Heb. 12:5). This is nothing but fatalism. It leads to questioning even the Lord's care for us. Again, we can grumble and complain about our troubles. This is what Paul warns us against in 1 Corinthians 10:10. Another option — we can indulge in

self-pity, thinking of no one but ourselves, and trying to get sympathy from others. Or better, we can be exercised by the difficulties and perplexities of life (Heb. 12:11). We can say, in effect, "God has allowed this trial to come to me. He has some good purpose in it for me. I don't know what that purpose is, but I'll try to find out. I want His purposes to be worked out in my life." This is what James advocates: **"My brethren, count it all joy when you fall into various trials."** Don't rebel! Don't faint! Rejoice! These problems are not enemies, bent on destroying you. They are friends which have come to aid you to develop Christian character.

God is trying to produce Christlikeness in each of His children. This process necessarily involves suffering, frustration, and perplexity. The fruit of the Spirit cannot be produced when all is sunshine; there must be rain and dark clouds. Trials never seem pleasant; they seem very difficult and disagreeable. But afterwards they yield the peaceable fruit of righteousness to those who are trained by them (Heb. 12:11). How often we hear a Christian say, after passing through some great crisis, "It wasn't easy to take, but I wouldn't give up the experience for anything."

1:3 James speaks of **the testing of your faith**. He pictures faith as a precious metal which is being tried by the Assayer (God) to see if it is genuine. The metal is subjected to the fires of persecution, sickness, suffering, or sorrow. Without problems, we would never develop endurance. Even men of the world realize that problems strengthen character. Charles Kettering, noted industrialist, once said, "Problems are the price of progress. Don't bring me anything but problems. Good news weakens me."

1:4 **"But let patience have its perfect work,"** says James. Sometimes when problems come we become desperate and use frantic means to cut short the trial. Without consulting the Lord as to His purposes in the matter, we rush to the doctor, for instance, and gulp down large doses of medicine in order to shorten the trial. By doing this, we actually may be thwarting God's program in our lives. And it is just possible that we may have to undergo a longer trial in the future before His particular purpose is realized in us. We should not short-circuit the development of endurance in our lives. By cooperating with God we will become mature, well-rounded Christians, **lacking** in none of the graces of the Spirit.

We should never become despondent or discouraged when passing through trials. No problem is too great for our Father. Some problems in life are never removed. We must learn to accept them and to prove His grace sufficient. Paul asked the Lord three times to remove a physical infirmity. The Lord did not remove it, but gave Paul the grace to bear it (2 Cor. 12:8–10).

When we face problems in life that God obviously isn't going to remove, we should be submissive to His will. The gifted blind hymn-writer wrote these lines as a girl of eight:

> O what a happy soul am I
>   Although I cannot see;
> I am resolved that in this world
>   Contented I will be.
> How many blessings I enjoy
>   That other people don't.
> To weep and sigh because I'm blind
>   I cannot and I won't.
> — *Fanny Crosby*

Peace comes through submission to the will of God.

Some problems in life are removed when we have learned our lessons from them. As soon as the Refiner sees His reflection in the molten metal, He turns off the heat. Most of us lack wisdom to view the pressures of life from God's standpoint. We adopt a short-range view, occupying ourselves with the immediate discomfort. We forget that God's unhurried purpose is to enlarge us through pressure (Ps. 4:1, JND).

1:5 We don't have to face the problems of life in our own wisdom. **If**, in the time of trial, we lack spiritual insight, we should go to God and tell Him all about our perplexity and ignorance. All who are thus exercised to find God's purposes in the trials will be **liberally** rewarded. And they need not worry that God will scold them either; He is pleased when we are teachable and tractable. We all lack **wisdom**. The Bible does not give *specific* answers to the innumerable problems that arise in life. It does not solve

problems in so many words, but God's word does give us general principles. We must apply these principles to problems as they arise day by day. That is why we need wisdom. Spiritual wisdom is the practical application of our Lord's teachings to everyday situations.

1:6–8 We must approach God **in faith, with no doubting**. We must believe He loves and cares, and that nothing is impossible with Him. If we doubt His goodness and His power, we will have no stability in time of trouble. One minute we might be resting calmly on His promises, but the next we will feel that God has forgotten to be kind. We will be like the surge **of the sea**, rising to great heights, then falling back into valleys — troubled **and tossed**. God is not honored by the kind of faith that alternates between optimism and pessimism. He does not give divine insight to such vacillating, unstable men (vv. 7, 8). In verses 5–8, the source of wisdom is God; it is obtained by prayer; it is available to everybody; it is given liberally and without reproach; the crucial condition is that we **ask in faith, with no doubting**.

1:9 At first glance, verses 9–11 seem to introduce a completely new subject, or at least a parenthesis. James, however, is continuing with the subject of holy trials by giving specific illustrations. Whether a man is poor or rich, he can derive lasting spiritual benefits from the calamities and crises of life. For instance, when a **lowly brother** finds himself dissatisfied and discouraged, he can always rejoice that he is an heir of God, and a joint heir with Jesus Christ. He can find consolation in the truth that all things are his, and he is Christ's and Christ is God's. **The lowly brother** probably has no control over his humble circumstances. There is no reason to believe he is lazy or careless. But God has seen fit to place him in a low income bracket and that is where he has been ever since. Perhaps if he had been rich, he never would have accepted Christ. Now that he is in Christ, he is blessed with all spiritual blessings in the heavenlies. What should he do? Should he rebel against his station in life? Should he become bitter and jealous? No, he should accept from God the circumstances over which he has no control and rejoice in his spiritual blessings.

Too many Christians go through life rebelling against their sex, their age, their height, and even against life itself. Girls with a flair for baseball wish they were boys. Young people wish they were older, and old people want to be younger. Short people envy those who are tall, and tall ones wish they weren't so conspicuous. Some people even say, "I wish I were dead!" All this is absurd! The Christian attitude is to accept from God things which we cannot change. They are God's destiny for us, and we should make the most of them for His glory and for the blessing of others. We should say with the Apostle Paul: "By the grace of God I am what I am" (1 Cor. 15:10). As we forget our disabilities and lose ourselves in service for others, we will come to realize that spiritual people love us for what we are, not for our appearance, for instance.

1:10, 11 Next James turns to **the rich**. But strangely enough he does not say, "Let the rich man rejoice in his riches." Rather he says that the rich can rejoice that he is made low. He agrees with Jeremiah 9:23, 24:

> Let not the wise man glory in his wisdom,
> let not the mighty man glory in his might,
> nor let the rich man glory in his riches;
> but let him who glories glory in this, that
> he understands and knows Me, that I am
> the LORD, exercising lovingkindness,
> judgment, and righteousness in the earth.
> For in these things I delight, says the
> LORD.

The rich man may actually find real cause for rejoicing should he be stripped of his material possessions. Perhaps business reverses would bring him to the Lord. Or if he is already a Christian, then he could take joyfully the spoiling of his goods knowing he has in heaven a better and more enduring possession (Heb. 10:34). Earthly riches are destined to pass away, like the **flower of the field** (Isa. 40:6, 7). If a man has nothing but material wealth, then all his plans will end at the grave. James dwells on the transiency of **grass** as an illustration of the fleeting life of a rich man and the limited value of his riches. He **will fade away in** the midst of **his pursuits**. The point is, of course, that neither sun nor

scorching wind can affect *spiritual* values. Any trial that weans us away from the love of passing things and sets our affections on things above is a blessing in disguise. Thus the same grace that exalts the lowly humbles the rich. Both are cause for rejoicing.

1:12 In concluding his discussion of holy trials, James pronounces a blessing on the person who stands up under afflictions. When such a man has stood the test or **has been approved, he will receive the crown of life. The crown** here is not the king's diadem but the victor's wreath, to be awarded at the Judgment Seat of Christ. There is no suggestion, of course, that eternal life is the reward for enduring testings, but those who have endured with fortitude will be honored for that kind of life, and will enjoy a deeper appreciation of eternal life in heaven. Everyone's cup will be full in heaven but people will have different sized cups — different capacities for enjoying heaven. This is probably what is in view in the expression **crown of life**; it refers to a fuller enjoyment of the glories of heaven.

Now let us make this section on holy trials practical in our own lives. How do we react when various forms of testing come into our lives? Do we complain bitterly against the misfortunes of life, or do we rejoice and thank the Lord for them? Do we advertise our trials or do we bear them quietly? Do we live in the future, waiting for our circumstances to improve, or do we live in the present, seeking to see the hand of God in all that comes to us? Do we indulge in self-pity and seek sympathy or do we submerge self in a life of service for others?

1:13 The subject now shifts to *unholy* temptations (vv. 13–17). Just as holy trials are designed to bring out the best in us, so unholy temptations are designed to bring out the worst in us. One thing must be clearly understood. When we are **tempted** to sin, the temptation does *not* come from **God**. God does test or try men, as far as their faith is concerned, but He never tempts a man to commit any form of evil. **He Himself** has no dealings with **evil**, and He does not entice to sin.

1:14 Man is always ready to shift responsibility for his sins. If he cannot blame God, he will adopt an approach of modern psychology by saying that sin is a sickness. In this way he hopes to escape judgment. But sin is not a sickness; it is a moral failure for which man must give account. Some even try to blame inanimate things for sin. But material "things" are not sinful in themselves. Sin does not originate there. James tracks the lion to its den when he says: **"Each one is tempted when he is drawn away by his own desires and enticed."** Sin comes from within us, from our old, evil, fallen, unregenerate nature. Jesus said, "Out of the heart proceed evil thoughts, murders, adulteries, fornications, thefts, false witness, blasphemies" (Matt. 15:19).

The word James uses for **desires**[1] in verse 14 could refer to any form of desire, good or evil. The word itself is morally neutral. But with few exceptions it is used in the NT to describe evil desires, and that is certainly the case here. Lust is likened to an evil woman here parading her allurements and enticing her victims. Every one of us is tempted. We have vile lusts and impure appetites constantly urging us on in sin. Are we helpless victims then, when we are **drawn away by** our **own desires and enticed**? No, we may expel all thoughts of sin from our mind and concentrate on subjects that are pure and holy (Phil. 4:8). Also in the moment of fierce temptation, we may call on the Lord, remembering that "The name of the Lord is a strong tower: the righteous run to it, and are safe" (Prov. 18:10).

1:15 If that is so, why then do we sin? Here is the answer: **Then, when desire has conceived, it gives birth to sin**. Instead of expelling the vile thought, we may encourage, nourish, and enjoy it. This act of acquiescence is likened to sexual intercourse. Lust conceives and a hideous baby named SIN is born. Which is another way of saying that if we think about a forbidden act long enough, we will eventually do it. The whole process of lust conceiving and bringing forth sin is vividly illustrated in the incident of David and Bathsheba (2 Sam. 11:1–27).

And sin, when it is full-grown, brings forth death, says James. Sin is not a barren, sterile thing; it produces a brood of its own. The statement that **sin** produces **death** may be understood in several ways. First of all, the sin of Adam brought physical death on himself and on all his posterity (Gen. 2:17). But sin also leads to eternal, spiritual death — the final separation of the person from God and from blessing (Rom. 6:23a). There is a sense also in which sin results in death for a believer. For instance, in 1 Timothy 5:6 we read that a believing widow who lives in pleasure is dead while she lives. This means that she is wasting her life and utterly failing to fulfill the purpose for which God saved her. To be out of fellowship with God is for a Christian a form of living death.

1:16, 17 It is not unusual for people who fall into sin to blame God instead of themselves. They say, in effect, to their Creator, "Why have you made me this way?" But this is a form of self-deception. Only good gifts come from God. In fact, He is the source of **every good and every perfect gift**.

James describes God as **the Father of lights**. In the Bible the word *Father* sometimes has the meaning of Creator or Source (see Job 38:28). Therefore God is the Creator or Source **of lights**. But what is meant by **lights**? Certainly it includes the heavenly bodies — the sun, moon, and stars (Gen. 1:14–18; Ps. 136:7). But God is also the Source of all spiritual light as well. So we should think of Him as the Source of every form of light in the universe. **With whom there is no variation or shadow of turning**. God is unlike the heavenly bodies He has created. They are undergoing constant changes. He never does. Perhaps James is thinking not only of the declining brilliance of the sun and stars, but also of their changing relation to the earth as our planet rotates. Variableness characterizes the sun, moon, and stars. The expression **shadow of turning** may mean **shadow** caused by **turning**. This could have reference to the shadows cast on earth by the rotation of the earth around the sun. Or it could refer to eclipses. A solar eclipse, for instance, is produced when the moon's shadow falls on the earth. With God it is quite different; there is no variableness in Him, or **shadow** caused by **turning**. And His gifts are as **perfect** as Himself. Therefore it is unthinkable that He would ever entice man to sin. Temptation comes from man's own evil nature.

Let us test our faith on the subject of unholy temptations. Do we encourage evil thoughts to linger in our minds, or do we expel them quickly? When we sin, do we say that we couldn't help it? Do we blame God when we are tempted to sin?

III. THE WORD OF GOD (1:18–27)

James has been speaking of God as the Father of lights. Now he reminds us that He is our Father also, and that He has given us a unique role in His vast creation. We can fulfill that role by obedience to the word of truth (vv. 19–27).

1:18 This passage outlines the part played in the new birth by the word of God as it is applied to us by the Holy Spirit. We are told that **"Of His own will He brought us forth by the word of truth, that we might be a kind of firstfruits of His creatures."** Of His own **will** — this tells us what prompted Him to save us. He was not forced to do it by any merit in us. He did it **of His own** free **will**. His love to us was unmerited, unbought and unsought. It was entirely voluntary on His part. This should cause us to worship! **He brought us forth** — this describes the fact of the new birth. By this spiritual birth we become His children — a relationship that can never be changed since a birth can never be undone. **By the word of truth** — the Bible is the instrument of the new birth. In every genuine case of conversion, the Scriptures are involved, whether orally or in printed form. Apart from the Bible, we would not know the way of salvation. Indeed, we would not even know that salvation was available!

That we might be a kind of firstfruits of his creatures — there are three prominent thoughts in connection with the word **firstfruits**. First, the **firstfruits** of a harvest was the first sheaf of ripened grain. The Christians to whom James was writing were among the first believers in the Christian Dispensation. Of course, all believers are **a kind of firstfruits** of His creatures, but the pri-

mary reference is to the Jewish Christians to whom James wrote. Second, **the firstfruits** were offered to God in gratitude for His bounty and in recognition that all comes from Him and belongs to Him. Thus, all believers should present themselves to God as living sacrifices (Rom. 12:1, 2). Third, the **firstfruits** were a pledge of the full harvest to come. James likened his readers to the first sheaves of grain in Christ's harvest. They would be followed by others down through the centuries, but they were set forth as pattern saints to exhibit the fruits of the new creation. Eventually the Lord will populate the whole earth with others like them (Rom. 8:19–23). The full harvest will come when the Lord Jesus returns to reign over the earth. In the meantime, they were to yield the same kind of obedience to Christ which all the world will yield during the Millennium. And though the passage refers primarily to first-century Christians, yet it has an application for each one of us who honors the name of Christ.

1:19a The rest of this chapter gives practical instructions as to how we can be firstfruits of His creatures. It sets forth the practical righteousness which should characterize those who have been born again by the Word of Truth. We know that we were begotten by the word in order to manifest the truth of God. **So then,**[2] let us now discharge our responsibility.

We should **be swift to hear**. This is an unusual command, with almost a trace of humor in it. It's like saying, "Hurry up and hear!" It means that we should be ready **to hear** the word of God, as well as all godly counsel and admonition. We should be teachable by the Holy Spirit. We should be **slow to speak**. It is surprising how much James has to say about our speech! He cautions us to be guarded in our conversation. Even nature itself teaches us this. Epictetus noticed so long ago: "Nature has given to man one tongue, but two ears, that we may hear from others twice as much as we speak." Solomon would have agreed heartily with James. He once said, "He who guards his mouth preserves his life, but he who opens wide his lips shall have destruction" (Prov.

13:3). He also said, "In the multitude of words sin is not lacking, but he who restrains his lips is wise" (Prov. 10:19). Compulsive talkers eventually transgress.

1:19b, 20 We should be **slow to wrath**. A man who is quick-tempered **does not produce the** kind of **righteousness** which **God** expects from His children. Those who lose their temper give people a wrong impression about Christianity. It is still true that "he who is slow to anger is better than the mighty; and he who rules his spirit than he who takes a city" (Prov. 16:32).

1:21 Another way to manifest ourselves as firstfruits of His creatures is to **lay aside all filthiness and overflow of wickedness**. These vices are likened to soiled garments which are to be set aside once for all. **Filthiness** includes every form of impurity, whether spiritual, mental, or physical. The expression **"overflow of wickedness"** may refer to those forms of evil which are a holdover from our unconverted days. It may refer to sins which **overflow** from our lives and touch the lives of others. Or it may refer to abounding evil, in which case James is not so much describing an excess of evil, but the intensely wicked character which evil has. The over-all meaning is clear. In order to receive the truth of the word of God, we must be morally clean.

Another requirement for the reception of divine truth is **meekness**. It is all too possible to read the Bible without letting it speak to us. We can study it in an academic way without being affected by it. Our pride and hardness and sin make us unreceptive and unresponsive. Only those with submissive, humble spirits can expect to derive the maximum benefit from the Scriptures. "The humble He guides in justice, and the humble He teaches His way" (Ps. 25:9). "But on this one I will look: on him who is poor and of a contrite spirit, and who trembles at My word" (Isa. 66:2).

James speaks of the Scriptures as **the implanted word, which is able to save your souls**. The thought is that the word becomes a sacred deposit in the Christian's life when he is born again. The margin of the RV reads "the inborn word." This word is able to **save your souls**. The Bible is the instrument God uses in the new birth. He uses it in saving the soul not only from the penalty of sin, but from its power as well. He uses it in saving us not only from damnation in eternity, but from damage in *this life*.[3] It is doubtless this present, continuing aspect of salvation James is speaking of in verse 21.

1:22 It is not enough to receive the implanted word; we must obey it. There is no virtue in possessing the Bible or even in reading it as literature. There must be a deep desire to hear God speaking to us and an unquestioning willingness to do whatever He says. We must translate the Bible into action. The word must become flesh in our lives. There should never be a time when we go to the Scriptures without allowing them to change our lives for the better. To profess great love for God's word or even to pose as a Bible student is a form of self-deception unless our increasing knowledge of the word is producing increasing likeness to the Lord Jesus. To go on gaining an intellectual knowledge of the Bible without obeying it can be a trap instead of a blessing. If we continually learn what we ought to do, but do not do it, we become depressed, frustrated, and callous. "Impression without expression leads to depression." Also we become more responsible to God. The ideal combination is to read the word and obey it implicitly.

1:23, 24 Anyone who hears **the word** but does not change his behavior **is like a man** who takes a fleeting glance in the mirror each morning, then completely **forgets what** he saw. He derives no benefit from the mirror or from looking into it. Of course, there are some things about our appearance that cannot be changed. But at least we should be humbled by the sight! And when the mirror says "Wash" or "Shave" or "Comb" or "Brush," we should at least do as we are told. Otherwise the mirror is of no practical benefit to us.

It is easy to read the Bible casually or because of a sense of duty without being affected by what we read. We see what we ought to be but we quickly forget and live as if we were already perfect. This type of self-satisfaction prevents spiritual progress.

1:25 In contrast is the man **who looks into the** word of God and who habitually reduces it to practice. His contemplative, meditative gazing has practical results in his life. To him the Bible is **the perfect law of liberty**. Its precepts are not burdensome. They tell him to do exactly what his new nature loves to do. As he obeys, he finds true freedom from human traditions and carnal reasonings. The truth makes him free. This is the man who benefits from the Bible. He does not forget what he has read. Rather he seeks to live it out in daily practice. His simple childlike obedience brings incalculable blessing to his soul. **This one will be blessed in what he does**.

1:26, 27 **Useless religion** and **pure and undefiled religion** are contrasted. **Religion** here means the external patterns of behavior connected with religious belief. It refers to the outward forms rather than the inward spirit. It means the outer expression of belief in worship and service rather than the doctrines believed.

Anyone who **thinks he is religious**, but cannot control **his tongue, . . . this one's religion is useless**. He might observe all kinds of religious ceremonies which make him appear very pious. But he is deceiving himself. God is not satisfied with rituals; He is interested in a life of practical godliness.

An unbridled **tongue** is only one example of futile **religion**. Any behavior inconsistent with the Christian faith is worthless. The story is told of a grocer who apparently was a pious fraud. He lived in an apartment above his store. Every morning he would call down to his assistant, "John!"

"Yes, sir."

"Have you watered down the milk?"

"Yes, sir."

"Have you colored the butter?"

"Yes, sir."

"Have you put chicory in the coffee?"

"Yes, sir."

"Very well. Come up for morning devotions!"

James says that such **religion is useless**.

What God is looking for is the practical type of godliness which takes a compassionate interest in others and keeps one's own life clean. As examples of **pure and undefiled religion**, James praises the man who visits needy **orphans and widows**, and who keeps himself **unspotted from the world**.

In other words, the practical outworking of the new birth is found in "acts of grace and a walk of separation." Guy King describes these virtues as practical love and practical holiness.

We should put *our own faith* on trial with the following questions: Do I read the Bible with a humble desire to have God rebuke me, teach me, and change me? Am I anxious to have my tongue bridled? Do I justify my temper or do I want victory over it? How do I react when someone starts to tell an off-color joke? Does my faith manifest itself in deeds of kindness to those who cannot repay me?

IV. CONDEMNATION OF PARTIALITY (2:1–13)

The first half of chapter 2 denounces the practice of showing respect of persons. Favoritism is utterly foreign to the example of the Lord or to the teachings of the NT. There is no place in Christianity for snobbishness or discrimination.

2:1 First of all, the practice is distinctly forbidden. Note first that the admonition is addressed to believers; we are assured of this by the salutation **"My brethren." The faith of our Lord Jesus Christ** refers to the Christian faith. It is not a question of His trust or dependence, but rather of the body of truth which He gave to us. Putting all these thoughts together, we find that James is saying, **"My brethren**, in your practice of the Christian **faith**, do not show **partiality."** Snobbery and caste distinctions are utterly inconsistent with true Christianity. Servility to human greatness has no place in the presence of the Lord of Glory. Contempt for others because of birth, race, sex, or poverty is a practical denial of the faith. This commandment does not contradict other portions of the NT where believers are taught to pay proper respect to rulers, masters, elders, and parents. There are certain divinely ordained relationships which must be recognized (Rom. 13:7). In this passage it is a matter of showing obsequious deference to people because of their expensive clothing or other artificial distinctions.

2:2–4 This is confirmed by the vivid illustration which James gives in verses 2–4. Guy King has cleverly entitled this section "The Shortsighted Usher." The scene is the local **assembly**[4] of Christians. A distinguished looking gentleman, with fashionable clothing and expensive **gold rings** has just arrived. The usher bows and scrapes, then escorts the notable visitor to a prominent, conspicuous seat in the front. As soon as the usher gets back to the door, he finds that another visitor has arrived. This time it is **a poor man** in humble attire. (The expression **filthy clothes** does not necessarily mean that the man's clothes needed cleaning. He is dressed poorly, in keeping with his humble circumstances in life.) This time the usher adroitly seeks to save the congregation from embarrassment by offering the visitor standing room at the rear, or a place on the floor, in front of his own seat. It seems incredible that anyone would ever act in this way. We would like to think that the illustration is overdrawn, but when we look into our own heart, we find that we often do make these artificial class distinctions among ourselves, and thus **become judges with evil thoughts**.

Probably the most glaring example of it in the church today is the discrimination shown against people of other races and colors. Black believers have been ostracized in many instances or at least made to feel unwelcome. Converted Jews have not always been accepted cordially. Oriental Christians have tasted discrimination in varying degrees. It is admitted that there are enormous social problems in the whole area of racial relations. But the Christian must be true to divine principles. His obligation is to give practical expression to the truth that all believers are one in Christ Jesus.

2:5, 6a Partiality is utterly incongruous with the Christian faith. James demonstrates this in verses 5–13. He gives four strong reasons why it is ridiculous for a believer to favor the rich and look down on the poor.

First of all, it means that we dishonor a man whom **God** honors. **God** has **chosen the poor** people **of this world** to be **rich in faith and heirs of the kingdom which He promised to those who love Him**. The poor are God's elect, God's elite, heirs of God, and lovers of God. Repeatedly we find in Scripture that it is the poor people, not the rich, who rally to the banner of Christ. Our Lord Himself said, "The poor have the gospel preached to them" (Matt. 11:5). It was the common people who heard Him gladly, not the wealthy or aristocratic (Mark 12:37). Not many noble are called, but the foolish, the weak, the base, the despised, and the insignificant (1 Cor. 1:26–29). Rich people are ordinarily poor in faith, because they trust their riches instead of the Lord. On the other hand, poor people have been **chosen** by God **to be rich in faith**. A survey of the citizens of His kingdom would reveal that most of them have been poor. In the kingdom, they will occupy positions of wealth and glory. How foolish, then, and how perilous it is to treat with contempt those who will one day be exalted in the kingdom of our Lord and Savior.

2:6b A second reason why it is foolish to show deference to **the rich** is that, as a class, they are the ones who have characteristically oppressed the people of God. The argument is involved, and even a little confusing at this point. The rich man referred to earlier in the chapter was undoubtedly a believer. That does not mean that the rich men mentioned in verse 6 are believers also. What James is saying is simply this: "Why show favoritism to people just because they are rich? If you do, you are honoring those who have been the first to bully you **and** to **drag you into the courts."** Calvin captured the argument tersely when he said, "Why honor your executioners?"

2:7 A third reason why it is foolish to be partial toward the rich is that they habitually use evil or harsh speech involving the name of Christ. This is the **noble name by which** believers **are called** — Christians, or followers of Christ. While railing against the Lord is not a sin on which the rich have a monopoly, yet it is true that those who persecute poor believers often accompany this persecution with the vilest language against the Savior. So why should believers show special favoritism toward anyone simply because he is rich? The traits which accompany riches are not ordinarily honoring to the Lord Jesus. The expression **that noble name by which you are called** might also be translated "that noble name which has been called upon you." Some see this as a reference to Christian baptism. Believers are baptized in the name of the Lord Jesus. This is the very **name** which the rich habitually **blaspheme**.

2:8 James' fourth argument is that showing deference to the rich violates **the law** that **"You shall love your neighbor as yourself."** It is called **the royal law** because it belongs to the King and because it is the king of all laws. Perhaps the usher excused his action toward the rich man by saying that he was just trying to love his neighbor as himself. But that wouldn't excuse his action toward the poor man. If we really loved our neighbors as ourselves, we would treat them all the way we would want to be treated. Certainly *we* would not want to be despised simply because we were poor. Then we should not show contempt to others for this reason.

Of all the teachings of the Bible this is certainly one of the most revolutionary — **You shall love your neighbor as yourself**. Think what it means! It means that we should care for others as we care for ourselves. We should be willing to share our material possessions with those who are not as privileged as we are. And above all, we should do all in our power to see that they have the opportunity to know our blessed Savior. Too often our decisions are based on how our actions affect ourselves. We are self-centered. We cater to the rich because of the hope of reward, either socially or materially. We neglect the poor because there is little prospect of their benefiting us in this way. **The royal law** forbids such selfish exploitation of others. It teaches us to **love** our **neighbor as** ourselves. And if we ask, "Who is my neighbor?" we learn from the story of the Good Samaritan (Luke 10:29–37) that our neighbor is any person who has a need which we can help to meet.

2:9 To **show partiality** is a violation of the royal law. It is both **sin** and transgression. **Sin** is any lack of conformity to the will of God, a failure to meet His

standards. Transgression is the breaking of a known law. Certain acts are sinful because they are basically and inherently wrong, but they become transgressions when there is a specific law which forbids them. **Partiality** is sinful because it is essentially wrong in itself. But it is also transgression because there is a law against it.

2:10 To break **one** part of the law is to be **guilty of all**. The law is like a chain of ten links. Break one link and the chain is broken. God does not allow us to keep the laws we like, and break others.

2:11 The same God who forbade **adultery also** forbade **murder**. A man may not be guilty of **adultery**, yet he may commit **murder**. Is he **a transgressor of the law**? Certainly he is! The spirit of the law is that we should love our neighbor as ourselves. **Adultery** is certainly a violation of this, but so is **murder**. And so is snobbishness and discrimination. If we commit any of these sins, we have failed to do what the law commands.

THE TEN COMMANDMENTS

Now we must pause in our discussion to consider a basic problem which arises at this point in James' argument. The problem is this: "Are Christians under the law or are they not?" It certainly seems that James has been enforcing the Ten Commandments on Christian believers. He specifically refers to the sixth and seventh commandments which forbid murder and adultery. Also he summarizes the last five commandments in the words: "You shall love your neighbor as yourself." Yet to put believers under the law, as a rule of life, contradicts other portions of the NT, such as Romans 6:14 — "You are not under law, but under grace"; Romans 7:6 — "We have been delivered from the law"; Romans 7:4 — "You also have become dead to the law through the body of Christ" (see also Gal. 2:19; 3:13, 24, 25; 1 Tim. 1:8, 9; Heb. 7:19.) The fact that Christians are not under the Ten Commandments is distinctly stated in 2 Corinthians 3:7–11.

Why then does James press the matter of the law on believers in this Age of Grace? First of all, Christians are *not* under the law as a rule of life. Christ, not the law, is the believer's pattern. Where there is law, there must also be penalty. The penalty for breaking the law is death. Christ died to pay the penalty of the broken law. Those who are in Christ are therefore delivered from the law and its penalty. But certain principles of the law *are* of abiding value. These precepts apply to all people of all ages. Idolatry, adultery, murder, and theft are basically and inherently wrong. They are just as wrong for believers as for unbelievers. Furthermore, nine of the Ten Commandments are repeated in the Epistles. The only one that is not repeated is the one concerning the Sabbath. Nowhere are Christians ever told to keep the Sabbath or seventh day of the week, for that commandment is ceremonial rather than moral. It was not basically wrong in itself for a Jew to work on the seventh day. It was wrong only because God set that day apart.

Finally, it should be mentioned that the nine commandments which are repeated in the Epistles are not given as *law* but as instruction in righteousness for the people of God. In other words, God does not say to Christians, "If you steal, you are condemned to death." Or "If you commit an immoral act, you will lose your salvation." Rather He says: "I have saved you by My grace. Now I want you to live a holy life out of love to Me. If you want to know what I expect of you, you will find it throughout the NT. There you will find nine of the Ten Commandments repeated. But you will also find the teachings of the Lord Jesus which actually call for *a higher standard of conduct than the law required*." So James is not really putting believers under the law and its condemnation. He is not saying, "If you show respect of persons, you are breaking the law, and are thus condemned to death." ‡

2:12 What James is saying is, "As believers, you are no longer under the law of bondage, but you are under **the law of liberty — liberty** to do what is right. The Law of Moses required you to love your neighbor but did not give you the power, and condemned you if you failed. Under grace, you are given the power to love your neighbor and are re-

warded when you do it. You don't do it in order to be saved but because you are saved. You do it, not through fear of punishment, but through love for Him who died for you and rose again. When you stand before the Judgment Seat of Christ, you will be rewarded or suffer loss according to this standard. It will not be a question of salvation but of reward." The expression **"So speak and so do"** refers to words and deeds. Both profession and life should agree. In speech and act, believers should avoid partiality. Such violations of the law of liberty will be judged at the Judgment Seat of Christ.

2:13 Verse 13 must be understood in the light of the context. James is speaking to believers. There is no question of eternal punishment here; that penalty was paid once for all at Calvary's cross. Here it is a question of God's dealing with us in this world as children. If we do not show **mercy** to others, we are not walking in fellowship with God and can expect to suffer the consequences of a backslidden condition.

Mercy triumphs over judgment may mean that God would rather show **mercy** to us than discipline us (Mic. 7:18); judgment is His "strange work." It may mean we can rejoice in the face of judgment if we have shown mercy to others, but if we have not shown mercy to those whom we might justly condemn, we will not be shown mercy. Or it may mean that **mercy triumphs over judgment** in the sense that it is always greater than judgment. The general idea seems to be that if we show mercy to others, the judgment which might otherwise fall on us will be replaced by mercy.

Let us test ourselves then on this important subject of partiality. Do we show more kindness to those of our own race than those of other races? Are we more kindly disposed to the young than to the old? Are we more outgoing to good-looking people than to those who are plain or homely? Are we more anxious to befriend prominent people than those who are comparatively unknown? Do we avoid people with physical infirmities and seek the companionship of the strong and healthy? Do we favor the rich over the poor? Do we give the "cold shoulder" to "foreigners," those who speak our language with a foreign accent?

As we answer these questions, let us remember that the way we treat the least lovable believer is the way we treat the Savior (Matt. 25:40).

V. FAITH AND WORKS (2:14–26)

These verses are perhaps the most controversial in James' Letter. Even such a great worthy of the church as Luther thought he saw an irreconcilable conflict between James' teaching on justification by works and Paul's insistence on justification by faith. These verses are commonly misused to support the heresy that we are saved by faith plus works, called "synergism." In other words, we must trust the Lord Jesus as our Savior, but that is not enough. We must also add to His redemptive work our own deeds of charity and devotion.

The section might actually be entitled "Justification by Works," because there is a sense in which we *are* justified by works. In fact, in order to grasp the full truth of justification, we should clearly understand that there are six aspects of justification. We are justified by *grace* (Rom. 3:24). This simply means that we do not deserve to be justified; in fact, we deserve the very opposite. We are justified by *faith* (Rom. 5:1). Faith is the human response to God's grace. By faith, we accept the free gift. Faith is that which appropriates what God has done for us. We are justified by *blood* (Rom. 5:9). Here blood is the price which had to be paid in order to procure our justification. The debt of sin was met by the precious blood of Christ, and now God can justify ungodly sinners because a righteous satisfaction has been made. We are justified by *God* (Rom. 8:33). The truth here is that God is the Person who justifies. We are justified by *power* (Rom. 4:25). Our justification is linked to the power that raised Christ from the dead. His resurrection proves that God is satisfied. And we are justified by *works* (Jas. 2:24). Works are the outward proof of the reality of our faith. They give outward expression to what would otherwise be invisible. From this we see that the person is justified by grace, by faith, by

blood, by God, by power, and by works. Yet there is no contradiction at all. These statements simply present different aspects of the same truth. Grace is the principle upon which God justifies; faith is the means by which man receives it; blood is the price which the Savior had to pay; God is the active Agent in justification; power is the proof; and works are the result.

2:14 James insists that a faith that does not result in good works cannot save. There are two keys which greatly help in the understanding of this verse. First of all, James does *not* say "What does it profit . . . though a man has faith . . . ." Rather he says, **What does it profit . . . if someone says he has faith**. In other words, it is not a question of a man who truly *has* faith, and yet is not saved. James is describing the man who has nothing but a profession of faith. He *says* he has faith, but there is nothing about his life that indicates it. The second helpful key is brought out in the NASB. There, the verse closes with the question "Can *that*⁵ faith save him?" In other words, can *that kind of faith* save? If it be asked what kind of faith James is referring to, the answer is found in the first part of the verse. He is speaking about a *say-so faith* that is not backed up by good works. Such a faith is worthless. It is all words, and nothing else.

2:15, 16 The futility of words without deeds is now illustrated. We are introduced to two people. One has neither adequate **daily food** nor clothing. The other has both, but is not willing to share them. Professing great generosity, the latter says to his poor brother, "Go and put on some clothing, and eat a good meal." But he doesn't raise a little finger to make this possible. What good are such words? They are positively worthless! They neither satisfy the appetite nor provide warmth **for the body**.

2:17 Thus also faith by itself if it does not have works, is dead. A **faith** without **works** is not real faith at all. It is only a matter of words. James is *not* saying that we are saved by faith *plus* works. To hold such a view would be to dishonor the finished work of the Lord Jesus Christ. If we were saved by faith plus works, then there would be two saviors — Jesus and ourselves. But the NT is very clear that Christ is the one and only Savior. What James is emphasizing is that we are not saved by a faith of words only but by that kind of faith which results in a life of good works. In other words, works are not the root of salvation but the fruit; they are not the cause but the effect. Calvin put it tersely: "We are saved by faith alone, but not by a faith that is alone."

2:18 True faith and good works are inseparable. James shows this by giving us a snatch from a debate between two men. The first man, who is genuinely saved, is the speaker. The second professes to have faith, but he does not demonstrate that faith by good works. The first is heard delivering an unanswerable challenge to the other. We might paraphrase the conversation: "Yes," the first man may correctly and justifiably **say, "you** say you **have faith**, but you do not have works to demonstrate it. I claim that faith must be backed up by a life of works. Prove to me that you have **faith without** a life of good **works**. You cannot do it. Faith is invisible. The only way others can know you have faith is by a life that demonstrates it. **I will show you my faith by my works.**" The key to this verse lies in the word *show*: To **show** faith apart from works is impossible.

2:19, 20 The debate continues. The first man is still the speaker. A man's professed faith may be nothing more than mental assent to a well-known fact. Such intellectual agreement involves no committal of the person, and does not produce a transformed life. It is not enough to believe in the existence of **God**. True, this is essential, but it is not sufficient. **Even the demons believe** in the existence of God and they shudder at the thought of their eventual punishment by Him. **The demons believe** the fact, but they do not surrender to the Person. This is not saving faith. When a person truly believes on the Lord, it involves a commitment of spirit, soul, and body. This commitment in turn results in a changed life. **Faith** apart from **works** is head belief, and therefore **dead**[6] belief.

2:21 Two examples of the faith which works are now given from the OT. They involve **Abraham** — a Jew, and Rahab — a Gentile. **Abraham** was **justified by works** in offering up **Isaac his son on the altar**. In order to see this truth in its proper perspective, turn to Genesis 15:6. We read that Abraham believed in the LORD, and He counted it to him for righteousness. Here Abraham was justified by believing; in other words, he was justified by faith. It is not till we come to Genesis 22 that we find Abraham offering up his son. It is then that he was **justified by works**. As soon as Abraham believed in the LORD, he was justified in the sight of God. But then, seven chapters later, God put Abraham's faith to the test. Abraham demonstrated that it was genuine faith by his willingness to offer up Isaac. His obedience showed that his faith was not merely a head belief, but a heart commitment.

It has sometimes been objected that there was no one else present when Abraham offered up Isaac, and there was therefore no one to whom he could prove the reality of his faith. But the young men who had accompanied Abraham were not far away, waiting for Abraham and Isaac to return from the mount. Moreover, Isaac was there. Also, Abraham's willingness to slay his son in obedience to God's command has been preserved in the Bible record, thus demonstrating to all generations the reality of his faith.

2:22, 23 It is clear then that Abraham's faith inspired his works, **and by** his **works** his **faith was made perfect**. True faith and works are inseparable. The first produces the second, and the second evidences the first. In the offering of Isaac we see a practical demonstration of the faith of Abraham. It was the practical fulfillment of **the Scripture** which said that **Abraham** was justified by believing. His good works identified him as **the friend of God**.

2:24 We conclude from this, **then, that a man is justified by works, and not by faith only**. Again, this does *not* mean that he was justified by faith *plus* works. He was justified **by faith** Godward, and **by works** manward. God justified him the moment he believed. Man says, "Show me the reality of your faith." The only way to do this is by good works.

2:25 The second OT illustration **is Rahab the harlot**. She certainly was *not* saved by good character (she was a prostitute!). But she was **justified by works** because **she received the messengers** (or spies) **and sent them out another way**. Rahab was a Canaanite, living in the city of Jericho. She heard reports that a victorious army was advancing toward the city, and that no opposition had been successful against this army. She concluded that the God of the Hebrews was the true God, and decided to identify herself with this God, whatever the cost might be. When the spies entered the city, she befriended them. In doing so, she proved the genuineness of her faith in the true and living God. She was not saved by harboring the spies, but this act of hospitality proved that she was a genuine believer.

Some people misuse this passage to teach that salvation is partly by good works. But what *they* mean by good works is giving to charity, paying your debts, telling the truth, and going to church. Were these the good works of Abraham and Rahab? Certainly not! In Abraham's case, it was willingness to kill his son! In Rahab's case, it was treason! If you remove faith from these works, they would be evil rather than good. "Strip them of faith and they were not only immoral and unfeeling, but they would have been sinful." Mackintosh well says, "This section refers to life-works, not law-works. If you abstract faith from Abraham's and Rahab's works, they were bad works. Look at them as the fruit of faith and they were life-works."

So this is a not a passage that can be used to teach salvation by good works. It puts the user in the untenable position of teaching salvation by murder and treason!

2:26 James ends the passage with the statement, **"For as the body without the spirit is dead, so faith without works is dead also."** Here the matter is summarized very beautifully. James compares **faith** to the human **body**. He likens **works** to **the spirit. The body without the spirit is** lifeless, useless, valueless. **So faith without works is dead**, ineffective, worthless. Obviously it is a spurious faith, not genuine saving faith.

To summarize, then, James tests our faith by our answers to the following questions. Am I willing like Abraham to offer the dearest thing in my life to God? Am I willing like Rahab to turn traitor to the world in order to be loyal to Christ?

VI. THE TONGUE: ITS USE AND ABUSE (3:1–12)

The first twelve verses of chapter 3 deal with the tongue (also mentioned in 1:19, 26; 2:12; 4:11; 5:12). Just as an old-fashioned doctor examined a patient's tongue to assist in diagnosis, so James tests a person's spiritual health by his or her conversation. Self-diagnosis begins with sins of speech. James would agree with the modern wit who said, "Watch your tongue. It's in a wet place where it's easy to slip!"

3:1 The subject is introduced by a warning against the hasty desire to be a teacher of the word of God. Although the tongue is not specifically mentioned, the underlying thought is that one who uses his tongue in teaching the Scriptures assumes added responsibility before God and man. The words **"Let not many of you become teachers"** may be paraphrased: "Do not become unduly ambitious to be a teacher." This should not be interpreted as a prohibition against the use of his gift by one who has actually been called of God to teach. It is a simple warning that this ministry should not be undertaken lightly. Those who teach the Word of Truth will receive heavier **judgment** if they fail to practice what they teach.

It is a great responsibility to teach the Bible. The teacher must be prepared to obey what he sees in the word. He can never hope to lead others beyond what he himself has practiced. The extent of his influence on others will be determined by how much he himself has progressed. The teacher begets others in his own image; he makes them like himself. If he dilutes or explains away the clear meaning of any Scripture, he hinders the growth of his students. If he condones sin in any form, he fosters lives of unholiness. No other book makes such claims on its readers as the NT. It calls for total commitment to Jesus Christ. It insists that He must be Lord of every phase of the believer's life. It is a serious matter to teach from such a book!

3:2 James now moves from the specific ministry of teaching to the general area of conversation. We are **all** prone to **stumble in many** areas but if anyone can control his tongue, so that he does not commit the various sins of speech, that person is truly well-rounded and well-disciplined. If one can exercise control in speech, he should not have difficulty in practicing self-control in other areas of life as well. Of course, the Lord Jesus Christ is the only One who ever did this completely, but there is a sense in which each of us can become **perfect**, that is, mature, complete, thoroughly disciplined.

3:3 Five figures of speech, or pictures of the tongue are given. First of all, it is compared to a bridle. Bridles are the harnesses which go over the horses' heads and hold the **bits in** the **horses' mouths**. Connected to the bit are the reins. Though the bit itself is a very small piece of steel, yet if a person can control that bit, he can control the behavior of the horse. So the tongue can direct the life — either for good or for evil.

3:4 The second picture is that of a **rudder**. Compared with the ship itself, a **rudder** is **very small**. It weighs only a fraction of the weight of the ship. For example, the Queen Elizabeth weighed 83,673 gross tons. The rudder of that ship weighed only 140 tons — less than two-tenths of one percent of the total. Yet when the rudder is **turned**, it controls the direction of the ship itself. It seems incredible that a man can control so huge a vessel with such a relatively small device; yet this is exactly what happens. Thus we should not misjudge the power of the tongue by its size. Though it is a very small member of the body, and relatively hidden, yet it can boast of great accomplishments, both good and evil.

3:5, 6 A third simile of the tongue is a **fire**. A lighted match, carelessly thrown, may start a brush fire. This in turn may ignite **a forest** and leave a charred mass of ruins. What possibilities, then, a small match holds of destruction and devastation! One of the great catastrophes of history was the Chicago fire of 1871. Tradition has it that it started when Mrs. O'Leary's cow kicked over her lantern. Whether or not that was true, the fire burned for three days over three and one half square miles of the city. It killed 250 people, made 100,000 homeless, and destroyed property valued at $175,000,000. The tongue is like a small lighted match or a turned-over lantern. Its potentials for wickedness are almost infinite. James speaks of it as **a world of iniquity . . . among our members**. The word *world* here is used to express vastness. We sometimes use it in this sense; for example, a world full of trouble. We mean a tremendous amount of trouble. The tongue, though so small, has vast possibilities of iniquity in it.

The manner in which the flame of evil-speaking spreads is illustrated by the conversation between two women in Brooklyn. One said, "Tillie told me that you told her that secret I told you not to tell her." The other replied, "She's a mean thing. I told Tillie not to tell you I told her." The first speaker responded, "Well, I told Tillie I wouldn't tell you she told me — so don't tell her I did."

The tongue can defile **the whole body**. A person can corrupt his whole personality by using his tongue to slander, abuse, lie, blaspheme, and swear.

Chappel writes:

> The faultfinder injures himself. . . . The mud slinger cannot engage in his favorite pastime without getting some of the mud that he slings both upon his hands and upon his heart. How often we have come away from such an experience with a sense of defilement! Yet that was not our intention at all. We were vainly hoping that by slinging mud upon others we might enhance someone's estimate of our own cleanliness. We were foolish enough to believe that we could build ourselves up by tearing another down. We were blind enough to imagine that by putting a stick of dynamite under the house of our neighbor we could strengthen the foundations of our own. But this is never the case. In our efforts to injure others we may succeed, but we always inflict the deeper injury upon ourselves.[7]

The tongue **sets on fire the course** (or the wheel) **of nature**. This is the "wheel" set in motion at birth. It describes the whole round of human activity. An evil tongue pollutes not only a man's personal life, but it contaminates all his activities as well. It affects "the whole of wickedness in the whole of man for the whole of life." A wicked tongue **is set on fire by hell**. All evil speech has its source there. It is hellish in its very character. The word used for **hell** here is Gehenna; apart from this instance, it is used only by the Lord Jesus in the NT.

3:7 The fourth figure to which the tongue is likened is a wild, untamable creature. All kinds of beasts, birds, serpents and marine life can be tamed. It is not uncommon to see tame elephants, lions, tigers, birds of prey, serpents, porpoises, and even fish. Pliny lists among creatures that were tamed by men in his day: elephants, lions and tigers, among beasts; the eagle, among birds; asps and other serpents; crocodiles and various fishes, among the inhabitants of the water. To argue that not every kind of creature has actually been tamed is to miss the point of James' argument; there is no reason to believe there is any kind of creature that could not be tamed by man, given sufficient time and persistence.

Robert G. Lee expresses it eloquently:

What has man done with huge elephants? He has invaded their jungle homes, trapped them, trained them — scores of them — in carrying lumber, in pushing heavily laden wagons, in all kinds of labor. What has man done with many green-eyed Bengal tigers? He has caught them, taught them, and made them his playmates. What has man done with fierce, furious, strong African lions? He has captured numbers of them and has trained them to jump through hoops of fire, to ride horseback, to sit on high pedestals, to leave untouched — when hungry — beef placed between their paws, to lie down, to stand up, to run, to roar in obedience to man's spoken word, in obedience to the crack of man's whip. Why, once I saw (years ago at a circus) a lion open wide his cavernous and ravenous mouth and hold it open while a man, his trainer, thrust his head far down into the lion's mouth and held it there a full minute.

What has man done with the huge boa constrictor? With the great python? Go to the circus and see little women, frail as flowers, coil these hideous monsters about their bodies with impunity. Go to the animal show, consider how man has made the spotted leopard and the bloodthirsty jaguar harmless and dumb before

him. Go to the show and see the trained fleas, see the hungry jackal lie down with the meek lamb, see the dove and the eagle nest together, see the wolf and the rabbit romp in play.[8]

3:8 But man's success with wild animals does not extend to the area of his own **tongue**. If we are honest, we will have to admit that this is true in our own lives. Because of the fall, we have lost dominion over this small piece of flesh. Human nature does not have the ability or strength to govern this little member. Only God can bring it under control.

James next characterizes the tongue as **an unruly evil**. Linking this expression with the words **full of deadly poison** we suspect that James has in mind a restless serpent, with exceedingly poisonous venom. A drop or two would be fatal. So the tongue can poison minds and assassinate characters. We all know how easy it is to gossip about others. How often we have engaged in mudslinging in order to get even for supposed wrongs. And often for no reason at all we have belittled others, criticized them, downgraded them. Who can measure the harm done, the tears that have flowed, the broken hearts, the ruined reputations? And who can measure the misery it has brought to our own lives and to our families? The inward bitterness that has been aroused, the shame of having to apologize, the bad effects on our health. Parents who have openly indulged in criticism of fellow-believers have had to watch their children adopt the same critical spirit and wander off from Christian fellowship. The price we have to pay for the undisciplined use of our tongue is enormous.

What is the remedy? Pray daily that the Lord will keep us from gossip, censoriousness, and unkind speech. Don't talk unfavorably about anyone; love covers a multitude of sins (1 Pet. 4:8). If we have something against another person, let us go to him directly, discuss it in love, and pray together (Matt. 18:15; Luke 17:3). Let us try to see Christ in our brethren instead of magnifying minor failures. If we start to say something unkind or unprofitable, let us stop in the middle of the sentence and explain that to continue wouldn't be edifying. Some things are better left unsaid.

3:9, 10 It is inconsistent to use the tongue for both good and evil purposes. It is completely unnatural; there is nothing like it in nature. One minute a man blesses **God** with his tongue, the next he curses those who are **made in the** image **of God.** How incongruous that a common source should ever produce such opposite results! Such a state of affairs should not exist. The tongue that blesses God should help men instead of wounding them. All that we say should be subject to the threefold test: Is it true? Is it kind? Is it necessary? Constantly we should ask the Lord to set a watch before our lips (Ps. 141:3), and pray that the words of our mouths and the meditations of our hearts might be acceptable in the sight of Him who is our strength and Redeemer (Ps. 19:14). We should remember that our members in Romans 12:1 include our tongue.

3:11 No **spring** gives **fresh water and bitter** at the same time. The tongue should not do so either. Its outflow should be uniformly good.

3:12 Just as water from a fountain speaks of refreshment, so fruit from **a fig tree** speaks of nourishment. A **fig tree** cannot produce **olives**, neither can a **grapevine** bear **figs**. In nature, a tree produces only one kind of fruit. How is it, then, that the tongue can produce two kinds of fruit — good and evil?

This passage should not be confused with a similar one in Matthew 7:16–20. There we are warned against expecting good fruit from bad trees. Evil men can only produce wicked works. Here we are warned against using the tongue to produce two opposite kinds of fruit.

No spring can yield **salt water and fresh** water at the same time. It must be one or the other. These lessons from nature are intended to remind us that our speech should be consistently good.

Thus James puts us on trial as far as our speech is concerned. Before leaving this section, let us ask ourselves the following questions. Do I teach others things that I have not obeyed myself? Do I criticize others behind their back? Is my speech consistently clean, edifying, kind? Do I use "minced oaths" such as gosh, golly, gee, jeepers, good heavens,

heck? After a solemn meeting, do I engage in levity or talk about football scores? Do I pun on the Scriptures? In retelling a story, do I exaggerate in order to make people more impressed? Do I habitually tell the truth, even if it means loss of face, friends, or finances?

VII. WISDOM: THE TRUE AND THE FALSE (3:13–18)

James now discusses the difference between true wisdom and false. When he speaks about wisdom, he is not thinking of how much *knowledge* a man has, but how he *lives* his life from day to day. It is not the possession of knowledge but the proper application of it that counts. We have here a portrait of the truly wise man. Basically, this man is the Lord Jesus Christ; He is wisdom incarnate (Matt. 11:19; 1 Cor. 1:30). But also the wise person is one who manifests the life of Christ, one in whom the fruit of the Spirit is evident (Gal. 5:22, 23).

We have also a portrait of the worldly-wise man. He acts according to the principles of this world. He embodies all the traits that men glorify. His behavior gives no evidence of divine life within.

3:13 If a man is **wise and understanding**, he will demonstrate it by his **good conduct** coupled with the humble spirit that comes from **wisdom**. The Lord Jesus, the embodiment of true wisdom, was not proud and arrogant; He was meek and lowly in heart (Matt. 11:29). Therefore, all who are truly wise will have the hallmark of genuine humility.

3:14 The worldly-wise man is characterized by **bitter envy and** selfish ambition in his heart. His one passion in life is to advance his own interests. He is jealous of any competitors and ruthless in dealing with them. He is proud of his wisdom that has brought success. But James says that this isn't wisdom at all. Such boasting is empty. It is a practical denial of **the truth** that the man who is truly wise is truly humble.

3:15 Even in Christian service, it is possible to be bitterly jealous of other workers, and to seek a prominent place for oneself. There is always a danger that worldly-wise men will be given places of leadership in the church. We must constantly guard against allowing worldly principles to guide us in spiritual affairs. James calls this false wisdom **earthly, sensual,** and **demonic**. There is an intended downward progression in these three adjectives. **Earthly** means that this wisdom is not from heaven, but from this earth. **Sensual** means that it is not the fruit of the Holy Spirit, but of man's lower nature. **Demonic** means that it stoops to actions that resemble the behavior of demons rather than of men.

3:16 Whenever you find **envy and self-seeking**, you will also find **confusion**, disharmony, **and every** other kind of **evil**. How true! Think of the unrest and agitation in the world today — all because men reject true Wisdom and act according to their own supposed cleverness!

3:17 **The wisdom that** comes from God **is first pure**. In thought, word, and deed, it is clean. In spirit and body, in doctrine and practice, in faith and in morals, it is undefiled. It is also **peaceable**. This simply means that a wise man loves peace, and will do all he can to maintain peace without sacrificing purity. This is illustrated by Luther's story of the two goats that met on a narrow bridge over deep water. They could not go back and they did not dare to fight. "After a short parley, one of them lay down and let the other go over him, and thus no harm was done. The moral," Luther would say, "is easy: be content if your person is trod upon for peace's sake; your person, I say, not your conscience." True wisdom is **gentle**. It is forbearing, not overbearing; courteous, not crude. A wise man is a gentleman, respectful of the feelings of others. Says A. B. Simpson, "The rude, sarcastic manner, the sharp retort, the unkind cut — all these have nothing whatever in common with the gentle teaching of the Comforter."

The next characteristic is **willing to yield**. It means conciliatory, approachable, open to reason, ready to give in when truth requires it. It is the opposite of obstinate and adamant. Wisdom from above is **full of mercy and good fruits**. It is **full of mercy** to those who are in the wrong, and anxious to help them

find the right way. It is compassionate and kind. There is no vindictiveness in it; indeed, it rewards discourtesy with benevolence. It is **without partiality**, that is, it does not produce favoritism. It is impartial in its treatment of others. Finally, true wisdom is **without hypocrisy**. It is sincere and genuine. It does not pretend to be other than it actually is.

Now let us put all these thoughts together to form the portraits of two men — the truly wise man and the man with false wisdom. The man who is truly wise is genuinely humble. He estimates others to be better than himself. He does not put on airs, but does put others at ease right away. His behavior is not like that of the world around him; it is otherworldly. He does not live for the body but for the spirit. In words and deeds, he makes you think of the Lord Jesus. His life is pure. Morally and spiritually he is clean. Then too he is peaceable. He will endure insult and false accusation but will not fight back or even seek to justify himself. He is gentle, mildmannered, and tenderhearted. And he is easy to reason with, willing to try to see the other person's viewpoint. He is not vindictive but always ready to forgive those who have wronged him. Not only so but he habitually shows kindness to others, especially to those who don't deserve it. And he is the same to all; he doesn't play favorites. The rich receive the same treatment as the poor; the great are not preferred above the common people. Finally, he is not a hypocrite. He doesn't say one thing and mean another. You will never hear him flatter. He speaks the truth and never wears a mask.

The worldly-wise man is not so. His heart is filled with envy and strife. In his determination to enrich himself, he becomes intolerant of every rival or competitor. There is nothing noble about his behavior; it rises no higher than this earth. He lives to gratify his natural appetites — just as the animals do. And his methods are cruel, treacherous, and devilish. Beneath his well-pressed suit is a life of impurity. His thought life is polluted, his morals debased, his speech unclean. He is quarrelsome with all who disagree with him or who cross him in any way. At home, at work, in social life, he is constantly contentious. And he is harsh and overbearing, rude and crude. People cannot approach him easily; he keeps them at arm's length. To reason with him quietly is all but impossible. His mind is already made up, and his opinions are not subject to change. He is unforgiving and vindictive. When he catches someone in a fault or error, he shows no mercy. Rather he unleashes a torrent of abuse, discourtesy, and meanness. He values people according to the benefit they might be to him. When he can no longer "use" them, that is, when there is no further hope of profit from knowing them, he loses interest in them. Finally, he is two-faced and insincere. You can never be sure of him — either of his words or actions.

3:18 James closes the chapter with the words, **"Now the fruit of righteousness is sown in peace by those who make peace."** This verse is a connecting link between what we have been discussing and what is to follow. We have just learned that true wisdom is peaceloving. In the next chapter we find conflict among God's people. Here we are reminded that life is like the farming process. We have the farmer (the wise man who is a peacemaker); the climate (**peace**); and the harvest (**righteousness**). The farmer wants to raise a harvest of righteousness. Can this be done in an atmosphere of quarrels and bickering? No, the sowing must take place under peaceful conditions. It must be done by those who are of a peaceful disposition. A harvest of uprightness will be produced in their own lives and in the lives of those to whom they minister.

Once again James has put our faith on trial, this time with regard to the type of wisdom we manifest in our everyday life. We must ask ourselves — "Do I respect the proud men of the world more than the humble believer in the Lord Jesus?" "Do I serve the Lord without caring who gets the credit?" "Or do I sometimes use questionable means in order to get good results?" "Am I guilty of flattery in order to influence people?" "Do I harbor jealousy and resentment in my heart?" "Do I resort to sarcasm and unkind remarks?" "Am I pure in thought, in speech, in morals?"

VIII. COVETOUSNESS: ITS CAUSE AND CURE (Chap. 4)

James has pointed out that the wise man is a peace-loving man. Now he is reminded of the tragic strife that often exists among God's people. What is the cause of it all? Why are there so many unhappy homes and so many churches torn by division? Why are there such bitter feuds among Christian workers in the homeland, and such conflicts among missionaries abroad? The reason is that we are ceaselessly striving to satisfy our lust for pleasures and possessions, and to outdo others.

4:1, 2a The sad fact is that there *are* **wars and fights** among Christians. To suggest that this paragraph does not apply to believers is unrealistic, and it robs the passage of all its value for us. What causes all this fighting? It arises from the strong **desires** within us which are constantly struggling to be satisfied. There is the lust to accumulate material possessions. There is the drive for prestige. There is the craving **for pleasure**, for the gratification of bodily appetites. These powerful forces are at work within us. We are never satisfied. We always want more. And yet it seems we are constantly frustrated in our desire to get what we want. The unfulfilled longing becomes so powerful that we trample on those who seem to obstruct our progress. James says, **"You murder."** He uses the word largely in a figurative sense. We don't literally kill, but the anger, jealousy, and cruelty which we generate are murder in embryo.

4:2b, 3 We **covet and cannot obtain**. We want to have more things and better things than others. And in the attempt, we find ourselves quarreling and devouring one another.

John and Jane have just been married. John has a fair job with a moderate salary. Jane wants a house as good as the other young couples at church. John wants a late model car. Jane wants fine furnishings and appliances. Some of these things have to be purchased on the installment plan. John's salary is hardly sufficient to bear the strain. Then a baby is born into the family; this means added expenses and a badly unbalanced budget. As Jane's demands mount, John becomes cross and irritable. Jane retaliates with backbiting and tears. Soon the walls of the house are vibrating with the crossfire. Materialism is destroying the home.

On the other hand, it may be that Jane is jealous. She feels that Bob and Sue Smith have a more prominent place in the assembly than she and John. Soon she makes snide remarks to Sue. As the battle between them increases in tempo, John and Bob become involved in the fighting. Then the other Christians take sides, and the congregation is divided — because of one person's lust for prominence.

Here then is the source of the bickering and strife among believers. It comes from the desire for more, and from jealousy of others. "Keeping up with the Joneses" is the polite name for it; more accurately we should call it greed, covetousness, and envy. The desire becomes so strong that people will do almost anything to gratify their lusts. They are slow to learn that true pleasure is not found in this way, but in contentment with food and clothing (1 Tim. 6:8).

Prayer is the right approach to this problem. "Don't argue. Don't fight. Pray." James says, **"You do not have because you do not ask."** Instead of taking these things to the Lord in prayer, we try to get what we want by our own efforts. If we want something which we do not have, we should ask God for it. If we do ask, and the prayer is unanswered, what then? It simply means that our motives were not pure. We did not want these possessions for the glory of God or for the good of our fellow men. We wanted them for our own selfish enjoyment. We wanted them to satisfy our natural appetites. God does not promise to answer such prayers.

What a profound lesson in psychology we have in these first three verses! If men were content with what God has given them, what staggering conflict and unrest would be avoided! If we loved our neighbors as ourselves, and were more interested in sharing than in acquiring, what peace would result! If we would follow the Savior's command to forsake all instead of to accumulate, to lay up treasures in heaven rather than on earth, what contentions would cease!

4:4 James condemns the inordinate love of material things as spiritual adultery.[9] God wants us to love Him first and foremost. When we love the passing things of this world, we are being untrue to Him.

Covetousness is a form of idolatry. It means that we strongly desire what God does not want us to have. That means that we have set up idols in our hearts. We value material things above the will of God. Therefore, covetousness is idolatry, and idolatry is spiritual unfaithfulness to the Lord.

Worldliness **is** also **enmity with God. The world** does not mean the planet on which we live, or the world of nature about us. It is the system which man has built up for himself in an effort to satisfy the lust of the eyes, the lust of the flesh, and the pride of life. In this system there is no room for God or His Son. It may be the world of art, culture, education, science, or even religion. But it is a sphere in which the name of Christ is unwelcome or even forbidden, except, of course, as an empty formality. It is, in short, the world of mankind outside the sphere of the true church. **To be a friend** of this system is to be **an enemy of God**. It was this world that crucified the Lord of life and glory. In fact, it was the *religious* world that played the key role in putting Him to death. How unthinkable it is that believers should ever want to walk arm-in-arm with the world that murdered their Savior!

4:5 Verse 5 is one of the most difficult in the Epistle: **Do you think that the Scripture says in vain, "The Spirit who dwells in us yearns jealously"?**

The first difficulty is that James seems to be quoting from the OT; yet these words are not found anywhere in the OT, or even in the Apocryphal books. There are two possible explanations. First of all, while the exact words are not found in the OT, James may have been quoting them as being the general teaching of the Scripture. The second solution of the problem is given by the RV. There the verse is broken into two questions: "Or think ye that the Scripture speaketh in vain? Doth the spirit which he made to dwell in us long unto envying?" Here the thought is that in condemning the competitive, worldly spirit, the Bible is not wasting words.

The second major difficulty in verse 5 is the meaning of the second part of the verse. The problem is whether the spirit is the *Holy* Spirit (as in the NKJV[10]) or the spirit of passionate *jealousy*. If the former is meant, then the thought is that the Holy Spirit whom God caused to dwell in us does not originate the lust and jealousy which cause strife; rather He **yearns** over us with jealousy for our entire devotion to Christ. If the latter is intended, then the meaning is that the spirit that dwells in us, that is, the spirit of lust and envy, is the cause of all our unfaithfulness to God.

4:6   But He gives more grace. In the first five verses we saw how wicked the old nature of the believer can be. Now we learn that we are not left to deal with the lusts of the flesh in our own strength. Thank God, **He gives more grace** or strength whenever it is needed (Heb. 4:16). He has promised, ". . . as your days, so shall your strength be" (Deut. 33:25).

> He giveth more grace when the burdens
>   grow greater,
> He sendeth more strength when the
>   labors increase,
> To added affliction He addeth His mercy,
> To multiplied trials His multiplied peace.
> – *Annie Johnson Flint*

To prove that God gives grace as it is needed, James quoted Proverbs 3:34, but here there is the added thought that it is **to the humble**, not the proud, that this **grace** is promised. **God resists the proud**, but He cannot resist the broken spirit.

4:7   In verses 7–10, we find six steps to be followed where there is true repentance. James has been crying out against the sins of the saints. His words have pierced our hearts like arrows of conviction. They have fallen like thunderbolts from the throne of God. We realize that God has been speaking to us. Our hearts have been bowed beneath the influence of His word. But the question now is, "What shall we do?"

The first thing to do is to **submit to God**. This means that we must be subject to Him, ready to listen to Him and

obey Him. We must be tender and contrite, not proud and stiff-necked. Then we must **resist the devil**. We do this by closing our ears and hearts to his suggestions and temptations. We do it also by using the Scriptures as the Sword of the Spirit to repel him. If we resist him, **he will flee from** us.

4:8   Next we should **draw near to God**. We do this by prayer. We must come before Him in desperate, believing prayer, telling Him all that is on our heart. As we thus approach Him, we find that He will **draw near to** us. We thought He would be far from us because of our carnality and worldliness, but when we **draw near to** Him, He forgives us and restores us. The fourth step is: **Cleanse your hands, you sinners; and purify your hearts, you double-minded.** **Hands** speak of our actions and **hearts** represent our motives and desires. We **cleanse** our **hands** and **purify** our **hearts** through confession and forsaking sins, both outward and inward. As **sinners** we need to confess evil acts; as **double-minded** people we need to confess our mixed motives.

4:9   Confession should be accompanied by deep sorrow for sin. **Lament and mourn and weep! Let your laughter be turned to mourning and your joy to gloom**. When God visits us in conviction of sin, it is not time for levity. Rather it is a time when we should prostrate ourselves before Him and **mourn** over our sinfulness, powerlessness, coldness, and barrenness. We should humble ourselves and weep over our materialism, secularism, and formalism. Both inwardly and outwardly, we should manifest the fruit of godly repentance.

4:10   Finally, we should **humble** ourselves **in the sight of the Lord**. If we honestly take our place in the dust at His feet, **He will lift** us **up** in due time.

This then is the way we should respond when the Lord exposes us to ourselves. Too often it is not the case, however. Sometimes, for example, we are in a meeting when God speaks loudly to our hearts. We are stirred for the moment, and filled with good resolves. But when the meeting closes, the people engage in animated and lighthearted conversation. The whole atmosphere of the service is dispersed, the power is dissipated, and the Spirit of God is quenched.

4:11, 12 The next sin James deals with is censoriousness, or speaking **evil** against **a brother**. Someone has suggested that there are three questions we should answer before indulging in criticism of others — What good does it do your brother? What good does it do yourself? What glory for God is in it?

The royal **law** of love says that we should love our neighbor as ourselves. To **speak evil** against a brother, therefore, or to judge his motives, is the same as speaking against this **law** and condemning it as worthless. To break a law deliberately is to treat it with disrespect and contempt. It is the same as saying that the law is not good, and not worthy of obedience. "He who refuses obedience virtually says it ought not to be law." Now this puts the one **who speaks evil of a brother** in the strange position of being **a judge** rather than one who is to be judged. He sets himself up as being superior to the law rather than subject to it. But only God is superior to the law; He is the One who gave it and the One who judges by it. **Who** then has the audacity to usurp the *place* of *God* and **judge another**?[11]

4:13 The next sin which James denounces is self-confident, boastful planning in independence of God (vv. 13–16). He pictures a businessman who has a complete plan laid out for the future. Notice the details. He thought about the time (**today or tomorrow**); the personnel (**we**); the place (**such and such a city**); the duration (**spend a year there**); the activity (**buy and sell**); and the anticipated result (**make a profit**). What is missing in this picture? He never once takes God into his business. In life, it is necessary to make some plans for the future, but to do so in self-will is sinful. To say "we will" or "I will" is the essence of sin. Note for instance, the "I wills" of Lucifer in Isaiah 14:13, 14: "For you have said in your heart: 'I will ascend into heaven, I will exalt my throne above the stars of God; I will also sit on the mount of the congregation on the farthest sides of the north; I will ascend above the heights of the clouds, I will be like the Most High.' "

4:14 It is wrong to plan as if **tomorrow** were certain. "Do not say . . . tomorrow" (Prov. 3:28). We do not know what tomorrow holds. Our lives are as frail and unpredictable as a "puff of smoke" (JBP).

4:15 God should be consulted in all our plans, and they should be made in His will. We should live and speak in the realization that our destinies are in His control. We should say, **"If the Lord wills, we shall live and do this or that."** Thus, in the book of Acts, we find the Apostle Paul saying, "I will return again to you, God willing" (18:21), and in 1 Corinthians 4:19 he wrote, "I will come to you shortly, if the Lord wills." Sometimes Christians employ the letters "D.V." to express this sense of dependence on God. These letters are the initials of two Latin words, *Deo volente*, meaning *God willing*.

4:16 **But now you boast in your arrogance**, writes James. The Christians were priding themselves in their boastful plans for the future. They were arrogant in their confidence that nothing would interfere with their time schedule. They acted as if they were the masters of their own fate. **All such boasting is evil** because it leaves God out.

4:17 **Therefore to him who knows to do good and does not do it, to him it is sin.** In this context, **to do good** is to take God into every aspect of our lives, to live in moment by moment dependence on Him. If we know we should do this, yet fail to do it, we are clearly sinning. Of course, the principle is of broader application. In any area of life, the opportunity **to do good** makes us responsible to do it. If we know what is right, we are under obligation to live up to that light. Failure **to do** so **is sin** against God, against our neighbors, and against ourselves.

In chapter 4, James has put us on trial with regard to covetousness and conflict, with regard to evil-speaking, and with regard to planning without consulting the Lord. Let us therefore ask ourselves the following questions — Am I continually anxious to get more or am I content with what I have? Am I envious of those who have more than I? Do I pray before purchasing? When God speaks to me, do I submit or resist? Do I speak against my brothers? Do I make plans without consulting the Lord?

IX. THE RICH AND THEIR COMING REMORSE (5:1–6)

In one of the most searching and piercing sections of his Letter, James now launches into a denunciation of the sins of the rich. The words fall like hammer-blows, blunt and unsparing. In fact, the denunciation is so strong that these verses are seldom preached on.

James is here seen in the role of a prophet of social justice. He cries out against the failure of the rich to use their money for the alleviation of human need. He condemns those who have become rich by exploiting their workers. He rebukes their use of wealth for self-indulgence and luxurious living. Finally, he pictures the rich as arrogant oppressors of the righteous.

5:1 First he summons the **rich** to **weep and howl** because of the **miseries** which they were about to experience. Soon they would meet God. Then they would be filled with shame and remorse. They would see that they had been unfaithful stewards. They would wail over the opportunities they had missed. They would mourn over their covetousness and selfishness. They would be convicted about their unfair employment practices. They would see the sin of seeking security in material things rather than in the Lord. And they would shed hot tears over the way they had indulged themselves to the full. James mentions four cardinal sins of the rich. The first is the sin of hoarding wealth.

5:2 "Your richest goods are ruined," says James, "your hoard of clothes is moth-eaten; your gold and silver are tarnished. Yes, their very tarnish will be the evidence of your wicked hoarding and you will shrink from them as if they were red-hot" (JBP).

The Bible never says that it is a sin to be rich. A person, for instance, may inherit a fortune overnight and certainly he has not committed any sin in thus becoming rich. But the Bible does teach that it is wrong to hoard riches. The Lord Jesus expressly forbade the hoarding of wealth. He said, "Do not lay up for yourselves treasures on earth, where moth and rust destroy and where thieves break in and steal; but lay up for yourselves treasures in heaven, where neither moth nor rust destroys and where thieves do not break in and steal. For where your treasure is, there your heart will be also" (Matt. 6:19–21).

James speaks of wealth in four forms: **riches, garments**, gold, and silver. In Bible times, wealth was generally in the form of grain, oil, and other produce: clothing, gold, and silver. Perhaps when James says **"Your riches are corrupted,"** he means that the grain had become wormy and the oil had become rancid. The point is that these things had been hoarded to the point where they were spoiled. They could have been used at one time to feed the hungry; now they were worthless. **"Your garments are moth-eaten,"** he says. This doesn't happen to clothing that is in regular use. But when the closet is so crowded with garments that they are used very infrequently, they are subject to moth damage. To James it is morally wrong to hoard clothes like this when so many people in the world are in desperate need.

5:3 **Your gold and silver are corroded, and their corrosion will be a witness against you, and will eat your flesh like fire**, he continues. **Gold and silver** do not rust, but they do tarnish and become discolored, and under unfavorable storage conditions, they could conceivably corrode. Instead of putting their money to work, feeding the hungry, clothing the destitute, providing medicines for the sick, and spreading the gospel, the rich were saving their money for a "rainy day." It benefited no one, and eventually rotted away.

Corrosion, speaking of disuse and decay, will be a condemning testimony against the rich. If this was true of the rich people of James' day, how much more true is it of believers in our day? What will be our condemnation if we have had the means of spreading the gospel and have failed to use it? If we have hoarded material things when they might have been used in the salvation of souls? The expression **their corrosion . . . will eat your flesh like fire** means that their failure to use their riches for the good of others would cause them the keenest suffering and remorse. When their eyes would at last be opened to see the cruelty of their selfishness and greed (costly jewelry, elegant clothing, luxurious homes, high-priced cars), it would be a scalding, scorching experience.

5:4 The second sin James attacks is acquiring wealth by failure to pay proper wages. **The laborers who mowed** the **fields** were deprived of their rightful pay. Though the workers might protest, they were quite helpless to get redress. They had no one on earth to plead their cause successfully. However, their **cries** were heard by the **Lord of Sabaoth** (Hebrew for "hosts"). He who commands the armies of heaven is strong on behalf of earth's downtrodden masses. The Lord God Omnipotent will help and avenge them. Thus, the Bible condemns not only the hoarding of wealth but the acquisition of wealth by dishonest means. In addition to the sin of paying inadequate wages, James could also have mentioned falsifying income tax returns, cheating on weights and measures, bribing local inspectors or other officials, false advertising, and falsifying expense accounts.

5:5 Next James denounces the luxurious living of the rich. Expensive jewelry, elegant clothes, epicurean foods, and palatial homes — how could they squander their wealth on self when multitudes were in desperate need? Or to bring it down to our own day, how can we justify the affluence and extravagance of the church and of Christian people? We live in a world where thousands die daily of starvation. Over half the world's population has never heard of the Lord Jesus Christ. In such a world, how can we justify our sports cars, limousines, speed boats? How can we spend the Lord's money in expensive hotels, in high-class restaurants, in any form of self-indulgence? The clear teaching of the Scriptures, the appalling need of the world, the example of the Savior, and the simple instinct of compassion tell us that it is wrong to live in comfort, luxury, and ease as long as there is a single soul who has not heard the gospel.

Those who live **in pleasure and** are unrestrained in **luxury** are likened to those who nourish their **hearts as in a day of slaughter** — like animals, fattening themselves just before their execu-

tion, or like soldiers who spend their time looting when others are perishing around them.

5:6 The final charge against the rich is that they **condemned** and **murdered the just**, and **he** did **not resist** them. Some think that this **just**, righteous one is the Lord Jesus. However, His death was brought about by the religious rather than by the rich. It is probably best to think of **the just** as representing innocent people in general. James is thinking of the rough, highhanded way in which rich people have characteristically behaved toward their subordinates. They **have condemned** them by false accusation, by harsh language, and by threats. They have killed them, not directly perhaps, but by overworking and underpaying them. The innocent offered no resistance. To protest might result in further brutality, or dismissal from their job.

X. EXHORTATION TO PATIENCE (5:7–12)

5:7 James now turns to believers who were being oppressed, and encourages them to **be patient**. The motive for patience is **the coming of the Lord**. This may refer either to the Rapture or to Christ's coming to reign. Both are used in the NT as incentives to patient endurance.

The farmer illustrates the need of patience. He does not reap on the same day that he plants. Rather there is a long period of waiting. First there must come the **early** rain, causing the seed to germinate. Then at the end of the season is the **latter rain**, needed to bring the crop to successful fruition. Some see in this reference to **early and latter rain** a promise that the blessings of Pentecost at the beginning of the Church Age will be repeated before the Lord's Return, but the overall tenor of NT Scripture seems to discourage such an expectation. However, there is nothing to forbid our looking for a faithful remnant of believers on fire for God and bent on world evangelization. What better way to welcome the returning Savior?

5:8 The wrongs of earth will be made right when the Lord returns. Therefore His people should **be patient**, like the farmer. Their **hearts** should be established with the certainty of His **coming**.

5:9 During times of persecution and distress, it is not uncommon for the victims to turn against one another. It is a curious twist of human nature that in times of pressure we build up wrath against those we love most. Hence the warning: **Do not grumble against one another, brethren, lest you be condemned**.[12] This verse has a voice for servants of the Lord working together under trying circumstances. We should not let resentment build up. After all, **the Judge is** already **at the door**! He knows what we think. Soon we will stand before the Judgment Seat of Christ to give an account. We should not judge lest we be judged.

5:10 **The** OT **prophets** are brought forth **as an example of suffering and patience**. Note that **suffering** precedes **patience**. "Tribulation produces perseverance" (Rom. 5:3). As explained previously, patience in the NT means fortitude or steadfastness. Because of their faithfulness in declaring the word of the Lord, the prophets were persecuted unmercifully. Yet "they endured as seeing Him who is invisible" (Heb. 11:27, 32–40).

5:11 We look back upon prophets such as Isaiah, Jeremiah, and Daniel with a great deal of respect. We honor them for their lives of zeal and devotion. In this sense we call them **blessed**. We agree that they were right and the world was wrong. Well, we should remember that they went through great trials and sufferings, and that they endured with patience. If we want to be blessed, it is only reasonable to conclude that we will be called upon to do the same.

Job is a fine example of **perseverance** or fortitude. Few if any men in the history of the world have ever suffered so much loss in so short a time as **Job**. Yet he never cursed God, or turned from Him. In the end, his endurance was rewarded. God revealed Himself, as He always does, to be **compassionate and merciful**.

If we did not know what James calls **the end intended by the Lord** (the final issue or result which **the Lord** brings to pass), we might be tempted to envy the wicked. Asaph was jealous when he saw the prosperity of the wicked (Ps.

73:3–17). The more he thought about it, the more perturbed he became. Then he went into the sanctuary of God and understood their latter end. This dispelled all his envy. David had the same experience. In Psalm 17:15 he describes the portion of the believer in the life to come. In view of this, it pays the believer to be steadfast. In Job's case, **the end intended by the Lord** was that God gave him twice as much as he had before (Job 42:10–15).

5:12 Impatience in times of trial is also manifested in swearing. Here it is not a question of profanity, or cursing, primarily. Neither is it a matter of taking an oath in a court of law. The practice forbidden is the thoughtless use of the Lord's Name or some other name to attest the truthfulness of one's speech. The Christian should **not** have to **swear** by anyone or anything, either in **heaven** or on **earth**. Those who know him should be able to depend on the fact that his **"Yes"** means **"Yes"** and his **"No"** means **"No."**

This passage could also be applied to forbid such needless expressions as "For heaven's sake," "As God is my Judge," "By Jove" and such minced oaths as "gee" (contraction for Jesus), "gosh" and "golly" (slang for God).

Lest you fall into judgment (or **hypocrisy**, NKJV margin[13]), says James, perhaps thinking of the third commandment: "You shall not take the name of the LORD your God in vain, for the LORD will not hold him guiltless who takes His name in vain" (Ex. 20:7).

XI. PRAYER AND THE HEALING OF THE SICK (5:13–20)

The theme of the closing verses of the Epistle is prayer. The word occurs seven times, either as a noun or verb.

5:13 In every circumstance of life, we should go to the Lord in prayer. When in trouble, we should approach Him with earnest entreaties. In times of rejoicing, we should lift our hearts to Him in praise. He wants to be brought into all the changing moods of our lives.

We should see God as the first great Cause of all that comes to us in life. We should not look into what Rutherford called the "confused rolling of the wheels of second causes." It is defeat to allow ourselves to be victims of circumstances, or to wait for our circumstances to change. We should see no hand but His.

This is one of the most disputed portions of the Epistle, and perhaps of the entire NT. It brings us face to face with the place of healing in the life of the believer today.

Before looking at the verses in detail, it should be helpful to review what the Bible teaches about sickness and healing.

DIVINE HEALING

1. Christians agree that all sickness is, in a general way, the result of sin in the world. If sin had never entered, there would be no sickness.

2. Sometimes sickness is a *direct* result of sin in a person's life. In 1 Corinthians 11:30, we read of certain Corinthians who were sick because they participated in the Lord's Supper without judging sin in their lives, that is, without confessing and forsaking it.

3. Not all sickness is a direct result of sin in a person's life. Job was sick in spite of the fact that he was a most righteous man (Job 1:8). The man born blind was not suffering for sins he had committed (John 9:2, 3). Epaphroditus was sick because of his tireless activity in the work of the Lord (Phil. 2:30). Gaius was spiritually healthy but apparently physically unwell (3 Jn. v. 2).

4. Sometimes sickness is a result of satanic activity. It was Satan who caused Job's body to be covered with boils (Job 2:7). It was Satan who crippled the woman in Luke 13:10–17 so that she was bent double, unable to straighten herself up: "This woman . . . whom Satan has bound — think of it — for eighteen years" (13:16). Paul had a physical infirmity caused by Satan. He called it "a thorn in the flesh . . . a messenger of Satan to buffet me" (2 Cor. 12:7).

5. God can and does heal. In a very real sense, *all* healing is divine. One of the names of God in the OT is *Jehovah-Ropheka* — "the LORD who heals you" (Ex. 15:26). We should acknowledge God in every case of healing.

It is clear from the Bible that God uses different means in healing. Sometimes He heals through natural bodily processes. He has placed within the human body tremendous powers of recuperation. Doctors know that most complaints are better by morning. Sometimes He heals through medicines. Paul advised Timothy, for instance, to "use a little wine for your stomach's sake and your frequent infirmities" (1 Tim. 5:23). Sometimes He heals through "deliverance from underlying fears, resentments, self-preoccupation, and guilts, all of which produce illness." Sometimes He heals through physicians and surgeons. Jesus explicitly taught that sick people need a physician (Matt. 9:12). Paul spoke of Luke as "the beloved physician" (Col. 4:14), which certainly recognizes the need of doctors among Christians. God uses doctors in the ministry of healing. As Dubois, the famous French surgeon said, "The surgeon dresses the wound; God heals it."

6. But God also heals miraculously. The Gospels contain many illustrations of this. It would be incorrect to say that God generally heals in this way, but neither should we say that He never does. There is nothing in the Bible to discourage us from believing that God can heal miraculously today.

7. Yet we must also be clear that it is not always God's will to heal. Paul left Trophimus sick at Miletus (2 Tim. 4:20). The Lord did not heal Paul of his thorn in the flesh (2 Cor. 12:7–10). If it were always God's will to heal, some would never grow old or die!

8. God has not promised to heal in every case; therefore, healing is not something we can demand from Him. In Philippians 2:27, healing is spoken of as a mercy, not something which we have a right to expect.

9. While it is true in a general sense that healing is in the "Atonement," yet not all the blessings that are in the Atonement have been given to us yet. For instance, the redemption of the body was included in Christ's work for us, but we will not receive it until Christ comes for His saints (Rom. 8:23). At that time also we will be completely and finally healed of all diseases.

10. It is not true that failure to be healed indicates a lack of faith. If it were, this would mean that some would live on indefinitely; but no one does. Paul, Trophimus, and Gaius were not healed,

and yet their faith was virile and active. ‡

5:14, 15 Returning to James 5, we see how it fits in with what the rest of the Bible teaches about healing:

Is anyone among you sick? Let him call for the elders of the church, and let them pray over him, anointing him with oil in the name of the Lord. And the prayer of faith will save the sick, and the Lord will raise him up. And if he has committed sins, he will be forgiven.

If these were the only verses in the Bible on healing, we would assume that a Christian could be assured of healing from every illness that comes in life, if he met the conditions listed. However, we have already seen from other Scriptures that it is not always God's will to heal. Therefore we are forced to the conclusion that James is not talking about *every* kind of illness, but only about a certain form of sickness, that is, a sickness which is the result of certain specific circumstances. The key to understanding the passage is found in the words **"And if he has committed sins, he will be forgiven."** Healing in this section is connected with the forgiveness of **sins**.

Here is a man who has committed some sin, probably involving the testimony of the local church. Shortly afterward he is stricken with illness. He realizes that this sickness is a direct result of his sin. God is chastening him in order to bring him back into fellowship. He repents of his sin and confesses it to God. But since the sin has also involved the public testimony of the assembly, he calls **the elders** and makes a full confession to them as well. They **pray over him, anointing him with oil in the name of the Lord**. This **prayer of faith** saves **the sick** man, **and the Lord will raise him up**. It is a definite promise of the Lord that where sickness is a direct result of sin, and where that sin is confessed and forsaken in the manner described, the Lord will heal.

Someone will say, "How do you know that the man has committed sins and that he is brought to the place of repentance and confession?" The answer is that the closing part of verse 15 speaks about his **sins** being **forgiven**. And we know that sins are forgiven only as a result of confession (1 Jn. 1:9).

Someone else will object, "It doesn't say he *has* committed sins. It says **if he has committed sins.**" This is true, but the whole context has to do with confession of sins and the restoration of a backslider. Notice the following: "Confess your trespasses to one another, and pray for one another, that you may be healed." The drought mentioned in verses 17, 18 was a judgment of God on Israel because of sin. It was lifted after they returned to the Lord, acknowledging Him as the true God (1 Kgs. 18:39). Verses 19, 20 clearly deal with the recovery of a backslider, as we shall see.

The entire context of James 5:13–20 implies that the healing promised by God is for a person whose sickness is a result of sin, and who confesses the sin to **the elders**. The responsibility of **the elders** is to **pray over him, anointing him with oil**. Some interpret **the oil** here as signifying the use of *medicinal means*, since oil was a form of medicine in the days when James was writing (Luke 10:34). Another view is that the *ritual use of oil* is meant. This view is strengthened by the words **in the name of the Lord**. In other words, the anointing was to be done by His authority and in obedience to His word. Oil was sometimes used by the apostles when effecting miraculous cures (Mark 6:13). The healing power was not in the oil, but the oil symbolized the Holy Spirit in His healing ministry (1 Cor. 12:9).

Some will object that the ritual use of oil is inconsistent with the Age of Grace, with its de-emphasis on ceremonies and rites. However, we do use the bread and wine as symbols of Christ's body and blood, and we use water in baptism. Also women use head coverings in the assembly as symbols of their submission to man. Why then should we object to the ritual use of oil?

In response to the **prayer of faith**, God will heal the person. It is a **prayer of faith** because it is based on the promise of God's word. It is not at all a question as to how much faith the elders have, or how much faith the sick man has. The elders can pray with complete assurance because God has promised to raise up the man when the conditions described have been fully met.

To summarize, then, we believe that verses 14, 15 apply to a case where a person is sick as a direct result of some sin. When he realizes this and repents, he should **call for the elders of the** assembly and make a full confession to them. They should then **pray over him, anointing him with oil in the name of the Lord**. They can pray for his recovery in faith, since God here promises to heal the man.

5:16a   Confess your trespasses[14] **to one another, and pray for one another, that you may be healed**. A casual reading of this statement might give the impression that we are to tell other people all about our secret sins. But that is not at all the thought! Primarily James means that when we sin against someone else, we should be prompt to confess this sin to the person we have wronged.

Also we should **pray for one another**. Instead of holding grudges and allowing resentments to build up, we should maintain ourselves in fellowship with others through confession and prayer.

Physical healing is linked with spiritual restoration. Notice how James links together confession, prayer, and healing. It is a clear intimation of the vital connection between the physical and the spiritual. Man is a tripartite being — spirit, soul, and body (1 Thess. 5:23). What affects one part of him affects all. In the OT, the priest was also the physician. It was he who diagnosed leprosy, and it was he who pronounced it cured, for instance. By thus combining the offices of priest and doctor in one person, the Lord indicated the close tie between the spirit and the body.

The field of psychosomatic medicine recognizes this link and searches for personal problems that might be causing physical troubles. But modern medicine does not have the remedy for sin. Deliverance from the guilt, defilement, power, and penalty of sin can come only on the basis of the blood of Christ, and through confession Godward and manward. More often than we are willing to admit, illnesses are caused by sin — such sins as gluttony, worry, anger, an unforgiving spirit, intemperance, jealousy, self-

ishness, and pride. Sin in the life brings sickness and sometimes death (1 Cor. 11:30). We should confess and forsake sin as soon as we are aware it has come into our lives. *All* sins should be confessed to God. In addition, sins against other people should be confessed to them as well. It is vital for our spiritual health and good for our physical health.

> **5:16b–18** Tremendous power is made available through a good man's earnest prayer. Do you remember Elijah? He was a man like us, but he prayed earnestly that it should not rain. In fact, not a drop fell on the land for three and a half years. Then he prayed again; the heavens gave the rain, and the earth sprouted with vegetation as usual (JBP).

This incident is recorded in 1 Kings 17:1–19:10. Ahab was king of Israel at the time. Through his wife Jezebel, he became a worshiper of Baal, and led the people into this vile form of idolatry. "Ahab did more to provoke the LORD God of Israel to anger than all the kings of Israel who were before him" (16:33). It was a direct result of sin that drought came upon Israel for three and a half years.

Then Elijah had the famous contest with the priests of Baal on Mt. Carmel. When the fire of the Lord fell and consumed the burnt offering, the altar, and the water, the people were convinced, and they turned back to the Lord. Elijah **prayed again** and the drought ended. The example of **Elijah** is given as an encouragement to us to pray for those who have sinned and wandered away from fellowship with God. **The effective fervent prayer of a righteous man avails much** or, as someone has paraphrased it: "The prayer of a man whose heart is right with God works wonders." Lest we be tempted to think of him as belonging to a higher creation than ourselves, James reminds us that **Elijah was a man** with the same kind of frail flesh. He was a mere man, subject to the same weaknesses and infirmities as other men.

5:19, 20   In the preceding verses we have seen the elders of the assembly being used in the restoration of a sinning saint. And we have seen Elijah being used in the restoration (partial and temporary) of a backsliding nation. Now we are exhorted to give ourselves to this far-reaching ministry.

Verse 19 describes a Christian brother who has wandered away **from the truth**, either in doctrine or in practice. Another brother makes this a matter of fervent, believing prayer, and thus lovingly **turns him back** to fellowship with God and with his brothers and sisters in Christ. How immense is the significance of this ministry! First of all, **he will save** his erring brother from dying prematurely under the chastening hand of God. Secondly, he will **cover a multitude of sins**. They are forgiven and forgotten by God. Also they are forgiven by fellow believers and veiled from the gaze of the outside world. We need this ministry today. In our zeal to evangelize the lost, perhaps we do not give sufficient attention to those sheep of Christ who have wandered from the fold.

Once again James has been prodding our consciences with regard to various areas of the Christian life. He has been asking us, for example: Do you lay up treasures on earth? Are your business methods strictly honest? Your income tax return, for instance? Do you live luxuriously, or do you live sacrificially so that others may come to know the Savior? When you sin against another person, are you willing to go to him and apologize? When you become ill, whom do you contact first — the doctor or the Lord? When you see a brother fall into sin, do you criticize him or try to restore him?

And so we come to the end of this practical, brief Epistle. In it we have seen faith on trial. We have seen faith tested by the problems of life, by unholy temptations, by obedience to the word of God. The man who says he has faith has been challenged to exhibit it by avoiding partiality or snobbishness and to prove it by a life of good works. The reality of faith is seen in a person's speech; the believer learns to yield his tongue to the lordship of Christ. True faith is accompanied by true wisdom; the life of envy and strife is exchanged for that of practical godliness.

Faith avoids the feuds, struggles, and jealousies that spring from covetousness and worldly ambition. It avoids a harsh, critical spirit. It avoids the self-confidence which leaves God out of life's plans. Faith stands trial by the way it earns and spends its money. In spite of oppression, it manifests fortitude and endurance in view of the Lord's Return. Its speech is uniformly honest, needing no oaths to attest it. Faith goes to God in all the changing moods of life. In sickness, it first looks for spiritual causes. By confession to God and to those who have been wronged, it removes these possible causes. Finally, faith goes out in love and compassion to those who have backslidden.

Your faith and mine are on trial each day. What is the Judge's verdict?

ENDNOTES

[1](1:14) The Greek word *epithumia* is just a strengthened form of "desire." The English word *lust* (cf. 1611 KJV) originally meant simply "strong desire" too, but has taken on definite sexual connotations.

[2](1:19) The words "So then" (Gk. *hōste*) are replaced by "Know" (*iste*) in some mss., and most modern versions that prefer the Alexandrian (NU) readings. However, the traditional reading best fits the context — a major break summing up what we should do in light of vv. 1–18.

[3](1:21) The same Greek word (*psuchē*) means both "life" and "soul" and it is not always certain which rendering is better. Also "save" (in Greek and English) does not necessarily refer to eternal salvation. It can refer to healing, deliverance, rescue, and other things. Thus, the expression "save your soul" could mean *in some contexts* "make a success of your *life*" (for Christ).

[4](2:2–4) The Greek word here is *sunagōgē* (congregation). Since this word later came to be used only for *Jewish* congregations ("synagogues"), this is an indication of the very early date of James. "Congregation" (Tyndale), "church" (KJV), and "assembly" (JND), are usually translations of the word *ekklēsia*, a (called-out) assembly. This was originally a political term (cf. General *Assembly* of the United Nations).

[5](2:14) However, in all fairness, it should be pointed out that the Greek does *not* have the word for "that" here,

but simply the definite article ("the"). While the article may sometimes have a demonstrative force, it could just be the ordinary article used with an abstract noun. Since this is admittedly interpretive, the NKJV, which had "that faith" in its 1st edition, reverted to the KJV reading in later editions.

[6](2:20) The NU text reads "useless" for "dead."

[7](3:5, 6) Clovis G. Chappel, *Sermons from the Psalms*, p.132.

[8](3:7) Robert G. Lee, *Lord I Believe*, pp. 166-168.

[9](4:4) Most mss. read "Adulterers and adulteresses," perhaps suggesting literal immorality in the congregations addressed. The Alexandrian mss. (NU) have only the feminine form "adulteresses," which would almost demand a non-literal meaning. The KJV and NKJV allow either meaning, physical and/or spiritual adultery.

[10](4:5) The most ancient mss. had not yet developed separate forms for capital and small letters. Ideally, there would be an "S" that was somewhere between upper case and lower case for the many places in the NT where a passage is not clearly Spirit or spirit. Since there is no such form, translators and editors must decide according to context. Here and elsewhere good Bible scholars are divided.

[11](4:11, 12) NU text reads *a neighbor*.

[12](5:9) Both NU and M texts read "judged," but the context does suggest a negative verdict, so "condemned" is still valid.

[13](5:12) The majority text has a most interesting variant reading here. The KJV (and NU) reading "into (lit. "under") judgment" is *hupo krisin*. The *majority* of mss., however, read *eis* ("into") *hupokrisin* ("hypocrisy"). If the little preposition "eis" were to drop out by mistake in copying, it would be natural to take the prefix on *hupokrisin* as a separate preposition and come up with "under judgment." While both expressions fit the immediate context, the whole Epistle of James, coming to a close here, could be said to be a warning against falling into religious *hypocrisy*.

[14](5:16a) The NU text reads "Therefore confess your sins."

BIBLIOGRAPHY

Adamson, James. *The Epistle of James* (NIC). Grand Rapids: Wm. B. Eerdmans Publishing Company, 1976.

Brown, Charles. *The General Epistle of James: A Devotional Commentary*. Philadelphia: The Union Press, 1907.

Gaebelein, Frank. *The Practical Epistle of James*. Great Neck, N. Y.: Doniger & Raughley, Inc., 1955.

Johnstone, Robert. *Lectures Exegetical and Practical on the Epistle of James*. Minneapolis: Klock & Klock Christian Publishers (Reprint of 1871 ed.).

Kelly, William. *The Epistle of James*. London: F. E. Race, 1913.

King, Guy H. *A Belief that Behaves*. London: Marshall, Morgan & Scott, Ltd., 1954.

Zodhiates, Spiros. *The Behavior of Belief*. Grand Rapids: Wm. B. Eerdmans Publishing Co., 1959.

THE FIRST EPISTLE OF PETER

Introduction

"Did we not know who wrote this letter we should be forced to say: 'This is a rocklike man who writes thus, whose soul rests on a rock foundation, and who with his mighty testimony undertakes to fortify the souls of others against the pressure of the storms of suffering advancing upon them and to establish them upon the true rock basis.' "

— Wiesinger

I. Unique Place in the Canon

Christians in Muslim and Marxist countries are so used to repression, hostility, and even downright persecution that they almost come to expect it. For them 1 Peter is a tremendous practical help in accepting suffering as allowed by the Lord and as beneficial in producing certain desirable qualities, such as perseverance.

Christians in the West, especially English-speaking believers with their great biblical heritage, have not yet adjusted to public opposition to the faith. Until recently the state at least smiled on the family unit as basic to society and even encouraged attendance at "the church of your choice." No longer. The government, especially local government, seems to use its judges, educational institutions, and especially the media, to misrepresent, ridicule, and even defame Bible-believing Christians. Radio, television, films, newspapers, magazines, and official communiqués promote immorality, liquor, cheating, and even blasphemy. Christianity is now "counter-culture," and the sooner believers learn the lessons the Apostle Peter teaches in his First Letter, the more prepared they will be for the last years of the twentieth and first years of the twenty-first centuries — if our Lord tarries.

II. Authorship[†]

External Evidence

The *external evidence* that Peter wrote this Epistle is early and well-nigh universal. Eusebius counts 1 Peter as among the books accepted by all believers (*homologoumena*). Polycarp and Clement of Alexandria accept the book. The fact that it is not in Marcion's "canon" should cause no wonder, as he only accepted *Paul's* Letters. The Muratorian Canon does not list 1 Peter, but this may be due to the fragmentary nature of that document.

It is quite possible that 2 Peter 3:1 is the earliest attestation to 1 Peter. Even those who believe Peter did not write 2 Peter (see Introduction to 2 Peter) still see the Letter as early enough to be a valid witness to 1 Peter, if indeed 2 Peter 3:1 is meant to refer back to this earlier Letter.

Internal Evidence

The *internal evidence* that causes some to doubt Petrine authorship is the very good Greek that is used. Could a Galilean fisherman write so well? Many say "No." However, as our own culture will amply illustrate, men with a flair for words and public speech often become outstanding users of the standard language without formal college or seminary training. Peter had thirty years' experience preaching, not to mention the Holy Spirit's inspiration and the probable help from Silvanus in composing the Letter. When Acts 4:13 says that Peter and John were unlearned it merely means they lacked formal rabbinical training.

References to Peter's life and ministry

†See p. i.

are ample in 1 Peter, as the following selection of details will demonstrate:

The writer implies in 1:8 that he had seen Jesus in a way his readers had not. He says, "whom having not seen *you* love," not ". . . *we* have not seen Him." We shall see in other passages that the writer had companied with the Lord.

The first ten verses of chapter 2 present Christ as the Cornerstone, and thus take us back to the incident at Caesarea Philippi (Matt. 16:13-20). When Peter confessed Jesus as the Christ, the Son of the living God, the Lord Jesus announced that His church would be built on that foundation, that is, on the truth that Christ is the Son of the living God. He is the Cornerstone and Foundation of the church.

The reference to living stones in 2:5 recalls the incident in John 1:42 where Simon's name was changed to Cephas (Aramaic) or Peter (Greek), which both mean *stone*. Through faith in Christ, Peter became a living stone. It is not surprising that he has so much to say about stones in chapter 2. In 2:7, the writer quotes Psalm 118:22: *"The stone which the builders rejected has become the chief cornerstone."* This is the same passage which Peter quoted when he was arraigned before the rulers, elders, and scribes in Jerusalem (Acts 4:11).

As we hear the apostle advising his readers to submit to governmental authorities (2:13-17), we think back to that time when Peter himself did not submit, but cut off the ear of the high priest's slave (John 18:10). So his advice, in addition to being inspired, has the ring of practical experience behind it!

Chapter 2:21-24 seems to indicate direct knowledge of the trial and death of the Lord Jesus. Peter could never forget the meek endurance and silent suffering of the Savior. In 2:24 we have a reference to the mode of the Savior's death — by crucifixion. The description seems to echo Peter's words in Acts 5:30 and 10:39.

When Peter spoke of his readers returning to the Shepherd and Overseer of their souls (2:25), he might well have been thinking of his own restoration (John 21:15-19), following his denial of the Lord.

The reminder that "love will cover a multitude of sins" (4:8) might refer back to Peter's questions, "Lord, how often shall my brother sin against me, and I forgive him? Up to seven times?" Jesus said to him, "I do not say to you, up to seven times, but up to seventy times seven" (Matt. 18:21, 22). In other words, indefinitely.

In 4:16 we are told that if anyone suffers as a Christian he should not be ashamed, but in that name should glorify God. Compare this with Acts 5:40-42 where Peter and the other apostles, after having been flogged, left the council, "rejoicing that they were counted worthy to suffer shame for His name."

The writer of the Epistle identifies himself as a witness of the sufferings of Christ (5:1). The expression, "a partaker of the glory that will be revealed," may be an allusion to the transfiguration. Peter was present, of course, on both occasions.

The gentle, pastoral counsel to "shepherd the flock of God which is among you" (5:2) reminds us of the Savior's words to Peter, "Feed My lambs. . . . Tend My sheep. . . . Feed My sheep" (John 21:15-17).

The language of 5:5, "be clothed with humility" is strongly reminiscent of the incident in John 13 where Jesus clothed Himself with the apron of a slave and washed His disciples' feet. In fact, the whole section on pride and humility (5:5, 6) is all the more meaningful when we remember Peter's proud assertion that he would never deny the Lord (Mark 14:29-31) and his subsequent threefold denial of the Savior (Mark 14:67-72).

A final reference that may relate to Peter's experience is found in 5:8: "Your adversary the devil walks about like a roaring lion, seeking whom he may devour." When Peter wrote this, was he thinking of the time when Jesus said to him, "Simon, Simon! Indeed, Satan has asked for you, that he may sift *you* as wheat . . . " (Luke 22:31)?

III. Date

Peter's teaching that government is generally helpful to those who wish to do right (1 Pet. 2:13-17) is thought by many to be too conciliatory to have been written *after* the start of Nero's fierce persecution of the Christians (A.D. 64). At any rate, the Letter cannot be very far removed from this period in time, probably 64 or 65.

IV. Background and Themes†

As has been noted, Peter is especially dealing with suffering in the Christian life. So far his readers seem to have undergone slander and ridicule for Christ (4:14, 15). Prison, confiscation of property, and violent death for many still apparently lay in the future. Suffering is not the only theme of this great Letter, however. The blessings inherited by accepting the gospel, the proper relationships of believers with the world, the state, the family, and the church, and instruction on elders and discipline are all included.

From "Babylon" — either the literal city on the Euphrates with its Jewish community, or spiritual Babylon on the Tiber (Rome) — the apostle sends this Letter to the eastern provinces of what is now Turkey.

OUTLINE

I. THE BELIEVER'S PRIVILEGES AND DUTIES (1:1–2:10)
  A. Salutation (1:1, 2)
  B. His Position as a Believer (1:3–12)
  C. His Conduct in the Light of His Position (1:13–2:3)
  D. His Privileges in the New House and Priesthood (2:4–10)

II. THE BELIEVER'S RELATIONSHIPS (2:11–4:6)
  A. As a Pilgrim in Relation to the World (2:11, 12)
  B. As a Citizen in Relation to Government (2:13–17)
  C. As a Servant in Relation to His Master (2:18–25)
  D. As a Wife in Relation to Her Husband (3:1–6)
  E. As a Husband in Relation to His Wife (3:7)
  F. As a Brother in Relation to the Fellowship (3:8)
  G. As a Sufferer in Relation to Persecutors (3:9–4:6)

III. THE BELIEVER'S SERVICE AND SUFFERING (4:7–5:14)
  A. Urgent Imperatives for the Last Days (4:7–11)
  B. Exhortations and Explanations Concerning Suffering (4:12–19)
  C. Exhortations and Salutations (5:1–14)

Commentary

I. THE BELIEVER'S PRIVILEGES AND DUTIES (1:1–2:10)

A. Salutation (1:1, 2)

1:1 The beloved fisherman introduces himself as **Peter, an apostle of Jesus Christ**. He had been commissioned by the Lord Jesus as one of the original twelve, called to be the herald of a glorious, transforming message. By responding to the divine tap on the shoulder, he had become a fisher of men.

All believers are called to represent Christ's interests here on earth. We are all supposed to be missionaries, whether at home or abroad. This is the central purpose of our life as Jesus' followers; all else is subordinate.

The Letter is addressed **to the pilgrims** or foreigners scattered throughout **Pontus, Galatia, Cappadocia, Asia, and Bithynia**. Who were these exiles?

Peter's use of the words **"of the Dispersion"** predisposes us to think that

†*See p. ii.*

they were Jewish believers because James uses that same word concerning believers from the twelve tribes of Israel (Jas. 1:1). Also the word in John 7:35 describes Jews who were scattered among the Gentiles.

But it is quite probable that Peter is writing to the Gentile believers who had been dispersed by persecution among the surrounding nations. In doing so, he takes many of the names that were formerly given to God's earthly people and applies them to God's new society, the church. He calls them elect (1:2), a chosen generation, a royal priesthood, a holy nation, a people of God's possession (2:9). He also gives three other indications that he is writing to Gentile believers. He speaks of the empty way of life which had been handed down to them from their forefathers (1:14, 18). He describes them as those who in time past were not a people (2:10). Finally, in 4:3 he says that they had lived in previous times like Gentiles. So there is strong evidence that the Diaspora or Dispersion to which Peter writes is the Christian church, composed largely of those who were Gentiles before their conversion. If it be objected that Peter was preeminently the apostle to the Jews, that did not preclude his ministering to Gentiles. Certainly Paul, the apostle to the Gentiles, spent time ministering to the Jews.

1:2 The recipients of the Letter are further designated by a fourfold progression of their salvation which involved all three Persons of the Trinity.

First of all, they were **elect according to the foreknowledge of God the Father**. This means that in a past eternity, God chose them to belong to Himself. The doctrine of divine election is not always popular, but it does have this virtue — it allows God to be God. Attempts to make it palatable to man only succeed in detracting from the sovereignty of God. Any difficulty in reconciling God's election and human responsibility lies in man's mind, not in God's. The Bible teaches both doctrines, and we should believe both. The truth lies in both extremes, not somewhere between them.

God's choice is said to be **according to** His **foreknowledge**. Some understand this to mean that God elected those

whom He foreknew would trust the Savior. Others say that God knew very well that, left to himself, no sinner would trust the Savior, and so in His foreknowledge He marked out certain ones to be trophies of His grace. While there is unutterable mystery in God's choice, we can be sure that there is nothing unjust about it.

The second step in salvation is **sanctification of the Spirit**. This aspect of **sanctification** takes place before conversion.[1] It is a ministry of the Holy **Spirit** by which He sets people apart to belong to God (see also 2 Thess. 2:13). It logically follows election by God the Father. In *eternity* God foreknew and chose men. In *time* the Holy Spirit operates to make that election real in the lives of the individuals concerned.

The third step in the soul's salvation is the sinner's response to the work of the Holy Spirit. It is described as **obedience** to **Jesus Christ**. This means obeying the gospel by repenting of one's sins and receiving Christ as Savior. The concept of the gospel as something to be obeyed is a common one in the NT (see Rom. 2:8; 2 Thess. 1:8).

Finally, there is the **sprinkling** with His **blood**. We must not take this with absolute literalness and insist that when a person is saved, he is actually sprinkled with the blood of Jesus. This is figurative language. What it does say is that as soon as a person obeys the gospel, he receives all the benefits which flow from the shedding of Christ's blood on Calvary. The Savior's blood was shed once for all over 1900 years ago; it will never be shed again. But we receive forgiveness, redemption, and the other innumerable blessings that flow from that crimson tide as soon as we believe on Him.

Having traced the four steps in his reader's spiritual birth, Peter now wishes that **grace** and **peace** might be **multiplied** to them. They have already experienced the grace of God in salvation and the resulting peace with God. But day by day they will need **grace** or strength for the Christian life, and **peace** in the midst of a turbulent society. That is what the apostle wishes for them here in fullest abundance. James Denney said that "grace is the first and last word of the Gospel; and peace — perfect spiritual soundness — is the finished work of grace."

B. His Position as a Believer (1:3–12)

1:3 In verses 3–12, Peter sets forth the unique glories of our salvation. He begins by calling for praise to be given to the Author of salvation — **the God and Father of our Lord Jesus Christ**. This title presents God in a twofold relationship to the Lord Jesus. The name **God ... of our Lord Jesus Christ** emphasizes the humanity of the Savior. The name **Father** underlines the deity of God's Son. The full name of the Son is given:

Lord — the One with the exclusive right to rule in hearts and lives.

Jesus — the One who saves His people from their sins.

Christ — God's Anointed One who has been exalted to heaven's highest place.

It is by God's **abundant mercy** that we have been born anew **to a living hope through the resurrection of Jesus Christ from the dead**. God is the source of this salvation. His great mercy is its cause. The new birth is the nature of it. A living hope is its present reward. **The resurrection of Jesus Christ** is the righteous basis of our salvation, as well as the foundation of our **living hope**.

As sinners, we had no hope beyond the grave. There was nothing ahead for us but the certainty of judgment and fiery indignation. As members of the first creation we were under the sentence of death. But in the redemptive work of Christ, God found a righteous basis upon which He can save ungodly sinners and still be just. Christ has paid the penalty of our sins. Full satisfaction has been made. The claims of justice have been met, and now mercy can flow out to those who obey the gospel. In the resurrection of Christ, God indicated His complete satisfaction with the sacrificial work of His Son. The resurrection is the Father's "Amen" to our Lord's cry, "It is finished!" Also, that resurrection is a pledge that all who die in Christ will be raised from among the dead. This is our **living hope** — the expectation of being

taken home to heaven to be with Christ and to be like Him forever. F. B. Meyer calls the **living hope** "the link between our present and future."

1:4 Verses 4, 5 describe this future aspect of salvation. When we are born again we have the certain hope of **an inheritance ... in heaven**. The **inheritance** includes all that the believer will enjoy in heaven for eternity, and all that will be his through Christ (Ps. 16:5). The inheritance is **incorruptible and undefiled and** unfading: (1) **Incorruptible** means that it can never corrode, crack, or decay. It is death-proof. (2) **Undefiled** means that the inheritance itself is in perfect condition. No tarnish or stain can dim its purity. It is sin-proof. (3) **That does not fade away** means that it can never suffer variations in value, glory, or beauty. It is time-proof.

Earthly inheritances are uncertain at best. Sometimes the value of an estate drops sharply because of market declines. Sometimes wills are successfully contested by parties not mentioned in them. Sometimes people are deprived of an inheritance because of legal technicalities. But this divine inheritance is not subject to any of the changes of time, and there are no loopholes in the believer's title to it. It is kept in the safety-vault of heaven for the child of God.

1:5 Not only is the inheritance guarded for Christians, but they **are kept** or guarded for *it*. In this life an heir may die before an inheritance is divided. But the same grace that preserves the heavenly inheritance preserves us as heirs to enjoy it. God's election of His people can never be frustrated. Those who were chosen in eternity past are saved in time now and kept for eternity to come. The believer in Christ is eternally secure.

But there is a human as well as a divine side to eternal security. We **are kept by the power of God** — that is the divine side, but it is **through faith** — that is the human side. This does not mean that a person is saved only as long as he exercises faith. Where there is true **faith**, there will be continuance. Saving faith *always* has the quality of permanence.

The child of God is guarded by the **power of God for salvation ready to be**

ting forth the manifold wisdom of God (Eph. 3:10). But it is not for them to know the joy that our salvation brings.

C. His Conduct in the Light of His Position (1:13–2:3)

1:13 Beginning here, there is a change in emphasis. Peter has been dealing with the glories of our salvation. At this point, he launches into a series of exhortations based on the foregoing. Jowett says: "The present appeal is based on the introductory evangel. . . . Spiritual impulse is created by the momentum of superlative facts. The dynamic of duty is born in the heart of the Gospel."[5]

First, Peter urges the saints to have a "girded" **mind**. The girding up of the **mind** is an interesting figure of speech. In eastern lands, people wore long, flowing robes. When they wanted to walk fast or with a minimum of hindrance, they would tie the robe up around their waist with a belt (see Ex. 12:11). In this way they girded up their loins. But what does Peter mean by **gird up the loins of your mind**? As they went out into a hostile world, believers were to avoid panic and distraction. In times of persecution, there is always the tendency to become rattled and confused. A girded mind is one that is strong, composed, cool, and ready for action. It is unimpeded by the distraction of human fear or persecution.

This state of mental solidarity is further encouraged by the words **be sober**. This means self-control in contrast to hysteria. The **sober** spirit is poised and stable.

Next, the saints are urged to have the optimistic, forward-looking mind: **rest your hope fully upon the grace that is to be brought to you at the revelation of Jesus Christ**. The assurance of Christ's Return is held out as a compelling motive for endurance through the storms and tribulations of life. **The revelation of Jesus Christ** is generally taken to refer to His coming back to earth when He will be revealed in glory. However, it could also refer to the Rapture when Christ will come for His saints.

1:14 In verses 14–16, the subject is the **obedient** mind. **Obedient children** should not indulge in the sins which characterized them in their former life. Now that they are Christians, they should pattern their life after the One whose name they bear. If they conform to the ungodly world, they are denying their heavenly character. The things they did in the days of their **ignorance** should be put away now that they have been illuminated by the Holy Spirit. **The former lusts** means the sins they indulged in while they were still ignorant of God.

1:15 Instead of imitating the ungodly world with its fads and fashions, our lives should reproduce the **holy** character of the One who called us. To be godly means to be Godlike. God is holy in all His ways. If we are to be like Him, we must be **holy** in all that we do and say. In this life we will never be *as* holy as He is, but we should **be holy** *because* He is.

1:16 Peter reaches back into the OT for proof that God expects His people to be like Himself. In Leviticus 11:44, the Lord said: **"Be holy, for I am holy."** Christians are empowered to live holy lives by the indwelling Holy Spirit. Old Testament saints did not have this help and blessing. But since we are more privileged, we are also more responsible. The verse Peter quotes from Leviticus acquires a new depth of meaning in the NT. It is the difference between the formal and the vital. Holiness was God's ideal in the OT. It has assumed a concrete, everyday quality with the coming of the Spirit of truth.

1:17 Not only are we exhorted to holiness but also to a reverent mind. This means a respectful **fear**, a deep appreciation of who God is. It especially means a realization that the One whom we address as **Father** is the same One who **judges** His children impartially **according to** their deeds. As we realize the extent of His knowledge and the accuracy of His judgment, we should live with a wholesome fear of displeasing Him. **The Father . . . judges** His own in this life; He has committed the judgment of sinners to the Lord Jesus (John 5:22).

Lincoln writes: "He is looking on, taking notice of all, whether there is integrity of purpose, intelligence of mind, and desire of heart to please Him."[6]

We are to pass **the time of** our **stay** on earth **in fear**. Christians are not at home in this world. We are living in a foreign country, exiled from heaven. We should not settle down as if this were our permanent dwelling. Neither should we imitate the behavior of the earth-dwellers. We should always remember our heavenly destiny and behave ourselves as citizens of heaven.

1:18 Before their conversion, believers were not different from the rest of the world. Their talk and walk were as empty and trivial as that of men around them. Their unconverted days are described as **your aimless conduct received by tradition from your fathers**. But they had been ransomed from that futile existence by a tremendous transaction. They had been rescued from the slavery of world-conformity by the payment of an infinite ransom. Was it by **silver or gold** that these kidnap victims had been freed (see Ex. 30:15)?

1:19 No, it was **with the precious blood of Christ** — like the blood of a perfect, unblemished **lamb**. Christ is **a lamb without blemish** or **spot**, that is, He is absolutely perfect, inwardly and outwardly. If a believer is ever tempted to return to worldly pleasures and amusements, to adopt worldly modes and patterns, to become like the world in its false ways, he should remember that Christ shed His **blood** to deliver him from that kind of life. To go back to the world is to re-cross the great gulf that was bridged for us at staggering cost. But even more — it is positive disloyalty to the Savior.

"Reason back from the greatness of the sacrifice to the greatness of the sin. Then determine to be done forever with that which cost God's Son His life."

1:20 Christ's work for us was no afterthought on God's part. The Redeemer was destined to die for us **before the** creation **of the world. But** at the end of the **times**, that is, at the end of the dispensation of law, He appeared from heaven to rescue us from our former way of life. Lincoln comments: "In these last times — the world's moral history was closed at the cross of Christ. It has shown itself fully and got to its end before God."[7]

Peter adds these considerations to impress us even more deeply with the importance of making a clean break with the world system from which Christ died to deliver us. We are in the world but not of it. We must not isolate ourselves from unregenerate men, but rather carry the gospel to them. Yet in our dealings and relationships with them, we must never share in or condone their sins. We are to show by our lives that we are children of God. The moment we become like the world, our testimony is weakened. There is no incentive for worldlings to be converted if they cannot see a difference — a change for the better in our lives.

1:21 Loyalty to the Lord Jesus is further demanded by the fact that it is **through Him** we have come to **believe in God**. He is the One who has revealed the Father's heart to us. As W. T. P. Wolston says: "it is not by creation nor providence nor law that man knows God, but by Christ."[8] The Father indicated His complete satisfaction with Christ's redeeming work by raising Him out **from** among **the dead** ones and honoring **Him** with the place of highest **glory** in heaven. The result of all this is **that** our **faith and hope are in God**. It is in Him, not in the present evil world system, that we live and move and have our being.

1:22 Now the Apostle Peter urges his readers to have the loving mind (1:22–2:3). First, he describes the new birth and points out that one of the changes that it brings is **love** for our **brethren** (1:22a). Next, he presses home the obligation to love (1:22b). Again he reverts to the new birth, and especially to the seed from which this new life has grown — the word of God (1:23–25). And once again he emphasizes the obligations that rest on those who have received the word (2:1–3).

In 1:22a, Peter first describes the new birth: **Since you have purified your souls. . . .** We understand, of course, that it is God who purifies our souls when we are saved; in the strict sense, we do not have the power for personal purity. But in this figure of speech those of us who have experienced purification are said to have attained it when we believed.

The means employed in this purification is **obeying the truth**. This is the second time Peter describes saving faith as an act of obedience (see 1:2). In Romans, Paul twice uses the phrase "the obedience of faith." In our thinking we should not try to separate belief and obedience. True faith is obeying faith. This can only be done **through the Spirit**.[9]

One of the goals of the new birth is **sincere love of the brethren**. In a very real sense, we are saved in order to love all our fellow Christians. By this **love**, we know that we have passed out of death into life (1 Jn. 3:14), and by it, the world knows that we are disciples of the Lord Jesus (John 13:35).

So the exhortation follows quite naturally — **love one another fervently with a pure heart**. This is one of the many instances in the NT where a declarative statement becomes the basis for an imperative. The declaration is this: **Since you have purified your souls ... in sincere love of the brethren. . . .** Then the command: **love one another fervently with a pure heart**. The positional forms the basis for the practical. Our love should be warm, wholehearted, with all our strength, earnest, unceasing, and **pure**.

The exhortation to **love one another** is especially timely for a people undergoing persecution because it is well known that "under conditions of hardship, trivial disagreements take on gigantic proportions."

1:23 Again Peter takes his readers back to their new birth, and this time to the seed of that birth **the word of God**. The exhortations in 2:1–3 will be based on this.

The new birth is **not** brought about by **corruptible seed**, that is, it is not produced in the same way as a physical birth. Human life is brought into being by means of seed that must obey physical laws of decay and death. The physical life that is produced has the same quality as the seed from which it sprang; it too is of a temporary character.

The new birth is brought about **through the word of God**. As men hear or read the Bible they are convicted of their sins, convinced that Christ is the sole and sufficient Savior, and converted to God. No one is ever saved apart from the instrumentality in some way of the incorruptible word of God.

Samuel Ridout notes in *The Numerical Bible:*

> . . . the three "incorruptible" things we have in this first chapter — an incorruptible inheritance (v. 4), an incorruptible redemption (vv. 18, 19), and an incorruptible word by which we are born (v. 23). Thus we have a nature which is taintless, fitted for the enjoyment of a taintless inheritance and on the basis of a redemption which never can lose its value. How the stamp of eternal perfection is upon all, and what a fitting companion to these is that "incorruptible" ornament of a meek and quiet spirit (chap. iii. 4).[10]

The word **lives and abides forever**.[11] Though heaven and earth pass away, it will never pass away. It is settled forever in heaven. And the life it produces is eternal also. Those who are born anew through the word take on the everlasting character of the word.

In the human birth, the seed which produces a child contains, in germ form, all the characteristics of the child. What the child will eventually be is determined by the seed. For our present purposes, it is enough to see that as the seed is perishable, so is the human life which results from it.

1:24 The transitory character of human nature is emphasized by a quotation of Isaiah 40:6, 7. Human life is as impermanent **as grass**. Physical beauty is as short-lived as the flowers of the field. **The grass withers**, and the flowers droop and die.

1:25 In contrast, **the word of the LORD endures forever** (Isa. 40:8). Therefore, the new life of the believer is equally incorruptible. This incorruptible word is the message of good news which **was preached** to Peter's readers and which caused them to be born again. It was the source of their eternal life.

2:1 Because they are partakers of the divine life, Christians should put away once for all the following unloving acts:

Malice — the harboring of evil thoughts against another person. **Malice** nourishes antagonism, builds up grudges, and secretly hopes that revenge, harm, or tragedy will overtake another. George Washington Carver was refused admission at a university because he was black. Years later, when someone asked him the name of the university, he replied, "Never mind. That doesn't matter now." He harbored no malice.

Deceit — any form of dishonesty and trickery (and what a variety of forms it takes!). **Deceit** falsifies income tax returns, cheats on exams, lies about age, bribes officials, and pulls shady deals in business.

Hypocrisy — insincerity, pretense, sham. The hypocrite is a play-actor, pretending to be someone he is not. He pretends to be happily married when his home is actually a battlefield. He pretends to be spiritual on Sundays but he is as carnal as a goat on weekdays. He pretends interest in others but his motives are selfish.

Envy — bare-faced jealousy. Vine defines it as the feeling of displeasure produced by observing or hearing of the advantage or prosperity of others. It was **envy** that caused the chief priests to deliver Jesus up to Pilate for death (Matt. 27:18). **Envy** is still a killer. Women can look daggers at others because of their better homes and gardens, smarter clothes, or superior cooking. A man can praise another fellow's new car or speedboat but what he is thinking is, "I'll show him. I'll get something better."

Evil speaking — backbiting, malicious gossip, recrimination. Slander is the attempt to make oneself look cleaner by slinging mud at someone else. It may take very subtle forms such as: "Yes, she is a lovely person but she has this one failing. . . ." and then the knife is deftly thrust into her back. Or it may even have a religious pose: "I mention this only for your prayer fellowship, but did you know that he. . . ." and then the character is assassinated.

All of these sins are violations of the fundamental commandment to love our neighbor as ourselves. No wonder Peter tells us to decisively rid ourselves of them.

2:2 A second obligation flowing from our new birth is to have an insatiable craving for the **pure** spiritual **milk of the word**. The sins mentioned in the previous verse stunt spiritual growth; the good word of God nourishes it.

The phrase **as newborn babes** does not necessarily mean that Peter's readers were new believers; they may have been saved for several years. But young or old in the faith, they should thirst for the word just as infants cry for **milk**. We get some idea of the thirst of the healthy baby by the impatient, aggressive, determined way he sucks and swallows.

By the **pure milk of the word**, a believer grows up spiritually.[12] The ultimate goal toward which all spiritual growth in this life is moving is conformity to the image of our Lord Jesus Christ.

2:3 **If indeed you have tasted that the Lord is gracious.** What a tremendous impetus for thirsting for the pure spiritual milk! The **if** does not express any doubt; we *have* tasted and seen that the Lord is good (Ps. 34:8). His sacrifice for us was an act of unspeakable goodness and kindness (Tit. 3:4). What we have already tasted of His kindness should whet our appetites to feed more and more on Him. The sweet taste of nearness to Him should make us dread the thought of ever wandering away from Him.

D. His Privileges in the New House and Priesthood (2:4–10)

2:4 Now Peter moves from exhortation to a consideration of believers' privileges in the new house (the church) and in the new priesthood.

In the new order, Christ is central, and so we come **to Him**. Because Peter is thinking in terms of a building and of building materials, we are not surprised to find the Lord presented figuratively as **a stone**. First, He is that **living stone** — not an inanimate or dead stone but One who lives in the power of an endless life (Heb. 7:16).

Incredible as it may seem, He is **rejected by men**. In their stupid, selfish, amateurish blueprints for life, insignificant, shortsighted men can find no place for their Creator and Redeemer. Just as there was no room for Him in the inn, so there is no place for Him in the plan of their lives!

But it is not man's opinion that counts. In God's sight the Lord Jesus is **chosen . . . and precious**. He is **chosen** as not only the suitable stone but the indispensable One. And His value to **God** is inestimable; He is **precious** beyond computation.

If we are going to be used in God's building program we must come to Christ. Our only suitability to be building materials is derived from our identification with Him. We are only important as we contribute to His **glory**.

2:5 The **spiritual house** is built up of all believers in Christ, and is therefore the same as the church. The church has this in common with the temple of the OT that it is the dwelling place of God on earth (1 Kgs. 6:11–13; Eph. 2:22). But it is contrasted with the temple, a physical, tangible building made of beautiful but lifeless, perishable materials. The church is a structure built of **living stones**.

Now the figure changes swiftly from **a spiritual house** to the **holy priesthood** that functions in connection with the house. Believers are not only **living** building blocks in the house; they are **holy** priests as well. Under the Mosaic Law, the priesthood was limited to the tribe of Levi and the family of Aaron. And even those who were priests were forbidden to approach the Presence of God. Only the high priest could do that on one day of the year (Yom Kippur, the Day of Atonement) following the precisely ordained procedure outlined for the event by the Lord.

In the new dispensation, all believers are priests with instant access to the Throne Room of the universe, day or night. Their function is **to offer up spiritual sacrifices** (in contrast to the animal, bird, and meal offerings of the Mosaic Law). The spiritual sacrifices of the NT priest are:

1. The presentation of the body as a living sacrifice, holy and acceptable to God. This is an act of spiritual worship (Rom. 12:1).
2. The sacrifice of praise. "That is, the fruit of our lips, giving thanks to His name" (Heb. 13:15).
3. The sacrifice of good works. "Do not forget to do good. . . . " This

sacrifice is pleasing to God (Heb. 13:16).
4. The sacrifice of possessions, or pocketbook. "Do not forget . . . to share." This sacrifice also is pleasing to the Lord (Heb. 13:16).
5. The sacrifice of service. Paul speaks of his ministry to the Gentiles as a priestly offering (Rom. 15:16).

These sacrifices are **acceptable to God through Jesus Christ**. It is only **through Jesus Christ**, our Mediator, that we can approach God in the first place, and it is only He who can make our offerings acceptable to God. All that we do — our worship and our service — is imperfect, flawed by sin. But before it reaches the Father, it passes through the Lord Jesus. He removes all the sin, and when it reaches God the Father it is perfectly acceptable.

The high priest in the OT wore a gold plate on his turban with the words HOLINESS TO THE LORD (Ex. 28:36) inscribed on it. It was for any sin that might be involved in the offerings of the people (Ex. 28:38). So our High Priest wears a miter for us, for any human failure that may be involved in our sacrifices.

The priesthood of all believers is a truth that should be understood, believed, and joyfully practiced by every Christian. At the same time, it must not be abused. Though all believers are priests, not every priest has the right to preach or teach in the assembly. There are certain controls which must be observed.

1. Women are forbidden to teach or to have authority over men; they are to keep silent (1 Tim. 2:12).
2. Men who speak should do so as the oracles of God (1 Pet. 4:11). That means they should have a distinct assurance that they are speaking the words which God would have them speak on that particular occasion.
3. All believers have some gift, just as every member of the human body has some function (Rom. 12:6; 1 Cor. 12:7). But not all gifts involve public speaking. Not all have the special service gifts of evangelist, pastor, or teacher (Eph. 4:11).
4. A young man should rekindle the

gift of God that is within him (2 Tim. 1:6). If that gift involves preaching, teaching, or some other form of public speaking, he should be given opportunity to exercise it in the assembly.

5. The priesthood of believers is seen in operation in 1 Corinthians 14:26: "How is it then brethren? Whenever you come together, each of you has a psalm, has a teaching, has a tongue, has a revelation, has an interpretation. Let all things be done for edification."

In that same chapter are many controls limiting the public exercise of gifts in a congregation to insure order and edification. The universal priesthood of Christians must not be used to justify abuses in the local church.

2:6 Still thinking of the building, Peter reverts to Christ the stone, and in particular, to Christ as the **chief cornerstone**. By quoting from Isaiah 28:16, he shows that Christ's role as **cornerstone** was foretold in Scripture. He points out that God has determined that Christ will have this unique position, that He is an **elect** and **precious** stone, and that He is completely dependable. No one who trusts in Him will ever be disappointed.

The word translated **cornerstone**[13] in this passage may be understood in at least three ways, and each applies with equal validity and force to the Lord Jesus.

1. **A cornerstone** in modern architecture is placed at the base of one corner, where it binds two walls together and symbolizes the foundation on which the entire building rests. Christ is the **cornerstone**, the only genuine foundation (1 Cor. 3:10, 11), the One who has united believing Jews and Gentiles (like two walls in one building) into one new man (Eph. 2:13, 14).

2. Some scholars think that this stone is the *keystone* in an arch. It is the stone which completes the arch and holds the rest of the building together. Our Lord certainly meets this description. He is the topmost stone in the arch, and without Him there would be no strength or cohesion to the building.

3. A third view is that the stone is the *capstone* in a pyramid, occupying the highest place in the structure. It is

the only stone of that shape in the structure. Its shape determines the shape of the entire pyramid. It is the last stone to be put in place. So Christ is the Capstone of the church, the truly unique Stone. The church gets its character from Him. When He returns, the building will be completed.

He is a stone **elect** and **precious**. He is **elect** in the sense that God has selected Him to occupy the place of chief honor; He is **precious** because there is not another like Him.

He **who believes on Him will by no means be put to shame**. The original passage in Isaiah from which this is quoted is rendered "he who believes will not act hastily." Put these two together and you have the wonderful promise that those who have Christ as their **cornerstone** are saved from frustrating humiliation and from frantic haste.

2:7 In the preceding verses the Lord Jesus has been presented as the *living* stone, a *rejected* stone, a *precious* stone and the *cornerstone*. Now, without using the word, Peter seems to picture Him as the touchstone. A touchstone reveals whether certain minerals rubbed against it are genuine or spurious. It shows, for instance, whether a nugget is gold or fool's gold.

When people come in contact with the Savior, they are shown for what they really are. In their attitude toward Him they reveal themselves. To true believers, **He is precious**; unbelievers reject Him. The believer can get some small indication of *how* **precious** He is by trying to imagine what life would be like without Him. Not all earthly pleasures are "worth comparing for a moment with a Christ-filled life." He is "Chief among ten thousand" and "altogether lovely" (Song 5:10, 16).

But what about **those who are disobedient** or disbelieve?[14] The writer of Psalm 118 predicted that this precious stone would be rejected by the builders, but would later become the head of the corner.

There is a persistent legend in connection with the building of Solomon's temple that perfectly illustrates this prophecy. The stones for the temple were prepared in advance in a nearby quarry. As they were needed, they were raised up to the building site. One day the workers in the quarry sent up a stone of unique shape and proportions. The masons saw no place for it in the building so they carelessly pushed it over the hill where, in time, it became overgrown with moss and surrounded with weeds. As the temple neared completion, the masons called for a stone of certain dimensions. The men in the quarry replied, "We sent that stone up to you long ago." After careful search, the discarded stone was found and was set in its proper place in the temple.

The application is obvious. The Lord Jesus presented Himself to the nation of Israel at His First Advent. The people, and especially the rulers, had no room for Him in their scheme of things. They rejected Him and delivered Him to be crucified.

But God raised Him from the dead and seated Him at His own right hand in heaven. When the Rejected One returns to earth the second time, He will come as King of kings and Lord of lords. He will then be publicly manifested as **the chief cornerstone**.

2:8 Now the figure changes from Christ the touchstone and the head of the corner to Christ the **stone of stumbling**. Isaiah predicted that for those who did not believe, He would be a stone that will make men stumble and **a rock** that will make them fall (Isa. 8:14, 15).

This was literally fulfilled in the history of the nation of Israel. When their Messiah came, the Jews were offended by His origins and His simple way of life. They wanted a political demagogue and a military strongman. In spite of the most convincing proofs, they refused to accept Him as the promised Messiah.

But this does not apply only to Israel. For any who will not believe on Jesus, He becomes **a stumbling stone and a rock** that trips them. Men either bow before Him in repentance and faith to salvation or stumble over Him into hell. "What might have been their salvation is made the cause of their deeper condemnation." There can be no neutrality; He must be either Savior or Judge.

They stumble, being disobedient to the word. Why do **they stumble**? Not because of honest intellectual difficulties. Not because there is anything about the Lord Jesus that makes it impossible to believe in Him. **They stumble** because they willfully disobey **the word**. The trouble is in the human will. The reason men are not saved is because they do not want to be saved (John 5:40).

The latter part of verse 8, **to which they also were appointed**, seems to say that they were destined to disobey **the word**. Is this what it means? No, this verse teaches that all those who willfully disobey **the word** are destined to **stumble**. The words **to which they also were appointed** refer back to the entire preceding clause, **they stumble, being disobedient to the word**. God has decreed that all who refuse to bow to the Lord Jesus will **stumble**. If a man insists on going on in unbelief, then he is appointed to stumble. "Unwillingness to obey makes stumbling a foregone conclusion" (JBP).

2:9 Peter now turns again to the privileges of believers. They are **a chosen generation, a royal priesthood, a holy nation**, God's **special people**. God had promised these very privileges to the nation of Israel if they would obey Him:

Now therefore, if you will indeed obey My voice and keep My covenant, then you shall be a special treasure to Me above all people, for all the earth is Mine. And you shall be to Me a kingdom of priests and a holy nation (Ex. 19:5, 6a).

Because of unbelief Israel failed to realize the promise of God, and the nation forfeited its place as God's own people. During the present age, the church occupies the favored place that Israel lost through disobedience.

Believers today are **a chosen generation, chosen** by God before the foundation of the world to belong to Christ (Eph. 1:4). But instead of being an earthly race with common ancestry and distinct physical characteristics, Christians are a heavenly people with a divine parentage and spiritual resemblances.

Believers are also **a royal priesthood**. This is the second **priesthood** mentioned in this chapter. In verse 5, believers are described as holy priests, offering up spiritual sacrifices. Now they are said to be **royal** priests, proclaiming the excellencies of God. As *holy* priests, they enter the sanctuary of heaven by faith to worship. As **royal** priests, they go out into the world to witness. This difference in priesthood is illustrated by the imprisonment of Paul and Silas at Philippi. As holy priests they sang praises to God at midnight; as **royal** priests they preached the gospel to their jailer (Acts 16:25, 31).

Believers are **a holy nation**. It was God's intention that Israel should be a nation distinguished by holiness. But the Israelites stooped to the sinful practices of their Gentile neighbors. So Israel has been set aside temporarily and the church is now God's **holy nation**.

Finally, Christians are a **people** for God's own possession. They belong to Him in a unique way and are of **special** value to Him.

The last part of verse 9 describes the responsibility of those who are God's new race, **priesthood, nation** and **people**. We should **proclaim** the excellencies **of Him who called** us **out of darkness into His marvelous light**. Once we were groping in the darkness of sin and shame. By a stupendous deliverance we have been transferred into the kingdom of His dear Son. The light is as clear and brilliant as the darkness was oppressive. How we should shout **the praises** of the One who did all this for us!

2:10 Peter closes this section by referring to the book of Hosea. Using the prophet's own tragic family life as an object lesson, God had pronounced judgment on the nation of Israel. Because of their unfaithfulness to Him, He said He would no longer have pity on them and that they would no more be His people (Hos. 1:6, 9). But the casting aside of Israel was not final, for the Lord also promised that in a future day, Israel would be restored:

". . . I will have mercy on her who had not obtained mercy; then I will say to those who were not My people, 'You are My people!' And they shall say, 'You are my God!' " (Hos. 2:23).

Some of the people to whom Peter was writing had once been part of the nation of Israel. Now they were members of the church. Through faith in Christ, they had become the people of God, while unbelieving Jews were still cast aside.

So Peter sees in the condition of the converted Jews of his day a partial fulfillment of Hosea 2:23. In Christ, they had become God's new people; in Christ, they had **obtained mercy**. This handful of saved Jews enjoyed the blessings promised to Israel through Hosea long before Israel nationally would enjoy them.

No one should conclude from this passage in Peter that because the church is now God's people, He is through with Israel as a nation. Neither should one assume that the church is now the Israel of God, or that the promises made to Israel now apply to the church. Israel and the church are separate and distinct entities, and an understanding of this distinction is one of the most important keys to interpreting the prophetic word.

Israel was God's chosen earthly people from the time of the call of Abraham to the coming of the Messiah. The nation's rebellion and faithlessness reached its awesome climax when Christ was nailed to the cross. Because of this crowning sin, God temporarily set aside Israel as His chosen people. They are His ancient earthly people today but not His chosen people.

During the present age, God has a new people — the church. This Church Age forms a parenthesis in God's dealings with Israel. When the parenthesis is closed, that is, when the church is caught away to heaven, God will resume His dealings with Israel. Then a believing portion of the nation will become God's people again.

The final fulfillment of Hosea's prophecy is still future. It will take place at the Second Advent. The nation that rejected its Messiah will "look on Me whom they pierced. Yes, they will mourn for Him as one mourns for his only son, and grieve for Him as one grieves for a firstborn" (Zech. 12:10). Then repentant, believing Israel will receive mercy and will become God's people once more.

The point Peter is making in verse 10 is that believing Jews today enjoy an advance fulfillment of Hosea's prophecy, while unbelieving Jews are still alienated from God. The complete and final fulfillment will take place when "the Deliverer will come out of Zion" and "turn away ungodliness from Jacob" (Rom. 11:26).

II. THE BELIEVER'S RELATION-SHIPS (2:11–4:6)

A. As a Pilgrim in Relation to the World (2:11, 12)

2:11 Most of the rest of 1 Peter concerns the conduct that should characterize the Christian in the various relationships of life. Peter reminds believers that they are **sojourners and pilgrims** in the world and that this fact should leave its stamp on all their behavior. They are **sojourners** in the sense that they are living in a foreign country where they do not have the rights of citizens. They are **pilgrims** in the sense that they are obliged to live for a while in a place which is not their permanent home.

The hymns of yesterday remind us of our pilgrimage. For instance:

Called from above, and heavenly men
  by birth
(Who once were but the citizens of earth),
As pilgrims here, we seek a heav'nly
  home,
Our portion in the ages yet to come.

We are but strangers here, we do not
  crave
A home on earth, which gave Thee but
  a grave:
Thy cross has severed ties which bound
  us here,
Thyself our treasure in a brighter sphere.
          – James G. Deck

But these sentiments have largely dropped from our hymnology. When the church has settled down in the world, it seems a bit hypocritical to be singing beyond our experience.

When we read the exhortation to **abstain from fleshly lusts which war against the soul**, we think immediately of sexual sins. But the application is wider than that; it refers to any strong desire that is inconsistent with the will of God. It would include over-indulgence in food or drink, catering to the body with excessive sleep, the determination to amass material possessions, or the hankering for worldly pleasures. All these things wage incessant warfare against our spiritual well-being. They hinder communion with God. They deter spiritual growth.

2:12 Not only must we exercise discipline in the area of fleshly indulgence, but we must also maintain our **conduct honorable**[15] **among the Gentiles**, that is, the pagan world. In our day we must not pattern our lives after the world. We should be marching to the beat of a different drummer.

Almost inevitably we will be criticized. At the time Peter wrote this Letter, writes Erdman:

. . . the Christians were being slandered as irreligious because of not worshiping the heathen gods, as morons and ascetics because of refraining from popular vices, as disloyal to the government because of claiming allegiance to a heavenly King.[16]

Such criticism cannot be avoided. But under no circumstances should believers give the world a *valid* reason for such reproach. All slanders should be refuted by an unbroken record of good deeds. Then the accusers will be compelled to **glorify God in the day of visitation**.

A **day of visitation** is any time the Lord draws near, either in grace or in judgment. The expression is used in Luke 19:41–44. Jesus wept over Jerusalem because it did not know the time of its visitation, that is, Jerusalem did not realize that the Messiah had come in love and mercy. Here it may mean: (1) The day when God's grace will visit the critics and they are saved, or (2) the day of judgment when the unsaved will stand before God.

Saul of Tarsus illustrates the first interpretation. He had shared in accusing Stephen, but Stephen's good deeds triumphed over all opposition. When God visited Saul in mercy on the road to Damascus, the repentant Pharisee glorified God and went forth, like Stephen, to influence others by the radiance of a Christ-filled life. Jowett says:

The beautiful life is to raise men's thoughts in homage to the glorious God. When they behold the Divine realized in the human, they too are to be wooed into heavenly fellowship. They are to be wooed, not by the eloquence of our speech, but by the radiance of our behavior. By the imposing grace of noble living we are to "put to silence the ignorance of foolish men,'' and that silence will be for them the first stage in a life of aspiring consecration.[17]

In the second interpretation, the thought is that unsaved people will be compelled to **glorify God in the day of** judgment. They will have no excuse, for they not only heard the gospel, they saw it in the lives of their Christian relatives, friends, and neighbors. God will then be vindicated through the blameless conduct of His children.

B. As a Citizen in Relation to Government (2:13–17)

2:13 The next five verses deal with the Christian's relation toward government. The key word here is **submit**. In fact, the injunction to submit is found four times in the Epistle.

Citizens are to **submit** to the government (2:13).

Slaves are to *submit* to their masters (2:18).

Wives are to *submit* to their husbands (3:1).

Younger believers are to *submit* to the elders (5:5).

Lyall says:

The ultimate Christian answer to persecution, detractors and critics is that of a blameless life, conduct beyond reproach and good citizenship. In particular . . . submission is a supremely Christlike virtue.[18]

Human governments are instituted by God (Rom. 13:1). Rulers are God's servants (Rom. 13:4). Even if the rulers are not believers, they are still God's men officially. Even if they are dictators and tyrants, their rule is better than no rule at all. The complete absence of rule is anarchy, and no society can continue under anarchy. So any government is better than no government at all. Order is better than chaos. Believers should **submit to every** human institution **for the Lord's sake**. In doing so, they are fulfilling His will and doing the thing that pleases Him. These instructions apply to the emperor or to whoever is the supreme ruler. Even if Nero happens to be occupying the imperial palace, the general exhortation is to be subject to him.

2:14 The injunction of obedience applies to subordinate officials such as **governors**. They are authorized by God to punish offenders and to **praise** those who keep the law. Actually, government officials have little time or inclination to do the latter, but that does not alter the responsibility of the Christian to obey! The historian Arnold Toynbee observed that ''as long as original sin remains an element in human nature, Caesar will always have plenty to do.''

Of course, there are exceptions. There is a time when obedience is not required. If a human government orders a believer to act contrary to the revealed will of God, then the believer must disobey the government. In that case he has a higher responsibility; he should obey God rather than men (Acts 5:29). If punishment is meted out for his disobedience, he should endure it courageously. Under no circumstances should he rebel or seek to overthrow the government.

Technically, those who smuggle Bibles into closed countries are breaking the law. But they are obeying a law that has precedence over any human law — the command to go into all the world with the gospel. So they cannot be condemned on scriptural grounds.

Suppose the government orders a Christian into the armed forces. Is he obligated to obey and to bear arms? If he feels that this is in direct violation of God's word, he should first exhaust any options that are open to him in the status of a non-combatant or a conscientious objector. If these fail, then he would have to refuse induction and bear the consequences.

Many Christians do not have conscientious scruples about serving in the military forces. It is a matter in which each one should be fully convinced in his own mind, and allow liberty for others to disagree.

The questions as to whether a Christian should vote or engage in politics are of a different order. The government does not demand these things, so it is not a question of obedience or disobedience. Each one must act in the light of the principles of conduct and citizenship found in the Bible. Here too we must allow liberty for differing viewpoints and not insist that others see eye to eye with us.

2:15 God's **will** is that His people should live so honorably and unblamably that the unconverted will have no legitimate basis for accusation. By lives of exemplary conduct, Christians can and should expose the **ignorance** of the charges made against Christianity by **foolish men**.

Christians and the Christian faith are ceaselessly bombarded by **the ignorance of foolish men**. It may be in the university classroom; it may be in the science laboratory; it may be in the pulpit. Peter says that one of the best answers to such blasting is a holy life.

2:16 Act **as free** men. We are not in bondage or slavery to civil authorities. We need not live in servility or terror. After all, we are the Lord's free men. But that does not mean we are free to sin. **Liberty** does not mean license. Freedom does not include lawlessness. So we must never use our freedom as a pretext for evil. Sinful disobedience should never be justified by some pseudo-spiritual excuse. The cause of Christ is never advanced by evil masquerading in religious clothes.

If we live as **bondservants of God**, our relationship with governmental authorities will fall into proper place. We are to act in the light of His presence, obey Him in all things, do all for His glory. The best citizen is a believer who lives as a slave of the Lord. Unfortunately, most governments don't realize how much they owe to Christians who believe and obey the Bible.

Ponder the expression **bondservants of God**. "Heaven takes our most dreaded terms," F. B. Meyer writes, "and makes them sparkle in its own light, till what seemed the synonym of terror becomes the target of our noblest aims."[19]

2:17 No relationship of life can be left outside the sphere of Christian responsibility. So Peter here runs the gamut with four crisp commands.

Honor all people. We cannot always **honor** their words or their behavior, but we can remember that every single life is of more value than all the world. We can recognize that every person was made in the image and likeness of God. We must never forget that the Lord Jesus bled and died for even the most unworthy.

Love the brotherhood. We are to **love** all men, but we are especially obligated to love the members of our spiritual family. This is a love like God's love for us. It is utterly undeserved, it goes out to the loveless, it looks for no reward, and it is stronger than death.

Fear God. We **fear** Him when we reverence Him as the supreme Lord. Glorifying Him then becomes our number one priority. We **fear** doing anything that would displease Him and we **fear** misrepresenting Him before men.

Honor the king. Peter returns to the subject of human rulers for a final reminder. We are to respect our rulers as officials appointed by God for the maintenance of an ordered society. This means we must pay "taxes to whom taxes are due, customs to whom customs, fear to whom fear" (Rom. 13:7). Generally speaking, the Christian can live under any form of government. The only time he should disobey is when he is ordered to compromise his loyalty or obedience to the Lord Jesus Christ.

C. As a Servant in Relation to His Master (2:18–25)

2:18 It is significant that the NT gives more instructions to **servants** than to kings. Many of the early believers were **servants**, and the Scripture shows that most Christians came from the middle or lower strata of society (Matt. 11:5; Mark 12:37; 1 Cor. 1:26–29).

This passage is addressed to domestic **servants**, but the principles apply to employees of any kind. The basic appeal is to submit to the master with all respect. It is a built-in fact of life that in any society or organization, there must be authority on the one hand, and obedience to that authority on the other. It is for any servant's own good to submit to his master, otherwise he would not have employment. But it is much more important for a *Christian* to submit. More than his paycheck is involved; his testimony depends on it.

Obedience should not vary according to the temperament of the employer. Anyone can submit to an employer who is **good and gentle**. Believers are called to go beyond that and be respectful and obedient to the **harsh**, overbearing boss. This stands out as distinctly Christian behavior.

2:19 When we suffer unjustly, we win God's approval. He is pleased when He finds us so conscious of our relation to Him that we endure undeserved pain without vindicating self or fighting back. When we meekly take unjust treatment, we display Christ; this supernatural life gains God's "Well done."

2:20 There is no virtue in patient suffering for our own misdeeds. Certainly there is no glory for God in it. Such suffering will never mark us out as Christians, or make others want to become Christians. But suffering **patiently** for well-doing is the thing that counts. It is so unnatural, so other-worldly that it shocks people into conviction of sin and, hopefully, into salvation.

2:21 The thought of believers' suffering for righteousness' sake leads inevitably to this sublime passage on our great **example**, the Lord Jesus. No one was ever treated as unjustly as He, or bore it as patiently.

We have been called to act as He acted, suffering for the wrongs of others. The word used here for **example** carries the idea of a copybook that contains flawless penmanship. The pupil seeks to reproduce the original as closely as possible. When he copies the model carefully, his writing is quite good. But the further he moves away from it, the more the copy worsens. Our safety is in staying close to the Original.

2:22 Our Lord did not suffer for His own sins because He had none. "He knew no sin" (2 Cor. 5:21); He **committed no sin** (this verse); "in Him there is no sin" (1 Jn. 3:5).

His speech was never tainted by **deceit**. He never lied or even shaded the truth. Think about that! A Person once lived on this planet who was absolutely honest, absolutely free from trickery or **deceit**.

2:23 He was patient under provocation. **When He was reviled**, He **did not** pay back in kind. When blamed He did not answer back. When accused He did not defend Himself. He was wondrously free from the lust of self-vindication.

An unknown author has written:

It is a mark of deepest and truest humility to see ourselves condemned without cause, and to be silent under it. To be silent under insult and wrong is a very noble imitation of our Lord. When we remember in how many ways He suffered, who in no way deserved it, where are our senses when we feel called to defend and excuse ourselves?

When He suffered, He did not threaten. "No ungentle, threatening word escaped His silent tongue." Perhaps His assailants mistook His silence for weakness. If they had tried it they would have found it was not weakness but supernatural strength!

What was His hidden resource in bearing up under such unprovoked abuse? He trusted God **who judges righteously**. And we are called to do the same:

> Beloved, do not avenge yourselves, but rather give place to wrath; for it is written, "Vengeance is Mine, I will repay," says the Lord. Therefore, "if your enemy hungers, feed him; if he thirsts, give him a drink, for in so doing you will heap coals of fire on his head." Do not be overcome by evil, but overcome evil with good (Rom. 12:19–21).

2:24 The Savior's sufferings were not only exemplary, but expiatory as well. We cannot imitate His sufferings in this respect, and Peter does not suggest that we should. Rather the argument seems to be as follows: The Savior's agony was not brought on by His own sins, for He had none. It was for **our sins** He was nailed to the cross. Because He has suffered for **our sins** once for all, we should never allow ourselves to get into the position where we have to suffer for them too. The fact that He died *for* them should cause us to die *to* them. And yet, it is not simply a matter of negative goodness; we should not only die to sin but **live to righteousness**.

By whose stripes you were healed. The word **stripes** is actually singular in the original, perhaps suggesting that His body was one massive welt. What should be our attitude toward sin when our healing cost the Savior so much? Theodoret comments: "A new and strange method of healing. The doctor suffered the cost, and the sick received the healing."

2:25 Before conversion, we **were like sheep going astray** — lost, torn, bruised, bleeding. Peter's mention of straying **sheep** is the last of six references to Isaiah 53 in this passage:

v. 21 *Christ . . . suffered for us* (cf. Isa. 53:4, 5).

v. 22 *He committed no sin, nor was deceit found in His mouth* (cf. Isa. 53:9).

v. 23 *When He was reviled, He did not revile in return* (cf. Isa. 53:7).

v. 24 *Who Himself bore our sins in His own body on the tree* (cf. Isa. 53:4, 11).

v. 24 *By whose stripes you were healed* (cf. Isa. 53:5).

v. 25 *For you were like sheep going astray* (cf. Isa. 53:6).

When we are saved, we return to the Shepherd — the good Shepherd who laid down His life for the sheep (John 10:11); the great Shepherd who "tends with sweet, unwearied care the flock for which He bled," and the Chief Shepherd who will soon appear to lead His sheep into the green pastures above — from which they will never stray.

Conversion is returning **to the** Guardian[20] **of our souls**. We were His by creation, but became lost through sin. Now we return to His keeping care, and are safe and secure forever.

D. As a Wife in Relation to Her Husband (3:1–6)

3:1 Peter has stressed the obligation of Christians to submit to human government and to earthly masters. He now takes up the submission of **wives** to their **husbands**.

Every wife is to **be submissive to** her husband, whether he is a believer or not. God has given to the man the place of headship, and it is His will that the woman should acknowledge the authority of the man. The relationship between husband and wife is a picture of that between Christ and the church. The woman should obey her husband just as the church should obey Christ.

This is considered passé in our society. Women are rising to places of authority over man, and our society is becoming increasingly matriarchal. In many churches, women seem to be more active and gifted than the men. But God's word stands. The headship of man is the divine order. No matter how reasonable the arguments may sound, nothing but trouble and chaos can ultimately result when woman usurps authority over the man.

Even when a woman's husband is an unbeliever, she should still respect him as her head. This will be a testimony to him of her faith in Christ. Her **conduct** as an obedient, loving, devoted wife may be used to win him to the Savior.

And she may win him **without a word**. This means that the wife need not be preaching to her husband constantly. Possibly great harm has been done by wives who nagged their husbands concerning the gospel, cramming it down their throats. The emphasis here is on the wife's winning her husband by living Christ daily before him.

But suppose a husband interferes with his wife in her Christian life. What should she do then? If he requires her to disobey a plain command of Scripture, then she must disobey her husband and be true to the Lord. If, however, the matter involves a Christian privilege rather than a clear duty, she should be subject to her husband and forego the privilege.

When Peter speaks about a Christian wife having a pagan husband, he does not thereby condone a believer's marrying an unbeliever. This is never God's will. The apostle is dealing primarily with cases where the wife was saved after marriage. Her obligation is to **be submissive** even to an unbelieving husband.

3:2 The unsaved husband may be impressed by the reverent and **chaste conduct** of his wife. The Spirit of God may use this to convict him of his own sinfulness, and he may come to faith in Christ.

George Müller told of a wealthy German whose wife was a devout believer. This man was a heavy drinker, spending late nights in the tavern. She would send the servants to bed, stay up till he returned, receive him kindly, and never scold him or complain. At times she would even have to undress him and put him to bed.

One night in the tavern he said to his cronies, "I bet if we go to my house, my wife will be sitting up, waiting for me.

She'll come to the door, give us a royal welcome, and even make supper for us, if I ask her."

They were skeptical at first, but decided to go along and see. Sure enough, she came to the door, received them courteously, and willingly agreed to make supper for them without the slightest trace of resentment. After serving them, she went off to her room. As soon as she had left, one of the men began to condemn the husband. "What kind of a man are you to treat such a good woman so miserably?" The accuser got up without finishing his supper and left the house. Another did the same and another till they had all departed without eating the meal.

Within a half hour, the husband became deeply convicted of his wickedness, and especially of his heartless treatment of his wife. He went to his wife's room, asked her to pray for him, repented of his sins, and surrendered to Christ. From that time on, he became a devoted disciple of the Lord Jesus. Won without a word!

George Müller advised:

> Don't be discouraged if you have to suffer from unconverted relatives. Perhaps very shortly the Lord may give you the desire of your heart, and answer your prayer for them. But in the meantime, seek to commend the truth, not by reproaching them on account of their behavior toward *you*, but by manifesting toward *them* the meekness, gentleness and kindness of the Lord Jesus Christ.[21]

3:3 The subject here seems to change to women's apparel, but actually the apostle is dealing primarily with the best ways for a wife to please and serve her husband. It is not her outward appearance that will influence him as much as her inner life of holiness and submission.

Various types of outward **adornment** are to be avoided:

1. **Arranging the hair**. Some think that this excludes even modest braids. It is more likely that Peter is speaking against the excess of mountainous coiffures with terraces of braids, which were popular in ancient Rome.
2. **Wearing gold**. Some interpret this as an absolute prohibition against any gold jewelry. Others see it as forbidding showy and extravagant displays.
3. **Putting on fine apparel**. Obviously, it is not the wearing of clothing that is forbidden, but the wearing of ostentatious dress. Read Isaiah 3:16–25 to see what God thinks about all forms of extravagant adornment.

CHRISTIAN DRESS

In the matter of clothing and jewelry, there are guidelines that apply to all believers, men as well as women. A first principle is expense. How much do we spend on clothes? Is it all necessary? Could the money be spent in better ways?

First Timothy 2:9 forbids expensive clothes: "not with . . . costly clothing." It is not a matter of whether or not we can afford them. It is sin for a Christian to spend money on expensive clothes, because God's word forbids it. Compassion forbids it too. The desperate plight of our neighbors in other lands, their enormous spiritual and physical needs, point up the callousness of spending money unnecessarily on clothing.

This applies not only to the quality of the clothes we buy but to the quantity as well. The closets of some Christians look like branch clothing stores. Often as they travel on vacation, a rod stretched over the back seat of the car holds an array of dresses, shirts, and suits that rivals the samples of a traveling clothing salesman.

Why do we do it? Is it not a matter of pride? We love to be complimented on our good taste, our fine appearance. The expense involved in buying clothes is only one principle that should guide us in its choice.

Another is modesty. Paul says "with propriety and moderation." One meaning of the word *propriety* is "decent." One of the functions of clothing is to hide man's nakedness. At least, that's the way it was in the beginning. But now clothing seems to be designed to reveal increasingly large areas of the anatomy. Man is thus glorying in his shame. It is not surprising to find ungodly men doing this, but it is rather shocking when Christians imitate them.

But modest can also mean attractive. This suggests that the Christian should dress neatly. There is no virtue in shabbiness, in untidiness. Oswald Chambers said that slovenliness is an insult to the Holy Spirit. The believer's clothes should be clean, pressed, in good repair, and well-fitting.

In general, the Christian must avoid fashions that attract attention to himself. That is not his function in life. He is not on earth as an ornament, but as a fruit-bearing branch of the Vine. We can attract attention to ourselves in many ways. Wearing clothes that are old-fashioned will do it. The Christian should also avoid wearing clothes that are uncommonly plain, or loud, or odd.

Finally, the Christian — and this may be a special problem for the young believer — should avoid clothes that are suggestive or provocative. We have already referred to fashions that are "revealing." But clothes can cover the whole body and still arouse unholy lust in others. Modern fashions are not designed to encourage spirituality. On the contrary, they reflect the obsession with sex in our age. The believer should never wear clothes that incite passions or make it hard for others to live a Christian life.

The great problem, of course, is the enormous social pressure to conform. This always has been true and always will be. Christians need plenty of spine to resist the extremes in fashion, to swim against the tide of public opinion, and to dress in a manner that befits the gospel.

If we make Christ the Lord of our wardrobe, all will be well. ‡

3:4 The clothing which makes a believer genuinely attractive is the beauty of **the hidden person**. Fashionable coiffures, costly jewelry, and fine clothing are perishable. In presenting this vivid contrast, Peter challenges us to make a choice. F. B. Meyer notes: "Plenty are there whose outward body is richly decked, but whose inner being is clothed in rags; whilst others, whose garments are worn and threadbare, are all glorious within."[22]

Men think jewels are precious; **God** considers **precious** the jewel of **a gentle and quiet spirit**.

3:5 Godly women of the OT **adorned themselves** by cultivating the moral and spiritual beauty of the inner life. One aspect of this beauty was a dutiful submission **to their own husbands**. These **holy women trusted in God**. They lived God-centered lives. Desiring to please Him in all things, they recognized His order in the home and were **submissive to their own husbands**.

3:6 Sarah is cited as an example. She **obeyed Abraham, calling him lord**. This takes us back to Genesis 18:12 where we read that Sarah said this "within herself." She did not go around and make a loud profession of submission to Abraham by publicly calling him *lord*. Rather, in her inward life, she recognized him as her head, and this recognition was displayed by her actions.

Those women who follow Sarah's example are her children. Jewish women are descendants of Sarah by natural birth. But to be her **daughters** in the best sense, they must imitate her personal character. Children should carry the family likeness.

They should **do good** and let nothing terrify them. This means that a Christian wife should fill her God-appointed role as an obedient helpmate, and not be terrified even if she must suffer the unreasonable conduct of an unbelieving husband, except, of course, when it becomes violent or life-threatening.

E. As a Husband in Relation to His Wife (3:7)

Now the apostle turns to **husbands** and shows the corresponding duties they must fulfill. They should live considerately with their wives, showing love, courtesy, and **understanding**. They should bestow the tender regard on their wives that is appropriate for members of the **weaker** sex.

In this day of the women's liberation movement, the Bible might seem out of step with the times in speaking of women as the **weaker vessels**. But it is a simple fact of life that the *average* woman is **weaker** than the man physically. Also, generally speaking, she does not have the same power to control her emotions and is more frequently guided by emotional reactions than by rational, logical thought. The handling of deep theological problems is not characteristically her forte. And, in general, she is more dependent than the man.

But the fact that a woman is **weaker** in some ways does not mean that she is inferior to man; the Bible never suggests this. Neither does it mean that she might not actually be stronger, or more competent in some areas. As a matter of fact, women are generally more devoted to Christ than men. And they usually are better able to bear prolonged pain and adversity.

A man's attitude toward his wife should recognize the fact that she is a fellow heir **of the grace of life**. This refers to a marriage in which both are believers. Though weaker than the man in some ways, the woman enjoys equal standing before God and shares equally the gift of everlasting life. Also she is more than her husband's equal in bringing new physical life into the world.

When there is discord, prayers are hindered. Bigg says: "The sighs of the injured wife come between the husband's prayers and God's hearing."[23] Also it is very difficult for a couple to pray together when something is disrupting their fellowship. For the peace and welfare of the home it is important for the husband and wife to observe a few basic rules:

1. Maintain absolute honesty in order to have a basis of mutual confidence.

2. Keep lines of communication open. There must be a constant readiness to talk things out. When steam is allowed to build up in the boiler, an explosion is inevitable. Talking things out includes the willingness for each to say, "I am sorry" and to forgive — perhaps indefinitely.

3. Overlook minor faults and idiosyncrasies. Love covers a multitude of sins. Don't demand perfection in others when you are unable to produce it in yourself.

4. Strive for unity in finances. Avoid overspending, installment buying, and the lust to keep up with the Joneses.

5. Remember that love is a commandment, not an uncontrollable emotion. Love means all that is included in 1 Corinthians 13. Love is courteous, for instance; it will keep you from criticizing or contradicting your partner in front of others. Love will keep you from quarreling in front of your children, which could undermine their security. In these and a hundred other ways, love creates a happy atmosphere in the home and rules out strife and separations.

F. As a Brother in Relation to the Fellowship (3:8)

That this verse deals primarily with the Christian and his relation to the fellowship seems evident from the exhortations to unity and brotherly love. The other three exhortations could have a wider application.

The word **Finally** does not mean that Peter is about to close his Epistle. He has been speaking to various classes of individuals such as servants, wives, and husbands. Now, as a finale, he has a word for **all of you**.

Let all of you be of one mind. It is not expected that Christians will see eye-to-eye on everything. That would be uniformity, not unity. The best formula is contained in the well-known expression: In fundamentals, unity; in nonessentials, liberty; in everything, love. We are to have **compassion for one another**. Literally, this means "to suffer with," and the admonition is especially appropriate when given to those undergoing persecution. The advice is for all times because no age is exempt from suffering.

Love as brothers. An unknown author writes:

Providence does not ask us whom we would like to be our brethren — that is settled for us; but we are bidden to love them, irrespective of our natural predilections and tastes. You say, "That is impossible!" But remember that true love does not necessarily originate in the emotions, but in the will; it consists not in feeling but in doing; not in sentiment, but in action; not in soft words, but in noble and unselfish deeds.

Tenderhearted means having a heart sensitive to the needs and feelings of others. It refuses to turn cold, callous, or cynical in spite of abuse.

Courteous[24] — It seems so proper

that courtesy should be taught as one of the Christian virtues. Essentially it means humbly thinking of others, putting others first, and saying and doing the gracious thing. Courtesy serves others before self, jumps at opportunities to assist, and expresses prompt appreciation for kindnesses received. It is never coarse, vulgar, or rude.

G. As a Sufferer in Relation to Persecutors (3:9–4:6)

3:9 This whole Epistle is written against a backdrop of persecution and suffering. From this verse to 4:6 the subject is the Christian and his relation to persecutors. Repeatedly, believers are urged to suffer for righteousness' sake without retaliating. We are not to repay **evil for evil or reviling for reviling**. Instead we are to bless those who mistreat us, and to repay insult with kindness. As Christians, we are not called to harm others but to do them good, not to curse but to bless. Then God rewards this type of behavior with **a blessing**.

3:10 In verses 10–12, Peter quotes Psalm 34:12–16a to confirm that God's blessing rests on the one who refrains from evil deeds and evil speech, and practices righteousness.

The force of the first verse is this: The one who wishes to enjoy **life** to the hilt and experience **good days** should **refrain** from speaking **evil** or **deceit**. He should not repay insult and lies in kind.

To **love life** is condemned in John 12:25, but there it means to live for self and disregard the true purpose of life. Here it means to live in the way God intended.

3:11 Not only evil speech, but **evil** deeds are forbidden. To retaliate only intensifies the conflict. It is stooping to use the world's weapons. The believer should repay **evil** with **good**, and promote **peace** by meekly enduring abuse. Fire cannot be fought with fire.

The only way to overcome evil is to let it run its course, so that it does not find the resistance it is looking for. Resistance merely creates further evil and adds fuel to the flames. But when evil meets no opposition and encounters no obstacle but only patient endurance, its sting is drawn, and at last it meets an opponent which is more than its match. Of course, this can only happen when the last ounce of resistance is abandoned, and the renunciation of revenge is complete. Then evil cannot find its mark, it can breed no further evil, and is left barren (Selected).

3:12 The LORD looks with approval on those who act righteously. He is attentive **to their prayers**. Of course, the Lord hears the prayers of all His people. But He undertakes in a special sense the cause of those who suffer for Christ's sake without returning evil for evil.

The face of the LORD is against those who do evil. This primarily refers to the persecutors of His people. But it may also include the believer who fights back against his foes with physical violence and intemperate language. **Evil** is evil, and God opposes it wherever He finds it — whether in the saved or in the lost.

In quoting Psalm 34:16, Peter left out the closing words: " . . . to cut off the remembrance of them from the earth." This omission was not an oversight. We are living in the dispensation of the grace of God; it is the acceptable year of the Lord. The day of vengeance of our God has not come as yet. When the Lord Jesus returns as King of kings and Lord of lords, He will punish evildoers and cut off the remembrance of them from the earth.

3:13 Peter resumes his argument with a question: **"And who is he who will harm you if you become followers of what is good?"** The answer implied is "No one." And yet the history of the martyrs seems to prove that enemies of the gospel do harm faithful disciples.

There are at least two possible explanations of this paradox:

1. Generally speaking, those who follow a path of righteousness are not harmed. A policy of nonresistance disarms the opposition. There may be exceptions, but as a rule, the one who is eager for the right is protected from harm by his very goodness.

2. The worst that the foe can do to a Christian does not give eternal harm. The enemy can injure his body but he cannot damage his soul.

During World War II a Christian boy of twelve refused to join a certain movement in Europe. "Don't you know that we have power to kill you?" they said. "Don't you know," he replied quietly, "that I have power to die for Christ!" He had the conviction that no one was able to harm him.

3:14 But suppose a Christian **should suffer** persecution because of his loyalty to the Savior. What then? Three results follow:

1. God overrules the suffering for His own glory.
2. He uses the suffering to bring blessing to others.
3. He blesses the one who suffers for His name.

Don't be afraid of men, or terrified by **their threats**. How well the martyrs lived out this policy! When Polycarp was promised release if he would blaspheme Christ, he said, "Eighty six years I have served Christ and He has never done me wrong. How can I blaspheme my King and my Savior?" When the proconsul threatened to expose him to the wild beasts, he replied, "It is well for me to be speedily released from this life of misery." Finally the ruler threatened to burn him alive. Polycarp said, "I fear not the fire that burns for a moment: You do not know that which burns forever and ever."

3:15 In the last part of verse 14 and in this verse, Peter quotes from Isaiah 8:12b, 13, which says: "Nor be afraid of their threats, nor be troubled. The LORD of hosts, Him you shall hallow; Let Him be your fear, and let Him be your dread." Someone has said, "We fear God so little because we fear man so much."

The Isaiah passage speaks of *The LORD of hosts* as the One to be reverenced. Quoting it, Peter by inspiration of the Holy Spirit, says, **sanctify the Lord God**[25] **in your hearts**.

To reverence the Lord means to make Him the Sovereign of our lives. All we do and say should be in His will, for His pleasure, and for His glory. The lordship of Christ should dominate every area of our lives — our possessions, our occupation, our library, our marriage, our spare time — nothing can be excluded.

Always be ready to give a defense to everyone who asks you a reason for the hope that is in you, with meekness and fear. This applies primarily to times when Christians are being persecuted because of their faith. The consciousness of the presence of the Lord Christ should impart a holy boldness and inspire the believer to witness a good confession.

The verse is also applicable to everyday life. People often ask us questions which quite naturally open the door to speak to them about the Lord. We should **be ready** to tell them what great things the Lord has done for us. This witnessing should be done in either case with gentleness and reverence. There should be no trace of harshness, bitterness or flippancy when we speak of our Savior and Lord.

3:16 The believer must have **a good conscience**. If he knows he is innocent of any crime, he can go through persecution with the boldness of a lion. If he has a bad conscience, he will be plagued with feelings of guilt and will not be able to stand against the foe. Even if a believer's life is blameless, the enemies of the gospel will still find fault with him and bring false charges against him. But when the case comes to trial, and the charges are found to be empty, the accusers will **be ashamed**.

3:17 If a Christian must **suffer**, which might sometimes be God's will for him, it should be **for doing good**. But he should not bring suffering on himself for his own misdeeds; there is no virtue in that.

3:18 The rest of chapter 3 presents **Christ** as the classic example of One who **suffered** for righteousness' sake, and reminds us that for Him, suffering was the pathway to glory.

Notice the six features of His sufferings: (1) They were expiatory, that is, they freed believing sinners from the punishment of their **sins**. (2) They were eternally effectual. He died once for all and settled the **sin** question. The work of redemption was completed. (3) They were substitutionary. **The just** died **for the unjust**. "The Lord has laid on Him the iniquity of us all" (Isa. 53:6b). (4) They were reconciling. Through His death we have been brought **to God**. The sin which caused alienation has been removed. (5) They were violent. His **death** was by execution. (6) Finally, they were climaxed by resurrection. He was raised from the dead on the third day. The expression **made alive by the Spirit** means that His resurrection was through the power of the Holy Spirit.

3:19 Verses 19, 20 constitute one of the most puzzling and intriguing texts in the NT. It has been made the pretext for such unbiblical doctrines as purgatory on the one hand and universal salvation on the other. However, among evangelical Christians, there are two commonly accepted interpretations.

According to the first, Christ went to Hades in spirit between His death and resurrection, and proclaimed the triumph of His mighty work on the cross. There is disagreement among proponents of this view as to whether **the spirits in prison** were believers, unbelievers, or both. But there is fairly general agreement that the Lord Jesus did not preach the gospel to them. That would involve the doctrine of a second chance which is nowhere taught in the Bible. Those who hold this view often link this passage with Ephesians 4:9 where the Lord is described as descending "into the lower parts of the earth." They cite this as added proof that He went to Hades in the disembodied state and heralded His victory at Calvary. They also cite the words of the Apostles' Creed — "descended into hell."

The second interpretation is that Peter is describing what happened in the days of Noah. It was the *spirit* of Christ who preached *through* Noah to the unbelieving generation before the flood. They were not disembodied spirits *at that time*, but living men and women who rejected the warnings of Noah and were destroyed by the flood. So *now* they are **spirits in** the **prison** of Hades.

This second view best fits the context and has the least difficulties connected with it. Let us examine the passage phrase by phrase.

By whom also He went and preached to the spirits in prison. The relative pronoun **whom** obviously refers back to *Spirit* at the end of verse 18. We understand this to mean the Holy Spirit. In 1:11 of this Letter the "Spirit of Christ," that is, the Holy Spirit, is described as speaking through the prophets of the OT. And in Genesis 6:3, God speaks of His Spirit, that is, the Holy Spirit, as nearing the limit of endurance with the antediluvians.

He went and preached. As already mentioned, it was Christ who preached, but he preached through Noah. In 2 Peter 2:5, Noah is described as a "preacher of righteousness." It is the same root word used here of Christ's preaching.

To the spirits *now* **in prison**. These were the people to whom Noah preached — living men and women who heard the warning of an impending flood and the promise of salvation in the ark. They rejected the message and were drowned in the deluge. They are now disembodied **spirits in prison**, awaiting the final judgment.

So the verse may be amplified as follows: **"by whom** (the Holy Spirit) **He** (Christ) **went and preached** (through Noah) **to the spirits** *now* **in prison** (Hades)."

But what right do we have to assume that **the spirits in prison** were the living men in Noah's day? The answer is found in the following verse.

3:20 Here the spirits in prison are unmistakably identified. Who were they? Those **who formerly were disobedient**. When **were** they **disobedient**? When **once the Divine longsuffering waited in the days of Noah, while the ark was being prepared**. What was the final outcome? Only **a few, that is, eight souls, were saved through water**.

It is well to pause here and remind ourselves of the general flow of thought in this Letter which was written against a general background of persecution. The Christians to whom Peter wrote were suffering because of their life and testimony. Perhaps they wondered why, if the Christian faith was right, they should be suffering rather than reigning. If Christianity was the true faith, why were there so few Christians?

To answer the first question, Peter points to the Lord Jesus. Christ suffered for righteousness' sake, even to the extent of being put to death. But God raised Him from the dead and glorified Him in heaven (see v. 22). The pathway to glory led through the valley of suffering.

Next Peter refers to **Noah**. For 120 years this faithful preacher warned that God was going to destroy the world with water. His thanks was scorn and rejection. But God vindicated him by saving him and his family through the flood.

Then there is the problem, "If we are right, why are there so few of us?" Peter answers: "There was a time when *only eight people in the world* were right and all the rest were wrong!" Characteristically in the world's history the majority has not been right. True believers are usually a small remnant, so one's faith should not falter because of the small number of the saved. There were only **eight** believers in Noah's day; there are millions today.

At the end of verse 20, we read that **a few, that is, eight souls, were saved through water**. It is not that they were saved *by* water; they were saved **through** the **water**. Water was not the savior, but the judgment **through** which God brought them safely.

To properly understand this statement and the verse that follows, we must see the typical meaning of the ark and of the flood. The ark is a picture of the Lord Jesus Christ. The flood of water depicts the judgment of God. The ark was the only way of salvation. When the flood came, only those who were inside were saved; all those on the outside perished. So Christ is the only way of salvation; those who are in Christ are as saved as God Himself can make them. Those on the outside could not be more lost.

The water was not the *means* of salvation, for all who were in the water drowned. The ark was the place of refuge. The ark went through the water of judgment; it took the full brunt of the storm. Not a drop of water reached those inside the ark. So Christ bore the fury of God's judgment against our sins. For those who are in Him there is no judgment (John 5:24).

The ark had water beneath it, and water coming down on top of it, and water all around it. But it bore its believing occupants **through the water** to safety in a renewed creation. So those who trust the Savior are brought safely through a scene of death and desolation to resurrection ground and a new life.

3:21 There is also an antitype which now saves us — baptism. Once again we are in difficult and controversial territory! This verse has been a battleground between those who teach baptismal regeneration and those who deny that baptism has any power to save.

BAPTISM

First let us see what it *may* mean, and then what it *cannot* mean.

Actually, there *is a baptism which saves us* — not our baptism in water, but a baptism which took place at Calvary almost 2000 years ago. Christ's death was a baptism. He was baptized in the waters of judgment. This is what He meant when He said, "I have a baptism to be baptized with, and how distressed I am till it is accomplished!" (Luke 12:50). The psalmist described this baptism in the words, "Deep calls unto deep at the noise of Your waterfalls; all Your waves and billows have gone over me" (Ps. 42:7). In His death, Christ was baptized in the waves and billows of God's wrath, and it is this baptism that is the basis for our salvation.

But we must accept His death for ourselves. Just as Noah and his family had to enter the ark to be saved, so we must commit ourselves to the Lord as our only Savior. When we do this, we become identified with Him in His death, burial, and resurrection. In a very real sense, we then have been crucified with Him (Gal. 2:20), we have been buried with Him (Rom. 6:4), and we have been brought from death to life with Him (Rom. 6:4).

All this is pictured in the believer's baptism. The ceremony is an outward sign of what has taken place spiritually; we have been baptized into Christ's death. As we go under the water, we acknowledge that we have been buried with Him. As we come up out of the water, we show that we have risen with Him and want to walk in newness of life.

An antitype which now saves us — baptism refers to Christ's baptism unto death on the cross and our identification with Him in it, which water baptism represents.

The verse *cannot* mean that we are saved by ritual baptism in water for the following reasons:

1. That would make water the savior, instead of the Lord Jesus. But He said, "I am the way" (John 14:6).

2. It would imply that Christ died in vain. If people can be saved by water, then why did the Lord Jesus have to die?

3. It simply doesn't work. Many who have been baptized have proved by their subsequent lives that they were never truly born again.

Neither can this verse mean that we are saved by *faith plus baptism*.

1. This would mean that the Savior's work on the cross was not sufficient. When He cried, "It is finished," it wasn't really so, according to this view, because baptism must be added to that work for salvation.

2. If baptism is necessary for salvation, it is strange that the Lord did not personally baptize anyone. John 4:1, 2 states that Jesus did not do the actual baptizing of His followers; this was done by His disciples.

3. The Apostle Paul thanked God that he baptized very few of the Corinthians (1 Cor. 1:14–16). This would be strange thanksgiving for an evangelist if baptism were essential for salvation! The fact that Paul did baptize some shows that he taught believer's baptism, but the fact that he baptized only a few shows that he did not consider it a requirement for salvation.

4. The penitent thief on the cross was not baptized, yet he was assured of being in Paradise with Christ (Luke 23:43).

5. The Gentiles who were saved in Caesarea received the Holy Spirit when they believed (Acts 10:44), showing that they then belonged to Christ (Rom. 8:9b). After receiving the Holy Spirit, that is, after being saved, they were baptized (vv. 47, 48). Therefore, baptism was not necessary for their salvation. They were saved first, then baptized in water.

6. In the NT, baptism is always connected with death and not with spiritual birth.

7. There are about 150 passages in the NT which teach that salvation is by faith alone. These cannot be contradicted by two or three verses that *seem* to teach that baptism is necessary for salvation. ‡

Therefore, when we read in verse 21, **Baptism . . . which now saves us**, it does not mean our baptism in literal water, but Christ's baptism unto death and our identification with Him in it.

Not the removal of the filth of the flesh. The ceremonial worship of the OT, with which Peter's Jewish-Christian readers were familiar, provided a sort of external cleansing. But it was not able to give the priests or the people a clear conscience with regard to sin. The **baptism** of which Peter is speaking is not a question of physical or even of ritual cleansing from defilement. Water does have the effect of removing dirt from the body, but it cannot provide a good conscience toward God. Only personal association with Christ in His death, burial, and resurrection can do that.

But the answer of a good conscience toward God. The question inevitably arises, "How can I have a righteous standing before God? How can I have a clear **conscience** before Him?" The answer is found in the baptism of which Peter has been speaking — Christ's baptism unto death at Calvary and one's personal acceptance of that work. By Christ's death the sin question was settled once for all.

Through the resurrection of Jesus Christ. How do I know that God is satisfied? I know because He raised **Christ** from the dead. A clear conscience is inseparably linked with **the resurrection of Jesus Christ**; they stand or fall together. The resurrection tells me that God is fully satisfied with the redemptive work of His Son. If Christ had not risen, we could never be sure that our sins had been put away. He would have died like any other man. But the risen Christ is our absolute assurance that the claims of God against our sins have en fully met.

As the hymn writer, James G. Deck, put it, "Our conscience has peace that can never fail: 'tis the Lamb on high, on the throne."

So it **now saves us — baptism . . . the answer of a good conscience toward God, through the resurrection of Jesus Christ**. My only claim for a good conscience is based on the death, burial, and resurrection of the Lord Jesus. The order is as follows:

1. Christ was baptized unto death for me at Calvary.
2. When I trust Him as Lord and Savior, I am spiritually united with Him in His death, burial, and resurrection.
3. Through the knowledge that He has risen, my request for a clear conscience is answered.
4. In water baptism, I give visible expression to the spiritual deliverance I have experienced.

3:22   Who has gone into heaven and is at the right hand of God, angels and authorities and powers having been made subject to Him. The Lord Jesus Christ not only arose from among the dead, but He ascended to **heaven** from where He had originally come. He is there today, not as an invisible, intangible spirit-being, but as a living Man in a glorified body of flesh and bones. In that body He bears eternally the wounds He received at Calvary — eloquent and everlasting tokens of His love for us.

Our Lord is **at the right hand of God**, the place of:

Power: Since the right hand is generally stronger than the left, it has come to be associated with power (Matt. 26:64).

Honor: Christ is "*exalted* to the right hand of God" (Acts 2:33; 5:31).

Rest: In virtue of His finished work Christ "*sat down* at the right hand of the Majesty on high" (Heb. 1:3; see also 8:1; 10:12). This *rest* is the *rest* of satisfaction and complacency, not the rest that conquers weariness.

Intercession: Paul speaks of Christ being at the right hand of God where He *intercedes* for us (Rom. 8:34).

Preeminence: "At His right hand in the heavenly *places*, (He is) *far above all* principality and power and might and dominion, and every name that is named, not only in this age but also in that which is to come . . ." (Eph. 1:20, 21).

Dominion: In Hebrews 1:13, God the Father says to the Son, "Sit at My right hand, *till I make Your enemies Your footstool*." Dominion is emphasized in 1 Peter 3:22: " **. . . at the right hand of God, with angels and authorities and powers having been made subject to Him.**"

Angels and authorities and powers are doubtless intended to cover all ranks of heavenly beings. They are all servants of the risen, glorified Christ.

This then was our Lord's experience in suffering for well-doing. Men rejected Him, both in His pre-incarnate testimony through Noah and in His First Advent as the Son of Man. He was baptized in death's dark waters at Calvary. But God raised Him from the dead and glorified Him at His own right hand in heaven. In the eternal purposes of God, suffering had to precede glory.

This was the lesson both for Peter's original readers and also for us. We should not be upset if we experience opposition and even persecution for doing good, for we do not deserve better treatment than our Savior had when He was on earth. We should comfort ourselves with the promise that if we suffer with Him, we shall be glorified with Him (Rom. 8:17). Furthermore, the sufferings now are not worthy to be compared with the glory that awaits us (Rom. 8:18). The afflictions are light and momentary; the glory is eternal and weighty beyond all comparison (2 Cor. 4:17).

4:1   There is a close connection between this section and the preceding (cf. 3:18). We have been considering **Christ** as an example of One who **suffered** unjustly. He **suffered** at the hands of wicked men for the cause of righteousness. Since this was so, His followers should **arm** themselves **with the same mind**. They should expect to suffer for His name. They should be prepared to endure persecution because they are Christians.

Whoever **has suffered in the flesh**, that is, in the body, **has ceased from sin**. The believer is faced with two possibilities — sin or suffering. On the one hand, he can choose to live like the unsaved people around him, sharing their sinful pleasures, and thus avoid persecution. Or he can live in purity and godliness, bearing the reproach of Christ, and suffer at the hands of the wicked.

James Guthrie, a martyr, said just before he was hanged, "Dear friends, pledge this cup of suffering as I have done, before you sin, for sin and suffering have been presented to me, and I have chosen the suffering part."

When a believer deliberately chooses to suffer persecution as a Christian rather than to continue in a life of sin, he has **ceased from sin**. This does not mean that he no longer commits acts of sin, but that the power of sin in his life has been broken. When a man suffers because he refuses to sin, he is no longer controlled by the will of the flesh.

4:2 During the remainder of a believer's earthly life, he is not controlled by human passions **but by the will of God**. He prefers to suffer as a Christian rather than to sin like the unbelievers. He would rather die than deny his Lord. **The rest of his time in the flesh** means the remainder of one's life here on earth. The believer chooses to live these years for the glory of God rather than for the gratification of sensual appetites.

4:3 Peter is writing to some who, before their conversion, had lived in all the moral corruption of the Gentile world. There had been **enough of** that kind of life! As Christians, they were new creatures, and the old sins should be abandoned. The remaining years of life belonged to God and should be given to Him.

The sins listed still characterize the Gentile non-Christian world today — the sins of sex, liquor, and false religion.

Lewdness — unrestrained indulgence, primarily in sexual immorality.

Lusts — gratification of unlawful appetites of any kind, but probably referring especially to sexual sins.

Drunkenness — giving oneself over to the control of intoxicating beverages with the resulting weakening of willpower to resist temptation. There is a close link between drunkenness and immorality.

Revelries — riotous parties and late-night merrymaking.

Drinking parties — drinking bouts which lead to debauchery and brawls.

Abominable idolatries — the worship of idols, with all the immorality that is associated with such worship.

People become like what they worship. When they abandon the true God, their moral standards are automatically lowered. These lowered standards permit them to engage in all sorts of sinful pleasures for which they have an appetite. This is why idolatrous religions breed sin and degradation.

4:4 This verse describes the common experience of those who are saved from lives of outward corruption. Their former cronies think they have gone mad and accuse them of being religious fanatics. They think it a form of insanity that the Christians will no longer participate in dances, worldly parties, and sex orgies. The clean, moral life of a believer condemns the sinner; no wonder he hates the change!

4:5 Though the ungodly blaspheme Christians in this life, **they will give an account** for every word and deed at the Judgment of the Great White Throne. The Lord **is ready to judge the living and the dead**. Clearly it is unbelievers whom Peter has in mind here. The judgment of the living unbelievers will take place before the Millennium begins; the wicked dead will be judged at the close of Christ's reign on earth. Their condemnation will be proof of the righteousness of the children of God.

4:6 **It is for this reason** — the vindication of the children of God — **that the gospel was preached also to those who are dead**. Here again we come to a difficult passage. Does this mean that the gospel was preached to people after they had died or while they were still alive? And who were these people?

We understand this verse to refer to people to whom the gospel was preached while they were still alive on the earth and who believed on the Lord. Because of their valiant stand for the truth, they suffered at the hands of wicked men, and in some cases were martyred. These believers, though **judged**, or condemned, **according to men in the flesh**, were vindicated by God. They are now enjoying eternal life with Him.

They were not dead when the gospel

was preached to them. But they **are dead now**, as far as their bodies are concerned. Though men thought them mad, **God** honored them, and their spirits are now in heaven.

Preaching the gospel brings two results to those who believe — the blame of men and the approval of God. Barnes explains:

> The design in publishing the Gospel to them was, that though they might be judged by men in the usual manner, and put to death, yet that in respect to their higher and nobler nature, *the spirit*, they might live unto God.[26]

III. THE BELIEVER'S SERVICE AND SUFFERING (4:7–5:14)

A. Urgent Imperatives for the Last Days (4:7–11)

4:7 A series of admonitions is now introduced by the statement **"The end of all things is at hand."** This has been taken to mean either (1) the destruction of Jerusalem, (2) the Rapture, (3) the return of Christ to reign, or (4) the destruction of the heavens and the earth at the end of the Millennium. We think it probably refers to the last of these.

The first admonition is to **be serious and watchful in your prayers**. This was written in a time of persecution and means that the believer's prayer life should be free from the distractions of panic and emotional instability brought on by stress: his fellowship with God should be undisturbed by discordant circumstances.

4:8 He must pay attention to his fellowship with other believers (vv. 8, 9), and **have fervent love** for all members of the household of faith. Such a love will not publicize the faults and failings of other believers, but will protect them from public view. Someone has said, "Hatred makes the worst of everything. Love is entitled to bury things out of sight."

The statement **"love will cover a multitude of sins"** (Prov. 10:12) should not be taken as a doctrinal explanation of how sins are put away. The guilt and penalty of sins can only be removed by the blood of Christ. Neither should the statement be used to condone sin or to relieve an assembly from its responsibility to discipline an offender. It means that true love is able to overlook minor faults and failures in other believers.

4:9 One means of demonstrating love to the brethren is by practicing hospitality ungrudgingly. This counsel is especially needed during times of persecution when food supplies might be running low and when those who harbor Christians are subject to arrest and imprisonment, if not death itself.

Hospitality is a tremendous privilege. In practicing it, some have entertained angels unwittingly (Heb. 13:2). Any kindness shown to a child of God is reckoned as shown to the Lord Himself (Matt. 25:40). No matter how slight the kindness, it will be rewarded handsomely; even a cup of cold water given in the Lord's name will be rewarded (Matt. 10:42). Those who receive a prophet because he is a prophet shall receive a prophet's reward (Matt. 10:41) which, in Jewish reckoning, was superlative. Many Christians testify to the blessing that has come to their homes and their children through hospitality shown to servants of the Lord.

Jesus taught that we should entertain those who cannot repay us (Luke 14:12). This does not mean that we should *never* entertain relatives, friends, or neighbors who might entertain us in return. But our purpose should be to show kindness in the name of the Lord Jesus with no thought of being repaid. Certainly it is questionable whether believers should keep up a continuing round of banquets and parties with their own clique, while great sections of the world are still unevangelized.

4:10 **Each** believer **has received a gift** from the Lord, some special function to perform as a member of the Body of Christ (1 Cor. 12:4–11, 29–31; Rom. 12:6–8). These gifts are a stewardship from God. They are not to be used for selfish gain but for His glory and for the good of others. We are not meant to be the *terminals* of God's gifts to us; His grace reaches us but should not end with us. We are intended to be *channels* through whom the blessing can flow to others.

We are to be **good stewards of the manifold grace of God**. The **grace of God** here refers to the undeserved favor which He offers to man. **Manifold** literally means *multi-colored* or variegated. Phillips translates it "magnificently varied."

4:11 Even if a man is gifted to preach or teach, he must be sure that the words he speaks are the very words **God** would have him say on that particular occasion. This is what is meant by **the oracles of God**. It is not enough for a man simply to preach from the Bible. He should also have the assurance that he is presenting the particular message intended by God for that audience at that time.

Anyone who performs any kind of service should do it with the humble recognition that it is **God** who empowers him. Then the glory will go to **God** — to whom it belongs.

A man should not become proud no matter how highly gifted he is in Christian service. The gift did not originate by his own effort, but was given to him from above. In fact, he has nothing which he did not receive. All service should be performed so that **God** gets the credit.

As Peter points out, this honor is presented to the Father **through Jesus Christ** as Mediator, and also because of what God has done for us through Him. To this blessed Savior belongs praise and power **forever and ever. Amen.**

B. Exhortations and Explanations Concerning Suffering (4:12–19)

4:12 The rest of chapter 4 contains exhortations and explanations concerning suffering incurred for the name of Christ. The word "suffering" and its derivatives are used twenty-one times in this Epistle.

The natural attitude for a Christian is to look on persecution as **strange** and abnormal. We are surprised when we have to suffer. But Peter tells us that we should consider it as normal Christian experience. We have no right to expect better treatment from the world than our Savior received. All who desire to live a godly life in Christ Jesus will be persecuted (2 Tim. 3:12). It is especially true

that those who take a forthright stand for Christ become the object of savage attack. Satan doesn't waste his ammunition on nominal Christians. He turns his big guns on those who are storming the gates of Hades.

4:13 The privilege of sharing **Christ's sufferings** should cause us great rejoicing. We cannot of course share His atoning sufferings; He is the only Sin-Bearer. But we can share the same kind of **sufferings** He endured as a Man. We can share His rejection and reproach. We can receive the wounds and scars in our bodies which unbelievers would still like to inflict on Him.

If the child of God can **rejoice** today in the midst of suffering, how much more will he rejoice and **be glad** when Christ's **glory is revealed. When** the Savior comes back to earth as the Lion of the tribe of Judah, He will be **revealed** as the Almighty Son of God. Those who suffer now for His sake will be honored then with Him.

4:14 The early Christians rejoiced that they were counted worthy to suffer shame **for the name of Christ** (Acts 5:41). So should every Christian who has the privilege of being reviled for Christ's sake. Such suffering is a true indication that **the Spirit of glory and of God rests upon** us. This is the Holy **Spirit** who **rests upon** persecuted Christians as the glory cloud rested on the tabernacle in the OT, indicating the presence of God.

We know that **the Spirit** indwells every true child of God, but He **rests** in a special way **upon** those who are completely committed to the cause of Christ. They know the presence and power of the Spirit of God as others do not. The same Lord Jesus who **is blasphemed** by the persecutors **is glorified** by His suffering saints.[27]

4:15 A Christian should never bring suffering upon himself for wrongdoing. He should never be guilty of murder, stealing, evil in general, or meddling **in other people's matters**. There is no glory for God in this — only shame for the testimony of Christ.

4:16 But there is no disgrace **if anyone suffers as a Christian**. F. B. Meyer says this is true whether it means "the loss of business, reputation, and home;

desertion by parents, children, and friends; misrepresentation, hatred and even death."[28] Under the name of **Christian** it is possible **to glorify God** in all these trials. G. Campbell Morgan admonishes as follows:

> This is more than glorying in the name. It is so living worthily of all it means as to glorify God. If a man is known as a Christian and does not live as one, he dishonors God. To bear the name is to take a responsibility, a great and glorious one, but none the less a very solemn one.[29]

4:17 Peter contrasts the suffering of God's people in this life with the sufferings of the wicked in eternity. **The time has come for judgment to begin at the house of God. The time** referred to is the dispensation of the church, which began at Pentecost and will continue to the Rapture. **The house of God** refers to the church. During this age, the church is undergoing **judgment** by the unbelieving world. Believers are experiencing their sufferings now, just as Jesus did when He was on earth.

If that is so, what will be the fate **of those who do not obey the gospel of God**? If Christians suffer now for doing good, what will the unsaved suffer in eternity for all their ungodly deeds?

4:18 The same argument is contained in this verse, quoted from Proverbs 11:31: **"If the righteous** will be recompensed on the earth, how much more **the ungodly and the sinner."**

The righteous person **is scarcely saved** or **saved** with difficulty. From the divine standpoint his salvation was purchased at enormous cost. From the human standpoint, men are told, "Strive to enter through the narrow gate" (Luke 13:24). Believers are taught that "We must through many tribulations enter the kingdom of God" (Acts 14:22). With all the dangers and temptations that beset a Christian, it is only a miracle of divine grace that preserves him for the heavenly kingdom.

That being so, what will be the doom of those who have died in their sins, unrepentant and unsaved? A vivid illustration of this truth is found in the following anecdote from the writings of F. B. Meyer:

It was the earnest wish of a holy man that his death might be so triumphant that his unconverted sons might be convinced and attracted by the evident power of the Gospel to sustain and cheer in the dark passage of the valley. Instead of this, to his deep regret, his spirit lay under a cloud; he was oppressed with fear and misgiving; and the enemy was permitted to torment him to the uttermost. But these very facts were the ones which most profoundly impressed his children. "For," said the eldest, "we all know what a good man our father was; and yet see how deep his spiritual sufferings were. What then may *we* not expect, who have given no thought to the concerns of our souls?[30]

4:19 Peter insists that sufferings must be **according to the will of God**. Religious zealots may *invite* suffering by acting impulsively without divine guidance. Those with a martyr complex tempt God in a way that leads to dishonor. But the true pathway of suffering for Christians leads to eternal glory. In view of that, they should continue to do right, no matter what the cost may be, and entrust **their souls** to the **faithful Creator**.

It seems somewhat strange that Peter should introduce the Lord as **Creator** here rather than as Savior, High Priest, or Shepherd. Christ is our Creator in a twofold sense — we are His as part of the original creation and of the new creation (Eph. 4:24; Col. 3:10). In either case, we are the objects of His love and care. It is only reasonable that we should entrust ourselves to the One who made our souls and who saved them.

C. Exhortations and Salutations (5:1–14)

5:1 This final chapter of 1 Peter contains exhortations and greetings. First there is a word for **the elders**. By way of authority for delivering such a charge, Peter introduces himself as a **fellow elder and a witness of the sufferings of Christ, and also a partaker of the** impending **glory. Fellow elder** — what a far cry from claiming to be "supreme pontiff" of the church! **A witness** — Peter saw the Shepherd die for the sheep, and the memory of such love constrains him to care for them as a faithful undershepherd. A **partaker** —

soon the glory will dawn, Christ will appear, and we shall appear with Him in glory (Col. 3:4). Till then the Savior's commission remains, "Feed My lambs! . . . Tend My sheep!" (John 21:15–17).

5:2 Elders are mature men of Christian character who are qualified by the Holy Spirit to provide spiritual leadership in the assembly. The NT presupposes a plurality of elders — not one elder over a church or over a group of churches, but two or more elders in one assembly (Phil. 1:1). For the qualifications of elders see 1 Timothy 3:1–7 and Titus 1:6–9. In the early church before the NT was available in written form, elders were appointed by the apostles and their representatives, but only after sufficient time had elapsed in a new church for it to be evident who had the qualifications. Today, Christians should recognize and obey those who have the qualifications and who do the work of elders.

Shepherd the flock of God which is among you. The flock belongs to **God** but elders have been given the responsibility to serve as undershepherds. **Not by compulsion but willingly.**[31] Overseeing the flock is not a work into which men are coerced by election or appointment. The Holy Spirit provides the burden and ability, and the elders must respond with a willing heart. So we read in 1 Timothy 3:1, "If a man desires the position of a bishop, he desires a good work." Coupled with divine enablement must be human willingness.

Not for dishonest gain but eagerly. Financial reward must not be the motive for being an elder. This does not mean that an elder may not be supported by the local church; the existence of such "full-time elders" is indicated in 1 Timothy 5:17, 18. But it means that a mercenary spirit is incompatible with true Christian ministry.

5:3 The third phase of Peter's exhortation is this: **nor as being lords over those entrusted to you, but being examples to the flock.** Elders should be **examples**, not dictators. They should be walking out in front of the flock, not driving them from behind. They should not treat the flock as if it belonged to them. This strikes at the very heart of authoritarianism!

Many of the abuses in Christendom would be eliminated by simply obeying the three instructions in verses 2, 3. The first would abolish all *reluctance*. The second would spell the end of *commercialism*. The third would be the death of *officialism* in the church.

5:4 An elder's work involves a tremendous expenditure of physical and emotional energy. He must sympathize, counsel, reprove, rebuke, teach, discipline, and warn. At times it may seem a thankless task. But a special reward is promised to the faithful elder. **When the Chief Shepherd appears,** he **will receive** an unfading **crown of glory.** Frankly, we don't know too much about the promised crowns of Scripture — the crown of rejoicing (1 Thess. 2:19), the crown of righteousness (2 Tim. 4:8), the crown of life (Jas. 1:12; Rev. 2:10); and the crown of glory. We do not know whether they will be literal crowns that we can cast at the Savior's feet; whether they simply indicate the extent of responsibility that will be given to us during the reign of Christ (Luke 19:17–19); or whether they are facets of Christian character which we will bear throughout eternity. But we do know that they will be ample recompense for any tears, trials, and sufferings we have experienced down here.

5:5 Those who are **younger,** whether in years or in the faith, should be submissive **to the elders.** Why? Because these overseers have wisdom that comes from years of experience in the things of God. They have a deep, experiential knowledge of the word of God. And they are the ones to whom God has given responsibility for the care of His sheep.

All believers should **be clothed with humility;** it is a great virtue. Moffatt says, "Put on the apron of humility." Very appropriate — since the apron is the badge of a servant. A missionary to India once said, "If I were to pick out two phrases necessary for spiritual growth, I would pick out these: 'I don't know' and 'I am sorry.' And both phrases are the evidences of deep humility." Imagine a congregation where all the member have this humble spirit; where they esteem others better than themselves; where they outdo each other in performing the menial tasks. Such a church need not be imaginary; it could and should be an actuality.

If there were no other reason for being humble, this would be enough: **God resists the proud, but gives grace to the humble**. (Peter is quoting from the Greek version of Prov. 3:34.) Think of it — the mighty God opposed to our pride and determined to break it, contrasted with the mighty God powerless to resist a broken and contrite heart!

5:6 This humility is to be shown not only in relation to others but to **God** as well. In Peter's day the saints were passing through the fires of affliction. These trials, though not sent by God, were permitted by Him. The best policy, Peter says, is to take them humbly from the Lord's hand. He will sustain His people and **exalt** them **in due time**.

5:7 Believers are privileged to cast **all** their anxieties on the Lord with the strong confidence that **He cares**. Once again Peter is quoting from the Greek version of the OT (Ps. 55:22).

J. Sidlow Baxter points out that there are two kinds of care here:

> There is *anxious* care, in the words: "Casting all your care upon Him"; and there is *affectionate* care, in the words: "He careth for you." Over against all our own *anxious* care is our Savior's never-failing *affectionate* care.[32]

Worry is unnecessary; there is no need for us to bear the burdens when He is willing and able to bear them for us. Worry is futile; it hasn't solved a problem yet. Worry is sin. A preacher once said: "Worry is sin because it denies the wisdom of God; it says that He doesn't know what He's doing. It denies the love of God; it says He does not care. And it denies the power of God; it says that He isn't able to deliver me from whatever is causing me to worry." Something to think about!

5:8 Although we should not worry, we must **be sober** and **vigilant, because** we have a powerful **adversary, the devil**. To **be sober** means to be serious-minded, to take a realistic approach to life, to be intelligent concerning the stratagems of Satan. Pentecost well says:

> An individual who takes no cognizance of the nature or character of the world, one who is unmindful of the purposes and attacks of our adversary, the Devil, can afford to live in a lighthearted or flippant way. But for one who sees life as Jesus Christ sees it, there must be an entirely

new attitude, an entirely new outlook characterized by sobriety.[33]

There must also be constant vigilance, a preparedness to meet every attack of the wicked one. Here the **adversary** is described as **a roaring lion, seeking** someone to **devour**. **The devil** has different poses. Sometimes he comes like a snake, seeking to lure people into moral corruption. Sometimes he disguises himself as an angel of light, attempting to deceive people in the spiritual realm. Here, as **a roaring lion**, he is bent on terrorizing God's people through persecution.

5:9 We are not to surrender to his fury. Rather we must **resist him** through prayer and God's word. We do not have strength in ourselves to oppose him, but as we are firm **in** our **faith**, in our dependence on the Lord, we can **resist him**.

One of Satan's devices is to discourage us with the thought that our sufferings are unique. As we pass through the fire of affliction, it is easy to faint under the mistaken idea that no one else has as much trouble as we do. Peter reminds us that **the same sufferings are experienced** by our Christian **brotherhood** throughout **the world**.

5:10 True victory in persecution is to see God behind the scenes working out His wonderful purposes. No matter what our trials, we should remember first of all that He is **the God of all grace**. This lovely title of our God reminds us that His dealings with us are not based on what we deserve, but on His thoughts of love to us. No matter how fierce our testing, we can always be thankful we are not in hell where we ought to be.

A second strong consolation is that He has **called us to His eternal glory**. This enables us to look beyond the sufferings of this life to the time when we shall be with the Savior and be like Him forever. Just think of it! We have been picked up from the scrap heap and **called to His eternal glory**!

A third comfort is that suffering is just for **a while**. When contrasted with the **eternal glory**, life's afflictions are less than momentary.

The final encouragement is that God uses suffering to educate us and mold our Christian character. He is training us for reigning. Four aspects of this training process are listed.

Perfect — Trials make the believer fit; they supply needed elements in his character to make him spiritually mature.

Establish — Suffering makes Christians more stable, able to maintain a good confession, and to bear up under pressure. This is the same word the Lord Jesus used with Peter: " . . .strengthen [or establish] your brethren" (Luke 22:32).

Strengthen — Persecution is intended by Satan to weaken and wear out believers, but it has the opposite effect. It strengthens them to endure.

Settle — This verb is related to the word "foundation" in the original. God wants every believer to be firmly planted in a secure place in His Son and in His word.

Lacey says:

The inevitable suffering of the Christian life always yields the same blessed result in the character of believers; it will refine the faith, adjust the character, establish, strengthen and settle the people of God.[34]

5:11 In view of the marvelous way in which God overrules persecution and suffering for His **glory** and our good, it is little wonder that Peter bursts into this doxology: **"To Him be the glory and the dominion forever and ever. Amen."** Only to such a One is **glory** due; only in the hands of such a One is **dominion** safe!

5:12 **Silvanus** (probably the same man called Silas, the shorter form of the name), was the **faithful brother** to whom Peter dictated this Letter, and probably the messenger who delivered it. Peter's object in this Letter was to assure the believers of the Dispersion that the Christian faith which they held was the true faith — or, as he calls it, **the true grace of God**. Perhaps in the heat of persecution, they might be tempted to wonder if they had been right to embrace Christianity. Peter declares that they were right. They had found *God's truth* and should stand fast in it.

5:13 **She who is in Babylon, elect together with you, greets you; and so does Mark my son.**

It is impossible to state with certainty who or what is meant by **"She who is in Babylon, elect together with you."** Some of the main interpretations are: (1) The "brotherhood" (2:17; 5:9). In the Greek this abstract noun happens to be feminine. (2) Peter's wife. (3) Some locally prominent lady. It is also impossible to know which **Babylon** is meant. It could be: (1) The famous city on the Euphrates, where there were many Jews; (2) The military station by the same name on the Nile (unlikely); (3) Rome. In Revelation, the city of Babylon is generally understood as referring to Rome (17:1–9; 18:10, 21).

A third question arises over the mention of **Mark**. Is this Peter's own **son** in the flesh, or is he referring to John **Mark**, the writer of the Gospel? The latter is more probable. If that is so, then we are left to decide whether Mark was Peter's son because the latter had led him to Christ or whether the word **son** merely designates the close spiritual relationship between an elder and a younger Christian. The word Peter uses for **son**[35] is not the same word which Paul uses to describe his spiritual relationship with Timothy and Titus, and fits the ancient tradition that Mark's very vivid Gospel is based on Peter's eyewitness accounts.

5:14 The elder closes with a charge and a benediction. The charge is, **"Greet one another with a kiss of love."** The obligation of brotherly **love** is a standing order for the church, though the manner of expressing it may vary in cultures and times.

The benediction is: **"Peace to you all who are in Christ Jesus."** It is a tranquil word to use with storm-tossed saints, who are enduring affliction for the name of Christ. Jesus whispers **peace** to His blood-bought flock as they suffer for Him in the midst of a turbulent society.

Peace, perfect peace, death shadowing
  us and ours?
Jesus has vanquished death and all
  its powers.
— *Edward H. Bickersteth*

ENDNOTES

[1](1:2) There are other forms of sanctification which take place later. When a person is born again, he becomes

positionally sanctified because he is "in Christ" (Heb. 10:10, 14). Throughout his Christian life he should experience *practical* sanctification, that is, the process of becoming more like Christ (1 Pet. 1:15). In heaven he will achieve *perfect* sanctification, for he will never again sin (Col. 1:22). See Excursus on Sanctification after Hebrews 2:11.

²(1:8) The majority of Greek mss. read "known" (*eidotes*) rather than "seen" (*idontes*). The resultant meaning is about the same; i.e., they had not been personally acquainted with Jesus on earth.

³(1:8) William Lincoln, *Lectures on the First and Second Epistles of Peter*, p. 21.

⁴(1:12) *Ibid.*, p. 23.

⁵(1:13) J. H. Jowett, *The Redeemed Family of God*, p. 34.

⁶(1:17) Lincoln, *Lectures*, p. 30.

⁷(1:20) *Ibid.*, p. 33.

⁸(1:21) W. T. P. Wolston, *Simon Peter: His Life and Letters*, p. 270.

⁹(1:22) The critical (NU) text omits "through the Spirit."

¹⁰(1:23) Footnote in F. W. Grant, "1 Peter," *The Numerical Bible*, Hebrews to Revelation, p. 149.

¹¹(1:23) The NU text omits "forever."

¹²(2:2) The Alexandrian Text (NU in NKJV footnotes) reads "grow up to salvation." However, this reading could cast doubt on assurance of salvation.

¹³(2:6) Biblical Greek *lithon* (stone) *akro-* (top or tip) *gōniaion* (of corner), hence *cornerstone* or *capstone*.

¹⁴(2:7) The NU text reads "disbelieve" for "are disobedient," but since *believing* the gospel is also called *obeying* the Gospel, the meaning is about the same.

¹⁵(2:12) A literal rendering is *noble* or *lovely* (Gk. *kalos*, cf. English *calligraphy*, beautiful writing).

¹⁶(2:12) Charles R. Erdman, *The General Epistles*, p. 66.

¹⁷(2:12) Jowett, *Redeemed Family*, pp. 88, 89.

¹⁸(2:13) Leslie T. Lyall, *Red Sky at Night*, p. 81.

¹⁹(2:16) F. B. Meyer, *Tried by Fire*, p. 91.

²⁰(2:25) The Greek word is *episkopos*, "overseer" or "bishop."

²¹(3:2) George Müller, in a periodical called *The Word*, edited by Richard Burson, date unknown, pp. 33–35.

²²(3:4) Meyer, *Tried*, p. 117.

²³(3:7) Charles Bigg, *A Critical and Exegetical Commentary on the Epistles of St. Peter and St. Jude* (ICC), p. 155.

²⁴(3:8) Instead of "courteous" (*philophrones*), the NU text reads "humble" (*tapeinophrones*). Both are fine virtues that fit the context; which is chosen as original depends on one's view of NT textual criticism. We follow the KJ tradition here.

²⁵(3:15) The NU text reads "Christ as Lord" for "the Lord God." This would suggest that the Christ of the NT is the Jehovah Sabaoth of the OT.

²⁶(4:6) Albert Barnes, *Notes on the New Testament: James, Peter, John and Jude*, p. 191.

²⁷(4:14) The NU text lacks the last sentence of verse 14. Since "rests upon you" and "glorified" both end with the same letters in Greek (*-etai*) it would be easy to omit it by accident. This is technically called omission by "homoeoteleuton" (similar ending).

²⁸(4:16)F. B. Meyer, *Tried by Fire*, p. 27.

²⁹(4:16) G. Campbell Morgan, *Searchlights from the Word*, p. 366.

³⁰(4:18) Meyer, *Tried*, pp. 180-181.

³¹(5:2) The NU text reads "according to God" for "willingly." The traditional reading of KJ and NKJV (found in TR and majority text) fits the context much better as a *contrast to compulsion*.

³²(5:7) J. Sidlow Baxter, *Awake, My Heart*, p. 294. The beautiful play on words of the KJ tradition is not in the original Greek, where the two "cares" are unrelated words. It comes from the first printed *English* NT (1526), the work of the outstanding translator and martyr of the Inquisition, William Tyndale (1484-1536). His text reads "cast all youre care to hym: for he careth for you."

³³(5:8) J. Dwight Pentecost, *Your Adversary the Devil*, p. 94.

³⁴(5:10) Harry Lacey, *God and the Nations*, p. 92.

³⁵(5:13) The ordinary Greek word *huios*; Paul uses *teknon*, literally "born one" (Scots *bairn*) or child.

BIBLIOGRAPHY
(1 and 2 Peter)

Barbieri, Louis A. *First and Second*

Peter. Chicago: Moody Press, 1975.

Bigg, Charles. *A Critical and Exegetical Commentary on the Epistles of St. Peter and St. Jude* (ICC). Edinburgh: T. & T. Clark, 1901.

Grant, F. W. "I and II Peter," *The Numerical Bible,* vol. 7. New York: Loizeaux Bros., 1903.

Ironside, H. A. *Notes on James and Peter.* New York: Loizeaux Brothers, 1947.

Jowett, J. H. *The Redeemed Family of God.* London: Hodder & Stoughton, n.d.

Lenski, R. C. H. *The Interpretation of the Epistles of St. Peter, St. John & St. Jude.* Columbus: Wartburg Press, 1945.

Lincoln, William. *Lectures on the First and Second Epistles of Peter.* Kilmarnock: John Ritchie Publ., n.d.

Meyer, F. B. *Tried by Fire.* Fort Washington, PA: Christian Literature Crusade, 1983.

Stibbs, Alan M. *The First Epistle General of Peter.* Grand Rapids: Wm. B. Eerdmans Publishing Co., 1959.

Thomas, W. H. Griffith. *The Apostle Peter: His Life and Writings.* Grand Rapids: Kregel Publications, 1984.

Westwood, Tom. *The Epistles of Peter.* Glendale, California: The Bible Treasury Hour, Inc., 1953.

Wolston, W. T. P. *Simon Peter: His Life and Letters.* London: James Nisbet & Co., 1913.

THE SECOND EPISTLE OF PETER

Introduction

"[Second Peter] breathes Christ and awaits His consummation."
— E. G. Homrighausen

I. Unique Place in the Canon

The above introductory quotation is especially significant because its author, like so many today, denies that Peter wrote the Epistle. He also admits that "what we have is Petrine in character and spirit."[1] Ironically, these two statements sum up the unique contribution of 2 Peter very succinctly.

Amid the encroaching darkness of apostasy this short Letter is looking forward to our Lord's Coming. It is personally reminiscent of Peter's life and personality, yet does indeed breathe Christ to those who will let the little Letter speak for itself.

II. Authorship†

A leading conservative American NT scholar recently said, "Second Peter, like Daniel and Isaiah in the OT, is where we separate the men from the boys as to strict orthodoxy in biblical criticism." Modern commentators often do not even seek to disprove the Petrine authorship of 2 Peter; they assume it is a proven fact that Peter did *not* write the Epistle. There are more serious problems in accepting this book as authentic than any other NT book, but they are definitely not as strong as they are presented.

External Evidence

The usual citations of Polycarp, Ignatius, and Irenaeus cannot be mustered for 2 Peter. However, if, as the early church taught, Jude is after 2 Peter, we have a *first century* attestation of 2 Peter in the Epistle of Jude (see Introduction to Jude). The German scholar Zahn thinks we need no other. Next to Jude,

Origen is the first one to quote 2 Peter, and he is followed by Methodius of Olympus (a martyr under Emperor Diocletian) and Fumilian of Caesarea. Eusebius admits that the *majority* of Christians accepted 2 Peter, whereas he himself had doubts.

The Muratorian Canon lacks 2 Peter — but it also lacks 1 Peter, and furthermore it is a fragmentary document. While Jerome was aware of doubts as to 2 Peter's authenticity, he, along with the other leading church fathers, Athanasius and Augustine, accepted it as genuine. The whole church followed suit till Reformation times.

Why is 2 Peter much more weakly attested *externally* than other books? First of all, it is short, apparently not widely copied, and does not contain much unique material. This latter point is an argument in its favor: books by heretics always *added* doctrine contradicting or at least strangely supplementing apostolic doctrine. This suggests perhaps the main reason for the caution regarding 2 Peter in the early centuries: there were several "pseudepigrapha" (false writings) using Peter's name to promote Gnostic heresies, such as "The Apocalypse of Peter."

Finally it is important to know that while 2 Peter was one of several books questioned by some (antilegomena), it was *never rejected as spurious by any church.*

Internal Evidence

Those who reject Petrine authorship emphasize the difference in style between 1 Peter and 2 Peter. Jerome explained this as due to Peter's using a different amanuensis. However, the difference is not really as great between

†See p. i.

1 Peter and 2 Peter as it is between the two Epistles together against the rest of the NT. Both Epistles use a wide, colorful vocabulary that has many coincidences with Peter's sermons in Acts and events in his life.

The references to events in Peter's past occurring in the book are used both *for* and *against* traditional authorship. Some who reject Petrine authorship say there should be *more allusions*; others say there are *too many* not to have been planned by a forger! But what would be the reason for forging such a book? While those rejecting authenticity have been most creative in attempting *theories*, no satisfactory ones have yet been produced.

But as we study the Epistle, we find several internal evidences that Peter was indeed the author:

In 1:3, the writer speaks of believers as having been called by the Lord's own glory and virtue. This takes us back to Luke 5:8 where the glory of the Lord so overpowered Peter that he cried, "Depart from me, for I am a sinful man, O Lord!"

When the writer gives a prescription whereby his readers may never stumble (1:5–10), we think immediately of Peter's fall, and of the sorrow it brought him.

Chapter 1 verse 14 is especially significant. The writer had been told of his death by the Lord Jesus. This fits perfectly with John 21:18, 19 where Jesus revealed to Peter that he would be killed in his old age.

In verses 13–15 of chapter 1, the words "tent" (tabernacle) and "decease" (exodus) are both words used by Luke in the account of the transfiguration (Luke 9:31–33).

One of the most convincing proofs that Peter wrote this Epistle is the reference in 1:16–18 to the transfiguration. The writer was present on the holy mountain. This means that he was either Peter, James, or John (Matt. 17:1). This second Letter claims to have been written by Peter (1:1), not by James or John.

In 2:14, 18 we find the words "enticing" and "allure." They come from the word *deleagō* — to catch with a lure. They are from the vocabulary of a fisherman, and are thus especially appropriate from Peter.

In 3:1 the author refers to a previous Letter, which is probably 1 Peter. He also speaks in 3:15 of Paul in very personal terms, which an apostle could certainly do.

A final word that harks back to Peter's experience is found in 3:17. The word "steadfastness" comes from the same root as the word "strengthen" which Jesus used in Luke 22:32. "When you have returned to Me, strengthen your brethren." It is also found as "establish" in 1 Peter 5:10 and 2 Peter 1:12.

Finally, as in the Pastoral Epistles, we suspect that Peter's trenchant condemnation of apostates has drawn out much of the modern hostility to 2 Peter as a genuine product of the apostle's life and pen.

As we study the Epistle, we may find other internal evidences that link it with the Apostle Peter. But the important thing is to turn to the Letter and see what the Lord is saying to us through it.

III. Date

The date of 2 Peter obviously hinges on its authenticity. Those who believe it is a forgery choose some date in the second century. Since we conclude that the church was correct in recognizing 2 Peter as canonical, both from a historical and a spiritual perspective, we would assign a date shortly before Peter's death (A.D. 67 or 68), that is, 66 or 67.

IV. Background and Themes[†]

Two main strands that militate against one another show up clearly in the fabric of the apostle's Letter: *the prophetic word* (1:19–21) and *libertinism* (chap. 2). Already on the horizon Peter sees false teachers who will bring in "destructive heresies" that allow loose and licentious lifestyles. These are people who ridicule the idea of coming judgment (3:1–7). What is seen as future in Peter's day is seen as having crept in by Jude's Epistle (v. 4). When Christendom lost its love for Christ's Coming and settled down in the world (under Constantine and following), the morals of the church went plummeting. The same is true today. The nineteenth century awakening of interest in prophetic truth is waning today in many circles — and the loose living in some churches shows that Peter was inspired to write much needed truth for the entire Christian era.

OUTLINE

    I. SALUTATION (1:1, 2)
   II. CALL TO DEVELOP STRONG CHRISTIAN CHARACTER (1:3–21)
  III. THE RISE OF FALSE TEACHERS PREDICTED (Chap. 2)
  IV. THE RISE OF SCOFFERS PREDICTED (Chap. 3)

Commentary

I. SALUTATION (1:1, 2)

1:1 **Simon Peter** introduces himself as **a bondservant and apostle of Jesus Christ**. At once we are struck by his simplicity and humility. He was a bondslave by choice; an **apostle** by divine appointment. He uses no pompous titles or symbols of status. He has only a grateful acknowledgment of his obligation to serve the risen Savior.

All we are told about those to whom the Letter was written is that they had **obtained** the same **precious faith** as Peter and his colleagues. This may indicate that he was writing to Gentile believers, the point being that they had received the same kind of **faith** as believing Jews, a faith that was in no way deficient. All who are saved by the grace of God enjoy equal acceptance before Him, whether they are Jews or Gentiles, male or female, slave or free.

Faith means the sum total of all they had received when they embraced the Christian faith. He goes on to explain that this **faith** is **by the righteousness of our God and Savior Jesus Christ**. He means that it was a righteous thing for **God** to give this **faith** of equal standing to those who believe on the Lord **Jesus**. Christ's death, burial, and resurrection provide a just basis upon which God can show grace to sinners through faith. The debt of sin has been fully paid and now God can justify the ungodly sinner who believes on His Son.

The title **our God and Savior Jesus Christ** is one of many in the NT which indicate the absolute deity of the Lord Jesus. If He is not God, then these words have no meaning.

1:2 The apostle's lofty prayer for his readers is that **grace and peace** might **be multiplied to** them **in the knowledge of God and of Jesus our Lord**. He wants them to have this **knowledge** by the sustaining, empowering **grace** of God in their everyday lives. He wants their hearts to be guarded by the **peace** of God that passes all understanding. But this is not to be given in small doses! He desires these blessings to **be multiplied** in volume, not added in small segments.

How can these blessings **be multiplied**? It is **in the knowledge of God and of Jesus our Lord**. The better we know God, the more we experience **grace and peace**. We do better by dwelling in the secret place of the Most High than by making occasional visits there. Those who live in the sanctuary rather than in the suburbs find the secret of God's **grace and peace**.

II. CALL TO DEVELOP STRONG CHRISTIAN CHARACTER (1:3–21)

1:3 This passage should be of immense interest to every Christian because it tells how we can keep from falling in this life and how we can be assured of a triumphal entry into the next.

First we are assured that God has made full provision for us to have a life of holiness. This provision is said to be an evidence of His **power**: **His divine**

power has given to us all things that pertain to life and godliness. Just as His power saves us in the first place, so His power energizes us to live holy lives from then on. The order is — first **life**, then **godliness**. The gospel is the power of God to save from the penalty of sin and from its power, from damnation and from defilement.

The **all things that pertain to life and godliness** include the high priestly work of Christ, the ministry of the Holy Spirit, the activity of angelic agencies on our behalf, the new life we receive at conversion, and the instruction of the word of God.

The **power** to live a holy life comes **through the knowledge of Him who called us**. Just as **His divine power** is the source of holiness, so **the knowledge of Him** is the channel. To know Him is eternal life (John 17:3) and progress in knowing Him is progress in holiness. The better we get to know Him, the more we become like Him.

Our calling is one of Peter's favorite themes. He reminds us that: (1) We have been called out of darkness into His marvelous light (1 Pet. 2:9). (2) We have been called to follow Christ in a pathway of suffering (1 Pet. 2:21). (3) We have been called to return blessing for reviling (1 Pet. 3:9). (4) We have been called to his eternal glory (1 Pet. 5:10). (5) We have been called **by glory and virtue** (2 Pet. 1:3). This last reference means that He **called us** by revealing to us the wonders of His Person. Saul of Tarsus was called on the road to Damascus when he saw the glory of God. A later disciple testified, "I looked into His face and was forever spoiled for anything that was unlike Him." He was **called by** His **glory and** excellence.

1:4 Included among the "all things" which God's power has **given** to promote a life of holiness are His **exceedingly great and precious promises** in the word. It is estimated that there are at least 30,000 promises in the Bible. John Bunyan once said, "The pathway of life is strewn so thickly with the promises of God that it is impossible to take one step without treading upon one of them."

The **promises** of God are the last of seven **precious** things mentioned by Peter in his Letters. Our faith is more precious than gold (1 Pet. 1:7). The blood of Christ is precious (1 Pet. 1:19). Christ, the Living Stone, is precious in God's sight (1 Pet. 2:4). He is precious also as the Cornerstone (1 Pet. 2:6). To all who believe, He is precious (1 Pet. 2:7). The imperishable jewel of a gentle and quiet spirit is very precious in God's sight (1 Pet. 3:4). And finally, the **promises** of God are **precious** (2 Pet. 1:4).

Think of some of the promises that relate to the life of holiness. (1) Freedom from sin's dominion (Rom. 6:14). (2) Grace that is sufficient (2 Cor. 12:9). (3) Power to obey His commands (Phil. 4:13). (4) Victory over the devil (Jas. 4:7). (5) Escape when tempted (1 Cor. 10:13). (6) Forgiveness when we confess our sins (1 Jn. 1:9) — and forgetfulness too (Jer. 31:34). (7) Response when we call (Ps. 50:15).

No wonder Peter says the **promises** of God are **precious** and very **great**! These promises enable the believer to escape **the corruption that is in the world through lust**. God has promised all that we need to resist temptation. When passionate cravings come, we can claim the promises. They enable us to escape from the world's corruption — its sexual sin, its drunkenness, its filth, its misery, its treachery, and its strife.

The positive side is that by these same promises we **may be partakers of the divine nature**. This takes place primarily at the time of conversion. Then as we live in the practical enjoyment of what God has promised, we become more and more conformed to His image. For instance, He has promised that the more we think about Him, the more we will become like Him (2 Cor. 3:18). We make this promise a reality by reading the word, studying Christ as He is revealed in it, and following Him. As we do this, the Holy Spirit changes us into His likeness from one degree of glory to another.

1:5 Verses 3 and 4 show that God has given us all that is necessary for the divine life. Because He has, we must be diligent in cultivating it. God does not make us holy against our will or without our involvement. There must be desire, determination, and discipline on our part.

In the development of Christian character, Peter assumes **faith**. After all, he is writing to Christians — to those who have already exercised saving **faith** in the Lord Jesus. So he does not tell them to furnish faith; he assumes that they already have it.

What *is* necessary is that **faith** be supplemented by seven elements of holiness, not adding these one after another, but manifesting all the graces all the time.

Tom Olson's father used to read the passage to his sons as follows:

> Add to your faith the virtue or courage of David; and to the courage of David the knowledge of Solomon; and to the knowledge of Solomon the patience of Job; and to the patience of Job the godliness of Daniel; and to the godliness of Daniel the brotherly kindness of Jonathan; and to the brotherly kindness of Jonathan the love of John.[2]

Lenski suggests:

> The list of seven is arranged with reference to the pseudo-prophets (2:1) and to the way in which they live according to their pretended faith. For praise they supply disgrace; for knowledge, blindness; for self-control, libertinistic license; for perseverance in good, perseverance in evil; for godliness, ungodliness; for fraternal friendliness, dislike for God's children; for genuine love, its terrible absence.[3]

The first characteristic is **virtue**. This may mean piety, goodness of life, or moral excellence, though these seem to be covered later by the word "godliness." It may also be that **virtue** here means spiritual courage before a hostile world, the strength to stand for what is right.

We think of the courage of the martyrs. Archbishop Cranmer was ordered to sign a recantation or be burned at the stake. At first he refused, but then under enormous pressure, his right hand signed the recantation. Later he realized his mistake and notified his executioners to start the fire. At his own request, his hands were untied. Then he held his right hand in the fire and said, "This is the hand that wrote it, and therefore it shall suffer punishment first. This hand hath offended! Perish this unworthy right hand!"[4]

Courage is to be supplemented with **knowledge**, especially the knowledge of spiritual truth. This emphasizes the importance of studying the word of God and obeying its sacred precepts.

> More about Jesus in His Word,
> Holding communion with my Lord.
> Hearing His voice in every line,
> *Making each faithful saying mine.*
> – Eliza E. Hewitt

Through an experiential knowledge of the Bible we develop what Erdman calls "practical skills in the details of Christianity."

1:6 God calls every Christian to a life of discipline. Someone has defined this as the controlling power of the will under the operation of the Spirit of God. There must be discipline in prayer, discipline in Bible study, discipline in the use of time, discipline in curbing bodily appetites, discipline in sacrificial living.

Paul exercised such **self-control**. "Therefore I run thus: not with uncertainty. Thus I fight: not as one who beats the air. But I discipline my body and bring it into subjection, lest, when I have preached to others, I myself should become disqualified" (1 Cor. 9:26, 27).

Audubon, the great naturalist, was willing to undergo prolonged discomfort to learn more of the world of birds. Let Robert G. Lee tell it:

> He counted his physical comforts as nothing compared with success in his work. He would crouch motionless for hours in the dark and fog, feeling himself well-rewarded, if, after weeks of waiting he secured one additional fact about a single bird. He would have to stand almost to his neck in the nearly stagnant water, scarcely breathing, while countless poisonous moccasin snakes swam past his face, and great alligators passed and repassed his silent watch.
>
> "It was not pleasant," he said, as his face glowed with enthusiasm, "but what of that? I have the picture of the bird." He would do that for the picture of the bird.[5]

Because of the example of others, the urgent needs of a perishing world, the personal peril of wrecking our testimony, we should discipline ourselves so that Christ will have the best of our lives.

Self-control should be supplemented with **perseverance**, that is, patient endurance of persecution and adversity. We need to be constantly reminded that the Christian life is a challenge to endure. It is not enough to start off in a blaze of glory; we must persevere in spite of difficulties. The idea that Christianity is an unending round of mountaintop experiences is unrealistic. There is the daily routine, the menial task, the disappointing circumstance, the bitter grief, the shattered plan. **Perseverance** is the art of bearing up and pressing on in the face of all that seems to be against us.

The next virtue is **godliness**. Our lives should be like God, with all that means in the way of practical holiness. There should be such a supernatural quality in our conduct that others will know we are children of the heavenly Father; the family likeness should be unmistakable. Paul reminds us, ". . . godliness is profitable for all things, having promise of the life that now is and of that which is to come" (1 Tim. 4:8).

1:7 Brotherly kindness identifies us to the world as Christ's disciples: "By this all will know that you are My disciples, if you have love for one another" (John 13:35).

Love of the brethren leads to **love** for all mankind. This is not primarily a matter of the emotions but of the will. It is not a sentimental exhilaration to experience but a commandment to obey. In the NT sense, love is supernatural. An unbeliever cannot love as the Bible commands because he does not have divine life. It takes divine life to love one's enemies and to pray for one's executioners. Love manifests itself in giving. For instance, "God so loved the world, that He gave . . . " (John 3:16). "Christ also loved the church and gave . . . " (Eph. 5:25). We can show our love by giving our time, our talents, our treasures, and our lives for others.

T. E. McCully was the father of Ed McCully, one of five young missionaries slain by Auca Indians in Ecuador. One night as we were on our knees together, he prayed, "Lord, let me live long enough to see those fellows saved who killed our boys, that I may throw my arms around them and tell them I love them because they love my Christ." That

is Christian love — when you can pray like that for the guilty murderers of your son.

These seven graces make a full-orbed Christian character.

1:8 There is either advance or decline in the pathway of discipleship — no standing still. There is strength and security in moving forward; danger and failure in retreat.

Failure to persevere in the development of Christian character leads to barrenness, unfruitfulness, blindness, shortsightedness, and forgetfulness.

Barrenness. Only the life lived in fellowship with God can be truly effective. The guidance of the Holy Spirit eliminates **barren** activity and insures maximum efficiency. Otherwise, we are shadow-boxing, or sewing without thread.

Unfruitfulness. It is possible to have considerable **knowledge of** the **Lord Jesus Christ** and yet to be **unfruitful** in that knowledge. Failure to practice what we know leads inevitably to barrenness. Inflow without outgo killed the Dead Sea, and it kills productivity in the spiritual realm as well.

1:9 *Shortsightedness.* There are various degrees of impaired vision which are spoken of as blindness. Shortsightedness here specifies the form of blindness in which man lives for the present rather than the future. He is so occupied with material things that he neglects the spiritual.

Blindness. Whoever lacks the seven characteristics listed in verses 5–7 is blind. He is not aware of what is central in life. He lacks discernment of true spiritual values. He lives in a dark world of shadows.

Forgetfulness. Finally, the man who lacks the seven virtues **has forgotten that he was cleansed from his old sins**. The truth of his redemption has lost its grip on him. He is going back in the direction from which he was once rescued. He is toying with sins that caused the death of God's Son.

1:10 And so Peter exhorts his readers to confirm their **call and election**. These are two facets of God's plan of salvation. **Election** refers to His sovereign, *eternal* choice of individuals to belong to

Himself. **Call** refers to His action *in time* by which the choice is made evident. Our **election** took place before the world was made; our **call** takes place when we are converted. Chronologically, there is first **election**, then **call**. But in human experience we first become aware of His **call**, then we realize we were chosen in Christ from all eternity.

We cannot make our **call and election** more **sure** than they already are; God's eternal purposes can never be thwarted. But we can confirm them by growing in likeness to the Lord. By manifesting the fruit of the Spirit, we can provide unmistakable evidence that we truly belong to Him. A holy life proves the reality of our salvation.

Living a holy life will keep us from stumbling. It is not a question of falling into eternal perdition; the work of Christ delivers us from that. Rather, it refers to falling into sin, disgrace, or disuse. If we fail to progress in divine things, we are in danger of wrecking our lives. But if we walk in the Spirit, we will be spared from being disqualified for His service. God guards the Christian who moves forward for Him. The peril lies in spiritual idleness and blindness.

1:11 Not only is there safety in constant spiritual progress, there is also the promise of a richly-provided **entrance** into **the everlasting kingdom of our Lord and Savior Jesus Christ**. Peter refers here not to the *fact* of our entry but to the *manner* of it. The only basis of admission to the heavenly **kingdom** is faith in the Lord Jesus Christ. But some will have a more abundant **entrance** than others. There will be degrees of reward. And the rewards are here said to depend on the degree of one's conformity to the Savior.

1:12 As he considered the present and eternal implications of this subject, Peter determined to keep on reminding the believers of the importance of the development of Christian character. Even if they already knew it, they needed to be constantly reminded. And so do we. Even though we **are established in the present truth**, there is always the danger of a preoccupied moment or a forgetful hour. So the truth must be constantly repeated.

1:13 Not only was it Peter's intention, but it was his duty **to stir** the saints **up** through frequent reminders **as long as** he lived. He felt the fitness of keeping them from spiritual drowsiness as he approached the close of his life.

1:14 The **Lord** had already revealed to Peter the *fact* that he would die and the *manner* in which he would die (John 21:18, 19). Many years had elapsed since then. The aging apostle knew that in the normal course of events, his death was near. This knowledge gave added impetus to his determination to care for the spiritual welfare of God's people during whatever time remained.

He speaks of his death as laying aside his earthly dwelling or putting off his body or **tent**. Just as a tent is a temporary dwelling for travelers, so the body is the structure in which we dwell during our pilgrimage on earth. In death the tent is taken down. At the Rapture, the body will be raised and changed. In its eternal, glorified form the body is spoken of as a building and a house (2 Cor. 5:1).

The fact that Peter knew he would die does not negate the truth of the imminent Return of Christ for His saints, as is sometimes argued. The true church has always expected that Christ may come at any moment. Only by a special revelation did Peter know that he would not be alive when the Lord returned.

1:15 Not only did the apostle determine personally to remind the saints of the importance of spiritual progress, he also arranged to leave **a reminder** behind in permanent written form. Through his writings, the believers would be able to remind themselves at any time. As a result, Peter's Letters have shed light on the path of men and women now for over nineteen centuries, and will continue doing so till the Coming of our Savior. Also, reliable ancient tradition says that the Gospel of Mark is essentially the eyewitness reminiscences of his spiritual leader, the Apostle Peter.

The importance of written ministry is clear here. It is the written word that lasts. Through the written word, a man's ministry goes on while his body is lying in the grave.

The word Peter uses for **decease** here

is the word from which we get *exodus*. It is the same word used to describe the death of Christ in Luke 9:31. Death is not the cessation of being but the departure from one place to another.

These verses have special value to us as they show what is important to a man of God who is living in the shadow of death. **These things** occurs four times — verses 8, 9, 12 and 15. The great, basic truths of the Christian faith have enormous value when seen from the borders of the eternal world.

1:16 The closing verses of chapter 1 deal with the certainty of Christ's coming in glory. Peter deals first with the certainty of the apostolic witness, then with the certainty of the prophetic word. It is as if Peter joins the NT and the OT, and tells his readers to cling to this united testimony.

He emphasizes that the apostles' testimony was based on fact, not on myth. They **did not follow** cleverly **devised fables** or myths **when** they **made known to** the readers **the power and coming of our Lord Jesus Christ**.

The specific event to which he refers is the Transfiguration of Christ on the mount. It was witnessed by three of the apostles — Peter, James, and John. **The power and coming** is a literary way[6] of saying "the coming in power," or "powerful coming." The Transfiguration was a preview of Christ's **coming** in **power** to reign over all the earth. This is made clear in Matthew's account of the event. In Matthew 16:28 Jesus said, "Assuredly, I say to you, there are some standing here who shall not taste death till they see the Son of Man coming in His kingdom." The very next verses (17:1–8) describe the Transfiguration. On the mount, Peter, James, and John saw the Lord Jesus in the same glory He will have when He reigns for one thousand years. Before they died, those three apostles saw the Son of Man in the glory of His coming kingdom. Thus the Lord's words in Matthew 16:28 were fulfilled in 17:1–8.

Now Peter is emphatic that the apostolic account of the Transfiguration was not based on **fables** (in Greek, myths). This is the word that some modern theologians are using in their attack on the Bible. They are suggesting that we should "demythologize" the Scriptures.

Bultmann spoke of the "mythological element" in the NT. John A. T. Robinson called on Christians to recognize that much of the Bible contains myths:

> In the last century a painful but decisive step forward was taken in the recognition that the Bible does contain "myth," and that this is an important form of religious truth. It was gradually acknowledged, by all except extreme fundamentalists, that the Genesis stories of the Creation and Fall were representations of the deepest truths about man and the universe in the form of myth rather than history, and were none-the-less valid for that. Indeed, it was essential to the defense of Christian truth to recognize and assert that these stories were not history, and not therefore in competition with the alternative accounts of anthropology or cosmology. Those who did not make this distinction were, we can now see, playing straight into the hands of Thomas Huxley and his friends.[7]

To refute the charge of myths, Peter gives three proofs of the Transfiguration: the testimony of *sight*; the testimony of *hearing*; and the testimony of *physical presence*.

As to *sight*, the apostles **were eyewitnesses of** the Lord's **majesty**. John testified, "We beheld His glory, the glory as of the only begotten of the Father" (John 1:14).

1:17 Then there was the testimony of *hearing*. The apostles heard the **voice of God** saying, **"This is My beloved Son, in whom I am well pleased."** This audible expression of honor for the Lord Jesus **came to Him from the Excellent Glory**, that is, from the bright, shining glory cloud, called the Shekinah, which symbolized the presence of God.

1:18 Speaking of James, John, and himself, Peter emphasizes that they distinctly **heard** the **voice** of God **when** they **were with** the Lord **on the holy mountain**. Here is the testimony of three witnesses, which according to Matthew 18:16 is authoritative and competent.

Finally, Peter adds the testimony of *physical appearance*: **we were with Him on the holy mountain**. It was a real-life situation; there could be no question about that.

We do not know the **mountain** on which the Transfiguration took place. If it were identifiable, it would probably be littered with shrines by now.[8] It is called the holy mountain not because it was intrinsically sacred but because it was set apart as the site for a sacred event.

1:19 And so we have the prophetic word confirmed. The OT prophets had predicted Christ's coming in power and great glory. The events on the mount of Transfiguration **confirmed** those prophecies. What the apostles saw did not set aside the OT prophecies or make them any more certain, but simply added confirmation to the predictions. The apostles were given an advance glimpse of the glory of Christ's future kingdom.

F. W. Grant's translation of the rest of verse 19 is helpful. ". . . to which ye do well in taking heed (as to a lamp that shineth in an obscure place, until the day dawn and the morning star ariseth) in your hearts." Notice Grant's use of the parenthesis. According to his translation, we should link **heed** with **in your hearts**. In other words, we should pay attention in our hearts. In the NKJV and many other versions, **the day dawns and the morning star rises in your hearts**, and this presents practical difficulties of interpretation.

The prophetic word is the shining **light**. The dismal or **dark place** is the world. The dawning of **day** signals the end of this present Church Age (Rom. 13:12). The rising of **the morning star** pictures Christ's coming for His saints. Thus the sense of the passage is that we should always keep **the prophetic word** before us, treasuring it **in our hearts**, for it will serve as a **light** in this dark world until the age is ended and Christ appears in the clouds to take His waiting people home to heaven.

1:20 In the final two verses of the chapter, Peter emphasizes that the prophetic Scriptures originated with God and not with man; they were divinely inspired.

No prophecy of Scripture is of any private interpretation (or **origin**, margin). This statement has given rise to a great variety of interpretations. Some are absurd, such as the view that interpretation of the Bible is the right of the church alone and that individuals should not study it!

Other explanations may be true statements, although not the meaning of this passage. For instance, it is true that no verse should be interpreted by itself, but

in the light of the context and of all the rest of Scripture.

But Peter here is dealing with the *origin* of the prophetic word, and not with the way men interpret it after it has been given. The point is that when the prophets sat down to write, they did not give their own **private interpretation** of events or their own conclusions. In other words **interpretation**[9] does not refer to the explaining of the word by those of us who have the Bible in written form; rather it refers to the *way* in which the Word came into being in the first place. D. T. Young writes:

> So the text, rightly understood . . . asserts that Scripture is not human in its ultimate origin. It is God's interpretation, not man's. We often hear of certain statements of Scripture as representing David's opinion, or Paul's opinion, or Peter's opinion. Yet, strictly speaking, we have no man's opinion in those Holy Writings. It is all God's interpretation of things. No prophecy of the Scripture represents an individual's interpretation: men spake as they were moved by the Holy Ghost.[10]

The translation in the NKJV margin, **origin**, is thus quite accurate, and, we believe, superior in context.

1:21 This verse confirms the explanation just given in verse 20. **For prophecy never came by the will of man**. As someone has said, "What they wrote was not a concoction of their own ideas, and it was not the result of human imagination, insight, or speculation."

The fact is that **holy men of God spoke**[11] **as they were moved by the Holy Spirit**. In some way which we cannot fully understand, God directed these **men** as to the very words to write, and yet He did not destroy the individuality or style of the writers. This is one of the key verses in the Bible on divine inspiration. In a day when many are denying the authority of the Scriptures, it is important that we stand firmly for the *verbal, plenary* inspiration of the *inerrant* word.

By *verbal* inspiration we mean that the *words* as originally penned by the forty or more human writers were God-breathed (see 1 Cor. 2:13). God did not give a general outline or some basic ideas, then let the writers phrase them as they wished. The very words they wrote were given **by the Holy Spirit**.

By *plenary* inspiration we mean that *all* the Bible is equally God-given from Genesis through Revelation. It is the word of God (see 2 Tim. 3:16). By *inerrant* we mean that the resultant word of God is totally *without error* in the original, not only in doctrine, but in history, science, chronology, and all other areas.

III. THE RISE OF FALSE TEACHERS PREDICTED (Chap. 2)

2:1 At the close of chapter 1 Peter referred to the prophets of the OT as men who spoke, not by their own will, but as moved by the Holy Spirit. Now he mentions that in addition to the true prophets in the OT period, **there were also false prophets**. And just as there will be bona fide teachers in the Christian era, **there will be false teachers** as well.

These **false teachers** take their place inside the church. They pose as ministers of the gospel. This is what makes the peril so great. If they came right out and said they were atheists or agnostics, people would be on guard. But they are masters of deception. They carry the Bible and use orthodox expressions — though using them to mean something entirely different. The president of a liberal theological seminary acknowledged the strategy as follows:

Churches often change convictions without formally renouncing views to which they were previously committed, and their theologians usually find ways of preserving continuity with the past through re-interpretations.

W. A. Criswell describes the false teacher as follows:

. . . a suave, affable, personable, scholarly man who claims to be the friend of Christ. He preaches in the pulpit, he writes learned books, he publishes articles in the religious magazines. He attacks Christianity from within. He makes the church and the school a lodging place for every unclean and hateful bird. He leavens the meal with the doctrine of the Sadducees.[12]

Where are these false teachers found? To mention perhaps the most obvious places, they are found in:

Liberal and Neo-Orthodox Protestantism

Liberal Roman Catholicism
Unitarianism and Universalism
Russellism (Jehovah's Witnesses)
Mormonism
Christian Science
Unity School of Christianity
Christadelphianism
Armstrongism (The "Radio Church of God")

While professing to be ministers of righteousness, they **secretly bring in** soul-destroying **heresies** alongside true Bible doctrine. It is a deliberately deceptive mixture of the false and the true. Primarily, they peddle a system of denials. Here are some of the denials which can be found among certain of the groups listed above:

They deny the verbal, plenary inspiration of the Bible, the Trinity, the deity of Christ, His virgin birth, and His death as a Substitute for sinners. They are especially vehement in their denial of the value of His shed blood. They deny His bodily resurrection, eternal punishment, salvation by grace through faith in the Lord Jesus Christ, the reality of miracles in the Bible.

Other false teachings common today are:

The Kenosis theory — the heresy that Christ emptied Himself of the attributes of deity. This means that He could sin, make mistakes, etc.

The "God is dead" fantasy, evolution, universal salvation, purgatory, prayers for the dead, etc.

The ultimate sin of false teachers is that they even deny the Master **who bought them**. While they may say nice things about Jesus, refer to His "divinity," His lofty ethics, His superb example, they fail to confess Him as God and as unique Savior.

Nels Ferré wrote, "Jesus never was or became God. . . . To call Jesus God is to substitute an idol for Incarnation."[13]

Methodist Bishop Gerald Kennedy agreed:

I am frank to confess that the statement (that Christ is God) does not please me and it seems far from satisfactory. I would much prefer to have it say that God was in Christ, for I believe that the testimony of the New Testament taken as a whole is against the doctrine of the deity of

Jesus, although I think it bears overwhelming witness to the divinity of Jesus.[14]

In this and in many other ways, **false teachers** deny **the Lord who bought them**. Here we should pause to remind ourselves that while these false teachers to whom Peter refers had been *bought* by the Lord, they had never been *redeemed*. The NT distinguishes between purchase and redemption. All are purchased but not all are redeemed. Redemption applies only to those who receive Jesus Christ as Lord and Savior, availing themselves of the value of His shed blood (1 Pet. 1:18, 19).

In Matthew 13:44 the Lord Jesus is pictured as a man who sold all He had to buy a field. In verse 38 of that same chapter, the field is distinctly said to be the world. So by His death on the cross, the Lord *bought* the world and all who are in it. But He did not *redeem* the whole world. While His work was *sufficient* for the redemption of all mankind, it is only *effective* for those who repent, believe, and accept Him.

The fact that these false teachers were never truly born again is indicated by their destiny. They **bring on themselves swift destruction**. Their doom is eternal punishment in the lake of fire.

2:2 Peter predicts that they will attract a large following. They do this by scuttling the biblical standards of morality and encouraging the indulgence of the flesh. Here are two examples:

Anglican Bishop John A. T. Robinson wrote:

> . . . nothing can of itself always be labeled as "wrong." One cannot, for instance, start from the position "sex relations before marriage" or "divorce" are wrong or sinful in themselves. They may be in 99 cases or even 100 cases out of 100, but they are not intrinsically so, for the only intrinsic evil is lack of love.[15]

In the book *Called to Responsible Freedom*, published by the National Council of Churches, young people are counseled:

> In the personal, individual sense, then, what justifies and sanctifies sexuality is not the external marital status of the people before the law but rather what they feel toward each other in their hearts.

Measured in such a way, holding hands can be very wrong indeed while intimate sex-play can be right and good.[16]

As a result of this type of behavior, taught and practiced by false teachers, **the way of truth** is maligned. Unbelievers develop a deep contempt for Christianity.

2:3 These false teachers are greedy, both in the sexual and financial realms. They have chosen the ministry as a lucrative profession. Their great aim is to build up a large following and thus to increase their income.

They **exploit** people with false **words**. Darby said, "The devil is never more satanic than when he carries a Bible." So these men, with Bible in hand, pose as ministers of righteousness, give out well-known evangelical hymns, and use scriptural expressions. But all this is camouflage for heretical teachings and corrupt morals.

An awful condemnation awaits these religious fifth-columnists. **Their judgment has not been idle**; it has been arming itself for the slaughter. **Their destruction** has **not** been nodding its head in sleep; it has been wide awake, ready to pounce like a panther.

2:4 In verses 4–10, we have three OT examples of God's judgment on apostasy — the angels, the antediluvians, and the cities of Sodom and Gomorrah.

We assume that **the angels who sinned** are those also mentioned in Jude 6. There we learn that: (1) They did not keep their position. (2) They left their proper dwelling. Though we cannot be certain, there is strong reason to believe that these are the same as "the sons of God" mentioned in Genesis 6:2: "The sons of God saw the daughters of men, that they were beautiful; and they took wives for themselves of all whom they chose." Angels are called sons of God in Job 1:6; 2:1. The inference in Genesis 6 is that these sons of God left the angelic position assigned to them, exchanged their dwelling in heaven for one on earth, and intermarried with human wives. The children born to them were *nephilim*, which means "fallen ones" (Gen. 6:4). It seems clear from Genesis 6:3 that God was extremely displeased with these abnormal sexual unions.

Against this view it is generally argued that angels are sexless and therefore cannot marry. But the Bible does not say this. All it says is that *in heaven* they do not marry (Mark 12:25). Angels often appeared in human form in the OT. For example, the two angels whom Lot entertained in Sodom (Gen. 19:1) are described as men in verses 5, 10, 12. They had feet (v. 2) and hands (v. 10); they could eat (v. 3); they had physical strength (vv. 10, 16). It is obvious from the perverted desires of the men of Sodom that these angels had bodies that were capable of sexual abuse (v. 5).

God was outraged by this gross apostasy of **the angels** from His established order. Their doom was to be thrown **down to hell**, committed to pits of utter gloom until the final **judgment**.

2:5 The second illustration of God's direct intervention in punishing sin relates to the people who perished in **the flood**. Their wickedness had been great. Every imagination of the thoughts of their heart was only evil continually (Gen. 6:5). In God's sight the earth was corrupt and filled with violence (Gen. 6:11–13). The Lord was sorry that He had made men on the earth (Gen. 6:6). He was so grieved that He determined to blot them out (Gen. 6:7). He **did not spare the ancient world**, but brought **the flood** upon it to destroy its ungodly inhabitants.

Only **Noah** and his family found favor in the eyes of the Lord. They sought and found refuge in the ark, and rode safely above the storm of God's wrath and indignation.

Noah is described as **a preacher of righteousness**. Doubtless as he built the ark, his hammer blows were interspersed with warnings to the mocking spectators to turn from sin or face God's righteous punishment for their wickedness.

2:6 The third example of God's unsparing judgment concerns the destruction of **Sodom and Gomorrah**. These two cities, somewhere near what is now the southern area of the Dead Sea, were cesspools of sexual perversion. The people accepted homosexuality as a normal way of life. This sin is described in Romans 1:26, 27:

Even their women exchanged the natural use for what is against nature. Likewise also the men, leaving the natural use of the woman, burned in their lust for one another, men with men committing what is shameful, and receiving in themselves the penalty of their error which was due.

God did not look upon this unrestrained degeneracy as sickness but as sin. In order to show to all succeeding generations His extreme hatred of homosexuality, He rained fire and brimstone on Sodom and Gomorrah (Gen. 19:24), reducing them to ashes. The destruction was so complete that there is considerable doubt today as to the exact location of the cities. They serve as an example to any who would legalize this sin or condone it as a disease.

It is significant that liberal clergymen today are becoming increasingly outspoken in favor of sexual perversion. One official of the United Church of Christ, writing in *Social Action*, recommended that the church cease to discriminate against homosexuals in admission to seminaries, in ordination, and in employment on church staffs. Ninety Episcopal priests recently decided that homosexual acts between consenting adults are morally neutral. False religious teachers are in the forefront of movements to legalize this sin.

It is no accident that this Epistle, dealing with *apostasy*, should have so much to say about *immorality*; the two often go together. Apostasy often has its roots in moral failure. For instance, a man may fall into serious sexual sin. Instead of acknowledging his guilt and finding cleansing through the blood of Christ, he decides to cast off the knowledge of God, which condemns his actions, and live in practical atheism. A. J. Pollock tells of meeting a young man who had once professed to be a Christian but who was now full of doubts and denials. Mr. Pollock asked him, "My friend, what sin have you been indulging lately?" The young man hung his head, brought the conversation to a quick halt, and went away shamefacedly.[17]

2:7 The same God who visits destruction on the ungodly rescues the **righteous**. Peter illustrates this by the experience of **Lot**. If we had only the OT account of Lot, we might not think him a true believer at all. In the Genesis account, he almost appears as a status-seeking opportunist, willing to put up with sin and corruption in order to make a place and name for himself in the world. But Peter, writing by inspiration, tells us that he was a **righteous** man **who was oppressed by the filthy conduct of the wicked**. God saw that Lot had genuine faith, and that he loved righteousness and hated sin.

2:8 To emphasize that Lot really was a **righteous man** in spite of appearances to the contrary, Peter repeats that his soul was **tormented** daily by the things he heard and saw in Sodom. The vile immorality of the people caused him deep suffering.

2:9 The conclusion is that **the Lord knows how to deliver the godly** and to punish the ungodly. He can rescue His people from trial, and at the same time **reserve the unjust under punishment for the day of judgment**.

The wicked are reserved for hell (v. 9) and hell for the wicked (v. 17). By way of contrast, an inheritance is reserved for believers, and they are kept for the inheritance (1 Pet. 1:4, 5).

2:10 God's ability to keep wicked men under restraints until their final trial is **especially** true of the class of people described in this chapter — false teachers whose lives are contaminated by sexual **uncleanness**, who advocate rebellion against governmental **authority**, and who boldly hurl insults at high officials.

It is no secret that false religious leaders, posing as ministers of Christ, are often characterized by low moral standards. They not only indulge in illicit sexual activities themselves, but they openly advocate libertinism. The Episcopal Chaplain of a girls' school in Baltimore, Maryland, wrote:

We all ought to relax and stop feeling guilty about our sexual activities, thoughts and desires. And I mean this, whether those thoughts are heterosexual, homosexual or autosexual. . . . Sex is fun . . . and this means that there are no laws attached which you ought to do or not to do. There are no rules of the game, so to speak.[18]

It is also significant that liberal religious leaders are commonly in the fore-

front of movements that advocate the violent overthrow of the government. Modernistic ministers have been frequently affiliated with subversive political causes. A director of church and community affairs for the Presbytery of Philadelphia said, "I don't think we preclude this (the use of bombs and grenades by the church) in the future, if all non-violent means prove ineffectual."

These men are bold and willful. Their brazen repudiation of all duly constituted authority seems to have no limits. No language is too extreme for them to use in reviling their rulers. The fact that human governments are ordained by God (Rom. 13:1) and that it is forbidden to speak evil of them (Acts 23:5) does not influence such men in the least. They seem to delight in shocking people by their belligerent denunciation of **dignitaries** (Greek: "glories" or "glorious ones"). This is a general term that could include all those, whether angels or men, who have been vested with governmental authority by God. Here it probably means *human* rulers.

2:11 The audacity of these professed ministers of religion is without parallel in the angelic realm. Although **angels . . . are greater** than men **in power and might**, they do not pronounce **a reviling accusation against** the glorious ones **before the Lord**. Here the reference to the glorious ones seems to apply to *angels* who are in positions of authority.

It is generally thought that this obscure allusion to angels is the same as that in Jude 9: "Yet Michael the archangel, in contending with the devil when he disputed about the body of Moses, dared not bring against him a railing accusation, but said, 'The Lord rebuke you.' " We are not sure as to why there was a controversy over the body of Moses. The important point for us is this: Michael recognized that Satan has a position of authority in the world of demons, and although Satan had no jurisdiction over Michael, yet the latter would not revile him. Think, then, of the boldness of men who dare to do what holy angels shrink from doing! And think too of the corresponding judgment that will repay such defiance!

2:12 **These** apostate religious leaders resemble irrational animals. Instead of using the powers of reasoning which distinguish them from animals, they live as if the gratification of their bodily appetites is the very essence of existence. Just as many animals seem to have no higher destiny than to be killed and butchered, so the false teachers lunge forward to destruction, heedless of what is their true calling — to glorify God and to enjoy Him forever.

They **speak evil of the things they do not understand**. Their ignorance is never more glaring than when they criticize the Bible. Because they are devoid of divine life, they are utterly unable to understand the words, ways, and works of God (1 Cor. 2:14). Yet they pose as experts in the spiritual realm. A humble believer can see more on his knees than they can see on their tiptoes.

They will be destroyed in the same destruction as the animals. Since they choose to live like animals, they will die like them. Their death will not mean extinction, but they will die ingloriously and without hope.

2:13 In death they will suffer for their **unrighteousness**. As Phillips paraphrases it, "Their wickedness has earned them an evil end and they will be paid in full."

These people are so shameless and abandoned that they carry on their sinful activities in full daylight. Most men wait for the cover of darkness to **carouse** (John 3:19); hence the dim lights of the bar and the brothel (1 Thess. 5:7). The false teachers have cast off the restraints that usually hide sin in the shadows.

When they eat with Christian people, they are blots **and blemishes**, that is, unsightly, impure intruders, who luxuriate in their excessive eating and drinking. In his description of these same people, Jude says: "These are spots in your love feasts, while they feast with you without fear, serving only themselves" (Jude 12). When the false teachers attended the love feasts held in connection with the Lord's Supper in the early days of the church, they were utterly intemperate and totally unmindful of the spiritual significance of the feast. Instead of thinking of others, which love always does, they selfishly looked after themselves.

2:14 Even more scandalous is the fact that their **eyes** are **full of adultery and that cannot cease from sin**. This describes men who preach supposedly religious sermons, administer the ordinances, counsel the members of their congregation; yet their **eyes** are constantly looking for women with whom they might have an adulterous affair. Their thirst for lechery, disguised perhaps under the ministerial "cloth," seems to be limitless.

They entice **unstable souls**. Perhaps they misuse passages of Scripture to condone sin. Or they explain that matters of right and wrong are largely determined by our culture. Or they suavely reassure their dupes that nothing is wrong if it is done in love. It is easy for unsteady souls to reason that if a thing is all right for a religious leader, it certainly must be all right for a member of the laity.

They have hearts **trained in covetous practices**. They are not rank amateurs, but are schooled in the art of seduction. While the word **covetous** may cover any kind of excessive craving, the context here seems to point primarily to sexual greed.

As Peter thinks of this enormous travesty of Christianity, of the sin that these apostates cause to be associated with the name of Christ, he exclaims, **accursed children**! It is not that he is cursing them; he is simply foreseeing that they will experience the curse of God in all its fury.

2:15 In several ways, these false teachers resemble the prophet **Balaam the son of Beor**. They falsely pose as spokesmen for God (Num. 22:38). They induce others to sin (Rev. 2:14). But the chief likeness is that they use the ministry as a means of financial enrichment. **Balaam** was a Midianite prophet hired by the king of Moab to curse Israel. His motive for doing this was money.

2:16 On one of his attempts to curse Israel, Balaam and his donkey met the angel of the Lord (that is, the Lord Jesus in one of His pre-incarnate appearances). The donkey repeatedly refused to go on. When Balaam whipped it, the **donkey** rebuked him in human language (Num. 22:15–34). This was an astonishing phenomenon — **a dumb donkey speaking with** a human **voice** (and showing better sense than its master!). But the miracle did not shock Balaam out of his **madness.**

Lenski says:

Balaam is a fearful example of a man who was "a prophet," whom God told what not to do, whom God hindered in his wrongdoing by even letting a dumb ass speak to him, but who in spite of everything secretly clung to his love for what he thought he could get out of unrighteousness, and so perished.[19]

God does not rebuke false teachers by dumb animals today. But there is every reason to believe that in other ways He often rebukes their madness and folly and encourages them to turn to the right way, which is Christ. God often uses the simple testimony of a humble believer to confound these men who pride themselves on their superior knowledge and on their ecclesiastical position. It may be by quoting a verse of Scripture or asking an incisive question, that a Spirit-filled "layman" leaves the modern-day Balaam to writhe in his humiliation and anger.

2:17 Peter likens the false teachers to waterless springs. Needy people go to them for refreshment and for relief from spiritual thirst but are disappointed. They **are wells without water.** They are also **clouds carried by a tempest.** The **clouds** hold promise of rain for land that has suffered from prolonged drought. But then a windstorm comes and drives the clouds away. Hopes are dashed; parched tongues are unsatisfied.

The nether gloom **of darkness** is **reserved for** these religious charlatans. Pretending to be ministers of the gospel, they actually have no good news to offer. People go to them for bread and get a stone. The penalty for such deception is an eternity[20] in **the blackness of darkness.**

2:18 **They speak great swelling words of emptiness,** or as Knox translates it, they use "fine phrases that have no meaning." This is an accurate description of the words of many liberal preachers and false cultists. They are accomplished orators, holding audiences spellbound by their grandiose rhetoric. Their erudite vocabulary attracts undiscerning people. What their sermons lack in content, they make up for in a dogmatic, forceful presentation. But when they have finished they have said nothing. As an example of this sort of sterile sermon, here is a quotation from a well-known theologian of our day:

It is not a relationship of either parity or disparity, but of similarity. This is what we think and this is what we express as the true knowledge of God, although in faith we still know and remember that everything that we know as "similarity" is not identical with the similarity meant here. Yet we also know and remember, and again in faith, that the similarity meant here is pleased to reflect itself in what we know as similarity and call by this name, so that in our thinking and speaking similarity becomes similar to the similarity posited in the true revelation of God (to which it is, in itself, not similar) and we do not think and speak falsely but rightly when we describe the relationship as one of similarity.

The strategy of these false teachers is to **allure** people by promising unrestrained indulgence in every form of lust and passion. They teach that since our bodily appetites are God-given, they should not be restrained. To do so, they say, would cause severe personality disturbances. And so they advocate sexual experimentation before marriage and relaxed morals after marriage.

Their victims are **the ones who have actually escaped**[21] **from those who live in error.** These unsaved people once indulged freely in sinful pleasures, but they've had a change of heart. They decide to reform, to turn over a new leaf, and to start attending church. Instead of going to a Bible-believing church, they wander into a service where one of these false shepherds is holding forth. Instead of hearing the gospel of salvation through faith in Christ, they hear sin condoned and permissiveness encouraged. It all comes as rather a surprise; they had always thought that sin was wrong and that the church was against it. Now they learn that sin is given religious approval!

2:19 The apostate ministers talk a lot about freedom, but they mean freedom from divine authority and freedom to sin. Actually, this is not **liberty** but the worst form of **bondage. They themselves are slaves of corruption.** Bound by the chains of evil lusts and habits, they are powerless to break free.

2:20 Verses 20-22 refer, not to the false teachers themselves, but to their victims. They are people who had reformed but who had not been born again. **Through** a partial **knowledge of . . . Christ** and of Christian principles, they had turned from a life of sin and begun a moral house-cleaning.

Then they come under the influence of false teachers who mock puritanical virtue and crusade for liberation from moral inhibitions. They become involved again in the very sins from which they had been temporarily delivered. As a matter of fact, they sink lower than before, because now that religious restraints are gone, there is nothing to hold them back. So it is true that their **latter** state is **worse than** the first.

2:21 The greater a person's privilege, the greater his responsibility. The more a person knows of Christian standards, the more obligated he is to live up to them. **It would** be **better** never **to have known** God's holy requirements, **than having known** them to turn back to the filth of the world.

2:22 These people illustrate **the true proverb** concerning **a dog** that **returns to his own** disgusting **vomit** (see Prov. 26:11) and a washed **sow** that goes back **to her wallowing in the mire**. It is significant that Peter uses the **dog** and **sow** as illustrations. Under the Law of Moses, both of these were unclean animals. There is no suggestion in the proverb that they had experienced any change in their natures. They were unclean before they were delivered from the **vomit** and the mud, and they were *still* unclean when they returned to them.

So it is with the people of whom Peter wrote. They had undergone a moral reformation but they had never received a new nature. In the language of Matthew 12:43–45, their house was empty, swept, and put in order, but they had never invited the Savior to dwell in it. The unclean spirit which was cast out went and found seven other spirits more evil than himself to occupy the empty house. And the last state of that house was worse than its initial condition.

This passage should not be used to teach that true believers may fall from grace and be lost. These people never were true believers. They never received a new nature. They demonstrated by their last state that their nature was still unclean and evil. The lesson is, of course, that reformation alone is not only insufficient, but is positively dangerous, because it can lull a person into a false security. Man can receive a new nature only by being born again. He is born again through repentance toward God and faith in our Lord Jesus Christ.

IV. THE RISE OF SCOFFERS PREDICTED (Chap. 3)

3:1 From the subject of false teachers in chapter 2, Peter turns to the certain rise of scoffers in the last days. In this Letter as in the previous one, he first encourages his readers to cling to the Bible.

3:2 They should remember the predictions of **the holy prophets** — found in the OT; and they should remember the teaching **of the Lord** as conveyed through **the apostles** — this is preserved in the NT. The Bible is the only true safeguard in days of declension.

3:3 The united testimony of the prophets and apostles was that **scoffers** would **come in the last days**, following **their own lusts**. Christians should remember this. They should not be bowled over by the arrogant and blasphemous denials of these men. Rather they should see in them a definite indication that the end of the age is nearing.

These mockers follow **their own** passions. Having rejected the knowledge of God, they fearlessly indulge their appetites. They advocate permissiveness with total disregard of any impending judgment.

3:4 Their primary scoff has to do with the coming of Christ. Their attitude is, **"Where is the promise of His coming?"** meaning, "Where is the *fulfillment* of the promise?" But what do they mean by **His coming**?

Do they mean Christ's coming for His saints, which we speak of as the Rapture (1 Thess. 4:13–18)? It is doubtful that these scoffers know anything about this first phase of the Lord's return.

Do they mean Christ's coming with His saints to set up His universal kingdom (1 Thess. 3:13)? It is possible that this could be included in their thinking.

But it seems clear from the rest of the passage that they are thinking of the *final judgment* of God on the earth, or what is commonly called the end of the world. They are thinking of the fiery destruction of the heavens and earth at the end of the Millennium.

What they really say is this: "You Christians have been threatening us with warnings about a terrible judgment upon the world. You tell us that God is going to intervene in history, punish the wicked, and destroy the earth. It's all a pack of nonsense. We have nothing to fear. We can live as we please. There is no evidence that God ever has intervened in history; why should we believe that He ever will?"

Their conclusion is based on the careless hypothesis that **"since the fathers fell asleep, all things continue as they were from the beginning of creation."** They say that nature invariably follows uniform laws, that there are no supernatural interventions, that there is a natural explanation for everything.

They believe in the law of uniformitarianism. This law states that existing processes in nature have always acted in the same manner and with essentially the same intensity as at present, and that these processes are sufficient to account for all the changes that have taken place.

There is a vital link between the law of uniformitarianism and the usual theories of evolution. The theory of the progressive development of living organisms from pre-existing types depends on the supposition that conditions have been fairly uniform. If this earth has been racked by cataclysms and catastrophes, then some of the presuppositions of Darwinian evolution are affected.

3:5 The scoffers deliberately ignore one fact — the flood. God *did* intervene at one time in the affairs of men, and the specific purpose of His intervention was to punish wickedness. If it happened once, it can happen again.

It is a withering indictment of these men that they are **willfully** ignorant. They pride themselves on being knowledgeable. They profess to be objective in their reasoning. They boast that they ad-here to the principles of scientific investigation. But the fact is that they deliberately ignore a well-attested fact of history — the deluge. They should take a course in geology!

For this they willfully forget: that by the word of God the heavens were of old, and the earth standing out of the water and in the water, . . . **perished. The heavens** and **the earth** were formed **by the word of God**; He spoke and they came into being (Heb. 11:3). The **earth** was formed, Peter says, **out of the water and in the water.** We confess that there are depths in this statement that we cannot fully understand. We do know from Genesis 1:2 that the face of the earth was once covered with water. Then in verse 6 we read that God made a firmament or expanse to separate the water on the earth from the mist or cloud-cover over the earth. We assume from this that the earth had been covered by a thick mist of water in which life could not have been sustained. The firmament provided the clear atmosphere in which we can breathe. In Genesis 1:9, the continents were separated from the oceans; this may be what is referred to by the expression **"the earth standing out of water"** (see also Ps. 24:2).

Whatever the scientific implications of Peter's statement, we do know that the earth is a watery, cloud-covered world; three quarters of the surface is ocean, and much of it is veiled by mists. As far as we know, the earth is the only watery planet, and therefore the only one that can sustain human life.

3:6 From its inception, the earth was stored with the means of its own destruction. It had water in its subterranean depths, water in the seas, and water in the clouds above. Finally God released the waters from below and above (Gen. 7:11), the land was inundated, and all life outside the ark was destroyed.

The critics willfully disregard this fact of history. It is interesting that the flood has emerged in recent years as the object of bitter attack. But the record of it is written in stone, in the traditions of ancient peoples and modern, and best of all, in God's Holy word.

3:7 When God created the earth, He seeded it with sufficient water to destroy it. In the same manner, He seeded the heavens and the earth with enough fire to destroy them.

In this nuclear age, we understand that matter is stored-up energy. The splitting of an atomic nucleus results in the fiery release of enormous quantities of energy. So all the matter in the world represents tremendous explosive potential. At present it is held together by the Lord (Col. 1:17, "in Him all things consist"). If His restraining hand were removed, the elements would melt. In the meantime the heavens and the earth are being reserved for fire until the day of judgment and perdition of ungodly men.

3:8 Why then the long delay in God's judgment? Well, first we should remember that God is timeless. He does not live in a sphere of time as we do. After all, time is determined by the relation of the sun to the earth, and God is not limited by this relationship.

With the Lord one day is as a thousand years, and a thousand years as one day. He can expand a day into a millennium, or compress a millennium into a day. He can either spread or concentrate His activities.

3:9 God has promised to end the history of ungodly men with judgment. If there seems to be delay, it is not because God is unfaithful to His promise. It is because He is patient. He does not want any to perish. His desire is that all should come to repentance. He purposely extends the time of grace so that men might have every opportunity to be saved.

In Isaiah 61:2 we read of the year of the Lord's favor and the day of His vengeance. This suggests that He delights to show mercy and that judgment is His strange work (Isa. 28:21). It may also indicate that He can extend His longsuffering 1000 years and condense His judgments into one day.

He waited 120 years before He sent the flood. Now He has waited several thousand years before destroying the world with fire.

3:10 But the day of the Lord will come. The day of the Lord refers to any period when God acts in judgment. It was used in the OT to describe any time when God punished evildoers and tri-

umphed over His foes (Isa. 2:12; 13:6, 9; Ezek. 13:5; 30:3; Joel 1:15; 2:1, 11, 31; 3:14; Amos 5:18, 20; Obad. 15; Zeph. 1:7, 14; Zech. 14:1; Mal. 4:5). In the NT it is a period of time with various stages:

1. It refers to the Tribulation, a seven-year period when God will judge unbelieving Israel (1 Thess. 5:2; 2 Thess. 2:2, NU Text).
2. It includes His return to earth when He will inflict vengeance on those who do not know God and who do not obey the gospel of the Lord Jesus (2 Thess. 1:7–10).
3. It is used of the Millennium when Christ will rule the earth with a rod of iron (Acts 2:20).
4. It refers to the final destruction of the heavens and the earth with fire. That is the meaning here in chapter 3.

It will come as a thief — that is, unexpectedly and destructively. The heavens will pass away. This certainly means the atmospheric heavens, and may mean the stellar heavens, but it cannot mean the third heaven — the dwelling place of God. As they pass away with a deafening explosion, the elements will be dissolved with fervent heat. The elements here refer to the constituent parts of matter. All matter will be destroyed in what resembles a universal nuclear holocaust.

Both the earth and the works that are in it will be burned up.[22] Not only the works of the natural creation, but all civilization will be consumed. The great capitals of the world, the imposing buildings, the phenomenal scientific productions are all marked for utter destruction.

3:11 Now Peter turns from the scoffers to the saints and presses home the obligations that devolve on them. Therefore, since all these things will be dissolved, what manner of persons ought you to be in holy conduct and godliness. Everything material has the stamp of oblivion upon it. The things of which men boast, the things for which they live are passing things at best. To live for material things is to live for the temporary. Common sense tells us to turn from the tinsel and toys of this world and live in holiness and godliness. It is a simple matter of living for eternity rather than time, of emphasizing the spiritual rather than the material, of choosing the permanent over the passing.

3:12 Believers should also be expectant. They should wait for and earnestly desire **the coming of the day of God**. Some use the words **"hastening the coming of the day of God"** to teach that we can hurry up the coming of the Lord by lives of devoted, unflagging service. But there are two difficulties in this teaching. First of all, the Day of God is *not* the coming of the Lord. Secondly, even if it were, there is real reason to question whether the time of Christ's coming can be altered by the zeal of His people.

The day of God refers to the eternal state. It follows the final phase of the Day of the Lord when the heavens and earth will be destroyed. **The day of God** is the Day of His complete and final triumph. For this reason it is a **day** we should wait for and earnestly desire.

In speaking of **the day of God**, Peter does not say "in which," but **because of which the heavens will be dissolved, being on fire, and the elements will melt with fervent heat. The day of God** is not the time in which the final destruction takes place. Instead, this ultimate judgment must occur before the Day of God can be ushered in.

3:13 In verse 12, believers were urged to wait for the Day of God. Here they are described as waiting **for the new heavens and a new earth in which righteousness dwells**. This supports the view that the Day of God refers to the eternal state when there will be **new heavens and a new earth**.

In Isaiah 65:17; 66:22, the **new heavens and new earth** are used to describe the Millennium as well as the eternal state. We know those passages include the Millennium because sin will be present (65:20) and children will be born (65:23). Peter applies the words exclusively to the eternal state; the existing heavens and earth will have already passed away.

Peter speaks of **righteousness** *dwelling* **in the new heavens** and **new earth**. At the present time grace reigns through righteousness (Rom. 5:21). In the Millennium righteousness will *reign* (Isa. 32:1); in eternity, righteousness will *dwell*. In the earthly kingdom, Christ will rule with a rod of iron and righteousness will be enforced by Him. In that sense righteousness will reign. But in eternity, there will be no need for an iron rod. **Righteousness** will be at home. No sin will enter to mar the peace or beauty of that scene.

3:14 The truth concerning the new heavens and the new earth should deepen our desire to live holy "as to the Lord." It is not only a truth that we should hold but one that should hold us. Knowing that we shall soon stand before God should create within us a desire to be **without spot and blameless**, that is, to be morally clean. It should make us zealous to be found in a state of **peace**, not strife.

3:15   And consider that the longsuffering of our Lord is salvation. His delay in judgment is to give men full opportunity to be saved. As we consider the multiplying wickedness of men, we often wonder how the Lord can put up with it any longer. His forbearance is astonishing. But there is a reason for it. He does not desire the death of the wicked. He longs to see people turn from their wicked ways and be saved.

As also our beloved brother Paul, according to the wisdom given to him, has written to you. Several interesting points emerge in this allusion to **Paul**:

1. First, Peter speaks of **Paul** as **our beloved brother**, and this in spite of the fact that Paul had publicly rebuked Peter in Antioch for acting insincerely (Gal. 2:11–21). Obviously Peter had accepted the rebuke humbly. We should all be able to accept correction without harboring animosities.

2. Peter acknowledged that Paul was **given** divine **wisdom** in writing his Epistles. This is surely an intimation that Peter considered Paul's writings to be divinely inspired.

3. Peter's readers had apparently read one or more of Paul's Epistles. This may mean that the Epistles were addressed directly to them or that they were circulated in that area.

Which of Paul's Letters says **that the longsuffering of our Lord is salvation**?

Romans 2:4 reads: "Or do you despise the riches of His goodness, forbearance, and longsuffering, not knowing that the goodness of God leads you to repentance?"

3:16 In all his epistles Paul spoke of the great truths with which Peter has been dealing in his two Letters; truths such as the new birth, the deity of Christ, His life of sinless suffering, His substitutionary death, His resurrection, His ascension, His coming again, the Day of the Lord and the eternal state.

Some Bible truths are **hard to understand**, such as the Trinity, God's election and man's free will, the mystery of suffering, etc. It should not disturb us if we find matters in the Bible which are above our understanding. The word of God is infinite and inexhaustible. In studying it we must always be willing to give God credit for knowing things which we can never fully fathom.

Peter is not criticizing Paul's writings when he speaks of **things hard to understand**. It is not Paul's style of writing which is difficult to understand but the subjects which he treats. Barnes writes: "Peter refers not to the difficulties of understanding what Paul *meant*, but to the difficulty of comprehending the great *truths* which he taught."[23]

Instead of accepting them simply by faith, **untaught and unstable people twist** some of these difficult truths **to their own destruction**. Some false cults, for instance, twist the law into a way of salvation rather than a revealer of sin. Others make baptism the door to heaven. They do this not only with Paul's writings but with other Scriptures as well.

Notice that Peter here puts Paul's writings on the same level **as the rest of the Scriptures**, that is, the OT and whatever portions of the NT were then available. He acknowledges that the Pauline Epistles were part of the inspired sacred Scriptures.

3:17 Believers must be constantly on guard against the peril of **error**. The knowledge that there will always be false teachers who corrupt and imitate the truth should keep us alert. It is easy for the unsuspecting to be swept off their feet by the **error of the wicked** and to lose their spiritual balance.

3:18 Once again Peter teaches that continued progress in divine things is a great protection against the peril of false teachers. There must be a twofold growth — **in grace and** in **knowledge. Grace** is the practical demonstration of the fruit of the Spirit. Growth in **grace** is not increased head knowledge or tireless activity; it is increasing likeness to the Lord Jesus. **Knowledge** means acquaintance with the Lord through the word. Growth in **knowledge** means increasing study of and subjection to His words, works, and ways.

But Peter cannot close his Epistle with an exhortation to the saints. The climax must be **glory** to the Savior. And so we find the lovely doxology: **To Him be the glory, both now and forever. Amen.** This, after all, is the ultimate reason for our existence — to glorify Him — and therefore no concluding note to this Epistle could be more fitting.

ENDNOTES

[1](Intro) E. G. Homrighausen, "The Second Epistle of Peter," *Exposition, IB,* XII, 1957, p. 166.

[2](1:5) From the spoken ministry of Tom Olson, a personal friend of the author.

[3](1:5) R. C. H. Lenski, *The Interpretation of the Epistles of St. Peter, St. John and St. Jude,* p. 266.

[4](1:5) This famous story is widely recounted. See, for example, S. M. Houghton, *Sketches from Church History,* pp. 114-116.

[5](1:6) Robert G. Lee, *Seven Swords and Other Messages,* p. 46.

[6](1:16) When we use two words to give one meaning, such as "good and mad" to mean *very* mad, it is called a *hendiadys* (from the Greek for "one through two"). The Bible uses this figure of speech frequently, as here, so it is good to be able to recognize it.

[7](1:16) John A. T. Robinson, *Honest to God,* p. 32, 33.

[8](1:18) Roman Catholic tradition makes Mt. Tabor the site of the Transfiguration, and it does indeed have shrines on it. Historically this tradition is impossible, as Tabor is not a high mountain and the Gospels say it was "exceedingly high." Also, there was probably a

Roman garrison on Tabor in the time of our Lord, a poor backdrop for a private revelation! Mt. Hermon, a high snow-capped range north of Galilee is a very likely site.

[9](1:20) The Greek word *epilusis* can be translated "origin" (NKJV margin) as well as "interpretation."

[10](1:20) Dinsdale T. Young, *The Unveiled Evangel*, pp. 13, 14.

[11](1:21) The critical text (NU) reads "but men spoke from God."

[12](2:1) Wallie Amos Criswell, further documentation unavailable.

[13](2:1) Nels Ferré, *The Sun and the Umbrella*, pp. 35, 112.

[14](2:1) Gerald Kennedy, *God's Good News*, p. 125.

[15](2:2) Robinson, *Honest*, p. 118.

[16](2:2) NCC, *Called to Responsible Freedom*, p. 11.

[17](2:6) A. J. Pollock, *Why I Believe the Bible is the Word of God*, p. 23.

[18](2:10) *Pageant Magazine*, October, 1965.

[19](2:16) Lenski, *Interpretation*, pp. 326, 327.

[20](2:17) The word "forever" is omitted by NU here but not in the close parallel in Jude 13.

[21](2:18) The NU text here reads "are barely escaping."

[22](3:10) Instead of "burned up" (*katakaēsetai*) the NU text reads "found" (*heurethēsetai*), perhaps meaning "laid bare."

[23](3:16) Albert Barnes, *Notes on the New Testament*, X:268.

BIBLIOGRAPHY

See Bibliography at the end of 1 Peter.

THE FIRST EPISTLE OF JOHN

Introduction

"It is not Christ walking on the sea, but His ordinary walk, that we are called on here to imitate."
— Martin Luther

I. Unique Place in the Canon

John's First Epistle is like a family photograph album. It describes those who are members of the family of God. Just as children resemble their parents, so God's children have His likeness too. This Letter describes the similarities. When a person becomes a child of God, he receives the life of God — eternal life. All who have this life show it in very definite ways. For instance, they acknowledge Jesus Christ as their Lord and Savior, they love God, they love the children of God, they obey His commandments, and they do not go on sinning. These, then, are some of the hallmarks of eternal life. John wrote this Epistle so that all who have these family traits may *know* that they have eternal life (1 Jn. 5:13).

First John is unusual in many ways. Although it is a real Letter that was actually sent, neither the author nor the addressees are named. Doubtless they knew each other well. Another remarkable thing about this lovely book is that extremely deep spiritual truths are expressed in such short, simple sentences, with a vocabulary to match. Who says that deep truth must be put into complex sentences? We fear that what some people foolishly praise as "deep" preaching or writing is merely muddy or *unclear.*

First John merits long meditation and sincere study. The apparently repetitious style actually repeats with slight *differences* — and it is these shades of meaning that must be noted.

II. Authorship†

The *external evidence* for the author-

ship of 1 John is early and strong. Specifically quoting the Epistle as by John, the author of the Fourth Gospel, are: Irenaeus, Clement of Alexandria, Tertullian, Origen, and his pupil, Dionysius.

Like the author of Hebrews, the writer of 1 John does not mention his name. Unlike Hebrews, however, 1 John has convincing *internal evidences* of its authorship.

The first four verses show that the writer knew Christ well and spent time with Him. This narrows down the possibilities of authorship considerably and coincides with the tradition that it is the Apostle John.

Strengthening this is the apostolic tone of the Letter: the author writes with authority, with the tenderness of an older spiritual leader ("my little children"), and even with a dogmatic note.

The thought, vocabulary ("abide," "light," "new," "commandment," "word," etc.), and expressions ("eternal life," "lay down one's life," "pass from death into life," "Savior of the world," "take away sins," "works of the devil," and others), coincide with the Fourth Gospel and the two other Epistles by John.

Likewise the Hebrew style of parallelism and simple sentence structure characterize both the Gospel and this Epistle. In short, if we accept the Fourth Gospel as by John the Apostle we should have no trouble crediting the Epistle to him as well.

III. Date

Some believe that John wrote his three canonical Letters in the 60's from

†See p. i.

1123

Jerusalem before the Romans destroyed it. More commonly, a date late in the first century is accepted (A.D. 80-95). The fatherly tone of the Epistles goes well with the ancient tradition of the aged Apostle John being carried into the congregation and saying, "Little children, love one another."

IV. Background and Theme†

At the time John was writing, a false sect had arisen which became known as Gnosticism (Gk. *gnōsis* = knowledge). These Gnostics professed to be Christians but claimed to have *additional knowledge*, superior to what the apostles taught. They claimed that a person could not be completely fulfilled until he had been initiated into their deeper "truths." Some taught that matter was evil, and that therefore the Man Jesus could not be God. They made a distinction between Jesus and the Christ. "The Christ" was a divine emanation which came upon Jesus at His baptism and left before His death, perhaps in the Garden of Gethsemane. According to them, Jesus *did* die, but the Christ did *not* die. They insisted, as Michael Green put it, that "the heavenly Christ was too holy and spiritual to be soiled by permanent contact with human flesh." In short, they denied the Incarnation, that Jesus is the Christ, and that Jesus Christ is both God and Man. John realized that these people were not true Christians, and so he warned his readers against them by showing that the Gnostics did not have the marks of true children of God.

According to John, a person either is a child of God or he is not; there is no in-between ground. That is why this Epistle is filled with such extreme opposites as light and darkness, love and hatred, truth and lie, death and life, God and the devil. At the same time, it should be noted that the apostle likes to describe people by their habitual behavior. In discerning between Christians and non-Christians, for instance, he does not base his conclusion on a single act of sin, but rather on what characterizes the person. Even a broken clock tells the correct time twice in every twenty-four hours! But a good clock tells the correct time regularly. So the general, day-by-day behavior of a Christian is holy and righteous, and by this he is known as a child of God. John uses the word "know" a great many times. The Gnostics professed to *know* the truth, but John here sets forth the true facts of the Christian Faith, which can be *known* with certainty. He describes God as light (1:5); love (4:8, 16); truth (5:6); and life (5:20). This does not mean that God is not a Person, but rather that God is the source of these four blessings. John also speaks of God as righteous (2:29; 3:7); pure (3:3); and sinless (3:5).

While John does use simple *words*, the *thoughts* he expresses are often deep, and sometimes difficult to understand. As we study this book, therefore, we should pray that the Lord will help us to grasp the meaning of His word and to obey the truth as He reveals it to us.

†See p. ii.

OUTLINE

Commentary

I. PROLOGUE: THE CHRISTIAN FELLOWSHIP (1:1–4)

1:1 The doctrinal foundation of all true fellowship is the Person of the Lord Jesus Christ. There can be no true fellowship with those who hold false views concerning Him. The first two verses teach His eternity and the reality of His Incarnation. The same One who existed from all eternity with God the Father came down into this world as a real Man. The reality of His Incarnation is indicated by the fact that the apostles **heard** Him, saw Him **with** their **eyes**, gazed upon Him with deep meditation, and actually **handled** Him. The **Word of life** was not a mere passing illusion, but was a real Person in a body of flesh.

1:2 Verse two confirms that the One who **was with the Father**, and whom John calls **that eternal life**, became flesh and dwelt among us and was **seen** by the apostles.

The following lines by an unknown author show the practical implications of these first two verses for our lives:

> I am glad that my knowledge of eternal life is not built on the speculations of philosophers or even theologians but on the unimpeachable testimony of those who heard, saw, gazed at, and handled Him in whom it was incarnate. It is not merely a lovely dream, but solid fact, carefully observed and an accurately recorded fact.

1:3 The apostles did not keep this wonderful news as a secret, and neither should we. They realized that the basis of all fellowship is found here and so they declared it freely and fully. All who receive the testimony of the apostles have **fellowship with the Father, with His Son Jesus Christ**, and also with the apostles and all other believers. How wonderful that guilty sinners should ever be brought into **fellowship with** God **the Father and with His Son Jesus Christ**! And yet, that is the very truth which we have here.

His Son Jesus Christ. Jesus and Christ are one and the same Person, and that Person is the **Son** of God. **Jesus** is the name given to Him at birth, and therefore speaks of His perfect humanity. **Christ** is the name that speaks of Him as God's Anointed One, the Messiah. Therefore, in the name **Jesus Christ**, we have a witness to His humanity and to His deity. Jesus Christ is very God of very God and very Man of very Man.

1:4 But why does John thus **write** concerning the subject of fellowship? The reason is that our **joy may be full**. John realized that the world is not capable of providing true and lasting **joy** for the human heart. This **joy** can only come through proper relationship with the Lord. When a person is in fellowship with God and with the Lord Jesus, he has a deep-seated **joy** that cannot be disturbed by earthly circumstances. As the poet said, "The source of all his singing is high in heaven above."

II. MEANS OF MAINTAINING FELLOWSHIP (1:5–2:2)

1:5 Fellowship describes a situation where two or more persons share things in common. It is a communion or a partnership. John now undertakes to instruct his readers as to the requirements for fellowship with God. In doing so, he appeals to the teachings of the Lord Jesus when He was here on earth. Although the Lord is not quoted as having used these exact words, the sum and substance of His teaching was **that God is light and in Him is no darkness at all**. By this He meant **that God is** absolutely holy, absolutely righteous, and absolutely pure. God cannot look with favor on any form of sin. Nothing is hidden with Him, but "all things are naked and open to the eyes of Him to whom we must give account" (Heb. 4:13).

1:6 Now it follows that in order for a person to be in **fellowship with** God, there can be no hiding of sin. Light and darkness cannot exist in a person's life at the same time, any more than they can exist together in the room of a home. If a man is walking **in darkness**, he is not in fellowship with God. A man who says he has **fellowship with Him** and habitually walks **in darkness** was never saved at all.

1:7 On the other hand, **if one walks in the light**, then he can **have fellowship with** the Lord Jesus and with his fellow Christians. As far as John is concerned in this passage, a man is either in the light or in darkness. If he is in the light, he is a member of God's family. If he is in darkness, he does not have anything in common with God because there is no darkness in God at all. Those who walk in the light, that is, those who are Christians, **have fellowship with one another, and the blood of Jesus Christ** continually **cleanses** them **from all sin**. All God's forgiveness is based on the blood of His Son that was shed at Calvary. That **blood** provided God with a righteous basis on which He can forgive sins, and, as we sing, "the blood will never lose its power." It has lasting efficacy to cleanse us. Of course, believers must confess before they can receive forgiveness, but John deals with that in verse 9.

1:8 Then again, fellowship with God requires that we acknowledge **the truth** concerning ourselves. For instance, to deny that we have a sinful nature means self-deception and untruthfulness. Notice that John makes a distinction between **sin** (v. 8) and *sins* (v. 9). **Sin** refers to our corrupt, evil nature. *Sins* refers to evils that we have done. Actually what we are is a lot worse than anything we have ever done. But, praise the Lord, Christ died for our **sin** and our *sins*.

Conversion does not mean the eradication of the sin nature. Rather it means the implanting of the new, divine nature, with power to live victoriously over indwelling sin.

1:9 In order for us to walk day by day in fellowship with God and with our fellow believers, we must **confess our sins**: sins of commission, sins of omission, sins of thought, sins of act, secret sins, and public sins. We must drag them out into the open before God, call them by their names, take sides with God against them, and forsake them. Yes, true confession involves forsaking of sins: "He who covers his sins will not prosper: but whoever confesses and forsakes them will have mercy" (Prov. 28:13).

When we do that, we can claim the promise that God **is faithful and just to forgive**. He is **faithful** in the sense that He has promised to forgive and will abide by His promise. He is **just to forgive** because He has found a righteous basis for forgiveness in the substitutionary work of the Lord Jesus on the cross. And not only does He guarantee to forgive, but also **to cleanse us from all unrighteousness**.

The forgiveness John speaks about here is parental, not judicial. Judicial forgiveness means forgiveness from the penalty of sins, which the sinner receives when he believes on the Lord Jesus Christ. It is called judicial because it is granted by God acting as Judge. But what about sins which a person commits after conversion? As far as the penalty is concerned, the price has already been paid by the Lord Jesus on the cross of Calvary. But as far as fellowship in the family of God is concerned, the sinning saint needs parental forgiveness, that is, the forgiveness of His Father. He obtains it by confessing his sin. We need judicial forgiveness only once; that takes care of the penalty of all our sins — past, present, and future. But we need parental forgiveness throughout our Christian life.

When **we confess our sins**, we must believe, on the authority of the word of God, that He forgives us. And if He forgives us, we must be willing to forgive ourselves.

1:10 Finally, in order to be in fellowship with God, we must not deny that we have committed acts of sin. God has stated over and over in His word that all have sinned. To deny this is to **make** God **a liar**. It is a flat contradiction of His word, and a complete denial of the reason the Lord Jesus came to suffer, bleed, and die.

Thus we see that fellowship with God does not require lives of sinlessness, but rather requires that all our sins should be brought out into His presence, confessed, and forsaken. It means that we must be absolutely honest about our condition, and that there should be no hypocrisy or hiding of what we really are.

2:1 John gives us God's perfect standard for His people, and His gracious provision in the event of failure. The **little children** refers to all the members of the family of God. God's perfect standard is then set forth in the words **these things I write to you, that you may not sin**. Because God is perfect, His standard for His people is absolute perfection. He would not be God if He said: "These things I write to you so that you sin just as little as you can." God cannot condone sin in the least degree, and so He sets perfection before us as the goal. The Lord Jesus did this with the woman who was caught in the act of adultery; He said, "Neither do I condemn you, go and sin no more."

At the same time, the Lord knows our frame. He remembers that we are dust, and so He has graciously made provision for us in the event of failure. This is expressed in the words, **"if anyone sins, we have an Advocate with the Father, Jesus Christ the righteous."** An **advocate** is one who comes to the side of another person in time of need in order to help. This is exactly what the Lord Jesus does for us when we sin. He immediately comes to us in order to restore us to fellowship with Himself. Notice that it does not say, "If any man confesses his sins. . . ." As our Advocate, the Lord seeks to bring us to the place where we do confess and forsake our sin.

There is something very wonderful in this verse which we should not overlook. It says, **"And if anyone sins, we have an Advocate with the Father."** It does not say *with God*, but rather *with the Father*. He is still our **Father** even if we sin. This reminds us of the blessed truth that though sin in a believer's life breaks fellowship, it does not break relationship. When a person is born again, he becomes a child of God. God is henceforth his **Father**, and nothing can ever affect that relationship. A birth is something that cannot be undone. A son may disgrace his father, but he is still a son by the fact of birth.

Notice that our **Advocate** is **Jesus Christ the righteous**. It is good to have a **righteous** Defender. When Satan brings some accusation against a believer, the Lord Jesus can point to His finished work on Calvary and say, "Charge that to My account."

2:2 And the Lord Jesus is not only our Advocate, but He is also **the propitiation for our sins**. This means that by dying for us, He freed us from the guilt of our sins and restored us to God by providing the needed satisfaction and by removing every barrier to fellowship. God can show mercy to us because Christ has satisfied the claims of justice. It is not often that an advocate (or lawyer) pays for his client's sins; yet that is what our Lord has done, and most remarkable of all, He paid for them by the sacrifice of Himself.

John adds that He is the satisfying sacrifice **not for** our sins **only, but also for the whole world**. This does not mean that the whole world is saved. Rather it means that the work of the Lord Jesus is *sufficient* in value to save all the **world**, but it is only *efficient* to save those who actually put their trust in Him. It is because His work is sufficient for all men that the gospel can be offered to all the world. But if all men were automatically saved, there would be no need of preaching the gospel to them.

It is interesting that the superscription on the cross was written in Hebrew — the language of God's chosen people — and in Greek and Latin, the principal languages of the then-known world. It was thus proclaimed to all the world that Jesus Christ is a sufficient Savior for all men everywhere.

III. MARKS OF THOSE IN THE CHRISTIAN FELLOWSHIP: OBEDIENCE AND LOVE (2:3–11)

2:3 John is about to give the true marks of those who are in the Christian fellowship. The first is obedience. We can have assurance concerning our relationship with God if our life is characterized by a loving desire to do His will. These verses are doubtless aimed at the Gnostics who professed to have a superior knowledge of God, but who showed little interest in keeping the **commandments** of the Lord. John shows that such knowledge is hollow and worthless.

John describes the believer's obedience in a threefold way — keeping **His commandments** (v. 3); keeping *His word* (v. 5); walking *as He walked* (v. 6). There is a definite progress in thought. To **keep His commandments** is to obey the teachings of the Lord Jesus as found in the NT. To keep *His word* means not only obedience to what is written, but a desire to do what we know would please Him. To walk *as He walked* is the full expression of God's standard for His people; it means to live as Jesus lived.

2:4 John does not imply that the Christian life consists in faultless obedience to the will of God, but rather that the Christian habitually desires to **keep His commandments** and to do those things that are pleasing in His sight. John is looking at the over-all tenor of a person's life. If someone says he knows God but **does not keep His commandments**, then it is clear that he is not telling **the truth**.

2:5 On the other hand, when we keep **His word**, then **the love of God is perfected in** us. **The love of God** does not refer to our love for God, but rather to His love for us. The thought is that God's **love** toward us has been brought to its goal when we keep **His word**. It accomplishes its aim and reaches its end in producing obedience to Him.

2:6 Therefore, whoever **says he abides in Him** should **walk just as** the Lord Jesus **walked**. His life, as set forth in the Gospels, is our pattern and guide. It is not a life which we can live in our own strength or energy, but is only possible in the power of the Holy Spirit. Our responsibility is to turn our lives over to Him unreservedly, and allow Him to live His life in and through us.

2:7 Another important mark of true believers is love for the brethren. John says that this is not a **new commandment** which he is writing, **but an old commandment which** they had **had from the beginning**. In other words, the Lord Jesus had taught His disciples to love one another **from the** very **beginning** of His earthly ministry.

The Gnostics were always parading their teachings as being new. But the apostle urges his readers to test everything by the teaching of the Lord Jesus when He was on earth. There is always the danger of drifting away from that which was in **the beginning**.[1] John says, "Get back to the beginning, and you will know what is true."

2:8 Yet this commandment is not only an old commandment, but there is a sense in which it is also **new**. When the Lord Jesus was here, He not only taught His disciples to love one another, but He gave them a living example of what He meant. His life was characterized by love for others. The commandment was thus **true in Him** when He was here on earth. But now there is a sense in which the Old Commandment is new. In this dispensation, it is not only **true in** the Lord Jesus, but in believers also. These Christians had formerly been heathens, living in hatred and passion. Now they illustrated and embodied the great law of love in their lives.

Thus **the darkness is passing away** whenever men receive the light of the gospel. The darkness has not all vanished because many have not come to Christ, but Christ, **the true light, is already shining**, and whenever sinners turn to Him they are saved, and henceforth love their fellow believers.

2:9–11 In verses 9–11 we have the contrast between love that is false and that which is true. If one professes to be a Christian and yet **hates** those who are truly Christians, it is a sure sign that such a one **is in darkness until now**. This latter expression shows that it is not a case of backsliding that is in view. The man continues to be what he always was, namely, unsaved. On the other hand, the one **who** characteristically **loves his brother abides in the light, and there is no cause for stumbling in him**. This may mean that the man himself is not in danger of stumbling, or that he will not cause others to stumble. Either interpretation is true. If the Christian is really living in touch with the Lord, the light illuminates his own pathway, and no one else is offended because of any discrepancy between his profession and his practice. The Gnostics had a deep hatred for those who were true to God's word. This proved that they were **in darkness** and walked **in darkness, and** that they did **not know where** they were **going, because the darkness** had **blinded** their **eyes**.

As if to illustrate the brotherly love about which he has been speaking, the apostle now stops to address loving greetings to those who are members of the family of God.

IV. STAGES OF GROWTH IN THE FELLOWSHIP (2:12–14)

2:12 First he embraces the whole family with the expression **little children**.[2] Here there is no thought of age or spiritual development. John is speaking to all who belong to the Lord, and this is proved by the rest of the verse, **because your sins are forgiven you for His name's sake**. This is true of all Christians. It is a wonderful thing to know, as a present possession, the complete remission of our sins. Notice, too, that our **sins are forgiven for His name's sake**. It is for Christ's sake that God forgives us our sins.

2:13 **Fathers** are described as those who **have known** the One **who is from the beginning**, mature believers who have known the sweet companionship of

the Son of God and are satisfied with Him. **Young men** in the spiritual family are characterized by vigor and by combat. This is the period of conflict and of wrestling with the foe. **Young men . . . overcome the wicked one** because they have learned the secret of victory, namely, "Not I, but Christ living in me." The **little children** are the babes in the faith. They do not know very much, perhaps, but they do know **the Father**.

2:14 When John repeats his address to the **fathers**, it is the same as at the first. This is because they have achieved maturity in spiritual experience. Again the **young men** are addressed as those who **are strong** in the Lord and in the power of His might. They **have overcome the wicked one** because **the word of God abides in** them. The Lord Jesus was able to defeat Satan in the wilderness by quoting the Scriptures. This emphasizes the importance of constantly feeding on the Bible and having it ready to repel the attacks of Satan.

V. TWO DANGERS TO THE FELLOWSHIP: THE WORLD AND FALSE TEACHERS (2:15–28)

In verses 15–17, we have a strong warning against the world and all its false ways. Perhaps this is addressed primarily to the young men, for whom the world often holds a special attraction, but it is a warning that applies to all the Lord's people. The world here is not the planet on which we live, or the natural creation about us. Rather it is the system which man has built up in an effort to make himself happy without Christ. It may include the world of culture, the world of opera, art, education — in short, any sphere in which the Lord Jesus is not loved and welcomed. Someone has defined it as "human society insofar as it is organized on wrong principles, and characterized by base desires, false values, and egoism."

2:15, 16 We are plainly warned **not** to **love the world or the things** that are **in the world**, for the simple reason that love for the world is not compatible with **love** for the **Father. All that** the **world** has to offer may be described as **the lust of the flesh, the lust of the eyes, and the pride of life. The lust of the flesh** refers to such sensual bodily appetites as proceed from within our evil nature. **The lust of the eyes** applies to such evil desires as may arise from what we see. **The pride of life** is an unholy ambition for self-display and self-glory. These three elements of worldliness are illustrated in the sin of Eve. The tree was good for food; that is **the lust of the flesh**. The tree was pleasant to the eyes; that is **the lust of the eyes**. It was a tree to be desired to make one wise; this describes **the pride of life**.

As the *devil* is opposed to *Christ*, and the *flesh* is hostile to *the Spirit*, so the *world* is antagonistic to the *Father*. Appetite, avarice, and ambition are **not of the Father, but of the world**. That is, they do not proceed from **the Father**, but find their source in **the world**. Worldliness is the love for passing things. The human heart can never find satisfaction with things.

2:17 The world is passing away, and the lust of it. When a bank is breaking, smart people do not deposit in it. When the foundation is tottering, intelligent builders do not proceed. Concentrating on this world is like rearranging the deck chairs on the Titanic. So wise people do not live for a **world** that **is passing away. But he who does the will of God abides forever.** It is **the will of God** that delivers us from the temptation of **passing** things. This, incidentally, was the life verse of D. L. Moody, the great evangelist, and is inscribed on his tombstone: "He who does the will of God abides forever."

2:18 Another test of those who are in the Christian fellowship is the test of doctrine. The subject is introduced by a warning addressed to those who are babes in Christ against false teachers. Those who are young in the faith are especially susceptible to the lies of **the Antichrist**. John's readers had been taught that an **Antichrist** would arise prior to the coming of Christ and pretend to be Christ. Just as coming events cast their shadow before them, so prior to the rise of **the Antichrist, many antichrists** appear. These are false teachers who offer a false christ and a false gospel. It is remarkable that the day in which we live is characterized by the existence of many Christ-denying cults, and these all bear testimony to the fact that the coming of the Savior is near.

2:19 These false teachers were professing Christians who once associated with the apostles. However, in heart they were not really one with true believers, and they showed this by going **out from** the fellowship. **If they had been of us, they would have continued with us.** Here we learn that true faith always has the quality of permanence. If a man has really been born again, he will go on for the Lord. It does not mean that we are saved by enduring to the end, but rather that those who endure to the end are really saved. The false teachers **went out that they might be made manifest, that none of them were of us.**

2:20 But this raises the question: "How can a young believer know what is truth and what is falsehood?" The answer is that we **have an anointing from the Holy One, and . . . know all things**, and this **anointing** refers to the Holy Spirit and **is from the Holy One**, the Lord Jesus Christ. When a person is saved, he receives the indwelling Holy Spirit, and He enables the believer to discern between truth and error. When John tells his young readers **"you know all things,"**[3] he does not mean this in an absolute sense. It is not that they have perfect knowledge, but rather that they have the capacity to recognize what is true and what is not. Thus the youngest, simplest believer has the capacity of discernment in divine things that an unsaved philosopher would not have. The Christian can see more on his knees than the worldling can see on his tiptoes. In the physical realm, when a baby is born, he is at once endowed with all the faculties of the human race. He has eyes, hands, feet, and brains. He never gets these later. Although they grow and develop, the whole person is there at the first. So it is when a person is born again. He has at that moment all the faculties that he will ever have, although there will be endless possibilities for developing them.

2:21 John did **not** write **because** his readers were ignorant of **the truth, but** rather to confirm them in the truth that they knew, and to remind them **that no lie is of the truth**. The Gnostics were teaching doctrines that were contrary to the word of God, and therefore they were lies. Their principal lie, the very basis of all their teaching, was their denial that Jesus is the Christ. As pointed out in the introduction, they taught that Jesus was a mere man and that the Christ came upon Him at His baptism. This is the great lie of some of the cults today. The Bible everywhere insists that the Jesus of the NT is the LORD (Jehovah) of the OT. It is not correct to say that the Christ came upon Jesus, but rather that Jesus is the Christ.

2:22 John is careful to point out that to deny the deity of the Lord **Jesus** is to deny **the Father** also. Some people like to believe that they worship God, but they do not want to have anything to do with the Lord Jesus Christ. The apostle says, **"He is antichrist who denies the Father and the Son."**

2:23 In John 8:19, 42, Jesus said that those who failed to recognize His deity and to love Him neither knew the Father nor had Him as their Father. Similarly, John says, **"Whoever denies the Son does not have the Father either; he who acknowledges the Son has the Father also."** Here we have the wonderful truth of the unity between **the Father** and **the Son**. You cannot have **the Father** unless you have **the Son**. This is a message which should be heeded by all Unitarians, Christian Scientists, Muslims, Modernists, Jehovah's Witnesses, and Jews.

2:24 The safeguard for young believers against the false teachers is to **let that abide in you which you heard from the beginning**. This refers to the teachings of the Lord Jesus and of all His apostles. Our great safety is to stay close to the word of God. We should test everything by "What do the Scriptures say?" If a teaching does not agree with the Bible, then we should reject it also. As Dr. Ironside used to say, "If it's new, it's not true, and if it's true, it's not new."

2:25 When we abide in the Christian doctrine, we give proof of the reality of our faith. And **the promise** of that faith is **eternal life**. When we accept the Lord Jesus, we receive His own life, namely, **eternal life**, and this life enables us to test all new and questionable doctrines.

2:26, 27 John wrote thus to the young believers concerning the false teachers by way of warning. He does not have any fear as to the eventual outcome when he remembers that his readers had **received . . . the anointing from** the Lord Jesus. As mentioned previously, **the anointing** is the Holy Spirit, and here we learn that the Holy Spirit **abides in you**. This is a positive statement that once the Holy Spirit is received, He will never be taken away. Because we have received the Holy Spirit, we **do not need any one** to **teach** us. This does not mean that we do not need Christian teachers in the church. God has made specific provision for such teachers in Ephesians 4:11. It means that the Christian does not need any teaching apart from what is found in the Word of God as to the truth of God. The Gnostics professed to have additional truth, but John is saying here that there is no need for additional truth. With the Word of God in our hands and the Spirit of God in our hearts, we have all that we need for instruction in the truth of God.

2:28 John addresses all the dear **children** of the family of God, and exhorts them to **abide in Him** so **that when He appears, we may have confidence and not be ashamed before Him at His coming.** The **we** here refers to the apostles, and the teaching is that if the Christians to whom John wrote did not go on faithfully for the Lord, the apostles who led them to Christ would **be ashamed** at Christ's **coming**. This verse emphasizes the importance of follow-up work in all evangelistic endeavors. It also suggests the possibility of shame when Christ comes.

VI. MARKS OF THOSE IN THE CHRISTIAN FELLOWSHIP (CONT.): RIGHTEOUSNESS, LOVE, AND THE CONFIDENCE IT BRINGS (2:29–3:24)

2:29 The fourth family trait is **righteousness**. We know in the physical realm that like begets like. So it is in the spiritual. **Everyone who practices righteousness is born of** God. Because God **is righteous**, it follows that all He does is righteous, and therefore everyone **born**

of Him is righteous. This is John's inescapable logic.

3:1 The thought of being born of
God arrests John with wonder, and he
calls on his readers to take a look at the
wonderful **love** that brought us into the
family of **God**. Love could have saved us
without making us **children of God**. But
the **manner of** God's **love** is shown in
that he brought us into His family as
**children. "Behold, what manner of love
the Father has bestowed on us, that we
should be called children of God!"**⁴

Now as we walk about from day to
day, **the world does not** recognize **us** as
children of God. The people of the world
do not understand us nor the way we
behave. Indeed, the world did not understand the Lord Jesus when He was
here on earth. "He was in the world,
and the world was made through Him,
and the world did not know Him. He
came to His own, and His own did not
receive Him." Since we have the same
characteristics as the Lord Jesus, we cannot expect the world to understand us,
either.

3:2 However, understood or not,
now we are children of God, and this
is the guarantee of future glory. It **has
not yet been revealed what we shall be,
but we** do **know that when** Christ **is revealed, we shall be like Him, for we
shall see Him as He is**. This does *not*
mean that we will be *physically* like Jesus
in heaven. The Lord Jesus will have His
own definite appearance, and will bear
the scars of Calvary throughout eternity.
Each of us, we believe, will have his own
distinct features and will be recognizable
as such. The Bible does not teach that
everyone will look alike in heaven. However, we will be morally like the Lord
Jesus Christ. We will be free from the
possibility of defilement, sin, sickness,
sorrow, and death.

And how will this marvelous transformation be accomplished? The answer
is that one look at Christ will bring it to
pass. **For we shall see Him as He is.**
Here in life, the process of becoming like
Christ is going on, as we behold Him by
faith in the word of God. But then the
process will be absolutely complete
when we **see Him as He is**: for to **see
Him** is to **be like Him**.

3:3 Everyone who has this hope of
seeing Christ and of being like Him, **purifies himself, just as He is pure**. It has
long been recognized by Christians that
the hope of the imminent return of
Christ has a sanctifying influence in the
life of the believer. He does not want to
be doing anything that he would not
want to be doing when Christ returns.
Notice that it says **"purifies himself, just
as He (Christ) is pure."** It does *not* say
"just as He (Christ) purifies Himself."
The Lord Jesus never had to purify Himself; He is pure. With us, it is a gradual
process; with Him, it is a fact.

3:4 The opposite of purifying oneself is found in verse four: **"Whoever
commits sin also commits lawlessness,
and sin is lawlessness."** The word **commits** is literally *does* (Gk., *poieō*). It is a
matter of continual behavior, expressed
by the present, continuous tense. It is
possible to have sin even if there is no
law. Sin was in the world between the
time of Adam and Moses, but this was
before God's law had been given. Thus
it is not entirely accurate to say "that sin
is a transgression of the law" (1611 KJV),
but rather that **sin is lawlessness**. It is
insubordination to God, wanting one's
own way, and refusing to acknowledge
the Lord as rightful Sovereign. In essence it is placing one's own will above
the will of God. It is opposition to a Living Person who has the right to be
obeyed.

3:5 A Christian cannot go on practicing sin, because that would be a complete denial of the purpose for which the
Lord Jesus came into the world. **He was
manifested to take away our sins.** To go
on in sin, therefore, is to live in utter disregard of the reason for His Incarnation.

Again, a Christian cannot go on in
sin because that would be a denial of the
One whose name he bears. **In Him
there is no sin.** This is one of the three
key passages in the NT dealing with the
sinless humanity of the Lord Jesus
Christ. Peter tells us that "He *did* no
sin." Paul tells us that "He *knew* no
sin." Now John, the disciple who knew the
Lord in an especially intimate way, adds
his testimony, "In Him *is* no sin."

**3:6 Whoever abides in Him does
not sin. Whoever sins has neither seen**

Him, nor known Him. This verse contrasts the true believer with one who has never been born again. It can definitely be said of the true believer that he does not go on sinning. John is not here speaking about isolated acts of sin, but rather continued, habitual, characteristic behavior. This verse does not imply that when a Christian commits an act of sin, he loses his salvation. Rather it says that when a person sins habitually, it is conclusive that he was never regenerated.

The question naturally arises, "When does sin become habitual? How often does a person have to commit it for it to become characteristic behavior?" John does not answer this. Rather he puts each believer on guard, and leaves the burden of proof on the Christian himself.

3:7 Now while the Gnostics made great pretensions as to their knowledge, they were very careless about their personal lives. Therefore, John adds, **"Little children, let no one deceive you. He who practices righteousness is righteous, just as He is righteous."** There should be no confusion on this point — a man cannot have spiritual life and go on living in sin. On the other hand, a man can only practice righteousness through having the nature of Him who **is righteous.**

3:8 Some children are so like their parents that you couldn't lose them in a crowd. This is true of God's children and of the devil's children. **He who sins is of the devil, for the devil has sinned from the beginning.** Here again the thought is, "He who practices sin is of the devil." The devil has been sinning (continuous, characteristic behavior) from the beginning, that is, from the first time that he did sin. All his children follow him in this broad way. It should be added here that men become children of God through the new birth, but there is no birth in connection with the children of the devil. A man becomes a child of the devil simply by imitating his behavior, but no one is begotten as a child of the devil.

In contrast, the coming of the Lord Jesus was in order to **destroy** (or annul) **the works of the devil.** The Lord could have destroyed the devil with a single word, but instead of that, He came down to this world to suffer, bleed, and die that He might annul **the works of the devil.** If it cost the Savior so much to put away sin, what should be the attitude of those who have trusted Him as Savior?

3:9 Verse nine repeats the impossibility of one who **has been born of God** going on in sin. Some Bible students think that this verse refers to the believer's new nature, and that while the old nature can and does sin, the new nature cannot sin. However, we believe that here again the apostle is contrasting the regenerate man with the unregenerate, and is speaking of constant or habitual behavior. The believer does not have the sin habit. He does not defiantly continue in sin.

The reason is that **His seed remains in him.** There is considerable disagreement among Bible students as to the meaning of this latter expression also. Some think that this **seed** refers to the new nature, others to the Holy Spirit, and still others to the word of God. All of these are true, and therefore are possible explanations. We take it that the **seed** refers to the new life which is imparted to the believer at the time of conversion. Here, then, is a statement that the divine life **remains in** the believer. He is eternally secure. Rather than being an excuse for the Christian to go out and sin, his eternal security is a guarantee he will not go on sinning. **He cannot sin** habitually **because he has been born of God.** This divine relationship precludes the possibility of continuance in sin as a lifestyle.

3:10a Here then is the fourth distinction of **the children of God and the children of the devil.** Those who do **not practice righteousness** are **not of God.** There is no in-between ground. There are none who are half-and-half. God's children are known by their righteous lives.

3:10b, 11 In this section we have a continuation of the second test of those who are in the family of God — the test of **love.** This is continued from 2:7–17. From the beginning of the Christian dispensation, it has been taught that **love** to one's brothers is a divine obligation. **Love** here is not used in the sense of friendliness or mere human affection, but it is *divine* **love.** It is loving others as Christ loved us. Actually, this cannot be done in one's own personal strength, but only as empowered by the Holy Spirit.

3:12 John goes back to the first recorded instance of a man who did not love his brother. **Cain** showed that he **was of the wicked one** by murdering **his brother**, Abel. The underlying reason for this is given in the words **"his works were evil and his brother's righteous."**

3:13 It is a basic principle in human life that wickedness hates righteousness, and this explains why **the world hates** the believer. The righteous life of the Christian throws the wickedness of the unbeliever into sharp relief. The latter hates this exposure and instead of changing his wicked behavior, he seeks to destroy what shows it up so clearly. It would be just as unreasonable for a person to destroy a ruler or straightedge for showing how crooked is the line that he has drawn.

3:14 **We know that we have passed from death to life, because we love the brethren.** It is a remarkable fact that when a person is saved, he has an entirely different attitude toward Christians. This is one of the ways he receives assurance of salvation. A person who does not love a true child of God may profess to be a Christian, but the Scripture says he **abides in death**. He always was dead spiritually, and that is what he still is.

3:15 In the eyes of the world, hatred is not a very wicked thing, but God calls it murder. A moment's reflection will show that it is murder in embryo. The motive is there, although the act might not be committed. Thus, **whoever hates his brother is a murderer**. When John says **that no murderer has eternal life abiding in him**, he does not mean that a murderer cannot be saved. He simply means that a man who characteristically hates his fellows is a potential murderer and is not saved.

3:16 Our Lord Jesus gave us the ultimate example of **love** when **He laid down His life for us**. Christ is here contrasted with Cain. He gives us love in its highest expression. In one sense, love is invisible, but we can see the manifestation of love. In the cross of Calvary we see the love that is love indeed. John draws the lesson from this that **we also ought to lay down our lives for the brethren**. This means that our lives should be a continual giving-out on behalf of other believers, and that we should be ready to die for them also if necessary. Most of us will never be required to die on behalf of others, but every one of us can manifest brotherly love by sharing our material things with those in need. That is what is emphasized in verse 17.

3:17 If verse 16 suggests the most we can do for our brethren, verse 17 suggests the least. John distinctly says that a man is not a Christian who **sees his brother in need** and yet withholds from him what is necessary to satisfy that need. This does not justify indiscriminate giving to everyone, because it is possible to harm a man by giving him money with which to buy what would not be good for him. However, the verse does raise very disturbing questions concerning the accumulation of wealth by Christians.

3:18 We should **not love in word or in tongue, but** rather **in deed and in truth**. In other words, it should not be a matter of affectionate terms only, neither should it be an expression of what is not true. But it should be manifested in actual deeds of kindness and should be genuine instead of false.

3:19 **By** the exercise of **this** real and active love to our brethren, we shall know **that we are of the truth**, and this will **assure our hearts** as we come **before Him** in prayer.

3:20 **For if our heart condemns us, God is greater than our heart, and knows all things.** The subject here is the attitude with which we come before God in prayer. This verse may be understood in two ways.

First of all, **if our heart condemns us, God is greater than our heart** in the sense that He is **greater** *in compassion*. While we may have intense feelings of unworthiness, yet God knows that basically we love Him and we love His people. He knows that we are His in spite of all our failures and sins.

The other view is that **if our heart condemns us, God is greater than our heart** in the matter of *judgment*. Whereas we only know our sins in a very limited way, God **knows** them fully and absolutely. He knows all that there is to blame in us, whereas we only know it in part. We lean to this latter viewpoint, although both are true and therefore possible.

3:21 Here is the attitude of one who has a clear conscience before God. It is not that this person has been living sinlessly, but rather that he has been quick to confess and forsake his sins. By doing this, he has **confidence** before **God** and boldness in prayer. Thus, **if our heart does not condemn us, we have confidence toward God**.

3:22 **And whatever we ask we receive from Him, because we keep His commandments and do those things that are pleasing in His sight.** To **keep His commandments** is to abide in Him. It is to live in close, vital intimacy with the Savior. When we are thus in fellowship with Him, we make His will our own will. By the Holy Spirit, He fills us with the knowledge of His will. In such a condition, we would not ask for anything outside the will of God. When we ask according to His will, **we receive from Him** the things **we ask for.**

3:23 **God's commandment** is **that we should believe on the name of His Son Jesus Christ, and love one another, as He gave us commandment.** This seems to summarize all the commandments of the NT. It speaks of our duty to God and to our fellow Christians. Our first duty is to trust in the Lord Jesus Christ. Then because true faith is expressed in right conduct, we should **love one another**. This is an evidence of saving faith.

Notice in this and other verses that John uses the personal pronouns **He** and **Him** to refer to both God the Father, and the Lord Jesus Christ without stopping to explain which one is intended. He dares to do this because the Son is as truly God as the Father, and it is no presumption to speak of Them in the same breath.

3:24a The first part of verse 24 ends the section on love as a test of the children of God: **Now he who keeps His commandments abides in Him, and He in him.** To obey Him is to abide in Him, and those who abide in Him are assured of His abiding presence also.

3:24b **And by this we know that He abides in us, by the Spirit whom He has given us.** The subject of confidence is in-

troduced by the statement that assurance of God's abiding in us comes **by the** Holy **Spirit**. All believers have the Holy Spirit. He is the one who guides them into all truth and enables them to discern error.

VII. THE NEED TO DISCERN BETWEEN TRUTH AND ERROR (4:1–6)

4:1 Having mentioned the Holy Spirit, John is reminded that there are other **spirits** abroad in the world today, and that the children of God need to be warned against them. Thus he cautions the believer not to trust **every spirit**. The word **spirit** here probably refers primarily to teachers but not exclusively so. Just because a man speaks about the Bible, God, and Jesus does not mean that he is a true child of God. We are to **test the spirits, whether they are of God; because many false prophets have gone out into the world.** These are people who profess to accept Christianity, but teach another gospel altogether.

4:2 John gives the actual tests by which these men are to be proven. The great test of a teacher is, "What do you think of Christ?" **Every spirit that confesses that Jesus Christ has come in the flesh is of God.** It is not so much the confession of the historical fact, namely that Jesus was born into the world in a human body, but rather it is the confession of a living Person, **Jesus Christ come in the flesh**. It is the confession that acknowledges **Jesus** as the **Christ** Incarnate. And confessing Him means bowing to Him as Lord of one's life. Now if you ever hear a person presenting the Lord Jesus as the true Christ of God, you will know that he is speaking by the Spirit of God. The Spirit of God calls on men to acknowledge Jesus Christ as Lord and to commit their lives to Him. The Holy Spirit always glorifies Jesus.

4:3 **And every spirit that does not confess that Jesus Christ has come in the flesh is not of God.**[5] This is how you can detect the false teachers. They do **not confess** the **Jesus** who was described in the previous verse. **This is the spirit of the Antichrist, which** has been prophesied **and which is now already in the world**. There are many today who are willing to say acceptable things about Jesus, but they will not confess Him as God Incarnate. They will say that Christ is "divine," but not that He is *God*.

4:4 Humble believers are able to **overcome** these false teachers **because** they have the Holy Spirit within them, and this enables them to detect error and to refuse to listen to it.

4:5 The false teachers **are of the world** and **therefore**, the source of all that they **speak** is **the world. The world** is the spring of all that they teach, and therefore **the world hears them**. This reminds us that the approval of the world is not a test as to the truthfulness of one's teachings. If a man simply wants to be popular, all he needs to do is to speak as the world speaks, but if he is to be faithful to God, then he must face the disapproval of the world.

4:6 In verse 6, John speaks as representing the apostles. He says, **"We are of God. He who knows God hears us."** This means that all who are really born of God will accept the teaching of the apostles found in the NT. On the other hand, those who are not of God refuse the testimony of the NT, or they seek to add to or adulterate it.

VIII. MARKS OF THOSE IN THE CHRISTIAN FELLOWSHIP (CONT.) (4:7–5:20)

A. Love (4:7–21)

4:7, 8 Here John resumes the subject of love for one's brother. He emphasizes that **love** is a duty, consistent with the character of **God**. As has been mentioned previously, John is not thinking of love that is common to all men, but of that love to the children of God which has been implanted in those who have been born again. **Love is of God** as to its origin, **and everyone who loves is born of God and knows God. He who does not love does not know God; for God is love.** It does not say that God loves. That is true, but John is emphasizing that **God is love**. Love is His nature. There is no love in the true sense but that which finds its source in Him. The words **"God is love"** are well worth all the languages in earth or heaven. G. S. Barrett calls them:

. . . the greatest words ever spoken in human speech, the greatest words in the whole Bible. . . . It is impossible to suggest even in briefest outline all that these words contain, for no human and no created intellect has ever, or will ever, fathom their unfathomable meaning; but we may reverently say that this one sentence concerning God contains the key to all God's works and way . . . the mystery of creation, . . . redemption . . . and the Being of God Himself.[6]

4:9, 10 In the verses that follow, we have a description of the manifestation of God's love in three tenses. In the past, it was manifested to us as sinners in the gift of **His only begotten Son** (4:9–11). In the present, it is manifested to us as saints in His dwelling in us (4:12–16). In the future, it will be manifested to us in giving us boldness in the day of judgment.

First of all, then, we have God's love to us as sinners. **God has sent His only begotten Son into the world that we might live through Him** and **to be the propitiation**[7] **for our sins.** We were dead needing life, and we were guilty needing **propitiation**. The expression, **"His only begotten Son"** carries with it the idea of a unique relationship in which no other son could share. This makes the love of God all the more remarkable, that He would send **His** unique **Son** into the world that we might live through Him.

God's love was **not** shown to us because **we** first **loved** Him. We did not; in fact, we were His enemies and hated Him. In other words, He did not love us because we loved Him, but He loved us in spite of our bitter antagonism. And how did He show His love? By sending His **Son** as **the propitiation for our sins. Propitiation** means satisfaction, or a settling of the sin question.

Some liberals like to think of the love of God apart from the redemptive work of Christ. John here links the two as not being in the least contradictory. Denney comments:

Note the resounding paradox of this verse, that God is at once loving and wrathful, and His love provides the propitiation which averts His wrath from us. So far from finding any kind of contrast between love and propitiation, the apostle can convey no idea of love to anyone except by pointing to the propitiation.[8]

4:11 John now enforces the lesson of such love on us: **"If God so loved us, we also ought to love one another."** The **if** here does not express doubt, but rather is used in the sense of "since." Since God so showered His love on those who are now His people, **we also ought to love** those who are members with us of His blessed family.

4:12, 13 God's love is manifested to us at the present time in dwelling in us. The apostle says, **"No one has seen God at any time. If we love one another, God abides in us, and His love has been perfected in us."** In John 1:18 we read: "No one has seen God at any time. The only begotten Son, who is in the bosom of the Father, He has declared Him." In John's Gospel we see that the invisible God is made known to the world through the Lord Jesus Christ. Here we have the expression **"no one has seen God at any time"** repeated in John's Epistle. But now God is manifested to the world, not through Christ, for He has gone back to heaven and is now at the right hand of God. Instead God is now manifested to the world through believers. How stupendous that now *we* must be God's answer to man's need to see Him! And when we love one another, **His love** is **perfected in us**. This means that God's love to us has achieved its goal. We are never intended to be terminals of God's blessings, but channels only. God's love is given to us, not that we might hoard it for ourselves, but that it might be poured out through us to others. When we do love one another in this way, that is proof that we are **in Him, and He in us**, and that we are partakers of **His Spirit**. We should pause to marvel at His dwelling in us and our dwelling in Him.

4:14 John now adds the testimony of the apostolic company: **"We have seen and testify that the Father has sent the Son as Savior of the world."** This is a grand statement of divine love in action. **"The Father has sent the Son"** describes the boundless scope of Christ's work. W. E. Vine wrote that "the scope of His mission was as boundless as humanity, and only man's impenitence and unbelief put a limit to its actual effect."[9]

4:15 The blessing of being indwelt by **God** Himself is the privilege of all who confess **that Jesus is the Son of God**. Here again it is not the confession of merely intellectual assent, but a confession that involves the commitment of one's person to the Lord Jesus Christ. No closer relationship is possible than for a person to abide **in God** and to have **God** abiding **in him**. It is hard for us to visualize such a relationship, but we might compare it, in the natural realm, to a poker in the fire, a sponge in the water, or a balloon in the air. In each case, the object is in an element and the element is in the object.

4:16 And we have known and believed the love that God has for us. God is love, and he who abides in love abides in God, and God in him. God is love, and that love must find an object. The special object of God's love is the company of those who have been born into the family. If I am to be in fellowship with God, then I must love those He loves.

4:17 Love has been perfected among us in this. It is not our love that is made perfect, but God's love is made perfect with us. John is now taking us on to that future time when we will stand before the Lord. Will it be with **boldness** and confidence or will it be with cringing terror? The answer is that it will be with **boldness**, or confidence, because perfect love has settled the sin question once and for all. The reason for our confidence in that coming day is given in the words **"because as He is, so are we in this world."** The Lord Jesus is now in heaven, with judgment completely behind Him. He came into the world once and suffered the punishment which our sins deserved. But He has finished the work of redemption and now will never have to take up the sin question again. **As He is, so are we in this world.** That is, our sins were judged at the cross of Calvary, and we can confidently sing:

> Death and judgment are behind me,
> Grace and glory lie before;
> All the billows rolled o'er Jesus,
> There they spent their utmost power.
> — *Mrs. J. A. Trench*

Just as judgment is passed for Him, so we are beyond the reach of condemnation.

4:18 Because we have come to know God's **love**, we have **no fear** of perishing. **There is no fear in love; but**

perfect love casts out fear. It is His **perfect love** that **casts out** our **fear**. I am assured of the Lord's love first of all, because He sent His Son to die for me. Secondly, I know He loves me because He indwells me at the present moment. Thirdly, I can look to the future with confidence and without fear. Truly, **fear involves torment**, and **he who fears is not made perfect in love**. God's love has not been allowed to operate in the lives of those who are afraid of Him. They have never come to Him in repentance and received the forgiveness of sins.

4:19 We love Him[10] **because He first loved us.** The only reason **we love** at all is **because He first loved us**. The Ten Commandments require that a man should love his God and neighbor, but the law could not produce this love. How then could God obtain this love which His righteousness required? He solved the problem by sending His Son to die for us. Such wonderful love draws out our hearts to Him in return. We say, "You have bled and died for me; from now on I will live for You."

4:20 John emphasizes the futility of professing to **love God** while at the same time hating one's **brother**. As spokes get nearer to the center of the wheel, so they get nearer to one another. Thus, as we get closer to the Lord, the more we will love our fellow believers. Actually, we do not love the Lord a bit more than we love the humblest of His followers. John argues the impossibility of loving God **whom** we have **not seen** if we do not love our brothers whom we have **seen**.

4:21 John closes the section by repeating the **commandment** which **we have from Him, that he who loves God must love his brother also.**

B. Sound Doctrine (5:1a)

John now concludes the tests of life. Here he resumes the test of doctrine, or we might also call it the test of faith. In the first three verses, we are given the results of faith. These are, first, the divine birth, then love for God, then love for one's fellow believers, and finally obedience to God's commandments. First of all, then, we have the divine birth: **Whoever believes that Jesus is the Christ is born of God.** Belief here is not a mere intellectual assent to the fact, but

rather a committal of one's life to Jesus as the Christ.

C. Love and the Obedience It Produces (5:1b–3)

5:1b If we have been truly **born of God**, then we will love **Him**. And not only so, we will love His children as well. It is good to notice here that we are to love all believers, and not just those of a certain earthly communion or fellowship.

5:2, 3 The fourth result of faith is obedience to God's **commandments. By this we know that we love the children of God, when we love God and keep His commandments.** Those who are truly saved will be characterized by a desire to do the will of God. Our **love** for **God** is expressed in willing obedience to His commands. The Lord Jesus said, "If you love Me, keep My commandments."

When John says that **His commandments are not burdensome**, he does not mean that they are not difficult, but rather that they are the very things which born again people love to do. When you tell a mother to take good care of her baby, you are only telling her what she loves to do. The **commandments** of the Lord are the things which are best for us, and the things in which our new nature takes a wholehearted delight.

D. Faith that Overcomes the World (5:4, 5)

5:4 Next we learn the secret of victory over **the world**. The world system is a monstrous scheme of temptation, always trying to drag us away from God and from what is eternal, and seeking to occupy us with what is temporary and sensual. People of the world are completely taken up with the things of time and sense. They have become the victims of passing things.

Only the man who **is born of God** really **overcomes the world**, because by **faith** he is able to rise above the perishing things of this world and to see things in their true, eternal perspective. Thus the one who really **overcomes the world** is not the great scientist or philosopher or psychologist, but the simple believer who realizes that the things which are seen are temporary and that the things which are not seen are eternal. A sight of the glory of God in the face of Jesus dims the glory of this world.

5:5 As we have seen, the subject of this section is faith as a test of eternal life. John has just mentioned that **he who overcomes** is **he who believes that Jesus is the Son of God**. He now goes on to expound the truth concerning the work of the Lord Jesus Christ.

E. Sound Doctrine (5:6–12)

5:6 He says, **"This is He who came by water and blood."** A great deal of discussion has arisen over the meaning of these words. Some feel that the **water and blood** refer to that which flowed from the Savior's side (John 19:34). Others feel that the **water** refers to the Spirit of God and that the **blood** refers to the blood shed on Calvary. Still others believe it is a reference to natural birth, where **water and blood** are present. We would like to suggest a fourth interpretation that takes particular account of the Gnostic heresy which the apostle is seeking to combat in this Epistle.

As mentioned earlier, the Gnostics believed that Christ came upon Jesus at His baptism and left Him before His passion, namely in the Garden of Gethsemane. In other words, they would say, "The Christ did not die on the cross, but Jesus the man died." This, of course, robs His work of any atoning value for the sins of others. We suggest that John is using **water** as an emblem of Jesus' baptism and **blood** as a symbol of His atoning death. These were the two terminals of His public ministry. John is saying that Jesus was just as much the Christ when He died on the cross as when He was baptized in the Jordan. **This is He who came by water and by blood — not only by water** (which the Gnostics would concede), **but by water and by blood**. It seems that the human heart is perpetually trying to rid itself of the doctrine of the atonement. Men would like to have the Lord Jesus as a perfect Man, the ideal Example, who has given us a marvelous code of morals. But John here insists that the Lord Jesus is not only Perfect Man, but Perfect God also, and that the same One who was baptized in the Jordan River gave His life as a sacrifice for sinners. Men say to Christ, "Come down from the cross and we will believe on You." If they can just eliminate the cross from their thinking, they will be happy. But John says, "No. You cannot have the Lord Jesus Christ apart from His perfect redemptive work at Calvary."

It is the Spirit who bears witness, because the Spirit is truth. This means that the Holy **Spirit** of God always testifies to the truth concerning the Lord Jesus which John has been unfolding. He bears witness that Christ came not with water only, but with **water and** with **blood**, because this is the truth of God.

5:7, 8 It always disturbs some devout Christians to learn that parts of verses 7, 8, as found in the KJV and NKJV, are actually found in only a handful of Greek manuscripts of the NT.[11] But this does not at all affect the truth of the inspiration of the Scriptures. Some people think it is important to retain the words because they mention the three Persons of the Trinity. However, the truth of the Trinity does not depend on this passage alone, but is found in many other portions of the Scriptures.

Having stated in the previous verses the Person and work of Christ, John now goes on to state the trustworthiness of our belief in Him. He says that **there are three that bear witness** (the words "in earth" should not be included), **the Spirit, the water, and the blood; and these three agree as one**. Although the word of God should be sufficient for us, as a basis of faith, He condescends to give us a threefold witness concerning the truth. First of all, **the Spirit** of God bears witness to the truth that Jesus Christ is God and that He is the only Savior of the world. The witness of the Spirit is found in the written word of God.

Then there is the witness of **the water**. We believe that this refers to what happened at the baptism of the Lord Jesus. At that event, God opened the heavens and publicly proclaimed, "This is My beloved Son, in whom I am well pleased." Thus God the Father added His own witness to God the Spirit concerning the Person of Christ.

Finally, there is the witness of **the blood**. On the cross, the Lord Jesus bore witness concerning Himself that He was the Son of God. No one took His life from Him; He laid it down by Himself.

If He were a mere man, He could not have done this. The **blood** of the Lord Jesus Christ witnesses that the sin question has been settled once and for all to the satisfaction of God. All **these three** witnesses **agree as one**. That is, they are united in the testimony concerning the perfection of the Person and work of Christ.

5:9 Now John comes in with a telling argument: **"If we receive the witness of men, the witness of God is greater."** In everyday life, we constantly accept the word of our fellow men. If we did not, business would be at a standstill and social life would be impossible. We accept the testimony of men who may be mistaken and who may be deceivers. Now if we do this in everyday life, how much more should we trust the word of God, who cannot fail and cannot lie. It is most unreasonable not to believe God. His witness is absolutely credible.

5:10 When a man does accept His testimony concerning His **Son**, God seals the truth by giving the man **the witness of the Spirit in himself**. On the other hand, if a man disbelieves God, he makes **Him a liar; because he has not believed the testimony that God has given of His Son**. People think they can accept or reject God's testimony concerning Christ, but John would have them know that to reject it is to accuse God of dishonesty.

5:11 John now summarizes the Christian message: **"This is the testimony: that God has given us eternal life, and this life is in His Son."** What tremendous truths these are, namely, that God has given **eternal life** to men, and that the source of this **life is in His Son**.

5:12 From this, the conclusion is inevitable. **He who has the Son has life; and he who does not have the Son of God does not have life.** The teaching is unmistakable. Eternal life is not found in education or philosophy or science or good works or religion or the church. To have **life**, one must **have the Son of God**. On the other hand, **he who does not have the Son of God does not have life**, that is, true life. *Eternal* **life** is inseparable from Jesus Christ.

F. Assurance Through the Word (5:13)

We have now come to the concluding portion of the Epistle. First of all, John states in the clearest terms why he has written the preceding passages. The purpose is that those **who believe in the name of the Son of God may know that** they **have eternal life**. If you have the marks of those who are children of God, then you can **know** that you have been born into the family of God. This verse also teaches another precious truth, namely, that assurance of salvation comes through the word of God. John wrote these things so that people **may know that** they **have eternal life**. In other words, the Scriptures were written that those who believe on the Lord Jesus may have *assurance* that they are saved. There is no need of hoping or guessing or feeling or groping in the dark. It is not presumption for one to say that he is saved. John states in the clearest possible manner that those **who** truly **believe in** the Lord Jesus **may know that they have eternal life**.

G. Confidence in Prayer (5:14–17)

5:14, 15 When we know that we have eternal life, needless to say, we can go before the Lord with **confidence**. John describes this **confidence** in verses 14, 15. We know **that if we ask anything according to** God's **will, He hears** those prayers and will answer them. Indeed we should fear to pray for anything that is *not* in accordance with His will. Perhaps someone will say, "But how can I know the will of God?" In a general way, the answer is that God's will is revealed to us in the Sacred Scriptures, and so we should study the word in order that we might know better what God's will is and how we can pray more intelligently.

5:16 John gives an instance in which the believer can have confidence in prayer, but he also cites an example in which confidence is not possible. **If anyone sees his brother sinning a sin which does not lead to death, he will ask, and He will give him life for those who commit sin not leading to death.** This apparently is a case where a Christian sees a fellow believer engaging in some sinful activity. It is not a sin of a nature as to bring death on the person committing it. In such an instance, the believer can ask for the recovery of the erring person, and God **will give** the petitioner **life** for those who do not sin unto death.

On the other hand, **there is sin leading to death**, and the apostle says, **I do not say that he should pray about that**.

THE SIN
LEADING TO DEATH

It is impossible to say with finality just what **sin leading to death** is, and so perhaps the safest course to follow is to list various accepted interpretations and then tell which one we feel is most correct.

1. Some feel that the **sin leading to death** refers to sin persisted in by a believer and unconfessed by him. In 1 Corinthians 11:30, we read that some had died because they partook of the Lord's Supper without judging themselves.

2. Others feel that the sin of murder is referred to. If a Christian should, in a moment of passion, murder another person, then we should not feel at liberty to pray for his release from the death penalty, because God has already stated that it is His will that "whoever sheds man's blood, by man his blood shall be shed."

3. Still others feel that the sin referred to here is blasphemy against the Holy Spirit. The Lord Jesus said that those who attributed His miracles which were done in the power of the Holy Spirit to Beelzebub, the prince of demons, had committed the unpardonable sin, and that there was no forgiveness for this sin either in that age or in the age to come.

4. Others believe that it is some special form of sin such as that committed by Moses or Aaron, Ananias and Sapphira, and which God visits with summary judgment.

5. A final explanation is that the sin of apostasy is in view, and we believe that this is the explanation which fits in best with the context. An apostate is one who has heard the great truths of the Christian Faith, has become intellectually convinced that Jesus is the Christ, has even made a profession of Christianity, although he has never been truly saved. After having tasted the good things of Christianity, he completely renounces them and repudiates the Lord Jesus Christ. In Hebrews 6 we learn that this is sin leading to death. Those committing this sin have no way of escape, since "they crucify again for themselves the Son of God, and put Him to an open shame." In this entire Epistle, John has been speaking with the Gnostics in view. These false teachers had once been in the Christian fellowship. They had professed to be believers. They had known the facts of the faith, but then they had turned their backs on the Lord Jesus and accepted a teaching which completely denied His deity and the sufficiency of His atoning work. A Christian cannot have liberty in praying for the restoration of such because God has already indicated in His word that they have sinned unto death. ‡

5:17 All unrighteousness is sin, and there is sin not leading to death. There are distinct differences in the degrees of **sin**, and there are sins which are **not** of such a serious nature as to result in **death**.

H. Knowledge of Spiritual Realities (5:18–20)

5:18 Beginning with verse 18, John brings his Epistle to a majestic close by reiterating the great certainties of the Christian Faith. **We know that whoever is born of God does not sin.** Of this we can be sure, that one who has the divine nature does not go on practicing sin. The reason follows: **He who has been born of God keeps himself,**[12] **and the wicked one does not touch him.** As in 3:9, this refers to the true believer who perseveres or keeps himself through his divine nature. It is only such a person who remains unscathed by the wicked one.

5:19 The Christian answer to those who profess to have superior knowledge is this: **We know that we are of God, and the whole world lies under the sway of the wicked one.** With John, there is no mincing of words. He sees only two spheres — in Him or **under the sway of the wicked one**. All people are either saved or lost, and their position depends on their relationship to Jesus Christ. Hear this, you Gnostics!

5:20 The third great truth is that of the Incarnation. **We know that the Son of God has come.** This is the theme with which John opened his Epistle and with which he is now about to close it. The coming of the Lord Jesus revealed to us **Him who is true**, that is, **the true God**. God the Father can only be known through the Lord Jesus Christ. "The only begotten Son, who is in the bosom of the Father, He has declared Him." Then John adds: **and we are in Him who is true, in His Son Jesus Christ**. Again the emphasis is that it is only as we are in Jesus Christ that we can be in God. "No one comes to the Father except through Me." **This is the true God and eternal life.** In other words, John is teaching what the Gnostics denied, namely, that Jesus Christ is God, and that eternal life is found only in Him.

IX. CLOSING APPEAL (5:21)

Lastly, we have John's final exhortation: **"Little children, keep yourselves from idols."** The apostle is saying in effect, "Beware of any teachings which are opposed to these realities." He wants believers to guard themselves from any ideas concerning God, other than those which have been handed down to us by the apostles. Jesus Christ is God. Any other thought is idolatry. Here John is not speaking primarily of idols carved out of wood. An idol is a substitute or false god taking the place of the true. Here an idol is not so much a material thing as a false teaching.

Archbishop Alexander spoke of this appeal as "an eloquent shudder." We can think of no language that could improve on such a description, and so we close this commentary with John's *eloquent shudder*:

> **"Little children, keep yourselves from idols. Amen."**

know." It is easy to see why the difficult reading would be changed to the easy-to-understand "you all know."

[4](3:1) The NU text adds "And we are."

[5](4:3) The NU text omits the second "that" and "Christ has come in the flesh."

[6](4:7, 8) G. S. Barrett, *The First Epistle General of St. John*, pp. 170-173.

[7](4:9, 10) *Propitiation* means satisfaction made for sin through a sacrifice. In the original, the word is related to the Greek word for "mercy seat." Under Britain's C. H. Dodd, a successful crusade was mounted against the word (and doctrine) so that, following the lead of the liberal RSV, most modern Bibles have changed the word. Since it is a standard "sound word" for a theological truth, we should maintain it (as in KJV and NKJV).

[8](4:9, 10) James R. Denney, *The Death of Christ*, 2d. ed., p. 276. The first part of the quotation is apparently from an earlier edition.

[9](4:14) W. E. Vine, *The Epistles of John*, p. 85.

[10](4:19) NU text omits *Him*.

[11](5:7, 8) Erasmus added these words to later editions of his Greek NT under pressure from the pope (they occur in the official Roman Catholic *Latin* Bible, the Vulgate). Only *four very late Greek* mss. have these words, so it is unsafe to use them. Those cultists who go door to door denying the Blessed Trinity are quick to point out these facts, so it is wise to be aware of the problem.

[12](5:18) If the NU text "him" is read instead of "himself," then "He who has been born of God" will refer to Christ.

ENDNOTES

[1](2:7) The critical (NU) text omits the second "from the beginning."

[2](2:12) The word *teknia* is from a word meaning *to bear* (children). The diminutive makes it "little born-ones," an exact counterpart to the tender Scots word "bairnies."

[3](2:20) The traditional (and majority) texts read "you know all things" (*panta*). The critical (NU) reads "you all (*pantes*

BIBLIOGRAPHY

Barrett, G. S. *The First Epistle General of St. John*. London: The Religious Tract Society, 1910.

Candlish, Robert S. *The First Epistle of John*. Grand Rapids: Zondervan Publishing House, n.d.

Findlay, George. *Fellowship in the Life Eternal*. London: Hodder & Stoughton, n.d.

Ironside, H. A. *Addresses on the Epistles*

of John. New York: Loizeaux Bros., n.d.

Kelly, William. *An Exposition of the Epistles of John the Apostle*. London: T. Weston, 1905.

Law, Robert. *The Tests of Life*. Edinburgh: T & T Clark, 1909.

Marshall, I. Howard. *The Epistles of John* (NIC). Grand Rapids: Wm. B. Eerdmans Publishing Company, 1978.

Mitchell, John G. *Fellowship: Three Letters from John*. Portland, Ore.: Multnomah Press, 1974.

Stott, John R. W. *The Epistles of John* (TBC). Grand Rapids: Wm. B. Eerdmans Publishing Company, 1964.

Vine, W. E. *The Epistles of John: Light, Love, Life*. Grand Rapids: Zondervan Publishing House, 1970.

Westcott, Brooke Foss. *The Epistles of St. John*. Cambridge: The MacMillan Company, 1892.

THE SECOND EPISTLE OF JOHN

Introduction

"[Second John] gives us a new aspect of the Apostle: it shews him to us as the shepherd of individual souls. . . . Whether it be addressed to a local Church, or . . . to a Christian lady, . . . it is for the sake of particular persons about whom he is greatly interested that he sends the letter."
— A. Plummer

I. Unique Place in the Canon

Along with 3 John this short note is all we have of the priceless *personal* correspondence of one of the most beloved early saints, the Apostle John.

Sometimes Christians are concerned about how "open" or "closed" they should be to others, especially to those who profess to be believers. Second and Third John answer this very practical question. Second John shows the importance of keeping our house (or house church) closed to heretics; 3 John encourages an "open door policy" to traveling preachers and missionaries.

II. Authorship†

The *external evidence* for 2 John is weaker than for 1 John, no doubt due to its size and private nature. Irenaeus quotes it, but, like several others, thought it was part of 1 John (chapter and verse divisions came centuries later). Origen doubted the Epistle, but Clement and Dionysius, both of Alexandria, quote it as John's. Cyprian specifically quotes verse 10 as by the Apostle John.

The *internal evidence* consists of the fact that the style and vocabulary match that of the Gospel and 1 and 3 John. Even though 2 and 3 John have different beginnings from 1 John, they are so similar that few would deny that they all came from the same hand and apparently from about the same time.

There is no compelling reason to doubt the traditional ascription of 2 John to the apostle (see Introduction to 1 John for more details).

III. Date

As in the case of 1 John, two general periods are possible. Either an early date (60's) before the destruction of Jerusalem, or a late date (85-90) is indicated. If the former, it would probably be from Jerusalem; if the latter, it would be from Ephesus, where the aged apostle ended his days.

IV. Background and Theme††

The background of this Epistle is the widespread ministry of itinerant preachers in the early church, still practiced somewhat in certain circles. These evangelists and ministers of the word would receive hospitality, food, and sometimes money at the Christian homes and congregations they visited. Unfortunately, false teachers and religious charlatans were quick to step in and use this custom as a means for easy gain and to spread their heresies, such as Gnosticism (see Introduction to 1 John).

If it was important in the first century to warn of heretics and "religious profiteers," what would the Apostle John say if he could see today's patchwork quilt of sects, cults, and false religions?

The central theme of 2 John is that we should give no cooperation whatever to a person who is spreading error regarding the Person of our Lord (vv. 10, 11).

†See p. i.
††See p. ii.

OUTLINE

Commentary

I. THE APOSTLE'S SALUTATION: GRACE, MERCY, AND PEACE (Vv. 1–3)

V. 1 In 2 John, the apostle introduces himself as **the elder**. This may refer to age or official position in the church. As to age, John was the last of the apostles who had companied with the Lord Jesus. As to official position, he surely was a bishop or overseer. Thus, we need not choose our explanation; both are correct.

The expression **"To the elect lady"** is not so easy to explain. Three views are commonly held. (1) Some believe that **the elect lady** is the church, elsewhere referred to as the Bride of Christ, or a particular local church. (2) Others think that the Letter was addressed to "the elect Kyria" — her name being Kyria. This name could be the Greek equivalent to the Aramaic name Martha (both mean "lady").[1] (3) Others feel that John is writing to an unnamed Christian **lady**, who with all other believers is among the **elect** of God — chosen in Christ before the foundation of the world.

We prefer the last view, and feel it is especially significant that this warning against anti-christian teachers should be found in a Letter addressed to a woman. Sin first entered the world through Eve's being deceived by Satan. "The woman being deceived, fell into transgression" (1 Tim. 2:14). Paul speaks of false teachers who make a special appeal to women; they get into the house and capture "gullible women loaded down with sins, led away by various lusts," who will listen to anyone and yet are "never able to come to the knowledge of the truth" (2 Tim. 3:6, 7). Even today the false cults visit homes during the daytime, when the man of the house is usually at work. Children need to be warned against false teachers also.

John states that he loves this **elect lady and her children . . . in truth**. Those who are saved find themselves in a wonderful fellowship, loving others whom they never would have loved, were it not for their common love for the truth of God. It is God's truth that binds hearts together — the hearts of **all those who have known the truth.**

V. 2 **Because of the truth** has two possible explanations. It may refer to the motive for loving all the saints, or it may give John's reason for writing this Letter. Both are valid meanings. **The truth which abides in us and will be with us forever**. Here **the truth** may refer to: (1) the Lord Jesus Christ. He said, "I am . . . the truth" (John 14:6); (2) the Holy Spirit. "The Spirit is truth" (1 Jn. 5:6; see John 14:16, 17); or (3) the Bible. "Your word is truth" (John 17:17). Should we not pause to marvel at our being sustained by these Three, and their being with us forever!

V. 3 John's greeting is **"grace, mercy, and peace will be with you."**[2] **Grace** is undeserved favor to those who deserve the opposite. **Mercy** is pity shown to those who are guilty and wretched. **Peace** is the harmonious relationship that *results from* God's **grace** and **mercy**. All three of these blessings are **from God the Father and from the Lord Jesus Christ**. The **Father** is the Source and the **Son** is the Channel. In addition, they are **in truth and love**, and never at the expense of either of these virtues.

II. THE APOSTLE'S JOY: OBEDIENT CHILDREN (V. 4)

Now John expresses his joy at hearing that some of the **children** of the elect lady were **walking in truth**. The **truth** is not just something to be believed with the mind, but something to be lived out in everyday behavior. Just as the Lord Jesus was the living embodiment of truth, so He expects our lives to be testimonies to the **truth**.

III. THE APOSTLE'S CHARGE: TO WALK IN LOVE (Vv. 5, 6)

V. 5 In verses 5 through 9, the apostle seems to give a short summary of his First Epistle. There he listed the tests of life. Now in these verses, he repeats at least three of them — the test of **love** (v. 5), the test of *obedience* (v. 6), and the test of *doctrine* (vv. 7–9).

V. 6 First, he reminds his readers of the commandment to **love** their fellow believers. **Love** here is essentially the unselfish giving of oneself for the benefit of others. It is not "What can I get out of that person?" but "What can I do for that person?" Then, **love** is shown to be a walking **according to His commandments**. We cannot truly love, in the divine sense, unless we are walking in obedience to the Lord and to the truth of God.

IV. THE APOSTLE'S CONCERN: ANTICHRIST DECEIVERS (Vv. 7–11)

V. 7 This brings us to the test of doctrine. The great question is: "Did God really become Man in the Person of Jesus Christ?" The answer is a resounding "Yes!" The Gnostics[3] believed that the divine Christ came upon Jesus of Nazareth for a period of time. But John insists that **Jesus Christ** was, is, and always will be God.

V. 8 Therefore, he warns his readers, **"Look to yourselves, that we do not lose those things we worked for, but that we may receive a full reward."** *In other words*, stand firm in the truth concerning the Lord Jesus Christ so that our labor

among you will not have been in vain, and so that **we** (the apostles and their followers) **will receive a full reward.**

V. 9 When John says, **"Whoever transgresses[4] and does not abide in the doctrine of Christ,"** he is speaking of false teachers. To transgress is to go beyond the allowed bounds. That is what the cults do; they claim to have new light and teach doctrines that God has not revealed in His word. They do not stay within the bounds of the Christian revelation, or abide **in the doctrine of Christ**, probably meaning the teachings which **Christ** Himself brought. It could also mean all that the Bible teaches *about* **Christ**. The apostle emphasizes in verse 9 that a cultist may claim to know God, but if he does not believe in the absolute deity and humanity of the Lord Jesus, he **does not have God** at all. God can only be known through His Son. "No one comes to the Father except through Me" (John 14:6).

Vv. 10, 11 This is the heart of the Epistle. It gives us valued advice on how to deal with false teachers who come to our doors. John does not refer to casual visitors but to anti-Christian propagandists. Should we invite them in? Give them a cup of coffee? Help them financially? Buy their literature? The answer is that we should **not receive** them or **greet** them. These people are enemies of Christ. To show them hospitality is to take sides with those who are against our Savior. It is possible that sometime we might let such a person into our house without knowing that he denies the Lord. These verses would not apply in such a case. But when we do know a man to be a false teacher, it would be disloyal to Christ to befriend him. These verses do not apply to visitors generally. We often have unbelievers as guests in an effort to win them to Christ. But here it is a question of religious teachers who deny the deity and humanity of Jesus Christ. C. F. Hogg explains:

Nothing should be done to give the impression that the offense against Christ is a matter of no great moment, or to put the delinquent in the way of influencing others.[5]

V. THE APOSTLE'S HOPE: A PERSONAL VISIT (Vv. 12, 13)

V. 12 John would have liked to say more to the elect lady. But he stops writing at this point in the hope of an early personal visit when he can speak **face to face**. How much more satisfactory it is to talk in personal encounter than to write **with paper and ink**! And how much more wonderful it will be to see the Savior face to face than to see Him by the eyes of faith, as at present! Truly then **our joy** will **be full**!

V. 13 So John closes: **"The children of your elect sister greet you."** We do not know who they were, but we shall meet them some day and enjoy fellowship with them and with the beloved Apostle John who penned this Letter, and best of all with the Savior Himself. **Amen.**

ENDNOTES

[1](V. 1) Less likely, the Greek word for elect (Eklektē, "Electa") could be taken as a proper name and the word "lady" as a title: "Lady Electa."

[2](V. 3) The critical (NU) and majority (M) texts read "us." The Greek words for *you/we*, for *you/us*, and *your/our* are only one letter different from each other, hence the copying problems in the mss. (See, e.g., V. 8, where the NU text reads *you*, not *we*.)

[3](V. 7) See Introduction to Colossians for a discussion of Gnosticism.

[4](V. 9) The NU text reads "goes ahead" or "progresses" (*proagōn*) instead of the "*transgresses*" (*parabainōn*) of the TR and majority text.

[5](Vv. 10, 11) C. F. Hogg, *What Saith the Scripture?*, p. 143.

BIBLIOGRAPHY

See Bibliography at the end of 1 John.

THE THIRD EPISTLE OF JOHN

Introduction

"Altogether this last glimpse of Christian life in the apostolic age is one on which the student may well linger. The state of things which is disclosed does not come near an ideal, but it witnesses to the freedom and vigour of a growing faith."
— B. F. Westcott

I. Unique Place in the Canon

Even 3 John, the shortest book in the NT (just one line shorter than 2 John in the original), illustrates the divine truth that "all Scripture . . . is profitable." Like 2 John, its key words are *love* and *truth*. But unlike 2 John, which shows the *firmness* of love in refusing to entertain those who do not teach the truth, 3 John shows the *tenderness* of love in helping those who have gone forward with the truth.

II. Authorship[†]

The *external evidence* for 3 John is similar to that of 2 John. These Letters are so short and so personal it is easy to see why they lack the greater spread of evidence that 1 John has.

Origen and Eusebius classed 3 John among the *antilegomena*, or disputed books. Clement and Dionysius, both of Alexandria, accepted 3 John, as did Cyril of Jerusalem. The evidence of the Muratorian Canon is unclear in this area.

The *internal evidence* couples this Letter very closely with 2 John, and also clearly with 1 John. Together the three support one another's authenticity.

There is no compelling reason to doubt the traditional view that John the Apostle wrote 3 John along with the other two Letters ascribed to him.

[†]*See p. i.*
[††]*See p. ii.*

III. Date

As in the case of 1 and 2 John, two general dates have been proposed. If John was writing from Jerusalem before the destruction of that city, a date in the 60's is likely. More commonly, scholars see the Letter as from a later period when John lived and served in Ephesus. Thus a date of 85-90 has been widely accepted.

IV. Background and Theme[††]

The historical backdrop of this little Letter gives us a vivid glimpse into church life in the latter half of the first century. With just a few concise strokes of the pen the apostle sketches in three characters: Gaius the hospitable and spiritual, Demetrius the commendable, and Diotrephes the self-seeking and unloving. Diotrephes may illustrate the strong self-willed personality that can show up in *any* church structure. On the other hand, he may show the trend toward one elder gaining precedence and rule over a formerly equal eldership. This latter trend evolved into the "monarchical episcopate" (rule of one dominant overseer, or bishop) of the second century and following.

OUTLINE

Commentary

I. SALUTATION (Vv. 1–4)

V. 1 As in his Second Epistle, John speaks of himself as **the elder**. He addresses the Letter to the **beloved Gaius, whom** he loves **in truth**. Although we do not know if this is the Gaius mentioned in Romans 16:23 or the one in Acts 20:4, it is surprising how much we do learn about him in these few verses. First of all, we gather that he was a much **beloved** believer, a man whose whole life commended him to his fellow Christians.

V. 2 But apparently he was not too well in body, since John wishes that his physical **health** might correspond to his spiritual vigor. When John says **I pray that you may prosper in all things** it is doubtful that he is thinking of wealth or material prosperity. Rather he is speaking of physical well-being, as suggested by the next phrase — **and be in health**.

Would we want *our* physical condition to correspond to our spiritual? Is it not sadly true that we take better care of our bodies than of our souls? That is why F. B. Meyer wryly remarked:

It would not be desirable to express the wish of verse 2 to all our friends, because if their bodies were to correspond to the condition of their souls, they would suddenly fall into ill-health.[1]

Verse 2 flatly contradicts what is taught by many so-called "faith-healers." They contend that all sickness is a result of sin in the life, and that if a person isn't healed, it's because of a lack of faith. This certainly wasn't true in Gaius' case. His spiritual condition was good, but his physical condition was not so good. This shows that one's spiritual state cannot be argued from the bodily one.

V. 3 The apostle **rejoiced greatly when** certain **brethren came and testified of the truth that** was **in** Gaius, and how he walked **in the truth**. It is good to have the truth in us but it is better to manifest the **truth** in our lives. We should not only hold the truth, but allow the truth to hold us. Men would rather see a sermon than hear one. Nothing counts more for God in an age of fact than a holy life.

V. 4 So important was this to John that he could say, **"I have no greater joy than to hear that my children walk in truth."** Perhaps most of us think of soul-winning as the greatest joy of the Christian life, and it is wonderful indeed to see men and women translated from the kingdom of darkness into the kingdom of the Son of His love. But who can measure the heartache to see those who professed to be saved, returning to their former life; like a sow returning to her wallowing in the mire and a dog to its vomit. On the other hand, what a thrill it is to see one's spiritual children going on for the Lord, from grace to grace. Again this emphasizes the importance of follow-up work in all our evangelistic endeavors.

II. THE GODLY GAIUS (Vv. 5–8)

V. 5 Gaius took a special delight in throwing open his home to those who had gone out preaching the gospel. He extended his gracious hospitality not only to those whom he knew, but to

strangers as well.[2] John says that he was faithful in this ministry. It appears from the NT that hospitality is very important in God's sight. If we entertain the Lord's people, it is the same as if we entertain the Lord Himself (Matt. 25:40). On the other hand, failure to entertain His servants is looked upon as failure to entertain Him (Matt. 25:45). Through entertaining strangers, "some have unwittingly entertained angels" (Heb. 13:2). Many can testify that through the practice of hospitality, meals have been turned into sacraments (Luke 24:29–35), children have been converted, and families have been drawn closer to the Lord.

V. 6 Rewards are involved. Gaius' kindness was known to all **the church**. But more than that, his name is forever enshrined in God's Holy Word as one who had an open home and an open heart. And even more, Gaius will yet be rewarded at the Judgment Seat of Christ, for "he who receives a prophet in the name of a prophet shall receive a prophet's reward" (Matt. 10:41). He will share in the reward of all those preachers he entertained. This is a good point to remember for those who cannot preach: You can receive a preacher's reward by showing hospitality to preachers in the name of the Lord. God will pay back all good deeds! His kindness will crown the kindness of men.

Now John reminds Gaius that he **will do well** to **send them forward on their journey in a manner worthy of God**. To **send them forward on their journey** means not just a friendly farewell, but adequate supplies. This surely sets a high standard for us as we share our material things with those who preach and teach.

V. 7 A special reason is given why Gaius should be helpful to these itinerant evangelists: **Because they went forth for His name's sake taking nothing from the Gentiles.** These men looked to the Lord alone for the supply of their needs. They would not accept support from the unconverted. To do so would imply that their Master was too poor to provide for them. It might also give the unsaved a false ground of self-righteousness on which to rest. What a rebuke this is to the money-raising methods of Christendom today! And how it should remind us of the special obligation we have toward those servants of the Lord who go out in faith in the living God and who make their needs known to no one but the Lord.

V. 8 **We therefore ought to receive such, that we may become fellow workers for the truth**. To **receive**[3] them means to do everything possible to help them, for when we do, we help **the truth** in its onward march.

III. THE DICTATORIAL DIOTREPHES (Vv. 9–11)

V. 9 Apparently John had written along this line **to the church**, but his Letter was intercepted by a man named **Diotrephes**, who had an exaggerated view of his own importance. He was a virtual dictator in the assembly. His sin was pride of place, an inflated ego, and a violent jealousy for what he regarded as his own rights — which he doubtless defended as the autonomy of the local church. Diotrephes had forgotten that Christ is the Head of the church — if he ever knew it! He had forgotten that the Holy Spirit is the Vicar or Representative of Christ in the church. No mere man has the right to take charge, to make decisions, to receive, or to refuse. Such conduct is popery, and God hates it. Doubtless Diotrephes excused his behavior on the ground that he was contending for the truth. But that was, of course, a lie! He was doing untold harm to the truth by refusing the apostle on the pretext of being faithful to God. And not only John, but other brethren as well.

V. 10 Not only did he refuse these true believers, but he excommunicated those who *did* receive them. He was a power-mad creature, **prating against** God's true servants **with malicious words**. John will remember him on his next visit to that assembly! Such self-styled popes cannot stand being openly denounced from the word of God. Their continuance in power depends upon secret meetings and upon a reign of fear and intimidation.

V. 11 Gaius is exhorted to turn away from such **evil** behavior and to follow **what is good**. Good works are an evidence of relationship with **God**. That being so, the apostle seems to cast grave doubts on the spiritual state of Diotrephes.

IV. DEVOUT DEMETRIUS (V. 12)

Perhaps **Demetrius** was the bearer of this Letter. At any rate, he had **a good testimony from all, and from the truth itself**. F. B. Hole says:

> Note, it is not that he bore witness to the truth, but that the truth bore witness to him. Demetrius was not the standard by which truth was tested. The truth was the standard by which he was tested; and having been so tested, he stood approved.[4]

V. THE APOSTLE'S PLAN AND BENEDICTION (Vv. 13, 14)

John closes in much the same way as he closed his Second Epistle — delaying discussion until **face to face** reunion. We are indebted to him for these Letters, giving us an insight into life in the early days of Christianity, and setting forth timeless instruction for the people of God. Soon we shall speak face to face in heaven, and then we shall understand more fully the occasional obscurities of divine revelation.

ENDNOTES

[1](V. 2) F. B. Meyer, *Through the Bible Day by Day*, VII:164, 165.

[2](V. 5) The critical (NU) text reads *"especially* (Gk. *touto*, lit. "this") strangers."

[3](V. 8) The NU text reads "support" *hupolambanein*) rather than the "receive" (*apolambanein*) of the TR and majority text.

[4](V. 12) F. B. Hole, further documentation unavailable.

BIBLIOGRAPHY

See Bibliography at the end of 1 John.

THE EPISTLE OF JUDE

Introduction

"An Epistle of few lines but full of the mighty words of heavenly grace."

— Origen

I. Unique Place in the Canon

Just as Luke begins Christian history with the Acts of the Apostles, Jude is chosen to write the next to the last book of the NT, which has been appropriately called "the Acts of the Apostates." Jude would have preferred to write about the common Christian Faith shared with his readers, but false teachings were becoming so prevalent that he was constrained to pen a plea to "contend earnestly for the faith which was once for all delivered to the saints."

Jude does not mince words! He pulls out all the stops, as it were, to unmask these notorious heretics, drawing illustrations from nature, the OT, and Jewish tradition (Enoch) to stir up the faithful.

In spite of its harsh language, the Epistle is a masterpiece of construction, studded with triads (e.g., the three evils in v. 11). The descriptions of the apostates are vivid and unforgettable.

The church is forever in debt to Jude for the beautiful benediction with which he ends his Letter. His Epistle may be short, but it is greatly needed in these days of ever-increasing apostasy.

II. Authorship†

External Evidence

In spite of its shortness, its use of non-canonical materials, and the fact that it is not by an apostle (v. 17), Jude is better attested as to *external evidence* than is 2 Peter.

Hermas, Polycarp, and probably Athenagoras use material borrowed from this Epistle. Tertullian specifically refers to Jude's use of Enoch. Eusebius puts Jude among the disputed books (*antilegomena*). The Muratorian Canon lists Jude as genuine.

Internal Evidence

Jude (same name as Judas and Judah, Hebrew *Yehudah*) was a very popular Jewish name. Of the seven Judes or Judases in the NT, three have been suggested as the "Jude, . . . brother of James" who wrote this Epistle:

1. The Apostle Judas (not Iscariot, who had committed suicide). Since verse 17 apparently differentiates the writer from the apostles, and since it would strengthen his position if he could claim apostleship, he is an unlikely candidate.

2. Judas, a leader sent to Antioch with Paul, Barnabas, and Silas (Acts 15:22). This is a possibility, but no evidence links this man with the Letter.

3. Judas (Jude), a younger half-brother of our Lord and a brother of James (see Introduction to James). He is the strongest candidate, sharing with the Lord Jesus and with James in his use of nature illustrations and a trenchant, colorful style. We accept this view.

Like his brother James, Jude was too modest to exploit his natural relationship to the Savior. After all, it is spiritual relationship to the Lord Jesus that counts. Did Christ not say, "Whoever does the will of My Father in heaven is My brother and sister and mother" (Matt. 12:50)? On another occasion He taught that it was more blessed to hear the word of God and do it than to be a close blood-relative of His (Luke

†*See p. i.*

11:27, 28). Like James, Jude took the place of "a bondservant." Since both brothers disbelieved in their divine Half-brother until after the resurrection, this was a suitable spirit to show. Jude was married and took his wife around on his itinerant preaching tours (1 Cor. 9:5). Jude's grandsons were brought before Emperor Domitian in the 90's on the charge of being Christians. Seeing their hands hardened from years of farming, the emperor released them as harmless Jews.

III. Date

Whether Peter used Jude, or Jude adapted 2 Peter (or both used a common source) is debated. The similarities between the two are too great to be coincidental. Since Peter writes in his Second Epistle (2:1 and 3:3) that there "*will be*" false teachers and scoffers, and Jude says such men "*have* crept in" (v. 4), it is probable that Jude is the later writer. A date between 67 and 80 is likely. Since Jude makes no mention of the destruction of Jerusalem (A.D. 70), this could suggest it was yet to happen, making a date of 67–70 likely. It could also mean that it had happened some time ago (if Jude was written in A.D. 80, or even 85 — assuming Jude lived that long). Another possibility is that the event was still too traumatic for a sensitive Hebrew Christian to use as an illustration.

IV. Background and Theme†

Jude is concerned with apostasy. Even in his day, the church was already being infiltrated by religious Quislings, men who posed as servants of God but who were actually enemies of the cross of Christ. Jude's purpose is to expose these traitors and to describe their ultimate doom.

An apostate is a person who professes to be a true believer but who, as a matter of fact, has never been regenerated. He may be baptized and participate fully in the privileges of a local Christian fellowship. But after a while, he willfully abandons the Christian faith and maliciously renounces the Savior. He denies the deity of Christ, His re-

demptive work at Calvary, His bodily resurrection, or other fundamental doctrines.

It is not at all a question of backsliding; the apostate was never converted at all. He has no qualms about his deliberate spurning of God's only way of salvation. He is hardened in his unbelief and stubbornly opposed to the Christ of God.

Apostasy is not simply a question of *denying* the Savior. Peter did that. Peter was a true believer who buckled under the pressures of a crisis. But he really loved the Lord and demonstrated the reality of his faith by his subsequent repentance and restoration.

Judas Iscariot was an apostate. He professed to be a disciple; he traveled with the Lord Jesus for about three years. He even served as treasurer of the team, but finally he revealed his true self by betraying the Lord for thirty pieces of silver.

Apostasy is a sin leading to death, one that lies beyond the responsibility of believers' prayers (1 Jn. 5:16b). It is impossible to renew an apostate to repentance, since he crucifies to himself the Son of God, and puts Him to open shame (Heb. 6:6). For those who thus sin willfully after receiving the knowledge of the truth, "there no longer remains a sacrifice for sins, but a certain fearful expectation of judgment, and fiery indignation which will devour the adversaries" (Heb. 10:26, 27).

The seeds of apostasy were already sown in the early church. Paul warned the Ephesian elders that after his departure savage wolves would come in, not sparing the flock, and that from among themselves, men would rise up, speaking perverse things, to draw away disciples after themselves (Acts 20:29, 30). In his First Epistle, John spoke of those antichrists who had been in the Christian fellowship but who manifested their unreality by leaving it, that is, by abandoning their faith (1 Jn. 2:18, 19).

In 2 Thessalonians 2:2–4 we learn that there will be a great apostasy prior to the Day of the Lord. As we understand it, the order will be this:

First, the Lord will come into the air to take the church to the Father's

†*See p. ii.*

house (John 14:1–3; 1 Thess. 4:13–18).

Then there will be a wholesale defection of those nominal Christians who are left behind.

Then the man of sin will make his public début on the world stage.

Then the Day of the Lord will begin — the seven-year Tribulation Period.

The man of sin will be the arch-apostate — not only opposing Christ but demanding that he himself be worshiped as God.

Peter gives a detailed portrait of the apostate false teachers who will arise in the last days (2 Pet. 2). In some respects his description closely parallels that which is given by Jude. The resemblance may be seen by comparing the following:

Jude	2 Peter
V. 4	2:1–3
V. 7	2:6
V. 8	2:10
V. 9	2:11
V. 10	2:12
V. 16	2:18

But actually the *differences* between the two passages are more significant than the *similarities*. Jude makes no mention of Noah, the flood, or Lot. Peter omits any mention of the Israelites who were saved out of Egypt, of Michael, Cain, Korah, or of Enoch's prophecy. He does not give as much information about the angels that sinned as Jude does. He speaks of the false teachers as denying the Master who bought them, whereas Jude elaborates by saying that they "turn the grace of our God into lewdness and deny the only Lord God and our Lord Jesus Christ" (Jude 4).

So instead of thinking of the two chapters as carbon copies, we should realize that the Holy Spirit has selected materials to suit his purpose in each case, and that the two chapters do not overlap as much as they might seem at first. Those who have studied the four Gospels and have compared Ephesians and Colossians realize that the Spirit of God never needlessly repeats Himself. There are spiritual meanings behind the similarities and differences, if only we have eyes to see them.

OUTLINE

I. SALUTATION (Vv. 1, 2)

II. THE APOSTATES UNMASKED (Vv. 3–16)

III. THE BELIEVER'S ROLE IN THE MIDST OF APOSTASY (Vv. 17–23)

IV. THE BEAUTIFUL BENEDICTION (Vv. 24, 25)

Commentary

I. SALUTATION (Vv. 1, 2)

V. 1 God used a righteous **Jude** to unmask the apostates, of whom another Jude, Judas Iscariot, was a prime example. All that we know *for certain* about the good **Jude** is that he was **a bondservant of Jesus Christ, and brother of James**.

In addressing the Letter, Jude gives three designations that are true of all believers. They **are called, sanctified**[1] **by God the Father, and preserved in Jesus Christ**. God has **called** these out of the world by the gospel to belong to Him-self. They are set apart **by God** to be God's special and pure people. And they are marvelously **preserved** from danger, damage, defilement, and damnation until at last they are ushered in to see the King in His beauty.

V. 2 Jude wishes for his readers **mercy, peace, and love**. The greeting is peculiarly suited to those who were facing the onslaught of those whose aim was to subvert the faith. **Mercy** means God's compassionate comfort and care for His beleaguered saints in times of conflict and stress. **Peace** is the serenity and confidence that come from reliance on God's word and from looking above circumstances to the One who overrules all circumstances for the accomplishment of His own purposes. **Love** is the undeserved embrace of God for His dear people — a super-affection that should then be shared with others.

He wishes that these three blessings **be multiplied**. Not measured out by mere addition, but by multiplication!

II. THE APOSTATES UN-MASKED (Vv. 3–16)

V. 3 Jude had originally intended **to write** about the glorious **salvation** that is the **common** possession of all believers. But God's Spirit so influenced this yielded scribe that he sensed a change of direction. A simple doctrinal essay would no longer do; it must be a fervent appeal that would strengthen the readers. They must be stirred up **to contend earnestly for the faith**. Attacks were being made on the sacred deposit of Christian truth, and efforts were already launched to whittle away the great fundamental doctrines. God's people must stand uncompromisingly for the inspiration, inerrancy, authority, and sufficiency of God's Holy Word.

Yet in contending for the faith, the believer must speak and act as a Christian. As Paul wrote: "A servant of the Lord must not quarrel but be gentle to all, able to teach, patient" (2 Tim. 2:24). He must **contend** without being contentious, and testify without ruining his testimony.

What we **contend earnestly for** is **the faith which was once for all delivered to the saints**. Notice that! Not "once upon a time" but **once for all**. The body of doctrine is complete. The canon is finished. Nothing more can be added. "If it's new it's not true, and if it's true it's not new." When some teacher claims to have a revelation which is above and beyond what is found in the Bible, we reject it out of hand. The faith has been delivered and we neither need nor heed anything else. This is our answer to the leaders of false cults with their books that claim equal authority with the Scriptures.

V. 4 The nature of the threat is unveiled in verse 4. The Christian fellowship was being invaded by subversive

elements. **Certain men** had wormed **in unnoticed**. It was an underground movement of stealth and deceit.

These fifth-columnists **long ago were marked out for this condemnation**. This seems to say that God selected these particular individuals to be doomed. But that is not the meaning. The Bible never teaches that some are chosen to be damned. When men are saved, it is through the sovereign grace of God. But when they are finally lost, it is because of their own sin and disobedience.

This expression teaches that the **condemnation** of apostates has been determined long beforehand. If men choose to fall away from the Christian Faith, then their **condemnation** is the same as that of the unbelieving Israelites in the wilderness, the rebel angels, and the Sodomites. They are not foreordained to fall away, but once they do apostatize by their own choice, they face the punishment predetermined for all apostates.

Two prominent features of these **ungodly** persons are their depraved conduct and their corrupt doctrine. In their behavior, they **turn the grace of God into lewdness**. They twist Christian liberty into license, and pervert freedom to serve into freedom to sin. In their doctrine, they **deny the only Lord[2] God and our Lord Jesus Christ**. They **deny** His absolute right to rule, His deity, His vicarious death, His resurrection — in fact, they **deny** every essential doctrine of His Person and work. While professing an expansive liberality in the spiritual realm, they are dogmatically and viciously opposed to the gospel, to the value of the precious blood of Christ, and to His being the only way of salvation.

Who are these men? They are supposed ministers of the gospel. They hold positions of leadership in Christendom. Some are bishops or church council members or seminary professors. But they all have this in common — they are against the Christ of the Bible and have invented for themselves a liberal[3] or Neo-Orthodox[4] "Christ", stripped of glory, majesty, dominion, and authority.

V. 5 There is no question about God's attitude toward these apostates. He has revealed it in the OT on more than one occasion. Jude now wants to **remind** his readers of three such example — the unbelieving Israelites, the angels that sinned, and the people of Sodom and Gomorrah.

The first example is Israel in the wilderness: **The Lord, having saved the people out of the land of Egypt, afterward destroyed those who did not believe** (see Num. 13, 14; 1 Cor. 10:5–10). God had promised the land of Canaan to the people. In that promise was all the enablement they needed. But they accepted the evil report of the spies at Kadesh and rebelled against the Lord. As a result, all those men who were twenty or over when they left Egypt perished in the wilderness, with the exception of Caleb and Joshua (see Heb. 3:16–19).

V. 6 The second example of rebellion and apostasy is **the angels** who sinned. All we know about them for certain is that they **did not keep** the **domain** that was assigned to them, they abandoned **their own abode**, and they are now restrained **in everlasting chains under darkness for** their final **judgment**.

It seems from Scripture that there have been at least two apostasies of angels. One was when Lucifer fell and presumably involved a host of other angelic beings in his rebellion. These fallen angels are not bound at the present time. The devil and his demons are actively promoting war against the Lord and His people.

The other apostasy of angels is the one referred to by Jude and also by Peter (2 Pet. 2:4). There is considerable difference of opinion among Bible students as to what event is referred to here. What we suggest is a personal viewpoint, not a dogmatic assertion of fact.

We believe that Jude is referring to what is recorded in Genesis 6:1–7. The sons of God left their proper estate as angelic beings, came down to the earth in human form, and married the daughters of men. This marital union was contrary to God's order and an abomination to Him. There may be a suggestion in verse 4 that these unnatural marriages produced offspring of tremendous strength and wickedness. Whether or not this is true, it is clear that God was exceedingly displeased with the wickedness of man at this time and determined to destroy the earth with a flood.

There are three objections to this

view: (1) The passage in Genesis does not mention angels, but only "sons of God." (2) Angels are sexless. (3) Angels do not marry.

It is true that angels are not specifically mentioned but it is also true that the term "sons of God" does refer to angels in Semitic languages (see Job 1:6; 2:1).

There is no Bible statement that angels are sexless. Angels sometimes appeared on earth in human form, having human parts and appetites (Gen. 18:2, 22; compare 19:1, 3–5).

The Bible does not say that angels do not marry but only that *in heaven* they neither marry nor give in marriage (Matt. 22:30).

Whatever historical incident may lie behind verse 6, the important point is that these angels abandoned the sphere which God had marked out for them and are now **in . . . chains** and in **darkness** until the time when they will receive their final sentence to perdition.

V. 7 The third OT apostasy which Jude mentions is that of **Sodom and Gomorrah and the cities around them** (Gen. 18:16–19:29). The introductory word **as** shows that the sin of the Sodomites had features in common with that of the angels. It was gross immorality that was utterly against nature and abhorrent to God.

The specific sin of perversion is discussed by Paul in Romans: "Their women exchanged the natural use for what is against nature. Likewise also the men, leaving the natural use of the woman, burned in their lust for one another, men with men committing what is shameful, and receiving in themselves the penalty of their error which was due" (Rom. 1:26b, 27). The men of Sodom, Gomorrah, Admah, and Zeboiim were greatly addicted to homosexuality. The sin is described here as **having . . . gone after strange flesh**, meaning that it is completely contrary to the natural order which God has ordained.

Is it mere coincidence that many modern day apostates are in the vanguard of those who publicly defend homosexuality and campaign for it to be legalized as long as it is done between consenting adults?

To all such libertines the cities of

Sodom and Gomorrah are exhibited **as an example** in **suffering the** punishment **of eternal fire**. That last expression **eternal fire** cannot mean that the fire which destroyed the wicked cities is eternal, but rather that in the thoroughness and vastness of its consuming power, it pictures the eternal punishment which will fall on all rebels.

V. 8 Jude reverts to the subject of present-day apostates, and launches into a description of their sins, their indictment, their counterparts in nature, their doom, and their ungodly words and deeds (vv. 8–16).

First of all is the matter of their sins. By dreaming **they defile the flesh**. Their thought life is polluted. Living in a world of filthy fantasies, they eventually find fulfillment of their dreams in sexual immorality, just like the men of Sodom.

They **reject authority**. They are rebels against God and against governmental institutions. Depend on them to be proponents of lawlessness and anarchy. Their names are on the membership rolls of organizations that are dedicated to the overthrow of government.

They **speak evil of** angelic **dignitaries**. It means nothing to them that "there is no authority except from God, and the authorities that exist are appointed by God" (Rom. 13:1b). They scorn the divine command, "You shall not . . . curse a ruler of your people" (Ex. 22:28). They speak contemptuously and spitefully against authority, whether it be divine, angelic, or human.

V. 9 In this respect they take liberties which even **Michael the archangel** would reject. When Michael disputed **with the devil about the body of Moses**, he did **not** dare rail **against him but** simply **said, "The Lord rebuke you!"** Here Jude shares with us an incident which is found nowhere else in the Bible. The question naturally arises, "Where did he get this information?"

Some say that the information was passed down by tradition. This may or may not be so.

The most satisfying explanation is that the information was supernaturally revealed to Jude by the same Holy Spirit who moved him to write the Epistle.

We have no definite knowledge why the dispute arose between Michael and Satan **about the body of Moses**. We do

know that Moses was buried by God in a valley of Moab. It is not unlikely that Satan wanted to know the spot so that he could have a shrine built there. Then Israel would turn to the idolatrous worship of Moses' bones. As the angelic representative of the people of Israel (Dan. 10:21), Michael would strive to preserve the people from this form of idolatry by keeping the burial site secret.

But the important point is this. Even if **Michael** is an **archangel**, the one whom God will use to cast Satan down from heaven (Rev. 12:7–9), still he did not presume to speak reproachfully to the one who rules in the realm of demons. He left all such rebuking to God.

V. 10 Headstrong and brazen, the apostates **speak** disrespectfully in areas of which they are ignorant. They do not realize that in any ordered society, there must be authority and there must be subjection to that authority. And so they surge forward and swagger around in arrogant rebellion.

The area in which they are most knowledgeable is that of natural instincts, the gratification of sensual appetites. With the mindlessness of unreasoning animals, they abandon themselves to sexual gratification, and in the process **they corrupt** and destroy **themselves**.

V. 11 A stinging indictment is pronounced upon them. **Woe to them!** Because of their stubborn and unrepentant heart, they store up wrath for themselves in the Day of wrath and revelation of the righteous judgment of God (Rom. 2:5).

Their career is described as a plummeting fall of ever increasing velocity. First **they have gone in the way of Cain**. They have **run greedily in the error of Balaam**. Finally they **perished in the rebellion of Korah**. Error and apostasy are never static. They lead people pell-mell to the precipice, then over it to destruction.

The way of Cain is basically the rejection of salvation through the blood of a sacrificial victim (Gen. 4). It is the attempt to appease God by human efforts. C. H. Mackintosh says, "God's remedy to *cleanse* is rejected, and man's effort to *improve* is put in its place. This is 'the way of Cain.' " But, of course, reliance on human effort leads to a hatred of grace and to the objects of grace. And that hatred eventually leads to persecution and even murder (1 Jn. 3:15).

The error of Balaam is the desire to become personally wealthy by making a business out of the service of God. Balaam professed to be a prophet of God, but he was covetous, and willing to prostitute his prophetic gift for money (Num. 22–24). Five times Balak paid him to curse Israel, and he was more than willing to do it, but he was forcibly restrained by God. Many of the things that he said were true and beautiful, but for all that, he was a hireling prophet. He couldn't curse the men of Israel, but he eventually succeeded in luring them into sin with the daughters of Moab (Num. 25:1–5).

Like Balaam, the false teachers of today are suave and convincing. They can speak out of both corners of their mouths at once. They suppress the truth in order to increase their income. The principal point is that they are greedy, seeking to make the house of God a house of merchandise.

Christendom today is leavened by the sin of simony. If the profit motive could somehow be removed, much of what passes as Christian work would come to a screeching halt. C. A. Coates warns:

> Man is so base that he makes gain for himself out of God's things. The ultimate point of man's baseness is that he will make gain out of God's things for himself. The Lord has a definite judgment on it all. We can see how Christendom is full of it, and we have to watch it in ourselves lest that element come in.[5]

The third reason for the **woe** pronounced by Jude is that these false teachers have **perished in the rebellion of Korah**. Along with Dathan and Abiram, Korah rebelled against the leadership of Moses and Aaron and desired to intrude into the priestly office (Num. 16). In this they were actually spurning the Lord. For their insubordination, they were swallowed alive in a great earthquake. God thus showed His extreme displeasure at **rebellion** against those whom He has set up as His representatives.

V. 12 Next Jude chooses five similes from the world of nature to picture the character and destiny of the apostates. Moffatt says that "sky, land and sea are ransacked for illustrations of the character of these men."

They **are spots in** the **love feasts**[6] which were held by the early Christians in connection with the Lord's Supper. They fear neither God nor man, and care for themselves rather than for the flock. They lure others to besmirch the faith.

They are clouds without water, appearing to hold promise of refreshment to the parched countryside, but then **carried along** (NKJV margin)[7] **by the winds**, and leaving disappointment and disillusionment.

They are **late autumn trees**, stripped of leaves and **fruit. Twice dead** may be an intensive form meaning thoroughly dead — or it may mean dead in the root as well as the branches. Also they are **pulled up by the roots**, as if torn out of the ground by a strong wind and leaving no stump as a possible future source of life and growth.

V. 13 They are **raging waves of the sea**, ungovernable, boisterous, and furious. For all their noise and motion, there is nothing to show but the foam of their **shame**. They glory in what they should be ashamed of and leave nothing of substance and value behind.

Finally, they are like **wandering stars, for whom is reserved the blackness of darkness forever. Wandering stars** are celestial bodies that do not move in regular orbit. They are worthless as navigational aids. How appropriate a description of the false teachers! It is impossible to get spiritual direction from these religious meteors, falling stars, and comets who blaze brightly for a moment, then fizzle out into darkness like firework rockets.

V. 14 The doom of the apostates was foretold by **Enoch** in **the seventh** generation **from Adam**. It is a prophecy that is found only in Jude's Epistle. Some think it is taken from the apocryphal Book of Enoch, but there is no proof that that spurious book existed in the time of Jude. Kelly said:

> It [Enoch] has every mark of having been written subsequent to the destruction of Jerusalem [and therefore after Jude's Epistle was written], by a Jew who still buoyed himself up with the hope that God would stand by the Jews.[8]

While we do not know how Jude learned of this ancient prophecy, a simple and plausible explanation is that the Holy Spirit revealed the words to him just as He guided in all the rest of the Epistle.

The prophecy begins: **"Behold, the Lord comes⁹ with ten thousands of His saints."** The prediction will have a preliminary and partial fulfillment when the Lord Jesus returns to earth after the Tribulation to destroy His foes and to reign as King. It will have its complete and final fulfillment at the end of the Millennium when the wicked dead are judged at the Great White Throne.

V. 15 Christ comes **to execute judgment on all**. The rest of the verse shows that the **all** here means all *the ungodly*. True believers will not be included. Through faith in Christ, they have been granted immunity from judgment, as promised in John 5:24: "Most assuredly, I say to you, he who hears My word and believes in Him who sent Me has everlasting life, and shall not come into judgment, but has passed from death into life." As the Son of Man to whom all judgment has been committed, the Lord Jesus will **convict all who are ungodly among them of all their ungodly deeds which they have committed in an ungodly way, and of all the harsh things which ungodly sinners have spoken against Him.** Four times in this one verse we find the word **ungodly** occurring. The people are **ungodly**, their deeds are **ungodly**, the manner in which they perform these deeds is **ungodly**, and they further manifest their ungodliness by their blasphemies against the Lord. He will convict them of the whole **ungodly** business, not just in the sense of making them feel a deep sense of guilt, but convicting them by pronouncing sentence as a result of their proven guilt.

V. 16 Their ungodly words and deeds are now described in more detail. They are **grumblers**, complaining against the providences of God instead of being thankful for His mercies. The fact that God hates such griping is abundantly proved by His punishment of Israel in the wilderness.

They are always finding fault with the Lord. Why does He permit wars and suffering? Why doesn't He put an end to all the social injustice? If He is all-powerful, why doesn't He do something about the mess the world is in? They also find fault with God's people for being narrow-minded in creed and puritanical in conduct.

They live lustfully, indulging the passions of the flesh and being the loudest in advocating permissiveness in the sexual realm.

Their arrogant speech proves a real attention-getter. By their shocking espousal of political, economic, and social extremism, they make the headlines. And their bold, shameless repudiation of basic Christian doctrines, such as their assertion that God is dead, give them a certain notoriety among liberal theologians.

Finally, they are masters in the art of flattery, thereby gaining a following for themselves and a comfortable income as well.

This portrait is true and accurate. It is confirmed almost every day by the news media of the world.

III. THE BELIEVER'S ROLE IN THE MIDST OF APOSTASY (Vv. 17–23)

V. 17 Jude now turns away from the apostates to the believers' role in the midst of these hireling shepherds. First he reminds them that they have been forewarned as to the oncoming peril. Then he encourages them to maintain themselves in a strong spiritual condition. Finally, he counsels them to use discernment in ministering to those who have been victimized by the apostates.

The **apostles** had predicted the rise of false teachers. This can be seen in the ministry of *Paul* (Acts 20:29, 30; 1 Tim. 4:1–5; 2 Tim. 3:1–9); *Peter* (2 Pet. 2:1–22; 3:1–4); and *John* (1 Jn. 2:18, 19).

Vv. 18, 19 The gist of their message was that **in the last time, mockers** would appear, following **their own ungodly lusts**.

To this testimony Jude now adds the explanation that these scoffers have three prominent characteristics. They are **sensual persons**, which means that they think and act as natural men. They **cause divisions**, drawing disciples after themselves and perhaps dividing people into various classes according to their progress in apostasy. They do not have **the Spirit**. They were never born from above and therefore have a total incapacity to understand the things of God.

V. 20 The believer's resource, of course, is to stay close to the Lord and live in unbroken fellowship with Him. But how is this done? Jude gives four steps.

The *first* is **building yourselves up on your most holy faith**, that is, the *Christian* faith. We build up ourselves on it by studying and obeying the Bible. Constant familiarity with the word guides us positively in the way of righteousness, and warns us against the perils along the way. "Men may decry doctrine," H. Pickering says, "but it is creed that produces character and not character that produces creed."

The *second* step is **praying in the Holy Spirit**. This means to pray as guided by the **Spirit**, in accordance with the will of God as revealed in the Bible or as privately revealed by the **Spirit** in a subjective way to the believer. It is in contrast to prayers which are recited mechanically or spun off without any real spiritual involvement.

V. 21 *Then again* believers are to **keep** themselves **in the love of God**. Here **the love of God** can be compared to the sunshine. The sun is always shining. But when something comes between us and the sun, we are no longer in the sunshine. That's the way it is with **the love of God**. It is always beaming down upon us. But if sin comes between us and the Lord, then we are no longer enjoying His love in practice. We can **keep** ourselves in His **love** first of all by lives of holiness and godliness. And if sin should come between, then we should confess and forsake that sin immediately. The secret is to let nothing come between us and God.

Nothing between my soul and the Savior,
Naught of this world's delusive dream;
Nothing preventing the least of His favor,
Keep the way clear, let nothing between.
— *Charles A. Tindley*

Finally, we should be eagerly **looking for the mercy of our Lord Jesus Christ unto eternal life. The mercy of our Lord** here refers to His imminent return to take His people home to heaven. In days of darkness and apostasy, we are to keep the light of the blessed hope burning in our hearts. It will prove a comforting and purifying hope (1 Thess. 4:18; 1 Jn. 3:3).

V. 22 A certain measure of spiritual discernment is necessary in dealing with victims of apostasy. The Scriptures make a distinction between the way we should handle those who are active propagandists of false cults and those who have been duped by them. In the case of the leaders and propagandists, the policy is given in 2 John 10, 11: "If anyone comes to you and does not bring this doctrine, do not receive him into your house nor greet him; for he who greets him shares in his evil deeds." But in speaking of those who have been deceived by false teachers, Jude counsels making a **distinction**[10] and gives two separate courses of action.

On some we should **have compassion**. That is, we should show a compassionate interest in them and try to guide them out of doubts and disputations into a firm conviction of divine truth.

V. 23 Then there are those who are on the verge of the precipice, ready to fall over into the flames of apostasy. These we are to **save** by strong, resolute warning and instruction, **hating even the garment defiled by the flesh**. In the OT the clothing of a leper was contaminated and had to be burned (Lev. 13:47–52). Today in dealing with people who have fallen into sexual sins, we must remember that material objects, such as clothing, for example, often excite the passions. As we see these things or feel them, there is a mental association with certain sins. So in dealing with people who have become defiled, we must be careful to avoid anything which might prove a temptation in our own lives. An unknown author expressed it like this:

The clothes that belong to a man have about them the association and infection of sin, the contagion of evil. Whatever is associated with a life of sin should be cast off and renounced, if we are to be safe from the infection and contagion of this soul-destroying disease.

J. B. Mayor warns, "While it is the duty of the Christian to pity and pray for the sinner, he must view with loathing all that bears traces of the sin."[11]

IV. THE BEAUTIFUL BENEDICTION (Vv. 24, 25)

V. 24 Jude closes with a beautiful benediction. It is the ascription of praise and worship **to Him who is able**. He is able to save (Heb. 7:25), able to establish (Rom. 16:25), able to aid (Heb. 2:18), able to subdue (Phil. 3:21) — and here He **is able to keep**. He is able to keep us in perfect peace (Isa. 26:3), He is able to keep that which we have committed to Him until that Day (2 Tim. 1:12), He is able to do exceedingly abundantly above all that we ask or think (Eph. 3:20), and **He is able to keep** us[12] **from stumbling**. This latter promise is especially timely for the days of apostasy to which Jude is referring.

But the promise doesn't stop there. He is able to make us stand **faultless** in **the presence of His glory with exceeding joy**. This is truly stupendous! When we think of what we were — dead through our trespasses and sins; when we think of what we are — poor, weak, failing servants; and then to think that one day we will stand absolutely **faultless** in the Throne Room of the universe, rejoicing **with exceeding joy** — what grace is this!

V. 25 He is not only our Keeper and Perfecter — He is **God our Savior**.[13] It is a marvel that **God** should be so interested in us that He would also become **our Savior**, in the sense that He devised the plan whereby we are saved and He provided His sinless Son as the sacrificial Lamb. **Who alone is wise** — ultimately all wisdom comes from God (cf. Jas. 1:5). Our wisdom is merely derived from the fount of wisdom, the only **wise** God.

If *worship* (Old English "worth-ship") means ascribing to God what He is *worthy of*, it will be **glory, and majesty, dominion, and power. Glory** — the superlative honor He deserves for all He is

and all He has done for us. **Majesty** — the dignity and splendor He deserves as the Supreme Monarch of the universe. **Dominion** — the unchallenged sway which is His by sovereign right. And **power** or authority — the might and prerogative to rule all that His hands have made.

He was worthy of such praise in the past, He is worthy at the present time, and He will be worthy of it throughout eternity. Apostates and false teachers may seek to rob Him of **glory**, detract from His **majesty**, grumble against His **dominion**, and challenge His **power**. But all true believers find their greatest fulfillment in glorifying and enjoying Him **both now and forever.**

Amen.

ENDNOTES

[1](V. 1) Instead of "sanctified" (*hēgiasmenois*) the critical (NU) text reads "beloved" (*ēgapēmenois*). The strong condemnation of immorality in this letter is probably better introduced by its opposite, "sanctified."

[2](V. 4) The word "God" is omitted by the NU text. The two "Lords" are different words in the original. In "Lord Jesus" the usual word *Kurios* is used. In "Lord God" a synonym, *Despotēs*, occurs. (Our derivative "despot" is not a good *translation* due to its bad connotation in *English*.) Both words mean "Lord," "Master," or "Owner."

[3](V. 4) "Liberal" means free, but in religion it refers to those who deny major doctrines of the faith, such as inspiration, the virgin birth, the deity of Christ, and the blood atonement. So-called liberals are often open to any doctrine or religion — as long as it is *not* the orthodox biblical teaching.

[4](V. 4) The Neo- ("New") Orthodox are not really orthodox. They accept some of the teachings of the Bible, but use orthodox terminology to mask unbiblical unbelief. For example, the Bible "becomes" the word of God to the Neo-Orthodox if it "speaks to him." To the orthodox believer, the Bible *is* the word of God.

[5](V. 11) C. A. Coates, *An Outline of Mark's Gospel and other Ministry*, p. 125.

6(V. 12) They called the feast an *agapē*, literally "love."

7(V. 12) The best reading is "carried away" or "along," as in the oldest (NU) and also the majority of mss. (majority text). The reading of the TR, KJV, and NKJV ("carried about") has weak support.

8(V. 14) William Kelly, "Lectures on the Epistle of Jude," *The Serious Christian*, I:123.

9(V. 14) "Comes" translates the aorist (*ēlthe*). This may translate a Semitic prophetic perfect, a future event seen as so certain that it is expressed in the past.

10(V. 22) The textual variants here are further complicated by the fact that the Greek verb *diakrinomai* can mean "doubting" or "making a distinction." See NKJV footnotes on vv. 22, 23.

11(V. 23) J. B. Mayor, *The Epistle of St. Jude and the Second Epistle of St. Peter*, p. 51.

12(V. 24) The majority text reads "them" for "you," meaning those sinning in the previous verses that spiritual Christians strive to save.

13(V. 25) As a constant reading of the textual notes in the NKJV NT will show, the NU text (largely Alexandrian) is very prone to be shorter ("omit") than the traditional and majority texts. Hence, when it *adds* something it is especially interesting. In verse 25, *three* additions are made, so that it reads:

"To the *only* God our Savior,
Through Jesus Christ our Lord,
Be glory and majesty,
Dominion and power,
Before all time," etc.

It *does* omit the word "wise," however. Perhaps Jude's perennially popular benediction was recited in this longer form in the Egyptian churches.

BIBLIOGRAPHY

Bigg, Charles. *The Epistles of St. Peter and St. Jude*. Edinburgh: T. & T. Clark Ltd., 1901.

Coder, S. Maxwell. *Jude: The Acts of the Apostates*. Chicago: Moody Press, 1958.

Green, Michael. *The Second Epistle General of Peter and the General Epistle of Jude*. Grand Rapids: Wm. B. Eerdmans Publishing Company, 1968.

Ironside, H. A. *Epistles of John and Jude*. New York: Loizeaux Bros., Inc., 1931.

Kelly, William. "Lectures on the Epistle of Jude," *The Serious Christian*. Vol. I. Charlotte, N.C.: Books for Christians, 1970.

Mayor, J. B. *The Epistle of St. Jude and the Second Epistle of St. Peter*. Grand Rapids: Baker Book House, 1965.

THE REVELATION OF JESUS CHRIST

Introduction

"Praise must fill our hearts when we read the words of this Prophecy and remember the grace which has saved us from all which is coming upon this age. Another blessing is the assurance of ultimate victory and glory."

— Arno C. Gaebelein

I. Unique Place in the Canon

The uniqueness of the last book of the Bible is apparent in the very first word — "Revelation," or in the original, *Apokalupsis*. This word, meaning *unveiling*, is the origin of our word *apocalyptic*, a type of writing found in Daniel, Ezekiel, and Zechariah in the OT, but only here in the New. It refers to the prophetic visions of the future that use symbols, figures, and other literary devices.

Not only does Revelation look *forward* to the *future* consummation of all things and the eventual triumph of God and the Lamb, but it also ties up the loose ends of the first sixty-five books of the Bible. In fact, that is how the book can best be understood, by knowing the whole Bible! The characters, symbols, events, numbers, colors, and so forth, are *nearly* all previously encountered in the word of God. Some have appropriately called the book "the Grand Central Station" of the Bible because it is here that the "trains" come in. What trains? The trains of thought begun in Genesis and the following books, such as the concepts of the scarlet line of redemption, the nation of Israel, the Gentile nations, the church, Satan the adversary of God's people, the Antichrist, and many more.

The Apocalypse (since the fourth century often erroneously labeled "The Revelation of St. John the Divine," but really "The Revelation of Jesus Christ" (1:1)), is the necessary culmination of the Bible. It tells us how everything is going to come out. Even a casual reading should be a stern warning to unbelievers to re-pent and an encouragement to God's people to persevere!

II. Authorship[†]

The book itself tells us the author is John (1:1, 4, 9; 22:8), writing at the command of his Lord, Jesus Christ. Ancient, strong, and widespread *external evidence* supports the view that the John meant is the Apostle John, the son of Zebedee, who labored for many years in Ephesus (in Asia Minor where all seven churches addressed in chapters 2 and 3 were located). He was exiled by Domitian to Patmos,[††] where he wrote the visions he was granted by our Lord. Later he returned to Ephesus, where he died at a ripe old age. Justin Martyr, Irenaeus, Tertullian, Hippolytus, Clement of Alexandria, and Origen, all ascribe the book to John. More recently a book called the *Apocryphon of John* (about A.D. 150), was found in Egypt that specifically attributes Revelation to John the brother of James.

The first opposition to the apostolic authorship was by Dionysius of Alexandria, but he didn't *want* it to be by John since he opposed the doctrine of the Millennium (Rev. 20). His vague and vacillating references first to John Mark and then to "John the Presbyter" as possible authors cannot counterbalance such strong testimony, although many modern scholars of the more liberal persuasion also reject John the Apostle as author. There is no evidence in church history of such an individual as "John the Presbyter" (Elder) other than the author of 2nd and 3rd John. These two Letters are in the same style as 1 John and also fit in well with John's Gospel in simplicity and vocabulary.

While the external evidence cited above is so strong, the *internal evidence* is not as clear. The vocabulary, rather rough "Semitic" Greek style (even containing a few expressions grammarians would call "solecisms"), and also the word order, convince many that the same person who wrote the Apocalypse could not have written the Gospel.

However, these differences can be explained, and are not without counterbalancing similarities between the two books.

Some, for example, accept an early date in the 50's or 60's for the *Revelation* (under Claudius' or Nero's reign) with the idea that John wrote his *Gospel* much later in the 90's when he had improved his mastery of Greek. However, this is not a necessary solution. It is quite possible that John had an amanuensis for his Gospel, and was strictly alone in his exile on Patmos. (The doctrine of inspiration is not affected either way, since God uses the individual style of the writer, not a generalized style for all Bible books.)

The general themes of light and darkness are found in both the Gospel of John and Revelation. Such words as "Lamb," "overcome," "word," "true," "living waters," and others tend to tie the two works together. Also, both John 19:37 and Revelation 1:7 quote Zechariah 12:10, yet do *not* use the word for "pierced" found in the Septuagint, but another word translated "pierced."[1]

A further reason for the differences in vocabulary and style in the Gospel and Revelation is the very different type of literature they represent. In addition, the great multitude of Hebraic phraseology in Revelation comes from drawing so widely upon the whole OT.

In conclusion, the traditional view that the Apostle John, the son of Zebedee and brother of James, wrote the Revelation has a firm historical foundation, and the problems can be explained without rejecting that authorship.

III. Date

An early date for Revelation is preferred by some, either in the 50's or late 60's. As was noted, this is partly to explain the less developed style of Revelation. Also, some believe that "666" (13:18) was a prediction of Nero,[2] who some believed would come back from the dead. This would suggest an early date. The fact that this did not happen did not affect the acceptance of the book. (Perhaps this suggests that it was written much *later* than Nero's time.)

Church fathers specifically indicate the latter part of Domitian's reign (about 96) as the time John was on Patmos receiving the Revelation. Since this is an early, informed, and widespread view among orthodox Christians, there is every reason to accept it.

IV. Themes and Scope[†]

A simple key to the understanding of the book of Revelation is to realize that it is divided into three main parts. Chapter 1 describes a vision in which John saw Christ robed as a Judge and standing in the midst of the seven churches. Chapters 2 and 3 have to do with the Church Age in which we now live. The remaining nineteen chapters have to do with future events following the close of the Church Age. We may divide the book as follows:

1. *The things which John saw*, that is, the vision of Christ as Judge of the churches.
2. *The things which are*: an outline of the Church Period from the death of the apostles to the time when Christ will take His saints to heaven (chaps. 2 and 3).
3. *The things which will take place after this*: an outline of future events from the Rapture of the saints to the Eternal State (chaps. 4–22). An easy way to remember the contents of this third section of the book is as follows:

a. Chapters 4 through 19 describe the Tribulation, a period of at least seven years during which God will judge the unbelieving nation of Israel and unbelieving Gentiles as well. These judgments are described under the figures of:

(1) Seven seals.
(2) Seven trumpets.
(3) Seven bowls.

†See p. ii.

b. Chapters 20–22 deal with Christ's Second Coming, His kingdom on earth, the Judgment of the Great White Throne, and the Eternal State.

In the Tribulation Period, the seventh seal contains the seven trumpets. Also the seventh trumpet contains the seven bowl judgments. Thus the Tribulation Period might be diagrammed as follows:

SEALS

1 2 3 4 5 6 7

TRUMPETS

1 2 3 4 5 6 7

BOWLS

1 2 3 4 5 6 7

The Parentheses in the Book

The above diagram gives the main line of thought through the book of Revelation. However, as the narrative proceeds, there are frequent interruptions to introduce the reader to various great personalities and events of the Tribulation Period. Some writers call these parentheses or insets. Some of the principal parentheses are:

1. The 144,000 sealed Jewish saints (7:1–8).
2. Gentile believers of this period (7:9–17).
3. The mighty angel with the little scroll (chap. 10).
4. The two witnesses (11:3–12).
5. Israel and the dragon (chap. 12).
6. The two beasts (chap. 13).
7. The 144,000 with Christ on Mount Zion (14:1–5).
8. The angel with the everlasting gospel (14:6, 7).
9. Preliminary announcement of Babylon's fall (14:8).
10. Warning to worshipers of the beast (14:9–12).
11. The harvest and the vintage (14:14–20).
12. The destruction of Babylon (17:1–19:3).

The Symbols in the Book

Much of the language of Revelation is symbolic. Numbers, colors, minerals, jewels, beasts, stars, and lampstands are all used to represent persons, things, or truths.

Fortunately some of these symbols are clearly explained in the book itself. For instance, the seven stars are the angels of the seven churches (1:20); the great dragon is the Devil, or Satan (12:9). Clues to the meaning of other symbols are found in other parts of the Bible. The four living creatures (4:6) are almost identical with the four living creatures of Ezekiel 1:5–14. In Ezekiel 10:20 they are identified as cherubim. The leopard, bear, and lion (13:2) remind us of Daniel 7 where these wild animals refer to the world empires of Greece, Persia, and Babylon respectively. Other symbols do not seem to be clearly explained in the Scriptures, and we must be extremely careful in seeking to interpret them.

The Scope of the Book

In studying Revelation, as in all Bible study, we must constantly keep in mind the distinction between the church and Israel. The church is a heavenly people, blessed with spiritual blessings, and called to share Christ's glory as His Bride. Israel is God's ancient, earthly people to whom God promised the land of Israel and a literal earthly kingdom under the rule of the Messiah. The true church is mentioned in the first three chapters, but is not seen again until the Marriage Supper of the Lamb in chapter 19:6–10. The Tribulation Period (4:1–19:5) is primarily Jewish in character.

Before closing this Introduction, it is only fair to say that not all Christians interpret the book of Revelation in the manner outlined above. Some think that the book was entirely fulfilled in the early history of the church. Others teach that Revelation presents a continuous picture of the Church Age from John's day to the end.

For all children of God, the book teaches the folly of living for things that will shortly pass away. It spurs us to witness to the perishing, and encourages us to wait with patience for the Lord's Return. For the unbeliever, the book is a solemn warning of the terrible doom that awaits all who reject the Savior.

its plentiful **works**, its arduous **labor**, and its patient endurance. It did not tolerate **evil** men in its midst. It had the ability to discern false apostles and to deal with them accordingly.

2:3, 4 For the sake of Christ's name, it had endured trial and adversity with **patience** and had **labored** tirelessly. But the tragedy of Ephesus was that it had **left** its **first love**. The fire of its affection had died down. The glowing enthusiasm of its early days had disappeared. The Christians could look back to better days when their bridal love for Christ flowed warm, full, and free. They were still sound in doctrine and active in service, but the true motive of all worship and service was missing.

2:5 They should **remember** the good days of their early faith, **repent** of their diminishing of **first** love, and repeat the devoted service which characterized the outset of their Christian life. Otherwise He would **remove** the **lampstand** at Ephesus, that is, the assembly would cease to exist. Its testimony would die out.

2:6 A further word of commendation concerns their hatred of **the deeds of the Nicolaitans**. We cannot be positive who these people were. Some think they were followers of a religious leader named Nicolas. Others point out that the name means "rule over the laity" and see in this a reference to the rise of the clerical system.

2:7 Those who have ears to hear God's word are encouraged to listen to **what the Spirit says to the churches**.

Then a promise is held out to the overcomer. In general, an overcomer in the NT is one who believes that Jesus Christ is the Son of God (1 Jn. 5:5), in other words, a true believer. His faith enables him to overcome the world with all its temptations and allurements. Perhaps in each of the letters the word has an additional thought, connected with the condition in that particular church. Thus an overcomer in Ephesus may be one who shows the genuineness of his faith by repenting when he has backslidden from his first love. All such **will . . .eat from the tree of life, which is in the midst of the Paradise of God**. This does not imply that they are saved by overcoming, but that their overcoming proves the reality of their conversion experience. The only way men are saved is by grace through faith in Christ. All who are saved will **eat from the tree of life**, that is, they will enter into eternal life in its fullness in heaven.

Ephesus is often taken to describe the condition of the church soon after the death of the apostles.

B. To Smyrna (2:8–11)

2:8 **Smyrna** means *myrrh* or *bitterness*. Here Christ presents Himself as **the First and the Last, who was dead and came to life**. This description would be particularly comforting to those who faced the threat of death daily.

2:9 With special tenderness, the Lord tells His suffering saints that He knows their **tribulation** thoroughly. To outward appearances, they might be **poverty**-stricken, but as far as spiritual things were concerned, they were **rich**. As Charles Stanley said, "There was peculiar honor in being near and like Himself, who had nowhere to lay His head. I have learned this: Jesus is specially the partner of His poor servants."

The saints at Smyrna were being bitterly attacked by the Jews. Historians tell of the eagerness with which these Jews sought to aid in the martyrdom of Polycarp, for instance. As **Jews**, they claimed to be God's chosen people, but by their blasphemous behavior they showed that they were **a synagogue of Satan**.

2:10 The Christians should **not fear any of those things** they would soon **suffer**. Some of them would be imprisoned and **tested** by **tribulation** for **ten days**. This time period may refer to **ten** *literal* **days**; to **ten** distinct persecutions under the Roman emperors who preceded Constantine; or to **ten** years of persecution under Diocletian.

The believers were encouraged to **be faithful until death**, that is, to be willing to die rather than renounce their faith in Christ. They would receive **the crown of life**, a special reward for martyrs.

2:11 Again the willing hearer is encouraged to listen to the Spirit's voice. The overcomer is promised exemption from **the second death**. Here an overcomer is one who proves the reality of his faith by choosing to go to heaven with a good conscience rather than stay on earth with a bad one. He will not be affected by **the second death**, the doom of all unbelievers (20:6, 14).

C. To Pergamos (2:12–17)

2:12 **Pergamos** (or Pergamum) means *high tower* or *thoroughly married*. This letter presents the Lord as the One **who has the sharp two-edged sword**. This is the word of God (Heb. 4:12) with which He will judge evildoers in the assembly (see v. 16).

2:13 Pergamos was the Asian headquarters for the cult of emperor-worship: hence it is called the place of **Satan's throne**. In spite of the surrounding paganism, the church had remained loyal to Christ, even though one of its members, **Antipas**, had been martyred for his confession of the Lord Jesus. He was the first known Asian to die for refusing to worship the emperor.

2:14, 15 But the Lord must reprove the church for permitting men with evil doctrine to continue in the Christian fellowship. There were **those who** held **the doctrine of Balaam** and **of the Nicolaitans. The doctrine of Balaam** sanctioned eating **things sacrificed to idols** and **sexual immorality**. It also refers to the practice of preaching for hire (Num. 22–25; 31).

The doctrine of the Nicolaitans is not defined. Many Bible scholars feel that these were libertines, teaching that those under grace were free to practice idolatry and sexual sins.

Dr. C. I. Scofield, however, links the doctrine with the rise of the clerical system:

It is the doctrine that God has instituted an order of "clergy" or priests, as distinguished from the "laity." The word is formed from two Greek words, *niko*, conqueror or overcomer, and *laos*, the people. The New Testament knows nothing of a "clergyman," still less of a priest, except as all sons of God in this dispensation are "a royal priesthood." In the apostolic church there were offices: elders (or bishops) and deacons; and gifts: apostles, prophets, evangelists, pastors and teachers (Eph. 4:11). These might or might not be elders or deacons. But late in the apostolic period there emerged a disposition to arrogate to elders alone authority to administer ordinances, and, generally, to constitute themselves a class between God and the people; they were the Nicolaitans. You will observe that what were "deeds" in the Ephesus or late apostolic period, had become a "doctrine" two hundred years later in the Pergamos or Constantine period.[8]

2:16 True believers are called on to **repent**. If they did, they would presumably expel the evil teachers from their midst. Otherwise the Lord Himself would **fight against** these evil men.

2:17 Obedient saints should **hear what the Spirit says to the churches**. The overcomer would be given **hidden manna** and a **white stone**. The overcomer in Pergamos may be the child of God who refuses to tolerate evil teaching in the local church. But what are **the hidden manna** and the **white stone**?

Manna is a type of Christ Himself. It may speak of heavenly food in contrast to foods offered to idols (v. 14). **Hidden manna** may be "some sweet, secret communion with Himself, known in the glory as the One who suffered here." The **white stone** has been explained in many ways. It was a token of acquittal in a legal case. It was a symbol of victory in an athletic contest. It was an expression of welcome given by a host to his guest. It seems clear that it is a reward given by the Lord to the overcomer and expressing individual approval by Him. Alford says that the **new name** indicates acceptance by God and title to glory.

Historically this church probably represents the time soon after Constantine, when the church was "thoroughly married" to the state. Thousands became nominal Christians, and the church tolerated pagan practices in its midst.

D. To Thyatira (2:18–29)

2:18 The name **Thyatira** means *perpetual sacrifice* or *continual offering*. In this letter the Son of God is seen as having **eyes like a flame of fire** and **feet like fine brass**. The **eyes** speak of piercing vision, and the brass **feet** speak of threatened judgment.

2:19 This church was outstanding in several ways. It was not lacking in good **works**, **love**, **service**, **faith**, and patient endurance. In fact, its **works** were increasing in quantity rather than declining.

2:20 But impure doctrine had been tolerated in the assembly with the result that **immorality** and idolatry were being practiced. The church had permitted a self-styled **prophetess** named **Jezebel**⁹ to lead God's servants into sin. Just as Jezebel in the OT had corrupted God's people with fornication and idolatry, so this woman taught that Christians could engage in these practices without sinning. Perhaps she encouraged the believers to join the trade guilds of Thyatira, even though this involved honoring the guild god or goddess and participating in festivals where food was **sacrificed to idols**. She doubtless justified this compromise with the world on the ground that it would allegedly advance the cause of the church.

2:21–23 Because she refused **to repent**, the Lord was going to give her a **sick bed** of tribulation in place of her bed of lust. **Those who** committed **adultery** with her would be thrown into a bed of **great tribulation** and death **unless they** forsook her and escaped from her **deeds**. Then **all the churches** would **know** that the Lord is watching and that He rewards according to man's deeds. There was probably a literal prophetess in Thyatira named Jezebel. But Bible students have also seen here a reference to the rise of a false church system with its adoration of images, sale of indulgences, and priestly absolution from such sins as fornication.

2:24, 25 There was a faithful remnant in Thyatira (**the rest . . . as many as do not have this doctrine**) which had not been initiated into the secret doctrines and rites of Jezebel, otherwise known as **the depths of Satan. No other burden** of responsibility was placed on them than to **hold fast** the truth until Christ's Coming.

2:26–28 The overcomer in Thyatira was the true believer who steadfastly maintained the **works** of genuine Christianity. His reward would be to reign with Christ during the Millennium. He would have authority **over the nations** and would **rule them with a rod of iron**. All sin and rebellion would be punished severely and promptly. The Lord promised to give to the overcomer **the morning star**. The Lord Jesus is the Bright and Morning Star (22:16). Just as the **morning star** appears in the heavens before the sun rises, so Christ will appear as the Morning Star to rapture His church to heaven before He appears as the Sun of Righteousness to reign over the earth (1 Thess. 4:13–18; Mal. 4:2). Thus the overcomer is promised a part in the Rapture. He does not earn this by his works, but his works demonstrate the reality of his faith. Because he is genuinely converted, he will be given **the morning star**.

2:29 In this and the following three letters, the formula **"He who has an ear, let him hear . . ."** follows the promise to the overcomer rather than preceding it. This may indicate that from this point on, only those who overcome are expected to have an ear to **hear what the Spirit says to the churches**.

E. To Sardis (3:1–6)

3:1 **Sardis** means *those escaping* or *renovation*. The Lord reveals Himself as the One **who has the seven Spirits of God and the seven stars**. It is in the power of the Holy Spirit that He controls the churches and their messengers. Sardis was a church of lifeless profession. It had a reputation as a Christian assembly, but for the most part, it simply went through a formal, dull routine. It did not overflow with spiritual life. It did not sparkle with the supernatural.

3:2, 3 The Lord called it to a new zeal and a new endeavor to **strengthen** what little there remained for Him, for even that was showing signs of dying. The people had often started projects for God but had never brought them to completion. Christ warned them to **hold fast** the sacred deposit of truth and to **repent** of their lifelessness. Unless they awoke, He would **come** unexpectedly and deal with them in judgment.

3:4 There was a remnant **even in Sardis** which had not lost its Christian testimony. These believers who had **not defiled their garments** with worldliness would **walk with** Christ **in white**.

3:5 They were the overcomers, whose righteous acts marked them as true believers. Their **white garments** speak of the righteousness of their lives. Because they were manifestly true Christians, their names would not be blotted out of **the Book of Life**.

Some think that the **Book of Life** contains the names of all who have been given *physical* life. According to this view, those who show by their lives that they have been truly born again will not be removed from the book whereas, by implication, all others will.

Others see the book as a register of those who have *spiritual* life. They are promised that their names will not be blotted out, that is, that they will never lose their salvation. According to this view, the fact that some names will not be blotted out does not require that others will.

Because of the consistent teaching of the Scriptures that salvation is by grace, not by works, and because of the clear statements that the true believer is eternally secure (John 3:16; 5:24; 10:27–29), verse 5 cannot imply the possibility of a child of God ever being lost.

Our Lord adds the promise that He **will confess** the names of the overcomers **before** His **Father** and the **angels** of heaven.

3:6 Again men are called to hear this solemn warning against having a religious profession without ever having been born again.

The assembly at Sardis is often taken as a picture of the Post-Reformation period when the church became formal, ritualistic, worldly, and political. The Protestant state churches of Europe and the American colonies were leaders in this drift.

F. To Philadelphia (3:7–13)

3:7 Philadelphia means *love for the brethren*. To this church the Lord appears as **He who is holy, He who is true, He who has the key of David, He who opens and no one shuts, who shuts and no one opens.**

In other words, He has administrative power and uncontestable control:

The open door which Jewish synagogue and pagan cults were powerless to shut is the God-given opportunity to preach Christ to all who will hear. The key of David is an Old Testament allusion to the absolute sovereignty of God in opening doors and shutting mouths. See Isaiah 22:22.[10]

3:8 The assembly at Philadelphia re-

ceived only words of praise from the Lord. The saints had been faithful. They had been zealous for good **works**. In their own human weakness, they had trusted in the Lord. As a result, they had been able to preserve the truth by living it out in their lives. They had **not denied** Christ's **name**. Therefore, He would **set before** them **an open door** of opportunity that **no one** would be able to **shut**.

3:9 Those self-styled **Jews** who had opposed them so bitterly would be humbled before these simple believers. Those who claimed to be God's chosen people, though actually a **synagogue of Satan**, would be forced to admit that the despised Christians were actually the chosen flock.

3:10 **Because** the Philadelphians had maintained God's truth by living it before men, the Lord would **keep** them **from the hour of trial** which is to come upon all **who dwell on the earth**. This is a promise of exemption from the Tribulation Period described in chapters 6–19. Note that they will be kept from the *hour* **of trial**, that is, from the whole time period. Also they will be kept *out of* that period (Gk., *ek*), not through it.

"Those who dwell on the earth" is a technical term, meaning those who make this earth their home, "men of the world who have their portion in this life" (Ps. 17:14b).

3:11 Christ's coming is held before the saints as a motive to steadfast endurance. They should not let anyone rob them of the victor's **crown** when it is so near at hand.

3:12 The overcomer will be made **a pillar in the** inner sanctuary of **God**. Whatever else this may mean, it certainly carries the thought of strength, honor, and permanent security. He shall never leave this place of safety and joy. The overcomer will have three names written **on him: the name of . . . God, the name of the New Jerusalem, which comes down out of heaven from . . . God**, and the **new name** of the Lord Jesus. He will thus be identified as belonging to all three.

3:13 **He who has an ear** should listen to this message from **the Spirit** to **the churches**.

The church of Philadelphia is often taken as a symbol of the great evangeliare variously understood as angelic beings, as the redeemed people of both the OT and NT, and as NT saints only. The fact that they are crowned and enthroned suggests that they are saints who have been judged and rewarded.

4:5 It is clear that **the throne** here is one of judgment, with its terrifying **lightnings, thunderings, and voices**. The **seven lamps of fire** represent the Holy Spirit in His fullness and majesty. There is only one Spirit of God, but the seven represents perfection and completeness.

4:6 **The sea of glass like crystal** tells us that the throne is located in a place that is undisturbed by the restless, wild tossings of this world, or by the opposition of the wicked, who are like a troubled sea.

At **the throne** were **four living creatures, full of eyes in front and in back**. This speaks of clarity, breadth, and depth of vision.

4:7, 8 **The four living creatures** are difficult to identify. All we can say for certain is that they are created beings because they worship God. They seem to be a combination of the cherubim in Ezekiel 10 and the seraphim in Isaiah 6. Verse 7 describes cherubim and verse 8 pictures seraphim. These angelic beings are guardians of the throne of God. The cherubim seem to be associated with burning judgment and the seraphim with burning purification.

The description in verse 7 parallels the way Christ is presented in the Gospels:

> **lion** — Matthew — King;
> **calf** or ox — Mark — Servant;
> **man** — Luke — Son of Man;
> **eagle** — John — Son of God.

The living creatures sing ceaselessly of the holiness and eternity of God. Most manuscripts actually have the word **holy** nine times here, a strong trinitarian touch.

4:9, 10 **Whenever the living creatures** worship the eternal One **on the throne, . . . the twenty-four elders** prostrate themselves, **worship** the eternal God, **and cast their crowns before the throne**.

4:11 Their worship acknowledges the **Lord** as **worthy** of **glory and honor and power** because He **created all**

things, and by** His **will they exist**.

The vision prepares us for what is to follow. God is seen as the Almighty Ruler of the universe sitting on the throne of His glory, surrounded by worshiping creatures, and about to send judgment on the earth.

B. The Lamb and the Seven-Sealed Scroll (Chap. 5)

5:1 God is seen holding **a scroll** which has **seven seals** binding it. The scroll contains a record of the judgments that must fall on the earth before the Lord Jesus can set up His kingdom.

5:2, 3 **A strong angel** sends forth an appeal for someone **worthy to open the scroll and** break the **seals**, one by one. **No one**, celestial, terrestrial, or subterranean, was found qualified to unroll it or to read it. No angel, man, or demon has the wisdom and knowledge to execute judgment.

5:4 John **wept** copiously when it seemed **that no one was found worthy**. Did that mean that the wrongs of earth would go unrighted, that the righteous would never be vindicated, that the wicked would go unpunished? Did it mean that the kingdom would not come because the necessary purging of the earth would be thwarted?

5:5 **One of the elders** comforted John with the glad news that **the Lion of the tribe of Judah, the Root** (Creator and Progenitor) **of David**, was qualified **to open the scroll**, break **the seals**, and thus release the judgments. Jesus is qualified to be the Judge by His infinite wisdom, by divine decree (John 5:22, 27), by personal excellence, and by His work at Calvary.

In Revelation our Lord is presented both as Lamb and Lion. As the Lamb of God, He is the sacrificial One, bearing away the sins of the world. As the Lion, He is the Judge, punishing His enemies. At His First Coming, He was the Lamb. At His Second Coming, He will be the Lion.

5:6 When John **looked**, he saw the **throne** surrounded **by the four living creatures** and **the elders. In the** middle **stood a** little **Lamb** which looked as if **it had been** freshly **slain**. The Lamb had **seven horns** (omnipotence) **and seven**

eyes (omniscience). His possession of **the seven Spirits of God** reminds us that the Lord Jesus was endued with the full measure of the Holy Spirit (John 3:34b). **The seven Spirits of God sent out into all the earth** suggest omnipresence.

5:7, 8 As soon as the Lamb **took the** judgment roll **out of the right hand of** God the Father, **the living creatures and elders** prostrated themselves **before the Lamb. Each had a harp and golden bowls full of incense**, representing **the prayers of the saints**, probably the prayers of martyrs crying to God to avenge their blood (6:10). Though they handled the prayers, there is no suggestion that they presented them to God or had any part in answering them.

5:9, 10 In their **new song**, they acclaimed the Lamb as **worthy** to execute judgment because of His redemptive work on the cross. There is a question whether they include themselves among the redeemed (**"have redeemed us to God"**) or whether it should read, as in some versions, "and did purchase for God with Your blood men from every tribe and tongue and people and nation".[13]

Beyond redemption, the Lord has made believers **kings**[14] **and priests** to worship Him, to witness for Him, and to **reign** with Him over **the** millennial **earth**.

5:11 The chorus widened as **many angels** joined **the living creatures and the elders**, a choir numbering millions, perhaps billions, all participating in perfect harmony.

5:12 Their tribute is one that believers will sing throughout eternity. **"Worthy is the Lamb who was slain to receive:**

power — over my life, the church, the world, the universe;

riches — all my silver and my gold;

wisdom — the finest of my intellectual powers;

strength — my physical strength for His service;

honor — a single, pure desire to magnify Him in all my ways;

glory — my entire life devoted to glorifying Him;

blessing" — all my powers of praise for Him.

5:13 Now the music becomes a diapason, a full, deep burst of harmonious song. **Every creature ... in heaven and on the earth** joins in heaping eternal **blessing and honor and glory and power** on God the Father and on **the Lamb**.

This verse parallels Philippians 2:10 and 11, which insists that every knee will bow at the name of Jesus and every tongue confess Him Lord. No single, specific time is mentioned, but it will obviously be after the saved are raised to everlasting life and then after the unsaved are raised to everlasting judgment. Believers will have already acknowledged Jesus as Lord; unbelievers will then be compelled to honor Him. Universal homage to the Father and the Son is an assured fact.

5:14 The finale! As **the four living ones** say **"Amen"**, the **elders** fall **down** and worship the enthroned Lord **who lives forever and ever**.

C. The Opening of the Six Seals (Chap. 6)

6:1, 2 **When the Lamb opened** the first seal, **one of the four living creatures** cried out **"Come and see."**[15] In response, a rider, possibly the Antichrist, carrying **a bow**, came forth on **a white horse ... conquering** and bent on conquest. This may represent what is known today as cold war. The **bow** poses the threat of war, but there is no mention of an arrow. Perhaps there is even the suggestion of missile warfare since the bow is a weapon of distant combat. This rider does not actually *cause* warfare; it is not until the second seal that peace is taken from the earth.

6:3, 4 **The second living creature** summoned the second rider to come forth. This one carried **a great sword** and rode on **a horse** which was **fiery red**. A **sword** is used in hand to hand combat. Thus the second seal contemplates invading armies in fierce person to person warfare. The second rider takes **peace from the earth**.

6:5, 6 In obedience to **the third living creature**, a rider holding a set **of scales** came forth on **a black horse**. This represents famine, which often follows war. **A voice in the** middle **of the four living creatures** announced that **wheat**

and **barley** were being sold at prohibitive prices. The **scales** were used to weigh the rationed grain and were thus a symbol of famine. The expression **do not harm the oil and the wine** is difficult. Some say that these were the food of the poor. If they were staple items, then they must be protected in order to preserve life. It seems more likely, however, that the luxury items of the rich are contemplated here: historically, even in famine the rich can get some luxuries.

6:7, 8 The fourth living creature called forth **a pale horse** with **Death and Hades** as its riders. **Death** is associated with the body and **Hades** with the spirit and soul. By means of war, famine, pestilence, and wild **beasts, a fourth of the earth's** inhabitants are destroyed. We might think that plagues are no longer a threat because of modern antibiotics and wonder drugs. However, the great killer diseases are not conquered but merely dormant. They can spread throughout the world as fast as jet aircraft can carry them.

6:9 Now we are introduced to the first martyrs of the Tribulation Period (Matt. 24:9), Jewish believers who go out and preach the gospel of the kingdom and who are **slain for** their **testimony**. Their **souls** are **under the altar** in heaven.

6:10 **They** cry out to the sovereign **Lord**[16] to **avenge** their **blood**. As mentioned previously, **"those who dwell on the earth"** refers to unbelievers who look upon the earth as their home.

6:11 **White** robes are **given to** the martyrs, a symbol of their righteousness. They are told to wait until the final complement of tribulation martyrs is **completed**.

6:12, 13 The opening of **the sixth seal** brought tremendous convulsions of nature. **A great earthquake** shook land and sea, and the starry heavens were thrown into disorder. **The sun** darkened and **the moon** turned red **like blood. Stars . . . fell to the earth** like ripe figs when the **fig tree is shaken** violently.

6:14 **The sky receded** as if it were a sheet of parchment being **rolled up. Every mountain and island was** displaced by tremendous upheavals.

6:15 Not surprisingly, all classes of society were seized with panic. Recognizing that God was pouring out His wrath, they **hid themselves in the caves and** among the **rocks of the mountains**.

6:16, 17 They preferred to be crushed by tumbling **mountains and rocks** than to endure the judgment of God and **the wrath of the Lamb**. Too late they realized that no rebel **is able to stand** up against the Lamb's indignation.

D. The Saved in the Great Tribulation (Chap. 7)

Chapter 7 comes between the sixth and seventh seals and introduces us to two important companies of believers. The chapter answers the question at the end of chapter 6, "Who is able to stand?" Those described in this chapter will stand in the sense that they will be spared to enter the Millennium with Christ.

7:1–4 The vision of **four angels standing at the four corners of the earth** and **holding** back **the four winds** means that a great storm is about to burst on the world. However, the angels are told to delay this terrible destruction until **the servants of God** have been **sealed on their foreheads**. Twelve thousand persons from each of **the** twelve **tribes** of **Israel** are then **sealed**.

7:5–8 The 144,000 are clearly Jewish believers, not members of some 20th century Gentile cult. These Jewish saints are saved during the early part of the Tribulation. The seal on their foreheads brands them as belonging to God and guarantees that they will be preserved alive during the ensuing seven years.

Two tribes are absent from the list: Ephraim and Dan. Perhaps they are omitted because they were leaders in idolatry. Some think that the Antichrist will come from Dan (Gen. 49:17). The tribes of **Joseph** and **Levi** are included in the list, **Joseph** doubtless taking the place of his son, Ephraim.

7:9 The people described in this section are Gentiles from **all nations, tribes, peoples, and tongues**. They stand **before the throne and before the Lamb with white robes** (the righteous acts of the saints, 19:8) and holding **palm branches**, which are a symbol of victory.

7:10 These are Gentiles who will be

saved during the Great Tribulation by trusting the Lord Jesus. In their song they celebrate their **salvation** and attribute it **to their God and to the Lamb**.

7:11, 12   The angels . . . and the elders and the four living creatures join in worshiping **God**, although the subject of redemption is missing from their praise. As the hymnwriter said, "Angels never felt the joy that our salvation brings." But they do chant His praises and pronounce Him worthy of seven distinct forms of **honor**.

7:13, 14   When **one of the elders** asked John **who** were **these** people **in white** and **where did they come from**, John confessed ignorance but a desire to know. Then the elder explained that they had **come out of the great tribulation, and** had **washed their robes and made them white in the blood of the Lamb**. "When we stand face to face with an inexplicable mystery," writes F. B. Meyer, "how comforting it is to be able to say in perfect faith, 'Thou knowest.' "

7:15   The elder went on to explain their present location and service. Bible students are not agreed as to whether this Gentile multitude is seen in heaven or on the millennial earth. The blessings described are true of either place. If the Millennium is in view, then the throne of God and **His temple** refer to the temple which will be located in Jerusalem during the Kingdom Age (Ezek. 40–44).

Notice the blessings that are described:

Perfect nearness: **Therefore they are before the throne of God**.

Perfect service: **and serve Him day and night in His temple**.

Perfect fellowship: **He who sits on the throne will dwell among them**.

7:16   Perfect satisfaction: **They shall neither hunger nor thirst anymore;**

Perfect security: **the sun shall not strike them, nor any heat;**

7:17   Perfect guidance: **for the Lamb who is in the midst of the throne will shepherd them and lead them to fountains of the waters of life** (NKJV margin).

Perfect joy: **God will wipe away every tear from their eyes**.

E.   The Seventh Seal and the Start of the Seven Trumpets (Chaps. 8, 9)

8:1   After the parenthesis of chapter 7, in which we saw two companies of Tribulation saints, we now come to **the seventh** and final **seal**. This is introduced by a thirty-minute **silence in heaven**, an awesome hush which precedes everdeepening judgments.

8:2   No specific judgment is mentioned when the seventh seal is broken. The narrative moves directly to seven trumpet judgments. From this we infer that the seventh seal *consists of* the **seven trumpets**.

8:3, 4   The **angel** in this verse is often understood to be the Lord Jesus. He is called the Angel of Jehovah in the OT (Gen. 16:13; 31:11, 13; Judg. 6:22; Hos. 12:3, 4). **The prayers of all the saints** ascend to the Father through Him (Eph. 2:18). He takes **much incense** to **offer it with the prayers**. The **incense** speaks of the fragrance of His Person and work. By the time **the prayers** reach God the Father, they are perfectly flawless and perfectly effectual.

In the context, **the prayers** are those of Tribulation **saints**, beseeching God to punish their enemies, although the order is true of all prayer.

8:5   In answer to their prayers, **the angel . . . threw** flaming coals **to the earth**, causing loud explosions, **thunderings, lightnings and an earthquake**. As H. B. Swete says, "The prayers of the saints return to the earth in wrath."[17] Thus the seven trumpet judgments are introduced with violent disturbances of nature.

8:6   We have now come to the middle of the Tribulation. These trumpet judgments take us on to the time when Christ descends to the earth, destroys His foes, and ushers in His kingdom. The first four judgments affect man's natural environment; the last three affect man himself. Many commentators note the resemblance between these plagues and the ones which fell on Egypt (Ex. 7–12).

8:7   When the **first angel sounded, a third** part **of the earth** (NKJV margin), **trees**, and **grass** were **burned up** by **hail and fire . . . mingled with blood**. It is

best to take this literally as a terrible calamity on the areas from which man gets
most of his food.

8:8, 9 **Something like a great** flaming **mountain . . . was thrown into the
sea**, turning **a third of the sea** into
blood, destroying **a third** of the marine
life, and wrecking **a third of the ships**.
This would not only decrease man's local
food supply still further but would reduce his means of obtaining food from
distant places.

8:10, 11 This third trumpet signaled
the fall of a blazing **star** called **Wormwood**, causing **a third** of man's **water**
supply to become **bitter** at its sources.
Apparently the **bitter** water was also
poisonous, since **many men died**. It is
difficult to identify **Wormwood**. When
the trumpet sounds, these verses will be
all too clear to earth-dwellers. In the
study of prophecy, it is good to remember that there are many things that will
not be clear until they actually take
place.

8:12 It appears that the **sun, . . .
moon**, and **stars** will be damaged in such
a way that they will give only two-thirds
of their usual light. This fourth trumpet
resembles the plague of darkness in
Egypt.

8:13 **An eagle** (NKJV margin)[18] **flying** in mid-heaven pronounces a threefold **woe to the inhabitants of the earth**,
that is, those whose outlook is utterly
worldly, who are at home on the earth,
who are not true believers. The three remaining judgments are also known as
three woes because of their dire effect on
men.

9:1, 2 **The star fallen from heaven**
may be a **fallen** angel or even Satan himself. He had the **key to** the shaft of **the
bottomless pit** (the *abyss* in Greek). This
is the dwelling place of demons. When
he opened the entrance to the abyss, billows of **smoke** poured forth, as if from
a huge **furnace**, veiling the landscape in
darkness.

9:3, 4 Swarms of **locusts** emerged
from **the smoke**, capable of inflicting excruciating pain like the sting of **scorpions**. But their **power** was restricted.
They were forbidden **to harm** vegetation. Their victims were those **who** did
**not have the seal of God on their fore-

heads**, that is, all who were unbelievers.

9:5, 6 Although their sting was not
fatal, it inflicted **torment** that lasted **for
five months**. It was so intense that **men**
wanted **to die**, but they could not.
These locusts probably represent demons which, when released from the
pit, took possession of unsaved men and
women. This demon-possession caused
the most intense physical suffering and
mental torture, as it did with Legion in
Mark 5:1-20.

9:7 The description **of the locusts** is
designed to create an impression of conquest and victory. **Like horses prepared
for battle**, they were a conquering host.
Wearing **gold**-like **crowns**, they were authorized to rule in men's lives. With
human-appearing **faces**, they were creatures of intelligence.

9:8–10 With **hair like women's**,
they were attractive and seductive. With
lion-like **teeth**, they were ferocious and
cruel. With armor-like iron **breastplates**,
they were difficult to attack and destroy.
With **wings** that made a great sound,
they were terrifying and demoralizing.
Tails like scorpions equipped them to
torture both physically and mentally. **Their power . . . to hurt men five
months** meant unrelieved suffering.

9:11 **They had** a **king . . . whose
name in Hebrew is Abaddon** (destruction), **but in Greek . . . Apollyon** (destroyer). This is generally understood to
refer to Satan.

9:12 **The first of three woes is past**.
The worst is yet to come. The judgments
increase in intensity.

9:13–15 The mention of **the golden
altar which is before God** links the following judgment to the prayers of God's
oppressed people. The sixth trumpeter
releases **four angels who are bound at
the great river Euphrates**. These **four
angels**, perhaps demons, had been held
in readiness for this exact moment to go
forth and **kill a third of mankind**.

9:16, 17 Following them were **two**[19]
hundred million riders on horses with
breastplates that were **fiery red, hya-
cinth blue, and sulfur yellow**. The
horses' **heads** were like lions', and their
mouths belched **fire, smoke**, and sulfur
(**brimstone**).

9:18, 19 These three: **fire, smoke**,

and brimstone, represent **three plagues** which kill **a third of mankind**. Not only do the horses kill with **their mouths**, but they also wound with **their** serpentine **tails**.

There are many unanswered questions in this passage. Are the four angels in verse 14 the same as those in 7:1? Are the riders real men, or do they represent demons, diseases, or other destructive forces? What are the three plagues that are pictured by **fire, smoke**, and sulfur?

It is worth noticing that death is inflicted by the horses, not the riders. One writer suggests that the mighty army of horsemen might symbolize "some irresistible delusion of the devil, coming from the East." Hamilton Smith says:

> "Their power is in their mouth" may indicate that this delusion will be presented with all the persuasive eloquence of speech. But behind the delusion is the power of Satan, symbolized by their tails being like serpents.[20]

9:20, 21 Although two-thirds **of mankind** survived **these plagues, they did not repent**, but continued to bow down to **demons** and handmade **idols**, lifeless and impotent. They did not turn from **murders, sorceries** (drug related[21]), **sexual immorality**, and **thefts**. Punishment and suffering cannot change a sinner's character; only the new birth can do that.

F. The Mighty Angel and the Little Scroll (Chap. 10, 11)

10:1 John now sees **another mighty angel coming down from heaven**. The description leads many to believe that He is the Lord Jesus. He had a **rainbow on his head**, the sign of God's covenant. **His face was like the sun**, an expression of unveiled glory. His **feet** were like **pillars of fire**, the **pillars** speaking of strength and the **fire** of judgment.

10:2 **He** held **a little book** or scroll, no doubt a record of impending judgments. With **his right foot on the sea and his left foot on the land**, He claimed His right to worldwide dominion.

10:3–6 When He called out **with a loud voice, . . . seven thunders** sounded. Apparently John could understand the message of these thunders, but when he was about to write, the angel forbade him. The angel then **swore by** God, the Creator, **that there should be delay no longer**.

10:7 **The mystery of God would be** fulfilled during the time of the seventh trumpet. **The mystery of God** has to do with God's plan to punish all evildoers and to usher in the kingdom of His Son.

10:8, 9 John was commanded to **eat** the **little book**, that is, he was to read and meditate on the judgments recorded in it.

10:10 As predicted by the angel, the scroll was **sweet as honey in** his **mouth, but bitter** in his **stomach**. For the believer, it is sweet to read of God's determination to glorify His Son where He was once crucified. It is sweet to read of the triumph of God over Satan and all his hosts. It is sweet to read of the time when the wrongs of earth will all be made right. But there is bitterness also connected with the study of prophecy. There is the bitterness of self-judgment which the prophetic Scriptures produce. There is the bitterness of viewing the judgments which must soon fall on apostate Judaism and Christendom. And there is the bitterness of contemplating the eternal doom of all who reject the Savior.

10:11 John was told that he **must prophesy again about many peoples, nations, tongues, and kings**. The remaining chapters of Revelation fulfill this mandate.

G. The Two Witnesses (11:1–14)

11:1, 2 John was now commanded to **measure the temple** and **the altar**, and to number the worshipers. Measuring here seems to carry the idea of preservation. He was *not* to measure **the court** of the **Gentiles** because it would be trampled by the nations **for forty-two months** — the latter half of the Tribulation Period (see Luke 21:24). **The temple** mentioned here is the one that will be standing in Jerusalem during the Tribulation. The act of numbering the worshipers may signify that God will preserve a remnant of worshipers for Himself. **The altar** pictures the means by which they will approach Him, that is, the work of Christ at Calvary.

11:3 God will raise up **two witnesses** during the last half of the Tribulation. **Clothed in sackcloth**, a symbol of mourning, they will cry out against the sins of the people and announce God's coming indignation.

11:4 The two witnesses are compared to **two olive trees** and **two lampstands**. As **olive trees** they are filled with the Spirit (oil). As **lampstands** they bear testimony to the truth of God in a day of darkness. (For an OT parallel see Zech. 4:2–14.)

11:5 For three and one half years, the witnesses are miraculously preserved from harm. **Fire** proceeding **from their mouth** consumes their foes, and even the effort **to harm them** is punished by death.

11:6 They **have power** to bring drought on the earth, **to turn** the waters **to blood, and to strike the earth with all plagues**. It is not surprising that they have been commonly associated with Moses and Elijah. Their power **to turn** the waters **to blood** and **to strike the earth with all plagues** reminds us of what Moses did in Egypt (Ex. 7:14–20; 8:1–12:29). Their power over fire and weather reminds us of Elijah's ministry (1 Kgs. 17:1; 18:41–45; 2 Kgs. 1:9–12).

McConkey says:

> They will warn the people who crowd the temple of the Man of Sin whom they come to worship. They will admonish them of the shortness of his time of triumph; of the coming of Jesus to destroy him; of the perils which the tribulation will bring; of the need of counting not their lives dear unto themselves when the test of life and death shall come; of their need to fear not him who can kill the body only but to fear Him who can cast both body and soul into hell; of the splendor and nearness of the King and His kingdom after they have suffered awhile; of the sureness that if they suffer with Him they shall reign with Him; and of the eternal peace, righteousness and glory that shall be theirs who endure unto the end, even though it may mean martyrdom in the great hour of trial through which they are passing. Mighty indeed will be their testimony from the Book.[22]

11:7 **When they finish their testimony, the beast** from the **bottomless pit** will **kill them**. This beast seems to be the same as the one in 13:8 — the head of the revived Roman Empire.

11:8 The **dead bodies** of the witnesses **lie in the street** of Jerusalem for three and one half days. Jerusalem is here **called Sodom** because of its pride, indulgence, prosperous ease, and indifference to the needs of others (see Ezek. 16:49). And it is called **Egypt** because of its idolatry, persecution, and enslavement to sin and unrighteousness.

11:9 People **from** all **nations** view **their dead bodies** but do **not allow** them to be buried, a tremendous indignity in almost all cultures.

11:10 Great rejoicing breaks out because their unpopular prophecies have been silenced, and people exchange **gifts**, much as they do today at Christmas time. The only prophets people love are dead ones.

11:11, 12 **After the three-and-a-half days, . . . God** raises them from the dead, much to the consternation of the populace, and takes them **to heaven** as **their enemies** watch.

11:13, 14 At **the same** time, Jerusalem is shaken by **a great earthquake**, one **tenth of the city** falls, and **seven thousand people** are **killed**. The survivors give **glory** to **God**, not genuine worship, but a grudging admission of His power. **The second woe is past**.

This does not mean that everything from 9:13 to 11:13 comprises the second woe. On the contrary, chapter 10 and 11:1–13 are a parenthesis between **the second woe** (sixth trumpet) and **the third woe** (seventh trumpet).

H. The Seventh Trumpet (11:15–19)

11:15 The blowing of the seventh trumpet reveals that the Great Tribulation is over and the reign of Christ has begun. **The kingdoms**[23] **of this world have become the kingdoms of our Lord and of His Christ, and He shall reign forever and ever!**

11:16, 17 Falling **on their faces** before **God**, the **twenty-four elders** express **thanks** to Him because He has assumed His **great power** and inaugurated His reign.

11:18 The unbelieving **nations** are **angry** with Him, and try to prevent His coronation. But now the time has come for Him to be angry with them, to judge those who do not have spiritual life, to **destroy** the destroyers. And it is time for the Lord to **reward** His own, **prophets** and people, **small and great**.

11:19 God has not forgotten **His covenant** with His people, Israel. When **the temple of God** is **opened in heaven, the ark of His covenant** appears, a symbol that all He promised to Israel will come to pass. There are **lightnings, noises, thunderings, an earthquake, and great hail**.

I. The Key Figures in the Tribulation (Chaps. 12–15)

12:1 A **great sign appeared in heaven**, namely, **a woman clothed with the sun, with the moon under her feet, and on her head a garland of twelve stars**. The **woman** is Israel. The **sun, moon** and **stars** depict the glory and dominion which has been promised to her in the coming kingdom, just as they pictured Joseph's ultimate rule over his father, mother, and brothers (Gen. 37:9–11).

12:2 The woman is **in labor**, awaiting the **birth** of a baby. Much of the history of Israel is telescoped in these verses, with no indication that time gaps exist between events, or that the events are necessarily in chronological order.

12:3 A second **sign** in heaven is **a fiery red dragon** with **seven heads and ten horns** and a diadem on each head. The **dragon** is Satan, but since the description parallels that of the revived Roman Empire in 13:1, it may be Satan energizing that world power.

12:4, 5 With a swish of **his tail**, the dragon sweeps **a third of the stars of heaven . . . to the earth**, a possible reference to war in heaven which takes place in the middle of the Tribulation and which results in fallen angels being cast from heaven to earth (see vv. 8, 9).

The dragon is ready **to devour** the **Child as soon as** He is **born** — fulfilled in the attempt of Herod the Great, vassal of Rome, to destroy the newborn King of the Jews. The **male Child** is clearly Jesus, destined **to rule all the nations with a rod of iron**. The record here jumps from His birth to His Ascension.

12:6 The present Church Age is passed over between verses 5 and 6. In the middle of the Tribulation, a portion of the nation of Israel flees to a secret place of refuge in **the wilderness** (some think it is Petra). These people remain in hiding for three and one half years.

12:7 **War** breaks out **in heaven** with **Michael and his angels** on one side and **the dragon and his angels** on the other. This is in the middle of the Tribulation. Michael, the archangel, is associated with the affairs of the nation of Israel (Dan. 12:1).

12:8, 9 The dragon is so thoroughly defeated that he loses any right of access to **heaven**. He and his minions are **cast** down **to the earth**. This is not his final fate, however (see 20:1–3, 10). Notice John's description of him: **the great dragon, that serpent of old, the Devil, Satan**, the one **who deceives the whole world**.

12:10 The eviction of the dragon is followed by **a loud** cry **in heaven** that God's triumph and the day of His people's conquest have come. This anticipates the Millennial Kingdom. In the meantime, it is a glorious event that **the accuser of our brethren . . . has been cast down**.

12:11 The announcement continues. Persecuted Jewish believers **overcame** the evil one **by the blood of the Lamb and by the word of their testimony**. Their victory was based on the death of Christ and **their testimony** to the value of that death. In faithfulness to Him, they sealed **their testimony** with their blood.

12:12, 13 The **heavens** can **rejoice** over the dragon's departure, but it is bad news for **the earth and the sea! The devil . . . knows** his **time** is **short** and he is determined to pour out his wrath as widely as possible. The dragon's spleen is vented especially against Israel, the nation from which the Messiah came.

12:14 The faithful Jewish remnant is **given two wings of a great eagle**, enabling it to escape quickly to its **wilderness** hideout. (Some have conjectured that these **wings** speak of a great Air Force.) There the remnant is cared for and protected from the serpent's attacks for three and one half years (**a time, times, and half a time**).

12:15, 16 In an effort to foil Israel's escape, **the serpent** causes a great **flood** to follow the people, but an earthquake swallows the water and the devil is outwitted.

12:17 Furious over this humiliation, he seeks to wreak vengeance on Jews who had remained in the land — Jews who show the reality of their faith by keeping **the commandments of God** and by bearing **testimony** to **Jesus**.

13:1 Chapter 13 introduces us to two great beasts: one **beast rising up out of the sea**, and one out of the earth or land, that is, the land of Israel. There is no doubt that these beasts symbolize men who will play prominent roles during the Tribulation Period. They combine the features of the four beasts of Daniel 7:3-7. The first beast is the head of the revived Roman Empire, which will exist in a ten-kingdom form. He rises **out of the sea**, a type of the Gentile nations. He has **ten horns**. Daniel predicted that the Roman Empire would be revived in a ten-kingdom form (Dan. 7:24). He has **seven heads**. In 17:9, 10 these are said to be seven kings, a possible reference to seven different types of rulers or seven different stages of the empire. He has **ten** diadems **on his horns**. These speak of the power to rule, which was given to him by the dragon, Satan. He has a **blasphemous name on his heads**, and he makes claims for himself as if he were God and not a mere man.

13:2 **The beast** is **like a leopard, his feet like** a bear's, and **his mouth like** a lion's. In Daniel 7, the **leopard** symbolizes Greece; the **bear** is a type of Medo-Persia; and the **lion** represents Babylon. The revived Roman Empire thus resembles its predecessors in that it is swift to conquer like **a leopard**, powerful as **a bear**, and greedy as **a lion**. In short, it combines all the evil features of the preceding world empires. The empire and its ruler receive supernatural strength from Satan.

13:3 The beast has a mortal **wound** in one of its heads. Scofield explains: "Fragments of the ancient Roman Empire have never ceased to exist as separate kingdoms. It was the imperial form of government which ceased; the one head wounded to death."[24] The **deadly**

wound is **healed**. In other words, the empire is revived with an emperor as head, namely, **the beast**.

13:4 **The beast** is **worshiped** by men. They are not only amazed at him; they actually worship him as God. They also worship **the dragon**.

13:5, 6 The beast makes proud boasts and utters unspeakable **blasphemies**. He is allowed **to make war** (NKJV margin) **for forty-two months**. He speaks with callous irreverence against God's **name, His tabernacle**, and the hosts of **heaven**.

13:7 He makes **war** with God's people and overcomes many of them. They die rather than submit to him. His rule extends over all the world — the last world empire before Christ's Reign.

13:8 Those who are not true believers readily **worship** the beast. Because they never trusted Christ, their names were never **written in the Book of Life of the Lamb**. And because their names are not found among those of the redeemed, they are given over to error. They would not believe the truth; now they believe a lie.

13:9 This should be a warning to everyone to accept the light of God's word when it is available. The consequence of rejecting light is to have light denied.

13:10 True believers are assured that their persecutors **shall go into captivity** and **be killed with the sword**. This enables **the saints** to wait in **patience** and **faith**.

13:11 The second **beast** is another prominent figure of the Tribulation Period. He works in close cooperation with the first beast, even organizing an international campaign for the worship of the first beast and of a huge idol representing the Roman emperor. The second beast comes **up out of the earth** or land. If the land of Israel is in view, then this leader is almost surely a Jew. He is the False Prophet (see 16:13; 19:20; 20:10). He has **two horns like a lamb**, giving the appearance of gentleness and harmlessness, but also suggesting that He impersonates the Lamb of God. He speaks **like a dragon**, indicating that he is directly inspired and empowered by Satan.

13:12–14 He exercises all the authority of the first beast, meaning that the Roman emperor gives him unlimited authority to act on his behalf. He has supernatural powers, even causing fire to fall from heaven. The purpose of his miracles, of course, is to deceive the people into worshiping a man as God.

13:15 He gives animation to the great image, the abomination of desolation, so that it can actually speak. The penalty for refusing to worship it is death.

13:16 The second beast insists that people indicate their allegiance to the Roman emperor by wearing the mark of the beast on their right hand or on their foreheads.

13:17 In addition to this mark, the beast has a name and a mystical number. Unless a person takes the mark, name, or number of the beast, he will not be able to buy or sell. It is an effort to force men by economic means to forsake Christ for idolatry. This will be a severe test, but true believers will prefer death to renouncing their Savior.

13:18 The number of the beast is 666. Six is the number of man. The fact that it is one less than seven may suggest that man has fallen short of the glory or perfection of God. The three sixes are a trinity of evil.

One of the biggest questions raised in connection with chapter 13 is whether the *first* or *second* beast is the Antichrist. Basically, the argument for the first being the Antichrist is that he insists on being worshiped as God. Those who hold that the second beast is the Antichrist point out that no Jew would ever accept a Gentile as Messiah, and that since the second beast is a Jew, He must therefore be the false messiah.

14:1 The Lamb is seen standing on Mount Zion with one hundred and forty-four thousand followers, all of whom were sealed on their foreheads. This looks forward to the time when the Lord Jesus will come back to the earth and stand in Jerusalem with this group of believers from each of the twelve tribes of Israel. The one hundred and forty-four thousand are the same ones mentioned in chapter 7. They are now about to enter the kingdom of Christ.

14:2, 3 John hears music coming from heaven like the voice of many waters, and like the sound of loud thunder, and like harpists playing their harps. Only the hundred and forty-four thousand could learn that song.

14:4, 5 They are described as virgins, those who have not defiled themselves with women. They had kept themselves free from the terrible idolatry and immorality of this period and followed the Lamb in unquestioning obedience and devotion. Pentecost says, "They are called 'the firstfruits unto God and to the Lamb', that is, they are the first of the harvest of the tribulation period that will come into the millennium to populate the millennial earth."[25] They did not accept the lie of the Antichrist — that a mere man was to be worshiped. They were blameless as far as their steadfast confession of Christ was concerned.

14:6, 7 The angel flying in midheaven with the everlasting gospel seems to correspond with Matthew 24:14: "And this gospel of the kingdom will be preached in all the world as a witness to all the nations, and then the end will come." The subject of the gospel is given in verse 7. Men are commanded to fear God rather than the beast; to give glory to Him rather than to the idolatrous image; and to worship Him rather than a mere man. Of course, there is only one gospel — the good news of salvation through faith in Christ. But there are different emphases in different dispensations. During the Great Tribulation, the gospel will seek to turn men away from worship of the beast and prepare them for Christ's kingdom on earth.

14:8 The second angel announces Babylon's fall. This anticipates chapters 17 and 18. Babylon represents apostate Judaism and apostate Christendom, which will be a vast commercial and religious conglomerate with headquarters in Rome. All nations will have become drunk with the wine of the wrath of her fornication.

14:9, 10 We can fix the time of the third angel's pronouncement as being at the middle of the Tribulation, which is the same as the beginning of the Great Tribulation. The angel warns that any who agree to beast-worship in any of its

16:18 When the last bowl is poured out, there are violent convulsions of nature: explosions, **thunderings, lightnings**, and an **earthquake** of unprecedented proportions.

16:19 **The great city** of **Babylon, divided into three parts**, drinks **the cup** of God's fury. He has not forgotten her idolatry, cruelty, and religious confusion. At this same time **the cities of the nations** are laid flat.

16:20 **Every island** and **the mountains** disappear as the earth reels.

16:21 One-hundred pound hailstones bombard the earth, but **men** blaspheme **God** rather than repent.

K. The Fall of Babylon the Great (Chaps. 17, 18)

17:1, 2 One of the **seven angels** invites John to witness **the judgment of the great harlot**. This is a great religious and commercial system with headquarters in Rome. Many believe that chapter 17 describes religious Babylon and chapter 18 the commercial aspect. Religious Babylon certainly includes apostate Christendom, both Protestant and Catholic. It may well represent the ecumenical church. Notice the description. The **harlot sits on many waters**, controlling great areas of the Gentile world. **The kings of the earth** have **committed fornication** with her; she has seduced political leaders with her compromise and intrigue. **The inhabitants of the earth** have become **drunk with the wine of her fornication**; vast numbers have come under her evil influence and have been reduced to staggering wretchedness.

17:3 The apostate church is seen **sitting on a scarlet beast**. We have already noted in chapter 13 that this beast is the revived Roman Empire (and sometimes the head of that empire). The beast is **full of** blasphemous **names** and has **seven heads and ten horns**.

17:4 For a while the false church seems to dominate the empire. She sits in full celestial state, wearing the symbols of her vast wealth and displaying **a golden cup full of** her idolatry and immorality.

17:5 **A name** of **mystery** is **on her forehead: Babylon the great, the mother of harlots and of the abominations of the earth**. This is the church that has shed the blood of Christian martyrs down through the centuries, and is still doing it. She is drunk with their blood.

17:6 Like many others, John **marveled** when he **saw the woman**, intoxicated **with the blood of the saints**. This refers to **the saints** of all eras of church history, but especially to **the martyrs of Jesus** during the Tribulation.

17:7, 8 **The angel** offers to explain to John **the mystery of the woman and of the beast. The beast** that John **saw was** (the Roman Empire existed in the past); it **is not** (it broke up and no longer exists as a world-empire today); it **will ascend out of the bottomless pit** (it will reappear in a particularly diabolical form); **and go to perdition** (it will be utterly and finally destroyed). The revival of the empire and the appearance of its charismatic leader will cause the world of unbelievers to **marvel**.

17:9 The angel says that this calls for a **mind** with **wisdom. The seven heads are seven mountains on which the woman sits.** A traditional interpretation is that the harlot has her headquarters in Rome, which is built on seven hills.

17:10 Some commentators explain these **seven kings** as seven forms of Roman government; others explain them as seven literal emperors. Others say that the kings represent great world powers: Egypt, Assyria, Babylon, Persia, Greece, Rome, and the future revived Roman Empire.

17:11 **The eighth** king has been variously identified as the head of the revived Roman Empire and the Antichrist. The exact meaning of this prophecy may never be perfectly clear until it is fulfilled.

17:12 **The ten horns** may symbolize the future **kings** who will serve under the Roman **beast**. They will rule **for one hour**, that is, a short time (see v. 10b).

17:13 The ten kings unanimously yield **their power and authority** to the Roman **beast**. In other words, ten countries (or governments) surrender their national sovereignty to him.

17:14 This ten-kingdom empire goes to war against the Lord Jesus when He returns to earth at the end of the

Tribulation. But they meet their Waterloo in this battle. Though He is **the Lamb, He is** also **Lord of lords and King of kings**. His followers **are called, chosen, and faithful**.

17:15 The angel goes on to explain that **the waters** in verse 1 are **peoples, multitudes, nations, and tongues. The harlot sits** on **the waters** in the sense that she dominates vast segments of the populace.

17:16 It appears that the revived Roman Empire allows itself to be controlled, or at least influenced by the harlot church for a while. Then, however, it throws off this intolerable yoke and destroys her. The hated **harlot** is stripped, consumed, and burned by the beast on which she sat.

17:17 **God** is behind the scenes in all of this. It is He who causes the kingdoms to unite under the Roman beast and then to turn against the harlot. It is all **to fulfill His** sovereign **purpose**.

17:18 **That great city** is Mystery Babylon, ruling **over the kings of the earth**. But as we have seen, the woman has her headquarters in Rome.

18:1 Chapter 18 consists primarily of a funeral song, celebrating the fall of Babylon. As mentioned, this refers to the harlot church which is not only a vast religious system but perhaps the greatest commercial establishment in the world. It apparently controls the world market.

When **another angel** with **great authority** comes **down from heaven** to break the news, it is as if the lights go on. **His glory** illuminates **the earth**.

18:2 **Babylon the great** has **fallen** and its ruins have become the haunt for **demons, every foul spirit**, and **unclean**, hateful **birds**.

18:3 The reason for her fall is the utter corruption she has practiced with the nations and their **merchants**. She has made **all the nations** drunk with her passionate **fornication**.

18:4 **Another voice from heaven** warns God's people to **come out of** the doomed system on the eve of its destruction. Intercourse with her would mean sharing **her plagues**.

18:5, 6 Her **sins have** piled up to **heaven, and God has remembered her iniquities**, and is lashing out against

them. She is to receive **double** payment for her wicked deeds, not from God's people, but from the angel who is the instrument of His vengeance.

18:7 **Her torment and sorrow** will be proportionate to her self-aggrandizement and luxurious lifestyle. She thinks of herself **as queen**, sitting on top of everything and safe from **sorrow**.

18:8 Her judgment **will come in one day** and will involve **death and mourning and famine**. It is the mighty **Lord God** who will punish her **with fire**.

18:9, 10 **The kings of the earth** will **lament** over the **burning** of their former mistress. Their mourning, however, is not unselfish. They sorrow over the loss of pleasure and luxury. **Standing at a distance**, they marvel at the extent of **her torment** and the suddenness of her end.

18:11–13 **The merchants mourn** principally because their hope of gain is gone. **No one buys their merchandise anymore**.

The list of products in which Babylon traded seems to compass world trade: precious metals, jewelry, fabrics, **wood, ivory, bronze, iron, marble**, spices, perfumes, **wine, oil**, grains, livestock, **chariots, and bodies and souls of men**. Both the apostate church and the business world are guilty of trafficking in the **souls of men**, the church by the sale of indulgences, etc., and the business world by exploitation.

18:14 The businessmen, addressing the fallen system, lament that its hoped-for profits have vanished, and its riches and splendor have disappeared suddenly and forever.

18:15, 16 Like the kings, **the merchants . . . stand** aghast, **weeping and wailing** that such profits were lost in an hour. They recount the former luxury of the city, how the people were finely **clothed** and **adorned with** jewels.

18:17, 18 Now all that opulence has suddenly come **to nothing**, and the threat of a great depression hangs low. Those engaged in maritime commerce stand **at a distance** and cry, "**What** could ever compare with **this great city?**"

18:19 They throw **dust on their heads**, weep and wail over the city that had enriched the world maritime indus-

ferent times. It occurs in several stages.

20:6 Those who participate **in the first resurrection** are **blessed** because they will not be included in **the second death**, when all unbelievers will be cast into the lake of fire (v. 14). True believers **shall be priests of God and of Christ and shall reign with Him a thousand years**.

20:7, 8 **When the thousand years have expired, Satan will be released from** confinement, **and will go out** to **the four corners of the earth** in order to **deceive the nations** that are hostile to Christ, here called **Gog and Magog**. This reference to **Gog and Magog** must not be confused with a similar reference in Ezekiel 38 and 39. There Magog is a great land north of Israel, and Gog is its ruler. Here the words refer to the nations of the world in general. In Ezekiel, the setting is premillennial; here it is postmillennial.

20:9 After recruiting an army of ungodly rebels, the devil marches against Jerusalem, **the beloved city**. But **fire** comes **down from God out of heaven** and consumes the troops.

M. The Judgment of Satan and All Unbelievers (20:10–15)

20:10 **The devil** himself is **cast into the lake of fire** to join **the beast and the false prophet**.

It may seem surprising that Satan would be able to assemble an army of unbelievers at the end of the Millennium. However, it should be remembered that all children born during Christ's Reign will be born in sin and will need to be saved. Not all will accept Him as rightful King, and these will scatter throughout the earth, trying to get as far away from Jerusalem as possible.

Note that **the beast and the false prophet** are still in hell after one thousand years. This disproves the doctrine of annihilation, as does the statement, **And they will be tormented day and night forever and ever**.

20:11 Next we are introduced to **the great white throne** judgment. It is **great** because of the issues involved and **white** because of the perfection and purity of the decisions handed down. The Lord Jesus is sitting as Judge (John 5:22, 27). The expression **from whose face the earth and the heaven fled away** indicates

that this judgment takes place in eternity, after the destruction of the present creation (2 Pet. 3:10).

20:12 **The dead, small and great**, stand **before God**. These are the unbelievers of all ages. Two sets of **books are opened**. **The Book of Life** contains the names of all who have been redeemed by the precious blood of Christ. The other books contain a detailed record of the **works** of the unsaved. No one who appears at this judgment is registered in **the Book of Life**. The fact that his name is missing *condemns* him, but the record of his evil **works** determines the *degree* of his punishment.

20:13 **The sea** will yield up the bodies of those who have been buried in it. The graves, here represented by **Death**, will deliver up the bodies of all the unsaved who have been interred. **Hades** will give up the souls of all who died in unbelief. The bodies and souls will be reunited to stand before the Judge.

Just as there will be degrees of reward in heaven, so there will be degrees of punishment in hell. This will be based on their **works**.

20:14 When we read that **Death and Hades** are **cast into the lake of fire**, it means the complete persons: spirit, soul, and body. The text explains **that this is the second death**, and the NKJV margin adds, *the lake of fire*.

There is a difference between Hades and hell. For the unconverted who have died, Hades is a disembodied state of conscious punishment. It is a sort of holding tank, an intermediate condition where they await the Judgment of the Great White Throne.

For believers who have died, Hades is a state of disembodied blessedness in heaven, awaiting the resurrection and glorification of the body. When Jesus died, He went to Paradise (Luke 23:43), which Paul equates with the third heaven (2 Cor. 12:2, 4), the dwelling place of God. In Acts 2:27 the Lord's disembodied state is called Hades. God did not leave His soul in Hades, but clothed it with a glorified body.

Hell is the final prison of the wicked dead. It is the same as the lake of fire, Gehenna, and the second death.

20:15 The deciding factor at this judgment is whether one's name is **written in the Book of Life**. Actually if a person's name had been inscribed there, he would have already been a part of the first resurrection. So this verse applies only to those who stand before the Great White Throne.

N. The New Heaven and the New Earth (21:1–22:5)

21:1 There is a question whether chapters 21 and 22 deal with the Eternal State alone or whether they alternate between the Millennium and the Eternal State. Since the Millennium and eternity are similar in many ways, it is not surprising if they seem to merge at times in the writings of the Apostle John.

Here the Eternal State is called **a new heaven and a new earth**. These are not to be confused with the new heaven and earth described in Isaiah 65:17–25. There the Millennium is in view, because sin and death are still present. These will be completely excluded from the Eternal State.

21:2 John sees **the holy city, New Jerusalem, coming down out of heaven, prepared as a bride adorned for her husband**. The fact that it is never said to land on the earth leads some to see it as hovering over the new earth. The fact that the names of the tribes of Israel are on the gates indicates that redeemed Israel will have access to the city, even if they are not part of the church itself. The distinction between the church (the Bride, the Lamb's Wife, v. 9), Israel (v. 12), and the Gentile nations (v. 24) is maintained throughout.

21:3 John hears an announcement **from heaven** that **the tabernacle of God is with men and** that **He will dwell with them**. As **His people** they will enjoy communion with Him closer than ever dreamed of. **God Himself will be with them and be their God** in a nearer and dearer relationship.

21:4, 5 The expression **"God will wipe away every tear from their eyes"** does not mean that there will be tears in heaven. It is a poetic way of saying that there will *not* be! Neither will there be **death, nor sorrow, nor crying**. For God's people, these will be forever ended.

The One who sits **on the throne** will **make all things new**. His **words are true and faithful**, and will surely come to pass.

21:6 The ushering in of the Eternal State marks the conclusion of God's purposes for the earth on which we live. As **Alpha** and **Omega** are the first and last letters of the Greek alphabet, so He is **the Beginning and the End**, the Creator and the Object of creation, the One who began and the One who finishes, the Eternal One. It is He who gives **the water of life** (salvation) **freely to** whoever **thirsts** for it.

21:7 It is He who blesses the overcomer with total inheritance and a new intimacy as between Father and **son**. As mentioned previously, an overcomer is one who believes that Jesus is the Son of God (1 Jn. 5:5). By faith he overcomes the world (1 Jn. 5:4).

21:8 But not all are overcomers. Some are **cowardly**, afraid to confess Christ; **unbelieving**, unwilling to trust the sinner's Savior; *sinners* (NKJV marginal reading found in most mss.), all those who remain in their sins, whether guilty of the gross iniquities listed here or not; **abominable**, given over to disgusting immorality; **murderers**, malicious and savage killers; **sexually immoral**, practicing fornication and other forms of sexual sins; **sorcerers**, those who traffic with evil spirits; **idolaters**, insulting God by worshiping images; **and all liars**, compulsive deceivers. These will be assigned to **the lake of fire** as their final destiny.

21:9 **One of the seven angels** involved in the bowl judgments offered to give John a further, more detailed view of the New Jerusalem, which he called **the bride, the Lamb's wife**. This may mean that the city is the residence of **the bride**.

21:10, 11 **Carried away in the Spirit to a great and high mountain**, John again saw **Jerusalem descending out of heaven**, radiant with **the glory of God** and sparkling like a costly gem.

21:12, 13 It was surrounded by a massive **wall** in which were **twelve gates**, graced by **twelve angels** and bearing **the names of the twelve tribes of . . . Israel. Three gates** faced each direction of the compass.

The number *twelve* is used twenty-one times in this book and seven times in this chapter. It is commonly understood to stand for *government* or administration.

21:14 The **twelve foundations** of the walls bore **the names of the twelve apostles of the Lamb**. This may have reference to the fact that they laid the foundation of the church in what they taught concerning Christ (Eph. 2:20).

21:15, 16 With a **gold** measuring rod, the angel determined that **the city** was approximately **twelve thousand furlongs** (1400-1500 miles) in **length, breadth, and height**. Whether shaped like a cube or a pyramid, it extended far beyond the bounds of restored Israel.

21:17 The **wall** was **one hundred and forty-four cubits** thick. The expression **"according to the measure of a man, that is, of an angel"** means that the angel of verses 9 and 15 used units of measure employed by man.

21:18 The description of the **wall** (**jasper**) **and the city** (**pure gold**), while hard for us to visualize, is designed to create an image of magnificence and brilliance. In that, it succeeds.

21:19, 20 The twelve **foundations** were adorned with twelve **precious stones**, similar to those on the breastplate of the high priest that represent the twelve tribes of Israel. It is not possible to identify all the jewels with precision or to determine their spiritual meaning.

21:21 The **twelve gates** are **twelve pearls**, a reminder that the church is the pearl of great price for which the Savior sold all that He had (Matt. 13:45, 46).

The street of the city was pure gold, like transparent glass, which speaks of unspotted glory.

21:22, 23 Certain things are missing from the city. **No temple** is necessary because **the Lord God Almighty and the Lamb** are there. There is no **sun** or **moon** because **the glory of God** illuminates it, and **the Lamb is** the lamp.

21:24 Gentile **nations** will enjoy its beauty, **and the kings of the earth** will come with their tribute to the Lord.

21:25 There are no closed **gates** because there is perfect security and freedom of access. There is **no night there**; it is a land of fadeless day.

21:26 As mentioned, the wealth of **the nations** will flow to the city, all their **glory** and **honor**.

21:27 Nothing unclean will ever **enter** there, **but only those who are written in the Lamb's Book of Life**.

22:1, 2 A pure river of water of life flows **from the throne of God and of the Lamb** through **the middle of** the **street. On either side of the river** grows **the tree of life** with its **twelve** kinds of fruit, no longer forbidden. This suggests God's ceaseless provision for every season. **The leaves of the tree** are **for the healing of the nations** is a figurative way of saying that they will enjoy perpetual health.

22:3–5 A. T. Pierson summarizes as follows:

"And there shall be no more curse," perfect sinlessness;

"but the throne of God and of the Lamb shall be in it," perfect government;

"and His servants shall serve Him," perfect service;

"They shall see His face," perfect communion;

"and His name shall be on their foreheads," perfect resemblance;

"And there shall be no night there," perfect blessedness;

"And they shall reign forever and ever," perfect glory.[31]

O. Closing Warnings, Comforts, Invitations, and Benedictions (22:6–21)

22:6 The interpreting angel reminds John again of the trustworthiness of all that he has revealed. **The Lord God** had **sent His angel to show His servants** the panorama of events that **must shortly take place**.

22:7 The climax, the high point of it all will be the glorious Advent of the Savior. He assures us that He will come **quickly**. This may mean either *soon* or *suddenly*, but *soon* is preferred. A special blessing is given to each one **who keeps the words of** this **prophecy**. We can do this by living in the hope of His Coming.

22:8, 9 When **John saw and heard these things**, he **fell down** at the angel's **feet**, but he was forbidden to do so. The **angel** was only a created being; only **God** should be worshiped.

22:10 John was **not** to **seal** up the **prophecy** because **the time** of fulfillment was near. To **seal** here means to postpone disclosure.

22:11 When the time of fulfillment comes, **the unjust** will be fixed in their impenitence. The **filthy** will have no further chance to change when the Lord returns to earth. But the **righteous** will continue to live righteously, and the **holy** to live in holiness.

22:12, 13 Again the Lord announces His soon Coming, this time with the promise of **reward to every one according to his work**. Again He identifies Himself as **the Alpha and the Omega**. The same One who created all things will draw the curtain on the stage of time.

22:14 This verse may read, **"Blessed are those who do His commandments"** or **"Blessed are those who wash their robes"** (margin). *Neither* reading teaches salvation by works but rather works as the fruit and proof of salvation. Only true believers have access **to the tree of life** and to **the** eternal **city**.

22:15 Forever excluded from heaven will be **dogs, sorcerers**, the **sexually immoral, murderers, idolaters**, and liars. **Dogs** here may refer to male prostitutes (Deut. 23:18), unclean Gentiles (Matt. 15:26), or Judaizers (Phil. 3:2).

22:16 The Lord **sent His angel** with this message to **the churches**. He speaks of Himself as **the Root and the Off-spring of David**. As to His deity, He is David's *Creator*; as to His humanity, He is David's *Descendant*. **The Bright and Morning Star** appears in the sky before the sun rises. Christ will first come to the church as **the Bright and Morning Star**, that is, at the Rapture. Later he will come to the earth as the Sun of Righteousness with healing in His wings (Mal. 4:2).

22:17 There are two ways of understanding this verse. First, it may be a gospel appeal throughout, with **the Spirit, the bride**, and the hearer urging the thirsty to **come** to Christ for salvation. Or the first three uses of the word **come** may be prayers for Christ to return, followed by two invitations to the unsaved to **come** to Him for **the water of life** (salvation) and thus be ready for His return.

22:18, 19 If men add to the things written in **this book** of Revelation, they will suffer **the plagues** described in it. Since the subjects in this book are woven throughout the Bible, the verse, in effect, condemns any tampering with God's word. A similar judgment is pronounced on **anyone** who **takes away from the words of this prophecy**. This does not apply to minor differences of interpreta-

tion, but to an outright attack on the inspiration and completeness of the Bible. The penalty is eternal doom. **God shall take away his part from the tree of life** (NKJV margin).[32] It means that he will never share in the blessings of those who have eternal **life**.

22:20 Revelation closes with a promise and a blessing. The promise is that the Lord Jesus is **coming quickly**. As mentioned previously, this could mean *soon* or *suddenly*. The hope of a *sudden* return would not excite the same anticipation or watchfulness as the hope of a *soon* return. Every redeemed person responds to the blessed hope, **"Amen. Even so, come, Lord Jesus!"**

Just as Genesis is the book of beginnings, so Revelation is the book of consummation. Subjects that were introduced in the first book are brought to fruition in the last. Note the following:

GENESIS	*REVELATION*
Creation of heavens and earth (Gen. 1:1).	Destruction of heavens and earth (Rev. 20:11b). Creation of new heavens and new earth (Rev. 21:1).
Start of Satan's reign on earth (Gen. 3:1–7).	Satan cast into the Lake of Fire (Rev. 20:10).
Entrance of sin (Gen. 3:1–7).	Sin banished (Rev. 21:27).
Pronouncing of the curse on creation (Gen. 3:17–19).	The curse removed (Rev. 22:3).
Right to tree of life forfeited (Gen. 3:24b)	Access to tree of life restored (Rev. 22:2, 19 marg.)
Eviction of man from the Garden of Eden (Gen. 3:24a).	Man welcomed back to [Paradise] (Rev. 22:1–7)
Entrance of death into the world (Gen. 2:17; 5:5).	Death forever removed (Rev. 21:4).
Marriage of the first Adam (Gen. 4:1).	Marriage of the last Adam (Rev. 19:7).
Sorrow comes to mankind (Gen. 3:16).	Sorrow eliminated (Rev. 21:4).

22:21 And now we come to the final blessing of this wonderful book of Revelation, and of the word of God. It is a peaceful close to a book filled with the thunders of divine judgment.

John wishes for **"The grace of our Lord Jesus Christ** to **be with** God's people." There are three interesting variant readings in the manuscripts here.

1. In the critical (NU) text John wishes Christ's grace to *all* — which hardly fits Revelation's theme of impending wrath on the majority.

2. The traditional (TR, KJV, NKJV) reading is better. Christ's grace is wished to "you all" — many of the hearers and readers of Revelation will be true believers.

3. The best reading in light of the sharp contrasts between saints and sinners in this book is found in the majority text and NKJV margin: **"The grace of our Lord Jesus Christ be with all the saints. Amen."**

ENDNOTES

[1](Intro) The verb used in the Gospel and Revelation is *ekkentēsan*; in the Septuagint of Zechariah the form is *katorchēsanto*.

[2](Intro) In Hebrew and Greek the letters of the alphabet have numerical value. For example, aleph and alpha are 1, beth and beta are 2, etc. Hence every name can be added up. The Greek name for Jesus (*Iesous*), interestingly enough, adds up to 888. (Eight is the number of new beginning and resurrection.) It is believed that the letters of the Beast's name will actually equal 666. By slightly adjusting the spelling, "Nero Caesar" can be made to add up to 666, using this system. Other names also add up to 666, however, and one should avoid wild speculation.

[3](1:5) The marginal reading here is the first of very many in the NKJV, of Revelation where both the oldest (NU) and majority (M) of readings agree against the reading of the TR, KJV, and NKJV. The reason for this is that Erasmus, who published the first Greek NT (1516), had only one copy of Revelation, and it was faulty. Hence, there are the many small variations in the footnotes or margin. Fortunately, the other books of the NT were represented by mss. that agreed largely with a yet-to-be discovered mass of mss. In this commentary, only crucial changes have been noted. The combination of NU and M will be the original reading, we believe. Where they differ from one another, the majority text is to be preferred.

[4](1:8) The NU and M texts omit "the Beginning and the End."

[5](1:10) "The Day of the Lord" is *hē hēmera tou Kuriou* in Greek; "the Lord's (lit. "lordly") Day" is *"hē Kuriakē hēmera"* (whence "kirk, church").

[6](1:13) James H. McConkey, *The Book of Revelation: A Series of Outline Studies in the Apocalypse*, p. 9.

[7](2:1) John F. Walvoord, *The Revelation of Jesus Christ*, pp. 50-100.

[8](2:14, 15) Ella E. Pohle, *Dr. C. I. Scofield's Question Box*, p. 89.

[9](2:20) The majority text reads, "your wife (or woman) Jezebel."

[10](3:7) *Daily Notes of the Scripture Union.*

[11](3:20) Richard Chevenix Trench, *Commentary on the Epistles to the Seven Churches in Asia*, p. 225.

[12](4:3) Walvoord, *Revelation*, p. 104.

[13](5:9, 10) Both the NU and M texts have "them" and "they," which would mean that the elders are not singing about themselves, but about *others*. This *might* suggest that they are angelic beings.

[14](5:9, 10) NU text reads "kingdom."

[15](6:1, 2) The NU and M texts omit "and see."

[16](6:10) The Greek word here is strong: *Despotēs* (but without the negative connotation of the English derivative).

[17](8:5) Henry Barclay Swete, *The Apocalypse of St. John*, p. 109.

[18](8:13) "Angel" and "eagle" look somewhat similar in Greek also (*angelos* and *aetos*), hence the copying error. "Eagle" is correct.

[19](9:16, 17) The majority of mss. read "one hundred million."

[20](9:18, 19) Hamilton Smith, *The Revelation: An Expository Outline*, p. 57.

[21](9:20, 21) The Greek word here is *pharmakon*, "medicine, potion, drug" (cf. English "pharmacy").

[22](11:6) McConkey, *The Book of Revelation*, pp. 68, 69.

[23](11:15) The NU and M texts read "kingdom . . . has become."

[24](13:3) *The Scofield Reference Bible*, p. 1342.

[25](14:4, 5) J. D. Pentecost, *Things to Come*, p. 300.

[26](15:3, 4) "Saints" is a very weakly supported reading. Both the NU and M texts support "nations."

[27](15:3, 4) Arthur T. Pierson, *Knowing the Scriptures*, p. 248.

[28](16:16) "Armageddon" comes from Hebrew "Har" (Mount) Megiddo. The majority text reads simply "Megiddo."

[29](19:8) The 1611 text reads "righteousness," often interpreted by preachers as that *righteousness of Christ* which is *imputed* to the saints. While this is a sound doctrine, the Greek word *dikaiō-mata* rules out that understanding. The word is plural (not the abstract singular which is *dikaiōsunē*). Furthermore, it has a "passive" ending, *here* denoting something *done* (in this case, "righteous deeds"). Salvation is not in view in this passage.

[30](19:10) Charles C. Ryrie, *The Ryrie Study Bible, New King James Version*, p. 1953.

[31](22:3–5) Pierson, *The Ministry of Keswick, First Series*, p. 144.

[32](22:18, 19) The reading "book of life" has *no* Greek mss. support here! The last six verses were missing in Erasmus' Greek copy of Revelation so he translated these verses back from the Latin Vulgate. This is a most unfortunate reading. It mars the literary "full-circle," that is, God's program from the banishment of man from the tree of life in Genesis 3 to its restoration to His saints at the end of the very last chapter in the Bible.

BIBLIOGRAPHY

Criswell, Wallie Amos. *Exposition of Sermons on Revelation*. Grand Rapids: Zondervan Publishing House, 1962.

Dennett, Edward. "The Seven Churches," *The Serious Christian*, Vol. XI. Charlotte, N.C.: Books for Christians, n.d.

Gaebelein, Arno C. *The Revelation*. New York: Publication Office "Our Hope," 1915.

Grant, F. W. *The Revelation of Christ*. New York: Loizeaux Brothers, n.d.

Ironside, H. A. *Lectures on the Revelation*. New York: Loizeaux Brothers, 1919.

Kelly, William. *Lectures on the Book of Revelation*, New Edition. London: G. Morrish, n.d.

Lenski, R. C. H. *The Interpretation of St. John's Revelation*. Minneapolis: Augsburg Publishing House, 1943.

McConkey, James H. *The Book of Revelation: A Series of Outline Studies in the Apocalypse*. Pittsburgh: Silver Publishing Co., 1921.

Morgan, G. Campbell. *The Letters of Our Lord*. Westwood, N.J.: Fleming H. Revell Co., n.d.

Morris, Leon. *The Revelation of Jesus Christ* (TBC). Grand Rapids: Wm. B. Eerdmans Publishing Co., 1969.

Mounce, Robert H. *The Book of Revelation* (NIC). Grand Rapids: Wm. B. Eerdmans Publishing Co., 1977.

Ryrie, Charles Caldwell. *Revelation*. Chicago: Moody Press, 1968.

Scott, Walter. *Exposition of the Revelation of Jesus Christ*. London: Pickering & Inglis Ltd., n.d.

Smith, Hamilton. *The Revelation: An Expository Outline*. Addison, IL: Bible Truth Publishers, n.d.

Stanley, Charles. *The Revelation of Jesus Christ*. New York: Loizeaux Brothers Publishers, n.d.

Swete, Henry Barclay. *The Apocalypse of St. John*. Grand Rapids: Wm. B. Eerdmans Publishing Company, n.d.

Tenney, Merrill C. *Interpreting Revelation*. Grand Rapids: Wm. B. Eerdmans Publishing Company, 1957.

Trench, Richard Chevenix. *Commentary on the Epistles to the Seven Churches in Asia*. Minneapolis: Klock and Klock Christian Publishers, 1978.

Walvoord, John F. *The Revelation of Jesus Christ*. Chicago: Moody Press, 1966.

General Bibliography

BOOKS

Alford, Henry. *The Greek Testament*. 4 vols. Revised by Everett F. Harrison. Chicago: Moody Press, 1958.

Anderson, Sir Robert. *Misunderstood Texts of the New Testament*. London: Nisbet & Co., Ltd., 1916.

Anderson-Berry, D. *Pictures in the Acts*. Glasgow: Pickering & Ingalis, n.d.

Arndt, William F. and F. Wilbur Gingrich. *A Greek-English Lexicon of the New Testament and Other Early Christian Literature*. Chicago: The University of Chicago Press, 1979.

Barker, H. P. *Coming Twice*. New York: Loizeaux Brothers, n.d.

Barnes, Albert. *Notes on the New Testament*. 10 vols. Grand Rapids: Kregel Publications, 1975.

Baron, David. *The New Order of Priesthood*. Findlay, Ohio: Dunham Publishing Company, 1955.

Barnhouse, D. G. *The Measure of Your Faith*. Book 69. Further documentation unavailable.

_____. *Words Fitly Spoken*. Wheaton: Tyndale House Publishers, 1969.

Baxter, J. Sidlow. *Awake My Heart*. Grand Rapids: Zondervan Publishing House, 1960.

_____. *Explore the Book*. 3 vols. London: Marshall, Morgan & Scott, 1955.

Bellett, James Gifford. *The Evangelists*. New York: Loizeaux Brothers, n.d.

Bonar, Andrew R. *Last Days of the Martyrs*. Kilmarnock: John Ritchie, Ltd., n.d.

Brookes, J. H. *I Am Coming*. Glasgow: Pickering & Inglis, 1895.

Chafer, L. S. *Systematic Theology*. 8 vols. Dallas: Dallas Seminary Press, 1947.

Chappel, Clovis G. *Sermons from the Psalms*. Nashville: Cokesbury Press, 1931.

Christenson, Larry. *The Christian Family*. Minneapolis: Bethany Fellowship, 1970.

Clow, W. M. *The Cross in Christian Experience*. New York: Hodder & Stoughton, 1908.

Cragg, H. W. *The Keswick Week, 1955*. London: Marshall, Morgan & Scott, 1955.

Darby, J. N. *The Collected Writings of John Nelson Darby*. Edited by William Kelly. 34 vols. and Index. Oak Park, IL: Bible Truth Publishers, 1971.

_____. *Synopsis of the Books of the Bible*. 5 vols. New York: Loizeaux Brothers, 1942.

Davidson, F., ed. *The New Bible Commentary*. Chicago: The InterVarsity Christian Fellowship, 1953.

Denney, James R. *The Death of Christ*. 2nd ed. Philadelphia: The Westminster Press, 1903.

Dillow, Joseph. *Speaking in Tongues*. Grand Rapids: Zondervan Publishing House, 1976.

Drury, T. W. *The Prison Ministry of St. Paul*. London: The Religious Tract Society, 1911.

*Eddy, Mary Baker. *Science and Health with Key to the Scriptures*. Boston: Allison V. Stewart, 1909.

Elliot, Elisabeth, ed. *The Journals of Jim Elliot*. Old Tappan, NJ: Fleming H. Revell Company, 1978.

Erdman, Charles R. *The General Epistles*. Philadelphia: The Westminster Press, 1919.

The Expositor's Greek Testament. 5 vols. Grand Rapids: Wm. B. Eerdmans Publishing Company, 1951.

Falwell, Jerry, ed. *Liberty Bible Commentary*. 2 vols. Lynchburg, Virginia: The Old-Time Gospel Hour, 1982.

*Ferré, Nels. *The Sun and the Umbrella*. New York: Harper & Brothers, 1953.

Fernald, James C., ed. *Funk & Wagnalls Standard Handbook of Synonyms, Antonyms, and Prepositions*. New York: Harper & Row, 1947.

Ford, Leighton. *The Christian Persuader*. New York: Harper & Row, 1966.

Gaebelein, Arno C. *The Annotated Bible*. 9 vols. Neptune, New Jersey: Loizeaux Brothers, rev. ed., 1970.

Gaebelein, Frank E., ed. *The New Scofield Reference Bible*. New York: Oxford University Press, 1967.

Gibbon, Edward. *The Decline and Fall of the Roman Empire*. Vol. II. Chicago: Belford, Charles and Co., n.d.

Gibbs, A. P. *Preach and Teach the Word*. Oak Park, IL: Emmaus Bible School, 1971.

Gook, Arthur. *Can A Young Man Find the Path?* London: Pickering & Inglis, 1949.

Grant, F. W. *Genesis in the Light of the*

New Testament. New York: Loizeaux Brothers, n.d.

———. *The Numerical Bible.* 7 vols. New York: Loizeaux Brothers, 1932.

Gray, James M. *Christian Workers' Commentary on the Whole Bible.* Westwood, NJ: Fleming H. Revell, 1953.

Grubb, Norman P. *C. T. Studd, Cricketer and Pioneer.* London: Lutterworth Press, 1957.

Guthrie, Donald. *New Testament Introduction.* 3 vols. London: The Tyndale Press, 1962.

Harrison, Everett F. *Introduction to the New Testament.* Grand Rapids: Wm. B. Eerdmans Publishing Company, 1964.

Havner, Vance. *Why Not Just Be Christians?* NY: Fleming H. Revell, 1964.

Hession, Roy. *The Calvary Road.* Philadelphia: Christian Literature Crusade.

Hodges, Zane C. and Arthur L. Farstad, eds. *The Greek New Testament According to the Majority Text.* Nashville: Thomas Nelson Publishers, 2d ed., 1985.

Hogg, C. F. *What Saith the Scripture?* London: Pickering & Inglis, 1947.

Hole, F. B. *Paul's Epistles, Volume Two.* Wooler, Northumberland, England: Central Bible Hammond Trust Ltd., n.d.

Houghton, S. M. *Sketches from Church History.* Edinburgh: The Banner of Truth Trust, 1980.

Hunter, Jack. *What the Bible Teaches, Galatians – Philemon.* Kilmarnock, Scotland: John Ritchie, Scotland: 1983, p. 78.

Ironside, Harry A. *Notes on James & Peter.* New York: Loizeaux Brothers, 1947.

Jamieson, Fausset and Brown. *A Commentary, Critical, Experimental, and Practical on the Old and New Testaments.* 6 vols. London: Wm. Collins and Co., n.d.

Jones, E. Stanley. *Christ's Alternative to Communism.* Nashville: Abingdon Press, 1935.

———. *Conversion.* Nashville: Abingdon Press, 1959.

———. *Growing Spiritually.* Nashville: Abingdon Press, 1978.

Jowett, J. H. *Life in the Heights.* London: Hodder & Stoughton, 1924.

———. *Things that Matter Most.* London: Jas. Clarke & Co., 1913.

Jukes, Andrew. *The Law of the Offerings.* London: Lamp Press, 1954.

*Kennedy, Gerald. *God's Good News.* New York: Harper & Brothers, 1955.

The Keswick Convention 1934, London: Pickering & Ingalis, 1934.

The Keswick Week 1955, London: Marshall, Morgan & Scott, Ltd., 1955.

Lacey, Harry. *God and the Nations.* Kilmarnock, Scotland: John Ritchie, 1944.

Lang, G. H. *The Churches of God.* London: Paternoster Press, n.d.

———. *The Parabolic Teaching of the Scripture.* Grand Rapids: Wm. B. Eerdmans Publishing Company, 1956.

Lange, J. P. *A Commentary on the Holy Scriptures.* 25 vols. Grand Rapids: Zondervan Publishing House, n.d.

Lee, Robert G. *Lord, I Believe.* Nashville: Broadman Press, 1927.

Lee, Robert G. *Seven Swords and Other Messages,* Grand Rapids: Zondervan Publishing House, 1958.

Lenski, R. C. H. *The Interpretation of the Epistle to the Hebrews and of the Epistle of James.* Minneapolis: Augsburg Publishing House, 1938.

———. *The Interpretation of St. Paul's Epistles to the Colossians, to the Thessalonians, to Timothy, to Titus and to Philemon.* Columbus, Ohio: The Wartburg Press, 1937.

———. *The Interpretation of St. Paul's Epistles to the Galatians, to the Ephesians, and to the Philippians.* Columbus, Ohio: The Wartburg Press, 1946.

Lyall, L. T. *Red Sky at Night.* London: Hodder & Stoughton, 1969.

Macartney, Clarence Edward. *Macartney's Illustrations.* New York: Abingdon Press, 1946.

Mackay, W. M. *The Men Whom Jesus Made.* London: Hodder & Stoughton, 1924.

Mackintosh, C. H. *Genesis to Deuteronomy: Notes on the Pentateuch.* 6 vols. New York: Loizeaux Brothers, 1879.

———. *The Mackintosh Treasury.* Neptune, NJ: Loizeaux Brothers, 1976.

Marsh, F. E. *Fully Furnished.* London: Pickering & Inglis, n.d.

Matheson, George. *Rest By the River.* London: Hodder & Stoughton, 1906.

McClain, Alva J. *The Greatness of the Kingdom.* Chicago: Moody Press, 1968.

Metzger, Bruce M. *The New Testament: Its Background, Growth, and Content.* Nashville: Abingdon Press, 1965.

Meyer, Frederick Brotherton. *Paul.* London: Morgan & Scott, n.d.

_____. *Through the Bible Day by Day.* 7 vols. Philadelphia: American S. S. Union, 1918.

Miller, J. R. *Come Ye Apart.* New York: Thomas Crowell & Co., 1887.

The Ministry of Keswick, First Series, 1892-1919. Grand Rapids: Zondervan Publishing House, 1963.

The Ministry of Keswick, Second Series, 1921-1956. Grand Rapids: Zondervan Publishing House, 1964.

Moorehead, William G. *Outline Studies in Acts and the Epistles.* Chicago: Fleming H. Revell, 1902.

_____. *Outline Studies in the New Testament: Acts to Ephesians.* Pittsburgh: United Presbyterian Board of Publications, 1902.

_____. *Outline Studies in the New Testament: Philippians to Hebrews.* Pittsburgh: United Presbyterian Board of Publications, 1905.

Morris, Leon. *Understanding the New Testament: 1 Timothy, 2 Timothy, Titus, Philemon, Hebrews, James.* Philadelphia: A. J. Holman Company, 1978.

Morrison, G. H. "Morrison on Luke," *The Glasgow Pulpit Series, Vol. I.* Chattanooga, TN: AMG Publishers, 1978.

Morgan, G. Campbell. *Searchlights from the Word.* London: Oliphants, 1970.

Murray, Andrew. *The Holiest of All.* Westwood, NJ: Fleming H. Revell, 1960.

Myers, F. W. H. *St. Paul.* London: Samuel Bagster & Sons Ltd., n.d.

Nee, Watchman. *Do All to the Glory of God.* NY: Christian Fellowship Publishers, Inc., 1974.

New and Concise Bible Dictionary. London: G. Morrish, 1897-1900.

Orr, J., ed. *International Standard Bible Encyclopedia.* 5 vols. Grand Rapids: Wm. B. Eerdmans Publishing Co., 1939.

Orr, William W. *Bible Hints on Rearing Children.* Wheaton, IL: InterVarsity Press, 1955.

Pentecost, J. D. *Your Adversary the Devil.* Grand Rapids: Zondervan Publishing House, 1969.

Pfeiffer, Charles F. and Everett F. Harrison, eds. *The Wycliffe Bible Commentary.* Chicago: Moody Press, 1962.

Phillips, J. B. *The Young Church in Action.* New York: The Macmillan Company, 1956.

Pierson, A. T. *"Knowing the Scriptures."* New York: Gospel Publishing House, 1910.

_____. "The Work of Christ for the Believer," *The Ministry of Keswick, First Series.* Grand Rapids: Zondervan Publishing House, 1963.

Pink, Arthur W. *The Attributes of God.* Swengel, Pennsylvania: Bible Truth Depot, n.d.

Pollock, A. J. *The Apostle Paul and His Missionary Labors.* New York: Loizeaux Brothers, n.d.

_____. *Modernism Versus the Bible.* London: Central Bible Truth Depot, n.d.

_____. *Why I Believe the Bible is the Word of God.* London: Central Bible Truth Depot, n.d.

Pohle, Ella E. *C. I. Scofield's Question Box.* Chicago: The Bible Institute Colportage Association, 1917.

Reid, R. J. *How Job Learned His Lesson.* New York: Loizeaux Brothers, n.d.

Robertson, A. T. *Word Pictures in the New Testament.* 6 vols. New York: Harper & Bros., 1930.

*Robinson, John A. T. *Honest to God.* Philadelphia: The Westminster Press, 1963.

Rogers, E. W. *Concerning the Future.* Chicago: Moody Press, 1962.

_____. *Jesus the Christ.* London: Pickering & Inglis, 1962.

Ryle, John Charles. *Expository Thoughts on the Gospels.* 3 vols. New York: Fleming H. Revell, 1858.

_____. *Holiness.* Grand Rapids: Baker Book House, 1979.

_____. *Practical Religion.* London: Jas. Clarke & Co., Ltd., 1959.

Ryrie, Charles C. *The Grace of God.* Chicago: Moody Press, 1975.

_____, ed. *The Ryrie Study Bible, New King James Version.* Chicago: Moody Press, 1985.

Salmon, George. *A Historical Introduction to the Study of the Books of the New Testament.* London: John Murray, 1894.

Sanders, J. Oswald. *A Spiritual Clinic.* Chicago: Moody Press, 1958.

_____. *Spiritual Problems.* Chicago: Moody Press, 1971.

Sauer, Erich. *The Dawn of World Redemption.* Grand Rapids: Wm. B. Eerdmans Publishing Company, 1953.

Scorer, C. G. *The Bible and Sex Ethics Today.* London: The Tyndale Press, 1967.

Scott, Walter. *Bible Handbook to the New Testament*. Charlotte, North Carolina: Books for Christians, 1977.

Scroggie, W. Graham. *Know Your Bible: A Guide to the Gospels*. London: Pickering & Inglis, 1948.

_____. "Paul's Prison Prayers," *The Ministry of Keswick, Second Series*. Grand Rapids: Zondervan Publishing House, 1964.

Spurgeon, Charles H. *The Treasury of the New Testament*. London: Marshall, Morgan & Scott, n.d.

Stalker, James. *Life of St. Paul*. Fleming H. Revell, 1912.

Stevens, G. B. *The Theology of the New Testament*. New York: Chas. Scribner's Sons, n.d.

Stewart, James A. *Evangelism*. Swengel, PA: Reiner Publications, n.d.

_____. *Pastures of Tender Grass*. Further documentation unavailable.

Stewart, James S. *The Life and Teaching of Jesus Christ*. Nashville: Abingdon Press, 1958.

_____. *A Man in Christ*. New York: Harper & Row, 1935.

_____. *Pastures of Tender Grass*, Philadelphia: Revival Literature, 1962.

Stonehouse, Ned B. *Origins of the Synoptic Gospels — Some Basic Questions*. Grand Rapids: Wm. B. Eerdmans Publishing Company, 1963.

Strombeck, J. F. *First the Rapture*. Moline, IL: Strombeck Agency, Inc., 1950.

Strong, A. H. *Systematic Theology*. Philadelphia: The Judson Press, 1943.

Swindoll, Charles. *Growing Strong in the Seasons of Life*. Portland: Multnomah Press, 1983.

Taylor, Mrs. Howard. *Behind the Ranges*. London: Lutterworth Press, 1944.

Thiessen, Henry Clarence. *Introduction to the New Testament*. Grand Rapids: Wm. B. Eerdmans Publishing Company, 1943.

Tozer, A. W. *That Incredible Christian*. India: Alliance Publications, 1964.

_____. *The Root of the Righteous*. Chicago: Moody Press, 1955.

Trench, Richard Chevenix. *Synonyms of the New Testament*. London: Kegan Paul, Trench, Trubner & Co., Ltd., 1901.

Unger, Merrill F. *Unger's Bible Dictionary*. Chicago: Moody Press, 1966.

_____. *Unger's Bible Handbook*. Chicago: Moody Press, 1966.

_____. *Zechariah*. Grand Rapids: Zondervan Publishing House , 1963.

Van Oosterzee, J. J. "The Pastoral Letters." *Lange's Commentary on the Holy Scriptures*. Vol. 23. Grand Rapids: Zondervan Publishing House, n.d.

Velikovsky, I. *Earth in Upheaval*. New York: Doubleday and Co., 1955.

Vincent, Marvin R. *Word Studies in the New Testament*. 4 vols. Grand Rapids: Wm. B. Eerdmans Publishing Company, 1957.

Vine, W. E. *The Divine Plan of Missions*. London: Pickering & Inglis, n.d.

_____. *Expository Dictionary of New Testament Words*. Old Tappan, NJ: Fleming H. Revell, 1966.

Walvoord, John F. and Roy B. Zuck, eds. *The Bible Knowledge Commentary: New Testament Edition*. Wheaton, Illinois: Victor Books, 1983.

Warfield, B. B. *Christology and Criticism*. New York: Oxford University Press, 1929.

Watson, David. *Discipleship*. London: Hodder and Stoughton, 1981.

Weatherhead, Leslie D. *Prescription for Anxiety*. London: Hodder & Stoughton, 1956.

Webb-Peploe, H. W. "Grace and Peace in Four Pauline Epistles," *The Ministry of Keswick, First Series*. Grand Rapids: Zondervan Publishing House, 1963.

Williams, George. *The Student's Commentary on the Holy Scriptures*. Grand Rapids: Kregel Publications, 1953.

Wuest, Kenneth S. *Ephesians and Colossians in the Greek New Testament*. Grand Rapids: Wm. B. Eerdmans Publishing Co., 1957.

_____. *In These Last Days*. Grand Rapids: Wm. B. Eerdmans Publishing Co., 1954.

_____. *Wuest's Expanded Translation of the Greek New Testament*. 3 vols. Grand Rapids: Wm. B. Eerdmans Publishing Co., 1956-1959.

Young, Dinsdale T. *The Enthusiasm of God*. London: Hodder & Stoughton, 1906.

_____. *Neglected People of the Bible*. London: Hodder & Stoughton, 1901.

_____. *Unfamiliar Texts*. London: Hodder & Stoughton, 1899.

_____. *The Unveiled Evangel*. London: Robert Scott, 1912.

Zahn, Theodor. *Introduction to the New Testament*. 3 vols. Minneapolis: Klock & Klock Christian Publishers, 1977.

ARTICLES AND PERIODICALS

Christian Truth Magazine. various dates.

Daily Notes of the Scripture Union. London: C.S.S.M., various dates.

*Homrighausen, E. G. "The Second Epistle of Peter," *Exposition*, IB, XII, 1957.

Our Daily Bread. Grand Rapids: Radio Bible Class, various dates.

The Sunday School Times. Homer L. Payne. "What Is a Missionary Church?" Feb. 22, 1964.

Toward the Mark. Weston-super-Mare, Vol. 5, No. 6 (1976).

PAMPHLETS

Cutting, George. "The Old Nature and the New Birth." New York: Loizeaux Brothers, n.d.

Green, Samuel. "Scripture Testimony to the Deity of Christ." Oak Park, Illinois: Bible Truth Publishers, 1959.

Hole, F. B. "The Administration of the Mystery." London: Central Bible Truth Depot, n.d.

*National Council of Churches. "Called to Responsible Freedom."

Scofield, C. I. "Rightly Dividing the Word of Truth."

N.B. Works marked with an asterisk (*) are quoted to illustrate false teaching.

Authors of the New Testament

Name	Nationality	Home Town	Occupation	Relationships	Chapters Written	Verses Written	Books Written
Matthew	Jew	Capernaum	Tax Collector	Apostle of Jesus Christ	28	1,071	Gospel of Matthew
Mark	Jew/Roman	Jerusalem	Missionary	Disciple of Peter	16	678	Gospel of Mark
Luke	Greek	Antioch	Physician	Disciple of Paul	52	2,158	Gospel of Luke Acts
John	Jew	Bethsaida or Capernaum	Fisherman	Apostle of Jesus Christ	50	1,414	Gospel of John 1 John 2 John 3 John Revelation
Paul	Jew	Tarsus	Tentmaker	Apostle of Jesus Christ	87 (100)*	2,033 (2,336)*	Romans 1 Corinthians 2 Corinthians Galatians Ephesians Philippians Colossians Philemon 1 Thessalonians 2 Thessalonians 1 Timothy 2 Timothy Titus (Hebrews?)
James	Jew	Nazareth	Carpenter?	Brother of Jesus Christ	5	108	James
Peter	Jew	Bethsaida	Fisherman	Apostle of Jesus Christ	8	166	1 Peter 2 Peter
Jude	Jew	Nazareth	Carpenter?	Brother of Jesus Christ	1	25	Jude

*Indicates total if Hebrews is assigned to Paul.

From *Talk Thru the Bible*. Reprinted by permission of Walk Thru the Bible Ministries.

THE THEMES OF THE NEW TESTAMENT LETTERS

PAUL'S LETTERS TO CHURCHES

BOOK	KEY WORD	THEME
Romans	Righteousness of God	Portrays the gospel from condemnation to justification to sanctification to glorification (1–8). Presents God's program for Jews and Gentiles (9–11) and practical exhortations for believers (12–16).
1 Corinthians	Correction of Carnal Living	Corrects problems of factions, immorality, lawsuits, and abuse of the Lord's Supper (1–6). Replies to questions concerning marriage, meat offered to idols, public worship, and the Resurrection (7–16).
2 Corinthians	Paul Defends His Ministry	Defends Paul's apostolic character, call, and credentials. The majority had repented of their rebellion against Paul, but there was still an unrepentant minority.
Galatians	Freedom from the Law	Refutes the error of legalism that had ensnared the churches of Galatia. Demonstrates the superiority of grace over law, and magnifies the life of liberty over legalism and license.
Ephesians	Building the Body of Christ	Extols the believer's position in Christ (1–3), and exhorts the readers to maintain a spiritual walk that is based upon their spiritual wealth (4–6).
Philippians	To Live Is Christ	Paul speaks of the latest developments in his imprisonment and urges his readers to a life-style of unity, humility, and godliness.
Colossians	The Preeminence of Christ	Demonstrates the preeminence of Christ in creation, redemption, and the relationships of life. The Christian is complete in Christ and needs nothing else.
1 Thessalonians	Holiness in Light of Christ's Return	Paul commends the Thessalonians for their faith and reminds them of his motives and concerns on their behalf. He exhorts them to purity of life and teaches them about the coming of the Lord.
2 Thessalonians	Understanding the Day of the Lord	Paul corrects false conclusions about the day of the Lord, explains what must precede this awesome event, and exhorts his readers to remain diligent.

PAUL'S LETTERS TO PEOPLE

BOOK	KEY WORD	THEME
1 Timothy	Leadership Manual for Churches	Paul counsels Timothy on the problems of false teachers, public prayer, the role of women, and the requirements for elders and deacons.
2 Timothy	Endurance in Ministry	A combat manual designed to build up and encourage Timothy to boldness and steadfastness in view of the hardships of the spiritual warfare.
Titus	Conduct Manual for Churches	Lists the requirements for elders and instructs Titus in his duties relative to the various groups in the churches.
Philemon	Forgiveness from Slavery	Paul appeals to Philemon to forgive Onesimus and to regard him no longer as a slave but as a brother in Christ.

LETTERS FROM OTHERS

BOOK	KEY WORD	THEME
Hebrews	Superiority of Christ	Demonstrates the superiority of Christ's person, priesthood, and power over all that preceded Him to encourage the readers to mature and to become stable in their faith.
James	Faith that Works	A practical catalog of the characteristics of true faith written to exhort James' Hebrew-Christian readers to examine the reality of their own faith.
1 Peter	Suffering for Christ	Comfort and counsel to those who were being maligned for their faith in Christ. They are encouraged to develop an attitude of submission in view of their suffering.
2 Peter	Guard Against False Prophets	Copes with internal opposition in the form of false teachers who were enticing believers into their errors of belief and conduct. Appeals for growth in the true knowledge of Christ.
1 John	Fellowship with God	Explores the dimensions of fellowship between redeemed people and God. Believers must walk in His light, manifest His love, and abide in His life.
2 John	Avoid Fellowship with False Teachers	John commends his readers for remaining steadfast in apostolic truth and reminds them to walk in love and avoid false teachers.
3 John	Enjoy Fellowship with the Brethren	John thanks Gaius for his support of traveling teachers of the truth, in contrast to Diotrephes, who rejected them and told others to do the same.
Jude	Contend for the Faith	This expose of false teachers reveals their conduct and character and predicts their judgment. Jude encourages his readers to build themselves up in the truth and contend earnestly for the faith.
Revelation	Revelation of the Coming Christ	The glorified Christ gives seven messages to the church (1–3). Visions of unparalleled judgment upon rebellious mankind are followed by the Second Advent (4–19). The Apocalypse concludes with a description of the new heaven and new earth and the marvels of the new Jerusalem (20–22).

From *Visual Survey of the Bible.* Reprinted by permission of the author.

Harmony of the Gospels

Date	Event	Location	Matthew	Mark	Luke	John	Related References
	Luke's Introduction Pre-fleshly state of Christ Genealogy of Jesus Christ		1:1–17		1:1–4 3:23–38	1:1–18	Acts 1:1 Heb. 1:1–14 Ruth 4:18–22 1 Chr. 1:1–4

BIRTH, INFANCY, AND ADOLESCENCE OF JESUS AND JOHN THE BAPTIST IN 17 EVENTS

Date	Event	Location	Matthew	Mark	Luke	John	Related References
7 B.C.	(1) Announcement of Birth of John	Jerusalem (Temple)			1:5–25		Num. 6:3
7 or 6 B.C.	(2) Announcement of Birth of Jesus to the Virgin	Nazareth			1:26–38		Is. 7:14
c. 5 B.C.	(3) Song of Elizabeth to Mary	{Hill Country {of Judea			1:39–45		
	(4) Mary's Song of Praise				1:46–56		Ps. 103:17
5 B.C.	(5) Birth, Infancy, and Purpose for Future of John the Baptist	Judea			1:57–80		Mal. 3:1
	(6) Announcement of Jesus' Birth to Joseph	Nazareth	1:18–25				Is. 9:6, 7
5–4 B.C.	(7) Birth of Jesus Christ	Bethlehem	1:24, 25		2:1–7		Is. 7:14
	(8) Proclamation by the Angels	{Near {Bethlehem			2:8–14		1 Tim. 3:16
	(9) The Visit of Homage by Shepherds	Bethlehem			2:15–20		
	(10) Jesus' Circumcision	Bethlehem			2:21		Lev. 12:3
4 B.C.	(11) First Temple Visit with Acknowledgments by Simeon and Anna	Jerusalem			2:22–38		Ex. 13:2 Lev. 12
	(12) Visit of the Wise Men	{Jerusalem & {Bethlehem	2:1–12				Num. 24:17
	(13) Flight into Egypt and Massacre of Innocents	{Bethlehem, {Jerusalem & {Egypt	2:13–18				Jer. 31:15
	(14) From Egypt to Nazareth with Jesus		2:19–23		2:39		
Afterward A.D. 7–8	(15) Childhood of Jesus	Nazareth			2:40, 51		
	(16) Jesus, 12 Years Old, Visits the Temple	Jerusalem			2:41–50		Deut. 16:1–8
Afterward	(17) 18-Year Account of Jesus' Adolescence and Adulthood	Nazareth			2:51, 52		1 Sam. 2:26

TRUTHS ABOUT JOHN THE BAPTIST

Date	Event	Location	Matthew	Mark	Luke	John	Related References
c. A.D. 25–27	John's Ministry Begins Man and Message His Picture of Jesus His Courage	Judean Wilderness	3:1 3:2–12 3:11, 12 14:4–12	1:1–4 1:2–8 1:7, 8	3:1, 2 3:3–14 3:15–18 3:19, 20	1:19–28 1:26, 27	Mal. 3:1 Is. 40:3 Acts 2:38

BEGINNING OF JESUS' MINISTRY IN 12 EVENTS

Date	Event	Location	Matthew	Mark	Luke	John	Related References
c. A.D. 27	(1) Jesus Baptized	Jordan River	3:13–17	1:9–11	3:21–23	1:29–34	Ps. 2:7
	(2) Jesus Tempted	Wilderness	4:1–11	1:12, 13	4:1–13		Ps. 91:11
	(3) Calls First Disciples	Beyond Jordan				1:35–51	
	(4) The First Miracle	Cana in Galilee				2:1–11	
	(5) First Stay in Capernaum	(Capernaum is "His" city)				2:12	
A.D. 27	(6) First Cleansing of the Temple	Jerusalem				2:13–22	Ps. 69:9
	(7) Received at Jerusalem	Judea				2:23–25	
	(8) Teaches Nicodemus about Second Birth	Judea				3:1–21	Num. 21:8, 9
	(9) Co-Ministry with John	Judea				3:22–30	

Date	Event	Location	Matthew	Mark	Luke	John	Related References
A.D. 27	(10) Leaves for Galilee	Judea	4:12	1:14	4:14	4:1–4	
	(11) Samaritan Woman at Jacob's Well	Samaria				4:5–42	Josh. 24:32
	(12) Returns to Galilee			1:15	4:15	4:43–45	

A.D. 27–29 — THE GALILEAN MINISTRY OF JESUS IN 55 EVENTS

Date	Event	Location	Matthew	Mark	Luke	John	Related References
A.D. 27	(1) Healing of the Nobleman's Son	Cana				4:46–54	
	(2) Rejected at Nazareth	Nazareth			4:16–30		Is. 61:1, 2
	(3) Moved to Capernaum	Capernaum	4:13–17				Is. 9:1, 2
	(4) Four Become Fishers of Men	Sea of Galilee	4:18–22	1:16–20	5:1–11		Ps. 33:9
	(5) Demoniac Healed on the Sabbath Day	Capernaum		1:21–28	4:31–37		
	(6) Peter's Mother-in-Law Cured, Plus Others	Capernaum	8:14–17	1:29–34	4:38–41		Is. 53:4
c. A.D. 27	(7) First Preaching Tour of Galilee	Galilee	4:23–25	1:35–39	4:42–44		
	(8) Leper Healed and Response Recorded	Galilee	8:1–4	1:40–45	5:12–16		Lev. 13:49
	(9) Paralytic Healed	Capernaum	9:1–8	2:1–12	5:17–26		Rom. 3:23
	(10) Matthew's Call and Reception Held	Capernaum	9:9–13	2:13–17	5:27–32		Hos. 6:6
	(11) Disciples Defended via a Parable	Capernaum	9:14–17	2:18–22	5:33–39		
A.D. 28	(12) Goes to Jerusalem for Second Passover; Heals Lame Man	Jerusalem				5:1–47	Ex. 20:10
	(13) Plucked Grain Precipitates Sabbath Controversy	En Route to Galilee	12:1–8	2:23–28	6:1–5		Deut. 5:14
	(14) Withered Hand Healed Causes Another Sabbath Controversy	Galilee	12:9–14	3:1–6	6:6–11		
	(15) Multitudes Healed	Sea of Galilee	12:15–21	3:7–12	6:17–19		
	(16) Twelve Apostles Selected After a Night of Prayer	{ Near Capernaum		3:13–19	6:12–16		
	(17) Sermon on the Mt.	{ Near Capernaum	5:1—7:29		6:20–49		
	(18) Centurion's Servant Healed	Capernaum	8:5–13		7:1–10		Is. 49:12, 13
	(19) Raises Widow's Son from Dead	Nain			7:11–17		Job 19:25
	(20) Jesus Allays John's Doubts	Galilee	11:2–19		7:18–35		Mal. 3:1
	(21) Woes Upon the Privileged		11:20–30				Gen. 19:24
	(22) A Sinful Woman Anoints Jesus	Simon's House, Capernaum			7:36–50		
	(23) Another Tour of Galilee	Galilee			8:1–3		
	(24) Jesus Accused of Blasphemy	Capernaum	12:22–37	3:20–30	11:14–23		
	(25) Jesus' Answer to a Demand for a Sign	Capernaum	12:38–45		{ 11:24–26, 29–36		
	(26) Mother, Brothers Seek Audience	Capernaum	12:46–50	3:31–35	8:19–21		
	(27) Famous Parables of Sower, Seed, Tares, Mustard Seed, Leaven, Treasure, Pearl, Dragnet, Lamp Told	By Sea of Galilee	13:1–52	4:1–34	8:4–18		Joel 3:13
	(28) Sea Made Serene	Sea of Galilee	8:23–27	4:35–41	8:22–25		
	(29) Gadarene Demoniac Healed	{ E. Shore of Galilee	8:28–34	5:1–20	8:26–39		
	(30) Jairus' Daughter Raised and Woman with Hemorrhage Healed		9:18–26	5:21–43	8:40–56		
	(31) Two Blind Men's Sight Restored		9:27–31				

Date	Event	Location	Matthew	Mark	Luke	John	Related References
A.D. 28	(32) Mute Demoniac Healed		9:32–34				
	(33) Nazareth's Second Rejection of Christ	Nazareth	13:53–58	6:1–6			
	(34) Twelve Sent Out		9:35—11:1	6:6–13	9:1–6		1 Cor. 9:14
	(35) Fearful Herod Beheads John	Galilee	14:1–12	6:14–29	9:7–9		
Spring A.D. 29	(36) Return of 12, Jesus Withdraws, 5000 Fed	Near Bethsaida	14:13–21	6:30–44	9:10–17	6:1–14	
	(37) Walks on the Water	Sea of Galilee	14:22–33	6:45–52		6:15–21	
	(38) Sick of Gennesaret Healed	Gennesaret	14:34–36	6:53–56			
	(39) Peak of Popularity Passes in Galilee	Capernaum				6:22–71 7:1	Is. 54:13
A.D. 29	(40) Traditions Attacked		15:1–20	7:1–23			Ex. 21:17
	(41) Aborted Retirement in Phoenicia: Syro-Phoenician Healed	Phoenicia	15:21–28	7:24–30			
	(42) Afflicted Healed	Decapolis	15:29–31	7:31–37			
	(43) 4000 Fed	Decapolis	15:32–39	8:1–9			
	(44) Pharisees Increase Attack	Magdala	16:1–4	8:10–13			
	(45) Disciples' Carelessness Condemned; Blind Man Healed		16:5–12	8:14–26			Jer. 5:21
	(46) Peter Confesses Jesus Is the Christ	Near Caesarea Philippi	16:13–20	8:27–30	9:18–21		
	(47) Jesus Foretells His Death	Caesarea Philippi	16:21–26	8:31–37	9:22–25		
	(48) Kingdom Promised		16:27, 28	9:1	9:26, 27		Prov. 24:12
	(49) The Transfiguration	Mountain Unnamed	17:1–13	9:2–13	9:28–36		Is. 42:1
	(50) Epileptic Healed	Mt. of Transfiguration	17:14–21	9:14–29	9:37–42		
	(51) Again Tells of Death, Resurrection	Galilee	17:22, 23	9:30–32	9:43–45		
	(52) Taxes Paid	Capernaum	17:24–27				Ex. 30:11–15
	(53) Disciples Contend About Greatness; Jesus Defines; also Patience, Loyalty, Forgiveness	Capernaum	18:1–35	9:33–50	9:46–62		
	(54) Jesus Rejects Brothers' Advice	Galilee				7:2–9	
c. Sept. A.D. 29	(55) Galilee Departure and Samaritan Rejection		19:1		9:51–56	7:10	

A.D. 29–30   LAST JUDEAN AND PEREAN MINISTRY OF JESUS IN 42 EVENTS

Date	Event	Location	Matthew	Mark	Luke	John	Related References
Oct. A.D. 29	(1) Feast of Tabernacles	Jerusalem				7:2, 11–52	
	(2) Forgiveness of Adulteress	Jerusalem				7:53—8:11	Lev. 20:10
A.D. 29	(3) Christ—the Light of the World	Jerusalem				8:12–20	
	(4) Pharisees Can't Meet the Prophecy Thus Try to Destroy the Prophet	Jerusalem—Temple				8:12–59	Is. 6:9
	(5) Man Born Blind Healed; Following Consequences	Jerusalem				9:1–41	
	(6) Parable of the Good Shepherd	Jerusalem				10:1–21	
	(7) The Service of the Seventy	Probably Judea			10:1–24		
	(8) Lawyer Hears the Story of the Good Samaritan	Judea (?)			10:25–37		
	(9) The Hospitality of Martha and Mary	Bethany			10:38–42		
	(10) Another Lesson on Prayer	Judea (?)			11:1–13		

Date	Event	Location	Matthew	Mark	Luke	John	Related References
A.D. 29	(11) Accused of Connection with Beelzebub				11:14–36		
	(12) Judgment Against Lawyers and Pharisees				11:37–54		Mic. 6:8
	(13) Jesus Deals with Hypocrisy, Covetousness, Worry, and Alertness				12:1–59		Mic. 7:6
	(14) Repent or Perish				13:1–5		
	(15) Barren Fig Tree				13:6–9		
	(16) Crippled Woman Healed on Sabbath				13:10–17		Deut. 5:12–15
	(17) Parables of Mustard Seed and Leaven	{Probably Perea			13:18–21		
Winter A.D. 29	(18) Feast of Dedication	Jerusalem				10:22–39	Ps. 82:6
	(19) Withdrawal Beyond Jordan					10:40–42	
	(20) Begins Teaching Return to Jerusalem with Special Words About Herod	Perea			13:22–35		Ps. 6:8
	(21) Meal with a Pharisee Ruler Occasions Healing Man with Dropsy; Parables of Ox, Best Places, and Great Supper				14:1–24		
	(22) Demands of Discipleship	Perea			14:25–35		
	(23) Parables of Lost Sheep, Coin, Son				15:1–32		1 Pet. 2:25
	(24) Parables of Unjust Steward, Rich Man and Lazarus				16:1–31		
	(25) Lessons on Service, Faith, Influence				17:1–10		
	(26) Resurrection of Lazarus	{Perea to Bethany				11:1–44	
	(27) Reaction to It: Withdrawal of Jesus					11:45–54	
A.D. 30	(28) Begins Last Journey to Jerusalem via Samaria & Galilee	{Samaria, Galilee			17:11		
	(29) Heals Ten Lepers				17:12–19		Lev. 13:45, 46
	(30) Lessons on the Coming Kingdom				17:20–37		Gen. 6—7
	(31) Parables: Persistent Widow, Pharisee and Tax Collector				18:1–14		
	(32) Doctrine on Divorce		19:1–12	10:1–12			Deut. 24:1–4 Gen. 2:23–25
	(33) Jesus Blesses Children: Objections	Perea	19:13–15	10:13–16	18:15–17		Ps. 131:2
	(34) Rich Young Ruler	Perea	19:16–30	10:17–31	18:18–30		Ex. 20:1–17
	(35) Laborers of the 11th Hour		20:1–16				
	(36) Foretells Death and Resurrection	{Near Jordan	20:17–19	10:32–34	18:31–34		Ps. 22
	(37) Ambition of James and John		20:20–28	10:35–45			
	(38) Blind Bartimaeus Healed	Jericho		10:46–52	18:35–43		
	(39) Interview with Zacchaeus	Jericho			19:1–10		
	(40) Parable: the Minas	Jericho			19:11–27		
	(41) Returns to Home of Mary and Martha	Bethany				{11:55— 12:1	
	(42) Plot to Kill Lazarus	Bethany				12:9–11	

Spring A.D. 30	JESUS' FINAL WEEK OF WORK AT JERUSALEM IN 41 EVENTS						
Sunday	(1) Triumphal Entry	Bethany, Jerusalem, Bethany	21:1–9	11:1–11	19:28–44	12:12–19	Zech. 9:9

Date	Event	Location	Matthew	Mark	Luke	John	Related References
Monday	(2) Fig Tree Cursed and Temple Cleansed	Bethany to Jerusalem	21:10–19	11:12–18	19:45–48		Jer. 7:11
	(3) The Attraction of Sacrifice	Jerusalem				12:20–50	Is. 6:10
Tuesday	(4) Withered Fig Tree Testifies	Bethany to Jerusalem	21:20–22	11:19–26			
	(5) Sanhedrin Challenges Jesus. Answered by Parables: Two Sons, Wicked Vinedressers and Marriage Feast	Jerusalem	21:23— 22:14	11:27— 12:12	20:1–19		Is. 5:1, 2
	(6) Tribute to Caesar	Jerusalem	22:15–22	12:13–17	20:20–26		
	(7) Sadducees Question the Resurrection	Jerusalem	22:23–33	12:18–27	20:27–40		Ex. 3:6
	(8) Pharisees Question Commandments	Jerusalem	22:34–40	12:28–34			
	(9) Jesus and David	Jerusalem	22:41–46	12:35–37	20:41–44		Ps. 110:1
	(10) Jesus' Last Sermon	Jerusalem	23:1–39	12:38–40	20:45–47		
	(11) Widow's Mite	Jerusalem		12:41–44	21:1–4		Lev. 27:30
	(12) Jesus Tells of the Future	Mt. Olives	24:1–51	13:1–37	21:5–36		Dan. 12:1
	(13) Parables: Ten Virgins, Talents. The Day of Judgment	Mt. Olives	25:1–46				Zech. 14:5
	(14) Jesus Tells Date of Crucifixion		26:1–5	14:1, 2	22:1, 2		
	(15) Anointing by Mary at Simon's Feast	Bethany	26:6–13	14:3–9		12:2–8	
	(16) Judas Contracts the Betrayal		26:14–16	14:10, 11	22:3–6		Zech. 11:12
Thursday	(17) Preparation for the Passover	Jerusalem	26:17–19	14:12–16	22:7–13		Ex. 12:14–28
Thursday P.M.	(18) Passover Eaten, Jealousy Rebuked	Jerusalem	26:20	14:17	22:14–16, 24–30		
	(19) Feet Washed	Upper Room				13:1–20	
	(20) Judas Revealed, Defects	Upper Room	26:21–25	14:18–21	22:21–23	13:21–30	Ps. 41:9
	(21) Jesus Warns About Further Desertion; Cries of Loyalty	Upper Room	26:31–35	14:27–31	22:31–38	13:31–38	Zech. 13:7
	(22) Institution of the Lord's Supper	Upper Room	26:26–29	14:22–25	22:17–20		1 Cor. 11:23–34
	(23) Last Speech to the Apostles and Intercessory Prayer	Jerusalem				14:1— 17:26	Ps. 35:19
Thursday-Friday	(24) The Grief of Gethsemane	Mt. Olives	26:30, 36–46	14:26, 32–42	22:39–46	18:1	Ps. 42:6
Friday	(25) Betrayal, Arrest, Desertion	Gethsemane	26:47–56	14:43–52	22:47–53	18:2–12	
	(26) First Examined by Annas	Jerusalem				18:12–14, 19–23	
	(27) Trial by Caiaphas and Council; Following Indignities	Jerusalem	26:57, 59–68	14:53, 55–65	22:54, 63–65	18:24	Lev. 24:16
	(28) Peter's Triple Denial	Jerusalem	26:58, 69–75	14:54, 66–72	22:54–62	18:15–18, 25–27	
	(29) Condemnation by the Council	Jerusalem	27:1	15:1	22:66–71		Ps. 110:1
	(30) Suicide of Judas	Jerusalem	27:3–10				Acts 1:18, 19
	(31) First Appearance Before Pilate	Jerusalem	27:2, 11–14	15:1–5	23:1–7	18:28–38	
	(32) Jesus Before Herod	Jerusalem			23:6–12		
	(33) Second Appearance Before Pilate	Jerusalem	27:15–26	15:6–15	23:13–25	18:39— 19:16	Deut. 21:6–9
	(34) Mockery by Roman Soldiers	Jerusalem	27:27–30	15:16–19			
	(35) Led to Golgotha	Jerusalem	27:31–34	15:20–23	23:26–33	19:16, 17	Ps. 69:21
	(36) 6 Events of First 3 Hours on Cross	Calvary	27:35–44	15:24–32	23:33–43	19:18–27	Ps. 22:18
	(37) Last 3 Hours on Cross	Calvary	27:45–50	15:33–37	23:44–46	19:28–30	Ps. 22:1
	(38) Events Attending Jesus' Death		27:51–56	15:38–41	23:45, 47–49		
	(39) Burial of Jesus	Jerusalem	27:57–60	15:42–46	23:50–54	19:31–37	Ex. 12:46
Friday-Saturday	(40) Tomb Sealed	Jerusalem	27:61–66		23:55, 56		Ex. 20:8–11
	(41) Women Watch	Jerusalem		15:47			

The Old Testament prophet Micah had predicted that the Messiah would be born in this city (Micah 5:2), Bethlehem. It is a small city just 10 km. (6 mi.) south of Jerusalem.

Bethlehem, in the hill country of Judah—the home of David and the birthplace of Jesus (1 Sam. 16:1, 4; Luke 2:11).

Photo by Gustav Jeeninga

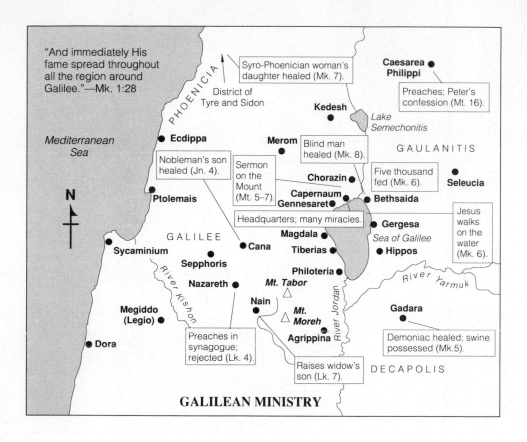

"And immediately His fame spread throughout all the region around Galilee."—Mk. 1:28

Mediterranean Sea

PHOENICIA

District of Tyre and Sidon

Syro-Phoenician woman's daughter healed (Mk. 7).

Caesarea Philippi

Preaches; Peter's confession (Mt. 16).

Kedesh

Lake Semechonitis

Ecdippa

Merom

Blind man healed (Mk. 8).

GAULANITIS

Nobleman's son healed (Jn. 4).

Sermon on the Mount (Mt. 5–7).

Chorazin

Five thousand fed (Mk. 6).

Seleucia

Ptolemais

Capernaum

Gennesaret

Bethsaida

Headquarters; many miracles.

Gergesa

Jesus walks on the water (Mk. 6).

N

GALILEE

Cana

Magdala

Sea of Galilee

Sycaminium

Tiberias

Hippos

Sepphoris

Philoteria

River Yarmuk

Nazareth

Mt. Tabor △

Megiddo (Legio)

Nain

Mt. Moreh △

Gadara

River Kishon

Dora

Preaches in synagogue; rejected (Lk. 4).

Agrippina

River Jordan

Demoniac healed; swine possessed (Mk.5).

Raises widow's son (Lk. 7).

DECAPOLIS

GALILEAN MINISTRY

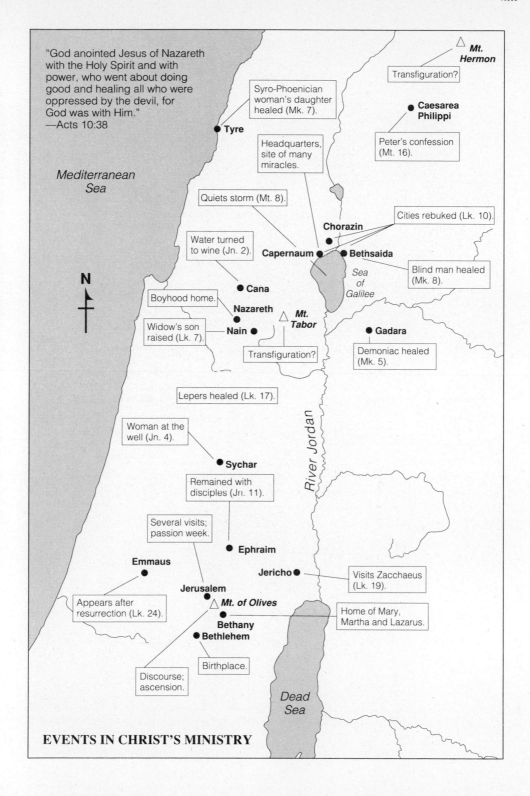

"God anointed Jesus of Nazareth with the Holy Spirit and with power, who went about doing good and healing all who were oppressed by the devil, for God was with Him."
—Acts 10:38

Mediterranean Sea

N

Syro-Phoenician woman's daughter healed (Mk. 7).

Tyre

Headquarters, site of many miracles.

Quiets storm (Mt. 8).

Water turned to wine (Jn. 2).

Boyhood home.

Cana

Nazareth

Widow's son raised (Lk. 7).

Nain

Mt. Tabor

Transfiguration?

Mt. Hermon

Transfiguration?

Caesarea Philippi

Peter's confession (Mt. 16).

Cities rebuked (Lk. 10).

Chorazin

Capernaum

Bethsaida

Blind man healed (Mk. 8).

Sea of Galilee

Gadara

Demoniac healed (Mk. 5).

Lepers healed (Lk. 17).

Woman at the well (Jn. 4).

Sychar

Remained with disciples (Jn. 11).

Several visits; passion week.

Ephraim

River Jordan

Emmaus

Jericho

Visits Zacchaeus (Lk. 19).

Jerusalem

Mt. of Olives

Appears after resurrection (Lk. 24).

Bethany

Bethlehem

Home of Mary, Martha and Lazarus.

Discourse; ascension.

Birthplace.

Dead Sea

EVENTS IN CHRIST'S MINISTRY

The Sea, or Lake, of Galilee, at the point where the Jordan River flows into the northern end of the lake.

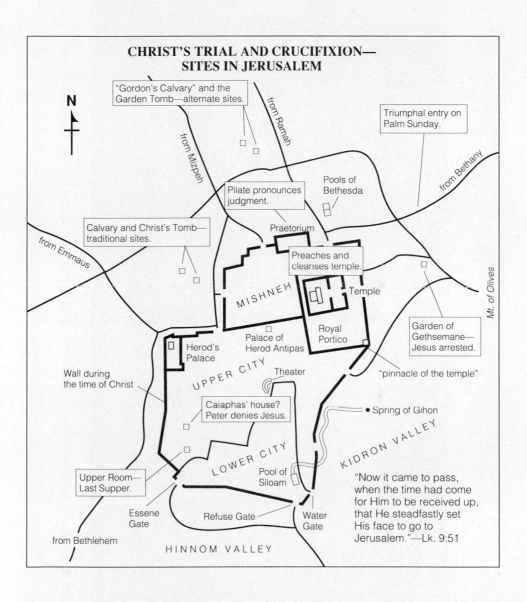

CHRIST'S TRIAL AND CRUCIFIXION—
SITES IN JERUSALEM

"Gordon's Calvary" and the
Garden Tomb—alternate sites.

N

from Ramah

from Mizpeh

Triumphal entry on
Palm Sunday.

from Bethany

Pilate pronounces
judgment.

Pools of
Bethesda

Praetorium

Calvary and Christ's Tomb—
traditional sites.

from Emmaus

Preaches and
cleanses temple.

MISHNEH

Temple

Mt. of Olives

Royal
Portico

Garden of
Gethsemane—
Jesus arrested.

Palace of
Herod Antipas

Herod's
Palace

UPPER CITY

Theater

"pinnacle of the temple"

Wall during
the time of Christ

Caiaphas' house?
Peter denies Jesus.

Spring of Gihon

KIDRON VALLEY

LOWER CITY

Upper Room—
Last Supper.

Pool of
Siloam

Essene
Gate

Refuse Gate

Water
Gate

from Bethlehem

HINNOM VALLEY

"Now it came to pass,
when the time had come
for Him to be received up,
that He steadfastly set
His face to go to
Jerusalem."—Lk. 9:51

Photo by Ben Chapman

A tomb carved out of limestone rock, similar to the tomb in which Jesus was buried. A large stone was rolled across the entrance to seal the tomb (Mark 15:46).

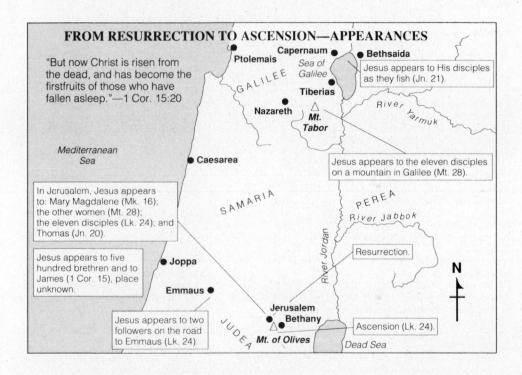

FROM RESURRECTION TO ASCENSION—APPEARANCES

"But now Christ is risen from the dead, and has become the firstfruits of those who have fallen asleep."—1 Cor. 15:20

Ptolemais

Capernaum

Bethsaida

Sea of Galilee

GALILEE

Jesus appears to His disciples as they fish (Jn. 21).

Tiberias

River Yarmuk

Nazareth

Mt. Tabor

Mediterranean Sea

Caesarea

Jesus appears to the eleven disciples on a mountain in Galilee (Mt. 28).

SAMARIA

PEREA

River Jabbok

In Jerusalem, Jesus appears to: Mary Magdalene (Mk. 16); the other women (Mt. 28); the eleven disciples (Lk. 24); and Thomas (Jn. 20).

River Jordan

Jesus appears to five hundred brethren and to James (1 Cor. 15), place unknown.

Joppa

Resurrection.

Emmaus

N

Jesus appears to two followers on the road to Emmaus (Lk. 24).

JUDEA

Jerusalem

Bethany

Mt. of Olives

Ascension (Lk. 24).

Dead Sea

PROPHECIES OF THE MESSIAH FULFILLED IN JESUS CHRIST

Presented Here in Their Order of Fulfillment

PROPHETIC SCRIPTURE	SUBJECT	FULFILLED
Gen. 3:15, p. 7 "And I will put enmity between you and the woman, and between your seed and her Seed; He shall bruise your head, and you shall bruise His heel."	seed of a woman	**Gal. 4:4, p. 1189** "But when the fullness of the time had come, God sent forth His Son, born of a woman, born under the law,"
Gen. 12:3, p. 14 "I will bless those who bless you, and I will curse him who curses you; And in you all the families of the earth shall be blessed."	descendant of Abraham	**Matt. 1:1, p. 973** "The book of the genealogy of Jesus Christ, the Son of David, the Son of Abraham:"
Gen. 17:19, p. 18 "Then God said, 'No, Sarah your wife shall bear you a son, and you shall call his name Isaac; I will establish My covenant with him for an everlasting covenant, *and* with his descendants after him.'"	descendant of Isaac	**Luke 3:34, p. 1040** "*the son* of Jacob, *the son* of Isaac, *the son* of Abraham, *the son* of Terah, *the son* of Nahor,"
Num. 24:17, p. 157 "I see Him, but not now; I behold Him, but not near; a Star shall come out of Jacob; a Scepter shall rise out of Israel, and batter the brow of Moab, and destroy all the sons of tumult."	descendant of Jacob	**Matt. 1:2, p. 973** "Abraham begot Isaac, Isaac begot Jacob, and Jacob begot Judah and his brothers."
Gen. 49:10, p. 50 "The scepter shall not depart from Judah, nor a lawgiver from between his feet, until Shiloh comes; and to Him *shall be* the obedience of the people."	from the tribe of Judah	**Luke 3:33, p. 1040** "*the son* of Amminadab, *the son* of Ram, *the son* of Hezron, *the son* of Perez, *the son* of Judah."
Is. 9:7, p. 687 "Of the increase of *His* government and peace *there will be* no end, upon the throne of David and over His kingdom, to order it and establish it with judgment and justice from that time forward, even forever. The zeal of the LORD of hosts will perform this."	heir to the throne of David	**Luke 1:32, 33, p. 1037** "He will be great, and will be called the Son of the Highest; and the Lord God will give Him the throne of His father David. And He will reign over the house of Jacob forever, and of His kingdom there will be no end."
Ps. 45:6, 7, p. 565; 102:25–27, p. 596 "Your throne, O God, *is* forever and ever; a scepter of righteousness *is* the scepter of Your kingdom. You love righteousness and hate wickedness; therefore God, Your God, has anointed You with the oil of gladness more than Your companions." "Of old You laid the foundation of the earth, and the heavens *are* the work of Your hands. They will perish, but You will endure; yes, all of them will grow old like a garment; like a cloak You will change them, and they will be changed. But You *are* the same, and Your years will have no end."	anointed and eternal	**Heb. 1:8–12, p. 1248** "But to the Son *He says:* 'Your throne, O God, is forever and ever; a scepter of righteousness is the scepter of Your kingdom. You have loved righteousness and hated lawlessness; therefore God, Your God, has anointed You with the oil of gladness more than Your companions.' And: 'You, LORD, in the beginning laid the foundation of the earth, and the heavens are the work of Your hands; they will perish, but You remain; and they will all grow old like a garment; like a cloak You will fold them up, and they will be changed. But You are the same, and Your years will not fail.'"

PROPHETIC SCRIPTURE	SUBJECT	FULFILLED
Mic. 5:2, p. 925 "But you, Bethlehem, Ephrathah, *though* you are little among the thousands of Judah, *yet* out of you shall come forth to Me the One to be ruler in Israel, whose goings forth *have been* from of old, from everlasting."	born in Bethlehem	*Luke 2:4, 5, 7, p. 1038* "And Joseph also went up from Galilee, out of the city of Nazareth, into Judea, to the city of David, which is called Bethlehem, because he was of the house and lineage of David, to be registered with Mary, his betrothed wife, who was with child. . . . And she brought forth her first-born Son, and wrapped Him in swaddling cloths, and laid Him in a manger, because there was no room for them in the inn."
Dan. 9:25, p. 879 "Know therefore and understand, *that* from the going forth of the command to restore and build Jerusalem until Messiah the Prince, *there shall be* seven weeks and sixty-two weeks; the street shall be built again, and the wall, even in troublesome times."	time for His birth	*Luke 2:1, 2, p. 1038* "And it came to pass in those days *that* a decree went out from Caesar Augustus that all the world should be registered. This census first took place while Quirinius was governing Syria."
Is. 7:14, p. 685 "Therefore the Lord Himself will give you a sign: Behold, the virgin shall conceive and bear a Son, and shall call His name Immanuel."	to be born of a virgin	*Luke 1:26, 27, 30, 31, p. 1036* "Now in the sixth month the angel Gabriel was sent by God to a city of Galilee named Nazareth, to a virgin betrothed to a man whose name was Joseph, of the house of David. The virgin's name *was* Mary. . . . Then the angel said to her, 'Do not be afraid, Mary, for you have found favor with God. And behold, you will conceive in your womb and bring forth a Son, and shall call His name JESUS.'"
Jer. 31:15, p. 776 "Thus says the LORD: 'A voice was heard in Ramah, lamentation *and* bitter weeping, Rachel weeping for her children, refusing to be comforted for her children, because they *are* no more.'"	slaughter of children	*Matt. 2:16–18, p. 974* "Then Herod, when he saw that he was deceived by the wise men, was exceedingly angry; and he sent forth and put to death all the male children who were in Bethlehem and in all its districts, from two years old and under, according to the time which he had determined from the wise men. Then was fulfilled what was spoken by Jeremiah the prophet, saying: 'A voice was heard in Ramah, lamentation, weeping, and great mourning, Rachel weeping for her children, refusing to be comforted, because they were no more.'"
Hos. 11:1, p. 892 "When Israel *was* a child, I loved him, and out of Egypt I called My son."	flight to Egypt	*Matt. 2:14, 15, p. 974* "When he arose, he took the young Child and His mother by night and departed for Egypt, and was there until the death of Herod, that it might be fulfilled which was spoken by the Lord through the prophet, saying, 'Out of Egypt I called My Son.'"
Is. 40:3–5, p. 713 "The voice of one crying in the wilderness: 'Prepare the way of the LORD; make straight in the desert a highway for our God. Every valley shall be exalted, and every mountain and hill shall be made low; the crooked places shall be made straight, and the rough places smooth; the glory of the LORD shall be revealed, and all flesh shall see *it* together; for the mouth of the LORD has spoken.'"	the way prepared	*Luke 3:3–6, p. 1039* "And he went into all the region around the Jordan, preaching a baptism of repentance for the remission of sins, as it is written in the book of the words of Isaiah the prophet, saying: *'The voice of one crying in the wilderness: "Prepare the way of the LORD, make His paths straight. Every valley shall be filled and every mountain and hill brought low; and the crooked places shall be made straight and the rough ways made smooth; and all flesh shall see the salvation of God."'"*

PROPHETIC SCRIPTURE	SUBJECT	FULFILLED
Mal. 3:1, p. 964 "'Behold, I send My messenger, and he will prepare the way before Me. And the Lord, whom you seek, will suddenly come to His temple, even the messenger of the covenant, in whom you delight. Behold, He is coming,' says the LORD of hosts."	**preceded by a forerunner**	**Luke 7:24, 27, p. 1046** "When the messengers of John had departed, He began to speak to the multitudes concerning John: 'What did you go out into the wilderness to see? A reed shaken by the wind? . . . This is *he* of whom it is written: *"Behold, I send My messenger before Your face, who will prepare Your way before You."*'"
Mal. 4:5, 6, p. 965 "Behold I will send you Elijah the prophet before the coming of the great and dreadful day of the LORD. And he will turn the hearts of the fathers to the children, and the hearts of the children to their fathers, lest I come and strike the earth with a curse."	**preceded by Elijah**	**Matt. 11:13, 14, p. 984** "For all the prophets and the law prophesied until John. And if you are willing to receive *it*, he is Elijah who is to come."
Ps. 2:7, p. 541 "I will declare the decree: the LORD has said to Me, "You *are* My Son, today I have begotten You."	**declared the Son of God**	**Matt. 3:17, p. 975** "And suddenly a voice *came* from heaven, saying, 'This is My beloved Son, in whom I am well pleased.'"
Is. 9:1, 2, p. 686 "Nevertheless the gloom *will* not *be* upon her who *is* distressed, as when at first He lightly esteemed the land of Zebulun and the land of Naphtali, and afterward more heavily oppressed *her, by* the way of the sea, beyond the Jordan, in Galilee of the Gentiles. The people who walked in darkness have seen a great light; those who dwelt in the land of the shadow of death, upon them a light has shined."	**Galilean ministry**	**Matt. 4:13–16, p. 976** "And leaving Nazareth, He came and dwelt in Capernaum, which is by the sea, in the regions of Zebulun and Naphtali, that it might be fulfilled which was spoken by Isaiah the prophet, saying: *'The land of Zebulun and the land of Naphtali, the way of the sea, beyond the Jordan, Galilee of the Gentiles: The people who sat in darkness saw a great light, and upon those who sat in the region and shadow of death light has dawned.'*"
Ps. 78:2–4, p. 582 "I will open my mouth in a parable; I will utter dark sayings of old, which we have heard and known, and our fathers have told us. We will not hide *them* from their children, telling to the generation to come the praises of the LORD, and His strength and His wonderful works that He has done."	**speaks in parables**	**Matt. 13:34, 35, p. 987** "All these things Jesus spoke to the multitude in parables; and without a parable He did not speak to them that it might be fulfilled which was spoken by the prophet, saying: *'I will open My mouth in parables; I will utter things which have been kept secret from the foundation of the world.'*"
Deut. 18:15, p. 191 "The LORD your God will raise up for you a Prophet like me from your midst, from your brethren. Him you shall hear."	**a prophet**	**Acts 3:20, 22, p. 1108** "And that He may send Jesus Christ, who was preached to you before, . . . For Moses truly said to the fathers, *'The LORD your God will raise up for you a Prophet like me from your brethren. Him you shall hear in all things, whatever He says to you.'*"
Is. 61:1, 2, p. 734 "The Spirit of the Lord GOD *is* upon Me, because the LORD has anointed Me to preach good tidings to the poor; He has sent Me to heal the brokenhearted, to proclaim liberty to the captives, and the opening of the prison to *those who are* bound; to proclaim the acceptable year of the LORD, and the day of vengeance of our God; to comfort all who mourn."	**to bind up the brokenhearted**	**Luke 4:18, 19, p. 1041** "*The Spirit of the LORD is upon Me, because He has anointed Me to preach the gospel to the poor. He has sent Me to heal the brokenhearted, to preach deliverance to the captives and recovery of sight to the blind, to set at liberty those who are oppressed, to preach the acceptable year of the LORD.*"
Is. 53:3, p. 727 "He is despised and rejected by men, a man of sorrows and acquainted with grief. And we hid, as it were, *our* faces from Him; He was despised, and we did not esteem Him."	**rejected by His own people, the Jews**	**John 1:11, p. 1075** "He came to His own, and His own did not receive Him." **Luke 23:18, p. 1068** "And they all cried out at once, saying, 'Away with this *Man*, and release to us Barabbas'"——

PROPHETIC SCRIPTURE	SUBJECT	FULFILLED
Ps. 110:4, p. 602 "The LORD has sworn and will not relent, 'You *are* a priest forever according to the order of Melchizedek.'"	**priest after order of Melchizedek**	*Heb. 5:5, 6, p. 1250* "So also Christ did not glorify Himself to become High Priest, *but it* was He who said to Him: *'You are My Son, today I have begotten You.'* As *He* also *says* in another *place: 'You are a priest forever according to the order of Melchizedek.'*";
Zech. 9:9, p. 955 "Rejoice greatly, O daughter of Zion! Shout, O daughter of Jerusalem! Behold, your King is coming to you; He *is* just and having salvation, lowly and riding on a donkey, a colt, the foal of a donkey."	**triumphal entry**	*Mark 11:7, 9, 11, p. 1023* "Then they brought the colt to Jesus and threw their garments on it, and He sat on it. . . . Then those who went before and those who followed cried out, saying: 'Hosanna! *Blessed is He who comes in the name of the LORD!'* . . . And Jesus went into Jerusalem and into the temple. So when He had looked around at all things, as the hour was already late, He went out to Bethany with the twelve."
Ps. 8:2, p. 544 "Out of the mouth of babes and infants You have ordained strength, because of Your enemies, that You may silence the enemy and the avenger."	**adored by infants**	*Matt. 21:15, 16, p. 995* "But when the chief priests and scribes saw the wonderful things that He did, and the children crying out in the temple and saying, 'Hosanna to the Son of David!' they were indignant and said to Him, 'Do You hear what these are saying?' And Jesus said to them, 'Yes. Have you never read, "*Out of the mouth of babes and nursing infants You have perfected praise*"?'"
Is. 53:1, p. 727 "Who has believed our report? And to whom has the arm of the LORD been revealed?"	**not believed**	*John 12:37, 38, p. 1091* "But although He had done so many signs before them, they did not believe in Him, that the word of Isaiah the prophet might be fulfilled, which he spoke: '*Lord, who has believed our report? And to whom has the arm of the LORD been revealed?*'"
Ps. 41:9, p. 563 "Even my own familiar friend in whom I trusted, who ate my bread, has lifted up *his* heel against me."	**betrayed by a close friend**	*Luke 22:47, 48, p. 1067* "And while He was still speaking, behold, a multitude; and he who was called Judas, one of the twelve, went before them and drew near to Jesus to kiss Him. But Jesus said to him, 'Judas, are you betraying the Son of Man with a kiss?'"
Zech. 11:12, p. 957 "Then I said to them, 'If it is agreeable to you, give *me* my wages; and if not, refrain.' So they weighed out for my wages thirty *pieces* of silver."	**betrayed for thirty pieces of silver**	*Matt. 26:14, 15, p. 1002* "Then one of the twelve, called Judas Iscariot, went to the chief priests and said, 'What are you willing to give me if I deliver Him to you?' And they counted out to him thirty pieces of silver."
Ps. 35:11, p. 558 "Fierce witnesses rise up; they ask me *things* that I do not know."	**accused by false witnesses**	*Mark 14:57, 58, p. 1029* "And some rose up and bore false witness against Him, saying, 'We heard Him say, "I will destroy this temple that *is* made with hands, and within three days I will build another made without hands."'"
Is. 53:7, p. 727 "He was oppressed and He was afflicted, yet He opened not His mouth; He was led as a lamb to the slaughter, and as a sheep before its shearers is silent, so He opened not His mouth."	**silent to accusations**	*Mark 15:4, 5, p. 1029* "Then Pilate asked Him again, saying, 'Do You answer nothing? See how many things they testify against You!' But Jesus still answered nothing, so that Pilate marveled."

PROPHETIC SCRIPTURE	SUBJECT	FULFILLED
Is. 50:6, p. 725 "I gave My back to those who struck *Me*, and My cheeks to those who plucked out the beard; I did not hide My face from shame and spitting."	spat on and struck	**Matt. 26:67, p. 1003** "Then they spat in His face and beat Him; and others struck *Him* with the palms of their hands,"
Ps. 35:19, p. 558 "Let them not rejoice over me who are wrongfully my enemies; nor let them wink with the eye who hate me without a cause."	hated without reason	**John 15:24, 25, p. 1094** "If I had not done among them the works which no one else did, they would have no sin; but now they have seen and also hated both Me and My Father. But *this happened* that the word might be fulfilled which is written in their law, *'They hated Me without a cause.'*"
Is. 53:5, p. 727 "But He *was* wounded for our transgressions, *He was* bruised for our iniquities; the chastisement for our peace *was* upon Him, and by His stripes we are healed."	vicarious sacrifice	**Rom. 5:6, 8, p. 1145** "For when we were still without strength, in due time Christ died for the ungodly. . . . But God demonstrates His own love toward us, in that while we were still sinners, Christ died for us."
Is. 53:12, p. 727 "Therefore I will divide Him a portion with the great, and He shall divide the spoil with the strong, because He poured out His soul unto death, and He was numbered with the transgressors, and He bore the sin of many, and made intercession for the transgressors."	crucified with malefactors	**Mark 15:27, 28, p. 1030** "With Him they also crucified two robbers, one on His right and the other on His left. So the Scripture was fulfilled which says, *'And He was numbered with the transgressors.'*"
Zech. 12:10, p. 957 "And I will pour on the house of David and on the inhabitants of Jerusalem the Spirit of grace and supplication; then they will look on Me whom they have pierced; they will mourn for Him as one mourns for *his* only *son*, and grieve for Him as one grieves for a firstborn."	pierced through hands and feet	**John 20:27, p. 1099** "Then He said to Thomas, 'Reach your finger here, and look at My hands; and reach your hand *here*, and put *it* into My side. Do not be unbelieving, but believing.'"
Ps. 22:7, 8, p. 551 "All those who see Me laugh Me to scorn; they shoot out the lip, they shake the head, *saying*, 'He trusted in the LORD, let Him rescue Him; let Him deliver Him, since He delights in Him!'"	sneered and mocked	**Luke 23:35, p. 1068** "And the people stood looking on. But even the rulers with them sneered, saying, 'He saved others; let Him save Himself if He is the Christ, the chosen of God.'"
Ps. 69:9, p. 576 "Because zeal for Your house has eaten me up, and the reproaches of those who reproach You have fallen on me."	was reproached	**Rom. 15:3, p. 1154** "For even Christ did not please Himself; but as it is written, *'The reproaches of those who reproached You fell on Me.'*"
Ps. 109:4, p. 601 "In return for my love they are my accusers, but I *give myself to* prayer."	prayer for His enemies	**Luke 23:34, p. 1068** "Then Jesus said, 'Father, forgive them, for they do not know what they do.' And they divided His garments and cast lots."
Ps. 22:17, 18, p. 551 "I can count all My bones. They look *and* stare at Me. They divide My garments among them, and for My clothing they cast lots."	soldiers gambled for His clothing	**Matt. 27:35, 36, p. 1005** "Then they crucified Him, and divided His garments, casting lots, that it might be fulfilled which was spoken by the prophet: *'They divided My garments among them, and for My clothing they cast lots.'* Sitting down, they kept watch over Him there."
Ps. 22:1, p. 550 "My God, My God, why have You forsaken Me? *Why are You so* far from helping Me, *and from* the words of My groaning?"	forsaken by God	**Matt. 27:46, p. 1005** "And about the ninth hour Jesus cried out with a loud voice, saying, 'Eli, Eli, lama sabachthani?' that is, *'My God, My God, why have You forsaken Me?'*"

PROPHETIC SCRIPTURE	SUBJECT	FULFILLED
Ps. 34:20, p. 558 "He guards all his bones; not one of them is broken."	no bones broken	*John 19:32, 33, 36, p. 1098* "Then the soldiers came and broke the legs of the first and of the other who was crucified with Him. But when they came to Jesus and saw that He was already dead, they did not break His legs. . . . For these things were done that the Scripture should be fulfilled, *'Not one of His bones shall be broken.'*"
Zech. 12:10, p. 957 "And I will pour on the house of David and on the inhabitants of Jerusalem the Spirit of grace and supplication; then they will look on Me whom they have pierced; they will mourn for Him as one mourns for *his* only *son,* and grieve for Him as one grieves for a firstborn."	His side pierced	*John 19:34, p. 1098* "But one of the soldiers pierced His side with a spear, and immediately blood and water came out."
Is. 53:9, p. 727 "And they made His grave with the wicked—but with the rich at His death, because He had done no violence, nor *was any* deceit in His mouth."	buried with the rich	*Matt. 27:57–60, p. 1005* "Now when evening had come, there came a rich man from Arimathea, named Joseph, who himself had also become a disciple of Jesus. This man went to Pilate and asked for the body of Jesus. Then Pilate commanded the body to be given to him. And when Joseph had taken the body, he wrapped it in a clean linen cloth, and laid it in his new tomb which he had hewn out of the rock; and he rolled a large stone against the door of the tomb, and departed."
Ps. 16:10, p. 547 "For You will not leave my soul in Sheol, nor will You allow Your Holy One to see corruption." *Ps. 49:15, p. 567* "But God will redeem my soul from the power of the grave, for He shall receive me. Selah"	to be resurrected	*Mark 16:6, 7, p. 1031* "But he said to them, 'Do not be alarmed. You seek Jesus of Nazareth, who was crucified. He is risen! He is not here. See the place where they laid Him. But go *and* tell His disciples—and Peter—that He is going before you into Galilee; there you will see Him, as He said to you.'"
Ps. 68:18, p. 575 "You have ascended on high, You have led captivity captive; You have received gifts among men; even *among* the rebellious, that the LORD God might dwell *there.*"	His ascension to God's right hand	*Mark 16:19, p. 1031* "So then after the Lord had spoken to them, He was received up into heaven, and sat down at the right hand of God." *1 Cor. 15:4, p. 1170* "And that He was buried, and that He rose again the third day according to the Scriptures." *Eph. 4:8, p. 1197* "Therefore He says: *'When He ascended on high, He led captivity captive, and gave gifts to men.'*"

JERUZALEM
BEGIN 1ᵉ EEUW

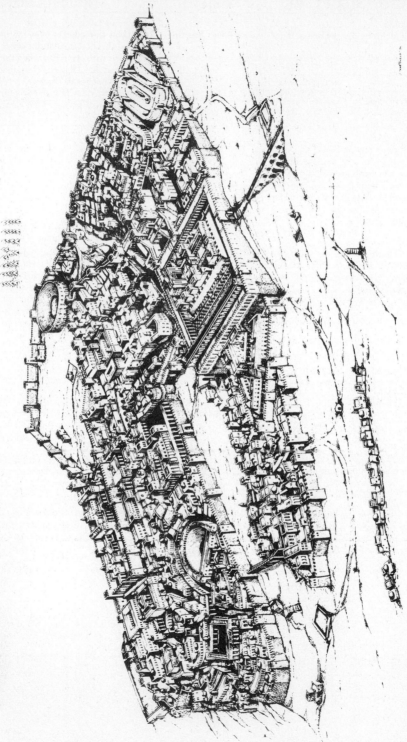

Photo: Amsterdam Bible Museum

An artist's sketch of what Jerusalem might have looked like in New Testament times. The beautiful Temple built by Herod appears within the square wall structure in the foreground.

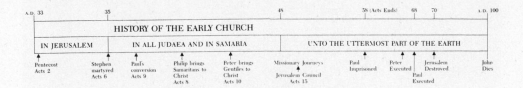

A.D. 33   35   48   58 (Acts Ends)   68   70   A.D. 100

HISTORY OF THE EARLY CHURCH

IN JERUSALEM	IN ALL JUDAEA AND IN SAMARIA	UNTO THE UTTERMOST PART OF THE EARTH

Pentecost
Acts 2

Stephen
martyred
Acts 6

Paul's
conversion
Acts 9

Philip brings
Samaritans to
Christ
Acts 8

Peter brings
Gentiles to
Christ
Acts 10

Missionary Journeys

Jerusalem Council
Acts 15

Paul
Imprisoned

Peter
Executed

Jerusalem
Destroyed

Paul
Executed

John
Dies

THE BOOK OF ACTS IN OVERVIEW

"But ye shall receive power, after that the Holy Ghost is come upon you: and ye shall be witnesses unto me both in *Jerusalem*, and in all *Judaea*, and in *Samaria*, and unto the *uttermost part of the earth* " (Acts 1:8).

Chapters	Acts 1–7	Acts 8–12	Acts 13–28
Spread of the Church	The church in Jerusalem	The church in all Judaea and Samaria	The church to all the earth
The Gospel	Witnessing in the city	Witnessing in the provinces	Witnessing in the world
Theme	Power and progress of the church	Expansion of the church	Paul's three journeys and trials
People Addressed	Jews	Samaritans	Gentiles
Key Person	Peter	Philip	Paul
Time	2 years (A.D. 33–35)	13 years (A.D. 35–48)	14 years (A.D. 48–62)
Development	Triumph	Transition	Travels and trials

From *Visual Survey of the Bible*. Reprinted by permission of the author.

The Areopagus (Mars' Hill) is a little hill near the acropolis in Athens where Paul may have been brought before the philosophers of this city (Acts 17:16-34).

Photo by Gustav Jeeninga

Photo by Ben Chapman

The great theater of the city of Ephesus, showing the marble boulevard leading to the nearby harbor, now silted in because of erosion.

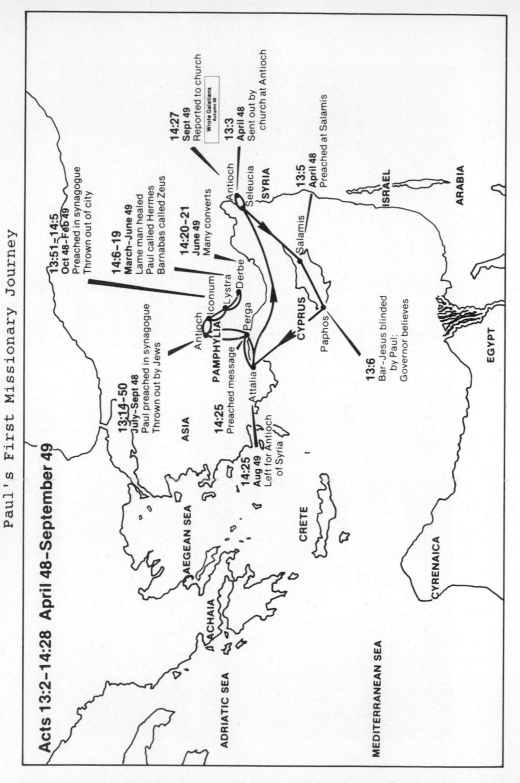

Paul's First Missionary Journey

Acts 13:2–14:28 April 48–September 49

13:51–14:5
Oct 48–Feb 49
Preached in synagogue
Thrown out of city

14:6–19
March–June 49
Lame man healed
Paul called Hermes
Barnabas called Zeus

14:20–21
June 49
Many converts

14:27
Sept 49
Reported to church

Wrote Galatians
Autumn 49

13:3
April 48
Sent out by
church at Antioch

13:5
April 48
Preached at Salamis

13:14–50
July–Sept 48
Paul preached in synagogue
Thrown out by Jews

14:25
Preached message

14:25
Aug 49
Left for Antioch
of Syria

13:6
Bar-Jesus blinded
by Paul;
Governor believes

Antioch   Iconium
                Lystra   Derbe
PAMPHYLIA   Perga
            Attalia

ASIA

Antioch
Seleucia
SYRIA

Salamis
CYPRUS
Paphos

ISRAEL

ARABIA

EGYPT

AEGEAN SEA

CRETE

ACHAIA

ADRIATIC SEA

MEDITERRANEAN SEA

CYRENAICA

From *Talk Thru the Bible*. Reprinted by permission of Walk Thru the Bible Ministries.

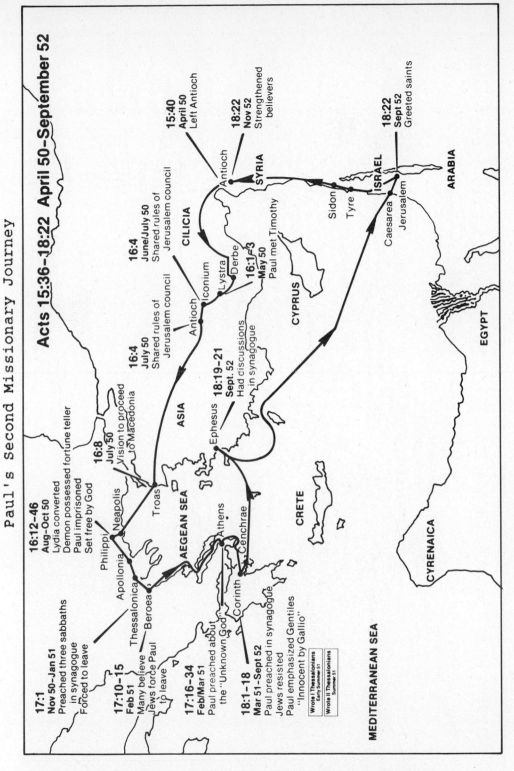

Paul's Second Missionary Journey

Acts 15:36–18:22 April 50–September 52

15:40
April 50
Left Antioch

18:22
Nov 52
Strengthened believers

18:22
Sept 52
Greeted saints

16:4
June/July 50
Shared rules of Jerusalem council

16:1–3
May 50
Paul met Timothy

16:4
July 50
Shared rules of Jerusalem council

16:8
July 50
Vision to proceed to Macedonia

18:19–21
Sept. 52
Had discussions in synagogue

16:12–46
Aug–Oct 50
Lydia converted
Demon possessed fortune teller
Paul imprisoned
Set free by God

17:1
Nov 50–Jan 51
Preached three sabbaths in synagogue
Forced to leave

17:10–15
Feb 51
Many believe
Jews force Paul to leave

17:16–34
Feb/Mar 51
Paul preached about the "Unknown God"

18:1–18
Mar 51–Sept 52
Paul preached in synagogue
Jews resisted
Paul emphasized Gentiles
"Innocent by Gallio"

Wrote I Thessalonians
Early Summer 51

Wrote II Thessalonians
Summer 51

SYRIA
CILICIA
ASIA
CYPRUS
ISRAEL
ARABIA
EGYPT
CRETE
CYRENAICA

Antioch
Iconium
Lystra
Derbe
Antioch
Sidon
Tyre
Caesarea
Jerusalem
Ephesus
Troas
Neapolis
Philippi
Apollonia
Thessalonica
Beroea
Athens
Corinth
Cenchrae

AEGEAN SEA
MEDITERRANEAN SEA

From *Talk Thru the Bible*. Reprinted by permission of Walk Thru the Bible Ministries.

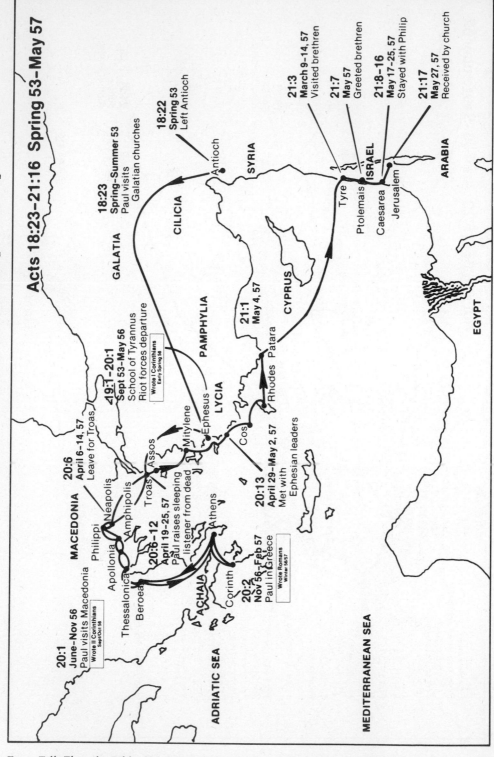

Paul's Third Missionary Journey

Acts 18:23–21:16 Spring 53–May 57

18:22
Spring 53
Left Antioch

18:23
Spring–Summer 53
Paul visits
Galatian churches

21:3
March 9–14, 57
Visited brethren

21:7
May 57
Greeted brethren

21:8–16
May 17–25, 57
Stayed with Philip

21:17
May 27, 57
Received by church

GALATIA

CILICIA

SYRIA

ISRAEL

ARABIA

Antioch

Tyre

Ptolemais

Caesarea

Jerusalem

CYPRUS

PAMPHYLIA

LYCIA

21:1
May 4, 57

Rhodes

Patara

Cos

EGYPT

19:1–20:1
Sept 53–May 56
School of Tyrannus
Riot forces departure

Wrote I Corinthians
Early Spring 56

Mitylene

Ephesus

20:13
April 29–May 2, 57
Met with
Ephesian leaders

20:6
April 6–14, 57
Leave for Troas

MACEDONIA

Neapolis

Philippi

Apollonia

Amphipolis

Thessalonica

Troas

Assos

20:6–12
April 19–25, 57
Paul raises sleeping
listener from dead

20:1
June–Nov 56
Paul visits Macedonia

Wrote II Corinthians
Sept/Oct 56

Beroea

Athens

ACHAIA

Corinth

20:2
Nov 56–Feb 57
Paul in Greece

Wrote Romans
Winter 56/57

ADRIATIC SEA

MEDITERRANEAN SEA

From *Talk Thru the Bible*. Reprinted by permission of Walk Thru the Bible Ministries.

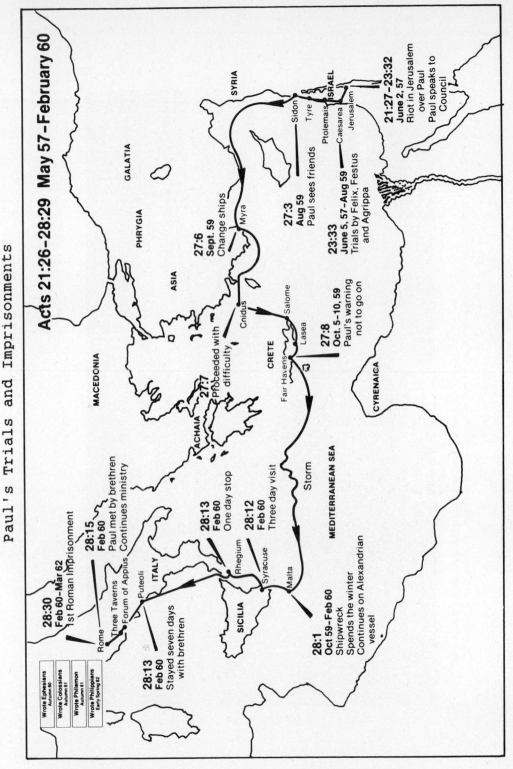

Paul's Trials and Imprisonments

Acts 21:26–28:29 May 57–February 60

21:27–23:32
June 2, 57
Riot in Jerusalem
over Paul
Paul speaks to
Council

23:33
June 5, 57–Aug 59
Trials by Felix, Festus
and Agrippa

27:3
Aug 59
Paul sees friends

27:6
Sept. 59
Change ships

27:7
Proceeded with
difficulty

27:8
Oct. 5–10, 59
Paul's warning
not to go on

28:1
Oct 59–Feb 60
Shipwreck
Spends the winter
Continues on Alexandrian
vessel

28:12
Feb 60
Three day visit

28:13
Feb 60
One day stop

28:13
Feb 60
Stayed seven days
with brethren

28:15
Feb 60
Paul met by brethren
Continues ministry

28:30
Feb 60–Mar 62
1st Roman Imprisonment

Wrote Ephesians
Autumn 60

Wrote Colossians
Autumn 61

Wrote Philemon
Autumn 61

Wrote Philippians
Early Spring 62

SYRIA
ISRAEL
Sidon
Tyre
Ptolemais
Caesarea
Jerusalem
GALATIA
PHRYGIA
ASIA
Myra
Cnidus
Salome
CRETE
Lasea
Fair Havens
CYRENAICA
MACEDONIA
ACHAIA
MEDITERRANEAN SEA
Storm
ITALY
SICILIA
Rome
Three Taverns
Forum of Appius
Puteoli
Rhegium
Syracuse
Malta

From *Talk Thru the Bible*. Reprinted by permission of Walk Thru the Bible Ministries.

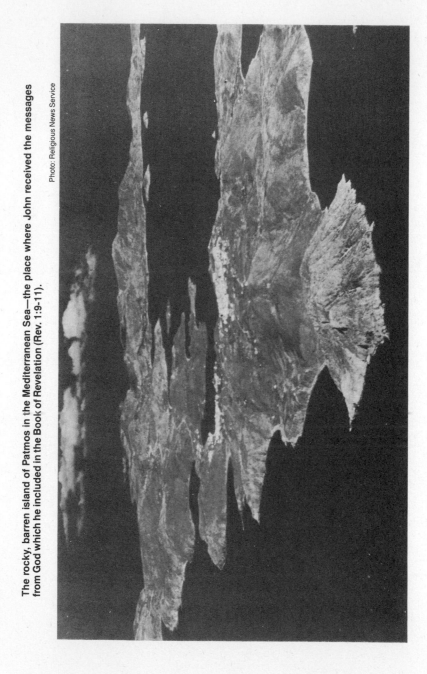

The rocky, barren island of Patmos in the Mediterranean Sea—the place where John received the messages from God which he included in the Book of Revelation (Rev. 1:9-11).

Photo: Religious News Service